W9-BOK-958
3 3420 00634 492 4

Christ on the road to Calvary, and St. George slaying the dragon, from the Psalter of St. Elizabeth, *thirteenth century.*
(© Gianni Dagli Orti/CORBIS)

NEW CATHOLIC ENCYCLOPEDIA

NEW CATHOLIC ENCYCLOPEDIA

SECOND EDITION

6
Fri–Hoh

Detroit • New York • San Diego • San Francisco • Cleveland • New Haven, Conn. • Waterville, Maine • London • Munich

in association with
THE CATHOLIC UNIVERSITY OF AMERICA • WASHINGTON, D.C.

The New Catholic Encyclopedia, Second Edition

Project Editors
Thomas Carson, Joann Cerrito

Editorial
Erin Bealmear, Jim Craddock, Stephen Cusack, Miranda Ferrara, Kristin Hart, Melissa Hill, Margaret Mazurkiewicz, Carol Schwartz, Christine Tomassini, Michael J. Tyrkus

Permissions
Edna Hedblad, Shalice Shah-Caldwell

Imaging and Multimedia
Randy Bassett, Dean Dauphinais, Robert Duncan, Leitha Etheridge-Sims, Mary K. Grimes, Lezlie Light, Dan Newell, David G. Oblender, Christine O'Bryan, Luke Rademacher, Pamela Reed

Product Design
Michelle DiMercurio

Data Capture
Civie Green

Manufacturing
Rhonda Williams

Indexing
Victoria Agee, Victoria Baker, Lynne Maday, Do Mi Stauber, Amy Suchowski

For more information, contact
The Gale Group, Inc.
27500 Drake Rd.
Farmington Hills, MI 48331-3535
Or you can visit our Internet site at
http://www.gale.com

LIBRARY OF CONGRESS CATALOGING-IN-PUBLICATION DATA

New Catholic encyclopedia.—2nd ed.
p. cm.
Includes bibliographical references and indexes.
ISBN 0-7876-4004-2
1. Catholic Church—Encyclopedias. I. Catholic University of America.
BX841 .N44 2002
282' .03—dc21
2002000924

ISBN: 0-7876-4004-2 (set)
0-7876-4005-0 (v. 1)
0-7876-4006-9 (v. 2)
0-7876-4007-7 (v. 3)
0-7876-4008-5 (v. 4)
0-7876-4009-3 (v. 5)
0-7876-4010-7 (v. 6)
0-7876-4011-5 (v. 7)
0-7876-4012-3 (v. 8)
0-7876-4013-1 (v. 9)
0-7876-4014-x (v. 10)
0-7876-4015-8 (v. 11)
0-7876-4016-6 (v. 12)
0-7876-4017-4 (v. 13)
0-7876-4018-2 (v. 14)
0-7876-4019-0 (v. 15)

Printed in the United States of America
10 9 8 7 6 5 4 3 2 1

For The Catholic University of America Press

EDITORIAL STAFF

CONTRIBUTING EDITORS

Foreword

This revised edition of the *New Catholic Encyclopedia* represents a third generation in the evolution of the text that traces its lineage back to the *Catholic Encyclopedia* published from 1907 to 1912. In 1967, sixty years after the first volume of the original set appeared, The Catholic University of America and the McGraw-Hill Book Company joined together in organizing a small army of editors and scholars to produce the *New Catholic Encyclopedia.* Although planning for the *NCE* had begun before the Second Vatican Council and most of the 17,000 entries were written before Council ended, Vatican II enhanced the encyclopedia's value and importance. The research and the scholarship that went into the articles witnessed to the continuity and richness of the Catholic Tradition given fresh expression by Council. In order to keep the *NCE* current, supplementary volumes were published in 1972, 1978, 1988, and 1995. Now, at the beginning of the third millennium, The Catholic University of America is proud to join with The Gale Group in presenting a new edition of the *New Catholic Encyclopedia.* It updates and incorporates the many articles from the 1967 edition and its supplements that have stood the test of time and adds hundreds of new entries.

As the president of The Catholic University of America, I cannot but be pleased at the reception the *NCE* has received. It has come to be recognized as an authoritative reference work in the field of religious studies and is praised for its comprehensive coverage of the Church's history and institutions. Although Canon Law no longer requires encyclopedias and reference works of this kind to receive an *imprimatur* before publication, I am confident that this new edition, like the original, reports accurate information about Catholic beliefs and practices. The editorial staff and their consultants were careful to present official Church teachings in a straightforward manner, and in areas where there are legitimate disputes over fact and differences in interpretation of events, they made every effort to insure a fair and balanced presentation of the issues.

The way for this revised edition was prepared by the publication, in 2000, of a Jubilee volume of the *NCE,* heralding the beginning of the new millennium. In my foreword to that volume I quoted Pope John Paul II's encyclical on Faith and Human Reason in which he wrote that history is "the arena where we see what God does for humanity." The *New Catholic Encyclopedia* describes that arena. It reports events, people, and ideas—"the things we know best and can verify most easily, the things of our everyday life, apart from which we cannot understand ourselves" (*Fides et ratio,* 12).

Finally, I want to express appreciation on my own behalf and on the behalf of the readers of these volumes to everyone who helped make this revision a reality. We are all indebted to The Gale Group and the staff of The Catholic University of America Press for their dedication and the alacrity with which they produced it.

Very Reverend David M. O'Connell, C.M., J.C.D.
President
The Catholic University of America

Preface to the Revised Edition

When first published in 1967 the *New Catholic Encyclopedia* was greeted with enthusiasm by librarians, researchers, and general readers interested in Catholicism. In the United States the *NCE* has been recognized as the standard reference work on matters of special interest to Catholics. In an effort to keep the encyclopedia current, supplementary volumes were published in 1972, 1978, 1988, and 1995. However, it became increasingly apparent that further supplements would not be adequate to this task. The publishers subsequently decided to undertake a thorough revision of the *NCE,* beginning with the publication of a Jubilee volume at the start of the new millennium.

Like the biblical scribe who brings from his storeroom of knowledge both the new and the old, this revised edition of the *New Catholic Encyclopedia* incorporates material from the 15-volume original edition and the supplement volumes. Entries that have withstood the test of time have been edited, and some have been amended to include the latest information and research. Hundreds of new entries have been added. For all practical purposes, it is an entirely new edition intended to serve as a comprehensive and authoritative work of reference reporting on the movements and interests that have shaped Christianity in general and Catholicism in particular over two millennia.

SCOPE

The title reflects its outlook and breadth. It is the *New Catholic Encyclopedia,* not merely a new encyclopedia of Catholicism. In addition to providing information on the doctrine, organization, and history of Christianity over the centuries, it includes information about persons, institutions, cultural phenomena, religions, philosophies, and social movements that have affected the Catholic Church from within and without. Accordingly, the *NCE* attends to the history and particular traditions of the Eastern Churches and the Churches of the Protestant Reformation, and other ecclesial communities. Christianity cannot be understood without exploring its roots in ancient Israel and Judaism, nor can the history of the medieval and modern Church be understood apart from its relationship with Islam. Interfaith dialogue requires an appreciation of Buddhism and other world religions, as well as some knowledge of the history of religion in general.

On the assumption that most readers and researchers who use the *NCE* are individuals interested in Catholicism in general and the Church in North America in particular, its editorial content gives priority to the Western Church, while not neglecting the churches in the East; to Roman Catholicism, acknowledging much common history with Protestantism; and to Catholicism in the United States, recognizing that it represents only a small part of the universal Church.

Scripture, Theology, Patrology, Liturgy. The many and varied articles dealing with Sacred Scripture and specific books of the Bible reflect contemporary biblical scholarship and its concerns. The *NCE* highlights official church teachings as expressed by the Church's magisterium. It reports developments in theology, explains issues and introduces ecclesiastical writers from the early Church Fathers to present-day theologians whose works exercise major influence on the development of Christian thought. The *NCE* traces the evolution of the Church's worship with special emphasis on rites and rituals consequent to the liturgical reforms and renewal initiated by the Second Vatican Council.

Church History. From its inception Christianity has been shaped by historical circumstances and itself has become a historical force. The *NCE* presents the Church's history from a number of points of view against the background of general political and cultural history. The revised edition reports in some detail the Church's missionary activity as it grew from a small community in Jerusalem to the worldwide phenomenon it is today. Some entries, such as those dealing with the Middle Ages, the Reformation, and the Enlightenment, focus on major time-periods and movements that cut across geographical boundaries. Other articles describe the history and structure of the Church in specific areas, countries, and regions. There are separate entries for many dioceses and monasteries which by reason of antiquity, size, or influence are of special importance in ecclesiastical history, as there are for religious orders and congregations. The *NCE* rounds out its comprehensive history of the Church with articles on religious movements and biographies of individuals.

Canon and Civil Law. The Church inherited and has safeguarded the precious legacy of ancient Rome, described by Virgil, "to rule people under law, [and] to establish the way of peace." The *NCE* deals with issues of ecclesiastical jurisprudence and outlines the development of legislation governing communal practices and individual obligations, taking care to incorporate and reference the 1983 *Code of Canon Law* throughout and, where appropriate, the *Code of Canons for the Eastern Churches.* It deals with issues of Church-State relations and with civil law as it impacts on the Church and Church's teaching regarding human rights and freedoms.

Philosophy. The Catholic tradition from its earliest years has investigated the relationship between faith and reason. The *NCE* considers at some length the many and varied schools of ancient, medieval, and modern philosophy with emphasis, when appropriate, on their relationship to theological positions. It pays particular attention to the scholastic tradition, particularly Thomism, which is prominent in Catholic intellectual history. Articles on many major and lesser philosophers contribute to a comprehensive survey of philosophy from pre-Christian times to the present.

Biography and Hagiography. The *NCE,* making an exception for the reigning pope, leaves to other reference works biographical information about living persons. This revised edition presents biographical sketches of hundreds of men and women, Christian and non-Christian, saints and sinners, because of their significance for the Church. They include: Old and New Testament figures; the Fathers of the Church and ecclesiastical writers; pagan and Christian emperors; medieval and modern kings; heads of state and other political figures; heretics and champions of orthodoxy; major and minor figures in the Reformation and Counter Reformation; popes, bishops, and priests; founders and members of religious orders and congregations; lay men and lay women; scholars, authors, composers, and artists. The *NCE* includes biographies of most saints whose feasts were once celebrated or are currently celebrated by the universal church. The revised edition relies on Butler's *Lives of the Saints* and similar reference works to give accounts of many saints, but the *NCE* also provides biographical information about recently canonized and beatified individuals who are, for one reason or another, of special interest to the English-speaking world.

Social Sciences. Social sciences came into their own in the twentieth century. Many articles in the *NCE* rely on data drawn from anthropology, economics, psychology and sociology for a better understanding of religious structures and behaviors. Papal encyclicals and pastoral letters of episcopal conferences are the source of principles and norms for Christian attitudes and practice in the field of social action and legislation. The *NCE* draws attention to the Church's organized activities in pursuit of peace and justice, social welfare and human rights. The growth of the role of the laity in the work of the Church also receives thorough coverage.

ARRANGEMENT OF ENTRIES

The articles in the *NCE* are arranged alphabetically by the first substantive word using the word-by-word method of alphabetization; thus "New Zealand" precedes "Newman, John Henry," and "Old Testament Literature" precedes "Oldcastle, Sir John." Monarchs, patriarchs, popes, and others who share a Christian name and are differentiated by a title and numerical designation are alphabetized by their title and then arranged numerically. Thus, entries for Byzantine emperors Leo I through IV precede those for popes of the same name, while "Henry VIII, King of England" precedes "Henry IV, King of France."

Maps, Charts, and Illustrations. The *New Catholic Encyclopedia* contains nearly 3,000 illustrations, including photographs, maps, and tables. Entries focusing on the Church in specific countries contain a map of the country as well as easy-to-read tables giving statistical data and, where helpful, lists of archdioceses and dioceses. Entries on the Church in U.S. states also contain tables listing archdioceses and dioceses where appropriate. The numerous photographs appearing in the *New Catholic Encyclopedia* help to illustrate the history of the Church, its role in modern societies, and the many magnificent works of art it has inspired.

SPECIAL FEATURES

Subject Overview Articles. For the convenience and guidance of the reader, the *New Catholic Encyclopedia* contains several brief articles outlining the scope of major fields: "Theology, Articles on," "Liturgy, Articles on," "Jesus Christ, Articles on," etc.

Cross-References. The cross-reference system in the *NCE* serves to direct the reader to related material in other articles. The appearance of a name or term in small capital letters in text indicates that there is an article of that title elsewhere in the encyclopedia. In some cases, the name of the related article has been inserted at the appropriate point as a *see* reference: (*see* THOMAS AQUINAS, ST.). When a further aspect of the subject is treated under another title, a *see also* reference is placed at the end of the article. In addition to this extensive cross-reference system, the comprehensive index in volume 15 will greatly increase the reader's ability to access the wealth of information contained in the encyclopedia.

Abbreviations List. Following common practice, books and versions of the Bible as well as other standard works by selected authors have been abbreviated throughout the text. A guide to these abbreviations follows this preface.

The Editors

Abbreviations

The system of abbreviations used for the works of Plato, Aristotle, St. Augustine, and St. Thomas Aquinas is as follows: Plato is cited by book and Stephanus number only, e.g., Phaedo 79B; Rep. 480A. Aristotle is cited by book and Bekker number only, e.g., Anal. post. 72b 8–12; Anim. 430a 18. St. Augustine is cited as in the Thesaurus Linguae Latinae, e.g., C. acad. 3.20.45; Conf. 13.38.53, with capitalization of the first word of the title. St. Thomas is cited as in scholarly journals, but using Arabic numerals. In addition, the following abbreviations have been used throughout the encyclopedia for biblical books and versions of the Bible.

Books

Acts	Acts of the Apostles
Am	Amos
Bar	Baruch
1–2 Chr	1 and 2 Chronicles (1 and 2 Paralipomenon in Septuagint and Vulgate)
Col	Colossians
1–2 Cor	1 and 2 Corinthians
Dn	Daniel
Dt	Deuteronomy
Eccl	Ecclesiastes
Eph	Ephesians
Est	Esther
Ex	Exodus
Ez	Ezekiel
Ezr	Ezra (Esdras B in Septuagint; 1 Esdras in Vulgate)
Gal	Galatians
Gn	Genesis
Hb	Habakkuk
Heb	Hebrews
Hg	Haggai
Hos	Hosea
Is	Isaiah
Jas	James
Jb	Job
Jdt	Judith
Jer	Jeremiah
Jgs	Judges
Jl	Joel
Jn	John
1–3 Jn	1, 2, and 3 John
Jon	Jonah
Jos	Joshua
Jude	Jude
1–2 Kgs	1 and 2 Kings (3 and 4 Kings in Septuagint and Vulgate)
Lam	Lamentations
Lk	Luke
Lv	Leviticus
Mal	Malachi (Malachias in Vulgate)
1–2 Mc	1 and 2 Maccabees
Mi	Micah
Mk	Mark
Mt	Matthew
Na	Nahum
Neh	Nehemiah (2 Esdras in Septuagint and Vulgate)
Nm	Numbers
Ob	Obadiah
Phil	Philippians
Phlm	Philemon
Prv	Proverbs
Ps	Psalms
1–2 Pt	1 and 2 Peter
Rom	Romans
Ru	Ruth
Rv	Revelation (Apocalypse in Vulgate)
Sg	Song of Songs
Sir	Sirach (Wisdom of Ben Sira; Ecclesiasticus in Septuagint and Vulgate)
1–2 Sm	1 and 2 Samuel (1 and 2 Kings in Septuagint and Vulgate)
Tb	Tobit
1–2 Thes	1 and 2 Thessalonians
Ti	Titus
1–2 Tm	1 and 2 Timothy
Wis	Wisdom
Zec	Zechariah
Zep	Zephaniah

Versions

Apoc	Apocrypha
ARV	American Standard Revised Version
ARVm	American Standard Revised Version, margin
AT	American Translation
AV	Authorized Version (King James)
CCD	Confraternity of Christian Doctrine
DV	Douay-Challoner Version

ERV	English Revised Version
ERVm	English Revised Version, margin
EV	English Version(s) of the Bible
JB	Jerusalem Bible
LXX	Septuagint
MT	Masoretic Text
NAB	New American Bible
NEB	New English Bible
NIV	New International Version
NJB	New Jerusalem Bible
NRSV	New Revised Standard Version
NT	New Testament
OT	Old Testament
RSV	Revised Standard Version
RV	Revised Version
RVm	Revised Version, margin
Syr	Syriac
Vulg	Vulgate

F

FRIARS

A term applied to the members of the mendicant orders founded in the 13th century and afterward. The friars represented a departure from the previous monastic tradition insofar as they lacked corporate possessions, a condition subsequently modified by the Council of Trent. They possessed a greater mobility insofar as they were not confined to a single monastery or abbey. The majority of their members were priests engaged in a direct apostolate to the faithful.

During the 13th century there was a remarkable growth in the number of mendicant orders until the Second Council of Lyons issued a decree on July 17, 1274, directed at the suppression of all but the four major orders: Dominicans, or Black Friars (1216); Franciscans, or Grey Friars (1223); Carmelites, or White Friars (1226); and Augustinians, or Austin Friars (1256). Of the other mendicants some, such as the Mercedarians (1235) and the Servites (1256), survived this proscription, while others, such as the Friars of the Sack (1251) and the Friars of the Blessed Mary, or Pied Friars (1257), gradually disappeared. Still others, such as the Order of the Holy Cross, or Crutched Friars (1248), evolved into an order of canons regular, known as the Crosier Fathers. Sometime after the Second Council of Lyons other orders of mendicants, such as the Minims (1435), were established.

Bibliography: T. SCHÄFER, *De religiosis ad normam codicis juris canonici* (4th ed. Rome 1947). R. W. EMERY, "The Second Council of Lyons and the Mendicant Orders," *Catholic Historical Review*, 39 (1953) 257–271.

[W. B. RYAN]

FRIDELLI, XAVER EHRENBERT (FRIEDEL)

China missionary and cartographer; b. Linz, Austria, March 11, 1673; d. Peking, June 4, 1743. He entered the Society of Jesus in 1688 and sailed for China in 1704. A skilled mathematician, he was one of the six to eight Jesuits who, working in groups of two and three, began in 1717 to map the Chinese Empire at the command of the Emperor. Because of the growing distrust of foreigners, the mandarin assistants served more as guards than advisers. Since the Jesuits were not permitted to enter Tibet or Korea, or go near the borders of Russia, they had to accept the information gathered by natives whom they trained for the task. In 1718 the huge map was presented to the Emperor, and later it was reproduced from 48 engraved plates. The work of the Jesuits remained the only reliable map of China until well into the 19th century. In 1720 Fridelli established a school, of which he was rector for six years, and in 1721 he opened St. Joseph's Church in Peking. His missionary work falls within the period of Christian persecution under Emperor Yum Tsching when his diplomacy, high esteem at court, and reputation for scholarship did much to soften the persecution.

Bibliography: C. W. ALLAN, *Jesuits at the Court of Peking* (Shanghai 1935) 222. A. ZERLIK, *Neue deutsche Biographie* 5 (Berlin 1961): 436.

[M. B. MARTIN]

FRIDESWIDE OF OXFORD, ST.

Abbess; b. *c.* 650–80; d. Oct. 19, 735. The legends describe Frideswide (Fredeswinda or, in Artois, Frévisse) as the daughter of an Anglo-Saxon *subregulus* who entered religious life after rejecting a princely suitor who was stricken blind when he continued to pursue her. For this reason, the legend contends, the English kings for centuries feared to approach Oxford, where she founded a monastery *c.* 727. The Danes burned her convent *c.* 1000, but it was refounded by Augustinian canons regular in 1122. St. Frideswide's relics were translated to splendid shrines in 1180 and 1289. She was the patroness of the city and the University of OXFORD by the late 12th century. Her cult was officially established at Oxford in 1434 and 1481 with special offices in the Breviary of the

Young friars study their prayers before an ordination ceremony, 1956. (©Bettmann/CORBIS)

Sarum Rite, and she was venerated also in parts of France as Frévisse. Her convent was transformed into Christ Church College *c.* 1526–46, and its church was made into a cathedral for the Anglican Diocese of Oxford in 1546. The shrine of St. Frideswide was dismantled in 1538, and her bones were mixed in 1561 with those of Catherine Cathie, the Protestant wife of Peter Martyr Vermigli. The tomb was restored in 1890 and is a popular shrine with English Catholics today.

Feast: Oct. 19.

Bibliography: *Acta Sanctorum* Oct. 8:379, 533–590. W. HUNT, *The Dictionary of National Biography from the Earliest Times to 1900,* 63 v. (London 1885–1900) 7:715–716. F. M. STENTON, ''St. Frideswide and Her Times,'' *Oxoniensia* 1 (1936) 103–112. E. F. JACOB, St. Frideswide, *The Patron Saint of Oxford* (Oxford 1953). A. M. ZIMMERMANN, *Kalendarium Benedictinum: Die Heiligen und Seligen des Benediktinerorderns und seiner Zweige,* 4 v. (Metten 1933–38) 3:197–200. A. BUTLER, *The Lives of the Saints,* ed. H. THURSTON and D. ATTWATER, 4 v. (New York 1956) 4:150–151.

[H. E. AIKINS]

FRIDOLIN OF SÄCKINGEN, ST.

Abbot, apostle of the Upper Rhine; b. Ireland; d. Säckingen, Germany, sixth or seventh century. Despite his noble Irish parentage, he exercised his sacerdotal ministry in Ireland by traveling from city to city, preaching the word of God. After crossing over to France, he continued his work as an itinerant preacher until he reached Poitiers, where he rediscovered the lost relics of St. HILARY OF POITIERS. Upon resuming his journeys, he went to Strasbourg, Constance, and Chur (Switzerland), establishing churches along the way. A vision finally directed him to the uninhabited island of Säckingen in the Rhine, where he founded a monastery and built a church. He is buried there. His cult is popular in Germany, Switzerland, and Ireland.

Feast: Oct. 18.

Bibliography: *Vita* (a somewhat extravagant legend written *c.* 1000 by Balther), *Acta Sanctorum* March 1:429–440; rep. as *Fridolin, der heilige Mann zwischen Alpen und Rhein. . . ,* ed. W. IRTENKAUF, tr. from the Late Middle High German by V. SCHUPP (Sigmaringen 1983). F. JEHLE, *Geschichte der Stadt Säckingen* (Säckingen 1968). *Monumenta Germaniae Scriptores rerum Merovingicarum* (Berlin 1825–) 3: 350–369. J. L. BAUDOT and L. CHAUSSIN, *Vies des saints et des bienheueux selon l'ordre du calendrier avec l'historique des fêtes* 12 v. (Paris 1935–56) 3:107–108. A. BUTLER, *The Lives of the Saints,* ed. H. THURSTON and D. ATTWATER, 4 v. (New York 1956) 1:499–500. H. BÜTTNER *Die Religion in Geschichte und Gegenwart,* 7 v. (3rd ed. Tübingen 1957–65) 2:1132.

[O. L. KAPSNER]

FRIEDEL, FRANCIS

Educator, author; b. Cleveland, Ohio, Aug. 8, 1897; d. Dayton, Ohio, Feb. 12, 1959. He received his B.A. at the University of Dayton (1917) and his S.T.D. at the University of Fribourg, Switzerland, where he was ordained a MARIANIST priest, April 2, 1927. He attended The Catholic University of America, Washington, D.C., receiving his M.A. in 1935; in 1950 the University of Pittsburgh, Pa., granted him a Ph.D. He was president and charter member of the American Catholic Sociological Society; President of Trinity College, Sioux City, Iowa (1943–49); and dean of the College of Arts and Sciences at the University of Dayton (1949–53). The *Dayton Journal* hailed him editorially for his ''interest in community welfare projects'' (Feb. 14, 1959). Among his many publications are *The Mariology of Cardinal Newman* (New York 1928), *Social Patterns in the Society of Mary* (Pittsburgh 1951), and *Necrology of the Society of Mary* (1952). He also contributed numerous articles to U.S. and foreign periodicals and wrote various religious pamphlets.

[G. J. RUPPEL]

FRIEDHOFEN, PETER, BL.

Chimney-sweep; founder of the Brothers of Charity of Mary Help of Christians; b. Feb. 25, 1819, Weitersburg (near Koblenz am Rhein), Germany; d. Dec. 21, 1860, Koblenz. A year after Peter's birth, his father died, leaving his wife to provide for seven children. Each of the children had to begin earning money for the family as soon as they were able. Peter, next to the youngest, and his older brother Jacob traveled around the region sweeping chimneys. Jacob died leaving a wife and 11 children whom Peter tried to assist financially. While continuing his work, Peter began to engage in his vocation—caring for the helpless, especially children. He established charitable projects in Adenau, Cochem, and Wittlich. From these charities evolved the Order of Brothers of Mercy of Mary the Helper (founded 1849) for the service of the poor, the sick, and the aged. Once Peter and his companion Karl Marchand were trained by the Alexian Brothers, adapted their Rule, and had the order's constitution approved by Bishop Arnoldi of Trier (July 2, 1848), the Brothers of Mercy opened their first house (June 21, 1850). The first brothers received the religous habit in 1851. The bishop of Trier and president of the Rheinland patronized the order and assisted in its work. At the time of Friedhofen's death from tuberculosis, the congregation had spread throughout Europe and into Brazil, China, and Malaysia. His body was interred at Trier am Mosel. He was beatified by John Paul II on June 23, 1985.

Bibliography: *Acta Apostolicae Sedis* (1985) 784. *L'Osservatore Romano,* Eng. ed. 29 (1985): 6–7.

[K. I. RABENSTEIN]

FRIEDRICH, JOHANN

Ecclesiastical historian; b. Poxdorf, Upper Franconia, Germany, June 5, 1836; d. Munich, Aug. 19, 1917. After his education at Bamberg and Munich, and his ordination, he taught on the theological faculty at Munich as *Privatdocent* from 1862, as professor of ecclesiastical history from 1872, and as a member of the philosophy faculty from 1882 until his retirement in 1905. At Vatican Council I he was theologian to Cardinal Gustav von Hohenlohe, and he used this opportunity to try to prevent the definition of papal infallibility, a doctrine that he considered historically indefensible, both by his own writings and by secretly supplying his former teacher and intimate friend DÖLLINGER with much of the material published in the *Letters from Rome* (1869–70) under the pseudonym Quirinus. After he refused to accept the conciliar definitions, he was excommunicated (1872), but he continued to exercise priestly functions as a member of the OLD CATHOLICS, a sect whose formation he influenced profoundly; he later withdrew from it when it ceased to insist on clerical celibacy. His historical writings concerning this period are highly subjective and tendentious. They include *Tagebuch während des Vatikanischen Konzils* (1871, 2d ed. 1873) and *Geschichte des Vatikanischen Konzils* (3 v. 1877–87), both on the Index, along with other of his works. His *Ignaz von Döllinger* (3 v. 1899–1901) is very well informed but one-sided and often indiscreet. Among his other works, the most important are an ecclesiastical history of Germany, completed only to the Merovingian period, *Kirchengeschichte Deutschlands* (2 v. 1867–69), and *Johann Adam Möhler, Der Symboliker* (1894).

Bibliography: T. GRANDERATH, *Geschichte des Vatikanischen Konzils,* 3 v. (Freiburg 1903–06). F. HACKER, ''J. Friedrich als Führer der altkatholischen Bewegung,'' *Internationale kirchliche Zeitschrift* 8 (1918): 252–274. C. B. MOSS, *The Old Catholic Movement* (2d ed. London 1964). S. LÖSCH, *Döllinger und Frankreich* (Munich 1955). W. KÜPPERS, *Neue deutsche Biographie* 5 (Berlin 1953–) 601.

[S. J. TONSOR]

FRIENDS, RELIGIOUS SOCIETY OF

One of the smaller Protestant denominations, referred to also as Quakers, or Friends, or Friends Church.

Origin and history. It originated about 1650 under the leadership of George FOX and other voluntary itinerant preachers. Within a decade, scores of these ''first publishers of Truth'' had carried their message throughout Great Britain and Ireland, to northern Europe, to the British colonies on the American seaboard, and to the West Indies. Regular meetings for worship were organized locally and continued to grow, although those in Holland, Germany, and the West Indies gradually died out.

Because of their rejection of compulsory church attendance and of military service and their deliberate disregard of minor social conventions, such as deference to superiors and judicial oaths, the Quakers met vigorous opposition nearly everywhere they went during their first half-century. At first this took the form of public disapproval or mob violence, but later special legislation against them was enforced by the courts. In Massachusetts, for example, four Quakers were executed between 1659 and 1661. Whatever the source of the nickname Quaker, it was used by the public in scorn. However, the unyielding pertinacity of the Friends, who refused to meet in secret, and their constant public nonresistance ultimately won them at least pity and toleration. In England their position improved after the Toleration Act of 1689, and by 1700 they had become a substantial segment of the total population both in Great Britain and the American colonies. In several of the latter they even held political control for a time. The areas of their greatest strength were Rhode Island, the Middle Colonies, and later Maine,

North Carolina, and Nantucket, Mass. During the westward expansion movement, many Friends migrated into Ohio, Indiana, and Iowa, partly to escape from the slave economy; later they moved farther west to the Pacific coast. After the Civil War, they made converts in the new Western settlements and undertook foreign missionary work in non-Christian cultures.

Doctrine. Arising as they did in England during the Commonwealth of Oliver CROMWELL, the Friends not only shared much of the prevailing antipapal bias of the PURITANS, but they went even further in rejecting formalism in worship and belief. They appealed to the absence of precedent in the New Testament for using ''Saint'' as in St. Paul's, for observing Christmas and other religious days, for giving tithes, for being married by a priest or with a ring, and for many other remnants of medieval ''superstition.'' They preferred ''divine immediate revelation'' to the authority of church, creed, or Bible. They have retained their emphasis on continuing first-hand religious experience. In one sense they have been at the opposite extreme from Roman Catholicism, but in other respects, such as their relative freedom from bibliolatry and their tendency to mystical or quietistic piety, they are more parallel to it than to Protestantism. Their emphasis on experience put them on guard against mere verbalism. They knew and used the Bible, but not as the chief rule of faith and conduct. Theological criticism from their contemporaries forced them into formulating a theology of their own. Robert BARCLAY in his classic *Apology* (1676) gave a logical defense of their views and practices, limiting himself to matters in which Quakers differed from the generality of Christians.

Freedom from a rigid creed has permitted great variety of belief in modern times and provided an excuse for inarticulateness. It has, however, posed problems to Friends and to members of other churches; ecumenical movements, otherwise congenial to Quaker participation, favor a statement of faith, no matter how simple or broad that statement may be. Meanwhile, what the early Friends called the Light Within or the Light of Christ is increasingly recognized as Christian experience in other groups.

Forms of worship. The Quakers early rejected most of the usual forms of Christian worship, Anglican or Roman, and even those of the Protestant sects. They fell into the practice of spontaneous, unprogrammed, cooperative worship. No human leader was designated and no formal ministry established to conduct worship. There were no consecrated buildings, persons, or objects; no hymns or other music; no reading or recitation; no ritual; no outward sacraments, not even baptism of water or the physical Eucharist. Women spoke and prayed as well as men, each whenever he felt moved. Silence was the background of worship and often its prevailing feature. This democratic and spontaneous type of worship is without much known parallel or precedent; it is one of the most distinctive features of Quakerism, still attractive to certain persons. In parts of America it has been superseded (except for the absence of sacraments) by something much like the usual type of nonliturgical Protestant service.

Organization. The Friends very early evolved a simple organization consisting of union in local meetings grouped into progressively larger units called respectively Monthly, Quarterly, and Yearly Meetings. These are largely autonomous. Various larger groupings of Yearly Meetings came into existence in America, two of them by coincidence in the same year, 1902. One was called the Friends General Conference, the other the Friends United Meeting. A third grouping, the Evangelical Friends International was founded in 1990, emerging out of the Evangelical Friends Alliance (established 1965). The Evangelical Friends seek to retrieve what they believe to be the Christ-centered evangelical character of the early Friends movement.

Although each Yearly Meeting has its own printed Book of Discipline, there is in fact worldwide similarity of practice in this kind of ''congregational'' polity, with no real distinction between clergy and laity, nor between men and women. Leadership is ''recognized'' as existing without human appointment.

The proceedings in the meetings for business are as democratic as in those held for worship. The matters discussed are decided not so much by debate and voting, as by the gradual emerging of a consensus, called ''the sense of the meeting,'' which it is the duty of the ''clerk'' who presides to wait for and to record. This kind of procedure has features as unfamiliar to most churches as is the distinctive Quaker worship. Communication among Friends and an indirect setting of standards have resulted from the regular presentation in the business meetings of a questionnaire called ''queries,'' concerning the behavior of the members of the meeting. The solidarity of Friends, prior to the present use of church periodicals, was promoted as well by the constant intervisitation by ''public Friends'' to the various Quaker communities.

Membership rests upon individual attachment to a local meeting either by birthright, automatically applied to children of Friends, or by ''convincement'' expressed by a request to be included. In neither case is adherence marked by any elaborate formality such as Baptism or Confirmation. For many years membership was lost if a member married a nonmember.

Recent Trends. The early persecutions, subsequent quietism, and intermarriage within a small group of

Friends, resulted in a close-knit, somewhat aloof culture. Outside contacts, secular and lately ecclesiastical, have changed this. Waves of political, social, and religious thought have penetrated the Religious Society of Friends; in America this led to actual schisms in 1827 and again later. Prominent figures in these alignments were Elias Hicks (1748–1830) of Long Island, N.Y., and Joseph John Gurney (1788–1846) of Norwich, England. In Gurney's thought, and in that of many Friends to this day, evangelical theology became more central and extreme than in early Quakerism (*see* EVANGELICALISM). On the other hand, intellectualism and social concern gained fresh support from many.

The continuance of numerous schools and colleges established by the Friends attests the Quaker concern for education, originally, but not now, chiefly for their own children. At all periods Quakerism manifested a sensitivity to social needs; this was exemplified in the work of Elizabeth FRY in prison reform and that of John WOOLMAN and John G. Whittier (the New England poet) in campaigns against slavery. Quakers also interested themselves in movements for justice for the Native Americans and for the humane treatment of the insane. Their opposition to war and their contributions to relief work, for which they received the Nobel Peace Prize in 1947, have made them widely known and given them an influence out of proportion to their small numbers.

In the 20th century, Friends from all countries were brought into fellowship by the Friends World Committee on Consultation (FWCC). Established in 1937, following the Second World Conference of Friends in Swarthmore, Pa., the FWCC promotes collaboration and exchange of resources at regional, national, and international levels through conferences, publications, consultations, studies, and meetings. Headquartered in London, England, the FWCC is registered as a non-governmental organization (NGO) with the United Nations (U.N.), and participates extensively in U.N. endeavors to promote world peace. In the ecumenical arena, the Friends United Meeting and the Friends General Conference are members of the WORLD COUNCIL OF CHURCHES, while the Philadelphia Yearly Meeting is a member of the NATIONAL COUNCIL OF THE CHURCHES OF CHRIST IN THE UNITED STATES OF AMERICA.

Bibliography: Classics first pub. at the dates indicated are accessible in various later editions: R. BARCLAY, *Apology* (1676). G. FOX, *Journal* (1694). W. SEWEL, *History of the . . . Quakers* (1722). J. WOOLMAN, *Journal* (1774). Modern works repr. or in print include W. C. BRAITHWAITE, *The Beginnings of Quakerism* (2d ed. Cambridge, Eng. 1955); *The Second Period of Quakerism* (2d ed. Cambridge, Eng. 1961). R. M. JONES et al., *The Quakers in the American Colonies* (New York 1962); *The Later Periods of Quakerism,* 2 v. (London 1921). H. H. BRINTON, *Friends for 300 Years* (New York 1952). F. S. MEAD, S. S. HILL and C. D. ATWOOD, *Handbook of Denominations in the United States* (Nashville, Tenn. 2001).

[H. J. CADBURY/EDS.]

FRIENDS OF GOD

A term that was used in a general sense from ancient times. It is found in the Old and New Testaments, in the works of the Fathers, and in early Christian and medieval writers to designate pious, devout, or saintly persons, such as Abraham, Moses, the Apostles, or martyrs, who gave themselves entirely to the service of God. Although the phrase continued to have a general meaning, during the 14th century, in the vocabulary of the mystics, it took on a more specialized sense, owing chiefly to its frequent use by Johannes TAULER. It was used to designate persons who were striving for or had attained mystical union with God, the highest state of the contemplative life. The Friends were not united by any formal ties or organization but were a free association of like-minded people held together by friendship, common aspirations, similar experiences, unity of purpose, and exchange of visits, letters, and spiritual writings. To this last activity are owed various spiritual classics, such as the correspondence of HENRY SUSO with Elsbeth STÄGEL and that of Henry of Nördlingen, a secular priest, with Margaret Ebner (considered by some authors the oldest collection of letters in the German language), and Margaret's *Revelations.* In this way the works of Suso and RUYSBROECK and the sermons of Tauler gained their widespread circulation.

Under the guidance of experienced and skillful leaders, notably Tauler, Suso, and Henry of Nördlingen, the Friends of God cultivated a life of interior devotion, intense prayer, austerity, and self-renunciation. By their edifying lives and spiritual practices, they hoped to reach intimate friendship with God and to counteract the political and moral evils of an age that was experiencing earthquake and famine, as well as political and religious strife between popes and emperors, the scandal of the papal residence at Avignon, chronic civic disorder in Italy, war between England and France, and would soon witness the Black Death and the consequent moral decay of Christendom. The Friends were heavily concentrated in Bavaria, Switzerland, the Rhineland, and the Low Countries (*see* SPIRITUALITY OF THE LOW COUNTRIES). Some of them lived alone, others in small groups, as at the former Benedictine monastery of Grüner Wörth near Strasbourg. Their principal centers were Strasbourg and Basel, with lesser areas of influence in Cologne and Constance, and at many of the Dominican monasteries of nuns, such as MARIA-MÖDINGEN near Nuremberg, Töss and Oetenbach in Switzerland, Adelhausen near Freiburg im Breisgau, and Unterlinden in Colmar.

Men and women of all ranks of society and every state of life, ''filled with a living love of God,'' moved with ''compassion for their fellow-men in affliction,'' and ''concerned about the corruption of the world and the faults of men which awakened the wrath of God'' (Tauler), embraced the ideals of the Friends and sought direction from their leaders. There were the friar and priest leaders; nuns, such as the Dominicans Margaret Ebner of Maria-Mödingen and Christine Ebner of Engelthal; layfolk, such as Margaret of the Golden Ring, Herman of Fritzlar, and Rulman Merswin (founder of the Grüner Wörth center); knights and ladies, such as Queen Agnes, widow of King Andrew III of Hungary, who had retired to a German monastery (*see* SPIRITUALITY, RHENISH).

The Friends of God were entirely orthodox in their beliefs and were devoted to the Church. Even when they venerated outstanding lay members of their company, they manifested no distrust of the hierarchy or the priesthood, nor did they exhibit any trace of ecclesiastical separatism. They set themselves apart from other clergy and layfolk in the Church only in their spiritual ideals, in their desire to live a truly spiritual life under the guidance of a spiritual master, and in their hope to rescue the Church and society from contemporary evils. They must also be clearly distinguished from the Brethren of the Free Spirit, WALDENSES, and heretical BEGUINES, who, glorying in a false liberty and preaching emancipation from the Church, concealed their heretical and separatist tendencies by assuming the name Friends of God.

The term ''Friends of God'' began to fall into disuse toward the end of the 14th century, probably because of the general decline of mysticism and its terminology.

Bibliography: A. CHIQUOT, *Dictionnaire de spiritualité ascétique et mystique. Doctrine et histoire,* ed. M. VILLER et al. (Paris 1932) 1:493–500. J. M. CLARK, *The Great German Mystics* (Oxford 1949) 75–97. A. G. SEESHOLTZ, *Friends of God: Practical Mystics of the 14th Century* (New York 1934). R. M. JONES, *The Flowering of Mysticism: The Friends of God in the 14th Century* (New York 1939).

[W. A. HINNEBUSCH]

FRIENDSHIP

A reciprocal relationship of affection or sympathy between persons of the same sex or at least independent of sexual attraction, and based on a community of nature and of interests, the latter of a spiritual kind. This article traces the historical development of the concept, presents a systematic analysis in traditional Catholic terms, and concludes with an evaluation of the role of friendship in Christianity.

History. The basic formulation of the definition of friendship took place in the context of Greco-Roman culture—the beginnings of the classical development in Greek antiquity and the remainder in Roman society. Later centuries added little to the essentials that were there discerned.

Greek Antiquity. The Greek naturalists were the first to speak of friendship, and this in connection with efforts to offer a rational explanation for changes going on in nature. They conceived of friendship as the basic principle of attraction and repulsion that governed the combining actions whereby material bodies were formed from their elemental constituents. Most of their discussions were concerned with the question of whether friendship was basically a union of contraries or a union of things with similar characteristics.

With SOCRATES, Greek thought began to restrict friendship to a relationship between persons and to give it a precise psychological meaning. In fact, friendship figured so importantly in Socrates's thought that he set himself to teach and to practice the art of acquiring friends. Following his example, both PLATO and ARISTOTLE attracted their disciples more as friends than as students, so much so that L. Dugas could remark that the philosophical schools of ancient Greece were ''not so much schools as they were associations of friends'' (23).

Aristotle presents perhaps the most complete analysis of friendship in classical antiquity in bk. 8 of his *Nicomachean Ethics.* Rejecting the equivocal usage of his naturalist predecessors, he restricts friendship (φιλία) to a type of accord among human persons and distinguishes it from the love (φίλησις) that is also properly human. He approaches its definition indirectly by considering it as a form of attraction and finds its basis in being liked, whether this be for interest, or pleasure, or virtue. He thus distinguishes three kinds of friendship: that based on utility, which unites opposites, and those based on pleasure and virtue, which unite similars. Friendships based on utility or on pleasure care less for the friend than for the good he affords, and for this reason are less stable, ceasing as they do when their motivation disappears. Friendship based on virtue, on the other hand, is more perfect; in fact it is friendship par excellence, for in its case the friends seek each other for what they are, rather than for what they give. Again, it is more stable than other friendships because it is based on virtue, which itself is enduring, and at the same time has all of their prerogatives, for those whom it unites are pleasurable and useful for each other. Yet it is rarely found, partly because there are few who are capable of it, and partly because of the time involved in discovering and cultivating those persons who may be worthy of it.

Finally, for Aristotle, friendship thrives only when there is some community in living (συνζῆν). Those who reciprocally and consciously seek the good in each other, but are unable to associate and communicate for one reason or other, cannot strictly become friends. The element of community involved in friendship was understood differently, however, by various Greeks: the Pythagoreans saw it as a community of resources; Aristotle, as a community of likes and interests; and the Epicureans and Stoics, as a community of philosophical beliefs.

Roman Society. Among the Romans, CICERO held a position analogous to that of Aristotle among the Greeks as their principal theorist of friendship. Less profound than Aristotle, perhaps, he made up for this by the charm and warmth of his treatment. He based his notion of friendship on the instinct for sociability that is found in man, defining it as a perfect agreement of wills, tastes, and thoughts accompanied by benevolence and affection. Nothing, in his estimation, is more adapted to human nature than this type of accord. Other goods such as riches, health, power, and honor are uncertain and defectible; only friendship is really enduring, because it is based upon virtue. It can be found only among good men, for they alone have the loyalty and integrity to sustain it and lack the cupidity and passion that destroy it. True friendship is not easily found, he admits; but once found, it is forever.

The reason why true friendships are rare, for Cicero, is that few are worthy of being loved in and for themselves and many seek to make friends purely for pleasure or for profit. A true friend must be another self; thus if one desires to find friends, he must become good himself and then seek out someone similar. Cicero saw friendship as an aid to virtue, since good people who are benevolent to each other become masters of their passions and preserve virtue in one another. This explains why Cicero insisted that one should choose his friends well, for a failure of judgment could cause one to become attached to a person who would later do him harm, and then would not be a true friend.

Later Centuries. The thoughts of Aristotle and Cicero on the subject of friendship have remained classic. They passed on to the Fathers of the Church, such as St. AUGUSTINE and St. AMBROSE; to scholastic doctors and theologians, such as St. AELRED, St. THOMAS AQUINAS, and St. FRANCIS DE SALES; and to secular writers, such as M. E. de MONTAIGNE. They thus constitute a heritage that has become traditional in the Western world. Modern psychologists have complemented their doctrines on points of detail, and philosophers have subjected them to searching analyses, but neither have contradicted them in their essential elements.

Systematic Analysis. With this historical background, it becomes possible to present an analysis of the concept of friendship that describes its psychological characteristics, its metaphysical nature, and its moral aspect.

Psychological Characteristics. Friendship is first of all an attraction; seen externally, its principal effect is one of dynamism, for friends seek one another out and are not happy unless they are together. When proximity is spatially impossible, the attraction manifests itself by the one's turning his thoughts and desires to the other.

Second, friendship involves affection, being based on an emotion known among the Greeks as φίλησις and among the Latins as *amatio.* It is because a man loves his friend that he is attracted to him in various ways. This emotion is more interior than exterior, and one senses it without always being able to see it; yet it is occasionally discernible, sometimes by gestures, sometimes by smiles or even by tears.

Third, friendship is a reciprocal affection. It is only when an ἀντιφίλησις responds to the φίλησις, or a *redamatio* to the *amatio,* that one can speak of true friendship (φιλία, *amicitia*). This explains why inanimate things cannot be friends or the object of friendship; a man may love wine, but wine cannot be his friend. Again, the reciprocity involved in friendship explains why it grows and deepens with each return of affection, for it involves a type of psychological resonance based on the phenomenon of love's provoking more love in ever-increasing proportions.

Fourth, friendship is a union of a spiritual kind. There are reciprocal affective responses even at the level of brute animals, and yet one does not speak of these as friendship. What is peculiar to friendship is its concern with the intellectual life, not with the life of sense. Its activity has a certain independence from matter, and it provokes a spiritual union, i.e., one based on intellect and will and feeling, and thus properly human. This is why Aristotle could maintain that friendship can exist only between persons.

Fifth, friendship is a disinterested type of relationship. Persons may voluntarily associate for a variety of reasons, such as for profit or for pleasure; but what these associations have in common is that they promote the interest of the one entering into them. The peculiar association that is friendship is more noble and ideal than these, for it sets aside personal gain and, in this sense, is disinterested. The true friend is such because of the qualities he finds in the other; this explains why he will make sacrifices for his friend and do things with no thought of what he himself gets out of them. This also explains why friendship has a lasting character, for monetary and sensual interests are subject to frequent change, whereas the virtuous qualities that attract a friend are stable and enduring.

Finally, perfect friendship is a fusion of souls. Spiritual and disinterested relationships can be more or less intimate, but at their best they encompass all the activities of the souls engaging in them. The effect of this perfect friendship, in the expression of Aristotle and Augustine (*Conf.* 4.6.11), is to put but ''one soul in two bodies.'' Then everything is held in common; the distinction between the ''I'' and the ''Thou'' disappears; and there results the highest type of unity to be found among men.

Metaphysical Nature. Friendship manifests itself by its acts, but such acts presuppose the reality that is friendship just as volition presupposes the will and judgment presupposes the intellect. This reality is not a power or faculty of the soul, because it is not inborn in man; rather it involves an acquired disposition, a HABIT, that exists in man's rational appetitive faculty, or WILL. This habit is actualized, as Aquinas teaches, when one friend ''informs'' the affection of the other. As HENRY OF GHENT and RICHARD OF MIDDLETON observed, however, habits of this type must exist in each person involved in the friendship, and thus the habits themselves must be numerically distinct. The reality that is friendship must therefore be a RELATION that is based on two absolute habits; one may refer to each habit as friendship in the person participating in it, but the notion is not complete unless it includes the relationship that unites one habit to the other.

Thomas Aquinas and other theologians who study friendship in the context of man's relationship with God generally speak of it as a kind of LOVE; they see the ''love of friendship'' as the highest form of love, and oppose it to the ''love of concupiscence'' (*Summa theologiae* 1a2ae, 26.3–4). From this viewpoint, one may define friendship as a love of benevolence, something held in common and based on the mutual regard of its participants. Lower forms of love are at the level of sense; they seek pleasure and self-gratification, and this is true even of the sexual love whereby man is prompted to conserve his species (*see* SEX). The love of friendship, on the other hand, is of a higher order; it is essentially spiritual, and thus serves well to explain the optimum relationship that unites man to God (*see* CHARITY).

Moral Aspect. Friendship as such is good, and therefore is legitimate for man. It is, in fact, beneficial for his soul: the companion of VIRTUE, it may itself be considered as a virtue in the one possessing it. Yet it places demands on those who embrace it, and in certain circumstances, particularly when too restrictive, can be harmful and even vicious. (For a fuller discussion, particularly as related to the spiritual life, *see* FRIENDSHIP, PARTICULAR.)

Role in Christianity. The fact of being a Christian in no way changes man's nature or his needs. It is thus possible for Christians, while living a supernatural life, to have purely human friendships among themselves. There is nothing distinctively Christian about such friendships, however, unless Christianity in some way enters into the relationships and transposes them to a higher level.

Some have seen an opposition between the teaching of the pagans on friendship and the New Law given to men by Jesus Christ. For example, Jesus prescribes charity toward man's neighbor, and this independently of one's particular feelings and personal likes or dislikes. Such a prescription seems to deprive friendship of its proper character; for, rather than seek something selective and personal, the Christian is urged to a universal attitude of love toward all men, and this by obligation rather than by free choice. Thus the pagan ideal of friendship seems to be absorbed in charity, and itself destroyed in the process. Again, the perfection of the love of God, as conceived by such spiritual writers as St. IGNATIUS OF LOYOLA, seems to demand of man that he transfer all of his affection from creatures to his Creator; thus the renunciation of human friendships seems to be the ideal toward which the perfect Christian should tend.

There is some element of truth in these considerations, but at the same time it is possible to oppose them by others that argue for the basic compatibility between friendship and charity. For one, Christianity has focused attention on the dignity of the individual independent of his place in society; it has liberated man more from matter by accenting the immortality of his soul. Such a liberation can only favor friendship, for it provides the basis for greater personal appreciation of one's fellow men. Much the same can be said for the teaching on the universality of the Redemption, for this too proclaims the equality of all souls in God's sight. Finally, by the gift of supernatural life, Christianity has made numberless human souls incomparably better and therefore more worthy of love; it has increased their resemblance to one another and has thus provided a new basis of community among them.

De facto, friendship does exist among Christians. It has never flourished so much as it has since the promulgation of the gospel, nor has it ever been so pure and so noble in its practice and its ideals.

Bibliography: G. VANSTEENBERGHE, *Dictionnaire de spiritualité ascétique et mystique. Docrine et histoire*, ed. M. VILLER et al. (Paris 1932–) 1:500–529. W. M. RANKIN and ST. GEORGE STOCK,

Encyclopedia of Religion and Ethics, ed. J. HASTINGS (Edinburgh 1908–27) 6:131–138. E. CENTINEO, *Enciclopedia filosofica* (Venice-Rome 1957) 1:168–169. E. BISER, *Lexikon für Theologie und Kirche*, ed. J. HOFER and K. RAHNER (Freiberg 1957–65) 4:363–364. J. DE VRIES and H. VAN OYEN, *Die Religion in Geschichte und Gegenwart* (Tübingen 1957–65) 2:1128–32. L. DUGAS, *L'Amitié antique* (2d ed. Paris 1914). P. PHILIPPE, *Le Rôle de l'amitié selon la doctrine de saint Thomas* (Rome 1937). A. ODDONE, *L'amicizia* (Milan 1937). M. NÉDONCELLE, *La Réciprocité des consciences* (Paris 1942). P. J. WADELL, *Friendship and the Moral Life* (Notre Dame, Ind. 1989). G. MEILAENDER, *Friendship, a Study in Theological Ethics* (Notre Dame, Ind. 1981).

[W. A. WALLACE]

FRIENDSHIP, PARTICULAR

Particular friendship is an exclusive association between two persons based upon emotional fascination. As such, it is a perversion of God's gift of good and wholesome friendship. In the very definition of particular friendship is found the distortion of truth that it is. It is an exclusive association and therefore detrimental to the universal charity due to all. It is a friendship based upon emotional fascination and motivated more by the selfish interests of the ''friends'' than the desire of each to promote the good of the other. Therefore, it does not deserve to be called FRIENDSHIP except in an extended sense of the term.

The danger of forming particular friendships is directly proportional to a person's emotional instability. Such an association exists most often between those who are emotionally insecure. Particular friendships are an expression of the human tendency to love and be loved, which in this case is applied wrongly. Such friendships can develop between those of the opposite sex, or those of the same sex.

The characteristics of particular friendship are: (1) Exclusiveness—all one's attention is focused on one person to the point that there is resentment of the intrusion of others. (2) Jealousy—because all attention is focused on one person, there is jealousy if that person has other friends. (3) Absorption of mind—the friends think of each other continually in much the same way that young lovers do. As a result, the freedom to pray, study, work, do one's duties, or be with others is hampered. (4) The tendency to manifest affection—because this type of friendship has all the marks of the relationship between young lovers, the friends feel more and more the desire to manifest affection. This they do by talking in a sentimental way and even by the physical expression of love. Because of this, it is obvious that particular friendship can easily lead to violations of chastity. This may not always happen, but even when it does not lead to this, the detrimental effects of particular friendship are numerous.

Avoidance of particular friendship and freeing oneself from it involve the use of means consistently recommended by spiritual writers. These are: (1) Conviction—the persons must be firmly convinced that such friendships are harmful and therefore must be avoided or eliminated. (2) Confidence—when emotion dominates a person, victory can seem impossible, but one must be convinced that victory is possible. (3) General self-discipline—just as an alcoholic cannot break his habit without a general practice of self-discipline, so neither can one break a particular friendship without a similar self-discipline. (4) Physical separation—one must carefully avoid all unnecessary association with this kind of ''friend,'' and when association is necessary, must be careful to control the emotional response that accompanies it. (5) Mental separation—one must avoid thinking about the other person as much as possible, for this only feeds the flame of emotional involvement. (6) Cultivation of other interests—such persons cannot succeed in a vacuum, as it were, but must substitute for the object sacrificed an interest in the right things. Only in this way is it possible to avoid or remedy a grave defect.

To see the so-called particular friendship for the perversion that it is, one need only compare it with the good and healthy friendship in which the friends grow mutually in goodness and the pursuit of higher ideals.

See Also: FRIENDSHIP.

Bibliography: G. A. KELLY, *Guidance for Religious* (Westminster, Md. 1956) 55–81. A. TANQUEREY, *The Spiritual Life* (Westminster, Md. 1945).

[C. BROWNING]

FRIENDSHIP HOUSE

A movement of Catholic lay men and women seeking to relate the Church to interracial justice, the poor and marginalized; founded in Toronto, Canada, in 1930 and in New York City in 1938. In 1938 Catherine DE HUECK DOHERTY, a Russian immigrant, took up residence and opened a store-front office and community center in Harlem; she attracted a group of young men and women to live and work with her there. The center became a source of emergency assistance for the poor, a recreational place for children, a meeting place to discuss and disseminate the Church's social doctrine, and a place where the liturgy became a daily way of life for the laity. Located as it was in the African-American ghetto, it was one of the pioneer efforts to arouse the consciences of Americans, particularly Catholic Americans, to the sinfulness of racial discrimination and segregation. Friendship House identified itself with the segregated and the insecure, not only through publications, demonstrations, and lectures, but by eschewing support from Church or community funds and relying upon voluntary contributions from interested clergy and laity. These contributions, though generous, were never sufficient to remove real poverty from the doors and tables of Friendship House workers.

By the early 1950s Friendship Houses had been established with the approval of local ordinaries in New York, Chicago, Washington, D.C., Shreveport, La., and Portland, Ore. The directors of each house, together with the chaplains, formed a national board to guide the activities and expansion of the movement. Meanwhile, Catherine de Hueck, who had married the journalist Eddie Doherty, returned to Canada in 1947, and began another apostolic effort known as Madonna House Apostolate. The Friendship House movement suffered one defeat in 1955 when the ordinary of the diocese asked that the Shreveport house be closed, after it had become the victim of a virulent attack by racists.

As the racial climate in the U.S. changed, so did Friendship House programs. Emphasis was redirected from social welfare and settlement house work, to social justice and equal opportunity; from Friendship House as a way of life, to the common vocation of all Christians to humanize the social order; from staff workers living a common life in poverty and under obedience, to staff people living a layman's life frugally and responsibly on a modest salary. By 1960 Friendship House had become a national movement for interracial justice with headquarters in Chicago; houses in all other centers had closed. The principal activities became: (1) social action, including joint efforts with civic and religious bodies to promote passage of national and state legislation in such areas as civil rights, employment, and housing; (2) publication of a monthly magazine (*Harlem Friendship House News* from 1941 to 1948, *The Catholic Interracialist* from 1949 to 1955, and *Community Magazine* from 1955 to 1983), and pamphlets on race relations and interracial justice; and (3) weekend retreats and conferences at Childerly Farm near Chicago where sisters, priests, seminarians, and lay men and women are brought together for prayer, study, and planning directed toward interracial justice and love.

In the face of declining participation and resources in the 1990s, the movement struggled to maintain its outreach programs. The day shelter for the poor and homeless in Chicago, which was opened in 1983, was finally closed at the end of March 2000. The movement vacated its historic premises on Division Street on Chicago.

Bibliography: C. DE HUECK, *Friendship House* (New York 1946).

[D. M. CANTWELL/EDS.]

FRIENDSHIP WITH GOD

That the just are in some sense friends of God is a dogma of faith defined by the Council of Trent (Denzinger, *Enchiridion symbolorum* [32d ed. Freiburg 1963] 1528, cf. 1535).

Scripture and the Fathers. Those individuals who are truly wise in the Old Testament sense, that is, those who perfectly observe God's law, are said to be the friends of God: ''For to men she [Wisdom] is an unfailing treasure; those who gain this treasure win the friendship of God, to whom the gifts they have from discipline commend them'' (Wis 7.14). ''And she, who is one, can do all things, and renews everything while herself perduring; and passing into holy souls from age to age, she produces friends of God and prophets'' (Wis 7.27). Accordingly, ABRAHAM (Jdt 8.22; cf. Jas 2.23) and MOSES (Ex 33.12) are called friends of God. In the New Testament Jesus calls His Disciples friends: ''You are my friends if you do the things I command you. No longer do I call you servants, because the servant does not know what his master does. But I have called you friends, because all things that I have heard from my Father I have made known to you'' (Jn 15.14–15; cf. Lk 12.4).

The Fathers of the Church frequently point to Abraham and Moses as men who fulfilled God's will and so showed themselves to be friends of God. But they also extend the title to all Christians. Thus St. Hilary writes: ''And indeed we know that Abraham was a friend to God. And the Law said that Moses was a friend to God. But the Gospels show that now many are friends of God . . .'' (*In ps.* 138, 38; *Patrologia Latina* 9:812). And St. Ambrose says: ''. . . charity makes a man a friend of God. Hence Christ says: 'But I call you friends''' (*Ep.* 37.23; *Patrologia Latina* 16:1090). Unlike the Hebrews, who considered FRIENDSHIP with God as the reward of a holy life, the Christian Fathers see it as a gratuitous election. Thus, St. Gregory the Great writes: ''O how great is the mercy of our Creator! We are unworthy servants and are called friends. How great is the dignity of men to be friends of God'' (*Hom. in evang.* 2.27.4; *Patrologia Latina* 76:1206). And St. Cyril of Alexandria writes: ''What greater or more honorable thing can be said than to be called and to be a friend of Christ. For observe how much this dignity exceeds the bounds of human nature. For all things serve the Creator . . . nor is there any created thing which is not subjected to Him by the yoke of servitude . . . the Lord has raised the saints who keep His commandments to a superatural glory . . .'' [*In Joan. evang.* 10 (Jn 15.14), *Patrologia Graeca* 74:384; cf. Irenaeus, *Adv. haer.* 4.13.4, *Patrologia Graeca* 7:1009; Clement of Alexandria, *Strom.* 7.10, *Patrologia Graeca* 9:481; Athanasius, *In ps.*

138.17, *Patrologia Graeca* 27:534; Augustine, *In ps.* 131.6, *Patrologia Latina* 37:1718–19; *In evang. Ioh.* 85, *Patrologia Latina* 35:1848–50].

Both Sacred Scripture and the Fathers describe the just man's relationship with God in other terms, which imply a state of friendship. St. Paul says that Christ has broken down the enmity and has established peace between God and men, who have become ''now no longer strangers and foreigners, but . . . citizens with the saints and members of God's household (οἰκεῖοι)'' (Eph 2.14–20). The image of spiritual nuptials is used as well to describe the relationship between God and His Church. Thus St. Paul writes to the Corinthians: ''I betrothed you to one spouse, that I might present you a chaste virgin to Christ'' (2 Cor 11.2; cf. Eph 5.22–32). The Fathers apply this symbol to the union between God and individual just souls. Basil of Ancyra, for instance, illustrates ''the union of the rational soul with the divine Word by the union of marriage'' (*De virginitate* 50; *Patrologia Graeca* 30:767). And St. Gregory of Nyssa interprets the Song of Songs as signifying a union of individual souls with God through CHARITY (*In cant.* 1.1, *Patrologia Graeca* 44:763; cf. 6, *ibid.* 44:891). Other titles also employed by Scripture and the Fathers, such as ''SONS OF GOD'' and ''brothers of Christ,'' imply a state of friendship.

Explanation of Theologians. In explaining the just man's friendship with God, theologians commonly have accepted the doctrine of St. Thomas Aquinas (*In 3 sent.* 27.1; *C. gent.* 4.19; *In Dion. de div. nom.* 4.9; *Summa Theologiae* 1a2ae, 26.4; 65.5; and especially 2a2ae, 23.1). Their notion of friendship is borrowed from Aristotle, who derived it from reflection on the common experience of human friendship (*Eth. Nic.* 8.1–8). Friendship supposes a similarity of nature and a community of life and interests, and consists in a stable, mutually known, and reciprocal love of benevolence. Although Aristotle had excluded the possibility of friendship between the gods and men for the reason that there is no similarity or common bond between them, Catholic theologians deny the validity of his argument in the SUPERNATURAL order: Thanks to the gifts of GRACE, the just man has been assimilated to God in a new, supernatural way, and through FAITH and the gifts of the Holy Spirit (*see* HOLY SPIRIT, GIFTS OF) he can come to an imperfect but adequate knowledge of God, who communicates to him through revelation and to whom he can speak in PRAYER. Moreover, between God and man there exists a reciprocal love of benevolence. God loves the goodness of the just man inasmuch as it is a participation of His own divine goodness, and He wills good to man for man's own advantage; and the just man, in turn, loves God above all else for His own sake, thanks to the supernatural virtue of charity. What is more, this selfless love is mutually known, since God can read man's heart, and the just man knows God's love for him by faith and his own love for God by the testimony of a good conscience. And it is stable, not only on the part of God, as is evident, but also on the part of man, since through charity he chooses God as the ultimate end of his whole life and being. Accordingly, in an analogous, but nonetheless true and proper, sense the just man is a friend of God.

All Catholic theologians agree that friendship with God is in some way rooted in the gifts of sanctifying grace. The most common explanation is that friendship with God flows as a formal effect from the very nature of grace, although Lessius, Duns Scotus, and Ripalda hold that this state of friendship arises from grace only because of some extrinsic element, such as the free ordination, disposition, or promise of God.

Suárez and some modern theologians who follow him see the just man's friendship with God as the precise reason under which the indwelling of the Holy Spirit (*see* INDWELLING, DIVINE) is to be understood. According to this theory, friendship demands the presence of the friend; hence, even if God were not already present by His immensity, He would come to be present with His friends because of His love for them. Therefore, they reason, the inhabitation of the Blessed Trinity in the soul of the just man consists precisely in this new presence of God as friend.

Ascetical Literature. Spiritual writers from the twelfth to the fifteenth centuries, such as Tauler, Suso, and the author of the *IMITATION OF CHRIST*, also speak of man's friendship with God. But their principal concern is not with friendship as the new relationship between God and man that is established by grace, but rather with man's growth in the spiritual life through the development and perfection of his friendship with Jesus, God incarnate. It is in this tradition that the author of the *Imitation* writes: ''Many are His visits to the man of inward life. With such a one He holds delightful converse, greeting him with sweet comfort, much peace, and an intimacy astonishing beyond measure. Come then, faithful soul, prepare your heart for this your Spouse, so that He may vouchsafe to come to you and dwell within you'' (2.1.1–2). ''Love Him, and keep Him for your friend, who, when all go away, will not forsake you, nor suffer you to perish finally'' (2.7.1; cf. 2.8.3). St. Ignatius Loyola, St. Teresa of Avila, and St. John of the Cross, through St. Francis de Sales and other modern writers after him down to St. Thérèse de Lisieux underline the just man's opportunity and responsibility to grow in God's friendship: ''It is a horrible irreverence to Him who with so much love and sweetness invites us to perfection to say, 'I do not want to be holy, or perfect, or to have a greater share in your friendship, or to follow the counsels you give me to advance in it''' (St. Francis de Sales, *On the Love of God* 8.8; cf. 2.22; 3.1–3; 8.9).

Bibliography: R. EGENTER, *Lexikon für Theologie und Kirche,* 10 v. (2d new ed. Freiburg 1957–65) 4:1104–06. E. DUBLANCHY, *Dictionnaire de théologie catholique,* 15 v. (Paris 1903–50) 2.2:2225–26. M. FLICK, *De gratia Christi* (Rome 1962) 342–429. N. D. PHILIPPE, *Le Mystère de l'amitié divine* (Paris 1949). L. M. BOND, ''A Comparison between Human and Divine Friendship,'' *Thomist* 3 (1941) 54–94. E. PETERSON, ''Der Gottesfreund,'' *Zeitschrift für Kirchengeschicte* 42 (1923) 161–202.

[J. F. DEDEK]

FRIGIDIAN OF LUCCA, ST.

Bishop; d. Lucca, Italy, *c.* 588. The chief source of information on his life is a vita (in manuscripts no earlier than the 11th century) claiming that he was of Irish origin and that he settled as a hermit in Italy. His reputation for sanctity caused him to be chosen bishop of Lucca. His cult spread through Tuscany into other regions of Italy and to Corsica, and his relics, miraculously discovered in the eighth century, are preserved in the church dedicated to his memory at Lucca. Recent scholars reject the legendary chronology and nationality, and one even puts him as far back as the third century. He should not be confused with another Irish traveler in Italy, St. FINNIAN of Moville.

Feast: March 18; March 20 (Ireland).

Bibliography: J. F. KENNEY, *The Sources for the Early History of Ireland:* v.1, *Ecclesiastical* (New York 1929) 1:184–185, 391. *Vita Sancti Fridiani,* critical edition, ed. G. ZACCAGNINI (Lucca 1989). A. M. TOMMASINI, *Irish Saints in Italy,* tr. J. F. SCANLAN (London 1937) 363–377. A. PEDEMONTE, ''S. Frediano,'' *Bollettino storico Lucchese* 9 (1937) 3–32; ''L'Antico catalogo dei vescovi di Lucca,'' *ibid.* 10 (1938) No. 2. J. HENNIG, ''A Note on the Traditions of St. Frediano and St. Silao of Lucca,'' *Mediaeval Studies* 13 (1951) 234–242. A. BUTLER, *The Lives of the Saints,* ed. H. THURSTON and D. ATTWATER, 4 v. (New York 1956) 1:626–627.

[C. MCGRATH]

FRIGOLET, MONASTERY OF

Premonstratensian abbey, Graveson, near Tarascon, France; Diocese of Aix, former Diocese of Avignon (patron, St. Michael). Founded as a cell of the Benedictine Abbey of MONTMAJOUR in 962, it later became a priory of CANONS REGULAR OF ST. AUGUSTINE who preserved there the old chapel of Notre-Dame du Bon-Remède. HIERONYMITES and Discalced AUGUSTINIANS served Frigolet successively, from 1647, until the monastery was suppressed in 1790. The buildings were preserved and, in 1858, a former Trappist, Edmond Boulbon, restored Frigolet as a house of the primitive observance of the PREMONSTRATENSIANS. In 1869 it became an abbey, and a sumptuous church and extensive new buildings were erected. After a short period of prosperity, the community was twice expelled (1880 and 1903). Its first refuge was Storrington, Sussex, England; its second, Leffe, Belgium.

Bibliography: N. BACKMUND, *Monasticon Praemonstratense,* 3 v. (Straubing 1949–56) 3:337–340. R. GAZEAU, *Catholicisme. Hier, aujourd'hui et demain,* ed. G. JACQUEMET (Paris 1947–) 4:1647–48.

[N. BACKMUND]

FRINS, VICTOR

Jesuit theologian and author; b. Aachen, Germany, April 17, 1840; d. Bonn, April 13, 1912. He entered the Society of Jesus in 1859, and studied at Münster and Maria Laach. After 1872 he taught philosophy and theology at Regensburg; scripture, and moral theology, and canon law at Ditton Hall near Liverpool; and scholastic theology at St. Bueno's, St. Asaph, Wales. He contributed to several periodicals, especially to *Stimmen aus Maria-Laach,* but is better known for his theological works: *Doctrina S. Thomae Aquinatis de cooperatione Dei* (Paris 1893), *De actibus humanis ontologice et psychologice consideratis* (Freiburg im Breisgau 1897), *De actibus humanis moroliter consideratis* (*ibid.* 1904), and *De formanda conscientia* (*ibid.* 1911).

Frins, well known in theological circles as a speculative and creative thinker, was an ardent disciple of Juan de LUGO, the Spanish cardinal and theologian of the 17th century.

Bibliography: L. KOCH, *Jesuiten-Lexikon* (Leiden 1962) 620.

[J. G. BISCHOFF]

FRITZ, SAMUEL

Missionary in the Amazon region; b. Trautenau, Bohemia, June 6, 1651; d. La Laguna, Amazon basin, 1724 or 1725. He entered the Society of Jesus on Oct. 28, 1673, and went to Ecuador in 1684. He made his profession on Aug. 15, 1687; for two years previously he had been at the mission on the Maranhão River, among the Omaguas, of the Tupí linguistic group, at 4° S. 74° W., in the Amazon basin. He eventually founded 38 settlements between the Napo and Negro Rivers and on islands of the Amazon. In 1688 he extended his activities to the Yarimaguas. Between 1690 and 1693 he served as a diplomat to the Portuguese, defending the thesis that the dividing line between the Portuguese and Spanish territories passed close to the Grão Pará, with Spain holding the lands west of that line. To this end he prepared a detailed and precise map that was influential with the Council of Indies. From 1704 to 1712 he was superior of the mission. As a missiologist, he left specific information and concrete pastoral suggestions in his diary. As a missionary, he was a valiant defender of his Indians against Brazilian incursions. As a geographer, he produced a map that even today is a primary source for the study of 17th-century geopolitics.

Bibliography: J. JOUANEN, *Historia de la Compañía de Jesús en la antigua provincia de Quito*, 1570–1774 [*i.e.* 1773] 2 v. (Quito 1941–43). J. DE VELASCO, *Historia moderna del Reyno de Quito y crónica de la provincia de la Compañía de Jesús del mismo Reyno,* ed. R. REYES Y REYES (Quito 1941–). J. CHANTRE Y HERRERA, *Historia de las misiones de la Compañía de Jesús en el Marañón Español,* ed. A. E. MERA (Madrid 1901).

[A. DE EGAÑA]

FRÖBEL, FRIEDRICH WILHELM

Educator and founder of the kindergarten system; b. Oberweissbach, Thuringia, April 21, 1782; d. Marienthal, June 21, 1852. Fröbel, son of a Lutheran pastor and motherless from infancy, was neglected in childhood and received little formal education. Apprenticed to a forester at 15, he was impressed by the beauty around him and with the idea of the oneness of nature. In 1800 he spent a short time at the University of Jena, and in 1805 he went to Frankfurt to study architecture. While there, Dr. Anton Gruner, master of the model school, persuaded him to teach in his school, which he conducted along Pestalozzian lines. Fröbel accepted and, during that year, spent two weeks in J. H. PESTALOZZI's school at Yverdon. Upon his return to Frankfurt he undertook a systematic study of Pestalozzianism under Gruner's guidance and spent two years (1808–10) at Yverdon studying the methods of the Swiss reformer. In 1811 he studied at Göttingen; in 1813 he entered military service; and in 1814 he went to Berlin to continue his studies. In 1816, with Heinrich Langenthal and Wilhelm Mittendorf, he organized an experimental school at Keilhau, and in 1826 published his most important work, *The Education of Man.* In 1835 the Swiss government invited him to superintend a public orphanage and organize courses for the training of teachers. He returned to Germany in 1837 and, at Blankenburg, established a school for small children to which, in 1840, he attached the name ''kindergarten.'' In 1843 he published *Mother Play and Nursery Songs* and from 1844 until his death devoted his time and talent to advancing the kindergarten idea in Germany and to training girls as kindergarten teachers.

Cloisters at St. Michel de Frigolet Abbey, Arles, France. (©Gail Mooney/CORBIS)

The aim of education, according to Fröbel, is the development of the child's inborn capacities and powers in accord with his nature, and the redirection of undesirable native impulses. Two basic principles, he maintained, underlie this aim: (1) the law of unity, for ''all things live and have their being in and through the Divine Unity, in and through God,'' which, applied to practical situations, involves the unity of knowing, feeling, and doing, as well as child development; and (2) symbolism, which shows itself in his deep interest in analogies between physical and spiritual phenomena.

Fröbel sums up his general method by the term ''self-activity,'' or the process of development from within by which the child expresses his impulses and thoughts and renders ''the inner, outer,'' as Fröbel terms it. Education, which, he held, should begin at birth, is most effective in a miniature community where children cooperate in active social participation induced by games and similar activities. Among his permanent contributions are the introduction into the curriculum of language, drawing, rhythm, and nature study based on observation of living things; the use of play materials; the simultaneous development of language, gesture, and constructive work; and his promotion of the kindergarten idea that was spread throughout Europe mainly through the efforts of his devoted pupil, the Baroness Bertha von Marenholtz Bülow, and reached the U.S. during the 1850s.

Bibliography: H. C. BOWEN, *Froebel and Education through Self-Activity* (New York 1893). F. P. GRAVES, *Great Educators of Three Centuries* (New York 1912). F. V. N. PAINTER, *Great Pedagogical Essays* (New York 1905). R. H. QUICK, *Essays on Educational Reformers* (new ed. New York 1896).

[W. G. WIXTED]

FROBEN, JOHANN

Printer and publisher; b. 1460?; d. 1527. Of Basel, Switzerland, he was a disciple of Johann AMERBACH, noted printer of humanistic works. From 1514 to his death, Froben was ERASMUS's major publisher, issuing many works in Scripture, patristics, and the classics. In 1491 he produced the first Latin Bible in small type and in 1516 issued the *editio princeps* of Erasmus's Greek New Testament; this, revised in subsequent editions before Erasmus's death, had an epochmaking influence in the early days of the REFORMATION. Hans Holbein (the younger) was associated with him for four years as a designer of borders and decorative material. Under his son Hieronymus and grandson Ambrosius, the firm continued until the end of the 16th century.

[E. P. WILLGING]

FROBERGER, JOHANN JAKOB

Internationally famous 17th-century composer and keyboard virtuoso; b. Stuttgart, Germany, May 19, 1616; d. Héricourt (Haute-Saône), France, May 6 or 7, 1667. Froberger was one of 11 children born to the conductor of the Protestant court chapel at Stuttgart. His brothers were active in this chapel, and his first musical training was undoubtedly a family affair. His professional training was completed under FRESCOBALDI in Rome (1637–41), and it is thought that his conversion to Catholicism occurred during this interval. At age 25 Froberger was appointed court organist in Vienna; he continued in this position and in other royal chapels until 1657, thus providing one of the chief channels through which Italian and French idioms passed into Germany. His final years were spent under the patronage of dowager Duchess Sibylla of Württemberg. Extant sources indicate that his creative activity was in large part confined to composition for keyboard instruments. Like Frescobaldi, he composed multisectional canzonas, ricercars, capriccios, and fantasias, in which each section presents the main theme in a particular shape; he applied this technique to toccatas as well. The pattern of his suites (allemande, courante, sarabande) is that of French composers, and the texture of these dances is regarded as a transformation of French lute technique. Froberger's music is a particularly rewarding field for study of the development of tonal organization in the 17th century.

Bibliography: *Gesammelte Ausgabe,* ed. L. G. ADLER (*Denkmäler der Tonkunst in Österreich* [1893– ; repr. Graz 1959–] 8, 13, 21). M. REIMANN, *Die Musik in Geschichte und Gegenwart,* ed. F. BLUME (Kassel-Basel 1949–) 4:982–993. G. FROTSCHER, *Geschichte des Orgelspiels und der Orgelkomposition,* 2 v. (2d ed. Berlin 1959). A. PIRRO, *Les Clavecinistes* (Paris 1924). W. APEL, *Masters of the Keyboard* (Cambridge, Mass. 1947). M. F. BUKOFZER, *Music in the Baroque Era* (New York 1947). G. J. BUELOW, "Johann Jacob Froberger," in *The New Grove Dictionary of Music and Musicians,* ed. S. SADIE, v. 6 (New York 1980) 858–862. F. LESURE, ed. *J. J. Froberger: Musicien Européen* (Montbéliard, France 1998). T. NORMAN, "Performance Practice of the Keyboard Music of Johann Jakob Froberger" (Ph.D. diss. Monash University 1991). D. M. RANDEL, ed., *The Harvard Biographical Dictionary of Music* (Cambridge, Mass. 1996) 285–286. H. SIEDENTOPF, *Johann Jakob Froberger: Leben und Werk* (Stuttgart 1977). N. SLONIMSKY, ed., *Baker's Biographical Dictionary of Musicians* (8th ed. New York 1992) 580.

[D. BEIKMAN]

FRÖBES, JOSEPH

Philosopher, psychologist, and author; b. Betzdorf, Germany, Aug. 26, 1866; d. Cologne, March 24, 1947. After brief public education, Fröbes entered a Catholic grammar school near Darmstadt; when this was suppressed by the Kulturkampf, he went to Stella Matutina, a Jesuit boarding school in Austria (1877–82). At age 16 he entered the Society of Jesus. He completed his philosophical studies in 1889, and spent five years teaching mathematics, physics, and chemistry; then he studied theology (1894–99), was ordained (1900), and was assigned to teach philosophy. Having been convinced that the teaching of psychology demanded revision, he undertook intensive training in experimental psychology under G. E. Müller at Göttingen (1902–04) and attended the lectures of Wilhelm Wundt at Leipzig. Fröbes then became professor of philosophy and founded a psychological laboratory at Ignatius College, a Jesuit house of studies in Holland. He taught there for more than 20 years, encouraging his students, notably, Johannes Lindworsky, to pursue scientific psychology. In Germany, Fröbes was *the* Catholic pioneer of experimental psychology. As the first to recognize the independence of experimental psychology from philosophical psychology, he wrote several textbooks in which the respective domains of these two fields were clearly distinguished.

Bibliography: J. FRÖBES, *Lehrbuch der experimentellen Psychologie,* 2 v. (3d ed. Freiburg 1923–29); *Psychologia speculativa in usum scholarum,* 2 v. (Freiburg 1927); *Brevior cursus psychologiae speculativae* (Paris 1933); *Compendium psychologiae experimentalis* (rev. ed. Rome 1948); *Tractatus logicae formalis* (Rome 1940). Literature. L. KOCH, *Jesuiten-Lexikon* (Louvain-Heverlee 1962) C. A. MURCHISON, ed., *A History of Psychology in Autobiography,* v. 3 (Worcester, Mass. 1934) 121–152. H. MISIAK and V. M. STAUDT, *Catholics in Psychology* (New York 1954).

[V. S. SEXTON]

FRODOBERT, ST.

Monk, founder of Montier-la-Celle; b. Troyes, 595; d. Dec. 31, 673. After being educated at the cathedral school and admitted as a cleric of the church of Troyes, he became a monk in LUXEUIL, returning to Troyes several years later to enter the bishop's service. Frodobert, wanting to satisfy his love of silence and humility, asked for and obtained from King Clovis II and BATHILDIS the Île Germanique, a marshy area on the outskirts of Troyes. There he founded a monastery (*c.* 650) dedicated to St. Peter. A charter of Clothar III and Bathildis (657) confirmed the gift. Frodobert's cult was recognized when, at the request of Abbot Bodo, Bishop Ottulph exhumed Frodobert's relics in 872 from the magnificent tomb to which they had been transferred by Abbot Bobinus in 790. Ottulph changed his feast from January1 to 8.

Bibliography: Sources. ADSO, *Vita S. Frodoberti, Patrologia Latina,* ed. J. P. MIGNE, 217 v. (Paris 1878–90) 137: 599–620. N. CAMUSAT, *Promptuarium sacrarum antiquitatum Tricassinae dioecesis* (Troyes 1610). *Gallia Christiana* 12:538–541. C. LALORE, *Cartulaire de Montier-la-Celle,* v.6 of *Collection des principaux cartulaires du diocèse de Troyes,* 7 v. (Paris 1875–90). **Literature.** A. È. PRÉVOST, *Le Diocèse de Troyes, histoire et documents,* 3 v. (Dijon 1923–26) v.1.

[P. COUSIN]

FROHSCHAMMER, JAKOB

Idealist philosopher; b. Illkhofen, Germany, Jan. 6, 1821; d. Bad Kreuth, Germany, April 14, 1893. He was ordained in 1847 and spent most of his life as a professor of philosophy at the University of Munich. His peculiar form of idealism is based on the conception of imagination, *phantasie,* as the basic principle of reality. In God this imagination is conscious and subjective and transcends the universe, which is the objective and unconscious manifestation of divine imagination. It is a creative and formative power governing the evolution of the universe and in man becomes individual and conscious as the principle of psychic life. Frohschammer was condemned specifically for attempting to bring within the scope of natural reason the supernatural mysteries of faith, and for asserting the absolute independence of philosophy from the authority of the Church (letter of Pius IX, *Gravissimas Inter,* Dec. 11, 1862). His failure to retract three of his works led to his suspension in 1862 (*see* SEMIRATIONALISM). His principal works are: *Über den Ursprung der menschlichen Seelen* (Munich 1854); *Einleitung in die Philosophie* (Munich 1858); *Die Phantasie als Grundprinzip des Weltprozesses* (Munich 1877).

Bibliography: J. G. WÜCHNER, *Frohschammer's Stellung zum Theismus* (Paderborn 1913). *Philosophen-Lexikon,* ed. W. ZIEGENFUSS, 2 v. (Berlin 1949) 1:369–370. A. W. ZIEGLER, *Dictionnaire de théologie catholique,* ed. A. VACANT, 15 v. (Paris 1903–50; Tables générales 1951–) 16.2:1753–54. J. HANSLMEIER, *Lexikon für Theologie und Kirche,* ed. J. HOFER and K. RAHNER, 10 v. (2d, new ed. Freiburg 1957–65).

[J. C. BUCKLEY]

FROILÁN, ST.

Patron and bishop of León; b. Lugo, Spain, 832; d. León, 905. With St. ATTILANUS he combined the life of a hermit in the mountains of Galicia with that of a preacher. In Viseu, at popular request, he founded a flourishing monastery of 300 confessors. Alfonso III of Oviedo authorized him to build large monasteries on his southern frontier to further repopulation. Two such monasteries were founded by 900, when Froilán, against his will, was made bishop of León. In his last years he had the gift of prophecy. His religious practices resemble somewhat those of the Mozarabs at this time. He was included in the Roman martyrology in 1724.

Feast: Oct. 3.

Bibliography: H. FLÓREZ, *España sagrada,* 54 v. (Madrid 1747–1957) 34:422–425. A. LAMBERT, *Dictionnaire d'histoire et de géographie ecclésiastiques,* ed. A. BAUDRILLART (Paris 1912–) 5:169–170. J. GONZÁLEZ, *San Froilán de León* (León 1946).

[E. P. COLBERT]

FROUDE, RICHARD HURRELL

A leader of the OXFORD MOVEMENT; b. Dartington, England, March 25, 1803; d. Dartington, Feb. 28, 1836. He was the eldest son of Robert Hurrell Froude, a vicar who became archdeacon of Totnes, and the brother of James Anthony Froude, a noted historian. He attended Oriel College, Oxford, where he was elected fellow (1826) and was ordained an Anglican priest (1829). At Oxford he came under the influence of John KEBLE, who converted him to HIGH CHURCH views. Froude was instrumental in bringing Keble and John Henry NEWMAN together, thus laying the foundations for the Oxford Movement. Froude contributed three tracts to the *Tracts for the Times* and several poems to the *Lyra Apostolica* (1836), but illness cut short his activities. The posthumous publication of his private papers, *Remains* (1838–39), revealed how far he had advanced toward a complete acceptance of Catholicism. Although he advocated clerical celibacy, was devoted to the Blessed Virgin and the saints, and was sharply critical of the Protestant Reformation, he still rejected Romanism at the time of his death.

Bibliography: *Remains of the Late Reverend Richard Hurrell Froude,* ed. J. H. NEWMAN and J. KEBLE, 2 v. in 4 (London 1838–39). L. I. GUINEY, *Hurrell Froude* (London 1904).

[T. S. BOKENKOTTER]

FRUCTUOSUS OF BRAGA, ST.

Monastic founder and archbishop of Braga, Portugal; d. San Salvador de Montelios, Spain, April 16, 665. Fructuosus, of a noble family, studied under Bishop Conantius of Palencia, then retired into a solitude near Astorga, Spain, where he founded the monastery of Complutum whence six further foundations were begun in Galicia and Baetica. He likewise organized double MONASTERIES. He was consecrated bishop and abbot of Dumium, and was named archbishop of Braga by the Tenth Council of Toledo (656). He devoted himself in particular to the spread of monasticism, writing a *Regula monachorum* and a *Regula communis* that were observed in the monasteries of Galicia and Portugal until the 11th century. His *Pactum,* or act of religious profession, shows the strong influence of Germanic law. A letter to BRAULIO of Saragossa and another to King Receswinth have been preserved. His life was written by the monk Valerius; in 1102 his relics were transported to Compostela, where they continue to repose in the church of S. Jerónimo de Real.

Feast: April 16.

Bibliography: *Opera omnia, Patrologia Latina,* ed. J. P. MIGNE, 217 v. (Paris 1878–90) 87:1087–1131; *Epistola ad Braulionen, Patrologia Latina,* ed. J. P. MIGNE, 217 v. (Paris 1878–90) 80:690–692. M. C. DÍAZ Y DÍAZ, *La vida de San Fructuoso de Braga* (Braga 1974). *San Fructuoso y su tiempo,* ed. F. A. DIEZ GONZÁLEZ et al. (León 1966). I. HERWEGEN, *Das Pactum des hl. Fruktuosus von Braga* (Amsterdam 1965). VALERIUS, *Vita,* tr. F. C. NOCK (Washington 1946). J. PÉREZ DE URBEL, *Los monjes españoles en la edad media,* 2 v. (Madrid 1933–34). G. BARDY, *Catholicisme* 4:1655–56.

[L. VEREECKE]

FRUCTUOSUS OF TARRAGONA, ST.

Bishop and martyr; d. 259. On being summoned before Aemilianus, Roman Governor of Tarragona, who was enforcing the second edict of the Emperors Valerian and Gallienus against the Christians, he did not hesitate to state that he was a bishop, and he and his two deacons, Augurius and Eulogius, steadfastly refused to offer pagan sacrifice. They were then condemned to be burned alive in the amphitheater of Tarragona. The *Acta SS. Fructuosi, Augurii et Eulogii,* the earliest documents of the kind for Spain, describe the trial and death of the martyrs in a simple and realistic manner. They have an authentic character, as they are clearly based on the official report filed in the archives of the Roman governor. The veneration of Fructuosus and his deacons began immediately, and their cult spread to Africa. In his Sermon 273, *In natali martyrum Fructuosi episcopi, Augurii et Eulogii diaconorum,* St. AUGUSTINE relates that their *Acta* were read also in the Church at Hippo, and Prudentius employed them as source material for his *Peristephanon* 6. In the Middle Ages St. Fructuosus of Tarragona was often confused with St. FRUCTUOSUS OF BRAGA (d. 665).

Feast: Jan. 21.

Bibliography: *Acta Sanctorum* Jan. 2:239–341. M. M. ESTRADE, *Sant Fructuós, bisbe de Tarragona i màrtir* (Barcelona 1960). T. RUINART, *Acta Primorum Martyrum* (Paris 1689) 220–223. P. FRANCHI DE' CAVALIERI, *Note agiografiche* 8 (*Studi e testi* 65; 1935) 127–194. G. LAZZATI, *Gli sviluppi della letteratura sui martiri nei primi quattro secoli* (Turin 1956). Z. GARCÍA VILLADA, *Historia eclesiástica de España,* 3 v. in 5 (Madrid 1929–36) 1:257–262. H. H. WARD, *A Dictionary of Christian Biography,* ed. W. SMITH and H. WACE, (London 1877–87) 2:571–572.

[M. R. P. MCGUIRE]

FRUMENTIUS, ST.

Venerated as the fourth-century apostle who converted Ethiopia to Christianity; life dates uncertain. The main Western source is RUFINUS OF AQUILEIA (*Histoire Ecclesiastique* 1.9). Meropius, a philosopher of Tyre, and his two young disciples, Frumentius and Aedesius, were en route to India when their ship was attacked by natives in an African harbor. The two youths were captured and kept as slaves in the personal service of the local king, after whose death Frumentius was appointed civil administrator by the queen regent; he then began his apostolate, giving full freedom of cult to Christian merchants from the Roman Empire.

When the prince and heir came of age, his mentor Aedesius returned to Tyre, where in 403 he met Rufinus. At the same time, Frumentius went to Alexandria, where St. ATHANASIUS consecrated him bishop for the region of his apostolate, to which he returned. Constantius II, who favored Arianism, wrote *c.* 356 asking the rulers of Aksum, the capital of Ethiopia, to expel Frumentius as a follower of the orthodox Athanasius. The Greek text of the letter, included in Athanasius's *Apology* (*Patrologia Graeca,* ed. J. P. Migne 25:656–657), is clear evidence that the events narrated about Frumentius by Rufinus, who does not name the country, took place in Ethiopia. Frumentius is known in Ethiopia as Ferēmenatos and as Kasātē Berhān (Revealer of the Light). His consecration by Athanasius is the historical link between the Ethiopian Church and the Coptic Patriarchate of Alexandria. Frumentius, a Syrian, probably intentionally avoided being consecrated by his own patriarch of Antioch, then favorable to Arianism.

Feast: Oct. 27; Aug. 1 (Hamlē); Aug. 26 (Ethiopian Church).

Bibliography: I. GUIDI, ed. and tr., *Synaxaire Ethiopien, Patrologia orientalis,* ed. R. GRAFFIN and F. NAU 7:427–429. E. CERULLI, ''Punti di vista sulla storia di Etiopia,'' *Atti del Primo Convegno Internazionale di Studi Etiopici* (Rome 1960) 21–22.

[E. CERULLI]

FRUTOLF OF MICHELSBERG

Historian and musicologist; d. Abbey of Michelsberg, Bamberg, Germany, Jan. 17, 1103. Probably a priest before becoming a Benedictine, Frutolf taught in the Michelsberg monastic school and possibly held the office of prior. During the last four years of his life he composed his *Chronicon* (autograph MS Jena 19), a history of the world to 1101. This work was overshadowed by the plagiarized and tendentious version of Ekkehard of Aura (d. 1125), and its author was forgotten. Yet, in its original form it ranks as one of the most distinguished world histories written in the Middle Ages. In its composition Frutolf drew from a staggering wealth of historical sources in bringing the account to his day, and with chronological and critical insight he produced an accurate, comprehensive, and readable narrative. The *Chronicon* is especially notable for its objectivity in the period for which its author is a contemporary witness, citing in evidence papal documents, letters, and official acts. Frutolf is credited also with the *De officiis divinis* and with several musicological works, viz, *Breviarium de musica, Tonarius,* and possibly the *Rithmimachia,* in which he depended on the work of BOETHIUS, GUIDO OF AREZZO, and HERMANNUS CONTRACTUS.

Bibliography: FRUTOLF-EKKEHARD, *Chronicon,* ed. G. WAITZ, *Monumenta Germaniae Scriptores* (Berlin 1825–) 6:33–267. H. BRESSLAU, *Neues Archiv der Gesellschaft für ältere deutsche Geschichtskunde* 21 (1895) 197–234. M. MANITIUS, *Geschichte der lateinischen Literatur des Mittelalters,* 3 v. (Munich 1911–31) 3:350–361. W. WATTENBACH, *Deutschlands Geschichtsquellen im Mittelalter. Deutsche Kaiserzeit,* ed., R. HOLTZMANN, v1.1–4 (3d ed. Tübingen 1948; repr. of 2d ed. 1938–43) 1:491–506. J. SCHAMLE-OTT, ''Die Rezension C der Weltchronik Ekkehards,'' *Deutsches Archiv für Erforschung des Mittelalters* 12 (1956) 363–387.

[O. J. BLUM]

FRUTTUARIA, ABBEY OF

Former BENEDICTINE monastery, near Volpiano, in the Piedmont, Italy, about ten miles from Turin. It was founded in the early 11th century by WILLIAM OF SAINT-BÉNIGNE OF DIJON and his uncle, Count Arduin of Ivrea, who died at Fruttuaria in 1015. William, a native of Volpiano, had been a monk of CLUNY and Saint-Bénigne in Dijon. The abbey enjoyed Episcopal EXEMPTION from 1029 on. The life of its monks was so exemplary that they were requested—even beyond the dependent houses Fruttuaria founded—to reform the older monasteries all over north Italy, Corsica, and as far away as Lorraine. Thus, was founded the great *Congregatio Fructuariensis.* Meanwhile, the arts and scholarship flourished at the motherhouse. The abbey became excessively rich, to the point where it had its own mint. This led to decline and ruin, and in 1477 Pope Sixtus IV gave it into COMMENDATION. In 1617 the abbey was secularized and became a collegiate church. The Savoys, who had been commendatories since the time of Emanuele Filiberto in 1577, occupied the abbatial territories in 1710 with troops; after a long fight and excommunication (1741) of the commendatory abbots, Pope Benedict XIV had to recognize the state of affairs by abolishing the abbatial fief. During the Napoleonic era, French invaders did irreparable damage to Fruttuaria: the library was destroyed, the school suppressed, the goods and chattels sold, and the territory of the Abbot *Nullius* abolished (1803). After a brief restoration of the abbey, the Piedmont government finally suppressed it in 1848. A Salesian Institute was later built on the site. The *Chronicon Fructuariense* has not yet been edited.

Bibliography: L. H. COTTINEAU, *Répertoire topo-bibliographique des abbayes et prieurés* 1:1227–28. F. UGHELLI, *Italia sacra,* ed. N. COLETI, 10 v. in 9 (2d ed. Venice 1717–22) 4:1066–68. G. PENCO, *Storia del monachesimo in Italia* (Rome 1961) 206–208.

[I. DE PICCOLI]

FRY, ELIZABETH

Philanthropist, prison reformer; b. Norwich, England, May 21, 1780; d. Ramsgate, England, Oct. 12,

Elizabeth Fry.

1845. Her father, John Gurney, a Quaker merchant and banker, provided her with no formal education. Although she was at first attracted to deism, she was converted to primitive Quakerism by an American, William Savery, and by Joseph Fry, whom she married in 1800, and by whom she had 11 children. Influenced by the deaths of her father and father-in-law, Fry entered the Quaker ministry in 1811. Her work at Newgate prison, which was prompted by her two Quaker brothers-in-law and facilitated by her husband's business reputation, began in 1817. She developed a program of prison reform that included education, paid employment, association by day, solitude by night, rewards, and women warders for female prisoners. While promoting her reforms through extensive travels, correspondence, and published reports, she found time for other philanthropic activities, the most important of which was founding an order of nursing sisters. Two of her daughters edited her *Memoirs, with Extracts from Her Journals and Letters.*

See Also: FRIENDS, RELIGIOUS SOCIETY OF.

Bibliography: J. WHITNEY, *Elizabeth Fry* (Boston 1936). J. KENT, *Elizabeth Fry* (New York 1963).

[E. E. BEAUREGARD]

FUCHS, JOSEF

Moral theologian; b. Bergisch Gladbach, Germany, July 5, 1912. Fuchs entered the diocesan seminary of Cologne in 1931 and was ordained a priest of that diocese in 1937. He studied at the Gregorian University, receiving licentiates in philosophy and theology. In 1938 he entered the German province of the Society of Jesus and received an S.T.D. from the Jesuit theologate at Falkenberg, Holland, in 1940. After four years in parish work, he returned to study, receiving a Th.D. from the University of Münster in 1946. Having taught moral theology at St. George Hochschüle from 1947, Fuchs was appointed to the faculty of the Gregorian University in Rome in 1954. Although he reached the mandatory retirement age of seventy in 1982, he remained active, providing consultation to faculty and students of the Gregorian.

A prolific author, Fuchs's writings include 14 books, several of which are collections of essays, as well as more than 50 other articles. Over the years, he gave extended attention to a wide variety of issues. His early writings focus on the theology of sexuality and marriage in St. Thomas Aquinas. Between 1958 and 1960 he published four textbooks on various areas of moral theology patterned on the classic ''manualist'' tradition but introducing new insights, which he used in his teaching at the Gregorian University and which were exported by his multinational student population. The early 1960s were especially fruitful, resulting in articles on new issues in sexual ethics, the place of law in human society, and a sundry other topics. In 1965 he published *Natural Law: A Theological Investigation,* a major work in the field of Catholic moral theology and a pivotal document in Fuchs's own intellectual history. It coincided with a long series of publications exploring the implications for moral theology of the vision of Vatican II, particularly as that vision is articulated in *Gaudium et spes.*

A major turning point in his career was Fuchs's membership on the Papal Commission on Family, Births, and Population of 1965–68. He is alleged to have been an author of the so-called ''majority report'' that Pope Paul VI ultimately rejected in the writing of *Humanae Vitae.* In any case, Fuchs's views on the permanence, universality, and exceptionlessness of concrete moral norms changed as a result of his reflections during these years.

Though Fuchs has addressed a variety of specific questions, his abiding focus, particularly in the years since Vatican II, has been the core commitments on which a Christian morality is based. He discussed the character of the natural law, the relationship of human morality and Christian life, the identity of the moral person, the shape and limits of moral norms, the role of conscience, issues of secularism and religious commitment, and the significance of moral community, especially the Catholic Church as an institution, for personal moral decision making. In many of these areas, Fuchs gives evidence of being deeply influenced by the theological anthropology of Karl RAHNER.

Fuchs's influence has been worldwide, thanks to his role at the Gregorian University. That influence is greater yet because he taught in the ecclesiastical period prior to, during, and since the Second Vatican Council. Indeed, he is both a commentator on and a major contributor to the renewal of moral theology occurring in this period. Along with his colleague at the Alphonsianum University, Bernard Häring (also born in 1912), Fuchs has been described as a ''revisionist'' and associated with the methodology of proportionalism.

Bibliography: F. FUCHS, *Natural Law: A Theological Investigation* (New York 1965); *Human Values and Christian Morality* (Dublin 1970); *Personal Responsibility and Christian Morality* (Washington 1983); *Christian Ethics in a Secular Arena* (Washington 1984); *Christian Morality: The Word Becomes Flesh* (Washington 1987); *Moral Demands & Personal Obligations* (Washington 1993). T. O'CONNELL, *Changing Roman Catholic Moral Theology: A Study in Josef Fuchs* (Ann Arbor 1974).

[T. E. O'CONNELL]

FUENTE, MICHAEL DE LA

Carmelite spiritual writer; b. Valdelaguna, a village between Madrid and Toledo, March 2, 1573; d. Toledo, Nov. 27, 1625 (Nov. 17, 1626?). He was professed as a Carmelite on May 29, 1594, and then studied philosophy and theology at the University of Salamanca. After the province of New Castile was separated from that of Old Castile, he retained the office of novice master in the new province. He spent the rest of his life in Toledo, where he wrote a rule for the Carmelite Third Order that was highly important in the development of that group. Especially devoted to the Eucharist, the Passion, the Immaculate Conception, and the Brown Scapular, he is said to have had the extraordinary graces of ecstacy, levitation, and prophecy. Miracles before and after his death are reported. Several years after he died, his body was found incorrupt; his cause for beatification was introduced at Rome shortly after death. A nephew (d. 1629) of the same name was also a Carmelite. La Fuente's principal writing, *Libro de las tres vidas del hombre corporal, racional y espiritual* (Toledo 1623), an ascetical and mystical work, has assured him of a significant place among spiritual writers in and outside of his order.

Bibliography: T. MOTTA NAVARRO, *Tertii Carmelitici saecularis ordinis historico-iuridica evolutio* (Rome 1960) 178–194. A. DE SAINT PAUL, *Dictionnaire de théologie catholique* 10 (Paris 1903–50) 2:1703–05. H. ERHARTER, *Lexikon für Theologie und Kirche* (Freiburg 1957–) 7: 395–396.

[K. J. EGAN]

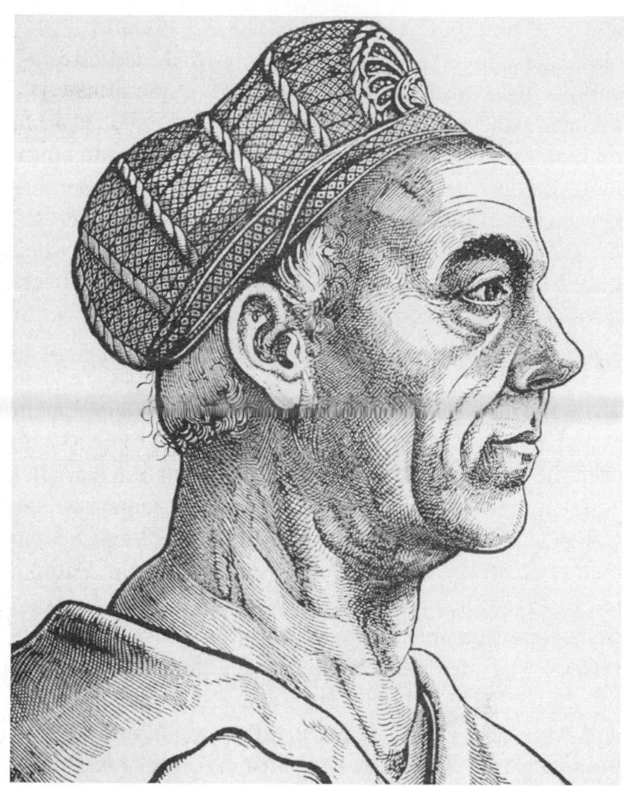

Jakob Fugger, from a woodcut by Hans Burgkmair. (©Bettmann/CORBIS)

FUGGER

Family of prominent early south German capitalists, enjoying immense wealth and great, if not commensurate, political influence. Ulrich Fugger, who moved to Augsburg in 1367, and his son Johann (d. 1409) were prosperous fustian weavers. Ulrich's grandsons, Jacob I (d. 1468) and Andreas (d. 1457), founded separate lines, though the latter soon died out. Through his in-laws, the Bässinger family, Jacob became interested in the silver mines of Schwaz in the Tyrol and extended his financial activity to the gold trade and to speculation in stock. During the last quarter of the 15th century the family wealth was increased enormously by Jacob's three sons, Ulrich I (d. 1510), Georg (d. 1506), and Jacob II (d. 1525). The acquisitive instincts of the youngest son, Jacob, made him an archetype of the early modern capitalist. He studied commerce in Venice, married the granddaughter of the merchant Ulrich Arzt the Rich, participated in the East India spice trade, and enlarged the family's mining and land holdings. The Fuggers became involved in ecclesiastical finance, organizing the transfer of money resulting from traffic in INDULGENCES and other revenues, financing the travels of papal legates and nuncios, and making large loans to churchmen. The Fuggers secretly lent ALBRECHT OF BRANDENBURG the 34,000 ducats that he needed in order to obtain the papal dispensation and the pallium, and to take care of related expenses, when he wished to add the archbishopric of MAINZ to his offices. This transaction led to the sale of indulgences for repayment and precipitated Martin LUTHER'S protest in 1517. Fugger money influenced papal elections and in 1519 was a decisive factor in securing the election of CHARLES V as Emperor of the Holy Roman Empire. Jacob remained neutral at the start of the Reformation, but after 1525 he became increasingly firm in his support of the Catholic Church. In Augsburg, he built the Fugger tomb chapel of St. Anna, hired Renaissance artists to decorate the Fugger palace, and in 1519 founded the Fuggerei, the first social settlement for poor workers, consisting of 106 houses at nominal rent. Jacob was childless and willed his holdings to his brother Georg's sons, Raymund (d. 1535) and Anton (d. 1560). Anton involved the family in risky political loans for the wars against the Turks and for the Hapsburg struggles with the Valois Kings of France. He supported Charles V against the German Protestants in 1546 and 1547 and again in 1552, losing large sums by default. Although Raymund's son, Ulrich II the Younger, decided in favor of the REFORMATION, the family as such remained with the Catholic Church, helping to establish a Jesuit College in Augsburg and supporting a number of prominent clergymen in later years, notably Sigmund Friedrich (d. 1600), Bishop of Regensburg, and Jacob (d. 1626), Bishop of Constance. Although lineal descendants of the family are still active today in finance and commerce, the family's power and influence waned rapidly after the THIRTY YEARS' WAR.

Bibliography: R. EHRENBERG, *Das Zeitalter der Fugger,* 2 v. (Jena 1896). A. SCHULTE, *Die Fugger in Rom, 1495–1523,* 2 v. in 1 (Leipzig 1904). J. STRIEDER, *Jacob Fugger der Reiche* (Leipzig 1926); Eng. tr. M. L. HARTSOUGH, ed. N. S. B. GRAS (New York 1931). E. HERING, *Die Fugger* (Leipzig 1939). G. VON PÖLNITZ, *Die Fugger* (2d ed. Frankfurt am Main 1960).

[L. W. SPITZ]

FULBERT OF CHARTRES

Bishop; b.*c.* 960; d. April 10, 1028. He was born of a poor and non-noble family, probably in northern France. He studied under Gerbert (SYLVESTER II) at Reims and then went to CHARTRES, where he taught in the cathedral school. He was ordained to the diaconate by 1004 and became bishop of Chartres in September or October 1006. As one of the principal churchmen in northern France and as bishop of a royal diocese, Fulbert was involved in the many ecclesiastical and secular controversies of his day. He was most anxious to remedy the abuses of SIMONY and clerical marriage and to free the Church from the control of the feudal nobility. Especially important were his efforts to uphold canonical regulations concerning episcopal elections and his attempts to reinforce the spiritual and temporal authority of the diocesan bishop. Yet Fulbert accepted the customary medieval notions of divine-right kingship and the longstanding traditions of royal influence within the French Church. He supported King Robert II of France in his struggle against the nobles and on several occasions actively intervened in an effort to restore peace. Fulbert was well educated for his time. He knew the standard classical and Christian authors and was exceptionally learned in ecclesiastical and secular law. There is no evidence to indicate that he continued to teach after his episcopal consecration, but he did maintain close contact with the students who came to Chartres. His advice was often sought on both scholarly and practical matters, and he corresponded with some of the most famous leaders of his time, including Abbots ABBO OF FLEURY and ODILO OF CLUNY, and Duke William V of Aquitaine. Fulbert was an ardent promoter of devotion to the Blessed Virgin, and he began the rebuilding of Chartres Cathedral, which had been destroyed by fire in 1020. In 1022 he made a pilgrimage to Rome and sometime later was made treasurer of St. Hilary's at Poitiers by Duke William. Fulbert was buried in the monastery church of St. Père-de-Chartres. Although he has long been popularly venerated as a saint, it was only in the mid-19th century that his cult was officially sanctioned for the Dioceses of Chartres and Poitiers.

Feast: April 10.

Bibliography: Collected works in *Patrologia Latina* 141:185–368. F. BEHRENDS, *The Letters and Poems of Fulbert of Chartres* (Oxford 1976). C. PFISTER, *De Fulberti Carnotensis Episcopi, Vita et Operibus* (Nancy 1885). L. C. MACKINNEY, *Bishop Fulbert and Education at the School of Chartres* (Notre Dame, Ind. 1957), with older bibliography. Y. DELAPORTE, "F. de C. et l'école chartraine de chant liturgique au XIe siècle," *Études Grégoriennes* 2 (1957) 51–81. J. R. GEISELMANN, *Lexikon für Theologie und Kirche,* ed. J. HOFER and K. RAHNER (Freiburg 1957–65) 4:443. J. M. CANAL, "Los sermones marianos de San Fulberto de C. (†1028)," *Recherches de théologie ancienne et médiévale* 29 (1962) 33–51; 30 (1963), 55–87, 329–333. H. BARRÉ, *Prières anciennes de l'occident à la mère du Sauveur* (Paris 1963) 150–162.

[F. BEHRENDS]

FULCHER OF CHARTRES

Crusade chronicler; b. *c.* 1059; d. *c.* 1127. Fulcher was raised at Chartres and was ordained before 1096. In

1095 he was present at the Council of Clermont when Pope URBAN II proclaimed the First Crusade (*see* CRUSADES). Fulcher's description of the Council and of the Pope's proclamation of the Crusade is an important eyewitness account. Fulcher joined the Crusade as chaplain to Count Stephen of Blois and Chartres. In 1097 Fulcher joined the retinue of another crusading prince, BALDWIN I, who later became Count of Edessa and King of Jerusalem. He accompanied Baldwin to Jerusalem when he assumed the throne of the Latin Kingdom on Nov. 9, 1100 (*see* CRUSADERS' STATES) and later appears as a royal chaplain and canon of the Holy Sepulcher. He may also have been appointed prior of Mt. Olivet. After the death of Baldwin I, Fulcher was also close to his successor, Baldwin II. Late in 1101 Fulcher began writing his *Historia Hierosolymitana,* on which he worked intermittently for more than a quarter of a century. Fulcher's account remains a major and unusually reliable source for the history of the First Crusade and of the Latin settlements in the Holy Land.

Bibliography: FULCHER OF CHARTRES, *Historia Hierosolymitana,* ed. H. HAGENMEYER (Heidelberg 1913); *Chronicle of the First Crusade*, tr. M. E. MCGINTY (Philadelphia 1941), Bk. I of the *Historia.* D. C. MUNRO, "A Crusader," *Speculum* 7 (1932) 321–335.

[J. A. BRUNDAGE]

FULCOIUS OF BEAUVAIS

Archdeacon, writer of Latin verse; fl. during the last half of the 11th century; b. Beauvais; d. Meaux, France. He composed three volumes of verse: *Uter* (epitaphs and letters), *Neuter* (lives of SS. Agil, Blandinus, Faro, and Maurus), and *Uterque* (Biblical narrative of Christ and His Church). Fulcoius's letters to ecclesiastical and political leaders reflect the moral-ethical condition of the time and show the nature of the obstacles facing Pope GREGORY VII in his reform. Familiarity with classical poets and the Church Fathers adds charm and value to his work, meriting for Fulcoius a place in the history of medieval poetry.

Bibliography: FULCOIUS OF BEAUVAIS, *Utriusque de nuptiis Christi et ecclesiae libri septem,* ed. M. I. J. ROUSSEAU (Washington 1960). Manitius 3:836–840. A. BOUTEMY, "Essai de chronologie des poésies de Foulcoie de Beauvais," *Annuaire de l'Institut de philologie et d'histoire Orientales et Slaves de l'Université Libre de Bruxelles* 11 (Mélanges Henri Grégoire 3; Brussels 1951) 79–96. M. L. COLKER, "Fulcoii Belvacensis epistulae," *Traditio* 10 (1954) 191–273.

[M. I. J. ROUSSEAU]

FULCRAN OF LODÈVE, ST.

Bishop; d. Feb. 13, 1006. Fulcran's great reputation for virtue led Bishop Thierry of his native Lodève, Languedox (southern France), to ordain him priest in spite of Fulcran's reluctance. By popular acclaim he was made Thierry's successor in 949. Through periodic episcopal visitations he insisted upon regular discipline in religious houses and outspokenly condemned the sins of the highborn as well as of the low. He befriended the poor, founded Saint-Sauveur for Benedictine nuns, and built the cathedral church of St. GENESIUS, in which he was buried. Once, upon hearing of a bishop who had fallen into Judaism, he remarked in emotion that he should be burned; and then, overwhelmed with remorse when taken literally, he undertook enormous penances and made a pilgrimage to Rome to seek forgiveness. His body was exhumed in 1127, but only some of his relics survived a Huguenot sack of his shrine in 1572.

Feast: Feb. 13 (Montpellier and Nîmes).

Bibliography: *Acta Sanctorum* Feb. 2:711–718, 898–900. A. BEC, *Vie de saint Fulcran* (Lodève 1858). H. REYNIS, *Les Reliques de St. F. de Lodève* (Lodève 1861). ABBÈ BOUTY, *Vie de St. F.* (Montpellier 1865). J. L. BAUDOT and L. CHAUSSIN, *Vies des saints et des bienheueux selon l'ordre du calendrier avec l'historique des fêtes* 12 v. (Paris 1935–56) 2:310–311.

[W. E. WILKIE]

FULDA, ABBEY OF

Former Benedictine monastery in the town of the same name, 54 miles northeast of Frankfurt am Main, Germany, Diocese of Fulda. It was founded March 12, 744, by STURMI, a disciple of St. BONIFACE. The Frankish mayor of the palace and Pope ZACHARY granted it special privileges, and it remained Boniface's own monastery until his martyrdom (754), after which his remains were translated to Fulda. Boniface and Sturmi had organized the abbey according to the BENEDICTINE RULE, combining elements of Anglo-Saxon origin with the monastic customs of Monte Cassino. Pepin made it a royal abbey (764–765). Fulda received numerous donations, and its territorial domain soon extended through all of what was then Germany.

By 780 CHARLEMAGNE had sent monks of Fulda on the mission to the Saxons. Construction on Fulda's great Holy Savior Basilica over the tomb of St. Boniface began *c.* 790, and the edifice, probably the first double-choired church in the West, was consecrated in 819. The smaller St. Michael's Chapel, still in use, was built in 822 in the monastery cemetery. Fulda, with more than 400 monks in the 9th century, possessed an important SCRIPTORIUM in which the Anglo-Saxon influence of the abbey's founding days lasted to *c.* 850. Notable abbots included Baugulf (780–802), Ratgar (802–817), and RABANUS MAURUS (822–842). Under their leadership, Fulda maintained an influential monastery school that produced such scholars of the 9th century as EINHARD, Lupus of Ferrières, WALAFRID STRABO, Baturich of Regensburg, Samuel of Worms, Rudolph of Fulda, Hartmut of Sankt Gallen, and GOTTSCHALK OF ORBAIS. In the Middle Ages its library had more than 2,000 MSS, containing works of ancient authors that have been preserved for the modern world only through the Fulda monks (e.g., the *Annales* and *Germania* of Tacitus); the MSS were scattered in the Thirty Years' War. Fulda was also a cradle of Old High German literature, e.g., the Vocabularius, the Hildebrandslied, the Wessobrunn Prayer(?), and the Muspilli(?).

Fulda became part of the reform movement of BENEDICT OF ANIANE (817–818). In 1013 the monastic reform of Lorraine (*see* GORZE) was instituted at Fulda by Emperor Henry II; Fulda became a model monastery, transplanting its observance to other monasteries in Hesse and Thuringia. From the 10th to the 12th century it was the most important imperial abbey in Germany; its abbot gradually became the abbot primate (969) of Germany and Gaul, assumed the office of archchancellor of the Empress, and was granted pontifical rights (1133). During this period MANUSCRIPT ILLUMINATION, such as that of the Fulda Sacramentary, murals as in the churches of Petersberg and Neuenberg, gold work, and sculpture, were at their zenith in Fulda.

The numerous privileges granted to Fulda made it easy for the abbey to organize its land holdings into a territorial state in the 13th century; the abbot held the rank of a prince of the Holy Roman Empire. Although the abbot had managed to quell the monastery's rebellious vassals during the 13th century, in 1353 and 1395 he was forced to grant them, as concessions to gain election, the right to participate in the government of the principality. When the household of the abbot became separate from the monastery proper (1294), grave irregularities in monastic discipline began to occur, especially as the community was accepting only noblemen as monks. Fulda was not affected by the numerous Benedictine reforms of the late Middle Ages.

The monastic state of Fulda was severely disturbed during the Peasants' War in 1525; simultaneously, the Protestant Reformation was penetrating the principality. Important abbots, such as Balthasar von Dernbach (1570–1606) and Schenk von Schweinsberg (1623–32), successfully resisted the dissolution of Fulda and worked toward a Catholic restoration. Monks from SANKT GALLEN helped reform the monastery. As early as 1571 the Jesuits had come to the town of Fulda, and thanks to them the principality had been restored to Catholicism by *c.* 1620. Franciscans established at the Frauenberg in 1620, and Benedictine nuns, from 1631, also played a part in revitalizing Catholicism throughout the principality. The Thirty Years' War (1618–48) severely damaged both the abbey and countryside, but abbots during the late 17th century laid the foundation for an artistic and intellectual revival. Among them were Athanasius KIRCHER, Christoph BROUWER, and Count Friedrich von SPEE. During the baroque period several important edifices were erected in the town of Fulda, including a new abbey church (the present cathedral), the orangery, and Schloss Adolfseck.

On Oct. 5, 1752, the abbot of Fulda was made bishop of the newly created exempt Diocese of Fulda; the monks, who were to function as the cathedral chapter, kept their monastic constitution. In 1755 the Diocese of Fulda was placed under the metropolitan of Mainz, while the abbey kept its exempt status. Under Bishop-Abbot Heinrich von Bibra (1759–88), the monastic state of Fulda experienced an economic revival, city development, and improvement in educational and pastoral care. As a result of the Treaty of Paris (1802) and the 1803 enactment of the delegates of the Empire the Diocese of Fulda was secularized, and the abbey was suppressed.

Bibliography: Sources. Annals. *Annales Fuldenses antiqui, Monumenta Germaniae Historica: Scriptores* 3:116–117. "Das Chronicon Laurissense breve." ed. H. SCHNORR VON CAROLSFELD, *Neues Archiv der Gesellschaft für ältere deutsche Geschichtskunde* 36 (1910) 13–39. *Annales Fuldenses,* ed. F. KURZE (*Monumenta Germaniae Historica: Scriptores: Scriptores rerum Germanicarum* 7; 1891). *Annales sancti Bonifatii, Monumenta Germaniae Historica: Scriptores* 3:117–118. *Catalogus abbatum Fuldensium, Monumenta Germaniae Historica: Scriptores* 13:272–274, 370. *Miracula sanctorum in Fuldenses ecclesias translatorum, Monumenta Germaniae Historica: Scriptores* 15.1:328–341. Biographies. *Vitae sancti Bonifatii archiepiscopi Moguntini,* ed. W. LEVISON (*Monumenta Germaniae Historica: Scriptores: Scriptores rerum Germanicarum* 57; 1905). *Eigilis vita sancti Sturmi, Monumenta Germaniae Historica: Scriptores* 2:365–377. *Vitae Leobae abbatissae Biscofesheimensis, Monumenta Germaniae Historica: Scriptores* 15.1:118–131. *Vitae Eigilis abbatis Fuldensis, ibid.* 221–233 and *Candidus de vita Aeigili, Monumenta Germaniae Historica: Poetae* 2:94–117. *Vita Bardonis archiepiscopi Moguntini, Monumenta Germaniae Historica: Scriptores* 11:321–342. *Monumenta Germaniae Historica Libri confraternitatum* (1884) 194–203. *Annales necrologici Fuldenses, Monumenta Germaniae Historica: Scriptores* 13:161–218. *Necrologium Fuldense,* ed. E. DÜMMLER, *Forschungen zur deutschen Geschichte* 16 (1876) 168–177. Charters. *Monumenta Germaniae Historica: Diplomata passim.* E. E. STENGEL, *Urkundenbuch des Klosters Fulda, 1.* (Marburg 1958). E. F. J. DRONKE. ed., *Traditiones et antiquitates Fuldenses* (Fulda 1844); *Codex diplomaticus Fuldensis,* 4 fasc. (Kassel 1847–50). Letters. S. *Bonifatii et Lulli epistolae,* ed. M. TANGL (*Monumenta Germaniae Historica: Espistolae selectae* 1; 2d ed. 1955). *Supplex Libellus monachorum Fuldensium,* ed. J. SEMMLER, in *Corpus consuetudinum monasticarum. I.,* ed. K. HALLINGER (Siegburg 1963) 319–327. *Hrabani Mauri . . . epistolae,* in *Monumenta Germaniae Historica: Epistolae Karolini aevi* 5.2:379–516. *Epistolarum Fuldensium fragmenta, ibid.* 517–533. *Thiotrochi diaconi epistola,* ed. W. WATTENBACH, *Neues Archiv der Gesellschaft* *für älterer deutsche Geschichtskunde* 4 (1879) 409–412. Titles and epitaphs. *Notae dedicationum Fuldenses, Monumenta Germaniae Historica: Scriptores* 15.2:1287–88. *Tituli ecclesiarum Fuldensium. Monumenta Germaniae Historica: Poetae* 2:205–217, 220–224. *Epitaphia Eigilis abbatis Fuldensis, ibid.* 117. *Epitaphium Hattonis abbatis Fuldensis, ibid.* 258. Sacramentary of Fulda. G. RICHTER and A. SCHÖNFELDER, *Sacramentarium Fuldense saeculi X.* (Quellen und Abhandlungen zur Geschichte der Abtei und der Diözese Fulda 9; Fulda 1912). Literature. *Quellen und Abhandlungen zur Geschichte der Abtei und Diözese Fulda,* eds. G. RICHTER and L. PRALLE (Fulda 1904–). *Veröffentlichungen des Fuldaer Geschichtsvereins* (Fulda 1899–). *Fuldaer Geschichtsblätter* (Fulda 1902–). C. BROWERUS, *Fuldensium antiquitatum libri IV* (Antwerp 1612). J. F. SCHANNAT, *Dioecesis Fuldensis cum annexa sua hierarchia* . . . (Frankfurt 1727); *Historia Fuldensis,* 2 v. (Frankfurt 1729). W. DERSCH, *Hessisches Klosterbuch* (2d ed. Marburg 1940) 39–52, with sources and literature up to 1939. A. SCHMITT, *Die Fuldaer Wandmalerei des frühen Mittelalters* (Fulda 1949). K. HALLINGER, *Gorze-Kluny,* 2 v. (*Studia anselmiana* 22–25; 1950–51), passim. P. J. JÖRG, *Würzburg and Fulda* (Quellen und Forschungen zur Geschichte des Bistums und Hochstifts Würzburg 1951). H. BEUMANN, ''Zur Fuldaer Geschichte,'' *Hessisches Jahrbuch für Landesgeschichte* 1 (1951) 211–217, with literature. L. PRALLE, *Die Wiederentdeckung des Tacitus* (Quellen und Abhandlungen zur Geschichte der Abtei und der Diözese Fulda 17; Fulda 1952). K. LÜBECK, *Fuldaer Studien,* 3 v. (Veröffentlichungen des Fuldaer Geschichtsvereins 27–29; Fulda 1949–51); *Die Fuldaer Äbte und Fürstäbte des Mittelalters* (*ibid.* 31; Fulda 1952). *Sankt Boniatius: Gedenkgabe zum 1200. Todestag* (Fulda 1954). T. SCHIEFFER, *Winfrid-Bonifatius und die christliche Grundlegung Europas* (Freiburg 1954). J. A. BORNEWASSER, *Kirche und Staat in Fulda unter Friedrich Wilhelm von Oranien, 1892–1906* (Quellen und Abhandlungen zur Geschichte der Abtei und der Diözese Fulda 19; Fulda 1956). H. HACK, *Der Rechtsstreit zwischen dem Fürstbischof von Würzburg und dem Fürstabt von Fulda . . . 1688–1717* (*ibid.* 18; 1956). R. GATTENS, *Das Geld- und Münzwesen der Abtei Fulda im Hochmittelalter* (Veröffentlichungen des Fuldaer Geschichtsvereins 34; Fulda 1957). A. HOFEMANN, *Studien zur Entwicklung des Territoriums der Reichsabtei Fulda und seiner Amter* (Schriften des Hessischen Landesamtes für geschichtliche Landeskunde 25; Marburg 1958). H. BÜTTNER, ''Das Diplom Heinrichs III. für Fulda von 1049 und die Anfänge der Stadt Fulda,'' *Archiv für Diplomatik* 4 (1958) 207–215. J. SEMMLER, ''Studien zum *Supplex libellus* und zur anianischen Reform in Fulda,'' *Zeitschrift für Kirchengeschichte* 69 (1958) 268–298. E. E. STENGEL, *Die Reichsabtei Fulda in der deutschen Geschichte* (Weimar 1948); ''Zur Frühgeschichte der Reichsabtei Fulda,'' *Deutsches Archiv für Erforschung des Mittelalters* 9 (1952) 513–534, with literature; ''Fuldensia I–V,'' *Archiv für Urkundenforschung* 5 (1913) 41–152; 7 (1920) 1–26; *Archiv für Diplomatik* 2 (1956) 116–124; 4 (1958) 120–182; *ibid.* 8 (1962) 12–67; *Abhandlungen und Untersuchungen zur hessischen Geschichte* (Veröffentlichungen der historischen Kommission für Hessen und Waldeck 26: Marburg 1960). W. A. MÜHL, *Die Aufkleärung an der Universität Fulda . . . 1734–1805* (Quellen und Abhandlungen zur Geschichte der Abtei und der Diözese Fulda 20; Fulda 1961). W. HESSLER, ''Zur Abfassungszeit von Eigils *Vita Sturmi,*'' *Hessisches Jahrbuch für Landesgeschichte* 9 (1959) 1–17; *''Petitionis exemplar,'' Archiv für Diplomatik* 8 (1962) 1–11. D. GROSSMANN, *Kloster Fulda und seine Bedeutung für den frühen deutschen Kirchenbau* v. 1 (*Das erste Jahrtausend* (Düsseldorf 1962) 344–370. K. WITTSTADT, *Placidus von Droste, Fürstabt von Fulda* (Veröffentlichungen des Fuldaer Geschichtsvereins 39; Fulda 1963). F. W. WITZEL, *Die Reichsabtei Fulda und ihre Hochvögte, die Grafen von Ziegenhain, im 12. und 13. Jahrhundert* (*ibid.* 41; 1963). W. HESSLER, ''Von Ratger zu Hraban: Fulda im Anfang des 9. Jahrhunderts,'' in *Archiv für Diplomatik* (1965–66).

[J. SEMMLER]

FULGENTIUS OF ÉCIJA, ST.

Bishop of Écija; b. Seville(?), Spain, *c.* 540–60; d. Écija(?), *c.* 619. He is one of four saints in an important Hispano-Roman family that had migrated, probably before his birth, from Byzantine-held Cartagena on the Mediterranean to Visigothic Seville on the Atlantic. He attended the Councils of Toledo (610) and Seville (619). His older brother, LEANDER, in his *De institutione virginum,* advised their sister FLORENTINA to pray for Fulgentius, whom he had sent to Cartagena. His younger brother, ISIDORE OF SEVILLE, wrote the *De officiis ecclesiasticis* at his request (*Patrologia Latina,* ed. J. P. Migne, 217 v. 83:737). Certain Spanish Breviaries attribute to Fulgentius writings by Fulgentius of Ruspe and Fabius Planciades Fulgentius; but N. Antonio in 1696 and E. Flórez in 1753 refuted these claims. A like attribution that he was bishop of Cartagena seems to have arisen about 1330 when his relics were discovered near Guadalupe. In 1593 the relics were shared with the Escorial and the See of Cartagena, of which Fulgentius is patron saint. His cult in Spain is immemorial.

Feast: Jan. 16.

Bibliography: *Bibliotheca hagiographica latina antiquae et mediae aetatis,* 2 v. (Brussels 1898–1901; suppl. 1911) 2:4810. N. ANTONIO, *Bibliotheca Hispana vetus,* 2 v. (Madrid 1788) 1:306–314. H. FLÓREZ, et al., *España Sagrada* (Madrid 1747–1957) 10:88–107. U. CHEVALIER, *Répertoire des sources historiques du moyen-âge. Biobibliographie,* 2 v. (2d. ed. Paris 1905–07) 1:1626. H. WARD, *A Dictionary of Christian Biography,* ed. W. SMITH and H. WACE, (London 1877–87) 2:584–585. *Enciclopedia universal ilustrada Europeo-Americana,* 70 v. (Barcelona 1908–30) 25:11. G. BARDY, *Catholicisme* 4:1668–69.

[E. P. COLBERT]

FULGENTIUS OF RUSPE

Sixth-century African bishop and theologian; b. Telepte, North Africa, 467; d. Jan. 1, 533. Fulgentius, the outstanding Western theologian of the early 6th century, came of a well-to-do family and received a sound education in Greek as well as Latin literature. He entered the civil service and was the procurator or tax collector of Telepte when, on reading Augustine's commentary on Psalm 36, he decided to become a monk. In 507 he was selected as bishop of Ruspe, a small seaside town in Byzacena; but in 508, with 60 other African bishops, he was exiled to Sardinia by the Vandal King Thrasamund. He returned to Ruspe in 515 but had to take up residence in Sardinia again from 517 to 523.

His writings were both dogmatic and polemic, the latter directed against the Arian doctrines of the Vandal rulers of Africa and against Pelagianism. His *Contra Arianos* is a reply to ten questions proposed by King Thrasamund, and his three books *Ad Thrasamundum regem* further elaborate the Catholic objection to Arian teaching. He composed also *Contra sermonem Fastidiosi Ariani, Contra Fabianum, De Trinitate ad Felicem,* and *De incarnatione ad Scarilam.* His tracts against SemiPelagianism include three books *Ad Monimum,* three books *De veritate praedestinationis,* and a *Contra Faustum Reiensem* in seven books, which has not been preserved.

His *De fide ad Petrum* is a compendium of dogmatic theology formerly attributed to Augustine. He wrote two books *De remissione peccatorum ad Euthymium* and a lost *Adversus Pintam.* The tract under that name (*Patrologia Latina*) is probably his *Commonitorium de Spiritu Sancto,* considered lost. He is also credited with a recently discovered *Psalmus abecedarius* against the Arians.

His letters are mainly long treatises dealing with virginity, marriage, and penance (*Epist.* 1–7); two are collective encyclicals of the exiled African bishops (15 and 17). The latter deals with the formula "one of the Trinity suffered in the Flesh" submitted for the bishops' judgment by the Scythian monks of Constantinople (*see* MONOPHYSITISM). Seven of the sermons attributed to him are authentic. The life of Fulgentius was written by the Carthaginian deacon Ferrandus soon after the bishop's death and is one of the finest biographies of the age.

Fulgentius followed Augustinian teaching faithfully. He defended Trinitarian teaching against the Arians and explained the problem of predestination in Augustine's terms: God's will determines one's predestination to glory or damnation; unbaptized infants are damned, but their punishment will be mitigated (*De veritate praed.* 1.1–31). Prayer and good works must be pursued, relying on the mystery of salvation. Parental concupiscence is the instrument for the transmission of original sin (*De veritate praed.* 3.14–23); hence he denied the Immaculate Conception of Mary (*Epist.* 17.6, 13).

Bibliography: *Patrologia Latina,* ed. J. P. MIGNE, 217 v. (Paris 1878–90) 65:105–1018. G. G. LAPEYRE, *L'Ancienne église de Carthage,* 2 v. (Paris 1932); ed. and tr., *Vie de saint Fulgence* (Paris 1929). G. KRUEGER, *Harnack-Ehrung* (Leipzig 1921) 219–223. B. NISTERS, *Die Christologie des hl. Fulgentius* (Münster 1930). A. D'ALÈS, *Recherches de science religieuse* 22 (1932) 304–316, Commonitorium. H. DELEHAYE, *Analecta Bollandiana* 52 (1934) 103–105. C. LAMBOT, *Revue Bénédictine* 48 (1936) 221–234, *Psalmus abecedarius.* F. DI SCIASCIO, *Fulgenzio di Ruspe* (Rome 1941). J. BEUMER, *Gregorianum* 23 (1942) 325–347, *de fide.* J. J. GAVIGAN, *Traditio* (1947) 313–322, Baptism. *Clavis Patrum latinorum,* ed. E. DEKKERS (2d. ed. Streenbrugge 1961) 814–846. A. GRILLMEIER and H. BACHT, *Das Konzil vom Chalkedon: Geschichte und Gegenwart* (Würzburg 1951–54) 2:807–814, Christology. B. ALTANER, *Patrology,* tr. H. GRAEF (New York 1960) 587–589.

[A. NEUWIRTH]

FULK OF NEUILLY, BL.

Preacher of the Fourth Crusade; d. March 2, 1201. Nothing is known of his early life, but from 1191 he was a priest in the church of Neuilly-sur-Marne near Paris. He was an eloquent speaker and served as a wandering missionary-preacher through Normandy, Picardy, and Burgundy. The historian Villehardouin stated that it was Fulk who had inspired Count Thibaut III of Champagne (d. 1201) to urge Pope INNOCENT III to organize the Fourth Crusade (1202–04), which resulted in the capture of CONSTANTINOPLE. Fulk then served as Innocent's chief recruiting agent in France, touring the country urging the people to follow their lords to the Holy War. He died, however, before the crusade got under way. Fulk was famed for his fearlessness before princes, and he reputedly ordered King RICHARD I of England to abandon his pride, avarice, and lust. Reference to Fulk can be found in Villehardouin, Roger of Hoveden, Ralph of Coggeshall, and JACQUES DE VITRY. He was buried in Neuilly-sur-Marne.

Feast: March 2.

Bibliography: Raynald's continuation of Baronius (1646) 1198, nn. 38–42. INNOCENT III, *Patrologia Latina,* ed. J. P. MIGNE, 217 v. (Paris 1878–90) 214:375–376. S. RUNCIMAN, *A History of the Crusades,* 3 v. (Cambridge, Eng. 1951–54) 3:107–109. U. CHEVALIER, *Répertoire des sources historiques du moyen-âge. Biobibliographie,* 2 v. (2d. ed. Paris 1905–07) 1:1553. A. BUTLER, *The Lives of the Saints,* ed. H. THURSTON and D. ATTWATER, 4 v. (New York 1956) 1:461–462.

[V. L. BULLOUGH]

FUNCTIONALISM

Because of its affinity with American pragmatism, functionalism is one of the most influential psychologies in education. Originally it was a reaction against the structuralism popular in Germany (Wundt), but its American proponents—James Angell, William JAMES, George Mead, and John Dewey—were responsible for its development and popularity.

Functionalists view man as a highly developed biological organism, and the mind as the result of the evolutionary process. Their work contains an explicit rejection of the traditional mind-body dualism, which attributes the activities of mind such as judgment and reasoning to a spiritual soul. In the late 19th century, Dewey argued against the separation of mind and body, structure and function, stimulus and response, sensation and idea. To him idea and body were of one and the same fabric. Thus, mind is a function of the organism enabling man to interact with and adjust to the environment. As such, its operations might be compared to breathing and other biological functions except that mental action, especially thought, is normally associated with conscious activity. Explanations are sought by this school for the purpose or function of consciousness itself.

Since mind is viewed as a dynamic function, functionalism is not purely mechanistic, and a simple stimulus-response explanation of behavior is inadequate. The psychologist must study mental operations and activities, the basic ''utilities'' of mind used in mediating between the organism and the environment (in the adaptive activities). What the mind does is more important than its contents. Psychological investigations must also view all functions in unison. As Angell says: ''Functionalism is a study of the responses of a whole individual rather than an investigation of the movements of any single part of an individual.'' The psychologist must give attention to phenomena as well as to behavior. Consequently, the subject matter of psychology, according to the functionalist, encompasses all acts such as seeing, hearing, tasting, thinking, and choosing as these relate to objects external to the knower and as such objects are related to other objects. However, psychology is not limited to the mere description of the physiological components of behavior, for psychology is concerned also with action, and a human act involves an awareness of a pattern of mental content, with adaptive significance, that will enable the organism to distinguish different acts through their consequences. Thus, an ''act is a group or pattern of contents exhibiting a unity from the standpoint of its meaningful implications as to end result'' (Angell). Because it includes so much in the psychology of behavior, functionalism lends itself readily to education and other areas of applied psychology.

The theory of learning is a central concern of the functionalist. For him, learning is not rooted in the faculty of intellect (or reason) but is conceived as a mode of reacting to problematic situations that confront the organism. However, the individual does not have to start from a clean slate in each new situation since an organic form of memory provides him with recollections of his own and others' experiences. Other factors that come into play include frequency, recentness, intensity, interest, emotion, moods, organic maturation, motivation, and forgetting with the sense receptors and the nervous system active in all phases.

Dewey's analysis of the complete act of thought reflects the principles of functional psychology. He argues that all thought or meaningful learning is initiated by a difficulty resulting from the organism's immediate inability to attain some goal. The situation is obscure and fraught with conflict and doubt. As the organism becomes aware of the difficulty it locates and defines the problem. A possible solution (or alternative solutions) is suggested, and each hypothesis is examined in terms of anticipated consequences. The hypothesis is put to the test of experience and is rejected or accepted. Acceptance follows when the situation becomes clear, coherent, settled, and harmonious; that is, when the organism has achieved a satisfactory adjustment to the environment or the difficulty disappears.

An important factor in Dewey's functionalism is the significance he gives to the role of habit in adaptive situations. Routine habits aid in adjustment where the environment is relatively static. Flexible habits, of which intelligence is one, are needed to aid the individual in his adjustment to changing environment, especially the social environment. Reflective thought, described above, is the most useful of the habits since it enables man to handle the highly complex problems of modern civilization.

Of all the theories of psychology, functionalism has had the greatest influence on modern American secular education. Adjustment, as an aim of education, the emphasis on skill in problem solving, and much of the emphasis on the ''whole child'' in education originated in functionalist thinking. The textbooks of adolescent and child psychology and those of educational psychology and methods used in teacher education demonstrate the influence of this school of psychology.

Its major weakness lies in interpreting human behavior in purely biological terms. It fails to recognize in man any activity, such as reasoning, that might transcend the purely organic. It fails also to provide an adequate explanation for the various states of consciousness. On the other hand, functionalism's emphasis on the dynamic nature of learning did much to break the strangle hold of purely mechanistic psychologies and their application.

Bibliography: J. R. ANGELL, *An Introduction to Psychology* (New York 1918). J. DEWEY, *How We Think* (Boston 1910); *Reconstruction in Philosophy* (New York 1950). J. DEWEY and A. F. BENTLEY, *Knowing and the Known* (Boston 1949). W. JAMES, *Pragmatism: A New Name for Some Old Ways of Thinking* (New York 1907). E. R. HILGARD, *Theories of Learning* (2d ed. New York 1956). G. MURPHY, *Historical Introduction to Modern Psychology* (rev. ed. New York 1949). A. ADLER et al., *Psychologies of 1930,* ed. C. A. MURCHISON (Worcester, Mass. 1930). B. B. WOLMAN, *Contemporary Theories and Systems in Psychology,* ed. G. MURPHY

(New York 1960). R. S. WOODWORTH, *Contemporary Schools of Psychology* (New York 1931); *Dynamic Psychology* (New York 1918).

[A. M. DUPUIS]

FUNDAMENTAL OPTION

The term fundamental option became popular in the 1960s. It represented an attempt to describe the basic orientation of one's moral life as a continuous process with a definite moral direction rather than as a sequence of discrete, unconnected actions. Particular acts are seen as expressing and modifying the fundamental option, confirming and developing it or diminishing and ultimately reversing it.

Existentialist and personalist analyses, combined with dynamic psychological insights, alerted theologians to the inadequacy of any atomistic picture of human actions, good or bad, into which the theological manuals had drifted. Thus the emphasis was shifted from the particular action to the living subject as the bearer of morality. The notion of a fundamental option has roots in several strata of the Christian tradition: in the prophet Jeremiah the new covenant is said to be written in the hearts of men; the New Testament insists on the interior dimension of morality; Paul frequently insists upon the centrality of a total conversion in expressions such as ''life in Christ''; and also in Thomas Aquinas's discussion of the new law (*Summa theologiae* 1–2, 106). Within this Christian perspective, grace and sin are regarded as states of existence—the result of a fundamental option.

On the level of moral analysis, discussion of the ''first moral act'' (*Summa theologiae* 1–2, 89, 5) has led to the recognition of a person's overall commitment through his actions, so that further actions expressed and reinforced or contradicted and weakened that commitment. To understand such a commitment it may be better to consider it as gradually gathering momentum through the responses of the agent. Depending upon whether the acts are predominantly other-centered or self-centered, the person is characteristically ordered toward an altruistic or selfish life-stance. In the Christian context of love of neighbor involving love of God, the predominantly other-centered person will also be open to the Absolute other and hence in the state of grace; the predominantly self-centered person will be closed to God and hence in sin. A transition from one state to the other through conversion or mortal sin will not occur easily, but will remain an actual possibility through some serious involvement of the agent and frequently as the climax of a process. Thus the term ''fundamental option'' has a definite value when describing the basis of one's overall commitment, although the actual state itself is better described as a basic orientation, thereby avoiding any implications of unique dramatic choice—an experience quite foreign to most people's moral lives.

The term appears in Church documents. The *Declaration on Certain Questions Concerning Sexual Ethics* issued by the Sacred Congregation for the Doctrine of the Faith (1975) and Pope John Paul II's encyclical *Veritatis splendor* adopt the concept of fundamental option but link it more closely to particular acts. They insist that mortally sinful acts, done with full knowledge and consent, constitute a turning away from God and, thereby, imply the exercise of a fundamental option.

Bibliography: E. J. COOPER, ''The Notion of Sin in Light of the Fundamental Option: The Fundamental Option Revisited.,'' *Louvain Studies* 9 (1983) 363–382. J. FUCHS, ''Basic Freedom and Morality'' *Human Values and Christian Morality* (Dublin 1970). E. MCDONAGH ''The Moral Subject,'' *The Irish Theological Quarterly* 39 (January 1972) 3–23. L. MONDEN, *Sin, Liberty and Law* (New York 1965). K. RAHNER, ''The Commandment of Love in Relation to the other Commandments,'' *Theological Investigations* 5 (Baltimore 1966) 439–460; ''Theology of Freedom'' and ''Reflections on the Unity of the Love of Neighbour and Love of God,'' *Theological Investigations* 6 (Baltimore 1969) 178–196, 231–252. H. REINERS, *Grundintention und Sittliches Tun* (Freiburg 1966).

[E. MCDONAGH/EDS.]

FUNDAMENTAL THEOLOGY

Fundamental theology has traditionally concerned itself with the two great Christian facts: God has revealed Himself to men, and this revelation was climaxed in Christ, who founded a Church that transmits the Christian revelation. The fundamentals, or foundations, or basic elements, in the Judeo-Christian tradition are the existence of divine revelation and the transmission of this revelation to and through the people of God. The method of fundamental theology has been philosophical, historical, and theological. Because methodological questions arise only after the theological work is in progress and because of the historicist and positivistic temper of the last century, there has been a certain ambivalence as to whether fundamental THEOLOGY is properly philosophical or theological. The tendency today is to regard the discipline as strictly theological, that is, the activity of man's human reason transformed by FAITH seeking an understanding of the WORD OF GOD transmitted in the Church. As fundamental theology is now structured, it is left to prior investigation to ascertain man's cognitional powers as well as to come to a knowledge of God's existence. Some theologians, however, prefer to begin fundamental theology with the existence of a personal and provident God as known by reason and confirmed by a study of the history of religions.

K. Rahner and other scholars have pointed out that the above presentation is one-sided because it does not explain how man is capable of receiving revelation without this revelation being necessary for man. Thus, Rahner has proposed that fundamental theology concern itself more with man's openness to all being. Fundamental theology would proceed from man's openness to all being by a study of the ANALOGY of being and a careful analysis of man's OBEDIENTIAL POTENCY for revelation. Precisely because man is spirit incarnated he is open to all being. He is capable of hearing the word of God, of receiving the divine self-disclosure. An analysis of this capability, both in the abstract and as it is fulfilled in the concrete, would be the task of fundamental theology. This discipline would study man in relation to the revelation in creation, in the personal word, and in the historical deeds of God as transmitted in Scripture. The *Thematik* of fundamental theology would be the ontological principles of natural and supernatural theology. Some of the categories to be examined are: the forms of revelation; the demand that revelation makes upon man; revelation as intersubjectivity or divine action in opposition to revelation as past external fact; the logos as address and as meaning; the social character of revelation; the nature of word, speech, writing; the mediation of revelation; the presence of revelation in the Church. This approach to fundamental theology might well answer the questions: How can man hear the word of God? What is the word of God that man hears? Where does man receive the word of God? This type of fundamental theology would be neither exclusively historical nor philosophical but rather completely and thoroughly theological. Fundamental theology would thus be the meeting point for FAITH AND REASON, theology and philosophy, revelation and the world.

See Also: APOLOGETICS; IMMANENCE APOLOGETICS; METHODOLOGY (THEOLOGY); REVELATION, CONCEPT OF (IN THE BIBLE); REVELATION, THEOLOGY OF; REVELATION, FONTS OF; WORD OF GOD.

Bibliography: G. SÖHNGEN and H. VORGRIMLER, *Lexikon für Theologie und Kirche*, ed. J. HOFER and K. RAHNER (Freiburg 1957–65) 4:452–460. S. TROMP, *De revelatione christiana* (Rome 1950) 11–22. K. RAHNER, *Theological Investigations*, tr. C. ERNST et al. (Baltimore 1961—) 1:19–23. B. LONERGAN, "Theology and Understanding," *Gregorianum* 35 (Rome 1954) 642–644. J. THORNHILL, "Towards an Integral Theology," *Theological Studies* 24 (Woodstock, Md. 1963) 264–277.

[P. J. CAHILL]

FUNDAMENTALISM

An interdenominational movement that originated in American Protestantism toward the end of the 19th century. It was a reaction against the liberal and modernistic currents of theology that infiltrated the seminaries and universities, especially in the Northern and Eastern parts of the United States. Drawing its strength principally from the rural areas and small towns of the "Bible belt" (the South and Midwest), old-fashioned evangelical faith found expression in various gatherings, notably in annual Bible conferences, at which the so-called "higher criticism" of the Bible was deplored. The Niagara Bible Conference of 1878 drew up 14 "fundamentals of the faith," which were later reduced to five: (1) the inspiration and inerrancy of the Bible; (2) the virgin birth and full deity of Christ; (3) Christ's death as a sacrifice to satisfy the divine justice; (4) Christ's bodily resurrection; and (5) Christ's return in bodily form to preside at the Last Judgment. In some lists the miracles of Christ in his public ministry took the place of his second coming as the fifth fundamental.

Origin and Development. In Los Angeles, California, two brothers, Milton and Lyman Stewart, promoted the movement by founding in 1908 the Los Angeles Bible Institute and establishing the Stewart Evangelistic fund to promote their conservative views. With their financial support a series of 12 small volumes, titled *The Fundamentals: A Testimony to the Truth*, were published between 1910 and 1915. The Stewarts mailed some three million copies of these books free of charge to pastors, missionaries, theology students, and church workers. These booklets, containing 90 articles by scholars from Europe and North America, defended the inspiration and total inerrancy of the Bible, opposed the "higher criticism," and attacked evolutionism and the "social gospel." Contrary to scientific biblical scholarship, they asserted that the Pentateuch (except Dt 34) was written by Moses himself.

The movement took another step forward in 1919, with the founding of the World's Christian Fundamentals Association, which published a quarterly review and conducted annual rallies in various North American cities during the next decade. About 1920 the title "Fundamentalist" first came into currency, signifying, as one newspaper expressed it, one who does "battle royal for the Fundamentals." This title was accepted by the adherents as a badge of honor. "Creation science," based on a strict interpretation of GENESIS, was promoted as an alternative to Darwinism.

During the 1920s many American Protestant churches, especially those with strong evangelical tendencies—such as the Presbyterians, Methodists, Baptists, and Disciples of Christ—became split into Fundamentalist and Modernist camps, with an amorphous group caught in the middle. The Lutherans and Episcopalians felt the contro-

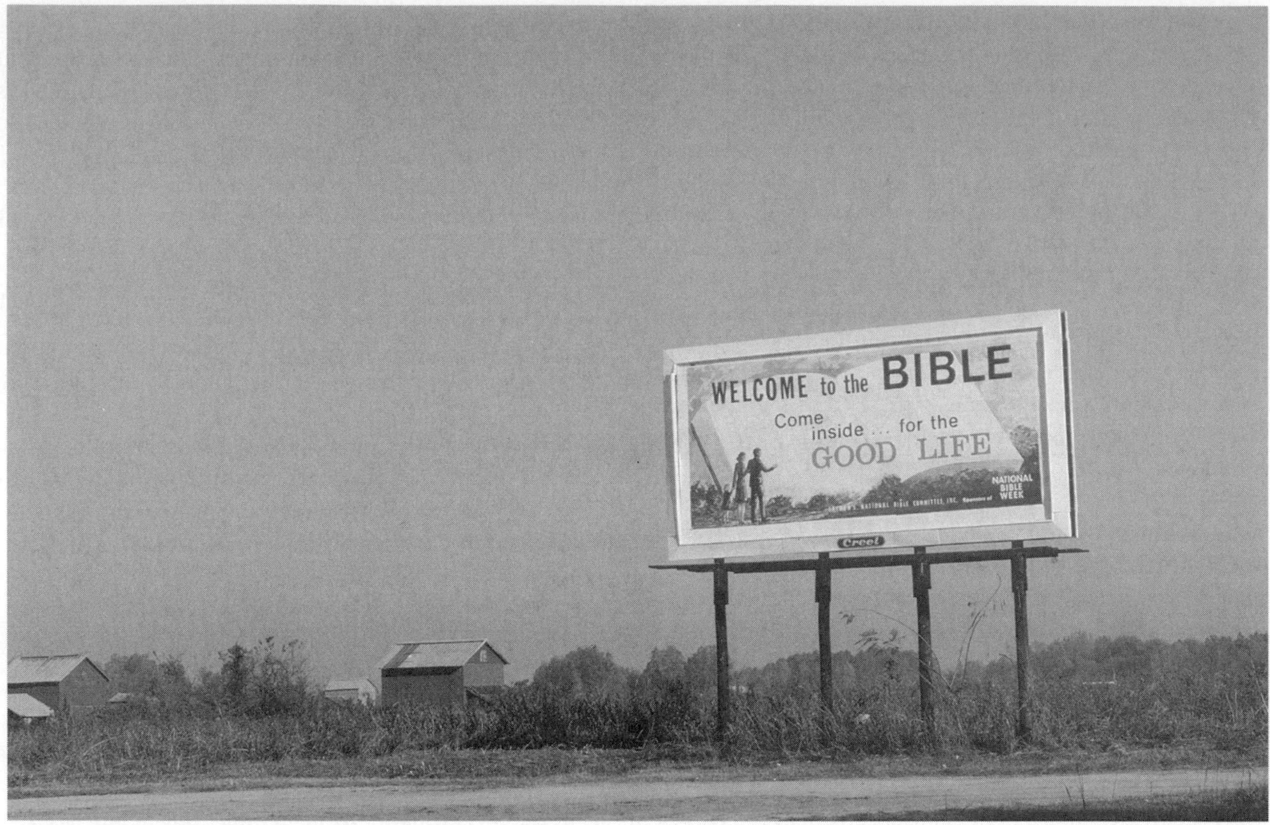

Religious billboard, South Carolina. (©Franken Owen/CORBIS)

versy less acutely, being more securely rooted in their confessional traditions.

Although Fundamentalism was primarily the fruit of simplistic popular thinking, it acquired intellectual respectability through the support of several distinguished theologians. Benjamin B. Warfield of Princeton Theological Seminary, perhaps the most eminent of America's conservative Presbyterian scholars, contributed to the first volume of *The Fundamentals*. John Gresham Machen, also of Princeton, while preferring to call himself simply a Calvinist, likewise supported the Fundamentalist cause.

Decline. Largely through Fundamentalist pressures, several state legislatures barred the teaching of evolution in public schools. In 1925 John T. Scopes, a high school biology teacher in Dayton, Tenn., was accused of teaching Darwinism in violation of the law. Behind the immediate question of evolution loomed the larger question whether the Bible was totally free of error in its obvious meaning, as understood by the ordinary reader. Although Scopes was convicted and the constitutionality of the statute upheld, William Jennings Bryan's feeble performance as a witness for the prosecution and the unfavorable publicity given to the case in the secular press resulted in a major setback for Fundamentalism.

In the mid-1920s the Fundamentalist tide began to recede. In 1927 Princeton Seminary, the traditional bastion of conservative orthodoxy, opened itself to other theological tendencies. In 1929 Machen resigned his post to found a new conservative seminary in Philadelphia, and ultimately (in 1936) his own Orthodox Presbyterian Church.

Although Fundamentalism lost much of its influence, important Protestant groups, especially in the Netherlands and the U.S., remain strongly committed to the view that the Bible, understood in its obvious literal meaning, is totally inerrant. The more sophisticated representatives of conservative Evangelicalism, such as Carl F. H. Henry and Edward J. Carnell, sought to shed the Fundamentalist label and to identify themselves with international conservative Protestant bodies, such as the World Evangelical Fellowship. But the Fundamentalist mentality continues to manifest itself in some parts of the United States. In 1981, for example, the State of Arkansas adopted a law requiring that ''creation science'' be taught alongside of evolutionary theory in public schools. That law was later ruled unconstitutional.

Catholic Responses. Fundamentalism properly so called can have no legitimate place in Catholic theology. Already in the 17th century the Catholic bishop J. B. Bossuet controverted the view of the Calvinist Pierre Jurieu that a few ''fundamental articles'' could be a sufficient test of orthodoxy. In his encyclical *Mortalium animos* (1928) Pius XI rejected the distinction between fundamental and nonfundamental articles. The ''five fundamentals,'' while true if rightly understood, do not mention all that Catholics consider basic to their faith. The omission of the Trinity, the Church, and the sacraments gives a markedly sectarian slant to the Fundamentalist platform.

Certain anti-Modernist trends in Catholic theology ran parallel to Protestant Fundamentalism. Catholics regarded by some as ultraconservative opposed the scientific study of the Scriptures and sought to defend every sentence of the Bible in what they took to be its obvious sense. They rejected the idea of human evolution as unbiblical and repudiated the practice of distinguishing between different ''literary forms'' in books deemed to be historical. Pius XII in his encyclical *Divino afflante Spiritu* (1943), correcting these tendencies, endorsed scientific literary and historical criticism and a prudent use of the method of form criticism. In 1993 the Pontifical Biblical Commission issued a document on *The Interpretation of the Bible in the Church*, which included a severe criticism of Fundamentalism for offering false certitudes and for confusing the divine substance of the Bible with what are in fact its human limitations. The United States Catholic Bishops' Conference in 1987 established an ad hoc committee on Biblical Fundamentalism that warned against the deceptive attractions of Fundamentalism, calling attention to its tendency to neglect the role of the Church in the transmission of Christian faith.

Bibliography: G. M. MARSDEN, *Fundamentalism and American Culture* (New York 1980); *Understanding Fundamentalism and Evangelicalism* (Grand Rapids, Mich. 1991). T. M. O'MEARA, *Fundamentalism: A Catholic Perspective* (New York 1990). PONTIFICAL BIBLICAL COMMISSION, *The Interpretation of the Bible in the Church* (Vatican City 1993). UNITED STATES BISHOPS' COMMITTEE, ''Pastoral Statement for Catholics on Biblical Fundamentalism,'' *Origins* 17 (Nov. 5, 1987) 376–77. H. A HARRIS, *Fundamentalism and Evangelicals* (Oxford 1998).

[A. DULLES]

FUNDAMENTALISM, BIBLICAL

The term fundamentalism is used in two related but clearly distinguished senses: (1) to designate what is more generally called a conservative type of Christian thought, as opposed to the liberal or modernist tendencies that became influential in the second half of the 19th and

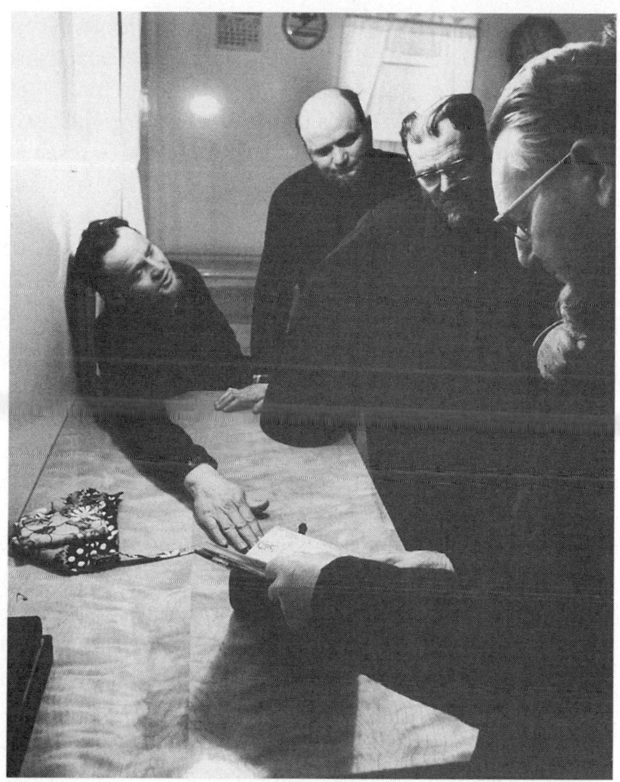

Hutterite elders gather around to re-examine their version of the Bible, Miller Colony, Montana, 1968. The Hutterites, a fundamentalist Christian sect founded by Hutter in Germany, immigrated to the Ukraine, Canada, South Dakota, and finally, Montana. (©Ted Streshinsky/CORBIS)

even more so in the first half of the 20th century; and (2) as the name of a specific conservative movement with it own organizations and agencies devoted to the propagation of a definite doctrinal program (the five points of fundamentalism) that, it was claimed, constitutes the true Christian faith. In the first sense the term is more often used by liberals to describe conservatives than by the conservatives to describe themselves.

Organized Movement. In the second sense fundamentalism is a religious movement that began in the U.S. in 1909 among very conservative members of various Protestant denominations (mainly Baptists). Its objectives were to resist the spread of modernism in theology and to maintain traditional interpretations of the Bible and what they believed to be the fundamental doctrines of the Christian faith. A series of 12 books or pamphlets was issued between 1910 and 1912, subsidized by two laymen, Milton and Lyman Stewart. Five points of doctrine were set forth as fundamental: (1) the literal inerrancy and infallibility of the Bible, (2) the virgin birth and full deity of Christ, (3) the physical Resurrection of Christ, (4) the atoning sacrifice of His death for the sins of the world, and (5) His second coming in bodily form to preside at the Last Judgment. The Stewart brothers also founded the Los Angeles Bible Institute and established the Stewart Evangelistic Fund in order to promote their tenets. In 1918 the World's Christian Fundamentals association was founded. Its chief objectives were to resist all anti-Christian influences throughout the world, especially in the U.S., and to defend the strict literal sense of the Bible. The main fundamentalist controversy was among the Baptists, though it spread to other denominations, in particular to the Presbyterians. At Dallas, Texas, in 1923, the bishops of the Episcopal Church issued a pastoral letter requiring strict conformity to the 39 Articles.

Repercussions. Tension between liberals and conservatives arose in many Bible colleges throughout the U.S. Dr. Harry Emerson Fosdick, a liberal Baptist preacher at the First Presbyterian Church, New York, refused to accept the church's required doctrinal positions and was forced to withdraw from his post. Repercussions were felt in other areas of public life. Laws against the teaching of evolution in the public schools were passed in some southern states of the U.S. In the famous Scopes trial at Dayton, Tenn., in 1925, William Jennings Bryan, a fundamentalist, won the state's case against John T. Scopes, a public high school teacher charged with teaching evolution. The influence of the fundamentalist movement was strong on both clergy and laymen in Protestant circles. It occasioned the organization of the American (now International) Council of Christian Churches in opposition to the Federal (now National) Council of the Churches of Christ in America (now in the United States of America). The fundamentalist movement exercised its strongest influence in the southern and agricultural areas of the U.S. in the 1920s. Fundamentalist theological seminaries were founded to counteract the influence of the more liberal theological schools of Crozer, Princeton, and Union, and Harvard University and the University of Chicago. By the late 20th century, fundamentalism had lost the extensive influence it once had. While no means extinct, the movement changed its methods and less frequently used that name.

Bibliography: J. W. JOHNSON, *Fundamentalism versus Modernism* (New York 1925). W. LIPPMANN, *American Inquisitors* (New York 1928). A. W. ROBINSON, *The New Learning and the Old Faith* (New York 1928). S. G. COLE, *The History of Fundamentalism* (New York 1931). J. L. NEVE and O. W. HEICK, *A History of Christian Thought,* 2 v. (Philadelphia 1943–46) 2:325–328. F. E. MAYER, *The Religious Bodies of America,* rev. A. C. PIEPKORN (4th ed. St. Louis 1961).

[T. A. COLLINS]

FUNERAL RITES

The Greco-Roman funeral procession—the *funus*—what everyone understood to be *the* funeral, was adopted by Christians as a metaphor for their journey as earthly church toward the heavenly Jerusalem. They spoke of this journey and its expression in the funeral procession as ''going to Christ'' (*ire ad Christum*). For ancient Christians, the mystery of divine incarnation and the promise of resurrection in the likeness of the risen Christ transformed superstitious concerns about the lot of the dead. Belief in the *sacredness of the human body*, the *mystery of Christ's incarnation and resurrection*, and the *resurrection of the dead* traditionally found expression in the care taken to prepare the bodies of the deceased for burial. The body that participated integrally in all the expressions of sacramental life became the primary object of liturgical attention in funeral liturgy. The prayers and ritual gestures of Catholic funeral rites affirm the Church's reverence for the mortal remains of her decreased members. Whatever form human mortal remains take, they are due Christian respect as the final form of the flesh and blood person who lived and died and will rise in relationship with God.

A Brief History. In the Greco-Roman culture of earliest Christianity burial and cremation existed side by side. Christians followed the Jewish custom of burial. By mid third century, burial became the preferred proper ritual attention to the dead, necessary to secure happiness in the afterlife. Throwing a handful of earth on the corpse or, in the case of cremation, cutting off a small bone to be buried later were essential rites. Even the dead stranger was to be given a ritual burial, and, when cremations did take place, burial of the ashes in the earth or a tomb was the norm.

The earliest Christian writings include examples of prayers and hymns for use at funerals, marking the beginning of the Christian *obsequiae* or services for the dead. Long before Christians had churches, they buried their dead brothers and sisters and kept their memory alive in their cemeteries (*koimeteria* or dormitories for the dead [*see* BURIAL II (EARLY CHRISTIAN)]). Later they constructed their first basilicas over the site of Jesus' death, burial, and resurrection and over the graves of martyrs. In time the Christian funeral developed into rites that took place ''at church,'' and burial in the churchyard or entombment in or along the walls of the church building itself became the tradition. These cemeteries are iconographic witnesses to Christian care of the dead. Their funerary decorations proclaimed that the dead had gone to the Paradise of the Shepherd, to the place of refreshment, light, and peace. They linked the ''refreshment'' of the funeral meal with the Eucharist, the food of life. Other decorations reflected singing and prayer on the part of individuals and the community.

In like manner Christians invested other funeral practices with their religious memory and faith. Activi-

Christian funeral service, Russia. (©David & Peter Turnley/CORBIS)

ties, such as washing and anointing of the dead, the solemn *funus* or funeral procession to the cemetery, and the tomb itself, became symbols of liturgy. To the Hebrew psalms they added Christian hymns; the eucharistic banquet came to supersede the memorial funeral meal; Jewish and pagan funerary art inspired still newer Christian representations expressing the mystery of redemption. Prayer for the dead became a duty in Christian charity. Augustine, for example, taught that prayer, almsgiving, and especially offering the Eucharist were efficacious for the dead before the judgment seat of God. In time, two attitudes of Christian faith, one hopeful of God's mercy, the other fearful of God's justice, marked the increasingly familiar ways Christians translated that faith into worship and constituted the origin of a Christian funeral liturgy.

Orders of funeral service survive from the ninth century. They reveal a pattern of prayerful preparation of the corpse (washing, clothing), vigil or wake with psalms, hymns and Scripture readings, a procession with the body to the church complex for burial to the accompaniment of psalms and prayers. Gradually, the celebration of Mass, associated with Christian death from the beginning, became a formal part of the funeral rites themselves and the church, the focal point of the liturgy. Throughout the Middle Ages, despite the different customs from region to region and between cathedral and monastic practices, a threefold structure of the classic Catholic funeral evolved as the norm. The *Rituale* ordered by the Council of Trent made it the universal practice of the Church. The *Order of Christian Funerals (OCF)* embodies this tradition as Vigil and Related Rites, Funeral Liturgy, Rite of Committal, like three panels of a triptych, and thus preserves the spirit of the funeral as metaphor for the Christian journey to Christ.

Vigil and Related Rites. The Vigil and Related Rites and Prayers are opportunities for liturgical prayer that may be celebrated during the time between death and the principal Funeral Liturgy or committal. They enable the specifically Christian expressions of faith and hope to find an appropriate place in the earliest moments of leave-taking. Although the term ''vigil'' in the *OCF* designates a particular liturgical rite of ''vigil for the deceased,'' the whole time span surrounding death is a liminal time of ''vigil'' or wake. Its purpose is to offer the Church's supportive ministry of gently accompanying the mourners in their initial adjustment, cognizant of their need to express the sorrow of bereavement and to enjoy the treasure of consolation their faith holds for them.

The Vigil for the Deceased is the principal celebration of the Christian community during the time before the funeral liturgy (or, should there be no funeral liturgy, before the rite of committal). It may take the traditional form of a liturgy of the Word or of some form of the Office for the Dead. The latter also introduces the community to the psalms, particularly the lament psalms, which effectively permit the bereaved to own the reality of grief in the context of faith and hope.

Custom and pastoral need determine where the vigil takes place. For bereaved confined to their homes or other residences, celebrating the vigil there may be preferred; for others, the vigil at the parish church (where the body might ''be waked'' until the Funeral Liturgy) will be the best solution. Finally, the funeral home, where the body has been prepared and laid out for visitation and last respects, offers a convenient, familiar location.

The vigil for a deceased child differs slightly from the vigil for adults. There is greater flexibility to adapt the rite to suit the occasion, with more appropriate texts, specifically adapted to the needs of the family suffering such a tragic loss. The Church commends the child to the love of God the author of life, and prays for the consolation of the immediate family.

The *OCF* restores the vigil as an integral part of the Catholic funeral, and the models proposed are familiar to today's faithful. The Church gathers to share the pain and suffering of the family by allowing the Word of God to transform their grief and to pledge support for them in the times ahead.

Besides the Vigil for the Deceased and the devotional prayer of parish groups (such as the traditional Rosary) during the wake, there are other critical times in the period soon after death when the Church wishes to pray with the family and close friends of the deceased. The *OCF* provides for this opportunity by including Related Rites and Prayers as models of liturgical pastoral care to be adapted according to the circumstances of time, place and culture. These moments include prayers after death, gathering in the presence of the body, and the transfer of the body to the church or place of committal. They are times when the intimate family and friends of the deceased ordinarily begin to confront the reality of death and loss and may start to feel grief and pain deeply. At such moments the *OCF* recognizes the need for paschal faith and the consolation of Christian hope as well as the support of the entire community embodied in the presence of those who gather.

The Funeral Liturgy. As Catholic leave-taking, the principal funeral rite in the church stands in direct continuity with the vigil and related rites during the time following death and presumes movement to final closure at committal. With its unique prelude (Reception of the Body) and postlude (Final Commendation and Farewell) the Funeral Mass is the principal Catholic funeral event: Eucharist, at one with Jesus dead and risen, toward which all has pointed, and from which closure and a new relationship with the deceased follows. The symbols surrounding the deceased are reminders of a living faith that cannot be quenched by death. Sprinkling with holy water, placing of the pall, lighting of the Easter candle are all signs of baptism. They mark the rite of passage not from but into the land of the living.

Models for Funeral Liturgy for both adults and children follow traditional patterns while still incorporating options for celebrating the Rite of Reception earlier at the Vigil liturgy as well as celebrating the Final Commendation later at the place of committal. Two forms accommodate pastoral circumstances: ''Funeral Liturgy'' (including a funeral Mass) and ''Funeral Liturgy outside Mass,'' with all elements of the former except the Eucharist. In all circumstances, a funeral Mass is preferred, and the *OCF* invites all to celebrate Mass soon in association with the death, whatever the circumstances of the funeral may have been. For the Eucharist is the sacrament that connects the mystery of the death and resurrection of the Lord to the death of this Christian.

The Final Commendation is very simple: an invitation to prayer, silence, signs and song of farewell, and prayer of commendation. Yet its explicit commendation of the deceased into God's hands at this closing moment of the Funeral Liturgy profoundly professes Christian belief that the living God, not the destruction of death, has the last word for this person of faith.

The Rite of Committal and Beyond. Nowhere do the paschal faith of Christians and the cross of human mortality meet more explicitly than beside an open grave or other final resting place. It is the authentic tradition of the Church to be present there. The liturgy of committal thus expresses the consolation of faith that gives meaning to this seemingly most meaningless experience of human loss and promises the continued presence of the Church.

What happens at the cemetery is a natural continuation of the funeral liturgy at church. The church complex and the cemetery form a liturgical unity, even when they are separated by time or distance. Formerly a short procession with the corpse from the church to the place of disposition—together with the prayers, psalms and rituals of committal—functioned primarily to conclude the rites of leave-taking. Today the procession with the body *from* the church is the same procession that *enters* the cemetery and proceeds to the grave or mausoleum. In this procession to the place of committal the *OCF* has restored the spirit of the classic Christian funeral. It is not distance but the movement of the Church with the deceased (*ire ad Christum*) as liturgical action that creates a ''funeral'' procession.

Rites of committal themselves follow the familiar pattern of spoken word and acted sign: gathering (preferably at the site of interment or preservation of cremated remains), short Scripture verses, prayer and, where pastorally appropriate, lowering the coffin into the grave or placing the cremation container in its resting place. The *OCF* affirms, ''Through this act (of committal) the community of faith proclaims that the grave or place of interment, once a sign of futility and despair, has been transformed by means of Christ's death and resurrection into a sign of hope and promise'' (209).

The liturgy now points beyond the funeral and professes the commitment of the assembled Church to walk with the bereaved on the long, often painful process of healing. In short, committal rites serve to bring the funeral liturgy to closure and open the official time of mourning.

Bibliography: NATIONAL CONFERENCE OF CATHOLIC BISHOPS, *Order of Christian Funerals*, 1989, including Appendix on Cremation. Available from three publishers: Catholic Book Publishing Co., The Liturgical Press, and Liturgical Training Publications. V. K. OWUSU, *The Roman Funeral Liturgy: History, Celebration, and Theology* (Nettetetal 1993). F. S. PAXTON, *Christianizing Death: The Creation of a Ritual Process in Early Medieval Europe* (Ithaca, NY 1996). G. ROWELL, *The Liturgy of Christian Burial* (London 1977). A. C. RUSH, *Death and Burial in Christian Antiquity* (Washington, DC 1941). R. H. RUTHERFORD, *The Death of a Christian. The Order of Christian Funerals* (Collegeville, MN 1990). D. SICARD, *La liturgie de la mort dans l'église latine des origins à la réforme carolingienne* (Münster 1978). J. M. C. TOYNBEE, *Death and Burial in the Roman World* (London 1971). F. VAN DER MEER and C. MOHRMANN, *Atlas of the Early Christian World* (London 1966).

[R. RUTHERFORD]

FUNERALS (CANON LAW)

Christian FUNERAL RITES have traditionally consisted of three parts: the escorting of the body to the church or cemetery; rites at the house, the church and the cemetery; and burial in ground set aside for the interment of the faithful.

Right to a Church Funeral. As to who may receive Church Funeral, *Codex iuris canonici* (CIC) 1 c., 1176, states that the Christian faithful departed must be given ecclesiastical funerals in accord with the norm of law. In addition to Catholic Christians, CIC c., 1183 allows for the celebration of Catholic funeral rites for certain other groups (confer, CCEO 1, 2 c., 876). Catechumens are to be given Catholic funeral rites, as are children whom the parents intended to baptize, but who died before baptism could be administered. A local ordinary may allow a Christian enrolled in a non-Catholic church or ecclesial community to have an ecclesiastical funeral, if the person's own minister is unavailable, and if such is not manifestly contrary to the person's intention.

Denial of Church Funerals. With regard to those who may not be given Christian burial, CIC c., 1184 expressly forbids ecclesiastical funerals to three classes of Catholics (confer, CCEO *c.* 877):

(1) Notorious apostates, heretics and schismatics. CIC c., 751 gives definitions for apostasy, heresy and schism. The offense must be publicly known. One who ceased the practice of Catholic religion without formally abandoning the Church does not fall under this heading, and should not be denied Catholic funeral rites.

(2) Those who have commanded that their body be cremated for reasons contrary to Christian faith. Officially forbidden for centuries, CREMATION is now permissible, so long as ''it does not demonstrate a denial of faith in the resurrection of the body'' (CCC, no. 2301). The Eastern Code permits cremation ''provided it does not obscure the preference of the Church for the burial of bodies and that scandal is avoided'' (CCEO c. 8763). In the Order of Christian Funerals approved for use in the United States, guidelines have been provided for funeral liturgies involving the cremated remains of the deceased.

(3) Other manifest sinners who cannot be granted ecclesiastical funerals without public scandal. The term manifest indicates that the person must be publicly known to have lived in a state of grave sin. For example, some who might qualify are those involved in the drug trade and those who have admitted to murder. It is also required that having an ecclesiastical funeral would provoke public scandal among the Christian faithful. Only when both conditions are verified would Catholic funeral rites be prohibited. Persons who have divorced and remarried do not come under this heading. Nor are persons who have committed suicide included under this heading. According to most medical authorities, a person who

Deán Gregorio Funes.

commits suicide is considered deprived at least temporarily of the full possession of his faculties.

Doubtful Cases. If the deceased has given any sign of repentance, he is not to be denied a Catholic funeral. Such a sign of repentance might be summoning a priest or making an act of perfect contrition. These signs show that the deceased in some way preserved an attachment to the Church.

Bibliography: M. CONTE, *De locis et temporibus sacris* (Turin 1922) 125–133, 150–151, 253–268. C. KERIN, *The Privation of Christian Burial* (*Catholic University of America Canon Law Studies,* 136; Washington 1941). A. BERNARD, *La Sépulture en Droit Canonique* (Paris 1933). J. M. HUELS, OSM in J. P. BEAL et al., *New Commentary on the Code of Canon Law* (New York 2000) 1412–1413.

[C. A. KERIN/J. STAAB]

FUNES, DEÁN GREGORIO

Argentine priest and political figure in the independence movement; b. Córdoba, May 25, 1749; d. Buenos Aires, Jan. 10, 1829. He was buried in the Cathedral of Córdoba.

Funes obtained his doctorate in theology at the University of Córdoba (1774), his degree in civil and Canon Law at Alcalá de Henares, Spain, and was admitted to the practice of law before the Royal Councils in 1778. He held numerous ecclesiastical posts in his native city, including that of dean of its cathedral (1804). He was also vicar-general and governor of the bishopric. Funes served as rector of the Colegio de Monserrat and of the University of Córdoba (then called San Carlos) between 1808 and 1813. His ideas and achievements in the field of education are set forth in his *Plan de Estudios* of 1813. In this work he included new ideas without breaking with tradition. Through education he tried to mold the student's personality, orienting his teaching around philosophy and theology.

In 1810 he joined the revolution that won Argentina its independence, and he performed many important services as a member of the first revolutionary governments and as deputy in the congresses that drafted the constitutions of 1819 and 1826. He advised the government on drafting decrees, such as those on freedom of the press and on the creation of provincial juntas foreshadowing federalism. He reformed ordinances and influenced public opinion through contributions to the newspapers *Gaceta, El Argos, El Centinela,* and *La Abeja Argentina.*

Funes was, above all, a politician concerned with the practical problems of his country in a time of great change, and he put his great learning into the service of his vocation, the independence of his country. His conception of the revolution was analogous to that of Bolívar. He was democratic and drew support for his ideas from the Spanish theological school, with influences from French ideology. As a liberal in politics, he advocated an ethical liberalism respectful of religion. He supported the organization of his country on a federal basis.

He was deeply concerned over the relations between Church and State, then disturbed by the PATRONATO REAL and the attitude of the Holy See, which continued to respect Spanish patronage and thus cut off the Argentine Church, with serious damage to its discipline. To Funes, the Patronato was tied to national sovereignty and therefore could be exercised by the revolutionary government. He felt the Church and the State differed in origins, means, and ends, but should act together and aid each other. The one, universal Church was subordinated to the pope, but within the Spanish tradition, the Church had granted to the State certain powers in the field of ecclesiastical discipline. He supported the intolerance of the Church but admitted State tolerance limited by the requirements of public order and due protection of religion.

Funes's writings are numerous and varied. They include articles on ecclesiastical matters and on civil rights, and a three-volume work, *Ensayo de historia civil del Paraguay, Buenos Aires y Tucumán* (Buenos Aires 1816–17).

Bibliography: G. FURLONG, *Bio-bibliografía del deán Funes* (Córdoba 1939). E. MARTINEZ PAZ, *El deán Funes: Un apóstol de la libertad* (Córdoba 1950).

[E. MARTÍNEZ PAZ]

FUNK, FRANZ XAVER VON

Church historian and patrologist; b. Abtsgmünd, Germany, Oct. 12, 1821; d. Tübingen, Feb. 24, 1907. Educated in the German school system, he obtained his doctorate in 1863, was ordained in 1864, and lectured as an instructor (repetent) in theology at Tübingen from 1866 to 1870. His early interests were devoted to moral theology and national economy, and he wrote monographs on usury, including *Zins und Wucher* (1868) and *Geschichte des kirchlichen Zinsverbotes* (1876). In 1870 he replaced C. HEFELE as lecturer in history and theology and in 1875 was named a full professor at Tübingen. He achieved an international reputation as a historian of the early Church, patrologist, and Christian archeologist. During his 37 years at Tübingen, his scientific method and devotion to scholarship helped further the reputation for excellence of the Catholic faculty at Tübingen. His edition of the post-Apostolic Fathers, *Opera Patrum Apostolicorum* (2 v. Tübingen 1878–81), has been reedited by his students and successors. His *Lehrbuch der Kirchengeschichte* (1886) was frequently revised and is the basis for the contemporary study by K. Bihlmeyer and H. Tüchle, *Church History* (tr. V. Mills, 3 v. Westminster 1956–65). He also published editions of the *Doctrina XII Apostolorum* (1887), *Didascalia et Constitutiones Apostolorum* (2 v. 1905), and a collection of articles and reviews, *Kirchengeschichtliche Abhandlungen und Untersuchungen* (3 v. 1897–1907).

Bibliography: K. BIHLMEYER, *Lexicon für Theologic and Kirche* 1 4:235. A. KOCH, *Theologische Quartalschrift* (Tübingen, 1908) 95–137. H. SCHIEL, *F. X. Kraus und die katholische Tübinger Schule* (Ellwangen 1958) 73–83. P. GODET, *Revue du Clergé* 56 (1908) 129–149; DTC 6.1:972–975.

[P. STEELS]

FURLONG, THOMAS

Bishop, founder of three religious institutes; b. Mayglass, County Wexford, Ireland, *c.* 1803; d. Wexford, Nov. 12, 1875. He entered St. Patrick's College, Maynooth, in 1819 and was ordained in 1826 after a Dunboyne theology course of two years. On June 28, 1827, he became junior dean in Maynooth, and then successively professor of humanities (1829), of rhetoric (1834), and of theology (1845). He was consecrated bishop of Ferns on March 22, 1857. As a bishop he strengthened ecclesiastical institutions and fostered a more personal and interior spirituality among his flock. Based on his deep personal spirituality, especially his devotion to the Blessed Sacrament, his labors produced results still in evidence both within the diocese and, through the work of the institutions he founded, far outside it. To promote the better observance of Sundays and holy days, he opposed the prevalent custom of holding fairs and transacting business on those days and also the intemperance so often associated with these practices. He developed the diocesan seminary, St. Peter's College, Wexford. For the education of girls, he introduced six convents of nuns into his diocese. He also completed the cathedral church of St. Aidan, Enniscorthy.

In 1866 he founded the Missionaries of the Blessed Sacrament, diocesan priests who live a common life and, from their headquarters in Enniscorthy, preach missions and retreats in the diocese and outside it. In 1871 he founded the Sisters of ST. JOHN OF GOD, a teaching and nursing order that has spread widely in Ireland and abroad. After various attempts to introduce an order of nuns devoted to perpetual adoration of the Blessed Sacrament, he secured papal approval in 1875 for the Institute of Perpetual Adoration, a diocesan congregation of sisters, which has ever since maintained vigil before the Blessed Sacrament in one of the parish churches of Wexford.

Bibliography: W. H. G. FLOOD, *History of the Diocese of Ferns* (Waterford 1916). *Irish Catholic Directory* (1857–75).

[P. J. CORISH]

FURSEY (FURSEUS), ST.

Irish missionary; b. near Lough Corrib, Ireland, possibly on the island Inisquin in that lake; d. Diocese of Amiens, France, *c.* 650. He became a religious and founded a monastery in the Diocese of Tuam (Cill Fursa) to which recruits came from all Ireland. Later he traveled in England and founded a monastery at Burgh Castle near Yarmouth. Between 640 and 644, having been driven out of England by Penda, he went to Gaul. There King Clovis II gave him land near Paris where he built a monastery at LAGNY-SUR-MARNE. At one time he served as vicar of the Diocese of Paris. He died while traveling in the Diocese of Amiens, and his remains were taken to Peronne, France; they were found incorrupt many years later. Fursey enjoyed great literary fame in the Middle Ages because of his celebrated visions (*see* VISION (DREAM) LITERATURE). These were first reported by BEDE (*Histoire Ecclesiastique.* 3.19) and by AELFRIC GRAMMATICUS, but the Latin vitae also devote much space to his mystical experiences.

Feast: Jan. 16 (Diocese of Northampton and throughout Ireland).

Bibliography: J. COLGAN, *The Acta sanctorum Hiberniae* (Louvain 1645; repr. Dublin 1948) 75–98. *Acta Sanctorum* Jan. 2:399–419. *Monumenta Germaniae Scriptores rerum Merovingicarum* (Berlin 1825–) 4:423–449. W. STOKES, *Three Months in the Forests of France: A Pilgrimage in Search of Vestiges of the Irish Saints in France* (London 1895); ed. and tr., "The Life of Fursa," *Revue Celtique* 25 (1904) 385–404. *Nova legenda Anglie,* ed. C. HORSTMANN, 2 v. (Oxford 1901) v.1. C. S. BOSWELL, *An Irish Precursor of Dante* (London 1908) 166–169. J. F. KENNEY, *The Sources for the Early History of Ireland:* v.1, *Ecclesiastical* (New York 1929) 500–503. L. GOUGAUD, *Gaelic Pioneers of Christianity,* tr. V. COLLINS (Dublin 1923) 17–19.

[R. T. MEYER]

FÜRSTENBERG, FRANZ VON

Priest, statesman, and educator who reformed education in the Diocese of Münster and influenced Catholic education throughout the Germanies; b. Herdringen, Westphalia, Aug. 7, 1729; d. Münster, Sept. 16, 1810. He attended the universities of Cologne and Salzburg and completed his studies in jurisprudence at the Sapienza in Rome. The Fürstenberg family, which takes its name from the castle of Fürstenberg on the Ruhr, ruled over large tracts of land in Westphalia and was among the most important Catholic lines in the Germanies. As a member of this family, Franz Friedrich Wilhelm had many paths of preferment open to him, but choosing to enter the service of the Church, he was ordained in 1757.

In 1761 the elector of Cologne, later the prince-bishop of Münster, appointed von Fürstenberg as a member of his curia. In 1770, after passing through numerous lower offices, von Fürstenberg became vicar-general of the diocese. Since the prince-bishop was also a temporal ruler, many secular administrative duties were attached to the office of vicar-general, in which capacity he effected several economic and agricultural reforms, improved the military system, and in 1773 established a college of medicine. His service on the curial staff also resulted in some administrative changes in church and state, accomplished by establishing a corps of educated and trained officials. The educational practices then in vogue, however, which leaned toward the classics and nonpractical subjects, seemed constructed to frustrate the vicar-general's purposes.

Von Fürstenberg's desire for administrative reforms focused his attention on education. Wishing to make the Gymnasium more practical, with greater emphasis on subjects that prepared young men for civil or Church service, he included the vernacular, German, in the curriculum; gave greater prominence to natural sciences and mathematics; and deemphasized the classics. To supply teachers for this new type of Gymnasium, in 1783 von Fürstenberg opened and entrusted to the priest-educator, Bernard OVERBERG, a normal school that became a model for the Catholic schools in the Germanies. The University of Münster received new financial grants and increased its influence during von Fürstenberg's tenure as vicar-general.

Bibliography: J. E. WISE, *The History of Education: An Analytic Survey from the Age of Homer to the Present* (New York 1964). J. ESTERHUES, *Lexikon der Pädagogik* 2:192–193.

[E. G. RYAN]

FÜRSTENBERG, FRANZ AND WILHELM EGON VON

Franz and Wilhelm Egon Von Fürstenberg were German churchmen and statesmen, sons of Egon von Fürstenberg–Heiligenberg (1588–1635), Bavarian Commander in Chief; Franz Egon, b. Bavaria, April 10, 1625; d. Cologne, Germany, April 1, 1682; and Wilhelm Egon, b. Bavaria, Dec. 2, 1629; d. Paris, April 10, 1704. The talents and the ambition of these brothers, who had their education by Jesuits in Cologne, were recognized early in their lives by the Bavarian Prince Maximilian Heinrich, later electoral prince of Cologne. They remained in his service until won over by Cardinal Mazarin with gifts, pensions, and benefices. They became energetic in furthering French interests and were instrumental in creating the *rheinischer Bund* between the rulers of important German cities and states and the crown of France. Later Louis XIV rewarded their loyalty with rich benefices and titles of honor, giving Franz the bishopric of Strassburg and Wilhelm the rich abbey of Saint–Michel. They also worked on the Francophile sympathies of Maximilia n Heinrich, with the result that the alliances on Oct. 22, 1666, and June 11, 1671, were favorable to the French monarch. During an annual carnival in Cologne, Wilhelm was apprehended by the troops of Emperor Leopold I. His execution for treason was averted by the intervention of the papal nuncio, but both he and Franz were deprived of incomes, privileges, and property. A provision of the treaty of Nijmegen in 1679, which closed the Franco-Holland wars, restored the Fürstenberg brothers to their possessions and titles. At the death of Franz, Louis XIV had Wilhelm elected to succeed to the See of Strassburg on June 22, 1682, and four years later obtained a cardinal's hat from Innocent XI for his loyal agent.

Wilhelm then intrigued to succeed the aged and ailing Maximilian Heinrich in the powerful See of Cologne. Against the warnings of Innocent XI, the cathedral chapter gave Wilhelm 17 of the 24 votes. Although the pope declared the election null and void, Fürstenberg headed the government on Maximilian Heinrich's death on June 3, 1688. Because his election had not been confirmed, another was set for July 19. Of the 24 votes, 13 fell to Wilhelm and nine to Joseph Clemens. Wilhelm entered the palace of the electoral prince and ordered a proclamation of his elevation. This precipitous action caused the assembly (September 15) to declare the postulation of Fürstenberg invalid and the election of Joseph Clemens legal. Preparations were made for the installation of Clemens, and Fürstenberg was commanded in severe terms to leave Bonn. On April 12, 1689, he left for his abbey, Saint–Germain–des–Prés in Paris, where he remained until his death.

Bibliography: L. ENNEN, *Allgemeine deutsche Biographie* (Leipzig 1875–1910) 7:297–306. *Der Grosse Brockhaus: Handbuch des Wissens*, 20 v. (15th ed. Leipzig 1928–35) 6:692. A. HASSAL, *Cambridge Modern History* (London-New York 1911–36) 5:32–63. H. S. WILLIAMS ed., *France 843–1715*, v. 11 of *The Historians' History of the World*, 27 v. in 15 (5th ed. New York 1926). M. BRAUBACH, *Lexikon für Theologie und Kirche*, ed. J. HOFER and K. RAHNER, 10 v. (2d, new ed. Freiburg 1957–65) 4:469–470.

[M. V. SCHULLER]

FUTURIBLE

That one of two possible contradictory acts that a free agent would perform if certain conditions were fulfilled. It is called pure futurible if they are not fulfilled. The reality of futuribles is apparent from an example: what a defeated electoral candidate would do if elected. At any given moment two contradictory actions would be possible to him, but only one would eventuate. Thus, every futurible is something that definitely ''would be'' and is therefore infallibly known by God. God's unerring providential government of human history is directed by His infallible knowledge of futuribles; admission of this divine knowledge is implied in all the Church's petitionary prayers. Few Catholic thinkers today question the reality of futuribles; but whether God knows the futuribles immediately, because of their definite intelligible being, or in Himself, is a disputed question.

See Also: PREDETERMINATION; SCIENTIA MEDIA; BÁÑEZ AND BAÑEZIANISM; MOLINISM; OMNISCIENCE; GRACE; PREDESTINATION; PROVIDENCE.

Bibliography: T. DE DIEGO DIÉZ, *Theologia naturalis* (Santander 1955).

[F. L. SHEERIN]

Johann Joseph Fux.

FUX, JOHANN JOSEPH

Preeminent baroque church musician in Austria; b. Hirtenfeld (Upper Styria), 1660?; d. Vienna, Feb. 13, 1741. His parents, simple country people, were Andreas and Ursula Fux. In 1680, as a young man, he began studies at the University of Graz, entered the Ferdinandeum, a Jesuit college, the following year, and apparently pursued further studies in Bologna. In 1696 he was appointed organist at the Schottenkirche, Vienna, maintaining this post until 1702; from 1698 he was also court composer to Emperor Leopold. From 1705 to 1715, when he became chief *Kapellmeister* to the court, he was music director at the cathedral of St. Stephen. His earliest composition (1697) is the Requiem for Archduchess Eleonora, Queen of Poland, performed also at the burial of Prince Eugene in 1737. This was followed by a seven-part *Concentus musico-instrumentalis* (1701) and his a cappella masterpiece, *Missa canonica,* both dedicated to the future Emperor Joseph I, and two operas (now lost), composed for saint's-day celebrations at court. His total compositions number more than 500 known items, some 300 of them for church use, including 60 Masses, 12 Requiems, 22 motets, 106 hymns, and several sonatas and settings of psalms and litanies, all distinguished by the perfection of his canonic writing, which even J. S. Bach admired. His great theoretical work, *Gradus ad Parnas-*

sum (1725, dedicated to Emperor Karl V), is a fundamental textbook of vocal counterpoint; it played an influential part in compositional training for more than a century and is still consulted in one or other of many editions and translations. The first English version appeared in 1791.

Bibliography: *Sämtliche Werke,* ed. JOHANN-JOSEPH-FUX GESELLSCHAFT (Kassel-New York 1959–); *Ausgewählte Kompositionen,* ed. J. MITTERER (*Denkmäler der Tonkunst in Österreich* [1893– ; repr. Graz 1959–] 3); *Messen,* ed. J. E. HABERT and G. A. GLOSSNER (*ibid.,* 1); *Steps to Parnassus,* ed. A. MANN (New York 1943), a new tr. of *Gradus ad Parnassum.* Also keyboard and instrumental works in various modern eds. O. STRUNK, ed., *Source Readings in Music History* (New York 1950) 535–563, with excerpts from *Gradus ad Parnassum.* A. LIESS, *Fuxiana* (Vienna 1958); *Die Musik in Geschichte und Gegenwart,* ed. F. BLUME (Kassel-Basel 1949–) 4:1159–75. J. H. VAN DER MEER, *Johann Joseph Fux als Opernkomponist,* 4 v. in 3 (Bilthoven 1961). A. LOEWENBERG and C. F. POHL, *Grove's Dictionary of Music and Musicians,* ed. E. BLOM, 9 v. (5th ed. London 1954) 3:527–575. P. H. LÁNG, *Music in Western Civilization* (New York 1941). D. J. GROUT, *A Short History of Opera,* 2 v. (2d, rev. and enl. ed. New York 1965). M. F. BUKOFZER, *Music in the Baroque Era* (New York 1947). H. FEDEHOFER, ''Johann Joseph Fux,'' in *The New Grove Dictionary of Music and Musicians,* ed. S. SADIE, v. 7 (New York 1980) 43–46. D. M. RANDEL, ed., *The Harvard Biographical Dictionary of Music* (Cambridge, Mass. 1996) 288. F. REIDEL, ''Johann Joseph Fux: Vor 250 Jahren starb Österreichs großer Barockkomponist,'' *Österreichische Musik Zeitschrift* 46 (1991) 450–457. N. SLONIMSKY, ed., *Baker's Biographical Dictionary of Musicians,* 8th ed. (New York 1992) 586. H. WHITE, ''Erhaltene quellen der oratorien von Johann Joseph Fux: Ein bericht,'' *Kirchenmusikalisches Jahrbuch,* 67 (1983) 123–131; ''The Oratorios of Johann Joseph Fux'' (Ph.D. diss. Trinity College, University of Dublin 1986); ed., *Johann Joseph Fux and the Music of the Austro-Italian Baroque* (Aldershot, Eng. 1992).

[F. HABERL]

G

GABON, THE CATHOLIC CHURCH IN

The Republic of Gabon is located in west central Africa. Featuring a narrow coastal plain to the west that rises to forested hills in the interior and a savanna in the east and south, Gabon was a territory in French West Africa from 1910 until it gained independence in 1960. Gabon is bordered by on the north by Equatorial Guinea and Cameroon, on the east and south by the Republic of the Congo, and on the west by the Atlantic Ocean.

With much of its territory covered by equatorial forest, Gabon's main products are agricultural: cocoa, plantains, coffee, cassava, palm oil, and soft timber. In addition, there are deposits of manganese, iron ore, uranium, and oil within its borders. Most of the population is ethnic Bantu, with tribal groupings of Fang, Eshira, Bapounou, and Bateke. Over 60 percent of the adult population is literate. Ecclesiastically, Gabon has an archdiocese located in Libreville, with diocese in Franceville, Mouila, and Oyem.

Although the Portuguese were the first Europeans to establish a presence on the coast of Gabon *c.* 1400, the region was settled by the French, who founded trading posts at the mouth of the Gabon estuary in 1839 and 1842. From these port cities, in 1839 France established a naval base to aid in its attempt to halt the slave trade. Ten years later Libreville was founded by French merchants from Senegal, and freed slaves settled there on a model plantation. The slow evangelization of Gabon's interior began in 1881 with the Mission of Lambaréné on the lower Ogooué River, which drains most of Gabon. Other missions were established at N'Djolé and Franceville in 1897 and at Sindara in 1899. An additional nine missions were founded in the region in 1925.

The immense Vicariate of the Two Guineas—Upper and Lower Guinea and Sierra Leone, called Gabon (1863) and Libreville (1947)—originally comprised all west Africa from Senegal to the Orange River (except Luanda), with no fixed inland borders. Eventually the vicariate was broken apart, with portions becoming the Prefecture of Fernando Po (1855) and the vicariates of Sierra Leone (1858), Dahomey (now Benin; 1860), Senegambia (now Dakar, Senegal; 1863), Congo (1865); the Gold and Ivory Coasts (now Cape Coast, Ghana and Abidjan; 1879), Upper Niger (now Benin City, Nigeria; 1884), the French Congo (now Brazzaville; 1886), the Lower Niger (now Onitsha, Nigeria; 1889), and Cameroon (now Yaoundé; 1890). American Bishop Edward BARRON became the first vicar apostolic of the Two Guineas in 1842, but withdrew from Africa three years later. Remy Bessieux, a Holy Ghost Father in Gabon (1844–76), became the second vicar apostolic in 1849.

By 1910 Gabon had become a colony of French West Africa, and in 1946 it gained territorial status. The Vicariate of Libreville became a diocese suffragan to Brazzaville in 1955, and in 1958 the suffragan See of Mouila was detached from Libreville, which became an archdiocese. In response to the nationalist movement that took shape during the late 1950s, French Prime Minister Charles de Gaulle granted increasing political autonomy to the region, and independence was granted to Gabon on Aug. 17, 1960. Unfortunately, the new government was quickly overthrown by the Gabonese military. With the help of French troops peace was restored by 1964, and a new constitution was adopted two years later. The first Gabon bishop, François Ndong, was appointed auxiliary bishop of Libreville in 1961. The Catholic Church continued to operate private schools in the country, although it received no aid from the government.

During the 1970s Gabon's attempts to develop its economy met with success due to the country's supply of natural resources—particularly oil. While multi-party elections were established in the republic in 1990, the nation's long-time president Omar Bongo, in power since 1967 and a member of the nation's Muslim minority, continued to win a majority of the votes, even defeating a Catholic priest in the 1993 election. In June 1999, after nearly two years of negotiations, Bongo's government

Capital: Libreville.
Size: 103,347 sq. miles.
Population: 1,208,436 in 2000.
Languages: French; Fang, Eshura, and local languages are spoken in various regions.
Religions: 664,640 Catholics (55%), 12,054 Muslims (1%), 752,537 Evangelical Protestants (5%), 459,205 indigenous religions (38%).

signed an accord with the Holy See that outlined the diplomatic and social functions of the Church within Gabon. The government also organized annual meetings between Church leaders and members of the Islamic Council to promote interfaith relations, which were amicable. Gabon, a member of the Central African Bishop's Conference, contained 65 parishes administered by 36 secular and 70 religious priests, and the nation' social welfare agencies benefitted from the efforts of its 23 brothers and 167 sisters.

In an effort to promote Christianity among the region's native peoples, Samuel Galley translated the New Testament (1925) and the whole Bible (1952) into the native Fang language. By this time, other faiths had begun evangelization efforts in the area, American Protestants having established a mission near Libreville as early as 1841. While Protestant activity subsided for several decades, the mission was revived by Presbyterians in 1870, and other missions were established with aid from French Protestants. In 1913 Nobel Prize-winning Alsatian theologian Albert Schweitzer revived the now-deserted mission at Lambaréné as a hospital devoted to treatment of leprosy and sleeping sickness. By the second half of the 20th century Gabon began to see an increase in Islamic non-citizens due to immigration from West African nations, and by 2000 Islamic worshipers were estimated to comprise as much as 12 percent of the actual resident population.

Bibliography: *Le missioni cattoliche: Storia, geographia, statistica* (Rome 1950) 129–130. *Bilan du Monde*, 2v. (Tournai 1964) 2:398–401.

[J. LE GALL/EDS.]

GABRIEL, ARCHANGEL

Gabriel is mentioned four times in the Bible (Dn 8.16; 9.21; Lk 1.19, 26). In the book of DANIEL he is the angel sent to explain to Daniel the meaning of his visions. In Luke's gospel he is the angel who foretells to Zechariah that he is to have a son (John the Baptist) and announces to Mary the coming birth of her son, Jesus. His name in Hebrew (*gabrî'ēl*) means ''hero of God.''

To Daniel, Gabriel appeared as ''a manlike figure'' (8.15). On another occasion ''a hand touched'' Daniel and raised him from his faint to a posture on hands and knees, and addressed him as ''Daniel beloved'' (10.9–12); presumably this also was Gabriel. Gabriel came to Daniel ''in rapid flight'' (9.21), though there is no explicit mention of wings. To Zechariah Gabriel appeared also in the form of a man standing and speaking (Lk 1.11, 13). Though there is no advertence to the form of the angel in his visit to Mary, the pericope (Lk 1.26–38) asserts personal identity between Mary's visitor and Zechariah's and presumes identical appearance.

In Daniel, ch. 8 to 10, the seer is professedly seeing visions; and in 10.7–8, the author asserts, ''I alone, Daniel, saw the vision''; the men who were with him fled ''although they did not see the vision.'' The objectivity of the appearances of Gabriel is not asserted. The internal and subjective character of these visions is quite possible. Moreover, Luke was not witness of either visitation of Gabriel that he records, and it is possible that he is using the literary form of haggadic MIDRASH, with his mind dwelling on the striking parallels existing between Daniel's visitation and Luke's own meditations on God's announcements to Zachary and to Mary of the impending parenthood of each.

Despite the scholarly doubts about the objective reality of Gabriel, Christian devotion venerates him as an archangel, a title never given him in the Bible, though perhaps suggested in Lk. 1.19 where Gabriel asserts he stands in the presence of God—possibly a Lucan reference to Tb 12.15. The universality and antiquity of representations of Gabriel (a 5th–century mosaic of Gabriel at the Annunciation is the oldest known representation of an angel with feet and two wings in St. Mary Major, Rome) testify to Gabriel's reality and power. The earliest liturgical recognition of Gabriel has been traced to a Greek litany of the Saints (7th century) where MICHAEL, Gabriel, and RAPHAEL occur in that order, and enjoy precedence over John the Baptist and the Blessed Virgin [see D. Bishop, *Liturgica Historica* (Oxford 1918) 142–151]. Gabriel has never been as popular or as versatile as Michael in Christian devotion. On Jan. 12, 1951, Gabriel was declared by Pius XII to be patron before God of people engaged in telecommunications (telephone, telegraph, television, radio).

In Jewish legend and apocrypha Gabriel has filled many functions: he is one of the four angels who stand at the four sides of God's throne, guardians of the four parts of the world and intercessors for the world at the time of the deluge; angel destroyer of Sodom; destroyer of the army of Sennacherib; foreteller of the birth of Samson. In Islamic literature, under the name Jibril (plus variants and other titles) Gabriel is the principal in many strange tales. He is supposed to have been the one who revealed the QUR'ĀN to the Prophet Muḥammad.

Historically, the Feast of Gabriel, Archangel was celebrated on March 24 in the Roman Rite. The post–Vatican II reform of the Roman liturgical calendar created a combined Feast of the Archangels Michael, Gabriel, and Raphael on September 29. In the Eastern Christian tradition, the Feast of the Archangels is celebrated on November 8.

Bibliography: D. KECK, *Angels and Angelology in the Middle Ages* (New York 1998). B. OTZEN, ''Michael and Gabriel,'' in *The Scriptures and the Scrolls*, ed. F. GARCIA MARTINEZ, A. HILHORST and C.J. LABUSCHAGNE (New York 1992).

[T. L. FALLON/EDS.]

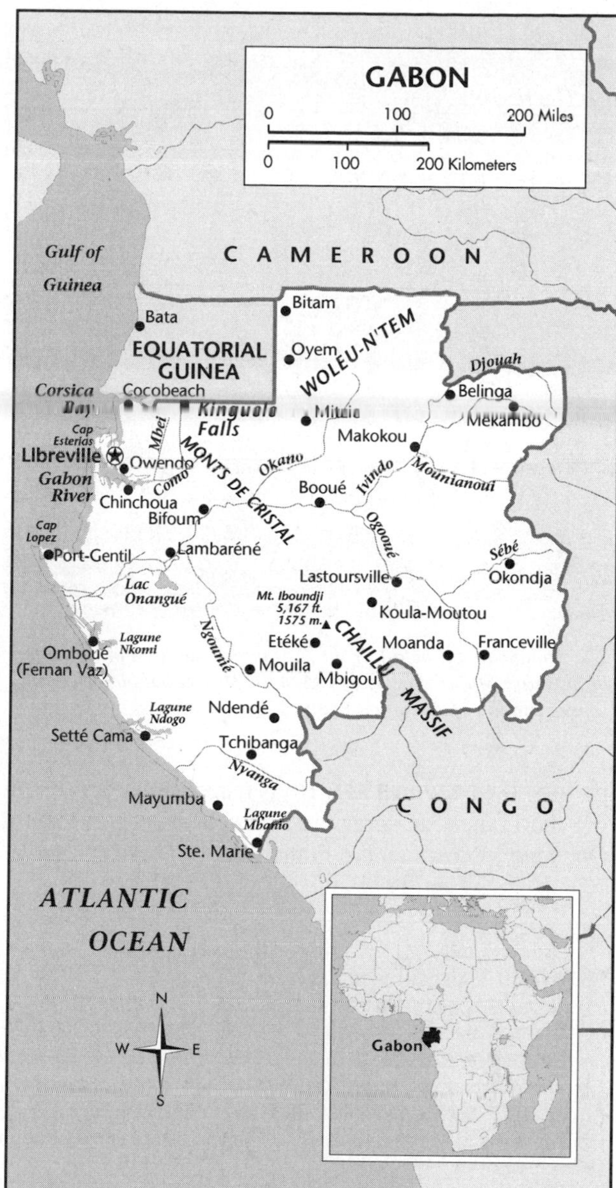

GABRIEL, COLOMBA JOANNA, BL.

Baptized Joanna Matylda (Matilda) Gabriel; Benedictine nun; founder of the Oblates of Saint Benedict and the Benedictine Sisters of Charity (*Sororum Ord. S. Benedicti a Caritate*); b. May 3, 1858, Stanislawow, Poland (now Ivano-Frankivsk, Ukraine); d. Sept. 24, 1926, Centacelle (suburb of Rome), Italy. Joanna, born into the Polish nobility, was known in her time as ''a woman born for love.'' She received her education locally and at Leopoldi, where she joined the Benedictines and became Sister Colomba. Called to serve poor working girls, she transferred to Rome (1900), spent time at Subiaco (1902), then returned to Rome (1903). Under the spiritual direction of Dominican Hyacinth CORMIER, Sister Colomba taught catechism and began visiting the sick and poor of the Roman Prati district. She gathered lay people to assist in her ministry, who became the Benedictine Oblates. In 1908, Colomba established the religious Benedictine Sisters of Charity to open homes and operate charitable programs for the needy of Rome. With the patronage of Italian Queen Elena, Pope Saint PIUS X and Pope BENEDICT XV, the congregation expanded throughout Italy, to Romania and Madagascar. Colomba was beatified by John Paul II, May 16, 1993.

Bibliography: *Acta Apostolicae Sedis* (1993): 601–03.

[K. I. RABENSTEIN]

GABRIEL FERRETTI, BL.

Responsible for the Franciscan crown; b. Ancona, Italy, 1385; d. there, Nov. 12, 1456. Born of the noble family of Ferretti, he joined the Franciscan Observants at the age of 18 (1403), and from the very beginning he was scrupulous in his observance of the smallest rules. He showed remarkable humility, a virtue that inspired his whole life. He was ordained and became a renowned preacher, and served both as guardian and as provincial. On his death bed in the Franciscan house in Ancona, he was assisted by Bl. George and by St. JAMES OF THE MARCHES. He was buried in the old church of St. Francis in Ancona. With the permission of INNOCENT VIII (1489), two relics were later interred at the right of the high altar in a marble Renaissance mausoleum. Shortly after his death his fellow citizens drew up an official account of his miracles—unfortunately lost—and sent it to Pope CALLISTUS III. A copy of this document was kept in the Franciscan convent; L. WADDING quoted from it and noted that it had been damaged. His cult was approved

The Annunciation, detail of the mosaic on the arch of the apse of St. Mary Major, Rome, c. 432–440. This is the oldest known representation of a winged Gabriel.

by BENEDICT XIV in 1753. He is responsible for promoting the Franciscan rosary in honor of the seven joys of Our Lady, known as the Franciscan or Seraphic crown.

Feast: Nov. 12.

Bibliography: L. WADDING, *Scriptores Ordinis Minorum* 12:546–550. S. MELCHIORRI, *Leggenda del b. Gabriele de' Ferretti d' Ancona* (Ancona 1844). A. BUTLER, *The Lives of the Saints,* ed. H. THURSTON and D. ATTWATER, 4 v. (New York 1956) 4:326–327. G. MENCARELLI, *L'angelo di Ancona: Vita del b. Gabriele dei conti Ferretti* (Ancona 1956). W. FORSTER, *Lexikon für Theologie und Kirche,* ed. J. HOFER and K. RAHNER, 10 v. (2d, new ed. Freiburg 1957–65) 4:92. M. A. HABIG, *The Franciscan Crown* (Chicago 1976).

[T. C. CROWLEY]

GABRIEL OF ST. MARY MAGDALEN

Also known as Adrian Devos; Discalced Carmelite, spiritual writer; b. Bevere-Audenaerse, Belgium, Jan. 24, 1893; d. Rome, March 15, 1953. After his studies in the humanities, he was professed in the Teresian Carmel of Bruges (Sept. 8, 1911) and studied philosophy at Courtrai (Belgium) and theology in Dublin. World War I forced his return to Belgium, where he was mobilized and served in the sanitation corps; twice wounded, he was awarded the military cross of honor. He was ordained Dec. 20, 1920, and then served as professor of philosophy and theology in his province (1920–26). He was called to Rome as professor in the International College of the Discalced Carmelites, of which he later became vice-rector (1926–36). As professor of spiritual theology and author of many lectures and writings, he acquired an international reputation. When the International College was granted the faculty of theology, he was appointed prefect of studies. He intensified his literary work in 1941 by founding the journal *Vita Carmelitana*, which became the *Rivista di Vita Spirituale* in 1947. He was cofounder of the scientific journal of the theological faculty *Ephemerides Theologicae-Carmeliticae* (1947). All his writings were in the field of mysticism.

Bibliography: C. DI S. GIUSEPPE, *Un Maestro di vita spirituale: P. Gabriel di S. M. Maddalena* (Rome 1959). B. DELLA SS. TRINITA, "Il fondatore della *'Revista de Vita Spirituale,'*" *Revista de Vita Spirituale* 7 (1953) 113–161. V. DI STA. MARIA, "Il P. Gabriele di Sta. M. Madd., Carm. Scalzo" *Vita Cristiana* 22 (1953) 249–258. BEDE OF THE TRINITY, "Fr. Gabriel of St. Magd., Exponent of Carmelite Mysticism," *Ephemerides Carmeliticae* 13 (1962) 758–767.

[O. RODRIGUEZ]

GABRIEL SIONITA

Maronite Orientalist; b. Edden, Lebanon, 1577; d. Paris, 1648. He studied Syriac and Hebrew, as well as Latin and theology, at the Maronite College in Rome. In 1614 he went, with John Hesronita, to Paris, where he collaborated on the Parisian POLYGLOT BIBLE and where he was soon given the chair of Semitic languages at the Sorbonne. He was ordained in 1622 at the age of 45. His collaboration on the Polyglot Bible from 1614 to 1645, marked by numerous disturbances mostly due to his abulic character, was limited to the revision and correction of almost all its Arabic and Syriac texts, most of which he also translated into Latin. For the Gospels, however, he merely revised the current Latin text, and he made no Latin translation from the Syriac for the Sapiential Books and Apocalypse. Among other works, he published also the Arabic text of the *Geographia Nubiensis* (Rome 1592, Paris 1619), with Latin translation, based especially on the geographical writings of Idrisi (1100–*c.* 1166), and in 1616 a short Arabic grammar.

Bibliography: J. LE LONG, *Bibliotheca sacra,* ed. A. G. MASCH, 2 v. (Paris 1778–90) 1:350–352. *Biographie universelle,* ed. L. G. MICHAUD, 45 v. (Paris 1843–65) 15:325–326. J. ASSFALG, *Lexikon für Theologie und Kirche 2* 4:482.

[J. M. SOLA-SOLE]

GABRIELI, ANDREA

Renaissance organist, teacher, and composer of the first magnitude; b. Venice, 1510 or 1520; d. Venice,

1586. He started out as a chorister at St. Mark's, and probably a pupil of its music director, WILLAERT. After travels in Germany and Bohemia, and various musical experiences such as serving as Bavarian court organist at the coronation of Maximilian II in 1562, he became organist at St. Jeremiah in Venice, then in 1566 at St. Mark's, where he remained until his death. His recitals with MERULO at the other organ on Sunday afternoons were high points in Venice's cultural life. He was a thoroughly Renaissance master, prolific and versatile, equally adept in sacred, instrumental, and social music, and he created masterpieces in all these categories. He left 4 Masses, 7 Penitential Psalms, 2 Magnificats, more than 100 motets, 260 madrigals, 4 *mascherate,* 4 dialogue-madrigals, choruses to Sophocles's *Oedipus* (performed at the opening of Palladio's Teatro Olimpico, Vicenza, in June 1585), some 30 *greghesche* and *justiniane* (comic part songs with dialect text), and many works for organ and instrumental ensembles.

He was a master of the divided-choir technique (*cori spezzati, coro battente*) and a pioneer in the new homophonic texture, reserving mainly to his madrigals his virtuosity in handling polyphony. His *canzoni francesi* for instrumental ensembles represent the climax of this species, as do his organ toccatas and ricercari in that field. His music mirrors the pompous and gay life of Venice at the close of the 16th century. Thus his madrigals have the lighter, more fanciful and good-humored spirit of that phase set off by V. Ruffo in Verona but brought to perfection by Gabrieli in the culturally superior and cosmopolitan atmosphere of Venice. Of his many pupils, the most famous were Hans Leo Hassler and his nephew Giovanni GABRIELI.

Bibliography: G. BENVENUTI, ed., *Andrea e Giovanni Gabrieli e la musica strumentale in San Marco,* 2 v. (Istituzioni e monumenti dell'arte musicale italiana 1–2; Milan 1931–32). A. EINSTEIN, *The Italian Madrigal,* tr. A. H. KRAPPE et al., 3 v. (Princeton N.J. 1949). D. ARNOLD, *Die Musik in Geschichte und Gegenwart,* ed. F. BLUME (Kassel-Basel 1949–) 4:1185–94; "The Significance of Cori Spezzati," *Music and Letters* (London 1920–) 40 (1959) 4–14. M. F. BUKOFZER, *Music in the Baroque Era* (New York 1947). D. ARNOLD and E. M. ARNOLD, "Andrea Gabrielli," in *The New Grove Dictionary of Music and Musicians,* ed. S. SADIE, v. 7 (New York 1980) 54–60. F. DEGRADA, ed., *Andrea Gabrieli e il suo tempo atti del Convegno Internazionale (Venezia 16–18 Settembre 1985)* (Florence 1987). D. KÄMPER, "Synkretismus der Formen und Annäherung an die Canzon da sonar bei Andrea Gabrieli," *Analecta Musicologica* 10 (1970) 152–155. D. M. RANDEL, ed., *The Harvard Biographical Dictionary of Music* (Cambridge, Mass. 1996) 289. N. SLONIMSKY, ed., *Baker's Biographical Dictionary of Musicians* (8th ed. New York 1992) 588–589.

[E. F. KENTON]

GABRIELI, GIOVANNI

Pioneer baroque church composer whose creative innovations forwarded virtually every musical form; b. Venice, *c.* 1557; d. Venice, Aug. 12, 1612. He was the nephew and pupil of Andrea GABRIELI, his only known relative, and rounded out his education in the Bavarian ducal chapel under LASSO. In 1585, when Andrea Gabrieli succeeded MERULO as first organist at St. Mark's in Venice, Giovanni succeeded his uncle at the second organ and kept this post until his death. He published chiefly his uncle's works and only a few of his own; many of his MSS disappeared during Napoleon's occupation of Venice. Preserved are 2 Mass fragments, 7 Magnificats (parts of 3 more), 1 litany, and some 85 *symphoniae sacrae,* choral works with or without instrumentation, destined for the Proper, Offices, and specifically Venetian holidays. Next in importance are his instrumental works: some 40 for organ and 37 for ensembles of from 8 to 22 parts. He produced also 30 madrigals (one a spiritual madrigal) and excelled in the Venetian dialogue and echo-madrigal.

The strong long-range influence of his printed output was in surprising contrast with its small quantity. The *sacrae symphoniae,* with their instrumental preludes and interludes, alternation of vocal solos, duets, and choirs, homophonic texture, and *basso per l'organo,* shaped the evolution of the baroque cantata perfected by J. S. BACH. His stylistic innovations appear in initial and end repetition, recapitulation of the beginning at the end, ritornels, and use of register levels developed in the divided-choir technique for structural purposes. He assigned instrumental parts to specific instruments (first attempt at orchestration) and was one of the first to use dynamic signs, and the first to differentiate between *canzone* and sonata and to use sequential episodes in *ricercari.* Two top parts in imitation foreshadow the trio-sonata form basic to later baroque composition. His harmony is clear and simple; chromaticism is reserved for expressiveness in vocal works, while chordal declamation used in choral works is transferred to instrumental ensembles. These and other departures from tradition were soon reflected in the work of his many northern pupils, especially that of Heinrich SCHÜTZ.

Bibliography: *Opera omnia,* ed. D. ARNOLD, 3 v. (*Corpus mensurabilis musicae,* ed. American Institute of Musicology, v. 1–12.1–12.3; 1956–62). C. G. A. VON WINTERFELD, *Johannes Gabrieli und sein Zeitalter,* 3 v. in 2 (Berlin 1834). E. F. KENTON, *Giovanni Gabrieli: His Life and Works* (Rome 1966); "The Late Style of G. Gabrieli," *Musical Quarterly* (New York 1915–) 48 (1962) 427–443. D. ARNOLD, "Music at the Scuola di San Rocco," *Music and Letters* 40 (1959) 229–241. G. REESE, *Music in the Renaissance* (rev. ed. New York 1959). *Histoire de la musique,* ed. ROLAND-MANUEL, 2 v. (Paris 1960–63); v. 9, 16 of *Encyclopédie de la Pléiade* v. 1. *Enciclopedia della Musica* (Milan 1963–). D. ARNOLD and E. M. ARNOLD, ''Giovanni Gabrielli,'' in *The New Grove Dictionary of Music and Musicians,* ed. S. SADIE, v. 7 (New York 1980) 54–60. R. CHARTERIS, ''Newly Discovered Manuscript Parts and Annotations in a Copy of Giovanni Gabrieli's *Symphoniae sacrae* (1615)'' *Early Music* 23 (1995) 487–496. H. PYUN, ''Modal Structure in Sixteen Instrumental Works from Giovanni Gabrielli's *Sacrae Symphoniae* (1597)'' (Ph.D. diss. Rutgers University 1994). D. M. RANDEL, ed., *The Harvard Biographical Dictionary of Music* (Cambridge, Mass. 1996) 289. N. SLONIMSKY, ed., *Baker's Biographical Dictionary of Musicians* (8th ed. New York 1992) 589.

[E. F. KENTON]

GADAMER, HANS-GEORG

Philosopher; b. Marburg, Germany, Feb. 11, 1900; d. March 14, 2002. The son of a pharmaceutical chemist, as a student in the classical gymnasium and at the University of Breslau, Gadamer was steeped in the study of the Greek and Latin classics and modern languages. He did his doctoral studies in philosophy at the University of Marburg under the neo-Kantian Paul Natorp. After completing his dissertation on Plato at the age of 22, Gadamer came under the spell of young Martin HEIDEGGER, newly arrived from Freiburg, who exercised a decisive influence on this thought.

During the almost 20 years he spent at Marburg as an assistant and Privatdozent (until 1938), Gadamer pursued the study of Plato and Aristotle, and began a study contrasting Sophistic and Platonic doctrine of the polis which led to the publication of ''Plato and the Poets'' (1934) and ''Plato's Educational State'' (1942). In those years Rudolf BULTMANN held Thursday evening *Graeca* sessions in his home where Gadamer came to know Heinrich Schlier, Günther Bornkamm, Gerhard von Rad and Erich Dinkler. It was also at Marburg that he collaborated in the preparation of Jacob Klein's masterwork *Greek Mathematical Thought and the Origin of Algebra* (1936), and came into contact with the circle surrounding the poet Stefan George. It was the George circle which produced the revolutionary, non-academic and political readings of Plato by Kurt Singer, Heinrich Friedemann and Kurt Hildebrandt. These influences, combined with the paramount role of Heidegger, are evident in Gadamer's Habilitationsschrift *Plato's Dialectical Ethics.*

In 1938 Gadamer began a distinguished career as Ordinary Professor of Philosophy at Leipzig where he became dean of the philosophical faculty and rector of the university in the immediate post–World War II years (1945–47) under the communist regime. In 1949 he succeeded Karl JASPERS at the University of Heidelberg. Named professor emeritus in 1968, Gadamer continued to write and lecture. He undertook an edition of his collected works (Tubingen: Mohr/Siebeck Verlag), and accepted appointments as visiting lecturer at The Catholic University of America in Washington, McMaster University in Hamilton, Ontario, and Boston College.

Thought. Gadamer's entire career was devoted to redefining the understanding of *Wissenschaft*, and the overcoming of defects in the Enlightenment notion of science and technology. Having been warned off Nietzsche by his father, young Gadamer while still in his teens was spurred to read a volume by the great philosopher from the paternal library. It was Nietzsche's anti-Platonic polemics that caused him to become intrigued with Plato. His youthful encounter with Nietzsche, moreover, coincided with the deep confusion wrought on the German scene by World War I. The crisis of the West, first proclaimed by Nietzsche and echoed by writers Oswald Spengler, Hermann Hesse and Thomas Mann, marked the end of the age of liberalism with its faith in progress. In seeking a new orientation and basis for cultural traditions, Gadamer turned to philosophy, while never relinquishing his predilection for literature, the arts and philology.

The Heideggerian Revolution. The prevalent philosophic approaches to which Gadamer was attracted before his encounter with Heidegger were: Paul Natorp's transcendental idealist approximations toward constructing comprehensive systems, bolstered by the Neo-Kantian conception of the history of supra-temporal problems that supposedly recur ''eternally'' within novel systematic context—what Gadamer called ''systems-games'' that lack evidential warrants from historical-critical method; Nikolai Hartmann's attempt to transform such systems-games into an open system of problems, categories, and values by means of an analysis of categories grounded in both a phenomenological investigation of essences and an idealistically tinged history of problems.

In stark contrast, in Heidegger's philosophizing ''the thought-formations of the philosophic tradition came alive, because they were understood as answers to real questions.'' As Gadamer later realized, Heidegger confirmed the rightness of abandoning eternally identical problems constructed with utter naivete out of the elements of idealist and Neo-Kantian philosophy for the alternative of using historical thinking to retrieve the questions of the tradition in such a way that the old questions became so intelligible and vivid as to become one's own. Gadamer described the pivotal hermeneutical experience as follows: ''The disclosure of these questions' historical motivation lends them something of inevitability. Questions as understood cannot just be treated as information. They become one's own questions.'' Once he appropriated such experiences, Gadamer became a lifelong opponent of any scholasticism—whether ancient, medieval, modern, or contemporary—whose characteristic bent from terminological fixity seeks to preserve traditional answers or positions without paying careful historical attention to the questions out of which they arise.

Heidegger, Plato, Aristotle. Heidegger undertook to criticize the metaphysical tradition dominant in Western philosophy and theology. For him both the premodern metaphysics of substance and the modern metaphysics of subject amount to a forgetfulness of being. In order to lay bare the questionable presuppositions of such metaphysics Heidegger returned to Plato and Aristotle. Even though Plato and Aristotle were more foils than exemplars for him, Heidegger nevertheless sought access to them in their originality beneath the encrustations of scholastic traditions. In this way Heidegger enabled Gadamer to recover what he called ''the mystery of the Platonic dialogue,'' namely, that philosophy's task of ''giving an account'' is not a matter of pursuing the guiding ideal behind the post-Cartesian notion of system to attain an ultimate foundation in some supreme principle or proposition; rather it is the dialogical task of trying to think through to the end the conceptual and perceptual force of the language in which we dwell by means of a repeated and further thinking through of our primordial experience of the world.

This opposition to the logical ideal of systematic grounding is central to Gadamer's hermeneutical resistance to the primacy of ancient *episteme* or of modern science, which he understood as approximating *techne* in Aristotle's sense. In the *Phaedo* the Platonic Socrates had argued that resistance to Sophism and the possibility of attaining a right orientation towards the whole resides not in a science of nature but in the ''flight into the *logoi,*'' or dialectic. Gadamer maintained that dialectical conversation lets something we hold in common come to light even through breakdowns in communication, misunderstandings, and the famed Socratic discovery that we do not know what is highest and best or the whole. But this sought-after commonality regarding our life-orientation—what the Platonic dialogues portray as the One, the Being, the Good at the basis of the order of the soul, of the city's regime, and of the cosmos—did not for Gadamer take the form of a logically established principle or of scientific or technical knowledge. Hence, the point of his hermeneutic philosophy was to make convincing in our time the Socratic legacy of ''human wisdom'' that, in comparison to the virtually godlike infallibility vulgarly ascribed to scientific knowledge, is nescience.

Gadamer's esteem for Platonic dialectic opened up for him by Heidegger led him to conclude that Aristotle is the first and perhaps the greatest Platonist. Under Heidegger's lead Gadamer grasped that Aristotle's analysis of practical knowing (*phronesis*) offers *the* model for linking the Socratic ''human wisdom'' (*docta ignorantia*) to the foundational problematic of the interpretative (*verstehende*) human sciences. Perhaps because he was less concerned than Heidegger to dismantle Plato and Aristotle as originators of Western metaphysics, Gadamer could see just how *Being and Time*'s analysis of the facticity of *Dasein* by way of disengaging the conditionedness of *Verstehen* (human understanding and interpretation) was dependent upon the earlier Aristotelian account of *phronesis*. Aristotle had shown how practical insight and practical reasonableness have little or nothing to do with the teachability of science's generalizations; and how they are made possible instead by practice itself in its concrete and indissoluble nexus with one's ethos. Thus, Gadamer's hermeneutical philosophy turns out to be a renewal of practical, social, and political rationality.

Gadamer's Dialectical Alternative. Gadamer spelled out his opposition to the knowingness of science specifically in terms of a rejection of idealism with its Romantic underpinnings in both aesthetic and historical consciousness. The incapacity of aesthetic consciousness to do justice to the truthfulness of art Gadamer exposed as merely the opposite side of the coin which degrades the existential value of the artistic, the mythic, and the poetic in the name of a mistaken overestimation of logic, conceptual rigor, and proof on the one hand, and of technical expertise on the other. Similarly, the dispassionate remoteness of the cultivated bourgeois consciousness that incarnates historical consciousness cannot do justice to the primordiality of our historical being. Both aesthetic and historical conceptions are based ultimately on the illusions of idealist conceptions of consciousness. Gadamer's antidote to these misconceptions was ''effective-historical consciousness.'' He elaborated this *wirkungsgeschichliches Bewusstsein* phenomenologically in his explication of the game or play (*Spiel*). And about it he made his famous claim that it is ''more being than consciousness.''

To counter the conceptualist hubris of idealist consciousness Gadamer underlined the primal significance of conversation. Against the conceptualist tendencies of the Greeks, against German idealism's metaphysics of the will, and against the methodologism of the NEO-KANTIANS and the Neo-Positivists, he pointed insistently toward our attempts at mutual understanding by which we are engaged in an unending conversation, a logic of question and answer in which no person will have the last word. To underscore this dialogical dimension Gadamer invoked the European traditions of rhetoric (Vico) and hermeneutics (SCHLEIERMACHER, DILTHEY) by way of reinforcing the truth of Plato's dialectic and of Aristotle's practical and political philosophy. At the heart of each of these is an art of holding a conversation, which entails holding this conversation with oneself and pursuing an internal harmony with oneself.

According to Gadamer's hermeneutic philosophy, focusing upon the experience of talking-to-each-other and listening-to-one-another means concentrating upon the linguisticality of human experience. Language, or better, language-in-use, has the signal advantage of highlighting the preschematization of our possible experience. In our use of language it becomes plain that human experience is enacted in a constant communicative build-up of our knowledge of the world. The linguistic entwinement of world-as-word and word-as-worlded also serves to decenter all subjectivistic illusions about consciousness; and it let Gadamer thematize the empirically verifiable reflective interiortry (which Bernard LONERGAN helpfully called ''consciousness as experience''). This awareness is prior to and irreducible to the mythic and exaggerated kind of awareness sponsored by Cartesian and Kantian idealism (which Lonergan identified as ''consciousness as perception''). Moreover, language as dialogical also makes clear the difference between advancing, enhancing, and illuminating the horizon of mutual understanding and the limited validity of the ideal of objective determinacy and its concern for logical consistency and univocity.

Hermeneutical philosophy teaches that linguisticality does not head towards the finality of propositional statements, of objective validity-claims, or towards totality as the to-be-completely-determined object. Rather it points in the direction of a mysterious and all-encompassing world-horizon in which we live and move and have our being. For Gadamer human language is not oriented towards a humanly inaccessible truth as ''full disclosure, whose ideal of fulfillment is ultimately the self-presence of the absolute spirit.'' This is why he repudiated ''any '*theoria*' whose ontological legitimation could only be found in an *intellectus infinitus* about which human experience unsupported by any revelation knows nothing.'' Gadamer tried to demonstrate that the finality warranted by language which is genuinely carried out in the infinite dialogue of the soul with itself is ''not to be characterized as the determination of an objective world to be known, either in the Neo-Kantian sense of an infinite task, or in the dialectical sense of transcending any given limit through thinking.'' For him what is expressed is not everything; and hermeneutical philosophy is out to help us acknowledge that what is unsaid ''first lets what is said become word and reach us.'' Thus, the infinity proper to dialogue has a finality consonant with the normative attainment of experience in human living: ''A plenitude of experiences, encounters, teachings, and disappointments culminate not in one's finally knowing everything, but in one's knowing something and in one's having learned modesty.'' In conversation we try to enter into the language of anyone who is thinking along with or thinking things out further than we are. In sum:

> ''Hermeneutical'' philosophy understands itself . . . not as an 'absolute' position, but as a way of experience. It insists that there is no higher principle than this: to open oneself up for conversation. But that constantly means acknowledging beforehand the possible correctness, and indeed the superiority of one's conversation partner. Is that too little? This seems to me the only kind of intellectual probity one can require of a professor of philosophy—but which one also ought to demand.

In articulating his hermeneutic philosophy in *Truth and Method* (1960), Gadamer gave a theoretical account of the style of his study, of his teaching in seminar and lecture hall, and of his personal hand in forming generations of Germany's leading teachers in philosophy. His published works stand as a witness to his teacher's efforts to establish sustained conditions for teaching and learning that embody the classic ideals of the German university and Western culture.

Bibliography: E. MAKITA, *Gadamer-Bibliographie: 1922-1994* (New York 1994). H.-G. GADAMER, *The Philosophy of Hans-Georg Gadamer* (Chicago 1997). Works.H.-G. GADAMER, *Gesammelte Werke* (Tübingen 1985-); *Kleine Schriften* (Tübingen 1967-1972); *Philosophical Hermeneutics*, tr. and ed. D. E. LINGE (Berkeley 1976); *Dialektik und Sophistik im siebenten platonischen Brief* (Heidelberg 1964); *The Relevance of the Beautiful*, tr. N. WALKER, ed. and intro. R. BERNASCONI (Cambridge 1986); *Hegel's Dialectic*, tr. and intro. R. C. SMITH (New Haven 1976); *Hermeneutik und Dialektik*, R. BUBNER, ed. (Tübingen 1970); *The Idea of the Good in Platonic-Aristotelean Philosophy*, tr. and intro. P. C. SMITH (New Haven 1986); *Idee und Wirklichkeit in Platos Timaios* (Heidelberg 1974); *Metaphysie XII: Übersetzung und Kommentar von Hans-Georg Gadamer* (Frankfurt am Main 1970); *Platos dialektische Ethik und andere Studien zur platonischen Philosophie* (Hamburg 1968); *Reason in the Age of Science*, tr. F. G. LAWRENCE (Cambridge, Mass. 1982); *Vernunft im Zeitalter der Wissenschaft: Aufsätze* (Frankfurt am Main 1976); *Truth and Method*, trs. G. BARDEN and J. CUMMING (New York 1975); *The Beginning of Knowledge*, tr. R. COLTMAN (New York 2001); *The Beginning of Philosophy*, tr. R. COLTMAN (New York 1998); *Hermeneutics, Religion, and Ethics*, tr. J. WEINSHEIMER (New Haven 1999); *Praise of Theory: Speeches and Essays*, tr. C. DAWSON (New Haven 1998); *Gadamer on Celan: ''Who Am I and Who Are You'' and Other Essays*, tr. R. HEINEMANN and B. KRAJEWSKI (Albany, N.Y. 1997); *The Enigma of Health: The Art of Healing in a Scientific Age*, tr. N. WALKER and J. GEIGER (Stanford 1996); *Heidegger's Ways*, tr. J. W. STANLEY (Albany, N.Y. 1994). Literature. J. GRONDIN, *Hans-Georg Gadamer: Eine Biographie* (Tübingen 1999). J. WEINSHEIMER, *Gadamer's Hermeneutics: A Reading of Truth and Method* (New Haven 1985). H. DIETER, et al., eds., *Die Gegenwart der Griechen im neueren Denken: Festschrift für Hans-Georg Gadamer zum 60* (Tübingen 1960). D. C. HOY, *The Critical Circle: Literature, History and Philosophical Hermeneutics* (Berkeley 1978). J. VANDENBUL-

CKE, *Hans-Georg Gadamer. Een filosofie van het interpreteren* (Utrecht 1973). L. K. SCHMIDT, *The Epistemology of Hans-Georg Gadamer. An Analysis of the Legitimization of Vorurteile* (New York 1985). M. R. FOSTER, *Gadamer and Practical Philosophy: The Hermeneutics of Moral Confidence* (Atlanta 1991). T. K. CARR, *Newman and Gadamer: Toward a Hermeneutics of Religious Knowledge* (Atlanta 1996). *Dialogue and Deconstruction: The Gadamer-Derrida Encounter,* tr. D. P. MICHELFELDER and R. E. PALMER (Albany, N.Y. 1989).

[F. G. LAWRENCE]

GAETANI (CAETANI)

Italian family descended, according to family tradition, from the consuls and dukes of Gaeta (ninth century to 1032). Genealogical documents for branches in Naples, Pisa, and Anagni date from the 12th century. *Benedetto* Gaetani, who became pope as BONIFACE VIII in 1294, made the family a GUELF power between the STATES OF THE CHURCH and the Kingdom of Naples, and used it combined with the ORSINI north of Rome to contain the Ghibelline COLONNA. The Naples branch, associated with the Angevins, disappeared in the 15th century, and the Pisa branch, which had four cardinals (including *Aldobrandino,* d. 1223, favored by Honorius III) and many prelates in the 12th and 13th centuries, lost importance after the time of the banker *James* (d. 1342), an intimate of Boniface VIII.

The Anagni branch at its peak (1350–1500) held 200 castles. Cardinal *Francis* (d. 1317) and JAMES GAETANI STEFANESCHI (d. 1343) defended the memory of Boniface VIII. As a papal legate, *Annibale de Ceccano* (d. 1350), a luxury-loving prelate with many benefices, sought to make peace between the kings of England and France in 1342. *Onorato I* was host to the dissident cardinals at Fondi, who in 1378 elected the antipope CLEMENT VII and began the Western Schism. *James II* (d. *c.* 1423) divided the Anagni branch (*c.* 1420) into the Gaetani d'Aragona, friendly to Spain, and the Gaetani di Sermoneta (near Rome), which ALEXANDER VI tried to exterminate in 1499. *Antonio I* (d. 1412), brother of Onorato I and of James II, became a cardinal in 1402. *Onorato IV* commanded papal troops in the Battle of Lepanto (1571). As papal envoy to France during the WARS OF RELIGION, Cardinal *Enrico* (d. 1599), Patriarch of Jerusalem, was accompanied by St. Robert BELLARMINE and his brother, *Camillo* Gaetani (d. 1602), Patriarch of Alexandria and later papal envoy to Emperor Rudolph II in Prague (1591) and to PHILIP II of Spain in Madrid (1592–99). Enrico's nephew, Cardinal *Antonio II* (d. 1624), was also an active papal diplomat. *Michelangelo* (d. 1882) was a moderate liberal politician and a DANTE scholar. *Honorato* (d. 1917) was a politician and geographer, whereas *Leone* (d. 1935) was a historian of Islam. *Gelasio* Caetani (d. 1934), ambassador to Washington from 1922 to 1925, rebuilt the castle of Sermoneta and published many volumes of documents from the family archives, now in the VATICAN, as well as a family history.

Bibliography: L. JANIN et al., *Dictionnaire d'histoire et de géographie ecclésiastiques*, ed. A. BAUDRILLART et al. (Paris 1912) 11:139–154. O. ENGELS, *Lexicon für Theologie und Kirche*, ed. J. HOFER and K. RAHNER (Freiburg 1957–65) 4:484. G. B. A. CAETANI, *Caietanorum genealogia* (Perugia 1920); *Regesta chartarum,* 5 v. (Perugia 1922–30); *Domus Caietana,* 2 v. (Perugia 1927–33). L. ERMINI, *Onorato I Caetani conte di Fondi, e lo scisma d'Occidente* (Rome 1938). C. MANFRONI, *La legazione del cardinale Caetani in Francia* (Turin 1893). E. CAETANI, *Alcuni ricordi di Michelangelo Caetani duca di Sermoneta* (Milan 1904). V. NOVELLI, *I Colonna e i Caetani, storia del medio-evo di Roma,* 2 v. (Rome 1892–93).

[E. P. COLBERT]

GAGARIN, IVAN SERGEEVICH

Writer; b. Moscow, Aug. 1, 1814; d. Paris, July 19, 1882. He belonged to a noble Russian family. In 1832 he joined the diplomatic corps and served as secretary to the embassy in Munich, Vienna, and Paris (from 1838). Mme. Swetchine, his aunt, brought him into contact with Chateaubriand, Falloux, Montalembert, Lacordaire, Donoso Cortes, and other leading Catholics who frequented her Parisian salon. Under the influence of Gustave de RAVIGNAN, SJ, he was converted from Orthodoxy to Catholicism and joined the JESUITS) (1843. From this time he used also the name John Xavier. After ordination he taught philosophy and ecclesiastical history in Brugelette (1849–51) and Laval (1854–55). From 1855 he lived mostly in Paris, where he engaged in writing and pastoral work, and sought chiefly to reunite the Russian Orthodox Church with Rome. Besides numerous periodical articles, he published in Paris *La Russie sera-t-elle Catholique* (1856), *Les starovères, L'Église russe et le Pape* (1857), and *L' Église russe et l'Immaculée Conception* (1868). With Charles Daniel he founded in 1856 the periodical *Études,* which still continues publication. Stories linking his name with the duel in which Aleksandr Pushkin, the Russian poet, was mortally wounded, lack foundation.

Bibliography: C. SOMMERVOGEL et al., *Bibliothèque de la Compagnie de Jésus* (Brussels-Paris 1890–1932) 3:1089–95. J. G. A. M. REMMERS, *De Herenigingsgedachte van Ivan S. Gagarin* (Tilburg 1951). L. KOCH, *Jesuiten-Lexikon: Die Gesellschaft Jesu einst und jetzt* (Paderborn 1934) 629.

[J. PAPIN]

GAGE, THOMAS

Missionary, apostate, and traveler; b. England, 1602 or 1603; d. Jamaica, 1656. Thomas, member of an old English Catholic family, joined the Dominican Order in Spain and went to Mexico in 1625. He spent 11 years in Guatemala, first in the capital, later as priest among the Pokoman Maya. He traveled overland to Panama and returned to England in 1637. Five years later he apostatized, joined the Puritans, and became violently anti-Catholic. Largely on his evidence three priests, including one who had been a schoolmate at St. Omer's, were executed, but he did testify so as to save the life of his former superior, Thomas MIDDLETON, OP, provincial of the small band of English Dominicans. In 1648 Gage published *The English-American, his Travail By Sea and Land or a New Survey of the West Indias,* an account of his travels and observations in Spanish America. This contained much anti-Catholic and anti-Spanish propaganda inserted to win support for an English invasion of the Spanish Main, but shorn of those features, it was a detailed, accurate, and fascinating picture by a first-class observer of that strange world forbidden to Englishmen, as the many editions and translations attest. The book helped establish the unhappy ''Black Legend.'' By exaggerating the weakness and corruption of Spanish rule and the supposed readiness of native peoples to revolt, Gage was partly, perhaps largely, instrumental in persuading Oliver Cromwell to attack the Spanish Main. Gage accompanied the expedition as chaplain and adviser and acted as interpreter in the negotiations for the surrender of Jamaica.

Bibliography: T. GAGE, *Travels in the New World,* ed. J. E. S. THOMPSON (Norman, OK 1958).

[J. E. S. THOMPSON]

GAGLIARDI, ACHILLE

Jesuit theologian and spiritual writer; b. Padua, 1537 or 1538; d. Modena, July 6, 1607. He entered the Society of Jesus on Sept. 29, 1559. After studying at the Roman College with Robert Bellarmine from 1561 to 1563, he taught philosophy and theology there from 1563 to 1579, except for the years 1568 to 1575, when he was rector of the Jesuit college at Turin. He taught at Padua and in 1580 was sent to Milan at the request of its archbishop, St. Charles BORROMEO, whom Gagliardi subsequently directed. He was superior of Milan's S. Fedele residence from 1584 to 1594. While there he published his *Catechismo della fede cattolica* (Milan 1584). He also participated in the revision of the Jesuit Ratio Studiorum in 1598 and composed ascetical works intended especially for Jesuits. Some of his reflections appear in his *Commentaria in exercitia spiritualia S. P. Ignatii de Loyola* (Bruges 1882); most of his *De disciplina interioris hominis* remains unpublished. As spiritual director of Isabella Bellinzaga Lomazzi (1551–1624), he collaborated with her on the *Breve compendio intorno alla perfezione cristiana* (Brescia 1611), a highly influential ascetical work and one whose French editions had an effect upon Bérullian spirituality. Because of the undue stress in the *Compendio* on spiritual passivity, Pourrat considered Gagliardi an unconscious precursor of Italian ''prequietism.'' P. Pirri has studied the difficult question of Gagliardi's share in the composition of the *Compendio,* and although the work reflects Gagliardi's spirituality and his conduct of retreats, it does not seem to be exclusively his creation. During Gagliardi's lifetime, its orthodoxy was questioned by the Holy Office, but a favorable judgment was given it in 1601, possibly because of Bellarmine's intervention. CLEMENT VIII forbade Gagliardi any further collaboration with Lomazzi and had him moved from Milan. The book was on the Roman Index from 1703 to 1800.

Bibliography: C. SOMMERVOGEL et al., *Bibliothèque de la Compagnie de Jésus* (Brussels-Paris 1890–1932) 3:1095–99. Brémond 11:3–56. J. DE GUIBERT, *The Jesuits: Their Spiritual Doctrine and Practice,* tr. W. T. YOUNG (Chicago 1964). *Directoria Exercitiorum Spiritualium,* ed. I. IPARRAGUIRRE (*Monumenta historica Societatis Jesu Madrid* 76; 1955). I. IPARRAGUIRRE, *Répertoire de spiritualité ignatienne* (Rome 1961). For the *Breve compendio,* consult M. VILLER, ''*L'Abrégé de la perfection de la dame milanaise,*'' *Revue d'ascétique et de mystique* 12 (1931) 44–89; ''Autour de l' *Abrégé de la perfection:* L'Influence,'' *ibid.* 13 (1932) 34–59; *Dictionnaire de spiritualité ascétique et mystique* 1:1940–42. M. VILLER and G. JOPPIN, ''Les Sources italiennes de l'*Abrégé de la perfection,*'' *Revue d'ascétique et de mystique* 15 (1934) 381–402. P. PIRRI, ''Il P. Achille Gagliardi, la Dama milanese, la riforma dello spirito e il movimento degli zelatori,'' *Archivum historicum Societatis Jesu* (1945) 1–72; ''Il *Breve compendio* di Achille Gagliardi al vaglio di teologi gesuiti,'' *ibid.* 20 (1951) 231–253; ''Gagliardiana,'' *ibid.* 29 (1960) 99–129.

[M. A. FAHEY]

GAGUIN, ROBERT

Humanist, poet, historian, and ecclesiastic; b. Callone-sur-Lys, Diocese of Artois, *c.* 1433; d. Paris, May 22, 1501. Although a Fleming by birth, he was French by nationality. Having been schooled by the TRINITARIANS (known also as Mathurins), he later joined the order and in 1473 was elected their general. He was a professor at the Sorbonne and dean of the Faculty of Canon Law. Much influenced by Guillaume Fichet, with him he celebrated the introduction of printing in Paris and was enthusiastic over Latin elegance. ERASMUS and REUCHLIN both studied with Gaguin in Paris. His correspondence, including letters to Erasmus and M. FICINO, is a storehouse of information concerning HUMANISM and reform in Paris at the end of the 15th century; the publication of his letters in 1498 was a significant event in the development of humanism in France.

After 1485 his energies were increasingly turned away from humanistic activities and given to diplomacy and various missions: Italy in 1486, England in 1489–90, and Germany in 1492. He was ambassador to England in 1489–90, at a time when Thomas MORE was in Archbishop MORTON'S household, and More's allusion, "Gaguin, who neither disparages the honor of the French nor broadcasts our honor," glances at this and at Gaguin's best-known work, *De origine et gestis Francorum compendium* (1495). He is also the subject of J. Skelton's *Recule ageinst Gaguyne.* His travels brought him into contact with BESSARION, Ermolao BARBARO, PICO DELLA MIRANDOLA, and Publio Fausto Andrelini—all distinguished humanists.

Theologically he is noteworthy for his writings in verse and in prose on the IMMACULATE CONCEPTION, and in 1497 he published the *Statuta ordinis fratrum sanctae Trinitatis et redemptionis captivorum.* In addition to his translations of Latin prose and verse, which included Caesar's *Commentaries* in 1485, he translated Alain Chartier's *Curial* into French and imitated him in his *Débat du laboureur, du prestre et du gendarme.*

Bibliography: R. GAGUIN, *Epistole et orationes,* ed. L. THUASNE, 2 v. (Paris 1903). A. RENAUDET, *Préréforme et humanisme à Paris . . .* (2d ed. Paris 1953). ANTONIO DE LA ASUNCIÓN, *Diccionario de los escritores trinitarios de España y Portugal,* 2 v. (Rome 1898–99) v. 2. K. GAQUOIN, *Denkschrift zum 400. Todestage des R. G.* (Heidelberg 1901). A. PALMIERI, *Dictionnaire de théology catholique* ed. A. VACANT et al. 15 v. (Paris 1903–50) 6:996–998. F. SIMONE, "R. G. ed il suo cenaculo umanistico," *Aevum* 13 (1939) 410–476. V. ZOLLINI, *Enciclopedia cattolica* 5: 1851. D. ERASMUS, *Opus epistolarum,* ed. P. S. ALLEN, 12 v. (Oxford 1906–58) 1:146, 241. *The Correspondence of Sir Thomas More,* ed. E. F. ROGERS (Princeton 1947) 36. H. M. FÉRET, *Catholicisme* 4:1699–1700.

[R. J. SCHOECK]

GAILHAC, PIERRE JEAN ANTOINE

Founder of the Religious of the SACRED HEART OF MARY; b. Béziers, France, Nov. 14, 1802; d. there, Jan. 25, 1890. He was born in modest circumstances and received his early education from a priest. After a brief apprenticeship to his uncle, a pharmacist, he entered the seminary of Montpellier. He remained there for eight years after ordination (1826) as professor of theology. When the government demanded that all professors of theology teach and defend the DECLARATION OF THE FRENCH CLERGY of 1682, Gailhac alone among the Montpellier faculty incurred diocesan disapproval by refusing (*see* GALLICANISM). While serving as hospital chaplain in Béziers (1830–49), he decided to devote himself to the sick poor. He opened a house of refuge for penitent women and later an orphanage. In 1849 he founded the Religious of the Sacred Heart of Mary. The immediate obligation of this congregation of women was the care of orphans, but the general purpose was the education of young women. A second foundation, the Priests of the Good Shepherd, did not endure. In 1860 Gailhac was anonymously accused of poisoning two nuns, subjected to an official investigation, and acquitted. Years later an obscure citizen sent a deathbed statement to the bishop confessing his responsibility for the false accusation. The decree introducing his cause for beatification was issued in 1953.

Pierre Jean Antoine Gailhac.

Bibliography: F. LERAY, *Un Apôtre: Le père Jean Gailhac* (Paris 1944). H. MAGARET, *Gailhac of Béziers* (New York 1946).

[H. MAGARET]

GAIUS (CAIUS), POPE, ST.

Pontificate: Dec. 17, 283 to April 22, 296. The biography of Gaius in the *Liber pontificalis* describes him as a Dalmatian and supposedly a relative of the Emperor Diocletian. He is said to have decreed that the hierarchical orders from lector to priest had to be observed before a bishop could be consecrated; he assigned deacons to administer the seven ecclesiastical districts of Rome. ANASTASIUS THE LIBRARIAN records Gaius's imprisonment with the future popes SIXTUS and DIONYSIUS in 257; legend connects him with the Diocletian persecution, and the *Passio S. Susannae* associates him in the martyrdom of Susanna, apparently identifying him with the donor of the title church Gaii near the Quirinal. The *Passio Sancti Sebastiani* says that Gaius encouraged SEBASTIAN, the famous Christian soldier who has been the subject of numerous paintings, to be firm in his martyrdom (the pagans shot him to death with arrows). However, his name appears in none of the martyrologies. It does head a trustworthy list of Roman ordination dates, and he is listed in the Liberian Catalogue as reigning from Dec. 17, 283 to April 22, 296, thus anticipating the Diocletian persecution. Eusebius cites him as a contemporary and credits him with a fifteen-year pontificate (*Ecclesiastical History* 7.32). According to the *Depositio episcoporum* Gaius was buried in the cemetery of St. Callistus in a room separate from the bishops' grotto, but this statement is unconfirmed by archeological research, although Pope URBAN VIII transported the body to the church of St. Caius in 1631. His epitaph, ''Burial of Gaius, bishop . . . April 22,'' has been reconstructed by G. de Rossi.

Feast: April 22.

Bibliography: G. SCHWAIGER, *Lexikon für Theologie und Kirche,* 3d. ed. (Freiburg 1995) 2:877. DUCHESNE, *Liber Pontificalis* 1:xcviii–xcix, 71–72, 154, 161. *Dictionnaire d'histoire et de géographie ecclésiastiques*, ed. A. BAUDRILLART, et al. (Paris 1912–) 11:237–238. H. LECLERCQ, *Dictionnaire d'archéologie chrétienne et de liturgie*. ed. F. CABROL, H. LECLERCQ and H. I. MARROU (Paris 1907–53) 2.2:1738–39. G. B. DE ROSSI, *La Roma sotterranea cristiana,* 4 v. (Rome 1864–97) 114–120; suppl 1, ns, J. WILPERT, *Die Papstgräber . . . in der Katakombe des hl. Kallistus* (Freiburg 1909). E. FERGUSON, ed., *Encyclopedia of Early Christianity* (New York 1997) 1:446. J. N. D. KELLY, *Oxford Dictionary of Popes* (New York 1986) 24.

[E. G. WELTIN]

GALAND, AGNÈS OF JESUS, BL.

Also known as Agnès de Langeac; Dominican nun; mystic; b. Nov. 17, 1602, Puy-en-Velay (near Langeac), France; d. Oct. 19, 1634, Langeac. Agnès, a vivacious and generous child, was educated by the Sisters of the Holy Virgin. She entered the Dominican convent at Langeac (1623) and, displaying the enthusiam that characterized her early life, was elected prioress in 1627. In accordance with her understanding of God's will revealed through a vision of the Virgin Mary (1631), Sister Agnès used her gift of prayer and her hidden penances for the good of Jean Jacques OLIER, abbot of Prébrac, who was then a young priest living irresponsibly and whom she had never met. She is said to have bilocated (1634) to the Church where Father Olier was praying during a retreat under the direction of Saint VINCENT DE PAUL. She met Olier just before her death. Twenty years later he founded the SULPICIANS. She was beatified by John Paul II on Nov. 20, 1994.

Feast: Oct. 19 (Dominicans).

Bibliography: *Mère Agnès de Langeac et son temps: une mystique dominicaine au grand siècle des âmes: actes du colloque du Puy* (Le Puy, France 1986). J. BOUFLET, *Petite vie de Agnès de Langeac* (Paris 1994). M. J. DORCY, *Saint Dominic's Family* (Dubuque, Iowa 1964) 386–87. E. PANASSIÈRE, *Mémoires sur la vie d'Agnès de Langeac* (Paris 1994). R. DE TRYON-MONTALEMBERT, *Agnès de Langeac: ''Qui a Dieu a tout''* (Paris 1994).

[K. I. RABENSTEIN]

GALANO, CLEMENTE

Theatine missionary, theologian, and Orientalist; b. Sorrento; d. Leopolis, May 14, 1666. He was professed at Holy Apostles Monastery, Naples, Feb. 25, 1628, and in 1636 appointed to the Georgian missions to reunite the Armenian Church with Rome. His negotiations with the Armenian patriarch, Ciriac of Erivan, ended short of success, cut off by the patriarch's death. In addition to his spiritual activities, Galano opened a college in Constantinople, publishing there his Armenian grammar and logic. He was forced to leave for Rome with his followers in 1645 because of the violent opposition of the newly elected Patriarch David. His group, made up of disciples and dignitaries converted from the Greek-Armenian Church, was warmly received by Pope Urban VIII. Shortly afterward, Galano was appointed professor of the Armenians in the college De Propaganda Fide, staffed by Theatines since 1641. In 1663 the Congregation for the Propagation of the Faith sent Galano and Louis Pidou to Poland to work toward reunion with the Church of Rome among the Polish-Armenians. They opened an Armenian college in Leopolis. On the eve of success, death overtook Galano, but Pidou completed the work and saw the end of the schism.

Bibliography: F. A. VEZZOSI, *Scrittori dei chierici regolari detti teatini,* 2 v. (Rome 1780). A. PALMIERI, *Dictionnaire de théology catholique* 6:1023–25. H. HURTER, *Nomenclator literarius theologiae catholicae* 6 v. (Innsbruck 1903–13) 4:118–119. F. ANDREU, *Enciclopedia cattolica* ed. P. PASCHINI et al. (Rome, 1949–54) 5:1853.

[A. SAGRERA]

GALANTINI, HIPPOLYTUS, BL.

Founder of the secular Institute of Christian Doctrine; b. Florence, Oct. 12, 1565; d. there March 20, 1619. The son of a silk weaver, Filippo Galantini (Galanti), he supported himself by this trade and remained a layman all his life. Although cured of a severe illness, he lacked health to enter the cloister; he decided at the age of 12 to devote himself to the service of God. Archbishop Alessandro de'Medici, recognizing his spiritual gifts, permitted him to use the church of S. Lucia al Prato to instruct children. Four years later Galantini established a confraternity for the religious education of poor children. Opposition, based on want of money and his own lack of secular education, delayed his plan until 1602. His work and his zeal came to the attention of CLEMENT VIII, who ordered that an oratory dedicated to St. Francis and St. Lucy should be built for his use. There at the age of 37, Galantini founded the Institute of Christian Doctrine and composed the rule for his associates. His own reputation for holiness and the ascetic spirit of his followers won for members of the institute the title ''Vanchetoni'' (unworldly ones). The practice of nocturnal adoration may be traced back to his use of this devotion to keep youth from dangerous entertainment. The Franciscans consider him as one of their tertiaries. He saw his work spread through northern Italy before he died of a painful illness. He was beatified by LEO XII in 1825.

Feast: March 20.

Bibliography: D. A. MARSELLA, *De beato Hippolyto Galantinio* (Rome 1826). A. BUTLER, *The Lives of the Saints,* ed. H. THURSTON and D. ATTWATER, 4 v. (New York 1956) 1:650.

[G. M. GRAY]

GALATIA

A region in central Asia Minor. The name Γαλατία (Galatia) is derived from that of the Γαλάται (Galatians), a variant form of Κελτοί (Celts), the name of a people speaking the Celtic language who came from the East into central and western Europe probably around the beginning of the first millennium B.C.

In History. In the first half of the 3rd century B.C. a group of this Gallic or Gaulish people invaded the Balkans, Macedonia, Thrace, and Greece. After they were repulsed from Greece, three of their tribes, embracing about 20,000 souls, crossed over into Asia Minor in 178 B.C. at the invitation of King Nicomedes I of Bithynia, who sought their military service. For the next half century they overran most of Asia Minor until they were subdued by King Attalus I of Pergamum (*c.* 232 B.C.). Thereafter they settled in central Asia Minor, both to the east and to the west of the great bend of the Halys River.

In this region, Galatia in the strict sense, the Gaulish invaders formed merely the ruling class, to whom the earlier inhabitants (Phrygians in the west and Cappadocians in the east) were subject. After Galatia had been a vassal state of Pergamum and a half-independent kingdom, it became a client state of Rome in 64 B.C. When King Amyntas of Galatia died in 25 B.C., the country was incorporated into the Roman Empire and formed part of a newly established province, which bore the same name. However, the Roman Province of Galatia as then constituted was much larger than the original region of Galatia; it included also the districts of Lycaonia and Pisidia in the south and the southern part of Phrygia in the southwest. When the Roman Emperor DIOCLETIAN reorganized the provinces of the empire (*c.* 295), he divided the Province of Galatia into two provinces, of which only the northern half (Galatia in the strict sense) was now called Galatia. In the 11th century the country was conquered by the SELJUKS, and in the 14th century it fell to the possession of the OTTOMAN TURKS.

In the Bible. Because the term Galatia was used by ancient writers to designate either Galatia in the strict sense or the Roman Province of Galatia or even southern Gaul (later France), the exact meaning of the term as used in the Bible is often uncertain and, in connection with the missionary activity of St. Paul, still much disputed. The Galatians who are mentioned in 2 Mc 8:20 are, no doubt, men from Galatia in the strict sense, who often served as mercenary troops. Those referred to in 1 Mc 8:2 as defeated by the Romans may well be the Gauls of northern Italy.

In the NT the Galatia mentioned in 1 Pt 1:1 is most likely the Roman province of that name, since all the other names mentioned in this verse are those of Roman provinces in Asia Minor. It is uncertain what district is meant by the Galatia to which Crescens went (2 Tm 4:10); it might be even southern Gaul. No mention of Galatia itself is made in the Acts of the Apostles, but according to Acts 16:6 St. Paul ''passed through Phrygia and the Galatian country [Γαλατική χώρα]'' on his second missionary journey, and according to 18:23 he ''traveled through the Galatian country and Phrygia in turn [better: one place after another in the Galatian country and Phrygia], strengthening all the disciples.'' Both passages probably refer to the southwest section of the Province of Galatia, which was inhabited by Phrygians and Galatians. In any case, there appears to be no clear reference in Acts to Paul's having ever evangelized Galatia proper. All available evidence seems to show that at the time of St. Paul Galatia in the strict sense was scarcely Hellenized, not even in its three main cities, Pessinus, Ancyra (modern Ankara), and Tavium, and very few Jews were settled there. The contrary is true of the southern section of the

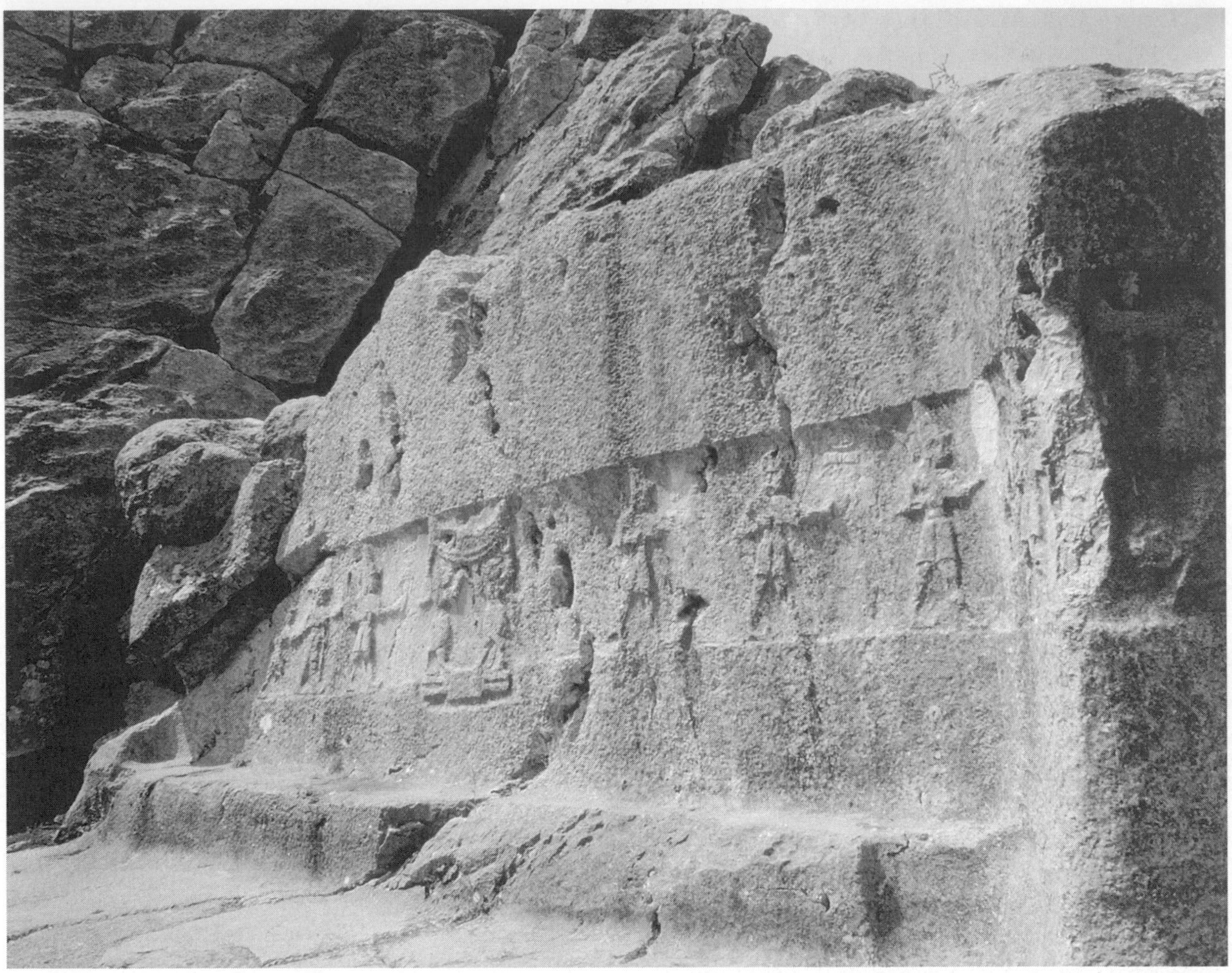

A Hittite Shrine near Ankara, Turkey, one of the three major cities of the former province of Galatia. (©Richard T. Nowitz/CORBIS)

Province of Galatia, which Paul evangelized on his first missionary journey (Acts 13:13–14:25).

However, there are many modern scholars who still defend vigorously the formerly unique opinion that ''the churches of Galatia'' (Gal 1:2) to which Paul addressed his Epistle to the GALATIANS were in Galatia proper. Among their arguments the strongest are (1) that Paul addressed the recipients of his letter as ὦ Γαλάται (O Galatians: Gal. 3:1), a term that would seem to fit the inhabitants of Galatia proper much better than those of the southern part of the Province of Galatia, and (2) that the ''Galatian country'' used in Acts 16:6; 18:23 (see above) can be understood as referring to Galatia proper.

Bibliography: W. RAMSAY, *Historical Geography of Asia Minor* (London 1890). *Paulys Realenzyklopädie der klassischen Altertumswissenschaft*, ed. G. WISSOWA et al. (Stuttgart 1893) 7.1:519–559. H. SCHLIER, *Lexicon für Theologie und Kirche* (Freiburg, 1957–66) 4:488–489. *Encyclopedic Dictionary of the Bible*, tr. and adap. by L. HARTMAN (New York 1963) 829–831.

[L. F. HARTMAN]

GALATIANS, EPISTLE TO THE

Paul's letter to the Galatians is a relatively brief writing. Its authenticity has seldom been put in doubt. It is often assumed that the addressees are, for the most part, believers converted from paganism; they live in Galatia, a region in central Asia Minor. Paul has visited and evangelized the population during his second missionary journey. Those ''who trouble'' (1:7) the Galatians are considered to be Jewish Christian missionaries who keep contact with the Jerusalem authorities. These opponents of Paul are compelling the Galatians to be circumcised and to observe (parts of) the Mosaic law. They also attack the legitimacy of Paul's apostleship. Paul tries to win back the Galatians who seem to side with his adversaries.

The letter to the Galatians was written, according to this common view, some time during Paul's third missionary journey in the mid-fifties, either during his stay at Ephesus or somewhere in Macedonia. The following outline provides a general overview of the letter's contents:

1:1–10 Salutation and Rebuke
(1) 1:11–2:21 Autobiography (Paul's apostleship)
(2) 3:1–4:31 Reflection (the Mosaic law)
(3) 5:1–6:10 Exhortation (freedom in love and Spirit)
6:11–18 Postscript

Overview of the Letter

Salutation and Rebuke (1:1–10). Paul introduces himself to the churches of Galatia and wishes them "grace and peace." He is an apostle sent not by humans but by God the Father and Jesus Christ (1:1–5). Paul omits his customary thanksgiving and at once expresses his astonishment that the Galatians, under the influence of troublemakers, are turning to a different gospel (1:6–10).

Autobiography (1:11–2:21). Paul's gospel came to him through a revelation of Jesus Christ. Paul relates how he was zealous for the traditions of the fathers and became a persecutor of the church. Yet God called him and revealed to him his Son so that he might preach Jesus Christ among the Gentiles. Only after three years did he go up to Jerusalem to visit Cephas and remained with him but 15 days; other apostles, except James the Lord's brother, he did not see (1:10–24). After 14 years he went up to Jerusalem a second time, in response to a revelation. He explained his Torah-free gospel privately to the three "pillars," James, Cephas, and John. They did not compel Titus, who came with him, and Barnabas to be circumcised, notwithstanding the pressure from the false brothers. Furthermore, the division of the apostolic work was recognized: Peter had been entrusted with the gospel for the Jews and Paul had been sent to the Gentiles. Paul, however, should remember the poor of Jerusalem (2:1–10). Later in Antioch Paul saw that, after the arrival of certain people from James, Cephas and with him other Jews and even Barnabas drew back and ate no longer with the Gentiles. According to Paul, Peter was no longer acting consistently with the truth of the Gospel. Therefore, Paul addresses Peter and emphasizes that Jews and Gentiles alike are justified by faith in Christ, not by works of the law (2:11–21).

Reflection (3:1–4:31). Already in 2:14b–21, the address to Peter, Paul was arguing in a theological way. At the beginning of chapter 3 he suddenly writes: "You foolish Galatians." Did they receive the Spirit by works of the law? Paul refers to Abraham who believed; his faith was reckoned to him as righteousness. So those who believe are the descendants of Abraham. Those who rely on works of the law are under a curse because they do not observe all the requirements of the law. But Christ redeemed us from that curse and in him the blessing of Abraham comes to the Gentiles (3:1–14). In fact, the promises made to Abraham belong to Christ, his only offspring ("seed" in Gn 12:7 is in the singular). The law came 430 years later than the covenant and cannot annul it. That law was added because of transgressions. The law was our custodian until Christ came: we were all imprisoned under the law. But now, since the Galatians belong to Christ, they are Abraham's offspring. There is no longer Jew or Greek, there is no longer slave or free, there is no longer male and female: the Galatians are one in Christ Jesus (3:15–29). We are no longer slaves and, as children, we are heirs of God. We were enslaved to the ruling powers of this world. But God sent his Son in order to redeem those who were under the law so that all might receive adoption as children. The Spirit of the Son cries in our hearts: "Abba! Father." Paul asks: how can you want to be enslaved again? He is afraid that his work will have been in vain (4:1–11). Paul now points to his first arrival in Galatia. Because of an ailment he remained there and preached the gospel. The Galatians received him with great love. He can testify to them that they would have torn out their eyes and given them to him. Has he now become their enemy? The opponents are courting the Galatians and want to separate them from Paul. But the believers are his children; he is again in childbirth until Christ be formed in them (4:12–20). Many Galatians desire to be under the law. But what is written in the law? Paul refers to the slave woman Hagar and the free woman Sarah and sees in them two covenants. Hagar, the covenant from Mount Sinai, bears children for slavery and corresponds to the present Jerusalem. The other woman corresponds to the Jerusalem above: she is free and is our mother. Like her child Isaac we are children of the promise and consequently heirs (4:21–31).

Exhortation (5:1–6:10). In 5:1 Paul begins his explicit exhortation: "For freedom Christ has set us free." The first item is: let yourselves not be circumcised, for you would cut yourselves off from Christ. In Christ Jesus neither circumcision nor uncircumcision means anything; what counts is faith working through love (5:1–12). The second item is: do not use your freedom as an occasion for the flesh but through love be enslaved to one another. The whole law is fulfilled in the one word "You shall love your neighbor as yourself." The Galatians must live by the Spirit and not gratify the desires of the flesh (5:13–24). In 5:24 Paul once again urges: "If we live by the Spirit, let us also follow the Spirit.'' The unifying factor of this section is the interweaving of mutual help and individual attentiveness, two complementary injunctions which throughout manifold themes dominate Paul's parenesis here. Bearing one another's burden is fulfilling the law of Christ (5:25–6:10).

Postscript (6:11–18). A final autograph warning against those who are trying to compel the Galatians to be circumcised comes at the end. Neither circumcision nor uncircumcision is anything. Believers are a new creation. Paul himself carries on his body the marks of Jesus. Wishes of peace and mercy as well as a blessing form the conclusion of the letter.

Hermeneutical Problems

The interpretation of Galatians is conditioned by the types of solutions one offers for the hermeneutical problems found in the letter. The second part of this article will deal with the rhetorical approach, addressees, and date of the letter, the identity of the so-called opponents, Paul's use of Scripture in this letter, and justification not by works of the law. Much more than a state of the questions cannot be offered. By way of conclusion a word about the current value of this letter will be said.

Rhetoric. Since about the 1970s the rhetorical approach to Galatians has been very much in vogue (cf. H. D. Betz). In writing his letter Paul uses persuasive language and is dependent on Greek rhetoric. Due attention must be given to the figures of style. As applied to Galatians, rhetorical criticism asks two basic questions: (1) To what kind of rhetoric does Galatians belong? (2) Is it possible to detect a rhetorical structure (*dispositio*) in the letter?

With regard to the first question few among those who favor this approach still defend the classification of Galatians as an apologetic letter. It would seem that a sustained deliberative rhetoric is present. Paul tries to persuade his addressees not to submit to the opponents' pressures. As to the second question, an example of rhetorical structure is proposed here. Within the epistolary frame (prescript and postscript) one finds an *exordium* (1:6–10), a *narratio* (1:11–2:10), a *propositio* (2:15–21), a *probatio* (3:1–4:31) and an *exhortatio* (5:1–6:10).

Yet many doubts remain. To what degree was Paul trained in Greek rhetoric? If so, does he apply the speech structure deliberately? Is a rhetorical division not forced upon the text? Moreover, there is a plethora of diverging structural proposals. Where does one find the *propositio?* Is Galatians not primarily a spontaneous and emotional letter? Does not Paul's way of reasoning and using Scripture indicate more Semitic than Greek influence?

Addressees and Date. There is no absolute certainty about the identity of the addressees. According to the North Galatian or territory hypothesis—the more traditional view—the Galatians are the inhabitants of the region Galatia (central Asia Minor) and Celtic by race. According to the more recent South Galatian or province hypothesis (cf. W. M. Ramsay), the addressees are the Christians about whom Luke writes in Acts 13–14. In Paul's time, the Roman province of Galatia included parts of Lycaonia, Pisidia, and Phrygia. During his first missionary journey Paul was in Antioch, Iconium, Lystra, and Derbe. The territory theory assumes that Paul preached the gospel in Galatia on his second missionary journey; that region (but no preaching) is mentioned in Acts 16:6 and, again, in Acts 18:23 at the beginning of the third journey. Yet not all consider the information found in Acts as trustworthy. Some exegetes are of the opinion that the first missionary journey took place after the Jerusalem conference and the Antioch incident (Gal 2:1–21) and that Acts 15—with its compromise decree that Paul does not mention—is from a later date. An early date for the letter has been proposed; some scholars even see Galatians as Paul's first letter.

It would seem that in Gal 4:12–14 Paul indicates the region, not the province, on his second journey (cf. Acts 16:6); moreover, *proteron* (former) in 4:13 possibly refers indirectly to the other visit (cf. Acts 18:23). Most probably the letter to the Galatians was written not long before that to the Romans that takes up the controversy about the law. So a preference for the North Galatian hypothesis and a date around 55 may be justified.

Opponents. The difficulty in identifying the opponents is because one has to rely on Pauline information alone (cf. 1:7; 3:1; 4:17; 5:7, 10, 12; and 6:12–13). Mirror reading is unavoidable; reconstruction proves delicate. The discussion about another name (e.g., agitators) is of minor importance. The opponents are hardly Gnostics. They do not consist of two categories or manifest a twofold, partly conservative and partly spiritual and liberal, mentality. They appear to have been Jewish Christian missionaries who arrived in Galatia after Paul and tried to impose circumcision and other Jewish regulations on the Gentile Christians. Therefore, they are called Judaizers; they may have had connections with the authorities in Jerusalem. According to Paul, the opponents are perverting the gospel of Christ.

Scripture. The way Paul uses the figure of Abraham for his main argumentation is disturbing to say the least. Paul's Jewish contemporaries assume that the works of Abraham, e.g., circumcision and the sacrifice of Isaac, are an integral part of his faith. He does more than just ''believe'' as Paul seeks to prove by means of Gen 15:6 cited in Gal 3:6. Jews are even more irritated by Paul's so-called allegory of Hagar and Sarah in Gal 4:21–31.

The question arises whether Paul's forced use of these Scripture passages is not caused by a previous use of them by the opponents against his understanding of faith. The same may perhaps also apply to the quotations present in Gal 3:10–13 (Dt 27:26; Hb 2:4; Lv 18:5; Dt 21:23).

Justification by Faith. In the traditional interpretation of Galatians, Paul was opposed by Judaizers who were legalists. They insisted upon "the works of the law," e.g., circumcision and other works prescribed by the law. The Galatians require more than faith in Christ in order to be saved. In accordance with the Jewish tradition, the Gentile Christians of Galatia must also earn their salvation by doing the works of the law. For Paul, however, one is justified by believing in Christ, by faith alone (i.e., by faith working through love, Gal 5:6).

It has been suggested that in Paul's days Judaism was not a legalistic religion of self-righteousness. For Jews the covenant is first of all grace and gift, and only then also human answer and work (E. P. Sanders). Furthermore, today many exegetes maintain that the problem in Galatia was not individual salvation but social discrimination: how can Galatians of pagan origin become true Christians? The opponents' answer is: by doing the works of the law that perhaps may be understood as specific signs of Israel's identity, such as circumcision, food prescriptions, and calendar regulations (J. D. G. Dunn). Paul's reaction is clear. One does not need to become a Jew in order to be an authentic Christian; one is not justified by the works of the law, but by faith in Christ (cf. 2:17).

Although the social dimension must not be neglected and it should not be assumed that Paul is criticizing Jewish pride and legalism, in Galatians the apostle reflects on the sinful condition of Jews and Gentiles alike. Christ alone is our redeemer, not the law. A final note: most probably the expression *pistis Christou* does not mean "Christ's faithfulness" (subjective genitive) but "faith in Christ" (objective genitive).

Galatians Today. Paul's letter to the Galatians constitutes one of the most basic documents of the New Testament. The letter offers a range of autobiographical details about Paul. Galatians emphasizes God's initiative in Christ, as well as justification for all peoples on the same condition. Last but not least, Galatians will remain the Magna Charta of Christian liberty.

Bibliography: J. M. G. BARCLAY, "Mirror-Reading a Polemical Letter: Galatians as a Test Case," *Journal for the Study of the New Testament* 31 (1987) 73–93; *Obeying the Truth: A Study of Paul's Ethics in Galatians* (Edinburgh 1988). C. K. BARRETT, *Freedom and Obligation: A Study of the Epistle to the Galatians* (Philadelphia 1985). H. D. BETZ, *Galatians* (Philadelphia 1979). J. BUCKEL, *Free to Love: Paul's Defense of Christian Liberty in Galatians* (Louvain 1993). J. D. G. DUNN, *The Epistle to the Galatians* (London 1993); *The Theology of Paul's Letter to the Galatians* (Cambridge 1993). I.-G. HONG, *The Law in Galatians* (Sheffield 1993). M. D. HOWARD, *Paul: Crisis in Galatia: A Study in Early Christian Theology* (Society for New Testament Studies Monograph Series 35; Cambridge 1990). P. H. KERN, *Rhetoric and Galatians. Assessing an Approach to Paul's Epistle* (Society for New Testament Studies Monograph Series 101; Cambridge 1998). L. J. MARTYN, *Galatians* (Anchor Bible 33A; New York 1998). F. J. MATERA, *Galatians* (SP 9; Collegeville, Minn. 1992). W. M. A. RAMSAY, *A Historical Commentary on St. Paul's Epistle to the Galatians* (New York 1900). B. WITHERINGTON, *Grace in Galatia: Commentary on St. Paul's Letter to the Galatians* (Edinburgh 1998).

[J. LAMBRECHT, S.J.]

GALBERRY, THOMAS

Bishop, first provincial of the AUGUSTINIANS in the U.S.; b. Naas, County Kildare, Ireland, May 28, 1833; d. New York City, Oct. 10, 1878. In 1836 the Galberry family came from Ireland to live in Philadelphia, Pa. Thomas graduated in 1851 from Villanova College (now University), Villanova, Pa., and joined the Augustinian Order in Jan. 1852. After ordination (Dec. 20, 1856) by Bp. John Neumann of Philadelphia, Galberry served as pastor, between 1858 and 1872, in Havertown, Pa.; Troy, N.Y.; and Lawrence, Mass. For the next three years he was president of Villanova College (1872–75). Meanwhile, in 1866, he was appointed superior (commissary general) of the Augustinian Order in the U.S., and in 1874 he was elected the first provincial of the newly erected province of St. Thomas of Villanova. Not long afterward Galberry was appointed to the See of Hartford, Conn.; he was consecrated March 19, 1876. His episcopate, like his life, was brief but filled with energetic labor; he laid the cornerstones of numerous churches and religious institutions and founded (1876) the diocesan newspaper, *Connecticut Catholic* (now the *Catholic Transcript*). While on a journey in 1878, Galberry became ill in New York and died suddenly.

Bibliography: T. PURCELL, "Thomas Galberry," *Tagastan* 5 (1941) 5–14.

[A. J. ENNIS]

GALBIS GIRONÉS, VICENTE, BL.

Lay martyr, lawyer; b. Sept. 9, 1910, Ontinyent (or Onteniente), Valencia, Spain; d. Sept. 21, 1936, Benisoda. Vicente (Vincent) was baptized in St. Charles Church in his hometown shortly after his birth. He received his early education at the hands of the Franciscan fathers, a baccalaureate degree at the National Institute of Murcia, and his law degree from the University of Valencia, where he was a member of the Catholic Student Union.

In 1922, Vicente became a founding member of the first Youth of Catholic Action in the Archdiocese of Valencia at Santa María Church. From that moment he was joined with the other martyrs of Ontinyent: Bl. Carlos DÍAZ GANDÍA, president, José María García Marcos, secretary, and Bl. Rafael Alonso Gutiérrez de Medina, president of the Men of Catholic Action.

In 1933, he moved into his family home, and began exercising his profession gratis in defense of the poor—a dream he had since childhood. A man of profound faith, he daily recited the rosary with his family, participated in the Mass, and received Holy Communion. He was also a member of the Apostleship of Prayer, Nocturnal Adoration Society, and the Society of St. Vincent de Paul.

On Sept. 5, 1935, Vicente married María de los Desamparados (called Amparo) Bonastre Oltra with whom he had one son, Vicente, born July 6, 1936—just three months before the father's death. He continued his devotional practices with his wife and joined various lay religious groups.

Although Vicente appeared to be timid, when religious persecution began and martyrdom seemed probable, he knew no fear in responding to blasphemy and detractors of the faith that it was his "greatest honor to be Catholic." Upon seeing the danger to the Church in the days just prior to the Revolution, he volunteered to spend some nights in vigil at the parish, despite the warnings of friends and family.

The Revolution began in Ontinyent with the burning of the churches and imprisonment of Catholics. Because Vicente openly professed his faith, his home was subjected to several searches. The last time the militants proposed that he abandon his current work with poor Catholic workers and become a well paid lawyer for the revolutionaries. He responded, "It would be impossible for me to defend people who profane religious images and destroy churches."

He was arrested in his home at 12:30 AM on Sept. 21, 1936. As his wife watched, he was taken to prison and held for two scant hours. From there he was taken with six youths, including Bl. Manuel TORRÓ GARCÍA, to Benisoda. En route they recited the rosary together. During his last moments before the firing squad, he shouted, "¡Viva Cristo Rey!" ("Long live Christ the King!").

At dawn Vicente's widow and her father obtained a safe conduct from the Committee to search the highways for the site of her husband's execution, where they were told to look for his body in Benisoda's cemetery. Overcoming the resistance of the militiamen, she searched among the bodies. When she found her husband's, she drenched a handkerchief in his blood and saved his scapular and rosary.

His wife, Amparo, and aunt, Ángeles Bonastre García, were present at the exhumation of his body and reburial in the new cemetery at Ontinyent (October 1959). He was beatified by Pope John Paul II with José APARICIO SANZ and 232 companions on March 11, 2001.

Feast: Sept. 22.

Bibliography: V. CÁRCEL ORTÍ, *Martires españoles del siglo XX* (Madrid 1995). W. H. CARROLL, *The Last Crusade* (Front Royal, Va. 1996). J. PÉREZ DE URBEL, *Catholic Martyrs of the Spanish Civil War*, tr. M. F. INGRAMS (Kansas City, Mo. 1993). R. ROYAL, *The Catholic Martyrs of the Twentieth Century* (New York 2000). Consejo Diocesano de los Hombres de Acción Católica de Valencia. *Possumus*, n. 108 (1960), 10; *Ánimos*, n. 12 (1945). *L'Osservatore Romano,* Eng. no. 11 (March 14, 2001) 1–4, 12.

[K. I. RABENSTEIN]

GALDINUS, ST.

Cardinal archbishop; b. Milan, *c.* 1100; d. Milan, April 18, 1176. Galdinus, of the noble Valvarsi della Sala family, was chancellor and archdeacon at Milan before becoming cardinal priest of Santa Sabina at Rome in 1165. The following year he was made archbishop of Milan (April 18, 1166), to which charge was added that of papal legate for Lombardy. In his diocese and throughout Lombardy, he strove vigorously to repair the ravages of the Victorine schism and to counteract the heresy of the CATHARI. He joined, also, in the rebuilding of Milan (destroyed by FREDERICK I BARBAROSSA), cared for the needs of the poor, and reformed and reorganized his clergy. He died literally on his feet while preaching, and he was canonized by the then-reigning pope, ALEXANDER III.

Feast: April 18.

Bibliography: *Acta Sanctorum* April 2:590–595. F. MEDA, *Galdino della Sala* (Bologna 1931). E. CAZZANI, *Vescovi e arcivescovi di Milano* (Milan 1955) 149–153.

[J. E. BRESNAHAN]

GALEN, CLEMENS AUGUSTINUS VON

Cardinal, bishop of Münster, Germany; b. Dinklage, Oldenburg, Germany, March 16, 1878; d. Münster, March 22, 1946. He was the son of Count Ferdinand

Heribert von Galen and Elizabeth, Countess of Spee. After being educated by the Jesuits in Feldkirch, he studied at the Catholic University in Freiburg, Germany, the Jesuit theological college in Innsbruck, Austria, and the diocesan seminary in Münster and was ordained in 1904. Following parish work in Berlin, he became pastor of St. Lambert's, Münster (1929). Having denounced the godlessness of Germany after World War I in his book *Die Pest des Laizismus und ihre Erscheinungsformen* (1932), Von Galen became an outspoken critic of the Hitler regime after his consecration as bishop of Münster (1933). His sermons attacked Nazi racial doctrines, totalitarian methods, and state confiscation of religious property. He was critical too of the Gestapo, the policy of euthanasia for insane and "unproductive" members of society, and the efforts to undermine youth. Von Galen displayed no concern for his personal safety, but Hitler, fearing that the support of Westphalia might be entirely lost, seems to have ordered that no restraints be placed on the "Lion of Münster." After World War II, the bishop continued his denunciation of injustices under the occupation authorities. He was created cardinal on Feb. 17, 1946, shortly before being stricken with a fatal attack of intestinal paralysis.

Bibliography: H. PORTMANN, *Cardinal von Galen,* tr. R. I. SEDGWICK (London 1957). G. RITTER, *The German Resistance,* tr. R. T. CLARK (New York 1959). M. A. GALLIN, *German Resistance to Hitler* (Washington 1961). H. ROTHFELS, *The German Opposition to Hitler,* tr. L. WILSON (Chicago 1962). M. BIERBAUM, *Staatslexicon* ed. Görres-Gesellschaft, 8 v. (6th, new and enl. ed. Freiburg 1957–63) 3:639–642.

[M. A. GALLIN]

Clemens Augustinus Von Galen.

GALERIUS, ROMAN EMPEROR

Reigned 305 to 311; b. Gaius Galerius Valerius Maximianus (Galerius Maximian), near Sardica, Illyricum, *c.* 250; d. 311. On March 1, 293, after a distinguished military career, he was chosen Caesar of the East by Diocletian. He was charged with the government and defense of the Danubian provinces, and was later sent against the Persian Narses. After an initial defeat at Carrhae, he achieved a complete victory (297) and was given command on the Danube. He went to Nicomedia early in 303, where he helped persuade DIOCLETIAN to issue the first of his four edicts against the Christians. During Diocletian's illness in 304, Galerius increased the intensity of the persecution. On May 1, 305, Diocletian and Maximian abdicated, probably at the urging of Galerius. Constantius and Galerius succeeded them as the Augusti, while Severus and Maximinus Daia were named the new Caesars. When Constantius died in 306, Galerius reluctantly recognized his son CONSTANTINE I as Caesar. After conferring the title of Augustus on Severus, he sent him against Maxentius in Rome. Severus was defeated, and Galerius himself had to retreat after an attempted invasion of Italy. In 308 a reorganization of the empire was effected at Carnuntum, where Licinius was named Augustus and Maxentius was declared a public enemy. In 310, Galerius was afflicted with cancer. One of his last acts, in April 311, was an edict issued in his own name and that of the other regents recognizing the failure of the persecution and allowing the Christians "to exist again and build the houses in which they used to assemble" (Eusebius, *Hist. Eccl.* 8.17.9). Galerius was by nature cruel and suspicious. His animosity toward the Christians may have been aroused by his mother, since she herself was known to have been extremely superstitious (Lactantius, *De mort. persec.* 11).

Bibliography: R. B. MOTZO, *Enciclopedia Italiana di scienzi, littere ed arti* 36 v. (Rome 1929–39), 16:270. A. AMORE, *Enciclopedia cattolica,* ed. P. PASCHINI et al. 12 v. (Rome 1949–54) 5:1867–68. W. ENSSLIN, *Paulys Realencyklopädie der klassischen Altertumswissenschaft* ed. G. WISSOWA et al. (Stuttgart 1893–) 14.2 (1930) 2516–28.

[M. J. COSTELLOE]

GALGANI, GEMMA, ST.

Italian mystic; b. Borgo Nuovo di Camigliano, near Lucca, Italy, March 12, 1878; d. Lucca, April 11, 1903. She was born of pious parents, Enrico and Aurelia (Landi) Galgani, and was educated by the Sisters of St. Zita, whose foundress, Bl. Elena GUERRA, was one of her teachers. Her mother died in 1886. Her father's death (1896) left her in extreme poverty. Her remaining years were spent in the large household of Matteo Giannini in Lucca. Serious recurring illnesses, which plagued her from childhood, prevented her from joining the Passionist nuns. From her early years she meditated on Christ's sufferings. Gemma had visions of Christ, the Blessed Virgin, and her guardian angel; she experienced STIGMATIZATION and other physical phenomena of Christ's Passion, such as the sweat of blood, scourging, and the crowning with thorns. At times she was disturbed by diabolical manifestations, but her life was for the most part retired and quiet. She was a model of humility, obedience, poverty, and especially of patience in illnesses and tribulations. She was beatified May 14, 1933, and canonized May 3, 1940. The cult of St. Gemma became quite popular after the publication in 1941 of her correspondence with her spiritual director, Germano di San Stanislao Ruoppolo, CP.

Feast: May 14.

Bibliography: *Gesù solo,* ed. G. POLLICE (Rome 1978); *Letters of St. Gemma Galgani,* ed. GERMANO OF ST. STANISLAUS, tr. Dominican nuns of Corpus Christi monastery (New York 1947); *Estasi, diario, autobiografia, scritti vari di s. Gemma Galgani,* ed. GERMANO OF ST. STANISLAUS (Rome 1943). J. JORGENSEN, *Gemma e altre storie lucchesi,* ed., L. DEL ZANNA (Lucca 1983). G. AGRESTI, *Ritratto della espropriata* (Lucca 1978). A. CARRARA, *Gemma Galgani* (Florence 1977). J. F. VILLEPELÉE, *La folie de la Croix* (Hauteville 1977). E. ZOFFOLI, *La povera Gemma* (Rome 1957). SISTER SAINT MICHAEL, *Portrait of St. Gemma, a Stigmatic* (New York 1950). J. L. BAUDOT and L. CHAUSSIN, *Vies des saints et des bienheueux selon l'ordre du calendrier avec l'historique des fêtes,* ed. by The Benedictines of Paris, 12 v. (Paris 1935–56) 4:272–275. A. BUTLER, *The Lives of the Saints,* ed. H. THURSTON and D. ATTWATER, 4 v. (New York 1956) 2:75–76.

[F. G. SOTTOCORNOLA]

GALILEI, GALILEO

Florentine philosopher, physicist, and inventor; most commonly remembered for his condemnation by the Holy Office as a result of his attempting to prove the Copernican theory of the universe; b. Pisa, Italy, Feb. 15, 1564; d. Florence, Jan. 8, 1642. The family name had originally been Bonajuti, but it had been changed in the 15th century to Galilei in honor of Galileo Bonajuti, a famous physician. The fortunes of the Galilei family had declined by the time Galileo was born. His father, Vincenzio Galilei, was a noteworthy, though impoverished, musician. At the age of 12, Galileo was enrolled in the monastery school at Vallombrosa. Subsequently, it seems, he entered the Vallombrosan order as a novice, but was withdrawn by his father before completing his novitiate training. In 1581 he entered the University of Pisa to pursue the liberal arts course as a prerequisite for entering the school of medicine. After four years of study, Galileo, who by then was more interested in mathematics and science than in medicine, had to withdraw from the university without completing his courses or graduating. He continued to study privately and began to write. In 1586 he wrote a treatise on the hydrostatic balance (*La Bilancetta*), and two years later he produced a work on the center of gravity in solids. By then he had attracted the attention of a wealthy patron, the Marquese Guidobaldo del Monte (1545–1607), who was also a very capable mathematician. Guidobaldo used his considerable influence to have Galileo appointed as a lecturer in mathematics at the University of Pisa.

Galileo seems to have made many enemies among the faculty members at the university. Although he probably taught within a framework of traditional mathematics and science, apparently he was not afraid to disagree with the standard doctrine when he had reason to do so. Although it is doubtful that Galileo ever did drop bodies of unequal weight from the Leaning Tower of Pisa to demonstrate that velocity of fall does not vary according to weight as Aristotle taught, the story does exemplify Galileo's spirit. To understand the opposition that Galileo faced at Pisa and throughout his life, it is necessary to review briefly the state of philosophy as generally taught in the universities of his time.

Philosophical Climate. It must be remembered that the philosophy of ARISTOTLE was the predominant system of thought in the 16th century. It had been introduced to the Western world in only the 13th century, but in a relatively short time it became the most widely accepted system, partly because of the commentaries of St. THOMAS AQUINAS and the scholastics. Aristotelian philosophy presented a logical, clear, and rational explanation of man and the world around him. By the 16th century, philosophical disputes more often than not were between schools advocating different interpretations of Aristotle. Scholastics, Averroists, and Alexandrists all claimed true intellectual descent from the Stagirite. Moreover, under the influence of Renaissance humanism, the tendency to attribute definitive authority to the texts of Aristotle grew even stronger, and philosophical writings were generally more textual and philological than original or creative. Intramural disputes on the interpretation of Aristotle replaced the empirical approach that Aristotle himself had championed centuries before as the beginning of philosophy.

The result was that those who opposed Galileo in the name of Aristotelian philosophy were neither Aristotelian in spirit nor philosophers in the true sense. Galileo described them as people who think that ''philosophy is a sort of book like the *Aeneid* or the *Odyssey,* and that the truth is to be sought not in the universe, not in nature, but by comparing texts.'' Galileo's willingness to speak out against Aristotle whenever he thought it necessary, coupled with the fact that he had never graduated from the university and had no academic degree, led his Aristotelian opponents on the faculty to oppose him bitterly as an upstart who dared to challenge their authority and that of ''the Philosopher.''

In 1592, after two years of teaching at Pisa, Galileo resigned. He returned to his family, then living in Florence and, when his father died, took over the duties of supporting them. Guidobaldo del Monte again came to Galileo's aid, and within a few months he was appointed by the Venetian senate to the chair of mathematics at the University of Padua, a post he held for 18 years. Soon after moving to Padua, Galileo began living in concubinage with a woman named Marina Gamba, who bore him a son, Vincenzio, of whom little is known, and two daughters, both of whom became nuns. Sister Marie Celeste was Galileo's greatest consolation during the trying years that followed.

Padua provided a congenial atmosphere for Galileo. It had a tradition of true philosophical inquiry as witnessed by the fact that 15th-century Paduans such as Paul of Venice, Gaetano da Thiene, and Johannes Marlianus had made significant changes and developments within the framework of Aristotelian science. There Galileo invented a thermometer, wrote many treatises dealing with his ideas and experiments in mechanics, and became deeply interested in astronomy.

Theories of the Universe. Through the ages, the geocentric system of the universe had been almost universally accepted. It had received its doctrinal formulation in the writings of Aristotle (378–322 B.C.) and PTOLEMY (fl. 150 B.C.). Both agreed that the earth was the motionless center of the universe; but whereas Aristotle accounted for celestial motions by postulating a squadron of concentric spheres to carry the planets and fixed stars around the earth, Ptolemy described the motions of the heavens in terms of eccentric spheres and epicycles. Elements of the Aristotelian and Ptolemaic views were combined in a treatise by JOHN DE SACROBOSCO (d. 1256) and the resulting eclectic system won widespread acceptance. The system did save the appearances, and it had physical support in the Aristotelian concepts of the quintessence,

Galileo Galilei. (©Bettmann/CORBIS)

the circular character of celestial motion, and the First Mover. It is true that there had been some opposition to the geostatic explanation. NICHOLAS ORESME, in the 14th century, conceived of a rotating earth at the center of an otherwise motionless universe. Cardinal NICHOLAS OF CUSA, in his *Docta ignorantia* (1440), supported Oresme's theory with a few modifications of his own. But it was not until Nicolaus COPERNICUS (1473–1543) that a rival system was sufficiently well formulated to challenge the Aristotelian-Ptolemaic position. In his great work *De revolutionibus orbium coelestium* (1543), Copernicus advocated a sun-centered universe in which the earth was a planet that revolved both on its axis and around the sun. Copernicus probably believed that his system described the real motions of the heavens, but, largely because of a spurious preface inserted in the *De revolutionibus* by Andreas OSIANDER in order to avoid religious opposition to the new system, it was commonly thought that Copernicus himself believed his system to be only a mathematical hypothesis and not necessarily representative of the actual constitution of the universe. Even though Copernicus had been unable to free himself of the idea that celestial motion must be circular and was therefore forced to employ eccentrics and epicycles, his system was a slight gain in simplicity over Ptolemy's. Galileo studied the *De revolutionibus* and, writing to Johann KEPLER in 1597, acknowledged that he had discarded the Ptolmaic position several years before and believed in the reality of the Copernican system. It was to be the passion of his life to demonstrate the truth of the new astronomy.

The Telescope. In 1608 a Dutchman, Hans Lippershey of Middleburg (1570?–1619), invented a fairly reliable telescope. When Galileo heard of the invention a year later, he began to construct one of his own. Within a short time, he built three telescopes, the largest of which made objects appear nearly 1,000 times larger and 30 times closer than when seen with natural vision. With this instrument Galileo searched the heavens. He made astounding discoveries, the most important of which were reported in his *Sidereus Nuncius,* or *Starry Messenger* (1610). In this work, which made him famous, Galileo revealed that the moon was not a perfect sphere as had been thought, but was marred with mountains and valleys. The Milky Way was seen to consist of a multitude of stars invisible to the naked eye. Most important, Galileo announced that the planet Jupiter had four moons revolving around it. These satellites of Jupiter could serve to answer an objection made against the Copernican theory to the effect that if the earth moved through space it would leave the moon behind. Here was a planet traveling a major orbit and carrying four moons with it. Galileo dedicated his *Starry Messenger* to Cosimo II de Medici (1590–1621), the Grand Duke of Tuscany. In return, Cosimo appointed him ducal philosopher and mathematician with a salary of 1,000 gold florins a year. Galileo left Padua in July 1610 and moved to a villa at Arcetri, near Florence. There he observed the heavens under the aegis of the Grand Duke.

There were strong reactions to the *Starry Messenger.* Some saw it as a great contribution to human knowledge, but the university Aristotelians came forth in defense of their master's cosmology. First, they said, no matter what Galileo saw through his telescope, the Copernican system seemed to contradict experience. Anyone with the sense of sight could see the sun rise in the east and set in the west. Second, they pointed out that a moving earth was completely opposed to all the known laws of physics. They had a point; a superior system of physics did have to be established before Copernicanism could win acceptance. Third, Aristotle had said long before that if the earth moved, stellar displacements or parallaxes would be observable, but none had ever been recorded. This was a strong objection, and it remained unanswered until F. W. Bessel (1784–1846) and others determined the parallax of the star 61 Cygni in 1838. Another objection raised was that, taken as a fact and not as a mere mathematical device for aiding astronomers in charting stellar positions, Copernican astronomy contradicted the explicit words of Sacred Scripture.

While the debate went on, Galileo made two more discoveries: the phases of Venus and the sunspots. The only explanation for the fact that Venus changes shape just as the moon does is that Venus moves around the sun and not the earth. The sunspots questioned the Aristotelian doctrine that celestial bodies were composed of an immutable quintessence.

While Galileo was formulating his arguments, he failed to adopt a discovery that might have helped the new astronomy win acceptance. In 1609 Johann Kepler published his *Astronomia nova,* in which he disclosed that planetary orbits were not circular but elliptical and that the sun is at a focus of the ellipse. This was the very thing needed to clear astronomy of epicycles and the dogma of perfect circles. Although it is fairly certain that Galileo knew of the discovery, he never made use of it.

In December 1610 Galileo received support from an unexpected source. Father Christopher CLAVIUS, chief mathematician and astronomer at the Jesuit Roman College, wrote to tell him that the Jesuit astronomers had confirmed all his discoveries. Galileo decided that it was time to go to Rome. If he could secure the support of the Jesuit astronomers, he might be able to win at least unofficial ecclesiastical backing for his position. He arrived in the Holy City in March 1611. His reception was most encouraging. Pope PAUL V granted him a long audience. Prince Federigo Cesi (1585–1630) appointed him a member of the Accademia de' Lincei, a society devoted to philosophical and scientific studies. The Jesuits of the Roman College held a day of ceremonies in his honor. Galileo returned to Florence in June confident that he had won some support.

Heliocentrism and Scripture. Despite his discoveries, Galileo still had no real proof that the Copernican system was anything more than a theory. His observations militated more against Aristotle and Ptolemy than for Copernicus. Had there been only two alternatives, either the Ptolemaic or Copernican, Galileo, by discrediting the first, would have shown the superiority of the second, but it was not that simple. A third system had been worked out by the Danish astronomer Tycho Brahe in 1588. In Brahe's scheme, the planets revolved around the sun while the sun was revolving around a motionless earth. This system could explain Galileo's chief discoveries, the moons of Jupiter and the phases of Venus, while keeping the earth as the motionless center of the universe.

Back in Florence, Galileo became involved in two minor controversies. One was over the question of why things float or sink; the other was an argument with the

Jesuit Christopher Scheiner as to who had discovered the sunspots first and how they were to be explained. The latter dispute prompted Galileo to write his *Letters on Sunspots* (1613), in which, despite his lack of proof, he endorsed the Copernican system. Cardinal Maffeo Barberini, later Pope URBAN VIII, was one of many who wrote to congratulate the author. The *Letters* were published in Italian rather than Latin, and the growing controversy now became a popular subject of discussion.

Interest passed from the complex problems of physics and astronomy and came to center on the scriptural difficulties raised by the new system. People wanted to know why Joshua would command the sun to stand still if it never moved anyway. (See Js 10.12–13.) They wondered how a moving earth could be reconciled with the statement that God ''fixed the earth upon its foundation, not to be moved forever'' (Ps 103.5). Also, they believed that the sun must be in motion, for the Book of Ecclesiastes states that ''the sun rises and the sun goes down: then it presses on to the place where it rises'' (Eccl 1.5). In December 1613 Galileo heard from Father Benedetto Castelli that these and other texts from Sacred Scripture were being invoked directly against the Copernican system. Galileo wrote a letter to Castelli in which he formulated his ideas on the relationship of the Bible and science. Copies of the letter were made and circulated freely. Now the dispute was in the open. In December 1614 a Dominican, Tommaso Caccini, preached a sermon at S. Maria Novella in Florence in which he strongly condemned the new astronomy. Before long, a copy of Galileo's letter to Castelli was forwarded to the Holy Office for examination. Although the Holy Office judged that the letter contained nothing contrary to the faith, Galileo decided to revise and expand it.

While he was working on this, a Carmelite, Paolo Antonio Foscarini (1565–1616), published a book that attempted to reconcile the Copernican system with Holy Scripture. He sent a copy to Cardinal Robert BELLARMINE, the leading theologian in Rome, and asked his opinion of it. Bellarmine's *Letter to Foscarini* expressed the unofficial but quite definite attitude of the theologians toward the new astronomy. Bellarmine admitted that the Copernican system saved the appearances better than the Ptolemaic and therefore could be considered a superior hypothesis, but, he pointed out, it was still not established as a fact. The cardinal explained that one is not allowed to interpret the Scriptures contrary to the common agreement of the Fathers of the Church, and the Fathers seemed to interpret the texts in question literally. To contradict their exegesis was to oppose the truth of the Scriptures themselves. There could be no departure from the interpretation of the Fathers in case of doubt, and there would always be a doubt unless Galileo could produce a true demonstration of his theory.

Bellarmine's opinion was wrong on several counts. First, he should have remembered that, as St. AUGUSTINE and St. Thomas Aquinas had said long before, the Bible was not intended to teach science and therefore its authority should not be invoked in scientific disputes. Second, although most of the Fathers did think that the earth was immobile and the sun moved, not one of them held that this had to be believed as a revealed truth. Third, although it is true that common interpretation by theologians of a text whose meaning is not defined makes that interpretation highly probable, there is still room for an alternative, if less probable, exegesis. However, Bellarmine demanded a physical demonstration before he would allow any other exegesis.

Galileo presented his position in the revised letter to Castelli, which he entitled *A Letter to the Grand Duchess Christina.* Galileo ably defended the fact that the Bible was not meant to teach science and that, when referring to the physical world around them, the sacred writers used the common conception of the universe in order to avoid confusing the minds of their readers and making them suspicious of the religious truths that the Holy Texts were meant to convey. However, Galileo then made the mistake of conceding to Scripture superior authority even in science, unless contrary physical arguments were demonstrative. ''As to the [physical] propositions which are stated but not rigorously demonstrated, anything contrary to the Bible involved in them must be considered undoubtedly false and should be proved so by every possible means.'' By granting Scripture precedence over probable physical arguments to the contrary and by his inability to prove the real truth of the Copernican system, Galileo was caught in a logical snare. The issue was still being debated when Galileo decided to go to Rome in December 1615 to plead his case personally. About this time, Cardinal Boniface Gaetani wrote to the Dominican Friar Tommaso CAMPANELLA, asking his views on the dispute. Campanella responded by writing an eloquent plea for scientific freedom entitled *Apologia pro Galileo;* and although it was undoubtedly the best theological analysis of the problem written at the time, it went largely unnoticed.

First Condemnation. Galileo's conduct in Rome was incredibly bold. He felt he had to convince anyone who would listen that his arguments supported ''realist'' Copernicanism. What particular incident brought the issue to a climax is a subject of debate; but early in 1616 Pope Paul V thought that the whole matter was getting out of hand, and he ordered the Congregation of the Holy Office to look into it. On Feb. 19, 1616, two propositions, clumsily worded, but representative of Galileo's position, were sent to a committee of 11 theologians who were consultors of the Holy Office. Five days later, they reported their decision to the authorities of the Holy Office.

Obviously, they agreed with Bellarmine's position. In their opinion the proposition that the sun is at the center of the universe and does not move was "philosophically foolish and absurd and formally heretical, inasmuch as it expressly contradicts the doctrines of Holy Scripture in many places, both according to their literal meaning and according to the common exposition and interpretation of the holy Fathers and learned theologians." As to the proposition that the earth is not the center of the universe, but that it moves with both an annual and daily motion, the consultors were agreed that this deserved "the same censure in philosophy, and, that, from a theological standpoint, it was at least erroneous in the faith." Galileo was ordered to appear before Cardinal Bellarmine and was told not to hold or defend the Copernican position any longer. Then, it seems, the commissary-general of the Holy Office, overzealous in his duty (for he was not instructed to intervene unless Galileo objected to Bellarmine's instruction), stepped forward and gave Galileo an absolute injunction not to hold, teach, or defend his opinion in any way, either verbally or in writing. The report of this meeting, found in the files of the Holy Office, has been the subject of a long controversy. It is quite possible that the commissary-general did serve this strict injunction but that Cardinal Bellarmine, knowing that it had not been called for, told Galileo that he was not bound by it. At any rate, with Galileo's promise to comply with the instructions, the case was closed before the Holy Office.

On March 5, 1616, the Congregation of the Index issued a decree suspending Copernicus's book *De revolutionibus orbium coelestium* until it could be rendered more hypothetical. (The corrections were made, and it was again permitted to be read within four years.) The decree further condemned outright all books that attempted to reconcile the heliocentric system with Holy Scripture, since that doctrine was "false and altogether contrary to Holy Scripture." The actions of the Holy Office and the Congregation of the Index in no way represented a commitment of the infallible teaching authority of the Church against the new astronomy. The decree of the Index received papal approval only *in forma communi* and therefore was only the fallible decision of a Roman Congregation. Still it did bind Catholics to at least external observance. The publication of the Index decree gave Galileo's enemies ample material for speculation about the theological orthodoxy of the Florentine scientist. Galileo appealed to Cardinal Bellarmine for a written statement that he could use in self-defense. The cardinal's certificate stated that Galileo had not abjured his opinion, nor had he been given a penance, but that he had been told not to hold or defend the Copernican system as true.

The Dialogue. Galileo returned to Florence discouraged but not defeated. For several years he stayed out of disputes. Then, in 1619, he backed a disciple, Mario Guiducci, in a bitter controversy with the Jesuit astronomer Horatio Grassi (1583–1654) over the nature and course of comets. This was still going on when, in 1623, Pope GREGORY XV died and Cardinal Maffeo Barberini was elected pope. Barberini, who was a good friend of Galileo and had opposed the actions of the Holy Office in 1616, took the name Urban VIII. Galileo dedicated *The Assayer* (1623), a polemic against Grassi, to the new Pope and then, a year later, went to Rome to see him. Galileo had six long audiences with Urban; and although the Pope refused to lift the ban against "realist" Copernican writings for fear of undermining the authority of the Congregations, he apparently told Galileo that as long as he treated the subject hypothetically and did not attempt to prove the Copernican system, he could go ahead and write.

Galileo decided to risk everything in the hope that he could demonstrate his theory. He spent most of the next six years (1624–30) working on what he thought would be final and conclusive proof that the Copernican system was true. By means of submission clauses in the preface and conclusion, the resulting book, entitled *Dialogue on the Two Great World Systems,* was approved by the censors and went to press in 1632. The main argument of the *Dialogue* was based on an erroneous theory of the tides: a theory that he thought would necessitate the motion of the earth. The other important argument of the book, that based on the motion of sunspots, was also faulty and undemonstrative, but the *Dialogue* still caused a storm. It was obvious that Galileo had attempted to prove the Copernican system. Not only that, but someone convinced Pope Urban that Galileo had made a fool of him and that he had never intended to heed the Pope's instructions. Urban appointed a special commission of theologians to investigate, and again Galileo was in trouble.

Second Condemnation. The special commission made two main charges against the famous scientist. First, Galileo had treated the Copernican system not as a hypothesis, but as an absolute fact. This was contrary to the decree of the Index and Bellarmine's admonition in 1616. Second, he had been fraudulently silent about a command given him in 1616 by the commissary-general during the audience with Bellarmine, not to hold, teach, or defend the new astronomy in any way, either verbally or in writing. The special commission found a record of this strict injunction in the files of the Holy Office, and news of it came as a surprise, even to the Pope. Galileo, then nearly 70 years old, was ordered to come to Rome.

After a long delay due to illness, he arrived on Feb. 13, 1633. He was received with kindness and given comfortable lodging. He was never imprisoned as some have claimed. During the trial, Galileo would not admit that he had tried to prove the Copernican system in his *Dialogue* despite the many passages from that book that could be cited to the contrary. Nor did he remember that any command had been given him by the commissary-general in 1616. He produced a copy of the certificate Bellarmine had given him years before, which stated that Galileo had been instructed only not to hold or defend the Copernican doctrine. Moreover, as he pointed out to the judges, his book had an imprimatur. It was a strong defense.

Still, he had disobeyed the decree of the Index, Bellarmine's admonition, and the explicit wishes of the Pope; and it seemed even to those who wanted to treat Galileo leniently that some token punishment was in order. There seem to have been two opposing views among officials in Rome regarding what action was to be taken against the old scientist. Cardinal Francesco Barberini, the Pope's nephew, led those who advocated leniency, but a stronger group wanted to humiliate Galileo completely, and they prevailed. They succeeded in having the *Dialogue* prohibited (the ban was lifted only in 1822) and in having Galileo condemned as ''vehemently suspected of heresy.'' Galileo was made to kneel and abjure the Copernican opinion, sentenced to imprisonment, and given a ''salutary penance'' to recite. The prison sentence was never imposed, although Galileo remained under house arrest in Florence for the rest of his life. The condemnation was the act of a Roman Congregation and in no way involved infallible teaching authority, but the theologians' treatment of Galileo was an unfortunate error; and, however it might be explained, it cannot be defended.

Last Days. Upon his return to Florence, Galileo went back to the study of dynamics. In 1636 he finished his greatest work, the *Discourses concerning Two New Sciences,* a clear statement of his thought on such subjects as the characteristics of solid bodies, accelerated motion, and the parabolic path of projectiles. In 1637, shortly after discovering the moon's libration, Galileo lost the sight of his right eye. A year later he was totally blind. He continued with the help of his disciples, E. Torricelli and V. Viviani (1622–1703), dictating addenda to his *Discourses* and experimenting. He was buried in the Church of S. Croce in Florence. Only in 1737 was permission finally obtained to erect a monument over his tomb.

Contributions to Scientific Thought. Galileo made many significant contributions to the progress of human thought. In astronomy his contributions were observational rather than theoretical. He made numerous discoveries, but was not a speculative astronomer, as was Kepler. Galileo used his discoveries to argue effectively against some Aristotelian and Ptolemaic doctrines. He showed that it was unnecessary to have one system of mechanics in celestial physics and another in terrestrial physics, and he definitely brought out the inadequacies of the Ptolemaic system. In addition, Galileo deserves to be considered one of the founders of the new mechanics. Some of his criticisms of Aristotelian mechanics had been anticipated by JOHN PHILOPONUS and JOHN BURIDAN, but these men made corrections within the framework of Aristotelian qualitative analysis, whereas Galileo, concentrating on the measure of motion, changed the emphasis from explaining why a body moves to why it ceases to move, Galileo formulated a rough approximation of the law of inertia that was later perfected by Sir Isaac Newton.

One of Galileo's most significant contributions to modern science was in the area of methodology. It would be an exaggeration to say that he alone founded a new method or that only he recognized the necessity of experimentation, but he did combine elements from the past and prepare the way for the future. Galileo's approach to a scientific problem was to begin by abstracting from concrete factors that were not easily controllable, for example, resistance. He could then formulate simple laws based on idealized description. These would subsequently be applied, making allowance for concrete, physical circumstances. In his method, the use of experiment was primarily to illustrate insights that were the result of prior scientific theorizing; secondarily, it provided the basis for theories where there were no original, pre-experimental insights.

Galileo's true originality, however, lay in his insistence that the book of nature is written only in mathematical characters such that the inner workings of nature can only be expressed mathematically. As far as Galileo was concerned, whatever could not be caught in mathematical abstraction, such as secondary sense qualities, essences, and causes, were either subjective or did not exist. Such a view denied the need for a natural philosophy in the traditional sense. Newton, who fully appreciated the mathematical approach to reality, did not accept Galileo's mathematical ''realism'' but allowed for the validity of the traditional qualitative, philosophical inquiry. Galileo, then, represents in many ways the culmination of certain scientific trends that existed before him, especially at Paris, Oxford, and Padua, and part of a new beginning for science that led to Newton and beyond.

Bibliography: *Le opere di Galileo Galilei,* ed. A. FAVARO, 20 v. (Florence 1929–39), contains Galileo's works and minor writings as well as many documents pertaining to his conflict with the theologians. Galileo's most important works are available in English: *Dialogue concerning the Two Chief World Systems,* tr. S. DRAKE (Berkeley 1953); *Dialogues concerning Two New Sciences,* tr. H. CREW and A. DE SALVIO (New York 1914; pa. repr. 1952); *Discoveries and Opinions of Galileo,* ed. and tr. S. DRAKE (New York 1957), contains translations of the *Sidereus Nuncius, Letters on Sunspots, Letter to the Grand Duchess Christina* and most of the *Assayer.* There is an enormous amount of secondary source material on Galileo. The philosophical background for his work is well handled in E. A. BURTT, *The Metaphysical Foundations of Modern Physical Science* (rev. ed. Garden City 1932; repr. Anchor Bks 1954) and J. A. WEISHEIPL, *The Development of Physical Theory in the Middle Ages* (New York 1960). Galileo's scientific work is analyzed in A. KOYRÉ, *Études Galiléenes* (Paris 1939) and clearly explained by I. B. COHEN, *The Birth of a New Physics* (Garden City 1960). The most important books recounting the events of the condemnation include J. J. LANGFORD, *Galileo, the Church and Science* (New York 1966), F. S. TAYLOR, *Galileo and the Freedom of Thought* (London 1938), and G. DE SANTILLANA, *The Crime of Galileo* (Chicago 1955), which is a very readable though not altogether fair account of the famous conflict. R. J. BLACKWELL, *Science, Religion and Authority: Lessons from the Galileo Affair* (Milwaukee 1998); *Galileo, Bellarmine, and the Bible: Including a Translation of Foscarini's Letter on the Motion of the Earth* (Notre Dame, Ind. 1991). T. CAMPANELLA, *A Defense of Galileo, the Mathematician from Florence: Which Is an Inquiry as to Whether the Philosophical View Advocated by Galileo Is in Agreement with, or Is Opposed to, the Sacred Scriptures*, tr. with intro. R. J. BLACKWELL (Notre Dame 1994). W. A. WALLACE, *Galileo's Logic of Discovery and Proof: The Background, Content, and Use of His Appropriated Treatises on Aristotle's Posterior Analytics* (Dordrecht; Boston 1992); *Galileo and His Sources: The Heritage of the Collegio Romano in Galileo's Science* (Princeton, N.J. 1984); W. A. WALLACE, ed., *Reinterpreting Galileo* (Washington, D.C. 1986). M. A. FINOCCHIARO, ed. and trans., *The Galileo Affair: A Documentary History* (Berkeley 1989). E. MCMULLIN, ed., *Galileo, Man of Science* (Princeton Junction, N.J. 1988). P. CARDINAL POUPARD, ed., *Galileo Galilei: Toward a Resolution of 350 Years of Debate, 1633-1983*, epilogue JOHN PAUL II, trans. I. CAMPBELL (Pittsburgh 1987). S. DRAKE, *Galileo at Work: His Scientific Biography* (Chicago 1981, c1978). D. SHAPERE, *Galileo: A Philosophical Study* (Chicago 1974).

[J. J. LANGFORD]

GALITZIN, ELIZABETH

Religious administrator; b. St. Petersburg, Russia, Feb. 22, 1797; d. St. Michael's, Louisiana, Dec. 8, 1843. Her father was Prince Alexsis Andrevitch; her mother, Countess Protasof, left the Russian Orthodox Church to embrace Catholicism. Four years later Elizabeth made her submission to Rome and entered the Society of the SACRED HEART at Metz, Lorraine. She received the habit in 1826, made her first vows in 1828, and made her final profession at Paris in 1832. Two years later she was appointed secretary general to the foundress, St. Madeleine Sophie BARAT. Mother Galitzin took an active part in the sixth general council of the order, held in Rome in 1839, and was elected assistant general. Sweeping changes in organization, designed to make the order resemble more closely the Society of Jesus, were approved for a three-year trial; and Mother Galitzin was sent (1840) as visitatrix to the American convents of the Sacred Heart to explain the new decrees and ensure their proper application. She reached New York early in September and traveled directly to Missouri to visit the convents in St. Louis, Florissant, and St. Charles, and then those in Louisiana. Although she was a conscientious and efficient visitor, her autocratic nature lacked sympathy and understanding. Before returning to France in 1842, she founded convents in New York City and McSherrystown, Pa., and approved the opening of a mission among the Potawatomi Indians at Sugar Creek, Kansas. When in March 1843 GREGORY XVI confirmed the original rules and constitutions of the society, Mother Galitzin became aware of the harm she had done in imposing too vehemently the changes she had championed and begged to be allowed to revisit America and restore the original organization as established there by St. Philippine DUCHESNE. Embarking from France, she visited convents in New York, Pennsylvania, and Canada, and then went to Missouri and Louisiana. At St. Michael's, where she found yellow fever raging, she nursed the sick with heroic devotedness until she herself was fatally stricken with the disease.

Bibliography: Archives, R.S.C.J., St. Michael's, Louisiana, housed at Maryville College of the Sacred Heart, St. Louis, Missouri. L. CALLAN, *The Society of the Sacred Heart in North America* (New York 1937). A. P. GALITZYN, *Vie d'une religieuse du Sacre-Coeur, 1795–1843* (Paris 1859). M. WARD, *Life of Bl. Madeleine Sophie Barat* (Roehampton, England, 1900; rev. 1911).

[L. CALLAN]

GALL, ST.

Irish missionary to the Continent; b. Ireland, *c.* 560; d. Switzerland, after 615, *c.* 630–35. Gall was known personally to JONAS OF BOBBIO, the biographer of COLUMBAN, Gall's religious superior. However, Jonas has little to say about Gall except to recount the incident when Columban ordered Gall to fish in the Breuchin, which flows into the Lanterne, and Gall decided to try the L'Ognan, a tributary of the Aar, instead. He caught nothing. On being reproved by Columban for his disobedience, he returned to the Breuchin and had a large catch. This account of Jonas is the only really authentic information available on Gall; for other details of his life one must depend on a vita written as late as *c.* 771 (which survives but in fragmentary form) and later accounts apparently based on it. According to these documents, Gall was offered to God as a child, in the Abbey of BANGOR, where he was placed under the guidance of Columban. When he set off for the Continent with Columban (*c.* 590), Gall was already a priest and so at least 30 years old (the canonical age for ordination). This places his birth in 560 or before. The history of his early years on the Continent is that of Columban. Gall's separate story begins with Columban's departure from Brigantium (present–day Bregenz), at the eastern extremity of Lake Constance, just after 610, for Italy. Gall's vita states that Gunzo, Duke of the ALAMANNI, was responsible for this departure, but he is not mentioned elsewhere. However, it is known that at that time, Theodoric, Columban's old enemy, had conquered his brother Theudibert and was controlling the Alamanni. In any case, Gall remained behind because of illness when Columban departed. Later Gall established a hermitage at the source of the Steinach, where he was joined by disciples. He spent the remainder of his life in meditation and in converting the Alamanni. The date of his death is uncertain, but apparently it was after that of Columban (d. 615). A genealogy makes Gall a relation of St. BRIGID, but this may safely be ignored. He is normally represented with a bear, mentioned in one of the legendary accounts of his life. His cult spread throughout Switzerland and into Alsace, Lorraine, Germany, and Italy. The famous Abbey of SANKT GALLEN was established nearly a century after his death on the site of his hermitage.

Feast: Oct. 16.

Bibliography: KENNEY, discusses the sources and gives a comprehensive bibliog. M. JOYNT, *The Life of St. G.* (London 1927), including an Eng. tr. of Gall's life by WALAFRID STRABO *c.* 833. B. and H. HELBLING, ''Der heilige Gallus in der Geschichte'', *Schweizerische Zeitschrift für Geschichte* 12 (1962) 1–62. L. HERTLING, ''Saint G. in Switzerland,'' in *Irish Monks in the Golden Age,* ed. J. J. RYAN (Dublin 1963) 59–72. L. GOUGAUD, *Gaelic Pioneers of Christianity*, tr. V. COLLINS (Dublin 1923) 124–126, on cult. A. M. TOMMASINI, *Irish Saints in Italy*, tr. J. F. SCANLAN (London 1937) 252–264, on cult. J. DUFT, *Die Gallus–Kapelle zu St. Gallen und ihr Bilderzyklus* (St. Gallen 1977), iconography at Saint Gallen. P. OSTERWALDER, *St. Gallus in der Dichtung* (St. Gallen 1983).

[C. MCGRATH]

GALL OF CLERMONT, ST.

Bishop; b. *c.* 486; d. 551. From the writings of his nephew, GREGORY OF TOURS (confirmed by an epitaph composed by Fortunatus and by the signatures of the councils), a meager biography of St. Gall can be gleaned. He came of a wealthy Gallo–Roman family, and became a monk at Cournon, where he distinguished himself by his fasts, love of reading, and fine singing voice. Because of his musical talent he was brought first to Clermont by Bishop QUINCTIAN, and then to the royal court at Trèves

Church of St. Gall, Prague, Czech Republic. (©Dave G. Houser/ CORBIS)

by King Theodoric I. In 526–527 he succeeded Quinctian to the See of Clermont. He took part in person or by proxy at four synods held in Orléans (533–549), and at one, which he himself assembled, in Clermont (535). His humility, his charity, and his miracles won the veneration of his people.

Feast: July 1.

Bibliography: GREGORY OF TOURS, *Historia Francorum,* 4:5, 6, 13; *Monumenta Germaniae Historica: Scriptores rerum Merovingicarum* 1.1:138–139, 144; Eng. tr. O. M. DALTON, 2 v. (Oxford 1927). *Vitae patrum*, 6. *Monumenta Germaniae Historica: Scriptores rerum Merovingicarum* 1.2. J. MABILLON, *Acta sanctorum ordinis S. Benedicti* 1:109–113. Epitaph by FORTUNATUS, *Monumenta Germaniae Historica: Auctores antiquissimi* 4.1:81. *Monumenta Germaniae Historica: Concilia* 1:65, 70, 84, 97, 109. L. DUCHESNE, *Fastes épiscopaux de l'ancienne Gaule* 2:36. H. LECLERCQ, *Dictionnaire d'archéologie chrétienne et de liturgie* 3.2:1917–18. J. L. BAUDOT and L. CHAUSSIN, *Vies des saints et des bienheureux selon l'ordre du calendrier avec l'historique des fêtes, by the Benedictines of Paris* 7:19–22. BUTLER *The Lives of the Saints* 3:3–4. J. DES GRAVIERS, *Catholicisme* 4:1718–19.

[G. M. COOK]

GALLAGHER, HUGH PATRICK

Missionary, editor; b. Donegal, Ireland, May 12, 1815; d. San Francisco, Calif., March 10, 1882. Leaving Ireland in 1832, he went to the U.S. and entered St. Charles Seminary, Overbrook, Pa., where he was assigned to teach Latin and Greek. After his ordination in 1840, he served as pastor in the coal regions of western Pennsylvania. There he defended the interests of the Irish immigrant and promoted the temperance movement begun in Ireland by Rev. Theobald MATHEW. In 1844 Gallagher was appointed rector of the Theological College of Pittsburgh, Pa. To combat nativist opposition to Irish Catholics in the state, he wrote editorials for the *Pittsburgh Catholic.* He was transferred to Loretto, Pa., and was named theologian to the First Plenary Council of Baltimore in 1852. There he met Bp. Joseph S. ALEMANY, OP, of Monterey, Calif., who persuaded him to obtain temporary leave from the Diocese of Pittsburgh to serve in the new Archdiocese of San Francisco.

Gallagher was sent as a missionary through northern California, serving in rapid succession at Benicia, Shasta, Weaverville, and St. Francis Church, San Francisco. Having founded (1853) the *Catholic Standard,* the first Catholic weekly on the Pacific Coast, he left for Europe in December 1853 to secure help for the California missions. In Ireland he enlisted several priests, 14 seminarians, the Sisters of Mercy of Kinsale, and the Presentation Sisters of Cork City. Having narrowly avoided sailing aboard the ill-fated *Arctic,* which sank in the Atlantic with the loss of all passengers, the party arrived in the U.S. in 1854. Released from Pittsburgh, Gallagher visited the gold and silver mining regions of the West. In Nevada he built (1861) the territory's first Catholic church at Genoa and purchased property for the churches in Carson City and Virginia City. In San Francisco he founded (1861) St. Joseph's, building the church, hall, and convent, and a free school that was the beginning of parochial education in the archdiocese. He was also one of the founders of St. Mary's Hospital, and of the Magdalen, a home for wayward girls. His civic influence was demonstrated when the state legislature adopted his plan to improve Golden Gate Park in 1869.

[M. J. HURLEY]

GALLAGHER, SIMON FELIX

Missionary; b. Ireland, 1756; d. Natchez, Miss., Dec. 13, 1825. As a priest of the Diocese of Dublin, Ireland, and, from his own statement, a graduate of the University of Paris, he presented himself to Bp. John CARROLL of Baltimore, Md., on Feb. 3, 1793, bearing a letter of recommendation from Bp. John Troy of Dublin. Carroll sent him as third pastor to Charleston, S.C., where organized Catholicism had begun in 1788. Gallagher immediately became a popular orator who made many friends, including Charles Carroll of Carrollton. He organized the Hibernian Society of Charleston and became an instructor at the College of Charleston, helping to enhance its reputation for learning.

Shortly after his arrival, Gallagher began to have trouble with TRUSTEEISM, which deprived him of real authority over the church at Charleston. In 1800, Gallagher was suspended for intemperance, and the vestry refused to acknowledge Carroll's new appointment. Gallagher's repentance and reinstatement relieved Carroll of action for the moment. In 1812 Carroll appointed Joseph Picot de Clorivière as an assistant to Gallagher to serve the large number of French in the congregation, and the two seemed to work amicably. But when Clorivière went to Europe in 1814, Gallagher called Rev. Robert Browne, pastor at Augusta, Ga., to assist him, and on Clorivière's return, Gallagher and Browne resisted the French priest's effort to take up his duties in Charleston. The vestry upheld Gallagher and, as holders of the incorporating charter, claimed the right to decide who would serve in the church.

Abp. Leonard NEALE, who had succeeded Carroll, confirmed Clorivière's appointment and suspended Gallagher and Browne. He also ordered Clorivière to open another place of worship for the faithful, placing under interdict the church controlled by Gallagher and the trustees. In 1818 the archbishop sent Rev. Benedict Fenwick to Charleston to effect a peace. During the negotiations Gallagher spent the winter of 1819–20 at Philadelphia, Pa., assisting Rev. Louis de Barth at St. Mary's Church. When Charleston was established as a diocese in 1820, its new bishop, John England, reinstated Gallagher, but considered him ''an old man to whom no duty can be committed.'' In August 1822, Gallagher requested a change to St. Augustine, Fla., where he remained until the following January, when he left for Havana, Cuba. While serving in New Orleans, La., in 1825, he preached at the cathedral for the annual commemoration of the Battle of New Orleans. By March 1825 he had moved to Natchez, Miss., and accepted the duties of pastor of St. Mary's Church, where he died the following December.

Bibliography: J. H. EASTERBY, *History of the College of Charleston* (Charleston 1935). P. K. GUILDAY, *The Life and Times of John England,* 2 v. (New York 1927). C. J. NEUSSE, *The Social Thought of American Catholics, 1634–1829* (Westminster, Md. 1945).

[R. C. MADDEN]

GALLANDI, ANDREA

Priest, canonist, and patristic scholar, whose writings contributed to the study of the development of the origins of Canon Law; b. Venice, Dec. 7, 1709; d. Venice, Jan. 2, 1779. He published a collection of treatises of such famous canonists as COUSTANT, De Marcha, BALLERINI, Berardi, QUESNEL, and Blasco. This work, entitled *De vetustis canonum collectionibus dissertationum sylloge,* was published at Venice in 1778. He compiled also the less-known writings of 380 ecclesiastical writers of the first seven centuries in *Biblioteca graeco-latina veterum Patrum antiquorumque scriptorum ecclesiasticorum.* This collection was published at Venice over a period of years between 1765 and 1781.

Bibliography: R. NAZ, *Dictionnaire de droit canonique,* (Paris 1935–) 5:931. H. HURTER, *Nomenclator literarius theologiae catholicae,* 6 v. (Innsbruck 3 1903–13; v. 1 4 1926) 5:111–112. J. C. HOEFER, *Nouvelle biographie générale,* 46 v. (Paris 1852–66).

[B. R. PISKULA]

GALLICAN RITES

Gallican is the name usually given to the liturgy that prevailed in Gaul from the beginnings of Christianity in that country to about the end of the 8th century, when Charlemagne imposed the Roman rite there. The difficulty of such a concept is that there was no single form of worship in the earliest times, but rather a diversity of liturgical forms, because Gaul was not a political or ecclesiastical unity. The characteristics that distinguish the so-called Gallican rite from that of Rome appear only in a later period, and many of them are then shared by other Western rites, such as the Spanish, Celtic, and Ambrosian. It is a serious mistake and, from a scholarly point of view, impossible to see these characteristics as belonging to the earliest period.

History. Unfortunately, the Gallican liturgy has so far not found its historian. There are a great number of problems regarding its origin that have escaped any solution. Several theories have been advanced, but none of them seems satisfactory. According to the oldest theory, the Gallican rite was brought to Lyons from Ephesus by St. Photinus and St. Irenaeus and was of apostolic origin, since they had received it through St. Polycarp from St. John the Apostle. This idea has been given up by all serious scholars because such an early beginning is absolutely improbable. It is the second theory, developed by L. Duchesne, that has found many adherents. According to this theory, the Gallican liturgy was strongly influenced by Milan, especially in its Oriental features. In fact, to Duchesne the Gallican liturgy is an Oriental liturgy introduced into the West toward the middle of the 4th century via Milan. This theory can no longer be regarded as convincing because Duchesne's reconstruction of the Gallican Mass of the 6th century is based on the assumption that the so-called *Letters of St. Germanus of Paris* are authentic. A. Wilmart, however, has clearly demonstrated that these letters have nothing to do with St. Germanus (d.576) or with Paris, but that they were composed in the south of France about the year 700. Thus Duchesne's reconstruction may give an idea of the Gallican liturgy of the 7th or 8th centuries, but not of the 6th, because these letters represent the Gallican rite, not in its early purity, but in the period of its decadence after it had been transformed by a number of foreign elements. One must take account of O. Faller's and H. Connolly's vindication of St. Ambrose's authorship of the treatise *De sacramentis.* There remains nothing to prove that the liturgy of Milan in the second half of the 4th century was a liturgy imported from the East. It was fundamentally a Roman rite, except for minor details. De *sacramentis* demonstrates that the Church of Milan was already using an early form of the Roman Canon. Hence Duchesne's theory that Milan was the center of diffusion for the Gallican rite in the West, which he supposed had been imported from the East by St. Ambrose's predecessor, Auxentius, about 360, must be discarded. Moreover, the greatest obstacle to a clear understanding of the beginnings of the liturgies in the West, Duchesne's theory of an Oriental origin for all non-Roman Western rites, has been eliminated, and the way has been opened for a new study of the beginnings of the Gallican rite.

E. Griffe, though fully aware of the remaining problems, has come to the conclusion that the early Gallican liturgy did not come from Milan, nor from the East, but from Rome. Far from being prolix and oratorical, this early liturgy was remarkable for its simplicity and sobriety of style. It was only in the course of the 6th and 7th centuries that the Gallican liturgy became enriched by new rites that had their origin in the Orient. Some of these rites were introduced via Rome, others via Spain, and others again directly from the East, especially Syria. In order to understand the beginnings of the Gallican liturgy, it will be necessary to leave these later additions aside.

Unfortunately, almost all the extant sources of the Gallican rite are of a later period and do not give any information for the 5th century and earlier. Hence, A. Wilmart was of the opinion that the liturgy of Gaul of that time must remain a myth. The so-called Gallican rite of that early period, if it existed at all, was not different from that of Rome.

If one wishes to get an idea of the liturgy for the period of 150 to 313, for which there are no Gallican sources at all, it may suffice to recall the description of the eucharist that St. Justin gave in his *Apology.* It provides an idea not only of the eucharist at Rome, but also for the other churches of primitive Christianity. The following order is found in ch. 65 and 67: (1) readings from the Old and New Testaments, (2) the homily, (3) the prayer of the faithful, (4) the kiss of peace, (5) the offering of bread and wine, (6) the Eucharistic Prayer, and (7) Holy Communion distributed by the deacons. The first Christian communities organized on the soil of Gaul most probably followed this order presented by the Church of Rome between 150 and 250. Its primitive structure can be recognized even in the later, more developed Gallican forms.

It was the 4th century that saw the Church of Gaul definitely organized, and this must have been the time that local differences in the liturgy began to appear. The *Consuetudines* of local synods of the 5th and 6th centuries testify to this development. Very soon this liturgical evolution led to the presence of two different types of liturgies in the West: the Roman, used in all Italy and in Africa, the Gallican, in Gaul and Spain. The writings of Gregory of Tours and Caesarius of Arles and the Merovingian councils enable one to get some idea of this early Gallican liturgy of the 6th century.

Sources. It is only after this period that there are available liturgical sources, such as Missals, Benedictionals, and Lectionaries. For the later form, there is the very valuable description found in the so-called *Letters of St. Germanus,* which show evidence of a definitely Eastern influence.

Mone Masses. Mass formularies have been published by F. J. Mone, *Lateinische und griechische Messen aus dem zweiten bis sechsten Jahrhundert* (Frankfurt 1850). They have been reprinted by J. M. Neale and G. H. Forbes, *The Ancient Liturgies of the Gallican Churches* (Burntisland 1855), by Migne, *Patrologia Latina* 138:863–882, and more recently by L. C. Mohlberg and P. Siffrin, *Missale Gallicanum Vetus* (Rerum Ecclesiasticarum Documenta, Series Maior, Fontes III; Rome 1958) 61–91. Mone discovered these Masses in a late 7th-century palimpsest manuscript belonging to the library of Karlsruhe, Germany, but originally from the Abbey of Reichenau. It contains 11 Masses of the pure Gallican type, notable for the absence of all reference to the cycle of liturgical feasts. One of them is in honor of St. Germanus of Auxerre, but the others do not specify any festival. H. Brewer [*Zeitschrift für katholische Theologie* 43 (1919) 603–703] is of the opinion that these Masses were composed by Venantius Fortunatus. This is highly improbable, except for one, *Sidera de sede nitens,* which is almost entirely in hexameter verse (the Post-Pridie is in prose). For the time of origin and the order of these Masses, see A. Wilmart, ''L'Âge et l'ordre des Messes de Mone,'' *Revue Bénédictine* 28 (1911) 377–399; for the place of origin and authorship, see P. Radò, ''Verfasser und Heimat der Mone-Messen,'' *Ephemerides liturgicae* 42 (1928) 58–65; for the sources used in their composition, see L. Eizenhöfer, *Revue Bénédictine* 43 (1953) 329–332.

Missale Gothicum. This is a Gallican Sacramentary, now in the Vatican Library (Cod. Vat. Reg. Lat. 317), written at the end of the 7th century and belonging formerly to the Petau Library. The misleading title, *Missale Gothicum,* was added to the manuscript in the 15th century and caused its first editor, G. M. Tommasi, to attribute it to Narbonne, then under Visigothic rule. The inclusion of the Masses for the feasts of St. Symphorian and St. Léger led L. Duchesne to believe that it was from Autun. Hence it is frequently called the *Sacramentary of Autun.* Following the order of the *Proprium de tempore,* it contains Masses from the Vigil of Christmas to Pentecost, interspersed with some saints' days, Rogation Days, and the Feast of the Finding of the Cross. It ends with Masses for the Common of Saints, six Sunday Masses, and a fragment of a Mass, *Missa Cotidiana Romensis,* for use of ferias. The arrangement throughout is that of the Gallican Mass, though for the Masses of the saints the formularies are Roman. It was first edited by G. M. Tommasi, *Codices Sacramentorum Nongentis Annis Vetustiores* (Rome 1680) 263–317, and by J. Mabillon, *De Liturgia Gallicana* (Paris 1685) 188–300; reprinted by L. A. Muratori, *Liturgia Romana Vetus* (Venice 1748) 517–558, by F. M. Neale and G. H. Forbes, *The Ancient Liturgies of the Gallican Church* (Burntisland 1855) 32–150, and by Migne, *Patrologia Latina* 72:225–318. Modern editions are: H. M. Bannister, *Missale Gothicum: A Gallican Sacramentary* (London 1917); facsimile edition by L. C. Mohlberg, *Missale Gothicum: Das gallikanische Sakramentar* (Cod. Vat. Regin. Lat. 317) *des VII.–VIII. Jahrhunderts* (2 v. Augsburg 1929). [For a study of the place of origin see G. Morin, ''Sur la provenance du Missale Gothicum,'' *Revue d'histoire ecclésiastique* 37 (1941) 424–430.]

Missale Gallicanum Vetus. The Sacramentary of Auxerre is preserved in a single manuscript, Codex Pal. 493 of the Vatican Library; it was written at the end of the 7th century or the beginning of the 8th and is in fragmentary condition. There is a certain disorder of arrangement that Tommasi tried to improve. The series of Masses begins with one for the feast of St. Germanus of Auxerre (Oct. 9), which is followed by prayers for the blessing of virgins and widows, two Advent Masses, a Mass for the Vigil of Christmas, the *Expositio, Traditio Symboli,* and other Lenten ceremonies preparatory to Baptism, the ceremonies for Holy Week and Easter Sunday including the baptismal liturgy, and Masses for the Sundays after Easter up to the Rogation Mass. Many prayers are identical with those in the *Missale Gothicum.* The Good Friday prayers are the same as in the Roman Missal, except for a few variations. The manuscript has been edited by Tommasi, 433–492; Mabillon, 329–378; Muratori, 697–760; Migne, *Patrologia Latina* 72:339–382; and Neale and Forbes, 151–204. There is a new edition by L. C. Mohlberg, L. Eizenhöfer, and P. Siffrin, *Missale Gallicanum Vetus* (Rome 1958).

Bobbio Missal. Now at Paris (B.N. MS lat. 13.246), this Missal is of the 8th century and represents an important collection of Gallican prayers, although it was compiled probably by an Irishman and written originally in Italy in the monastery of Bobbio, where Mabillon found it. The original edition was published by J. Mabillon, *Museum Italicum seu Collectio Veterum Scriptorum ex Bibliothecis Italicis eruta* (Paris 1687) 1.2:278–397. It was reprinted by L. A. Muratori, *Liturgia Romana Vetus* (Venice 1748) 775–968, and Migne, *Patrologia Latina* 52:451–580. A modern critical edition was published by E. A. Lowe, *The Bobbio Missal, A Gallican Mass Book* (Henry Bradshaw Society 56; London 1920). There is a facsimile edition by J. Wickham Legg, *The Bobbio Missal, Facsimile of MS Paris. lat. 13.246* (Henry Bradshaw Society 53; London 1917). A volume of notes was added later by A. Wilmart, E. A. Lowe, and H. A. Wilson, The *Bobbio Missal, Notes and Studies* (Henry Bradshaw Society 61; London 1923). [For a description see A. Wilmart, *Dictionnaire d'archéologie chrétienne et de liturgie* 2.1:939–962; ''Une Curieuse instruction liturgique du missel de Bobbio,'' *Revue Charlemagne* 2 (1912) 1–6.]

Mass Fragments. Fragments of Masses of the Gallican rite have been found by a number of scholars. D. de Bruyne edited from a Gospel manuscript of the 7th century (BN Codex 256) prayers and a *contestatio* of a *Missa pro defuncto* [D. de Bruyne, ''Une Messe gallicane inédite pro defuncto,'' *Revue Bénédictine* 34 (1922) 156–158; repr. L. C. Mohlberg, *Missale Gallicanum Vetus* (Rome 1958) 96–97]. G. Bickell published a fragment of a Gallican Christmas Mass from a codex of Gonville and Caius College at Cambridge (No. 820) of the middle of the 8th century [G. Bickell, ''Ein neues Fragment einer gallikanischen Weihnachtsmesse,'' *Zeitschrift für katholische Theologie* 6 (1882) 370–372; repr. L. C. Mohlberg, *Missale Gallicanum Vetus* 370–372, and K. Gamber, *Sakramentartypen* (Beuron 1958) 28–29]. There are fragments from a codex of the monastery of St. Gall in Switzerland (Stiftsbibliothek Codex 194). Six palimpsest pages of this MS contain a *Benedictio populi* and a Postcommunion that seems to be the end of a Pentecost Mass (see K. Gamber, *Sakramentartypen* 29). A. Dold has published fragments of a Sacramentary from Codex M 12 of the Ambrosian Library at Milan that represent a mixture of Gallican and Visigothic type of the 7th century. The framework is more Gallican, the formularies more Visigothic [A. Dold, *Das Sakramentar in Schabkodex M 12 Sup. der Bibliotheca Ambrosiana mit hauptsächlich altspanischem Formelgut im gallischen Rahmenwerk* (Texte und Arbeiten 43; Beuron 1952)]. J. Mabillon edited a *Missa in honorem S. Remigii* from Codex Reims 1395 of the 9th century [*Annales Ordinis S. Benedicti* 1 (Paris 1703) 63, 680; repr. L. C. Mohlberg, *Missale Gallicanum Vetus* 91–92; see also F. Baix, ''Les Sources liturgiques de la Vita Remigii de Hincmar,'' *Miscellanea A. De Meyer* 1 (Louvain 1946) 222–227]. A. Dold also published, from Codex Sangallensis 908 of the 6th or 7th century, a series of *Missae defunctorum et exhortationes matutinales* [*Palimpsest-Studien* 1 (Texte und Arbeiten 45; Beuron 1955) 1–36; see J. A. Jungmann, ''Die vormonastische Morgenhore im gallisch-spanischen Raum des 6. Jahrhunderts,'' *Zeitschrift für katholische Theologie* 78 (1956) 306–336]. W. J. Anderson published fragments of a Gallican Sacramentary from Codex London W. Merton of the 8th century [''Fragments of an Eight-Century Gallican Sacramentary,'' *Journal of Theological Studies* 29 (1928) 337–345; repr. L. C. Mohlberg, *Missale Gallicanum Vetus* 98–102]. A *Praefatio Missae* from Codex latinus Monacensis 14429 of the 7th or 8th centuries was published by Dold [''Liturgie-Fragmente aus Clm 14429,'' *Revue Bénédictine* 38 (1926) 277–287; see M. Frost, ''A Prayer-Book from St. Emmeran, Ratisbon,'' *Journal of Theological Studies* 30 (1929) 32–45; H. Frank, ''Die Briefe des hl. Bonifatius und das von ihm benutzte Sakramentar,'' *Sankt Bonifatius: Gedenkgabe zum 1200. Todestag* (Fulda 1954) 75]. P. Siffrin published fragments of a Calendarium from Codex Berlin lat. fol. 87 and Regensburg Graf Walderdorff of the 8th century [P. Siffrin, ''Das Walderdorffer Kalendarfragment saec. VIII,'' *Ephemerides liturgicae* 47 (1933) 204–209; repr. L. C. Mohlberg, *Missale Francorum* (Rome 1957) 71–85]. Fragments of a Cologne Codex GB Kasten B 24.123, 124 of the 8th century were published by H. M. Bannister [''Fragments of an Anglo-Saxon Sacramentary,'' *Journal of Theological Studies* 12 (1911) 451–455]. Two Postcommunions were discovered in Codex Parisinus Bibl. Nat. MS. lat. 242 of the 9th century and edited by A. Wilmart [*Archivum latinitatis medii aevi* 15 (1940) 207; repr. L. C. Mohlberg, *Missale Gallicanum Vetus* 102–103]. In addition, L. C. Mohlberg published *Fragmentum diptychorum ex regula S. Aureliani* (92–93) and *Priscilliani benedictio super fideles* (103–105) from Codex Würzburg, Univ. M.p.th. Q.3 of the 5th or 6th centuries and reprinted (93–94) the fragment of a lost Codex of Fulda of the 8th century, which was first edited by A. Ruland [*Theologische Quartal-*

schrift 39 (1857) 420–421]. *Missae in honorem S. Samsonis* were edited by F. Duine [*Inventaire liturgique de l'hagiographie bretonne* (Paris 1922) 20–23, 236–237].

Benedictionalia. Pope Zacharias, in a letter (*Monumenta Germaniae Historica: Epistolae* III, Merov. et Karol. aevi 1:371) addressed to St. Boniface in 751, criticized the custom that the bishops of Gaul had of inserting blessings after the Our Father at Mass as against apostolic tradition, and exhorted him to remain loyal to the Roman custom, which did not have such blessings. A number of such prayers are preserved in collections called *Benedictionales.* The oldest of them seems to be the *Benedictionale Frisigense vetus* composed in Gregorienmünster at the end of the 7th century and later used in Freising [W. Dürig, ''Das Benectionale Frisigense Vetus (Clm 6430 fol. 1–14),'' *Archiv für Liturgiewissenschaft* 4 (1955) 223–244; for a later Freising collection see W. Dürig, ''Die Typologie der Osterwoche im jüngeren Freisinger Benedictionale,'' *Paschatis Sollemnia,* ed. B. Fischer and J. Wagner (Freiburg 1959) 197–207].

A shorter Gallican collection is the *Benedictionale Friburgense* found in the 9th-century Codex 363 of the University of Freiburg [M. J. Metzger, *Zwei karolingische Pontifikalien vom Oberrhein* (Freiburg 1914) 87–92, 18*–25*]. A third collection is the *Benedictiones Gallicanae* found in MS Clm 29163m of the 9th or 10th centuries in the Munich Library [W. Dürig, ''Die Bruchstücke einer Sammlung von Benedictiones Gallicanae in CL 29163,'' *Revue Bénédictine* 64 (1954) 168–175]. For further Gallican *Benedictiones Episcopales* see *Dictionnaire d'archéologie chrétienne et de liturgie* 2.1:717–720; W. Lüdtke, ''Bischöfliche Benediktionen aus Magdeburg und Braunschweig,'' *Jahrbuch für Liturgiewissenschaft* 5 (1925) 97–122; R. M. Wooley, *The Benedictional of John Longlonde* (London 1926); A. de Vasconcelos, ''Notas liturgico-bracarenses,'' *Opus Dei* 5 (1930–31) 21–28, 46–54; G. Manz, *Ausdrucksformen der lateinischen Liturgiesprache* (Beuron 1941) 25–36; J. Leclercq and J. Laporte, ''Bénédictions épiscopales dans un manuscrit de Huesca,'' *Hispania Sacra* 5 (1952) 79; L. Eizenhöfer, ''Nochmals Spanish Symptoms,'' *Sacris Erudiri* 4 (1952) 32–42; and L. Brou, ''Encore les Spanish Symptoms et leur Contre-Partie,'' *Hispania Sacra* 7 (1954) 467–485.

Gallican Lectionaries. The oldest Gallican Lectionary is that discovered and edited by A. Dold from the palimpsest Codex Weissenburgensis 76 of the 5th or 6th century in the Herzog August Bibliothek at Wolfenbüttel [*Das älteste Liturgiebuch der lateinischen Kirche* (Beuron 1936)]. This Lectionary is the oldest document of liturgical Scripture lessons that has been preserved. The Lessons are taken partly from a pure Vulgate text, partly from an older Latin Scripture text, partly from a mixture of both. A very interesting feature is the fact that the ecclesiastical year of this Lectionary begins with Easter and ends with Holy Saturday. Hence the first Lessons are those of the Easter Vigil. There follow those of Easter and Easter week, including the Octave of Easter (Low Sunday), the Gallican Rogation Days, and the feasts of the Ascension and Pentecost. In between Ascension and Pentecost, the Lectionary gives the Lessons for the anniversary of the Dedication of the Cathedral. Then follow the Lessons for the Nativity of St. John the Baptist, for the feasts of St. Peter and St. Stephen, Epiphany, the feast of the *Cathedra Petri,* and Lent, including Holy Week, ending the ecclesiastical year with a liturgy for Holy Saturday. An appendix contains the Lessons for special liturgical occasions (e.g., the consecration of a bishop and the ordination of a priest), the Lessons of the Common of one or several martyrs, of a confessor, of a dedication of a church, of the birthday of the diocesan bishop, of the funeral of a bishop and of Christians in general, of the consecration of a virgin, and for the offering of tithes. The order of the Lessons for the ecclesiastical year may reach down even to the period before the Council of Ephesus. The Lectionary was written in southern France in the old Septimania.

The Luxeuil Lectionary, part of MS 9427 of the Bibliothèque Nationale in Paris, was discovered by J. Mabillon in the Abbey of Luxeuil. It is of the 7th century and contains, among its very few saints' days, the feast of St. Genevieve, a feature that induced G. Morin to attribute it to Paris. Beginning with Christmas Eve, it gives the prophetical Lessons, Epistles, and Gospels of the liturgical year, followed by the Lessons for a few special Masses, for the burial of a bishop, for the dedication of a church, for when a bishop preaches, for the giving of tithes, for when a deacon is ordained and when a priest is blessed, and for starting on a trip, and *lectiones cotidianae.* J. Mabillon [*De Liturgia Gallicana* (Paris 1685) 106–173] gives only the references to all the Lessons and the beginnings and endings of the texts. A critical edition of the entire text was published by P. Salmon [*Le lectionnaire de Luxeuil I-II* (Collectanea Biblica 7, 9; Rome 1944–53); for the place of origin see C. Charlier, ''Note sur les origines de l'écriture dite de Luxeuil,'' *Revue Bénédictines* 58 (1948) 149–157; E. Masai, ''Pour quelle église éxécuté le lectionnaire de Luxeuil?'' *Scriptorium* 2 (1948) 37–46; 3 (1949) 172; P. Salmon *Le Lectionnaire de Luxeuil: Étude Paléographique* (Rome 1953)].

For other Gallican Lectionaries see E. Chatelain, ''Fragments palimpsestes d'un lectionnaire mérovingien,'' *Revue d'histoire et de littérature religieuse* 5 (1900) 193–199 (palimpsest Codex of Paris, B.N. lat. 10863 of the 7th century); P. Salmon, ''Le Systéme des lectures liturgiques contenu dans les notes marginales du MS. Mp. Th.Q. la de Wurzbourg,'' *Revue Bénédictines* 61 (1951) 38–53 (Evangelium S. Kiliani); G. Morin, *Études, textes, découvertes* (Maredsous 1913) 440–456 (Lectionary of Schlettstadt of the 8th century), 446 (Epistolary of Schlettstadt of the 8th century); P. Salmon, ''Le Texte biblique de l'Évangéliaire de St. Denis,'' *Miscellanea Mercati* 1 (1946) 103–106 (Gospel book of St. Denis in Codex Paris, B. N. MS lat. 256 of the 8th century); D. de Bruyne, ''Les Notes liturgiques du manuscrit 134 de la Cathédral de Trèves,'' *Revue Bénédictines* 33 (1921) 46–52 (Gospel book of the 8th century); A. DOLD, *Die im Codex Vat. Reg. lat. 9 vorgeheftete Liste paulinischer Lesungen für die Messfeier* (Texte und Arbeiten 35; Beuron 1944) 39–52 (Lectionary of Tegernsee in Clm 19126 of the 8th century); C. H. Turner, *The Oldest MS. of the Vulgate Gospels* (Oxford 1931) 217 (Gospel books of Durham in MS of the 8th or 9th century); U. Robert, *Pentateuchi versio latina antiquissima e cod. Lugdunensi I* (Paris 1881) XIX-XLI; *II* (Lyons 1900 XIII; E. A. Lowe, *Codices Lugdunenses antiquissimi* (Lyon 1924) 32–33; A. Wilmart, ''Une Lectionaire d'Aniane,'' *Revue Mabillon* 13 (1923) 40–53 (Epistolary in Codex Montpellier, Bibl. mun. 6 of the 9th century); B. Bischoff, ''Gallikanische Epistelperikopen,'' *Studien und Mitteilungen aus dem Benediktiner und Zistertienser-Orden* 50 (1932) 515–519 (Epistolary of Freising in Clm 6229 of the 8th century).

The Letters of St. Germanus of Paris. The most important source for knowledge of the late Gallican liturgy is the so-called *Expositio Brevis Antiquae Liturgiae Gallicanae.* It is preserved in a codex from the Abbey of St. Martin at Autun, at present in the library of the Seminary of Autun, the only manuscript of this valuable document that exists. The *Expositio* consists of two letters, the first of which describes the rite of the Gallican Mass, while the second deals with *diversa ecclesiae carismata,* i.e., with the baptismal rite, liturgical vestments, antiphons, responses, etc. The first to edit this text was A. Martène, *Thesaurus novus anecdotorum* 5 (Paris 1717) 91–100; repr. Migne, *Patrologia Latina* 72:83–98. A separate edition was published by J. Quasten, *Expositio antiquae liturgiae Gallicanae Germano Parisiensi ascripta* (Münster 1934). The question naturally arises as to the authorship of these letters and as to the time of origin. The *Epistula prima* seems to answer this question, because it starts with the following sentence: *Capitula patrum traditionum suscipimus. Quomodo solemnis ordo ecclesiae agitur quibusve instructionibus Kanon ecclesiasticus decoratur, Germanus episcopus scripsit de missa* (*Expositio* 10.4–7). Germanus was born about 496 near Autun, and he was ordained in 530. From 555 until his death, May 28, 576, he was bishop of Paris. The *Expositio* would therefore belong to the 6th century if the introductory sentences are correct in attributing these letters to Germanus of Paris. A. Martène, P. Lebrun, L. Duchesne, A. Franz, and others did not question this statement. L. Duchesne went so far as to state: ''I do not believe that there is the slightest reason to doubt the authenticity of this heading'' [*Christian Worship* (5th ed. London 1919) 155]. Today very few scholars dare to think of Germanus as the author. A critical analysis proves that the letters make use of Isidore of Seville's *De ecclesiasticis officiis,* a work that originated about the year 620. It is therefore more probable that the two letters were composed by an anonymous author of the 7th or 8th century. The liturgy that they describe seems to be not the liturgy of Paris, but perhaps that of Autun, where the manuscript was found. The Gallican rite as described in these letters shows strong influence of Oriental liturgies [see A. Wilmart, ''Germain de Paris (Lettres attribuées à Saint),'' *Dictionnaire d'archéologie chrétienne et de liturgie* 6.1: 1049–1102; A. Gaudel, ''Le Problème de l'authenticité des Lettres attribuées à St. Germain de Paris,'' *Revue des sciences religieuses* 7 (1927) 299; J. Quasten, ''Oriental Influence in the Gallican Liturgy,'' *Traditio* 1 (1943) 55–78].

Points of Difference. From these sources, especially from the letters attributed to Germanus, the following specialities can be pointed out for the late form of the Mass and Baptism in the Gallican rite.

Mass. The ceremony begins with an antiphon, an entrance chant, and a greeting, after which comes the *Aius,* i.e., the *Trisagion* sung in Greek and Latin, well known from all Oriental Liturgies. Both the letters of Pseudo-Germanus and Bobbio Missal mention the *Trisagion* as part of the introduction to the Mass. According to Pseudo-Germanus, this hymn occurs three times during the Mass, the second and third time before and after the Gospel. The *Trisagion* was not reported in Gaul until the very end of the 6th century, the period when importations from Syria became evident in the liturgy of France.

Upon the *Aius* there follows a threefold Kyrie, which in turn is followed by the Benedictus. The use of the Benedictus is attested by the *Missale Gothicum,* the Bobbio Missal, and the letters of Pseudo-Germanus. In the Gallican Mass of the 6th century it held the position that the Gloria held at that time in the Roman liturgy. According to Pseudo-Germanus, after the Epistle the Canticle of the Three Children, or the Benedicite, is sung. The Lectionary of Luxeuil mentions it once after the OT Lessons and once after the Epistle. In the Roman Mass it appears on Ember Saturdays after the last OT Lesson.

The Diptychs and the Kiss of Peace occurred before the Canon. In the Roman Mass the Diptych for the dead did not exist at that time. It appeared in the Gallican Mass in the 7th or 8th century. The Roman Mass did not adopt the commemoration of the dead in all Masses before the 9th century.

Of special interest in the Gallican Mass is the fact that the Canon, except for the words of Institution, varied with the season. The words of Institution were followed in many Gallican Masses by a prayer Post-Pridie. In 11 of the Mone Masses that represent such an early state of the Gallican liturgy, four contain a form of an EPICLESIS in this Post-Pridie.

The letters of Pseudo-Germanus state that the Fraction takes place while an antiphon is sung. In the Ambrosian rite, this antiphon is called *Confractorium.* The *Pater Noster* followed the Fraction but was preceded by a variable introduction and followed by a variable EMBOLISM. During the Communion, the *Trecanum* was sung; this is a Trinitarian hymn, which seems to be a counterpart of the Trinitarian acclamation preceding Holy Communion in Oriental Liturgies.

Baptism. The authorities for the Gallican baptismal service are the *Mixssale Gothicum* and the *Missale Gallicanum Vetus.* The baptismal formula was: ''Baptizo in nomine . . . Patris et Filii et Spiritus Sancti in remissionem peccatorum, ut habeas vitam aeternam.'' The *Missale Gallicanum Vetus* and the Bobbio Missal mention the ceremony of Feet-washing. The letters of Germanus mention too that Baptism was not administered during Lent; for this reason the baptistery was closed. The Gallican rite here accords with the liturgy of Spain and Syria.

Bibliography: H. NETZER, *L' Introduction de la messe romaine en France sous les carolingiens* (Paris 1910). J. B. THIBAUT, *L'Ancienne liturgie gallicane, son origine, et sa formation en Provence aux Ve VIe siècles* (Paris 1929). F. CABROL, ''Les Origines de la liturgie gallicane,'' *Revue d'histoire ecclésiastique* 30 (1930) 951–962. G. NICKL, *Der Anteil des Volkes an der Messliturgie im Frankenreich von Chlodwig bis Karl den Grossen* (Innsbruck 1930). H. G. J. BECK, *The Pastoral Care of Souls in South-East France during the 6th Century* (*Analecta Gregoriana* 51; 1950). È. GRIFFE, ''Aux origines de la liturgie gallicane,'' *Bulletin de littérature ecclésiastique* 52 (1951) 17–43. H. ASHWORTH, ''Gregorian Elements in Some Early Gallican Service Books,'' *Traditio* 13 (1957) 431–443. W. S. PORTER, *The Gallican Rite* (London 1958). A. A. KING, *Liturgies of the Past* (Milwaukee 1959) 77–185. J. KOVALEVSKY, *Le canon eucharistique de l'ancien rite des Gaules* (Paris 1957). GERMANUS OF PARIS, *Expositio antiquae liturgicae gallicanae* (London 1971). J. A. FRENDO, *The ''post secreta'' of the ''Missale Gothicum'' and the eucharistic theology of the Gallican anaphora* (Malta 1977). K. GAMBER, *Ordo antiquus Gallicanus; der gallikanische Messritus des 6. Jahrhunderts* (Regensburg 1965). K. GAMBER, *Die Messfeier nach altgallikanischem Ritus* (Regensburg 1984). K. GAMBER, *Der altgallikanische Messritus als Abbild himmlischer Liturgie* (Regensburg 1984).

[J. QUASTEN/EDS.]

GALLICAN RITES, CHANTS OF

Chants of the ancient liturgies practiced in French Gaul from the beginning of the 5th century to the early part of the 9th century. Four important regions, each revolving around important churches and corresponding roughly to the old civil divisions made by the Romans in Gaul, established centers of their provincial rites. The regions of Narbonne and Aquitaine (with Narbonne and Toulouse as mother churches) had much in common with the Mozarabic liturgy and chant. The region of Lyons and Provence influenced the churches of Lyons, Autun, Vienne, and Arles. The churches of the west, center, and north came under the influence of Tours. Sharing a basic liturgy, each developed its own provincial rites, and perhaps its own particular chants.

Because of the royal edicts of unity these ancient liturgies and chants were suppressed in favor of the Roman liturgy and chant. The movement of suppression, begun by Pepin at the instigation of his cousin St. CHRODEGANG, fully ensured by the strong measures of Charlemagne, reached its consummation under Charles the Bald. Unfortunately for the preservations of Gallican chant, its suppression occurred at a time when neume notation was not widely used. No single musical MS of the Gallican liturgy has been preserved. Authentic examples of Gallican chant are those that have been absorbed into the Roman rite and enshrined in Gregorian MSS, especially those of the school of Aquitaine. The best examples of chants absorbed into the Roman rite are those incorporated in the Good Friday liturgy: the *improperia, Crux fidelis, Pange lingua . . . certaminis,* and *Vexilla regis.* Principal among the MSS is the Graduale written in the 11th century for the cathedral of Albi (Paris: Bibl. nat. lat. 776). This magnificent specimen of Aquitainian diastematic notation contains the Gregorian Mass repertory plus supplementary chants, tropes, proses, and some pieces taken from the Gallican and Mozarabic liturgy. It is from this source and from MSS originating at St. Martial of Limoges that extant transcriptions of Gallican chants, mostly from the Mass and Office, have been made. Thus in the *Variae Preces* of Solesmes are found Compline antiphons, *Preces,* and the antiphon *Venite populi.* The Solesmes *Processionale monasticum* contains the *Hodie illuxit nobis* for the feast of SS. Peter and Paul, the *Hodie nobis beata illuxit* for the feast of Epiphany, the *Ascendit Christus* for the feast of the Assumption. Still other examples are found in the *Ordinaire des Saluts* and the *Histoire du chant liturgique à Paris* of A. Gastoué.

The musical study of these absorptions and transcriptions—frequent cadences on *ut;* the use of *si* natural in a large number of cadences; the use of recitational pitches on *mi* and *si;* frequent intonations of *ut-re-mi, ut-*

mi-sol; and a preference of *si* natural—indicates that Gallican chant is a dialect of its own, with characteristics of style, modality, and melodic development different from the Gregorian. Walafrid Strabo (d. 849) mentions that in his day the discerning cantor could still distinguish Gallican pieces in the Roman chant books (*Patrologia Latina,* ed. J. P. Migne, 114:956).

Bibliography: J. M. NEALE and G. H. FORBES, *The Ancient Liturgies of the Gallican Church* (Burntisland 1855–67). L. DUCHESNE, ''Sur l'origine de la liturgie gallicane,'' *Revue d'histoire et de littérature religieuses* 5 (1900) 31–47. A. GASTOUÉ, *Histoire du chant liturgique à Paris, des origines à la fin des temps carolingiens* (Paris 1904). A. WILMART, ''L'âge et l'ordre des messes de Mone,'' *Revue bénédictine* 28 (1911) 377–90. H. LIETZMANN, *Ordo missae romanus et gallicanus* (Bonn 1923). F. CABROL, ''Les origines de la liturgie gallicane,'' *Revue d'histoire ecclésiastique* 25 (1930) 951–62. A. GASTOUÉ, *Le chant gallican* (Grenoble 1939). J. QUASTEN, ''Oriental Influence in the Gallican Liturgy,'' *Traditio* 1 (1943) 55–73. W. S. PORTER, *The Gallican Rite* (London 1958). H. HUCKE, ''Toward a New Historical View of Gregorian Chant,'' *Journal of the American Musicological Society* (1980) 437–67. K. LEVY, ''Toledo, Rome and the Legacy of Gaul,'' *Early Music History* 4 (1984) 49–99. K. LEVY, ''Charlemagne's Archetype of Gregorian Chant,'' *Journal of the American Musicological Society* 40 (1987) 1–31. K. LEVY, ''Gallican Chant,'' *New Oxford History of Music* 2 (1990) 93–101. J. CLAIRE, ''Le cantatorium romain et le cantatorium gallican: etude comparée des premières formes de la psalmodie,'' *Orbis musicae* 10 (1990–91) 50–86. J. MCKINNON, ''The Eighth Century Frankish-Roman Communion Cycle,'' *Journal of the American Musicological Society* 45 (1992) 179–227. J. MCKINNON, ''Lector Chant versus Schola Chant: a Question of Historical Plausibility,'' in *Laborare fratres in unum: Festschrift László Dobszay zum 60. Geburtstag,* ed. J. SZENDREI and D. HILEY (Berlin 1995) 201–11. Y. HEN, ''Unity in Diversity: the Liturgy of Frankish Gaul before the Carolingians,'' in *Unity and Diversity in the Church,* ed. R. N. SWANSON (Oxford 1996) 19–30. Y. HEN, *Culture and Religion in Merovingian Gaul, A.D. 481–751* (Leiden 1995).

[I. WORTMAN/EDS.]

GALLICANISM

A complex of theological and political doctrines, administrative and judicial practices, and religious passions, which characterized the life of the Catholic Church in FRANCE from the late Middle Ages to the French Revolution. The adjective *Gallican,* derived from the Latin *gallicanus,* was for a long time in common usage without connoting a doctrine suspected of heresy; it was not, however, a synonym for *French* except in a few expressions such as Gallican Breviary, Gallican Church, Gallican liturgy, Gallican Flanders, and the Gallican province of the Third Order of St. Francis. *Gallicanisme* was not introduced into the French language as a noun until *c.* 1900. Soon after this it appeared in other languages. It was a convenient word because it replaced several other expressions in use since the 15th century, such as ''maxims and immunities of the Gallican Church.'' A lawyer in the Paris Parlement *c.* 1800, taking his inspiration from Pierre Pithou, began an article dealing with the liberties of the Gallican Church thus: ''The word *Libertés,* which proclaims to servile ultramontane minds exorbitant privileges, merely denotes the ancient right common to all churches, which the French have succeeded in defending against the court of Rome with more steadfastness than the magistrates and doctors of other Catholic nations.'' This jurist merely echoed a tradition when he opposed Gallicanism to ULTRAMONTANISM (opinions commonly held beyond the mountains, in Italy, and more precisely, those held by Roman theologians and canonists, who had only a small number of representatives in France). The defenders of the liberties of the Gallican Church were and wished to remain Catholics. There were, in fact, many ways of interpreting the term ''liberties,'' and of utilizing them. ''We have found far less evidence of a developing Gallican system than of Gallican systems that succeed one another'' (M. Dubruel, *Dictionnaire apologétique de la foi catholique* 2:201); but this author and his collaborator, H. X. Arquillière, multiplied in this famous article, examples of successions and traced Gallicanism as far back as the Carolingian period (*ibid.*). In any case, the best contemporary historian is explicit: ''There is not one Gallicanism but Gallicanisms, so different are the interpretations of doctors, bishops, magistrates, and kings'' (A. G. Martimort, *Le Gallicanisme de Bossuet* 7). If Gallicanism terminated with the end of the alliance between throne and altar during the FRENCH REVOLUTION of 1789, the revival during the 19th century of some theses dear to Gallicanism can be called neo-Gallicanism.

Despite the varieties of Gallicanism, Victor MARTIN has attempted to establish a common source for all of them, which consisted of three basic ideas: independence of the king of France in the temporal order; superiority of general COUNCILS over the pope; and union of king and clergy in France to limit papal intervention within the kingdom, in the name of ancient canons (*Les Origines du gallicanisme* 1:7). This appeal to ancient canons, or to rights acquired in ancient times by the Church of France, seems to be the distinctive trait of a certain French anti-Romanism; it eliminated the possibility of confusing Gallicanism with other similar movements that were spreading over Europe long before the appearance of FEBRONIANISM and JOSEPHINISM.

Gallicanism is inseparable from a certain pride of French Catholicism. It did not believe in the DONATION OF CONSTANTINE. It knew that PEPIN III, Charlemagne's father, helped Pope Stephen II (753) and had permitted him to lay the foundations for the STATES OF THE CHURCH. Since then, France has been called the eldest daughter of the Church, with St. Petronilla, daughter of

St. Peter, as her patron saint. The king of France was consecrated with oil said to have been brought from heaven by an angel and believed to have the miraculous power of healing the king's evil (scrofula). He was not elected; he believed that his power came to him directly from God. "The king of France and the emperor are not one and the same thing," wrote an author in the service of King Charles V, in *Le Songe du verger* (1376). Independent of the emperor and an emperor in his own kingdom, the king claimed to be dependent on the pope only in spiritual matters, not at all in temporal affairs. The conflict of PHILIP IV the Fair with Pope BONIFACE VIII demonstrated this in striking and brutal fashion.

First Manifestations (1398–1438). It was during the attempts to end the WESTERN SCHISM that the ancient immunities of the Gallican Church were evoked and discovered. Following a national synod, Charles VI decided (July 27, 1398) to sever relations with Benedict XIII, the Avignon pope, and to do so without any recognition of Boniface IX as pope. The end of the royal ordinance read thus: "The king intends to take the necessary measures to make certain that in the future the Gallican Church will, under all circumstances, retain its original immunities and liberties to use them and enjoy them" (V. Martin, *Origines* 288–289). In accord with his clergy, the king of France had, therefore, passed judgment on the pope (or at least on the one he thought to be pope), because this pontiff, too eager for money, was no longer fulfilling his proper function as servant of the common good of all the faithful. The national synod of 1398 was not a general council, but because of the dangers threatening the Church it was considered to be virtually a general council (V. Martin, *Origines* 1:283). The Church in France, which was making use of its original immunities to assume full liberty, freed itself from the demands of the papal treasury only to fall under royal fiscal control; it escaped papal abuses in the distribution of benefices only to submit its litigations to the Paris parlement. After undergoing other difficulties, the Church in France rejoiced to see the Western Schism terminated with the election of Pope Martin V (1417). But the ancient immunities and privileges, which were used merely as an expedient during a crucial period, became, as Charles VI had desired, a permanent institution.

The desire to end abuses once again brought about a national synod, this time at Bourges, to legislate as a general council. A royal ordinance, the PRAGMATIC SANCTION (1438), collected the decisions concerning the authority of general councils, the conferring of benefices, elections, expectancies, appeals, ANNATES, the celebration of Divine Office, and other ecclesiastical matters (F. A. Isambert, *Recueil général des anciennes lois françaises* 9:3–47). According to the Pragmatic Sanction ecumenical councils must convene every 10 years, as the Councils of CONSTANCE and BASEL had ordained; an ecumenical council is superior to the pope; bishops must be elected by cathedral chapters, and abbots, by their abbeys. Some of these articles undoubtedly anticipated the reform work of the Council of TRENT a century later, but the Pragmatic was a document of debatable canonical value and also a condemned one; yet it had considerable value. Members of the parlements, who were charged with supervising the observance of the Pragmatic, long regarded it as the special constitution of the Gallican Church. Doctors on the various faculties of theology were wary of it for fear lest graduates lose their privileges, which allowed them to obtain benefices more easily than could other clerics. Bishops were of two minds about it. They approved the independence it afforded the Church in France; but they did not like it when they were themselves elected by chapters and then found these chapters too powerful. (*See* CONCILIARISM.)

Ramifications of Gallicanism (1438–1594). Gallicanism assumed several different aspects: rigid among members of the parlements, nuanced among theologians, hesitant among bishops, and opportunist among kings.

Gallicanism of Parlement. As guardians of the holy decrees of the Gallican Church and of the Pragmatic Sanction of Bourges members of the parlements wished to establish their own courts as a supreme ecclesiastical court and as the necessary intermediary between the national Church and the pope. Every summons to Rome, *omisso medio,* was considered by them an abuse. No papal document and no papal legate could enter France without the consent of the Paris parlement. In 1465 this parlement presented the king with a remonstrance composed of 89 articles. In them it was sorrowful as it recalled the years from 1407 to 1439, but joyful as it evoked the years from 1439 to 1461 (the year in which Louis XI suppressed the Pragmatic). During this latter period, it claimed, the Pragmatic had brought prosperity to the king and his kingdom and rendered the Church in France illustrious with saintly prelates and numerous miracles. To repeal it, according to articles 18 and 19 of the remonstrance, would expose both king and kingdom to every evil, and especially to four: the whole ecclesiastical order would be thrown into confusion (art. 20–61); the kingdom would become depopulated (art. 62–66); the currency would be sent abroad (art. 67–80); and all dioceses would be ruined (art. 81–89). It was held necessary, therefore, to maintain "the freedom of elections and the exoneration of the Church from the heavy burden of annates" (E. Maugis, *Histoire du Parlement de Paris de l'avènement des rois Valois à la mort d'Henri IV* [Paris 1913] 1:707–708). Logical in its own interests, parlement opposed the official registration of the concordat of 1516 and had to be compelled before it registered the pact in 1518. Its remonstrances of 1579–80, for example, still pleaded for the reestablishment of the Pragmatic as something very praiseworthy and desired by all royal subjects (*ibid.* 1:710).

Theological Gallicanism. Just as the Parlement of Paris set the tone for the other parlements, so the Faculty of Theology of the University of PARIS set the tone for the provincial universities. Its doctors were the spiritual heirs of PETER OF AILLY and Jean GERSON, who played a decisive role at the Council of Constance and contributed to ending the Western Schism. These doctors revered the pope, but above all they loved the Church. They believed that a pope might err but not the Church. To the latter, united in general council, "each one owes obedience, no matter what rank or dignity he may hold, even papal." This decree of the fifth session of the Council of Constance was one that met with unanimous approval among French theologians. They liked to repeat, with St. Jerome, "orbis major est urbe." University, or theological, Gallicanism claimed that if the papal power was not limited in itself, it was in its use and exercise by natural law, by the very constitution of the Church, and by the ancient statutes that governed various churches. "We do not read," said Gerson, "that Christ conferred on the pope the power to dispose of benefices, dignities, bishoprics, domains, or ecclesiastical properties. We read nowhere that Peter ever exercised this power." (P. Imbart de la Tour, *Les Origines de la Réforme* 2:77–83; Martimort, *op. cit.* 17–56). This tradition was presented by French bishops at the Council of Trent, but it nearly disappeared later as a consequence of the Counter Reformation. In 1611 the *Syndic* of the Faculty of Theology of Paris, Ed. Richer revived it in order to oppose ultramontanism. His extreme views were rejected but theological Gallicanism subsisted in the faculty, expressed in a succession of pronouncements, the most important of which are the Six Articles of 1663, the source of the 1682 Gallican Articles, and the censure of J. Vernant (1664), "the most somplete synthesis of what the faculty achieved againts the Ultramontanes for many centuries" (A. G. Martimort, *Le gallicanisme de Bossuet* 245). It was renewed by the opponents to the bull *Unigenitus* and was eventually condemned by *Auctorem fidei.*

Episcopal Gallicanism. French theologians spoke rarely of the liberties of the Gallican Church but the bishops made much of them. They claimed for themselves the exercise of a threefold liberty: administrative, permitting them to deliberate among themselves, especially in provincial councils; fiscal, allowing them to levy taxes (tithes) and to dispose of the income; and judicial, giving them the right to have diocesan officials and to be the sole judges of fellow bishops, when these have failed to fulfill their duties. Should parlements encroach on episcopal jurisdiction, the prelates appealed to the king's council, nor did they overlook the pope. In the 15th century an archbishop of Toulouse composed a whole treatise against the validity of the Pragmatic and in favor of papal supremacy, while an archbishop of Tours published another treatise, *Contre la constitution impie des Gallicans appellée Pragmatique.* In 1487 the bishop of Autun published some papal bulls without having them officially registered and invited the clergy and faithful to obey them. Two years later, the bishop of Luçon refused to have certain briefs revoked; in 1491 the bishop of Beauvais placed a papal interdict on the lands of the priests belonging to the Archdiocese of Narbonne. Others accepted mandates from delegated judges, general collectors of tithes. After the Council of Trent, the bishops came into conflict with statesmen. The conviction that further entreaties were useless led the bishops to distinguish between the role of a prince and the duties of the episcopate. It was, then, the struggle precipitated in France by the introduction of the Tridentine reforms that allowed for the acceptance of the "separating of powers:" the religious power, the guide of consciences, whose domain is the supernatural; and the civil power, engaged mainly with temporal affairs and endowed with physical force to put its will into effect.

Royal Gallicanism. After the appearance of the Pragmatic Sanction, the king sought much less to keep aloof from the pope than to negotiate with him; but the royal motivation was more self-interest than religion. In 1442 Charles VII agreed to renounce the Pragmatic and to conclude a concordat with Pope Eugene IV. Negotiations broke down, but reopened in 1449. King Louis XI made known to Pope Pius II his intention of abrogating the Pragmatic (1461) and proclaimed its abrogation in 1462. But the ordinances issued in 1463 and 1466 nullified the significance of this spectacular act. After Louis XI came to an understanding with Pope Sixtus IV (1472), a concordat, which remained in force for three years, provided that major benefices should be at the king's disposal, while minor benefices should be conferred by the pope in the uneven months and by the king in the even months. After 1475 the king avoided the strict application of the Pragmatic and allowed electors to select their own candidates. After a new attempt at a concordat (1485), King Francis I and Pope Leo X signed at Bologna in 1516 a concordat that was observed until 1790. This concordat put an end to the Pragmatic, which had been praised as "the palladium of national liberties." The concordat granted the king in perpetuity the unique privilege of naming to consistorial benefices but said nothing about the papal right to collect annates. Later papal demands that the Tridentine decrees be received officially in

France went unheeded. The kings could no doubt have overcome the obstinacy of the parlements. It was not fear of excessive papal power that deterred them but rather the fear of being deprived of the privilege of COMMENDATION. The Blois ordinance (1579) tried to introduce a part of the Tridentine reform into French legislation but Pope Gregory XIII could not allow France once again to legislate as in 1438.

Pithou. Pierre PITHOU, a lawyer in the Paris parlement, published in 1594 a 54-page treatise (*Les Libertés de l'Église gallicane*) that had astounding success well into the 19th century. This booklet was divided into 83 articles. This catalogue of propositions, arranged to attract French readers, was doubtless less logical than was claimed in article three where the author affirmed that all the following liberties stemmed from two maxims only: "The first is that the popes can neither command nor ordain anything, be it general or particular, that bears on the temporal affairs of countries or lands under obedience to the Most Christian King, and should they command or decree any such thing, the subjects of the king, even though they be clerics, are therefore not bound to obey" (art. 4); "The second, although the pope is recognized as sovereign in spiritual matters, nevertheless absolute and infinite power has no place in France, but is restricted and limited by the canons and rules of the ancient councils of the Church accepted in this kingdom" (art. 5). To exemplify these maxims Pithou continued: "The prelates of France may not leave the kingdom without his majesty's permission" (art. 13). "The king's officers cannot be excommunicated for the exercise of their duties" (art. 16). "The bull *In coena Domini* is not accepted in France" (art. 17). "The Church of France does not accept all the decretals" (art. 41).

Pierre Dupuy (1582–1651), state counselor and curator of the royal library, republished Pithou's book as part of *Traitez des droits et libertés de l'Église gallicane,* and commented on it in *Preuves des Libertés de l'Église gallicane.* These two works appeared in 1639; a second edition came out in 1651. Jean Louis Brunet (1688–1747), a lawyer in the Paris parlement, added considerably to these two books in 1731. Pierre Toussaint Durand de Maillane (1729–1814), lawyer in the Aix-en-Provence parlement, organized the material accumulated by Dupuy and Brunet and called his compilation, increased by new commentaries, *Les Libertés de l'Église gallicane prouvées et commentées suivant l'ordre et la disposition des articles dressés par M. Pierre Pithou* (5 v. Lyon 1771). It was a summary of Parlementary Gallicanism with all its excesses. No work could give a clearer and more complete idea of this teaching. Without being guilty of rash judgment, one could apply to it what the French bishops said in 1639 of Dupuy's two volumes: "a hateful work, full of the most venomous propositions and presenting formal heresies under the fair name of freedoms . . . . Never has the Christian faith, the Catholic Church, ecclesiastical discipline, the safety of the kingdom been attacked by more pernicious doctrines." In the same tone, but with a touch of humor, Claude FLEURY, a canonist and a moderate Gallican, observed in his *Discours sur les libertés de l'Église gallicane* (1723): "Any bad Frenchman, who could flee to safety outside France, could write a *Traité des servitudes de l'Église gallicane,* as has already been done in regard to its liberties, and he need not lack for proofs."

Declaration of 1682. At the meeting of the Estates General (1615) the clergy rejected the first maxim of Parlementary Gallicanism, that of the absolute independence of the king in relation to the pope in temporal affairs. A meeting of the Assembly of French Clergy (*see* ASSEMBLIES OF FRENCH CLERGY) some months later accepted decrees of the Council of Trent. These two important decisions did not imply that the French clergy, with the bishops at their head, had ceased to defend the Gallican liberties. If such was the intent, repentance was made in 1682. Victor Martin has devoted an entire book, *Le Gallicanisme politique et le clergé de France* (1929), to explaining how this reversal came about. Nevertheless, the declaration of 1615 at the Estates General pertained only to the first of the four articles of 1682.

The declaration of March 19, 1682, the manifesto of episcopal Gallicanism, was approved by an extraordinary meeting of the Assembly of the French Clergy. King LOUIS XIV permitted this reunion of 52 bishops and priests to settle the affair of the REGALIA and to condemn a book. The Second General Council of Lyons (1274) had tolerated the continuance of the regalia in the dioceses in which it already existed, but forbade bishops, under pain of excommunication, to permit it to be introduced into dioceses in which it did not already exist. Louis XIV wished to extend the regalia throughout his kingdom (1673–75). It might seem that the king, as a good Gallican, would want to obey the prescriptions of a general council, but this would confuse royal Gallicanism, which had little concern for doctrine, with the Gallicanism of the theologians. Royal Gallicanism had only to accept the principles of Parlementary Gallicanism as established by Dupuy, which held that the canons and decrees subsequent to the 9th century were not obligatory. In any event, two French bishops took their stand on the Second Council of Lyons and opposed Louis XIV. Pope INNOCENT XI approved them. After the death of these two bishops, the conflict between the French court and the Holy See still perdured in 1681.

The condemnation of a book by Jean Gerbais, *Dissertatio de causis majoribus ad caput concordatorum* (1679), did not improve matters. A brief of Innocent XI (Dec. 18, 1680) reproved the book's contents as ''schismatic, suspect of heresy, and injurious to the Holy See.'' Gerbais had written his book at the request of the 1665 Assembly of the Clergy, and in it he defended some of the ideas cherished by episcopal Gallicanism, namely, that bishops have the right to judge matters relative to faith and also to judge, as courts of first instance, their fellow bishops.

The extraordinary assembly of 1681–82 believed that it could contribute to the reestablishment of peace between the king and the pope by determining clearly the respective powers of popes, kings, and bishops. J. B. BOSSUET, Bishop of Meaux, was charged with drafting a declaration in Latin. The preamble demonstrated the conciliatory purposes of the document, which sought to avoid the excesses of those who were attacking the decrees and liberties of the Gallican Church (i.e., the ultramontanists) and also the excesses of those who magnified these liberties even to the point of casting aspersions on the PRIMACY OF THE POPE and the obedience due to the Holy See by all Christians. The essentials of the first article have been noted above. The second article admitted the papal plenitude of power and also accepted as permanently valid the decrees of the fourth and fifth sessions of the Council of Constance regarding the superiority of ecumenical councils over popes. The third article insisted that the papal power must be exercised in conformity with the ancient canons and with the customs of the Gallican Church. The fourth article admitted that in decisions on matters of faith the pope enjoys the principal role but claimed that his judgments are not irreformable without the consent of the universal Church (*see* DECLARATION OF THE FRENCH CLERGY).

Louis XIV was pleased to accept this declaration and issued an edict (March 1682) that enjoined the professors of theology to subscribe to it and to teach it each year, and required bishops to make known its contents in their dioceses. Once the king had won the clergy to his side, he believed that Innocent XI would finally yield to his wishes, but he was mistaken. A new conflict, which began because of other royal demands relative to the quarters of the French embassy in Rome, aggravated the situation. Innocent XI continued to refuse to confirm the bishops whom Louis XIV proposed to him. As a result there were 35 dioceses vacant in France in 1689 when Innocent XI died.

In 1690 Pope Alexander VIII condemned the declaration of 1682 (see below). In a letter to Innocent XII (Sept. 14, 1693), Louis XIV denounced his own edict of March 1682. The declaration could have been condemned much sooner, in accord with its own principles, if foreign bishops had followed the example given them in 1682 by the primate of Hungary. Bossuet sensed the danger and composed between 1683 and 1685 an extensive defense in Latin: *Defensio declarationis cleri gallicani,* which did not appear in print until 1745. Despite the withdrawal of Louis XIV's edict, the declaration of 1682 continued to be widely taught in France during the 18th century. In 1772 Jacques ÉMERY wrote: ''To avoid the least suspicion of ultramontanism, we add that we adhere fully to the maxims of the French clergy contained in the declaration of 1682. We consider this declaration to be a precious monument, valuable even to the Holy See, which we do not doubt will one day recognize its wisdom'' (cited by J. Leflon, *Monsieur Emery* [Paris 1947] 2:302).

Last Manifestations. In the 18th century, royal and episcopal Gallicanism became circumspect. Thus the king himself forbade (1720, 1730) his subjects to bring the topic of an APPEAL TO A FUTURE COUNCIL. Parlementary Gallicanism, on the other hand, became more and more violent and repeatedly had recourse to the appeal from an abuse (*appel comme d'abus*). Theological Gallicanism was divided. There were moderates, who sided with the bishops, and Jansenists, who made common cause with the Gallicans of the parlements. In JANSENISM could be found something of Presbyterianism, parochialism, and even of LAICISM, as well as of Gallicanism. Gallicanism died with the CIVIL CONSTITUTION OF THE CLERGY (1790), which broke the bond between the king and his clergy. The situation then was far different from that under the Pragmatic Sanction. After the parlements had discredited Gallicanism, they were themselves abolished during the French Revolution. J. E. M. Portalis, who thought he could conciliate his admiration for the declaration of 1682 with the decisions of the 18th-century parlements, tried to revive the liberties of the Gallican Church by adding 77 Organic Articles to the 17 articles of the French CONCORDAT OF 1801. This, however, was merely one of the means of controlling the Church open to Napoleon. Furthermore, nothing was more contrary to episcopal Gallicanism than the resignation of the entire French hierarchy in obedience to the demand of PIUS VII. Associated as it was with Bossuet's name, the declaration of 1682 continued to have admirers. Between 1824 and 1860, A. Dupin published five editions of Pithou's book; but his *Manuel du droit public ecclésiastique française,* which contained Pithou's work, was condemned by the majority of French bishops, even by those who were Gallicans; it was also placed on the Index (1845). Between 1845 and 1865 the French clergy withdrew their attachment to Gallicanism and adhered in great numbers to ultramontanism. Henri MARET tried to conciliate Gallicanism with LIBERALISM in his book, *Du concise général et de la paix religieuse* (1869). After the complete separation of Church and State in France (1905), the upholders of laicism, although indifferent to the Catholic Church or hostile to it, regretted more than the Catholics themselves the abrogation of the concordat of 1801 and its attached Organic Articles.

Papal Condemnations. The papal condemnations of the *appel comme d'abus,* the appeal to a future council, the exequatur, and the *placet* also affected Gallicanism. When Leo X promulgated the concordat of 1516 with the bull *Pastor aeternus* (1516), he also attacked Gallican conciliarism (*Enchiridion symbolorum* 740). Alexander VIII's constitution *Inter multiplices* (1690) decreed the Four Gallican Articles void (*Enchiridion symbolorum* 1322–26). Pius VI renewed Alexander VIII's condemnation in his constitution *AUCTOREM FIDEI* (1794) against the Synod of Pistoia, which had, among other things, adopted Gallicanism (*Enchiridion symbolorum* 1599). The *SYLLABUS OF ERRORS* (1864) included an attack on Gallicanism. The solemn definitions of the papal primacy and infallibility at VATICAN COUNCIL I (1870) rendered impossible any revival of the old Gallican claims, which were by then a faded memory.

Bibliography: V. MARTIN, *Les Origines du gallicanisme,* 2 v. (Paris 1939); *Le Gallicanisme et la réforme catholique: Essai historique sur l'introduction en France des decrets du Concile de Trente, 1563–1615* (Paris 1919); *Le Gallicanisme politique et le clergé de France, 1615–1682* (Paris 1929). J. LECLER, ''Qu'est-ce que les libertés de l'Église gallicane?'' *Recherches de science religieuse* 23 (1933) 385–410, 542–568; 24 (1934) 47–85. A. FLICHE and V. MARTIN, eds., *Histoire de l'église depuis les origines jusqu'à nos jours* (Paris 1935–) v. 7–21, esp. 7, 14, 15, 18–21. P. IMBART DE LA TOUR, *Les Origines de la Réforme* v. 2, ed. Y. LANHERS (2d ed. Melun 1944) 73–125. G. MOLLAT, ''Les Origines du gallicanisme parlementaire aux XIVe et XVe siècles,'' *Revue d'histoire ecclésiastique* 43 (1948) 90–147. A. G. MARTIMORT, *Le Gallicanisme de Bossuet* (Paris 1953). J. R. PALANQUE, *Catholiques libéraux et gallicans en France face au concile du Vatican, 1867–1870* (Aix-en-Provence 1962). R. THYSMAN, ''Le Gallicanisme de Mgr. Maret et l'influence de Bossuet,'' *Revue d'histoire ecclésiastique* 52 (1957) 401–465. L. BÉRARD, ''Séparation, gallicanisme et concordat,'' *Revue des deux mondes* (July–August 1957) 193–216. E. PUYOL, *Edmond Richer. Etude historique et critique sur la renovation du Gallicanisme au commencement du XVIIe siècle* (Paris 1876). M. VÉNARD, ''Ultramontane or Gallican? The French Episcopate at the End of the Sixteenth Century,'' *Jurist* 52 (1992), 142–161. P. BLET, *Les assemblées du Clergé et Louis XIV, de 1670 à 1693* (Rome 1972). R. DUCHON, ''De Bossuet à Febronius,'' *Revue d'histoire ecclésiastique* 65 (1970) 375–422. J. M. GRES-GAYER, *Le Gallicanisme de Sorbonne* (Paris 2001). W. J. BOUSWSMA, ''Gallicanism and the Nature of Christendom,'' *A Usable Past: Essays in European Cultural History* (Berkeley) 308–324. H. G. RULE, ''Louis XIV and the Church,'' *Louis XIV and the Craft of Kingship,* ed. J. C. RULE (Ohio 1969) 240–263. P. SONNINO, *Louis XIV's View of the Papacy* (Berkeley 1966). P. BLET, *Le clergé de France en ses assemblées (1615–1717)* (Paris 1995). M. DUBRUEL and H. X. ARQUILLIÈRE, *Dictionnaire apologétique de la foi catholique,* ed. A. D'ALÈS, 4 v. (Paris 1911–22; Table analytique 1931) 2:193–273. M. DUBRUEL, *Dictionnaire de théologie catholique,* ed. A. VACANT et al., 15 v. (Paris 1903–50; Tables générales 1951–) 6.1:1096–1157. C. CONSTANTIN, *Dictionnaire de théologie catholique,* ed. A. VACANT et al., 15 v. (Paris 1903–50; Tables générales 1951–) 4.1:185–205, s.v. ''Déclaration de 1682.'' R. LAPRAT, *Dictionnaire de droit canonique,* ed. R. NAZ, 7 v. (Paris 1935–65) 6:426–525, s.v. ''Libertés de l'Église gallicane.''

[C. BERTHELOT DU CHESNAY/J. M. GRES-GAYER]

GALLIENUS, ROMAN EMPEROR

Emperor 253 to 268; b. Publius Licinius Egnatius Gallienus, *c.* 218; d. Milan, Aug.(?) 268. His mother was Gnatia Mariniana. In 253, when his father, P. Licinius Valerianus, became emperor, Gallienus was named Augustus and given the West to defend. In successful campaigns along the Rhine, he saved Gaul from the attacks of Germanic tribes, and in 258 at Milan checked an invasion of Italy by the Alamanni. On the death of his father VALERIAN, in 259 or 260, the defense of the Empire, complicated by numerous rebellions among his generals, fell upon Gallienus. In 267 he gained a brilliant victory over the Heruli, who were ravaging Greece, and returned to Italy to check the revolt of Aureolus. He was murdered by his officers during the siege of Milan in July or August 268. Gallienus introduced a number of important political, military, and religious reforms; excluded senators from military commands; and created an independent cavalry corps with its base at Milan. In 260 he issued edicts that ended the persecution of the Christians, recognized their bishops and restored their churches and cemeteries (Eusebius, *Hist. Eccl.* 7.13). His tolerance followed a realization of the failure of his father's policy and reflected the influence of his wife, Salonina, who had a high esteem for Christians. This was the first Roman declaration of tolerance for Christians. Though later tradition made a tyrant of Gallienus, he was a man of high culture and boundless energy, keenly aware of the essential needs of his times. Many of his political reforms anticipated those of Diocletian.

Bibliography: U. WICKERT, *Paulys Realencyklopädie der klassischen Altertumswissenschaft,* ed. G. WISSOWA et al. 13.1 (Stuttgart 1926) 350–369. G. M. BERSANETTI, *Enciclopedia Italiana di scienzi, littere ed arti.* 36 v. (Rome 1929–39) 16:326–327.

[M. J. COSTELLOE]

GALLIFET, JOSEPH FRANÇOIS DE

Theologian; b. Aix, France, May 3, 1663; d. Lyons, Aug. 31, 1749. He entered the Society of Jesus at Avignon in 1678. He had as spiritual director Bl. Claude la Colombière, who first taught him devotion to the Sacred Heart. As a young priest during his third year of probation at Lyons (1690), he fell critically ill. As he lay near death, one of his brethren, probably Jean Croiset, another early promoter of the devotion, made a vow in his name that should he live, Gallifet would spend his life in promoting this devotion. He recovered fully, ratified the vow, and devoted all his activities to fulfilling it. Gallifet held important positions: he was rector at Vesoul, Lyons, Grenoble, and Besançon; provincial (1719–23) and French assistant to the superior general in Rome (1723–30). He built chapels of the Sacred Heart, wrote several books, and established more than 700 confraternities of the Sacred Heart in his lifetime. He is best known for his efforts in Rome to obtain approval for the public cult and establishment of a liturgical feast of the Sacred Heart. As promoter of the cause before the Congregation of Rites, he composed the *De cultu sacrosancti Cordis Dei ac Domini nostri Jesu Christi* (1726), a Latin theological treatise with the autobiography of St. Margaret Mary ALACOQUE appended, later revised and published in French as *De l'Excellence de la dévotion au Coeur adorable de Jésus-Christ* (1733). Its weakness, which contributed to the negative reply of the Congregation of Rites, was the explanation of the heart as seat of the emotions. Final victory came only after his death with the establishment of the feast in 1765.

Bibliography: P. MECH, *Catholicisme* 4:1739–40. P. BERNARD, *Dictionnaire de théologie catholique,* ed. A. VACANT, 15 v. (Paris 1903–50; Tables générales 1951–) 6.1:1137–40. C. SOMMERVOGEL, *Bibliotèque de la Compagnie de Jésus,* 11 v. (Brussels-Paris 1890–1932) 3:1124–31. A. HAMON, *Histoire de la dévotion au Sacré-Coeur,* 5 v. (Paris 1923–41) 4:5–31.

[C. J. MOELL]

GALLITZIN, AMALIA

Leader of the Münster circle in the German Catholic revival; b. Berlin, Aug. 28, 1748; d. Münster, April 27, 1806. Adelheid Amalia, Countess von Schmettau, the daughter of the Prussian Count von Schmettau, was baptized a Catholic but was raised in an atmosphere of religious indifference. In 1768 she married the Russian Prince Dimitri Gallitzin, from whom she separated (1775) after bearing two children. With the encouragement of Franz Hemsterhuis, the Dutch philosopher, she settled in Münster (1779), retired from high society, and devoted herself to study. She and Franz von FÜRSTENBERG established the Münster circle, which discussed philosophy, pedagogy, and Christian perfection and maintained a fruitful intellectual exchange with Catholic groups in southern Germany. Its members included Johann HAMANN, Friedrich von STOLBERG, Clemens von DROSTE ZU VISCHERING, and Bernard OVERBERG. Through the influence of Overberg (much more than that of Hamann), Princess Gallitzin ceased to be a disciple of the French ENLIGHTENMENT, returned to Catholicism (*c.* 1786), and became an active promoter of Catholic life in Westphalia. Later she became an intimate friend of GOETHE. Her son Demetrius GALLITZIN was a missionary in Maryland and Pennsylvania.

Head of Gallienus from Museo delle Terme, Rome. (Alinari-Art Reference/Art Resource, NY)

Bibliography: S. SUDHOF, ed., *Der Kreis von Münster: Briefe und Aufzeichnungen Fürstenbergs, der Fürstin Gallitzin und ihrer Freunde* (Münster 1962–64) 1:1769–88, in process. J. GALLAND, *Die Fürstin Amalia von Gallitzin und ihre Freunde* (Cologne 1880). P. BRACHIN, *Le Cercle de Münster (1779–1806) et la pensée religieuse de F. L. von Stolberg* (Lyons 1952). E. REINHARD, *Die Münsterische "Familia sacra"* (Münster 1953). W. H. BRUFORD, *Fürstin Gallitzin und Goethe* (Cologne 1957).

[A SCHRÖER]

GALLITZIN, DEMETRIUS AUGUSTINE

Pioneer missionary; b. The Hague, Holland, Dec. 22, 1770; d. Loretto, Pa., May 6, 1840. He was the son of the Russian Prince Demetrius, a scientist, and Countess Amalia Gallitzin, daughter of a Prussian field marshal. Although his mother had been baptized a Roman Catholic, she had lost interest in her religion before the birth of her son. Soon after his birth, the parents separated and Demetrius was raised in the Orthodox Church of his father. His mother, after a critical illness in 1786, returned to the Roman Catholic Church, and young Demetrius followed her the next year. He completed his education and served for a time as aide-de-camp to the Austrian general Von Lillien. Instead of making the customary grand tour of Europe, Gallitzin was sent by his mother on a trip to the U.S.

His arrival in Baltimore, Md., on Oct. 28, 1792, was a turning point in his life. He presented himself to Abp. John CARROLL, asking to be admitted to the seminary. On March 18, 1795, he was ordained—the first priest to receive all his training and orders in the U.S. He first served the mission stations of Port Tobacco, Md., and Conewago, Pa., and the German community in Baltimore. However, like many of his contemporaries, he desired to go to the West. On a trip to the Allegheny Mountains in 1796, he visited Capt. Michael McGuire's settlement in Cambria County, Pa. The captain offered him a tract of land if he would settle in the area, but it was several years before Gallitzin obtained the permission from his bishop. He built a church at what came to be known as Loretto, Pa., and celebrated Mass there on Christmas Day, 1799. Wishing to create an ideal Catholic frontier settlement, Gallitzin encouraged migration by purchasing land and offering it to settlers at a low cost. His early years at Loretto were stormy, for his masterful personality and strict moral standards antagonized the local settlers. In the beginning he supported his activities with money received from his father during the latter's lifetime. When he inherited little of his father's estate, he sought funds by a public appeal for aid in 1827.

Gallitzin declined several episcopal appointments in order to direct his colonization project. He eventually became vicar-general for Western Pennsylvania. Although his ''ideal'' community subsequently disappeared, the strong Catholicism he established in Cambria County is reflected in that area's present heavily Catholic population.

Bibliography: P. H. LEMCKE, *Life and Work of Prince Demetrius Augustine Gallitzin,* tr. J. C. PLUMPE (New York 1940). G. MURPHY, *Gallitzin's Letters: A Collection of Polemical Works . . .* (Loretto, Pa. 1940). D. SARGENT, *Mitri, or the Story of Prince Demetrius Augustine Gallitzin, 1770–1840* (New York 1945).

[T. V. HARTZEL]

GALLO, ANDRÉS MARÍA

Colombian patriot; b. Tuta, Boyacá, Colombia, Feb. 2, 1791; d. Bogotá, April 14, 1863. He studied in Tunja and Bogotá and graduated in law, Oct. 4, 1815. During the war for independence he served in the republican army, rising from captain to commander of a unit, but after his brief army career he had returned to the university. Gallo was an alcalde in Tunja when the royalist forces regained power in 1816 and condemned him to death for his republican activities. That sentence was canceled. He served as a member of the court of justice and of the legislature in Tunja and as representative from Tunja in the federal congress. He received a doctorate in theology from the University of Santo Tomás in 1818 and was ordained April 25 that same year. As pastor of Ramiriquí he helped provide supplies for Bolívar's troops; he was named chaplain of the military staff and was active in the battle of Pantano de Vargas (July 25, 1819). Later he served as pastor of Viracachá, Firavitoba, Genesano, Guatavita, and Tenza. At various times he served as representative and as senator in the congress. Three times he was proposed for a bishopric: for Pasto, Cartagena, and Pamplona; however, he did not accept a see. In 1856 he was canon of the cathedral of Bogotá, and in 1859 he became vicar-general of the archdiocese. In that position he defended the rights of the Church against the dictator Gen. Tomás C. de Mosquera, while Abp. Antonio Herrán was in exile. Gallo had a reputation as a preacher and often preached on patriotic themes. By keeping up his political activities he became vice president of the senate, but he also acquired many political enemies. He was interested in promoting education in Colombia. He left his memoirs: *Reminiscencias del Canónigo doctor Andrés M. Gallo.*

Bibliography: J. ACOSTA ORTEGÓN, ''El doctor Andrés María Gallo y su época,'' *Boletín de historia y antigüedades* 33 (1946) 477–505.

[J. M. PACHECO]

GALLO, MARIA FRANCESCA OF THE FIVE WOUNDS, ST.

Italian mystic; b. Naples, March 25, 1715; d. there, Oct. 8, 1791. At a very early age she began to practice penances and to meditate on Christ's Passion. After resisting her father's urging to marry, she joined the Third

Order of Franciscans (1731) and changed her baptismal name, Anna Maria Rosa Nicoletta. Continuing to live at home, she devoted herself to charitable works for the poor and sick. She was favored with extraordinary mystical graces and was reputed to be endowed with the gift of prophecy. On Fridays, especially, she experienced in a physical manner the agonies of the Passion and STIGMATIZATION. Her deep devotion to the suffering Christ and to the Eucharist helped her to endure severe illnesses, misunderstandings by her relatives and by her spiritual directors, and spiritual aridity. She was beatified Nov. 12, 1843, and canonized June 29, 1867.

Feast: Oct. 6.

Bibliography: M. P. ADAMI, *S. Maria Francesca delle cinque piaghe di N. S.* (Naples 1970). A. BUTLER, *The Lives of the Saints* 4:46–47. J. L. BAUDOT and L. CHAUSSIN, *Vies des saints et des bienheureux selon l'orde du calendrier avec l'historique des fêtes, by the Benedictines of Paris* 10:177–182.

[F. G. SOTTOCORNOLA]

GALLUP, DIOCESE OF

Established Dec. 16, 1939, the Diocese of Gallup (*Gallupensis*) is suffragan of the Metropolitan See of Santa Fe, N.M. It embraces 55,468 square miles of northwestern New Mexico and northern half of the state of Arizona, including the Navajo and Hopi Reservations, with a 15 percent Catholic population. The diocese included a larger Native American population than any other diocese in the U.S.

History. The region, proclaimed "the new kingdom of St. Francis" in 1539 by the Franciscan friar Marcos de Niza, is the home of the Pueblo people of Acoma, Laguna, Zuñi, and other villages, the Jicarilla Apaches, located in New Mexico; the Whiteriver Apaches, the Havasupais, Hualapais, and Mohaves; the Pueblo people of the three Hopi Mesas in Arizona; and the Navajos whose reservation extends over 25,000 square miles in both New Mexico and Arizona. When the diocese was established in 1939 it had a population of about 50,000 Native Americans. There were 30,000 Catholics in 1939, including 23,000 Hispanic Americans, 6,000 Caucasian Americans and 1,000 Native Americans.

The first bishop, Bernard T. Espelage, O.F.M., of the Province of St. John the Baptist, Cincinnati, Ohio, was consecrated Oct. 9, 1940. He was succeeded by Jerome J. Hastrich, Auxiliary bishop of Madison, who was installed as second bishop on Dec. 3, 1969. The third bishop, Donald E. Pelotte, S.S.S, Ph.D., of the Congregation of the Blessed Sacrament of Cleveland, Ohio, and a Native American, was appointed coadjutor bishop of Gallup on Feb. 24, 1986, and succeeded to the see on March 20, 1990. The diocese's 56 parishes and 35 missions are served by 91 diocesan and religious priests, 26 permanent deacons, 13 religious brothers, and 139 religious sisters. The prominent Romanesque cathedral of the Sacred Heart is visible from all highways entering the city of Gallup.

Bibliography: O. FELLIN, *Yahweh, the Voice that Beautifies the Land: A Brief Historical View of the Diocese of Gallup, New Mexico* (Gallup, NM 1976).

[E. TROCKUR/A. ESPELAGE]

GALLUPPI, PASQUALE

Italian philosopher; b. Tropea, Calabria, April 2, 1770; d. Naples, Dec. 13, 1846. His fame as a philosopher went beyond the confines of the kingdom of Naples and Italy; he was known by E. B. de CONDILLAC, A. ROSMINI-SERBATI, V. COUSIN, and W. HAMILTON, among others. In 1831 he gained the professorial chair of logic and metaphysics at the University of Naples. The French Academy of Sciences named him "corresponding socius" and Louis Philippe granted him the Cross of the Legion of Honor.

For Galluppi, immediate consciousness of oneself is the first truth that necessarily serves as the first principle. The perception of myself, through its modifications, grasps what is outside of me. Upon this is focused the activity of the mind, which decomposes and then recomposes its elements "in analysis and synthesis, that is, in the faculties which isolate and decompose perceptions, and in that which unites and composes them" [*Saggio filosofico sulla critica della conoscenza,* SIX v. (Naples 1819–23) 1:2.10]. Judgment is distinct from feeling; analysis and synthesis are the basis for every universal judgment.

Along with KANT, he accepts a priori practical synthetic judgments as precepts without which it is "impossible to establish the morality of actions" [*Filosofia della volontà,* four v. (Naples 1832–40) 4:147]. He criticizes any form of EUDAEMONISM or Utilitarianism as a morality not based upon disinterested action, the sole guarantee of all public and private virtue. Virtue is not a means, but an aim: "the consciousness of having practiced it should be a pure pleasure distinct from, and independent of, the pleasure resulting from the reward" [*Elementi di filosofia,* six v. (Messina 1820–27) 5:37]. Nevertheless, Galluppi maintains that the useful can accompany duty, as long as the former is subordinated to the latter.

Bibliography: G. DI NAPOLI, *Enciclopedia filosofica* 2:576–581; *La filosofia di Pasquale Galluppi* (Padua 1947).

[M. F. SCIACCA]

GALTIER, PAUL

Theologian; b. Jouanesq (Aveyron), France, Feb. 9, 1872; d. Rome, Jan. 20, 1961. He entered the Jesuits in 1892 and was ordained in 1904. He taught dogmatic theology at Enghien, Belgium (1907–38), and at the Gregorian University, Rome (1939–57). Galtier contributed greatly to the understanding of the divine indwelling. In explaining this mystery he did not admit a special relation of the just to each person of the Trinity [*De SS. Trinitate in se et in nobis* (Paris 1953), *L'Habitation en nous des trois personnes* (Paris 1950), *Le Saint Esprit en nous d'après des Pères grecs* (Paris 1946)]. In Christology, the most original aspects of his doctrine are the conception of Christ the Redeemer as the end of creation, and the explanation (much disputed later) of the unity between the divine and human conscience of Christ by means of the beatific vision [*De incarnatione et redemptione* (Paris 1947), *Les deux Adam* (Paris 1947), *L'Unité du Christ: Être, personne, conscience* (Paris 1939)]. Galtier's research was especially esteemed in the history of Christian penance. He demonstrated in a very convincing manner that the Church of the Fathers reconciled sinners and attributed to this act a value analogous to that of Baptism, i.e., the remission of sins [*De paenitentia tractatus dogmatico-historicus* (Rome 1957), *L'Église et la rémission de péchés aux premiers siècles* (Paris 1932), *Aux Origines du sacrement de pénitence* (Rome 1951)].

Bibliography: G. JACQUEMET, *Catholicisme* 4:1742–43. *Liber annualis Pontificiae Universitatis Gregorianae* (Rome 1962) 103–107.

[Z. ALSZEGHY]

GALUPPI, BALDASSARE

Early classical composer of church music and opera; b. Burano Island, near Venice (hence his nickname Il Buranello), Oct. 18, 1706; d. Venice, Jan. 3, 1785. His father, a barber and theater orchestra violinist, provided his first music training. After Galuppi's first opera failed in 1722, Benedetto MARCELLO arranged for him to study composition with Antonio Lotti, and this resulted in a steady flow of commissions (112 operas in all). In 1748 he was named vice chapelmaster at St. Mark's, Venice, becoming first chapelmaster in 1762. He was invited to Russia by Catherine the Great, and he spent three years there (1765–68), composing and producing operas, teaching (Bortniansky was a pupil), and serving as the Czarina's adviser on music. By 1773 he had stopped composing operas in favor of oratorios (27) and church music. His sacred works (very few of which have been published) were projected in both an austere *A CAPPELLA* style and in a contemporary style like that of his operas, in which the solo parts are filled with elaborate coloratura passages and the role of the large orchestra is quite important. A gifted harpsichordist, Galuppi also wrote 51 keyboard sonatas, as well as a number of concerti.

Bibliography: No complete modern ed. of his music, but selected arias, sonatas, and Masses have been transcribed. A. DELLA CORTE, *Baldassare Galuppi* (Quaderni dell'Accademia Chigiana 18; Siena 1948). W. BOLLERT, *Die Musik in Geschichte und Gegenwart*, ed. F. BLUME (Kassel-Basel 1949–) 4:1342–48. E. BLOM, *Stepchildren of Music* (London 1925). *Baker's Biographical Dictionary of Musicians*, ed. N. SLONIMSKY (5th, rev. ed. New York 1958) 532–533. R. EITNER, *Quellen-Lexikon der Musiker und Musikgelehrten*, 10 v. [Leipzig 1900–04; New York n.d. (1947)] 4:138–141. JAMES L. JACKMAN, "Baldassare Galuppi" in *The New Grove Dictionary of Music and Musicians*, v. 7, ed. S. SADIE (New York 1980) 134–138. D. MONSON, "Baldassare Galuppi" in *International Dictionary of Opera*, 2 v., ed. C. S. LARUE (Detroit 1993) 483–486. M. T. MURARO and F. ROSSI, eds., *Galuppiana 1985: Studi e ricerche atti del Convego Internazionale (Venezia, 28–30 ottobre 1985)* (Florence 1986). N. SLONIMSKY, ed., *Baker's Biographical Dictionary of Musicians* (New York 1992) 596–597. R. WIESEND, *Studien zur opera seria von Baldassare Galuppi* (Tutzing 1981).

[R. STEINER]

GALVÁN BERMÚDEZ, DAVID, ST.

Martyr, priest; b. Jan. 29, 1881, Guadalajara, Jalisco, Mexico; d. there, Jan. 30, 1915. Entered Guadalajara's seminary at age 14, but he became disillusioned. A year later he returned a new man. Even before his ordination (1909) he taught at Guadalajara's seminary and continued thereafter. He was arrested, but later released, during the Carrancista revolution for being a priest. Because of his great love for the poor and for workers, he organized a workers union. Defender of the sanctity of marriage, he helped a young woman pursued by a married soldier by pretending to be her spouse. This act earned him the enmity of his executioner. He and Araiza were arrested as they ministered to wounded soldiers (Jan. 30, 1915) following a confrontation between Pancho Villa's supporters and the Carrancistas. Lieutenant Colonel Enrique Vera ordered them shot. Fr. Galván was both beatified (Nov. 22, 1992) and canonized (May 21, 2000) with Cristobal MAGALLANES [*see* GUADALAJARA (MEXICO), MARTYRS OF, SS.] by Pope John Paul II.

Feast: May 25 (Mexico).

Bibliography: J. CARDOSO, *Los mártires mexicanos* (Mexico City 1953). R. HARO LLAMAS, *El padre Galván: una vida sacerdotal en el marco histórico de su tiempo* (Guadalajara, Jalisco 1977).

[K. I. RABENSTEIN]

GALVÃO DE FRANÇA, ANTÔNIO DE SANT'ANA, BL.

Franciscan priest; founder; b. 1739, Guaratinguetá, São Paulo, Brazil; d. Dec. 23, 1822, São Paulo. Antonio's socially prominent, devout father encouraged his son's religious vocation by sending him to study at the Jesuit seminary of Belém (1752–56). Eventually, Antonio entered the novitiate of the Alcantarine Franciscans at Macacu near Rio de Janeiro (1760), professed his solemn vows (1761), and was ordained priest (1762). Upon completing his studies (1768), he was appointed porter at St. Francis Friary in São Paulo and engaged in priestly ministry. While serving as chaplain to the Recollects of St. Teresa (1769–70), Father Galvão met the mystic Sister Helena Maria Espirito Santo. With her he founded the convent of Our Lady of the Conception of the Divine Providence in 1774, a women's religious community that initially required no vows. Following Helena's death (1775), he continued to nurture the community—the *Recolhimento de Nossa Senhora da Luz* (Recollects of Our Lady of Light)—by writing its rule, ensuring the completion of its convent and church (dedicated in 1802), and guiding its incorporation into the Order of the Immaculate Conception (1929). In addition to this work, Galvão served as novice master in Macacu (1781), guardian of St. Francis Friary in São Paulo (1798, 1801), definitor (1802), visitator general, and chapter president (1808); he founded St. Clara Friary in Sorocaba (1811). Above all, he responded to his religious vocation by caring for the poor, sick, afflicted, and enslaved. In his declining years the priest lived at the Recolhimento da Luz, where his mortal remains are enshrined in its church. On March 8, 1997, he was declared venerable. He became the first native Brazilian *beatus* when he was beatified by Pope John Paul II on Oct. 25, 1998.

Feast: Oct. 25.

Bibliography: C. E. MARCONDES DE MOURA, *Os Galvao de França no povoamento de Santo Antonio de Guaratinguetá* (Sao Paulo 1993). V. WILLEKE, *Franciscanos na história do Brasil* (Petrópolis, Brazil 1977). *L'Osservatore Romano,* Eng. ed., no. 43 (1998): 3.

[K. I. RABENSTEIN]

GALVIN, EDWARD J.

Bishop, founder of the COLUMBAN FATHERS; b. Crookstown, County Cork, Ireland, Nov. 23, 1882; d. Navan, Ireland, Feb. 23, 1956. One of nine children of John and Mary (Lorden) Galvin, he entered St. Patrick's College, Maynooth, and was ordained in 1909. He went to Brooklyn, N.Y., where he was a curate in Holy Rosary parish for three years. When he learned of vast missionary opportunities in China, he volunteered his services there. After landing in Shanghai (April 1912) he worked with the French Vincentians. When French priests were ordered home to be drafted into the army upon the outbreak of World War I (1914), Galvin wrote to Ireland for volunteers. In 1915 two Irish priests joined him. In the following year he returned to Ireland seeking further recruits. The result was the foundation of St. Columban's Foreign Mission Society in 1916, with the approval of the Irish hierarchy and the blessing of Pope Benedict XV. The first house was opened at Delgan Park, Galway (January 1918). Recruits from the U.S. soon joined, and the first American house was started in Omaha, Nebr. (1918). When the Holy See assigned the Columban Fathers mission territory in Hanyang, Hupeh Province, China, 600 miles from the mouth of the Yangtze River, Galvin went there with two colleagues (1920). During 1920 they were joined by 15 more priests. Some Sisters of Loretto from the U.S. soon arrived to help. In Hanyang Galvin became prefect apostolic (1924), vicar apostolic (1927), and first head of the see when it became a diocese (1946). Hanyang was the scene of much misery because of the frequent air raids and the capture of the city by the Japanese in 1938. By 1949 Communists gained control of the area, and the bishop was left with six priests to care for the 50,000 Catholics of the diocese. After a house arrest lasting three years and frequent interrogations, Bishop Galvin was tried and was expelled from China (Sept. 15, 1952). He spent the following year visiting Columban houses in the U.S., and then he returned to Ireland, where he died of leukemia.

Bibliography: R. T. REILLY, *Christ's Exile: Life of Bishop Edward J. Galvin* (Dublin 1958). P. CROSBIE, *March Till They Die* (Westminster, Md. 1956). E. FISCHER, *Journeys Not Regretted: The Columban Fathers' Sixty-Five Years in the Far East* (New York 1986). J. MCCASLIN, *The Spirituality of Our Founders: A Study of the Early Columban Fathers* (1986).

[E. MCDERMOTT]

GAMALIEL

Name of six Palestinian rabbis of the early Christian centuries, all of them descendants of Hillel; the most important among these rabbis are the following.

Gamaliel I or the Elder, active in Jerusalem from *c.* A.D. 20 to *c.* 50. According to Josephus (*Life* 38.190–191), Gamaliel belonged to "a highly respected family"; there is no good reason to reject the early Jewish tradition that he was the grandson (or perhaps the son) of Rabbi Hillel. In any case, he was the leading Hillelite as well as the most highly esteemed PHARISEE of his time.

Since the early Tannaim (''repeaters''), such as Gamaliel the Elder, are usually cited anonymously in the TALMUD, relatively few sayings are ascribed to him expressly by name. But it seems that he took a special interest in social reform, particularly in bettering the legal status of women. This is the Gamaliel from whom St. Paul received his rabbinical education (Acts 22.3). He is also the one mentioned in Acts 5.34: when the Apostles were arrested and brought to trial before the Sanhedrin, ''a Pharisee named Gamaliel, a teacher of the law respected by all the people,'' counseled caution before condemning the Apostles; his speech at this trial (Acts 5.35–39) shows that he was skeptical of messianic movements. Because he seemed so well disposed toward the Apostles on this occasion, early Christian legends imagined that he himself later became a Christian (Pseudo-Clement, *Recog.* 1.65–67), even a saint martyred for Christ [*see* STEPHEN (PROTOMARTYR), ST.], and an apocryphal Gospel was attributed to him.

Gamaliel II, ben Simeon, known also as Gamaliel of Jabneh to distinguish him from his grandfather Gamaliel the Elder, was active toward the end of the 1st and perhaps the beginning of the 2d century. After the death of JOHANAN BEN ZAKKAI (*c.* A.D. 80), Gamaliel II succeeded him as president of the Sanhedrin at Jabneh. In his efforts to establish a uniform rabbinical law based on the teaching of the Pharisees, he settled all the disputes between the Hillelites and the Shammaites in favor of the former. He drew up the definitive form of the Shemone Esre (the ''Eighteen Blessings''), one of the oldest Jewish prayer formulas, to which he added the ''prayer against heretics,'' i.e., Judeo-Christians (*Ber.* 28b). Because of his harsh use of the ban (excommunication) against scholars who disagreed with him, he was temporarily deposed from the presidency of the Jabneh Sanhedrin.

Gamaliel III (3d century) was the eldest son and successor of JUDAH HA-NASI (grandson of Gamaliel II) as president of the Sanhedrin. During his term of office the final form was given to the MISHNAH of Juda Ha-Nasi.

Bibliography: D. J. BORNSTEIN, *Encyclopedia Judaica* 7:80–89. R. GORDIS, *Universal Jewish Encyclopedia* 4:506–508. W. BACHER, *Jewish Encyclopedia* 5:558–562. K. SCHUBERT, *Lexikon für Theologie und Kirche*, ed. J. HOFER and K. RAHNER, 10 v. (2d new ed. Freiburg 1957–65) 4:510. C. H. HUNZINGER, *Die Religion in Geschichte und Gegenwart*, 7 v. (3d ed. Tübingen 1957–65) 2:1197. G. F. MOORE, *Judaism in the First Centuries of the Christian Era: The Age of the Tannaim,* 3 v. (Cambridge, Mass. 1927–30).

[J. J. DOUGHERTY]

GAMBACORTA, PETER, BL.

Known also as Peter of Pisa, hermit, founder of the Poor Hermits of St. Jerome; b. Pisa, Feb. 16, 1355; d. Venice, June 17, 1435. Born of the ruling family of Pisa, he became a hermit in the wilderness near Urbino. When he was joined by other hermits he formed the congregation of the Poor Hermits of St. Jerome, at Montebello. The congregation was approved in 1421, and further foundations were made at Venice, Pesaro, and Treviso. Peter's zealous asceticism brought him before the Inquisition. He was beatified in 1693; an Office and Mass in his honor were approved in 1729. In 1933 Pius XI suppressed the Poor Hermits because of the smallness of the congregation.

Feast: June 17.

Bibliography: *Acta Sanctorum* June 4:436–451. *Bibliotheca hagiographica latina antiquae et mediae aetatis* 2:6710. A. POTTHAST, *Bibliotheca historica medii aevi* 2:1522. W. MARSCHALL, *Lexikon für Theologie und Kirche*[2] 8:376. For suppression of order, see *Acta Apostolicae Sedis* 25 (1933) 147–149.

[C. DAVIS]

GAMBIA, THE CATHOLIC CHURCH IN

The smallest nation on the African continent, the Republic of the Gambia is located on the northwest coast of Africa, extending west to east for 200 miles in a narrow strip along both banks of the Gambia River and surrounded by SENEGAL. The fertile floodplain region along the length of the river allows for the production of groundnuts and the raising of livestock, while fishing and tourism also contribute to the Gambian economy. Ethnically the Gambians are members of Mandingo, Fulani, Wolof, Dyola and Serahuli tribes, as are the surrounding Senegalese.

The mouth of the Gambia River was discovered by Portuguese traders traveling the Atlantic Ocean in the mid-15th century, although the river would not be traversed by Europeans until the British did so *c.* 1618. Granted to the British in the Treaty of Versailles in 1783 and incorporated into Sierra Leone, the Gambia provided a means of fighting the slave trade through its fort at Banjul (1816). It became a British colony in 1843, and a protectorate in 1893, in part because of tribal wars in nearby Senegal. Gambia became an independent member of the British Commonwealth on Feb. 18, 1965. Gaining its independence in 1970, it joined Senegal as the federation of Senegambia in 1982, but that association lasted only seven years. In July of 1994 President Dawda Kairaba Jawara was overthrown in a military coup led by Lieutenant Yahya Jammeh, but peace was quickly restored and in August of 1996 civilian elections were resumed under a new constitution.

Christianity was introduced into the region in the wake of the Portuguese explorers, although evangelization efforts did not meet with any real success until the early 19th century. By 2000 Catholicism remained a minority faith in Gambia, a country that had thus far remained immune to the religious and ethnic conflicts proliferating in that part of Africa. During a meeting in 2001, Pope John Paul II encouraged Gambia's new ambassador to the Vatican to ''make courageous decisions that will lead people along the road to peace,'' a reference to Gambian efforts to mediate the violence in nearby Senegal. The faithful in the country's 52 parishes were tended by 11 diocesan and 12 religious priests, while 13 brothers and 65 sisters aided in maintaining the Gambia's 41 primary and 11 secondary Catholic schools as well as hospitals, clinics, shelters and other humanitarian efforts. The government put no limits on religious instruction, which was made available in both public and private schools.

Capital: Banjul.
Size: 4,127 sq. miles.
Population: 1,367,120 in 2000.
Languages: English; Mandingo, Fulani and other languages are spoken in various regions.
Religions: 41,700 Catholics (3%), 1,298,950 Muslims (95%), 13,850 Protestants (1%), 12,620 follow indigenous religions or other faiths.
Ecclesiastical organization: Gambia was part of the Vicariate Apostolic of Senegambia in Senegal until 1931, when it became a mission sui juris. It was entrusted then, together with its 3,000 Catholics, to the Irish province of the Holy Ghost Fathers. In 1951 this mission became the Prefecture Apostolic of Bathurst, which in 1957 was made a diocese (Banjul) directly subject to the Holy See.

Bibliography: *Bilan du Monde,* 2v. (Tournai 1964) 2:401–402. *Annuario Pontificio*. For additional bibliography, *see* AFRICA.

[J. BOUCHAUD/EDS.]

GAMBLING

The staking of something of value, usually money, on some fact or the outcome of some event, the determination of which is due solely to chance or to contingency not predictable with certainty. The term is used here to include: (1) gaming, in which skill plays a part in determining the outcome; (2) wagering, in which the event or fact upon which the bet is laid is beyond the power of the wagering parties to affect; (3) lotteries, in which prizes are distributed by lot to some of those who have paid a premium for the chance of having their names or the numbers of their tickets drawn from a mass of names or tickets of other competitors. Gambling is a type of aleatory contract and as such is licit provided that there is a reasonable equality between the parties, that the transaction is conducted without fraud, and that the particular type of contract is not prohibited by law.

A person is entitled to dispose of his own property as he wills, so long as in doing so he does not render himself incapable of fulfilling duties incumbent upon him by reason of justice or charity. Gambling, therefore, though a luxury, is not considered sinful except when the indulgence in it is inconsistent with duty. Thus it can be sinful when a person has no right to risk the money he bets, either because it is not his own, or because he needs it for the support of his family or for the discharge of other obligations. It is sinful also when he knows the person with whom he bets ought not to risk his money. Moreover, since with some types of personality gambling readily becomes a compulsive activity, damaging to the individual and a disruptive influence in family and other social relationships, excessive indulgence is sinful, especially when it is marked by passionate infatuation.

Gambling may be sinful also on the part of one who cheats or engages in other dishonesty in the transaction, or who bets upon a certainty, unless the rules of a game, understood by all participants, make this permissible. Moreover, the gambling contract is unjust if there is no reasonable proportion between what is risked and what may possibly be gained. A disproportion, however, is admissible in state lotteries conducted for purposes of revenue, or in lotteries held to gather money for charity. In these cases the participants understand that only a portion of what is taken in will be returned to winners in the form of prizes, and they are presumed to consent to the arrangement.

Because gambling can become a major social evil, most societies have laws restricting, controlling, or prohibiting certain forms of it. Generally speaking, these laws appear to be just, and defiance of them on a large or professional scale seems incompatible with Christian morality.

Bibliography: D. M. PRÜMMER, *Manuale theologiae moralis*, ed. E. M. MÜNCH (Freiburg-Barcelona 1955) 2:267–271. H. DAVIS, *Moral and Pastoral Theology*, rev. and enl. ed. by L. W. GEDDES (New York 1958) 2:373–376. M. ZALBA, *Theologiae moralis summa* 3 v. (*Biblioteca de autores cristianos* 93, 106, 117; 2d ed. 1957). F. DESHAYES, *Dictionnaire de théologie catholique*, ed. A. VACANT et al. (Paris 1903–50) 1.1:695–703.

[F. O'HARE]

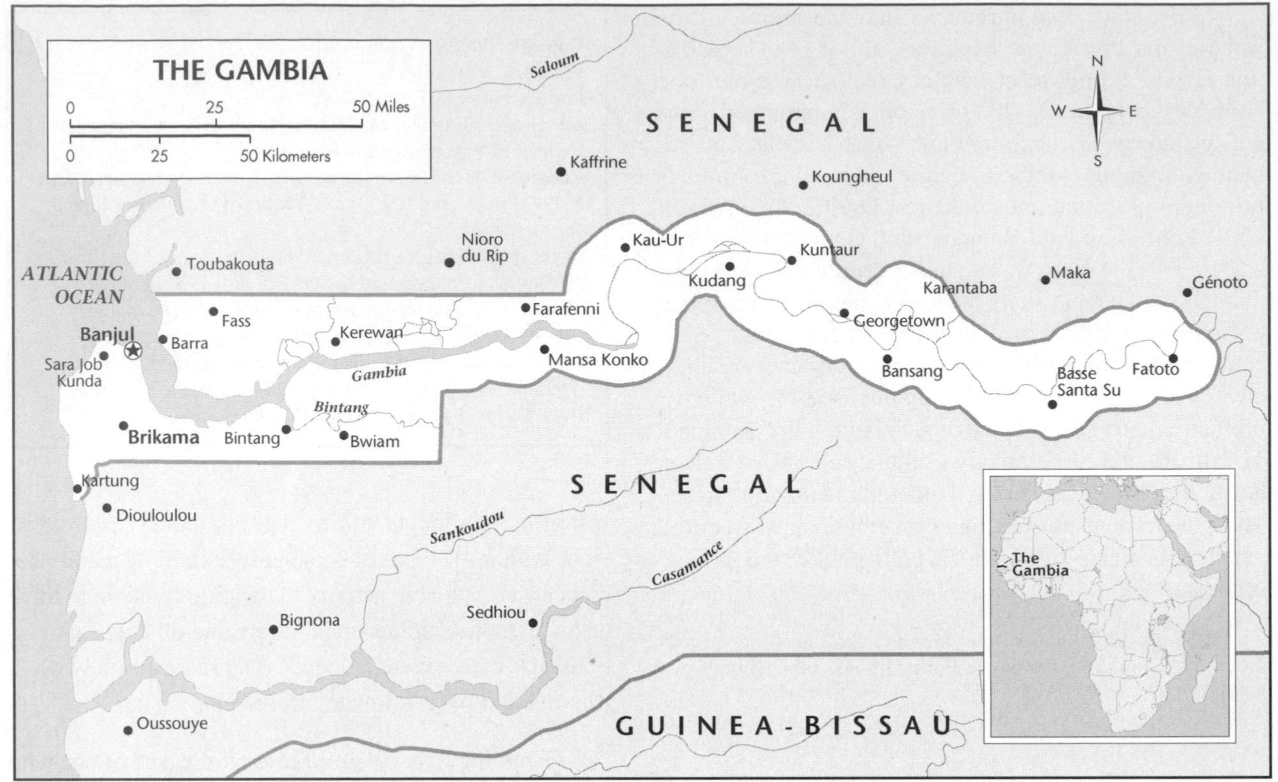

GAMS, PIUS

Church historian; b. Mittelbuch (Württemberg), Germany, Jan. 23, 1816; d. Munich, May 11, 1892. He studied in Tübingen (1834–38), was ordained in 1839, and became professor of history and theology at Hildesheim (1847–55). In 1855, he entered the Benedictine Abbey of St. Boniface in Munich. Four of the five volumes of his *Kirchengeschichte von Spanien* (1862–79; Graz 1959) deal with the period before 1492. At times the work becomes an ecclesiastical chronicle, but it includes many valuable studies of difficult problems. His gigantic *Series episcoporum* (1873; Leipzig 1931; Graz 1957), brought up to date in two supplements (1879, 1886), lists all bishops known in the history of the Church.

Bibliography: F. LAUCHERT, *Studien und Mitteilungen zur Geschichte des Benediktiner-Ordens* 27 (1906) 634–649; 28 (1907) 53–71, 299–315. B. HEURTEBIZE, *Dictionnaire de théology catholique*, ed. A. VACANT et al. 15 v. (Paris 1903–50) 6.1:1141–42. H. LANG, *Lexikon für Theologie und Kirche,* ed. J. HÖFER AND K. RAHNER, 10 v. (1957–) 4:511.

[E. P. COLBERT]

GANDERSHEIM, CONVENT OF

A former BENEDICTINE establishment in the Diocese of Hildesheim located in the town of Bad Gandersheim, Lower Saxony, Germany. It was founded in Brunshausen in 852 as a free imperial abbey of canonesses by Margrave Liudolf of Saxony (d. 866), ancestor of the Ottonian dynasty, and was moved to Gandersheim in 856. Three daughters of Liudolf ruled their family's foundation: Hathumod (d. 874), Gerberga (d. 896), and Christina (d. 919). Under Abbess Gerberga II (959–1001), daughter of Duke Henry I of Bavaria, the abbey school achieved great fame through the poetic works of ROSWITHA. In her *Primordia coenobii Gandeshemensis*, the important donations of Bishop Altfried of Hildesheim (852–874), which resulted in proprietary rights for the Diocese of Hildesheim, are passed over in silence. To break the ties with Hildesheim, OTTO III's sister, Sophie, abbess from 1002 to 1039, persuaded Archbishop WILLIGIS OF MAINZ to claim the abbey for his see on the basis of Fulda's ancient rights over Brunshausen and Gandersheim. After a struggle of more than seven years, Bishop BERNWARD OF HILDESHEIM saw his rights recognized by his metropolitan, Willigis, in 1007. However, Archbishop ARIBO renewed the claims against GODARD, Bernward's successor, in 1023, and a final settlement was not reached until 1028. Emperor HENRY II added a county to the possessions of the wealthy abbey in 1021, and the Salic emperors continued to entrust the convent, together with other Saxon abbeys, to an imperial princess because of its political importance. A Low-German adaptation of an early 12th-century Latin chronicle, made by Eberhard, deacon of Gandersheim (*c.* 1216), reflects the abbey's century-long struggle for independence from the bishop. Pope INNOCENT III's privilege finally brought Gandersheim exemption from Hildesheim in 1208. The free imperial abbey became a Protestant convent in 1589 and was dissolved in 1810.

Bibliography: L. H. COTTINEAU, *Répertoire topo-bibliographique des abbayes et prieurés* 1:1250. L. WOLFF, *Die deutsche Literatur des Mittelalters* 1:470–474. W. WATTENBACH, *Deutschlands Geschichtsquellen im Mittelalter* 1:37–38, 61–62. H. GOETTING, ''Die Gandersheimer Originalsupplik an Papst Paschalis II. als Quelle für eine unbekannte Legation Hildebrands nach Sachsen,'' *Niedersächs. Jahrbuch* 21 (1949) 93–122; ''Zur Kritik der älteren Gründungsurkunde des Reichsstifts Gandersheim,'' *Mitteilungen des Österreich. Staatsarchivs* 3 (1950) 362–403. O. PERST, ''Die Kaisertochter Sophie, Äbtissin von Gandersheim und Essen, 975–1039,'' *Braunschweig. Jahrbuch* 38 (1957) 5–46. H. ENGFER, *Lexikon für Theologie und Kirche* 2 4:511–512.

[A. A. SCHACHER]

GANDHI, MOHANDAS KARAMCHAND

The greatest and most widely admired of 20th-century Indian leaders; b. Porbandar, Kathiawad, Oct. 2, 1869; assassinated, New Delhi, Jan. 30, 1948. Gandhi came from a well-to-do Hindu family and studied in India and England. He was admitted to the bar (1891) and practiced as a lawyer in South Africa (1893), where he became involved in the struggle of the South African Indians against the white rulers. He divided his time between India and South Africa (1896–1902), established *Indian Opinion* and Phoenix Farm (1904), contested through *satyāgraha* (civil disobedience) the policies of the South African government, and was jailed more than once between 1907 and 1913. On his return to India, Gandhi established the Sabarmati Ashram (1915) and was gradually drawn into the vortex of Indian politics—for example, he organized an all-India *hartal* (work stoppage) on April 6, 1919. He also edited the periodicals *Young India*, in English, and *Navajivan*, in Gujarati.

On gaining control of the Indian National Congress, Gandhi launched the noncooperation movement and inaugurated mass civil disobedience (December 1921). He suspended it (February 1922), but launched another satyāgraha, this time against the government salt monopoly, by marching to Dandi (1930). He signed a pact with the viceroy (1931) and attended the Round Table Conference at London. In 1933 he began *Harijan,* a weekly paper, and worked for civic integration of the untouchables. He launched limited individual satyāgraha (1940), gave the call for the ''Quit India'' movement (August 1942), and was imprisoned.

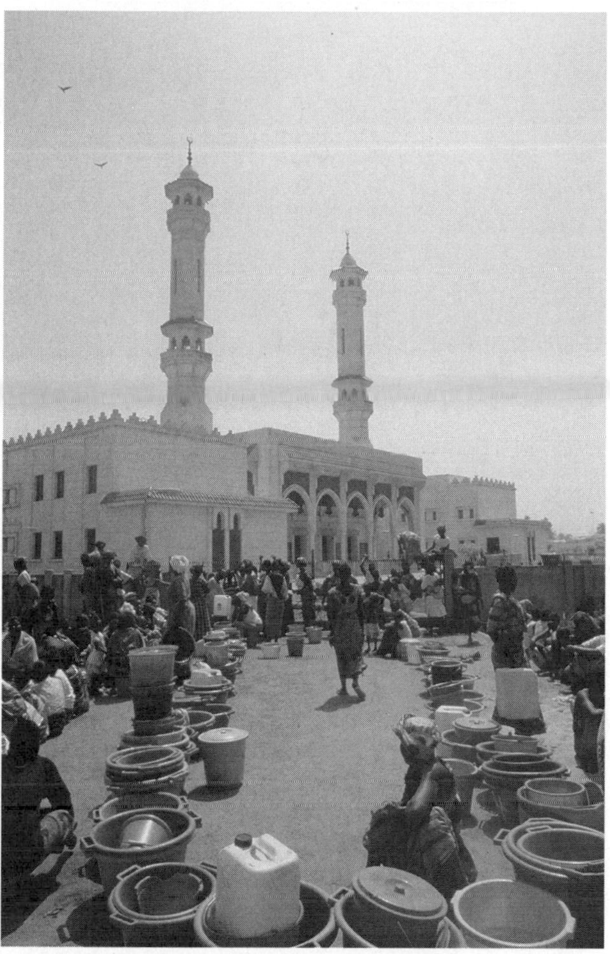

Central mosque, Banjul, Gambia. (©Nik Wheeler/CORBIS)

Gandhi's talks with Jinnah, the Muslim leader, ended in failure (1944), and he was deeply distressed by the Hindu-Muslim riots in 1946–47. While opposing the partition of India, he repeatedly fasted and prayed to avert communal frenzy. He was acclaimed ''Father of the Nation'' by free India, and acted as adviser to J. Nehru's government on crucial matters. He was assassinated while on his way to prayer. The title *Mahatma* (great-souled) was popularly accorded to him.

Gandhi wrote in Gujarati, his mother tongue, and in English. While his succinct *Hind Swaraj* (1909) became the *locus classicus* of the Gandhian philosophy of life and action, his *Autobiography* (1927) revealed to millions with complete fidelity the contours of his mind and the impulses of his heart. He was deeply influenced not only by the Hindu scriptures, but by the New Testament and the writings of THOREAU, RUSKIN, and TOLSTOI. His philosophy of action comprised *sarvōdaya* (happiness for all) to be achieved through *satyāgraha* (action based on fearlessness, truth, and the abjurement of violence). He pleaded for inner purification through celibacy or chasti-

Mohandas Karamchand Gandhi. (AP/Wide World Photos)

ty, dietetic regulation, fasting, silence and prayer, the adoption of a simple life, the ready acceptance of manual labor, and the voluntary rejection of material possessions. His asceticism and strength were reflected in his speech and writing; in Gandhi, the style was truly the man.

Bibliography: *Collected Works* (New Delhi 1958–94); *An Autobiography: The Story of My Experiments with Truth,* tr. M. DESAI (2d ed. Washington 1948); comp. and tr., *Songs from Prison* (New York 1934); *A Gandhi Reader: A Source Book of His Life and Writings,* ed. H. A. JACK (New York 1956). V. SHEEAN, *Lead, Kindly Light* (London 1950), biog.

[K. R. SRINIVASA IYENGAR]

GANDOLF OF BINASCO, BL.

Franciscan hermit; b. village of Binasco, near Milan, Italy, late 12th century; d. Polizzi Generosa, Sicily, *c.* 1260. He joined the FRANCISCANS during the lifetime of FRANCIS OF ASSISI, and his observance of the rule was so perfect that he advanced rapidly in holiness of life and the practice of virtue. His food was coarse, his dress rough; he spent long night vigils in prayer, and he severely disciplined his body. His quest for solitude took him from Palermo to a hermitage near the small town of Polizzi Generosa, where, even during his lifetime, his conspicuous sanctity, his inspired eloquence, and his reputation for miracles won him the enthusiastic veneration of the people of the town and surrounding countryside. He had great devotion to the Passion, as well as to the Blessed Mother, and as he lay dying, he embraced the crucifix, punctuating his sobs with the ejaculation ''Ave.'' A vita, in dialogue form, written not long after his death by James of Narni, bishop of Cefalù (d. 1324), was published in 1632 in the *Processus pro canonizatione,* and his cult was confirmed by Pope GREGORY XV in 1621.

Feast: April 3 (Franciscans).

Bibliography: *Acta Sanctorum* September 5:701–728. *Bibliotheca hagiographica latina antiquae ct mediae aetatis,* 2 v. (Brussels 1898–1901; suppl. 1911) 1:3261–64. O. BONMANN, *Lexikon für Theologie und Kirche,* ed. J. HOFER and K. RAHNER, 10 v. (2d, new ed. Freiburg 1957–65) 4:513. L. WADDING, *Scriptores Ordinis Minorum* (3d ed. Quaracchi-Florence 1931–) 4:165–170.

[T. C. CROWLEY]

GANGOLF, ST.

Historically, an uncertain figure: either the attorney and defender of the abbey of Beza in the Côte d'Or, France, d. 670; or the friend of St. CEOLFRID and of St. BEDE, d. 716; or—as is usually believed—a virtuous and valiant warrior, descendant of a noble family of Burgundy and friend of PEPIN III. He was murdered at the instigation of his unfaithful wife and is honored as a martyr of conjugal fidelity. The traditional place of his burial is Varennes–sur–Amance (Haute–Marne). His cult is popular in western and central Europe, e.g., at Florennes in Belgium. The account of his martyrdom, first written toward the end of the ninth century, was rewritten by ROSWITHA in the tenth century.

Feast: May 11; May 12 (Langres).

Bibliography: J. P. MIGNE, *Patrologiae latina,* 137:1083–94. *Acta Sanctorum,* May 2:643–652. *Monumenta Germaniae Historica: Scriptores rerum Merovingicarum,* 7.1:142–174. *Monumenta Germaniae Historica: Scriptores,* 15.2:791–796. E. MARTIN, *Histoire des diocèses de Toul, de Nancy et de S. Dié,* v.1 (Nancy 1900), *passim.* F. MAYER, ''Der heilige Gangolf,'' Freiburger *Diözesan–Archiv* 67 (1940) 90–139. P. VIARD, *Catholicisme* 4:1831–32.

[É. BROUETTE]

GANGRA

Gangra, the capital of the Roman province of Paphlagonia, today Cankiri, northeast of Ankara, Turkey. It probably had a bishop at the Council of NICAEA in 325, but the story of the stoning of Bishop Hypatius by the Novatians after his return from that council is not based on historical data [Roman martyrology Nov. 14, *Acta Sanctorum* dec. Propyl. 521–522, *Analecta Bollandiana* 51 (1933) 392–395]. Its first bishop was probably Eusebius, who presided at the Council of Gangra (J. D. Mansi *Sacrorum Conciliorum nova et amplissima collectio* 2:1095–1122). Although the date is uncertain, the council is the most important event of Gangra's Christian history. Sozomen (*Church History* 3.24 and 4.24) dated it before the synod of Antioch in 341. Twenty canons of the council described and condemned the exaggerated asceticism of EUSTATHIUS OF SEBASTE, who would have required all Christians to follow monastic discipline with regard to dress, marriage, and abstinence. He also ordered fasting on Sunday rather than according to the practice of the Church, and he claimed that rich or married people could not be saved. The 20 canons were sent to all Armenian bishops and were later included in GRATIAN'S *Decretum*. After the Turkish conquest of 1423, the metropolitan See of Gangra along with its five suffragan sees was suppressed. Its ancient cathedral of St. Demetrius has since been converted into a mosque.

Bibliography: C. J. VON HEFELE and H. LECLERCQ, *Histoire des conciles d'après les documents originaux* (Paris 1907–38) 1.2:1029–45. *Paulys Realenzyklopädie der klassischen Altertumswissenschaft*, ed. E. WISSOWA (Stuttgart 1893—) 7.1:707. G. BARDY, *Dictionnaire de droit canonique*, ed. R. NAZ (Paris 1935–65) 5:935–938. *Catholicisme* 4:1745–46. A. BIGELMAIR *Lexikon für Theologie und Kirche* ed. J. HOFER and K. RAHNER (Freiburg 1957–65) 4:514.

[J. VAN PAASSEN]

GANSFORT, JOHANNES WESSEL

Theologian, philosopher, humanist; b. Groningen, Netherlands, *c.* 1419; d. Groningen, Oct. 4, 1489. He was probably baptized Wessel, and later, when he was identified erroneously with Johannes Rucherath von Wesel, Johannes was added to his name. After studying under the direction of the BRETHREN OF THE COMMON LIFE, Gansfort taught at Zwolle from 1432 to 1449, and was deeply influenced by the DEVOTIO MODERNA. His desire for more learning led him to Cologne (1449), where he studied Greek, Hebrew, philosophy, and theology and familiarized himself with the works of Augustine, BERNARD OF CLAIRVAUX, and RUPERT OF DEUTZ. After a brief stay in Heidelberg, Gansfort went to Paris *c.* 1458, became involved in the nominalist controversy, and called into question the infallible teaching authority of the pope and of the ecumenical councils, the power of priestly absolution, the teachings on indulgences, purgatory, and the efficacy of the Sacraments. After a brief visit with Italian humanists *c.* 1470, Gansfort returned to Paris, and some five years later he departed for his native land. He has at times been called a precursor of the Reformation. Luther is even quoted as saying that his enemies might accuse him of having copied from Gansfort *(poterat . . . videri Lutherus omnia ex Wesselo hausisse)*. The writings of Gansfort, however, are occasional treatises, rather than a systematic presentation of a body of teachings, and can be open to several interpretations, as was noted by his contemporaries. To his friends he seemed the ''light of the world'' (*lux mundi*), while his enemies dismissed him as ''the master of contradictions'' (*magister contradictionum*). Enjoying the protection of David, Bishop of Utrecht, Gansfort spent the last years of his life in study and in the writing of several ascetical works, such as the *Scala meditatoria* and the *Exemplum scalae meditatoriae,* which gained for him as a layman an honored position among the teachers of the Devotio Moderna. His works were published for the first time by A. Hardenberg at Gröningen in 1614.

Bibliography: S. D. VAN BEEN, *Realencyklopädie für protestntische Theologie*, ed. J. J. HERZOG AND A. HAUCK, 24 v. (Leipzig 1896–1913) 21:131–147. L. CRISTIANI, *Dictionnaire de théologie catholique*, ed. A. VACANT et al. 15 v. (Paris 1903–50) 15.2:3531–36. M. GOOSENS, *De Katholieke Encyclopaedie,* ed. P. VAN DER MEER et al., 25 v. (2d ed. Amsterdam 1949–55) 11:263–264. P. DOYÈRE, *Catholicisme* 4: 1746. E. BARNIKOL, *Die Religion in Geschichte und Gegenwart,* 6 v. (Tübingen 1957–63) 2:1199–1200. A. FRANZEN, *Lexikon für Theologie und Kirche,* ed. J. HÖFER AND K. RAHNER (1957–) 5:1034–35.

[H. DRESSLER]

GANTE, PEDRO DE

Franciscan missionary, founder of the first school in Mexico; b. Ayghem-Saint-Pierre, Gante, Flanders, 1486; d. Mexico City, April 1572. He studied first with the Brothers of the Common Life (whose emphasis on broad humanistic principles probably strongly influenced his own pedagogical principles), and later studied also at the University of Louvain before he entered the Franciscans as a brother. He stammered, and this defect may have restrained him from becoming a priest. However, while his fellow friars claimed they could not understand him in either Spanish or Nahuatl, the indigenous people never had that difficulty. Hence Pedro often served as an interpreter and frequently, on Sundays when a priest was not available, preached to the natives in their own language. His special realm was that of teacher, and modern authors have called him the ''first teacher of the Americas.'' The revolutionary regime of modern Mexico, planning its program to teach the indigenous people to read and write, restudied Pedro's methods and applied them to modern circumstances.

Fray Pedro arrived in Veracruz, New Spain, Aug. 13, 1523, with the Franciscan friars Juan Dekkers and Juan

Van der Auwera. He established his Colegio de San José (called also Colegio de San Francisco) in Texcoco. Late in 1526 or early in 1527 it was transferred to a site next to the Convento de San Francisco in Mexico City. At the time it was customary to have a doctrinal school in each Franciscan friary in Mexico. This particular school was a school of doctrine, but from the beginning it was something much more for the 800 to 1,000 students it housed and fed. In the mornings the pupils were taught reading, writing, and singing. The afternoons were devoted to learning Christian doctrine and to rehearsals of the sermons, songs, or plays that selected young men would present on the following Sunday or feast day in a neighboring pueblo. Because of the shortage of priests, Pedro had selected about 50 of the students to act as catechists. Whenever he heard that the pagans were to have a festival, he prepared songs or a tableau on Christian themes, trained his students, and led the group to the fiesta to counteract pagan influences and to arouse interest in the Catholic faith.

By 1529 Pedro wrote that he had built more than 100 churches in the environs of Mexico City. To build, ornament, and staff them, he expanded his curriculum. Latin was added, as was instrumental music, to supply the chanters and musicians needed for Church services. Painting, sculpture, and embroidery were introduced to supply the vestments and images; and among other crafts, carpentry, iron working, leather working, and stonecutting were taught. By 1533 there were at least 13 courses being taught successfully to more than 1,000 natives. A hospital had been added in which natives could be trained in European medical practices while refining the use of their older medicinal herbs. The chapel these students built for their school—Capilla de San José de los Naturales—was for many decades the largest and best in Mexico. Even though it was the parish church of the natives, the Spaniards liked to use it for their greater festivals.

After the death of Archbishop Zumárraga, Pedro de Gante wrote in one of his letters that he was tempted to return to Europe to prepare for death. The affection of the native people drove away this idea, and he remained with them as their friend and protector. Archbishop Montúfar, Zumárraga's successor, once exclaimed: ''I am not the archbishop of Mexico; Fray Pedro de Gante is.'' He is buried in San Francisco church; his statue is in the monument to Columbus on the Paseo de la Reforma.

Bibliography: V. M. GRACIA, *Fray Pedro de Gante, primer maestro del continente iberoamericano* (Valencia 1989). P. R. VÁZQUEZ, *Fray Pedro de Gante: El primero y más grande maestro de la Nueva España* (Mexico 1995). J. C. CASTELLANOS, *El catecismo en pictogramas de fray Pedro de Gante: Estudio introductorio y desciframiento del Ms. Vit. 26-9 de la Biblioteca Nacional de Madrid* (Madrid 1987). R. C. CARVAJAL, *La obra educativa de Pedro de Gante en Tezcoco* (Tezcoco 1986). *Cartas, compiladas de diversas obras,* ed. F. DE J. CHAUVET (Mexico City 1951). E. A. CHAVEZ, *El ambiente geográfico, histórico y social de fray Pedro de Gante, hasta el año 1523* (Mexico City 1943); *El primero de los grandes educadores de la América, fray Pedro de Gante* (2d ed. Mexico City 1943).

[L. CAMPOS]

GAPP, JAKOB, BL.

Priest of the Society of Mary (SM); b. Wattens, Tyrol, western Austria, July 26, 1897; d. Plötzensee Prison, Berlin, Germany, Aug. 13, 1943.

Jakob Gapp, the seventh child of Martin Gapp and Antonia Wach, completed secondary school under the tutelage of the FRANCISCANS at Hall, Tyrol. During World War I Gapp served in the military on the Italian front; received the silver medal of Courage Second Class after being wounded in 1916; and was a prisoner of war at in the Italian Piedmont from Nov. 4, 1918 to Aug. 18, 1919.

After Gapp made his vows as a Marianist at Greisinghof, Upper Austria, he worked for four years in Graz. He entered the seminary at Fribourg, Switzerland, where he was ordained on April 5, 1930. His first eight years as a priest, Gapp worked as a primary school teacher, director of religious education, and chaplain in Marianist schools in Austria.

During the depression following World War I, he collected and distributed food and funds to those in need, and helped the unemployed to find jobs. He refused to heat his own room in winter in order to give his allotment of coal to poor families. This sense of justice led to his final demise.

Gapp came to recognize the incompatibility of National Socialism and Christianity after reading Nazi publications, particularly Alfred Rosenberg's *Myth of the Twentieth Century,* the statements of the Austrian bishops, and Pius XI's encyclical *Mit brennender Sorge.* He boldly denounced the ''abhorrent and totally irreconcilable'' ideology when German troops occupied Austria in March 1938. Because of his notoriety as an enemy of Nazism, in October 1938, the Gestapo forbade him to teach. Despite the ban, he continued to advise parishioners to ignore German propaganda and defended Pope Pius XI against Nazi slander in a sermon on Dec. 11, 1938. Advised to leave Austria, Gapp served as librarian and chaplain at the Marianist motherhouse in Bordeaux for several months before being reassigned to Spain (May 1939).

In Spain Gapp found himself isolated among the Marianists because his confrères could not understand his insistence that Catholics must vocally oppose injustice in all forms, particularly that of the Nazis. During his three years in Spain, Gapp was transferred to San Sebastián, Cádiz, Lequeitio, and finally Valencia.

In August 1942 Gapp received messages from two German agents posing as refugee Jews from Berlin in need of his help. They were living just across the border at Hendaye in southern France. When he drove over the border to meet them on November 9, Gapp was immediately arrested by the Gestapo. He was detained at several French prisons before being taken to Berlin. There he was tried before the infamous *Volksgerichtshof* and condemned to death on July 2, 1943 on the charge of high treason. The sentence specified that his remains were not to be returned to his family for burial because Gapp had "defended his conduct on expressly religious grounds. For a religious people Fr. Gapp would be considered a martyr for the faith, and his burial could be used by the Catholic population as an opportunity for a silent demonstration in support of an already judged traitor."

In the six hours between being informed of his execution and his decapitation by guillotine, Gapp wrote moving letters to his superior and his family. Gapp's body was sent to the Anatomical-Biological Institute of the University of Berlin on the grounds that it would be used for research. The only known relic is the ring Gapp received upon his religious profession, which is kept in the Marianist novitiate at Greisinghof, Austria. Gapp was respected even by his enemies. Himmler had remarked to Gapp's judge that Germany would easily win if there were more party members as committed to the cause as Gapp was to his Christian faith.

Gapp was beatified by Pope John Paul II on Nov. 24, 1996.

Feast: Aug. 13 (Society of Mary).

Bibliography: *Blessed Jakob Gapp, Marianist* (Dayton, Ohio 1999). *L'Osservatore Romano,* Eng. ed., no. 48 (1996). J. LEVIT, *Jakob Gapp: Zeuge seines Glaubens* (Innsbruck 1988). J. M. SALAVERRI, *Jakob Gapp Martyr de la Foi* (Saint-Augustin 1997).

[K. I. RABENSTEIN]

GARABITO, JUAN DE SANTIAGO Y LEÓN

Bishop of Guadalajara, Mexico; b. Palma, Andalucia, Spain, July 13, 1641; d. Guadalajara, July 11, 1694. He was a member of a distinguished Spanish family related to St. PETER OF ALCÁNTARA. He received a doctorate in theology from Salamanca and held various ecclesiastical offices, including positions as preacher to Charles II, preaching canon of the cathedral of Badajoz, visitor general of the diocese, and censor of the Holy Office. In 1676 he was named bishop of Puerto Rico and in the following year was nominated to the See of Guadalajara. He took possession of the diocese on Jan. 7, 1678, and was consecrated in Puebla on May 22. Garabito is considered one of the most distinguished bishops of Guadalajara. Although the diocese gave him a rich annual rent of 17,000 pesos, he set aside about two-thirds of it for the needy and lived in relative poverty himself. Zealous in his care for souls, he acquired a wide reputation for sanctity. He introduced the Oratorians into his diocese. He fostered devotion to the Blessed Virgin Mary, especially to the Virgin of Guadalupe and the Virgin of Zapopan. He insisted that all priests in the diocese be instructed in Nahuatl so that they could better serve the people.

Bibliography: J. I. P. DÁVILA GARIBI, *Apuntes para la historia de la iglesia en Guadalajara* (Mexico City 1957, 1961).

[E. J. GOODMAN]

GARAKONTHIE, DANIEL

Iroquois chieftain; b. *c.* 1600; d. Onondaga, N.Y., 1676. When he visited Montreal in 1654 as a member of a delegation of Native Americans seeking peace with the French, he remained there as one of the hostages left by the Iroquois as a pledge of their good faith. On his return to his home territory, Garakonthie became an ardent admirer of the French. In 1661 he met Simon le Moyne, SJ, and a close friendship developed between them. When Le Moyne returned to Canada, he was accompanied by Garakonthie and nine French captives whom the native American had rescued from hostile tribes. Garakonthie made frequent trips between Onondaga, the headquarters of the Iroquoian Confederacy, and Quebec, seeking to lessen tensions between the French and the Iroquois and urging that additional missionaries be sent. Although for many years he was sincerely interested in spreading the Gospel, it was not until 1670 that he was baptized and confirmed by Bp. François Laval in the Immaculate Conception Cathedral, Quebec. He took Daniel as his Christian name. Firm in his new faith, he desired to read the Scriptures, and before long, had learned both reading and writing. He was attended at his death in 1676 at Onondaga by Jacques de Lamberville, a Jesuit missionary.

[R. C. NEWBOLD]

GARAMPI, GIUSEPPE

Cardinal, archivist, diplomat; b. Rimini, Oct. 29, 1725; d. Rome, May 4, 1792. Garampi, born of a noble family and well educated, drew his passion for historical studies from Ludovico MURATORI. In Rome he belonged to the Academy of Church History founded by BENEDICT XIV, who employed him in the Papal Secret Archives in 1749 and appointed him prefect in 1751. CLEMENT XIII twice sent him to Germany. In 1761 there was talk of calling a peace conference in Augsburg. Awaiting it, Garampi studied and traveled until 1763. After careful observation he made a proposal that had some influence—namely, that in order to counteract anti-Church books, such as those of Febronius, Catholic theologians should themselves publish books. In 1764 he accompanied Niccolò Oddi, the nuncio, to Frankfurt for the election of Archduke Joseph as King of the Romans. Appointed nuncio to Warsaw by CLEMENT XIV in 1772, he arrived there just after the first partition of Poland and was faced with the difficulties that arose concerning the status of Catholic churches in the portions annexed by Prussia and Russia, and the dissolution of the Society of Jesus by CLEMENT XIV in 1773. He served also as nuncio to Vienna, and he was there during PIUS VI'S visit to Joseph II. He was created a cardinal in 1785, and was also bishop of Montefiascone and Corneto, as well as protector of the German College in Rome.

Wherever he was he pursued three objectives: the study of the history of the Church, the betterment of the state of religion and of scholarship, and the acquisition of manuscripts and books for his library. He left a library of 16,630 items, 4,225 of them theological and 7,812 historical subjects. A number of his studies and one diary have been published; others are among the Vatican manuscripts.

Bibliography: G. GARAMPI, *Viaggio in Germania, Baviera, Svizzera, Olanda e Francia . . .*, ed. D. G. PALMIERI (Rome 1889), journal. Pastor v.35–40, scattered statements and quotations from Garampi's official letters in v.38. F. CANCELLIERI, "Notizia sul Cardinale Giuseppe Garampi," *Memorie di Religione, di Morale e di Letteratura* 11 (Modena 1827) 385–442, written by a contemporary who knew Garampi, with 12 of his personal letters included. G. AMATI, *Bibliothecae Josephi Garampii Cardinalis Catalogus,* 5 v. (Rome 1796) 1:3–14, biog. sketch. J. WODKA, *Lexikon für Theologie und Kirche,* ed. J. HÖFER AND K. RAHNER (1957–) 4:515.

[M. L. SHAY]

GÁRATE, FRANCISCO, BL.

Jesuit brother, affectionately called "Brother Courtesy"; b. Feb. 3, 1857, Azpeitia (near Loyola Castle), Spain; d. Sept. 9, 1929, Bilbao. Francisco Gárate, the second of seven siblings, was raised in a devout farming family in which three sons became JESUITS. He entered domestic service (1871) as a house servant at the new Jesuit College of Nuestra Señora de la Antigua at Orduña. Because the Jesuits had been expelled from Spain (1868), Francisco sought entrance into the Society of Jesus (1874) at the novitiate in Poyanne in southern France. After professing his initial vows in 1876 and spending another another year in Poyanne, he was assigned as infirmarian and sacristan (1877–87) at the College of Santiago Apostolo in La Guardia, Pontevedra in western Spain, where he was known for his extreme kindness. He professed his final vows in August of 1887. In March of 1888, he was transferred to Bilbao in northern Spain because his service in the infirmary was affecting his health. For the next 41 years, Brother Francisco was doorkeeper at the Jesuit university in Duesto Bilbao. There he became renowned for the evangelizing power of his humble, joyful service to all he encountered. Pope John Paul II beatified Francisco on Oct. 6, 1985 for his Christian perfection in the way of humble service.

Feast: Sept. 10 (Jesuits).

Bibliography: J. ITURRIOZ, *H. Francisco Garate, S.I.: "Portero" de Deusto* (Bilbao 1985). J. A. DE SOBRINO, *Tres que dijeron 'si'* (Madrid 1985). *Acta Apostolicae Sedis* 79 (1987): 7–10. J. N. TYLENDA, *Jesuit Saints and Martyrs* (Chicago 1998) 297–9. *L'Osservatore Romano,* Eng. ed., no. 42 (1985): 6–7.

[K. I. RABENSTEIN]

GARCÉS, FRANCISCO TOMÁS HERMENEGILDO

Franciscan missionary and martyr; b. Morata del Conde, Spain, April 12, 1738; d. on the banks of the Colorado River, July 19, 1781. As a child he was taught by an uncle who was a priest. In 1753 he entered the Franciscan province of Aragon. Upon his ordination in 1763, he asked for mission work and was sent to the Missionary College of Santa Cruz de Querétaro the same year. In 1767 he was assigned to the missions in Sonora and went with other friars to Tepique to await transportation. After months of delay there followed by a stormy voyage, he arrived at San Xavier del Bac (near modern Tucson, Arizona) on June 30, 1768. He went on four *entradas*: to the Gila River in 1768 and again in 1770; to the Gila and the Colorado in 1771; and over the same territory and on to the Mission of San Gabriel in California in 1774. He did missionary work among the Pápagos, Pimas, Yumas, and Apaches. His missionary travels took him many miles—in one 11-month period he covered about 3,600 miles through hostile territory. In August 1779, when the rebellion broke out among the Yuma people, he returned to the Pueblo de la Concepción on the Colorado River to try to pacify them. There he was martyred by the Yuma. He wrote *Diario y Derrotero,* dated 1777, which has been translated into English.

Bibliography: E. COUES, ed., *On the Trail of a Spanish Pioneer: The Diary and Itinerary of Francisco Garcés,* 2 v. (New York 1900)

[E. DEL HOYO]

GARCÉS, JULIÁN

First bishop of Tlaxcala, Mexico; b. Munébrega, Aragón, Spain, 1447; d. Puebla, 1542. He was born of a noble family, was educated by a tutor and later at the Sorbonne, and then entered the Dominican convent of San Pedro Mártir in Calatayud. His erudition and fame as a preacher led to a call to the court of Charles V as royal chaplain and confessor to Bp. Rodríguez de Fonseca. The See of Cozumel (later named Yucatán) was established in 1518, and Rodríguez de Fonseca recommended his confessor as bishop. Since there were neither Spaniards nor churches in that diocese, a new see was established at Tlaxcala in 1526, and Garcés was named bishop by Charles V. Early in 1527 he embarked for New Spain. The King conferred on Garcés the title of Protector of the Indians, and ordinances of the Council of the Indies gave him powers necessary to enforce penalties against violators. The fact that the *audiencia* was persecuting the native Mexicans (between 1528 and 1531) at the same time it was supposed to aid the bishop complicated his work. However, Garcés' exemplary life and zeal resulted in numerous conversions. He wrote Charles V that he baptized no fewer than 300 native Mexicans each week. His championship of native rights won him the enmity of the *encomenderos,* but ultimately he was successful. His strong letter to the Pope favoring the indigenous peoples is believed responsible for Paul III's bull (1537) declaring them to be truly men with all the rights of men. He was buried in the cathedral of Puebla, where the see was transferred in 1539.

Bibliography: M. CUEVAS, *Historia de la Iglesia en México,* 5 v. (5th ed. Mexico City 1946–47). W. E. SHIELS, *King and Church: The Rise and Fall of the Patronato Real* (Chicago 1961).

[E. J. GOODMAN]

GARCIA DIEGO Y MORENO, FRANCISCO

First bishop of the Californias; b. Lagos, Jalisco, Mexico, Sept. 17, 1785; d. Santa Barbara, Calif., April 30, 1846. He was the son of Francisco Diego and Ana Maria Moreno. After completing his studies at St. Joseph's Conciliar Seminary, Guadalajara, Mexico, he entered the Franciscan Order, taking his vows on Dec. 21, 1802. He then attended the Franciscan College of Our Lady of Guadalupe, Zacatecas, Mexico, and he was ordained on Nov. 14, 1808. In addition to doing missionary preaching and to writing a handbook for mission priests, *Metodo de misionas,* he held various posts at the Franciscan College, including those of prefect (1822–25) and vicar (1832). When the Mexican government decided to replace Spanish missionaries in California with native Mexicans, García Diego and ten friars from Zacatecas were sent to take charge of the missions of Upper California. The Zacatecans, with García Diego as prefect, arrived Jan. 15, 1833 and established their headquarters at Mission Santa Clara. They were preparing to take over eight missions north of Monterey, Calif., when the Mexican congress, on Aug. 17, 1833, enacted a bill converting the mission churches into parishes under secular clergy. Opposing this secularization of the missions, García Diego traveled to Mexico City, where he persuaded the government to suspend secularization until diocesan organization could be obtained. On April 27, 1840, Gregory XVI separated Upper and Lower California from the Diocese of Sonora, establishing them as a single suffragan diocese with San Diego, Calif., as the see city. Consecrated as first bishop of the new diocese on Oct. 4, 1840, García Diego hoped to secure financial assistance from the PIOUS FUND, but this was not forthcoming and the promise of financial support induced the bishop to move to Santa Barbara. García Diego was unable to check the steady decay that confronted his diocese, although he did succeed in founding a seminary at Santa Ines on May 4, 1844, and in ordaining his first three priests on Jan. 1, 1846, shortly before his death and the American conquest of California.

Bibliography: F. J. WEBER, *A Biographical Sketch of Right Reverend Francisco García Diego y Moreno* (Los Angeles 1961). Z. ENGELHARDT, *The Missions and Missionaries of California,* 4 v. (San Francisco 1908–15). A. R. BANDINI, ''A Bishop Comes to California,'' *American Ecclesiastical Review* 103 (1940) 253–267.

[M. J. GUILFOYLE]

GARCÍA OF TOLEDO

Pseudonym of the author of the antipapal tract *De reliquiis preciosorum martirum Albini et Rufini* (generally recognized after 1076 as *Silver and Gold*). In the tract, García in 1099 happens to accompany Archbishop Grimoardus (actually Bernard) of Toledo, who hopes to be confirmed as legate for Aquitaine after offering ''relics'' to the Roman Curia. URBAN II and the cardinals received Grimoardus during a drinking feast and, impressed by his prowess as a drinker, granted his request. Throughout the tract the author parodies the words of the Bible and the liturgy in rude but witty satire, using homiletic and dramatic techniques with skill. Much of the work is modeled after classical Latin comedy. Although García calls himself a canon of Toledo in the title, the Pope addresses him in the tract as ''brother,'' i.e., bishop.

Bibliography: *Libelli de lite* 2:423–435. *Geschichte der lateinischen Literatur des Mittelalters* 3:46.

[E. P. COLBERT]

GARCIA VILLADA, ZACARIAS

Historian; b. Gatón de Campos (Valladolid), March 16, 1879; shot and killed by Leftist militia in Vicálvaro, near Madrid, Oct. 1, 1936. As a Jesuit after 1894, he studied at Rome, Innsbruck, and Vienna. He taught historical method (*Methodología,* 1912) in Barcelona, continued Lowe-Hartel's *Bibliotheca patrum latinorum Hispaniensis* (1913), edited the *Chronicle of Alfonso III* (1918), and published a catalogue of the codices and documents of the cathedral of Léon (1919) and a textbook of Spanish paleography (1925). His small volumes on Cisneros (1920), Covadonga (1922), St. ISIDORE THE FARMER (1922), and the Battle of Pavia (1925), have more value than their popular format indicates. His main work, *Historia eclesiástica de España,* 3 v. in 5, (1929–36), represents his many years of study. It was interrupted in May 1931, when material he had been collecting since 1902, much not available in Spain, was destroyed in the burning of the Jesuit Instituto Católico in Madrid, where he resided. He published lectures on the life of Spanish medieval writers (1926), and (upon his entry into the Real Academia de la Historia in Madrid in 1935) on the organization of the Church in Spain from 711 to 1085. In *El destino de España en la historia universal* (1936), he rejects atheistic materialism in favor of divine providence, showing that when Spain was great, she traditionally associated herself with Catholicism.

Bibliography: *Razón y Fe* 8–103 (1904–33), *passim.*

[E. P. COLBERT]

GARCÍA XEREZ, NICOLÁS

Bishop of Nicaragua; b. Murcia, Spain, 1746; d. Guatemala, July 31, 1825. He entered the Dominican monastery in his native city, where he studied and graduated as master of sacred theology. He then went to the Indies as a missionary. There he was elected prior of the monastery in Cartagena. One author says that before he came to America he had renounced the archbishoprics of Zaragoza and Valencia. This is not very probable for he accepted the bishopric of Nicaragua in 1807 and took possession in 1810. His see city of León disavowed the governor intendant of Nicaragua Don José Salvador when the revolutionary movement in New Granada asked that all Spaniards be deprived of office. Although García Xerez was a Spaniard, he was accepted by the people as magistrate until 1814. García Xerez could do no less than join in proclaiming the independence of Nicaragua from the Spanish crown. However, he took a very moderate position, which was interpreted by Liberal authors as ambiguous. He calmed impulsive men and warded off riots and excesses; he brought under his influence the committee presided over by Miguel González Saravia. He inspired the proclamation of Oct. 11, 1821, known as the Acta de los Nublados, which declared that Nicaragua freed itself not only from Spain but from every other nation. Saravia altered his stand at the end of 1821 and supported annexation with Mexico. This started a fight between the inhabitants of New Granada, who were unwilling, and the people of León, who because of their leader were ready to compromise. In the political-religious confusion stirred up in Nicaragua in 1824, García Xerez was banished to Guatemala, and he died there in the Dominican monastery. His remains were brought back to Nicaragua on Sept. 12, 1854, and rest in the cathedral of León.

García Xerez had finished the towers and façade of the monumental cathedral and rebuilt the church and monastery of La Merced; he built a bridge of stone and mortar, which joined the city of León with its suburb of Guadalupe.

Bibliography: V. SANABRIA MARTÍNEZ, *Episcopologio de la diócesis de Nicaragua y Costa Rica* (San José 1943). F. ORTEGA, *Nicaragua en los primeros años de su emancipación política* (Paris 1894). A. AGUILAR, *Reseña histórica de la diócesis de Nicaragua* (León 1927).

[L. LAMADRID]

GARDEIL, AMBROISE

Dominican theologian; b. Nancy, March 29, 1859; d. Paris, Oct. 2, 1931. Gardeil joined the Dominican Province of France in 1878 while it was in exile. He began his long teaching career on the Gold Coast in 1884; his lifelong specialty was theological methodology. In 1893 he assisted Father Coconnier in founding the *Revue Thomiste,* and became provincial regent of studies. Meanwhile, he continued to instruct young Dominicans, eventually covering the whole of the *Summa Theologiae* twice in class. Although he was probably his order's best theologian at the time, Gardeil gave up teaching in 1911 to have more time for writing and preaching. Apart from his many articles in the *Dictionnaire de théologie catholique,* the *Revue Thomiste,* etc., he is best known for his trilogy: *La Crédibilité et l'apologétique* (1908), *Le Donné révélé et la théologie* (1910), and *La Structure de l'âme et l'expérience mystique* (1926).

Bibliography: H. D. GARDEIL, *L'Oeuvre théologique du Père Ambroise Gardeil* (Paris 1956). R. GARRIGOU-LAGRANGE, ''Le Père A. Gardeil,'' *Revue thomiste* 36 (1931) 797–808.

[P. CANGELOSI]

GARDINER, GERMAN, BL.

Layman, last martyr under Henry VIII; d. Tyburn (London), England, March 7, 1544. The Cambridge educated German was secretary to Bp. Stephen Gardiner of Winchester and an able apologist. He wrote a tract against John Frith (Aug. 1, 1534) after which little is heard of his career. He was inspired by the English martyrs who preceded him, especially St. Thomas More. When Henry VIII waivered in his Protestant convictions, Cranmer fell under suspicion and Gardiner was employed to draw up a list of his errors in faith. The king's whim then turned on Gardiner, who was indicted for endeavoring ''to deprive the king of his dignity, title, and name of Supreme Head of the English and Irish Church.'' He was beatified by Pope Leo XIII.

Feast of the English Martyrs: May 4 (England).

See Also: MARTYRS OF ENGLAND AND WALES.

Bibliography: B. CAMM, ed., *Lives of the English Martyrs,* (New York 1904), I, 543–47. R. CHALLONER, *Memoirs of Missionary Priests,* ed. J. H. POLLEN (rev. ed. London 1924; repr. Farnborough 1969). J. H. POLLEN, *Acts of English Martyrs* (London 1891).

[K. I. RABENSTEIN]

GARDINER, HAROLD CHARLES

Editor, journalist, author; b. Washington, D.C., Feb. 6, 1904; d. Denver, Colorado, Sept. 3, 1969, the son of Ignatius and Lillian (Bechtel) Gardiner. He graduated from Gonzaga High School, Washington, D.C., and entered the Society of Jesus on Aug. 14, 1922, at St. Andrew-on-Hudson, Poughkeepsie, New York. He subsequently spent two periods of philosophical (1926–29) and theological (1932–36) study at Woodstock College, Maryland, in the course of which he earned his A.B., M.A., and S.T.L. degrees. In between (1929–31), he taught Latin, Greek, and English literature at Canisius College in Buffalo.

Gardiner was ordained to the priesthood on June 21, 1945. After a year (1936–37) of study in ascetical theology at Tronchiennes, Belgium, he began graduate studies in English literature at Cambridge University, and received his Ph.D. in 1941. In the summer of 1940 he joined the editorial staff of *America,* the Jesuit-edited national Catholic weekly review, in New York City. He served as literary editor of *America* from 1940 to May 1962, when he took a leave of absence to become a staff editor, with responsibility for all materials dealing with literature, of the 15-volume *New Catholic Encyclopedia,* then in preparation in Washington, D.C. After completing this task in 1966, he took on the editorship of Corpus Books until his death. In addition to his work as an editor and author, Gardiner lectured widely before university audiences and on radio and television. From 1948 to 1962, he was chairman of the editorial board of the Catholic Book Club. He also served frequently as a consultant to publishers and film directors.

Gardiner promoted literary excellence among Catholic authors and pioneered the formulation of a new understanding among Catholics of the relation between morality and literature, art and the censor. His books include: *Mysteries' End* (1945), *The Great Books* (ed. 4 v., 1947–53), *Fifty Years of the American Novel* (ed., 1951), *Norms for the Novel* (1953), *Imitation of Christ* (tr. and ed., 1955), *Edmund Campion* (1957), *Catholic Viewpoint on Censorship* (1958), *American Classics Reconsidered* (ed., 1958), *In All Conscience* (1959), *Movies, Morals and Art* (jt. auth., 1961).

[D. R. CAMPION]

GARDINER, STEPHEN

Bishop of Winchester and lord chancellor of England; b. Bury-St.-Edmund's, West Suffolk, England, between 1483 and 1493; d. Whitehall, London, Nov. 12, 1555. He was educated in canon and civil law at Trinity Hall, Cambridge, where he later became master. From Cambridge he passed into Cardinal Thomas WOLSEY'S household and in 1528 was sent to the papal court on an embassy (concerning HENRY VIII'S divorce) with which he made his mark. He survived Wolsey's fall, became the King's secretary, and in November 1531 became bishop of Winchester. In the spring of the next year he temporarily lost favor by upholding the cause of the clergy against the combined attack of Commons and King, but he was soon back in royal service, being present the next year at the court in which Thomas CRANMER, Archbishop of Canterbury, declared Henry's marriage to Catherine null.

Despite some hesitation, which cost him the secretaryship in 1534, Gardiner became an enthusiast not only for the divorce but also for Henrician caesaropapism. It was such bishops as he who made Henry's theological revolution so easy, and his *De vera obedientia* (1535) was an important piece of propaganda for the Royal Supremacy. From then onward, though a keen rival of Cromwell, he served Henry unquestioningly, above all as a diplomat, without, however, acquiring high office, probably because he was a bishop.

Gardiner was a typical Henrician, convinced that the King was, by God's law, his spiritual and temporal overlord, to whom he owed all obedience; but otherwise he was theologically conservative. He was one of those behind the swing back to orthodoxy in 1539, and he took a leading part in the unsuccessful attempt to unseat Cranmer with a charge of heresy in 1543. For the rest of Henry's reign he was a major figure in the conservative party and was keenly engaged in the jockeying for power that filled the last months of Henry's reign. Shortly before Henry died, Gardiner had been worsted, and the new reign finally brought him down. Gardiner opposed the Protestant reforms of Cranmer (particularly his *Book of Homilies*) and was promptly imprisoned. He was released in early 1548 but was arrested again a few months later and sent to the Tower. He had then taken a firm stand on behalf of the Real Presence and the Mass against the reformers. Not till late 1550 was he brought to trial, then, being found guilty of opposing "godly reformations of abuses in religion," he was deprived of his bishopric. Had Edward VI lived, Gardiner might have ended his days in the Tower. But in 1553 MARY TUDOR came to the throne, and he was released, restored to his see, and created lord chancellor. Despite his past, he was the sort of man upon whom Mary had to rely to carry out the restoration of Catholicism. Whether he had any real grasp of the size or nature of the problem confronting him and his fellow bishops, whether he had become more than the ecclesiastical politician of old is not easy to say. But he gave Mary good advice when he boldly opposed the Spanish marriage and, though his hand was behind the restoration of the heresy laws, he was not particularly active as a persecutor, even trying to soften the blows against Cranmer and John Dudley, Duke of Northumberland. Furthermore, his own conversion seems to have been sincere. The former Henrician and trimmer seems to have declared his true self when in 1554 he made his peace with Rome. Late the next year he died at Whitehall with the following words on his lips: "I have denied with Peter, I have gone out with Peter, but I have not wept with Peter"; we may accept this as his epitaph.

Bibliography: S. GARDINER, *Obedience in Church and State,* ed. and tr. P. JANELLE (Cambridge, Eng. 1930); *Letters,* ed. J. A. MULLER (New York 1933). J. A. MULLER, *Stephen Gardiner and the Tudor Reaction* (New York 1926). H. M. SMITH, *Henry VIII and the Reformation* (New York 1962). L. B. SMITH, *Tudor Prelates and Politics, 1536–1558* (Princeton 1953). P. HUGHES, *The Reformation in England* (New York 1963) v.2. H. O. EVENETT, *Lexikon für Theologie und Kirche,* ed. J. HOFER and K. RAHNER, 10 v. (2d, new ed. Freiburg 1957–65) 4:518. A. GATARD, *Dictionnaire de théologie catholique,* ed. A. VACANT, 15 v. (Paris 1903–50; Tables générales 1951–) 6.1:1156–58. J. B. MULLINGER, *The Dictionary of National Biography from the Earliest Times to 1900,* 63 v. (London 1885–1900) 7:859–865.

[J. J. SCARISBRICK]

GARESCHÉ, EDWARD FRANCIS

Author and mission-aid organizer; b. St. Louis, Missouri, Dec. 27, 1876; d. Framingham, Mass., Oct. 2, 1960. He was a member of one of the old Catholic families of St. Louis, was a graduate of St. Louis University (1896), and received a law degree from Washington University in St. Louis (1898). After practicing law for two years, he entered the Society of Jesus at Florissant, Missouri, on Sept. 7, 1900 and was ordained on June 27, 1912. Garesché's first assignment was a summer's work on the staff of the Jesuit weekly *America.* He was then assigned in 1913 to intensify the promotion of the Sodality of Our Lady on a national scale. In 1914 he founded the Sodality publication *The Queen's Work,* and before he left the promotion work in 1922 the magazine had a circulation of 160,000. Daniel A. LORD, SJ, succeeded him as promoter; *The Queen's Work* ceased publication in June 1964.

After leaving the Sodality, Garesché became associated with the Catholic Hospital Association. In 1927 he was engaged by the Catholic Medical Mission Board, of which he was director from 1929 until his death. In 1928 he founded the International Catholic Guild of Nurses, with himself as permanent spiritual director, a position that caused considerable controversy in 1936. In 1935 Garesché founded a congregation of mission sisters, the Daughters of Mary Health of the Sick, and after much opposition he founded a companion community of brothers, SONS OF MARY HEALTH OF THE SICK, at Framingham, Mass., in 1952. After this foundation he spent half of his time with the brothers and half in New York City. Although he remained a member of the Jesuit Missouri province, many found his status anomalous, since he went his own way most of the time. A bibliography of his works lists 37 books of prose, six books of poetry, and eight booklets. He also published millions of leaflets during World War II and numerous articles in Catholic periodicals. His literary efforts were more devotional than learned; his true title to fame rests on the tons of medical supplies he was able to send to missions all over the world.

[E. R. VOLLMAR]

GARESCHÉ, JULIUS PETER

Union soldier; b. near Havana, Cuba, April 26, 1821; d. Murfreesboro, Tenn., Dec. 31, 1862. He was the son of a Huguenot father, Vital Marie, and a Catholic mother, Louisa (Bouday) Garesché; he and the family resided chiefly in Delaware. After attending Georgetown College (later University), Washington, D.C., from 1833 to 1837, during which time he became a Catholic, he was appointed to the U.S. Military Academy, and he graduated 16th in his class in 1841. Garesché was first commissioned second lieutenant in the Fourth U.S. Artillery. He served in various frontier posts and in the war with Mexico before becoming brevet captain (assistant adjutant general) on Nov. 9, 1855. In 1862 as a lieutenant-colonel, he was assigned to the staff of Gen. William S. Rosecrans, Commander of the Army of the Cumberland, and became his chief of staff. He was killed early in the Battle of Stones River, Tenn., while riding beside Rosecrans. As a resident of Washington, D.C., Garesché helped to establish the St. Vincent de Paul Society in St. Matthew's parish, the first such unit in that city. He contributed to the New York *Freeman's Journal* and to *Brownson's Quarterly Review.* In September 1851 he was vested with the Order, Knight of St. Sylvester, by Pius IX.

Bibliography: U.S. War Dept., *The War of Rebellion: A Compilation of the Official Records of the Union and Confederate Armies,* 70 v. in 128 (Washington 1880–1901). G. W. CULLUM, *Biographical Register of the Officers and Graduates of the U.S. Military Academy, 1802–1890* (3rd ed. rev. Boston 1891–). L. GARESCHÉ *Biography of Lieut. Col. Julius P. Garesché* (Philadelphia 1887). W. M. LAMERS, *The Edge of Glory: A Biography of General William S. Rosecrans* (New York 1961).

[J. W. COLEMAN]

GARET, JEAN (GARETIUS)

Theologian; b. Louvain, early 16th century; d. Belgium, Jan. 21, 1571. After completing a course in philosophy, he joined the Canons Regular of St. Augustine at Saint-Martin in Louvain. After his ordination, he served as subprior of the monastery of Saint-Martin. He also assumed the spiritual direction of two convents of religious women at Antwerp and Ghent. He devoted all his free time to writing and preaching against Protestantism. His writings manifest vast erudition, sane judgment, and ardent attachment to the traditional truth. For reasons of ill health, he refused the bishopric of Ypres. His masterpiece was a work on the Eucharist proving the Real Presence from patristic texts: *De vera praesentia corporis Christi in sacramento Eucharistiae* (Antwerp 1561). It was the source which A. ARNAULD and P. NICOLE used in the compilation of their famous *La Perpetuité de la foi* (Paris 1669–76). Garet also published works on the invocation of saints and suffrages for the dead.

Bibliography: J. FORGET, *Dictionnaire de théologie catholique* 6.1:1158–60.

[C. R. MEYER]

GARIBALDI, GIUSEPPE

Italian military and nationalist leader; b. Nice, France, July 4, 1807; d. Caprera Island, near Sardinia, June 2, 1882. After receiving a Catholic upbringing, he went to sea as a youth and came into contact with exiles and conspirators. By 1832 he was certified as a ship's captain. While a member of the Young Italy movement of Mazzini, he joined the Sardinian navy (1833) and plotted to seize the frigate ''Euridice'' and occupy the arsenal in Genoa. For his involvement in this abortive conspiracy he was condemned to death. He escaped and went to South America, where he fought in behalf of Brazil's rebellious province of Rio Grande do Sul. From 1841 to 1847 he assisted Uruguay in its war against Argentina, organizing an Italian legion in Montevideo. This experience in guerrilla warfare proved very useful to him in Italy, to which he returned during the revolution of 1848 and led a volunteer army against Austria in the struggle to unify Italy. After the Italian defeat at Custozza, Garibaldi became the general for the forces of the short-lived Roman Republic against the Neapolitans at Palestrina and Velletri and against the French at San Pancrazio. When the republic collapsed he went into exile, landing in New York in 1850 and then following the sea as a sailor (1851–54).

Garibaldi returned to Piedmont in 1854 and purchased half of the barren island of Caprera, off the coast of Sardinia, and made his home there. During the Austro-Sardinian War (1859) he commanded a successful volunteer army (*Cacciatori delle Alpi*) against the Austrians. Garibaldi's conquest of the Kingdom of the Two Sicilies was his most famous exploit. Despite the strong disapproval of CAVOUR, Garibaldi and his Red Shirts invaded Sicily and defeated General Landi at Calatafimi (May 15, 1860). Suppressing his animosity toward the Church, Garibaldi participated in religious exercises and impressed the Sicilians as a defender of Catholicism. He entered Naples in September, but upon the arrival of Victor Emmanuel II in November, he surrendered his dictatorial position and retired to Caprera. When the Civil War erupted in the U.S., Abraham Lincoln offered him the command of a corps in the Union army but Garibaldi refused to accept unless the President appoint him supreme commander and abolish slavery. In 1862 Garibaldi led a march on Rome that was halted by royal troops at Aspromonte. He defeated the Austrians in several engagements in northern Italy during the Austro-Prussian War (1866).

A renewed attempt by Garibaldi to overthrow the STATES OF THE CHURCH met defeat at Mentana (Nov. 2, 1867). In the Franco-Prussian War he served with the French.

Garibaldi devoted his later years to revising his autobiography, composing irreligious novels, and engaging in other literary activities. His religion was a vague compound of DEISM, PANTHEISM, and what he called the religion of humanity. Bitter ANTICLERICALISM was characteristic of his outlook to the close of his life. His political testament explicitly repudiated the priesthood. Although he was a member of every Italian parliament, except one, elected after 1860, he rarely occupied his seat because of his scorn for legislative assemblies, at least as they functioned in Italy. His own preference was for temporary dictatorship. He possessed a keen sense of justice and identified himself with the common man. As a military leader he was noted for his valor and ability. For his services in the RISORGIMENTO he is honored as a national hero of Italy.

Bibliography: G. GARIBALDI, *Edizione nazionale degli scritti di Giuseppe Garibaldi,* 6 v. (Bologna 1932–37); *Autobiography,* ed. A. WERNER, 3 v. (London 1889). G. SACERDOTE, *La vita di Giuseppe Garibaldi* (Milan 1933). D. MACK SMITH, *Garibaldi* (New York 1956).

[E. A. CARRILLO]

GARICOÏTS, MICHAEL, ST.

Founder of the BÉTHARRAM FATHERS; b. Ibarre (Basses-Pyrénées), France, April 15, 1797; d. Bétharram (Basses-Pyrénées), May 14, 1863. He came of a poor peasant family, which reared him in profoundly Christian surroundings. To follow his priestly vocation he worked as a domestic while a student. After ordination (1823) he renewed a parish while a curate. As professor (from 1825) and superior (1831–33) of the seminary in Bétharram he reestablished discipline and piety. After the transfer of the seminary to Bayonne he remained at Bétharram, where he founded (1832) and directed under enormous difficulties a congregation of missioners and teachers. By his foundations of schools and colleges he was a pioneer in Christian education, and through his missioners and his own activity he helped re-Christianize the region. An adversary of JANSENISM, he favored frequent communion, devotion to the Sacred Heart and to the Blessed Virgin Mary. An exemplary priest, firm, obedient to the point of heroism, zealous, he was a peerless and supernaturally enlightened director of souls—called the Seer of Bétharram. He was beatified May 10, 1923; canonized July 6, 1947.

Feast: May 14.

Bibliography: *Life of Blessed Michael Garicoïts*, ed. BÉTHARRAM FATHERS, tr. C. OTIS-COX (London 1935). D. BUZY, *Saint Michel Garicoïts, le saint de Bétharram* (Lourdes 1967). P. DUVIGNAU, *Un Maître spirituel du XIXe siècle: Saint Michel Garicoïts* (Paris 1963); *La Doctrine spirituelle de saint Michel Garicoïts* (Paris 1949). D. INNAMORATI, *The Life of St. Michael Garicoïts* (Leigh, U.K. 1997).

[P. DUVIGNAU]

GARIN, ANDRÉ

Missionary; b. Côte-Saint-André, Isère, France, May 7, 1822; d. Lowell, Mass., Feb. 16, 1895. After studies in the local seminary of his birthplace, he entered the Oblates of Mary Immaculate on Nov. 1, 1842 and was sent to Canada to be ordained on April 25, 1845, in Montreal by Bp. I. Bourget. Garin's 12 years as a missionary to the Native Americans from the Saguenay to Hudson Bay and Labrador were filled with hardships, but also with great apostolic achievement. When he went to Springfield, Mass., in October 1866 to preach a mission for Canadians, he attracted the attention of Bp. J. J. Williams of Boston, who invited the Oblates to found a parish in Lowell for Franco-Americans. Within a month after Garin and a companion visited Lowell on April 19, 1868 to explore the question, the bishop bought a former Unitarian chapel, naming it St. Joseph's. Three other churches were built under Garin's direction during his 27 years in Lowell. Two years after his death, the parishioners honored him by erecting a statue of him.

Bibliography: *Missions de la Congrégation des Missionaires Oblats de Marie-Immaculée* (Paris 1862) 7.

[T. F. CASEY]

GARLICK, NICHOLAS, BL.

Priest, martyr; b. ca. 1555 at Dinting, Glossop, Derbyshire, England; hanged, drawn, and quartered July 24, 1588 on St. Mary's Bridge at Derby. He finished his studies at Gloucester Hall, now Worcester College, Oxford, but did not take a degree, perhaps because it required taking the Oath of Supremacy. For the next seven years he was schoolmaster at Tideswell in the Peak (Derbyshire), where his personal holiness so influenced his pupils that three of them, including Bl. Christopher BUXTON, followed him to Rheims in June 1581. He was ordained in 1582 and returned to England the following January. After working for a year in the Midlands, he was arrested and sent into exile (1585). Although he knew that he would be shown no mercy should he be found again in England, he was soon back at work in the same neighborhood. In 1588, he was apprehended with Bl. Robert LUDLAM by the infamous Topcliffe at Padley

Hall, the home of John Fitzherbert, whose son betrayed the priests. They were confined in the verminous Derby Gaol with Bl. Richard SIMPSON until execution. Garlick was beatified by Pope John Paul II on Nov. 22, 1987 with George Haydock and Companions.

Feast of the English Martyrs: May 4 (England).

See Also: ENGLAND, SCOTLAND, AND WALES, MARTYRS OF.

Bibliography: R. CHALLONER, *Memoirs of Missionary Priests,* ed. J. H. POLLEN (rev. ed. London 1924). J. H. POLLEN, *Acts of English Martyrs* (London 1891).

[K. I. RABENSTEIN]

GARNERIUS OF ROCHEFORT

Also known as Garnier of Rochefort or Langres; monk, bishop, monastic author; b. *c.* 1140; d. Clairvaux, after 1225. He was an active and influential man, related to the lords of Rochefort-sur-Brévon of the Côte d'Or, France. A CISTERCIAN of Longuay Abbey, he became prior of CLAIRVAUX *c.* 1175 and abbot of Auberive in 1180 and then of Clairvaux in 1187. He preached the Third CRUSADE, and it was to Garnerius that RICHARD I, the Lion-Heart, wrote on Oct. 1, 1191, telling of his successes and asking for reinforcements. Garnerius was bishop of the important See of Langres by 1193 at the latest, but he was soon in conflict with his cathedral chapter. Pope Innocent III demanded his resignation; after a delaying action, he complied in 1199 and retired to Clairvaux. He has left a letter and some sermons (crit. ed. in prep.). In all likelihood he wrote the treatise *Contra Amaurianos* and compiled an onomastic list beginning with *angelus.* Numerous charters signed by him have been preserved. A fervent monk, a worthy bishop, and a distinguished humanist, Garnerius should be studied also as a representative of the monastic theology of the late 12th century. For a long time scorned, he now attracts more attention, particularly for his exegetical method and his mystique of numbers.

Bibliography: *Gallia Christiana* 4:591–594 and *Instrumenta:* 194–195. J. C. DIDIER, ''Garnier de Rochefort: Sa Vie et son oeuvre,'' *Collectanea Ordinis Cisterciensium* 17 (1955) 145–158; ''Une Lettre inédite de G. de R.,'' *ibid.* 18 (1956) 190–198; ''Quelques précisions sur G. de R.,'' *Les Cahiers haut-marnais* 46 (1956) 164–166; *Dictionnaire de théologie catholique Tables générales* 1:1775. J. LECLERCQ, ''Manuscrits cisterciens dans diverses bibliothèques,'' *Analecta Sacri Ordinis Cisterciensis* 11 (1955) 139–148. M. D. CHENU, ''Erigène à Citeaux. Expérience intérieure et spiritualité objective,'' *La Philosophie et ses problèmes: Recueil d'études . . . offert à R. Jolivet* (Paris 1960) 99–107.

[J. C. DIDIER]

Henry Garnet.

GARNET, HENRY

Jesuit superior in England; b. Heanor, Derbyshire, 1555; d. London, May 3, 1606. Garnet, son of the headmaster of a school in Nottingham, was not brought up a Catholic. After attending Winchester School, he studied law, but on his conversion he journeyed to Rome to enter the Jesuit novitiate (September 1575). Later, he taught Hebrew in the Roman College and also, for a time, mathematics. On May 8, 1586, with Robert SOUTHWELL, he left Rome for England, landing there July 17. Father William Weston, his superior, was soon captured, and on Weston's removal from the Clink to Wisbech, January 1588, Garnet became superior. He fixed his headquarters near London, but he made several missionary journeys in the country. He gradually increased the number of Jesuits in England, enrolling several seminary priests, until by 1605 there were more than 40. He placed his priests near one another for mutual help and held periodic meetings for spiritual exercises and renewal of vows. As no one was attending to organization within the English mission, Garnet realized the need and filled it. Newly arrived seminary priests were received and supported until they could safely journey to relatives or be otherwise placed. To priests in poorer districts he afforded such monetary aid as was available. Many lay-helpers were employed and supported by him. One, a carpenter, traveled the country making hiding-places. Some accompanied Jesuits and priests on their journeys and, when traveling was dangerous for priests, acted as messengers. Others worked the press, which he set up, printing spiritual books that were dispersed throughout the country. Such work not only left him frequently in debt, but also caused a few to think, quite unjustly, that the Jesuits wished to dominate the clergy.

When strife broke out among the prisoners at Wisbech and 18 priests begged to have Weston as their superior, Garnet refused, though he would not condemn the priests' association. He worked to end the strife, and through his persistence a pacification was agreed to in November 1595.

On Cardinal William ALLEN's death in October 1594, many students in the English College, Rome, got out of hand, until Robert Persons, recalled to Rome (1597), restored peace and discipline. Fuel had been added to these troubles in 1596 by letters, still extant, of W. Gifford, dean of Lille, full of calumnies against English Jesuits. To spread these calumnies in England and bring back further charges, students were sent to England. The last of these, Robert Fisher, on returning to the Continent, drew up a paper containing these charges, purporting to be in the name of the clergy; the Flanders nuncio, persuaded by Gifford and Charles Paget, forwarded it to Rome. While Persons dealt with these calumnies in Rome and Flanders, Garnet did so in England. A circular letter to the clergy in March 1598 resulted in nearly 200 seminary priests testifying in favor of the Jesuits. Fisher's confessions in Rome, also in March, further revealed what was a combined effort to get the Jesuits withdrawn from England and from the seminaries.

Partly in consequence of these disturbances, Clement VIII, in March 1598, appointed George BLACKWELL archpriest and superior of the clergy in England. Some few priests refused to recognize his authority; in the ensuing controversy Garnet supported Blackwell and at one time considered severe measures from Rome necessary (*see* ARCHPRIEST CONTROVERSY). After the pope's decision in October 1602, Garnet worked for a general pacification, enjoining on his brethren strict observance of the papal brief.

In James I's reign, Garnet, advocating peaceful means, eventually obtained from the pope a prohibition of violent measures. Convinced that most Catholics would bear the increasing persecution patiently, he yet doubted his power to restrain some of them. Strongly suspecting some plot, he desired the pope to issue a brief adding excommunication to the prohibition. In confession he obtained a knowledge of a plot, which knowledge he was allowed to use only if called in question by the pope, his general, or the state. Apprehended at the end of January 1606, Garnet denied any cooperation in the Gunpowder Plot. According to a letter of W. Baldwin, SJ (May 27, 1606), the Spanish ambassador's interpreter, present at Garnet's execution, had affirmed that on the scaffold Garnet, solemnly protesting his innocence, declared that he received the confessional knowledge only five days before the plot was discovered.

Bibliography: H. FOLEY, ed., *Records of the English Province of the Society of Jesus,* 7 v. in 15 (London 1877–82). T. FITZHERBERT, *Letters,* ed. L. S. HICKS (*Publications of the Catholic Record Society* 41; London 1948); *The Wisbech Stirs, 1595–1598* (*ibid.* 51; London 1958). J. GERARD, ''Contributions Towards a Life of Father Henry Garnet, S.J.,'' *Month* 91 (1898) 6–21, 121–130, 238–246, 356–367, 458–467, 603–610. T. G. LAW, ed., *The Archpriest Controversy,* 2 v. (Camden Society 56, 58; London 1896–98). For his writings, A. F. ALLISON and D. M. ROGERS, *A Catalogue of Catholic Books in English . . . 1558–1640,* 2 v. (London 1956). T. COOPER, *The Dictionary of National Biography from the Earliest Times to 1900* (London 1885–1900) 7:881–884.

[L. HICKS]

GARNET, THOMAS, ST.

English martyr; b. Southwark, in the parish of St. Mary Overies, *c.* 1575; d. Tyburn, June 23, 1608. He attended grammar school at Horsham in Sussex, where in 1588 his father, Richard Garnet, brother of Henry GARNET, was imprisoned for his faith with his wife and children. For a time Thomas was a page to Lord William Howard, half-brother to Bl. Philip HOWARD. At the age of 15 or 16 he crossed to Saint-Omer to complete his education at the Jesuit college. On Feb. 21, 1596, he entered the English seminary at Valladolid, where he was a fellow student with Andrew White, later the founder of the Maryland mission. In July 1599, Garnet, a priest, left for England, and there in September 1604 he became a Jesuit. Arrested and imprisoned in the Gatehouse at the time of the Gunpowder Plot, he was stringently examined by Lord Salisbury for evidence that might implicate his uncle, Henry Garnet. When he proved himself innocent he was banished with other priests in June 1606, but, after a brief novitiate at Louvain, returned the following September. Five or six weeks later he was again arrested and imprisoned, first in the Gatehouse, then in Newgate. After several examinations he was tried at the Old Bailey on June 19, 1608, and condemned for his priesthood. A crowd estimated at more than 1,000 witnessed his execution at Tyburn four days later. On the scaffold he mentioned by name all who were responsible for his execution and prayed God's forgiveness for them. He was beatified by Pius XI on Dec. 15, 1929, and canonized by Paul VI in 1970. He is the protomartyr of St. Omer's College, now Stonyhurst.

Feast: June 23.

Bibliography: H. FOLEY, ed., *Records of the English Province of the Society of Jesus,* 7 v. (Quarterly Ser. 75; London 1877–82) 2.2:475–505. A. BUTLER, *The Lives of the Saints,* rev. ed. H. THURSTON and D. ATTWATER, 4 v. (New York 1956) 2:627. J. H. POLLEN, *Acts of the English Martyrs* (London 1891). R. CHALLONER, *Memoirs of Missionary Priests,* ed. J. H. POLLEN (rev. ed. London 1924). J. GILLOW, *A Literary and Biographical History or Bibliographical Dictionary of the English Catholics from 1534 to the Present Time,* 5 v. (London–New York 1885–1902; repr., New York 1961) 2:395–397.

[G. FITZHERBERT]

GARRAGHAN, GILBERT JOSEPH

Historian; b. Chicago, Ill., Aug. 14, 1871; d. Chicago, June 6, 1942. His parents, Gilbert and Bedelia (Kehoe) Garraghan, sent him to St. Ignatius College, Chicago, where he earned his A.B. in 1889. He entered the novitiate of the Society of Jesus at Florissant, Mo., Sept. 1, 1890, taking vows in 1892 and pursuing classical studies there for a year. After three years of philosophy at St. Louis University, Mo., he became instructor in Latin at Xavier University, Cincinnati, Ohio (1896–1901). Garraghan returned to St. Louis University for theology, was ordained on June 29, 1904, and made his tertianship at Florissant (1905–06).

Garraghan spent the next year teaching English literature in Creighton University, Omaha, Nebr., and then four years teaching young Jesuits in the juniorate at Florissant. From 1911 to 1921, and again from 1927 to 1928, he served as assistant to the provincials of the Missouri province of the Society. Residing at St. Louis University during these years, he used the opportunity to engage in historical studies and was awarded the doctorate in history in 1919. Research on the beginnings of the Catholic Church in the Midwest occupied him from 1921 to 1925. Garraghan was professor of history in the graduate school of St. Louis University (1925–32), and editor of *Mid-America,* a historical quarterly (1929–33). In 1932 he was made research professor at Loyola University, Chicago.

In Europe from 1933 to 1935, he collected an extensive file of documents from the archives of Italy, France, Belgium, and England. Returning to Loyola University, he completed his monumental work on the Middle Western missionary and educational activities of the Jesuits from 1673 to 1919. His historical works include *Catholic Beginnings in Kansas City* (1919), *Catholic Church in Chicago* (1921), *Chapters in Frontier History* (1934), *Catholic Beginnings in Maryland* (1934), *Marquette, Ardent Missionary, Daring Explorer* (1937), *Jesuits in the Middle United States* (3 v. 1938), and *Guide to Historical Method,* edited by Jean Delanglez (1946).

[J. V. JACOBSEN]

St. Thomas Garnet.

GARRIGOU-LAGRANGE, RÉGINALD

Dominican theologian and philosopher; b. Auch (France), Feb. 21, 1877; d. Rome, Feb. 15, 1964. Before entering the Dominican Order (1897) he studied medicine at the University of Bordeaux. When he completed his ecclesiastical studies under the direction of A. GARDEIL, he was assigned to teach philosophy and theology at Le Saulchoir, Belgium (1905). From 1909 until 1960 he taught fundamental, dogmatic, and spiritual theology at what is now called the Pontifical University of St. Thomas Aquinas in Rome, and served during the latter part of his career as a consulter of the Holy Office and of other Roman congregations. He began to write for publication in 1904, and produced in all more than 500 books and articles published in scholarly periodicals, many of which have been translated from the original French or Latin into other tongues. He was a zealous proponent of the doctrine of St. Thomas Aquinas as expounded by the classical commentators of the Dominican school— CAJETAN (TOMMASO DE VIO), Báñez, JOHN OF ST. THOMAS, and Charles BILLUART. He combined a great respect for the past with an understanding and appreciation of the intellectual and spiritual needs of his own time. His principal theses are set forth systematically in his *La Synthese thomiste* (Paris 1946).

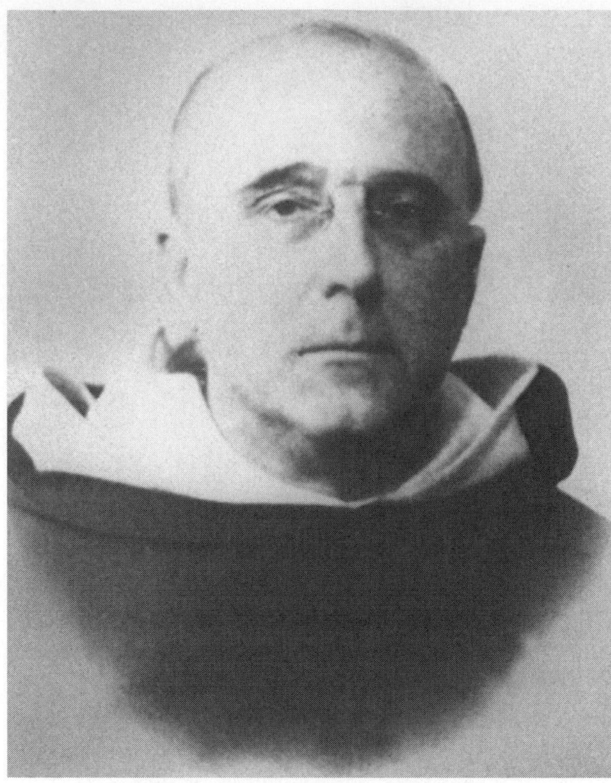

Réginald Garrigou-Lagrange.

In the field of philosophy his first outstanding work was his *Le Sens commun, la philosophie de l'être et les formules dogmatiques* (Paris 1909). This was written against Modernism and its conception of the evolution of dogma. Reaffirming the validity of the philosophy of being, of moderate realism and of Aristotelian-Thomistic metaphysics, which is simply the development of elementary and primordial ideas by natural intelligence, Garrigou-Lagrange showed how the human mind grasps first and self-evident principles in intelligible being, which is the first object apprehended by the intellect in the data of the senses. Turning then to dogmatic formulas, which he did not wish to enfeoff to any philosophical system, he showed their rational value and stability. Knowledge of dogma and of dogmatic expressions and formulas can progress, but the dogma remains always immutable in itself. Among his other philosophical works were *Le Réalisme du principe de finalité* (Paris 1932) and *Le Sens du mystère et le clair obscur intellectuel* (*Nature et Surnaturel*) (Paris 1934). His most important philosophical work was *Dieu, son existence et sa nature* (Paris 1915). In this study, by which he hoped to provide a solution to the antinomies of agnosticism, he explained first principles, defending their ontological and transcendental validity. Then, basing his argument on them, he advanced the Thomistic proofs of the existence of God and of certain truths regarding the divine nature, laying great stress on the Thomist doctrine concerning the identity of essence and existence in God and the real distinction of essence and existence in the creature.

The major part of Garrigou-Lagrange's work, however, was theological. His classic *De revelatione ab ecclesia proposita* (Rome 1918; rev. ed. Rome 1932), fixed for his generation the main lines of Catholic apologetics. For him apologetics was a theological rather than a philosophical science, because he conceived it as a rational defense of divine revelation made by reason under positive direction by faith. Thus he tried, on the one hand, to protect the notion of faith as a gratuitous gift of God, a grace, and, on the other, to avoid the pitfalls of a fideism that ignores reason and human study. Faith, essentially a supernatural gift, transcends by far the elaborations of human thought and cannot be the fruit of a rational syllogism, which can lead the mind no farther than to the judgment of credibility.

Garrigou-Lagrange's magisterial commentary on the *Summa Theologiae* of St. Thomas (7 v. Paris-Turin 1938–51) is a comprehensive development and treatment of the truths of faith according to the theology of St. Thomas Aquinas. Other theological works worthy of mention were *La Prédestination des saints et la grâce* (Paris 1935); *L'Éternelle vie et la profondeur de l'âme* (Paris 1950), his articles in the *Dictionnaire de théologie catholique*—''Prédestination,'' ''Promotion physique,'' ''Providence selon la Théologie,'' ''Thomisme''—and the article ''Predestinazione'' in the *Enciclopedia cattolica*.

In spiritual theology the principal points in his doctrine were established in the light of Thomistic teaching. Adopting the position of Juan Gonzalez ARINTERO, he insisted vigorously on the universal call to holiness and therefore to infused contemplation and to the mystical life as the normal ways of holiness, or of Christian perfection. Among his most fundamental works in this field are *Perfection chrétienne et contemplation* (Paris 1923), *Les trois conversions et les trois voies* (Paris 1933), *Les trois âges de la vie intérieure* (Lyons 1941), *De sanctificatione sacerdotum secundum exigentias temporis nostri* (Turin 1947), and *De unione sacerdotis cum Christo Sacerdote et Victima* (Turin 1948).

Bibliography: ''Essai de bibliographie du R. P. Garrigou-Lagrange,'' *Angelicum* 14 (1937) 5–37. C. MAZZANTINI, ''Nota a proposito del principio d'identità . . . nella filosofia del G.-L.,'' *ibid.* 318–322. H. D. GARDEIL, *Catholicisme* 4:1764. B. LAVAUD in *Sacra Doctrina* 2 (1957) 14–20. *Dictionnaire de théologie catholique*, Tables générales 1:1776–77. ''Reginaldi Garrigou-Lagrange: In memoriam,'' *Angelicum* 42.1–2 (1965).

[R. M. PIZZORNI]

GARVIN, JOHN E.

Author; b. San Antonio, Texas, Feb. 24, 1865; d. Washington, D.C., Oct. 7, 1918. He joined the Marianist brothers and received his B.A. from the University of Dayton, Ohio (1886), and a licentiate in physics and mathematics from Stanislaus College, Paris, France (1891). Although trained in science, he is remembered also for his speeches and conferences on religious topics. His chief publications were the translation of Henry Rousseau's *Life of Guillaume Joseph Chaminade,* from French to English, and *The Centenary of the Society of Mary in America* (Dayton 1917). A methodical teacher, he addressed meetings of the National Catholic Educational Association and was a frequent contributor to the *Apostle of Mary* and other publications. His notes on the teaching of composition in elementary and high schools are preserved in the archives of Mt. St. John, Dayton.

[G. J. RUPPEL]

GASPARRI, PIETRO

Cardinal, secretary of state under two popes, codifier of Canon Law; b. Ussita (Macerata), Italy, May 5, 1852; d. Rome, Nov. 18, 1934. At the Apollinare in Rome he received doctorates in philosophy, theology, and civil and Canon Law. After ordination (1877), he was secretary to Cardinal Mertel, the prefect of the Apostolic Signatura, and he lectured on Canon Law at the college of Propaganda in Rome. At the request of Leo XIII he accepted (1890) the newly established chair of Canon Law at the Institut Catholique in Paris, and remained there 18 years. During this period he published the fruits of his research: *Tractatus canonicus de Matrimonio* (1892), *De sacra Ordinatione* (1893–94), and *De Sanctissima Eucharistia* (1897). He joined the commission examining the validity of ANGLICAN orders. At first he favored their validity, but he modified his opinions somewhat in *De la valeur des ordinations anglicanes* (1896). He was sent as apostolic delegate to Peru, Bolivia, and Ecuador (1898–1901), and was consecrated titular archbishop of Caesarea (March 6, 1898). He returned to Rome (1901) as secretary of the Congregation for Extraordinary Ecclesiastical Affairs. His greatest accomplishment was the codification of Canon Law. As secretary of the cardinalitial commission of codification and as presiding officer of the two groups of scholars who did the research and actual formulation of the canons, he was the man most responsible for the completion of the tremendous task. Work began Nov. 13, 1904 and was expected to require 25 years. However, Gasparri handed Benedict XV the first printed copy of the new Code of CANON LAW on Dec. 4, 1916. It was solemnly promulgated on Pentecost 1917. Gasparri was elevated to the cardinalate Dec. 16, 1907.

Pietro Gasparri. (The Catholic University of America)

Gasparri succeeded Cardinal FERRATA as secretary of state (Oct. 13, 1914) a few months after the outbreak of World War I. No detail of Benedict XV's many projects to end hostilities and to alleviate human misery was too insignificant for the cardinal's wholehearted attention. When Benedict XV died (Jan. 22, 1922), Gasparri said: ''Every man has his special mission in life. Mine was the codification of Canon Law and the support of Benedict during the war. These two tasks are now completed.'' Pius XI, however, pleaded with the weary camerlengo to continue as secretary of state. On Feb. 11, 1929, in the Lateran Palace, Gasparri and Mussolini signed the Lateran Pacts on which Gasparri had worked painstakingly for some years, and which ended the ROMAN QUESTION. The pope finally acquiesced to Gasparri's pleas for permission to resign (Feb. 7, 1930). The remaining four years of his life he spent in a modest residence overlooking the Colosseum, enjoying his library and completing his *Cathechismus Catholicus* (1930). He lived to see the completely edited manuscript of the seventh volume of his celebrated *Fontes Iuris Canonici.* On

Italian Premier Alcide De Gasperi, second from left. (AP/Wide World Photos)

Nov. 14, 1934, he gave a brilliant address to the international jurists, assembled at the Apollinare for the 14th centenary of the Code of JUSTINIAN I. He suffered a heart attack immediately after and died four days later. Gasparri, descended from a family of shepherds, was always a simple, devoted priest, practical rather than theoretical in his approach to problems. His inexhaustible capacity for work, his disarming amiability, humor, tact, and imaginative resourcefulness were qualities that contributed to his greatness. His diary remains unpublished.

Bibliography: P. GASPARRI, "Storia della codificazione del diritto canonico per la Chiesa latina," *Acta Congressus iuridict internationalis,* 5 v. (Rome 1935–37) 4:1–10. L. FIORELLI, ed., *Il cardinale Pietro Gasparri* (Rome 1960). F. M. TALIANI, *Vita del Cardinale Gasparri, segretario di Stato e povero prete* (Milan 1938). W. SANDFUCHS, *Die Aussenminister der Päpste* (Munich 1962). C. LEDRÉ, *Catholicisme* 4:1765–68. W. H. PETERS, *The Life of Benedict XV* (Milwaukee 1959).

[W. H. PETERS]

GASPERI, ALCIDE DE

Italian statesman; b. Pieve Tesino (Trentino), Austria-Hungary, April 3, 1881; d. Sella, Italy, Aug. 19, 1954. After receiving his secondary education in Trent, he studied in the University of Vienna (1900–05), where he specialized in philosophy and philology. While there he devoted much time to organizing Catholic students and workers and instilling in them the principles of Leo XIII's social encyclical *RERUM NOVARUM*. After graduation he edited *Il Trentino* and made it the journal of the Popular party, which advocated Catholic solutions to socioeconomic problems and autonomy for the Trentino region. De Gasperi was elected to the Austrian Reichsrat in 1911. During World War I he supervised relief activities in the camps peopled with Italians who had been expelled from the Trentino by the Austrian authorities.

After Italy annexed the Trentino (1919), De Gasperi joined the Popular party of Don STURZO and was elected to the Italian parliament (1921). As an opponent of fascism, De Gasperi was arrested and charged with clandestine attempts at expatriation (1927). He received a four-year prison sentence, but illness and royal intervention effected his release (1928). From 1929 until 1943 he worked in the VATICAN LIBRARY, first as a cataloguer and later (1939–43) as the secretary of the library. In 1942 he revived the Popular party, which was known henceforth as the Christian Democratic party. He was premier of Italy (Dec. 1945 to July 1953), the first practicing Catholic to hold the post. Communists and left-wing Socialists were part of his coalition cabinets until June 1947, but they were excluded thereafter and membership was restricted mostly to his own party. As premier De Gasperi supported industrial and agrarian reforms, continuation of the Lateran Pacts, alliance with the West, and European unity. He is buried in Rome in the Church of S. Lorenzo.

Bibliography: A. DE GASPERI, *I Cattolici dall'opposizione al governo* (Bari 1955). I. GIORDANI, *Alcide De Gasperi* (Milan 1955). G. ANDREOTTI, *De Gasperi e il suo tempo* (Milan 1956). E. A. CARRILLO, *A. De Gasperi* (Notre Dame, Ind. 1965).

[E. A. CARRILLO]

GASQUET, FRANCIS NEIL AIDAN

Cardinal, historian, and in his time leading authority on English monasticism; b. London, Oct. 5, 1846; d. Rome, April 4, 1929. The son of a French emigré father and a Scots mother, he was educated at DOWNSIDE ABBEY, near Bath. In 1866 he entered the Benedictines at Belmont Abbey, Hereford. After his novitiate Gasquet (now Dom Aidan) returned to Downside, where he taught mathematics and history and was ordained in 1874. In 1878 his community elected him prior, but he resigned in 1885 because of ill health. Enforced convalescence led him to historical research, and much of his time was spent in the British Museum and the Public Record Office. His two volumes, entitled *Henry VIII and the English Monasteries* (1888–89) were welcomed as a vindication of English monks and nuns of the Reformation period and established him as an authority on monastic history in England. His *Edward VI and the Book of Common Prayer* (3d ed., London 1891) won him nomination to the Commission on Anglican Orders set up by Pope Leo XIII. After taking a prominent part in the reorganization of the English monasteries, he was elected (1900) abbot-president of the English Benedictine Congregation. During his term of office, the monasteries of Downside, Ampleforth, and Douai were raised to the ranks of abbeys, and houses of studies were opened in London and Cambridge. The international commission for the revision of the Vulgate had Gasquet as its first president. He raised $10,000 for the project on a lecture tour of the United States.

Pope Pius X, in the last consistory of his pontificate, created Abbot Gasquet a cardinal-deacon with the title of St. George in Velabro. Subsequently, his titular church was changed to Santa Maria in Campitelli, and in 1924 he was promoted to cardinal-priest. At the beginning of World War I (December 1914), the British government, anxious about Austrian and German influence in Roman ecclesiastical circles, secured the acceptance of a special envoy to the Vatican. Cardinal Gasquet was concerned in the establishment of these diplomatic relations. He was a member of the Congregations of Rites, *De Propaganda Fide,* of Religious, and of the Oriental Church. He became prefect of the Vatican archives in 1917 and, two years later, librarian of the Holy Roman Church. By his own wish, he was buried at Downside Abbey. Gasquet's published works include *A History of the Catholic Church in England,* 2 v. (London 1897), *Parish Life in Medieval England* (3d ed. London 1909), *Religio religiosi, the Object and Scope of the Religious Life* (4th ed. London 1924), and *A History of the Venerable English College, Rome* (London 1920). Some of his works have been translated into other languages.

Bibliography: E. C. BUTLER, *The Dictionary of National Biography from the Earliest Times to 1900* (1922–30) 330–332. D. KNOWLES, *Cardinal Gasquet as an Historian* (London 1957). S. LESLIE, *Cardinal Gasquet: A Memoir* (New York 1953). J. C. FOWLER, ''Cardinal Gasquet at Downside,'' *Downside Review* 47 (1929) 123–131. B. KUYPERS, ''Cardinal Gasquet in London,'' *ibid.* 132–149. U. BUTLER, ''Cardinal Gasquet in Rome,'' *ibid.* 150–156. A. BAER, ''The Careers of Cardinal Gasquet,'' *American Benedictine Review* 5 (1954) 113–122; *A Benedictine Bibliography: An Author-Subject Union List* 1:4112a–4212.

[B. EGAN]

GASSENDI, PIERRE

Philosopher whose works influenced the growth of mechanics and theoretical astronomy from GALILEO to Newton; b. Champtercier, Jan. 22, 1592; d. Paris, Oct. 24, 1655.

Exposed to, but not convinced by, the Aristotelianism presented during his student days at the University of Aix (1609–12), the philosophically hungry Gassendi taught rhetoric in the college at Digne. In 1614 he received minor clerical orders, was granted a doctorate in theology by the University of Avignon, and was elected canon-theologian of the cathedral chapter at Digne. In 1616 Gassendi joined the philosophical faculty of the Royal Bourbon College at Aix and was ordained a priest at Marseilles. Gassendi's courses at Aix were ambiguous, for he countered each presentation of an ''official'' Aristotelian thesis with objections calculated to weaken, if not destroy, its acceptability. When in 1621 the Bourbon College was entrusted to the Jesuits, Gassendi returned to Digne.

In 1624 at Grenoble, en route to Paris on chapter business, Gassendi published the first of his projected seven *Unpopular Essays against the Aristotelians (Exercitationes paradoxicae adversus Aristoteleos . . .).* At Paris Gassendi consolidated an intimate friendship with Marin Mersenne, who, fearful of the inroads of magical pseudonaturalism, counseled Gassendi to discontinue the *Exercitationes* series and search instead for a sounder philosophy to fill the intellectual vacuum created by the impending dissolution of Aristotelianism. Gassendi chose Epicurus to replace Aristotle. To explore and expound the philosophy of Epicurus, as compatible with both the demands of orthodox Christian faith and the needs of the new science, thenceforth became Gassendi's goal as scholar and scientist.

Gassendi's choice entailed two consequences: (1) *epoche* and (2) acceptance of both atoms and the void. The first consequence, as a conscientious refusal to commit oneself to any one of several competing theories, allowed Gassendi, in his 1643 *Disquisitio metaphysica,* to controvert powerfully the purportedly certain deductive system of Descartes's 1641 *Meditationes de prima philosophia* and to write (*indeterminatamente*) another book, his 1647 *Institutio astronomica.* Galileo had received papal authorization for such a book, but instead had produced his passionately partisan 1632 *Dialogo* in defense of Copernicus. Gassendi's espousal of atomism exorcised that theory from the curse of popular prejudice and made it respectable in a Christian milieu, but scientific development of it needed the quantitative and experimentally analytic results of Robert Boyle, not the qualitative and imaginatively synthetic descriptions of Gassendi's ''compounds.'' Gassendi's acceptance of the void, however, allowed him to set the mechanics of Galileo's 1638 *Discorsi* into an isotropically neutral space, and hence to publish for the first time (1649) a scientifically adequate formulation of the principle of inertia.

Bibliography: *Opera omnia,* ed. H. L. HABERT DE MONTMOR and F. HENRI, 6 v. in 4 (Lyons 1658–75); repr. in 6 v. (Stuttgart 1964), introd. T. GREGORY. B. ROCHOT, ed., *Pierre Gassendi: Sa vie et son oeuvre* (Paris 1955). Comité du Tricentenaire de Gassendi, *Actes du Congrés du Tricentenaire de Pierre Gassendi* (Paris

1957). T. GREGORY, *Scetticismo ed empirismo: Studio su Gassendi* (Bari 1961). J. T. CLARK, "P. G. and the Physics of Galileo," *Isis* 54 (1963) 352–370.

[J. T. CLARK]

GASSER, VINZENZ FERRER

Prince-bishop of Brixen; b. Inzing (Tirol), Oct. 30, 1809; d. Brixen, April 6, 1879. After ordination (1833), he taught dogmatic theology and Oriental studies in the seminary at Brixen (1836–55). In 1848 he was elected to the Frankfort national assembly. Pius IX approved his nomination by Emperor Franz Joseph I as prince-bishop of Brixen (1856). As bishop he was an example of asceticism and scholarship for his clergy, for whom he also provided the necessary vocations by founding a seminary at Brixen, the Vincentinum, which still carries his name. As a member of the Tirol parliament (Landes-parlament), by virtue of his ecclesiastical position, he fought successfully for the exclusive recognition of the Catholic religion in Tirol, which had been guaranteed by ancient state laws. He became world famous during VATICAN COUNCIL I as an outstanding theologian. As a member of, and speaker for, the commission on faith, which had the responsibility of rewriting the first schema on the Catholic faith, he defended successfully the first part of the new schema, prepared by himself. Later during the commission's discussions on the essential nature of the primacy of the pope, he was responsible for having inserted in the schema the explanation that the papal primacy does not limit the ordinary and immediate governing authority of bishops, but protects and strengthens it. Finally (July 11, 1870), he presented to the Council fathers the decree, composed by himself, on papal infallibility in a four-hour Latin speech with such conviction that the decree was approved by a majority of the bishops with only minor changes, and was solemnly defined a week later.

Bibliography: J. ZOBL, *Vinzenz Gasser* (Bressanone 1883). C. BUTLER, *The Vatican Council*, 2 v. (New York 1930), with photo. A. SPARBER, *Lexicon für Theologie und Kirche* 4:525–526.

[F. MAASS]

GASTON, WILLIAM JOSEPH

Judge, statesman; b. New Bern, N.C., Sept. 19, 1778; d. Raleigh, N.C., Jan. 23, 1844. He was one of three children of Alexander, a physician, and Margaret (Sharpe) Gaston. In 1781 his father, an ardent rebel, was killed by Tories. William became the first student of Georgetown College, Washington, D.C., but after two years withdrew because of ill health. He graduated from Princeton in 1796, studied law with François X. Martin, and in two years was admitted to the bar. His election to the North Carolina Senate at 22 was the beginning of a 30-year career of service that included four terms in the state Senate and seven in the state House of Commons. He drafted many of North Carolina's important statutes and was chairman of the joint committee that in 1818 created the new supreme court of the state. He was trustee of the state university for 42 years. In 1840 he wrote the song "The Old North State."

In 1808 Gaston was a Federalist presidential elector. He was twice elected to Congress (1813, 1815), where he was a leader of the antiwar Federalists. Among the speeches that gained for him a national reputation, the best known was that on "The Previous Question," directed against Henry Clay. It has been frequently reprinted as a masterpiece of parliamentary oratory. In 1815 he obtained from Congress the charter for Georgetown University. Despite a prohibition of the state constitution against anyone holding office "who did not believe in the truths of the Protestant religion," Gaston was elected by the legislature in 1833 to the state supreme court. Two years later he was elected to the state constitutional convention, where his eloquence effected the substitution of the word "Christian" for "Protestant" in the constitution.

Gaston was known for his humanitarianism and ready defense of minority causes. He dared to speak against slavery and did so in 1832 in delivering the commencement address at the University of North Carolina, Chapel Hill. Three years later he spoke at Princeton against the nativist movement. As a member of the state supreme court he handed down opinions that were models of clarity, logic, and vigor of expression. His judgment in *State v. Will* established the rights of slaves against brutal treatment; another concerning the citizenship of the colored freemen (*State v. Manuel*) was cited by Judge Benjamin Curtis in the Dred Scott case. Gaston was awarded honorary doctorates by Harvard and Princeton Universities and the University of Pennsylvania. He served Bp. John England of Charleston as legal and financial advisor and saved the *U.S. Catholic Miscellany* from destruction on several occasions. Gaston was married three times and was survived by five children. He died on the bench while presiding over a session of the North Carolina supreme court in Raleigh and was buried in New Bern.

Bibliography: P. K. GUILDAY, *The Life and Times of John England,* 2 v. (New York 1927). J. H. SCHAUINGER, *William Gaston: Carolinian* (Milwaukee 1949).

[J. H. SCHAUINGER]

GATES OF HELL

This phrase occurs in the New Testament only at Mt 16.18: ". . . upon this rock I will build my Church, and the gates of hell shall not prevail against it." The Greek word here rendered "hell" is ᾅδης (HADES), which in the Septuagint regularly translates the Hebrew šeʾôl (SHEOL). In the Old Testament Sheol was conceived as the dark, underworld abode of all the dead; in later Judaism it came to be thought of as a place of punishment for the souls of the wicked, whereas the souls of the just awaited the resurrection in paradise. The earlier idea is seen in the New Testament at Acts 2.27, 31; the latter notion is found in Lk 16.22–26, where the rich man is buried in Hades and there suffers torments, whereas Lazarus is carried by angels into Abraham's bosom.

The phrase "the gates of Hades–Sheol" occurs in the Old Testament at Is 38.10 and Wis 16.13, where it is a figurative expression for death. This is likewise its meaning in the apocrypha (*Psalms of Solomon* 16.2; 3 Mc 5.51) and in classical Greek literature (Homer, *Iliad* 5.646; 9.312; *Odyssey* 14.156; Aeschylus, *Agamemnon* 1290; Euripides, *Hippolytus,* 56). Since death is seen as the passage through the gates of hell, which then shut to prevent all escape, the gates can stand, as *pars-pro-toto,* for the whole realm.

Exegetes differ as to the exact sense of the promise in Mt 16.18 that "the gates of hell shall not prevail." Noting that in the Old Testament and its apocrypha the gates of Sheol meant death, A. von Harnack and P. Schepens take it as a promise of immortality. (Von Harnack's conjecture that the original saying contained no reference to the Church, but only a promise that PETER would not die, lacks solid foundation.) Schepens argues that a promise of immortality is a figurative way of promising the Church's INDEFECTIBILITY. J. Schmid [*Regensburger Neues Testament,* ed. A. Wikenhauser and O. Kuss, (Regensburg 1955–) 1:249–250] likewise takes the gates of Hades to mean the power of death, and the promise to mean that the Church will endure to the end of time. O. Cullmann agrees that Hades is the realm of the dead, but takes the promise to mean that its gates will not withstand the assault of the Church, which will force Hades to release its dead at the resurrection (*Theological Dictionary of the New Testament,* 6:107). Against this, J. Jeremias (*ibid.* 6:926) argues that the promise in v. 18c must be understood as developing the theme of the rock, which he explains in the light of the contemporary image of the cosmic rock that bars the flood of the nether world. Hence he concludes that the gates of Hades stand for the hostile power in the lower world, which will storm in vain against the rock. Until now there has been no general acceptance of the conjecture of R. Eppel and J. B. Bauer that the original Aramaic word meant gate keepers rather than gates.

William Joseph Gaston, engraving by A.B. Durand, from portrait by George Cooke.

Bibliography: J. JEREMIAS, TDNT 6:924–928. M. SALLER, *Lexikon für Theologie und Kirche,* ed. J. HOFER and K. RAHNER, 10 v. (2d, new ed. Freiburg 1957–65) 4:1305. J. DUBLIN, "The Gates of Hades," *The Expositor* 11 (1916) 401–409. P. SCHEPENS, "L'Authenticité de S. Matt. 16,18," *Recherches de science religieuse* 10 (1920) 267–302. L. E. SULLIVAN, "The Gates of Hell," *Theological Studies* 10 (1949) 62 64. R. EPPEL, "L'Interpretation de Matt. 16:18b," *Mélanges offerts à M. Goguel* (Paris 1950) 71–73. J. B. BAUER, "Ostiarii inferorum," *Biblica* 34 (1953) 430–31.

[F. A. SULLIVAN]

GĀTHĀS

The hymns of ZOROASTER preserved as part of the Avesta, are short poems, comparable to those of the Rig-Veda in India. Although their language is fairly intelligible, being closely akin to Vedic Sanskrit, their style and contents make them excessively difficult to understand and translate. Their burden is the praise, untiringly repeated and varied, of the god Ahura Mazda and of his court or family of Entities, who bear abstract names and are, at the same time, human (moral and social) qualities

"The Gates of Hell," sculpture by Auguste Rodin. (©Vanni Archives/CORBIS)

personified. On the other hand, the cult of the ancient gods or daevas (cf. Sanskrit *deva* "god") and of the Evil Spirit [*see* AHURA MAZDA (OHRMAZD) AND AHRIMAN] and his entourage is unrelentingly combatted. It is not clear whether the sacrifice of the sacred liquor (*see* AVESTA) and the bull sacrifice were prohibited as such, or only special, repulsive forms of them. Anyhow, a destiny of woe in a dark hell with nauseous food is promised to the daevas-worshipers, whereas the followers of Ahura Mazda and his Holy Spirit, i.e., all those who rally to Truth, Justice, etc., against the forces of evil, will hereafter enjoy bliss, either in heaven or on a renovated earth. This renovation, entailing a resurrection of the body, will be brought about by coming saviors.

Bibliography: J. DUCHESNE-GUILLEMIN, *The Hymns of Zarathustra,* tr. M. HENNING (London 1952); *La Religion de l'Iran ancien* (Paris 1962).

[J. DUCHESNE-GUILLEMIN]

GATTERER, MICHAEL

Jesuit pastoral theologian; b. Oberrasen (south Tirol), Sept. 21, 1862; d. Innsbruck, June 6, 1944. He studied theology at Innsbruck as a disciple of Josef Jungmann and was ordained in 1885. After three years of experience in pastoral work, he entered the Society of Jesus in 1888 and began his teaching career at Innsbruck in 1892, where he became professor of moral theology, homiletics, and catechetics. His writings include: *Katechetik* (Innsbruck 1909); *Die Erstkommunion der Kinder* (Innsbruck 1911); *Elementarkatechesen* (Innsbruck 1923), a work in collaboration with A. Gruber; and *Das Religionsbuch der Kirche* (4 v. Innsbruck 1928–30). Establishing this Augustinian goal for himself, Gatterer held that love of God is the beginning, middle, and end of every religious inquiry. In keeping, however, with the declaration on faith of Vatican Council I, he maintained that the authority of the Church is the point of departure for every investigation. During the famous dispute about catechetical methods that arose about 1900, Gatterer insisted that catechesis should begin with the actual concerns of the child about his soul and should teach him to live devoutly.

Bibliography: *Bibliotèque de la Compagnie de Jésus* 3:1265–68. J. A. JUNGMANN, *Lexicon der Pädagogik* 2:214–215. W. CROCE, *Lexicon für Theologie und Kirche* 4:529–530.

[F. C. LEHNER]

GATTINARA, MERCURINO ARBORIO DI

Grand chancellor of Emperor CHARLES V, cardinal; b. Castello di Arborio, Vercelli (Piedmont), Italy, June 10, 1465; d. Innsbruck, Austria, June 5, 1530. Gattinara, orphaned at 14, was raised at Vercelli in the household of his uncle Pietro di Gattinara. His studies in jurisprudence began under the distinguished lawyer Bartolomeo Ranzo and were completed at the University of Turin. He became a successful advocate, then a professor of law at the University of Dôle and a jurisconsult for Philibert II, Duke of Savoy. After the Duke's death in 1504, he served the Duke's widow, Margaret of Austria (1480–1530). When Margaret was chosen by Emperor Maximilian I to be regent of the Netherlands and guardian of his grandson Charles, Gattinara remained in her court. There he oriented the political interests of the future Charles V away from the narrow dynastic traditions of the Burgundian court and toward the principles of universal monarchy, which he had himself learned from Dante's *De Monarchia.* In 1513 Gattinara was named president of the Council of the Netherlands; he was later accused of treason, and after defending himself he retired to a Carthusian monastery. Maximilian, needing his services, returned him to power and sent him on diplomatic missions to France, Italy, and Spain. Charles, after his accession to the throne of Spain (1516), made Gattinara his grand chancellor to succeed Jean de Sauvage, who died June 7, 1518. In this office, which he kept until his death, Gattinara influenced Charles's statecraft concerning the need of a general council as a political and religious move, and an Italian policy that would oust French control from northern Italy. He was created a cardinal and bishop of Ostia by Clement VII in 1529.

Gattinara's concept of imperial power is expressed in a memorandum sent to Charles after his election on June 28, 1519. It reminded the new Emperor that he now had power hitherto possessed only by Charlemagne, and that he "was on the way to world sovereignty and the gathering of all Christendom under one shepherd." He left a large correspondence, essays on political subjects, and an autobiography edited by C. Bornate, "Historia vitae et gestorum per dominum magnum cancellarium . . . ," *Miscellanea di storia italiana,* 3d ser. 17 (Turin 1915) 231–585.

Bibliography: K. BRANDI, *The Emperor Charles V: The Growth and Destiny of a Man and a World-Empire,* tr. C. V. WEDGWOOD (New York 1939). Jedin Trent 1. C. BORNATE, *Enciclopedia Italiana di scienzi, littere ed arti* 16:451. P. MIKAT, *Lexicon für Theologie und Kirche* 4:530. P. SANNAZZARO, *Enciclopedia cattolica* 5:1960–61.

[E. D. MCSHANE]

GATTORNO, ROSA MARIA BENEDETTA, BL.

Also known as Anna Rosa Gattorno; widow, mother, founder of the Institute of Daughters of St. Anne; b. Oct. 14, 1841, Genoa, Italy; d. May 6, 1900, Rome. One of six children born to Francesco Gattorno and Adelaide Campanella, Rosa was educated at home. She married her cousin Gerolamo Custo (November 5, 1852) and gave birth to three children (1853–57). Gerolamo's death from tuberculosis (1858) left her with continued financial problems and a sickly, deaf-mute eldest daughter. Her youngest child died the same year. Though grief-stricken, Rosa offered herself in charitable service and care of her two surviving children. She privately vowed perpetual chastity and obedience (1858), then added a vow of poverty (1861). Even during her marriage, Rosa grew spiritually through daily Communion and the gift of a hidden stigmata. As her reputation for holiness increased, she was chosen president of the Pious Union of the New Ursuline Daughters of Mary Immaculate and revised its rule (1864).

This revision led her to consider founding a new religious order, but she was torn between her duty to her children and her new heightened sense of religious vocation. She sought advice from her confessor, the archbishop of Genoa, St. Francis of Camporosso and Pope Pius IX (1866), and then decided to establish the Institute of Daughters of St. Anne. The new foundation was made in Piacenza, Dec. 8, 1866, with the help of Giovanni Battista Tornatore, CM. Rosa received the habit in 1867 and was professed with 11 other sisters in 1870. The institute, dedicated to working with disadvantaged youth, received approval in 1879, as did the rule in 1892. She collaborated with Giovanni Battista SCALABRINI in ministering to the speech and hearing impaired. She contracted a virulent influenza in February 1900, died the following month, and was buried in the church adjoining the generalate.

The institute expanded before and after Mother Rosa's death throughout Europe to South America, Africa, the Middle East, Asia, and Oceania, where the sisters have been engaging in evangelization, catechesis, and assistance to the poor including drug rehabilitation centers, schools, daycare centers, and homes for the elderly. Her charism has expanded to include contemplative sisters, an association of priests (Sons of St. Anne), a secular institute, and a lay association (Movement of Hope). She was beatified by Pope John Paul II on April 9, 2000.

Feast: May 6.

Bibliography: *L'Osservatore Romano,* Eng. ed., no. 16 (2000): 3.

[K. I. RABENSTEIN]

GAUCHERIUS, ST.

Augustinian canon, abbot; b. Meulan-sur-Seine, *c.* 1060; d. near Limoges, April 9, 1140. Having received a fine education, Gaucherius retired to the forests near Limoges to live the contemplative life of a hermit when he was about 18 years old. Gradually cells of other devout men were erected in the vicinity, and Gaucherius founded a priory there (*c.* 1078) that came to be called Saint-Jean of Aureil. A daughterhouse of Saint-Rufus et André, founded earlier by Gaucherius's kinsman, Rufus, in Avignon, it followed the Rule of St. Augustine (*see* CANONS REGULAR OF ST. AUGUSTINE). Gaucherius's disciples included such saints as Lambert of Angoulême, Faucherius, and STEPHEN OF MURET. He also founded a convent for women and gave it the rule of the Canonesses Regular of St. Augustine. He was canonized in 1194.

Feast: April 9

Bibliography: *Acta Santorum* April 1:841–844. A. LECLERQ, *Dictionnaire d'histoire et de géographie ecclésiastiques,* ed. A.

BAUDRILLAT et al. (Paris 1912–) 5:710–713. J. L. BAUDOT and L. CHAUSSIN, *Vies des saints et des bienheureux selon l'ordre du calendrier avec l'historique des fêtes,* 12 v. (Paris 1935–56) 4:218–219. A. BUTLER, *The Lives of the Saints,* rev. ed. H. THURSTON and D. ATTWATER, 4 v. (New York 1956) 2:59–60.

[E. J. KEALEY]

GAUDENTIUS OF BRESCIA, ST.

Fl. 400; date of birth, episcopal consecration, and death unknown. The chief source for his life is his own *Sermo de ordinatione sua.* He was on a journey to the East when he received the news that he had been chosen bishop of Brixia (Brescia) to succeed Filastrius (d. 397). Despite his opposition to the nomination, he was finally persuaded by St. AMBROSE and other northern Italian bishops to accept it. He was one of the Latin bishops who were requested by the Emperor Honorius and Pope INNOCENT I to go to Constantinople to plead with the Emperor Arcadius for the return of St. JOHN CHRYSOSTOM from exile, but this mission failed (*see* Palladius, *Dial. de vita Chrys.*, 4; Chrysostom, *Epist.,* 184). Of his 21 extant sermons, ten were delivered during Easter week, and the last (*De vita et obitu Philastrii*), on the 15th anniversary of the death of his predecessor in the See of Brescia. The sermons show that Gaudentius had a remarkably sound knowledge of theology. Sermon 2 contains an important treatment of the Eucharist. Sermon 9 defends the virginity of the Blessed Virgin, and Sermon 5 contains an interesting passage on the episcopal staff and the duties of the bishop as a guide and corrector of the faithful. Since he knew Greek, Gaudentius in his exegesis was able to compare Latin Biblical readings with those of the Greek text. His style is simple and clear and much closer to the best school standard of the age than that of Filastrius. The sermons of Gaudentius were much admired for their style and content by his flock. Those extant owe their preservation to the fact that a high official, Benivolus, a *magister memoriae* and friend of Gaudentius, furnished the bishop with stenographic copies, which the bishop revised for circulation in written form. The influence of his classical training is concretely revealed by borrowings from Terence, Cicero, Vergil, and Ovid. There is a modern critical edition of the Sermons (*Tractatus*) by A. Glueck, *Corpus scriptorum ecclesiasticorum latinorum* 68 (1956).

Feast: Oct. 25.

Bibliography: G. M. BRUNI, *Teologia della storia secondo Gaudenzio da Brescia* (Vicenza 1967). C. TRUZZI, *Zeno, Gaudenzio e Cromazio: testi e contenuti della predicazione cristiana per le chiese di Verona, Brescia e Aquileia* (Brescia 1985). A. JÜLICHER, ''Gaudentius (9),'' *Paulys Realenzyklopädie der klassischen* 7.1 (1910) 859–861. O. BARDENHEWER, *Geschichte der Altkirchlichen Literatur* 3:485–486. U. MORICCA, *Storia della letteratura cristiana,* 3 v. in 5 (Turin 1923–1935) 2.1:585–590. F. SAVIO, *Gli antichi vescovi d'Italia,* 4 v. (Bergamo 1898–1932) 3:149–156.

[M. R. P. MCGUIRE]

GAUDENTIUS OF GNIEZNO, ST.

First metropolitan of Gniezno, younger brother of St. ADALBERT; b. *c.* 960–70; d. *c.* 1006–11. Having joined the BENEDICTINE order in Rome in 988, he was later ordained priest there. About 996 he accompanied Adalbert on his missionary journey into Prussia, where he witnessed Adalbert's martyrdom. When Gaudentius returned to Rome for his brother's CANONIZATION process, the matter of the first archbishopric for Poland came to the fore. In late 999 he was consecrated with the title *archiepiscopus sancti Adalberti martyris.* The following March, papal legates enthroned him as archbishop in Gniezno in the presence of Emperor OTTO III and King Boleslaw Chrobry. Details of his episcopal activity are vague. His relics were translated to Prague in 1039. His cultus is immemorial, but without formal ratification.

Feast: Jan. 5, Aug. 25.

Bibliography: G. LABUDA, in *Polski Słownik Biograficzny,* v.7 (Cracow 1949) 308–309. F. DVORNIK, *The Making of Central and Eastern Europe* (London 1949) 101–105, 143–144. Z. SZOSTKIEWICZ, ''Katalog Biskupów obrz. łac. Przedrozbiorowej Polski,'' *Sacrum Poloniae Millennium* 1 (1954) 450. W. MEYSZTOWICZ, ''Koronacje Pierwszych Piastów,'' *ibid.* 3 (1956) 294.

[L. SIEKANIEC]

GAUDERICH OF VELLETRI

Bishop; fl. second half of 9th century; d. before 897. One of the chief counselors of Pope John VIII, he had probably been consecrated bishop of Velletri by Pope Nicholas I *c.* 865. Shortly after Nicholas's death (Nov. 13, 867), Gauderich, together with Bp. Stephen of Nepi and JOHN THE DEACON (Hymmonides), was unjustly exiled by Duke Lambert of Spoleto, but was soon recalled to Rome by Pope ADRIAN II (December 867). In 868 Adrian had Gauderich and Bishop FORMOSUS (later pope) ordain the Slavic disciples of St. Cyril who had just arrived in Rome. In the Roman synod of 869, Gauderich, as spokesman for the bishops, urged severe action against PHOTIUS. In the following decade, he performed several important legations for Pope JOHN VIII. In 879 he was instrumental in securing the rehabilitation of Photius; and, apparently in gratitude, Photius sent him a very friendly letter and a gift (probably an enameled cross) in spring 880. Though Gauderich died before 897, there is no substantial proof that he had retired to Monte Cassino. To honor Pope St. CLEMENT I, patron of his cathedral, he asked John Hymmonides to compile an account of Clement's miracles and the translation of his relics to Rome. He received a description of this translation from ANASTASIUS the Librarian (*Epistolae* 7:435–438). Hymmonides died before finishing the work, which was then completed by Gauderich himself [Bibliotheca Casiniensis IV (Monte Cassino 1874) 373–390]. Although only partially preserved, this work was used by later authors, and is one of the chief sources for the lives of SS. CYRIL and Methodius.

Bibliography: F. DVORNIK, *The Photian Schism* (Cambridge, Eng. 1948). P. MEYVAERT and P. DEVOS, ''Trois énigmes cyrillo-méthodiennes de la *Légende italique,*'' *Analecta Bollandiana* 73 (1955) 375–461; ''Autour de Léon d'Ostie et de sa *Translatio s. Clementis,*'' *ibid.* 74 (1956) 189–240. P. DUTHILLEUL, *L'Évangélisation des Slaves: Cyrille et Méthode* (Tournai 1963) 20–25, 119–120.

[G. T. DENNIS]

GAUL, EARLY CHURCH IN

Earliest evidence of the existence of Christianity in Gaul stems from the middle of the 2d century; the legends tracing evangelization to the Apostles and Disciples are totally unhistorical. In about 150 a Christian community was organized in the Roman colony of Lyons to care for a large group of Greek settlers, but in 177 a popular uprising caused persecution to break out there. Among some 48 known victims were the first bishop of the city, Pothinus, who died in prison; the deacon Sanctus of Vienne; the young slave girl Blandina; and the youth Ponticus. The details of the persecution are known from a letter sent by the Christians of Lyons and Vienne to their brethren in Asia Minor (Eusebius, *Hist. eccl.* 5.1–4).

Foundation of the Episcopacy. The successor of Pothinus was IRENAEUS OF LYONS, who in his youth had been a disciple of POLYCARP at Smyrna. Christianity spread from Lyons into the valley of the Rhône and penetrated northward toward Treves and the Rhine Valley. Irenaeus wrote to Pope VICTOR (*c.* 190) to give him the collective opinion of the parishes of Gaul on the EASTER CONTROVERSY (*Hist. eccl.* 5.23). Although Irenaeus suffered martyrdom under Septimius Severus (*c.* 202), according to GREGORY OF TOURS (*Hist. Franc.* 1.27), Eusebius makes no reference to the death of the great bishop. The Greek epitaph of PECTORIUS discovered at Autun indicates that there were Christians in that city by the second half of the 2d century or at the beginning of the 3d; by 250 there were some 30 episcopal sees, including Lyons, Arles, Marseilles, Autun, Vienne, Toulouse, Narbonne, Treves, Reims, and Paris.

A letter from CYPRIAN OF CARTHAGE to Pope STEPHEN on the severity of Bp. Marcion of Arles, in dealing with the lapsi of the Decian persecution, names several Gallic bishops (Cyprian, *Epist.* 68.2–3). Faustinus of Lyons had informed the Pope of the schismatic attitude of Marcion and appealed to Cyprian to solicit the intervention of Rome. According to Gregory of Tours (*Hist. Franc.* 1.30), Bp. Saturninus of Toulouse suffered martyrdom in the persecution of Decius (249–251); in that case, the bishopric of Toulouse was anterior to 250. Bishoprics were established also in Belgian and Celtic Gaul; but the western region, less Romanized, seems to have been neglected. The account of seven bishops sent to Gaul by Pope Fabian (*c.* 250) is found only in Gregory of Tours (*Hist. Franc.* 1.28) and has no other evidence, nor is there any proof that the churches of Tours, Limoges, and Clermont were founded at this time. The later persecutions had only a few victims in Gaul; under Valerian (257), Denis of Paris suffered martyrdom. But thanks to the benevolent policy of Constantinus Chlorus, the persecution of Diocletian was not carried out in Gaul.

There were 36 episcopal sees in Gaul when CONSTANTINE I granted peace to the Church. Sixteen of these were represented at the Council of Arles (314), 12 of them by their bishops: Arles, Lyons, Vienne, Marseilles, Vaison, Bordeaux, Eauze, Autun, Rouen, Reims, Treves, and Cologne. In the 30 years following this council, efforts were made toward ecclesiastical organization. By the middle of the 4th century, the number of episcopal sees had doubled the number listed for the year 313. By the time of the death of THEODOSIUS I (395), the Church in Gaul was fully organized in diocesan structure and hierarchy; but it was only in the last third of the 4th century that the Nicene provision for provincial grouping was effectively adopted. According to the *Notitia Galliarum*, Gaul counted 17 provinces in 375.

Administration and the Control of Heresy. Conflict in the southwest over the attempt to follow the framework of the civil administration in provincial grouping led to controversy between the metropolitan of Vienne and the bishop of Arles. The latter claimed to be the metropolitan, since the prefecture of Gaul had been transferred from Treves to Arles. In 398 the bishops of Gaul submitted the matter to the bishops of the province of Milan, meeting in synod at Turin. They suggested a division of the province between the two bishops. The same synod was asked to settle the claims of the bishops of the Narbonnaise against Bp. Proclus of Marseilles, who had assumed the office of metropolitan of that province.

Only one bishop from Gaul had assisted at the Council of Nicaea; but after the sojourn in Treves of ATHANASIUS OF ALEXANDRIA, who had been exiled by Constantine I (335–337), the bishops of Gaul participated in the controversies that had their rise in the political Arianism of Constantius. At the Council of SARDICA (343) that restored Athanasius, bishops were present from Lyons and Treves. Although Saturninus of Arles sided with the Arianizing Emperor, HILARY OF POITIERS and Phebadus of Agen strongly supported the orthodox position. After the Council of Béziers (356), Hilary spent four years in exile in Phrygia (356–360). On his return, in spite of the wavering of almost all the bishops of Gaul at the Council of Rimini (359), Hilary succeeded in having the episcopate of Gaul assembled about him at the Council of Paris (360). ''Everyone knows,'' wrote Sulpicius Severus, ''that Gaul is indebted to Hilary alone for the benefit of freedom from heresy'' (*Chron.* 2.45). In 380 two bishops of Aquitaine took part in the Council of Saragossa that condemned PRISCILLIANISM; the next year, six Gallic bishops assisted at the Council of Aquileia that dealt with two bishops accused of Arianism.

Parishes and Monasteries. Since a bishop was an official personage, he installed his cathedral inside the city. In the suburbs, cemeterial basilicas were built to honor the tombs of martyrs and confessors. The apostolate in the countryside began only with the peace of the Church. It was carried out through the erection of parishes in the villages. St. Martin of Tours, who was noted for evangelizing the rural areas, created the first six parishes of his diocese (371–397). At the beginning of the 5th century, the number of pagans, almost insignificant in the cities, was still high in the country places. The oratories established by the lords of rural estates were often transformed into parochial churches. In the second half of the 4th century, following the example of the East, hermitages and monasteries were established. The oldest known was the modest monastery that Martin of Tours organized at Ligugé near Poitiers. Later as bishop, Martin gathered his numerous disciples at Marmoutier near his episcopal city. Many women embraced a life of virginity; some lived in common, others, such as St. GENEVIÈVE OF PARIS, lived at home. There were also recluses among them (Sulpicius Severus, *Dial.* 2.12). Monastic life gained in prestige during the 5th century. Among the monasteries were Lérins, established by HONORATUS OF ARLES (*c.* 410), and that of St. Victor at Marseilles founded by John CASSIAN (*c.* 416) on the model of Egyptian monasticism.

Consolidation. The 5th century witnessed the struggle to consolidate the power of the episcopate of Gaul and to preserve communication with Rome in the midst of barbarian inroads. Under Pope Siricius (384–398) a number of decrees were sent to bishops in Gaul, and the popes were frequently called upon to preserve discipline and uphold the rights of sees and bishops. In 417 jurisdictional conflicts arose when Pope ZOSIMUS, pressed by Bp. Patroclus of Arles, placed under the metropolitan authority of Arles all the ancient Narbonnaise, to which was annexed the provinces of the Maritime Alps. Although this attempt to create the primacy of Arles was not sustained by the successors of Zosimus, the city remained a great ecclesiastical center, especially under Bishop HILARY OF ARLES (429–449), whose encroachments were severely censured by Pope LEO I in 445 (*Epist.* 10). Before attracting the unfavorable attention of the Pope, Hilary had tried more than once to assemble all the bishops of the southeast in inter-provincial council: Riez (439), Orange (441), and Vaison (442).

The VANDALS raged through Gaul between 407 and 408, but the invasions of the VISIGOTHS, Burgundians, FRANKS, and Alamanni were of more serious consequence. These peoples, at first established as *foederati* of the Roman Empire, set up independent kingdoms and destroyed what remained of imperial authority. The bishops, among whom were Aignan of Orléans, GERMAIN OF AUXERRE, and Lupus of Troyes, tried to alleviate the hardships of the time. The Church adapted itself to the rule of barbarian kings: Visigoths in Aquitaine and a part of the Narbonnaise, Burgundians in the valleys of the Rhine and the Saine, and Franks in Belgian Gaul and in the Rhine region. With the baptism of Clovis and about 3,000 of his retainers (*c.* 496), the conversion of the Frankish nation was soon an accomplished fact.

Scholars and Defenders of the Faith. Gaul produced some of the foremost writers of early Christianity. Two works of Irenaeus of Lyons (originally from Asia Minor, however) are extant: *Proof of the Apostolic Preaching* and *Adversus haereses*. Hilary of Poitiers (d. 367), the first to write in Latin, composed *De Trinitate, Commentarium in s. Mattheum,* and *Tractatus super Psalmos,* as well as controversial tracts in defense of Nicene orthodoxy. St. Jerome reports that Hilary also composed a *Liber hymnorum*. PAULINUS OF NOLA (353–431) composed most of his poetry after he had left Gaul for Italy. SULPICIUS SEVERUS (d. 420) wrote excellent Latin prose, as his *Dialogues, Chronicle,* and *Vita Martini* prove. The latter work (*Ancient Christian Writers* 7) popularized the cult of the famous bishop and attracted pilgrims to his tomb. John Cassian (d. 435) wrote *De Incarnatione* at the request of the deacon, later Pope Leo I, and composed his *Institutes* and *Collations* as a stimulus to monastic spirituality. His Semi-Pelagian tendencies provoked a lay theologian, PROSPER OF AQUITAINE, to come to the defense of St. Augustine in works of prose and verse. VINCENT OF LÉRINS (d. 450) exhibited Semi-Pelagian leaning in his *Commonitorium*, and Salvian of Marseilles (*c.* 400) wrote his famous *De gubernatione Dei* (*Ancient Christian Writers* 7). The hagiography that developed in the 6th century with Gregory of Tours' eight books of miracles is not trustworthy, although his *History of the Franks*, despite its credulous and moralizing tendency, is an indispensable source for the early history of Christian Gaul and one of the major historical works of the Middle Ages.

The zeal of CAESARIUS OF ARLES (502–542) was exercised in an attempt to vivify the Church in Gaul by means of popular preaching and a reform of ecclesiastical discipline. Some 238 of his sermons have been preserved and reveal him to have been the greatest popular preacher in the Latin Church after St. Augustine. The synod at Orange (529), presided over by Caesarius, submitted its 25 canons rejecting PELAGIANISM and Semi-Pelagianism to Pope BONIFACE II (530–532). The papal confirmation of the decisions was accepted throughout the Church, and thus the first great Western controversy in regard to grace was brought to a close. With the death of Caesarius, a new phase in the Gallican Church began.

Bibliography: J. LEBRETON and J. ZEILLER, *The History of the Primitive Church,* tr. E. C. MESSENGER, 4 bks. in 2 (New York 1949) 1:360–363; 2:717–728, 772–778, 1193–96. J. R. PALANQUE et al., Fliche-Martin v.3–4, Eng. *The Church in the Christian Roman Empire,* tr. E. C. MESSENGER, 2 v. in 1 (New York 1953) 1:272–283; 2:634–647. H. LECLERCQ, *Dictionaire d'archeologie chrétienne et de liturgie,* eds. F. CABROL, H. LECLERCQ, and H. I. MARROU (Paris 1907–53) 5.2:2116–2575; 6.1:310–473, s.v. Gallicane église; 8.2:2357–2440, s.v. Légendes Gallicanes; 12.2:1717–27, s.v. Notitia Galliarum. É. GRIFFE, *La Gaule chrétienne à l'époque romaine* v.1–2.1 (Paris 1947–57; rev. ed. 1965-); *Catholicisme* 4:1775–82; *Lexikon für Theologie und Kirche,* eds. J. HOFER and K. RAHNER (Freiburg 1957–65) 2 4:504–506. L. SCHMIDT and M. C. PFISTER, Cambridge Medieval History, 8 v. (London-New York 1911–36) 1:277–303. S. DILL, *Roman Society in Gaul in the Merovingian Age* (London 1926). GREGORY OF TOURS, *The History of the Franks,* ed. and tr. O. M. DALTON, 2 v. (Oxford 1927). C. J. VON HEFELE, *Histoire des conciles d'après les documents originaux* (Paris 1907–38) 1.1:192–193, on legendary synod of Narbonne; 1.2, *passim;* 2.1–2, *passim.* References to the pertinent councils may be checked through the *Table Analytique* at end of pt. 2 in each v. A. LATREILLE et al., *Histoire du catholicisme en France,* 3 v. (Paris 1957–62) v.1. E. MÂLE, *La Fin du paganisme en Gaule* (Paris 1950).

[M. C. HILFERTY]

GAUZELIN OF TOUL, ST.

Bishop; d. Sept. 7, 962. Of a noble Frankish family, he entered the chancery of Charles the Simple as notary (913); he was chosen bishop of Toul, March 17, 922. His episcopate was disturbed by various political problems. In his time Lorraine came under the control of Abp. BRUNO OF COLOGNE, brother of OTTO I, who created the duchies of Upper and Lower Lorraine (959). The city and Diocese of Toul, part of Upper Lorraine, also suffered from the Hungarian invasions of 928 and 954. Standing free of these contentions, Gauzelin tried to maintain and develop the patrimony of his church and favored monastic reform. Einold, the archdeacon of Toul, started the reform of GORZE, and Gauzelin encouraged various foundations, personally introducing the observance of SAINT-BENOÎT-SUR-LOIRE at the Abbey St. Aper. He was buried near Nancy, in the Abbey of Bouxières-aux-Dames, which he founded.

Feast: Sept. 7.

Bibliography: *Gesta episcoporum Tullensium,* J. P. NIGNE, *Patrologia latina* 157:459–463. *Acta Sanctorum,* Sept. 3:143–144. E. MARTIN, *Histoire des diocèses de Toul, de Nancy et de Saint–Dié,* 3 v. (Nancy 1900–03) v.1.

[J. CHOUX]

GAVAN, JOHN, BL.

Jesuit priest and martyr; b. London, England, 1640; d. hanged, drawn, and quartered at Tyburn (London), June 20, 1679. Affectionately called ''Angel'', Gavan studied at the Jesuit college at St-Omer, Flanders, before his entrance into the Society of Jesus at Watten (September 7, 1660). Prior to his ordination (1670), he studied philosophy at Liège and theology at Rome. Upon returning to England (1671), he ministered fruitfully for eight years in Staffordshire, until he was implicated by Stephen Dugdale in the fictitious Titus Oates Plot to kill the king. When a bounty of 50 pounds was placed on his head, he planned to escape to the Continent disguised as a servant. He was discovered in the imperial ambassador's stables, arrested on Jan. 23, 1679, and imprisoned at the Gatehouse (London), then at Newgate Prison.

During his trial at the Old Bailey with Frs. Thomas WHITBREAD, Antony TURNER, William HARCOURT, and John FENWICK, he served at spokesman. They were found guilty of high treason based on perjured testimony with the judge's prodding of the jury. On the gallows he again protested his innocence, then said: ''I am contented to undergo an ignominious death for the love of you, my dear Jesus, seeing you have been pleased to undergo an ignominious death for the love of me.'' He was beatified by Pius XI on Dec. 15, 1929.

Feast of the English Martyrs: May 4 (England); December 1 (Jesuits).

See Also: ENGLAND, SCOTLAND, AND WALES, MARTYRS OF.

Bibliography: R. CHALLONER, *Memoirs of Missionary Priests,* ed. J. H. POLLEN (rev. ed. London 1924; repr. Farnborough 1969). J. H. POLLEN, *Acts of English Martyrs* (London 1891). J. N. TYLENDA, *Jesuit Saints & Martyrs* (Chicago 1998) 179–81.

[K. I. RABENSTEIN]

GAY, CHARLES LOUIS

Ascetical theologian and spiritual writer; b. Paris, Oct. 1, 1815; d. Paris, Jan. 19, 1892. As a young man Gay led an indifferent religious life, but the sermons of Lacordaire began his conversion, and he decided to study for the priesthood. Ordained in 1845, he soon became extremely popular as a preacher and spiritual director. He based his direction on a clear exposition of Christian dogma, insisting that instruction must precede advice. He belonged to the Oratorian school of spirituality and followed the footsteps of Pierre de BÉRULLE. Among his chief writings are *De la vie et des vertus chrétiennes* (2 v. Paris 1874), of which 10,000 copies were sold in 18 months, and *Elévations sur la vie et la doctrine de Notre Seigneur Jésus Christ* (2 v. Paris 1879). He was appointed vicar general of Poitiers and later auxiliary bishop and attended Vatican Council I as a theologian. In addition to his many books, several volumes of sermons and six of letters witness to his great influence on the France of his day.

Bibliography: G. LIÉVIN, *Enciclopedia cattolica* 5:1969. P. POURRAT, *Christian Spirituality,* tr. W. H. MITCHELL et al., 4 v. (Westminster, Md. 1953–55) 4:493–499. B. DU BOISROUVRAY, *Mgr. Gay . . . sa vie, ses oeuvres,* 2 v. (Tours 1922–27).

[M. J. BARRY]

GEBHARD II OF CONSTANCE, ST.

Bishop; b. 949; d. Aug. 27, 995. He was the son of Count Udalrich VI of Bregenz and was educated in Constance under Bp. CONRAD OF CONSTANCE. In 979 Emperor OTTO II made him Conrad's second successor. Like Conrad he was concerned with monastic reform, and in 983 he founded the Abbey of PETERSHAUSEN opposite Constance. From Pope JOHN XV he obtained relics of Pope St. GREGORY THE GREAT, under whose title he consecrated the abbey church in 992; however, since the church was modeled on ST. PETER'S BASILICA in Rome, the abbey came to be known as Petershausen. Gebhard called an abbot and BENEDICTINE monks from EINSIEDELN, thus introducing the customs of that great reform center, but Petershausen never played the important role he had hoped for. Gebhard was buried in his foundation, and his cult is allowed in the former Diocese of Constance.

Feast: Aug. 27.

Bibliography: Vita (*c.* 1134), *Monumenta Germaniae Historica: Scriptores,* 10:582–594. *See Casus Monasterii Petrishusensis,* bk. 1, *Monumenta Germaniae Historica: Scriptores* 20:627–639. Two Sequences in *Analecta hymnica* 54:61–64. J. L. BAUDOT and L. CHAUSSIN, *Vies des saints et des bienheurex selon l'ordre du calendrier avec l'historique des fêtes, by the Benedictines of Paris* 8:518. A. M. ZIMMERMAN, *Kalendarium Benedictinum: Die Heiligen und Seligen des Benediktinerorderns und seiner Zweige* 2:630. H. TÜCHLE, *Kirchengeschichte Schwabens,* 2 v. (Stuttgart 1950–54) 1:156–157. O. FEGER, *Geschichte des Bodenseeraumes,* 4 v. (Lindau 1956–) 1:205–211. A. M. ZIMMERMANN, *Lexicon für Theologie und Kirche*[2] 4:555. K.SCHMID, *Neue deutsche Biographie* 6:114.

[A. A. SCHACHER]

GEBHARD III OF CONSTANCE

Bishop; b. *c.* 1050; d. Constance, Germany, Nov. 12, 1110. The future leader of the papal party in Germany was the son of Berthold I of Zähringen. He was provost in Xanten and then a simple monk in the Abbey of HIRSAU before Otto of Ostia, later Pope URBAN II, consecrated him bishop of the largest diocese in the Empire. Gebhard supported WILLIAM OF HIRSAU in the reform or foundation of numerous monasteries while he imposed the customs of Hirsau on the Abbey of PETERSHAUSEN near Constance, which flourished under Abbot Theodorich (1086–1116). Named papal LEGATE by Urban II in 1089, Gebhard became the principal legate for Germany after the death of ALTMANN OF PASSAU in 1091. As such, he won his brother Berthold II, Duke of Carinthia and Swabia, and Duke Welf IV of Bavaria for the papal cause. During a princes' meeting at Ulm in November 1093, Gebhard and Berthold were given religious and political leadership in Swabia. A reform synod at Constance during Easter 1095 followed. Driven from his see in 1103, Gebhard, at the request of Pope PASCHAL II, rallied the papal party behind the Emperor's rebellious son, HENRY V. At the Diet of Mainz during Christmas 1105, he denied the Emperor the absolution for which he had asked. In the cause of Henry V who had returned him to his see in 1105, he went to Rome the following year. Gebhard was reprimanded in absentia by Paschal II at the Synod of Troyes in 1107 for having acquiesced to Henry V's nomination of the bishop of Halberstadt, and thus his legation came to an end. He devoted his last years exclusively to the care of his diocese.

Bibliography: E. HOFMANN, ''Die Stellung der Konstanzer Bischöfe zu Papst u. Kaiser während des Investiturstreites,'' *Freiburger Diözesanarchiv* 31 (1931) 181–242, esp. 218–242. H. TÜCHLE, *Kirchengeschichte Schwabens,* 2 v. (Stuttgart 1950–54) 1:219–221; *Lexicon für Theologie und Kirche* 4:555–556. O. FEGER, *Geschichte des Bodenseeraumes,* 2 v. (Lindau 1956–58). K. SCHMID, *Neue deutsche Biographic* 6: 114–115, bibliog.

[A. A. SCHACHER]

GEBHARD OF SALZBURG, BL.

Archbishop; d. Salzburg, June 15, 1088. A member of the Suabian nobility, and chaplain to Emperors HENRY

III and HENRY IV, he served also as royal chancellor and ambassador to the Greek court (1057–59). Having become archbishop of Salzburg in 1060, he founded the Diocese of Gurk (1072) and the Abbey of ADMONT (1074), organized parishes, suspended the tithe of the Slavs, and effectively supported GREGORY VII. He wrote a reliable description of the INVESTITURE struggle (now known only from second-hand sources) and a letter answering Bp. Herman of Metz regarding the election of antipope GUIBERT OF RAVENNA (*Monumenta Germaniae Scriptores* 8:459–460). He was driven from his see by Henry IV and could return only in 1086. His remains rest in Admont; his canonization process was begun in 1629.

Feast: June 15.

Bibliography: *Monumenta Germaniae Scriptores* (Berlin 1825–) 11:17–19, 25–50. *Acta Sanctorum* June 6:147–154. W. STEINBÖCK, *Erzbischof Gebhard von Salzburg* (Vienna 1972). *Salzburger Urkundenbuch,* eds. W. K. HAUTHALER and F. MARTIN, v.2 (Salzburg 1916) 160–180. P. KARNER, *Die Heiligen und Seligen Salzburgs (Austria Sancta* 12; Vienna 1913). E. TOMEK, *Kirchengeschichte Österreichs* v.1 (Innsbruck 1935) 138–139, 143–149. R. BAUERREISS, *Kirchengeschichte Bayerns* (2d ed. Munich 1958–) v.2. J. WODKA, *Kirche in Österreich* (Vienna 1959); *Lexikon für Theologie und Kirche,* ed. J. HOFER and K. RAHNER, 10 v. (2d, new ed. Freiburg 1957–65) 4:556. W. OHNSORGE, *Abendland und Byzanz* (Darmstadt 1958) 342–363.

[V. H. REDLICH]

GEBIZO, ST.

Monk; d. Oct. 21, 1078 or 1087. About 1060 he left Cologne and made a pilgrimage to MONTE CASSINO with the advice and assistance of the Empress Agnes (d. 1077). Abbot Desiderius, later Pope VICTOR III, received him into the BENEDICTINE Order. Gebizo was a lover of prayer and silence, and he practiced great self–denial, taking no foods with oil or animal fat. He was confused with the future bishop of Cesena and thus falsely reported to have been sent in 1076 as the legate of GREGORY VII to crown the Croatian king, Demetrius Zvonimir (d. 1089). At the end of his life Gebizo suffered great pain from an abscess on his chest, but he continued to beg God for additional sufferings. The bishop of Venafro treated him but could not help him. He was always called a saint, even in his earliest biographies, but there is no trace of any liturgical veneration. He is mentioned in the monastic martyrology, but not in the Roman, although his cult has been approved. His picture may be seen in Cesena in the church of S. Maria del Monte.

Feast: Oct. 21.

Bibliography: *Acta Sanctorum*, Oct. 9:397–405. J. P. MIGNE, *Patrologia latina*, 173:1107–10. A. M. ZIMMERMANN, *Kalendarium Benedictinum: Die Heiligen und Seligen des Benediktinerorderns und seiner Zweige* 3:205–207.

[G. SPAHR]

GEDDES, ALEXANDER

Catholic Biblical scholar pioneering in the literary criticism of the Pentateuch, known especially for his ''fragment hypothesis''; b. Ruthven, Banffshire, Scotland, Sept. 14, 1737; d. London, Feb. 26, 1802. He received his higher education at the Scots' College in Paris, where he also attended lectures at the Sorbonne. Having become proficient in Hebrew, he took a deep interest in the Tübingen school of Biblical criticism. After ordination in 1764, he carried out parochial duties in Scotland until 1779, when his liberal views, expressed with uncompromising frankness and imprudence, brought him into difficulties with his bishop. Helped by his munificent patron, Lord Petre, he established himself in London, where he devoted the rest of his life to Biblical and literary studies. In the preface to his English translation of the Hexateuch (1792), Geddes propounded such extreme views on the origin of the Pentateuch that Protestants as well as Catholics were shocked. He denied that the mission of Moses was divine, held that not all of Scripture was inspired, and, in general, showed strongly rationalistic tendencies. For his views he was suspended from exercising his priestly functions. Of a brilliant but erratic character, Geddes was one of the first scholars in England to recognize the inadequacy of the traditional notions about the Mosaic authorship of the Pentateuch, but he went to excess in his ardor for the new theories. Always claiming to be a Catholic, though of his own strange variety, he received the Last Rites and died in the Church. Among his better-known works are: *The Holy Bible . . . Faithfully Translated from the Corrected Texts of the Original . . .* (2 v., containing the Pentateuch and the historical books; London 1792–97); *Critical Remarks on the Hebrew Scriptures* (London 1800); *A Modest Apology for the Roman Catholics of Great Britain* (London 1800); *A New Translation of the Psalms from the Original Hebrew . . .* (posthumously edited by J. Disney and C. Butler; London 1807).

Bibliography: *A Literary and Biographical History or Bibliographical Dictionary of the English Catholics from 1534 to the Present Time* 2:410–415. J. GOOD, *Memoirs of the Life and Writings of Alexander Geddes* (London 1803). T. K. CHEYNE, *Founders of Old Testament Criticism* (London 1893) 3–12.

[K. O'SULLIVAN]

GEHENNA

A valley in Jerusalem where refuse was burned, later becoming a symbol for the place of punishment in the nether world. The NT term γέεννα is a Greek-influenced form of Aramaic *gêhinnām,* corresponding to Hebrew *gê'hinnōm* (the Valley of Hinnom: Neh 11.30, a shortened form of *gê' bᵉnê-hinnōm,* the Valley of the Sons of Hinnom: Jos 15.8; 18.16; etc.); the ravine (modern Wâdī er-Rabâbeh) is situated at the southern end of Jerusalem. During the monarchy the place called Thopheth in this valley was the scene of an idolatrous cult involving the burning of children as sacrificial victims to Moloch (Jer 7.31; 2 Kgs 16.3; 21.6). Later, perhaps because of its reputation as a place of idolatrous worship, it became the dumping ground where the refuse of the city was burned. In Jeremiah's time it was known simply as ''the valley'' (Jer 2.23).

By the time of Christ, however, the word Gehenna had evolved from a topographical designation to an eschatological one; it became the place of chastisement for the wicked immediately after death or in the eternity that was to follow the resurrection and the Judgment. The eschatological imagery of Gehenna came from Jer 7.30–8.3; 19.2–13; and Is 66.24. Jeremiah foretold that this place would one day be called the Valley of Slaughter, for in the destruction of Jerusalem so many of its inhabitants would be killed that their corpses would be cast, unburied, into the valley to rot or be burned. In short, Gehenna would be a symbol of divine chastisement, although this would not be definitive, for Jeremiah predicted also that the valley of dead bodies and ashes would eventually be holy to Yahweh (Jer 31.40).

In Is 66.24, the last verse of an eschatological oracle coming from the period of reconstruction after the Exile, YAHWEH proclaimed that He would vindicate Himself by restoring ZION and by having all the nations come there to pay Him honor. Outside its gates the nations would see the cadavers of all who had rebelled against Him. Although Gehenna was not mentioned in the oracle, there was an obvious allusion to Jer 7.30–8.3, but now the chastisement is described as definitive (''Their worm shall not die, nor their fire be extinguished''). As a rubbish dump, Gehenna was a place where fire burned constantly and where worms feasted on the garbage, and these images were transferred to the never-ending punishment of the rebellious. The references to fire in Is 31.9 and Is 33.14 envisioned Yahweh's power as bringing vengeance on Israel's oppressors (Is 33.10–12) rather than a fire punishing the damned.

The apocryphal literature used the image of Gehenna as a symbol of everlasting punishment but not in a uniform way. The Book of Enoch (ch. 6–36, *c.* 150 B.C.) still envisaged a terrestial eschatology: the resurrected just would rejoice on the earth (ch. 25) and evildoers would rise and be thrown into the fire of Gehenna (ch. 22). In ch. 83 to 90 of Enoch, Gehenna was not named, but it was alluded to in an apparently transcendental eschatology. The fallen angels after the Judgment would be cast into a fiery abyss (90.24–27). This concept was not so developed an eschatology as that of Matthew in which Gehenna was conceived in cosmic terms as belonging exclusively to the world beyond and as having always been in existence (Mt 25.41).

In ch. 37 to 71 of Enoch (beginning of the Christian Era) SHEOL and Gehenna were used interchangeably (54.1–2). The darkness of Sheol was thus added to the fire of Gehenna, which was thought of as a fire that burns without giving light. Such confusion between Sheol and Gehenna is found also in the NT, e.g., ''the darkness outside'' (Mt 8.12; 22.13; 25.30). Gehenna had thus become disengaged from its ancient topography and transferred to the NT eschatology of the world beyond. In Enoch 90.26–27; 54.1–2; and 56.3–4 Gehenna was destined only for apostate Jews; elsewhere it was the destiny for all the wicked, including pagans. Later Judaism, however, regarded Gehenna as a sort of purgatory for faithless Jews and a place of eternal perdition for the Gentiles.

Other NT texts that mentioned Gehenna are Mt 5.22, 29; 10.28; 18.9; 23.15, 33; Mk 9.43–47; Lk 12.5; and Jas 3.6. Synonyms such as ''furnace of fire'' (Mt 13.42, 50), ''everlasting fire'' (Mt 18.8; Jude 7), and ''pool of fire'' (Rv 19.20; 20.9, 14–15; 21.8) were employed as well to signify eternal punishment.

See Also: HADES; HELL (IN THE BIBLE); HELLFIRE; JUDGMENT, DIVINE (IN THE BIBLE).

Bibliography: *Encyclopedic Dictionary of the Bible* (New York 1963) 847–850. J. JEREMIAH, *Theologisches Wörterbuch zum Neuen Testament,* ed. G. KITTEL (Stuttgart 1935) 1:655–656. A. WIKENHAUSER, *Lexikon für Theologie und Kirche,* ed. J. HOFER and K. RAHNER (Freiburg 1957–65) 4:598. T. H. GASTER, *The Interpreters' Dictionary of the Bible* (Nashville, Tenn. 1962) 2:361–362. J. BONSIRVEN, *Palestinian Judaism in the Time of Jesus Christ,* tr. W. WOLF (New York 1964) 226–251.

[I. H. GORSKI]

GEILER VON KAYSERSBERG, JOHANNES

Theologian and preacher; b. Schaffhausen, Switzerland, March 16, 1445; d. Strassburg, March 10, 1510. In 1446 his father went to Ammerschweier, Upper Alsace, as city clerk; he was killed in an accident when Johannes was three years old. The boy's grandfather in nearby

Kaysersberg brought him up. At the age of 15 he began the study of philosophy at the recently established University of Freiburg im Breisgau, and in 1465 he taught philosophy and grammar there and for a brief period was dean of the philosophical faculty. In 1470 he resigned his position in order to study theology at the University of Basel, which had also been founded a short time before. He obtained his doctorate in 1475, and the following year he returned to the University of Freiburg, where he had received an appointment and where he was elected rector the next year. Teaching, however, was less congenial to him than preaching, and in 1478 he accepted an invitation to go to Strassburg as cathedral preacher, an office in which he continued until his death. He was buried under a magnificent late-Gothic pulpit built especially in his honor.

Geiler was a man of broad humanistic, philosophical, and theological learning. With his teacher, John Heynlin—an outstanding teacher, preacher, and university administrator—and many other friends and acquaintances, he belonged to a group of early German humanists. Despite his classical and national historical interests, he was steadfast in his adherence to the fundamentals of the old faith. In his theological inspiration he was chiefly dependent upon J. GERSON, and although he vigorously criticized the ecclesiastical conditions of his time, he was in no way a revolutionary. His tie with late medieval scholasticism shows itself externally in the ramified classifications that characterized his sermons. He possessed an extraordinary knowledge of the Fathers, and made abundant use of the Bible. He also had recourse to profane authors, and was given to the use of literary patterns in his preaching. He preached, with great acclaim, a series of sermons that had the *Narrenschiff* (*Ship of Fools*) of his friend Sebastian Brant for their theme.

Die vorred
Doctor Keiserspergs predig

Nimwar du gü
ter hirt. Hochwirdiger
vatter. Du fleissiger bisch
off dises wirdigen stifftes
Straßburg. Nimwar/deine iüger sein
alle versamlet/ sie seind sammenthafft
zů dir kommen/nit vß forcht der iuden
sunder vß gehorsame. Sie seind nit als
irrige schefflin sunder sie haben sich ge/
kert/zů dir/irem hirten vnd bischoffen
irer selen. Du stest auch mittē vnder inē
als ein gůter hirt/vnd folgst nach den
fůßstapffen des obersten hirtē/der mit/
tel vnder seinen iungern gestanden ist.
Du hirt stost mittel vnder dē hirten.
Dan wan du sie fragst wer sie seien/so
gebürt inē/das sie mit den kindern Ja
cob dir antwurteten. Wir seind schaff
hirtē. Got wolt auch/das inen vñ ir ye
dem das ewangelisch wort gezim. Ich
bin ein gůter hirt / der sein sel gibt für
seine schefflin/ia für die schefflin dy da
die wort des künigs David zů got dē

Johannes Geiler von Kaysersberg preaching, woodcut from "Ein heilsam kostiche Predig Doctor Iohans Geiler von Keisersperg."

He could, when he wished, preach well upon dogmatic topics, but for the most part he preferred moral subjects, and in treating of these he gave less attention to the building up of positive ideals than to the condemnation of the moral decadence of his time. From his pulpit there flowed a richly colored picture of the moral corruption of the world he knew. He excoriated the obscene conversation of the bath houses, the ridicule of the Sacraments, and the sexual mores of the times with shocking frankness. From his mordant observations about their inordinate preoccupation with dress and finery one could write a book of fashions for the times around the year 1500. Indeed, his sermons are an important source of knowledge of the speech, customs, and beliefs of the common people at the beginning of the 16th century.

He cast an especially critical eye upon the social evils of the time. He denounced the avarice of the lawyers, the injustice of certain laws, the raising of prices, and the practice of usury. With great apostolic courage he attacked the laxity of monasteries and the concubinage practiced by the clergy, and he did not hesitate to pillory the patrons in high places whom he considered to be mainly responsible. The influence of the nobility in securing for their offspring ecclesiastical offices, especially bishoprics, he considered to be a cancerous social evil.

Geiler prepared his sermons with great care, writing them out beforehand, but these compositions were drawn up in Latin rather than in German. Few of the sermons that have been published under his name came directly from his pen; most of them were taken down by others and later published.

As was true also of Berthold of Regensburg and ABRAHAM OF SANCTA CLARA, Geiler's homeliness and originality of speech lent power to his words and contributed to his popularity. But, like the other two great popular preachers, he yielded sometimes to the coarseness of his age.

From the fact of his popularity and from the testimony of contemporaries it is evident that Geiler's sermons produced a marked effect upon those who heard him. Still, for all his apostolic zeal and his strenuous labors, this effect fell far short of his target. He lamented that neither clergy nor laity could be persuaded to join in an effort toward reform. His preaching appears to have produced no lasting effect. Perhaps his manner was too gruff, his language too hard, his criticism too merciless, or his moralizing sermons too negative, to bring about the results he wanted. Or perhaps it was too late. A few years after his death Strassburg became Protestant.

Bibliography: N. SCHEID, *The Catholic Encyclopedia* 6:403–405. E. BARNIKOL, *Die Religion in Geschichte und Gegenwart* 2:1266–67. J. M. B. CLAUSZ, "Kritische Übersicht der Schriften über Geiler von Kaysersberg," *Historisches Jahrbuch der Görres-Gesellschaft* 31 (1910) 485–519. E. F. ROEDER VON DIERSBURG, *Komik und Humor bei Geiler von Kaisersberg* (Berlin 1921).

[J. F. GRONER]

GEISERIC, KING OF THE VANDALS

Reigned 428–477. Geiseric (also Genseric or Gaiseric) became king over the Vandals, Alans and a polyglot group of barbarians in Spain in 428. He was the illegitimate son of King Godagisel, born of a slave woman in 389. Of short stature, Geiseric walked with a limp as a result of a fall from a horse. The circumstances of his accession to the kingship are unknown, as is the cause of death of Geiseric's half–brother Guntharic, who preceded him as king.

In May 429 Geiseric led the most bold and successful expedition of any barbarian leader of his time. Having acquired a fleet, he effected the large–scale migration of 80,000 men, women and children across the strait of Gibraltar. With a fighting force estimated at a maximum of only 16,000 men, he proceeded to break the Roman Empire's hold over all of North Africa and install himself as king in Carthage within ten years. Styling himself *rex Vandalorum et Alanorum* (the King of the Vandals and Alans), he instituted a new calendar that began with the seizure of Carthage and minted coins in honor of his reign.

In politics and war, Geiseric was thoroughly Machiavellian. He avoided major conflicts with Roman forces but exploited Roman weakness wherever it was evident. On Oct. 19, 439, Geiseric entered Carthage, left undefended by virtue of a 435 treaty with the Western emperor Valentinian III. Valentinian recognized the *fait accompli* in a second treaty signed in 442. That same year Geiseric bloodily suppressed a revolt of his soldiers and nobles. From Carthage Geiseric ruled a large part of North Africa and many Mediterranean islands. He enjoyed tranquil relations with the indigenous African tribes, even enlisting their aid in military expeditions. His fleets engaged in piracy and raids along the coastlands of the Roman Empire; Italy and the Balkan peninsula were particularly afflicted. In June 455 Geiseric seized the opportunity afforded by the murder of Valentinian III to pillage Rome. He carried off the treasures of Rome (including the vessels that had been captured from the Temple in Jerusalem in A.D. 70) and many Romans, among them Valentinian's widow and daughter Eudoxia, whom he married to his son Huniric. In 468 Geiseric destroyed a large fleet sent by Emperor Leo I. Under the pretext of taking several days to consider peace, he awaited the proper wind and attacked by night, hurling burning ships into the anchored imperial fleet. In 474 Geiseric signed a treaty of perpetual peace with Leo's successor Zeno.

Geiseric attempted to completely replace the Catholic Church in Africa with the Arian creed and ecclesiastical structure. He employed bribery, forced re–baptism, torture, death and exile on Catholics—especially the bishops—but was met by the fortitude of Catholic Trinitarian faith. Because of his political success, cruelty, and persecution of the Catholic faith, some contemporaries saw Geiseric as Antichrist. Hydatius relates a rumor that Geiseric was an apostate who left Catholicism for Arianism. He died of natural causes on Jan. 24, 477.

Bibliography: C. COURTOIS, *Les Vandales et l'Afrique* (Paris 1955). H.-J. DIESNER, *Das Vandalenreich, Aufstieg und Untergang* (Stuttgart 1966). E. F. GAUTIER, *Genséric, roi des Vandales* (Paris 1951). H. GOURDIN, *Genséric: soleil barbare* (Paris 1999). F. MARTROYE, *Genséric: la conquête vandale en Afrique et la destruction de l'empire d'Occident* (Paris 1907). L. SCHMIDT, *Geschichte der Wandalen* (1942, repr. Munich 1970).

[D. VAN SLYKE]

GEISSEL, JOHANNES VON

Cardinal, archbishop of Cologne; b. Gimmeldingen (Rhine Palatinate), Germany, Feb. 5, 1796; d. Cologne, Sept. 8, 1864. After studying in the diocesan seminary in Mainz, he was ordained (1818). He was much influenced in an ultramontane direction by the theological circle at Mainz and maintained close ties with the Holy See throughout his life. He became bishop of Speyer (1836), coadjutor to Abp. DROSTE ZU VISCHERING of Cologne (1841), archbishop (1845), and cardinal (1850). While coadjutor he administered the archdiocese and helped end the Cologne mixed marriage dispute. He was one of the outstanding German bishops of his century, an energetic and far-sighted leader who fostered clerical education, the introduction of religious orders into his archdiocese, and the founding of Catholic societies; and he vigorously combated the followers of GÜNTHER and HERMES. Under King Friedrich Wilhelm IV (1840–61), who was well disposed to Catholics, he notably improved Church-State relations. In the King's presence he laid the cornerstone for continuing construction of the cathedral of Cologne, and saw its completion in 1863. Geissel organized and directed the first conference of the German episcopate at Würzburg, which proved very important for Church renewal. He was also responsible for the Cologne provincial council (1860), whose decrees were heeded elsewhere. He also won esteem as a preacher and writer.

Bibliography: J. VON GEISSEL, *Schriften und Reden Geissels,* ed. K. T. DUMONT, 4 v. (Cologne 1869–76). *Cardinal Geissel,* 2 v. (Freiburg 1895). A. BECK, *Die Kirchenpolitik des Erzbischofs von Köln, Johannes Kardinal von Geissel* (Geissen 1905). F. SCHNABEL, *Deutsche Geschichte im neunzehnten Jahrhundert,* v.4 (2d ed. Freiburg 1951) 76–80, 149–155, 251–259. R. LILL, *Die Beilegung der Kölner Wirren 1840–1842* (Düsseldorf 1962); *Die ersten deutschen Bischofskonferenzen* (Freiburg 1964). R. HAAS, *Lexikon für Theologie und Kirche* 2 4:608.

[R. LILL]

GELASIAN DECREE

So-called, consists of 5 chapters concerned with (1) the Holy Spirit and the names of Christ, (2) the canon of Sacred Scripture, (3) the primacy of Peter and of the apostolic see, as well as the precedence of patriarchal sees, (4) the authority of the decrees of general (ecumenical) councils, and (5) the authority of patristic and papal writings, along with the acceptability of other Christian works available at the time (see Denz 178, 179–180, 350–354). A compilation of documents of probably different periods, it is thought by many scholars to have been put together privately by a cleric of southern Gaul or northern Italy at the beginning of the 6th century.

Bibliography: E. VON DOBSCHÜTZ, *Das Decretum gelasianum de libris recipiendis et non recipiendis* (TU 3d ser. 8.4; 1912). G. BARDY, *Dictionnaire de la Bible,* supplement (Paris 1928–) 3:579–590. T. CAMELOT, *Catholicisme* 4: 1804.

[M. O'CALLAGHAN]

GELASIAN LETTER

This letter, often referred to by its opening words *Famuli vestrae pietatis* (Ep. 8, PL 59:41–47; *Ep.* 12, Thiel's *Epistolae rom. pont.* 1:349–358), was written by Pope GELASIUS I (492–496) in 494 to the Byzantine Emperor Anastasius I. Its importance is in the fact that it is held to be ''the most famous document of the ancient Church concerning the 'two powers' that exist on earth'' (Denz 347) and that it states what has come to be called the Gelasian theory on relations between Church and state. The oft-repeated sentence runs: ''Duo quippe sunt, imperator auguste, quibus principaliter mundus hic regitur: auctoritas sacra pontificum et regalis potestas—There are indeed, Your Majesty, two [powers] by which this world is mainly ruled: the sacred authority of pontiffs and the royal power.''

Though this central thesis of Gelasius is plainly enough stated, one who would derive from it a complete theory on the exact relations between the Church and civil societies under all circumstances would hardly escape the charge of rashness. The judgment of S. Z. Ehler and J. B. Morrall can perhaps be endorsed: ''Silence on the question of what were in practice the limits of each sphere made it [letter and theory] ambiguous when borderline instances occasioned a clash between the two powers. This ambiguity is shown by the fact that both papalist and imperialist supporters in the medieval controversies appealed to Gelasius with equal freedom'' [*Church and State through the Centuries* (Westminster, Md. 1954) 11].

The point of Gelasius' teaching is better appreciated if one recalls that the letter forms one incident in the whole series of incidents that occurred after and in consequence of the Council of Chalcedon (451) and more precisely during the ACACIAN SCHISM. This split between East and West arose out of the deposition (484) by Pope Felix III of Acacius, Patriarch of Constantinople, and was not healed until 519. It was then, during this period of friction, that the Pope wrote the letter to the Emperor, reproaching Anastasius for his support of the schismatical tendencies of the patriarchs of Constantinople.

If the occasion demanded a frank statement of the autonomy of the episcopate in deciding the doctrine and the discipline of the Church, an independence for which the Church had been struggling since the days of Constantine (cf. similar declarations of Athanasius, Ambrose, Augustine, Gregory of Nazianzus, and John Chrysostom in Lo Grasso Eccl), it did not suggest to Gelasius that a ''distinction'' of powers should evolve into a ''separation'' of powers. Gelasius' view of the relationship between the two powers can be read in that passage of the letter in which he states that ''in the interests of their salvation much more will the people of Constantinople necessarily obey you, if you lead them back to the catholic and apostolic communion. For, Your Majesty, if you would not permit a man under any pretext to act against the laws of the State, don't you think that it is a matter of conscience for you to restore the people subject to your authority to an unsullied and genuine devotion to God?'' For Gelasius the Emperor will be acting properly if he exerts his not inconsiderable influence to effect at the public level Christian religious unity on the lines laid down by the legitimate authority of the combined episcopate under the leadership of the successor of Peter.

The letter therefore is composed within the framework of a theory of two distinct ''powers'' in a Christian world rather than of two distinct ''societies.'' It takes for granted a close cooperation between these two powers as well as a profession of religion on the part of the State. It does not examine the problem it treats in the light of the religious liberties of the individual nor does it envisage the relations between the Church and a State of divided religious allegiance. One of its main purposes is to insist that bishops are not mere ministers for public worship in the imperial ''cabinet,'' but are immediately empowered in matters of religion by a distinct divine disposition, a disposition that entitles them to determine without interference from the other ''power'' the sense of Christian revelation and to enact all appropriate disciplinary measures.

See Also: AUTHORITY, ECCLESIASTICAL.

Bibliography: Y. M. J. CONGAR, *Catholicisme* 3:1430–41. P. T. CAMELOT, *ibid.* 4:1801–03. K. BAUS, *Lexikon für Theologie und Kirche* 4:630. J. LECLER, *The Two Sovereignties* (New York 1952). J. MARITAIN, *Man and the State* (Chicago 1951). J. C. MURRAY, *We Hold These Truths* (New York 1960).

[S. E. DONLON]

GELASIAN SACRAMENTARY

Also known as Old Gelasian Sacramentary (Latin: *Gelasianum Vetus*), Gelasian Sacramentary is the popular name for the Vatican manuscripts *Reginensis latinus* 316. Muratori gave this convenient but misleading label to the Vatican manuscript *Reginensis* 316 in his edition of 1748, and it has been in usage ever since. But its most recent editor, Mohlberg, despite adverse criticism, has rightly restored the actual title of the manuscrpt: *Liber Sacramentorum Romanae Aeclesiae Ordinis Anni Circuli* (Rome 1960). However, since that title, though accurate, is cumbersome, it will be referred to as *Reg* 316.

Date. Besides being the oldest and most complete extant manuscript of the Roman Sacramentary, albeit a Frankish-Roman hybrid, it is also a beautiful example Merovingian manuscript and calligraphy. The authorship of the *Reg* 316 can no longer be attributed to Pope GELASIUS (492–496), because ''that theory rests upon a faulty interpretation of a passage in the *Liber pontificalis* and from an expression in the *Vita Gregorii* by the Roman deacon John which is too late to be helpful'' (Vogel, *Medieval Liturgy*, 68). The Old Gelasian Sacramentary is to be distinguished from the so-called 8th-century Gelasian Sacramentary or the Frankish-Gelasian Sacramentaries, a different family of sacramentaries which is discussed as a topic under GREGORIAN SACRAMENTARY.

C. Vogel suggests that the ancestor of the *Reg* 316 ''must have been composed between 628 and 715, i.e., between the oldest possible date of the most recent feast and the beginning of Gregory II's pontificate.'' The *terminus ad quem* can be determined from the fact that in the *Reg* 316, the Thursdays of Lent are liturgical, i.e., it did not yet have the Masses which Gregory II (715–731) introduced into the Roman liturgical calendar. As for the *terminus a quo*, Vogel observes that the *Reg* 316:

> already has a *Capitulum S. Gregorii papae* (†604), the *Canon actionis* contains the Gregorian embolism of the *Hanc igitur: Diesque nostros in tua pace disponas atque ab aeterna damnatione nos eripe et in electorum quorum iubeas grege numerari* and the *Pater noster* is situated immediately after the Canon — exactly where St. Gregory I put it. The Sanctoral Cycle has both feasts of the Cross, although the *Exaltatio Crucis* was introduced at Rome after the death of Gregory the Great, probably after the recovery of the True Cross from the Persians by the Emperor Heraclius in 628. The Sanctoral also contains the four feasts of the Blessed Virgin (*Purificatio*, Feb. 2; *Annunciatio*, Mar. 25; *Assumptio*, Aug. 15; *Nativitas*, Sept. 8) unknown at Rome in the time of Gregory but which were being celebrated during the reign of the Syrian pope, Sergius I (687–701).

History. This manuscript is the only one of its kind known to exist. A. Wilmart and Lowe were inclined to the view that it was written in northeastern France, its ornamentation suggesting Corbie. But in 1953 Lowe drew attention to B. Bischoff's suggestion that the *Reg* 316 belongs to the same school as a group of 8th-century Cologne manuscripts written for Bishop Hildebald of that see (785–819). In Lowe's opinion the scriptorium that produced such manuscripts must have been of some importance, and in all probability Bischoff is right in thinking of the convent of Chelles near Paris, whose abbess was Gisela, sister of Charlemagne and lifelong friend of Alcuin.

Description. The *Reg* 316 is divided into three distinct parts or books. Book 1 contains the Mass formularies from Christmas Eve to the Octave of Pentecost. Book 2 consists of the Sanctoral throughout the year, the Common of Saints, and an appendix of Advent Masses. Book 3 contains a well-known series of 16 Sunday Masses, which have found their way into the Roman Missal, the Canon of the Mass, a series of votive Masses and various blessings. Different interpolations of Gallican origin are found within the body of the book and have been the object of a serious examination by Chavasse [*Le Sacramentaire Gélasien* (Paris 1958)].

Authorship. Ever since Muratori's edition of the *Reg* 316, it has been called the Gelasian Sacramentary. An examination of its contents, however, makes it difficult to believe that in its present state it is an exact copy of the work of Gelasius. In 1945 Capelle drew attention to the fact that the LEONINE SACRAMENTARY contains material that, in all probability, was composed by Gelasius in very precise circumstances; but this material is absent from the Sacramentary that bears his name. This of itself is a reason for rejecting its attribution to Gelasius [''Retouches Gélasiennes dans le Sacramentaire Léonien,'' *Revue Bénédictine* 61 (1951) 3–14]. Numerous studies by such scholars as Coebergh and Chavasse served only to confirm Capelle's verdict. The Gelasian Sacramentary is not the work of Pope Gelasius, although it may contain isolated prayers and prefaces that are his and that found their way into the body of the text, perhaps through the Leonine Sacramentary.

Character. Concerning its character and contents, earlier scholars such as E. Bishop and M. Andrieu were inclined to look upon it as the official Roman Mass Book of the 6th century. Duschesne, Baumstark, and more recently Schmidt consider it to be a Frankish compilation of the 8th century, the compiler having used both Roman and Gallican material. More recently the prestige of Chavasse's learning has led the majority of scholars to accept his conclusions presented in his major work on the subject referred to above. In his view the Roman source of the *Reg* 316 is a Sacramentary now lost (but incorporated into this work by the 8th-century scribe of the *Reg* 316) that was used by the clergy of the Roman *tituli.* This lost source, in Chavasse's view, provided a quarry also for the Gregorian Sacramentary and the earlier Gallican service books. Not all scholars, however, have followed Chavasse in every detail. Capelle more cautiously suggested that the evidence could point to the *Libelli Missarum* preserved in the Lateran Archives as a probable source of the Merrovingian service books [*Revue d'histoire ecclésiastique* 54 (1959) 877–879]. Coebergh expressed himself unconvinced by the author's arguments and objected that insufficient use had been made by Chavasse of the material provided by J. P. Kirsch in his *Die römischen Titelkirchen im Altertum,* ignorance of which had led Chavasse into some grave errors of judgment. Coebergh considers it more likely that the *Reg* 316 is a compilation made by two Frankish priest-monks, of progressive tendencies, who drew upon a series of Lateran *Libelli Missarum* during the course of the 7th century [''Le Sacramentaire Gélasien Ancien, une compilation de clercs romanisants du VIIe siècle,'' *Archiv für Liturgiewissenschaft* 7 (1961) 45–88].

Whatever the case may be, what is clear is the fact that the *Reg* 316 is a hybrid sacramentary, comprising the most primitive extant Roman substratum with Frankish additions. The Roman substratum itself is not entirely homogeneous, but ''is the result of an intermingling of a variety of Roman *libelli* belonging to different periods and representing both papal and presbyteral usages'' (Vogel, *Medieval Liturgy*, 66).

Bibliography: Critical Edition: *Liber Sacramentorum Romanae Aeclesiae Ordinis Annis Circuli* (Cod. Vat. Reg. lat. 316; Paris Bibl. Nat. 7193 41/56), ed. L. C. MOHLBERG, L. EIZENHÖFER, and P. SIFFRIN (Rerum Ecclesiasticarum Documenta, Series Maior, Fontes 4; Rome, 1960). **Color Photo–reproduction:** *Sacramentarium Gelasianum: e Codice Vaticano Reginensi Latino 316 Veritente Anno Sacro MCMLXXV,* iussu Pauli PP. VI, phototypice editum (Vatican 1975). This important reproduction contains two important introductory essays: B. NEUNHEUSER, ''The Manuscript,'' 5–29; and ''The 'Sacramentarium Gelasianum' (*Reg. lat. 316*) and its Significance in Liturgical History,'' 30–49. **Commentary:** A. CHAVASSE, *Le Sacramentaire Gélasien* (Tournai 1958). For overview and further bibliographies, see: C. VOGEL, *Medieval Liturgy: An Introduction to Sources* (Washington, D.C. 1986); and E. PALAZZO, *A History of Liturgical Books: From the Beginning to the Thirteenth Century* (Collegeville, Minn. 1998).

[H. ASHWORTH/EDS.]

GELASIUS I, POPE, ST.

Pontificate: March 1, 492, to Nov. 19, 496. A strong-willed archdeacon of the Roman Church, Gelasius apparently came from an African lineage but there is a debate over whether he was born in Africa or in Rome. The *Liber pontificalis* states that he was ''natione Afer'' whereas in a letter to Emperor Anastasius (Ep. Xii, n.1) he described himself as ''Romanus natus.''

He was the dominant figure in Rome during the reign of Felix II and draftsman of that pope's letters. His own letters and treatises reveal him as the chief Roman theoretician in the quarrel with Constantinople, known as the ACACIAN SCHISM. Technically, the dispute concerned the flouting of the authority of the Roman Church through the intrusion of heretics in certain Eastern sees. In this light, he became an active defender of the historical importance of the sees of Antioch and Alexandria against the see of Constantinople. Actually, more was at stake. The popes were increasingly alarmed by the manifestations of caesaropapism in the late 5th century, exemplified by the heretical *Henoticon* of Emperor Zeno, who attempted to appease the Monophysites with a statement of faith devised by the Patriarch Acacius without consulting Rome. Though he was not attacked directly, Zeno became the real object of papal strictures.

Papal Supremacy. When faced by a new threat to orthodoxy, the popes of the time reacted instinctively by exalting the divine origin and apostolic basis of the papal office. If Leo I can be said to have laid the juridical foundations of papal authority for all time, Gelasius I applied those principles in letters that read very much like legal briefs. There was little that subsequent generations could add to his explicit statements about papal supremacy or the relations between church and state, except a spelling out of what was contained in his thought. The fame of Gelasius I rests on the great influence exercised by his letters and treatises on later generations; this influence they owed to the wide currency that they acquired through being excerpted and incorporated in a series of contemporary canonical collections, which began to be compiled about that time in the West, the products of the so-called Gelasian Renaissance, which he helped to inspire. One of the most famous of these early canonists, the Scythian Dionysius Exiguus, paid tribute to the learning and virtue of the pope in the preface to his early 6th-century collection of papal decretals. The inflexible attitude of Gelasius toward Constantinople was influenced by the pope's good relations with the Arian, Theodoric, who replaced Odoacer as king in Italy. Attempts were made by the Constantinopolitan patriarchs, Flavita and Euphemius, to restore communion with Rome, but the pope's demand that the name of Acacius be stricken from the diptychs caused the negotiations to break down.

The Two Powers. Zeno's successor as emperor, Anastasius II, inclined as he was to Monophysitism, was even less likely to countenance any concession on this point. However, he recognized the importance of cultivating good relations with Rome in the interests of protecting his vague suzerainty over Italy and took the occasion of an embassy from King Theodoric to Constantinople to remind the pope that he had received no greetings from him. In his respectful but firm reply Gelasius outlined his views on the two powers that govern the world, the consecrated authority of bishops (*auctoritas sacrata pontificum*) and the royal power (*regalis potestas*). Gelasius made clear that, in his opinion, it was the duty of the emperor to learn about ''divine things'' from bishops, not vice versa. His implicit claim that the papal power was superior to the civil marked a significant step toward the formation of the medieval hierocratic ideal.

Vicar of Christ. At a Roman synod held in 494, Gelasius decreed that the revenue from church property should be apportioned four ways, among the bishop, the clergy, and the poor and for the maintenance of buildings. (It should be noted, however, that in Ep. Xiv, n.27 he notes this practice as ''dudum rationabiliter decretum,'' which would seem to indicate that it had been a common practice, at least in Rome, for some time). This rule was incorporated in the oath that all bishops under the metropolitan jurisdiction of Rome were required to make on the day of their consecration (*Liber diurnus*); and other churches adopted somewhat similar arrangements. A Roman synod the following year, whose acts have survived, is remembered as the first-known occasion when the pope was hailed as Vicar of Christ. Gelasius I warned against a resurgence of Pelagianism in Dalmatia and Picenum, and was active in routing out the last vestiges of paganism in Rome. Most notable in this respect is his treatise against the Lupercalia (a penitential and fructifying festival in which young men with whips cavorted about the city and struck women) which the senator Andromachus had tried to reform. He was also zealous in rooting out the last vestiges of Manichaeanism at Rome. A cache of Manichaean books was discovered and burned before the doors of St. Mary Major's. To this end, he also mandated, at least for a time, the celebration of the Holy Eucharist under both species because the Manichaeans would have rejected wine, seeing it as impure and sinful.

Gelasian Sacramentary. More than 100 of his letters and treatises have been preserved. Although Gelasius apparently wrote Mass formulas later incorporated in the so-called Leonine, or Verona, Sacramentary, a 6th-century compilation, he can hardly have had anything to do with the 7th-century Roman presbyteral Sacramentary that commonly bears his name. Gelasius I was buried in St. Peter's, although the exact location of his tomb is unknown.

Feast: Nov. 21.

Bibliography: *Clavis Patrum latinorum*, ed. E. DEKKERS (Streenbrugge 1961) 1667–76. *Patrologiae cursus completus, series latina*, suppl. ed. A. HAMMAN (Paris 1957—) 3:739–. G. POMARÈS, ed., *Lettre contre les Lupercales et dix-huit messes du sacramentaire Léonien* (*Sources Chrétiennes* 65; 1960). *Patrologia Latina*, ed. J. P. MIGNE (Paris 1878–90) 59:13–190. A. THIEL, ed., *Epistolae romanorum pontificum*, v.1 (Branieno, Ger. 1868) 287–510. S. LOEWENFELD, ed., *Epistolae pontificum romanorum ineditae*, repr. (Graz 1959) 1–12. *Liber pontificalis*, L. DUCHESNE (Paris 1886–92) 1:255–257; 3:87. H. LECLERCQ, *Dictionnaire d'archéologie chrétienne et de liturgie* (Paris 1907–53) 13.1:1212. E. CASPAR, *Geschichte de Papsttums von den Anfängen bis zur Höhe der Weltherrschaft* (Tübingen 1930–33) 2:44–81, 749–752, 758. K. BAUS, *Lexikon für Theologie und Kirche*, ed. J. HOFER and K. RAHNER (Freiburg 1957–65) 4:630. G. BARDY, *Dictionniare de droit canonique*, ed. R. NAZ (Paris 1935–65) 5:940–945. A. FLICHE and V. MARTIN, *Histoire de léglise depuis les origines jusqu'à nos jours* (Paris 1935—) 4:339–340. H. ANTON, ''Kaiserliche Selbstverstandnis in der Religionsgestezgebung der Spatantike und papstliche Herrschaftsinterpretation im 5 Jahrhundert,'' *Zkirchgesch* 88 (1977) 38–84. A. COTTRELL ''Auctoritas and Potestas: A Reevaluation of Gelasius I on Papal-Imperial Relations,'' *Medieval Studies* 55 (1993) 95. F. DVORNIK, *The Idea of Apostolicity in Byzantium* (Cambridge, MA 1958). J. GAUDEMET, *L'Église dans l'Empire ro-*

main (Paris 1958). J. TAYLOR, ''Early Papacy at Work: Gelasius I (492–6),'' *Journal of Religious History* 8 (1975) 317–32. W. ULLMANN, *The Growth of Papal Government in the Middle Ages* (New York 1962); *Gelasius I. (492–496): das Papsttum an der Wende der Spatantike zum Mittelalter* (Stuttgart 1981). A. K. ZIEGLER, ''Pope Gelasius I . . . the Relation of Church and State,'' *American Catholic Historical Review* 27 (1942) 3–28.

[J. CHAPIN/EDS.]

GELASIUS II, POPE

Pontificate: Jan. 24, 1118 to Jan. 28, 1119; b. John of Gaeta; d. Abbey of Cluny. The son of John Coniulo of Gaeta, Italy (not a member of the Gaëtani family), he entered Monte Cassino as an oblate *c.* 1060 under Abbot Desiderius (1058–87), the future Pope VICTOR III. As his master John had Alberic of Monte Cassino, whose teachings influenced the style of his Lives of SS. Erasmus, Eustasius, and Hypolistus. Pope URBAN II called the young subdeacon as *prosignator* to his chancery as early as 1088, promoted him in the same year to deacon and cardinal, and made him chancellor in 1089. In this office John carried out important improvements in the papal chancery, increasing its personnel and reforming the style (revival of the *Cursus Leoninus*) and the dating of papal documents. Probably in 1111 he received from Pope PASCHAL II the church of S. Maria in Cosmedin, whose reconstruction was begun by him.

John was unanimously elected pope on Jan. 24, 1118, in the church of S. Maria in Pallara on the Palatine. At the end of the ceremony the pope and the cardinals were attacked by Cencius II FRANGIPANI, who imprisoned the pope and released him only after an uprising of the other nobles and the people. The arrival in Rome of Emperor HENRY V early in March forced the pope to withdraw to his home town, Gaeta, where he was consecrated priest, bishop, and pope, and assumed the name Gelasius II (March 10). Meanwhile, Henry V, supported by the celebrated IRNERIUS of Bologna, had the disgruntled Abp. Mauritius of Braga proclaimed antipope, with the name of Gregory VIII. Gelasius excommunicated him together with Henry V. The approach of Robert of Capua's army caused Henry to leave Rome, and Gelasius was able to return to Rome, whence he fled to France in September after a new attack by Cencius. He stayed briefly at Saint-Gilles near Nîmes and elsewhere in southern France and held a synod in Vienne. He died at Cluny, where he was buried on the following day.

Bibliography: Vita Gelasii by PADULF, in *Liber pontificalis,* ed. L. DUCHESNE (Paris 1886–1953) 3:157–166, 135–136; see also 2:311–321. *Annales Romani, ibid.* 2:347. P. JAFFÉ, *Regesta pontificum romanorum ab condita ecclesia ad annum post Christum natum 1198,* ed. S. LOWENELD (Graz 1956) 1:6631–81. For John's lives of saints, O. ENGELS, *Römische Quartalschrift für christliche Altertumskunde und für Kirchengeschichte* 51 (1956) 16–33, Erasmus; *Quellen und Forschungen aus italienischen Archiven und Bibliotheken* 35 (1955) 1–45, Eustasius and Hypolistus; *The Historical Journal* 76 (1957) 118–133. C. ERDMANN, ''Mauritius Burdinus (Gregor VIII),'' *Quellen und Forschungen aus italieniscchen Archiven und Bibliotheken* 19 (1927) 205–261. R. ELZE, ''Die päpstliche Kapelle im 12. und 13. Jahrhundert,'' *Zeitschrift der Savigny-Stiftung für Rechtsgeschichte, Kanonistische Abteilung* 36 (1950) 145–204. J. HALLER, *Das Papsttum* (Stuttgart 1950–53) 2:503–504. F. X. SEPPELT, *Geschichte der Päpste von den Anfängen bis zur Mitte des 20. Hr.* (Munich 1954–59) 3:151–154. W. ULLMANN, *The Growth of Papal Government in the Middle Ages* (2d ed. New York 1962) 327–331. G. ANDRISANI, ''Gelasio II a Capua,'' *Benedictina* 40 (Rome 1993) 35–47. O. ENGELS, *Lexikon für Theologie und Kirche,* 3d. ed. (1995). R. VOLPINI, ''Documenti nel 'Sancta sanctorum' del Laterno. I resti dell' 'Archivio' di Gelasio II,'' *Lateranum* 52 (1986), 215–64. J. N. D. KELLY, *Oxford Dictionary of Popes* (New York 1986) 163.

[H. BLOCH]

GELASIUS OF CAESAREA

Bishop and church historian; b. before 335; d. *c.* 395. His mother was the sister of CYRIL OF JERUSALEM. Gelasius became bishop of Caesarea (Palestine) in 367, was ousted by Valens in 372 for his attachment to the faith of Nicaea, but regained his see in 378. He was among the 150 fathers of the Ecumenical Council of CONSTANTINOPLE I (381). None of his writings have survived. Jerome praised their style and stated that Gelasius kept them in his desk (*De vir. ill.* 130). Some of them were published, however, as is proved by the testimony of Photius (*Bibl. cod.* 88, 89) and by fragments quoted in the writings of THEODORET OF CYR, Leontius of Byzantium, and Severus of Antioch. Gelasius wrote also a polemical treatise against the Anomoeans and a collection of at least 20 instructions on the fundamental teachings of the Church that probably paralleled the famous Catechetical Instructions of his uncle, Cyril of Jerusalem. An *Explanation of the Symbol,* mentioned in fragment four, may have formed part of the above collection. His main work was an *Ecclesiastical History,* a continuation of Eusebius's work. According to F. Scheidweiler, it can be reconstructed for the most part from later church historians who borrowed from it: RUFINUS OF AQUILEIA, Gelasius of Cyzicus, SOCRATES, and the author of the *Vita Metrophanis et Alexandri.* The literary dependence between Gelasius's *History* and that of Rufinus of Aquileia has been greatly debated. The fragments of Galasius's dogmatic writings have been edited by F. Diekamp in *Analecta patristica* 42–49.

Bibliography: F. DIEKAMP, *Analecta patristica* (*Orientalia Christiana Analecta* 117; 1938) 16–49. J. QUASTEN, *Patrology,* 3:347–348. B. ALTANER, *Patrology,* 272–273. F. SCHEIDWEILER,

Byzantinische Zeitschrift 46 (1953) 277–301; 48 (1955) 162–164; 49 (1956) 2–6; 50 (1957) 74–98. F. X. MURPHY, *Rufinus of Aquileia* (Washington 1945) 61–63.

[V. C. DE CLERQC]

GEMARAH

The discussion of the Jewish legal opus, the MISHNAH, with which it forms the TALMUD. The term is from the Aramaic word *ge mārā',* meaning completion, but it is used also in the derived senses of tradition, study, or even Talmud. In the technical sense the Gemarah is a commentary on the Mishnah. In it the rabbis known as Amoraim (plural of the Hebrew-Aramaic word *'ămôrâ',* speaker, lecturer) seek to interpret the teachings of the earlier rabbis, the Tannaim (plural of the Aramaic word *tannā',* repeater, recounter), that are recorded in the Mishnah and to reconcile them with the Baraitot (plural of the Aramaic word *baraitā',* external thing), the Tannaitic teachings that are not recorded in the Mishnah but are often held as equally authoritative. There are two Gemarahs (and therefore two Talmuds): the Palestinian, composed between A.D. 200 and 400 and written in western Aramaic, and the Babylonian, completed *c.* A.D. 500 and written in eastern Aramaic; both, however, are interspersed with Hebrew. The Babylonian is the larger work and is held by Judaism as the more authoritative. About a third of it consists of HAGGADAH (homiletic and folkloristic material), and the remainder of HALAKAH (legal exposition).

For bibliography, *see* TALMUD.

[R. KRINSKY]

GEMBLOUX, ABBEY OF

Benedictine abbey near Namur, Belgium; founded *c.* 922 by St. Guibert (Wibert), monk from the Abbey of GORZE. On Sept. 20, 946, Emperor Otto I approved the foundation against the feudal claims of Guibert's relatives. Erluin (d. 986) succeeded Guibert after the latter's retirement to Gorze and obtained a charter of exemption from Pope Benedict VII. This right was surrendered to the friendly Notger, Bishop of Liège by Abbot Heriward (d. 990). Gembloux (Gemblours, Gemblacum) began its period of greatness under Olbert, who ruled from 1012 to 1048. He enlarged the monastery, built a new church, organized the library, and restored the discipline of the house, which had lapsed during the rule of his predecessor, Erluin II. During the rule of Abbot Thietmar, the Benedictine historian Sigebert (d. 1112) wrote the important chronicle of the world, and commenced the history of the abbots of Gembloux, which was continued by his disciple Gottschalk (*see* SIGEBERT OF GEMBLOUX). Prior Guerin, his contemporary at Gembloux, won fame at this time as a monastic teacher. In 1505 Abbot Arnold II of Solbrecg (d. 1511) affiliated his jurisdiction of Gembloux with the Abbey of BURSFELD in Hildesheim. During the religious wars, Gembloux was pillaged by Calvinists. In addition to this devastation in 1598, damage by fires threatened its ruin in 1678 and 1712. It was suppressed in 1796, but the buildings are used as a state agricultural institute.

Bibliography: L. H. COTTINEAU, *Répertoire topobibliographique des abbayes et prieurés,* 2 v. (Mâcon 1935–39) 1:1263–65. *Sigeberti gesta abbatum Gemblacensium et vita Wicberti, Patrologia Latina,* ed. J. P. MIGNE, 271 v., indexes 4 v. (Paris 1878–90) 160:591–678 (to 1136). R. FORGEUR, *Lexikon für Theologie und Kirche,* ed. J. HOFER and K. RAHNER, 10 v. (2d, new ed. Freiburg 1957–65) 4:643, bibliog.

[E. D. MCSHANE]

GEMELLI, AGOSTINO

Franciscan philosopher and psychologist; b. Milan, Jan. 18, 1878; d. July 15, 1959. He was a founder of the Catholic University of the Sacred Heart in Milan, and its rector; professor of psychology, and director of a psychological research center; president of the Papal Academy of Sciences; and a promoter of neoscholasticism in Italy. Gemelli first studied medicine and received a doctorate in medicine and surgery at the University of Pavia in 1902. As a young man he lost his faith and thought that science alone could solve all "the riddles of the universe." Eventually disillusioned with philosophy, which he studied for a while, he returned to Catholicism, entered the Franciscan Order, and was ordained in 1908. He continued to study biology, physiology, and philosophy at various universities in Europe. In 1911 he completed his doctorate in philosophy at the University of Louvain, but his dominant interest soon became psychology.

Gemelli's extensive research and publications and his active participation in psychological congresses made him one of the most prominent psychologists in Europe. The scope of his studies and writings included areas such as perception, feeling and emotion, developmental psychology, clinical psychology, psychoanalysis, and electrolinguistics. One of his recurring themes was the nature of psychology and its relation to philosophy and biology. Much of his research was devoted also to practical problems, such as vocational selection and guidance, accident prevention, delinquency, education, and working conditions in industry. During World Wars I and II he rendered valuable services to the Italian armed forces, especially in regard to the selection and training of pilots. Through these activities Gemelli contributed considerably to a better understanding and appreciation of psychology among Catholics and attracted Catholics to the study of psychology.

Gemelli also published works in theology, philosophy, and ethics. Deeply interested in current religious, moral, and scientific issues, he discussed such issues in his writings and ably presented the Catholic point of view. He thereby exerted a profound influence on the intellectual life of Catholic Italy.

Bibliography: Autobiography in *A History of Psychology in Autobiography,* v.4 (Worcester, Mass. 1952). H. MISIAK and V. M. STAUDT, *Catholics in Psychology* (New York 1954). D. MORANDO, *Enciclopedia filosofica* 2:603. P. BONDIOLI, *Il P. Agostino Gemelli* (Milan 1926). *Vita e Pensiero* 42 (1959) 505–716, entire issue about Gemelli with his bibliog. A. MANOIL, *La Psychologie expérimentale en Italie: École de Milan* (Paris 1938).

[H. MISIAK]

GENEALOGIES, BIBLICAL

The Israelites share with other Semitic peoples the tendency to trace the ancestry of the tribe, clan, or individual back through the male line to a historical or legendary figure of the distant past. Frequently he is eponymous; i.e., from him they take their name—e.g., the individuals of a social group would be known as the sons of Israel (Heb. *b*ᵉ*nê yiśrā'ēl*) and the group as the house of Israel (*bêt yiśrā'ēl*). Membership in a tribe or clan means to be descended from such a common ancestor either really or by legal fiction. When those who are not of natural descent are amalgamated to the group (Jos 15.13), they are genealogized into it by adoption of its ancestors.

The Old Testament genealogies are mostly the work of the Pentateuchal PRIESTLY WRITERS in the Persian period from the 6th to the 4th century. They are found especially in the Pentateuch, Chronicles, Ezra, and Nehemia. Some, such as Genesis ch. 4–5, have parallels in Babylonian literature, where there is also an artificial listing of ten generations between the first man and the flood. The Priestly Writers frequently utilized genealogies as mnemonic aids, bridging the important epochs of history. Writing for a nation that was no longer independent, they wished to show the links of the present community with the past and Yahweh's special intervention in Israel's history. Israel's role and God's choice of Israel were shown to be no accident of history; they were in Yahweh's plan from the creation of the ancestor of all men, Adam. The genealogy showing the descent of all nations from Noah (Gn ch. 10) continued the same line of thought, indicating the relationship of the chosen people to the Gentiles.

After the Exile, genealogies became so important that ancient figures, such as Samuel, who previously had none, were given lines of ancestors. Every effort had to be made to preserve the identity and faith of the nation, continually threatened by syncretism. One solution was to insist that the priests and other leaders be of pure Jewish blood (Neh 7.5) as proved by genealogical charts. Levites who lacked authentic genealogies were excluded from the service of the Temple. The effort to preserve the nation developed into a nationalism and exclusivism opposed by works such as Jonah and Ruth. Finally, John the Baptist told the Jews that genealogy did not bring salvation: "God is able out of these stones to raise up children to Abraham" (Mt 3.9).

Studies of the individual genealogies often show their artificial nature. There are symmetrical patterns of names and periods of time. Words such as son and brother are used for distant relatives and for those joined only by covenant. Doublets occur showing great variation in the genealogy of the same person. After the period of conquest when the Israelites settled the land of Canaan, names of villages and towns often replaced personal names. All of this points to the fact that the author felt that the history of Israel is the history of God's chosen ones. Study of the genealogies shows that he was more interested in theology than chronology, more concerned with salvation history than the narration of names and dates.

See Also: GENEALOGY OF JESUS.

Bibliography: R. DE VAUX, *Ancient Israel, Its Life and Institutions,* tr. J. MC HUGH (New York 1961) 4–6. J. PEDERSEN, *Israel, Its Life and Culture,* tr. A. MØLLER and A. I. FAUSBØLL, 2 v. (New York 1926–1940; rev. ed. 1959) 1:257. L. WATERMAN, "Some Repercussions from Late Levitical Genealogical Accretions in P and the Chronicler," *American Journal of Semitic Languages and Literatures* 58 (1941) 50. R. A. BOWMAN, *The Interpreters' Dictionary of the Bible,* G. A. BUTTRICK, ed., 4 v. (Nashville 1962) 2:362–365.

[S. C. DOYLE]

GENEALOGY OF JESUS

The two lists of Jesus' ancestors are given in the Gospels, one in Mt 1.1–17 and one in Lk 3.23–38. The importance of Christ's genealogy and the differences between the two lists will be considered here.

Importance. Besides the importance attached in general to genealogies in the ancient Near East (*see* GENEALOGIES, BIBLICAL), the genealogy of Jesus is of particular significance in support of His claim to be the MESSIAH, the son of David. The Old Testament (e.g., Is 11.1–9; Jer 23.5–6; Ez 34.23–24) foretold that the promised Messiah would be David's descendant, and as such have a legitimate claim to the restored throne of the Davidic dynasty. That the terms ''Messiah'' and ''son of David'' were considered synonymous at the time of Christ is clearly shown in Mt 22.41–46; Mk 12.35–37; and Lk 20.41–44. There can be little doubt that the Savior's Davidic descent was part of the primitive KERYGMA (cf. Acts 13.22–23; Rom 1.3), and it was eventually incorporated into the written gospel.

Matthew (1.1–17) and Luke (3.23–38) both give formal genealogies, the primary aim of which is to identify Jesus as Son of David and, secondarily, as Son of Abraham (Mt) or Son of God (Lk).

Differences Between the Lists. It is immediately apparent to anyone who places the two lists side by side that they differ widely in particulars. These difference may signify that one (or perhaps both) of the genealogies is more concerned with something beyond biological lineage, for the genealogical table in antiquity could fulfill more than a single function. It served to legitimate a royal or cultic line and to reveal character, on the assumption that descendants inherit the traits of their ancestors. The differences between the lists may signify, however, no more than the presence of two traditions that may or may not be reconcilable.

First List. Matthew (1.17) makes it clear that the genealogy he gives has been schematically arranged; it is divided into three sections, each of 14 generations. To achieve this, he has omitted four of the kings between Solomon and Jechonias, and other names have also no doubt been dropped. Perhaps the number 14 was chosen because it is twice seven (the perfect number), or possibly because the Hebrew consonants (the letters of the alphabet having numerical value) that make up the name David add up to 14. A major problem posed by this genealogy is that the descendants of Zorobabel whom it enumerates do not apparently correspond to those given in 1 Chr 3.19–24.

A final observation on this genealogy concerns the mention of four women (five if we include Mary): Tamar, Rahab, Ruth, and Bathsheba. St. Jerome maintained that these ''sinful'' women were mentioned to remind us that ''He who came for the sake of sinners'' was born of sinners. This explanation fails. Ruth was in no way a sinner. Although Tamar and Rahab were prostitutes, and Bathsheba was an adulteress, each of these women was honored in later Judaism; Tamar (Gn 38), as a proselyte to Judaism and because she upheld Judah's family line by seducing her father-in-law; Rahab (Jos 2, 6), because she aided Israel's victory at Jericho (cf. Heb 11.31); Bathsheba, because she gave birth to Solomon. A more plausible explanation for the inclusion of women is that what all of them have in common is a foreign background: Tamar and Rahab were Canaanites, Ruth was a Moabite, Bathsheba was the widow of a Hittite. Matthew aimed accordingly, to emphasize the universality of Messianic salvation and to appeal to the Gentile members of the community addressed by his gospel

A final explanation for the inclusion of women in Matthew's genealogy makes sense of the biblical texts, on their own historical and literary terms, while offering a perspective compatible with modern convictions. In each case divine intervention occurs, through a woman, by ''irregular'' or even ''scandalous'' means (R. Brown), thus foreshadowing Mary's role in Jesus' birth. To become pregnant out of wedlock (Matt 1.18) would have been scandalous at the time, while Jesus' conception by the holy spirit, rather than by natural means, is irregular. Tamar, Rahab, Bathsheba, and Ruth may be viewed, moreover, as examples of ''higher righteousness'' (Amy-Jill Levine). Their distance from positions of social and cultural privilege, and the initiative they take to advance divine purposes, qualifies them as models for a kind of justice inaccessible to their male counterparts (Judah, the king of Jericho, David, Boaz).

Second List. Luke's genealogy is much longer than Matthew's (giving the descent of Abraham from Adam) and is regressive in structure (moving backward from Jesus rather than forward to Him). Between David and Joseph only two names, Zorobabel and Salathiel, correspond to any found in Matthew's table. The descent from David is traced through the line of Nathan, one of his numerous sons (2 Sm 5.14) about whose issue the Bible tells us nothing save that it was extant in the time of Deutero-Zechariah (Zec 12.13).

If this were the only point at issue, we should have no hesitation in accepting one of the two ancient proposals to harmonize the Matthean and Lucan genealogies. Julius Africanus, in his *Letter to Aristides,* explained that the Jacob of Matthew's genealogy and the Heli of Luke's were uterine brothers, and that upon the death of Heli without any children, Jacob, following the levirate law (Dt 25.5–10) married his brother's widow and begot Joseph, the legal father of Jesus. This has long been considered the traditional answer to the problem of divergent genealogies, but it is highly doubtful that the levirate law applied to uterine brothers. The alternative suggestion, usually credited to Annius of Viterbo (*c.* A.D. 1490) but traceable to the 5th century and possibly even to the writings of Justin Martyr (*Dial.* 100), regards Luke's genealogy as that of Mary. On this supposition we should read Lk 3.23 as follows:''And Jesus Himself, when He began His work, was about thirty years of age, being—as was supposed—the son of Joseph [but in reality the grand-] son of Heli. . . .'' Against this hypothesis it is frequently alleged that descent through a woman was of no account to the Jews and that the genealogy of women is never given. This is not true. The lineage of heiresses is recorded (e.g., Nm 26.33; 1 Chr 2.16–17) and the lengthy genealogy of Judith (Jdt 8.1), whatever one may choose to make of it, shows that a woman's importance entitled her to the same distinction. The real difficulty with the Marian hypothesis, as with that of Africanus, is that neither explains how Salathiel and Zorobabel appear as descendants of Nathan in Luke's genealogy. It is useless to invoke the solution of a levirate marriage again, for we know the names of all the sons of Jechonias and none of them is called Neri (cf. 1 Chr 3.17–18).

Yet the inclusion of Salathiel and Zorobabel in this pedigree may point to its having a wider function than the purely genealogical. Closer study reveals that it consists of 11 sets of seven names each and, more significantly, that the last name in all but the earliest two groupings marks a sort of climax: Jesus, Joseph, Mathathias, Salathiel, Jesus, Joseph, David, Aram, and Thare. These names constitute a kind of historical panorama calling to mind the departure from Ur, the enslavement in Egypt, the first monarchy and the long period of Messianic expectation (the early Joseph and Jesus paralleling the later Joseph and Jesus), the Babylonian exile, the second monarchy, and finally the era of the true Messiah. Some of the other names may have been suggested to the compiler by Zec 12.12–13; some may be fragments of an actual genealogy. We cannot say that the Lucan genealogy has yielded up all its secrets, but we are closer to understanding it.

Bibliography: J. OBERNHUMER, ''Die menschliche Abstammung Jesu,'' *Theologisch-praktische Quartalschrift* 91 (1938) 524–527. R. T. HOOD, ''The Genealogies of Jesus,'' *Early Christian Origins,* ed. A. WIKGREN (Chicago 1961). L. NOLLE, ''Old Testament Laws of Inheritance and St. Luke's Genealogy of Christ,'' *Scripture* 2 (1949–50) 38–42. S. SANDMEL, ''Myths, Genealogies and Jewish Myths and the Writing of the Gospels,'' *Hebrew Union College Annual* 27 (1956) 201–211. R. E. BROWN, *The Birth of the Messiah* (Garden City, NY 1977). A.-J. LEVINE, ''Matthew,'' *The Women's Bible Commentary,* eds. C. A. NEWSOM and S. H. RINGE (Louisville, KY 1992) 253–54.

[J. E. BRUNS/M. STEVENSON]

GÉNÉBRARD, GILBERT

Exegete and Hebraist; b. Riom, Auvergne, France, Dec. 12, 1537; d. Semur, Bourgogne, France, March 14, 1597. He entered the Benedictine monastery at Mausac as a youth, received the doctorate of theology in Paris (1563), and there became professor of Hebrew and Scripture (1569). Consecrated a bishop (April 4, 1592), he was appointed archbishop of Aix-en-Provence (Oct. 9, 1593). A staunch supporter of the Catholic League in opposing the succession of the Protestant Henry of Navarre to the throne of France, Génébrard suffered for his resistance, even though, soon after Henry became a Catholic and was crowned HENRY IV of France (1593), he rendered his submission to the new king. In 1596 the parliament of Provence accused him of lese majesty, had his work *De sacrarum electionum jure* (Paris 1593) publicly burned, and banished him from the region. After a brief exile in Avignon, he was allowed to retire to his priory *in commendam* at Semur, where he soon died.

Génébrard was rightly regarded by his contemporaries as one of the outstanding savants of the 16th century. Among his numerous published works are studies in the fields of OT exegesis, rabbinical literature, Patristics, dogmatic and moral theology, Canon Law, liturgy, and chronology.

Bibliography: H. HURTER, *Nomenclator literarius theologiae catholicae,* 3:116–117. B. HEURTEBIZE, *Dictionnaire de théologie catholique* 6.1:1183–85; *Dictionnaire de la Bible* 3.1:171–172. Y. CHAUSSY, *Catholicisme* 4:1813. A. VACCARI, *Lexicon für Theologie und Kirche* 4:662–663.

[L. F. HARTMAN]

GENERAL DIRECTORY FOR CATECHESIS

Catechetical directories are a new genre of writing in the Roman Catholic religious education that emerged at the Second Vatican Council. They furnish guidelines that delineate theological-pastoral principles, describe the nature and purpose of catechesis, set goals, outline structures, and suggest strategies for catechetical programs. The *General Directory for Catechesis* (GDC) promulgated in 1997 by the Congregation for the Clergy updates the *General Catechetical Directory* published in 1971. Composed originally in Spanish and Italian, the GDC exists in Latin (the *editio typica*), English, French, German, and other translations. The new edition reflects the orientation given to catechesis in the apostolic exhortations *Evangelii nuntiandi* of Pope Paul VI (1974) and *Catechesi tradendae* of Pope John Paul II (1979) by yoking catechesis and evangelization in the Church's mission to proclaim the Gospel. It encourages the baptismal catechumenate, restored in the Rite of Christian Initiation of Adults (1972), as the model for all catechesis. The 1979 Directory, considerably longer than the earlier edition, consists of five parts. Part 1 explains the nature, object, and the duties of catechesis in the context of the Church's mission of evangelization. Part 2 recapitulates the norms and criteria for presenting the Gospel found in the 1971 edition of the Directory and explains the contents and use of the Catechism of the Catholic Church. Part 3 describes ''the pedagogy of God'' as the source and model of the pedagogy to be adopted in catechesis. Part 4 focuses on the recipients of catechesis, explaining how the methods and even the message needs to be adapted according to age groups, special needs, the socio-religious context, and cultural background of those being catechized. Part 5 addresses catechesis in the local church. It outlines principles that should guide the formation of catechesis, the need to be sensitive to the surroundings where it is carried on, and the importance of coordinating catechetical and other pastoral programs for their mutual support. The 291 numbered paragraphs of the GDC are not all of the same importance. The sections deal with divine revelation, the nature of catechesis, and the criteria governing the proclamation of the Gospel message are ''universally valid.'' Paragraphs that refer to particular circumstances, methodology, and to the manner of adapting catechesis to diverse age groups and cultural contexts are by way of guidelines and suggestions. The immediate aim of catechetical directories is to assist in the composition of national and regional directories and the writing of catechisms.

Bibliography: *General Directory for Catechesis*. Washington, D.C.: United States Catholic Conference, 1998. C. BISSOLI, ''Il Direttorio Generale per la Catechesi (1997),'' *Salesianum* 60 (1998) 521–547. B. L. MARTHALER, *Sowing Seeds: Notes and Comments on the General Directory for Catechesis* (Washington, D.C. 2000).

[B. L. MARTHALER]

GENERAL INTERCESSIONS

General intercessions are also called universal prayer, prayer of the faithful, or prayers of the people. Christian tradition has always given an important place to intercessory prayer. St. Paul exhorts to the offering of ''prayers, petitions, intercessions and thanksgiving for all: for rulers and all in authority, so that we may be able to live quiet and peaceful lives in the full practice of religion and of morality'' (1 Tm 2.1–4). Intercessory prayer is a natural part of the liturgy in which the Church, in the name of Christ, continues to offer the prayer and petition which he poured out in the days of his earthly life. Already by the 2nd century the origins of the General Intercessions appear. St. Justin Martyr writes (*c.* 155) that ''on the Lord's day, after the reading of Scripture and the homily, all stand and offer the prayers'' (*First Apology* 67). Vatican Council II's Constitution on the Liturgy called for the restoration of these General Intercessions which in the course of time had disappeared from the Roman Mass (*Sacrosanctum Concilium* 53).

At Mass. The structure of the General Intercessions has three parts. First, after the Homily the one presiding invites the people to pray. Second, the deacon (or another person) announces the intentions to the people and they pray for that intention in silence or by a common response, recited or sung. Third, the one presiding concludes with a prayer (GenInstrRomMissal 47). As a rule the sequence of intentions is: (1) for the needs of the Church; (2) for public authorities and the salvation of the world; (3) for those oppressed by any need; and (4) for the local community (*ibid.* 46).

Liturgy of the Hours. The Church praises God throughout the course of the day by celebrating the Liturgy of the Hours. The tradition does not separate praise of God from petition and ''often enough praise turns somehow to petition'' (GenInstrLitHor 179). Consequently, the General Intercessions have been restored to Morning and Evening Prayer, however with some nuance to avoid repetition of the petitions at Mass. The intentions at Morning Prayer are to consecrate the day to God (*ibid.* 181); those at Evening Prayer stress thanksgiving for graces received during the day. The intentions found in the *Hours Book* are addressed directly to God (rather than to the people, as at Mass) so that the wording is suitable for both common celebration and private recitation (*ibid.* 190). Although ''the Liturgy of the Hours, like other liturgical actions, is not something private but belongs to the whole body of the Church'' (*ibid.* 20), it must be acknowledged that it is still often prayed privately. In every case, however, the petitions should be linked with praise of God and acknowledgement of his glory or with a reference to the history of salvation, as in the Lord's Prayer (*ibid.* 185).

Bibliography: Consilium, *De Oratione Communi seu Fidelium: Natura, momentum ac structura. Criteria atque specimina coetibus territorialibus episcoporum proposita* (Vatican City 1966). P. DE CLERCK, *La ''prière universelle'' dans les liturgies latines anciennes: Témoignages patristiques et textes liturgiques* (Liturgiewissenschaftliche Quellen und Forschungen 62 Münster, Westfalen 1977). D. CONNORS, ed. Issue on ''General Intercessions,'' *Liturgical Ministry* 2 (1993) 1–33. J. B. MOLIN, ''Quelques textes médiévaux de la prière universelle,'' in *Traditio et progressio* (Rome 1988) 333–358.

[T. RICHSTATTER/EDS.]

GENERATION-CORRUPTION

The change or passage from a negative term to a positive term, from not existing to existing, is called generation (Lat. *generatio*); the change or passage from a positive term to a negative term, from existing to not existing, is called destruction or corruption (Lat. *corruptio*). Because there is no intermediary between the contradictories ''existing'' and ''not existing,'' between ''affirming'' and ''denying,'' generation and corruption are called changes according to contradiction. They are therefore instantaneous. Either one may be ''absolute'' (*simpliciter*) or merely ''with respect to something'' (*secundum quid*). An example of the former is the coming into existence of Socrates, a man, or his ceasing to exist; of the latter, his becoming white or his ceasing to be white, whether he, too, comes to be or ceases to be or not.

Neither generation nor corruption, whether absolute or with respect to something, is MOTION in the strict sense of the word. Motion requires something already in existence that can be moved gradually from one positive term to another positive term contrary to the first.

In living beings, substantial or absolute generation is a vital operation that proceeds from within the parent as a conjoined principle producing an offspring specifically like itself.

See Also: SUBSTANTIAL CHANGE; MATTER AND FORM.

[A. ROBINSON]

GENERATION OF THE WORD

The topic here is the origin of the Son from the Father within the Godhead. As such that origin is not an object of direct consideration in the New Testament. This is not, however, to say it has no background there; quite the contrary is the case. The Father and Son (prescinding from the Holy Spirit) appear on the same side of the dichotomy between Creator and everything else. And precisely in this frame of reference they are still related to each other in the way their very names imply (*see* GOD [SON]). To speak of the Son as being generated is to continue further the Biblically inspired analogy of paternity-filiation in the Deity. The Latin version of the Scriptures gives reason for so doing in applying *unigenitus* to the Son (Jn 1.14, 18; 3.16, 18; 1 Jn 4.9), although the Greek μον ογενής has more the sense of unique, sole, or only one of its kind, than only-begotten. All this has importance as it indicates the type of origin ascribed to the Son before the Incarnation, namely, GENERATION. The Bible being what it is, its authors were not concerned with giving a description of the preconditions, constituents, and consequences of that intra-Trinitarian generation. Its factual character is, however, asserted, namely, a dependence of Son on Father in a way that is diverse from that of all other realities.

If the Scriptures did not enter into the precise manner of the origin in question, the case was decidedly otherwise in the postapostolic Church. It was no small task to find a formula that would express both the origin and dependence of Jesus on the Father and also not imply that He was on the other side of the above-mentioned dichotomy. The difference between γίνομαι and γεννάω was difficult to grasp and explain, this due to a resemblance at once literal and ideological. At the instance of Arius, the Council of Nicaea I entered more directly into the implications of the Son's eternal generation. Excluding origin from nothing and origin from other preexistent beings, He was said to be generated (not made) from the Father's own reality, or substance (*Enchiridion symbolorum*, 125–126). When later the Holy Spirit was proposed as the creature of the Son, the orthodox reaction affirmed His origin from the Father by way of procession (*Enchiridion symbolorum*, 150) distinguished from the Son's generation (*Enchiridion symbolorum*, 75, 800). Finally the connection between the conception of the Son in time and His eternal birth from the Father entered very much into the Nestorian controversy of the 5th century [cf. A. Grillmeier, *Christ in Christian Tradition,* tr. J. S. Bowden (New York 1965) 369–399].

The assertion that the Father's personal note (αγεννησία) was connected of utter necessity with the nature of Deity excluded not only the Son (as generated) but also much mystery from the Godhead (Eunomius, *Apol.; Patrologia Graeca* 30:842–847). By reaction, the incipient theology of the beatific vision found some Greek Fathers qualifying the intellectual union of man with God even in glory so as to preserve the transcendence of the Deity [Chrysostom, *Incomprehens., Patrologia Graeca* 48:704; Theodoret, *Eran.* (*Dial.*) 1, *Patrologia Graeca* 83:49].

In dependence on Augustine, scholastic theologians considered the human psychology of knowing and loving analogous to the divine processions (*see* WORD, THE). The difference between the two in man provided intelligibility to an increased degree for the article of faith that in the Godhead only the Son arises, or takes origin, by way of generation (intellection). Contemporary Christian theology, with its emphasis on CHRISTOLOGY, is attempting to investigate or consider the procession of the Son (generation) as continued in His temporal mission (*see* MISSIONS, DIVINE) and as a possible precondition for the concession of revelation and grace by God to man (*see* LOGOS).

See Also: CONSUBSTANTIALITY; FILIATION; HOMOOUSIOS; TRINITY, HOLY, ARTICLES ON.

For bibliography, *see* GOD (SON); WORD, THE; LOGOS; TRINITY, HOLY.

[C. J. PETER]

GENESIS, BOOK OF

The first book in the Bible. As with all their sacred books, the Jewish people called the first book by its opening words b^e^rē'šît The name commonly used in modern European languages is derived from the Vulgate adaptation of the Septuagint (LXX) title, which refers to the story of creation, or the ''genesis,'' of the world.

The main topics considered in this article concerning the Book in the Bible are its historical character, its place in the Church's doctrine, and its most important teachings. Before these are considered, however, it will be helpful to outline its contents and say a word about its composition.

Contents and Division. Genesis is divided into two main parts. As the first book of the Pentateuch, Genesis is an introduction to Israel's history. The main division is between ch. 1–11, which treat of the primeval age, and ch. 12–50, which treat of the patriarchal history. The latter section is an immediate introduction to the story of Israel (beginning with Abraham), and the former is a prologue to the whole Pentateuch, explaining the need for a divine intervention in mankind's history. Both are interpretative analyses, but they differ in their type of material. The history of the primeval age is a conflation of two traditions, the YAHWIST (J) and the Priestly (P). (*See* PRIESTLY WRITERS, PENTATEUCHAL.) In the patriarchal history a third tradition, the ELOHIST (E), appears. The following division of the book into literary units and their attribution to the three traditions are somewhat tentative and subject to revision on the basis of further scholarly work.

1. 1.1–11.32: Primeval Age
   - *a.* 1.1–2.4a: creation of world and man (P)
   - *b.* 2.4b–25: creation of man and woman (J)
   - *c.* 3.1–24: the Fall (J)
   - *d.* 4.1–16: Cain and Abel (J)
   - *e.* 4.17–26: genealogy of Cain (J)
   - *f.* 5.1–32: genealogy of Adam to Noah (P)
   - *g.* 6.1–22: prologue to the Flood (J and P)
   - *h.* 7.1–8.22: the Flood (J and P)
   - *i.* 9.1–17: covenant with Noah (P)
   - *j.* 9.18–27: sons of Noah (J)
   - *k.* 10.1–32: peopling of the earth (P and J)
   - *l.* 11.1–9: tower of Babel (J)
   - *m.* 11.10–32: concluding genealogies (P and some J)
2. 12.1–25.18: The Patriarch Abraham
   - *a.* 12.1–9: call of Abram (J, some P)
   - *b.* 12.10–20: Abram and Sarai in Egypt (J)
   - *c.* 13.1–18: separation of Abram and Lot (J, some P)
   - *d.* 14.1–24: Abram and the four kings (?)
   - *e.* 15.1–20: promises renewed (J, some E?)
   - *f.* 16.1–16: Hagar's flight (J, some P)
   - *g.* 17.1–27: covenant of circumcision (P)
   - *h.* 18.1–19.38: Sodom and Gomorrah (J)
   - *i.* 20.1–18: Abraham and Sarah in Gerar (E)
   - *j.* 21.1–21: Isaac and Ishmael (J and P)
   - *k.* 21.22–34: Abraham and Abimelech (E)
   - *l.* 22.1–24: sacrifice of Isaac (E, some J)
   - *m.* 23.1–20: purchase of cave of Machpelah (P)
   - *n.* 24.1–67: wife of Isaac (J)
   - *o.* 25.1–18: Abraham's descendants (P and J)
3. 25.19–36.43: Patriarchs Isaac and Jacob
   - *a.* 25.19–34: birth of Esau and Jacob (J, some P)
   - *b.* 26.1–35: Isaac in Gerar and Bersabee (J, some P)
   - *c.* 27.1–45: Isaac's blessing of Jacob (J)
   - *d.* 27.46–28.9: Jacob's departure for Phadan-aram (P)
   - *e.* 28.10–22: vision at Bethel (J and E)
   - *f.* 29.1–30: Jacob's marriages (J and E?)
   - *g.* 29.31–30.24: Jacob's children (J and E)
   - *h.* 30.25–43: Laban outwitted by Jacob (J, some E)
   - *i.* 31.1–21: Jacob's departure (E, some J)
   - *j.* 31.22–42: Laban's pursuit (E, some J)
   - *k.* 31.43–32.3: contract between Jacob and Laban (J and E)
   - *l.* 32.4–22: preparation for Jacob's meeting with Esau (J and E)
   - *m.* 32.23–33: Jacob's struggle with God (J)
   - *n.* 33.1–20: Jacob's meeting with Esau (J, some E?)
   - *o.* 34.1–31: rape of Dinah (J and E)
   - *p.* 35.1–29: Jacob at Bethel (E and P, some J)
   - *q.* 36.1–43: descendants of Esau (P?)
4. 37.1–50.26: History of Joseph
   - *a.* 37.1–36: Joseph sold into Egypt (J and E)
   - *b.* 38.1–30: Judah and Tamar (J)
   - *c.* 39.1–23: Joseph's temptations (J)
   - *d.* 40.1–23: Joseph's interpretation of prisoners' dreams (E)
   - *e.* 41.1–57: Joseph's interpretation of Pharaoh's dreams (E, some J)
   - *f.* 42.1–38: first encounter of Joseph with his brothers (E, some J)
   - *g.* 43.1–34: second journey to Egypt (J, some E)
   - *h.* 44.1–34: Judah's plan for Benjamin (J)
   - *i.* 45.1–28: recognition of Joseph (J and E)
   - *j.* 46.1–34: Jacob's journey to Egypt (J, E, and P)
   - *k.* 47.1–31: Hebrews in Egypt (J and P)
   - *l.* 48.1–22: Jacob's adoption of Joseph's sons (J and E, some P)
   - *m.* 49.1–33: Jacob's blessings (J)
   - *n.* 50.1–26: burial of Jacob and final acts of Joseph (J, E, and P)

The principles for the literary analysis of the Pentateuch were first applied to Genesis, where the documenta-

"Lot and His Daughters," painting by Wolfgang Krodel, 16th century. (©Archivo Iconografico, S.A./CORBIS)

"The Expulsion from Eden," fresco by Masaccio, 1427, the Brancacci Chapel of S. Maria del Carmine, Florence, Italy.

ry traditions were quite apparent. In the history of the primeval age (ch. 1–11) J provided the narrative continuity, while P, for the most part, supplied the chronological and ethnological framework. The same roles were generally continued in the patriarchal history (ch. 12–50), although here E added its theological insights with a parallel narrative. The narrative was probably more extensive in its original form, but was reduced when conflated with J.

Historical Character. Genesis presents a theological interpretation of history, intended to throw light on later Israelite history. It does not purport to be a disinterested presentation of facts, but a religious illustration of the divine plan of salvation. As such it is highly selective in its use of material and freely adapts it to its purpose.

The basic facts in the patriarchal history correspond, at least in a general way, to the findings of modern archeology that provide information and insight about the political, social, juridical, and religious conditions in the first half of the 2nd millennium B. C. Similar conditions are reflected in Genesis ch. 12–50. The general lines of the patriarchal activity, from the migration from Upper Mesopotamia, through their varying adventures in Canaan, to the descent of at least a representative group into Egypt, are true to historical reality.

This basic family history was first recorded and preserved in oral form. The original purpose was generally one of entertainment and tribal pride, resulting in the story's popular form. Thus, popular explanations were given to the meaning of names; family incidents were put into ballad form; and, at times, local cult legends were used to give a deeper insight into mysterious happenings. Gradually the stories tended to concentrate on certain individuals or, especially, to become liturgical elements for certain shrines, thus assuring their preservation. Cycles of stories arose, frequently with a geographical link. During this period of their shrine history, the stories underwent a development that emphasized religious elements and reflected confessional interests that added luster to the local shrine or tribe. Only after this development did the Pentateuchal editors adapt them to their purposes. Such adaptation necessitated adjustments at times in order to stress religious lessons for each story or dominant themes for the entire history. In the gradual conflation of the traditions and in the final redaction of the canonical book, still more editorial work was done in keeping with the purposes of the inspired authors. Despite this long and varied history, which must be taken into account in interpreting Genesis, the basic historical character of the patriarchal narratives was preserved. (For the historical nature of Genesis ch. 1–11, *see* PRIMEVAL AGE IN THE BIBLE.)

The Church and Genesis. Many stories and figures in the Book of Genesis have become part of general western culture. The story of creation, the tower of Babel, and the flood are ready points of reference, as are the names of Adam and Eve, Cain and Abel, Noah, and the patriarchs Abraham, Isaac and Israel. Within Christianity, however, there are sharp differences in the interpretation of the text, especially of the first 11 chapters, both as regards the origin of the material and its historical value. In the 18th and 19th centuries the study of linguistics and comparative religion as well as the newborn sciences of archeology, geology, and anthropology brought into question the historicity of the first chapters of Genesis and caused some to raise doubts about the reliability of the Bible itself. In reaction Christian apologists defended the veracity of the biblical accounts even to the point of insisting of a literal interpretation of six days of creation. Catholic scholars for the most part, steering a middle course between FUNDAMENTALISM and rationalism, advocated forms of concordism, that is, interpretations of the text that were consonant with the findings of anthropology and geology.

The common Christian belief that the Bible mediates the revealed word of God is fundamental to the official Catholic interpretation of Genesis, and it was to safeguard this truth that the Church was at times tenacious in defending its Mosaic authorship and the historical value. This was especially the case in early decisions of the PONTIFICAL BIBLICAL COMMISSION in repudiating rationalist and Modernist interpretations of the text. By the time Pope Pius XII published his important encyclical *DIVINO AFFLANTE SPIRITU* in 1943, leading Catholic scholars had reexamined the tradition. The encyclical set down basic principles for a sound Christian exegesis and encouraged scholars to apply them to all parts of the Scriptures without fear. There followed, not long after this, scholarly articles and several complete commentaries on Genesis that made full use of scientific methodology. That these were not contrary to the mind of the Church was implied in the letter of the secretary of the Pontifical Biblical Commission to the cardinal archbishop of Paris (E. Suhard) on Jan. 16, 1948. Concerning the first 11 chapters of Genesis, the letter said in part, ''They relate in simple and figurative language, adapted to the understanding of a less developed people, the fundamental truths presupposed for the economy of salvation, as well as the popular description of the origin of the human race and of the chosen people'' (*Enchiridion biblicum*, 4th ed., 581).

There was a similar development in the understanding of the origin of the material used in the opening chapters. Catholic scholars came to agree that the truths contained in these 11 chapters were the fruit of Israel's faith and that the narrative form in which the truths were preserved can be traced, in part at least, to extra-Biblical sources that antedate Israel. Northern Mesopotamia is the likeliest place for the narratives' origin, since this was the immediate home of the Patriarchs' ancestors, and the suggestion is confirmed by a comparison of the Genesis stories with those of Mesopotamia. Israel's theology, of course, radically affected the stories and made them vehicles for teaching Israelite religious truths. Most Catholic scholars accepted some form of the documentary thesis that attributes the Genesis text to a conflation of the Yahwist (J) and Priestly (P) traditions that were given final form by the Elohist (E) editor.

The *Catechism of the Catholic Church* acknowledges that the natural sciences have ''splendidly enriched our knowledge of the age and dimensions of the universe'' (n.283), and at the same time it emphasizes the ''unique place'' that the first three chapters of Genesis occupy in the Church's teaching on creation. ''From a literary standpoint,'' the Catechism says, ''these texts may have had diverse sources. The inspired authors have placed them at the beginning of Scripture to express in their solemn language the truths of creation—its origin and its end in God, its order and goodness, the vocation of man, and finally the drama of sin and salvation'' (n. 289). Elsewhere it states, ''the account of the fall in *Genesis 3* uses figurative language'' to affirm ''a primitive event, a deed that took place at the beginning of the history of man'' (n. 390; see also, 375).

Importance of Genesis. The abundant references and allusions to Genesis in the NT, the Fathers, and the official documents of the Church attest to its importance as the background for many Christian doctrines. Dependent on Genesis, for instance, are the Pauline doctrines of original sin, of the new Adam, and of the role of faith in justification. In 1 Peter the waters of the flood become a type of baptismal waters, and the author of Hebrews has greatly developed and applied the symbolism of the figure of Melchisedek.

Its importance is even more clearly shown by a summary of the principal teachings of the book. The primary purpose of Genesis is to explain the saving actions of God on Israel's behalf. These actions are seen, first of all, as the fulfillment of the patriarchal promises recorded in ch. 12–50 and, ultimately, as necessitated by man's religious and moral deterioration as described in ch. 1–11. The book is, therefore, wholly soteriological in aim. (For a summation of the doctrine of ch. 1–11, *see* PRIMEVAL AGE IN THE BIBLE.)

The scattering of the peoples over the face of the earth, which marks the climax of man's alienation from God (11.1–9), forms the background for the divine intervention in the favor of Abraham. The Patriarch is called from his Mesopotamian homeland and given the promise of a great posterity and of special divine blessings (12.1–3). This promise, made by the personal God of the fathers (31.5, 29, 42, 53), is constantly renewed (13.14–16; 26.2–5; 28.13–15) and is to be fulfilled in the people of Israel (15.13–16, 18–21). Together with the conviction of the one personal Lord, the promise of a great nation possessing one land ties the patriarchal narratives intimately to the rest of Israel's history.

All that is recorded in these narratives has its final relevance to the divine plan of salvation. Dependent on it, therefore, are the manifestations of divine power (12.17; 14.19–20), divine justice (19.24–29; 38.7), and divine mercy (18.23–32; 19.19–22). It is likewise within this context of the divine saving plan that human virtues are presented: faith (12.4a; 15.6; ch. 22), sacrificial worship and the invoking of God's name (12.7–8; 13.4, 18; 26.25; 31.54; 33.20; 35.1, 7; 46.1), sexual morality (ch. 19–20; 38.24; 39.7–12), hospitality (19.1–8; 24.17–20), forgiveness of offenses (50.15–21), abhorrence of murder (37.21–22), and respect for the dead (cb. 23; 25.8–10; 35.19–20, 29; 50.1–14).

Bibliography: C. WESTERMAN, *Genesis 1–11, Genesis 12–36, Genesis 37–50* 3 vols. (Minneapolis, 1984–86) [Noteworthy for its comprehensive bibliography based on the work of the University of Heidelberg Genesis- Research Institute]. G. VON RAD, *Genesis: A Commentary,* tr. J. H. MARKS (Philadelphia 1961). E. A. SPEISER, *Genesis* (Anchor Bible 1; Garden City, NY 1964). B. VAWTER, *On Genesis: A New Reading* (New York 1977). W. BRUEGGEMANN and W. WOLFF, *The Vitality of the Old Testament Traditions* (Atlanta, 1975).W. BRUEGGEMANN, *Genesis* (Atlanta, 1982). M. NOTH, *A History of Pentateuchal Traditions* (Englewood Cliffs, NJ 1972). J. VAN SETERS, *Abraham in History and Tradition* (New Haven, CT 1975). C. L'HEUREUX, *In and out of Paradise* (Ramsey, NJ 1983).

[E. H. MALY/EDS.]

GENESIUS, SS.

There are four saints by this name of whom any details are known.

Genesius (Genès) of Arles, martyr; d. 303? This catechumen, as notary of Arles, refused to transcribe an edict ordering the persecution of Christians. Fleeing the city, he sent the bishop a request for baptism, but before he could receive the sacrament, he was beheaded near the river Rhône. He is often confused with Genesius the Comedian.

Feast: Aug. 25.

Genesius, bishop of Clermont; d. *c.* 660. When chosen unanimously by the populace to fill the bishopric on the death of St. Proculus, Genesius reluctantly accepted. After five years he made a pilgrimage to Rome seeking permission to resign and lead a solitary life, but his people forced him to return. He built the church of St. Symphorian (where he was buried and which later bore his name), a hospice, and a monastery, Manglieu or Grandlieu. A later bishop of Clermont, St. Praejectus (Prix; d. 676), was his ward.

Feast: June 3.

Genesius the Comedian, legendary martyr, patron of actors; of unknown origin. The *passio* relates that, a pagan actor, he was ''baptized'' while performing a burlesque of Christian rites for the Emperor DIOCLETIAN and publicly confessed the faith. Diocletian immediately put him to torture and had him beheaded.

Feast: Aug. 25.

Genesius, bishop of Lyons; d. Nov. 11, 678. He was an abbot and chaplain of Queen St. BATHILDIS, becoming bishop of Lyons in 658. In 677 he presided over the Council of Malay.

Feast: Nov. 1.

Bibliography: S. CAVALLIN, ''Saint Genès le notaire,'', *Eranos Löfstedtianus* 43 (1945) 150–175. P. FRANCHI DE' CAVALIERI, *Note agiografiche* 8 (*Studi e Testi* 65; 1935) 203–210. H. LECLERCQ, *Dictionnaire d'archéologie chrétienne et de liturgie* 6.1:903–909. A. BUTLER, *The Lives of the Saints* 2:465; 3:398–400. A. M. ZIMMERMANN, *Kalendarium Benedictinum: Die Heiligen und Seligen des Benediktinerorderns und seiner Zweige* 3:247. G. of Arles. G. PRETE, *Trittico stenografico* (2d. ed. Asti 1970). J. VERT I PLANAS, *La reliquía de Sant Genís* (Torroella de Montgrí1982). G. the Comedian. M. PERRIN, *Saint Genès et comediens convertis* (Paris 1966). C. RAMBAUD, *Le comedien aux liens* (Saint–Etienne 1983). H. GALINDO, *Genesio: obra fársica en quince cuadros* (Monterrey, Mexico 1995).

[A. M. SHEA]

GENEVIÈVE, ST.

Patroness of Paris, France; b. Nanterre, outside Paris, *c.* 422; d. *c.* 500. According to the ancient vita, Geneviève, or Genovefa, on hearing an inspiring sermon by St. GERMAIN OF AUXERRE, promised to consecrate her life to God. She was only seven years old at the time. When she was 15, she was received as a virgin before a certain Bishop Vilicus. Her parents died soon after, and Geneviève moved to Paris to live with her godmother. In 451, when Attila's troops were on the outskirts of the city, Geneviève persuaded the citizens of Paris to hold fast and not to leave the city. Her prediction was correct. Attila's troops switched their offensive from Paris and turned toward Orléans, where they were defeated by the Romans and the Franks on the Catalonian fields. Geneviève was buried in the church of the Holy Apostles Peter and Paul, popularly known as the church of St. Geneviève. When the church that had been built in her honor (in 1764) became the Pantheon (1793), most of her relics were destroyed; a center of her veneration today is the church of St. Étienne–du–Mont. Frequent claims of her miraculous protection of the city of Paris, including delivery from a pestilence in 1129, contributed to both the literature of devotion and legend during the Middle Ages. The vita has been preserved in three recensions and has been the object of vigorous historical research. Some competent scholars defend its authenticity.

Feast: Jan. 3.

Bibliography: *Vita*, ed. B. KRUSCH, *Monumenta Germaniae Historica: Scriptores rerum Merovingicarum* 3 (1896) 204–238. M. HEINZELMANN, J. C. POULIN, and M. FLEURY, *Les vies anciennes de sainte Geneviève de Paris études critiques* (Paris 1986). C. KOHLER, *Étude critique sur . . . Sainte Geneviève* (Paris 1881) 5–47. K. KÜNSTLE, ed., *Vita Sanctae Genovefae* (BT; 1910). G. KURTH, *Études franques,* 2 v. (Brussels 1919) 2:1–96. *Acta Sanctorum*, Jan. 1:137–153. H. LECLERCQ, *Dictionnaire d'archéologie chrétienne et de liturgie* 6.1:960–990. P. VIARD, *Catholicisme* 4:1829–31. E.

BOURASSIN, *Sainte Geneviève* (Monaco 1997). J. DUBOIS and L. BEAUMONT-MAILLET, *Sainte Geneviève de Paris: la vie, la culte, l'art* (Paris 1982). H. LESÊTRE, *Sainte Geneviève* (Les Saints 191; Paris 1900). A. RICHOMME, *Sainte Geneviève: patronne de Paris* (Paris 1979). A. D. SERTILLANGES, *Sainte Geneviève* (Paris 1917). M. SLUHOVSKY, *Patroness of Paris: Rituals of Devotion in Early Modern France* (Leiden 1998). Y. Z. ZHANG, *Der Legendenstoff der heiligen Genoveva in dramatischen Bearbeitungen vom Barock bis zum Realismus* (Frankfurt am Main 1998). F. L. CROSS, *The Oxford Dictionary of the Christian Church.*

[D. KELLEHER]

GÉNICOT, ÉDOUARD

Jesuit moral theologian; b. Antwerp, June 18, 1856; d. Louvain, Feb. 21, 1900. Génicot entered the Society of Jesus on Sept. 27, 1872. He took over the chair of moral theology at Louvain in 1889, teaching first Canon Law and then moral theology until his death in 1900. His teaching was marked by great clarity and the avoidance of subtleties, and by the careful pursuit of principles to their legitimate conclusions. His *Theologiae Moralis Institutiones,* first published in 1896, went through numerous revised editions and became the standard moral text in many seminaries. It draws its inspiration mainly from the large work of Ballerini-Palmieri, and was in turn frequently edited and adapted, especially after the promulgation of the Code of Canon Law, by Génicot's nephew, Joseph Salsmans. Génicot judiciously popularized, for the use of students and the general public, the work that Ballerini had written for scholars. Génicot's other well-known work, *Casus Conscientiae,* published posthumously at Louvain in 1901, was also brought up to date by Salsmans.

Bibliography: P. BERNARD, *Dictionnaire de théologie catholique* 6.2: 1223–24. H. HURTER, *Nomenclator literarius theologiae catholicae* 5.2:2056.

[J. H. CAMPANA]

GENIZA

The Hebrew name for a room in a synagogue in which damaged manuscripts of the Bible or other writings with sacred associations are preserved when withdrawn from use. It is also a collective term designating writings so preserved. The Hebrew verb *gānaz* means ''to conceal,'' and, consequently ''to preserve carefully.'' The setting apart of the ''holy'' from the ''profane'' being one of the main tenets of the Jewish religion, sacred objects worn beyond usefulness were concealed instead of being destroyed. This practice was observed in Biblical times in respect to the knife used in the temple for killing sacrificial animals and the linen garments worn by the high priest on the Day of Atonement. The command to conceal applies especially to canonical Scriptures and other writings in which the divine name appears. An exception is made regarding writings of heretics, especially Christians, which may be destroyed by fire even if the name of God is found in them (*Bab. Talmud, Sab.* 116a). Books whose canonicity was contested or held suspect were equally concealed: ''Originally, it is said, Proverbs, Song of Songs, and Ecclesiastes were concealed [*gᵉnûzîm*] . . . , until the men of the Great Synagogue [variant: the men of Hezekiah] came and interpreted them'' (*Aboth de R. Nathan*, 1). No mention is made in the Talmud of the mode of concealment, except a remark of Rabba (4th-century Babylonian sage) that a Torah roll unfit for use was concealed by being placed in a scholar's grave. Maimonides (1135–1204) makes the authoritative pronouncement: ''A Torah roll which has become old or unfit for use is to be laid in an earthen vessel and buried beside a scholar. In this consists its concealment''

''Saint Geneviève,'' 15th-century sculpture by Hugo van der Goes. (©Archivo Iconografico/CORBIS)

(*Mishnēh Tôrâ, Hilkôth Sēfer Tôrâ,* 10.3). Fortunately, this prescription was not always carried out. Today "the Geniza" refers to the ancient storeroom of the now rebuilt Ezra Synagogue (once the Melkite Church of St. Michael) in Old Cairo (Egypt), belonging to the Karaites and containing valuable documents accumulated for centuries. Solomon Schechter, U.S. Jewish theologian and Talmudist, in 1896 brought over to Cambridge University Library from Cairo about 100,000 of these treasured fragments, the bulk of the collection, although other portions of it reached Oxford, Paris, and New York. A broad survey of its significance is given by Paul E. Kahle in his *The Cairo Geniza* (2d ed. New York 1960). The two most notable finds were the original Hebrew text of the book of SIRACH (Ecclesiasticus), known until then only in Greek and Syriac translations, and the Zadokite Document, the true character of which did not appear clearly until the discoveries in the Judean Desert in 1947 (*see* DEAD SEA SCROLLS). It should be noted that the title given by E. L. Sukenik to his first edition of the scrolls found in the Judean Desert, *Megilloth Genuzoth* (v.1–2, Jerusalem 1948, 1950), is misleading, as these scrolls were indeed stored away, but not concealed.

Bibliography: S. SCHECHTER, *Studies in Judaism* (2d ser. Philadelphia 1908) 1–30.

[M. J. STIASSNY]

GENNADIUS I, PATRIARCH OF CONSTANTINOPLE, ST.

Episcopacy 458 to 471, theologian and exegete; b. place and date unknown; d. Constantinople. In his extant works he opposes Alexandrian Christology and interprets Scripture literally. As a young man he vigorously attacked (431) CYRIL OF ALEXANDRIA's *Twelve Anathemas* and in a later work (*Ad Parthenium*) accused Cyril of blasphemy. Fragments of his encomium on LEO I THE GREAT's *Ad Flavianum* establish his own orthodoxy on the Incarnation. He wrote commentaries on Genesis, Exodus, Daniel, Psalms, and the Pauline Epistles; surviving fragments show him to have been an exegete of the Antioch school. He became patriarch of Constantinople (458), and he removed the Monophysite bishop of Alexandria, Timothy Aelurus, on the admonition of Leo I (*Ep.* 170). At a synod (460) called to curb simony in ordinations, he issued an encyclical anathematizing this abuse. He was conspicuous for learning and sanctity, and his power of prayer was a legend in his own lifetime. When an unruly lector heeded neither reprimand nor flogging, Gennadius prayed that he might mend his ways or leave this world; to the terror of all, the lector died the next day. An artist who had presumed to paint Christ as Jupiter found his right hand withered, but at Gennadius's prayer it was restored to use. He administered his see ably and successfully.

Feast: Aug. 25.

Bibliography: *Patrologia Graeca* 85:1613–1734. *Acta Sanctorum* Aug. 5:148–155. J. QUASTEN, *Patrology* 3:525–526. F. L. CROSS, *The Oxford Dictionary of the Christian Church* 547.

[P. W. HARKINS]

GENNADIUS II SCHOLARIUS, PATRIARCH OF CONSTANTINOPLE

Byzantine lay theologian and scholar, patriarch of Constantinople as Gennadius II (1453–*c.* 1466); b. George Courtesis, Constantinople, *c.* 1405; d. Constantinople, after 1472.

Scholarius early devoted himself to the study of philosophy, and he had Mark EUGENICUS as one of his teachers in theology. His preference for Aristotelianism led him to learn Latin and to admire St. Thomas Aquinas, several of whose works he translated into Greek. He opened a school of grammar and philosophy, became imperial secretary, judge general of the Greeks, and, though a layman, preacher-in-ordinary at the court. Sanguine about the projected council of union in Italy, he participated in the preliminary discussions in Constantinople and wrote a letter of congratulations to Pope EUGENE IV. He served the Emperor John VIII (1392–1448) as theological adviser at the Council of Florence but, to judge from the documents, was not very active. From the start he would have preferred to discuss the doctrine, not the legitimacy, of the FILIOQUE. In April 1439 he addressed a strong exhortation to the Greeks for agreement with the Latins, since the Fathers of both Churches agreed in doctrine, and thus to win military assistance for Constantinople. On May 30 he stated publicly that he considered the Council ecumenical, and the Latin "from" and the Greek "through" he considered equivalent in respect to the procession of the Holy Spirit from the Father. At the same time he presented two treatises in support of that position. He left Florence on June 25, 1439 for Venice but returned to Constantinople with the other Greeks.

He resumed his former activities and for a time took no part in the controversy for or against the union. In June 1445, however, he acceded to the request of the dying Mark Eugenicus and replaced him as leader of antiunionism. To that end he directed all his undoubted talent, defending his position in 15 debates in Constantinople with the Latin legate Lapacci (1445) and later began the series of writings that made him the outstanding leader of the antiunionists. With the death of the Emperor John VIII (Oct. 31,1448), Scholarius lost his protector and in 1450 became a monk, with the name Gennadius. However, he continued as leader and propagandist for the antiunionists, redoubling his efforts when ISIDORE OF KIEV arrived in Constantinople (Oct. 26, 1452) to promulgate the decree officially. In the fall of the city (May 29, 1453) Gennadius was taken prisoner, but was chosen as patriarch by Mohammed, who wished to use the Church to stabilize his new empire. The Sultan presented him with the insignia of the patriarchal office. Gennadius, unhappy in his position, was nevertheless reinstated, once after resigning and again after flight. He was finally allowed to abdicate and spent the last half-dozen years of his life in a monastery near Serres, reediting old writings and producing new ones, among them translations of St. Thomas's *Summa Contra Gentiles* and the *Prima* and the *Prima Secundae* of the *Summa Theologiae*. His literary and theological production was enormous and included countless pamphlets against the union, two long treatises on the procession of the Holy Spirit, a profession of faith (1446), several anti-Latin dialogues, an apology for his part in the Council of Florence, and others. He wrote a tract in favor of Palamism (*see* PALAMAS, GREGORY), a dialogue against the Jews (1464), and a collection of prophecies, and he engaged in controversy with Gemistos PLETHON in defense of Aristotle and early Christianity and against fatalism and polytheism. As the result of conversations with Sultan Mohammed II, he composed several tracts on the divinity of Christ and an address to Islam. He also published sermons; eulogies; pastoral letters on the Sacraments, liturgy, and penance; a treatise on simony; and prayers in verse and prose.

Bibliography: *Oeuvres complètes,* ed. L. PETIT et al., 8 v. (Paris 1928–36), with biog. 8: 15–47. M. JUGIE, *Dictionnaire de thèologie catholique,* 14.2:1522–70; ''La Polémique de Georges Scholarios contra Pléthon,'' *Byzantion* 10 (1935) 517–530. S. SALAVILLE, *Échos d'Orient* 23 (Paris 1924) 129–136. K. BAUS, *Lexicon für Theologie und Kirche* 2 4:676–677. J. GILL, *Personalities of the Council of Florence* (New York 1964) 79–94. H. G. BECK, *Kirche und theologische Literatur im byzantinschen Reich,* 760–763. F. BABINGER, *Mehmed der Eroberer* (Munich 1953).

[J. GILL]

GENNADIUS OF ASTORGA, ST.

Bishop of Astorga (Spain) from 899 and patron saint, fostered Benedictine monasticism in Bierzo; date and place of birth unknown; d. Bierzo, 936. As a priest in 895 he restored the monastery of San Pedro de Montes. In 920 he built an oratory for hermits and resigned his see to lead the eremitic life. He is buried at Santiago de Peñalba, one of three hermitages he founded, where his feast was celebrated as early as 1311. There is no vita; data derive from documents. In his testament he left to his monasteries copies of liturgical books and other important manuscripts. His Benedictines flourished next to immigrant Mozarab monks from the south.

Feast: May 25.

Bibliography: *Acta Sanctorum* May 6:93–99. H. FLÓREZ ET. AL. *España sagrada* (Madrid 1747–1957) 16:129–147. A. LAMBERT, *Dictionnaire d'histoire et de géographie ecclésiastiques* (Paris 1912) 4:1218–19; 8:1443. F. C. NOCK, *Vita sancti Fructuosi* (Washington 1946). C. M. AHERNE, *Valerio de Bierzo* (Washington 1949).

[E. P. COLBERT]

GENNADIUS OF MARSEILLES

Fifth-century priest and theological writer of unknown origin; d. Marseilles, between 492 and 505. Gennadius is the author of a *De viris illustribus,* written between 467 and 480 as a continuation of a similar work by St. JEROME. It contains 101 notices of fourth- and fifth-century Christian writers, nine of which (92 to 100) were added by a later hand. While the biographical detail is limited, these notices are invaluable for their bibliographical information regarding such authors as EVAGRIUS PONTICUS, Gennadius of Constantinople (89), Isaac of Antioch (66), Eutropius of Spain (50), Fastidius of Britain (56), NICETAS OF REMESIANA (22), Commodian (15), PROSPER OF AQUITAINE (84), and MAXIMUS OF TURIN (40). Chapter 101 is devoted to his own writings, and lists works against NESTORIUS, PELAGIUS, and Eutyches, none of which have been preserved. His *Liber ecclesiasticorum dogmatum* gives an indication of Semipelagian leanings, but it appears to have been rewritten during the 6th century. It is probable that the final section of his unpreserved eight books *Adversus omnes haereses* is contained in the *Liber.* The pseudo-Augustinian *Commentary on the Apocalypse* (*Patrologia Latina,* ed. J. P. Migne, 217 v. 5:2417–52) ascribed to Gennadius is actually a work of CAESARIUS OF ARLES; and the *Confessio* likewise attributed to his authorship is of much later origin. The information he provided concerning the authors he cited, as well as the Pelagian and early Monophysite controversies, has been the subject of much recent study.

Bibliography: *Patrologia Latina,* ed. J. P. MIGNE, 217 v. (Paris 1878–90) 58:979–1054, 1059–1120. JEROME, *De viris illustribus,* ed. E. C. RICHARDSON (*Texte un Untersuchungen zur Geschichte der altchristlichen Literatur* 14.1; 1896); *De viris illustribus,* ed. G. HERDING (*Bibliotheca scriptorum Graecorum et Romanorum Teubneriana* 1924). A. FEDER, *Scholastik* 2 (1927) 481–514; 3 (1928) 238–243; 8 (1933) 380–399. C. H. TURNER, ed., *Journal of Theological Studies* 7 (1905–06) 78–99 8 (1907)

Bl. Edmund Gennings, antique engraving made the year of his martyrdom.

103–114, *Liber ecclesiasticorum dogmatum.* G. MORIN, *Revue Bénédictine* 24 (1907) 445–455. B. CZAPLA, *Gennadius als Litterarhistoriker* (Münster 1898). J. MADOZ, *Razon y Fe* 122 (1941) 237–239. G. BARDY, A. GRILLMEIER and H. BACHT, *Das Konzil von Chalkedon: Geschichte und Gegenwart,* 3 v. (Würzburg 1951–54) 2:771–789, Christology. H. A. SANDERS, ed., *Beati in Apocalipsin libri XII* (Rome 1930). B. ALTANER, *Patrology,* tr. H. GRAEF from the 5th German ed. (New York 1960) 567–568. O. BARDENHEWER, *Geschichte der altkirchlichen Literatur,* 5 v. (Freiburg 1913–1932) 4:595–599.

[A. NEUWIRTH]

GENNINGS, EDMUND, BL.

English martyr; b. Lichfield, 1567; d. Gray's Inn Fields, London, Dec. 10, 1591. When Edmund was 16, Mr. Sherwood, a much persecuted Catholic gentleman, came to Lichfield and inquired of the local schoolmaster if there were a youth in the town who would make a good page. The schoolmaster recommended Edmund, who had been brought up a Protestant, but under his new master's influence became a Catholic. In 1584 he fled from England to study for the priesthood at Reims. Overwork and austerity broke his already delicate health, but he recovered and was ordained in 1590 by special dispensation because he was only 23 years old.

On his way back to England as a missionary he was captured and imprisoned for three days by French Huguenots. Edmund adopted the alias Ironmonger, and eventually landed at Whitby and made his way to Lichfield only to find all his family dead except his brother John, who was in London. Determined to convert John, Edmund set out for London. After a month's search he met him on Ludgate Hill; John, however, was very hostile and frightened of being compromised. Edmund, seeing there was no hope of his brother's conversion for the moment, left for the country.

On Nov. 7, 1591, he returned to London, where he met Father Polydore Plasden, a fellow student at Reims. They decided to say Mass the next day in the Gray's Inn Lane at the house of the devout Catholic layman Swithin Wells. While Edmund was saying Mass, Topcliffe, the pursuivant, arrived and arrested the two priests and the congregation. They were accused of treason and all tried together. On December 10 Edmund and Swithin Wells were executed together at Gray's Inn Fields in front of Swithin's house. After Edmund's martyrdom John Gennings, who had wished his brother dead, had a sudden change of heart and could not rid his mind of his brother's image. He decided to become a Catholic; he joined the Franciscans and was appointed the first provincial of the restored English Franciscan province. Edmund was beatified on Dec. 15, 1929. (*See* ENGLAND, SCOTLAND, AND WALES, MARTYRS OF.)

Feast: Dec. 10.

Bibliography: J. H. POLLEN, *Acts of English Martyrs* (London 1891). *A Literary and Biographical History or Bibliographical Dictionary of the English Catholics from 1534 to the Present Time* 2:415–419. A. BUTLER, *The Lives of the Saints* (New York 1956) 4:532–534.

[G. FITZHERBERT]

GENNINGS, JOHN

English Franciscan provincial; b. Lichfield, Staffordshire, 1570; d. Douai, Nov. 12, 1660. The martyrdom of Edmund GENNINGS, John's older brother, inspired John to remorse and the renunciation of Protestantism for Roman Catholicism. Leaving England, John entered Douai and was ordained (1607). When sent on the English mission, he zealously served English Catholics until shortly after 1610, when he decided to become a Franciscan. By 1614 he had been admitted and in conjunction with several English Franciscans was seeking to revive the defunct English Franciscan province. Aided by their Belgian and French confreres, the group began a provincial college at Douai, which was to serve as their motherhouse. They petitioned for the canonical erection of the

English province, and Gennings was first appointed *custos* and then provincial (1629) when the petition was granted. After 1621 Gennings was also assisted by English Franciscan nuns of the convent of St. Elizabeth, Brussels. He was subsequently elected and re-elected provincial in 1634 and 1640; Gennings provided effective leadership and inspiration for the revived English province until his death.

Bibliography: THADDEUS, *The Franciscans in England, 1600–1850* (London 1898). R. CHALLONER, *Memoirs of Missionary Priests,* ed. J. H. POLLEN (rev. ed. London 1924). J. GENNINGS, *Life and Death of Ven. Edmund Gennings* (London 1887). J. GILLOW, *A Literary and Biographical History or Bibliographical Dictionary of the English Catholics from 1534 to the Present Time,* 5 v. (London and New York, 1885–1902) 2:419–423.

[P. S. MCGARRY]

GENTILE, GIOVANNI

Italian idealist philosopher, educator, and statesman; b. Castelvetrano, Sicily, May 30, 1875; d. Florence, April 15, 1944. He was a student of the Hegelians D. Jaja and B. Spaventa and was a collaborator with B. CROCE on *La Critica.* As minister of public instruction (1922–24) he wrought an extensive transformation in the Italian educational system, inspired by the principles of his own philosophy—to which he gave the name actual idealism. Gentile consciously related his philosophical position to his interpretation of the history of Western philosophy; thus actual idealism can best be understood as Gentile's response to the basic quest of Western thought, the establishment of the immanent rationality of concrete existence. Actualism draws its profoundest inspiration from the insight of G. VICO: *verum factum convertuntur;* the immanent rationality of concrete existence can be grasped only through the principle of its becoming. Gentile develops this insight into the proposition that reality is a process of ''autoctisi'' involving position, distinction, and unification, by which all immediacy, dualisms, and transcendence are overcome. Relying on the critique of Spaventa, Gentile concluded that Hegel had misconceived the dialectic through his faulty notion of becoming. The clues to a rectification of this error are to be found in a purified form of the Kantian synthesis a priori and in Spaventa's conception of the dialectic of actual thought.

This correction of Hegel gives rise to Gentile's theory of the spirit as ''pure act'': reality that ''is'' insofar as ''it is not yet,'' but ''becomes,'' or ''makes itself''; this reality is the ''I,'' the individual that becomes by the process of universalizing itself. This ''I'' is the only concrete reality; it is not a subject that ''is'' as an object, a ''fact,'' but an ''act.'' Gentile develops the notion of ''I'' and of ''pure act'' in two directions: the existential and moral, which terminates in his theory of education, and the abstract, which is expounded in the *Sistema di Logica* (1917–23). The *Logica* distinguishes the ''logic of what is thought'' from the ''logic of the act of thinking''; since ''what is thought'' has its whole being from the act of thinking, the logic of the latter is more basic and the ground of the former. The former is the realm of the concept and is governed by the principle of identity; the latter is pure becoming and is governed by the dialectic. These are united in the concrete existence of the ''I.'' The self generation of the ''I'' is not an abstract process; it is concrete, and as such is the fulfillment of a duty or project, which is identical with the self; the ''I'' is a moral reality, a value and a generator of values. The process by which the ''I'' realizes itself in its own universalization is education. As a consequence, pedagogy is the highest reach of philosophy and *paideia* the purest form of concrete existence under its rational aspect.

See Also: HEGELIANISM AND NEO-HEGELIANISM; IDEALISM.

Bibliography: Works. *Opere complete,* 60 v. (Florence 1957–) Literature. Istituto di Studi Filosofici, *Bibliografia filosofica italiana dal 1900–1950,* 4 v. (Rome 1950–56) 2:111–133. V. A. BELLEZZA, *Bibliografia degli scritti di G. Gentile* (Florence 1950); *Enciclopedia filosofica,* 4 v. (Venice-Rome 1957) 2:631–643; *L'esistenzialismo postivo di G. Gentile* (Florence 1954). *Giovanni Gentile: La vita e il pensiero,* 8 v. (Florence 1948–57). E. CHIOCCHETTI, *La filosofia di G. Gentile* (Milan 1922). U. SPIRITO, *Note sul pensiero di G. Gentile* (Florence 1954). M. M. THOMPSON, *The Educational Philosophy of G. Gentile* (Los Angeles 1934). H. S. HARRIS, *The Social Philosophy of G. Gentile* (Urbana 1960). R. W. HOLMES, *The Idealism of G. Gentile* (New York 1937).

[A. R. CAPONIGRI]

GENTILES

A term used in the Bible to designate those who are not Israelites. In the OT the words *gôyīm* and *'ammîm* were the terms most commonly used for peoples or nations other than the chosen people. The Greek Septuagint rendered these words as ἔθνη, and the Latin, in its turn, as *gentes.* The NT employed the same terminology, using ἔθνη (*gentes*) to indicate non-Jews. In a more general sense, the term indicated all those who had not been converted to the true faith (Mt 10.18; Acts 21.21; 26.17).

The attitude of the Israelites of the OT was determined by religious rather than racial considerations. Social and political contacts with Gentiles always involved the danger of religious contamination, and since the Israelites were the sole champions of pure moral monotheism, this was a consideration of prime importance. It explains some of the harsh strictures against Gentiles in the OT (Dt 7.1–5; 20.16; Ex 23.27; 34.15–16). The entrance of a Gentile into the Temple was tantamount to desecration (Acts 21.28). Food grown or prepared by Gentiles was unfit for Israelite consumption (Ez 4.13; Hos 9.3; Dn 1.8; Tb 1.10–12; Jdt 10.5; 12.2). A fortiori, marriages between Israelites and Gentiles were strictly forbidden (Ex 34.16; Dt 7.3; Ezr 9.1–10.44). In the prophetic and postexilic periods a more universalist attitude developed. The Book of JONAH is an expression of this attitude. The blessings conferred on the Israelites could be extended to Gentiles also, but only through entrance into the chosen people and its worship (Is 4.2–4; 19.18–25; 56.3–8; 66.18–21).

The apostolic Church was at first, as might be expected, exclusively Jewish. It took much time and trouble—and, indeed, a divine intervention—to clarify the question of the admission of Gentiles into the Church and the manner of their admission. The principle was clear enough: Jesus had indicated that salvation was to be extended to all. The first recorded conversion of a Gentile was that of Cornelius, a proselyte, by Peter (Acts 10.1–48). This act, however, was viewed with alarm by the Jerusalem community, and Peter felt it necessary to justify his action (11.1–18). At Antioch Christianity was preached for the first time to Gentiles who were not proselytes. Some Judaeo-Christians thought converted Gentiles should be required to observe the Mosaic Law, but the Council of JERUSALEM rejected this suggestion. The Judaizers, however, were not so easily discouraged, and the problem forms the background of St. Paul the Apostle's Epistle to the ROMANS and his Epistle to the GALATIANS. Chiefly through his efforts the Church became the wholly universal kingdom envisioned by its Founder.

Bibliography: *Encyclopedic Dictionary of the Bible*, tr. and adap. by L. HARTMAN (New York 1963) 857–861. A. VOGEL, *Lexikon für Theologie und Kirche*, ed. J. HOFER and K. RAHNER, 10 v. (2d new ed. Freiburg 1957–65) 5:67–68. H. CONZELMANN, *Die Religion in Geschichte und Gegenwart*, 7 v. (3d ed. Tübingen 1957–65) 3:128–141. G. BERTRAM and K. L. SCHMIDT, in G. KITTEL, *Theologisches Wörterbuch zum Neuen Testament* (Stuttgart 1935–) 2:362–379. H. LESÊTRE, *Dictionnaire de la Bible*, ed. F. VIGOUROUX, 5 v. (Paris 1895–1912) 3.1:189–192. T. W. MANSON, *Jesus and the Non-Jews* (London 1955). J. JEREMIAS, *Jesus' Promise to the Nations*, tr. S. H. HOOKE (Naperville, Ill. 1958). G. DIX, *Jew and Greek* (Westminster 1955).

[J. J. CASTELOT]

GENTIS POLONAE GLORIA

An office hymn formerly sung at Vespers on the feast of JOHN CANTIUS; its division, *Corpus domas ieiuniis,* is used for Matins. The *Te deprecante, corporum* used at Lauds is possibly still another division of the hymn. Each division has 5 four-line Ambrosian stanzas. The author is unknown but the text is found as early as 1772, the saint's canonization having taken place in 1767. The hymn—especially in stanzas 1 and 3 of the *Corpus* section—enumerates John's virtues, i.e., his teaching, his devotion to the divine law, his ascetic practices, and his Christian charity. Three main episodes of the saint's life are recounted: his teaching at the university, his four visits to the tomb of the Apostles in Rome, and his pilgrimage to the Holy Land (cf. the lessons for the feast). The author probably modeled his work on the hymns of St. Dominic, especially *Gentis Hispanae decus* (1525), and of St. Teresa of Avila (1616). It should be compared also with the *Gentis Hispanae pater* in honor of Isidore of Seville (1659).

Bibliography: J. CONNELLY, *Hymns of the Roman Liturgy* (Westminster MD 1957) 240–241. H. LAUSBERG, *Lexicon für Theologie und Kirche*, ed. J. HOFER and K. RAHNER (Freiburg 1957–65) 4:682.

[J. SVÖVÉRFFY]

GENUS

(Gr. γένος) refers first to the principle of generation (Gr. γένεσις), the genus or stock, then to the multitude of things springing from one principle. In logic genus refers first to the universal that is predicable of many things differing in species; like SPECIES, it answers the question ''What is it?'' Whereas species predicates the whole ESSENCE, genus predicates the common and determinable part of the essence of its subject. The genus that is contained under no higher genus is called supreme genus or category. Those contained under higher genera are called subaltern genera.

In Aristotelian DIALECTICS genus is one of the four predicates, constituting one kind of dialectical problem (*Topica* 101b 37–102b 27; 128b 14–139a 20). Genus refers also to the *genus subjectum* of a science, the limited subject-matter considered by a given science (*Anal. post.* 76b 11–16).

In things composed of matter and form, MATTER is remotely the principle of genus inasmuch as it is the principle of all POTENCY. It is also the principle of diverse genera within a category, insofar as in the category of substance matter receives the perfection of ACT to different degrees. As actuated to one degree, say ''sensitive life,'' it will be the basis of a genus and be in potency either to the further perfection, ''rational,'' or to the imperfection, ''non-rational'' (St. Thomas Aquinas, *In Boeth. Trin.*, 4.2).

The genus of the logician is, moreover, to be distinguished from the genus of the natural philosopher. The former looks merely for a common ratio, the latter requires in addition a common matter (physical genus).

See Also: PREDICABLES; PORPHYRIAN TREE; DEFINITION; MATTER AND FORM.

[W. BAUMGAERTNER]

GEOFFREY HARDEBY

Augustinian theologian; b. England; d. May 21, 1385. He entered the AUGUSTINIANS at Leicester and studied at Oxford. Appointed master regent at the Oxford monastery in 1357, he engaged in the controversy caused by Abp. RICHARD FITZRALPH's *De pauperie salvatoris.* Both in his lectures and in his posthumously published *De vita evangelica* (1385), Hardeby not only ably and courteously answered Fitzralph's arguments on the nature of poverty, property, and jurisdiction, but also defended the Augustinian Friars against the charges of the Augustinian CANONS REGULAR. Bale credited him also with the authorship of *Quodlibeta Oxoniensia, Ordinariae questiones, Determinationes, Postillae Scripturarum, Lectiones Veteris et Novi Testamenti, Sermones de tempore* and *de sanctis,* and a historical record of the Augustinians. Hardeby was also active in the affairs of his order. He served as a delegate for the English province to the general chapter at Padua in 1359. Having been granted a papal dispensation for illegitimacy, he was elected prior provincial of England in 1360, and it would seem that he served in this office for six years. After being out of office for three years, he was reelected in 1369. Hardeby was favored by King EDWARD III with pensions and acted as confessor to Richard, Prince of Wales, 1376–77. On his death he was buried at the Austinfriars in London.

Bibliography: R. L. POOLE, *The Dictionary of National Biography from the Earliest Times to 1900,* 63 v. (London 1885–1900; repr. with corrections, 21 v., 1908–09, 1921–22, 1938; suppl. 1901–) 8:1213–14. A. GWYNN, *The English Austin Friars in the Time of Wyclif* (London 1940). A. B. EMDEN, *A Biographical Register of the Scholars of the University of Oxford to A.D. 1500,* 3 v. (Oxford 1957–59) 2:869, xviii.

[E. J. SMYTH]

GEOFFREY OF CLAIRVAUX

Or Geoffrey of Auxerre, Cistercian abbot, author; b. Auxerre, France, *c.* 1120; d. Hautecombe Abbey, after 1188. A student of ABELARD in Paris, he became a CISTERCIAN monk at CLAIRVAUX in 1140 after hearing BERNARD OF CLAIRVAUX preach his famous *De conversione ad clericos.* As St. Bernard's secretary, Geoffrey accompanied him on many journeys (1145–48) and was present at the Council of Reims presided over by Pope EUGENE III (1148), which centered on the GREGORIAN REFORM. Certain scholars hold that he succeeded Bl. GUERRIC as abbot of Igny in 1155; it is certain, however, that he was elected abbot of Clairvaux (1161 or 1162) but had to resign this office in 1163 because of the hostility of certain monks. He retired to CÎTEAUX, was sent on various missions, and later became abbot of Fossanova, near Rome (1170), and then of HAUTECOMBE (1176). Geoffrey's main work was his collection of Bernard's letters and the completion of Bernard's biography begun earlier by WILLIAM OF SAINT-THIERRY and ARNOLD OF BONNEVAL (*Patrologia latina* 185:301–368, 523–530). Geoffrey tells of Bernard's work in Languedoc among the ALBIGENSES (*Patrologia latina* 185:410–416) and of his preaching the Second Crusade in Germany in 1146 (*Patrologia latina* 185:395–410). From Bernard's sermons he extracted the *Declamationes de colloquio Simonis cum Iesu* (*Patrologia latina* 184: 435–476). One of Geoffrey's sermons on an anniversary of the death of Bernard is extant (*Patrologia latina* 185:573–588).

Geoffrey also wrote a refutation of GILBERT DE LA PORRÉE, the *Libellus contra capitula Gilberti Pictaviensis* (*Patrologia latina* 185:595–618), and two letters to Cardinal Henry of Albano, one in 1188 about Gilbert's condemnation at the Council of Reims (*Patrologia latina* 185:587–595), and the other *Super transsubstantiatione aquae mixtae vino in sanguinem Christi* (Baronius, *Annales,* year 1188, n.28). Also extant are a commentary on the *Our Father* (*Patrologia latina* 184:617–620), the *Tractatus de contemptu mundi* (formerly attributed to Bernard), sermons for the feast of John the Baptist and Martin of Tours (F. Combefis, *Bibliotheca concionatoria* 7:1470; 8:480; Tissier, *Bibliotheca patrum Cisterciensium* 4:261), and a vita of PETER OF TARENTAISE (*Acta Sanctorum* May 2:322–345). The library of Troyes, France, has several of his unpublished MSS: a *Liber contra Abaelardum,* 17 sermons, a *Commentaria in Canticum Canticorum,* and sermons on the Apocalypse (*Catalogue général des MSS des bibliothèques des départements* v.2).

Bibliography: *Patrologia latina,* ed. J. P. MIGNE, 217 v. (Paris 1878–90) 185.1:221–224. *Histoire Littéraire de la France,* 14:430–451. B. HEURTEBIZE, *Dictionnaire de théologie catholique,* 6.1:1227–28. DTC Tables Générales 16:1795–96. F. STEGMÜLLER, *Repertorium commentariorum in Sententias Petri Lombardi,* 1:111. F. STEGMÜLLER, *Repertorium biblicum medii aevi,* 2:332–334. J. LECLERCQ, ''Les Écrits de G. d'Auxerre,'' *Revue Benedictine,* 62 (1952) 274–291; ''Le Témoignage de G. d'A. sur la vie cistercienne,'' *Analecta monastica* ser. 2 (*Studia anselmiana* 31; Rome 1953) 174–201. M. S. LENSSEN, ''L'Abdication du Bx. G. d'A. . . . Clairvaux,'' *Collectanea Ordinis Cisterciensium Reformatorum,* 17 (1955) 98–110. M. A. DIMIER, *Catholicisme* 4:1849.

[J. DAOUST]

GEOFFREY OF DUNSTABLE

Abbot; b. Maine, France; d. St. Albans, 1146. Geoffrey studied at the University of Paris and then directed a school at Dunstable, England. For a stage production of the miracle play *Ludus de S. Catherina,* in 1119, he borrowed several copes from ST. ALBANS, and to compensate for their loss in a fire Geoffrey joined the community, where he became prior and then abbot. His extensive building program included a guest hall, an infirmary, a lepers' hospital, and a shrine to which he translated the remains of St. ALBAN in 1129. Geoffrey's efforts saved his abbey from demolition during the Civil Wars of King STEPHEN.

Bibliography: T. WALSINGHAM, comp., *Gesta abbatum monasterii Sancti Albani,* 3 v., ed. H. T. RILEY, *Rerum Britannicarum medii aevi scriptores* (Rolls series; London 1867) 1:72–105. W. HUNT, *The Dictionary of National Biography from the Earliest Times to 1900,* 7:1011–12. *Ghellinck Essor* 2:269.

[M. L. MISTRETTA]

GEOFFREY OF MONMOUTH

Historian, bishop; b. Monmouth, England, *c.* 1100; d. 1155. Little is known of his career except that he seems to have been ''magister'' at Oxford and was consecrated Bishop of SAINT ASAPH, Wales, Feb. 21, 1152. Because of the Welsh rebellion in 1150, he probably never visited his see. He is chiefly remembered for his literary activity as a writer of pseudo-history. His first completed work, *Prophetiae Merlini,* an obscure series of prophecies in a highly apocalyptic style, may well contain native Welsh vaticinal material. It is included as Book 7 of his major work, *Historia regum Britanniae,* completed probably between 1136 and 1139. Geoffrey said he translated the *Historia* from a British book given him by Walter, Archdeacon of Oxford, but there is no other evidence for the book's existence. Starting from the barest hints in the ninth-century *Historia Brittonum* attributed to Nennius, Geoffrey combined materials from the Old Testament, Latin writers, Continental and insular historians, and an undetermined amount of Welsh tradition (though this is vigorously denied by some scholars) with other materials and contemporary events, to trace in full and convincing detail the history of Britain from the fall of Troy to the invasions of Julius Caesar and on to the final conquest of the island by the Anglo-Saxons. His greatest achievement, the reign of King Arthur, occupies about a fifth of the whole. There is no reason to believe that the work has any value as history. Though it had little direct influence on the ARTHURIAN legends, it was widely read, and scarcely an English chronicler for the next 500 years failed to make use of it. It is found in over 200 MSS and in at least three distinct versions, only two of which have yet been published. The *Vita Merlini, c.* 1150, is in verse and more certainly contains Celtic material.

Bibliography: E. FARAL, *La Légende Arthurienne* (Paris 1929). GEOFFREY OF MONMOUTH, *The Historia Regum Britanniae. . . ,* ed. A. GRISCOM (New York 1929); *Historia Regum Britanniae: A Variant Version,* ed. J. HAMMER (Cambridge, Mass. 1951); *History of the Kings of Britain,* tr. S. EVANS, rev. C. W. DUNN (New York 1958). A. B. EMDEN, *A Biographical Register of the University of Oxford to A.D. 1500,* 2:1294–95. J. S. P. TATLOCK, *The Legendary History of Britain: Geoffrey of Monmouth's Historia Regum Britanniae and Its Early Vernacular Versions* (Berkeley 1950). J. J. PARRY and R. A. CALDWELL, ''Geoffrey of Monmouth,'' *Arthurian Literature in the Middle Ages,* ed. R. S. LOOMIS (Oxford 1959).

[R. A. CALDWELL]

GEOFFREY OF VENDÔME

Benedictine abbot, cardinal, staunch defender of the GREGORIAN REFORM; b. Angers, France, *c.* 1070; d. Angers, March 26, 1132. Geoffrey (Goffridus) was born of a noble family, entered the monastery of Sainte-Trinité at VENDÔME, and in 1093, while only a deacon, was elected abbot and consecrated by Bp. IVO OF CHARTRES. Hearing of the plight of Pope URBAN II in his struggle against the antipope GUIBERT OF RAVENNA, Geoffrey traveled to Rome and became a strong ally of the Pope. In 1094, with Urban finally in the Lateran palace, Geoffrey was consecrated cardinal priest of St. Prisca on the Aventine. An intimate of Urban and the succeeding popes, PASCHAL II and CALLISTUS II, Geoffrey was soon caught up in the INVESTITURE STRUGGLE. In a series of eight polemics (*libelli*), he followed the lead of Cardinal HUMBERT OF SILVA CANDIDA and advocated that SIMONY and lay INVESTITURE be branded as heretical. Geoffrey frequently served as papal legate and was present at the Councils of Clermont (1095), Saintes (1096), and REIMS (1131). He stayed true to his monastery and maintained the privileges of Vendôme in a period of great unrest. His letters (more than 185) remain a precious source of information for 12th-century Church politics. Other writings include several short tracts (e.g., on Baptism, on the Eucharist), 11 sermons, a few hymns, and a commentary on the Psalms (unpublished).

Bibliography: Editions. *Patrologia latina,* ed. J. P. MIGNE, 33–290. *Monumenta Germaniae Historica: Libelli de lite,* 2:680–700, *libelli.* MS Paris, BN lat. 12959, for the commentary on the Psalms. Biography. L. COMPAIN, *Étude sur Geoffroi Vendôme* (Paris 1891). E. SACKUR, *Monumenta Germaniae Historica: Libelli de lite,* 2:676–680; ''Zur Chronologie der Streitschriften des Gotfried von Vendôme,'' *Neues Archiv der Gesellschaft für altere deutsche Geschichte Kunde,* 17:329–347; ''Die Briefe Gotfrieds von Vendôme,'' *ibid.* 18:666–673. J. J. HERZOG and A. HAUCK, eds., *Realencycklopädie für protestantische Theologie* 7:37–38. H. MEI-

NERT, "Die Fälschungen Gottfrieds von Vendôme," *Archiv für Urkundenforschung* 10 (1928) 232–325. A. WILMART, "La Collection chronologique des écrits de Geoffroi abbé de Vendôme," *Revue Benedictine* 43 (1931) 239–245. *Dictionnaire de théologie catholique* (DTC), Tables générales 1:1795–96.

[R. B. PALMER]

GEOFFREY OF YORK

Chancellor of England, archbishop of York; b. England, 1152 or 1153; d. Grandmont, near Rouen, France, Dec. 18, 1212. An illegitimate son of King HENRY II, he was acknowledged by the king and reared with Eleanor of Aquitaine's children. Geoffrey's mother is unknown. His life was the stereotypical life of a royal bastard. Forced early into an ecclesiastical vocation, he received the diaconate and lucrative preferments. In April 1173 he was elected bishop of Lincoln. Supported by papal dispensations, he delayed ordination and consecration while he aided Henry against his unfaithful sons and insurgent barons. In 1182, still unconsecrated, Geoffrey resigned his bishopric, and in 1183 he became chancellor of England. In Henry's last struggle with King PHILIP II AUGUSTUS OF FRANCE, (1187–89), Geoffrey proved himself the only faithful son. As a reward he was named archbishop of YORK. His half-brother, King RICHARD I, honored the nomination, and Geoffrey was ordained (Sept. 23, 1189) and consecrated at Tours (Aug. 18, 1191). Geoffrey's undesired return to England (September 1191) and his subsequent arrest made him a potential Becket and precipitated the downfall of William de Longchamp. But Geoffrey, even though a man of abstinence and purity, was too temperamental and tactless to be a leader. His episcopacy was marked by continuous royal and ecclesiastical arguments and litigations. In 1207 he withstood King JOHN of England's demands for clerical taxes and was forced to flee England. He died in exile.

Bibliography: GIRALDUS CAMBRENSIS, "De vita Galfridi archiepiscopi Eboracensis," *Opera,* ed. J. S. BREWER, 8 v. (*Rerum Brittannicarum medii aevi scriptores* [Rolls series] 21; London 1861–91) 4:355–431. W. STUBBS, *Historical Introductions to the Rolls Series,* ed. A. HASSALL (London 1902) 173–309. K. NORGATE, *The Dictionary of National Biography from the Earliest Times to 1900,* 7:1018–1024. A. L. POOLE, *From Domesday Book to Magna Carta* (2d ed. *Oxford History of England* 3; 1955). C. R. CHENEY, *From Becket to Langton* (Manchester, Eng. 1956).

[E. J. SMYTH]

GEORGE, ST.

Martyr. In the Canon of Pope Gelasius (d. 496) St. George is mentioned in a list of those "whose names are justly reverenced among men, but whose acts are known

"St. George and the Dragon," woodcut by Albrecht Dürer, 15th century. (© Corbis-Bettmann)

only to God." The only historical element in the intricate tradition that has grown around his name is his martyrdom. The dubious elements include his rapid advance to high military rank, his organization of the Christian community at Urmiah (modern Iran), and his visit to Britain on an imperial expedition. The connection of St. George with the dragon, familiar since the Golden Legend of JAMES OF VORAGINE, can be traced to the close of the sixth century. At Jaffa, near Lydda, Perseus had slain the sea monster that threatened the virgin Andromeda, and George acquired the inheritance of veneration previously enjoyed by the pagan hero.

According to a sixth-century local tradition George came originally from Lydda in Palestine, and his remains were brought back from Nicomedia to his native city, but Eusebius of Caesarea (*c.* 322), relating the martyrdom of a noble soldier who confessed Christ at Nicomedia before Diocletian in April 303, neither names the saint, nor mentions his country or place of burial. The deacon Theodosius (*c.* 530) is the first pilgrim to mention the tomb of St. George in Lydda. The fifth-century passio is pure fantasy.

St. George was popular in the East, and the crusaders revived his cult in Europe. The Synod of Oxford in 1222 ordered that his feast be kept as a national festival, but it was only in Edward III's time that he was made patron of the kingdom. He is also patron of Portugal, Aragon, Catalonia, Georgia, Lithuania, and several cities; in Italy 118 communes carry his name. In the Middle East, it is difficult to identify St. George, for at times he has replaced Adonis; more often he is linked with the Prophet Elias, under the name *El Khader* (the living). Until modern times, he played a most important role in popular feasts and folklore, the date of his festival being connected with the arrival of spring.

Feast: April 23.

Bibliography: *Acta Sanctorum* April 3:101–165. H. DELEHAYE, *Les Légendes grecques des saints militaires* (Paris 1909) 145–176. E. HOADE, *Guide to the Holy Land* (Jerusalem 1962).

[E. HOADE]

GEORGE HAMARTOLUS

Also George the Monk, Byzantine historian; fl. mid-ninth century. Nothing is known of his life. His *Chronicle,* which treats the period from the creation to 842, is edificatory in purpose; his interest is mainly ecclesiastical—he is bitterly opposed to ICONOCLASM—and his conception of historical causation is naïvely theological. His value lies in the many and varied sources from which he uncritically copied or excerpted, some of which are now lost. His *Chronicle* has independent value only for the first half of the ninth century. Simple in concept and popular in language and style, it was highly esteemed in the Middle Ages and often excerpted by later chroniclers. It was translated into Old Slavonic and Georgian, and a continuation to 948 was added, probably by a supporter of the deposed Emperor Romanus Lecapenus.

Bibliography: *Georgii monachi chronicon,* ed. C. DE BOOR, 2 v. (Leipzig 1904). Latin tr. of chronicle in *Patrologia Graeca,* 110:41–1260, no tr. into any mod. lang. G. MORAVCSIK, *Byzantinoturcica,* 2 v. (2d ed. Berlin 1958) 1:277–280, full bibliog.

[R. BROWNING]

GEORGE (THE BEARDED) OF SAXONY

Referred to also as "the Rich," duke of Saxony, opponent of LUTHERANISM; b. Dresden, Aug. 27, 1471; d. there, April 17, 1539. The son of Albert the Brave, founder of that line of the Wettin house that bore his name, and Sidonia, daughter of Bohemian King George of Podiebrad. George was the cousin of Frederick the Wise, Elector of Saxony, who became Martin Luther's protector and strongest supporter. His excellent education was heavily weighted toward theology because he was a younger son and destined for service in the Church rather than for political life. But the death of his older brother made George the heir apparent. When he was 17, his father, while fighting in Friesland, left him behind as regent of the duchy (1488). On Nov. 21, 1496, he was married to Barbara, the daughter of the Polish king, Casimir IV. The marriage was prolific; but only one daughter survived George. Upon the death of his father (Sept. 12, 1500) George inherited the Duchy of Saxony, the Margravate of Meissen, and the cities of Leipzig and Dresden. His brother Henry was given the hereditary governorship of Friesland, which their father had received from the Emperor Maximilian. But Henry was unable to control rebellious Friesland and in 1505 traded this claim to his brother George for a pension and the districts of Freiberg and Wolkenstein. George soon found that he could control the high-spirited population no better than his brother could and sold Friesland to the Count of Burgundy for a meager 100,000 florins.

When Luther posted his attack on indulgences in 1517, George did not immediately oppose him. He was very much aware of the need for reform and spoke out against abuses in the monasteries and those surrounding the granting of indulgences. In his pursuit of truth he sponsored the Leipzig debates (1519) between John Eck, a leading German theologian, and Luther. As Luther became a defined heretic and split with Rome, George turned against the reformers. As one of the Church's strongest supporters in Germany, he did all that he could to prevent the spread of Lutheranism into his territories. Even so he did not lose sight of the fact that there was a need for reform within the Church. When the German princes of the Empire presented the Emperor with a list of grievances at the Imperial Diet of Worms in 1521, George included 12 additional complaints of his own against indulgences and annates. His opposition to Luther steadily increased as the Protestant movement grew. To counter Luther's translation of the Bible, he ordered his secretary, Hieronymus EMSER, to prepare a new translation. To this work George added a staunchly orthodox preface. He also added a ban not merely on the works of Luther but on those of known Lutheran sympathizers. He banished those holding anti-Catholic views from the Duchy of Saxony and even delivered unfaithful ecclesiastics to the bishop of Merseburg. Apostates were denied the right of Church burial.

George was a strong advocate of a universal council that would define beyond doubt Christian doctrine and introduce long overdue reforms. Until such a council could be convoked, he sought to introduce reforms in his own lands. To this end he made formal appeals to Rome for the right to make formal visits and investigations of the monasteries in the duchy. But since the Curia was not yet ready for the reforms, the Duke did not receive the authority he sought. Thus the reforms he was able to introduce, such as the consolidation of half-empty monasteries and the supervision of monastic lands turned over to the secular authority, had little effect in staving off the tide of Protestantism sweeping across northern Germany. Though he united with Protestant princes—the most notable being his cousin Frederick the Wise and his less exalted brother-in-law, the Landgrave Philip of Hesse—to put down the Peasants' Revolt (1525), he was one of the main organizers and supporters of the League of Dessau (1525), a group of German princes who defended the interest of the Church against the encroachments of the reformers and their secular allies. In 1533 it was superseded by the League of Halle with George again playing a prominent part in the organization. The League of Halle in its turn gave birth to the Holy League of Nuremberg (1538). This league was dedicated to the preservation of the religious peace of Nuremberg, which temporarily prevented open war between growing hostile parties.

One of George's greatest disappointments was that he died without sufficient assurance that the Duchy of Saxony and his other holdings would remain Catholic. His last son, Frederick, died without an heir, though he had been married to Elizabeth of Mansfeld shortly before his death, and the ducal holdings passed to George's Lutheran brother Henry. A belated attempt was made by the Duke in 1539 to secure from his brother a promise to give up his Lutheran beliefs as a condition to the inheritance, but this was unsuccessful.

Bibliography: J. JANSSEN, *History of the German People at the Close of the Middle Ages,* tr. M. A. MITCHELL and A. M. CHRISTIE, 17 v. (London 1896–1925). W. GOERLITZ, *Staart und Stände unter den Herzögen Albrecht und Georg,* 1485–1539 (Leipzig 1928). O. VOSSLER, ''Herzog Georg der Bärtige und seine Ablehnung Luthers,'' *Historische Zeitschrift* 184 (1957) 272–291. J. LORTZ, *Die Reformation in Deutschland,* 2 v. (Freiburg 1949). H. HOLBORN, *A History of Modern Germany: The Reformation* (New York 1959). F. SCHWARZBACH, *Lexicon für Theologie and Kirche* 2 4:695, bibliog. F. LAU, *Die Religion in Geschichte und Gegenwart* 3 2:1395–96.

[J. G. GALLAHER]

GEORGE SYNCELLUS

Byzantine chronicler; d. after 810. What is known about him is derived entirely from his chronicle and its introduction by THEOPHANES THE CONFESSOR. George was honored with the high ecclesiastical title of syncellus. Earlier in his career he had lived in the Holy Land; then during the patriarchate of TARASIUS (784–806) he acted as the patriarch's private secretary. He later retired to a monastery where he composed his chronicle. He was still alive in 810. His world chronicle relates to the period from the creation of the world to the reign of Diocletian (284). Its coverage is quite uneven: the birth of Christ and the happenings of the era of the New Testament are treated rather extensively, but the age that follows this is given only in barest outline. Its importance lies in the fact that next to the chronicle of EUSEBIUS OF CAESAREA, it is the most important work for the understanding of Christian chronography, particularly the work of the two Alexandrians, Panodoros and Annianos. Indeed what is known of these chronographers, who established the Alexandrian era but whose works have not survived, is derived almost entirely from George Syncellus.

Bibliography: K. KRUMBACHER, *Geschichte der Byzantinischen Literatur* (Munich 1890 and 1897), 339–342. V. GRUMEL, *La Chronologie* (Paris 1958), 86–95. M. E. COLONNA, *Gli storici bizantini dal sec. IV al sec. XV* (Naples 1956—).

[P. CHARANIS]

GEORGETOWN UNIVERSITY

Situated in Washington, D.C., Georgetown University, founded in 1789, is the oldest Catholic institution of higher education in the United States. Its story is one of a traditional European *collegium* transplanted into a new republic on American soil, shaping and being powerfully shaped by its new environment.

Founding. On March 30, 1787, John CARROLL (1735–1815), who was shortly to become the first Catholic bishop of the United States, issued a broadside entitled ''Proposals for establishing an Academy at George-Town, Patowmack-River, Maryland.'' Carroll had entered the Society of Jesus in 1753 and was ordained a priest in 1761. When Pope Clement XIV suppressed the order in 1773, Carroll emerged as the leader of the former Jesuits in the Maryland area who banded together to continue their apostolic work.

Carroll's ''modest academy'' at the beginning followed the traditional plan of studies in Jesuit schools, the *Ratio Studiorum*, a five- or six-year program intended for boys from the ages of ten to sixteen. It was designed to take students who had learned the ''first Elements of Letters'' and provide them with a classical humanities education, fitting them for entrance into a university.

The staff was largely composed of former Jesuits, though four Sulpicians, exiles of the French Revolution, were crucial to the survival of the school in the early years. Carroll appointed one of them, William Louis DUBOURG, to serve as president from 1796 to 1798. In 1805, after a partial restoration of the Society of Jesus, Jesuits assumed the direction of the school. Through the good offices of its first student, William GASTON, who became a representative from North Carolina, the school was chartered by an act of Congress in 1815.

Carroll had no intention of restricting admission to Catholics. In keeping with the religious liberty guaranteed to all Christians in 1776 in the Maryland Constitution, he wished his school to be ''open to students of every religious profession.''

Though Carroll's 1787 ''Proposals'' failed in their purpose of raising funds for the academy, 69 students were enrolled for 1791 and 1792, the first year of its operation. Enrollments gradually increased over the years so that through its first hundred years they averaged about 145 students, most of whom were in the preparatory division. The college division conferred its first bachelor's degree in 1817 and awarded an average of seven A.B. degrees each year throughout the nineteenth century.

In 1806, Georgetown College acquired a theology faculty, which was set up to teach Jesuit seminarians. The theology faculty remained at Georgetown until 1869 when the seminary was relocated to Woodstock, Maryland.

In 1849, four Washington physicians wrote a letter to James Ryder, the president of Georgetown College, indicating their intention to establish a medical school and requesting that its degrees be conferred in virtue of Georgetown's charter. Since the physicians agreed to pay all the expenses of the venture, Ryder graciously acceded to their request.

By mid-century, the training of lawyers was beginning to shift from private apprenticeships in law offices to programs in an academic setting. In 1865, Columbian College, now George Washington University, established the first law school in Washington, prudently scheduling all its classes in the late afternoon and early evening to make it possible for federal workers to attend. Five years later, Georgetown inaugurated its own law school in the same ''sunset'' style.

Second Founding. When Patrick F. Healy became prefect of studies in 1868, he increased substantially the role of sciences and mathematics in the curriculum, while raising standards in the study of Latin and Greek. As president (1873–82), this son of a white planter in Georgia, Michael Healy, and his wife, Mary Eliza, a former slave, boldly moved to the task of turning Georgetown into a university on the model that emerged in the United States in the post-bellum period. In 1877, he undertook the construction of a massive building that would proclaim his ambition to make Georgetown a center of higher education in the nation's capital. Healy, however, experienced great difficulty in finding donors for the project and, though much of the building was in use in 1881, areas like the library and the assembly hall were not completed until the end of the century. Subsequently named Healy Hall, it remains a monument to the man referred to as the ''second founder'' of the school and provides the architectural signature of the main campus.

New ventures followed with a certain regularity. The Graduate School of Arts and Sciences was formally inaugurated in 1893. The Dental School was added in 1901 and the School of Nursing was established in 1903. After World War One, Edmund A. Walsh began the School of Foreign Service to prepare people not only for diplomatic service but also for international business careers. This initiative led to the development of the School of Languages and Linguistics (1949) and the School of Business Administration (1950).

Tradition in Transition. The Second Vatican Council (1962–65), together with the social and political upheavals in the 1960s, set in motion a dramatic series of changes at Georgetown as the university sought to discern ''the signs of the times.''

The impact of the council was felt immediately in the Theology Department, which until 1966 was staffed almost entirely by Jesuits with seminary training in Catholic theology. The department responded to the call for ecumenical openness and dialogue by hiring men and women with university training in the world's major religious traditions. This resulted in a major revision of the department's course offerings, enabling all students to choose from a wide variety of elective courses.

At the same time, the office of campus ministry carried one step further John Carroll's desire that the school be open to students ''of every religious profession'' by bringing to campus clergy and pastoral counselors to meet the needs of a religiously diverse student body.

The School of Foreign Service made a notable contribution to interreligious dialogue by founding in 1993 with the blessing of Pope John Paul II the Center for Muslim-Christian Understanding, which is at present the only academic institution in the United States dedicated to exploring the cultural, historical, political, and theological interactions of Christianity and Islam.

The college, which had from its founding been all-male, welcomed the first women students in 1969, and in a short while became fully co-educational. A policy of open recruitment brought increasing numbers of women into the faculty and into positions in the administration previously held only by men (provost, executive vice president and dean of the Law Center, dean of the College, treasurer, general counsel).

Prominent during this period of growth was the figure of Timothy S. Healy, president from 1976 to 1989, who embarked on an ambitious plan of construction, greatly increased minority enrollments, and provided much of the incentive for Georgetown to strive for excellence in its graduate programs, giving rise to the saying that the ''second Healy was Georgetown's third founder.'' It was during his tenure that Georgetown became the only Catholic member of the Consortium on the Financing of Higher Education, a group of 31 major private American universities, including Harvard, Yale, Stanford, and Chicago.

The relatively rapid rise of the university's profile in the last third of the twentieth century was sustained by alumni support that would have gladdened the hearts of John Carroll and Patrick Healy, through great growth in annual giving and in a series of successful fund-raising campaigns. Of great significance was the change in the composition of the board of directors. What had been a board composed entirely of Georgetown Jesuits, serving under a president who was also their religious superior, who in turn reported to the provincial superior in Baltimore and the general superior in Rome, became in 1969 an autonomous external board composed of 40 to 50 men and women, including 10 or 12 Jesuits not from Georgetown, who accepted responsibility for carrying out the unfolding purposes of the university.

When in 2000 the university needed to recruit a new president, it conducted an open search, inviting applications from all qualified candidates, specifying that each ''should understand and be committed to the Catholic and Jesuit tradition of higher education.'' In February of 2001, the board appointed John J. DeGioia to be the first lay president of Georgetown.

Mission Statement. In September of 2000 the board of directors approved a new mission statement in which Georgetown is described as ''a Catholic and Jesuit, student-centered research university . . . founded on the principle that serious and sustained discourse among people of different faiths, cultures, and beliefs promotes intellectual, ethical, and spiritual understanding.'' The university is committed to justice and the common good as well as to providing education in the Jesuit tradition, ''for the glory of God and the well-being of humankind.'' The changes that have taken place in John Carroll's ''modest academy'' could not have been foreseen, but he might recognize in this mission statement the same end he proposed for his school in a letter he wrote in 1787: ''to diffuse knowledge, promote virtue & serve Religion.''

Bibliography: J. M. DALEY, *Georgetown University: Origin and Early Years* (Washington 1957). J. T. DURKIN, *Georgetown University: The Middle Years, 1840–1900* (Washington 1963). J. D. G. SHEA, *Memorial of the First Centenary of Georgetown College, D.C., Comprising a History of Georgetown University* (New York 1891). W. C. MCFADDEN, ed., *Georgetown at Two Hundred* (Washington 1990). R. E. CURRAN, *The Bicentennial History of Georgetown University: From Academy to University, 1789–1889*, v. 1 (Washington 1993), v. 2 (forthcoming).

[W. C. MCFADDEN]

GEORGETOWN VISITATION

Founded in 1799, the monastery and schools of the Visitation Nuns at Georgetown, D.C., in 1895 became officially known as the Georgetown Visitation Convent.

Growth of the Academy. The founders of this community numbered only three: Miss Alice Lalor (*see* LALOR, TERESA, MOTHER), and two widows, Mrs. McDermott and Mrs. M. Sharpe, all of them immigrants from Ireland who had come under the direction of Leonard NEALE, SJ, in Philadelphia. When, near the close of 1798, Bp. John CARROLL appointed Neale to the presidency of Georgetown College, the latter was deeply stirred by the total want of Catholic schools for ''female youth.'' (*See* GEORGETOWN UNIVERSITY.) He, therefore, invited his three spiritual daughters to Georgetown for the purpose of forming a religious society and of educating the young girls of Maryland. On their arrival he lodged them with a small community of Poor Clare Nuns, exiles from the French Terror. Finding the austerities and the spirit of the Poor Clares incompatible with his ideals of religious life for these women and unsuited to the task of teaching young Americans, he soon rented another dwelling nearby, where on June 24, 1799, he opened the first Catholic academy for girls in the original 13 states. The three women and their later companions, known as ''The Pious Ladies,'' were directed by Neale according to a modified Jesuit rule. He persisted, however, in his determination that they should be Visitandines and thus fulfill a prophetic dream he had experienced during his missionary days in British Guiana, but he was unsuccessful in his attempts to obtain Visitation Nuns from Europe or documents of affiliation with the order. Finally, in 1815, on the death of Archbishop Carroll, whose coadjutor he had been for 15 years, he petitioned the Holy See for admission of the community into the Visitation Order. Pius VII readily acceded to the request, and on Dec. 28, 1816, Mother Josephine Teresa Lalor and two others pronounced solemn vows. Six months later, on June 18, 1817, the archbishop died. It was not until Jan. 19, 1819, that the sisters received a new spiritual director, Joseph Picot de Clorivière, who saw at once the plight of both community and school, whose enrollment had dwindled alarmingly.

Reorganization. Aided by an excellent teacher, recently admitted to the community, Mrs. Jerusha Barber,

Clorivière set to work to train the sisters in both the matter and the methods of education. Soon a one-page prospectus of the school was issued, which listed French, music, and drawing in addition to subjects usually offered in a good grammar school: English grammar, arithmetic, geography, history, reading, and writing. To provide finer accommodations, he drew plans for a new academy, which was completed in 1823. He also carried out two of Neale's cherished dreams, the establishment of a ''Benevolent School'' and the erection of a chapel in honor of the Sacred Heart. The former, built in 1819 and known as St. Joseph's School, continued to give free education to an average of 130 girls a year until 1918, when the Sisters of Mercy assumed the direction of the new Holy Trinity parochial school. The chapel was blessed on Nov. 1, 1821, and became a center of devotion to the Sacred Heart. Clorivière died in 1826, two years before the legal incorporation of the community by act of the 20th Congress.

Almost immediately he was succeeded by Michael Wheeler, SS, who thoroughly understood the Visitandine religious life. Aware of the demands of education in the United States, on his journey to Europe in 1829 he obtained from PIUS VIII indults permitting the sisters certain dispensations necessary for carrying out their work. As the community grew, it established foundations and schools in cities throughout the United States.

The 20th Century. In 1919 the sisters added a junior college that continued in existence until 1964. In 1975 the boarding school was closed and nonresident student enrollment increased. A fire in July 1993 destroyed the main academic building, 80 percent of the school's teaching area, but did not touch the monastery. Proud of its tradition of uninterrupted instruction, the school closed for only one day of summer school following the fire, and resumed classes as usual the following September. As Georgetown Visitation continued to flourish, its bicentennial in 1999 was marked by the restoration of Founders Hall and the dedication of several new buildings and programs.

Bibliography: G. P. and R. H. LATHROP, *A Study of Courage: Annals of the Georgetown Convent of the Visitation* (Cambridge, Mass. 1895). Archives of the Georgetown Visitation Convent, especially MS histories of the foundation and of the lives of the first Sisters by M. J. BARBER and M. S. JONES. These were compiled sometime after the Civil War and before 1879.

[M. L. WHIPPLE/M.-A. GELL]

GEORGIA, CATHOLIC CHURCH IN

Georgia was the southernmost of the 13 original English colonies in America, and was admitted to the Union as the fourth state in 1788. Its 58,876 square miles extend westward from the Atlantic Ocean to the Appalachian Mountains. The Archdiocese of ATLANTA covers the northern part of the state, at the end of the Appalachian chain. At the ''fall line,'' where the rivers drop precipitously to the southern alluvial plain, the Diocese of SAVANNAH begins, taking in the ''fall line'' cities of Columbus, Macon and Augusta and everything to the south. If the Archdiocese of Atlanta is centripetal, focused on the city of Atlanta, the Diocese of Savannah is centrifugal, with no geographical center; the abovementioned cities plus Savannah itself, Brunswick, Valdosta and Albany form an irregular outer circle ringing a rural interior.

The history of the Church in Georgia begins in the 16th century when the Spanish were in control of the region, but when it fell under the rule of the British early in the 18th century, Catholics were not welcome. It was only after the American Revolution that the Church structures began to take shape and parish life began to flourish.

Spanish Control. Catholic Spain sought to spread its civil and religious influence beyond its lucrative colonies in Central and South America into North America. During the 16th and 17th centuries, what later became Georgia formed part of the Spanish province of *La Florida*. Franciscan friars on Hernando de Soto's expedition performed the first baptisms of Native Americans east of the Mississippi River, near what is now Macon, in 1540. Father Pedro Martínez, S.J., became the first ''Georgia martyr'' when natives killed him on Cumberland Island in 1566. Other Jesuits followed Martínez to work among the Guale, a strong tribe with a vibrant culture whose predominance in the region led the Spanish to call the whole coastal area ''Guale.'' Various Franciscan friars succeeded the Jesuits. In 1587, Father Pedro de Corpa, O.F.M., founded a mission dedicated to Our Lady of Guadalupe near present-day Darien, and Franciscan Father Blas de Rodríguez established another in honor of Saint Clare ten miles further north. Their efforts led to the conversion of more than 1,500 Guale. In 1595, three more missions were founded on the Golden Isles. These missions were not only religious centers, but were Christian towns where the inhabitants' physical as well as spiritual needs were met. But language barriers and the lack of necessities often caused tensions, as did Catholic moral teaching, when it ran counter to human failings or tribal customs. In 1597, when Juanillo, the heir apparent to the *cacique* or chief of Guale, relapsed into polygamy, a long-held native custom, Fathers de Corpa and de Rodríguez reminded him that Christian doctrine required monogamy. Refusing to give up his additional wife, Juanillo systematically planned the slaughter of the missionaries,

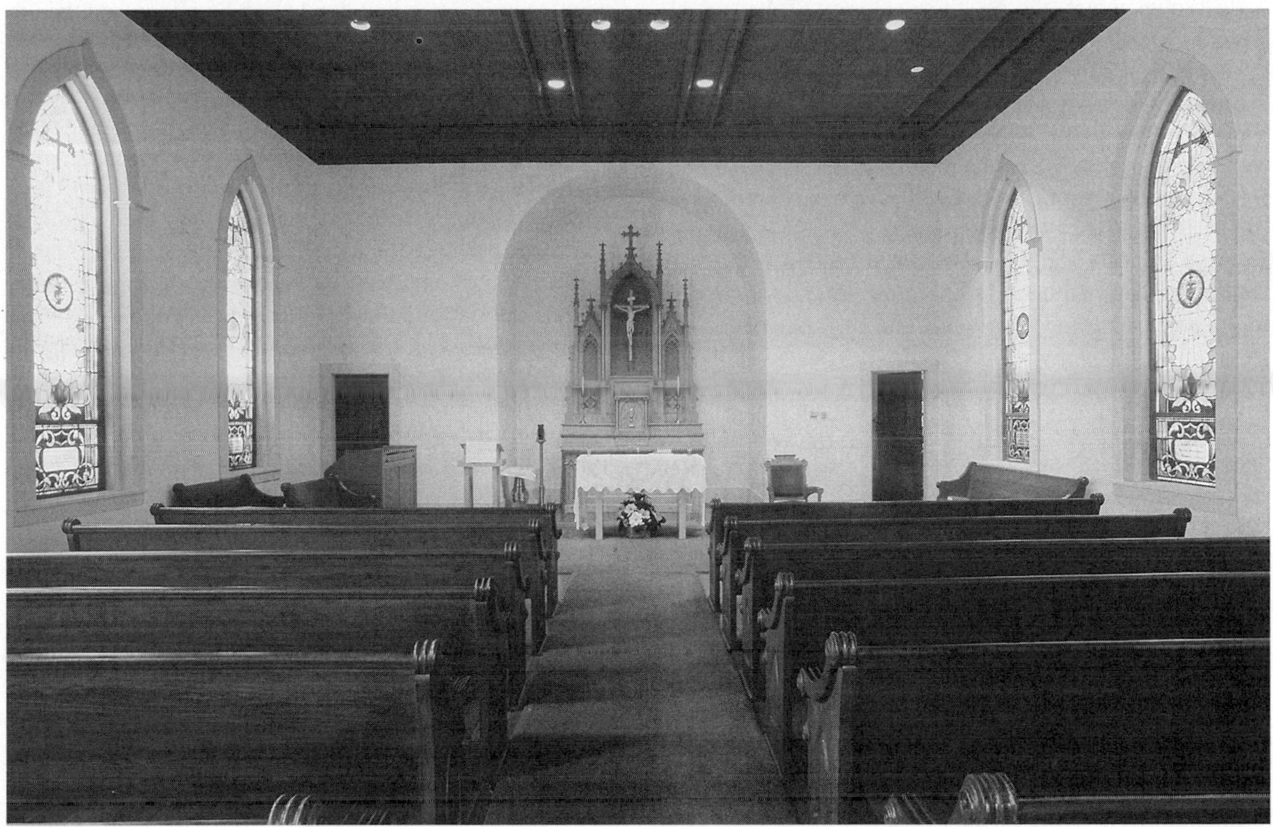

Interior of St. Teresa's Catholic Church, built in 1859, Albany, Georgia. (©Kevin Fleming/CORBIS)

all but one of whom were killed in mid-September 1597. On Jekyll Island, Father Francisco de Avila was held captive and enslaved for nine months before he was rescued by Spanish forces from Saint Augustine. (Nearly 300 years later, Savannah Bishop Raymond W. Lessard opened the official cause for the beatification of the Georgia Martyrs on Feb. 22, 1984.)

After the Juanillo revolt, the Spanish governor and his forces took revenge on the Guale and managed to ''pacify'' the area enough to allow the re- establishment of the missions. In 1606, Bishop Altamirano of Cuba visited the Florida missions to confirm converts and ordain priests. In Guale, he confirmed more than 1,000. In 1635, Fray Francisco de Ocana reported great numbers of Spanish and Guale coming to church because of miracles worked through the martyrs' relics.

The War of the Spanish Succession (1701–1714) led to the destruction by British forces of all but one of the 14 Spanish missions in the Apalachee (northern Florida-southern Georgia) area. British settlers from South Carolina thereafter built forts in what was then Spanish territory, on the Savannah, Santee and Altamaha rivers, to protect themselves from the Spanish and their native allies.

British Rule. After the Anglo-Spanish war in 1727–28, General James Oglethorpe (1696–1785) founded the British Colony of Georgia in 1733—named after King George II—as a Utopian refuge for debtors, many of whom were Irish, and as a bastion of protection for the British colonies against the Spaniards in Florida. Although not himself anti-Catholic (indeed, there is some evidence that he may have been baptized a Catholic in infancy), Oglethorpe adhered to British law and prejudice: his colony's charter outlawed the Catholic Church along with rum, slaves and lawyers. Georgia intended as a refuge for poor ''persecuted Protestant sects'' as well as for ''the unfortunate but worthy indigent classes.'' Austrian Lutherans, known as ''Salzburgers,'' and Jews were among those welcome in the colony. Catholics were not. Oglethorpe brought Anglican chaplains to his colony, including some of the leading evangelists of the day, John and Charles Wesley and George Whitefield. A Spanish attack on Saint Simons was repulsed by Oglethorpe's forces at the Battle of the Bloody Marsh (1742). The Spanish threat to British domination of the area was effectively ended.

The idealistic provisions of the charter stood in the way of economic growth, and in 1751 the colony passed to the crown, which allowed the institution of slavery. Although Catholicism remained outlawed in Georgia until the American Revolution, a few Catholics seem to have resided in Savannah from time to time. Some 400 French Catholic ''Acadians'' (''Cajuns'') landed there after they were expelled from their homes in Nova Scotia by the British government in 1755, on the eve of the French and Indian War. At first they were only given permission to stay the winter. Many were then separated from their children and sent inland, while their children were distributed among Protestant families to be raised as Protestants.

U.S. Statehood. During the American Revolution, the British occupied Savannah, a hotbed of revolutionary discontent, from 1778 until 1782. Catholics on the whole distinguished themselves in the revolutionary armies, in supply and in Congress. The vital alliance of the colonies with Catholic France under Louis XVI and eventually with Catholic Spain helped dampen anti-Catholic feeling in the new United States. More than 600 Catholic French and Haitians died alongside Irish and American soldiers trying to wrest control of the city of Savannah from loyalist forces in 1779. The Catholic heritage of the Marquis de la Fayette and of Count Casimir Pulaski, who died in the Battle of Savannah, enhanced the reputation of their co-religionists. Georgia's first state constitution (1777) granted religious toleration to its citizens, but had no effect in Savannah while it remained under British control from 1778–1782. Dissenting Protestants and even Jews were tolerated in British-controlled areas, provided they paid tithes in support of the Anglican Church, but Catholics remained officially proscribed. By the time of Georgia's second constitution (1789), the Revolution was over, the British were gone and the last official discrimination against Catholics—a religious test required of office holders that obliged them to deny the key Catholic doctrine of transubstantiation—had been abolished. But as the plantation system prevailed, most of the arable land ended up in the hands of Protestant landowners, who in turn determined the religion of their dependents. In effect, Catholics could practice their faith only in towns and in small settlements of their own.

English-speaking Catholics from Maryland founded the first Catholic congregation in Georgia at Locust Grove about 1793 even though there was no resident priest. They built the first Catholic church in Georgia, dedicated to the Purification of Mary. Not long after the Marylanders arrived, a group of French Catholics, fleeing the insurrection of slaves in Santo Domingo, moved into the area with their priest, Father Souze, about whom little is known. Around 1793–94 another French priest, Father Jean (John) le Moyne, settled in the community as its first ''parish priest,'' although nothing is known about his appointment. He, too, had fled to San Domingo and then to Georgia. From Locust Grove, he traveled to Augusta and Savannah, ministering to the Catholics in both towns, and dying in Savannah in 1794.

Other Catholics soon arrived from Ireland, after Theobald Wolfe Tone's abortive revolt against British rule (1798), and from Germany, after the Napoleonic invasion and the ensuing secularization of Church lands (1803). Around 1820, a larger group of Irish settlers, leaving the deprivations of their native land, arrived at Locust Grove. The Irish remained in the area.

At first, one priest was responsible for all Georgia. Baltimore Bishop John Carroll authorized Father Olivier le Mercier, who also came via Santo Domingo, to exercise his priestly ministry in Savannah in 1796. Father le Mercier came to be known as the ''Missionary of Georgia.'' By November 1796 he had settled in Locust Grove, with Savannah, Augusta, and the Golden Isles as missions. But in May 1798, Father le Mercier made the parish of Saint John the Baptist in Savannah his headquarters. The little congregation grew through the addition of immigrants and on May 30, 1799, the Mayor and Aldermen of Savannah passed a resolution reserving half a trust lot for its use. When the state of Georgia incorporated a church, it did so in the name of lay leaders, and not in the name of the pastor, giving the lay trustees legal control. This situation was not unique to Georgia, and the trustee quarrels in Georgia were minor compared to those elsewhere.

When in 1803, Father le Mercier was named pastor of the troubled Saint Mary's Church in Charleston, the Reverend Antoine (Anthony) Carles replaced him in Savannah as ''Rector and Priest'' for over 16 years.

A petition for an extra lot in 1811 highlighted the parish's growth ''owing to continued emigrations from Europe and the West Indies, settling on these shores to escape death and persecution.'' Augusta received a pastor in about 1810, when Augustinian Father Robert Browne arrived in Georgia's ''Second City.''

In 1820, the Holy See established the Diocese of Charleston, comprising both Carolinas and Georgia. the Reverend John England, of Cork, Ireland, became its first bishop. The presence of a bishop in the vicinity, rather than in far-off Baltimore, was of great benefit to the Catholics of Georgia. The financial support of prosperous Irish immigrants such as Dominick O'Byrne of County Mayo, who came to Savannah in 1820 and made a fortune in the lumber business, was also vital to sustaining the Catholic faith in a largely Protestant area. When he died in 1850, O'Byrne reputedly left his wife the richest widow in the South.

The growth of public works in Georgia in the 1820s, '30s and '40s brought large numbers of less prosperous Irish settlers. Arriving to work on canals and railroads, those who survived the dangerous work usually settled in the worst housing in the most unsanitary parts of Georgia's towns. The terrible living conditions of the majority of Georgia's Irish also concerned the state's priests. When Father Jeremiah O'Neill, Sr., for example, brought the Sisters of Charity of Our Lady of Mercy, many of whom were Irish, from Charleston to Savannah in 1845, he intended for them to meet the educational needs of his rapidly growing congregation. In 1835 Bishop England laid the cornerstone of a new Church of Saint John the Baptist in Savannah. On April 1, 1839, Bishop England dedicated the new brick edifice capable of seating 1,000 people. The parish at that time included about one-third of the Catholics in Georgia.

On July 19, 1850, Pope Pius IX erected the Diocese of Savannah, as the seventh provincial Council of Baltimore had requested in May 1849. At its creation, the diocese included all of Georgia and most of Florida, with a total Catholic population of 5,500, with parishes in Savannah, Locust Grove, Atlanta, Augusta, Macon and Columbus. Father Francis X. Gartland, a native of Dublin, Ireland, and vicar general of the Diocese of Philadelphia, was appointed to the new see on July 23, 1850.

In 1937 the name of the see was changed to Savannah-Atlanta, and in 1956 Atlanta was designated a separate diocese. About that time Bishop Hyland in a public statement said, ''The Catholic Chruch has always, and will always, condemn racism in all its various shapes and forms.'' In 1961 he, along with the bishops of Savannah and Charleston, issued a pastoral letter announcing their intention to integrate the Catholic schools within a year. In 1962 Atlanta was raised to the dignity of a metropolitan archdiocese, with Savannah, Charlotte, Raleigh and Charleston as suffragan sees. The provincial bishops meet twice yearly and the priests are invited to an annual gathering, as are various diocesan officials.

The population of Georgia in 2000 was about 7,500,000, of whom only 397,000 (5.3%) were Catholic (320,000 out of 5,000,000 or 6.4% in the Archdiocese of Atlanta and 77,000 out of 2,500,000 or 3% in the Diocese of Savannah). Both Catholic dioceses, Atlanta and Savannah, belonged to the Georgia Christian Council, an ecumenical conference of the judicatory heads of and other delegates from the ecclesial communions in the state.

Bibliography: J. T. LANNING, *The Spanish Missions of Georgia* (Chapel Hill, N.C. 1935). R. M. MILLER and J. L. WAKELYN, eds., *Catholics in the Old South* (Macon, 1983). M. V. GANNON, *Rebel Bishop: The Life and Era of Agustine Verot.* (Milwaukee, 1964).

[D. K. CLARK]

Carving depicting a member of the noble family that built the church kneeling before St. Stephen, 6th-century church, Georgia, Russia. (©Dean Conger/CORBIS)

GEORGIA, CHURCH IN ANCIENT

Georgia (Georg. *Sakartvelo,* Russ. *Gruziya*) is located south of the main ridge of the Caucasus, between the Caspian and Black seas. Located to the south of Russia, Georgia was part of the Soviet Union until 1991. Georgia's historical development is part of the rich history of the east Mediterranean world.

ORIGINS

The Georgian nation emerged between the 7th and the 4th century B.C. as a result of the mingling of several older peoples of pre-Indo-European (Japhetite) linguistic affinities and is thus related to the ancient Urartians, proto-Hattians, and Hurrians (Mitannians). Historical Georgia stretched from the Caucasus Mountains in the north to Armenia in the south, and from the Black Sea eastward toward the Caspian Sea. On its soil numerous cultural and political influences met and overlapped: Mesopotamian, Anatolian, Aegean, Iranian, Greek, and

Hellenistic. From the start the territory of the Georgians was divided into two units, East and West Georgia (Kartli and Egrisi). The earliest political formation took place in West Georgia in the 7th century B.C. as the kingdom of Colchis, whose connection with the myth of the Argonauts is an indication of early Caucasian-Greek contacts. This was followed, in the 4th century B.C., by the rise of the East Georgian kingdom of Iberia (Kartli).

PRE-CHRISTIAN GEORGIA

In the 1st century B.C. Colchis was annexed to the kingdom of Pontus; this left Iberia as the point of historical continuity of the Georgian nation. In 65 and 64 B.C., as a result of the Mithridatic wars, both Iberia and Colchis became vassals of Rome and bulwarks of the Pax Romana against Iran. But in the 3rd century A.D. the Iberian throne passed to the Chosroids, a dynasty of Iranian origin. This Iranian political success was thwarted by the acceptance of Christianity, almost simultaneously with the Roman Empire's acceptance of it, on the part of the first Chosroid king of Iberia, Mirian III. It brought Iberia into a religious as well as political conformity with the Roman Empire, and sowed discord between it and Mazdaist Iran.

CHRISTIANITY IN GEORGIA

Georgian paganism was an amalgam of local astral and ancestor cults, worship of the forces of nature, imported Hellenistic syncretism, and Mazdaism introduced from Iran. Christian influences also found their way to Georgia, preceding official conversion. This was especially the case of West Georgia, a Roman province after A.D. 63, with Greek coastal cities and widely developed economic contacts with the Mediterranean world. It is, however, the conversion of East Georgia (Iberia) that is better known as the result of the apostolate of a Roman captive woman, St. Nino, Christiana of the Roman Martyrology (d. 338). Freed from the superimpositions of Georgian and Armenian legends, her story goes back to a version by RUFINUS OF AQUILEIA, who derived it near the end of the 4th century from the Iberian prince Bacurius. It is corroborated by the seemingly independent Iberian version as well as by archeological data.

Arriving in Iberia in 324 and beginning her preaching in 328, St. Nino converted first the Queen of Iberia (333) and then King Mirian himself (334). The King then asked Emperor Constantine I for clergy to organize the Church in his country, and in 337, with the baptism of the King, his family, the princes of the realm, and many of the people, Iberia became officially Christian. Though its first bishop, whose see was at the capital city of Mtskheta, received his consecration from Constantinople, the Iberian Church was under the jurisdiction of Antioch. In addition to Greek influences, the youthful Iberian Church came under the influence of Palestinian, Armenian, and Syro-Iranian Christianity.

The earliest Biblical texts, traceable to the 5th century, show a dependence on Armenian and Syriac versions; and the earliest liturgical monuments show the prevalence in Iberia of the Hierosolymitan liturgy of St. James, first in Greek, and after the end of the 6th century, in Georgian. In spite of the resistance of local paganism and especially of Mazdaism sponsored by Iran, Christianization progressed steadily, and by the beginning of the 6th century there were some 30 bishops in Iberia.

The evangelization of West Georgia was less the work of historical personages than part of the general Christianizing of the Roman Empire. Among the fathers of Nicaea I (325) there was a bishop from West Georgia, Stratophilus of Pityus (modern Pitsunda); another, the bishop of Trebizond, considered Georgian by some historians, belonged to Pontus and not to Colchis, and it was only after the 10th century that his diocese came to be called Lazica by the Byzantines, after the neighboring Georgian land of Lazica (Chaneti). By the 5th century the whole of West Georgia had become Christian, except the land of Abkhazia in the north and that of Lazica in the south, which were evangelized in the 6th century. In the 7th century West Georgia was divided into two ecclesiastical units, the Metropoly of Phasis (Poti), with four suffragan sees, and the Archdiocese of Sebastopolis (Dioscurias, modern Sukhum), both under the jurisdiction of Constantinople. Here, the liturgy was that of Constantinople, in Greek at first, but from the 8th and 9th centuries in Georgian.

BUFFER STATE

The history of Georgia hinged largely on its position as a buffer between two hostile empires, Roman and Iranian, each trying to control it. With West Georgia firmly in Roman hands, this was particularly the case of Iberia, which, though an autonomous kingdom, passed from the one imperial suzerainty to the other. The Iberian monarchy, in its endeavor to assert its authority over its great vassals, gravitated toward the centralized and autocratic Roman Empire; on the other hand, the local princes, though Christians, tended in their opposition to the crown to be pro-Iranian. King Vakhtang I Gorgasal (*c.* 466–522), a strong monarch, concluded an alliance with Emperor ZENO, ending Iranian suzerainty over Iberia, and accepted the pro-Monophysite *HENOTICON* (484). In return, Zeno recognized (between 486–488) the head of the Iberian Church as an autocephalous catholicos, but still dependent on Antioch. Mtskheta, his see, was now superseded as political capital by Tiflis. And in 505 Iberia, together with Armenia and Caucasian Albania, officially adhered to the *Henoticon* at a council at Dvin in Armenia.

In the course of the 6th century, East and West Georgia returned to Catholicism in the wake of Byzantium's reconciliation with Rome in 519; Armenia and Albania, however, clung to the *Henoticon.* In 555, at another council at Dvin, Armenia openly accepted Monophysitism, whereas Albania was to waver between it and Catholicism. The political alliance with the empire ended with the death of Vakhtang I in 522, and his successors fell once more under the control of Iran, which in 580 abolished the Iberian monarchy.

The successful anti-Iranian war of Emperor MAURICE brought Iberia back to the Roman sphere of influence and in 588, the Emperor established the office of presiding prince to replace the Iberian kingship. Within a decade, a new change in the balance of power brought Iberia momentarily under Iranian suzerainty, causing a resurgence of Monophysitism. It was due to Catholicos Cyrion I that in the 600s Iberia returned to Catholicism, as it did to the imperial political allegiance, breaking with the stanchly Monophysite sister-church of Armenia.

Although Georgian monastic communities are known to have already existed in the Holy Land in the 5th century, monasticism began to flourish in Georgia only in the 6th century. The earliest monastic foundations are ascribed to the activity of the so-called 13 Syrian Fathers, who arrived there in the decade of 560–570 and who were probably Monophysites. But the Monophysitic tinge soon vanished, and the Georgian monasteries became centers of missionary and cultural activity that greatly contributed to the growth of the Church in Georgia. A blossoming of monastic life was reached in the southwestern provinces of Iberia (Tao-Klarjeti) in the 8th and 9th centuries, owing particularly to the activity of St. Gregory of Khandzta (d. 861), as well as in the Georgian monastic communities on Mt. ATHOS, Mt. SINAI, and in the Holy Land. It was to monasticism that organized education, traceable to the 5th century, owed its growth after the 10th century.

ARAB CALIPHATE

From the mid-7th to the 9th century, Iberia, along with Armenia, was an autonomous vassal state of the Arab caliphate, and so became a buffer between the latter and Byzantium, as it had been between Rome and Iran. Tiflis was the seat of an Arab emir. In 813 the office of presiding prince became hereditary in the Bagratid dynasty, a branch of the Armenian princely house of the same name. Profiting by the temporary weakness of the Abbasid caliphate, Ashot I the Great (d. 830), first Bagratid prince of Iberia, accepted the suzerainty of the Byzantine Empire along with the title of Curopalate; and in 888 his descendant Adarnase IV assumed the title of king, restoring the monarchy.

The history of West Georgia was no less turbulent. In the mid-5th century Colchis was conquered by the Lazic princes from the south, and from a Roman province it became a vassal kingdom of Lazica, which lasted until the late 6th century and which served as a battleground for Justinian's Persian wars. From the 6th to the 8th century Lazica was again a province of the empire, but in the 790s it was conquered by the Princes of Abkhazia and became the kingdom of Abasgia (Apkhazeti), though still under imperial suzerainty. In 978 the crown of Abasgia was inherited by Bagrat III of Iberia (d. 1014), who in 1008 united Abasgia and Iberia into one kingdom of Georgia. Simultaneously the West Georgian Church was united with that of Iberia under the catholicos of Mtskheta. But Constantinople was compensated in influence for this loss in jurisdiction. The Byzantine liturgy of the West Georgian Church now passed to East Georgia replacing the ancient Hierosolymitan liturgy of Iberia.

Arab overlordship had considerably weakened Byzantine influence. This and the unification of the two Georgias contributed to the birth of national consciousness, which now expressed itself in the field of religion in the purely Georgian system of chronology with a new *annus mundi,* a purely Georgian order of ecclesiastical feasts, of the Lessons, and of the Divine Office, as well as in a distinct character of Georgia's Byzantine rite in general. Georgian church music, traceable back to the beginnings of Georgian Christianity, has a distinct flavor.

THE GOLDEN AGE

The period of more than two centuries following the unification of 1008 is considered the golden age of Georgia. The Bagratid sovereigns, among whom the most notable were David III(II) the Builder (1089–1125) and Queen Thamar (1184–1212), both recognized as saints by the Georgian Church, transformed the country into a powerful military state. The onslaught of the Seljuk Turks, who now spearheaded Islam and who, between 1060 and 1070, had nearly destroyed Georgia, was now repelled, and Tiflis was regained from the Muslims (1122).

PAN-CAUCASIAN EMPIRE

Georgia became a pan-Caucasian empire, stretching from sea to sea, controlling non-Georgian states, and enjoying the zenith of culture and prosperity. Among its vassals it counted at different times the Greek empire of Trebizond and the Muslim kingdom of Shirvan on the Caspian. Georgia even launched a counteroffensive against the Seljuk empire, a Georgian crusade, which by diverting to the north a part of Seljuk power contributed to the First Crusade. This success was grounded in the predominance achieved by the crown over the highly feudalized nobility and to the use of mercenary troops to supplement the feudal levies. Georgia's industries and commerce profited by the unification under one sovereignty of all the important Transcaucasian commercial and industrial centers and by its participation in two great economic systems, the Saracen (transCaspian) and the Byzantine (Black Sea region). In the golden age, Georgian literature reached its apogee and the arts flourished. Georgian architecture, chiefly ecclesiastical, was marked at this period by the blending of the two hitherto distinct types, the centralized domed edifice and the basilica, into the new cruciform domed type.

A happy balance was reached between the absolutist tendencies of the crown and the feudal society of Georgia. The emergence of the Council of the State, an embryonic parliament, was a manifestation of this balance. In this great epoch the Church played a leading role. Although national success obliterated vestiges of Byzantine suzerainty, Byzantine influence was again on the increase in the domain of religion and culture, with the Georgian monasteries as centers of diffusion. The imposition of the Byzantine liturgy on East Georgia was one aspect; in the literary output of the time, likewise, translations from the Greek tended to outnumber original productions. The monasteries organized centers of higher education. In them the study of philosophy was accompanied by the Byzantine tension between anti-intellectual clericalism, admitting only mystical experience, and philosophy, especially Neoplatonist and verging on laicism. There was a struggle among the philosophers themselves, as the Georgian academies became battlefields between the Neoplatonists (led by John Petritsi, d. *c.* 1125) and the Aristotelians (led by Arsenius of Iqalto, d. *c.* 1130). This submission to Byzantinism did not fail to evoke a nationalist reaction, even among the monks themselves, both at home and on Mt. Athos.

It was in the golden age that the Church-State relations began to be formulated. Ultimately the catholicos was regarded as the spiritual king of the country, theoretically the king's equal. But he was also a temporal prince, possessed of territory, noble vassals, subjects, and armed forces, and as such he was subordinate to the king. The bishops and abbots ranked with the princes of the realm and were endowed with feudal rights. The office of Grand Chancellor of Georgia, for example, belonged ex officio to the archbishop of Chqondidi in West Georgia. The power and wealth of the Church, its involvement in the feudal order, and its national character had many negative effects. Its high offices became the nobles' monopoly. In his struggle with the nobility David III (II) attempted also to break the monopoly. With this in view he convoked in 1103 the Council of Ruisi-Urbnisi. But he was not successful. Altogether, as in Byzantium, the Church in Georgia had become a mere venerable adjunct of the nation and of the state.

Two waves of barbarian invasions abruptly terminated the golden age. The first wave, that of Genghis Khan's Mongols and of the Khwarizmian Turkomans in the first half of the 13th century, devastated Georgia and enforced on Queen Rusudan (1223–45) the suzerainty of the Great Khan. The second wave was the series of campaigns of Tamerlane at the end of the 14th and the beginning of the 15th century. It completed the ruin of the kingdom. Under the weight of the earlier wave, Georgia had lost its unity; in 1258 it split into two kingdoms, Georgia (Iberia) and Abasgia (also called Imeretia). This split was momentarily healed by George VI(V) the Illustrious (1314–46).

After Tamerlane, decline set in definitively, in spite of the countermeasures of Alexander I (1412–42). His son and third successor, George VIII (1446–65), offered to take part in Pope PIUS II's projected anti-Ottoman crusade (1458–60). But the impoverishment of the country through constant warfare and exactions of the conquerors, the general economic collapse, and the weakening of the crown furthered by the strife within the royal family, which broke out under George VIII, led to a new and final division of Georgia. It split into three kingdoms: Georgia proper (Iberia), Abasgia-Imeretia, and Kakhetia (eastern Iberia); as well as five independent principalities: Abkhazia, Guria, Meschia, Mingrelia, and Suania. This division became definitive in the years 1490–91. The Georgian Church actually anticipated this trend, since by 1390 West Georgia had withdrawn from the jurisdiction of the catholicos of Iberia and formed a rival catholicate of Abasgia with its seat at Pitsunda (ancient Pityus). Antioch sought to profit by this disunion to establish its authority over the new catholicate.

RELATIONS WITH THE HOLY SEE

The relations of the Georgian Church and the Holy See, which after the former's lapse into Monophysitism were strengthened by the catholicos Cyrion I in the 600s, seem to have continued unchanged well into the golden age. The distance and the intermediary position of Byzantium must account for the paucity of evidence regarding them. We do know that St. Hilarion the Iberian in the 9th century journeyed to Rome to venerate the tombs of the Apostles and the popes, and appears to have been responsible for the translation into Georgian—from the Latin, it seems, rather than the Greek—of the liturgy of St. Peter. The few annalistic references to the popes assign to them a place above the Eastern patriarchs, as is the case also with the dating of some manuscripts, and almost invariably apply to them the adjective holy.

Anti-Byzantine reaction in the golden age may have in part prevented the Georgian Church, which had kept aloof from the iconoclastic and the Photian upheavals, from following Cerularius in 1054. Thus, in 1065 St. George the Hagiorite, Abbot of the Iberian monastery on Mt. Athos, asserted in the presence of Emperor Constantine X the ancient belief in the inerrancy of the Roman Church. However, the isolation, aggravated by the Byzantine schism and Seljuk conquests, the nationalization of Georgian Christianity, and the continued communion with the Byzantines, with whom the Georgians shared the same rite—all this made Georgia, almost imperceptibly, drift into schism. Yet there was no formal break. In his letter of 1224, Pope HONORIUS III, replying to Queen Rusudan's announcement of her accession of 1223, invited her to participate in a crusade and granted to her and her people an apostolic indulgence. Gregory IX continued this correspondence, asking the Queen in 1233 for assistance to some Friars Minor. But when in 1240 the Queen appealed to the same Pope for help against the Mongols, she promised reunion with the Holy See; and in his reply, of that year, Gregory IX urged her to return to the union with the See of Peter. It was, accordingly, between 1224 and 1240 that the Holy See became apprised of the fact of separation.

The Friars Minor, who came to Georgia in the 13th century, were followed by the Dominicans; and their missionary effort was so successful that in 1328 Pope John XXII, who seven years previously had written to King George the Illustrious urging reunion, transferred the See of Smyrna to Tiflis and in 1329 named the Dominican John of Florence the first Latin-rite bishop of the capital. The See of Tiflis continued until the beginning of the 16th century. In 1330 an English Dominican, Peter Gerald, was named Catholic bishop of Sukhum (Sebastopolis-Dioscurias). All this hinged, obviously, on royal sanction.

There is much here that is unknown, but that may explain the curious fact that one of the titles officially accorded to the king of Georgia by the contemporary Mamluk Court of Egypt was ''Supporter of the Pope.'' In spite of this and of the exchange of communications between the Holy See, the kings and the catholicoi that were to continue for centuries to come, no reunion was effected, and the two Georgian representatives at the Council of FLORENCE did not sign the Act of Union (1439).

SILVER AGE

The receding Mongol waves revealed what was still left standing of the cultural and political structure of Georgia. Slowly the work of restoration began. Politically, indeed, the situation had hardly improved. The internal division and consequent weakness continued; the Mongol pressure had been succeeded by two simultaneous pressures of Safavid Iran and the Ottoman Empire. It was, however, precisely the rivalry of the two empires, both claiming suzerainty over Georgia, a geopolitical inheritance of the struggle between Rome and Iran, that made possible, despite sporadic violence, the survival and renaissance of Georgia, its so-called silver age (*c.* 1500–1800). The violence took the shape of religious persecution; and although there were many apostasies, there were also numerous martyrdoms, such as that of the Dowager Queen Ketevan of Kakhetia, who suffered for her Christian faith at the hands of Shah Abbas I, at Shiraz on Sept. 22, 1624, and who has since been regarded as a saint by the Georgian Church.

RELATIONS WITH THE WEST

In the silver age, under the enlightened guidance of the governing class, education was reorganized, new centers of learning were established, and literature was revived. Byzantium had long been dead and other influences now gave shape to this renaissance. In the face of the renewed Moslem danger Georgia sought a *rapprochement* with the West and with Russia. The post-Tridentine development of missionary activity sent numerous religious to Georgia: Augustinians, Carmelites, and especially Theatines, to whom the Georgian mission was entrusted in 1628 by Urban VIII. They were followed by the Capuchins, who remained active from 1661 to 1845, when the Russians, then masters of Georgia, expelled them.

CATHOLIC REVIVAL

Like the Byzantine elite at the end of the empire, a number of distinguished Georgians, including kings and catholicoi, were drawn to Catholicism. In 1629 the first Georgian printing press was set up at Rome. Thomism found its way to Georgia in the works of Antony Dadiani, Archbishop of Chqondidi. The greatest figures of this Catholic revival were also those of Georgian literature: Orbeliani and Catholicos Antony I. It should be mentioned that the silver age saw a considerable decline of the Georgian Orthodox Church, worldliness of the prelates, and ignorance and immorality of the clergy in general.

RUSSIAN INFLUENCE

Georgian relations with Russia were at first exclusively political, motivated, on the Georgian side, by the need of protection against Islam—and only as a last resort after the attempts to secure the aid of the West had failed—and on the Russian side by the need of a springboard for the eventual expansion in the eastern Mediterranean. That both Russia and Georgia belonged to the Greek Orthodox communion was an additional factor; and Georgia changed somewhat, under the cultural influences of Russia, and, through Russia, of the ENLIGHTENMENT of the West.

Politically the Russian empire played an increasingly predominant role. Its growing expansionism coincided with Georgia's growing dependence on it in the face of resumed Iranian expansionism. In these circumstances on Aug. 3, 1783, King Heraclius II of Georgia (Georgia and Kakhetia had been united since 1762) concluded a treaty of protectorate with Empress CATHERINE II of Russia, which guaranteed the integrity of both the kingdom and its church. George XIII(XII), who succeeded him in 1798, was pressed by Emperor Paul I and showed a willingness to increase Georgia's dependence on Russia, but his death, on Jan. 9, 1801, before he could sign the projected new treaty, left it without legal force. Nevertheless, in that same year, Paul I proceeded to annex Georgia, weakened by the Iranian war of retaliation of 1795, in violation of the guarantees of 1783. His successor, Alexander I, ratified this act. In 1804 a protectorate was in turn imposed on Imeretia, which was annexed in 1810. The pattern of protectorate and annexation was applied to other Georgian states (Guria, 1829; Suania, 1858; Abkhazia, 1864). In 1867 the Prince of Mingrelia was allowed to abdicate in favor of Emperor Alexander II. Meschia, no longer a princedom, was acquired from the Turks in 1878.

In 1811 Russian annexationism affected the Georgian Church as well. The catholicate of Iberia was abolished, while that of Abasgia had been in abeyance from 1795. The last catholicos, Antony II, was deported to Russia and the Church became part of the Russian Church, to be ruled by the Holy Synod through an exarch. All the exarchs, save the first one, were Russians. The Georgian episcopal sees, which had numbered some 77 in the 17th century and some 30 on the eve of the annexation, were reduced to 5. The Church was impoverished through governmental confiscations of Church property (amounting to some 140,000,000 rubles) and the rapacity of the Russian-appointed hierarchs. Ecclesiastical art treasures were decimated through neglect and the rapacity of lay officialdom. The Georgian language was suppressed in seminaries, in schools, and even in the liturgy, and replaced by Russian or Palaeoslavic. The Church, no less than the country, was subjected to Russification, a trend that was resented by the people. The collapse of the Russian empire in 1917 brought about the restoration of Georgia's political independence, if only momentarily.

In 1917 the Georgian Orthodox Church declared its independence from the Russian Holy Synod and reestablished a catholicos-patriarch of All Georgia. In 1921, however, Georgia was reabsorbed into the new Soviet empire, though accorded the status of a Soviet socialist republic, while two West Georgian lands, Abkhazia and Achara, were given that of autonomous republics. The catholicate was allowed to continue.

After the Russian expulsion of the Capuchins in 1845 the Georgian Catholics were cared for by local Catholic clergy, later principally members to the Georgian Congregation of the Servants of the Immaculate Conception, founded at Constantinople in 1861. They were placed under the Catholic bishop of Tiraspol in Russia. At the outbreak of World War I there were some 40,000 Catholics of the Latin, as well as of the Armenian rite in Georgia (the Byzantine rite was always especially persecuted in the Russian Empire) out of the population that has since risen to over 4,000,000. After the war the Holy See appointed an administrator apostolic of Tiflis and Georgia.

Bibliography: W. E. D. ALLEN, *A History of the Georgian People* (London 1932). M. TAMARATI, *L'Eglise géorgienne: Des origines jusqu'à nos jours* (Rome 1910). M. TARCHNIŠVILI, *Muséon* 73 (1960) 107–126, autocephalous church; ''Sources arméno-géorgiennes de l'histoire ancienne de l'Eglise de Géorgie,'' *ibid.* 60 (1947) 29–50; *Geschichte der kirchlichen georgischen Literatur* (Rome 1955); *Orientalia Christiana* 39 (1955) 79–92, church and state. C. TOUMANOFF, *Studies in Christian Caucasian History* (Washington 1963); ''Christian Caucasia between Byzantium and Iran,'' *Traditio* 10 (1954) 109–189.

[C. TOUMANOFF]

GEORGIAN BYZANTINE CATHOLICS

Historians cannot tell with precision when the Georgian Church broke ties with Rome. When contact with Rome became impossible because of the domination of the Mongols from the 13th to 15th centuries, there occurred a gradual estrangement from Rome and a turning toward the East. In the schism that had earlier separated Constantinople from Rome, Georgia remained neutral. It is known only that George of Mthatsminda (11th century), the official speaker of the Georgian Church, defended before the emperor the position of Rome. Until the middle of the 13th century it did not appear likely that the Georgian Church would be separated from Rome. In their letters to the pope, both Queen Rusudan and her minister (122–345) recognized the primacy of the pope. Thus one can conclude only that separation from Rome was not an official, juridical act. Support of Constantinople was favored by political conditions and encouraged by the century-old traditions that Georgia shared with Byzantium. However, notwithstanding the actual separation, Georgia's kings from the 13th to the 19th century always kept a desire for communion with the Roman Church.

Several Latin religious orders, chiefly the Franciscans and Dominicans, worked in Georgia for reunion. In 1329 Pope John XXII erected a Catholic see at Tiflis and appointed the first Latin bishop of Georgia, thus beginning a line that continued until 1507. The Theatines and

Capuchins worked until the 18th and 19th centuries establishing a nucleus of Latin Catholics. They numbered about 50,000 before World War I. A smaller nucleus of Georgian Catholics at the end of the 19th century embraced the Armenian rite because it was forbidden by Russian law until 1917 for any Catholic to follow the Byzantine rite. In 1917, when Georgia cut off ecclesiastical bonds from the Moscow patriarchate, a small group of Georgians sought communion with the See of Rome as a fledging Georgian Byzantine Catholic community. This was a very small group that numbered at its peak 10,000 in 1920, whereas there were 40,000 of the Latin rite during that period. Two religious congregations of the Immaculate Conception were founded in 1861 in Constantinople by Father Peter Karishiaranti to work among the Catholics of Georgia of both Byzantine and Latin rites, but they had died out by the 1960s.

The nascent Georgian Byzantine Catholic community of the early 20th century was impeded by the fact that no hierarchy was ever established for them. The small Georgian Byzantine Catholic parish in Constantinople is the only surviving vestige of the small community. After Georgia regained its independence in 1991, the Latin Catholics and Armenian Catholics experienced a resurgence and renaissance. The future of the incipient Georgian Byzantine Catholic community remains uncertain.

Bibliography: R. ROBERSON, *The Eastern Christian Churches: A Brief Survey*, 6th ed (Rome 1999)

[A. S. MANVEL/EDS.]

GERALD OF AURILLAC, ST.

Patron of Upper Auvergne, France; b. 855; d. Oct. 13, 909. He was born into an old noble family at Aurillac and succeeded his father as count of that region, although he had wished to enter religious life and had been educated as a cleric. He made several pilgrimages to Rome and, despite many difficulties, in 894 established the Abbey of AURILLAC, which he placed under papal protection. He was celebrated for his justice as a ruler, his many devotions (including recitation of the Divine Office), his lifelong chastity, and his gift of healing. Gerald was buried in the church at Aurillac which now bears his name. Although his popular cult began immediately and has been confirmed, he is little known outside France.

Feast: Oct. 13.

Bibliography: *Acta Sanctorum* Oct. 6:277–331. ODO OF CLUNY, ''De vita Sancti Geraldi,'' *Patrologia Latina* 133:639–704. E. JOUBERT, *Saint Geraud d'Aurillac* (Aurillac 1968). G. SITWELL, ed. and tr., *St. Odo of Cluny . . . St. Gerald of Aurillac* (New York 1958). A. BUTLER, *The Lives of the Saints* (New York 1956) 4:104–105.

[F. BEHRENDS]

GERALD OF BRAGA, ST.

Monk, bishop; d. Dec. 5, 1108. Gerald became a Benedictine of the Cluniac observance at the Abbey of MOISSAC. In 1086, another Cluniac, Bernard of Salvetat, abbot of Sahagún, was promoted to the archbishopric of Toledo, which had been recovered from the Moors by King Alfonso VI of León-Castile in the previous year. Then, in 1088, Bernard was named primate of Spain by Pope URBAN II. In the process of developing a capable and learned hierarchy, Bernard invited Gerald to join him, consecrating him bishop of Braga, 1096. This see, the metropolitan of Galicia before the Moslem conquest, had been reestablished by King García in 1070, and on Dec. 28, 1099, it was restored to metropolitan status by Pope PASCHAL II. On Dec. 5, 1100, at the national council of Palencia, Gerald's cult was formally recognized by his suffragans.

Feast: Dec. 5.

Bibliography: M. DE OLIVEIRA, *Lexikon für Theologie und Kirche*. (Freiburg 1957–65) 4:707.

[A. G. BIGGS]

GERALD OF MAYO, ST.

Abbot; b. Northumbria, England; d. Mayo, Ireland, 732. When the synod of WHITBY (664) banned the observance of the Celtic date of Easter in Northumbria, St. COLMAN left LINDISFARNE with all the Irish monks and with some 30 of the English monks, including Gerald. In Ireland they founded a monastery at Inishbofin off the Mayo coast. Strife between the Irish and English monks led Colman to establish a house on the mainland (Mayo) for the English monks. He acted for a time as superior of both houses, but then Gerald succeeded him as abbot of Mayo, which became a great sanctuary for saints. Gerald's vita, though legendary, contains valuable material on the relations of Christians and Druids in early Ireland.

Feast: Mar. 13.

Bibliography: *Acta Sanctorum* March 2:284–288. J. COLGAN, *Acta sanctorum Hiberniae* (Louvain 1645; repr. Dublin 1948) 599–704. J. F. KENNEY, *The Sources for the Early History of Ireland* (New York 1929) 463–464. C. PLUMMER, comp., *Vitae sanctorum Hiberniae*, 2 v. (Oxford 1910) 1:lxxi–lxxii; 2:107–115. A. BUTLER *The Lives of the Saints* (New York 1956) 1:584.

[R. T. MEYER]

GERALDINI, ALEJANDRO

Italian humanist, second bishop of Santo Domingo; b. Italy, date unknown; d. Santo Domingo, March 8,

1524. Titular bishop of Vultutara from 1494, Geraldini spent almost 40 years in the service of the crown of Castile as a diplomat, priest, and cultured man. He brought the spirit of the Italian Renaissance to the palace of the Catholic kings. He was a prolific writer of Latin verse and prose. On Jan. 26, 1516, he was nominated for the See of Santo Domingo and personally delivered the royal letter to the Pope. Confirmed and consecrated, he left for America and wrote a letter to Charles V from Santo Domingo on Oct. 6, 1519. He described his arrival in *Itinerarium ad regiones sub aequinoctiali plaga constituas* (Rome 1631) in which he gave an enthusiastic picture of the city, its culture, and its wealth. Geraldini's greatest accomplishment as bishop was the construction of the cathedral of Santo Domingo, the first in America, started in 1522. He wrote a Latin ode in honor of his beloved cathedral, in which he was buried, but nothing in the building today reflects his description of it.

Bibliography: CIPRIANO DE UTRERA, *Episcopologio dominico-politano* (Ciudad Trujillo 1956). P. HENRÍQUEZ UREÑA, *La cultura y las letras coloniales en Santo Domingo* (Buenos Aires 1936).

[E. RODRÍGUEZ DEMORIZI]

GERARD, JOHN

Jesuit missionary; b. Etwall Hall, Derbyshire, Oct. 4, 1564; d. Rome, June 27, 1637. During his education at Exeter College, Oxford, where he matriculated in December 1575, he left for Douai in August 1577 to avoid taking the oath of supremacy; he later continued his studies at the Jesuit College in Clermont, Paris. After returning to England in the spring of 1583, he was imprisoned in the Marshalsea. Shortly after his release, about May 1586, he left England and went to Rome, where on August 5 he entered the English College. About a month after his ordination (six weeks short of the required canonical age), he joined the Society of Jesus on Aug. 15, 1588. The same year, in company with Edward Oldcorne, he returned to England, landing at night in early November on a deserted stretch of beach near Happisburgh on the Norfolk coast between Great Yarmouth and Cromer. His adventures during the next 18 years are recorded in his *Autobiography,* perhaps the most remarkable and exciting narrative of adventure in Elizabethan literature. Between 1588 and 1594 he worked in East Anglia, first in Norfolk and then in Suffolk, Cambridgeshire, and Essex; he made many converts and established a large number of Catholic centers in the houses of the gentry. Several times he narrowly escaped arrest, but finally he was caught in London, on April 23, 1594. After close imprisonment in the Counter-in-the-Poultry he was transferred to the Clink on July 6, 1594; there he was able to say Mass, instruct converts, and establish in London a house for priests entering England from the seminaries. His success led to stricter confinement and to his transference to the Tower on April 12, 1597. He was never brought to trial; but he was tortured twice, principally that he might reveal the names of the persons who had sheltered him and the whereabouts of his superior, Henry GARNET. With the help of friends in London, with whom he communicated by letters written in orange juice, he organized his escape by means of a rope slung from the roof of the Cradle Tower over the moat to the wharf below. This was on the night of Oct. 5, 1597.

Thereafter, though closely pursued, he continued his apostolate in Northants, Bucks, and Oxfordshire. At the time of the Gunpowder Plot a proclamation was issued ordering Gerard's arrest along with that of Garnet and Father Oswald Tesimond. Although innocent, Gerard was a friend of several of the conspirators, notably Sir Everard Digby. Gerard eluded capture and on May 3, 1606, crossed from Dover to the Continent disguised as a retainer to the Spanish ambassador. Later he wrote his *Narrative of the Gunpowder Plot,* which remains a primary historical source. Early in 1607 he was appointed English Penitentiary at St. Peter's, and two years later he was sent to Flanders to help in the training of the novices in the English novitiate established at Louvain. In 1614 a Jesuit house of philosophy and theology was established at Liège, and Gerard became its first rector. He built it from the foundations in a fine style with alms collected from all quarters. In 1622 he visited Rome to get papal support for the new Institute of Religious Women founded by Mary WARD; and on his return to Belgium was made rector of the house of the English Jesuits at Ghent, where the newly ordained priests made their ''third year'' of probation under his direction. From 1627 to 1637 he was confessor to the English College in Rome, where he died.

Bibliography: J. GERARD, *The Autobiography of a Hunted Priest,* tr. P. CARAMAN (New York 1952). T. COOPER, *The Dictionary of National Biography from the Earliest Times to 1900,* 7:1101–02.

[P. CARAMAN]

GÉRARD, JOSEF VALENCIA, BL.

Oblate missionary priest; b. March 12, 1831 Bouxières-aux-Chênes (near Nancy), France; d. May 29, 1914, Roma, Lesotho, Africa. Josef, son of peasants Jean Gérard and Ursula Stofflet, studied at Pont-à-Mousson and Nancy seminary (1851–52) before pronouncing his final vows as an oblate of Mary Immaculate (1852). After completing his studies at Marseilles, he left for Natal (1853), South Africa, where he was ordained nearby at

Pietermaritzburg (February 1854). His first efforts as a missionary among the Zulus were unsuccessful. In 1862, he traveled on horseback to establish a mission in Basutoland (now Lesotho) at the ''Village de la Mère de Jésus'' (also known as Roma). There he won the heart of the great warrior king Moshoeshoe, baptized his first converts (1865), and established a flourishing school and convent. He labored alone to found St. Monica's Mission in the northern part of the country (1876), before returning to Roma in 1898. The Basuthos remember Gérard as a man whose prayer led him to care for the sick and weak. After praying at his tomb in Maseru, Lesotho, Pope John Paul II beatified Gérard on Sept. 15, 1988.

Bibliography: *Father Joseph Gérard, O.M.I., Speaks to Us from South Africa and Lesotho, 1854–1914*, ed. M. FERRAGNE, tr. G. BROSSARD (Maseru, Lesotho 1980). J. MORABITO, *Jamais plus comme lui!: vie et vertus du serviteur de Dieu, le père Joseph Gérard* (Rome 1980). *Acta Apostolicae Sedis* (1988): 961.

[K. I. RABENSTEIN]

GERARD, MILES, BL.

Priest, martyr; *alias* William Richardson; b. ca. 1550, Ince, near Wigan, Lancashire, England; hanged, drawn, and quartered at Rochester, April 13 or 30, 1590. Before beginning his seminary studies at Douai, then Rheims, Gerard was tutor to the children of Sir Edward Tyldesley, at Morleys, Lancashire. He was ordained at Rheims, April 7, 1583, then was a professor at the English College there for several years. On Aug. 31, 1589 (O.S.), he started for England with five companions. When the sailors at Dunkirk refused to take more than two passengers, the priests flipped a coin. Gerard and Bl. Francis Dickenson won passage. Upon landing at Dover (November 24, N.S.), they were arrested. At first they hid their true identities. After confessing that they were Catholic priests, they were brutally tortured and condemned as traitors in London. Jesuit Father John Curry wrote shortly after their execution that they ''gave a splendid testimony to the Catholic Faith.'' Gerard and Dickenson were beatified by Pius XI on Dec. 15, 1929.

Feast of the English Martyrs: May 4 (England).

See Also: ENGLAND, SCOTLAND, AND WALES, MARTYRS OF.

Bibliography: R. CHALLONER, *Memoirs of Missionary Priests*, ed. J. H. POLLEN (rev. ed. London 1924; repr. Farnborough 1969). J. H. POLLEN, *Acts of English Martyrs* (London 1891).

[K. I. RABENSTEIN]

GERARD, RICHARD

Recusant and confessor; b. probably Staffordshire, *c.* 1635; d. London, March 22, 1680. Counting among his antecedents both the solicitor general under Elizabeth I (Gilbert Gerard) and the famous Jesuit missioner (John Gerard), Richard seems representative of the lesser English peerage of the mid-17th century, on whom both recusant Catholicism and conformity to the Established Church laid rival traditional claims. How he himself became a Catholic is not known, but certainly by the 1670s he had become identified as a friend of the Jesuits, having three sons at Saint-Omer and administering some small properties on behalf of the society. This friendship was to prove convenient for the anti-Catholic purposes of the ''Whig'' opposition to the Duke of York, for when Gerard came to London to testify in favor of the five Catholic peers who had been impeached following Titus Oates's revelation of the Popish Plot, he found himself arrested on a similar charge of conspiracy. His acknowledged contact with Father John Gavan on Aug. 15, 1678, at Bascobel in Worcestershire, was cited by the informer Stephen Dugdale as evidence of treason; and on this charge he was committed to the Gatehouse prison by the Lords' committee on May 19, 1679. Ten months later, in the meantime removed to Newgate prison and still awaiting trial, he died.

Bibliography: J. GILLOW, *A Literary and Biographical History or Bibliographical Dictionary of the English Catholics from 1534 to the Present Time,* 2:432–433. H. FOLEY, ed., *Records of the English Province of the Society of Jesus,* 7 v. (London 1877–82), 5:434–436.

[R. I. BRADLEY]

GERARD OF ABBEVILLE

Secular master in theology at Paris; b. Abbeville, near Amiens, *c.* 1220; d. Nov. 8, 1272. Mentioned as a master of the university and papal subdeacon in 1254 (*Chartularium Universitatis Parisiensis* 1:374), he was regent master in theology and archdeacon of Ponthieu in 1262 (*ibid.* 1:436). His entire career was devoted to the academic life at Paris. An intimate friend of WILLIAM OF SAINT-AMOUR, he became one of the leaders of the movement to expel mendicants from the university and to suppress their privileges. After the exile of William of Saint-Amour in 1257, Gerard preserved contact by correspondence and became the recognized leader of the opposition to the mendicant orders, particularly in the second stage of the conflict. In 1256 he had already written *Contra adversarium perfectionis Christianae,* but it was not circulated until late summer of 1269. This was answered by both BONAVENTURE and THOMAS AQUINAS.

In January 1269 Gerard inaugurated renewed opposition in a sermon affirming that use of material goods for the sake of the Church does not place secular clerics in a less perfect state than that of religious. In his Lenten quodlibet (March 1269), he attacked the Franciscan concept of absolute poverty. In this he received strong support from his colleague Nicholas of Lisieux. Early in 1270 he addressed two critical questions to JOHN PECKHAM that were answered both in Peckham's *Tractatus pauperis* and in Aquinas's *Quodl.* 3.11–12. Later Gerard published a list of 110 false, dangerous, and heretical propositions from the Franciscan pamphlet *Manus quae contra omnipotentem* attributed to THOMAS OF YORK or Bertrand of Bayonne. Gerard in turn became the object of constant attack from the mendicants, particularly the Franciscans; he replied twice in 1270 to anonymous Franciscan attacks. His last defense, *Liber apologeticus,* appeared about the middle of July 1270. After his death the controversy relaxed somewhat. Literature directed against Gerard and his supporters has come to be known as *contra Geraldinos.*

Bibliography: P. GLORIEUX, *Répertoire de maîtres en théologie de Paris au XIIIe siècle* 1:356–360. P. GLORIEUX, ''Les Polémiques *contra Geraldinos,*'' *Recherches de théologie ancienne et médiéval* 6 (1934) 5–41. G. BONAFEDE, *Enciclopedia filosofica* 2:664–665. S. CLASEN, ''Die *Duplez quaestio* de Gerhard von Abbeville über den Ordenseintritt Jugendlicher,'' *Antonianum* 22 (1947) 177–200; ''Tractatus Gerardi de Abbatisvilla *Contra adversarium perfectionis Christianae,*'' *Archivum Franciscanum historicum* 31 (1938) 276–329; 32 (1939) 89–200. Y. M. J. CONGAR, ''Aspects ecclésiologiques de la querelle entre mendiants et séculiers dans la seconde moitié du XIIIe siècle et le début du XIVe,'' *Archives d'histoire doctrinale et littéraire du moyen-âge* (1961) 35–151.

[A. J. HEIMAN]

GERARD OF BROGNE, ST.

Abbot, monastic reformer; b. Stave, Namur, Belgium, *c.* 880; d. Brogne Abbey, Oct. 3, 959. His father, Santio, was of noble birth, and his mother, Plectrude, was a sister of Bp. Stephen of Liège. While in the service of Berengar, count of Lomme, Gerard rebuilt an old oratory that was in the freehold of Brogne on the edge of the forest of Marlagne. There he placed the relics of St. Eugene that he had received from Leutger, abbot of Deuil (Seine-et-Oise, France) and from the monks of SAINT-DENIS. The translation took place on Aug. 18, 914, presided over by the Archdeacon Adelhelm, delegated by Bishop Stephen. By an act of June 2, 919, Gerard endowed this church, rededicated to SS. Peter and Eugene, with land and replaced its clerics with monks. In a charter of 923 Gerard himself appears as abbot of the new monastery; some sources say he had meanwhile made his novitiate at Saint-Denis. In 934, while his own rather small monastery was at peace and enjoying prosperity, Gerard was commissioned by Duke Gislebert of Lorraine to restore regular observance of the BENEDICTINE RULE at the Abbey of Saint-Ghislain in Hainaut. Later, at the suggestion of Bishop Transmar of Noyon and Tournai, Arnulf I, Count of Flanders, entrusted Gerard with the reform of the monastery of Saint-Bavon of Ghent (partially rebuilt after 937) and then with Saint-Pierre on Mont-Blandin at Ghent (where Arnulf reserved to himself the confirmation of the abbot elected by the monks) as well as SAINT-BERTIN, SAINT-AMAND-LES-EAUX, and SAINT-REMI in Reims. Soon Gerard's followers reformed SAINT-RIQUIER and the great Norman Abbeys of FONTENELLE (SAINT-WANDRILLE), MONT-SAINT-MICHEL, and SAINT-OUEN in Rouen. In 953 Gerard resigned as abbot of Mont-Blandin and returned to BROGNE. His only concern had been to aid princes in restoring regular observance of the Rule in monastic communities; he had never thought of founding a new congregation. Gerard's reform ideas, derived from BENEDICT OF ANIANE, differed substantially from the CLUNIAC REFORM ideal, of which he must have been ignorant. But he did, in any case, prepare the ground for the great GREGORIAN REFORM. In 1131 Alexander of Juliers, bishop of Liège, delegated by Pope INNOCENT II, elevated the body of Gerard, a ceremony equivalent to canonization. Since the 17th century, Brogne has had the name of Saint-Gerard.

Feast: Oct. 3.

Bibliography: Vita (written 1050–70) *Monumenta Germaniae Historica: Scriptores* 15:655–673. *Translatio s. Eugenii* (written *c.* 935) *Analecta Bollandiana* 3:29–54; 5:385–395. *Acta Sanctorum* Oct. 2 220–320. U. BERLIÈRE, ''Étude sur la *Vita Gerardi Broniensis,*'' *Revue Benedictine* 9 (1892) 157–172. F. BAIX, *Dictionnaire d'histoire et de géographie ecclésiastiques* 10:818–832. P. SCHMITZ, *Histoire de l'ordre de saint-Benoît*, 7 v. (Maredsous, Bel. 1942–56) 1:150–151. É. DE MOREAU, *Histoire de l'èglise en Belgique*, v.2 (2d ed. Brussels 1945) 142–154. A. BUTLER, *The Lives of the Saints* (New York 1956) 4:17–18. J. M. DE SMET, ''Recherches critiques sur la Vita G. abbatis B.,'' *Revue Benedictine* 70 (1960) 5–61. J. WOLLASCH, ''G. von B. und seine Klostergründung,'' *ibid* 62–82.

[J. DAOUST]

GERARD OF CAMBRAI

Theologian; b. Saxony, *c.* 975; d. Cambrai, March 14, 1051. After being attached to the imperial chapel and having been named bishop of Arras and Cambrai on Feb. 1, 1012, by Emperor St. Henry II (1002–24), Gerard was ordained at Nijmegen and consecrated at Reims. In loyal feudal service he accompanied Henry on several expeditions and for a while refused to enter a pact with French bishops favoring the Truce of God (*see* PEACE OF GOD). His relations with Henry's successors were less close. He aided the monastic reform begun in Lotharingia by Gerard of Brogne (d. 959) and turned over to Richard of St. Vanne (d. 1046) some abbeys he and his brothers had supported or founded. In Arras early in 1025 Gerard learned of the arrival of some Cathari-type heretics from Italy. He brought them before a synod there and secured the retraction of their anti-sacramental and anti-ecclesial errors. He sent, with a covering letter, his long discourse and an account of the synod to a Bishop R., who was probably Roger, Bishop of Châlons-sur-Marne (d. 1042). Book 3 of the *Gesta episcoporum Cameracensium* (*Monumenta Germaniae Historica: Scriptores* 7.402–498; *Patrologia latina* 149:21–176) is Gerard's *Vita.* The *Acta* of the synod is printed in different editions (Mansi 19:423–460; *Patrologia latina* 142:1269–1312). Gerard's letters, preserved in the *Vita*, are reprinted in *Patrologia latina* 142:1313–22 and 149:159–160.

Bibliography: T. SCHIEFFER, ''Ein deutscher Bischof des 11. Jahrhunderts: Gerhard I. von Cambrai (1012–1051),'' *Deutsches Archiv für Erforsheung des Mittelalters* 1 (1937) 323–360. É. DE MOREAU, *Histoire de l'Église en Belgique*, v.2 *La Formation de l'Église médiévale* (2d ed. Brussels 1947). H. PLATELLE, *Catholicisme* 4:1867–68. H. SILVESTRE, ''À propos de l'épithaphe de l'évêque de Liège, Durand (+ 1025),'' *Revue belge de philologie et d'histoire* 41 (1963) 1136–45.

[J. N. GARVIN]

GERARD OF CLAIRVAUX, BL.

Second eldest brother of BERNARD OF CLAIRVAUX; d. June 13, 1138. He originally refused to follow Bernard into the CISTERCIAN order; but after being wounded in battle, taken prisoner, and miraculously freed as his brother had foretold, he took the monastic habit at CÎTEAUX in 1112. He accompanied Bernard to the foundation of CLAIRVAUX (June 11, 1115), almost abandoned the project because of the difficulties encountered, but remained to fill the office of cellarer until his death. Bernard's lament at his loss, now sermon 26 of the *Sermones in Cantica,* is one of the most moving tributes to be found in medieval Latin literature.

Feast: June 13 (formerly Jan. 30).

Bibliography: *Acta Sanctorum* June 3:192–195. BERNARD OF CLAIRVAUX, ''Sermo XXVI,'' *Sermones in Cantica, Patrologia Latina* 183:903–912. J. B. JOBIN, *Saint Bernard et sa famille* (Paris 1891). R. LECHAT, ''Les *Fragmenta de vita et miraculis s. Bernardi,*'' *Analecta Bollandiana* 50 (1932) 83–122.

[C. H. TALBOT]

GERARD OF CREMONA

Translator from Arabic into Latin; b. Cremona, Italy, *c.* 1114; d. Cremona, 1187. After completing early studies in Italy, he was attracted by the new learning available in Toledo, which had been recaptured by the Christians in 1085. Under the auspices of Raymond of Sauvetât, Archbishop of Toledo (1126–51), the city became a lively center of scientific studies and translations. By 1134 Gerard was already in Spain, first as a student of Arabic, then as a prolific translator of works that would transform SCHOLASTICISM. Unlike his contemporary DOMINIC GUNDISALVI, he was a translator exclusively.

Ancient catalogues credit him with more than 70 works, although some listed were done by Gerard Sabionetta (13th century). Almost every branch of learning was renewed and reformed because of his translations of ARISTOTLE, some of the Greek commentators transmitted through Arabic, Avicenna, Al-KINDI, ALFARABI, Euclid, and Ptolemy. Among his more important contributions were his translation of Aristotle's *Posterior Analytics,* with the paraphrase of Themistius; Aristotle's *De naturali auditu* (*Physics*), *Liber caeli et mundi, De generatione,* and *Meteora* (bks. 1–3); the pseudo-Aristotelian *Liber de causis or Liber bonitatis purae* (a compilation of extracts from the *Elementatio theologica* of PROCLUS); *Canones medicinae* of Avicenna, as well as a substantial part of Avicenna's philosophical work, *Shifa;* the *Almagest* of Ptolemy; the best complete translation of Euclid's *Elementa geometriae*; Alkindi's *De intellectu* and *De quinque essentiis;* and Alfarabi's *De intellectu.* Through these translations the West came to know a new Aristotle and the best of Greek medicine, astronomy, and mathematics that had long been known and developed by the Muslim.

Bibliography: E. H. GILSON, *History of Christian Philosophy in the Middle Ages* (New York 1955) 376–377. G. BONAFEDE, *Enciclopedia filosofica* (Venice-Rome 1957) 2:665. B. BONCOMPAGNI, *Della vita e delle opere di Gherardo Cremonese* (Rome 1851). H. BEDORET, ''L'Auteur et le traducteur du *Liber de causis,*' *Revue néo-scolastique de philosophie* 41 (1938) 519–533.

[P. GLORIEUX]

GERARD OF CSANÁD, ST.

Bishop and martyr; b. Sagrado, near Venice, Italy, *c.* 980; d. Buda (Budapest), Hungary, Sept. 24, 1046. A native of a Slav village in northern Italy, he spent a few years of his youth in the Benedictine Abbey of San Giorgio at Venice and returned as abbot after studies at Bologna. The beginning of the 10th century found him in the hermitage of Bel, Hungary, whence King STEPHEN I of Hungary sought him to tutor his son EMERIC *c.* 1015–23.

Stephen established the Diocese of Csanád in 1035 and appointed Gerard its first bishop with the task of Christianizing southeastern Hungary. Gerard founded mission parishes, entrusting them to monks from various countries; and at the monastery of Csanád he founded a school where monks were trained to convert the Hungarian tribes. Because of the close relations between the Polish and Hungarian monks and hermits at that time, Gerard was until the last century frequently confused with the famous Polish hermit ZOËRARDUS. All of Gerard's writings are lost except the *Deliberatio Gerardi Moresanae episcopi supra hymnum trium puerorum.* He was martyred at Buda by the idolatrous opponents of the deceased King Stephen as he was attempting to cross the Danube. In 1333 the Hungarian king sent the major portion of Gerard's relics to Venice, where he is revered as that city's protomartyr.

Feast: Sept. 24.

Bibliography: *S. Gerardi scripta et acta,* ed. I. BATTHYAN (Karlsburg 1790). *Bibliotheca hagiographica latina antiquae et mediae aetatis* 1:3424–28. M. MANITIUS, *Geschichte der lateinischen Literatur des Mittelalters* (Munich 1911–31) 2:74–83. L. C. DEDEK, *Leben des hl. Gerhard* (Budapest 1900). J. KARÁCSONYI, *Szent Gellért* (2d ed. Budapest 1925). A. M. ZIMMERMANN, *Kalendarium Benedictinum: Die Heiligen und Seligen des Benediktinerorderns und seiner Zweige* (Metten 1933–38) 3:96–101. A. BUTLER, *The Lives of the Saints* (New York 1956) 3:629. J. SZALAY, *Catholicisme* 4:1868–69. A. L. GABRIEL, ''The Conversion of Hungary to Christianity,'' *Polish Review* 6.4 (1961) 31–43, esp. 41–42. H. KAPISZEWSKI, ''Eremita Swirad w Panonii,'' *Nasza przeszłość* 10 (1959) 17–69, esp. 65–68. V. D'AMBROSIO, *L'uomo che asservo Satana: S. Gerardo Maria Maiella* (Naples 1964). G. SILAGI, *Untersuchungen zur ''Deliberatio supra hymnum trium puerorum'' des Gerhard von Csanád* (Munich 1967). G. R. ZITAROSA, *San Gerardo Maiella mistico* (Naples 1969).

[L. SIEKANIEC]

GERARD OF SAUVE-MAJEURE, ST.

Benedictine abbot; b. near Corbie, France, *c.* 1025; d. April 5, 1095. Having been a child oblate of CORBIE ABBEY, he was cellarer there by 1050. Shortly thereafter he accompanied Abbot Fulk on a pilgrimage to Monte Cassino and Rome, where both were ordained by Pope LEO IX. Disturbed by bad health, he was cured through the intercession of St. ADALARD, a former abbot, to whom he fostered devotion and whose biography he directed. After a pilgrimage to the Holy Land in 1073, he was called by the monks of Saint-Vincent, Laon, to succeed his recently deceased brother, Raynier, as form abbot. (Some would also identify Gerard with the ''Abbot Gerald'' of Saint-Médard, Soissons, who lived about this time.) After five years of futile effort to reestablish regular observance at Saint–Vincent, Gerard and two monks from the abbey joined a hermit and his party of five knights, who had originally come to Gerard for advice about a new foundation. On a pilgrimage to Tours the group encountered William VIII, duke of Aquitaine and count of Poitou, who offered them a choice of land for an abbey. On Oct. 28, 1079, they took possession of a forested area, Sauve–Majeure (*Silva Major*), or Grande–Sauve, just east of Bordeaux, and construction began on May 11, 1081. The foundation, free from all lay feudal control and directly under the Holy See, prospered immediately under Gerard's guidance. A priory at Sémoy near Orléans was begun in 1081, and an abbey at Broqueroie, Hainaut, Belgium, in 1082. Gerard's cult began almost immediately after his death, and he was canonized by CELESTINE III on April 27, 1197.

Feast: April 5; June 21 (Poitou).

Bibliography: *Acta Sanctorum* April 1:407–431. J. MABILLON, *Annales Ordinis S. Benedicti,* 6 v. (2d ed. Lucca 1739–45) 4:469; 5:100–101, 151–153. ABBÉ CIROT DE LA VILLE, *Histoire de l'abbaye . . . de La Grande-Sauve,* 2 v. (Paris 1844–45) v.1. R. GAZEAU, *Catholicisme* 4:1869–70. *Monumenta Germaniae Historica: Scriptores* 15.2:859–865.

[W. E. WILKIE]

GERARD OF TOUL, ST.

Bishop; b. Cologne, *c.* 935; d. Toul, France, April 23, 994. Having been a canon in Cologne, he was designated by Abp. Bruno of Cologne to replace Bishop GAUZELIN OF TOUL in 963. Gerard completed there the foundation of Saint-Mansuy Abbey, begun by his predecessor. He erected a convent for women in honor of St. Gengoult, transformed *c.* 986 into a chapter of canons. The founding of the Maison–Dieu of Toul is also attributed to him. The cathedral consecrated in 981, a vast edifice characteristic of Ottonian art, was rebuilt through his care. His pastoral activity on behalf of parish life is not well known but seems to have been fruitful. His successor at Toul, Bruno of Egisheim, who became Pope LEO IX, arranged for the elevation of Gerard's relics on Oct. 21, 1050.

Feast: April 23.

Bibliography: *Bibliotheca hagiographicae latina antiquae et mediae aetatis* 1:3431–34. *Acta Sanctorum* April 3:207–215. A. MICHEL, *Die Akten Gerhards von Toul als Werk Humberts und die Anfänge der päpstlichen Reform* (Munich 1957). E. MARTIN, *Histoire des diocèses de Toul, de Nancy et de Saint–Dié* 3 v. (Nancy 1900–03) v.1. P. VIARD, *Catholicisme* 4: 1870–71.

[J. CHOUX]

GERARD OF VILLAMAGNA, BL.

Hermit; b. Villamagna, near Florence, Italy, *c.* 1174; d. there, May 13, 1245. Orphaned at an early age, he took service as a page in a knightly Florentine family. As an attendant to his master, he went on CRUSADE (1220–28), was captured by the Saracens, and, after his release, traveled as a pilgrim to Jerusalem. It is possible that he may also be identified with a lay brother of the Knights of Malta named Micaty (Mercatti). After returning to Italy he joined the Third Order of St. Francis and lived as a hermit in his native town. His cult was approved in 1833.

Feast: May 23; May 13 (Florence).

Bibliography: *Acta Sanctorum* May 3:247. L. WADDING, *Scriptores Ordinis Minorum* 5:19. A. BUTLER, *The Lives of the Saints* 2:378–379. L. BOEHM, *Lexikon für Theologie und Kirche*[2] 4:723.

[O. J. BLUM]

GERARD OF YORK

Archbishop of York; d. Southwell, England, May 21, 1108. Gerard was probably a distant relative of England's Norman royal house; one of his uncles was bishop of Winchester, another abbot of Ely; he himself was a resolute supporter of the royal policy, a beneficiary of royal favor and for most of his career lined up as an opponent to Abp. ANSELM OF CANTERBURY. Called from the precentorship of Rouen to serve King WILLIAM II Rufus in chancery and chapel, he was entrusted with a secret mission to Rome in 1095. His success brought him the bishopric of HEREFORD, though he was not yet in deacon's orders. Anselm ordained him deacon and priest and then consecrated him bishop the next day (June 8, 1096). On the accession of King HENRY I of England in 1100, Gerard was made archbishop of YORK, but it was only after a dispute that Anselm issued the necessary letters of confirmation for presentation to the Pope. The rivalry between Henry and Anselm soon permeated the wider issues of the INVESTITURE struggle in England. Church and State, archbishop and king, each presented his case before the Pope. Three prelates, led by Gerard, represented the King, but though Gerard earned Pope PASCHAL II's praise for his able and eloquent presentation of Henry's cause, the verdict was for Anselm. It was conveyed in peremptory letters requiring the King's submission. But on his return Gerard claimed to have secret assurances that these stern demands would not be enforced. The Pope vigorously denied this and excommunicated Gerard and his associates until they had confessed the fraud and made satisfaction. At the same time Gerard was forced to profess canonical obedience to CANTERBURY, though he continued to claim coequality of dignity. This Canterbury-York quarrel over primacy was further embittered when Gerard was ordered (1103) by the King to consecrate three bishops whom Anselm had refused to consecrate on the grounds that they had received investiture from the King. When Gerard attempted to begin the ceremony, it was interrupted, his presence was challenged, and the ceremony broke up in confusion. During Anselm's exile Gerard busied himself in restoring order and discipline in his own extensive province. He received from Pope Paschal a severe rebuke for having supported the king against Anselm, and this may explain Gerard's change of attitude, for he was among those who entreated Anselm to return. And the reconciliation seems to have been complete: Gerard took his place among the prelates who officiated in the long-deferred consecration of bishops (August 1107). His conflict with Anselm and his consistent support of the royal policy made him many enemies; he is charged by the chroniclers with licentiousness, avarice, and the practice of magic. His cortege was pelted with stones on entering York; his canons refused him burial within the cathedral; his body was ignominiously buried outside its walls but later it was interred within the cathedral by one of his successors. Two of his letters are printed among Anselm's correspondence; some mediocre verses written by him are contained in a MS in the British Museum (Cotton, Titus D. xxiv. 3).

Bibliography: RAINE, *Fasit Eboracenses,* sources. ANSELM OF CANTERBURY, *Opera Omnia,* ed. F. S. SCHMITT, 6 v. (Edinburgh 1946–61). *The Dictionary of National Biography from the Earliest Times to 1900,* 7:1087–89. R. W. SOUTHERN, *Saint Anselm and His Biographer* (New York 1963), 35–138.

[J. H. BAXTER]

GERASIMUS, ST.

Famous Palestinian anchorite; b. Lycia, date unknown; d. Palestine, March 5, 475. Gerasimus went on pilgrimage to the Holy Land *c.* 451 and met St. EUTHYMIUS THE GREAT, who became his fast friend and purged him of the Eutychian (*see* EUTYCHIANISM) errors that Gerasimus had unwittingly embraced. Disciples flocked to Gerasimus, and in 455 he founded a monastery near the Jordan. He instituted a strict formation program for his followers. At the end of this training, those who preferred the common life remained in the monastery; those desiring solitude lived in hermitages that Gerasimus had built nearby. These hermits spent five days each week in prayer and labor, without fire or food except bread, palm dates, and water. Weekends they had to return to the common life of the monastery.

Gerasimus took only the Eucharist for nourishment during Lent and at all times set his monks a stern example of fasting and poverty. Legend tells how, like Androcles, he removed a thorn from the paw of a lion, which then served him and the monastery until Gerasimus' death.

Confusion of his name with Hieronymus (Jerome) led to the lion being an emblem for St. JEROME.

Feast: March 5.

Bibliography: *Acta Sanctorum* March 1:384–387. G. MARSOT, *Catholicisme* 4:1873. H. GRÉGOIRE, ''La Vie anonyme de S. Gérasime,'' *Byzantinische Zeitschrift* 13 (1904) 114–135.

[P. W. HARKINS]

GERBERON, GABRIEL

French Benedictine, Jansenist theologian and historian; b. Saint-Chalais, Vendôme, Aug. 12, 1628; d. Paris, March 29, 1711. He studied philosophy under the Oratorians at Vendôme, joined the Benedictines at Rennes, and taught in several monasteries. While stationed at Saint-Germain-des-Prés in Paris, the center of Maurist erudition, he prepared the works of St. Anselm for publication (Paris 1675; *Patrologia latina* 158–159). This excellent work caused no difficulties. However through this contact with the Church Fathers, the author had acquired a taste for sources and a taste for scholastic thinkers. He was coming closer to the view of the Jansenists, among whom he had friends, and was arousing the mistrust of his superiors. His antiroyalist position made his situation worse. In 1682, he fled to Amiens, settled in the Low Countries, and by 1689 was in Holland. In 1690, he returned to Brussels, where he was in close contact with Arnauld and Quesnel. He published many theological, ascetical, and historical works and later prepared a list of them himself. The following are worth mention: *Michaelis Baii . . . opera,* (Cologne 1694); *Lettres de M. Cornelius Jansenius* (Cologne 1702); and especially the work published anonymously, *Histoire générale du jansénisme* (3 v. in 12, Amsterdam 1700). This history, obviously not complete but based on a rich documentation, still deserves to be juxtaposed with Rapin's.

By their active intervention in the polemical disputes of the Low Countries, Gerberon and his friends aroused the hostility of the bishops. On May 30, 1704, Gerberon was arrested in Brussels, incarcerated, and then condemned on the evidence of his confiscated documents. He was extradited into the hands of French authorities and remained in prison until 1710.

Bibliography: C. FILLIATRE, *Gerberon* (Paris 1921); ''Gerberon: Bénédictin Janséniste du XVIIe Siècle,'' *Revue historique* 146 (1924) 1–54. B. HEURTEBIZE, *Dictionnaire de théologie catholique* 6.1:1290–94.

[L. CEYSSENS]

GERBERT VON HORNAU, MARTIN

Liturgist whose collection of medieval music-theory texts, *Scriptores ecclesiastici de musica sacra potissimum,* opened the way for scholarship in medieval music; b. Horb am Neckar, Germany, Aug. 12, 1720; d. St. Blaise (Schwarzwald), May 13, 1791. He studied philosophy and theology at the Abbey of St. Blaise and there was professed as a Benedictine (1737), ordained (1744), and elected abbot (1764). As abbey librarian he was intrigued by its MS treatises dealing with music theory and history, and thereafter he made extensive researches in France, Switzerland, southern Germany, and Italy, gathering musical and liturgical MSS of the Middle Ages (his *Iter Alemannicum,* 1765, recounts his travels). He projected a scholarly history of chant and sacred music, but its first printing and almost all his materials were lost in a fire at the abbey in 1768. Finally, in 1774 it appeared in two volumes as *De cantu et musica sacra a prima ecclesiae aetate usque ad praesens tempus.* The second volume of J. N. Forkel's *Allgemeine Geschichte der Musik* borrows heavily from this work. In 1784 Von Hornau issued the three-volume *Scriptores . . . ,* considered one of the greatest single achievements in the monastic tradition. It was continued in Coussemaker's *Scriptorum de musica mediiaevi* (1864). Von Hornau published also several important liturgical works, such as *Vetus liturgia Alemannica* (2 v. 1776) and *Monumenta veteris liturgiae Alemannicae* (2 v. 1777), and anticipated 19th-century church-music reforms by restoring plainchant in his own community. His position as prince-abbot, together with his musicological achievement, engaged him in correspondence and contact with many great personalities of his time, among them G. B. ''Padre'' MARTINI, J. J. ROUSSEAU, Empress MARIA THERESA, and Pope PIUS VI.

Bibliography: M. GERBERT VON HORNAU, *Die Korrespondenz des Fürstabts,* ed. G. PFEILSCHIFTER, 3 v. (Karlsruhe 1931–34). C. GROSSMANN, ''Fürstabt M. Gerbert als Musikhistoriker,'' *Kirchenmusikalisches Jahrbuch* 27 (1932) 123–134. F. NIECKS, ''Martin Gerbert: Priest, Prince, Scholar and Musician,'' *Musical Times* (1882) 585–588, 646–649. H. HÜSCHEN, *Die Musik in Geschichte und Gegenwart* 4:1783. H. LECLERCQ, *Dictionnaire d'archéologie chrétienne et de liturgie* 6.1:1036–49. B. HEURTEBIZE, *Dictionnaire de théologie catholique* 6:1294–96. C. F. POHL, *Grove's Dictionary of Music and Musicians* 3:598–599. F. L. HARRISON et al., *Musicology* (Englewood Cliffs, N.J. 1963). G. REESE, *Music in the Middle Ages.*

[I. WORTMAN]

GERBET, OLYMPE PHILIPPE

Philosopher, theologian, bishop, precursor of social Catholicism in France; b. Poligny (Jura), Feb. 5, 1798; d. Perpignan, Aug. 8, 1864. He studied at the Académie and the Grand Seminaire of Besançon, at Saint-Sulpice, and at the Sorbonne, and was ordained in 1822. He was an enthusiastic admirer of Félicité de Lamennais and collaborated with him in *L'Avenir* until its suppression in 1834; he withdrew from his circle in 1836. Meanwhile, he published several philosophical works. The first of importance, *Des Doctrines philosophiques sur la certitude, dans leurs rapports avec les fondements de la théologie* (Paris 1826), was a critique of Cartesianism in philosophical explanations of the acquisition of faith. His concern for the social question was evident in two published conferences, each titled *Introduction à la philosophie de l'histoire* (Paris 1832); anticipating the *Communist Manifesto,* as it were, he argued that the workers had ended feudalism by their revolutionary activity but had been deprived of the fruits of this victory. He is credited with responsibility for the initial social emphasis of *L'Université catholique.* In 1839 he went to Rome, where he spent ten years, publishing *Esquisse de Rome chrétienne* (2 v. Paris 1844–50) and adopting increasingly conservative views. After returning from Rome, he became successively professor of sacred eloquence at the Sorbonne, vicar-general of Amiens, and, in December 1853, bishop of Perpignan. He gave expression to his timidity about social change in essays published in 1850 under the title ''Rapports du rationalisme avec le communisme,'' in which he was especially apprehensive about the organizational implications of socialism. His episcopate was marked by the holding of a synod, the reorganization of clerical studies, various religious foundations, and above all a famous pastoral instruction of 1860 *sur diverses erreurs du temps present,* which pleased PIUS IX and influenced the preparation of his SYLLABUS OF ERRORS.

Bibliography: *Oeuvres,* 2 v. (Paris 1876). C. DE LADOUE, *Monseigneur Gerbet: Sa vie, ses oeuvres et l'école menaisienne,* 3 v. (Paris 1870). L. FOUCHER, *La Philosophie catholique en France au XIXe Siècle* (Paris 1955).

[E. T. GARGAN]

Olympe Philippe Gerbet.

GERBILLON, JEAN FRANÇOIS

Second superior general of the French Mission to China, 1700–06; b. Verdun, June 11, 1654; d. Pekin, March 22, 1707. He entered the novitiate at Nancy of the Champagne Province of the Society of Jesus on Oct. 6, 1670. Chosen by Father de Fontaney, the superior, to be a member of the first group of French Jesuits sent to China by Louis XIV, he arrived there in July 1687. He gained the esteem of Emperor K'ang-Hsi, lived at the court in Pekin, and instructed the emperor in the elements of geometry and philosophy. He was sent by the emperor with Father Tomás PEREIRA to accompany the Chinese ambassadors to Nerchinsk, where in 1689 the first Russo-Chinese peace treaty was concluded. In the negotiations that led up to the signing of the treaty the two Jesuits were interpreters and advisers. Gerbillon, who accompanied the emperor eight times into Tartary, supervised the building and ornamentation of the French Church at Pekin. After its completion in 1703 Gerbillon did ministerial work in Pekin until his death.

Bibliography: C. SOMMERVOGEL, *Bibliotèque de la Compagnie de Jésus* 3:1346–48. L. PFISTER, *Notices biographiques et bibliographiques,* 2 v. (Shanghai 1932–34).

[E. HAGEMANN]

GERHARD, JOHANN

German Lutheran theologian; b. Quedlinburg, Oct. 17, 1582; d. Jena, Aug. 17, 1637. Although strongly influenced by the theologian and mystic Johann Arndt, he became one of the staunchest supporters of Lutheran orthodoxy. After completing his studies (philosophy, medicine, and theology) at Wittenberg, Marburg, and Jena, he was appointed superintendent of the churches of Heldburg in the Duchy of Coburg in 1606. He became professor of theology in 1616 at Jena where he remained, despite many calls from other universities, until his death.

He played a prominent role from 1621 to 1630 in directing the unsuccessful work of the movement to develop a supreme tribunal of the Lutheran Church. His theological system, as contained in his *Loci theologici* (9 v. 1610–22), is the culmination of Lutheran dogma initiated by Melanchthon and, as such, the most authoritative work of the age of orthodoxy following the *Formula of Concord* (1577). His *Confessio catholica* (four parts, 1634–37) is an extensive apology and polemic of the Evangelical creed, in which an attempt is made to prove the truth of Lutheran doctrine by citing the testimony of Roman Catholic writers. He is noted also for his exegetical and devotional writings.

Bibliography: J. GERHARD and M. CHEMNITZ, *The Doctrine of Man in Classical Lutheran Theology,* ed. H. A. PREUS and E. SMITS, tr. M. COLACCI et al. (Minneapolis 1962). E. R. FISCHER, *Vita I. Gerhardi* (Leipzig 1723). F. LAU, *Die Religion in Geschichte und Gegenwart* 2: 1412–13. Y. CONGAR, *Catholicisme: Hier, aujord'hui et demain* 4:1880. H. RENNINGS, *Lexikon für Theologie und Kirche* 4:724.

[C. J. BERSCHNEIDER]

GERHARDINGER, KAROLINA ELIZABETH FRANCES, BL.

In religious life, Maria Theresia of Jesus, Theresa of Jesus, founder of the School Sisters of Notre Dame; b. June 20, 1797, Stadtamhof (near Regensburg), Bavaria, Germany; d. May 9, 1879, Munich, Bavaria, Germany.

Karolina was the only child of Willibald Gerhardinger, a ship master on the Danube, and Frances Huber. She attended the cloister school of the Congregation de Notre Dame until they were forced to disband by government order in 1809. Michael Wittmann, cathedral pastor and later bishop of Regensburg, continued the King's School for Girls with three apprentice teachers, including Karolina. At 15 she received her government certificate and began teaching in the parish school at Stadtamhof. At 18 she told the bishop she would like to become a nun. Only then did he reveal his wish to see founded the kind of religious institute that St. Peter FOURIER had planned but that the Church and the world of the 17th century had been unready to accept—a community of teaching sisters who would not be confined to monasteries and thus could teach in poor villages.

Rev. Matthias Siegert, who was commissioned by Bishop Wittmann to study the new pedagogy pioneered by Pestalozzi, became educational and spiritual director of the new congregation, in which Karolina's ''Teresian spirit'' flowered and her teaching genius matured. Only in 1833 was she allowed to take her vows, after the state and ecclesiastical authorities were convinced her community could maintain itself. Gerhardinger opened the first house in Neunburg vom Wald (Oberpfalz) joined by two other women, Maria Blass and Barbara Weinzierl. They lived a common life in poverty dedicated to the Blessed Virgin Mary, the model for her sisters and young girls. The congregation received episcopal sanction in 1834 and spread quickly to small towns and villages throughout Germany, 13 other European countries, and abroad. In 1843 the mother house was established at Munich in a convent given to them by King Louis Philippe. In 1847, Mother Gerhardinger and five sisters migrated to the mountains of Pennsylvania to teach children of German immigrants. Although they were unwelcome there, St. John NEUMANN paved the way for a better reception in Baltimore. In America they endured hunger and other hardships, but nevertheless spread throughout the eastern United States. After two years in the United States Gerhardinger returned to Bavaria.

Gerhardinger pioneered a new form of religious life. The sisters were sent out in twos or threes so that they could serve in many small communities. Mother Maria Theresia insisted that the sisters be allowed to direct themselves under a central government, rather than being placed under the control of the local bishop, in order to maintain a common spirituality without a physical community life. Although the sisters found opposition to the new concept, the institute was formally recognized by the Vatican in 1854. Pope Pius IX in 1865 approved the constitution which was the first to allow a sister to govern the members of the women's congregation. For the rest of her life she actively fostered the education of girls and oversaw the growth of her community. Pope John Paul II beatified her on Nov. 17, 1985 and named her patron of Christian educators.

Feast: May 9.

Bibliography: *Acta Apostolicae Sedis* 79 (1987): 243–247. *L'Osservatore Romano,* Eng. ed., no. 47 (1985). F. FRIESS, *Life of Reverend Mother Mary Teresa of Jesus Gerhardinger* (Baltimore 1921). C. GRÖN, *Eine Frau steht am Steuer* (Munich 1962). M. D. MAST, *Through Caroline's Consent* (Baltimore 1958). *Mother Caroline and the School Sisters of Notre Dame in North America,* 2 v. (St. Louis 1928). T. SCHMIDKONZ, *Du Gott. Gebets–Meditationen zu Worten von M. Theresia von Jesu Gerhardinger* (St. Ottilien, Germany 1985). *Selige Theresia von Jesu Gerhardinger (1797–1879): ein Leben für Kirche und Schule zum 200. Geburtstag . . .* (Regensburg 1997).

[M. D. MAST]

GERHOH OF REICHERSBERG

Polemist, Gregorian reformer, statesman, theological writer; b. Polling, Bavaria, 1093–94; d. Reichersberg, June 27, 1169. He studied in Freising and Moosburg and in the school at Hildesheim. Bishop Herman of Augsburg appointed him master of the school in Augsburg and canon of the cathedral, though Gerhoh was only a deacon (1118–19). For years Gerhoh was deeply involved in the turbulent conflicts of the Church and the Holy Roman Empire (*see* GREGORIAN REFORM), and while still at Augsburg he sided with Pope CALLISTUS II against his simoniacal bishop who favored the imperial party. In 1122, however, Gerhoh was influential in reconciling the bishop to the Pope. After the First LATERAN COUNCIL rejected his proposal for a reform of the clergy based on a communal life for all clergy, Gerhoh withdrew (1124) to the monastery of the CANONS REGULAR OF ST. AUGUSTINE in Rottenbuch. There he immediately became an enthusiastic reformer, making a special journey to Rome with several confreres to obtain a true and complete version of the Rule of St. AUGUSTINE for the monastery. Two years later (1126) Gerhoh left this monastery and went to Regensburg at the request of Bishop Kuno, who ordained him priest. But Church-State conflict there compelled Gerhoh to flee the diocese (1128); at this time he began his literary career with the *Liber de aedificio Dei,* on reform of canons. After the death of Kuno, he was received into the Church of Salzburg by Archbishop Conrad I. In 1132 Gerhoh was appointed provost of the Austin monastery of Reichersberg, a position he held until his death. A frequent emissary to Rome, Gerhoh came to know BERNARD OF CLAIRVAUX. During the schism of 1160, Gerhoh refused to support the imperial papal candidate, antipope Victor IV, and adhered instead to Pope ALEXANDER III. For this he was banned in 1166 by Emperor FREDERICK I and forced to flee his monastery.

Gerhoh's works (many of which are in *Patrologia latina* 194, 198) deal especially with the reform of the clergy and relations between CHURCH AND STATE. They discuss the validity of Sacraments conferred by excommunicated priests. Gerhoh generally opposed such prescholastics as ABELARD, GILBERT DE LA PORRÉE, PETER LOMBARD, and Folmar; his polemical writings against Abelard and Gilbert caused him often to consider the human nature assumed by Christ (*see* INCARNATION). His numerous letters are a valuable source of knowledge concerning Church-State relations in his epoch. Gerhoh's lengthiest and most important work, *Expositio in Psalmis* [ed. D. van den Eynde and A. Rijmersdael (Rome 1955–56)], is a commentary divided into ten parts of unequal length, the fifth part of which is now lost. This work, begun in 1144 or early 1145, and finished in 1169, is full of digressions that often have little connection with the Biblical text but that amount to actual treatises on dogmatic and moral theology, Church discipline, Canon Law, liturgy, and monastic life. Gerhoh borrowed his views on these matters mostly from the writings of his contemporaries RUPERT OF DEUTZ, HUGH OF SAINT-VICTOR, and Bernard. For the commentary itself he depended especially on Augustine, Gregory the Great in the collection of Paterius, and the glosses of Rupert, Gilbert, and ANSELM OF LAON.

Bibliography: Sources. GERHOH OF REICHERSBERG . . . , *Libelli selecti,* ed. E. SACKUR, *Monumenta Germaniae Historica: Libelli de lite* 3:131–525. *Magni presbyteri annales Reicherspergenses,* ed. W. WATTENBACH, *Monumenta Germaniae Historica: Scriptores* 17:490–499. *Vita,* in *Patrologia latina* E. MARTÈNE and U. DURAND, *Thesaurus novus anecdotorum* 193:481–488. E. MARTÈNE and U. DURAND, *Thesaurus novus anecdotorum* 5:1457–60. Literature. *Dictionnaire de théologie catholique* Tables générales 1802. D. VAN DEN EYNDE, *L'Oeuvre, littéraire de Géroch de Reichersberg* (Rome 1957); *Lexicon für Theologie und Kirche* 2 4:725–726. E. MEUTHEN, *Kirche und Heilsgeschichte bei Gerhoh von R.* (Leiden 1959).

[C. E. SHEEDY]

GERLACH, ST.

Hermit; b. Houthem, Limburg, Netherlands, *c.* 1100; d. Houthem, *c.* 1177. Like most young nobles of his class he was trained in CHIVALRY and knighted, but after the tragic accidental death of his wife, he disposed of his estates and set out as a poor pilgrim for Rome. Pope EUGENE III listened to his story of repentance and approved of his plan to spend seven years in the Holy Land caring for the poor and sick. On his return he sought the permission of the new pope, ADRIAN IV, to allow him to return to his native town and there continue his life of reparation and good works. At Houthen, in a PREMONSTRATENSIAN habit, he lived as an anchorite in a huge hollow oak tree. His life of mortification and prayer aroused suspicion, and on the rumor that he had gold hidden in his cell some of his critics with episcopal approval razed the oak. Only after his death did his neighbors begin to recognize his virtues, and *c.* 1200 Goswin IV of Heinsberg-Valkenburg was instrumental in the establishment of a church and hospital at Houthem dedicated to Gerlach. The Premonstratensians claim the saint as one of their own, although at best he could only have been a member of the Third Order by wearing the habit. Pope PIUS IX approved his feast for the Dioceses of Cologne, Liège, and Roermond.

Feast: Jan. 5.

Bibliography: *Acta Sanctorum* Jan 1:304–321. G. CRIPIO, *Vita sancti Gerlaci* is summarized in J. LE PAIGE, *Bibliotheca Praemonstratensis ordinis* (Paris 1633) 496. F. WESSELMAN, *Der hl. Gerlach von Houthem* (Steyl 1897). F. A. HOUCK, *The Life of Saint Gerlach* (London 1900). C. DAMEN, *Publications de la Société historique dans le Limbourg* (Limburg 1956–57) 92; 93:49–113. *Bibliotheca hagiographica latina antiquae et mediae aetatis* 3449.

[L. L. RUMMEL]

GERMAIN, ST.

Germain, St., 6th-century bishop of Paris; b. near Autun, France, *c.* 496; d. Paris, May 28, 576. Germain became an anchorite early in life, was ordained by Bishop Agrippinus (*c.* 530), and appointed administrator by Bp. Nectarius of Paris and then abbot of the monastery of St. Symphorian near Autun. In 555 Germain was elected bishop of Paris; during his episcopate he continued to practice the rigorous life he had begun in the monastery as abbot. He presided over the third and fourth Councils of Paris (557 and 573) and attended the second Council of Tours in 566. He was credited with having miraculously restored King Childebert to health; with the monarch's aid he founded the celebrated abbey later known as Saint-Germain-des-Pres. Noted for his charity and learning, Germain befriended SS. Radegunda and Fortunatus and exerted great pressure to bring peace and stable government to the MEROVINGIAN kingdom. The last years of his life were shadowed by the crimes and scandals of Clotaire's sons. In fact he had to excommunicate Charibet as an incorrigible adulterer. Germain died in his 81st year and was buried in the chapel of St. Symphorian in the vestibule of the abbey. In 754 his relics were solemnly moved into the body of the church by Bishop Eligius, in the presence of King Pepin and his son Charlemagne, who was then only a boy of seven. The relics were destroyed in 1795. His vita was written in verse by Venantius FORTUNATUS.

Feast: May 28.

Bibliography: VENANTOUS FORTUNATUS, *Vita*, ed. B. KRUSCH (*Monumenta Germaniae Historica, Scriptores rerum Merovingicarum* 7.1; 1919) 332–428. *Analecta Bollandiana* 2 (1883) 69–98. A. RODEWYK, *Lexikon für Theologie und Kirche* (Freiburg, 1957–66) 4:756–757. O. HOLDER-EGGER, *Neues Archiv der Gesellschaft für ältere deutsche Geschichtskunde* 18 (1893) 274–281. J. L. BAUDOT and L. CHAUSSIN, *Vies des saints et des bienheureux selon l'ordre du calendrier avec l'historique des jêtes,* ed. by the Benedictines of Paris (Paris 1935–56) 5:546–550. Y. CHAUSSY, *Catholicisme* 4:1885–86. A. WILMART, *Dictionnaire d'archéologie chrétienne et de liturgie,* ed. F. CABROL, H. LECLERCQ, and H. I. MARROU (Paris 1907–53) 6.1:1049–1102.

[D. KELLER]

GERMAIN OF AUXERRE, ST.

Bishop of Auxerre; b. Auxerre, *c.* 378; d. Ravenna, July 31, 448. This son of a distinguished Gallo-Roman family received the best education available in Gaul, completed his training in rhetoric and law at Rome, and entered the imperial civil service. In Rome he married a lady of high station. Some time later he was sent to northwestern Gaul (Armorica) as a *dux*, or military governor. On the death of St. AMATOR, bishop of Auxerre, in 418, he was elected, much against his will, as his successor. Germain adopted an austere way of life and spent his ample private fortune in erecting or endowing churches and monasteries and on works of charity. With St. MARTIN OF TOURS he was the founder of cenobitic monasticism (*see* CENOBITISM) in Gaul. In 429 he and St. LUPUS OF TROYES were sent by Pope CELESTINE I and the Gallic bishops to combat Pelagianism in Britain; and in 447 he went on a second mission for the same purpose. He felt that an educated clergy was needed to deal effectively with heretics and stressed the formation of clerics in both Britain and Gaul. He went to Arles to plead with the highest Roman authority in Gaul for an alleviation of tax burdens for his people and apparently was successful in obtaining redress. In 448, to prevent government reprisal for a revolt in Armorica, he made the long journey to RAVENNA to seek a pardon from Emperor VALENTINIAN III and his mother, Galla Placidia, who had a strong influence on the young emperor. Germain died there as he was preparing to return to Auxerre. There is a probability that St. PATRICK spent some years at Auxerre and was ordained by Amator and consecrated by Germain. Germain's vita was written by Constantius of Lyons only some 30 years after his death.

Feast: Aug. 3; July 31.

See Also: MARTYROLOGY, ROMAN.

Bibliography: CONSTANTIUS, *Vita,* ed. W. LEVISON. *Monumenta Germaniae Historica: Scriptores rerum Merovingicarum* 7.1:1919 225–283. R. BORIUS, ed. and tr. *Constance de Lyon: Vie de saint Germain d' Auxerre* (*Sources Chrétiennes* 112; 1965). *Bibliotheca hagiographica latina antiquae et mediae aetatis* 3453–64. P. VIARD, *Catholicisme* 4:1882–84. A. BUTLER, *The Lives of the Saints* (New York 1956) 3:251–253. W. LEVISON, ''Bischof Germanus von Auxerre und die Quellen zu seiner Geschichte,'' *Neues Archiv der Gesellschaft für ältere deutsche Geschichts Kunde* 29 (Hanover 1904) 95–175. *St. Germain et son temps* (studies pub. by Assoc. Bourguignonne des Sociétés Savantes after its 1948 meeting; Auxerre 1950). M. MIELE, *La Vita germani di Costanzo di Lione: realt storica e prospettive storiografiche nella Gallia del quinto secolo* (Rome 1996). E. A. THOMPSON, *Saint Germanus of Auxerre and the End of Roman Britain* (Woodbridge, Suffolk 1984). L. BIELER, *The Life and Legend of St. Patrick* (Dublin 1949) 93–96, 104–106. P. GROSJEAN, ''Notes d'hagiographie celtique,'' *Analecta Bollandiana* 75 (1957) 158–175.

[M. R. P. MCGUIRE]

GERMAINE OF PIBRAC, ST.

Virgin; b. Pibrac, France, 1579; d. there, June 1, 1601. Her mother died when she was eight. Her stepmother hated Germaine, and under the pretense of protecting her own children from scrofula, which Germaine had contracted, forced her to sleep in the stable with the sheep. For most of the rest of her life the shepherdess suffered the rigors of the seasons and family neglect. Among legendary accounts is one of Germaine's placing her staff on the ground while she attended daily Mass, her sheep remaining unharmed in a wolf-infested area. Extraordinary incidents and the girl's unusual patience and kindness brought respect and reverence from derisive villagers. Her stepmother relented also, and shortly before Germaine's death permitted her to rejoin the family. However, Germaine preferred the solitude of the stable, where she died. In 1644 when Germaine's grave was opened to receive another corpse, her body was incorrupt. The movement for beatification, interrupted by the French Revolution, was later resumed. In 1854 PIUS X proclaimed her blessed and in 1857, a saint.

Feast: June 15.

Bibliography: H. GHÉON, *St. Germaine of the Wolf Country*, tr. F. J. SHEED (London 1932). A. STOLZ, *The Life of St. Germana*, tr. N. GROTH (Little Falls, Minn. 1936).

[C. LYNCH]

GERMANIC RELIGION

The sources for the study of the religion and mythology of the old Germanic (Teutonic) peoples are few. They consist chiefly of Greek, Roman, and medieval writings, runic inscriptions, folklore, laws, and the vitae of early missionaries. The *Germania* of Tacitus is especially important as a source. It took more than 700 years, from the 4th century in the South (Gothi) to the end of the 10th century in the North (Scandinavia), to displace the pagan Germanic religion by Christianity, and some superstitions continued to flourish much longer. Despite the progressive differentiation in language and customs that developed among the many Germanic tribes in the course of centuries, there are many religious traits shared by all.

Gods and Forms of Worship. From the earliest times the Germani believed in a number of gods in anthropomorphic form. Although there was no uniform cult among the various tribes, many of the same deities seem to have been known to all tribes. The central figure of the cult, taking the highest place among all gods, was Wodan, the All-Father, the Scandinavian Odin. After him came Donar, the North Germanic Thor. Another important deity was Tiu or Ziu (Alemannic Zîstac), the Nordic Týr. Next to these male deities was Freya, Wodan's wife, the Scandinavian Frigga. The names Tiu, Wodan, Thor, and Freya are preserved in our days of the week: Tuesday, Wednesday, Thursday, and Friday.

The forms of worship for these and many other deities were prayers, and sacrifices of fruit, animals, and even human beings. The Germani first worshipped under the open sky in forests and groves and later, under Roman influence, in houses and temples. Unlike the Celts, they had no special class of priests. Nevertheless, because of the intimate relationship of state, law, and religion, priests enjoyed great prestige and exercised much power; they directed the sacrifices and consulted the oracles in public assemblies.

Minor Divinities and Spirits. Common to all tribes was the primitive belief in the magic power of nature and of the spirits of the dead. Almost every natural element was personified, given human or animal form, and worshipped as a divinity. Among the unfriendly divinities were the giants of the mountains, the nixes and nixies, or water sprites, the kobolds or trolls of house and cave, the elves of the wind, the brownies of the field, the mermen and mermaids of the sea, the dwarfs under the earth, and many other demon-like creatures. Friendlier divinities or supernatural beings of lower degree were the Norns (the Norse Fates), the Valkyries (Choosers of the Slain), and numerous other familiar and attendant spirits.

According to Germanic cosmogony, in the beginning there was an original profound abyss, out of which first came Niflheim (frozen reaches), Muspellsheim (arid reaches), and then finally the giants, gods, and ultimately men. In Norse eschatology, the stars will fall from heaven, the earth will sink into the ocean; and in a bloody battle all gods, giants, and men will perish in flames, but a new and better world will be born out of the ashes.

Bibliography: D. E. M. CLARKE and N. KERSHAW, *Encyclopedia of Religion and Ethics* ed. J. HASTINGS (Edinburgh 1908–27) 12:246–259. A. CLOSS, *Christus und die Religionen der Erde: Handbuch der Religionsgeschichte*, ed. F. KÖNIG (Vienna 1961) 2:267–366. G. DUMÉZIL, *Mythes et dieux des Germains* (Paris 1939). M. BOUCHER, "Les Germains," in *Histoire des religions*, ed. M. BRILLANT and R. AIGRAIN (Paris 1953–56) 5:135–199. E. TONNELAT, "La Religion des Germains," *"Mana": Introduction à l'histoire des religions* (Paris 1944—) 2.3:321–385. C. CLEMEN, ed., *Fontes historiae religionis Germanicae* (Bonn 1928). R. MUCH, *Paulys Realenzyklopädie der klassischen Altertumswissenschaft*, ed. G. WISSOWA, et al. (Stuttgart 1893—) 3:579–585. W. BAETKE, *Die Religion in Geschichte und Gegenwart* (Tübingen 1957–65) 2:1432–40. J. DE VRIES, *Altgermanische Religionsgeschichte* (Berlin 1956–58).

[C. SELMER]

GERMANUS I, PATRIARCH OF CONSTANTINOPLE, ST.

Patriarchate 715–730, Mariologist and controversialist; b. Constantinople, *c.* 634. His father, Justinian, of a noble family, was a favorite of Emperor HERACLIUS (610–641) but lost favor with succeeding emperors and was executed for conspiracy in 668. Germanus was made an eunuch and forced to join the clergy of HAGIA SOPHIA, where he gradually rose to a leading position. He exercised great influence on the Emperor CONSTANTINE IV in the convocation of the Ecumenical Council of CONSTANTINOPLE III (681), which condemned MONOTHELITISM.

Germanus was appointed to the metropolitan See of Cyzicus *c.* 706, but was accused of yielding to the threats of Emperor Philippicus and of signing the Monothelite decrees of a synod in 712. He was made patriarch of Constantinople on Aug. 11, 715, by the Orthodox Emperor Anastasius II and in the same year rejected Monothelitism in a local synod. Germanus was deposed *c.* 730 for his opposition to Emperor Leo III's (the Isaurian) edict favoring ICONOCLASM. He later wrote his only extant historical work (many of his works were destroyed by iconoclastic emperors), *De haeresibus et synodis,* treating of the major heresies from Simon Magus to the iconoclasm of his own day. He was posthumously condemned by the iconoclastic synod of 754, and his name was erased from the diptychs, but it was finally reinstated by the seventh ecumenical council (787). Three of his ''dogmatic'' letters controvert iconoclasm and are cited in the decrees of the eighth ecumenical council; the fourth letter, *Ad Armenos,* defends the Council of CHALCEDON. He is credited with nine homilies, seven witnessing the development of Marian doctrines.

Feast: May 12.

Bibliography: *Germano di Capua: ambasciatore ecumenico a Costantinopoli e modello di santit per il Cassinate* (Venafro, Isernia 1999). L. LAMZA, *Patriarch Germanos I. von Konstantinopel* (Wörzburg 1975). *Patrologia Graeca* 98:39–454. F. CAYRÉ, *Dictionnaire de théologie catholique* (Paris 1903–50) 6.2:1300–09. B. ALTANER, *Patrology* (New York 1960) 634–635. F. L. CROSS, *The Oxford Dictionary of the Christian Church* (London 1957) 552.

[F. DE SA]

GERMANUS II, PATRIARCH OF CONSTANTINOPLE

1222 to 1240; b. Anaplai (Propontis), *c.* 1175; d. Constantinople, 1240. As a deacon of HAGIA SOPHIA, he took refuge in the monastery of St. George of Achyranus during the Latin siege of Constantinople in 1204. The Emperor JOHN III Ducas Vatatzes had him elected patriarch in 1222. Following the fall of Constantinople to the Latins (1204) the Byzantine Empire was in danger of being split into many independent principalities; that fate threatened the Byzantine Church. Germanus attempted to prevent such schisms, and wrote to Pope GREGORY IX with a view toward union of the Churches. At the instigation of the emperor, he received envoys from Rome at Nicaea in 1231, but soon concluded to the impossibility of an understanding. In Cyprus he favored the conciliating attitude of Archbishop Neophytus, which caused difficulties between 1229 and 1231. He recognized the title of patriarch of the Bulgarians assumed by the archbishop of Trnovo in 1235, but would not concede that the Bulgarian Church should become autocephalous. He worked for reunion with the Armenians, but his death prevented a successful conclusion. He was buried in the monastery of Kyriotissa in Nicaea. Of his writings, many still unedited, those dealing with the azymes, purgatory, and the filioque display an anti-Latin feeling; but his letters and homilies testify to his zeal and pastoral care; and he may have been the author of some poetry.

Bibliography: GERMANUS II, *Homiliae, Patrologia Graeca,* ed. J. P. MIGNE (Paris 1857–66) 140:621–751; *Orationes, ibid.* 98:221–384. K. BAUS, *Lexikon für Theologie und Kirche,* ed. J. HOFER and K. RAHNER, 10 v. (2d, new ed. Freiburg 1957–65) 4:754–755. J. A. FRABRICIUS and C. C. HARLES, *Bibliotheca Graeca,* 12 v. (4th ed. Hamburg 1790–1809) 9:162. M. RONCAGLIA, *Les Frères mineurs et l'Église orthodoxe au XIIIe siècle* (Cairo 1954). D. M. NICOL, *The Despotate of Epiros* (Oxford 1957).

[P. JOANNOU]

GERMANUS OF MÜNSTER-GRANFELDEN, ST.

Abbot; b. Trier, *c.* 610; d. Feb. 21, 675. Son of a senator and reared, after his father's death, by St. Modoald, bishop of Trier (d. *c.* 640), Germanus first became a disciple of St. ARNULF OF METZ. He later transferred from Arnulf's monastery at REMIREMONT to LUXEUIL, whose abbot, St. Walbert (d. *c.* 668), recommended him to Duke Gondo, who was seeking an abbot for a new monastery founded at Münster-Granfelden. Germanus ruled the abbey for 35 years. He vigorously opposed the oppression of the peasants by Boniface, Gondo's brother and successor. Boniface murdered Germanus and his companion Randoald *c.* 675. Germanus's relics, along with his crosier, are preserved in the parish church of Helsberg.

Feast: Feb. 21.

Bibliography: *Monumenta Germaniae Historica: Scriptores rerum Germanicarum* 5:25–40. *Bibliotheca hagiographica latina antiquae et mediae aetatis* 3467. *Acta Sanctorum* Feb3:266–269. A. REIS, *Moutier-Grandval* (Biel 1940). A. BUTLER, *The Lives of the Saints* (New York 1956) 1:385. G. HASELOFF, *''Der Abtsstab des hl. G.,'' Germania* 33 (1955) 210–235. R. MOSSBRUGGER, *Ur-Schweiz* 20 (1956) 54–60. S. KOFFER, *La crosse merovingienne de Saint Germain, premier abbé de Moutier-Grandval* (Porrentruy 1996).

[M. B. RYAN]

GERMANY, THE CATHOLIC CHURCH IN

Located in western Europe, the Federal Republic of Germany is bordered on the north by the Baltic Sea and Denmark, on the northeast by the North Sea, on the east by Poland and the Czech Republic, on the southeast by Austria, on the southwest by Switzerland and France, and on the west by Luxembourg, Belgium and the Netherlands. Containing a wealth of natural resources—coal, lignite, salt, natural gas, iron ore and other minerals—as well as some of the most beautiful forests and meadowlands, Germany is also the wealthiest nation in western Europe. Heavily industrialized, its exports include electronics, automobiles, chemicals, optical and scientific instruments, and pharmaceutical products. With its fertile soil, Germany also produces agricultural crops of potatoes, sugar beets, wheat, barley and grapes, the last of which provides the basis for another of the country's chief exports: wine.

Capital: Berlin.
Size: 138,000 sq. miles.
Population: 82,797,408 in 2000.
Languages: German.
Religions: 31,463,015 Catholics (38%), 1,407,555 Muslims (1.7%), 30,975,440 Protestants (38%), 75,000 Jews (.01%), 900,000 Orthodox (1%), 17,976,398 other or without religious affiliation.

The following essay is in four parts. The first part treats the history of the Catholic Church in Germany from the period of Christian origins to 1500, the second from 1500 to 1789, the third from 1789 to 1900, and the fourth from 1900 to the present.

From the Beginnings to the Reformation

Throughout its early history, Germany and the Teutonic tribes of its traditional territory were subjected to a variety of influences from the civilizations to the south.

The Roman Period. From 58 to 38 B.C. Julius Caesar and then Agrippa forced the Germanic Ubii tribes west of the Rhine, resulting in the colonization of that area by Germans and remnant Celtic peoples. A similar situation occurred in the area of the confluence of the Rhine and the Main. Military conquests Romanized the new provinces of Belgica, Germania inferior ("Lower Rhine") and Germania superior ("Upper Rhine"), as well as the newly won provinces south of the Danube, Raetia and Noricum. To these were added the Agri Decumates, protected by the limes running from the Rhine to the Danube. Like other parts of the Roman Empire, these provinces were now opened to Christianity, which, in the period of peace and prosperity following the 2d century, gained a scattered foothold in the larger settlements through the efforts of merchants and soldiers from Lugdunum.

By the end of the 3d century there were bishops in the imperial city of Trier, and at the beginning of the 4th century in Cologne (probably also in Mainz and Augsburg). The flowering of Christianity after the Church attained her freedom (313) is seen in the participation of the bishops of Worms, Speyer, Strassburg, Augst (Basel), Metz and Tongeren in the synods of the later Arian period; the mention of bishops from Noricum by Athanasius; the erection of churches (St. Severin, St. Gereon, St. Ursula in Cologne); and in numerous archeological finds (bowls and gold glasses with Christian symbols and inscriptions). The creation of a metropolitan organization (COLOGNE, TRIER, Mainz, Milan and AQUILEIA) can only be conjectured; but the center of missionary activity was probably Trier. The migrations of the 5th century were indeed a catastrophe for these areas had apparently been completely Christianized. The succession of bishops for Mainz, Augsburg, and other cities was broken, but small Christian communities somehow managed to survive.

Christianization of Germanic Tribes. The Romanized Germans of these provinces were opposed to the independent pagan tribes of Germania Magna, which, after the ALAMANNI had breeched the limes, had been moving to the southeast since the 3d century. These wandering tribes, by penetrating farther into the Roman Empire, could not, in the long run, avoid the strong influence of Christianity and its culture. The first contact of Christianity with these tribes was with the VISIGOTHS in connection with the border fighting along the Lower Danube. At Nicaea a Gothic bishop, Theophilus, signed the conciliar decrees. After 341 ULFILAS, Bishop of the Goths, led his people to Christianity in its Arian form, because the Visigoths were at that time allies of an Arian emperor.

This superficial form of ARIANISM was retained by the Visigoths in Spain, from whom it spread to the other Germanic tribes, the Ostrogoths (*see* GOTHS), Suevi, VANDALS, LOMBARDS and Burgundians. These tribes looked upon Arianism as a national characteristic, in opposition to the Catholic faith of the natives of conquered countries, and stressed their variant outlook on Church-State relations, rather than their theological differences. From the beginning, the king ruled the Church among the Germans, and Church property remained under landlords (*see* PROPRIETARY CHURCHES). Whereas THEODORIC THE GREAT was, in general, tolerant toward Catholics in the Ostrogothic kingdom, they were subjected to bloody persecution in the Vandal kingdom of Africa. However, both the Ostrogoth and Vandal states disappeared by the mid-

Metropolitan Sees	Suffragans
Bamberg	Eichstätt, Speyer, Würzburg
Berlin	Dresden-Meissen, Görlitz
Cologne	Aachen, Essen, Limburg, Münster, Trier
Freiburg im Breisgau	Mainz, Rottenburg-Stuttgart
Hamburg	Hildesheim, Osnabrück
Munich and Freising	Augsburg, Passau, Regensburg
Paderborn	Erfult, Fulda, Magdenburg.

A military ordinariate is also located in Germany.

dle of the 6th century, the Visigoths and Lombards became Catholic *c.* 600, and by 532 the Burgundians were forced to accept the domination of the Catholic FRANKS.

By the end of the 5th century, the last shreds of Roman authority in Catholic Gaul were eliminated by the Franks. The baptism of CLOVIS (498?) quickly heralded that of the nobility, whereas the people were not thoroughly Christianized until probably the 7th century. Thus the German conquerors and their Roman subjects in the Frankish kingdom were for the first time of one faith, greatly facilitating their merger into one people and making Clovis, in the eyes of Catholics living under Arian rule, the champion of the Church. Also by virtue of this merger, the uninterrupted blending of the culture of late antiquity with German folk custom was made possible. The Frankish kingdom thus became the means of fusing the various tribes, which were henceforth to be held together by the bond of their common Catholic faith and ancient Christian culture. Accordingly, Burgundians, Visigoths and Suevi were quickly incorporated into Frankland, whose Church, to be sure, was forced to serve the political purposes of the nobility in the 8th century. The other great tribes—Alamanni, Bavarians, Thuringians and Saxons—came under the influence of Christianity after the conversion of the Franks as a result of Frankish conquest and missionary activity. So, in the case of the Alamanni after the loss of their political freedom, the estates of the king and of the Frankish nobility became Christian strongholds, and the ties of Alamannic magnates with the Frankish court occasioned many conversions. But the native missionary strength of the Frankish national Church, entirely dependent on the king, was quickly exhausted by upheavals from within the dynasty.

Nevertheless, the Merovingian court, as well as Austrasian Metz, became the base and starting point for Celtic and other missionaries. It was especially due to COLUMBAN, GALL and later PIRMIN that the mission to the Alamanni in the 7th century succeeded, leading to their conversion. The famous foundations of SANKT GALLEN, REICHENAU and others provided access to Christian culture and educational centers for these new converts. A Frankish migration to the area of the Main followed upon the conquest of the Thuringian kingdom in 531. The mission to this people reached its peak in the 7th century through the efforts of KILIAN, and *c.* 700, the East Frankish kingdom was definitively won over to Christianity. When the Bavarians entered the area bearing their name in the early 6th century, they were exposed to the strong influence of the native Roman Christian population. Nevertheless, only after they had lost political independence to the Franks was the tribe fully converted, through the efforts of Frankish (RUPERT) and Celtic (EMMERAM and CORBINIAN) missionaries. But the Church was not fully organized until the time of St. BONIFACE, the "apostle of Germany."

The completion of the mission and the organization of the Church in Germany begun by other ANGLO-SAXON missionaries was due primarily to the efforts of Boniface. The well-organized Anglo-Saxon mission among the various Germanic tribes on the Continent marked Willibrord as the apostle of the Frisians and Winfrid-Boniface as the apostle of Germany. Having worked independently in Hesse and Thuringia since 721, Boniface declared his allegiance to the pope, and according to his native custom, sought support for his work from civil authority, viz, the Frankish mayor of the palace. As archbishop and as papal legate for Germany, he created the diocesan organization that still exists in Bavaria (Freising, Passau, Regensburg, Salzburg); founded the Sees of Buraburg, Erfurt and Eichstätt; and revised Würzburg. Newly founded monasteries (e.g., FULDA) were the first centers of mission activity, and convents (e.g., Lioba) became the first institutions for the Christian education of women. As a reformer of the Frankish Church, Boniface fought SECULARIZATION OF CHURCH PROPERTY, COMMENDATION and lay control, as well as the moral degradation of bishops and priests in the Merovingian kingdom. In numerous synods, both local and general, he worked for the restitution of CHURCH PROPERTY and the establishment of the metropolitan system, but was only partly successful. On the other hand, he was able to bring the Church, entirely dependent on sectional chieftains, into closer union with Rome at the general synod of 747, and accustomed the Frankish mayors to this association with the pope.

While Boniface's role in the anointing of PEPIN may be doubted, the participation of his disciple BURCHARD OF WÜRZBURG in the legation to Rome that negotiated the change of authority with the pope was significant. With

unselfish dedication Boniface led the mission territories to independence, revived the Frankish Church and made further efforts of foreign missionaries more or less superfluous, since the Franks themselves were henceforth capable of converting the last of the German tribes, the Saxons. This had been planned by Boniface as a later objective and had already been unsuccessfully attempted by several skilled missionaries. After 30 years of military campaigns and the preaching of the faith, the Saxons finally entered the Carolingian Empire and the Catholic Church when national-pagan opposition lost its leader through the baptism of WIDUKIND. Henceforth this territory could be organized with the help of sponsoring bishoprics and abbeys. Thus *c.* 800, no less than eight sees were successively established (Bremen, soon thereafter transferred to Hamburg, Verden, Minden, Paderborn, Münster, Osnabrück, Halberstadt and Hildesheim). While these new bishoprics coincided with the territory

Cologne Cathedral, c. 1870, Cologne, Germany. (Hulton/Archive Photos)

of the various Saxon tribes, the organization of dioceses in older areas generally conformed to boundaries established in the Roman period, with the exception of Windisch, which disappeared in the south, and Constance, the largest German bishopric, which came into existence in the early 7th century. Parishes with baptismal rights also began gradually to make their appearance.

The Church in the Carolingian and Ottonian Empires. Merovingian royal control of the Church, which the Frankish king had based on Old Testament authority, and the union with Rome created by Boniface, were the foundations upon which CHARLEMAGNE, son of Pepin III, built the Church of the empire (*Reichskirche*). As king he had already assumed the task of expanding missions to the Saxons and to the Slavs on the upper Main and in the Alps, defending the faith against Arabs and Avars, and restoring and ordering the internal administration of the Church and the development of its cultural activities. Besides establishing bishoprics, he also completed the metropolitan system (Mainz, Cologne, Trier and Salzburg). Under his son Louis the Pious, Bremen-Hamburg would also become an archdiocese. The position of bishops was strengthened when Charlemagne ordered regularly held diocesan synods and employed the bishops as his *missi dominici.* He himself presided at imperial synods that made decisions on dogmatic questions, such as the FILIOQUE and the veneration of IMAGES. A passion for order prompted him to unify the LITURGY and monastic observance. Using his father's plans, Louis would make the BENEDICTINE Rule mandatory for the empire.

Above all Charlemagne interested himself in furthering the spiritual life and the education of both clergy and people. By numerous CAPITULARIES, he provided for sermons, Sunday observance and the erection of CATHEDRAL, MONASTIC and parish schools. The policies of Charlemagne's long administration, permeated with ideas dedicated to the advance of culture, created the ''Empire of the West,'' over which he presided after his coronation as emperor in 800, crowned by Pope Leo III. Prescinding from Charlemagne's personal interpretation of his office, his crowning meant not only the revival of the ROMAN EMPIRE and the dawning of the Middle Ages, but also the opportunity for him and his successors to influence the occupancy of the Roman See by confirming the election of the pope. For centuries to come, this coronation also made Germany the intellectual center of Europe and the heartland of the Church. But this event likewise caused Germany, in the following centuries, to be more deeply involved in theoretical controversies and armed conflicts over the relationship between Church and empire, pope and emperor.

The spiritual unity of the West revealed the flourishing cultural life of Charlemagne's realm, and, despite later Carolingian decline, also that of his successors. It is possible to speak of a CAROLINGIAN RENAISSANCE, even though it was hardly a creative and artistic impulse, but was rather a movement that, following the example of antiquity, confined itself to organization and collection. The court school at AACHEN and the monastic school of TOURS, under the supervision of ALCUIN, were the training grounds for generations of officials and ecclesiastical dignitaries. Here they learned classical Latin, the intellectual tool needed for their profession and also for literary work. In the academic circle of Aachen, scholars gathered from all corners of the vast empire. In his *Vita Caroli magni,* EINHARD produced the model historical biography. RABANUS MAURUS, Abbot of Fulda and Archbishop of Mainz, made the accumulated knowledge of his century accessible to his contemporaries in great anthologies. Living in the monasteries, surrounded by valuable libraries that had been enriched by copies of ancient works produced in their own SCRIPTORIA, were Otfrid of Weissenburg, the author of a Gospel harmony; the poet and liturgist WALAFRID STRABO, at Reichenau; and among the recently converted Saxons, the author of the *HELIAND*—the most significant work in the German language of that early Christian period. In theology also, the first independent attempts were made to present and defend the Augustinian theory on PREDESTINATION and to settle the controversies that had risen over the EUCHARIST (GOTTSCHALK OF ORBAIS). In Church architecture, the new form of early Romanesque came under German influence (Aachen, Seligenstadt).

While Germany's contribution to liturgy and art may be considered important, its impact on the youthful Church in the area of law was even more significant. The mentality of this era was primarily realistic and intuitive. Abstract intellectual concepts could be grasped only after lengthy and involved discussions. Thus, when a church was established, emphasis was placed, not on the singular blessings attached to the new location, but on the rights

Speyer Cathedral, c. 1030, Speyer, Germany. (©Carmen Redondo/CORBIS)

of the owner of the foundation and its property. Similarly with Church appointments, it was not so much the spiritual duties of the office that were of importance as the associated benefices and the investment with rights of office. Church property, which accumulated as a result of numerous donations, was considered a special kind of crown property, to be used by the king only in time of need. The old view of a society divided by class distinctions determined at birth was carried into the Church. The most prestigious monasteries accepted only the highest nobility, and bishops were increasingly chosen only from this class. With this practice, imperial influence grew, especially in the northwest. This influence of the king seemed justifiable, since bishops and prelates, as the administrators of sizable fiefs, were gradually endowed also with political responsibility and sovereignty.

The first climax of this development was reached in Germany under King OTTO I. In his struggle against the centrifugal tendencies of the hereditary duchies, Otto won the solid support of bishops and abbots. He gener-

St. Hedwig's Cathedral, Berlin. (©Eye Ubiquitous/CORBIS)

ously invested them with royal prerogatives (REGALIA), particularly with the title and dignity of counts, entrusted them with important offices of the realm, and demanded execution of clearly defined economic and military obligations. Among the German hierarchy were a number of outstanding personalities distinguished in the affairs of both Church and State who were able to harmonize their secular and ecclesiastical functions. Nevertheless, this double role of the lords spiritual—who actually became territorial princes by the 13th century and remained such until the Reformation, and in some cases, down to the secularization of 1803—brought with it dangers and conflicts. Despite the possibility of the effectual cooperation of both authorities, to the mutual interest of Church and State, the danger continued. Both Episcopal INVESTITURE with secular possessions and sovereign rights, and the concomitant feudalization of Church property resulted from the bestowal by the king of the symbols of spiritual power: the staff and, after HENRY III, also the ring. Such investitures were not only indicative of proprietary Church law and feudal sovereignty, but also, in the light of the theories of uniformity current in the period, seemed to deny the independence of spiritual authority and to derive that authority from royal prerogative, thus making the Church dependent upon the crown.

For years no one raised an objection to this situation. Otto I, who had saved Germany from the pagan Hungarian invasion of 955, revived the empire in 962 and consciously identified it with the German nation. With the new responsibility of an anointed and consecrated ruler, he and his successors frequently freed the papacy from the ignominious control of the factional Roman nobility (*see* CRESCENTII; TUSCULANI). While papal authority had declined, the preeminence of the emperor increased, evidenced by numerous imperial appointments of popes. Nevertheless, the Ottos and Henry III chose only worthy men. But such intervention seemed to give the appearance of dominance over the See of Peter and brought about a canonically oriented reaction against the institution of the proprietary Church and the inveterate practice of lay investiture.

The High Middle Ages. The Salian imperial house, which had recently led the CLUNIAC REFORM in Germany to victory, now witnesses a sudden outbreak of hostilities. The PAPAL ELECTION decree of 1059, by failing to mention the emperor's right of nomination, sparked the struggle, which smoldered until the days of GREGORY VII and the autocratic intervention of HENRY IV in Milan. The general investiture prohibition, decreed in 1075 for the reestablishment of ''proper order'' in the world, represented, in fact, a revolutionary attack on the foundations of the German empire. Its political structure was shaken and the source of the emperor's military and financial power was mortally threatened. The conflict between the two legal concepts and the empire's concern for survival explain the extreme bitterness of both sides in the INVESTITURE struggle. The undignified attitude of Henry hindered his party from reaching a peaceful compromise. The reform monasteries (e.g., HIRSAU) vigorously defended the papacy, whereas the bishops, with few exceptions, supported the emperor. Only after numerous defeats on both sides (the deposition of Gregory, the excommunication of Henry and his submission at Canossa) was the struggle provisionally settled in the Concordat of WORMS (1122). During the conflict both sides had learned to distinguish the secular from the religious elements involved and to assign them their respective officers.

The investiture controversy had thrust the anointed king into the secularized world, even though the age of St. BERNARD would again show how in practice the papacy and the empire could be harmonized. It is not surprising, therefore, that the Hohenstaufen attempted to trace kingship back to antiquity, whereas the popes continued to cling to the constitutional significance of coronation as performed by them. This opposition, strengthened by the problem of the enduring bond between the Sicilian crown and the empire, caused the controversy between the two supreme powers to flare up once again. In less than a century the struggle reached such uncontrolled dimensions under FREDERICK II and INNOCENT IV that it could be concluded only by the exhaustion of one of the factions. It ended with the fall of the Hohenstaufen. The dependence of the papacy on France, which followed the victory, strengthened the religious estrangement of the German Empire from the Curia. In the course of the AVIGNON PAPACY, a double imperial election led to new controversies. During the imperial interregnum, JOHN XXII claimed the right to administer the empire in Italy and to intervene decisively in the controversy over the throne. The victorious LOUIS IV, the Bavarian, was excommunicated and extensive areas of Germany were placed under interdict. As a national reaction grew against the excessive demands of the Curia, the German imperial election was made legally independent of the papacy at the Electoral Diet of Rhense in 1338 (Golden Bull, 1356).

In spite of these controversies between Church and State, the German Church remained strong. Beginning in the Carolingian period, evangelization was vigorously pursued. Christianity spread from Germany into the north, to Denmark, Sweden and Iceland; in the east to the Avars; and especially from Regensburg to the Moravians and Bohemians; from Passau it spread to Hungary; and from Salzburg to the Carentanians (Slovenes). The Diocese of Bamberg, founded by HENRY II, oversaw the evangelization of the Wends along the Main and Regnitz. The mission to the Slavs on the Elbe (Wends), whose racial animus and love of freedom constituted great obstacles, was carried out by the Archdiocese of Magdeburg, founded by Otto I, but would not be successful until after the crusade against them in the Hohenstaufen period, when the Dioceses of Merseburg, Naumburg-Zeitz and Meissen were established. Like Havelberg, Brandenburg and Lübeck, founded earlier, these dioceses, too, came under the jurisdiction of Magdeburg. OTTO OF BAMBERG was occupied with the conversion of the Pomeranians, while the Prussians and Lithuanians were Christianized principally through the efforts of the TEUTONIC KNIGHTS. Since the Second Crusade, the German rulers led CRUSADES for over a century, and both secular and religious princes participated enthusiastically and in great numbers.

The religious orders in Germany played a significant role in sustaining cultural and religious life. Among the monasteries, the most outstanding were SANKT EMMERAM in Regensburg, CORVEY, WERDEN and TRIER. The reforms of GORZE and HIRSAU eventually included almost all the German Benedictine monasteries. The CISTERCIANS and the MENDICANT orders spread quickly throughout Germany. Efforts to reestablish common life among priests led to numerous organizations of CANONS REGULAR, the best known of which were the PREMONSTRATENSIANS, founded by NORBERT OF XANTEN. Cistercians and Premonstratensians earned special recognition for colonizing and developing the north and the northeast. In the north, foundations of canonesses soon surpassed the convents of Benedictine sisters. Throughout Germany the great martial and charitable efforts of the MILITARY ORDERS were supported by donations and volunteers. In the flourishing cities, the mendicant orders were intensively active in the care of souls (*see* DOMINICANS; FRANCISCANS). They successfully guided the POVERTY MOVEMENT, threatened by heresy and radicalism, back into the fold of the Church (Tertiaries). Thus, along the Rhine and in southern Germany, heretical tendencies were easily contained by preaching and religious instruction. The convents, especially the numerous houses of DOMINICAN SISTERS, became outstanding schools and centers of mysticism. The mendicants succeeded the Benedictines, among whom special mention should be made of NOTKER LABEO and HERMANNUS CONTRACTUS, as the leaders in ecclesiastical learning. ALBERT THE GREAT won for the philosophical thought of emerging SCHOLASTICISM its earliest universal recognition. His circle of students and the Dominican general house of studies at Cologne, where Albert the Great, THOMAS AQUINAS and Meister ECKHART lectured, gave direction to the new philosophy and theology. From the beginning,

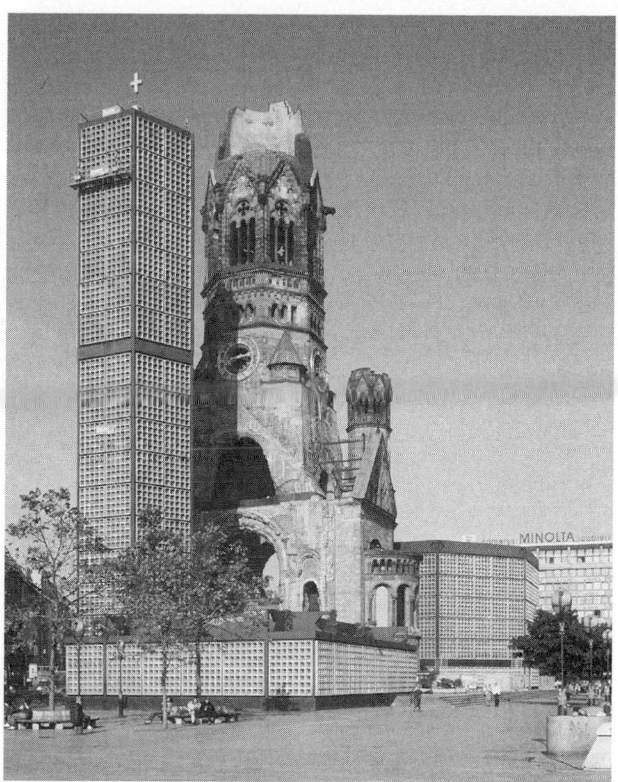

Kaiser-Wilhelm-Gedachtniskirche, Berlin. (©Vanni Archive/ CORBIS)

Cologne Cathedral, with twin Gothic spires standing unscathed among war-damaged buildings. (©Hulton/Archive Photos)

the young universities of PARIS and BOLOGNA attracted German students in great numbers. In 1348 CHARLES V founded the first German university at Prague and within the next two generations six others were established.

As a counterpart to the scholastic *summae* (*see* SENTENCES AND SUMMAE), German artistic skill in adopting Gothic style created magnificent cathedrals and churches, with a wealth of sculpture and brilliant windows. Since the days of the Hohenstaufen, a lay culture developed side by side with clerical education, often outspokenly critical of the Church (e.g., Walter von der Vogelweide).

The Pre-Reformation Crisis. During the WESTERN SCHISM almost all of Germany stood behind the Roman popes. The efforts of Emperor SIGISMUND on behalf of the Council of CONSTANCE led to the end of division within the Church. The Council of BASEL was recognized in Germany until 1438, but after a period of neutrality the emperor and the electors gave their support to EUGENE IV, who, in turn, agreed to at least some of the German demands to limit papal patronage and financial exactions (*see* GRAVAMINA). The Concordat of Vienna (1448) remained in force until the secularization of 1803. In the following decades, emperors and popes frequently shared the same political views. In contrast to France, Germany no longer officially promoted the tenets of CONCILIARISM.

On the other hand, while true reform of the Church was recognized as a necessity, the reform councils proved too weak to carry it out. The concordats with various princes settled only a few of the problems while creating others. The reform programs of outstanding churchmen, such as NICHOLAS OF CUSA and zealous preachers, such as GEILER OF KAYSERSBERG, had only local success. After the troops of the HUSSITES had invaded Germany, eschatological and revolutionary ideas were disseminated by pamphlets and even by more substantial works, giving expression to general dissatisfaction with both Church and empire. The princes, as far as it was possible within the limits of their concordats and privileges, carried out reform only if it could be effected in their own name and to the advantage of their dynasty. The papacy, on the other hand, was completely occupied with the urgency of combating the Turks, and spent tremendous sums of money promoting the arts and enhancing its own court. The general weakening of papal authority and the prejudiced attitude toward everything that came from Rome made the efforts of even sincere popes futile. The religious orders undertook to reform themselves, and were at least temporarily successful. Various reforms among the Benedictines (e.g., at BURSFELD and MELK) and among the mendicant Observants fought against the abuses of proprietorship, disregard of papal enclosure, etc. But the secular clergy, despite their attendance at the new universities, where generally they followed courses only in the arts, lacked thorough education and ecclesiastical training. Concubinage was widespread. The higher clergy, even the bishops, were excessively involved in disputes over property and benefices, were enmeshed in politics, and often led a wholly secular life. Among the people, there was much superstition (WITCHCRAFT) and superficial, often exaggerated, piety. Theology, moreover, was preoccupied with controversy between the various schools of thought. NOMINALISM, after its revival, sometimes associated with WILLIAM OF OCKHAM, soon became the vogue. Among its consequences were the destruction of the medieval harmony between faith and reason, and the weakening of the doctrines on grace and the sacrifice of the Mass. These were also instrumental in emphasizing excessively such nonessential practices of the faith as PILGRIMAGES, veneration of RELICS and INDULGENCES.

In opposition to numerous serious abuses, however, a great, if only superficial upsurge of piety marked the pre-Reformation era. Numerous new churches were built in town and country, and altars, chapels and tabernacles were endowed. Artists, constantly in demand, were unable to fill orders for ecclesiastical sculpture and altarpieces. Foundations of benefices, as well as of votive and anniversary Masses, multiplied. The increase in the number of specific preaching offices bore witness to the hunger for the word of God. The distribution of food, the founding of hospitals, and other charitable works testify to the self-sacrificing fraternal charity of the age, as well as to its concern for personal salvation. The new art of printing produced valuable devotional and catechetical writings, and the Bible was printed in many German translations. Compendia, Biblical commentaries (*postillae*) and Bibles for the poor (*Biblia pauperum*) also made their appearance, providing religious education for the unlettered. The BRETHREN OF THE COMMON LIFE devoted themselves to education, especially in more advanced schools, and sought to impart a deep, personal piety (*IMITATION OF CHRIST*). There was no lack of mystical experience and prayer, if only in the unpretentious garb of personal spirituality. New forms of devotion, such as the ROSARY and the ANGELUS, spread rapidly, and German hymns were sung with great enthusiasm. Stern DANCES OF DEATH and MORALITY PLAYS were evidence of popular piety, and in the upper class Christian humanists attempted to relate the new scientific ideas to faith and loyalty to the Church. But pre-Reformation piety was altogether too subjective, and, when scandalized by the worldly life of the clergy, gradually led to a deep and insuperable alienation from the Church as a formal institution and from its teachings. The time was ripe for the great catastrophe.

Mid-13th-century grave effigy of Henry the Lion, Duke of Bavaria, in the cathedral Church of St. Blasius, Braunschweig, Germany. (Marburg-Art Reference, Art Resource, NY)

Bibliography: Sources and collections. *Patrologia Latina,* ed. J. P. MIGNE, 217 v., indexes 4 v. (Paris 1878–90). *Monumenta Germaniae Historica* (Berlin 1826–). J. F. BÖHMER et al., *Regesta imperii* (Innsbruck-Graz 1889–). P. F. KEHR, *Regesta Pontificum Romanorum. Germania Pontificia,* ed. A. BRACKMANN, 3 v. (Berlin 1911–). *Deutsche Reichstagsakten* (Munich-Göttingen 1867—), 17 v. to 1963. J. F. SCHANNAT and J. HARTZHEIM, *Concilia Germaniae,* 11 v. (Cologne 1759–90). *Repertorium Germanicum. Verzeichnis der in den päpstlichen Registern und Kameralakten vorkommenden Personen, Kirchen und Orte des deutschen Reiches 1318–1517* (Berlin 1916—). *Die deutschen Inschriften* (Stuttgart 1942–). Source studies and bibliographies. A. POTTHAST, *Bibliotheca historica medii aevi* (2d ed. 1896; repr. Graz 1954). W. WATTENBACH, *Deutschlands Geschichtsquellen im Mittelalter. Vorzeit und Karolinger,* Hefte 1–4, ed. W. LEVISON and H. LÖWE (Weimar 1952–63). *Die Rechtsquellen,* ed. R. BUCHNER (Wattenbach-Levison suppl. 1953). W. WATTENBACH, *Deutschlands Geschichtsquellen im Mittelalter. Deutsche Kaiserzeit,* ed. R. HOLTZMANN, v.1.1–4 (3d ed. Tübingen 1948; repr. of 2d ed. 1938–43). K. JACOB, *Quellenkunde der deutschen Geschichte im Mittelalter,* 3 v. (5th–6th ed. Berlin 1952–61). F. C. DAHLMANN and G. WAITZ, *Quellenkunde der deutschen Geschichte* (9th ed. Leipzig 1932). Literature. H. RÖSSLER and G. FRANZ, *Biographisches Wörterbuch zur deutschen Geschichte* (Munich 1952); eds., *Sachwörterbuch zur deutschen Geschichte* (Munich 1958). *Deutsche Geschichte im Überblick,* ed. P. RASSOW (2d ed. Stuttgart 1962). B. GEBHARDT, *Handbuch der deutschen Geschichte,* ed. H. GRUNDMANN, 4 v. (8th ed. Stuttgart 1954–60) v.1. K. JORDAN, *Handbuch der deutschen Geschichte,* ed. L. JUST (Constance 1956—). W. NEUSS, *Die Kirche des Mittelalters* (2d ed. Bonn 1950). K. BHILMEYER and H. TÜCHLE, *Kirchengeschichte,* 3 v. (17th ed. Paderborn 1962) v.1–2. J. LORTZ, *Geschichte der Kirche in ideengeschichtlicher Betrachtung* (21st ed. Münster 1964—) v.1. A. HAUCK, *Kirchengeschichte Deutschlands,* 5 v. (9th ed. Berlin-Leipzig 1958). *Germania sacra: Historisch-statistische Darstellung der deutschen Bistümer* (Berlin 1929–41); *Historisch-statistische Beschreibung der Kirche des alten Reiches* (NS Berlin 1962–). G. SCHNÜRER, *Kirche und Kultur im Mittelalter,* 3 v. (3d ed. Paderborn 1929–36), Eng. *Church and Culture in the Middle Ages,* tr. G. J. UNDREINER (Paterson, N.J. 1956–), only v.1 tr. F. ZOEPEL, *Deutsche Kulturgeschichte,* 2 v. (2d ed. Freiburg 1931–37). K. D. SCHMIDT, *Die Bekehrung der Germanen zum Christentum,* 2 v. (Göttingen 1939–40). T. SCHIEFFER, *Winfrid-Bonifatius und die christliche Grundlegung Europas* (Frieburg 1954). L. HALPHEN, *Charlemagne et 'empire carolingien* (Paris 1947). J. FLECKENSTEIN, *Die Bildungsreform Karls des Grossen als Verwirklichung der norma rectitudinis* (Freiburg 1953). K. VOIGT, *Staat und Kirche von Konstantin dem Grossen bis zum Ende der Karolingerzeit* (Stuttgart 1936). K. HAMPE, *Das Hochmittelalter (900–1250)* (4th ed. Münster 1953); *Deutsche Kaisergeschichte in der Zeit der Salier und Staufer* (10th ed. Heidelberg 1949). A. SCHULTE, *Der Adel und die deutsche Kirche im Mittelalter* (3d ed. Darmstadt 1958). K. EDER, *Deutsche Geisteswende zwischen Mittelalter und Neuzeit* (Salzburg 1937). L. A. VEIT, *Volksfrommes Brauchtum und Kirche im deutschen Mittelalter* (Freiburg 1936). W. ANDREAS, *Deutschland vor der Reformation* (6th ed. Stuttgart 1959). *Die deutsche Literatur des Mittelalters: Verfasserlaxikon,* eds., W. STAMMLER and K. LANGOSCH, 5 v. (Berlin-Leipzig 1933–55). M. MANITIUS, *Geschichte der lateinischen Literatur des Mittelalters,* 3 v. (Munich 1911–31).

[H. TUCHLE]

1500 to 1789

With the ascent of the house of HAPSBURG at the beginning of the 16th century, Germany, after a long absence, returned to the center of European history during what became known as the confessional period. There she remained until the shift in power effected by the Peace of WESTPHALIA (1648) and the Peace of the Pyrenees (1659).

Hapsburg Power. Emperor MAXIMILIAN I's grandchildren CHARLES V (emperor 1519–58) and FERDINAND I (emperor 1558–64) united in themselves the Spanish-Burgundian-Hapsburg inheritance, along with the colonies of the New World. Germany opposed the house of Valois, which, since 1498, had been struggling for supremacy in Italy and had, in sporadic military expeditions, penetrated the western boundary of the Holy Roman Empire. Since 1558 the eastern flank of the empire was exposed to the constant threat of the Moscovite Empire and its expansion toward the sea; it was also threatened by the Turks, who were moving in the direction of Hungary. Within the empire there was need for domestic reform. To achieve this, a supreme court for maintaining public peace (*Reichslandfrieden*) and an imperial chamber of justice (*Reichskammergericht*) were established in 1495. These measures, together with the formation of Administrative Circles (*Kreiseinteilung, 1500*) and a general reorganization of the empire through changes made by the Peace of AUGSBURG (*Reichsexecutionsordnung, 1555*), were elements in the imperial constitution that kept their essential validity until the end of the Holy Roman Empire in 1806. The ever-increasing power of the territorial state became a dangerous rival for imperial central authority, and its striving for regimentation and particularism weakened imperial control, sometimes completely stifling it.

Need for Religious Reform. The conflicting religious intellectual thought of the period could not be reconciled: along with a strong sense of personal piety—which in itself showed signs of sterility, even forms of degeneration—there were evident, to an alarming extent, incidents of decline in Church life. This was manifested to some extent in the reduced vigor and productivity of theology, as well as in the absence of learning and morality among a not insignificant number of the secular and religious clergy. Strong anti-Roman sentiment in Germany increased when the papacy, under LEO X and his successors, steadfastly postponed the thorough Church reform demanded repeatedly by the intellectual class and which the parasite-ridden Curia made impossible. The *Gravamina of the German Nation*, first formulated in 1458 and repeatedly strengthened at the diets of Augsburg (1518), Worms (1521) and Nuremberg (1522–23), were conveyed with national emotion to large audiences by the German humanists, especially Ulrich von HUTTEN.

Role of Martin Luther. Thus the foundation was laid for an ecclesiastical revolution, which the religious genius of Martin LUTHER introduced according to his theory of subjective justification as he saw it in Pauline theology. As a result, the Protestant REFORMATION became a movement that encompassed Europe. Essentially of a religious nature and scope, the Reformation soon digressed from its original subjective-individualistic elements and led to new confessions, thereby shattering the ecclesiastical unity of the Western Church (*see* CONFESSIONS OF FAITH, PROTESTANT). It received political assurances and at the same time considerable outside encouragement from the sovereign state, which was ecclesiastically oriented. Luther's friends and benefactors, Frederick the Wise, the Landgrave PHILIP OF HESSE, Duke Christoph von Württemberg and many other princes, utilized religious strength to expand their territories, for which the confiscation of extensive Church property provided a welcome increase of power. Its popular nature was sacrificed when Luther, in his pamphlet *Wider die räuberischen Rotten der Bauern* (1525), turned against the peasants, who adopted the principles of the Reformation in order to realize social emancipation. With their defeat in the PEASANTS' WAR (1524–25) this issue was eliminated as an active factor in the political life of Germany.

In the *Summepiscopat* (Supreme Protestant Episcopate), where the sovereign was also highest bishop, the Reformation sharply increased the absolutist thinking of the modern state; it created important external prerequisites for the development of the idea of tolerance, which stemmed from different intellectual sources (*see* CHURCH AND STATE). Its strongest influence in Germany was on language, schools and national culture; in the spiritual realm, it liberated numerous intellectual powers, foremost of which was the religious autonomy of the individual's conscience. However, it did not attain its original objective of Church reform, since, on the one hand, wide areas (the Rhine principalities, southern Germany) remained steadfast in their Catholic faith, and, on the other hand, the rejection of the magisterium of the hierarchical Church, resulting from the exaggeration of the Protestant principle of *sola scriptura,* soon led to division within the reform movements themselves (Ulrich Zwingli, John Calvin) and to a colorful variety of religious enthusiasts (Anabaptists, Socinians, Anti-Trinitarians).

Confessional Debate. The movement that followed in the wake of Luther and Philipp MELANCHTHON split, after Melanchthon's death, into different groups; the succeeding generation of theologians discarded the traces of the dialectic-existentialist theological language of Luther in order to form an alliance with Aristotelian philosophy. This led to the scholastic solidification of doctrine in Lutheran orthodoxy. The formation of a "particular" ecclesiastical system and the doctrinaire isolation of the Reformation from the existing Church only gradually made itself evident, despite the sharp antipapal polemics of Luther—indeed, many people, engulfed by the new religious mainstream, were not at all conscious of any such separation. Consequently, the defensive battle of the Catholic Church was handicapped from the very beginning. The majority of defensive measures taken were halfhearted and indecisive, generally failing in their evaluation of the scope of the revolutionary ideas and often applied with apathy by the bishops. The threat of excommunication for Luther in the bull *Exsurge Domine,* which Johann ECK brought from Rome in 1519, made evident the gravity of the situation, but the means used by the Curia were completely incapable of meeting the adamant demands for ecclesiastical reform. The Curia adopted an anti-Spanish policy and tried to stop the election of Charles V as emperor in deference to the candidacy of Frederick III the Wise, Duke of Saxony (1463–1525), hoping thereby to win his powerful support within Germany. This delayed the process against Luther, and gave the movement a head start of two years (1518–20), which later could not be overcome, either by the Diet of Worms (1521) or by any other measures that were taken.

Imperial Concessions. Initiative in defending Catholicism in the first half of the century lay chiefly with the emperor and the Catholic princes. Whereas the diets referred the religious question to a council or a German national meeting (Nuremberg 1523–24; Speyer 1526), the emperor and Catholic elements attempted to suppress the movement by means of political force (the treaties of Regensburg, 1524, and Dessau, 1525). As a result, political parties were formed among church factions, and evangelical princes gave them life, both in the Torgau (1526) and in the SCHMALKALDIC LEAGUE (1531). The emperor, isolated from the Empire until 1530 by the French wars, threatened by the Turks, and dependent upon Protestant support, was forced to repeatedly postpone enactment of his policies and grant further concessions. Only after the Treaty of Crépy (1544) did he win a free hand. Following initial successes in the Schmalkaldic War (1546–47), the revolt of Protestant princes, led by Moritz of Saxony, forced him to make further concessions, which, first in the Treaty of Passau (1552) and then in the Religious Peace of Augsburg (1555), led to the recognition of the ecclesiastical status quo and sealed the dualism of the confessions (*see* INTERIMS; PROTESTANTISM).

Territorial Churches. The fundamental principle that henceforth found common acceptance among German princes (*cuius regio, eius religio*) interjected a territorial and materialistic principle into the religious question, allowing them to choose Lutheranism or Catholicism as the religion of their state. This gave only a provisional foundation, one later to be repeatedly shaken by religious wars, to the coexistence of the two confessions. Another aspect of this agreement, that of ecclesiastical reservation (*reservatum ecclesiasticum*), should have hindered the progress of the Reformation in that it denied the prince bishop, who wanted to become Protestant, his Reformation rights and forced him to resign; this, however, proved to be an aid for Catholicism only in the Rhine-Main area, in Westphalia and in Bavaria. In northern and central Germany, two archbishops and 15 bishops were lost to the Church; by 1570, approximately seven-tenths of the population was Protestant. The literary-theological defense of Catholicism in the Reformation was led by polemical theologians, such as Johann Eck, Johannes COCHLAEUS, Johannes Fabri and Friedrich NAUSEA, but it rarely penetrated the fundamental issues of the Reformation. In general, such polemic was content to assume an air of superiority on the individual issues strongly attacking Catholic doctrine. The unsuccessful religious discussions at Hagenau, Worms and Regensburg (1540–41) could be traced to Charles V, who was aided by Gasparo CONTARINI. Confessional debate had become impotent by the time the Council of TRENT (1545–63) awakened Catholic thought and introduced reform. There could no longer be a general reform council embracing Christianity; it could only attain the lesser goal of Catholic reform.

Catholic Reawakening. The indefatigable efforts of Jesuits such as Peter CANISIUS, established a bulwark of the old faith in numerous foundations in Germany. Not only was Catholicism saved, but its consciousness was so strengthened that gradually a new spiritual feeling could grow, giving birth to the BAROQUE, the last stage of general European culture. Hand in hand with this inner spiritual reawakening was the movement of the COUNTER REFORMATION, whose strongest political leaders were the Bavarian Dukes Albrecht V (1550–79) and William V (1579–97). In the forceful personalities of Archbishop Jacob von Eltz in Trier (1567–81) and Julius ECHTER VON MESPELBRUNN in Würzburg (1573–1617) appeared a new type of religious sovereign, guided by a reinvigorated ecclesiastical spirit.

Thirty Years' War. Within the empire itself the religious parties expanded. Meanwhile, the new confession, LUTHERANISM, within its political context, was strongly weakened by the third confession, CALVINISM, which gained ground and made itself politically effective, especially in the Palatinate. Toward the end of the 16th century, the constitution of the empire was rendered powerless. The contradictions in the interconfessional politics led them from confessional treaties (Protestant Union, 1608; Catholic League, 1609) to the calamities of the THIRTY YEARS' WAR (1618–48). The latter spread, as a result of Spanish-French rivalry, into a power struggle that engulfed Europe. Although the cultural tradition of Europe was not destroyed in this war, a great social and economic debility was felt during the succeeding decades. The Peace of Westphalia (1648) definitively shifted political emphasis from the Holy Roman Empire to the territories; it supplemented, from the religious-political viewpoint, the Peace of Augsburg to the extent that it gave confessional recognition to the reform religions, which had not been recognized until then, and it abolished the principle that the subjects of territories should continue to be affected by the change of religion of the territorial princes after the key year of 1624.

Secular Absolutism and the Church. The Hapsburg monarchy was faced with two tasks at the outset of the 17th century: to defend itself against the conquest policies of LOUIS XIV in the west, and to defend Europe against the Turks. After the Austro-Hungarian power thrust was temporarily secured by the Peace of Ryswick (1697) and Karlowitz (1699), it suffered a new threat in the War of the Spanish Succession (1701–14). The subsequent relatively short period of tranquility was brought to an end in 1740 by the War of the Austrian Succession, from which Prussia emerged a great power in the Peace of Hubertusburg (1763). The dualism between Catholic Austria and Protestant Prussia determined the course of German politics far into the 19th century. In the age of absolutism, the structure of a unified central state began to take shape in Prussia under Frederich William I and FREDERICK THE GREAT, as well as in Austria during the reigns of MARIA THERESA and JOSEPH II. The ENLIGHTENMENT contributed less toward the intellectual downfall of feudalism in Germany than it did in France and England; it did not turn against Christianity, whose morality it sanctioned, but it did reject its claim on absolute truth (G. LESSING, Johann HERDER). Its concept of the state, which opposed a religious doctrine of an authoritative teaching mission and supreme authority over and above the state, such as in Catholicism, theoretically and practically underscored the state's supreme authority in religious matters. This theory developed, on the Catholic side, in JOSEPHINISM, a system of state protectorship of the Church that alleviated many Church abuses as a result of state aid and thus cannot be judged wholly negative. The consciousness of the scandal of the Church schism did not escape the best minds of the period. While Gottfried LEIBNIZ engaged Jacques BOSSUET in polemical correspondence, the Franciscan Bishop Cristóbal de Rojas y SPÍNOLA and the Capuchin Dennis of Werl (d. 1709) struggled in the great cause of reconciliation.

The same cause motivated the publications of the Trier auxiliary bishop, Johann Nikolaus von HONTHEIM, who, in order to re-win Christians who had lost their faith, demanded that the Church return to its original state in Christian antiquity. His vague theological position based on his practical, canonical views led to the condemnation of his works, but this by no means resolved the important problems he posed. Episcopalism, a movement that identified itself with the FEBRONIANISM of HONTHEIM as expressed in the Congress of EMS (1786), offers sufficient proof of this. Hontheim's goal was not a national church freed from Rome, but rather the curtailment of papal rights and claims by a reevaluation of the episcopacy. The structure of the German imperial Church, as it again flourished culturally in the 18th century, after the losses of the 16th century, was stamped by the mark of feudalism; the nobility, who comprised the cathedral chapters, again elected the bishop, whom the pope approved. As a conservative element of the constitution of the empire, the prince bishops were strongly favored and protected by the emperor, but nevertheless this did not prevent some of the Rhenish-Westphalian dioceses, which had become refuges for the descendants of Bavarian princes, from carrying on independent anti-imperial politics. Along with their dynastic rise to power, the bishops of the house of Schönborn (Speyer, Mainz, Bamberg, Würzburg) were especially active in cultural matters. The main Catholic contribution in the epoch of the baroque and the rococo lies in decorative art, especially architecture (Vierzehnheiligen, Wieskirche, OTTOBEUREN, St. Paulin in Trier, WEINGARTEN). The historical research inspired by the French MAURISTS gained ground in southern Germany and reached its peak in the literary work of Abbot Martin Gerbert of St. Blaise. To what extent the Enlightenment was felt either positively or negatively in the theological realm remained an area debated by scholars.

The Fall of the Empire and Reconstruction: 1789–1900

The severe treatment by the armies of the FRENCH REVOLUTION, which occupied the left bank of the Rhine until 1798, brought about the collapse of the HOLY ROMAN EMPIRE of the German Nation. The chief beneficiaries in Germany were the lay rulers who had for many years utilized Protestant and ENLIGHTENMENT propaganda to speed the downfall of the ecclesiastical principalities and the secularization of their possessions. In 1803 an enactment of the Imperial Delegation (*Reichsdeputationshauptschluss*) caused ecclesiastical principalities and Church property to be seized and given to secular princes, partly as indemnification for the property they had lost to France west of the Rhine. The Archdiocese of Salzburg, the three Rhenish ecclesiastical electorates, 80 abbeys and foundations, and more than 200 monasteries lost their civil independence. More than three million Catholics changed territorial rulers and generally found themselves living in Protestant states. The immediate result for Catholicism was a great loss of political and social influence, which could only be regained slowly by internal renewal. Leadership in the German Confederation, founded in 1815, was assumed by predominantly Protestant Prussia, which had been strengthened by reforms since the struggle against Napoleon for freedom. After successful wars with Denmark (1864) and Austria (1866) under the leadership of BISMARCK, Prussia established in 1870 the German Empire, in which it was the strongest state.

Protestant Domination of 19th-Century Culture. Of perhaps most serious concern to intellectual German Catholics was the Protestant domination of German cultural life. Until World War I the intellectual accomplishments of Catholics remained on the periphery of the nation's creative activity. The ideas of German IDEALISM, as represented by men like Goethe, Schiller, Hegel, Hölderlin, Schleiermacher and Wilhelm von Humboldt, were very influential in establishing the *Weltanschauung* of educated Germans, at least in the first half of the 19th century; but they did not penetrate Catholic circles. German Catholic poets and writers of this period, such as Joseph von Eichendorff, Annette von Droste-Hülshoff and Adalbert Stifter, lived in isolation and were little known outside the Catholic ghettos. The philosophically less well-defined thought of ROMANTICISM did, however, affect Catholic renewal at the beginning of the 19th century. The proximity of various religious confessions resulted in numerous conversions to Catholicism or in vitalizing tensions that enriched Catholicism. Since Catholic universities and cultural centers of formation were nonexistent during this period, Catholics gathered around well-known personalities or in circles of similarly disposed friends. Thus in Münster the circle of Princess Amalia GALLITZIN included Bernard OVERBERG, Franz von FÜRSTENBERG and Friedrich von Stolberg. In Mainz the principal figures in the circle around Bishop Joseph Colmar were the Alsatian theologians Bruno Liebermann, A. Räss and Nikolas Weis. The founding of the *Katholik* (1821) assured the Mainz Circle of a permanent publication, primarily theological in its orientation, which was influential among Catholics.

In southern Germany the devout and mild pastoral theologian Johann SAILER, who was, together with Karl von DALBERG, the outstanding personality in the German episcopate of that period, had a wide influence on the care of souls, which was felt long afterward, thanks to his numerous pupils. The Munich Circle (or Round Table), which formed around the highly gifted Joseph von GÖRRES, was the most influential of these groups by virtue of the versatility of its members, the originality of their ideas, and their political stance. To it belonged the lay theologian and philosopher Franz von BAADER, who sought closer relations between the Catholic and Orthodox Churches; the theologian Johann MÖHLER; the jurist George PHILLIPS; and, above all, the Church historian Johannes Ignaz von DÖLLINGER, who cultivated international Catholic contacts, especially with England and France and who, as the eminent Catholic scholar in the 1860s, engaged in ecumenical endeavors. During the rule of Louis I (1825–48), Bavaria was a center of Catholic life and saw the revival of Benedictine monasteries. The *Historische Politische Blätter,* founded in Munich by Joseph and Guido Görres (1837), became the leading publication of the German Catholic press in the 19th century. Its development was especially notable under the direction of Josef JÖRG. Munich had a theology faculty from 1825, and the theology faculty in Tübingen, established in 1817, took inspiration from Protestant scholarship and flourished under Möhler, Johann HIRSCHER, Heinrich KLEE, Carl von HEFELE and Johannes KUHN. The *Tübinger Theologische Quartalschrift* began publication in 1819.

Ecclesiastical Reorganization. The juridical reorganization of the German Church was a slow process resulting from bilateral agreements with the Roman Curia or from unilateral decrees emanating from Rome or from the German state. Thus, a concordat was concluded with Bavaria in 1817, with Austria in 1855, and with Baden in 1859. Ecclesiastical affairs in Prussia were regulated by the papal circumscription bull *De salute animarum* (1821) for the ecclesiastical provinces of Cologne and Gnesen-Posen; and in Hanover, by *Impensa Romanorum Pontificum* (1824), for the Dioceses of Hildesheim and Osnabrück. The bull *Provida sollersque* (1821) erected the metropolitan see of Freiburg im Breisgau, with Rottenburg, Mainz, Fulda and Limburg as suffragans; it concerned Baden, Hesse, Darmstadt, Württemberg, Kurhessen and Nassau.

In the meeting at Cologne during the mixed marriage controversy (1837), German Catholicism for the first time became conscious of its social and political potential in the life of the nation (*see* COLOGNE, MIXED MARRIAGE DISPUTE IN). The pilgrimage to the Holy Garment in TRIER, which attracted a half million pilgrims in 1844, demonstrated a religiously vital Catholicism striving for a political voice in order to break the fetters of state control (*Staatskirchentum*). The revolution of 1848, warmly greeted by many Catholics, gave the Church new strength. Catholic representatives in the Frankfurt National Assembly even advocated separation of Church and State, as in Belgium and the United States. Although this goal had to be deferred, the Church was able to attain considerable freedom from state control.

Freedom of the press and freedom of assembly opened to the Church new possibilities of religious activity. In Mainz Catholics took the initiative by founding the Pius Associations (Piusvereine), and, under the leadership of Adam Lennig, strove successfully to unite German Catholics in the Catholic Union of Germany. The first Katholikentag met in Mainz (October 1848); it would become a permanent institution in German Catholic life. The German Bishops Conference in Würzburg (1848) was the first general meeting of German bishops; it would continued to meets in Fulda.

The project of a permanent federation of dioceses on the national level was not successful. Diocesan particularism and distrust in Rome, which was horrified by the term ''National Church,'' destroyed Döllinger's plan, perhaps too advanced for its time. The liturgical and pastoral reforms proposed by Ignaz von WESSENBERG and the scripturally and theocentrically orientated moral theology of the conciliatory Hirscher unfortunately were rejected. Georg HERMES in Bonn and Anton Günther in Vienna sought in vain for points of departure in contemporary philosophical systems in order to overcome disbelief and to arrive at an independent theological understanding of Christian revelation. Hermes was loyal to the Church during life, but after his death his system was condemned by Rome in 1835, and his writings placed on the Index. Günther's work was placed on the Index in 1857. NEOSCHOLASTICISM won recognition in Germany in the latter half of the century under the impulse of the Mainz *Katholik,* whose editor was Joseph Kleutgen, SJ, and whose most eminent contributor was Matthias SCHEEBEN. After mid-century tensions developed between the Roman school, which favored SCHOLASTICISM, and German theology, whose orientation was predominately historical. This divergence led to a crisis in Vatican Council I, and to the defection of such important Catholic theologians as Döllinger and Franz REUSCH, and lay professors Friedrich von Schulte and Karl von Cornelius. It also resulted in the schism of the OLD CATHOLICS. Like Deutschkatholizismus, founded a quarter-century earlier by Johann CZERSKI and Johann RONGE, the Old Catholic sect never constituted a danger to Church life; yet it led able scholars into a defection the effects of which would be perceptible into the 20th century.

Social and Political Projects. In the social movement the work of Adolf KOLPING was extremely successful. Bishop Wilhelm von KETTELER, who made the public aware of the labor question, became the intellectual inspiration for the guilds of Catholic workers that came into being after 1892. The political organization of German Catholics found a voice after the Catholic CENTER party gained a seat in the Prussian parliament in 1852. This party attained increasing political importance in the parliaments of various states, including, after successful German Empire reunification, Jan. 18, 1871, the Reichstag under the leadership of Ludwig WINDTHORST, Hermann von Mallinckrodt and Ernst Lieber.

The self-consciousness of German Catholicism received a great stimulus from the KULTURKAMPF, which was directed by Otto von Bismarck and Adalbert Falk. The Kulturkampf's objectionable effects, somewhat overdramatized by Catholics, were more often in the intellectual than the practical life of the Church, insofar as Catholicism became more isolated intellectually than before. Directly stimulating this struggle was the concept of the state, which had grown increasingly stronger since the founding of the empire; but in the background, the driving power was LIBERALISM's concept of nationalism, which was *a priori* suspicious of ultramontane Catholicism, and which considered it a natural enemy of the state following the 1864 publication of the SYLLABUS OF ERRORS and the development of the movement favoring a definition of papal primacy and infallibility. Bismarck considered Catholics enemies of the empire, lacking in patriotism. Discrimination against them socially and politically was most apparent at universities and in government administrative circles. Until 1918 Catholics in the higher ranks of imperial officialdom corresponded to less than a tenth of the numerical strength of the Catholic population.

Catholic Intellectual Life during the Second Empire. A way out of this ghetto appeared in 1876 with the founding of the GÖRRES-GESELLSCHAFT and its goal of the pursuit of learning. Other scholarly accomplishments, primarily by historians such as Johannes Janssen, Ludwig von PASTOR and Franz KRAUS, were acclaimed by the public. A second generation of historians succeeded them in the 20th century: Albert EHRHARD, Heinrich DENIFLE, Franz EHRLE, Heinrich Finke, Gustav Schnürer, Sebastian Merkle and Martin GRABMANN. Much more difficult was acceptance by the nation's intellectual and literary circles, the leading representatives of which had a negative relationship with Catholicism. A new Catholic literature developed whose literary merit was dubious. Carl MUTH was the first to bring Catholic culture into a meaningful relationship with Catholic faith by founding *Hochland* (1903). MODERNISM made slight impression on Catholic Germany, which was still weak as a result of the intellectual losses in the Old Catholic schism. The censuring of the Würzburg theologian Hermann SCHELL (1898), who came to grips passionately with the problem of the Church and progress, did not solve the important problems he confronted.

German Church Enters the Modern World

In 1900 the German Second Empire, which consisted of 25 German states united by Bismark, was now under the rule of Emperor von Büow, an imperialist. Now the greatest industrial power in Europe and hungry for new markets, the Second Empire was viewed with concern by Great Britain and France, who felt their colonial holdings in Africa and elsewhere threatened. Germany's strong political/military alliance with the Austro Hungarian Empire to its south threatened the balance of power on the continent. In addition, the greatly expanded German navy, now a rival of the formerly invincible British fleet, also gave Germany's European neighbors cause for concern. Against this sense of Germany as a growing menace, the assassination of Austrian Archduke Franz Ferdinand and his wife in Sarajevo on June 28, 1914 would act as a spark on dry, brittle leaves.

Growth of Religious Orders. As Germany grew in economic strength under the Second Empire, so the religious spirit of German Catholicism strengthened also. At the turn of the 20th century this was most evident in the religious orders and societies. The fruits of this revival were reaped by the Jesuits, Redemptorists, Franciscans and Benedictines, as well as newer missionary congregations, such as the Society of the DIVINE WORD founded in 1875 by Arnold JANSSEN. Among the congregations founded abroad that now flourished in Germany were the Pallottines, Marian Hill Missionaries, Salesians, White Fathers and Sacred Heart Missionaries. Still more remarkable was the growth of congregations of religious women dedicated to education and nursing: the Sisters of Charity of Münster, the Borromeans of Nancy, the Ladies of Loretto, the Gray Sisters, the Vincentian Sisters of Charity and also the congregations founded by Pauline von MALLINCKRODT, Clara FEY and Franziska SCHERVIER. Inspiring examples of Christian perfection were given by Clemens von DROSTE ZU VISCHERING, St. CONRAD OF PARZHAM and Rupert Mayer, SJ (d. 1945). Peter CAHENSLY, general secretary of the St. Raphael Union, founded in 1871, was tireless in aiding German emigrants, despite great opposition from the state. Numerous secular priests cared for these emigrants and settled with them in North America.

The St. Vincent de Paul conferences were devoted to the practical aid of the poor. The Volksverein in München-Gladbach, founded in 1890, undertook the social and political education of German Catholics; it had 850,000 members by 1914, and 380,000 by 1932. Influential social theorists, such as the Jesuits Viktor CATHREIN and Heinrich Pesch, also appeared; their traditions would be successfully continued on a wider scale by Oswald von Nell-Breuning, SJ, after 1945.

The Rise of Nazi Socialism. After Germany joined the Austro-Hungarian Empire in declaring war on the Allied powers in 1914, German Catholic leaders unwaveringly supported their political and military leaders, putting aside long years of discrimination by the imperial government. After the collapse of 1918, members of the Catholic hierarchy and influential noblemen regretted the fall of the monarchy. During the moderate socialist Weimar Republic (1919–33) the Center party, with 20 percent of the deputies, gained control of the government for the first time, and supplied the chancellors Karl Joseph Wirth (1921–22), Wilhelm Marx (1923–25; 1926–28) and Heinrich Brüning (1930–32). As minister of labor (1920–28), Heinrich Brauns, a Catholic priest, improved social legislation along the lines that the Center party had been advocating since Bismarck's time.

The post-World War I generation was especially receptive to religious values and responsive to the LITURGICAL MOVEMENT, which centered on Abbot Ildefons HERWEGEN, an energetic promoter, whose organizational center was Maria Laach Abbey. Theodor Haecker, who entered the Church under the influence of NEWMAN and KIERKEGAARD, had great influence as a spiritual educator. Karl Adam, Theodor Steinbüchel and F. Tillmann contemplated dogmatic and moral theology from the viewpoint of contemporary problems.

One consequence of Germany's industrialization had been the growing neglect of spirituality and religion among the working classes. The owners of industry, even in predominantly Catholic areas, were primarily Protestant, and industrial cities, while Protestant, became increasingly affected by the drift toward dechristianization. Less affected were the Rhenish and southern German cities, which were predominately Catholic. By the 1930s, with the Weimar economy in chaos as a result of its requirement to pay large war reparations, unemployment rose throughout Germany, and the working classes searched for guidance as poverty tore apart their lives.

Communism and National Socialism filled the intellectual vacuum in these dechristianized circles. National socialism, taking advantage of the misery of the working classes, took control of the government under the leadership of Adolf Hitler (March 1933), who directed the terrorism of an unjust regime for 12 years. Hitler's success in decreasing unemployment and in other domestic policies could hardly disguise the totalitarian character of his regime. The warmongering of the Nazis, revealed in propagandist demands for the revision of the Versailles Treaty, led in 1939 to the catastrophe of World War II.

Hitler, once a Catholic, played opportunistic politics with the German Catholic hierarchy; he reserved the definitive solution of the religious question until after the war.

The German bishops incessantly warned against national socialism and threatened Church members with serious ecclesiastical penalties, especially after 1930; but once the Nazis were in power, it became necessary to establish a modus vivendi that would preserve at least the appearance of legality. The hierarchy accordingly accepted the concordat of July 20, 1933 concluded between Pope Pius XI and the National Socialist government (*see* PIUS XI), under which the Church could sustain Catholic education and maintain communication with Rome. This agreement was soon violated both overtly and covertly, but it gave the Church during this period of dictatorship a basis for existence. It was, to be sure, a precarious and ever more restricted basis, but it did make possible the Church's continued functioning.

Very frequently the bishops felt obliged to protest the violation of Catholic rights and the ruthless suppression of Catholic organizations. Cardinal Michael von FAULHABER, the leading figure in the German episcopate in the first half of the 20th century, protested in his Advent sermons of 1933 against the disparaging of the Old Testament. In 1941 Bishop Clemens von GALEN of Münster publicly denounced the race legislation, especially the destruction of ''useless lives.'' Urged by the German hierarchy, a dying Pius XI composed the encyclical *Mit Brennender Sorge,* denouncing Nazi racial theory and other government actions and set it to German priests to be read on Palm Sunday, 1937; meanwhile, bishops Sproll of Rottenburg and Konrad von Preysing of Berlin were expelled from their dioceses in 1938. As the Nazi policies continued, thousands of Catholic laymen and priests would be sentenced to concentration camps or to prisons. Among those put to death were the secular priest Max Metzger (1887–1944) and Alfred Delp, SJ (1907–45). However, the tacit acceptance by many bishops and numerous Catholic laymen of the barbarous Jewish persecution by the National Socialists, especially after *Kristallnacht* in 1938, revealed, an undeniable moral blindness. Responsibility for this silence can be ascribed to personal factors and to special circumstances in some individual cases, but ultimately it must be sought in the historical roots of Germany's national mythology. In addition, the inability of the newly elected Pope Pius XII to take a firm stand against the German government for fear it would endanger more Jews, frustrated both the Allied powers and Catholics around the world. When he finally spoke out—in late 1942—his words sounded impotent in the face of the horrors of the Nazi Final Solution. While many felt Pius XII damaged the moral credibility of the Church, historians continued to debate the subject into the next century.

A Country, Church Divided. At the close of World War II, Germany was divided into two regions: the Federal Republic of Germany (West Germany; proclaimed May 23, 1949) and the Soviet-backed German Democratic Republic (East Germany; proclaimed Oct. 7, 1949). With the German capital now in East German territory, the city was divided into East and West Berlin; ultimately political tensions would prompt the building of the Berlin Wall in 1961, which separated families for decades before its destruction in November of 1989. While West Germany hoped for eventual reunification, East Germany gradually declined into a Soviet-backed police state, which continued until popular protest and the fall of the USSR signaled the reunification of the German republic on Oct. 3, 1990. A visit by Pope John Paul II to Germany in 1987 encouraged all Germans to come together, and he was considered to be a major leader in the effort to bring the two Germanys back under one flag.

In the years after 1945, defeated and demoralized by war, West Germany's political and intellectual reorganization depended heavily for support on Christian forces. These were organized in the Christian Democratic Union under Catholic chancellor Konrad Adenauer (1948–63). The Christian Democrats formed the governing party in the republic and in numerous states after 1948. Between the end of World War II and German reunification, West German Catholics participated intensively in the ECUMENICAL movement. Their acceptance of responsibility for underdeveloped countries and peoples was shown by generous Catholic contributions to the works of charity carried on by the organizations Misereor and Adveniat. In intellectual dialogues, Catholic academies, especially the one in Munich, served as discussion and training centers. The Federal Republic retained a Christian government despite trends among the population toward materialism and spiritual indifference.

The situation was much different in East Germany, where Catholics now found themselves living in a communist country with no way to leave. The atheistic communist-controlled government placed great restrictions on Christian life and doomed it to isolation, although fervent Catholics continue to keep the torch of faith lighted. In the 1946 census this so-called Diaspora region was 12.2 percent Catholic and 81.6 percent Protestant, with 6.2 percent belonging to other religious groups or to none.

Church Moves into 21st Century. In March of 1990 the first free elections were held in East Germany, with a Christian Democrat winning the vote. While the election results proved immaterial—the region was reclaimed by a united Germany months later—it showed that the conservative Catholic mindset had not been destroyed by more than 40 years of communist oppression. While proceedings were held against those accused of human rights abuses, of more concern to all Germany was the poverty and unemployment of the former East Germany, which had survived on state-controlled industry that no longer existed. Cases of right-wing extremism, sometimes focused against Jews and foreign citizens, followed as Germans grew frustrated with the economic downturn reunification had cost their country. Government efforts to refund the eastern Germany became increasingly successful, and a center-right wing coalition under Christian Democratic leader Helmut Köhl retained control throughout the reunification effort. In elections in 1998 Social Democratic party candidates gained control of the government. In January of 1999 Germany joined together with ten other European Union countries to adopt the euro as their common currency.

While Köhl's government was politically right of center, it supported social policies far more liberal than those advocated by the Church. In April of 1996 the German Catholic Church joined with Lutheran leaders to oppose the practice of Euthanasia by sponsoring a ''Week for Life'' to attract attention to the growing problem. Even more politically sensitive was the growing debate on birth control, as German Chancelor Köhl made a public statement criticizing the pope's unwillingness to allow artificial birth control. With the unification of Germany, liberal East Germany laws were expanded to permit legal abortions in Germany. Pope John Paul II responded to the changes in German law by ordering Church representatives not to involve themselves in a mandatory abortion counseling program established by the government in 1995 that in essence involved the Church in the legal abortion process through its pro-life counsel. While Catholic bishops upheld the pope' wishes, there were some defectors among the clergy.

When the pope made what would be his third trip to Germany in June of 1996, he received an unpleasant welcome from abortion activists and gay and lesbian groups that opposed many of the Church's social doctrines in support of the family. Between vehement, often ugly vocal protests, red paint was thrown at the pope's vehicle. Visiting the site of the Brandenburg Gate and the Berlin Wall, condoms and paint bombs were thrown at the pope's entourage; despite this he called on listeners to respect human rights around the world. Reflecting on this visit in 2000, the pope noted that Germany, ''one of the pillars of the European house,'' bore a particular responsibility for promoting social and political unity. In a letter to German cardinals, dated March 2001, the pope also expressed concern over the secularization of the German Church, and observed that while Catholicism in Germany ''may appear strong on the outside, . . . [it] has no inner vitality, and has lost credibility in the process.''

As a minority religion within a predominately Lutheran nation, the German Catholic Church continued to expand its ecumenical efforts. Such efforts were aided by the work of the Pontifical Council for Christian Unity in October of 1996, when it was announced that after a quarter century of discussion, Catholic and Lutheran leaders had reached a consensus on the question of justification; that justification results from the mercy of God, rather than from good works. Participating as well in the 1996 Council of European Bishops conference, Mainz Archbiship and future Karl Cardinal Lehmann considered Germany's future. ''The credo of individualism should not come to mean isolation from the community,'' Lehmann noted, adding that while democratic governments should value diversity of all kinds, the strength created by a unity among the Christian faiths would create the moral and spiritual foundation required for modern society to flourish. Less successful than works with German Lutherans were the Church's efforts to reconcile with its own Old Catholic schism, which, in May of 1999, in its continued rejection of Catholic doctrine went even further afield by ordaining two women into the priesthood.

Bibliography: K. SCHOTTENLOHER, *Bibliographie zur deutschen Geschichte im Zeitalter der Glaubensspaltung,* 1517–85, 6 v. (Leipzig 1933–40; repr. Stuttgart 1956–58, v.7 1962–). G. PFEILSCHIFTER, *Acta Reformationis Catholicae . . .* (Regensburg 1959—). M. RITTER, *Deutsche Geschichte im Zeitalter der Gegenreformation und des Dreissigjährigen Krieges,* 3 v. (Stuttgart 1889–1908). G. SCHNÜRER, *Katholische Kirche und Kultur im Zeitalter des Barock* (Paderborn 1937); *Katholische Kirche und Kultur im 18. Jahrhundert* (Paderborn 1941). K. EDER, *Die Geschichte der Kirche im Zeitalter des konfessionellen Absolutismus (1555–1648)* (Vienna 1949). G. BARRACLOUGH, *The Origins of Modern Germany* (2d ed. Oxford 1957; pa. New York 1963). L. PETRY, *Die Gegenreformation in Deutschland* (Braunschweig 1952). A. L. VEIT and L. LENHART, *Kirche und Volksfrömmigkeit im Zeitalter des Barock* (Freiburg 1956). B. GEBHARDT, *Handbuch der deutschen Geschichte,* ed. H. GRUNDMANN, 4 v. (8th ed. Stuttgart 1954–60) v.2–4. J. LORTZ, *Die Reformation in Deutschland,* 2 v. (4th ed. Freiburg 1962). K. BHILMEYER and H. TÜCHLE, *Kirchengeschichte,* 3 v. (17th ed. Paderborn 1962) v.3. H. HOLBORN, *A History of Modern Germany,* v. 1, 2 (New York 1959–64). H. BRÜCK, *Geschichte der katholischen Kirche in Deutschland im 19. Jahrhundert,* with additions by J. B. KISSLING, 4 v. (2d ed. Münster 1902–08). G. GOYAU, *L'Allemagne religieuse,* 5 v. (Paris 1898–1908) v.1–4; *Le Catholicisme,* v.5; *Le Protestantisme; Bismarck et l'Église: Le Culturkampf 1870–78,* 4. v. (Paris 1911–13). C. BACHEM, *Vorgeschichte, Geschichte und Politik der deutschen Zentrumspartei,* 9 v. (Cologne 1927–32). L. A. VEIT, *Die Kirche im Zeitalter des Individualismus, 1648–1932,* 2 v. (Freiburg 1931–33). J. LEFLON, *La Crise révolutionnaire, 1789–1846. Histoire de l'église depuis les origines jusqu'à nos jours,* eds., A. FLICHE and V. MARTIN, 20 (1949). R. AUBERT, *Le Pontificat de Pie IX, 1846–1878,* (*ibid.* 21; 2d ed. 1964). F. SCHNABEL, *Deutsche Geschichte im 19. Jahrhundert,* 4 v. (2d–4th eds. Freiburg 1948–55), esp. v.4 *Die religiösen Kräfte* (3d ed. 1955). H. HERMELINK, *Das Christentum in der Menschheitgeschichte von der Französischen Revolution bis zur Gegenwart,* 3 v. (Stuttgart 1951–55). K. BHILMEYER and H. TÜCHLE, *Kirchengeschichte,* 3 v. (17th ed. Paderborn 1962). K. S. LATOURETTE, *Christianity in a Revolutionary Age: A History of Christianity in the Nineteenth and Twentieth Centuries,* 5 v. (New York 1958–62) v. 1, 2, 4. A. DRU, *The Contribution of German Catholicism* (New York 1963). J. NEUHÄUSLER, *Kreuz und Hakenkreuz,* 2 v. (Munich 1946). E. ALEXANDER, ''Church and Society in Germany,'' *Church and Society, 1789–1950,* ed. J. N. MOODY (New York 1953) 325–583. G. G. WINDELL, *The Catholics and German Unity, 1866–71* (Minneapolis 1954). J. ROVAN, *Le Catholicisme politique en Allemagne* (*Histoire de la démocratie chrétienne,* 2; Paris 1956). *Catholicisme Allemand* (Paris 1956). K. BUCHHEIM, *Ultramontanismus und Demokratie: Der Weg der deutschen Katholiken im 19. Jahrhundert* (Munich 1963). H. LUTZ, *Demokratie im Zwielicht: Der Weg der deutschen Katholiken aus dem Kaiserreich in die Republik 1914–25* (Munich 1963). G. LEWY, *The Catholic Church and Nazi Germany* (New York 1964). See review by W. M. HARRIGAN, *American Catholic Historical Review,* 50 (1965) 605–608. *Deutscher Katholizismus nach 1945,* ed. H. MAIER, (Munich 1964). K. S. PINSON, *Modern Germany: Its History and Civilization* (New York 1954). M. DILL, *Germany: A Modern History* (Ann Arbor 1961). R. W. SOLBERG, *God and Caesar in East Germany* (New York 1961). H. HOLBORN, *A History of Modern Germany,* v.2 (New York 1964). N. MICKLEM, *National Socialism and the Catholic Church* (New York 1939). G. C. ZAHN, *German Catholics and Hitler's Wars* (New York 1962). F. ZIPFEL, *Kirchenkampf in Deutschland, 1933–45* (Berlin 1965). P. RICHARD et al., *Dictionnaire d'histoire et de géographie ecclésiastiques,* ed. A. BAUDRILLART et al. (Paris 1912—) 2:494–591. A. BIGELMAIR, *Dictionnaire d'histoire et de géographie ecclésiastiques,* ed. A. BAUDRILLART et al. (Paris 1912—) 6:1524–1626. F. VERNET, *Dictionnaire de spiritualité ascétique et mystique. Doctrine et histoire,* ed. M. VILLER et al. (Paris 1932—) 1:314–351. H. BORNKAMM et al., *Die Religion in Geschichte und Gegenwart*[3], 7 v. (3d ed. Tübingen 1957–65) 2:133–154. E. MEYNEN et al., *Staatslexikon,* ed., Görres-Gesellschaft, 8 v. (6th, new and enl. ed. Freiburg 1957–63) 2:673–880. H. TÜCHLE et al., *Lexikon für Theologie und Kirche*[2], eds., J. HOFER and K. RAHNER, 10 v. (2d, new ed. Freiburg 1957–65) 3:280–304. *Bilan du Monde* 2:49–70. *Kirchliches Handbuch,* v.25, *1956–61* (Cologne 1963). Catholic directory and statistical record for Germany. *Annuario Pontificio* has annual statistics on all dioceses.

[V. CONZEMIUS/EDS.]

GERMERIUS, ST.

Statesman, abbot; b. Vardes, France, *c.* 610; d. Saint-Germer-de-Flay, *c.* 660. Of noble Frankish blood, he served as a statesman at the court of Dagobert I and Clovis II. Upon the advice of St. OUEN, bishop of Rouen, Germerius (or Germier) founded the monastery of Isle (now Saint-Pierre-aux-Bois). As was somewhat customary in his day, he left a secular career and the married state to embrace the religious life, entering the monastery of Pentale (now Saint-Samson-sur-Risle), where he became abbot. Because of misunderstandings with his flock he left the abbey and pursued the eremitic life for five years, then he founded the Abbey of Flay (now Saint-Germer-de-Flay), where he was again made abbot.

Feast: Sept. 24.

Bibliography: *Acta Sanctorum* Sept. 6:692–708. J. MABILLON, *Acta sanctorum ordinis S. Benedicti* 2:455–462. *Monumenta Germaniae Historica: Scriptores rerum Merovingicarum* 4:628–633. J. L. BAUDOT and L. CHAUSSIN, *Vies des saints et des bienheureux selon l'ordre du calendrier avec l'historique des fêtes* (Paris 1935–56) 9:496–498. A. BUTLER, *The Lives of the Saints* (New York 1956) 3:628–629. G. MARSOT, *Catholicisme* 4:1891–92.

[O. L. KAPSNER]

GERO OF COLOGNE, ST.

Archbishop of Cologne; d. June 28, 976. He was the son of the Margrave Christian of Lausitz and a nephew of Otto I's chaplain, Gero, who had defended the Saxon borders against the Wends. He was invested in 969 at Pavia by OTTO I and sent to CONSTANTINOPLE in 971 to request the Byzantine Princess Anna, daughter of Romanus II (d. 963), as bride for the emperor's son, later OTTO II. He received, instead of Anna, Theophano (d. 991), niece of the Eastern Emperor John I Tzimisces. At the same time Gero brought back the relics of St. Pantaleon for the monastery of that name in Cologne. With his brother Thietmar he founded a Benedictine monastery in Thankmarsfeld that was soon transferred to Nienburg on the Saale. In 972 he founded the Abbey of Gladbach. His name is associated with the beautifully ornamented Gero-codex of the Gospels, now in Darmstadt, given to the Cologne cathedral possibly by the archbishop.

Feast: June 28.

Bibliography: W. NEUSS, ed., *Geschichte des Erzhistums Köln* (Cologne 1964–) 1:172–173. J. TORSY, *Lexikon für Theologie und Kirche,* ed. J. HOFER and K. RAHNER (Freiberg 1957–65) 4:757–758. W. WATTENBACH, *Deutschlands Geschichtsquellen im Mittelalter bis zur Mitte des 13. Jh.* (Stuttgart-Berlin 1904) 1:362. R. HOLTZMANN, *Geschichte der sächsischen, Kaiserzeit,* 900–1024 (4th ed. Munich 1961). A. SCHÜTTE, *Handbuch der deutschen Heiligen* (Cologne 1941) 140, bibliog. L. BERG, *Gero, Erzbischof von Köln* (Freiburg 1913).

[M. F. MCCARTHY]

GEROLD, ST.

Hermit; b. *c.* 920; d. Friesen, Germany, April 10, 978. Descended from the Rhetian family of the counts of Sax, he became a recluse at 38. He bestowed his land on the BENEDICTINE Abbey of EINSIEDELN, in which his sons Bl. Cuno and Bl. Ulric were monks, and built a hermitage on a small plot of forest ground that his friend, OTTO I, gave to him. After his death, his sons occupied his cell and watched over his tomb. Later the forest was cleared and the abbots of Einsiedeln, several of whom were of

Gerold's family, established a church on the site. During the REFORMATION the church was destroyed, but in 1662 Abbot Placid erected a new structure to house the relics of Gerold, Cuno, and Ulric, as well as a six-monk priory at the village of Sankt-Gerold near Mitternach in the Walgau. The iconography of St. Gerold pictures him in ducal dress with his two haloed sons beside him, or as freeing a trapped bear from attacking hounds while the bear bows to him.

Feast: April 19.

Bibliography: *Acta Sanctorum* April 2:625–627. A. BUTLER, *The Lives of the Saints* (New York 1956) 2:129. A. M. ZIMMERMANN, *Kalendarium Benedictinum: Die Heiligen und Seligen des Benediktinerorderns und seiner Zweige* (Metten 1933–38) 2:73–75. O. RINGHOLZ, *Geschichte des fürstlichen Benediktinerstiftes U. L. F. von Einsiedeln* (New York 1904) 661–667.

[B. CAVANAUGH]

GEROSA, VINCENZA, ST.

Cofoundress of the Sisters of Charity of Lovere; b. Lovere (Lombardy), Italy, Oct. 29, 1784; d. Lovere, June 28, 1847. Vincenza's family was well-to-do and noted for its charities to the poor and to the Church, but it suffered so much from domestic disharmony that Vincenza's mother died away from the household alone and poor. Priests advised the daughter not to exchange her home for that of her uncles, lest she forfeit her patrimonial rights. Once she fell heir, with her sister, to the family fortune, she indulged her charitable zeal by transforming a house belonging to her into a hospital. In it she performed the humblest duties, leaving control to Bartolomea CAPITANIO.

Learning of the latter's intention to found a religious institute that would enable her to expand her charitable endeavors, she became cofoundress and ceded all her wealth to the new congregation. When Capitanio died (1833) a year later, Vincenza, in her humility, thought herself totally incapable of carrying on the work. Local priests, however, dissuaded her from returning to secular life.

Vincenza proved sensible, penitent, and courageous enough to surmount every obstacle. To her belongs the credit for drawing up the constitutions of the Sisters of Charity, winning ecclesiastical approval for the institute, guiding it in its early years, and developing its characteristic spirit of amiability, humility, and charity. Against her wish she was elected superior when the first community was juridically established (Nov. 21, 1835). At her death there were 243 members in 24 houses. Her most characteristic saying was: ''One who knows the Crucified knows all. One who does not know the Crucified knows nothing.'' She was beatified May 7, 1933, and canonized May 18, 1950.

St. Vincenza Gerosa.

Feast: June 28.

Bibliography: A. STOCCHETTI, *Le Sante Bartolomea Capitanio e Vincenza Gerosa* (Vicenza 1950).

[M. C. BIANCHI]

GERSON, JEAN

Chancellor of the University of Paris; b. Jean Charlier, in Gerson, near Rethel, Champagne, Dec. 14, 1363; d. Lyons, July 12, 1429. He became a master of theology Dec. 8, 1392, after study at the College of Navarre in Paris. Having received a D.Th., he succeeded PETER OF AILLY as chancellor of the University of Paris (*see* PARIS, UNIVERSITY OF) (Apr. 13, 1395). He kept this title until his death, although after the Council of CONSTANCE (1414–18) he was unable to return to Paris, taking refuge in Lyons with his brother, a Celestine. In the tradition of the great humanists, he was one of the masters of the French language. He was a renowned theologian, a spiritual writer of note, the tireless artisan of the peace of the Church. He was a poet when the muse inspired him, a recognized pedagogue, a proven mystic. His chancellorship gave unity to these varied activities, for Paris exercised great influence, and her chancellor was expected to take a stand on all the problems that touched the life of the state, the Church, or the intellectual and moral life of society. Though living in a period of bloody civil crises, e.g., Armagnacs vs. Burgundians, the Cabochian Revolution, *Ordonnance Cabochienne*, compounded by the Hundred Years' War, Gerson remained loyal to legitimate authority. He urged the reconciliation of the Armagnac and Burgundian parties, but did not hesitate to condemn the excesses of the French court and defend the poor against all oppressors. He opposed Jean Petit's *Apologia* for tyrannicide and had it condemned in both Paris and Constance, thus incurring the hatred of the Burgundians, who prevented his return to Paris after 1418.

Living in the midst of the WESTERN SCHISM, Gerson labored to effect Church unity. He opposed the use of violence, favoring voluntary resignation of the papal candidates or compromise. He did not support the withdrawal of obedience from antipope BENEDICT XIII (1398–1403), and after its restoration he was a member of the delegation (1408) sent to both popes urging an entente. Of his treatises on the Church, e.g., *De unitate ecclesiae,* written between 1391 and 1415, 27 are extant. At the Council of Constance, where he was head of the French delegation, his addresses created a sensation. He maintained the thesis of the superiority of the council over the pope, which was actually defined at the fifth session, but he was not an extremist. Though he applauded the election of Pope MARTIN V, he spoke very frankly on the limitation of papal power and insisted on the necessary reform of prelates, of the Curia, and of pontifical finances. During his exile from Paris (1419–29) he continued to write; at least 25 of his works, some of great length, are from this period.

In 1400, while considering resigning his chancellorship, Gerson set forth his conception of teaching in *Mémoire sur la réforme de la faculté de théologie.* Here he rejected purely speculative science and all theological research cut off from spiritual life or accessible only to an intellectual elite. He felt theological study should be coupled to spiritual and pastoral concerns.

This same tendency appeared in his more than 66 works on the spiritual life, e.g., *De vita spirituali animae* and *De theologia mystica.* Never losing sight of practical applications, he warned against deviations from accepted standards (his letters to Bartholomew Clantier on Jan van RUYSBROECK's *De ornatu spiritualium nuptiarum*), against vain curiosity, and against illusions (his correspondence with the Carthusians). He tried above all to bring such problems within the grasp of the simplest minds, especially in his informal writings, such as *Miroir de l'âme, Montagne de contemplation,* and *Mendicité spirituelle,* as well as in letters or treatises of spiritual direction, such as those he wrote for his sisters. Many of these latter writings were in French instead of Latin. He did not write *The Imitation of Jesus Christ.*

Gerson penned more than 100 sermons and addresses, of which some 60 were in French. He was a renowned orator, accustomed to great occasions and noble audiences, but he was equally at ease speaking to his parishioners at St-Jean-de-Grève. His series of *Poenitemini* and his great sermon *Ad Deum vadit* on the Passion are excellent examples of his direct and compelling style. Though an outstanding humanist, he avoided excesses, protesting against the paganism of the *Roman de la Rose*, because care for souls outweighed his concern for style. His personal life was in harmony with his teachings.

Bibliography: *Opera omnia,* ed. E. DU PIN, 5 v. (Antwerp 1706); centenary edition, ed. P. GLORIEUX, 11 v. in progress, v.1–6 (Tournai 1960-), biographical essay 1:105–139: bibliog. notes 1:153–166. J. B. L'ECUY, *Essai sur la vie de Jean Gerson,* 2 v. (Paris 1832). H. JADART, *Jean de Gerson: Recherches sur son origine* (Rheims 1881). R. THOMASSY, *Jean Gerson, chancelier de Notre Dame* (Paris 1843). J. B. SCHWAB, *Johannes Gerson, Professor der Theologie und Kanzler der Universität Paris* (Würzburg 1858). B.P. MCGUIRE, tr., *Jean Gerson: Early Works* (New York, 1998). J. L. CONNOLLY, *John Gerson: Reformer and Mystic* (Louvain 1928). E. VANSTEENBERGHE, ''Quelques écrits de Jean Gerson: Textes inédits et études,'' *Revue des sciences religieuses* 13 (1933) 165–185, 393–424; 14 (1934) 191–218, 370–395; 15 (1935) 532–566; 16 (1936) 33–46. L. MOURIN, ''L'Oeuvre oratoire française de Jean Gerson,'' *Archives d'histoire doctrinale et litéraire du moyen-âge* 21 (1946) 225–261; *Jean Gerson, prédicateur français* (Bruges 1952); ed., *Six sermons français inédits de Jean Gerson* (Paris 1946). A. COMBES, ''Études gersoniennes,'' *Archives d'histoire doctrinale et litéraire du moyen-âge* 14 (1939) 291–385; 21 (1946) 331–482; *Essai sur la critique de Ruysbroeck par Gerson* (Paris 1945–). M. LIEBERMAN, ''Chronologie gersonienne,'' *Romania* 70 (1948–49) 51–67, continued irregularly in subsequent volumes. P. GLORIEUX, ''L'Activité littéraire de Gerson à Lyon,'' *Recherches de théologie ancienne et médiévale* 18 (1951) 238–307; ''Autour de la liste des oeuvres de Gerson,'' *ibid.* 22 (1955) 95–109; ''L'Enseignement universitaire de Gerson,'' *ibid.* 23 (1956) 88–113. A. AMPE, ''Les Rédactions successives de l'apologie schoonhovienne pour Ruusbroec contre Gerson,'' *Revue d'histoire ecclésiastique* 55 (1960) 401–452. D. C. BROWN, *Pastor and Laity in the Theology of Jean Gerson* (Cambridge, England, 1987). M. S. BURROWS, *Jean Gerson and De Consolatione Theologiae* (Tübingen, 1991). J. L. CONNOLLY, *John Gerson: Reformer and Mystic* (Louvain, 1928). J. B. MORRALL, *Gerson and the Great Schism* (Manchester, 1960). L. B. PASCOE, *Jean Gerson, Principles of Church Reform* (Leiden, 1973).

[P. GLORIEUX]

GERTRUDE (THE GREAT), ST.

A German nun and mystic; b. Jan. 6, 1256; d. Helfta, near Eisleben, Saxony, Nov. 17, 1302, or possibly 1301.

Nothing is known of her birthplace, family, or the circumstances of her entrance into the monastery. She was committed to the care of the nuns at the monastery of Helfta at the age of five, and in the company of other oblates such as herself received a careful education. Unusually talented, she gave herself zealously to study. At the age of 25 she discovered the mystical life. She enjoyed visions and interior graces, but apart from that, little is known of her life. She certainly worked as a copyist in the monastic scriptorium. Although often too ill to be present at all the choral Offices, she served as second chantress with St. Mechtild of Hackeborn (1241–98), who was also favored with revelations. In fact, the experiences of these two saints were inseparable; both belonged to the same mystical school of the 13th-century spiritual renaissance of the Cistercians. The nuns of Helfta, however, were independent and never juridically attached to the Cistercian Order.

Gertrude's ''conversion,'' a mystical experience that took place Jan. 27, 1281, was for her a living encounter with Christ and the revelation of a bond of love between Him and herself. The entire spirituality of the mystics of Helfta was centered on that type of union with the person of Christ. Their spirituality was essentially what is called by some theologians a *Brautmystik*, or a nuptial mysticism. Gertrude certainly knew the school of abstract and speculative spirituality current at the time in the Low Countries and the Rhineland, but she did not belong to it. Union with Christ was the way by which her contemplation progressed toward the life of the ''resplendent and completely calm Trinity.'' Her Christocentric perspective found expression in a devotion to the SACRED HEART, upon the later development of which the revelations and lyrical outpourings of SS. Mechtild and Gertrude had an important influence. Another essential characteristic of Gertrude's spirituality was the unity that constant attention to God established among the activities in her monastic life—Scripture study, spiritual reading, prayer, and choral Office. For her the liturgy was not simply a duty to be fulfilled at certain hours but rather the rhythm of her life of prayer. The liturgy and Scripture furnished her with the doctrinal themes of her piety, the best of her images, and even the form of her lyricism. But more than that, it was a ''mystery,'' a sacrament of the presence of Christ. Hence instead of being in contradiction, her liturgical and personal prayer were in profound harmony.

Three Latin works are attributed to St. Gertrude. (1) The *Exercitia spiritualia*. This title was probably not given to the work by Gertrude herself. These exercises represent seven affective meditations. They tend to renew in the soul a consciousness of the work of holiness accomplished by grace from baptism up to the preparation for death. (2) The *Insinuationes* (called also *Revelationes* or *Legatus divinae pietatis*), which is composed of five books. The essential point is to be found in bk. 2, written by Gertrude herself in 1289 as a memorial of her mystical experiences over an eight-year period. In the following years she wrote in the sense that she dictated, or perhaps simply inspired, other confidences and recollections. After her death the whole corpus of her other writings was reassembled in three other books (3, 4, 5) by a companion, another nun of the same monastery who also wrote an introduction to justify the entire work (bk. 1). This introductory book is in the manner of a biographical study. (3) *Preces Gertrudianae*, which is the book through which most people have known her. However, the work is not really authentic. It was composed in the 17th century, and is a flowery collection of loving effusions impregnated with the spirit and lyricism characteristic of St. Gertrude, but only some of the passages represent a faithful reproduction of her actual texts.

Feast: Nov. 16.

Bibliography: Works. *Revelationes Gertrudianae ac Mechtildianae*, ed. L. PAQUELIN and J. POTHIER (Poitiers 1875–77) v.1. *The Exercises of St. Gertrude*, ed. and tr. a Benedictine of Regina Laudis (Westminster, Md. 1960). *The Life and Revelations of St. Gertrude, Virgin and Abbess, of the Order of St. Benedict*, tr. M. F. C. CUSACK (Westminster, Md. 1949). *Prayers of St. Gertrude and St. Mechtilde of the Order of St. Benedict* (Philadelphia 1955), spurious. Literature. A. M. ZIMMERMANN, *Lexikon für Theologie und Kirche*, ed. J. HOFER and K. RAHNER (Freiburg 1957–65) 4:761. J. L. BAUDOT and L. CHAUSSIN, *Vies des saints et des bienheureux selon l'ordre du calendrier avec l'historique de fêtes*, ed. by the Benedictines of Paris (Paris 1935–56) 11:520–536, extensive bibliog. *The Love of the Sacred Heart*, pref. A. GOODIER (New York 1922), contains excerpts from her writings. M. J. FINNEGAN, *Scholars and Mystics* (Chicago 1962). ''Similitudes in the Writings of St. Gertrude of Helfta,'' *Mediaeval Studies* 19 (1957) 48–54. P. DOYÈRE, ''St. Gertrude, Nun and Mystic,'' *Worship* 34 (1960) 536–543.

[P. DOYÈRE]

GERTRUDE OF NIVELLES, ST.

Abbess; b. 626; d. between 653 and 659. The daughter of Pepin of Landen and St. Iduberga, she entered the double MONASTERY of Nivelles (Belgium) that her mother, a widow, had just founded (640). There she succeeded her mother as superior (652), ruling a house in which, according to Celtic custom, the nuns and monks were subject to an abbess. Gertrude was an example of virtue and a defender of Irish monasticism; her abbey later sent the first nuns to Andenne, founded by her sister, St. BEGGA. Gertrude is invoked against mice, then the bane of the countryside. Her remains are preserved in a reliquary, a masterpiece of silverwork (dating from 1272–98), now in the collegiate church of Nivelles. The vita of St. Gertrude of Nivelles was written *c.* 670, and it was rewritten sometime in the 11th century.

Feast: March 17.

Bibliography: Life. *Acta Santorum* March 2:590–603. *Monumenta Germaniae Scriptores rerum Merovingicarum* (Berlin 1826–) 2:447–474. Literature. L. VAN DER ESSEN, *Étude . . . des saints mérovingiens* (Louvain 1907). P. WENZEL, *Die Frauenstifte der Diözese Lüttich* (Bonn 1909). B. DELANNE, *Histoire . . . Nivelles* (Nivelles 1944). J. HOEBANX, *L'Abbaye de Nivelles . . .* (Brussels 1952). A. BUTLER, *The Lives of the Saints,* rev. ed. H. THURSTON and D. ATTWATER, 4 v. (New York 1956) 1:620–621. R. FORGEUR, *Lexikon für Theologie und Kirche,* ed. J. HOFER and K. RAHNER, 10 v. (2d, new ed. Freiburg 1957–65) 4:761–762. A. WAUTERS in *Biographie nationale de Belgique,* v.7 (1880–83) 680–684.

[É. BROUETTE]

GERULF, ST.

Martyr; b. Meerendra, Belgium, *c.* 732; d. near Ghent, Belgium, *c.* 750. A 10th-century legend reports that Gerulf was confirmed at the age of 18 in the monastery of St. Bavon at Gand. After the ceremony, while Gerulf and his godfather were riding home, the devil possessed the godfather, who threatened to kill Gerulf. The boy protested that he would go to hell if he did, but the man pierced him with his sword. Gerulf's mother saw the bloody and riderless horse return and instinctively knew what had happened. His body was buried first in the church of Bl. Redegund in Meerendra, but after several miracles it was moved in the 9th century to the monastery at Dronghem, Flanders, where Gerulf was venerated as a saint. His relics were frequently translated and gradually suffered dispersal until, after the Catholic restoration of 1584, only the head was left to be enshrined again at Dronghem, which was under the care of the PREMONSTRATENSIANS.

Feast: Sept. 21.

Bibliography: *Acta Sanctorum* Sept. 6:250–270. A. SANDERUS, *Hagiologium Flandriae* (Antwerp 1625) 72–83. W. LAMPEN, *Lexikon für Theologie und Kirche*, ed. J. HOFER and K. RAHNER (Freiburg 1957–65) 4:763.

[B. CAVANAUGH]

GERVAISE, FRANÇOIS ARMAND

Historian, abbot of La Trappe; b. Paris, 1660; d. Le Reclus, 1751. He was the son of a Parisian physician and was educated by the Jesuits. He joined first the Discalced Carmelites, then in 1695, the reformed Cistercians at LA TRAPPE. He was Armand de RANCÉ's successor as abbot of La Trappe (1696–98) but his restless and quarrelsome temper forced his resignation. He drifted from monastery to monastery until the end of his long life. Seeking compensation for his personal calamities in writing, he published a large number of biographies and critical studies composed with skill but with conspicuous lack of balance and objectivity. Of these only one has retained an undeserved popularity with monastic historians, the *Histoire générale de la réforme de l'ordre de Cîteaux* (Avignon 1746). It was printed clandestinely in Paris as a savage attack against the unreformed Common Observance of CISTERCIANS and is responsible for the transmission to posterity of a wholly unjust and distorted view of the process of reform during the 17th century. By the demand of the indignant Cîteaux a royal *lettre de cachet* relegated the octogenarian author to the monastery of Le Reclus for the remaining five years of his life. His two-volume biography of Rancé remained in manuscript form for more than a century and was edited only in 1866 by Abbé Dubois, *Histoire de l'Abbé de Rancé et de sa réforme* (Paris).

Bibliography: For a full list of works see: J. BESSE, *Dictionnaire de théologie catholique* 6:1339–40. L. J. LEKAI, "The Unpublished Second Volume of Gervaise's 'Histoire générale de la réforme de l'ordre de Cîteaux en France'," *Analecta Sacri Ordinis Cisterciensis* 17 (1961) 278–283; "The Problem of the Authorship of De Rancé's 'Standard' Biography," *Collectanea Ordinis Cisterciensium Reformatorum* 21 (1959) 157–163.

[L. J. LEKAI]

GERVASE, GEORGE, BL.

Benedictine priest and martyr; b. Bosham, Sussex, England, *c.* 1569–71; d. hanged, drawn, and quartered at Tyburn (London), April 11, 1608. Although born into two well-established families (Jervis and Shelly) of Suffolk, George suffered much in his short life. He was orphaned while young. Thereafter he was kidnapped to the West Indies. During his 12–year captivity, he lost his faith. Upon returning to England he learned that his brother Henry was suffering voluntary exile in Flanders so that he could continue to practice his religion. George tracked him down and was reconciled to the Church, entered the seminary at Douai (1595), and was ordained a priest at Cambrai (1603). Immediately thereafter he began his ministry in England, which was interrupted in June 1606 by arrest and banishment. After making a pilgrimage to Rome and unsuccessfully seeking admittance to the Society of Jesus, he returned to Douai, where he received the Benedictine habit at St. Gregory's. He was arrested soon after arriving in England and condemned under the statute 27 Elizabeth. Some authorities say he did not receive the Benedictine habit until a short time before his death from Fr. Augustine Bradshaw. He is the protomartyr of St. Gregory's Abbey (now Downside). He was beatified by Pius XI on Dec. 15, 1929.

Feast of the English Martyrs: May 4 (England).

See Also: ENGLAND, SCOTLAND, AND WALES, MARTYRS OF.

Bibliography: R. CHALLONER, *Memoirs of Missionary Priests,* ed. J. H. POLLEN (rev. ed. London 1924; repr. Farnborough 1969). J. H. POLLEN, *Acts of English Martyrs* (London 1891).

[K. I. RABENSTEIN]

GERVASE OF CANTERBURY

English chronicler; d. *c.* 1210. The first certain date in his life, Feb. 16, 1163, marks his profession as a monk of Christ Church, CANTERBURY, in the presence of Abp. Thomas BECKET, whose burial he was to attend seven years later. Gervase seems to have spent most of his life at Canterbury, composing the historical works that are his claim to fame. A typical monastic historian of that age, he filtered all events through the screen of his own monastery's interests. His earliest work was an analysis of the controversy between his archbishop, RICHARD OF CANTERBURY, and the monks of the neighboring abbey of ST. AUGUSTINE (1179–83). This was followed by an account of a struggle between Christ Church and Archbishop BALDWIN OF CANTERBURY (1185–91) in which Gervase was an active participant, probably drawing up some of the letters justifying the stand of Christ Church. It was at this time that Gervase began his major work, the *Chronica,* which covered the period from 1100 to 1199; the narration was carried to 1209 by his lesser work, *Gesta regum,* which is especially valuable for the history of King JOHN. Gervase wrote also *Actus pontificum Cantuariensis ecclesiae,* a history of the archbishops of Canterbury from AUGUSTINE OF CANTERBURY to HUBERT WALTER; a topographical work, *Mappa Mundi,* on ecclesiastical foundations in the British Isles; and a graphic account of the burning of Canterbury cathedral, Sept. 5, 1174.

Bibliography: *Historical Works,* ed. W. STUBBS, 2 v. *Rerum Brittanicarum medii aevi scriptores* (*Rerum Britannicarum medii aevi scriptores* 1879–80). D. M. KNOWLES, ''*The Mappa Mundi* of Gervase of Canterbury,'' *Downside Review* 48 (Yeovil, England 1930) 237–247.

[D. NICHOLL]

GERVASE OF REIMS

Archbishop; b. Coémont, Sarthe, France, Feb. 2, 1008; d. July 4, 1067. He was the son of Aimon and Hildegard (Hildeburg), sister of Bishop Avesgand of Le Mans (d. in 1036). Gervase succeeded his uncle in the See of Le Mans and was consecrated bishop Dec. 18, 1036. He was impeded in the exercise of his episcopal office particularly by Geoffrey of Anjou (d. 1060), who imprisoned him for seven years, but in a synod at Reims in 1049 Pope LEO IX threatened to excommunicate the Count of Anjou if he did not release the bishop (Mansi 19:742). Geoffrey yielded, but only after the prisoner had turned over to him Château-du-Loir. In 1055 Gervase was promoted to the archbishopric of REIMS, in which office he functioned also as chancellor and primate of the realm. On Pentecost, May 23, 1059, he solemnly crowned PHILIP I, who swore to guarantee and defend the rights of the Church. In 1063 Gervase petitioned Pope ALEXANDER II to come to Reims on important ecclesiastical matters, but the pontiff sent PETER DAMIAN, ''our eye and redoubtable bulwark of the Apostolic See,'' as his legate (P. Jaffé, *Regesta pontificum romanorum ab condita ecclesia ad annum post Christum naturm 1198* L 1:5416).

Bibliography: J. D. MANSI *Sacrorum Conciliorum nova et amplissima collectio* 31 v. (Florence-Venice 1757–98). *Patologia latina* 143:870, 1397–1404, 1547–49. *Gallia Christiana* 9:68–70. R. CEILLIER, *Histoire générale des auteures sacrés et ecclésiastiques* 13:263–266. C. J. HEFELE, *Histoire des conciles d'aprés les documents originaux,* tr. H. LECLERCQ, 4.2:1024. A. FLICHE and V. MARTIN eds., *Histoire de l'église depuis les origines jusqu'à nos jours* 8:22. H. G. KRAUSE, *Studi gregoriani* 7 (1960) 52. H. GLASER, *Lexicon für Theologie und Kirche*[2] 4:764.

[H. DRESSLER]

GERVASE OF TILBURY

Author of a medieval book of universal knowledge; b. probably Tilbury, Essex, England, *c.* 1140; d. probably England, *c.* 1220. He studied and briefly taught law at the University of Bologna; in 1177 he was an eyewitness to the peace talks between Emperor FREDERICK I BARBAROSSA and Pope ALEXANDER III. Shortly afterward he seems to have returned to England, where he had high connections at court and where he attached himself to King HENRY II's son, Henry (d. 1183), for whom he wrote the now-lost *Liber facetiarum.* Gervase next entered the service of King William II of Sicily (d. 1189), the son-in-law of Henry II, and it is known that he was in Salerno during the siege of Acre (1190–91). Subsequently, through his various English connections, he was taken into the service of Emperor OTTO IV, the grandson of Henry II. Otto made Gervase marshal of the kingdom of ARLES, and there he seems to have married. In 1209 he accompanied Otto IV to Rome for his imperial coronation, and in 1211, when Otto was excommunicated by Pope INNOCENT III, Gervase was already writing his famous *Otia imperialia* for Otto. He finished the work in 1214, the year the emperor met disastrous defeat at Bouvines, which forced him to retire to his own principality of Brunswick, while Gervase seems to have returned to England. The *Otia imperialia,* a book written for the instruction and entertainment of the monarch, was divided into three sections. The first, in 24 chapters, beginning with the creation of the world, includes a physical description of the earth and traces world history up to the Flood. The second section, in 36 chapters, begins with Noe and his sons and the division of the world into Asia, Europe, Africa, etc., and describes certain areas in detail, especially the regions of western Europe, listing and discussing various lines of kings. Section three, in 119 chapters, is quite eclectic, treating of such diverse topics as stones, trees, animals, serpents, the British Sea, Christ's cross, Thomas the Apostle, and water that becomes salt. The *Otia* is of special interest because of the insight it gives into the mental equipment of a man whom contemporary society held to be well educated, and because of its moderate stand in discussing the proper relationship of pope and emperor.

Bibliography: *Otia imperialia,* ed. G. W. LEIBNIZ, in his *Scriptores rerum Brunsvicensium,* 3 v. (Hanover 1707–11) 1:884–1004; 2:751–784; complete third section, ed. F. LIEBRECHT (Hanover 1856); selections, *Monumenta Germaniae Historica: Scriptores* 27:359–394. W. HUNT, *The Dictionary of National Biography from the Earliest Times to 1900* 7:1120–21. J. R. CALDWELL, ''The Autograph MS of G. of T.,'' *Scriptorium* 11 (1957) 87–98; ''MSS of G. of T.'s *Otia imperialia,*'' *ibid.* 16 (1962) 28–45; ''The Interrelationship of the MSS of G. of T.'s *Otia imperialia,*'' *ibid.* 246–274; ''G. of T.'s Addenda to his *Otia imperialia,*'' *Medieval Studies* 24 (1962) 95–126. K. SCHNITH, ''Otto IV und Gervasius von Tilbury: Gedanken zu den *Otia imperialia,*'' *Historiches Jahrbuch der Gö-Gesellschaft* 82 (1963) 50–69.

[M. J. HAMILTON]

GERVASE AND PROTASE, SS.

Ss. Gervase and Protase, martyrs, are patrons of Milan; dates unknown. Nothing is known of the life or martyrdom of these saints; even their existence has been questioned. The tradition that they were martyred during the persecution of Nero is unreliable, since there is no evidence for a Christian community in Milan before the end of the 2nd century. Their tombs were in the church of SS. Nabor and Felix, which was rebuilt after the Peace of the Church (313). In this church St. AMBROSE OF MILAN discovered the bodies on June 17, 386, and he translated the relics to the newly dedicated basilica named after him. The identification of the bodies was based on their extraordinary size, the finding of an ampula, and the miraculous cure of a blind man. Ambrose himself described the rediscovery of the relics in an extant letter to his sister Marcellina. The cult of Gervase and Protase spread rapidly in Italy, in Gaul, and throughout Western Christendom. In the 5th century a legend describing their martyrdom was forged and ascribed to St. Ambrose. Without historical merit, the legend connects them with Nazarius and Celsus as sons of Vitalis and Valeria, who had a church dedicated to her in Milan. The earliest extant representation of Gervase and Protase is in S. Vitale, Ravenna. The relics of the martyrs are now venerated in a silver reliquary in the cathedral of Breisach in Baden, where Emperor FREDERICK I BARBAROSSA's Chancellor, Rainald von Dassel, is alleged to have translated them. The original relics, however, are still under the main altar of the Basilica of St. Ambrose in Milan.

Feast: June 19.

Bibliography: *Acta Sanctorum* June 4:680–704. P. FRANCHI DE'CAVALIERI, *Nuovo Bullettino di archeologia cristiana,* 9 (1903) 109–126. G. RAUSCHEN, *Jahrbücher der christlichen Kirche unter dem Kaiser Theodosius dem Grossen* (Freiburg 1897) 243–. E. LUCIUS, *Die Anfänge des Heiligenkults,* ed. G. ANRICH (Tübingen 1904) 153–. H. DELEHAYE, *Analecta Bollandiana* 49 (1931) 30–35; *Les Origines du culte des martyrs* (2d ed. Brussels 1933) 75–78. H. GÜNTER, *Die Psychologie der Legende* (Freiburg 1949) 348–.

[J. BRÜCKMANN]

GERVIN OF OUDENBURG, ST.

Abbot; b. Flanders, 11th century; d. Forest of Cosfort, Flanders, April 17, 1117. He had traveled to Rome and had also made two pilgrimages to JERUSALEM, before he became a BENEDICTINE monk and priest at Bergues-Saint-Winoc. He left the monastery to lead the life of a hermit; but while he was in the vicinity of the abbey of Oudenburg (Aldenburg) in 1095, he was elected abbot by the monks. About 1105 he resigned his office to spend his last years living alone in the forest near the abbey. The holiness of his life soon won him a reputation for sanctity.

Feast: Apr. 17.

Bibliography: *Acta Sanctorum* April 2:492. *Patrologia Latina* 174: 1480. A. M. ZIMMERMANN, *Kalendarium Benedicinum: Die Heiligen und Seligen des Benediktinerorderns und seiner Zweige* 2:61–62. G. MARSOT, *Catholicisme* 4:1898–99. S. HILPISCH, *Lexikon für Theologie und Kirche*, ed. J. HOFER and K. RAHNER (Freiburg 1957–65) 4:765.

[E. J. KEALEY]

GÉRY OF CAMBRAI, ST.

Bishop and patron of Cambrai; b. Carignan, France, mid-6th century; d. Aug. 11, *c.* 625. He was the son of

Gaudentius and Austadiola. Because of his exemplary life, Magneric, Bishop of Trier (d. 596), conferred the TONSURE on Géry and according to report, he promised to ordain him a deacon as soon as he knew the Psalter by heart. Upon the death of their bishop, the inhabitants of CAMBRAI chose Géry for the episcopal office. With the approval of Childebert II (d. 596), Archbishop Giles of Reims consecrated him *c.* 584. Géry appears fourth in the list of bishops of Cambrai, but it is unclear whether he or his predecessor moved the episcopal residence from Arras to Cambrai. The 7th-century vita of Géry, written by a cleric at Cambrai, is too preoccupied with reported miracles to give much biographical detail. The saint was zealous in uprooting paganism, compassionate to prisoners and to the poor. He built a church in honor of St. MÉDARD, made a pilgrimage to Tours, and attended a council held at Paris in 614.

The beginnings of Géry's cult are unclear, but by the 9th century his name was in the Litany of All Saints used in Cologne.

Feast: Aug. 11.

Bibliography: *Monumenta Germaniae Historica: Concilia* (Berlin 1826) 1:191. C. J. VON HEFELE, *Histoire des conciles d'après les documents originaux* 3.1:251. *Monumenta Germaniae Historica: Scriptores rerum Merovingicarum* (Berlin 1826—) 3:649–658. P. GAMS, *Series episcoporum ecclesiae catholicae* (Regensburg 1873) 526. *Acta Sanctorum* Aug. 2:664–693. L. VAN DER ESSEN, *Étude critique et littéraire sur les Vitae des saints mérovingiens de l'ancienne Belgique* (Louvain 1907) 206–211. J. L. BAUDOT and L. CHAUSSIN, *Vies des saints et des bienheureux selon l'ordre du calendrier avec l'historique des fêtes* 8:198–199. H. PLATELLE, *Catholicisme* 4:1901. B. GAIFFIER, *Analecta Bollandiana* 79 (1961) 288. M. COENS, *ibid.* 77 (1959) 386; 80 (1962) 153.

[H. DRESSLER]

GESTA ROMANORUM

A collection of exempla, or anecdotes, arranged for the use of preachers in the late 13th century. The title, which suggests historical material and Roman origin, is misleading, for the narratives are of many kinds including Oriental tales, classical fables, and Christian saints' legends, all supplied with moral application for sermon use. According to scholarly opinion, the collection was originally gathered in England, but was soon imitated on the Continent in sets of stories considerably different from the contents of the English manuscripts. The Anglo-Latin version is one of the finest of all the European EXEMPLUM books and well deserved the copying and imitation that it received. It has sometimes been attributed to John of BROMYARD, the known author of another such collection called the *Summa predicantium,* but he flourished too late for authorship of the *Gesta.* The Continental version has also been uncertainly associated, usually with the names of Hélinand or of Berchorius, a French Benedictine. The Latin narratives were subjected to translation in the late Middle Ages into various vernacular languages, the earliest English versions being made in the reign of Henry VI, *c.* 1430.

With the invention of movable type, the tales of the *Gesta* spread rapidly. The collection was first printed at Utrecht in 1472 in its Latin form and soon elsewhere in various translations. One of the most precious of such editions survives in a unique copy bearing the imprint of Wynkyn de Worde, dating from *c.* 1510. Containing 43 of the stories in English, it became the basis of Richard Robinson's version printed in Elizabeth's reign and possibly was known to Shakespeare, who immortalized three of the tales in *King Lear, Pericles,* and *The Merchant of Venice.*

Bibliography: *Gesta Romanorum,* ed. H. OESTERLEY (Berlin 1872) Lat. text; Eng. tr. C. SWANN, ed. W. HOOPER (London 1877). *The Early English Versions of the G. R.,* ed. S. J. H. HERRTAGE (EEngTSoc 33; 1879; repr. 1962). J. T. WELTER, *L'Exemplum dans la littérature religieuse et didactique du moyen âge* (Paris 1927). G. R. OWST, *Literature and Pulpit in Medieval England* (2d ed. New York 1961).

[E. C. DUNN]

GESUALDO, CARLO

Prince of Venosa, progressive Renaissance composer; b. Naples, *c.* 1560; d. Naples, Sept. 8, 1613. He lived chiefly at his country estate of Venosa, although his travels in Italy (especially a three-year sojourn in Ferrara) brought him into contact with poets and musicians of the highest rank. He knew Tasso and set several of his poems as madrigals, of which seven books have been preserved. At Ferrara he probably met MARENZIO, Luzzaschi, and VICENTINO, whose experiments with subtleties of tuning and temperament may have influenced Gesualdo's sometimes bizarre harmonic vocabulary. This he used as a means of heightening expression in already vivid verbal texts, applying this in some degree to his religious music, most of which he had published in two books of *Sacrae cantiones* (1603) and a volume of Responsories and other compositions for Holy Week (1611). These are all of excellent quality, although somewhat eclipsed by the subsequent fame of the madrigal books. His reputation has always been clouded by the story, based on substantial evidence, that he ordered the murder of his wife and her lover.

Bibliography: *Gesamtausgabe*, ed. W. WEISMANN et al. (Hamburg 1960–). *Tres sacrae cantiones*, completed I. STRAWINSKY (New York 1960). C. GRAY, *Carlo Gesualdo* (London 1926).

Thomas Merton dipping his hand in holy water, Abbey of Gethsemani, Louisville, Kentucky. (©Horace Bristol/CORBIS)

G. R. MARSHALL, *The Harmonic Laws in the Madrigals of Carlo Gesualdo* (doctoral diss. microfilm: New York U. 1956). H. F. REDLICH, *Die Musik in Geschichte und Gegenwart*, ed. F. BLUME (Kassel-Basel 1949–) 5:41–45. ''Gesualdo and the Italian Madrigal,'' *Listener* 48 (1952) 481. E. LAWTON, *Enciclopedia della musica* (Milan 1963–65) v.1. A. EINSTEIN, *The Italian Madrigal*, tr. A. H. KRAPPE et al., 3 v. (Princeton 1949) 2:688–717. D. ARNOLD, *Gesualdo* (London 1984). L. BIANCONI, ''Carlos Gesualdo'' in *The New Grove Dictionary of Music and Musicians*, v. 7, ed. S. SADIE (New York 1980) 313–324. H. MEISTER, ''Ausdruck und musikalische Gestalt der Madrigale Gesualdos'' (Ph.D. diss. Köln, 1973); ''Untersuchungen zum Verhältnis von Text und Vertonung in den Madrigalen Carlo Gesualdos,'' *Kölner Beiträge zur Musikforschung* 74 (1973), 1–205. D. M. RANDEL, ed., *The Harvard Biographical Dictionary of Music* (Cambridge, Mass. 1996) 304. N. SLONIMSKY, ed. *Baker's Biographical Dictionary of Musicians*, (New York 1992) 616.

[D. STEVENS]

GETHSEMANI, ABBEY OF

A monastery of Cistercian Monks of the Strict Observance (Trappists) situated about 15 miles south of Bardstown, Ky., and considered one of the historical monuments of the Commonwealth. Unsuccessful attempts had been made in 1805 by Dom Urban Guillet and Trappist refugees from revolutionary France to establish a permanent community in this part of Kentucky. On Dec. 21, 1848, a colony of 44 monks from the Breton Abbey of Melleray, near Nantes, settled on this site which had been purchased from the Sisters of Loretto. Gethsemani was the first monastic community in the U.S. to be raised to abbatial rank (1851). The first abbot, Eutropius Proust, was blessed in Bardstown cathedral on Oct. 26, 1851, by Bp. Benedict Flaget.

During this early period, the strict rule, plus the rigors of the primitive and isolated life of the monks, discouraged postulants from entering or persevering. Under its third abbot, Edward Chaix Bourbon (resigned 1898), the Gethsemani community was on the point of expiring when it was revived by the energetic administration of Edmond OBRECHT (1898–1935).

Gethsemani's history in the mid–20th century was marked by an extraordinary influx of vocations, reaching a climax in 1952 when the community numbered 279. Although it is often wrongly stated that this unusual growth began suddenly after World War II, in actual fact it had already begun by the late 1930s. Under the fifth abbot, Frederick DUNNE (1935–48), the first American-born postulant to persevere as a choir monk at Gethsemani, the first two foundations of Gethsemani were made at Conyers, Ga. (1944) and at Huntsville, Utah (1947). The next abbot, James Fox, made foundations on the Luce Plantation at Mepkin, S.C. (1949), at Piffard, N.Y. (1951), and on Vina Ranch in the Sacramento Valley of California (1955). The abbatial church of Gethsemani was elevated to the rank of a minor basilica on May 3, 1949.

Bibliography: T. MERTON, *The Waters of Siloe* (New York 1949). M. RAYMOND, *The Man Who Got Even with God* (Milwaukee 1941); *Burnt out Incense* (New York 1949); *The Less Traveled Road* (Milwaukee 1953).

[T. MERTON/EDS]

GEULINCX, ARNOLD

Cartesian philosopher; b. Antwerp, Jan. 31, 1624; d. Leyden, November 1669. He studied at the University of Louvain, where he was named professor and later dean (1654). His frankly Cartesian sympathies and his attachment to JANSENISM and later to CALVINISM obliged him to resign (1658) and take refuge in Leyden. Deeply impressed by his reading of Descartes's works, Geulincx rediscovered in them the decisive stages of doubt and of the *cogito*. But he linked these with the results of an inspiration very different from that of Descartes. The *cogito* is not so much the affirmation of a thinking substance as the consciousness of entire dependence with regard to God: the individual spirits of men are only modes of the infinite spirit of God, just as particular things are only modes of universal extension. Whence it follows that of himself man can perceive only what God allows him to perceive and that if he himself can will, this willing is limited by the absolute inefficiency of a passive perception. ''Nihil est in me praeter cognoscere et velle; nudus sum hujusce mundi contemplator: spectator sum in hac scena, non actor'' (*Ethica,* 1). The principle of this sharing between things and self, as between God and self, is given in one of the fundamental propositions of the doctrine: ''qua fronte dicam, id me facere, quod quomodo fiat, nescio'' (*ibid.*). From this is also derived the first rule of morality: ''ubi nihil vales, ibi nihil velis'' (*ibid.*). This governs all the obligations that the rule prescribes and the unity of the virtues it retains, the main one of which is humility.

See Also: CARTESIANISM; OCCASIONALISM.

Bibliography: *Opera philosophica,* ed. J. P. N. LAND, 3 v. (The Hague 1891–1893). *Arnold Geulincx,* trans. A. DE LATTRE (Paris 1970). A. DEL NOCE, *Enciclopedia filosofica* 2:693–699. V. VAN DER HÄGHEN, *Geulincx: Étude sur sa vie, sa philosophie et ses ouvrages* (Ghent 1886). J. P. N. LAND, *Arnold Geulincx* (The Hague 1895). E. TERRAILLON, *La Morale de Geulincx dans ses rapports avec la philosophie de Descartes* (Paris 1912). B. ROUSSET, *Geulincx entre Descartes et Spinoza* (Paris 1999).

[A. DE LATTRE]

GEZELINUS, BL.

Cistercian lay brother; d. *c.* 1137. According to the legend of his life, he was a CISTERCIAN lay brother in the Abbey of Altenberg. He supposedly spent some time as a shepherd and hermit in the Rhineland. He was buried in Leverkusen-Schlebusch, and in 1814 his relics were translated to the parish church of Sankt Andreas.

Feast: Aug. 6.

Bibliography: *Acta Sanctorum* Aug. 2:172–173. A. HEINTZ, *Lexikon für Theologie und Kirche*, ed. J. HOFER and K. RAHNER, 10 v. (2d, new ed. Freiburg 1957–65); suppl., *Das Zweite Vatikanische Konzil: Dokumente und Kommentare*, ed. H. S. BRECHTER et al., pt. 1 (1966) 4:878. P. OPLADEN, *Heimatbuch Leverkusen-Schlebusch* (Leverkusen 1952) 2:79–88.

[B. J. COMASKEY]

GEZZELINUS, BL.

Hermit; d. Aug. 6, 1138. He was a hermit in Grünenwald near Luxembourg and for almost 14 years lived without shelter or clothing in the mountains and forests. With incredible patience and endurance he bore the summer heat and winter cold with herbs and roots as his only food. The monk ACHARD of Clairvaux is supposed to have met Gezzelinus while staying at the Abbey of HIMMEROD as a master builder and to have given him the habit of BERNARD OF CLAIRVAUX. On the basis of this the CISTERCIANS number him as one of their own, but in fact he never assumed the habit. He was buried in the Benedictine abbey church of Maria–Münster in the city of Luxembourg, but his relics have disappeared since the destruction of the abbey church in 1544.

Feast: Aug. 6.

Bibliography: A. M. ZIMMERMANN, *Kalendarium Benedictinum: Die Heiligen und Seligen des Benediktinerorderns und seiner Zweige* 2:544; 4:88. B. GRIESSER, ed., *Exordium magnum Cisterciense* (Series scriptorum sancti ordinis cisterciensis 2; Rome 1961) 202. *Patrologia Latina* 185.1:455–459.

[C. SPAHR]

GHANA, THE CATHOLIC CHURCH IN

Capital: Accra.
Size: 92,100 sq. miles.
Population: 19,533,560 in 2000.
Languages: English; Akan, Moshi-Dagomba, Ewe, and Ga are spoken in various regions.
Religions: 4,102,505 Catholics (21%), 4,300,830 Muslims (22%), 4,884,333 Protestants (25%), 6,245,892 practice indigenous faiths (32%).

Formerly the British Colony of the Gold Coast, the Republic of Ghana is located in West Africa bordering the Gulf of Guinea on the south, Côte d'Ivoire on the west, BURKINA FASO on the north and northwest, and TOGO on the east. A flat region with a predominately tropical climate, Ghana rises to mountains in the southeast. The north is primarily grassland, while in the south are dense forests. Agricultural products include coco, cassava, corn and palm oil, while natural resources consist of bauxite, diamonds, gold and manganese. Harmattan winds visit the region in late winter, and periods of drought are not uncommon.

Ghana, which was formed from a merger of several British colonial holdings—on the west the Gold Coast and on the east the Togoland Trust Territory—was granted internal autonomy in 1954 and independence in 1957. In 1960 it became a republic within the British Commonwealth, and fell under a series of civilian regimes before beginning multi-party elections in 1993. Despite the wealth of natural resources in the region, by the start of the 21st century Ghana remained dependent on foreign aid due to its continued instability.

Archdioceses	Suffragans
Accra	Ho, Jasikan, Keta-Akatsi, Koforidua
Cape Coast	Goaso, Konongo-Mampong, Kumasi, Obuasi, Sekondi-Takoradi, Sunyani, Wiawso
Tamale	Damongo, Navrongo-Bolgatonga, Wa, Yendi

The Developing Church. Encompassing an ancient African kingdom known as ''the land of gold'' as early as 800, Ghana was discovered by Portuguese traders in 1471. Portuguese priests arrived at the coast beginning in 1482, although their efforts were hampered by the developing slave trade in the region. Ghana was captured by the Dutch in 1637, but was returned to the Portuguese in trade for Brazil five years later. Sporadic missionary work was carried on by the Augustinians (1572–76), the Capuchins (1637–84) and the Dominicans (1687–1704), although these early efforts were seriously hampered by tribal hostilities, a myriad of native languages, an unhealthy climate and the now-booming slave trade carried on by competing Dutch, British, Danish and French interests. Accra had an African priest from 1679 to 1682.

The Vicariate of the Two Guineas, created in 1842, included Ghana. In 1879, four years after the region became a British colony, the Prefecture Apostolic of the Gold Coast was erected and entrusted to the Society of the AFRICAN MISSIONS. Catholic missionary work began in earnest in 1880, following active Protestant evangelization efforts begun as early as 1737 and growing in strength through the efforts of Presbyterian and Methodist missionaries in the 1800s. In 1901 Ghana expanded northward and by 1906 the White Fathers began to evangelize this new region. In 1943 the Prefecture Apostolic of Accra was established and entrusted to the Society of the DIVINE WORD. In 1950, with 300,000 Catholics in the country, the hierarchy was established, with Cape Coast (formerly Vicariate of the Gold Coast, 1901–50) as archdiocese and metropolitan see. The Ghana Catholic Bishop's Conference was established in 1960.

In 1956 the territory of Togoland voted for union with Ghana, and the region achieved independence from Great Britain a year later, on March 7, 1957. A republic was established under the leadership of Kwame Nkrumah in 1960, but was overthrown by a military coup in 1966. Although the civilian government was restored in 1969, its fall again within three years foreshadowed the political unrest that would plague the region for several decades.

Bibliography: R. M. WILTGEN *Gold Coast Mission History: 1471–1880* (Techny, IL 1956). *Bilan du Monde*, 2 v. (Tournai 1964) 2:403–408.

[R. M. WILTGEN]

The Modern Church. The Second Vatican Council, held from 1962–65, inspired a re-evaluation of the Ghanaian Church's relationship to its cultural milieu. Taking account of the socio-religious traditions shaping the country, the Church recognized the need for a dynamic interaction between the Gospels and native traditions. As a result, meaningful symbols from local cultures were introduced into the liturgy, and in catechesis Ghanaian concepts were used to transmit the message of the Gospel. Another postconciliar development was the resurgence of spiritual activity among lay people. The Spiritual Renewal Center in Kumasi and the Wanye Renewal Center at Wa were organized to support the formation of lay groups in their regions. As a result of diocesal training, lay people soon staffed national and diocesan departments and commissions.

Church Weathers Political Upheaval. Through a series of coups, a succession of governments held short-term control of the country following the fall of Nkrumah. Then, in 1979 a military government under Jerry Rawlings took power through brutal means. On Dec. 31, 1981 the brutality of Rawlings and his cadre of junior military officers reached extreme proportions, including the murder of three judges and a retired army major. The constitution was suspended, and freedom of speech curtailed. Catholic schools had been nationalized in 1950; in 1987 the teaching of Christian religion within Ghana's public schools was further curtailed by the state, and by the late 1990s the Church role in education had been reduced to appointing and supervising teachers. In 1985 the government forced the shut-down of the Church-run *Catholic Standard* after it criticized state policy, and four years later, in June of 1989, required the registration of all religious bodies, although this law was later repealed. The *Catholic Standard* resumed publication in 1992. The Church remained active in the areas of education, medical care and socio-economic well-being. Under pressure from international organizations, Rawlings eventually restored democracy, although he won the first multiparty election, held in November of 1992 amid some controversy.

Continues Active Role in Politics, Society. The growing presence of native bishops in the Ghana Catholic Bishops' Conference during the 1970s enabled it to play an active role in the protection and defense of human rights. The Conference maintained a good working relationship with the Christian Council of Ghana and on several instances worked together to jointly protest

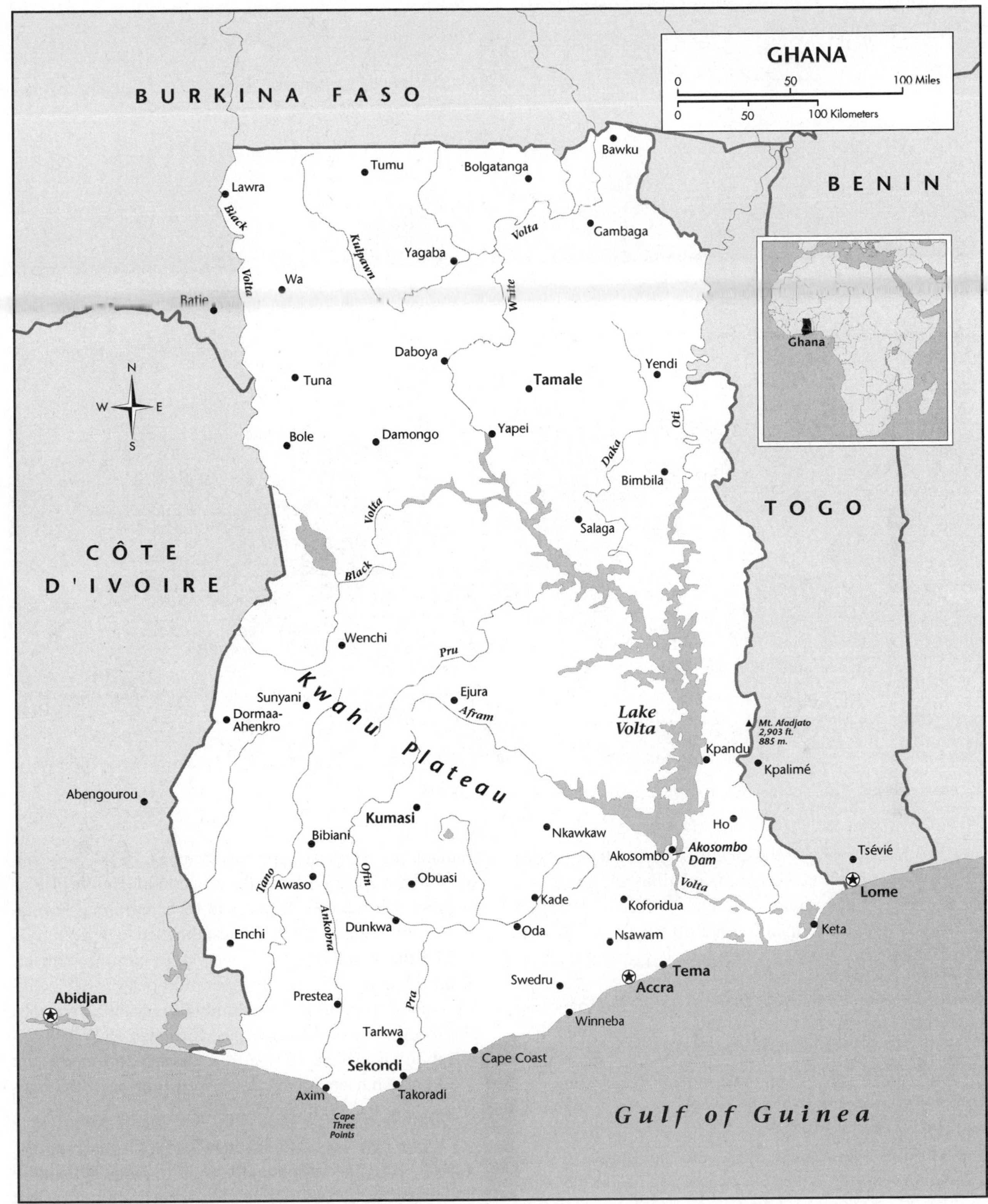

government injustices. In 1972 the bishops published a statement on family planning to express concern about public policy. A pastoral letter in December of 1973 stressed the right to life as fundamental to human beings. In September of 1982, a Justice and Peace Commission document drew the nation's attention to the causes of the

Pope John Paul II, Kumasi, Ghana, May 1980. (©Vittoriano Rastelli/CORBIS)

steady desertification of the country. To stop the process, it made some important recommendations and suggested measures for their implementation. In July of 1988 the bishops issued a statement on the effects of the government's Economic Recovery Program, expressing their indignation at high taxes, the importation of drugs forbidden in the countries of their origin and the vast funds being used for Family Planning. And in 1991 they published *The Catholic Church and Ghana's Search for a New Democratic System*, a document that strongly advocated the promotion of human rights, the harmonization of aspects of structures and norms of traditional constitutions with modern ones, party politics and the enshrinement of the freedom of expression and of the press in a future constitution. Ghana's April 1992 constitution reflected most of the concerns in this document.

Into the 21st Century. By 2000 Ghana had 289 parishes, tended by 684 secular and 169 religious priests. Three major seminaries were in operation: St. Victor's at Tamale, St. Peter's at Cape Coast and St. Paul's in Accra. In 1990 the Holy Ghost Fathers opened a House of Philosophy at Ejisu and an Institute for Continuing Formation for the religious was also established. The country's 172 brothers and 767 sisters were active in the ministry of the Church, aiding in the operation of hospitals, clinics, nurses' training colleges, midwifery training schools, pharmacies and orphanages. The Christian Hospitals Association of Ghana (CHAG), Catholic and Protestant served as a liaison between religious-run service organizations and the Ministry of Health.

Among the issues facing the Church by 2000 was the continued conflict between local cultures and Christianity caused by the proliferation of syncretic churches that adopted some Christian doctrines while placing them within a native faith. Financial self-reliance, the treatment of leprosy, AIDS and other diseases, and efforts to maintain public health through the preservation of safe drinking water also received Church attention. Of particular concern to Catholics with regard to tribal religions was the prevalence of a form of religious slavery known as ''trokosi'' which violated the human rights of thousands of young women and children in the Ewe tribe. A pastoral letter issued in 1997 calling for an end to ethnic tensions and political corruption was followed up by Pope John Paul II in February of 1999, when he encouraged Ghanaian bishops to help the nation's weakest people, adding that ''Rivalries based on race or ethnic origin have no place in the Church of Christ.''

Bibliography: J. G. AMAMOO *The New Ghana: The Birth of a Nation* (2000). *Common Journey, Different Paths,* ed. S. RAKOCZY, (Maryknoll, NJ 1992). CHRISTIAN COUNCIL OF GHANA AND GHANA CATHOLIC BISHOPS' CONFERENCE, *The Election of President and Parliamentarians for the Fourth Republic* (Accra 1992). GHANA CATHOLIC BISHOPS' CONFERENCE, *The Catholic Church and Ghana's Search for a New Democratic System* (Accra 1991). J. S. POBEE, *Religion and Politics in Ghana* (Asempa, 1992); *Kwame Nkrumah and the Church in Ghana: 1949–66* (Chicago, IL 2000). *Mission in Dialogue,* eds., M. MOTTE and J. LANG (Maryknoll, NJ 1982) 537–43. K. SHILLINGTON, *Ghana and the Rawlings Factor* (London 1991). *Missiology,* 19 (1991) 59–68. *Pro Mundi Vita Dossiers: Africa,* 32 (1985) 2–38. *PMV Bulletin,* 53 (1975) 1–36. AFER, 23 (1981) 37–39. *Journal of Religion in Africa,* 17/1 (1987) 44–62. *Annuario Pontificio* has data on all diocese.

[G. A. MANTE/EDS.]

GHEBREMICHAEL, BL.

Ethiopian martyr and theologian (known also as Gabra Micha'el); b. Mertoulé Mariam, Ethiopia, *c.* 1790; d. Cerecia Ghebaba, Ethiopia, Aug. 28, 1855. Of Portuguese-Ethiopian ancestry, Ghebremichael (servant of Michael) was a Monophysite monk renowned for his holiness and theological learning. During a mission in 1841 to the Coptic patriarch of Alexandria to seek the election of an Abyssian metropolitan, he became acquainted with the Italian Vincentian, Giustino de JACOBIS. Afterward he visited Rome and was received by Pope Gregory XVI. Impressed by Catholic Christology, he began to recast his own theology and soon became suspect of Arianism to the new metropolitan, Abuna Salama. In 1844 he was received into the Catholic Church by De Jacobis and assisted him in the establishment of a Catholic seminary at Gaula. Ghebremichael began translating the catechism and Catholic theological works into Ethiopic languages. In 1851 he was ordained secretly by De Jacobis and was afterward admitted to the VINCENTIANS. He was imprisoned by the usurper Theodor in 1855 at the urging of Salama. After months of harsh treatment he died in chains. He was beatified Oct. 31, 1926.

Feast: Sept. 1.

Bibliography: G. GOYAU, in *The Golden Legend Overseas,* ed. M. M. VAUSSARD, tr. W. B. WELLS (London 1931). *Acta Apostolicae Sedis* 12 (1920) 123–127; 18 (1926) 407–411. J. L. BAUDOT and L. CHAUSSIN, *Vies des saints et des bienheureux selon l'ordre du calendrier avec l'historique des fêtes.* ed. by the Benedictines of Paris (Paris 1935–56) 9. 35–39. D. ATTWATER, *The Golden Book of Eastern Saints* (Milwaukee 1938) 136–147. A. BUTLER, *The Lives of the Saints,* rev. ed. H. THURSTON and D. ATTWATER (New York 1956) 3:465–466.

[T. P. JOYCE]

GHETTO

An enclave within a city or on its outskirts to which the Jews were confined by law. During the Middle Ages most Jews in any city lived by themselves in a special quarter (known in English as Jewry, in German as *Judengasse*), to which no legal restrictions were attached. But beginning with the COUNTER REFORMATION of the 16th century and lasting well into the 19th century, the ghetto in the strict sense, in which all the Jews of a city were compelled to live and in which no Christian could reside, was a well-established institution throughout southern and central Europe. Rome, Prague, and Frankfurt am Main were some of the cities that had important ghettoes.

Usually located in the worst section of a town, a ghetto often suffered serious epidemics, and its surrounding walls severely limited the living room of its inhabitants. Egress was prohibited after sunset, and its gates were closed on Sundays. Yet religious activities flourished under the stimulus of segregated adversity. Self-contained economically and culturally, the ghetto was largely autonomous, having its own councils and its own courts, in both the secular and the rabbinical spheres.

The derivation of the term is uncertain. It is generally derived from the Italian word *getto* (with a soft ''g''), meaning foundry, since the term was first used of the ghetto of Venice (founded in 1516), which was near the city's foundry; yet in the Venetian dialect the word would be *zetto.* Less likely are the derivations from Italian *borghetto* (little suburb) or the Hebrew *get* (with a hard ''g''—bill of divorce).

Bibliography: L. WIRTH, *The Ghetto* (Chicago 1928; pa. 1956). G. KISCH, *The Jews in Medieval Germany* (Chicago 1949). H. LEHMANN and R. PO-CHIA HSIA, *In and Out of the Ghetto: Jewish-Gentile Relations in Late Medieval and Early Modern Germany* (Cambridge, England 1995). A. LEWIN, *A Cup of Tears: A Diary of the Warsaw Ghetto* (Oxford 1988). D. A. SIERAKOWIAK, ed., K. TUROWSKI, KAMIL, tr. *The Diary of Dawid Sierakowiak: Five Notebooks from the Lódz Ghetto* (Oxford 1996). A. TOAFF, *The Ghetto of Rome in the 16th Century: Ethnical and Social Conflicts* (Ramat-Gan, Israel 1984). Y. ZUCKERMAN, *A Surplus of Memory: Chronicle of the Warsaw Ghetto Uprising* (Berkeley 1993).

[R. KRINSKY]

Aurobindo Ghose.

GHOSE, AUROBINDO

Indian philosopher and poet who wrote in English, best known under his title, Sri Aurobindo; b. Calcutta, Aug. 15, 1872; d. Pondicherry, Dec. 5, 1950. He was the third son of Dr. Krishnadhan Ghose and was educated at the Loretto Convent School, Darjeeling, and at St. Paul's School, London; he then went on to King's College, Cambridge, England, where he took first–class honors in classics. After returning to India (1893), he taught French and English at Baroda College, and while engaging in literary and political journalism he published two volumes of poetry, *Songs to Myrtilla* (1895) and *Urvasie* (1896). He married Mrinalini in 1901. He entered active politics in 1906 in order to combat English efforts to partition Bengal, but his opposition led to his arrest. His practice of YOGA enabled him to achieve an inner peace, which sustained him during his arrest, trial, and acquittal (1908–09). He thereafter withdrew from politics and retired to Pondicherry (then in French India), where he remained until his death. He edited *Arya*, a philosophical journal (1914–21), and published serially *The Life Divine, The Synthesis of Yoga, The Ideal of Human Unity,* and other works. He established an *ashram* (a retreat for spiritual aspirants) in 1922 and in his last years was mainly engaged on *Savitri*, an immense symbolic epic based on the ancient story of Savitri and Satyavan as related in the Sanskrit epic *Mahābhārata.*

Ghose was a poet, a mystic, and a philosopher whose ideas bear some resemblance to those of St. THOMAS AQUINAS and Pierre TEILHARD DE CHARDIN. In *The Life Divine* Ghose tried to synthesize all knowledge into an integrated whole; and as Teilhard posited the ''omega point,'' Ghose envisioned the ''supermind''—arduous spiritual striving inevitably shaping the New Man in whom the divine is radiantly revealed. Ghose's English prose is rich and sweeping; his poetry includes translations, blank verse dramas (*Perseus the Deliverer, Vāsavadutta, Rodogune, Eric*), philosophical poems (e.g., *Ahana*), lyrics (e.g., *Thought the Paraclete*), the unfinished *Ilion*, a sequel to the *Iliad*, and the 24,000-line *Savitri*. In this last work the heroine symbolizes the divine force that frees the light of truth from the darkness of death. It contains (in Canto 2 of ''The Book of Fate'') a significant reference to Christ's drinking the bitter cup and signing salvation's testament with His blood.

Bibliography: A. GHOSE, *The Life Divine* (Pondicherry 1955); *Collected Poems and Plays,* 2 v. (Pondicherry 1942); *Savitri* (Pondicherry 1954). K. R. SRINIVASA IYENGAR, *Sri Aurobindo* (2d ed. Calcutta 1950). P. NANDAKUMAR, *A Study of ''Savitri''* (Pondicherry 1962). D. A. CAPPADONA, ''Poetry as Yoga: The Spiritual Ascent of Sri Aurobindo,'' *Horizons* 7 (Fall 1980) 265–284. R. A. MCDERMOTT, ed., *Six Pillars: Introductions to the Major Works of Sri Aurobindo* (Chambersburg, PA 1974). R. N. MINOR, ''Sri Aurobindo's Integral View of Other Religions,'' *Religious Studies* 15 (1979) 365–377. S. H. PHILLIPS, *Aurobindo's Philosophy of Brahman* (Leiden, 1986). K. R. SRINIVASA IYENGAR, *Sri Aurobindo: A Centenary Tribute* (Pondicherry, India, 1974). F. THOMPSON, *A New Look at Aurobindo* (Delhi, 1990).

[K. R. SRINIVASA IYENGAR]

GIACCARDO, TIMOTEO, BL.

Baptized Giuseppe Domenico Vicenzo Antonio (Joseph Dominic Vincent Anthony) Giaccardo; publisher, Pauline priest, founder of the Pious Disciples of the Divine Master; b. June 13, 1896, Narzole (diocese of Alba), Cuneo, Italy; d. Jan. 24, 1948, at Rome.

His parents were peasant farmers who began instilling in their son a strong spirit of prayer from infancy. Giaccardo met Fr. James Alberione, founder of the Society of St. Paul, while serving Mass at St. Bernard's Church in Narzole in 1908. Giaccardo entered the diocesan seminary in Alba (1917), but he received his bishop's permission to join the Paulines, despite the bishop's initial caution about the new society. Giaccardo was ordained in 1919 as the first priest of the new order, taking the name Timothy upon his profession in 1920.

Giaccardo's ministry consisted of writing, editing, and distributing religious material. In addition, he helped in the formation of younger members of the order as a teacher of theology, and served as vocation director. In 1926, he was entrusted with founding the society's first house in Rome. There he edited the weekly *The Voice of Rome* and managed the pressroom. He was recalled to Alba to direct the motherhouse, but sent back to Rome in 1946 as provincial superior of the Society of St. Paul and vicar general of the congregation. Recognizing the importance of prayer to support the active ministries of the Pauline Family, he established the nucleus of the contemplative branch, the Sister Disciples of the Divine Master. When the Holy See opposed the division of the Daughters of St. Paul, Giaccardo was given the delicate task of persuading Vatican authorities to approve the community, which happened in 1948.

Although Giaccardo was Alberione's chosen successor, he died shortly after the approbation of the new contemplative order. His body was laid to rest in the lower crypt of the Basilica of Mary, Queen of Apostles, next to the house he founded. He was beatified by Pope John Paul II on Oct. 22, 1989. He is the patron of publishers.

Bibliography: E. FORNASARI, *Bl. Timothy Giaccardo: An Obedient Prophet*, tr. K. D. WHITEHEAD (New York 1991). G. PAPÀSOGLI, *Il beato Timoteo Giaccardo della Società San Paolo* (Turin 1989).

[K. I. RABENSTEIN]

GIANELLI, ANTHONY, ST.

Bishop, religious founder; b. Cereta (Liguria), Italy, Apr. 12, 1789; d. Piacenza, June 7, 1846. Born of a poor family, he attended the seminary at Genoa due to the generosity of a benefactress, and was ordained (1812). The following year he began a decade of teaching rhetoric. In 1826 he became archpriest at Chiavari, and in 1838 bishop of Bobbio. While a professor, he developed a new method of education. He gained a wide reputation as an eloquent, tireless, popular preacher, and conductor of retreats to the clergy. As a writer he published nine valuable tracts on varied subjects. Four volumes of his discourses have been printed; nine others remain in MS. His correspondence was also very extensive and helped promote many vocations. He was a member of the Società Economica, whose aims were cultural and charitable. In 1829 he founded the Daughters of OUR LADY OF THE GARDEN, or Gianelline; and in 1839, the Oblates of St. Alfonsus for clerical formation, but this group did not survive him. As bishop he continued his zealous activities, held two diocesan synods, and proved himself both a saintly prelate and a capable administrator, firm in principles. He was beatified April 19, 1925, by Pius XI, and canonized Oct. 21, 1951, by Pius XII.

Feast: June 7.

St. Anthony Gianelli.

Bibliography: C. SANGUINETI, *Il beato A. M. Gianelli* (Turin 1925). G. FREDIANI, *S. Antonio Maria Gianelli: Profilo biografico* (2d ed. Rome 1951); *Bibliotheca sanctorum* (Rome 1961–) 2:211–216.

[A. FERRAIRONI]

GIBAULT, PIERRE

Missionary; b. Montreal, Canada, April 7, 1735; d. New Madrid, Mo., Aug. 15, 1802. He was the eldest of five children of Pierre and Marie Madeleine (Brunet) Gibault, peasants whose ancestors had come to New France in 1663. Sometime in his youth he visited the Mississippi Valley with a fur brigade. Gibault received two years of theological training in the diocesan seminary of Quebec, where he was ordained at the age of 25. In June 1760 he went to the Illinois country, where, from the time of the expulsion of the Jesuits, the aging Sebastian Meurin, SJ, was the only priest to care for the French and indigenous people residing between Michilimakinac and the Arkansas River. Gibault settled at Kaskaskia, and from there he visited Vincennes, Ste. Genevieve, Cahokia, St. Louis, Peoria, St. Joseph (Michigan), and Michilimakinac. In 1777 he was left alone in the ministry when Meurin died at Prairie du Rocher.

When the War of Independence began, Bp. Joseph Briand of Quebec forbade any of the clergy or laity of his diocese to offer help to the revolutionists, threatening suspension of offenders among ecclesiastics and denial of the Sacraments to the laity. However, Gibault lent his support to Gen. George Rogers Clark when the Virginian appeared on July 4, 1778, to persuade the citizenry and the native Americans at Kaskaskia, Cahokia, and Vincennes to join the American cause. The priest's courageous action was the deciding factor in the success of General Clark's campaign. Gibault continued on friendly terms with American officials, but in 1782, when lawless easterners drifted into the Illinois country, making Kaskaskia their center, he left there, taking up residence in Ste. Genevieve. From there he continued to care for the religious needs of the Catholics in the Mississippi Valley. In 1789 when Bp. John Carroll acquired episcopal jurisdiction over the territory, Gibault was in a quandary regarding the source of his ecclesiastical faculties. Though Carroll treated the veteran missionary kindly, Gibault preferred to leave Ste. Genevieve in favor of New Madrid, Mo., which was then clearly within Spanish territory. He applied to Spanish civil authorities as well as to the newly appointed bishop of the See of Louisiana, and in 1792 became the pastor of New Madrid, where he died ten years later.

Bibliography: Archives of the Archdiocese of Baltimore. Archives of the Archdiocese of St. Louis. The New Madrid collection in the Missouri Historical Society of St. Louis. J. C. DUNN, JR. ''Father Gibault,'' *Transactions of the Illinois State Historical Society* (1905) 15–34.

[J. P. DONNELLY]

GIBBONS, JAMES

Cardinal, ninth archbishop of Baltimore; b. Baltimore, Md., July 23, 1834; d. Baltimore, Md., March 24, 1921. He was the oldest son of Irish immigrant parents and was taken to Ireland at the age of three when his family returned, hoping to improve his father's health. However, Thomas Gibbons died in 1847, and in 1853 Bridget (Walsh) Gibbons returned to the U.S. and settled in New Orleans with her five children. For two years James worked as a clerk in a grocery store, but having decided to be a priest, he entered St. Charles College, Ellicott City, Md., in 1855. In 1857, he proceeded to St. Mary's Seminary, Baltimore, and was ordained for that archdiocese on June 30, 1861, by Abp. Francis Patrick Kenrick.

After about six weeks as an assistant priest at St. Patrick's Church, Baltimore, Gibbons became pastor of St. Bridget's Church, Canton, and the mission of St. Lawrence O'Toole across Chesapeake Bay. For four years he attended his two congregations and assisted as a volunteer chaplain to the Civil War troops at Fts. McHenry and Marshall. In 1865 he was appointed secretary to Martin John SPALDING, seventh Archbishop of Baltimore, and a year later named assistant chancellor of the archdiocese and made responsible for some of the preparations for the Second Plenary Council, which convened at Baltimore in October 1866. This council recommended to the Holy See the erection of new ecclesiastical jurisdictions in the U.S., among them the Vicariate Apostolic of North Carolina to which the 32-year-old James Gibbons was named. He was consecrated with the title of bishop of Adramyttium *in partibus infidelium* by Archbishop Spalding on Aug. 16, 1868.

North Carolina, nearly 50,000 square miles in area, had over a million people of whom only about 700 were Catholics. Although Gibbons found there only three priests and no Catholic institutions, he soon infused new life into his scattered flock. In October 1869 he left for Rome to attend Vatican Council I (December of 1869 to July of 1870), where he was the youngest of more than 700 bishops from all over the world. When he returned to North Carolina in October 1870, he found it plagued by carpetbagger rule. In 1872, upon the death of Bp. John McGill of Richmond, Gibbons was named administrator of the vacant see and in the following July was appointed successor to McGill while still being left in charge of North Carolina. Despite this double burden, which he carried for the next five years, the Church made marked progress in both states.

Gibbons drew on his missionary experiences in North Carolina and Virginia to write a simple exposition of the teaching of the Catholic Church designed to enlighten Catholics and to instruct prospective converts and Protestants. Published in 1876, *The Faith of Our Fathers* proved to be the most successful work of its kind in the apologetical literature of American Catholicism. When James Roosevelt Bayley, eighth Archbishop of Baltimore, sought a coadjutor, Gibbons was named in May of 1877 and given the right of succession. Bayley died on October 3, and 16 days later Gibbons arrived in Baltimore, where, at the age of 43, he assumed charge of the premier see of the U.S.

Archbishop of Baltimore. As archbishop of Baltimore, Gibbons automatically became one of the principal leaders of the American Church. Even during the eight years (1877–85) when he was outranked by Cardinal John McCloskey, Archbishop of New York, this leadership continued to grow because of McCloskey's retiring manner and increasingly ill health. In the period before the establishment of the Apostolic Delegation (1893), the occupants of the See of Baltimore performed many of the

James Cardinal Gibbons with President Theodore Roosevelt, 1918, Baltimore, Md.

functions of that institution, acting as a clearing house for American business with the Holy See. All of this Gibbons continued to do, although in a routine way, since it was not his nature to initiate new policies or inaugurate new undertakings. Thus the event that won him a national reputation in ecclesiastical circles, the Third Plenary Council of 1884, over which he presided as apostolic delegate, was in no sense owed to his initiative, any more than was the institution that may be said to have been born during the sessions of that council.

The Catholic University of America. In both cases the initiative was in other hands; in fact, Gibbons was distinctly cool to the proposal for a council, and when the time came for the bishops to vote on the location of the university, he voted for Philadelphia, not wishing it in his archdiocese. However, once the more progressive and daring bishops of the West had forced the issue of a council by appeals to Rome, Gibbons assumed the leadership that his office demanded and effectually managed the difficult and protracted preparatory plans for the council. And once the council itself had voted favorably on the project of a university, he presided with balance and fairness to all groups over the committee appointed to bring into being a university.

As archbishop of Baltimore he automatically became the first chancellor of the University once it had been determined to locate it in Washington, which was within his archdiocese. Thus from a presiding official who had somewhat reluctantly attended its birth and supervised its early life, Gibbons passed to the role of a promoter and, indeed, literally a savior of the University in the dark days of 1904 when bankruptcy overtook the treasurer and threatened to close the institution. The success with which Gibbons presided over the council for four weeks to the satisfaction of the 71 bishops in attendance made him a probable candidate for further honors, and his name was mentioned for cardinal after the death of McCloskey in 1885. In May 1886 Leo XIII designated him for the cardinalate and the red biretta was conferred on him on June 30 in Baltimore's cathedral.

Cardinal. Shortly after Gibbons's advent to Baltimore the American Church entered upon the two stormiest decades in its history. The last 20 years of the 19th century were marked by an unprecedented influx of Catholic immigrants from Europe, whose coming magnified existing problems and created new ones which the bishops had to meet. Into every major problem the archbishop of Baltimore was projected, first, by reason of his office, secondly, because after 1886 he was the ranking national dignitary of the Church, and finally, because his grasp of the affairs of Church and State was commanding. While he had no part in creating the controversies of the 1880s and 1890s within Catholic ranks, he had a major share in the solution of most of them.

Secret Societies and McGlynn Affair. The problem of membership of Catholic men in secret societies reached an acute stage in the 1880s. The cardinal was anxious that Catholic men should remain apart from any secret groups that would endanger their religious faith, but he was strongly opposed to the Church's banning these groups unless there was positive proof of their harmful character, as in the case of the Free-masons. He believed that hasty condemnations were injurious to the Church's prestige in the eyes of non-Catholics, and that they often failed to attain their objectives. Accordingly, he defended the Knights of Labor (K of L) when they came under the scrutiny of the Catholic bishops of the U.S. in 1886, and of Rome in February 1887. His defense prevented the public condemnation of the K of L in the U.S., a happy contrast to what had happened in Canada three years before.

This same spirit characterized his approach to the question of whether to put the works of Henry George, author of the single tax movement, on the Index, as Abp. Michael A. CORRIGAN of New York and others advised. Gibbons was not at all in sympathy with George's economic theories, any more than he was with the action of Edward MCGLYNN, New York priest. McGlynn's defiance of his archbishop in support of George's candidacy for mayor of New York and of his economic doctrines had led to his suspension by Corrigan and his later excommunication by the Holy See. Gibbons deplored both the fallacies of George's theories and the intransigence of McGlynn, but he insisted that a condemnation of George's books would do more harm than good, since it would afford him and his constituents a publicity that they had not merited.

These views were embodied in the documents that Gibbons addressed in February of 1887 to Cardinal Giovanni Simeoni, Prefect of the Congregation de Propaganda Fide. The one prevented a public condemnation of the K of L, while the other succeeded in keeping George's books off the Index and their author from receiving a public condemnation from the Holy Office. Gibbons's action in these two cases helped to set the American Church's future policy toward the rising industrial society of which Catholic laborers were so important a part. Gibbons knew the value that his fellow Americans attached to democratic procedures. He was sensitive, too, to the danger that might arise from officials of the Roman Curia acting in a manner that would put weapons into the hands of the enemies of the American Church. Therefore, he had said to Simeoni, ''To speak with the most perfect respect, but also with the frankness which duty requires of me, it seems to me that prudence suggests, and that even the dignity of the Church demands that we should not offer to America an ecclesiastical protection for which she does not ask, and of which she believes she has no need.''

Nationality Conflicts and School Controversy. It has often been said that Gibbons's major contribution was his ability to interpret the U.S. to the Holy See and the Catholic Church to the U.S. This was illustrated in the controversy of the late 1880s between quarreling groups of Catholics of differing national backgrounds, mostly Irish and German, which constituted a severe internal strain on the American Church. Throughout this crisis Gibbons emphasized the oneness of their common American citizenship and its obligations, as well as the oneness of their religious faith. In the sermon he preached in Milwaukee (Aug. 20, 1891) at the conferring of the pallium on Abp. Frederick X. KATZER, the cardinal warned, ''Woe to him who would breed dissension among the leaders of Israel by introducing a spirit of nationalism into the camps of the Lord! Brothers we are, whatever may be our nationality, and brothers we shall remain.'' In the same spirit he had sought to quiet the misgivings of President Benjamin Harrison when the latter revealed to him his uneasiness over the threat of foreign interference in the nationalist disputes of the American Catholics; Gibbons succeeded in convincing the President that the policies of German extremists would find no countenance with Pope Leo XIII.

He worked to calm his coreligionists during the controversy over parochial schools in the early 1890s while agreeing substantially with the proposals of Abp. John IRELAND of St. Paul. At the same time he made clear to his non-Catholic fellow citizens why the Catholic Church was compelled to insist on having its own school system. Finally, as the 19th century was closing, Gibbons did his share to reassure Leo XIII that there was no justification for the charges made by a few conservative Catholic writers in France that there was, within American Catholic circles, a movement tinged with heresy called AMERICANISM.

Other Contributions. Gibbons and his fellow bishops faced the problems of a growing secularization of American society along with the highly varied character of the Catholics themselves, composed, as they were, of men and women of numerous national backgrounds. When he took possession of his titular Church of Santa Maria in Trastevere on March 25, 1887, he sought in his sermon to harmonize as far as possible conflicting elements in American Catholic life. Acknowledging that the U.S. was not without defects, he stated, nonetheless, "I proclaim with a deep sense of pride and gratitude, and in this great capital of Christendom, that I belong to a country where the civil government holds over us the aegis of its protection without interfering in the legitimate exercise of our sublime mission as ministers of the Gospel of Jesus Christ." The cardinal's remarks on separation of Church and State in the U.S. on that occasion have since been echoed many times by clerical and lay representatives of the American Church.

Patriotism was a favorite theme of Cardinal Gibbons. Of few things was he more proud as an American than his country's Constitution, of which he said in January 1897, "I would not expunge or alter a single paragraph, a single line, or a single word . . . ." The last article he published only a month before he died stated that as the years passed he had become "more and more convinced that the Constitution of the United States is the greatest instrument of government that ever issued from the hand of man." This conviction endeared Gibbons to Americans of all religions. On June 6, 1911, President William Howard Taft and former President Theodore Roosevelt were among the 20,000 people assembled in Baltimore to commemorate the 50th anniversary of his ordination. Gibbons's interest in national, state, and municipal questions led Theodore Roosevelt to remark to him in 1917, "taking your life as a whole, I think you now occupy the position of being the most respected, and venerated, and useful citizen of our country."

Gibbons lived to within three months of the 60th anniversary of his ordination as a priest; his 52 years as bishop and 35 years as cardinal and dean of the American hierarchy made him a symbol of the American Church, which he represented at hundreds of functions, ecclesiastical and secular, in Europe and the U.S. He was a spiritual guide for men of his time. He ordained 2,471 priests and consecrated 23 bishops, a record for the American Church until 1945. In addition to conducting the affairs of his own see, and functioning as dean of the American hierarchy in the founding of the National Catholic War Council (1917), forerunner of the National Catholic Welfare Conference at whose birth he presided (1919), he fostered the Catholic Foreign Mission Society of America, better known as Maryknoll (1911). He wrote articles for secular and Catholic periodicals and newspapers, and besides *The Faith of Our Fathers,* he was the author of four other works: *Our Christian Heritage* (1889), *The Ambassador of Christ* (1896), *Discourses and Sermons* (1908), and *A Retrospect of Fifty Years* (1916).

Bibliography: J. T. ELLIS, *The Life of James Cardinal Gibbons,* 2 v. (Milwaukee 1952), especially "An Essay on the Sources," 2:651–659, where all the leading manuscript and printed sources for Gibbons's life are listed with critical comments.

[J. T. ELLIS]

GIBERTI, GIAN MATTEO

Bishop of Verona and advocate of Church reform; b. Palermo, Sept. 20, 1495; d. Verona, Dec. 30, 1543. He was the son of Francesco Giberti, Grand Admiral of Genoa. As a young priest he served in the secretariat of Cardinal Giulio de Medici and rose rapidly in the papal service. He was associated with the Oratory of DIVINE LOVE, a group devoted to the promotion of the austere life and reform of the Church. He was appointed datary by CLEMENT VII in 1523 and bishop of Verona in 1524. He remained in Rome for the first years after this appointment and was represented by a vicar-general in Verona. In 1527 he was taken hostage during the sack of Rome. Upon his release he took up his residence in Verona (1528).

Giberti established his reputation as a reformer by close supervision of all the responsibilities of his position. He insisted that the clergy perform their duties and live in the proper religious manner. He promoted measures of relief for the poor and the establishment of charitable institutions. His support of intellectual activity was carried out through the printing of religious works by his own printing press. He encouraged the study of Scripture and supported the work of learned men. In his own letters and in *Constitutiones Ecclesiasticae* he suggested various means of reform for the improvement of the Church. He was also a member of the reform commission appointed by Pope PAUL III in 1536. The report of this commission severely criticized many papal policies and recommended specific measures of reform. In 1540 Giberti served as papal legate to the conference of Catholic and Protestant theologians at Worms. His sudden death in 1543 prevented his participation in the Council of Trent.

Bibliography: M. A. TUCKER, "Gian Matteo Giberti, Papal Politician and Catholic Reformer," *English Historical Review* 18 (1903) 24–51, 266–286, 439–469. G. B. PIGHI, *Gianmatteo Giberti, vescovo di Verona* (Verona 1900). H. JEDIN, *Il tipo ideale di vescovo* *secondo la riforma cattolica* (Brescia 1950). L. BOPP, *Lexikon für Theologie und Kirche*, (2d, new ed. Freiburg 1957–65) 4:885.

[W. J. STEINER]

GIBIEUF, GUILLAUME

Philosopher and theologian; b. Bourges *c.* end of the 16th century; d. Paris, June 6, 1650. Gibieuf joined the Oratory in 1612, and became a valuable assistant to its founder, Pierre de BÉRULLE. Upon the death of Bérulle in 1629 Gibieuf became superior, then visitor of the Carmelite nuns. In 1641 after having refused the See of Nantes, he became superior of Saint-Magloire, the archdiocesan seminary of Paris, where he died nine years later. Gibieuf is important in the fields of spirituality, philosophy, and theology. His teaching and practice of the Christian life are very much of the Bérullian school. His Marian work, *Vie et grandeurs de la très sainte Vierge Marie* (2 v., Paris 1637), is noteworthy for its original insights, its elevated mysticism, and its theological exactitude. In philosophy and theology, his *De libertate Dei et creaturae* (Paris 1630) was a new attempt to solve the problem of free will and the divine concursus. Some philosophers, including É. Gilson, hold that this work possibly influenced the thinking of R. DESCARTES, particularly in the Cartesian concept of the divine freedom; others believe that Gibieuf's influence is limited to the Neoplatonic and Augustinian elements found in Descartes. Gibieuf's work has also been called a precursor of C. O. JANSEN's *Augustinus.* However, even if it is true that his ideas on liberty are somewhat similar to those later held by Jansen, Gibieuf was himself no Jansenist: he adhered completely to the decisions of the Church, and he took steps to preserve his Carmelite subjects from Jansenist influence.

Bibliography: É. GILSON, *Liberté chez Descartes et la théologie* (Paris 1913). A. INGOLD, *Dictionnaire de théologie catholique,* ed. A. VACANT, 15 v. (Paris 1903–50; Tables générales 1951–) 6.2:1347–48. G. MARAFINI, *Agli albori del Giansenismo: Guillaume Gibieuf e il suo pensiero intorno alla libertà* (Rome 1947), with good bibliog.

[M. A. ROCHE]

GIBSON, WILLIAM, BL.

Lay martyr; b. near Ripon, Yorkshire, England; d. Nov. 29, 1596, hanged, drawn, and quartered at York. Arrested for his involvement in an uprising in the North, he spent many years imprisoned at York Castle where he gained a reputation for piety. He was sentenced with BB. George ERRINGTON and William KNIGHT for trying to ''persuade to popery'' a Protestant prisoner, who indicated an interest in Catholicism, but used it as a tool to gain freedom for himself and intelligence for the authorities. Gibson was beatified by Pope John Paul II on Nov. 22, 1987 with George Haydock and Companions.

Feast of the English Martyrs: May 4 (England).

See Also: MARTYRS OF ENGLAND AND WALES.

Bibliography: R. CHALLONER, *Memoirs of Missionary Priests,* ed. J. H. POLLEN (rev. ed. London 1924). J. H. POLLEN, *Acts of English Martyrs* (London 1891). YEPES, *Historia Particular de la persecucion de Inglaterra* (Madrid 1599). STAPLETON, *Post-Reformation Catholic Missions in Oxfordshire* (London 1906).

[K. I. RABENSTEIN]

GIDEON

A ''major'' judge from western Manasses who saved Israel from disaster *c.* 1070 B.C. (Jgs 6.1–8.28). Gideon's vocation to save Israel involved first the vindication of the unique cult of Yahweh against syncretist tendencies (Jgs 6.25–32). His struggle against religious assimilation was summarized in the popular explanation of his second name, Jerubbaal, ''Let Baal take action against him, since he destroyed his altar'' (Jgs 6.32), although the correct meaning of the name is ''May Baal defend him.'' Through Gideon, then, the cult of Yahweh ousted that of Baal, because Baal was powerless to defend his rights. That Gideon's name was formed with Baal, while his father's, Joash, with Yahweh, illustrates the confused religious situation of the time. Many had adopted the cult of local gods, the Baals; only a few along with Gideon remained faithful to Yahweh, and through them monotheism finally triumphed.

Annually, at harvestime, camel-riding nomads—''Midianites, Amalekites, and the Kedemites'' (Jgs 6.3)—irrupted into Palestine from the Arabian desert, ravaging the land. The avalanche of marauding nomads threatened to drive Israel from Palestine. The story of Gideon's war against Midian—the second stage in his liberation of Israel—combines a series of distinct episodes; hence, reconstruction is difficult. Yahweh's intervention and leadership were the sacred author's primary affirmation and concern. The Lord delivered Midian into Israel's hands. He was the real victor. The timid were sent away, and the army was reduced to 300 men to make the divine intervention even more striking. ''For Yahweh and for Gideon!'' was their battle cry. Yahweh threw the enemy camp into confusion and victory followed. The victorious Israelites, sensing their military weakness, offered Gideon hereditary principality: ''Rule over us—you, your son and your son's son.'' He refused because, ''The Lord must rule over you'' (Jgs 8.22–23). That he

"Gideon Testing His Soldiers," engraving. (©CORBIS)

did, however, exercise some type of authority is indicated by his large harem, a mark of power and rule (Jgs 8.30). The eventual ruin of Gideon's family was occasioned by an EPHOD made from the spoils of victory. Though he intended it for Yahweh's cult in the sanctuary at Ophrah, "all Israel paid idolatrous homage to it" (Jgs 8.27).

The story of Gideon poses some delicate problems. There are, apparently, two different traditions concerning the origin of the worship of Yahweh in Ophrah. A double convocation of the tribes is recorded and discrepancies appear in the narrative of the campaign against Midian. Many commentators attribute these apparent inconsistencies to the intermingling of two sources. Perhaps a basic narrative has been enriched by independent pieces, with several documents being used in a complementary fashion.

Bibliography: *Encyclopedic Dictionary of the Bible*, tr. and adap. by L. HARTMAN (New York 1963) 846–847. H. CAZELLES, *Dictionnaire de la Bible,* suppl. ed. L. PIROT, et al. (Paris 1928–) 4:1403–04. R. G. BOLING, *Judges* Anchor Bible 6A. (Garden City, NY 1975).

[J. MORIARITY]

GIFFARD, BONAVENTURE

Vicar Apostolic of the (English) Midlands district (1688–1703) and of the London district (1703–34); b. Wolverhampton, 1642; d. Hammersmith, 1734. The most prominent of the early vicars apostolic, and greatly venerated, he lived through the reigns of 12 popes and of eight rulers of England. The second son of Andrew Giffard of Chillington, Staffordshire, he was educated at Douay College, and was the first student to enter St. Gregory's, Paris. After taking his doctorate he went to England and began his long career of danger and hardship in the Midlands and in the London slums. He was made the first vicar apostolic of the Midland district, having been consecrated titular bishop of Madura at Whitehall on April 22, 1688. In the same year he was appointed by James II to be president of Magdalen College, Oxford, after the king had ejected the Protestant fellows. A few months later Giffard and his Catholic fellows were in turn ejected. Captured while trying to escape to the Continent, he suffered for nearly two years in Newgate prison. Fifteen years later, on the death of Bp. John Leyburn, he returned to London where until his death he remained the leader of the persecuted Catholics. Hunted by government agents, he constantly had to change his lodgings, and was five times arrested. In extreme old age he retired to the disguised convent of the Institute of Mary at Hammersmith, where he died.

Bibliography: J. GILLOW, *A Literary and Biographical History or Bibliographical Dictionary of the English Catholics from 1534 to the Present Time,* 5 v. (London-New York 1885–1902; repr. New York 1961) 2:454–456. W. M. BRADY, *The Episcopal Succession in England, Scotland, and Ireland,* A.D. *1400 to 1875,* 3 v. (Rome 1876–77) v.3 passim. B. HEMPHILL, *The Early Vicars Apostolic of England, 1685–1750* (London 1954).

[B. WHELAN]

GIFFORD, WILLIAM

English party leader, Benedictine, and prelate; b. Gloucestershire, 1554; d. Reims, April 11, 1629. He was educated at Lincoln College, Oxford, the University of Louvain, the English College at Douay, and the English College at Rome. After ordination in 1582 as a protégé of Cardinal William Allen, he taught theology at Reims until 1593, then served Allen in Rome and Flanders (1593–94). Upon Allen's death he was made dean of Lille in 1595. His long and violent disagreement with Robert PERSONS, SJ, was at that time well advanced.

Until all the evidence of the intricate quarrels of the English exiles is published, much will remain obscure, although this tentative character of our knowledge has not prevented widely varying partisan judgments on the protagonists. Persons accused Gifford of fomenting opposition in the seminaries to Jesuit direction and policies, and of corresponding secretly and treacherously with the English government and agents. It is generally certain that Gifford did foment trouble and conduct such a correspondence. What is still uncertain is the degree of irresponsibility and factiousness he showed, and how far he was justified in his opposition to Persons' policies. Moreover, there is no real doubt about the firmness of his Catholic faith throughout these troubles. In 1606 he was mysteriously expelled from the Spanish Netherlands and lived in Paris (1606–08) and then in Reims as a professor at the university. In 1608 he did what an increasing number of seminarian opponents of Persons were doing—joined the English Benedictines. From his profession in 1609 until 1617 he was remarkably active: in rapid succession he became Prior of Dieulouard, founded the English monasteries of St. Malo and St. Edmund's Paris, helped to form the English Benedictine Congregation, and became first president of and helped to reform Fontrevault. He was a close friend of the Guise family and supporter of the Ligue, and through their influence he was consecrated in 1617 coadjutor to Louis of Lorraine, cardinal de Guise, and archbishop of Reims. In 1622 he succeeded to the see, clearly as a Guise nominee, and ruled it until his death. After Allen and Persons, he was undoubtedly the most celebrated English Catholic of his day. His achievements included the decisive reestablishing of the English Benedictine Congregation, much solid teaching of theology and effective preaching, and a good deal of hard work to help restore the French Church after the religious wars.

Bibliography: T. FITZHERBERT, *Letters,* in *Publications of the Catholic Record Society,* v. 41, ed. L. HICKS (London 1948). *The Wisbech Stirs, 1595–1598* in *Publications of the Catholic Record Society,* v. 51, ed. P. RENOLD (London 1958). J. MCCANN, ''William Gabriel Gifford,'' *Ampleforth and Its Origins,* ed. J. MCCANN and C. CARY-ELWES (London 1952). T. H. CLANCY, *Papist Pamphleteers: The Allen-Persons Party and the Political Thought of the Counter-Reformation in England, 1572–1615* (Chicago 1964)

[H. AVELING]

GIGLI, GIOVANNI

Bishop, English agent at the Roman Curia; b. Bruges, 1434; d. Rome, Aug. 25, 1498. Gigli, son of a merchant of Lucca, was a doctor of civil and canon law by 1477, when he became a naturalized Englishman. He served as a papal collector in England, and became papal subdeacon by 1483 and prothonotary apostolic by 1488. These curial connections led to his appointment as resident English proctor at Rome (1490–98). His services were rewarded by substantial preferments after 1477: he held canonries in Wells, St. Paul's, London, Lichfield, Lincoln, and Salisbury and was archdeacon of London (1482–90) and of Gloucester (1489–97). Having been provided on Aug. 30, 1497, to the See of WORCESTER, he was consecrated at Rome on September 10, and held the see until death. Although he enjoyed some reputation as a humanist, he used his literary abilities chiefly to further his career.

Bibliography: B. BEHRENS, ''The Origins of the Office of English Resident Ambassador at Rome,'' *English Historical Review* 49 (1934) 640–656. R. WEISS, ''Lineamenti di una biografia di G. Gigli . . . ,'' *Rivista di storia della Chiesa in Italia* 1 (1947) 379–391. A. B. EMDEN, *A Biographical Register of the Scholars of* *the University of Oxford to A.D. 1500,* 3 v. (Oxford 1957–59) 2: 764–765.

[C. D. ROSS]

GIGOT, FRANCIS ERNEST

Scripture scholar and professor; b. Lhuant (Indre), France, Aug. 21, 1859; d. New York City, June 14, 1920. After his studies at the Christian Brothers' college, Le Dorat, Vienne, the diocesan seminary of Limoges, and the Catholic Institute of Paris, he joined the Society of St. Sulpice. He was ordained on Dec. 22, 1883. In 1883 he came to America, and until 1899 he was on the faculty of St. John's Seminary, Brighton, Mass., as professor, successively, of dogmatic theology, philosophy, and Scripture. In 1899 he was transferred to St. Mary's Seminary, Baltimore, and in 1904 to St. Joseph's Seminary, Dunwoodie, Yonkers, New York. In both of these institutions he was professor of Scripture, and he remained in that field until his death. In 1906 he resigned from the Sulpicians and joined the diocesan clergy of New York. At the time it was stated in the public press that his resignation resulted from the fact that his researches and the publication of them were being curtailed by his Sulpician superiors who were fearful of criticism from ultraconservative Vatican circles. The rector of Dunwoodie denied that interpretation of the resignation. Gigot's competence as a scripturist was acknowledged by scholars of various faiths. He contributed articles to Vigouroux's *Dictionnaire de la Bible,* the *Catholic Encyclopedia,* and the *New York Review,* and he translated the Apocalypse for the Westminster version of the NT. He was the author of several books on Biblical subjects, which reflected the best contemporary scholarly trends and were models of their type. The ecclesiastical spirit of the time was not favorable to the scholarship that Gigot represented, but his method and approach to scriptural study were amply vindicated two decades after his death by the *DIVINO AFFLANTE SPIRITU* of PIUS XII. Once widely used manuals were Gigot's *General Introduction to the Study of the Holy Scriptures* (New York 1900) and *Special Introduction to the Study of the Old Testament* (2 v. 1903–06).

[M. M. BOURKE]

GIKATILLA, JOSEPH BEN ABRAHAM

Eminent Spanish mystic; b. Medinacelli, Old Castile, Spain, 1248; d. Peñafiel, Spain, after 1305. As a youth he had studied Talmud and philosophy, but later, under the influence of Abraham Abulafia (1241–after 1291), he began his literary activity as a zealous follower of the school of prophetic cabalism (*see* CABALA). Throughout his life Gikatilla remained a prolific writer, and although he considered cabalism a science superior to, and the basis of, philosophy, his writings generally sought to reconcile the two and indicate that he tried to further the mystic science by philosophic speculation.

As did Abulafia, Gikatilla believed that religious doctrines and prophetic concepts can best be explained through the mystic symbolisms of the Hebrew letters, vowels, and numbers; his development of this phase of the cabala and the profundity of his cabalistic knowledge soon earned for him the reputation of being a miracle worker, and he was accordingly referred to by many as Joseph Ba'al ha-Nissim (the master of miracles).

His first work, *Ginnath Egoz* (Garden of Nuts, from Ct 6.11), in three parts (the various names of God, the twenty-two letters of the Hebrew alphabet, and the vowels and accents are discussed and given special interpretation in parts one, two, and three, respectively), was completed at the age of 26 and deals with the three elements of cabala: Gematria, Notarikon, and Themurah; the initials of these terms form the word *Ginnath,* and *Egoz* symbolizes the study of mysticism.

His second important work, *Sha'are Orah* (Gates of Light), which attempts to correlate the names of God with the ten Sefiroth of Divine manifestation, was translated into Latin by Paulo Riccio under the title *Porta Lucis* and quoted by Johann REUCHLIN in support of his thesis against his adversaries that the cabala was in agreement with the tenets of Christianity.

Gikatilla's other writings include: *Sefer ha-Nikkud* (Book of Vocalization), a cabalistic interpretation of the vowels; *Sod ha-Hashmal* (Secret of the Electrum), a mystic commentary of Ezechiel's vision; *Sodoth ha-Mitzvoth* (Secrets of the Commandments), a cabalistic explanation of various commandments; *Tsofnath Pa'aneah* (Revealer of Hidden Things; Gn 41.45), a commentary on the Passover HAGGADAH; and *Hassagoth* (Criticisms; unpublished), which consists of strictures on Maimonides's *Moreh Nevuhim* (Guide of the Perplexed).

Bibliography: G. G. SCHOLEM, *Major Trends in Jewish Mysticism* (3d ed. New York 1954; repr. pa. New York 1961) 194–195. H. H. GRAETZ, *History of the Jews,* ed. and tr. B. LÖWY, 6 v. (Philadelphia 1945) 4:10, 466. M. STEINSCHNEIDER, ''Catalogus Librorum Hebraeorum,'' in *Bibliotheca Bodleiana codicum manuscriptorum orientalium,* 2 v. (Oxford 1787–1833) 1461–70. G. JELLINEK, *Beiträge zur Geschichte der Kabbala* (Leipzig 1852) 2:57–64. S. A. HORODEZKY, in *Encyclopaedia Judaica: Das Judentum in Geschichte und Gegenwart,* 10 v. (Berlin 1928–34; incomplete) 7:408–411. K. SCHUBERT, in *Lexikon für Theologie und Kirche,* ed. J. HOFER and K. RAHNER, 10 v. (2d new ed. Freiburg 1957–65) 4:889.

[N. J. COHEN]

GIL VALLS, ENCARNACIÓN, BL.

Lay martyr, teacher; b. Jan. 27, 1888, Onteniente (Ontinyent), Valencia, Spain; d. Sept. 24, 1936, L'Ollería, Valencia. Gaspar Gil and Adriana Valls had their daughter María Encarnación baptized at St. Mary's Church, Onteniente, the day following her birth. From them she and her siblings learned how to live and die as Christians. She was confirmed May 24, 1893 and received her First Communion in 1899.

Encarnación received private instruction until she studied in Valencia to become a teacher. Thereafter she was tutor in the household of Pasquala Enríquez de Navarra y Mayans de Calatayud de Valencia and a teacher at Albuixech (Valencia; 1915–22). She was beloved by her students. On the hour she would orally pray an Ave Maria, followed by some pious ejaculation. As the children did their work each afternoon, she prayed the Rosary. On Saturdays she reminded her charges of their obligation to attend Sunday Mass. She often allowed some of her students to accompany her on Saturdays when she visited her brother Gaspar at the seminary in Valencia where he was studying.

In 1922, the ownership of the school changed hands and Encarnación went to live with her brother Gaspar and assist him in his parish work. With him she founded the Patronato de la Infancia (Foundation of Infancy) and taught catechism to children. Personally she was distinguished by her simplicity, self–sacrifice, apostolic fervor, and charity, especially towards children.

She was known to rise early to spend time in meditation and to attend Mass daily. Encarnación belonged to the Nocturnal Adoration Society, Third Order of Carmelites, Daughters of Mary, and other Catholic groups. She was also secretary of Catholic Action. She exercised her social apostolate as a teacher of woman workers.

Shortly after the Spanish Revolution began, her brother Gaspar was imprisoned and their home confiscated. Undaunted, Encarnación said that they had offered their lives to God for the salvation of Spain; all she asked was that she die with her brother. On September 24, the militia came to her door telling her to accompany her imprisoned brother to Porta Coeli Hospital. She asked that a friend, Juan Recatalá Fuertes, also accompany them. They were taken instead to the marble quarry near the port of Ollería, where the brother and sister were summarily executed and buried in the cemetery of Canals. Their bodies were transferred to the cemetery of Onteniente after the war and later translated to San Carlos Church. She was beatified by Pope John Paul II with José Aparicio Sanz and 232 companions on March 11, 2001.

Feast: Sept. 22.

Bibliography: V. CÁRCEL ORTÍ, *Martires españoles del siglo XX* (Madrid 1995). W. H. CARROLL, *The Last Crusade* (Front Royal, VA 1996). J. PÉREZ DE URBEL, *Catholic Martyrs of the Spanish Civil War*, tr. M. F. INGRAMS (Kansas City, MO 1993). R. ROYAL, *The Catholic Martyrs of the Twentieth Century* (New York 2000). *L'Osservatore Romano,* Eng. Ed. no. 11 (Mar. 14, 2001), 1–4, 12.

[K. I. RABENSTEIN]

GILBERT, WILLIAM

English scientist and physician, whose book on magnetism founded the study of geomagnetism and established electricity as a separate discipline; b. Colchester, England, May 24, 1544; d. London, Nov. 30, 1603. William, the son of Jerome Gilbert, lawyer and recorder of Colchester, and Jerome's first wife, Elizabeth Coggeshall, matriculated as a member of St. John's College, Cambridge, in 1558. He received the B.A. degree in 1560–61, the M.A. in 1564, and the M.D. on May 13, 1569. He held a number of offices in St. John's College, and became a senior fellow in December 1569. Nothing is known of Gilbert's life for the next eight years. In 1577 arms were "confirmed" to him by Robert Cooke, an Elizabethan herald who had a reputation for complaisance in such matters.

By 1581 Gilbert was beginning to climb the ladder of social success in London medical circles. He lived at Wingfield House, inherited from his stepmother, Jane Wingfield Gilbert. This home, on St. Peter's Hill close to St. Paul's Cathedral, was only a few doors from the buildings housing the College of Arms and the Royal College of Physicians. Gilbert was censor of the Royal College of Physicians (1581, 1582, 1584–87, 1589, 1590), treasurer (1587–94, 1597–99), consilliarius (1597–99), and elect (1596–97). In 1600 he reached the peak of social success in his profession, becoming president of the College of Physicians and one of the physicians to Queen Elizabeth I. At her death in 1603 he was appointed physician to James I, but he died within a year, presumably of the plague.

Gilbert left, in manuscript, an unfinished cosmological work, *De mundo nostro sublunari philosophia nova,* which was published half a century later and consequently had little influence. His notable work, the *De magnete, magneticisque corporibus, et de magno magnete tellure; Physiologia nova, plurimis et argumentis, et experimentis demonstrata* (London 1600), was probably completed about 1583, before Gilbert became involved in the London medical world. His views were heavily influenced by the 13th-century *Epistola de magnete* of Peter of Maricourt, from which he got the idea that the "natural" shape for a lodestone or natural magnet is round. Gilbert created the idea that the earth is a giant lodestone and that a spherical lodestone was a *terrella* (little Earth). Specific ideas published in the *De magnete* that influenced later scientists were: (1) The possibility of conducting magnetic experiments in the laboratory and thereby learning about ''the great lodestone, the Earth.'' (2) The suggestions that weight is due to the magnetic attraction of the earth, that the strength of a magnet is proportional to its *mole* (mass), and that the earth exerts a magnetic force on the moon. All of these ideas affected the development of gravitational theory. (3) The clear distinction between magnetic and electric phenomena, thereby eliminating the confusion between them and establishing electricity as a field of study separate from magnetism. (4) The creation of the concept of a class of substances that behave like amber, when rubbed. He coined the name *electrica* (electrics) for this class, from the Greek name, ''elektron,'' for ''amber,'' thereby introducing the root ''electric'' into the language.

The *De magnete* is a highly experimental work, and Gilbert consciously appealed to experiments in support of his theories, marking his ''experiments and discoveries'' with marginal asterisks and urging his readers to try the experiments for themselves. His education was a classical, scholastic one, and Gilbert's approach to the study of natural phenomena is in accord with his education. Many of his ideas, in the hands of such men as Johann Kepler and Galileo Galilei, were developed far beyond anything Gilbert had imagined.

Bibliography: D. H. D. ROLLER, *The De magnete of William Gilbert* (Amsterdam 1959). M. S. KELLY, *The 'De mundo' of William Gilbert* (Amsterdam 1965).

[D. H. D. ROLLER]

GILBERT CRISPIN

Benedictine monk at BEC, abbot of WESTMINSTER, 1085; d. *c.* 1117. Gilbert was in frequent contact with St. ANSELM and, while maintaining his intellectual independence, was deeply influenced by him. While in London with Anselm, probably during the winter (1092–93), he met a Jew of Mainz. This meeting occasioned the writing of the *Disputatio Iudaei et Christiani,* his most important work. He wrote also various other historical and doctrinal works, particularly *De simoniacis, De Spiritu Sancto, De casu diaboli, De anima,* and the *Disputatio Christiani cum gentili.* He is the author also of a sermon for Palm Sunday, two conferences on *The Three Marys of the Gospel,* and another on *The Monastic Life and Profession.* He was a skilled writer, more at ease in Biblical exegesis and in the handling of commonsense argumentation than in philosophical speculation. We are indebted to him for a better understanding of Anselm's influence on his environment, his friends, and disciples. In his *De anima,* Gilbert tried to complete the ideas of his master on a subject that Anselm had hoped one day to elaborate. His writings, especially those in which he intervened in controversy with the Jews, give an idea—and this is their principal interest—of the intellectual milieu in which Anselm wrote the *Cur Deus homo,* as well as of the kind of problems he wished to resolve.

Bibliography: Gilbert Crispin's works are in part unedited. Critical ed. of *Vita Herluini* in J. A. ROBINSON, *Gilbert Crispin* (Cambridge, Eng. 1911) 87–110; *Patrologia Latina* 150:695–714; *De nobili Crispinorum genere, Patrologia Latina* 150:735–744; *Disputatio Christiani cum gentili,* ed. C. C. J. WEBB, *Mediaeval and Renaissance Studies* 3 (1954) 55–77; *Disputatio Iudaei et Christiani,* ed. B. BLUMENKRANZ (Utrecht 1956). Minor works ed. in part or completely by Robinson, *op. cit.* and R. W. SOUTHERN, in *Mediaeval and Renaissance Studies* 3 (1954) 99–115. The letter on monastic life, ed. J. LECLERCQ, *Analecta monastica* 2 (1953) 118–123. Literature. R. W. SOUTHERN, *Saint Anselm and His Biographer* (New York 1963). J. LECLERCQ, ''Une Doctrine de la vie monastique dans l'école du Bec,'' *Spicilegium Beccense* 1 (1959) 477–488. S. G. A. LUFF, ''Norman Sense and Sensibility: Abbot Gilbert Crispin at Westminster,'' *Wiseman Review* 235 (1961) 374–384.

[J. LECLERCQ]

GILBERT DE LA PORRÉE

Scholastic theologian and philosopher; b. Poitiers, France, *c.* 1075; d. there, Sept. 4, 1154.

Life. Gilbert first studied under Master Hilary at the cathedral school of Poitiers, then became the student of BERNARD OF CHARTRES, and later went to Laon. Before 1124 he returned to Chartres, where he was made chancellor of the cathedral several times (1126–36). For a short time he taught in Paris, where in 1141 JOHN OF SALISBURY ''heard him in logic and theology'' (*Metal.* 2.10). In 1142 he was consecrated bishop of Poitiers and seems not to have continued to teach theology.

When Gilbert spoke on the Trinity at a diocesan synod at Poitiers in 1146, two archdeacons, Calon of Thouars and Arnold of Brioux, denounced his doctrine to Pope Eugenius III, who convened a consistory in Paris shortly after Easter of 1147. The accusations were supported by the Parisian Master Adam of Petit Pont and by Hugh of Champfleury. Two witnesses, Rotold, bishop of Evreux, and a Master Ivo of Chartres, denied the charges. The pope ordered Godescalc, Abbot of St. Martin, to examine Gilbert's commentary on Boethius's *Tractate on the Trinity* and adjourned the inquiry until the Council of Reims. The council opened on March 21, 1148. The trial took place at a consistory convened after the closing of the council. But since Gilbert and his followers appeared before the consistory thoroughly prepared, the debates again threatened to end in a deadlock. In order to reach a decision, Bernard drew up a profession of faith as a reply to the four errors (*capitula*) of which Gilbert was accused. To ensure their acceptance he arranged a meeting in his own quarters and put the matter to a vote. The cardinals of the papal court reacted indignantly to this procedure and "agreed among themselves to support the cause of the Bishop of Poitiers, saying that the Abbot had attacked Master Peter [Abelard] in exactly the same way" (John of Salisbury, *Hist. pont.* 9).

Gilbert was accused of saying that the divine essence is not God (Otto of Freising, *Gesta Frid.* 1.56; Geoffrey of Auxerre, *C. Gilb.* 64), of rejecting the statement that God is the divinity (*Hist. pont.* 8), and of saying that the divine nature was not made flesh and that it did not assume human nature (*C. Gilb.* 67). Another accusation was directed against Gilbert's assertion that no divine Person can be made the predicate of a sentence (*Gesta Frid.* 1.50).

Gilbert agreed with St. Bernard's profession of faith; the pope commanded him to correct any conflicting statements that might occur in his book on the Trinity. Gilbert concurred and was acquitted of the charges but made no change in his commentary. He pardoned his two archdeacons and returned to his diocese "with fulness of honor" (*Gesta Frid.* 1.57). Gilbert was nearly 70 years old when he faced his accusers.

Thought. Gilbert's apparently novel views are based on his principles of speculative grammar. Following Boethius, he divided the speculative sciences into natural, mathematical, and theological. Beginning with concrete composite objects, human language or scientific terminology follows two levels of reality. Concrete terms, such as substance, animal, white, person, and Plato, belong to the first level, the realm of natural science. But the human mind cannot grasp a concrete object unless it perceives the immediate reason why the object is a substance, or an animal, or white, etc. So the mind separates the concrete object from the numerous forms that make it what it is. Abstract terms such as substantiality, corporeality, and whiteness best express the abstract realm of mathematical science. But every concrete noun or adjective connotes its form just as every abstract term connotes the corresponding concrete reality in which it inheres. The direct meaning of a concrete or abstract work is called its substance, the connotation, its quality. Grammatical position and context indicate whether the intention is to express the substance or the quality of a word. Since the predicate is always universal, the word "man" in the sentence "Plato is a man" expresses the universal form that causes Plato to be a man. However, in the sentence "A man spoke" or "I saw a man," the same word expresses a concrete human being or even a person.

Although Gilbert was willing to make concessions to traditional patterns of speech, he transferred these rules of speculative grammar to theology. The sentence "The Father is God" would mean that He is God through His divinity and not, for instance, through His goodness or His eternity. Gilbert insisted that such insufficiency of human language must not be interpreted to the detriment of the absolute simplicity of God. According to him the sentence "The divine essence is God" is open to misunderstanding because Scripture uses the word "God" to designate either the divine nature (Mk 12.29) or a divine Person (Ps 46.6). If "God" is used in the sense of person, the statement is false. Gilbert could not accept the sentence "God is the divinity," for the abstract term "divinity" in the predicate would convey the idea that God causes God to be God.

As John of Salisbury relates, Gilbert's opponents maintained that his "novelty of speech" was "inconsistent with accepted beliefs" (*Hist. pont.* 8). He declares further that Gilbert's "doctrine seemed obscure to beginners, but all the more compendious and profound to advanced students" (*ibid.* 12); Gilbert himself, however, professed in his prologue to Boethius that he thought his teaching was so traditional "that it appeared that he had stolen rather than invented it." His doctrine continues to be the object of controversy.

Works. At his trial in Reims Gilbert demanded that he be judged on the evidence of his writings on the Psalms, on the Epistles of St. Paul, and on Boethius (*Hist. pont.* 10). He must have written them in that order. There are indications that his commentary on the Psalms was compiled before the death of ANSELM OF LAON (1117). It is still unpublished. The numerous manuscripts of this work are listed in F. Stegmüller, *Repertorium biblicum medii aevi,* 7 v. (Madrid 1949–61) 2:2511. Gilbert's commentary on St. Paul, written before 1140 and still unpublished, is a more mature work. The many manuscripts listed in *Repertorium biblicum medii aevi* 2:2528 attest to its popularity. His commentary on four Sacred Tractates of Boethius, written in the early 1140s, was first published in the Basel edition (1570) of the works of Boethius (*Patrologia Latina,* 217 v. [Paris 1878–90] 64:1247–1412). More than 40 manuscripts of the work are known to exist. A critical edition by N. M. Haring is found in *Studies and Texts* 13 (Toronto 1966). Two of Gilbert's letters are extant, one to his beloved teacher Bernard of Chartres [*Bibliothèque de l'École de Chartres 16* (1855): 461], the other to Abbot Matthew of Saint-Florent de Saumur (*Patrologia Latina* 188:1258). Much remains to be done concerning the authenticity of numerous other works attributed to Gilbert.

Bibliography: A. BERTHAUD, *Gilbert de la Porrée, évêque de Poitiers, et sa philosophie* (Poitiers 1892). R. L. POOLE, *Illustrations of the History of Medieval Thought and Learning* (2d ed. rev. Gloucester, Mass. 1961). A. HAYEN, ''Le Concile de Reims et l'erreur théologique de Gilbert de la Porrée,'' *Archives d'histoire doctrinale et littéraire du moyen-âge* 10–11 (1935–36): 29–102. M. E. WILLIAMS, ''The Teaching of Gilbert Porreta on the Trinity,'' *Analecta Gregoriana* 56 (Rome 1951). N. M. HARING, ''The Case of Gilbert de la Porrée, Bishop of Poitiers, 1142–1154,'' *Mediaeval Studies* 13 (1951): 1–40; ''Das sogenannte Glaubensbekenntnis des Reimser Konsistoriums von 1148,'' *Scholastik* 40 (1965): 55–90. S. GAMMERSBACH, ''Gilbert von Poitiers und seine Prozesse im Urteil der Zeitgenossen,'' *Neue Münstersche Beiträge zur Geschichtsforchung* 5 (Cologne 1959). F. VERNET, *Dictionnaire de théologie catholique,* 15 v. (Paris 1903–50) 6.2:1350–1358. M. MANITIUS, *Geschichte der lateinischen Literatur des Mittelalters,* 3 v. (Munich 1911–31) 3:210–215.

[N. M. HARING]

GILBERT OF HOLLAND (HOYLAND)

Cistercian abbot cited frequently as a source of monastic theology and medieval exegesis; place and date of birth unknown; d. at the Cistercian Abbey of Rivour, Diocese of Troyes (France), 1172. Little is known of Gilbert, called ''one time abbot of Hoyland'' by the Clairvaux Chronicle. The earliest record of him is in documents he attested (*c.* 1150–58) when he was already abbot of Swineshead, an abbey in the region of Holland, in Lincolnshire. He was still abbot there when in his *Sermones in canticum* (41) he referred to the ''recent'' death of St. AELRED (d. 1167). Claims that he was either from Clairvaux or from Scotland-Ireland appear to be unsubstantiated; he may have been sent from Rievaulx (*c.* 1148–49) by St. Aelred to ensure an orderly changeover to the Cistercian rule at Swineshead, and he was perhaps exiled about 1170 in the controversy over St. THOMAS BECKET. He wrote 48 *Sermones* (*Patrologia Latina* 184:11–252), continuing St. Bernard's commentaries on the Canticle of Canticles. He remains known and memorable by these sermons, which, though lacking St. Bernard's genius and grace, reveal not only practical and personal details but the developed literary culture set to serve the Biblical mysticism of the 12th century. The Bollandists [May 6 (1688) 3F] and the 1952 *Menologium Cisterciense* (117) list him as ''Blessed Gilbert.''

Bibliography: J. LECLERCQ, ''Théologie traditionelle et théologie monastique,'' *Irénikon* 37 (1964) 50–74. C. L. KINGSFORD, *The Dictionary of National Biography from the Earliest Times to 1900,* 7:1194. E. MIKKERS, ''De vita et operibus Gilberti de Hoylandia,'' *Cîteaux* 14 (1963) 33–43, 265–279. J. MORSON, ''The English Cistercians and the Bestiary,'' *Bulletin of the John Rylands Library* 39 (1956) 146–170. J. VUONG-DINH-LAM, ''Le Monastère . . . les observances monastiques . . . d'après G. de H.,'' *Collectanea ordinis Cisterciensium Reformatorum* 26 (1964) 5–21, 170–199. B. SMALLEY, *The Study of the Bible in the Middle Ages* (2d ed. New York 1952, repr. Notre Dame, Ind. 1964). H. DE LUBAC, *Exégèse médiévale,* 2 v. in 4 (Paris 1959–64).

[P. EDWARDS]

GILBERT OF NEUFFONTAINES, ST.

Premonstratensian prior; b. Auvergne, *c.* 1100; d. abbey of Neuffontaines (Neuffons), June 6, 1152. After the failure of the Second CRUSADE (1147–49) he gave half his possessions to the poor, and with the other half he rebuilt a convent for women at Aubeterre in 1150 and a monastery for men at Neuffontaines, both PREMONSTRATENSIAN houses. The hospital and monastery completed, he joined the order in 1150 and in 1151 became the first prior, ruling wisely and living virtuously. Many cures are attributed to his intercession, especially benefiting children. In 1159 Gilbert's body was transferred to the abbey church, renamed for him. It was lost during the French Revolution. His cult was officially approved in 1725, his feast being observed on June 1 at Clermont in the Norbertine church, to which some relics had been transferred in 1615.

Feast: June 6 (formerly Oct. 26).

Bibliography: *Acta Sanctorum* June 1:749–754. C. L. HUGO, *S. Ordinis Praemonstratensis annales* 1:743–746. G. MARSOT, *Catholicisme* 5:9.

[M. J. MADAJ]

GILBERT OF SEMPRINGHAM, ST.

Founder of the Gilbertines; b. Sempringham, Lincolnshire, England, *c.* 1083; d. Sempringham, Feb. 4, 1189. The son of a Norman knight who had settled in Lincolnshire, Gilbert was destined for the Church from an early age, and to this end he was sent to study at Paris. On his return home he received the benefices of Sempringham and Tirington from his father and opened a school. He took service for a short while with the bishops of LINCOLN and was ordained a priest by Bishop Alexander in 1123. By 1131 he had returned to Sempringham as a parish priest and in that year organized seven young women who wished to dedicate themselves to a religious life into a community based on the Cistercian model. This convent was the beginning of the GILBERTINES, the only exclusively English religious order. Gilbert soon found it necessary to associate with the nuns a number of lay sisters and lay brothers to work the convent's estates. The community grew and a second foundation was made in

1139; it had reached such size by 1147 that Gilbert journeyed to CÎTEAUX to ask the CISTERCIANS, assembled in a general chapter, to assume its administration, but they were unwilling to undertake the responsibility for supervising communities of women. Gilbert then sought spiritual direction for his nuns from CANONS REGULAR OF ST. AUGUSTINE, who henceforth formed an integral part of the Gilbertine double MONASTERIES. Pope EUGENE III gave his approval to the order in 1148 and a short time later confirmed Gilbert as its master general. In 1165 Gilbert was charged by officials of King HENRY II with giving aid to the exiled Thomas BECKET, Archbishop of CANTERBURY; but he refused to clear himself of the groundless charge, as he insisted on his right to have given such support if opportunity had presented itself. Advancing age forced Gilbert to resign the office of master general to Roger of Malton; at the time of his death the order had grown to nine double monasteries and four distinct houses of canons. He was canonized by Pope INNOCENT III in 1202, and his relics were enshrined in the church at Sempringham.

Feast: Feb. 16.

Bibliography: *Acta Sanctorum* Feb. 1:576–578. W. DUGDALE, *Monasticon Anglicanum* 6.2: *v-*xxix (between pages 946 and 947), with Eng. tr. in *John Capgrave's Lives of St. Augustine and St. Gilbert of Sempringham,* ed. J. J. MUNRO (Early English Text Society 140; 1910) 61–142. *Bibliotheca hagiographica latina antiquae et mediae aetatis* 3529–38. T. A. ARCHER, *The Dictionary of National Biography from Earliest Times to 1900* 7:1194–96. R. GRAHAM, *S. Gilbert of Sempringham and the Gilbertines* (London 1901). R. FOREVILLE, ed., *Un Procès de canonisation à l'aube du XIIIe siècle, 1201–1202: Le Livre de saint Gilbert de Sempringham* (Paris 1943). F. L. CROSS, *The Oxford Dictionary of the Christian Church* 558. A. BUTLER, *The Lives of the Saints,* ed. H. THURSTON and D. ATTWATER 1:351–352. D. KNOWLES, *The Monastic Order in England, 943-1216.* D. KNOWLES, *The Religious Orders in England.*

[B. J. COMASKEY]

GILBERTINES

An extinct medieval religious order for men and women founded in England by GILBERT OF SEMPRINGHAM. The order originated in 1131 with seven young women who, under Gilbert's direction and with the support of Bp. Alexander of LINCOLN, formed a convent at Sempringham, on property belonging to their founder's estate. Gilbert seems to have copied Cistercian customs rather closely, but a general chapter of the CISTERCIANS meeting at CÎTEAUX in 1147 refused to assume the government of the community of nuns. At the suggestion of William, Abbot of RIEVAULX, Gilbert had already added lay sisters to attend to the needs of the nuns, and lay brothers for the heavy agricultural labor on their property. He then proceeded to introduce a small number of CANONS REGULAR OF ST. AUGUSTINE, who would undertake the spiritual direction of the community, and thereafter the Gilbertines usually lived in double MONASTERIES, marked by great austerity in style and decoration. Papal approval of the new order came from the Cistercian Pope EUGENE III in 1148. The nuns were to live by the BENEDICTINE RULE, the canons by the Rule of St. AUGUSTINE, and the lay brothers were to be governed by a modification of the usages of the *conversi* of Citeaux. The Gilbertines founded their second house in 1139 and numbered some 13 communities in 1189, when Gilbert died. The order continued to receive special favors from the English crown, for, unlike the Cistercians and the monks of Cluny, it had no foreign connections, its priories being located for the most part in Lincolnshire, with one house in Scotland and two in Westmeath, Ireland. In time the order began to decline, and its financial status was so critical that King HENRY VI found it necessary to exempt all its foundations from payments of any kind. Even so, the Gilbertines still controlled some 25 houses, with 150 canons and 120 nuns, when HENRY VIII forced them to surrender all property in the dissolution (1538–40).

A master general, who was elected and could also be deposed by a chapter general, ruled the order with authority to make all appointments, to receive novices into the community, and to pass on all contracts entered into by the various houses. He was assisted by a number of priests and nuns who acted as visitors, as well as by the chapter general, which met yearly at Sempringham during the ROGATION DAYS and consisted of the prior, prioress, and cellarer of each house. The chief difficulty in the government of the order grew out of the continued attempts of the lay brothers to work in their own interest, and even in the founder's lifetime a serious revolt developed. The Gilbertine habit consisted of a black tunic and a scapular with a white cloak and hood for the canons; the nuns, also with a scapular, were dressed in white.

Bibliography: W. DUGDALE, *Monasticon Anglicanum* 6.2:947–982. R. GRAHAM, *S. Gilbert of Sempringham and the Gilbertines* (London 1901). *The Gilbertine Rite,* ed. R. M. WOOLLEY, 2 v. (Henry Bradshaw Society 59, 60; 1921–22). D. KNOWLES, "The Revolt of the Lay Brothers of Sempringham," *English Historical Review* 50 (1935) 465–487. D. KNOWLES and R. N. HADCOCK, *Medieval Religious Houses: England and Wales* (New York 1953) 171–175.

[B. J. COMASKEY]

GILBERTUS ANGLICUS

Bolognese canonist of the late 12th and early 13th centuries, date and place of birth in England unknown; with ALANUS ANGLICUS he may have entered the Dominican Order (at Bologna) after 1220.

His chief work is a collection (*c.* 1202) of decretal letters from the pontificate of Alexander III (1159–81) to 1202 (fourth year of Innocent III). It had two stages. In a first version he included in an appendix, outside the framework of the titles, some 32 decretals of Innocent III that in a second, definitive recension he inserted into the body of the collection under their appropriate headings; some of these texts appear to have been copied from registers in Innocent III's chancery (*see* PAPAL REGISTERS). In all, the collection contains some 258 decretals in 290 chapters; it falls into five books, following the classic division (*iudex, iudicium, clerus, connubia, crimen*) of the *Breviarium* (or *Compilatio prima antiqua*) of Bernard of Pavia, 1181–82 (*see* QUINQUE COMPILATIONES ANTIQUAE). A critical list of the collection has been published by Von Heckel. Gilbertus's collection was utilized by other collections, e.g., that of BERNARD OF COMPOSTELLA, THE ELDER (1208), by means of which it influenced the official *Compilatio* (*tertia antiqua*) of Innocent III's decretals (1210). With the collection of Alanus Anglicus it was the formal source of the compilation of JOHN OF WALES (*Compilatio secunda antiqua*, 1210–12); it influenced also the *Compilatio quarta* of JOANNES TEUTONICUS (1216–17). Gilbert glossed his own collection [one short gloss was printed by J. Junker, *Summen und Glossen, Savigny-Stiftung f. Rechtsgeschichte* Kan Abt. 15 (1926) 486], and these glosses were used by Albert and TANCRED when composing their apparatuses on the *Compilatio secunda.*

Bibliography: J. F. SCHULTE, ''Die Compilationen Gilberts und Alanus,'' *Sitzungsberichte der Akademie der Wissenschaften im Wein*, Philos.-hist. Klasse 65 (1870) 595–698. *Repertorium der Kanonistik* 223, 225, 302, 309, 310–313, 345, 348. R. VON HECKEL, ''Die Dekretalensammlungen des Gilbertus und Alanus nach den Weingartner Handschriften,'' *Zeitschrift der Savigny-Stiftung für Rechtsgeschichte Kanonistische Abteilung* 29 (1940) 116–357, 180–225 (critical register), 340. *Historia iuris canonici latini* v. 1, *Historia fontinum* 231. C. LEFEBVRE, *Dictionnaire de droit canonique* 5:966–967. See also the *Bulletin of the Institute of Research and Study in Medieval Canon Law* in *Traditio* 14 (1958) 464–466; 17 (1961) 534.

[L. E. BOYLE]

GILBY, THOMAS

English Dominican theologian, author, editor; b. Birmingham, Dec. 18, 1902; d. Cambridge, Nov. 29, 1975. Gilby was a member of Emmanuel College, Cambridge, when he chose to become a Dominican in 1919. After ordination in 1926, he did graduate work at Louvain in philosophy. He was a lector at Hawkesyard Priory (Staffordshire) and Blackfriars, Oxford; until 1935, he served as editor and frequent contributor for *Blackfriars.* At this time, he published his *Poetic Experience* (1934), and *Marriage and Morals* (1936, pseudonym I. G. Wayne; repr. 1952).

From 1939 to 1948, Gilby served as chaplain in the Royal Navy. With the experience of naval warfare behind him, he then acted as a representative of the British government, lecturing in American universities. During the war he wrote one book on logic, *Barbara Celarent* (1949) and another on epistemology, *The Phoenix and the Turtle* (1950). From 1948 until his death, Gilby lived in Blackfriars, Cambridge, where he served several terms as prior and published several books: *Between Community and Society* (1953); *Principality and Polity* (1958, U.S. title, *Political Thought of St. Thomas Aquinas*); *Up the Green River* (1955), and a military history, *Britain at Arms: A Scrapbook from Queen Anne to the Present Day* (1953).

Gilby completed his greatest work acting as editor, translator, annotator, and commentator of St. Thomas Aquinas's writing. He began modestly with an arrangement, translation, and annotation of *St. Thomas Aquinas, Philosophical Texts* (1955) and *St. Thomas Aquinas, Theological Texts* (1955). The English-Latin edition of the *Summa theologiae* (60 v., 1965-76) occupied him until his death. He translated, edited, and annotated vv. 1, 5, 8, 16, 17, 18, 28, 36, 43, 44, and 59 and, as general editor, handled each page of copy in all of the 60 volumes. Throughout his life, Thomas Gilby was dedicated to his quiet convert apostolate: reconciling the strayed and counseling the anguished. The greatest of his theological contributions remain in the pages of ''the Gilby Summa.''

[T. C. O'BRIEN]

GILDAS, ST.

Called ''the Wise''; author of a history of the Britons; b. early sixth century; d. *c.* 570. He appears to have been a native of Scottish Strathclyde, but his early life is obscure. He was an ecclesiastic, probably a monk; he worked in Wales, visited Ireland, and is at least reputed to have founded the monastery of SAINT-GILDAS-DE-RHUYS in Brittany. Sometime before 547, at the age of 44, Gildas wrote what BEDE refers to as a ''tearful discourse concerning the ruin of Britain,'' that is, the *De excidio et conquestu Brittaniae*. Intended as an indictment of Gildas's contemporaries in Britain for their moral shortcomings, the work relates a course of events that seems probable. Once the Roman occupation ended, the Britons appealed for aid against Pict and Scottish marauders to the Consul of Gaul, Aetius (*c.* 446). When he refused aid, the Britons used their own resources against these enemies until a ''proud tyrant,'' usually considered to be Vortigern, invited Saxons led by Hengist and Horsa to become the Britons' *foederati*—a common practice throughout the empire. Gildas then recounts the settling of the Saxons on the Isle of Thanet and their ensuing revolt against the Britons. He discusses the precarious condition of life in Britain and seems to suggest that town life was destroyed only at this time, a very questionable conclusion as archeological evidence points to a much earlier date. He makes no mention of permanent German settlements, though here, too, evidence indicates their existence. Much more probable is Gildas's description of a temporary British resurgence led by a certain Ambrosius Aurelianus, which culminated in the Saxon defeat at the Battle of Mons Badonicus (Mount Badon) *c.* 500. His failure to mention King Arthur in connection with the battle does not discount his existence since Gildas was strangely reluctant to use personal names. Gildas remained a popular saint in Brittany, where a monastery (Saint-Gildas-du-Bois) was founded near Nantes as late as 1026. He may also have written a Penitential, the hymn *Lorica*, and a travel prayer.

Feast: Jan. 29.

Bibliography: *Analecta hymnica* 51:358–364. *Monumenta Germaniae Historica: Poetae* 4:618–619. *Monumenta Germaniae Historica: Auctores Antiquissimi* 13:1–85. T. F. TOUT, *The Dictionary of National Biography from the Earliest Times to 1900* (London 1885–1900) 7:1223–25. R. G. COLLINGWOOD and J. N. L. MYRES, *Roman Britain and the English Settlements* (2d ed. London 1937). C. E. STEVENS, ''Gildas Sapiens,'' *English Historical Review* 56 (1941) 353–373. F. M. STENTON, *Anglo-Saxon England* (2d ed. Oxford 1947). C. GROSS, *Sources and Literature of English History from the Earliest Times to About 1485* (2d ed. New York 1915; repr. 1952) 245–246. G. O. SAYLES, *The Medieval Foundations of England* (2d ed. London 1952). P. GROSJEAN, ''Notes d'hagiographie celtique,'' *Analecta Bollandiana* 75 (1957) 158–226. N. K. CHADWICK et al., *Studies in the Early British Church* (Cambridge, Eng. 1958).

[B. F. BYERLY]

GILES, ST.

Hermit, abbot, and one of the FOURTEEN HOLY HELPERS; d. *c.* 720. According to the 10th-century vita, Giles (Aegidius) was an Athenian who came to Marseilles and became a hermit near the mouth of the Rhone. He influenced a certain Flavius, King of the Goths, to build an abbey there, and later became confessor to King Charles of France. This most untrustworthy biography was composed to satisfy pilgrims on the road to Rome and SANTIAGO DE COMPOSTELA; the bulls for the founding of the abbey are 9th century, and seem to be forgeries invented to help the monks of SAINT-GILLES to free themselves from the authority of the bishop of Nîmes. However, the tomb of the saint at the abbey became a great pilgrimage place, making the town of Saint-Gilles prosperous. The cult of the saint spread throughout western Europe, and especially to England; he was invoked as patron of cripples, beggars, and blacksmiths. His emblem is a hind with an arrow. Because of the dubious quality of the sources, Pope Benedict XIV's commission proposed removal of this feast from the general calendar.

Feast: Sept. 1.

Bibliography: *Acta Santorum* Sept. 1:284–304. *Analecta Bollandiana* 8 (1889) 103–120. F. BRITTAIN, *Saint Giles* (Cambridge, Eng. 1928). A. FLICHE, *Aigues-Mortes et Saint-Gilles* (Paris 1950). G. JACQUEMET, *Catholicisme* 5:19–20. A. M. ZIMMERMANN, *Lexikon für Theologie und Kirche,* ed. J. HOFER and K. RAHNER, 10 v. (2d, new ed. Freiburg 1957–65) 1:190. A. BUTLER, *The Lives of the Saints,* rev. ed. H. THURSTON and D. ATTWATER, 4 v. (New York 1956) 3:457–458.

[G. J. DONNELLY]

GILES OF ASSISI, BL.

Third companion of St. Francis of Assisi; b. Assisi, c.1190; d. Perugia, April 22, 1262. Coming from peasant stock, he joined Francis at the Portiuncula on April 23, 1208, and was with him in his early missions. Very early on, Giles undertook pilgrimages to the main shrines of the times, the Holy Land, as well as an aborted trip to Tunisia where he wanted to die as a martyr. Shortly after the death of Francis, Giles spent prolonged periods in various hermitages where visions and mystical states took place. The early sources painted a conflicting picture of him. The official Legends (e.g., Celano, Bonaventure) highlighted his contemplative gifts, while the non-official sources, (e.g., the *Leonine Corpus, The Chronicle of the Twenty-four Generals*) saw him not only as a mystic but also as an exemplar of the early Franciscan ideal and a dissident of the evolution of the Order and its abandonment of poverty. Giles is also remembered for his pithy and pungent *Dicta*, or *Golden Sayings* (300 or so) reminiscent in style and spirit of the *Admonitions* of Francis and the *Apopthegmata* of the Desert Fathers. Pius VI beatified him in 1777.

Feast: April 23.

Bibliography: *Dicta Beati Aegidii Assisiensis* (Quaracchi-Florence 1905); *The Golden Words,* trans. I. O'SULLIVAN (Chicago 1966); *La Sapienza di Frate Egidio Compagno di San Francesco con I Detti,* ed. and trans. E. MARIANI (Venice 1981). R. BROWN, *Franciscan Mystic* (Garden City, N.Y. 1962).

[P. LACHANCE]

GILES OF FOSCARARI

Canonist; b. probably Bologna; d. Bologna, 1289. His family was prominent in Bolognese society. From

1252 to 1269 he is frequently mentioned in official documents as *magister* and *doctor decretorum.* He was the first layman to teach Canon Law at the University of Bologna. In 1267 he spent a short time in the service of Charles I of Naples. Because of the great esteem in which he was held, it was directed at his death that those assisting at his funeral or at the funeral of any canonist thereafter could be vested in scarlet, an honor usually reserved for the funerals of knights and professors of civil law. His works include *De ordine iudiciario*, written about 1260, which is valuable for understanding judicial practice during this period (William Durantis copied much of it in his *Speculum*), *Lectura in Decretales;* and many *quaestiones* and *consilia*, which remain scattered in various manuscripts.

Bibliography: M. SARTI and M. FATTORINI, *De claris Archigymnasii Bononiensis a saeculo XI usque ad saeculum XIV*, 2 v. (2d ed. Bologna 1888–96; repr. Turin 1962). 1:447–452. F. K. V. SAVIGNY, *Geschichte des römischen Rechts im Mittelalter,* 7 v. (2d ed. Heidelberg 1834–51; repr. Darmstadt 1958) 5:520–526. J. F. VON SCHULTE, *Die Geschichte der Quellen und der Literatur des kanonischen Rechts,* 3 v. in 4 pts. (Stuttgart 1875–80; repr. Graz 1956) 2:139–143. J. DESHUSSES, *Dictionnaire de droit canonique,* ed. R. NAZ, 7 v. (Paris 1935–65) 5:967–968.

[C. M. ROSEN]

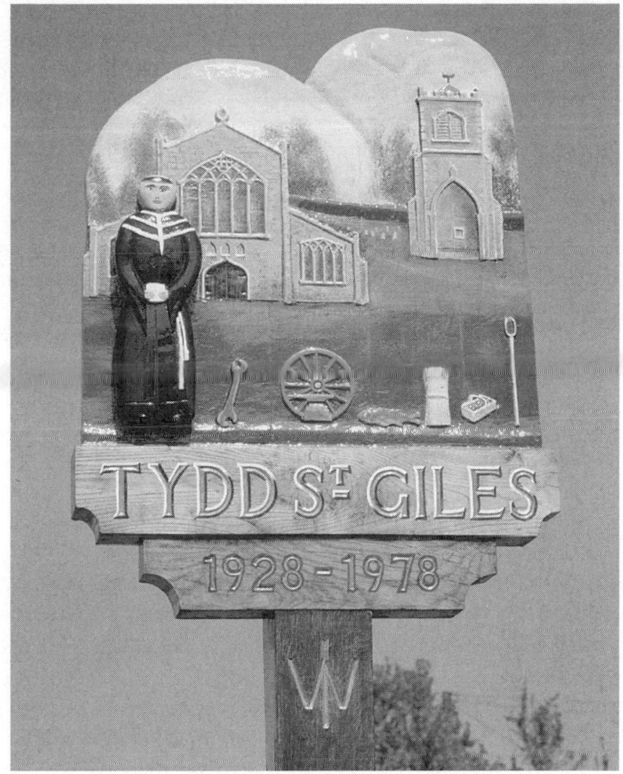

Village sign depicting St. Giles. (©Robert Estall/CORBIS)

GILES OF LESSINES

Dominican philosopher and scientist; b. probably Lessines (Hainaut, Belgium), *c.* 1230–40; d. 1304 or later. He entered the order perhaps at the convent of Valenciennes. His relations with ALBERT THE GREAT suggest that he studied under this master, probably at Cologne. His later residence at Paris and the strong Thomistic character of some of his writings make it very likely that he attended the lectures of St. THOMAS AQUINAS during Aquinas's second regency at the University of Paris (1269–72). He is known in the early lists of Dominican authors as a bachelor, so he seems not to have been a master in theology. Various treatises are attributed to him. The first is *De essentia, motu et significatione cometarum*, on the occasion of the comet of 1264, in which the author shows an interest for natural sciences not uncommon in the school of Albert the Great. He made use of the *LIBER DE CAUSIS* and propounded the common doctrine on providence and on the influence of the heavenly bodies. The *De concordia temporum,* or *Summa de temporibus,* gives a concordance of historical chronology up to the beginning of the 14th century; its authenticity is not yet entirely demonstrated. A *Tractatus de crepusculis*, attributed to Giles by P. Mandonnet, is in the same field of scientific investigation. The two last mentioned treatises exist in MS [University of Bologna, 957 (1845)]. There are no texts for the following works attributed to Giles: *De geometria, Quaestiones theologicae, In 1 et 2 sententiarum, Flores casuum, Tractatus de (decem) praeceptis*, and *De immediata visione divinae essentiae;* the last may be a confusion with a similar treatise attributed to WILLIAM DE HOTHUM.

Three other writings are certainly authentic. (1) He wrote a letter to Albert the Great asking his judgment about 15 points of doctrine that were discussed among the masters of Paris. Items one to 13 coincide with points contained in the condemnation promulgated by Bishop É. TEMPIER of Paris on Dec. 10, 1270. (2) The *De unitate formae* is a strong defense of the doctrine of the unity of the substantial form, one of the most violently attacked Thomist teachings. Its first three chapters expose the opinion of the plurality of forms; the next seven chapters are devoted to the concept of form and its relation to matter; and the final six chapters establish the unity of form and answer the arguments of the pluralists. The treatise was directed especially against ROBERT KILWARDBY and was most likely written in 1278. HENRY OF GHENT tried to refute it, and HARVEY NEDELLEC made use of it. (3) The *De usuris* is the most complete study of usury in the Middle Ages. It is against the more backward theories of Henry of Ghent, and thus must have been written between 1278 and 1284 (F. Veraja). It was first attributed to Thomas Aquinas.

Bibliography: M. DE WULF, *Le Traité "De unitate formae" de Gilles de Lessines* (Les Philosophes Belges 1; Louvain 1901). P. MANDONNET, "Giles de Lessines et son Tractatus de crepusculis," *Revue néo-scolastique* 22 (1920) 190–194. M. GRABMANN, "Einzelgestalten aus der mittelalterlichen Dominikaner- und Thomisten-theologie," *Mittelalterliches Geistesleben*, v.2 (Munich 1936) 512–530. L. THORNDIKE, *Latin Treatises on Comets between 1238 and 1368* (Chicago 1950). F. VERAJA, *Le origini della controversia teologica sul contratto di censo nel XIII secolo* (Rome 1960) 83–99. P. M. M. DUHEM, *Le Systéme du monde*, 5v. (Paris 1913–17), repr. 10 v. (1954–59).

[J. C. VANSTEENKISTE]

GILES OF ROME

Augustinian theologian, general, archbishop of Bourges; b. Rome, *c.* 1243; d. Avignon, France, 1316. He joined the Hermits of St. AUGUSTINE at the age of 14 and was sent to the order's house in Paris in 1260 for basic studies. He obtained the equivalent of a master in arts degree in 1266 and studied theology in the university, probably attending the lectures of THOMAS AQUINAS. As a bachelor he commented on the *Sentences* (1276), but his commentary was not published until many years later (bk. 1 after 1285; bks. 2, 3, *c.* 1300). He, like Aquinas, maintained that there could not be many individual angels in a single species in his *Theoremata de ente et essentia* (ed. E. Hocedez, Louvain 1930). This view, attacked by HENRY OF GHENT in 1276, was one of the propositions condemned by Étienne TEMPIER in 1277. Forced to leave Paris, Giles resided in Bayeux (1278–80). On returning to Italy, he was definitor of the Roman province in 1281, provincial in 1283, and vicar-general of the order in 1285. At the intervention of HONORIUS IV on July 1, 1285, he was reinstated at the University of Paris, where he became the first Augustinian master in theology. He taught as regent master from 1285 until 1291; two years later he was succeeded by his disciple, JAMES OF VITERBO. Giles was a prodigious writer, and he conducted numerous disputations rejecting the views of Henry of Ghent and of GODFREY OF FONTAINES and reflecting the concerns of his day. In 1287 the general chapter of Florence imposed his doctrines on all teachers in his order. As tutor to the young PHILIP IV OF FRANCE he wrote *De regimine principum* (ed. Venice 1585). His important commentary on *LIBER DE CAUSIS* (ed. Venice 1550) reveals a strong predilection for Proclus's theory of participation.

He left Paris in 1291 and was elected general of his order on Jan. 6, 1292. A frequent visitor to France, he was highly esteemed by the King of France, by CELESTINE V, and by BONIFACE VIII, who frequently employed his services. On April 25, 1295, he was appointed archbishop of Bourges by Boniface. When the abdication of Celestine V and the election of Boniface VIII were contested in 1257, Giles wrote a long treatise in defense of their validity, *De renuntiatione papae* (ed. Rome 1554). In the quarrel between Boniface and Philip he sided with the Pope, writing in 1301 his *De ecclesiastica potestate* (ed. R. Scholz, Weimar 1929), which inspired the bull *UNAM SANCTAM* of 1302. Relying on the analogy of the soul's supremacy over the body, he saw in papal theocracy fulfillment of the Augustinian ideal of the city of God. Although he championed the theory of the "two swords," his own fanaticism and pedantry helped to eliminate an outdated papal theocracy.

The legend that Giles was an authentic disciple of Thomas Aquinas originated in the 15th century, when Coriolano attributed to him authorship of *Correctorium "Quare"* (ed. Venice 1486; *see* CORRECTORIA). It is true that Giles was almost alone in upholding publicly the Thomistic doctrine of the unicity of substantial form in material creatures (*see* FORMS, UNICITY AND PLURALITY OF). But as E. Hocedez has shown, Giles was not condemned for this doctrinal position. Even in his defense of the doctrine of unicity, he criticized Aquinas on many points with a sharpness that later shocked DENIS THE CARTHUSIAN.

His distinction between essence and existence in finite creatures was recognized as novel even among his contemporaries. Giles admitted that it was close to the doctrine of hylomorphism. His description of essence and *esse* as "two things" (*duae res*) has been interpreted as (1) an ultrarealist caricature of Aquinas's view (Hocedez); (2) a forceful reaction to the intentional distinction proposed by Henry of Ghent and hence compatible with the Thomistic explanation (G. Suárez, A. Pattin); (3) a fundamentally essentialist position derived from BOETHIUS, PROCLUS, and AVICENNA, in which *esse* is metaphysically posterior and complementary to essence as a second act (P. W. Nash).

Giles's doctrine of creation seems to confirm the metaphysical priority of essence. Following St. Augustine and fearing Greek necessitarianism, he insisted on the absolute contingency of all creatures. Since creatures can be annihilated, they must of themselves tend to nothingness. Nowhere does Giles admit, as did Aquinas, any inner necessity either to the material universe as a whole or to spiritual beings. For Giles, this contingency demonstrates the rear distinction between essence and *esse*, since in annihilation the "two things" are actually separated. The real distinction exists only between essence or *forma totius* (e.g., humanity) and its corresponding *esse*, whereas only a modal distinction is to be found between substantial form or *forma partis* (e.g., soul) and the *esse* it gives to matter. Thus Giles kept the universal validity of the formula *forma dat esse* by interpreting it to mean that a really distinct *esse* corresponds only to essence, whereas all forms, substantial and accidental, possess a modality of being.

In theology Giles was conscious of being a professional defender of the doctrines of St. Augustine. The real distinction served to differentiate creatures from God as the mutable from the immutable, the composite from the simple. For him the ultimate goal of theology is affective and the formal constituent of beatitude is an act primarily of the will.

Giles is an important witness to the unique position of Thomas Aquinas in the last quarter of the 13th century. Not only had he studied under him, but he also read his works extensively and used almost identical expressions with regard to unity of form and the metaphysical composition of creatures. Nevertheless, his use of sacred Scripture and St. Augustine distinguish his thought and that of the Augustinian school.

To his contemporaries he was known variously as *Doctor beatus, Doctor fundatissimus*, and *Doctor verbosus*.

Bibliography: P. GLORIEUX, *Répertoire des maîtres en théologie de Paris au XIIIe siècle* 2:293–308. É. H. GILSON, *History of Christian Philosophy in the Middle Ages, passim.* P. W. NASH, ''G. of R: Auditor and Critic of St. Thomas,'' *The Modern Schoolman* 28 (1950) 1–20. ''G. of R. on Boethius' *Diversum est esse et id quod est,*'' *Medaevil Studies* 12 (1950) 57–91. ''The Accidentality of Esse according to G. of R.,'' *Gregorianum* 38 (1957) 103–115. E. HOCEDEZ, ''La condemnation de G. de R.,'' *Recherches de théologie ancienne et médiévale* 4 (1932) 34–58. Z. K. SEMIATKOWSKA, ''Avant l'exil de G. de R. au sujet d'une dispute sur les Theoremata de esse et essentia de G. de R.,'' *Medievalia Philosophica Polonorum*, 7 (1960). A. ZUMKELLER, *Theology and History of the Augustinian School in the Middle Ages* (Villanova 1996). ''Aegidius von Rom,'' *Marienlexicon* I (1988) 42. ''Aegidius Romanus,'' *Lexicon des Mittelalters* I (1978) 178. D. GUTIERREZ, ''Gilles de Rome, ermite de Saint-Augustin, theologien et Eveque, 1243–1316,'' *Dictionnaire de Spiritualite* VI (1967) 385–390.

[P. W. NASH]

GILES OF SANTAREM, BL.

Dominican preacher and ecclesiastical superior; b. Vaozela, Portugal, *c.* 1184; d. Santarem, Spain, May 14, 1265. Having been endowed in youth with five ecclesiastical benefices, he used their proceeds to live a dissipated life. He went to Paris to study medicine, but gave up this interest to take up necromancy, which he practiced with some attendant fame. After experiencing a religious conversion, he returned to Spain, about 1220, where he entered the Dominican Order at Palencia. When sent to study the sacred sciences, he made the acquaintance of Bl. JORDAN OF SAXONY, Bl. HUMBERT OF ROMANS, and other prominent friars. He taught and preached after he returned to Spain, and was twice elected provincial of the Spanish province. BENEDICT XIV ratified his cult on March 9, 1748.

Feast: May 14.

Bibliography: *Acta Sanctorum* May 3:400–436. J. QUÉTIF and J. ÉCHARD, *Scriptores Ordinis Praedicatorum* 1:241–244. P. ÁLVAREZ, *Santos, bienuventurados, venerables de la orden de los Predicadores* 4 v. (Vergara, Spain 1920–23) v.1.

[A. H. CAMACHO]

GILES OF VITERBO

Augustinian friar, Renaissance scholar, reformer, cardinal; b. Viterbo, 1469; d. Rome, Nov. 11–12, 1532. His family name was Antonini, not Canisius as many historians (including L. von Pastor) state. Giles (Aegidius) joined the Augustinians at Viterbo and in 1493, while still a student at Padua, published an edition of three works of Aegidius Romanus. From this time dates his hostility to AVERROISM; it was confirmed when he studied under Marsilio FICINO at Florence. Plato, St. Augustine, and the Bible were three sources from which he drew liberally. He became an outstanding member of the Pontanian Academy at Naples, and gave his name to Giovanni Pontano's dialogue, *Aegidius.* He was perhaps the most sought after preacher of his day—Popes Alexander VI and Julius II, Kings Frederick and Ferdinand of Naples, the cities of Florence and Venice, demanded his services. His most memorable oration was the appeal for reform at the opening of the Fifth LATERAN COUNCIL on May 3, 1512. His preaching had both the polish and defects of Renaissance style.

In 1503 he joined the observant movement within the Augustinian Order, became affiliated with the famous monastery of Lecceto near Siena, and on June 27, 1506, to his own dismay, was appointed vicar-general of the AUGUSTINIANS by Julius II. Thereafter, his main concern until he resigned from office (Jan. 25, 1518) was reform of the order. He secured the much-coveted *Bulla Aurea* in favor of the Augustinians from Julius II in June 1507 and in 1508 authorized the first printed edition of the constitutions of the order. He halted the growing division between Augustinian observants and conventuals; early in 1511 he won over a young German friar, Martin Luther, to the cause of unity. He insisted on a return to the full common life and greatly encouraged higher studies. To ensure the success of reform he personally visited houses and provinces or sent his own delegates with wide powers. He did not hesitate to suspend or dismiss priors and provincials, and he demanded monthly reports from each province. But all his efforts were hampered by the general laxity of Church affairs at that time.

His intellectual versatility was amazing: he wrote both Latin and Italian poetry, edited philosophical works, compiled a major theological commentary, attempted a survey of Christian history, and was indefatigable in his scriptural studies, particularly Hebrew, the cabala, and rabbinical literature. He defended Johann REUCHLIN and will always be remembered as the generous patron of Elijah Levita (*c.* 1468–1549), who later became the leading Hebrew scholar of Renaissance Europe. Aegidius was a linguist of rare ability and was credited with being the only person in Europe with a competent knowledge of Arabic. The first complete printed edition of the Bible in Greek was published at Venice in 1518, and was dedicated to Aegidius. Most of his own works remained unpublished during his lifetime; he suffered from an intellectual meticulosity.

He went as papal agent to the Emperor Maximilian in 1515, was nominated a cardinal in July 1517, and was sent as papal legate to Spain in 1518. He was a serious candidate for the papal tiara at the conclave in 1521. In 1523 he was appointed bishop of Viterbo by Clement VII. The remainder of his life he devoted mainly to scholarship, but he made one notable political effort in May, 1527 when he led an army of 2,000 soldiers to free CLEMENT VII, then besieged by the imperial troops in the CASTEL Sant' Angelo in Rome. To the end he continued to be an advocate for reform of the Church.

Bibliography: *Letters as Augustinian General,* ed. C. O'REILLY (Rome 1992). *Lettere familiari,* ed. A. M. VOCI ROTH, 2 vols. (Rome 1990). *Scechina e libellus de litteris Hebraicis,* ed. F. SECRET, 2 vols. (Rome 1959). J. W. O'MALLEY, ''Fulfillment of the Christian Golden Age under Pope Julius: Text of a Discourse of Giles of Viterbo, 1507,'' *Traditio* 25 (1969) 265–338. F. GIACONE and G. BEDOUELLE, ''Une lettre de Gilles de Viterbe á Jacques Lefèvre d'Étaples (c. 1460–1536) au sujet de l'affaire Reuchlin,'' *Bibliothèque d'Humanisme et Renaissance: Travaux et Documents* 36 (1974) 335–45. F. X. MARTIN, ''Egidio da Viterbo, 1469–1532: Bibliography, 1510–1982,'' *Biblioteca e societé* (Viterbo) 4 nos. 1–2 (June 1982) 5 91. A. DE MEIJER, ''Bibliographie historique de l'ordre de Saint Augustin,'' *Augustiniana* 35 (1985), 39 (1989), 43 (1993), 47 (1997). F. X. MARTIN, *Friar, Reformer and Renaissance Scholar: Life and Work of Giles of Viterbo 1469–1532,* ed. J. ROTELLE (Villanova 1992). J. W. O'MALLEY, *Giles of Viterbo on Church and Reform: A Study in Renaissance Thought* (Leiden 1968). A series of papers in English on Giles as Renaissance scholar, scripture scholar, classical scholar, and prior general, is published in *Egidio da Viterbo, O.S.A., e il suo tempo,* ed. Analecta Augustiniana (Rome 1983).

[F. X. MARTIN]

GILGAMESH EPIC

The longest extant Babylonian poem, an epic narrating the heroic exploits of Gilgamesh, a semilegendary Sumerian king of the 3d millennium B.C. In its latest and most elaborate redaction (7th century B.C.) the poem (Babylonian title: *ša naqba īmuru,* ''he who experienced all things'') probably consisted of 12 tablets of approximately 300 lines each. The discovery that this late version contained a Babylonian story of the Flood closely paralleling the deluge narrative in Genesis was announced by George Smith in December 1872 and aroused widespread interest not only in this poem and its relation to the Bible but also in the whole new field of cuneiform studies in general. This article will treat of the contents and versions of the epic, its flood narratives, and its hero.

Contents. Despite many lacunae in the present-day editions of the ancient text, the general contents of the tale may be reconstructed with reasonable accuracy. It begins by praising the knowledge and wisdom of Gilgamesh, his long journeys in quest of adventure and immortality, and his building of the monumental walls and temple in his native city, Uruk. At the outset of the story, the people of Uruk are dissatisfied with Gilgamesh and his oppressive rule: he appropriates the young girls of the city for his court and burdens the young men with heavy labor on his building projects. The people of the city pray to the gods for deliverance, and they respond by creating a foil for Gilgamesh: Enkidu, a wild man from the steppe, who is initiated into the arts of civilization by a prostitute, comes to Uruk, and, after engaging in a heroic wrestling match with Gilgamesh, proves his constant companion in adventures, thus diverting Gilgamesh's attention from the harried people of his city.

The first adventure of Gilgamesh and Enkidu is against the giant Humbaba, appointed by the god Enlil as guardian of a great cedar forest (probably to be localized in northern Syria). When they succeed in tracking down the ogre and overcoming his magic defenses, he begs Gilgamesh for mercy, only to have the latter persuaded by Enkidu to kill the giant. When the two heroes return to Uruk, the goddess Ishtar (*see* ASTARTE) asks Gilgamesh to become her lover; but he refuses, tauntingly reminding her of the brutal treatment she has accorded her previously discarded lovers. Enraged, Ishtar persuades Anu, the father of the gods, to send down the ''Bull of Heaven,'' a monster personifying seven years of drought, to punish Gilgamesh. After killing hundreds of Gilgamesh's men, the bull attacks Enkidu and is then slain by Gilgamesh and Enkidu. The subsequent triumph through the jubilant throngs in Uruk is short-lived, for that same night Enkidu sees in a dream the gods deliberating which of the two who had killed Humbaba and the bull should perish. The god Shamash comes to their aid, but can save only Gilgamesh. Enkidu becomes ill and dies.

Gilgamesh broods over the sudden death of his companion and, reflecting on his own mortality, decides to seek the secret of eternal life from Utnapishtim, the only human being who had survived the Flood. He makes a perilous journey to the far-off land ''at the mouth of the rivers'' and hears from Utnapishtim's own lips the tale of how the gods in wrath had tried to destroy mankind through the Flood. But the god Ea had secretly warned Utnapishtim, who constructed a large boat and saved himself and various species of fauna from destruction. Gilgamesh inquires how he too may gain immortality, but fails to remain awake when he is put to the test. Finally, after being given the Plant of Life, Gilgamesh while bathing in a pond loses it to a snake that steals it from the shore. Dejected and disheartened, Gilgamesh returns to Uruk, recognizing in the end that his utmost achievement as a mortal will be his monumental building activities.

The 12th and final tablet of the epic is an artificial appendage to the tale and describes the descent of Enkidu into the nether world to obtain two precious possessions lost by Gilgamesh.

Versions of the Poem. The preceding synopsis of the contents of the Gilgamesh epic is based on the Ninevite recension, as known from the library of Assurbanipal, King of Assyria (668–*c.* 627 B.C.). This was probably the latest and most detailed redaction of the epic, and roughly half its lines are now known—with new tablet discoveries continually increasing the total.

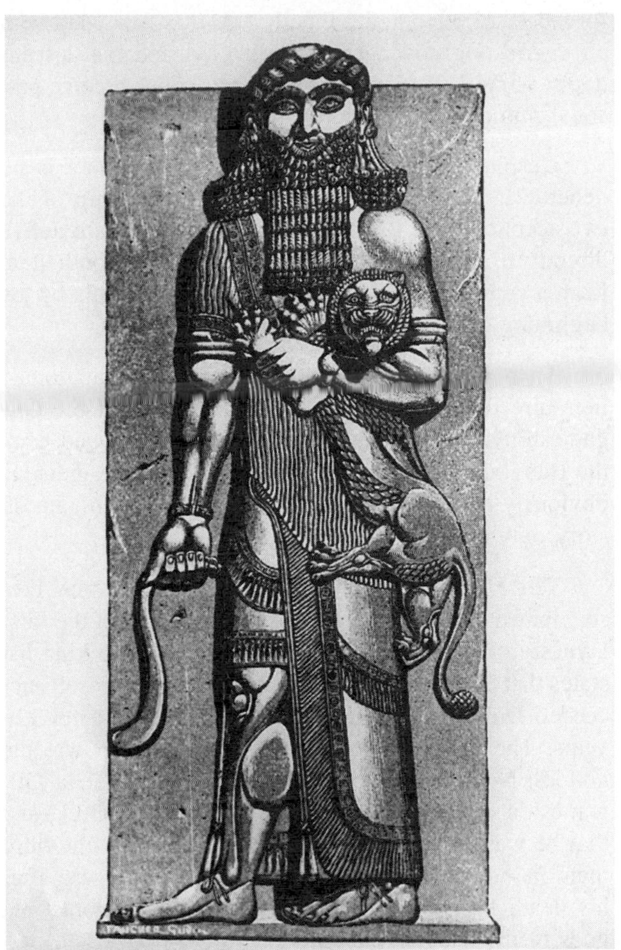

Gilgamesh, from sculupture in alabaster found in Khorsabad. Illustration, Louvre, Paris. (© CORBIS/Bettmann)

Other redactions of the tale of Gilgamesh are known to exist. The earliest fragments are contained in Sumerian literature of the late 3d millennium, when at least five separate sagas concerning the exploits of Gilgamesh were current. By the Old-Babylonian period (18th century B.C.) some of these stories had been woven into a single larger poem; but as yet its contents are known only from five small fragments. The work enjoyed great popularity in Mesopotamia and spread through the Near East. Fragments have been found at Boghazköy, the Hittite capital, at Mageddo in Palestine, at Sultantepe in (ancient) Syria, at Nineveh and Assur in Assyria, and at Ischali, Nippur, Sippar, Ur, and Uruk in Babylonia. Hittite and Hurrian translations are known to have been made. The Old-Babylonian and Hittite versions especially differ from the later Ninevite recension in their arrangement of the various episodes and by including material not in the later edition (and, apparently, omitting tales later incorporated into the poem).

Flood Narrative. The common framework of the Flood narratives in the Gilgamesh Epic and in Genesis has attracted much attention. Both deluges are the result of divine decisions to destroy mankind and are announced in advance to a selected hero, who is directed to build a large boat of specified dimensions and to save himself, his family, and a representative selection of living creatures from impending catastrophe. The floods are both caused primarily by heavy rains, which cover the entire land with water, submerging even the mountain peaks and killing all living creatures. When the rains cease and the flood waters subside, the heroes each dispatch several birds to test whether the ground is exposed sufficiently to sustain life. Both boats ground on mountain tops, and each hero descends and offers sacrifice to his god(s), who then bestow(s) blessings on the survivors.

There are also many disagreements in detail between the two versions. In Gilgamesh, mankind is destroyed primarily because of the caprice of the gods and only secondarily because of the fault of man (the primary motive in Genesis). In Genesis, mankind is given a chance to repent before the Flood, while no such opportunity is afforded in Mesopotamia. Finally NOAH is rewarded with an everlasting covenant between God and his descendants, while Utnapishtim and his associates receive personal immortality.

Despite the great number of parallels, there is no general agreement as to the genetic relationship of the two accounts. The Biblical story does not seem to derive directly from the Gilgamesh saga. They may both stem from a common account, current in Mesopotamia by the beginning of the 2d millennium B.C.

There is good reason for thinking that in Babylonian literature the Flood was not originally part of the Gilgamesh cycle. It is probable that it was borrowed from the Babylonian Atrahasis epic, where the flood theme is obviously more central, and inserted into the Gilgamesh story only after the Old-Babylonian period.

The Hero. Little is known about the historical person named Gilgamesh, who was the fifth king of the First Dynasty of Uruk (*c.* 2600 B.C.). The Sumerian king list states that his father was a demon and that he himself succeeded Dumuzi (TAMMUZ) as king and reigned for 126 years. The epic, however, tells that his mother was the goddess Ninsun (supposedly the wife of Lugalbanda, Gilgamesh's second predecessor on the throne of Uruk) and that he was, consequently, two-thirds god and one-third man. In Assyro-Babylonian mythology, Gilgamesh after his death became king and judge over the people and gods of the underworld.

Bibliography: A. HEIDEL, *The Gilgamesh Epic and Old Testament Parallels* (2d ed. Chicago 1949). *The Epic of Gilgamesh,* ed. and tr. N. K. SANDARS (Baltimore 1960). *Gilgameš et sa légende,* ed. P. GARELLI (Paris 1960). E. SOLLBERGER, *The Babylonian Legend of the Flood* (London 1962). J. P. PRITCHARD, *Ancient Near Eastern Texts Relating to the Old Testament* (2d, rev. ed. Princeton 1955) 72–99.

[J. A. BRINKMAN]

GILIJ, FILIPPO SALVATORE

Italian Jesuit missionary and ethnographer of the Orinoco region; b. Legona (Norcia), Italy, July 26, 1721; d. Rome, 1789. He entered the Society of Jesus in 1740 and went to the New Kingdom of Granada (today Colombia) in 1743. He was a missionary in the Orinoco area from the time of his ordination (1748) until the Jesuit expulsion in 1767; he then returned to Italy and lived in Rome until his death. While in Orinoco he saw much of the famous Father Gumilla; in Italy he collaborated with Hervas and Panduro; and Humboldt frequently appealed to his authority. His *Saggio di Storia Americana* (4 v. Rome 1780–84) made him famous. The first three volumes concern the Orinoco: religious and civil history, inhabitants and customs, religion and language; volume four is about Tierra Firme, and is a fundamental source for the history of Colombia. *Saggio* became a source of Americanist information in Europe, but was almost unknown to Americans until 1947. In 1782 Veigl translated into German the linguistic section; volume four was translated into Spanish by Mario Germán Romero and Carlos Buscantini (Bogotá 1955).

Bibliography: J. A. SALAZAR ORSA, "El padre Gilij y su *Ensayo de historia americana,*" *Missionalia Hispanica* 4 (1947) 249–328. G. GIRALDO JARAMILLO, *Estudios históricos* (Bogotá 1954).

[J. A. SALAZAR ORSA]

GILLESPIE, MOTHER ANGELA

U.S. foundress of the Congregation of Sisters of the Holy Cross (CSC); b. Brownsville, Pa., Feb. 21, 1824; d. Notre Dame, Ind., March 4, 1887. She was the daughter of John and Mary (Miers) Gillespie and was baptized Eliza Maria. In her early years she moved to Lancaster, Ohio, with her widowed mother, her sister, and her brother (later Rev. Neal Gillespie, CSC). While attending Georgetown Visitation School, Washington, D.C., Eliza, as niece of Sen. Thomas EWING, participated actively in the social life of the capital. She was interested also in the apostolate and organized a parochial school, taught at a Maryland state school where her tact won acceptance of religious instruction for Catholics, opened a Sunday school for African Americans, and acted as visiting nurse for the poor.

In 1853 Eliza entered the community of Holy Cross Sisters at Bertrand, Mich., and, as Sister Angela, was sent to the novitiate in Caen, France. After taking her vows, she returned to Bertrand to direct the academy, which in 1855 was transferred to St. Mary's, Notre Dame, Ind. There she introduced advanced courses in science and higher mathematics, foreign languages taught by teachers instructing in their native tongues, art and music offered by recognized artists, and a program of philosophy and theology. In April 1860 she began to publish the *Metropolitan Readers* (continued as the *Excelsior Series*), a literature series graded for elementary, secondary, and college levels. As a translator of foreign writers and as unofficial editor of *Ave Maria* after 1866, she was instrumental in presenting such authors as Charles de Montalembert, François Chateaubriand, Louis Veuillot, Frédéric Ozanam, Orestes Brownson, and Isaac Hecker to American readers.

During the Civil War, Mother Angela established eight military hospitals, staffed two hospital ships, and provided for the direction of 80 sister-nurses. She was appointed provincial superior in 1869, and she founded St. Catherine's Institute, a teacher-training institution in Baltimore, Md., in 1874, staffing it with religious and lay teachers from St. Mary's and elsewhere. During the period 1855–82, Mother Angela made 45 foundations from New York to California and from Michigan to Texas.

Bibliography: M. MCCANDLESS, *Family Portraits* (Notre Dame, Ind. 1952). M. RITA, *A Story of Fifty Years* (Notre Dame, Ind. 1905). A. S. MCALLISTER, *Flame in the Wilderness: Life and Letters of Mother Angela Gillespie* (Paterson 1944).

[M. R. DAILY]

Mother Angela Gillespie.

GILLIS, JAMES MARTIN

Editor, author; b. Boston, Mass., Nov. 12, 1876; d. New York City, March 14, 1957. He was the son of James and Catharine (Roche) Gillis. After early education at Boston Latin School, he attended St. Charles College, Baltimore, Md., and St. John's Seminary, Brighton, Mass. In 1900 he joined the Paulist fathers; he was ordained the following year and sent to the Catholic University of America, Washington, D.C., where he earned a licentiate in theology (1903). He taught at St. Paul's College, Washington, D.C., until 1910, when he left to engage in missionary work.

In 1922 Gillis was named editor of the Paulist periodical the *Catholic World,* a post he filled until 1948. Under his direction the *Catholic World* retained the reputation it had acquired under such predecessors as Isaac HECKER and Augustine F. HEWIT. Gillis was noted for his vigor as a controversialist and for his outspoken and conservative opinions on political issues, which were frequently quoted. After 1928 he produced also a newspaper column called "Sursum Corda: What's Right with the World," which was syndicated in 50 diocesan papers. From 1930 to 1941 he attracted notice as a popular radio speaker on the "Catholic Hour," produced by the National Broadcasting Company. He was a prolific author, publishing his first book, *False Prophets,* in 1925 and *My Last Book* in 1957. His other works included: *The Catholic Church and the Home* (1928), *The Ten Commandments* (1931), *Christianity and Civilization* (1932), *The Paulists* (1932), *This Our Day* (2 v. 1933, 1949), *So Near Is God* (1953), *On Almost Everything* (1955), and *This Mysterious Human Nature* (1956). His numerous articles appeared in leading Catholic magazines, and he wrote for the old *Catholic Encyclopedia* and the *Encyclopedia Americana.* He was an academy member of the Gallery of Living Catholic Authors and received many honorary degrees from American Catholic colleges, including Fordham University, Fordham, N.Y. (1935), and the University of Detroit, Mich. (1940). In 1951 he received an honorary doctorate in theology from the Angelicum (Pontifical University of St. Thomas Aquinas), Rome. Illness forced him to retire in 1948, but he continued to serve as contributing editor of the *Catholic World* until his death. He was buried in the Crypt Church at St. Paul the Apostle, New York City.

Bibliography: J. F. FINLEY, *James Gillis, Paulist* (Garden City, N.Y. 1958).

[J. L. MORRISON]

GILLOW Y ZAVALZA, EULOGIO GREGORIO

Mexican archbishop; b. Puebla, Mexico, March 11, 1841; d. Ejutla, Mexico, May 18, 1922. His parents were Tomás Gillow, of English origin, and María Zavalza y Gutiérrez, Marchioness of Selva Nevada. At age ten Gillow went to England and spent three years at Stonyhurst School. He then studied philosophy at Namur in Belgium. On a visit to Rome in 1862, he was received and honored by Pope Pius IX. In Rome he studied theology. In 1865 he returned to Mexico and was ordained in Puebla by Bp. Carlos M. Colina. Returning to Rome in 1869, he obtained a doctorate in canon law. On May 26, 1887, Pope Pius IX appointed Gillow bishop of Antequera, Oaxaca, to succeed the late Márquez Goyeneche. Gillow was consecrated on the feast of St. Ignatius, July 31, 1887, by Archbishop Labastida of Mexico; he took possession of his diocese in November. In 1890 he again went to Rome with five students for the Latin American College. Gillow returned to Mexico the following year with a papal bull elevating Antequera to an archbishopric, for which he had been made archbishop. He called a provincial council, which met in Oaxaca from Dec. 8, 1892, to March 12, 1893. His outstanding ability led to his consideration for a cardinalate, but he did not receive the appointment because of political opposition. He also assisted at the plenary council on Latin America in Rome.

In addition to his pastoral duties, Gillow worked for the material betterment of his archdiocese and helped in the development of the Mexican railway system. During a visit to San Antonio, Texas, he proposed the construction of a seminary that could be used by Mexicans in case of new persecutions. He was forced into exile when the Revolution broke out in 1910. For some time Gillow lived in San Antonio and later in Los Angeles, where he prepared his memoirs before returning to Mexico.

Bibliography: E. VALVERDE TÉLLEZ, *Bio-bibliografía eclesiástica mexicana, 1821–1943,* 3 v. (Mexico City 1949).

[L. MEDINA ASCENSIO]

GILMOUR, RICHARD

Second bishop of the Cleveland, Ohio, Diocese; b. Glasgow, Scotland, Sept. 28, 1824; d. St. Augustine, Fla., April 13, 1891. The Gilmour family, of Scotch Covenanter stock, came to Cumbola, Pa., when Richard was 13. At a Father Mathew temperance rally, the boy became interested in the Catholic Church (*see* MATHEW, THEOBALD). He was baptized in 1842 by Father Patrick Rafferty and, under this Pennsylvania missionary, began studies for the priesthood, completing them at Mt. St. Mary's, Emmitsburg, Md. He was ordained Aug. 30, 1852, by Abp. John B. Purcell in Cincinnati, Ohio. Assigned to the Ohio River area, Gilmour built churches at Portsmouth and Ironton, Ohio, visited counties in Kentucky and Virginia, and served parishes in Cincinnati and Dayton.

On April 14, 1872, he was consecrated bishop of Cleveland, where the growing Catholic population faced a bitter nativism, especially in the newspapers. Gilmour's first pastoral in 1873 showed that he would provide leadership: ''Catholics are too timid; they seem to go on the principle that if they are tolerated, they are doing well.'' He stressed the rights of Church and conscience, yet in all civic matters, obedience to the state. He demanded Catholic schools that were ''equal to the best,'' and a just share of public school funds. In 1874, to strengthen the Church's voice, he founded the *Catholic Universe* and the Catholic Central Association for the betterment of social and religious conditions. After a two-year illness that kept him away from the diocese, he returned in 1876 to continue his leadership.

During his episcopate the number of churches increased from 160 to 233, and schools from 90 to 142; many earlier structures were replaced and four new hospitals were built. He introduced the Dominicans of New Jersey, Felicians, and Sisters of St. Joseph, Notre Dame, Charity of Cincinnati; he brought the Jesuits to Cleveland to open St. Ignatius College (later John Carroll University) in 1886. Gilmour encouraged native vocations to the priesthood: 122 priests, 55 of them American-born and about 27 of them from the diocese, were ordained from 1872 to 1892.

At this time, the question of public funds for private schools was being bitterly debated in the United States. In Ohio, Gilmour joined other bishops in calling for distribution of funds to parochial as well as to public schools; in 1873 he offered a plan of ''shared control'' of Catholic schools in his diocese. As secularization of public schools continued, the bishop told the American Congress of Churches at Cleveland in 1886: ''Catholics object neither to State schools, nor to religion in State schools. However, they do object that any other than the Catholic religion be taught Catholic children.'' By 1872, Ohio, with 16 other states, had already forbidden religious school aid. Aware of this, Gilmour turned to the multiplication and improvement of Catholic schools, and required Catholic children to attend them. He successfully fought attempts to tax Catholic school property (*Gilmour v. Pelton*, Ohio, 1883), established a diocesan school board, and argued effectively at the Third Plenary Council of Baltimore for strong sanctions for Catholic education. The bishop himself produced the popular textbooks known as ''Gilmour Readers,'' and the ''Gilmour Bible History,'' published by Benziger Brothers. Gilmour participated forcefully in the discussions of the Baltimore Plenary Council in 1884, especially those on church property, secret societies, education, and the controversial subjects of irremovable rectors and consultors.

Generally conservative, he upheld the authority of the bishops. As he expressed it to Abp. (later Cardinal) James Gibbons: ''The clergy need to be strengthened against the people, and the people against the irresponsible ways of the clergy, and the bishop against both.'' At Gibbons's request, he joined bishops Joseph Dwenger of

Fort Wayne, Ind., and John Moore of St. Augustine, Fla., in presenting the conciliar acts and decrees at Rome. When the Congregation of Propaganda vetoed the decree requiring the bishop in property transactions to have only the counsel, not the consent, of the consultors, Gilmour led the American bishops in persuading Leo XIII to retain the original decree.

Experience in cosmopolitan Cleveland gave Gilmour an understanding of the dangers of nationality conflict. Although, when possible, he provided immigrant Catholics with churches and priests of their own language, he urged them to be American Catholics. While in Rome in 1885, he and Moore strongly opposed the Germanizing influence in a ''Memorial on the Question of the Germans in the Church in America.'' In his concern over secret societies, Gilmour required the Ancient Order of Hibernians in Cleveland to break with the Ireland-based Fenians.

Gilmour's voice was that of a strong bishop, conscious that the Church's problems in the 19th-century United States could be best solved by candor, discipline, and unity. Although generally conservative, he was among the midwestern bishops advocating a plenary council and a Catholic university. He supported the first American Catholic Lay Congress (1889) and Cardinal Gibbons in his defense of labor unions. After his death in 1891, 5,000 citizens honored him at a memorial service.

Bibliography: M. J. HYNES, *History of the Diocese of Cleveland 1847–1952* (Cleveland 1953). J. T. ELLIS, *The Life of James Cardinal Gibbons,* 2 v. (Milwaukee 1952). C. J. BARRY, *The Catholic Church and German Americans* (Milwaukee 1953). P. D. JORDAN, *Ohio Comes of Age 1873–1900,* v.5 of *History of the State of Ohio,* ed. C. WITTKE, 6 v. (Columbus, Ohio 1941–44). R. D. CROSS *The Emergence of Liberal Catholicism in America* (Cambridge, Mass. 1958).

[P. J. HALLINAN]

GILSON, ÉTIENNE HENRI

Historian of philosophy, Christian philosopher, Thomist; b. Paris, June 13, 1884; d. Cravant, Sept. 19, 1978. The third son of five boys born to Paul Anthelme Gilson, a Parisian shopkeeper, and Caroline Juliette Rainaud, the daughter of a Burgundian (Cravant) innkeeper, Étienne was educated in the parish school of Sainte-Clotilde, in the classical Collège de Notre-Dame-des-Champs and in Lycée Henri IV.

After a year of military service, during which he began to read R. DESCARTES, he studied philosophy at the Sorbonne under Victor Delbos (1862–1916) and Lucien Lévy-Bruhl (1857–1939) and at the Collège de France under H. BERGSON, obtaining the *Diplôme* in philosophy in 1906. In 1907 he married Thérèse Ravisé of Melun.

Academic Career. From 1907 to 1913 Gilson taught philosophy at *lycées* in Bourg-en-Bresse, Rochefort-sur-Mer, Tours, Saint-Quentin, and Angers. In 1913 he received the *Doctorat-ès-Lettres* from the University of Paris and taught at the University of Lille. During World War I, Gilson was mobilized in a Lille regiment and assigned to instructing recruits in central France. A year later, qualified as a machine gunner, he was sent to the Verdun front where he became a lieutenant. He was taken prisoner at Verdun in 1916 and awarded the Croix de Guerre. In 1919 he taught at the University of Strasbourg, and in 1921 he was appointed professor of medieval philosophy at the Sorbonne. The same year he became director of studies for medieval philosophy at the École Pratique des Hautes Études in Paris. In 1922 he was on a relief mission in Russia. In 1926 a chair in medieval philosophy was created specifically for Gilson at the Sorbonne. Also in 1926 he made the first of his many trips to America, lecturing at Harvard University and the University of Virginia. In 1929 he was cofounder of the Institute of Mediaeval Studies in Toronto, Canada, and became its director of studies. In 1932 he was appointed professor of the history of medieval philosophy at the Collège de France. In 1942 he was annoyed to learn that Père CHENU's brochure on Saulchoir methods had been placed on the Roman Index. He was soon to be equally disturbed at attempts to have de LUBAC's *Surnaturel* condemned. He was elected to the Académie Française in 1947, and the same year he was appointed Conseiller de la République. After resigning from the Collège de France in 1951, he became full-time professor at the institute in Toronto, a position he retained until 1968. Gilson retired to Cravant in 1971.

Gilson's reputation during his lifetime was nonpareil: unsurpassed respect for and trust in advanced scholarly research and commitment to the primacy of the oldest materials, read always in the language in which they were written down, in view of what the original author intended to say, and with critical distrust of intervening interpretations. He wanted medieval studies to make a fresh start, functioning primarily at the post-graduate level, rediscovering the riches of a neglected and only too-often despised Christian civilization between late classical times and the early Renaissance.

Christian Philosophy. Gilson came to medieval philosophy and to Thomism in particular through his study of CARTESIANISM. While examining the vocabulary and ideas borrowed from scholasticism by Descartes, he discovered in the medieval schoolmen an unsuspected wealth of philosophy, the knowledge of which is essential for the understanding of modern philosophy. After this discovery Gilson devoted much of his life to the study of medieval philosophy. His voluminous writings cover the whole range of philosophy in the Middle Ages, and he expounded with objectivity and sympathy the ideas of its leading thinkers, from St. Augustine to Duns Scotus. He also wrote extensively on facets of medieval humanism and modern philosophy.

In his Gifford Lectures of 1930–31, entitled *The Spirit of Mediaeval Philosophy,* Gilson showed that during the Middle Ages, under the influence of Christianity, new philosophical ideas were created that passed into modern philosophy. Hence he called philosophy in the Middle Ages "Christian philosophy," which he defined as "every philosophy which, although keeping the two orders [of faith and reason] formally distinct, nevertheless considers the Christian revelation as an indispensable auxiliary to reason."

Gilson rejected the notion of a common philosophical synthesis, or "scholasticism," in the Middle Ages. In his view there were several scholastic syntheses in the 13th century, each of which was highly original and often in opposition to the others. The doctrinal syntheses of masters such as St. BONAVENTURE, St. THOMAS AQUINAS, DUNS SCOTUS, and WILLIAM OF OCKHAM were not primarily philosophical but theological. They philosophized as theologians and within the context of their theologies.

Gilson was a philosophical historian, seeking truth through the history of philosophy. His historical studies led him to the truth of Thomism. In Thomism he found a metaphysics of existence that conceives God as the very act of being (*ipsum esse*) and creatures as beings whose center is an act of existing (*esse*). He refused to modernize Thomism by treating its rational content as a philosophy independent of theology or by expounding it according to a philosophical order. He also distinguished between the Thomism of St. Thomas and that of his followers, such as Tommaso de Vio CAJETAN, who sometimes distorted Aquinas's doctrine. He opposed attempts to synthesize Thomism with philosophies contrary to its spirit, such as Cartesianism and KANTIANISM. In his view Thomistic realism is irreconcilable with the methodic doubt of Descartes and the critique of I. Kant.

While seeking to understand Thomism in its medieval setting, Gilson called for the revival of its creative spirit. He championed a living Thomism that will interpret, criticize, and put into order, in the light of the Thomistic metaphysics of being, the enormous data accumulated since the Middle Ages (*The Spirit of Thomism,* 96). Among Gilson's outstanding contributions to living Thomism are his philosophical analyses of the fine arts.

See Also: CHRISTIAN PHILOSOPHY; EXISTENTIAL METAPHYSICS; SCHOLASTICISM, 3; THEOLOGY, NATURAL.

Bibliography: Works. A complete bibliography of Gilson's writings up to 1958 is contained in *Mélanges offerts à Étienne Gilson de l'Academie française* (Toronto 1959) 15–58. M. MCGRATH, *Étienne Gilson, A Bibliography* (Toronto 1982). Among his works are: *La Liberté chez Decartes et la théologie* (Paris 1913); *Le Thomisme* (Strasbourg 1919; 6th ed. Paris 1965), Eng. *The Christian Philosophy of St. Thomas Aquinas,* tr. L. K. SHOOK (New York 1956); *La Philosophie au moyen âge,* 2 v. (Paris 1922; 2d ed., 1 v. 1944); *La Philosophie de s. Bonaventure* (Paris 1924; 2d ed. 1942), Eng. tr. I. TRETHOWAN (New York 1938); *Introduction à l'étude de s. Augustin* (Paris 1929; 2d ed. 1943), Eng., *The Christian Philosophy of Saint Augustine,* tr. L. E. M. LYNCH (New York 1960); *Études sur le rôle de la pensée médiévale dans la formation du système cartésien* (Paris 1930); *The Spirit of Medieval Philosophy,* tr. A. H. C. DOWNES (New York 1936). *Les Idées et les lettres* (Paris 1932); *La Théologie mystique de s. Bernard* (Paris 1934), Eng. tr. A. H. C. DOWNES (New York 1940); *Le Réalisme méthodique* (Paris 1935); *Christianity and Philosophy,* tr. R. MACDONALD (New York 1939); *The Unity of Philosophical Experience* (New York 1937); *Héloise and Abelard,* tr. L. K. SHOOK (Chicago 1951); *Reason and Revelation in the Middle Ages* (New York 1938); *Dante et la philosophie* (Paris 1939), Eng. tr. D. MOORE (New York 1949); *Réalisme thomiste et critique de la connaissance* (Paris 1939); *God and Philosophy* (New Haven 1941); *L'Être et l'essence* (2d ed. Paris 1962); *Being and Some Philosophers* (2d ed. Toronto 1952); *L'École des muses* (Paris 1951), Eng.; *Choir of Muses,* tr. M. WARD (London 1953); *Jean Duns Scot* (Paris 1952); *Les Métamorphoses de la cité de Dieu* (Louvain 1952); *History of Christian Philosophy in the Middle Ages,* (New York 1955); *Painting and Reality* (Bollingen Ser. 35; New York 1957); *Peinture et réalité* (Paris 1958); *Elements of Christian Philosophy* (New York 1960); *Le Philosophe et la théologie* (Paris 1960), Eng. tr. C. GILSON (New York 1962); *Modern Philosophy: Descartes to Kant* (with T. LANGAN) (New York 1963); *Les Arts du Beau* (Paris 1963); *Matières et formes* (Paris 1964); *The Spirit of Thomism* (New York 1964); *The Art of the Beautiful* (New York 1965); *Dante et Béatrice: Études dantesques* (Paris 1974); *Thomist Realism and the Critique of Knowledge*, tr. M. A. WAUK, foreword by F. D. WILHEMSEN (San Francisco 1986). Literature. L. K. SHOOK, *Étienne Gilson* (Toronto, Ont. 1984). C. J. EDIE, *The Philosophy of Étienne Gilson,* 3 v. (Doctoral diss. unpub., Institut Supérieur de Philosophie, Louvain 1958). J. MARITAIN et al., *Étienne Gilson: Philosophe de la chrétienté* (Paris 1949). A. C. PEGIS, "G. and Thomism," *Thought* 21 (1946) 435–454. *A Gilson Reader,* ed. A. C. PEGIS (New York 1957) 7–20. H. DE LUBAC, *Lettres de M. Étienne Gilson au père Henri de Lubac et commentaire par celui-ci* (1986), L. A. KENNEDY and J. C. MARLER, eds., *Thomistic Papers II* (Houston 1986).

[A. MAURER/L. K. SHOOK]

GIMÉNEZ MALLA, CEFERINO, BL.

Also know as "El Pele," married gypsy, martyr, lay Franciscan; b. Aug. 26(?), 1861, Fraga, Huesca, Catalonia, Spain; d. Aug. 9, 1936, in the cemetery of Barbastro, Spain. Ceferino (Zeferino) was one of over 500,000 gypsies to suffer racial and religious persecution in the 20th century. Following his marriage to Teresa Giménez Castro of Lérida, Ceferino moved with his new wife to Barbastro. The marriage, a gypsy union that was regularized in 1912 in the Catholic Church, resulted in no children of their own, but the couple adopted Teresa's niece Pepita. A successful horse trader, Giménez used his negotiating skills to settled disputes and gained a reputation for fairness. He was also known for his charity and piety. Ceferino's illiteracy and humility belied his great wisdom, which led even his bishop, Blessed Florentino ASENSIO BARROSO, who was martyred hours after Ceferino and beatified with him, to seek his counsel. He was a member of the city council of Barbastro and, as one of the first 159 Franciscan tertiaries of Barbastro (initiated by the Capuchins in 1926), elected to the advisory council of the society. Ceferino was arrested for defending a young priest who was being harassed. During his 15 day imprisonment in the Capuchin friary with 350 other detainees, Ceferino incited the guards by daily praying the Rosary. Despite the intervention of Eugenio Sopena, an influential member of the revolutionary committee and Ceferino's neighbor, he was shot by a Republican firing squad for refusing to renounce his faith. Eighteen others, mainly priests and religious, died with him and were buried in unmarked graves. Ceferino's cause was opened in Barbastro in 1993, and the decree of martyrdom was issued in Rome on Dec. 17, 1996. When Pope John Paul II beatified him on May 4, 1997, he became the first gypsy blessed and second lay martyr of the Spanish Civil War. Patron of gypsies.

Feast: Aug. 2.

Bibliography: *Acta Apostolicae Sedis* 12 (1997) 599. *L'Osservatore Romano,* Eng. ed. 42 (1995): 8.

[K. I. RABENSTEIN]

GINOULHIAC, JACQUES MARIE ACHILLE

French bishop and theologian; b. Montpellier, Dec. 3, 1806; d. there, Nov. 17, 1875. In 1830, immediately after ordination, he was appointed professor of philosophy and natural sciences and in 1833 professor of theology at the seminary of Montpellier. In 1839 he became vicar-general of Aix. While bishop of Grenoble (1852–70) he conducted a careful investigation during the controversy concerning LA SALETTE before deciding in favor of the credibility of the apparitions there. In 1870 he was promoted to the archbishopric of Lyons, where in 1873 he laid the cornerstone for the basilica of Notre Dame de Fourvière. He was a good administrator in both sees and issued pastoral letters of high theological caliber. Although he was always very devoted to the Holy See, upheld the papal temporal power, and repulsed attacks on the SYLLABUS OF ERRORS, he gained the reputation of being a supporter of LIBERALISM and GALLICANISM. His intent, however, was to prevent misunderstanding between the Church and modern society. At VATICAN COUNCIL I he delivered a remarkable address advocating freedom of theological investigation. Along with Félix DUPANLOUP he was a leader among the French bishops in the minority group opposed to the definition of papal primacy and infallibility. He voted *non placet* (July 13, 1870) and absented himself from the public session (July 18) that promulgated the doctrines, but he subscribed to them on August 16. Ginoulhiac's reputation as a theologian was established with his *Histoire du dogme catholique pendant les trois premiers siècles* (2 v. 1852; 2d ed. in three v. 1865), in which he asserted that the doctrine of the Trinity did not result from rationalistic speculation but from the theological development of teachings contained in revelation. His other writings include *Sermon sur la montagne* (1873) and *Les origines du christianisme* (1878).

Bibliography: E. MANGENOT, *Dictionnaire de théologie catholique* 6.2:1371–73. C. BUTLER, *The Vatican Council,* 2 v. (New York 1930).

[V. CONZEMIUS]

GIOBERTI, VINCENZO

Nineteenth-century Italian philosopher and statesman; b. Turin, April 5, 1801; d. Paris, Oct. 26, 1852. Gioberti was ordained in 1825. Exiled in 1830, he stayed first at Paris, then at Brussels, where he taught for ten years in a private institute. NEO-GUELFISM seemed to triumph in the 1846 election of Pius IX to the papacy; so in 1848 Gioberti returned to Turin and became president of the chamber, then president of the ministers. In his *Il Rinnovamento civile d'Italia* (2 v. Turin 1851) he manifested his abandonment of neo-Guelfism and adoption of liberalism. Retiring to Paris in voluntary exile, he passed the last year of his life there.

Gioberti maintained a complete identity between the first psychological principle and the first ontological principle, a consequence of his embracing the teaching of A. ROSMINI-SERBATI concerning the intuition of being as the principle of intelligibility in reality and of objectivity in consciousness. Indeed, his whole philosophy can be summarized in the formula ''Being creates the existent and the existent returns to being.'' All of his philosophical investigation was centered upon the union-distinction of Being and the existent. At one time he emphasized the distinction between them, at another he so emphasized their unity that he resolved Being into the existent, and his philosophy became a divination about the existent, a philosophy of a simultaneously divine and human mind. Although it is disputed whether his teaching was one of

THEISM OR PANTHEISM, he did, in fact, end up in pantheism. His ''substantive'' distinction between Being and the existent is expressed in the following way: ''The term 'exist' precisely indicates the divine reality inasmuch as, with creation, it goes outside itself, as it were, transplants itself, expresses itself, and manifests itself'' [*Protologia* 2 v. (Naples 1861) 1:16–17]. The two cycles, namely, creation and palingenesis, are conjoined and, as it were, united: ''The first act of creation and the last act of palingenesis do not subsist in themselves, since they are interminable; hence they are nothing. Therefore, they are immediate to each other; nothing is Being, Being is nothing, but only in respect to the existent. . . . However, they subsist in God, in Being, by means of His capacity to fill and reoccupy the infinite'' (*ibid.* 1:251).

Gioberti's concept of the history of humanity as a continuous revelation of God and elevation of man led him, especially in his *Riforma cattolica* (ed. G. Balsamo-Crivelli, Florence 1924), to view revelation, not as completed in the preaching of the Apostles, but as perennial and ever open, manifesting itself in history and in man's consciousness. This doctrine has been condemned by the Church, and Gioberti's works were placed on the Index of Prohibited Books.

See Also: ONTOLOGISM.

Bibliography: U. BENIGNI, in *The Catholic Encyclopedia,* ed. C. G. HERBERMANN et al., 16 v. (New York 1904–14; supplement 1922). C. MAZZANTINI, in *Enciclopedia filosofica,* 4 v. (Venice-Rome 1957).

[M. F. SCIACCA]

GIOTTO DI BONDONE

Florentine painter; b. Vespignano, near Florence, *c.* 1266 or *c.* 1276; d. Florence, *c.* 1336. Giotto effected a revolution in Florentine painting that was to reach its apogee in the work of Michelangelo. Florentine painters had traditionally used the flat two-dimensional figures of the Romanesque and Byzantine styles as models for their forms. Giotto broke with this tradition by using sculpture as his models. He thereby gave his figures greater three-dimensional substance and enhanced the dramatic content of the episodes depicted. The Gothic style with its naturalism in painting and sculpture had begun to invade Italy. It appears in the works of Arnolfo di Cambio and of Niccolò and Giovanni Pisano, whose sculptures were to influence Giotto's style. Giotto's hulking ''Ognissanti Madonna'' in the Uffizi, for example, seated on her flimsy Gothic throne, resembles the blocky portraits of Boniface VIII by Arnolfo.

In the Arena Chapel frescoes (Padua 1303–05), the earliest authenticated frescoes by Giotto, Gothic influence is apparent not only in the figure style and the cascading drapery but also in the iconographic program of the decoration. The scenes from the life of the Virgin and of Christ, the monochrome personifications of virtues and vices painted to resemble sculpture, and the huge Last Judgment are elements characteristically present in the portal sculptures of Gothic cathedrals.

Giotto was a mature artist between 30 and 40 years of age when he painted in the Arena Chapel. What his earlier style might have been, how and where he made the break with the Byzantinized style of CIMABUE, his supposed master, and turned to sculpture as models for his figures, and where he acquired the technique of fresco painting are still matters of conjecture. The answer might well be that he went to Rome, where the fresco tradition was at home and where he would have come in contact with both classical sculpture and that of contemporary Italian Gothic artists. At any rate, his reputation there was such that he was commissioned in 1298 to execute the great mosaic of the Navicella—now completely redone—in St. Peter's.

Ever since the 16th century the fresco cycle of scenes from the life of St. Francis in the upper church of San Francesco at ASSISI has been considered as in Giotto's early style. This claim has been disputed pro and con in more recent times, since several hands can be distinguished in the work. The earliest literary evidence for Giotto's presence at Assisi is an entry for the year 1305 in a contemporary chronicle. It states that Giotto's greatness as an artist is proven by his work in the church of the Minorites at Assisi, at Rimini, and at Padua. The question then arises, where in San Francesco is Giotto's work if not in the St. Francis cycle? Certain NT scenes, such as the ''Deposition,'' the ''Ascension,'' the ''Pentecost,'' and the ''Madonna'' roundel among the frescoes of the Roman school in the upper areas of the nave above the St. Francis series, have been attributed to him. Most recently the attempt has been made to identify him with the Isaac Master.

In the 1320s Giotto decorated four chapels in Santa Croce, FLORENCE. The frescoes of two of these are still preserved: the scenes from the life of St. Francis—recalling the Assisi ones—in the Bardi Chapel, and those from the lives of St. John the Baptist and St. John the Evangelist in the Peruzzi Chapel. These furnish examples of Giotto's late style. The frescoes in both these chapels were restored in the 19th century, but this restoration was recently removed.

In the early 1330s, Giotto was called to Naples by Robert of Anjou to decorate the great hall of the Castelnuovo with figures of famous men. These frescoes no longer exist. The same is true for the frescoes in Santa

Chiara commissioned at the same time. In 1334 Giotto was recalled to Florence to take charge of the construction of the campanile of the cathedral. Some of the relief sculptures there have been attributed to him.

Bibliography: W. HAUSENSTEIN, *Giotto* (Berlin 1923), lists all bibliog. before 1923. R. SALVINI, *Giotto: Bibliografia* (Rome 1938). R. OFFNER, "Giotto, non-Giotto," *Burlington Magazine* 74 (Jan.–June 1939) 259–268; 75 (July–Dec. 1939) 96–113. P. TOESCA, *Giotto* (Turin 1945). M. MEISS, *Giotto and Assisi* (New York 1960). E. T. DeWald, *Italian Painting, 1200–1600* (New York 1961) 119–141.

[E. T. DE WALD]

GIRALDUS CAMBRENSIS

Archdeacon, historian, prolific writer; b. Manorbier Castle, Pembrokeshire, Wales, *c.* 1147 or 1148; d. 1223. Welsh by his mother and Norman by his father, William de Barri, Giraldus was of the royal family of Wales. In his early years he showed a strong interest in the religious life and in study. Since Wales lacked good schools, he first studied under Peter Comestor and then lectured on the liberal arts at Paris, returning to England in 1172. Made archdeacon of Brecknoch, he worked vigorously to reform the Church in WALES. When his uncle David Fitzgerald, Bishop of SAINT DAVIDS, died in 1176, Giraldus was proposed as the new bishop, but HENRY II, KING OF ENGLAND, would allow only Norman bishops. Giraldus thereupon returned to Paris to study theology, civil, and Canon Law. After returning to England in 1180 as a master of theology, he was made a royal chaplain in 1184. He was assigned first to pacify Wales and then to accompany Henry II's son John on a military expedition to Ireland. Giraldus described his experiences in Ireland in his popular *Topographia Hiberniae* [first version tr. J. J. O'Meara (Dundalk 1951)], dedicated to Henry II in 1188, while his *Expugnatio Hibernica* (History of the Conquest of Ireland) is the most valuable of all his works. In 1188 he accompanied Abp. BALDWIN OF CANTERBURY to Wales to preach the crusade proclaimed by Henry II; he described this trip in *Itinerarium Cambriae* (1191). When Henry died in 1189 and Giraldus received no preferment, he decided to retire to a life of prayer and study at LINCOLN. With the death of Peter de Leia, Bishop of Saint Davids, in 1198, and his election by the chapter as Peter's successor, Giraldus tried to win the necessary approval of Abp. Hubert Walter of Canterbury. When Hubert refused, Giraldus appealed to Pope INNOCENT III and became involved in five years of litigation that ended in failure (1203). He revisited Ireland (1205–06) and made a pilgrimage to Rome (1207). He is buried in Saint Davids cathedral.

Giraldus wrote numerous works including an autobiography [tr. H. L. Butler (London 1937)] in which he explained his career and his long struggle to become bishop of Saint Davids. He was a vain man who liked to boast of his charm, of his ability as a teacher in Paris, and of the rightness of his cause. His letters, poems, and speeches are in his *Symbolum electorum.* His works have been published in eight volumes in the Rolls Series (ed. J. S. Brewer and J. F. Dimock, 1861–1891).

"Vision of the Fiery Chariot," detail from the Life of St. Francis of Assisi fresco cycle by Giotto di Bondone, Assisi, Italy, 1297–1299. (©Elio Ciol/CORBIS)

Bibliography: Eng. tr. of historical works, T. FORESTER and R. C. HOARE, rev. and ed. T. WRIGHT (London 1863). M. MANITIUS, *Geschichte der lateinischen Literatur des Mittelalters,* 3 v. (Munich 1911–31) 3:622–637. H. R. LUARD, in *The Dictionary of National Biography from the Earliest Times to 1900,* 63 v. (London 1885–1900; reprinted with corrections, 21 v., 1908–09, 1921–22, 1938; supplement 1901–) 7:1268–72. F. M. POWICKE, "Gerald of Wales," *The Bulletin of John Rylands Library* 12 (1928) 389–410. J. CONWAY DAVIES, "Giraldus Cambrensis, 1146–1946," *Archaeol. Cambrensis* 99 (1946). A. B. EMDEN, *A Biographical Register of the University of Oxford to A. D. 1500,* 3 v. (Oxford 1957–59) 1:117–118.

[J. A. CORBETT]

GIRALDUS OF SALLES, BL.

Monastic founder; b. Salles, Bergerac, France, *c.* 1070; d. abbey of Châtelliers, near Poitiers, France, April 20, 1120. He was a canon regular of the monastery of St. Avit-le-Senieur at Bergerac near his home, and late in life he became a student of Robert of Arbrissel in the Diocese of Périgueux. With great reforming zeal, he founded seven monasteries for men and two for women, most no-

"St. Francis Expels the Devils from Arezzo," 13th-century fresco painting by Giotto di Bondone, Assisi, Italy. (©Archivo Iconografico, S.A./CORBIS)

tably Notre Dame des Châtelliers, where he was buried. Although some miracles were reported after his death, his feast is not widely celebrated. The *Acta Sanctorum* [Oct. 10 (1869) 249–267] includes details on each of the monastic foundations and a laudatory 13th-century biography.

Feast: Oct. 23.

Bibliography: J. LAVIALLE, *Vie du Bx. Géraud de Sales* (1907). A. BORST, *Lexikon für Theologie und Kirche*[2] 4:900. M. B. BRARD, *Catholicisme* 4:1874.

[E. J. KEALEY]

GIRARD OF ANGERS, ST.

Monk; b. Diocese of Angers, *c.* mid-11th century; d. Nov. 4, 1123. He was at first a secular cleric and then became a BENEDICTINE monk at the Abbey of Saint-Aubin in Angers *c.* 1085. In 1097 he founded the priory of Sainte-Madeline in Brossay, and then another at Bois-de-Jarze. Apparently he was much given to fasting and reported having visions after prolonged fasts. Among other things, he reputedly predicted the death of Pope GELASIUS II in 1119 and of King HENRY I's son, William, in 1120. A number of miracles were attributed to him, and he was canonized in 1468. His relics were enshrined in a chapel of the abbey church but were lost during the French Revolution.

Feast: Nov. 4.

Bibliography: *Acta Sanctorum* Nov. 2.1 (1894) 491–509. A. M. ZIMMERMANN, *Kalendarium Benedictinum: Die Heiligen und Seligen des Benediktinerorderns und seiner Zweige* (Metten 1933–38) 3:258–260. E. C. A. LITOU, *Vie de s. Girard, apôtre du pays de Brossay* (Angers 1903).

[E. J. KEALEY]

GIRY, FRANÇOIS

A Minim, author of ascetical, historical, and hagiographical works; b. Paris, Sept. 15, 1635; d. there, Nov. 29, 1688. His father, Louis Giry, lawyer, scholar, and translator, was among the first members of the Académie Française. François entered the MINIMS in 1652 and made profession the following year. Under the direction of Nicolas BARRÉ (founder of the Charitable Schools of the Saint-Enfant-Jésus), he progressed in virtue and knowledge. A professor of theology and master of novices, he held the most important positions in his order. Father Barré, while dying (1686), commissioned him to care for his charitable schools, and Giry fulfilled this trust for the rest of his life. His spiritual treatises are: *Entretiens de Jésus-Christ avec l'âme chrétienne; Livre des cent points d'humilité; Explications . . . sur la Règle du tiers-ordre de St. François de Paule; Méditations pour les soeurs . . . du Saint-Enfant Jésus.* Among his hagiographical works are the *Dissertio chronologica . . . de anno natali et aerate s. Francisci de Paula* (Paris 1680), and above all his edition (following L. Lippomano, L. Surius, P. Ribadeneyra) of *Les Vies des saints dont on fait l'office dans le cours de l'année,* 2 v. (Paris 1683, 1687, 1715, 1719). This work, begun by Simon Martin, though lacking a critical approach, was a marked advance over earlier collections and is still in use.

Bibliography: C. RAFFRON, *Vie du R. P. François Giry* (Paris 1691). L. MORÉRI, *Grand dictionnaire historique* (new ed. Paris 1759). E. D'ALENÇON, *Dictionnaire de théologie catholique,* ed. A. VACANT, 15 v. (Paris 1903–50; Tables générales 1951–) 6.2:1377–79.

[J. DAOUST]

GISELA, BL.

Queen of Hungary; b. *c.* 973; d. *c.* 1060. She was the daughter of St. Henry II (d. 995), duke of Bavaria, and became the wife of St. STEPHEN I, king of Hungary. The tradition according to which she died in 1095 in Passau cannot be taken seriously, nor can the tombstone preserved there be regarded as hers. She died probably in exile or in the seclusion of a convent at an uncertain date. She married Stephen *c.* 996 and gave birth to several children, including St. EMERIC OF HUNGARY. After the death of her husband she became deeply involved in the intrigues created by the problems of his succession. Stephen's successor, the Italian Peter I (d. 1041), is traditionally depicted as a villain, and it is possible that many of the virtues ascribed to Gisela were meant to emphasize the shortcomings of Peter, with whom she came in growing conflict. Gisela has not been canonized and is not normally honored as a saint, although her case is still under consideration by the Holy See.

Feast: May 7.

Bibliography: *Acta Sanctorum* May 2 (1863) 132. J. MABILLON, *Acta sanctorum ordinis S. Benedicti,* 9 v. (Paris 1668–1701; 2d ed. Venice 1733–40) 7:803. A. M. ZIMMERMANN, *Kalendarium Benedictinum: Die Heiligen und Seligen des Benediktinerorderns und seiner Zweige,* 4 v. (Metten 1933–38) 2:159, 161. J. SZALAY, *Catholicisme* 5:36. J. ROKA, *Leben der heil. Gisela* (Vienna 1777). W. M. SCHMID, *Das Grab der Königin Gisela von Ungarn, Gemahlin Stephans I. des Heiligen* (Munich 1912). F. ZSUZSA, ed., *Gizella és kora: felolvasóülések az Árpád-korból* (Veszprém, Hungary 1993).

[D. SINOR]

GISLENUS, ST.

Abbot: b. *c.* 650; d. Oct. 9, *c.* 681. Gislenus (Ghislain in French) was a hermit in a forest of Hainault, France. Near Mons he founded and governed the monastery of SS. Peter and Paul, called locally ''The Cell'' and since renamed Saint-Ghislain. It was also originally known as Urisdongus, that is, the bear's den, from the legend that a bear he saved from the hunt showed him the site of his future monastery. It is said he influenced St. VINCENT MADELGARIUS and his wife, St. WALDETRUD, whom he helped found a convent at Mons. He also helped Waldeturd's sister, St. ALDEGUNDIS found a convent at Maubeuge and was her close friend, for they visited at each other's monasteries and, in old age, at a convenient oratory. Another legendary account of the saint's life states that he was born in Attica, became a BASILIAN monk and then bishop of Athens. He is supposed to have resigned his see after a vision, gone to Rome and then to Hainault by divine instruction, met St. AMANDUS, and settled on the river Haine.

Feast: Oct. 9.

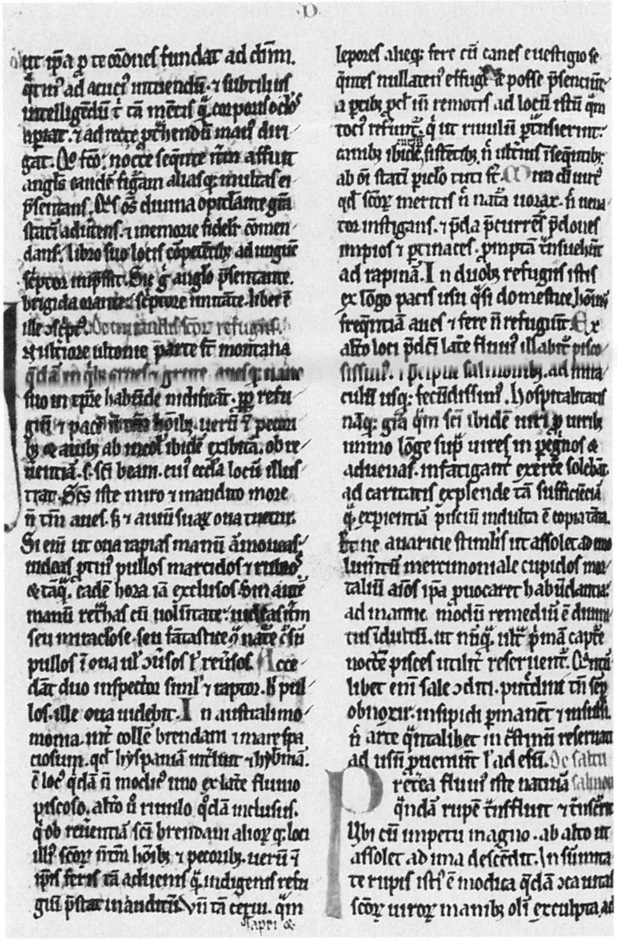

Bibliography: *Acta Sanctorum* Oct. 4:1010–37. A. BUTLER, *The Lives of the Saints* (New York 1956) 4: 71. A. M. ZIMMERMANN, *Kalendarium Benedictinum: Die Heiligen und Seligen des Benediktinerorderns und seiner Zweige* (Metten 1933–38) 3:154–157. J. DUBOIS, *Catholicisme* 4:1910.

[B. CAVANAUGH]

Manuscript page from ''Topographia Hiberniae,'' 12th century, by Giraldus Cambrensis (British Museum MS Royal 13 B viii, fol. 22v).

GIULIANI, MARIANNA, ST.

In religion Maria della Pace (Eng: Mary of Peace; Fr.: Marie de la Paix); martyr, religious of the Franciscan Missionaries of Mary (FMM); b. Dec. 13, 1875, Aquila, Italy; d. July 9, 1900, Taiyüan, China. Although Marianna's father was dogmatically anti–religious, her mother covertly taught her the faith. Her father abandoned the seven children to the care of neighbors after her mother's death in 1885. Marianna's uncle, a Franciscan priest, commended her to the care of Mother Mary of the Passion. Upon completing her studies in France, she joined the Franciscan Missionaries of Mary (1892) and took the name Sr. Marie de la Paix. At the novitiate in Paris she worked with difficult girls. Thereafter she was assigned consecutively to Vanves, where she made her first vows, Austria, and China, where she was responsible for organizing the orphanage and using her beautiful voice to enhance the beauty of the liturgy. She was killed during the Boxer Uprising. Sr. Marie de la Paix was beatified with her religious sisters by Pope Pius XII, Nov. 24, 1946, and canonized, Oct. 1, 2000, by Pope John Paul II with Augustine Zhao Rong and companions.

Feast: July 4.

Bibliography: G. GOYAU, *Valiant Women: Mother Mary of the Passion and the Franciscan Missionaries of Mary*, tr. G. TELFORD (London 1936). M. T. DE BLARER, *Les Bse Marie Hermine de Jésus et ses compagnes, franciscaines missionnaires de Marie, massacrées le 9 juillet 1900 à Tai–Yuan–Fou, Chine* (Paris 1947). L. M. BALCONI, *Le Martiri di Taiyuen* (Milan 1945). *Acta Apostolicae Sedis* 47 (1955) 381–388. *L'Osservatore Romano*, Eng. Ed. 40 (2000): 1–2, 10.

[K. I. RABENSTEIN]

GIULIANI, VERONICA, ST.

Capuchin Poor Clare, stigmatic, and mystical writer; b. Mercatello, Italy, Dec. 27, 1660; d. Città di Castello, Italy, July 9, 1727. She was the daughter of Francesco Giuliani, a financier, and Benedetta Mancini; she was baptized Ursula. In 1677, after brief opposition from her widowed father, she joined the austere Capuchin POOR CLARES at Città di Castello, taking the name Veronica in honor of the Passion. She was favored with mystical experiences and received the visible impression of the crown of thorns on April 4, 1694. On April 5, 1697, she received the stigmata; this recurred several times later. For a time this led to misunderstanding in the convent, yet she was respected to such an extent that she was novice mistress for 34 years and was afterward elected abbess. She remained in this post from 1716 until her death in 1727. A post-mortem showed that her heart bore the imprint of the cross. She was beatified June 17, 1804, and canonized by GREGORY XVI, May 26, 1839. Besides her personal sanctity and close adherence to the ideals of St. Francis, Veronica is known for her *Diary* of ten volumes, written at the direction of her confessor; it is one of the most interesting accounts of mystical phenomena known to hagiographers. Her total works cover 44 volumes, of which 42 were written in her own hand. She had great devotion to the Eucharist and the Sacred Heart, and she offered her suffering for the promotion of the missions. She is usually represented crowned with thorns, holding a cross and a heart imprinted with the instruments of the Passion.

Feast: July 9.

Bibliography: *Diario di S. Veronica Giuliani,* ed. P. PIZZICARIA, 10 v. (Prato and Città di Castello 1895–1928). G. CITTADINI, *Lineamenti di dottrina ascetico-mistica secondo gli scritti di santa Veronica Giuliani* (Turin 1992); *Vita di Santa Veronica Giuliani e del suo tempo* (Città di Castello 1992). M. COURBAT, *Dico e ridico e non dico niente: il fenomeno del diario sdoppiatio in santa Veronica Giuliani* (Siena 1994). R. PICCINELLI, *La teologia della croce nell'esperienza mistica di S. Veronica Giuliani* (Assisi 1989).

[J. CROSBY]

GIUSTINIANI

A celebrated family, which, according to Bernardo Giustiniani in his vita of his uncle St. Lawrence, was driven from Constantinople by sedition and migrated to Istria and Venice. The Venetian branch is found in Chioggia and Fermo. A Genoese branch spread to Corsica, Naples, Sicily, and Lipara, as well as to Chios, an Aegean island ruled by Genoa. The first member of whom there is record was Bl. *Nicholas,* a Benedictine monk (d. *c.* 1180). He entered the monastery of San Niccolò del Lido at Venice in 1153. When all the male members of his family perished in a disaster at sea, he was dispensed from his monastic vows by Pope Alexander III. He married Anna Michieli, daughter of the Doge of Venice, and fathered nine children. He returned to the monastery before his death. Although he is honored on November 21 in the Benedictine Order, there has been no formal beatification.

Venetian Branch. *Lawrence* (*see* LAWRENCE JUSTINIAN, ST.), the most famous member of the family, an ascetical and mystical writer, entered the CANONS REGULAR OF ST. AUGUSTINE in 1400 and led a humble, mortified life, showing special love for the poor. From 1409 on, he served in various administrative posts in his order and in the Church, ultimately becoming superior general (1424–31), bishop of Castello (1433), and finally patriarch of Venice (1451–56). Beatified in 1524 by CLEMENT VII, Lawrence was canonized by ALEXANDER VIII in 1690.

Leonardo, statesman and poet; b. Venice, *c.* 1388; d. there, Nov. 10, 1446. Leonardo was the brother of Lawrence. He became head of the Council of Ten (1443) and the procurator of SAINT MARK'S. He is noted for having restored the *canzonetta* as a popular lyric.

Bernardo, statesman and historian; b. Venice, Jan. 6, 1408; d. there, March 10, 1489. He was the son of Leonardo, and became ambassador to Louis XI of France, PAUL II, and SIXTUS IV, as well as a member of the Council of Ten. He is known for his biography of his uncle St. Lawrence (Venice 1475) and for his history of Venice, the *De origine urbis Venetiarum* (Venice 1492).

Paolo, Bl., monk and spiritual author, known also as Tommaso; b. Venice, June 15, 1476; d. Abbey of St. Sylvester of Mt. Sorate, June 28, 1528. He studied philosophy and theology at the University of Padua and then *c.* 1505 took up a solitary existence at Murano near Venice. He was the founder of the Camaldolese Hermits of Monte Corona and in 1513 succeeded Pietro DELFINO as general of the order. Paolo is known also as the author of numerous ascetical works and the *Regula vitae eremiticae* (Camaldoli 1519). His cult has not been officially confirmed.

Innocenzio, scholar; d. Aug. 10, 1563. He was a Camaldolese monk, a noted theologian and the author of a vita of Bl. Paolo.

Nicolò Antonio, bishop; b. 1712; d. 1796. A Benedictine, he was named to the See of Torcello in 1754, Verona in 1759, and Padua in 1772. He also translated and edited the works of St. ATHANASIUS and of St. Lawrence Giustiniani. Two Jesuit authors, *Fábrice* (1530–1604) and *Gerolamo* (b. 1698), also are from this branch of the family.

Genoese Branch. *Paolo de Moneglia,* curialist and diplomat; b. Genoa, 1444; d. Budapest, Hungary, 1502. A Dominican since 1463, he became provincial for Lombardy in 1485, master of the Sacred Palace in 1490, and inquisitor general for Genoa in 1494 (*see* INQUISITION). In 1499 he became bishop of Chios and was named legate for Hungary by Pope ALEXANDER VI.

Agostino, bishop and Orientalist; b. Genoa, *c.* 1470; d. at sea off Liguria, Italy, 1536. He became a Dominican, was named bishop of Nebbio in Corsica in 1514 and participated in the Fifth LATERAN COUNCIL (1516–17). In 1517 he became the first professor of Hebrew at the University of Paris. A friend of PICO DELLA MIRANDOLA, ERASMUS, and Thomas MORE, Agostino was the first in Europe to publish a POLYGLOT BIBLE (1516), and in it, commenting on Ps 18.5, he inserted a brief notice on Christopher COLUMBUS. Quétif ascribes 15 works to his authorship.

Vincenzo, a classicist; d. 1599. He took up residence at Valencia, Aragon, and was the author of *Commentaria in universam logicam* and editor of the works of VINCENT FERRER. *Decio* (1580–1642), another Dominican, came from Messana and was bishop of Aleria, Corsica, from 1612.

Benedetto, Jesuit exegete; b. Genoa, March 16, 1551; d. Rome, Dec. 19, 1622. He served seven years as rector of the Roman College and was appointed theologian of the Sacred PENITENTIARY in 1606. Twelve works are ascribed to his authorship, of which his commentaries on the Epistles of St. Paul (2 v. Rome 1612–13) and on the Catholic Epistles (Lyon 1621) are best known.

Six other Giustiniani are numbered among the Jesuit writers: *Agostino* (1551–90), *Giorgio* (1569–1644), *Vincenzo* (1593–1661), *Pietro* (1628–1707), *Gerolamo* (1656–1734) and *Ottaviano* (1689–1768).

Giovanni, a military commander; d. Chios, 1453. He brought a Genoese contingent to Constantinople in 1453 and played a leading part in the brave but unsuccessful defense of that city against the Turkish attack.

Michele, (1612– *c.* 1680) was vicar to his cousin Decio, Bishop of Aleria, and also a historian of Italian affairs. *Lorenzo* (1761–1824 or 1825) was a distinguished scholar who became librarian of the Biblioteca Nazionale (1805) and professor of critical diplomatics at the University of Naples.

Members of the Hierarchy. There were five cardinals from the Giustiniani family.

Vincenzo of Chios, scholar; b. Chios, Aug. 28, 1519; d. Rome, Oct. 28, 1582. He was master general of the Dominican Order from 1558 to 1571 and participated in the Council of TRENT (1562–63). He was the legate of Pope Pius V in Spain and was created a cardinal in 1570. He edited the first complete edition of the works of St. THOMAS AQUINAS (17 v. Rome 1570).

Benedetto of Chios, bishop of Porto; b. 1554; d. 1621. He served under the popes from GREGORY XIII to GREGORY XV and was noted for his zeal and charity to the poor of his diocese.

Orazio of Chios, scholar and curialist; b. Chios, Feb. 28, 1580; d. Rome, July 25, 1649. He was an ORATORIAN and became librarian of the Vatican (*see* VATICAN LIBRARY) under URBAN VIII. He was made bishop of Montalto in 1640 and a cardinal in 1645. He also served as consultor of the Congregation for the PROPAGATION OF THE FAITH and of the Holy Office, as well as grand penitentiary.

Giacomo, curialist and papal diplomat; b. Rome, Dec. 29, 1769; d. Rome, Feb. 24, 1843. He was vicelegate at Ravenna in 1794, governor of Perugia in 1797, and vice-governor of Rome until he was forced to withdraw before Napoleon's troops. Reinstalled in Rome by PIUS VII, he was created archbishop of Tyre in 1817 and served as nuncio to Spain until raised to the cardinalate in 1826 by LEO XII. He was among the candidates for the papacy after the death of PIUS VIII but was opposed by the Spanish government.

Allesandro, papal diplomat; b. Genoa, Feb. 3, 1778; d. Genoa, Oct. 11, 1843. He was instrumental in the negotiation of the Concordat of 1818 with the Kingdom of the Two Sicilies and was in Naples during the revolution of 1820–21. He was created archbishop of Petra in 1822, named nuncio to Naples the same year, reassigned as nuncio to Lisbon in 1826, and raised to the cardinalate in 1832.

Two archbishops and four bishops are listed among the Giustiniani of Chios. *Leonardo* (*c.* 1395–1459), a Dominican, was vicar-general of the Congregation of Fratres Peregrinati until appointed archbishop of Mytilene in 1444. He is widely known through the account of the capture of Constantinople (*Patrologia Graeca* 159:923–944) that he sent to Pope NICHOLAS V. *Antonio* (1505–71) became archbishop of Naxos in 1562, assisted at the Council of Trent, and was later transferred to the See of Lipari. *Timoteo* (*c.* 1502–71), a Dominican, was bishop of Aria in Crete (1550), of Chios (1564), and later of Stromboli in Calabria. *Angelo* (1520–96), a famous Franciscan preacher, was bishop of Geneva (1568) and assisted with the edition of the Greek Fathers produced under Pope Gregory XIII. *Gerolamo* (1554–1618) was made bishop of Chios in 1597. *PietroMario,* a Benedictine, was bishop of Sagona in Corsica (1726) and of Ventimiglia (1741). He also composed a history of the Abbey of MONTE CASSINO to the 10th century.

Bibliography: General. J. KRAUS, *Lexikon für Theologie und Kirche,* ed. J. HOFER and K. RAHNER (Freiburg 1957–65) 4:904–905. M. L. FENOGLIO, *Dizionario ecclesiastico* 2:209. Nicholas. A. M. ZIMMERMAN, *Kalendarium Benedictinum: Die Heiligen und Seligen des Benediktinerorderns und seiner Zweige* 3:343. J. L. BAUDOT and L. CHAUSSIN, *Vies des saints et des bienheureux selon l'ordre du calendrier avec l'historique des fêtes*, ed. by the Benedictines of Paris (Paris 1935–56) 11:703. Leonardo. M. T. DAZZI, *Leonardo Giustiniani, poeta popolare d'amore* (Bari 1934). G. BILLANOVICH, ''Alla scoperta di L. G.,'' *Annali della R. Scuola normale superiore di Pisa* 8 (1939) 99–129. Bernardo. *Enciclopedia ecclesiastica,* ed. A. BERNAREGGI (Milan 1942) 4:156. Paolo. P. LUGANO, ed., *L'Italia benedettina* (Rome 1929) 273–279. A. DES MAZIS, *Dictionnaire d'histoire et de géographie ecclésiastiques* 11:519–536. J. LECLERCQ, ''Le Bx. Paul Giustiniani et les ermites de son temps,'' *Problemi di vita religiosa in Italia nel cinquecento: Atti del convegno di storia della chiesa in Italia (Bologna, 2–6 sett. 1958)* (Padua 1960) 225–240; *Un Humaniste ermite: Le Bx. Paul Giustiniani, 1476–1528* (Rome 1951). Innocenzio. J. FRANÇOIS, *Bibliothèque générale des écrivains de l'Ordre de Saint Benoît,* 4 v. (Bouillon 1777–78; repr. Louvain 1961) 1:550. Nicolo Antonio. *Enciclopedia ecclesiastica, op. cit.* 4:156–157. Fabrice and Gerolamo. C. SOMMERVOGEL et al., *Bibliothèque de la compagnie de Jésus* (Brussels-Paris 1890–1932) 3:1491–94. Paolo de Moneglia. J. QUÉTIF and J. ÉCHARD, *Scriptores ordinis Praedicatorum* (Paris 1719–23) 2.1: 3–4. Agostino. *ibid.* 2.1:96–100. R. A. VIGNA, *I vescovi domenicani liguri ovvero in Liguria* (Genoa 1887) 216–244. Benedetto. *Bibliothèque de la Compagnie de Jésus op. cit.* 3:1489–91. P. BERNARD, A. VACANT et al, ed. *Dictionnaire de théologie catholique* (Paris 1903–50) 6.2:1381. Other Jesuits. *Bibliothèque de la Compagnie de Jésus op. cit.* 3:1491–94. Giovanni. S. RUNCIMAN, *The Fall of Constantinople, 1453* (New York 1965), *passim.* Michele and Lorenzo. N. CORTESE, *Eruditi e giornali letterari nella Napoli del settecento* (Naples 1922) 36–59. *Enciclopedia ecclesiastica,* op. cit. 4:156. Vincenzo of Chios. J. QUÉTIF and J. ÉCHARD, *Scriptores ordinis Praedicatorum* (Paris 1719–23) 2.1:164–165. Orazio. É. D' ALENÇON, A. VACANT et al, ed. *Dictionnaire de théologie catholique* (Paris 1903–50) 6.2:1381–82. Giacomo. A. EISLER, *Das Veto der katholischen Staaten bei der Papstwahl* (Vienna 1907) 240–242. J. BECKER, *Relaciones diplomáticas entre España y la Santa Sede durante el siglo XIX* (Madrid 1908), *passim.* J. M. MARCH, *La exclusiva dada por España contra el cardinale Giustiniani* (1932). Alessandro. W. MATURI, *Il Concordato del 1818 tra la Santa Sede e le due Sicilie* (Florence 1929), *passim.* J. H. BRADY, *Rome and the Neapolitan Revolution of 1820–21* (New York 1937), *passim.* G. M. MONTI, ''Stato e Chiesa durante la rivoluzione napoletana del 1820–21,'' in *Studi storici,* v.1 of *Chiesa e Stato,* 2 v. (Milan 1939) 335–405. Leonardo. S. RUNCIMAN, *op. cit., passim.* R. LOENERTZ, *La Société des Frères Pérégrinants* (Rome 1937–) 1:66–70. Angelo. L. WADDING, *Scriptores Ordinis Minorum* (Lyons 1625–54) 23:275–278. G. MATTEUCCI, *Due illustri minoriti del sec. XVI* (Venice 1949). Pietro-Mario. J. FRANÇOIS, *op. cit.* 1: 550–551.

[M. G. MCNEIL]

GLADSTONE, WILLIAM EWART

English statesman; b. Liverpool, Dec. 29, 1809; d. Hawarden, Wales, May 19, 1897. The fourth son of a wealthy merchant of Scottish ancestry, he was educated at Eton and at Oxford University, where he took a double first in classics and mathematics (1831). He was drawn to TRACTARIANISM and made friends with a number of its leaders. His selection of a political rather than an ecclesiastical career was solely in deference to his father's wishes. In December 1832, he was elected to Parliament as the member from Newark. Within a comparatively short time he became a trusted member of Peel's government. The poverty he witnessed in Naples during a visit there in 1851 is said to have led him to cast off his innate Toryism. He was prime minister four times (1868–74, 1880–85, 1886, 1892–94).

In *The State in its Relations with the Church* (1838), Gladstone declared that the State, no less than the individual, is bound by moral law; and that the State must have a Christian awareness. Originally, this belief led him to advocate a theocracy. His changed attitude appeared later when he led the successful struggles to disestablish the Church of IRELAND (1867) and to remove the religious tests in the universities, thereby opening positions in them to all creeds. His education Act of 1870, however, embittered the Church of England and failed to satisfy Nonconformists. It also antagonized Catholics, who were already suspicious of Gladstone for his early opposition to the Maynooth Grant and to the Irish hierarchy's schemes for university education. Gladstone's friendship with Cardinal MANNING dated from their undergraduate days. They corresponded regularly on Irish affairs, education, and social matters. It was largely Manning's influence that dissuaded Gladstone from attempting to break up VATICAN COUNCIL I by force. Gladstone's polemical pamphlets against the Council elicited written replies from Manning and one from Bishop ULLATHORNE. Relations between Gladstone and Manning became especially strained in 1885 when Cardinal McCabe of Dublin died. Gladstone was anxious to have an amenable prelate appointed. Lord Granville, Gladstone's foreign secretary, employed ''Mr. George Errington . . . an active, officious, though not an official agent'' to work for the British government at Rome. The matter became notorious. It was Manning, acting on information supplied by Sir Charles Dilke, who prevented the appointment of a government candidate.

Bibliography: J. MORLEY, *The Life of William Ewart Gladstone,* 3 v. (New York 1903). G. T. GARRATT, *The Two Mr. Gladstones* (London 1936). J. L. HAMMOND, *Gladstone and the Irish Nation* (London 1938). C. C. O'BRIEN, *Parnell and His Party, 1880–90* (Oxford 1957). V. A. MCCLELLAND, *Cardinal Manning: His Public Life and Influence, 1865–1892* (New York 1962). D. MCELRATH, *The Syllabus of Pius IX: Some Reactions in England* (Louvain 1964).

[V. A. MCCLELLAND]

GLASTONBURY, ABBEY OF

Former BENEDICTINE monastery in Somerset, England. The origins of Glastonbury are remote and obscure. The legendary founder was Joseph of Arimathea. This and other legends, e.g., that St. Patrick the Younger, King Arthur, the HOLY GRAIL, and St. BRIGID OF IRELAND were buried there, made Glastonbury a perennial pilgrimage center. In fact, Celtic monks were at Glastonbury from at least the 5th century; the BENEDICTINE RULE was instituted there probably in the early 8th century. During the Danish invasions, regular life disappeared, but Glastonbury served as the center of the great monastic revival in 10th-century ENGLAND that followed St. DUNSTAN's installation as abbot there in 940. Glastonbury's reformed abbots and monks served as bishops and missionaries and were instrumental in spreading Benedictine life and the spirit of reform throughout England and Scandinavia.

At the Conquest, Glastonbury was the wealthiest monastery in England. The new Continental customs were resisted there, and as a result, some of the monks were killed by Norman men-at-arms. Not until the rule of HENRY OF BLOIS (1126–71) did Glastonbury obtain an administrator who was able to reorganize its finances, embark on an extensive building program, and introduce reform discipline. But Henry's rule was not entirely beneficent; he was also bishop of Winchester and more a patron than a father to his monks. Misfortune followed; in 1184 the abbey buildings were destroyed by fire, and in 1194 the bishop of Bath began his attempts to make Glastonbury an episcopal monastery. Not until 1234 was the abbey completely independent once again.

William Ewart Gladstone.

The 13th century was a golden age for Glastonbury, which reached a high point under John of Taunton (1274–90). The economic basis for this revival was the abbey's scientific farming. Glastonbury was a proponent of monastic reform in provincial meetings and led the way in eliminating many liturgical accretions and in emphasizing intellectual development. Glastonbury's library had become large and very early included works of modern theology, such as those of Thomas Aquinas. An extensive building program was completed and charitable services were extended during this period.

In the 14th and 15th centuries discipline declined at Glastonbury, though scandals were few. Community life was marred by the increasing separation of abbot and monks, the decentralization of finances, and the presence of a wasteful or superfluous household staff. However, liturgical life remained essentially unaltered.

The last abbot, Richard WHITING (1524–39), kept good order in the monastery, though he was not a disciplinarian. Despite the abbot's acquiescence in the gradual assumption of control of the English Church by HENRY VIII, the great wealth of Glastonbury made it a rich prize, and the King's spoilers were sent in. Whiting was sent to the Tower. He was executed in 1539, the abbey was dissolved, its monks were pensioned, and its treasures

Ruins of Glastonbury Abbey, Cornwall, England. (©Tim Hawkins/CORBIS)

were delivered to the King. The abbey buildings became a quarry for the area, so that little survives today. The Church of England has owned the property since 1907 and has sponsored archeological excavations on the site.

Bibliography: Sources. A. WATKIN, ed., *The Great Chartulary of Glastonbury,* 3 v. (Somerset Record Society 59, 63, 64; London 1947–56). ADAM OF DOMERHAM, *Historia de rebus gestis Glastoniensibus,* ed. T. HEARNE, 2 v. (London 1727). JOHN OF GLASTONBURY, *Chronica: sive historia de rebus Glastoniensibus . . .*, ed. T. HEARNE (Oxford 1726). WILLIAM OF MALMESBURY, *De antiquitate Glastoniensis ecclesiae* (*Patrologia Latina,* ed. J. P. MIGNE, 179:1681–1734); *De gestis regum Anglorum,* ed. W. STUBBS, 2 v. (Rerum Britannicarum medil aevi scriptores 90; London 1887–89). Literature. W. DUGDALE, *Monastitcon Anglicanum* (London 1655–73); best ed. by J. CALEY et al., 6 v. (1817–30) 1:1–79. F. B. BOND, *An Architectural Handbook of Glastonbury Abbey* (4th ed. Glastonbury 1925). G. ASHE, *King Arthur's Avalon: The Story of Glastonbury* (New York 1958), with good bibliog. A. WATKIN, *The Story of Glastonbury* (London 1960), short introd. D. KNOWLES and R. N. HADCOCK, *Medieval Religious Houses: England and Wales* (New York 1953) 66. D. KNOWLES, *The Monastic Order in England, 943–1216* (2d ed. Cambridge, Eng. 1962). D. KNOWLES, *The Religious Orders in England,* 3 v. (Cambridge, Eng. 1948–60), scattered, but excellent references.

[J. R. SOMMERFELD]

GLENDALOUGH, MONASTERY OF

Former monastery in the heart of the Wicklow Hills, Ireland, founded by St. KEVIN *c.* 570. The original buildings were on a level patch of ground between two lakes (*glenn-dá-locha,* the valley of the two lakes). When the area became too small, the community moved to a wider plain further down the valley, where the round tower and a remarkable group of churches still stand. The community's long list of abbots stretches from the death of Kevin in 618 to St. LAWRENCE O'TOOLE in the 12th century. Mention of bishops, priests, hermits, professors, and royal burials there shows that the monastery continued to flourish despite two centuries of attacks by the Scandinavian invaders after 835. In 1111 Glendalough became the see of a large diocese, which was in turn united with Dublin (1214). The monastic buildings, which dot the valley here and there for some two miles, remained more or less intact until 1714, when they were razed by the high sheriff, at the head of troops, and by the local Protestant settlers. Glendalough was the center of a famous pilgrimage, culminating on the feast of St. Kevin (June 3), that survived until the middle of the 19th century.

Bibliography: *Vita s. Coemgeni* (Kevin), in *Vitae sanctorum Hiberniae,* comp. C. PLUMMER, 2 v. (Oxford 1910) 1:234–257. J. F. KENNEY, *The Sources for the Early History of Ireland*: v. 1, *Ecclesiastical* (New York 1929) 403–404. L. PRICE, ''Glendalough: St. Kevin's Road,'' *Essays and Studies Presented to Professor Eain McNeill,* ed. J. RYAN (Dublin 1940) 244–271.

[J. RYAN]

GLENMARY HOME MISSION SISTERS

(G.H.M.S., Official Catholic Directory #2080); a diocesan congregation canonically established in Cincinnati, Ohio, in 1952 and devoted exclusively to home mission work in the United States. In 1936 Father William Howard BISHOP, the founder, published a plan for a society of priests, brothers, and sisters to work in the then 1,000 U.S. counties without resident priests. Assigned to areas where there were few or no Catholics, the sisters were to perform social work and home and clinical nursing, and to teach religion. The first two women candidates joined Father Bishop in 1941. Eleven years later the community was officially established by Archbishop Karl J. Alter of Cincinnati. In 1953 Mother Mary Catherine Rumschlag was appointed superior general, and she then received the vows of 14 new members. In 1955 the community of 41 professed sisters elected Mother Catherine at their first general chapter. The congregation follows the Rule of St. Augustine and constitutions adapted from those of the Dominican Sisters of Adrian, Michigan, under whom the first sisters were trained. The motherhouse is in Owensboro, Kentucky.

[J. SCHMID/EDS.]

GLENMARY HOME MISSIONERS

(Official Catholic Directory #0570) The Home Missioners of America (*Societas Missionarium Domesticorum Americas*), popularly known as the Glenmary Home Missioners, was established by Father William Howard BISHOP to work in United States areas without resident priests. The society is composed of secular priests, living in community under oath to their superior general, and brothers, who assist as catechists, parish administrators, counselors, pastoral associates, and youth directors.

In 1937 there were more than 1,000 counties in the United States without resident priests, located largely in the southeastern states where the birth rate is proportionately higher than the national average. That year, under the patronage of Archbishop John T. MCNICHOLAS of Cincinnati, Ohio, Bishop began publishing *Glenmary's Challenge* to mobilize forces to meet the urgent need of providing a Catholic priest for every U.S. community. His movement became a society when he was joined by five seminarians and Reverend Raphael Sourd in 1939.

In their evangelical outreach, the Glenmary missioners care for both the spiritual and daily needs of the people under their care. When the congregation is adequate to support a resident priest, the parish is returned to the diocese and the missioners are released for intensive activity elsewhere. Glenmary Missioners have worked in Ohio, Kentucky, Virginia, West Virginia, Oklahoma, Georgia, and North Carolina. The national Glenmary's headquarters is Cincinnati, Ohio.

Bibliography: W. H. BISHOP, ''A Plan for an American Society of Catholic Home Missions to Operate in Rural Sections of the United States,'' *Ecclesiastical Review* 94 (1936) 337–47. H. W. SANTEN, *Father Bishop, Founder of the Glenmary Home Missioners* (Milwaukee 1961). C.J. KAUFFMAN, *Mission to Rural America: The Story of W. Howard Bishop, Founder of Glenmary* (New York 1991).

[R. P. O'DONNELL/EDS.]

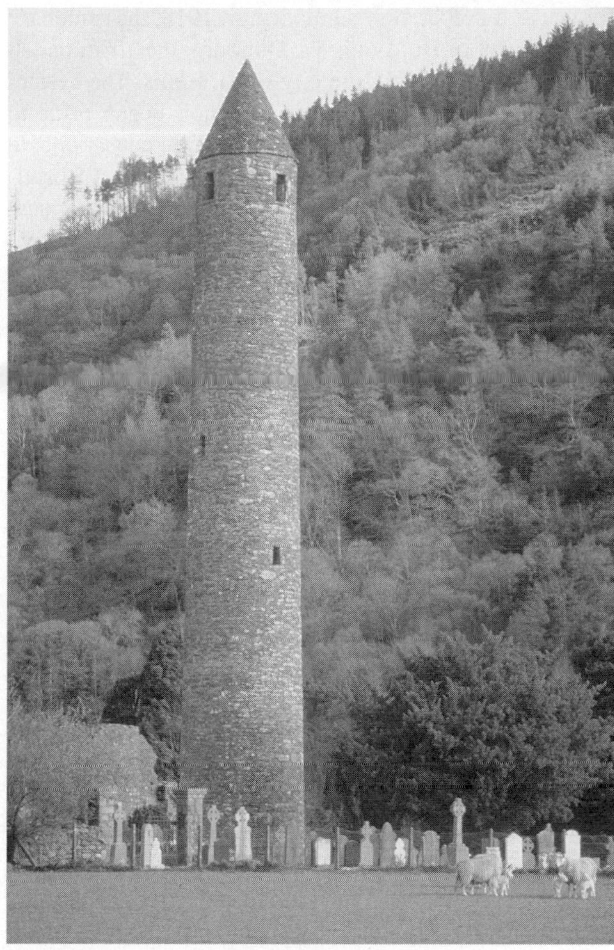

The Round Tower, St. Kevin Monastery, Glendalough, Ireland. (©Michael St. Maur Shell/CORBIS)

GLENNON, JOHN JOSEPH

Cardinal; b. County Meath, Ireland, June 14, 1862; d. Dublin, Ireland, March 9, 1946. Although he was born in Ireland, the previous residence of his father in New Jersey brought him U.S. citizenship at birth. He completed his courses at All Hallows College, Dublin, at the age of 21, and went to Kansas City, Mo., to work under Bp. John J. Hogan until he had attained the canonical age for ordination. Glennon was ordained in Kansas City's cathedral on Dec. 20, 1884. A year at the University of Bonn gave him knowledge, valuable later, of the German language and people. After returning to Kansas City, he became successively vicar-general, administrator, and finally coadjutor bishop of the diocese.

Less than seven years after his consecration on June 29, 1896, he was transferred to the coadjutorship of St. Louis, Mo. When Abp. John J. Kain died on Oct. 13, 1903, Glennon succeeded as the youngest resident archbishop in the U.S. The need for a new cathedral had been recognized by his two predecessors. Abp. John Ireland has been credited with suggesting its construction at the conferring of Glennon's pallium, the insignia of office, in 1905. However, Glennon himself had already called on his clergy for contributions. A St. Louis architect, George D. Barnett, was chosen; Glennon turned the first spadeful of earth in 1907; and the first Mass was offered in the uncompleted structure seven years later. Although the building was finished in his lifetime, the adornment of the massive cathedral continued after his death.

The new Kenrick Seminary was opened in 1915 and at the same time Glennon purchased a home in St. Louis for use as a preparatory seminary. In 1918, the centenary of the advent of Bp. Louis W. Dubourg, the 100th parish was established within the city of St. Louis. The system of diocesan high schools that Glennon began prior to World War I contributed much to Catholic education. He used his episcopal jubilee gifts in 1921 to erect Rosati-Kain High School for girls. Shortly thereafter a new boys' school, McBride Memorial, was built with a large benefaction connected with his jubilee. Through all these projects the archdiocese remained free of debt and Glennon's economic acumen caused his advice to be sought extensively.

Second only to Glennon's reputation as a builder was his nationwide fame as an orator. Best remembered is his address at the Eucharistic Congress in his native Ireland in 1932, although he preached also at congresses in Chicago, Montreal, Buenos Aires, and Budapest. Less well known were his significant activities in the field of immigration and colonization. He organized the Colonization Realty Company in 1905 to attract Catholic colonists from overcrowded cities of the U.S. East Coast and from Europe to the farmlands of Missouri. He also encouraged the National Catholic Rural Life Movement. In 1911 he began the organization of charity in his archdiocese through the Catholic Charities and Kindred Activities of St. Louis. He sponsored also such institutions as Father Dempsey's Hotel for the homeless and Father Dunne's Newsboys' Home and Protectorate, and he was one of the founders of the National Catholic War Council, which was later transformed into the National Catholic Welfare Conference. He was still active in his eighth decade, when he was elevated to the College of Cardinals at the age of 83. During the trip to Rome he was afflicted by bronchitis, and he died while stopping at the home of President Sean O'Kelly of Eire on his way back to the U.S. His body was buried in the crypt of the Cathedral of St. Louis.

Bibliography: Archives, Archdiocese of St. Louis. J. E. ROTHENSTEINER, *History of the Archdiocese of St. Louis,* 2 v. (St. Louis 1928). T. B. MORGAN, *Speaking of Cardinals* (New York 1946).

[P. J. RAHILL]

GLODESINDIS, ST.

Benedictine abbess; b. Metz, France, *c.* 570; d. *c.* 600. Her father, Duke Wintron of Champagne, tried to give her in marriage against her wishes; she fled and sought refuge in the cathedral of Metz. Her abbess aunt, Rotlinda, succeeded in calming the father's wrath and brought the young girl to Trier. There she was so well instructed in the rule and customs of monastic life that, returning to Metz, she founded a monastery that became known as Subterius (lower monastery) in contrast to the monastery above, Saint-Pierre de la Citadelle. Glodesindis united under her rule about 100 nuns. Her life was written at the end of the ninth century. In 840 Bp. DROGO OF METZ had her relics placed in the church in Metz that now bears her name; SS. Peter and Sulpicius had formerly been the patrons of the church.

Feast: July 25 and 27.

Bibliography: *Acta Sanctorum* July 6:198–225. A. M. ZIMMERMANN, *Kalendarium Benedictinum: Die Heiligen und Seligen des Benediktinerorderns und seiner Zweige* (Metten 1933–38) 2:496. J. L. BAUDOT and L. CHAUSSIN, *Vies des saints et des bienheureux selon l'ordre du calendrier avec l'historique des fêtes* (Paris 1935–56) 7:609–610. W. GRUNDHÖFER, *Lexikon für Theologie und Kirche* (Freiburg 1957–65) 4:966–967.

[É. BROUETTE]

GLORIA

One of the most ancient examples of hymnody in the early Church. Like its biblical counterparts, the Psalms and Canticles, it was not written on rhythmic and metrical principles. It was so highly esteemed in the early Church that it was able to withstand the later reaction against church hymns created ''by merely human endeavor'' [cf. Fourth Council of Toledo (633), c.13; J. D. Mansi, *sacrorum Conciliorum nova et amplissima collectio* (Florence-Venice 1757–98) 10.622].

The textual origin can be traced to three principal sources: (1) the Syrian version from the East Syrian (Chaldean) liturgy; ((2) the Greek version from the *Apostolic Constitutions* 7.47 (*c.* 380); and (3) the Greek version found in the *Codex Alexandrinus* (Fifth century) among the Septuagint *Odes of Solomon.*

The oldest witness for the Latin text, the *Antiphonary of Bangor* [*c.* 690; ed. Warren, *HGS* 4; *HBS* 10 (London 1892–95)], presents an almost literal translation of the Greek version of the *Codex Alexandrinus.* The first complete version of the present-day text, however, is found in the ninth-century *Psalter of Abbot Wolfcoz* of St. Gall (St. Gall MS 20).

The earliest names for the Gloria were numerous and varied. The title ''Greater Doxology'' (*see* DOXOLOGY, LITURGICAL) was used to distinguish it from the Gloria Patri or ''lesser doxology.'' The titles *Hymnus angelicus, Laus angelorum,* and *Laus* (or *Hymnus*) *angeli cum carmine* refer to the song of the angels heard by the shepherds at the birth of Christ (Lk 2.13–14), used as the opening phrases of this hymn. The title ''morning hymn'' was used in the *Codex Alexandrinus* and by St. Athanasius (controverted) in *De virginitate* 20 (*Patrologia Graeca* ed J. P. Migne [Paris 1857–66] 28:276). The Gloria was used also as a festive hymn of thanksgiving (*see* GREGORY OF TOURS, *De gloria martyrum* 1.63; *Patrologia Latina* ed. J. P. Migne [Paris 1878–90] 71:762) comparable to present-day usage of the *Te Deum* (*ibid.* 78:570). The *Antiphonary of Bangor* lists the Gloria as a hymn for Vespers and Matins.

From its usage in the Office and on festivals, the Gloria passed into the Roman rite Mass. An ancient tradition has it first inserted as the angelic announcement of the birth of Christ into the Christmas Mass at Rome (*see Liber pontificalis*, ed. L. Duchesne [Paris 1886–92] 1:56–57, 129–130, n.5). The usage itself is highly probable, though its origin with Telesphorus (d. early second century; *ibid.* 1:56–57) is unlikely. A more trustworthy account of the dispositions concerning the Gloria is the notice in the *Liber pontificalis* (1:263) about Symmachus I (d. 514). Symmachus is said to have permitted the Gloria to be used (outside of Christmas) on Sundays and martyrs' festivals but only at the bishop's Mass [bishop = shepherd (pastor of the Church) or angel (messenger to the Church)]. The *Ordo of St. Amand* in the nineth century allowed a priest to intone the Gloria but only at the Mass of the Easter Vigil and on the day of his ordination [*see* L. Duchesne, *Christian Worship, Its Origin and Evolution,* tr. M. L. McClure (5th ed. New York 1903) 471, 477]. When the Gloria was no longer considered proper only to the bishop's role, its insertion into all festive Masses was demanded (*see* BERNOLD OF CONSTANCE, *Micrologus* 2; *Patrologia Latina* 151:976). By the end of the 11th century the present usage was established (*Const. Cluniac* 1.8; *Patrologia Latina* 149:653).

During the Middle Ages, many churches in the West were accustomed to sing the Gloria in Greek as well as in Latin. The *Anonymous Turonensis* [ed. E. Martène, *De antiquis ecclesiae ritibus,* v. 1 (Rouen 1700) 102] ascribes this practice to the influence of the large number of Greek clerics in Rome during the seventh and eighth centuries. The usage is verified by the existence of some 16 medieval MSS containing both the Greek and Latin texts. Notable instances are two MSS of the *Winchester Troper* (Corpus Christi College MS 473; Bodley MS 775), and a *Troparium, Prosarium,* etc., of St. Martial in Limoges (Paris B.N. lat. 1120). Three MSS contain not only the Greek text with a Latin interlinear translation but also the Greek melody that served as the model for Gloria 14 in the *Graduale Romanum* (Paris B.N. lat. 2291, nineth century; lat. 1118, tenth century, lat. 9436, 11th century).

Out of some 341 medieval MSS, a total of 56 different melodies for the Gloria have been found (cf. Bosse, 73–82). The most ancient known melodies with a reciting tone are the simple and the elaborate settings of the Milanese (Ambrosian) Gloria (*Graduale Romanum* 89*). The melody listed as Gloria 15 in the *Graduale Romanum* is an example of psalmodic recitation, parallel to the Mozarabic setting of the Pater Noster. It is generally thought to be the oldest extant Roman Gloria. Nonetheless, the richly ornamented melodies, whether using melodic motifs or completely freely composed, were already very widespread at the time of the earliest melodic notation (11th–12th century; Bosse 45–56). On the other hand, there are simple Gloria melodies extant in later MSS that are strictly syllabic but not psalmodic in form in their treatment of the text (D. Bosse, *Untersuchung einstimmiger mittelalterlicher Melodien zum ''Gloria in excelsis,''* melodies 16, 50, and 54 of the 15th century; 35 of the 16th century; 4 and 8 of the 17th century). Simplicity and syllabic melodies, therefore, are not the ultimate criteria of the antiquity of the melodies.

Bibliography: C. BLUME, ''Der Engelhymnus Gloria in excelsis Deo: Sein Ursprung und seine Entwicklung,'' *Stimmen aus Maria-Laach* 73 (1907) 43–62. D. BOSSE, *Untersuchung einstimmiger mittelalterlicher Melodien zum ''Gloria in excelsis''* (Regensburg 1954). J. FROGER, *Les Chants de la Messe aux VIII*e*–IX*e *siècles* (Tournai 1950). A. GASTOUÉ, ''Le Chant du Gloria in excelsis,'' *La Tribune de St. Gervais* 3 (1897) 6–10, 41–44. M. HUGLO, ''La Mélodie grecque du *Gloria in excelsis . . .*,'' *Revue Grégorienne* 29 (1950) 30–40. J. A. JUNGMANN, *The Mass of the Roman Rite,* tr. F. A. BRUNNER, 2 v. (New York 1951–55). J. BOE, ''Gloria A and the Roman Easter Vigil,'' *Musica Disciplina* 36 (1982) 5–37.

[C. KELLY/EDS.]

GLORIA, LAUS ET HONOR

A processional hymn for PALM SUNDAY, written in the early ninth century, probably by THEODULF OF ORLÉANS, a native of Spain. The original text has 39 distichs, of which the first six are now sung at the procession. The first distich serves as a refrain after each verse. According to legend (recorded by Hugh of Fleury; *Monumenta Germaniae Historica: Scriptores* 9:363–64), Theodulf wrote this hymn while a prisoner at Angers. When the Palm Sunday procession, in which Emperor Louis the Pious took part, halted beneath the tower where Theodulf was kept, Louis heard Theodulf singing his hymn. The Emperor was moved and pardoned him. Raby regards the story as a ''testimony to the popularity of this magnificent hymn, the crown of Theodulf's poetry.'' The text has Biblical background (Mt 21.1–3, 8–11) and Christ's reception into Jerusalem is interpreted in a mystical-allegorical sense (see the last distich of the original poem). The quantitative distichs display the influence not only of the classical tradition on Carolingian poetry, but also of the Resurrection poem *Tempore florigero* (*Salve festa dies*) of Venantius FORTUNATUS, the chief model for later processional hymns down to the close of the Middle Ages.

Bibliography: *Analecta hymnica* 50:160–163. *Monumenta Germaniae Historica: Poetae* 1:558–559. J. CONNELLY, *Hymns of the Roman Liturgy* (Westminster MD 1957) 84–86. F. J. E. RABY, *A History of Christian-Latin Poetry from the Beginnings to the Close of the Middle Ages* (Oxford 1953) 174–176. J. GAILLARD, *Catholicisme* 5:58–59. F. BRUNHÖLZL, *Lexikon für Theologie und Kirche*, ed. J. HOFER and K. RAHNER (Freiburg 1957–65) 4:967. J. SZÖVÉRFFY, *Die Annalen der lateinischen Hymnendichtung* (Berlin 1964–65) 1:202–204.

[J. SZÖVÉRFFY]

GLORIFIED BODY

Here understood as the physical body of the just reunited at the RESURRECTION OF THE DEAD with the soul that formerly animated it and that at the moment of reunion is already enjoying the BEATIFIC VISION.

Fact. That at the end of time there is to be a universal resurrection of both the good and the evil is a dogma of the Church. This truth is explicitly set forth in all the major creeds and symbols, and formally defined in the *BENEDICTUS DEUS* of BENEDICT XII (H. Denzinger, *Enchiridion symbolorum*, ed. A. Schönmetzer [32d ed. Freiburg 1963] 1000–02). It is found in the formal teaching of Christ: ''. . . the hour is coming . . . when the dead shall hear the voice of the Son of God. . . . And they who have done good shall come forth unto resurrection of life; but they who have done evil unto resurrection of judgment'' (Jn 5.25–30). St. Paul's teaching is replete with references to the resurrection; for instance, he witnesses to the common faith: ''. . . I serve the God of my fathers; believing all things that are written in the Law and the Prophets, having a hope in God which these men themselves also look for, that there is to be a resurrection of the just and the unjust'' (Acts 24.14–16). The classic text for the resurrection of the just is, of course, 1 Cor 15 (see below).

Besides the two dogmas mentioned above, namely, the fact of the resurrection, and its universality, there is a third truth, also dogmatic, the identity of the risen body with that which each individual now has as his own. Thus Lateran Council IV defined that Christ ''will come at the end of the world . . . and all will rise with their own bodies which they now have so that they may receive according to their works, whether good or bad'' (H. Denzinger, *Enchiridion symbolorum* 801). How this identity is to be explained has exercised theologians over the centuries. It is clear from St. Paul that Christ's own Resurrection is not only the cause but also the model of the Christian's (1 Cor 15). Finally, the body of the just man, while remaining in some mysterious way materially identical with his body of the present life, will, nevertheless, be transformed and made immeasurably superior to its present condition; the fact of this at least is the unambiguous teaching of St. Paul (*ibid.*). What can be said about the nature of this transformation can now be set forth; here theologians are sometimes in the realm of speculation and conclusions that carry no more doctrinal weight than is warranted by the intrinsic validity of the argumentation itself.

Nature of the Glorification. In light of 1 Cor 15 theologians traditionally teach that the characteristic qualities of the glorified body are four: impassibility—''What is sown in corruption rises in incorruption''; clarity—''what is sown in dishonor rises in glory''; agility—''what is sown in weakness rises in power''; and subtilty—''what is sown a natural body rises a spiritual body.'' These qualities follow from the body's repossession and complete dominance by the soul already in full blessedness.

It is against the nature of the soul, the form of the body, to exist without its body (*C. gent.* 2.68, 83; 4.79); indeed the soul separated from the body is in one way imperfect, as is every part existing outside its whole, for the soul is naturally a part of the human composite. The scholastics accordingly speak of the separated soul as *in statu violento.* For this reason Aquinas says the resurrection is natural in that its purpose is to reunite soul and body, though of course the cause of the reunion is supernatural (*C. gent.* 4.81). Since, however, the soul of the just person, once completely free from all stain of sin, is from that moment in the state of perfect beatitude (H. Denzinger, *Enchiridion symbolorum* 1000), it follows that, reunited with the body, it shares with it its glory. St. Thomas says repeatedly that the glory of the body derives from that of the soul. He lays down the principle ''In perfect happiness the entire man is perfected, but in the lower part of his nature by an overflow from the higher'' (*Summa theologiae* 1a2ae, 3.3 ad 3). Concretely, ''it is by divine appointment that there is an overflow of glory from the soul to the body, in keeping with human merit; so that as man merits by the act of the soul which he performs in the body, so he may be rewarded by the glory of the soul overflowing to the body. Hence not only the glory of the soul but also the glory of the body is merited'' (*Summa theologiae* 3a, 19.3 ad 3; cf. 3a, 7.4 ad 2). On the other hand, the body now perfectly vivified will also be most fully responsive to the soul. No longer impeded by the imperfections and limitations of matter still in captivity to sin (cf. Rom 8.23), it will be not only the soul's docile instrument but also most completely itself. St. Thomas addresses himself to this point:

> The soul which is enjoying God will cleave to Him most perfectly, and will in its own fashion share in His goodness to the highest degree; and thus will the body be perfectly within the soul's dominion and will share in what is the soul's very own characteristics so far as possible—in the perspicuity of sense knowledge, in the ordering of bodily appetite, and in the all-round perfection of nature; for a thing is the more perfect in nature the more its matter is dominated by its form . . . just as the soul of man will be elevated to the glory of heavenly spirits to see God in His essence . . . so also will his body be raised to the characteristics of heavenly bodies—it will be lightsome, incapable of suffering, without difficulty and labor in movement, and most perfectly perfected by its form. For this reason the Apostle speaks of the bodies of the risen as heavenly, referring not to their nature, but to their glory [*C. gent.* 4.86].

Since the RESURRECTION OF CHRIST is not only the cause of the Christian's but also its model, what the Scriptures relate concerning the perfections of His body are also to be predicated, with due proportion, of the body of everyone who shares in His victory and with Him rises to glory: ''For as in Adam all die, so in Christ all will be made to live. But each in his own turn, Christ as first-fruits, then they who are Christ's'' (1 Cor 15.22–23). St. John perhaps has given the best epitome of the whole man's future glory: ''We know that, when he [Christ] appears, we shall be like him for we shall see him just as he is'' (1 Jn 3.2–3).

See Also: HEAVEN; SOUL, HUMAN; IMMORTALITY; SOUL-BODY RELATIONSHIP; TRANSFIGURATION.

Bibliography: J. RATZINGER, *Lexikon für Theologie und Kirche*, ed. J. HOFER and K. RAHNER, 10 v. (2d new ed. Freiburg 1957–65) 1:1052–53. A. CHOLLET, *Dictionnaire de théologie catholique* 3.2:1879–1906. A. MICHEL, *Dictionnaire de théologie catholique* 13.2:2501–71. A. WINKLHOFER, ''Eschatologie,'' H. FRIES, ed., *Handbuch theologischer Grundbegriffe,* 2 v. (Munich 1962–63) 1:327–336; *The Coming of His Kingdom* (New York 1963). F. X. DURRWELL, *The Resurrection: A Biblical Study,* tr. R. SHEED (New York 1960). M. A. GENEVOIS, *Entre dans la joie* (Paris 1960). R. GUARDINI, *The Last Things,* tr. C. E. FORSYTH and G. B. BRANHAM (New York 1954).

[C. J. CORCORAN]

GLORY (IN THE BIBLE)

In English versions of the Bible, glory stands for various words in the original languages, but basically it construes the word *kābôd* in Hebrew and δόξα in Greek. This article traces the use of these words through the OT and NT.

In the Old Testament. Every OT writer knew that to see God was beyond man's capacity; as Moses had

''Eternal Father,'' by Pordenone. (©Elio Ciol/CORBIS)

been told, ''But my face you cannot see, for no man sees me and still lives'' (Ex 33.20). Yet in very primitive times God was thought by the Hebrews to manifest Himself somehow in spectacular thunderstorms.

> The earth swayed and quaked; the foundations of the mountains trembled and shook when his wrath flared up. Smoke rose from his nostrils, and a devouring fire from his mouth that kindled coals into flame. And he inclined the heavens and came down, with dark clouds under his feet. He mounted a cherub and flew, borne on the wings of the wind. And he made darkness the cloak about him; dark, misty rain-clouds his wrap. From the brightness of his presence coals were kindled to flame. And the Lord thundered from heaven, the Most High gave forth his voice; He sent forth His arrows to put them to flight, with frequent lightnings he routed them (Ps 17 [18].8–15). Fire goes before him and consumes his foes round about. His lightnings illumine the world; the earth sees and trembles. The mountains melt like wax before the Lord, before the Lord of all the earth. The heavens proclaim his justice, and all peoples see his glory (Ps 96 [97].3–61).

To express this awesomeness of YAHWEH's self-disclosure, the Hebrews favored the word *kābôd* in this special sense, although it originally meant weightiness or impressiveness. Some of the same lightning-storm imagery is used to describe the Lord's presence on Mt. Sinai: ''On the morning of the third day there were peals of thunder and lightning, and a heavy cloud over the mountain, . . . Mount Sinai was all wrapped in smoke, for the

Lord came down upon it in fire. The smoke rose from it as though from a furnace, and the whole mountain trembled violently'' (Ex 19.16, 18). ''After Moses had gone up, a cloud covered the mountain. The glory of the Lord settled upon Mount Sinai. The cloud covered it for six days, and on the seventh day he called to Moses from the midst of the cloud. To the Israelites the glory of the Lord was seen as a consuming fire on the mountaintop'' (Ex 24.15–17).

God's glory—a formless, flashing fire—is always cloaked in cloud to protect man from gazing directly upon it, lest it overwhelm him. Another site of divine encounter was the TENT OF MEETING, where God would descend to render judgment, deliver an oracle, or entertain some request: ''As Moses entered the Tent, the column of cloud would come down and stand at its entrance while the Lord spoke with Moses'' (Ex 33.9).''When he came down from offering the sin offering and holocaust and peace offering, Moses and Aaron went into the Meeting Tent. . . . Then the glory of the Lord was revealed to all the people. Fire came forth from the Lord's presence and consumed the holocaust'' (Lv 9.22–24).

Another ancient tradition pictured the *kābôd* as abiding permanently in the cloud-enveloped fire upon the ARK OF THE COVENANT. The top of this wooden chest was a plate of gold surmounted by two golden cherubim, whose outstretched wings formed a throne for God's glory. The Lord came to be called ''He who sits upon the Cherubim'' (2 Kgs 19.15). Later when the Ark was brought to grace the sanctuary of Solomon's new Temple (*see* TEMPLES [IN THE BIBLE]), the glory took up residence there: ''And it came to pass, when the priests were come out of the sanctuary, that a cloud filled the house of the Lord. And the Priests could not stand to minister because of the cloud: for the glory of the Lord had filled the house of the Lord'' (1 Kgs 8.10–11).

As time went on the idea of the glory was developing. I. Abrahams observes: ''The clouds have gone, the earthquake, the wind. Out of the primitive storm associations the only physical feature that endured was the illumination'' (56). Ezekiel adds a further insight; in his inaugural vision he sees the glory riding a heavenly chariot in fiery tumult, drawn by four chimeric creatures: ''Upon it was seated, up above, one who had the appearance of a man. Upward from what resembled his waist I saw what gleamed like electrum; downward from what resembled his waist I saw what looked like fire; he was surrounded with splendor. Like the bow which appears in the clouds on a rainy day was the splendor that surrounded him. Such was the vision of the likeness of the glory of the Lord'' (Ez 1.26–28). Thus a further step has been taken toward personalizing the glory. Some years later the author of Isaiah ch. 56 to 66, while not abandoning the ancient fire symbol for a simply spiritual *kābôd,* does begin to blend into it the ideas of God's power and lordly majesty:

> Rise up in splendor! Your light has come, the glory of the Lord shines upon you. See, darkness covers the earth, and thick clouds cover the peoples; But upon you the Lord shines, and over you appears his glory. Nations shall walk by your light, and kings by your shining radiance (Is 60.1–3).

After returning from Exile the Jews grew to realize that Yahweh's rule must somehow extend over all the earth, and the sense of ''glory'' overflowed more and more the bounds of the old fire-and-cloud imagery, to become a symbol for His universal triumph: ''Be exalted above the heavens, O God; above all the earth be your glory!'' (Ps 56 [57].12). ''Tell his glory among the nations; among all peoples, his wondrous deeds'' (Ps 95[96].3). Very late in the OT period the author of Daniel foresees that the oppressed Jewish people (portrayed as ''One like a SON OF MAN'') would one day be invited to share in the Lord's glory:

> I saw One like a son of man coming, on the clouds of heaven; When he reached the Ancient One and was presented before him, He received dominion, glory, and kingship; nations and peoples of every language serve him. His dominion is an everlasting dominion that shall not be taken away, his kingship shall not be destroyed. (Dn 7.13–14)

Already in the 3d century B.C., the existing books of the OT were being translated into Greek for the numerous Jews living abroad in Greek-speaking areas. This version, called the Septuagint (LXX), proved more than a simple translation; the added resources of Greek language and thought permitted even further continuance of theological development begun in Hebrew. The word *kābôd* had become a highly technical term; its Greek equivalent, δόξα, became even more specialized. Δόξα, stripped of its original meaning of ''opinion,'' served in the LXX to signify only such meanings as might be included within the span of *kābôd.* More and more emphasis was laid on God's power to work wonders and to save, and on His majesty as King.

In the New Testament. The term in the NT is still found in its classic sense of the radiant fire of Yahweh's presence, e.g., ''my brethren, who are my kinsmen according to the flesh; who are Israelites, who have the adoption of sons, and the glory and the covenants and the legislation and the worship and the promises'' (Rom 9.3, 4). Yet the remarkable development in the NT is that the traditional glory of Yahweh becomes the glory of Christ; indeed, the application of δόξα to Jesus is one of the chief literary techniques used to suggest His Divinity. The SYNOPTIC GOSPELS, recognizing that Jesus' divine radiance was concealed during His earthly ministry, observe its outburst only after the Resurrection: "His countenance was like lightning, and his raiment like snow" (Mt 28.3). See also Mk 14.61–62. Yet on certain occasions the presence of the divine δόξα is suggested in a cloud or radiance: at His baptism, when Jesus was commissioned as Savior, and at the Transfiguration, when His disciples were shown the significance of His coming death. Also, Luke in his infancy narratives inserts several allusions to the δόξα designed to hint at Jesus' divine origins: "the power of the Most High shall overshadow thee" (Lk 1.35); "an angel of the Lord stood by them and the glory of the Lord shone round about them, and they feared exceedingly" (Lk 2.9; the presence of angels, perhaps reminiscent of the Ark's cherubim, and the fearful reaction are standard biblical accompaniments to the δόξα). John, on the other hand, considers that Jesus' glory is always there to be perceived, but only by those who believe. His works are not presented so much as miracles, as in the Synoptics, but as "signs," which mysteriously show forth His glory to the eyes of faith: "He manifested his glory and his disciples believed in him" (Jn 2.11). "'Have I not told thee that if thou believe thou shalt behold the glory of God?'" (Jn 11.40). Yet John also realizes that only after the Resurrection will Jesus be glorified with the glory he had with the Father before the world existed (Jn 17.5). Paul, who had been called to apostleship by a vision of Jesus surrounded with glory, makes frequent references to Ex 34.27–35, where Moses has to veil his face, so dazzling is the radiance beaming from it after he has spoken with the Lord. So, too, the Apostolic life is a reception of light in order to reflect the "glory of God, shining on the face of Christ Jesus" (2 Cor 4.6). "But we all, with faces unveiled, reflecting as in a mirror the glory of the Lord, are being transformed into his very image from glory to glory, as through the Spirit of the Lord" (2 Cor 3.18).

See Also: SHEKINAH; THEOPHANY.

Bibliography: G. KITTEL, *Theologisches Wörterbuch zum Neuen Testament* (Stuttgart 1935–) 2:236–256. G. VON RAD, *Old Testament Theology,* tr. D. M. G. STALKER (New York 1962–) v. 1. L. H. BROCKINGTON, "The Septuagintal Background to the New Testament Use of 'Doxa,'" *Studies in the Gospels,* ed. D. E. NINEHAM (Oxford 1955). C. MOHRMANN, "Note sur 'doxa,'" *Sprachgeschichte und Wortbedeutung; Festschrift Albert Debrunner* (Bern 1954). I. ABRAHAMS, *The Glory of God* (London 1925).

[J. T. BURTCHAELL]

GLORY OF GOD (END OF CREATION)

The glory of God is a favorite theme of the Old and New Testaments. Its roots lie in the presence of the *k^e^bôd* Yahweh, the δόξα τοῦ θεοῦ. The theological interpretation of the glory of GOD as the purpose of CREATION must reflect the scriptural data, which basically reveals two mutually related and complementary themes: the glory of God as the divine perfection and as the divine praise.

Divine Perfection. Scripture identifies the glory of God with God Himself, with His power whereby He tramples His enemies underfoot and terrifies men, with His beauty, with the image of light and splendor that includes a sweetness and attraction, so that whoever beholds the glory of God is filled with joy and lightness. This sweetness and attraction is especially perceived in God's generous benevolence, in the pouring out of His divine goodness, in His mercy and fidelity toward all His creatures. It takes shape in the production of a likeness or an image of the divine goodness in creatures. The Old Testament expresses this in describing the wisdom of God as the pure emanation of the glory of the Most High (Wis 7.25–26). Isaiah says that "all the earth is filled with his glory!" (Is 6.3). Creatures, therefore, are the image and glory of God. All created things, especially men, are filled from the expansive fullness of the glory of God (cf. Eph 3.16). By their very existence they announce this glory [Ps 18(19).2].

The glory of God is poured forth in Jesus Christ in a very special way. He is the image of the invisible God, the firstborn of every creature (Col 1.15). He is the effulgence of His splendor and the stamp of God's very being (Heb 1.3). In Him and through Him all things are (Col 1.16–17), and are redeemed (Eph 1.3–14). Through the knowledge of Christ the Savior, the glory of God is diffused to all Christians. The gospel of the glory of Christ, who is the very image of God, dawns upon us and brings us to the revelation of the glory of God in the face of Jesus Christ (2 Cor 4.4, 6). The result of this influence of the Lord who is spirit (2 Cor 3.17) is that we all reflect "as in a mirror the glory of the Lord" (2 Cor 3.18). Christ Himself tells us that He shares with us, His friends, the glory He has received from the Father (Jn 17.22). Our life in Christ is not merely a new birth—it is a new way of life. The glory of God in the just is not only the divine INDWELLING (1 Cor 6.19) but likewise all the good actions of the just (1 Cor 10.31).

Divine Praise. The most frequent meaning of the word glory is the fame, praise, and good reputation that comes with the recognition of one's excellence. Frequently Scripture exhorts man "to give glory to the

Lord.'' Revelations tells us that the Lord is worthy of receiving glory (4.9–11). The glory of God is contrasted with and opposed to the glory of men (Is 42.8; Jn 7.18; Rom 1.23). Here the glory of God is the admiration of the grandeur of God, an admiration that is expressed in praise, not only by the words of men, but much more by the Christian way of life. For our lights are to shine before men, so that they may see our good works and give praise to the Father (Mt 5.16). Indeed, all creatures ''declare the glory of God'' [Ps 18(19).2]; and in this sense all the works of the Lord ought to bless Him, to praise and exalt Him (Dn 3.52–88). It is because of this dumb, yet eloquent, praise that the greatness of God is so visible in creation that for man not to recognize it and to join in it is inexcusable (Rom 1.21–23).

Glory of God and the Purpose of Creation. Confronted with this double facet of the glory of God as identified both with the divine perfection and the divine praise, the theologian must beware lest he give undue importance to one over the other.

The supreme purpose of God in creating is the divine intrinsic goodness and glory. God's purpose in creating cannot be any created good because God cannot be moved by anything outside Himself. Rather, God's purpose or intended end in creating is Himself, His divine intrinsic goodness and glory. For the divine goodness is the sole adequate object of the divine volition, and love and is the sole adequate reason for which God freely willed to produce creatures. Creatures exist because of the divine goodness, because God wishes in His superabundance of love freely to communicate this same divine goodness to them and to manifest it externally through them. The finite communication and manifestation of the divine intrinsic goodness and glory in creation are but conditions for the production of creatures and are not to be identified with the purpose or object of the creative will as such. Hence, God does not create because He desires some gain for Himself from creation. His extrinsic glory is in no wise the good on account of which He produced creatures.

The supreme purpose of creation is God Himself. The divine intrinsic goodness and glory is also the ultimate good toward which all creatures are ordered as their supreme purpose. For God's own supreme purpose in creating and the ultimate purpose of creation must be one and the same. In fact, all creatures by their innate sensitive or rational appetites tend toward God as the supreme GOOD, as that which ultimately perfects them. Thus, all creatures have the very same ultimate objective end, God Himself. They do, however, have specifically different ultimate intrinsic ends, for each attains God in its own way. Only man, because of his spiritual faculties, is capable of attaining God directly as He is in Himself. All other creatures attain God in their service of man.

The extrinsic glory of God is a true end of creation (H. Denzinger, *Enchiridion symbolorum*, ed. A. Schönmetzer [Freiburg 1963] 3025). God's extrinsic glory is a reflection and manifestation through creatures of the intrinsic and substantial glory that is God Himself. As such, God could not create without ordering all things to His extrinsic glory. He is free, nonetheless, to choose any universe with any extrinsic glory, because extrinsic glory is something on which He in no way depends. Extrinsic glory, however, is a consequence of creation and at the same time is the last created end of creatures. For in attaining its ultimate intrinsic perfection, a creature attains that participation in and manifestation of God's goodness to which it is ordered by God as a part of the total universe. In this way the creature's own intrinsic perfection is really the same as the extrinsic glory of God.

See Also: GLORY (IN THE BIBLE).

Bibliography: *Dictionnaire de théologie catholique*, ed. A. VACANT et al. (Paris 1903—50) Tables générales 1:1817. E. PAX, ed. H. FRIES, *Handbuch theologischer Grundbegriffe* (Munich 1962–63) 1:680–685. M. FLICK and Z. ALSZEGHY, *Il creatore: L'inizio della salvezza* (2d ed. Florence 1961); ''Gloria Dei,'' *Gregorianum,* 36 (1955) 361–390. P. J. DONNELLY, ''St. Thomas and the Ultimate Purpose of Creation,'' *Thological Studies,* 2 (1941) 53–83; ''The Vatican Council and the End of Creation,'' *ibid.* 4 (1943) 3–33. D.-J. EHR, *The Purpose of the Creator and of Creatures according to John of St. Thomas* (Techny, Ill. 1961). G. PADOIN, *Il fine della creazione nel pensiero di S. Tommaso* (Rome 1959).

[D. J. EHR]

GLOSSA ORDINARIA

A designation given during the Middle Ages to certain compilations of ''glosses'' on the text of a given manuscript. The earliest *glossa ordinaria* is that made on the Bible, probably in the 12th century (*see* GLOSSES, BIBLICAL). However, the term *glossa ordinaria* was most commonly used in the field of law, particularly Canon Law.

Several *glossa ordinaria* (also referred to by medieval canonists as the *glossa*) were produced in the field of law during the 13th and 14th centuries. These works were generally held by the schools and courts as containing the best selection of commentaries and explanations on the legal texts contained in various collections. These glosses were endowed with a certain authority, though not of an official nature. Presumed to be the most correct, they were the ones most likely to be adopted by the Roman Curia and the ones every student had to know and of which every author had to take cognizance. These legalistic *glossa ordinaria* had their immediate origins in the works of the glossators from the middle of the 12th century, and particularly in their *apparatus glossarum* (systematic compilations of glosses: *see* GLOSSES, CANON LAW).

The *glossa ordinaria* of this period are among the most important and influential treatises of the classical period of Canon Law. They are based upon those collections of law that formed the principal legal texts of the period. The first canonical *glossa* to become known as a *glossa ordinaria* is that of JOANNES TEUTONICUS. It was completed shortly after Lateran Council IV (1215–16) and is a commentary written in the form of a marginal gloss on the text of GRATIAN's *Decretum.* It is not printed as Joannes made it. Another Bolognese master, BARTHOLOMEW OF BRESCIA, *c.* 1245 adapted it to the later decretals. It was later included in the printed text of Gratian's *Decretum.*

The work that came to be considered as the *glossa ordinaria* on the *QUINQUE COMPILATIONES ANTIQUAE* was that of TANCRED OF BOLOGNA. This commentary covered only the first three *compilationes*; its final edition came out *c.* 1220. Joannes Teutonicus also produced the *glossa ordinaria* for the *Compilatio quarta*, *c.* 1217; JAMES OF ALBENGA produced the one for the *Compilatio quinta.* This latter is probably the least important of all, since the *Compilatio quinta* was in force only a short time.

The *glossa ordinaria* on the Decretals of GREGORY IX was produced by BERNARD OF PARMA. It underwent at least four recensions (1234–63) during Bernard's lifetime, and it later received several additions, especially from Joannes Andreae. The *glossa* on the *LIBER SEXTUS* was produced by JOANNES ANDREAE *c.* 1301. He produced also the *glossa ordinaria* on the Constitutions of Clement V shortly after they appeared (1322). The remaining part of the *CORPUS IURIS CANONICI*, i.e., the *Extravagantes*, had glosses on individual sections, but none became known as the *glossa ordinaria* (*see* CANON LAW, HISTORY OF, 4).

The practice of glossating texts was popular also in the schools of Roman law. The *glossa ordinaria* on the basic text of Roman law, the *Corpus Iuris Civilis*, was produced by Accursius (d. *c.* 1260), a professor of the Roman law school of Bologna. It was produced at the same time as the first *glossa ordinaria* of Canon Law.

Bibliography: J. SCHMID and A. M. STICKLER, *Lexikon für Theologie und Kirche*, ed. J. HOFER and K. RAHNER (Freiburg 1957–65) 4:968–971. G. MOLLAT, *Dictionnaire de droit canonique*, ed. R. NAZ (Paris 1935–65) 5:972–974. A. VAN HOVE, *Commentarium Lovaniense in Codicem iuris canonici 1*, v.1–5 (Mechlin 1928—); v.1, Prolegomena (1945) 1:412 and *passim.* J. F. VON SCHULTE, *Die Geschichte der Quellen und der Literatur des kanonischen Rechts* (Graz 1956) 2:86–88. W. M. PLÖCHL, *Geschichte des Kirchenrechts*, v.2 (Vienna 1962) 504 and *passim.*

[J. M. BUCKLEY]

GLOSSES, BIBLICAL

The term ''gloss,'' it has been said, may be applied to almost every form of biblical exposition. This article points out the several ways in which it has been used.

A biblical gloss may be defined as one or more words, usually only a few, added in the margin or between the lines of a text, in explanation of an obscure word. Although generally helpful to the exegete, it cannot always be relied on as a correct clarification. The glossator, or author, of the gloss may be well intentioned but in error or purposely tendentious.

As glosses multiplied it was found convenient to gather them into separate books, either in the order of their occurrences or alphabetically. A collection of this sort forms a glossary, also at times called a gloss. Among the principal glossaries containing biblical terms are the lexicon (preserved in a much interpolated MS of the 15th century) of the fourth-century Alexandrian lexicographer Hesychius, the nineth-century lexicon of PHOTIUS, the tenth-century lexicon of the Suidas, and the 12th- or 13th-century *Etymologicum Magnum.* For a printed collection, *see* F. W. Sturz, *Glossae sacrae N.T. illustratae* (Leipzig 1818–20).

Although glosses originally consisted of only a few words, they grew in length as glossators enlarged them with their own comments and quotations from the Fathers. Thus the tiny gloss evolved into a running commentary of an entire book. The best-known commentary of this type is the vast *Glossa ordinaria* of the 12th and 13th centuries. Its marginal glosses were formerly ascribed to WALAFRID STRABO (d. 849), but recent studies demonstrate that both its marginal and interlinear glosses were compiled from Latin translations of Origen and Hesychius, from Latin Fathers, and from medieval glossators under the direction of ANSELM OF LAON (d. 1117). In appearance, a page contains a very few words of the Latin Vulgate text at the center surrounded by extensive marginal and interlinear glosses. So great was the influence of the *Glossa ordinaria* on biblical and philosophical studies in the Middle Ages that it was called ''the tongue of Scripture'' and ''the bible of scholasticism.'' Of the many printed editions, one of the best is that of Leander a St. Martin (6 v. Antwerp 1634).

The term ''gloss'' is also used of words in the Bible itself that were not part of the original writing but were accidentally or intentionally embodied into the text by a transcriber. The existence of glosses in biblical manuscripts is universally admitted but often difficult to discern. Differences in style and vocabulary or an introductory phrase (e.g., ''that is'') are signs of a possible gloss. It is one of the tasks of the textual critic, frequently quite difficult, to disentangle a gloss from the genuine text.

See Also: EXEGESIS, MEDIEVAL.

Bibliography: J. SCHMID, *Lexikon für Theologie und Kirche*, ed. J. HOFER and K. RAHNER (Freiberg 1957–65) 4:968–970. B. SMALLEY, *Die Religion in Geschichte und Gegenwart* (Tübingen 1957–65) 2:1627–28; *The Study of the Bible in the Middle Ages* (2d ed. New York 1952; repr. Notre Dame, Ind. 1964) 46–66. F. VIGOUROUX, *Dictionnaire de la Bible*, ed. F. VIGOUROUX (Paris 1895–1912) 3.1:252–258.

[C. O'C. SLOANE]

GLOSSES, CANON LAW

The practice of glossing owes its chief popularity among medieval jurists to the specifically juridical turn of mind and method of operation requisite for the interpretation of laws, the chief function of jurisprudence. When Canon Law as such began to flourish after the *Decretum* of GRATIAN and the inception of papal decretal legislation, the canonists borrowed from the civil jurists who were treating Roman law the method of glossing that seemed the most promising way to cope with the growing mass of ecclesiastical legislation. Each individual passage of any source had to be given a meticulously accurate interpretation, and the gloss was the most appropriate method.

Form and Content. The glosses were entered either between the lines of the text (interlinear gloss) or in the margin (marginal gloss) beside the word being glossed; as the glosses became more extensive, they were entered also in the free space at the top and bottom of the page. If there was still space available, later copyists often added further glosses; in this process older glosses were often erased and new ones were entered in their place. There are manuscripts that have three, four, and even more layers of glosses.

With regard to content, the glosses developed very quickly from a primitive form to the highest degree of perfection. The earliest glosses are the *allegationes,* collections of concordant or discordant *capitula* (*concordantiae* and *contraria,* respectively). These glosses, representing simple citations, became the basis and set the problems for later presentations. The passage glossed is made to yield a brief legal rule, usually in the form of an *argumentum,* and parallel passages are adduced. Especially important legal axioms are prefixed with such notations as *nota.* The glosses give rise, upon addition of *contraria,* to the later *Brocarda* or *Generalia* collections. The content of the chapter being glossed or sections with still wider implications are briefly summarized. This sort of purely reportorial gloss is closely allied with the *casus,* which gives the facts of a case and the ruling of a passage in a law. But this summarizing individual gloss also becomes the nucleus for the systematic textbook *summae.* *Continuationes* elaborate the connection with preceding material. Individual words are explained philologically or juridically.

Glossing arrives at a more advanced stage as soon as it proceeds to the interpretation of the law itself, to a commentary that is analytic as well as systematic. This kind of gloss examines the internal connection of the parallel passages adduced, subsumes one passage under another, or deduces one from another. The collection of discordant passages is accompanied by a gloss offering a solution that will reconcile the contradictions, usually by way of distinctions. These steadily increasing commentary glosses become more and more important; instead of providing explanations of individual words, they might enter into greater detail on a legal question touched upon in the passage being glossed. Here it is often difficult for the modern historian of law to grasp the connection seen by the medieval jurist between the problem treated in the gloss and the legal text being glossed; this is why it is difficult to find the *sedes materiae* of a legal problem in the glosses. These discursive glosses take various forms. The individual glosses containing a simple statement of content are enriched by explanations of the juridical significance of that content; and this gives rise to the *summae* on the individual chapters (*capitula*) and to *summae* on still more extensive sections of the text (the *causae, quaestiones,* and *distinctiones* of Gratian and the titles of the decretal collections). Summaries of these sections necessarily entail a summary and systematic presentation of the maxims drawn from them. Other glosses contain the distinction in the form of a schema or continuous text. A generic concept in the source, a legal rule, is analyzed into subordinate specific concepts by the use of distinctive characteristic features. Finally, many glosses contain juridical explanations having no definite form.

Apparatus Glossarum. Eventually the glosses of all sorts became more numerous and extensive until the more connected commentaries and finally the outright glossary apparatuses developed. The glosses of many authors (DECRETISTS, DECRETALISTS) are sometimes anonymous; sometimes they bear the initial or initials of the author. These logograms are not very reliable, and it is not known in many cases for what name they stand. The master writes the glosses in his copy of the text, so that they can then be transferred into other copies and disseminated. The universities provide another opportunity for their dissemination, the students copying glosses into their own texts from the copy loaned out by the master. The students also make copies of the lectures (*reportationes*). And finally, there are manuscripts with glosses privately authored by their owners.

About the end of the 12th century, there began a collection of the glosses that had by then become quite extensive; less important elements were deleted, and the remainder was systematized, the compiler and reviser adding his own glosses, so that there came into existence a continuous comprehensive commentary, a melting pot of the glosses, the *apparatus glossarum.* This *apparatus* was subject to constant revision and expansion; thus there are several editions of many *apparatus glossarum.* The schools and courts recognized as the *GLOSSA ORDINARIA* the one that was generally held to have made the best selection and provided defensible original opinions, while preserving completeness and distinguishing itself by succinctness and clarity. Such recognition was often very swiftly forthcoming, and the *glossa ordinaria* for the most part quickly and almost totally supplanted the preceding pertinent glossaries to become the final authority. Later canonists comment on the *glossa ordinaria* on an equal footing even with the text it glosses.

The importance of the glosses for medieval Canon Law can hardly be overestimated. Almost all the types of writing of medieval jurisprudence have their origin in the activity of glossing. The gloss was for the student the door to the whole realm of law; for the scholar, the prime means for coping with the material and enriching it with his own thoughts; for the judge, a tool to be used to prepare for and facilitate the application of the law. The glosses written from mid-12th century to the first half of the 14th century represent, in form and content, the foundation of the prodigious edifice of medieval Canon Law, the classical law of the Church.

Bibliography: F. K. V. SAVIGNY, *Geschichte des römischen Rechts im Mittelalter*, 7 v. (2d ed. Heidelberg 1834–51; repr. Darmstadt 1958) 3:552–574. J. F. VON SCHULTE, *Die Geschichte der Quellen und der Literatur des kanonischen Rechts*, 3 v. in 4 pts. (Stuttgart 1875–80; repr. Graz 1956) 1:212–220; 2:456–484; and *passim.* J. JUNCKER, ''Summen und Glossen,'' *Zeitschrift der Savigny-Stiftung für Rechtsgeschichte, Kanonistische Abteilung* 14 (1925) 384–474. E. GENZMER, ''Die Iustinianische Kodifikation und die Glossatoren,'' in *Atti del Congresso internazionale di diritto Romano, Bologna e Roma, 1933*, 4 v. (Pavia 1934–35) *Bologna,* 1:345–430. S. KUTTNER, *Repertorium der Kanonistik* (Rome 1937) 1–12 and *passim.* A. VAN HOVE, *Commentarium Lovaniense in Codicem iuris canonici 1*, v. 1–5 (Mechlin 1928–) 1:412–465, esp. 412. A. M. STICKLER, *Lexikon für Theologie und Kirche*, ed. J. HOFER and K. RAHNER, 10 v. (2d new ed. Freiburg1957–65) 4:970–971. *Bulletin of the Institute of Research and Study in Medieval Canon Law,* ed. S. KUTTNER, in each v. of *Traditio* since 1955.

[K. W. KNÖRR]

GLOSSOLALIA

Glossolalia denotes the gift of speaking in a language in which facility has not been achieved through the process of human learning. The phenomenon appears three times in Acts (2.4, 6; 10.46; 19.6), where it is always a ''corporate, church-founding, group-conversion phenomenon, and never the . . . Spirit-experience of an individual'' (cf. Bruner p. 192). In 1 Corinthians 12 to 14 there is a different understanding of glossolalia. It is presented as an individual prayer gift to be used in private devotion for personal edification (1 Cor 14.2–4) or, if there is an interpreter, in the public assembly. It is considered inferior to prophecy (1 Cor 14.5). Mk 16.17 speaks of ''new tongues'' but 16.9–20 seems to be addition to the Gospel. Some scholars hold that Rom 8.26 refers to tongues but this is unlikely as here the Spirit is said to pray within one ''with sighs too deep for words'' (*stenagmois alalētous*).

Glossolalia has accompanied many religious revivals throughout history and is not unknown outside Christian circles. There appear to be three sources of the phenomenon: First, the genuine gift received from God and as experienced by such Christians as Teresa of Avila, Catherine of Siena, Francis Xavier, etc. Secondly, a ''hypnotically'' induced glossolalia which is not the authentic gift but probably akin to *xenophoneo* (strange speech) found among the second century Montanists (Eusebius, *Ecclesiastical History* 5, 16, 167). Similar to this are the ecstatic utterances acknowledged within many religious traditions. Thirdly, ''tongues'' may be due to diabolical obsession or possession.

The phenomenon in the Roman Catholic Church has become widespread since the recent public manifestations of the neo-pentecostal movement. Both the genuine and the hypnotic type appear to be present. The hypnotic type produces the characteristics of divisiveness, projection of anger, group camaraderie, histrionic display, preoccupation with glossolalia and, most importantly, a regression of the ego which results in subordination to the authority figure who introduces the recipient to ''tongues.'' In the light of this danger it would seem advisable to refrain from imposition of hands and repetition of syllables after leaders in order to help in yielding to tongues lest the hypnotic element be inadvertently introduced.

When the gift is genuine it facilitates prayer, especially that of praise and intercession, and is accompanied by fruits of the Spirit, especially peace and joy. Sometimes it endows the recipient with poetic and musical powers which he did not originally possess. Private interpretation may also be received. The gift is under the control of the will and may be used or not as desired (cf 1 Cor 14.27). According to Samarin even the genuine gift of tongues does not appear to be a language in the technical sense of the term but it is a ''non-cerebral'' means of communicating with God akin to silent prayer, well-known liturgy, the Jesus Prayer or the rosary (Baer).

See Also: PENTECOSTALISM.

Bibliography: R. BAER ''Quaker Silence, Catholic Liturgy and Pentecostal Glossolalia—Some Functional Similarities,'' *Logos International* (1973). F. D. BRUNER, *A Theology of the Holy Spirit* (Michigan 1970). S. D. CURRIE, '''Speaking on Tongues' Early Evidence outside the New Testament bearing on 'Glossais Lalein,''' *Interpretation* 19 (1965) 274–294. J. D. DAVIES, ''Pentecost and Glossolalia,'' *Journal of Theological Studies* 3 (1952) 228–231. J. M. FORD, *Baptism of the Spirit* (Illinois 1971) 79–133, or *Theological Studies* 32.1. R. H. GUNDRY, ''Ecstatic Utterance,'' *Journal of Theological Studies* 17.2 (1962) 329–360. M. KELSEY, *Speaking with Tongues* (1964). J. P. KILDAHL, *The Psychology of Speaking in Tongues* (New York 1972). W. J. SAMARIN, *Tongues of Men and Angels* (New York 1972). F. STAGG, E. G. HINSON, and W. E. OATES, *Glossolalia* (1967). J. P. M. SWEET, ''A Sign for Unbelievers: Paul's Attitude to Glossolalia,'' *New Testament Studies* 6 (Nov. 1968) 173–179.

[J. M. FORD]

GLOUCESTER, ABBEY OF

Monastery dedicated to St. Peter in the county of Gloucester and the Diocese of WORCESTER, England. The site was occupied *c.* 681 by a nunnery established by Osric of Mercia, and later by seculars and Benedictine monks. It never flourished until William the Conqueror appointed his chaplain, Serle, as abbot in 1072. The king and his sons gave ample endowment for 80 monks. The abbey was noted for fine building, especially when funds were obtained from pilgrims visiting the tomb of Edward II (d. 1327), whose body was brought there by Abbot Thokey. The builders were pioneers of the perpendicular style (*see* CHURCH ARCHITECTURE). The abbey was dissolved in January 1540, and the following year the church became the cathedral of the new diocese established by HENRY VIII.

Bibliography: W. H. HART, ed., *Historia et cartularium monasterii sancti Petri Gloucestriae,* 3 v. (*Rerum Britannicarum medii aevi scriptores* 33; 1863–67). *The Victoria History of the County of Gloucester,* ed. W. PAGE (London 1907–) v. 2.

[F. R. JOHNSTON]

GLUBOKOVSKIĬ, NIKOLAĬ NIKANOROVICH

19th- and 20th-century Russian lay theologian; b. N. Russia, Dec. 6, 1863; d. Sofia, March 18, 1937. Of a poor family, Nicholas studied at the Moscow Ecclesiastical Academy and obtained a degree in theology. He became a professor in the Ecclesiastical Academy of Petersburg, but left Russia in 1921 and taught at the University of Belgrade (1921–23), then at Sofia until his death. He also lectured at the Orthodox Russian Institute of St. Sergius in Paris. His theological teaching was traditional in tendency, but he took an active part in Russian Church affairs and in the nascent ecumenical movement.

His first important work was a study of THEODORET OF CYR (2 v. Moscow 1890). On the death of A. P. Lopukhin (1905) he became the responsible editor of the Russian Theological Encyclopedia, and published down to the letter L. A commentary he wrote on the Epistle to the Hebrews was published in the Theological Annual of the University of Sofia (Godišnik 6.1–14: 1923–37); he wrote also a tract on the Orthodox Church and the Reunion of Christians (1924). He also published exegetical essays in *Pravoslavnaja Mysl'* (Orthodox Thought) on St. John's Gospel 1.1–18 (Paris 1928) and on the Epistle to the Philippians 2.5–11 (Paris 1930).

Bibliography: I. LAGOVSKY, *Viestnik* 3–4 (Paris 1937) 17–21.

[B. SCHULTZE]

GLUCK, CHRISTOPH WILLIBALD

Eminent composer whose operatic reform initiated the classical operatic style; b. Weidenwang (Upper Palatinate), Germany, July 2, 1714; d. Vienna, Nov. 15, 1787. He studied music privately in Prague and later, for four years, in Milan with Sammartini. His first dozen operas (1741–46), some with librettos by Metastasio, contained the conventional features of the current Italian style. With a new librettist, Calzabigi, he initiated his ''reform'' with *Orfeo ed Euridice* (1762). His principal goals were to subordinate musical effects to dramatic truth by avoiding complicated plots, superfluous melodic ornamentation, and vocal display; and to unify the hitherto disparate elements of aria and *recitativo secco.* Encouraged by the marriage of Marie Antoinette, his former pupil, to the heir of the French throne, Gluck composed a series of works for the Paris Opéra incorporating these reforms: *Iphigénie en Aulide* (1774), *Orphée* and *Alceste* (revisions of earlier works), *Armide* (1777), and *Iphigénie en Tauride* (1779). The last named won out in the bitter controversy between Gluckists and Piccinists that climaxed the ''war'' between French buffonists (partisans of traditional Italian opera) and antibuffonists (admirers of Lully and Rameau). Irritated by the failure of *Echo et Narcisse* (1779), Gluck retired to Vienna. Apart from its historical importance Gluck's music is outstanding. His symphonic instrumentation, dramatic use of the chorus, and incorporation of the overture into the general mood of the work are particularly noteworthy.

Bibliography: *Sämtliche Werke,* ed. R. GERBER (Kassel 1951–); O. STRUNK, ed., *Source Readings in Music History* (New York 1950) 673–675, 681–683. M. COOPER, *Gluck* (New York 1935). P. HOWARD, *Gluck and the Birth of Modern Opera* (New York 1964). A. A. ABERT, *Die Musik in Geschichte und Gegenwart,* ed. F. BLUME (Kassel-Basel 1949–) 5:320–380. N. SLONIMSKY, ed., *Baker's Biographical Dictionary of Musicians* (5th ed. New York 1958) 574–577. D. J. GROUT, *A Short History of Opera,* 2 v. (2d, rev. and enl. ed. New York 1965). I. A. BRANDENBURG, ''*Le Cinesi* di Pietro Metastasio e Christoph Willibald Gluck: Un primo avvicinamento del futuro riformatore al genere comico,'' *Esercizi: Musica e Spettacolo* 13 (1994) 17–32. G. CROLL, ''Glucks *Alceste* in Wien und Paris,'' *Österreichische Musik Zeitschrift* 48 (1993) 231–236; '''. . . mit Leben und Geschick arrangiert . . .' Zu Glucks *Iphigénie en Tauride,*'' *Österreichische Musik Zeitschrift* 49 (1994) 283–288. P. HOWARD, *Gluck: An Eighteenth-Century Portrait in Letters and Documents* (Cambridge, Eng. 1995).

[R. W. LOWE]

Christoph Willibald Gluck, painting by Carl Jaeger. (©Austrian Archives/CORBIS)

GLUTTONY

The sin and vice opposed by way of excess to the virtue of abstinence, whose function it is to control the desire and use of food and non-intoxicating drink. The virtuous man will take nourishment of proper quality and sufficient quantity to maintain his physical life and well-being (somatic, psychic, and social), but without exceeding the limit set by PRUDENCE with a view to that same end.

In the OT little is said with direct bearing on the vice of gluttony. Fasting is commended in connection with prayer and repentance, but not so much, it would seem, as a corrective of intemperance in eating as a kind of self-humiliation, a bowing down of the soul, likely to lend strength to one's prayers. In Sirach gluttony is called an evil (31.13), and moderate eating that ensures sound slumber and a clear mind next day on arising is encouraged (v. 20). However, it is understood in the context that food is good, and blessings are invoked on the man who is generous with it (v. 23). Although immoderateness brings distress and anguish, gives offense to others, and causes a man to be looked down upon (31.17–18), the pleasures associated with good meals, so long as they are indulged with moderation, are considered with approval (v. 29). In Deuteronomy, God's mercy to His chosen people was illustrated by the good things He had given them to eat—honey oozing from the rocks, olive oil, butter, milk, fat cattle, the finest wheat, and the foaming blood of the grapes—although, to be sure, there is warning in the passage, too, for God's gifts were abused; His darling became fat and gross and gorged and then spurned the God who made him (32.13–15). The good things provided by God's extraordinary providence were also delectable to the taste: the bread He sent in the desert was endowed with all delights and conformed to every taste (Wis 16.20), and, later, the wine at Cana was excellent (Jn 2.10).

The NT records Our Lord's fast at the beginning of His public ministry, but this appears to have been an event of religious and perhaps even messianic significance and not merely a disciplining of the sense appetite (see Vann and Meagher, 54–55). For the rest, little stress is laid upon fasting in the NT, though Jesus did say that His Disciples would fast when the Bride-groom was no longer with them (Mt 6.16–18). Not much is said about excessive eating. The rich man who feasted every day in splendid fashion was buried in hell, but more, it would seem, because he was so preoccupied with his self-indulgence that he had no compassion toward the poor who were in need (Lk 16.19–31) than because of simple gluttony. In St. Paul, however, gluttony is more explicitly

"Gluttony," mid-19th century drawing by Louis Boilly. (©Historical Picture Archive/CORBIS)

condemned, and the Philippians were exhorted not to imitate those whose god is the belly, who mind the things of earth, and whose end is ruin (3.19).

As the various forms of ascetical practice evolved among Christians, particularly under the influence of the eremitical and monastic ways of life, fasting and abstinence from particular kinds of nourishment, especially meat, assumed a prominent place among them. It is a simple and effective way to practice MORTIFICATION and SELF-DENIAL and to subdue the powerful stirrings of the sense appetite. The Fathers of the Church, the theologians, and ascetical writers urged its practice and have been vigorous in their condemnation of gluttony, which has been traditionally classified among the capital SINS.

However, in spite of the disfavor with which gluttony was viewed because of its status as a capital sin and particularly because it was supposed to contribute to sexual disorder, it was nevertheless not considered to be *per se* a grave sin even when carried to disgusting lengths (*ad vomitum*). It consists in the excessive use of things in themselves legitimate. It does not therefore necessarily involve a basic disorder with regard to the goal of human life or imply the pursuit of an end unworthy of a Christian or a man. Hence it lacks the element of aversion from God that is always present in mortal sin. Nonetheless, because of incidental circumstances, aversion from God may in fact occur in gluttony, and in that case it becomes mortally sinful. This happens if one prefers the satisfaction of his appetite for food to God, and, in effect, makes his belly the god he serves (Phil 3.19). This he could do by preferring high living to the payment of his just debts, or by being so dedicated to the pleasures of eating that he is prepared to commit acts of injustice, or to violate serious obligations, rather than to forgo them.

There are many ways, as the scholastic theologians pointed out, that one can fail to keep his eating or his will to eat within reasonable bounds. One can offend by eating: *praepropere,* i.e., by anticipating the time or hour when eating is allowable; *laute,* i.e., more sumptuously than is appropriate to one's means; *nimis,* i.e., too much; *ardenter,* i.e., in a voracious manner; and *studiose,* i.e., with an excessive fastidiousness about what one eats.

The virtuous mean that gluttony violates does not consist in an indivisible point short of which there is culpable defect and beyond which there is culpable excess. It has, on the contrary, a certain amplitude within the limits of which there can be a considerable variation of more and less without fault. Again, the mean is not static, but varies from occasion to occasion according to one's needs. Moreover, it has a certain elasticity. Festive occasions and the special need for relaxation and agreeable fellowship can justify at times a more generous interpretation of how much and what kinds of food fall within its limits.

Much that is said in ascetical literature on the subject of gluttony should be understood as directed not against the sin of gluttony as such, but against the imperfect dispositions of those who are unreasonably reluctant ever to mortify or deny themselves in matters of food or drink. Voluntary self-denial of some legitimate satisfactions has a value that no Christian can afford to overlook, and pleasures of the table provide obvious and acceptable material for sacrifice. Recognizing the common tendency to neglect this opportunity, the Church imposes on the faithful the laws of fast and abstinence.

Bibliography: THOMAS AQUINAS, ST 2a2ae, 148. G. VANN and P. K. MEAGHER, *The Temptations of Christ* (New York 1957). V. OBLET, *Dictionnaire de théologie catholique*. ed. A. VACANT et al., (Paris 1903—50) 6.2:1520–25. G. JACQUEMET, *Catholicisme* 5: 124–125.

[P. K. MEAGHER]

GLYCAS, MICHAEL

Twelfth-century Byzantine theologian and exegete, called also Sicidites; b. Corfu, *c.* 1118; d. *c.* 1200. Glycas came into prominence as secretary to Emperor Manuel I Comnenus (1143–80). In 1159 he was accused of practicing magic and was condemned and half blinded. His crime seems rather to have been an attack on the emperor for his addiction to astrology and the use of false patristic citations in one of Manuel's writings. In prison Glycas was allowed to seek the authentic citations. On release, he became a monk and participated in the theological controversies of the era.

He wrote a World Chronicle from Creation to the death of Emperor ALEXIUS I COMNENUS (1118), in which he combined a rare blend of theology and antiquarian curiosities. His *Kephulula,* or Chapters of Scriptural Difficulties (*Aporiai*), is a complex work that is devoted both to exegesis of the Bible and to a sort of universal theology. It contains 95 solutions (*Luseis*) to problems and includes historical and cultural information; it is of great interest for its sound skepticism as well as for its illumination of the humanistic concerns of its age. In an orthodox manner, he treated of the Assumption of Mary, the Immaculate Conception, the procession of the Holy Spirit, and the interpretation of Christ's statement ''The Father is greater than I.'' His teaching regarding the presence of Christ in the Eucharist was challenged as unorthodox, however, for he maintained that the liturgical celebration reenacted the life of Christ and that the pre-Resurrection body of Christ was present before Communion and became the resurrected body at the moment of Communion. A patriarchal synod (1199–1200) dealt with this doctrine, ascribing it to Myron Sicidites, who was identical with Glycas. Glycas wrote also political verse and letters; many of his writings are still unedited.

Bibliography: *Patrologia Graeca* 158:648–958. *Catalogus codicum astrologorum graecorum,* ed. F. CUMONT and F. BOLL, 5.1 (Brussels 1904) 125–140. S. EUSTRATIADES, ed., *Aporiai* v.1 (Athens 1906), v.2 (Alexandria 1912), in Gr. V. GRUMEL, *Dictionnaire de théologie catholique* 10.2:1705–07. H. HUNGER, *Lexikon für Theologie und Kirche* 2 7:396. M. JUGIE, *Theologia dogmatica christianorum orientalium ab ecclesia catholica dissidentium* 1:413–414. K. KRUMBACHER, *Michael Glykas* (*Sitzungsberichte der Bayerischen Akademie der Wissenschaften zu München* 1894). H. PACHALI, *Byzantinische Zeitschrift* 18 (1909) 422–423. *Kirche und theologische Literatur im byzantinischen Reich* 343, 654–655, 665.

[F. CHIOVARO]

GNECCHI SOLDO, ORGANTINO

Jesuit missionary; b. Casto (Brescia, Italy), 1532; d. Nagasaki, April 22, 1609. He entered the Society of Jesus at Ferrara in 1555, was ordained in 1561, and became rector of the College of Loreto in 1565–66. Assigned to Goa, he arrived there in 1567. He was assigned to Macao in 1568 and Japan in 1570; there he remained until his death. He settled in Miyako (Kyoto), the capital at that time, where he was local Jesuit and remained superior, even during the anti-Catholic persecution. He was distinguished for his administrative skill, prudence, zeal, and care of Christians. He gained the confidence of the local rulers and was able to build a beautiful church, dedicated by him Aug. 15, 1576, to the Assumption (this was the day in 1549 when Francis Xavier landed in Japan). In 1582 at Azuchi he opened a seminary for the education of native clergy. He was a decided friend of adaptation and integration of native practices with Christian teaching. A number of his letters are extant.

Bibliography: R. STREIT and J. DINDINGER, *Bibliotheca missionum* (Freiburg 1916–) 4:405, 564; 5:1030. J. F. SCHÜTTE, *Valignanos Missionsgrundsätze für Japan,* (v.1.1–1.2; Rome 1951–58), best study. C. SOMMERVOGEL, *Bibliotèque de la Compagnie de Jésus,* 11 v. (Brussels-Paris 1890–1932) 5:1932–34.

[J. WICK]

GNESIOLUTHERANISM

A term used since *c.* 1700 to designate pure Lutheranism as opposed to the conciliatory and moderate interpretation of Luther's theology made by Philipp MELANCHTHON, and adopted by many during the 16th and 17th centuries (*see* PHILIPPISM). Mainly concerned with keeping the church faithful to Luther without Melanchthonian additions, the tendency of the Gnesio (genuine) Lutherans was less generous than that of Luther, who considered Melanchthon indispensible to his reform, even when not altogether in agreement with him. In the ensuing controversies were discussed the questions of the necessity of good works for the believer (*see* MAJOR, GEORG; MAJORISTIC CONTROVERSY), the Lord's Supper (*see* CRYPTOCALVINISM), freedom of the will (*see* SYNERGISM), and ecumenism (*see* CALIXTUS, GEORG). The heat and bitterness of some Gnesiolutherans, at times matched by their opponents, likely owed something to the fear of the German princes of Philippism as a danger to their power. While they put ecumenism in peril, Gnesiolutherans helped preserve some of the essential Protestant emphases for a later era in which the spiritual climate was more properly favorable to it. The leading Gnesiolutherans were: Matthias FLACIUS ILLYRICUS, Nikolaus von AMSDORF, Joachim Westphal (1510–74), Johannes Timan (?–1557), Tilemann Heshusius (1527–88), Nikolaus Gallus (1516–70), Johannes Wigand (1523–87), Joachim Mörlin (1514–71), Aegidius Hunnius (1550–1603), and his son, Nikolaus Hunnius (1585–1643).

Bibliography: O. RITSCHL, *Dogmengeschichte des Protestantismus* v.4 (Göttingen 1908–27). H. W. GENSICHEN, *Damnamus: Die*

Verwerfung von Irrlehre bei Luther und im Luthertum des 16. Jahrhunderts (Berlin 1955). W. LOHFF, *Lexikon für Theologie und Kirche*, ed. J. HOFER and K. RAHNER (Freiburg 1957–64) 4:1018–19.

[Q. BREEN]

GNOSEOLOGY

From the Greek γνῶσις, a term used to designate the science or the study of KNOWLEDGE. Originally signifying any investigation of a cognitive procedure, it took on a more specific meaning as the critique of knowledge assumed importance in philosophical inquiry; eventually its cognate forms in Italian, Spanish, and French came to have the same meaning as the German *Erkenntnistheorie* and the English EPISTEMOLOGY. This shift from a purely psychological signification to one stressing the value of knowledge began, however, only after R. DESCARTES and I. KANT had emphasized the critique of knowledge as primary and essential—an emphasis that not all philosophers have been able to accept. The term gnoseology is frequently used in Italy and Spain to designate the study of knowledge in general, and in this sense it is opposed to epistemology, which is usually applied in these countries to the study of knowledge deriving from modern science alone. With the introduction of the term criteriology by J. L. BALMES and its popularization by Cardinal D. J. MERCIER, the use of the term gnoseology has tended to decline among Catholic philosophers.

See Also: CRITERION (CRITERIOLOGY).

Bibliography: P. COFFEY, *Epistemology,* 2 v. (New York 1917; repr. Gloucester, MA 1958). D. J. MERCIER, *Critériologie générale ou théorie générale de la certitude* (His *Cours de philosophie* 4; 8th ed. Louvain 1906). P. PRINI, *Enciclopedia filosofica,* 4 v. (Venice-Rome 1957) 2:813–840.

[G. C. REILLY]

GNOSIS

Of the several Greek words for knowledge, γνῶσις is frequently left untranslated, as Gnosis, when referring to early Christian literature, to indicate a particularly significant form of knowledge of God, of Christ, of heavenly ''mysteries'' and the like. In heterodox circles this was the esoteric, salvific knowledge of GNOSTICISM. Whether in reaction to Gnosticism or independently of it, some New Testament and other early Christian writers also developed a doctrine of Gnosis.

Gnostic Influence on the New Testament. No passage of the New Testament can be said with clear certainty either to be directed expressly against Gnosticism on the one hand or to have derived its vocabulary from Gnostic sources on the other. There are many more or less probable instances of Gnostic background, however. The logion of Mt 11.25–27, though difficult to interpret in its Matthean setting, may be traced to a Jewish background without appeal to Gnostic ideas or language [see W. D. Davies, '''Knowledge' in the Dead Sea Scrolls and Matthew 11:25–30,'' *Harvard Theological Review* 46 (1953) 113–139]. The early heresiologists attributed the founding of Gnosticism to the Samaritan SIMON MAGUS, and yet nothing in Acts 8.9–24 unmistakably marks him as a Gnostic. St. Paul's Corinthian opponents (1 and 2 Cor), who gloried in their charismatic ''Gnosis,'' may have been affected by an early form of Gnosticism or may simply have been other errant Judeo-Christians; the many allusions are not decisive and are still disputed. The ''Colossian heresy'' corresponds much more closely to what is known of some types of Jewish Gnosticism (*see* GNOSTICISM, JEWISH), and it is not improbable that in both Colossians and Ephesians some of the vocabulary is adapted in conscious opposition to at least an early form of such Gnosticism. In 1 Tm 6.20 there is a specific warning against a ''falsely named Gnosis,'' and many references in the Pastoral Epistles can be understood of some early form of Jewish Gnosticism. In Jude 5–19; 2 Pt 2.1–22; Rv 2.2, 6, 14–15, 20–23, groups that may very probably be identified as antinomian (Jewish) Gnostic ones are vehemently opposed; one group, the NICOLAITES, are named in Rv 2.6, 15. The extent of Gnostic influence upon the Johannine writings has been a very disputed question. St. John repeatedly uses the verb ''to know'' but never the noun ''Gnosis''; he does not betray familiarity with Gnostic mythology any more than does St. Paul. Increased recognition (partly through the Dead Sea Scrolls) of the Palestinian elements in the Fourth Gospel does not preclude some material influence on his vocabulary from the side of early Gnosticism. But the Johannine Epistles openly combat ''false prophets'' (1 Jn 4.1), who can perhaps best be understood as Gnostics.

Meaning of Gnosis for Paul and John. Whatever their debt to nascent Gnosticism, both Paul and John evolved doctrines of Christian Gnosis that could well have been partly inspired by elements current in the syncretistic world about them but are certainly original because they focus on the person of Christ. The principal sources of New Testament Gnosis are in fact the Old Testament and Jewish concept of knowing God and the revelation of God made by Jesus Christ. Unlike the Gnostics, Paul understands Gnosis as directed toward God, not toward self; it is self-knowledge only insofar as knowing God, and thus being known by Him, place one's awareness of self in a new perspective (1 Cor 8.2; Gal 4.9). In the Old Testament, knowledge was practical, not theoretical; it was personal, not discursive; it was mediated by knowledge of the Law, not mystically infused. So for Paul it involves man's personal religious response, his attitude as well as his conviction (Col 1.9–10); it is a gift of God communicated through knowledge of the gospel message (1 Cor 1.4–6). Thus true knowledge of God is first and necessarily knowledge of Christ (2 Cor 4.6; Phil 3.8–10). Gnosis in the New Testament is distinct from Gnosticism also in that it has historical and eschatological dimensions (Ti 1.1–3; Phil 3.10–11; 1 Cor 13.12). Paul further presents Gnosis as pertaining to the mysteries of God, a higher degree of contemplation of the same gospel message that is the object of faith (Rom 16.25–26; Eph 3.2–12; Col 1.25–28; 2.2–3). But precious as it is, the gift of knowledge must yield before the higher gift of love of God (1 Cor 8.2–3; 13.2, 8).

The Johannine ''Gnosis'' is fundamentally the same as the Pauline; if anything it assumes an even more prominent role (Jn 17.3) and is more closely allied to love (1 Jn 4.7–8). Knowing God is eternal life; it is loving God, obeying His commandments (1 Jn 2.3–4), entering into communion with Him (Jn 14.20). John's juxtaposition of knowledge and vision is a Hellenistic rather than an Old Testament feature (Jn 14.7–9), but it is unique in its association with faith (Jn 8.28–32; 10.38; 17.8) and especially with John's insistence on the mediation of knowledge by the incarnate Son of God (Jn 8.54–55; 10.14–15; 17.3; 1 Jn 5.20).

Christian Gnosis of Early Church Fathers. In the early patristic period, the APOSTOLIC FATHERS and the Greek APOLOGISTS for the most part continued the understanding of Christian Gnosis found in the New Testament. The most distinctive development comes with the Alexandrians CLEMENT and ORIGEN who, though bitterly opposed to Gnosticism, nevertheless profess doctrines of ''orthodox'' Gnosis that have their roots in a blending of Biblical tradition, Jewish apocalyptic, and Hellenistic philosophy (Middle Platonism). For Clement, Gnosis is related to faith, but is a higher knowledge of God and all revelation leading to perfection in love and unitive vision. It is based on an understanding of Scripture and an esoteric secret tradition supposedly handed down from Christ. Knowledge of the angels and of the ascent of the soul is derived from a Hellenization of Jewish apocalyptic themes. Origen professes a similar higher degree of knowledge reserved for the ''perfect,'' but he derives it exclusively from an esoteric exegesis of the mysteries concealed in Scripture.

Bibliography: R. BULTMANN, ''Gnosis,'' tr. J. R. COATES, in *Bible Key Words,* ed. G. KITTEL, v.1–5 (New York 1951). L. CERFAUX, *Dictionnaire de la Bible,* suppl. ed. L. PIROT et al. (Paris 1928–) 3:659–701. R. SCHNACKENBURG, *Lexikon für Theologie und Kirche,* ed. J. HOFER and K. RAHNER, 10 v. (2d, new ed. Freiburg 1957–65) 3:996–1000. F. NÖTSCHER, ''Gnosis,'' *Zur theologischen Terminologie der Qumran–Texte* (Bonn 1956) 15–79. R. P. CASEY, ''Gnosis, Gnosticism and the New Testament,'' *The Background of the New Testament and Its Eschatology,* ed. W. D. DAVIES and D. DAUBE (Cambridge, Eng. 1956) 52–80. J. DUPONT, *Gnosis: La Connaissance religieuse dans les épîtres de saint Paul* (Louvain 1949). C. H. DODD, ''Knowledge of God,'' *The Interpretation of the Fourth Gospel* (Cambridge, Eng. 1953; repr. 1960). L. BOUYER, ''Gnosis: Le Sens orthodoxe de l'expression jusqu'aux Pères alexandrins,'' *Journal of Theological Studies* NS 4 (1953) 188–203. J. DANIÉLOU, *Message évangélique et culture hellénistique aux IIe et IIIe siècles* (Tournai 1961) 405–460. T. CAMELOT, *Foi et Gnose: Introduction à l'étude de la connaissance mystique chez Clément d'Alexandrie* (Paris 1945). W. VÖLKER, *Der wahre Gnostiker nach Clemens Alexandrinus* (*Texte und Untersuchungen zur Geschichte der altchristlichen Literatur* 57; 1952). H. CROUZEL, *Origène et la ''connaissance mystique''* (Bruges 1961).

[G. W. MACRAE]

GNOSTICISM

The term Gnosticism usually designates a widespread religious philosophy, current especially in the early centuries of the Christian era, which was characterized by the doctrine that salvation is achieved through knowledge or γνῶσις.

Problem of Definition

The obvious inadequacy of this definition is necessitated first by the historically changing views of what Gnosticism is and secondly by the extreme complexity of the religious phenomenon itself. The term was first applied by 2nd- and 3rd-century patristic writers to a large number of pseudo-Christian teachers and sects such as VALENTINUS, BASILIDES, and many others, all of whom were regarded as Christian heretics. In various forms their ''heresies'' persisted up to the 7th century, and the name Gnosticism was limited to them until modern times. In the 18th and 19th centuries the term began to receive a much broader scope when historians observed many of the distinguishing features of Gnosticism, particularly its myths and its images, in a host of other religious movements, some of them decidedly non-Christian.

Hermetic and Mandaean Writings. A purely pagan body of philosophico-religious literature, the Hermetic writings, had come to be classified as a pagan Gnosis. HERMETIC writers, it was found, needed but some mention of Christ, and the role Gnostics traditionally ascribed to Him, in order to parallel very accurately some of the Christian heresies. Mandaeism also, the anti-Christian baptist sect of Iraq which continues to exist even today, falls in the broader category of Gnosticism. The name MANDAEAN is itself derived from a word in the Mandaean dialect of Aramaic meaning ''knowledge.'' Though the time and place of origin of this religion are still matters of uncertainty and dispute, Mandaeism may safely be regarded as a late form of Gnostic religion, perhaps originating in the 5th century A.D. The great and dangerous heresy of the 3rd and subsequent centuries, Manichaeism, is generally regarded as the direct heir of some of the leading Gnostics. Its origins lie in a mingling of seemingly Christian ideas with Iranian, and possibly even Buddhist, ones.

Among the Jews, too, there were traces of Gnostic ideas, first in the DEAD SEA SCROLLS and some of the Jewish apocrypha, as well as in the writings of the Hellenistic-Jewish mystic PHILO; then in Christian times in the Merkabah speculations of the school of Rabbi JOHANAN BEN ZAKKAI, in the Hekalot treatises, and in the medieval Cabala. Certain late heterodox forms of Islam, some aberrant forms of medieval Christianity such as CATHARISM, and even several modern types of occultism or theosophy deserve inclusion in the broader category of Gnosticism.

Gnosticism in the broadest sense that would embrace all the above-mentioned religions and sects over the past 2,000 years can be distinguished from Gnosticism in a much stricter sense that rejoins in extent, if not precisely in intent, the usage of the Church Fathers. Since Hermeticism, Mandaeism, Manichaeism, and Jewish mysticism are treated elsewhere, the present article will limit itself to the pseudo-Christian sects of the 2nd to the 7th centuries A.D.

Gnosticism Not a Christian Heresy. But even with this limitation, is Gnosticism correctly viewed as a Christian heresy? Here again modern scholarship has effected a significant change, one which can best be illustrated by the general rejection of Harnack's famous description of Gnosticism as ''the acute Hellenization of Christianity.'' The Gnostics can no longer be considered Christians, half-formed ones perhaps, who tried to absorb into Christianity certain mythological and speculative currents of the Hellenistic world at large. The process was almost the reverse, described in the phrase of one modern scholar as ''the verbal Christianizing of paganism.'' However many Christian ideas are used or misused by the Gnostics, Gnosticism remains essentially a form of paganism. Its Christian elements are on the surface only. The language and images of Christianity are used, but the essence of the Christian message is ignored completely. One must think of a vast religious spirit or atmosphere, the origins of which will be treated later in this article, a spirit essentially pagan which absorbed select elements from Christianity as indeed it absorbed something from most of the other religions it encountered.

The rejection of the patristic understanding of the Gnostic movement is not meant, however, to minimize the danger that Gnosticism offered to early Christianity in its own confrontation with the Hellenistic world. Gnosticism was assuredly one of the worst dangers ever faced by Christianity, one which the efforts of the Church Fathers managed to overcome successfully only after a prolonged struggle. Yet, like all great threats to Christian faith, it provoked many theological precisions and clarifications of value to the Church's own development within the world of Hellenistic thought.

The Sources

The documents that furnish information on the Gnostic sects and doctrines fall readily into two main categories distinct not only in nature but in the time in which they have become known to scholarship. The first category consists of the descriptions, fragments, and short works of Gnostics contained in the extant refutations of the great patristic writers. The second category embraces the highly significant Gnostic works themselves that have been discovered in recent decades.

Patristic Polemics against Gnosticism. The first and greatest of these works to come down to us in its entirety is the *Adversus Haereses or Unmasking and Refutation of the False Gnosis,* written late in the 2nd century by St. IRENAEUS OF LYONS, and extant in Latin translation. A somewhat earlier foe of Gnosticism was HEGESIPPUS, whose extensive travels gave him firsthand knowledge of Gnostics. His major work, the *Memoirs* (*Hypomnemata*), is lost but is quoted frequently in Eusebius's *Ecclesiastical History.* TERTULLIAN (d. after A.D. 220) wrote five books against MARCION, one against Valentinus, and the *Scorpiace* (''remedy for the scorpion's sting'' of Gnosticism). Besides numerous quotations from Valentinus and other Gnostics in his *Stromata,* CLEMENT OF ALEXANDRIA (d. before 215) preserved extensive Gnostic passages in an appendix to that work, the *Excerpta ex Theodoto.* HIPPOLYTUS OF ROME (d. 235) is very probably the author of the long collection of *Philosophoumena* or *Refutatio omnium haeresium,* which is partly dependent on Irenaeus. This last-mentioned refutation of the Gnostics came to light in 1851 and was for a time wrongly attributed to ORIGEN. The works of Origen (d. 253–254), especially his *Commentary on John,* contain relevant citations from the Gnostic HERACLEON and others.

From the 4th century come the attack on the Manichaeans in the *Acts of Archelaus* of Hegemonius, much useful information in the *Ecclesiastical History* of Eusebius, and the monumental *Panarion* (medicine-box) or *Haereses* of St. EPIPHANIUS OF SALAMIS (d. 403). The last-named refutation, which combines firsthand information with wide use of the earlier writers on heresies, cites in full a valuable Gnostic composition, the *Letter of Ptolemy to Flora.* There is also much information on Gnostic heresies in the Syriac works of St. EPHREM (d. 373) and on the survival of Gnosticism in a later Syrian author, Theodore bar Konai, who lived in the 8th century.

Original Gnostic Writings. As sources for our knowledge of Gnosticism, all the above works suffer from a double disadvantage. Not only are they all second-hand sources, but the picture of Gnosticism they give is one seen through the eyes of its resolute enemies. Such a picture had to suffice, however, until in the mid-18th century there began a series of discoveries of original Gnostic texts culminating in the great collection of Gnostic documents found near the site of the ancient village of CHENOBOSKION (modern Nag-Hammadi), Egypt, in 1946. All of these papyri are written in Coptic, but are presumably translations from Greek originals. What is most significant is that they are the writings of the Gnostics themselves, many of them known already by title or in fragments. Though detailed study of them will continue for a long time, it is already established that they reinforce the reliability of the patristic descriptions of the sects.

The first of the three codices found prior to the Chenoboskion collection is the Askew Codex, acquired by the British Museum in 1785 and published in translation some 65 years later. Of the five works contained in it the best known is the *Pistis Sophia,* named after a mythical figure in the Gnostic world of Aeons. The work, in two books, purports to narrate conversations of the risen Jesus with His disciples, revealing esoteric knowledge of the world. The contents of this codex were composed probably in the 3rd century by members of one of the popular and somewhat decadent Gnostic sects. Equally fantastic in content is the Bruce Codex, discovered in 1769 and first published in 1891. It contains two principal works, the two books now generally recognized as the *Books of Jeû* cited in the *Pistis Sophia,* and an anonymous treatise apparently of the Sethian Gnostic sect. The third document is Berlin Codex 8502, discovered in 1896. It contains a *Gospel of Mary,* a *Sophia of Jesus Christ,* and a very important *Apocryphon,* or *Secret Book, of John,* which was used as a source by Irenaeus in his description of the Barbelo-Gnostics. By the time this codex was finally published in 1955, all previous Gnostic material was dwarfed in extent and importance by the Chenoboskion discoveries.

The Chenoboskion find consists of 13 codices containing some 51 Gnostic works in Coptic dialects. Included in this collection are two works previously known, the *Apocryphon of John* and another writing of the Berlin Codex; several works known by name but thought lost, such as the very important *Gospel of Truth* of Valentinus; and others hitherto completely unknown, such as the now celebrated *Gospel of Thomas.* The codices seem to have formed the library of a 4th-century Sethian group but include Hermetic as well as Valentinian compositions.

Gnostic Elements in Apocryphal Gospels and Acts. A third category of sources for knowledge of Gnosticism, which is not, however, on a par with the others, is some of the apocryphal gospels and acts which remain from that vast post-Biblical pseudonymous literature that circulated so widely in the early Church. It is not easy to distinguish in this literature what is definitely Gnostic and what is merely part of the speculative world of early Christianity. The *Acts of Thomas* fall into the Gnostic category, and the famous ''Hymn of the Pearl'' contained in them marks a high point in Gnostic literature—which, in general, is of very poor literary quality. It is still a matter of dispute whether the apocryphal *Odes of Solomon,* a 2nd-century work extant in Syriac, is predominantly Gnostic or not.

Gnostic Doctrines

In speaking of only one of the many Gnostic sects, the Valentinians, St. Irenaeus begins: ''Let us look now at the inconstant opinion of these, how when they are two or three they do not say the same things about the same subject, but give answers contrary both in words and in meanings'' (*Adv. Haer.* 1.11.1). Such diversity is both a symptom of the disorder of Gnostic teachings and a logical consequence of one of its basic doctrines. If knowledge is given absolute salvific value and is counted the prerogative of a minority, then there is nothing to prevent the multiplication of esoteric systems of knowledge wherever the movement takes root. And that is precisely what happened, especially after the first generations of Gnostic teachers.

It must be understood, then, that it is impossible to sketch the contents of Gnostic teaching in such a way as to include all the pseudo-Christian forms, much less the later Christian and non-Christian forms. One can, however, detach from these many systems a series of assertions and attitudes that reflect the common atmosphere of Gnosticism. The scheme suits no one branch but is not completely foreign to any of them. The basic structure of Gnosticism may be grouped around five headings: God, the world, man, salvation, and morality. Through these categories are indicated what are commonly considered distinguishing traits of Gnosticism: dualism, emanationism, and salvation through esoteric knowledge.

Theology. The God of the Gnostics is often described as the alien God, the unknown God, the nonexistent God, the absolutely transcendent God, or the totally

Other. All these expressions are an attempt to stress the complete separation of God from the world of men and angels and semidivine beings. God is not the creator of the world and has nothing to do with the world's continued existence or its government, despite the fact that the powers responsible for the world in some systems have issued from God in some mysterious way. He is unknown in the sense that man in the world cannot really know Him, and even when the spark of divinity in man is enlightened by revelation he cannot make any positive assertion about God. It is in this sense that God is said to be nonexistent.

The Gnostic concept of God presents the first facet of the absolute ontological DUALISM that in some form or other underlies every Gnostic tendency. God and the universe of other beings are unalterably opposed as light to darkness and as good to evil.

Cosmogony. It is proper to speak of the Gnostics' ''COSMOGONY'' rather than ''cosmology'' because their speculation most often took the form of a mythological explanation of the origin of the universe rather than a philosophical consideration of its composition. The first element of this cosmogony was a vast area of beings intermediate between God and men in which the Gnostic delighted to multiply names, personages, and relationships. Sometimes there is a fairly coherent distinction between the two worlds: the noumenal one in which a series of such beings, the purely spiritual Aeons, inhabit the Pleroma (fullness) near God Himself, and the phenomenal, the visible universe and its rulers. The creator of the visible world, if an individual, is called the Demiurge, after Plato's Craftsman, or if a group, the Archons, ''rulers.'' These are often seven in number (the Hebdomad), patterned on the Babylonian planetary gods, but often given names derived from Old Testament names for God such as Iao, Adonai, and El Shaddai. They rule over the spheres that successively envelop the earth. All these powers come into being by a series of emanations, sometimes traceable back to God Himself, but without compromising His transcendence.

The shaping of the material world results, according to a frequently recurring myth, from the fall of one of the higher powers, Sophia (often called Achamoth from the Hebrew word for wisdom). As a result of her fatal attraction to evil matter, Sophia brings into being or into action the Archons who in turn produce by emanation the material world.

The powers of the spheres and the world of matter are all essentially and primordially evil, and here again appears the basic dualism. Their evil nature results primarily from the fact that they represent separation from the alien God, and each plays his role in preventing man's ascent to God. They are darkness compared with the God of light. The Archons rule the world with an almost inexorable fatality which grips men and binds them to the earth even through successive reincarnations.

Anthropology. There is a divine spark in man, according to Gnostic anthropology, which descends from the Pleroma, from God Himself; and the problem of human existence is the struggle to ascend again from the evil world of matter to the good God through knowledge. Man is in fact composed of not two but three elements: a material body, a soul (psyche), and spirit (pneuma). According to whichever of these elements dominates in him, he falls into a particular category of existence. The ''hylics,'' the material ones, are those dominated by the body, swallowed up in the cares of life on earth. The ''psychics,'' dominated by the soul, are but one short step removed from the hylics, for the soul like the body is created by the lower powers, is subject to their rule, and is basically evil. The pseudo-Christian Gnostics identified the psychics with the majority of Christians who aspired by faith and obedience as well as by the sacramental life to join their God in eternal bliss. But those in whom the spirit or the divine spark had been rekindled, the ''pneumatics,'' the Gnostics themselves, were destined to rejoin the divine world to which they really belonged, once they had been liberated from this world.

There can be no mistake about this process of liberation: it takes place through the instrumentality of Gnosis, knowledge. It has been observed that Gnosticism in contrast to other religions is more outspokenly man-centered than God-centered. A celebrated passage from the *Excerpta ex Theodoto* (no. 78.2) illustrates this tendency and describes the object of Gnosis: ''It is not the bath [baptism] alone which liberates, but it is knowledge of who we were, what we have become, where we were, into what we have been cast, whither we hasten, whence we are redeemed, what birth is, and what rebirth is.'' The process of divine descent and reascent in Gnostic anthropology provides the answers to these questions.

Soteriology. Gnosticism is a religion of redemption, salvation, liberation. Its most distinguishing feature is that salvation is accomplished, not by the power of God nor by human faith nor by cooperation with the will of God, but by the assimilation of esoteric knowledge. The various Gnostic systems gave a central place to the figure of a redeemer whose essential task was to come among men and communicate or reveal to them the saving knowledge. The Gnostic savior is scarcely recognizable from the New Testament point of view. He is a semidivine personage, a messenger from God Himself. But Christ does not become man; Gnosticism is Docetic in holding that the redeemer merely seems to become incarnate. Various devices are used to explain away the Passion and death of Jesus.

The necessity of a redeemer tells us something more about the nature of Gnosis. For the Gnostics, knowledge is not philosophical speculation but a revelation from God, hence the popularity of the many ''revelations'' and discourses of Christ or other divine and semidivine powers to the disciples or the legendary heroes of Gnosticism. Further, Gnosis is an esoteric knowledge; not only is it not available to everyone, but it is intended only for those capable of being saved by it. Thus, unhampered by the demands of rigorous philosophical coherence and cloaked by esotericism, the Gnostics' imaginations could be given free rein to create and develop new systems.

Morality. One of the most common charges leveled against the Gnostics by patristic writers was immorality, made more heinous because the Gnostics defended their practice. St. Irenaeus says of them in a memorable passage: ''As gold sunk in filth does not lose its beauty but preserves its own nature, the filth being unable to harm the gold, so they say of themselves that even if they be immersed in material deeds, nothing will injure them nor will they lose their spiritual essence. Therefore 'the most perfect' among them do unafraid all the forbidden things of which Scripture tells us that 'they who do such things will not inherit the kingdom of God''' (*Adv. Haer.* 1.6.2–3). This practical attitude, which has been called an antinomian libertinism, is but a consequence of the Gnostic theory.

In their role as pneumatics, the Gnostics considered themselves withdrawn from the domain of the world and its powers. Their true life was the divine life of the spark of Pneuma within them. Their life on earth was meant to be an ever more complete withdrawal from matter. Paradoxical though it may seem, this withdrawal could be practiced in the two opposite extremes of severe ascetical abstention from the pleasures of life, such as we find in Marcionism, or reckless indulgence in them, which was the more common attitude of the popular sects. Contempt for the material and the laws that govern it, the latter felt, could best be shown by almost systematic flouting of all earthly standards of morality. There was no law but that of the spirit within them. While Gnostic writings show disdain for marriage and sexual relations, their authors practiced sexual promiscuity without fear of either convention or consequences. Precisely how widespread was the actual practice of immorality among the Gnostic sects, however, it is impossible to say.

Information on the religious life of the Gnostic groups is likewise very limited. It is clear that they all practiced baptism but in various disguises. Widespread among the later sects especially were the performance of magic rites and the use of magic formulas. Inscriptions and drawings of the period illustrate their delight in repeating magical names, or formulas (e.g., *Abraxas*), series of vowels, phrases, and the like. There is evidence also that many were devoted to astrology and that some sects carried on mystery rites similar to those of the pagan mystery religions.

Gnostic Leaders and Sects

After this general sketch of Gnostic teachings and practice, it will be useful to mention some of the leading ancient Gnostic teachers and schools or sects. No effort will be made to be complete in the enumerations as they are found in the patristic sources, since in many cases the groups are known by name only.

Early Gnostics. According to the Fathers the founder of the Gnostic movement was SIMON MAGUS, the Samaritan, who appears in the New Testament in Acts 8.9–24 as a magician interested in Christianity. He was said by the Fathers to have written a work called the *Great Tidings* and to have influenced numerous disciples toward a Gnosticism with a practical libertine aspect. One of these was Menander, a Samaritan who taught in Antioch and claimed to be a savior sent from above. Simon probably represents the transition between the general current of Gnostic ideas in the 1st century and what we have called pseudo-Christian Gnosticism.

Another forerunner of the classical Gnosis was Nicolas, originator of the sect of NICOLAITES mentioned in Rv 2.6, 15. Little else is known of him. Another Samaritan pre-Gnostic leader was Dositheus, founder of a sect of Dositheans and said to be the teacher of Simon Magus.

Classical Period of Gnosticism (2nd Century). Simon's pupil Menander had two outstanding disciples, Saturnilus and Basilides, at Antioch according to the patristic accounts. Our knowledge of the former comes from Hippolytus, who attributes typically Gnostic themes to him. Saturnilus may have been the first of the Gnostics to find a place for Jesus Christ within his system.

Basilides. About BASILIDES we are much better informed. He and his son Isidore inaugurated a sect at Alexandria in Egypt. The Fathers provide sharply contrasting descriptions of Basilides' teaching, which seems to have been characterized by some philosophical subtlety.

Carpocrates. St. Irenaeus reports that it was an Alexandrian contemporary of Basilides, CARPOCRATES, who with his son Epiphanes established the sect called simply ''the Gnostics'' (*Adv. Haer.* 1.25). Among other things, they were noted for their reverence for Epiphanes, who died in his youth, and for their veneration of icons and the practice of magic.

Valentinus. The most famous and probably the most influential Gnostic teacher of the 2nd century was the Egyptian VALENTINUS who taught at Rome. He was the author of many works, all lost except the *Gospel of Truth* and a *Letter to Rheginus,* possibly from Valentinus, in the Chenoboskion collection. His mature doctrine, as described by the Fathers, was based on a careful distinction between the spiritual and phenomenal worlds and on the tripartite classification of men. Valentinus's numerous disciples formed two schools that differed in considering the body of Jesus as psychic (the Western or Italian School) or spiritual (the Oriental School). To the former group belonged Ptolemy, author of the *Letter to Flora* preserved by Epiphanes; HERACLEON, who wrote the first known commentary on John often cited by Origen; and a Roman presbyter named Florinus. Among the teachers of the Oriental group were THEODOTUS, excerpts of whose work are found in Clement of Alexandria, and Marcus, who taught in Asia Minor and whose disciples were said to have penetrated as far as Gaul.

Marcion. One of the most distinctive of the heretics commonly included among the Gnostics was MARCION, a native of Pontus who came to Rome in A.D. 140. Unlike many of the other teachers mentioned, Marcion aimed not merely at devising a saving doctrine, but at founding an organized church. His only known work, the *Antitheses,* has not survived. The New Testament of his sect was one which he had revised with many omissions from the traditional one. Though his system lacked many of the familiar Gnostic ideas, Marcion taught that the evil material world was the work of a Demiurge whom he identified with the God of the Old Testament. Whatever the Gnostic views of Marcion himself, there is no doubt that the sect of Marcionites, spread by a disciple Apelles, and others, was plainly Gnostic. Strong opposition to the Old Testament and rigid asceticism were two of its characteristics.

Bardesanes. Doubt has been cast also on the classification of the Syrian Bar Daisan (Bardesanes) as a Gnostic, but here again the sect founded by him and much later opposed by St. Ephrem was undeniably Gnostic. BARDESANES himself, author of various hymns and treatises including the extant *Book of the Laws of the Countries,* may once have been a Valentinian, but he opposed this sect later. His most notable disciple was his son Harmonius.

The Popular Gnostic Sects. It is neither feasible nor useful to enumerate all the Gnostic sects listed by Irenaeus, Epiphanius, and the other patristic writers against heresies. In many cases it is possible that individual sects were known by more than one name or that many of the names designate only minor variations within the same general groups. The date of origin of these sects is uncertain; some of them may have paralleled the work of the great Gnostic teachers, and many of them certainly lasted for a few centuries longer. As far as is known, they all seem to be characterized by excessive and fantastic mythologies and by elaborate, often repugnant rites.

Some of the sects were named after an Old Testament personage who was held to be the first prophet of their particular teachings and, therefore, was especially venerated. Thus there are such groups as the Cainites, the Sethians, and the Melchisedekians. The Sethians especially are now becoming much better known through the library of one of their adherents found near Chenoboskion in Upper Egypt. Another group, the Barbelo-Gnostics, takes its name from a mythical figure prominent in its cosmogony, the female word for the Father, Barbelo. Irenaeus infers that the *Apocryphon of John* stems from this sect, which appears to some to be a popular outgrowth of Valentinianism.

Several descriptions are available of groups called Ophites and Naassenes, whose names reflect respectively Greek and Hebrew words for ''serpent.'' A cult of the serpent, presumably borrowed from the mystery religions, was a prominent part of their ritual. It is a matter of dispute whether these were really distinct sects. The Peratae described by Hippolytus may have been a branch of a more general category of Ophites. Among the sects mentioned by the 8th-century writer Theodore bar Konai were the Audians, followers of the Syrian heretic Audius.

Gnostic Origins

The uncertainty and vagueness encountered in the effort to define Gnosticism reappears in a related but more exaggerated manner in the task of discovering the origins of the Gnostic movement. Here a careful distinction must be made between the psychological origins of Gnosticism as it has been described above and the ideological origins of the syncretistic movement behind it.

The Question of Jewish Origins. It has been proposed that the great Gnostic systems arose out of the disappointed apocalyptic hopes of late Judaism. In New Testament times the messianic expectations of Judaism were high, and the fall of Jerusalem and consequent scattering of the Jews dealt them a decisive blow. Out of their profound discouragement over their present situation in the world, many Jews turned for religious solace to a sort of other-worldliness, imagining the true life of man to be lived on another plane entirely. Esoteric knowledge of this life supplanted fidelity to the faith of Israel. Novelty was sought in the religious currents abroad in the Hellenistic world, including the current of nascent Christianity.

There appears to be much truth in this sort of explanation of the origins of Gnosticism, but it prompts two cautionary remarks. The first is that it explains only the psychological state which made certain types of men receptive to the phenomenon of Gnosticism. It does not explain the origins of the varied religious and philosophical ideas which go to make up Gnostic doctrine. Secondly, this explanation runs the risk of exaggerating the role played by Judaism in Gnostic origins. It cannot be denied that there are Jewish elements in the pseudo-Christian forms of Gnosticism even though these sometimes show a strong anti-Jewish bias. Moreover, Jewish influence is often present in non-Christian *Gnoseis,* and there is a characteristically Gnostic strain even in heterodox Judaism itself. While the question remains a disputed one, the limited information available does not warrant the attribution of a primary role in the movement to Judaism.

Other Sources. As for the sources upon which Gnosticism drew for its strange mixture of ideas, only the following general observations can be made. Gnosticism grew out of the confrontation of a broad syncretistic movement which flourished especially in Egypt, Syria, and Asia Minor, and eventually in Rome, with Christianity. The syncretism consisted in a tendency to adopt into one pattern of thought elements from all the religions and philosophies current in the Hellenistic world. To this amalgam ancient Iranian religion contributed the cosmic dualism that forms a basic element of nearly all varieties of Gnosticism. From Egypt came elements of the cult of Isis and Osiris; from Babylonia the influence of astrology and the planetary gods; from Syria, Greece, and Rome cultic features of the mystery religions and magic; from Judaism a host of Old Testament figures and many variations on the creation story; and from Greece, again, the philosophical currents of Stoicism and Neo-Pythagoreanism. Platonic influences felt in Gnosticism were transmitted only through the medium of later popularizations; Gnosticism was never a rigorously philosophical system of thought. Finally, Christianity lent to the syncretistic movement the role of the Savior Christ.

This is but a brief list of the currents that entered the syncretistic movement of Gnosticism, but little more can be said with certainty at the present stage of research. It is disputed whether or not there was a pre-Christian Jewish Gnosticism or even whether it is proper to speak of Gnosticism at all before the encounter with Christianity. The second question may be resolved in part by adopting the terminological distinctions suggested at the beginning of this article.

See Also: GNOSTICISM, JEWISH; GNOSIS.

Bibliography: Sources. W. VÖLKER, ed., *Quellen zur Geschichte der christlichen Gnosis* (Tübingen 1932). R. M. GRANT, *Gnosticism: A Sourcebook of Heretical Writings from the Early Christian Period* (New York 1961). C. SCHMIDT and W. TILL, *Koptisch-gnostische Schriften* (Die griechischen christlichen Schriftsteller der ersten drei Jahrhunderte 45; 3d ed. Berlin 1959). W. TILL, *Die gnostischen Schriften des koptischen Papyrus Berolinensis 8502* (Texte und Untersuchungen zur Geschichte der altchristlichen Literatur 60; Berlin 1955). G. HORNER, *Pistis Sophia* (London 1924). Studies. C. COLPE, et al., *Die Religion in Geschichte und Gegenwart* (3rd ed. Tübingen 1957–63) 2:1648–61. K. PRÜMM, et al., *Lexicon für Theologie und Kirche* (Freiburg, 1957–66) 4:1021–31. J. QUASTEN, *Patrology* (Westminster 1950) 1:254–277. J. DORESSE, *The Secret Books of the Egyptian Gnostics,* tr. P. MAIRET (New York 1960). R. M. GRANT, *Gnosticism and Early Christianity* (New York 1959). H. JONAS, *The Gnostic Religion* (2nd. ed. Boston 1963). R. M. WILSON, *The Gnostic Problem* (London 1958). W. C. VAN UNNIK, *Newly Discovered Gnostic Writings* (Studies in Biblical Theology 30; Naperville, Ill. 1960). H. CORNÉLIS and A. LÉONARD, *La Gnose éternelle* (Je sais, je crois 146; Paris 1959). H. A. WOLFSON, *The Philosophy of the Church Fathers,* v.1 (Cambridge, Mass. 1956) 495–574. F. L. SAGNARD, *La Gnose valentinienne et le témoignage de saint Irénée* (Paris 1947). G. G. SCHOLEM, *Jewish Gnosticism, Merkabah Mysticism, and Talmudic Tradition* (New York 1960). H. C. PUECH, "Gnosis and Time," *Man and Time: Papers from the Eranos Yearbooks* (Bollingen Series 30, v. 3; New York 1957) 38–84. R. M. WILSON, "Some Recent Studies in Gnosticism," *New Testament Studies* 6 (1959–60) 32–44. S. SCHULZ, "Die Bedeutung neuer Gnosisfunde für die neutestamentliche Wissenschaft," *Theologische Rundschau* 26 (1960) 209–226, 301–334.

[G. W. MACRAE]

GNOSTICISM, JEWISH

Under the influence of Hellenism certain Jews of the Greco-Roman period indulged in speculations that can rightly be called Gnostic, even though this Gnosticism had its own typically Jewish character. Its early manifestations can be seen in the esoteric traditions contained in the Jewish apocalyptic writings and in the DEAD SEA SCROLLS; its later development is evident in the mystical speculations of the rabbis of the Talmudic period and in the so-called *merkābâ* mysticism; its climax is reached in the Book of YESIRAH and in the Gnostic elements of the Book of Bahir.

Jewish Hellenism and the Phenomenon of Gnosis. After the 3rd century B.C., Judaism came in contact with Hellenism. The first result of this contact was the Septuagint, the Greek translation of the Bible made in Egypt. In the field of philosophy, Stoicism and Platonism had an especially strong influence on Judaism. The Platonic concept of God came the closest to the Jewish concept of a divine Creator supreme over all, while Stoicism allowed Judaism to identify the laws of the Torah (Mosaic Law) with the laws of the universe according to which nature is governed and man should live; God conceived the order that, as the natural law, is inherent in the world and, as the Torah, is binding for man. This idea, intimated as early as the middle of the 2nd century B.C. in the commentary on the Pentateuch by the Alexandrian Jew Aristobulus, was then further developed by PHILO JUDAEUS. Following the speculation on wisdom in Prv 8.22–30 (see also Jb 28.27) according to which wisdom was created by God before the creation of the world as "the firstborn of His ways," Jesus ben Sirach, at the beginning of the 2nd century B.C., equated this wisdom with the Torah (Sir 24.22–27). This led then in rabbinical speculation to the notion, already present in a similar form at the beginning of Philo's *De Opificio Mundi*, that the Torah was the instrument used by God in creating the world (e.g., *Pirke Avoth* 3.14; *Midrash Gen. rabba* 1.2). Similar ideas were in the Manual of Discipline of the QUMRAN COMMUNITY (1QS) 3.15–17; 11.11 (see Schubert, *Die Religion*, 13–25).

Especially clear was the influence of Hellenism on the anthropology of Judaism. Ancient Israel, as the ancient Near East in general, did not yet have the concept that became current in Greek philosophy, of the soul as a vital principle existing independently of the body. The rabbis, however, were already familiar with the idea, as seen, for instance, in *Sanh* 91b (2nd Christian century): "Antoninus asked Rabbi, 'When does the soul enter into man? At the time of conception or during the formation of the embryo?' He answered, 'During the formation of the embryo.' But the other objected: 'Without salt can any piece of meat be kept for three days without spoiling? It must be at the time of conception.' Rabbi said that Antoninus had convinced him in this matter." [See R. Meyer, *Hellenistisches in der rabbinischen Anthropologie, Beiträge zur Wissenschaft vom Alten (und Neuen) Testament* 4.22 (Stuttgart 1937).] Also in the field of art the influence of Hellenism was unmistakable. [See B. Kanael, *Die Kunst der antiken Synagoge* (Frankfurt am Main 1961).]

Motifs Common to Jewish and Non-Jewish Gnosticism. Jewish Hellenism had the following seven distinctive motifs of Gnostic thought, without, however, their having here the specific significance that they had for the pagan or Christian-pagan Gnosticism. (1) Aristobulus and Philo made a distinction between the all-high God outside the world and a divine power that produced the world; in Gnosticism there was a radical opposition between the all-high God and the power that created the world. (2) A distinction was made between body and soul whereby the body was judged the lower and the soul the higher; thus, e.g., in *Midrash Lev. rabba* 4.5 (end of the 2nd century B.C.): "Rabbi Hiyyah said . . . , 'In the world to come soul and body will stand before the judgment seat. What then will the Holy One (glory be to Him!) do? He will leave the body aside and deal with the soul. Then the soul will say to Him, 'Lord of the world, we both sinned together; why do You put the body aside and deal only with me?' He will say to it, 'The body is of the lower regions where sin is committed, but you come from the upper regions where no sin is committed before me. That is why I leave the body aside and deal with you.''' The idea, however, that the soul, in order to be free, must release itself from its confinement in the body, remained alien to the Jews. In clear opposition to this, Judaism developed the idea of the resurrection of the body. (3) Radically dualistic ideas appeared in the apocalyptic literature and the Dead Sea Scrolls. Here, however, in opposition to Gnosticism, dualism was eschatologically limited, whereas Gnosticism, instead of postulating an apocalyptic waiting, purported to show the way here and now to the transcosmic realm of light. The dualism of Gnosticism was absolute and cosmic and, therefore, in many cases entailed the removal of moral teachings, whereas the dualism of the apocalyptic writings and the Dead Sea Scrolls was more relative and ethical and sought a strict compliance with the traditional law. (4) Gnosticism and apocalypticism had an equally negative attitude toward the concrete world; however, whereas the Gnostic wanted to flee from the world, the apocalyptic writer hoped for a glorified world, a "new" world. (5) Both Gnosticism and apocalypticism, especially in the Dead Sea Scrolls, entertained the notion of a hidden knowledge that was limited to a small group of the saved. In Gnosticism, however, this knowledge meant salvation itself or at least the way to salvation, whereas in the apocalyptic writings and the Dead Sea Scrolls salvation was the possession of the elect community exclusively. Here the emphasis lay less on knowledge or knowing in itself than on the idea of election. The knowledge proper to apocalypticism was the insight of those who belonged to the remnant of Israel. (6) Both apocalypticism and Gnosticism had a keen interest in angelology and cosmology. To be sure, Judaism, too, had the notion of fallen angels who seduced men and ensnared them in sin. But according to Judaism, their power was not absolute, and as they were created by God, they would be stripped of their power and destroyed at the end of time. (7) In individual Jewish texts, to be treated later more in detail, certain motifs appeared that were current in pagan Gnosticism, but they were regularly adapted in the Jewish texts to the presuppositions of Biblical monotheism.

It is impossible to determine here with certainty whether in these cases the Jewish texts were influenced by developed forms of pagan Gnosticism, or whether, on the contrary, the influence was in the direction from Jewish circles to Gnosticism, or whether it was merely a matter of parallel developments. In one basic case, however, that of the portrayal of man's ascent to the vision of God's throne, this motif, which later became important in Gnosticism, though in a form adapted to specifically

Gnostic dualism, can be traced back in Judaism as far as the first half of the 2nd century B.C. (e.g., in Ethiopic Enoch 14). On the basis of this fact, much can be said for the statement of Scholem: "Initially, Jewish esoteric tradition absorbed Hellenistic elements similar to those we find in Hermetic writings. Such elements entered Jewish tradition before Christianity developed, or at any rate before Christian Gnosticism as a distinctive force came into being" (*Jewish Gnosticism,* 34).

Possible Development of Gnosticism under Jewish Influence. Several attempts have been made to regard Judaism as the source of Gnosticism as such, since this is first evidenced in the Syro-Palestinian and Anatolian area. But all these efforts, plausible though they may seem individually, are not entirely satisfactory. G. Quispel [*Gnosis als Weltreligion* (Zurich 1951); "Der gnostische Anthropos und jüdische Tradition," *Eranos* 22 (1953) 195–234; "Christichliche Gnosis und jüdische Heterodoxie," *Evangelische Theologie* 14 (1954) 474–484] calls attention to Jewish anthropological speculations according to which the fall of Adam was conceived of as a falling from Paradise's realm of light into the world of birth and death. In this, however, he is relying heavily on rabbinical citations that are more recent than the Gnostic teachings that are supposed to depend on them. In these cases it is a matter of rabbinical HAGGADAH being influenced by Gnostic material rather than of Gnostic concepts being influenced by Jewish motifs. J. Doresse himself [*Les Livres secrets des gnostiques d'Egypte* (Paris 1958) 324–329] describes as merely hypothetical his theory according to which the Essene settlement of Qumram may probably be meant by the place name Gomorra in the so-called Holy Book of the Great Invisible Spirit that is found among the still unpublished Coptic texts of Chenoboskion. R. M. L. Wilson ["Simon, Dositheus and the Dead Sea Scrolls," *Zeitschrift für Religions- und Geistesgeschichte* 9 (1957) 21–30] and, following him, J. Daniélou [*Théologie du Judéo-Christianisme* v.1 (Tournai 1958) 82–85] see in the strange and much-discussed figure of DOSITHEUS OF SAMARIA the missing link between the Essene community of the Dead Sea Scrolls and later Gnosticism. Although the theory is certainly intriguing, the evidence, nevertheless, appears too weak to permit its being followed without reservation. The statement of the PSEUDO-CLEMENTINE Homilies that SIMON MAGUS and Dositheus were disciples of John the Baptist does not bear an unqualified stamp of historic credibility [see T. Caldwell, "Dositheus Samaritanus," *Kairos* 4 (1962) 105–117]; moreover, the historical contact in ideas that no doubt existed between John the Baptist and the Dead Sea Scrolls should not be overrated. R. M. Grant [*Gnosticism and Early Christianity* (New York 1959) esp. 34–35, 41] is of the opinion that the collapse of the apocalyptic eschatological hopes in Judaism, especially after the destruction of the Temple in A.D. 70, had a stimulating effect on Jewish Gnosticism. Here, indeed, the psychological agreement between apocalypticism and Gnosticism in relation to the concrete world has been rightly perceived; but sufficient consideration has not been given to the fact that, although the year 70 is a landmark in the history of the Jews, such is not the case in the history of Gnosticism. The thesis, nevertheless, is supported further by the fact that between apocalypticism and the special phenomenon of Jewish Gnosticism there is an undeniable relationship At any rate, the relationship of "Jewish" Gnosticism to the rest of the Gnosticism is much less clear than would be wished.

K. Rudolf [*Die Mandaer* v.1 (Göttingen 1960) 266] sees in the community of the Dead Sea Scrolls "a heretical Judaism already influenced by Gnostic trends." The Qumran people offer, according to Rudolf, "a valuable example for showing the existence of a syncretistic form of Judaism that lost essential roots of its own parentage and therefore gave in to other influences." However, one cannot speak of a heretical Judaism in these early times, because there was no normative "orthodox" Judaism until after A.D. 70. However, since the Essenes, about whose APOCALYPTIC character the Hellenizing Flavius JOSEPHUS is silent, went back to the movement of the HASIDAEANS or so-called early *ḥăsîdîm* (pious) more radical than the Maccabees, the Essenes were deeply rooted in the apocalyptic tradition of Judaism. They cannot therefore be taken as an example of a form of uprooted syncretistic Judaism. In spite of this, however, it is again admittedly difficult to overlook the fact that there is an intimate connection between the Dead Sea Scrolls and Jewish Gnosticism. Moreover, many ideas in the Dead Sea Scrolls go back to foreign influence also. All these theses attempt, therefore, to offer explanations for the state of the case that is not yet completely explainable concerning the relationship of Judaism to Gnosticism, and so it is well for the time being to treat Jewish Gnosticism as a phenomenon *sui generis;* only as such was it, in any case, of significance for the development of the later CABALA.

Esoteric Traditions in the Apocalyptic Writings and the Dead Sea Scrolls. In Dn 11.33, 35; 12.3 the members of the group behind the historico-apocalyptic parts of the Book of Daniel (most likely the Hasidaeans) are called *maśkîlîm* (the wise, the understanding ones), which is equivalent to saying that they were those who were initiated into the apocalyptic traditions of the community of the elect. In the ten-week apocalypse of Ethiopic Enoch, which, like the historico-apocalyptic parts of Daniel, was written about the time of the Maccabean revolt (168–164 B.C.) and likewise arose in a Hasidaean milieu, it is stated that, at the end of the period represented by the seventh week, ''the just elect of the eternal plant of justice [cf. Is 60.21] will be chosen to receive the sevenfold instruction on the whole creation'' (Enoch 93.10). The apocalyptic groups were, therefore, of the opinion that they were the guardians and preservers of esoteric traditions. Included among these traditions were speculations on the heavenly world, the related questions about the calendar, and detailed accounts of the fall of the angels and the destructive power of these fallen spirits. The Essenes of Qumran carried this esoteric character to the extreme. Flavius Josephus spoke of this in his well-known account of the Essenes (*Bell. Jud.* 2.8.7), and in the Manual of Discipline of Qumran [1QS (DSD) 4.5–6] it is said of the just: ''They conduct themselves humbly with all prudence and with ability to conceal the true secrets of knowledge.'' The word knowledge has a strongly Gnostic character in the Thanksgiving Psalms of Qumran. The Qumran psalmist, for instance, thanked God that He let him ''know the mystery of His truth and understand His marvelous deeds'' [1QH (DST) 11.4].

In connection with Ezechiel ch. 1 the motif of the ascent to God's throne is found already in the older apocalyptic writings. The oldest piece in question, Enoch 14.8–25, which most likely was written in the first half of the 2nd century B.C. and knew only three heavens, in contrast to the later notion of seven, is composed as follows. After traversing the first two divisions of the heavens, the heavenly wanderer enters the third and highest heaven. ''Its floor was like fire, its upper part was formed by lightning flashes and whirling stars, and its ceiling was blazing fire.'' There stood the throne of God, on which the *kābôd,* the Splendor of God, was visible. ''His raiment was more splendent than the sun and whiter than pure snow. None of the angels could enter this house and look upon His face because of the glory and majesty, nor could flesh behold Him. Blazing fire was all around Him, and none of the angels drew near Him.'' A similar motif is found also in the Testament of Levi ch. 2–3 and in Enoch ch. 71. In the Dead Sea Scrolls that are so far known such description of an ascent to God's throne, with God's glory made visible, has not yet been found. But there is indirect testimony to it in the Manual of Discipline. There [1QS (DSD) 11.3–8] it is said that the initiated man ''beholds a salvation that is hidden from the man of knowledge . . . a fountain of justice, a pool of strength, and a spring of glory'' (*ma'yan kābôd*). The spring of glory is apparently the same as the glory of God revealed on the heavenly throne and surrounded by angels. This knowledge is exclusively the secret salutary possession of the elect, for ''to those whom God chose from among the men of flesh He gave this knowledge as an eternal possession; He let them participate in the lot of the saints and united their community with the sons of heaven (i.e., the angels) to form the council of the assembly.'' Possibly a certain angelic liturgy, which is supposed to be an early form of the later rabbinical *merkābâ* visions, belongs in this context. See J. Strugnell, *Vetus Testamentum* Supplement 7 (1960) 318–345.

Mystical Speculation of the Rabbis. While the notions discussed in the preceding section reach back as far as the 2nd century B.C., the corresponding rabbinical traditions are known from the 1st Christian century on. Apart from individual, and in parts very obscure, data in the TALMUD and in the great midrashim (*see* MIDRASHIC LITERATURE), there are available a number of smaller tractates from rabbinical circles that are of inestimable value as references. (They are cited and briefly discussed by Scholem, *Jewish Gnosticism,* 5–7). It is advisable not to date the ideas contained in these tractates too recently. The oldest ones come probably from the tannaic or early amoraic period, i.e., from the 1st to the 3rd century (Scholem, *Jewish Gnosticism,* 40). These texts belong to the Gnosticizing circles of normative Judaism that was the successor of Pharisaism, while the apocalyptic writings and the Dead Sea Scrolls came from non-Pharisaical circles. Like the latter, the rabbinical Gnostics were pure monotheists who rejected the absolutely dualistic character of pagan Gnosticism. Even if these rabbinical Gnostics may have been able to form their own separate conventicles, they shared with the whole of Judaism the high esteem for the Mosaic Law and rejected every kind of antinomianism. In one of the rabbinical Gnostic tractates (*Hekalot rabbati* 20.1) it is expressly demanded of one who aspires to a vision of the divine throne-world that he should apply himself to the whole Bible, as well as the Mishnah and Midrash, and he should strictly observe all the commands and prohibitions of the Jewish law. Rabbinical tradition knew quite well how to distinguish such Gnostic teachings as were possible within the framework of official Judaism from those that would necessarily lead from it to general Gnostic dualism and antinomianism. The example of the great scholar of the 2nd century, Elisha ben Abuya, who, after his fall into dualism and antinomianism, was known only as Aher (another), shows this quite clearly. The fact, however, that Aher (according to *Hagigah* 14b), like other authorities who remained within the bounds of normative Judaism, entered ''into paradise'' and thereby became a sinner, proves how close to its pagan counterpart official rabbinical Gnosticism must have stood.

Speculations on the ''Glory.'' In the Mishnah *Ḥagigah* 2.1 it is stated: ''One is not permitted to lecture to three on the laws of incest, to two on *ma'ăśê bᵉrê'sît* (story of creation, i.e., esoteric speculations in connection with Genesis ch. 1), or to one on *merkābâ* (chariot, i.e., esoteric speculations in connection with Ezekiel ch. 1), unless he is wise and knowing because of his own knowledge. For anyone who speculates on [the] four [following] things, it would have been better if he had never been born: what is above, what is below, what is ahead, and what is behind [cf. Eph 3.18]. For anyone who does not have the proper respect for the glory [*kābôd*] of his Creator, it would have been better if he had never been born.'' Therefore, the special subject of rabbinical Gnosis pursued in the esoteric circles was again the *kābôd,* the ''glory'' of God. As is perfectly clear from a comparison of Tosephta *Ḥagigah* 2.1 with *Ḥagigah* 14b, the concepts of *kābôd* and *ma'aśê merkābâ* (story of the chariot) could be used synonymously. Studies on *kābôd* or *merkābâ,* therefore, were considered unusually dangerous and were thought possible only when extraordinary measures of prudence were employed. As in Enoch 14, so here again fire was a characteristic accompaniment of the sphere of the *kābôd.* Used synonymously with *kābôd* and *merkābâ* was the term paradise, a concept that was already used in the oldest esoteric literature as a technical term for the heavenly paradise (Scholem, *Jewish Gnosticism,* 16–17, where reference is made to 2 Cor 12.2–4). According to Syriac Baruch ch. 51, the resurrected just ones dwell in the heights of the heavenly world and are like the angels and the stars. Also, ''the expanse of paradise will be spread before them, and the beauty of the greatness of the living beings under the [divine] throne will be shown them'' (51.11). What the just all together will come to know after the resurrection, the rabbinical Gnostic wished to attain in his own lifetime. Only in this sense can the well-known passage of the Tosephta, *Ḥagigah* 2.3–4 and *Ḥagigah* 14b be understood: ''Four entered into paradise: Ben Aṣai, Ben Ṣoma, Aḥer, and Rabbi Akiba.'' That this is concerned with nothing else than the notion of an ascent to the glory (*kābôd*) of God that appears on the heavenly throne surrounded by the heavenly living beings, follows from two definite indications. In the tractate *Ḥagigah* 15b it is stated in this connection: ''Rabbi Akiba ascended in peace and in peace descended again''; and shortly after that it is said: ''The ministering angels also wanted to drive even Rabbi Akiba out again. Then the Holy One (praised be He!) said, 'Let this old man, who is worthy, enjoy my glory (*kābôd*).'''

Speculation on the Seven Heavens. The scanty information in the Talmud and Midrash is supplemented in a valuable manner by a few remnants of the rabbinical Gnostic literature that have been preserved. In the *Hekalot rabbati* ch. 15–23 the journeys of the Jewish Gnostics are extensively described as leading through the seven palaces that are in the seven heavens, in the seventh of which stands the throne of God. Just as in the non-Jewish absolutely dualistic Gnosticism the one ascending is hindered by the hostile rulers of the seven planetary spheres, so in monotheistic Judaism, the one ascending is restrained by the ministering angels who guard the gates to God, unless he can show seals inscribed with secret names. In *Hekalot rabbati* 15.1 it is stated: ''According to Rabbi Yishmael, Rabbi Neḥunyah ben Hakanah said, 'In the seven palaces lives Totrosiah, the Lord, the God of Israel, in room inside of room. At the entrance of each palace are eight gate keepers, four to the right of the threshold and four to the left.''' The further the Gnostic advances, the greater become the dangers that threaten him. The sixth and seventh palaces are especially dangerous. According to the *Hekalot sutrati,* the dangers at the gate of the sixth palace consist in the fact that the shimmering marble stones there are mistakenly taken for water (Scholem, *Jewish Gnosticism,* 14–15). That a well-known motif from as early as the 2nd century is involved here is clear from *Ḥagigah* 14b: ''Rabbi Akiba said to them, 'When you come to the stones of pure marble, do not say,''Water, water!'' For he who tells lies has no standing in my eyes.''' However, in *Hekalot rabbati* 23.4 it is said of him who passes the dangers that he ''enters and stands before the throne of His glory (*kābôd*).'' Another dangerous moment in the ascent to *kābôd* of God is the fire of the *merkābâ* sphere. In *Hekalot rabbati* 3.4 it is said: ''The fire that issues from the man who looks down burns him and consumes him.'' This fiery characteristic is especially stressed in Hebrew Enoch, which is evidently somewhat more recent than the *Hekalot sutrati* and the *Hekalot rabbati,* since it comes from the 5th or 6th century (Scholem, *Jewish Gnosticism,* 7): ''Rabbi Yishmael said, 'Metatron, the prince of the [divine] presence, said to me, ''When I was taken from the sons of the Deluge generation, I was brought up to the highest heaven on the pinions of the breath of the SHEKINAH. I was allowed to enter the great palaces that are in the heights of the *arabot* heaven [*arabot* being, according to *Ḥagigah* 12b, the seventh heaven], where there were the throne of glory [*kābôd*], the Shekinah, and the *merkābâ,* the hosts of fire, the flaming armies, the blazing sparks, the fiery Cherubim, the glowing Ophanim [angelic ''wheels''], the flaming ministering angels, the flashing lightnings, and the Seraphim. There I was placed, to serve day by day before the throne of glory [*kābôd*'' [A. Jellinek, *Bet ha-Midrash* 2nd ed. (Jerusalem 1938) 173–174].

The connection between the rabbinical Gnostic speculations on the ascent to the *kābôd-merkābâ* sphere and the old apocalyptic writings is becoming clear through the eschatological significance of the *kābôd-merkābâ* vision. In *Hekalot rabbati* 16.5 it is said: ''When will he descend who descends to the *merkābâ?* When will he see the heavenly Majesty? When will he hear the last day of redemption? When will he see what no eye has yet seen?''

Gnosticism in the Book of Yeṣirah. The book of Yeṣirah (creation), *c.* A.D. 500, is, in spite of its short length, one of the most difficult works of all Jewish literature to understand. It shows strong late-Hellenistic and Gnostic influence. It is based on a magical picture of the world. In the view of its author, the numbers and letters, as well as their combinations into different words, have creative power. The abstract figures are considered as metaphysical principles of the universe and stages of creation. In the Yeṣirah they are called Sephirot, a term that later in the Cabala signified the stages of the divine creative development. The creative letters are called *'ôtīyôt yᵉsôd* (element letters), that is, letters of the alphabet that represent the elements and correspond, therefore, to the Hellenistic-Gnostic idea of στοιχεῖα, which can mean also elemental spirits and constellations, as well as elements (cf. Gal 4.3; Col 2.8, 20). God achieved the work of creation with the help of 32 hidden ways of divine wisdom, 10 Sephirot and the 22 letters of the Hebrew alphabet. The latter were subdivided into three ''mothers'' (aleph, mem, and shin), seven letters with double pronunciations (the six *begathkephat* letters and *rēš*), and 12 simple letters. It is said of them in Yeṣirah 2.2: ''He engraved, fashioned, purified, evaluated, and exchanged the 22 letters, and He formed with them the entire creation and whatever else was to be created.'' The idea behind this is evidently ideal creation through ideal and abstractly conceived Sephirot (Sephirot *bᵉlîmâ,* of abstraction) and real creation through the combination of the letters as elements of speech.

Although the Sephirot doctrine includes no logically developed theory of emanation, yet for the first four Sephirot the emanation of one out of the other is expressly affirmed. The first Sephirah is the ''breath [spirit] of the living God,'' the second is ''the breath of the breath'' and is considered the principle of the air, which results from the condensation of the ''breath of the living God.'' To it correspond the 22 letters of the alphabet. The third Sephirah, the principle of water, proceeds from the air. Here is the place of cosmic chaos. The fourth Sephirah, the principle of fire, proceeds from the water. Here is the world of God's throne that is described in Ezechiel ch. 1; the fourth Sephirah corresponds, therefore, to the *merkābâ* sphere. Particularly the three ''mother'' letters correspond to the functions of the second, third, and fourth Sephirot. The points of correspondence are *aleph* for *'ăwîr* (air), *mem* for *mayim* (water), and *šin* for *'ēš* (fire). The remaining six Sephirot correspond to the six directions of space (up, down, east, west, south, and north). To the six spatial dimensions correspond six of the seven letters with double pronunciations, while the seventh, the ''Place of the Sanctuary,'' contains them all. The ten Sephirot are not Neoplatonic stages of emanation, but rather dynamic powers that, even where explicit mention is made of an emanation process, are united with each other, despite the distinction into stages, to form a single unit. In Yeṣirah 1.7 it is said of them: ''Their end lies in their beginning, and their beginning in their end, just as the flame is united to the coal.'' In all of them the one God is operating.

Combined in different ways, the letters, which are all consonants, can give opposite meanings, e.g., *' n g* can be either *'onēg* (pleasure) or *nega'* (plague). To the three ''mother'' letters of air, water, and fire correspond, in the universe, heaven (fire), earth (water), and air, which lies in between. Likewise in correspondence to them are summer (fire), winter (water), and the temperate seasons (air), as well as the head (fire), the stomach (water), and the trunk of the body (air). The seven letters with double pronunciations give occasion for the Yeṣirah to develop the doctrine of the opposing pairs, which is already evidenced in the dualistic doctrine of the Manual of Discipline (1QS) of Qumran and *Ḥagigah* 15a. In Yeṣirah 4.1 (4.3) it is said: ''Doubles that complement each other: the complement of life is death, the complement of peace is evil, the complement of wisdom is stupidity, the complement of riches is poverty, the complement of attractiveness is ugliness, the complement of sowing is destruction, and the complement of lordship is servility.'' To the seven letters with double pronunciations correspond also the seven planets, the seven days of the week, and the seven organs of sense (two eyes, two ears, two nostrils, and one mouth). The 12 simple letters, too, have their equivalents in the cosmos, in time, and in man.

Certain traditions, as they are developed in the Yeṣirah, are evidenced as early as the time of the Talmud (3rd to 4th centuries), e.g., in *Sanhedrin* 65b, 67b. They are connected with the Golem doctrine, that is, with the notion according to which living creatures can be produced from lifeless matter by the proper recitation of the creative letter combinations. See G. Scholem, ''Die Vorstellung vom Golem in ihren tellurischen und magischen Beziehungen,'' *Zur Kabbala und ihrer Symbolik* (Zürich 1960) 209–259.

Gnosticism in the Book of Bahir. In the early cabalistic book of Bahir are contained elements of an otherwise forgotten Jewish Gnosticism. While in the Hekalot tractates the Gnostic doctrine of Pleroma (fullness) was modified into the realm of the ''Throne of Glory'' and the doctrines of the AEONS, in connection with Ezekiel ch. 1, into the ''*merkābâ* world,'' in the Bahir the originally Gnostic terminology is found extensively. The Greek word πλήρωμα (Pleroma, fullness) is rendered in Hebrew either literally as *hammālē'* (the fullness) or as *hakkōl* (the entirety, all). In Bahir ch. 14 ''all'' is equated with the cosmic tree from which the spirits proceed, and in Bahir ch. 85 it is written: ''And what is this tree? He said to him, 'All the powers of the Holy One (blessed be He!) lie one above the other and resemble a tree. As this tree brings forth its fruit by means of water, so the Holy One (blessed be He!) increases the strength of the tree with water. And what is the water of the Holy One (blessed be He!)? That is wisdom.''' In contrast to the idea of the Pleroma, there is no exact Hebrew equivalent for the concept of the Gnostic Aeons, the powers of the Pleroma, even though the Aeon doctrine is distinctly and extensively evidenced in the Bahir. Instead of the term Aeon, a number of symbolic designations are used. The Sephirot of the Book of Yeṣirah are the Aeon for the Bahir. Although the term Sephirot itself is found only in Bahir ch. 87, it is presumed as something well known. The ten fingers on the hand are ''indications of the ten Sephirot with which heaven and earth are sealed.'' These ten Sephirot correspond also to the ten commandments, which include the 613 commandments. The Bahir is acquainted with the ten Aeons. Like the older rabbinical Gnostic texts, the Bahir rejects all absolute dualism. Evil comes from the left side of God. Out of these assumptions the later Cabala developed the concept of *sitrā aḥera* ''the other side'' of God, a concept that became decisive for its image of the world.

Bibliography: L. BAECK, ''Zum Sepher Jezira,'' *Monatsschrift für Geschichte und Wissenschaft des Judentums* 70 (1926) 371–376; ''Die zehn Sephirot im Sepher Jezira,'' *ibid.* 78 (1934) 448–455. M. FRIEDLÄNDER, *Der vorchristliche jüdische Gnosticismus* (Göttingen 1898). L. GOLDSCHMIDT, *Das Buch der Schöpfung* (Frankfurt am Main 1894). G. G. SCHOLEM, *Das Buch Bahir* (Leipzig 1923); *Major Trends in Jewish Mysticism* (3rd ed. New York 1954); *Jewish Gnosticism, Merkabah Mysticism, and Talmudic Tradition* (New York 1960); *Ursprung und Anfänge der Kabbala* (Berlin 1962). K. SCHUBERT, *Die Religion des nachbiblischen Judentums* (Vienna 1955); ''Problem und Wesen der jüdischen Gnosis,'' *Kairos* 3 (1961) 2–15; J. HÖFER and K. RAHNER *Lexicon für Theologie und Kirche,* (Freiburg, 1957–66) 4:1024–26. J. MAIER, *Vom Kultur zur Gnosis* (Salzburg 1964).

[K. SCHUBERT]

GOA

A former Portuguese enclave on the west coast of India, a metropolitan see since 1558. Captured by Affonso de Albuquerque from the Muslims of Bijapur on Nov. 25, 1510, Goa was once the capital of Portuguese India and of the entire Portuguese empire in the East. In 1759 cholera epidemics forced the removal of the capital five miles west to Pangim (New Goa), and Old Goa became a city of ruins. With the rise of the Dutch and English as maritime powers in the late 17th century, Goa declined. It was annexed by India on Dec. 18, 1961, and attained full statehood within India in 1987.

Fresco painting, depicting a male saint holding a sword, Goa, India. (© Paul Seheult: Eye Ubiquitous/Corbis/Bettmann)

Beginnings. After Vasco da Gama's arrival in India in 1498, Portugal began to acquire small coastal areas (Goa in 1510 and Daman [Damão] in 1559) to create Portuguese India. Until 1514 the area was ecclesiastically under vicars-general of the Order of Christ, which was entrusted with the overseas Church. In 1514 it came under the newly created diocese for overseas lands, Funchal on Madeira Island, whose bishop resided in Lisbon. Pope Clement VII erected the Latin See of Goa on Jan. 31, 1533. In 1534 Goa was made a suffragan see to Funchal with territory reaching from the Cape of Good Hope to the Moluccas. On Feb. 4, 1558, Pope Paul IV detached Goa from the province of Lisbon and raised it to a metropolitan archdiocese, having as suffragans the dioceses of Cochin and Malacca (Melaka). On March 15, 1572, Pope Gregory XIII acknowledged the archbishop of Goa as the Primate of the East. As Goa grew in prestige, other suffragans were added: Macau (1576), the short-lived Funai in Japan (1588), the former Syro-Malabar Metropolitan See of Angamaly (1600), and Mylapore (1606). In 1612 the prelacy of Mozambique was attached to Goa. In 1690 the newly created sees of Peking (Beijing) and Nanking (Nanjing) in China were made suffragan to Goa, which with its suffragans came under the Portuguese *padroado* (*see* PATRONATO REAL). Provincial Councils of Goa have established ecclesiastical discipline for Catholics in the East (1567, 1575, 1585, 1592, 1606, and 1894). The Inquisition was established in Goa in 1560 and operated until its suppression in 1812.

Goan (Indo-Portuguese) Schism. The apostolic vicariates established by the Congregation for the Propagation of the Faith from 1637 conflicted with the padroado jurisdiction of Goa. In Bombay, which Portugal had earlier ceded to England in 1661, this conflict became particularly acute and resulted in the Goan Schism of 1838. The immediate cause of the schism was Pope Gregory XVI's decision in the papal bull *Multa praeclare* (April 24, 1838) which withdrew Cochin, Cranganore, and Mylapore (all of which were British colonial territories) from the jurisdiction of Goa and assigned them to vicars apostolic under the Congregation for the Propagation of the Faith. Subsequent interpretation and enactments further restricted Goa's jurisdiction to the Portuguese territory. The bull was rejected as spurious or surreptitious by the *padroado* clergy in these three suffragan sees who were loyal to the archbishop of Goa. They had argued that even the Holy See could not legislate thus without the consent of the king of Portugal, as was stated in original earlier bulls.

The resistance that ensued in Bombay and elsewhere in India was called the Goan (or Indo-Portuguese) Schism by many historians; and the term ''schism'' appears frequently in papal pronouncements, which, however, do not call the Goans schismatic (except four priests in Bombay), only ''openly disobedient.'' The padroadists consistently rejected the label ''schism,'' arguing that the vicars misinformed the Holy See and that they were only defending their canonical and natural rights. The basic difficulty was the inability of the Portuguese crown and the Holy See to communicate with each other, let alone negotiate an acceptable solution to the crisis. The Concordat of 1857 brought some peace, but opposition continued until 1862. The Concordat of 1886 restored jurisdiction over Cochin and Mylapore and added a new suffragan, Daman (Damão). On Jan. 23, 1886, Pope Leo XIII invested the archbishop of Goa with the title of Patriarch of East Indies. After the diocese of Daman (Damão) was merged with Goa in 1928, the reconstituted See became known as the archdiocese of Goa and Daman (Damão).

Delinkings and Restructurings. The 20th century witnessed further delinkings of suffragan sees from Goa. Mozambique was detached in 1940. In the wake of India achieving its independence in 1957, it became increasingly untenable for suffragan sees to remain under the jurisdiction of a past colonial power. Therefore, Cochin and Mylapore were separated in 1950, and the vicariates general of the Ghats (covering Belgaum, Sindhudurg, Ratnagiri and Sangli) and of Canara were separated in 1953. The Indian annexure of Goa and its dependencies of Daman (Damão) and Diu resulted in the collapse of the last vestiges of the padroado system in India. In 1962, the last Portuguese patriarch-archbishop of Goa and Daman, Jose Vieira Alvernaz, resigned and returned to Portugal. On Jan. 1, 1976, the Holy See restructured the archdiocese of Goa and Daman as an archdiocese immediately subject to the Holy See.

Historical Churches. The Chapel of St. Catherine (1512–31) was the first of many religious edifices in Old Goa. In Bom Jesus Church (1594–1605), a minor basilica in 1946, are the relics of the Jesuit St. Francis Xavier. The churches of St. Francis of Assisi (1517–21, rebuilt in 1661) and St. Cajetan's (1651, once Theatine) are noteworthy. The Augustinian convent of St. Monica (1606) and the Jesuit College of St. Paul, taken over from the Franciscan College of Santa Fé in 1542 and made the headquarters of Jesuit missions in the East, are in ruins.

Bibliography: For bibliography, *see* INDIA, CHRISTIANITY IN.

[J. WICKI/K. PATHIL]

GOAR, JACQUES

Historian of Eastern liturgies; b. Paris, 1601; d. Sept. 23, 1653. He joined the Dominican Order in 1619. As prior of Chios in Greece, he studied the Greek liturgy for nine years. In 1637 he was prior of St. Sixtus in Rome and in 1642 at Paris. Of his many works on the Greek rite, his greatest was *Euchologium seu Rituale Graecorum* (Paris 1647), which has not yet been superseded. It reproduces the original texts and provides a Latin translation and valuable notes.

Bibliography: J. QUÉTIF and J. ÉCHARD, *Scriptores Ordinis Praedicatorum* 2:574–575. H. HURTER, *Nomenclator literarius theologiae catholicae* 3:121. H. LECLERCQ, *Dictionnaire d'archéologie chrétienne et de liturgie* 6.1:1368–74. A. STRITTMATTER, ''The Barberinum S. Marci of J. Goar,'' *Ephemerides liturgicae* 47 (1933) 329–367. R. COULON, *Dictionnaire de théologie catholique* 6.2:1467–69.

[J. H. MILLER]

GOAR OF TRIER, ST.

Priest and hermit; d. *c.* 575. The *Vita Goaris*, written probably by a monk of PRÜM in the eighth century, states that the saint came from Aquitaine in the days of Childebert I (d. 558), king of the Franks; and with the permission of the bishop of TRIER (Fibicius or Felicius), he built a chapel and hermitage along the Rhine near Oberwesel. Reports of Goar's hospitality allegedly aroused the suspicions of a later bishop of Trier named Rusticus, who decided to put the hermit to the test. Summoned to Trier, Goar was ordered by the bishop to command a three-day-old foundling to name its father and mother, but the test proved to be the undoing of Rusticus, who was named as the infant's father. The problems of fitting the persons named in the vita into a chronologically accurate account have given rise to conflicting opinions on the dates of Goar, for some place him in the sixth century while others put him as late as the eighth century. The difficulties are compounded by Wandelbert's reworking of the vita in 839, but in spite of these uncertainties, the local cult of Goar, venerated as the patron of innkeepers, is one of long standing.

Feast: July 6; July 9 (Diocese of Limburg); July 24 (Diocese of Trier).

Bibliography: *Patrologia Latina* ed. J. P. MIGNE 71:639–654. *Acta Sanctorum* July 2:327–346. *Monumenta Germaniae Historica: Scriptores rerum Merovingicarum* 4:411–423. A. SCHÜTTE, *Handbuch der deutschen Heiligen* (Cologne 1941) 145. E. EWIG, *Trier im Merowingerreich* (Trier 1954) 88. M. COENS, "Un Martyrologe de Saint-Géréon de Cologne" *Analecta Bollandiana* 79 (1961) 78; "Coloniensia" *ibid.* 80 (1962) 152, 159, 162. J. DUBOIS, "Le Martyrologe de Wandelbert" *ibid.* 79 (1961) 288. R. GAZEAU, *Catholicisme* 5:75. F. PAULY, "Der heilige Goar und Bischof Rustikus" *Trierer Theologische Zeitschrift* 70 (1961) 47–54. H. E. STIENE, *Wandalbert von Prüm, Vita et miracula Sancti Goaris* (Frankfurt am Main 1981).

[H. DRESSLER]

GOBAT, GEORGE

Jesuit moral theologian; b. Charmoille, France, July 1, 1600; d. Constance, Germany, March 23, 1679. Gobat entered the Society of Jesus on June 1, 1618, and was ordained in Eichstadt in 1629. He taught humanities and sacred sciences at Fribourg (1631–41) and moral theology at Munich (1641–44), at Ratisbon (1651–54), and finally at Constance (1656–60). Appointments as rector at Halle (1647–51) and at Fribourg (1654–56) interrupted his career as professor of moral theology. During his last period of teaching at Constance, he was made penitentiary at the cathedral at Constance. In addition to various other writings, Gobat published a number of works on moral topics. He answered the attack upon the Jesuits' use of probabilism contained in Pascal's *Provinciales with Clypeus clementium iudicum* (1659). At the end of his teaching career he began a series of casuist studies on the Sacraments and the vows; these appeared between 1659 and 1672 under the title *Alphabetum.* Some of these he revised and republished together in *Experientiae theologicae sive experimentalis theologia* (1669). Still later, in the year of his death, these reappeared in *Opera moralia* (v. 1, 1679) and in the second and third volumes, published posthumously (1681). His writings reflect vast experience in the confessional and in the classroom, where he taught candidates for the priesthood who, for want of money or talent, could not go on to the universities. Pedagogical techniques acquired through teaching supplied the format he used in his books in which he presented first the conscience problem and then the general theory and principles by which it was to be solved. Although he based his opinions on solid authority, his cases, enriched by profound knowledge of local customs, were criticized as unsuitable for theological writing; and some of his solutions, based upon principles of probabilism, were judged too lenient. Accordingly, on March 2, 1679, three weeks before his death, Innocent XI condemned several of his doctrines. More than two decades later, when a Douai firm republished *Opera moralia* (1700–01), Bp. Guy de Sève de Rochechouart of Arras censured 32 of its propositions (1703) and thereby sparked adversaries to further attacks on the moral teaching of the Jesuits. Springing to their defense, and that of Gobat among others, Gabriel Daniel, SJ, published *Apologie pour la doctrine des Jésuites* at Liège (1703). Specifically in defense of Gobat, Christopher Rassler, SJ, wrote *Vindiciae Gobatianae* at Ingolstadt (1706). Despite the dispute, *Opera moralia* appeared afterward in Venice (1716) and again for the last time in the same city (1744).

Bibliography: C. SOMMERVOGEL et al., *Bibliothèque de la Compagnie de Jésus,* 11 v. (Brussels-Paris 1890–1932 v. 12, supplement 1960) 3:1505–12; 9:417. W. KRATZ, *Zeitschrift für katholische Theologie* 39 (1915) 649–674. P. MECH, in *Catholicisme. Hier, aujourd'hui et demain,* ed. G. JACQUEMET (Paris 1947–) 5:76. R. HOFMANN, in *Lexikon für Theologie und Kirche,* ed. J. HOFER and K. RAHNER, 10 v. (2d new ed. Freiburg 1957–65) 4:1032–33. P. BERNARD, in *Dictionnaire de théologie catholique,* ed. A. VACANT et al., 15 v. (Paris 1903–50; Tables générales 1951–) 6.2:1469–70.

[J. D. MORRISSY]

GOBEL, JEAN BAPTISTE JOSEPH

Constitutional bishop of Paris; b. Thann, Alsace, Sept. 1, 1727; d. Paris, April 26, 1794. He became a canon in Moutiers-Grand-Val in 1741, studied at the German College in Rome, gained a doctorate in theology, and was ordained. In 1755 he was made a canon in Basel and vicar-general of the diocese and, in 1772, coadjutor for Alsace to the bishop of Basel. His ambition led him to scheme for the detachment from the Diocese of Basel of that section of Alsace that was under its jurisdiction, and for the creation of Colmar as a diocese with himself as bishop. In recompense for these efforts, the French government gave him a pension of 8,000 livres. He was a deputy to the Estates-General (1789). In the Constituent Assembly he tried vainly to conciliate the three orders and to have the Assembly reach an agreement with the Holy See before instituting religious reforms. Once the CIVIL CONSTITUTION OF THE CLERGY became law, Gobel supported it, took the oath to uphold it (Jan. 3, 1791), and was elected metropolitan bishop of the Seine, whose seat was in Paris. He was enthroned in Paris at Notre-Dame (March 27, 1791) and became vice president of the Jacobins. His efforts in starting an uprising in the principality of Basel against its prince bishop, resulting in its union to France, caused him to be sent there by the National Convention as commissioner when a republic was proclaimed at Porrentruy. He was too lacking in firmness to resist the attempt at dechristianizing France under the Terror. After displaying his weakness by disregarding the protests of several other constitutional bishops and giving a cure of souls to a married priest (May 1793), he abdicated his priesthood to the tribune of the Convention (Nov. 7, 1793). Along with the Hébertists he was handed over to the Revolutionary Tribunal by Robespierre (April 13, 1794) and was condemned to death. While in prison, Gobel was reconciled to the Church just before his decapitation. He died courageously, crying: ''Vive Jésus-Christ.''

Bibliography: P. PISANI, *Répertoire biographique de l'épiscopat constitutionnel, 1791–1802* (Paris 1907); *L'Église de Paris et la Révolution*, 4 v. (Paris 1908–11) v.1–2. G. GAUTHEROT, *Gobel, évêque métropolitain constitutionnel de Paris* (Paris 1911).

[J. LEFLON]

GOD, ARTICLES ON

The principal theological articles are GOD (which treats of the one God as He is considered in revelation and in Christian tradition) and TRINITY, HOLY (for subsidiary and related articles, see TRINITY, HOLY, ARTICLES ON). The principal philosophical article is GOD IN PHILOSOPHY (the place, existence, and nature of God in philosophy); see also GOD, PROOFS FOR THE EXISTENCE OF and GOD IN PAGAN THOUGHT. There are articles on the divine attributes (e.g., OMNIPOTENCE; OMNISCIENCE; INEFFABILITY OF GOD) and the divine operations (e.g., WILL OF GOD, PROVIDENCE OF GOD [IN THE BIBLE]; PROVIDENCE OF GOD [THEOLOGY OF]; PREDESTINATION [IN CATHOLIC THEOLOGY]). The main articles on Jesus Christ are JESUS CHRIST (IN THE BIBLE) and JESUS CHRIST (IN THEOLOGY). For articles subsidiary to or related to these, see JESUS CHRIST, ARTICLES ON.

[G. F. LANAVE]

GOD

The Supreme Being, Pure Act, First Cause of all, provident conserver and governor of the universe; the Absolute—infinite, eternal, immutable, intelligent, omniscient, all-powerful, and free; the Creator, to whom creatures owe homage, respect, and obedience; the Sovereign Good, diffusive of all goodness, toward which everything tends as to its ultimate final cause; the supernatural source of revelation; the Godhead composed of three Divine Persons in one divine nature—Father, Son, and Holy Spirit. This article treats of God in revelation and in the Christian tradition. Christian philosophical reflection on God is described here as flowing from the Christian tradition; for a fuller treatment of the place, existence, and nature of God in philosophy see GOD, PROOFS FOR THE EXISTENCE OF.

1. In Revelation

The Christian Scriptures present for us the God of revelation, the God who makes himself known and gives himself to mankind through his words and deeds. The content of this revelation is nothing other than the personal self-disclosure of God himself, calling forth a corresponding self-giving to God from those with ears to hear it. God's self-communication invites and requires a response of covenant and communion. Yet God's unveiling of himself as love and mercy in the Scriptural narrative never occurs at the loss of God's fundamental mysteriousness and incomprehensibility; the God revealed is the present but hidden God. In this way the God who speaks and acts in creation and history is both one who humbles and accommodates himself for his people, and also one who in that self-revelation remains beyond man's power to categorize and control. Divine self-disclosure never reduces God to man's disposal. In freely revealing himself God remains free; in being present in the midst of his people and acting on their behalf God remains transcendent. The corresponding anthropological truth is that every glimpse of the glory of God and every taste of the divine sweetness inspires within the human person an ever-increasing desire to behold God's beauty and savor his mystery. Revelation therefore also reveals man to be made for the God who exceeds him. Though the human mind and heart are created with a dynamic capacity for self-transcendence, only the self-disclosure and gift of the ever-mysterious God can fulfill their deepest aspirations.

The very notion of revelation implies some fundamental truths about God not generally found in pagan religious myths: that God has an ongoing concern for creation and a special regard for man, that he wishes to be known and loved, that he takes the initiative and is active in developing this relationship, and that this relationship has a crucial moral dimension. It also presupposes certain premises not generally accepted in the modern view of the notion of revelation: that it is ultimately God, not man, who is the author of the human words and historical deeds attributed to him in the Scriptures, that man cannot have sufficient knowledge of either God or the meaning of human existence simply on the basis of reason's grasp of the natural world, and that the primary concern of human life ought to be coming to know and be known by this God who discloses his mystery in revelation (cf. Jer 32:34; 1 Cor 8:3, 13:12). The reduction of God to simply an idea to be understood, especially when it assumes that one can truly know God apart from a wholehearted response to him, is completely antithetical to the nature and purpose of the revelation in both the Old and New Testaments.

OLD TESTAMENT

Basis for a Theology of God. The God of the Old Testament is primarily and always *Yahweh*, the God of Israel (Ex 5:1, Is 45:15). The revelation and understanding of God contained therein is thus inseparable from the history of that people, rooted in the covenantal relationship between the Lord God and the people he has chosen to be his own. Its historical and covenantal character means that God reveals himself gradually in the ongoing encounter with his people, through a series of divine manifestations and actions on their behalf that in turn also shape and define the people's identity. Since the medium includes a history of events, Israel's understanding of God is expressed, as one might expect, in functional terms, in contrast to the essentialist approach (i.e., divine being or nature) of Greek philosophy. Likewise, Israel's knowledge of God grows and deepens as the history of God's actions unfolds. This progression is organic and, significantly, never requires rectification or refutation of earlier theological affirmations. In general, biblical understanding of God develops from a more immediate understanding of God as the Lord of the nation of Israel and active in its history to include a more universal understanding of God as the Lord of all creation and beyond all history.

Biblical language is well suited to express the dynamic character of God and the intensity of his love for Israel, and hence is often unabashedly anthropomorphic—e.g., God is said to have eyes (Am 9:4) and see (Gn 1:4), ears (Ez 8:18) and hear (Nm 11:18), a mouth (Jer 9:12) and speak (Gn 1:3), etc. There are even striking anthropopathisms—e.g., "I the Lord your God am a jealous God" (Ex 20:5; Dt 4:24; Zec 8:2), and, "the Lord was sorry that he had made man on the earth, and it grieved him to his heart" (Gn 6:6; Jon 3:10). Yet any tendency to take this simple and direct way of speaking about God as literal descriptions is countered by the commandment forbidding all images and representations of him (Ex 20:4), and the recognition that God's ways and thoughts are as high above human ways and thoughts as the sky is above the earth (Is 55:8-9; cf. Hos 11:9). Biblical language never intends to reduce God to human characteristics but simply to make God accessible to human beings, even to those with the simplicity of children (Mt 11:25). The concreteness and immediacy of its style demonstrate that God is the personal and living God who is known through his interactions with the people dear to him.

God of the Covenant. *Promise to Abraham.* The history of the people of God begins with Abraham and his call by God to walk in his presence and be blameless (Gn 17:1). From the beginning God reveals himself as a God of blessing, promise and covenant. The blessings are concrete—land and posterity—and reflect the major concerns of a semi-nomadic people and God's intimate involvement in the lives and fortunes of the patriarchs. In promising a son to an elderly Abraham and a sterile Sarah, God demands trust that there is nothing "too difficult for him to do" (Gn 18:14). Then in testing Abraham to sacrifice this son, God demands an obedience which withholds nothing from him (Gn 22). God demonstrates his freedom and the primacy of his election in favoring Jacob (Israel) over Esau (Gn 25:21–23; cf. Mal 1:2–3 & Rom 9:10–13), and Joseph over his brothers. The story of Joseph (Gn 37–50) exhibits how God's providential foresight brings Joseph through the many betrayals of his life to saving stewardship in time of famine (Gn 45:5–8, 50:20). These early stories of God's presence and activity in the lives of their ancestors provide the foundation for the theology of Israel. Appropriately, Israel will continue to know their God as the "God of your ancestors, the God of Abraham, the God of Isaac, and the God of Jacob" (Ex 3:15, 4:5), reflecting the tribal character of their faith and that even across the generations their God is one and the same. Addressing God this way reminds them that their own history is a fulfillment of the promises God made to their ancestors, inspiring a confident assurance that God will in turn be true to all his future promises.

These early narratives in some ways borrow, and in many ways transcend, the diverse understandings of deity found in the ancient near East. Abraham's ancestors worshipped many gods (Jos 24:3), and God's call to him to leave the land of his fathers (Gn 12:1) is also a call to faith in the one God. The patriarchs used common words and ancient titles for God (cf. Ex 6:3), such as *El* (likely from the Semitic for ''strength''), the father of the gods and lord of heaven in Ugaritic and Canaanite religions. This name was readily combined with various modifiers: *El Elyon* – ''God most high'' (Gn 14:18–19), *El Shaddai* – ''God almighty'' / ''God of the mountains'' (Gn 17:1), *El Ro'i* – ''God of seeing'' (Gn 16:13), and *El Olam* – ''the everlasting God'' (Gn 21:33). Early Israel continued to use these ancient names because they invoke divine greatness and transcendence. However, what was not appropriated from the surrounding religions were the ideas that God was head of a pantheon of other gods, had a consort or equal, or could be identified with some element or force of nature. Again in contrast to the norm in ancient religions and cosmogonies, never is there an attempt to explain God's origins, or any suggestion that there are powers that threaten him. God is one and supreme, and Abraham's faith was monotheistic at least in the tribal and personal sense: if the existence of the gods worshipped by other peoples was never explicitly denied, nonetheless they have no meaning or value to those whose only Lord is the God almighty. Even the word *Elohim*, used more than 2,500 times in the texts to indicate not only ''God'' and ''the God'' specifically, but also ''a god'' and the ''gods'' generically (e.g., Ex 20:3), need not imply any genuine form of polytheism. When used to refer to the God of Israel's faith (Gn 1:1) the plural *Elohim* always takes a singular verb, indicating that, like the royal *we*, the plural of excellence, not number, is meant. ''To you it was shown, that you might know that the Lord is God (*Elohim*); there is no other besides him (Dt 4:35).

Yahweh. The most definitive event of Israel's history, the exodus from Egypt, and the revelation of the most prominent name for God in the Hebrew Scriptures coincide. *Yahweh* (scholarship has proven ''Jehovah'' to be a mispronunciation) is revealed to Moses in the great theophany of the burning bush (Ex 3–4), and thus in the context of God's solicitous regard for his people enslaved in Egypt. *Yahweh* occurs over 6,700 times and appears in almost every book of the Old Testament. Unlike other names of ancient deities, like ''Baal'' (possessor) or ''Adon'' (master), ''Yahweh'' is not also a title or derived from one; it is only a name, and unlike a title, cannot be transferred to another. Etymologically related to *hwh* (''hayah''), the Hebrew verb ''to be,'' Exodus 3:14 renders the name as ''I am who am,'' and more simply as ''I am.'' The meaning is mysterious as well as manifold, depending upon the sense given the verb. Indicatively, *Yahweh* means ''He who is,'' a meaning which later Christian theology will find particularly significant when it engages Greek philosophy. But the verb can also be taken in the causative sense (which conforms more closely with the Hebrew understanding of God as active Creator), in which case *Yahweh* can mean: ''I cause to be what ever comes to be.'' The richness of the name allows even a third possibility: ''I will be there as who I am (will I be there).'' This meaning fits closely with the context in which it appears—that is, with God telling Moses his intentions to deliver Israel from slavery and to be with Moses as he contends with Pharaoh and leads the people. Every sense, however, suggests that God is unique and incomparable, and therefore his very name is beyond comprehension. In their great reverence for God, and the Semitic mentality that the name itself is identical to the reality named, the Israelites avoided pronouncing the name *Yahweh.* Their substitution for the name, *Adonai*, meaning Lord, expresses the power and reign of *Yahweh* over all things, as well as the claim he has on his people. At the same time, the substitution respected the ineffability of God's name and mystery, while avoiding the risk of taking the name in vain (Ex 20:7).

Moses and the Israelites quickly learn that *Yahweh* is the God who does great deeds on their behalf. Initially, God's acts include the deliverance from slavery in Egypt, the giving of the law and covenant on Mt. Sinai, leading Israel into the promised land, and granting victory or defeat in Israel's battles. Through these deeds Israel comes to understand God to be in their midst (Ex 40:34–38), demonstrating his supreme greatness and power (Dt 4:32–40), acting for their good (Dt 5:33, 8:2–10), fulfilling his promises to their forefathers (Dt 5:37, 9:5), and expressing his choice for them as a people for his own possession (Dt 7:6–8). These saving deeds become the foundation for the covenant, not only in the sense that God plagues Egypt because of Pharaoh's refusal to let Israel go and worship God on Mt. Sinai (Ex 7:16, 8:25–28), but also in that the favor God shows to Israel in these wondrous deeds serves as the basis for the covenantal obligations God expects from them (Dt 6:21–25, 11:1ff.). ''I am the Lord your God, who brought you out of the land of Egypt, to be your God: I am the Lord your God'' (Nm 15:41). As acts expressive of his gracious favor, they invite Israel to respond with likeminded love and loyalty. As acts expressive of his power, they give Israel reason to revere and fear him, and to believe that there is no other god like him. God's merciful goodness is reason to pay him heed, as is evident in the great and intimate theophany given to Moses upon Mt. Sinai during the making of the covenant: ''The Lord, the Lord, a God merciful and gracious, slow to anger, and abounding in steadfast love and faithfulness, keeping steadfast love for the thousandth generation, forgiving iniquity and transgression and sin, yet by no means clearing the guilty, but visiting the iniquity of the parents upon the children and the children's children, to the third and fourth generation. And Moses made haste to bow his head toward the earth, and worshiped'' (Ex 34:6–7; cf. Dt 7:9–11 & Jon 4:2).

Through their encounter with God in history and covenant Israel learns that God is holy (Ps 99:3, 5, 9; Is 6:3), ''the holy one of Israel'' (Is 1:4, 5:19, 30:15, 31:1). Originally referring to ritual items reserved and set apart for worship, holiness applied to God designates his uniqueness, his exalted otherness, his incomparability (Hos 11:9). One of *Yahweh*'s most distinguishing characteristics, divine holiness sets him apart from all other gods, from all that he has made, from the wicked and from every evil. It means that God is unapproachable, that no one can see his face and live (Ex 33:20; Is 6:5). ''Who is able to stand before the Lord, this holy God?'' (1 Sm 6:20). As exalted in holiness over all, he is not to be tested or provoked (Dt 6:16; Ps 95:8–9), nor his determinations gainsaid (Jb 38–41; Is 45:9–13; Jon 4). As holy, his name is great and terrible (Ps 99:3), and the earth trembles at his approach (Jgs 5:4). *Yahweh* is ''the great, the mighty, and the terrible God'' (Dt 10:17; Dn 9:4), in the sense of inducing awe and fear by his powerful deeds on behalf of his people (Dt 10:21; 2 Sm 7:23; Ps 106:22), and the fearful natural events of violent thunderstorm and earthquake (Ex 19:16–19; Ps 29; Is 10:33). Thus, a decisive feature of the biblical understanding of *Yahweh* is that the same God who is immanently present and compassionate towards Israel is transcendently exalted far above the heavens in glory.

Israel's Response. Because ''great in your midst is the Holy One of Israel'' (Is 12:6), the people of God are set apart as well: to be holy unto the Lord (Nm 15:40; Dt 7:6), and to be a light to the nations (Is 42:6, 49:6). In the covenant God commands Israel to be holy because *Yahweh* is holy (Lv 11:44–45, 19:2), just as he demanded their forefather Abraham before them (Gn 17:1). Their call to holiness is contained in the twin obligations of the covenant: the religious commandments in regards to God and the moral ones concerning neighbor. Though fittingly expressed in the form of law, since obedient action is the heart of the matter, the covenantal demands of the *Torah* are essentially a teaching of wisdom, a way of acting that leads to life and blessing (Dt 30:15–20; Ps 1). Israel was called to listen to God, and respond with the whole of heart and life, as the daily praying of *Shema* reminded them: ''Hear, O Israel: The Lord is our God, the Lord alone. You shall love the Lord your God with all your heart, and with all your soul, and with all your might'' (Dt 6:4–5). The covenantal relationship requires them ''to fear God''—that is, to walk in all his ways, to love him, serve him, and keep all his commandments and statutes (Dt 10:12–13). Living truthfully is to seek the face of the Lord (Ps 24:6). The fear of God, the reverential acknowledgement of God's claims upon man (Ex 20:20), is the beginning of wisdom (Ps 111:10), for the carrying out of God's commands is the whole duty of man (Eccl 12:13). In contrast, it is the fool who says in his heart there is no God (Ps 14:1), who convinces himself that God does not see human behavior or will require an accounting for it (Ps 36:1–2, 94:4–11; Is 47:10–11). This is not atheism in the strict and ideological sense, where the existence of God is denied outright, but a functional or performative kind of atheism that ignores God and thereby denies his Lordship and right to judgment.

Israel's theology of God, therefore, is a lived one, formed and sustained by moral obedience to God's commands. Equally important in this formation are the cultic practices required by the covenant: the offering of sacrifices of expiation and thanksgiving, the petitions, praise and prayers of the psalms, and the rites of the yearly calendar of feasts through which they remembered the saving deeds of God and sang: ''Praise him for his mighty deeds, praise his surpassing greatness'' (Ps 150:2). These religious rituals were performed in the family setting, at specific religious shrines of ancestral significance, and eventually in the temple of Jerusalem above all. Central too is the conviction that *Yahweh* is present in the midst of the people (Ex 25:8), especially in his *shekinah* (presence) over the ark of the covenant, at first in tent (Ex 40:34–38), later in temple (1 Kgs 8:10–11). This deep confidence that God was with them communally is an ongoing realization that the name of *Yahweh* means, ''I am he who will be there for you.''

God of Creation. As Israel understands *Yahweh* as the author of wonderful historical deeds on their behalf, in like fashion they conceive the coming to be of all things as a great work of *Yahweh*. The making of the heavens and the earth by calling them into existence and placing all things in their proper setting is the first of Yahweh's saving deeds, and thus the beginning of salvation history. Creation is a divine act integrated with, and never separate from, the divine work of the covenant. As his own proper act—the Hebrew verb to create, *bārā* (Gn 1:1), is chiefly reserved for God alone—the work of creation displays God's power and gives evidence of his greatness, beauty, and artistry (Wis 13:1–9). Creation gives God glory (Ps 19:1), and like his saving historical deeds, inspires Israel to worship and praise him (Ps 95:5–6, 104:31–35).

The work of creation is accomplished by the powerful word (*dabar*) and wind or breath (*ruah*) of God (Gn 1; Ps 33:6), and the resultant good depends upon God's wisdom and love (Prv 8:22–31; Wis 11:24–26). While one can find early mythopoetic representations of God's act of creation as a victory over the restless sea (Ps 93:3–5), personified as the sea-monster Leviathan (Ps 74:12–15) or Rahab (Jb 26:12; Is 51:9–10), the first chapter of Genesis presents it more simply as God bringing order to what is unformed (Gn 1:1). Only after contact with Greek thought is creation expressed as a making *ex nihilo* (2 Mc 7:8). In striking contrast to other cosmogonies, biblical creation is never portrayed in the terms of some life-giving process found within the world—i.e., sexual reproduction or the natural cycle wherein death leads to life. Because *Yahweh* has no consort or rival, the creation account is conspicuously monotheistic. The transcendent *Yahweh* creates without strain by simply commanding, and thus like the lawgiver Israel knew him to be.

As a work of the Lord, creation has a definite beginning, yet it never means a cessation of divine activity. By the same command and power he made all things, God sustains all things in being, prevents their disintegration, and provides for their needs. As the ''living God'' (Dt 5:26; Jer 10:10), he is the source of life (Nm 27:16; Ps 38:9), who gives breath (Gn 2:7) and takes it away (2 Sm 12:14–23; Ps 104:29). In his untiring stewardship over creation *Yahweh* is the cause of daily events and changes in nature: he authors day and darkness (Am 4:13, 5:8); he calls forth the movements of the heavens (Is 40:26, 45:12, 48:13); even the wind, rain and snow go forth at his command (Jb 37:9–11; Ps 147:15–18). In particular, Psalm 104 praises the Creator for his ongoing care of creation, in watering the earth, giving food for the hungry, sending and taking away the breath of life (cf. Jb 38:39–39:30).

Since nature is completely subject to the God who made it, and natural events can spell either blessing or misfortune for man, timely rains that bring forth the earth's bounty indicate God's reward for Israel's covenantal fidelity (Lv 26:4; Dt 11:13–14), while drought and natural disasters are punishments from God for the people's unfaithfulness (Jer 5:24–25; Am 4:7; Jl 2:1–11). Therefore God's relation to creation, too, is covenantal (Gn 9:9–17; Hos 2:18). This understanding of the world stands in stark contrast to, and often intentionally subverts, the pagan tendency to identify natural forces with gods. It is also differs markedly from later conceptions of nature as autonomous, mechanical and impersonal. Creation manifests God's wisdom and goodness, but the order discernible in its unfolding is not due to absolute, inviolable natural laws, but to the constancy and justice of *Yahweh*. Not only does Hebrew lack a word for ''nature,'' there is little Semitic concern to distinguish between natural causality and divine agency. The one prominent exception is that genuine human deliberation and moral responsibility is always recognized, since it is a necessary presupposition for Israel's participation in the covenant.

Israel's Disobedience and God's Response. As the history of Israel unfolds *Yahweh* continues to act according to the covenantal relationship, both in the communal fortunes of the nation and in the personal lives of individuals. At the forefront of the covenant is the commandment to worship *Yahweh* alone (Ex 20:1–6), and the events of Israel's history are interpreted in respect to the people's wavering fidelity to their one God, so that a cycle of apostasy, divine punishment, petition, divine deliverance, and repentance is repeated over the generations. God raises up ''judges'' who deliver Israel from their idolatry and thus from their subjection to their enemies (Judges). Though *Yahweh* is Israel's true King (1 Sm 8:7), he allows the establishment of a monarchy, himself appointing the first kings, and, in response to David's religious loyalty and obedience, secures his lineage as a dynasty (2 Sm 7:8–16). When the kings and people of Israel succumb to the polytheism present in and around Israel, God responds by sending prophets. Led by the spirit of God to proclaim his judgment, they call Israel back to the demands of the covenant: to worship *Yahweh* alone, to trust him exclusively for the nation's welfare, and to act justly toward neighbor. Since *Yahweh* is the protector of widows, orphans and aliens (Dt 10:18; Ps 68:5–6), acts of injustice to the poor, innocent and defenseless of society are especially condemned by the prophets. The history of Israel proves that the abandonment of the coherence of covenantal monotheism leads inevitably to ritual hypocrisy (Is 1:10–17; Am 5:21–25), moral degradation (Is 5:20; Hos 4:1–2; cf. Rom 1:18–32), societal injustice (Jer 6:13; Am 8:4–8), and loss of the nation's identity and independence (2 Kgs 24–25; Is 5).

Certainly Israel's disobedience provides the context for one of the most misunderstood and maligned anthropopathisms in the Old Testament: the fierce anger of God (e.g., Ez 5:13–17). God's anger in the Scriptures expresses and personifies the justice of God, but this divine displeasure, unlike parallels in ancient Near Eastern religions, is never capriciously without grounds or purpose. The anger of *Yahweh* is always in response to covenantal unfaithfulness, and always presupposes the holiness of God wholly incompatible with sin. On account of his righteousness which the covenant must manifest (Is 5:7, 16), the holy God is intolerant towards disobedience in the people he desires and commands to be like him, for their own good and that they may be a blessing to the nations (Gn 12:3; Is 19:24). It is always and only as a consequence of their unfaithfulness to the covenant that God punishes the people of Israel (Jer 21:11–22:9). They come to experience his ''wrath'' (Jer 6:11; Ex 7:8; Hos 5:10)—that is, the negative consequences of their own idolatry, immorality and injustice. In this way the natural and human disasters of their history (e.g., famine and conquest) are understood theologically. It is *Yahweh* who through natural calamities and foreign armies accomplishes the demands of his covenantal justice, even to the point of the destruction of Jerusalem and the temple, and the deportation of the people into exile (Is 46:6; Jer 21:3–7, 27:5–11). Again this reflects and affirms the radical monotheism of Israel, who is Lord over every natural and human power.

Yet the drama of Israel's failure to keep the covenant and God's punishing mercy upon his people allows for a deepening of the Bible's portrayal of *Yahweh* as the one and holy God. The divine quality that comes most to the fore through all this turmoil is the *hesed* of *Yahweh*: God's loving faithfulness or steadfast love (Ex 34:6; Ps 106:45, 108:4). The prophets, especially Hosea, characterized Israel's exclusive covenantal relationship with God as that of a marriage of love and fidelity between husband and bride. Even as they equate Israel's idolatrous pursuit of other gods with adultery and harlotry (Ez 16; Hos 4:10–19), the prophets affirm the constancy of *Yahweh*'s love and tenderness for Israel his beloved (Is 62:1–5; Hos 2:14–20). While Israel repeatedly breaks the covenant, God remains true to it, certainly by justly punishing wickedness, yet more so by mercifully forgiving, preserving and restoring Israel. Though God always acts for the good of his people, he acts on account of who he is: justice and mercy and love. ''For my own sake, for my own sake, I do it, for why should my name be profaned? My glory I will not give to another'' (Is 48:11; cf. Ez 36:22–23). Thus, after originally choosing Israel as his own, God ever after favors them because his love for Israel has become inseparable from faithfulness to his own name. Having punished Israel's idolatry, *Yahweh* forgets their iniquity but remembers his loving faithfulness which cannot pass away. As the reason for Israel's hope in the goodness of God to them, the *hesed* of *Yahweh* elicits Israel's gratitude and praise: ''O give thanks to the Lord, for he is good; his steadfast love endures forever'' (Ps 107:1, 117:2, 118:1–4, 138:2).

Thus the prophets who foretell Israel's pending destruction always also proclaim God's subsequent mercy upon them (e.g., Jer 33; Hos 2:14–23; Am 9:11–15). Indeed, in the very nadir of Israel's history, the exile of Judah into Babylon, there occurs a profound renewal in theological thought, particularly evident in Second Isaiah (Is 40–66), towards a more universal and eschatological understanding of *Yahweh*'s steadfast love for Israel. At this time, after the bankruptcy of religious syncretism, Israel's faith becomes explicitly and absolutely monotheistic—not only is *Yahweh* the only God for Israel, he is the only God, period. ''I am the Lord, and there is no other'' (Is 45:18; cf. 44:6–8; 46:9). As the Creator of all things, he can be Israel's savior outside the confines of the Promised Land, even in the midst of a people whose gods are nothing more than lifeless idols (Ps 134:15–18; Is 44:9–20; Jer 10:14). Because *Yahweh* alone is God, he is the Lord of history ruling over all nations, commissioning foreign powers in the work of returning Israel to the land as surely he had used them to drive them from it (Is 45:1–7; Jer 29:4–14; Zec 10:3–12). Rejecting the common belief that the gods of each nation were responsible for its fortunes, the prophets dare to ascribe the destinies of all peoples to the one and only Lord of heaven and earth.

God and the Future Hope. In the honest acknowledgement of Israel's guilt a hope is born for a future great work of the Lord. This hope of the prophets looks forward to a messianic and eschatological future in which God will definitively act to deliver Israel from its own unfaithfulness and establish an everlasting covenant of God's universal reign. In order to express this future hope of what the Lord will do, the prophets speak in terms of what he had done in the past; hope is grounded in and transforms memory. God will act and there will be a new creation of justice and peace (Is 11:6–9), a new heavens and earth (Is 65:17–19), and the desert representing human spiritual lifelessness will become verdant and fruitful (Is 42:17–20; Ez 47:1–12). God will establish a new covenant (Jer 31:31–34), so that his people, with a new heart and spirit (Ez 36:22–32), will all have knowledge of and steadfast love for God (Is 11:9; Hos 2:18–20, 6:6). There will be a new Jerusalem (Is 66:7–16) and temple (Ez 40–47), honored and sought by the nations. God will send his anointed and chosen one, his Messiah, who as a suffering servant (Is 52:13–53:12), will expiate faithlessness by his redemptive suffering, and as a king in the line and example of David (Jer 33:14–18; Ez 34:23–24, Zec 9:9–10) will restore Israel to glory. In these ways not only God's original intentions for Israel will be realized, but through Israel's restoration, the whole world will come to salvation (Is 2:2–4, 49:6; Zep 3:8–13). For the new deliverance of Israel will lead all nations to acknowledge and worship *Yahweh* alone (Is 45:8–25, 56:6–8; Jer 16:19–21), and so demonstrate the universal dominion of the one God.

The true character of the God of the Old Testament, *Yahweh*, is thus to be known through his intimate regard for Israel, which in its very particularity opens up to a true universality, and in its activity in time moves forward to a future beyond history. God is present among and active for his people, yet in his very immanence God remains wholly transcendent. Even as he reveals his glory to Israel (Dt 5:24), he remains hidden, mysterious (Is 45:15). In antithesis to the disregard of pagan deities for what is beneath them, *Yahweh* is mindful of Israel, with the tenderness of a mother's love for her child (Is 49:15, 66:13). He is their personal and communal shepherd (Ps 23; Ez 34), rock (Ps 18:2; Is 17:10), refuge and shield (Ps 3:3, 27:1).

Yet his closeness to those who fear him involves no reduction of his greatness but always affirms his otherness. God has power over all he has made (Jb 12:7–25), does whatever he pleases (Ps 115:3), and is in no way subject to the constraints that limit the actions of creatures, such as frustration of will (Jb 42:2; Ps 135:5–7; Is 55:11) or weakness (Is 40:28; Jer 32:17). Responsive to the choices of men and women, still, in contrast to them, God does not change his mind but remains resolute in his determinations (Nm 23:9; Ps 110:4, 132:11; Ez 24:14). While the human heart and its secret thoughts are completely open to him (Ps 139:1–4, 12, 15), God's own thoughts and ways remain incomprehensible to human minds (Jb 42:3; Ps 139:6; Is 40:28). Even as he abides in the temple that cannot contain him (1 Kgs 8:27), God is enthroned above the heavens, and the earth is his footstool (Is 66:1). God is present everywhere (Ps 139:7–10; Jer 23:23–24), unchanging and everlasting in every age (Ps 90:1–4, 102:26–27), and blessed forever (Ps 41:13, 89:52, 106:48). Thus, while no other god than *Yahweh* acts so solicitously, yet in doing so *Yahweh* acts as he is, which is unlike all that he has made.

In summary, the God of the Old Testament is the only living God, before whom all other gods are naught (Is 34:18, 46:9), to whom nothing compares. ''Who is like the Lord our God, who is seated on high, who looks far down upon the heavens and the earth?'' (Ps 113:5–6). He is *Yahweh*, the one true God, maker of heaven and earth, Lord of all that he has made. Eternal, almighty, dwelling in the heavens, he chooses Israel as his own people, and delivers them from slavery to live his *Torah* in the land he promised their ancestors. Even as they fail to love the Lord alone and their neighbor in justice, the God of Israel remains true to his name, punishing iniquity while remaining merciful. In loving faithfulness he preserves a remnant of his people until the day when, in a new act of deliverance that establishes a universal and everlasting covenant, all nations will acknowledge, worship and obey the one true God.

NEW TESTAMENT

Continuity and Difference with the Old Testament. In the New Testament the God of the Old Testament is confessed in light of a new revelation and praised for a new work of salvation. Many passages make it clear that ''God'' designates the same one attested by the Scriptures and believed by the Jewish people (e.g., Mt 4:10; Mk 7:8; Jn 8:54; Rom 3:2). The Jewish faith is the foundation for the Christian, and the Scriptures of the former are essential to the latter, precisely because the same God acts in a way that reflects but also transcends what he did before. The God of the New Testament is the same God ''in whom [Abraham] believed, who gives life to the dead and calls into existence those things that do not exist'' (Rom 4:17). He is the ''living and true God'' distinct from all idols (1 Thes 1:9; Heb 3:12), the ''God of Israel'' who has fulfilled the promises he made to their ancestors by doing something amazing and scarcely to be believed (Acts 13:17–41).

All the key elements of the Old Testament theology of God are present (often operating to clarify who Christ is): the oneness of God (Jn 17:3; 1 Cor 8:4–6; Eph 4:6; Jude 25), God's holiness (Mt 6:9; Heb 12:10, 14, 29; 1 Pt 1:15–16), condemnation of idolatry (Acts 14:10–17, 15:29; 1 Cor 8:4–6; 1 Thes 1:9), God working wonders and delivering his people (Acts 2:22–36; Rom 6:15–23; Col 1:13–14; 1 Pt 1:18), the presence of God dwelling in the midst of his people (Jn 1:14, 2:21; 1 Cor 3:16–17; Rv 21:3), the theme of election (Lk 9:35; Eph 1:4; 1 Pt 1:2), the establishment of a covenant (Mt 26:26–28; Heb 9:11–28, 13:20), communal identity centered around the praise and worship of God (Acts 2:42–47; 1 Cor 11:23–32; Eph 5:18–20), a spiritual and moral way of life in accordance with the covenant (Mt 5–7; Col 3:1–4:6), divine judgment and punishment as a real possibility to be feared (Mt 13:40–42, 18:7–9; Mk 9:42–48; Rv 20:11–15), a still greater emphasis upon divine mercy (Jn 3:16–17; Rom 4:20–21; Ti 3:3–7; 1 Jn 3:19–22), and an eschatological hope for a final glory (Rom 8:22–25; 1 Cor 15:51–57). As before, the God who saves in time is also the God who creates, sustains and rules over all things as Lord of heaven and earth (1 Cor 1:15–20; Heb 2:10–11). Not only is God understood as remaining faithful to the covenantal promises made to the patriarchs and people of Israel (Rom 11:25–32), but all the promises put forth by the prophets of God's future work of salvation are understood as reaching fulfillment in the advent and life of Jesus Christ (Jn 19:28; 2 Cor 1:18–20). Indeed, a deep, inspired understanding of the Old Testament Scriptures is considered absolutely essential for understanding Christ and his mission (Lk 19:31, 24:27, 45; Jn 5:39, 45–47).

Yet the New Testament bears the additional influence of Greek modes of thought and expression, reflecting the language it was written in, the Greek translation of the Old Testament (LXX) it often quotes, and the cultural background of its main audience. In contrast to the Hebrew Scriptures, anthropomorphic and anthropopathic language is atypical (yet cf. Lk 11:20; Rom 1:18; Ti 3:4). The positive vitality of Old Testament descriptions of God are sometimes refined into simple negations of divine imperfections—e.g., ''the living God,'' ''whom no man can see and live,'' is ''immortal'' and ''invisible'' (Rom 1:20, 23; 1 Tm 1:17). The God enthroned on the clouds of heaven is ''the blessed and only Sovereign, the King of kings and Lord of lords, who alone has immortality and dwells in unapproachable light, whom no man has ever seen or can see'' (1 Tm 6:15–16). When familiarity with Old Testament history cannot be presumed, emphasis is given to the universal dominion of God the Creator and Savior (1 Cor 15:24–28; Eph 1:20–23), ''who desires all men to be saved and come to the knowledge of the truth'' (1 Tm 2:4). God is *Pantokrator*, the Almighty (2 Cor 6:18 [citing the LXX]; Rv 4:8), whose power and reign is expressed more generally and on a cosmic scale. ''For from him and through him and to him are all things'' (Rom 11:36). As the ''Alpha and Omega who is, and who was and who is to come, the Almighty'' (Rv 1:8), God ''accomplishes all things according to the counsel of his will'' (Eph 1:11; cf. Rom 8:28). The divine favor shown to the Gentiles is not part of the particular election of Israel, but the manifestation of a mystery hidden for all ages (Col 1:26), a plan of God from the foundation of the world to predestine them to glory (Rom 8:28–30; Eph 1:4; 2 Thes 2:13; 2 Tm 1:9). This appropriation of Greek modes of thought about God in the task of evangelization can be seen in Paul's sermon to the Athenians at the Areopagus: ''The God who made the world and everything in it, being Lord of heaven and earth, does not live in shrines made by man, nor is he served by human hands, as though he needed anything, since he himself gives to all men life and breath and everything. And he made from one every nation of men to live on all the face of the earth, having determined allotted periods and the boundaries of their habitation, that they should seek God, in the hope that they might feel after him and find him. Yet he is not far from each one of us, for, 'In him we live and move and have our being;' as even some of your poets have said, 'For we are indeed his offspring.' Being then God's offspring, we ought not to think that the Deity is like gold, or silver, or stone, a representation by the art and imagination of man . . .'' (Acts 17:24-29).

God as Father. Given this foundation in the Old Testament and context in the Greco-Roman world, the New Testament is entirely distinctive in its theology of God because of its confession of faith in Jesus Christ. The revelation of God in these Scriptures is grounded in the relationship that Jesus Christ has with God, and the work of salvation God accomplishes in and through him. While ''God'' (*theos*) is used a few times to refer to Jesus (Jn 1:1, 20:28; Rom 9:5; Ti 2:13; 1 Jn 5:20), ''the God'' (*ho theos*) is always used in reference to his Father; this usage is evidence that the primary meaning of ''God'' in the New Testament is ''Father.'' First and foremost, God is ''Father'' in relation to Jesus Christ, his Son. Paul especially speaks this way in his greetings: ''the God and Father of our Lord Jesus Christ'' (Rom 1:7; 1 Cor 1:3; Gal 1:3; Thes 1:1). ''Father'' is the most common appositive for God, and ''God'' alone or ''God the Father'' alternate in being frequently paired with ''Jesus Christ'' (Jn 17:3; 1 Cor 8:6; 2 Thes 2:16; 2 Tm 4:1). In the Johannine writings, ''the Father'' and ''the Son'' are indissolubly linked (Jn 5:19–23, 14:13; 1 Jn 1:3; cf. Mt 11:27). In an important secondary sense, dependent upon the first and which encapsulates the meaning of salvation in the New Testament, God is ''Father'' of all those who through faith in his Son become his children by the Holy Spirit (Rom 8:14–17; Gal 3:26). Hence, God is frequently named and invoked as ''God our Father'' (Mt 6:9; Eph 1:2; Col 1:2; Philm 3).

To understand the God of the New Testament, then, requires understanding both these meanings to God the Father. As much as the Old Testament theology of God is rooted in the meaning of *Yahweh*, so the theology of God in the New Testament centers on the meaning of ''God the Father.'' Again as before, the revelation of this most definitive name for God occurs through great works in history that bring about deliverance and salvation, albeit now universal and eternal in scope. The revelation of God as Father occurs in and through the life, death, resurrection, ascension, glorification of his Son, and his sending of Holy Spirit in the Father's name to make us children of the Father by grace. Moreover, as in the Old Testament too, the fullness of the divine mystery, while truly active and immanent in of salvation of his people, remains transcendent and irreducible throughout that great work. God saves as God is, which means that the temporal and finite conditions under which he saves us are not the conditions of his own eternal being.

Although ''Father'' as a designation of God is found in the Old Testament (Is 63:16; Tb 13:4; Sir 23:1, 4), it is not foundational or prevalent. God is ''Father'' for being the Creator and source of all life (Dt 32:6), and in terms of the election of Israel. The angels are ''sons of God'' because their life is directly from God (Gn 6:4; Dt 32:8; Ps 82:6). God is the ''Father of Israel'' (Jer 31:9), and Israel his ''son'' (Ex 4:22; Hos 11:1), not because he has sired them in any natural sense, but because of the covenant in which he claims them as his own, like a father adopting a child into his family, with all the responsibilities and blessings that accrue therefrom. This sense of God's Fatherhood, specific to the chosen people of Israel, continues in the New Testament (Rom 9:4, 11:29). Yet it is radically surpassed in regard to the identity of Jesus Christ, who is the Son of God (Mt 16:16; Mk 1:1; Rom 1:3–4), indeed the *only* Son of God (Jn 1:14, 18, 3:16, 18; 1 Jn 4:9). Though he is, like Israel, chosen (Lk 9:35, 23:35) and beloved (Mt 17:5; Col 1:13), more than this he alone is begotten by or born of God (Acts 13:33; Heb 1:5–6, 5:5; 1 Jn 3:9, 4:2, 5:1), chosen before the foundation of the world (1 Pt 1:20), and ''in the bosom of the Father'' (Jn 1:18).

The Father of Jesus. Foundational to the New Testament, therefore, is the unique relationship that exists between the Father and the Son, one that preexists before his becoming man, one that defines everything the incarnate Son does and says, and one that reigns in glory after his death and exaltation. The Father acts towards his Son in a distinctive manner, authorizing and empowering the Son through the Holy Spirit to act in the Father's name as the agent of our salvation. God the Father sends the Son into the world (Lk 4:43; Jn 6:29; Gal 4:4; 1 Jn 4:9–10), declares him to be his chosen beloved (Mt 12:18; Mk 1:11; Lk 20:13; 2 Pt 1:17), commands the Son what to do and say (Jn 5:36, 12:49–50, 14:31, 17:4, 8), gives all things to the Son (Mt 11:27; Jn 3:35, 13:3, 16:15) including all those who believe in him (Jn 6:44,17:2, 11), gives up his Son to death (Acts 2:22, 3:18; Rom 8:32), raises the Son from the dead (Acts 2:24, 10:40; Rom 10:9; Col 2:12), and glorifies him by seating him at his right hand in heaven (Jn 17:5; Acts 3:13; Eph 1:20; 1 Pt 1:21), thereby giving him perfect authority over all powers and peoples (Mt 18:18; 1 Cor 15:24–28; Phil 2:9–11; Eph 1:21, Col 2:10; 1 Pt 3:22), as well as all judgment (Mt 25:31–46; Jn 5:22–23, 27; 2 Cor 5:10).

Conversely, in relation to the Father the Son is said to be the perfect image and radiance of the Father's glory (2 Cor 4:4; Col 1:15; Heb 1:3), and the fullness of God dwells in him (Col 1:19, 2:9; cf. Jn 1:14; Eph 1:23; Phil 2:6). It is from his fullness that we receive the riches of his grace, life, truth and love (Jn 1:16–17; Phil 4:19; Col 2:9–10). Anointed in full with the Holy Spirit (Mk 1:10; Lk 4:1; Jn 3:34), Jesus reveals the Father whom he alone knows and sees (Lk 10:22; Jn 1:18, 6:46, 10:15). In a striking and unprecedented manner, Jesus addresses God as ''Abba,'' evocative of his great intimacy with one whom he spent long hours in prayer (Lk 5:16, 6:12, 11:1). To express the uniqueness of his relation to God, he says, ''my Father'' (Mt 7:21, 10:32–33), while to his disciples he says, ''your Father'' (Mt 5:16, 45); never does he collectively say with them, ''our Father'' (Jn 20:17). The Father and Son are so inseparably conjoined (Jn 10:30), that to accept and receive the Son is to accept and receive the Father (Lk 9:48; Jn 13:20), to deny or reject the Son is to deny or reject the Father (Lk 10:16; 1 Jn 2:22–23, 5:10–11). In short, one's relationship to God is in and through one's relationship with Jesus Christ, for ''through him we have access in one Spirit to the Father (Eph 2:18; cf. 2 Cor 1:20). ''For there is one God, and there is one mediator between God and men, the man Christ Jesus, who gave himself as a ransom for all'' (1 Tm 2:5–6).

In his teaching, especially the Sermon on the Mount, Jesus expresses who God the Father is. God the Father is in heaven (Mt 6:9, 18:14), enthroned (Mt 5:34; Rv 7:10), in secret (Mt 6:6, 18), Lord of heaven and earth (Mt 11:25). The Father is perfect and holy (Mt 5:48, 6:9; 1 Pt 1:15–16), for whom all things are possible (Mk 14:36; cf. 9:23), and nothing impossible (Lk 1:37). God the Father, who knows everything (1 Jn 3:20) because everything is open and laid bare before him (Heb 4:13), even the hearts of men (Acts 1:24; Rom 8:27), knows what we need before we ask him (Mt 6:8, 32). The Father knows how to give good things to his children, and thus can be trusted to provide for daily needs (Mt 6:25–34), give abundantly for every good work (2 Cor 9:8), and to reward what is done for love of him (Mt 6:6, 18). ''If you then, who are evil, know how to give good gifts to your children, how much more will the heavenly Father give the Holy Spirit to those who ask him!'' (Lk 11:13).

God alone is good (Mt 19:17; Lk 18:19; Jas 1:5), blessed (1 Tm 1:11, 6:15), even ''kind to the ungrateful and the selfish'' (Lk 6:35), making his sun to rise and his rain to fall on the just and the unjust (Mt 5:45). Jesus' miracles of healing ''the lame, the maimed, the blind, the dumb, and many others'' (Mt 15:30) reveal that the Father is compassionate (Lk 6:36). Jesus' eating with tax collectors and forgiving the repentant (Mt 9:9–13; Lk 7:36–50) demonstrate that God is forgiving (Mt 6:14; Mk 11:25). Indeed, the Father is superlatively merciful (Lk 1:72, 78, 6:36; 2 Cor 1:3; Eph 2:4; Ti 3:5; 1 Pt 1:3), and the source of grace, mercy and peace (1 Tm 1:2; 2 Jn 3; Jude 2). He is patient with sinners (Rom 2:4; 2 Pt 3:9), desiring that all repent and come to salvation, unwilling that any should perish (Mt 18:14; 1 Tm 2:4; 2 Pt 3:9). Still, he is to be feared because he ''has the power to cast into hell'' (Lk 12:4–5; 1 Pt 2:17). Most of all, the Father is gracious (Mt 11:26), for it pleases him to give the greatest gift: ''Fear not, little flock, for it is your Father's good pleasure to give you the kingdom'' (Lk 12:32). In sum, there is simply nothing that we have that we have not received from God our Father (1 Cor 4:7), for ''every good endowment and every perfect gift is from above, coming down from the Father of lights with whom there is no variation or shadow due to change'' (Jas 1:17).

The Father of All. In his passion and death Jesus reveals the depths of his Father's generous love and mercy. Divine love for men and women in danger of perishing in death is the motive for the sending of the Son (Jn 3:16), and his sacrifice for the unworthy the fitting manifestation of the depth of that love: ''God shows his love for us in that while we were yet sinners Christ died for us'' (Rom 5:8; Eph 2:4–7). ''In this the love of God was made manifest among us, that God sent his only Son into the world, so that we might live through him. In this is love, not that we loved God but that he loved us and sent his Son to be the expiation for our sins'' (1 Jn 4:9–10). In this way the ''God of love'' (2 Cor 13:11) reveals himself to be love itself: ''God is love, and he who abides in love abides in God, and God abides in him'' (1 Jn 4:16). The sacrificial suffering and death of Jesus is thus the definitive divine act expressing the mystery of God and his immeasurable love for the human race. Upon this ''rock'' (cf. 1 Cor 10:4) lies the Christian faith and hope in God which cannot disappoint (Rom 5:1–11; Heb 11:1). It is a love which no tribulation or power can overcome (Rom 8:31–39), which promises all good things: ''He who did not spare his own Son but gave him up for us all, will he not also give us all things with him?'' (Rom 8:32; cf. Eph 1:3).

Through Jesus' suffering and death, the Father, the ''God of peace'' (Rom 15:33; Phil 4:9; 1 Thes 5:23), reconciles the world to himself (2 Cor 5:19; Col 1:20), and all peoples to one another (Eph 2:13). ''God our Savior'' (1 Tm 1:1; Ti 1:3, 2:11; cf. Lk 1:47) has freed men and women from the reign or power of sin and death (Rom 8:2), ransomed them from a futile way of living (1 Pt 1:18), and in the end, will deliver them from death and bodily corruption (Rom 7:24; 1 Cor 15:53–57; 2 Cor 5:4–5). This work of salvation is accomplished in us by the Holy Spirit, ''the promise of the Father'' (Lk 24:49), sent by the glorified Jesus exalted at the right hand of the Father (Jn 7:39, 16:7; Acts 2). ''God's love has been poured into our hearts through the Holy Spirit which has been given us'' (Rom 5:5). Through the Holy Spirit believers are able to cry, ''Abba, Father,'' for as the ''spirit of sonship'' he makes us children of God, fellow heirs with Christ (Rom 8:14–17). Through the Holy Spirit abiding in us the Father of Jesus Christ is truly our Father as well, who in the gift of the Spirit pledges his promised inheritance to his children (Rom 8:17; 2 Cor 1:21–22; Gal 3:18, 29; 1 Pt 1:3–5), nothing less than the a sharing in the eternal glory of his Son (Jn 17; Rom 8:29–30), a graced participation in the divine nature itself (2 Pt 1:4). ''See what love the Father has given us, that we should be called children of God; and so we are . . . Beloved, we are God's children now; it does not yet appear what we shall be, but we know that when he appears we shall be like him, for we shall see him as he is.'' (1 Jn 3:1–2).

To truly know God as Father and be his child requires living the commandment of his Son to love others (Jn 13:34–35, 15:8–17; Rom 13:8–10; 1 Jn 4:7; 5:1–2), and thus imitate the Son of the Father. ''By this we know love, that he laid down his life for us; and we ought to lay down our lives for the brethren'' (1 Jn 3:16, 4:11). Those who despise their neighbor cannot be said to be children of the loving Father, for it is impossible to know and to love God unless one love and serve others (1 Jn 4:8, 20–21). Because Jesus is the definitive revelation and saving work of God, the response must be wholehearted, transforming the mind (Rom 12:1), and bearing fruit in good works (Gal 5:13–25). ''Only let your manner of life be worthy of the gospel of Christ'' (Phil 1:27). The calling is from repentance (Mk 1:15; Lk 13:1–9; 2 Cor 7:10) to the Father's perfection (Mt 5:48; Eph 5:1; Heb 12:23), to be holy, by the power of the Holy Spirit, as God is holy (2 Cor 7:1; 1 Pt 1:16). Since ''our God is a consuming fire'' (Heb 12:29; cf. 1 Cor 3:12–15), nothing less than absolute purity of heart and freedom from all sin is required for the children of the Father to see God and enter into his glory (Mt 5:8; Heb 12:14).

For this purpose, our loving Father treats us as his children when he chastises and ''disciplines us for our good, that we may share in his holiness'' (Heb 12:7, 10). Suffering and trials, persecution and the world's rejection, are to be expected of followers of the Son whose destiny was the cross (Mt 5:11, 16:21–28; Jn 15:18–21). Suffering purifies faith (1 Pt 1:6–7, 4:1–2, 12–16), for through the trial of affliction humbly accepted one places God the Father's will over one's own (Mk 14:36; 1 Pt 4:1–2). Since ''all who desire to lead a godly life in Christ Jesus will be persecuted'' (2 Tm 3:16), suffering is the great opportunity to follow the Son in trusting in the goodness of the Father, by repaying evil with good (Mt 5:28–42; Rom 12:14–21), forgiving, blessing and praying for one's enemies (Mt 5:43–48; Mk 11:25), and rejoicing that one's reward from the Father will be great (Mt 5:12; Jn 16:33; Jas 1:2–3). ''Therefore let those who suffer according to God's will do right and entrust their souls to a faithful Creator'' (1 Pt 4:19). God, who protects and guards those who believe (1 Pt 1:5), will sustain them with a peace that surpasses all understanding (Phil 4:7; cf. Jn 14:27), for he is the ''God of steadfastness and encouragement'' (Rom 15:5). And after having tested them through temptation or suffering, God ''will restore, establish and strengthen'' his children (1 Pt 5:10; cf. Mt 4:11).

The Father is worthy of such trust because ''God is light and in him is no darkness at all'' (1 Jn 1:5). Though no one can know the mind of the Lord for no one can counsel him (1 Cor 2:16, quoting Is 40:13), his judgments are just and true (Rv 16:7, 19:2), and he judges impartially (1 Pt 1:17). ''O the depth of the riches and wisdom and knowledge of God! How unsearchable are his judgments and how inscrutable are his ways!'' (Rom 11:33). He alone is wise (Rom 16:27), and he is incapable of deceit, for lying and being proved false are impossible for him (Ti 1:2; Heb 6:18). God is faithful (1 Cor 1:9; 2 Cor 1:18; Heb 10:23), and even when we are faithless, ''he remains faithful, for he cannot deny himself'' (2 Ti 2:13; cf. Rom 3:3). Therefore, even in the experience of anguish and tragedy one is called to trust and ''know that in everything God works for good with those who love him, who are called according to his purpose'' (Rom 8:28). We ''must consider that the sufferings of this present time are not worth comparing with the glory that is to be revealed in us'' (Rom 8:18), ''an eternal weight of glory beyond all comparison'' (2 Cor 4:17). We must be patient and hope for what is beyond our understanding: '''what no eye has seen, nor ear heard, nor the heart of man conceived, what God has prepared for those who love him''' (1 Cor 2:9, quoting Is 64:4). In the end, God, ''the Father of mercies and of all comfort'' (2 Cor 1:3–4, 6:6), ''will wipe away every tear'' and ''make all things new'' (Rv 21:4–5).

In summary, the God of the New Testament is revealed to be the Father of an only Son, Jesus Christ, whose life, death and glorification manifest the Father's great love for us. God is also Father of those redeemed by his Son, and this relationship is realized in us by the work of the Holy Spirit, who makes us children of the Father in the Son. The word ''Father'' expresses simultaneously that God is the source and destination of all things, the authority over all things, the merciful and compassionate provider for every good, and the giver of an eternal and glorious inheritance to his children. The greatness of his love for us means that God does not in this life deliver us from suffering, but saves us through suffering, so that the perfection of the Father's love for all and the Son's self-denial for others may be realized in us. This God cannot be truly known or rightly understood apart from the experience and living of the salvation won for us. And yet because this salvation is the Father's eternal plan accomplished by his Son and Spirit sent from heaven, God acts for us as God truly is in his own mystery. Therefore, the God of the New Testament, though nearly always addressed simply as ''Father,'' is indeed the one God with the single name of ''Father, Son and Holy Spirit'' (Mt 28:19).

Bibliography: W. KASPER, *The God of Jesus Christ*, tr. M. J. O'CONNELL (New York 1997). L. KÖHLER, *Old Testament Theology*, tr. A. S. TODD (Philadelphia 1957). K. RAHNER, ''*Theos* in the New Testament,'' *Theological Investigations*, v. 1, tr. C. ERNST (Baltimore 1961) 79–148. E. L. MASCALL, *He Who Is: A Study in Traditional Theism* (London 1962). R. SOKOLOWSKI, *The God of Faith and Reason: Foundations of Christian Theology* (Washington, D.C. 1982, 1995). G. WAINWRIGHT, *Doxology: The Praise of God in Worship, Doctrine and Life: A Systematic Theology* (New York 1980). T. G. WEINANDY, *Does God Change? The Word's Becoming in the Incarnation* (Still River, Mass. 1985). T. E. FRETHEIM, *The Suffering of God: An Old Testament Perspective* (Philadelphia 1976). J. LAMBRECHT and R. COLLINS, eds., *God and Human Suffering* (Louvain 1990).

[M. A. HOONHOUT]

2. In Christian Tradition

The formation of an intellectually mature concept of God is one of the principal goals of theology. This notion has been the fruit of a long evolution of human reason seeking to understand divinely revealed truths. The evidences of this progress and development are present in the writings of the Fathers and ecclesiastical authors as well as in the formal statements of the Church. This development occurs within a process where the subject and methodology of theology itself, as well as the philosophical wisdom it employs, evolves and changes. While this growth in understanding is organic, building upon the achievements of earlier generations, still, it is not without regression—over time there occur various failures to maintain the multi-faceted fullness of who and what the God of Christian faith is. Thus one must attend to the overall dynamics of each era that shapes and limits the way the one, enduring Christian faith in God is explained theologically. This section will trace this development through four distinct periods: patristic, medieval or scholastic, modern, and contemporary, as it focuses upon the growing understanding of God's attributes and existence, his relation to the world, and in what sense his ineffable mystery can be understood and expressed by us.

The Patristic Period. In the early centuries the Church had the double task of transposing the Hebraic, biblical portrait of God to fit the cultural mindset of the Greco-Roman world and defending the faith against external criticisms and internal corruptions. While remaining devoted to and grounded in the revelation of the Sacred Scriptures, early Christian writers appropriated the reasoned wisdom of Greek philosophy as they engaged in controversies with Judaism, paganism, and heretical alterations of Christian belief. The polemics of the time required both clear presentations and forceful arguments, and it is not surprising that the most literate and able apologists for the faith often had learning in classical philosophy and rhetoric. At this point faith is seeking primarily the understanding needed to refute the criticisms put against the faith. Because the philosophy used in these first theological endeavors was for the most part that of Plato (ORIGEN and AUGUSTINE) and NEOPLATONISM (PSEUDO-DIONYSIUS), the mystery of God was primarily expressed in essentialist terms. This usage, however, was not uncritical, for naïve appropriations of philosophical ideas judged to compromise the revelation of God always merited vigorous opposition by the Church fathers.

In the first few centuries of the Church, Christian writers such as the apologists had much to do in defending the monotheism, and thus the overall integrity, of the Christian faith. Against Jewish critics and in a wider climate of pagan polytheism they had to refute the charge that Christians believed in three gods. Against the dualism of gnosticism which disparaged the material creation, they had to affirm that creation and salvation are the work of the one God revealed in both Testaments. Emphasis is given to the one monarchy of God, ruling over all things. Thus the creeds of the Church begin the confession of the faith by declaring the one God is *Pantokrator*, the Almighty, who redeems and restores that which he made. To counter widespread belief in fate and astrology, the Church fathers spoke of the divine economy of salvation and the mystery of divine providence—God's *pronoia* or foresight to order all things so that his plan for creation is accomplished. In God they knew of a hope beyond fatalism, and emphasized human responsibility against those who used the alignment of celestial bodies or the existence of evil gods as excuses for immoral behavior.

Early patristic literature was content to describe God by his attributes of omnipotence, goodness, and mercy—i.e., those which God must have to be the one Author of creation and salvation. At this stage little attempt was made at transforming the metaphorical language of the Scriptures themselves. The first conciliar creeds (Nicene and First Constantinople) reflect this language in their simple affirmation of divine unity, omnipotence, and causality (H. Denziger, *Enchiridion symbolorum,* 32nd ed. 125, 150). But by the fourth century there is evidence of both wider investigation and more penetrating analysis into God's nature and the proper expression of it. Both Eastern and Western fathers, writing in Greek and Latin respectively, worked towards a purification of thought regarding the understanding of God. The eternity of God beyond all change comes to the fore, and more abstract language regarding the perfection of the divine essence in itself becomes more common. This is in large part owing to the controversies with Arius and Eunomius. The Arian controversy required the Church to unequivocally declare the absolute equality of the three divine persons, and thus their possession in common of one eternal divine substance or nature. Whatever transcendent, essential qualities that had tended to be reserved to God the Father (*ho theos*)—eternity, unknowability, absolute unity and supremacy—now passed to the divine nature according to the demands of *homoousios*. In contrast to Eunomius who taught that the divine essence could be adequately comprehended, orthodox theologians stressed the utter mysteriousness and ineffability of God's nature, a position confirmed in the later creedal statements (D.S. 294, 501).

In order to speak of the eternal mystery of God and not betray his incomprehensibility Christian thinkers contrasted God with the world that he made, using terms of negation that excluded from the divine nature the conditions and limitations that mark our existence. Creatures suffer, but God is impassible; creatures die, but God is immortal, etc. Theologians also took the various positive qualities or faculties present in the world and applied them to God in a supreme manner: an elder may be wise, but God is supremely wise; a king may be powerful, but God is all powerful. Now it is natural to give special prominence to one aspect above all others that is most uniquely true of God, the quality proper to him whereby he is distinguished from all other beings. In the light of the revelation of God's name in Ex 3:14, the Fathers considered existence to be that which is most characteristic of him. EPHREM THE SYRIAN, commented, ''by this one exclusive name [God] let it be known that he alone is Being, which can be said of no other'' (*Adversus haereses serm.*; Assemani ed. 2:555, cf. *Enchiridion patristicum* 729). After reading the words of this passage Hilary of Poitiers confessed that:

> I was amazed to find in them an indication concerning God so exact that it expressed in the terms best adapted to human understanding an unattainable insight into the mystery of the Divine nature. For no property of God which the mind can grasp is more characteristic of Him than existence, since existence, in the absolute sense, cannot be predicated of that which shall come to an end, or of that which has had a beginning, and He who now joins continuity of being with the possession of perfect felicity could not in the past, nor can in the future, be non-existent; for whatsoever is Divine can neither be originated nor destroyed. Wherefore, since God's eternity is inseparable from Himself, it was worthy of Him to reveal this one thing, *that He is*, as the assurance of His absolute eternity. (*De Trinitate* 1.5; *Patrologia Latina* 10:28)

Recognizing the parallels between the God of revelation and the God of the philosophers and scholars, Augustine too was intrigued that God revealed his name as a declaration of his existence. Reflecting on this passage from Scripture he wrote, ''perhaps it ought to be said that God alone is essence. For He alone truly is, because He is unchangeable, and it is this He declared to Moses, His servant, when He said, 'I am who am''' (*De Trinitate* 7.5.10; *Patrologia Latina* 42:942). In Augustine's judgment the name ''I Am'' is best translated by the abstract term essence, meaning above all else, God's perfect immutability. If God is *that which* is then God is beyond the flux of coming into and passing out of existence, and to be contrasted with all things that have their existence from him:

> I considered all the other things that are of a lower order than yourself, and I saw that they have not absolute being in themselves, nor are they entirely

> without being. They are real in so far as they have their being from you, but unreal in the sense that they are not what you are. For it is only that which remains in being without change that truly is. (*Confessions* VII, 11)

While Augustine clearly recognized the incomprehensibility of God's being, he also labored to correct misconceptions of God's mystery, remembering from his own experience the tendency to apply spatial and temporal categories to our thinking about God. With the help of philosophy he had come to realize that what is immaterial is more genuinely real, true and good, and from the sorrows of loving the mutable good of fleeting pleasures and friends who had passed away, he learned the attractiveness of the beauty which cannot fade and the good that cannot be lost. It is important to appreciate, therefore, that Augustine stressed divine immutability because it ensured the incomparable desirability of God's goodness. As the unchanging Good, the "Beauty ever ancient, Beauty ever new" (*Confessions* X, 27), God alone could be sought as the true light and love of the human mind and heart, the one alone in whom our restless hearts can finally find peace. God's immaterial greatness means he must always be pursued because he cannot be comprehended, while his immutability guarantees that he cannot disappoint when he is finally beheld in glory. "Eternal Truth, true Love, beloved Eternity—all this, my God, you are, and it is to you that I sigh by night and day" (*Confessions*, VII, 10). In this way God serves to anchor all human aspirations and pursuits, in that he alone is to be enjoyed and loved for his own sake. In turn, all other things are to be used only insofar as they help one attain the enjoyment of God, and all other persons loved only for the sake of the love of God. "For he is the best man who turns his whole life toward the immutable life and adheres to it with all his affection" (*De Doctrina Christiana*, I, 22).

A representative expression of the understanding of God found in the thought of the Fathers can be found in this quotation from Augustine, one which underscores that in all that God is and does for his creatures he remains perfect and unchanging in his transcendent greatness:

> What, then, is the God I worship? He can be none but the Lord God himself, for *who but the Lord is God? What other refuge can there be, except our God?* (Ps 18:31). You, my God, are supreme, utmost in goodness, mightiest and all-powerful, most merciful and most just. You are the most hidden from us and yet the most present amongst us, the most beautiful and yet the most strong, ever enduring and yet we cannot comprehend you. You are unchangeable and yet you change all things. You are never new, never old, and yet all things have new life from you. You are the unseen power that brings decline upon the proud. You are ever active, yet always at rest. You gather all things to yourself, though you suffer no need. You support, you fill, and you protect all things. You create them, nourish them, and bring them to perfection. You seek to make them your own, though you lack for nothing. You love your creatures, but with a gentle love. You treasure them, but without apprehension. You grieve for wrong, but suffer no pain. You can be angry and yet serene. Your works are varied, but your purpose is one and the same. You welcome all who come to you, though you never lost them. You are never in need yet are glad to gain, never covetous yet you exact a return for your gifts. We give abundantly to you so that we may deserve a reward; yet which of us has anything that does not come from you? You repay us what we deserve, and yet you owe nothing to any. You release us from our debts, but you lose nothing thereby. You are my God, my Life, my holy Delight, but is this enough to say of you? Can any man say enough when he speaks of you? Yet woe betide those who are silent about you! For even those who are most gifted with speech cannot find words to describe you. (*Confessions* I, 3)

The Medieval Period. The medieval period of Western Christianity sees the emergence of theology as a distinct field of study with its own highly developed methodology. Whereas within the patristic period development in theological understanding is closely connected with the process of clarifying the faith against heretical distortions, development in the Scholastic period is free to be more purely speculative, the pursuit of theological understanding and subtler distinctions for their own sake. Like the early Fathers, the great medieval theologians continue to write commentaries on Scripture, but this primary responsibility is at first supplemented with, and only much later supplanted by, the task of writing highly organized summaries of theology. The systemization of scholastic theology began with Peter Lombard who collected and arranged by topic biblical and patristic statements on the diverse elements of the faith. His *Sentences* set off a new application of dialectical reasoning, in which seemingly contradictory statements from different sources were reconciled according to higher, more distinguished, viewpoints. In the process a method of discussion evolved: an article of faith was broken down into a series of questions, an authority quoted supporting the proper conclusion, counter-arguments arrayed against it, an answer developed elaborating the principles at stake, and refutations of the objections given. Through the theological influence of Augustine and Pseudo-Dionysius, theology continues to depend upon Platonic and neo-Platonic philosophical ideas for its expression. Yet at this time theology begins to make use of the philosophy of Aristotle, and through the exemplary achievement of THOMAS AQUINAS his metaphysics will provide the standard explanatory categories employed by Catholic theology for centuries to follow.

The *Sentences* of PETER LOMBARD begins with the mystery of God, discussing the one divine nature and the three divine persons together. As his ordering of the subject matter of theology came to be improved upon, these different aspects of our knowledge of the one divine mystery came to be delineated into two distinct treatises. In part this was justified as a better way to handle the material; another justification was that the delineation made clear what could be known by the demonstrations of reason, and what could be known only by revelation. The discussion of the divine nature, which concerns us here, focused upon the attributes and operations of that nature which express why God is wholly other than all things in this world. As the Fourth LATERAN COUNCIL of 1215 confessed, ''We firmly believe and profess without qualification that there is only one true God, eternal, immense, unchangeable, incomprehensible, omnipotent, and indescribable, the Father, the Son, and the Holy Spirit; three Persons but one essence, substance, or nature that is wholly simple'' (H. Denziger, *Enchiridion symbolorum,* 800). Other essential attributes include his goodness, beatitude and omnipresence, while perfections of his eternal operations of knowing and willing include his omniscience and wisdom, and the benevolence, justice, mercy and absolute efficacy of his will. These affirmations about God say as much about our inability to comprehend God's essence as they truly point to what God must be, for they are put forth with an awareness of how we may properly speak of God. What the early Fathers practiced often implicitly is now itself discussed and made explicit: all human knowledge of God, whether by way of reason or by faith, is analogical: whatever perfections found in creation are present in God in a manner that completely transcends all limitations in creation, including the way we understand them. ANALOGY affirms a positive correspondence of what is true and good in creation to its Maker, for it can only reflect its Source, while maintaining a much stronger denial: no thing in creation or concept in human understanding is in any way comparable to God, who is not delimited in any way. Again the Fourth Council of Lateran: ''between Creator and creature there can be found no similarity in which an even greater dissimilarity cannot be found'' (H. Denziger, *Enchiridion symbolorum,* 806).

The key difference between the perfections of creatures and that of God is not intensity of degree, as if creatures and Creator could be placed in the same scale of proportion. Rather, the difference lies in God's absolute simplicity. Whereas perfections like wisdom and goodness in a creature are qualities that enhance, and thus are added to, its basic constitution, wisdom and goodness in God are identical to the whole of his very essence, for he cannot but be perfectly wise and good. Therefore, God does not have a quality that makes him wise or good; rather, God is his wisdom and God is his goodness. The one and indivisible God is his every perfection. Although we must distinguish every attribute in God from every other because our minds can grasp only what has been delineated, in the divine mystery, every perfection we name is in the reality of God absolutely and simply identical to God himself. God is mercy and God is justice, and because it is his essence to be both perfect and simple, his mercy is his justice and his justice his mercy. What in human situations are often irreconcilable opposites are in God one mystery without requiring any reconciliation or dilution.

Theological refinement of the understanding of God advanced by the double process of removing all imperfections from the divine essence (the way of remotion), and by affirming the incomparable manner in which God simply is his every perfection (the way of eminence). For ANSELM OF CANTERBURY, this process of correcting and uplifting our thoughts about God is expressed in his judgment that God is *aliquid quo maius nihil cogitari potest*—that than which nothing greater can be thought. In addition to serving in his demonstration that God must exist or else he would not exceed the best we can think of him, this principle inspired a theological pursuit of the reasons we can surmise why God has revealed himself and saved us as he has. Since theology is faith seeking understanding, Anselm strived to show, for example, how the humiliation of God in becoming man and dying on the cross does not disparage but is indeed in perfect accordance with God's transcendent greatness. Other theologians influenced by Anselm would probe divine mysteries further.

For Thomas Aquinas, the utter simplicity and fullness of perfection that is the divine essence are also central to his theological presentation of God's mystery. Demonstrating God's existence, not from the idea of God as with Anselm, but from the insufficiency of created reality to explain why anything exists, is good, and acts in an orderly fashion, Thomas concludes that only as the simple, pure act of existence itself can God be the true cause of all that is. His judgment is that God is *ipsum esse subsistens*—subsistent existence itself—utterly without composition, potency or imperfection since any of these conditions would render God in need of something greater to perfect him (*Summa theologiae*, I, q. 3, a. 4). ''Existence'' here is not a quality or even a state but the dynamic act of *be-ing*—''what God is'' is that he *is*. Like the Fathers before him, St. Thomas appealed to the revelation of God's name in Ex 3:14 to confirm this demonstration of reason.

> God's essence is therefore His act of being. Now this sublime truth God taught Moses, when Moses asked what to reply if the children of Israel should ask His name. Thus He showed that His proper name is ''Who is.'' Now every name is intended to signify the nature or essence of something. It remains then that the divine act of being itself [*ipsum esse divinum*] is the essence or nature of God. (*Summa Contra Gentiles*, Bk I, 22)

The judgment that God's essence is ''active existing'' functions as the foundational premise for the rest of Thomas' theology. First of all, it is the touchstone for all theological judgments about what is and is not true about God. Every perfection is contained simply and every limitation excluded absolutely in the *Is* that God is. Secondly, it sets God apart from all else, for everything created is a composition of its essence (what it is) and its existence (that it is). God alone *is* existence itself; all created things *have* existence. In contrast to God who is *ipsum esse per se subsistens*, creatures have *esse per participationem*—existence by a direct participation in God's own existence (*Summa theologiae* I, q. 44, a. 1). Thirdly, since God is pure Act, he actively relates to creation in the most dynamic manner conceivable, and creation is nothing apart from the continuous extension of God's Act to it. It is true that Thomas repeatedly affirms that God has no ''real relation'' to creation (*Summa theologiae* I, q. 6, a. 2, ad 1; q. 28, a. 1, ad 3; q. 45, a. 3, ad 1)—meaning that it is not necessary for God to create in order to be truly God. Yet the whole of his thought is suffused with the active presence of God operating in, through and with all things, for to Aquinas the subject of theology concerns God and all things in their relation to God as their origin and end (*Summa theologiae* I, q. 2, a. 7). Even as he labors to express more than any other theologian before him the integrity and causal responsibility of the natural order, he always sees all things in their fundamental dependence upon God's active *esse*. Given that Thomas consciously developed the systematic order of the *Summa theologiae* so that primacy is given to that which is most fundamental and consequential, the entire discussion begins with God so that all things distinct from God can be understood as always inherently and necessarily related to God.

With Thomas there occurs a fundamental shift in theological thinking, away from an essentialist understanding of God and things which tends to see created reality primarily as symbolic representations of the divine essence, to a metaphysical approach that emphasizes the existence and causality of things as instruments of God's agency. Thomas puts to wide-ranging theological use the different kinds of causality outlined in Aristotle's metaphysics in order to give expression to how God actively relates to his creation. God is the First, Exemplary and Final Cause of all that is: the universal Cause of all causes, the one Exemplar of all diverse forms and perfections, and the ultimate End to which all things tend. Every existence, every nature, every action, every good pursued is such because of its created participation in God. Created reality proceeds forth from God the Creator endowed with natural capabilities which make them genuinely coresponsible for the perfecting of the universe under the direction of God's providence. Human beings, through the further perfection of God's grace, are called to the redemption and perfection of their nature in their living, knowing and loving, so that through them, creation returns to God. Since God is *Act*, the world and the human are dynamically conceived: the realization of creation's perfection and human salvation is a matter of acting well, and in the end the final state of the glorified is the perfect activity of knowing and loving God in the beatific vision.

Thomas has been appropriately described as a theologian of the Creator, since everything in his thought is always considered as so radically related to and dependent upon God's agency, even as created nature is acknowledged to be distinct and integral in its own existence and operation. His use of ARISTOTLE was controversial at the time, however, not just because it moved beyond the neo-Platonism of Augustinian theology, but especially because some Christian thinkers were using Aristotle to demonstrate that the world was eternal and necessary. Ironically, the philosophy Thomas used to give deeper expression to the meaning of the relationship of creation to God came under ecclesial condemnation for denying the gratuitous non-necessity of the creation. These censures and their emphasis upon the Creator's freedom and omnipotence to make all things as he pleased contributed to the rise of nominalism. This was a late medieval mode of thought that in theology preserved the transcendent freedom of the Creator at the expense of his other attributes—namely, the wisdom and goodness of God to act providentially and purposefully through the created natural order. Thinkers like WILLIAM OF OCKHAM gave such theological precedence to God's absolute will and power to do anything that little could be said about the character of God from the nature of things, since God could just have easily made all things differently than he did. This loss of a proper theology of the Creator and his providence would have a deleterious effect in the ensuing periods as the relation of the world to God came to be such a crucial issue with the rise of modern science.

In organizing the subject matter of theology into a discipline, scholastic theology of the Medieval period tended to discuss God and the works of God not in the historical order of the economy of salvation, but in a systematic or synthetic order in which terms and topics are related to one another. The dialectical reasoning and the metaphysical framework gave precision in defining and relating theological doctrines for the sake of clarity in understanding. A natural consequence of its abstract, universal and technical language was that it was hardly suited to express the immediacy and vitality of the experiential, concrete and historical through which God is encountered. Since its rational investigation of the divine mystery always presupposed the foundational necessity of faith and never claimed to comprehend the ineffable God, scholastic theology in no way replaced the God of revelation with the God of philosophy. Even as the task of interpreting Scripture remained the primary responsibility of the medieval theologian, theology sought not to reiterate the historical manifestation of God in the economy of salvation but to explicate the attributes and operations of God such an economy presupposes.

The Modern Period. The period from the Reformation to the First VATICAN COUNCIL at the end of the nineteenth century sees a gradual break-up of the medieval synthesis, as new discoveries and new questions lead to fundamental revisions in how the world, society and the human individual are conceived. In an era that saw the loss of the religious unity of western society, the emergence of the modern scientific understanding of nature, and the development of nation states, political rights, and the industrial economy, the centrality and universality of God for the understanding of the world and the human weakens over time. The emergence of secular society and atheistic totalitarian states by the twentieth century will be due in large part to a growing opposition between reason and faith and a more autonomous understanding of the world and human existence. Over time the idea of God becomes a ''problem'' for intellectuals who have difficulty considering revelation as anything more than a primitive, man-made conception of God, and who deny human reason the ability to know anything definitive about God, including whether he exists.

In the heritage left by NOMINALISM, it is not surprising that major Reformation writers like Martin LUTHER and John CALVIN have little place in their thought for a theology of creation. In their defense of the utter gratuity of salvation they tended to exalt God over and against natural causality, with the God of revelation placed in opposition to the God of philosophy and the life of grace opposed to the life of natural virtue. Luther was dismissive of the contribution Aristotle or philosophy could make to theology, and sought to develop a purely Scriptural *theologia crucis* which in its focus upon the paradox and foolishness of the crucified God overturned the *theologia gloriae* of scholastic theology. For Calvin, the sovereignty of God, divine honor and glory, and the determinations of his will are central to his theology. Providence is not the Creator working through and with creatures so that they might act for the greater good, but God acting arbitrarily either with, without or even against natural means in order to manifest his sovereign glory (*Institutes of the Christian Religion*, Bk 3, 17). The clear opposition in Reformation thought between grace and nature, faith and reason reflects an assumption that affirmations of the created good come at the expense of God's greatness. The ''world'' in their thinking is not the goodness of God's creation, but another sense found in Scripture: the world as ''all that is opposed to God.''

From its beginnings and throughout much of its progress modern science was the achievement of men who were quite religious in their thinking. They saw nature as the creative work of God, and studying it as a way to know the ways of God. Yet their tendency to conceive of nature as inert matter subject to mechanical forces ordered by absolute, universal and immutable laws ultimately fostered a worldview in which the historical actions of the personal God of the Scriptures could only be an alien interference. As science endeavored more and more to explain all reality with totally natural explanations, the universe came to be understood as a closed system, the cosmos a giant mechanism of rigidly determined outcomes, with God's role reduced simply to setting things up. This was the God of deism, and as science advanced further and found the origins of the universe and life to be different than that of the biblical account, nature came to be seen as the only necessary and reliable ''revelation'' of God. Miracles were denied outright not only because the biblical accounts could not be trusted in their historical accuracy or understanding of nature, but also because they were seen only as violations of the laws of nature, reflecting badly on God the perfect engineer and lawgiver. Even though the theories and discoveries of twentieth-century science led to a correction of the closed, mechanical worldview of early science, there survives the propensity to limit reality only to what is material (i.e., natural materialism) and knowledge only to what science can demonstrate (i.e., positivism or scientism). Gradually the cosmos loses its sacred character, as science no longer considers it to be the creation authored by a personal God, the arena in which God is providentially active, and the symbol and image of a greater, heavenly reality that is the true home for the human spiritual animal. Religion and science come to be seen as opposed or irrelevant to one another, to the detriment of both.

Parallel to the development of modern science is the emergence of modern philosophy which again at first was the work of believers but contained within it principles that tended toward atheism. Modern philosophy was concerned most of all with epistemological questions and politics, and in both a dualism develops between what is rational and what is religious. God was central to the thought of early modern philosophers like René DESCARTES and Benedict Spinoza, who variously endeavored to demonstrate his existence and the implications God has for knowledge and ethics. But Descartes would contribute to the future split between reason and faith by rejecting all previous philosophy, espousing a radical dualism between mind and matter, and practicing a radical skepticism of all that is not innately clear to the mind or demonstrably proven. In his pantheism Spinoza would collapse the distinction between God and the world and labor to replace what he considered to be the weaknesses of Scriptural revelation with a more rational philosophical conception of God. In both thinkers faith is not an admirable form of knowledge, and the incomprehensibility of God's mystery does not temper the reliance upon reason.

The philosopher Immanuel KANT, on the basis of his epistemological critique of pure reason, came to deny the very legitimacy and value of metaphysics, throwing into doubt whether it is possible to know any reality beyond the appearances of things. Because his position ruled out all cosmological proofs for God's existence, Kant developed one on the basis of practical reason. Moral behavior depends upon an absolutely universal or ''categorical imperative'' which points to the existence of a God who alone is in position to posit such a law. The net effect is to remove God from the dimension of what is true to what is valued. Eventually the fact that human knowledge is acquired in a subjective process leads to the conclusion that objective knowledge of God is impossible; the human encounter with God can only take place in the will and the emotions. By the nineteenth century, this agnosticism flowers into an explicit atheism of radical autonomy. Ludwig FEUERBACH reduces theology to anthropology by claiming God is the projection and image of human ideals and aspirations. Karl MARX considers religion to be a man-made illusion, numbing mankind to tolerate political and economic injustices in the false hope of a heavenly kingdom to come. Friedrich NIETZSCHE proclaims that ''God is dead for we have killed him,'' an indictment of the insignificance God has for modern culture as much as an acknowledgement that the idea of God is no longer tenable. In all of these ideologies there lies an assumption that atheism indicates a new maturity in human thought, and a hope that men and women emancipated from their childish dependency on God can create an ideal human future.

The ecclesial divisions arising after the Reformation and the warfare between Catholics and Protestants initiated a search for civil peace and social cohesion that did not have to depend upon a unity in belief, a major contributing factor to the eventual displacement of God from the center of human political life. The bad example of violent persecution given by both sides promoted a distrust of religious authority and extremism, and as tolerance of diversity in belief became a social necessity religious faith moved from the category of universal, binding truth to that of personal opinion. The Reformation's call for emancipation from religious authority was extended to unwanted civil authority, and over time a theory of individual, inalienable rights and government established by the will of the people replaced the more medieval politics of monarchial rule established by the will of God. The organization of industrial production and the application of scientific discoveries in new technologies supported the new hubris that man has mastery over nature and can redeem himself from problems and miseries that in the past he could only pray to God to alleviate. These great political and economic changes confirmed that the modern world was indeed a new age, making it easier for many to believe more in human progress than in any religion from the past.

Catholic theology in this period solidified into a practice and a posture better able to critique the erroneous than appreciate and engage what was novel and worthwhile in the modern era. Theology corrected the mistaken notions concerning God's nature, existence and action, refuting PANTHEISM, DEISM, ATHEISM and denials of revelation and the supernatural. It also challenged the opposition modernity put between faith and reason in human knowledge of God, countering the RATIONALISM, FIDEISM and AGNOSTICISM of the age. Yet even as theology disputed modern ideas and values there was often an unrecognized assimilation of some of its principles or perspectives. For example, the Cartesian quest for indubitable certainty influenced theological practice as it became as much concerned about the varying degrees of credibility and authority of different doctrines as their understanding. And the arguments theologians gave for God's existence and relevance favored the abstract, universal and thus rather impersonal ways of reasoning that were closer to the tone and language of their opponents than that of the biblical revelation. There was much reliance upon demonstrations of the truth and refutations of error to convince, less upon showing the meaning, beauty and contemporary significance of divine mysteries in order to inspire and move the heart. The success of scholastic theology in organizing the subject of theology discouraged different ways of arranging and discussing the material more suitable for the times, and eventually its distinctions calcified into divisions that often left the doctrines isolated from one another and their interconnections.

Vatican Council I, echoing the teaching of St. Paul in the Epistle to the Romans, declared that God's existence can be ''known with certainty by the natural light of human reason from the things that have been made.'' In response to the extreme IMMANENTISM so conducive to agnosticism and the equally perilous fideism of extreme traditionalism, ecclesiastical documents were forthcoming to express Catholic teaching more specifically. Against traditionalism, Gregory XVI taught that ''reason can prove with certainty the existence of God'' (H. Denziger, *Enchiridion symbolorum,* 2751; cf. Pius IX, Denziger 2812). Pope Pius IX taught that ''human reason . . . perceives and well understands . . . many truths such as the existence of God . . . [and] demonstrates these by arguments drawn from its own principles'' (H. Denziger, *Enchiridion symbolorum,* 2853). Pope LEO XIII in the encyclical letter *Aeterni Patris* taught that ''certain truths that are either divinely proposed for belief, or are bound by the closest ties to a doctrine of faith, were known by pagan sages with nothing but their natural reason to guide them, were, moreover, demonstrated and proved by suitable arguments'' (H. Denziger, *Enchiridion symbolorum,* 3136). He affirmed that the demonstration of God's existence is a great and noble fruit of human reason. With particular reference to the Modernists, Pope St. PIUS X insisted on this explicit statement of Catholic belief ''that God, the origin and end of all things, can be known with certainty by the natural light of reason 'from the created world' [cf. Rom 1.20], that is, from the visible works of creation, as a cause from its effects, and that His existence can even be demonstrated'' (H. Denziger, *Enchiridion symbolorum,* 3538). Pope Pius XI in his encyclical *Studiorum ducem* [*Acta Apostolicae Sedis* 15 (1923) 317] called this an outstanding statement of the dogma solemnly defined by Vatican I, although it is true that the Council for reasons of its own used its own expression and omitted the word demonstration. Yet to say that man can know God with certainty by the light of human reason by means of things that are made implies at least the kind of intellectual operation that man ordinarily calls proof.

Nevertheless, Vatican I reminded theology that its primary task is to shed light upon the mysteries of the faith and their interrelations, not to determine their credibility: ''Nevertheless, if reason illumined by faith inquires in an earnest, pious and sober manner, it attains by God's grace a certain understanding of the mysteries, which is most fruitful, both from the analogy with the objects of its natural knowledge and from the connection of these mysteries with one another and with our ultimate end'' (Vatican I, *Dei Filius*, chap 4; H. Denziger, *Enchiridion symbolorum,* 3016).

The Contemporary Period. As with the preceding eras, the contemporary understanding of God is an understanding of the Christian revelation of God by means of certain forms of thought characteristic of the times. The contemporary way of thinking theologically is well represented in VATICAN COUNCIL II, a pastoral, as distinct from a dogmatic, council, called for the purpose of better communicating the Gospel to the modern world. Although the council did not concern itself with a further elaboration of the Church's doctrinal teaching about God's nature in himself, in its declaration on Divine Revelation (*Dei Verbum*) the council presented a summary of the biblical revelation of the God of salvation. While the council considered its teaching in perfect conformity with that of Vatican I, there is a marked shift in the style and language of theological presentation. Instead of listing the essential attributes of the eternal God in the terminology of scholastic theology, Vatican II returns to language of Scripture to emphasize who God is for us and how the good news remains relevant for the modern world. Vatican II acknowledges that Christian understanding of the faith has undergone historical development, and that communication of the truth of God must include a process of enculturation in order to be effective. In the Pastoral Constitution on the Church in the Modern World (*Gaudium et spes*), the Church enters into dialogue with the modern world, distinguishes different kinds and causes of modern atheism, and through a theological anthropology revealed in the humanity of Jesus Christ makes the counter-argument that only faith in God manifests, preserves and upholds the greatness of human dignity.

This conciliar change in theological presentation is symbolic of a wider, methodological shift within the contemporary practice of theology: a change from metaphysical formulations and categories (being, causality, relation) to historical descriptions and the categories of personal experience (event, meaning, relationship). In the effort to promote the relevance and meaning God should have for the modern person, and thus to counteract modern ideological atheism and secularism, theology after the Council has made great effort to connect the mystery of God with the mystery of the human person and salvation. This is done with explicit attention to the human contribution in the mediation of revelation and tradition and consideration of the way God is experienced within the conditions of human subjectivity. Consequently, God is considered less in terms of the eternal perfections of his own being expressed in an unchanging, technical vocabulary purged of historical referents, and more in terms of the meaning and transformative effect he has upon those whom he encounters. The challenge is to reaffirm God's active immanence in the world without compromising his transcendence, and to express the meaning he represents while not reducing his mystery to that meaning or making it entirely relative to the disparities of times, cultures, and individual experiences.

Within contemporary Catholic theology there are different approaches that try to bridge the gulf that has appeared between God and modern experience. Historical theologians like Henri DE LUBAC and Yves CONGAR contributed much to the renewal of theology by initiating a project of *ressourcement* that sought to recover the richness and diversity within the long Catholic tradition. De Lubac in particular argued against atheism and secularism not by rational demonstrative proofs of God's existence but by giving expression to the deep-seated experience of and orientation to God, fundamental to the human creature made in the image of God. The principle that it is natural and constitutional, not extrinsic or supplemental, for the human person to desire and seek God is the premise of his repudiation of a dualistic conception of the natural and supernatural within neo-Thomistic theology, a dualism that facilitated and reflected the modern tendency to divorce the human good from eternal blessedness.

In a manner more epistemological and psychological, Karl RAHNER and Bernard LONERGAN also made the openness of the human person to the transcendent fundamental to their theological approach. For Rahner, human experience in the world involves an engagement with finite being that presupposes an unrestricted openness of the human mind to Absolute Being; God is the transcendental *a priori*—the condition for the very possibility—of human knowing. Because of his infinite transcendence beyond all human conceptions, God who is Absolute Being is also Absolute Mystery. In order for man to fulfill his inherent orientation to God he stands in need of divine revelation, in which God communicates himself while remaining wholly mysterious. Along similar lines, Lonergan built upon his historical research in the thought of Thomas Aquinas on grace and the word of understanding (*verbum*) in order to represent and advance that achievement within the modern context. His work on grace and freedom resolved the centuries old *De auxiliis* controversy between the positions of Luis de MOLINA and Domingo BAÑEZ on how to reconcile God's eternal knowledge and will with the contingent free acts of human beings, and prepared for further work that outlined how a world that develops according to statistical probabilities and the dynamics of human behavior can be understood in a theology of God's providence. His work in epistemology recovered the critical realism lost in modern philosophy's collapse into subjectivism, reaffirmed the possibility of metaphysics, and showed how human reasoning retains its natural authenticity as it moves on to and is transformed by the act of faith.

All these theologians whose work straddle Vatican II were aware of the inadequacies of neo-scholastic theology, and they developed new theological methods in order to overcome its deficiencies. Though they considered a strictly metaphysical approach incomplete, still they did not doubt its legitimacy. It is evident, however, that many theologians after them are less discriminating in their dismissal of this earlier theological method and its achievements. One finds today a rather widespread rejection of the God of ''classical theism'' (i.e., medieval scholasticism) and its philosophical presentation of the attributes of God's being. As theology has become so firmly rooted in human experience that God is only considered in relation to us, an approach that seeks to relate God and creation through the universal category of being is found to be rather alien and too impersonal. Yet the God of classical theism is primarily rejected for more specific reasons: the attributes of absolute divine immutability and impassibility central to its understanding of God are denounced as incompatible with the God of Christian faith. A fundamental theological revision of God's perfection first proposed at the end of the nineteenth century has been embraced by a growing majority of both Protestant and Catholic theologians at end of the twentieth. Much of recent contemporary theology is beholden to the idea that God indeed changes and suffers, whether in the sense that it is his eternal nature to do so, or because he freely chooses to make himself be affected by creation and its outcomes. There are many and various contributing causes for this, including biblical hermeneutics, process philosophy, and an extension of the dynamics of relationship which constitute the Trinity to God's relationship with the world.

The justification for divine mutability and passibility in some contemporary biblical exegesis arises when the anthropopathisms of the biblical language are considered not as an accommodation to its human audience but as expressive of the true character of God. The Old Testament revelation of a God who so intimately covenants with his people that he grieves over their infidelity is taken to mean that the Scriptures reveal God to be truly affected and changed by his relationship with humanity. Similarly, the crucifixion of Jesus in the New Testament, when considered as the definitive moment of God's self-revelation, indicates that suffering is at the very center of the mystery of God. Influential here are Luther's theology from the cross (*kreuzestheologie*) and kenotic Christology of the nineteenth century, leading Eberhard Jüngel, Jürgen Moltmann and others to argue that the passion and death of Jesus, one who is God, occurs in and impacts the divine nature. For God to truly suffer on the cross, he must suffer divinely, and so the cross becomes expressive of the mysterious nature of divine suffering itself.

These readings of Scripture are bolstered by the historical claim that the Christian tradition compromised biblical revelation when it accepted the influence and principles of Greek philosophy. Briefly stated, the early Church fathers replaced the passionate God of the Hebrews with the more rationally appealing Unmoved Mover of the Greeks, and only now is theology correcting this mistake by once again daring to uphold that God truly changes and suffers. Despite the growing acceptance of this understanding of revelation and tradition, it is ultimately untenable. Biblically, it fails to account that *Yahweh* is always immanent in creation and covenant in a completely transcendent manner, and that the kenosis of the Logos is the assumption of a human nature which according to Chalcedon remains integral and unconfused with his divine nature (H. Denziger, *Enchiridion symbolorum,* 300–302). (On the cross God did indeed suffer and die, but precisely as a man did the Son of God do so.) And in regard to the early tradition, not only would such a fundamental distortion of the Gospel be impossible to reconcile with the Holy Spirit's guidance of the Church, it is wholly incongruent with the great effort of the Church fathers to refute many Greco-Roman ideas about God precisely in order to remain true to the Scriptural revelation.

In process thought, developed by Alfred WHITEHEAD and applied to theology by Charles HARTSHORNE and John Cobb, Jr., "becoming" replaces "being" as the fundamental category of reality. God is reconceived as absolute infinite possibility in the process of realization through the world's becoming. Though distinct from the world in his necessary primordial nature, God in his conditional consequent nature is identified with the world (PANENTHEISM), as he actualizes his possibilities in and through the good that comes into concrete existence in the world. Process thought is favored by many endeavoring to rework theology in the light of modern science, convinced that a God in process with the world corresponds to the current scientific worldview of the natural world as fundamentally evolutionary. The immutability, omniscience and omnipotence of the classical God of theism may have fit a static world proceeding whole and complete from its Creator, but such attributes could only preclude a true divine openness to and involvement in a world of random, undetermined outcomes. Thus process theology is considered a better alternative for contemporary theology than traditional metaphysics for explaining the God-world relation, even though it is incompatible with official Church teaching on the absolute perfection and immutability of God. Yet in compromising the transcendence of God for the sake of his immanence, process theology loses the full sense of God as Creator and Lord (*Pantokrator*), and changes the meaning of salvation from a free work on our behalf to a necessary process needed as much by God as by us. And in preferring the God of becoming over the God of pure act, process theologians sacrifice the distinction between God and the created order, that which is precisely so crucial for a genuine dialogue between theology and science.

Finally, the God of absolute perfection without need of or real relation to the world is also critiqued and dismissed upon the basis of the renewal in Trinitarian theology. One of the positive developments in contemporary theology has been to make the TRINITY once again central to all theological discussion. Yet following Rahner's rejection of the traditional procedure in Western tradition to discuss the divine essence before the distinction of the divine persons, contemporary discussion of the Trinity usually begins and stays focused upon the dynamics of the divine persons in relation to one another. While this allows a proper characterization of divine nature within the terms of relationship and being-for-the-other, it is not complemented with discussion of the divine essence in contrast to the created order. Instead, under the influence of Rahner's axiom that the immanent Trinity is the economic Trinity and vice versa, the essence of God to be intrinsically relational is often applied without proper qualification to the God-world relation. It is argued that since God is love, and to love is to be for the other, for God to truly love the world as he has revealed is for him to make himself open to its response and vulnerable to its rejection. The relationship between God and the world must therefore be genuinely mutual, co-defining to both, in which each is deeply affected by the other. Classical theism, therefore, was mistaken to place God's perfection in his being complete in himself and unaffected by the world, for divine immutability and impassibility are antithetical to his Triune nature as pure relationship and love.

The current judgment within theological circles that divine IMMUTABILITY and IMPASSIBILITY are actually imperfections, suggesting that God is aloof, apathetic and unsympathetic to the tragic suffering in the world, is, however, simply mistaken. It reflects a failure to truly engage and appreciate the concerns and achievement of patristic and medieval theology, which focused upon the revelation of God as existence (Ex 3:14) in order to relate all creation, including that which is impersonal and thus outside the category of relationships, with the transcendent and actively immanent Creator. The strength of traditional theism to properly express the dynamics of the Creator-created relation should not be abandoned. The created order is the necessary foundation for rightly understanding the economy of salvation in which God is revealed as Trinity. Without the judgment that God is pure Act, achieved through the analogical contrast of God and his creation, the perfection of the triune God as purely relational risks the reduction of God's transcendent mystery to the conditions of human experience and finite existence. As God is, so does God save us, but under conditions that are not the equal of him; *Yahweh* is indeed present in the midst of his people, but always as wholly other.

What is needed today is a theology of God that can effectively combine the traditional and contemporary emphases together: the one God who as the act of existence itself is also and therefore the triune God of pure relation. God *is*, and so the Father, Son and Holy Spirit who *are for each other* so perfectly that their love cannot be lessened or augmented, act through the missions of Son and Spirit to bring human creatures into the fullness of who they are. Divine immutability and impassibility function here in the positive manner in which they were originally affirmed: as a safeguard which preserves divine transcendence and consequently allows the immanent Trinity to act economically, not by readjusting their nature but in complete conformity to it. In this way salvation is the perfection of human creatures by graced participation in the perfect life God is as Trinity, not the completion of God by what human beings can do to God. How much the world matters to God is shown not by how much it changes him, but that in perfect fidelity to his unconditional mystery God the Father has loved us with and in the love he always has for the Son. In turn, his receptivity to the perfect love of the Son has always included an eternal openness to the love of those whom his Son redeems.

Bibliography: Y. CONGAR, *A History of Theology* (Garden City, N.Y. 1968). G. L. PRESTIGE, *God in Patristic Thought* (London 1936). L. SCHEFFCZYK, *Creation and Providence* (New York 1970). D. F. FORD, ed., *The Modern Theologians: An Introduction to Christian Theology in the Twentieth Century*, 2nd ed. (Oxford 1997). T. G. WEINANDY, *Does God Suffer?* (Notre Dame, Ind. 1999). H. DE LUBAC, *The Discovery of God*, tr. A. DRU; footnotes tr. M. SEBANC and C. FULSOM (Grand Rapids, Mich. 1996); *The Mystery of the Supernatural*, tr. R. SHEED (New York 1967). M. J. BUCKLEY, *At the Origins of Modern Atheism* (New Haven 1987). D. B. BURRELL, *Aquinas: God and Action* (Notre Dame, Ind. 1979). W. J. HANKEY, *God in Himself: Aquinas' Doctrine of God as Expounded in the Summa theologiæ* (New York 1987). A. F. KIMEL, JR., ed., *Speaking the Christian God: The Holy Trinity and the Challenge of Christian Feminism* (Grand Rapids, Mich. 1992). B. J. F. LONERGAN, *Philosophy of God, and Theology* (London 1973). T. C. ODEN, *The Living God: Systematic Theology, Volume 1* (San Francisco 1987). K. RAHNER, ''The Concept of Mystery in Catholic Theology'' in *Theological Investigations*, v. 4, pp. 36–73, tr. K. SMYTH (New York 1982). J. M. STEBBINS, *The Divine Initiative: Grace, World-Order, and Human Freedom in the Early Writings of Bernard Lonergan* (Toronto 1995). P. S. FIDDES, *The Creative Suffering of God* (New York 1988). C. HARTSHORNE, *Omnipotence and Other Theological Mistakes* (Albany 1984). E. JÜNGEL, *God as the Mystery of the World: On the Foundation of the Theology of the Crucified One in the Dispute between Theism and Atheism*, tr. D. L. GUDER (Edinburgh 1983). J. MOLTMANN, *The Crucified God: The Cross of Christ as the Foundation and Criticism of Christian Theology*, tr. R. A. WILSON and J. BOWDEN (London 1976).

[M. A HOONHOUT/J. R. GILLIS/R. J. BUSCHMILLER]

GOD (FATHER)

The order of treatment is God as father in the Old Testament, God as father in the New Testament, and, finally, God as father in doctrinal development and theology.

God as Father in the Old Testament. Contrary to what one might be inclined to presume, explicit use of the father symbol to designate the Deity was extremely rare in the Old Testament. Nor was explicit use, when and as it did occur, original with the Hebrew people. However, neither of these considerations is so significant as would appear, for, quite aside from instances of formal designation, there is the far more important personal and clearly paternalist dimension that marked such concepts as that of lord and sovereign, creator, deliverer, and partner in covenant relationship. But this brings one to the heart of what was both distinctive and original in the Hebrew monotheistic faith.

The simple fact of more ancient, as well as broadly contemporary, parallels—Babylonia's Father of the Land, Greece's Father Zeus—points up the ultimate normalcy and spontaneity of conceiving a god as a father in human psychology. Further, this basic expectation is intensified when one turns to the cultural ancestors of the Hebrews specifically. For, as J. Jeremias has noted (*The Lord's Prayer* 17–18), here the paternal deity is no mere procreator but a merciful and gracious father. Nevertheless, all of this is still quite remote when compared with the highly developed and nuanced father symbol that emerged from within the strictly Hebraic concept of a God of history—a history that was itself conceived not as of men exactly but as of Yahweh-with-us.

A God who was lord and sovereign was by that alone, implicitly, and to some minimal extent, father. But the sovereignty of this God extended to the activity of universal creation, thus making His fatherhood more concrete and more meaningful. Finally, though in the revelation of SALVATION HISTORY it was actually prior, this Creator-Lord was Israel's very special deliverer and covenant partner. This specification of the fatherhood of Israel's God is brought out very neatly in Mal 2.10: ''Have we not all one father? Has not one God created us? Why then are we faithless to one another, profaning the covenant of our fathers?'' It was in the Sinaitic covenant that Israel was bound together as sacred family whose head

Scenes from Genesis showing God (the Father) with Adam and Eve in the Garden of Eden, detail of a 13th-century mosaic in the narthex of the Basilica of St. Mark, Venice.

and father was the God who had delivered them from the bondage of Egypt and taken them unto His own. Hence, it is only in the same covenant relationship that the divine fatherhood as conceived by the Israelites—with its overtones of unique beneficence, intimacy, personalness—can really be appreciated. Even the righteousness of God, since essentially it was fidelity to His covenant promises, was reduced to the sustaining, as it were, of this fatherhood of unique and gratuitous election.

God as Father in the New Testament. The New Testament witnesses a twofold development. First, there is a highly significant deepening of the symbolism in the area of intimacy and familiarity. From the studies of J. Jeremias, who relies mainly on the testimony of the Antiochene Fathers, it appears (*op. cit.* 18–21) that the Aramaic term *'abbā'* must have been used by Jesus Himself and that the intimacy which it connoted was of far-reaching theological importance. ''He, to whom the Father had granted full knowledge of God, had the messianic prerogative of addressing Him with the familiar address of a child'' (*ibid.* 20). But Jesus did not reserve this prerogative to Himself. If Jeremias is correct (*ibid.* 17), Jesus Himself authorized His disciples to address the heavenly Father with this same term when He gave them the famous Lord's Prayer instruction. In any case, in Rom 8.15 and Gal 4.6 it is the name the believer is empowered to utter in virtue of the indwelling Spirit.

It would be incorrect, however, to consider the evidence for this deepening of the father symbol as resting exclusively, or even chiefly, on the interpretation of a single word. The argument would seem to be strong that *'abbā'*, the child's name for its father, is the form of address, and behind that the mentality, authentically distinctive of the new covenant. But as such, it merely condenses and renders explicit what is already present in the essential features of the new covenant even apart from the term *'abbā'*. For over and above the covenant intimacy characteristic of the Old Testament, it is the key message of the New that the believer, made one with Christ through possession of Christ's very own imparted Spirit, is thereby rendered adopted and true son of the Father. As in the Old Testament, so likewise in the New, the father symbol is a function of covenant relationship.

But the New Testament makes another and far more radical addition. Yahweh is father in the Old Testament exclusively with respect to creatures. In the New Testament His fatherhood is revealed as extending back into the recesses of the Godhead itself. It is only now that the Father as one distinct first emerges for to say that the Father was revealed in the Old Testament, Son and Spirit in the New, is actually, but perhaps unwittingly, to presume knowledge of the Trinity for the Old Testament. In referring to the Old Testament, it is more correct to say not that the Father was revealed but that God was revealed as father.

From the New Testament, however, one learns that God is father not only with respect to creatures but also, first and foremost—eternally—with respect to His own divine Son. It is this eternal sonship upon which the sonship of adoption, the sonship of the new covenant, is based and in which it is made to share.

God as Father in Doctrinal Development and Theology. In the great period of the evolution of Trinitarian dogma leading up to Constantinople I in 381, and thereafter, attention became focused on what might be called the ontological, rather than historical, concept of divine fatherhood. This happened as the Christian consciousness began to wrestle with the problem of a true plurality in the Godhead. In a sense God was one. In another and necessarily different sense God was nevertheless three—Father, Son, and Holy Spirit. God was one, it was eventually determined, in the sense of being, majesty, power; or somewhat more technically, in the sense of NATURE or essence. And God was three in the sense of Person or HYPOSTASIS. The reason, moreover, why this was not a contradiction, though it remained very much a mystery, was that Father and Son, to take the first two members, differed from one another not in nature or essence but only in the relative property of fatherhood and sonship respectively. Everything the Father was, the Son was also, excepting only fatherhood.

Two things can be said in historical retrospect of this concentration on the ontological aspect of the divine fatherhood. First, it was necessary. The ancient Christian spirit could not go on confessing one God, distinctly Father, Son, and Holy Spirit, if there were no satisfactory reply to both the subordinationist and Sabellian oversimplifications. Second, however, the concentration meant that everything else that was to be said of God's fatherhood—as drawn from the revelation of both the Old and New Testaments—was being presupposed or taken for granted. But this created a risk. Eventually one can lose sight of what is presupposed and taken for granted in matters of Christian belief and theology. It simply has to be recalled, quite explicitly. A proof of such a need, and one that touches directly on the subject of God the Father, is seen in the strange fact that Roman Catholics often take the fatherhood of God and the brotherhood of man to be a Protestant rather than a Catholic point of doctrine. Fortunately, however, and with profound ecumenical consequences, this naive attitude is in the process of being corrected in the wake of the Roman Catholic, as well as Protestant, Biblical revival.

The fatherhood of God has a special significance in the question of the divine plurality, but this is neither its only nor its primary significance. In the drama of salvation we return to the Father—and return is the right word inasmuch as the Father is source as well as end of all reality, even in the Godhead—we return, therefore, to the Father, to *our* Father, as one with Christ Jesus, sharing by adoption in His own sonship in virtue of His indwelling Spirit (*see* INDWELLING, DIVINE). Such is the ultimate perfection and consummation of the Old Testament covenant relationship as achieved in the New.

See Also: AGENNĒTOS; GOD, 1, 2; LORD, THE; PATERNITY, DIVINE; PERSON (IN THEOLOGY); PERSON, DIVINE; REDEMPTION (IN THE BIBLE); TRINITY, HOLY; TRINITY, HOLY, ARTICLES ON.

Bibliography: B. W. ANDERSON, in G. A. BUTTRICK, ed. *The Interpreters' Dictionary of the Bible,* 4 v. (Nashville 1962) 3:407–430. J. JEREMIAS, *The Lord's Prayer,* tr. J. REUMANN (Philadelphia 1964), esp. 16–21; *The Parables of Jesus,* tr. S. H. HOOKE (New York 1963), esp. 190–191. J. MUILENBURG, *The Way of Israel* (New York 1961), esp. 38–40.

[R. L. RICHARD]

GOD (HOLY SPIRIT)

The entire teaching of the Church regarding the Holy Spirit, the Third Person of the Blessed Trinity, is contained formally, either explicitly or implicitly, in Sacred Scripture (*see* SPIRIT OF GOD). Early Christian writers, the Fathers, and theologians of the Church under the guidance of the teaching authority of the Church, gradually made more explicit that which was contained only implicitly in the original revelation. Thus the infallible Church, in the course of time, penetrated more deeply into and became more acutely conscious of what it possessed and, gradually, solemnly defined its faith.

Catholics have always believed that the Holy Spirit is true God, a distinct Person of the Blessed Trinity, consubstantial with the Father and Son, eternal, and in every respect equal to the other two Divine Persons. Such is the profession of the earliest CREEDS (H. Denzinger, *Enchiridion symbolorum* 1–75), including the so-called Creed of Epiphanius (ibid. 42–45) and the so-called ATHANASIAN CREED (ibid. 75–76). It is also the profession of the NICENE (ibid. 125–126) and Constantinopolitan (ibid. 150) Creeds. In the early Church, however, there were not yet formulated clearly the manner of the Spirit's procession, the source from which He proceeds, and the role of the Son in the procession of the Holy Spirit.

Patristic Teaching. The early Christian writers, St. Clement of Rome (*d.* 95) and St. Ignatius of Antioch (d. 107) join the Holy Spirit with Father and Son as one God. Justin Martyr (d. *c.* 167) and Athenagoras (*c.* 177), relying on the baptismal formula (Mt 28.19), clearly teach that the Spirit is God. Tertullian (d. *c.* 222) adds that the Holy Spirit proceeds from the Father through the Son. Gregory Thaumaturgus (d. 270) stresses the inseparability of the Divine Persons. From the Holy Spirit's giving man a share in the divine nature St. Athanasius (373) proves His divinity and says that the Spirit has the same relation to the Son as the Son to the Father. St. Cyril of Jerusalem (386) insists on the one nature in three Persons and that the Father works through the Son in the Spirit. In the West, St. Hilary (366) continues this teaching in his *De Trinitate.* In the East, the Cappadocian Fathers, SS. Basil (*c.* 379), Gregory of Nazianzus (*c.* 390), and Gregory of Nyssa (Basil's brother, *c.* 394), develop past teaching by stressing that the Spirit proceeds and is not begotten as is the Son. In the West, St. Augustine (430) develops the doctrine of the Spirit. As true God, He proceeds from Father and Son as from one principle, as their bond of union in love. St. Cyril of Alexandria (444), like Athanasius, puts his doctrine of the Spirit into the context of sanctification. St. John Damascene (end of 7th century to before 754) emphasizes the equality of the Spirit with Father and Son, since the Son and Spirit have everything the Father has except to be unbegotten. The Spirit is not the son of the Father, but His Spirit, and the Son's, also, because He proceeds from the Father through the Son. This patristic teaching developed in the life of the Church and later was embodied in conciliar teaching.

Conciliar Formulations. The first adversaries of the dogma were the Macedonians or *Pneumatomachoi* (Adversaries of the Spirit) condemned as heretics by the Second Ecumenical Council, Constantinople I, in 381 (*Enchiridion symbolorum* 151).

In 382 Pope St. Damasus presented a collection of canons (the famous *Tome of Damasus*) to bishops gathered at a local council in Rome. In these canons the Holy Spirit is said to be of one power and substance with the Father and the Son. The Spirit is eternal, from the Father, of the divine substance, and true God. The Holy Spirit can do all and knows all and, as Father and Son, is everywhere. The three Persons, having everything in common, are perfectly equal to one another in all things and have complete dominion over all creatures. Hence, the Holy Spirit must be adored by all creatures, just as must Father and Son (ibid. 153, 162, 169, 170, 173, 174).

In 675 the Eleventh Council of Toledo (*see* TOLEDO, COUNCILS OF) proposed:

> We also believe that the Holy Spirit, the Third Person in the Trinity, is God, and that he is one and equal with God the Father and God the Son, of one substance as well as of one nature. However, he is not begotten nor created, but he proceeds from both and is the Spirit of both. We believe that the Holy Spirit is neither unbegotten nor begotten: lest, if we said unbegotten we should be asserting two Fathers; and if we said begotten we should appear to be preaching two Sons. He is called the Spirit, not only of the Father nor only of the Son but equally of the Father and of the Son. He proceeds not from the Father into the Son nor from the Son to sanctify creatures; but he is shown to have proceeded from both equally, because he is known as the love or the sanctity of both. This Holy Spirit therefore, is believed to be sent by the two together as the Son is sent [by the Father]; but he is not considered inferior to the Father and the Son in the way in which the Son, because of the human nature which he has assumed, testifies that he is inferior to the Father and the Holy Spirit. (ibid. 527)

The Fathers in the East had long held that the Holy Spirit proceeds from the Father through the Son. It was in the West, however, that the word *FILIOQUE* was added to the symbol of Constantinople by the Fourth Council of Braga (675; *Lexikon für Theologie und Kirche* 2 4:126); subsequently it was put into the liturgy of the Western churches. Rome, although holding the *Filioque,* hesitated and only later on incorporated it into her liturgy, probably around 1013.

The abbot JOACHIM OF FIORE (1130–1202) accused Peter Lombard (d. 1160) of introducing four elements into the Blessed Trinity. The Fourth Lateran Council (1215) first stated the doctrine of the Trinity against the ALBIGENSES and other heretics:

> . . . there is only one true God . . . the Father, the Son, and the Holy Spirit: three persons, indeed, but one essence, substance, or nature that is wholly simple . . . the Holy Spirit is from both the Father and the Son equally. (*Enchiridion symbolorum* 800)

Then, against the Abbot Joachim the council maintained its belief in that

> . . . certain one supreme reality . . . which truly is the Father, and the Son, and the Holy Spirit. That reality is the three persons taken together and each of them taken singly; and hence, there is in God only a trinity, not a quaternity . . . the same reality is the Father, and the Son, and the Holy Spirit who proceeds from both. (ibid. 804–805)

The Second Council of LYONS (1274) is most explicit:

> . . . we confess that the Holy Spirit proceeds eternally from the Father and the Son, not as from two principles, but as from one; not by two spirations but by one . . . we condemn and reprobate those who presume to deny that the Holy Spirit proceeds eternally from the Father and the Son, or those who injudiciously dare to assert that the Holy Spirit proceeds from the Father and the Son as from two principles, and not as from one. (ibid. 850.)

And the council concludes:

> And we believe that the Holy Spirit, completely and perfectly true God, proceeding from the Father and from the Son, is coequal, consubstantial, coomnipotent, and coeternal with the Father and the Son in all things. (ibid. 853)

The Council of FLORENCE (1439–45), sums up the doctrine:

> . . . there is one true God, all-powerful, unchangeable, and eternal. Father, Son, and Holy Spirit, one in essence, but three in persons. The Father is not begotten; the Son is begotten of the Father; the Holy Spirit proceeds from the Father and the Son.

After carefully teaching the distinction of one Person from another, the council says:

> . . . the Holy Spirit alone proceeds both from the Father and equally from the Son. These three persons are one God, not three gods; for the three persons have one substance, one essence, one nature, one divinity, one immensity, one eternity. And everything is one where there is no distinction by relative opposition. (ibid. 1330)

The council then teaches the doctrine of CIRCUMINCESSION, that the three persons are wholly within one another without losing their distinction. And, finally we read:

> All that the Holy Spirit is and all that he has, he has from the Father and equally from the Son. Yet the Father and the Son are not two principles of the Holy Spirit, but one principle, just as the Father and the Son and the Holy Spirit are not three principles of creation but one principle. (ibid. 1331)

In conclusion, the council condemns, among others, those who say that only God the Father is true God and classify the Son and the Holy Spirit as creatures (ibid. 1332).

Summary of Conciliar Teaching. It is the teaching, therefore, of the Church (1) that the Holy Spirit is true God is of faith from the various creeds, as well as from the Fourth Lateran Council, the Second Council of Lyons, and the Council of Florence; (2) that the Holy Spirit is not begotten (*see* GENERATION OF THE WORD) but proceeds is a dogma of faith contained in the so-called Athanasian Creed (*Ouicumque*), the Eleventh Council of Toledo, and equivalently from the Fourth Lateran Council and the Council of Florence; (3) that He proceeds from the Father is set forth in the anathemas of Pope Damasus and in the Constantinopolitan Creed. The procession of the Holy Spirit from both Father and Son was defined (and that according to the Latin formula *Filioque,* not just *per Filium*) in the Fourth Lateran, Second Lyons and the Council of Florence; and (4) That the Holy Spirit proceeds from the Father and the Son as from one principle and by one SPIRATION has been defined by the Second Council of Lyons in a formula repeated by the Council of Florence.

Manner of Spiration, Work of the Spirit. The manner of the breathing forth of the Holy Spirit is not a matter of faith. Theologians commonly hold that, whereas the Son is begotten by intellectual generation, the Holy Spirit proceeds from the mutual love and will of Father and Son. The Eleventh Council of Toledo repeats the saying of St. Augustine that the Holy Spirit proceeds from both Father and Son, because He is the love or holiness of them both (ibid. 527). *The Catechism of the Council of Trent* (1.9.7) speaks of the Holy Spirit as proceeding from the divine will inflamed by love. The encyclical *DIVINUM ILLUD MUNUS* of LEO XIII speaks of the Holy Spirit as being the love between the Father and the Son (*Enchiridion symbolorum* 3326).

The Holy Spirit is the SOUL OF THE CHURCH, the MYSTICAL BODY OF CHRIST and dwells (*see* INDWELLING, DIVINE) within the soul of the person in the state of sanctifying grace (*Divinum Illud Munus, Enchiridion symbolorum* 3329–3331; Pius XII, *MYSTICI CORPORIS, Enchiridion symbolorum* 3807–3808; 3814–3815). This does not mean that the Father and Son do not also give life to the Mystical Body. This activity is appropriated to the Holy Spirit, because the work of sanctifying the Mystical Body and the individual soul bears a special resemblance to the particular personal character of the Holy Spirit (love and sanctification).

The doctrine of the Holy Spirit is developed in the works of the great theologians, such as St. Thomas's *In 1 sent.* of Peter Lombard (dd. 10–18; 31–32); *C. gent.* 4.15–25; *Comp. theol.* 45–49, 58; *Summa theologiae* 1,

36–38; 1, 43. Modern theologians, in general, follow the teaching of St. Thomas, adding to their treatises further developments that have been motivated by the authentic teaching of the Church.

See Also: TRINITY, HOLY, ARTICLES ON; GOD (FATHER); GOD (SON); MISSIONS, DIVINE.

Bibliography: A. PALMIERI, *Dictionnaire de théologie catholique,* ed. A. VACANT et al., 15 v. (Paris 1903–50; Tables générales 1951–) 5.1:676–829. R. HAUBST, *Lexikon für Theologie und Kirche,* ed. J. HOFER and K. RAHNER, 10 v. (2d, new ed. Freiburg 1957–65) 5:108–113. J. GALOT, *L'Esprit d'amour* (Paris 1959). A. HENRY, *The Holy Spirit,* tr. J. LUNDBERG and M. BELL (New York 1960). E. LEEN, *The Holy Ghost* , (New York 1937). G. GENNARO, *Lo Spirito di Cristo* (Rome 1957). R. KOCH, *Geist und Messias: Beitrag zur biblischen Theologie des Alten Testaments* (Vienna 1950). L. LABAUCHE, *Traité du Saint Esprit* (Paris 1950). J. LEBRETON, *History of the Dogma of the Trinity,* tr. A. THOROLD (New York 1939). M. JUGIE, *De processione Spiritus Sancti ex fontibus revelationis et secundum Orientales dissidentes* (Rome 1936). J. MCMAHON, *The Gift of God* (Westminster, Md. 1958). T. MAERTENS, *Le Souffle et l'Esprit de Dieu* (Paris 1959). F. BOURASSA, ''Le Saint-Esprit unité d'amour du Père et du Fils,'' *Sciences Ecclésiastiques* 14 (1962) 375–415. M. A. FATULA, *The Holy Spirit: Unbounded Gift of Joy* (Collegeville, Minn. 1998). A. HOLL, *The Left Hand of God: A Biography of the Holy Spirit,* tr. J. CULLEN (New York 1998). *The Holy Spirit, Lord and Giver of Life,* tr. A. BONO (New York 1997). Y. CONGAR, *I Believe in the Holy Spirit,* tr. D. SMITH (New York 1997); *The Word and the Spirit,* tr. D. SMITH (San Francisco 1986). J. MOLTMANN, *The Source of Life: The Holy Spirit and the Theology of Life,* tr. M. KOHL (Minneapolis 1997); *The Church in the Power of the Spirit: A Contribution to Messianic Ecclesiology,* tr. M. KOHL (Minneapolis 1993). H. U. VON BALTHASAR, *Creator Spirit,* tr. B. MCNEIL (San Francisco 1993). *On the Holy Spirit in the Life of the Church and the World: Encyclical Letter of the Supreme Pontiff John Paul II* (Boston 1986). P. B. T. BILANIUK, *Theology and Economy of the Holy Spirit: An Eastern Approach* (Bangalore 1980). K. RAHNER, *The Spirit in the Church* (New York 1979).

[M. J. DONNELLY]

GOD (SON)

The following consideration deals with the Father-Son relationship Christian faith professes to be found within the immanent life of God Himself. The context is thus Trinitarian; the one to whom both FILIATION and divinity are attributed is such independently of the INCARNATION since God cannot but be Father and Son, each distinct from the other. And yet man encounters that strictly divine Son of a natural, divine Father only in the historical figure Jesus of Nazareth. Until enfleshed in the latter, that relation of filiation, or concretely God the Son in His distinction from the Father, is simply not a reality affecting man sufficiently to evoke recognition and acceptance. It may be asked whether, prescinding from God as the Word of Revelation to man historically, there *is* within the Deity a Word distinct from the Father. An affirmative reply does not by any means deny the fact that God the Son is *known* in His eternal and necessary relationship to GOD THE FATHER only through the manifestation, or Word, that He is not merely in relation to the Father's thought but also in reference to historical man.

Sacred Scripture. The New Testament in particular serves as source for human knowledge of God's inner life; its perspective, however, is anything but direct in this case. The preoccupation quite clearly is not with divine vitality in itself and in its implications. Far more than being, action is in focus; and that is divine action. The question ''Who is Jesus of Nazareth?'' is answered in response to the query ''What does He do in relation to mankind?'' For it is precisely His salvific-illuminative creative function that presents Him in a frame of reference in which He occupies an utterly unique relation with God His Father or the Father.

His preexistence is asserted (Jn 1.1–3). If He is already the WORD before creatures exist, He is no less Son (Jn 1.14, 18). That same state is not one of inertia; it is represented as involving activity. In this way, Scripture associates Him with Creator rather than creature (Col 1.15–17; Heb 1.1–3, 10–12). Let it be noted that He is the intermediary or guide through whom all things have their reality, in distinction to the Father as the source, or one *from whom* (1 Cor 8.6). Both are said to be goal, or one *to whom* all things are ordered (Col 1.16; Rom 11.36), without a denial that even in this the Son depends on the Father (1 Cor 15.28). Nor is His function of guide or intermediary denied of God (the Father)—Romans 11.36.

Thus Jesus stands in relation to God before becoming a son of Mary (Phil 2.6–7). Before the world came to be, the Son was in glory with the Father, who loved Him (John 17.1, 5, 24).

The glorified Jesus is also presented, in retrospect, as endowed with a role in universal origins, and therefore not only in terms of a preexisting Son but as well in those of a preexisting Lord actually reigning (1 Cor 8.6). If all this points to equality with the Father in the order of operation (Jn 5.17, 26) and unity with Him (Jn 10.28–30; 14.10), it unmistakably as well implies a definite dependence in the Son (Jn 5.19).

The perspective of the Synoptics is somewhat different. Still Jesus is presented as Son in a unique sense (Mk 12.1–11; 13.32). Though SON OF MAN appears frequently, it introduces Him into contexts where He exercises divine prerogatives: forgiveness of sins (Mk 2.10), mastery over the law of Moses (Mk 2.28), Redemption (Mk 10.45; Mt 26.28), ultimate jurisdiction (Mk 13.26), exigence of love from men for their salvation (Mt 19.17–18; 25.40; Lk 10.27–28). His sonship is not the same as that of others in relation to the same Father.

It has not only ontological implications but psychological repercussions. Concretely this involves a mutual interchange between personal beings, at once intellectual and affective (Mt 11.25–27; Lk 10.21–22). United completely with His Father (Jn 4.34; 6.38; 10.17; 10.29–30), He is convinced that He has ready access to that Father's hearing (Jn 11.42), approval (Mk 1.11), and efficacious assistance (Mt 26.53). Thus His sonship is found connected with reverence and obedience (Heb 5.7–8).

To ask whether the New Testament presents Jesus as God the Son (see the variant reading of Jn 1.18; see also Jn 3.16, 18; 1 Jn 4.9) is to inquire about His CONSUBSTANTIALITY and seek a frame of reference for Him that was developed only later. In the Biblical context a preexistent Son is related uniquely to the Father in counterdistinction to creatures; this in terms of their mutual activity with regard to the welfare of mankind. Consubstantiality, however, is a different perspective; in it Father and Son are related to each other as identified with a single divine substance and prescinding from their relations with humanity. To assert a difference of perspective is necessary; it is, however, the same utterly unique relationship that is expressed in both.

Patristic-Conciliar Development. If the New Testament identified Jesus with God's eternal Son, the Fathers early asserted His divinity [see Ignatius of Antioch: F. X. Funk, *Patres apostolici* (Tübingen 1901) 1:218, 226; *Patrologia Graeca*, ed. J. P. Migne, 5:649, 660]. Divine sonship involved divinity but also origin from God. To this the Apologists applied themselves and drew a similarity between the Son or Word originating from the Father and speech arising from mind or thought in man (see Theophilus of Antioch, *Ad Autolychum* 2.22; *Enchiridion patristicum*, ed. M. J. Rouët de Journel, 182). Such attempts were accompanied by protests that to inquire into the Son's generation was beyond man (see Irenaeus, *Adversus haereses* 2.28.6; *Patrologia Graeca* 7:808–09). If the Son was still considered in relation to the Father, His filiation as prior to and independent of creatures was of far more direct concern than was the case in the New Testament.

It was, however, at the Council of NICAEA that the Church was constrained by circumstances to introduce non-Biblical categories into its authentic description of the Son's relation to the Father. The Arian controversy occasioned this determination. Consubstantial; taking origin neither from nothing nor from preexisting beings but from the Father's own substance; begotten, not made—these are His characteristics (H. Denzinger, *Enchiridion symbolorum*, ed. A. Schönmetzer, 125–26). The Cappadocians emphasized that the difference between Father and Son rests not in the one's positing and verifying in Himself a perfection the other lacks; rather in a relation by which the same Godhead exists in Father and Son, but in the latter from the former (see Gregory of Nazianzus, *Orat.* 29.16; *Patrologia Graeca* 36:96). Augustine sought in man's psychology or way of knowing the natural analogate for understanding the eternal generation of the Son (*Trin.* 12.6.6 and 15.11.20; *Patrologia Latina*, ed. J. P. Migne, 42: 1001, 1072).

Subsequent Theology. It was the contribution of the Latin Middle Ages to develop this analogy further. The Son's consubstantiality and procession were put into an intelligible and interrelated whole by Thomas Aquinas when he introduced the hypothesis of intellectual emanations within the Godhead (*Summa theologiae* 1a, 27.1; *see* PROCESSIONS, TRINITARIAN).

Contemporary Christian theology has focused attention on the danger that exaggerated emphasis of the immanent aspect of Trinitarian life may be detrimental to a balanced view of the roles played by Divine Persons in the economy of salvation. Special interest has been regenerated in the fact that man's sonship of adoption is connected with the sonship of Jesus Himself. The former is a share in the latter, man acquiring a filial relation to the Father. This, however, involves no divine action of the Son distinct from that of the Father (*Enchiridion symbolorum* 1330).

What is required for God the Son to become man in Jesus Christ, what, in other words, the mission of God the Son involves besides His eternal procession, is another theological question that has aroused interest in the past few decades; the hypotheses of quasi-formal causality and contingent predications have been introduced in this context (see B. Lonergan, *De Deo trino* v.2:217–60).

If the modern world has investigated the relationship between person and consciousness, the same question has been asked about Divine Persons (*ibid.* 186–93). The answers that have been given indicate a diversity in the way consciousness is understood.

See Also: TRINITY, HOLY, ARTICLES ON; GENERATION OF THE WORD; HOLY SPIRIT; LOGOS

Bibliography: P. RICHARD, *Dictionnaire de théologie catholique*, ed. A. VACANT et al., 15 v. (Paris 1903–5) 5.2:2353–2476. H. DE LAVALETTE et al., *Lexikon für Theologie und Kirche*, ed., J. HOFER and K. RAHNER, 10 v. (2d, new ed. Freiburg 1957–65) 3:543–62. S. MORENZ et al., *Die Religion in Geschichte und Gegenwart*, 7 v. (3d ed. Tübingen 1957–65) 6:118–25. F. BÜCHSEL G. KITTEL, *Theologisches Wörterbuch zum Neuen Testament* (Stuttgart 1935–) 4:747–49. B. LONERGAN, *De Deo trino,* 2 v. (v.1 2d ed., v.2 3d ed. Rome 1964). V. TAYLOR, *The Person of Christ in New Testament Teaching* (New York 1959). P. MCSHANE, "The Hypothesis of Intelligible Emanations in God," *Theological Studies* 23 (1962) 545–68.

[C. J. PETER]

GOD, INTUITION OF

The intuition of God refers to an immediate apprehension of God as He is in Himself. Since God is a spirit, this intuition cannot be a sense perception, but must be an act of the intellect knowing God directly, immediately, as object.

Some modern philosophers speak of an obscure intuition of God in that primordial intuition of self as contingent being (being-with-nothingness) and as part of a larger whole that is also being-with-nothingness. This whole demands as sufficient reason for its existing, the existence of another being, who is being-without-nothingness, Absolute Being. This is not a direct apprehension of God as object, however, but rather an intuitive experience of the contingency of being-with-nothingness, which leads the mind to recognize the necessary existence of Absolute Being.

The mystics speak of an intuition of God in infused CONTEMPLATION, but all admit that this supernatural experience of God as He is in Himself is given in the darkness of faith and is not an immediate, direct apprehension of the divine essence. If this is so, is intuition of God possible for a created intellect?

Revelation. Man's vocation to the intimacy of friendship with God is found in the OT. The full revelation that those who love God will so share in His life and beatitude that they will ''see'' Him in His Godhead is not given until the coming of the WORD into the world as God-Man, and the special mission of the Holy Spirit to the New Israel. The intuition of God, in the strict sense, is realized only in this supernatural intellectual vision of God as He is in Himself, known as the BEATIFIC VISION, because it gives its possessor a created share in God's own happiness. This immediate and intimate knowledge of the triune God and of the Word Incarnate is, in fact, the fullness of eternal life (cf. Jn 17.3; 1 Jn 3.2). Except for Christ [*see* JESUS CHRIST, III (SPECIAL QUESTIONS), 1, 6], the God-Man, this vision is reserved to the next life and is given only to those who die in the friendship of God and after their purification, should they need such purification (cf. 1 Cor 13.12; Mt 5.8; Heb 12.14).

Development. The Church's faith in the beatific vision as the ultimate end of all who die in Christ was firm from the beginning. In the development of this doctrine, she became fully aware that since the Ascension of Christ into heaven, the beatific vision is given to souls who die in grace as soon as they have been purified and before their resurrection. In his definition of the immediacy of the beatific vision, since the Passion and death of Christ, for all who die in grace (including those who died before the Incarnation), Pope Benedict XII declared that even before the resumption of their bodies and the general judgment, these souls ''have beheld and do behold the divine essence with intuitive and face-to-face vision, with no creature mediating in the manner of object seen, but the divine essence immediately showing itself to them plainly, clearly, and openly, and seeing in this way, they have full enjoyment of that same divine essence.'' Moreover, this ''intuitive, face-to-face vision and enjoyment . . . exists continuously without any interruption . . . to the last judgment and from then on forever'' (H. Denzinger, *Enchiridion symbolorum*, ed. A. Schönmetzer [32d ed. Freiburg 1963] 1000 01). The Council of Florence gave further precision to this doctrine by defining that these souls ''see clearly the triune and one God Himself, just as He is, yet one more perfectly than another, according to the diversity of merits'' (*Enchiridion symbolorum* 1304–05).

Theology. All knowledge requires a union of knower and known on the ontological level of the knower, but no created idea of God can be God known as He is in Himself. Therefore, for a created intellect to know the divine essence, that intellect must be united directly to God so that the divine essence itself, as the object understood, actuates the intellect to the act of knowing. For such an act of knowing, the knower must be assimilated supernaturally to the triune God. Now all created gifts of grace are effected in the soul by God both as the consequence of, and the disposition for, His gift of Himself to His intellectual creature. Grace and charity are a beginning of assimilation to the Godhead and have as their finality the beatific vision. For this vision, however, the intellect must be further strengthened and perfected by the light of glory, that supernatural actuation of the created intellect which disposes it for the *act* of seeing God and for immediate union with *God seen.* Although only God can know Himself as much as He is knowable, all the blessed know God as He is in Himself, but some more perfectly than others. Those who love God more, share more in the light of glory, and so have a greater power of knowing Him (cf. Council of Vienne, *Enchiridion symbolorum* 895; *Summa theologiae* 1a, 12; 2a2ae, 23–28; 3a Suppl., 92, 93; *C. gent.* 3.52, 53; *Comp. theol.* 2.8–10).

See Also: BENEDICTUS DEUS; CREATED ACTUATION BY UNCREATED ACT; DESTINY, SUPERNATURAL; ELEVATION OF MAN; GLORIFIED BODY; ONTOLOGISM; RESURRECTION OF THE DEAD.

Bibliography: A. MICHEL, *Dictionnaire de théologie catholique* 7.2:2351–94. R. SCHNACKENBURG and K. FORSTER, *Lexikon für Theologie und Kirche*, ed. J. HOFER and K. RAHNER, 10 v. (2d new ed. Freiburg1957–65) 1:583–591. M. J. SCHEEBEN, *The Mysteries of Christianity,* tr. C. VOLLERT (St. Louis 1946). M. DE LA TAILLE, *The Hypostatic Union and Created Actuation by Uncreated Act* (West Baden, Ind. 1952). K. RAHNER, ''Some Implications of the Scholastic Concept of Uncreated Grace,'' *Theological Investigations,* tr. C. ERNST (Baltimore 1961) 1:319–346.

[M. J. REDLE]

GOD, NAME OF

The biblical use of the names for God provides a valuable insight into the richness and complexity of Semitic thought. For the Semitic peoples, an unnamed thing was a nonexistent thing; names were considered to identify and describe the very being and function of their bearers (Eccl 6.10; Gn 1.3–10; 27.36; Is 40.26). A man's name represented him wholly, was his alter ego. To know a name was to be able to exercise influence over the owner by using it. To change a man's name was to show one's power and authority over him (2 Kgs 23.34: cf. Gn 2.19–20; Dt 28.10). To cut off a man's name was the same as destroying him (Jer 11.19; Ps 82[83].5).

In religious matters, knowledge of the name of a god was considered the most effective way of establishing contact with him. The priests of BAAL tried to obtain Baal's intervention by the repeated shouting of his name (1 Kgs 18.26–28). In Israel, where one also called upon the name of the Lord (1 Kgs 18.36–37), belief in the magical properties of the divine name never took root. The divine name was not a carefully guarded secret, whereas secrecy was an essential feature of magical names and formulas. Moreover, the Lord had freely revealed His name and commanded that He be addressed by it and by no other (Ex 3.15; 23.13). It was a name that should not be profaned (Ez 36.21). Legislation against its misuse was quite explicit (Ex 20.7).

The divine name was evocative, not only of God's being, but of His relationship with His people. He was not the God of a land, nor of a particular city, but the God of the people of Israel, into whose life He intimately penetrated. In Israel His name was held in great esteem, and became an all-embracing part of the religious life of the nation. The ''name of the Lord'' was loved (Ps 5.12), praised (7.18; 148.13), and used in prayer (Jer 14.21); it was blessed (Jb 1.21), proclaimed (Dt 32.3), and thanked (Ps. 96[97].12). Israel lived and acted in His name (Mi 4.5), trusting in His help and interest (Ps 123[124].8). The divine name was synonymous with God's glory (Is 42.8; Jer 10.6; Ps 101[102].16). Prophets spoke ''in the name of the Lord,'' with all His authority and power (Jer 11.21).

The Temple was built to honor the Lord's name (2 Sm 7.13; 1 Kgs 8.16, 29). Not only did the Temple bear His name (Jer 7.10, 14); it was also His name's abode (Dt 12.5, 21). All nations would honor the Lord's name in Jerusalem (Jer 3.17). Isaiah declared (30.27) that the divine name comes from afar to punish Assyria. Such personifications reconciled the transcendence of Yahweh with His presence in the Temple. Eventually, Yahweh was referred to simply as ''the Name'' (Lv 24.11) without any further specification.

See Also: ADONAI; EL (GOD); ELOHIM; ELYON; JEHOVAH; SHADDAI; YAHWEH.

Bibliography: H. GROSS, *Lexikon für Theologie und Kirche,* ed. J. HOFER and K. RAHNER, 10 v. (2d, new ed. Freiburg 1957–65) 4:1127–29. W. EICHRODT, *Theology of the Old Test.,* tr. J. A. BAKER (London 1961–). E. JACOB, *Theology of the Old Testament,* tr. A. W. HEATHCOTE and P. J. ALLCOCK (New York 1958). J. P. E. PEDERSEN, *Israel: Its Life and Culture,* 4 v. in 2 (New York 1926–40; repr. 1959). P. VAN IMSCHOOT, *Théologie de l'Ancien Testament,* 2 v. (Tournai 1954–56). T. VRIEZEN, *An Outline of Old Testament Theology,* tr. S. NEUIJEN (Newton Centre, Mass. 1958).

[R. T. A. MURPHY]

GOD, PROOFS FOR THE EXISTENCE OF

The classic text presenting proofs for the existence of God is that of St. THOMAS AQUINAS (*Summa theologiae* 1a, 2.3). Known as the *quinque viae* or ''five ways,'' these demonstrations are proposed by Aquinas as a foundation for his systematic development of sacred theology. This article analyzes the arguments of each of the five ways, prefacing this by an introduction that explains the need for the proofs, the methodology that underlies them, and the general characteristics of the line of their argument.

Introduction

Many feel that man's innate desire for happiness, which can be only satisfied in God, makes sufficiently evident the existence of God. Although God truly implants this desire in man, the fact is that many men do not seek their happiness in God. Hence, this desire for happiness of itself is too vague to evince conclusively and clearly the existence of God (*Summa theologiae* 1a, 2.1 ad 1). The same must be said to those who hold that the existence of truth, which in general is self-evident, makes God's existence obvious (*ibid.* ad 3). Men, particularly in recent times, have frequently rejected the proposition that God exists, which could not be the case if the statement were immediately evident.

Need for proof. A self-evident proposition is one wherein ''the predicate forms part of what the subject means'' (*Summa theologiae* 1a, 2.1). ''God exists'' is such a proposition in itself since the divine essence and existence are identical. Yet, the statement is not self-evident to the human intellect because man does not grasp the divine nature as such. Clear-cut evidence of God's existence is so apparently lacking that the genuine problem concerns whether His existence can in any way be shown.

On the other hand, God's existence is not so deeply embedded in mystery that only faith can make it known. Rather, God's existence is attainable through the natural powers of human reason and is a presupposition to revealed truths (*Summa theologiae* 1a, 2.2 ad 1). In other words, both philosophy and theology may ask the question of God's existence. Philosophy asks the question in the supreme branch of natural wisdom called metaphysics and does so in order to discover the principles of its own subject matter, being in common (*ens in commune*). In theology the question is asked to ascertain whether the science has a subject matter at all. Whereas philosophy terminates its investigations of truth by arriving at God, theology initiates its study with God and uses revealed principles as it analyzes all of reality.

Since the five ways are found in a treatise that is theological and not philosophical, to expect the proofs as given in the *Summa* by St. Thomas to expound the full metaphysical implications would be to confuse theology with philosophy. Yet the five ways are truly proofs; "way" is not meant to indicate some weak expression, but rather the strong work of the theologian in his rational approach.

The five ways are meant to be demonstrations of the conclusion: God exists. Demonstration is needed when some fact or truth is not evident. Proving the obvious is not merely a waste of argument but quite impossible. God's existence is not obvious. The danger seems to be that the supposition of His existence is so remote and beyond man's intellectual capabilities that no method can be found to establish it. The difficulty would be insurmountable were the proofs to go beyond the fact that God exists. Once an attempt is made to investigate the very nature of God, the limits of the proofs for His existence are exceeded.

Methodology. The question, then, is not why God exists, which rationally cannot be asked, but whether or not God exists. St. Thomas follows an Aristotelian methodology based on the Greek philosopher's logic, physics, and metaphysics. Having answered affirmatively the question whether God's existence is demonstrable, St. Thomas presents the five ways.

DEMONSTRATION is a categorical SYLLOGISM that intends to produce certain knowledge. This syllogistic device employs a middle (or connecting) term to establish the fact that a designated predicate belongs to the subject under consideration. This middle term, called the medium of demonstration, is a DEFINITION. If the definition is based on one of the four causes, the demonstration is a priori in the sense that it gives the reason or cause why the predicate can be said of the subject. Clearly demonstration of this kind is impossible relative to God, who is beyond definition, exceeding as He does all human categories of thought.

Instead, the demonstration must be *a posteriori;* it must proceed from effect to cause and employ a nominal definition rather than a causal one. In the present consideration an effect serves as a nominal definition of the cause. St. Thomas concedes that the effect is by no means proportionate to the cause; yet, no difficulty arises since the only point the proof intends to establish is the existence of the cause (*Summa theologiae* 1a, 2.2 ad 3). For example, one who detects a fragrance need not know what the nature of the odoriferous object is in order validly to conclude that some fragrance-giving thing does exist. One author (O'Brien) suggests a brief outline of the demonstration of the first way as follows:

> God is the First Unmoved Mover (nominal definition imposed from movement); But the First Unmoved Mover exists (effect, movement demands this); Therefore God exists.

General Characteristics. All five ways begin with evidences of sense experience that are effects, as it develops, of God. Basic to the cogency of the proofs is the fact of limitation within the actualities studied, a concretion of act and potency that means dependence and thus leads to an independent being free of potency in any form. The first, second, and fifth ways consider the world of operation: motion, efficient causes, and finality. The third and fourth ways start from the actuality of being and show its extremes of contingent and necessary, and of more and less good, true, or noble.

Since all the proofs deal with effects, the notion of efficient causality is present not only in the second, as is obvious, but also in the other four. Nevertheless, in the resolution of each proof, the particular effect leads to a determined actuality of the cause that alone adequately explains the effect. The five ways are therefore truly distinct, not mere variations of one proof.

Each proof terminates in a cause that alone sufficiently explains the effect used as the middle term of the demonstration and as the nominal definition of God. In particular, this means that (1) motion is explained only by a mover not subject to motion; (2) subordinated causes are intelligible as causing only if there is a cause that is uncaused; (3) the possible or contingent must depend on a cause not merely necessary, but with no cause of its own necessity; (4) graded perfections are limited perfections, and only an unlimited perfect cause could be responsible for them; and (5) directed things moving toward determined ends depend on an intelligent ruler. In each way the crux of the proof lies in the truth that the cause reached produces a formality in the effect that the cause itself transcends. If this were not the case, the problem would still remain for solution.

Two observations from the commentary of CAJETAN on the five ways are worthy of mention. Although each proof establishes a predicate that in truth is proper to God, the proof as presented in this theological context merely establishes the need of a first mover unmoved, a first efficient cause uncaused, etc., without caring what else can be said of its nature. Secondly, the direct conclusion of the five ways is simply ''God exists'' and not ''God as God exists,'' for the latter assertion would exceed the premises; each way concludes to the proper cause of the effect adopted as the middle term, but God as God is much more than that.

Proof from Motion

The point of departure is the fact of experience that MOTION exists. ''The senses clearly perceive that some things in the world are being moved.'' Local motion is the most obvious, although as the proof unfolds, every motion or change in its totality is embraced, that is, any transit from potency to act. Were the proof restricted to physical movement, the demonstration could stop at some physical first mover. Yet any going from potency to act constitutes a real change and so falls within the definition of motion.

Argument. The force of the proof rests on the nature of motion as an incomplete act, an actualization of what is potential. Unless motion is understood to be a dependent actuality requiring something else already in act to explain it, the cogency of the proof is lost. The argument depends upon the Aristotelian concept of motion and its corollary, ''Whatever is being moved is being moved by another.'' Also rooted in the proof is the doctrine of potency and act (*see* POTENCY AND ACT). Nothing can be at the same time in potency and in act relative to the same reality, and consequently nothing can reduce itself to act in respect to that potentiality. To do so would be a contradiction. To produce motion is to give act, but nothing can give what it does not possess. Hence, the mobile thing cannot produce its own motion; it cannot give itself the very act it lacks, for otherwise it would not be in potency to it.

Motion is an effect that depends intrinsically on a cause. In other words, without the cause here and now causing, the motion would not exist. Thus the proof is not considering a motion given independent existence, as when one man generates another and he in turn generates a third, and so on. The father can die and his son continue to live and even generate, for the dependence here is accidental, limited to communicating the original viable material for conception within the mother. An immediately subordinated motion, on the other hand, ceases with the cessation of the prime mover; for example, ''if the hand does not move the stick, the stick will not move anything else.'' In moved movers an infinite regress is repugnant. St. Thomas succinctly states his reasons: ''We must stop somewhere, otherwise there will be no first cause of the change, and, as a result, no subsequent causes.''

The conclusion of the proof is that a first mover exists who is not subject to change but who is the source of all motion: and in the time of St. Thomas, at least, ''all understand this to be God.'' The causality of the first mover is necessary for every motion that occurs; for whatever may seem to be an ultimate mover within some frame of reference is itself also subject to the definition of motion and thus in the end is dependent on another mover.

The first mover must be completely above the limitations of motion. If not, the problem would still remain. From the first mover comes the act that is responsible ultimately for all motion here and now occurring. To appreciate the implications of the first way, as conceived by St. Thomas, the first mover has to be viewed as the principal agent of motion; all other agents are secondary. The divine causality of motion is seen as universal and necessary, and the prime mover is but one since He is PURE ACT, devoid of the potency that makes for multiplicity.

The first proof does not rest on this or that motion, but treats of motion in itself as something that by nature depends on a cause. Consequently, the proof from motion does not depend on the positive physical sciences, which deal with particular cases and kinds of motion. Difficulties raised against the proof on the basis of positive science should, of course, be faced; but they can be given more adequate treatment under a separate heading (*see* MOTION, FIRST CAUSE OF).

Difficulties. At this point, it may be useful simply to mention a few common difficulties, most of which pertain to the other ways as well as to the first. One such objection is based on a misconception of what is being proved. It is asked: Why not arrive at a finite being? Why could there not be many unmoved movers? Why is not nature itself a sufficient answer to motion? These questions are really not concerned with the fact of the existence of God, but attempt instead to discuss the nature of God. In the theological context of the proofs, St. Thomas takes up the question of God's nature immediately after establishing his affirmative answer to the question of God's existence. In metaphysics, on the other hand, these objections would be ridiculous; they would indicate that the philosopher had not even reached the heart of the problem concerning the principles of his science. Finitude, multiplicity, and a self-contained reality themselves encourage the quest for a more profound solution.

A second series of difficulties claims that the proofs are arbitrary. If everything requires a mover, why contradict that statement by concluding to an unmoved mover? Or if everything has a cause, why does not God need a cause? These objections arise from an inaccurate reading of the proofs. The first way maintains that whatever is being moved is being moved by another; in no way does it claim that everything must be in a state of being moved. The second way, as will be noted below, is not a study of causality as such, but is restricted to the order of efficient causality.

Thirdly, a most frequent difficulty is that if God is outside nature, that is, completely unlike it, man has no way of knowing Him. Knowledge based on nature would be insufficient, inadequate to attain the supranatural. In reply it has to be said that all knowledge of God is analogical. ANALOGY is an intellectual construct whereby the human reason touches, at least in some way, on areas of reality otherwise closed to it. Thus man's very intellect is not an observed organ as is his eye. As a result, philosophers employ analogy to make evident something of the operations and even the nature of the intellect by comparing it to the functions of the better-known eye. A man says he ''sees'' a truth; and by this he means that—just as his eye perceives its object after its fashion of knowing, sense knowledge—the mind comprehends its object in its proper mode, intellectual knowledge. Thus to talk of God's existence does not mean equating the finite existences of beings known in the universe to God's existence; it means, rather, that as existence is a perfection found in a limited way in things, it is also found in an unlimited way in God. Man talks, writes, and thinks of God in this dark manner called analogy. Even faith does not remove analogy.

Finally, a word of caution may save time and prevent confusion. The first way concludes eventually to the truth that God is always involved in the reality of motion. However, to pick out a falling leaf and ask how God is immediately implicated in its motion is to ignore the world of secondary causes also at work. Further, particular mobile things do not yield certitude in and of themselves. For incontrovertible truth, the universal and necessary are required. Demonstration takes its initial step at the sense level, but has to soar high above this level to produce a stable body of certain knowledge.

Proof from Efficient Causality

Once again St. Thomas appeals to the evidence of experience wherein men find an order of efficient causes in the things they observe. No claim is made that every cause must have a cause. In fact, the consideration of efficient causality is made not in any way whatsoever, but precisely under the aspect of the order among such causes discovered in reality. Although this activity is evident to the senses, the intellect must reason over it and comprehend its meaning to give the proof metaphysical depth.

Argument. Two important truths are prerequisite to the proof. The first is that nothing is its own efficient cause, either in being or in operating, since this would involve a contradiction—the thing would be prior to itself, in order to cause itself to be or to operate. The second is that in an ordered arrangement of efficient causes, an infinite regress is impossible. When efficient causes are in an ordered series, one cause is the cause of the next; thus, were the first or an earlier or middle cause removed in the series, the final effect also would be removed. If there were no first efficient cause, no middle efficient causes would be communicating their act, and thus no effects would be produced—a condition that man's senses clearly perceive as false. One need but think of a mechanical device such as an automobile to see the implications of efficient causality operating in a subordinated series; or one can look within himself for endless examples of subordinated efficient causality. For instance, each man is the cause of his own speaking, and this involves his intellect, will, brain, nervous system, emotions, vocal cords, mouth, and tongue. Remove the first efficient cause and none of the middle causes will function; consequently no effect will result. While the effect is being produced, it should be noted, the entire series of causes is operating.

An observation of Cajetan can be added for clarification. An intermediate cause must be under the influence of the first cause; otherwise the full efficacy of the intermediate cause is lacking. The intermediate cause is by definition not merely a prior cause but a *medium* (Lat.), that is, a means, for communicating the causality of the first efficient cause. From this it also follows that if there were no first cause, any discussion of intermediate or middle causes would be pointless. Without a first there is no intermediate cause, for the first cause is alone the cause of the intermediate's causing.

Clarification. St. Thomas's own words are the clearest reply to the repeated objection against the first two ways that if the world were eternal an infinite regress would be possible. ''In efficient causes it is impossible to proceed in infinity *per se*. Thus, there cannot be an infinite number of causes that are *per se* required for a certain effect, for instance, that a stone be moved by a stick, the stick by the hand, and so on to infinity. But it is not impossible to proceed to infinity accidentally as regards efficient causes. For instance, if all the causes thus infinitely multiplied should have the order of only one cause, their multiplication being accidental, as an artificer acts by means of many hammers accidentally, because one after the other may be broken. It is accidental, therefore, that one particular hammer acts after the action of another. Likewise it is accidental to this particular man as generator to be generated by another man; for he generates as a man, and not as the son of another man. For all men generating hold one grade of efficient causes, namely, the grade of a particular generator. Hence, it is not impossible for a man to be generated by man to infinity. Yet such a thing would be impossible if the generation of this man depended upon this man, and on an elementary body, and on the sun, and so on to infinity'' (*Summa theologiae* 1a, 46.2 ad 7).

In this way, as in the first, only the existence of the first efficient cause is established by the proof. No implication as to the nature of the first cause is mentioned, although philosophically a number of notions are derivable from the demonstration. Clearly, God is an uncaused efficient cause; otherwise the same contradiction would be involved in Him as in any cause that is a cause to itself. Pushed further, this proof as well as the others is meant to establish that God is the total cause of all being, even though secondary causes genuinely exercise causality. The secondary causes are only partial; the activity of God as first efficient cause is constant. Hence the concept of God as ''winding up'' the universe (as though it were a toy top) and letting it go to unwind is erroneous; for the proof from efficient causality makes it clearly evident that intermediate causes really depend on the first cause here and now. The first efficient causality's act always has an influx into whatever is or operates, since the dependence of the secondary causes on the first efficient cause never ceases. (*See* CAUSALITY; EFFICIENT CAUSALITY.)

Proof from Contingency

Of the five ways, the third is the least popular and probably the most controverted—both by reason of the argument proffered and because of textual difficulties. Nevertheless, eventually modern scientists may well find this proof closest to their own kind of thought. The demonstration is based on being rather than on operation and has at least a remote affinity to notions of probabilities.

Argument. The third way begins from the observable fact that some things have a CONTINGENCY surrounding their existence. Contingent in the present context is understood as meaning possible to exist and not to exist. An obvious illustration of contingent existence is the constant generation and corruption of plant life. If all things have this intrinsic potency to be and not to be, then, carrying the supposition to its ultimate limits, at some moment in the past nothing at all existed. This validly follows because whatever has an intrinsic existential contingency has a limited duration, a beginning and an end.

St. Thomas has deliberately placed a false hypothesis: ''If all things (that exist) are possible to exist and not to exist, at some time nothing existed in reality.'' The assumption that nothing existed at one time leads to the absurdity that nothing exists now; for nothing can come to be except through something already existing, and this has by supposition been ruled out. Only after squarely facing reality does St. Thomas deny universal contingency and draw the obvious inference that some necessity is demanded in things.

Difficulties. Conveniently, at this phase of the demonstration a number of difficulties can be mentioned. First of all, some have objected that the doctrine of creation is a necessary element for the cogency of the proof. On the contrary, introducing creation would mean penetrating into the nature of God when only His existence is at issue; further, the doctrine of creation is not required for the force of the proof, since the next step of the demonstration leads to the cause behind contingency. Secondly, St. Thomas cannot be accused of arguing gratuitously that all things are contingent or even that contingent things cease to be through annihilation. The argument looks to the past and not to the future in its first premise; its forward motion comes as the reasoning seeks out the necessary element in reality. Finally, the objection that St. Thomas is guilty of the error he himself noted as a weakness in the ontological argument, that is, that he argues from the possible order and concludes at the level of reality, is not justified; for the hypothesis is presented as false.

Contingent beings, then, are not sufficient to explain the existence of reality. Also, an infinite regress among contingent things of this kind is impossible. This would demand a series of infinite duration composed of things having only a finite duration; such a concept is absurd. Appeal must therefore be had to NECESSITY in things. Things are said to be necessary if they cannot not be, that is, there is not present in them a potency not to be.

Necessary Being. Many philosophers unable to discover any evidence of necessity in things protest that the proof is therefore invalid. Necessity in propositions they concede, but not necessity in existence. Nor can their objection be refuted by recourse to necessity in operations, as breathing is necessary for life. The third way rests on necessity in being, not in operation. One accepting the hylomorphic theory might point to primary matter, not as necessary in being, but as the necessary underlying principle of change. One can offer the human soul as an illustration of a being that has a necessary existence by reason of its simplicity in essence.

However, the validity of the demonstration does not demand an unequivocal answer to the question of the existence of some necessary being in the universe of immediate experience. The proof has led to the conclusion that necessity is demanded in things because contingency is inadequate for the work of sustaining dependent beings. Once this is established, then the next step is that whatever is necessary is so either from another or not. As in efficient causality, likewise here, nothing can be the cause of its own necessity, and an infinite regress is impossible. This means that a being must be posited that is intrinsically necessary, with no dependence from outside to account for its own necessity in existence. Indeed, this being is the cause of necessity in others; it is the being men call God.

The argument treats mainly of necessity in regard to existence as such. Whether some observable things always existed or not does not affect the course of the reasoning. If planets were eternal, that is, have had an infinite duration in existence, the problem of what caused their existence and permitted this endless duration would still remain. On the other hand, if all things really are contingent in their existence then a necessary being is still needed to explain how they came into existence at all and continue to be.

Textual Variants. As mentioned above, the proof has various readings. The Leonine (1880 edition) has: *Impossibile est autem omnia quae sunt talia, semper esse: quia quod possibile est non esse, quandoque non est.* ''It is impossible, however, for all things which are such (possibles), always to be: because what is possible not to be, sometimes is not.'' All the other codices, dating back to Vaticanus of the 13th century, read: *Impossibile est autem omnia quae sunt, talia esse, quia quod possible est non esse quandoque non est.* ''It is impossible that all things are, be such as these (possibles): because what is possible not to be sometimes is not.'' This second reading seems the more accurate because it follows the movement of the thought of the demonstration more closely. In practice, commentators using either version come to the same conclusion.

Proof from Grades of Perfection

Man clearly sees that some things are better than others. Much advertising is based on this truth—even the same kind of product, such as soap, will have claimants declaring one brand superior to all others. The point under consideration is a perfection that admits of more and less, not one that is indivisible such as humanity, which one either has or does not have. Further, in the realm of transcendental perfections involving analogical concepts—such as good, true, and noble—degrees of perfection are even more pronounced.

Argument. The fourth way is clearly in the setting of these TRANSCENDENTALS, which are perfections without any intrinsic limitation in themselves and yet are found in diverse things in different degrees or modes. These perfections of good, true, and noble as found in sensible reality do not flow from the nature of the things themselves. Whatever flows from the nature of a being cannot be had according to more or less; thus all men by nature have the perfection of humanity absolutely, whereas beings that are not men do not have this perfection at all. If the things of experience possessed the transcendental perfections in the way that man possesses humanity, they would have these perfections in a full, absolute way; in other words, one should expect the things he encounters to be good, true, and noble without limitation. Since this is evidently not the case—since the things of this world have goodness, truth, and nobility in varying degrees—one must conclude that these things do not possess the transcendental perfections by their nature. And, therefore, they must receive these perfections from outside, from some absolutely perfect cause that is not merely exemplary but also efficient.

The conclusion that the being of supreme perfection must be the efficient cause of perfection in all others is reached with the help of an Aristotelian principle: Whatever is the greatest in any kind (genus) of being is the cause of all that are of this kind (genus). Since this principle is somewhat subtle, St. Thomas introduces a vivid illustration. Fire is hot by its very nature, while other things, such as water and metal, become hot by participating in the heat of the fire, more or less intensely so by reason of their proximity to the fire. This participated perfection can be retained only so long as the being in which the perfection properly exists is efficiently causing the perfection in others; as soon as the fire is withdrawn, the water begins to cool. Likewise, the being in which all transcendental perfections are realized absolutely must be the efficient cause of whatever participation of these perfections is found in other things. And this supreme source of all perfection is the being men call God.

Use of Plato and Aristotle. Although the reference to efficient causality and the example of the fire are based on ARISTOTLE, a Platonic notion is really at the heart of this fourth way. In the *Summa* St. Thomas does not mention PLATO, but in another work (*De pot.* 3.5) he acknowledges his indebtedness to the author of the *Dialogues.* St. Thomas actually invokes an analogy of proper proportionality, and Plato's doctrine supplies him with the basic insight.

Plato's own words should make evident what St. Thomas took from him. "He who has been instructed thus far in the things of love, and who has learned to see the beautiful in due order and succession, when he comes toward the end will suddenly perceive a nature of wondrous beauty . . . a nature which in the first place is everlasting, not growing and decaying, or waxing and waning; secondly, not fair in one point of view and foul in another . . . but beauty absolute, separate, simple, and everlasting, which without diminution and without increase, or any change, is imparted to the ever growing and perishing beauties of all other things" (*Symp.* 211). As with beauty, so too with good, true, noble, a supreme or greatest must exist.

Plato carried his theory to what is known as the world of Forms and Ideas, some kind of separate world where genuine archetypes apparently existed as distinguished from the "shadows" of them in this material world. Whatever Plato really meant is not at issue in this proof. St. Thomas does not accept any extreme presentation of the Platonic theory. What he does see in it are the elements basic to the analogy of proper proportionality and the truth made evident through this analogy, namely, that there is some one First to which all others are referred and from which they derive their share of truth, goodness, beauty, etc.

Having discovered, or perhaps inserted, analogy in Plato's doctrine, St. Thomas turns to Aristotle in order to show that what is supremely true and good must be supremely being. In the text explicitly cited at this point (*Meta.* 993a 30-b 30), Aristotle's context is different from that of St. Thomas. Aristotle is discussing the arduous effort involved in investigating truth and concludes with the observation that "the principles of eternal things must be always most true . . . so that as each thing is in respect of being, so is it in respect of truth." St. Thomas borrows this thought in order to arrive at God, who is First Truth and First Being. Finally, as has already been noted, it is to Aristotle that St. Thomas appeals in order to establish that the God who is First Truth and First Being is the efficient source of the truth and the very existence of all other things.

Proof from Order

Another evident fact of experience is the orderly operation of nature. In the overwhelming majority of cases, the earth brings forth her fruits and is thoroughly predictable as to her activities. Although lacking knowledge, the acorn is moved almost without exception toward its proper end of becoming an oak. Such uniform and consistent attainment of goals by nescient beings requires an explanation. To attribute it all to CHANCE would be hopelessly naive, since chance by its own connotation means something out of the ordinary, something not within the normal order of procedure. A more profound explanation must be sought.

Argument. The fifth way is carefully restricted to natural things lacking knowledge. Hence the proposition that a watch requires a watchmaker to design and make it is really not pertinent to the present demonstration, nor indeed is it the most helpful illustration with which to suggest the existence of God. For one thing, unlike nature, the watch continues to exist independently of the watchmaker once he has made it. Likewise the present proof is based rather on the notion of the government or guidance of natural things, rather than on design as such.

St. Thomas's example, chosen with his customary precision, is that of an arrow moving toward a target. The arrow is directed toward its end; so is nature. The arrow depends entirely on the archer for its operation; nature depends entirely on something outside herself. Lack of knowledge is a definite limitation in a being acting for an end; the lack must be supplied in some way from without by a knowing being.

Thus the orderly movement of natural things toward their proper ends indicates the presence of an intelligent being. Order demands intelligence, because order is the arrangement of things in a definite series according to a norm, and only an intellect can conceive the relationships involved in such arrangement. The establishment of means to an end requires some foresight, some comprehension of relations, and even more primary, a conception of the end itself. Only an intelligent being satisfies these conditions.

A deeper insight into the argument is obtained when it is recalled that GOOD and END are convertible terms. For St. Thomas, the best evidence that natural things act for an end is the fact that they tend to act in such a way as to achieve what is best for them. The conclusion to an intelligent being rests, in the final analysis, on the need for an agent by whose intention the things of nature are directed toward their good. Thus the proof begins by considering natural things as passively governed in their movement and ends with an intelligent agent or efficient cause that actively governs them.

Clarifications. Certainly there are numerous cases in which natural things fail to attain their end, but the failure is due to what may be called accidental interference; thus the acorn will die in the earth if conditions for its survival are not present. At any rate, instances of failure can never outweigh the overwhelming evidence that exists for order and finality. The fact that nature does consistently attain her goals argues to the existence of an intelligent being. Furthermore, the constant achievement of the end means that the intellect responsible for the operations is never idle, but is exercising its causality continuously. And the intelligent ruler who exercises universal and constant direction over nature is the being men call God.

Much confusion over the fifth way is avoided if one remembers that the demonstration is concerned only with internal finality, not with external finality. An acorn is of its own intrinsic nature potentially an oak tree; it has a tendency to attain that end in a favorable environment. Later the tree may be chopped down and made into toothpicks; but that involves another scheme of things not pertinent to the fifth way. Hence the answer to the question whether the purpose or end of the egg is to be a chicken or an egg sandwich is: the intrinsic end of the egg is to be a chicken; the external ends of the egg are as limitless as its possibilities (*See* FINAL CAUSALITY).

See Also: GOD IN PHILOSOPHY, 2; AGNOSTICISM.

Bibliography: Thomas Aquinas, *Summa theologiae* 1a, 2, Eng. tr. and comment. v. 2, ed. T. MCDERMOTT (New York 1964–), 60 v.; *Suma teologica,* 16 v. (*Biblioteca de autores cristianos* dispersed nos. 29–197; 1947–60) v. 1, q. 1–26, with notes on the proofs by F. MUÑIZ. T. C. O'BRIEN, *Metaphysics and the Existence of God* (Washington 1960). J. MARITAIN, *Approaches to God,* tr. P. O'REILLY (New York 1954). R. GARRIGOU-LAGRANGE, *God: His Existence and His Nature,* tr. B. ROSE, 2 v. (St. Louis 1934–36).

[R. C. SMITH]

GOD IN PAGAN THOUGHT

The concept of God in primitive religions has been the subject of considerable dispute. Suffice it to say that the evolutionary theory whereby all primitive peoples are regarded as slowly developing from an initial polytheism toward a gradual monotheism has met with sufficient modifications in actual case studies as to have fallen somewhat out of favor. In addition to belief in a plurality of spirits, many primitive groups give evidence of a belief in a high god, in the sky or at a great distance, supreme, uncreated, molder of the present world, but often somewhat remote, and not regarded as interfering much, if at all, with the lives of men. Such a high god appears early in the creation myths of such peoples as the Australian aborigines and primitive Indians.

Primitive Religions. From Egypt come more sophisticated accounts of creation, with the self-emergence of the creator-god Atum and his organization of a preexisting chaos represented by four pairs of primordial

''Polyphemus and Galatea'' by Annibale Carracci, c. 1604, detail of ''Love Scenes of the Pagan Gods,'' on the ceiling of the Farnese Palace, Florence, Italy. (Alinari-Art Reference/Art Resource, NY)

''gods.'' A cosmogony is effected by Atum's production from himself of another four pairs of gods who represent air and moisture, earth and sky, and the creatures of this world. In the so-called Memphis Theology, an attempt is made to go behind these physical terms to an account that stresses internal thought and external utterance as the process of creation, although the originator of the process, the Memphite god Ptah, is equated with the primeval waters out of which Atum emerged.

In Mesopotamian myth there is a gradual overcoming of the powers of chaos, culminating in the decisive victory of the god Marduk, a later version of the storm god Enlil, and himself to be replaced by the god Assur in subsequent accounts, when the power of Assyria had become dominant.

The Sumerian, Egyptian, and Assyro-Babylonian myths are of considerable interest to Hebrew scholars, and their literary forms provide parallels with the Book of GENESIS. More information on this subject is found elsewhere, as also on the Indian concept of Brahman and the origins of JAINISM, BUDDHISM, and HINDUISM. Space limits the scope of this article to a survey of Greek thought.

Ten avatars of the Hindu God of Vishnu. (Archive Photos)

Pre-Socratic Thought. The Babylonian, Egyptian, and Hittite myths are not without parallels in the earliest Greek cosmogonies, as found in Homer, Hesiod, Pherecydes of Syros, and the Greek lyric poets. The account of Oceanus as a broad stream encircling the earth and as the ''begetter of gods'' and the story of the mutilation of Ouranos by Kronos strongly suggest common sources. Again, the paramount figure to emerge from a succession of deified cosmic constituents is the god of thunder and lightning, Zeus, on a par with the storm gods Enlil and Marduk.

The pre-Socratic philosophers present no sharp break with the mythologists and cosmogonists who were their forerunners. They are representative of a gradual change toward processes of discursive reasoning in accounting for physical phenomena. Thus the view of Thales that the earth rests on water or that water is the principle of all things and that ''all things are full of gods'' has obvious parallels in Egyptian creation myths and in the typical Mesopotamian attitude to the surrounding physical world. To his first principle, the ''Indefinite,'' Anaximander applies the Homeric epithets reserved for the gods, i.e., ''eternal (or immortal) and free from old age.'' For Anaximenes ''air'' or ''mist'' was divine and the source of all the gods. Thus the Milesian thinkers closely identified their prime cosmological constituents with the divine, apparently while continuing their adherence to the gods of traditional religion.

With Xenophanes of Colophon and HERACLITUS OF EPHESUS, however, one meets with some outspoken criticism of accepted religious belief and practice. Xenophanes criticized the concept of the gods in Homer and Hesiod as anthropomorphic, and their behavior as immoral. In their place he posited one God, completely unlike mortals, who moves all things by the thought of His mind. Heraclitus, on the one hand, identified God with the Logos, or principle of balance in all things, and with cosmic fire or Zeus; on the other hand, he criticized the excesses of superstition and obscenity in traditional cults.

Other thinkers, such as PYTHAGORAS and PARMENIDES, do not seem to have made any explicit equation between their first principles or view of reality and any divinity. EMPEDOCLES personified the cosmic forces of love and strife and made Aphrodite prior to the other gods, but he was sharply critical of the anthropomorphism and cruel bloodshed embodied in religious mythology. ANAXAGORAS made the important contribution of considering that the whole cosmological process is controlled by a transcendent Mind, which he termed "infinite" and "self-ruled," but did not explicitly describe as "divine." Finally Diogenes of Apollonia reverted to the notion of "air" as the basic substance, but this "air" is both intelligent and divine.

In summary, these pre-Socratic thinkers tended to identify God with their primary cosmological principles, much in the tradition of the earlier mythologies, but criticism of traditional religion and refinement of the notion of deity was also current among some of them, as among some of the Greek poets who were their contemporaries. The poets had received from Homer and Hesiod the notion of Zeus as a god of justice and retribution, along with less edifying stories about the Olympian deities. All of this was accepted more or less uncritically by Pindar; but especially with the Greek tragedians problems of human suffering, in particular fortuitous suffering on the part of the innocent, and questions of conflicting obligations in the moral order became paramount. There was a deep interest in human pride and in the workings of divine justice. The idea of the supreme deity was exalted and criticism of the inconsistencies of traditional religion became evident.

Greek Religions. Before going any further with this account, it is necessary to stress that the distinctive views of the Greek philosophers on God represent the thought of only a select minority. Throughout the period from the seventh century B.C. to the fourth century A.D. the various Greek communities lived a life that included social and personal religious worship, centered around a traditional plurality of gods, with special local cults and various modifications and accretions over the centuries, as well as the various equations made with Roman deities in the late republic and under the empire. The traditional Olympian gods, as established by Homer and Hesiod and hymned by later Greek poets, continued to be objects of worship, with Zeus assuming the role of father figure. The ecstatic worship of Dionysos, the cult of Demeter and Persephone at Eleusis, the teachings of ORPHISM, the consultation of Apollo at Delphi, and the religious brotherhood of the Pythagoreans were more particular manifestations of the religious spirit in close association with individual figures and localities. Alongside the legalistic and ritualistic relationship between the god and his worshiper ran an element of personal devotion and the desire to achieve purification of the soul by initiation into the mysteries, or even to achieve ecstatic union with the deity. This vast area of religious belief and practice provided a constant background to the views of the Greek thinkers. [*See* GREEK PHILOSOPHY (RELIGIOUS ASPECTS).]

Socrates and Plato. With SOCRATES, one finds a belief in the conventional plurality of gods going hand in hand with references to "God" or "the god" in the singular. Socrates was too wise a man to think that human reason could settle every question; some matters were beyond it and needed the help of divine guidance (*Xen. mem.* 1.1). The final passage of Plato's *Apology* contains references to both "gods" and "God," and Socrates's last words in the *Phaedo,* "Crito, we owe a cock to Asclepius; do not neglect the debt but pay it," are no doubt meant to show his careful observance of traditional ritual.

In the writings of PLATO the role assigned to God gradually becomes more prominent. The Ideas, including the Idea of the Good, are universals or natures, whereas God is a being having a nature in a supreme degree. He is thus not to be confused with the Ideas, nor does he appear to be the cause of them, in spite of *Republic* 597, where for the sake of comparison God is said to have wrought the Ideal Bed. As the demiurge or "creator" of the *Timaeus,* it is his function to take over the chaos of disorder and reduce it to order, but he is limited by "necessity" and has to work with materials not created by him. The WORLD SOUL and the heavenly bodies are also divine, although in a lesser degree. Man as the microcosm is to achieve happiness by regulating his actions on the model of the universe. This is what "becoming like to God as far as possible"—originally a reference to righteousness and wisdom (*Theaet.* 176A)—tends to become in the *Timaeus,* and this cosmic view of religion is emphasized in the *Epinomis.* Yet God is not merely some impersonal cosmic principle, but a person who is good and providential, the cause of good but not of evil, with whom a relationship of love may be cultivated (*Leges* 716). Indeed in some sense man's highest purpose is to be God's plaything (*Leges* 803C–E).

Certainly the overall impression given by Plato's writings is an atmosphere of great reverence for the divine, an exalted notion of it, and a strong desire for assimilation to it in some intimate personal relationship. To be more precise than this would be to state explicitly what Plato merely hints at implicitly.

Aristotle. There may be something of an evolution in the theology of Aristotle. Fragments of his early dialogues give evidence of an argument from the degrees of being for the existence of God, an argument from the order within the universe, and arguments from human experience in dreams, premonitions, and inner presentiment. There may be some traces of a divine providence in the early theory of star souls endowed with sight and hearing, and in the *Eudemian Ethics* the ultimate norm of human action is the service and knowledge of God. In several texts, however, Aristotle links nature and the divine and so paves the way for Stoic insistence on "life according to nature." In his later emphasis on cosmic religion, Aristotle undoubtedly follows the lead given by Plato in his *Timaeus and Laws.* God becomes the ''Unmoved Mover'' of the *Physics,* as required by current astronomical theories, a pure Intellect who moves the outermost sphere by desire, the desire finding realization in the perfection of circular movement as an imitation of the eternal ''thinking upon thinking.'' God is identical with eternal life, because the actuality of thought is life, and this life is most good and self-sufficient. He is His own well-being, whereas man's good lies outside himself. Each of the heavenly spheres requires its own unmoved mover to account for its particular motion; what relationship exists between the Prime Mover and these other unmoved movers is not clear. There are traces in Aristotle of an interest in mystery religions and of a personal approach to God, but the main emphasis in his treatises is on a cosmic principle removed from any preoccupation with the universe or the men in it.

Stoicism and Epicureanism. The Stoics followed the emphasis in the later Plato and Aristotle on cosmic religion, while at the same time they looked back to Heraclitus. For them God is the active principle in the universe, the Logos, Fate, but also a creative fire, immanent and material in the sense of not separable from matter. The Logos contains within itself the seminal grounds of all things. God is also called Zeus and ''Nature,'' as the law of the universe and universal providence. Other gods are admitted as names for the different aspects of the world. (*See* STOICISM.)

For EPICURUS, perhaps influenced by Aristotle's Unmoved Mover, God is a living, incorruptible, and blessed being. Epicurus rejects popular theology as attributing to the gods qualities and characteristics incompatible with their nature. They are not concerned with the universe or with human affairs, since freedom from toil and disturbance are necessary prerequisites of happiness. In any case the universe contains so much evil that it could not be a work of the gods. Man is aware of the gods by means of fine mental images or effluences that come to him from them in sleep. They are an example for him to imitate in achieving tranquillity of soul. The wise man marvels at their nature and disposition, tries to draw near it, and even desires to achieve contact and union with it. Thus he is a friend of the gods, and they of him. Epicurus admits the gods of popular religion, suitably purified from superstitious notions, and even many deities besides. (*See* EPICUREANISM.)

Later Greek Thought. The last century B.C. and the first two centuries A.D. were a period of conflation in Greek thought. The resurgence of interest in Plato's dialogues and Aristotle's treatises resulted in attempts to harmonize their views on God on the part of the Middle Platonists, who adopted the ways of negation, eminence, and analogy in speaking of the deity, and described the Platonic Ideas as the ''thoughts of God.'' It remained for PLOTINUS to bring this process to its culmination, but he was not an adherent of popular religion. He was more the philosopher of optimistic rational contemplation than a religious person. He refers to his supreme principle, the One and the Good, as ''God'' almost incidentally and uses both neuter and masculine pronouns with reference to it. The second hypostasis, ''Nous,'' is referred to as ''God'' somewhat more readily. Yet the culmination of the soul's return is undoubtedly a personal and mystical union in the highest degree. PORPHYRY says that Plotinus actually attained this state four times while in his company.

The tendency to make God ineffable and totally transcendent, evident even among the Middle Platonists, was pushed much further by the Gnostics, Hermetic writers, and later Neoplatonists. Faced with the task of reconciling Greek thought with a strictly monotheistic and creationist theology, the Arab thinkers who followed in the footsteps of the later Neoplatonists and Aristotelian commentators were the first, apart from St. Augustine, to build up a body of thought describing God's essence, causality, and relation to the world and men in philosophical terminology. The Christian medieval theologians and philosophers owe them a debt far greater than is generally appreciated. (*See* NEOPLATONISM; PATRISTIC PHILOSOPHY.)

Yet, throughout the long history of Greek thought, the notion of a strict monotheism does not seem evident. In company with other, more primitive peoples, the Greeks preserved a tradition of belief in a plurality of gods, with a special position assigned to Zeus as ''high god.'' The tendency to deify cosmic forces carried over from mythology into rational thought. In addition, some of the foremost Greek thinkers produced concepts of supreme metaphysical entities, hardly personal at all, whose identification with the deity is somewhat casual, although the notion of the deity itself underwent considerable refinement.

See Also: RELIGION; GREEK PHILOSOPHY.

Bibliography: F. M. CORNFORD, *From Religion to Philosophy* (New York 1912). W. W. JAEGER, *The Theology of the Early Greek Philosophers,* tr. E. S. ROBINSON (Oxford 1947). R. K. HACK, *God in Greek Philosophy to the Time of Socrates* (Princeton 1931). W. K. C. GUTHRIE, *The Greeks and Their Gods* (London 1950). E. R. DODDS, *The Greeks and the Irrational* (Berkeley 1951). A. M. J. FESTUGIÈRE, *Personal Religion among the Greeks* (Berkeley 1960); *La Révélation d'Hermès Trismégiste,* 4 v. (Paris 1944–54); *Epicurus and His Gods,* tr. C. W. CHILTON (Cambridge, Mass. 1956); *Contemplation et Vie contemplative selon Platon* (2d ed. Paris 1950). F. SOLMSEN, *Plato's Theology* (Ithaca 1942). P. MERLAN, ''Aristotle's Unmoved Movers,'' *Traditio* 4 (1946) 1–30. A. H. ARMSTRONG and

R. A. MARKUS, *Christian Faith and Greek Philosophy* (New York 1962).

[W. H. O'NEILL]

GOD IN PHILOSOPHY

This article deals with the place, existence, and nature of God in philosophy, as philosophy has come to be understood since the High Middle Ages. For the ancient Greek philosophical views of God, *see* GOD IN PAGAN THOUGHT. For the rise of Christian philosophical reflection on God, *see* GOD, 2. CHRISTIAN TRADITION.

1. Place

A survey of views on the place of God in philosophy would have to be as universal as the history of philosophy itself. While there is no consensus on this matter, one generalization based on the history of the question does seem valid. The term or idea ''God'' has most often been a religious, cultural, or theological presupposition accepted anteriorly to the philosophical enterprise. Philosophers have built their systems on this presupposition; or they have sought to justify it or to demolish it or to show that it lies outside reason's grasp. Often enough the prephilosophical assumption has led to nonphilosophical procedures and conclusions. There is, then, need to separate what is assumption from what is truly philosophical discovery in dealing with this question.

Catholic Views. Among Catholics there are widely accepted attitudes toward God's place in philosophy. For the Catholic to speak of God at all means the one true God, Creator of all things, visible and invisible. ''God in philosophy'' means this much before any particular philosophical endeavor, namely, that the God of the Creed can, by the resources of reason alone, be shown to exist and to have certain attributes, that this knowledge can be knowledge derived only through God's effects, and that it is not a direct understanding of His proper nature. These are religious teachings, the principal points of Catholic doctrine on the question of God and human reason [H. Denzinger, *Enchiridion symbolorum,* ed. A. Schönmetzer (Freiburg 1963) 3026, 3041; cf. 2841–47]. They need not jeopardize the authenticity of the philosophical procedures; they should, however, be acknowledged as presuppositions that serve to orient the Catholic who philosophizes about God toward reaching God the Creator, to disorient him from any alleged direct experience of the divine, and to suggest the search for proofs that proceed from sensible effects to a transcendent cause.

The way in which the neo-scholastic tradition in philosophy among Catholics has matched these indications came to be quite common, at least in its general lines. God is reached through METAPHYSICS, in its highest phase, called natural theology (*see* THEOLOGY, NATURAL). There is also basic agreement that metaphysics attains a knowledge of God by its answer to the question: Does God exist? From the way this question is answered, the rest of reason's yield about God is shaped. The methodology employed in facing the basic problem is simple. A PROOF rising from effect to cause is required. The conclusion of the proof is a proposition, ''God exists,'' ''God'' being the subject and ''exists'' the predicate. In such a proof the medium of DEMONSTRATION, the middle term, is a nominal DEFINITION of the subject, i.e., one that merely expresses what the term ''God'' means. The proofs developed amount to this: God is first mover, or first cause, or first necessary being, or most perfect being, or governor of the universe; now one, or more, or all of these exist; therefore God exists. The burden of the proof is in establishing the second, or minor proposition; this is usually done by referring to the ''five ways'' of St. THOMAS AQUINAS (*see* GOD, PROOFS FOR THE EXISTENCE OF). What is involved is an analysis of the dependencies found in the beings of experience, which the terms themselves suggest. The conclusion signifies God under all these ''names,'' and from its implications the rest of the philosophical discoveries about the divine nature and attributes are derived.

There is no doubt that this mode of proceeding satisfies the religious presuppositions of Catholics. But the demand has been felt to justify a philosophical encounter with God on the basis also of philosophy's own epistemological canons. Generally this has been done by stating that the question of God belongs to metaphysics, since God is ''given'' in the very division of being into created and uncreated; thus a part of philosophy must be devoted to God. But since this way of proceeding seems already to presuppose God's existence, at least implicitly, another has been more recently espoused. A Christian philosophizes as a Christian; the Christian experience of God is the basis for philosophy and should be frankly admitted. On this basis any proof of God's existence must lead to the ''I am who am'' of Exodus. Thus, in the one case a questionably ''pure'' philosophical approach to God rests on an implicit religious assumption; in the other, the religious assumption is made explicit in a CHRISTIAN philosophy of God.

Thomistic Teaching. One can, however, formulate a philosophical approach different from the foregoing. This views metaphysics as a purely rational, philosophical account of experienced reality that proceeds along lines demanded by the human mind's gradual opening upon the world of experience. The statement of Aquinas that the SCIENCE (*scientia*) of metaphysics considers God not as its subject, but as a PRINCIPLE of its subject, implies this sort of inquiry about God (*In Boeth. de Trin.* 5.4). Metaphysics does not set for itself the task of discovering God; the task is thrust upon it by its subject, BEING. But this is not based on a presupposition that being is created or uncreated. Nothing is presupposed; metaphysics remains a process of discovery throughout.

The first step is the discovery of being as an intelligible value of the experienced real, one that is not attained properly by the natural philosopher's consideration of the things of experience as changeable or animate. With this initial discovery comes the realization that things need to be evaluated as they are existents, and further that through this distinctive grade of intelligibility something of the nature of any reality whatsoever can be known and expressed. At this point metaphysics is already self-conscious of its status as first philosophy, of its being an ultimate and absolute account of all reality. In its apprehension of being as such, it is already on the way to being self-vindicating through its awareness of being's own evidence. On the basis of the distinctive character of the subject of the science, metaphysics proceeds to evaluate the beings of experience, those at the level of the corporeal and the human. Through observation and experience of the ways in which these are beings, there is a discovery of composition, imperfection, and limitation. With this comes the knowledge that such beings are not self-explanatory. It is then that the inquiry for an explanation leads to the affirmation of their dependence on a first cause. This very dependence demands that the first cause be free of the same dependence; as cause, the first cause must be a being not composed of essence and existence (*esse*) as really distinct principles. From this truth, in turn, metaphysics is in a position to demonstrate that being in every other case is so composed, and thus must necessarily manifest all the aspects of limitation that started the inquiry in the first place.

Such a process does lead to philosophical knowledge about God, but not by presuppositions of a non-philosophical nature. No nominal definition of God need be tailored to fit these assumptions. The knowledge of God is really the knowledge of the dependence of all being upon Him. The Christian's recognition of God in this discovery does not have to be incorporated into the philosophical enterprise. The basis and vindication of metaphysics are autonomous, relying on the self-assurance afforded by being, the subject of the science. A metaphysics that remains true to itself and has its own interior criterion does lead to certitude about its affirmations concerning God, that these are not pure equivocation, and to the awareness that the proper being of God can be neither experienced nor directly known by reason alone. It faces any denial of God's existence with the resources of its own apprehension of being. The religious presuppositions of the Catholic are served; but they do not substitute for, or distort the fulfillment of, the task to which they point, viz, to achieve an authentically philosophical knowledge of God.

Contemporary Thought. The problem of knowing God shifted in the late twentieth century from metaphysics to the question of religious language, i.e., whether non-empirical language can express any meaning whatsoever. Ever since Ludwig Wittgenstein overthrew Hume's epistemological principle (that the meaning of any assertion can be sought only in its verification) by distinguishing truth from meaning and locating meaning in usage, theistic endeavor has been directed to establishing the truth value of God-talk as something more than emotive or performative language by authenticating how it can refer to a Transcendent which really exists outside consciousness. This has had implications for both theology and philosophy.

Faith Alone. The classical Protestant distrust of natural theology continues to allow affirmations of God's existence and nature only from within an ambit of faith, even though the discussion has recently moved beyond the Barth-Bultmann axis into hermeneutical and eschatological theology. The former emphasizes faith as language event and, using categories of the later Heidegger, allows for knowing God not as object but as subject, to which the believer relates himself (by way of Scripture and exegesis) in a stance of nonobjectified ''primal thinking'' (Heinrich Ott). Eschatological theology prefers to equate faith with universal history, refusing the distinctions between the events of history (*Historie*) and their appropriated meaning (*Geschichte*), and contends that history delivers its own interpretation. According to this view, the ultimate meaning of all human history is proleptically offered in the Resurrection of Christ, in which God manifests who he is for man (Wolfhart Pannenberg).

Reason Alone. Some theologians have dismissed the above approaches as fideism, and have sought to ground the knowledge of God in human rationality. Negatively, this has issued in new dismissals of the logic and intellectualism of traditional theism (Anthony Kenny). Positively, these efforts have taken several directions: 1) Charles Hartshorne and Norman Malcolm have tried to rehabilitate the ontological argument by arguing that if ''necessary being'' has any meaning then what it means must actually exist. 2) Process thought establishes a knowledge of God by extrapolating from a metaphysics of becoming in which God, who really exists in both a primordial nature and a nature which undergoes change through the processes of finite existents, is understood to perfect the world and himself through realizing in himself whatever of value is achieved within the world (Alfred Whitehead, Charles Hartshorne, John Cobb, Jr.). 3) In Anglo-Saxon circles linguistic analysis often substitutes for metaphysics, but presses beyond the narrow positivism inherited from Hume (Bertrand Russell, early Wittgenstein) to justify a rational but nondemonstrative "logic of reasoned beliefs." This approach employs epistemological techniques of emergent probabilities, etc., in an empirically based knowledge of the nonempirical in which knowing God is regarded as interpretative knowledge, analogous to knowing, for instance, that something is beautiful (John Wisdom, Anthony Flew, James Richmond).

Reason under Faith. By and large contemporary solutions have assumed some form of coherence between faith and reason. In the tradition of *American Empiricism* the notion of experience has been broadened to include the encounters of faith, experienced as offering answers to questions of ultimacy posed by human existence on the plane of immediacy (John Smith). In phenomenology, human existence comes to appearance within consciousness as radically contingent and precarious, thereby pointing to God as necessary, not by way of rational inference *from* the finite but as a discernment *within* the finite of clues of a Transcendent. God is signaled in a purely symbolic knowledge, therefore, not as Cause but as Presence (Langdon Gilkey, Louis Dupré). The empirical approach suggests Tillich's principle of correlation between the evident realities of man's existential situation and any philosophical/theological solution, reduced, however, from the ontological to the ontic realm. Phenomenology, on the other hand, seems to surmise God somewhat after the fashion in which the Transcendental Ego is surmised as undergirding the Empirical Ego (Husserl).

Among Catholic thinkers, this outlook surfaces in a marked tendency to understand Romans 1:18–20 and the dogmatic constitution *Dei Filius* of Vatican Council I (DS 3004), in which the natural knowability of God is asserted, as referring to something that is achieved, historically and in fact, only by those who already believe; the claim then is one of possibility not of fact. This amounts to reconstruing natural theology as a movement wherein prior faith knowledge, through conscious reflection, articulates itself in structures which in themselves are not rationally convincing or probative.

Significant attempts at implementing this project are represented by Karl Rahner, Bernard Lonergan, and Emerich Coreth. Each has, in his own way, evolved a critical epistemology, loosely designated as Transcendental Thomism. In this approach, all explicit knowledge is a conceptual explicitation of a prior nonconceptual preunderstanding of the totality of Being. This preunderstanding is rooted in a prehension (*Vorgriff*) by finite spirit of Being as the unrestricted horizon of its consciousness, on which basis knowing is a "performing" of Being. Thus, all knowledge is a subjective dynamism of spirit toward God, affirmed not by demonstrative logic in service of faith but by the method of transcendental reduction. An analysis of this unthematic preknowledge, insofar as it is the condition for the very possibility of all other knowledge, enables the believing theologian to recognize this unlimited horizon as materially identifiable with God (Rahner). So conceived, knowledge is heuristic, first posing the question of God conditionally and then, upon intelligent satisfaction of the conditions, rendering the affirmation of God as a condition for the intelligibility of the real which is only virtually unconditioned (Lonergan).

Dominic DePetter and Edward Schillebeeckx have presented an alternative to this approach, rejecting the analysis of subjectivity in favor of an objective dynamism of knowing wherein judgment is a nonconceptual activity that implicitly intuits, in its own order of intentionality, the realm of real, extramental, finite Being. This implicit intuition of the real in its very finiteness and contingency releases a dynamism on which basis the intellect is led to affirm God as Infinite Cause. The intellect is led to this affirmation objectively and noetically, i.e., from within the intelligible contents of its own concepts (the transcendentals) as these provide a perspective out of which God can be designated without being represented. Underlying this is a metaphysics of participation whose epistemological counterpart is analogy, sc., the expansive and projective power latent in human intelligence to affirm the Unknown in its pure relationality to what it does know.

Bibliography: T. C. O'BRIEN, *Metaphysics and the Existence of God* (Washington 1960) 264–269, complete bibliog. W. A. WALLACE, "Metaphysics and the Existence of God," *The New Scholasticism,* 36 (1962) 529–531. J. OWENS, "Existential Act, Divine Being, and the Subject of Metaphysics," *ibid.* 37 (1963) 359–363. W. J. HILL, *Knowing the Unknown God* (New York 1971). L. GILKEY, *Naming the Whirlwind* (Indianapolis, New York 1969). J. RICHMOND, *Theology and Metaphysics* (New York 1971). L. DUPRÉ, *The Other Dimension* (Garden City, N.Y. 1972). R. J. ROTH, ed., *God: Knowable and Unknowable* (New York 1973).

[T. C. O'BRIEN/W. J. HILL/EDS.]

2. Existence

God is not an object of human experience, and hence His existence is not immediately evident to man and must be demonstrated. Thus arises the problem of God's existence, a problem that lies at the summit of philosophical endeavor and whose solution has direct bearing on the meaning and purpose of human life. If God does not exist, then man becomes a law to himself and the norm of his own acts; but if God exists, man must acknowledge his essential dependence on a creator, who is also his conservator, legislator, and judge, to whom he is responsible for all his acts and operations. This is the striking disjunction that somehow or other confronts every individual with a cogency that admits no delay or alternative.

Philosophers are acutely aware of the importance of this problem and attempt to offer a solution in line with their own systems. Their attitudes toward God's existence may be reduced to three: theists affirm it, atheists deny it, and agnostics question it. Along with these three main positions there are systems of philosophy that admit the existence of God but deny some of the basic characteristics of the Supreme Being, such as His personal nature, transcendence, and providence. There are also those who refuse to admit the problematic nature of the issue and claim that man has a quasi-intuitive knowledge of God or a direct experience of His presence. This article sketches, in broad outline, various philosophical errors regarding the existence of God, alternative approaches to the existence of God that have been advanced by philosophers, and philosophical proofs for God's existence.

Philosophical Errors. The chief errors of philosophies with regard to the existence of a Supreme Being may be classified under the headings of atheism, agnosticism, and ontologism.

Atheism. ATHEISM is the theory of those who deny the existence of God. This definition does not apply to practical atheism, which is a way of life rather than a philosophical theory, or to negative atheism, i.e., the attitude of those who have no knowledge of God or do not care to acquire it. The definition applies only to positive theoretical atheism, or the kind of atheism that presents a problem to the philosopher inasmuch as it attempts to destroy belief in God by demolishing its rational foundation. Whether or not it is possible for a man to be absolutely convinced of the nonexistence of God, at least for an extended time, is questionable. But the fact remains that there have always been philosophers who have challenged belief in a Supreme Being and who have worked to recast and reconstruct their thought and estimation of human values on a purely atheistic, or antitheistic, basis. This is particularly true in an age that has witnessed the tragic and solitary atheism of a man such as F. W. NIETZSCHE, the literary and fashionable atheism of some extreme existentialists, and the revolutionary atheism of dialectical materialism.

Agnosticism. The major threat to theistic belief is not so much atheism, with its ruthless and irrational attacks on God, as it is the more subtle and therefore more insidious form of error named AGNOSTICISM. The term means literally ''lack of knowledge,'' and was coined by T. H. Huxley in 1869 to describe the attitude of a person who asserts the inability of the mind to know the realities corresponding to man's ultimate scientific, philosophical, and religious ideas. There are various types of agnosticism. Modern religious agnosticism assumes two principal forms, the rigid and the moderate. Rigid, or pure, agnosticism considers the problem of God as being entirely beyond the reach of human intelligence. Man can know absolutely nothing about God, not even whether He exists or not. Moderate or dogmatic agnosticism believes in the existence of God, but denies any rational foundation for such a belief. As far as the nature of God is concerned, moderate agnosticism goes along with rigid agnosticism in professing complete ignorance.

Two antimetaphysical schools of thought have contributed to the affirmation and spreading of modern agnosticism, viz, Comte's POSITIVISM and Kant's criticism (*see* CRITICISM, PHILOSOPHICAL). Although the two doctrines differ widely from each other, both are indebted to Hume's subjective EMPIRICISM and both attempt to reduce the notion of knowledge to scientific knowledge. Since God is not the object of empirical observation, it follows that in their view man cannot have any concept of Him. But whereas for COMTE the belief in God is useless and even harmful to mankind, inasmuch as it hampers the natural development of human reason, for KANT it becomes an act of faith for which no rational justification is given. Comte is a pure agnostic; Kant a dogmatic agnostic.

The impact of these two philosophies is manifest in Herbert Spencer's theory of the Unknowable. SPENCER admits the existence of the ABSOLUTE as a necessary postulate for the intelligibility of the relative objects of human experience, but he denies any knowledge of the Absolute. The mentality created by Spencer and his predecessors influenced the religious theory of William JAMES. Following the pragmatic principle that an idea is true if it works and produces good results, James maintains that the belief in God, which is largely a matter of feeling, is true because it has a definite value in concrete life. The empirical study of such belief shows in effect that it expresses confidence in the promise of the future and has beneficial results for one's life, both as an individual and as a member of society. James spurns the traditional proofs of God's existence and settles for the ''hypothesis of God'' as more satisfactory than any alternative hypothesis. Truth is thus sacrificed to expediency; and belief in God, whom James prefers to consider as a finite Being with limited power, is deprived of any metaphysical foundation.

The intellectual movement known as Modernism was influenced by similar ideas. As St. Pius X's encyclical *PASCENDI* indicates, agnosticism is at the basis of the religious philosophy of Modernism. Because of their fundamental PHENOMENALISM, the Modernists make it impossible for human reason to attain any supersensible and transcendent reality. While eliminating all rational demonstration of God's existence, they also attempt to discredit the historical fact of God's actual intervention in the world. Hence Modernism is a theological error as well as a false philosophical system.

Among more recent versions of agnosticism mention may be made of LOGICAL POSITIVISM, according to which a proposition is meaningful, and therefore true, only if its composing elements can be reduced to experimental data by careful linguistic analysis. In this conception of philosophy—if one can still speak of philosophy—all statements about God are meaningless because they are incapable of experimental verification.

Modern agnosticism, under whatever form, distrusts the power of human reason. Such distrust is based on an erroneous conception of the limits and value of KNOWLEDGE in general and of inferential knowledge in particular. Thus in the last analysis agnosticism is the consequence of a false epistemology. By way of criticism it may be pointed out that although human knowledge starts with the particular data of sense experience, man can form ideas that abstract from all individuating notes and represent the nature of a thing as it is in itself. These ideas have the characteristic of universality, which is in direct contrast with the datum of sense experience. Just as man can form ideas of the essence of sensible things, so he can form ideas of spiritual substances, such as the soul and God. The existence of these substances is proved by rational inference from the nature of their effects. Since every effect demands an adequate cause, from the nature of an effect one can infer the nature of its cause. The fundamental principle of positivism, as well as of Kantian criticism, viz, that the sensible alone is knowable, is a gratuitous assumption that is neither demonstrated nor demonstrable. It is in effect a self-destroying principle, for all attempt at demonstration leads to a rejection of the principle itself.

Ontologism. At the other extreme from agnosticism stands ONTOLOGISM, which maintains that since man has a quasi-intuitive knowledge of God, all rational demonstration of His existence is unnecessary. According to one of its chief exponents, Nicholas MALEBRANCHE, man envisions all things by means of a direct intuition of God's ideas. Since there is no distinction between the divine essence and its ideas, it seems to follow that God is present to the human mind in every act of knowledge. Vincenzo GIOBERTI defined and developed Malebranche's mild ontologism and identified the ontological order with the logical order of knowledge. Thus, for him, God is the first object known by man's mind. Antonio ROSMINI-SERBATI, whose name is often associated with the ontologists, held that all knowledge is through the innate idea of being in its supreme ideality (*l'essere ideale*), and this makes the soul intelligent. The idea is not the result of abstraction or reflection, nor is God Himself. Rosmini called it an ''appurtenance of God,'' or something divine and pertaining to God, which may be compared to the impression of the divine light on man's soul. Since the ideal being is for man the vehicle of ascent to the Real Being (*Essere Reale*), God, it is only improperly that Rosmini is classified as an ontologist.

Ontologism in the strict sense of the term has never been a popular system. It runs against man's experience and does not account for men's persistent errors concerning the existence and nature of God. Moreover, if man had an intuitive knowledge of God or the divine ideas, his knowledge would always be infallibly true, which evidently is not the case.

Approaches to the Existence of God. Although there are many approaches to the problem of God's existence, not all have the same value and appeal. Along with the highly rationalized metaphysical arguments suitable to a philosophically trained mind, there are other approaches of a more subjective nature, as well as a spontaneous, prephilosophical knowledge of God that precedes any scientific elaboration. The nature and value of such knowledge is the subject of the present discussion.

Prephilosophical Knowledge. Knowledge of God's existence is so deeply rooted in human nature that St. JOHN DAMASCENE speaks of it as being ''implanted in man'' (*De fide orthodoxa* 1.1.3), St. BONAVENTURE calls it ''innate to the rational mind'' (*De mysterio Trinitatis* 1.1), and St. THOMAS AQUINAS explains that ''it is through principles which are innate in us that we are able to perceive that God exists'' (*In Boeth. de Trin.* 1.3 ad 6). Aquinas goes so far as to say that ''all knowing beings know God implicitly in every known object'' (*De ver.* 22.2 ad 1), while Duns Scotus affirms even more emphatically that ''in the knowledge of any being as this particular being, God is conceived in a most indistinct manner'' (*Opus Oxon.* 1.3.2.3). While it is wrong to interpret these statements as meaning that the idea of God is innate to man in the way that the idea of the infinite is for R. DESCARTES, they do point to the natural and innate facility with which the human mind can attain the knowledge of the Supreme Being.

In the teaching of the schoolmen, such knowledge is at first obscure and confused, and is the result of INTU-

ITION rather than of an inferential JUDGMENT. It becomes gradually more distinct as man begins to think of the magnitude and wonders of the universe, the inexorable laws of nature and his own helplessness in the face of natural events and calamities, the many evils that go unpunished, and his unsatisfied craving for unlimited truth, goodness, and happiness. These reflections, which arise naturally in the mind of every man regardless of his background, milieu, and education, suggest the idea of a superior Being who is the cause of the universe and judge of mankind. This is roughly the idea of a personal and transcendent God, whom man has tried to propitiate by prayer and sacrifice from the dawn of history up to the present. As man progresses and develops his intellectual abilities, this primordial idea of God acquires new traits and more closely approximates the reality of the Supreme Being. Imperfect though it may be, this spontaneous, prephilosophical notion of God can hardly be overrated, since upon it a large segment of humanity will be judged by the same God who chose this way to reveal Himself to their minds.

Subjectivist Approaches. Many persons are content with the idea of God obtained as a result of spontaneous thought or acquired through faith and education. A philosopher wishes to go further and analyze the contents and ultimate foundation of such an idea. In so doing he may start from himself and his personal experiences, or from the nature and existence of extramental reality. In the first case, one has the subjectivist approach to God; in the second, the objective, traditional approach of scholastic philosophy. The subjectivist approach, which goes back to St. AUGUSTINE and is strongly emphasized by Descartes, has assumed various forms in modern and contemporary philosophy. One of these is the sentimental school of thought, so called because of the importance attached to sentiment or subjective feeling in human knowledge. Its chief exponents are Pascal, Schleiermacher, Ritschl, and Otto.

B. PASCAL challenges the demonstrative value of traditional metaphysical proofs of God's existence on the ground that their abstract and purely intellectual character fails to convince man in his state of fallen nature. Instead he appeals to the heart, which grasps intuitively the truths that escape rational demonstration. The heart is for Pascal a complex faculty having the immediacy and certainty of sense perception and the intellectual apprehension of first principles, as well as the appetitive acts of desire and love. The heart has a logic of its own that includes all the foregoing acts but consists preeminently in supernatural faith. Here is where Pascal's sentimentalism comes close to FIDEISM, a system holding that faith alone is the source of man's knowledge of God.

F. D. E. SCHLEIERMACHER, a 19th-century German theologian, reduces the essence of religion to what he calls ''a sense and taste for the Infinite,'' or ''a feeling of absolute dependence.'' God's existence cannot be demonstrated by human reason, but man feels and experiences his dependence on God, whose existence he admits only because of the inclination of his heart and will. Schleiermacher is considered a forerunner of Modernism. So also is Albrecht RITSCHL, for whom the idea of God is the result neither of intuition nor of rational inference, but is rather a necessary postulate of human nature in its attempt to establish spiritual supremacy over the inferior world. Rudolf OTTO distinguishes between the rational and nonrational elements in religious experience, the unique quality of which is holiness. While the rational element is indispensable for understanding some characteristics of the ''holy'' or the divine, it tends to overshadow the deeper nonrational core, which he calls the ''numinous,'' the ''awe-inspiring and fascinating mystery.'' To grasp the nonrational element in the divine, man has a *sensus numinis.* This is not mere emotion or natural feeling but an affective state of mind involving some kind of preconceptual knowledge. Otto links it to the ''faculty of divination,'' a special faculty enabling man to know the ''holy'' in its appearance. Both the rational and nonrational elements of religion are described in Kantian terms as an a priori category.

Another subjectivist approach to God is contained in the philosophy of IMMANENCE of H. BERGSON, who conceives reality as a dynamic, creative becoming, a vital impetus (*élan vital*). In its evolutionary process the vital impetus is continuously striving to overcome the drag of inert matter, which in a way is its own by-product. In so doing, it gives rise to different levels of being, inanimate nature, plants, animals, and men. Thus the vital impetus appears to be the source of all reality, the God of Bergson's philosophy (although not all interpreters agree on this point), whom he describes metaphorically as a center from which worlds shoot out like rockets in a display of fireworks. Man grasps this all-embracing reality by intuition, a self-conscious instinct that can actually feel the flow of becoming because of a certain ''sympathy.'' Intuition is superior to intellect, the chief function of which is to form concepts that furnish mere ''snapshots'' of reality. To prove his doctrine of man's knowledge of God, Bergson appeals to the experience of the great Christian mystics and attempts to show the superiority of a dynamic religion stemming from vital intuition over the static religion of conceptualized knowledge.

Edouard LE ROY, Bergson's disciple and a leading figure in the Modernist movement, tried unsuccessfully to reconcile the doctrine of immanence with Catholic teaching. Like his master, he reduces all reality to becoming. God himself is not, He becomes. After questioning the ontological validity of abstract knowledge and attacking the classical arguments for God's existence, he claims that the only way to arrive at God is by analyzing CONSCIOUSNESS. This manifests to man an exigency for a growing realization, an infinite progress, and a perfect spiritual life. At the root of such moral exigency there is an absolute: to recognize this is to affirm the existence of God. Briefly, there is no metaphysical certitude of God's existence but merely "a moral certitude based upon a direct experience of a moral reality." Yet Le Roy, like Bergson, rejects the charge of PANTHEISM.

Still another form of subjectivist approach to God is the "method of immanence" of M. BLONDEL; this may be defined as a psychological way of stating all religious and philosophical problems, starting from the self. It differs from the "theory of immanence" in that the source of religious truth is held to be internal observation rather than consciousness or subconsciousness. According to Blondel, man arrives at God not by mere speculative thought but by action. Action includes thought, but it is much more than that. It is the entire human experience conceived within the framework of man's basic needs and tendencies; it is the synthesis of thought, will, and being itself, the activity of the whole man. The infinite disproportion that man observes between his exigencies in life and his ideals makes him realize his deficiencies and the need for a transcendent and necessary Being. Thus the order of nature finds its integration in the supernatural order of grace and revelation as manifested in the Christian religion.

The foregoing theories must be credited for their emphasis on the important role that subjective factors play in man's knowledge of God. However, they overlook the fact that feelings and emotional states are relative to individuals and subject to change, while intuition and, especially, mystical experience are the privilege of the few. Hence it is wrong to consider them as a universal criterion of man's knowledge of God. The traditional theistic arguments of scholastic philosophy retain their demonstrative value even without subjective elements. This holds true also with regard to Blondel's method of immanence; although of unquestionable merit, it cannot be considered a substitute for more objective reasoning.

Phenomenological and Existentialist Views. PHENOMENOLOGY, worked out chiefly by Edmund HUSSERL and Alexius Meinong and consisting in a descriptive analysis of the essence of the given, the phenomenon, is explicitly applied to the problem of God by Max SCHELER. Scheler holds that God, like any other essence, is reached by man through emotional acts of a religious nature, such as faith, worship, fear, and love. By these acts man attains to God, not merely as being in the ideal order but as a supreme value in the order of existence. The starting point of man's knowledge of God may be any object of human experience, for all things are effects of God in such ways that they have a symbolic relation to Him. This relation is grasped by an intuitive emotional act apart from any discursive reasoning. Yet a religious predisposition is necessary, and God has to reveal Himself through some sort of illumination.

The phenomenological method of investigation has found supporters even among the existentialists, who apply it to existence rather than essence, and especially to man in his concrete existing reality. The results of their investigation are quite different, just as their systems are different, for one can hardly speak of a unique and homogeneous EXISTENTIALISM. As far as the problem of God is concerned, one can roughly draw a line between theistic and atheistic existentialists, even though some existentialist philosophers defy any strict classification. Theistic existentialists, such as S. KIERKEGAARD, G. Marcel, L. Chestov (1866–1938), and N. BERDÎAEV, have certain traits in common. They all believe that God is discovered or encountered by the individual as he strives for the free realization of his true self rather than as the term of impersonal objective reasoning. Thus God is for them the foundation of existence in which man, like all other beings, participates. Atheistic existentialists, such as J. P. Sartre and A. Camus, consider the idea of God as contradictory and describe, in vivid and often crude terms, the irrationality and ABSURDITY of the world and human existence. M. Heidegger and K. Jaspers, the two main representatives of German existentialism, seem not to exclude God from their philosophy and strongly resent the charge of atheism, but at the same time they develop a system in which there seems to be no room for the God of traditional philosophy. Heidegger's "Being" and Jasper's "Transcendent" are such vague and ambiguous terms that they inevitably perplex the reader as to their real meaning. Inadequate as it is, existentialism under all its forms has served at least one purpose: it has proved beyond doubt that God is at the center of all solutions to the problem of human existence. With God, life has a meaning and a purpose; without God, life and the world itself become meaningless as well as absurd.

Proofs for the Existence of God. In his *Summa theologiae* (1a, 2.2) St. Thomas asks whether it can be demonstrated that God exists. He answers in the affirmative, explaining that from the knowledge of the effect it is possible to infer the existence of its proper cause, since no effect can exist without a preexisting cause. Hence, insofar as the existence of God is not self-evident to man, it can and must be demonstrated from effects that are known to man. Such DEMONSTRATION must utilize arguments *a posteriori,* i.e., from effect to cause, and thus presupposes the ontological and transcendental validity of the principle of CAUSALITY.

Traditional Arguments. Using this principle, St. Thomas sets forth his ''five ways'' (*Summa theologiae,* 1a, 2.3; *Summa contra gentiles,* 1.13, 15), or ''the arguments by which both philosophers and Catholic teachers have proved that God exists'' (*Summa contra gentiles,* 1.13). The structure of each of the five ways is basically the same. Each starts from a fact of experience—motion or change, caused existence, corruptibility, composition and imperfection, finality—and they all lead to the existence of a self-subsistent Being considered as the ultimate cause or explanation of that particular experimental datum—Immovable Mover, Uncaused Cause, Necessary Being, Absolute Perfection, Supreme End. Aquinas applies the principle of causality when showing that in a series of essentially subordinate causes one cannot proceed in infinity, but must rather come to a first cause that is independent of all other causes and responsible for the causality of the entire series. In such a series the causes are so dependent on one another that no inferior cause can exert its causality without the actual influence of the superior cause. If no first cause existed over and above the entire series and as the actual source of all causality, there would be no effect now, and hence no being, which is obviously not the case. The five ways can perhaps be reduced to one single proof expressed by the axiom that ''the greater cannot proceed from the less,'' or that a limited and contingent being finds its ultimate explanation only in an infinite and self-subsistent Being. (*See* GOD, PROOFS FOR THE EXISTENCE OF.)

As to whether, in view of the many discoveries of modern science, the traditional arguments for God's existence are still valid, the answer can only be in the affirmative. Philosophy and science are two distinct fields of knowledge; they follow different methods and pursue distinct objectives. The problem of God's existence is philosophical, and its solution rests on metaphysical principles that are not subject to change. Thus to reject the existence of God in the name of physical science is to give a scientific answer—and a wrong one at that—to a philosophical question. Besides, far from invalidating the traditional theistic arguments, the findings of modern science seem to confirm their conclusions. (*See* GOD AND MODERN SCIENCE.)

Confirmatory Arguments. Other arguments for God's existence do not have the cogency of the traditional metaphysical proofs but perhaps have greater appeal to the philosophically untrained and to thinkers who are not metaphysically oriented. The argument from moral obligation, also known as the argument from conscience, is a case in point. It is a fact of experience to which the conscience bears witness that man perceives within himself a law commanding him to do certain acts because they are good and avoid others because they are evil. This law is not merely subjective and artificial; it is imposed upon man by virtue of his very nature, and violation of it brings a sense of guilt and remorse. It is an absolute command, a CATEGORICAL imperative, to use Kant's terminology, that admits of no exception, and is found in every man having the use of reason. Training and environment may help to develop knowledge of this law, but a general agreement seems to exist among men concerning its most universal principles. Since there is no law without a lawgiver, and man cannot possibly be held responsible for imposing upon himself an obligation that restricts his own freedom, it must be concluded that the natural law owes its origin to the author of human nature, a supreme lawgiver, God.

The same conclusion can be arrived at from consideration of the need of sanctions to ensure the observance of the natural law. A law that cannot be enforced loses all practical value, and the only way to enforce it is by adequate rewards and punishments. Yet cases in which the good suffer and the wicked prosper throughout life are not rare, showing that proper sanctions are not attached to the natural law in this life. Must one admit that in this world—where all things act according to a rational plan obeying the laws of nature—only man is free to violate with impunity the natural law he discovers within himself? An affirmative answer would be inconsistent with the entire plan of the universe. The only explanation is that since perfect justice is not done in this life, there must be a future life where adequate justice is done by a supremely wise and all-powerful judge, namely, God.

A related theistic proof is man's desire for happiness. Man is so constituted that he always strives for happiness but never completely attains it. He does not seek just any kind of happiness but happiness to the utmost degree. Since this tendency cannot be fully satisfied in this life, where all goods are limited and imperfect, a supreme good must exist that completely satisfies man's aspirations, and that is God. To hold the contrary is to admit in man a natural tendency destined for frustration rather than for fulfillment because of the absence of an object to satisfy it. Man would find himself in a more miserable condition than brutes and animals, since they can obtain in this life all the satisfaction of which they are capable, whereas man would be prevented from attaining the good toward which he strives.

Another subsidiary proof for the existence of God is the argument from universal consent. The human race as a whole has always recognized the existence of a superior

Being deserving of worship and on whom man and the world depend. But mankind cannot be wrong in a matter of such importance without jeopardizing the trustworthiness of the human mind and man's final destiny. Hence God's existence is demanded as a sufficient reason for that universal conviction. Needless to say, this argument, like all other confirmatory proofs, has only a relative value inasmuch as no strict metaphysical reasoning goes to support it. However, it cannot simply be dismissed on the ground that universal convictions, such as popular belief that the sun revolves about the earth, have later proved to be wrong. A scientific theory of this type has no direct bearing on man's final destiny. It is therefore conceivable that man be mistaken about it as long as no adequate means of verification are available. Nor can it be objected that individual persons or tribes may never have had a notion of a Supreme Being, and that many people even today refuse to accept the existence of God as a well-established doctrine. Universal consent does not preclude the existence of individual men or groups of men who do not share the common belief. The credence of the vast majority of the human race is a sufficient ground for the argument under discussion.

Ideological Argument. Known originally as the argument from eternal truths, which was hinted at by PLATO and suggested by St. Augustine in *De libero arbitrio* (2.2–15), the ideological argument has assumed different forms in the course of history. Its proponents seem to agree that the argument is an attempt to prove the existence of God from the nature of the intelligibles. These are either the possible essences of things (argument from the possibles), or the eternal truths, namely, those statements that express necessary relations among the possibles or the first principles of reason (argument from eternal truths). The argument may be stated as follows. There are intrinsically possible beings whose essence and essential principles are necessary, immutable, and eternal. But such beings demand as their ultimate foundation an actually existing being that is absolutely necessary, immutable, and eternal. Therefore such a being exists, and men call this being God.

The ideological argument, its defenders maintain, is not based on ideas considered only in their logical or analytical order. Rather, ideas are considered from the point of view of mental concepts with a foundation in reality; not inasmuch as they represent an actually existing thing or the truth of an actually existing object, but inasmuch as their content reflects a being or truth in the essential order. They are ideas of a possible or potential essence for which an ultimate reason is sought in a necessary and eternal being. Thus understood, the argument keeps its distinctive feature as an argument from the ideal order, and at the same time it obviates the inconsistency of involving an illicit passage from the ideal to the real order. The ideal, in this case, is also real; it belongs to the realm of the intelligibles, and the transition is simply from one order of reality to another order of reality. The principle of demonstration used for such a transition is either the principle of sufficient reason or the principle of causality. When the principle of causality is used, then the argument is conceived within the framework of St. Thomas's five ways, especially the fourth way, which argues to God from the various degrees of being.

To the objection that the possibles and their characteristics of necessity, immutability, and eternity can be sufficiently explained through an abstractive intellect and the object, the upholders of the argument answer that the human mind and the object are the proximate causes and foundation of the possibles, but not their ultimate reason. Indeed, by their very nature, the possibles transcend all created mind and reality; they are such even if no contingent being or human intellect ever existed. Far from being the ultimate foundation of the possibles, the human mind and all created beings would not exist at all, were they not intrinsically possible.

A similar answer is given to the objection that truth depends on the existence of contingent being and is therefore purely hypothetical. The existence of contingent things, the defenders of the argument rebut, is the immediate cause of man's knowledge of truth, but it is not the ultimate foundation of truth, which prescinds from both contingent reality and the human mind. If nothing ever existed, there would be no truth; but there is TRUTH, and so there must be an eternal and necessary foundation without which truth and its properties of eternity and necessity are inconceivable. The foundation is God.

See Also: DEISM; THEISM.

Bibliography: R. GARRIGOU-LAGRANGE, *God: His Existence and His Nature,* tr. B. ROSE, 2 v. (St. Louis 1934–36). É. H. GILSON, *God and Philosophy* (New Haven 1941). F. J. SHEEN, *God and Intelligence in Modern Philosophy* (New York 1925); *Philosophy of Religion* (New York 1948). C. HARTSHORNE and W. L. REESE, eds., *Philosophers Speak of God* (Chicago 1953). *American Catholic Philosophical Association. Proceedings of the Annual Meeting* (Baltimore 1926) 28 (1954). J. MARITAIN, *Approaches to God,* tr. P. O'REILLY (New York 1954). J. D. COLLINS, *God in Modern Philosophy* (Chicago 1959). M. R. HOLLOWAY, *An Introduction to Natural Theology* (New York 1959). T. C. O'BRIEN, *Metaphysics and the Existence of God* (Washington 1960). J. A. BAISNÉE, *Readings in Natural Theology* (Westminster, Md. 1962). G. L. ABERNETHY and T. A. LANGFORD, eds., *Philosophy of Religion* (New York 1962). J. MACQUARRIE, *Twentieth-Century Religious Thought* (New York 1963). B. M. BONANSEA, "The Ideological Argument for God's Existence," *Studies in Philosophy and the History of Philosophy* 1 (1961) 1–34. M. CHOSSAT, *Dictionnaire de théologie catholique,* ed. A. VACANT et al., 15 v. (Paris 1903–50; Tables générales 1951) 4.1:874–948. P. ORTEGAT, *Philosophie de la religion,* 2 v. (Gembloux 1948). F. VAN STEENBERGHEN, *Dieu caché* (Louvain 1961). M. F. SCIACCA, *Il problema di Dio e della religione nella filosofia attuale* (Brescia 1953).

[B. M. BONANSEA]

3. Nature

The proofs for God's existence, each in its own way, lead one to knowledge of God as first on all levels of existence, as *Ipsum Esse Subsistens.* The aim of the present section is to make explicit what is implicitly contained in this concept. One may well wonder to what extent such explicit knowledge is possible. All Christian thinkers have recognized the depth of this "sublime truth," possessing as it does an infinity of intelligibility—far more than man can grasp. Thus GREGORY OF NYSSA wrote: "To have true knowledge is to understand that seeing is really not seeing, because God transcends all knowledge." God, moreover, cannot be defined. Man may indeed name Him, but this is not to define Him. For DEFINITION would assign Him to a GENUS, and since God calls Himself "He who is," the genus would have to be BEING. Now being is not a genus, for a genus is determined by specific differences that are not contained within itself. Nothing can be added to being, since outside of being there is nothing (St. Thomas Aquinas, *Summa theologiae,* 1a, 3.5). Is one therefore constrained to silence and reduced in the final analysis to affirming that in a philosophical sense man can know nothing of God? Catholic thinkers respond in the negative: God can be known, to a certain degree, yet not to His innermost depths. This reply need offer no stumbling block to reason; rather the human mind's inability to comprehend God may itself be taken as a sign of truth.

Extreme Views. Though man is unable to define God, he may at least indirectly "characterize" Him, using the conclusions of the proofs of His existence. In this attempt, however, two extremes are to be avoided, viz, ANTHROPOMORPHISM and AGNOSTICISM.

Anthropomorphism. The first consists in thinking of God and man under the same univocal concept. Sometimes such univocity is mythological and psychological in origin: this is the anthropomorphism of the masses who attribute to God the feelings and reactions of man and judge Him according to human standards. At other times the conception presents itself under an intellectual guise, crediting God with all the perfections of which man has knowledge. Between God and man, in this view, there is no difference of nature but only one of degree—a position very close to that of PANTHEISM, which identifies God and the world of human experience. To avoid this extreme, one must constantly refine his concept of God, who is in fact far beyond man's representations and concepts. The safeguard against anthropomorphism is therefore purification; but solicitude for purification should not lead to the other extreme, that of agnosticism.

Agnosticism. This maintains the possibility of a type of demonstration of the existence of God, but denies that man is able to affirm anything about God's nature. It invokes EQUIVOCATION rather than univocity. What one says of God, in this view, is either attributed to Him in a purely negative fashion or signifies only that He is a cause; for God is unknowable in His nature. Certainly this position is not new; it was found among the Neoplatonists and during the Middle Ages, especially in MAIMONIDES. But in recent times it has assumed a new form, that of Modernism. One should, of course, seek always to refine his concept of God, but must beware of refining that concept to nothingness in the process. Analogy is the surest means to attain such refinement, for it allows man to consider the universe as a screen through which he may come to know divine being and life (cf. Rom 1.20).

Means of Knowing God. To know God philosophically, two means are available: negation and analogy. The passage from the world to God is assured by a twofold dialectic, one negating and the other constructing. One is suppressive, the other progressive; yet their movements enmesh so that the one cannot function without the other.

Negation. The way of negation consists in denying of God anything that belongs to a contingent being as such. Thus, to know God through this way is not to show what He is, but rather what He is not. Instead of beginning with an inaccessible essence to which are added positive differences leading to better and better understanding, one collects rather a series of negative differences that indicate what this essence is not. Such a method leads to knowledge that, admittedly, is not positive; it is imperfect. Yet, by denying all the limitations found in creatures, it allows one to say with ever greater precision what God is not and what He cannot possibly be. Thus, by distinguishing God from what is not God, one attains some knowledge of His essence (see St. Thomas Aquinas, *Summa contra gentiles,* 1.14).

Analogy. The way of ANALOGY consists in attributing to God, to an eminent degree, everything that can be considered as a PERFECTION pure and simple, that is, a perfection that is without any trace of imperfection. To describe the nature of God is to name Him variously as just, powerful, wise, etc. The principle behind such predication is this: because God is First Cause, He must possess to an eminent degree all the perfections found in creatures. The problem is to discover how these perfections may be predicated of God. One may not attribute them in a univocal sense, for God does not produce creatures as one man engenders another. The human offspring has the same nature as his parents, whereas the effects produced by God do not conform to the divine nature. Nor is the equivocal sense applicable, for the mere sharing of a name implies no real relation, no resemblance at all between the things compared. When it obtains, knowledge of one through the other becomes impossible.

A certain likeness, however, must exist between things and God, and this is the likeness of an effect to its cause. This relationship is the basis for analogy—the only way one may speak of the Uncreated while avoiding both anthropomorphism, which pretends to understand God as He knows Himself, and symbolism. Analogy is a relationship between two beings that, while different, bear a certain likeness to each other. Just as there are different types of resemblance, so too there are different analogies: metaphorical analogy, analogy of simple attribution, and analogy of proper proportionality. In speaking of God, there is no question of metaphorical analogy, which involves a simple likeness of relations. Such a comparison reveals no more than the accidental aspects of things. Nor can analogy of attribution be involved; things said to be analogical in this sense share in the relationship to a single term that properly, by its intrinsic nature, possesses the perfection being considered. Between God and man there are no common denominators. The only type of analogy left is that of proper proportionality: the application of a concept that is analogous in itself to two subjects that are essentially different; an application based on their proportionate participation in the ontological reality signified by the concept. It is this analogy that allows one to say, for instance, that in God there is something that bears the same kind of relationship to the divine nature as intelligence does to human nature. This expresses a parallel relationship between divine nature and divine intelligence on one hand and between human nature and human intelligence on the other.

Since effects manifest their causes, those perfections that denote positive realities in creatures (e.g., life, intelligence, and will) are found also in God. It is not sufficient, however, to affirm that God is intelligent, just, or wise simply as man might be. The likeness between divine and human perfections must be stated in these terms: a perfection that is realized in a finite being to the degree consonant with its proper mode of being is similar to that found in God according to His mode of being. This analogy is legitimate, for any being or perfection that can be assigned to a creature must have its root in God. Consequently, one cannot remove from God the positive value of this being or perfection, no matter what the form (or lack of form) it may take in God.

Divine Attributes. The foregoing furnishes a basis for understanding what is meant by a divine attribute. In general, a divine attribute may be defined as an absolutely simple perfection that exists in God necessarily and formally, and that, according to man's imperfect mode of knowing, either constitutes the essence of the Divine Being or is deduced from this essence. Divine attributes that do not constitute the divine essence are further divided into entitative attributes and operative attributes. Entitative attributes relate to the very being of God; they are perfections such as unicity, truth, goodness, infinity, immensity, ubiquity, and eternity that in themselves bespeak no relation to contingent being. Operative attributes, on the other hand, relate to the divine operations, i.e., to the immanent operations of God's intellect and will, from which proceed effects that are extrinsic to God, namely, creation and conservation.

The divine attributes do not designate perfections really distinct from one another; rather there is only a virtual distinction among them, in the sense that each perfection explicitly states what is implied in the others (*see* DISTINCTION, KINDS OF). Thus, all the divine attributes designate one and the same, absolutely unique, Entity, but as understood under multiple and diverse aspects. Moreover, such multiplicity does not impair the divine perfection, because if God appears to human reason as simultaneously one and many, this is owing only to the limitations of man's intellect.

Divine Essence. Among the divine attributes it is possible to isolate one or more that can be said to be the formal constituent of the divine essence. This manner of speaking refers only to a logical determination of the divine essence, for in God all reality is His very essence. The formal constituent, in this sense, is the fundamental perfection from which all others can be logically deduced. Such a perfection must appear to man as absolutely first, prior to any other attribute, and should be the basis for his distinguishing God from what is not God.

It is commonly taught that God is Being itself, subsistent by itself, and that this ASEITY (*ASEITAS*), or ''by-itself-ness,'' is the constitutive perfection of God. Aseity is fundamental, for God's fundamental perfection consists in being absolutely independent, self-sufficient, and self-existent. Everything else is said of God precisely because He exists of Himself. The perfection of aseity, furthermore, properly belongs to God and distinguishes Him clearly from His creatures. Though all other divine perfections can be imitated analogically, only existence of Himself is absolutely proper to God. This perfection, moreover, does not allow any equivocation. Finally, it can be said that the divine attributes are implied one in the other only because each one contains being. Infinity, for example, implies intelligence, eternity, etc., because infinity is nothing more than an infinity of being. ''Absolute being contains all other perfections eminently within itself'' (St. Thomas, *Summa theologiae,* 1a2ae, 2.5 ad 2). Divine aseity thus fulfills all the conditions necessary for it to be considered the formal constituent of the divine essence. God is indeed *Ipsum Esse Subsistens,* and St. Thomas adds that the name most proper to God is ''He who is'' (*Summa theologiae,* 1a, 13.11), that is to say: He in whom essence and existence are one.

There are some, however, who do not accept this teaching. The nominalists, following WILLIAM OF OCKHAM, deny that in God one attribute can be the source of all other perfections, since the divine essence is the complexus of all these perfections. From the nominalist point of view, the universal is but a collective term; thus, the formal constituent of the divine nature serves only to designate the collection of divine perfections. Moreover, for them, this synonym for the ensemble of divine attributes is purely equivocal and has no proper content. It is only a symbol for a reality that is in itself unknown and unknowable. Such a position borders on agnosticism.

Duns Scotus maintains that the formal constituent consisted in a radical infinity, that is, in a demand for all the perfections possible (*Op. Oxon.* 1.3.2). It must be admitted that infinity is one of the concepts that better explain the divine nature, for all God's perfections do flow from it. But one can say as much for any of the divine attributes, since each implies all others. The logical essence must not only imply all the divine perfections, but must express their radical source and basic explanation.

JOHN OF ST. THOMAS places the formal constituent of the divine essence in subsistent intellection; for in God, as in man, intelligence is the perfection upon which all others depend (In *Summa theologiae,* 1a, 16.2.10). Yet intellection presupposes a subject or essence, as John of St. Thomas undoubtedly intends when he speaks of *subsistent* intellection. But if one considers essence as more fundamental than its operation, then one must hold that Subsistent Being itself is the formal constituent of the divine essence.

Entitative Attributes. Among the attributes related to the very being of God, simplicity and infinity give man direct knowledge of God's personal nature.

Simplicity. God is absolutely one in Himself, perfectly simple, that is to say, excluding any composition, whether physical, metaphysical, or logical. (1) Since God is PURE ACT, He cannot, on the physical level, be composed of matter and form, both of which necessarily imply potentiality and essential imperfection. A fortiori, He is not composed of quantitative parts since these indicate indetermination and passivity. (2) On the metaphysical level, God cannot be composed of essence and existence since He is Being of Himself (*Esse per se*); neither can He be composed of substance and accident, since He is Pure Act and thus not in potency to further determination. (3) On the logical level, God is not contained in a genus or a species because, as universal principle, He transcends all genera and all differences of being. (*See* SIMPLICITY OF GOD.)

One must understand clearly the significance of this divine simplicity. It is not by eliminating the limitations found in creatures that one arrives at *Esse Subsistens per se;* this would be to place this Being in the same genus with creatures, undoubtedly to an eminently superior degree, but nonetheless sharing a common nature with them. Such a position leads directly to contradictions. Thus, to pretend to eliminate any limitation is to consider essence and existence as two realities, separable at will. Similarly, one cannot consider Subsistent Being as entering into the genus of created being. For created being is properly characterized as a composition of essence and existence, of potentiality and actuality. Consequently, if Pure Act were found in this genus, it would no longer be Pure Act, that is to say, identifiable with itself, which is obviously a contradiction. Thus, divine simplicity is the mark of a Being in which essence and existence are identified without any limitation. Here one is no longer concerned with a relation between essence and existence; such a relation is swallowed up in identification—the essence of God is none other than His existence (St. Thomas, *De ente* 5).

The UNICITY OF GOD is a necessary result of the absolutely divine simplicity. If divinity were multiple, one would have to distinguish, in divine beings, the divinity common to all as well as their individual differences. In consequence, one would find in these beings a composition of genus and difference; thus, no one of them could be termed *Ipsum Esse Subsistens,* and no one would be God. Moreover, on these terms God, being His very nature, would have no cause to multiply Himself. If a man were what he is by reason of human nature rather than by reason of individual characteristics that distinguish him from other men, he would be humanity itself; thus, there could be no other men besides him. The same reasoning applies to God: He is His very nature. Thus there can be only one God (*Summa theologiae,* 1a, 3.3).

Infinity. Infinity means the same as ''without limits.'' But there are many ways of being without limits. Thus, matter is infinite in a privative sense: it cannot be completed by itself. In this sense, the infinite connotes indefiniteness or basic indetermination, and therefore essential imperfection. In a contrary sense, the infinite can also bespeak something that is without limits by reason of its very perfection. From this point of view, one can distinguish (1) the relative infinite, which has no limits within the genus of a certain perfection, and (2) the absolute infinite, which has no limits within the genus of all perfections possible.

The latter infinity of perfection is the type attributed to God. In fact, God is infinitely perfect insofar as He is *Esse per se.* In Him, existence is not received as in an essence capable of existing; God is unreceived, and therefore absolutely unlimited existence. From another viewpoint, moreover, one can say that if God had limitations, He would be susceptible to some new perfection; He would be composed of act and potency, which is a contradiction. Again, if He had limitations, He would be subject to them, and therefore, in a sense, passive. In either case, He would no longer be Pure Act. God is therefore infinite by His essence and by the fulness of infinity. His infinity is not to be understood as indetermination, since all indetermination is imperfection. Divine infinity, since it is that of Pure Act, is rather absolute determination; that is to say, it implies the total and perfect actuality of all perfections. (*See* INFINITY OF GOD.)

Operative Attributes. These attributes refer to God's immanent operations, or, in other words, to the divine life as this is known to natural reason. Emphasis here is on God's intellect and will, for these attributes enable man to conceive of God as a personal being.

Divine Intelligence. God's intelligence can be deduced from His infinite perfection and supreme actuality. Since God possesses all perfections to an absolute degree, science, the perfection of the intellect, is His first operative attribute—it specifies the divine nature, the principle of divine operation. Again, God is known to be immaterial from His excluding all potentiality. Now knowledge is proportionate to the degree of immateriality, and a being is intelligent to the degree that its being is pure. God, the Pure Spirit, therefore possesses supreme and absolute knowledge (*Summa theologiae,* 1a, 14.1). Furthermore, since the act of knowing is essentially immanent and since whatever is in God is the divine essence, divine intelligence is identified with the divine essence; it is, properly speaking, subsistent intellection.

To say that divine intelligence is subsistent intellection is to affirm that God understands Himself perfectly, that He is Thought Thinking Itself (cf. Aristotle, *Meta.* 1072b 13–30). Knowing that the degree of a being's intelligibility increases with its immateriality, one may conclude that any being that is fully immaterial is fully intelligible. In God the supreme degree of knowledge and the ultimate degree of intelligibility merge within His essence. It is quite true to say, then, that God knows Himself perfectly (*De ver.* 2.2). This is not to say that God knows nothing apart from Himself. To know a thing perfectly is to be fully aware of its power, and consequently, to grasp fully the effects to which this power extends. In knowing Himself, God knows everything else. He knows things in His essence, which He understands to be imitable to different degrees of PARTICIPATION. He knows all singular beings, since whatever shares in being finds its origins in the divine essence: *Ipsum Esse Subsistens.*

To clarify further the field of objects comprehended by divine knowledge, one may inquire whether God knows (1) possibles, that is to say, things that do not actually exist but can exist and (2) future contingents, namely things that can be made to exist or not, at will. As for the first type of objects, it is commonly taught that since God is the source of all existence, and knows everything that exists, whatever the kind of existence it may possess, He does know possibles. The teaching with regard to contingents is more complicated. Since God is by nature outside of time, His knowledge bespeaks a relation to ETERNITY. Now eternity embraces all of time in an immobile present. God, therefore, knows future contingents as actually present and realized (*Summa theologiae,* 1a, 14.13); yet the necessary knowledge He has of them does not in any way affect their contingent character.

Divine Will. From the fact that God has the power to know, one may conclude that He also has the power to will. Indeed, since the GOOD as known constitutes the proper object of the WILL, once any good becomes known it must also come to be desired. Thus, a being that knows the good must be endowed with a will. Now God, as perfectly intelligent, knows being under its formality of goodness. From the very fact that He knows, He also wills (St. Thomas Aquinas, *Summa contra gentiles,* 1.72). Just as God's intellect is identical with His essence, so too is His will, since He wills insofar as He is intelligent. The will of God is His very being.

Since the object of the will is the good as apprehended by the intellect and since the divine intellect apprehends the divine essence directly, this essence is in consequence the primary object of the divine will. Further, every being endowed with a will naturally tends to communicate to others the good it possesses. But if natural beings communicate to others their own proper good, with greater reason does the divine will communicate its perfection to others, to the extent that such perfection is communicable. To say this is to assert that God loves all being, for LOVE is nothing other than the first movement of the will in its tendency toward the good. Again, for God to love His creatures is for Him to love Himself. For creatures possess goodness only to a degree proportionate to their being, i.e., a degree that corresponds to their perfection (*Summa theologiae,* 1a, 20.2).

Thus is God's FREEDOM manifested. In fact, God is supremely free: on the one hand, God is free relative to all contingent beings, for divinity as the absolute good is sufficient unto itself; on the other, God is free regarding the means He uses to achieve the goals of His infinite wisdom. One could say that God is bound only by His science, by His wisdom, and by the natural necessity of things. God's science and wisdom, however, are not something foreign or superior to Him, for they are His very self. In like manner, the natural necessity of things cannot limit God's liberty, for this necessity flows from His perfection and from His free decision. God is therefore not only supremely free, He is freedom, for this also is His very being.

Transcendence and Immanence. From the foregoing it is evident that God, if He exists at all, must be Infinite Being, radically distinct from the universe He has created and maintains in existence. The conception of this distinction became a matter of much discussion in the late twentieth century. The specific problem connected with divine transcendence and immanence is not God's existence but His identity in relationship to the world, i.e., does His reality bear some continuity to things of the finite order or is it so disparate in kind as to remain unknown?

Biblical man, in the immediacy of religious experience, encountered God at work effecting salvation within a people's concrete history, but a history God entered only at His own initiatives. This assumed God's transcendence of first, history, and second of the natural world He had summoned into being. Beyond this the question was not urged until later confrontation with Hellenic thought necessitated posing the ontological question. Here, the Platonic categories adopted, in preference to Stoic ones that tended to divinize the logos element immanent in the cosmos, allowed a dualistic conception of God who was independent of the cosmos in Himself, yet operative in it by way of a divinely decreed "economy." Thomas Aquinas, modifying Aristotle's metaphysics into a notion of being as "act" (*esse*), viewed God as the Pure Act of Being, qualitatively different from all finite essences yet necessarily omnipresent within them as the exclusive cause of their beingness (*Summa theologiae,* 1a2ae, 3, 8), thus emphasized the simultaneity of God's transcendence and immanence. The Reformation, insisting upon the absolute autonomy of faith, introduced a new dichotomy: God, remaining transcendent in His wrath, becomes immanent only in the offer of forgiveness in Christ (Luther). In the nineteenth century, Schleiermacher's Pietism compromised this absolute otherness of God by allowing for a religious a priori within human consciousness, a "feeling" (*Gëfuhl*) of dependence upon the Infinite. This led to a collapse into pure immanentism, notably with the use of Hegelian thought by thinkers such as Feuerbach; God was now constrained to remain within the processes of human consciousness as Absolute Idea objectifying itself in the dialectical moments of thought.

A restoration of transcendence, inaugurated by Kierkegaard, was achieved within Protestant theology with Karl Barth's *Church Dogmatics* in the twentieth century, and furthered in the U.S. by H. Richard Niebuhr. Barth urged an understanding of God's Word as antithetical to any word of man. Thus God's radical otherness makes impossible any disclosure of Himself from within the structures of nature or culture. Encounter occurs only through God's initiatives in faith (not religion) in which language itself is "appropriated" to bear meaning discontinuous with that available outside of faith-experience. Rudolf Bultmann, accepting this faith, founded in the existential meaning of history, insisted upon rendering the "message" into the language of contemporary man, in such a way however that its content became existential self-understanding rather than understanding of God's own reality. Paul Tillich pushed this approach into the search for the God beyond theism.

An abrupt reversal to this radical removal of God from nature, history, and culture occurred in the 1960s with what was known in the U.S. as the "Death of God Movement" (Paul Van Buren, Thomas Altizer, William Hamilton). Theology, already collapsed into Christology, collapsed further into anthropology in which the New Testament was interpreted as summoning man to authentic living with Jesus independently of all theistic considerations. The emptying kenosis of God in the man Jesus was meant to denote a shift in the meaning of the name "God," sc., from designating an existing Transcendent Being to a mere symbol of human values realized in Christ as the "man for others."

An alternative to this was Christian secularity in which the death of God was recast in terms of understanding only a cultural eclipse of the *idea* of God, but one manifesting the intentions of God Himself for mankind come of age. God's transcendence was affirmed not in categories of power posing a threat to the autonomy of the world, but outside all perspectives of nature or cosmos and primarily in categories of love and freedom; God's immanence within the finite order was precisely His freeing of the world to be worldly, i.e., nondivine, and to pursue its own values in true evolution rather than merely executing the predetermined designs of Divinity. Yet the pursuit of these values would ultimately bring the world to God as its "Omega point" (Dietrich Bonhoeffer, Teilhard de Chardin, J. B. Metz, Edward Schillebeeckx).

A distinct nuancing of man's historicity gave birth to "theologies of hope" in which the utter transcendence of God is preserved precisely by deferring it to the future.

God is thus seen not as the Totally Other but as the Totally New. Immanence is explained as God's presence within the radically altering processes of history, operative in a proleptic way in fidelity to His promises (Jürgen Moltmann, Wolfhart Pannenberg).

Vastly different in kind are theological adaptations of Whitehead's philosophy of becoming in which the transcendence of God is acknowledged to be merely relative. God, while superior to the world, is necessarily dependent upon it, forming with it the larger whole which is process itself. Within the metaphysical system reintroduced here, the notion of God is no exception but a component part extrapolated from it. Obviously, this Christian use of process thought marks a new return to immanentism (Norman Pittenger, John Cobb, Jr.).

Recent Catholic thought continues to affirm the simultaneity of God's transcendence and immanence through the use of classical metaphysics, shifted however to the plane of subjectivity in which Being is viewed more as Meaning, of which man is coconstitutor (Karl Rahner, Bernard Lonergan). This transcendental THOMISM defines man as ''spirit in the world,'' as God's self-communication into the Void, so that God is at once immanent to man's process of bestowing meaning and at the same time the Infinite and Transcendent Meaning always ''intended.''

Conclusion. At a philosophical level, one cannot penetrate into the intimacy of the divine nature. Although man can know that God exists, that He is perfect, intelligent, free, etc., he does not know what it means for God to exist or to be perfect, intelligent, and free. The ''how'' of all these attributes escapes him. In view of this, one can say that the more man penetrates into the infinite, the better he understands that it is beyond him. What little he knows of God is but a small fraction of all there is to know. And yet his intellect, in its philosophical search, neither destroys nor diminishes the mystery, but rather deepens it. Doubtless, this is the justification for his intellectual efforts, for reflection is always a deepening of thought, a springboard to higher truth.

See Also: PERFECTION, ONTOLOGICAL; OMNIPOTENCE; OMNIPRESENCE; OMNISCIENCE.

Bibliography: M. CHOSSAT, *Dictionnaire de théologie catholique,* ed. A. VACANT et al., 15 v. (Paris 1903–50; Tables générales 1951) 4.1:1152–1243. R. GARRIGOULAGRANGE, *God: His Existence and His Nature,* tr. B. ROSE, 2 v. (St. Louis 1934–36); *Les Perfections divines* (Paris 1937). R. JOLIVET, *The God of Reason,* tr. M. PONTIFEX (New York 1958). H. DE LUBAC, *The Discovery of God,* tr. A. DRU (New York 1960). J. DANIÉLOU, *God and the Ways of Knowing,* tr. W. ROBERTS (New York 1957). G. WEIGEL and A. G. MADDEN, *Religion and the Knowledge of God* (Englewood Cliffs, N.J. 1961). D. J. B. HAWKINS, *The Essentials of Theism* (New York 1949). É. H. GILSON, *God and Philosophy* (New Haven 1941); *The Philosophy of St. Thomas Aquinas,* ed. G. A. ERLINGTON, tr. E. BULLOUGH (St. Louis 1939). J. MARITAIN, *Approaches to God,* tr. P. O'REILLY (New York 1954). C. TRESMONTANT, *Essai sur la connaissance de Dieu* (Paris 1959). C. JOURNET, *Connaissance et inconnaissance de Dieu* (Fribourg 1943). W. J. HILL, *Knowing the Unknown God* (New York 1971). E. L. MASCALL, *The Openness of Being* (London 1971). J. COBB, JR., *A Christian Natural Theology* (Philadelphia 1965).

[R. LE. TROCQUER/W. J. HILL/EDS.]

GOD-MAN

The term expresses the fundamental Christian belief in the one Lord, Jesus Christ, who is both God and man—man, born of Mary of David's lineage, and God, the only begotten Son of the Father. The special claim that Christianity makes for its founder can thus be distinguished from those of other religions. Jesus is more than a man specially favored by God, one in whom God dwells in a higher degree than in any other human being. This does not mean that He is a marvelous being higher than man, yet still less than the almighty God, one who is neither God nor man. Jesus is fully God as well as fully man. His being God does not imply any denial of His manhood. One sometimes speaks of God dwelling among men, sanctifying humanity by the HYPOSTATIC UNION, but this is not meant to signify that God only pretended to be man, as if He simply put on the outward appearance of man as one reads about in some of the legends of the pagan gods. No, He is like us in all things except sin. This mysterious nature of Jesus impressed itself from the beginning on those with whom He came in contact. Later theological reflection expressed it in terms of two natures, the divine and the human, united in the one Person of the Word. This formulation simply serves to preserve accuracy in speaking of Christ. The mystery of the God-Man remains.

See Also: JESUS CHRIST, ARTICLES ON.

[M. E. WILLIAMS]

GOD THE FATHER, ICONOGRAPHY OF

By God the Father is understood the creator of the world and sole reigning deity of the Old Testament as well as the first Person of the Holy TRINITY. He has been represented in successive periods of Christian art chiefly as the divine hand, a beardless young man, the Ancient of Days, and the celestial pope or emperor. In the late Middle Ages in representations attempting a literal translation of the consubstantiality of the Trinity the physical traits of God the Father are identical with those of Christ.

"God the Father," ceiling painting c. 19th century. (©Paul Almasy/CORBIS)

In the earliest Christian iconography God is symbolized by a hand issuing from a cloud or nimbus. This was a workable compromise between the injunction of the Second Commandment and the need in art for an effective symbol of the divine power in its various manifestations. The hand appears expressively in a variety of scenes from the Old Testament. It orders Noah to build the ark; it prevents Abraham from sacrificing Isaac; it delivers the Commandments to Moses on Sinai; and it transports the Prophet Ezekiel from the valley of the dry bones (3d–century fresco, Dura–Europos, Syria). On the bronze doors of Hildesheim the hand of God presides in a scene depicting the offering of Cain and Abel. The appearance of the divine hand is not so common in New Testament scenes. Still, it blesses Christ at the moment of baptism in the Jordan, consoles Him during the Agony in the Garden, and assists Him in the Ascension. The hand of benediction occurs also in many scenes of dying saints.

The representation of God the Father as the most venerable of Patriarchs, the Ancient of Days, stems from a graphic passage in the Book of Daniel (7.9): "As I watched, thrones were set up and the Ancient One [*Antiquus dierum*] took his throne. His clothing was snow bright, and the hair on his head as white as wool." A full beard completed the figure in the Middle Ages. The earliest examples occur in Byzantine art of the 11th century, and by the end of the 12th century the type had taken hold in western Christendom (fresco in the crypt of the chapel of Saint Blaise, Brindisi).

With the heightening of realism in the later Middle Ages God the Father was represented in the guise of a pope or emperor, wearing the papal tiara or imperial crown. The celestial ruler of all thus was endowed in art with the costly and impressive garb of His temporal delegates. This lavish iconographic type was abandoned in the Renaissance. Michelangelo combined the medieval type of the Ancient of Days, revivified by antique portrayals of Jupiter, with the divine hand of early Christian art. In his remarkable synthesis of elements in the SISTINE CHAPEL creation scene the whole figure of God in a supreme gesture of divine creativity issues from heaven with right arm, hand, and forefinger outstretched in a dramatic moment of imparting life to the form of Adam. The Michelangelesque type of God the Father remained dominant in his own time and provided the model for later generations of artists.

See Also: TRINITY, HOLY, ICONOGRAPHY OF.

Bibliography: A. N. DIDRON, *Christian Iconography,* tr. E. J. MILLINGTON, completed by M. STOKES, 2 v. (London 1886). A. JAMESON and LADY EASTLAKE, *The History of Our Lord as Exemplified in Works of Art* (4th ed. London 1888). H. LECLERCQ, *Dictionnaire d'archéologie chrétienne et de liturgie,* ed. F. CABROL, H. LECLERCQ, and H. I. MARROU, 15 v. (Paris 1907–53) 4:821–824. L. HEIMAIER, *Die Gottheit in der älteren christlichen Kunst* (Munich 1922). K. KÜNSTLE, *Ikonographie der christlichen Kunst,* 2 v. (Freiburg 1926–28) 1: 221–239. L. RÉAU, *Iconographie de l'art chrétien,* 6 v. (Paris 1955–59) 2:3–29.

[L. P. SIGER]

GODARD OF HILDESHEIM, ST.

Benedictine abbot and bishop; b. Reichersdorf, lower Bavaria, 960; d. near Hildesheim, May 5, 1038. Godard (Godehard, Gothard, or Gotthard) was a monk at NIEDERALTAICH, where he became abbot in 996. Because of his advocacy of the exemplary spiritual life of the CLUNIAC reform, he was made reform abbot of TEGERNSEE (1001) and HERSFELD (1005) abbeys. In 1022, Emperor HENRY II induced him to succeed BERNWARD as bishop of HILDESHEIM. Godard defended Hildesheim's rights against ARIBO OF MAINZ in the GANDERSHEIM dispute initiated by St. WILLIGIS OF MAINZ. Although a gifted administrator, builder, and promoter of learning, Godard was primarily a stern spiritual ruler. INNOCENT II canonized him in 1131. The Saint Gotthard Pass bears his name.

Feast: May 4.

Bibliography: *Vita, Monumenta Germaniae Historica: Scriptores* (Berlin 1926–) 11:167–218. A. HAUCK, *Kirchengeschichte Deutchlands* (Berlin-Leipzig 1958) 3:451–455, 549–552. W. WATTENBACH-R. HOLTZMANN, *Deutchlands Geschictquellen im Mittelater bis zur Mitte des 13, Jh* (Stuttgart-Berlin 1904)

1.1:62–65; 1.2:287–288. A. BUTLER, *The Lives of the Saints* (New York 1956) 2:231–232. O. J. BLECHER, *Das Leben des heiligen Godehards* (2d ed. Hildesheim 1957). J. FELLENBERG GEN. REINOLD, *Die Verehrung des Heiligen Gotthard von Hildesheim in Kirche und Volk* (Bonn 1970). W. HALLER, *Bischofsamt im Mittelalter* (Hildesheim 1970).

[R. H. SCHMANDT]

GODDEN, THOMAS (TYLDEN)

Catholic controversialist; b. 1624; d. 1688. He was educated at Oxford and then Cambridge, where he was converted to Catholicism by John SERGEANT, himself a convert. In 1642 both went to the English College in Lisbon, where they were ordained. There, after 1650 Godden became successively lecturer in philosophy, lecturer in theology, prefect of studies, vice president and president, and also won fame for his eloquent sermons in Portuguese. In 1661 he was appointed chaplain and tutor to Princess Catherine of Braganza, destined consort of Charles II, and accompanied her to London, where he engaged in controversy with Edward Stillingfleet, the king's chaplain. In 1678 Godden was falsely accused of complicity in the murder of Sir Edmund Berry Godfrey at the time of Titus Oates's alleged Popish Plot. Godden escaped to Paris, but returned, under James II, as chaplain to the Queen Dowager. In 1686, in the presence of the king, he publicly defended the Catholic doctrine of the Real Presence against Dr. William Jane, the Protestant dean of Gloucester.

Bibliography: J. GILLOW, *A Literary and Biographical History or Bibliographical Dictionary of the English Catholics from 1534 to the Present Time,* 5 v. (London-New York 1885–1902; repr. New York 1961) 2:503–506, lists and summaries of Godden's writings. J. D. CARR, *The Murder of Sir Edmund Godfrey* (London 1936). J. LANE, *Titus Oates* (London 1949).

[G. ALBION]

GODEAU, ANTOINE

Bishop, man of letters, orator, one of the first members of the Académie Française; b. Dreux, Sept. 24, 1605; d. Vence, April 21, 1672. While still in his early 20s Godeau settled in Paris, where he eventually became one of the favorite habitués of Hôtel Rambouillet. He was known as ''*le nain de princesse Julie,*'' and his wit, good cheer, and literary criticism generally overcame his physical unattractiveness. Surprisingly, Godeau turned to the Church and was ordained in 1636. That same year Richelieu appointed him to the rather small but strategically located Diocese of Grasse. Godeau became also bishop of Vence in 1644, but he relinquished the See of Grasse in 1653 to quiet the dissatisfaction of the clergy of Venice. From 1636 to his death, Godeau was a pious and model bishop. By sermons, synods, visitations, and publications he sought the welfare of his entire flock. Godeau's pastoral outlook followed closely the theology of the Council of Trent. As a layman and as a prelate, Godeau demonstrated remarkable literary productivity. Among his better known works are *Discours sur les oeuvres de Malherbe* (1629), *Oeuvres chrétiennes, vers et prose* (1633), and *Histoire de l'Église* (2 v., 1653).

Bibliography: G. GRENTE *Dictionnaire des letters françaises* (Paris 1954–60) A. ADAM, *Histoire de la littérature française au XVII* 5 v. (new ed. Paris 1958–62). P. BROUTIN, *La Réforme pastorale en France au XVII* 2 v. (Tournai 1956). K. HOFMANN, *Lexicon für Theologie und Kirche* 4:1034. P. SAGE, *Catholicisme* 5:78. G. DOUBLET, *Dictionnaire de thèologie catholique* 6.2:1470–71.

[R. J. MARION]

GODFREY, WILLIAM

Cardinal, seventh archbishop of Westminster; b. Liverpool, Sept. 25, 1889; d. London, Jan. 22, 1963. The younger son of George and Maria (Garvey) Godfrey, he was educated at Ushaw College and at the English College in Rome. After ordination (1916) he gained his doctorate in theology (1917) before returning to England. He taught successively classics, philosophy, and theology at Ushaw between 1918 and 1930 and then served as rector of the English College in Rome from 1930 to 1938. Appointed the first apostolic delegate to Great Britain, Gibraltar, Malta, and Bermuda (1938), he fulfilled this difficult assignment with notable tact. Godfrey was archbishop of Liverpool from 1953 until 1956, when he succeeded Cardinal GRIFFIN at Westminster. To this position he brought wide experience, and in it he distinguished himself by his gentleness, dignity, deep spirituality, broad sympathy, and inflexibility on matters of principle. His publications, *The Young Apostle* (1924) and *God and Ourselves* (1928), reflected his constant preoccupation with priestly education and the care of souls. He was raised to the cardinalate in 1958.

Bibliography: D. WORLOCK, *Wiseman Review* 237 (1963–64) 3–15.

[D. MILBURN]

GODFREY GIFFARD

Chancellor of England, bishop of Worcester; b. *c.* 1235; d. Jan. 26, 1302. The son of Hugh Giffard of Boyton in Wiltshire, a royal justice, he was the younger brother of WALTER GIFFARD. When Walter was appointed chancellor of England (1265), Godfrey was soon thereafter chancellor of the exchequer. Walter's translation to YORK (1266) and resignation from the chancellorship opened the way for Godfrey's appointment to that high office (1267–68). Godfrey was elected to the See of WORCESTER in 1268. King EDWARD I subsequently employed him on diplomatic missions and as an itinerant justice. As bishop of Worcester, Godfrey engaged in long-drawn controversies with the monastic chapter of the cathedral about control of properties. He disputed with the abbot of WESTMINSTER over the right of visitation at MALVERN. Joining with other suffragans, including THOMAS OF CANTELUPE, he resisted Abp. JOHN PECKHAM's excessive claims of metropolitan jurisdiction within the province of CANTERBURY. Litigation with his chapter troubled his last years: William of Gloucester charged him on some 36 counts before Abp. ROBERT OF WINCHELSEA. Among other things, it was claimed that Giffard had manumitted serfs without the consent of the chapter. But this and other charges he answered satisfactorily. Giffard contributed to the decoration and pavement of Worcester cathedral and completed and fortified Hartlebury Castle.

Bibliography: *Register of Bishop Godfrey Giffard,* ed. J. W. W. BUND, 2 v. (Oxford 1898–1902). *Annals of Worcester* in *Annales Monastici,* ed. H. R. LUARD, 5 v. (*Rerum Britannicarum medii aevi scriptores* 36; 1864–69) v.4. J. C. CAMPBELL, *Lives of the Lord Chancellors . . . ,* 12 v. (7th ed. Jersey City 1881–85). T. F. TOUT, *The Dictionary of National Biography from the Earliest Times to 1900,* 7:1172–73. A. B. EMDEN, *A Biographical Register of the University of Oxford to A.D. 1500* 2:761–762.

[A. R. HOGUE]

GODFREY OF AMIENS, ST.

Bishop, abbot; b. near Soissons, France, mid-11th century; d. Saint-Crépin Abbey, near Soissons, Nov. 8, 1115. At the age of five, Godfrey entered the Benedictine abbey of Mont-Saint-Quentin; he was later professed and ordained there. Despite the opposition of the previous superior, Godfrey was elected abbot of Nogent-sous-Coucy, a small house in Champagne that prospered under his rule. He was elected bishop of Amiens in 1104, partly because he was so adept in business affairs. Godfrey's successor at Nogent, GUIBERT, praised Godfrey's career as abbot but suggested that as bishop his promise was greater than his performance. Godfrey's severity made him unpopular. Attempting to resign his see, he retired to La Grande Chartreuse. Despite the opposition of his clergy and people, he was summoned back to Amiens by his archbishop but died within the year. During the GREGORIAN REFORM, he was particularly zealous in combating the prevalent evil of SIMONY

Feast: Nov. 8.

Bibliography: GODFREY OF AMIENS, Letters, *Patrologia Latina* (Paris 1878–90) 162:683,735–748. *Acta Sanctorum,* Nov. 3:889–944. C. BRUNEL, ''Les Actes faux de l'abbaye de Saint-Valery,'' *Moyen-âge* 22 (1909) 179–196. J. L. BAUDOT and L. CHAUSSIN, *Vies des saints et des bienheureux selon l'ordre du calendrier avec l'historique des fêtes* (Paris 1935–56) 11:274–278.

[E. J. KEALEY]

GODFREY OF BOUILLON

First Crusader king of Jerusalem; b. probably *c.* 1060; d. July 18, 1100. Godfrey, the second son of Eustace II, Count of Boulogne, and Ida, daughter of Godfrey II, ''the Bearded,'' of Upper Lorraine, could trace his descent on each side from Charlemagne. In 1076 his maternal uncle Godfrey, the ''Hunchback'' of Lower Lorraine, named him his heir. Thus he acquired the castle of Bouillon, about 50 miles north of Verdun, and certain other smaller allodial holdings. In 1087 he was invested with the Duchy of Lower Lorraine by Emperor Henry IV. Although not, perhaps, as deeply religious as contemporary chroniclers indicated, Godfrey did possess a simple piety. This, combined with the spirit of adventure, which was then strong among his French neighbors, no doubt prompted him—alone among the major princes of the Empire—to join the First CRUSADE. The army that he led across Europe through Hungary numbered about 1,000 cavalry and 7,000 infantry. Notable among his associates were BALDWIN, his younger brother and successor as King of Jerusalem, and Baldwin of Bourg. Godfrey's role in the Crusade reveals him as somewhat lacking in administrative capacity and as capable of occasional pettiness and obstinacy. Nevertheless, he won general respect; and when RAYMOND OF TOULOUSE refused the crown of Jerusalem, he was the choice of the other leaders. He was doubtless entirely sincere in believing that the Holy City should be under ecclesiastical rather than lay jurisdiction, and thus in also assuming the modest title of Advocate of the Holy Sepulcher (July 22, 1099). Similar feelings, combined with his desperate need for reinforcements, no doubt prompted him to accept the investiture of Jerusalem from the patriarch and papal legate, Daimbert of Pisa. Godfrey was not a strong ruler, but with extremely limited resources he preserved and stabilized a state that, despite his promises to Daimbert, was to survive him as a lay kingdom (*see* JERUSALEM, KINGDOM OF). He died after governing the infant state a few days less than one year.

Bibliography: J. C. ANDRESSOHN, *The Life and Ancestry of Godfrey of Bouillon* (Bloomington 1947). S. RUNCIMAN, *A History of the Crusades,* 3 v. (Cambridge, Eng. 1951–54) v.1. M. W. BALDWIN and K. M. SETTON, eds., *A History of the Crusades* (Philadelphia 1955) v.1.

[M. W. BALDWIN]

GODFREY OF FONTAINES

Scholastic philosopher and theologian, known as *Doctor venerandus;* b. Liège, before 1250; d. Paris, Oct. 29, 1306 (1309?). Studying arts at the University of Paris during the second regency of THOMAS AQUINAS, he may have been a student of SIGER OF BRABANT in Arts and HENRY OF GHENT in Theology. A master in theology by 1285, he taught at Paris until 1304 or thereafter, apparently with an interruption for some time after 1297. Together with Henry of Ghent he took an active part in opposing the privileges of MENDICANT ORDERS. On March 15, 1292, he was appointed by Pope Nicholas IV to examine the complaints of the university against its chancellor, Berthaud of Saint-Denis. In 1300 he was proposed for the See of Tournai, but renounced his rights before the appointment of Guy of Boulogne.

His most important contribution to scholasticism consists of 15 *Quodlibeta,* all of which have been published (Louvain 1904–37), and a number of disputed questions, only some of which have been edited. He rejected the real distribution between essence and existence, apparently as defended by GILES OF ROME, and Henry's theory of intentional distinction. Identifying essence and existence, he multiplied existences to correspond to substantial and accidental essences. For him, nature is merely the abstract term for the concrete supposit, and SUBSISTENCE is simply the existence of a substantial nature that has not been assumed by a higher supposit. In Christ, in whom human nature was assumed by a divine person, there is only one supposit and one subsistence, but two existences.

In his theory of knowledge, he was strongly Aristotelian and highly critical of Augustinian and Neo-Augustinian theories of knowledge (*see* KNOWLEDGE, THEORIES OF). Insisting on the impossibility of created powers to reduce themselves to act, he emphasized the passivity of sense and intellect in cognition and of will in volition. For him, an object as ultimately presented to the will by the intellect is the efficient cause of volition. Agreeing with Aquinas that no created substance is immediately operative, he maintained a real distinction between the soul and its powers (*see* FACULTIES OF THE SOUL). While open to the possibility of an eternal world, he rejected the possibility of an actual infinite multitude of souls that might result there from, proposing instead the possibility of TRANSMIGRATION OF SOULS.

For Godfrey, as for Aquinas, primary matter is pure potentiality, incapable of existence without substantial form. He opposed every form of universal HYLOMORPHISM defended by 13th-century AUGUSTINIANISM. Since primary matter is the root of corruptibility, he suggested that the incorruptible heavenly bodies had no primary matter. He was sharply critical of the various theories of plurality of forms (*see* FORMS, UNICITY AND PLURALITY OF). For him, despite possible theological difficulties concerning Christ's body in the tomb, plurality of forms tends to destroy the substantial unity of matter-form composites. Since substantial form serves as the principle of transcendental unity in created substances, it is also the formal principle of INDIVIDUATION. However, since quantity is the principle of numerical unity in material substances, it is also the material dispositive cause of individuation.

Among his followers may be listed John of Pouilly, PETER OF AUVERGNE, Gerard of Bologna, and Guy Terrena of Perpignan. Among his criticis were BERNARD OF AUVERGNE and John DUNS SCOTUS. His influence declined after the middle of the 14th century, perhaps because there was no religious community to espouse his cause.

Sometimes styled a Thomist, sometimes an eclectic, he was an independent and critical thinker, often favorable to THOMISM. More Aristotelian and no less platonic than Aquinas, he sometimes departed radically from Aquinas because of a more extreme interpretation of Aristotle, frequently that of Averroës. Generally he was highly critical of the Neo-Augustinian tradition, especially of HENRY OF GHENT.

Bibliography: *P. Glorieux, Répertoire des maîtres en théologie de Paris au XIII de siècle* 1:396–399. B. NEUMANN, *Der Mensch und die himmlische Seligkeit nach der Lehre Gottfrieds von Fontaines* (Limburg 1958). É. H. GILSON, *History of Christian Philosophy in the Middle Ages* (New York 1955). R. J. ARWAY, "A Half Century of Research on Godfrey of Fontaines," *New Scholasticism* 36 (1962) 192–218. P. STELLA, *Enciclopedia filosofica* 2:854–855. O. LOTTIN, "Le Libre arbitre chez Godefroid de Fontaines," *Revue néo-scholastique* 40 (1937) 213–241; "Le Thomisme de Godefroid de Fontaines en matière de libre arbitre," *ibid.* 554–573. J. F. WIPPEL, "Godfrey of Fontaines and the Real Distinction between Essence and Existence," *Traditio* 20 (1964) 385–410; *The Metaphysical Thought of Godfrey of Fontaines* (Washington DC 1981). M. DE WULF, *Un Théologien-philosophe du XIII siècle: Étude sur la vie, les oeuvres et l'influence de Godefroid de Fontaines* (Brussels 1904).

[J. F. WIPPEL]

GODFREY OF SAINT-VICTOR

Philosopher, theologian, and poet, b. *c.* 1125; d. after 1190. Godfrey studied the arts at Paris, where he was influenced by the dialectician Adam of Balsham (Adam Parvi Pontis). After his theological studies, he probably taught a few years prior to entering the Abbey of Saint-Victor, before 1160. He is to be distinguished from Godfrey of Breteuil, who lived in the second half of the 12th century and was subprior of Sainte-Barbe-en-Auge in Normandy. The abbey in which Godfrey became a canon was a center of piety and of the intellectual life; the influence of HUGH OF SAINT-VICTOR was maintained by the prior, RICHARD OF SAINT-VICTOR, and Godfrey could develop his cultural humanism. However, in 1173, at the death of Richard, the priorship was given to WALTER OF SAINT-VICTOR, a narrow-minded and violent character. Walter hounded Godfrey for his humanistic tendencies, and finally obliged him to leave the abbey for the solitude of a rural priory *c.* 1180. It was there that Godfrey wrote his principal work, the *Microcosmus*. After Walter's death *c.* 1190, Godfrey returned to the abbey and took up the duties of sacristan until his death.

Works. Godfrey's literary legacy is varied. Still extant are 32 of his sermons, one series dating from his early stay in Paris, the other after his return from exile; these use doctrinal explanations to excite devotion to the person of Christ, the Virgin Mary, and the saints. Godfrey was also a poet, composing a panegyric to St. Augustine that paraphrases the principal subjects treated by that doctor and a canticle of the Virgin Mary, inspired by Biblical themes. Shortly before 1176 Godfrey dedicated to his friend Stephen of Tournai a compilation of works that are varied in form and content. The collection is called the *Fons philosophiae* after the first of the works, an allegorical account of the sources of Godfrey's formation symbolized as a flowing stream from which he drew water as a student. It presents an interesting tableau of Parisian schools in the mid-12th century and epitomizes the ideals of Victorine culture as formulated by Hugh. Also noteworthy is the third work, the *Anatomy of the Body of Christ,* a long poem wherein Godfrey describes in detail each member and organ of Christ's body. This merits a place in the history of Christian symbolism, especially since it gathered together a long series of allegories used by the Fathers and helped form medieval devotion to the humanity of Christ.

Godfrey's masterpiece, however, is the *Microcosmus*. The work's theme is traditional in philosophy and in the Fathers, viz, that man is a miniature of the universe, a microcosm. The first part is an allegorical exposition of the Hexaemeron (the account in Genesis describing creation within six days) to explain how God produces each human soul. The work of the first three days corresponds to the nature God gives man; that of the last three days, to the crowning of man's nature by supernatural grace. The second part explains the gifts of God's grace and their relation to man's affective life, showing how the Christian regulates his affections and conforms their movements to God's will.

Influence. Godfrey represents the flowering of the richest elements in the Victorine tradition concerning man. His work, however, neither enjoyed a wide reading nor exercised direct influence on later thinkers. It came too late, at the moment when the brightness of the great abbey of Paris had begun to dim, but Godfrey's basic points, the distinction between grace and nature and the positive value of nature in a unified Christian and religious life, were to be recognized and reaffirmed in the high SCHOLASTICISM of the 13th century.

Bibliography: GODEFROI DE SAINT-VICTOR, *Fons philosophiae*, ed. P. MICHAUD-QUANTIN (Namur 1956); *The Fountain of Philosophy: A Translation of the Twelfth-Century Fons philosophiae of Godfrey of Saint Victor*, trans. E. A. SYNAN (Toronto 1972); *Godefroy de Saint-Victor: Microcosmus. Texte*, ed. P. DELHAYE (Lille 1951). F. BONNARD, *Histoire de l'abbaye royale et de l'ordre des chanoines réguliers de Saint-Victor de Paris*, 2 v. (Paris 1907). J. CHATILLON, ''Sermons et prédicateurs victorins de la seconde moitié du XIIe siècle,'' *AHDLMA* 32 (1965) 7–60. P. DAMON, ''The Preconium Augustini of Godfrey of Saint Victor,'' *Mediaeval Studies* 22 (1960) 92–107. P. DELHAYE, *Le Microcosmus de Godefroy de Saint-Victor: étude théologique*, (Lille 1951); ''Les sermons de Godefroy de Saint- Victor: leur tradition manuscrite.'' *RTAM* 21 (1954) 194–210.

[P. MICHAUD-QUANTIN]

GODO, ST.

Abbot; d. Oyes, Belgium, May 26 *c.* 690. He was the nephew of St. WANDRILLE, founder of the monastery of FONTENELLE (now Saint-Wandrille). Godo (or Goan) was a member there until 661. He left to found a new monastery at Oyes, later known as Saint-Gond. His relics were transferred to the cathedral at Langres. He is patron of glove makers.

Feast: July 24.

Bibliography: *Acta Sanctorum* May 6:440–442. *Gesta sanctorum patrum fontanellensis coenobii,* ed. F. LOHIER and J. LAPORTE (Rouen 1936) 9–10. J. L. BAUDOT and L. CHAUSSIN, *Vies des saints et des bienheuruex selon l'ordre du calendreir avec l'historique des fêtes* (Paris 1935–56) 5:514–515. A. M. ZIMMERMANN *Kalendarium Benedictinum: Die Heiligen und Seligen des Benediktineorderns und seiner Zwige* (Metten 1933–38) 2:493–494. R. GAZEAU, *Catholicisme. Hier, au jourd'hui et demain,*, ed. G. JACQUEMET, 5:94.

[O. L. KAPSNER]

GODOY, PEDRO DE

Dominican philosopher and theologian; b. Aldeanneva, Spain, *c.* 1600; d. Segontia, Nov. 2, 1677 (1687?). He studied at the College of St. Gregory at Valladolid and, in 1638, held the first chair of theology at the University of Salamanca. After 25 years there, King Philip IV rewarded him with the appointment to the bishopric of Osma (1663), a choice ratified by Pope Alexander VII on March 31, 1664. In 1672 Godoy left Osma to become bishop of Segontia, a position he held until July 12, 1677, when Pope Innocent XI named the Dominican Thomas Carbonel his successor. Included in his writings, some of which are lost, are three collections of *Disputationes theologicae in 1am, 1am 2ae, et 3am partem D. Thomae,* published separately between 1666 and 1672 (composite ed. Venice 1686, 1696, 1763). The last edition contains appendices by J. B. GONET, sometimes considered a plagiarist of Godoy's lecture notes, but credited with providing the stimulus that Godoy needed to publish his work at all.

Bibliography: J. QUÉTIF and J. ÉCHARD, *Scriptores Ordinis Praedicatorum* (New York 1959) 2.2:673–674. R. COULON, *Dictionnaire de théologie catholique* 6.2:1472–1473. G. GIERATHS, *Lexicon für Theologie und Kirche* 4:1036. L. GETINO, *Enciclopedia Universal Ilustrada Europa-Americana* 26:453. H. HURTER *Nomenclator literarius theolgiae catholicae* 4:7. P. GAMS, *Series episcoporum Ecclesiae Catholicae* 57, 75. V. M. FONTANA, *Sacrum theatrum dominicanum* (Rome 1666).

[F. J. ROENSCH]

GOESBRIAND, LOUIS DE

Bishop, author; b. St. Urbain, France, Aug. 4, 1816; d. Burlington, Vt., Nov. 3, 1899. He was the son of Marquis Henri de Goesbriand and Emilie de Bergean. After his education at the seminaries of Quimper, France, and Saint-Sulpice, Paris, he was ordained on July 13, 1840. His interest in the American missionary field brought him to the U.S., where he engaged in parochial work in the Diocese of Cincinnati, Ohio, from 1840 to 1847. When Cleveland, Ohio, became a diocese in 1847, Goesbriand became its vicar-general and served until he was named first bishop of the newly established Diocese of Burlington, Vt., on July 29, 1853. He was consecrated on Oct. 30, 1853 in New York City, and arrived in Burlington on November 5. At that time there were only 20,000 Catholics and five priests in Vermont. With the exception of eight churches and a small parochial school taught by lay teachers, there were no institutions of any kind. Between 1853 and 1891 the number of priests increased to 52 and the number of churches to 78; eight academies and 16 parochial schools were established; and seven congregations of nuns were brought into the diocese to teach. In addition to his work as bishop, Goesbriand also wrote or translated a number of books and pamphlets, among which were: *Catholic Memoirs of Vermont and New Hampshire* (1886); *Christ on the Altar* (1890); *History of Confession* (1889); and *St. Peter's Life* (1893).

[J. D. SULLIVAN/G. E. DUPONT]

Johann Wolfgang Goethe. (Archive Photos, Inc.)

GOETHE, JOHANN WOLFGANG VON

Poet, dramatist, philosopher, scientist, and statesman; b. Frankfurt am Main, Aug. 28, 1749; d. Weimar, March 22, 1832. Goethe grew up in an atmosphere of enlightened, refined cosmopolitan culture. His father, a well-to-do Frankfurt lawyer who bore the honorary title of imperial councilor and who lived in self-imposed retirement, was a well-educated man of a serious and rational bent. From his mother Goethe inherited a ''gaiety of spirit and delight in story-telling.'' He received his early education from his father, later from private tutors, concentrating on humanistic studies, chiefly French and Latin literature, but enjoying enough freedom to pursue his own intellectual and spiritual interests.

Early Work. At the age of 16 Goethe went to Leipzig to study law but he had little motivation to acquire systematically an abstract body of knowledge. He enjoyed Leipzig's society and its enlightened rococo style that was fashioned after Parisian patterns. His early lyrics were some elegant Anacreontic poems with little originality. A delirious love affair with an innkeeper's daughter, Käthchen Schönkopf, inspired a short pastoral play, *Die Laune des Verliebten* (1767), a collection of songs titled *Annette,* and later another play with moralistic overtones, *Die Mitschuldigen* (1769). His earliest lyrical diction was distinguished by a striking visual quality; Goethe was aware that ''it was particularly the eye with which I conceived the world.'' He gained a number of lasting impressions of Greek art from A. F. Oeser, who taught drawing and etching at the Leipzig art academy. In 1768 Goethe returned to Frankfurt gravely ill and exhausted. During a long period of recovery he was influenced by a pietistic circle headed by Susanne von Klettenberg, an intimate of his mother. He also became interested in mystical philosophers, including Paracelsus, SWEDENBORG, and Giordano BRUNO. (*See* PIETISM.)

New Perspectives. A new period of life began in 1770 with his departure for Strassburg to complete his juridical studies. Goethe shook off the influence of the artificial social conventionalism of rococo culture, encountered the beauty of nature, and found grandeur in simplicity of life and the direct appeal of art. He wrote an enthusiastic essay praising the Gothic architecture of the Strassburg minster as characteristic German style. Of lasting consequence was his friendship with J. G. von HERDER, a young theologian and budding literary critic. Herder's aesthetic and historical writings were rooted in the *Sturm und Drang* reforms, were directed against the arid enlightened rationalism of his time, and pleaded for genuine expression of feeling and the truly human creative forces. Herder acquainted Goethe with the more realistic and effective concepts of art; these Herder recognized in the religious and poetic creativity of the human soul whose expression he found in history, in the symbolic language of folk songs, and in the works of great genius, such as Homer, Ossian, Sophocles, and Shakespeare. Under these influences and inspired by his affection for Frederike Brion, a pastor's daughter from the village of Sesenheim, Goethe created a new lyric diction that united the expression of strong personal feelings with an intense experience of the immediate situation. Among these early poems, *Willkommen und Abschied* and *Mailied* are notable.

Goethe concluded his legal studies, was awarded the licentiate, and returned to Frankfurt to practice law, but devoted insufficient time to develop his practice. Instead, he worked on the dramatization of the autobiography of the 16th-century knight Götz von Berlichingen, whom he portrayed in a series of dramatic pictures. *Götz von Berlichingen* (1771) reflects the revolt of the young Goethe against stagnant institutionalism and courtly egotism, against inhuman betrayal, suppression, and anarchy. As such, and as the first drama with a national subject matter and a penetrating ethical spirit, it was enthusiastically received by the younger generation when it appeared anonymously in 1773. Other similar works, with such titles as *Caesar, Mahomet,* and *Prometheus,* remained fragments. Goethe was quite aware of the historical and social necessities that prevented him from idealizing self-centered individualism and demonic heroism. The motif of the wanderer, the man in search of an immediate and formative experience as the central principle of his creativity, recurs frequently in the large hymnic poems of these years. This seeker does not simply strive to assert his ego but to liberate the true impulses of his soul in response to all operative natural and cosmic forces, through which he tries to share the rapture of creative enjoyment. Here lie the beginnings of *Faust,* which were ''stormed out'' in these months: a compulsive yearning for growth within his boundless urge to be active and creative, an attempt to embrace the totality of existence through restless aspiration and to fuse knowledge and feeling, nature and spirit.

Fame with Werther. While spending a few months in Wetzlar at the imperial court, Goethe fell in love with Charlotte Buff, the fiancée of his friend Kestner; a similarly confusing infatuation with Maximiliane Brentano, together with the suicide of a Wetzlar colleague, gave the impetus to his first novel, *Die Leiden des jungen Werthers* (1774). This epistolary novel, written in the manner of Richardson and Rousseau, but more intensely personal and psychological, reflects the painful contrast between sentiment and the reality of life, between inner vitality and the moral principles of society. This book made him at 25 the most popular author in Europe. Such powerful emotional impulses, such vibrating interrelations between internal and external forces had never before been depicted in a language so succinct and emotionally saturated. Goethe was admired by his younger contemporaries, and especially by the writers of the *Sturm und Drang* movement. He won new friends, such as the theologian Johann LAVATER, the pedogogical writer Johann Basedow, the philosopher Friedrich JACOBI, and the brothers C. and F. Stolberg. He was greatly attracted by the philosophy of SPINOZA, with whom he believed that one could ''visualize God in nature, nature in God.'' Closer to LESSING's ideas of dramaturgy were the two plays Goethe completed at Frankfurt, *Clavigo* (1774) and *Stella* (1775), both of which reflect the conflict between individual freedom and middle-class morality.

Two Tragedies. More significant, however, than these pieces were the beginnings of the two tragedies, *Faust* (1790) and *Egmont* (1787). The old moralistic legend of Faust's sin and damnation, which Goethe knew through the chapbook of 1725 and a popular puppet play on this theme, was now converted into a symbolic drama of man's inner struggle toward light and his restless search for a greater creativity. Faust's urge to comprehend ''what holds this world together in its in-most fold'' leads him to tragic error and destruction; this striving for the highest stage of human perfection, however, transcends mere titanic self-assertion and appears in Goethe's metaphysical perspective as an essential development toward a superior form of capability, finally achieved through love and grace. (*See* FAUST LEGEND.) The tragedy *Egmont* shows a significant transition in the hero's development from youthful individualism to self-sacrificing altruism within the context of the historical and political reality that is characteristic of Goethe's classical style. Egmont realizes a truly creative mission by defending the rights of his Dutch people against the increasing suppression by the Spanish duke Alba. Egmont's attitude culminates in an inner struggle to convert his zest for life into the highest ethical activity of committing himself uncompromisingly to the principle of freedom and human integrity that alone justifies and impels his people's liberation.

Public Offices. Goethe developed such idealistic concepts and images of personal fulfillment during his first decades in Weimar. The young duke Carl August (1757–1828) had in 1775 invited the author whom he admired so greatly to his small provincial residence, where the duke and his mother had gathered a group of intellectuals. This chance companionship with the duke soon grew into a more serious relationship when Goethe accepted a series of administrative responsibilities. He became a member of the minister's council, was put in charge of the departments of mining, military affairs, and public improvements, and later was given charge of the financial affairs of the state. He received his patent of nobility in 1782. In conjunction with his offices he engaged in various scientific studies, which finally led to important morphological treatises. Of great significance for his personal development was his friendship with Charlotte von Stein, the wife of the court equerry; she helped him establish a more mature perspective and to appreciate inner beauty and social decorum. Being convinced that ''we all have to complete our life's circle according to eternal, unchangeable, and all-encompassing laws,'' Goethe became increasingly receptive to universal problems and social demands that transcend personal initiative. His lyric poems began to reflect a new sense for classical simplicity and beauty as well as a genuine feeling for all fundamental forms of human destiny. The drama *Iphigenie auf Tauris* (1786) is conceived in the idealistic and ethical spirit of these years. Its climax is Iphigenie's decision to choose personal sacrifice to atone by her ''pure humanity'' for her family's guilt rather than expediently abandon her moral integrity. The tragedy of the passionate, oversensitive artist in *Torquato Tasso* (1789) also originates in these productive years, indicating Goethe's own inner danger in his attempt to practice restraint and achieve his proper place in the social and ethical order. The geniuslike exuberance and demonic drive of the young poet, whom Goethe later called an ''exaggerated Werther,'' tragically disrupts the context of life at court but also reveals the stagnant limitation of an unproductive formalism imposed upon a creative mind.

Italian Experience. Overwhelmed by the suppression of his literary and scholarly pursuits under his mounting official duties and the demands of personal relationships, Goethe secretly departed for Italy. ''I count a true rebirth from the day I entered Rome,'' he wrote in 1786. He acquired a new and immediate relationship with the objective world as he visualized an identity between the human mind and the intrinsic principles of nature. He not only gained a more tangible appreciation of antique beauty but also found an intensive perceptiveness of the fundamental forms of life. Realizing that ''one should seek nothing behind the phenomena—they themselves are the theory,'' he conceived the idea of ''Urphänomene'' or symbolic principles that contain all developmental possibilities of any given species. Close to nature, to the simplicity and grandeur of classical art, and to the unpretentious life of the people, he developed firmer concepts of humanity and aesthetic perspectives.

A unique precipitate of the Italian experience were the *Römische Elegien* (1788), which combine classical plasticity and sensual fullness of life, spiritual rigor and realistic feelings. These distichs also reflect the new love for Christiane Vulpius, whom he took into his home shortly after his return to Weimar in 1788. She became the mother of his son August, and Goethe married her in 1806. The following years were marked by a period of social isolation. With the consent of the duke, he devoted more time to cultural than to administrative functions and also assumed the directorship of the Weimar theater. He felt keenly the spreading unrest caused by the French Revolution and experienced its aftereffects when he accompanied the duke into the campaign of the Coalition against the revolutionary forces that ended in the defeat of Valmy (1793). In the midst of the far-reaching social and historical changes that evolved from these events, Goethe remained skeptical, supported peaceful evolution rather than revolution, and concerned himself primarily with preserving all distinctly human values. The idyllic epos *Hermann und Dorothea* (1797) depicts the overcoming of external danger through simple human bonds and sound social conditions. Similar expressly humane ideas appear in novelistic form in *Unterhaltungen deutscher Ausgewanderten* (1797) and in some shorter plays. He later attempted to give lasting expression to his experience of the revolution in the drama *Die Natürliche Tochter* (1803).

New Creative Impulse. His friendship with the great dramatist Johann Friedrich von Schiller began a new creative phase in Goethe's life. Their famous correspondence attests to their mutually inspiring search for aesthetic principles in accord with the cultural and philosophical tenor of the time. They wrote a series of ballads, chiefly in 1797, and collaborated in the epigrammatic *Xenien* and some theoretical essays. Schiller gave Goethe a greater awareness of his intellectual mission; he urged him to complete *Faust I* (1808) and particularly the ''novel of development'' *Wilhelm Meister* (1796), which evolved from an earlier 1786 fragment. In the first part, *Wilhelm Meisters Lehrjahre,* Goethe recognized art and the theater as significant means of education, but more personal commitments and social functions lead the hero to mature humanistic ideals. The center of Goethe's concern is the formative influence of all the effective, aesthetic, intellectual, and ethical spheres of life, radiating the conviction that ''deep in us lies the creative power which enables us to bring forth what ought to be.'' The second part, *Wilhelm Meisters Wanderjahre* (1829), shows the hero in a more advanced industrial world that had outgrown the old aristocratic order. Broad universal education is replaced by practical specialization designed to cope with the technical and social problems of a new era. In his final stage, Meister leads an active and altruistic existence within a thriving community that serves broadly human rather than individualistic needs.

In the tendencies of the new Romantic movement, arising in neighboring Jena, Goethe saw a return to the individualism of the *Sturm und Drang* period in spite of the homage that the young generation of poets and critics paid to his *Wilhelm Meister.* The attempt of the Romantics to identify life and art seemed to contradict the notion of form that he fervently upheld in his later years. His novel *Die Wahlverwandtschaften* (1809) can be taken as a protest against the Romantics' disregard for social institutions. Even the most passionate content, the theme of adultery and divorce, could be combined with a stern adherence to objective moral demands and inner beauty. In depicting an intense struggle between the elemental power of love and the binding moral order, Goethe symbolically recognized the tragic incompatibility of these opposing forces but found no other human solution than renunciation and either ethical, religious, or self-immolating transformation of the basically insoluble dilemma.

Biographical Work. After the death of Schiller in 1805 Goethe began to see his own life in a historical and symbolic way. This stimulated his *Dichtung und Wahrheit* (1809–14; 1830–31), a synthesis of autobiography and philosophical interpretation of his life in its essential interrelations with the determining currents of his time. This autobiography, which covers only the period of his youth, is supplemented by other biographical writings: *Italienische Reise* (1816–17), *Campagne in Frankreich* (1822), and his correspondence and conversations with Schiller, Zelter, Riemer, Von Müller, and Eckermann. The style of his old age was determined by problems of wide human application expressed in a symbolic and allegorical language whose aim was the fullest possible representation of reality. His lyric poetry now achieved a complete unity of thought and form. Characteristic of this phase is the lyric cycle *Westöstlicher Divan* (1819), inspired by his love for Marianne von Willemer, and the *Marienbad Elegie* (1823), where his unrequited feelings for the young Ulrike von Levetzow found sublime expression. Creative and spiritually transcending renunciation, and not withdrawn resignation, is the key to this late expression of love and wisdom.

Faust, Part 2. As Goethe was writing the final books of *Wilhelm Meister,* he began the ''principal occupation'' of his last years, the second part of *Faust,* completed a few months before his death. This enormous tragedy had absorbed all the essential impulses and insights of his life. It began as a subjective ''fragment of a grand confession'' revealing his youthful convictions about knowledge, love, nature, and God; its second phase, after 1788, includes more mature views on moral and religious problems. Individualistic expressionism changed to a symbolic drama of mankind, a mystery play in its own right. Schiller praised its ''duality of human nature and the tragically miscarried attempt to unite divine and earthly realities in man.'' Goethe, however, regarded such a discrepancy as the basis for any creative development. Higher maturity means an infinitely active search for the realization of new forms of existence. The polarity between Faust and Mephistopheles, between active, spiritual longing on the one hand, and the arresting power of sensual drives on the other, forms a creative rhythm, a productive interplay and intensification of his potentials. Since, for Goethe, God does not stand outside the creative process of life but moves the world from within, constant activity and aspiration draw Faust closer to perfection. This positive and partly redemptive aspect of Faust's destiny, which Goethe added in his middle years, is countered by the destructive boundlessness of his actions, the passionate urge to experience and enjoy ''whatever is allotted to all mankind.'' Such a spiritual titanism can only lead to self-destruction and despair. The tragedy of Gretchen is the most intense objectivation of this process.

Part 2 leads Faust into the world at large, to higher and purer spheres of activity. Goethe admits that allegorical and ideological elements prevail: ''The treatment had to proceed from the specific to the generic, because specification and variety belong to man's youth.'' All persons and actions presented are to be understood as symbols of comprehensive experiences or universal ideas. Faust travels through an expansive and multiform world, at first as an artist exploring the life of the court, then as a wanderer through the mythological world of the classical Walpurgis Night in search for beauty and knowledge; he allies himself in ancient Greece with Helen of Troy, the symbol of womanly perfection. The climactic but tragically limited union of Faust and Helen indicates Goethe's own synthesis of classical and northern elements. Fulfillment is attained only momentarily beyond time and space, and the continuing development is represented by their allegorical offspring, Euphorion, whose boundless flight and self-destruction again reflect the fate of Faust himself as well as that of the advancing times.

In his final phase of life Faust is shown as warlord, colonizer, engineer, free and absolute master of his own territory, yet still unsatisfied and full of inner conflicts. He cannot achieve his goal without destroying part of the inner realization of the divine power of man's soul. Guilt, error, and care accompany him to his death and remind him of the earthly limitation of all human existence. Goethe saw in the full acceptance of the limits imposed by the formative part of man's nature and in the compromises that his existence requires the prerequisite conditions for his attaining perfection. Freedom to act, ceaseless striving, keen awareness of change and continuity throughout the universe are his means of approaching the creative process of life that is one with the divine principle. Faust finally ''dies to live anew,'' his spiritual entelechy becoming part of the all-embracing powers of existence, and with the help of love and divine grace he transcends the sphere of mundane tragedy. His transformation and ascent to heaven can be affected insofar as his inner substance, the impetus of his aspiration, is not sacrificed to the expansion of his being in total action and blind enjoyment. Goethe thus concludes his life's work with the poetic representation of the mystery of human salvation, shrouded in the symbols of Christianity and reaffirming his belief in the continuation of life after death. But the poetic symbolism of heavenly harmony and perfection also contains an element of mystical silence and inexpressible awe before the inscrutable, which Goethe revered and acknowledged throughout his long and unusually productive life.

Religious Attitudes. In all phases of his development Goethe expressed deep religious convictions without binding himself to any of the traditional denominations; neither did he practice a mere theological eclecticism. Fundamental to his faith is his concept of God's omnipotence within the process of nature, and of man's inborn ability to recognize God both as force and mind, substance and form, uninterruptible motion and fixed order. For Goethe, God and world, spirit and matter were neither identical nor could they exist separate from one another; they formed, as it were, a ''united polarity of being.'' Within the dynamic order of life, man's spiritual growth depends upon his active participation in God's continuous self-realization in the phenomenological world. Any particular form of religion or image of God, in Goethe's thought, would mean a narrow humanization of God's greatness: ''Being engaged in natural sciences, we are pantheists, in poetry polytheists, morally monotheists.'' He believed in various forms of revelation that correspond to man's characteristic realms of activity. He admitted that the ''worshipful awe'' of the ''highest principle of morality'' as revealed in Christ was as natural to him as his reverence of the sun as the mightiest revelation of God's procreative power. He considered this attitude as ''world piety.'' In contrast to most of the 18th-century European philosophers, Goethe developed a complex of religious feelings and insights; he saw no need, however, to confess more than his resignation to God's incomprehensible will and he remained convinced that man is made to see what is illuminated but not the light itself, to behold God in his works, not God himself. In Christian thought, this is true for this world, but it denies, or at least prescinds from, the ultimates of revelation, which promises a face-to-face vision of God. In this sense, Goethe was no nearer to Christianity than some of the great pagan thinkers had been.

Bibliography: Editions. *Werke: Vollständige Ausgabe letzter Hand,* 40 v. (Stuttgart 1827–30), continued as *Nachgelassene Werke,* 20 v. (Stuttgart 1832–42); *Weimarer Ausgabe,* 133 v. (Weimar 1887–1919); *Jubiläums-Ausgabe,* ed. E. VON DER HELLEN, 40 v. (Stuttgart 1902–07; index v. 1912); *Propyläen-Ausgabe,* ed. C. HÖFER and C. NOCH, 49 v. (Munich 1909–32), in chronological order; *Gedenkausgabe,* ed. E. BEUTLER, 24 v. (Zurich 1948–54; suppl. 1960); *Hamburger Ausgabe,* ed. E. TRUNZ, 14 v. (Hamburg 1948–60); *Akademie-Ausgabe,* ed. E. GRUNACH et al. (Berlin 1952–). Literature. G. H. LEWES, *The Life and Works of Goethe,* 2 v. (London 1855). H. GRIMM, *Goethe* (Berlin 1887). R. M. MEYER, *Goethe* (Berlin 1895). A. BIELSCHOWSKY, *Goethe,* 2 v. (3d ed. Munich 1902–04). G. WITKOWSKI, *Goethe* (Leipzig 1899). G. SIMMEL, *Goethe* (Leipzig 1913). F. GUNDOLF, *Goethe* (Berlin 1916). P. H. BROWN, *Life of Goethe,* 2 v. (New York 1920). G. MÜLLER, *Kleine Goethebiographie* (2d ed. Bonn 1947). B. FAIRLEY, *Goethe as Revealed in His Poetry* (London 1932); *A Study of Goethe* (Oxford 1947). K. VIËTOR, *Goethe, the Poet,* tr. M. HADAS (Cambridge, Mass. 1949); *Goethe, the Thinker,* tr. B. Q. MORGAN (Cambridge, Mass. 1950). E. STAIGER, *Goethe,* 3 v. (Zurich 1952–59). H. A. KORFF, *Geist der Goethezeit,* 5 v. (Leipzig 1956–62), various eds. R. FRIEDENTHAL, *Goethe: His Life and Times* (London 1965). LOEWEN, H., *Goethe's Response to Protestantism* (Berne and Frankfurt, 1972). H. PLENDERLEITH, ''An Approach to Goethe's Treatment of Religion in *Dichtung und Wahrheit*'' *German Life and Letters,* v. 46, no. 4 (1993), 297. J. J. PELIKAN, *Faust the Theologian* (New Haven, Conn. 1995).

[K. SCHAUM]

GOGARTEN, FRIEDRICH

Theologian and defender of secularization; b. Jan. 13, 1887; d. Oct. 16,1967. Gogarten was educated at the universities of Berlin, Jena, and Heidelberg in the typically liberal Protestant theology characteristic of German university faculties at the turn of the century. During his time as pastor in a small country parish in Thuringia, he steeped himself in the thought of Martin Luther and began to question the optimistic assumptions of liberal thought. In an intellectual shift similar to that of Karl Barth, Gogarten rejected the historicism of theologians such as Ernst Troeltsch which seemed to be based upon an individualistic understanding of man and an identification of the Word of God with human conscience. Instead, especially during his career at the University of Göttingen (1935–55), Gogarten insisted that Christianity is not found in a realm of ideals or universal truths but in a summons to historical self-understanding in which the believer accepts responsibility for his existence under the Word of God addressed to him in Christ. Thus human beings encounter God not in abstract categories but in a personal Thou-I relationship within the relativity of history and the gratuity of the divine initiative.

Gogarten departed somewhat from his earlier neoorthodoxy by supporting the demythologizing of Rudolf Bultmann. He affirmed the existentialist position that faith is not the affirmation of objective historical truths but the personal acknowledgment of the efficacy of God's present action within the believing community.

Gogarten later came to insist on the value of secularization. The Christian must avoid any divinization of the historical process and is thereby rendered free to assume a radical concern for the world in its meaning-filled yet less-than-ultimate significance.

Bibliography: F. GOGARTEN, *Demythologizing and History* (New York 1955); *Christ the Crisis* (Richmond 1970); *The Reality of Faith* (Philadelphia 1959). L. SHINER, *The Secularization of History* (Nashville 1966).

[T. M. MCFADDEN]

GÓIS, DAMIÃO DE

Portuguese humanist, musician, composer; b. Alenquer, 1502; d. Alenquer, 1574. While still a page at the court of King Manuel I, Góis found his interest in Eastern Christianity stimulated by Matthew, the Ambassador from Ethiopia (1514). This interest was further stirred in 1523, when, after his appointment to the Portuguese commercial headquarters at Antwerp, he became more directly familiar with the Eastern and Portuguese deeds therein. In 1529 he journeyed briefly through Eastern Europe and obtained information about the Lapps from John Magnus Gothus, Archbishop of Uppsala, then in exile in Danzig. This information inspired him to call attention to the missionary opportunities among the Lapps at a time when the Reformation was imminent. He also made information about the Ethiopians available in a Latin treatise, published without his knowledge in 1532 in Antwerp (printed in London the following year in an English translation by St. Thomas More's son, John).

After visiting Denmark and Poland, Góis registered (1531) at the University of Louvain. In 1533 he visited Erasmus in Freiburg im Breisgau, returning to Lisbon in expectation of his appointment as treasurer of India House. He became dissatisfied, however, and returned to Flanders the following year, spent several months with Erasmus in Freiburg, and proceeded to Padua, where he stayed until 1538. He returned to Flanders, married, and studied again at Louvain, where his definitive work, *Fides, Religio, Moresque Aethiopum,* was published in 1540 (English translation in Joannes Boemus, comp., *The Manners, Lawes, and Customes of All Nations,* tr. Edward Aston, London 1611). In it he incorporated material gathered in Lisbon from Ethiopia's second ambassador, Zagazabo, who had arrived in 1527 with Francisco ÁLVARES.

Although the great book was reprinted several times in Northern Europe, its charity toward non-Latin Christianity displeased the Inquisition in Portugal, and it was condemned (1541). Moreover, Góis, who had been recalled to Lisbon from Belgium in 1543, returned only in 1545, an object of suspicion because of allegations concerning his Protestant associations abroad. In the meantime, however, a number of his brief works on Portugal and Portuguese deeds in the East were being published in Louvain: *Commentarii Rerum Gestarum in India citra Gangem a Lusitanis Anno 1538* (1539); *Hispania* (1542); and *De Bello Cambaico Ultimo Commentarii Tres* (1549).

Góis's greatest work, *Chrónica do Felicíssimo Rei Dom Emanuel,* a long history of the reign of King Manuel (4 v. 1566–67), was followed in 1567 by his one-volume chronicle of Prince João (later King João II), *Chronica do Principe Dom Ioam.* Disparaging references in these works to the royal family and various nobles brought about his arrest by the Inquisition in 1571; the charges went back to his friendships with Protestants. He repented after a year and a half in prison, was released as a penitent, and died shortly afterward.

Bibliography: G. J. C. HENRIQUES, ed., *Ineditos Goesianos,* 2 v. (Lisbon 1896–98). M. BATAILLON, *O cosmopolitismo de Damião de Góis,* tr. C. B. CHAVES (Lisbon 1938); this originally appeared as "Le Cosmopolitisme de Damião de Góis," in *Revue de littérature* *comparée* 18 (1938) 23–58, and was reprinted in his *Études sur le Portugal au temps de l'humanisme* (Coimbra 1952). F. M. ROGERS, *The Quest For Eastern Christians: Travels and Rumor in the Age of Discovery* (Minneapolis 1962).

[F. M. ROGERS]

GOLDEN AGE

A theme common to all the myths concerned with the early history of mankind is the assumption of a continuous deterioration. Its ultimate source is the pessimistic feeling of regret for a lost paradise and of sorrow for a fall from a high estate. The first age of the world is thought of as a period of innocence and happiness. This ''Golden Age'' is one of the oldest ideas of mankind. In Greece it is certainly earlier than the *Odyssey,* for the narrative of Eumaeus (15.403–) seems to be an ironic imitation of a tale on the Golden Age. The oldest tradition probably, as in the Sanskrit texts, distinguished four ages or stages in the steady deterioration of mankind, the Ages of Gold, Silver, Bronze, and Iron.

In Hesiod and Later Greek Poets. In Hesiod (*Op.* 109), the earliest Greek source, the races of gold and silver are mythical human beings, closer to the gods than to men, whom the earth supported in miraculous fashion. Hesiod's description of this Eden-like existence assumes an original human state of happiness and piety. The use of meat is not forbidden, but a ''Pythagorean'' tradition of vegetarianism is found in Empedocles (*Frag.* 128D) and in Theophrastus (*ap.* Porph. *Abst.* 2.20). On the other hand, the comic poets Pherecrates in his *Wild Men,* and Moschio, in *Frag.* 6 (ed. Nauck TGF[2]), echo legends of a primitive life in which there is a ceaseless struggle for animal flesh as a food, with human flesh even being substituted for it in case of necessity. This is the ἀλληλοφαγία (an eating of one another) mentioned in Plato's *Epinomis* (975A; cf. *Orphica, Frag.* 292, ed. O. Kern). The transition from savagery to civilization was made only very slowly, and the process was even interrupted by catastrophes.

In Plato. Plato's *Laws* (bk. 3) opens with a tableau of mankind immediately after the Flood, again forced to start from the very beginning. With this description it is necessary to compare the myth of the *Protagoras* (321C), and that of the *Statesman* (*Politicus* 274A–D), which depicts the world without God. Earlier, the *Statesman* had given an idyllic description of a life of men with God as their shepherd (271D–272B)—the Golden Age that is sketched more briefly in bk. four of the *Laws* and in the *Critias.* In his narrative of the rule of Cronus in the *Statesman* and in *Laws* (bk. 4), as well as in his account of the beginnings of Zeus's reign in the *Statesman* and of the survivors of the Flood in the *Laws* (bk. 3), Plato does not hesitate to give his own form to traditions that were differently presented by earlier writers.

Among the Romans. In the Latin world, bk. three of the SIBYLLINE ORACLES, which dates from *c.* 140 B.C., spread the idea of a peace among animals (verses 788–794), an idea from Isaiah (11.6–). This feature of the Golden Age reappears in the descriptions of Vergil (*Ecl.* 4) and Horace (*Epod.* 16; cf. *Od.* 3.18.13). Saturn succeeds Cronus, the reign of Cronus becomes the *Saturnia regna* (*Georg.* 4.6); the *Cumaeum carmen* of verse 4 alludes to the Cumaean Sibyl, and the *gens aurea* of verse nine refers to the first race of men in Hesiod. However, there is no warrant for attributing to Vergil the role of pagan prophet of the Messiah; the tradition that leads him to the Manger in company with the prophets of Israel is to be regarded not so much as a ''presentiment'' as rather a certain ''delicacy and fineness of feeling on the part of souls who were soon to receive the gift of God'' [M. J. Lagrange, RB 35 (1922) 572].

Bibliography: W. K. GUTHRIE, *In the Beginning: Some Greek Views on the Origins of Life and the Early State of Man* (London 1957). H. GRAY, et al., J. HASTINGS, ed., *Encyclopedia of Religion and Ethics* 13 v. (Edinburgh 1908–27) 1:183–210. J. HAEKEL, *Religionswissenschaftliches Wörterbuch,* ed. F. KÖNIG (Freiburg 1956) 641–644. M. ELIADE, *Myths, Dreams, and Mysteries,* tr. P. MAIRET (New York 1960). H. JEANMAIRE, *Le Messianisme de Virgile* (Paris 1930). J. CARCOPINO, *Virgile et le mystère de la IVe églogue* (Paris 1930). W. H. ROSCHER, ed., *Ausführliches Lexikon der griechischen und römischen Mythologie,* 6 v. (Leipzig 1884–1937) 6:375–430. S. THOMPSON, *Motif-Index of Folk-Literature,* 6 v. (rev. and enl. ed. Bloomington, Ind. 1955–58) 1:A1101–03.

[E. DES PLACES]

GOLDEN ROSE

The golden rose is the symbol of papal recognition of some outstanding service to the Church. Its symbolism is linked with the mid–Lent (or *Laetare Jerusalem*) Sunday, on which the pope traditionally blessed a golden rose in the church of Sta Croce in Gerusalemme and bore it in procession to the LATERAN PALACE. In modern times the ceremony takes place within the Vatican, the blessing in the Hall of Vestments and the solemn Mass in the papal chapel. At first (from the late 11th century) the rose was a single flower of red–tinted gold, but it was later embellished with gems, and at least from the mid–15th century it comprised a branch of gold with leaves and roses and a principal rose at the top. The meaning of the rose was explained by Pope ALEXANDER III to King LOUIS VII in *Ex antiqua* (L. Jaffé, *Regista pontificum romanrun ad condita ecclesia ad annum post Christum natum 1198,* ed. S. Löwenfeld, 882–1198; 10826) in 1163: the flower

Golden Rose presented to the Republic of Siena by Pope Pius II, made by goldsmith Simone da Firenze in 1459. (©Alinari-Art Reference/Art Resource, NY)

is the symbol of Christ the King, the gold of His kingship, the red of His passion, its fragrance prefiguring His Resurrection and glory. The practice grew of dispatching this rose to a Catholic king or ruler, basilica or sanctuary, republic or city, indeed to any place or person, and most commonly in modern times to Catholic queens, in recognition of some outstanding service to the Church. The origin of the tradition is uncertain; the earliest sure reference dates from 1049, when Pope LEO IX described it as an ancient custom; and the first recorded example dates from 1096, when URBAN II dispatched a rose to Fulk of Anjou. The more recent recipients have included the American M. G. CALDWELL, who gave $300,000 to the Catholic University of America in 1887, the Queen of the Belgians in 1925, the Queen of Italy in 1937, and the shrine of Our Lady of FATIMA in 1964.

Bibliography: A. SHIELD, ''The Golden Rose,'' *Month* 95 (1900) 294–304. E. MÜNTZ, ''Les Roses d'or pontificales,'' *Revue de l'art chrétien* 44 (1901) 1–11. J. KREPS, ''La Rose d'or,'' *Questions liturgiques et paroissiales* (Louvain 1921–) 11 (1926) 71–104; 149–178. F. L. CROSS, *The Oxford Dictionary of the Christian Church* (London 1957) 570. J. A. JUNGMANN, *Lexikon für Theologie und Kirche*[2], ed. J. HOFER and K. RAHNER, 10 v. (Freiburg 1957–65) 4:1041. E. BARNIKOL, *Die Religiion in Geschichte und Gegenwart*[3], 7 v. (Tübingen 1957–65) 5:1183.

[C. DUGGAN]

GOLDSTEIN, DAVID

Apologist, author; b. London, England, July 27, 1870; d. Boston, Mass., June 30, 1958. He was the son of poor Dutch Jewish parents who were married in London. They brought him to New York City in 1871, where he lived for 17 years attending public school, the Hebrew Free School, and the Spanish Jewish Synagogue, where he studied Hebrew. At the age of 11, Goldstein began work as a cigar maker, following his father's trade. He was allowed to attend the meetings of the Cigar Makers' International Union, with which he became affiliated, and continued his membership for life.

In 1888, the family moved to Boston, where David joined the Socialist Labor Party. He became the party's first candidate for mayor of Boston and one of the seven members of its national board of appeals. Here he met Mrs. Martha Moore Avery, prominent in the Socialist movement, who ultimately influenced him toward Catholic principles. Impressed with Catholic teaching on marriage and divorce, he undertook considerable reading and instruction, which culminated in his baptism in the Immaculate Conception Church, Boston, in 1905.

Goldstein had resigned from the Socialist Party in 1903 (the year Mrs. Avery joined the Church) after eight years of campaigning upon the soapbox and Lecture–debating platform. In 1906 he began, with Mrs. Avery, the first modern lay apostolate to the man in the street, first known as the Catholic Truth Guild (since 1935 Catholic Campaigners for Christ). As the first Catholic layman to devote full time to defending the Church against attack, he spent more than 25 years lecturing across the country.

Among the honors he received were a degree of doctor of literature (1939) from Niagara University, Niagara, N.Y.; the Catholic Action Medal (1946) from St. Bonaventure's College, St. Bonaventure, N.Y.; the Distinguished Service Medal of the Franciscan Order (1947); and Knight of the Order of St. Gregory (1955). He was a columnist for the *Boston Pilot* (1945–58), and his other published works include *Socialism: The Nation of Fatherless Children,* an exposé of false doctrines of Socialism (with Mrs. Avery); *Bolshevism: Its Cure* (1919); *Campaigner for Christ Handbook* (1934); and *Letters of a Hebrew-Catholic to Mr. Isaacs* (1943).

Bibliography: D. GOLDSTEIN, *Autobiography of a Campaigner for Christ* (Boston 1936).

[J. LLOYD]

GOLDWELL, JAMES

English canonist, civil servant; b. Great Chart, Kent; d. Feb. 15, 1499. Son of the lord of the manor, he became a fellow of All Souls College, Oxford, in 1441, and doctor of Canon and civil law by 1461. Goldwell was commissary general of John KEMP when Kemp was archbishop of Canterbury (1452–54) and subsequently enjoyed the patronage of his nephew Thomas KEMP, Bishop of London. In 1460 Goldwell appears to have been appointed secretary to King HENRY VI by the King's "Yorkist" captors. He afterward served King Edward IV as registrar of the Order of the Garter, master of requests, clerk of the council, and diplomat to several European monarchs. He was the King's orator at the Roman Curia in 1468–69 and 1471–72, and was consecrated there as bishop of Norwich, England, in 1472. Thereafter he was occasionally a councilor of Edward IV and King HENRY VII. Goldwell was a munificent benefactor to Norwich Cathedral, Leeds Priory, Great Chart Church, and All Souls College library (MSS listed in Emden 2:785).

Bibliography: *The Dictionary of National Biography From the Earliest Times to 1900* 8:96–97. A. B. EMDEN *A Biographical Register of the University of Oxford to A. D. 1500* 2:783–786. J. R. LANDER, "Council Administration and Councillors, 1461 to 1485," *Bulletin of the Institute of Historical Research* 32 (1959) 138–180.

[R. L. STOREY]

GOMARUS, FRANCISCUS

Calvinist theologian; b. Bruges, Jan. 30, 1563; d. Groningen, Jan. 11, 1641. He studied at Strasbourg under Johann STURM, at Neustadt under Franciscus Junius, Zacharius URSINUS, and Hieronymus Zanchius, and at Oxford and Cambridge. He became pastor of the Dutch congregation at Frankfurt am Main (1586–94), then professor of theology at Leiden (1594–1611), and was pastor and teacher in Middelburg (1611–14), when at the invitation of Du Plessis Mornay he became professor of theology at Saumur. Here, as a right-wing Calvinist, he felt uncomfortable, and returned to the Netherlands, where he taught theology at Groningen. He was now the leading opponent of the followers of ARMINIUS, whose appointment to succeed Junius at Amsterdam he had hesitatingly approved in 1602. He was prominent at the Synod of Dort (1618–19), which condemned the Arminians but did not affirm his own supralapsarian position. His numerous writings are learned but chiefly polemical. In 1594 he edited, with a commendation to Henry IV, the *Defensor Pacis* of Marsilius of Padua. Some of his weightier treatises, including the *De divinae praedestinationis hominum objecto* (1650), were posthumously published.

Bibliography: *Opera theologica omnia,* 3 v. (Amsterdam 1644; 2d ed. 1664). G. P. VAN ITTERZON, *Franciscus Gomarus* (The Hague 1929). W. F. DANKBAAR, *Die Religion in Geschichte und Gegenwart* 2:1691–92.

[J. T. MCNEILL]

GOMBERT, NICOLAS

Renaissance polyphonist of the Franco-Flemish school; b. Bruges or south Flanders?, *c.* 1500; d. Tournai?, 1556. This distinguished disciple of Josquin DESPREZ became first a singer (1526), then master of the children (1530) in the chapel of Charles V, and traveled in Spain, Italy, Austria, and Germany. He obtained ecclesiastical benefices in Lens, Courtrai, Béthune, and Metz and a canonry in Tournai (1534). His works comprise ten parody Masses for four to six voices (including one for the coronation of Charles V), 169 motets for four to eight voices (mostly Marian, but occasionally political), about 60 chansons for three to six voices, one Italian piece, and one Spanish piece. Hermann Finck (1527–58) praises Gombert for his technique of imitation (*fugas*) as well as for his avoidance of *pausas* (variously interpreted to mean rests, paired imitation, or full cadences that would interrupt the polyphonic continuity). Indeed, his voices are almost constantly active in points of pervading imitation. By amalgamating traditional Franco-Flemish characteristics with his personal style, Gombert greatly developed the art of polyphony and may be considered one of its leading exponents in the generation preceding PALESTRINA.

Bibliography: *Opera omnia*, ed. J. SCHMIDT-GÖRG, *Corpus mensurabilis musicae*, v. 6 (Rome 1951–). J. SCHMIDT-GÖRG, *Nicolas Gombert* (Bonn 1938). R. MANIATES, "The Sacred Music of Nicolas Gombert," *The Canadian Music Journal* 6.2 (1962) 25–38. H. EPPSTEIN, *Nicolas Gombert als Motettenkomponist* (Würzburg 1935). D. VON BARTHA, "Probleme der Chansongeschichte im 16. Jahrhundert. Nicolas Gombert—Benedictus Appenzeller," *Zeitschrift für Musikwissenschaft* 13 (1930–31) 507–530. A. EINSTEIN, *The Italian Madrigal*, tr. A. H. KRAPPE et al., 3 v. (Princeton 1949). J. RAVELL and S. BROMAN, *Grove's Dictionary of Music and Musicians*, ed. E. BLOM (London 1954) 3:705–706. *Histoire de la musique*, ed. ROLAND-MANUEL, v. 1 (Paris 1960–63). G. REESE, *Music in the Renaissance*, (rev. ed. New York 1959). E. JAS, "Nicolas Gombert's *Missa Fors Seulement*: A Conflicting Attribution," *Revue Belge de Muiscologie* 46 (1992) 163–177. G. NUGENT, "Nicolas Gombert" in *The New Grove Dictionary of Music and Musicians*, v. 7, ed. S. SADIE (New York 1980) 512–516. D. M. RANDEL, ed., *The Harvard Biographical Dictionary of Music* (Cambridge 1996) 321. N. SLONIMSKY, ed. *Baker's Biographical Dictionary of Musicians* (New York 1992) 647.

[I. CAZEAUX]

GOMENSORO, TOMÁS XAVIER DE

Argentine priest and supporter of Uruguayan independence; b. Buenos Aires, Dec. 20, 1770; d. there, April 2, 1841. He studied at the Real Colegio de San Carlos, was ordained to the priesthood in 1799, and in 1803 was appointed vicar of Santo Domingo de Soriano, in the Banda Oriental. Having taken part in the Soriano uprising known as *Grito de Asencio* on Feb. 28, 1811, Gomensoro was persecuted and finally replaced in his own church. He moved to Buenos Aires and engaged in agriculture and cattle raising near Rosario. He was appointed priest of Canelones in 1814, and remained there for nine years. Recognized as a ''worthy man by reason of his distinguished accomplishments and great learning,'' in 1824, he was appointed acting rector of the Colegio de Estudios Eclesiásticos. He was also professor at the university founded by Rivadavia. With his brother Loreto, delegate of the revolutionary government, Gomensoro worked in Buenos Aires with great zeal for the revolutionary cause that led to the independence of the Republic of Uruguay in 1825. He served in the Argentine Congress in 1825, voted for Rivadavia for president of the United Provinces, and in 1826 was appointed pastor of the San Ignacio church in Buenos Aires. He was acting pastor of the cathedral of the same city and was appointed honorary canon in 1840.

Bibliography: J. GOMENSORO, ''El canónigo Tomás Xavier de Gomensoro,'' *Revista Nacional* 30 (Montevideo 1945) 257–281.

[A. D. GONZÁLEZ]

GOMES, ANTONIO CARLOS

South American opera composer; b. Campinas, Brazil, July 11, 1836; d. Belem, Sept. 16, 1895. Gomes, son of a band director, had composed a Mass by the time he was 18. At 23 he entered the Rio de Janeiro Conservatory and, after winning the favor of Emperor Pedro II with a Calvary cantata and two youthful operas, continued at the Milan Conservatory (1864–66). Of his six mature operas—*Il Guarany* (1870), *Fosca* (1873), *Salvator Rosa* (1874), *Maria Tudor* (1879), *Lo schiavo* (1889), and *Condor* (1891)—four had their premieres at La Scala, Milan, gaining for him the greatest international renown ever won by an American opera composer. Although *Il Guarany*, his greatest success, was South American in its subject, his operatic idiom was purely italianate. He also composed songs, piano works, and, for the fourth centenary of America's discovery, an oratorio, *Colombo* (1892). In 1895, after many years in Italy, he made his last trip to Brazil to head the Pará Conservatory, but died within six months of arriving.

Bibliography: *Revista Brasileira de Música*, special centenary number, 1936. M. DE ANDRADE, Carlos Gomes (Rio de Janeiro 1939). K. PAHLEN, *Die Musik in Geschichte und Gegenwart*, ed. F. BLUME (Kassel-Basel 1949–) 5:512–513. G. BEHAGUE, ''Carlos (Antônio) Gomes'' in *The New Grove Dictionary of Music and Musicians*, v. 7, ed. S. SADIE (New York 1980), 517–518. W. J. COLLINS, ''Antônio Carlos Gomes'' in *International Dictionary of Opera*, 2 v., ed. C. LARUE (Detroit 1993) 535–536. M. GÓES, *Carlos Gomes: A Força Indômita* (Bélem 1996). D. M. RANDEL, ed., *The Harvard Biographical Dictionary of Music* (Cambridge 1996) 321–322. N. SLONIMSKY, ed. *Baker's Biographical Dictionary of Musicians* (New York 1992) 647–648.

[R. STEVENSON]

GOMEZ, JOSÉ VALENTIŃ

Argentine ecclesiastic and political figure; b. Buenos Aires, Nov. 3, 1774; d. there, Sept. 20, 1839. He began his studies at the Colegio de San Carlos and took his doctorate in theology at the University of Córdoba in 1795. He received his bachelor's degree in Canon and civil law in Chuquisaca. At the age of 23 he was an ecclesiastical attorney general, and in 1799, through competition, he obtained the professorship of philosophy at the Colegio Carolino, which he held for three years. He was a canon of the cathedral of Córdoba. From 1805 he was in the parish of Morón, until he took over that of Canelones in the Banda Oriental in 1808. Gómez served as military chaplain in the armies of the revolution and fought as a soldier in the battle of Las Piedras in 1811. Then he became a canon of the cathedral of Buenos Aires. In 1813 he was one of the deputies of the National Assembly, where he became known as a great political orator. He was chosen governor of the bishopric. The Directorate was created at his suggestion and became a part of the Council of State in 1814. Gómez was very active until the fall of Alvear, when Álvarez Thomas had his property seized and exiled him to Europe in 1815. He returned to become a councilor of state in the government of Pueyrredón, and in 1818 he was sent to Brazil and to the courts of London and Paris to gain recognition of independence. Gómez represented Buenos Aires in the general constitutional assembly of 1824 and was one of the signers of the constitution adopted in 1826.

[V. O. CUTOLO]

GONÇALVES, VITAL MARÍA OLIVEIRA DE

Capuchin bishop of Olinda and Recife; b. Pedras de Fogo, Pernambuco, Brazil, Nov. 27, 1844; d. Paris, July 4, 1878. Vital, the son of Capt. Antonio Gonçalves and Antonia Albia de Oliveira, attended school in Itambá and Recife, the seminary in Olinda, and Saint-Sulpice in Paris. On July 16, 1863, he entered the Capuchin Order in Versailles, and on Aug. 15, 1863 received the habit and the name Frei Vital María de Pernambuco. He was ordained on Aug. 2, 1863 and returned to Brazil in November. Frei Vital taught philosophy in the seminary of São Paulo until he was nominated by Pedro II to the bishopric of Olinda and Recife on May 21, 1871. He was consecrated in the cathedral of São Paulo on March 17, 1872, and made his solemn entrance into his diocese on May 24. As bishop he was destined to play a pivotal role in the major Church-State crisis of the Brazilian empire, the religious question that disturbed Brazil between 1872 and 1875. The first overt attack of Masonry on a Brazilian bishop was occasioned after the disciplinary action Bp. Pedro Maria de Lacerda of Rio de Janeiro took against a priest in March 1872 for public participation in a Masonic festival. Brazilian Freemasonry began an all-out campaign against what the fraternity called the ultramontanism of the Brazilian hierarchy, with the French-educated Vital as the chief target. The second phase began when the Masonic press of Recife announced that on the Feast of SS. Peter and Paul, June 30, 1872, the Masonic lodge of Recife would commemorate the anniversary of its founding by having a Mass celebrated in St. Peter's church. Vital ordered the clergy not to participate, and no Mass was celebrated. In reprisal, the fraternity published the names of clerical and lay members of the Catholic brotherhoods who were affiliates of Masonry. Bishop Vital ordered all clerics to abjure Masonry and directed the brotherhoods to expel members who refused to abandon Masonry. When a brotherhood challenged the bishop's directive by availing itself of its constitutional safeguard, the right of recourse to the crown, the crisis moved from a contest between Freemasonry and the episcopacy to a Church-State issue involving the right of the government to control the spiritual prerogatives of the Catholic hierarchy.

The imperial government attempted settlement by an indirect appeal to Vital, presented to him by an imperial minister who was also a relative, urging him not to meddle in the affairs of the Masonic lodges. Vital, unintimidated by the government's action, placed recalcitrant religious associations under interdict. The imperial committee that reviewed the brotherhoods' recourse to the crown charged Vital with violation of the constitution. He was tried Feb. 18, 1874, found guilty, and sentenced to four years of hard labor, which was commuted to a four-year imprisonment. Vital had been joined by Bp. Antonio de MACEDO COSTA of Pará, who was similarly charged, indicted, tried, and then imprisoned.

Popular reaction embarrassed the imperial government to the point that it dispatched a special mission to Rome to persuade the Holy See to force the bishops to retract their spiritual penalties against the Masonic-infiltrated brotherhoods. The mission failed and the Emperor extracted himself from the impasse by granting amnesty to the two bishops, Sept. 17, 1875.

Vital, knowing that many false impressions had been created in Rome, left on Oct. 5, 1875 to present his case at the Vatican. He died in Paris. In 1882 his body was returned to Brazil and buried in Recife. On July 25, 1953, the diocesan process for his beatification was initiated.

Bibliography: F. GUERRA, *A questão religiosa do segundo império brasileiro* (Rio do Janeiro 1952). F. DE OLÍVOLA, *Um grande brasileiro* (Recife 1936).

[C. THORNTON]

GONDULPHUS OF METZ, ST.

Bishop; d. Gorze Abbey, Sept. 6, 823. The See of Metz fell vacant after the death of Bishop ANGILRAMNUS (791). It was filled only upon Gondulphus's accession, probably Dec. 28, 816, although the *Annales S. Vincentii Mettensis* give the date as 819. During Gondulphus's episcopate, which lasted six years, eight months, and seven days according to the old episcopal catalogue, ALDRIC OF LE MANS spent five years in Metz. Gondulphus attended the synod held at Thionville in 821. He was buried in GORZE ABBEY, where his relics are still honored. His successor was DROGO OF METZ.

Feast: Sept. 6 (Metz).

Bibliography: *Monumenta Germaniae Historica, Scriptores* (Berlin 1926—)2:269. *Acta Sanctorum*, Sept. 2:782–784. L. DUCHESNE, ed. *Fastes épiscopaux de l'anncienne Gaule* (Paris 1907–15) 33:58. H. LECLERCQ, *Dictionnaire d'archéologie chretienne et de liturgie*, ed. F. CABROL, H. LECLERQ, and H. I. MARROU (Paris 1907–35) 1:831–832.

[G. J. DONNELLY]

GONET, JEAN BAPTISTE

Dominican theologian; b. Béziers, in southern France, *c.* 1616; d. there Jan. 24, 1681. After receiving his early education in his native Languedoc, he entered the Toulouse province of the Dominicans at the age of 17. He received his doctorate in theology from the University of Bordeaux, where he was to spend the major portion of his life as professor of theology and where he became famous as a champion of Thomistic theology. He retired from teaching in 1677 and spent his remaining years in Béziers, where he corrected his writings.

In 1660 Gonet was one of three professors who, free of Jansenism themselves, declared Blaise PASCAL's *Lettres provinciales* exempt from the heresy of Jansenism. When some bishops and the University of Paris found heresy in the work, it was condemned, and the King suspended Gonet and his companions from teaching for three years. They had not approved the contents of Pascal's work, but had merely stated that the work contained no heresy. In 1663 Gonet joined his colleagues in signing the six Gallican articles promulgated by Louis XIV. This did not imply a denial of papal authority, however, for in 1665 Gonet and the others signed Alexander VII's formulary demanding acceptance of papal condemnations of Jansenism.

Gonet is best known for his *Clypeus theologiae thomisticae contra novos ejus impugnatores* (Bordeaux 1659–69; Lyons 1681, contains corrections made by the author and is his definitive work; Paris 1875, six volumes). In this work Gonet was especially indebted to his contemporary Peter Godoy (d. 1677), a Dominican professor at Salamanca until his elevation to the See of Osma. Even before Godoy's commentaries were published, manuscript copies of his lectures spread his fame as a theologian throughout Spain, France, and Italy. One of these manuscripts reached Gonet, who was then composing *Clypeus.* Finding agreement with his own ideas, he incorporated Godoy's works into his own. Gonet was most conscious of his debt to Godoy and in his prologue he had the highest praise for him. Without the stimulus provided by the incorporation of his works into Gonet's writings, perhaps Godoy would never have published his *Disputationes theologicae* (Venice 1686).

Gonet was one of the Neo-Thomists who preferred to compose theological treatises on various subjects rather than to comment upon each article of St. Thomas. His work was intended to shield Thomism from the charge of Calvinism, to reply to the questions raised by JANSENISM, and to defend PROBABILIORISM against what he took to be the laxities of certain casuists who were probabilists.

Bibliography: R. COULON, *Dictionnaire de théologie catholique* 6:1487–89. Quétif–Échard 2.2: 692–693. J. FINKENZELLER, *Die Lehre von den Sakramenten der Taufe und Busse nach J. B. Gonet, O.P.* (Munich 1956).

[R. P. STENGER]

GONFALONIERI

An archconfraternity under the name of the Mother of God, founded in 1264 at St. Mary Major in Rome by 12 noblemen, or standard-bearers (*gonfalonieri*), as the *Compagnia de' Raccomandati di Madonna S. Maria.* It undertook the ransom of the Christian captives of the Saracens. Until forbidden by PAUL III IN 1549, it presented a dramatization of the Passion of Christ during Holy Week in the Colisseum. In 1588, SIXTUS V made it a kind of third order. Today it exists under the name *Arciconfraternita del Gonfalone* at S. Lucia del Gonfalone. The garb is a white habit with a red cross on the right shoulder. Its works now include marriage counseling, caring for the sick, and attending funerals. Similar confraternities, affiliated with the one at Rome, exist throughout the world, especially in France.

Bibliography: M. NOIROT, *Catholicisme* 5:99. R. HINDRINGER, *Lexikon für Theologie und Kirche*, J. HOFER and K. RAHNER, eds. (Freiburg 1957–65) 4:1050.

[J. F. JOLLEY]

GONSALVUS HISPANUS

Philosopher, theologian, and the 15th general of the Franciscan Order; b. province of Galicia, Spain; d. Paris, April 13, 1313. He is not to be identified with another Spanish Franciscan, Gonsalvo de Vallebona or de Balboa, with whom he was confused by a 16th-century chronicler, Mariano da Firenze (L. Amorós). After preparatory studies in Spain, Gonsalvus became a bachelor of theology at Paris (1288), where he commented on the *Sentences* of Peter Lombard; his commentary, however, is not extant. In 1289 he was member of a delegation sent by Sancho IV, King of Castile, to Pope Nicholas IV; the following year he was elected provincial minister for the Franciscan province of Santiago of Compostela. He returned to Paris (*c.* 1297) to become a master of theology, and in 1302–03 was regent master of the Franciscan *studium;* there John DUNS SCOTUS commented on Lombard's *Sentences* during his regency. On June 25, 1303, both Gonsalvus and Duns Scotus were obliged to leave France because they had refused to sign Philip the Fair's appeal against Boniface VIII (E. Longpré). Shortly thereafter Gonsalvus became provincial minister for the province of Castile and, on March 17, 1304, general of the order.

Gonsalvus's literary legacy is not extensive. He compiled the *Conclusiones metaphysicae* (once attributed to Scotus), whose importance lies more in their practical usefulness than in their doctrinal content. His *Quaestiones disputatae et de quolibet,* dating from his regency in Paris, reflect heated discussions with the Thomists JOHN (QUIDORT) OF PARIS and PETER OF LA PALU, with Meister ECKHART, and with GODFREY OF FONTAINES and his students. Gonsalvus supported the traditional Augustinian theses on the supremacy of the will, the hylomorphic composition of angels and souls, the plurality of forms in the human compound, etc., but denied the need for divine illumination in intellectual knowledge, as PETER JOHN OLIVI had done before him and as Scotus would do later.

Gonsalvus's generalship, which lasted until April 13, 1313, was eventful. The conflict over Franciscan poverty had reached a new high, and Gonsalvus was obliged to combat not only laxity but also the extreme austerity of the spirituals and of the fraticelli. Some of his letters, most of them to various provincials of the order, have been preserved. He wrote also a small treatise concerning the precepts of the Franciscan rule, and engaged in polemics with the followers of Olivi [*see Archivum Franciscanum historicum* 7 (1914) 659–675; 8 (1915) 56–80; 10 (1917) 116–122]. He sponsored the compilation of the *Catalogus Generalium Ministrorum,* known as the *Gonsalvinus,* and the catalog of the cardinal protectors of the order. He also took an active part in the Council of Vienne (1311–12).

Gonsalvus's merit as general lies in his success in having preserved the order, during extraordinarily difficult times, from the dissolution that threatened it.

Bibliography: GONSALVUS HISPANUS, *Quaestiones disputatae et de quodlibet*, ed. L. AMORÓS *Bibliotheca Franciscana scholastica medii acvi* 9: 1935, complete bibliog. to 1935. For later additions, see E. MÜLLER, *Das Konzil von Vienne 1311–1312: Seine Quellen und seine Geschichte* (Vorreformationsgeschichtliche Forschungen 12; Münster 1934). *Archivum Franciscanum historicum* indexes to v. 1–50 (1908–1957), where Gonsalvus appears 38 times. E. LONGPRÉ, *Le B. Jean Duns Scot, OFM, pour le Saint Siège et contre le Gallicanisme* (Quaracchi-Florence 1930). R. LÓPEZ DE MUNAÍN, ''El problema de la libertad y los doctores franciscanos del siglo XIII,'' *Verdad y Vida* 5 (1947) 283–307. B. MENDIA, ''Influentia de los maestros franciscanos en la psicologéa del conocimiento intellectual de Suarez,'' *ibid.* 6 (1948) 421–453. A. PISVIN, ''Die Intuitio und ihr metaphysischer Wert nach Vitalis de Furno (+ 1327) und Gonsalvus Hispanus (+ 1313),'' *Wissenschaft und Weisheit* 12 (1949) 147–162. G. MURANA, ''Il pensiero de Gonsalvo di Spagna,'' *Italia Franciscana* 26 (1951) 25–37; ''Cenni sul pensiero di Gonsalvo di Spagna,'' *Revista Rosminiana* 47 (1953) 15–21. É. H. GILSON, *History of Christian Philosophy in the Middle Ages* (New York 1955) 698.

[G. GÁL]

GONZAGA

Ruling family of Mantua, Italy. It was a century and a half after the family arrived in Mantua that *Luigi* was

Painting of Vincenzo I. Gonzaga, Duke of Mantua, by Frans, Pourbus the Younger, 1600. (©Ali Meyer/CORBIS)

elected captain general of the city (1328). This was the beginning of almost 400 years of Gonzaga rule there: the years 1328 to 1407 were marked by four Gonzaga captains general; the years 1407 to 1587 were a brilliant period in which the family produced rulers of ability; and the years 1587 to 1707 were a period of decline. Mantua's very location demanded vigilance and often involved the city in war, yet the rulers built palaces and churches and made Mantua a cultural center.

Gianfrancesco (ruled 1407–44) was the first marquis in the family (under Emperor SIGISMUND) and was also the first ruler to bring an eminent personage to Mantua, namely the educator VITTORINO DA FELTRE. *Ludovico* (1444–78) brought Leone Battista Alberti and Andrea Mantegna; *Federigo II* (1519–40), Giulio Romano; *Vincenzo I* (1587 1612), Peter Paul Rubens. *Francesco* (1484–1519) and Isabella d'Este were the parents of three able sons: the above-mentioned Federigo II, Cardinal Ercole (see below), and *Ferrante* (d. 1557), who became viceroy of Naples and governor of Milan. Federigo II, who became the first Gonzaga duke in 1530, added Montferrat to the family domain. It was under his second son, *Guglielmo* (1550–87), that Mantua had its greatest prosperity. Competition in industry from other states and the extravagance of Vincenzo I precipitated the decline of the family. After the reigns of Vincenzo's three sons, the main branch ended in 1627. One evidence of the family's status was the sale of paintings from the Gonzaga gallery in that same year. The Gonzaga-Nevers or French branch ruled from 1627 to 1707, when the last duke went into exile and Austria annexed Mantua.

Rivalry between Ludovico and his brother *Carlo* just prior to 1444 resulted in the practice—common in noble families—of having the second son and sometimes other younger sons seek careers in the Church. Hence, in four of six consecutive reigns the second son became a cardinal; in the other two reigns there was a valid reason for the exceptions. In all, while the family ruled, there were ten cardinals (the first date given being that of their cardinalate); *Francesco* (1461, d. 1483), son of Ludovico, served as bishop of Mantua and as legate in Bologna and Ferrara. He has been criticized for his worldly ways and for his friendship with Angelo Poliziano. His nephew *Sigismondo* (1505, d. 1525) was bishop of Mantua and legate in the Marches and Bologna. Sigismondo's nephew *Ercole* (1527, d. 1563) was appointed bishop of Mantua in 1521. He spent the next three years studying at the University of Bologna. After 1527 he held appointments in four minor cities and was legate to Emperor CHARLES V when he came to Italy in 1530. The ideas of two friends, Gasparo CONTARINI and Gian Matteo GIBERTI, Bishop of Verona, guided Cardinal Ercole in reforming the Diocese of Mantua: e.g., before the decrees of the Council of Trent, Ercole ordered a careful visitation of churches in his diocese and repeated the visitation at intervals to ensure that proposed improvements had been made. When Duke Federigo died, the cardinal was the chief regent for his two nephews (1540–56). He governed the duchy well, improving the city, promoting industry, curbing extravagance, and systematizing weights and measures. His last appointment was as legate and president of the Council of TRENT (1561–63), but he died before it closed. Esteemed by his contemporaries and historians for his administration of diocese and duchy, he has also been praised for less public actions. He paid for the education of young men who were not his relatives. In his will he left money for the MONTES PIETATIS. *Pirro* (1527, d. 1529) became bishop of Modena. *Francesco* (1561, d. 1566) and *Gianvincenzo* (1578, d. 1591) were the sons of Ferrante and nephews of Cardinal Ercole. Francesco was bishop of Mantua. Duke Guglielmo valued particularly the advice of Gianvincenzo. *Federico* (1563, d. 1565) became bishop of Mantua. *Ferdinando* (1607, d. 1626) and *Vincenzo* (1615, d. 1627) were sons of Vincenzo I, and they renounced their cardinalates to become the last two dukes of the main branch of the Gonzaga family.

Scipione (1587, d. 1593) was the son of the marquis of Gazzolo, a collateral branch. Well educated and generous with his time, Scipione advised several writers, among them Torquato Tasso. He supported the entrance of his nephew ALOYSIUS GONZAGA into the JESUITS. His brother *Annibale* (Francesco) was the minister general of the Franciscan Observants (1579–87; d. 1620) who wrote the *De origine Seraphicae religionis et progressibus* (Rome 1587).

Bibliography: P. LITTA, *Famiglie celebri italiane,* 14 v. (Milan 1819–1923) v.7. G. MORONI, *Dizionario de erudizione storico0ecclesiastica*, 103 v. in 53 (Venice 1840–61) 31:282–288. L. PASTOR, *The History of the Popes From the Close of the Middle Ages*, 40 v. (London-St. Louis 1938–61): v.11 (3d ed.) 11:505–508. A. LUZIO, *La Galleria dei Gonzaga . . .* (Milan 1913). S. J. C. BRINTON, *The Gonzaga—Lords of Mantua* (London 1927). G. FOCHESSATI, *I Gonzaga di Mantova e l'ultimo duca* (rev. ed. Milan 1930).

[M. L. SHAY]

GONZÁLEZ, ROQUE, ST.

Jesuit missionary and martyr; b. Asunción, Paraguay, 1576; d. Rio Grande do Sul, Brazil, Nov. 15, 1628. He was probably ordained on March 25, 1599; he dedicated his life to the evangelization of the Native South Americans. He was appointed priest of the cathedral and, in 1609, vicar-general of the diocese. On May 9, 1609, he entered the Society of Jesus. In 1615 he began his missionary work by founding the Reduction of Itapúa and in subsequent years other such settlements, until in 1620 he was appointed by his superiors to give religious instruction to the inhabitants of the area that is now the Brazilian state of Rio Grande do Sul. There he was martyred at the Reduction of Todos los Santos, the last one he founded. He was beatified in 1934 and canonized in 1988. He had two companions in his martyrdom. The first, Alonso Rodríguez, was born in Zamora, Spain, on March 10, 1598. He entered the Society of Jesus on March 25, 1614, and arrived in Buenos Aires on February 15, 1617. After completing his studies, he gave religious instruction to the native peoples for four years. Two days later, Juan del Castillo died at the Reduction of La Asunción. He was born in Belmonte, Spain, September 14, 1596, and he entered the Society of Jesus on March 22, 1614. Assigned to Paraguay, he arrived in Buenos Aires with Rodríguez and worked among the natives there for three years.

Feast: Nov. 17

Bibliography: H. THURSTON, ''The First Beatified Martyr of Spanish America,'' *Catholic Historical Review* 20 (1934–35) 371–383. L. G. JAEGER, *Os-bem aventurados Roque González, Alfonso Rodríquez e João del Castillo: Mártires do Caaró e Pirapó* (2d ed. Pôrto Alegre 1951).

[H. STORNI]

GONZÁLEZ DÁVILA, GIL

Historian of Spain and the New World; b. Avila, *c.* 1570; d. there, April 25, 1658. He was the son of Agustín González and María Morales. While still a boy, he went to Rome in the service of Cardinal Pedro de Deza and studied there. In 1592 he returned to Spain with the papal appointment as prebendary of the cathedral of Salamanca. He was appointed archivist of the cathedral chapter in 1607 and was given the task of writing books or registers about the houses and estates of the cathedral. He published *De la antigüedad del Toro de piedra de la puente de Salamanca y de otros que se hallan en otras ciudades y lugares de Castillo* (Salamanca 1596), *Historia de las antigüedades de la ciudad de Salamanca* (1606), and *Vida de Don Alonso Tostado de Madrigal* (1611). He then began working on his principal work, an ecclesiastical history of Spain. He published the volume on Salamanca in 1617, the year in which he was appointed chronicler of the kingdoms of Castile. This work was also contained in the first volume of the *Teatro eclesiástico de las ciudades e iglesias catedrales de España: Vida de sus obispos y cosas memorables de sus obispados* (1618). Later he went to the court, and there in 1623 he published *Teatro de las grandezas de la villa de Madrid,* then gradually published sections of his *Teatro eclesiástico* (1643, 1647, 1650), the last volume of which did not appear until 1700. In 1643 he had been named chief chronicler of the Indies "to write the ecclesiastical history of those areas and what the Gospel and its ministers have done to augment the honor of the Holy Catholic Faith and the number of those it had saved by religious instruction." As part of his work on Spain he had had to work on the New World, since it was impossible to study one independently of the other, and this background enabled him to finish the study on the Church in Michoacán by 1644. In 1649 appeared the first volume of the *Teatro eclesiástico de la primitiva iglesia de las Indias Occidentales, vida de sus arzobispos, obispos y cosas memorables de sus sedes,* and in 1655 the second volume. By then, González Dávila, almost 90, was deaf and blind; in April 1656 he suffered an attack of paralysis that left him unable to speak.

Bibliography: A. MILLARES CARLO, *Tres estudios biobibliográficos* (Maracaibo 1961). F. ESTEVE BARBA, *Historiografía Indiana* (Madrid 1964).

[H. PEREÑA]

GONZÁLEZ DE SANTALLA, TIRSO

Theologian and 13th general of the Society of Jesus; b. Arganza, Spain, Jan. 18, 1624; d. Rome, Oct. 27, 1705. He entered the Jesuits in 1643 and taught philosophy and theology at Salamanca (1655–65, 1676–87). He preached popular missions (1667–76) and was general of the Jesuits from 1687 to 1705.

In the late 17th century the Jesuits, most of whom held probabilism, were under attack for a lax interpretation of moral matters. In 1674 González wrote a book strongly opposing probabilism in favor of stricter doctrine. The book was refused publication by Jesuit reviewers. He continued to urge probabiliorism and received the support of Innocent XI. At the urging of Innocent, Gonzalez was elected general of the Society of Jesus. He then attempted to publish his previously rejected book, but his assistants blocked publication. The controversy caused considerable dissension in Jesuit circles. Innocent XII ordered a new examination, and a much-revised edition was published in 1694, a work applauded by the strict Bossuet, but judged excessively rigorist by St. Alphonsus Liguori. When the controversy continued, a general congregation of the Jesuits considered the case in 1696. A solution reaffirmed the freedom of Jesuit moral theologians to hold either system. Although muted for several years by this controversy, Jesuit moralists recovered to continue among the foremost advocates of probabilism.

González's most important work was the controversial *Fundamentum Theologiae Moralis* (Rome 1694). He also composed apologetical works, among which are *Selectae disputationes ex universa theologia* (4 v. Salamanca, 1680–86), directed against Neothomists and Jansenists; *Manductio ad conversionem Mahometanorum* (2 v. Madrid 1687); and treatises on the Immaculate Conception and on papal infallibility.

Bibliography: A. ASTRAIN, *Historia de la Compañia de Jesús,* 7 v. (Madrid 1902–25) 6:172–372. Pastor 32:435–441, 621–633. M. P. HARNEY, *The Jesuits in History* (New York 1941; repr. Chicago 1962). Sommervogel 3:1591–1602. P. BERNARD, *Dictionnaire de théologie catholique* 6.2:1493–96.

[W. R. CALLAHAN]

GONZÁLEZ FLORES, ANACLETO

Mexican journalist, orator, organizer of Catholic lay action; b. Tepatitlán, Jalisco, July 13, 1888; d. Guadalajara, 1926. He was the son of poor parents, second in a family of 12. He attended the Seminary of San Juan de los Lagos but decided that he did not have a vocation to the priesthood and left for Guadalajara to study law. Because the state schools refused to validate his seminary courses, he was obliged to resume his studies on the preparatory level. He taught history and literature in private schools, while organizing Catholic worker groups on the principles of Pope Leo XIII. From 1914 to 1916 he formed a series of Catholic study circles in sociology, philosophy, and literature, inspired by such figures as Ketteler, Wind-horst, Manning, Count de Mun, Daniel O'Connell, García Moreno, and even Mahatma Gandhi. This activity was interrupted when the revolution spread to Guadalajara, and he took refuge with a brother who had settled in the southern part of the state. There he joined the troops of Delgadillo, a partisan of Villa, as secretary. In December 1915 Delgadillo was captured and shot for treason, and González returned to Guadalajara, disillusioned with warfare.

By 1916, he had become a local leader, popularly known as *El Maestro,* in the *Asociación Católica de la Juventud Mexicana,* a national organization aimed at restoring a Christian social order in Mexico. He was admitted to the practice of law in 1922, and shortly thereafter he married. Upon the government's closing of the Conciliar Seminary of Guadalajara, he organized the Catholic Committee of Defense, and in early 1925 he consolidated this into a permanent *Unión Popular,* or united front, against the antireligious campaigns that raged from 1926 to 1929. He edited the weekly *Gladium,* which reached a circulation of 100,000.

When in 1926 the national government under CALLES determined to exterminate the Church through enforcement of the antireligious articles of the 1917 Constitution, González called upon Catholics in an article in the national newspaper *El País* to resist. He led the ensuing passive resistance to the government program, which accompanied the hierarchy's decision to suspend public worship. When the intransigent attitude of Calles made it appear that passive resistance was inadequate, Catholic leaders decided to resort to armed resistance. From this came the *Liga Nacional Defensora de la Libertad Religiosa,* setting off the *Cristeros* rebellion, so-called from the cry of the Catholic guerrilla warriors "Viva Cristo Rey." González found himself swept into this movement. Working from secret quarters in the home of Dr. Vargas González, he was discovered and arrested on April 1, 1926. After being brutally tortured in a vain effort to extract his secrets, he was bayoneted and shot, together with his companions Luis Padilla and Jorge and Ramón Vargas González. The public funerals accorded him and his associates were a spontaneous general reaction to his final words: "For a second time, may the Americas hear this holy cry: I die, but God does not die. 'Long live Christ the King!'"

Bibliography: A. GÓMEZ ROBLEDO, *Anacleto González Flores: El maestro* (2d ed. Mexico City 1947). A. RÍUS FACIUS. *Méjico cristero: Historia de la ACJM, 1925 a 1931* (Mexico City 1960). J. H. SCHLARMAN, *Mexico: A Land of Volcanoes* (Milwaukee 1950). J. HERRERA ROSSI, *Cinco retratos* (Mexico City 1949).

[J. A. MAGNER]

GONZÁLEZ GARCÍA, MANUEL, BL.

Bishop of Málaga (1920–35) and Palencia (1935–40), founder of the Eucharistic Missionaries of Nazareth; b. Feb. 25, 1877, Sevilla, Andalucia, Spain; d. Jan. 4, 1940, Palencia, Castille y Léon. Manuel was the fourth of the five children of Martín González Lara, a carpenter, and his wife, Antonia. He paid for his education by working as a domestic servant in the seminary. Following his priestly ordination (Sept. 21, 1901) at the hands of Bl. Marcelo SPÍNOLA Y MAESTRE, he was assigned to a mission in Palomares del Rio (1902–05) near Sevilla, then Huelva (1905–16).

Profoundly affected by the vision of an abandoned tabernacle, the bishop dedicated his life to promoting the Real Presence in the Eucharist. On March 4, 1910, he petitioned a group of his faithful collaborators to undertake the "Obra para los Sagrarios-Calvarios" (Work of Sacred Calvary) to make reparations to the Eucharistic Jesus. From this Eucharistic Union for Reparations developed Marys of the Tabernacle for lay women, the Disciples of St. John for laymen, the Children's Eucharistic Reparation Society, Eucharistic Missionaries for priests (1918), Eucharistic Missionaries of Nazareth for women religious (1921), the Institute of Nazarene Missionary Helpers (1932), and the Youth Eucharistic Reparation Society (1939). These societies quickly spread to other dioceses in Spain and the Western Hemisphere through the periodical *El Granito de Arena* (*The Grain of Sand*). Fr. Manuel's work received the approval of Pope Pius X in 1912. This love of the Eucharist also moved the priest to relieve the suffering of his flock and open schools.

On Jan. 16, 1916, Fr. Manuel received episcopal ordination as the auxiliary bishop of Málaga. His elevation to bishop of the same diocese (1920) was celebrated with a banquet for 3,000 poor children—served by dignitaries, priests, and seminarians—rather than the usual gala for the elite. As bishop he visited each parish, improved the educational system for both secular and religious training, and labored to encourage more priestly vocations.

The arrival of the Spanish Republic threatened the work he had accomplished. On May 11, 1931, the episcopal palace was burned, forcing the bishop to direct his diocese from Gibraltar, then Madrid (1932–35). On Aug. 5, 1935, Pope Pius XI named him bishop of Palencia.

Throughout his career, González shared his love of the Eucharist through his writings, which include *Lo que puede un cura hoy, El abandono de los Sagrarios acompañados, Oremos en el Sagrario como se oraba en el Evangelio, Artes para ser apóstol, La gracia en la educación*, and *Arte y liturgia.*

He died after patiently enduring years of ill health. The epitaph marking his remains in the Blessed Sacrament Chapel in Palencia's cathedral reads: "I ask to be interred next to a Tabernacle, so that my bones after death, as my tongue and pen during life, will always say to those who pass by: Jesus is there! He is there! Do not abandon him!" Pope John Paul II declared him venerable (April 6, 1998), approved a miracle attributed to his intercession (Dec. 20, 1999), and beatified him (April 29, 2001).

Bibliography: *L'Osservatore Romano,* Eng. Ed. 18 (2001), 1, 6–8; 19 (2001), 7, 10.

[K. I. RABENSTEIN]

GONZÁLEZ HOLGUÍN, DIEGO

Jesuit linguist; b. Cáceres, Spain, 1552; d. Mendoza, Argentina, 1617 or 1618. He entered the Society of Jesus in 1568. In May 1581, he arrived in Lima and in 1584 he went as a missionary to Cuzco. Assigned to the group who were to establish the society in Ecuador, he went to Quito in 1586. In 1600 he was rector at Chuquisaca (today Sucre, Bolivia), and later held the same post at Asunción, Paraguay. Devoted by preference to academic work, on occasional excursions as a missionary he made close contacts with the Indian world, and became a specialist in Quechua. He composed a grammar of the language and a dictionary, along with an account of the privileges granted to the Indians. As a moralist, in 1611 he published a treatise defending the compulsory character of obedience to royal orders and an instruction on "the conduct that should be observed in the tribunal of penance with the encomenderos." He achieved a balanced Indianist judgment, rare among the extreme tendencies usually shown by jurists dealing with the disputes over the encomiendas at the beginning of the 17th century.

Bibliography: A. DE EGAÑA, *Monumenta Peruana* (Rome 1954–61). E. TORRES SALDAMANDO, *Los antiguos jesuítas del Perú* (Lima 1882).

[A. DE EGAÑA]

GONZÁLEZ SUÁREZ, FEDERICO

Ecuadorian bishop and historian; b. Quito, April 12, 1844; d. Quito, Dec. 1, 1917. González, grew up during the upheaval of civil war that followed the Wars of Independence. As a young man he witnessed the power struggles between García Moreno and his opponents, Julio Arboleda and Tomás Cipriano Mosquera. González left the army and joined the Society of Jesus. By temperament he was unsuited for community life; he left the society after ten years and was later ordained by the bishop of Cuenca. Thereafter, he devoted himself to historical studies and to preaching, distinguishing himself not only by his eloquence but also by his strict judgments, which at times occasioned violent reaction from opponents.

Federico González Suárez.

His years in Cuenca were marked also by an interest in the prehistory of the aborigines of the region. His *Estudio sobre los Cañaris* was the fountainhead of new research into the past of America. Before publishing his study, González had been elected to Congress. He moved to Quito and became a well-known and respected figure in public life. He planned to write the history of the Church in Ecuador and published the first volume in 1881. Then he became interested in a general history of the nation. The archeological study in volume one (1890) failed again to attract readers. Only when volume four appeared did González's work gain attention, because of the scandal created by his description of the bad conditions prevalent in convents during the colonial period. The Roman Curia, to which the matter had to be referred, required no changes. Even before the decision, Pope Leo XIII had, in 1894, designated him bishop of Ibarra. González wrote his response in the work, published posthumously in 1937, *Defensa de mi criterio histórico.*

As bishop of Ibarra, he was forced to the political upheavals of the time. The ousted Ecuadorean party tried to regain power with the aid of Colombians who fought the war in the name of religion. When required by the goverment to take part in a patriotic celebration, the bishop left his vicar instructions for action in case of emergency, saying, ''We eccclesiastics must never sacrifice the Fatherland in order to save religion.'' He opposed a bishop of a neighboring diocese who had tried to interfere in a school in Tulcán and had threatened its members with excommunication. González made it clear that he and he alone would dictate policy in the diocese and that all other orders were void. His position was upheld by Rome.

Seven volumes of his history, covering the whole colonial era, were published. Later he published *Estudios literarios* on well-known figures whose lives somewhat resembled his own.

[I. J. BARRERA]

GONZÁLEZ Y DÍAZ TUÑÓN, CEFERINO

Dominican cardinal and philosopher; b. San Nicolás de Villoria, Asturias, Jan. 28, 1831; d. Madrid, Nov. 29, 1894. Entering the Dominican Order for the province of the Philippines in 1844, he was sent to Manila in 1849, where he studied and was ordained in 1859. He taught at the University of Santo Tomás (1859–66) and returned to Spain in 1867. Consecrated bishop of Córdoba in 1875, he was made archbishop of Seville in 1883, cardinal in 1884, and archbishop of Toledo in 1886. Through his teaching and many publications he contributed substantially to the restoration of THOMISM prior to *AETERNI PATRIS*. To a profound knowledge of Thomistic philosophy he added a wide knowledge of modern thinkers and a deep interest in the physical sciences. For him, Thomism was not a closed system, but a progressive, living tradition capable of renewing itself and of assimilating the progress of science. His first work was *Estudios sobre la filosofia de Santo Tomás* (Manila 1864). Later he wrote *Philosophia elementaria,* 3 v. (Madrid 1868; Spanish tr., 2 v. Madrid 1873); *Estudios religiosos, filosóficos, científicos y morales* (Madrid 1873); and *Historia de la filosofia,* 3 v. (Madrid 1878–79). In his last publication, *La Biblia y la ciencia,* 2 v. (Madrid 1891, 1894), he presented the scriptural problem clearly and formulated solid principles of resolution that were adopted by J. LAGRANGE in his preface to *Revue Biblique* (1892) and by Leo XIII in his *PROVIDENTISSIMUS DEUS.*

Bibliography: A. FRÜHWIRTH, *Analecta Sacri Ordinis Praedicatorum* 2 (1895–96) 34–41. N. DEL PRADO, *Revue thomiste* 3 (1895) 85–94. G. FRAILE, *Revista de Filosofia* 15 (1956) 465–488. F. DIAZ DE CERIO, *Pensamiento* 20 (1964) 27–70.

[G. FRAILE]

GOOD

In general the term ''good'' refers to something of value, or anything that fills a need or desire and thus affords satisfaction. Philosophers refine this notion and use it in several different senses. In speculating about God as Absolute Perfection, the ultimate end of man and the universe, they refer to the Supreme Good (*see* GOOD, THE SUPREME). In the context of social and political thought they sometimes speak of the motivating force behind all human activity as the common good. In metaphysical analysis they identify the good with being considered precisely as an object of desire or appetition, and thus enumerate it among the TRANSCENDENTALS. In ethics, finally, they speak of any action in conformity with a norm of MORALITY as itself good, and thus conducive to man's fulfillment and happiness. In what follows major consideration will be given to the last two meanings, under the headings of ontological good and moral good, respectively.

Ontological Good

The good, viewed metaphysically, expresses something so fundamental that it is impossible to define it in terms of anything more basic. The unsuspected depth and diversity of meaning that follow man's initial understanding of what constitutes the good can best be exposed by tracing the development of this concept throughout the long history of philosophy.

Platonic Origins. Discussing the good primarily in an ethical context, PLATO sees it as the action man ought to perform. If a man acts for the sake of something, this something is what he wills and seeks precisely as conducive to his good. The good is what will make him happy. This may be the useful or the pleasurable; but even the unpleasant, e.g., punishment, can be good if it is the remedy that cures diseases of the soul, such as injustice or intemperance. The good then is primarily a virtue of the soul, a kind of knowledge: the knowledge of good counsel, or of the just and unjust, the temperate or intemperate, etc. This knowledge is a certain synthesis of all the virtues, but one according to a pattern elaborated through reason. A knowledge so elaborated implies for Plato knowledge of an absolute norm or form of good action. This norm defines the good.

Yet Plato is aware that this does not fully solve the problem. Though it seems reasonable that a man should be just and act justly, yet when such action presents many and immediate disadvantages there must be some reason why virtuous action is good in spite of these. This requires a deeper notion of the good that makes the goodness of virtuous action a good in itself. In the *Symposium*

Plato indicates that the ultimate principle is some nature that is absolute unity, harmony, and perfection. Again, in the *Republic,* he specifies that the unity of knowledge is founded in the good, for the good is the author of all known things and is their very essence. Yet the good itself is not essence, but transcends it in dignity and power. He does not further elaborate the character of this ultimate good, nor does he explain how it is related to the multiple virtues of the soul.

Aristotelian Development. For Aristotle, since every act, inquiry, or pursuit seems to tend to some good, the good is said to be that at which all things aim. The good is the end of human action, and as such might be either a product of that activity or the activity itself. Among good ends, Aristotle notes a hierarchy in which the lower is desired as a means to the ultimate. The existence of lower ends permits him to identify some good things with the useful. But there must be a highest good or ultimate end, for otherwise man would never wish to act. This ultimate end is a good not identified with the useful but one desired for its own sake.

The Highest Good. Aristotle sees the supreme good as the end of man's highest action or the end of that action that is the reason of all other actions. For Aristotle, as for Plato, man's highest activity is knowing. But the former makes a clear distinction between speculative knowledge and practical knowledge. Speculative knowledge bases its principles in things, and its end is the truth of these things. Practical science, or the knowledge of doing or making, takes its principles from the one knowing and the goal envisaged, and its end is the truth of something yet to be done or made. Again, for Aristotle, man is not an isolated individual but a social animal who cannot achieve his end independent of society. So the good of man's highest practical activity is not an individual good but the good of man. Thus he identifies the good of man with the good of the state. Man, see what should be his aim or end as a member of a city-state, thereby determines his highest good.

Aristotle realizes that the term good has as many meanings as being. Yet, even though it can be predicated of all the categories, it somehow transcends them. Moreover, if some one good exists that is itself totally good, it cannot be reached by man; nor can knowledge of it, transcending as it does the field of action, clarify knowledge needed by man to achieve a particular end or good.

Human Happiness. Such considerations, however, lead Aristotle to the question: Is there one final end for man, or are there many? In his understanding, ''final'' is something not desired for the sake of something else, although not necessarily ultimate in the sense of transcendent. He answers that happiness is such a good, since it is always chosen for its own sake, and he equates this with virtuous action that is the strictly human good. However, this action cannot consist in just one act, but entails action of the highest virtue during a ''complete life.'' Nor can this happiness of virtuous action be complete without some other gifts of FORTUNE such as health, a certain prosperity, friends, and a long life. The whole complex state entitled ''happiness'' varies somewhat with different abilities and types of men, and thus is not identical for all.

For Aristotle, then, the good is what man rationally judges should be done to achieve his happiness as a social being in this life. He does not develop the notion of an independent existing object, such as that implied by Plato, which would be ultimate in the order of good.

Epicureans and Stoics. The Epicureans saw the good as relative bodily pleasure; the Stoics identified it and virtue with passionless nature lived rationally (*see* EPICUREANISM; HEDONISM; STOICISM).

Plotinus and the Good. It is PLOTINUS who stresses the good in terms of the ultimate ontological principle suggested by Plato. His whole philosophy is a search not merely for the good as moral but also for the supreme principle of both speculative and practical knowledge. This principle he terms the nature of the good. It is the ultimate source of all things.

Plotinus speaks of being as a Platonic form, i.e., as an object that is logically prior to intelligence even though correlative to it. Yet intelligence and the objects it understands constitute a multitude; they are unintelligible unless reduced to some unity. This unity, because it is above being and intelligence, cannot be grasped by intellect, since this would immediately delimit it and make it a ''this'' and not ''that.'' The resulting One he identifies with the Good. It is the source of the being of all other things, for these are beings by emanation, obtaining their perfection from the Good.

Plotinus thus teaches that: first, the good is identified primarily with reality in the fullness of its perfection; second, all other things, as emanations, are in that degree good; and third, a comprehension (not of the existence, but) of the nature of the Supreme Good is beyond the capacity of intelligence; which is itself a limited emanation. The meaning of the nature of the Supreme Good is therefore reached by man only in a negative way, by a sort of intuitive experience.

Augustinian Teaching. St. AUGUSTINE synthesizes Plotinian philosophy with Christian Revelation, for the latter clearly reveals the notion of a sovereign transcendent good and identifies this with God. All other things, having been created, are by God but not of Him. They are good but not as an emanation of God's goodness. Rather, God creates a being, making it this nature or that; since it is a nature, it is good. For St. Augustine the good is not primarily end or something desired, but rather being and a degree of perfection. He holds that being has measure, form, and order.

First, all natures are ordered, that is, are intelligible and related in an intelligible fashion to all other beings. If a nature dynamically maintains its order it should attain its end. The mode of a being implies order: it also expresses the measure of being, while form, or species, expresses the particular character of that measure. Each nature, as a kind of ordered measure, is in itself a degree of reality and so ''good.''

St. Augustine does not identify this objective order of the good with the *de facto* end of man and his knowledge of that end. Revelation tells him that man's end or good is unattainable by natural powers. Only by the assurance of Revelation is the objective Supreme Good, hinted at by Plato and considered as out of man's reach by Aristotle, reintegrated into the objective moral order. The supernatural order requires man to love God for Himself as The Good, and all else as means.

Neither does St. Augustine identify the morality or goodness of human action with man's practical knowledge of the good. Such knowledge and virtue are not the same thing. He recognizes the difference between knowledge of what is, knowledge of what ought to be done, and the willing of the directive to action. Unlike earlier thinkers he sees voluntary choice rooted in knowledge as basic to virtue. This distinction between knowledge and will gives rise to the thorny problem of the difference between the objective moral good and that which, in the light of a good intention, may be mistakenly judged to be a means and so a good. From this distinction one can understand how conscience can make its demands to be itself respected as a good.

Thomistic Doctrine. St. THOMAS AQUINAS's meaning of the good, often identified with the Aristotelian phrase as ''that which all things desire,'' is rather one that embodies not merely Aristotle's thought but also the further contributions of PSEUDO-DIONYSIUS and St. Augustine. His essential contribution lies partly in his treatment of the good in general, making it an integral part of his metaphysics, and partly in his subtle explanation of the connection between the first principles of ethics and those of metaphysics, and so of the relation between ontological good and the good of moral action.

Being and the Good. St. Thomas seems to make two approaches to the understanding of being. The first is a deepening of experience through which he sees that ''to be'' is to be this something, which, through change, can become other; and again, that ''to be'' is to be many kinds, measures, or modes.

The second view develops when, from the fact of change and multiplicity, he establishes that there must be a First Cause, a First Necessary Being, a First Truth, etc. (*see* GOD, PROOFS FOR THE EXISTENCE OF). Considering the character of this ''First,'' he then establishes its utter simplicity by way of negation. Simplicity in being is to be the Act Itself of Existing, the principle of all other modes. This leads him to reflect on finite things and see them as beings precisely because, by creative act, they are given existence.

Emphasizing existence as the perfection of all perfections, St. Thomas attains a deeper understanding of being and its transcendental properties. First, he holds that ''to be'' is to be an existing something; but this exists as itself and not other: thus it is one. The mind also apprehends being as intrinsically intelligible and, in its highest mode, as an intellect in act: thus being is true. As true, it is correlative to mind and the good of mind. But the true as good is not good merely for the intellect, but also as existent in its own right; it is that to which the intellectual appetite or will tends, and in which it rests. Being is thus seen as both perfective and perfection. It is good because it perfects and fills the intellectual appetite; it is good and loved because its actuality is perfection. In its highest mode the good of the will is seen as identical with its love.

Aquinas thus shows that the Highest Being, God, Existence Itself, is at the same time a pure act of intellectual understanding and a pure act of delight and love. Existence Itself, as perfectly lucid Love, is the Good. But its mode of existence transcends our positive comprehension.

Ontological and Moral Good. For man, to be is not only to exist, but also to develop, and this by the absorption of being. Yet, though all things can be seen intellectually as good in themselves, not all ontological goods are good for man's development here and now. Thus the ontologically good is morally good only insofar as, in a given situation, it becomes a proper means to man's ultimate end. Man by his choice so relates other beings to his being that he develops his own being in the process. In so doing he gives expression to the primary principle of being, viz, that being must be and is good. Seeking through action this affirmation of being, man has it in his power to tend toward his ultimate end and good.

But man cannot use being for his development by a mere mechanical relating of the ontological good to himself; rather, through understanding and choice, he must employ a limited creative act. Man's free action is based on a spiritual synthesis made by himself as a distinct person. Thus the moral good must be seen as bearing the stamp of his personality. Respect for the person and his action, which depends in turn on complicated judgments inspired by love of the good and yet is perfectible in various degrees by moral and intellectual virtues, causes St. Thomas to hold that the conscientious judgment is itself good—even though from the theoretical and objective point of view it might be judged erroneous and imperfect. Following St. Augustine, St. Thomas regards the personal act of conscience as a good to be respected. The moral good, then, is not necessarily identical with the ontological. In a certain sense, the ordering of the ontological good to the ultimate end is potential to man's creative act of choice.

Spinoza and the British Moralists. Among modern philosophers SPINOZA makes almost complete identification between moral and ontological good. His philosophy is based on the principle ''that the order and connection of ideas is the same as the order and connections of things'' (*Ethics* 2, prop. 7). We seek, through reflection on our understanding of things, a knowledge of the intelligible principle involved in their intelligibility. For example, various figures or modes of thought involve intelligible extension or thought respectively. Both extension and thought can be conceived as intelligible expressions of substance; yet substance itself, a principle implied in the understanding of everything else, implies no further principle. The order of thought and reality being the same, the ultimate principle, substance, is also the Supreme Reality. And man finds his good, contentment, and peace in the gradual comprehension of what is, which reaches its culmination in an intuition of the unitive whole of substance, or God. This intuition, being a conscious affirmation of mind, is identical with love, which is the very spontaneity of the mind. The wise man being ''conscious of himself and of God and of things by a certain eternal necessity, never ceases to be, but always possesses true acquiescence of spirit'' (*Ethics* 5, prop. 42n). This is man's Good: to be absorbed in what is.

The BRITISH MORALISTS of the 18th century attempted to found their idea of the good on moral phenomena experienced in the life of the ordinary man rather than on a metaphysical basis. All agreed that happiness was the good sought. The intellectualist school saw happiness as resulting from man's respect for reasonable relations that express things as they are; the sentimentalists stressed those relations they felt were apt to produce the well-being of oneself or the majority. The good was really the state from which happiness results.

Kant's Notion of Good. Immanuel Kant regarded this phenomenal idea of the good as relativistic and purely subjective. Instead, he sought a moral relation that would be universally valid and based on something absolute in the person. This he found in the good will or good intention. Kant's will is a subjective extreme opposed to Spinoza's objective position. Hegel synthesizes both views.

In his *Critique of Pure Reason* Kant criticized all metaphysical knowledge of being; in his view, we know only the effects or appearances of things. Both nature and the self become syntheses of appearances. Therefore it is meaningless to say that one understands or loves a thing because of its inherent perfection. The moral good cannot be based on the ontological good. The only good is a will that wills with all its power, even if it fails of its purpose. There is ''an absolute value in the mere will'' [*Fundamental Principles of the Metaphysics of Morals*, sec. 1; tr. T. K. Abbott (London 1927) 10].

Such a will is not an act of love but an imperative expressing itself in a dictate of the rational will determined solely by itself; it is an autonomous dictate, an ''ought'' that is absolutely pure when it is expressible in a categorical imperative (*see* CATEGORICAL IMPERATIVE). Such a spontaneous dictate of the will, being independent of objects or consequences and thus purely formal, is the only absolute good. It is a demand that the ''will'' be ''will,'' for only thus can man be man. The good as end is not a norm but a subjective good, such as the useful or pleasurable; this is relative to the individual in the changing conditions of sense and so is not good in itself.

In a priori fashion Kant holds that a good will should produce happiness. But happiness is not the result of one act alone. It is possible only on the supposition ''of an endless duration of the existence and personality of the same rational being,'' i.e., on the supposition of immortality [*Critique of Practical Reason*, 2.2.4; tr. T. K. Abbott (London 1927) 218]. Moreover, although the virtuous man is worthy of happiness, experience shows that happiness is not necessarily connected with virtue. Happiness can in fact follow virtue only if one also assumes the existence of an intelligent cause of both nature and rational being. On such a supposition the *Summum Bonum,* the sum of virtue and happiness, is possible. These suppositions are thus the a priori condition of the possibility of the Highest Good, although they are not the a priori conditions of a good will as such.

Hegelian Teaching. With HEGEL there is no dichotomy between knowledge and the real. Knowledge is knowledge of the real and the real is what is known. Like Spinoza, Hegel has no criterion of the truth beyond reflective consciousness of truth itself. The life of the mind is nothing other than reason, or reality, expressing itself in a dialectical process of understanding, reflecting, distinguishing through reflection, and synthesizing to form a higher object that leads to Idea or Reason as the Absolute. In other words, consciousness through self-reflection transcends itself and its object. As limited, such action is autonomous and free insofar as it becomes an expression of Spirit and Reason, or a manifestation of the Absolute.

The recognition of this unity of self-consciousness and being is also a recognition of ''ethical substance.'' Self-consciousness at different levels yields moments of this substance and so ''the healthy natural reason knows immediately what is right and good.'' A healthy reason knows the law immediately as: ''this is right.'' But the right is never something related to an individual as individual; it must be an expression of the universality or community of Reason. Yet Reason at the stage of ethical action, since this stage is a moment in process, is an autonomous, universal willing of several things. It intends, first, the consciousness of the family as a community; this consciousness secondly involves seeing the family in relation to the greater community, the nation; and this in turn is related or absorbed in the unity of Absolute Spirit.

The Hegelian position is thus much like that of Spinoza: a metaphysical explanation is also an ethical view of reality. The Ultimate Good is Reason, or Absolute Spirit, or the spiritual as embodying all reality. Every expression of that Reality can be said to be good since each is implicitly Reason. Moral life is the progressive effort consciously to realize Spirit, just as for Spinoza it is progress toward the understanding of the Ultimate Principle, Substance. Virtue becomes identified with this dynamic understanding. But, for Hegel as for Kant, progress is an act of the self and is one entailing a hierarchy of levels. On each level the understanding makes the self explicit in its universal communal relations, and this too progresses in time, rather than unfolding in the Spinozistic mode in a linear series of implications.

Bergson and Sartre. Contemporary philosophy sees all of reality from an evolutionary, dynamic viewpoint. For the most part, the existentialist, creative character of action is stressed in reaction to the over-rationalized character of the Hegelian concept. In the philosophy of BERGSON the ontological good consists in action begetting the new through the *élan vital.* In line with this the moral good is embodied in the life of the model person or saint. Just as being or action expresses the unique, original character of existence, so it expresses the good.

The most radical expression of the existentialist trend is found in the work of Sartre (*see* EXISTENTIALISM). For him being is neither consciousness nor object, but what is presupposed to both thought and phenomena. It simply *is,* without meaning, and is identical with the absurd. Though being is neither good nor evil, Sartre speaks of it in terms of disgust. Man's act of consciousness or decision generates something intelligible, or an essence. In the order of moral action spontaneous decision is the free creation of the good bound by no rule. This is inherently contradictory and the negation of the good in its own terms.

See Also: PERFECTION, ONTOLOGICAL; OPTIMISM; EVIL; PESSIMISM.

Bibliography: E. G. SALMON, *The Good in Existential Metaphysics* (Milwaukee 1953). E. SMITH, *The Goodness of Being in Thomistic Philosophy and Its Contemporary Significance* (Catholic University of America Philosophical Studies 98; Washington 1947). C. HOLLENCAMP, *Causa causarum: On the Nature of Good and Final Cause* (Quebec 1949). L. DE RAEYMAEKER, *The Philosophy of Being,* tr. E. H. ZIEGELMEYER (St. Louis 1954). R. EISLER, *Wörterbuch der philosophischen Begriffe*, 3 v. (4th ed. Berlin 1927–30) 1:611–18. M. J. ADLER, ed., *The Great Ideas: A Syntopicon of Great Books of the Western World*, 2 v. (Chicago 1952) 1:605–38.

[E. G. SALMON]

Moral Good

Man's ontological good is his corporeal-spiritual being with its existent perfections and activities. An individual's good, in this sense, can be compared to an anthropological exemplar to see whether he falls short of the average, as would a blind, maimed, or insane person. But we do not say that a man is good or bad on the basis of such perfection or defect. For, although one's ontological good is desirable for its own sake, it is impermanent and does not represent the ultimate state of human well-being. Moral good refers to a man's ultimate good and whatever is directly connected therewith.

Notion of Moral Good. Moral goodness is the goodness of man as man, and basically consists in a relationship to his ultimate end. This relationship can exist: (1) in man's total being, (2) in his acts, and (3) in his habitual dispositions. Now the whole man is correctly and habitually related to his last end only when he possesses sanctifying GRACE. However, a radical orientation to this end is not enough in the case of the adult. For ends are actually attained by acts proper to the agent; and the characteristic act of man is the human act, the act of which man is master. An act of man is human when done with knowledge of the purpose of the act and freely placed (*see* HUMAN ACT). As a free being, man has the power to affirm his being and choose what leads to the end; or he can deny his being and choose what defeats his end. The former acts are good and right; the latter bad and wrong.

Without freedom there is no man; so, without freedom there is neither moral good nor moral evil. We ordinarily speak of moral good as existing in man's rational choices. These, however, will lead to the vision of God only if they are vivified by actual grace. In another common meaning moral good refers to the person of the human agent; thus he is called morally good (virtuous) if habitually disposed to perform good acts; he is called morally bad (vicious) if habitually disposed to perform bad acts (*see* VIRTUE).

Moral theology studies human acts and habits in relation to the last end. It teaches how one may maintain himself in the state of grace, acquire virtues, and identify the chief good and evil acts. Since early Greek times, philosophers have concerned themselves with problems about the virtues and the acts. The following discussion is for the most part about acts.

Theories about Moral Goodness. The perennial problem is one of determining the ultimate difference between right and wrong conduct. In theory, that is right which leads to the end, that is wrong which defeats the end, so that attainment of the end is incontestable proof of the rightness of a given course of action. We cannot, however, use attainment of the end to judge the rightness of conduct, because we have no experiential knowledge of people attaining their last end. Although the concepts of goodness and rightness differ (for goodness is suitability to nature, rightness rectitude toward an end), nevertheless, in the concrete the good act is the right act and the bad act is the wrong act. Hence the problem is soluble only if one finds why good acts are good and bad acts are bad.

Non-Normative Systems. The answers that they give to this question have been used to characterize some moral systems (*see* ETHICS, HISTORY OF). Thus the intuitionists are those who say that we simply see one act to be good and another to be bad. Some forms of this theory postulate a special moral sense that enables us to discern moral goodness in much the same way as sight tells yellow from blue. This doctrine is moral sensism. Phenomenologists, following HUSSERL, say that we immediately perceive the negative or positive value of a human act, not by operation of an intellect, but by an emotional act of value-appreciation. Some existentialists say that in a given situation we create the morally good act by our choice of whatever in a given situation promotes our value as existent persons. This is a form of situational ethics. These views dispense with a norm of morals.

Normative Systems. Many systems, however, hold a norm. Thus WILLIAM OF OCKHAM said that the positive will of God denominates certain acts as good and certain others as bad, and these labelings He could change at pleasure. Some modern Protestants reecho this doctrine and say that the sovereign Will of God, which may differ with each occasion and which can neither be contained within universal principles nor known by reason, is the sole norm of goodness. This function HOBBES attributes to the law of the state. According to Kant an act is good if it conforms to a dictate of the autonomous reason from the sole motive of devotion to duty. The supreme dictate upon which he based all others is: So act that thy motive may be made a universal law for all men. The hedonist, ancient and modern, judges the goodness of an act by its capacity to afford him pleasure (*see* HEDONISM). The 19th-century utilitarian pronounced an act good on the basis of its utility to serve the greatest good of the greatest number of men and animals. One of the most commonly accepted norms is the current practice of a given community based upon public approvals and disapprovals.

Naturalism and Positivism. The naturalists hold that morals is a natural science akin to biology or psychology, that moral goodness is a physical property inhering in some object, and of the same kind as color, shape, or feeling, to which many give the name of ''V-property.'' This is identified by some as a bodily process such as a pleasant titillation of the nerves, as that which the agent likes or prefers or which arouses his interest, as that which assists evolution, or the life-process, or the continuing social process by relief of tensions. Nearly all such systems are at one in shying away from the question of man's ultimate end. (*See* INSTRUMENTALISM.)

Logical positivists think that the problem of moral goodness is a pseudo problem on the ground that moral concepts and statements are not addressed to the intellect and make no sense; they merely evince emotion. Hence a statement asserting an action to be good or bad is either an exclamation of approval or disapproval, a hidden command, a gerundive, or a prescription. (*See* LOGICAL POSITIVISM.)

Scholastic Analysis. Scholastics commonly teach that the basic difference between good and bad is natural and not arbitrary. First, some actions of themselves defeat human ends and are bad and must be forbidden; others are so necessary to human existence that they are good in themselves and must be commanded. Not even God could sanction the former and prohibit the latter; for in that event human life would be impossible. Second, the reason why some acts are good in themselves and others bad in themselves is because human nature is what it is. Consequently the norm of human goodness is the complete nature of MAN. Here is obvious application of the ontological principle that action is proportionate to being. As the activities that allow a plant or an animal to come to maturity and perfection are only those that accord with the nature of the plant or animal, so man, if he is to arrive at the perfection of his nature, must choose to do only that which accords with his nature.

The Norm of Nature. To say that the norm of moral goodness is man's nature is a fuller explication of: (1) Aristotle's thought that the golden mean of virtue is right reason; for whoever acts in accordance with his nature is following right reason; and (2) St. Thomas's doctrine that the ultimate rule of conduct is the eternal LAW. For the provident Creator guides His creatures to their destiny by means befitting the nature of each. It is fitting that the rational creature be directed by moral law addressed to his intelligence and guiding his free will; and the content of this law is the prohibition of those actions that run counter to man's nature, and the command to do those things essential to the realization of that nature.

Moral Evil. The norm that discerns the good discerns the EVIL; for evil is the contrary of good. Ontologically evil is a nothing, the absence of a perfection that ought to be present. Man's ontological evil is lack of being, such as pain, mutilation, death, loss of power, that militates against his wholeness as a natural unitary being. Moral evil exists only in human choices; it consists in a lack of rectitude whose basis is that the act is not befitting the nature of the agent. Appetite must seek good, but in choosing moral evil it seeks what is only apparently good. While this may be an ontological perfection of the faculty whence it proceeds, it is unbecoming the total man and cannot be ordered to the last end. Formal moral evil is choice of what the agent thinks to be wrong; material moral evil is the choice of a wrong object that the agent thinks to be right.

Moral Objectivity. The essential goodness or badness of the will-act does not depend upon the subjective perfection by which it issues from the agent, as might an act of singing or running, but upon the object directly chosen, for the object specifies the will-act. This statement contradicts those existentialists who say that what a man chooses is of little or no consequence if only he chooses freely, sincerely, authentically. But the intensity or remissness of the will adds only accidental perfection or defect to the human act. The act is good if a morally good object is chosen; it is bad if a morally bad object is chosen. We carefully note that the total object of the will includes both what a man chooses to do and why he does so. The why is the motive that prompts the action; the what is the action, with its modifying circumstances, by which a motive is to be realized. Now in order to be good the act must accord with the norm, both as to what a man does and why he does it. This common teaching is also contested by existentialists who say that the nature of our action is not to be reckoned, if only one acts from the motive of the love of God. The most fundamental rule of morals is that the will may never seek, or rest in, moral evil. Therefore, an action wrong in itself does not become good when it is chosen as a means to a noble end; and an action good in itself is vitiated whenever it is made a means to an ignoble end. (*See* MORALITY; CIRCUMSTANCES, MORAL.)

Morality of Consequences. While certain moderns, contrary to Kant, consider consequences to be of the essence of morality, scholastics do not teach a morality of consequences except so far as consequences known and willed are part of the nature of the moral act. Since, therefore, the true human act is the inner act of the will, whenever one intends to do a wrong external act he is at once guilty of a moral wrong, even though he may later fail to carry out his wrong intention. Fulfillment of a wrong or right intention adds nothing essential, only a quantitative goodness or badness, to the right or wrong intention elicited. Consequences, however, have this peripheral importance: bad consequences, which though unintended are foreseen as following from what is directly intended, may be reason for forbidding an act innocent in itself. The principle of double effect, based on equal immediacy of resultant good and on proportion of evil allowed, illumines difficult cases in this area (*see* DOUBLE EFFECT, PRINCIPLE OF).

Good as the Goal of Human Action. Even though no law enjoined it, right reason must ever direct man to choose his real good in preference to his apparent good. Man is in a situation where he must constantly choose, for he is a complex being with many needs and many corresponding goods. Conflicting desire is the universal experience. How is such conflict resolved? While an immediate rule of thumb is that necessary good (i.e., what is required to prevent moral evil here and now) is to be preferred to good that is not so required, yet the general principle of solution is that goods are to be esteemed not for their power to attract but for the place they hold in the hierarchy of being. Since every good chosen adds a peculiar human luster to the agent, the act that affords more being is, other things being equal, more to be preferred than the act that affords less being. The nobler the object chosen, the nobler will be the act.

Varieties of Good. The Greeks distinguished perfective, delectable, and useful good. Perfective good is that object of desire that when had makes a man more a man. Man's perfections are his substance with its faculties, acquired skills, and all acts that improve his substance, faculties, and skills. These are intrinsic values desirable for their own sakes. Each man's problem is to recognize what things are worthy of choice, and the order and measure in which they are to be sought.

Delectable good is the pleasure or satisfaction one experiences upon the fulfillment of a want or the exercise of a faculty. Since nature attaches pleasure to our activities in order to induce us to seek our proper perfective goods, pleasure is a natural object of desire. One ought not to be without some measure of pleasure, but pleasure sought merely for pleasure's sake is unreasonable.

Useful good is a pure means to a perfective good or pleasure. Useful good and delectable good become moral good when they are sought in subordination to perfective good and directed by reason to the last end. A man ought not to regard useful good as having intrinsic value nor make pleasure the sole end of action.

Subordination of Goods. In dealing with self, the rule is that what satisfies vegetative needs is less important than what satisfies sensitive needs; both of these in turn are subordinate to rational and spiritual needs. Moreover, each man requires a skill whose highest exercise is wisdom in discerning the true ends of life and the appropriate means of attaining them. Another needed skill is restraining within the bounds of reason appetite striving after sensitive pleasure. Still another skill is spurring on or restraining appetite that is faced with difficulty.

In dealing with things less than himself, a man should comport himself as a faithful steward of the divine bounty. Dealing with other men he must maintain the natural equality of all men and do justice by respecting their goods. Justice regulates not only the private good of each but especially the common good of all. The common good implies two things: (1) the one goal toward which the Creator draws all men; a common nature requires that men love one another by helping, never hindering, each other in their quest of this goal; (2) that sum of helps and advantages to be produced by mutual cooperation that is necessary for the individual to realize himself and his potentialities. Foremost among these helps is society in general and all particular natural and supernatural societies. Each one is to contribute his due share to the common good as determined by law of God or man; each one is entitled to a proportionate share in the social advantage.

One is to prefer the common good to his individual good except when he would be called upon to lose or endanger his supreme good. In dealing with God, one must observe the relation of complete dependence upon the source of all being. Since God is Infinite Goodness, things that directly unite man to God, such as acts of faith, hope, and charity, are better for man than those whose purpose is human perfection, such as acts of prudence, justice, temperance, and fortitude. Charity is the supreme skill uniting one most closely to God and directing all activities to the final end.

Highest Good. By observing these relations to self, to lower beings, to his fellow man, and to God, a man moves toward his final end, which is his supreme good (*see* GOOD, THE SUPREME). This is, first, a state of perfect happiness consisting in the unflawed exercise of his characteristically human faculties of knowledge and love, and the delight resulting therefrom. Second, since man cannot make himself happy, his happiness is in the possession of some all-satisfying object, which can be only God. For man has unlimited yearnings that only God can satisfy.

This final end is above man's nature and exceeds his natural capacities. It is wholly supernatural, for it is a sharing in the proper life of God, a knowing of God as the Triune God knows, and a loving of God as the Persons of the Most Blessed Trinity love one another. We call it the vision of God because God is known, not as He is reflected in creation, but as He is in Himself (*see* BEATIFIC VISION). Now in order that man may do what is proper to God he must be lifted to the divine level. This happens when sanctifying grace, a share in the divine nature, is infused into a man. The infusion of this grace in this life is the real beginning of the vision hereafter. The practical aspiration of the Christian and the sole criterion of a successful life is to die when in the possession of sanctifying grace.

No naturally good acts have a direct bearing on attainment of the beatific vision. What is required is good acts elevated to the supernatural by either actual or sanctifying grace, i.e., supernatural acts. Yet the vision is granted as a reward for a good life. Hence arises the concept of the meritorious act. Not every supernatural act bears the character of MERIT, because the agent performing it may have the support of actual but not of sanctifying grace; he may not be a friend of God. To be meritorious, then, the act must be done by one who has sanctifying grace, it must be morally good, and in some way directed to the beatific vision. Hence the highest type of moral act is the meritorious act. Meritorious acts differ among themselves accordingly as one act is more free, more intense, aimed at a nobler object, more permeated with charity, and produced by a more worthy moral agent.

Relation of Good to Value. The modern tendency is to substitute the term ''value'' for ''good,'' and evolve a philosophy of value (*see* AXIOLOGY). Although no fresh insights into the problems of the good have come from introducing the word ''value,'' yet ''value'' is a more manageable term. Thus one could not convey what is meant by a VALUE JUDGMENT (which is opposed to a judgment of fact) by calling it a ''good'' judgment. ''Goods'' has become obsolete except where it designates articles of commerce; whereas ''values'' now covers the whole field of human desires.

When this philosophy first arose, value usually meant a pleasant reaction to experience, a subjective state like delectable good. Later theorists, however, attribute an objective character to values, and divide them into instrumental and intrinsic values corresponding to the scholastic useful and perfective goods. They identify the chief intrinsic values as truth, beauty, talent, meaning, health, rest, play, morality, and religion. A value then represents a wide area of interest and desire, and not merely single acts or single objects of desire. But it refers to fewer things than good; for value belongs only to persons capable of appreciating and distinguishing sub-human, human, and moral values.

See Also: END; MAN, NATURAL END OF; FINAL CAUSALITY.

Bibliography: T. J. HIGGINS, *Man as Man* (Milwaukee 1963). T. E. HILL, *Contemporary Ethical Theories* (New York 1950). A. C. EWING, *The Definition of the Good* (New York 1947). D. VON HILDEBRAND, *Christian Ethics* (New York 1953) 23–166. M. V. MURRAY, *Problems in Ethics* (New York 1960) 72–178. J. A. OESTERLE, *Ethics* (Englewood Cliffs, New Jersey 1957) 101–15. H. RENARD, *The Philosophy of Morality* (Milwaukee 1953). M. CRONIN, *The Science of Ethics,* 2 v. (Dublin 1939) v. 1. J. WILD, *Introduction to Realistic Philosophy* (New York 1948) 39–175.

[T. J. HIGGINS]

GOOD, THE SUPREME

The positive reality of anything is considered as GOOD when it is viewed as the fulfillment of some inclination or tendency. If the inclination in question is that of each thing to its own full REALITY, the comparison of goods is identical with the comparison of beings, and the highest good is the first being, GOD. If the inclination in question is the human WILL, the comparison of goods is preference or desirability, and the highest good is the ultimate perfection to which man can aspire. The expression, "the supreme good," is used in both of these senses.

Supreme Good in reality. The question of the supreme good in reality arises only if the whole of BEING is viewed as a single, orderly system. POSITIVISM and pragmatism generally involve a rejection of such a synoptic view. PANTHEISM and dialectical philosophies like that of HEGEL, on the other hand, insist so strongly on the unity of being that only reality as a whole or the ABSOLUTE is considered to be good.

Creator and Creatures. PLATO and ARISTOTLE both attempted in different ways to understand reality as a hierarchy of really diverse beings unified in an orderly system. Christian thinkers, working in the light of divine revelation, perfected these philosophical conceptions by developing a balanced notion of the TRANSCENDENCE and IMMANENCE of God, and by clarifying the relationship of the Creator and provident Lord to His creatures.

God has in Himself the fullness of being that includes all perfections. He creates freely out of pure generosity, merely as a self-expression of His own perfection, and He directs all things to their own full reality, which is an imitation of His infinite perfection. Thus God is good in Himself, and in comparison with creatures He is the supreme good, for all created goods preexist in Him in a perfect way, and the fulfillment of every creature is a likeness of His fullness. (*See* PERFECTION, ONTOLOGICAL.)

Hierarchy of Goods. Two implications of this understanding of the supreme good should be noted. First, because God is the supreme good in virtue of His fullness of being, the dualism of MANICHAEISM, which posits a supreme evil opposed to and struggling with the supreme good, is excluded. Second, because God exists in His own uniquely perfect way and gives His creatures a way of being of their own, created beings have a real goodness that belongs to them in themselves. Hence a real hierarchy of goods exists, for each creature has a genuine goodness of a certain degree, while God has the fullness of perfection without measure.

Among created things, the highest good belongs to the order of creation as a whole, for this includes every created perfection. Insofar as it relates creatures to God in a special way, each supernatural gift of God is a higher good than every natural perfection. Comparing the kinds of created beings with one another, we consider that angels and men, who have intelligence and freedom, surpass other creatures in worth and dignity, for only intellectual beings can extend their own perfection in order to encompass in some way the full range of reality.

Supreme good for man. In the history of moral thought, the first question in most theories has concerned the supreme good for man. Since KANT, positions on this question have divided between eudaemonistic and deontological theories—i.e., those that put the highest human perfection in satisfaction and those that put it in the fulfillment of moral obligation (*see* EUDAEMONISM; DEONTOLOGISM). For Kant, the highest good combines virtue and happiness, but morally good action is determined solely by moral law, not by a desire for the good.

Many ancient philosophical theories—e.g., EPICUREANISM and STOICISM—are characterized chiefly by their theories of the supreme good for man. The best classical theories, those of Plato and Aristotle, transcend the modern distinction between satisfaction and morality by uniting both in a view of the end of man. Christian thought, with its conception of HEAVEN, transcends this antimony even more perfectly.

According to Catholic faith, the highest good for man is that of being admitted by divine GRACE to a share in God's own inner life. The fullness of this supernatural life is variously called beatitude, eternal life, the kingdom of God, and heavenly glory.

See Also: MAN, NATURAL END OF; BEATIFIC VISION; GOD; CREATION; PARTICIPATION; GOOD.

Bibliography: G. P. KLUBERTANZ and M. R. HOLLOWAY, *Being and God* (New York 1963) 171–183, 202–208, 334–336. J. MOUROUX, *The Meaning of Man* (New York 1948). J. BUCKLEY, *Man's Last End* (St. Louis 1949). THOMAS AQUINAS, *Summa theologiae* 1a, 5–6; 1a2ae, 1–5; *C. gent* 1.37–41; 2.45; 3.1–63.

[G. G. GRISEZ]

GOOD FRIDAY

From earliest times this has been a day given over to the remembrance of the Crucifixion of Our Lord. The official, somewhat redundant name for Good Friday since 1955 is ''Friday of the Passion and Death of the Lord''; before then it was ''Friday of Preparation [for the Pasch].'' This name was derived from Jewish usage. In the third century Good Friday was known as the Pasch of the Crucifixion as Easter was the Pasch of the Resurrection; the Eastern Churches have retained this use up to the present time. St. Ambrose called it ''Day of Bitterness.''

As it now stands in the Roman rite, the liturgical celebration of Good Friday differs little from what it has been for centuries. The dominant theme of the whole Good Friday liturgy is the mystery of the cross and its place in the overall paschal mystery of Redemption.

The solemn evening liturgical action consists of three distinct parts: (1) the service of readings and prayers, (2) the veneration of the cross, and (3) the Communion service. Until the late Middle Ages the aliturgical synaxis was held in the afternoon, but by the sixteenth century it had been pushed back into the morning hours. The decree of Pius XII in 1955 restored the earlier custom, allowing the service to begin between 3 P.M. and 8 P.M.

Service of Readings and Prayers. On this one day of the year, the Roman Church has retained the ancient custom of having only a service of reading and prayer on the stational days. Not only that, the first part of the Good Friday service has preserved many features of the first part of the early Roman daily eucharistic liturgy.

The first part of the service (except for the Prayers of the People) recalls the Passion of Our Lord. The reading service concludes with the Prayers of the People according to the ancient Roman solemn collect form. Certain significant changes were made in this Service of the Word by Pius XII's Holy Week Ordinal. The celebrant remains at the bench for everything except the Solemn Prayers; he sits and listens to the Lessons and joins in the chants. The people kneel for a short time before he says the Collects, and so forth.

Veneration of the Cross. When the Solemn Prayers of the People are over, the deacon brings from the sacristy a large veiled crucifix. The celebrant receives it from him and unveils it in the sight of the people singing the *Ecce lignum crucis,* inviting all to contemplate the mystery of the cross and the world's salvation. All venerate the sacred sign of our Redemption. After this general adoration of the cross, three times repeated, an individual veneration is made by all present.

While this is going on, the Reproaches or *IMPROPERIA* are sung, then other antiphons and the splendid hymn of ''Venantius Fortunatus,'' *Pange lingua,* which sings of the triumph of the cross and the victory of Christ. The rite concludes with *Crucem tuam,* borrowed from Byzantine sources.

The veneration of the cross, like other Holy Week rites, had its beginning in Jerusalem, where at first it was a popular devotion in the true sense of the term. The Spanish pilgrim nun Egeria (see under EGERIA, ITINERARIUM OF) tells us that in Jerusalem toward the end of the fourth century all the faithful of the city went out to Golgotha on Good Friday morning. There the bishop was seated on his chair surrounded by the deacons while a table covered with a white linen cloth was placed before him, and on that the relic of the true cross. He held the ends of the cross in his hands, while the deacons stood guard around the table. Then the faithful and the catechumens filed past and venerated the cross. All this was done in complete silence; no hymns or prayers accompanied the action [*Ethérie, Journal de Voyage,* ed. Hélène Pétré (*Sources Chrétiennes* 21; Paris 1948) 37.1–3].

In time other churches imitated the pious custom of the Church of Jerusalem, especially those fortunate enough to possess relics of the true cross. Those who did not used a wooden cross instead. It is important to remember that the rite of Veneration of the Cross was originally directed to the true cross itself.

We do not know for certain when this practice spread to Rome, but it must have been sometime about the middle of the seventh century, probably under Byzantine influence. The first description of the veneration as an element in the Good Friday services in Rome occurs in the eighth-century Roman Ordinal 23 (12–17; M. Andrieu, *Les 'Ordines Romani' du haut moyen-âge,* 5 v. [Louvain 1931–61] 3:270–271).

At two o'clock in the afternoon, the pope and the clergy went in procession from St. John Lateran to the nearby basilica of Holy Cross, carrying the relic of the cross in a silver casket, the pope walking barefoot before it, carrying a smoking censer. During the procession Psalm 118 was sung with *Ecce lignum* as a refrain.

When they arrived at Holy Cross, the stational church for Good Friday, they placed the relic upon the altar, where it remained while the pope and the clergy venerated it. The subdeacons then carried the relic to the people. While the adoration by the people was in progress, the synaxis began. Like the original practice of the Church of Jerusalem, the Roman veneration of the cross was really a private devotion.

Only gradually were psalms, hymns, and antiphons introduced to accompany the veneration. Most of the elements of the modern rite appeared for the first time in the tenth-century Romano-Germanic Pontifical of Mainz. During the twelfth century the showing of the cross to the people, with the *Ecce lignum,* was added; not long after that this showing took the threefold progressive form we know today. The evolution of the rite was completed in the fourteenth century by the change of place and the progressive raising of the voice during the singing of the *Ecce lignum.*

Communion Service. The last part of the Good Friday action is the Communion service. Historically, as a sign of mourning there was no Eucharistic celebration of any kind throughout the ancient Church on Good Friday, nor did anyone even receive Communion. Yet it would seem that on the day that recalled Our Lord's Passion, Christians would want to receive communion. And indeed it appears that in the course of time the consciousness of its fitness did bring about the desire to receive Communion on this day. Nevertheless there is no mention of Communion in the Roman rite before the eighth century; even then it appears to have been a custom recently introduced in the environs of Rome. Roman Ordinal 23 (21–22; Andrieu, 3:272) says that while neither the pope nor the clergy received Communion, the people could do so if they wished; if they did not go at Holy Cross they might go at any of the other ''titles'' in the city. Evidently then while Communion had no official place in the papal service, it was allowed to people in their parish churches. They were free to receive or not. But by the end of that same century, the Gelasian Sacramentary states simply, ''all communicate'' [ed. H. A. Wilson (Oxford 1894) 77], which seems to indicate that it was expected. Later the thirteenth-century Papal Pontifical says ''only the Pontiff communicates'' (43, 18; Andrieu, *Le Pontifical Romain au moyen-âge,* 4 v. [Rome 1938–41] 2:469). The Communion of the faithful had become increasingly rare by the thirteenth century. So at first they just stayed away and finally were *forbidden* to go at all. This prohibition was repeated several times during the seventeenth century, showing that at least in some places people continued to receive.

During the Middle Ages the earlier Communion service, much like that of today, was transformed under Gallican influence into the Mass of the Presanctified, which was obviously designed to give the service the appearance of a real Mass. Pius XII's Holy Week Ordinal suppressed this and restored the original Communion service with the significant difference that Communion is not distributed in silence as it once was, but accompanied by singing. Here we see the influence of the liturgical revival, which has tried to bring into relief the fact that the Eucharist is a communal Sacrament and so should be received in a communal setting.

Bibliography: W. J. O'SHEA, *The Meaning of Holy Week* (Collegeville, Minn. 1958). J. GAILLARD, *Holy Week and Easter,* tr. W. BUSCH (Collegeville, Minn. 1954). L. BOUYER, *The Paschal Mystery: Meditations on the Last Three Days of Holy Week,* tr. M. BENOIT (Chicago 1950). A. LÖHR, *The Great Week,* tr. D. T. H. BRIDGEHOUSE (Westminster, Md. 1958). H. A. SCHMIDT, *Hebdomada Sancta,* 2 v. (Rome 1956–57). T. J. TALLEY, *The Origins of the Liturgical Year* (Collegeville, Minn. 1991). A. J. MARTIMORT, ed., *The Church at Prayer IV: The Liturgy and Time* (Collegeville, Minn. 1986); A. NOCENT, *The Liturgical Year* (Collegeville, Minn. 1977) v. 1. Advent, Christmas, Epiphany.—v. 2. Lent.—v. 3. The Paschal Triduum, the Easter Season.—v. 4. Sundays nine to thirty-four in ordinary time. J. M. PIERCE, ''Holy Week and Easter in the Middle Ages,'' in *Passover and Easter: Origin and History to Modern Times*, eds. P. F. BRADSHAW and L. A. HOFFMAN (Notre Dame, Ind. 1999) 161–185. A. ADAM, *The Liturgical Year: Its History and Its Meaning after the Reform of the Liturgy* (New York 1981).

[W. J. O'SHEA/EDS.]

GOOD SHEPHERD

One of the oldest and most favored subjects of early Christian art is the Good Shepherd. It appears among the paintings of the catacombs of Rome, Naples, Sardinia, and Sicily and on sarcophagi of the East and West. However, it is by no means limited to the sepulchral field. As early as 210, Tertullian (*De pud.* 7.1; 10.12) spoke of chalices decorated with the picture of the Good Shepherd, and the number of lamps showing the same is considerable. It is found on ancient rings and gems, on glasses, and on medals. Among the remains of early Christian sculpture, statuettes of the Good Shepherd are the most beautiful pieces, such as the famous marble statuette now in the Lateran Museum in Rome. The picture of the Good Shepherd appeared at an early time among the paintings of liturgical buildings. Thus the frescoes of the baptismal chapel on the rear wall above the font at DURA-EUROPOS (Before 256) depict the Good Shepherd standing behind his flock, carrying a huge ram. About a century and a half later, four mosaics decorating the interior of the baptistery of S. Giovanni in Fonte (Naples) are representations of the Good Shepherd.

Though the picture of the Good Shepherd carrying the lamb on his shoulders is the most frequent type, He is depicted from the beginning in a great variety of scenes. The paintings of the catacombs display the Good Shepherd usually as a young and beardless man wearing a tunic, a shoulder cape, and high stockings—sometimes seated among his flock, sometimes with the shepherd's flute, sometimes protecting his lambs from aggression, and sometimes carrying a milk pail. But the favorite picture is that of the Good Shepherd with the animal on his shoulders. This figure has a long pre-Christian tradition. In early Christian art the Good Shepherd illustrates the Gospel parable of the lost sheep carried back to the fold (Lk 15.3–7; Jn 10.1–18) in a time-honored type.

Archeologists have drawn attention to many surviving statuettes of Hermes Criophoros, the protector of flocks, who carried a ram on his shoulders; and the representation of this subject is found not only in Greco-Roman times, but much earlier. In Syria and Assyria, reliefs have been discovered from the 8th and 10th centuries B.C. that portray a man bearing a gazelle on his shoulders. These older figures represent worshipers bringing animals for sacrifice. At least by the time of the ram-bearing Hermes of Greece, and perhaps even earlier, the thought of the Good Shepherd was introduced as a symbol of *philanthropia,* the great civil virtue. This explains the appearance of the figure of a good shepherd on pagan sarcophagi. In Christian art the type was conceived anew and filled with Christian meaning. The good shepherd became Christ Himself, especially as the Savior of the soul and of mankind.

Bibliography: J. QUASTEN, *Heilige Überlieferung: Festschrift Ildefons Herwegen,* ed. O. CASEL (Münster 1938) 51–58, Logos theology; *Pisciculi: Festschift Franz Joseph Dölger* (AntChr Suppl 1; 1939) 220–244, baptismal liturgy; "The Waters of Refreshment," *The Catholic Biblical Quarterly* 1 (1939) 325–332; *Miscellanea Giovani Mercati,* 6 v. (Rome 1946) 1:373–406, Liturgy of the Dead; *Mediaeval Studies* 9 (1947) 1–18, Dura–Europos. A. PARROT, *Mélanges Syriens offerts à R. Dussaud,* v.1 (Paris 1939) 171–182. P. BRUUN, *Acta Instituti Romani Finlandiae* 1.2 (1963) 146–149.

[J. QUASTEN]

GOOD SHEPHERD, SISTERS OF OUR LADY OF CHARITY OF THE

The Religious of Our Lady of Charity of the Good Shepherd (RGS, Official Catholic Directory #1830), popularly known as Sisters of the Good Shepherd, traces its origin to a group of women organized by (St.) John EUDES at Caen, France, in 1641 to reach out to wayward women and girls. This institute became known as Religious of Our Lady of Charity of the Refuge. Seven Houses of Refuge, each an autonomous community, had been established but were dispersed at the time of the French Revolution. The Refuge at Tours was struggling to reestablish itself when Rose-Virginie Pelletier entered the community in 1814. As Sister Maria Euphrasia, she revitalized the community when she became its superior at the age of 29 (*see* PELLETIER, MARIA EUPHRASIA, ST.). In 1829 she established a flourishing convent at Angers, followed by four additional foundations within five years. So successful was Mother Euphrasia's work among her charges that a complete transformation of life was effected for many of the girls. For some of these young women who wished to devote themselves to a life of prayer and penance, Mother Euphrasia established the religious community of Sisters Magdalens, which she regarded as the crown of her work.

Through her experience Mother Euphrasia recognized that a central motherhouse and novitiate would ensure unity in religious spirit and a sharing of resources and personnel. Her plans met with bitter opposition because some felt that her efforts were motivated by personal ambition. In 1835 Gregory XVI granted permission for a unified administration; and the convents of Angers, Grenoble, Poitiers, and Metz were united under the title of Sisters of Our Lady of Charity of the Good Shepherd. This new development, alive with the spirit of St. John Eudes and the zeal of Mother Euphrasia, enjoyed a phenomenal growth. In Mother Euphrasia's own lifetime, 110 foundations were made. In December 1842, five sisters, each of a different nationality, arrived from Angers to make the first American foundation at Louisville, Kentucky. Within 25 years convents were established at St. Louis, Missouri; Philadelphia, Pennsylvania; Cincinnati and Columbus, Ohio; New York and Brooklyn, New York; New Orleans, Louisiana; Chicago, Illlinois; Baltimore, Maryland; Boston, Massachusetts; and St. Paul, Minnesota.

The apostolate of the Sisters of the Good Shepherd is rooted in the appreciation of the dignity and worth of each individual. Mother Euphrasia taught each of her sisters how to be a true mother to the girls in her charge. Included in the heritage of the foundress is detailed advice regarding the approach to girls of varied emotional needs, in some ways anticipating modern psychotherapeutic techniques. For their specialized work, the sisters are trained as social workers, group mothers, psychologists, guidance counselors, teachers, recreation leaders, nurses, chaplains, and youth ministers.

Bibliography: B. STASIEWSKI, *Lexikon für Theologie und Kirche*, ed. J. HOFER and K. RAHNER, 10 v. (2d, new ed. Freiburg 1957–65) 5:389. G. BERNOVILLE, *Saint Mary Euphrasia Pelletier: Foundress of the Good Shepherd Sisters* (Westminster, Maryland 1959).

[M. ANDREOLI/EDS.]

GOOD SHEPHERD SISTERS OF QUEBEC

A congregation whose official title is Sisters, Servants of the Immaculate Heart of Mary (SCIM, Official Catholic Directory #3550). They were founded in Quebec, Canada, in 1850 by Genevieve Fitzbach Roy, who became first superior as Mother Mary of the Sacred Heart. The U.S. province with headquarters in Saco, Maine, was established in 1933, but the sisters have been in New England since 1882. Besides the personal sanctification of its members by the faithful observance of the three vows of religion, the chief work of the institute is the rehabilitation of wayward girls and the Christian education of youth. In the United States, the sisters work in parishes, schools, hospitals, homes for the aged, homes for unmarried mothers and adoption agencies. Their ministries include catechesis, youth ministries, counseling, retreat and spiritual direction.

Bibliography: ST. B. UPHAM, *Years of Shepherding* (Quebec 1950).

[M. G. LIRETTE/EDS.]

GOOD WORKS

Human acts, either internal or external, that are in conformity with the norms of morality are good works. This article discusses the nature of such good works and certain doctrinal questions about the relation of GRACE to these works.

Nature of Good Works. In some of his actions man acts by necessity. Thus sensation, respiration, and similar acts proceed indeed from man but not in his distinctively human mode of conduct. Other actions, properly called HUMAN ACTS, come from him precisely as he is intelligent and capable of free choice. These actions are expressions of his spiritual nature and are also called moral acts, for such deliberate choices involve a relationship to the norms of morality. Acts that conform to the norms of morality are called good; those that do not are evil. Theologians dispute whether INDIFFERENT ACTS form a distinct category of morality. Such human, or moral, acts include purely interior acts, as a particular act of choice, and external actions, as giving alms.

A standard, or rule, by which the goodness or evilness of an act is measured is called a norm of morality. Besides the immediate, subjective norm—the particular act of moral judgment called CONSCIENCE—there are objective standards of morality. The proximate, or created, norm is described in various ways by different Catholic theologians: for St. Thomas Aquinas it is right reason (*Summa theologiae,* 1a2ae, 19.3), for F. Suárez it is human nature. This norm is subject to a higher standard: the eternal law, which is the ordering by divine wisdom of all things to their goal. Aquinas explains the relation of the two norms: ''Now it is from the eternal law, which is divine reason, that human reason is the rule of the human will, that is, that from which its goodness is measured'' (*Summa theologiae,* 1a2ae, 19.4).

Various aspects of the human act must be examined in determining its morality: its object, the circumstances in which it is done, and its purpose, or motive. For an act to be morally good, all three aspects must conform to the norms of morality. Catholic theology recognizes that the most basic of these moral determinants is the object of the act, that to which the act by its nature is ordered. In recent years new emphasis was given to this recognition by the Holy See's condemnation of the theory of morality known as ethical existentialism or situational ethics. This theory tends to ignore objective moral standards and judge the moral act purely in terms of its individual circumstances [*see* J. C. Ford and G. A. Kelly, *Contemporary Moral Theology,* v.1 (Westminster, Md. 1958) 104–140].

Relation of Grace to Good Works. Pelagianism (5th century) and the teaching of the reformers (16th century) occasioned sharp controversies concerning the relationship of grace to good works. Three questions need to be answered: (1) Can any good works be done without grace? (2) Is grace necessary for every SALUTARY ACT (work)? (3) Are the good works of one already justified meritorious of SALVATION? This discussion is limited to the case of subjects capable of human acts and does not treat the question of the salvation of infants or others incapable of moral acts.

The answer to the first of these questions involves the distinction between natural and SUPERNATURAL acts. The validity of this distinction, common to Catholic theologians, is affirmed by the condemnation [H. Denzinger, *Enchiridion symbolorum,* ed. A. Schönmetzer (32d ed. Freiburg 1963) 1934, 1961] of the doctrine of Michel de Bay—known commonly by the Latin form of his name, BAIUS. Man, even in a state of fallen nature, can do some naturally good works, although he cannot do all natural good works collectively taken. At least part of this teaching may be restated thus: Not every act of a sinner is a sin. The reason advanced by theologians for the sinner being able to do some, but not all, naturally good works is that man's nature is not totally corrupted by sin, even though his inclination to virtue is weakened (cf. St. Thomas, *Summa theologiae* 1a2ae, 85.1–2; 109.2). St. Paul teaches that Gentiles did good works (Rom 2.14), and St. Augustine notes that sinners do some good works even though these do not lead to eternal salvation [*Spir. et litt.* 28.48; *Corpus scriptorum ecclesiasticorum latinorum* (Vienna 1866–) 60:203]. Exaggerated notions about the necessity of grace for every ethically good work have been rejected by the Church in the condemnation of the doctrine of Hus (H. Denzinger, *ibid.,* 1216), Luther (H. Denzinger, *ibid.,* 1481–82, 1486), Baius (H. Denzinger, *ibid.,* 1927–28, 1930, 1937), the Jansenists (H. Denzinger, *ibid.,* 2308, 2311), and Quesnel (H. Denzinger, *ibid.,* 2401, 2438).

The second question is concerned with the necessity of grace for salutary works, that is, those that are ordered in some way to supernatural happiness, or salvation. The impossibility of any supernaturally good work without the assistance of grace is clearly part of Catholic doctrine. For example, Christ explicitly affirms dependence on Himself (Jn 15.5), and St. Paul reminds his readers of their dependence on divine assistance (Phil 2.13; 2 Cor 3.5). St. Augustine, faithful witness to tradition, writes: ''We can do nothing toward the good works of piety without Him [God] either working that we will or working with us when we will'' [*Grat. et lib. arb.* 17.33; *Patrologia Latina,* ed. J. P. Migne, 217 v., indexes 4 v. (Paris 1878–90) 44:901]. In particular the Church teaches the necessity of actual grace for the beginning of justification. The good acts that dispose for habitual, or sanctifying, grace are the result in men of actual grace. See, for example, the doctrine of the Second Council of Orange (H. Denzinger, *ibid.,* 375–377) and the Council of Trent (H. Denzinger, *ibid.,* 1525, 1553, 1559).

The third question concerns the good works done after JUSTIFICATION. This particular problem received great attention because of Luther's assertion that man is saved by faith alone (*sola fide*) and that good works contribute nothing to salvation. In part this position represents a violent reaction to the writings of some theologians who tended toward Semi-Pelagianism. More basic, perhaps, is the Lutheran idea of justification, which denies any intrinsic transformation of man by God's justifying grace. Thus Luther would deny that man, when justified, is capable of performing works truly proportioned to his supernatural DESTINY.

Catholic theology, on the other hand, stresses the fact that the meritorious works are truly proportioned to man's supernatural goal but that they are possible only as a result of grace (*see* MERIT). They presuppose an ELEVATION and perfection of man and his powers through habitual grace and the infused virtues. Thus, justification intrinsically modifies man, changing him from a sinner to one who is holy (i.e., one who loves God above all). Divine assistance (i.e., actual grace) is also required for the actual performance of meritorious works. The Council of Trent sets forth the doctrine of justification in a prologue, 16 chapters, and 33 canons (H. Denzinger, *ibid.,* 1520–83). Canons 26 and 32 (H. Denzinger, *ibid.,* 1576, 1582) especially regard meritorious action.

See Also: IMPUTATION OF JUSTICE AND MERIT; GRACE, ARTICLES ON.

Bibliography: THOMAS AQUINAS, *Summa theologiae* 1a2ae, 18–21, 109–114. J. RIVIÈRE, ''Justification,'' *Dictionnaire de théologie catholique,* ed. A. VACANT et al., 15 v. (Paris 1903–50; Tables générales 1951–) 8.2:2164–92; ''Mérite,'' *Dictionnaire de théologie catholique,* ed. A. VACANT et al., 15 v. (Paris 1903–50; Tables générales 1951–) 10.1:574–785. L. MARCHAL, ''Moralité de l'acte humain,'' *Dictionnaire de théologie catholique,* ed. A. VACANT et al., 15 v. (Paris 1903–50; Tables générales 1951–) 10.2:2459–72. C. JOURNET, *The Meaning of Grace,* tr. A. V. LITTLEDALE (New York 1960). ''Joint Declaration on the Doctrine of Justification,'' *Origins* 28:8 (1998): 120–127.

[J. HENNESSEY]

GOODIER, ALBAN

Archbishop and spiritual writer; b. Great Harwood, Lancashire, England, April 14, 1869; d. St. Scholastica's Abbey, Teignmouth, March 13, 1939. He was educated at Stonyhurst, joined the Society of Jesus in 1887, was ordained in 1903, and made his solemn profession in 1906. In 1915, when superior of the Jesuit students in London, he was called to face the wartime crisis caused at the Jesuit Bombay University by the withdrawal of the entire professorial staff of German Jesuits. His tact in management soon established him as fellow and syndic of the university and a justice of peace. Appointed archbishop of Bombay in 1919, he was consecrated in Westminster Cathedral and took possession of his see Jan. 27, 1920. The administration of the Poona Diocese was added to his responsibilities in 1924. In Bombay, he was much loved by the people for his practical charities. However, the thorny politico-religious situation weighed heavily upon his sensitive nature, and on his quinquennial visit ad limina, he reported the facts to Pius XI. Advised not to return, he resigned Sept. 8, 1926, becoming titular archbishop of Hierapolis in Phrygia. After acting as auxiliary in London for Cardinal Bourne, he finally made St. Scholastica's Abbey his headquarters, and devoted himself to writing and to the giving of retreats, lectures, and sermons. His scholarly bent, simplicity, and deep piety are revealed in his writings, which have exercised a profound influence on many. Among his better-known works are: *The Public Life of Our Lord Jesus Christ* (1931); *The Passion and Death of Our Lord Jesus Christ* (1933); and *Introduction to the Study of Ascetical and Mystical Theology* (1939).

Bibliography: E. GRAF, "The Archbishop of Hierapolis," *Dublin Review* 205 (1939) 1–15. H. KEAN, "Alban Goodier (1869–1939)," *Month* 173 (1939) 408–415.

[W. PEERS-SMITH]

GOODMAN, GODFREY

Protestant bishop of Gloucester, only bishop of an English see since the Reformation reputed to have died in the Roman Catholic Church; b. Ruthin, Denbighshire, March 10, 1583; d. Westminster, Jan. 19, 1656. He was born of wealthy parents, Godfrey Goodman and his second wife, Jane Cruxton, and was educated at Westminster School (1592–99), under the care of his uncle Gabriel, who was dean. Godfrey took the B.A. (1604) and M.A. (1607) degrees at Trinity College, Cambridge. From 1606 to 1620 he was rector of a country parish at Stapleford Abbots in Essex. He held a number of livings in Berkshire, Gloucester, and Wales. An excellent preacher, writer, and stylistic disciple of Lancelot Andrewes, Goodman first achieved notice at court with the publication of *The Fall of Man* (1616). Appointed a canon of Windsor in 1617, he quickly rose in preferments to dean of Rochester (1621), then bishop of Gloucester (1625). His appointment to the bishopric through the influence of George Villiers, Duke of Buckingham, rather than by the nomination of William LAUD, then bishop of St. David's, later archbishop of Canterbury, earned him Laud's lifelong enmity. A sermon Goodman delivered before the King in 1626 "pressed so hard upon the point of the Real Presence, that he was supposed to trench too near the borders of Popery" (Peter Heylin, *Cyprianus Anglicus*). Although censured in convocation by Laud for the sermon, Goodman continued in good standing in the House of Lords. In 1628, the Puritan element in Commons (William Prynne, Henry Burton, and John Bastwick) petitioned against his Romanism. Lucius Cary, Viscount Falkland, undoubtedly referred chiefly to Goodman in his speech against bishops in the Long Parliament some years later, when he spoke of some who have "found a way to reconcile the opinions of Rome to the preferments of England, and to be so absolutely, directly, and cordially Papist, that it is all £1,500 a year can do to keep them from confessing it." Only in his will did Goodman openly confess his spiritual allegiance to Rome.

The date of his conversion is not known, although it is thought to be as early as 1636, through his longtime friend the Jesuit William Claybrooke (alias Hanmer). In that same year, Gregorio PANZANI, papal emissary to England, noted Goodman's great desire for reunion with the Church of Rome. In convocation in 1640, Goodman refused to sign, or accept, canons requiring greater efforts in the detection and punishment of Catholics. He was deprived of his see by Laud, and committed to the Gate-House, where he was kept until he subscribed to the canons three months later. Ironically, Goodman was then impeached, committed to the Tower, and fined £2,000 by the House of Commons for his share in framing the same canons, which was considered an illegal infringement on Parliamentary rights. Goodman joined in the protest of the bishops in the House of Lords in December 1641, and was again committed to the Tower on a charge of high treason. While he was imprisoned, his property at Gloucester was plundered, and he was ejected from his canonry and bishopric. On regaining his freedom, Goodman retired to the home of a Catholic, Mrs. Silbylla Agliomby, at Westminster, where he died, attended by his friend and confessor, the Franciscan Christopher Davenport. Though wanting in moral courage, Goodman was noted for kindliness, tolerance, and great charity. A noted historian, he wrote *The Court of King James the First,* which is still of considerable historical value.

Bibliography: G. GOODMAN, *The Court of King James the First,* ed. J. S. BREWER, 2 v. (London 1839). G. I. SODEN, *Godfrey Goodman, Bishop of Glouster, 1583–1656* (London 1953), bibliog. S. LEE, *The Dictionary of National Biography From the Earliest Times to 1900* (London 1885–1900), 8:131–134. J. GILLOW, *A Literary and Biographical History or Bibliographical Dictionary of the English Catholics from 1534 to the Present Time* (London and New York, 1885–1902), 2:528–530, some errors.

[J. O. HANLON]

GOOSSENS, PIERRE LAMBERT

Archbishop of Mechelen, organizer of Catholic education in Belgium; b. Perck, Belgium, July 17, 1827; d. Mechelen, Jan. 2, 1906. From his family, which was in comfortable circumstances, he inherited distinguished manners. After a solid humanistic training, and his ordination (Dec. 25, 1850), he acted as professor (1851) and pastor at St. Rombaut in Mechelen, where he demonstrated great pastoral zeal and administrative ability. He became secretary to the archbishop of Mechelen (1856), vicar-general (1878), bishop of Namur (1883), archbishop of Mechelen (24 March 1884), and cardinal (1889).

During the politicoreligious difficulties in Belgium caused by the pressures of secular liberalism, and the disagreement between liberal and ultramontane Caththolics, he was entrusted on different occasions with conciliatory missions by the government and the Holy See. As archbishop he upheld the Catholic party. He maintained unity by taking inspiration, although only after some delay, from Leo XIII's *RERUM NOVARUM;* and by keeping peace between conservatives and democrats. He promoted social works and favored the political advancement of the working class. Convinced, however, of the necessity of having the bourgeoisie in the directing role, he created for their benefit ten establishments for instruction in the humanities. Penetrated as he was with a sense of authority, he slowed the renewal of THOMISM and the personal efforts of Mercier.

Bibliography: J. MUYLDERMANS, *Zijn Eminentie Kardinaal Goossens* (Mechlin 1922). P. PIRRI, *Lexikon für Theologie und Kirche* (Freiburg 1957), 2 4:1055.

[A. SIMON]

GORDIAN AND EPIMACHUS, SS.

Martyrs; d. *c.* 362 and 250, respectively. The cult of Gordian and Epimachus has been well attested in Western Christendom since the sixth century; the Roman MARTYROLOGY and most of the other martyrologies commemorate them on May 10. There is no doubt about their historic existence and early cult, but their legends are fictitious and even their identity is uncertain. Gordian is known to have been a young boy, but legend made him a judge in Rome who embraced Christianity during the reign of JULIAN THE APOSTATE and was decapitated in 362. He was buried in the tomb of St. Epimachus.

Epimachus may have been an Alexandrian martyr thrown into a lime kiln in 250 whose remains were subsequently translated to Rome, or a Roman martyr of the same name of whom nothing is known. Another unsubstantiated legend states that the relics of Gordian and Epimachus were subsequently translated by Bl. HILDEGARD OF KEMPTEN, Charlemagne's wife, to the Abbey of Kempten in Bavaria.

Feast: May 10.

Bibliography: *Acta Sanctorum*, May 2:549–553. E. JOSI, *Revista de archeologia cristiana* 16 (1939) 21–37, 42–47; 17 (1940) 31–35. W. HOTZELT, *Römiske Quartalschrift für christliche Altertumskunde und für Kirchengeschichte* 46 (1938) 1–17.

[J. BRÜCKMANN]

GORDON RIOTS

The Gordon Riots occurred in June 1780, beginning as an anti-Catholic demonstration and ending in mob violence that terrorized London for ten days. The proximate excuse was the first Catholic Relief Act of June 1778, a moderate measure that freed priests from the threat of imprisonment and enabled Catholics to take an oath of loyalty to the Crown. Catholics were apprehensive of the effect of the Act on extreme Protestants, but at first all seemed to pass quietly. When it was proposed in the following year to apply the Act to Scotland, these fears were justified. The rioting that broke out in Edinburgh and Glasgow was suppressed with difficulty and caused the Scottish Act to be withdrawn. Opposition to the English Act was stimulated by this Scottish success. A Protestant association was formed in London in February 1779 led by Lord George Gordon, 27-year-old Member of Parliament, whose eccentric behavior often amused his fellow members and indicated a mental unbalance verging on derangement. The association was supported by many middle-class nonconformists who had no thoughts of violence, including John Wesley, who wrote a pamphlet in its support.

It was decided to draw up a petition and present it to Parliament in the most public manner. Supporters gathered in St. George's Fields, Southwark (where the Catholic cathedral now stands) on Friday, June 2, 1780. The petition, said to contain 120,000 signatures, was taken in procession to Westminster. The participants in the march, variously estimated from 20,000 to 50,000, were at first orderly, but by the time they reached the Palace yard they had been joined by riffraff who turned the march into a mob, assaulting Peers and Commoners as they entered the Houses of Parliament. Gordon presented the petition in the Commons, but his hysterical rushing back and forth to report to the mob incited it to violence and alienated his more respectable supporters who returned to their homes. While a troop of guards cleared the approaches of the besieged Parliament, detachments of the mob looted and burned the Catholic chapels in Golden Square, Lincoln's Inn Fields, and Moorfields. The Lord Mayor, the Council of the City of London, and the magistrates took no serious steps to quell the rioting. Many refused to act, as they sympathized with the ''No-popery'' cry. Some of the mob sought out 89-year-old Bp. Richard CHALLONER, Vicar Apostolic, but he was taken to a friend's house in Finchley.

The rioting, which was less violent on Saturday and Sunday, increased during the next two days, making it clear that by now anti-Catholic feeling was being replaced by mob hooliganism. Newgate prison as well as the houses of magistrates and of unpopular public figures were burned. Even Lambeth Palace was threatened. Lord Stormont, the Secretary of State, had urged from the beginning that the Lord Mayor and the military authorities take firm action, but his repeated appeals resulted in the ineffective use of inadequate forces. The military believed they could act only at the request of a magistrate.

Caricature depicting soldiers marching over victims in the Gordon Riots, 1787. (©Corbis)

At a privy council on Wednesday, June 7, this idea was corrected and King George III gave orders that the utmost vigor be used to restore peace. Troops were at once moved to London, and that night they drove off an attack on the Bank of England, but not before the three prisons—the King's Bench, the Clink, and the Fleet—had been set in flames. A distillery in Holborn was also set on fire, resulting in an orgy of drunkenness. Meanwhile, now that private property was endangered, the citizens organized patrols for their own protection. On Thursday the troops took effective control and the worst was over. The official number of those killed or dead of injuries was 285, certainly an underestimate. Fifty-nine prisoners were sentenced to death, of whom 21 were hanged.

Lord George Gordon was sent to the Tower on June 9, brought to trial on Feb. 5, 1781, and acquitted of the charge of treason, a verdict endorsed by modern legal opinion. He was later converted to Judaism and died in the rebuilt Newgate in 1793 during imprisonment for libel. Though the riots were confined generally to London, there were minor outbreaks in Hull and Bath, where Catholic chapels were burned. The Common Council of the City of London petitioned Parliament without success to repeal the Relief Act. The riots made Catholics more circumspect than ever in the exercise of their religion, and a decade was to pass before another modest installment of relief from penal legislation was granted.

Bibliography: T. HOLCROFT, *A Plain and Succinct Narrative of the Late Riots* (2d ed. London 1780). W. MAWHOOD, *The Mawhood Diary* (London 1956). T. R. HOWELL, ed., *A Complete Collection of State Trials and Proceedings for High Treason and Other Misdemeanours* 22 (London 1814) 485–652. J. P. DE CASTRO, *The Gordon Riots* (London 1926). *The Dictionary of National Biography From the Earliest Times to 1900*, 63 v. (London 1885–1900; repr. with corrections, 21 v., 1908–09, 1921–22, 1938) 8:197. C. HIBBERT, *King Mob* (London 1958). R. WATSON, *The Life Of Lord George Gordon* (London 1795). P. COLSON, *The Strange History of Lord George Gordon* (London 1937).

[E. E. REYNOLDS]

GORE, CHARLES

Anglican bishop, theologian; b. Wimbledon, Surrey, England, Jan. 23, 1853; d. London, Jan. 17, 1932. Of aristocratic descent, Gore was educated at Harrow and at Balliol College, Oxford (1870–75). After ordination (1878) he served as a curate in various parishes until he became vice principal of Cuddesdon Theological College (1880). As warden of Pusey House at Oxford (1884–93), he made a notable impact on the undergraduates, took an interest in social questions, and was active in the Christian Social Union. His visit to the Oxford Mission in Calcutta and his resultant experience of India profoundly influenced his life and spirituality. He founded at Oxford in 1892 an Anglican religious order, the Community of the Resurrection (which moved later to Mirfield, Yorkshire), and acted as its superior until 1901. In 1894 he became a canon of Westminster, where his preaching drew large crowds. Despite protests of conservative churchmen, he was named bishop of Worcester (1902). After a division of his diocese, he became the first bishop of Birmingham (1905). He was bishop of Oxford from 1911 until 1919, when he resigned to become dean of theology at Kings College, London. Gore's Anglo-Catholicsm was tinged with a degree of Modernism that distressed conservatives such as Henry Parry Liddon. They were disturbed especially by Gore's views on the limitation and growth of Our Lord's human knowledge (kenotism). Gore was strongly anti-Roman; indeed his rigidity as episcopal visitor of the Anglican Benedictine community at Caldey contributed to their submission to the Holy See in 1913. Abp. Randall DAVIDSON sent him to the MALINES CONVERSATIONS to exert a moderating influence on the more extreme ANGLO-CATHOLICS there. Gore also opposed the Lambeth Conference of bishops in their plans for reunion with the church of South India and on contraception. Gore edited LUX MUNDI (1889) and *A New Commentary on Holy Scripture* (1928), both expressive of a somewhat Modernist viewpoint. Among his own writings, the most notable are *Roman Catholic Claims* (1888), *The Ministry of the Christian Church* (1888, new ed. 1919), *The Incarnation of the Son of God* (1891), *The Body of Christ* (1901), and *The Reconstruction of Belief* (1926).

Bibliography: G. L. PRESTIGE, *Life of Charles Gore* (London 1935). A. DUNELM and A. T. P. WILLIAMS, *Dictionary of National Biography from the Earliest Times to 1900* (London 1931–40) 349–353. F. L. CROSS, *The Oxford Dictionary of the Christian Church* (London 1957) 571–572.

[W. HANNAH]

Charles Gore. (©CORBIS/Bettman)

GORETTI, MARIA, ST.

Martyr; b. Corinaldo (Ancona), Italy, Oct. 16, 1890; d. Nettuno (Roma), Italy, July 6, 1902. Maria, or Marietta as she was familiarly known, was born of poor, pious parents. Luigi, the father, moved with his family to Colle Gianturco in the region of the Pontine marshes and in 1899 to Ferriere di Conca, where he lived as a tenant farmer on the estate of Count Mazzolini. In 1900 Luigi died, leaving his wife Assunta with six small children. While the mother labored in the fields, Maria took care of the household. She never had the opportunity to attend school and was unable to read or write. The pious young girl received her first Communion May 29, 1902. The neighboring Serenelli family had a son Alessandro, aged 19, who sought in vain to seduce Maria and threatened her with death if she revealed his designs. On July 5, 1902, Alessandro entered the Goretti home with a dagger during the mother's absence. Maria repulsed his advances and told him: ''No, God does not wish it. It is a sin. You would go to hell for it.'' The youth then stabbed the girl repeatedly. She died the next day in the hospital at Nettuno after forgiving her murderer. Many miracles were reported at her tomb. For some years Alessandro was noted by the prison authorities for his surly, brutal disposition. When he eventually repented, he attributed his conversion to the intercession of his victim. After his release from prison he worked to advance her cause for beatification. Maria was beatified April 28, 1947, and canonized June 24, 1950, at a ceremony held (unprecedently) in St. Peter's Square and attended by some 250,000 persons, including the saint's mother. Maria's remains repose in the church of Our Lady of Grace in Nettuno.

Feast: July 6.

Bibliography: M. C. BUEHRLE, *Saint Maria Goretti* (Milwaukee 1950). A. MACCONASTAIR, *Lily of the Marshes: The Story of Maria Goretti* (New York 1951)

[M. C. BUEHRLE]

GORGONIA, ST.

Matron and martyr; d. *c.* 375. Gorgonia was the daughter of St. Gregory Nazianzen the Elder (bishop of Nazianzos, *c.* 328–374; b. *c.* 276; d. 374) and of St. Nonna (d. 374); she was also the sister of St. GREGORY OF NAZIANZUS. The only significant source for her life is her funeral oration, which was preached by her brother, Gregory (*Patrologia Graeca* 35:789–817). Gorgonia appears to have been married and the mother of at least three children. She is said to have been twice cured of severe illness through faith in the will of God, but appears to have put off baptism until the end of her life. An incident described by Gregory has been taken to refer to the reservation of the Blessed Sacrament, but modern scholars question its significance.

Feast: Dec. 9.

Bibliography: F. L. CROSS *The Oxford Dictionary of the Christian Church* (London 1957) 572. H. THURSTON, *Journal of Theological Studies* 11 (1909–10) 275–279, Eucharist.

[J. BRÜCKMANN]

GORKUM, MARTYRS OF

Nineteen priests and religious hanged by Calvinists because of their Catholic beliefs, in Briel near Dordrecht, Holland, July 9, 1572. They were beatified Nov. 24, 1675, and canonized June 29, 1867: Nicholas Pieck and Jerome Weerden, guardian and vicar of the Franciscan monastery of the Observance in Gorkum, and nine other Franciscans from Gorkum; a Canon Regular of St. Augustine, John Van Oosterwyk; a Dominican, John Van Hoornaer from Cologne, who had gone to the aid of the Franciscans when he heard they had been taken; two Premonstratensians, Adrian Van Hilvarenbeek and James Lacops; and four secular priests, Godfrey Van Duyen, Nicholas Janssen-Poppel, Leonard Vechel, and Andrew Wouters Van Heynoert. The anti-Spanish Calvinist ''Sea Beggars,'' in the struggle for independence from Spain, seized Gorkum June 26, 1572, and imprisoned the religious, who were treated with cruelty by soldiers on the hunt for sacred vessels. On July 7 at the order of Admiral Lumaye, Baron de la Marck, they were marched to Briel half-naked in procession, singing the Litany of the Saints. There they were confronted with Calvinist ministers and subjected to lengthy interrogation. They were offered their liberty if they would abandon belief in the Real Presence and papal primacy. The magistrates of Gorkum and the Prince of Orange protested the illegal detention of the prisoners and demanded their release, but the admiral refused unless they would abjure the primacy of the pope. When they again refused, they were taken to a sacked and deserted monastery on the outskirts of Briel and hanged. One of the Franciscans was 90 years old, and two other martyrs were 70.

Feast: July 9.

Bibliography: *Acta Sanctorum*, July 2:736–847. F. VAN DEN BORNE, *De Katholieke Encyclopaedie* 12:96–97. W. LAMPEN, *Lexikon für Theologie und Kirche* 2 4:1057–58. G. MARSOT, *Catholicisme* 5:104.

[F. D. S. BORAN]

GÖRRES, JOHANN JOSEPH VON

German Catholic publicist, lay theologian, political philosopher, and romantic mystic; b. Coblenz, Jan. 25, 1776; d. Munich, Jan. 29, 1848. He was the single most influential and formative force in the 19th-century German Catholic thought. Although he was a typical product of the ENLIGHTENMENT, hostile to all religion, and an enthusiastic supporter of the French Revolution, his books and editorial activities mark his progress toward a deep Catholic mysticism and a moderate conservatism. He was the author of *Glauben und Wissen* (1805), *Mythengeschichte der asiatischen Welt* (1810), *Deutschland und die Revolution* (1819), *Die christliche Mystik* (1836–42), *Athanasius* (1837), and *Die Wallfahrt nach Trier* (1845). He founded (1814) and edited the *Rheinische Merkur* until its suppression in 1816, and published a collection of folktales, *Deutsche Volksbücher* (1807). In 1827 he became professor and dominating spirit at the University of Munich. Here, he and his circle published two journals, *Eos* (1828–32) and the *Historischpolitische Blätter* (from 1838). Görres became a leader in the renewal of Catholic life and thought that accompanied the Romantic movement. He demanded a free Church, independent of the State, but at the same time he rejected ULTRAMONTANISM. His thought was vague and sentimental and his mysticism verged on the fanciful, but his ''Munich circle'' energized the whole of German Catholic Life.

Bibliography: *Gesammelte Schriften,* ed. M. GÖRRES, 9 v. (Munich 1854–74); critical ed. W. SCHELBERG (Cologne 1926–). J. GALLAND, *Johann von Görres* (2d ed. Freiburg 1876). J. N. SEPP, *Görres und seine Zeitgenossen* (Nördlingen 1877). A. DRU, *The Church in the Nineteenth Century: Germany 1800–1918* (London 1963). L. JUST, *Lexikon für Theologie und Kirche* (Freiburg 1957–), 2 4:1058–60, esp. bibliog.

[S. J. TONSOR]

GÖRRES-GESELLSCHAFT

A German Catholic society devoted to scholarly research and publication. It was founded by Georg von Hertling in 1876, the centenary of the birth of Johann von GÖRRES. It soon formed a bulwark of Catholic scholarly resistance to the KULTURKAMPF. The presidents of this private organization have been: Georg von Hertling (1876–1919), Hermann von Grauert (1919–24), Heinrich Finke (1924–38), and Hans Peters (1940-). The society relies on scientific teamwork and international collaboration continued from generation to generation. The original four sections have increased to 12: philosophy, natural science and technology, history, civil and canon law and political science, economics and social sciences, pedagogy, psychology and psychotherapy, archeology, linguistics and literature, Christian Oriental studies, fine arts, and folklore. Theological topics are pursued solely in their historical aspects. After being suppressed in 1941 by the Nazis, the society revived after World War II. In 1964 it had 1,650 members. Annual meetings are held in various German cities or outside the country (as in 1963 at Trent). Abroad the society maintains the Roman Institute (since 1888), the Oriental Institute in Jerusalem (1908), and the Spanish Institute in Madrid (1926). In 1957 the International Institute for Relations between Natural Science and Faith opened in Munich.

The society continues to publish the following periodicals: *Historisches Jahrbuch* (founded in 1880), *Römische Quartalschrift* (1887), *Philosophisches Jahrbuch* (1888), *Oriens Christianus* (1911), *Literaturwissenschaftliches Jahrbuch* (1926), *Kunstwissenschaftliches Jahrbuch* (1928), *Volk und Volkstum. Jahrbuch für Volkskunde* (1936), and *Jahrbuch für Psychologie und Psychotherapie* (1952). Between 1887 and 1963 the society sponsored six editions of the *Staatslexikon* (6th ed. 8 v. 1957–63). It also sponsored the first three volumes of Konrad EUBEL, *Hierarchia catholica medii aevi* (1898–1910). Between 1901 and 1965 the society published 12 volumes of the acts of the Council of TRENT, *Concilium Tridentinum.* Other collections of sources and results of research that have appeared under the same auspices are: *Quellen und Forschungen aus dem Gebiet der Geschichte* (1900–), *Studien und Darstellungen aus dem Gebiet der Geschichte* (1901–), *Studien zur Geschichte und Kultur des Altertums* (1907–). *Collectanea Hierosolymitana* (1917–), *Schriften zur deutschen Literatur* (1926–), *Spanische Forschungen* (1928–), and *Forschungen zur Geschichte der Philosophie der Neuzeit* (1931–). Utilizing the Vatican Archives, the society has been publishing *Vatikanische Quellen zur Geschichte der päpstlichen Hof- und Finanzverwaltung im 14 Jahrhundert* (1910–) and *Veröffentlichungen zur Kirchen- und Papstgeschichte der Neuzeit* (1929–). The society's section for legal and political studies has issued volumes since 1908, and the section for social and economic subjects, since 1927. Sixteen volumes have appeared since 1926 in the complete edition of the works of Görres.

Bibliography: W. SPAEL, *Die Görres-Gesellschaft, 1876–1941* (Paderborn 1957) J. SPÖRL, *Staatslexicon* 3:1007–09.

[N. BACKMUND]

GORRITI, JUAN IGNACIO DE

Argentine priest and politician; b. Jujuy, Argentina, 1766; d. Sucre, Bolivia, 1842. After receiving his doctorate in Córdoba, he served in various parishes. Later he was archdean of the Cathedral of Salta and for several years served as chaplain in the army of Belgrano. Gorriti was one of the most able political thinkers in the Argentine independence movement of 1811, winning many capable men to the cause through his political tracts. He was one of the first to support the idea of a federal form of government for the new nation, similar to that of the U.S., but reserving autonomy to the states. He served as deputy to Buenos Aires from Jujuy and later was active as a member of the house of representatives in Salta. In 1829, having changed to the Unitarian party, he was elected governor of Salta. Soon afterward he fled to Bolivia for fear of reprisals by the Federalists. In Bolivia he was protected by Santa Cruz and became rector of the Colegio Junín in Sucre. In exile he wrote his famous *Reflexiones* on sociology, pedagogy, and government (1836). As a governor, he was concerned with the general well-being of the people and with furthering public education. He was an effective political orator and an excellent preacher.

Bibliography: J. I. DE GORRITI, *Papeles del Dr. Juan Ignacio de Gorriti,* ed. M. A. VERGARA (Jujuy, Arg. 1936).

[M. A. VERGARA]

GORZE, ABBEY OF

A former BENEDICTINE monastery on the Gorze River in the *arrondissement* and Diocese of Metz,

France. It was founded in 749 by Bp. CHRODEGANG OF METZ and soon flourished. It was responsible for the reform of Gengenbach in 761 and the settling of LORSCH in 765, and soon over 25 villages and 45 parishes made up its secular and religious domain. Decline set in with the introduction of COMMENDATION in 825 until finally Bp. Adalbero I of Metz in 933 gave the ruined monastery to the archdeacon Einold of Toul and to JOHN OF GORZE, who wished to establish a more austere community. The reform movement that had its start in Gorze as well as in Saint-Evre in Toul and SAINT-MAXIMIN in Trier came to be known as the reform of Gorze when numerous communities adopted its customs under the Abbots Einold (933–967), John of Gorze (967–976), Immo (976–1016), Siegfried (1016–55), and Henry the Good (1055–93). This monastic federation, eventually counting over 170 houses, did not seek exemption from episcopal authority, nor did it tend toward centralization, as was the case with the equally famous reform movement instituted by CLUNY. Besides Gorze, whose immediate affiliation counted 31 monasteries, the principal centers of the movement were Saint-Maximin in Trier, SANKT EMMERAM in Regensburg, NIEDERALTAICH, Lorsch, Fulda, Mainz-St. Alban, EINSIEDELN, Schwarzach on the Main, and Ilsenburg. Emperor HENRY II imposed the customs of Gorze on several unwilling communities such as the Abbey of REICHENAU in 1006. As Gorze's spiritual power declined, it became a feudal principality, gaining the right of minting in 1095 and of fortifying the abbey in 1173. The monastery, again under commendatary abbots after 1468, saw French and Spanish troops fight over its territories from 1543 to 1552. At the request of Gorze's abbot, Cardinal Charles I of Lorraine (d. 1574, *see* LORRAINE, CARDINALS OF), Pope GREGORY XIII secularized the monastery in 1572. In 1580, 12 canons with their abbot took the place of the monks. Duke Charles IV of Lorraine ceded the territory of Gorze to France in 1661, and the chapter was suppressed in 1790. The various buildings that still remain have been put to other uses.

Bibliography: Sources. *Monumenta Germaniae Historica: Scriptores* (Berlin 1826–) 4:333–377; 15:973–977. Literature. L. H. COTTINEAU, *Répertoire topobibliographique des abbayes et prieurés*, 2 v. (Mâcon 1935–39) 1:1303–04. C. WOLFF, "Die Gorzer Reform in ihrem Verhältnis zu deutschen Klöstern," *Elsass-lothringisches Jahrbuch* 9 (1930) 95–111. W. WATTENBACH, *Deutschlands Geschchtsquellen im Mittelalter. Deutsche Kaiserzeit*, ed. R. HOLTZMANN, v.1.1–4 (3d ed. Tübingen 1948; repr. of 2d ed. 1938–43) 1:180–186, 596–597. K. HALLINGER, *Gorze-Kluny*, 2 v. (*Studia anselmiana* 22–25; 1950–51); *Die Religion in Geschichte und Gegenwart*, 7 v. (3d ed. Tübingen 1957–65) 2:1695–96. H. BÜTTNER, "Verfassungsgeschichte und lothring. Klosterreform," in *Aus Mittelalter und Neuzeit: Festschrift G. Kallen* (Bonn 1957) 17–27. L. GAILLARD, "Gorze et St-Riquier," *Mélanges de science religieuse* 17 (1960) 143–151. J. FLECKENSTEIN, *Lexikon Für Theologie und Kirche*, ed. J. HOFER and K. RAHNER, 10 v. (2d, new ed. Freiburg 1957–65) 4:1061–62. R. GAZEAU, *Catholicisme. Hier, aujourd'hui et demain*, ed. G. JACQUEMET (Paris 1947–) 5:110–111.

[A. A. SCHACHER]

GOSLING, SAMUEL

Liturgist; b. Stone, Staffordshire, England, April 18, 1883; d. Oct. 8, 1950. He was ordained in 1908. While serving as an army chaplain in World War I, he became convinced that the retention of Latin as the sole liturgical language of the Roman rite was a serious handicap to pastoral work. In those days, such a view was so novel as to seem revolutionary and even shocking. For some years Gosling spread it only by word of mouth among trusted friends, but in 1942 he ventured to write an article on the subject and offered it to the English *Catholic Herald.* The editor risked publishing it, and the result was such a spate of letters in the correspondence columns that Gosling felt the time was ripe for action.

In 1943, he founded the English Liturgy Society for priests and laity who "desired to promote the use of the mother tongue in public worship so far as is consonant with the doctrines and traditions of the Church." In 1944, he launched a small periodical, *The English Liturgist,* which he edited until his death. He wrote many articles for other periodicals, courageously advocating, against bitter opposition, the need for English in the liturgy. After his death his views continued to spread, and were finally vindicated by Vatican Council II in its *Constitution on the Sacred Liturgy,* Dec. 4, 1963. The foundation of the American Vernacular Society in 1946 is attributed largely to the influence of this far-sighted and apostolic priest.

[C. W. HOWELL]

GOSPEL

The good news about Jesus Christ and the salvation that He brings to mankind. The English word gospel comes from the Anglo-Saxon term *gōd* (good) *spell* (tale), a correct translation of the Greek word εὐαγγέλιον (good news), which was taken over bodily into Latin as *evangelium.*

In the New Testament. The New Testament usage of the term εὐαγγέλιον depends less on the usage of the word in classical literature, where it seldom has a religious connotation, than on its usage in the Septuagint, where the cognate verb εὐαγγελίζω (to announce good news) is employed to translate the Hebrew verb *bissēr,* especially in the Deutero-Isaian sense of announcing the glad tidings of Yahweh's eschatological salvation (Is 40.9; 52.7; 60.6; 61.1).

Jesus used the word gospel only in this sense, as the fulfilling of the prophecy of Deutero-Isaiah: He was God's messenger announcing the good news of divine salvation to the poor (Lk 4.16–19; 7.22; Mt 11.5). The good news that He proclaimed was ''the gospel of the KINGDOM OF GOD'' (Mk 1.14–15; See also Mt 4.23; 9.35; 24.14). It was a message, not of something that had happened (the ordinary non-Biblical sense of the word), but of what was about to take place.

For the Apostles, however, the gospel was the glad tidings of the divine salvation that Jesus as the Messiah had won for men by His Passion, death, and Resurrection (Acts 5.42; 14.6, 20; 15.20; etc.). Such use of the term is common especially in the writings of St. Paul, who employed the noun εὐαγγέλιον about 60 times (Rom 1.1, 9, 15–16; etc.) and the verb εὐαγγελίζω about 20 times. He called his message ''the gospel of God'' (Rom 1.1; 15.16; 2 Cor 11.7; etc.) because it came from God, ''the gospel of Christ'' (Rom 15.19; 1 Cor 9.12; 2 Cor 2.12; 9.13; etc.) because it concerned Jesus Christ and His redemptive work, and ''my gospel'' (Rom 2.16; 2 Tm 2.8; etc.), not as if Paul's message of salvation differed in any essential way from that of the other Apostles (Gal 1.6–9), but because he received it directly from Christ (Gal 1.11–12; 1 Cor 15.3), who made him an outstanding ''minister of the gospel'' (Col 1.23).

Although the gospel that the Apostles proclaimed was concerned primarily with the mystery of Redemption, the earthly life of Jesus as far as it was known to them, i.e., His public ministry, formed part of their preaching also (Acts 10.34–43). This is the meaning of the word gospel as it is used in verse 1 of St. Mark's Gospel: ''The beginning of the gospel of Jesus Christ, the Son of God,'' which means: this is how the good news concerning Jesus Christ begins. Neither here nor anywhere else in the New Testament is the term used in the sense of a written Gospel. The custom of using the term as the name of a book began in the second century (Justin, *Apol.* 1.66; *Dial.* 10.2). The early Church always remembered that there was only one gospel; the New Testament never employed the term in the plural. Therefore it spoke only of the four-fold form of the one gospel: ''the Gospel according to Matthew [κατὰ Ματθαῖον],'' ''the Gospel according to Mark,'' etc.

In the Liturgy. The public reading or singing of a PERICOPE or selection from the Gospels before the celebration of the Eucharist forms part of the liturgy in all Christian rites. The importance of this ceremony is shown by the special reverence that is given to the Gospel Book, e.g., by its being carried in procession with candles and incense at more solemn services, by its being read from a special ambo or pulpit, by its reader having to be at least a deacon, by the standing of the congregation during its reading, and by other ceremonies (at least in the Roman rite, the greeting to the faithful before the reading, the doxology—''Glory be to you, Lord!''—at the end, and the kissing of the book by the reader). The term Gospel is also applied to the selection read.

Bas-relief with gospel scenes from Cathedral of Altamura, Altamura, Italy, 1232. (©Vanni Archive/CORBIS)

In the 13th century the custom arose of reading Jn 1.1–14a as the so-called Last Gospel at the end of the Roman Mass as an additional blessing on the people. Later, some other selection from the four Gospels was occasionally substituted for Jn 1.1–14a as the Last Gospel. The Roman Missal (1570) of PIUS V made the reading of the Last Gospel obligatory for almost all Masses of the Roman rite, but this custom was abolished in the liturgical reform of 1964.

See Also: EVANGELIST; LECTIONARIES.

Bibliography: J. HUBY, *L'Évangile et les Évangiles* (3d ed. Paris 1954). J. SCHMID and J. A. JUNGMANN, *The Mass of the Roman*

Rite, 2 vols. (New York 1950). *Encyclopedic Dictionary of the Bible*, tr. and adap. by L. HARTMAN (New York 1963) 888–890.

[L. F. HARTMAN]

GOSPEL SONG

A type of popular religious song that emerged in the U.S. during the 19th century (also called gospel hymn or gospel music). As early as 1644 the term ''Gospel Musick''—used as the title of a Puritan tract by Nathaniel Homes—was taken to mean the kind of popular congregational song inspired by ''Not Art, but heart'' (Homes's phrase). In the early 1800s gospel hymns were published in the U.S. by Seth Y. Wells (*Millenial Praises, Containing a Collection of Gospel Hymns . . .* , 1813) and by John Putnam (*Revival Melodies, or Songs of Zion,* 1842), but it was in the last quarter of the century that the form achieved widespread acceptance in the U.S. and Great Britain as a feature of the revivalist movement dominated by Dwight L. MOODY (1837–99) and Ira D. Sankey (1840–1908) and continued into the 20th century in the work of such men as William A. (Billy) SUNDAY and H. A. Rodeheaver. The name ''gospel'' was assigned to these songs because their texts were often directly taken from the Gospels, or dealt with the teachings of Jesus and his Church.

The gospel song is evangelical and nonsectarian, and its popularity cuts across racial boundaries. Unlike the spirituals, whose roots lay in the cotton fields and rural camp meetings, the gospel song took root in urban settings. Since its purpose is to admonish and instruct the listener, the gospel song makes judicious use of biblical texts and frequent repetition to convey its message. To appeal to its urban audience, its musical style is often patterned after familiar sounds and genres, e.g., marches, waltzes, sentimental ballads, and even jazz rhythms. While more dignified Protestant denominations regarded gospel songs as common and vulgar, they were beloved by many, especially the poor for whom the power lyrics and attractive music were their comfort and strength. From the mid-20th century onwards, the popularity of the gospel song spread to the more sophisticated churches. During the 1950s and 1960s, many professional gospel groups emerged and toured the country, leaving a lasting imprint on the musical consciousness of many churches. In the wake of the Second Vatican Council, many African-American Catholic parishes started using the gospel song and forming gospel choirs. Gospel songs are prominently featured in the African-American Catholic Hymnal, *Lead Me, Guide Me* (Chicago: GIA, 1987), as well as the African-American Episcopal Hymnal, *Lift Every Voice and Sing: An African American Hymnal* (New York: Church Hymnal Corporation, 1993) and the ecumenical Black hymnal, *African American Heritage Hymnal* (Chicago: GIA 2001).

Bibliography: M. P. BANGERT, ''Black Gospel and Spirituals: A Primer,'' *Currents in Theology and Mission* 16 (1989) 173–179. J. J. CLEVELAND, ''A Historical Account of the Black Gospel Song,'' in *Songs of Zion* (Nashville, 1981). P. K. MAULTSBY, *Afro-American Religious Music: A Study in Musical Diversity* (Springfield, Ohio 1981). J. R. HILLSMAN, *The Progress of Gospel Music: From Spirituals to Contemporary Gospel* (New York 1983). C. M. HAWN, ''A Survey of Trends in Recent Protestant Hymnals: African-American Spirituals, Hymns, and Gospel Songs,'' *Hymn* 43 (January 1992) 21–28. D. LARSON, '''When We All Get to Heaven': The Ecumenical Influence of the American Gospel Song,'' *Restoration Quarterly* 36 no. 3 (1994) 154–172. P. K. MAULTSBY, ''The Use and Performance of Hymnody, Spirituals, and Gospels in the Black Church,'' *The Hymnology Annual* (Berrien Springs, Mich., 1992) 11–26.

[A. M. GARRETT/EDS.]

GOSSEC, FRANÇOIS JOSEPH

Early symphonist of the classical school (also Gossé); b. Vergnies (Hainaut), France, Jan. 17, 1734; d. Passy, Feb. 16, 1829. Gossec had been a choir boy at the Antwerp cathedral and at age 17 was sent to Paris with an introduction to RAMEAU. Through him he was accepted by a musical patron, Le Riche La Pouplinière, a rich ''fermier général'' who maintained a private theater and a fine instrumental ensemble. For this ''veritable musical laboratory,'' as it has been called, Gossec composed some of Europe's first symphonies (his early works predate F. J. Haydn's), as well as string quartets and trio sonatas, and also conducted the orchestra. At the patron's death in 1762, Gossec (then 28) embarked on a career of royal then public acclaim. He served princes through the monarchy, conducted the National Guard band during the Revolution, and became a director of the Conservatoire in 1795. He was also associate director of the Opéra, founded Le Concert des amateurs (1770), and helped reorganize Le Concert Spirituel (1773). In 1802 he became a Chevalier of the Legion of Honor. Despite political upheavals he maintained a prodigious output. His symphonic works were famous for their instrumentation. He introduced horns and clarinets into the opéra orchestra and experimented with multiple groups, in a Mass (1762) and an oratorio, *La Nativité*.

Bibliography: J. G. PROD'HOMME, *François Joseph Gossec* (Paris 1949). L. DE LALAURENCIE, *La Musique française au XVIIIe siècle* (Paris 1910). G. CHOUQUET et al., *Grove's Dictionary of Music and Musicians*, ed. E. BLOM (5th ed. London 1954) 3:720–722. B. BROOK, D. CAMPBELL, and M. COHN, ''François-Joseph Gossec'' in *The New Grove Dictionary of Music and Musicians*, v. 7, ed. S. SADIE (New York 1980) 560–563. D. M. RANDEL, ed., *The Harvard Biographical Dictionary of Music* (Cambridge

1996) 324–325. N. SLONIMSKY, ed. *Baker's Biographical Dictionary of Musicians* (New York 1992) 651–652. W. THIBAUT, *François-Joseph Gossec: Chantre de la Révolution Française* (Brussels 1970).

[E. BORROFF]

GOSWIN, ST.

Benedictine abbot, scholar (known also as Gossen, Goduin); b. Douai; d. ANCHIN, Oct. 9, 1165 or Oct. 10, 1166. Goswin studied at Paris. Despite the attempts of his master Joscelin, later bishop of Soissons, to dissuade him, he became a fierce opponent of Peter ABELARD on Mont St. Geneviève. Goswin then taught as a canon in DOUAI. He entered the monastery of Anchin, near Douai, *c.* 1112, under Abbot Alvisus and took an interest in monastic reform, notably in the monasteries of St. Crispin and St. Médard of Soissons, and of St. Remigius of Reims. As prior of St. Médard, Goswin received Abelard after the latter's condemnation at the Council of Soissons in 1121. In 1131, Goswin succeeded Alvisus as abbot of Anchin. During his abbacy, Goswin encouraged his monks to produce manuscripts and to illuminate them. Some splendid examples survive in the library of the city of Douai. He remained at Anchin until his death. Goswin's cult was propagated early at Douai and Saint-Amand.

Feast: Oct. 7 and 9.

Bibliography: *Acta Sanctorum* Oct. 4:1084–94, two vitae written very soon after his death, excerpts. V. COUSINS, ed., *Petri Abaelardi opera,* 2 v. (Paris 1849–59) 1:43–58. L. H. COTTINEAU *Répetoire topobibliographique des abbayes et prieurés* (Mâcon 1935–39) 1:91–92. J. L. BAUDOT and L. CHAUSSIN, *Vies des saints et des bienheureux selon l'ordre du calendrier avec l'historique des fêtes* (Paris 1935–56) 10:294–295. M. G. BLAYO, *Dictionnaire d'historie et de géographie ecclésiastiques* (Paris 1912) 2:1516–24. A. M. ZIMMERMANN, *Kalendarium Benedictinum* (Metten 1933–38) 3:149–151.

[V. I. J. FLINT]

GOTHS

An East German tribe that migrated into southern Russia in the 2d century A.D. and overflowed into Dacia after the Romans left, *c.* 271. They split into the western Visigoths (Ammianus' Thervingi) and the more progressive eastern Ostrogoths (Greutungi), on separate sides of the Dniester River.

The Ostrogoth King Ermanarich (*c.* 350–370) created a huge empire that fell to the Huns, who dominated the Ostrogoths until 455. Allowed into the Roman Empire, the Ostrogoths settled in Pannonia until THEODORIC THE GREAT accepted Emperor Zeno's commission in 488 to attack Odovacar in Italy, where the Goths established themselves. Theodoric's wise reign (489–526) marked the apogee of Ostrogoth power. Although his successors, Witigis and Totila, fought Justinian's armies bitterly (535–554), they were defeated and the Ostrogothic state and people disappeared together.

The Visigoths at first lacked tribal unity. They were ruled by petty chieftains or "judges," such as Athanaric, who warred against the Emperor Valens (367–369) and cast off the status of *foederati.* Unsuccessful against the Huns, Athanaric was replaced. In 376 Fritigern led the Visigoths into Moesia as *foederati.* In 378 they rebelled because of bad treatment and defeated Valens at Adrianople. By 382 Theodosius I came to terms with them. Under Alaric they rebelled repeatedly, invading Italy and in 410 sacking Rome. Athaulf (410–415) and Wallia (415–418) won lands around Toulouse in Aquitaine. Under Euric (466–484) conquests expanded their rule from the Loire to the Alps and central Spain. Alaric II (484–507) promulgated the important *Lex Romana Visigothorum* for Roman subjects. Defeated by Clovis in 507, the Visigoths concentrated their kingdom in Spain, where it lasted until 711 to 712.

Early archeological evidence of Christianity in Gothic lands of Eastern Europe pertains probably to pre-Gothic Christians, not to the Goths. Bishop Theophilus of Gothia at the Council of Nicea came from the Crimea, where there may have been some Christian Goths. The Goths learned of Christianity from missionaries in the 3d century and from Roman prisoners of war. Bishop Ulfilas (311–*c.* 381), an Arian who was the grandson of such a prisoner, was the most important figure in the Christianization of the Goths. There were Christian martyrs in the persecution by the Visigoths (348, 369–375). Ulfilas led many Christians into the empire, where they were known as Little Goths. It is not clear when the Visigoths as a tribe embraced Christianity, which played a part in the controversy between the pagan Athanaric and the Christian pro-Roman Fritigern. By 400 the Visigoths and by 450 the Ostrogoths were Christian. Through the Goths other German tribes accepted Arianism, which was an impediment to assimilation into Roman society. The Ostrogoths never abandoned Arianism. The Visigoth King Leovigild (571–586) persecuted Catholics, but his son Recared (586—601), under the influence of St. LEANDER OF SEVILLE, officially adopted Catholicism in Spain in 589.

Bibliography: E. SCHWARZ, *Germanische Stammeskunde* (Heidelberg 1956). E. A. THOMPSON, "The Date of the Conversion of the Visigoths," *The Journal of Ecclesiasitical History* 7 (1956) 1–11. P. B. GAMS, *Die Kirchengeschichte von Spanien,* 5 v. (Regensburg 1862–79; reprinted Graz 1956).

[R. H. SCHMANDT]

GOTTI, VINCENZO LODOVICO

Dominican philosopher, theologian, apologist, cardinal priest of St. Sixtus, and patriarch of Jerusalem; b. Bologna, Sept. 5, 1664; d. Rome, Sept. 18, 1742. The son of Jacob Gotti, professor of law at the University of Bologna, he entered the order at 16 and studied philosophy at Forli and theology at Salamanca. He lectured in philosophy at Mantua, the Roman College of St. Thomas (Minerva), and Bologna, and in theology at Faenza and Bologna. Gotti was three times prior of the Dominican convent at Bologna and twice provincial of the Lombardy province. His first significant work in apologetics dates from his two-year sojourn in Milan (1715–17) as inquisitor general; entitled *La vera chiesa di Cristo* (Bologna 1719, 1750; Milan 1734), this is a systematic treatise refuting the errors of the Swiss Calvinist minister Jacques Picenini. On April 30, 1728, Pope Benedict XIII named him titular patriarch of Jerusalem and added him to the college of cardinals, conferring the red hat on June 10 of the same year. In addition to his administrative duties as a member of no fewer than ten sacred congregations, Gotti continued writing on questions of clerical reform and in defense of the authority of the pope. In all his works the apologetical method predominated; he drew his dogmatic defense against Jansenistic, sectarian heresies from the writings of St. Thomas Aquinas.

Bibliography: V GOTTI, *Colloquia theologica polemica in tres classes distributa* (Bologna 1727); *Theologia scholastico-dogmatica juxta mentem Divi Thomae Aquinatis ad usum discipulorum* (Bologna 1727–35; 2d ed. Venice 1750; 3d ed. 1783); *De eligenda inter dissentientes Christianos sententia adversus Joannem Clericum reformatae. . .*, 2 v. (Vienna 1750). R. COULON, *Dictionnaire de théologie catholique.*, ed. A. VACANT et al. (Paris 1903–50) 6.2:1503–07. H. HURTER, *Nomenclator literarius theologiaea catholicae* (Innsbruck 1903–13) 4:1353–57. J. QUÉTIF and J. ÉCHARD, *Scriptores Ordinis Praedicatorum* (New York 1959) 2.2:814. A. WALZ, *Lexikon für Theologie und Kirche*, ed. J. HOFER and K. RAHNER (Freiburg 1957–65) 4:1142. T. A. RICCHINI, *De vita et studiis Pr. Vincentii Ludovici Card. Gotti. . .* (Rome 1742).

[F. J. ROENSCH]

GOTTSCHALK, ST.

Martyr; d. Lenzen on the Elbe, June 7, 1066. He was an Abodrite prince and was educated at St. Michael's monastery in Lüneburg, but left *c.* 1030 to avenge the murder of his father, Uto, killed by the Saxons. After this uprising had been put down, Gottschalk was forced into exile and went to England in the service of King Canute, whose daughter he married. In 1043 he was able to return and rule his people. He administered an extensive area that he attempted to Christianize, with the help of ADALBERT OF BREMEN; the Dioceses of Mecklenburg and Ratzeburg were founded during his reign. Upon the collapse of Adalbert's political fortunes in 1066, Gottschalk fell victim to the pagan reaction and was martyred.

Feast: June 7.

Bibliography: *Acta Santorum* June 2 (1867) 40–42. ADAM OF BREMEN, *Monumenta Scriptores rerum Germanicarum* (Berlin 1826–) v. 7. HELMOLD OF BOSAU, *ibid.* STEINDORFF, *Allgemeine deutsche Biographie* (Leipzig 1875–1910) 9:489–493. K. JORDAN, *Neue deutsche Biographie* (Berlin 1953–) 6:684. B. STASIESSKI, *Lexikon für Theologie und Kirche*, ed. J. HOFER and K. RAHNER, 10 v. (2d, new ed. Freiburg 1957–65) 4:1144. W. BRÜSKE, *Untersuchungen zur Geschichte des Lutizenbundes* (Münster 1955). W. H. FRITZE, in *Siedlung und Verfassung der Slawen zwischen Elbe, Saale und Oder*, ed. H. LUDAT (Giessen 1960). F. DVORNIK, *The Slavs: Their Early History and Civilization* (Boston 1956) 297–300.

[L. KURRAS]

GOTTSCHALK OF LIMBURG

Monk and poet; b. *c.* 1010 to 1020; d. Nov. 24, 1098. Information concerning this poet comes from three sources. From his own works it is known that Gottschalk (*Godescalcus*) was a monk at the monastery of Limburg, studied under the direction of a monk named Henry, preached to the community, and was criticized by his fellow monks for some of his sermons. He also wrote that he composed and set to music an Office in honor of SS. IRENAEUS and ABUNDIUS, patrons of his monastery, as well as several SEQUENCES, five of which he cited by their opening words. From the *De hymnorum et sequentiarum auctoribus brevissima eruditiuncula*, published by Jakob WIMPFELING in 1499, it is known that there was in the monastery at Klingenmünster a collection of Sequences dedicated to HENRY IV written by Gottschalk, court chaplain and provost of AACHEN, but only five Sequences were published in this work. The date of the author's residence at Klingenmünster is uncertain. The *Anonymus Mellicensis* (ed. E. Ettlinger, 1896) states that Gottschalk wrote, among other works, a book of sermons. Gottschalk's claim to renown rests primarily on his authorship of 22 or possibly 23 Sequences. These compositions, almost all handed down with their melodies, were written for use at Mass on the feast days of angels and saints, particularly the Blessed Virgin, and for the feasts of Christmas, Epiphany, Pentecost, Transfiguration, and the Exaltation of the Cross. The content of the Sequences is at times heavily dogmatic; yet a certain mystical approach and a touch of tender poetic feeling are not lacking. The use of biblical imagery is truly impressive, and rhetorical figures frequently enhance the compositions. There is a great striving for assonance both within and at the end of the line. Gottschalk was no innovator, but his work is in no way inferior to the great tradition of NOTKER BALBULUS.

Bibliography: H. A. DANIEL, *Thesaurus hymnologicus*, 3 v. in 1 (Leipzig 1855) 2:37–49. *Analecta Gregoriana* (Rome 1930–) 50:339–369; 53:274–276. M. MANITIUS, *Geschichte der lateinischen Literatur des Mittelalters* (Munich 1911–31) 3:998–1000. F. J. E. RABY, *A History of Secular Latin Poetry in the Middle Ages* 2 v. (2d ed. Oxford 1957) 224–225. J. SZÖVÉRFFY, *Die Annalen der lateinischen Hymnendichtung. Ein Handbuch* 2 v. (Berlin 1964–65) 1:409–414. B. STÄBLEIN, *Lexikon für Theologie und Kirche*, ed. J. HOFER and K. RAHNER (Freiburg 1957–65) 4:1143–44. *Godescalcus Lintpurgensis*, ed. G. M. DREVES (Leipzig 1897). L. GUSHEE, ''Gottschalk von Limburg'' in *The New Grove Dictionary of Music and Musicians*, v. 7, ed. S. SADIE (New York 1980) 574.

[H. DRESSLER]

GOTTSCHALK OF ORBAIS

Benedictine theologian and poet, whose teaching on predestination disquieted the Church in France and Germany; b. *c.* 803; d. Abbey of Hautvillers, near Reims, France, between 867 and 869. The son of Berno, a Saxon noble, Gottschalk was offered by his father as an OBLATE in the Benedictine abbey of Fulda. After reaching his majority, he was released at his own request from his monastic obligations by the Synod of Mainz in 829, but LOUIS I THE PIOUS, on the appeal of his abbot, RABANUS MAURUS, reversed this decision. Gottschalk was forced to lead a monk's life and moved to the monastery of Orbais in the Diocese of Soissons, where he studied diligently the writings of St. AUGUSTINE and Fulgentius of Ruspe. With disregard for the rights of the bishop of Soissons, he was raised to the priesthood by the chorbishop Rigbold of Reims. He made a pilgrimage to Rome (*c.* 847) and on his return journey discussed with Count Eberhard of Friuli and Bp. Noting of Brescia his views on the twofold PREDESTINATION of the elect to life and of the reprobate to death. Shortly afterward Noting alerted Rabanus Maurus, then archbishop of Mainz, of these theories and the danger of their diffusion in upper Italy. After a period of missionary activity in the Balkan regions, Gottschalk appeared before the Synod of Mainz, which in 848 condemned him for HERESY and committed him to his metropolitan, HINCMAR OF REIMS. In 849 Hincmar convoked another synod at QUIERCY-SUR-OISE, which again condemned Gottschalk; he was degraded from the priesthood, flogged until he was half dead, and imprisoned for life in the monastery of Hautvillers in the Diocese of REIMS. Toward the middle of 849 Hincmar wrote a small work to counteract Gottschalk's influence and to explain the passages from Scripture and the Fathers of the Church that he had used. This work aroused a storm of opposition from illustrious churchmen who, without openly siding with Gottschalk, defended twofold predestination; but Hincmar prevailed at the synod of Quiercy-sur-Oise in 853, and the doctrine of twofold predestination was condemned. His opponents declared against his teaching at the synods of Valence (855) and Langres (859) and proclaimed the doctrine of twofold predestination. The controversy ended with the deliberations of the national councils of Savonnières (859) and especially of Toucy (860), which enunciated generally acceptable principles and avoided explicit reference to the predestination of the reprobate to death. During this phase of the dispute over Augustinian predestination Gottschalk languished in prison almost overlooked; but, as his reputation became more widely known, his plight was brought to the attention of Pope NICHOLAS I. When pontifical envoys were sent to Metz in June of 863 to discuss the divorce of King Lothair II, they were commissioned to get further information on the imprisoned monk. On their return to Rome the citation of Gottschalk before the Roman Curia was discussed; and in 866 a monk of Hautvillers, Guntbert, fled the monastery to bring to Rome an appeal on behalf of Gottschalk. Hincmar charged his representative at Rome to present to the Holy See in a favorable light his role in Gottschalk's imprisonment, but Nicholas's death ended the desires of the Roman Curia to have the controversial monk brought to Rome for a review of his trial and condemnation. From his arrival at Hautvillers Gottschalk had been deprived of the Sacraments; and as his end approached, Hincmar was anxious to admit him to their reception but only on condition he abjure what he considered his errors. Despite increasing insistence he remained inflexible. Stubbornly adhering to his views and embittered by the harsh treatment accorded him, the cause of the hallucinations that clouded his last years, Gottschalk resisted his archbishop to the end and died unreconciled. He taught a positive reprobation that supposed the prevision of future misdeeds, denied a universal salvific will in God after the sin of Adam, and limited the efficacy of the sufferings of Christ for salvation to those predestined to life. The interpretation of his words and the exact import of his theses needed more explanation and clarification than he was able to give them and are subject to discussion. He opposed the Eucharistic teaching of PASCHASIUS RADBERTUS and attacked Hincmar for replacing with *Summa deitas* the expression *Trina deitas* in the Vesper hymn *SANCTORUM MERITIS,* from the common of many martyrs. Gottschalk left several well-written poems that rank among the best Carolingian verse and reveal depths of poetic feeling and a delicately sensitive use of rhyme.

Bibliography: *Monumenta Germaniae Poetae* (Berlin 1825–) 3:707–738; 4:934; 6:86–106. C. LAMBOT, *Oeuvres théologiques et grammaticales de Godescalc D'Orbais* (Spicilegium sacrum Lovaniense 20; Louvain 1945). M. MANITIUS, *Geschichte der lateinischen Literatur des Mittelalters* (Munich 1911–1931) 1:568–574. B. LAVAUD, *Dictionaire de théologie catholique* (Paris 1903–1950) 12:2901–35. F. CHATILLON, ''Augustine in G. and Peter the Venerable,'' Revue de moyen-âge latin 3 (1949) 234–237. K. VIELHABER, *Gottschalk der Sachse* (Bonn 1956). J. JOLIVET, *Godescalc d'Orbais et la Trinité* (Paris 1958). K. VIELHABER, *Lexicon für Theologie und Kirche* (Freiburg 1957–) 2 4:1144–45. SZÖVÉRFFY, *Die Annalen der lateinischen Hymnendichtung* (Berlin 1964–65) 1:235–244.

[J. M. O'DONNELL]

GÖTTWEIG, ABBEY OF

Benedictine abbey in the Diocese of St. Pölten, near Krems, Lower Austria. It was founded (1083) for Augustinian canons by Bishop St. ALTMANN OF PASSAU, who is buried there. Bishop Ulrich I of Passau (1092–1121) settled it with Benedictines from SANKT BLASIEN; an attached convent of nuns survived to *c.* 1550. SANKT LAMBRECHT in Styria, Garsten, and SEITENSTETTEN were founded in part by Göttweig, which participated in Benedictine reforms of the 15th and 17th centuries. The abbey was always devoted to pastoral care and warded off the inroads of Protestantism under Abbots Michael Herrlich, Georg Schedler, and David Corner. Scholarship flourished in the 18th century, especially under Abbots Gottfried von Bessel and Magnus Klein. Only the church and a tower survived a fire of 1718. The grandiose plan of baroque reconstruction by Johann Lukas von Hildebrand (1668–1745) was not completed. The library has 60,000 volumes, 1,100 incunabula, 1,111 MSS, music archives, and important collections of prints and coins. In 1964 the 38 monks included 32 priests; the abbey cares for 34 parishes.

Bibliography: L. KOLLER, *Abtei Göttweig* (Göttweig 1953). *Österreichische Ordensstifte* (Vienna 1961) 24–27. E. RITTER, ''Neue Forschungsergebnisse zur Bau-und Kunstgeschichte des Stiftes Göttweig,'' *Mitteilungen des Kremser Stadtarchivs* (Krems 1961) 57–104. M. SCHMID, *Lexikon für Theologie und Kirche,* ed. J. HOFER and K. RAHNER, 10 v. (2d, new ed. Freiburg 1957–65) 4:1145–46. L. H. COTTINEAU, *Répertoire topobibliographique des abbayes et prieurés,* 2 v. (Mâcon 1935–39) 1:1307–08.

[M. H. SCHMID]

GOUDIMEL, CLAUDE

Renaissance composer and music editor; b. Besançon, France, *c.* 1514; d. Lyon, 1572. He studied at the University of Paris and was Du Chemin's music editor and partner until 1555. His residences include Metz, where he became a Huguenot (1557– *c.* 1565), Besançon, and Lyon, where he died in the St. Bartholomew's Day Massacre. Among his works were five Masses, three Magnificats, about ten Latin motets, psalm-motets (1551–66), psalms, about 60 chansons, Horatian odes (lost), Muret's spiritual songs (lost), and bowdlerizations of Arcadelt chansons. Although he composed for the Catholic church, his Calvinist psalms in the Marot-Bèze translations (some homorhythmic, with the Genevan melodies in the tenor, and others, more florid, with the tunes in the *superius cantus*) are his most famous works.

See Also: PSALTERS, METRICAL; HYMNS AND HYMNALS.

Bibliography: C. GOUDIMEL, *Psaumes de David,* ed. H. EXPERT, 3 v. (Les Maîtres musiciens de la renaissance française 2, 4, 6; Paris 1895–97). F. LESURE, ''Claude Goudimel, étudiant, correcteur et éditeur Parisien,'' *Musica Disciplona* 2 (Rome 1948) 225–230. E. M. LAWRY, *The Psalm Motets of Claude Goudimel* (Doctoral diss. microfilm; New York U. 1954). P. PIDOUX, ''Notes sur quelques éditions des psaumes de Claude Goudimel,'' *Revue de musicologie* 42 (Paris 1958) 184–192. P. A. GAILLARD, *Die Musik in Geschichte und Gegenwart,* ed. F. BLUME (Kassel-Basel 1949–) 5:584–589. G. REESE, *Music in the Renaissance* (rev. ed. New York 1959). M. EGAN-BUFFET, *Les Chansons de Claude Goudimel: Analyses modales et stylistiques* (Ottawa 1992). P.-A. GAILLARD, ''Claude Goudimel'' in *The New Grove Dictionary of Music and Musicians,* v. 7, ed. S. SADIE (New York 1980) 578–579. R. HÄUSLER, *Satztechnik und Form in Claude Goudimelss lateinischen Vokalwerken* (Bern 1968). D. M. RANDEL, ed., *The Harvard Biographical Dictionary of Music* (Cambridge 1996) 325. N. SLONIMSKY, ed. *Baker's Biographical Dictionary of Musicians* (New York 1992) 654.

[I. CAZEAUX]

GOUDIN, ANTOINE

Dominican philosopher and theologian; b. Limoges, *c.* 1639; d. Paris, Oct. 25, 1695. He entered the order in 1657 and achieved recognition first as a student and later as a master at the Limoges convent. Sent to Avignon to reorganize theological studies, Goudin rendered a considerable service to scholastic philosophy in his interpretations and expositions of the schoolmen. In 1669 he was elected prior at Brives. He taught theology at Saint-Germain, Paris, and later became a doctor of theology at the University of Paris. He joined the faculty at Saint-Jacques and subsequently became its prior. Goudin remains a controversial figure in the 17th-century struggle between Molinists and Thomists over physical PREMOTION and efficacious GRACE. In spite of the famous letter of R. Simon remonstrating with Goudin for his theological treatises, an exact evaluation of Goudin's position in reference to St. Thomas's doctrine awaits the discovery and publication of his own MSS. His most frequently published work is *Philosophia juxta inconcussa tutissimaque divi Thomae dogmata* (Lyons 1671; Paris 1674, 1692, 1851, etc.), which constitutes a representative compendium of scholastic-Thomistic philosophy. At the time of his death, Goudin was preparing a *Cursus theologiae;* its doctrine on such subjects as knowledge, ideas, will, freedom, providence, predestination, grace, and reprobation may be gleaned in part from certain *Tractatus theologici* published posthumously in Cologne (1723) and Louvain (1874).

Bibliography: QUÉTIF-ÉCHARD, *Scriptores Ordinis Praedicatorum* (New York 1959) 2.2:739–740. R. COULON, *Dictionaire de Théologie Catholique* (Paris 1903–1950) 6.2:1508–1515. E. FILTHAUT, *Lexikon für Theologie und Kirche* (Freiburg 1957–) 2 4:1149. L. PAGELLO, *Enciclopedia Filosofica* (Venice-Rome 1957) 2:871. H. HURTER, *Nomenclator literarius theologiae catholicae* (Innsbruck 1903–1913) 4:320. *Enciclopedia Universal Ilustrada Europa-Americana* (Barcelona 1908–1930) 26:778.

[F. J. ROENSCH]

GOUNOD, CHARLES FRANÇOIS

Prominent figure in romanticist music; b. Paris, June 17, 1818; d. Saint-Cloud, Oct. 18, 1893. The boy was heir to a long artistic tradition; his father was a Prix de Rome painter; his mother, an excellent pianist. Young Gounod took his B. ès Lettres at the Lycée Saint-Louis, then entered the Paris Conservatory, winning the Prix de Rome in 1839. After experience as church organist in Rome and Paris, he studied theology for two years before deciding finally upon a career as composer. As with his life, his creative work moved along two lines—the opera and the Church. Among many operatic failures, his *Faust* remains a landmark of the lyric stage despite its theatrical absurdities, and *Romeo et Juliette* was one of the first French coloratura operas. His religious works—notably the four Masses and the oratorios *Rédemption* and *Mors et Vita*—have certain fine moments, and betray a marvelous gift for vocal writing as well as unfailing workmanship and earnestness of purpose; but they lack virility and humility and are aesthetically banal. After a period of Victorian popularity they have all but disappeared. His best (because simple and unpretentious) church music may be found in the Anglican anthems and other pieces composed while he was in England during the Franco-Prussian War.

Apart from his fine musicianship, he had a serious musical outlook unusual for the period. His first *envoi* as a Prix de Rome winner was an unaccompanied *Te Deum* for ten soloists and two choruses in Palestrina style, at a time when Palestrina was an unknown quantity in France. When he discovered Bach's *Well-Tempered Clavichord* and brought it back to Paris, he caused consternation at the conservatory. He was also generous and encouraging toward young composers. Church music has since acquired a dignity that cannot be detected in Gounod's Masses; yet these works remain emblematic of the romanticist period.

Charles François Gounod.

Bibliography: C. F. GOUNOD, *Memories of an Artist*, tr. by A. E. CROCKER (New York 1895); *Autobiographical Reminiscences, with Family Letters and Notes on Music,* tr. W. H. HUTCHINSON (London 1896). N. DEMUTH, *Introduction to the Music of Gounod* (London 1950). H. BUSSER, *Charles Gounod* (Lyons 1961). E. HARASZTI, *Die Musik in Geschichte und Gegenwart,* ed. F. BLUME (Kassel-Basel 1949–) 5:593–604. G. CHOUQUET and A. JULLIEN, *Grove's Dictionary of Music and Musicians,* ed. E. BLOM, 9 v. (5th ed. London 1954) 3:729–735. N. SLONIMSKY, ed., *Baker's Biographical Dictionary of Musicians* (5th ed. New York 1958) 594–596. M. COOPER, ''Charles Gounod and His Influence on French Music,'' *Music and Letters* 21 (1940) 50–59; *French Music* (London 1951; pa. New York 1955). A. G. GANN, ''Théophile Gautier, Charles Gounod, and the Massacre of *La Nonne sanglante,*'' *Journal of Musicological Research,* 13 (1993) 49–66. C. F. GOUNOD, ''Composers as Conductors,'' introduced by M. KELKEL, tr. W. ASHBROOK, *Opera Quarterly,* 12/1 (1996) 5–17. W. E. GRIM, ''*Faust,*'' in *International Dictionary of Opera* ed. C. S. LARUE, 2 v. (Detroit 1993) 421–423. J.-M. GUIEU, ''*Mirèio* and *Mireille:* Mistral's Poem and Gounod's Opera,'' *Opera Quarterly,* 10/1 (1993) 33–47. S. HUEBNER, *The Operas of Charles Gounod* (Oxford 1990). L. SNYDER, ''*Mireille,*'' in *International Dictionary of Opera* ed. C. S. LARUE, 2 v. (Detroit 1993) 880–882. L. A. WRIGHT, ''Gounod and Bizet: A Study in Musical Paternity,'' *Journal of Musicological Research,* 13 (1993) 31–48.

[N. DEMUTH]

GOVERNANCE, POWER OF

Since the Second Vatican Council, the expression ''power of governance'' is preferred in place of ''power of jurisdiction.'' The broad concept ''power in the Church'' (of governance and of orders) formed a greatly debated topic at Vatican II. This debate continues today and certain important questions remain unanswered.

Presupposition. Traditionally, the power of jurisdiction (or of governance or of government) refers to the ''public power of governing or ruling belonging to a supreme and independent society'' (Abbo – Hannon, I, 251). The change in terminology to ''power of governance'' better reflects the Vatican II teaching concerning the triple *munera* (functions) of Jesus Christ as priest, prophet and ruler. All of the faithful, in virtue of baptism, participate in the mission of the Church through sharing in these functions of Jesus Christ. Thus, all of the Christian faithful, depending on each one's particular condition, exercise the common or ministerial priesthoods; share in the proclamation of the Word of God; and cooperate in the governance of the People of God.

The power of governance is distinct from the power of orders, which derives from the sacrament of order and is the power to celebrate the sacraments. Both powers exist in the Church by the intention of Jesus Christ. *Lumen gentium* 8 establishes an analogy between the Incarnation of Jesus Christ and the Church as incarnated in the world. Through the will of Jesus Christ, the Church exists both as a hierarchically structured society and the mystical body of Christ; both a visible assembly and a spiritual community. The two cannot be separated from each other. The distinction between power of governance and power of orders fundamentally reflects the nature of the Church as one reality consisting of both dimensions. As an organized society, the Church requires the power of governance in order to fulfill its divine mandate to proclaim the gospel of Jesus Christ. But priority must be given to proclamation of the gospel: governance exists to serve this mission.

A major debate both theologically and canonically continues concerning the relationship between the power of jurisdiction and the power of orders. Canon 129 states that the ordained ''are qualified for the power of governance'' whereas the laity ''can cooperate in the exercise of this same power.'' To what extent, therefore, may the laity exercise the power of governance? The answer to this question incorporates complex theological, canonical, and historical issues as well as differing ecclesiologies and ecclesiological pre-suppositions. Vatican II, which generally referred to ''power'' (either alone or with the adjective ''sacred'') neither explicitly addressed the issue nor resolved it, and it would appear that debate will continue for the foreseeable future. Nonetheless, two significant points must receive due emphasis. (1) According to the present canon law, lay people may hold ecclesiastical offices; these are no longer limited only to clergy. Further, lay members of institutes of consecrated life, societies of apostolic life, and secular institutes may hold offices within these institutes and societies. (2) The present law seems to imply (at the very least) that lay men and women do exercise some power of governance in certain offices, for example, the diocesan bishop may appoint a lay person a judge on a collegiate tribunal (c. 1421, §2); he may also entrust the pastoral care of a parish to a lay person (c. 517, §2); a lay person may be appointed the administrator of ecclesiastical goods (c. 1279). The type of power exercised by lay superiors and moderators in societies and institutes of consecrated life forms another greatly discussed topic (c. 596).

Exercise of the Power of Governance. The power of governance is subdivided into legislative, executive, and judicial powers. In distinction to the common law tradition, the civil law tradition does not necessarily accept the 'separation of powers' as evidenced, for example, in the United States (on the federal level, for example, the President exercises executive power; the Congress, legislative power; and the Supreme Court, judicial power). All three powers may be held and exercised by one individual, for example, a diocesan bishop (although he usually exercises judicial power through judges whom he appoints).

Usually, the power of governance is exercised in the external forum, that is, in the realm of public, juridically verifiable activity, for example, the celebration of baptism. However, the power of governance may also be exercised in the internal forum, which is either the sacramental internal forum (that is, the sacrament of penance) or the internal non-sacramental forum.

'Ordinary power of governance' is power ''joined to a certain office by the law itself'' (c. 131). This ordinary power is *proper* if it is exercised in one's own name; *vicarious*, if exercised in the name of another person. For example, a diocesan bishop, through appointment to and installation in the office of bishop, receives all the ordinary, proper and immediate power necessary to fulfill this function (*see* c. 381 which also includes the important nuance, ''except for cases which the law or a decree of the Supreme Pontiff reserves to the supreme authority or to another ecclesiastical authority.'' ''Immediate'' indicates that he can exercise this authority directly over the Christian faithful, not through a mediator). A vicar general, on the other hand, has ordinary but vicarious power: ordinary, because it is attached to the office by the law itself; vicarious, because he exercises it in the name of the diocesan bishop. Ordinary power—both proper and vicarious—ceases when the office is lost (c. 143).

''Delegated power of governance'' is power granted to a person by means other than appointment to an office

(c. 131). The delegation of power generally applies only to executive power—legislative and judicial power can be delegated only in limited cases: when the law specifically allows for the delegation of legislative power or for the performance of certain activities preparatory to the issuance of a judicial decree or judicial sentence (canon 135). Further, in general and unless specifically disallowed by the law, delegated power can also be subdelegated. The specific subject of who may receive delegated power is not resolved by the Code; therefore, the question remains debated as to whether or not lay persons can receive the power of governance through delegation. According to canon 142, delegated power ceases in a variety of ways, dependent upon the grant of delegation – by the completion of the mandate; by lapse of time; by cessation of the purpose of the delegation; by revocation (of the one delegating); by resignation (of the one delegated).

The exercise of the power of governance also involves subjects, that is, individuals subject to such exercise. As a general rule, laws bind those for whom they were enacted (canons 11–13) and canons 1404–1416 and 1673 establish competency for judicial matters. Executive power is exercised only over those who are subject to the one exercising this power.

In his apostolic constitution promulgating the new code, Pope John Paul II described the purpose of the Code as ''to create such an order in the ecclesial society that, while assigning the primacy to love, grace, and charisms, it at the same time renders their organic development easier in the life both of the ecclesial society and the individual persons who belong to it.'' (*Sacrae disciplinae leges* in *The Code of Canon Law*). This same rationale underlies the exercise of the power of governance.

Bibliography: M. WIJLENS, ''The Power of Governance [cc. 129–144],'' in *New Commentary on the Code of Canon Law*, ed. J. BEAL, J. CORIDEN, T. GREEN (New York and Mahwah 2000), 183–194. J. ABBO and J. HANNAN, *The Sacred Canons* (St. Louis and London 1952). J. BEAL, ''The Exercise of the Power of Governance by Lay People: State of the Question,'' *The Jurist* 55 (1995) 1–92.

[R. J. KASLYN]

GOVERNMENT

The terms ''government'' and ''STATE'' are frequently confused. Broadly considered, government is the concrete system through which the objective of the state—the common good—is attained. This article discusses the definition of government, the nature of political power, and historic classifications of the forms of government.

Definition. Man is a social animal, and he requires various kinds of social organization to achieve his specific and varied objectives. One of these is the state, whose end is broader than that of any other element of society. As Jacques Maritain says, ''it specializes in the interests of the whole'' (*Man and the State* [Chicago 1951] 12). Nevertheless, it is to be distinguished from society, whose discrete and varied objectives are only partially achieved by the state as such. Traditionally, the state is conceived as including population, territory, SOVEREIGNTY, independence, and government. Robert MacIver defines it as ''an association which, acting through law as promulgated by a government endowed to this end with coercive power, maintains within a community territorially demarcated the universal external conditions of social order'' (*Modern State* [Oxford 1926] 22).

Government, as one of the several elements that constitute the state, is the machinery through which the state operates. Concretely, it consists of the combined organisms and mechanisms such as the legislature, the courts, the executive branch, the bureaucracy, and the political parties that shape and implement public policy. While government is an apparatus, it is also a process through which the people of the state seek to meet the common problems that inevitably arise in the course of social living. Since the problems that face man in the course of history change and since government is a social invention of man designed to meet his needs, it is obscurantist to conceive of government as unchanging in form or frozen in its functions.

Power and Government. While man is a social animal, as Aristotle described him, he is also, in Christian terminology, the product of original sin. The extent to which man's social nature predisposes him to orderly living in society and the extent to which his individual egoism prompts him to seek personal aggrandizement at the expense of others have become opposite poles of reference for political theorists in expanding or contracting the extent of power to be allowed to government. Thus, Thomas HOBBES (1588–1671) conceived of man as reflexively selfish, compelled only through fear of coercion to live an orderly life in society. On the other hand, Jean Jacques ROUSSEAU (1712–78) in some of his works conceived of man as naturally good and presaged the Jacksonian view of man as fully capable of self-government and properly subject only to minimal restraints.

If power is defined generally as the capacity to make and enforce decisions (rules and regulations) affecting the behavior of individuals or groups, it is apparent that it is possessed by many individuals and subsocieties, including the family. Without the ability to enforce decisions, one cannot speak realistically of power or of government. But power is not to be conceived of solely in terms of physical coercion. Custom, tradition, education, and habit develop attitudes of compliance as well as pomp, pageantry, and charisma of leadership. Power is more than force, and the state is more than power. And although these are shared with other groups in society besides government, nevertheless, in modern times only the government in the name of the state may legitimately use physical coercion. Government is distinguished in this facet of power both by the intensity and the extent to which it may apply it.

The philosophical tradition of the West has admitted the need for some kind of coercive power to be possessed by government as a necessary condition for minimal order. Individual interests no less than those of corporate bodies within the state must bow to the legitimate broader ends of the state, preferably through conviction, but if necessary through coercion. In his *Disquisition on Government* even John Calhoun (1782–1850), who was congenitally concerned about checks and balances in government, defined government as ''controlling power'' in society (*Works* [6 v. New York 1854] 1.4).

But while most schools of political thought grant the use of coercive power to government, few grant it without qualification. PLATO (*c.* 427–347 B.C.) believed that until philosophers are kings and kings are philosophers, the world will never cease from ill. In this view, wisdom rather than consent of the people is the legitimate condition for the exercise of power. For a considerable period of history primogeniture in hereditary succession was the badge of legitimacy. In more modern times and under the influence of the modern natural right school, selection by the people and acceptance of contractual limitations are the necessary conditions for the exercise of coercive power. Thus, for most nations of the West (Russia included) some kind of constitution, written or unwritten, forms the basis for government and spells out the structure and conditions of governing. What that structure is and what the conditions are depend upon the historical experience of the people, the prevailing political philosophy, and perhaps the social milieu in which the government is formed. To invest the political power with authority, that is, to make it legitimate by meeting the expectations of the governed concerning the wielding of authority, is the central goal of all government and politics.

In Western culture, the basic condition for the legitimate use of power has been that it be used for the good of the people. What that good is depends, of course, upon the particular nature of man as conceived by any particular society. The Greco-Roman-Christian tradition would reject a concept of absolute sovereignty in the state. Government has to be morally responsible and its powers are limited by the nature of man and the common good. As the Apostle Paul said, ''There exists no authority except from God, and those who exist have been appointed by God'' (Rom 13.1) and are responsible to a higher power. Even Plato's philosopher-king, who is above positive law, remains subject to the moral law. The right to power, therefore, in the Western tradition—ignoring the aberrations of some of the German idealists and of MACHIAVELLI (1469–1527) and Hobbes among others—has always been a qualified right. Absolute sovereignty, as Maritain says, is not a characteristic of government in the West. Might never makes right. (*See* AUTHORITY, CIVIL.)

Historic Classifications. Governments have been grouped according to different criteria ever since Aristotle attempted the first systematic classification in his famous studies of Greek constitutions. The great Greek classified them according to the number of men involved in governing, ranging from one-man rule (MONARCHY) to rule by the majority (polity). He also distinguished government according to the interests served. Thus, one man rule in the interest of the whole community is called monarchy; but if it is conducted in the interest of the ruler himself, it is termed ''TYRANNY.'' By the same reasoning, ARISTOCRACY is opposed to oligarchy and polity to DEMOCRACY, then defined as the rule of the many for their own selfish benefit. This classification persisted through many centuries, being used variously by Roman political theorists and by many medieval writers, including St. THOMAS AQUINAS (*c.* 1225–74).

Logically, there are other possible classifications that might more accurately reflect the true nature of contrasting governmental forms. For instance, the parliamentary form may be distinguished from the presidential form, best exemplified by England and the United States, respectively. The parliamentary system fuses legislative and executive powers by making the executive in theory the creature of the legislative body, but often in practice, because of party discipline, the executive actually is master. Also, the titular head of the government is most often a purely ceremonial figure without power, such as the monarchy in England. Only the maximum time is fixed for terms of office and the legislative product is not subject to judicial review.

The presidential system, on the other hand, makes the president independent of the legislative branch and elects him or her from a different constituency than that of the legislators. Terms of office are fixed, judicial review is provided in some instances, and separation of powers is prescribed in the basic instrument. There is no guarantee that the same party will control both the presidency and the Congress, or even both houses of Congress.

Another classification is made according to the concentration or dispersal of authority over a geographical area. The so-called unitary state, for example, has a central source of authority. Local governments are merely the creatures of the central government and owe their legal existence to it. Their powers and even their boundaries are subject to the higher authority, as is the case in the relationship of municipal government to state governments in the United States. Great Britain and France have unitary governments. It should be noted that unitary government does not necessarily imply highly centralized government, since authority may be freely decentralized through delegation to subunits.

In contrast is a form by which unity is achieved, in the midst of diversity, through federalism. The United States is one example; Canada and Russia are others. Federalism is simply the distribution of powers and functions of government between two or more semi-independent levels of government in the same state. It is differentiated from the separation of powers, which is the division of powers and functions at a particular level of government.

Normally, all levels of government in a federal system have some independence of action and each possesses its own three organs. Like the separation of powers, federalism poses some obstacles to the solution of modern problems that are intergovernmental in character but the solutions to which are not legally located at any single level. Such problems as control and conservation of river systems, labor-management relations, and interstate crime have perplexed the advocates of strict federalism, since the problems transcend the jurisdiction of state governments but are not clearly the responsibility solely of the central government. A cooperative approach is sometimes called "cooperative federalism," although both Congress and the federal courts have in recent years been willing to concede rather large areas of jurisdiction to the central government where the jurisdiction is not legally clear-cut, or where the states are obviously incapable of attacking the problem effectively. In the cases of some states, such as Russia, the system is formally federal but actually highly centralized because of the tight discipline of a pervasive party system.

A fourth classification is made according to the groups that exercise power in the state, namely, political parties. This involves a description of the basic party system as a one-party, two-party, or multiparty structure. A one-party system such as that of the Soviet Union or Nazi Germany obviously can corrupt the formal structure of the government as defined in the constitution. The existence of a single party state is considered by most political scientists as more revealing of the real dictatorial nature of the state than the existence of traditional checks on power such as judicial review or representative assemblies. Two-party systems have proved to promote stability more than multiparty systems; France prior to Charles de Gaulle provided the best modern illustration of party-induced instability.

Finally, governments have been classified according to the scope of power resident in them. Anarchy at one extreme considers coercive power in government as an undiluted evil and reserves to society itself or to associations within it the functions normally given to government. Underlying ANARCHISM is a denial of fallen human nature. As Thomas Paine put it, "Government, like dress, is the badge of lost innocence" ("Common Sense," *Complete Writings,* ed. P. S. Foner [New York 1945] 1.4).

Totalitarianism, on the other hand, places the totality of functions that society has to perform for man in the hands of the government rather than judiciously distributing them between the government and subsocieties within the state. Nothing is properly exempt from government regulation; voluntary groupings such as church and school are regarded in Hobbesian terminology as "worms in the entrails of a natural man" (*Leviathan* 2:29).

All types of government line up somewhere between these two extremes including the laissez-faire government of the classical economists. Philosophically the battle continues to rage over whether government is, as Jefferson regarded it, "a necessary evil," or whether, as in Aristotle, Thomas Aquinas, and modern papal teaching, it is a positive help in reaching the good life.

Bibliography: R. RIENOW, *Introduction to Government* (3d ed. New York 1964). S. H. BEER and A. ULAM, *Patterns of Government* (2d ed. New York 1963). R. M. MACIVER, *The Web of Government* (New York 1947). A. D. LINDSAY, *The Modern Democratic State* (New York 1943). R. W. BREWSTER, *Government in Modern Society* (2d ed. Boston 1963). C. J. FRIEDRICH, *Constitutional Government and Democracy* (rev. ed. Boston 1950). W. ELLIOTT and N. MCDONALD, eds., *Western Political Heritage* (New York 1949). J. MARITAIN, *Man and the State* (Chicago 1951). G. SABINE, *A History of Political Theory* (rev. ed. New York 1950). E. S. CORWIN, *The "Higher Law" Background of American Constitutional Law* (Ithaca, N.Y. 1955).

[E. L. HENRY/EDS.]

GOWER, JOHN

English poet; b. probably in Kent, *c.* 1330; d. 1408. It is untenable that he was a member of the clergy, a lawyer, or a physician; records would indicate, rather, that he must be identified with the merchant class. He was a friend of Chaucer, and was known to Richard II and Henry IV. He became blind seven years before his death, and was buried in the chapel of St. John the Baptist in St. Savior's Church (Southwark Cathedral), originally the church of the Priory of St. Mary Overey, of which he had been a substantial benefactor. The effigy on his tomb represents him resting his head on three large volumes entitled *Vox Clamatis, Speculum Meditantis,* and *Confessio Amantis.* Each is a major work in a different language, and in each he is a moralist concerned with the ills of contemporary society, particularly in England, brought on by man's departure from virtue, reason, and good order.

Speculum Meditantis or *Mirour de l'Omme,* the earliest work, consists of about 30,000 octosyllabic lines of French verse. Through allegory it treats the vices and virtues, reviews the state of society since the time of Rome, and finds all classes corrupt because of man himself; it urges repentance and amendment through the intercession of the Blessed Virgin Mary and concludes with a life of her and a series of praises to her under various titles.

Vox Clamantis, in Latin elegiacs, consists of more than 10,000 lines. Introducing his subject with a dream allegory picturing the Peasants' Revolt of 1381, Gower pointedly exposes corruption on the various levels of society, and laments the loss of ideals and the evils of the country.

Confessio Amantis, written in English and comprising more than 34,000 lines in short couplets, also advocates a moral order preserved by wisdom and virtue, but the book is intended for pleasure as well as instruction. The poet, or lover, is told by Venus to confess to Genius, her priest, who instructs him concerning the Deadly Sins as applied to love. There is a profusion of illustrative stories drawn from classical and medieval sources. Gower was a poet, not of revolt, but of reform within the existing framework of society. His talent was notable, but he lacked genius; he did not transcend his own time and his reputation has waned.

Bibliography: *Complete Works,* ed. G. C. MACAULAY, 4 v. (London 1899–1902); *The Major Latin Works of John Gower,* tr. E. W. STOCKTON (Seattle 1962). G. R. COFFMANN, ''John Gower in His Most Significant Role,'' *University of Colorado Studies Series B* 2.4 (1945) 52–61.

[P. E. BEICHNER]

GOYAU, GEORGES

Ecclesiastical historian; b. Orléans, France, May 31, 1869; d. Bernay (Eure), France, Oct. 25, 1939. After studying at the Lycée Louis le Grand and the École normale, he received his university degree in history and was sent to the École française in Rome for further studies. During World War I he served in the Red Cross because his physique was too frail for combat duty. From 1927 until 1938 he was professor of mission history at the Institut Catholique de Paris. He served the Roman Congregation of Rites as a consultor in historical matters. He married Lucie Félix-Faure (b. 1866), a writer, in 1903. After her death in 1913 he married Juliette Heuzey (1862–1952), also a well-known writer, who later published a biography of her husband.

Goyau's prolific pen produced nearly 100 works on diverse topics of religious history, including biographies, the missions, and social Catholicism. His *Histoire religieuse de la France* (1922) formed the seventh volume of the *Histoire de la nation française,* edited by Gabriel Hanotaux. His best-known books were his nine volumes on the Church in modern Germany, *Allemagne religieuse* (1898–1913). Goyau contributed about 170 articles to the *Catholic Encyclopedia.* Many of his writings were aimed at a wide popular audience, but all of them were characterized by accuracy and by esteem for the Church. He was elected to the French Academy in 1922 and was the recipient of many other honors, including membership in the Order of Leopold, in the Order of St. Gregory as a commander, and in the Legion of Honor as a chevalier. Throughout his life he was a fervent Catholic. After his death Pius XII praised him as a model of charity.

Bibliography: F. VEUILLOT, *G. Goyau* (Paris 1942). J. P. HEUZEY, *G. Goyau: Sa vie, son oeuvre* (Paris 1948). J. MORIENVAL, *Catholicisme* 5:128–129, 711; 4:1161–62.

[M. H. QUINLAN]

GOYENECHE Y BARREDA, JOSÉ SEBASTIÁN DE

Peruvian prelate; b. Arequipa, Peru, Jan. 20, 1784; d. Lima, Feb. 19, 1872. He was successively in charge of the Diocese of Arequipa and the Archdiocese of Lima for 54 years during the period of transition between the viceroyalty and the republic. He completed his studies in Lima, and in 1804 and 1805 the University of San Marcos granted him the licentiate and the doctorate in theology and law. He practiced law for some time, but, having a vocation to the priesthood, he received Holy Orders in 1807. He was appointed bishop of Arequipa on April 14, 1817, and was consecrated on Aug. 2, 1818; he took over his see three months later. He rendered invaluable services to both Church and State as a participant in the historical process of the country's emancipation, contributing, at the ecclesiastical level, to the consolidation of the republican institutions. In contrast with many

Seal and signature of José Sebastián De Goyeneche Y Barreda.

others, he knew how to separate the highest interests of religion from political events. Once the revolution was accomplished, he collaborated loyally with the authorities. Because of the prudence of his actions and his tact, he was respected by all, even though he was occasionally forced to maintain inflexibly the rights of the Church to safeguard the integrity of faith and discipline. In all conflicts provoked by the regalist civil power he showed his pastoral virtues and canonical knowledge.

As one of the few bishops who remained at their posts during the crisis of emancipation, he was able to attend to the needs of the other dioceses of Peru and neighboring republics. This task became easier when Pope Gregory XVI designated him apostolic delegate to Peru in 1832. He was promoted to the Archdiocese of Lima on Sept. 26, 1859, where he undertook the reform of the religious orders and continued the restoration of the seminary that had been started by his predecessors.

Bibliography: P. J. RADA Y GAMIO, *El arzobispo Goyeneche y apuntes para la historia del Perú* (Rome 1917), with an appendix containing documents and some illus. R. VARGAS UGARTE, *Historia de la Iglesia en el Perú* 5 v. (Lima 1953–62) v.5.

[E. T. BARTRA]

GRABMANN, MARTIN

Theologian and historian of scholasticism; b. Winterzhofen, Bavaria, Jan. 5, 1875; d. Eichstätt, Jan. 9, 1949. After his philosophical and theological studies in the seminary at Eichstätt, he was ordained in 1898. In 1900 he was sent to Rome to specialize in medieval theology; he obtained his doctorate from the College of St. Thomas in 1902, writing on *Die Lehre des hl. Thomas von Aquin von der Kirche als Gotteswerk* (Ratisbon 1903). In Rome he enjoyed the esteem of F. EHRLE and H. DENIFLE. During his parochial assignment in Eichstätt, he continued to study and publish. His desire for study destined him to an academic career. He became professor of dogma at Eichstätt (1906–13), of Christian philosophy at the University of Vienna (1913–18), and of dogma at the University of Munich (1918–39; 1945–48). Through assiduous research in European libraries, he unearthed a wealth of original material in MSS containing lost works of Siger of Brabant, St. Albert the Great, Peter of Spain, Boethius of Sweden, Peter Abelard, and Meister Eckhart. His principal interests centered on the works of St. Thomas Aquinas, the development of SCHOLASTICISM, ARISTOTELIANISM, THOMISM, and German mysticism. He received honorary degrees from the universities of Louvain, Innsbruck, Milan, and Budapest; in 1935 Pius XII made him an apostolic prothonotary. M. Schmaus, his successor, founded the Grabmann-Institut at the University of Munich in 1954 to promote the study of medieval philosophy and theology.

Bibliography: Works. *Die Geschichte der scholastischen Methode,* 2 v. (Freiburg 1909–11); *Thomas Aquinas,* tr. V. MICHEL (New York 1928); *Introduction to the Theological Summa of St. Thomas,* tr. J. S. ZYBURA from 2d rev. Get. ed. (St. Louis 1930); *Die Werke des heiligen Thomas von Aquin* (3d ed. Münster 1949); *Mittelalterliches Geistesleben,* 3 v. (Munich 1925–56) bibliog. 3:1–35. Literature. J. VAN DER MEERSCH, *Dictionnaire de théologie catholique* (Paris 1903–1950) 16.1:1843–44. R. BÄUMER, *Lexikon für Theologie und Kirche* (Freiburg 1957–) 2 4:1156.

[A. M. WALZ]

GRACE, ARTICLES ON

The articles on grace deal with various aspects of the divine gift whereby God intervenes in the created universe and transforms the human person. The principal articles are: GRACE (IN THE BIBLE) and GRACE (THEOLOGY OF); see also CHRISTIAN ANTHROPOLOGY. Shorter articles treating of the nature of grace include GRACE, CREATED AND UNCREATED; INDWELLING, DIVINE; HABIT (IN THEOLOGY). There are also individual articles on grace in its various infused forms: e.g., FAITH; HOPE; HOLY SPIRIT, GIFTS OF.

Many of the articles on grace are grouped around the antinomies that prompted the great historical controversies (see GRACE, CONTROVERSIES ON; CONVERSION AND GRACE, CONTROVERSIES ON). There are primarily three such antinomies. For grace and human cooperation, see, e.g., JUSTIFICATION; JUSTICE, DOUBLE; PELAGIUS AND PELAGIANISM; SEMI-PELAGIANISM; IMPUTATION OF JUSTICE AND MERIT; SYNERGISM; see also MERIT. For grace and human freedom, see, e.g., FREE WILL AND GRACE; BAIUS AND BAIANISM; JANSENISM; MOLINISM; BÁÑEZ AND BAÑEZIANISM; CONGRUISM; CONGREGATIO DE AUXILIIS; PREMOTION, PHYSICAL; GRACE, EFFICACIOUS; GRACE, SUFFICIENT; PREDESTINATION (IN CATHOLIC THEOLOGY); PREDESTINATION (IN NON-CATHOLIC THEOLOGY). For grace and human nature, see, e.g., GRACE AND NATURE; PURE NATURE, STATE OF; SUPERNATURAL EXISTENTIAL; ELEVATION OF MAN.

There are other articles as well that deal with the acquisition of grace and its effect on the human person. See especially CONVERSION, II (THEOLOGY OF); CONVERTS AND CONVERSION; REDEMPTION (THEOLOGY OF); and the numerous articles in sacramental theology (see SACRAMENTS, ARTICLES ON).

[G. F. LANAVE]

GRACE (IN THE BIBLE)

The concept of grace as it appears in the Bible is treated here by considering its terminology, its effects, its recipients, the condition for its reception, and the problem of grace and merit.

Terminology. In the New Testament the Greek word that corresponds to the English word grace is χάρις, when used in the technical sense of a gratuitous supernatural gift of God to man (e.g., Jn 1.14, 16; 2 Cor 12.9; Rom 1.5). Etymologically, χάρις denotes that which causes joy (χαρά), hence, graciousness, attractiveness, a common meaning of the term in non-Biblical Greek that is also found in Lk 4.22 and Col 4.6. From this basic meaning, χάρις developed the notion of gracious care or help, goodwill, or favor, often with special signification in the New Testament, such as the favor of the new Christian economy of grace (Rom 5.2; 6.14; Gal 2.21; 5.4), the favors of God's external providence that dispose to grace (1 Pt 2.19), divine help on a mission (Acts 14.25; 15.40), and divine favor in itself, which is the source of grace (Lk 1.30; 2.40). The word χάρις can also mean favor of men (Acts 2.47), favor of a collection (1 Cor 16.3), and even gratitude for a favor received, as in the phrase χάριν ἔχειν (to give thanks, to be grateful: Lk 17.9).

In the Old Testament there is no term to match the New Testament technical sense of χάρις. The Septuagint (LXX), however, often (61 times) uses χάρις to translate the Hebrew word *ḥēn,* which sometimes means grace in the sense of charm, attractiveness (e.g., Prv 11.16; 22.1; 31.30), but more often denotes favor, goodwill, especially in the phrase *māṣā' ḥēn bᵉ'ênê,* "to find favor in the eyes" of someone, i.e., to be pleasing to someone who thereby becomes favorably disposed (e.g., Gn 6.8; 18.3; 19.19;30.27; etc.). The Hebrew noun *ḥēn* is connected with the Hebrew verb *ḥānan* (to be gracious, kind, compassionate), used especially with God as the subject (Gn 33.11; 43.29; Ex 33.19; etc.). These Hebrew terms, however, never reach the technical sense of New Testament χάρις. In the LXX, χάρις is used at times also for other Hebrew words, e.g., twice for *raḥămîm* (tender mercy, compassion), three times for *rāṣôn* (benevolent love), and twice for *ḥesed* (loyalty, the dutiful love by which kinsmen or those bound by COVENANT should help one another, or the deeds rising therefrom). The Hebrew word *ḥesed,* however, is generally rendered in the LXX by ἔλεος (mercy). Although the concept of mercy fails to express the mutual bond God entered into through His covenant with Israel, yet, since He did make His covenant out of mercy and does not owe anything to men (although He does owe it to Himself to keep His covenanted word), ἔλεος is not an entirely unfitting term, and it approaches the New Testament concept of grace.

Effects of Grace. In describing the effects of divine favor, Scripture speaks at first chiefly of exterior and general effects, but in time it comes to penetrate increasingly into particular effects within man's soul. The Old Testament first stresses the favor of being God's chosen people, who lived in the *ḥesed* bond with Him, since by covenant—as the sprinkling of blood in Ex 24.8 testified, for life is in the blood [Lv 17.11]—He bound Himself to act toward them as a blood kinsman and as the *gō'ēl* (redeemer) who is committed by covenant to rescue them from their straits. Yet the Old Testament speaks at times of other effects of divine favor. The most general word is *b^e rākâ* (blessing) by which men receive joy, strength, fullness of life, and a special relationship to God. More specific interior effects are mentioned at times, especially wisdom, which makes one spiritually perfect.

In the Synoptic Gospels, χάρις occurs rather rarely (eight times in Luke, never in the others). The picture of grace in the Synoptics is much like that of the Old Testament in that God's favor invites men to belong to His kingdom (Mt 22.1–14; 13.3–50), to be under a new covenant (Mt 26.28), and to be His children (Mt 6.9–10). They must imitate Him (Mt 5.48) and bear much fruit (Mt 7.17; Lk 8.4–15).

The Epistles of St. James and St. Jude do not penetrate further to describe effects of grace interior to man. James, like the Old Testament, speaks much of wisdom and the law. The Petrine Epistles for the most part remain at the same level, speaking of the effects of grace as salvation (1 Pt 1.10), light (1 Pt 2.9), and sanctification (1 Pt 1.2). Some texts go further, speaking of a sanctification that must be interior since it imitates the sanctity of Him who called the faithful (1 Pt 1.15–16) and is a rebirth (1 Pt 1.3). The penetration is deeper if the words about a Christian's participation in the divine nature (2 Pt 1.4) refer to the present life.

The Johannine writings speak of effects of grace as light and truth, but also as passing from death to life (Jn 5.24; 1 Jn 3.14) and an abundant sharing in Christ's life (Jn 10.10) through a rebirth in the Spirit (Jn 3.3). Insofar as man lives this divine life, he cannot sin (1 Jn 3.6, 9). The Father and Son (Jn 14.23), and the Holy Spirit too (1 Jn 4.13), dwell in him.

By far the deepest and richest penetration of grace is described in the Pauline Epistles. In a progressive transformation (2 Cor 3.18) men dedicated to the Christ-mystery become a new creation (Gal 6.15; 2 Cor 5.17) and the temples of God (1 Cor 3.16–17). They live as members of Christ (1 Cor 6.15). They are sons of the Father (Rom 8.14–17; Gal 3.26) and are no longer coerced by the Mosaic Law from without (Rom 7.4–6), but rather are moved interiorly by God's Spirit (Rom 8.14, 26–27) who moves the faithful, not only to the exterior performance of good works, but even to the inner act of will, which God works in them (Phil 2.13). On Him Christians depend for the very thought of good (2 Cor 3.5). Paul distinguishes different effects of grace: there are the greater gifts (1 Cor 12.31), accessible to all, i.e., the abiding state of transformation and the movement to good acts spoken of above. There are also other CHARISMS or charismatic gifts, that are not given to all. Some receive diverse external roles, as those of apostles, prophets, and teachers (1 Cor 12.27–29; Eph 4.7–13); some receive the gifts of tongues, of interpretation, of healing, etc. (1 Cor 12.30)

Recipients of Grace. The Old Testament does not teach clearly to whom God shows favor or gives grace. Two themes, at first sight contradictory, run through the entire Old Testament. Israel knows itself to be the special possession of God, dearer than other nations, because God has bound Himself by covenant to show favor to them (Ex 19.5). The favor of belonging to the chosen people is not extended to all; rather, God says to Moses, "I . . . show favors to whom I will, I . . . grant mercy to whom I will" (Ex 33.19), and to Malachi (1.3), "I loved Jacob, but hated Esau." Yet, the apparently opposite theme also is primitive. Already in the call of Abraham, Israelite tradition represents God as saying, "In you shall all the nations of the earth be blessed" (Gn 12.3). Of the Servant of the Lord, God says, "I will make you a light to the nations, that my salvation may reach to the ends of the earth" (Is 49.6; cf. Is 42.6–7; Jer 16.19–21), for "the Lord's mercy reaches all flesh" (Sir 18.11). He loves even the Assyrians, the worst of men (Jon 4.11).

The theme of the restriction of divine favor appears but little in the Gospels (Mt 10.5–6, 15.24), and then only in such a way that it seems to be but a temporary arrangement. The parable in Lk 17.7–10 seems to imply that one cannot earn a place in the kingdom. In contrast, the theme of universal favor, grace, and mercy is strongly reaffirmed and developed in the Gospels. The Father's love is such that He gave His only Son (Jn 3.16). He loves all, including sinners (Mt 5.45), even the greatest sinners (Mt 18.23–5; Lk 15.12–32; 18.13–14). He searches for sinners (Lk 15.3–9). He is not content merely with doing good to men, but, like a man whose intensity of love leads him to bind himself by a vow, the Father wills to bind Himself by a new and eternal covenant in the blood of His Son, for the "many" (Mt 26.28; the concept of *rabbîm,* "many," is more extensive and forceful than the English connotation). Although He does not really owe anything to man, He does owe it to Himself to keep His covenanted word. The Apostles are ordered to preach to all nations (Mt 28.18–20).

Both themes appear in clearly marked fashion in St. Paul. God wills all men to be saved (1 Tm 2.4), for He has bound Himself in a new covenant (1 Cor 11.25) in which an infinite price (1 Cor 6.20; 7.23) testifies to infinite love, in favor of each individual man (Gal 2.20) so that He who has not spared even His Son will also give to believers all things with Him (Rom 8.32). He will give even the grace to persevere until the end (1 Cor 1.5–8; 1 Thes 5.23–24; Phil 1.6), for He who has begun a good work in them will not leave it unfinished. The theme of restriction appears chiefly in Paul's teaching (Romans ch. 9; 1 Cor 1.26–31) that God's call and predestination are not given to all, and that it is not given according to human merits. The rule is: "I will have mercy on whom I have mercy" (Rom 9.15), as seen in the Old Testament example: "Before the children had yet been born or had done aught of good or evil . . . , it is written: 'Jacob I have loved, but Esau I have hated'" (Rom 9.11–13). Yet Paul does not contradict himself. The quite diverse statements belong to different contexts, and refer to quite different effects of divine favor. The texts of universal grace, considered in their context, refer to eschatological salvation; while in Romans ch. 9 the problem is: How does God choose nations for membership in the chosen people of both covenants? The solution is: Not by merits does God choose them [although those who do receive the special call can cut themselves off by infidelity, as did the Jews (Rom 11.20)]. Even without the privileged condition of full membership in the chosen race, a man can be saved (Rom 2.14–16). Paul knows that God wants all men to have even this privileged state, for He has sent Paul to preach to all the Gentiles (cf. Mt 28.18–20). In view of the limitations of human means, not all can have it; a choice must be made. Thus, the clarity of Paul explains and illumines the merely apparent contradiction in earlier Scriptural passages.

Condition for the Reception of Grace. St. Paul stresses greatly the gratuity of the call to full membership in the chosen people and of the grace of justification, the first step to eschatological salvation (Rom 11.5–6; 4.1–6;). Justification does not depend on the works of the Law (Rom 3.20, 28). Yet, with John (Jn 6.29; 3.18–21; 8.44–47), Paul teaches also that the reception of justification depends on man's recognition and acceptance of God's favor, i.e., on FAITH (Rom 3.28; 4.3; Gal 3.6). Grace comes to man through faith; the just man lives by faith (Rom 1.17). This faith is not just an assent of mind, but includes also an act of obedience of one's will adhering to God (Rom 10.16; 2 Thes 1.8) and active charity (Gal 5.6; cf. 1 Cor 7.19).

A seeming contradiction appears in the scriptural teaching on this faith. On the one hand, all Scripture takes for granted that man can decide whether or not he will adhere to God in faith. Otherwise, all the exhortations of the Prophets, the Apostles, and Christ Himself would be vain. Nor could one deserve to be condemned (Mk 16.16) for that about which he could not do anything. Paul, too, presents faith as a condition in man's power, and exhorts all "not to receive the grace of God in vain" (2 Cor 6.1; cf. Jn 6.28–29). He urges the believers not to grieve the Spirit (Eph 4.30).

On the other hand, faith is a gift of God (Jn 6.37, 43–47, 65–66; Eph 2.8; Phil 1.29) and, inasmuch as Pauline and Johannine faith involves an act of the will, Paul adds that it is God who works in man both the will and the performance (Phil 2.13) and even the good thought by which man sees the good that grace presents for his acceptance (2 Cor 3.5). The seeming contradiction vanishes if one holds fast to the precise words of St. Paul and does not go beyond them: unaided, one cannot earn the gift of grace (Eph 2.8); but it is offered abundantly to all, for God wills all men to be saved (1 Tm 2.4), and His love has even engaged itself in a new covenant (1 Cor 11.25) with its price in Christ's blood (1 Cor 6.20) in order to offer all graces (Rom 8.32) to every man. He is faithful and will do this. It is true, then, that without His aid man cannot even move his will to accept God's grace or conceive the good thought of doing what leads to salvation; it is God who works in man both the will and the performance (Phil 2.13) and gives man the good thought (2 Cor 3.5).

Yet the outcome is in man's control, for man can reject God's offered gift. Paul entreats the faithful not to reject it (2 Cor 6.1). If man does not reject it, God will work in him both the will and the performance. Paul does not mean, of course, that man can of himself make a decision saying, as it were, "I will not reject this grace," for that decision would be a good will. It is God who works such a good will in man. There must be another sense in which man can keep from receiving grace in vain, for Paul urges man to do just that. It is not hard to see; it is grace that begins the work, showing man a good thought, and giving him a favorable attitude. Grace can and does go thus far without man's aid (although it will not go as far as consent without him). Since grace is already at work making this start without man, no decision, nothing at all from man is needed for the good thought and favorable attitude that grace makes to continue (although men could do something to remove them). This lack of interference, without any decision, is enough to be a condition on which grace will continue and work both the will and the performance. Of course, man cooperates in this completion even though grace began without him. Other interpreters, adhering less closely to the precise words of St. Paul, simply say that grace at once, at the outset, makes man able to move his will to accept it. In both views, although without grace man is helpless (Rom

7.14–25), man can do all things in Him who strengthens him (Phil 4.13).

Grace and Merit. The gratuity of grace does not preclude merit. For although the word merit is found neither in the Old Testament nor in the New Testament, yet the chief foundation of the notion of merit, God's promise to reward good, is already seen throughout all the Old Testament (although retribution in a future life is not clearly mentioned until the second century B.C.). Paul's emphasis on the gratuity of grace does not prevent him from teaching that, after gratuitously receiving the means of merit, grace, the Christians who long for the PAROUSIA are given a crown of justice from the just Judge (2 Tm 4.8; 2 Cor 5.10). However, Paul insists that man does not earn reward in the same full and fundamental sense in which he earns punishment. He merits in a lesser, secondary sense, since the graces that make him holy and move him to do good are a gift: ''The wages of sin is death, but the gift of God is life everlasting in Christ Jesus Our Lord'' (Rom 6.23).

In making this distinction, Paul is bringing out an implication of the fact that God is the Father from whom all fatherhood takes its name (Eph 3.15; Gal 3.26). Children can, in the fullest sense, earn punishment, even disinheritance, but they need not and cannot merit the basic love and care of their father. Similarly, man's hope of reaching the Father's mansions is based on the truth, ''if we are sons, we are heirs also'' (Rom 8.17; Col 3.24). However, the Father requires that the faithful be conformed to His Son, Jesus Christ (which entails merit), for they are ''joint heirs with Christ, provided however we suffer with him that we may also be glorified with him'' (Rom 8.17). Just as the very merit of Christ did not strictly move the Father to grant mercy and grace (for He did not need to be moved, since He always loved men, and His spontaneous love sent His Son), so neither do man's works move the Father. His unearned love is the basic explanation of all the good men are and have. Meritorious obedience is a human condition, which, in His love of goodness and of mankind, the Father wills to regard (although He gains nothing) as man's fulfillment of the covenant founded by and on God's love that man has not earned.

Bibliography: *Encyclopedic Dictionary of the Bible*, tr. and adap. by L. HARTMAN (New York 1963) 897–903. R. BULTMANN, G. KITTEL, *Theologisches Wörterbuch zum Neuen Testament* (Stuttgart 1935–) 2:475–479. J. HASPECKER and F. MUSSNER, *Lexikon für Theologie und Kirche*, ed. J. HOFER and K. RAHNER (Freiberg 1957–65) 4: 977–984. P. BONNETAIN, *Dictionnaire de la Bible*, suppl. ed. L. PIROT, et al. (Paris 1928–) 3:701–1319. E. WÜRTHWEIN and G. STÄHLIN, *Die Religion in Geschichte und Gegenwart* (Tübingen 1957–65) 2:1632–37. J. GUILLET, *Themes of the Bible*, tr. A. J. LAMOTHE (Notre Dame, Ind. 1960) 26–93. L. CERFAUX, ''La Théologie de la grâce selon saint Paul,'' *La Vie spirituelle* (Paris 1919–) 83 (1950) 5–19. J. BONSIRVEN, *The Theology of the New Testament*, tr. S. F. L. TYE (Westminster, Md. 1963) 34–127, 130–139, 251, 270–351.

[W. G. MOST]

GRACE (THEOLOGY OF)

The theological usage of the term ''grace'' directly corresponds with that of its Latin equivalent, *gratia,* from which it is derived. It is notable that the English word has also absorbed the peculiarly Christian character given by St. Paul to the Greek word χάρις. Thus grace is ''the free and unmerited favour of God as manifested in the salvation of sinners'' (*A New English Dictionary,* ed. J. A. H. Murray, 5.1:326), or simply ''the free and unmerited favour of God'' (*The Shorter Oxford English Dictionary,* ed. C. T. Onions, 817), or even, according to the Shakespearean usage, the very source of favor, God (cf. the phrase ''grace of Grace,'' *Macbeth* 5.8.72). It is this fundamental emphasis on the total gratuity of grace that effectively relates the totality of its Catholic theological exposition to the affirmations of Christian revelation.

Yet, in addition to this common note, there are connotations. Generally these arise from the fact that historically there are certain problematics that have brought other aspects than gratuity to the fore. As a result, a full grasp of the notion of grace must indicate these emphases. Perhaps the broadest of these would be the antithesis of grace and sin, which has frequently tended to emphasize and even overemphasize the medicinal aspect of grace. Almost equally important has been the problematic of GRACE and nature, which at times would move in the direction of making grace simply an aid or completion or perfection of nature. Correlative to this would be the controversies engendered by Calvinism, Baianism, and Jansenism concerning ''corrupt'' nature and ''pure'' nature (*see* PURE NATURE, STATE OF), and thus the concern with naturally, or ethically, good acts. Noteworthy too are the lengthy debates over JUSTIFICATION, which often seem to equate grace and justification. The long, heated conflict over freedom and grace in terms of divine and human causality accentuates grace and the specific concrete act or the divine motion involved and the human response to that motion (*see* FREE WILL AND GRACE). Added to this would be the trend of the manuals to encompass all of the doctrine of grace under the scholastic categories and so conceive of it almost solely in terms of habitual and actual grace [*see* HABIT (IN THEOLOGY)]. Finally, there is the extensive discussion that begins with Denis PETAU (d. 1652) on the role of the Holy Spirit in the divine indwelling and His relation to grace. The interchange becomes quite concentrated on this point and appears eventually to give a kind of tangential character to the relation between the divine INDWELLING and grace, the uncreated almost obscured by the created. Some other historical contrasts could be included, but these are central and suffice to set the scene for the modern understanding and emphasis.

For in the light of biblical theology and a deeper appreciation of the history of theology, a much larger perspective has been given. In it the term ''grace'' is seen not only as a personal gift but as a whole economy. Seen in this perspective, the various aspects stressed as a result of particular historical situations are judged to be derivative and secondary. Grace, then, rather comprises the whole history of God's saving dealing with man. It signifies essentially an economy of love. As such it denotes the Holy Trinity—Father, Son, and Holy Spirit—giving itself freely to man and calling for man's free response through faith, hope, and charity. It connotes at the same time Christ in the supreme moment of the encounter and this in turn embodied in the Sacraments and the Church, His Body. This approach is thus more comprehensive and more fully expressive of the theology of Scripture and the fullness of the Christian tradition.

History of the Catholic Doctrine of Grace

The Catholic doctrine of grace calls for a considerable history of its theological development if it is to be fully understood. In fact, it may well be argued that this historical aspect is more necessary to the understanding of grace than to the understanding of any other doctrinal area in Catholic teaching. Yet, if such a history is to look to understanding rather than be a mere cataloging of events, this development must be regarded as a properly theological enterprise. This means that for the Catholic this theological development results from the effort undertaken by the believer to understand better what he believes. By faith he assents and consents to God's revealing Himself through Christ and the Church, and seeks to understand the divine meaning by bringing to bear rational and philosophical notions and perspectives. Because of this, his theologizing will necessarily have an element of relativity and contingency. In any age the theologian is bound to time, to history, and to the vital exigency of development in understanding. This contingent aspect stands in relation to a permanent element, i.e., the DOGMAS defined by the Church, all that is contained in Scripture, as well as the total Catholic doctrinal tradition. To this will be added certain fundamental metaphysical acquisitions that constitute the basis of a Christian metaphysical horizon. In seeking to understand or apply these, the theologian will make use of contingent representations or notions or even systematizations, for the theologian must draw upon what he knows. He must seek intelligibility through the natural structures that are open to him in his own cultural milieu. In view of this, a few generalizations may help in understanding the very complex history of the theology of grace in the compressed form in which it must be treated here.

First, there is always a hazard that in the light of an effort of genius men will be tempted to bind the revealed and defined affirmations to a particular theology. It is easy to forget that there can be a number of theologies developed about them and that the only fully realized theology is that of the blessed in heaven. This does not deny the fact that a particular theological effort may arrive at understanding, in particular areas, which becomes a permanent part of the Catholic doctrinal tradition.

Second, often and particularly in the matter of grace the theological formulations rise out of a contemporary and immediate concern, confusion, controversy, or error. Frequently, therefore, the theological representations and formulations may concentrate on only one aspect of the doctrine and so form themselves into counterpositions to the positions taken by the opposition. As a result, both Scripture and the Catholic doctrinal positions may very well be read and understood in the light of these counterpositions. This understanding may then tend to set other elements of the doctrine into the background or to obscure them.

Third, to understand the history of a theological development it is of the essence to ask precisely what the problem was that was the central concern. Why was it a problem, and exactly what were the questions being asked about it? How far was the answer given circumscribed by the particular problem or controversy out of which it came? Finally, were all the biblical possibilities open to the theologians, and were they acquainted with the full doctrinal tradition on the matter?

Fourth, necessarily integrated into this whole approach is the underlying historical fact of development, namely, the theological acceptance that growth in Christian understanding finds its dynamism in the revealed Word of God manifesting itself to men. Hence, for the believer, its past is necessarily incorporated into the living Church here and now. The theologian thus judges, evaluates, enlarges, and reconstructs the theological presentations of the past in the light of this development at once truly historical and truly theological (*see* DOCTRINE, DEVELOPMENT OF).

General patristic. Central to understanding the teaching of the early Church on grace is a grasp of the basic problematic that determines much of its form: how to harmonize the religion received out of the Jewish-Christian religious life with the Greco-Roman culture? [see J. Daniélou, *Message évangélique et culture hel-*

lénistique au IIe et IIIe siècles (Tournai 1961)] The Christian teachers were faced with an abundance of religious and philosophical ideas and images and representations out of the Greco-Roman world. Among these they endeavored to find ways to affirm and present what was primarily an experienced way of life rather than a theory (*see* THEOLOGY, INFLUENCE OF GREEK PHILOSOPHY ON). And so, in the earliest writings, what is stressed is that a new life, a new kind of knowledge and immortality, are revealed through Jesus Christ (cf. Didache 9.3; 10.2). Ignatius of Antioch presents salvation as actually achieved through union with Christ, through whom newness of life flows into men so that He is their true and inseparable life (cf. *Eph.* 15.3; 3.2; *Magn.* 14; *Rom.* 6.3; *Smyrn.* 4).

Greek Fathers. It is with Justin Martyr that two main themes are opened up that directly relate the patristic teaching to the Pauline doctrine on grace. The first is the notion of freedom and responsibility, which will be seen presently. The second thematic comes to the fore in Justin's explanation of the redemptive character of Christ's death on the cross.

Divinization-Recapitulation. Justin explains that because of His redemptive work, Christ has become the source of a new humanity that He has regenerated through water, faith, and the cross (cf. *Dial.* 40). It is this profoundly biblical perspective that Irenaeus takes up from Justin and develops into a comprehensive theory of RECAPITULATION: ''He recapitulated in Himself the long history of man, summing up and giving us salvation in order that we might receive again in Christ Jesus what we had lost in Adam, that is, the image and likeness of God'' (*Adversus haereses* 3.18.1; cf. J. Quasten, *Patrology* 1:295–297). It is this basic theme set deeply into a Trinitarian context that gives meaning to the whole patristic emphasis on divinization (θέωσις, θεοποιεῖν). Thus it is the Son who makes men participate in His eternal generation through the gift of filial adoption. This runs through from Irenaeus (cf. *Adversus haereses* 3.19.1) to Cyril of Alexandria [cf. *Jo.* 1.9 (on Jn 1.13)]. Into this notion of divinization is assumed the understanding of 2 Pt 1.4, ''sharers of the divine nature.'' This is understood as a participation in and a communion with the Triune life itself [e.g., by Cryil of Alexandria, *Jo.* 9.1 (on Jn 14.11–20)]. Integrated into it is the Johannine and Pauline theme of REBIRTH and regeneration. To be noted also is the explanation of this participation in terms of a form impressed on the soul as in Basil of Caesarea and Gregory of Nyssa (*Hom. 2 in Cant.*). Throughout, as H. de Lubac, SJ, has noted, the SUPERNATURAL character of grace is developed with increasing clarity [*Surnaturel: Études historiques* (Paris 1946) 325–394].

Grace and Liberty. Here again the teaching of the Greek Fathers is closely related to a basic affirmation of St. Paul. It is the proclamation that the economy of grace has made the Christian truly free, has freed his liberty that he may act in love. In part this emphasis is to confront the widespread and contemporary Greek fatalism with clarity and assurance. However, its inner emphasis has its source in the conviction that it is precisely through his liberty that man is in the image of God (see, e.g., Irenaeus, *Adversus haereses* 4.4.1, *Patrologia Graeca* 7:981; Gregory of Nyssa, *Hom. opif.* 16, *Patrologia Graeca* 44:184). Accordingly, it is by man's free choice of light instead of darkness that he renews himself and remodels himself (Gregory of Nyssa, *V. Mos.* 2.54). It is God's love that places His liberty on the same level as man's (cf. Basil).

As can be seen, the Greek Fathers (with many nuances that cannot be treated here) clearly delineate the main lines that will structure the history of the theology of grace. The notion of divinization and the notion of Christian liberty will be obscured in various ways. At times, aspects of each of these themes will be so emphasized as to distort them, even dangerously so. Yet around these two poles the doctrinal history of grace will revolve.

St. Augustine. The name of St. AUGUSTINE rather than that of the Latin Fathers in general is used here simply because in fact for the Western Church he is the ''Doctor of Grace.'' As with the Greek Fathers, divinization through grace is a basic theme in St. Augustine, although his Trinitarian context has another accent. The theme of grace and liberty is integrated in a very important way with the dimension of sin.

Divinization. Of special importance here is the Christological aspect that Augustine stresses. In a sense, it is the development of one aspect of recapitulation. This is found in his teaching on the *totus Christus,* the whole Christ. For Christ is not only in the head and so not in the Body, but the whole Christ is in the head and Body (cf. *In evang. Ioh.* 28.1). ''So the Word was made flesh and dwelt among us, and to that flesh the Church is joined so that there comes into being the whole Christ, head and Body'' (*In epist. Ioh.* 1.2). This solidarity and community of the redeemed with Christ is a very important element in the theology of Augustine concerning grace, as will be seen shortly.

In the specifically Trinitarian aspect of the economy of grace, St. Augustine gives a prominent place to the presence or indwelling of the Trinity in the souls of the just. It is this indwelling proper to the regenerated that enables the Christian in grace to know and love God in a special way (*Trin.* 4.20.28–29). In this life of grace he attributes to the Son, or Word, illumination, which the Greek Fathers attribute to the Holy Spirit. To the Holy

Spirit, following St. Paul (Rom 5.5), he attributes charity, since the Holy Spirit is the gift by which men love God. "Love itself which is of God, which is God, is especially the Holy Spirit, by which the love of God is diffused in our hearts, by which love the whole Trinity dwells in us" (*Trin.* 15.18.32). And so, according to Augustine, to live well is to adhere to the whole Trinity by Christ and the Spirit. In this very personal reflection on the mystery of the Trinitarian indwelling, St. Augustine gives to his doctrine of grace an orientation that will deeply color later Latin theological thought. On this point, however, a number of theologians following De Régnon have felt that Augustine is attempting to balance unity and transcendence, and that this has led to far too strict a formulation of APPROPRIATION [see H. Rondet, *Gratia Christi* (Paris 1948) 162]. In addition to these aspects peculiar to himself, St. Augustine clearly teaches other elements that are found in the Greek Fathers; e.g., men's union in brotherhood with Christ by reason of a filial adoption by God. They are divinized because they are sharers of the divine nature of the Son, who has become a sharer of men's nature (*Epist.* 140.10).

Grace and Liberty. It is in the development of this Pauline thematic that St. Augustine exerts his deepest and most pervasive tutorial influence on Western theological thought. For reasons both personal and doctrinal, the grace of Christ strikes him above all as liberative. It is the grace of Christ that heals the effects of ORIGINAL SIN and personal sin and so frees men to live a genuinely Christian life. More than anyone else, St. Augustine elaborates the Pauline teaching on the supernatural polarity of original sin and the grace of Christ. Yet it is evident that in the doctrinal history of grace his teaching on this polarity has been a source of deeply divisive debate. In the name of his teaching on grace, erroneous positions have been formulated, and in some cases those claiming him as their authority have been authoritatively condemned by the Catholic Church. In view of these facts, therefore, it might be well to apply specifically the principles set down earlier in this article. First, in studying the texts of St. Augustine it must be kept in mind that he is to be read historically, i.e., in the light of his own preoccupations. He is not trying to formulate a theory of sufficient and efficacious grace. Neither is he trying to construct the metaphysical elements proper to the free act. Finally, he is not, as such, concerned with the basic problematic of the Jansenists: to establish a theory reconciling free will with the primacy of predestination. In fact, St. Augustine simply does not eliminate free will as the Jansenists would like to have him do but insists on it even when he insists most strongly on the necessity and power of grace. At the same time, he admits frequently the difficulty of reconciling both these insistences [*Grat. Christi* 47.52; see G. de Broglie, "Pour une meilleure intelligence du 'De correptione et gratia,'" *Augustinus magister* (Paris 1954) 2:317–337].

Perhaps the best view of the problematic as St. Augustine himself sees it is found in his *De correptione et gratia.* Here he affirms that it is the sin of Adam that calls forth the just wrath of God and that man renews his solidarity with sinful Adam by his own personal sins and thus evokes God's wrath on them (*Corrept.* 7.12, 16; 9.25). All this involves, then, a hereditary and collective responsibility along with personal responsibility. Augustine is not concerned with human nature in the abstract but specific man in a concrete historical situation. In Augustine grace, therefore, refers to the actual states of man: Adam before sin acting in accord with his God-given powers fully free; the present state of man called to eternal life so that any salutary activity absolutely requires the grace of Christ; lastly, redeemed humanity joined with God in the heavenly city. In this present state, then, sin or salvation, merit or demerit, must be recognized as the fruit of men's solidarity with the first Adam or with Christ. Only the grace of Christ enables men to tend freely to eternal life (G. de Broglie, *op. cit.* 334–335). It is in the light of these doctrinal perspectives drawn from Scripture itself that the Augustinian teaching on grace and liberty must be weighed.

Basic to this perspective on Augustine is his distinction between freedom (*libertas*) and free will or free choice (*liberum arbitrium*). Freedom, or *libertas,* is the effective engagement of all man's powers in tending to his only true end, God; it is love fully implemented. Thus, fallen man possesses free choice (*liberum arbitrium*), but he is not truly free (*libertas*) to accomplish his true purpose. And this purpose is to participate in God's freedom and love Him as He loves us. Only through the grace of Christ can he overcome sin and be free to love God. As long as free choice remains, this freedom can be regained through grace (see *Enchir.* 32; *C. Iulian.* 6.11; *C. Pelag.* 1.3.5; *Quaest. Simpl.* 1.1.14). Fallen man can act or not act under grace; but if his action is to be free in the Christian (and what one may term supernatural) sense, then grace is absolutely necessary. Sin has caused the loss of freedom, the power to do that which deserves eternal life, the freedom to love God (*Corrept.* 12.33). Only God can restore this because God is love and only God can give love (*Lib. arb.* 2.20.54).

This approach serves to bring out a matrix of the conflict with the Pelagians (*see* PELAGIUS AND PELAGIANISM). It is not a question of the Pelagians championing free will and Augustine rejecting it, but rather of Augustine insisting on degrees of freedom rather than a *simpliste,* undifferentiated idea of it. For Augustine freedom is what St.

Paul calls Christian freedom, the freedom of the children of God. Man is in sin, hereditary and personal in solidarity with Adam. Through divinely engraced solidarity with Christ, he is healed and is now truly capable of exercising the freedom of a son of God through love (*Corrept.* 11.32). For a Pelagian such as Julian, liberty is a matter of indetermination of choice, but for Augustine it is the manifestation of the very nature of man himself, the option that determines his whole fulfillment. Grace alone can give this to sinful man so that, while it is difficult, he is truly free.

Once this is seen, it is also clear why Augustine places so much stress on the gratuity of grace. ''After man's fall God willed that man's approach to Him should only be because of His grace, and it was only because of His grace that man did not depart from Him'' (*Persev.* 7.13). So the power of free choice is healed by grace, but man is not exempt from willing—but to will the good and to achieve it, this is the work of grace (*libertas; Corrept.* 2.4).

It is in this properly Augustinian context that his usage of *delectatio victrix* and the so-called *gratia indeclinabilis* must be evaluated. The *delectatio victrix* has to be set in the framework of Augustine's own psychological theory of choice. First, the will never decides anything without a motive, and evidently some motives are more effective than others (*Spir. et litt.* 34.60). Second, it is from God that one receives his first thoughts, and so the providential design of God makes it opportune that certain thoughts enter one's mind (*Persev.* 8.20). Finally, God knows what reaction a man will have to a particular motive. Grace does not cause one to act but evokes the desire to act. It does not dispense with willing but brings one to love the true good and so to act. The *delectatio* is part of the total free act. In the case of indeclinable grace, or what some have called irresistible grace, the passage in question reads: ''Aid has been brought to the weakness of the human will so that divine grace might act indeclinably and invincibly [*indeclinabiliter et insuperabiliter ageretur*]'' (Corrept. 12.38). This has been treated as though the antithesis rested on the adverbs, whereas, in fact, as De Broglie points out, in the light of the total theology of Augustine, the emphatic word is *ageretur.* It is this that centers the distinction between the primitive state of Adam in his full power and man's present condition enabled to act by grace but without loss to his power of free choice (*liberum arbitrium*) [see G. de Broglie, *op. cit.* 334; M. T. Clark, *Augustine: Philosopher of Freedom* (New York 1959) 55–75.]

St. Anselm. The ''father of scholastic theology'' is introduced here for two reasons. First, because of his mediatorial relationship between the world of Augustine and the scholastic world that is on the horizon. Second, in this matter of grace he reflects and brings to the fore the thematic on grace and liberty present in the traditional teaching. This second point is of considerable importance because the later debates over sufficient and efficacious grace have served frequently to obscure the primary doctrine with a secondary issue.

Anselm's organized treatment of grace and liberty takes both the Augustinian perspective and the patristic tradition and roots them deeply in the soil of Western theology. Like Augustine, he sees freedom from the standpoint of purpose. For him as for Augustine the right will is an engraced will and the only true freedom is a will rightly ordered. As with Augustine, Anselm never considers man except in his actual historical state, called to beatitude and absolutely in need of grace to attain it. Thus, to be free, one must preserve that rectitude whereby man wills what God wills. No creature, however, has such rectitude of will save through the grace of God (*De concordia praescientiae et praedestinationis et gratiae Dei cum libero arbitrio* 3.3). Yet this grace does not do away with free choice (*liberum arbitrium*) because man must choose to cooperate with grace. Grace enables the will to accomplish what it was created to do (*libertas*), but the will has the power to refuse this grace. The rectitude that comes with grace results from free choice and joins the free will to its proper supernatural end (*ibid.* 3.3). As Augustine, Anselm affirms that it is the union of grace and free choice that brings about salvation. Either by itself does not suffice (*ibid.* 3.5), but the primacy lies with grace (*ibid.* 3.4). All this explanation is informed with what has been seen as central to the patristic tradition, namely, that true human freedom is a participation in the divine freedom. St. Augustine saw this as the work of love. St. Anselm finds it in the rectitude whereby one seeks justice and so wills what God wills.

St. Thomas Aquinas. With St. Thomas there comes one of the most deeply decisive moments in the history of the doctrine of grace. His work represents a synthesis of the Christian tradition with the resources and perspectives of Greek philosophical thought. It is also, in a sense, the doctrine of Augustine rethought and reformulated in the perspective of his own theological synthesis, which is quite properly called Thomism [see F. Van Steenberghen, in A. Fliche and V. Martin, eds. *Histoire de l'église depuis les origines jusqu'à nos jours* (Paris 1935) 13:253]. It is this speculative instrument of Christian thought that has been the common basis for the majority of theological treatises on grace since the 16th century. For this reason the teaching of St. Thomas must be considered in some detail.

In Overall Synthesis. To evaluate properly the teaching of St. Thomas on grace, it must be recognized that this doctrine is subordinate to his overall theological synthesis and so dispersed throughout his *Summa theologiae.* Yet the full patristic tradition finds proper place in his work. The thematic of recapitulation, already noted, finds full place in the *Summa theologiae.* The ecclesial emphasis of St. Augustine as to the relation of head and members is properly emphasized in his treatment of the redemption (*Summa theologiae* 3a, 19.4; 48.2 ad 1). The theological tradition on divinization he expresses by saying that men are beatified through participation, so that in this sense they may be called gods (*ibid.* 1a2ae, 3.1 ad 1). Through grace and the work of charity man is incorporated into the familial life of the Father, the Son, and the Holy Spirit. Accordingly, as sharer in the divine nature man enjoys the Divine Persons (*ibid.* 1a2ae, 65.5; 1a, 43.3 ad 1) and is therefore deified by them (*ibid.* 1a2ae, 112.1). And so for St. Thomas grace is seen as the favor of God, the action of His merciful or gracious disposition. God, therefore, gives Himself to humanity by reason of a vital, creative act of love. This in turn effects a responsive action in the creature so engraced (*ibid.* 1a2ae, 110.1 ad 1; *De ver.* 27.1). Finally, taking man in his actual historical situation, he incorporates the Augustinian emphasis on the medicinal character of grace as derived from the fact of original sin (*Summa theologiae* 1a2ae, 109.2; 109.4).

Grace Synthesis. It is grace as understood in the synthesis based on St. Thomas's notion of nature that has been most decisive in the history of the theological doctrine of grace as it has come down to modern times. Negatively, this influence manifests itself in the counterpositions taken to it particularly in the nominalist tradition. Positively, it is evidenced in what since the 16th century has been the common scholastic tradition formed in terms of the *Summa theologiae.* This in turn, in a variety of forms, has been the structure of the manuals of theology that have been the medium of the tradition down to the present time. There are, of course, other and quite different theological traditions, but in the limits of this article St. Thomas alone is the concern because his influence is central to the understanding of the common theological tradition on grace.

To evaluate his role in the history of the doctrine as well as the relationship of his theological work to the modern systematic theology on grace, some preliminary considerations are necessary. First, building on the scholarly achievements in the history of scholastic thought laid by such men as M. Grabmann, A. Landgraf, and É. H. Gilson, such specialists as H. Bouillard, SJ, H. Redon, SJ, and J. Auer have brought about an extensive historical reevaluation of the theological formulations of St. Thomas. The result of these studies, strongly undergirded, is the contention that St. Thomas's own theology of grace has been given perspectives and emphases by his disciples that are not necessarily present in his actual work. For example, the central role given to the problem of grace and liberty as it culminates in the *De auxiliis* debate is not found in St. Thomas. The compression of the treatment on grace into the categories of habitual and actual grace is alien to St. Thomas. The historical situation that made the topics of justification and MERIT treatises in themselves is equally foreign to his synthesis. It becomes clear, too, that the extensive and supple use of Aristotelian metaphysical positions results from a deep personal reflection on them so that they might serve the traditional Christian doctrine on grace. His purpose is theological, and so it is the traditional doctrine coming through the Greek Fathers and especially St. Augustine that is rethought and elucidated in terms of its ontological exigencies. Making use of the Greek philosophical resources and synthesizing them with the Christian tradition through the medium of his own personal reflection and judgment, St. Thomas endeavored to employ them to probe the depths of the doctrine of grace. In this he represents with St. Albert the transition from a refined and highly nuanced biblical theology to a deeply speculative enterprise [see J. Auer, *Entwicklung der Gnade in der Hochacholastik,* 2 v. (Freiburg 1942–51) 1:109–123].

Central to St. Thomas's speculation on grace is the notion of a fixed and stable nature. It is this philosophical conception of nature with its dynamism or principle and the ends proper to it that enabled St. Thomas to formulate the idea of the absolutely supernatural. In harmonizing the received theological tradition with these philosophical considerations, he makes the case that the supernatural end actually given to the intelligent being gives consistency and orientation to the NATURAL ORDER itself. Yet it should be noted that it is this very concern with nature that tends to make him give heavy emphasis in his thought to what the scholastics were beginning to call created grace (*see* GRACE, CREATED), a position taken up in opposition to Peter Lombard's identification of charity and the Holy Spirit [see J. Auer, *Entwicklung der Gnade in der Hochacholastik,* 2 v. (Freiburg 1942–51)]. St. Thomas thus explains the life of grace in terms of nature and its operations. The nature of man, according to his teaching, has three principles or dynamisms of operation, the very being of the soul (*essentia animae*) and the faculties of reason and will. Since God does not act less perfectly in the works of grace than of nature, there is, he finds, a parallel (see *Summa theologiae* 1a2ae, 65.3; 110.4 and ad 1). Just as nature, so the life of grace has principles whereby it achieves its proper end: grace itself as the supernatural principle of existence in the soul and the theological virtues perfecting the faculties [see O. Lottin, *Psychologie et morale aux XIIe et XIIIe siècles,* 3 v. (Louvain 1942–49) 3:468–472].

It is in the light of this parallelism that St. Thomas's notion of grace as a habit, or, more accurately, as a habitual gift (*donum habituale*), must be seen. Lottin traces the development of this conception of grace as a habit to two main currents. One of these, a theological conception, stems from Hugh of Saint-Victor and is Augustinian in inspiration. The other is given currency by Peter Abelard and is Aristotelian in source (*ibid.* 103–115). It is this second line of emphasis for which Thomas opts. It is the application of the thesis noted above that God must provide for the life of grace as He does for the natural life. And so in the natural order God gives forms and virtues that are the principles of action and incline the nature to the movements proper to it. Equally, to achieve the supernatural good, God infuses forms as supernatural qualities to accomplish it. Hence the gift of grace is a kind of quality, *qualitas quaedam* (*Summa theologiae* 1a2ae, 110.2). As such, it is a permanent habitude, which is the root of the infused virtues. This idea of a permanent habitude might well signify not so much the Aristotelian habit but a permanent hold of God in man's very being; or, as C. Moeller indicates, in St. Bonaventure, to hold is to be held [see ''Théologie de la grâce et oecuménisme,'' *Irénikon* 28 (1955) 32–37; H. Bouillard, *Conversion et grâce chez s. Thomas d'Aquin* (Paris 1944) 211–219].

In connection with St. Thomas's formulation of grace as a habitual gift, a word is in order on its correlative in the later Thomistic tradition, actual grace. St. Thomas himself makes the distinction between the habitual gift and divine aid, *divinum auxilium* (*Summa theologiae* 1a2ae, 111.2; 110.2). He speaks in these places of God moving the soul of man to know or to will or to act. Yet he would also say that commonly the term ''grace'' means the habitual justifying gift. Moreover, he recognizes in the preparation for justification a divine aid by which God moves man (*ibid.* 1a2ae, 112.1 ad 1). Whether this divine aid is to be equated with the usage of the term ''actual grace'' has been a source of considerable debate since the study of H. Bouillard on the subject (*op. cit.*). Bouillard argues quite persuasively that the whole matter must be studied in the light of St. Thomas's own development as a theologian. The issue is a peculiarly subtle one, and St. Thomas's expressions do leave themselves open to divergent interpretations. However, in the light of Bouillard's work and subsequent debates about it, it would appear legitimate to presume this highly complex problematic historically an open issue [see H. Rondet, *Gratia Christi* (Paris 1948) 218–220; J. Auer, *Entwicklung der Gnade in der Hochacholastik,* 2 v. (Freiburg 1942–51) 1:211–219].

With regard to the relationship between grace and liberty, St. Thomas brings to its theological structuring a whole philosophical and speculative instrument unavailable to his predecessors. At no point, however, does he treat this relationship for its own sake. His concern is to integrate it into the more universal framework of his metaphysics. Grace does not violate liberty, and God will not save man without the movement of free will (*Summa theologiae* 1a2ae, 113.3). However, God is absolutely the first cause and moves all other things (*ibid.* 1a, 19.8). Grace and liberty thus are set into the ontological order of the relationship between the first cause and a secondary one. Hence St. Thomas places emphasis on the fact that this first cause is neither necessary nor contingent but transcendent (*In 1 perih,* 14). Accordingly, while a good deal of the later debate on sufficient and efficacious grace will center on the interpretation of St. Thomas, nonetheless it will center on a question that he neither raises nor in its essence considers. It will involve also an understanding of actual grace that possibly may not have been present in his work. See in addition to the works already noted: W. A. Van Roo, *Grace and Original Justice according to St. Thomas* (Rome 1955); G. Lafont, *Structures et méthode dans la Somme Théologique de saint Thomas d'Aquin* (Bruges 1961); J. Alfaro, *Lo natural y lo sobrenatural: Estudio historico desde santo Tomas hasta Cayetano* (Rome 1952).

Nominalist tradition. Recent scholarship has tended to see in the nominalist tradition a much more constructive character than has hitherto been conceded it [see H. A. Oberman, ''Some Notes on the Theology of Nominalism,'' *Harvard Theological Review* 53 (1960) 46–76]. More and more it is emphasized that its accepted historical title, nominalism, is based on an epistemological conception that is not central to the tradition itself but derivative from its religio-theological perspectives and preoccupations. It is because of these theological presuppositions that its teaching on grace is included here. They serve to bring out the continuing evolution and emphasis on the gratuity of grace and help to evaluate properly many of the discussions at the Council of Trent.

Essential to the understanding of the nominalist development is the fact of its very heavy accentuation on the sovereignty of God and its correlative, His absolute freedom. This accentuation, as nominalists see it, is a necessary antidote to a prevailing and dangerously deterministic Aristotelianism (represented for many of them by St. Thomas). Opposed to this must be a return to the only law open to the Christian—the law of love proposed by Augustine, wherein alone true liberty acts. For God's work is one of absolute freedom. He gives Himself in total freedom out of love and not by reason of any created structure or exigency such as a stable order of nature would set up [see R. Guelluy, *Philosophie et théologie chez Guillaume d'Ockham* (Paris 1947) 266–267].

In the realm of grace, this absolute sovereignty and freedom of God is preserved by what is the central religio-theological motif of the whole tradition. This is the *potentia absoluta-potentia ordinata* principle. The nominalists through this principle clearly articulate ''the contingence of the whole order of nature as well as grace, and thus emphasize the dependence of all things with regard to a Principle that acts with a sovereign liberty and gratuity'' [P. Vignaux, *Nominalisme du XIVe siècle* (Montreal 1948) 22]. Through the interaction of the *potentia absoluta* and the *potentia ordinata,* divine mercy and divine justice are reconciled. Man becomes just, as he must in order to be saved, but it is solely through divine acceptance.

The stress of the nominalist tradition on acceptance in order to preserve absolute gratuity leads to a further step in the rejection of the medieval, and particularly the Thomistic, explanation of grace as a kind of habit or habitude. For, as nominalists see it, God's acceptance alone makes man and his works worthy of heaven and thus makes the whole notion of *habitus* superfluous [see H. A. Oberman, ''Some Notes on the Theology of Nominalism,'' *Harvard Theological Review* 53 (1960) 65]. In addition, as William of Ockham specifically indicates, this notion of grace as a habit, a structuring of the will itself, can interfere with the concept of human freedom, which is the cause of the meritoriousness of the act. God, after all, can accept this action without any grace, since grace is only a status required by God in man's actual situation (*de potentia ordinata*) (see H. A. Oberman, *ibid.* 64–65). This point is important in the history of the theology of grace, since attention to it can help to explain the strong counterposition taken by the 16th- and 17th-century Thomistic commentators who make of the notion of habit so central an element in their theology of grace.

Great debates. For methodological purposes this article bypasses at this point the Council of Trent and takes it up rather in the consideration of the systematic theology of grace. The next stage is represented by Baianism, the Catholic theological debate over efficacious grace, and Jansenism. These are three chronologically interrelated phases in the development of this stage. Each of them interacts on the other, and all of them affect very deeply both the direction and emphasis of subsequent theologizing on grace.

Baianism. The fundamental characteristic of Baius's teaching may be summed up as follows. He is directly, even bitterly, opposed to the scholastic development on grace, particularly as represented by St. Thomas; and so he draws his own explanation from what he conceives to be the thought of St. Augustine. The result is that Baius rejects the whole notion of grace as a created and totally gratuitous gift that permanently elevates man and makes him a sharer of the divine nature—an understanding of grace strongly emphasized by St. Thomas (*see* ELEVATION OF MAN). Yet while claiming Augustine as his master, Baius ignores the role that divinization plays in the theology of the Augustine. Likewise, in his distaste for philosophical conceptions, he does not appear to see in St. Augustine's teaching the distinction between freedom (*libertas*) and free choice (*liberum arbitrium*). He thus equates the two and gives man no freedom of choice, so that in man's present state grace becomes a necessitating thing. In this way he opens the way to the debate on sufficient and efficacious grace and prepares the way for Jansenism as well [see X. Le Bachelet, ''Baius,'' *Dictionnaire de théologie catholique* 2.1:81–89; H. Rondet, *Gratia Christi* (Paris 1948) 287–293]. Finally, with all of his objections to philosophical formulas, he in fact begins with a conception of nature that desupernaturalizes Augustine's whole conception of the relationship between grace and nature. Whereas St. Augustine sees human nature finding its fulfillment and completion in God's gracious gifts, Baius looks upon the informing work of the Holy Spirit as being of the very nature of man and the gifts given to Adam as serving the ends of nature and not a gratuitous elevation and divinization. And thus in so radically denying the gratuity of the SUPERNATURAL ORDER, he denies the supernatural order itself. When he comes to grace in the case of fallen man, then he sees it as only extrinsic and being only a matter of mode, not of substance [see H. de Lubac, *Surnaturel: Études historiques* (Paris 1946) 30–37; *see* BAIUS AND BAIANISM].

De Auxiliis Controversy. The Latin phrase *De auxiliis,* meaning ''On the matter of aids,'' has come to be the historical title of one of the most extensive theological controversies in Western Catholic theology. It had its source in the opposing theories employed by the Jesuits and the Dominicans to harmonize grace, predestination, and human liberty. In its early stage the issue was, for the Jesuits, a decidedly practical affair. Confronting both Calvinism and Baianism in the Low Countries, their emphasis is on the role of man's freedom in salutary activity. To be noted also is the role given to voluntary effort in the Jesuit method of spiritual direction. Likewise, in the ascetical orientation of the *SPIRITUAL EXERCISES* of St. Ignatius, while the initiative belongs to grace, there is a mutual interaction and development with voluntary activity. It is this approach that finds in the work of the Jesuit theologian Luis de MOLINA many points that are attractive. The orientation is also particularly notable in the case of Leonard LESSIUS, who is teaching in Louvain during this period [see H. Rondet, *Gratia Christi* (Paris 1948) 294–295].

Essentially, the concern of Molina is with the concrete SALUTARY ACT; his aim is to preserve the free activity of man without undermining God's governance of the economy of salvation. To accomplish this aim, Molina maintains that free will cannot be touched or moved from within without destroying freedom itself. Rather, grace must look only to attracting the will to move itself. And so all grace as it is offered to man is called *gratia oblata.* If the will by its innate liberty consents to the proferred grace, it becomes efficacious. If the will resists the grace, then it remains merely sufficient (*see* GRACE, EFFICACIOUS; GRACE, SUFFICIENT). There is, therefore, only one grace offered; whether or not it efficaciously attains a salutary act derives ultimately from man's free choice. On the other hand, the divine governance of the salutary economy for humanity is preserved through the introduction of a theological concept that becomes the touchstone of much of the subsequent controversy. This is the famous *SCIENTIA MEDIA*, the middle knowledge, between God's knowledge of all possibles and His knowledge of what actually is. By this *scientia media* God knows all the futuribles, i.e., all the possibilities of a free will under an infinite variety of circumstances. Thus when God chooses a particular order, He knows infallibly how a given man will respond to grace. The divine governance then looks to infallible knowledge and in no way enters into human causality [L. de Molina, *Concordia liberi arbitrii cum gratiae donis, divina praescientia, providentia, praedestinatione, et reprobatione* (Paris 1876); see E. Vansteenberghe, ''Molinisme,'' *Dictionnaire de théologie catholique* 10.2:2094–2187; H. Rondet, *Gratia Christi* (Paris 1948) 294 and following] (*See* MOLINISM).

While accepting with reservation the notion of *scientia media,* neither Bellarmine nor Suárez felt that Molina's explanation satisfies the biblical affirmations or sufficiently protects God's role in predestination. Bellarmine held that, while the efficacy of grace is exterior to the will, still the grace itself has a moral congruity that so accommodates it to the circumstances, the character, and the dispositions of the man that he unfailingly consents even though he could resist [R. Bellarmine, *De gratia et libero arbitrio 1.12; Opera omnia,* 12 v. (Vivès ed. Paris 1870–74) 5.529–531]. Suárez would accept congruent grace, but this congruency for him would appear to stem from extrinsic circumstances rather than from any special adaptation of the grace itself (*see* CONGRUISM). It should be noted too that Suárez's acceptance of the *scientia media* is reserved and is to be understood in the light of his own philosophical perspectives (F. Suárez, *De gratia* 5.21; Vivès ed. 8: 498–500).

Domingo Báñez and those who follow him place their emphasis on the divine will as absolute in priority if the gratuity of God's salvific economy is to be preserved. They therefore reject totally the whole idea of *scientia media,* describing it as a pure construct without any real object in the order of divine knowledge. God knows infallibly what will be because He has decreed that it should be. Since God is absolutely the first cause, then He must be the mover of every second cause and in the order of existence the first mover of every act. On the basis of this metaphysical position, it is maintained that the grace that moves man to a salutary act must be efficacious by its very nature and so must enter into the very structure of the free act. The reconciliation of this affirmation with man's freedom calls for a subtle and complex analysis of the interaction of intellectual judgment as formal cause and the will as efficient cause (see R. Garrigou-Lagrange, ''Thomisme,'' *Dictionnaire de théologie catholique* 15.1:823–1023, esp. 979–985; *see* BÁÑEZ AND BAÑEZIANISM).

The presentation here on the *De auxiliis* debate is admittedly but a sketch of a controversy that has permeated and frequently dominated the scholastic tradition down to the present (*see* CONGREGATIO DE AUXILIIS). However, enough had to be said to throw light on the reasons why the consideration of actual grace has been so much to the fore in the scholastic treatment and in so many of the manuals. As has already been noted, this emphasis on actual grace calls for a good deal more historical perspective than is as yet available. It seems too that the penetration of the unique causal relationship between God and man in the supernatural order calls for the development of further speculative resources than are presently at hand.

Jansenism. While JANSENISM may be better remembered for its ultrarigid moral outlook, its teaching on grace has the same character. It is the work of Cornelius JANSEN, who lived, reflected, and wrote his work in the turbulent atmosphere engendered by the debates over efficacious grace. Like Baius, he is the product of the Louvain atmosphere and harbors an even deeper resentment of the Jesuits and shares his antipathy for scholasticism. The future bishop of Ypres is totally committed to Augustine and entitles his book *AUGUSTINUS.* Yet, as happens so often to the disciples of the bishop of Hippo, in attempting to draw out a synthesis from the master's work, he ended up forcing his own construction on St. Augustine's thought. At the heart of his position, as well as at that of the Jansenist school throughout its history, is the same distortion that blinds Baius to the meaning of Augustine. It is his conception of nature before the Fall, Adam in the state of innocence. It may be argued that the notion of Jansen does not expressly exclude the gratuity of the original state of grace, but it surely caricatures it beyond recognition. For Jansen man is created in a state of innocence and rectitude; his will is naturally turned toward God as his last end. The first man possesses liberty of indifference toward good and evil but is naturally turned toward good. Grace is given to man to accomplish the good but it waits upon man's consent. It is, in fact, the sufficient grace of the contemporary theologian (see J. Carreyre, ''Jansenisme,'' *Dictionnaire de théologie catholique* 8.1:345–348).

However, when Adam falls all this is radically changed. Adam and his descendants are now committed to concupiscence-self-love and have no freedom of choice. The will is free only from outside intervention. Interiorly the will is determined either to sin or to charity. If man is to be saved, then the all-powerful grace of Christ will do it of itself. In such a conception, Jansen sees sufficient grace as a monstrosity, for fallen man has no power either to consent or to resist if the grace of Christ is bestowed upon him. Once again St. Augustine's distinction between liberty and free choice is not understood, and an absolutely irreconcilable opposition is seen between man's original state and his fallen state in the matter of grace [see J. Carreyre, *ibid.* 349–367; H. Rondet, *Gratia Christi* (Paris 1948) 309–314; R. Knox, *Enthusiasm* (New York 1950) 204–230]. For understanding the subsequent history of the theology of grace, it is important to recognize that it was the effort to soften this radical opposition of the original to the fallen state posed by Baius and Jansen that led to so much stress on ''pure nature'' in contemporary and later theology [see J. Carreyre, ''Jansenisme,'' *Dictionnaire de théologie catholique* 362–363; H. Rondet, ''Le Problème de la nature pure et la théologie du XVIe siècle,'' *Recherches de science religieuse* 35 (1948) 481–521; H. de Lubac, *Surnaturel: Études historiques* (Paris 1946) 101–127].

Petavius. The French Jesuit Denis Petau (Petavius, d. 1652) is singled out because he restores a perspective to the theology of grace that will be most important in its modern development. By the time the controversy over efficacious grace has reached its climax, and in part due to it, the whole emphasis is on created grace. The aspect of uncreated grace, of the divinization of the Christian, is being presented as a formal effect of habitual grace. The indwelling of the Holy Spirit as well as the ecclesial aspect of the grace of Christ have both been placed in the background of theology. It is due to the work of Petau, even while the Jansenist struggle is continuing under Antoine ARNAULD, that these deeply biblical and traditional aspects of the theology of grace begin to be restored to their proper proportion.

Petau himself is the first of the great positive theologians, deeply erudite in the history of dogma and particularly well versed in the Greek Fathers and Scripture. It is from the standpoint of positive theology that he studies the mission of the Holy Spirit. His guide is St. Cyril of Alexandria. As a result, he is convinced that the Holy Spirit has a far more personal role in the divinization of the Christian than his contemporaries propose [*De Trinitate* 8.4; *Dogmata theologica,* 8 v. (Paris 1865–67) 3:453–465]. The data as he interprets it seems to require that the work of sanctification be proper to the Holy Spirit. Accordingly, he maintains that the scholastic doctrine of appropriation does not suffice to explain either Scripture or the Greek patristic tradition of the role of the Holy Spirit (see *ibid.* 8.6; 3:481–487).

It must be admitted that the speculative capacities of Petau are limited and that he is not really able to answer the question he has posed. He frankly leaves the problem for someone else to answer and makes of his own proposal simply a tentative. His tentative is vigorously criticized in his own time as well as in modern times [see A. Michel, ''Trinité,'' *Dictionnaire de théologie catholique* 15.2:1851–55; P. Galtier, *Le Saint Esprit en nous d'après les pères grecs* in *Analecta Gregoriana* 35 (Rome 1946)].

The problem raised by Petau is treated again by M. J. SCHEEBEN, whom Grabmann described as the greatest speculative theologian of the 19th century. Scheeben is a dedicated disciple of St. Thomas Aquinas and is also deeply influenced by the Fathers and especially the Greek patristic tradition. Like Petau, he studies the mission of the Holy Spirit in the light of Cyril of Alexandria's thought. As a result, it is his Trinitarian theology that determines his theology of grace. Avoiding any simplistic commitment to the hypostatic character of the Holy Spirit's mission of sanctification, nonetheless he maintains that each of the Divine Persons dwells in us in a manner that is personal and proper. They are present formally by what constitutes them as Persons [M. J. Scheeben, *The Mysteries of Christianity,* tr. C. Vollert (St. Louis, Mo. 1946) 158–180]. While more developed and nuanced speculatively than the tentatives of Petau, Scheeben's position does not find much favor and is generally rejected by the manuals. The importance of Scheeben, however, lies less in his theory than the fact that he gave very strong impetus to the return to the tradition that emphasizes the Trinitarian ground of the doctrine and theology of grace. This return is given a further impulse by the extensive and detailed patristic studies of T. de Régnon [*Études de théologie positive sur la Sainte Trinité,* 4 v. (Paris 1892) 4:466–498; 524–572]. While De Régnon's own resolution of the issue raised by Petau receives very little popular assent, his work insures that the study of the Greek tradition will become a theological exigency.

Contemporary. In the mid-20th century, the emphasis on the study of the Fathers joined with a renewal of biblical theology began to bring about a considerable change in the systematic treatment of the theology of grace. As has been already implied, there was considerable emphasis of the Pauline and patristic insistence on the Trinitarian ground of the whole doctrine of grace. Biblical theology as well as the history of theology more and more made theologians conscious that the categories of habitual and actual grace are unable to encompass fully the revealed reality of grace. Hence the trend in theologizing on grace was to give primacy to the supernatural economy of God's personal and saving activity. Along with this was an effort to disengage the treatment of grace from the limitations imposed on it by the polemics of the Reformation, Baianism, and Jansenism. There was also a strong trend to set the long debate over sufficient and efficacious grace into a historical perspective where it no longer dominates the treatment of grace and freedom. In the place of this emphasis, many contemporary theologians sought to restore the Augustinian distinction between liberty, or Christian freedom, and freedom of choice. By this distinction they sought to give to Christian freedom a dimension that touches the very roots of man's personal supernatural relation with the Triune God.

Even before Vatican Council II, theologians such as Hans Küng were rethinking historic Protestant-Catholic controversies about grace in the light of contemporary developments. Increasingly, both Catholic and Protestant theologians showed a willingness to recognize elements in each others' traditions as valid. Thus Catholics sought acceptable interpretations of such phrases as ''justification through faith,'' ''simultaneously justified and sinful,'' etc. Meanwhile, they found inspiration for their thinking in the works of such Protestant theologians as Barth, Bultmann, Tillich, and Bonhoeffer.

At the same time, Catholic thought on grace became more ''secular.'' That is, grace was seen as the all-pervasive reality of God's love to be found in every dimension of life in this world, rather than as a discrete entity transmitted only through ''sacred'' channels. All constructive human activity is in some sense supernatural insofar as it is carried out under the force of God's call to friendship with Himself, and grace is thus available to all men everywhere. Reexamination of the distinction between natural and supernatural, and the discussions of ''anonymous'' Christianity, led to a greater appreciation of the universality of grace.

The influence of ecumenical discussions and of the secularizing trend converged in the development of personalist theologies of grace. Personalist theology offered not a new doctrine of grace but a new approach to understanding and expressing the realities found in Scripture and tradition. Grace was to be understood as an interpersonal relationship between God and man, the appreciation of which stands at the very heart of the theological endeavor. The impact of grace on consciousness, on acts of faith and hope and love, and on human psychology in general received greater and greater attention, and theologians' vocabularies and frames of reference were likely to be drawn from existential philosophy and contemporary psychology.

Finally, the need for a social theology of grace became clear in light of developments in other areas of theology. For example, Vatican II reiterated the biblical notion that God does not call us as individuals but as a people. In moral theology, the deprivatization of sin calls for a corresponding deprivatization of grace. In addition, sacramental and liturgical theology shifted their focus to the social, viewing Baptism as the initiation of a person into the Christian community, and Eucharist as the sharing of a communal meal. Traditionally, the impact of grace has been a major factor in the study of each of these areas. However, a purely personalist approach to grace proved an inadequate grounding for these social understandings. This inadequacy, in turn, led many theologians to ignore the topic of grace.

Liberation theologians were among the first to point out the general neglect of the social dimensions in theological tracts on grace. Not only did they develop a social theology of grace to counterbalance their notion of sin as systemic evil, but they claimed that human beings receive grace within society and by transforming society. More specifically, for them, grace is liberation, the freeing action of God in society.

Systematic Treatment of Grace

In the biblical perspective, grace is the generous kindness and favor of God that He witnesses to by His personal action in the PEOPLE OF GOD and each of its members. St. Thomas Aquinas speaks for this theological tradition when he declares that grace is fundamentally God's gracious disposition. This disposition for St. Thomas is, above all, an act of love that produces in the very being of man a correlative response and activity (see *Summa theologiae* 1a2ae, 110.1–3).

This favor and love of God that makes man pleasing to Him is not an abstract but a personal reality that finds its full manifestation in the historical reality of Jesus Christ, the Son of God. The incarnate Word is *the* grace and *the* favor of God appearing for the SALVATION of all men and ''of his fullness we have all received grace upon grace'' (Jn 1.16). It is the grace of the Father in Jesus Christ that is given men by the Holy Spirit. This whole approach is beautifully phrased in the Tridentine decree on justification.

> The commencement of justification itself in adults must be understood as coming from the prevenient grace of God through Christ Jesus, i.e., from His vocation, by which He summons them without any anterior merits on their part so that those who have been averted from God through their sins are turned to their own justification through His grace that excites and aids. In freely consenting and cooperating with this grace [these sinners] are so disposed that God touches their heart in such a way through the illumination of the Holy Spirit that it cannot be said that man does nothing at all when he receives this inspiration, for he can reject it; neither may it be said that without the grace of God he can move himself to justice before God by his own free will. (H. Denzinger, *Enchiridion symbolorum* 1525)

In this magisterial statement are the two poles central to the systematic theology of grace: the absolute primacy of God as savior and the realism of regeneration. As C. Moeller has so cogently brought out, these two poles must orient any theology of grace if it is to be true to God's revealed word and at the same time be as genuinely ecumenical as the present age demands [''Théologie de la grâce et oecuménisme,'' *Irénikon* 28 (1955) 21–23].

Absolute primacy of God in the work of salvation. ''The Eternal Father by a free and hidden plan of His own wisdom and goodness created the whole world. His plan was to raise men to a participation of the divine life. God the Father did not leave men fallen in Adam to themselves but ceaselessly offered helps to salvation for the sake of Christ the Redeemer, 'who is the image of the invisible God, the firstborn of every creature' (Col 1.15). All the elect, before time began, the Father 'foreknew, and He predestined them to become conformed to the image of His Son so that He should be the firstborn among many brethren' (Rom 8.29)''—Vatican Council II, *Dogmatic Constitution on the Church* 2; *Acta Apostolicae Sedis* 57 (1965) 5–6. In these words the Church reaffirms both the gratuity and the supernaturality of God's gracious favor and salutary activity.

In the conception of grace outlined above, there is found in direct focus what the Greek Fathers described as the divinization of the Christian. God became man that men might share in the divine life. By the love of the Father man is introduced into the life of the three Divine Persons. Through this freely given love is communicated to the redeemed a share (although in a human degree) of the love of the Son for the Father. It is this love of the Father in the image of the Son that is realized and vitally sustained by the Holy Spirit.

Supernaturality. In this context of grace, considered as an absolutely free and personal act through which God communicates Himself to men, the traditional usage of supernatural must be understood. Man through God's love is endowed with the divine through a personal act of God's own self-giving. Such an act by its very nature must be absolutely free; it cannot be necessitated. On the other hand, the spiritual creature must respond to this divine self-donation freely. Hence, the doctrine of grace supposes a creature already constituted in its own being in such ways that it has the possibility of entering into a free and personal relationship with the Divine Persons or of rejecting that relationship. The fact of a completely gratuitous operation on the part of God and the possibility of a free response or refusal on the part of the creature makes God's self-communication supernatural. For it means that it cannot be something owed or necessitated. God can deny it to man since it is a participation in the divine life, which belongs and is proper only to the Father, Son, and Holy Spirit. The scholastic terminology describes it as that which by its very nature goes beyond the essence, capacity, or claim of any creature (cf. K. Rahner, *Lexikon für Theologie und Kirche* 4:993).

The Church in its official teaching has given considerable emphasis to both the idea and the term ''supernatural.'' The idea itself first appears in Benedict XII's exposition of the BEATIFIC VISION (H. Denzinger, *Enchiridion symbolorum* 1000–01). The term itself is employed in the condemnation of Baius (*ibid.* 1921, 1923; cf. 1926). The same notion is to be found in the statements issued against QUESNEL (*ibid.* 2435) and in 1794 against the Synod of Pistoia (*ibid.* 2616). Pius IX employed the term ''supernatural'' to bring out the semirationalist errors of J. Frohschammer (*ibid.* 2851, 2854). In its constitution on the Catholic faith, Vatican Council I makes the supernaturality of God's will to give Himself to man the foundation of the necessity of grace as well as a necessary property of divine faith (*ibid.* 3005, 3008). The encyclical of Pius XII *HUMANI GENERIS* gives heavy emphasis to the absolute gratuity of the supernatural order (*ibid.* 3891).

Grace and Nature. The correlative aspect of God's self-revelation that is man's free response to it is also set into focus by the absolute gratuity of grace. By the very nature of the relationship of love, man must enter into communion with God freely. Yet as both the Councils of Orange and Trent affirm, he is incapable of either earning this grace of response, or preparing himself positively for it, or ever attaining it by his own acts (*ibid.* 373–397, 1523, 1525). For the very nature of God's personal communication of Himself requires that man's actual ability to respond freely be itself the action of God's unnecessitated grace.

While insisting on this supernaturality, one is also to be aware that, since man must respond freely, even without grace there is in the spiritual creature a capacity for this self-disclosure of God in Christ. It is this capacity that theologians have termed an OBEDIENTIAL POTENCY (*potentia obedientialis*). This term simply formulates this fact: what God can achieve in and with man can be impossible for man himself to do. Yet, because man is God's creature, then inherent in his created nature is the possibility of becoming what God can and does will. Although this implies no capacity for self-realization, there is a real possibility that God has the power to actualize if He so wills.

Modern theology has devoted considerable attention to the actual nature of this obediential power as found in historical man called to grace. A number of theologians have felt that the relationship between nature and grace has been too much confined to the discussions of the relationship of the supernatural with man's natural desire to see God. This itself is a source of extensive debate in the Thomistic tradition [see, e.g., W. O'Connor, *The Eternal Quest* (New York 1947)]. By focusing on this perspective, it is maintained, the whole relationship is reduced to a kind of extrinsicism. For one of the elements involved, viz, pure nature, is solely a speculative construct that has never had any existence. This extrinsicism would, it is maintained, make of human nature so determinable and thus so self-enclosed a system that the supernatural adds only a veneer or an extrinsic layer. Hence really to understand the relationship constructively one must return to the fact that the one thing revelation tells man is that God has created him with the purpose of giving Himself in Christ. The sole final end that is given in fact to the creation of spiritual creatures is the possession of God Himself, and this with the fact of sin foreseen.

In view of such judgments, a number of theologians have striven to reconstruct the relationship between nature and grace by centering it on historical man called to grace from the beginning of human history. Implicitly this point of view reaches back to the early part of the 20th century and the work of M. Blondel and J. Maréchal, SJ. Later it was given prominence by H. de Lubac, SJ, K. Rahner, SJ, and H. U. von Balthasar [see L. Malevez, ''La Gratuité du surnaturel,'' *Nouvelle revue théologique* 75 (1953) 561–586, 673–689; H. de Lubac, *Surnaturel: Études historiques* (Paris 1946); K. Rahner, ''Concerning the Relationship between Nature and Grace,'' *Theological Investigations,* v. 1, tr. C. Ernst (Baltimore, Md. 1961) 297–317; H. von Balthasar, *Karl Barth: Darstellung und Deutung seiner Theologie* (Cologne 1951) 278–335; J. P. Kenny, ''Reflections on Human Nature and the Supernatural,'' *Theological Studies* 14 (1953) 280–287].

The best-elaborated and most carefully balanced exposition of this position is that offered by K. Rahner. As he sees it, the divine decree that calls all men to the beatific vision must have a real effect on each man so called. God could not will to make men adopted sons unless there resulted an interior orientation to this actual end that would oblige men to choose or reject it. To conceive of the call as a purely extrinsic, juridical reality is to leave an actual historical decree of God without a corresponding historical term. For the possession of God is men's only true end in fact. How, therefore, can this be if there is no actual attraction or tension in regard to this *de facto* situation? As a vocation, it is totally God's gift, His gracious intervention; and the resonance it strikes in man is thus the work of His own free gift. It is this supernatural DESTINY, freely conferred, that in turn engenders in man an affinity to the end for which he was in fact made. This affinity touches the very source of man's existence so that man never ceases to be called by God's love. It is this that Rahner terms the SUPERNATURAL existential, an *attrait*, a resonance, that results from an unconditioned and positive tendency to the vision of God derived from God's gift of a vocation to supernatural life.

It should be remarked here that Rahner is aware that some have pushed this position to extremes, as indicated in the encyclical *Humani generis.* He emphasizes that this position in no way attenuates the absolute gratuity of the supernatural. He insists that the concept of pure nature is necessary to defend this divine gratuity. He also accepts the validity of the notion represented by obediential power but maintains that it is not mere nonrepugnance but an inner ordination. He would, however, make it plain that because of this supernatural existential, the concept pure nature is not something clearly determinable or open to exact definition. Pure nature can only be described as what would remain in concrete human nature after the existential has been abstracted as not due. Since one does not know the full impact of the supernatural existential, one cannot say definitively what this pure nature would be.

As might be expected, this position has not gone unchallenged. Perhaps the best critique is offered by H. E. Schillebeeckx, OP. He sees the whole tentative as a shifting of the problematic from the relationship between nature and grace to a relationship between nature and a medium between nature and grace, a medium that is neither natural nor supernatural as such. He would hold that the basic error arises from a false perspective. By reason of this false perspective, the proponents of the supernatural existential hold that a sinner can be really and actually called in the concrete and yet still remain a sinner. Hence he maintains that Rahner would place in human nature as the term of man's destiny a reality present in both man in the state of grace and man a sinner. Schillebeeckx would claim that the actual and real destination to the supernatural order is sanctifying grace since only this in fact places man in the supernatural order. Hence in actuality the distinction is either acceptance and personal relationship with God or a deliberate refusal and thus being truly a sinner—these are the only terms of God's call. Vocation by its nature remains extrinsic to man because it cannot become actual save by free response or rejection. For the destination to the supernatural order is the fruit of God's will to save; this involves either effective assumption into FRIENDSHIP with God or, if one is not in the state of grace, the reality of being a sinner. There is no other possibility [see H. E. Schillebeeckx, ''L'Instinct de la foi selon s. Thomas d'Aquin,'' *Revue des sciences philosophiques et théologiques* 48 (1964) 396–400].

Reality of regeneration. Theology has systematized the various aspects of grace insofar as it affects man. The variety of categories and formulas represents the effort by theologians to grasp and give intellectual precision to the scriptural affirmations that the man in grace is a new creature, a sharer of the divine nature, a son of God not only nominally but in truth.

Created and Uncreated Grace. This terminology and division has been very prominent in Western Catholic theology since the early 13th century. As the historical treatment indicated, this terminology came into use in order to signify the effect that God's self-giving in grace produces in man. Peter Lombard had resolved the issue by identifying charity in the justified man with the Holy Spirit Himself. Since the *Sentences* of Peter Lombard was the textbook for theologians until the 16th century, his answer to the problematic demanded an explanation. To the great theologians who followed him, it seemed evident in Scripture that God in giving Himself to man had pledged an enduring and transforming result in man. Yet it was also apparent that if this effect was simply God Himself, one must ultimately deny any personal activity to the Christian in grace. This problematic was ultimately resolved by introducing the distinction of uncreated and created grace (*see* GRACE, CREATED AND UNCREATED). In this formula, uncreated grace stands for the Father, the Son, and the Holy Spirit as out of love they communicate themselves to man. Created grace is seen correlatively as signifying the effect of this divine communication. Employing this distinction, the scholastics sought to keep clearly in the forefront the reality or the realism of man as regenerated. As they used it, they stressed the incapacity of man as regards justification and the actual reality of the sanctification that God works in man. In such a context, the concept created grace simply marks the continuous influence of God's personal and sanctifying activity in man.

It is in the light of this same problematic but raised in the context of Lutheran teaching that the Council of Trent's teaching on inherent grace must be understood. The Tridentine fathers deliberately eschewed the term ''created grace'' and used ''inherent grace'' and infused grace. Both of these Tridentine usages looked to emphasizing the fact that when God justifies man a true inner transformation takes place. This emphasis was given primacy because, as they saw it, the Lutheran teaching clearly appeared to deny or, at least, jeopardize the Catholic teaching on this point. In view of this, the Council of Trent taught: ''Finally the unique formal cause [of justification] is the 'justice of God, not the justice whereby He is just but that by which He makes us just.' And this means that by this gift of His we are renewed in the spirit of our mind so that justice is not merely reputed to us but we are truly called just and indeed are just by the fact that each one receives his own justice in the measure that the 'Holy Spirit destines to each one' and in accord with each one's disposition and cooperation'' (H. Denzinger, *Enchiridion symbolorum* 1529). In the light of this statement, the subsequent declaration on inherent grace should be understood: ''through the Holy Spirit charity is poured forth in the hearts of those who are justified and inheres [*inhaer et*] in them'' (*ibid.* 1530). Again: ''For the justice that is called ours, because we are justified by its inhering in us, is God's justice because He infuses it into us through the merit of Christ'' (*ibid.* 1547).

The doctrine of grace in the Council of Trent, then, concentrates on the results of God's sanctifying activity in man. This emphasis stems from the conviction that it is grace as it affects man that is threatened by the reformers. Yet, as so often happens after a conciliar decision, what had been intended as a specific response to a determined problematic becomes in the post-Tridentine theologians the important element in the whole treatise on grace. Thus created grace viewed only in the light of the scholastic and Counter Reformation perspectives gradually was isolated from its necessary correlative, uncreated grace. The dominant Aristotelian emphasis on causality then began to show how created grace was an effect; thus it insisted on attributing grace to God not as triune in Person but as one in nature. Conceived of in this fashion, grace is seen as uniting one to the Godhead and not so much to the individual Divine Persons. Hence, to share in the divine nature is not to enter into personal relationship with the three Divine Persons but with what makes God to be God [see R. Garrigou-Lagrange, *Grace* (St. Louis, Mo. 1952) 153–156]. Such a position leads to a further consequence in the history of the theology of grace: the indwelling of the Blessed Trinity is described as a formal effect of sanctifying grace.

As the historical treatment in this article has indicated, the position delineated above has had a very articulate, though minority, opposition. That opposition, at best, served only to keep the question alive. It is only in recent years that it has been recognized that the notion created grace demands as its proper correlative uncreated grace (see K. Rahner, ''Some Implications of the Scholastic Concept of Uncreated Grace,'' *Theological Investigations* 1:319–346; this article contains a good bibliography of contemporary articles). Richer and more profound biblical and patristic studies, a more perceptive understanding of the history of the theology of grace, as well as ecumenical exigencies have combined to bring this about. Rahner sums up this contemporary situation by pointing out that in Scripture it is the Father in the Trinity who is man's Father, while the Spirit dwells in man in a particular and proper way. Such expressions of Scripture and the monuments of tradition are first of all in possession. It is necessary to prove that they may be merely appropriations and that the contrary interpretation is impossible; this cannot be taken for granted. So long as this has not been achieved, one must understand Scripture and its expressions quite precisely (cf. *ibid.* 345–346).

This contemporary effort to give to the notion of uncreated grace its due primacy has given rise to a number of theological tentatives. Chronologically, the first of these is the proposal of M. De la Taille [*The Hypostatic Union and Created Actuation by Uncreated Act,* tr. C. Vollert (West Baden Springs, Ind. 1952)]. De la Taille postulates as his point of departure the scholastic concepts of obediential power and the composition of the finite being as act and potency. He would then maintain that God as pure act can communicate Himself as perfection to this obediential power. This communication, however, is not as a form but nevertheless as an act, or actuation, and so it is capable of transforming the creature [see P. de Letter, ''Created Actuation by the Uncreated Act,'' *Theological Studies* 18 (1957) 60–92; M. J. Donnelly, ''The Inhabitation of the Holy Spirit,'' *Catholic Theological Society of America* 4 (1949) 39–77; *see* CREATED ACTUATION BY UNCREATED ACT]. K. Rahner urges as an interpretation of the scholastic conception of uncreated grace the notion of quasi-formal causality. This notion and its context of theory relate glory and grace. In this relationship, uncreated grace is not just a consequence of grace but the central gift in the life of grace (''Some Implications of the Scholastic Concept of Uncreated Grace,'' *Theological Investigations* 319–346). More recently he has maintained that this central gift is specifically the Incarnation of the Word because this is the only way in which divine self-communication can take place [see ''Zur Theologie der Menschwerdung,'' *Schriften zur Theologie* (Einsiedeln 1960) 4:137–155]. B. Lonergan, SJ, in treating of the sanctifying mission of the Holy Spirit, objects to the idea of immanent actuation. He takes the position that the divine indwelling is caused efficiently by the three Divine Persons. This indwelling, however, is constituted intrinsically by the divine relation of origin that constitutes the Person of the Holy Spirit. Yet, because this indwelling is in a creature, it has a created term (sanctifying grace), which is received in the soul as an obediential potency. This created term does not enter in any way into the constitution of the indwelling but is consequent upon the union of the Holy Spirit with the soul [*Divinarum personarum conceptio analogica* (2d ed. Rome 1959) 206–215].

Habitual Grace. Very widely used in theology since Trent, the term ''habitual grace'' has frequently designated one of the basic divisions of the treatise on grace. Like the term ''created grace,'' it too is an effort that after Trent would emphatically formulate both the reality of the effect of God's grace and the permanence of that effect in man. Martin Luther had strongly rejected this notion of *habitus* partly by reason of his nominalistic background and partly by reason of his own preoccupation with the absolute gratuity of grace. In the face of this, the Council of Trent placed strong insistence on the real transformation wrought in man through justification. Hence, while it did not employ the terms ''created grace'' or ''habit,'' it did speak of a grace that is infused in the justified and inheres in them (H. Denzinger, *Enchiridion symbolorum* 1530, 1561). This, in turn, was taken by the post-Tridentine theologians as a confirmation of the fact that the term ''habit'' is descriptive of the reality of grace. By reason of this and of what they conceived to be the polemical exigencies of the Counter Reformation, the notion of habitual grace became a central aspect of their presentation.

Contemporarily there has come to the fore a strong trend that would nuance much more carefully the term ''habit'' when it is applied to the life of grace. It is the contention of some theologians that this term, if properly nuanced, can in fact fulfill a valuable theological role. Properly understood, it can help one keep clearly in view the fact that regenerated man is truly and actually a new creature. It also enables the theologian to give proper stress to the fact that grace's transformation is a continuing reality involving a dynamic and developing intimacy of knowledge and love of the Trinity. Finally, it can be seen as a divinely conferred instrumentality through which one participates continually, vitally, and immediately in the active and continual presence of God [''Théologie de la grâce et oecuménisme,'' *Irénikon* 28 (1955) 36–38].

Actual Grace. While there has been a flood of discussion and debate on the nature and notion of actual grace, the explicit teaching of the Church about actual grace is relatively limited. The Church distinguishes between actual grace and habitual grace (as seen above) only to the extent that it teaches that elevating grace is absolutely necessary for the supernaturally good acts through which the nonjustified man prepares himself for justification (H. Denzinger, *Enchiridion symbolorum* 375). The Church also teaches against the Pelagians and Semi-Pelagians that supernatural grace is absolutely necessary for every supernaturally good act (*ibid.* 238–249, 373–380). In treating the acts that positively prepare for faith and justification, the Council of Trent teaches that this grace comes to man without any merit on his part whatsoever (*ibid.* 1525). In general, the First Vatican Council makes clear the supernaturality of these graces by affirming their absolute necessity for supernaturally good acts (*ibid.* 3008–10).

In affirming God's will to save all men as well as the sinfulness of man, the theologians conclude that there is a sufficient grace. The sufficient grace is constantly offered by God but is not always efficacious. This theological position is clearly the significance of the teaching of the Council of Trent in chapter 5 of the decree on justification as well as the fourth canon that is attached (*ibid.* 1525, 1544, 1554). The same doctrine is to be seen explicitly in the series of condemnations issued against Baius and the Jansenists (*ibid.* 2002, 2305–06, 2621). The correlative of sufficient grace, which is efficacious grace, has been the object of decades of unresolved dispute. The crux of the debate is the determination of how the free salutary act of man can also be God's gift. As far as Catholic doctrine is concerned, the theological consensus is that although man's freedom to accept or resist remains, still the efficacy has its source in God's gratuitous election.

From the standpoint of systematic theology, several points about actual grace should be mentioned. First, whatever be the resolution of the discussion about St. Thomas's position on actual grace [see historical section of this article; also M. C. Wheeler, ''Actual Grace According to St. Thomas,'' *Thomist* 16 (1953) 334–360], there is no question that beginning with the post-Tridentine theologians the general teaching is quite clear. Almost unanimously the position has been that actual graces are distinct supernatural motions ordained to man's sanctification. Additionally, in what has been the more dominant tradition of Thomism, these actual graces are held to be given for each supernatural act and to elevate man's powers in such ways that the act is at once truly supernatural yet freely placed by man.

Commonly in post-Tridentine theology a further distinction has been introduced with regard to actual graces. It is the division between indeliberate and deliberate acts. Indeliberate acts, in this theological context, are those that are produced by grace independently of any deliberation or free election on man's part. They are, as it were, calls or invitations to salutary action that can be consented to or rejected. The way in which actual grace accomplishes this illumination of the intellect and inspiration of the will radically divides the Thomists and the Molinists. Deliberate acts are, then, those acts of the will that, consequent upon intellectual deliberation, constitute man's free choices as well as the acts commanded by such free choices. The theological debate here has centered on the free act of the will and its relationship with the absolutely gratuitous character of God's efficacious grace. Lastly, it is in view of this distinction between indeliberate and deliberate acts that modern theology has generally tended to limit the traditional Augustinian division of grace to actual graces. Thus *gratia praeveniens, excitans,* and *operans* would apply to the indeliberate act, and *gratia subsequens, adjuvans,* and *cooperans* to the deliberate act (cf. J. Van der Meersch, ''Grâce,'' *Dictionnaire de théologie catholique* 6.2:1654).

Account, however, must be taken of the fact that some theologians have questioned this whole systematic development. The questions raised by H. Bouillard in his study of St. Thomas, already cited, plus historical studies on the Council of Trent, as well as the Trinitarian dynamism of the traditional doctrine of grace have been the source of a number of reservations. This contemporary position recognizes the legitimacy of the distinction between actual and habitual grace insofar as the term ''actual grace'' is applied to the supernatural acts of the nonjustified man preparing himself for justification. These theologians hold, however, that it is an open question whether this actual grace is distinct from the self-communication of God that, when accepted, is called habitual. They also hold that there is no agreement as to whether actual grace as distinct from justifying grace in man is necessary for every supernatural act.

To sum up: ''Grace is called habitual insofar as the supernatural self-communication of God is offered to man (from Baptism on) permanently and insofar (with regard to adults) as it is freely accepted—to the particular degree possible, to the particular degree accepted. This same grace is called actual insofar as it actually produces the act of its acceptance and actualizes itself in it. This act of acceptance by its very nature is existentially gradated and ever to be renewed'' (K. Rahner,''Gnade,'' *Lexikon für Theologie und Kirche* 4:996).

With regard to this contemporary opinion on actual grace, it should be kept in mind that it is tentative. As yet there has not been any confrontation either in extent or depth with the common theological teaching. Likewise, it must not be lost sight of that, whatever be the ultimate foundations of these distinctions in the manifold reality that is grace, such distinctions are inescapable if the complex reality of grace is to be opened to any systematic understanding [see M. Schmaus, *Katholische Dogmatik,* v. 3.2 (Munich 1951) 16]. Finally, in the present state of historical research and biblical theology, the common theological teaching on actual grace is supported by a legitimate and defensible interpretation of Scripture and the magisterial documents. Therefore, though the question may be an open one, in the present state of the case the weight of theological opinion rests with the common teaching.

Medicinal Grace. Ever since Augustine's controversies with the Pelagians, the medicinal aspect of Christ's grace has had an essential place in Western theology. Essentially this medicinal aspect of grace simply brings to the fore the fact of original sin and the redemptive character of Christ's saving work. In the history of theology, however, this fact has required a whole series of correlative affirmations. On the one hand, concupiscence as of sin and tending to sin (H. Denzinger, *Enchiridion symbolorum* 1515) can only be overcome by the special help of God. On the other hand, it must also be held that this teaching does not mean that each new act of the unjustified man is thereby a sin. Out of this arises the distinction between elevating grace and medicinal grace (see St. Thomas, *Summa theologiae* 1a2ae, 109.2, 3, 4, 8). Magisterially this distinction is implied by the Councils of Orange and Trent (e.g., H. Denzinger, *Enchiridion symbolorum* 384, 1541, 1572). Trent specifically condemns the teaching that all works done before justification are sins (*ibid.* 1557). Against Baius and the Jansenists the Church teaches that those not yet justified can perform genuinely holy acts with the help of grace and correlatively that their (presumed) sinful state does not make each act of theirs a mortal sin (see *ibid.* 1925, 1935, 1937, 2307, 2311, 2445, etc.). This teaching led to a further theological distinction: supernatural grace is absolutely necessary for supernaturally good acts, but for simply honest acts, i.e., those that fulfill the natural law, medicinal grace need not be supernatural in the fullest sense but only relatively, and might even be only external. This matter is still a debated point, as well as its further refinement as to whether it need be the grace of Christ at all. The theologians in the Thomist tradition, however, have always held firmly that the perfect fulfillment of the natural law demands that this healing grace be justifying grace.

A further consequence has followed upon the condemnations of Baius and Jansen that affirm the possibility of naturally good acts that have no bearing on salvation. In view of this teaching, the greater number of theologians have maintained the existence, in fact, of such naturally good actions that have no relation to the grace of Christ. Only a small minority of theologians, including Ripalda, for example, have taught that free will could do no good without some kind of grace [see J. M. de Ripalda, *De ente supernaturali,* 4 v. (Paris 1870–71) 1:209–269].

In recent years there has been a strong trend toward the reconsideration of this whole point of view. It begins with Hefele's study of the councils. In his treatment of the Council of Orange, he puts forward the opinion that canon 22 must be taken in its Augustinian context. He therefore holds that when only the natural forces of man are involved, the result is the opposite of morality, namely, sin and falsehood. Thus sin is what man has on his own and not by virtue of grace in its widest sense [see C. J von Hefele, *Histoire des conciles d'après les documents originaux* (Paris 1907–38) 2.2:1100–03]. This would be correlated with proposition 27 in the condemnation of Baius (''Free will without the aid of grace avails for nothing save sinning,'' H. Denzinger, *Enchiridion symbolorum* 1927) by interpreting grace here as meaning the grace of justification [see H. Küng, *Justification,* tr. T. Collins et al. (New York 1964) 178; H. Rondet, *Gratia Christi* (Paris 1948) 161]. The whole thing is summed up by Schmaus: ''[S]o it must be stressed that the Church's doctrinal statements only declare the possibility of a natural morality and not its actuality. The Church's teaching, therefore, leaves the way open for the position that no purely natural act exists in fact . . . . The proposition that on a purely natural level there is no such thing as a good action finds support in the fact that the whole creation is centered on Christ and nothing stands apart from this relationship with Jesus Christ. The result of this relationship with Christ is that mankind was never without grace; grace was never absent regardless of how sparingly it might have been given. Thus, humanity never had to live under a situation totally without grace nor to bear sin in its entire horror. Baius erred in thinking unbelievers to be without grace. This error gave rise to the other that all works of the unbeliever and the pagan are sins and the virtues of the philosophers vices'' [M. Schmaus *Katholische Dogmatik,* v. 3.2 (Munich 1951) 3.2:274–275; cf. K. Rahner, ''Nature and Grace,'' *Nature and Grace,* tr. D. Wharton (New York 1964) 131–134].

Grace and freedom. As the historical part of this article indicated, the question of grace and freedom is being treated in the context of a much broader horizon contemporarily. Historical studies have served to remove layers of controversy that have tended to confine the whole discussion to the matter of free choice. Contemporary biblical theology has studied freedom in Scripture independently of these controversial presuppositions as well as of the politico-philosophical formulations of the Enlightenment. Accordingly, the treatment of grace and freedom takes as its point of departure the scriptural horizon. Biblically, human freedom is opposed not to necessity but to bondage. Only those who are naturally free can suffer bondage. In the realm of the spiritual, such bondage is sin, whereby man orders his life without reference to God. Modern thinkers have tended to correlate freedom with independence, so that the greater the freedom, the greater the independence and therefore the self-sufficiency. In Scripture, however, the reverse is true. To love and be loved gives to freedom both its meaning and its development. Yet man cannot attain this of himself. It is God who out of love delivers man from sin and through His Spirit incorporates him into the redeemed community of free men enjoying the freedom of the children of God [E. La B. Cherbonnier, ''Liberty,'' *Dictionary of the Bible,* et. J. Hastings, rev. F. C. Grant and H. H. Rowley (New York 1962) 582–583; J. Marsh, ''Liberty,'' *The Interpreters' Dictictionary of the Bible* (Nashville 1962) 3:122–123; J. Dheilly, ''Liberté,'' *Dictionnaire biblique* (Tournai 1964) 664–666].

Both St. John and St. Paul give much prominence to this theme of Christian freedom. ''[E]very one who commits sin is a slave of sin. The slave has no permanent standing in the household, but the son belongs to it forever. If the Son sets you free, you shall be truly free'' (Jn 8.35–36). ''Christ set us free; to be free men stand firm then and refuse to be tied to the yoke of slavery again'' (Gal 4.31–5.1). Starting with this biblical perspective, a number of theologians have begun to give prominence to St. Augustine's distinction between Christian liberty (*libertas christiana*) and free choice (*liberum arbitrium*). From this standpoint, only the Christian in grace really possesses liberty since only the Christian united with God in love is able to accomplish the ends for which he was created. In terms of systematic theology with a strong personalist emphasis, this has been particularly well expressed by P. Fransen, SJ, in ''Towards a Psychology of Divine Grace,'' *Cross Currents* 8 (1958) 211–232. He states that if one's exercise of free will is to become truly human, then ''this early form of liberty [free will] must be directed by something deeper, more stable, supported and directed by a profound and total commitment, by a fundamental option in which *I express myself wholly* with all that I wish to be in this world and before God'' (214). It is this fundamental, spontaneous orientation of a man's life that is at the same time actualized in a series of particular actions forming the visible woof of his life. This involves a constant interaction between one's conscious actions of the moment and his fundamental option and orientation.

Man, however, is born a sinner, and it is precisely at the depth of this fundamental option that the problem of sin is most acute. Fransen finds the essential alternative facing man's personal liberty posed by St. Augustine: love of God or love of self. Either the love of God through others and the forgetfulness of self or the love of self to the denial of God and the inclusion of all the forms of pride and hate. Only grace can overcome this solitude of sin. For the grace of Christ is first of all a call of divine love to man to make the fundamental option by which alone he will be fully free. This grace calls and urges from without and from within, and if man consents to it he is restored to that liberty that wells up out of the very center of his existence. Man, in grace, is free and able to actualize in union with the Father, Son, and Holy Spirit the total gift of himself that is God's call and grace for man. Thus grace as the love and mercy of God is the soul of Christian freedom, the very gift of the Spirit. The vocation of the Christian is the vocation to freedom, for the Christian law is the law of love, ''the glorious liberty of the sons of God'' (Rom 8.21) [see also A. M. Henry, OP, ''The Law of the Spirit and Freedom,'' *The Holy Spirit,* tr. J. Lundberg and M. Bell (New York 1960) 119–138; R. Guardini, *Freedom, Grace and Destiny,* tr. J. Murray (New York 1961)].

Grace and the Church. Once grace is viewed in its full scriptural reality as the supernatural economy of God's personal and saving activity, then the ecclesial dimension of grace must also be taken into account. As the *Dogmatic Constitution on the Church* of Vatican Council II states, ''He [the Father] planned to assemble in the holy Church all those who would believe in Christ. Already from the beginning of the world the foreshadowing of the Church took place. It was prepared in a remarkable way throughout the history of the people of Israel and by means of the old covenant. In this present era of time the Church was constituted and by the outpouring of the Spirit made manifest. At the end of time it will gloriously achieve completion, when, as is read in the Fathers, all the just from Adam and 'from Abel the just one to the last of the elect' will be gathered together with the Father in the universal Church'' [*Lumen gentium* 2; *Acta Apostolicae Sedis* 57 (1965) 6].

Underlying this magisterial statement is the clear proclamation of Scripture that the grace of the Father in Christ working through the Spirit establishes a communion of fellowship with Christ. The whole economy of grace is established to draw men into the Church, the gathering together of all those who believe. Grace, therefore, cannot be seen as distinct from the Church, since both are indivisible aspects of the one saving design of God. The Church is the very heart of the redeeming work of God. Through it the Father has gathered for Himself a people sanctified in Christ through the Holy Spirit. This people, freed from sin and united with God through grace, constitutes a family of divinely adopted sons, the Body of Christ. As P. Fransen has written: ''It ought to be plain that the being and substance of the Church ought not to be thought of as distinct from grace. In fact, the Church is grace *par excellence* insofar as she manifests visibly that aspect of grace which binds us all like brothers and sisters into a true and everlasting people of the promise and the inheritance'' [*Divine Grace and Man,* tr. G. Dupont (New York 1962) 111].

This ecclesial aspect of grace finds its central manifestation in the worship of the Church. For in the liturgy ecclesial, communal worship is offered by the MYSTICAL BODY OF CHRIST—head and members. The liturgical action of the Church is the supreme expression of grace in the Church. To this loving worship of the community of Christ all the actions of the Church are ultimately ordered—authority, Sacrament, and ministry of the Word. It is from this worship that the saving activity of the Church itself flows. ''The liturgy in its turn moves the faithful, filled with 'the paschal sacraments,' to be 'one in holiness'; it prays that 'they may hold fast in their lives to what they have grasped by their faith'; the renewal in the Eucharist of the covenant between the Lord and man draws the faithful into the compelling love of Christ and sets them on fire. From the liturgy, therefore, and especially from the Eucharist, as from a fount, grace is poured forth upon us; and the sanctification of men in Christ and the glorification of God, to which all the other activities of the Church are directed as towards their end, is achieved in the most efficacious way possible'' [Vatican II, *Constitution on the Sacred Liturgy* 10; *Acta Apostolicae Sedis* 56 (1964) 102].

Bibliography: *Dictionnaire de théologie catholique*, ed, A. VACANT (Paris 1951) Tables générales 1:1844–68. N. J. HEIN et al., *Die Religion in Geschichte und Gegenwart* (Tübingen 1957–65) 2:1630–45. J. HASPECKER et al., *Lexikon für Theologie und Kirche,* ed. J. HOFER and K. RAHNER (Freiburg 1957–65) 4:977–1000. F. STEGMÜLLER, *ibid.* 1002–10. K. RAHNER, *ibid.* 1010–14. J. AUER, *ibid.* 1014–15. F. LAKNER, *ibid.* 1015–16. I. HERMANN and J. AUER, H. FRIES, *Handbuch theologischer Grundbegriffe* (Munich 1962–63) 1:548–562. J. GUILLET et al., *Catholicisme* 5:135–172. C. BAUMGARTNER, *La Grâce du Christ* (Tournai 1963). J. DAUJAT, *The Theology of Grace* (New York 1959). S. DOCKX, *Fils de Dieu par grâce* (Paris 1948). F. CUTTAZ, *Our Life of Grace,* tr. A. BOUCHARD (Chicago, Ill. 1958). R. W. GLEASON, *Grace* (New York 1962). C. JOURNET, *The Meaning of Grace,* tr. A. V. LITTLEDALE (New York 1960; pa. 1964). H. LANGE, *De gratia* (Freiburg 1929). L. LERCHER, *Institutiones theologiae dogmaticae,* 4.1 (5th ed. Barcelona 1951). J. H. NICOLAS, *The Mystery of God's Grace* (pa. Dubuque, Iowa 1960). G. STEVENS, *The Life of Grace* (Englewood Cliffs, N.J. 1963). H. BOUILLARD, ''La Théologie de la grâce au XIIIe siècle,'' *Recherches de science religieuse* 35 (1948) 469–480. G. DE BROGLIE, ''De gratitudine ordinis supernaturalis,'' *Gregorianum* 29 (1948) 435–463. H. RONDET, ''La Divinisation du chrétien,'' *Nouvelle revue théologique* 71 (1949) 449–476, 561–588. F. COLBORN, ''The Theology of Grace,'' *Theological Studies* 31 (1970) 692–711. P. FRANSEN, *The New Life of Grace* (Tournai 1969). G. GUTIERREZ, *A Theology of Liberation* (Maryknoll 1973). H. KÜNG, *Justification: The Doctrine of Karl Barth and a Catholic Reflection* (New York 1964). J. MACKEY, *The Grace of God, The Response of Man* (Albany, N.Y. 1966). W. MEISSNER, *Foundations for a Psychology of Grace* (Glen Rock, N.J. 1966). J. METZ, *Theology of the World* (New York 1969). K. RAHNER, ''Grace: Systematic,'' *Sacramentum Mundi* 2.415–421; ''Justified and Sinner at the Same Time,'' *Theological Investigations* 6 (1969) 218–230: ''Questions of Controversial Theology on Justification,'' *ibid.* 4 (1966) 189–218. J. L. SEGUNDO, *Grace and the Human Condition* (Maryknoll 1973). B. J. F. LONERGAN, *Grace and Freedom: Operative Grace in the Thought of St. Thomas Aquinas* (Collected Works of Bernard Lonergan 1; Toronto, Ont. 1988). P. C. PHAN, *Grace and the Human Condition* (Message of the Fathers of the Church 15; Wilmington, Del. 1988). D. COFFEY, *Grace: the Gift of the Holy Spirit* (Faith and Culture 2; Manly, N.S.W. 1979). J. P. WAWRYKOW, *God's Grace and Human Action: ''Merit'' in the Theology of Thomas Aquinas* (Notre Dame, Ind. 1995). S. J. DUFFY, *The Dynamics of Grace: Perspectives in Theological Anthropology* (New Theology Studies 3; Collegeville, Minn. 1993).

[E. M. BURKE/F. COLBORN/S. KENEL]

GRACE, CONTROVERSIES ON

A series of disputes through the history of the Church over various aspects of the theology of GRACE.

Early Centuries. The Catholic doctrine of grace was first attacked by Gnostics, against whom St. Jude seemed to be writing ''godless men . . . are perverting the life of grace our God has bestowed on us. They even deny Jesus Christ, our one Lord and Master'' (Jude 4); ''animal natures without the life of the Spirit'' (Jude 19). St. Irenaeus continued to defend the doctrine of grace against GNOSTICISM, insisting on the presence of the Holy Spirit in souls. Origen emphasized Christ's presence in the Christian (*Patrologia Graeca,* ed. J. P. Migne, 161 v. [Paris 1857–66] 14:1037–39). Macedonianism, which attacked the divinity of the Holy Spirit, caused St. Basil to describe the role of the Holy Spirit as sanctifier and to develop the theology of grace (*Patrologia Graeca* 29:660, 725). Gregory of Nyssa also treated the Holy Spirit as sanctifier (*Patrologia Graeca* 45:1328–29) but further emphasized the divine INDWELLING in the souls of the just (*Patrologia Graeca* 44:1248). This doctrine became a favorite theme of St. Cyril, who even said that catechumens having the faith are already indwelt by the Holy Spirit (*Patrologia Graeca* 33:344). Ever since, the Greek Church has generally been content to concentrate on the divine indwelling in its doctrine of grace without trying to develop a fuller theology of grace.

St. AUGUSTINE, father of Western theology, under the stimulus of Pelagian opposition, developed a doctrine of grace and predestination that still is very influential in the West. In it he emphasized the remedial character of grace and its necessity, the gratuity of grace and of predestination, the fewness of the elect, and the divine indwelling (*Corpus scriptorum ecclesiasticorum Latinorum* 12:1–571). He himself retracted his initial erroneous belief in man's ability to reach unaided the *initium fidei* (*Retract.* 1.23.2; *see* FAITH, BEGINNING OF).

Pelagius was a Celtic monk who visited Rome (*c.* 400), and Africa (410). At first St. Augustine respected him but then opposed him vigorously (410) in *De peccatorum meritis* and *De spiritu et littera.* For Pelagius nature, free will, and moral law, the example or doctrine of Christ, and forgiveness of sins are grace. Man should ask God's pardon but not His help, for there is no free will if it needs other help of God. If other grace is needed, it is due to men's efforts and comes to crown their merits. For Augustine grace is a collection of gifts pertaining to salvation, really distinct from nature and natural perfections. Man is dependent on such grace to do good. Such grace is not only necessary but gratuitous, a free gift of God not due to man's efforts. Pelagius considered all sins mortal but held that men not only could and should achieve sinlessness but had. Augustine denied this. By making no distinction between pagan and Christian, Pelagius saw more clearly than others that men before Christ could be saved; the mistake he made was in understanding them to be saved without Christ's grace. He withdrew to Palestine, where an inconclusive investigation of his doctrine was made. His treatise on free will was condemned at Carthage (416). Nine canons dealing with Pelagianism survive from the Council of CARTHAGE in 418 (H. Denzinger, *Enchiridion symbolorum,* ed. A. Schönmetzer [32d ed. Freiburg 1963] 222–230; *see* PELAGIUS AND PELAGIANISM).

John Cassian and others in southern France modified Pelagius's ideas but developed the error later called SEMI-PELAGIANISM, which ascribed more to nature and less to grace than had Augustine. To unaided human nature it attributed ''a certain beginning of good will'' (*Patrologia Latina,* ed. J. P. Migne, 271 v., indexes 4 v. [Paris 1878–90] 49:912–913) and the power to merit or impetrate salutary graces and to ''initiate faith.'' Prosper of Aquitaine opposed these errors, and they were rejected in the *Indiculus* (H. Denzinger, *Enchiridion symbolorum* 238–249). They were finally and effectively condemned by the Second Council of Orange (529), under Caesarius of Arles, which asserted vigorously that grace anticipates man's SALUTARY ACTS and causes them (H. Denzinger, *Enchiridion symbolorum* 370–397); these conciliar pronouncements now have dogmatic value.

Medieval Period. The Carolingian era experienced a revival of Augustinian theology under Alcuin (*Patrologia Latina* 100: 934). But shortly afterward the Benedictine Gottschalk of Orbais taught an uncompromising predestination that permitted the letter of Augustine's thought to triumph over the spirit. Denounced by Rabanus Maurus, he passionately defended himself (*Patrologia Latina* 121:368) at Mainz (848) but was condemned at Quiercy (849) and imprisoned for life. At this time Frankish bishops and abbots and the Sees of Reims and Lyons differed sharply in their interpretations of Augustine. Hincmar of Reims enlisted the dubious aid of John Scotus Erigena. But John's emphasis on human liberty was so strong and his reduction of predestination to prescience was so evident that to the opposition he seemed to be a pure Pelagian (*Patrologia Latina* 119:101–250; 121:985–1134). Still, Hincmar's views prevailed at Quiercy-sur-Oise (853), where it was declared that God predestines the good and foresees the loss of the wicked, that man can choose if preserved and helped by grace, and that Christ died for all without exception (*Enchiridion symbolorum* 621–624). But a rival council at Valence (855) maintained a double predestination (*Enchiridion symbolorum* 625–633). This protracted struggle brought some profit to the theology of grace by its insistence on God's universal salvific will. (*See* OMNISCIENCE.)

In the 12th century, Abelard briefly espoused Pelagianism and argued that since original sin did not remove man's free will, pagan philosophers could have practiced supernatural virtues. But St. Bernard secured his condemnation (1140) at Sens (H. Denzinger, *Enchiridion symbolorum* 725), and Abelard retracted (*Patrologia Latina* 178:707).

The great schoolmen, especially St. Thomas Aquinas, while remaining Augustinian, revived the Greek emphasis on the divine indwelling. But some extreme and erroneous views appeared in the 14th and 15th centuries. Eckhart, the German mystic who identified men in grace so absolutely with God as to say, ''God's eyes are his eyes,'' was condemned in 1329 (*Enchiridion symbolorum* 950–980). The Beghards, who had identified God with grace-filled souls, were also condemned (1312) at Vienne (*Enchiridion symbolorum* 891–899). William of Ockham (d. *c.* 1349), whose ideas later had a profound influence on Biel and Luther, promoted nominalism and voluntarism to such an extent as to deny any connection between grace here and glory hereafter. Thus, according to Ockham, God could arbitrarily give or refuse either, and JUSTIFICATION is extrinsic. Biel, a Pelagian, insisted that man unaided by grace could love God supernaturally and that God could declare sinners just. Nominalism thus laid a foundation for Reformation theology.

Reform and Counter Reform. Martin Luther, Ockham's heir, taught man's radical corruption through original sin, which poisons good works. Hence when one is justified by faith and Christ's merits are imputed to him, sin remains. Luther's theories answered his agonized cry, "How shall I find a gracious God?" His answer, erected into a universal system, is salvation through trust in Christ's efficacious Redemption, through grace (i.e., mercy), through God's gracious disposition to accept sinners unconditionally through baptism (whence Luther's triumphant retort in temptation to despair, "Baptizatus sum!"). The divine love and mercy live in Christ. All is given in Him. He is the word divine, i.e., the fullest expression of who God is and what God wills (Skydsgaard, 135). The word itself operates as a means of grace through which the new world comes into existence here and now. Nevertheless, although grace alone saves men, it changes nothing (*see* IMPUTATION OF JUSTICE AND MERIT).

Luther conceived justifying faith as a leap upward in confidence to the terrifying God who damns whom He wills but saves those abandoning themselves to His infinite mercy. Luther scorned the *justitiarius* obsessed with the law (Skydsgaard, 134). Justification is not through common beliefs and observances but comes from a divine decree of justification that renders the mortally sinful actions of those thus justified only venial. Hence man is saved by a juridical fiction in a once-and-for-all event when a man grasps by faith the fact of his election by God. In *De servo arbitrio* (1525) Luther taught double predestination, using the analogy of a beast ridden by God or the devil, but later Lutheran theologians rejected this doctrine. In *De captivitate babylonica* and *De libertate christiana* Luther aimed to separate souls from the Church that he felt would stifle them once the means of grace became an end in themselves. He separated absolutely grace here from glory hereafter since grace is only imputed but never really belongs to the soul.

John Calvin carried Lutheran justification to its logical conclusion: absolute antecedent predestination and reprobation. Though God calls all to salvation through exterior preaching, this affects only the predestined (*Institutes of the Christian Religion* 3.24.8), and they cannot lose grace. Man cannot keep the law (2.5) and is incapable of merit (3.15). Yet the Church is not intangible: to obey it is to obey God.

The Council of Trent's comprehensive decrees on original sin and justification (*Enchiridion symbolorum* 1510–16; 1520–83) were the Catholic dogmatic answers to the errors of Luther and Calvin. The council rejected the idea of extrinsic justification and maintained that man is justified by an interior justice infused by the Holy Spirit. It declared that man genuinely cooperates through his free will in the work of his own justification and, with the grace of Christ, merits his final reward. Thus it condemned the subjectivism in justification that would stand "man alone before God alone" and emphasized strongly (1) justification's radical, ontological transformation of man and (2) the need for man's cooperation in it. But it left unsolved many problems, such as the identification of grace with charity, the existence of infused moral virtues, and the value of works done before justification.

Baius (d. 1589), a Louvain theologian, was nominalist and Protestant in his views of fallen man: grace only restores man's natural powers. Without grace fallen man can only sin, and so all the works of infidels are sins. Man must be satisfied with imperfect justice that God mercifully accepts as true justice. Condemned (1567) by Pius V (*Enchiridion symbolorum* 1901–80), Baius submitted and died in the Church, but his theories survived in Jansenism (*see* BAIUS AND BAIANISM).

De Auxiliis. The most dramatic controversy on grace, although happily not the most disastrous, was the struggle between Dominicans and Jesuits over Molinism. Luis de MOLINA, SJ (1536–1600), theologian and teacher, was opposed by Domingo Báñez, OP. The controversy revolved around the questions of predestination and, more narrowly, the infallible efficacy of grace, which both sides accepted absolutely. With regard to the former, is it antecedent or consequent upon God's knowledge of man's merits? With regard to the latter, is grace infallibly efficacious because efficacious grace is intrinsically different from merely sufficient grace, or because of the knowledge God has prior to man's foreseen acts of what use each man will make of all possible graces? Molina postulated in God middle knowledge (*SCIENTIA MEDIA*), a knowledge of the FUTURIBLES; the existence of this middle knowledge is basic to his whole theory.

Báñez and the theologians of Salamanca opposed Molinism, for Molina's efforts to save human liberty seemed to them, among other things, an oversimplification of the divine action. In a series of public discussions beginning in 1582 at Valladolid, Diego Nuño, OP, attacked Molina's theories; Antonio de Padilla, SJ, defended them. Nuño declared Molina a heretic when Padilla quoted the latter, saying, "With the same grace given to many, one man is converted, another is not." Bitter quarreling broke up the discussion. On May 17, 1583, a second disputation likewise ended in a battle. The struggle was augmented when Báñez published his course (1584), and Molina, extracts from his called *Concordia liberi arbitrii cum gratiae donis . . .* (Lisbon 1588). The reception of the *Concordia* was very diverse. Báñez had tried in vain to prevent its publication. The Spanish Inquisition attacked it, and the fight spread beyond theological circles (*see* MOLINISM; BÁÑEZ AND BAÑEZIANISM).

Ultimately Clement VIII intervened (1594), suspended the Spanish investigation, and commanded the superiors of both orders to send him statements of their teachings on grace. He decided then to hear both parties; thus began the famous *Congregationes de [divinae gratiae] auxiliis,* which met in 120 sessions from 1598 to 1607. They were terminated inconclusively by Paul V, who forbade further public discussions (Dec. 1, 1611). A formula for ending the dispute was imposed (*Enchiridion symbolorum* 1997). Paul V denied the alleged Calvinism of the Dominicans and the Pelagianism of the Jesuits and affirmed the orthodoxy of both orders. With the publication of Cardinal H. Noris's *Historia pelagiana* (1673), the Augustinian Order became involved in the grace controversy. J. H. Serry, OP, in 1699 and L. de Meyer, SJ, in 1705 wrote histories of the controversy from their respective viewpoints. In 1748 Benedict XIV stated that all three views of grace, the Dominican, the Jesuit, and the Augustinian, could be held (*Enchiridion symbolorum* 2564–65). This controversy on grace helped to clarify the question of God's universal salvific will just when the West was becoming conscious of the existence of countless pagans. (*See* CONGREGATIO DE AUXILIIS.)

Jansenism. Cornelius JANSEN (1585–1638), ignoring the theological labors of centuries, tried to present a purely Augustinian theology of grace in his *AUGUSTINUS*, which was published posthumously (Louvain 1640). In book 3, ''De gratia Christi Salvatoris,'' Jansen said that man is not really free—as Bañezians and Molinists claimed—but only extrinsically so, being interiorly necessitated by grace and consequently absolutely predestined. There is no truly but merely sufficient grace. The only true grace of Christ the Savior is efficacious grace, and this is given to the predestined alone, for Christ died for the salvation of the predestined alone. All humanity logically could have been damned, and the majority will be, including unbaptized infants and infidels. Jansen's errors were condemned in 1653 (*Enchiridion symbolorum* 2001–10) and in 1656 (*Enchiridion symbolorum* 2010–12). A formula of submission was offered the Jansenists (*Enchiridion symbolorum* 2020), but they continued to resist and their errors were condemned again by Alexander VIII (*Enchiridion symbolorum* 2301–32), and by Clement XI in 1705 (*Enchiridion symbolorum* 2390). Finally the bull *Unigenitus* (*Enchiridion symbolorum* 2400–2502) condemned the Jansenist errors as elaborated by P. Quesnel, who was called the second founder of Port-Royal. (*See* JANSENISM.)

Later Developments. The Jesuit D. Petau (1583–1652) recognized the fact of development of doctrine and the imperfections in patristic teaching. Though many of his views were almost universally rejected, he opened up again vistas on the divinization of the Christian by grace that prepared the way for the ''theology *in excelsis*'' of M. J. Scheeben (1835–88). Scheeben, a fervent Thomist, revived the scholastic tradition. But while agreeing that works of the Godhead *ad extra* must be attributed to the common unitary activity of the three Persons, he still felt that St. Thomas suggests that the divinization of souls is not merely a work *ad extra* (*Summa theologiae* 1a, 43.3 ad 1). Hence he taught that the Trinity dwells in the soul in grace in such a way as to set up in it personal relations with each member of the Trinity. He was sharply criticized, especially by T. Granderath. Today the nature and mode of the divine indwelling are matters of liveliest controversy; cf. e.g., the theories of P. Galtier, S. Dockx, M. De la Taille, K. Rahner, P. De Letter, M. Donnelly, T. Mullaney, and B. Lonergan.

Many 20th-century Protestant theologians, such as K. Barth and T. F. Torrance, differed sharply from Catholic theologians on matters of grace. Contemporary Lutheran theology comes closer to the Catholic position, though there are differences.

See Also: GRACE, ARTICLES ON; GRACE, EFFICACIOUS; GRACE, SUFFICIENT; VIRTUE; SUPERNATURAL.

Bibliography: J. FERGUSON, *Pelagius: A Historical and Theological Study* (Cambridge, Eng. 1956). R. HEDDE and É. AMANN, *Dictionnaire de théologie catholique,* ed. A. VACANT et al., 15 v. (Paris 1903–50) 12.1:675–715. Augustine's anti-Pelagian works, ed. C. F. URBA and J. ZYCHA, *Corpus scriptorum ecclesiasticorum Latinorum* 12:1–571. C. LAMBOT, *Godescalc d'Orbais: Oeuvres théologiques et grammaticales* (Louvain 1946). J. ANCELET-HUSTACHE, *Master Eckhart and the Rhineland Mystics,* tr. H. GRAEF (pa. New York 1958). G. BIEL, *Quaestiones de justificatione,* ed. C. FECKES (Aschendorff 1929). H. A. OBERMAN, *The Harvest of Mediaeval Theology: Gabriel Biel and Late Mediaeval Nominalism* (Cambridge, Mass. 1963). M. LUTHER, *Works,* ed. J. PELIKAN (St. Louis-Philadelphia 1955–64). H. JEDIN, *Lexikon für Theologie und Kirche,* ed. J. HOFER and K. RAHNER, 10 v. (2d, new ed. Freiburg 1957–65) 6:1223–30. F. STEGMÜLLER, *Lexikon für Theologie und Kirche,* ed. J. HOFER and K. RAHNER, 10 v. (2d, new ed. Freiburg 1957–65) 4:1002–07. L. MOLINA, *Concordia . . . ,* ed. J. RABENECK (Madrid-Oña 1952). P. MANDONNET, *Dictionnaire de théologie catholique,* ed. A. VACANT et al., 15 v. (Paris 1903–50) 2.1:140–146. J. BRODRICK, *The Life and Work of Blessed Robert Francis Cardinal Bellarmine,* 2 v. (London 1927–28). J. H. SERRY, *Historia congregationum de auxiliis divinae gratiae* (Venice 1740). L. DE MEYER, *Historia controversiarum ab objectionibus H. Serry vindicata* (Brussels 1715; Venice 1742). N. DEL PRADO, *De gratia et libero arbitrio,* 3 v. (Fribourg 1907). V. MUÑOZ, *Nuevos documentos acerca de las controversias ''de auxiliis'' en Salamanca: Salmanticenses* 1 (Salamanca 1954) 440–449. G. GERBERON, *Michaelis Baii opera* (Cologne 1696). X. LE BACHELET, *Dictionnaire de théologie catholique,* ed. A. VACANT et al., 15 v. (Paris 1903–50) 2.1:38–111. J. CARREYRE, *Dictionnaire de théologie catholique,* ed. A. VACANT et al., 15 v. (Paris 1903–50) 8.1:377–448; 13.2:1460–1535. H. DE LUBAC, *Surnaturel: Études historiques* (Paris 1946). H. RONDET, *Gratia Christi* (Paris 1948). M. J. FARRELLY, *Predestination, Grace, and Free Will* (Westminster, Md. 1964). L. BOUYER, *The Spirit and Forms of Protestantism,* tr. A. V. LIT-

TLEDALE (Westminster, Md. 1956). K. E. SKYDSGAARD, *One in Christ,* tr. A. C. KILDEGAARD (Philadelphia 1957). W. M. HORTON, *Christian Theology, an Ecumenical Approach* (rev. ed. New York 1958). M. LACKMANN, *The Augsburg Confession and Catholic Unity,* tr. W. R. BOUMAN (New York 1963). R. NIEBUHR, *The Nature and Destiny of Man,* 2 v. (New York 1941–43) 2:98–126, 127–212. C. MOELLER, "Théologie de la grâce et oecumenisme," *Irénikon* (1955) 19–56.

[C. M. AHERNE]

GRACE, CREATED AND UNCREATED

Created grace is any grace that results from God communicating Himself beyond nature's demands, such as the beatific vision and all supernatural creatures positively leading to it. It may be actual or habitual, external or internal, medicinal or elevating, or anything else, so long as it is a creature positively undue to the person it enhances. Since the reality signified by the term grace is found properly both in God and in created things given to creatures beyond their due, the term grace applies truly to some created gifts of the supernatural order. It is therefore some gratuitous gift of God, distinct from God Himself, positively leading to the beatific vision of God.

God Himself, given to a creature beyond any of its demands, is uncreated grace. Examples are primarily: the Blessed Trinity indwelling in the just as distinct from created gifts, the Son of God given in the Incarnation, the Holy Spirit sent men by the Father and the Son, the love of God for men that is God Himself beyond the demands of nature, and predestination, or God's decree to glorify those who shall be saved. This concept of grace is commonly admitted by theologians; for every supernatural gift is rightly called grace, and preeminent among these is God Himself.

Bibliography: C. BAUMGARTNER, *La Grâce du Christ* (Tournai 1963). I. WILLIG, *Geschaffende und Ungeschaffende Gnade* (Münster 1964). H. RONDET, *Gratia Christi* (Paris 1948). P. FRANSEN, *Divine Grace and Man,* tr. G. DUPONT (rev. ed. New York 1965).

[F. L. SHEERIN]

GRACE, EFFICACIOUS

A division of actual internal grace, efficacious grace means today grace that infallibly obtains the free cooperation of the will. It is considered in two senses: (1) as actually producing, together with the will, the election of a free act—efficacious grace has this connection with the free act from the consent of the will; (2) as already having infallible connection with a future free act of the will prior to that free action absolutely foreseen by God.

Grace Efficacious before Will's Consent. Some have questioned whether all efficacious grace has this efficacy. St. Alphonsus Liguori and others speak of a grace of prayer, given to everyone and rendered efficacious by the recipient's consent. It has no more prior connection with consent rather than dissent; it gets its efficacy entirely from the recipient's response. With this grace all can pray. If they pray, they infallibly receive grace of its nature efficacious, which is necessary for more difficult deeds.

Some modern theologians simply assert that efficacious grace means that the performance of a good act by man is due to God's primacy in grace manifesting itself in man's good act. Others identify efficacy with the infallibility of grace in obtaining God's absolute will in creation prior to man's absolute consent: the city of the blessed. Thus, grace is efficacious in obtaining good acts from mankind as a whole, the acts of individuals being left out of the direct consideration.

But the majority of theologians hold that all efficacious grace has infallible power to obtain the consent of the will prior to the will's consent; for otherwise there could be no providence in God, nor any certain and infallible predestination of the elect, nor would there be any certain and infallible means of implementing the divine will.

Places in Scripture (Prv 21.1; Jer 31.33; Ez 11.9; Jn 10.29; Phil 2.13) bear out the idea that grace has efficacy prior to the consent of the will, but not all has; however, Christian humility has always understood that the difference between one and another in the work of salvation is always due to God's action, which would not be true if the reason why grace is efficacious in one and not another is sometimes the consent of the will. From this follows the corollary that every good act performed by man is a special benefit of God.

Freedom under Efficacious Grace. But despite this priority of the efficacy of grace, it in no way necessitates the will's consent, but leaves intact the ability to dissent, under the action of the most powerful grace; it does not move the will irresistibly to will that to which it solicits it. Man, even under the action of grace, which is infallibly going to obtain the will's consent, retains the power of self-determination to will or not will deliberately that to which he is solicited by preceding indeliberate acts; infallibly he will consent, but he can dissent—efficacious grace does not remove this power. It should be noted that to predetermine the will is not the same as to necessitate it; the former effects that man will infallibly consent, but it does not thereby remove the power of dissent, which is freedom of choice.

In view of recent Catholic writing a distinction should be made between acting freely under grace, with the power not to act, and acting spontaneously, gladly, willingly. The latter is spontaneity, not freedom; a free act may be made with great reluctance, as it was in the agony in the garden.

The reformers held that every grace necessitates the will; it acts spontaneously, but not freely. The Jansenists also held that efficacious grace, stronger than the opposite concupiscence, necessitates the will. But the freedom of the will under the influence of efficacious grace is a dogma of faith; (*see* H. Denzinger, *Enchiridion symbolorum,* 1554, 2002–03). For Biblical reference (*see* Sir 31.8–11; 2 Cor 6.1); they show that man is able to dissent from the very grace to which he consents.

One meets here two facts. The efficacy of grace is not derived from the consent of the will, yet it leaves the will free. Theologians have striven over this problem for centuries without definite conclusion.

Bibliography: ALPHONSUS LIGUORI, *The Great Means of Salvation and of Perfection,* ed. E. GRIMM (Brooklyn 1927). B. BERAZA, *De gratia Christi* (Bilbao 1929). J. FARRELLY, *Predestination, Grace and Free Will* (Westminster, Md. 1964). P. FRANSEN, *Divine Grace and Man,* tr. G. DUPONT (New York 1965). R. GARRIGOU-LAGRANGE, *Grace,* tr. Dominican Nuns, Menlo Park, Calif. (St. Louis 1957). S. GONZÁLEZ, *Scarae theologiae summa,* ed. Fathers of the Society of Jesus, Professors of the Theological Faculties in Spain, 4 v. (Madrid), v. 1 (1962), v. 2 (1958), v. 3 1961), v. 4 (1962); *Biblioteca de autores cristianos* (Madrid 1945) 3.3:295–312. H. LANGE, *De gratia* (Freiburg 1929). J. POHLE, *Grace, Actual and Habitual,* ed. and tr. A. PREUSS (St. Louis 1942). H. RONDET, *Gratia Christi* (Paris 1948).

[F. L. SHEERIN]

GRACE, SACRAMENTAL

This article discusses the nature and the objective efficacy of the Sacraments, and the special questions of the efficacy of infant Baptism and reviviscence from the perspective of scholastic theology. Other theological approaches to these questions may be found in the entry SACRAMENTAL THEOLOGY. See also: EX OPERE OPERANTIS; EX OPERE OPERATO; BAPTISM OF INFANTS; REVIVISCENCE, SACRAMENTAL.

Nature of Sacramental Grace

In the history of sacramental theology several opinions have been offered to explain the nature of sacramental grace. Some theologians teach that sacramental and sanctifying grace are identical; others maintain a strict and real distinction between them but explain this distinction in various ways.

Sacramental and Sanctifying Grace Really Identical. There is no distinction whatsoever between them. Although held centuries ago, this position is no longer held by any reputable theologian, for several reasons. First, it would call into serious question the wisdom of God's having instituted seven Sacraments instead of one, if they all give exactly the same kind of grace or the same grace. Moreover, it does not adequately explain the Church's official teaching that the Sacraments "are not equal to one another and that there is a diversity of worth among them" (Denz 1603).

Sacramental and Sanctifying Grace Not Really Identical. But this distinction between the two is not understood by all theologians in exactly the same way. The following variant explanations are the most common.

A Right to Actual Graces. Sacramental grace differs from common sanctifying grace insofar as it confers a right to the actual graces to be received in accordance with the demands of the Christian situation in life into which one is introduced by the reception of a particular Sacrament. This opinion was so widespread until recently that it was the one most commonly accepted by theologians. This right is something juridical, effecting nothing real in the person or his powers, not even the grace-reality or life that he receives through the Sacrament. Thus the various Sacraments would not really give a different grace or permanent Christian elevation of a peculiar kind. Rather, they would seem to give the same grace plus a juridical title to actual graces needed by the person because of his having received a Sacrament. The sacramental grace would be only this juridical title (J. de Lugo, G. Vazquez, F. Suárez, J. Gonet, D. de Soto).

Special Habitus. Another group of theologians, declaring that this explanation does not satisfy the teaching of the Council of Trent, offered another. Sacramental grace differs from common sanctifying grace insofar as it adds one or several special habitus through the intermediary of which sanctifying grace performs the acts to which the Sacraments commission a person and by which the deficiencies of the powers of the soul are partially counteracted. These additional habitus so strengthen these powers that they easily perform the acts demanded by their new sacramental status, and they formally and immediately heal the wounds inflicted on the soul by sin (J. Capreolus, B. Brazzarola, B. Leeming).

Special Mode of Sanctifying Grace. Still a third opinion claims that sacramental grace is a special mode of sanctifying grace acting as a basis or fundament for correlative actual graces to be received in view of the purposes for which the Sacrament is given. The reasoning lying behind this position is quite clear. Because the different Sacraments have different purposes for which they have been instituted and because they have a distinct signification, causality, and necessity, they seem to communicate distinct graces for their effects. Sacramental grace is distinct from sanctifying grace not as one reality is distinct from another reality, but as a reality is distinct from a peculiar mode or orientation that it has or that it assumes in order to meet new demands. Insofar as the various Sacraments make us members of Christ according to a variety of offices and commissions and functions within His Body, the Church, they confer on us those effects of this new life in Christ necessary to meet the demands of our peculiar ecclesial mission. This permanent orientation of sanctifying grace also establishes a basis or fundament, or it connotes a right to all the actual graces that will be needed to fulfill the new Christian life-situation for which we have been sacramentalized (John of St. Thomas, Salmanticenses, A. Piolanti, H. Boüessé, R. Garrigou-Lagrange, E. Schillebeeckx).

At the heart of all sacramentalism there occurs an encounter with God. But this takes place within the framework of a visible and an ecclesial action, that is, through a visible sacramental action of Christ and the Church, which is His earthly Body or Self. Grace, or communion and encounter, is made real in a liturgical action that shows both the nature of the gift and the demands that it makes on the recipient. Thus sacramental grace is the grace of the redemption, but grace in its direction and application to the seven different situations in which a Christian can find himself within the Church. Or it is the grace of redemption having a peculiar function with reference to a particular ecclesial and Christian situation of life and to a particular need of man. We might speak of grace as being modified or tailored to meet these needs. The Anointing of the Sick, for example, has as its ecclesial effect a more specific incorporation into the Church that has been given power over death. The Church's anointing gives one in serious suffering a share in the suffering of Christ and the Church. And thus the anointed has a special ecclesial status making him the object of the special prayer and solicitude of the Church.

From this it should be clear that sacramental grace is sanctifying grace itself, but as coming to us visibly in the Church in the fullness of its power, specifically ordered and aimed to meet the particular ecclesial needs of life and the special commissions of a Christian in the Church. It is because the Sacraments give positive commissions or functions within the Church that the grace they communicate is permanently oriented to receive the actual graces needed to fulfill such functions.

Of course, extrasacramental graces are also possible to man, but these are meant to grow in the recipient to a culminating point—a personal and decisive communion with God that is had through the activity of the Church. A certain grace can be present for man apart from the Sacraments, but this would seem to have some orientation toward one or other of them. It would be a kind of inchoate grace that normally reaches full development only in the Sacraments; for it is only there that communion in grace is achieved within an ecclesial context within the Church as the fullness of Christ or as His earthly Body.

Objective Efficacy of the Sacraments

The Council of Trent has defined that "the Sacraments of the New Law confer grace EX OPERE OPERATO," on those who place no obstacle in the way of this grace (Denz 1606, 1608). This notion *opus operatum* has often been misunderstood, especially by those not of the Catholic faith. For these it means automatic conferral, such that the Sacraments are considered to possess a kind of magical force that the recipient cannot resist and that does not at all require dispositions on the part of either the minister or the recipient. This, however, is not the true Catholic position.

Ex opere operato is a technical phrase opposed to *EX OPERE OPERANTIS.* It admits of an older interpretation dating especially from Trent up to recent times; and of a newer interpretation that is really not so new but is a return to the full meaning of the term. The older view limits the expression to the level of validity. So understood, *ex opere operato* means that the correct bringing together of the matter and form, or the action and formula or word, brings about the sacramental effect. While this mode of presenting the Catholic position is not inexact, it is incomplete. That is why the newer view is attempting to see the expression as having a very definite Christological character. It means exactly the same as "by the power of Christ and God." It means that the sacramental action as an act, done in virtue of a character, is objectively and ministerially an act of Christ, an objective celebration-in-mystery of the historical redemptive mystery of Christ. This action brings about the unmerited application of the redemption and is a work of pure mercy toward the person involved. If the bringing together of the matter and form of a Sacrament communicates grace, this happens because this action in the hands of the Church and her ministers is an act of Christ by which He works His redemption in a member of His Body, and this independently of the *merits* (not the dispositions) of the subject, or minister, or both.

Ex opere operantis refers to the work of the minister, or the subject of the Sacrament, or both in sacramental actions. While the dispositions of these do not play or constitute a part of the sacramental action (since this is an action of Christ and the Church), still these dispositions do have a very necessary part to play in sacramentalism considered as the actual reception of grace given through a Sacrament. A sacramental event is intended to bring about communion with Christ, and for this the religious attitude of the recipient is most important. If the sacramental action, the advent of Christ, is not personally desired and met (in keeping with the state of the recipient, of course) communion or encounter with Christ cannot occur. This implies that a Sacrament that is fully such (fruitful as well as valid) does not consist only in the visible manifestation of Christ's redemptive action or only in the visibility of the Church's will to sanctify. It must consist also in the visible expression of the recipient's personal desire for grace and his will to be sanctified. We can speak of a minimum and an optimum and intermediate grades of disposition on the part of the recipient that account for the varying degrees of encounter or fruitfulness. Moreover, there must also be some active dispositions on the part of the minister, if the Sacrament is to be effective. Here also we have a minimum and an optimum (and varying grades between) that enter in some way into the effect produced by the sacramental action. While no positive loss will necessarily occur in the case in which a minister is merely minimally disposed, still the ministration is not everything that it ought to be when the prayer of the minister is not a real personal prayer.

Efficacy of Infant Baptism. The BAPTISM OF INFANTS has at times presented a problem, especially to some Protestant exegetes and theologians. K. Barth, for example, writes: ''From the standpoint of a doctrine of baptism, infant baptism can hardly be maintained without exegetical and practical artifices and sophisms—the proof to the contrary has yet to be supplied'' [*The Teaching of the Church regarding Baptism* (London 1959) 49]. The Church teaches that infant Baptism is profitable to children (Denz 1626), and requires that it be administered to them soon after birth since in the ordinary plan of God there is no other way open. [*See* BAPTISM, SACRAMENT OF; LIMBO.]

The possibility of infant Baptism's being profitable stems from the fact that not all the Sacraments necessarily on all occasions suppose a psychological awareness on the part of the recipient. This does not mean that any dispensation from a condition otherwise necessary has been granted. Rather, it follows from the very nature of the symbolic action precisely as performed for one who is psychologically an infant, just as the very nature of a symbolic action performed for a conscious adult requires his response. While it is true that the dormant personality of the child is still not capable of interpersonal rational encounter, God can still love it with His preventive grace. That a child is not yet capable of a similar encounter with its mother does not mean that its mother will wait to bestow her love on the child when the latter is capable of freely returning it. She loves it and cares for it from the very first instant, and it is just this care and love that evokes a response from the child when it is capable of such. In like manner the Sacrament of Baptism produces within the child an ontological foundation (the grace of the virtues and the gifts) for encounter with God, making this encounter possible when the child has attained the maturity to achieve it. While a person must freely will and accept the divine initiative immediately, an infant is expected to do so in its own time and then to make personally its own the grace that it received previously, in a similar way as it does its own existence. The obligation for our seeing to infant Baptism stems from the social coresponsibility that all of us have for the realization of the goal of life of our fellowmen. The Church, as the earthly prolongation of the Lord and the mother of men, has this desire and aim for all, and she realizes it concretely and visibly both in the parents and in the minister of the Sacrament.

Reviviscence. As we have seen, there are two sides to sacramentality. There is first the objective side—the ecclesial expression of God's will to link Himself with us, the *opus operatum,* which we discussed above. And there is the subjective side—the individual's personal acceptance of God's grace-giving intent, at least in the case of the adult. Thus some movement toward God's approach is required (part of the *opus operantis*). This movement can be of different kinds: that which is sufficient to make this approach valid (sufficient to establish the ecclesial link proper to the Sacrament), and that which is needed to make this approach fruitful (required to establish a personal link or encounter with God). REVIVISCENCE refers to those instances in which a sacramental action produces its personal link with God (sacramental grace) only some time after its ecclesial link because of an imperfect movement on the part of the recipient. While the possibility of a Sacrament's accomplishing this has never been defined, it has been taught from the time of the Church Fathers, and is universally accepted in the Church (at least in regard to some of the Sacraments). The reason is simple. If some of the Sacraments (those especially that are either absolutely or relatively unrepeatable) could not revive, impossible consequences would follow. For if a person did not receive the grace of these Sacraments at the time of their reception, he would be forever excluded from this benefit regardless of what he might do later in regard to his religious dispositions. Thus reviviscence of some kind or other seems to be almost a necessary postulate in such instances.

Bibliography: B. BRAZZAROLA, *La natura della grazia sacramentale nella dottrina di San Tommaso* (Grottaferrata 1941). E. DORONZO, *De sacramentis in genere* (Milwaukee 1946). B. LEEMING, *Principles of Sacramental Theology* (new ed. Westminster,

Md. 1960). H. LENNERZ, *De sacramentis Novae Legis in genere* (Rome 1950). R. R. MASTERSON, ''Sacramental Graces: Modes of Sanctifying Grace,'' *Thomist* 18 (1955) 311–372. J. H. MILLER, *Signs of Transformation in Christ* (Englewood Cliffs, N.J. 1963). K. RAHNER, *The Church and the Sacraments,* tr. W. J. O'HARA (New York 1963) E. SCHILLEBEECKX, *Christ: The Sacrament of the Encounter with God* (New York 1963) C. SCHLECK, ''On Sacramental Grace,'' *University of Ottawa Review* 24 (1954) 227–251; ''St. Thomas on the Nature of Sacramental Grace,'' *Thomist* 18 (1955) 1–30; 242–278. C. S. SULLIVAN, ed., *Readings in Sacramental Theology* (Englewood Cliffs, N.J. 1964). J. H. NICOLAS, ''La Grâce sacramentelle,'' *Revue tomiste* 61 (1961) 165–192, 522–540.

[C. A. SCHLECK/EDS.]

GRACE, SUFFICIENT

A division of internal actual grace, sufficient grace is used in two senses: (1) grace that gives sufficient ability to perform a salutary act, prescinding from the result (grace efficacious with the efficacy of power)—grace is always sufficient in this sense or it would not be grace; (2) purely sufficient grace, which does not obtain a good, free act, but gives sufficient power to produce one—grace inefficacious in the production of a good, free act.

In the First Sense. The conferral of sufficient grace in this sense upon all human beings for their various needs is a corollary of the doctrine of a sincere universal salvific will.

Here one must distinguish between grace proximately and remotely sufficient for a good act. Grace is proximately sufficient if it gives sufficient power to perform the act without additional aid (H. Denzinger, *Enchiridion symbolorum,* 1536); it is remotely sufficient for an act if further aid is needed—but a grace remotely sufficient for a future good act, e.g., of confession, is always proximately sufficient for another good act, e.g., salutary fear. Thus, sufficient grace is not always given for undergoing martyrdom, because martyrdom is not always impending; but there is always given proximately sufficient grace, which may eventually lead to the heroic act of fortitude that undergoing martyrdom is. Grace is always sufficient for a good act now impending, or it would not be grace, but only remotely for good acts of the future, which may require additional grace.

Grace proximately sufficient to perform a given good act, e.g., to suffer martyrdom, may never be given, because need for it never arises, but everyone receives grace proximately sufficient for present needs. Today a person has not proximately sufficient grace to perform a difficult act that may impend in future, but that person can through today's graces perform today's duties. By doing what is possible now the person sets no obstacles to future graces and is in a position later infallibly to obtain proximately sufficient grace for greater deeds. This is God's understanding of His own word, ''sufficient for the day is its own evil'' (Mt 6.34).

Purely Sufficient Grace. Grace is also called purely sufficient or inefficacious. That there is such grace, which gives full power to perform a good, free act, even in the presence of contrary difficulties, but which lacks effect due to the will's resistance, is Catholic doctrine; it seems implied by the Second Council of Orange (H. Denzinger, *Enchiridion symbolorum,* 397) and also by the condemnation of the first two propositions of Jansen (*ibid.,* 2001–02). This is also the meaning of Is 5.1–7, Mt 11.21, 2 Cor 6.1, and is a corollary of the fact that grace is given to men without result.

Purely sufficient (inefficacious) grace was not recognized by the reformers, who recognized no grace but efficacious, nor by the Jansenists, who did not recognize relatively, though purely, sufficient grace. For them all grace relatively sufficient is efficacious. It is *gratia magna,* more intense than the contrary concupiscence, necessarily drawing the fallen will. *Gratia parva,* though producing velleities, is insufficient for a free salutary act. It may be called ''absolutely'' sufficient, because it gives power of action prescinding from contrary concupiscence. Hence, for the Jansenists, purely sufficient grace, which does not work, is not a benefit and is not given with the intention of benefiting.

However, in Catholic doctrine, purely sufficient grace is a grace that is capable of benefiting, a quality not nullified by the recipient's unwillingness. It is given with the sincere intention that the recipient receive good. The grace given is of its nature beneficent, and it is given with the sincere intent of benefiting. This intention is compatible with God's knowledge of the grace's inefficacy, because this is not intended, and with the possibility of giving another grace, for God in order to intend a benefit sincerely need not give one graces he would accept, but those he truly can.

Purely sufficient grace is given by God not because of its inefficacy, nor with the intention of inefficacy, but although it is inefficacious. It is given with knowledge of its inefficacy, but with sincere desire that it be efficacious; for the grace given is truly sufficient, and lacks efficacy only through man's unwillingness, which God does not intend, though He intends to permit it.

Catholic theologians differ in their explanations of the nature of sufficient grace in its relation to efficacious grace (*see* BÁÑEZ AND BAÑEZIANISM; MOLINISM).

See Also: JANSENISM.

Bibliography: B. BERAZA, *De gratia Christi* (Bilbao 1929). P. FRANSEN, *Divine Grace and Man,* tr. G. DUPONT (New York 1965).

R. GARRIGOU-LAGRANGE, *Grace,* tr. Dominican Nuns, Menlo Park, Calif. (St. Louis 1957). S. GONZÁLEZ, *Sacrae theologiae summa,* ed. Fathers of the Society of Jesus, Professors of the Theological Faculties in Spain, 4 v. (Madrid), v. 1 (1962), v. 2 (1958), v. 3 (1961), v. 4 (1962); *Biblioteca de autores cristianos* (Madrid 1945–) 3.3:117–142, 284–294. H. LANGE, *De gratia* (Freiburg 1929). J. POHLE, *Grace, Actual and Habitual,* ed. and tr. A. PREUSS (St. Louis 1942). H. RONDET, *Gratia Christi* (Paris 1948).

[F. L. SHEERIN]

GRACE, THE STATE OF

The phrase ''state of grace'' refers to that permanent disposition of soul in which the divine life of sanctifying or habitual grace is present. This condition of soul is marked by sinlessness and by the fulfillment of God's will and, once obtained, remains unless it is destroyed by willful mortal sin. It is contrasted to the state of sin in which such grace is absent. Habitual grace is first obtained through the Sacrament of Baptism in the case of infants or through either Baptism or an act of perfect contrition in the case of adults. If lost by serious sin it may be recovered through an act of perfect contrition or through ATTRITION coupled with sacramental absolution.

Unless a soul is in the state of grace at the moment of death, it cannot attain the Beatific Vision. Even in this life the state of grace is necessary for the performance of any supernatural act, for the accomplishment of acts that are meritorious *de condigno* of grace and glory, for the gaining of indulgences, and for the licit administration of the Sacraments. Particularly is the state of grace required as a necessary disposition for the fruitful reception of the Sacraments of the living (at least *per se*), since these Sacraments have been instituted to increase grace and therefore presuppose that the soul is already in the state of grace. (One says *''per se''* since, at least according to most theologians, if one in mortal sin receives a Sacrament of the living in good faith and with attrition, sanctifying grace will be conferred upon him *per accidens.*) Canon Law (1917 CIC cc. 807, 856) demands that one who is conscious of having committed serious sin ordinarily confess that sin and obtain sacramental absolution before celebrating Mass or receiving the Holy Eucharist. (The law makes an exception for those cases in which there is some necessity for celebrating Mass or receiving Holy Communion and no confessor is available.) For the reception of other Sacraments, the state of grace may be recovered either through confession or through an act of perfect contrition. The question arises as to how certain a person must be that he is in the state of grace before he can legitimately approach the Sacraments.

The problem of what knowledge a person can have of his own possession of the state of grace is a matter of considerable controversy. Lutherans and Calvinists insist that a man is justified by faith alone and that therefore he can know with certitude that he possesses grace. Catholic theologians, on the other hand, make distinctions in answering this question. All agree with St. Thomas Aquinas (*Summa theologia* 1a2ae, 112.5.c) that one cannot have the certitude of faith concerning this matter except by a special revelation from God, at least in the case of adults. Nor can an adult possess the certitude of a theological conclusion in this matter (although some theologians have defended this position), since such certitude arises only from a reasoning process in which one premise is a revealed truth and the other is an absolutely certain natural truth. Moreover, an adult cannot have the certitude of ''scientific'' knowledge that he is in the state of grace, since such certitude comes from a syllogism in which both premises are either self-evident or demonstrable. Man can have, however, what St. Thomas calls ''conjecture'' or what modern theologians refer to as moral certitude: that is, a knowledge that excludes all prudent or positive doubt. Such moral certitude is reached through definite signs that are incompatible with a state of sin: the testimony of a well-formed conscience, sincere love of God, delight in the things of God, fervor in prayer, solicitude in avoiding sin, zeal for souls, contempt for the world, the practice of mortification, etc. From such indications a prudent man can generally exclude all objectively probable doubt concerning the state of his soul. St. Thomas also taught (*Summa theologiae* 3a, 80.4 ad 5) that one who has committed mortal sin can possess only conjecture (moral certitude) concerning his recovery of grace, since he cannot be absolutely certain of the supernatural quality of his contrition. It suffices that he possess such signs of sorrow as regret for his past action and a firm purpose of amendment.

It does not follow, however, that it is always easy or even possible to come to a morally certain judgment regarding one's state of soul. The scrupulous are frequently troubled by anxieties that are an obstacle to ready and confident judgment in this matter. Moreover, the data upon which judgment must be based can sometimes be obscure even to one not prone to scruple. Now a reasonable degree of positive assurance of being in the state of grace is unquestionably desirable in a recipient of a Sacrament of the living, but doubt is not *per se* a disqualifying state of mind. The law of the Church as formulated by the Council of Trent (H. Denzinger, *Enchiridion symbolorum*, ed. A. Schönmetzer [Freiburg 1963] 1647) and stated by the Code of Canon Law (*Codex iuris canonici* [Graz 1955] c.916) does not require the recipient of Holy Communion to be certain that he is in the state of grace; rather it forbids the reception of Communion by one who is certain that he is not in the state of grace, which is quite another thing. Moralists and canonists agree that ''conscious of grave sin'' in this case means a morally certain consciousness of being in grave sin, and it cannot be understood to include a state of doubt about one's state of soul.

Bibliography: J. VAN DER MEERSCH, *Dictionnaire de théologie catholique*, ed. A. VACANT et al., (Paris 1903–50) 6.2:1616–87. H. MOUREAU, *Dictionnaire de théologie catholique*, ed. A. VACANT et al., (Paris 1903—50) 3.1:503–505. T. ORTOLAN, *Dictionnaire de théologie catholique*, ed. A. VACANT et al., (Paris 1903—50) 3.1:955. A. TANQUEREY, *Synopsis theologiae dogmaticae*, 3 v. (25th ed. Paris 1947) 3:62–64. P. GAUCHER, *Le Signe infallible de l'état de grâce* (Le Perreux 1907).

[J. P. BROWNE]

GRACE AND NATURE

The relationship between GRACE and NATURE is one of the most fundamental problems of Christian anthropology. Grace is something really distinct from nature, wholly undue to nature, yet divinely given to nature. It confers on man a participation in the divine nature and divine life.

Historical Perspectives. The question of grace and nature's mutual relationship has taken shape in and through a long history. The summary of the principal positions of Catholic theology on the relationship gains significance and clarity from a survey of the more important moments in this history.

Augustine and Pelagianism. In polemic with Pelagianism, the Church made explicit her belief in the absolute necessity of grace if man is to attain eternal life or perform any action positively tending to it (H. Denzinger, *Enchiridion symbolorum,* ed. A. Schönmetzer [32d ed. Freiburg 1963] 225–230, 370–397, 1551–53). Pelagius's denial of ORIGINAL SIN, and his consequent practical ignoring of the sinful condition of man conditioned the approach of St. Augustine (*see* PELAGIUS AND PELAGIANISM). Augustine used by preference terms that proclaimed man's indigence. ''Nature'' was one such. The term derives from *natus,* a participial form of the verb meaning ''to be born.'' Hence it can sustain the meaning of ''that which belongs to a being's pristine condition.'' When Augustine spoke of nature in a proper sense, he had in mind that graced condition that should have been his and should have been passed on by natural generation. Thus he could write that man's nature is ''wounded, hurt, damaged, destroyed'' by the willful disobedience of sin (*Nat. et grat.* 53.62, *Patrologia Latina,* ed. J. P. Migne, 271 v., indexes 4 v. [Paris 1878–90] 44:277). Actually St. Augustine knew that man's natural being remained intact, and that freedom of choice was inalienably his. Centuries later this expression and his analogous usage of ''free will'' would be used in support of a pessimism alien to the doctrine of Augustine.

St. Thomas Aquinas. The introduction of Aristotelianism into the West in the 13th century brought the philosopher's clear and precise concept of nature into the Catholic theology of grace. St. Thomas is to be credited with exploiting this notion for its theological accuracy. He clearly affirmed that while grace now is necessary to heal wounded nature, its primary function, which it would have in any hypothesis, is to elevate nature to a share in the properly divine nature (*Summa theologiae* 1a, 95.4 ad 1). Grace is supernature, rooted in nature and making nature transcend itself. St. Thomas affirmed the existence in every intellectual nature of a capacity for this elevation—a teaching that would subsequently find many different interpretations.

Nominalism and the Reformation. The Thomist synthesis did not gain the loyalty of the centuries immediately following. A juridic mentality and a nominalist philosophy were in the ascendant (*see* NOMINALISM). Under these influences theological inquiry tended to fragment men's view of the ontological union and harmony of grace and nature. The results were diffused in the schools by the works of Gabriel BIEL. The grace of adoption was seen to consist in an arbitrary divine decree and hence to be an extrinsic adornment of nature. Mere nature's capacity to observe the moral law was extolled in a way that smacked of Pelagianism. The sense of grace as a participation in divine life practically disappeared. The Reformation burst into this atmosphere of nominalist theology. Although they were heirs of nominalism's concept of an extrinsic grace, and its ignorance of divinizing grace, still Martin LUTHER and the reformers reacted strongly against its Pelagian tendency. Augustine's strong indictment of sinful nature was resumed and given new dimensions. Not only had sin destroyed the liberty of the children of God, but free will itself was henceforth capable of nothing but sin. The Church countered with the teaching and the anathemas of Trent, affirming the truly inherent character of justifying grace by which nature is elevated in Christ, and its authentic healing is begun (H. Denzinger, *Enchiridion symbolorum* 1525–31, 1554–61). An attenuated version of Luther's teaching appears in the works of BAIUS and JANSEN and their disciples. The common note that binds them together is their inability to conceive of justifying grace as something that makes man transcend the order of nature. At best, grace is a medicinal agent that restores man to the primitive (natural) state that sin had destroyed. Particularly in correction of Baius the teaching Church intervened to establish the authentic gratuity of the order of grace (H.

Denzinger, *Enchiridion symbolorum* 1921, 1923, 1924, 1926, 1942).

Contemporary Orientations. Passing over the intervening centuries to the 20th, one finds after World War II a new theological orientation that gave rise to excesses that compromised the transcendent gratuity of the order of grace. Theologians sought to probe the link that binds man's nature to a supernatural destiny. They judged the usual conception of this link to be vitiated by an ''EXTRINSICISM'' that makes grace a mere superstructure added to nature and to be unable to explain how grace is inserted into nature and fulfills it. A number of historical studies appeared investigating the notion of the SUPERNATURAL, the OBEDIENTIAL POTENCY (capacity) for the supernatural, and St. Thomas's teaching on the natural desire for the vision of God. This tendency came to be spoken of as the ''new theology.'' It tended to affirmations incompatible with the absolute gratuity of the order of grace by making an interior ordination and openness to grace a constituent of man's nature, and hence reducing the notion of ''pure nature'' to an unrealizable abstraction. Pope Pius XII reacted strongly against this position, speaking of it as a ''deadly fruit'' of theological novelties. In the encyclical *Humani generis* he declared: ''Others destroy the gratuity of the supernatural order, since God, they say, cannot create intellectual beings without ordering and calling them to the beatific vision'' (H. Denzinger, *Enchiridion symbolorum* 3891). Catholic theologians are continuing the task of penetrating the nature of man's actual destiny to the order of grace.

Theological Positions. The principal positions of Catholic theology on the relationship between grace and nature may be outlined under three headings.

Grace Elevates Nature. For Christian philosophy, nature signifies the essence of a thing considered as the fundamental principle of every activity and receptivity that belongs to it because of what it is. Nature is a fixed and well-determined reality with stable laws of a necessary character. A being must have certain determined constitutive elements, as well as its own powers, properties, and goals if it is to be of a particular nature. Although created nature comes into existence by a sovereignly free act of God, yet God cannot create a man without making him a finite intellectual being endowed with all the essential characteristics of human nature. Now, the fundamental revelation concerning grace is that the blessing God has granted the world through Christ constitutes a true *divinization* of sinful man. This emerges as the clear meaning of the Pauline and Johannine Scriptures concerning men's adoption as sons and heirs of God in Christ. The REDEMPTION means not only the remission of sin, but also a positive sharing of the divine nature. Man's divinization is revealed as an unfolding thing begun in faith, hope, and charity, and ending in the glory of face-to-face vision of God (1 Jn 3.1–2; 1 Cor 13.8–13). Obviously this completion is not within the scope of man's native powers; only a divine nature has natural powers capable of entering into an immediate union of knowledge and love with the divine being. Consequently, to divinize man means to elevate him to a level of perfection transcending his own nature. Since it entirely transcends the powers and exigencies of man's nature, divinizing grace is something to which nature can lay no claim. Arising in the mystery of God's self-giving love, grace can be received only in grateful wonder at the eternal miracle of love that it is.

Grace Heals Nature. Catholic teaching has always held that the nature of man is not totally destroyed by original sin. This is based on the Scriptures (Wis 13.1–9; Rom 1.17–28), which credit man with the radical capability of knowing God by means of his natural reason. Were nature truly destroyed by sin, how would man be capable of responding to the divine call in faith, or how could he be held accountable for his refusal to respond? (H. Denzinger, *Enchiridion symbolorum* 1554–55.) While Catholic doctrine refuses to admit a total destruction of nature, it does not minimize the damage sin has wrought in man's nature (H. Denzinger, *Enchiridion symbolorum* 371, 400). There are two different explanations of this wounding. With Suárez and Bellarmine, many theologians teach that as a consequence of original sin mankind lost the supernatural gift of grace and the gratuitous PRETERNATURAL gifts, but that its natural perfections are undiminished. The Thomist school emphasizes more forcefully the reality of sin's havoc by holding that the loss of ORIGINAL JUSTICE brings in its wake a profound diminution of nature's tendency to virtue (*Summa theologiae* 1a2ae, 85.1). The grace that divinizes man as man and does it progressively also heals the wounds of nature by restoring the elevation sin negated and by removing the obstacle that hinders nature's gravitation toward virtue. Only when divinization is total will its healing restore the equivalent of the lost preternatural gifts.

Harmony of Grace and Nature. The adequate distinction between grace and nature brings no artificial dualism with it. The Creator of nature and grace has ordered the creation of the world and of man to Christ, in whom and through whom all humanity is called to a participation in the inner life of God. This unity of the divine economy of salvation orders nature to grace, creation to Redemption. In the very structure of his nature man is ''IMAGE OF GOD''; there is in him an openness to grace that no lower creature has. It is because man is an intellectual creature that he is basically capable of beatific vision—for as intellectual he is open to the total breadth of being, which includes even the Supreme Being. Consequently, unaided natural reason could conclude that it is probably possible for man to be elevated to this undue, supernatural, face-to-face vision of God. Revelation assures us that this is a real possibility and meant to be fulfilled. Not all theologians understand in the same way this basic tendency of the finite spirit toward the supernatural. Some affirm a mere nonrepugnance to being elevated, i.e., apart from the free gift of grace there is no positive tendency or desire in the finite will to possess the being of God as its supreme beatitude, though there is a natural tendency or desire in the finite intellect to come to see the real essence of the First Cause of being, who is God. This appears to be the meaning of St. Thomas's references to a natural desire to see God (he never speaks of a natural desire for the beatific vision). Others (Scotists, Suárez, Alfaro), assuming that there is an innate human longing for perfect beatitude, note that the perfect beatitude of the intellectual creature can be had only in the satisfaction of his unlimited capacity for being and goodness. Nothing short of beatific vision can satisfy this natural longing, and hence they conclude that there is in man's nature an innate natural desire for the beatific vision, though it can reach its goal only through the gracious intervention of God. Finally there are those (Mersch, K. Rahner) who consider the problem in the actual historical situation of man. By the free determination of God, man was actually created in grace and has never had any real destiny other than a supernatural one. A determination of this kind must imply a real change in the creature (the ''SUPERNATURAL EXISTENTIAL'' in Rahner's terminology), otherwise the supernatural order labors under the liability of remaining artificially juxtaposed to the natural order. According to this view, although human nature as such has no exigency for the supernatural order of grace, the concrete natures of men do have such an exigency, and because of it the absence of grace in the unjustified is not a mere absence but a true privation. This notion may be implicit in Thomas Aquinas's *suasio* for the existence of original sin (*C. gent.* 4.52).

See Also: DESIRE TO SEE GOD, NATURAL; HABIT; IMPUTATION OF JUSTICE AND MERIT; JUSTICE OF MEN; PURE NATURE, STATE OF.

Bibliography: H. RONDET, *Gratia Christi* (Paris 1948). J. ALFARO, *Lexikon für Theologie und Kirche,* ed. J. HOFER and K. RAHNER, 10 v. (2d, new ed. Freiburg 1957–65) 7:830–835; ''Trascendencia e inmanencia de lo sobrenatural,'' *Gregorianum* 38 (1957) 5–50. K. RAHNER, ''Concerning the Relationship between Nature and Grace,'' *Theological Investigation,* v. 1, tr. C. ERNST (Baltimore 1961) 297–317. W. R. O'CONNOR, *The Eternal Quest* (New York 1947). P. J. DONNELLY, ''On the Development of Dogma and the Supernatural,'' *Theological Studies* 8 (1947) 471–491; ''Discussions on the Supernatural Order,'' *ibid.,* 9 (1948) 213–249; ''A Recent Critique of P. De Lubac's *Surnaturel,*'' *ibid.,* 9 (1948) 554–560; ''The Gratuity of the Beatific Vision and the Possibility of a Natural Destiny,'' *ibid.,* 11 (1950) 374–404; ''The Surnaturel of P. Henri de Lubac, S.J.,'' *Catholic Theological Society of America. Proceedings* 3 (1948) 108–121. S. DUFFY, ''The Graced Horizon: Nature and Grace in Modern Catholic Thought,'' *Theology and Life* 37 (Collegeville, Minn. 1992). D. J. M. BRADLEY, *Aquinas on the Twofold Human Good: Reason and Human Happiness in Aquinas's Moral Science* (Washington, D.C. 1997). S. A. LONG, ''On the Possibility of a Purely Natural End for Man,'' *Thomist* 64 (2000) 211–237.

[C. REGAN]

GRADUAL

In the medieval Roman Rite of the Mass, the term ''Gradual'' had a double usage:(1) the first of two chants sung between the readings in the Liturgy of the Word; and (2) the book containing the entire collection of chants for the Mass.

This article concerns only the chant sung after the first Scripture reading. The term is derived from early Christian usage: at one time a soloist sang this chant from the steps (Latin, *gradus*) of the ambo, the platform reserved for the deacon's singing of the Gospel. Yet in the oldest MSS (up to the 11th and 12th centuries), the chant known as the Gradual was called Responsorium (responsorial psalm).

History. The RESPONSORIAL PSALM is a very ancient and very simple musical form once widely used in the early Church, and it was revived in the wake of the liturgical reforms of Vatican II. A soloist intones a text in strophe form (the psalm, among the Jews), and the choir repeats a very short refrain after each strophe (Greek ὑπαχόη, or *responsa*). In the synagogue service there was a psalm or a canticle to be sung after the readings; the first Christians continued the same custom. In the earliest form of the Mass in the West, there were three readings: one from the Old Testament followed by a psalm, one of the New Testament epistles followed by the Alleluia verse, and finally the Gospel. The responsorial singing of the psalm is witnessed to from earliest times: *Const. Apost.* (2:57.6), St. Augustine (*In Psalm.* 119; *Patrologia Latina* 37:1596), St. Leo (*Serm.* 3; *Patrologia Latina* 54:145). The Roman Council of 595 deprived deacons of the privilege of singing the Gradual psalm. Probably it was at this time that the *responsa* lost its simple syllabic form and became enriched musically into an ornate selection, while its execution became the business of the specialists of the *SCHOLA CANTORUM*.

Historically, the Gradual was sung like a responsory in the Office, i.e., the first part was repeated after the verse. This system has been preserved in certain MSS for

''Flagellant Brothers of the Fraternity of Santa Maria degli Carita,'' manuscript illumination, from 14th-century gradual. (©Gianni Dagli Orti/CORBIS)

the Gradual that was traditionally assigned to June 24—*R:* Priusquam te formarem . . . sanctificavi te. *V:* Misit Dominus . . . et dixit mihi. *Rep.:* Priusquam . . . sanctificavi te. The Gradual *Ecce quam bonum* (that was assigned to the 22d Sunday after Pentecost in the Tridentine Missal) formerly had a second verse that has now disappeared. The Gradual *Haec dies* (Easter) has seven distinct verses that were distributed throughout Easter week during the medieval period, but they were originally part of a single gradual. In the 9th and 10th centuries the Graduals (and alleluias) were often copied into a special collection, the *cantatorium,* a book elongated in form, with a cover sheathed in plaques of carved ivory. In Milan the Gradual has the name of *Psalmellus* (short psalmody); its composition is much more elaborate than the Gregorian Gradual of Rome. In the ancient Hispanic liturgy it was called the *Psallendo;* after the versicle only the second part of the responsory was repeated, from the section marked ''P.'' (*presa, repeat*).

Musical Aspects. The gradual, although an ornate chant, was not composed without rules proper to spontaneous improvisation. It has a musical timbre for each mode, adapted, according to rigorous rules, to texts of varying lengths. In the modes of D, a single timbre (of the type of *Justus ut palma*) has been adapted to 18 other texts; in the modes on E, a single timbre serves for 12 graduals; in the modes on F, 44 verses of graduals are constructed according to the same melodic outline. Whatever the mode of the Gradual, the versicle has a more extended range than does the response, as its melodic weaving is carried higher.

Bibliography: J. A. JUNGMANN, *The Mass of the Roman Rite,* tr. F. A. BRUNNER, 2 v. (New York 1951–55). W. APEL, *Gregorian Chant* (Bloomington, Ind. 1958) 344–63. H. HUCKE, ''Towards a New Historical View of Gregorian Chant,'' *Journal of the American Musicological Society* 30 (1980) 437–67. R.-J. HESBERT, ''Le graduel, chant responsorial,'' *Ephemerides liturgicae* 95 (1981) 316–50. M. HUGLO, ''Le répons-graduel de la messe: Évolution de la forme: permanence de la function,'' *International Musicological Society Congress Report* 13 (1982) 53–77. P. JEFFERY, ''The Introduction of Psalmody into the Roman Mass by Pope Celestine I (422–432): Reinterpreting a Passage in the Liber pontificalis,'' *Archiv für Liturgiewissenschaft* 26 (1984) 147–55. J. MCKINNON, ''The Fourth-Century Origin of the Gradual,'' *Early Music History* 7 (1987) 91–106. R. CROCKER, ''Chants of the Roman Mass,'' *New Oxford History of Music* 2 (2/1990) 196–214. D. HILEY, *Western Plainchant: A Handbook* (Oxford 1993). J. MCKINNON, ''Preface to the Study of the Alleluia,'' *Early Music History* 15 (1996) 213–49.

[M. HUGLO/EDS.]

GRAFT

Graft is the acquisition of money, position, or favor through dishonest means by a person who takes advantage of his official position. Graft is a sin against legal justice, according to which an official is bound to promote the common good of the community. It is also against distributive justice, by which rulers are bound to act toward individual persons and classes in accord with their merits, needs, and capacities. Graft is also a violation of commutative justice, by which a person is bound to the faithful discharge of the obligations he assumes in taking employment.

Elected public office holders are the usual offenders in this form of dishonesty, though the injustice may be committed by those who are appointed to public office rather than elected.

In the United States a spoils system is sometimes used, according to which political offices are filled by the members of the party that is in power. It is not wrong to make appointments on a party basis, but it is wrong to appoint persons who are not qualified for office. It is sinful for a politician to demand graft of another in exchange for appointment to a lesser public office. The sin of selling an appointment is worse when the appointee is in no way worthy.

If a public official, upon compensation, favors the evasion of a law, he is bound to make restitution to the state; he is also bound to make restitution to the wronged private citizen when money is involved. If a minor official is obliged by his superior to rubber stamp an evasion of the law he should offer resistance in whatever way possible; however, he is not bound to restitution as the superior official would be.

A public servant may sin by accepting graft for an appointment or by obtaining money, favor, or position through the awarding of devious contracts for services private companies perform for the state or country. He may sin by giving secret information, e.g., to real estate companies in return for compensation or a share in their profit.

The first duty of a public official who has sold immunity is to restore the graft. If the violation of the right cannot be repaired by a recall of the immunity and by bringing of the offender to trial or punishment, the money for which the right was exchanged should be given to the public treasury as restitution. If the public official abuses his function and forces someone to give or promise graft, the prime offender acquires a greater guilt. In our modern penal code such action is called extortion.

Normally, the acceptance of gifts by judges from attorneys who practice law before them and by public officials from companies who do business with the government is not morally offensive, unless it is specifically proscribed by civil legislation.

The public official, if he is Catholic, also commits an additional sin of scandal by taking graft. Today it seems almost impossible that he could be in good faith.

See Also: BRIBERY.

Bibliography: J. AERTNYS and C. A. DAMEN, *Theologia moralis,* 2 v. (16th ed. Turin 1950). B. HÄRING, *The Law of Christ,* tr. E. G. KAISER, 3 v. (Westminster, Md. 1961–). F. J. CONNELL, *Morals in Politics and Professions* (Westminster, Md. 1946).

[T. CRANNY]

GRAIL, THE

Founded as a movement of Catholic laywomen in Holland in 1921 by Jacques van Ginneken, SJ, a professor at the University of Nijmegen, and a group of his students. The movement unites married and single women of all races, backgrounds, and professions in a common effort to deepen Christian life and bring spiritual values to all areas of modern society. It was guided by concepts of worldwide spiritual renewal; of the share of the laity among the People of God in Christ's redeeming mission; and of woman's untapped capacities to inculcate God-centeredness, love, peace, and human dignity in contemporary life. The Grail extended to Great Britain, Germany, Australia, and the U.S. by 1940, but it was driven underground in Holland during the Nazi occupation. The postwar period brought its worldwide expansion to the Third World.

Grail spirituality emphasizes personal commitment to Christ and to His mission, the recognition of the primacy of personal prayer and community worship, concern for the dignity of the person and for the building of the community, readiness for service and sacrifice, and joy in the goodness of material creation. Although participation varies according to talent and state of life, it requires of every member a commitment to the spirit and goal of the Grail; active association, wherever possible, with work in a Grail center or in personal contact with other members; and participation in formation programs. Every local Grail chapter works with the approval and guidance of the local ordinary.

Grail teams work in areas of adult education and apostolic formation; religious education and teacher-training in catechetics; community development and social action, especially through work with cooperatives and credit unions; medical services; cultural programs, including book- and art-shops, production and distribution of contemporary works of art and music; ecumenism, through promotion of social and cultural collaboration with other Christians.

Bibliography: L. VAN KERSBERGEN, *Woman* (Loveland, Ohio 1956). E. REID, *I Belong Where I'm Needed* (Westminster, MD 1961).

[D. MYERS/EDS.]

GRANDE ROMÁN, JUAN, ST.

In religion Juan (Grande) Pecador (John the (Great) Sinner), religious of the Hospitaller Brothers of St. John of God; b. March 6, 1546, Carmona (near Seville), Andalusia, Spain; d. June 3, 1600, Jerez de la Frontera (near Cadiz), Spain.

Like his father before him, Juan Grande was a cloth merchant in Carmona until he left home to discern his vocation in solitude near Marcena. Upon discovering God's will for his life, Grande moved to Jerez de la Frontera (1566). He tended prisoners and the elderly poor, first in a room off the chapel of La Virgen de los Remedios, then in a hospital (Nuestra Señora de la Candelaria) that he established next to the Church of San Sebastian. He became known for his extreme austerity, intense prayer life, and service to anyone in need including prisoners, prostitutes, and even 300 fugitive Spanish soldiers after the English stormed Cadiz. During an epidemic in 1574, he successfully mounted a campaign to help victims that involved many people, even the city council. That same year he adopted the rule of the Hospitallers of St. John of God and gathered others to assist in his apostolate. In 1576, he took the habit of the Hospitallers and transferred Candelaria into their hands. At the request of Bishop Rodrigo de Castro of Seville, he reorganized the local hospital system to provide better care to the poor. He contracted the plague which was ravaging Jerez in 1600 and offered himself to God in atonement. The epidemic ended with his death in Candelaria Hospital. He was originally buried in the hospital courtyard, but later was transferred to his titular shrine in the hospital of the Brothers of St. John of God in Jerez.

St. John the Sinner was beatified in 1853. On June 2, 1996, Pope John Paul II canonized this patron of Jerez.

Feast: June 3.

Bibliography: *L'Osservatore Romano,* Eng. ed., no. 29 (1995): 5; no. 23 (1996): 1–2, 5, 12. J. L. REPETTO BETES, *El hermano Juan Pecador: biografía crítica del beato Juan Grande O.H., fundador del Hospital Jerezano de la Candelaria* (Jerez de la Frontera 1984). H. SANCHO DE SOPRANIS, *Biografía documentada del beato Juan Grande, O.H., fundador del Hospital de Candelaria de Jerez de la Frontera* (Jerez de la Frontera 1960).

[K. I. RABENSTEIN]

GRANDERATH, THEODOR

German Jesuit ecclesiastical historian; b. Giesenkirchen (Westphalia), June 19, 1839; d. Valkenburg, Netherlands, March 19, 1902. After joining the JESUITS (1860), and completing his studies, he taught Canon Law (1874–76), then dogmatic theology and apologetics (1876–87) to Jesuit scholastics at Ditton Hall, England. His main scholarly contribution, which occupied his subsequent years, was the publication of the documents of VATICAN COUNCIL I and the writing of its history. After going to the Netherlands (1887), he succeeded Father SCHNEEMANN in editing the *Acta et Decreta Concilii Vaticani* (1890), which forms the seventh and final volume of the *Collectio Lacensis* (1870–90). The tome remains indispensable for its official conciliar documents and wealth of extracts from extraconciliar sources. This labor kept him in Rome much of the time between 1893 and his retirement in 1901. While there he also lectured (1897–98) at the Gregorian University.

His three-volume history of the synod, *Geschichte des Vatikanischen Konzils,* published posthumously (1903–06) by Konrad Kirch, was the first scholarly Catholic account. A French version also exists. It was regarded as an official history because the author gained special papal permission to consult rarely accessible conciliar documents. He refuted the biased accounts of OLD CATHOLICS, but glossed over the divergent outlooks of the bishops. His outlook on the majority group among the prelates was often uncritically favorable. The positive role and devoutness of the minority group eluded him. Later theologians have found his work lacking in theological penetration.

He also published many articles in *Stimmen aus Maria Laach, Zeitschrift für Katholische Theologie,* and the second edition of the Kirchenlexikon (1881–86) edited by Wetzer and Weltes.

Bibliography: H. HURTER, *Nomenclator literarius theologiae catholicae* (Innsbruck 1903–1913) 3 5.2:1988–99. P. BERNARD,

Dictionnaire de théologie catholique (Paris 1903–1950) 6.2:1693–94. L. KOCH, *Jesuiten-Lexikon* (Leiden 1962) 723.

[V. CONZEMIUS]

GRANDIN, VITAL

Missionary, bishop of St. Albert, Canada; b. St. Pierre-la-Cour, France, Feb. 8, 1829; d. St. Albert, June 3, 1902. After a brief trial period with the Foreign Missions of Paris, he entered the Oblates of Mary Immaculate in 1851 and was ordained April 23, 1854. He was sent to the missions of Rivière-Rouge, Canada, took up residence in Île-à-la-Crosse, Saskatchewan (1855), and visited the Northwest Territories (1856). On Dec. 21, 1857, Grandin was named auxiliary bishop of St. Boniface, but he did not hear of the appointment until 1859. After consecration in Marseilles, France, Nov. 30, 1859, he settled first in Île-à-la-Crosse (1860–69) and then in St. Albert, to which he was appointed bishop in 1871. His efforts during the Métis revolt (1855) and in defense of the rights of native North Americans and of Catholic schools were dynamic and effective. The case for his canonization was presented in Rome in 1937.

Bibliography: P. E. BRETON, *Vital Grandin* (Paris 1960).

[G. CARRIÈRE]

GRANDMAISON, LÉONCE DE

Theologian, defender of the Church's teaching against the incursions of relativism and Modernism; b. Le Mans, Dec. 31, 1868; d. Paris, June 15, 1927. He entered the Society of Jesus in 1886, studied on the Isle of Jersey from 1890 to 1893, then completed his studies while a teacher at Le Mans. In 1899, the year following his ordination, he became professor of apologetics, first at Fourvière, France, then at Hastings, England. In 1908 he was appointed editor of *Études,* and in 1910, inspired by the anti-Modernist encyclical *PASCENDI* (1907), he founded the periodical *Recherches de science religieuse.* He was a prolific writer, whose forte was apologetic writing, and who composed over 150 extensive treatises in the various fields of religion and theology. His most significant work, *Jésus Christ: sa personne, son message, ses épreuves,* was published in two volumes, after his death, by his friend Jules Lebreton. His article ''Jésus Christ,'' in the *Dictionnaire apologétique de la foi catholique* 2: 1288–1538, is also a significant work. For a list of his works, see Geuser, 281–295.

Bibliography: J. GEUSER, ''Mélanges Grandmaison,'' *Recherches de science réligieuse* 18 (1928) 281–295. J. LEBRETON, *Le Père Léonce de Grandmaison* (Paris 1932). L. KOCH, *Jesuiten-Lexikon: Die Gesellschaft Jesu einst und jetzt* 723–724.

[B. F. SARGENT]

GRANDMONT, ABBEY AND ORDER OF

The name of a religious order of men founded by STEPHEN OF MURET at Muret, north of Limoges, France, whose motherhouse was moved from there to a new house a few miles away at Grandmont soon after the founder's death in 1124. The original community, which Stephen formed from his followers, was planned along severe lines inspired by the monastic life that the founder had seen flourishing among eremetical houses in southern Italy. At first the brethren lived in cells, but fairly soon conventual buildings of the usual, contemporary pattern were adopted. Houses were in secluded places and adopted a rule of poverty as rigorous as that which later characterized the MENDICANT ORDERS. For their subsistence, the religious relied on alms and on the agricultural labors of the *CONVERSI.* These latter were always a major element in the order, generally outnumbering the clerical brethren; at first almost complete control of the administration of the monastic property was entrusted to them, but this arrangement soon proved unwise and was accordingly modified. For those who were not lay brothers enclosure was complete. Monastic buildings remained small and simple, and the order's lack of parochial responsibilities partially explains why the nave of their churches was narrower than the choir, which had no aisle. The founder's way of life drew empirically on the Rule of St. AUGUSTINE, the BENEDICTINE RULE, and the Rule of St. Basil (*see* BASILIAN MONASTICISM), but the order came to be classed among Benedictine orders. At first it did not have elaborate regulations, but these were supplied under the fourth prior, Stephen de Liciac (1139–63), and show signs of both CISTERCIAN and CARTHUSIAN influence. A custumal was produced in 1170–71.

The major reason for the spread of the order was its high spiritual reputation, but expansion was aided also by the proximity of the motherhouse to the great pilgrimage routes to SAINT-LÉONARD-LE-NOBLAT, Our Lady of Rocamadour, and SANTIAGO DE COMPOSTELA. Notable early patrons included both the Empress Matilda, who left Grandmont a large legacy, and her son King HENRY II of England, whose generous benefactions included a large gift of English lead for the church roof of Grandmont, which, local tradition avers, arrived in 800 carts drawn by English horses of the same color. About two-thirds of the houses of the order were in Henry's French lands;

there were only three houses in England, all founded in the early 13th century. Stephen's priorate had seen a phenomenal expansion of the Order of Grandmont, some 60 houses having been founded by the time of his death. At its peak (mid-13th century) the order had *c.* 140 houses and 2,000 members.

Reform was found necessary in the time of Guillaume Pellicier (1317–36); he was made the first abbot of Grandmont by Pope John XXII, and the order was reorganized. Its subsequent history was generally uneventful, but more reforms were instituted with the help of VINCENT DE PAUL. In 1768 the order was suppressed by the Commission des Réguliers of France, at which time its membership had shrunk to about 100.

Bibliography: *Patrologia Latina*, ed. J. P. MIGNE (Paris 1878–90) v.204, for most of the principal documents concerning the early history of the order. J. BECQUET, *Dictionnaire de spiritualité ascétique et mystique. Doctrine et histoire*, ed. M. VILLER et al. (Paris 1932–) 4.2:1504–14, for evaluation and augmentation of these documents. J. LEVESQUE, *Annales ordinis grandimontis* (Troyes 1662). L. H. COTTINEAU, *Répertoire topobibliographique des abbayes et prieurés*, 2 v. (Mâcon 1935–39) 1:1326–28.

[J. C. DICKINSON]

GRANVELLE, ANTOINE PERRENOT DE

Churchman and diplomat in the service of the Hapsburgs; b. Ornans, Franche-Comté, Aug. 20, 1517; d. Madrid, Spain, Sept. 21, 1586. After studies at Padua and Louvain, the 21-year-old Granvelle, younger son of Nicholas Granvelle, minister of Charles V, already holder of a canonry at Arras, was named bishop of that diocese. Entering the imperial diplomatic service, he acted as the Emperor's representative at the opening of the Council of TRENT in 1545. In Charles's military campaign against the Protestant princes of the SCHMALKALDIC LEAGUE, Granvelle drew up the peace terms after the League's defeat at the hands of the Emperor at Mühlberg (1547). One of the chief results of the imperial victory had been the removal of John Frederick the Magnanimous from the electorate of Saxony. His successor, Elector Maurice of Saxony, quickly followed his relative in treason against the Emperor, joining with Henry II of France in a twofold attack on the imperial forces in 1551. Bishop Granvelle was in the company of Charles V when the latter was almost captured by Maurice's forces at Innsbruck. Subsequently, Granvelle negotiated the Treaty of Passau in August 1552, which brought this conflict to an end.

After Emperor Charles V's abdication and retirement in 1555, Granvelle continued as advisor to his son PHILIP II OF SPAIN. In 1559, when Margaret of Parma was named Philip's regent in the Netherlands, Granvelle accompanied her as chief counsellor. While Granvelle was serving in this post, Pope Paul IV named him archbishop of Malines (1560) and cardinal (1561). Devoting himself to the double objectives of making Spanish authority absolute and of uprooting the rapidly spreading Protestant movement, Granvelle quickly drew on himself the enmity of the dissatisfied Netherlands nobility and their leader, William the Silent of Orange. An opposition party, the Ligne Anticardinaliste, was formed, later to evolve into the confederation known as Gueux. Because of Granvelle's increasing unpopularity, Philip relieved him of his office in 1564 and the cardinal retired to Besançon, an imperial city in his native Franche-Comté. In 1565 Granvelle was transferred to Rome; in 1570 he assisted in drawing up the Holy League, an alliance between Spain, the Holy See, and the Republic of Venice against the Turks. From 1571 to 1575 he served King Philip as viceroy of Naples, being promoted in 1575 to the presidency of the Council for Italy, a post he held till 1579. In that year, Granvelle was summoned to Spain to replace the recently dismissed Antonio Perez as Philip's secretary of state. One of his administration's first acts was to put a price on the head of William of Orange and to intensify the campaign against the Dutch Protestants (January 1580). Single-handed, Granvelle administered the Spanish government that year during the military campaign against Portugal and was responsible, after the cessation of hostilities, for negotiating the formal union of the Spanish and Portuguese crowns that was to last for the next 60 years (1580–1640). In 1584 Granvelle renounced his See of Malines and was named to the Diocese of Besançon, though he never returned to take possession of his new benefice.

Bibliography: *Correspondance du Cardinal de Grandvelle 1565–1586,* ed. E. POULLET and C. PIOT, 12 v. (Brussels 1877–96); *Papiers d'état du Card. de Grandvelle,* ed. C. WEISS, 9 v. (Paris 1841–61). Jedin Trent. P. GEYL, *The Revolt of the Netherlands, 1555–1609* (2d ed. New York 1958). B. CHUDOBA, *Spain and the Empire, 1519–1643* (Chicago 1952). R. PALMAROCCHI, *Enciclopedia cattolica* 6:1002. M. DIERICKX, *Lexikon für Theologie und Kirche* 4:1166, bibliog. E. HASSINGER, *Die Religion in Geschichte und Gegenwart* 2:1825.

[W. KELLER]

GRANZOTTO, CLAUDIO, BL.

Baptized Riccardo, Franciscan friar; sculptor; b. Aug. 23, 1900, Santa Lucia di Piave, Treviso, Italy; d. Aug. 15, 1947, Padua, Italy. Riccardo was the youngest of nine children in a family of modest means. After the death of his father (1909), he worked in the field and as a carpenter and bricklayer to help support his family. He developed a passion for art at age 15, but had to set it aside to complete his military service (1918–22). Upon discharge, he studied at the Academy of Fine Art in Venice, where he earned a diploma in sculpture (1929). He was a moderately successful artist with his own studio when he joined the Franciscans in Venice (Dec. 7, 1933) and received the name Claudio. Thereafter he expressed ''the infinite beauty of divine contemplation in sculpture'' (John Paul II, beatification homily, Nov. 20, 1994), completing four grottos of Lourdes, one of which in Chiampo is identical in proportion to that in Massabielle, France. The man dedicated to prayer, beauty, and compassion died of a brain tumor in the hospital at Padua and was buried at the foot of the Grotto of Lourdes in Chiampo. Bishop Albino Luciani, the future Pope John Paul I, opened the diocesan process for Claudio's beatification (Dec. 16, 1959).

Feast: Sept. 2 (Franciscans).

Bibliography: C. CIATTAGLIA and E. PAPINUTTI, *Vinto dal Signore* (Chiampo n.d.). Collegio Serafico, *Fede e arte di Fra Claudio* (Chiampo n.d.). R. FUSATI, *Beato Claudio Granzotto* (Chiampo n.d.). E. URBANI, *Oltre l'arte* (Chiampo n.d.).

[K. I. RABENSTEIN]

GRASSEL, LORENZ

First coadjutor-elect of the U.S. Church; b. Ruemansfelden, Bavaria, Aug. 18, 1753; d. Philadelphia, Pa., October 1793. He entered the Jesuits, but the suppression of the Society of Jesus prevented him from completing his novitiate. After ordination as a secular priest in Germany (*c.* 1780), he went to Philadelphia, Pa. (1787), at the request of Rev. Ferdinand FARMER. Grassel was initially attached to St. Mary's Church, Philadelphia; in addition, he made missionary excursions into New Jersey. In Philadelphia he ministered with prudence and devotion to German immigrants and to descendants of the English and Irish settlers. At St. Mary's he upheld the authority of John Carroll as prefect apostolic of the U.S.; Grassel was retained at St. Mary's Church (1788) over the opposition of the German board of trustees, who in time built Holy Trinity Church, insisting on the right to choose their own pastors. In the midst of these embroilments Grassel joined in an unsuccessful effort to petition the restoration of the Society of Jesus. His pastorate soon won the recognition of his fellow priests as well as that of Bishop Carroll. In 1791 he was a promoter at the first national synod. On Sept. 24, 1793, he was nominated as coadjutor bishop to Carroll and confirmation was asked from Pius VII at an audience on Dec. 8, 1793. Formal letters of his appointment as bishop of Samosata were sent Jan. 18, 1794, but Grassel did not live to see these official acts accomplished. Within a month of his nomination, he died ministering to the afflicted in the Philadelphia yellow fever epidemic.

Bibliography: P. K. GUILDAY, *The Life and Times of John Carroll, Archbishop of Baltimore,* 1735–1815, 2 v. (New York 1927).

[T. O. HANLEY]

GRASSI (DE GRASSIS)

The family name of a number of prominent Italian ecclesiastics in the 16th century, of whom the most noteworthy were the following.

Antonio, bishop, papal diplomat; b. date and place unknown, d. 1491. He was appointed auditor of the Rota in 1462 by Pope PIUS II. In 1478–79 he served as Sixtus IV's nuncio to Emperor Frederick III. In 1485, Pope INNOCENT VIII appointed him bishop of Tivoli, in which office he remained until his death.

Achilles (the Elder), Italian cardinal, statesman, and canonist; b. Bologna, 1463; d. Rome, Nov. 27, 1523. He was an auditor of the Rota and bishop of Civitá de Castello; Pope JULIUS II sent him as envoy to Louis XII of France to ask Louis to withdraw his protection from the Bentivogli, a rival Bolognese family, who were plotting to poison the pope. Achilles was nominated cardinal of S. Sisto by Julius II on March 10, 1511; this was done to please the people of Bologna, where he was then bishop. The chaplain to Julius II as well as a canonist, Achilles wrote a collection of the decisions of the Tribunal of the Rota.

Paris, brother of Achilles De Grassis, master of ceremonies for Popes Julius II and LEO X; b. Bologna 1470; d. Rome, June 10, 1528. He was successively a canonist, governor of Orvieto, master of ceremonies, prelate of the Pontifical Palace, and bishop of Pesaro (1515). Julius II had promised De Grassis a bishopric on the occasion of the solemn opening of the Council of the Lateran in 1512; he was promised the bishopric for the admirable way in which he had organized and conducted the function in St. John Lateran. Paris is chiefly known for his close association with Julius II during most of his pontificate, and with Leo X during all of his reign. His *Diarium* is one of the major sources for the day-by-day account of the lives of these popes. A laconic man with a dry wit who was exact in regard to ceremonies, Paris is known for such remarks as the following, made concerning Leo X: ''He left Rome without a stole, and what is worse without his rochet, and worst of all with boots on. That is quite improper, for no one can kiss his feet'' (*Diarium,* Roscoe-Henke, III, 520, quoted in Pastor, VIII, 162). He is the author of *De*

Caeremoniis Cardinalium et Episcoporum in eorum diocesibus (1564) and *Ordo Romanus et Diarium Curiae Romanae* (1504–21).

Achilles, bishop of Montefrascona, nephew of Achilles, and secretary of the Council of Trent; b. Bologna, 1498; d. Rome, 1555. He was sent from Trent to Rome to inform Pope PAUL III of the difficulty with Emperor Charles about translating the Council from Trent.

Bibliography: L. PASTOR, *The History of the Popes from the Close of the Middle Ages* (London–St.Louis 1938–61) 12:248, 309. F. WASNER, *Lexikon für Theologie und Kirche*, ed. J. HOFER and K. RAHNER (Freiburg 1957–65) 4:1167–68.

[R. L. FOLEY]

GRASSI, ANTHONY, BL.

Priest, Confessor, Provost b. Fermo, Italy, Nov. 13, 1592; d. there, Dec. 13, 1671. He grew up in a devout Catholic family and in close contact with the priests of the Fermo Oratory. He joined the community in 1609 and remained in it till his death. He lived a mortified life, eating and sleeping little, and praying much. He usually spent five hours daily hearing confessions. In 1625 he made a pilgrimage to Rome, to the places made holy for him by St. Philip NERI, founder of the Oratory, and he returned home with the intention of imitating this saint, who had been canonized in 1622. In 1635 Grassi became provost (an office filled every three years by election), and remained in this office till his death, being reelected no fewer than 12 times, despite regular protestations of unworthiness. As provost, he gave few orders, preferring to request and to suggest, and by his excellent example he brought to the Fermo Oratory the reputation of outstanding faithfulness to the rule and spirit of St. Philip.

Feast: Dec. 13.

Bibliography: C. ANTICI, *Vita del beato Antonio Grassi* (Rome 1900). A. KERR, *A Saint of the Oratory* (London 1901).

[J. CHALLENOR]

GRASSI, GREGORIO, ST.

Bishop and martyr; b. Castellazzo Bormida (Alessandria), Italy, Dec. 13, 1833; d. Taiyüanfu (Shanxi), China, July 9, 1900. Grassi joined the Franciscans in 1848 and was ordained in 1856. In 1861 he went to the Shanxi Province in northern China, where he labored for four decades. He became titular bishop of Ortosia and coadjutor with right of succession (1876), then vicar apostolic of northern Shanxi (1891). During the Boxer Rebellion he was imprisoned in his residence at Taiyüanfu and put to death four days later. Martyred with him were Bp. Francesco FOGOLLA, his coadjutor; seven sisters, Franciscan Missionaries of Mary; five Chinese seminarians; and nine servants. All were beatified Nov. 24, 1946, and canonized on Oct. 1, 2000.

Feast: July 9.

Bibliography: *Acta Apostolicae Sedis* 41 (1949) 84, 472–473; 39 (1947) 213–221, 307–311. *Les Vingt-neuf martyrs de Chine, massacrés en 1900, béatifiés par Sa Sainteté Pie XII, le 24 novembre 1946* (Rome 1946). A. BUTLER, *The Lives of the Saints*, rev. ed. H. THURSTON and D. ATTWATER (New York 1956) 3:59–62.

[J. KRAHL]

GRATIAN, DECRETUM OF *(CONCORDIA DISCORDANTIUM CANONUM)*

The *Decretum* of Gratian was composed in the first half of the 12th century by a Camaldolese monk about whom there exists no precise information, except that he was born in Chiusi and resided in the monastery of SS. Felix and Nabor. The work appeared in the earliest manuscripts under the title of *Concordia discordantium canonum.* It is one of the most important canonical collections in the history of Canon Law, despite the fact that it was never officially adopted as an ''authentic'' source of Canon Law by papal authority (*see* CORPUS IURIS CANONICI).

Contents. The *Decretum* is a vast compilation that includes about 4,000 *capitula* and is divided into three parts. Part one comprises 101 *distinctiones:* the first 20 define the sources of law; the remainder may be looked upon as a sort of canonical illustration of pastoral problems, dealing with clerics and various aspects of ecclesiastical discipline. The second part is composed of 36 *causae,* which in turn are divided into a certain number of *quaestiones.* Each *causa* ordinarily deals with a specific question, but occasionally several *causae* treat of the same matter, forming a distinct treatise. For example *causae* 2 to 7 constitute an *ordo judiciarius; causae* 12 to 14 are a treatise on temporal goods of the Church and of the clergy; *causae* 16 to 20 present a section on monks; and *causae* 27 to 36 constitute a treatise on Matrimony. The third part, titled *De consecratione,* is generally divided into five *distinctiones* and is a treatise on the Sacraments.

The *Decretum* of Gratian is composed of texts of different origin: APOSTOLIC CONSTITUTIONS, canons of the councils, decretals and patristic texts, all of which constitute the *auctoritates.* Hence Gratian's work does not differ from the collections that immediately preceded it, namely those of ANSELM OF LUCCA, BURCHARD OF

WORMS, and IVO OF CHARTRES (*see* CANONICAL COLLECTIONS BEFORE GRATIAN). A thorough study of the *auctoritates* cited in the *Decretum* has determined that the collections of Ivo of Chartres, particularly the *Decretum* and the *Panormia,* were Gratian's main sources. However there remain a certain number of *auctoritates,* taken especially from patristic texts, the origin of which has not been determined.

Gratian did not simply collect texts with rubrics in a skillful manner. He accompanied them with an original commentary, which, in a certain sense, represents the unifying element of his work. Each division and subdivision is preceded by a brief summary of the subject matter to be treated. The *auctoritates* or groups of *auctoritates* are likewise connected by means of commentaries (*dicta*), which vary in length. Gratian realized that the *auctoritates* cited often contradicted one another, and in his commentary he attempted to reconcile these oppositions. As a general rule his commentary underlines the particular features of the various opinions presented and draws the conclusion to which they lead. In addition Gratian sought to demonstrate that the conflicts among the various doctrines were more apparent than real and were frequently attributable to a different interpretation of terms. Finally, he attempted to formulate a general conclusion. It was indeed a *Concordia discordantium canonum.*

Gratian's *Decretum* was the object of commentaries from the middle of the 12th century. Among the first commentators were PAUCAPALEA and Roland Bandinelli, who in 1159 became Pope ALEXANDER III. The *Decretum* was used in the schools of law from the end of the 12th century, and it rapidly achieved a universal recognition that had not been enjoyed by any previous canonical collection.

Textual Questions. The *Decretum* of Gratian poses a number of technical problems that modern criticism is endeavoring to solve.

There is considerable discussion as to the origin of Gratian's treatment of Penance (*De penitentia*) and his *De consecratione.* His treatment of Penance is introduced without explanation in the middle of *causa* 33. Both treatises, and particularly the one on Penance, differ noticeably from the rest of the work. A study of the manuscripts has revealed numerous anomalies in the transcription of these two treatises, with the *De penitentia* appearing in some ancient manuscripts as an addition. At any rate, if the *De penitentia* and the *De consecratione* were not an integral part of Gratian's work, they must have been added to it shortly following publication since they were known to the first commentators.

It is not certain whether the summaries or rubrics, which precede the *auctoritates,* are to be attributed to Gratian or rather, as A. Vetulani suggests, to one of the first commentators whose summary of the *Decretum* is contained in a manuscript of the library of Gdansk. A careful examination of these summaries reveals the following facts: certain rubrics reproduce either the *dictum* that precedes them or the first word of the text that follows them; several others reproduce the summaries of the *Panormia* of Ivo of Chartres; finally some rubrics were formed over a period of time, as is demonstrated by the numerous differences which are found in the manuscripts.

The *paleae* by themselves present several problems: the origin of the term, which texts may be considered as *paleae,* and how they were introduced into the *Decretum.*

Various explanations have been given for the origin of the term *palea:* some see it as coming from the name Paucapalea; others, such as Huguccio, see in it a reference to straw (*palea*), indicating that which must be separated from the good grain; still others, in modern times, noticing that a large number of doublets are found in the *paleae,* see this word as deriving from the Greek *palin.* This last explanation seems to be hardly probable; nonetheless it is difficult to accept with certainty either one of the first two.

The *paleae,* which are *auctoritates* like all the others, present four essential characteristics: they do not appear in all the manuscripts; they frequently appear to have been transcribed in the margin at a date later than that of the manuscript; they are found scattered throughout various sections of the *Decretum;* from the second half of the 12th century they were often accompanied by the word *palea* or by a note calling them to the attention of the reader.

It has been established that all the texts considered as *paleae* antedate Gratian. Furthermore, even though individual manuscripts from the end of the 12th century contain fewer *paleae* than those of the 14th century, almost all the *paleae* existed as such in the 12th century. Moreover, small collections of *paleae* used to complete the *Decretum* were found in certain manuscripts dating from the end of the 12th and early 13th centuries. The collections that have been examined indicate 162 fragments taken from collections prior to Gratian and from the decretals of the popes prior to the years 1170–73; 64 of them were incorporated into the *Decretum,* 13 of which cannot be classified as *paleae.* The *paleae* of the *Decretum* probably came from these collections. The collections prepared the way for the first compilations of decretals, which flourished from the last quarter of the 12th century.

There is some doubt as to whether the texts of the *Corpus iuris civilis* and the treatises of Roman Law, which are found in the *Decretum* in a rather large number, are later additions. Most of the fragments of the *Corpus iuris civilis* inserted in the *Decretum* possess the four essential features of the *paleae,* even though the indication *palea* is often replaced by the word *lex.* Moreover, in many instances the interpolation is evident. However, the texts appear to have been introduced into the *Decretum* by a process entirely different from that used for the *paleae.* In the earliest glosses are often found references to the *Code* or the *Digest.* Later on there is found a marginal transcription of the text thus selected, and then the addition into the very body of the *Decretum.*

See Also: CANON LAW, HISTORY OF, 4.

Bibliography: Editions. A. ADVERSI, ''Saggio di un catalogo delle edizioni del 'Decretum Gratiani' posteriori al secolo XV,'' *Studia Gratiani* 6 (1959) 285–451, 164 eds. A. VILLIEN and J. DE GHELLINCK, *Dictionnaire de théologie catholique*, ed. A. VACANT et al. (Paris 1903–50) 6.2:1727–51. F. TORQUEBIAU, ''Corpus juris canonici,'' *Dictionnaire de droit canonique*, ed. R. NAZ (Paris 1935–65) 4:611–627. Critical studies. *Studia Gratiana,* ed. J. FORCHIELLI, and A. M. STICKLER (Bologna 1953–). G. LEBRAS et al., eds., *Histoire du droit et des institutions de l'Église en Occident* (Paris 1955–) v.7 *L'Âge classique (1140–1378): Sources et théorie du droit* (Paris 1965) 51–129.

[J. RAMBAUD-BUHOT]

GRATIAN, JEROME

Theologian, collaborator with St. Teresa, and writer; b. Valladolid, 1545; d. Brussels, Sept. 21, 1614. His father was Diego Gracián, secretary to Philip II. After finishing his studies at the University of Alcalá, Jerome was ordained (1570). Attracted to the Teresian Reform, he took the habit at Pastrana (April 25, 1572), and was professed there the following year. Although professed only four months, he was appointed apostolic visitor to Andalusia and filled that office with courage, prudence, and diligence amid many difficulties. At his first meeting with the mother foundress (May 1575), he won her confidence and kept it until she died (1582). His misfortunes began with the death of St. Teresa. He was elected first provincial of the Discalced Carmelites by a narrow margin at Alcalá (1581). Soon after completing his term of office, he found himself at odds with Nicholas Doria, his successor, concerning the regime and observance; as a result, he was prosecuted on charges of rebellion and was finally expelled from the Reform (Feb. 17, 1592), in the establishment of which his collaboration had been so important to St. Teresa. After his expulsion, his misfortunes increased: his appeal to the Holy See failed; he was rejected by various religious orders; he was captured by Turkish pirates (1593). After two years of hard labor in prison, he was rescued. Finally, the pope authorized him to live among the Calced Carmelites (1596); from 1596 to 1600 he remained in Rome as private theologian of Cardinal Deza. Returning to Spain, he engaged in an intensive apostolate until 1607, when he accompanied the ambassador of Philip II to the Low Countries and took up residence with the Calced Carmelites of Brussels, where he died. He has remained a controversial figure down to the present time, although all agree that he was one of the most important persons in the first 25 years of the Teresian Reform.

Bibliography: A. DEL MARMOL, *Excelencias, vida y trabajos del P. Jerónimo Gracián . . .* (Valladolid 1619). SILVERIO DE SANTA TERESA, *Historia del Carmen Descalzo en España, Portugal y América,* 15 v. (Burgos 1935–49) 6:5–606. ALBERTO DE LA VIRGEN DEL CARMEN, ''Doctrina ascético-mística del V. P. Gracián,'' *Revista de Espiritualidad* 1 (1941) 73–88; 2 (1942) 156–185. ALLESANDRO DI S. GIOV., ''Spiritualitá cristocentrica del P. Graziano,'' *Vita Carmelitana* 3 (1942) 57–65. J. HUIJBEN, ''Gratien et les perfectistes,'' *Études Carmélitaines* 18 (1933) 237–243.

[O. RODRIGUEZ]

GRATIAN, ROMAN EMPEROR

367 to 383; b. Sirmium, 359; d. (assassinated) Lyons, Aug. 25, 383. Flavius Gratianus, to use his Latin name, son of VALENTINIAN I, was proclaimed Augustus at Amiens in 367 and, on the sudden death of his father in 375, became emperor in the western half of the empire in his 16th year. His uncle Valens continued to rule in the East. He had to share his own rule, in theory, with his four-year-old half brother Valentinian II, who had been proclaimed Augustus at Aquincum a few days after his father's death. However, during Gratian's reign, Valentinian II continued to occupy a subordinate position. From 369 the famous rhetor Ausonius served as Gratian's tutor and advisor. As a boy and as emperor, Gratian spent most of his life at Treves. Under the influence of Ausonius he adopted a policy of mildness, as compared with the harsh government of his father, and in his first years as emperor he issued a series of laws that in part remedied abuses and in part annulled or mitigated the actions that had been taken by Valentinian against his opponents. In 377 he won an important victory over the Alamanni. He was on his way to Sirmium when he heard the news of the disastrous defeat and the death of Emperor VALENS at Adrianople (Aug. 9, 378). Unable to rule both East and West, Gratian made General Theodosius—whose father had been executed by Valentinian—Augustus and emperor of the East (Jan. 19, 379). In the domestic sphere, Theodosius I adopted a rigorous policy of suppression against pagans and heretics, making Christianity the official religion of the state. It is precisely from this time that Gratian also adopted a similar policy under the influence

of new advisors, namely, Theodosius, Pope DAMASUS, and especially St. Ambrose, the great bishop of Milan. In 379 (rather than in 375 or 382) he was the first emperor to reject the title of Pontifex Maximus, and in 382 he abolished public support for the pagan priesthoods, confiscated temple properties, and had the altar of victory removed from the Senate house in Rome, a decision that he refused to change despite the formal protest made by SYMMACHUS, the leader of the pagan party. In 379 and 380 he issued strong laws against heresy. Early in 383, Magnus Maximus was proclaimed Augustus by his troops in Britain and crossed into Gaul. Gratian hastened from Italy to suppress the revolt, but most of his own troops abandoned him and he was assassinated at Lyons as he was fleeing southward from Paris. Gratian was a young man of high moral character, but he lacked the qualities of leadership, above all, the power of independent, firm, and prompt decision, that were required of an emperor in that turbulent age.

See Also: AMBROSE, ST.; THEODOSIUS I.

Bibliography: O. SEECK, *Paulys Realencyklopädie der klassischen Altertumswissenschaft* (Stuttgart 1893) 7.2 (1912) 1831–39. J. WORDSWORTH, *A Dictionary of Christian Biography* (London 1877–87) 2:721–727, old but still valuable. E. STEIN, *Histoire du Bas-Empire* (Paris 1949–59) 1:172–202, and ''Notes'' 507–526. G. BARDY and J. R. PALANQUE, in *Histoire de léglise depuis les origines jusqu'á nos jours* (Paris 1935–) 3:276–296, 513–524. M. FORTINA, *L'imperatore Graziano* (Turin 1955).

[M. R. P. MC GUIRE]

GRATITUDE

Gratitude, one of the social virtues, a potential part of justice. It falls short of the notion of justice because it does not suppose strict indebtedness nor require a full measure of equality in what is returned for benefits received. In a broad sense, gratitude can be considered as the acknowledgment of a favor received from a superior and so includes religion, piety, and observance. In these, however, a strict but not an equal payment is required. Properly, gratitude refers to a debt that is not legal but moral. It inclines men to acknowledge private favors with appreciation and to repay them with kindness.

A benefactor has no strict claim to the gratitude of the beneficiary. Because a gift is freely given, it does not give rise to an obligation in justice to repay it. There is, however, a moral obligation, in decency, to acknowledge the favor and to make some kind of return for it. This repayment involves an attitude of will rather than a material *quid pro quo*. Hence no one is so destitute that he cannot exercise gratitude. Like beneficence, it is measured by the disposition of the heart: ''Since kindness depends on the heart rather than on the deed, so too gratitude depends chiefly on the heart'' (ST. THOMAS AQUINAS, *Summa theologiae,* 106.3 ad 5). It is to be directed to all from whom favors are received: ''However, well off a man may be it is possible to thank him for his kindness by showing him reverence and honor'' (*ibid*). Repayment by affection should be made at once. A return gift, however, should wait for an opportune occasion. Indeed, if repayment is hurried, it could indicate unwillingness to be indebted, which is itself a form of ingratitude. It is better to return more than received, because there is nothing gratuitous or generous in giving back the equivalent or less. However, repayment of more should not be made from the selfish motive of making others dependent, but should rather spring from the benevolent love of charity. The debt of gratitude never becomes onerous because it flows from the debt of love.

Gratitude can be violated by excess, as when thanks are given for something that should be thankless, e.g., for cooperation in evil, or when repayment is too prompt; by defect, when there is ingratitude. When it is deliberate, ingratitude involves contempt for the favor rendered or for the benefactor. There are various degrees of gratitude: recognizing the favor received, expressing appreciation, and repaying suitably. So also there are degrees of ingratitude: not acknowledging a favor, especially by evaluating it as an unkindness. Speculatively, men consider ingratitude as contemptible; practically, however, it is not uncommon.

Bibliography: THOMAS AQUINAS, *Summa theologiae,* 2a2ae 8–, 106, 107. F. L. W. R. FARRELL, *Companion to the Summa* (Dubuque 1959). W. L. DAVIDSON, J. HASTINGS, ed., *Encyclopedia of Religion and Ethics,* 13 v. (Edinburgh 1908–27) 6:390–392. J. A. MCHUGH and C. J. CALLAN, *Moral Theology,* rev. E. P. FARRELL, 2 v. (New York 1958) 2:2143–2380. B. H. MERKELBACH, *Summa theologiae moralis,* 3 v. (8th ed. Paris 1949) 2:836–839.

[P. J. KELLY]

GRATIUS, ORTWIN (VAN GRAES)

Theologian and humanist; b. Holtwick, near Münster, 1480; d. Cologne, May 22, 1542. He was educated in the school of the Brethren of the Common Life in Deventer under Alexander Hegius. He studied in Cologne (B.A., 1501; M.A., 1506) and subsequently taught in the arts faculty, serving at the same time as an editor for the Quentell publishing house. He was ordained in 1514. His humanist learning was evident in his *Orationes quodlibeticae* (Cologne 1508), nine orations in support of the seven liberal arts, poetry, and philosophy, containing citations from the classics. He soon alienated the humanists, however, by opposing Hermann von dem Busche, who had attacked traditional authorities; by translating into Latin various books by Johann PFEFFERKORN, who favored burning Jewish books (1507–09); and by displaying his hostility to Johann REUCHLIN. Against Reuchlin he wrote a Latin poem to accompany Arnold von Tungern's *Articuli* (1512); the *Praenotamenta* (1514), a collection of documents presenting a slanted version of the Reuchlin controversy; and a *Defensio* (1516). Consequently Crotus Rubeanus and Ulrich von Hutten made him the chief target of their ridicule of the Cologne scholastics in their *Letters of Obscure Men* (1515). His inept rejoinder, more wordy than witty, *Lamentationes obscurorum virorum* (1518), merely unleashed another barrage of pamphlets and letters from which Gratius' reputation has suffered unjustly ever since. He published a *Fasciculus rerum expetendarum ac fugiendarum* (Cologne 1535), a collection of documents from Aeneas Sylvius, Lorenzo Valla, Wyclif, Poggio, the Waldenses, and others favorable to reform and critical of conditions within the Church, a work later placed on the Index.

Bibliography: D. REICHLING, *Ortwin Gratius: Sein Leben und Wirken* (Heiligenstadt 1884). F. ZOEPFL, *Lexikon für Theologie und Kirche* (Freiburg 1957–65) 2 4:1171–72.

[L. W. SPITZ]

GRATRY, AUGUSTE JOSEPH ALPHONSE

French theologian and philosopher; b. Lille, March 30, 1805; d. Montreux, Feb. 7, 1872. Gratry was indifferent to religion until 1822, when he received a kind of illumination concerning the nothingness of worldly ambitions. His secondary education, begun at Tours, was completed at the Collège Henry IV. While studying at the Polytechnique (1826–27), he returned to the Sacraments; soon afterward, he went to study theology under the Abbé Bautain in Strasbourg (1828), and in 1834 he was ordained. Gratry returned to Paris in 1840 as director of the Collège Stanislas. Thence, he became chaplain at the École Normale (1846–51). He entered the Oratory in 1852 and was appointed professor of moral theology at the Sorbonne in 1863. In 1867, he was elected to the French Academy.

By reason of his many works, both apologetic (*De la Connaissance de Dieu,* 1855; *Les Sources,* 1862) and polemic (*La Sophistique contemporaine,* 1861; *Les Sophistes et la critique,* 1864), Gratry contributed to the renascence of CHRISTIAN PHILOSOPHY. But while his avowed intention was to oppose both rational ECLECTICISM and FIDEISM with the Augustinian tradition of the Oratory, his thought is more poetic than precise, more prayerful than profound. He assigned an excessive role to emotion and to ''heart'' in the discovery of truth; in considering the knowledge of God, he appealed to ''a sense of the infinite'' that is superior to intellect. In politics and in morals (*La Morale et la loi de l'histoire,* 1868) he sought to associate Catholicism with the movement toward indefinite progress, wherein he saw the law of history operating.

See Also: SPIRITUALISM.

Bibliography: R. CRIPPA, *Enciclopedia filosofica* (Venice-Rome 1957) 2:891–892.

[R. JOLIVET]

GRAVAMINA

Complaints of any kind, but especially ecclesiastical protests made formally to a superior authority such as pope or legate or council or king, and setting out the ''burdens'' (*gravamina*), secular or ecclesiastical, which the church or the realm had to support. Thus, in 13th-century England, *gravamina* listing secular infringements of church liberties were put before the legate Otto in 1239 and were later presented by representative groups of clergy (synod or council) to the king; the royal replies (e.g., of 1258, 1280, 1300) are extant. These *gravamina* form the substance of those submitted by the English Church to the Council of Vienne in 1311: usurpation of ecclesiastical jurisdiction; the capture, torture, and sometimes the execution of criminous clerks; the frustration of decisions of ecclesiastical courts. Complaints of this nature were, in fact, sent in to the Council of Vienne from various provinces of the church (Ehrle), but only a few received conciliar attention, chiefly because a committee eliminated many beforehand (Göller). Furthermore, official memoranda censuring the conduct of the papacy itself were not uncommon, particularly in respect of papal PROVISIONS. The practice of beneficing foreign clergy in England was the burden of English *gravamina* at the First Council of Lyons in 1245; and papal provisions in general occasioned the *gravamina ecclesiae gallicanae*, or ''Protestation of St. Louis,'' in 1247, when, foreshadowing GALLICANISM, it was alleged that there was no canonical authority for such practices. In the 15th and 16th centuries spirited *gravamina* that protested curial extortions through the COLLATIO of benefices and the collection of TITHES and annates were drawn up by German clergy, e.g., at diets in Mainz (1451, 1455), Frankfurt (1456, 1458, 1479), Worms (1521), and Nuremberg (1522–23).

Bibliography: MATTHEW PARIS, *Chronica majora*, ed. H. R. LUARD, 7 v. *Rerum Britannicarum medii aevi scriptores* 57:1872–83, 6:99–112. F. EHRLE, ''Ein Bruchstück der Akten des Concils von Vienne,'' *Archiv für Literatur und Kirchengeschichte* *des Mittelalters* 4 (1888) 361–470. E. GÖLLER, ''Die Gravamina auf dem Konzil von Vienne und ihre literarische Überlieferung,'' *Festgabe Heinrich Finke* (Münster 1904) 197–221. G. MOLLAT, ''Les Doléances du clergé de la Province de Sens au concile de Vienne, 1311–1312,'' *Revue d'histoire ecclésiastique* 6 (1905) 319–326. G. J. CAMPBELL, ''The Protest of Saint Louis,'' *Traditio* 15 (1959) 405–418. H. RAAB, *Lexikon für Theologie und Kirche*, 10v. (2d, new ed. Freiburg 1957–65) 4:1174–75. F. M. POWICKE and C. R. CHENEY, *Councils and Synods* (Oxford 1964–) v.2 *passim*.

[L. E. BOYLE]

GRAY, WILLIAM

Bishop of Ely, treasurer of England, bibliophile; d. Downham, Cambridgeshire, Aug. 4, 1478. He was the son of Sir Thomas Gray of Heton, Northumberland, and nephew of Humphrey (Stafford), Duke of Buckingham. While resident in Balliol College, Oxford (*c.* 1430–42), he obtained the degree master of arts (1434) and became chancellor of the university (1441). To further his interest in theology he went to the University of Cologne (1442) and there added to an already unusual library by purchasing humanistic texts, as well as theological and legal works. From Cologne he traveled to Florence; he acquired books from Vespasiano da Bisticci, and moved on to Padua to secure the D.Th. degree (1445). Later, in Ferrara, Gray attended lectures by the humanist Guarino da Verona and befriended Niccolò Perotti. Upon receiving an appointment as king's proctor at the papal Curia, Gray began a period of residence in Rome. NICHOLAS V formed a high opinion of him, appointed him prothonotary apostolic, and eventually secured for him the bishopric of ELY (1454). Thereafter he was often prominent in national affairs, serving as treasurer of England (1469–70) and in diplomatic and political matters of the highest importance. A lifelong collector of MSS, Gray frequently employed scribes to make copies of books. Clearly, his main interests were theology and philosophy, but his library contained many Latin classics, among which the works of Cicero were preeminent. He left his large book collection to Balliol College, where it furthered the classical interests of younger scholars and contemporaries.

Bibliography: W. F. SCHIRMER, *Der englische Frühhumanismus* (2d ed. Tübingen 1963). R. WEISS, *Humanism in England during the Fifteenth Century* (2d ed. Oxford 1957) 86–97. A. B. EMDEN, *A Biographical Register of the University of Oxford to A.D. 1500* (Oxford 1957–59) 1:809–814.

[A. R. HOGUE]

GREAT AWAKENING

A movement in Protestantism in the thirteen North American colonies and precursor of the revivalism that was a major characteristic of much of the Protestantism of the U.S. The Great Awakening was an outgrowth of the PIETISM of Europe and of the Puritanism and EVANGELICALISM of the British Isles (*see* PURITANS). It first appeared in the Dutch Reformed Churches in the Raritan Valley in New Jersey as a result of the preaching of Theodore Jacobus FRELINGHUYSEN, who had been educated under Pietist influences (*see* REFORMED CHURCHES, II: NORTH AMERICA). In 1720 Frelinghuysen came to America, where he found the religion of the churches formal and conventional. In Pietist fashion he insisted on a personal experience of conversion that would issue in moral transformation. Under him the Raritan revival reached its peak in 1729 and spread to other Dutch Reformed Churches. Another contribution came from Irish-born William Tennent, a Presbyterian pastor who came to America in 1716. He began training young men for the ministry and for that purpose erected, opposite his residence in Neshaminy, Pa., a log house, called derisively by its critics the Log College. In it were educated a number of men who became preachers of the revival. Outstanding among them was Tennent's son, Gilbert, who was long a pastor in New Brunswick, N.J., and who preached widely as an itinerant. He became a close friend of Frelinghuysen and cooperated with him. Another leader, Jonathan EDWARDS, of Northampton, Mass., in 1734 preached an awakening that had wide repercussions not only in America but also in the British Isles. The preaching of George WHITEFIELD profoundly influenced the Great Awakening also. In his first months in America (1739–40) Whitefield traveled from Georgia to New England; later he made repeated tours of the colonies; he died in Newburyport, Mass., in 1770. He was an amazing orator, with a voice that could reach an audience of many thousands in the open air and with a wide range of pathos, humor, and compelling earnestness; he profoundly influenced both Great Britain and the thirteen colonies. By his preaching throughout the length of the entire Atlantic seaboard, he helped to give a degree of geographic and interdenominational unity to the movement. In addition to the leaders, scores of other preachers contributed to the Awakening.

The Great Awakening gave rise to controversy. The emotional scenes—faintings, cryings, and bodily agitations—that accompanied many of the meetings, and the condemnation by numbers of its preachers of ''unconverted'' ministers and the ''unconverted'' members of their flocks led to dissensions and divisions. For a time the PRESBYTERIANS were split; in New England the ''new lights,'' as the advocates of the Awakening were known, and the ''old lights,'' who opposed it, denounced each other. Their differences led to the division of many local congregations. Numbers of the dissidents gathered into

Baptist churches. The Great Awakening continued in many parts of the country until the political controversies that emerged in the Revolution diverted attention. In the 1790s and early 1800s, after the independence of the U.S. and peace with Great Britain, New England experienced what was called the Second Awakening, and revivals occurred in many other parts of the country.

The Great Awakening brought about a marked increase in church membership and various humanitarian undertakings; created a more democratic spirit; stimulated the founding of colleges, notable among them the College of New Jersey (later Princeton) and Dartmouth; and contributed to missions to the Native Americans, particularly the work of David Brainerd, Eleazer Whealock, and Samuel Kirkland.

Bibliography: J. TRACY, *The Great Awakening* (Boston 1842). W. M. GEWEHR, *The Great Awakening in Virginia* (Durham, N.C. 1930). E. S. GAUSTAD, *The Great Awakening in New England* (New York 1957). C. H. MAXSON, *The Great Awakening in the Middle Colonies* (Chicago 1920). R. J. COX, ''Stephen Bordley, George Whitefield, and the Great Awakening in Maryland,'' *Historical Magazine of the Protestant Episcopal Church* 46 (1977) 297–307. F. LAMBERT, ''The Great Awakening as Artifact: George Whitefield and the Construction of Intercolonial Revival, 1739–1745,'' *Church History* 60 (1991) 223–246. B. F. LE BEAU, '''The Acrimonious, Controversial Spirit' among Baptists and Presbyterians in the Middle Colonies during the Great Awakening,'' *American Baptist Quarterly* 9 (1990) 167–183. M.A. NOLL, ''From the Great Awakening to the War for Independence: Christian Values in the American Revolution,'' *Christian Scholar's Review* 12, no. 2 (1983) 99–110.

[K. S. LATOURETTE]

GREAT SAINT BERNARD HOSPICE

A refuge conducted by CANONS REGULAR OF ST. AUGUSTINE on the 8,114-foot high Great St. Bernard Pass over the Pennine Alps from Martigny, Valais, Switzerland, to Aosta, Italy (50 miles); it is in the Diocese of Sion, Switzerland. The pass, where there was a Celtic and then a Roman shrine (*Mons Jovis*), has long been used by armies, merchants, pilgrims, kings, and popes. There was a Carolingian Hospice of St. Peter, probably under Benedictines, at nearby Bourg-Saint-Pierre. The hospice founded *c.* 1050 by St. BERNARD OF AOSTA, with a chapel of St. Nicholas, came to be dedicated to St. Bernard by the 12th century. It was cared for by brothers (1145), canons (1191), and Augustinians of Martigny (13th century). Medieval popes and emperors who used the pass favored the hospice with privileges and benefices in many lands. In 1752 the hospice was made a provostship independent of that of Aosta, which had been commendatory (1465–1586); and the provost received pontifical privileges of miter and crozier. Napoleon favored the hospice after passing there with his army to the battle of Marengo (1801). A highway (1903–05) and a tunnel (1963) have reduced the rescue duties of the canons, many of whom gave their lives in their work; the hospice now serves tourists and skiers. In 1933 the canons extended their work to the evangelization of Tibet and China. Hospice buildings comprise a church (1669), a convent, and guest houses; the archives, library (30,000 volumes), and museum are notable. In 1964 there were 20 canons. The famous St. Bernard dogs have been used in rescue work since the 17th century.

Bibliography: L. H. COTTINEAU, *Répertoire topobibliographique des abbayes et prieurés*, 2 v. (Mâcon 1935–39) 1:1320–21. L. QUAGLIA, *La Maison du Grand St. Bernard, des origines aux temps actuels* (Aosta 1955). A. PELLOUCHOUD, *Le Grand-St-Bernard* (Lausanne 1954); *Der Grosse Sankt Bernhard* (Grand-St-Bernard 1964). M. GIROUD, *Lexikon für Theologie und Kirche*, ed. J. HOFER and K. RAHNER, 10 v. (2d, new ed. Freiburg 1957–65) 9:135.

[A. MAISSEN]

GREBEL, CONRAD

Founder of the New Testament-oriented pacifist ANABAPTISTS (Swiss Brethren); b. Zurich, *c.* 1498; d. Maienfeld, *c.* 1526, Grebel, of a patrician family, was a humanist who had studied in Basel, Vienna, and Paris (1514–20); he was interested mainly in philology and the natural sciences. Upon his return to Zurich (1520) he became associated with Ulrich Zwingli and other Swiss humanists with whom he engaged in Biblical studies in the original languages. In 1522 Grebel's marriage to a girl of more humble origin caused a break with his family. Soon after, still under the influence of Zwingli, he experienced a conversion to a personal Christian faith. Unwilling, however, to accept Zwingli's inclusive view of the church, Grebel soon broke with his mentor (1523), hoping to establish a voluntary and disciplined Christian community conforming to his idea of New Testament Christianity. This meant also the abolition of infant baptism and the introduction of ''believer's baptism.'' Attempting to rally all groups similarly inclined, he wrote a letter to Thomas MÜNZER seeking to form an alliance and warning him at the same time against the use of force, thus distinguishing his group clearly from the revolutionaries. The letter never reached its destination and the effort to establish an alliance failed. Grebel remained a leader of the Swiss Anabaptists, sharing their trials until his death from the plague at the age of 28.

Bibliography: H. S. BENDER, *Conrad Grebel* (Goshen, Ind. 1950). G. H. WILLIAMS, *The Radical Reformation* (Philadelphia 1962). H. FAST, *Die Religion in Geschichte und Gegenwart* (Tübingen 1957–63) 3 2:1834.

[G. W. FORELL]

GRECO, EL (DOMENICO THEOTOCOPULI)

Great religious painter of a visionary nature; b. Candia, Crete (a Venetian possession), 1541; d. Toledo, Spain, 1614. While popularly known as El Greco (Spanish article with Italian substantive), he signed his paintings Doménikos Theotokópoulos (in Greek letters), and on Spanish documents used the half-Italian, half-Spanish Domenico Theotocopuli.

Probably he went first to Venice (*c.* 1560) to study with Titian. The triptych in the Modena Gallery combining Cretan-Venetian elements, signed "cheir Doménikou" (sic) is accepted as El Greco's by some critics, while this writer and others attribute it to another artist with the same forename. The attribution to El Greco of religious panels by hack painters (Madonneri) is now discredited by responsible historians. His Italian works of *c.* 1560 to 1576 include two signed versions of the "Purification of the Temple" (National Gallery of Art, Washington D.C., and Minneapolis, Minn., Institute of Arts); those after 1570 display a knowledge of Florentine-Roman art as exemplified in "Christ Healing the Blind" (Parma Museum), and the "Pietà" compositionally dependent on Michelangelo (Philadelphia, Pa., Museum of Art; Hispanic Society of America, New York). The first two subjects are symbolic of the Counter Reformation.

Early in 1577 he departed for Spain, then the dominant world power, and in Toledo he painted his first masterpieces: three altars in Santo Domingo el Antiguo, whose major picture, the "Assumption," is now in the Art Institute, Chicago, Ill.; and "Espolio" (Disrobing of Christ), in the Toledo cathedral sacristy. Although its pictorial sources are Italian, the "Espolio" demonstrates a resurgence of medieval Byzantine iconography. Emotional power is projected by the dominating figure of Christ in a brilliant red tunic, surrounded and oppressed by a massive crowd of revilers. Philip II gave him only two commissions, and was dissatisfied with these: the "Allegory of the Holy League" (oil study, National Gallery of Art, London; large version, Nuevos Museos, Escorial) and the "Martyrdom of St. Maurice" (Escorial); the latter masterpiece combines startling effects of color with the Counter-Reformation ideal of glorifying martyrdom. Henceforth El Greco eliminated time and space in emphasis on spiritual exaltation, as in the "Crucifixion with Two Donors" (Louvre, Paris). His greatest achievement, the "Burial of Count Orgaz" (1586; Santo Tomé, Toledo), displays an earthly funeral with an extraordinary array of portraits of black-garbed Toledo dignitaries; an apparition of SS. Stephen and Augustine in brilliant crimson and gold vestments; and, in the vision of glory above, an assembly of saints suggesting the Last Judgment, with a white-robed Christ accompanied by the Virgin and St. John the Baptist.

El Greco, self-portrait. (©CORBIS-Bettmann)

El Greco created a vast new iconography of religious art, fully in the COUNTER REFORMATION spirit. His various interpretations of Francis of Assisi (ten different compositions), Peter in tears, Dominic, Mary Magdalen, and Jerome symbolize miracle and repentance. Other devotional subjects are the Holy Family, the Agony in the garden, Christ carrying the cross, Christ crucified, and the Apostles series. All his late compositions stress the supernatural: the "Fifth Seal of the Apocalypse" (1608–14, Metropolitan Museum of Art, New York); "Annunciation" (1596–1600; Museum, Villanueva y Geltrú, near Barcelona); and the "Adoration of the Shepherds" (*c.* 1612–14; Prado, Madrid), in which tall distorted figures, shadowy setting, and sharply contrasted vivid colors create intensity of mood. The last picture was planned for the altar of his tomb in Santo Domingo el Antiguo.

El Greco was equally great as portraitist, beginning in Italy in pure Venetian style with "Giulio Clovio" (Capodimonte Museum, Naples) and "Vincenzo Anastagi" (Frick Collection, New York). Later portraits of Spanish dignitaries and churchmen have remarkable psychological insight and superlative technique, e.g., "Cardinal Niño de Guevara" (Metropolitan Museum of Art) and

"Fray Hortensio Paravicino" (Museum of Fine Arts, Boston) are surpassingly great in characterization and pictorial beauty. His sculpture includes the "Miracle of St. Ildefonso" (cathedral, Toledo) and "Risen Christ" (Hospital Extramuros, Toledo). His architectural designs begin with altars, Palladian in style, in Santo Domingo. Late Mannerist design appears subsequently in the high altar (1597) of the chapel of St. Joseph, Toledo, high altar at Illescas (1603), and sepulchral retable, Santo Domingo el Antiguo (1612).

Differences of opinion prevail about the importance of his Byzantine heritage in iconography and style. Some critics (as Kelemen) regard it as predominant, whereas others consider his Venetian color and technique and his knowledge of MICHELANGELO and Italian mannerism (precedent for tall figures) as the basis of his art. All agree that El Greco was a unique genius of unparalleled visionary nature, one of the greatest religious painters of all time.

Bibliography: H. E. WETHEY, *El Greco and His School,* 2 v. (Princeton 1962), monograph, classified catalogue, bibliog. P. KELEMEN, *El Greco Revisited* (New York 1961), supports Byzantine thesis. H. SOEHNER, "Greco in Spanien," *Münchener Jahrbuch der bildenden Kunst,* 3d ser., 8 (1957) 123–194; 9–10 (1958–59) 147–242; 11 (1960) 73–217, catalogue of pictures in Spain. M. B. COSSÍO, *El Greco* (Madrid 1908). E. ARSLAN, *Encyclopedia of World Art* (New York 1959–87) 6:835–845.

[H. E. WETHEY]

GRECO-ROMAN SCHOOLING

The Greco-Roman school exerted a profound influence on ancient culture as it evolved between the 5th century B.C. and the 3d century A.D. It first appeared in ancient Athens, developed with the early SOPHISTS, and then, thanks to Plato and especially to Isocrates, assumed a form that it kept through the whole Hellenistic period. The Romans had only to adapt an already perfected institution to their own use. As they expanded, they introduced it into all sections of the empire.

Organization. The school of the *magister ludi* or *litterator* (elementary school) accepted a child at seven and taught him to read according to the analytical method (letters, syllables, words). First he read short moral texts, fables, or the *DISTICHA CATONIS*. At the same time, he learned to write by copying words on wax tablets. Then he was taught basic arithmetic, in particular how to calculate on his fingers (digital computation). The techniques of instruction at this stage were rather basic and the rod was not spared (Augustine, *Conf.* 1.9.14–15).

When about 12 years old the child went to the school of the *grammaticus* (grammarian), who taught him the mechanics of language and introduced him to the classical authors: Homer and Hesiod in the East; Vergil, Terence, Sallust, and Cicero in the West. For three years the student devoted much time to the poets. The *Iliad* or the *Aeneid* were studied verse by verse, both for form (verbal expression and scansion) and for content. As the people and events treated by the poets were identified, broad excursions were made into mythology, history, geography, and even the sciences. The student thus acquired a knowledge that made him "a bright young man." Then, in accord with the ideas of the Greek masters, he embarked on studies preparatory to rhetoric, designed to help him learn to write and speak well.

He began his "higher studies" in the school of the rhetor, Greek σοφιστής, where his goal was to master the art of oratory. Quintilian in his *Institutio oratoria* offers a complete picture of the stages of this study upon which the student was engaged between the ages of 16 and 20. The rhetor taught the various steps involved in the composition of a discourse: how to find topical material or common places (*topoi*) and construct a speech (*dispositio*) from the exordium to the peroration; and how to deliver it in words (*elocutio*) with gestures (*actio*). A study of ancient orators (Isocrates, Cicero) and historians taught him to use *exempla* (fictitious legal cases, commentaries on historical subjects) with which to enrich the exercises assigned by the rhetor. Studies in dialectic prepared the student to overcome the objections of future adversaries. He left the rhetor's class a well-versed lecturer or, as the case might be, a formidable lawyer.

Studies. To understand the school of antiquity at the moment during the 3d century when Christians began to take an interest in it, one must distinguish developments in the West from those in the East. Studies in Roman schools were essentially literary and oratorical, diverging from the Greek tradition, which placed a high value on the liberal arts, the three literary disciplines (grammar, rhetoric, dialectic) and the four sciences (arithmetic, geometry, music, astronomy). These seven branches of learning were introductory to the supreme art, philosophy. Among the Romans, however, scientific and philosophical studies gradually disappeared as the knowledge of Greek came to be restricted to an elite. In the East, on the other hand, the philosophical tradition continued. There, the student learned logic, physics, and especially ethics that prepared him to attain the supreme good and happiness, the goal of all his studies. Under the Later Empire, however, the school was employed to produce officials for the constantly increasing governmental bureaus, and the state became more and more interested in the municipal schools, favoring them even in the farthest reaches of the empire. The more totalitarian the state became, the more it encroached in this area. After JULIAN THE

APOSTATE, only persons approved by the municipal council, or even the emperor, could teach. In the 5th century Theodosius II founded an imperial university in CONSTANTINOPLE and gave it a monopoly in higher education.

Early in its development, Christianity was faced with a dilemma. Could the Church ignore this Greco-Roman school and develop its own religious schools, as the Jews had done with the Synagogue? Or would they try to enter into the school and Christianize it? Would they find another solution? The matter was important, for on the decision of the Church would depend the future of Mediterranean culture.

Christianity and the School

Two possible positions confronted each other from the beginning: to reject the school or to compromise. Opposition between Christian principles and those of the school of antiquity seemed absolute. Christianity as a religious way of life apparently had nothing in common with Hellenism. ''Where is the 'wise man'? Where is the scribe? Where is the disputant of this world? Has not God turned to foolishness the 'wisdom' of this world?'' Paul had asked (1 Cor 1.20).

Rejection. At first the wisdom of the Greeks was considered incompatible with the true wisdom of the Gospel, and the early Christians who were regarded with contempt as ''barbarians'' by learned pagans took great pride in that epithet (Tertullian, *Test. anim.* 1). The Christian seeking an education had no need to go to the school of the pagans. The third-century *DIDASCALIA APOSTOLORUM* represents the attitude of the early Christian communities: ''Do not even touch the books of the gentiles. What have you to do with these alien words and laws, or these false prophets who so easily bestow error on inconstant men? What do you lack in the word of God that you should turn to pagan fables? If you wish to read history, you have the Book of Kings; if you need philosophy or poetry, you have the Prophets. . . . If you desire songs, you have the Psalms; if you wish to know the beginning of the history of the world you have Genesis. . . . Abstain therefore absolutely from all these profane and diabolical works'' [1.6, Latin fragment, ed. Connolly (Oxford 1920) 13]. This rigorist idea of Christian culture was originally adopted by the monks, for whom true philosophy was not to be learned in the school but in solitude, by meditating on sacred writings. What would the Christian student find at the pagan school but immorality in the legends of mythology, and idolatry in the cult of false gods? As John Chrysostom said, ''Why send Christian youths to masters where, before the art of speaking, they will learn evil?'' (*Adv. opp. vitae monast.* 3.95).

The Dialogue Begins. If Christianity had developed apart from the Hellenic world, all Christians would probably have taken the position of the rigorists. But the Gospel had been written or translated into Greek, and borrowed much of its vocabulary from Hellenism, beginning with the all-important concept of the LOGOS (Jn 1). Thus Christianity simply could not escape the influence of the cultural atmosphere in which it developed. From the second century learned men who had been graduated from the school of antiquity had been turning to the new religion. In their writings they could not abandon their early training. In his *Dialogue with Trypho* JUSTIN MARTYR (d. *c.* 163) recalls how he arrived at the knowledge of the God of the Gospel by stages, following the development of pagan philosophy, and in his Apologies, he proves that Christianity provided answers for the questions posed by Greek thinkers. The Christian apologists (*see* APOLOGISTS, GREEK), who created the first Christian philosophy, took over many ideas from ancient philosophies, especially from Stoicism.

Christian Schools. GNOSTICISM showed that the encounter of Christianity with ancient philosophy was not without dangers, and many Christians felt that the philosophers were ''the patriarchs of the heretics'' (*Test. anim.* 3). In order to refute heretical teaching in Rome, Justin opened a school (a Didaskaleion) where he taught in a toga, ''the dress of a philosopher'' (Eusebius, *Hist.* 4.11.8). At the beginning of the third century, HIPPOLYTUS, a Roman priest and possibly a disciple of Irenaeus, author of the *Philosophumena* (Refutation of all Heresies), was honored with a statue representing him as a philosopher (*Dictionnaire d'archéologie chrétienne et de liturgie*, ed. F. Cabrol, H. Leclerq, and H. I. Marrou, 6.2:419–60).

In this same period, St. Clement of Alexandria, a former philosopher and student of the Stoic PANTAENUS, gathered a group of disciples whom he advised to study the pagan disciplines with a view to entering more deeply in the mystery of the faith. For him education and culture were ''the most beautiful and the most perfect goods that we possess in this life'' (*Paedag.* 1.16.1). Like an earlier Alexandrian, PHILO JUDAEUS, Clement found material in secular culture with which to improve his scriptural studies. He too sought ''to dress as a philosopher'' in order to demonstrate the proofs of the true wisdom to the pagan philosophers.

Again in Alexandria, in the middle of the third century, the former grammarian ORIGEN founded a school that became famous, and taught more than philosophy. Less favorable than Clement to the currents of ancient thought, he saw in classical studies a propaedeutic or preparation for understanding the Scriptures. The school he directed was a center of higher religious studies where students, Christian and non-Christian, after having studied the liberal arts and the philosophical systems, received exegetical and theological instruction. Eusebius of Caesarea describes Origen's school (*Hist.* 6.18.3–4): ''Many well educated men came to him to test his competence. Thousands of heretics and a large number of the most distinguished philosophers studied under him and quite openly learned not only divine truths but even things concerning secular philosophy. The disciples whom he saw to be naturally gifted he directed also to the study of philosophy, geometry, arithmetic, and other fundamental studies. Then he conducted them further into the teachings of the sects found among the philosophers, explaining, commenting upon, and examining their writings one by one.'' When he left Alexandria and took his school to Caesarea in Palestine, Origen had among his disciples the future saint GREGORY THAUMATURGUS, for whom he explained the principle that to reach Christianity more surely the student must ''take over from Greek philosophy the course of disciplines that can serve as an introduction to Christianity and those theories in geometry and astronomy that may be useful in the explanation of the Sacred Books.'' Then, employing a favorite image, he compares the Christians making use of the learning of the pagans to the Hebrews in Exodus who took with them the spoils of the Egyptians with which to adorn the Tabernacle (*Patrologia Graeca*, ed. J. P. Migne, 11:88–89). For the first time a Christian scholar had worked out the elements of Christian culture, and the lesson was not to be forgotten.

Christians Attend the School

Such was the synthesis of Christianity and classicism that in the end Christians had no choice but to send their children to the Greco-Roman school. Not to attend this school was not only to cut oneself off from the general culture but to make it impossible to take part in any activity within the empire. Even Tertullian, who had severely criticized pagan classicism, saw that it was necessary to attend the school: ''How would one do anything according to human prudence, or receive any mental formation without literature, the instrument of life?'' (*Idol.* 10). The Christian youth had to receive instruction from the pagan masters, but care had to be exercised lest the poison harm him, as Jerome would point out in his observations on education in the 4th century *in pueris necessitas* (*Epist.* 21.13.9). It seems that Christian children had continued in the schools even during the persecutions, occasionally being subjected to anti-Christian propaganda, such as resulted from an edict of Maximian requiring teachers to make their students learn the *Acts of Pilate,* which were filled with blasphemies against Christ (Eusebius, *Hist.* 9.5.1).

Christian Professors. Tertullian had been a rigorist; discouraging Christians from teaching in the pagan school. He judged that the risks run by the Christian teacher would be too great: he would have to lecture in detail about the pagan gods and take part in their ceremonies and feasts (*Idol.* 10). But the Church did not follow the African apologist. Thus, the *Apostolic Tradition* (*see* APOSTOLIC CONSTITUTIONS), composed in the circle of HIPPOLYTUS OF ROME, lists as professions that prevented catechumens from entering the Church: procurers, actors, and those who make idols; in regard to teachers, however, the text states (16): ''If anyone teaches children the learning of this world he should give it up, but if he has no other means of livelihood he will be excused.''

A number of Christians were teachers by profession. PRUDENTIUS speaks of a Cassian of Imola martyred by his students who stabbed him with their pens. Origen had opened a school of grammar to support himself after his father died. In 264 Anatolius, future bishop of Laodicea, held a chair of philosophy at Alexandria. In 268 the priest Malchion directed a school of rhetoric in Antioch. The Africans Arnobius and Lactantius were rhetors. LACTANTIUS was even invited to teach rhetoric at Nicomedia under Diocletian. For the fourth century the evidence in texts and inscriptions is plentiful. In Rome the conversion of the rhetor MARIUS VICTORINUS caused a scandal in pagan circles. Prohaeresius in Athens and the grammarian APOLLINARIS OF LAODICEA were Christian teachers, as were St. Basil and his father in Caesarea of Cappadocia. It is easy to understand, then, the painful surprise of the Christians when Julian the Apostate, intent upon reviving the pagan cults, forbade Christian masters to teach in the public schools.

Julian's Persecution. In a law of June 17, 362, Julian ruled that professors should be nominated by the municipalities and appointed by the emperor, who thus could pass sentence on their morality. In an accompanying letter, Julian explained what he meant by morality: a perfect accord between what one preached and what one practiced. For Christian teachers were explaining Homer and Hesiod, in whose words they saw only a tissue of diabolical fabrications. They were thus hypocrites and unworthy to teach: ''If they believe that these authors are mistaken with regard to beings of the greatest veneration, let them go to the churches of the Galileans and explain Matthew and Luke'' (*Epist.* 42).

This step created consternation in university circles, among both Christians and pagans. GREGORY OF NAZIANZUS, in his *Invectives against Julian* echoed the feelings of the Christians, while even pagans were disturbed to see the state interfering with the schools (Ammianus Marcellinus, 22.10.7; 25.4.20), for fear lest, in the service of a pagan revival, that institution might become a denominational school. Many Christian professors gave up their positions rather than abjure their faith. Others attempted to adorn the sacred writings of the Scriptures with a classical grace. The historian SOCRATES gives an account of a father and son named Apollinaris: ''Since they were both scholars, the father in grammar, the son in sophistic, they proved of great use to the Christians at this pass. The father composed a Christian grammar by rendering the books of Moses and everything of a historical character in the Old Testament in the meter called heroic, employing now the dactylic meter and now the tragic style to treat the subjects dramatically. The son, skilled in eloquence, presented the Gospels and the apostolic beliefs in dialogues, after the manner of Plato among the Greeks'' (*Hist.* 3.16, *Patrologia Graeca* 57:417). Since these writings are lost, the results of this endeavor cannot be evaluated. But at least it shows that Christian professors were devoted to the classicism of antiquity. When the edict of Julian was rescinded on Jan. 11, 364, thanks to the succession of a new emperor, Christian masters resumed their activities in the schools of the state. It should be noted that the scholastic persecution of Julian did not cause the Christians to open denominational schools. The only scholastic centers where the Psalms were learned instead of the short classical texts used in the schools were on the outskirts of the empire, in upper Egypt (the school of Protogenes at Antinoe discussed by Theodoret of Cyr, *Ecclesiastical History* 4.18. 7–14) and in the ''barbarian'' lands ignorant of classical culture.

Christian Classical Culture

Even before the undertaking of the two Apollinarises, some learned Christians decided that the language of the Bible was too crude and attempted to provide their contemporaries with the sacred texts in classical form. The Spanish priest Juvencus *c.* 330 put the Gospels into verse so that the content of the divine message could be remembered better. The Roman Proba succeeded in translating biblical stories in hemistichs of Vergil. In Gaul, Cyprian offered a versified translation of the Heptateuch. His exploit was repeated by the rhetor Marius Victorinus in the 5th century and by AVITUS OF VIENNE in the 6th. Christian poetry of the fourth and fifth centuries flowed effortlessly in the classical mold giving new life to a literary genre that had been dying out.

Christian Oratory. Sacred preachers also availed themselves of the devices of the traditional rhetoric when they presented their message. In the East a renaissance of pagan eloquence had a great influence in learned Christian circles. JOHN CHRYSOSTOM, student of Libanius the rhetor of Antioch, Basil of Caesarea and GREGORY OF NAZIANZUS, former students at the school of Athens, did not forget the lessons of their masters. Gregory of Nazianzus, apropos of the school law of Julian, cried: ''I have given up riches, nobility, glory, power, but I hold fast to eloquence'' (*Or.* 4.100, *Patrologia Graeca* 35:636). In the West in the sermons of St. Ambrose and St. Augustine, appear the *topoi* (common places) dear to rhetors. To be sure, the Fathers of the Church as a rule avoided the bad features of rhetoric, but many preachers of the period sought to please rather than to instruct and courted applause in their own churches.

Christian Learning. The presence of Christian professors in the school of antiquity not only enabled them to present Christian thought in classical guise, but offered them the means to construct a basically Christian scholarship. Following principles proposed by Origen, they saw in the program offered in the school a propaedeutic for the scientific study of Holy Scripture. In his *Admonitions to Young Men on the Profitable Use of Pagan Literature,* Basil of Caesarea suggested that ''as dyers begin by exposing an object to be dyed to certain preparations, if we wish our idea of the good to be indelible, we will demand of these external sciences a preliminary initiation whereby we can better understand the holy teachings of the mysteries.'' Clearly, one had to know how to choose what was good for the soul and reject what was harmful. JEROME took the same position: ''When books of worldly wisdom come into our hands, if we find something useful we take it over for our doctrine, but what is in excess or alludes to idols, love, or worldy matters we cut out'' (*Epist.* 21.13.6). Jerome, caught between his classical education and his monastic vocation, did not want to be ''more Ciceronian than Christian.'' While he cautioned his correspondents against the dangers of profane literature, he realized nevertheless that neither Christians nor clerics could be ignorant of secular branches of knowledge. He compared this learning to the comely captive that the Israelite could marry after shaving her head and paring her nails (*Epist.* 21.13.5, 70.2.5).

Augustine had the same concern to take over from classical culture everything suitable for the building of a Christian body of knowledge. He had been a brilliant student in the schools of Africa and had taught at Thagaste, Carthage, and Rome. He got his passion for philosophical inquiry from the *Hortensius* of Cicero (*Conf.* 3.4). At the end of the 4th century, pursuing ideas already broached in his *De Trinitate* and *De Ordine,* he set forth in the *De Doctrina Christiana* his convictions on the use of profane literature. He presented this treatise, which has been called ''the charter of Christian culture,'' as an initiation to the reading of the Scriptures. In Book 2 he demonstrates the use that the exegete must make of ancient languages, grammar, rhetoric, dialectic, and also the sciences—history, botany, mathematics, astronomy, and music—in order not only to be able to understand Holy Scripture, and to recognize the figures of style there employed, but to explain all the literary and scientific allusions found there (animals, herbs, trees, plants, numbers, etc.). The only things to be rejected absolutely are the arts that serve the cult of demons, in particular astrology and the fables of the poets. Likewise, philosophy not only should initiate the mind into the handling of abstractions but should prepare it for the spiritual life. Rhetoric should be taught not ''to plead both truth and falsehood'' but to preach Christian truth with artistry. Augustine thought, as did Jerome, that Christians in using the liberal arts were only reclaiming the riches that divine Providence had given to mankind but which had been wrongly used by the pagans.

The Counter-Offensive

The Fathers of the Church in the 4th century gradually evolved a *via media* between the exigencies of Christian morality and the necessity for a worldly education. But hardly had they laid the bases for a Christian culture, when a violent attack was directed against Greco-Latin classicism and even against Christian classicism.

Hostile Monks. The development of MONASTICISM dates from the 3d century, first in the East, then in the West. From the start, the abbots organized schools offering only religious instruction for the pupils admitted to the monasteries. The students learned to read and write, and their first reader was the Psalter. When Jerome devised a course of instruction for a young nun, he centered it on Holy Scripture and excluded literature and secular arts. Theoretically, the monastic school was for monks only, but SS. Basil and John Chrysostom thought that resident students should be accepted who after their studies would return to the world. They could obtain a purely religious education, which would protect them from the dangers of the world. But the further hope of influencing secular education was not fulfilled, and the monasteries remained primarily centers of asceticism for centuries.

During the barbarian invasions in the West many former monks were selected as bishops, and their ideas about Christian culture began to prevail. While the political crisis had grave repercussions on the ancient school system, it is not true to say that the barbarians caused the school of antiquity to disappear. In Milan, Ravenna, Rome, and Carthage the traditional instruction was still given in the 6th century; but the standards declined. The grammarian and the rhetor could impart to a few aristocrats a mundane culture in which form was considered to be of more importance than content. It was natural then for men coming from monastic circles to react against the vanity of the intellectual trifles with which learned men, even Christians, were amusing themselves. The monks, with only a superficial knowledge of classicism, regarded it as a block to the reception of the evangelical message. Classical studies seemed to them to be a danger to morals. Cassian deplored the fact that the monk who had studied the pagan poets would remember this poison all his life (*Conl.* 14.12) and felt that such studies were also a danger to faith, for philosophical speculation gave birth to heresies (*Inc. Dom.* 3.15.2).

The important work of CLAUDIANUS MAMERTUS and BOETHIUS, who put philosophy at the service of Christian truth, was not understood by many of their contemporaries. Classical studies, moreover, threatened to raise a wall in the Christian community between the learned and other Christians. Hence it was felt that to be understood by all, preacher and writer had to abandon the florid style (*sermo scholasticus*) and adopt a plain and forthright one (*sermo rusticus*), for salvation had been preached not by orators but by fishermen (Sulpicius Severus, *Mart.* 1.4). Cassian (*Inst.*, pref.), SALVIAN OF MARSEILLES (*Gub.* 3), POMERIUS of Arles (1.24), and PETER CHRYSOLOGUS (*Serm.* 43) manifested a desire to break with the traditional rhetoric, which was more concerned with words than facts (*verba,* non *res*). At a time when the Church was bringing its efforts to bear on the evangelization of the masses who were still pagan and when rural churches were multiplying, it seemed necessary to adopt a new way of speaking.

Prohibitions. Going back to the prohibitions of the 3d century in the *Didascalia apostolorum,* the *Statuta ecclesiae antiqua,* attributable perhaps to GENNADIUS OF MARSEILLES [ed. C. Munier (Strasbourg 1960)], forbade bishops to read pagan books (*ut episcopus gentilium libros non legat,* can. 5). Some historians have held that this canon was not binding upon the whole Church and that it did not prevent learned bishops of the 5th century from occupying their leisure with literature. But at the end of this century and at the beginning of the next, cultured ecclesiastics such as SIDONIUS APOLLINARIS, AVITUS OF VIENNE, and ENNODIUS of Pavia had scruples about returning to books they had read previously. For Ennodius of Pavia, this prohibition applied to clerics as well: ''Christ does not reject those who come to Him from liberal studies (*disciplina saecularia*), but He will not suffer anyone who leaves His splendor for them'' (*Epist.* 9.9, *Monumenta Germaniae Historica: Auctores antiquissimi* 7:297). He wrote this apropos of a young cleric who wanted to pursue classical studies. Influenced by the example of the monks, clerics began to regard secular learning as unworthy of their religious vocation, and they no longer dared to participate in the interests of the world of students. To deal with the problem of providing future clerics with the minimum instruction necessary before they could proceed to religious learning, recourse was had to the monastic solution.

Thus were created the first parish schools in the West (Council of Vaison in 529) and the first episcopal schools (Council of Toledo in 527). These were boarding schools with a course similar to that of the monastic schools: the study of sacred texts beginning with the Psalter, chant, and exegesis for the more advanced. Moreover, to make it unnecessary for youths to waste time in the schools of rhetoric, CASSIODORUS and Pope Agapetus thought of founding in Rome a school of higher religious studies modeled after the 3d-century school of Alexandria and the school of theology that was open in NISIBIS under Persian rule. The wars that afflicted Italy made this "Christian University" impossible, but Cassiodorus took up his plan again for his monks at Vivarium. Unfortunately, after his death this project disappeared. The end of the Roman Empire in the West was marked by a predominance of Christian culture and a return to the rigorist principles of early Christianity. Not until the CAROLINGIAN RENAISSANCE would the synthesis of classicism and Christianity again take place.

In the East. Things were different in the East, for the empire there was able to withstand the invasions, and the public schools were able to maintain the quality of instruction. The University of Constantinople, founded in 425, was the chief center of studies until the Turkish invasion in the middle of the 15th century. Relations between learned circles of clerics and laymen continued to be close. THEODORET OF CYR (d. 458) showed in his "Cure for the Pagan Diseases" that, on a basis in ancient philosophy, one could discover the truth of the Gospel. LEONTIUS OF BYZANTIUM in the 6th century sought to adapt the philosophy of Aristotle to Christian dogma, while a revival of Neoplatonism served as a basis for the predominantly mystical elements in the theology of PSEUDO-DIONYSIUS.

Only in the 10th century is there certain evidence for a school of religious learning founded in connection with the cathedral of Constantinople. But the patriarchs who were professors in this school did more than give courses in exegesis. They taught the liberal arts and philosophy as a propaedeutic to the study of Sacred Scripture, resuming the curriculum that Origen had followed many centuries earlier.

Bibliography: M. ROGER, *L'Enseignement des lettres classiques d'Ausone à Alcuin* (Paris 1905). H. I. MARROU, *Saint Augustin et la fin de la culture antique* (Paris 1938); *A History of Education in Antiquity,* tr. G. LAMB (New York 1956). C. N. COCHRANE, *Christianity and Classical Culture* (New York 1957). P. DE LABRIOLLE, *Histoire de la littérature latine chrétienne,* ed. G. BARDY (3d ed. Paris 1947). E. IVÁNKA, *Hellenisches und Christliches im frühbyzantinischen Geistesleben* (Vienna 1948). P. COURCELLE, *Les Lettres grecques en Occident de Macrobe à Cassiodore* (new ed. Paris 1948). G. L. ELLSPERMANN, *The Attitude of the Early Christian Latin Writers Toward Pagan Literature and Learning* (Washington 1949). M. L. W. LAISTNER, *Christianity and Pagan Culture in the Later Roman Empire* (Ithaca, N.Y. 1951). M. SPANNEUT, *Le Stoïcisme des Pères de l'Église* (Paris 1957). H. HAGENDAHL, *Latin Fathers and the Classics* (Göteborg 1958). A. M. J. FESTUGIÈRE, *Antioche païenne et chrétienne* (Paris 1959). P. RICHÉ, *Éducation et culture dana l'Occident barbare, VII*e*-VIII*e *siècles* (Paris 1962).

[P. RICHÉ]

GREDT, JOSEPH AUGUST

Benedictine philosopher of the Thomistic revival inaugurated by LEO XIII; b. Luxembourg, July 30, 1863; d. Rome, Jan. 29, 1940. The son of a teacher, he made his philosophical and theological studies in Luxembourg, was ordained in 1886, and studied in Rome under F. SATOLLI, A. LEPIDI, T. ZIGLIARA, and G. Pecci. He became a Benedictine in 1891 at Seckau, Austria, and served as philosophy professor at San Anselmo, Rome, from 1896 to his death. His main work, based on T. de VIO CAJETAN and FERRARIENSIS, is the comprehensive manual *Elementa philosophiae aristotelico-thomisticae* (2 v. Rome 1899–1901). Under the influence of some neoscholastics, the SALMANTICENSES, and especially JOHN OF ST. THOMAS, he notably altered the second edition in arrangement and in several theses, while retaining the rigidly scholastic method. Long quotations from Aristotle and Aquinas are of special value. The emphasis is on metaphysics; Gredt argues that *aliquid* is one of the TRANSCENDENTALS and proposes a *sexta via* to God's existence from the ordering of the soul toward the Infinite. In cosmology he makes extensive use of the positive sciences. His "natural realism" (*De cognitione sensuum externorum,* 2d ed. Rome 1924) defends the objectivity of all sense qualities against experimental psychologists and "critical realists." His criticisms of other philosophers, however, are not always reliable. His articles are concerned mostly with cosmology and psychology, and develop Aquinas's doctrine of the real distinction between act and potency.

See Also: SCHOLASTICISM.

Bibliography: J. A. GREDT, *Miscellanea philosophica R. P. Josepho Gredt* (Rome 1938); *Divus Thomas* (Fribourg) v.16–18 (1938–40) *passim.;* "De entitate viali qua in schola thomistica explicatur causalitas instrumentalis," *Divus Thomas* (Piacenza) 41:413–424; "De activitate creaturarum," *ibid.* 43:339–344; *Acta Pontificiae Academiae Romanae S. Thomae Aquinatis* v.3–5 (1936–38); *Elementa philosophiae aristotelico-thomisticae* (13th ed. rev. Barcelona 1961).

[A. W. MÜLLER]

Capital: Athens.
Size: 50,944 sq. miles.
Population: 10,601,525 in 2000.
Languages: Greek, English, French.
Religions: 10,389,465 Greek Orthodox (96%), 62,000 Catholics (.6%), 99,800 Muslims (1%), 30,000 Protestants (.3%), 20,260 follow other faiths or are without religious affiliation.
Archdioceses: Athens and Rhodes, both of which are directly subject to the Holy See; the Ionian Islands of Corfu, Zante, and Cephalonia; and Naxos, Andros, and Mikonos, with suffragans Chios, Melos and Syros, Santorino, and Candia (on the island of Crete). There is an apostolic vicariate in Thessaloniki on the Greek mainland. The Greek Byzantine Catholic Church has an apostolic exarch in Athens. There is also an ordinariate in Athens for the Armenian Catholic Church.

GREECE, THE CATHOLIC CHURCH IN

The Hellenic Republic, or Greece, is a peninsular region located in southern Europe bound on the north by the former Yugoslavian Republic of Macedonia and Bulgaria, on the northeast by Turkey, on the east by the Aegean Sea, on the southeast by the Sea of Crete, on the south by the Mediterranean Sea, on the west by the Ionian Sea, and on the northwest by Albania. A mountainous country with ranges transforming into small islands at the coast, Greece has a temperate climate, characterized by hot summers and mild, rainy winters. Earthquakes are common and range in severity. Natural resources include bauxite, lignite, magnesite, oil and marble. Wheat, corn, barley, sugar beets, olives, tomatoes and dairy products comprise the bulk of Greece's agricultural sectors.

THE EARLY CHURCH

The region was inhabited as early as the Paleolithic period and by 3000 B.C. had become home to a sophisticated people. Crete was home to the Minoan empire by 2000 B.C. and gained connections to Egypt and Sicily. The Mycenaeans eventually replaced the Minoans, establishing a system of small city-states, which became the basis for the Roman organization following its incorporation into the Roman Empire.

The name Greece occurs but once in the New Testament (Acts 20.2), and refers to the Roman province Achaia. The exact boundaries of this administrative unit of the Roman Empire varied, but at the beginnings of Christianity it most probably comprised the area of ancient Hellas that extended northward from the southern tip of the Peloponnesus to the borders of Thessaly, Aetolia and Acarnania (Strabo, *Geography* 17.3.25). Euboea and most of the Cyclades also belonged to this province. Corinth was the capital, where the Roman proconsul had his residence.

The Apostolic Age. The scriptural record concerning the beginnings of Christianity in Greece is limited mainly to the Acts, which discusses Athens and Corinth; Cenchrae, the eastern seaport city of Corinth, is mentioned only briefly in passing. In the course of his second missionary journey, St. Paul stopped for a time in Athens (Acts 17.16–34), where he had ''discussions in the synagogue with the Jews and those who worshiped God, and in the market place with those who were there.'' Some Epicurean and Stoic philosophers debated with him. The scriptural narrative reports the address Paul delivered on the Areopagus and notes: ''certain persons became believers; among them Dionysius the Areopagite,'' the first bishop of Athens, according to Eusebius (*Hist. eccl.* 4.23.3), ''and a woman named Damaris, and others with them.'' From Athens Paul traveled to Corinth, where he lodged at first with Aquila and Priscilla and preached in the synagogue every Sabbath (Acts 18.1–18). After the arrival of Silas and Timothy from Macedonia Paul spent his time preaching to the Jews until they contradicted him and blasphemed. Thereafter he preached to the Gentiles and resided with Titus Justus. ''Crispus the president of the synagogue believed in the Lord and so did his household, and many Corinthians . . . believed and were baptized.'' After some time the Jews made a concerted attack against Paul, who was summoned before the tribunal of Gallio, Proconsul of Achaia. The case, however, was dismissed, and after he had spent 18 months in Corinth, Paul departed. He stopped briefly at Cenchrae, where Phoebe ''was in the ministry of the church'' (Rom 16.1). During his third missionary journey Paul came once more to Greece (Achaia) and remained for three months (Acts 20.2, 3). The Apostle's two letters to the Corinthians close the scriptural account of events in Achaia.

Other sources attempt to complete the narrative about apostolic times. As quoted by Eusebius, DIONYSIUS, bishop of Corinth (*c.* 170), made a surprising statement about Peter and Paul: ''both of them taught together in our Corinth and were our founders'' (*Hist. eccl.* 2.25.8). The apocryphal *Acta Andreae* (*c.* 260) and the still later *Passio,* purporting to be a letter of the priests and deacons of Achaia, claim that Andrew preached in that province, suffered martyrdom on November 30 in Patras, and was buried there. In spite of doubts about the historicity of these events, a strong local tradition still links Andrew with Achaia and Patras, as Pope Paul VI's decision in 1964 to return the head of St. Andrew to the reputed place of his martyrdom supports. According to still other traditions, Saints Matthew, Thomas and Luke are reputed to have visited Greece in the course of their missionary journeys.

The Post-apostolic Age. Very little is known about the Church in Greece during the period immediately following the apostolic age. Only the Church of Corinth with its deplorable factions is mentioned in the first *Epistle of Clement* of Rome. Persecution severely afflicted the Church of Athens during the 2d century. While its Bishop Publius died as a martyr, his successor, Quadratus, worked successfully to revive the faith of the sorely tried Christian community. ARISTIDES, the philosopher who wrote an *Apology* addressed to Emperor Hadrian and ATHENAGORAS, who composed the *Supplication for the Christians* directed to Marcus Aurelius and Commodus, brought glory to the Church of Athens.

Corinth was famous for two of its illustrious bishops. Dionysius rendered special service by his letters to the churches in Athens, Sparta, Nicomedia, Crete, Amastris, Pontus and Rome. He considered the Church at Rome worthy of special praise for its efforts in behalf of the needy and of those Christians who had been condemned to the mines (Eusebius, *Hist. eccl.* 4.23.10). Bacchylus was an active participant in the EASTER CONTROVERSY and wrote a useful letter concerning this question (Jerome, *De viris illustribus,* 44).

In the first half of the 3d century ORIGEN visited Athens, where he completed his commentary on Ezekiel (Eusebius, *Hist. eccl.* 6.32.2) and was edified by the exemplary conduct of the Athenian Christians, as he later wrote (*Contra Celsum* 3.30). The Decian persecution, however, dominated the history of the Church in Achaia at this time. Because of fragmentary evidence, the names of only a few who died for the faith are recorded: Leonides, Bishop of Athens and his companions from Corinth; QUADRATUS (CODRATUS) and his Corinthian companions; Irene and Adrian from a city in Achaia, whose feast day is kept March 10.

Surviving evidence for the progress of the Church in the 4th century is meager for Achaia. From this province two bishops were present at the First Council of NICAEA: Pistus of Athens and Strategius of Hephaistia on the island of Lemnos. The presence of Strategius at Nicaea is the earliest extant evidence for the Christianization of the islands in the Aegean Sea.

During the 5th and 6th centuries ecclesiastical jurisdiction in Greece shifted with the political alignment between Rome and Constantinople. The metropolitan of Thessalonika served as vicar of the pope, while Thrace was taken under the control of Constantinople. Emperor Leo III (717–741) made eastern Illyria part of the Byzantine Empire, and Basil I (867–886) directed a missionary enterprise for the full Christianization of the Peloponnesus. With the Eastern Schism in 1054, Greece became part of the Orthodox Church and was gradually subdued by the Ottoman Turks, who gave the hierarchy a limited independence in their elections and internal activities, as well as in their relations with the patriarch of Constantinople.

In 1209, during the occupation of Greece as part of the Crusade against Constantinople, Pope Innocent III created a Latin archiepiscopal see in Athens with 11 suffragan sees. The Cistercians, Dominicans, Franciscans and other orders founded residences in Greece and particularly in Crete. After the Council of FLORENCE, Catholic colonies flourished in Crete, Methone, and Coronea with Greek-rite Catholic priests. The invasion of the Ottoman Turks in 1453 sent the Church into decline under an Islamic government.

Bibliography: C. BRANDIS, *Paulys Realenzyklopädie der klassischen Altertumswissenschaft,* ed. G. WISSOWA et al., 1.1 (1893) 193–198. A. VON HARNACK, *The Mission and Expansion of Christianity in the First Three Centuries,* ed. and tr. J. MOFFAT, 2 v. (2d ed. New York 1908) v.2. H. LECLERCQ, *Dictionnaire d'archéologie chrétienne et de liturgie,* eds., F. CABROL, H. LECLERCQ and H. I. MARROU, 15 v. (Paris 1907–53) 1.1:321–340. S. VAILHÉ, *Dictionnaire d'histoire et de géographie ecclésiastiques,* ed. A. BAUDRILLART et al. (Paris 1912—) 1:300–304. R. JANIN, *ibid.* 5:16–18; 13:876–878. F. DVORNIK, *The Idea of Apostolicity in Byzantium and the Legend of the Apostle Andrew* (Cambridge, MA 1958) 181–222. O. VOLK, *Lexikon für Theologie und Kirche*[2], eds., J. HOFER and K. RAHNER, 10 v. (2d, new ed. Freiburg 1957–65) 6:553–554. J. BAYOT, *Catholicisme,* 5:215–216. H. JEDIN, *Handbuch der Kirchengeschichte,* 6 v. (Freiburg 1962–) 1:122–123, 241. J. DANIÉLOU and H. I. MARROU, *The First Six Hundred Years,* tr. V. CRONIN v.1 of *The Christian Centuries* (New York 1964–) 1:26, 33, 51. E. HONIGMANN, ''La Liste originale des Pères de Nicée,'' *Byzantion,* 14 (1939) 27–76.

[H. DRESSLER/EDS.]

THE MODERN CHURCH

In 1821 a holy war led by the Lavra Monastery of Patras culminated in the defeat of Turkish rule in Greece. A year later the country's first National Assembly proclaimed the Greek Church autocephalous, breaking its dependence on Constantinople. After nine years of revolt aided by France, England and, later, Russia, in February of 1830 the Protocol of London recognized the Peloponnesus, certain Aegean Islands, and the mainland as far as Epirus and Thessaly as an independent country, with Greek Orthodoxy as the state religion. Under the authority of the Bavarian-born King Otto, over 400 monasteries were abolished, their goods distributed among the fighters for freedom. The Megali concept, which involved uniting all Greeks of the declining Ottoman Empire within an independent Greek State, began to come to fruition during the mid-19th century. The Ionic Islands were given to Greece by England in 1863, Thessaly was annexed in 1881 through the Conference of Berlin and in 1897 Crete gained its independence, but reverted to Greece in 1913. During the Balkan War of 1912–13 Greece took possession of South Macedonia, West Thrace and the Aegean Islands; it gained Western Thrace in 1918 and the Dodecanese Islands in 1947.

World War I brought great suffering to both the Greek Church and State. After the war Greece joined the Allied occupation of Turkey. During a 1921 attack on Ankara, Greek forces were defeated by Mustafa Kemal (later Ataturk), and the resulting refugee problem ended the Megali push. From now on Greeks focused on the constant struggle between monarchists and republicans. In 1924 Greece was proclaimed a republic, and during the early 1930s the government attempted to interfere with the Orthodox Church by systematizing the control of parishes and the idiorhythmic or self-ruling monasteries. With the reestablishment of the monarchy under George II (1934), the Orthodox Church came under royal control.

On Oct. 28, 1940 the Italians invaded Greece, forcing the nation into World War II. The Greeks successfully repulsed the Italians, but were not as fortunate against the Germans when Hitler attacked in April of 1941. With Greece under the dictatorial control of General J. Metaxas, German forces remained in the country until October of 1944. During the war, the country's Jewish population, which had numbered 75,000, was decimated, as 60,000 Greek Jews were sent to Auschwitz or executed. Following World War II, several communist resistance groups began a struggle for power that escalated into civil war by 1946. Violence continued, killing thousands, until in August of 1949 a government-led offensive forced the remaining insurgents to flee into Yugoslavia. On Jan. 1, 1952, the monarchy was restored under King Paul I, and from 1952 to 1965 the country experienced relative stability. In 1967 a military dictatorship under Colonel George Papadopoulos took power in Greece, forcing the king into exile and suspending many liberties granted under the constitution. On Dec. 8, 1974, the country returned to civilian rule, drafted a new constitution, held democratic elections, abolished the monarchy and created a parliament. Greece joined the European Union in 1981.

Under the constitution of June 1975, the Greek Orthodox Church was the prevailing religion of the state. As such, it received financial benefits such as state payment of clergy salaries, the funding of church buildings and tax exemptions. The Muslim minority, concentrated in Thrace, which was given legal status by provisions of the Treaty of Lausanne in 1923, was Greece's only officially recognized minority faith. As a faith unrecognized by the state, the Roman Catholic Church in Greece was not allowed to own property except through a created legal entity, although in 1999 the government extended legal recognition to those Catholic churches in existence prior to 1946.

Relations between the Faiths. During the 17th century many Orthodox prelates wrote to the Holy See for assistance, as did the monasteries of Athos, Chios and Patmos. The Jesuits, Capuchins and Lazzarists (Vincentians) founded schools in Athens, Piraeus, Salonika, Crete, Chios, Naxos, Syros and Corfu. Relations with the Orthodox, however, became increasingly difficult because of accusations of attempts at proselytism and Latinization. In 1938 laws were passed to prevent proselytism among the Orthodox by Catholics, and difficulties arose over mixed marriages. Such laws were reinforced by the 1975 constitution, which stipulated that the practice of non- Orthodox worship should not offend or disturb public order.

After World War II many younger monks from Mt. Athos and the monasteries became involved in parochial activities, creating an atmosphere that translated into a move toward Christian reunion. In 1965 Pope Paul VI and Patriarch Athenagoras I began a dialogue that planted the seeds of reconciliation by nullifying the mutual excommunications imposed during the schism of 1054. The government's decision, in 2000, to remove religious affiliation from national identity cards, reflected a growing tolerance for religious diversity among some Greek people, although such tolerance was not reflected by the Orthodox leadership, which opposed the government's move. While Orthodox Ecumenical Patriarch Bartholomew, head of the Orthodox Church, began a discourse with the Vatican, Greek leaders were among those objecting to his efforts at bridging the two divergent faiths. In response to a request by Pope John Paul II to visit Greece in 2001, a metropolitan objected to the proposed visit, noting the efforts of the Catholic Church to aggressively proselytize in Greece. The Eastern Catholic churches, noted Metropolitan Kallinkos, in September of 1999, ''are the Trojan Horse of the Catholic Church.'' The pope's visit, which took place in May, was done as part of a trip retracing the steps of St. Paul. During his historic meeting with Orthodox Archbishop Christodoulos, the pope apologized for the treatment of the Orthodox by Latin Catholics, beginning with the sacking of Constantinople.

Into the 21st Century. By 2000 there were 64 parishes tended by 50 diocesan and 45 religious priests. Other religious included 35 brothers and 127 sisters, although foreign religious, such as members of the Missionaries of Charity, had difficulty obtaining or renewing visas. Most Catholics, who were descendent from Venetian settlers, resided in Athens, Thessaloniki or Patrias, or on the islands of Tinos, Naxos, Syros and Corfu. Polish and Philippine immigrants also comprised part of the Catholic community.

Bibliography: P. JOANNOU, *Lexikon für Theologie und Kirche*, eds., J. HOFER and K. RAHNER, 10 v. (2d, new ed. Freiburg 1957–65) 4:1231–34. C. KONIDANS, *Christian Greece* (Athens 1953) 1–22. P. HAMMOND, *The Waters of Marah* (London 1956). R. JANIN, *Catholicisme,* 3:1456–57. J. KARAYANNOPULOS, *Die Religion in Geschichte und Gegenwart*, 7 v. (3d ed. Tübingen 1957–65) 2:1857–60. *Staatslexikon,* ed. Görres-Gesellschaft, 8 v. (6th, new and enl. Ed. Freiburg 1957–63) 3:1023–24. *Oriente Cattolico* (1962) 420.

[F. X. MURPHY/EDS.]

GREEK CATHOLIC CHURCH (EASTERN CATHOLIC)

The Greek Catholic Church is a very tiny church that owes its existence to the reunion movement launched by Father John Marango (d. 1885) among Greek Orthodox in Istanbul. Father Isaias Papadopoulos formed a small group of zealous Greek Catholics in northern Greece. Bishop George Calavassy succeeded him and worked until his death in 1957 to make the Greek Catholic Church known in Greece by the works of corporal and spiritual mercy that he launched. The Catholic group in Turkey was practically dissolved when the Greeks were repatriated to Greece. Since 1957 the exarchate in Turkey has been directed by an apostolic administrator. In Greece the Greek Catholic Church has a resident Greek bishop in Athens. The Greek Orthodox Church has never warmed up to the Greek Catholic Church in its territory, viewing it as an intruder. It remains illegal for Greek Catholic priests to dress in Byzantine clerical style.

Bibliography: R. ROBERSON, *The Eastern Christian Churches: A Brief Survey*, 6th ed (Rome 1999).

[G. A. MALONEY/EDS.]

GREEK LANGUAGE, BIBLICAL

This term is used for the language of the Greek Old Testament and the Greek text of the New Testament. It is a form of Koine (''common'') Greek that evolved in the time of Alexander the Great from the diverse dialects of classical times through leveling and assimilation and became the everyday commercial and cultural language of the Mediterranean world for more than ten centuries. Spoken in many lands by peoples with different native languages, it was subject to variations caused by foreign influences. Biblical Greek shows many types of Semitic interference phenomena, not only in the use of words with different meanings than in classical or Hellenistic authors, but also in the use of many non-Greek grammatical constructions.

The Greek Old Testament circulated most widely in the Septuagint (LXX) translation, which also preserves the original text of some (deutero)canonical books (Wisdom, 2 Maccabees) and the basic form of others, either in whole (Tobit, Judith, Baruch, 1 Maccabees) or in part (Esther, Daniel, Sirach). Hardly a unity, its style varies in quality from a faithful translation of the Hebrew (Pentateuch) to a slavishly literal rendering (Qoheleth), which was the result of periodic revisions that culminated in the later word-for-word translations of (proto-) Theodotion and Aquila and the more idiomatic version of Symmachus.

The Greek of the New Testament is similarly diverse. The letters, especially those of Paul and Hebrews, represent good Koine Greek, not unlike that found in documentary papyri from Roman Egypt. The Gospels and Acts preserve more of a Semitic tone and flavor, though the Gospel according to Luke begins with a well-constructed prologue in contemporary literary style. The Gospel according to John is written in simple but elegant language. Revelation is written in the poorest Greek.

Bibliography: W. BAUER, F. W. GINGRICH, and F. W. DANKER, *A Greek–English Lexicon of the New Testament and Other Early Christian Literature*, 3rd ed. (Chicago 2001). F. BLASS and A. DEBRUNNER, *A Greek Grammar of the New Testament and Other Early Christian Literature*, tr. R. W. FUNK (Chicago 1961). F. C. CONYBEARE and S. G. STOCK, *A Grammar of Septuagint Greek* (Grand Rapids 1980). J. W. MOULTON, W. F. HOWARD, and N. TURNER, *A Grammar of New Testament Greek*, 4 v. (Edinburgh 1908–76). J. VERGOTE, ''Grec Biblique,'' *Dictionnaire de la Bible*, suppl. ed. L. PIROT et al. (Paris 1928–) 3:1320–69. M. ZERWICK, *Biblical Greek Illustrated by Examples*, tr. J. SMITH (Rome 1963).

[F. T. GIGNAC]

GREEK LANGUAGE, EARLY CHRISTIAN AND BYZANTINE

At the beginning of the Christian era, Greek was widely spoken in the Mediterranean basin. In morphology, syntax, and vocabulary it was derived from the Attic-Ionic dialect, but it bore the imprint of subsequent linguistic developments. Contacts with other languages and cultures in the Hellenistic world left their mark, especially in vocabulary and syntax. Two factors in particular helped mold this spoken Greek into the vehicle for the dissemination of Christian teaching.

Basic Elements. First, the Septuagint (LXX) translation of the OT crystallized Greek terminology for theological concepts completely foreign to ancient Greek, added Hebrew and Aramaic loanwords to the vocabulary, and through literal renderings of the Hebrew, introduced Semitisms into Christian Greek. Second, the books of the NT, deeply influenced by LXX terminology, gave specifically Christian meanings to current words and coined words to explain new concepts. Other formative elements of early Christian Greek are the language of the early liturgy, the terminology of the mystery religions, and the ethical and moral contexts of pagan philosophy. The earliest extant works of Christian literature outside the NT, those of the Apostolic Fathers and their immediate successors, were written primarily to instruct Christian converts. In language and style they generally echo the OT and NT. Rhetorical figures and balanced sentence structure, characteristic of classical Greek, yielded to an almost unmitigated parataxis. This unadorned diction became the norm and was later approved in the dictum of Isidore of Pelusium (d. *c.* 435): ''If they seek elaborate diction let them know that it is better to learn truth from an unlettered man than falsehood from a sophist'' (*Letter to Theognostus, Patrologia Graeca*, ed. J. P. Migne, 161 v. (Paris 1857–66) 78:1124).

Apologists. The apologists of the 2nd century addressed a different audience, their non-Christian contemporaries, and defended Christianity against its enemies. Accordingly, the content rather than the literary style of their works was affected. St. Justin Martyr is not conspicuous for style or orderly arrangement of thought, but he knew Homer, Plato, Euripides, and Menander. The notable exception to the usual disregard of style, the *Supplication for the Christians* of Athenagoras of Athens addressed to Marcus Aurelius and Commodus, in spite of its literary merit, was soon forgotten in Christian antiquity. The apologies, ranging from friendliness to open hostility toward the content of Hellenism, made a contribution in theology but not in the development of an artistic Christian Greek literature. This literary development did not appear before the beginning of the 3rd century.

Christian Literature. As Christianity penetrated the ancient world, it gained more converts from educated circles. The need for teachers competent to instruct such catechumens on a level commensurate with their culture gave rise to the catechetical schools. The most famous of these was at Alexandria, where Eastern, Egyptian, and Greek cultures had long ago met and commingled. Here the LXX in large part had been translated. A Hellenistic Jewish literature flourished and culminated perhaps in the works of Philo, who exerted a great influence on early Christian writers. Such a cultural environment conditioned the Alexandrian catechetical school for an interest in the philosophy of Plato, the allegorical interpretation of Scripture, and the metaphysical investigation of the content of faith. The content of Hellenism soon appeared in Christian writings that began to rival ancient artistic prose. This was the age of Clement, ''the pioneer of Christian scholarship,'' and of Origen, whose influence extended to Asia Minor, Syria, and Palestine where he founded the famous school of Caesarea. Christian Greek was indebted to Eusebius of Caesarea more for an encyclopedic learning that preserved excerpts from pagan and Christian works no longer extant than for his literary excellence. Chronologically he falls in the age of Constantine, but he was not significantly influenced by the new literary developments characteristic of that period.

Epideixis. Pagan Greek was dominated by the New or Second Sophistic with its emphasis on pure Attic diction and its preoccupation with rhetorical devices and adornment. The influence of the New Sophistic was felt in Christian Greek at the time of Constantine and reached a climax in Basil the Great, the two Gregories, and John Chrysostom (d. 407), all of whom had studied at famous pagan schools of rhetoric. When Gregory of Nazianzus became bishop of Constantinople (*c.* 379), hostile factions objected to his sermons, which were richly adorned with pagan rhetoric. Gregory's answer, it may be noted, implied that the rhetorical devices compensated for his lack of the gift of miracles (*Oratio* 36, *Patrologia Graeca*, 36:266). A generation later Christians expected to hear a display of oratory in church, at least in the larger cities, and applauded the speaker when the rhythmical cadences of his sentences pleased their ears. Chrysostom says that he met opposition when he sought to ban applause and that many speakers deliberately sought acclaim and keenly felt the lack of approval from their hearers (*Homilia 30 in Actus Apostolorum*, *Patrologia Graeca*, 60:225,266). The impact of pagan epideictic oratory on Christian Greek was certainly paramount. Other pagan literary genres, however, such as the letter, the dialogue, and the consolation, were also cultivated. In artistic form they rival, and in content surpass, their pagan counterparts. Gregory of Nazianzus, the ''Christian Demosthenes,'' is known also for poetry of genuine feeling and beauty. Gregory of Nyssa, the ''Father of mysticism,'' illustrates how Christian ascetical authors pressed into service Platonic and Neoplatonic terminology.

Thus was Hellenism Christianized. The masters of Christian Greek were profoundly influenced by Hellenic thought and culture; consequently, Christian Greek literature cannot be appreciated apart from the Hellenic background against which it was written.

Bibliography: J. QUASTEN, *Patrology*, 3 v. (Westminster, Md. 1950–), in progress. 1:186-253; 2: 1–152. W. SCHMID and O. STÅHLIN, *Geschichte der griechischen Literatur* (Munich 1924) 2. Teil, 2. Hälfte 1105–1492, esp. 1106–22 and 1274. L. R. PALMER, *The Greek Language* (2nd ed. London 1980). L. RADERMACHER, ''Koine,'' *Sitzungsberichte der Akademie der Wissenschaften in Wien* 224 (1947) 1:74. G. BARDY, *La Question des langues dans l'église* ancienne, 2 v. (Paris 1948) v. 1. E. SCHWYZER, *Griechische Grammatik*, 3 v. (2nd ed. Munich 1950–53) 1:116–130.

[H. DRESSLER/F.T. GIGNAC]

GREEK PHILOSOPHY

Greek philosophy gave the first strictly rational answers in Western thought to basic questions about the universe and man. The origin and nature of the visible universe concerned the earliest philosophers, the pre-Socratics, from Thales in the 6th century B.C. to Democritus in the 5th, with a gradual shift to dominant interest in ethical or political life. In reaction against Sophistic relativism and the rhetorical basis of traditional Greek education, Socrates emphasized virtue as scientific knowledge. His disciple Plato and, in turn, Plato's student, Aristotle, mark the peak of Greek philosophy. Both attempted, in different ways, to establish firm scientific principles as guides for the investigation of the universe, the human mind, and human conduct. Other influential

Aristotle teaching Alexander the Great, after a painting by J.L.G. Ferris. (©Bettmann/CORBIS)

philosophies, such as Stoicism and Epicureanism, arose in the wake of this period of keen intellectual activity. Finally, Plotinus's fusion of Platonic spirit with Aristotelian doctrines and some elements from Stoic thought is the last great movement in Greek philosophy.

The term ''philosophy'' itself is of Greek origin. Meaning ''love of wisdom,'' it was attributed in biographical tradition (Diogenes Laërtius, *Lives* 1.12; 8.8) to Pythagoras, and suggested that wisdom is something divine and a man cannot be truly wise but only a lover of wisdom. Designating men who pursue wisdom, the term ''philosophers'' appears in a fragment of Heraclitus cited in the 2d or 3d century A.D. (H. Diels, *Die Fragmente der Vorsokratiker: Griechisch und Deutsch,* ed., W. Kranz, 3 v. [10th ed. Berlin 1960–61] 22B 35). At any rate, it was used in the 5th century B.C. by Herodotus as an established Ionian word. At that time the Greek term for wisdom (σοφία) signified skill in a quite general sense, while philosophy (φιλοσοφία) seems from the start to have been restricted to the intellectual. Yet it was never divorced by the Greeks from its bearing on practical and moral life. In its ancient use it also included natural history. In the time of Isocrates it could mean the proficiency given by rhetoric, and for Aristotle it still embraced mathematics and literary theory. (*See* PHILOSOPHY.)

Ionia. Western philosophy originated in the Greek city-states of Ionia, along the coast of Asia Minor. By both ancient and modern historians it is seen assuming its distinctive form either with Thales of Miletus (fl. *c.* 585 B.C.) or with his townsman and pupil Anaximander (*c.* 610–546 B.C.). For generations, it is true, various conceptions of the world's origin had been handed down in mythological lore, and a treasury of aphoristic wisdom had accumulated with the traditional customs and laws. But none of these teachings had reached a level that could be called genuinely philosophical. With the better opportunities and greater leisure for thought in the progressing culture of the city-states, however, these active traditions helped to focus the attention of inquiring Greek minds upon the problems of the nature and origin of the visible universe and upon the questions of human destiny. The efforts to answer the questions from an all-embracing viewpoint and in strictly rational rather than in mythological terms constituted the beginnings of Greek philosophy.

Thales and Anaximander. To Thales is attributed an attempt to explain the whole universe in terms of development from one basic nature, water. For him the visible universe seemed to grow from water as from a seminal plasm, and to be continually nourished by water in the manner of a living organism. His teachings are known only through a vague oral tradition preserved in writings that do not go back further than Aristotle (4th century B.C.). Of his successor Anaximander there remains but one continuous fragment. In mythological language it proclaims that all existing things come from and pass away into a basic nature, indeterminately described as ''the unlimited'' (Gr. τὸ ἄπειρον), in a process by which they ''make amends to one another for their injustice, according to the ordering of time'' (Diels, 12B 1). Detailed testimonia in later tradition ascribe to Anaximander a well-developed rational explanation of this process of becoming and perishing. The continual cosmic change takes place through an eternal and intrinsic motion, conceived apparently after the manner of living development.

Anaximenes. In a short extant fragment the philosophical successor of Anaximander, Anaximenes of Miletus (fl. *c.* 525 B.C.), located the primitive vital nature in the air that surrounded the visible universe and that sustained it and kept it together as soul does body. Anaximenes explained the changes in the universe by rarefaction and condensation. His philosophical successors, Anaxagoras of Clazomenae and Archelaus (5th century B.C.) transferred their activities to Athens. Together with Diogenes of Apollonia (5th century B.C.), these men continued or deepened Anaximenes's conception of the universe as developing from a basic vital principle conditioned in one way or another by the character of air. From Anaximenes on, there was present the notion of soul as something of an airlike nature that guides and controls a living being.

Anaxagoras. With ANAXAGORAS, the greatest of the Ionian physicists, there emerges the notion of mind (Nous) as a principle that regulates the whole cosmos and is participated by some things but not by all. For him, however, mind like soul seems to have remained on the level of a material thing in its nature and functioning. The philosophical notion of the spiritual was not yet present to be either affirmed or denied. The conception of the universe as growing from an original plasm in the manner of a living organism implied failure to encounter the problem of a first extrinsic cause such as a creator. At least in point of fact the question of an outside cause did not arise among the Ionians.

Heraclitus. The best known of all the Ionians, HERACLITUS OF EPHESUS, was classed as a ''sporadic'' philosopher because he did not fit in with the Ionian or any other philosophical succession. He is the earliest philosopher the fragments of whose works are sufficiently numerous to exhibit a thoroughly meditated philosophy. These fragments reveal a penetrating view of the unity of things in the cosmos, a dynamic unity worked out through an all-pervading common direction and maintained by a continually changing balance of opposite tensions. The moral wisdom of Heraclitus in striving to establish a common pattern of action amid the perpetually varying circumstances of human conduct is astonishingly profound and has proved abiding in its philosophical appeal.

Italy. In the latter half of the 6th century B.C. an Ionian, Pythagoras of Samos, had emigrated to the southern coast of Italy and founded there a religious and cultural organization (*see* PYTHAGORAS AND PYTHAGOREANS). The history of the Pythagoreans is very obscure. They cultivated the study of mathematics, and tried to explain the cosmos on a mathematical basis. Their efforts are rightly seen as the beginnings of the quantitative account of the physical universe. They emphasized education and moral guidance, explaining the virtues in mathematical terms. They are credited with a doctrine of transmigration of souls, and of the imprisonment of soul in body as in a tomb. In accord with the general pre-Socratic mentality, however, they do not seem to have reached any notion of the supersensible, nor to have shown any interest in seeking a creator for the cosmos.

Parmenides. Further north along the west coast of Italy, probably early in the 5th century B.C., PARMENIDES of Elea wrote hexameters giving a vivid account of the universe in terms of being. From the viewpoint of being, all things formed for him one strictly limited and continuous whole, everywhere equal in respect to their being, without origin, change, or end. Through ordinary human cognition, nevertheless, a multiple and changing cosmos is set up for men by the ever varying proportions of two basic forms, light and darkness. This may be called the world of seeming (δόξα). Parmenides's achievement began a long chain of attempts to explain things in terms of being, proceeding through different types of dialectic and culminating in the development of metaphysics as a science.

Eleatics. In the middle of the 5th century B.C. the dialectical phase was operative in the teaching of ZENO OF ELEA, whose paradoxes on motion are still controversial, and in the doctrines of Melissus of Samos. Melissus, about whose life nothing is known with certainty, seems to have applied the Eleatic dialectic of being to the unlimited basic reality as conceived by the earlier Ionians. For that reason he is classed as an Eleatic. Xenophanes of Colophon (570–478? B.C.), an Ionian rhapsodist who traveled throughout the mainland of Greece, has been regarded traditionally as the founder of the Eleatic school, though without strictly historical foundation.

Other Centers. In Sicily, EMPEDOCLES of Acragas stereotyped the four traditional Ionian opposites, hot and cold, dry and wet, into the more concrete fire, earth, air, and water. He called them the ''roots of all'' (πάντων ῥιζώματα), as though the cosmos grew from them in the fashion of living things. They became known in later tradition as the four Empedoclean elements. They were composed of ingenerate and indestructible particles, in accord with the Parmenidean doctrine that a being could not be generated or destroyed. Through mixture continually changing under the impulse of the two fundamental cosmic forces, love and strife, they were always combining and separating to form the actual universe.

Atomists. At Abdera in Thrace, Leucippus (5th century B.C.) and DEMOCRITUS gave a more profound explanation of the physical world in a doctrine known as ATOMISM. The basic particles were ''atomic'' in the sense of indivisible, and were not subject to generation or alteration or destruction. In this way they were ''being,'' and were in perpetual motion in a void that was existent yet characterized as ''nonbeing.'' They were all of the same nature, differing only in shape, position, and arrangement. By joining and separating through the perpetual cosmic motion they constituted the universe. The soul consisted of spherical atoms, which on account of their shape were most mobile, and were identified with fire and heat. Most of the 300 and more fragments attributed to Democritus, however, are concerned with moral matters. They teach an ethics in which cheerfulness, coinciding with self-sufficiency and imperturbability and well-being, is the goal of human action. This goal is attained by moderation in accordance with the mean between excess and deficiency, and is promoted by wisdom just as health is promoted by the science of medicine.

Sophists. Protagoras of Abdera (*c.* 490–420 B.C.) and Gorgias of Leontini (*c.* 480–380 B.C.), a pupil of Empedocles, were outstanding representatives of the career teachers known in the 5th century as SOPHISTS or professors of wisdom. Throughout the cities of the Greek world they taught the rhetoric that could sway public assemblies and lead to political power. The fragments that remain from Protagoras and Gorgias indicate a conception of the universe in which everything is changing and relative, as though set up by ever-changing human cognition in the fashion of Parmenides's cosmos; this provided an excellent philosophical basis for a world that could be ruled by rhetoric.

Athens. In the last half of the 5th century B.C. Athens became the center of Greek philosophical activity. SOCRATES, about whom very little detail is known except chronology and the manner of his death, exercised through his conversations a profound influence upon Athenian youth. He emphasized virtue, and taught that it consisted in knowledge. He wrote nothing, but became the central figure in a literary genre known as ''Socratic discourses.'' In these discourses various writers exploited him, using him as a mouthpiece for their own teachings. His insistence on virtue as knowledge meant, according to Aristotle's comments, that virtuous conduct had to be based upon common and abiding notions of what virtue is, notions that could be expressed in stable definitions. This was in direct opposition to the rhetorical training given by the Sophists.

Lesser Socratics. The influence of Socrates's name was spread through the writings and teachings of his disciples. A number of these such as Aristippus of Cyrene (*see* CYRENAICS), Euclides of Megara, and Antisthenes of Athens, are grouped under the designation ''Lesser Socratics.'' In this way they are distinguished from Socrates's greatest pupil, Plato. Followers of Euclides, such as Eubulides of Miletus, Diodorus Cronus, and Philo of Megara, made notable contributions to the development of logic as a science (*see* LOGIC, HISTORY OF).

Plato and Aristotle. In PLATO and ARISTOTLE Greek philosophy reached its greatest splendor. The philosophical conception of realities above the whole order of extension and time, and therefore completely immaterial, made its first appearance in Western thought. For Plato these were the Ideas, the eternal natures of things. For Aristotle they were forms separate from matter, and different from the natures of any sensible things. The Platonic Idea and the Aristotelian form provided philosophical bases for the common definition urged by Socrates, and for the scientific knowledge built upon it. Both Plato and Aristotle developed highly articulated moral doctrines that aimed to achieve the common good by virtuous action, and in which one's private good was attained in the common political good. For both philosophers the norm of virtue was the mean between excess and defect. In the teaching of Aristotle, logic and the classification of the sciences reached a form that endured for centuries. The philosophical schools that stem from Plato and Aristotle are called respectively the Academy and the Peripatos (*see* PLATONISM; ARISTOTELIANISM).

Other Schools. In Aristotle's time a movement known as Cynicism (*see* CYNICS) had been started by Diogenes of Sinope (*c.* 410–320 B.C.). It rejected Greek social conventions and advocated living in accord with the simplicity of nature. It was a type of life made possible only by rigorous ascetic training, and was offered as a shortcut to virtue and happiness. Two other widespread schools originated at Athens toward the close of the 4th century B.C., the Garden, or school of EPICURUS, and the Stoa, or school of Zeno of Citium (*see* EPICUREANISM; HEDONISM; STOICISM). Both rejected the supersensible. Further, two types of SKEPTICISM developed among the Greeks, the one taking its name from Pyrrho of Elis (*c.* 365–275 B.C.), the other from the Platonic Academy in the 3d and 2d centuries B.C. (*see* PYRRHONISM). During the first two centuries of the Christian Era the period of the Academy called ''Middle Platonism'' carried on the original Platonic traditions with the incorporation of teachings from other schools, while interest in Pythagorean doctrines resulted in a tendency called Neopythagoreanism. An eclectic school is reported (Diogenes Laërtius, *Lives* 1.21) to have selected its teachings from all the other schools (*see* ECLECTICISM). Finally, the last Greek form of Platonism, called in the 19th century NEOPLATONISM, was developed by PLOTINUS. It penetrated deeply into Patristic thought. In A.D. 529 the schools at Athens were closed by Justinian and original movements in Greek philosophy came to an end.

Influence on Christian Thought. Philosophy was consistently looked upon as a way of life by the Greeks. Accordingly it was regarded by St. Paul (Col 2.8) as opposed to the new and divinely inspired way of life, Christianity. Nevertheless the influence especially of Stoic and Neoplatonic philosophy soon made itself felt in the vocabulary and external structure of Christian thinking, and in the 13th century direct contact with the works of Aristotle made a profound and lasting impression on the molds of Christian teaching. Acquaintance with Greek philosophy is therefore necessary to understand the written tradition of Christian thought. In this contact, however, Christian genius proved equal to the task of profiting by Greek intellectual methods without imbibing the accompanying pagan doctrines. The revival of scholastic methods in Catholic theology and philosophy during the late 19th and the 20th centuries has given renewed importance to Greek philosophy as an indispensable tool for the study and presentation of Christian doctrine on an intellectual basis.

See Also: PHILOSOPHY, HISTORY OF; GREEK PHILOSOPHY (RELIGIOUS ASPECTS); GREEK RELIGION.

Bibliography: The only general history of Greek philosophy remaining from ancient times is DIOGENES LAËRTIUS, *Lives of Eminent Philosophers,* tr. R. D. HICKS, 2 v. (*Loeb Classical Library*; New York 1925, reprint Cambridge, Mass. 1950). The fragments of the pre-Socratics are edited in H. DIELS, *Die Fragmente der Vorsokratiker: Griechisch und Deutsch,* ed. W. KRANZ, 3 v. (8th ed. Berlin 1956), and those of the early Stoics by H. F. VON ARNIM, *Stoicorum veterum fragmenta,* 4 v. (Leipzig 1903–24). The best established modern history of Greek philosophy is E. ZELLER, *Die Philosophie der Griechen,* 3 v. in 6 (5th–7th ed. Leipzig 1920–23). In English, a comprehensive history was undertaken by W. K. C. GUTHRIE, *A History of Greek Philosophy,* of which the first volume (Cambridge, England) was published in 1962. Shorter surveys are numerous, e.g.: E. C. COPLESTON, *Greece and Rome,* v. 1 of *A History of Philosophy* (Westminster, Md. 1946–). A. H. ARMSTRONG, *An Introduction to Ancient Philosophy* (3d ed. London 1957). I. C. BRADY, *A History of Ancient Philosophy* (Milwaukee 1959). J. OWENS, *A History of Ancient Western Philosophy* (New York 1959). On the significance of Greek philosophy, see C. J. DE VOGEL, ''What Philosophy Meant to the Greeks,'' *International Philosophical Quarterly* 1 (1961) 35–37. *Phronesis* (1955–), a journal appearing twice a year, is dedicated largely to Greek philosophy. Studies in the field are listed in the Louvain quarterly *Répertoire Bibliographique de la Philosophile,* ''Antiquité Grecque et Romaine'' section.

[J. OWENS]

GREEK PHILOSOPHY (RELIGIOUS ASPECTS)

Two viewpoints respecting philosophy are in evidence from the 5th century B.C. to the end of antiquity. On the one hand, philosophy was regarded as a subject in higher education that should receive the attention of students completing their course in rhetoric and interested, to some extent at least, in metaphysical and ethical questions. The tenets of the various philosophical schools were examined in a sterile manner, and in the end many students took refuge in skepticism. For the majority of the educated class, philosophy remained a fashionable subject for discussion rather than a really vital one affecting their lives and conduct. The Emperor Marcus Aurelius undoubtedly wished to develop a more serious attitude toward philosophy when in A.D. 176 he established four chairs of philosophy at Athens, thus giving official recognition and support to the teaching of Platonism, Aristotelianism, Stoicism, and Epicureanism.

On the other hand, philosophers themselves, beginning with Socrates and Plato, had insisted that philosophy should be concerned with all aspects of life if it was to form men useful to the state and capable of living a happy life, to say nothing of earning the rewards of an existence beyond the grave (cf. Plato, *Republic* 497C–498C). This text alone suffices to suggest that Greek philosophy presented religious aspects during its history.

Main Religious Aspects. The religious aspects of Greek philosophy can be illustrated by four general views: 1. The philosopher as superior being, He can be considered a divine messenger and a miracle worker. His death can resemble that of a martyr, and he can become the object of worship as a hero or god. 2. The philosopher as teacher and missionary. The philosopher conforms his life to his principles, separating himself from the world and its possessions. He goes about preaching his doctrine and tries to convert others. He may become even a founder or member of a kind of pagan monastic community. 3. Philosophy as a school for life. Among intellectuals, especially, it often held the place occupied by religion in modern times. Conversion to philosophy often signified a radical change in values and the beginning of a new existence. 4. Philosophy as an explanation of the world and a way of salvation. It offered its adherents a clear and certain explanation of the world. For some centuries philosophers were the only men who pondered over the composition of the universe and its laws. At times it taught a way of salvation, in rivalry with or parallel to that presented by religions. The philosopher was a physician who took care of souls, and he was sometimes capable of achieving a mystical union with God.

It must be understood, however, that these different aspects are not found in all periods and at the same time in all the philosophical systems. They evolved gradually, and it is important to be precise with respect to the date at which any particular philosophy is being studied. However, it is not absolutely necessary to examine the teaching of each sect in detail throughout its history for two reasons. On the one hand, complex reactions of one system on another entailed syncretism respecting certain points of doctrine; and on the other, in the case of each sect, there were periods of decline followed by periods of renewed vitality.

Important Historical Facts. In the perspective of primary concern to this article, four historical facts must be explained and emphasized:

Major Interest in Moral Questions. From the time of SOCRATES, there was a current that, according to Cicero, ''forced the descent of philosophy from heaven to earth'' (Cicero, *Tusc. disp.* 5.4.10) or, in other words, assured the priority of moral questions over metaphysical problems. This current was the chief factor in the success of Stoicism in the Roman world to the end of the second century A.D. The moralists of the Roman period were not really attached to any precise system. The maxim''hidden life'' was adopted with enthusiasm by the Platonists and the Pythagoreans, and, although it was Epicurean, the Platonists attributed it to Pythagoras. The inscribing of Epicurean thoughts on tombstones became a common custom. Seneca admired the counsels of Epicurus as much as those of the Stoics, and Epictetus used to warn his disciples not to devote too much study to Stoic logic and physics, as he considered these subjects useless for the improvement of morals. Marcus Aurelius did not think that moral precepts should be changed according to one's belief in Providence or atoms, and Cicero's *De officiis* does not contain a word on Stoic physics. Thus, the ideal of human wisdom, divested of all social, political, or metaphysical complications, exercised a great influence not only on thinkers in the last period of antiquity, Christian as well as pagan, but also on those in the modern world, for Descartes returns repeatedly to the Stoic theme of philosophical resignation.

Common Agreement on World and World Order. In the first centuries A.D., philosophical and religious systems, however diverse, were in accord in their view of the world and the order of its parts. The universe was an organized whole, in which each part had its place as in a living organism; the universe was conceived of as finite and harmoniously arranged, a worthy object of religious contemplation, a model of order and regularity, to which all have the duty to conform their conduct. This vision of the universe was first presented by Plato in his *Timaeus,* and was accepted by Aristotle, who proclaimed the eternity of the world. The Stoics emphasized the living character of the universe, maintaining that it was inhabited by a soul that extended into all its parts. The doctrine of universal sympathy made the parts of this universe members, as it were, of the same body, and thus gave the Stoics a foundation for their astrological predictions and other forms of divination. Finally, Plotinus made a synthesis of earlier systems. He excluded the demiurge, but he did not exclude the intelligible model. He retained the world soul, but he was at pains to show that this soul was not an absolute principle, and he put the transcendence of the Aristotelian intellect above the immanent soul of the Stoics. [See J. Moreau, *L'Idée d'univers dans la pensée antique* (Turin 1953)].

Mystic Element in Pagan Philosophy. At the beginning of the Christian era, there was present, in the very heart of Hellenism, a body of ideas that can be called mystical. There are echoes of them in Cicero, Seneca, Plutarch, and Philo, and, among modern scholars, the name of Posidonius long sufficed to explain them. P. Boyancé has shown, however, that, while this current was opposed to the clearest teaching in the systems dominating thought after Aristotle, it had its roots in an idea found in philosophy itself, an idea connected with the social organization among the guilds of the Muses. The conception of music as having power to free and purify, a concept fundamentally ancient and Greek, played an essential role in the appearance of mystical ideas [see P. Boyancé, *Le Culte des Muses chez les philosophes grecs* (Paris 1937)].

Vogue of Religion in Second Century. In the 2d century A.D., the vogue for religion was evidenced at all levels of culture. The masses gave themselves over to Oriental and Egyptian cults and embraced magic with enthusiasm. Philosophers found in Plato the strongest encouragement to fuse philosophy and religion, so that the religious spirit among educated people in this period was colored by Platonism—a Platonism, it must be admitted, that was rather questionable and spiritless. In the literature of the age, texts repeatedly proclaim the identity of religion and philosophy. For Maximus of Tyre (A.D. 125–185), philosophy is man's sole faculty for prayer (*Disc.* 5.8). According to Apuleius, in commenting upon Plato (*De Platone* 2.7; 2.23), justice, queen of the virtues, is often identified with holiness, and the last word of wisdom is ''Follow the footsteps of God.'' See M. Caster, *Lucien et la pensée religieuse de son temps* (Paris 1937). All Greek philosophy was hardly summed up in Neoplatonism, but that school did finally bring together all the religious forces of paganism, and it did last as long as ancient Greek culture itself, i.e., down to the 6th century.

Philosopher as a Superior Being

Veneration of the philosopher as a superior being and his deification are apparent in several schools. The best-known examples are Pythagoras, Socrates, and Plato.

Deification of Pythagoras. from the age of Aristotle, Pythagoras was regarded as a miracle worker who became renowned for numerous prodigies and prophecies (Aristotle, *Rhetoric* 1398b). It may be surmised that he was honored as a hero. In any event, the Pythagoreans played an important role in the development of hero worship (Boyancé, *op. cit.,* 223–247). According to Aristoxenus (4th century B.C.), they thought of heroes as disembodied souls and as intermediaries between God and mortals. From the end of the Roman Republic, study of astral eschatology by intellectuals increased (see Cicero's *Dream of Scipio*), and the subject was influencing public opinion. The name of Pythagoras was connected with that of the Pythian Apollo, and this alone was enough to reveal his divine mission and put into relief the Apollonian origins of his teachings (Diogenes Laertius, *Vita Pyth.* 8.21). His disciples called him divine, and, while not wishing to make him a god in the strict sense, they regarded him as belonging to an intermediate category between the divine and the human Aristotle, *Fragments* 187).

By the 1st century B.C. there was no longer any doubt about the divinity of Pythagoras, and his house at Metapontum (in Sicily) had become a temple in which he was worshiped (see Pompeius Trogus *ap.* Just. 20.4.17–18). His legend was continually enriched, and its progress can be easily traced from Heraclides Ponticus (*c.* 390–310 B.C.) to PORPHYRY and Iamblichus. The *Life of Pythagoras* by Iamblichus, followed by the detailed account of the subject's virtues, inaugurated a type of biography that was destined to become a vogue (see Marinus's *Vita Procli*, 5th–6th centuries). The Pythagoreans claimed they had a supernatural knowledge (*gnosis*) and had no need of proof beyond the word of the master; ''He said it'' (αὐτὸς ἔφα), was an affirmation that could not be questioned (see Cicero, *Nat. deor.* 1.5.10).

Among the later Pythagoreans, special mention should be made of P. Nigidius Figulus, a friend of Cicero, who devoted himself to astrology and assumed a prophetic role, and Apollonius of Tyana, the famous miracle worker and seer. Both gloried in being Pythagoreans and prided themselves on their divinely inspired prophecies.

Religious Veneration of Socrates, Plato, and Others. Pythagoreanism undoubtedly should be regarded as a religion supported by philosophy rather than a religious philosophy proper. But similar phenomena are found in Platonism.

Socrates. From the day that the oracle at Delphi told Chaerephon that Socrates was the wisest of men, Socrates began to question his fellow citizens about the principles governing their conduct; he considered this inquiry a mission assigned to him by the god at Delphi. He was aware of signs that warned him against certain actions (Plato, *Apol.* 31 A–D) and could experience a kind of ecstasy (cf. Plato, *Symp.* 175 A–B). All antiquity venerated Socrates almost as a divine being.

Plato. Plato in turn was honored as a hero, doubtless not long after the eulogy delivered by Speusippus. Speusippus had related in his *Life of Plato* that wise men from the Orient had built an altar to the master. This homage was connected with the number of years in Plato's life, namely, 81, the Apollonian number obtained by multiplying the number of the Muses (9) by itself. Legends at once arose on the Apollonian birth of Plato, and, thus, like Pythagoras, he was deified after his death.

Epicurus. Even the most irreligious of the philosophers adored their founder as a god. Undoubtedly, as Boyancé assumed (*op. cit.*), the Epicurean school remained a religious society, and Epicurus became the object of a formal cult in both Greece and Rome. Epicurus had provided by will for annual commemorations of his birth, and four centuries later, according to Pliny the Elder, they were still being celebrated (Pliny, *Hist. nat.* 35.2.5). Although the Epicureans did not believe in the survival of the soul, they offered to it the customary sacrifices. They even venerated the physical features of Epicurus, and, again according to Pliny, they had images of him in their bedrooms and carried his effigy on the stones of their rings. This veneration really had a very precise spiritual meaning, for Epicurus had counseled his disciples: ''Act always as if Epicurus were looking at you.''

Other Examples. These are the most important examples, but there are many others. For Cercidas, Diogenes the Cynic (*c.* 400–329 B.C.), 100 years after his death, was a celestial being. Epictetus (*c.* A.D. 55–*c.* 135) became the object of a cult. CELSUS believed that Orpheus, Anaxarchus, and Epictetus were men truly worthy of homage. The Carpocratians, a Gnostic sect, kept images of Christ beside those of Pythagoras, Plato, and Aristotle (see Irenaeus, *Adversus haereses* 1.20.4). Porphyry did not hesitate to attribute a thaumaturgic power to Plotinus, stating that he was aided by a demon (*Vit. Plot.* 10). Iamblichus, finally, is represented as one inspired, living among the gods, causing spirits to appear in fountains, and giving rise to the belief that when he prayed his garments took on a beautiful gold color, and his body was raised 10 cubits above the ground. In short, he was a wonder-worker (see Eunapius, *Vit. soph.* 458–).

All the schools are not represented, but Pythagoreanism, Platonism, Epicureanism, and Neoplatonism furnish the chief witnesses. Two schools, in particular, were more concerned with the exact sciences than with religion, namely the Skeptics and the Peripatetics. The Skeptics especially were accused of ruining thought and morality. The Emperor Julian forbade his priests to read Sextus Empiricus, the famous Skeptic philosopher of the 2d century A.D. The school of Aristotle studied nature objectively and avoided the temptation of mixing magic with the natural sciences.

Philosopher as Teacher and Missionary

The pagan priest did not preach. However, philosophers, beginning with Pythagoras, taught or preached their doctrines, especially to their followers or disciples.

Pythagoras and Plato. Despite the skepticism of A. J. Festugière [''Sur une nouvelle édition de la Vita Pythagorica de Jamblique,'' *Revue des études greques* 50 (1937) 470–494], Iamblichus's description of the ''rule'' of the Pythagorean community would seem to be substantially reliable. The group of converts around T. Statilius Taurus, by whose order the Pythagorean basilica at Rome was built, deserves special mention. See J. Carcopino, *La Basilique pythagoricienne de la Porte Majeure* (Paris 1927). Plato conducted his school in the gardens of the Academy at Athens and admitted only selected listeners. So far as is definitely known, he was the first philosopher to attempt to frame political constitutions and to become an advisor to princes. Aristotle became the tutor of Alexander the Great, and Alexander's successors in the Hellenistic kingdoms had philosophers as consultants or advisors. See, e.g., F. Ollier, ''Le philosophe stoïcien Sphaeros et l'oeuvre réformatrice des rois de Sparte Agis et Cléomène,'' *Revue des études grecques* 49 (1936) 536–570.

Plotinus, Porphyry, Iamblichus. Plotinus, the founder of Neoplatonism, experienced a revelation while listening to Ammonius Saccas, and became a convert to philosophy. He followed the lectures of his master for 11 years and agreed to keep the teachings secret (Porphyry, *Vit. Plot.* 3)—a proof that they were considered to be concerned with the whole spiritual life. Plotinus attracted a number of enthusiastic disciples, among them Amelius, who followed his instruction for 24 years, and Porphyry, who introduced beginners to the study of logic and wrote numerous commentaries on Plato and Aristotle. Plotinus encouraged his disciples to ask questions and conducted his lectures in an informal and friendly manner.

Iamblichus, according to Eunapius (*Vit. soph.* 455), had a large following and exercised a kind of fascination on his hearers. That he must have played the role of a director of souls is indicated in the extracts from his moral epistles preserved in Stobaeus. One of his correspondents compares him to Aesculapius; he was regarded as a savior-god of Hellenism in peril. See J. Bidez; ''Le philosophe Jamblique et son école,'' *Revue des études grecques* 32 (1919) 29–40.

Cynics. Socrates, as it has been noted, carried out his apostolate in a quite different fashion from those already mentioned. In this respect, the true successors of Socrates were the Cynics, with Diogenes as their ideal type. They formed a part of the street scene. Throughout antiquity they were seen traveling about, in short mantles, with long hair and beards, barefoot, with staff in hand and knapsacks on their backs. Everyone heard their simple talks interspersed with witticisms and jokes, and witnessed their capricious and histrionic conduct. They enriched the public squares with their character sketches and sonorous diatribes. St. Augustine mentions them along with the Platonists and Pythagoreans as the sole survivors of paganism. From the outset they created a tradition of public preaching, which had an influence on a famous New Testament incident: when the philosophers heard St. Paul debating in the synagogue, they brought him to the Areopagus so that he could explain his ideas publicly.

Undoubtedly there were many charlatans among the Cynics; however, their unselfishness, their call to human brotherhood, and their promise of a better future made a deep impression. One of the greatest converts was the famous orator Dion Chrysostom (*c.* A.D. 40-after 112). He regarded himself as a vigilant physician of souls, and he fulfilled his mission with evident sincerity. His Cynicism was closely related to Stoicism. Cf. L. F. François, *Essai sur Dion Chrysostome, philosophe et moraliste cynique et stoïcien* (Paris 1921).

Stoics. Stoicism lasted at least five centuries (from the 3d century B.C. to the end of the 2d century A.D.), but only late Stoicism, represented especially by Seneca, Epictetus, and Marcus Aurelius, is well known through complete extant writings. That was the age also when Stoicism was concerned almost exclusively with preaching and moral meditation. The Stoic philosopher became a spiritual director. For a long time at Rome, private instruction was given to the sons of great houses by a philosopher in residence, and leading statesmen regularly attached such persons to themselves as friends and counselors. Let it suffice to mention as examples: the association of Metrodorus with Aemilius Paulus, of C. Blossius with Tiberius Gracchus, of Panaetius of Rhodes with P. Scipio, of Athenodorus of Tarsus with Cato of Utica, of the Stoic Diodotus with Cicero, of Athenodorus and Theon with Augustus, and later, of Rusticus with Marcus Aurelius.

Yet the real center of Stoicism in the 1st century A.D. was the family. Tacitus was at his best in describing the death scene of Thrasea Paetus, who, after conversing with friends and relatives in his gardens, withdrew to his bedchamber, opened his veins, made a libation with his blood to Jupiter the Liberator, and died with his eyes fixed on the Cynic Demetrius (Tacitus, *Ann.* 16.34–35). Seneca did not limit his activity to a single family, but became the guide of Paulinus, Marcellinus, Serenus and Lucilius. He made the letter the medium of psychological and moral consultation, and he gave advice in the manner of a private physician (see Seneca, *Epistles* 22.1). His contemporary, Cornutus, played a similar role, and the poet Persius has described this beloved master [Sat. 3.66–; 5.34–44; see R. Chevallier, ''Le Milieu stoïcien à Rome au premier siècle après Jésus-Christ,'' *Lettres d' humanité* 19 (1960) 534–562].

Epicureanism. Epicurus founded a kind of community fired with a great urge to win souls, and his influence spread not only over Greece and Italy but even over barbarian lands (see Cicero, *De fin.* 2.15.49). He addressed himself to both intellectuals and the masses, and included women and slaves among his disciples. As the Christian Lactantius said many centuries later, he invited all men to accept his philosophy (*Div. inst.* 3.25.4). The famous 2d-century inscription of Diogenes of Oenoanda in Asia Minor, with its detailed presentation of Epicurean principles, gives an excellent idea of the form and spirit of Epicurean propaganda. [See *Paulys Realenzyklopädie der Klassischen Altertumwissenschaft*, Suppl. 5 (1931) 153–170].

The Epicurean school must have had a formal organization somewhat like that of a monastic order, with novices subject to the counsels of the older and more advanced members. See M. N. De Witt, ''Organization and Procedure in Epicurean Groups,'' *Classical Philology* 31 (1936) 205–211. This life in common had an important educational value that Seneca emphasized by saying that this *contubernium* had made great men out of the disciples of Epicurus (*Epistles* 6.6.). Epicureanism sought to give peace to the soul by overcoming certain fears, especially that of death, and found no better means than fostering friendship. It had a long life, and its continued influence in their time provoked the repeated attacks of Plutarch and Galen. At the beginning of the 4th century, Dionysius, Bishop of Alexandria, still considered it necessary to refute Epicurus in a book, *On Nature.* The Emperor Julian, however, states that by the middle of that century the sect had died out.

Philosophy as a School for Life

In the Imperial age all the philosophies more or less agreed on the practical answers to apply to the problems of existence. From the moment a man became a philosopher he knew that he must bear pain, scorn death, be patient with sickness, keep an untroubled soul, and content himself with the happiness achieved through a virtuous life. These five rules are summarized, for example, in the five books of Cicero's *Tusculans.* About 140 B.C., the Stoic Panaetius wrote a treatise *On Duty.* This treatise inspired Cicero in the first two books of his *De Officiis;* and Cicero's work, in turn, inspired St. Ambrose to write a Christian treatise under the same title.

Epicureans. In spite of widespread rumors that the Epicureans were debauched, Epicureanism actually required an exacting morality. The peace that they offered could be achieved only by imposing a strict discipline over physical desires, and by rejecting all that was neither natural nor necessary. A man could turn to Epicureanism if he were seeking to free himself from the burden of human miseries. Epicurus deserves recognition for developing a fine sense of interior contemplation and harmony within the soul. It is against this background that the conversions—sometimes transitory—of men like Maecenas, Horace, or Vergil, can be explained. [See P. Boyancé, ''L'Épicurisme dans la société et la littérature romaines,'' *Lettres d'humanité,* 19 (1960) 499–516].

Cynics. The Cynic sect experienced a revival in the 1st century, probably as a reaction against the luxury of Rome and political oppression. Cynicism refused to take seriously either family or state conventions. In social relations this attitude was demonstrated by their outspokenness; they had to be self-sufficient and unencumbered with material goods. The wise man lived by reason, and knew no other happiness than its realization through hard effort. Above all, Cynicism despised the body. Although their sect was founded on pride in human strength, the Cynics had a strong feeling of the baseness of man under the sway of his body, and an equally strong feeling that happiness was possible for the man who was able to make his soul prevail. A distinguishing feature of their doctrine was its conciseness. Their philosophy of life was so simplified that their ideal could be realized by a man in his lifetime.

Stoics. Stoicism was distinguished from Cynicism, from which it derived, by its scientific work; when this work passed into its second plane of interest, the Cynic base reappeared. Moreover, the attitude of the Stoic wise man had changed: pride, and the paradoxical proclamations concerning the royalty of the wise man, had given place to a certain humility. The wise man must neither hurt nor scandalize people. Panaetius had repeatedly advised his followers to be polite; the Stoic must not be insulting, pedantic, or dirty (Epictetus, *Discourses* 3.2.89). For Epictetus, the origin of philosophy was the awareness of human misery and the passionate desire to overcome it. Yet, in spite of all, Stoicism retained its taste for a certain pedantry, tortuous reasoning, and detailed interrogations.

Although undeniably eclectic, the teaching of the Stoics remained rigid in its morality and seems to have ignored true charity; egotism and pride were essential elements. The Stoic ethic achieved its end in mysticism by a resigned acceptance of natural laws and submission to destiny. The same was later true of the Neoplatonists.

Philosophical Resignation and Courage. The philosophers quite often showed examples of resignation and courage in their personal lives. Socrates, the first martyr to wisdom, was a perfect model of courage before death, furnishing antiquity with an almost inexhaustible theme. Philosophy was often looked on with suspicion and its practitioners exiled or put to death. About the year A.D. 65 the Stoics Musonius Rufus and Cornutus were exiled; in 71, under Vespasian, all philosophers were banished from Rome; in 85, Domitian had Maternus, Rusticus Arulinus, and Herennius Senecio executed (Dion Cassius, *Hist. Rom.* 66.12–19; 67.13). In 93, the same emperor again banished the philosophers from Italy. Epictetus thereupon retired to Epirus and opened a school at Nicopolis. There were probably religious motives behind the banishment, as the Stoics appeared to violate the official religion. It was also possible to confuse their doctrine with certain foreign cults. An Oriental seer, e.g., the Egyptian Chaeremon, proclaimed himself a Stoic (Martial 11.57).

Even under the worst emperors, philosophers stood for the affirmation of virtue and taught people how to die gracefully. The death of Thrasea Paetus has already been mentioned. Seneca reports the peaceful death of Julius Canus (*Dialogues* 9.14.7–9), and the example of Rubellius Plautus can be added. One of his freedmen advised him to resist the order to die sent by Nero, but the philosophers Coeranus and Musonius persuaded him to prefer death (Tacitus, *Ann.* 14.58–9). Seneca himself died nobly (*ibid.* 15.62–3). Epictetus, while a slave, suffered without complaining. There should be no cause for wonder at the declaration of Marcus Aurelius that philosophy is necessary to accept death (*Med.* 12.5).

Ethics was based on a psychological analysis, which, for example, creates the charm of Seneca's *Letters to Lucilius.* Among all philosophers the practice of asceticism is evident. E. Bréhier noticed, even in Plotinus, what he called alarming symptoms of fatigue and nervous weariness [*Plotinus: Ennéades* (2d ed. Paris 1954) 1.8]. When Porphyry knew Plotinus, bad eating habits, intellectual overwork, and lack of sleep had impaired his health. ''A man must reduce and weaken his body . . . he will even want to have the experience of suffering'' (*Ennead* 1.4.14). This sentence, taken from one of the last writings of Plotinus, goes beyond Stoic indifference because it actually reaches the point of desiring pain. See L. Robin, *La Morale antique* (Paris 1938).

Explanation of the World and Way of Salvation

Even after Socrates had given philosophy the essential goal of knowing man's inner nature, and positive sciences had developed outside philosophy, philosophers continued to search for the inner nature of things. Some who, it seems, like the physicians, must have remained detached from metaphysical speculation more than others, often continued to devote themselves more or less to philosophy. The Methodist School, for example, claimed that it followed Zeno. The extraordinary and complex activity of Apuleius shows clearly the compromises that continued to befall science. This is perhaps one of the reasons that can be given for the astonishing fact that the Romans contributed practically nothing to ancient science. Science and philosophy were borne along on the mystical current that was the chief phenomenon of the 2d century A.D. Men were more preoccupied with their salvation than with scientific knowledge of things; they sought only an explanation of the world with a view toward salvation and decided to use the least rational means to achieve the saving vision. This grave deterioration of Greek thought was occasioned by the development of the mystery religions and Oriental cults.

Stoics. Religious feeling among the Stoics came from a rational conception of the universe. They achieved the paradox of teaching a religious philosophy combined with materialism. In fact, this philosophy became entirely religious when the later Stoics spoke of God as a personal being, as Providence. Zeno of Citium was a pantheist and a materialist; to him the world and God were one. God, who is fire, was the active element in the world, the rational and organizing force. From him emanated the gods of the stars, the divine forces of nature, heroes, and even man's reason. Stoicism thus furnished a material explanation of polytheism. Since the gods originated in the manner indicated, they were not eternal, and would be reabsorbed into the Whole at the time of the world conflagration. Stoicism kept the spiritual life absolutely separate from any religious interference. The purpose of man, they believed, was to live in conformity with nature, to accept fate, and to live according to reason as manifested by nature, and through its impetus, which is virtue. See A. Jagu, *Zénon de Cittium* (Paris 1946).

Consequently, when the distinction between soul and body was sharpened by philosophers like Epictetus, ancient monistic materialism was practically at an end. The germ of dualism, which Posidonius had introduced, began to develop; and the mystic tendency, to assert itself. The soul, feeling itself exiled in the body, sought to rejoin the divinity of which it was a spark. Stoicism thus became colored by Platonism and Pythagoreanism. Marcus Aurelius, through his bent for contemplation, was on the way to achieving Neoplatonic ecstasy.

The soul of the Stoic was sustained by the conviction that God loved it and watched over it, that He had created the world for man, and that His providence was perpetually concerned with the world. All this was a bold development and interpretation of ancient fatalism. The messengers of Providence were spirits, as were the gods of the popular legends. By adoring them with proper understanding, the Stoic rendered homage to God; the wise man was thus a sort of priest.

M. Spanneut has shown the influence of Stoicism among the Fathers of the Church [*Le Stoïcisme des Pères de l'Église de Clément de Rome à Clément d'Alexandrie,* (Paris 1957)]. Even without considering the purely moral aspects of Stoic influence, such as the points on which there was general agreement among the sects (cosmology has been mentioned) and the clearly related influence of Neoplatonism, the Stoic influence appears to have been profound. In their theodicy, the Fathers owe the idea of an intimate link between God and the world to the Stoics. In physics, they appreciated the monism of the early Stoics, and consequently became receptive to the idea of a universal kinship and a cosmic sympathy among all things. The most intellectual among them took the trouble to read Soranus or Musonius for themselves, and then used their ideas, incidentally, without mentioning their names.

Syncretism in Various Philosophies. In the syncretism made by the Romans, Stoicism and Epicureanism were only in conflict with each other as religious systems. Epicureanism recognized the official cults, but only as social conventions. Cynicism, for its part, was not interested in the afterlife. It was opposed to polytheism and to the various cults, and scorned oracles because they denied man's freedom. The Peripatetics merged Providence strictly with the order of the universe. Alexander of Aphrodisias declared that Providence, as generally understood, would be incompatible with the ideas of God and the world, for man would become the end and God the means (*De fato* 30). He admitted divination, but the gods left men free to use their oracles or not as they chose (*ibid.* 31). He believed in prayer and magic, but remained fully aware of the majesty of natural laws (*ibid.* 16–17).

Revival of Mystic Aspect of Platonism. The Neoplatonists brought out the mystic side of Plato's doctrine, a Plato seeking, like Plotinus, the foundation of the hierarchy of realities in the intuition of pure being (the Good or the One). A number of texts support this phase of Plato's thought, and the Neoplatonists were the first to make use of them. Plato was unable to speak of the knowledge of the supreme reality without employing the terminology of the mysteries. For instance, in the *Symposium,* he speaks of the unexpected and immediate knowledge that makes the complete ascent toward the beautiful and that in the *Republic* attains, in the good, the common cause of the thought and of the realities that it knows. But for Plotinus, intuition of the first cause does not call for intuition of the intelligible world, as if the first were necessarily to draw enrichment from the second. On the contrary, intuition of the intelligible world can arise only through a marked change in conditions. Far from suggesting the intuition of the world of which it is the first cause, the vision of the One causes the man who attains it to forget all else, including himself. Neoplatonism developed out of Platonism when mystical contemplation had been isolated from progressive dialectic, and when this dialectic had become "procession."

The dialectic of Plato perceived in the tangible world deficiencies that did not meet the requirements of the intelligible. The multiplicity of changeable things was organized into species, each with a realizable model, which could be explained only through entities outside itself. These entities were forms that themselves constituted an ordered multiplicity, their order being explained by a higher unity, the form of the Good. In the famous text of the *Republic* (508b–), Plato asserted that the Good, the sun of the intelligible world, was at once producer of knowledge and of being (the same Good that was the object of mystical contact); however, he never developed this theory further.

On the other hand, the constructions that he erects in the *Philebus,* in the *Sophist,* or in the *Timaeus* take their point of departure below the Good in a multiplicity of elements; such as the five types in the *Sophist,* the four species of being in the *Philebus,* or the geometrical and arithmetic schemata in the *Timaeus.* Between the point of arrival in the ascent, the One or the Good, and the point of departure in the descent, the multiplicity of the elements of being, there is a hiatus; so much so that, in Plato, the contemplative life and scientific knowledge remained detached from each other. In other words, there was a mystic Plato and a scientist Plato.

Neo-Pythagoreanism and Its Influence. In the 2d century A.D. the mystic trend of Platonism was subjected to strong contamination, mainly from Pythagoreanism. The best known of its representatives mixed the two doctrines without scruple. Numenius (*c.* A.D. 150–200) considered himself a Pythagorean and extolled the union of Pythagoras and Plato as heirs to the wisdom of the Brahmans, the Egyptians, and Moses. Wishing to keep the idea of God pure, they removed the divinity as far as possible from the material world, although that same divinity, at the time of its creation, had arranged the world by means of number-ideas. Here Pythagorean speculations revealed themselves. This pronounced dualism between God and the world required spirit intermediaries; it saw in the soul a divine particle, and in the body an evil spirit. Through asceticism, the purification of the body and return to God could be hastened. There was a marked development in the role of spirits or demons in Pythagoreanism, a fact that confirms the extent to which its thought was imbued with religious and other influences from the East. Pythagorean monotheism had become very complaisant. The true god, according to Apollonius of Tyana (cf. Eusebius, *Praep. evang.* 4.13), could be honored only by an uplifting of the soul; but lesser gods were quite satisfied with ceremonies. Furthermore, since most mythological legends had an allegorical meaning [see J. Pépin, *Mythe et allégorie: Les Origines grecques et les contestations judéo-chrétiennes* (Paris 1958)], the Pythagoreans carefully refrained from criticizing them. The basis of their thought was that man was a god in power. The doctrine of μετενσωμάτωσις, or transmigration, was traditional with the Pythagoreans.

Plotinus and Neoplatonism. The change that Plotinus made in Platonism had connections with Gnostic speculations. Plotinus did not reject hypostases or lower steps of divinity, nor allegorical myths; nor did he exclude the names or the myths of polytheism. The One could be called Uranus, the Intelligence, Cronus, and the Soul of the World, Zeus. But both his metaphysics and his conception of the inner life were original. He believed that the life of suprasensible principles, the One, Intelligence, the Soul, was independent of the sensible world. All teaching suspected of assigning human feeling or attributes to these divine beings was rejected. Plotinus gave no place to astrology, although he did not deny the influence of the stars. He showed the magicians and the astrologers that their techniques could succeed only in the sensible world, which was subject to determinism. It was not right that divine being should depart from its proper character. Plotinus likewise condemned the Gnostic theory of salvation (*Ennead.* 2.9; 2.3). Man should not wait for God to bend down to him; rather, man should ascend to God. On the other hand, it is not by freeing oneself from nature, but by uniting with it, that the soul can rise above material things. The inner life above all consists in coming out of itself. It is not the life of an individual soul that is isolated, but the innermost life of all things. The peak of the inner life is complete ecstasy, a union with the One, in which the feeling of unity alone persists, without any further distraction. [See M. de Gandillac, *La Sagesse de Plotin* (Paris 1952)].

An episode related by Porphyry is very instructive in this regard. When Amelius wanted to lead Plotinus to the sacrifices that formed a part of the ceremonies for the new moon, he received this answer: "It is for the gods to come to me, not for me to go to them" (*Vit. Plot.* 10). This is not really in contradiction to what has just been said, but it shows the gap that separated Plotinus from his disciples and that widened further with Iamblichus.

Before the time of Iamblichus (*c.* A.D. 250–*c.* 325) the Chaldean oracles—a sort of higher form of magic—was considered only as a second-rank instrument of initiation. See S. Eitrem, "La Théurgie chez les néoplatoniciens et dans les papyrus magiques," *Symbolae Osloenses* 22 (1942) 49–79. Iamblichus was the first to raise this theurgy to the point of regarding it as the true means of bringing souls to God. See J. Bidez, "Le Philosophe Jamblique et son école," *Revue des études grecques* 32 (1919) 29–40. Bidez supposed that the Neoplatonists had organized genuine mysteries, but this is a hypothesis only. There is no solid reason for believing that the hymns of Proclus (*c.* A.D. 410–484) served any other purpose than to furnish intellectual entertainment at the meetings of the school. In any case, from this time on, philosophy is completely merged with some form of religion. The African Martianus Capella (early 5th century A.D.) in his *Marriage of Mercury with Philology* described the apotheosis of mystical knowledge, and reconstituted beneath "the Abyss of the Father" a whole pantheon of gods presiding over the intellectual world: a triad, seven astral divinities, a Virgin-Fountain, powers "beyond," the Flower of Fire, and Primordial Truth. All this is done as if polytheism were going to be reintroduced into the framework of monotheism.

See Also: CYNICS; EPICTETUS; EPICUREANISM; GREEK PHILOSOPHY; NEOPLATONISM; NEO-PYTHAGOREANISM; PLATO; PLATONISM; PLOTINUS; STOICISM.

Bibliography: H. I. MARROU, *A History of Education in Antiquity,* tr. G. LAMB (New York 1956) 206–216. A. D. NOCK, *Conversion: The Old and the New in Religion from Alexander the Great to Augustine of Hippo* (New York 1933). G. BARDY, *La Conversion au christianisme durant les premiers siècles* (Paris 1949) 46–649. P. AUBIN, *Le Problème de la "conversion": Étude sur un terme commun à l'hellénisme et au christianisme des trois premiers siècles* (Paris 1963). A. E. TAYLOR, *Plato: The Man and His Work* (6th ed. London 1949; reprinted 1955). M. POHLENZ, *Die Stoa: Geschichte einer geistigen Bewegung,* 2 v. (2d ed. Göttingen 1955). A. JAGU and M. SPANNEUT, *Dictionnaire de spiritualité ascétique et mystique*, ed. M. VILLER et al. (Paris 1932–) 4.1:822–849. N. W. DE WITT, *Epicurus and His Philosophy* (Minneapolis 1954). D. R. DUDLEY, *A History of Cynicism from Diogenes to the 6th Century A.D.* (London 1937). A. H. ARMSTRONG, *An Introduction to Ancient Philosophy* (London 1947) 175–204. P. MERLAN, *From Platonism to Neoplatonism* (The Hague 1953). P. COURCELLE, *Les Lettres grecques en Occident de Macrobe à Cassiodore* (new ed. rev. Paris 1948) 3–36, 195–209. H. A. WOLFSON, *Religious Philosophy: A Group of Essays* (Cambridge, Mass. 1961).

[P. LANGLOIS]

GREEK RELIGION

The term is employed to designate all the religious practices and beliefs of the ancient Greeks throughout their hundreds of communities in the Mediterranean world and the adjacent areas. The study of ancient Greek religion embraces the long span of time from the Mycenaean period (1600–1100 B.C.) to the age of the Emperor Justinian (A.D. 527–565).

INTRODUCTION

At the outset it must be emphasized that the ancient Greeks and Romans were religious people and convinced believers, and that among the Greeks the Athenians especially should be so characterized. Let it suffice to cite the testimony of St. Paul in his Areopagus discourse, in which the Latin word *religiosiores* would be a better translation for the Greek δεισιδαιμονεστέρους than the Vulgate *superstitiosiores* (Acts 17.22; cf. Festugière, ''Aspects de la religion populaire grecque,'' 28).

Religion of the Masses and of the Philosophers. The pagan Greek differed from the Christian (*ibid.* 28–29) in two essential ways: he lacked a sense of sin as an offense against God [(cf. É. des Places, ''Péché dans la Grèce antique,'' *Dictionnaire de la Bible*, suppl. ed. L. Pirot, et al., 7:471–480 (Paris 1928–)], and he was a polytheist. On the latter point, a distinction must be made between the masses and the philosophers. Although even Plato remained a polytheist in many respects, from the period of the pre-Socratics, both Ionians and Eleatics, all Greek philosophy tended toward monotheism, while the popular religion continued to tend toward polytheism. Accordingly, the distinction made between ''popular religion'' and the ''religion of the sages or philosophers'' provides in the study of Greek religion a convenient division, which, in the long run, is quite justified.

Sources. The sources themselves actually fall into two categories, namely, archeological monuments, epitaphs, ex-voto inscriptions, and oracles; and literary works in the strict sense. The latter rarely furnish detailed information on current religious beliefs and practices, except when Plato, e.g., toward the end of his life, undertook to codify them in his *Laws* [cf. Festugière, ''Aspects . . . ,'' 19; *id.*, ''Le fait religieux dans la Grèce ancienne,'' in *Permanence de la Grèce* (Paris 1948) 77–87]. But the literary sources have a deeper significance. A. Harnack goes so far as to say: ''Real, deep devoutness, such as controls the whole life, is certainly a power that is only to be found in a few. But it is on the basis of those few that the nature of an age's piety must be determined, just as we must determine the art of a period on the basis of the real artists. For in those devout men, as in those artists, lives the eternal, ever-moving spirit of religion and of art, and they compel the rest, even though slowly and gradually, to follow after them, and at least to acknowledge as form and authority that which they cannot receive as spirit. But many out of the throng do receive a ray of the spirit, and warm their cold life with it'' (*The Hibert Journal* 10 70).

Homeric religion occupies a place between popular religion and philosophic religion; it is closer to the first, but the second is in part dependent upon it, just as all Greek literary genres are indebted to the epic [cf. É. des Places, ''Style parlé et style oral chez les écrivains grecs,'' *Mélanges Bidez* (Brussels 1934) 267–286].

POPULAR RELIGION

Characteristic features of popular religion are (1) faith in the power and omniscience of the gods—nothing can be achieved without them; they are consulted on all doubtful matters (e.g., Zeus at Dodona); (2) trust in the god who is served well; (3) gratitude for the gifts that he sends; (4) friendship (φίλος is a favorite word of Euripides and Theocritus) and even intimacy with him; (5) an atmosphere of joy and festivity that surrounds worship, a ''respite'' in the hard routine of daily life (cf. Plato, *Laws* 2.653C-D, 654A; Festugière, ''Aspects . . . ,'' 20–21, 23–24, 26–27).

The Olympian gods were honored in a spirit of gladness (cf. Plato, *Epin.* 980B), while the chthonian deities (the *inferi* of the Latins) inspired fear primarily and had their own special rites (cf. Plato, *Laws* 828C). Each category accordingly had its corresponding ritual, one of service and the other of aversion.

Homeric Religion. The gods of the *Iliad,* and their counterparts, more highly conceived characters, in the *Odyssey,* already comprise the pantheon of Olympus, which retains its worshippers until the end of paganism; and the principal forms of sacrifice and prayer are likewise established from Homer on. Homeric morality, which is less closely bound to religion than in other systems, juxtaposes elevated concepts—honor, hospitality, and the solidarity of the *genos* or clan—and ideas and practices that are vestiges of barbarism.

Zeus. In Hellenic polytheism the supreme god is called Zeus. He is a combination of the Cretan Zeus, a god of fertility, and the Indo-European god of the sky and of lightning, thus reconciling Aegean religion, the sun-cult of the indigenous farmers, and the sky-cult of the aristocratic conquerors. He is the ''father of gods and men.'' As father of the gods, he is like a patriarch among his own people, the sovereign divinity to whom all others show a profound respect. He is also the father of men, although the *Iliad* opposes the race of men to that of the gods (5.441–442), and Pindar does the same at the beginning of *Nemean Ode* 6.

But at all times, the Greeks tended to bring themselves closer to their gods or to bring their gods closer to themselves. This dual movement produces either anthropomorphism or a tendency toward perfection. Between man and divinity, assimilation could operate in two directions, from above to below or from below to above. In the case of the Greeks of the Homeric Age, it operated from below to above; they fashioned gods in the image of man, debasing divinity by attributing to it the crimes of mankind and thereby justifying them. But the origin of anthropomorphism can be found also in the feeling of kinship with God: ''Anthropomorphism involves theomorphism'' (cf. Adam, *Vitality of Platonism,* 124). The solidarity of the family in Greece, strongly knit through the conception of the *genos* or clan, favored the idea of an intimacy with God that reached even the point of likeness. Since the ideal of parents was to have children like themselves (cf. Hesiod, *Works* 182 and 235), kinship with divinity would necessarily be expressed by a resemblance.

Other Gods. Besides Zeus, two goddesses have dominant positions, Hera in the *Iliad* and Athena in the *Iliad* and *Odyssey.* Hera never stops reminding Zeus that he agreed to let Troy be destroyed. Her affection for the Achaeans is not altered by their quarrels; she loves equally Agamemnon and Achilles (*Iliad* 1.196–209). Hera, an Argive goddess, appears in the Feudal Age as the consort of the Father of the Gods and the protectress of marriage. Her sacred union (hierogamy) with Zeus, which a metope of one of the temples at Selinus (Sicily) represents under the aspect of her unveiling, consecrates the marriage of Sky and Earth. Athena helps Achilles to achieve self-control, and in describing her role in the *Iliad,* which is a little like that of grace in the Christian sense, one could construct a tableau of the highest stages of psychological life. It is especially in the *Odyssey,* however, that the solicitous assistance that she gives to Odysseus makes it possible for the poet to attribute to her the noblest sentiments, thoughts, and advice, which are far more elevated than the capricious interventions of the gods of the *Iliad* in favor of or against a specific human personage.

The other Homeric divinities of the ancient pantheon are: Poseidon, ruler of the sea; Hades, king of the Lower World; Demeter, also a chthonian divinity, the Earth-Mother; Artemis and her brother Apollo, ''masters of beasts'' (πότνιοι θηρῶν), great protectors of the Trojans; Hermes, the shepherd god who multiplies flocks, god of travelers, and guide of souls that he leads to Hades (ψυχοπομπός).

Apollo is also the brother of Dionysus. These two relatively recent foreign gods represent two aspects of Greek religion, the difference between which has often been exaggerated. Actually, the devotees of Apollo, beginning with the Pythia of Delphi, pass through states of trance or ecstasy that connect his worship with that of Dionysus and explain the ultimate reconciliation of the two brothers and their association at Delphi. It is not possible to oppose the Dionysian to the Apollonian—to use the terminology of Nietzsche—in such a way that the Apollonian element does not contain germs of its opposite. The rational and the irrational have always coexisted. The religion of Apollo with its ritual observances and maxims may approach Jewish legalism, yet the mystic movement depends more on the cult of Dionysus, although the bacchants did not regard themselves as exalted or spiritually regenerated. The religious thought of the Greeks always wavered between a feeling for the human condition, beyond the limits of which it was not possible to rise, and assimilation with God, the goal of the philosophers and mystics. A wise man like Empedocles was a combination of both and, as E. R. Dodds (156) put it, the double ''Orphic'' faith in metempsychosis and in an original offense reconciles ''the 'Apolline' sentiment of remoteness from the divine and the 'Dionysiac' sentiment of identity with it.''

Destiny. In Homer, Zeus tends to merge with destiny, which is called μοῖρα, μόρος, αἶσα, literally ''part, portion'' [cf. K. von Fritz, *Review of Religion* 15 (1950–51) 50–51]. Destiny and divinity, while often independent or juxtaposed, can come into conflict; sometimes the gods are subordinated to destiny, but much more frequently destiny expresses their will, Διὸς αἶσα. A scene like the weighing of lots (or of souls, *psychostasia*), which precedes the death of Hector, furnishes a good example of the interpenetration of the personal will of Zeus and the anonymous force that presides over the destinies of men (*Iliad* 22.209–). The Homeric idea of destiny can be clearly comprehended in the long labor of synthesis that produced the Homeric religion in its totality. In the Homeric poems there is not merely a compromise between the concept of destiny and the concept of divine power, for the idea itself of destiny is an idea of compromise.

Prayer. The prayers found in ''Homer are ordinarily formulary and traditional. Those of Chryses in bk. 1 of the *Iliad* contain the three essential parts of all liturgical prayer in Greece: (1) invocation of the god, ''hear me'' (κλῦθί μευ, 1.37, 451); (2) the reasons for being heard: sacrifices offered, services rendered, favors already obtained; (3) conclusion: statement of the petition. Those of Diomedes to Athena, in bks. 5 and 10, begin in the same way: κλῦθί μοι (5.115), κέκλυθι ἐμεῖο (10.284). Odysseus, before Diomedes, had prayed in the same terms (10.278, 282), and Nestor and Achilles also address Zeus in like manner. Priam (24.108) employs numerous epithets (''Father,'' ''Master of Ida,'' ''most glorious,'' ''very great''), in accordance with the style that was to become that of all hymns down to the *Hymn to Zeus* of the Stoic Cleanthes.

There are also less official prayers, outside all ritual and sacerdotal presence, and perhaps more intimate, such as those of Hector (*Odyssey* 5; *Iliad* 6). Hector takes his son Astyanax in his arms and asks Zeus and all the other gods to give him a valor even greater than that of his father (*Iliad* 6.474–481). The shipwrecked Odysseus calls on the god of the river to give him access to the shore: ''Hear me, O Lord, whose name I do not know [again κλῦθί] . . . receive in your pity, O Lord, the suppliant who calls out to you'' (*Odyssey* 5.445–450). On Homeric prayer and on Greek prayer in general, see K. von Fritz, ''Greek Prayers,'' *Review of Religion* 10 (1945–46) 5–39.

Conclusion. A religious character cannot be denied to poems where the interpretation of the world and life is completely religious, and where the gods intervene in almost all experiences of physical and psychological life. While one may hardly speak of a religious morality in Homer, it must be acknowledged that the ancient bard never ceased emphasizing the divine, in spite of the obscurities or seamy elements in the mythology of which he sang.

RELIGION OF THE PHILOSOPHERS

While it is possible roughly to contrast the popular religion with that of the ''sages,'' it does not necessarily follow that all philosophers professed the same religion. Their belief in a single principle, which tended toward monotheism, took various forms, and among most of them it did not exclude a residue of faith in the traditional gods. On the other hand, the term ''philosopher'' is used here in a very broad sense. Originally the term ''sage'' (σοφός) was applied to poets. These sometimes had a theology—if Hesiod or Pindar did not, probably at least Euripides and certainly Aeschylus did.

Aeschylus. Aeschylus developed to perfection the idea of a morality at the same time divine and human. The idea had been elaborated by Hesiod in his *Works and Days* and by Solon in his *Elegies* (cf. Solmsen), but neither Hesiod nor Solon transferred justice to Olympus. On the contrary, the transformation of a system of violence into a system of divine justice is the problem underlying the two trilogies, *Prometheus* and the *Oresteia*. In the *Oresteia,* particularly in the third play, the *Eumenides,* the coming of justice upon earth depends on the gods; the reconciliation of the chthonian goddesses with the gods of Olympus, as with the judges of the Areopagus, requires fairness in human decrees. The conflict of *Prometheus Bound,* which opposes an older god, a Titan, to the new master Zeus, shows a trend toward a compromise and gives, besides, the noble lesson that the gods, like men, learn through suffering.

Xenophanes and Parmenides. Xenophanes and especially Parmenides were poets, but poet-philosophers in the full sense of the word. To Xenophanes religious philosophy owes a lofty conception of the dignity of God, of ''what is suitable to him'' (θεοπρεπές); to Parmenides, the idea of an unconditioned existence of being on which the epithets, lavished as in a hymn, are those bestowed on the ''Infinite'' (ἄπειρον) by Anaximander, ''unbegotten,'' ''deathless,'' ''without beginning or end.'' The attitude of Parmenides regarding Being is truly a religious one. Even if this Being is not a personal God, it is divine, as later was the Platonic form of the Good.

Plato. Of an eminently religious mind, Plato professed at the same time: (1) the traditional religion, (2) a religious philosophy, and (3) an astral religion.

Adherence to Traditional Religion. Whatever the importance of an ''Orphic'' or ''Pythagorean'' element in the Platonic myths, which for the most part are eschatological, Plato, beginning with his *Euthyphro,* but particularly in his *Republic* and the *Laws,* revised traditional beliefs and mythology. In all his writings, without breaking with the heritage of his ancestors, ''the inherited conglomerate'' (G. Murray), he purified the legends, which were only too often immoral, in order to restore a religious meaning. Plato was scandalized by the denial of the existence of the gods, by the denial of Providence (the gods exist, but they are not interested in human affairs), and by attempts at corruption of the gods (they occupy themselves with men, but the latter can buy and seduce them by sacrifices and offerings). This is the triple impiety exposed by Adimantus in bk. 2 of the *Republic* (365D–E), and refuted in the *Laws,* bks. 10 (888A–D, cf. 885B) and 12 (948C), and in the *Epinomis* (980D). Plato resented less the gods of mythology than the fables that disfigured them, such as the mutilation of Uranus and other horrors (*Euthyphro* 5E–6C; *Rep.* 2.377E–378E). Cult itself was not condemned. On the contrary, Plato, like Socrates, seems to have accepted it in good faith along with the names of the gods. In this regard he said: ''One must conform to the law'' (*Tim.* 40E), and all the more so ''because men are ignorant of the true name of the gods'' (*Crat.* 400D–E).

Among all the Olympian gods, Socrates and Plato revered Apollo most. His importance, which is so marked in Plato's ideal state, increased even more in the ''Apollonian'' city of the *Laws.* In both, the following order governs worship: (1) Olympians, (2) chthonian divinities, (3) demons (δαίμονες), (4) heroes (cf. *Laws* 4.717A–B). The demons, who were above heroes, served as intermediaries between the gods and men, as is clear from corroborative narratives in the *Banquet* (202E) and in the *Epinomis* (984E–985A).

Religious Philosophy. The religious philosophy of Plato is based on the relationship of the soul to the Forms—a relationship that implies the soul's immortality. Metempsychosis and reminiscence, which flows from metempsychosis, postulate a former life where the soul contemplated the Forms. On earth, joined to a body, which Pythagoreanism represents as a prison, the soul retains a yearning for the other world where it lived as in its true family. Indeed, spiritual relationship, συγγένεια, is at once the foundation for worship of the gods and for the intuitive knowledge of the Forms. To indicate the stages of religious knowledge, four steps are differentiated in the *Republic:* opinion, faith, reasoned knowledge, and pure intelligence (bk. 6 end, bk.7); and at the end of the dialectic process in *Epistle* 7, the superior degree of intelligence that apprehends the real object is likewise intuitive knowledge.

Eternal being, perpetually the same, is grasped through the intellect and reasoning, while becoming is the object of opinion combined with unreasoning sensation. Is this eternal being God? The Form of the Good is never identified with God by Plato, although it does have godlike attributes. This Form, ''which gives to the objects of knowledge their essence and their being, while not itself essence, is still above essence in power and in dignity'' (*Rep.* 6.509B), sometimes appearing even superior to God, who only contemplates it and imitates it in his operations. If one sticks to the letter of the texts, ''the fact remains that Plato himself has never called the Good a god. . . . The reason for it might be that he never thought of it as of a god. And why, after all, should an Idea be considered as a god? An Idea is no person; it is not even a soul; at best it is an intelligible cause, much less a person than a thing'' (Gilson, 26).

Astral Religion. Late in his life, perhaps under the influence of a Chaldean associate at the Academy, Plato seems to have been converted to the astral religion. Having once accepted, and as early as his *Phaedrus,* that motion is caused by a soul, nothing prevented him from identifying the Olympian gods with the souls of the sun, moon, planets, and other celestial bodies. This doctrine, which is found in the *Timaeus* and in the *Laws,* was expanded in the *Epinomis* (e.g., 982B–E). As the Greeks know how to embellish and bring to perfection everything they receive from the barbarians, so the oracles of Delphi will teach them to honor these new gods with a care that will surpass that given them by their Eastern worshippers (987E–988A).

Although a faithful adherent of the traditional religion right up to his conversion, Plato nevertheless introduces the astral religion into the whole framework of his ideal city, concerned only with establishing it in conformity with the Delphic oracles. The worship of the stars is thus to coexist with that of the Olympians, even if little by little it is to supplant the latter. To Eusebius (*Dem. evangel.* 4.9, 10–11), worship of the stars was not far from monotheism and could soon lead to the pure and true origin of things. There remained, however, an essential difference between the attitude of the Jew, who saw in the heavenly body a creation of the one God, and that of Plato, who worshipped the star itself as a god. There was always an obstacle for the Greeks, namely, that they had so many gods that it was practically impossible for exclusive monotheism to take root among them. What must be remembered at least is that there was a very strong tendency toward monotheism, even though it did not reach a full development. It remained a polytheism oriented in some respects toward the one true God.

The Stoics. As compared with their predecessors, the Stoics emphasize at least the appearances of a monotheism. God is universal reason present everywhere. Men, each of whom possesses a particle of this divine reason, must consider each other as brothers. On the other hand, this God allows neither temples nor statues; his true sanctuary is the sky filled with stars. If Zeno thus rejected polytheism, it was scarcely out of a feeling of intimacy with God. This feeling is more evident in Cleanthes' *Hymn to Zeus* (so well commented on by Adam in his *Vitality of Platonism,* 108–189); Zeus is presented not merely as the master of nature, but as a father who saves men from fatal ignorance of true goods. In its religious feeling as in its poetic quality, the hymn of Cleanthes anticipates Epictetus, the nightingale and swan of God (*Diatribes* 1.16.20–21). For Epictetus even more than for Plato, philosophic religion expresses itself in a filial piety, of which the principal elements are perhaps (1) submission to the will of God, (2) pride in one's condition as man, and (3) the feeling of one's divine affiliation. The wisdom of consent, which in the beginning sums up Stoicism, changes with Cleanthes into prayer, and with Epictetus it rises to the height of a mystical doctrine. What he lacks is an understanding of human weakness and sin, the meaning of human misery; Plato had a greater sense of our misery, at least in the *Laws.* No Greek philosopher, any more than the Greeks in general, had a clear conception of sin in the Judeo-Christian sense.

See Also: CRETAN-MYCENAEAN RELIGION; DELPHI, ORACLE OF; GREEK PHILOSOPHY (RELIGIOUS ASPECTS); MYSTERY RELIGIONS, GRECO-ORIENTAL; SACRIFICE.

Bibliography: L. R. FARNELL, J. HASTINGS, *Encyclopedia of Religion and Ethics* (Edinburgh 1908–27) 6:392–425. É. DES PLACES, ''Les Religions de la Grèce Antique,'' *Histoire des religions,* ed. M. BRILLANT and R. AIGRAIN (Paris 1955–) 3:159–292. F. R. WALTON, *Die Religion in Geschichte und Gegenwart* (3d ed.

Greek Orthodox bishop carries Mary's Icon, Jerusalem. (©Hanan Isachar/CORBIS)

Tübingen 1957–65) 2:1860–67. A. J. FESTUGIÈRE, "La Grèce: I, La Religion," *Grèce et Rome,* in *Histoire générale des religions,* ed. M. GORCE and R. MORTIER, 4 v. (Paris 1944–51) v.2; *Personal Religion among the Greeks* (Berkeley 1960); "Aspects de la religion populaire grecque," *Revue de théologie et de philosophie* 11 (Lausanne 1961) 19–31. J. E. HARRISON, *Prolegomena to the Study of Greek Religion* (3d ed. Cambridge, Eng. 1922). E. R. DODDS, *The Greeks and the Irrational* (Berkeley 1951). W. K. C. GUTHRIE, *The Greeks and Their Gods* (London 1950). G. MURRAY, *Five Stages of Greek Religion* (2d ed. New York 1930). M. P. NILSSON, *Greek Popular Religion* (New York 1940); *Greek Piety,* tr. H. J. ROSE (Oxford 1948); *Geschichte der griechischen Religion* (Munich, v.1, 2d ed. 1955; v.2, 2d ed. 1961). J. ADAM, *The Religious Teachers of Greece* (Edinburgh 1909); *The Vitality of Platonism and Other Essays* (Cambridge, Eng. 1911). W. JAEGER, *The Theology of the Early Greek Philosophers* (Oxford 1947). F. SOLMSEN, *Hesiod and Aeschylus* (Ithaca, N.Y. 1949). É. H. GILSON, *God and Philosophy* (New Haven, 1941). H. J. ROSE, *A Handbook of Greek Mythology* (6th ed. New York 1958).

[É. DES PLACES]

GREEK THEOLOGY

On May 29, 1453, when the Muslim Turks captured Constantinople and put an end to the Byzantine Empire, the development of Byzantine theology ceased. From 1500 on theology was written by Greek-speaking Orthodox and Catholics inhabiting what had been the Byzantine Empire. This body of material that is often designated Byzantine theology, but a more exact term would be Greek theology of the Byzantine tradition.

This article deals with Greek theology: (1) from 1500 until the patriarchate of Cyril LUCARIS (1612); (2) from Cyril Lucaris to the Synod of Constantinople (1723); (3) from 1723 to the constitution of the autocephalous Church of Greece (1833); (4) from 1833 until 1923; and (5) from 1923 to the beginning of the ecumenical movement.

First Period: 1500 to 1612. Even though the patriarchal school continued to function in Constantinople under the guidance of Matthaeus Kamariotas during the reign of Muḥammad II, theological centers of learning were gradually suppressed. Among the Orthodox, the Slavs, especially in Kiev and Moscow, utilized their independence of Constantinople and began to develop their own Slav theology (*see* RUSSIAN THEOLOGY). Greek students migrated to theological universities in the West, especially in Germany, Italy, and England. Their initiation into non-Orthodox theology resulted eventually in grouping into three types of theologian depending upon one or another emphasis: (1) the conservative, rigid followers of early Byzantine theology who would accept no influence from the West and assumed a polemical attitude in the attempt to preserve their traditional Orthodoxy; (2) those who came under the influence of Protestant doctrines and incorporated them into Oriental theology; and finally (3) those who favored Latin theology and strove to introduce Latin concepts and terminology into Orthodoxy.

The abortive attempt made by the Council of Florence (1439) to heal the schism between the Western and Eastern Churches had prepared the ground for fresh, anti-Latin writings. Catholic missionaries entered Orthodox countries intent on proselytizing to bring about unity of faith and practice particularly in the Near East and in the Polish kingdom. The reunion of Brest-Litovsk (1595), which united millions of Orthodox Ukrainians with Rome, further stiffened Greek opposition to Latin theology. From the middle of the 16th century many Byzantine writers who had studied in Italy and Germany manifested interest in Catholic as well as Protestant theology. This development was looked upon with disfavor by the conservative Greek theologians.

Augsburg Confession. Early Protestant leaders, beginning with MELANCHTHON, had sought the friendship of the Orthodox. The Reformers were eager to obtain Greek approval of their AUGSBURG CONFESSION. When Patriarch Joasaph II sent his deacon Demetrius Mysos to Wittenberg to investigate the newly reformed Christianity, Melanchthon gave him a Greek version of the Augsburg Confession, but the patriarch quickly rejected its teaching (1559). In 1573 the professors of the University of Tübingen, through Stephan Gerlach, tried to obtain approval for their doctrines from Jeremias II. Three documents sent by way of response, in 1578, 1579, and 1581, completely rejected the Lutheran Confession. These were the first Greek writings to sound the alarm at Protestant infiltration.

The principal author of these responses was Patriarch Jeremias, but others collaborated, such as Joannes and Theodosius Zygomalas, Leonarus Mindonios, Damascene the Studite, and probably Gabriel Severus. The Council of TRENT's doctrine was upheld in the Orthodox presentation of their teaching on justification and free will, on the Sacraments, on the invocation of the saints, and on the monastic life. However, with regard to procession of the Holy Spirit, the FILIOQUE doctrine was rejected. In general, the fundamental tenets of the Augsburg Confession were repulsed with an exhortation that the Protestants return to the doctrine of the Church Fathers and the definitions of the first seven ecumenical councils.

Meletius Pigas. Catholic influence is seen more in the Orthodox theologians after Jeremias, who remained up to his death strongly anti-Catholic and attacked the Roman authorities for their forceful tactics in bringing about the union of Brest. But many of the Greek theologians who had studied at the University of Padua openly accepted Catholic teachings. The first Greek theologian of note to study in Italy was Meletius Pigas (1601). He was born on the island of Crete, and after completing his studies at Padua he took the monastic habit and began to preach and teach. He was made patriarch of Alexandria in 1590.

After the union of Brest Pigas turned from his earlier Catholic sympathies and began to write sharply against Roman teaching. ''Concerning the Primacy of the Pope in the Form of Letters'' was his first polemical attack. Three of these letters were sent to the Ukrainians living in the Polish kingdom, urging them to repudiate the union of Brest, while the fourth was directed to the Orthodox faithful on the island of Chios where there was a similar movement in favor of reunion with Rome. Little originality is shown by Pigas, who repeated the standard objections of his Byzantine predecessors against the primacy of the pope, filioque, Communion under one species, purgatory, fasting on Saturday, and use of unleavened bread. His main theological works are ''The Orthodox Christian,'' a long discussion on the procession of the Holy Spirit, Penance, and purgatory (published at Vilna in 1596 and later at Jassy, Rumania, 1769), and ''Concerning the True Catholic Church and Its Genuine and True Head and Concerning the Primacy of the Pope of Rome'' (1585). His archdeacon Maximus of Peloponnesus followed in his footsteps leaving among his other anti-Latin writings an ''Enchiridion against the Schism of the Papists'' in which, like Pigas, he attacked the doctrine of the primacy, procession of the Holy Spirit from the Son, and the use of unleavened bread. But both Pigas and Maximus follow the Catholic position in presenting the Sacraments.

Two other alumni of Padua University were Maximus Marguinios (1602) and Gabriel Severus (1616). Maximus had disputed with Gabriel Severus at Venice in favor of the Catholic doctrine expressed in the word filioque. He presented his arguments in three treatises, which he sent to the Patriarch Jeremias II in 1683, and staunchly supported Jeremias II against Protestant influences in Orthodoxy. Gabriel Severus, Metropolitan of Philadelphia, spent most of his writing career in Venice where he was in charge of the Greek Orthodox church of St. George. In his ''Brief Tract on the Holy Sacraments'' (Venice 1600) he used terminology borrowed chiefly from the Latin scholastics to describe the theology of the Sacraments in a refutation of the doctrines of the Protestants.

Second Period: 1612 to 1723. The 17th century was a period of controversy both within the Greek Orthodox

Church itself and on the part of Catholics and Protestants who fought to draw the Orthodox to themselves. The Protestants seemed to have had the first success in attracting Cyril Lucaris to Calvinistic doctrines, which he expressed in his *Confession* of 1629; but soon both Russian and Byzantine theologians reacted strongly, and, in various synods and confessions of faith, the Orthodox rejected Protestant errors.

Cyril Lucaris. Of the theologians sympathetic to Protestantism, Cyril Lucaris was the most influential. Born in 1572 on the island of Crete, Cyril studied at Padua and Venice where he became proficient in Latin and Italian. Meletius Pigas in 1584 sent him to the Ukraine where he took part in the Council of Brest. He became patriarch of Alexandria in 1601 and held this office until 1620. In various letters to Calvinists he showed his sympathy toward their doctrine, especially in the matter of the Eucharist, free will, and justification. He was elected patriarch of Constantinople in 1620, a dignity he held on and off six different times, until, by order of the Turkish ruler, he was drowned in the sea.

In violation of the traditional teaching of the Orthodox Church, his *Confession* (1629, augmented 1633) accepts Calvinistic teaching: Holy Scripture is the only rule of faith (art. 2); justification comes by faith alone (art. 13); free will is abolished (art. 14); predestination is presented according to the teaching of Calvin (art. 3); consequently a false concept of the Church is taught (art. 11). He admitted only two Sacraments, Baptism and Eucharist, and believed that Christ is present only at the time of Holy Communion (arts. 15, 17). He rejected purgatory (art. 18), the cult of images (q. 4), and the deuterocanonical books of the Old Testament (q. 3). Some Orthodox, such as Chrysostomos Papadopoulos, claimed that Cyril was not the author of the *Confession.* But his correspondence with Calvinist theologians demonstrates his sympathies toward their doctrines, and an extant autographed codex leaves little doubt that Cyril Lucaris was its author.

Lucaris gave the impetus to other Orthodox theologians who openly proclaimed their Protestant teachings. Theophilus Corydalleos, Zacharias Gerganos, Joannes Caryophyllos, Maximus Callipolita, and METROPHANES CRITOPOULOS all followed this example. Critopoulos was a pupil of Lucaris, who sent him to universities in England, Germany, and Switzerland. In his travels he strove to bring about a union of Orthodox and Protestants. On his return to Greece he was created patriarch of Alexandria and abstained from manifesting Protestant tendencies. He even took part in the Synod of Jassy (1642), which condemned the *Confession* of Lucaris. His adherence to Protestantism is clear, however, from his *Confession of Faith of the Catholic and Apostolic Oriental Church*, composed in Helmstadt in 1624 but printed only in 1661. There has been much discussion about the *Confession.* A. Palmieri maintains that it is a clear expression of Lutheran faith; others, with I. Mihalcescu, concede that in some points Critopoulos deviated from common Orthodox opinion. Finally there are those who hold it as one of the chief symbols of Orthodox faith and quite genuinely in keeping with the Byzantine theological tradition.

A synod held in 1925 on Mt. Athos vindicated Critopoulos and his *Confession.* Yet an influence from Protestant theology cannot be denied, e.g., in his definition of the Church, in his treatment of the Sacraments, in his accepting only three (Baptism, Eucharist, and Penance), and in his rejection of the deuterocanonical books. Critopoulos's *Confession* is valued highly by contemporary Greek theologians who accept his Protestant opinions and his arguments against Roman Catholicism concerning the filioque, the Immaculate Conception, and the Roman primacy. They favor the mystical concept of the Church, which is derived mostly from Protestant sources.

Polemicists. A chief characteristic of Greek theology in the 17th century was the role played by polemical writings against both Catholics and Protestants. Meletius Syrigos (d. 1667) had studied both at Padua and Venice and was commissioned by Parthenios I, Patriarch of Constantinople, to correct the *Confession* of Peter MOGHILA and translate it into modern Greek. It was his corrected version that was accepted as a confession of faith for all the Orthodox in the Council of Jassy (Romania) in 1642. Moghila had protested the changes made in his original Latin text by Syrigos, and the Greek text was not edited until 1667, after the death of Moghila. D. Balanos claims that the original *Confession* of Moghila was a compendium of the *Catholic Catechism* of St. Peter CANISIUS. But Syrigos removed most of the Tridentine doctrine found in the original text and brought it into closer harmony with the Greek thinking of his day. His chief theological work was a polemical monograph against Calvinist doctrine: *Orthodox Refutation of the Chapters and Questions of the Confession of Cyril Lukaris.* Except for the chapter concerning the procession of the Holy Spirit, most of this work is consonant with Catholic theology. Both Greek and Latin Fathers as well as Scripture are quoted frequently.

Dositheus of Jerusalem. Syrigos was employed by Dositheus, Patriarch of Jerusalem (d. 1707), one of the leading Byzantine figures in the polemics against non-Orthodox groups. His own *Confession* proved of great importance in checking Protestant infiltration into Orthodoxy when it was accepted at a synod in Jerusalem (1672) by all the Orthodox patriarchs. More intent on fighting

Calvinistic errors than Latin Catholicism, Dositheus demonstrated his dependence on Latin theology, not only in the opinions expressed but even in terminology, particularly in the theology of the Sacraments where words never before used by Byzantine theologians, such as confirmation, satisfaction, and transubstantiation, were introduced into Greek theology. As expressed in the *Confession*, his doctrine on free will and predestination (decrees 3, 14), on justification and good works (decree 13), and on the seven Sacraments (decree 15) is in perfect harmony with the teaching of the Council of Trent. He did not use the word purgatory, yet he holds a third state between heaven and hell that would correspond to Catholic teaching on purgatory. Dositheus is the author of *An Enchiridion against the Errors of Calvinism* (Bucharest 1690); he established a printing press at Jassy, Rumania, to spread the polemical works of both earlier and contemporary Byzantine writers against Calvinism and the Roman Church.

Other theologians include George Coressios (d. 1641), who studied medicine in Pisa and returned to Greece to write polemical tracts against both the Protestants and the Catholics; and Paisy Ligarides (d. 1678), who embraced Catholicism as a boy in Rome but later left the Church to become a sharp controversialist against Protestant and Catholic theological doctrine. Nectar, Patriarch of Jerusalem (d. 1676), wrote a tract *Concerning the Primacy of the Pope*, which Dositheus printed at Jassy. The two Lichudes brothers, Joannes (d. 1717) and Sophronius (d. 1730), both studied in Venice and Padua. Dositheus sent them as instructors to the seminary of Moscow where they wrote polemical tracts attacking the theological school of Kiev for its Catholic tendencies. Sevastus Kymenites (d. 1702), Elias Meniates (d. 1714), and Nicolaus Kerameos (d. 1672) must also be listed among the polemicists of this period.

Catholic Sympathizers. Amidst so many Greek theologians dedicated to polemics, a few with Catholic sympathies wrote works that never became popular. Agapius Landos, with his ascetical writings printed at Venice, was the most esteemed of this group. Among his writings are: *Salvation of Sinners* and *New Paradise* (lives of the saints taken from Symeon Metaphrastes), and *Eklogion* and *New Eklogion* (more selected lives of the saints). Gregorius of Chios published a compendium of the *Divine and Sacred Dogmas of the Church* (Venice 1635). Nicolaus Kursulas (d. 1652), an alumnus of St. Athanasius Greek College founded in Rome by Pope Gregory XIII to bring about concord between the West and East, wrote a *Synopsis of Sacred Theology* using the scholastic method and permeated by a Catholic mentality. Nicolaus the Bulgar studied in Padua and edited his *Sacred Catechism* (Venice 1681), which has been used by more recent Greeks in an effort to correct errors in later Orthodox speculation.

Two outstanding Byzantinists, also alumni of St. Athanasius College, Rome, were Peter Arcudius (d. 1633) and Leo Allatius (d. 1669), who held various offices in the Vatican and used their Oriental background in the service of the Church. Arcudius was mainly responsible for effecting the union of Brest while Allatius collected innumerable Greek and Syrian manuscripts under Pope Gregory XV, thus preserving in the Vatican Library an important Eastern heritage that otherwise would have been lost.

Third Period: 1723 to 1833. The nadir of modern Greek theology, the period from 1723 to 1833 was typified by an increase in theological compendia, polemical writings against Roman Catholics, and synopses of Byzantine spirituality. In the 18th century many Christians of the Antiochene patriarchate united with Rome and constituted the Melkite Greek Catholic Church. Hatred against Catholics mounted. In 1755 the Ecumenical Patriarch Cyril V declared Baptism by infusion, as administered by the Latins, invalid. The chief theologian of the period was Eugenius the Bulgar, even though he showed no great talent. His main writing, a theological compendium called *Theologikon*, was printed in Venice in 1872. Other authors who collected the past theological traditions into compendia were Vincent Damodos (d. 1752), Antonius Moschopoulos (d. 1788), Joannes Kontones (d. 1761), and Theophilus Papaphilos (d. *c.* 1785).

The chief compiler of Byzantine spiritual writings was Nicodemus, the Hagiorite of Mr. Athos (d. 1809). Together with Agapius Leonardos he compiled *The Pedalion* (Rudder), which today is the most famous Byzantine collection of commonly accepted (in the Greek-Slavic Churches) canons from ancient ecumenical or local councils. The two authors also provided commentaries on the canons. But Nicodemus is more popularly known as the editor of the *Philokalia*, a five-volume collection of ascetical writings, drawn mostly from the spiritual writers of the Hesychastic tradition. This was first printed in Venice in 1782; a third edition was printed in Athens in 1957.

Fourth Period: 1833 to 1923. There followed a period chiefly of eclecticism. Political freedom had been won in 1833, and the Greeks were able to form their own nation. This brought them freedom to have their own universities and faculties of theology. The University of Athens' theology faculty was founded in 1837. Theology in the other Orthodox patriarchates of Antioch and Alexandria was practically nonexistent, due again to Muslim oppression. The theology that did develop in the newly liberated Greece was not very original but came under the influence of three principal sources: some theologians favored positions held by Protestant theologians; others, those of Catholics; while a third group became followers of the more creative Russian theologians, especially of the Khomiakovian school. Thus their eclecticism brought about many diverging opinions. Meanwhile, from 1867 onward, many sought reunion with the Anglicans.

Count Protasov. In 1833 Greece won autocephaly for its own Church and took as its model the independent Church in Russia. Protestantism had been spreading, but, recognizing the possibility of having its own theology schools, the Greek Church, like the Russian Church under Count Protasov, the procurator of the Holy Synod of Moscow, began to react against the infiltration of Protestant thinking in Orthodox theology. In 1836 Patriarch Gregorios VI of Constantinople issued an encyclical in which he condemned the errors of Luther, Zwingli, Calvin, and followers. The Greek Orthodox faithful were forbidden to read Protestant books and, above all, to read the Protestant versions of the Holy Scripture.

Encyclical of the Four Patriarchs. A document that exacerbated relations with the Catholics was the *Encyclical of the Four Patriarchs* of 1848. On Jan. 6, 1848, PIUS IX in his encyclical *In Suprema Petri Apostoli Sede* had addressed himself to the Orientals, inviting them to reunion with the Roman Church. In May 1848 the four chief Greek-speaking Orthodox patriarchs, Anthimus VI of Constantinople, Hierotheus II of Alexandria, Methodius of Antioch, and Cyril II of Jerusalem, along with 29 metropolitans, signed the *Encyclical of the Four Patriarchs.* The author of this document was Constantius I, Patriarch of Constantinople, who several years before (1834) had written an anti-Latin document as M. Popescu has shown. The contents of this encyclical summarized all the main points of the polemical literature of the prior centuries. Papism is claimed as a heresy that embraces several errors: that expressed by the word filioque; Baptism by aspersion; the defect of an epiclesis; Communion under one species; and the use of unleavened bread. The chief difficulty was the confusion of religious with civil power, which the Roman pontiffs abused by imposing an intolerable yoke on others. Thus the encyclical appeared more as a violent diatribe against the Roman pontiff than an answer to Plus IX.

Another document that became the source of authority for polemical writers of the period was the *Encyclical of Anthimus VII.* Pope Leo XIII, who was respected by many Orthodox for his zeal in promoting unity, sent to the Orientals his encyclical *Praeclara gratulationis* (June 20, 1894). Anthimus VII, Patriarch of Constantinople, answered at the end of 1894 with a long list of denunciations against the innovations of Latin Catholics. The list repeated the charges of the former 1848 Orthodoxy encyclical and added an attack on the idea of the fire of purgatory, immediate retribution, the newly defined dogma of the Immaculate Conception (1854), and that of the primacy of the pope and his infallibility, which had been declared dogma in the Vatican Council of 1870.

Theological Compendia. Russian theologians at this time excelled in theological manuals, and many of these were translated into Greek and used by the Greek Faculties. Popular Russian compendia that had great use in Greece included that of Antony Amphiteatrov, rector of the Academy of Kiev, *Dogmatic Theology of the Eastern Catholic Church* (Kiev 1848), and that of Macarius Bulgakov, *Introduction to Orthodox Theology* (St. Petersburg 1847). It was not long, however, before the Greek theologians were producing their own compendia. Nicolaus Damalas, Zikos Rhosis, Crestos Andrutsos, K. J. Dyovuniotis, D. S. Balanos, I. Mesoloras, Nectarios Kephalas, and Nicolaus Ambrazis all made useful compendia for use in Greek-speaking seminaries.

Meanwhile, during this period internecine controversies arose among the Greeks concerning the relation of the newly liberated Church and State in Greece and the primacy of the patriarch of Constantinople in ruling this Church. The Greek Orthodox divided into two factions: those, led by Theoclitus Pharmakides (d. 1860), who favored full ecclesiastical autonomy and autocephaly rendering the Church subject to the State in all that pertained to external administration and jurisdiction; the others, led by Constantinus Economos (d. 1857), who favored complete independence of the State and submission in all Church jurisdiction to the ecumenical patriarch of Constantinople. These two factions quarreled among themselves concerning the use of Protestant Bibles. In 1823 Protestant Bible societies began to disseminate Bibles printed in the modern Greek tongue. Pharmakides and Neophyte Vamvas (d. 1855) upheld the usefulness of these versions, while Economos argued theologically that the Protestant translations from the Hebrew had many discrepancies from that of the Septuagint, which alone he held to be infallible.

Theosevia. A new religion appeared in Greece about this time, a mystical rationalism promulgated by Theophilus Kairis (d. 1853). It was a type of the Modernism later condemned in the West by Pius X. The Synod of Greece condemned this so-called *Theosevia* religion as heretical, and Kairis was expelled in 1841. He returned only to be imprisoned by the state and soon died.

Theological journals began to appear as a greater spirit of creative speculation awoke among the Greek theologians. The Constantinople patriarchate published *Ekklesiastike Aletheia* (''Church Truth''), which was suppressed in 1923 when the majority of Greeks emigrated from Turkey. It was replaced by *Orthodoxia* in 1925 and *Apostolos Andreas*, the latter being the official voice of the ecumenical patriarch; but it printed theological articles also. Both of these periodicals were suppressed in 1964 by the Turkish government. Holy Cross Seminary in Jerusalem prints *Nea Sion;* the former *Ekklesiastikos Pharos* by the Alexandrian Patriarchate has been replaced by Pantaios.

Fifth Period: 1923 to the Ecumenical Movement. The modern era witnessed a renaissance in Greek theology. Under the inspiration of two leading archbishops of Athens, Meletius Mataxakis and Papadopoulos, theological studies and learning among the clergy and laity were fostered. Yet much of this modern Greek theological literature displays certain common defects. The majority of the older professors studied abroad, particularly in Germany. They mastered the critical techniques of the German schools of theology of the latter part of the 19th century, but because of nationalistic circumstances they had little contact with the more relevant theology developed in the 20th century among the Russian Orthodox *émigrés* and the Western Catholic world. They produced a theology almost wholly academic, confined to manuals and bearing little relation either to the spiritual contemporary world or to the patristic tradition of the past.

Contemporary Development. Paradoxically, in the 1950s and early 1960s the professors of the two leading theological faculties in Greece were almost exclusively laymen. They included Chrestos Androutsos, P. N. Trembelas, P. I. Bratsiotis, A. Alivisatos, B. Vellas, I. N. Karmiris, B. Joannides, C. Bonis, G. Konidaris, and Archimandrite Jerome Kotsonis, all of whom taught in the theological faculties of the universities of Athens and Salonika, and produced many serious theological writings.

A suspicion grew among the monks and pastors of souls as well as among the members of new movements such as *Zoe* (Life), *Aktines* (Action), and the two *Apostoliki Diakonia* (Apostolic Services) of Athens and Salonika, that this academic theology was irrelevant for confronting the materialism of modern Greece. A gradual change became noticeable among these Greek theologians, especially with the impetus received from the *Zoe* movement, also known as the ''Brotherhood of Theologians.'' This was started by Father Eusebius Matthopoulos in 1907 as a semimonastic order whose members remain celibate but take no formal vows. A quarter of the brothers are monks, the rest are laymen. Through their teaching of theology in the two faculties of Greece and in their innumerable printed works, they are making theology less academic and more Biblical, liturgical, and relevant for modern men in a rapidly changing society.

Ecumenical Interests. Active participation in the various ecumenical discussions launched throughout Europe in the 20th century, especially in the World Council of Churches from the very first assembly of 1948 in Amsterdam, brought closer contact with Protestants and Roman Catholics. Greek theologians sought to emerge from the national narrowness in an attempt to understand forms of Christianity other than their own. The late 20th century witnessed in Greek theology a flexible approach to theology, a return to the Bible, the Eastern liturgies, and the writings of the early Fathers. The new Greek theology aimed for relevance to the modern Christian developments.

Bibliography: C. ANDROUTSOS, *Dogmatic Theology of the Orthodox Eastern Church* (2d ed. Athens 1956), in Greek. H. G. BECK, *Kirche und theologische Literatur im byzantinischen Reich* (Munich 1959). P. I. BRATSIOTIS, ''Greek Theology in the Last 50 Years,'' *Theologia* 19 (1941–48) 83–112, 271–86, in Greek; ed., *Die orthodoxe Kirche in griechischer Sicht,* 2 v. (Stuttgart 1959–60). F. GAVIN, *Some Aspects of Contemporary Greek Thought* (Milwaukee 1923). M. JUGIE, *Theologia dogmatica christianorum orientalium ab ecclesia catholica dissidentium*, 5 v. (Paris 1926–35) v.1. E. S. KIMMEL, *Monumenta fidei ecclesiae orientalis*, 2 v. (Jena 1850). K. KRUMBACHER, *Geschichte der byzantinischen Literatur* (Munich 1890; 2d ed. 1897). A. PALMIERI, *Theologia dogmatica orthodoxa*, 2 v. (Florence 1911–13). D. SAVRAMIS, ed., *Aus der neugriechischen Theologie* (*Das östliche Christentum*, Neue Folge 15; Würzburg 1961).

[G. A. MALONEY]

GREEN, HUGH, BL.

Priest, martyr; *alias* Ferdinand Brooke; b. London, England, *c.* 1584; d. hanged at Tyburn (London), Aug. 19 (or 28?), 1588. Hugh, son of Protestant gentry, took his degree at Peterhouse, Cambridge (1605), and was converted to Catholicism while a student at Gray's Inn. Thereafter he undertook seminary studies at the English College, Douai (1610–12). Following his ordination (1612) he tested a religious vocation as a Capuchin, but left for reasons unknown. Instead he became chaplain to Lady Arundel of Lanherne at Chideock Castle, Dorsetshire. Although he attempted to comply with Charles I's banishment of priests (March 8, 1641), he was late in embarking for the Continent. He was arrested, tried, and condemned in August. He had a profound effect on fellow prisoners, who sought his absolution before mounting the gallows. Green made a public confession of his sins and was absolved by a disguised Jesuit. Contemporary descriptions expound on the barbarity of his execution. The disembowelment took one-half hour, then witnesses played football with his severed head. Fr. Green was beatified by Pius XI on Dec. 15, 1929.

Feast of the English Martyrs: May 4 (England).

See Also: ENGLAND, SCOTLAND, AND WALES, MARTYRS OF.

Bibliography: R. CHALLONER, *Memoirs of Missionary Priests,* ed. J. H. POLLEN (rev. ed. London 1924; repr. Farnborough 1969), II, 113. J. H. POLLEN, *Acts of English Martyrs* (London 1891).

[K. I. RABENSTEIN]

GREENE, GRAHAM

Novelist; b. Berkhamsted, England, Oct. 2, 1904; d. Vevey, Switzerland, April 3, 1991.

After completing public school Greene was sent to Balliol College at Oxford in 1922, where he studied modern history. In 1925, he began a career in journalism, first with the *Nottingham Journal* for six months and then as subeditor with the *Times* of London, where he stayed until 1930. His efforts at getting published were ineffectual until his third novel, *The Man Within* (1929), which proved a success with both readers and critics.

Among Greene's early successes were *Stamboul Train* (1932; American title, *Orient Express*), *A Gun for Sale* (1936; American title, *This Gun for Hire*), and *The Confidential Agent* (1939). During this early period Greene experienced two important changes: his conversion to Roman Catholicism and his marriage. The events were linked by the fact that his future wife, Vivien Dayrell-Browning, was Catholic. He took instructions from Father Trollope at the cathedral in Nottingham and was accepted into the Church in 1926. The next year he married Vivien, and from that marriage came a daughter, Lucy Caroline (m. Bourget), and a son, Francis. By the close of 1939, however, the marriage had begun to disintegrate, and after the war Greene and his wife separated permanently.

The publication and reception of *Brighton Rock* in 1938 pointed the way toward Greene's strengthening grip on stories that brought issues of faith and politics to bear on each other. *Brighton Rock* was followed by *The Power and the Glory* (1940), *The Heart of the Matter* (1948), and *The End of the Affair* (1951). In each of these novels Greene depicts a character whose actions and beliefs force the reader to question the nature of the life of faith, of the ways in which saint and sinner are two halves of one being, and the difficulties that lie in the way of defining goodness and evil in conventional moral terms. In *Brighton Rock* that character is the malevolent teenage hoodlum Pinkie; in *The Power and the Glory,* the deeply flawed but committed whisky priest; in *The Heart of the Matter,* the excruciatingly conscientious Major Scobie; and in *The End of the Affair,* the emotionally trapped and burdened Sarah Miles. In these protagonists and in others in his later fiction Greene created personalities that speak to readers of all faiths about abiding issues of religious belief and commitment.

Graham Greene. (AP/Wide World Photos)

During World War II Greene was an air-raid warden and later an agent in MI6, the counterintelligence arm of the British Secret Service. From 1941 to 1943 he served in Freetown, Sierra Leone, and from 1943 to 1944 he served in London in the Iberian section under the notorious Kim Philby. Greene remained a friend and staunch defender of Philby after the latter's defection to the Soviet Union in 1963. Greene's career in intelligence came to an end in 1944, but his fascination with it found voice in several novels, most notably *The Ministry of Fear* (1943), *The Third Man* (1950), *The Quiet American* (1955), *Our Man in Havana* (1958), and *The Human Factor* (1966).

In the 1950s and 1960s Greene continued to produce novels and short stories, plays, children's books, and essays. He also wrote two remarkable film scripts (*The Third Man* and *The Fallen Idol*), and accounts of journeys to areas of political and social crisis, such as Malaya, Kenya, Indochina, Haiti, Cuba, and the Congo. He reported on events for *Life, Paris-Match,* the *Sunday Times, Le Figaro,* and the *Sunday Telegraph,* and conducted a soberer but no less distinguished career as a director of the publishing firm the Bodley Head. His retirement from the business side of publishing came in 1968, but his writing career continued unabated until 1985, when he experienced a waning of his writing powers. Most of his last years were spent in residence in a small flat in Antibes, France, writing and giving occasional interviews. To the time of his death from complications caused by a blood disease at age 86, Greene remained a dedicated writer, producing late in life one of his finest books, *The Honorary Consul* (1973), in which he blends his usual concerns with both politics and religion in a tale of terrorism. Greene considered it his best work, though many readers continue to prefer the earlier novels of faith and disillusionment.

Although Greene came to detest the epithet "Catholic novelist," it is difficult not to think of him as one of the preeminent Catholic novelists of the twentieth century. Like his fellow authors Georges Bernanos, Ignazio Silone, and François Mauriac, Greene brought issues of faith and creed to bear powerfully on the lives of his characters. In his writings he raised important questions about the nature of evil, of God, of sin, and the relationship between conventional moral imperatives and the deeper, more profound question of the reality of evil. Although his fictional techniques strike many critics today as conventional and "high modern," it is no secret that his works continue to draw large readerships and to increase yearly in stature.

Bibliography: J. ADAMSON, *Graham Greene and Cinema* (Norman, OK 1984). M.F. ALLAIN, *The Other Man: Conversations with Graham Greene,* G. WALDEMAN, trans. (New York 1983); originally published in French as *L'autre et son double* (Paris 1981). M. COUTO, *Graham Greene: On the Frontier* (New York 1988). A. A. DEVITIS, *Graham Greene* (rev. ed.; Boston 1986). S. HYNES, ed., *Graham Greene: A Collection of Critical Essays* (Englewood Cliffs, NJ 1973). R. H. MILLER, *Understanding Graham Greene* (Columbia, SC 1990). R. SHARROCK, *Saints, Sinners, and Comedians: The Novels of Graham Greene* (Notre Dame, IN 1984). N. SHERRY, *The Life of Graham Greene,* Vol. I (London and New York 1989). P. STRATFORD, *Faith and Fiction: Creative Process in Greene and Mauriac* (Notre Dame 1964).

[R. H. MILLER]

GRÉGOIRE, HENRI BAPTISTE

French Constitutional bishop; b. Vého, near Lunéville (Meurthe-et-Moselle), Dec. 4, 1750; d. Paris, May 28, 1831. He was the son of a poor tailor. After his ordination (1775), he was a teacher at Pont-à- Mousson, a curate at Marimont, and in 1782 a pastor at Embermenil. Grégoire was at once a Jansenist and an admirer of the Enlightenment, who was distinguished by his tolerance and by his campaign in favor of the Jews. His election as representative of the clergy to the Estates-General in 1789 started his political career. In the Estates-General his aversion for the aristocracy led him to oppose the nobles among the bishops. He was one of the first clerical deputies to rally to the third estate, and he participated in the Oath of the Tennis Court. In the Constituent Assembly Grégoire campaigned for the liberation of Negroes and pronounced in favor of the CIVIL CONSTITUTION OF THE CLERGY. He opposed putting a limitation on the authority of the pope or on that of the bishops. After taking the oath to support the Civil Constitution, he was elected constitutional bishop of Blois, and was consecrated by Jean GOBEL (March 13, 1791). He scarcely ever resided in his diocese, except during the Legislative Assembly (1791–92), from which members of the Constituent Assembly were excluded. Grégoire was a member of all the remaining assemblies during the FRENCH REVOLUTION, with which he wished to reconcile the Church in order to save religion. When he was summoned in 1793 to abdicate his ecclesiastical functions, he imperiled his life by his refusal to do so. Even during the Terror he retained his episcopal costume. In the National Convention he was prominent especially on the Committee of Public Instruction, where he contributed to the foundation of the Academy of Arts and Crafts, the Central Astronomical Office, and the Institute of France. Also, he helped save from vandalism the treasures of religious art. A mission to Savoy saved him from voting on the execution of Louis XVI. After Thermidor, Grégoire defended religious liberty in the National Convention, and labored to restore the Constitutional Church, of which he became the effective head. He animated the two synods of this Church in 1797 and 1801.

During the Directory he was a member of the Five Hundred; and during the Consulate and Empire he was a member of the Legislature and then of the Senate. Grégoire opposed the Napoleonic regime and the CONCORDAT OF 1801. In the Senate he spoke in 1804 against the establishment of the Empire; and in 1814 he proposed that the Senate vote for Napoleon's deposition. Grégoire showed himself no less indomitable toward the Bourbons after the restoration. He was elected a deputy from Isére in 1819, but was excluded from the Chamber.

Grégoire resigned as bishop of Blois in 1802, but remained faithful to the Constitutional Church. He was responsible for the continuance of contacts between former Constitutional bishops and priests, and maintained an active correspondence with them and with the Jansenist Church of Utrecht. When Pius VII came to Paris in 1804 for Napoleon's coronation, Grégoire refused to approach him. Repeatedly he declined to retract his oath to the Civil Constitution. Despite the pleas of Archbishop de Quelen of Paris, the ''patriarch of the Gallican Church'' died unreconciled with the Holy See. Although the Archbishop forbade it, Abbé Guillon, the Queen's chaplain, administered to Grégoire the Last Rites. De Quelen also prohibited religious ceremonies at the funeral, but they were celebrated in the *Abbaye-au-bois,* Paris, by order of King Louis Philippe. Grégoire's theology was doubtfully sound and his outlook was somewhat confused, but his disinterestedness and his dignified priestly life deserve some recognition. Most of his numerous publications were polemical. His *Histoire des confesseurs des empereurs, des rois, et d'autres princes* and *Histoire des sectes religieuses* were placed on the Index (1827, 1828).

Bibliography: A. POUGET, *Les idées religieuses et réformatrices de l'évêque constitutionnel Grégoire* (Paris 1905). J. TILD, *L'Abbé Grégoire d'aprés ses mémoires* (Paris 1946). P. F. J. GRÜNEBAUM-BALLIN, *Henri Grégoire, l'ami des hommes des toutes les couleurs,* 1789–1831 (Paris 1948). P. PISANI, *Dictionnaire de théologie catholique*, ed. A. VACANT et al., 15 v. (Paris 1903–50) 6.2:1854–63. J. A. G. TANS, *Lexikon für Theologie und Kirche*, ed. J. HOFER and K. RAHNER, 10 v. (2d, new ed. Freiburg 1957–65) 4:1177.

[J. LEFLON]

GREGORIAN CHANT

The revival of monasticism in the 19th century by Dom P. GUERANGER of SOLESMES ABBEY and the concomitant revival in liturgical studies brought about a renewed interest in the history of Gregorian chant. This chant was seen as belonging to the golden age of the formation of Roman liturgy and thus as holding priority of place in the history of sacred music. Although terms such as plainsong or plainchant (*cantus planus,* unmeasured chant, in contradistinction to *cantus mensuratus* or rhythmically organized song) also are used, Gergorian chant has become the most popular term because it can be easily differentiated from AMBROSIAN, MOZARABIC, GALLICAN, and BYZANTINE chant. Gregorian chant was first written down in the 9th century and has continued in unbroken use in the Roman rite to the present day. In each period of music history it has been influenced by the contemporary musical idiom, and constant attempts to find out what its original character was like have bee made during the centuries. Present scholarship has unearthed many problems that remain unsolved. More important historical perspectives have been opened up by: M. Huglo, H. Hucke, J. Handschin, B. Stäblein, D. Levy, D. Hughes and J. McKinnon. Valuable contributions have been made by E. Wellesz, Dom L. Brou, and O. Strunk on the relationship between Gregorian chant and other

Illumination of the nativity annotated in Gregorian chant, from Pius II Book of Psalms, Orvieto Cathedral, Bethlehem. (©David Lees/CORBIS)

Eastern and Western chants. Scholars such as E. Jammers, J. Vollaerts, S. Corbin, and H. Husmann have probed specific areas such as paleography, rhythm, rhymed Offices, drama, Sequence, and trope. Work on the medieval theorists has not ceased, and valuable reediting and interpreting of texts has been done by J. Smits van Waesberghe, H. Oesch, and H. Hüschen. A most comprehensive and complete study on Gregorian chant, bringing together all of the information thus far arrived at by scholars and offering a balanced judgment on recent theories, was made by Willi Apel (*Gregorian Chant,* Bloomington, Indiana 1958). This present brief survey of mid-20th-century scholarship indicates the renewed interest in the field and the areas that are the subject of most concern.

Problem of Origin. General histories of music had too easily assumed that Gregorian chant dates back to at least the 6th century and was put in its present form by Pope Gregory the Great (590 to 604). Although this theory was often seriously challenged (see F. Gevaert, *Les Origines du chant liturgique de l'église latine,* Ghent 1890), it persisted in vogue, carried along by centuries of tradition. It must, however, be recalled that the first manuscripts containing Gregorian chant came from the 9th century from the Frankish empire. Many of these manuscripts, especially the *Graduales,* contain a famous introductory trope, *Gregorius praesul.* It is a kind of Carolingian publicity technique to advertise the fact that the new chants were in the Roman style, the *cantilena romana.* It cannot be proved that Gregory the Great is the Gregory here alluded to, and the possibility that it refers to Gregory II (715 to 731) must also be considered. Even if one accepts the assumption that Gregory the Great is referred to, it remains dubious how much of the music that is first written down in the 9th century goes back to Gregory's time in an oral tradition.

Gregory's Role. What can be said with certitude concerning the activity of Gregory the Great is that he sought to bring order into the liturgical texts by compiling from various sources the *antiphonarius cento.* This could not have been done without reference to the music accompanying the texts, but about this nothing is known. His concern for music can be seen also in the founding of monastic groups to serve the basilicas and in the impetus he gave to the *SCHOLA CANTORUM.* The general principles of music-making that lead to Gregorian chant and especially the principles of formulae that form its psalmodic structure must have existed in his day, but there is no way of proving that any given piece of Gregorian chant goes back to that date. In the lists of popes in the Liber pontificalis, other pontiffs also are included as contributing to the history of the annual liturgical cycle (*annalis cantus omnis*), but the lack of accurate musical examples from the period makes its impossible to assess the contribution of any particular individual to the formation of the chant corpus.

The Role of Rome. The problem of the origin of Gregorian chant is complicated by the difficulty of ascertaining the nature of chant at the Roman basilicas until the 11th century. It can be accurately documented that Roman chant from the 11th to the 13th century was not the same as Gregorian chant. Five manuscripts dating from that time contain a tradition that is unique. They are: Vat. lat. 5319, a *Graduale* from the last quarter of the 11th century; a *Graduale* dated 1071 and written for Santa Cecilia in Trastevere, now in the M. Bodner collection, Cologny-Genève, Switzerland; Vat. Bas. F22, a *Graduale* from the first half of the 13th century; Vat. Bas. B79, an antiphonary, 12th century; and British Museum, Add. 29, 988, an antiphonary from the 12th century. The theory that the tradition contained in these manuscripts dates back to the Carolingian period and beyond and is thus the ''Old-Roman'' repertoire has had strong support among scholars ever since the theory was seriously proposed by Bruno Stäblein (see *Die Musik in Geschichte und Gegenwart,* ed. F. Blume, 2:1265–1303). In general, Old-Roman chant is more ornate than Gregorian chant, but the melodic contours and formulae are too close to deny some original relationship between the two. That the Gregorian was simply derivative from the Old Roman without other influences seems impossible. It is also impossible to assert that the Old-Roman is simply an ornamented version of the Gregorian. Other solutions proposed make both chants of Roman origin, the Gregorian being the ''monastic'' practice that was carried northward by the monks into England and France. Such a solution does not explain the relationship between the two chants, however. The best solution still seems to be that proposed by M. Huglo and arrived at also by W. Apel, that the Old-Roman version comes closest to the Roman practice at the time of Charlemagne and that it combined with the Gallican usage to give birth during the 8th century to the version now called Gregorian. The testimony of Amalarius of Metz (early 9th century) certainly supports this view. The role of Gregory in the formation of the Old-Roman repertoire remains just as dubious. A solution to the problem, without the unexpected discovery of yet-unknown documents containing the Old-Roman version and dated before the 11th century, will have to rely on internal evidence and comparative studies not yet completed.

Repertoire. When Gregorian chant was first written down in the 9th century, the type of notation employed merely indicated the direction the melody was to take, up or down, without accurate pitch differences. Until that time the repertoire had to be retained by memory without such an aid. It is remarkable, nevertheless, that the oral tradition, written down almost simultaneously throughout the vast area of present-day France, Germany, and Italy, showed such great uniformity. The retention of this repertoire by memory must have been an ever-increasing burden to the choirmaster, and the necessity of teaching it to the monks and succeeding cantors gave added impetus to the search for a system of notation. The repertoire for Mass and Office at the beginning of the 9th century must have comprised well over 2,000 pieces. These pieces were not all different one from another, and the early cantors and chant theorists exploited such similarities in inventing didactic processes.

The Recitative and Psalmody. Since the texts for most of the liturgical services are taken from the Old and New Testaments, musical systems for their proclamation had to be devised that could be altered to suit prose texts of various lengths. Simple formulas for the Old Testament reading, the Epistle and Gospel at Mass and for the readings at Matins consisted of a single recitation pitch with variants from the pitch to indicate inner and final pauses in the texts. More solemn tones were devised for the greater solemnities. Special tones were reserved for the lamentations on Good Friday and the reading of the Passion. The tones for the orations of the Mass and the Prefaces followed the same general principles of a recitation tone with cadential figures but respected the nature of the text by having two types of inner cadences. This simple principle served also for the frequent singing of Psalms at Mass and Office, where the antithetical structure of the text was clearly outlined by the musical cadences. There is some indication that the second half of the verse was not always sung on the same pitch as the first and that the text structure was delineated more clearly by a second reciting tone.

Responsorial and Antiphonal Chants. Although Gregorian chant may have arisen out of the recitation system just described, individual pieces—at first derived almost exclusively from the Psalter—became a part of the entire system. The greatest body of these pieces are the antiphons of the Mass and Office. Their counterpart are the responsories. The antiphons may originally have been sung as a kind of refrain after two groups alternated verses of the Psalter; but this practice had disappeared before the 9th century, and the antiphons that are found in Gregorian chant are larger and more elaborate and were sung only before and after the Psalm. At Mass the Introit and Communion were sung in this fashion; at the Office the many Psalms of all the hours had antiphons to be sung with them. The tonary of Regino of Prüm (d. 915) contained 1,235 such Office antiphons. It was evident to the Carolingian cantors that these antiphons could be catalogued according to certain melodic characteristics. From this one can surmise that the preceeding oral tradition for the antiphons must have had a kind of repertoire of melodic formulae to which new texts were adapted. These formulae, it can be seen, often have a kind of psalmodic structure to them, consisting of a recitation tone with cadential figures. If such was the primitive state of the music of the antiphons, with the passing of time they tended to become independent pieces in their own right.

In origin the Responsory too consisted of a refrain sung after verses of a Psalm, but this time the verses were sung by a solo cantor. By the time Gregorian chant was written down, this form had lost much of its primitive shape, except that its soloistic nature had tended to make the responsory more elaborate, especially the psalmodic verses. At Mass the Gradual and Alleluia are responsorial in nature. The Offertory seems to have passed from being antiphonal to responsorial in character shortly before the chant repertoire was written down. Even in the responds, especially in the substructure of the elaborate verses, one can see the original psalmodic principle of reciting tone and cadential figures. At Matins the responsory follows the scripture readings as a kind of musical commentary on the Scriptures. Their original improvisational nature had been lost before the 9th century.

Other Pieces. The chant repertory included other specific pieces that were needed to complete the Mass and Office services. Some of these chants may originally have been quite simple in nature, somewhat in the style of a litany, but later developed into full-blown, ornate pieces. This had become true of the Ordinary of the Mass by the late Carolingian period. Elaborate Kyrie's, Gloria's, Sanctus's, and Agnus Dei's can be found in all *Graduales* and form one of the most complicated groups of the chant repertoire. Only the Ordinary and the Alleluia cycle seem to have remained areas for new compositions after the 9th century. They were the last pieces of the standard repertory to be fixed; the composition of new chant Ordinaries continued even after the high Middle Ages. All of these items were affected by the new forms of the TROPE and SEQUENCE.

Sources. Various claims have been made periodically by scholars that they have found fragments of musical notation that go back to the 8th century. But each of these items, such as the *Orationale* of Verona, when subjected to closer scrutiny, has been declared as non-musical in nature or as additions by later hands. The first verified fragments are still from the mid-9th century with the first full manuscript from the end of the century. The fragments are usually of isolated pieces that do not belong to the standard repertoire or are newly composed—evidence that these first attempts at mnemonic notation had a practical, didactic purpose. The treatise of Aurelian of Réomé (written about 850) has several passages that imply a knowledge on his part of a primitive notation. Of special interest are the paleofrankish fragments from the end of the 9th century that show a different system from that which became standard throughout the West. A treatise such as Hucbald's *De institutione harmonica* (written about 900) shows the growing concern on the part of cantors for a more precise notation than that of the mnemonic neumes then in use. (A list of full manuscripts from about 900 can be found in Suñol, *Introduction* . . . 32.) Not until a century later (about 1000) was the staff invented, and then it required another half century before it was perfected to the point where melodic accuracy could be perfectly ascertained. For this reason chant scholars must search for the pieces of the earlier MSS in later 11th- and 12th-century manuscripts to transcribe with accuracy. In sum, the first manuscripts containing Gregorian chant in an accurate unequivocal melodic notation came from shortly after the year 1000; the repertory can be traced back to 900 in a mnemonic notation, but only in fragments and descriptions befor that.

Theorists. In addition to the manuscripts containing the chant repertory, there exist the chant theorists, who furnish invaluable information on the repertory and how it was performed. The first such theorist is Aurelian of Réomé, who wrote his *Musicá disciplina* about 850. A fragment of this treatise has been erroneously attributed to Alcuin. Aurelian in the first eight chapters of his work gives a résumé of the theory of music inherited from the ancient Greeks through Boethius and Cassiodorus. He makes no attempt to reconcile this theory with the chant practice of his day. Boethius in particular was used in the Carolingian schools as the *auctor itas* in music. From chapters 9 to 20, however, Aurelian makes a first attempt of cataloguing the chant repertory according to the *toni.* For the first time he speaks of the Byzantine octoechos, or eight modes, and of the manner in which the Psalms sung in these modes are to be joined to the antiphons and responds. Subsequent chant theorists, such as Regino of Prüm (d. 915), Hucbald of St. Armand (d. 930), and Remy of Auxerre (end of 9th century), began the arduous task of trying to combine these two divergent theoretical systems and to use them for an explanation of Gregorian chant. The octoechos became identified for the first time with the eight-mode Boethian system in the treatise *De alia musica* (late 9th century). It is not until the 11th century that the amalgamation is completed in the treatises of GUIDO OF AREZZO, BERNO OF REICHENAU, and HERMANNUS CONTRACTUS. There is evidence that the inherited Boethian theory had an effect on the chant that may have been altered at times to fit the *auctoritas.* Boethius continued to be taught as the authority in the schools and universities of the Middle Ages, while Guido became the infallible guide to the cantor.

Gregorian Chant Style. To the 20th-century ear, accustomed to the gigantic sounds of the orchestra of the romanticist period and the striking contrasts of dynamics and timbre inherent in the romanticist style, Gregorian chant seems unemotional and less expressive. To a listener of the Middle Ages, however, this was not true. The Gregorian style was broad in its expressive content, even though more austere than the music of recent centuries. Since it had to accommodate so many prose texts, it ranged from formulalike patterns such as psalmody and antiphon types to highly expressive melismatic passages such as the *jubilus* of the Alleluia. These extremes in the style have often been labeled syllabic and melismatic, or *accentus* and *concentus.* Such terms, however, are not synonymous. Syllabic chant refers to those pieces in which each syllable has predominantly one note, seldom more; melismatic chant has expressive vocalises on important syllables. In between these two lie most of the chant pieces. The Sequence, for example, is syllabic; the Alleluia is melismatic. Most of the Introits, Offertories, and Communions lie in between. *Accentus* refers to the recitative formulas used for orations and thereadings—the heightened speech patterns, while the *concentus* refers to true melody. In the latter the laws of music itself have their role.

Chant Rhythm. Perhaps no other aspect of Gregorian chant has been so feverishly debated by scholars as that of the original rhythm of the chant. The following facts are accepted by all: The earliest chant manuscripts (from *c.* 900) show various ways of writing the same neume and these variants imply rhythmic differences. Many of these manuscripts reinforce this notational difference with letters (called Romanian letters) to signify rhythmic alteration. Other differences in notation involve vocal phenomena (such as the liquescents and the quilisma) that also have rhythmic implications. The basic diference in interpretation of these signs among scholars centers around the length of the altered notes in relationship to a given pulse. Further dispute arises as to the rhythmic organization of the given pulse. It was in answer to this latter question that Dom MOCQUEREAU developed the theory of rhythm, usually called the Solesmes theory, in which the basic pulses are related by groups of two or three and with the unifying factor being called the ictus. This ictus is conceived as the end of rhythmic motion in its fundamental state of movement—repose. Mocquereau attempted to show at great length that this is the natural rhythm of the Latin word, which gave its rhythm to the chant. Such a theory has much merit in dealing with psalmody and other pieces belonging to the *accentus* group; it proves more difficult to maintain in dealing with the *concentus.* Here the ictus, or rhythmic subdivision, corresponds at times with the end or repose of the Latin word, at times with accent or force (as when it corresponds in larger phrases with the accent of the text), at times with length, or even at times with melodic contour. There is no doubt that Mocquereau's theory grew out of the accentualist or oratorical theory of Dom Pothier, where the textual accent of the Latin word was the organizing principle, and that he broadened the concept so that it could serve also for the melismatic passages. To introduce it into present books, an elaborate system of vertical and horizontal bars was invented.

The Solesmes theory was rejected at the turn of the 19th century by most German scholars who ranked themselves among the mensuralists, i.e., those favoring various time values with accent as the chief unifying factor. The former mensuralist theories of Dechevrens, Peter Wagner, Dom Jeannin, and Bonvin have all but been forgotten. Chief exponents of mensuralism today are E. Jammers and J. Vollaerts, although their theories admit of only two or three time values and are a kind of free rhythm with irregular occuring accents. It can be said that the weakness of the Solesmes theory lies in its historical justification in the nature of the Latin word since it presupposes that this rhythm was established for chant in the 5th and 6th centuries during its formative period, a supposition that is hard to maintain. The historical evidence in favor of the long and short time values comes chiefly from the theorists, and it seems a less forced interpretation of the early neumes and the different ways in which they are written. More recent rhythmic studies by T. Agostoni and E. Cardine are tending to a modification of the Solesmes theory that brings it closer to the interpretation of J. Vollaerts. It is unfortunate that the introduction of polyphony and the tendency to clearer pitch indications in notation saw at the same time a less accurate rhythmic care. The notation *in campo aperto,* i.e., without lines, and thus mnemonic in character, is less accurate in pitch but more accurate in rhythm, while the later diastematic manuscripts, i.e., with lines, are more accurate in pitch but less so in rhythm and vocal nuances.

Formal Aspects of Gregorian Chant. All patterns found in later Western music are found also in chant. Musicologists have taken great pains to find ABA and Rondo forms in various chant pieces. All of this is true but says little about the formal structures of the chant melody. Being pure melody, the chant relies on purely melodic motives for its formal structure. In general, the high point of the line is arrived at rather rapidly and tapers off gradually. The length of the line is frequently dictated by the text and its components. There is no music where the shape of the text so affects the shape of the line. Sequential structures are found but never stressed as formative elements. The general punctuation of the text determines the inner cadences, which, as a rule, do not stress the final tone. Later melodies tend to have larger leaps in succession, while the older melodies use the leap beyond a third with great discretion. The word accent does not always receive musical development but frequently is higher in pitch than the unaccented syllables. There is some evidence that interest in the Latin rhythmic cursus may have had some influence in cadential formulas, especially of the psalm tones. The manner in which a typical pattern can be altered to fit a new text shows a keen appreciation of text declamation and a freedom within a given form that is always expressive and sensitive. The subtlety was lost or obscured by the advent of polyphony.

The Modal System. The chief unifying element in Gregorian chant is its modal structure. The oral tradition from which chant arose was undoubtedly one of a group of melodic formulae or phrases that could be adapted to various texts. These formulae were traditionally grouped into eight divisions depending on the melodic contour, the manner of beginning, and the relationship between the reciting or dominant tone and the ending formula. There is reason to believe that originally the beginning was most important in such a grouping, but certainly after the influence of the classical Greek theories inherited through Boethius the ending or final note and its relationship to the reciting or dominant note proved the vital factor in determining mode. Also from Boethius is derived the influence of range as an important element. The Byzantine theory that was inherited spoke of four authentic modes and four plagal or derivative modes. A plagal mode shared with its respective authentic mode the same final but usually had a lower dominant or reciting tone, thus throwing the whole range somewhat lower. In the authentic modes the final or cadential figure comes at the bottom of the range; in the plagal modes, it is in the middle. The accompanying table presents the standard modal theory as it was fully developed in the treatises of the 11th century. This theory cannot be applied rigidly to all chants. By the introduction of the B♭ the general flavor of a mode can be altered and transpositions can be effected. There are no other accidentals possible in chant, and thus chromaticism is impossible. The tritone (interval of the augmented fourth) was avoided also in later chant, although the treatise of Hucbald *De institutione harmonica* cites this interval without prejudice and gives examples of it. Later tonaries give model modal melodies that embody the characteristics of each mode and served didactic purposes, but the repertory itself is much freer in its adherence to modal structure. Some of the more elaborate verses of the soloistic responsories use both the plagal and authentic ranges of the same mode and thus exploit all of the melodic possibilities of the mode.

Subsequent History of Gregorian Chant. After the Carolingian period the interests of the chant composer turned to tropes and Sequences and the rise of polyphony. The standard repertory remained in use, but it lost its rhythmic piquancy and became the source for polyphonic treatment. Several new Offices were written that exploited the modal theories by presenting the antiphons of the night Office in modal succession, but general interest in chant composition waned.

The Council of Trent. By the 16th century the condition of chant was truly lamentable, and a reform was badly needed. Unfortunately the Medicean edition that resulted from an attempt at reform (*see* CHANT BOOKS, PRINTED EDITIONS OF) was not founded on scholarly principles and reflected more the aesthetics of the late Renaissance than the early Middle Ages. This edition, however, remained the source for all subsequent editions until the 19th century. Pioneers in musical research in the 19th century, such as Lambillotte, La Fage, D'Ortigue, and Nasard, laid the basis for the subsequent more accurate work of the Solesmes school. To this latter, under the directorship of Dom Pothier and Dom Mocquereau, belongs the lasting credit of making available the original mnemonic manuscripts in facsimile editions in the series *Paléographie musicale grégorienne* and of initiating a series of monographs that made scholars search out the original documents. The treatises of the theorists were gathered together by M. GERBERT and E. Coussemaker. The controversies that arose in opposition to the Solesmes theories, with P. Wagner and F. Gevaert as chief protagonists, gave rise to intensive chant studies that are still accurate sources for information.

Present Practice. As a result of chant scholarship since the mid-19th century, the present practice can be said to come closer to the original in its melodic precision than that of any previous century. However, the rhythmic controversies still continue; there are more performances in the mensuralist style, and there is less adherence to the Solesmes school. Frequently the chant is accompanied on the organ, which thus adds a third dimension never intended by the original composers. Often this accompaniment totally falsifies the underlying modal structure. True chant must be unaccompanied. Attempts at congregational use of the chant repertory in the 20th century have been limited to the simple Mass Ordinaries and have not been universally successful. It is generally found to be too alien to 20th-century aesthetic tastes. Various systems of arm and hand motions also have been invented to direct chant (called chironomy) and have been most successfully used. With the increase of the vernacular in the liturgy, less interest has been shown in Gregorian chant, although many attempts at adapting its melodies to new English texts have been made.

Bibliography: A complete bibliography of Gregorian chant to 1935 can be found in G. M. SUÑOL, *Introduction à la paléographie musicale grégorienne* (Tournai 1935), and an extension of the same *Bibliographie grégorienne, 1935–1937* (3d ed. Solesmes-Rome 1958). A further extensive bibliography is found in B. STÄBLEIN, "Choral," *Die Musik in Geschichte und Gegenwart*, ed. F. BLUME (Kassel-Basel 1949–) 2:1265–1303. The two most extensive works on Gregorian chant are P. WAGNER, *Einführung in die gregorianischen Melodien*, 3 v. (Leipzig), v.1 (3d ed. 1911), v.2 (2d ed. 1912), v.3 (1921); repr. (Hildesheim 1962) and W. APEL, *Gregorian Chant* (Bloomington, Indiana 1958). The following works in English are comprehensive and useful: G. REESE, *Music in the Middle Ages* (New York 1940). J. SMITS VAN WAESBERGHE, *Gregorian Chant* (London 1949). H. ANGLÈS, "Latin Chant before St. Gregory" and "Gregorian Chant," *New Oxford History of Music*, ed. J. A. WESTRUP, 11 v. (New York 1957–) 2:58–127. Indispensable sources are: M. GERBERT, *Scriptores ecclesiastici de musica sacra potissimum*, 3 v. (Milan 1931). H. COUSSEMAKER, *Scriptorum de musica medii aevi nova series*, 4 v. (Paris 1864–76). *Paléographie musicale* (Solesmes 1889–). H. M. BANNISTER, *Monument Vaticani di paleografia musicale latina*, 2 v. (Leipzig 1913). Selective list of other important works follows. R. J. HESBERT, ed., *Antiphonale missarum sextuplex* (Brussels 1935). W. H. FRERE, ed., *Antiphonale Sarisburiense* (London 1901–26); *Graduale Sarisburiense* (London 1894); *The Winchester Troper* (London 1894). P. M. FERRETTI, *Esthétique grégorienne* (Paris 1938). A. GASTOUÉ, *L'Antiphonaire grégorien* (Paris 1907); *Le Graduel et l'antiphonaire* (Paris 1913); *Les Origines du chant romain* (Paris 1907). F. A. GEVAERT, *La Mélopée antique dans le chant de l'Église latine* (Ghent 1895); *Les Origines du chant liturgique de l'Église latine* (Ghent 1890). A. MOCQUEREAU, *Le Nombre musical grégorien*, 2 v. (Tournai 1908–27). J. POTHIER, *Les Mélodies grégoriennes* (Tournai 1880). P. WAGNER, *Einführung in die gregorianischen Melodien*, 3 v. (Leipzig), v.1 (3d ed. 1911), v.2 (2d ed. 1912), v.3 (1921); repr. (Hildesheim 1962). O. URSPRUNG, *Die katholische Kirchenmusik* (Potsdam 1931). R. VAN DOREN, *Étude sur l'influence musicale de l'Abbaye de Saint-Gall, VIIIe au XIe siècle* (Brussels 1925). F. TACK, *Gregorian Chant* (Cologne 1960). L. AGUSTONI, *Gregorianischer Choral* (Freiburg 1963). *Études grégoriennes*, 5 v. (Solesmes 1954–62). W. APEL, *Gregorian Chant* (Bloomington, Indiana 1958). H. HUCKE, "Toward a New Historical View of Gregorian Chant," *Journal of the American Musicological Society* 33 (1980) 411–87. H. VAN DER WERF, *The Emergence of Gregorian Chant* (Rochester, New York 1983). D. HUGHES, "Evidence for the Traditional View of the Transmission of Gregorian Chant," *Journal of the American Musicological Society* 40 (1987) 377–404. K. LEVY, "Charlemagne's Archetype of Gregorian Chant," *Journal of the American Musicological Society* 40 (1987) 1–30. J. MCKINNON, "The Emergence of Gregorian Chant in the Carolingian Era," *Antiquity and the Middle Ages* (London 1990) 88–119. D. HILEY, *Western Plainchant: A Handbook* (Oxford 1993).

[R. G. WEAKLAND/EDS.]

GREGORIAN REFORM

This term is traditionally used to designate the vast movement of reform of the Church, beginning toward the middle of the 11th century and continuing into the 1st decade of the 12th. GREGORY VII, who has been made the patron of this movement, was neither its initiator nor its final consummator. Yet the importance of his reign, the measures taken by this pope and implemented by his legates under his impetus and the prestige that he was able to restore to the PAPACY justify in large measure the application of the adjective Gregorian to the reforming movement. The works to which Augustin FLICHE devoted the greater part of his academic labors have contributed to popularizing the expression. In recent years new studies have underscored the part played by CLUNY in this reform movement (especially K. Hallinger, *Gorze-Kluny*) and have restored to their proper proportions the contributions of Gregory VII.

The history of the Gregorian reform could be traced from the PAPAL ELECTION DECREE (1059) of NICHOLAS II to the First LATERAN COUNCIL (1123). Such an exposition would cover a period of moderate reform (1049–73), the harder Gregorian line (1073–85) and the conciliatory tendency after URBAN II (1088–1123). The narrative, however, would exceed the scope of this article. But three lines along which the reformers were working must be distinguished: (1) reaffirmation of papal primacy; (2) reform of the clergy; and (3) freeing the Church from lay ascendancy. Nor is this the place to discuss the important reform that progressed simultaneously in the monastic establishment or in canonical renewal; for these, although essential aspects of the Gregorian movement, are such vast and complex subjects as to require special studies [J. F. Lemarignier, *Histoire des institutions françaises au moyen-âge,* 3 (Paris 1962) 115–138].

Although for the sake of clarity the three problems have been held distinct, it is evident that in actual fact these questions were intimately connected and that measures considered for any one of them could not but have an effect on the others. All these measures tended in fact to substitute for the Carolingian and Ottonian dream of an *ecclesia universalis,* grouping *sacerdotium* and *regnum* into one politico religious community, the organization of a Church independent of secular powers, having its own institutions and law and profiting from the weakness of princes to assume the leadership of Western Christendom.

REAFFIRMATION OF PAPAL PRIMACY

The Gregorian age marks a crucial stage in the history of papal PRIMACY. This primacy had indeed been strongly asserted in the fifth century by INNOCENT I and LEO I. The CANONICAL COLLECTIONS of the Gelasian era were at once a manifestation and an assertion of it. But the papacy in the tenth and in the first half of the 11th century had experienced a period of crisis, weakness and at times disgrace. A prize contested by the factions of Rome, dependent on the will of the German emperor, given over to men who were often mediocre and at times unworthy, the papacy could not exercise its role of leadership in the Church.

Pre-Gregorian Reforms. Thus the decree of Nicholas II, promulgated at the Lateran Synod (April 13, 1059), a few weeks after his accession, was of crucial importance. It reserved to the cardinal bishops the *tractatio* culminating in the designation of a new pope. The other cardinals were to be consulted only after the fact and the clergy and the Roman people were merely to acclaim the candidate so designated [*Monumenta Germaniae Historica, Constitutiones,* 1:529; the imperial version of this text (*ibid.* 1:543) is a forgery dating probably from 1084]. In practice, the rights of the emperor simply disappeared. Despite the opposition of the Roman nobility and the emperor, the new procedure was confirmed and even stiffened the following year in another Lateran Synod (April of 1060; *ibid.* 1:550). Thus the papacy recovered an independence that was the preliminary condition to any reform in the Church.

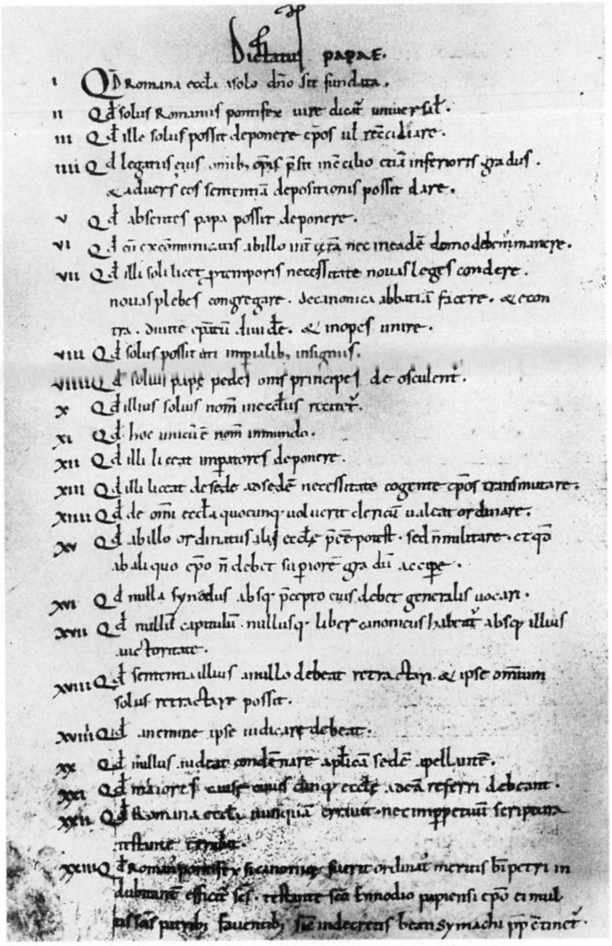

"Dictatus Papae," list of 27 propositions, possibly titles for Gregorian canonical collections, manuscript folios from a Register of Gregory VII.

Although the decree of 1059 was crucial, it was not a complete innovation. The election of STEPHEN IX (1057) had already been effected without German intervention and the *Adversux simoniacos* of HUMBERT OF SILVA CANDIDA [*Monumenta Germaniae Historica, Libelli de lite* (Berlin 1826—) 1:95–253] had demanded freedom of ecclesiastical elections. Nicholas II's successor, ALEXANDER II, had, as bishop of Lucca, striven against the immorality of the clergy. His advisers, PETER DAMIAN (Opusc. 4: *Disceptio synodalis;* Opusc. 5: *De privilegiis Romanae ecclesiae*) and Hildebrand, were convinced that the reform could come only from Roman authority, and the pope strongly asserted the Roman primacy in his bulls. The legates, among them Peter Damian, HUGH OF REMIREMONT and Gerard of Ostia (d. 1077), made it felt in France, Spain, England and even in Scandinavia, Bohemia and Dalmatia. In Germany the pope profited from the minority of HENRY IV and gained control of the Church in the empire. Finally, Robert Guiscard

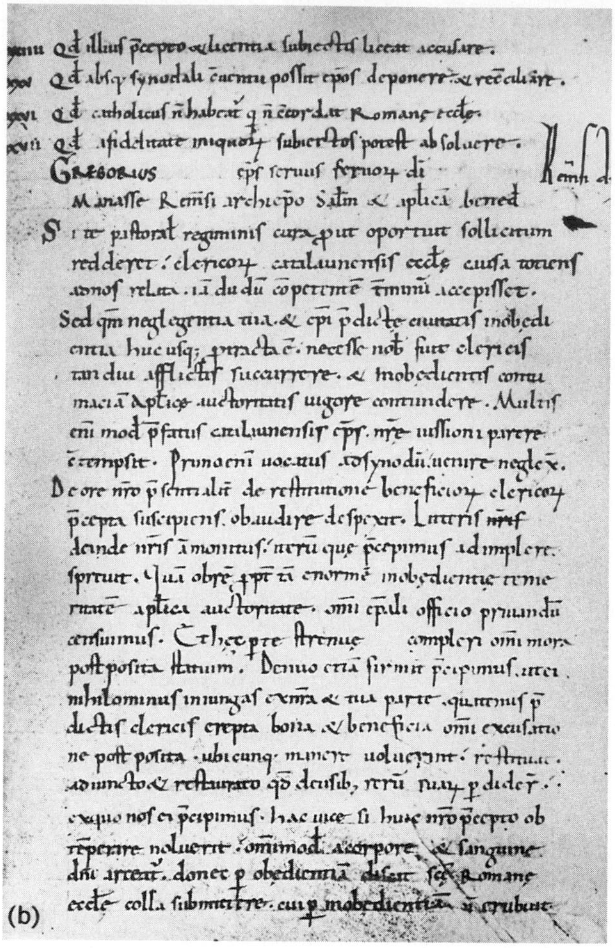

(b)

Page 2 of the ''Dictatus Papae.''

had some years previously declared himself a vassal of Nicholas II for the Norman lands in southern Italy and Alexander II, who organized the French crusade in Spain, reserved to the Holy See the overlordship of lands that might be retaken from the infidels.

Gregory VII. But it was GREGORY VII (1073–85) who by his policy toward the princes, especially the German sovereign, as well as by his doctrinal pronouncements, maintained most dramatically the Roman primacy. At the beginning of the reign his letter to the faithful of Lombardy (*Reg.* 1.15; July 1, 1073) and later the *DICTATUS PAPAE* (*Reg.* 2.55a; 1075) and the letters to Hermann of Metz (*Reg.* 4.2; 7.21; Aug. 25, 1076, and May 15, 1081) set forth the foundation, the principles, and the practical consequences of the primacy. It is of divine origin: the pope is only the intermediary, charged with making known the will of the Trinity and of the Apostles Peter and Paul. As Leo the Great before him, Gregory identified himself with Peter. The 27 propositions constituting the *Dictatus papae* articulate in lapidary and unrestrained terms the universal power of the pope; his authority over bishops, clerics and councils; and his right to depose the emperor, to certify every canonical text, to make law and to deliver judgments from which there is no appeal. ''Founded by the Lord alone'' (*Dict.* 1), the Roman Church cannot err (*Dict.* 22). The judge of all, the pope cannot be judged by anyone (*Dict.* 18–21). Thus the pope is overlord of the Church; he controls the hierarchy and can modify its institutions. The authority of Rome is no less with respect to secular princes and Gregory demonstrated papal power in the struggle with Henry IV, as well as in several letters that formulate the theory of the supremacy of the Holy See over temporal rulers (Dec. 8, 1075 and May 8, 1080; *Reg.* 3.10, 7.25, etc.). Gregory exercised this authority over the Church in councils in which he achieved the adoption of his reforming views and by the action of his legates who were his representatives all over Christendom and, as such, took precedence over all local authority (*Dict.* 4).

The Gregorian policy was given significant support in a series of occasional, politically inspired writings (especially the *Liber ad Gebehardum* of MANEGOLD OF LAUTENBACH, *c.* 1084; *Monumenta Germaniae Historica, Libelli de lite,* 1) and still more in the so-called Gregorian collections (P. Fournier and G. Lebras, *Histoire des collections canoniques en occident depuis les fausses décrétales jusqu'au Décret de Gratien,* 2). To the collections of the preceding period, stressing the powers of the bishop (especially the *Decretum* of BURCHARD OF WORMS, beginning of the 11th century) were added a series of collections, mostly Italian in origin, which had been inspired by the desire for reform and by the concern that reform be founded on a restoration of papal authority. Some of these collections appeared prior to the pontificate of Gregory VII [the *Collection in 74 Titles* under LEO IX, called by Fournier the ''first canonical manual of the reform''; it may actually have been preceded by the *Collection in Two Books,* which its recent editor, J. Bernhard (Strasbourg 1962), dates for *c.* 1053]. The most important collections date from Gregory's pontificate and were often composed at his urging: the *Capitulare* of ATTO OF VERCELLI; the *Collection in 12 Books* of ANSELM OF LUCCA, close collaborator with the pope, *c.* 1083; the *Collection* of DEUSDEDIT, begun under Gregory, but published only *c.* 1085; later under Urban II, the *Liber de vita christiana* of BONIZO OF SUTRI, etc. All these collections exalt the Roman primacy. Often they commence with a section titled *De primatu romanae ecclesiae.* They are in accord with papal policy and serve its purposes. The texts produced by these compilers establish the divine institution of the Roman Church, the dogmatic primacy of the sovereign pontiff, his right to legislate for the whole Church, to judge any case, to direct all the members of the hierarchy and all the faithful, including secular rulers.

The stockpile of texts thus collected corresponded to the tenets of the *Dictatus papae* and was to be of great service to the Roman policy in the difficult years following the death of Gregory VII.

The exaltation of Roman primacy was continued by the successors of Gregory VII. It led the papacy, especially under Urban II, to accede to the requests for exemption of monasteries that were thus removed from Episcopal jurisdiction and put directly under Rome. Accordingly, the renewal of the privileges of Cluny occurred in 1088; so too the exemption of La Cava, 1089 and especially 1093; of Saint-Victor de Marseilles, 1089; Marmoutier, 1090; Fécamp, c. 1093 etc. [see J. F. Lemarignier, *Privilèges d'exemption . . . des abbayes normandes . . .* (Paris 1937); P. Jaffé, *Regesta pontificum romanorum ab condita ecclesia ad annum post Christum natum 1198,* 5714, 5715, 5773, 5782, 5783, 5787, 5791, 5792, 5802]. Urban II, moreover, continued the centralizing efforts of Gregory VII and declared: "The important matters of individual churches must be judged by Apostolic authority" (*Regesta pontificum romanorum ab condita ecclesia ad annum post Christum natum 1198,* L 5519).

REFORM OF THE CLERGY

In furthering clerical reform, another major objective of the Gregorian movement, the papacy continued along lines set by the Cluniac reformers. Lay intrusion into the assignment of bishoprics, abbeys and parishes had entailed two evils affecting the clergy: acquisition of ecclesiastical dignities for money or some material advantage (SIMONY) and immorality of the clergy, who were often married or living in concubinage (Nicolaitanism).

Simony. This abuse had been denounced by Cardinal Humbert in his treatise *Adversus simoniacos.* The author considered simony a heresy and denied any validity to the consecration of a bishop who had bought his see. Consequently, any ordination conferred by a simoniacal prelate was null and void. This was a rigorously logical solution but one that ran the risk of setting aside a great portion of the hierarchy. For many had been branded as simonists either by their own act, or by that of the prelate who had given them orders, or via some preceding prelate (see the possibly excessive but alarming estimates made by Bonizo of Sutri, *Liber ad amicum,* 6). Peter Damian was more moderate and perhaps more realistic: he contented himself with imposing on simoniacal clerics a severe penance and suspension from the exercise of their office. But the rigorous position was still being defended by Bonizo of Sutri (*Liber de vita christiana,* 1089–94) and Deusdedit (*Libellus contra invasores et simoniacos,* prior to 1095).

The fight against simony was joined by c.6 of the Lateran Synod of 1059, which forbade anyone "to receive a church from the hands of a layman, either gratis or for money" (see c.9 which speaks of "simoniacal heresy"). The prohibition of simony was renewed in the synods of 1060 (J. D. Mansi, *Sacrorum Conciliorum nova et amplissima collectio,* 19:899) and November of 1078. The legates were energetic in citing the prohibition and in having it respected in Italy, France (Council of Vienne and Tours, 1060) and Germany, where simony was general during the minority of Henry IV. The fight waged by Gregory VII was continued by Urban II, who in several bulls proclaimed the deposition of simonists (*Regesta pontificum romanorum ab condita ecclesia ad annum post Christum natum 1198,* L 5381, 5396, 5743). The Council of Melfi (1089) renewed the condemnation (c.1). However, in several cases the pope showed a sometimes excessive tolerance, which was reproved by Bonizo of Sutri. As against the rigorist stand of the Italian canonists, IVO OF CHARTRES, though reproducing the canons against simony and Nicolaitanism (*Decretum* 5.81—), authorized in the prologue of the *Decretum* (where he took up again the theory of dispensation expounded some years previously by BERNOLD OF CONSTANCE) certain relaxations justified by the *necessitas temporis* or by considerations of mercy. Simony was again condemned by the Councils of Autun (1094), Piacenza (1095; c.2–7), and Clermont (1095; c.6–8), which again adopted the rigorist doctrines of the Italian canonists.

"Simoniacal heresy" continued to rage, however, in the final years of the 11th century, especially in France. CALLISTUS II denounced it again at the Councils of Toulouse (1119; c.1, 6, 8, 9) and of Reims (1119; c.1, 4). In Hungary the Council of Gran (1114) likewise forbade simony (c.42–43). Simony was solemnly condemned in c.1 of the First Lateran Council (1123). The large number of such measures shows how difficult they were to implement pratically. However, the persevering action of the popes and their legates, the end of the INVESTITURE STRUGGLE in the Empire and the gradual decrease of lay pressure resulted, toward the first quarter of the 12th century, in a noticeable improvement in the recruitment of the episcopate. Although simony had not ceased entirely, it was no longer the scourge that a half-century previously had discredited the hierarchy.

Celibacy. Simultaneously with their fight against simony, legislators and reforming prelates attacked the immorality of the clergy. The Synod of 1059 forbade priests living in concubinage to celebrate Mass and ordered the faithful not to assist at the offices of an unworthy minister (c.3). This assembly recalled the regulation, traditional in the Latin Church, imposing CELIBACY on clerics from the subdiaconate onward. Contrary to these norms, a pamphlet of 1060, probably the work of Bishop Ulric of Imola, maintained that the only means of averting clerical immorality was to permit the clergy to marry [*Monumenta Germaniae Historica, Libelli de lite* 1:254–60; A. Fliche, *Revue des sciences religieuses,* 2 (1922) 127–139]. This pamphlet was revised and expanded in a Norman version [*ibid.* 5 (1925)] and again in the *Tractatus Eboracenses* (*Monumenta Germaniae Historica, Libelli de lite* 3:645). It was against such tendencies that Peter Damian published his *De celibatu sacerdotum* [*Patrologia Latina,* ed. J. P. Migne, 217 V., indexes 4 v. (Paris 1878–90) 145:379–388]. Gregory VII fought energetically against the incontinence of the clergy [Council of Rome, Lent 1074 [see *Studi gregoriani,* ed. G. B. Borino (Rome 1947—) 6:277–295]; by letters of the pope to bishops, for example, *Reg.* 2.61, 64, 66, 67, 68; 3.3, 4; by excommunication of unworthy prelates; and by local action by legates]. The reform work was carried on by Urban II [Councils of Melfi (1089), c.2, 37; of Constance and Autun (1094); of Clermont (1095), c.9–10; of Nîmes (1096), c.12], by Callistus II [Council of Reims (1119), c.5, again adopted by the Council of Rouen (November 1119) and by the First Lateran Council (1123), c.7]. In England ANSELM OF CANTERBURY convoked a council in London (1108), which recalled the precepts of ecclesiastical celibacy and renewed the traditional measures to assure its observance. In Hungary the Council of Gran (1114) also proclaimed the law of celibacy but with certain mitigations.

FREEING THE CHURCH FROM LAY ASCENDANCY

By mid-11th century the dominant institution of the PROPRIETARY CHURCH allowed feudal lords to appoint the clergy serving such churches, which were considered a part of their domain. Parochial functions were thus too often exercised by mercenary and ignorant priests who were married or living in concubinage. Emperors, kings and feudal lords disposed of bishoprics to their relatives or liegement, without any great concern for their value to the episcopate. The goods of parishes, dioceses and abbeys were for the most part in the hands of laymen. Deflected from their pious or charitable purposes, CHURCH PROPERTIES thus became the object of traffic, feudal concession, hereditary transmission and partition. The Gregorian reform strove to free the hierarchy and the goods of the Church from this lay control.

Selection of Pastors. The decree of 1059 had restored to the Roman Church the selection of the sovereign pontiff. The struggle against lay INVESTITURE restored the independence of the episcopate. That of the lower clergy would come later. Sketched in outline form in mid-12th century by the Decretum of GRATIAN (*Corpus iuris canonici* ed. E. Friedberg, C.16 q.7), which limited the effects of lay dominium on the churches (U. Stutz, "Gratian u. die Eigenkirche," *Zeitschrift der Savigny-Stiftung für Rechtsgeschichte, Kanonistische Abteilung*), it was to be fully actualized only by ALEXANDER III at the end of the 12th century and by the first decretists who would substitute the *ius patronatus* for the *dominium.* In the Gregorian era, however, various measures had aimed at restoring the authority of the bishop over the local clergy (for example, the letters of Alexander II, Pascal II and Callistus II for Lucca in L. Nanni, *La parrochia nei documenti lucchensi*). The creation of collegiate churches was likewise an effective means of organizing and controlling the local clergy. Renewing the decrees of 1059 (c.6–7), the reforming councils of the late 11th and early 12th century [Rome (1078); (1080), c.2; Clermont (1095), c.15; Rome (1099)] decreed excommunication for laymen who granted investiture of churches, clerics who accepted such churches and bishops who ordained such clerics. The Councils of London (1106), Troyes (1107), etc., forbade clerics to receive a church from the hands of a layman (GRATIAN, *Corpus iuris canonici,* C.16 q.7 c.16–20). The First Lateran Council (c.3, 4) removed episcopal elections and selection of pastors from lay interference. Toward the middle of the 12th century the principles advocated by the reform movement concerning election of bishops by chapters and the designation of local clergy by the bishop had triumphed in almost every diocese.

Recovery of Temporalities. This was likewise a cardinal concern of the reform. The restitution of churches, church lands and tithes that had been usurped by the laity was ordered by numerous councils from mid-11th century [for example, Toulouse 1056, Tours 1060, Avranches 1072, Rouen 1074, 1096, Rome 1078, 1080, Gerona 1078 and Lillebone 1080; see Schreiber, *Zeitschrift der Savigny-Stiftung für Rechtsgeschichte, Kanonistische Abteilung* (1947) 31–171]. Placid of Nonantola and Deusdedit declared that after the consecration of a church, a layman can have no right to it [thus, the Council of Reims (1131), c.10]. An attempt to draw a distinction between *ecclesia* (building) and *altare* (altar and revenues thereto attached) was to have no success. ABBO OF FLEURY refused to admit any distinction, and finally the Lateran Councils of 1123, c.15, and of 1179, c.14 (*Corpus iuris canonici,* C.10 q.1 c. 14; X 3.38.4), anathematized unlawful holders of church goods (Thomas, *Le droit de propriété des laïcs sur les églises*).

The recovery of churches and tithes was the work of the reforming bishops. Feudal lords and kings sometimes helped (see, for example, numerous charters of Philip I, in the Acts of Philip I, published by Prou). Often the goods were restored not to the parishes themselves but to monasteries, chapters and bishops in whom persons making restitution had more confidence.

Thus the long fight waged for more than a century by the reformers had by 1130 led to tangible results regarding Roman centralization, ecclesiastical buildings and patrimonial rights.

Bibliography: General. A. FLICHE, *La Réforme grégorienne,* 3 v. (Louvain 1924–37). *Histoire de l'église depuis les origines jusqu'à nos jours,* eds., A. FLICHE and V. MARTIN (Paris 1935—) 8–9. E. VOOSEN, *Papauté et pouvoir civil à l'époque de Grégoire VII* (Gembloux 1927). E. DE MOREAU, *Histoire de l'Église en Belgique* (2d ed. Brussels 1945—) v.1–3. A. HAUCK, *Kirchengeschichte Deutschlands,* 5 v. (9th ed. Berlin-Leipzig 1958) 3–4. G. TELLENBACH, *Church, State, and Christian Society at the Time of the Investiture Contest,* tr. R. F. BENNETT (Oxford 1959). F. X. SEPPELT, *Geschichte der Päpste von den Anfängen bis zur Mitte des 20. Jh.* v.1, 2, 4, 5 (Leipzig 1931–41) 3. J. F. LEMARIGNIER, "L'Influence de la réforme grégorienne" in *Histoire des institutions françaises au moyen âge,* ed. F. LOT and R. FAWTIER, v.3 (Paris 1962) 78–139. *Studi gregoriani,* ed. G. B. BORINO, v.1–7 (1947–60), esp. studies by G. BARDY, O. J. BLUM, G. B. BORINO, L. DE LA CALZADA, G. DRIOUX, H. E. FEINE, G. and K. HOFMANN, N. N. HUYGHEBAERT, S. KUTTNER, L. DE LACGER, A. MICHEL, G. MICCOLI, and W. ULLMANN. Gregory VII. *Das Register Gregors VIII,* ed. E. CASPAR, *Monumenta Germaniae Historica, Epistolae selectae* (Berlin 1826—) 2. W. WÜHR, *Studien zu Gregor VII. Kirchenreform und Weltpolitik* (Munich 1930). R. MORGHEN, . . . *Gregorio VII* (Turin 1942). H. X. ARQUILLIÈRE, *Saint Grégoire VII* (Paris 1934); "La Deuxième lettre de Grégoire VII á Hermann de Metz (1081)," *Recherches de science religieuse,* 40 (1951–52) 231–242. Special studies. G. MOLLAT, "La Restitution des églises privées au patrimoine ecclésiastique en France du IXe au XIe siècle," *Revue historique de droit français et étranger,* 27 (1949) 399–423. A. MICHEL, *Die Sentenzen des Kardinals Humbert: Dos erste Rechtsbuch der päpstlichen Reform* (Stuttgart 1943; repr. 1952). J. CHOUX, *Recherches sur le diocèse de Toul au temps de la réforme grégorienne: L'Épiscopat de Pibon (1069–1107)* (Nancy 1952). J. J. RYAN, *Saint Peter Damiani and His Canonical Sources* (Toronto 1956). E. MAGNOU, "L'Introduction de la réforme grégorienne à Toulouse," *Cahiers de l'Association Marc Bloch* (Toulouse 1958). H. G. KRAUSE, *Das Papstwahldekret von 1059 und seine Rolle im Investiturstreit, Studi gregoriani,* ed. G. B. BORINO, 7 (1960). R. MORGHEN, "Richerche sulla formazione del Registro di Gregorio VII," *Annali di storia del diritto* 3–4 (1959–60) 35–65. M. MACCARRONE, "I papi del secolo XII e la vita comune e regolare del clero," *La vita comune del clero,* 1 (1962) 349–411. G. MICCOLI, "Pier Damiani e la vita comune del clero," *ibid.* 186–219. J. T. GILCHRIST, "Canon Law Aspects of the Eleventh Century," *Journal of Ecclesiastical History,* 13 (1962) 21–38. K. HALLINGER, *Gorze-Kluny* (2 v. Rome 1950–51). *Monumenta Germaniae Historica, Constitutiones* (Berlin 1826—). P. JAFFÉ, *Regesta pontificum romanorum ab condita ecclesia ad annum post Christum natum 1198,* ed. S. LÖWENFELD, 882–1198, 2 v. (2d ed. Leipzig 1881–88; repr. Graz 1956). J. D. MANSI, *Sacrorum Conciliorum nova et amplissima collectio,* 31 v. (Florence-Venice 1757–98).

[J. GAUDEMET]

GREGORIAN SACRAMENTARY

The history of this service book is a complex one. It is convenient to deal with its evolution by reference to three distinct books: (1) the primitive or pre-Hadrian Sacramentary, (2) the eighth-century group of service books commonly known as the Eighth-Century Gelasian or Frankish-Gelasian Sacramentaries, and (3) the *Hadrianum* and Supplement of Alcuin. To have a clear idea of the problems involved in the course of its history, the table of dates and events may be useful.

Dates/Events

590–604 Reign of Gregory I, traditionally regarded as the author of the primitive Gregorian Sacramentary.

c. 614 Dedication by Boniface IV of the Pantheon, in which he imitated Gregory's style in composing the collect.

625–638 Reign of Honorius I, date of an early primitive Gregorian Sacramentary (Gamber's *Urgregorianum*).

715–731 Reign of Gregory II, under whom the Gregorian Sacramentary was reorganized.

747 Council of Cloveshoe in England decreeing the use of a Sacramentary lately received from Rome.

741–768 Reception by Pepin, King in the Frankish dominions, of liturgical books from Rome.

772–795 Reign of Pope Adrian I, who sent a copy of the Gregorian Sacramentary to Charlemagne. This is called by scholars the *Hadrianum.*

c. 730–804 Lifetime of Alcuin, traditionally held to have adapted the *Hadrianum* to the needs of the Frankish clergy by giving it a Supplement. This book is known as the Gregorian Sacramentary of Charles the Great.

10th–11th centuries A period during which the *Hadrianum* and Alcuin's Gregorian were fused, with numerous additions that eventually evolved into diverse types of mixed Sacramentaries.

The Primitive or Pre-Hadrian Sacramentary. The name of Gregory the Great has been linked with the composition of a Sacramentary ever since the mid-eighth century. A tradition to this effect is found at York at the time of Archbishop Egbert (732–766) and at Rome when John the Deacon wrote his life of St. Gregory in the years 873 to 875. It is unfortunate that no MS of this service book has survived. Two centuries elapsed between the death of Gregory and the earliest extant copy of a Gregorian Sacramentary. The Cambrai MS 164, written for Hildoard, bishop of that see in 811–812, is in all probability, according to N. Abercrombie, [*Archiv für Liturgiewissenschaft* 3 (1953) 99–103], a direct copy of the Sacramentary sent by Pope Adrian I to Charlemagne sometime between 784 and 791; hence its title the *Hadrianum* [H. Lietzmann, ed., *Das Sacramentarium Gregorianum nach dem Aachener Urexemplar* (*Liturgiesgeschichtliche Quellen* 3, Münster in Westfalen 1921)]. It has long been the goal of liturgical scholars to get behind this text and to find the primitive form of the Gregorian Sacramentary. This quest seemed to have met with some success in 1927, when Mohlberg edited the famous MS D. 47 of the Chapter Library of Padua. In his introduction, Mohlberg expressed his opinion that the ''Gregorian archetype used by the compiler of MS D. 47 was probably the oldest attainable form of the primitive Gregorian text,'' and he added that he thought St. Gregory had composed his Sacramentary for the year 595. Not all scholars were convinced. In his *Wage zum Urgregorianum [Texte und Arbeiten* 46 (Beuron 1956)], K. Gamber rejected the thesis and claimed that the Paduan MS D. 47 was nothing more than a new type of the eighth-century group of Sacramentaries. In this he was in agreement with W. H. Frere, who looked upon D. 47 as ''a somewhat eccentric member of the group representing the eighth Century Mixed Sacramentaries'' [*Studies in Early Roman Liturgy, I: The Calendar* (*Alcuin Club Collections* 28, Oxford 1930) 59].

Date and authenticity are the main subjects of debate today concerning the Gregorian Sacramentary. If scholars such as Mohlberg, Gamber, and Chavasse have taken the authenticity for granted and have suggested the years 595, 593, and 594 to 596 as the probable time of its composition, others have been far from convinced by the evidence they have produced. G. Baron d'Eckhart expressed doubts concerning the authenticity of the Gregorian Sacramentary as long ago as 1729, and the controversy flared up once more in 1890, when the traditional view was vigorously defended by G. Morin. More recently Capelle and H. Ashworth have examined the text of the *Hadrianum* for evidence of Gregory's authorship. From this examination it became evident that a certain number of prayers must be definitely assigned to St. Gregory, yet a good deal of caution is still needed in assessing the value of this evidence. The Sacramentary, as it stands, is not the work of one person, and therefore not of Gregory alone. There are grounds for the inference that the Sacramentary may well have been drawn up after his death (Ashworth, ''The Liturgical Prayers'' 107–161). No very precise answer can be given to the question of how soon after. It may well be that Boniface IV first began the process. Mohlberg and Gamber may well be right when they trace the archetype of Padua D. 47 to the pontificate of Honorius I (625–638). The Gregorian Sacramentary certainly received its definitive form under Gregory II (715–731), for this is evidently the book spoken of by the Council of Cloveshoe in 747 as having been ''lately received from Rome,'' the companion volume of Gregory II's *Antiphonale Missarum,* or *Cantatorium,* i.e., the Gradual (See S. J. P. Van Dijk, 338).

Eighth-Century Gelasian Sacramentaries. Long before the Carolingian liturgical reform, that is before the *Hadrianum* reached Charlemagne at Aachen, numerous copies of a new type of service book were being made in monastic scriptoria. This book was a hybrid, for it mixed material drawn from the old Gelasian Sacramentary, the archetype of *Reg. 316*, and from a seventh-century Gregorian Sacramentary. E. Bishop christened it the Missal of King Pepin, under the impression that it was the service book enforced by Pepin and St. Boniface. It is more commonly known as the Eighth-Century Gelasian Sacramentaries or the Frankish-Gelasian Sacramentaries. Extant copies of this book differ widely in their content. The earlier MSS have drawn most of their material from the Old Gelasian; the later MSS have a more Gregorian character about them.

Concerning the date and origin of this hybrid service book, there is a good deal of disagreement. The earliest-known MS of the type is Paris, Bibl. Nat. Lat. 12048, the famous *Sacramentarium Gellonense.* Wilmart and P. de Puniet have dated it 770 to 780. Lowe was content with saying ''end of the eighth century.'' More recently Chavasse and J. Deshusses placed it in the last decade of that century. Various guesses have been made concerning the place of its origin. Leroquais and Bourque pointed to the scriptorium of Flavigny. Lowe suggested Saint-Croix of Meaux. The latest opinion, that of Chavasse and Deshusses, ascribes it to Cambrai, on the grounds that Bishop Hildoard was one of the ardent supporters of the Carolingian reform. Thanks to Hildoard's zeal the Cambrai library possesses the only copy of Alcuin's Lectionary without the Supplement (Cambrai MS 553) and the earliest-known copy of Hadrian's Sacramentary (Cambrai MS 164). Indeed, if these authors are right, the earliest-known copy of the eighth-century service book (*Gellonense*) should be added to the list. As to the date and origin of this type of service book, it is difficult to give a precise answer. As the work of modern scholars proceeds, it becomes evident that all extant copies of this type of service book depend on a lost archetype. It can be conjectured with some confidence that it existed before the reign of Pepin. It is significant that all extant liturgical fragments emanating from the Anglo-Saxon Church or Continental Anglo-Saxon centers point to a liturgical service book of a type represented either by the Old Gelasian Sacramentary or this eighth-century Gelasian Sacramentary. It was evidently known in northern Italy [Gamber, ''Il sacramentario di Paolo Diacono. La redazione del Gelasiano s. VIII in Pavia,'' *Rivista di storia della Chiesa in Italia* 16 (1962) 412–438].

The Hadrianum and Alcuin's Supplement. The common opinion of liturgical scholars is that the aim and purpose of the Carolingian renaissance and reform was one of unification. Charlemagne's policy was to unify his empire, and one of the chief means of doing so, it is said, was adoption of Roman liturgical books that were to be made obligatory throughout his realm. It is commonly supposed that he accordingly sought from Pope Adrian I a copy of a Sacramentary, which Adrian described as *immixtus* (pure) and as being in accord with the tradition of the Roman See. This Sacramentary reached Aachen some time between 772 and 795, and in the judgment of Abercrombie the Cambrai MS 164 is an exact copy of it [''Alcuin and the Text of the Gregorianum: Notes on Cambrai Manuscript No. 164,'' *Archiv für Liturgiewissenschaft* 3 (1953) 99–103]. This interpretation of the motives behind the Carolingian liturgical reform has been questioned by recent writers. Van Dijk (p. 336) has argued convincingly that Carolingians were eager to establish a western empire that would rival Byzantium, and therefore they adopted and propagated papal liturgical books with impressive ceremonial. Be this as it may, the *Hadrianum* was found insufficient for the aims of Charlemagne. Alcuin was commissioned to bring it up to date. This he did by adopting a good deal of material found in the eighth-century type of service book and forming it into a supplement. Nor did he hesitate to use material from Gallican and Mozarabic sources. Between the material of the *Hadrianum* and his Supplement, he placed a preface beginning with the word *Hucusque,* in which he stated that the first part of the Sacramentary was that of St. Gregory the Great and the Supplement was his own to be used at each priest's discretion. This Supplement contained the following items: (1) additional matter for the rites of Baptism, Ordinations, and the Paschal vigil and vigil of Pentecost; (2) Masses for the Sundays after Epiphany, Easter, and Pentecost; (3) a full extract from the Pontifical contained within the pages of the eighth-century service book; (4) the full series of prefaces contained therein; and (5) a series of episcopal blessings, very close to those still found in the eighth-century Sacramentaries of Angoulême and Godelgaudus, but with an edited and corrected text.

This use of the eighth-century service book and the fact that such books were still being produced in the Carolingian monasteries well into the nineth and tenth centuries demands an explanation. It is no longer sufficient to repeat what has been so confidently stated without very precise evidence for too long: that the *Hadrianum* was immediately copied on its arrival at Aachen, given a Supplement by Alcuin, and subsequently imposed by royal decree. C. Hohler has observed well that what evidence there is points to no such interpretation. What the evidence does suggest is that Mass had to be celebrated according to the *Ordo Romanus,* and that all Gregory's prayers had to be used [*Journal of Ecclesiastical History* 7 (1957) 233–234]. In this he is supported by Deshusses, who has deduced that the service book imposed by royal decree, probably at the Council of Frankfurt in 794, was in effect the eighth-century service book. All early extant copies of this book date from the last decade of the eighth century. Alcuin's Supplement was not written until toward the end of his life (d. 804). Nor does it seem to have been known at Cambrai in 811 and 812, for the copy of the *Hadrianum* made at that date for Bishop Hildoard was not modeled on the text of Alcuin's edition with its Supplement, but on the older and faulty text of the book received from Adrian. H. A. Wilson based his edition of Alcuin's Gregorian Sacramentary on two ninth-century Vatican MSS: Reginensis 337 and Ottobonianus 313 (HBS 1915). It was only during the reign of Louis the Pious (814–841) that Alcuin's edition of the Gregorian Sacramentary began its career. Nor did it keep for long the form given it by Alcuin. During the course of its reproduction, the copyists found it more convenient to omit the preface *Hucusque* or to push it further and further toward the end of the book. Others simply inserted portions of the Supplement into their logical places during the course of the liturgical year. The result was the fusion of the original material from the *Hadrianum* and that of Alcuin's Supplement, and it is this form that, after being supplemented during the ninth and tenth centuries, found its way back to Rome and was subsequently adopted there.

Bibliography: Critical Edition. *Le sacramentaire grégorien: Ses principales formes d'après les plus anciens manuscrits,* ed. J. DESHUSSES, v. 1 (Fribourg 1971), v. 2 (Fribourg 1979), v. 3. **Commentaries.** E. BOURQUE, *Études sur les sacramentaires romains,* pt. 1, *Les Textes primitifs* (Rome 1948); pt. 2, *Les Textes remaniés,* v. 1, *Le Gélasien du VIIIe siècle* (Quebec 1952), v. 2, *Le Sacramentaire d'Hadrien: Le Supplément d'Alcuin et les Grégoriens mixtes* (Rome 1958). B. CAPELLE, ''La Main de S. Grégoire dans le sacramentaire Grégorien,'' *Revue Bénédictine* 49 (1937) 13–28. H. ASHWORTH, ''The Liturgical Prayers of St. Gregory the Great,'' *Traditio* 15 (1959) 107–161. Concerning St. Gregory and the Chant see S. J. P. VAN DIJK, ''Gregory the Great Founder of the Urban *Schola Cantorum,*'' *Ephemerides liturgicae* 77 (1963) 336–356. B. MORETON, *The Eighth-Century Gelasian Sacramentary* (London 1976). For overview and further bibliographies, see: C. VOGEL, *Medieval Liturgy: An Introduction to Sources* (Washington, DC 1986); and E. PALAZZO, *A History of Liturgical Books: From the Beginning to the Thirteenth Century* (Collegeville, Minn. 1998).

[H. ASHWORTH]

GREGORIUS AKINDYNOS

14th-century Byzantine monk, priest, and theologian; b. Prilep, Bulgaria, *c.* 1300; d. *c.* 1349. Akindynos studied under Thomas Magistros and Gregory PALAMAS in Thessalonika and taught grammar in Beroea. A friend of both BARLAAM OF CALABRIA and Palamas, he tried to mediate between them in 1335 during their controversy over HESYCHASM. However, in 1338 he sided with Palamas and wrote against Barlaam, who was condemned (June 10, 1341) as an outsider who had no appreciation of the Taborite Illumination and was intent upon destroying the monastic ideal.

Further study, however, convinced Akindynos that Barlaam's theological approach in dealing with the distinction between the divine essence and the divine energies was correct, but he failed in his attempt to win Palamas over to his views. After the political changes of October 1341, the patriarch of Constantinople, John XII Calecas, encouraged Akindynos to write against Palamas. Between March and April 1343 Akindynos prepared a report on the origins of his dispute with Palamas and by 1344 had composed seven treatises against the Palamite doctrine. Abetted by Theodore Dexios, he combatted the Palamite teaching in Thessalonika. Then, although he had been considered for the bishopric in Thessalonika, he was condemned instead by a synod in 1347. Again in 1351, two years after his death, his writings were condemned by a synod and his name was placed in the list of heretics anathematized on Orthodox Sunday. He was considered a most dangerous opponent of hesychastic monasticism, and his teachings were combatted by the Emperor John IV Cantacuzenus, the Patriarch Philotheus Coccinus, and Nilus Cabasilas.

Some supposed that he had knowledge of scholastic philosophy, because of a confusion between himself and Prochorus CYDONES. Akindynos rejected the teachings of Palamas that the light of Mt. Tabor was uncreated and visible, and he defended the simplicity of God, the identification of the divine essence and operations, and other anti-Palamite theses. Among his works, which are still mainly unedited, are a Tract in five books against Barlaam, a Diatribe in six books directed against Palamas, two professions of faith most probably submitted to the Empress Anne of Savoy, and a corpus of letters connected with the Palamite controversy. He is credited also with 509 iambic verses describing the errors of Palamas and an Apology to the Patriarch John Calecas.

Bibliography: H. G. BECK, *Kirche und theologische Literatur im byzantinischen Reich* (Munich 1959) 716–717. M. JUGIE, *Dictionnaire d'histoire et de géographie ecclésiastiques*, ed. A. BAUDRILLART et al. (Paris 1912) 1:340–341. M. T. DISDIER, *Dictionnaire de spiritualité ascétique et mystique. Doctrine et histoire*, ed. M. VILLER et al. (Paris 1932–) 1:263–268. V. LAURENT, *Lexikon für Theologie und Kirche*, ed. J. HOFER and K. RAHNER, 10 v. (2d, new ed. Freiburg 1957–65) 4:1205. R. J. LOENERTZ, *Orientalia Christiana periodica* 23 (Rome 1957) 114–144, 18 letters. M. CANDAL, *ibid.* 25 (1959) 215–264, confession of faith. J. MEYENDORFF, *A Study of Gregory Palamas,* tr. G. LAWRENCE (London 1964).

[H. D. HUNTER]

GREGORY

The name of many ecclesiastics and statesmen in church history. Among the more prominent not given separate articles were the following.

Gregory of Agrigentum (Agrigento), St., 6th-century Byzantine prelate and writer; b. near Agrigentum, Sicily, *c.* 559; d. after 603 (Feast: Nov. 23). At 18 he traveled through northern Africa and the Near East, and at the age of 31, became bishop. By defamatory accusations, his enemies had him imprisoned; but when he appealed to Rome, Pope GREGORY I adjudged him innocent, and he was received with honor by the Emperor MAURICE. His ten-book commentary on Ecclesiastes has been preserved, and he is known to have written many sermons. He had an influence on the development of Byzantine ecclesiastical and literary styles. His vita was written by Leontius, hegumen of St. Sabas Monastery in Rome.

Gregory of Antioch, patriarch from 570 to 593, Byzantine preacher and writer. Gregory was a monk at the Byzantine monastery in Jerusalem and Sinai and at the Laura of Pharan; Justin II elected him as patriarch of Antioch after the deposition of ANASTASIUS I. He calmed a rebellion of a Byzantine army at Litarba with a speech preserved by Evagrius (*Historia ecclesiastica* 6.12), and he was esteemed by the Emperors Maurice and Tiberius as well as by Pope Gregory I. Of his many sermons and writings, one discourse on the Resurrection and two on the Baptism (theophany) of Christ have been preserved.

Gregory Dekapolites, St., Byzantine monk; b. Eirenopolis, in the Isaurian Dekapolis, *c.* 780; d. Constantinople, 842 (Feast: Nov. 20). He became a monk and hermit in Isauria and entered into the dispute over ICONOCLASM. Displaced from the monastery, he traveled to Greece, Sicily, Rome, Thessalonika, and Constantinople, where he resided during the reign of Leo V, the Isaurian. His biography was written by Ignatius the Deacon. A short ''History of the Conversion of an Arab,'' attributed to him, was later enlarged with dragon legends of St. GEORGE.

Gregory Magistros, Armenian prince; b. Armenia, *c.* 990; d. 1058. The son of Prince Vassak Pahlavuni, he became Prince of Betšni (1021), but under Turkish pressure surrendered his dominions to Emperor Constantine IX Monomachus (1045) and dedicated his last years to letters. He taught at the University of Constantinople and wrote poetry, including a verse paraphrase of the Bible, a panegyric on the Holy Cross, and a collection of 88 letters of dogmatic, philosophical, and literary content. He also translated into Armenian some works of Plato, Euclid, and Olympiodorus the Younger and a commentary on the Grammar of Dionysius Thrax.

Gregory Narek, Armenian mystical theologian and poet; b. 951; d. 1001 (feast, Armenian Church, Feb. 27). He was the son of Bishop Chosrov the Great; he lived and died in the monastery of Narek in Eastern Armenia. Gregory became a priest and *Vardapet* (prelate) and wrote a commentary on the Canticle of Canticles, influenced by GREGORY OF NYSSA, a commentary on ch. 38 of the Book of Job, an Epistle against the Thondrakians (Armenian Paulicians), a history of the Cross of Aparan, liturgical hymns, and prayers. His writings are characterized by deep thought and the use of mystical imagery. His most important work is a collection of sacred elegies, or *Book of Lamentations.*

Gregory II Vkajaser, or Martyr-lover, Armenian catholicos and translator; d. 1105 (feast in the Armenian Church, Aug. 3). Gregory Vkajaser, related to the family of Gregory the Illuminator, was the son of Gregory Magistros, and became catholicos in 1065. He journeyed to Rome in 1074 to discuss union with Pope GREGORY VII and remained in correspondence with Rome. As a result of further travels in Palestine and Egypt he collected and published the Armenian acts of the martyrs and with his disciples translated into Armenian a commentary on the Apocalypse and the panegyric and the life of JOHN CHRYSOSTOM by Proclus.

Gregory III Pablav, Armenian catholicos (1113–66) and ecclesiastical writer; b. *c.* 1093; d. 1166. The nephew of GREGORY II, he was elected catholicos in 1113, and was faced with a schism on the part of Abp. David of Aghtamar. Pursuing the contacts with Rome initiated by his predecessor, he corresponded with Popes HONORIUS II and INNOCENT II. With his brother Bishop Nerses he attended the Latin Councils of Antioch (1139) and Jerusalem (1142), and accepted the doctrine of the Council of Chalcedon. Upon rejection of his advances by the Greeks, he sent an embassy to Pope EUGENE III at Viterbo and received the pallium in return. He retired in old age and appointed his brother Nerses IV Schnorhali as successor. He left a legacy of correspondence, hymns, and liturgical writings.

Gregory IV Tegha, Armenian catholicos and writer; b. 1133; d. 1193. He was the nephew and successor (1173) of Nerses IV Schnorhali as catholicos, and he pursued union with the Byzantine Church. In the Synod of Hromcla (1179), with 33 bishops, he subscribed to a profession of faith that was rejected by the Greeks on the death of Manuel I Comnenus (1143–80) but accepted by Pope LUCIUS III, (1184) who sent Gregory the pallium. His Elegy on Jerusalem decries the Islamic siege of that city in 1187, and his letters describe his difficulties with antiunionist priests and monks.

Gregory of Tat'ew, 14th-century Armenian theologian, b. Vayo Jor, 1340; d. Tat'ew, 1411. He is honored as a saint by the Orthodox Armenian Church. A pupil of John Kachik, he had studied both Eastern and scholastic philosophy and theology in the monastery schools of Aprakouniq, Tat'ew, and Mecop', and achieved renown as a preacher. He opposed both the Armenian Catholics and the schismatics of Aghtamar and wrote commentaries on almost all the books of the Old Testament, as well as on Porphyry, Aristotle, and the Armenian philosopher David.

Bibliography: Gregory of Agrigentum. *Patrologia Graeca*, ed. J. P. MIGNE, 161 v. (Paris 1857–66) 98:741–1182. J. KRAUS, *Lexikon für Theologie und Kirche*, ed. J. HOFER and K. RAHNER, 10 v. (2d, new ed. Freiburg 1957–65) 4:1205. H. G. BECK, *Kirche und theologische Literatur im byzantinischen Reich.* **Gregory of Antioch.** *Patrologia Graeca*, ed. J. P. MIGNE, 161 v. (Paris 1857–66) 88:1847–66, H. G. BECK, *Kirche und theologische Literatur im byzantinischen Reich* (Munich 1959) 399. O. VOLK, *Lexikon für Theologie und Kirche*, ed. J. HOFER and K. RAHNER, 10 v. (2d, new ed. Freiburg 1957–65) 4:1206. **Gregory of Decapolis.** *Patrologia Graeca*, ed. J. P. MIGNE, 161 v. (Paris 1857–66) 100:1199–1212. H. G. BECK, *Kirche und theologische Literatur im byzantinischen Reich* (Munich 1959) 579. F. DVORNIK, *Le Vie de saint Grégoire Décapolite* (Paris 1926). F. HALKIN, *Analecta Bollandiana* 69 (1951) 393–394. H. HUNGER, *Lexikon für Theologie und Kirche*, ed. J. HOFER and K. RAHNER, 10 v. (2d, new ed. Freiburg 1957–65) 4:1206. **Gregory Magistros.** H. HUNGER, *Lexikon für Theologie und Kirche*, ed. J. HOFER and K. RAHNER, 10 v. (2d, new ed. Freiburg 1957–65) 4:1208. V. LANGLOIS, ''Mémoire sur la vie et les écrits du prince Grégoire Magistros,'' *Journal Asiatique*, ser. 6, ser. 13 (1869) 5–64. M. LEROY, ''Grégoire Magistros et les traductions arméniennes d'auteurs grecs,'' *Annuaire de l'Institut de Philologie et d'Histoire Orientales et Slaves* 3 (1935) 263–294. **Gregory Narek.** J. SALAVILLE, *Cathoticisme* 5:255. M. VAN DEN OUDENRIJN, *Lexikon für Theologie und Kirche*, ed. J. HOFER and K. RAHNER, 10 v. (2d, new ed. Freiburg 1957–65) 4:1209. **Gregory II Vkajaser.** H. F. TOURNEBIZE, *Histoire politique et religieuse de l'Arménie* (Paris 1910) 163–167. H. HUNGER, *Lexikon für Theologie und Kirche*, ed. J. HOFER and K. RAHNER, 10 v. (2d, new ed. Freiburg 1957–65) 4:1209. **Gregory III Pahlav.** H. F. TOURNEBIZE, *op. cit.* 235–239. V. INGLISIAN, *Lexikon für Theologie und Kirche*, ed. J. HOFER and K. RAHNER, 10 v. (2d, new ed. Freiburg 1957–65) 4:1213–14. **Gregory IV Tegha.** H. F. TOURNEBIZE, *op. cit.* 253–258. V. INGLISIAN, *Lexikon für Theologie und Kirche*, ed. J. HOFER and K. RAHNER, 10 v. (2d, new ed. Freiburg 1957–65) 4:1215–16. **Gregory of Tat'ew.** M. VAN DEN OUDENRIJN, *Lexikon für Theologie und Kirche*, ed. J. HOFER and K. RAHNER, 10 v. (2d, new ed. Freiburg 1957–65) 4:1215.

[E. EL-HAYEK]

GREGORY II CYPRIUS, PATRIACH OF CONSTANTINOPLE

1283 to 1289; b. Cyprus, 1241; d. Constantinople, 1290. He was baptized George. Gregory studied at a Frankish school in Cyprus, but traveled to Ephesus, Nicaea, and Constantinople in search of the learning of his Greek heritage, which he found under Gregory Acropolites (1266–73). He became lector and cleric in Constantinople, and under the Emperor MICHAEL VIII PALAEOLOGUS (1259–82) strongly supported the movement for reunion with Rome.

However, in 1283 he changed his position; he supported the Emperor ANDRONICUS II, took part in the synod that condemned John Beccos, and wrote against Beccos. On the death of the Patriarch Joseph (1283), Gregory was selected to succeed him. In his attempt to refute Beccos on the procession of the Holy Spirit, he published a new theory in his Tome on Faith (*Tomos pisteos*), and was attacked by both the enemies and supporters of reunion. He defended himself in an apology, a confession (*homologia*), and a letter to Andronicus II; but in 1289 he had to resign as patriarch and retire to a monastery, where he died the following year. Gregory composed *encomia* in honor of his patron St. Gregory, St. Marina, Dionysius the Areopagite, and St. Euthymius of Madyta. He wrote also a life of the monk St. LAZARUS THE CONFESSOR of Mt. Galesius. He wrote an autobiography (*Diegesis Merike*) as an introduction to a collection of his letters and several treatises on rhetoric and mythology.

Bibliography: *Patrologia Graeca*, ed. J. P. MIGNE, 161 v. (Paris 1857–66) 142-19-30, autobiography, 233–300. F. CAYRÉ, *Dictionnaire de théologie catholique*, ed. A. VACANT et al., 15 v. (Paris 1903–50; Tables Générales 1951–) 6.1:1231–35. H. G. BECK, *Kirche und theologische Literatur im byzantinischen Reich* (Munich 1959) 677–679, 685–686. K. BAUS, *Lexikon für Theologie und Kirche*, ed. J. HOFER and K. RAHNER, 10 v. (2d, new ed. Freiburg 1957–65) 4:1207–08. G. MISCH, *Zeitschrift für Geschichte der Erziehung* 21 (1931) 1–16. W. LAMEERE, *La tradition de la correspondance de Grégoire de Chypre* (Brussels 1937). *Acta Sanctorum* Nov. 3:588–606, St. Lazarus. His letters have been edited by S. EUSTRATIADES (Alexandria 1910).

[F. CHIOVARO]

GREGORY III, PATRIACH OF CONSTANTINOPLE

1443 to 1451, apostle of reunion; b. Constantinople, 1400; d. Rome, 1459. Of the family of the Melissenoi, called Mamme, Gregory became a monk (1415–20), superior of the monastery of the Pantocrator, and confessor to the Emperor JOHN VIII PALAEOLOGUS (1425–48), who selected him to represent the patriarch of Alexandria at the Council of Ferrara-Florence (1439–41). At first, strongly opposed to Rome, he countered the unionistic efforts of the Emperor at Ferrara. However, in 1439 he accepted and signed the formula of union and engaged in a campaign to offset the antiunion opposition in Byzantium, particularly that on the part of Mark EUGENICUS, Metropolitan of Ephesus, and George Scholarius (later Patriarch Gennadius II). He composed the Emperor's letter to the patriarch of Alexandria on the reunion of the Churches, two Apologies against Eugenicus, a commentary on the Creed for the Emperor of Trebizond, and still unedited tracts on the primacy of the pope, the use of unleavened bread, and celestial beatitude. As patriarch of Constantinople, he encountered the hostility of the antiunionists, particularly among the monks and his own clergy. In 1450 he retired to the Peloponnese Islands and then (1452) to Rome, where he presided over the Greek territories under Venetian control until his death.

Bibliography: *Patrologia Graeca*, ed. J. P. MIGNE, 161 v. (Paris 1857–66) 160:13–248. L. MOHLER, *Kardinal Bessarion* 3 v. (Paderborn 1923–42); "Zwei unedierte griechische Briefe über das Unionskonzil von Ferrara-Florenz," *Oriens Christianus* 6 (1916) 213–222. L. PETIT "Documents relatifs au Concile de Florence," *Patrologia orientalis*, ed. R. GRAFFIN and F. NAU (Paris 1903–) 17 (1923) 309–524. J. GILL, *The Council of Florence* (Cambridge, Eng. 1959). H. G. BECK, *Kirche und theologische Literatur im byzantinischen Reich* (Munich 1959) 763–764. V. LAURENT, *Catholicisme* 5:273–274; "Le Vrai surnom du Patriarche de Constantinople Grégoire III," *Revue des études byzantines* 14 (1956) 201–205. K. BAUS, *Lexikon für Theologie und Kirche*, ed. J. HOFER and K. RAHNER, 10 v. (2d, new ed. Freiburg 1957–65) 4:1208.

[L. VEREECKE]

GREGORY (THE GREAT) I, ST. POPE

Pontificate: Sept. 3, 590, to March 12, 604; Doctor of the Church; b. Rome, *c.* 540.

Early Years. The son of Gordian, a minor official in the Church, and Sylvia, Gregory belonged to a patrician family that had ties to the papacy. FELIX III (483–492) was Gregory's grandfather, and Gregory may also have been related to Pope AGAPETUS (535–536). Considering the tumultuous nature of his time, Gregory received an excellent education, especially in law. Gregory of Tours said that he was dedicated to God from his youth; and his Christian alignment was fostered by the holiness of his mother and two aunts, Aemiliana and Tharsilla. Having entered the civil service, Gregory was prefect of the city by 573. In this position he provided for the defense, food supply, finances, and policing of Rome, as well as handling judicial matters for member of the Senatorial order (the Senate having ceased to function by this time). The experience thus garnered gave him a knowledge of business affairs as well as a sense of responsibility and a respect for authority. He had been in office for only a short while when his father died and he decided to become a monk and follow "the grace of conversion that he had put off for a long time." Soon after 573 he turned his family home, on the Clivus Scauri of the Coelian Hill, into a monastery dedicated to St. Andrew and provided for the founding of six monasteries on his family's property in Sicily. By meditation and study he acquired a wide knowledge of the Latin Fathers and a profound acquaintance with the Scriptures. His excessive fasting undermined his health and brought on the stomach trouble that remained a lifelong trial for him.

Apocrisiarius in Constantinople. Gregory was called back to public life in the service of the Church. Between 575 and 578 he was ordained a regionary deacon by either Benedict I (575–8) or by Pelagius II (578–590). In 579 he was sent to Constantinople as APOCRISIARIUS, the papal representative at the Byzantine court under the emperors Tiberius II and Maurice. While the extent of his knowledge of Greek learned here is debated, he did acquire wide experience of the problems both political and ecclesiastical then troubling the empire, vainly sought Byzantine military aid against the Lombards who had invaded Italy, and made the acquaintance of many outstanding personalities of the time, including LEANDER OF SEVILLE, John the Faster (patriarch of Constantinople) and Anastasius (ex-patriarch of Antioch). He had acquaintances in the royal court and served as godfather to Emperor Maurice's eldest son. During this time, he also entered into a theological debate with the patriarch Eutychius over the nature of the resurrection body. It seems that Eutychius held an Origenistic understanding of the subtlety of the resurrection body, which Gregory found unorthodox. In Constantinople Gregory lived a monastic life with the monks he had brought with him. At their request he delivered a series of conferences in the form of a commentary on the Book of Job. These conferences were later developed into his largest work, the *Moralia*.

Return to Rome. Gregory was recalled to Rome *c.* 585/6, and while it seems that he did not assume direction of the monastery of St. Andrew, as deacon of the Roman Church he served as counselor to Pope Pelagius II. He was involved in the effort to heal the schism between Rome and the bishops of Istria, which had endured since the condemnation of the Three Chapters by Pope Vigilius I at the Council of Constantinople II (553). During 587 the tenuous peace held with the Lombards was broken and war ensued. This was followed in 589 by an overflow of the Tiber that brought a new outbreak of the plague during which Pelagius II died (January 590). Gregory was elected as his successor by popular acclaim, but he insisted upon waiting for the approval of the Byzantine Emperor Maurice before being consecrated. Gregory dedicated himself to the people, who were dying off as though they were "shot down by arrows from the sky." He organized a three-day penitential procession in which the clergy and laity, arranged in seven groups, met at designated churches, then, under the leadership of the clergy of the seven regions, marched "to meet together at the basilica of the Blessed Mother." Gregory suggested to

Pope Gregory I.

the people that the plague was a divine affliction that they should accept as a means of turning to God, and with fatherly encouragement he raised their panic-stricken spirits. His reluctance to assume the papal office gave rise to legends, particularly the story of an attempt to flee Rome hidden inside a basket. With the emperor's approval Gregory was consecrated. His early letters as pope betray his acute consciousness of the oppression he experienced in leaving the safety of life as a contemplative monk and being preoccupied with business matters and the care of the whole Church, which he felt had been entrusted to so weak an agent. In the language of the times, however, he confessed that he "obediently followed what the merciful hand of the Lord had been pleased to bring about in his regard," and sent his synodical letter to the patriarchs of the East, together with a brief profession of faith. Gregory's letter was addressed to considerations of the pastoral and priestly office, enunciating a concerted program of high ideals for the universal Church.

The Lombards. Italy had been invaded by the Lombards in 568; they set up their kingdom in the north and succeeded in establishing duchies near Rome in Spoleto and Benevento. The territory embracing Rome and Ravenna, in which the exarch (the emperor's representative) lived, was still an imperial possession. While Emperor Maurice did not send help, he refused to enter a truce lest this legalize the presence of the barbarians, and the exarch was entrusted with this unrealistic policy. After vain representations, Gregory made a truce with Ariulf of Spoleto, who threatened an invasion of Rome in 592. When the Byzantine exarch broke this agreement, Agilulf, the Lombard king, descended on Rome from Turin bent on destroying the city (593). Gregory rallied the defenders and personally dealt with Agilulf. He saved Rome by paying out a large sum of money and agreeing to a yearly tribute. Intent on achieving a general peace, Gregory appealed to the exarch, who turned a deaf ear to the pope's plans and wrote a critical report to the emperor. Maurice replied in what has been termed the ''Fool'' letter. Under the euphemistic word ''simple'' (*fatuus*), Gregory claimed, Maurice had called him a fool, and in return he sent off a letter ''such as few emperors had ever received from one of their subjects'' (Dudden 2.26). The pope admitted he was a fool for staying at his post and suffering ''amid the swords of the Lombards.'' But he defended his work ''for *my* country,'' and informed the emperor that his trust was in the mercy of Jesus Christ at His coming, rather than in the justice of the emperor. The restoration of peace had to wait until 598. Gregory's dealing with the Lombards led to important consequences. The people thereafter looked to the pope as their true protector since he had recognized the failure of the civil government and had saved Italy by personally assuming responsibility. This action made him a *de facto,* but not *de jure,* civil ruler and constituted one of the steps leading to the creation of the Papal States when the pope became a *de jure* temporal ruler.

The Papal Patrimony. The papal patrimony consisted of lands in Italy, Sicily, Corsica, Sardinia, Gaul, Africa, and Illyricum. The pope was the landlord of these properties, whose revenues were used for the many needs of the Church. Each patrimony was controlled by a rector appointed by the pope. With his fine sense of justice as an administrator, Gregory rebuked agents who enlarged the estates by ruthlessly disregarding the rights of others or who kept back goods in time of plenty to sell them at a higher price in time of need, and he insisted that the purse of the Church was ''not to be polluted by sinful gain.'' The patrimonies were Gregory's means of helping the poor, the destitute, and families displaced or separated by war. Upon his appointment, Gregory had admonished each rector ''to care for the poor,'' and ''to promote not so much the worldly interests of the Church but the relief of the needy in their distress.'' Gregory insisted that he was dispensing not his own property, but the property of the poor, that the goods belonged to St. Peter, who was caring for his flock through Gregory. The papal treasury was used to ransom captives and restore them to their families and to buy peace by paying off the Lombards. In this respect, he ironically called himself the paymaster of the Lombards and the Emperor's paymaster.

The Liturgy. Gregory's contributions to the liturgy have been extremely difficult to assess. His involvement in the Gregorian Sacramentary continues to be hotly debated. The Gregorian Sacramentary, basically a modification of the Gelasian Sacramentary, was continually worked and reworked until the ninth century thus making any definitive statements very difficult. Gregory seems to have been involved in a revival of the station churches as is seen in his ordering of a penitential procession upon Pelagius' death and his election. At various times it has been posited that he was perhaps responsible for standardizing the practice of having the *Kyrie Eleison* and the *Christe eleison* sung alternately by the clergy and laity; decreeing that the *Alleluia* should be used throughout the entire year except on penitential days; limiting the deacons to the singing of the Gospel; stressing the importance of the homily; and adding to the *Hanc igitur* these words: ''Dispose our days in your peace. Also, save us from eternal damnation and command that we be numbered in the flock of your Elect.'' The present position of the *Pater Noster* is most likely his work. Others have also asserted that many of the prayer texts in use today stem from Gregory, for example, the Christmas Preface, the Oration for Epiphany, and the Prefaces of Easter and Ascension [J. A. Jungmann, *The Mass of the Roman Rite* 2 v. (New York 1951–55) 1:63].

Gregory and the East. The synodical letter to the patriarchs of Constantinople, Alexandria, Antioch, and Jerusalem indicates that Gregory accepted the precedence of the sees, ranking Constantinople first. From at least the fourth century, ecclesiastical union was achieved among the sees by the acceptance of such letters, and each patriarch ruled in his own jurisdiction. Gregory continued this custom and would not directly contact the bishop of another patriarchate without going through the patriarch. However, the right of appeal over the patriarch to Rome was generally recognized, and Gregory did reverse the decision against two priests handed down at Constantinople. Friction between Rome and Constantinople was occasioned by John IV the Faster's use of the title ''ecumenical patriarch.'' Pelagius II had refused to acknowledge a council held at Constantinople in 587 since it was held without his authorization and because in the acts of the council the patriarch was called ecumenical. Great import was attached to the title since the council had cited the patriarch of Antioch to appear before it. Actually, the title was not new. It had been used by the Constantinopolitan patriarchs during the Acacian Schism (484–519) and the reign of Justinian I (527–565). In 595 Gregory received an appeal from two priests condemned at Constantinople. In the acts he saw that "practically on every page the patriarch of Constantinople was designated as ecumenical." His opposition to the term was not mere ecclesiastical sensitivity, but reflected pastoral and ecclesiological concerns. Gregory appears most of all to have been upset by the "pride" he felt was entailed in the title. In apocalyptic tones he compares this title to the "name of blasphemy" (Ep.V.37; cv V.44). Gregory taught that all bishops were in one sense "ecumenical" and that the use of this term to refer to a specific bishop was "robbing" another of his due. In response to the Patriarch of Constantinople who, in calling Gregory 'universal pope' had misunderstood Gregory's problem with the term, he wrote, "I am correctly honored when each is not denied the honor due him; for if you call me 'universal pope,' you deny that you are what you call me universally" (Ep. VIII.29). In his counterclaim he asserted the universal jurisdiction of the Bishop of Rome, but made it clear that this should be used with humility, and he referred to himself constantly as the Servant of the Servants of God. Although not new, this title was typically Gregorian and was incorporated into the list of titles of the popes. As Servant of the Servants of God, Gregory taught that the Apostolic See is "the head of all the churches." It is the See of Peter "to whom was committed the care and primacy of the whole Church"; as such it is the *caput fidei.* Gregory asserted that "the See of Constantinople is subject to the Apostolic See," and that there was no bishop who was not subject to the See of Rome, "which is set over all the churches." He also recognized the fact that other churches had their own accepted territories of jurisdiction. If he defended his own rights, he was careful "to observe the rights of the different churches." The jurisdiction of each of his brother bishops had to be safeguarded, otherwise "the ecclesiastical order is destroyed by us through whom it ought to be preserved." Gregory further contended (and has been quoted with satisfaction by Pope Paul VI): "My honor is the honor of the universal Church. It is also the solid authority of my brothers. I am truly honored only when the honor due to each and every one of them is not denied to them."

Gregory and the West. As Patriarch of the West, Gregory's jurisdiction embraced the three prefectures of Italy, the two Gauls, and Eastern Illyricum. In this vast territory, his jurisdiction was complicated by the civil rule of the Byzantine exarch in Africa and by the independent kingdoms resulting from the barbarian nations who invaded Gaul and elsewhere. He met this challenge generally by acting through the metropolitans, whom he recognized as adequate in their proper jurisdictions.

Italy and Africa. As Bishop of Rome and metropolitan of the suburban regions, Gregory had immediate ecclesiastical control of all Italy from Tuscany south. He looked to the canonical regularity of the election of bishops, who were then consecrated in Rome; he supervised their lives, championed their rights, and helped them in need. Charges against bishops were judged in Rome by the pope, usually during their annual assembly in Rome on the feast of St. Peter. The bishops from Sicily came every three years; aware of the difficulties of traveling such a distance, Gregory changed this to every five years. The other Italian metropolitan sees were Ravenna, Milan, and Aquileia. Aquileia called for special attention. Istrian bishops in that province were still in schism because of the condemnation of the Three Chapters. By insisting that the belief of Rome was the teaching defined at Chalcedon and that the Council of Constantinople II did not reverse the work of Chalcedon, Gregory succeeded in winning over some of these bishops, but the schism was finally healed only after his death. In his dealings with Africa Gregory acceded to the request of the bishops of Numidia that their local customs be maintained, and insisted only that no convert from Donatism be made primate. Regarding ecclesiastical privileges, he informed Donatus of Carthage that the pope not only defends his own rights but respects those of others. His aim was "to honor my brothers" and "to maintain the honor of each one, provided there is no conflict." Letters to Africa were frequent and called for episcopal vigilance, the holding of councils, and the help of civil and church leaders in curbing the troublesome Donatists.

Spain, Gaul, and England. To Gregory, the conversion of the Arian Visigoths in 589 was "a great miracle." Relations with Spain had been delicate because of Visigothic nationalism and the token of Byzantine power in the south. But with St. Leander as bishop of Seville, Gregory found the Church in Spain in good hands. A request from Gaul in 593 to restore the papal vicariate at Arles was well received by Gregory, who "was glad of the opportunity to extend his influence in the kingdom of the Franks, and too clever not to profit by it" (Batiffol, 203). The Merovingians had split the kingdom into separate units, and each ruler looked upon the Church as "his church." In restoring the vicariate, Gregory linked the Church in Gaul with Rome and the Church universal. Numerous letters were sent to the vicar, bishops, and rulers denouncing simony, lay interference, and ordinations of laymen without the proper preparation. Gregory called for a council to carry out Christian renewal. The council, held in 614, ten years after his death, reflected Gregory's program for reform and peace, even though the Merovingians kept their hold over the episcopate of each kingdom. The mission to the Anglo-Saxons was inaugurated when Gregory discovered that these invaders had not been evangelized by the native clergy of Britain. Stirred to action, he decided to use monasticism in furthering the missionary projects of the papacy. From his monastery of St. Andrew he sent St. Augustine of Canterbury and 40 monks to carry out his project. The work began in 597 and was helped by Bertha, the Catholic wife of King Ethelbert and a descendant of Clovis. In time, Celtic monks from Iona joined in the evangelization being carried on by the Benedictine monks from Rome, and the Byzantine Theodore of Tarsus was sent from Rome in 668 to reorganize the mission.

Gregory as a Writer. In a period of decline, Gregory stands out as the proclaimer of the Christian message accommodated to every situation and class. He is a bridge over which the wisdom and culture of the past were passed on and preserved. To have done this in an age of chaos is a significant achievement. In a special way he was the expounder of the Christian way of life, reaching to the heights of mysticism and contemplation. He presented his teaching not in a speculative or theoretical manner, but in the existential setting of the concrete human person with his immediate capacity for greatness and smallness, for response and refusal.

Scriptural Homilies. Gregory's textbook was the Bible, and many of his writings are scriptural homilies or conferences. The 40 *Homilies on the Gospel,* delivered in 590–592, show the importance of the homily in the liturgical celebrations of Sundays and feasts. These are pastoral talks in which he often introduces stories to make the doctrine graphic. In this he is a pathfinder. The historical conditions in which he lived, with wars and plagues as constants, explain his stress on the end of the world, death, hell, and heaven. His aim was to have the people constantly ready to meet their Judge. The 22 *Homilies on Ezekiel* (592), revised eight years later, are much more profound. Based on the first four and the fortieth chapters of Ezekiel, these sermons contain sublime passages dealing with Christ, the Church, the active and contemplative life, suffering, ideals of the priesthood, and the Christian life as rooted in faith, hope, and charity. They contain precious historical eyewitness accounts of Italy and the Lombards. The concluding passage is a literary masterpiece. With Agilulf's army at the gates of Rome, Gregory dispensed with instruction and turned to comfort his terrified people, urging them to give thanks even in the midst of their tears and sorrows, ''for He who created us has also become a Father to us by the spirit of adoption that He gave us.'' The *Homilies on the Canticle of Canticles* are now generally agreed to be genuine, although only a portion of the work seems to have survived. (See Ep. XII.6) This work is similar to the *Moralia* in tone and, like it, seems to have been compiled as spiritual reflections to be delivered to a monastic audience. It most likely dates from just prior to his pontificate to shortly thereafter (593–597). There is another work titled *Expositions on the First Book of Kings* which is most likely Gregorian, although its authenticity has recently been questioned. This work seems to date from the middle period of his pontificate. It was revised by the Abbot Claudius as well as retouched again by Gregory toward the very end of his life.

Moralia. Gregory's longest work is the *Book of Morals*, an exposition of the Book of Job. The text was begun during or shortly after 579 in Constantinople, but not completed until at least 595 when Gregory sent an early copy to his friend Leander of Seville. The work must have been revised again after this time as well because the final edition of the work in 35 books mentions the Augustinian mission to England which was not begun until 596. Begun as conferences to the monks when Gregory was in Constantinople, the work opens with the literal meaning of the Scriptures, delves most liberally into the mystical and allegorical interpretation, and then points out moral applications. Although it is not strictly a work of scriptural exegesis by today's standards, it is impossible to follow it without constant reference to the Book of Job. The texts are used as starting points for spiritual conferences. It is a *summa* or storehouse of dogma, moral asceticism, and mysticism. It deals with the totality of Christian doctrine from God the Creator to God the Rewarder. These truths are not treated in a topical and unified manner; nevertheless there is unity in the work because moral teaching and asceticism are not fragmented disciplines but vital parts of the one, undivided science of theology, whose object is God. As a storehouse of theology, the *Morals* was a *vade mecum* for the later centuries.

Pastoral Care. In the *Pastoral Care*, written in the first months of his pontificate, Gregory defended his attempt to escape the papacy by setting forth his ideas on the office of bishops and the care of souls. In four books he delved into (1) the type of person and the proper motives for the pastoral office, (2) the virtues required in a pastor, (3) the manner of preaching to different types of people (40 types in all, described with psychological acumen), and (4) the need for an examination of conscience so that the pastor will not neglect himself in caring for others. During Gregory's lifetime this book was translated into Greek. Under King Alfred the Great it was translated (901) into Old English (West Saxon). During the Middle Ages Gregory's *Pastoral* was for bishops and priests what the Rule of St. Benedict was for monks. The *Pastoral* parallels the *Dialogues*, for the *Dialogues* were to the simple and uneducated people what the *Pastoral* was for bishops and priests.

Dialogues. The authenticity for the dialogues has been recently brought into question by Francis Clark, however, most scholars are comfortable in maintaining Gregorian authorship. In 593–594 Gregory wrote *The Four Books of Dialogues on the Life and Miracles of the Italian Fathers* [i.e., Saints] *and on the Immortality of Souls*. In the form of a conversation between Gregory and Peter the Deacon, the first three books detail, with emphasis on the miraculous, the holiness of sixth–century saints. The entire second book deals with the greatest of them all, St. Benedict. Gregory insisted that the true value of life is measured in virtue and not in miracles and that there are saints who, even if they do not work miracles, are just as good as those who do (*Dial.* 1.12). In these stories he shows that holiness is not confined to the days of old, that God is wonderful in His saints, and that the intercession of holy people is powerful with God even to the working of miracles. The fourth book, on the immortality of the soul, treats of death, purgatory, heaven, and hell. This book is important both psychologically and doctrinally. To the simple-minded people, driven to despair regarding not only this life but also the next, Gregory insisted upon the immortality of the soul and life everlasting by vividly describing the death scenes of the wicked surrounded by devils and of the good surrounded by saints and angels. Visions of saints point to the immortality of the soul in everlasting happiness. His goal was to encourage people to bear the trials of life and to fix their sights on heaven. Gregory's doctrine on heaven is important because he was the first to teach categorically the possibility of the immediate entrance of the soul into heaven. For him there was no intermediate stage where saintly souls wait to enter heaven only on the last day. For those not yet ready to behold God face to face after death, there is purgatory. Gregory explained this very clearly and pointed out the value of the Eucharistic Sacrifice in helping these souls to attain heaven more speedily. Frequently misinterpreted as oversimplifications and miracle-filled legends, the *Dialogues* are basically a literary genre in which Gregory used stories to give doctrinal information and moral and ascetical stimulation to the simple and uneducated. The stories show that God is still with His own, always present and helpful, despite human wickedness and opposition. ''The *Dialogues* were *The City of God* rewritten for the simple'' (Batiffol, 182).

Letters. The 14 books of Gregory's *Letters* are a source of information of the first order for his pontificate. They deal with the Church, the empire, the Germanic invaders, bishops, monasticism, and the missionary and social aspects of the Church, and are a rich source for an understanding of the theology, liturgy, history, psychology, and sociology of the age. The letters reveal Gregory as a capable administrator and throw light on his teachings as they were applied to particular persons and situations. Most of all, they reveal Gregory in his accomplishments and failures, his talents and limitations; they portray the sixth–century Roman who became the saintly man of God. It should be cautioned, however, that the papal scrinium, which was responsible for the correspondence of the popes, had established a system for writing ''form letters'' and one must be careful in teasing out any great doctrinal or spiritual truths from a few letters.

History. By his position as the bridge between the ancient and the medieval world, Gregory was an instigator of the Anglo-Saxon and the Carolingian culture. The Benedictines looked to Gregory as their own and gave his works worldwide diffusion. To the Middle Ages he was the mouthpiece of the Christian way of life and was a first-class authority in moral, ascetical, and mystical theology. In moral theology Gregory is the most frequently cited of the Latin Fathers. In 242 articles of the second part of the *Summa theologiae*, St. Thomas Aquinas cited him 374 times; and Gratian showed the influence of Gregory in the field of Canon Law. Gregory was officially named among the ''great Doctors of the Church'' by Boniface VIII in 1298. Gregory's influence continued in the age of the German and Spanish mystics and on through the Enlightenment and declined only in the 19th century, with its emphasis on nationalism in historical method and research. The rediscovery of Gregory was a phenomenon of the 20th century. In 1904 Pope (St.) Pius X wrote an encyclical to commemorate the 13th centenary of Gregory's death. Gradually, deconfessionalized research recaptured the mentality of the ages that called him great. H. Marrou remarked: ''We can understand why writers in the Middle Ages. . .accorded him a place beside and equal to St. Ambrose, St. Jerome, and St. Augustine as one of the four Doctors of the Latin Church. . . .Only in our own day are we beginning to recognize the truth of this judgment.''

Art. The representation of Gregory in art continues a tradition widespread in the Middle Ages that he received his teachings directly from the Holy Spirit. He is usually pictured as writing or dictating to Peter the Deacon, with a dove, the symbol of the Holy Spirit, resting on his head, and its beak in his mouth. Peter the Deacon of Rome affirmed that he saw this happen. A passage in Gregory's *Homilies on Ezekiel* (2.2.1) supplied a further basis for this tradition. He said there that often the meaning of a scriptural text came to him while he was actually preaching, that God gave it to him for the sake of the people, and that he himself was learning while he was teaching.

Feast: March 12.

Bibliography: *Opera omnia*, *Patrologia Latina*, ed. J. P. MIGNE (Paris 1878–90) v.75–79. *Gregorii Magni opera = Opere* *di Gregorio Magno* CCSL text. 7 volumes, (Rome, 1992). *Registrum epistolarum*, ed. P. EWALD and L. M. HARTMANN, *Monumenta Germaniae Historica* (Berlin 1826–) division: Epistolae, v.1–2; *Expositiones in Canticum Canticorum et in Librum Primum Regum*, ed. P. VERBRAKEN (*Corpus Christianorum. Series latina* [Turnhout, Belg. 1953–] 144; 1963). *Commentaire sur le Cantique des cantiques*, ed. and tr., R. BELANGER, *Sources chretiennes* 314. *In Librum primum Regum expositionum*, ed. and tr., A. DE VOGUE, *Sources chretiennes* 351, 391, 432, 449. *Dialogues*, tr. O. J. ZIMMERMAN, Fathers of the Church Series (New York, 1959). *Homiliae in Hiezechihelem prophetam*, ed. and tr. C. MOREL, Sources Chretiennes 327, 360. *Moralia in Iob*, ed. and tr. A. DE GAUDEMARIS, Sources chretiennes 32, 212, 221. *Ibid.* ed. and tr. M. ADRIAEN, Corpus christianorum series latina 143. *Morals on the Book of Job*, tr. J. BLISS, (Oxford, 1844–50) Library of Fathers of the Holy Catholic Church, vol. 18, 21, 23, 31. *Liber regulae pastoralis*, ed. F. ROMMEL, tr. C. MOREL, Sources chretiennes 381, 382. *XL Homiliarum in Evangelia*, ed. and tr. R. ETAIX, Corpus christianorum series latina 141. *Forty Gospel Homilies*, tr. D. HURST, (Kalamazoo, Mich. 1990). *The Book of Pastoral Rule and Selected Epistles of Gregory the Great*, tr. J. BARMBY (Grand Rapids 1979). *Pastoral Care*, ed. and tr. H. DAVIS (*Ancient Christian Writers*, ed. J. QUASTEN et al. [Westminster, MD 1946–] 11; 1950). R. GODDING, *Bibliografia di Gregorio Magno (1890/1989)* (Rome 1990); and, ''Les dialogues. . .de Gregoire le Grand. A Propos d'un livre recent,'' *Analecta Bollandiana* 106 (1988): 201–29. P. AUBIN, ''Interiorite et exteriorite dans les *Moralia in Iob* de saint Gregoire le Grand'' *Recherches de science religieuse* 62 (1974): 117–66. F. CLARK, *The Pseudo-Gregorian Dialogues* 2 vols. (Leiden 1987). C. DAGENS, *Gregoire le Grand: culture et experience chretiennes* (Paris 1977). F. H. DUDDEN, *Gregory the Great*, 2 v. (London 1905). L. BRÉHIER and R. AIGRAIN, *Gregoire le Grand* (A. FLICHE and V. MARTIN, eds., *Histoire de l'église depuis les origines jusqu'à nos jours* [Paris 1935–] 5; 1938). N. SHARKEY, *St. Gregory the Great's Concept of Papal Power* (Washington 1956). M. FRICKEL, *Deus totus ubique simul* (Freiburg 1956). J. LECLERCQ, ''La doctrine de saint Gregoire,'' *Histoire de la spiritualite chretienne*. Vol. 2 (Paris 1961): 72–83. J. P. MCCLAIN, *The Doctrine of Heaven in the Writings of St. Gregory the Great* (Washington 1956). R. A. MARKUS, *Gregory the Great and His World* (Cambridge 1997). P. MEYVAERT, ''The Enigma of Gregory the Great's Dialogues: A Response to Francis Clark,'' *Journal of Ecclesiastical History* 39 (1988) 335–81. C. STRAW, *Gregory the Great: Perfection in Imperfection* (Los Angeles 1988); and, *Gregory the Great* (Brookfield, VT 1996). L. M. WEBER, *Hauptfragen der Moraltheologie Gregors des Grossen* (Fribourg 1947); *Lexikon für Theologie und Kirche*, ed. J. HOFER and K. RAHNER (Freiburg 1957–65) 4:1177–80. *Clavis Patrum latinorum*, ed. E. DEKKERS (Streenbrugge 1961). A. C. RUSH, *Theological Studies* 23 (1962) 569–589, martyrdom.

[A. C. RUSH/K. HESTER]

GREGORY II, POPE, ST.

Pontificate: May 19, 715 to Feb. 11, 731. Born *c.* 669, Gregory was a member of a wealthy noble Roman family. At a young age he entered the papal curia where he was educated for service in the papal bureaucracy. He was made a subdeacon and appointed to a major financial office (*sacellarius*) responsible for dispensing the funds of the papal government by Pope SERGIUS I (687–701); subsequently he served the curia as librarian (*bibliothecarius*). As a deacon he accompanied Pope CONSTANTINE I (708–715) to Constantinople in 710 where he played an important role in negotiations with Emperor JUSTINIAN II that addressed issues arising from the disputed canons of the QUINISEXT Council *in Trullo* of 692.

Gregory II's pontificate was one of the most important of the 8th century, marked by the confluence of several trends that redefined the position of the papacy in the political and religious scene. The forces that had been working for some time to dissolve the ties linking the papacy to the imperial regime in Constantinople were dramatically accentuated during Gregory II's pontificate, a development that pointed toward greater independence for the papacy but also threatened to deprive Rome of its long-time protector, the emperor. In no small part because of the decline of imperial power in Italy, the Lombard kingdom became increasingly aggressive to the point where it threatened to absorb the duchy of Rome and to reduce the Pope to the status of a regional bishop. But there were new opportunities that allowed the papacy to expand its influence north of the Alps into the world dominated by the Franks. Gregory II responded to the changing scene with actions that marked a decisive point in establishing the independence of the papacy, securing its control over Rome and the surrounding territory, and expanding its ties with the Frankish world.

The Clash with Constantinople. The most dramatic events of Gregory II's pontificate centered around his confrontations with the eastern Roman emperor. The relationship between Rome and Constantinople had been relatively peaceful since the settlement of the Monothelete dispute at the Council of CONSTANTINOPLE in 680–681. In part, the peace was due to the weakness of the eastern Roman Empire, under attack from external enemies, especially the triumphant Muslim forces, and torn by internal dissent. All that changed with the accession of Emperor LEO III (717–741). His reign began with a decisive victory over the Muslim forces besieging Constantinople that blunted their westward advance into the heart of the empire. Following that victory, he initiated measures to restore internal order in the empire, including reforms of the military and administrative systems. In 717 he decided to replenish the imperial treasury by imposing new taxes, especially on his Italian subjects. Faced with a major loss of revenue resulting from the new burden on the papal patrimonies, Gregory II refused to comply with imperial orders. His defiance earned him a hero's role among all in Byzantine Italy who were opposed to paying taxes imposed by a distant ruler whose policies had little bearing on their interests or well-being in Italy. Leo III and his agents responded by organizing plots aimed at murdering Gregory II, but those plans were repeatedly thwarted by local military forces in Rome and elsewhere in Italy which came to the defense of the Pope. That resistance made it clear that the imperial military establishment in Italy could no longer be trusted to defend imperial interests or enforce imperial policies; its concerns, interests, and allegiances had become local.

Leo III soon provided an even stronger cause for challenging his authority. In 726 he undertook on his own authority to introduce a major change in religious policy aimed at ending the use of images (icons) in religious ceremonies and church decoration. This was a policy fraught with major doctrinal implications, certain to threaten deeply rooted cult practices sacred to many of the faithful, and destined to alienate important elements in the Byzantine ecclesiastical system, especially the monastic establishment. In the face of an imperial order to recognize the new policy, Gregory II denounced ICONOCLASM as heresy. He dispatched two letters to the emperor the authenticity of which is highly doubtful in the form in which they have survived, but which likely reflected the papal position on the theological error involved in Leo's position on icons and the papal challenge to the competence of a secular ruler to define orthodox doctrine. For the remainder of his pontificate the pope stood fast in his opposition to iconoclasm, denouncing Leo's decree of 730 making iconoclasm official policy, protesting his deposition of Patriarch GERMANUS for resisting iconoclasm, and refusing to recognize the new patriarch chosen by Leo. Gregory II's stance won wide approval in Italy, greatly enhancing the papal position as defender of orthodoxy and further weakening the ability of the emperor to direct affairs in Italy. However, despite the hostility between the Pope and the emperor over taxation, doctrine, and ecclesiology, Gregory II repeatedly acted in ways that demonstrated his deep commitment to the papacy's traditional place in Roman imperial structure and his respect for the imperial office as the key agency sustaining civilized Christian society. Among other things, he thwarted an attempt by Italian separatist factions to elect a new emperor to replace Leo III, and he brought pressure to bear on the Lombards to restore to their rightful owner territories seized from the empire, including Ravenna. In reality, however, Rome and Constantinople were parting company politically and religiously, and the papacy as represented by Gregory II was increasingly a major force in shaping and giving momentum to that trend.

Gregory II's somewhat ambivalent relationship with the imperial regime in Constantinople was due in part to his deep commitment to the Roman imperial tradition. But it was also prompted by his concern with the growing power of the LOMBARDS and the consequent threat to the autonomy of Rome and its *de facto* ruler, the Pope. That prospect forced Gregory to be hesitant in cutting off all ties with Rome's long-time protector, the eastern emperor. Although Gregory II's relations with the Lombards was generally peaceful, in part because the Lombards shared papal opposition to iconoclasm, the Lombard threat became ever clearer as Gregory's pontificate advanced. For the papacy the matter of finding a new protector loomed ever more urgent.

Growing Ties with the North. Gregory II contributed in significant ways to expanding ties with northern Europe from whence a papal protector would eventually come. He received numerous pilgrims from north of the Alps, including King INE of Wessex, whose visit to Rome symbolized a growing reverence throughout the West for St. Peter and his successors. Duke Theodo of Bavaria came to Rome to pray and to seek papal assistance in organizing the church in his still not completely Christianized principality. Of especially great significance was the support that Gregory II gave to St. BONIFACE for his missionary work in Germany. Even before the Anglo-Saxon monk began his evangelizing effort there, he came to Rome in 719 to seek papal blessing, which he received along with letters authorizing him to preach in Germany. Upon learning of Boniface' successes in Germany, Gregory II commanded him to return to Rome in 722 to receive consecration as bishop and to swear an oath of allegiance to the Roman pontiff; the new bishop left Rome with canon law books containing guidelines for imposing discipline on his converts and with a letter of introduction to CHARLES MARTEL, mayor of the palace in the kingdom of the Franks, who in turn provided letters indicating his support of Boniface's missionary effort. On several occasions Gregory II supplied Boniface with directions on how to proceed in winning converts and in drawing them into full participation in Christian life; in their substance these instructions demonstrated Gregory's firm grip on Christian tradition relative to such matters as marriage, liturgy, and theology. His guidance assured that the religious establishment which Boniface was creating in Germany would bear a strong Roman mark. Eventually, Boniface utilized that model when he became the directive figure in the CAROLINGIAN REFORM of the Frankish church, thereby establishing another important link between the papacy and the Franks.

Gregory II was active in other spheres. He undertook to strengthen the fortifications of Rome. He continued the work of his predecessors as a builder and restorer of churches, contributing substantially to the physical transformation of Rome into a Christian city. He took an interest in promoting monastic life in Rome and elsewhere. His action in coping with a major flood of the Tiber demonstrated the extent to which the papacy had assumed responsibility for civil administration and public welfare in Rome. His ability to muster resources for such activities indicates that he was an effective manager of papal revenues. He was willing to intervene in ecclesiastical affairs outside Rome to assure the well-being of the Church, illustrated not only by his support of Boniface but also his role in ending a conflict between the sees of Aquileia and Grado. In every way his pontificate marked a strengthening of the papal role as ruler of Rome and its surrounding territory, as a moving force in the tangled web of Italian politics, and as an authority figure in spiritual affairs affecting Christian life in the West

Feast: Feb.13.

Bibliography: *Le Liber Pontificalis*, ed. L. DUCHESNE, 3 v., 2nd ed. (Paris 1955–1957), 1: 396–414, English translation in *The Lives of the Eighth-Century Popes (Liber Pontificalis). The Ancient Biographies of Nine Popes from AD 715 to AD 817*, trans. with intro. by R. DAVIS (Liverpool 1992) 1–16. *Regesta Pontificum Romanorum ab condita ecclesia ad annum post Christum MCXCVIII*, ed. P. JAFFÉ, 2 v. (2nd ed. Leipzig 1885–88) 1:249–257. P. CONTE, *Regesto delle lettere dei papi del secolo VIII: saggi* (Milan 1984) 46–79; 192–200. *Epistolae Langobardicae collectae*, Epp. 8–12;, ed. W. GUNDLACH, *Monumenta Germaniae Historica, Epistolae: Epistolae Merowingici et Karolini aevi* (Berlin 1892; reprinted 1994) 697–702. *Concilia aevi karolini,* Part 1, ed. A. WERMINGHOFF, *Monumenta Germaniae Historica, Concilia,* v. 2.1 (Hannover and Leipzig 1906; repr. 1997) 19–20. *Die Briefe des heiligen Bonifatius und Lullus (S. Bonifatii et Lulli epistolae)*, ed. M. TANGL, *Monumenta Germaniae Historica, Epistolae Selectae* 1 (Berlin 1916; repr.1989), English translation as *The Letters of St. Boniface*, tr. E. EMERTON (New York 2000). *Vita sancti Bonifatii archiepiscopi Moguntini*, ed. W. LEVISON, *Monumenta Germaniae Historica, Sriptorum rerum Germanicarum in usum scholarum* 57 (Hannover and Leipzig 1905; repr. 1999), English translation as ''Willibald, The Life of Saint Boniface,'' tr. C. H. TALBOT, in *Soldiers of Christ. Saints and Saints' Lives from Antiquity and the Early Middle Ages*, ed. T. F. X. NOBLE and T. HEAD (University Park, Penn. 1985) 107–140.

[R. E. SULLIVAN]

GREGORY III, POPE, ST.

Pontificate: March 18, 731 to Nov. 28, 741. Of Syrian origin, Gregory was ordained to the priesthood before his election as Pope. He was the last Pope who sought confirmation of his election from the emperor in Constantinople or his agent, the exarch of Ravenna; thereafter, the emperor had no role in the process which determined who would serve as the successor to St. Peter. At the time of his election, Gregory III faced a tenuous situation, marked by an aggressive Lombard ruler seeking to dominate Italy and by an emperor attempting to impose his iconoclastic policy at a moment when imperial power in Italy was eroding. At stake for the papacy was the quasi-independent position of Rome and its surrounding territory that Gregory III's predecessors had succeeded in establishing. That position required a protector for the papacy, a role that had long been filled by the Byzantine emperor. But at the moment the emperor's attitude toward Rome was sorely tested by the leadership role taken by Pope GREGORY II (715–731) in resisting the attempts of Emperor LEO III (717–741) to impose new taxes and to enforce his policy of ICONOCLASM. And those same imperial policies had sorely tested the allegiance to the emperor not only of the Pope but also of many of the emperor's subjects in Italy.

Immediately upon assuming office Gregory III moved to reaffirm his predecessor's repudiation of iconoclasm. Perhaps hoping to persuade Emperor Leo III to abandon his iconoclastic policy, Gregory III attempted to establish a dialogue with Leo III by letter. Receiving no response, he summoned a Roman synod which met in 731–732, attended by a large number of bishops from Italy who in a show of solidarity with the Pope condemned iconoclasm and decreed that anyone who destroyed or profaned sacred images would be excommunicated. Leo III responded by sending a fleet to Italy to force the submission of Gregory III, a venture that came to naught when the fleet was wrecked by a storm. Then he confiscated papal patrimonies in Sicily and Calabria and transferred the ecclesiastical province of Illyricum, embracing most of the Balkan Peninsula, Sicily, and southern Italy, from the jurisdiction of the pontiff of Rome to that of the patriarch of Constantinople. The loss of income from the properties in Sicily and Calabria was a major blow to the papacy. But Gregory III apparently found ways of offsetting his losses, since he had the revenue to build and decorate many churches in Rome. Thus he contributed substantially to the effort begun by his predecessor that led to the physical transformation of classical Rome into a medieval Christian city. Although the papal claims on the province of Illyricum became a bone of contention between Rome and Constantinople in the 9th century, there is no evidence that Gregory III saw its loss as a major papal setback. In fact, papal authority was negligible there. Leo III's measures were interpreted by many in Rome as another sign of his tyranny; however, his action more likely represented a move to solidify his position in a place where imperial control was still effective and to abandon Italy, where his power was growing weaker. During the remainder of Gregory III's pontificate there was little interaction between Rome and Constantinople; Rome had gained *de facto* freedom from imperial control.

During the first part of Gregory III's pontificate papal relations with the LOMBARDS were relatively quiet; the agreement of 728 between Pope Gregory II and King LIUTPRAND (712–744) served to keep the peace. Gregory remained aware of the Lombard threat, as indicated by his restoration of the walls of Rome and his efforts to regain strategic strongholds seized by the Lombards. In 738 Liutprand seized Ravenna and forced the exarch into exile; Gregory III played an important role in restoring the exarch, an act that Liutprand considered hostile. Liutprand's main objective was the subjugation of the dukes of Spoleto and Benevento, whose efforts to remain independent threatened Liutprand's plans to unify the Lombard kingdom. Gregory III's support of a rebellion of the dukes increased the hostility of the Lombard king. Liutprand's success against the dukes and subsequent march on Rome with the intention of forcing Gregory III to abandon his alliance with dukes prompted the Pope to send an embassy to CHARLES MARTEL in 739, pleading for Frankish intervention to save St. Peter's church and his ''special people'' (*peculiarem populum*). Charles declined to act in defense of Rome, probably because Liutprand was a Frankish ally who at the moment was providing invaluable help to Charles in his effort to check Muslim intrusions into Provence. But Charles did send an embassy to Rome that prompted a second appeal from Gregory III. In his letters to Charles, Gregory spoke in terms that suggested that he and most Romans believed that a Roman political entity had come into existence whose leader could deal with other princes as an independent agent. In the meantime, Liutprand retired from the Roman scene, perhaps because of the intercession of Charles Martel on behalf of the Pope, but more likely because his threat to Rome had convinced the Pope to give up his alliance with the Lombard dukes of Spoleto and Benevento. Peace, albeit tenuous, had been restored in Italy.

Meanwhile, Gregory III continued expanding papal ties with the world north of the Alps. Already noted was his interaction with Charles Martel, a step in establishing closer relationship with the kingdom of the Franks. He became involved in ecclesiastical affairs in England when he responded favorably to a request by Bishop EGBERT OF YORK to restore that see to the metropolitan status that had originally been awarded it by Pope Gregory I (590–604). He continued to follow closely the missionary work of BONIFACE in Germany. On the basis of reports of Boniface's successes in Hesse and Thuringia and his continued requests for guidance, in 732 Gregory III elevated Boniface to archiepiscopal status without a fixed see but closely linked to Rome; Boniface was instructed to proceed with the establishment of bishoprics in Germany and to appoint qualified clerics to serve as bishops in the new sees. Boniface gave his immediate attention to establishing an episcopal structure in Bavaria to which Gregory III gave his approval, and then he continued his organizational work by establishing episcopal sees in Hesse and Thuringia. As his work progressed, the Pope provided his legate with letters soliciting support for his work and providing guidance on a wide range of disciplinary, liturgical, and theological matters pertaining to the establishment of Christian life among the partially Christianized and newly converted peoples in Bavarian, Hesse, and Thuringia. On occasion, Boniface responded by reminding his spiritual mentor of rumors about religious matters in Rome that needed correction. In 737 at the Pope's command Boniface visited Rome for the third time, and then returned north armed with papal letters to various parties urging support for his work and with instructions to continue organizing the lands in which he had been working. By the time this phase of his career was completed in the early 740s, Boniface was ready to move into a new realm that would involve the papacy, the reform of the Frankish church along lines that promised to increase papal influence in the Frankish realm.

Gregory III died in 741, a year that also witnessed the deaths of Emperor Leo III and Charles Martel. New leaders would now continue to transform the power structure in Italy, which had changed considerably during the pontificate of Gregory III. It was marked especially by his exploration of new ways to replace the eastern Roman emperor as protector of the Pope and the territories he controlled against the Lombards.

Feast: Nov. 28.

Bibliography: *Le Liber Pontificalis*, ed. L. DUCHESNE, 3 v., 2nd ed. (Paris 1955–1957) 1: 415–425, English translation in *The Lives of the Eighth-Century Popes (Liber Pontificalis). The Ancient Biographies of Nine Popes from AD 715 to AD 817*, tr. with intro. by R. DAVIS (Liverpool 1992) 17–28. *Regesta Pontificum Romanorum ab condita ecclesia ad annum post Christum MCXCVIII*, ed. P. JAFFÉ, 2 v. (2d ed. Leipzig 1885–1888) 1:257–262. P. CONTE, *Regesto delle lettere dei papi del secolo VIII: saggi* (Milan 1984) 200–207. *Codex Carolinus*, Epp.1–2, ed. W. GUNDLACH, *Monumenta Germaniae Historica, Epistolae: Epistolae Merowingici et Karolini aevi* (Berlin 1892; repr. 1994) 475–479. *Epistolae Langobardicae collectae*, Epp. 12–17, *ibid.*, 702–709. *Die Briefe des heiligen Bonifatius und Lullus (S. Bonifatii et Lulli epistolae)*, ed. M. TANGL, *Monumenta Germaniae Historica, Epistolae Selectae* 1 (Berlin 1916; reprinted, 1989), English translation as *The Letters of St. Boniface*, tr. E. EMERTON (New York 2000). *Vita sancti Bonifatii archiepiscopi Moguntini*, ed. W. LEVISON, *Monumenta Germaniae Historica, Sriptores rerum Germanicarum in usum scholarum* 57 (Hannover and Leipzig 1905; repr.1999), English translation as ''Willibald, The Life of Saint Boniface,'' tr. C. H TALBOT, in *Soldiers of Christ. Saints and Saints' Lives from Antiquity and the Early Middle Ages*, ed. T. F. X. NOBLE and T. HEAD (University Park, Penn. 1985) 107–140.

[R. E. SULLIVAN]

GREGORY IV, POPE

Pontificate: Sept. 827 to Jan. 25, 844. A native Roman, he was cardinal priest of St. Mark's at the time of his election. His consecration (March 29, 828?) was

Christ with Saints, mosaic in the apse of the church of St. Mark in Rome. Pope Gregory IV is at the left; St. Peter is the center figure (the mosaic was commissioned by Pope Gregory IV in 833).

delayed until a *missus* of LOUIS THE PIOUS had reviewed the election in accord with the *Constitutio Romana* of 824 (*see* EUGENE II, POPE).

Subsequent to the revolt of Louis's older sons, LOTHAIR I, Pepin, and LOUIS THE GERMAN (830), and the veiling of the Empress Judith at a convent in Poitiers, a diet at Aachen (Feb. 2, 831) restored Judith to her husband on the mandate of the pope and other bishops (Thegan: *Vita Ludov.* 37; *Patrologia latina* 106:419). Two years later, during another uprising of the imperial sons, Gregory was present in the camp of Lothair [*Ann. Xantenses* 833; R. Rau, ed., *Quellen z. karoling. Reichsgesch.,* 2 (1958) 340], whence at Easter 833 he appealed to Abp. AGOBARD OF LYONS and Abbot WALA OF CORBIE for aid in bringing concord to the royal family. To the reluctance of the imperial bishops to meet with him, Gregory replied by strongly justifying his intervention (*Monumenta Germaniae Historica: Epistolae* 5:228–232). A conference of pope and emperor near Colmar (June 24, 833) was followed closely by Lothair's perfidious seizure of power and Gregory's acquiescence in Louis the Pious's deposition (*Vita Walae* 2.18; *Patrologia latina* 120:1640). After Louis's restoration as Emperor (Mar. 1, 834) and Lothair's harassment of church property in Italy, Louis censured his son and in 837 sent Abbot Adrebald to Rome to consult with the ailing pope. A papal embassy of gratitude to Louis was turned back by Lothair at Bologna, though Gregory's letters secretly reached the emperor (Astronomer: *Vita Ludov.* 55–56; *Patrologia Latina* 104:970). After Louis's death Gregory tried in vain to keep peace among the sons by dispatching Abp. George of Ravenna as his legate (*Ann. Bertiniani* 841; Rau, ed., *Quellen* 2:54; but cf. Agnellus. *Liber pontificalis episc. Raven.; Patrologia latina* 106:747–750).

He endowed Roman churches and fortified Ostia (called Gregoriopolis in his honor) against Saracen pirates from Africa. AMALARIUS OF METZ [*De ordine antiphonarii,* prol. (J. M. Hanssens, ed., 1948)] notes that in 831, on his visit to Rome, Gregory assigned an archdeacon to instruct him in Roman liturgical usages. Four years later, at the pope's urging, Louis the Pious extended the Feast of All Saints (November 1) to the Frankish domains (*Chron. Sigeberti* 835; *Patrologia latina* 160:159). In 831–832 this pope bestowed the pallium upon (St.) ANSGAR and named him papal legate to Scandinavia [Jaffé E 2574; F. Curschmann, *Die ältesten Papsturkunden d. Erzb. Hamburg* (1909) 13–15].

Bibliography: *Liber pontificalis,* ed. L. DUCHESNE (Paris 1886–92; 1958) 2:73–85; 3:122–123. P. JAFFÉ, *Regesta pontificum romanorum ab condita ecclesia ad annum post Christum natum 1198,* ed. S. LÖENFELD et. al. (2d ed. Leipzig 1881–88; repr. Graz 1956) 1:323–327. H. K. MANN, *The Lives of the Popes in the Early Middle Ages from 590 to 1304* (London 1902–32) 2.1:187–231. A. HAUCK, *Kirchengeschichte Deutschlands* (9th ed. Berlin-Leipzig 1958) 2:513–521. P. BREZZI, *Roma e l'Impero medioevale* (Bologna 1947). L. HALPHEN, *Charlemagne et l'empire carolingien* (Paris 1947). F. X. SEPPELT, *Geschichte der Päpste von den Anfängen bis zur Mitte des 20. Jh.* (2d ed. Munich 1955) 2: 214–221. H. X. ARQUILLIÈRE, *L'Augustinisme politique* (2d ed. Paris 1955). R. BENERICETTI, *La cronologia dei Papi dei secoli IX–XI secondo le carte di Ravenna* (1999) 23–24. P. JOHANEK, *Lexikon für Theologie und Kirche,* 3 (3d ed. Freiburg 1995). J. N. D. KELLY, *Oxford Dictionary of Popes* (New York 1986) 102–103.

[H. G. J. BECK]

GREGORY V, POPE

Pontificate: May 3, 996 to February or March 999; b. Bruno, 972, the second son of Duke Otto of Carinthia, and the great-grandson of the Emperor OTTO I. Destined for the clerical life, he received an excellent education and served in the imperial chapel. After the death of JOHN XV, who had previously requested OTTO III to invade Italy in opposing Crescentius (*see* CRESCENTII), the emperor appointed his 24-year-old chaplain as pope and presented him to the Roman legation that had come to Ravenna (996). Accompanied by his teacher, Archbishop WILLIGIS OF MAINZ, and by the Chancellor Hildibald, Gregory was accepted at Rome without opposition—the first German and the first non-Italian pope in more than a century. One of his first acts was to crown Otto III (Ascension Day, May 3, 996). In the fall of 996, however, the pope had to flee Rome because of aristocratic oppression, headed by Crescentius, whom the emperor had previously pardoned at Gregory's request. In early 997 Abp. John Philagathos of Piacenza was promoted as antipope John XVI; but even with Byzantine aid he was unable to secure his hold on Rome. On his second campaign into Italy (February 998), Otto assisted Gregory's return to the city and there dealt severely with the insurgents: Crescentius was beheaded; John XVI was blinded and kept in a monastery. Gregory, however, reigned for barely more than a year and died suddenly. His personal integrity and strong reforming purpose produced the first notable example of harmonious cooperation between pope and emperor. Yet Gregory's awareness of the need for independent decision and of the rights of the Holy See often produced a degree of tension in his relations with the emperor. His independence is evident in his handling of affairs in the Church of REIMS, where he supported the claims of Archbishop Arnulf against the opposition of Gerbert (SYLVESTER II), suspending the French bishops who cooperated (Synod of Pavia, 997). Overlooking the incident, however, Gregory sent Gerbert the pallium upon his appointment by Otto as archbishop of Ravenna (998). Also against the will of the emperor, he restored the See of Merseburg after it had previously been absorbed into the metropolitan See of Magdeburg.

Bibliography: *Liber pontificalis,* ed. L. DUCHESNE (Paris 1886–92) 2:261–262. P. JAFFÉ, *Regesta pontificum romanorum ab condita ecclesia ad annum post Christum natum 1198,* ed. S. LÖWENFELD (882–1198) 1:489–495. A. FLICHE and V. MARTIN, eds., *Histoire de l'église depuis les origines jusqu'à nos jours* (Paris 1935—) 7:64–67. F. X. SEPPELT, *Geschichte der Päpste von den Anfängen bis zur Mitte des 20. Jh.* (Munich 1955) 2:387–392. K. and M. UHLIRZ, *Jahrbücher des Deutschen Reiches unter Otto II und Otto III* v.2 (Berlin 1954). H. ZIMMERMANN, "Papstabsetzungen des Mittelalters," *Mitteilungen des Instituts für österreichische Geschichtsforschung* 69 (1961) 270ff. K. GÖRICH, "Der Gandersheimer Streit zur Zeit Otto III. Ein Konflikt um die Metropolitanrechte des Erzbishofs Willigis von Mainz," *Zeitschrift der Savigny-Stiftung für Rechtsgeschichte. Germanistiche Abteilung* 110 (Vienna 1993) 56–94. K. GÖRICH, "Otto III. Romanus, Saxonicus et Italicus. Kaiserliche Rompolitik und sächische Historiographie," *Roxznik Historyczne* 59 (1993) 132–35. V. HUTH, *Erzbischof Arnulf von Reims und der Kampf um das Königtum im Westfrankreich. Zugleich ein Beitrag zur Geschichte der Reimser Remigius-Fälschungen* (Sigmaringen 1994) 85–104. T. E. MOEHS, *Pope Gregory V (996–999): A Biographical Study,* (Stuttgart 1972) A. SOMORJAI, "Sant' Adalberto e il Cristianesimo ungherese nel contesto centroeuropeo," *La civiltà Ungherese e il Cristianesimo. Atti del IV Congresso Internazionali di Studi Ungheresi* (Rome-Naples 1996) 36–43. J. WARMINSKI, *Encyklopedia Katolicka* (Lublin 1993). H. ZIMMERMANN, *Lexikon für Theologie und Kirche* 4 (1995). J. N. D. KELLY, *Oxford Dictionary of Popes* (New York 1986) 134–35.

[F. DRESSLER]

GREGORY VI, POPE

Pontificate: May 1, 1045 to Dec. 20, 1046; b. John de Gratiano; d. probably Cologne, Germany, *c.* November 1047. He was possibly related by marriage to both the converted Jewish family of Benedict the Christian (*see*

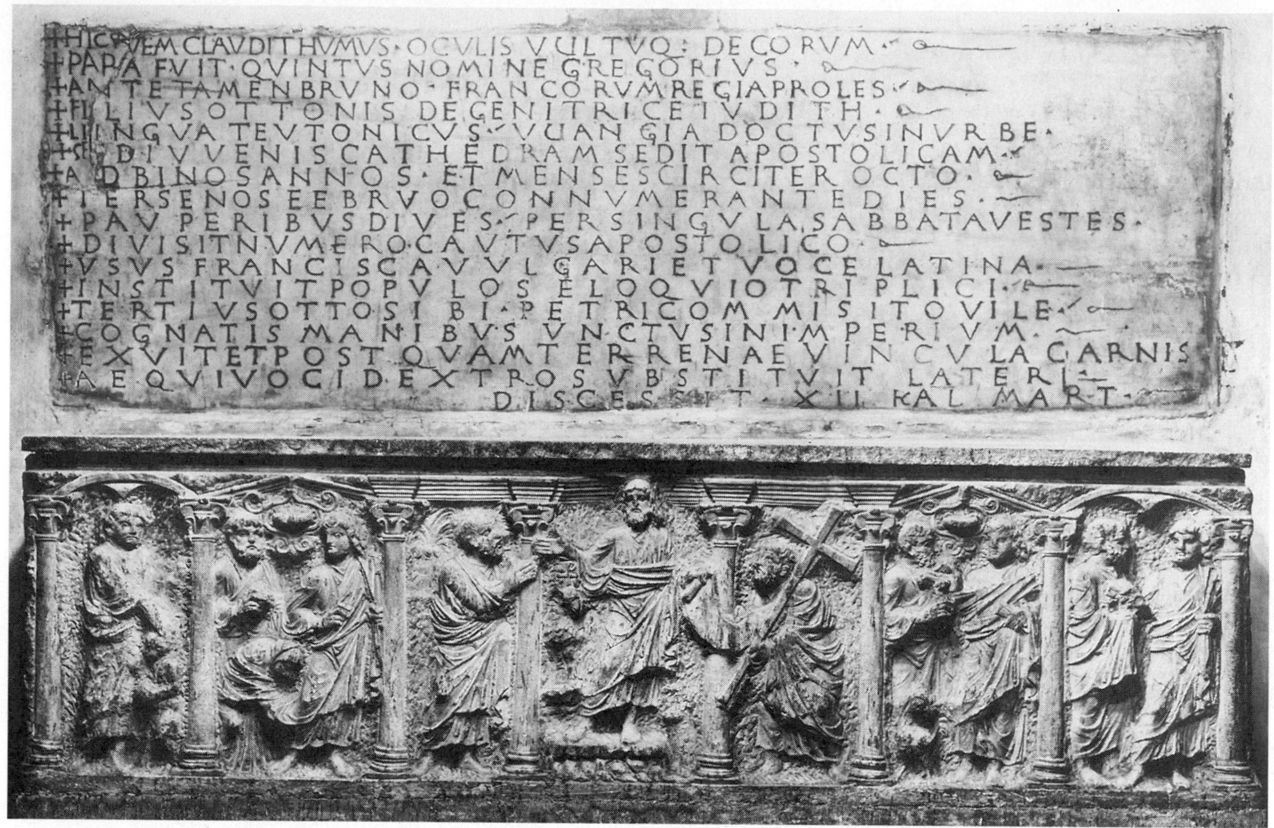

Sarcophagus and inscription of Pope Gregory V, located in the Grotto of St. Peter's Basilica, Rome, 6th century. (Alinari-Art Reference/Art Resource, NY)

PIERLEONI) and to Hildebrand (*see* GREGORY VII, POPE). John was a respected member of the Roman reformers and archpriest of the church of St. John at the Latin Gate. The godfather (?) of the reigning Pope BENEDICT IX, he was already past middle age, and was a man of unblemished character when, deeply disturbed by Benedict's unworthiness, he arranged to provide the pope with the money that would induce his resignation. Benedict reportedly accepted the sum of 1,000 to 2,000 pounds of silver pennies of Pavia (about $150,000) and departed. Gregory was elected pope the same day. At first his accession was hailed by PETER DAMIAN and other reformers; but as it became evident to the German party that SIMONY had been involved in the transaction, (Emperor) HENRY III was persuaded to intervene, especially as both the CRESCENTII and the TUSCULANI threatened the peaceful rehabilitation of Rome. Henry was perhaps further motivated by the desire to materialize in a somewhat altered form the dream of OTTO III: he would not rule the Empire from Rome, but would govern the affairs of Italy through his proxy, a German pope. Coming south with his army and a great assembly of churchmen from Germany, Burgundy, and Italy, Henry held a synod at Pavia (October 1046). Learning of Henry's approach, Gregory traveled north and met the king at Piacenza. Henry received the pope courteously but denied him recognition, demanding an investigation of his title to the papacy. At the synod of SUTRI (Dec. 20, 1046), about 26 miles north of Rome, the pope's claims were judged. Since Benedict IX and the antipope Sylvester III had months before departed from the scene, it was necessary only to declare them removed from office. After due consideration of the charges of simony brought against the pope, Henry and the synod deposed the well-intentioned Gregory, opening the way for the selection of the first German pope in 50 years (*see* CLEMENT II). At Henry's order, Gregory was taken into exile in Germany (January 1047), accompanied by his chaplain Hildebrand.

Bibliography: P. JAFFÉ, *Regesta pontificum romanorum ab condita ecclesia ad annum post Christum natum 1198*, ed. S. LÖWENFELD (882–1198) 1:524–525. G. B. BORINO, "L'elezione e la deposizione di Gregorio VI," *Archivio della Società Romana di Storia Patria* 39 (1916) 142–252, 295–410. "Invitus ultra montes cum domno Papa Gregorio abii," *Studi gregoriani*, ed. G. B. BORINO (Rome 1947—) 1:3–46. R. L. POOLE, "Benedict IX and Gregory VI," *Proceedings of the British Academy* 8 (1917–18) 199–235. J. HALLER, *Das Papsttum* (Stuttgart 1950–53) 2:572–576. F. X. SEPPELT, *Geschichte der Päpste von den Anfängen bis zur Mitte des 20. Jh.* (Munich 1955) 2:415–418. R. AUBERT, *Diction-*

naire d'histoire et de géographie ecclésiastiques 21 (Paris 1986), s.v. ''Grégorie VI.'' H. H. ANTON, ''Die Synode von Sutri, ihr zeitgeschichtlicher Kontext und Nachklang,'' *Zeitschrift der Savingny-Stifung für Rechtsgeschichte. Germanistische Abteilung* (Wien 1997) 576–84. J. LAUNDAGE, *Lexikon für Theologie und Kirche* 4 (1995), s.v. ''Gregor VI., Papst.'' T. STRUVE, *Lexikon des Mittelalters*, 7 (München-Zürick 1992), s.v. ''Sutri Synode v. 1046.'' O. WIDDING, ''An Old Norse Version of a Pamphlet on the Papacy of Gregor VI,'' *Analecta Romana Instituti Danici* 15 (Odense 1986) 51–65. J. N. D. KELLY, *Oxford Dictionary of Popes* (New York 1986) 144–145.

[O. J. BLUM]

GREGORY VI, ANTIPOPE

Pontificate: May to December 1012. Nothing is known of Gregory until he emerges as the Crescentius family's choice for pope during a period when Rome was free from imperial control. After the death of Emperor Otto III in 1002, the Crescentii had nominated and installed three popes (John XVII, John XVIII and Sergius IV) under the leadership of John II Crescentius, who had been acting as dictator of Rome from 1003. When Pope Sergius IV (1009–12) died less than a week before John II Crescentius (they died May 12, and May 18, respectively), there was a struggle for control of the city between the Crescentii and their rivals, the Tusculan family. In a successful bid to wrest power away from the Crescentii, the Tusculans selected Benedict VIII (1012–24) to be pope, while the weakened Crescentii chose Gregory. Gregory's position was precarious from the start, and by the end of summer he had been forced to leave Rome. He went to Germany and appealed to King Henry II (1002–24) for help. Henry promised to investigate Gregory's claim, but he was already in the process of negotiating an agreement with Benedict, whom he soon recognized. From this point we hear no more of Gregory, and the Tusculans began a decades-long rule in Rome.

Bibliography: L. DUCHESNE, ed. *Liber Pontificalis* (Paris 1886–92; repr. 1955–57) 2.268. THIETMAR OF MERSEBURG, *Chronicon* 6.101, in *Monumenta Germaniae historica, Scriptores* (new series) 9.394–95. H. JEDIN and J. DOLAN, eds. *Handbook of Church History* (New York 1965–81) 3.249. K. J. HERRMANN, *Das Tuskulanerpapsttum, 1012–1046* (Stuttgart 1973) 5, 7, 25–7. J. N. D. KELLY, *The Oxford Dictionary of Popes* (Oxford 1986) 141. P. VIARD, *Dictionnaire d'histoire et de géographie ecclésiastiques* (Paris 1986) 21.1423. T. STRUVE, *Lexikon des Mittelalters* (Munich 1989) 4.1668 for additional bibliography.

[P. M. SAVAGE]

GREGORY VII, POPE

Pontificate: April 22, 1073, to May 25, 1085; b. Hildebrand, probably at Sovana (Tuscany) c. 1015; d. Salerno. He became a monk, probably at S. Maria on the Aventine at Rome where he had relatives, and there he seems to have attracted the attention of the papal household in the Lateran palace—the household of St. Peter to whom he always professed an overriding loyalty. It is improbable that he was ever a monk at CLUNY, although its great abbot, HUGH OF SEMUR (1049–1109), was his friend and confidant. In 1046 he accompanied GREGORY VI into exile, going to Cologne and then encountering the Lorraine circle of reformers. When Bp. Bruno of Toul in 1049 became Pope LEO IX, he took to Rome with him a number of personally and morally outstanding churchmen; amongst them was Hildebrand, whom Leo made subdeacon and also *economus* (administrator) of the basilica of ST. PAUL-OUTSIDE-THE-WALLS. From this time Hildebrand's activities multiplied both in Rome and more widely. In 1054, he presided as papal legate over the synod of TOURS which considered the eucharistic teaching of BERENGARIUS. Visits to Germany established a strong link with the Salian royal house. Hildebrand was concerned in the elections of NICHOLAS II in December 1058 and of ALEXANDER II in 1061. Probably in 1059 he became archdeacon of the Roman church; in the same year he was present at Melfi when Nicholas concluded an alliance with the South Italian Normans. Under Alexander, Hildebrand seemed to many to be the power behind

Pope Gregory VII, 1844, drawing by Karl Herman. (Christel Gerstenberg/CORBIS/Bettmann)

the papal throne. As his own register shows, his eventual election as pope was a tumultuous affair which bore no resemblance to the procedure envisaged in the PAPAL ELECTION DECREE (1059); he was promoted by popular acclamation. The considerable delay before his consecration (he was ordained priest on May 22, 1073, and raised to the episcopate and to the full exercise of the papal office on June 30) had nothing to do with a wish to obtain confirmation of his election from the German king, HENRY IV, who had in fact incurred excommunication by association with counselors banned by Alexander II.; he postponed his consecration until the Sunday after the feast of St. Peter (June 29), thereby emphasizing his life-long devotion to the Prince of the Apostles.

The Program of Reform. Gregory took his papal name, and in many respects his vision of the papal office, from Pope GREGORY THE GREAT. Yet in him, a man of exceptional caliber, wisdom, vision, and single-mindedness ascended the throne of St. Peter (Gregory habitually referred to himself as vicar of St. Peter, never as vicar of Christ); in many respects he is unique among the popes, and with much justification has been called ''the great innovator who stands alone'' (E. Caspar). Such a preeminence is reflected in the style of his letters and decrees, many of which are preserved in his register but some only elsewhere (his *epistolae vagante*). As W. Peitz showed and others have confirmed, the register is the original working record of the papal household; it is the earliest entire and contemporary papal register to survive, and many letters both in and outside it bear the marks of Gregory's personal dictation. His letters testify to the profoundly spiritual and religious motivation of his pontificate. In the spirit of Gregory the Great he aspired to preach the claims of Christianity to all peoples, near and far, and to revive the pristine fervor of a church in which the faith of its early years had become tarnished. Near the end of his life he declared that ''I have above all sought that holy church, the bride of God and our mistress and mother, should return to her proper glory and should stand free, chaste, and catholic'' (Ep. vag. 54).

In such terms, few popes have had so clear a vision of their duty and of their program; but much remained to be done in order both to establish and warrant assured principles of papal authority and to apply them in practice and reality. Gregory's thinking developed over the years. While archdeacon, he asked Cardinal PETER DAMIAN to work through the decrees of ancient popes and to abstract and arrange systematically whatever seemed especially to bear upon the authority of the apostolic see. The 27 lapidary formulations of papal prerogatives inserted in the register in 1075 and headed *Dictatus papae* (II.55a) are perhaps best understood as headings under which ancient canonical material might usefully be sought, deployed, and appraised. Progressively more assured and documented statements occur in the letters in which Gregory justified to Bp. Hermann of Metz his sentences of 1076 and 1080 against King Henry IV (*Reg.* IV.2, VIII.21). In the second letter especially, Gregory proclaimed the immeasurable superiority of the priestly dignity (*sacerdotium*) over the kingly (*regnum*) on account of the powers that they respectively exercised. He also drew a moral contrast between secular rulers as driven by human pride and religious popes made holy by the merits of St. Peter. Kings like bishops owed a duty of obedience to the pope as the upholder of a Christian righteousness (*justicia*) which was the power and purpose of God in action upon a fallen world. The force of Gregory's thought led him, in the case of Henry IV, to deviate from his usual advocacy of strong and hereditary—and obedient—monarchy into an argument for election.

A necessary condition for the realization of Gregory's vision of a renewed church which should be ''free, chaste, and catholic'' was the moral purification of both clergy and laity. Especially at his Lent synods of 1074 and 1075, he reinforced the requirement that all clerks in major orders (subdeacons and above) should refrain from marriage and practice chastity (*see* CELIBACY, CLERICAL HISTORY OF). Laity were to marry only within the permitted degrees of kinship. (For Gregory, this was a safeguard of the vitality of princely lineages.) Upon clergy and laity alike, Gregory rigorously imposed a duty of refraining from SIMONY (the buying and selling of orders and offices in the church); this was an aspect of Gregory's progressively intensified concern for ''free'' ecclesiastical elections, i.e. elections from which improper lay intervention was excluded. Such demands upon clergy and laity had been made during preceding pontificates, but especially in Germany and France Gregory's requirement of strict clerical chastity gave rise to anger and resistance.

The synods in the Lateran at which decrees for reform were often passed were held during Lent during most years of Gregory's pontificate, and occasionally also in the autumn. They were usually well attended by clergy and laity who experienced Gregory's reforming zeal first hand and their decrees were widely disseminated. If the Lateran synods brought many from throughout Latin Christendom to Gregory in Rome, an increased use of papal legates who represented the apostolic see brought its authority to bear in localities of Christendom. Gregory often dispatched legates, in pairs, to perform and report back on specific matters. Of especial usefulness to Gregory were the standing papal vicars who represented his authority in extensive areas for periods of years, especially Bp. HUGH OF DIE (later Abp. of Lyons) and Bp. Amatus of Oloron in France, Bp. ANSELM II OF LUCCA in Lombardy, and Bp. ALTMANN OF PASSAU in South

Germany; all were staunch Gregorians who did much to implement and commend Gregory's reforming purposes. As for archbishops, Gregory expected them normally to come to Rome for their PALLIUM—the vestment which signified their participation in the pope's pastoral office. They were also expected to pay regular visits to Rome and thus to confirm their solidarity with papal purposes; when paid, such visits anticipated the AD LIMINA journeys which later would become general practice. By such means as these Gregory sought to add effectiveness to his apostolic authority over the church.

Gregory and Henry IV of Germany. At the outset of his pontificate, Gregory wished to build upon his regard for the Salian royal family by training Henry IV not only for the royal but also for the imperial office; this was despite Henry's youthful peccadilloes and Alexander II's excommunication of his five counselors. But a major problem arose over filling the Lombard metropolitan see of Milan: when Henry nominated a royal candidate, the PATARINES of the city elected a rival whom the papacy warmly supported. At his Lent synod of 1075 and in the context of Milanese affairs, Gregory probably passed the first of his decrees against lay INVESTITURE, to which he had not hitherto in principle objected. Henry persisted with his establishment of bishops, not only at Milan, but at Fermo and Spoleto. Upon receiving a menacing rebuke from Gregory in December 1075 (*Reg.* III.10), Henry sought to seize the initiative by summoning an assembly at Worms for the end of January 1076; an assembly of 26 bishops initiated a series of impassioned Henrician manifestos which denounced "the monk Hildebrand," calling for his deposition. Soon after, at his Lent synod, Gregory suspended Henry from the government of the Kingdom of Germany and Italy, absolving all Christians from their oaths to him and forbidding them to serve him; thereafter he excommunicated him. The falling away of his support in Germany compelled Henry to seek and receive absolution from Gregory at Canossa in January 1077, though Gregory did not consider that he had restored him to the exercise of the kingship. Matters were greatly complicated when, on March 15, 1077, without Gregory's permission, an assembly of German princes elected an antiking, Duke Rudolf of Swabia. In Germany there followed a complex period of civil war, propaganda, and negotiation. Gregory sought to act as arbitrator. His desired means was an assembly or *colloquium* over which he or his legate would preside; its aim would be to establish which of the rival kings divine righteousness favoured (*cui parti magis justicia faveat*). However, by 1080, Gregory became convinced that by renewed disobedience Henry had revived the sentence of excommunication against himself. At his Lent council he himself excommunicated Henry and then took from him his whole kingdom and office; the reversal of order of the sentence and its intensification by comparison with 1076 should be noted. He proclaimed Rudolf of Swabia for his proven humility and obedience to be king of the Germans.

Henry's response came on June 25, 1080, when his synod of Brixen chose Abp. GUIBERT OF RAVENNA to be antipope; this betokened a papal schism. In an age that deemed the outcome of battle to be a judgement of God, it was a grave blow to Gregory when, on the following October 25, Rudolf of Swabia suffered mortal injuries in the battle of Hohenmölsen; it was some nine months before a new antiking was elected—the unimpressive Count Hermann of Salm. The upshot of the momentous events of 1080 was that from being a would-be arbiter in the settlement of the German kingdom Gregory became a protagonist: Gregory against Henry. Henry had learned some of the skills of kinship, and to a papal sacrality patronized by St. Peter, prince of the Apostles, he sought to oppose a royal sacrality under the yet more exalted patronage of Mary, Queen of Heaven. In a Germany racked by war and war-weariness, the rival parties contended by words and by arms with results that, by 1085, were not to Gregory's advantage—this despite a heroic effort by Cardinal-Bp. Odo of Ostia, later Pope URBAN II, to rally the Gregorian cause. In 1081, 1082, and 1083–4, Henry undertook campaigns in Italy. In 1084, after the defection from Gregory of 12 or 13 cardinals, Henry entered Rome. He declared "Hildebrand" deposed; Guibert was acclaimed pope with the name Clement III, and on Easter Day (March 31) he crowned Henry as emperor. Gregory took refuge in the Castel Sant'Angelo whence he was rescued by the Norman duke Robert Guiscard. The Normans sacked the city so savagely that Gregory accompanied Guiscard home to Salerno where he spent his last months in active furtherance of his cause. His reported last words, "I have loved righteousness (*justicia*) and hated iniquity, therefore I die in exile," are probably to be regarded as expressing, not bitterness and disillusion, but invincible confidence in the blessedness of those who suffer persecution for righteousness' sake (Mt 5.10).

France. The very large number of Gregory's letters that concern France testifies to its importance for him. Broadly, whereas in his dealings with Germany the demands of righteousness were emphasized, with France he gave fuller scope to restraint and to the exercise of apostolic mercy. Except for a tempestuous few months in 1074 when he canvassed the deposition of King PHILIP I, he was conspicuously reticent about his shortcomings; he did not press such decrees as those concerning lay investiture, so that in France there was no "investiture controversy," let alone "contest." He was conspicuously sparing of French bishops. His patience with Abp.

MANASSES I OF REIMS before his eventual deposition in 1080 is remarkable. Accused bishops who appealed to Gregory at Rome found there a mercy that contrasted with the rigor of a legate like Hugh of Die; the effect was to commend Roman authority and to encourage direct recourse to it.

Other Regions. Gregory corresponded with most of the rulers of Christendom; besides the Norman princes of South Italy who were papal vassals, letters were sent to the Spanish kings and to kings of England and Ireland in the west, to the Scandinavian kings in the north, and in the east to rulers of Poland, Russia, Bohemia, Hungary, and lands across the Adriatic. Gregory sought to foster strong, hereditary dynasties which, in obedience to the papacy, built up the church and provided peace and justice for their subjects. He sought good relations with the emperors of Byzantium and the fostering of concord between the Eastern and Western Churches. In 1074, his projected military expedition to the East to defend Christian peoples against the savagery of the Seljuk Turks was part of a re-evaluation of Christian warfare which helped to prepare for the CRUSADE. A somewhat different approach is apparent in Gregory's letters to a subject Christian community and to a well disposed Muslim ruler in North Africa.

Other Concerns. Gregory was zealous in promoting the defense, good order, and well-being of monasteries and monks whose intercessory and other services he valued. His relations were especially strong with MONTE CASSINO as a southern bastion of papal security (its great abbot, Desiderius, briefly succeeded him as Pope VICTOR III) and with Cluny as an exemplar of ecclesiastical liberty. Gregory's support of the HIRSAU reform was a major feature of his impact upon South Germany. Indirectly he was instrumental in promoting the CARTHUSIANS, founded by BRUNO OF COLOGNE, who in 1084 started his first community near Grenoble. Of his many other concerns mention may particularly be made of liturgical matters. He defended and promoted the ROMAN RITE, especially against the MOZARABIC (Hispanic) usage in Spain. He permanently fixed the EMBER DAYS for fasting throughout the Latin Church. He was influential with respect to the practice and understanding of penance.

Conclusion. Gregory undoubtedly ranks amongst the greatest popes of all time and makers of the Middle Ages, but in modern times, no less than his own, the most contrasting judgements have been passed on him. He is perhaps best regarded as a bridge figure between the outstanding popes of Christian antiquity whose pastoral and moral authority he aspired to renew and the papal monarchy of the central Middle Ages. His comprehensive view of Christendom and exploration of the prerogatives of the apostolic see effectively prepared the way in principle and in practice.

From his death until the Reformation, he was referred to surprisingly seldom in sources of all kinds, but in the sixteenth century interest revived amongst both Protestants and Catholics. His canonization, therefore, came slowly: in 1583, Pope Gregory XIII caused him to be included in the Roman Martyrology; in 1609, Pope Paul V authorized his commemoration at Salerno; in 1728, Pope Benedict XIV extended his feast to the whole Church.

Feast: May 25.

Bibliography: L. JAFFÉ *Regesta pontificum romanorum a condita ecclesia ad annum post Christum natum 1198* (Leipzig 1881–88) 1:594–649. E. CASPAR ed., *Registrum Gregori VII Monumenta Germaniae Historica,* Epistolae selectae, 2 (Berlin 1920–3), Eng. tr. H. E. J. COWDREY (2000). H. E. J. COWDREY ed. and tr., *The Epistolae vagantes of Pope Gregory VII* (1972). L. SANTIFALLER ed., *Quellen und Forschungen zum Urkunden- und Kanzleiwesen Papst Gregors VII,* 1: *Quellen: Urkunden. Regesten. Facsimilia* (Studi e Testi 190). H. E. J. COWDREY *Pope Gregory VII, 1073–1085* (Oxford 1998). I. S. ROBINSON, *The Papacy, 1073–1198* (Cambridge 1990) *Studi gregoriani,* ed. G. B. BORINO. W. ULLMANN, *The Growth of Papal Government in Middle Ages: A Study in the Ideological Relation of Clerical to Lay Power* 3d ed. (London 1970).

[W. ULLMANN/H. E. J. COWDREY]

GREGORY VIII, POPE

Pontificate, Oct. 21 to Dec. 17, 1187; Canon of St. Augustine, b. Alberto de Morra, Benevento, *c.* 1110, d. Pisa. Prior to his election to the papacy at Ferrara, Gregory had been a canon regular at Laon and a professor (*magister*) of law at Bologna, before becoming cardinal in 1155–56 and chancellor of the Roman Church in 1178.

As cardinal Gregory was sent on important missions to England, Dalmatia, and Portugal by Pope Alexander III. He was involved in settling the dispute between the Curia and King HENRY II of England after the murder of Archbishop Thomas BECKET in 1170. It is no longer certain if, as Roman chancellor, Gregory wrote the *Forma dictandi*, an influential tract on the rhythmic prose of papal documents, which has in the past been attributed to him. Shortly before becoming pope, Gregory asserted his reformist tendencies by founding a monastery at Benevento and providing it with a rule based on austerity and evangelical simplicity.

Gregory's 57-day pontificate was dominated by his response to the Muslim conquest of Jerusalem (Oct. 2, 1187). Only eight days into his pontificate Gregory announced a major new crusade to the Holy Land. Gregory sought speedy conciliation between the Curia and Emperor Frederick I and promoted peace between Genoa and Venice in order to gather support for his crusade project. Despite his short pontificate, the impact of Gregory's policies were far-reaching. His crusading bull *Audita tremendi* not only marked an important stage in the development of crusading thought, it eventually also triggered what was perhaps the greatest crusading effort in aid of the Holy Land ever to occur, known as the Third Crusade.

Bibliography: *Patrologia Latina,* comp. J. P. MIGNE (Paris 1844–64) 202: 1537–64. P. JAFFÉ, *Regesta pontificum Romanorum,* ed. G. WATTENBACH (Leipzig 1885–88) 2: 528–35. *Liber pontificalis,* ed. L. DUCHESNE (Paris 1886–92) 2: 349, 451. H. K. MANN, *The Lives of the Popes in the Early Middle Ages* (London 1902–32) 10: 312. G. KLEEMANN, *Papst Gregor VIII* (Bonn 1913). P. KEHR, "Gregor VIII. als Ordensgrönder," *Miscellanea F. Ehrle* vol. 2 (Studi e Testi 38; Rome 1924) 248–75. W. HOLTZMANN, "Die Dekretalen Gregors VIII" *Mitteilungen des Instituts für österreichische Geschichtsforschung* 58 (1950) 113–123. F. X. SEPPELT, *Geschichte der Päpste* (Munich 1954–59) 3: 301–4. A. DALZELL, "The *Forma Dictandi* attributed to Albert of Morra and related texts," *Mediaeval Studies* 39 (1977) 440–65. V. PFAFF, "Sieben jahre päpstlicher Politik. Die Wirksamkeit der Päpste Lucius III., Urban III., Gregor VIII.," *Zeitschrift der Savigny–Stiftung für Rechtsgeschichte. Kanonische Abteilung* 67 (1981) 148–212. J. N. D. KELLY, *The Oxford Dictionary of the Popes* (Oxford 1988) 182–3. P. AUBERT, *Dictionnaire d'histoire et de géographie ecclésiastiques* (Paris 1912) 21: 1436. U. SCHMIDT, *Lexikon für Theologie und Kirche* 3d ed. (Freiburg 1995) 4:1018. B. ROBERG, *Lexikon des Mittelalters* 4: 1671.

[C. MAIER]

GREGORY VIII, ANTIPOPE

Pontificate: March 10, 1118 to April 22, 1121. He died *c.* 1140. Mauritius Burdinus (Bordinho or Bourdin, meaning "donkey") was born in southern France and became a Cluniac at Limoges, but he was educated in Spain, where he had traveled with Archbishop Bernard of Toledo. He was archdeacon of Toledo, and was made bishop of Coimbra in 1099. After spending part of the next decade on a nearly four-year pilgrimage in the Holy Land, he was made archbishop of Braga by Paschal II in 1109. As archbishop he appeared before the pope twice to defend his rights, once in a boundary dispute with Archbishop Bernard of Toledo, and again to protest decisions that benefited Santiago de Compostela at a cost to his diocese. In 1116, Paschal sent Mauritius on an embassy to Henry V (1106–25); while on this mission he defected to the emperor's cause. After Paschal had been forced from Rome by pressure from the Frangipani family in 1117, Henry appeared in the city with a large entourage, and on Easter Sunday (March 25) Mauritius solemnly crowned Henry emperor. In response, Paschal held a synod in Benevento where he deposed and excommunicated Henry and removed Mauritius as bishop of Braga.

Paschal died within a year (Jan. 24, 1118) and was succeeded by Gelasius II (1118–19). Henry immediately returned to Rome in the hope he could negotiate an end to the INVESTITURE CONTROVERSY. Gelasius, however, remained in the town of Gaeta and had no intention of returning for negotiations with the emperor. Upon the advice of Irnerius of Bologna and other jurists, the imperial party anulled Gelasius' election, and on March 8, 1118 Mauritius was proclaimed pope with the support of the Frangipani. He took the name Gregory VIII, an odd choice if one considers Gregory VII's strong opposition to imperial involvement in the church. Gelasius excommunicated Henry and Gregory on April 8, and began to circulate letters throughout Europe denouncing Gregory's elevation.

Gregory's position became even weaker when Henry returned to Germany and dropped his support for the antipope upon the election of Callistus II (Feb. 2, 1119). Callistus and Henry began negotiations in 1119 while Callistus made consistent progress in controlling Lombardy and Tuscany. As a result, Gregory had to leave Rome for Sutri in 1119. In June 1120, Pope Callistus entered Rome, and in April 1121 he besieged Sutri. The citizens of the town turned Gregory over to the increasingly popular pope, and Callistus, in a final show of victory, forced Gregory to proceed through Rome seated backward on a camel. Gregory was then confined in various locations until his death. They include monasteries in Rome and Passerone, Holy Trinity at La Cava (near Salerno, and the place of confinement for antipopes Theodoric, 1100, and Innocent III, 1179–80), Rocca Iemolo (near Monte Cassino), and finally Castel Fumone. We know that he was alive at La Cava as late as August 1137; after this he disappears from the historical record.

Bibliography: L. DUCHESNE, ed. *Liber Pontificalis* (Paris 1886–92; repr. 1955–57) 2.315, 347; 3.162–69. P. JAFFÉ, *Regesta pontificum Romanorum* (Leipzig 1885–88; repr. Graz 1956) 1.821–22; 2.715. I. M. WATTERICH, *Pontificum Romanorum* (Leipzig; repr. Aalen 1862) 2.15, 119ff. C. ERDMANN, "Mauritius Burdinus (Gregor VIII)," *Quellen und Forchungen aus Italienischen Archiven und Bibliotheken* 19 (1927) 205–61. P. DAVID, "L'énigme de Maurice Bourdin," in *Études historiques sur la Galice et le Portugal* (Lisbon 1947) 441–501. F. X. SEPPELT, *Geschichte der Päpste von den Anfängen bis zur Mitte des zwanzigsten Jahrhunderts* (Munich 1954–59) 3.152–159. C. SERVATIUS, *Paschalis II* (Stuttgart 1979) 128–131, 332. R. AUBERT, *Dictionnaire d'histoire et de géographie ecclésiastiques* (Paris 1986) 21.1433–36. J. N. D. KELLY, *The Oxford Dictionary of Popes* (New York 1986) 163–64. K. SCHREINER, "Gregor VIII, nackt auf einem Esel," in *Ecclesia et Regnum...Festschrift für F.J. Schmale* (Bochum 1989) 155–202. T. STRUVE, *Lexikon des Mittelalters* (Munich 1989) 4.1671.

[P. M. SAVAGE]

Gregory IX consecrating the chapel of St. Gregory, detail of a 12th-century fresco in the lower church of the Sacro Speco at the monastery of Subiaco, Italy.

GREGORY IX, POPE

Pontificate: March 19, 1227, to Aug. 22, 1241; b. Hugo[lino] at Anagni, *c.* 1170; d. Rome. Hugolino was a member of the family of the counts of Segni. His father was a certain Mathias, who died prior to 1192, and his brother Adenulphus served as rector of Anagni. Hugolino was educated in Paris. There is no contemporary evidence that he studied in the law schools of Bologna, despite later tradition.

He was named cardinal deacon of St. Eustachius in 1198 and emerged as one of the leading cardinals in the reign of Innocent III, to whom he was closely related. He served in the negotiations with Markward of Anweiler in the kingdom of Sicily, and, in 1206, he became cardinal bishop of Ostia and was recognized as a leading figure in the papal curia. Under Honorius III, his influence increased. He was papal legate in Liguria and Tuscany in 1217 and remained Honorius's chief representative in this region and in his negotiations with the young emperor, FREDERICK II, whose confidence he enjoyed through most of Honorius's pontificate. Hugolino worked tirelessly to bring about peace among the warring factions in the communes of northern Italy and to recruit contingents for the crusade.

Following the death of Cardinal John of St. Paul, who had been one of St. FRANCIS OF ASSISI'S key supporters in the curia, in 1220, Hugolino became the first cardinal protector of the Franciscan order. He assisted Francis in the composition of the Franciscan rule, the *regula bullata* of 1223. He was also a supporter of St. Dominic and the Dominicans.

On the death of Honorius III, he was immediately elected pope. It was a critical period. The last years of Honorius's reign had seen not merely the defeat of the crusader army at Damietta, but the continued frustration of the papal effort to persuade Frederick II to fulfill his vow to undertake a crusade. The emperor delayed past the August 1227 deadline for his departure, using illness in the army as his excuse. His explanation may have been true, since there was illness in the army, but this delay triggered his automatic excommunication under the terms to which he had agreed in 1225. The excommunication was renewed in early 1228, while he was involved in delicate negotiations with the Egyptian Sultan, al-Kāmil, that were aimed at reviving the sultan's offer, made during the Fifth Crusade, to surrender Jerusalem and other holy places in return for a truce. The excommunicated emperor had little choice but to go to the Holy Land to attempt to reach an agreement with al-Kāmil and to rescue his reputation in the West. It was only after the re-fortification of Jaffa and a show of force that Frederick succeeded in getting an agreement with the sultan. Despite the propaganda efforts of both sides, there was no denying that it was a flawed treaty. Moreover, Frederick, who was regent of the kingdom of Jerusalem for his son, was unpopular with many in the kingdom, both because of his intervention in Cyprus before his arrival in the Latin Kingdom, and for his strained relations with many of the nobles, as well as with the Templars and Hospitalers. In the meantime, trouble erupted in Italy, where Gregory claimed that Count Rainald of Spoleto, who represented Frederick, was invading the Patrimony of St. Peter. Leaving a *bailli* in the Latin Kingdom, Frederick returned to Italy and quickly defeated the papal forces under John of Brienne and entered into negotiations with the pope, which resulted in the Treaty of Ceprano in 1230.

For the most part, Gregory and Frederick cooperated during the 1230s. Among the most notable accomplishments of this period was the promulgation of the *Liber Extra (vagantium),* compiled by Raymond of Peñafort in 1234. The *Decretales,* as it was called, was the most important collection of canon law down to modern times. It established the central role of the papacy in the legal structure of the Roman Catholic Church, marking the completion of the work begun by Gratian in the mid-twelfth century. In this connection, it was formerly thought that the promulgation of the *Decretales* represented Gregory's reaction to Frederick II's promulgation of the Constitutions of Melfi for the Kingdom of Sicily in 1231, but that was not the case. In fact, Frederick came to the aid of the pope in 1234 when the Romans rebelled, and Gregory supported Frederick's effort to re-assert imperial authority in northern Italy.

Inevitably papal and imperial interests clashed. Only after imperial forces invaded Sardinia, over which the papacy claimed feudal overlordship, however, did the rupture become permanent. The ensuing propaganda war brought out some of the strongest letters of condemnation from both sides. Frederick himself was excommunicated on March 20, 1239. Behind the rhetoric lay the influence of some members of the mendicant orders, particularly the Dominicans, who were quite influential at the papal court. Brother Elias, the deposed minister general of the Franciscans, sided with Frederick, but seems not to have had a direct role in the propaganda war. The correspondence on both sides, however, reflects some Joachimite imagery that was beginning to be felt in the mendicant orders. It should not be surprising that both Gregory and Frederick, as well as their chanceries, adopted some of the current strands of thought.

Emphasis on papal-imperial conflicts has distorted our view of Gregory's pontificate. To some extent, the same is true of his approach to the issue of heresy. He is regarded as the founder of the papal Inquisition, although both of his predecessors have received some credit or blame, and the full-blown Inquisition only developed after 1250. Gregory's views on heresy were deeply influenced by those of Innocent III that combined strong legal sanctions with a willingness to work for healing. To some degree he favored the rights of the counts of Toulouse, although they were regarded by many as supporters of heretics. On the other hand, he was very much caught up in the wave of religious enthusiasm that swept through Europe in the 1230s. One aspect of this, represented in the extreme anti-heretical activities of Conrad of Marburg and Robert le Bougre, received considerable support from the pope. He enlisted the Dominicans as preachers against heresy in Provence and was passionately involved in its suppression. This region, where the French monarchy was taking the lead in the suppression of heresy, at the same time integrating this with Capetian France, was a central focus of his concerns. There, as in other parts of Europe, it was often difficult to separate charges of heresy from political rivalries and personal quarrels. If some of those pursuing heretics went far beyond their authorization, Gregory's efforts were sometimes their justification. One difficult problem not easily dealt with is the degree to which concern over heresy was exaggerated by an intensification of religious zeal and the preaching of the friars. Perhaps Gregory more accurately reflected the attitudes of his time rather than attempting to moderate them.

The pope was also involved in the missionary efforts of his time, especially in the Baltic. These had been going on for many years, but were increasingly complicated by the political interests of secular rulers. Moreover, the military orders intended to maintain peace and security in the region, the Sword Brothers and the Teutonic Order, were themselves rivals and sources of conflict. The latter order would, in fact, emerge as a secular principality in the latter part of the thirteenth century. Gregory supported the DOMINICANS as preachers and tried to protect converts from economic and political exploitation. His concerns were chiefly pastoral, but they had almost no long-term impact.

The major achievement of Gregory's pontificate was the firm backing he gave to the FRANCISCANS and Dominicans, as well as to other new religious orders. He was deeply imbued with the spirit of reform that motivated these communities. He issued privilege after privilege aimed at freeing them from episcopal jurisdiction, encouraging their preaching, and drawing on them for the work of the church. He was chiefly responsible for using them as a kind of special force in the employ of the papacy against heresy. He admired the educational attainments of the Dominicans and saw in them a way to educate and persuade those who might otherwise fall into heresy. He also participated in an abortive discussion with the Greek Church, but his adherence to the Latin position on the *azymes* and *filioque* questions resulted in disappointment. A man of strong and emotional character, he was more capable of flexibility than some have thought. For example, in spite of his breaks with Frederick, he was capable of recognizing specific imperial and royal rights.

Bibliography: Sources: L. AUVRAY, *Registre de Gregoire IX: recueil des bulles de ce pape publièes ou analysèes d'après les manuscrits originaux du Vatican,* 4 v. (Paris 1890–1955). J. L. A. HUILLARD-BRÉHOLLES, *Historia Diplomatica Friderici II Romanorum imperatoris,* 6 v. in 12 (Paris 1852–51). G. LEVI, *Registri di Cardinali Ugolino d'Ostia e Ottaviano degli Ubaldini* (Rome 1890). *Monumenta Germaniae Historica, Leges,* 2.1. *Monumenta Germaniae Historica, Epistolae,* 1. *Monumenta Germaniae Historica, Scriptores,* 16:22. B. GUI, *Rerum Italicarum Scriptores,* III. (Life of Gregory by Bernard Gui). Secondary Works: P. BALAN, *Storia di Gregorio IX e dei suoi tempi,* 2 v. in l (Modena, 1872–73). J. FELTEN, *Papst Gregor IX* (Freiburg 1886). H.K. MANN, *The Lives of the Popes in the Early Middle Ages from 590 to 1304* (London 1902–32) 13: 165–441. F.X. SEPPELT, *Geschichte der Päpste von den Anfängen bis zur Mitte des 20. Jahrhunderts* (Munich 1956) 3: 411–52. J. HALLER, *Das Papsttum* (2d. rev. ed. Stuttgart 1950–53) 4:47–160. C. THOUZELLIER, ''La legation en Lombardie du cardinal Hugolin,'' *Revue d'histoire ecclésiastique,* 45 (1950), 508–542. J. M. POWELL, *Anatomy of a Crusade, 1213–1221* (Philadelphia 1986). C. MORRIS, *The Papal Monarchy: The Western Church from 1050 to 1250* (New York 1991). J. STRAYER, *The Albigensian Crusades* (Ann Arbor 1992). B. SCHIMMELPFENNIG, *The Papacy* (New York 1992) 174–187. M. LAMBERT, *The Cathars* (Oxford 1999). E. CHRISTIANSEN, *The Northern Crusades* (New York 1997).

[J. M. POWELL]

GREGORY X, POPE, BL.

Pontificate: Sept. 1, 1271, to Jan. 10, 1276; b. Teobaldo or Tedaldo Visconti, Piacenza, Italy, 1210; d. Arezzo, Italy. The death of Clement IV was followed by one of the longest interregnums to occur in the history of the papacy. The conclave at Viterbo lasted nearly three years, largely because of the inability of French and Italian factions to agree upon a suitable candidate. As the debate continued, public indignation grew, and in the summer of 1270 the civic authorities of the town of Viterbo attempted to force the vote by locking the cardinals in the papal palace, removing the roof, and threatening to withdraw daily rations of food. These stern measures failed to secure a compromise, however, and the stalemate continued. After royal intervention the deadlock was eventually broken and the fifteen-member Sacred College of Cardinals agreed to designate six of their body to cast the final vote. On Sept. 1, 1271 Tedaldo Visconti was elected to the See of Peter.

By most accounts, Tedaldo Visconti was a remarkable man, who had a peaceful and conciliatory spirit. The English historian David Knowles even went so far as to describe him as the most spiritual pope after Celestine V. Yet when he was elected, Tedaldo was neither an ordained priest nor a cardinal. Nevertheless, he had served the church for several years outside of Italy, and by the time of his election he had earned an excellent reputation as an archdeacon of Liège. As a young man, Tedaldo had worked for years with Cardinal James of Praeneste, and he had helped to organize the first council of Lyons in 1245. Between the years 1245 and 1248, Tedaldo attended the University of Paris, where he may have met both St. Thomas Aquinas and St. Bonaventure. In 1265, Tedaldo traveled with Cardinal Ottobono on his mission to England, while there he served as the confidant of both the French and English royal families. Five years later, Tedaldo left England and accompanied the future King Edward I on a crusade to the Holy Land. They were in Saint-Jean d'Acre when they heard the news of the papal election. Responding to the summons of the Cardinals to return home immediately, Tedaldo left Acre on Nov. 19, 1271 and reached Viterbo on Feb. 12, 1272. Upon his arrival, Tedaldo Visconti accepted the papal office and took the name Gregory X. One month later, the pope-elect traveled to Rome, where he was ordained to the priesthood on March 19. His consecration took place in St. Peter's on March 27, 1272.

When Gregory ascended to the papal office, he was immediately confronted with a set of potentially dangerous political situations remaining from the reign of his predecessor. For example, the execution of Conradin in 1268 ended the Hohenstaufen line and held the possibility for the end of imperial authority in Germany with the resulting instability. Charles of Anjou, the brother of Louis IX of France and the Count of Provence, who had defeated Conradin at the Battle of Tagliacozzo, became king of both Sicily and southern Italy. He was now a powerful neighbor of the pope with the potential to recover Constantinople for the West. Yet this possibility had to be balanced against the cause of Church unity, which the Byzantine emperor, Michael Paleologos, dangled before the pope in the hope of keeping King Charles at bay.

On May 1, 1274, approximately four days after his coronation, Gregory called a general council at Lyons (Council of Lyons II) to deal with what he perceived as a serious situation. Gregory himself sought wide support for his council, whose significance is perhaps best reflected by the postponement of Edward I's coronation in order to ensure the attendance of a large delegation from England. In fact, Thomas Aquinas died on route to the council. Gregory remained a crusader at heart and the deliverance of the Holy Land was a central concern. At his request, the Council called for a new crusade, and Gregory laid the plans to fund it by adopting a resolution by which one tenth of all benefices accruing to all churches would be set aside for a period of six years. To create the necessary conditions for a crusade, the new pope needed to secure greater unity within Europe. In Lombardy and Tuscany this meant making peace between the Guelphs, a pro-papal party, and the Ghibellines, a pro-imperial party. Gregory also worked toward stability by encouraging the election of a new German king. Although there were a number of rival claimants to the crown, Gregory was instrumental in securing the election of Rudolf of Habsburg on Oct. 1, 1273. This action undoubtedly annoyed Charles of Anjou, who favored Philip III of France, but by supporting the Habsburgs, Gregory managed to prevent Angevin domination in Italy.

Gregory was an enthusiastic advocate of Church unity, which he saw as desirable in its own right, but which would have strategic value for a crusade. So despite protestations from King Charles, the pope sent envoys to Constantinople as early as October 1272. Gregory openly expressed his desire for unity and invited Michael Paleologos to send a delegation to the Council of Lyons. The union that Gregory wanted was accomplished when the Emperor Michael renounced the schism, and the eastern ambassadors agreed to the Roman creed, including the double procession of the Holy Spirit. Yet the patriarch of Constantinople was not represented in the Greek delegation, and the results of the Council were not accepted in the East. Despite all of his preparations, Pope Gregory's crusade never took place.

Nevertheless, Gregory's pontificate was successful, since many of his other policies had consequences that were far reaching and positive. He is particularly remembered for his famous bull *Ubi Periculum,* that established the rules for the election of popes and was intentionally designed to prevent prolonged vacancies in the papacy, like the one that preceded his election. It was proclaimed at the Council of Lyons on July 7, 1274. In the interest of wider moral reformation, Gregory also attempted to curtail long vacancies of benefices; he attacked pluralism, and he placed restrictions on the religious orders, with the exception of the Dominicans and Franciscans.

In October 1275, Gregory traveled to Lausanne to meet Rudolf of Habsburg and to discuss plans for his coronation as emperor. Gregory then crossed the Alps and visited Milan, Florence, and Arezzo. In the latter city, he was stricken by fever and he died on Jan. 10, 1276. He was buried in the Duomo and is revered as a saint in Arezzo, Placenza, and Lausanne. In fact, he was declared blessed by the Church in 1713. He is remembered as a pope who de-emphasized the temporal authority of the papacy and concentrated on spiritual revival and the restoration of Christian unity.

Feast: Jan. 28 and Feb. 4.

Bibliography: *Registres de Grégoire X,* ed. J. GUIRAUD (Paris 1892–1906). *Vita* in L. A. MURATORI, *Rerum italicarum scriptores, 500–1500* (Milan 1723–51) 3.1:597–598; 3.2:424–426. G. PACHYMERES, *Michael Palaeologus, Patrologia Graeca* ed. J. P. MIGNE (Paris 1857–66) 143:822–854. C. J. VON HEFELE, *Histoire des conciles d'après les documents originaux,* tr. and continued by H. LECLERECQ (Paris 1907–38) 6:153–209. J. D. MANSI, *Sacrorum Conciliorum nova et amplissima collectio* (Graz 1960–) v. 24. H. K. MANN, *The Lives of the Popes in the Early Middle Ages from 590 to 1304* (London 1902–32) 15:361–454. S. KUTTNER, ''Conciliar Law in the Making,'' *Miscellanea Pio Paschini,* 2 v. (Rome 1948–49) 2:39–81. A. FLICHE and V. MARTIN, eds., *Histoire de l'église depuis les origines jusqu'à nos jours* (Paris 1935–) 10:487–503. *Dictionnaire de théologie catholique,* ed. A. VACANT et al., (Paris 1903—50) Tables générales 1925. D. J. GEANAKOPLOS, *Emperor Michael Palaeologus and the West, 1258–1282* (Cambridge, MA 1959) 258–304. L. GATTO, *Il pontificato di Gregorio X, 1271–1276* (Rome 1959). B. ROBERG, *Das Zweite Konzil von Lyon* (Paderborn 1990) 17–31. *The New Cambridge Medieval History,* ed. D. ABULAFIA (Cambridge 1999) 107–163. G. SCHWAIGER, *Lexikon für Theologie und Kirche,* ed. J. HOFER and K. RAHNER (Freiberg 1957–65) 4:1187–88.

[J. A. SHEPPARD]

Allegory in praise of Gregory XI, detail of the pope's tomb in Sta Maria Nova, Rome, carved by the Roman sculptor Pier Paolo Olivieri in 1584. (Alinari-Art Reference/Art Resource)

GREGORY XI, POPE

Pontificate: Dec. 30, 1370 to March 26, 1378; b. Pierre Roger de Beaufort, in the Limousin, 1329; d. Rome. This final representative of the AVIGNON PAPACY studied law at Perugia after having been made cardinal (May 1348) by his uncle, Pope CLEMENT VI. When elected pope in Avignon, Gregory was considered a pious, knowledgeable, and modest priest bothered by a weak constitution. He proved, however, a more resolute pope than he has often been credited with being. His reign was preoccupied with three problems, primarily with peace. Arbitration between the houses of Anjou and Aragon resulted in the recognition of the latter's right to the Kingdom of Trinacria, on condition of homage to the pope (1374). Negotiators were dispatched to the Anglo-French talks at Bruges. In Italy, where there was already violent fighting against the Visconti, Gregory alarmed Florence when he sent agents to reassert papal power in central Italy; Florence, backed by the Visconti, went to war, unleashing a general revolt in the STATES OF THE CHURCH (1375). The pope was compelled to wage a painful war to recover his lands; Florence ended it by negotiation in December 1377. The second concern of Gregory was for the reform of the religious orders, especially the DOMINI-

CANS and HOSPITALLERS. His third problem was heresy. The INQUISITION was reactivated, especially against the WALDENSES in the Alps. Certain of WYCLIF's theses were condemned.

Like Pope URBAN V before him, Gregory always cherished the idea of taking the papacy back to Rome, and in September 1376 he actually left Avignon, entering Rome on Jan. 17, 1377. His death there 14 months later marked the beginning of the dissension that gave rise to the WESTERN SCHISM.

Bibliography: *Lettres . . . se rapportant à la France*, ed. L. MIROT et al. (Paris 1935–57); *Indices*, ed. G. MOLLAT and E. R. LABANDE; *Lettres . . . intéressant les pays autres que ta France*, ed. G. MOLLAT (Paris 1962). É. BALUZE, *Vitae paparum Avenionensium*, ed. G. MOLLAT, 4 v. (Paris 1914–27). P. AMEILH, ''Itinerarium domini Gregorii papae XI'' in *Rerum italicarum scriptores, 500–1500* 3.2:690–712; Fr. tr. P. RONZY (Florence 1952). J. P. KIRSCH, *Die Rückkehr der Päpste Urban V. und Gregor XI. von Avignon nach Rom* (Paderborn 1898). G. MOLLAT, ''Grégoire IX et sa légende,'' *Revue d'histoire ecclésiastique* 49 (Louvain 1954) 873–877; *The Popes at Avignon*, tr. J. LOVE (New York 1963). F. CARDINI, ''L'idea di crociata in santa Caterina da Siena,'' *Studi sulla storia e sull'idea di crociata* (Rome 1993) 423–56. M. HARVEY, ''The Household of Cardinal Langham,'' *The Journal of Ecclesiastical Studies* 47 (1996) 18–44. U. NICOLINI, ''Perugia e l'origine dell' osservanza francescana,'' *Scritti di Storia* (Naples 1993) 447–58. A. I. PINI, *Città medioevali e demografia storica: Bologna, Romagna, Italia* (Bologna 1996). H. SCHMIDINGER, ''Die Rückkerhr Gregors XI. Nach Rom in den Berichten des Cristoforus von Piancenza,'' in *Ecclesia peregrinans. Josef Lenzenweger zum 70. Geburtstag* (Vienna 1986) 133–41. P. R. THIBAULT, *Pope Gregory XI: The Failure of Tradition* (Lanham, MD 1986). ST. WEISS, ''Kredite europäischer Fürsten für Gregor XI. Zur Finanzierung der Rückkehr des Papsttums von Avignon nach Rom,'' *Quellen und Forschungen aus Italienschen Archiven und Bibliotheken* (Tübingen 1997) 176–205. J. N. D. KELLY, *Oxford Dictionary of Popes* (New York 1986) 225.

[E. R. LABANDE]

GREGORY XII, POPE

Pontificate: Nov. 30, 1406 to July 4, 1415; b. Angelo Correr, at Venice, *c.* 1325; d. Recanati, Italy, Oct. 18, 1417. During his pontificate the Western Schism was finally ended. Little is known about his early life and career. In 1380 he became bishop of Castello and in 1390 was named Latin patriarch of Constantinople. Becoming associated with Pope INNOCENT VII, he was made apostolic secretary, then legate of Ancona, and, in 1405, cardinal. Each cardinal who met in Rome in 1406 to elect a successor to Innocent VII promised that if elected he would resign the papal see providing the schismatic antipope in AVIGNON would do likewise: the dual resignations would free both Avignon and Roman cardinals to elect a new pontiff and thereby end the paralyzing WESTERN SCHISM in the Church. Gregory XII was elected on Nov. 30, 1406, and accordingly on December 12 he informed the antipope at Avignon, BENEDICT XIII, of his election and asked for a meeting at which the resignations could be arranged. Benedict agreed to meet with Gregory, but difficulties arose over the location of the conference. Benedict was in fact unwilling to resign despite his announced intention of discussing the matter, and Gregory, although sincerely interested in doing so at the outset, gradually lost interest in the project. Angered at the failure of the two popes to resolve their differences and end the schism, cardinals from both parties met at a ''council'' at PISA in 1409 and proceeded to declare both popes deposed and to elect a third, who took the name ALEXANDER V. The Pisan pope died in the following year and was succeeded by antipope JOHN XXIII. On Dec. 12, 1413, at the insistence of Emperor SIGISMUND, John XXIII called a council to convene at CONSTANCE. When the council met (Nov. 5, 1414), John XXIII was deposed (May 29, 1415) and Gregory XII was recognized as the lawful pope. Gregory in turn reconvoked the council and then resigned the papal office (July 4, 1415), paving the way for the eventual election of a new pope, MARTIN V, by the assembled cardinals. The Avignon pontiff, Benedict XIII, still refused to recognize the proceedings at Constance, but the Council declared him guilty of heresy and deprived him of all rights to the papacy (July 1417), whereupon he fled to Spain and remained there until his death. Gregory XII was made cardinal bishop of Porto and legate of the March of Ancona for life.

Bibliography: *Acta Concilii Constanciensis*, ed. H. FINKE, 4 v. (Münster 1896–1928). L. PASTOR, *The History of the Popes from the Close of the Middle Ages* (London-St. Louis 1938–61) 1:166–202. M. DE BOÜARD, *Les Origines des guerres d'Italie: La France et l'Italie au temps du grand schisme d'Occident* (Paris 1936). F. X. SEPPELT, *Geschichte der Päpste von den Angfängen bis zur Mitte des 20. Jh.* (Munich 1957) 4:228–248. A. FLICHE and V. MARTIN, eds., *Histoire de l'église depuis les origines jusqu'à nos jours* (Paris 1935—) 14. L. R. LOOMIS, J. H. MUNDY and K. M. WOODY, *The Council of Constance* (New York 1961). R. AUBERT, *Dictionnaire d'histoire et de géographie écclesiastiques* 25 (Paris 1994), s.v. ''Hugolin de Camerino, OP.'' M. FANUCCI, *L'estimo di Pisa nell'anno del Concilio (1409)* (Pisa 1986). M. GAIL, *The Three Popes: An Account of the Great Schism—when Rival Popes in Rome, Avignon and Pisa Vied for the Rule of Christendom* (London 1972). D. GIRGENSOHN, *Theologische Realenzyklopedie* 26 (Berlin 1996), s.v. ''Pisa, Konzil von (1409).'' D. GIRGENSOHN, ''Über die Protokolle des Pisaner Konzils von 1409.'' *Annuarium Historiae Conciliorum* 18 (Paderborn 1986). M. KINTZINGER, *Lexikon für Theologie und Kirche* 6 (1997), s.v. ''Konrad v. Susato.'' A. W. LEWIN, '''Cum Status Ecclesie Noster sit': Florence and the Council of Pisa (1409),'' *Church History* 62 (Chicago 1993) 178–89. J. N. D. KELLY, *Oxford Dictionary of Popes* (New York 1986) 234.

[J. M. MULDOON]

GREGORY XIII, POPE

Pontificate: May 14, 1572, to April 10, 1585; b. Ugo Buoncompagni, Bologna, Jan. 1, 1502. The fourth son of Cristoforo, a merchant, and of Angela Marescalchi, he studied at Bologna under celebrated jurisconsults and became a doctor of canon and civil law at 28. From 1531 to 1539 he taught at Bologna as professor of law, including among his pupils Otto TRUCHSESS, Cristoforo MADRUZZO, Reginald POLE, Francesco Alciati, and Alessandro FARNESE. In 1539 Cardinal Pietro Paolo Parisio brought him to Rome. Paul III made him successively judge in the Capitol, abbreviator (secretary) of the Council of Trent, and vice-chancellor in the Campagna. Until that time he had not been ordained to the priesthood, and while at Bologna, he had a natural son, Giacomo. He was ordained when he was about 40 years of age. Under Paul IV Buoncompagni was made datary to Cardinal Carlo CARAFA, the pope's nephew, whom he accompanied twice on important legations, namely, to France in 1556 and to Brussels in 1557. In July 1558 he was made bishop of Viesti. Despite his association with the Carafa family, he escaped being involved in their downfall after the death of Paul IV. In 1561 Pius IV sent Buoncompagni, as an expert in Canon Law, to Trent with Cardinal Ludovico SIMONETTA, the legate.

When the Council of Trent ended in 1563, he returned to Rome. On March 12, 1565, Pius IV created him cardinal priest with the title of St. Sixtus. He was then sent to Spain to review the case of the Archbishop of Toledo, Bartolomé de CARRANZA, whom the Inquisition had imprisoned on suspicion of heresy. Felice Peretti (later Sixtus V) accompanied him as theologian on this mission. Pius IV died while Buoncompagni was in Spain. He did not reach Rome for the conclave that elected Pius V. The new pope gave Buoncompagni the Segnatura of Briefs (1566). In the conclave that followed the death of Pius V, Cardinal Antoine Perrenot de GRANVELLE dissuaded those who favored the election of Cardinal Alessandro Farnese and helped secure, with the favor of Philip II, the election of Buoncompagni on May 14, 1572. He took the name Gregory in honor of Pope Gregory the Great, on whose feast day he had been made cardinal.

Gregory XII, engraving by Panvinio.

Religious Restoration. Gregory was fervently concerned with religious restoration. Some of his efforts were inconclusive, as in France, where the outcome in favor of Catholicism would not be decided until after Gregory's death. But the massacre of ST. BARTHOLOMEW'S DAY occurred barely three months after Gregory's election. The letters of Antonio Maria Salviati, the legate in Paris, were read in consistory on Sept. 6, 1572. These alleged, on testimony of the French court, that the HUGUENOTS had plotted to kill Charles IX and the royal family and that they had therefore been sentenced to death. Cardinal Charles de Lorraine (1524–1574), a GUISE, then urged the Pope and Sacred College to join in a *Te Deum* the following week. The event was celebrated not merely as the defeat of a political treason, but as defeat of a conspiracy against the Church. Although Gregory continued to support the League in France, he sensed the ambition of the Guises. He stressed that members of the League should work primarily for religious and not for political ends.

He failed in moves against England and the Turks, and his efforts in Sweden and Russia were likewise fruitless. He acted against Elizabeth mainly because of her persecution of Catholics, but also because she was aiding the Huguenots surreptitiously and because of MARY STUART's situation. He was unsuccessful in his hopes for an Irish invasion, when the first attempt, organized by Thomas Stucley (Stukeley), became abortive in 1578 and the second ended in the killing of his confederate James (Fitzmaurice) Fitzgerald in a skirmish after landing in 1579. In Sweden John III (reign 1568–92) secretly ab-

Pope Gregory XIII, statue by the 16th-century sculptor Pier Paolo Olivieri, in S. Maria in Aracoeli, Rome. (Alinari-Art Reference/Art Resource, NY)

jured Lutheranism and began negotiating with the papacy, but his stipulations (including clerical marriage and suppression of the invocation of saints and of prayers for the dead) were unacceptable. John III then reverted to Lutheranism. The efforts of the pope to secure union of the Russian Church with Rome failed because Gregory and his envoys, mediating between Stephen BÁTHORY of Poland and Ivan IV, underestimated the religious inflexibility of the Russians. Gregory failed also in the attempt to sustain a crusade against the Turks. Despite the victory of Lepanto in 1571, Venice made peace with the Turks in 1573, the Spaniards were driven out of Tunis in 1574, and Spain negotiated a peace in 1581. Hope of organizing a combined Polish-Russian crusade, however, was never realized.

The religious restoration succeeded in Poland, the Low Countries, and parts of Germany. Poland was definitively won for Catholicism. The southern provinces of the Netherlands remained predominantly Catholic, and Michel Baius at Louvain abjured his errors. In Germany Duke Albert of Bavaria and Emperor Ferdinand II halted and reversed Protestant gains in Austria, Carinthia, and Styria. The Jesuits flourished in Ingolstadt, Regensburg, and at the University of Graz. Fulda, Mainz, and Cleves were held for Catholicism. Cologne was saved from the attempt of Gebhard Truchsess to convert that ecclesiastical principality into a holding for his family.

Gregory's nepotism was limited. His son Giacomo was made governor of Castel Sant'Angelo and gonfalonier of the Church. Two of his nephews were made cardinals. But the persons who most influenced his decisions were men imbued, like Cardinal Charles BORROMEO, with the ideals of Trent.

Reforms. Gregory supported the Jesuits both in Europe and in such lands as India, China, Japan, and Brazil. He also favored the Franciscans, the Trinitarians, and the Capuchins. In 1575 he sanctioned establishment of the Oratory under Philip NERI, and approved the reform of the Spanish Carmelites under Teresa of Avila. Wishing to defend the faith with an effectively trained clergy, he fostered such schools as the German, the Greek, and the English colleges. In 1572 he reconstructed the Roman College, later known as the Gregorian University. Many schools outside Rome also owed their foundation to him. He enriched the Vatican Library by donating his own private library to it and opening it to scholars. Calendar correction, undertaken by a commission of scientists, provided a unique memorial to Gregory. The reformed calendar, which dropped ten days and interjected a lead year, was solemnly published in February 1582. Gregory continued and completed Pius IV's commission for a new edition of the *Corpus Iuris Canonici,* and produced a new edition of the Martyrology. He established the feast of the Most Holy Rosary (1573) and that of St. Anne (1584). In 1575 a jubilee brought over 300,000 pilgrims to Rome.

His stand against Henry of Navarre, against Elizabeth of England, and against the Turks cost great sums. So, too, did his support of schools and missions. He constructed, among many works in Rome, the Quirinal palace, the Gregorian chapel in St. Peter's, and the fountains in the Piazza Navona. His expenditures exhausted the papal treasury and led him to seek additional revenues from papal monopolies and customs. But he also charged escheatments and arrearages against extensive feudal holdings so that many fiefs were reclaimed by the papacy. Widespread banditry then arose on the part of dispossessed nobles, but the pontifical government was lax in countering disorder, and lawlessness came to prevail through the Papal States, even in Rome itself. Commerce declined. Despite the economic and administrative failures at the end of the reign, Gregory's was a great pontificate, especially in the actualizing of the aims of the Council of Trent.

Bibliography: M. A. CIAPPI, *Compendio delle attioni et vita di Gregorio XIII* (Rome 1591). P. HERRE, *Papsttum und Papstwahl im Zeitalter Philipps II* (Leipzig 1907). L. KARTTUNEN, *Gregoire XIII comme politicien et souverain* (Helsinki 1911). G. LEVI DELLA VIDA, *Documenti intorno alle relazioni delle chiese orientali con la S. Sede durante il pontificato di Gregorio XIII* (Studi e Testi 143; Rome 1948). P. MONCELLE, *Dictionnaire de théologie catholique,* ed. A. VACANT et al., 15 v. (Paris 1903–50; Tables générales 1951–) 6.2:1809–15. L. PASTOR, *The History of the Popes from the Close of the Middle Ages* (London–St. Louis 1938–61) v.19–20. G. SCHWAIGER, *Lexikon für Theologie und Kirche,* ed. J. HOFER and K. RAHNER, 10 v. (2d, new ed. Freiburg 1957–65) 2 4:1188–90. G. JACQUEMET, *Catholicisme* 5:245–248. C.A. FERNANDEZ, *Gregory XIII y Felipe II* (Toledo 1991). J. DULUMEAU *Catholicism between Luther and Voltaire* (London 1977). P. CARAMAN, *University of Nations: The Study of the Gregorian University* (New York 1981). J.W. O'MALLEY *The First Jesuits* (Cambridge, Mass. 1993).

[D. R. CAMPBELL]

GREGORY XIV, POPE

Pontificate: Dec. 5, 1590, to Oct. 16, 1591; b. Niccolò Sfondrati, Somma (near Milan), Feb. 11, 1535, of an ancient noble family from Cremona, which transferred to Milan. His father, Francesco, after the death of his wife, Anna Visconti, entered religion and in 1550 was named cardinal by Pope Paul III. Niccolò studied law at Perugia and Padua, received his doctorate at Pavia, and then entered clerical life. He was a follower of (St.) Charles Borromeo, who had an important influence upon him. At the age of 25 he was named bishop of Cremona by Pius IV (March 12, 1560). As bishop he participated in the third period of the Council of Trent (1561–63) and sought to execute its decrees in his diocese. He was named cardinal of St. Cecilia by Pope Gregory XIII on Dec. 12, 1583; as a cardinal he was a close friend of (St.) Philip Neri, whom he tried to imitate. On Dec. 5, 1590, after a conclave lasting for more than two months and marked by intrigue, Niccolò was elected to succeed Urban VII, largely because he was favored by the Spanish party. Though honest and pious, Gregory was not suited by disposition or by experience for the heavy burden of the pontificate; moreover, he was often in bad health. Most unwisely he chose his nephew Paolo Emilio SFONDRATI as his secretary of state, creating him a cardinal at the age of 29 on Dec. 19, 1590. Both the pope and his secretary were ignorant of political affairs.

Gregory tried to free Rome from the triple scourge of epidemic, scarcity of food, and brigandage. During the pestilence of 1590 he received the aid of (St.) Camillus de Lellis, whose congregation he erected into a religious order the next year. He gave his support to the French League, which was guided by the Guise family and Spain, and took measures against Henry of Navarre, renewing on March 1, 1591, the sentence of excommunication of Sixtus V and ordering the French to renounce him (*see* HENRY IV, KING OF FRANCE). In this action he was influenced by his nephew Paolo Emilio, who was pro-Spanish and quite dependent on the Spanish ambassador in Rome. The pope granted a monthly subsidy of 15,000 gold scudi to the city of Paris and dispatched his nephew Ercole Sfondrati to France at the head of the papal troops, followed by Marsilio Landriano as special nuncio to unite the Catholics against the Protestant Henry. The French, however, rejected the papal edicts; Landriano was not permitted to present the papal brief either to Cardinal Philippe de Lenoncourt or to Cardinal Charles Bourbon. At this time the pope was taken ill and removed to the Quirinal. Although still sick in August 1591, he moved to the Palace of S. Marco to discuss with Duke Alfonso II of Ferrara the succession to the throne of Ferrara, since the duke had no children. This question and its connection with the bull of Pius V on the alienation of the fiefs of the Church disturbed the pope until his death.

The pontificate of Gregory XIV, though brief, was important in furthering the internal reform of the Church. Gregory enforced more strictly the rules of episcopal residence and visitations of religious houses, and required an examination of the worthiness of those aspiring to episcopal office. He forbade the celebration of Mass in private homes and the making of wagers on papal elections. He assigned commissions to revise the Pian Breviary and the Sistine Vulgate. The latter had been edited by his predecessor, Sixtus V, but withdrawn from circulation because of errors. On May 24, 1591, he published a constitution regulating the right of sanctuary, suspending all previous enactments. He also gave orders for the completion of the work at St. Peter's and for the erection of a chapel at St. Mary Major for his own tomb. His friend Giovanni Pierluigi da PALESTRINA dedicated several of his musical works to the pope's memory. However, his nepotism disturbed the cardinals while the masses in the Papal State resented the prevailing lawlessness.

Bibliography: M. FACINI, *Il Pontificato de Gregorio XIV* (Rome 1911). L. CASTANO, *Nicolò Sfondrati, vescovo di Cremona al concilio di Trento 1561–1563,* (Turin 1939). L. PASTOR, *The History of the Popes from the Close of the Middle Ages,* (London–St. Louis 1938–61) 22:351–408 and *passim.* G. SCHWAIGER, *Lexikon für Theologie und Kirche,* ed. J. HOFER and K. RAHNER, 10 v. (2d, new ed. Freiburg 1957–65) 4:1190. P. PARTNER, ''Papal Financial Policy in the Renaissance and Counter-Reformation'' *Past and Present* (August 1980) 17–62. M. CARAVELE and A. CARACCIOLO, *Lo stato pontificio de Martino V a Pio IX* (Turin 1978).

[R. L. FOLEY]

GREGORY XV, POPE

Pontificate: Feb. 9, 1621, to July 8, 1623; b. Alessandro Ludovisi, Bologna, Jan. 9, 1554. Alessandro came from a noble family that had been in Bologna since the twelfth century. In 1567 he went to Rome to study under the Jesuits. On account of his health he returned home in 1569, but later that year he was again in Rome. In 1571 he began studying law at the University of Bologna and received his degree in 1575. Then he decided to become a priest.

Early Career. Gregory XIII gave him his first appointment, that of chairman in the College of Judges. Sixtus V selected him to accompany the legate to Poland, but illness prevented his going. When Clement VIII was a cardinal, he became Ludovisi's patron. Pope Clement VIII appointed him to the Segnatura di giustizia, where he solved the difficult cases. He advised the pope and settled disputes: one between the French and Spanish ambassadors; another between the Farnese family and the pope; another, with the assistance of Cardinal Maffeo Barberini, later Urban VIII, between the pope and Naples over Benevento. Paul V appointed him vicegerent for the cardinal vicar; in this office he arbitrated disputes among Romans. He also helped in settling the disagreement between the pope and the Venetian government. He was appointed archbishop of Bologna in 1612, but did not remain there long, since the pope needed him as a negotiator between Charles Emmanuel I of Savoy and Philip III of Spain about Monferrato. His assistance pleased both rulers and the pope. On his return to Bologna he began reforms, especially for the training and supervision of his clergy. Paul V made him a cardinal in 1616.

Pontificate. When elected pope, Gregory appointed his brother Orazio general of the Church and created his

25-year-old nephew Ludovico Ludovisi cardinal secretary of state. The favors bestowed on the cardinal made him very wealthy.

In spite of the shortness of this pontificate, there were two important and far-reaching reforms of this first Jesuit-trained pope. The first changed the method of electing a pope, thereby abolishing abuses. The practice of electing by adoration or acclamation had several weaknesses, especially the influence some cardinals or rulers wielded over timid cardinals. Sometimes there had been bargaining before the death of a pope. Immediately after the election of Gregory XV, which had some abuses, several cardinals proposed a reform. The first bull, published November 26, contained the following major changes: an election could take place only after the closing of the conclave and a candidate must receive at least two-thirds of the votes by secret ballot; no candidate could vote for himself; each cardinal must take an oath that would prevent the casting of votes as compliments. The second bull, March 12, 1622, amplified the first by regulating every part of an election. These provisions were followed in all succeeding elections until the time of Pius X.

The second important reform established the Congregatio de Propaganda Fide (*see* PROPAGATION OF THE FAITH, CONGREGATION FOR THE) for missionary work on January 6, 1622. Three preceding popes, Pius V, Gregory XIII, and Clement VIII, had seen the need for improvement and had started plans, but nothing was done by Paul V. The new Congregation consisted of 16 persons: two bishops, 13 cardinals, and a secretary. Juan Vives, one of the bishops, gave his palace in Piazza di Spagna as a center. The cardinals appointed were outstanding. One was Cardinal Maffeo Barberini, who as Gregory's successor continued the reform. On January 14, only eight days after its foundation, the Congregation met. From its meetings twice a month and once a month with the Pope, there followed the bull of June 22 and later additional provisions by Gregory XV. The Congregation brought unity. It gathered information, decided the regions to which missionaries would go, settled disputes, supervised colleges in Rome, and restricted the claims of Spain and Portugal to patronage (*see* PATRONATO REAL). The work of the Congregation was not limited to the non-Christian parts of the world, as it sought to revive faith and to extend it in the European countries. These were divided into groups, and each group was placed under a nuncio. In 1922 he canonized several heroes of the Catholic revival including Ignatius Loyola, Francis Xavier, Teresa of Avila and Phillip Neri.

Two other achievements were in keeping with Gregory XV's religious goals. Since the restoration of Elector Frederick in the Palatinate in the first phase of the THIRTY YEARS' WAR would have extended the Protestant faith, the pope greatly increased his subsidies to the Catholics. Catholicism was restored in Bohemia, and Maximilian of Bavaria became the Palatine elector. In gratitude he gave the Palatine library to the pope. In the quarrel between France and Spain over the territory of the Valtellina, there was the possibility of war, and of Catholics losing their religious rights. The pope succeeded in preventing war by having the Valtellina placed temporarily under the Holy See. He also sought to improve the status of Catholics in the British Isles by granting a dispensation for the marriage between Prince Charles of England and a Spanish princess. The marriage never took place.

Bibliography: L. PASTOR, *The History of the Popes from the Close of the Middle Ages,* (London–St. Louis 1938–61) v. 27, *passim.* L. VON RANKE, *The History of the Popes During the Last Four Centuries*, tr. MRS. FOSTER, ed. G. R. DENNIS, 3 v. (London 1913) 2:209–259, 3:220–243. D. ALBRECHT, *Lexikon für Theologie und Kirche,* ed. J. HOFER and K. RAHNER, 10 v. (2d, new ed. Freiburg 1957–65) 4:1190. P. MONCELLE, *Dictionnaire de théologie catholique,* ed. A. VACANT et al., 15 v. (Paris 1903–50; Tables générales 1951–) 6.2:1815–22. F. HAMMOND, *Music and Spectacle in Baroque Rome* (New Haven 1994). G. LABROT, *L'Image de Rome: Une arme pour la Contre-Reforme, 1534–1677* (Seyssel 1987). J.W. O'MALLEY, ed. *Catholicism in Early Modern History* (St. Louis, Mo. 1988).

[M. L. SHAY]

GREGORY XVI, POPE

Pontificate: Feb. 2, 1831, to June 1, 1846; b. Bartolomeo Alberto (Mauro) Cappellari, at Belluno (in Venetia), Italy, Sept. 18, 1765.

Prepapal Career. He was the son of Giovanni Cappellari, a lawyer, and Giulia (Cesa-Pagani) Cappellari, both of noble birth. In 1783 he joined the monastic order of CAMALDOLESE and entered the monastery of San Michele di Murano near Venice, taking Mauro as his religious name. After ordination (1787), he became in 1790 professor of science and philosophy. Sent to Rome in 1795 to assist the order's procurator general, he was chosen abbot of the monastery of San Gregorio on the Caelian Hill in 1805. In 1807 he became procurator-general of the Camaldolese. His opposition to the French during the Napoleonic occupation led to his expulsion from the Eternal City (1807). He went then to his monastery in Murano and later dwelt in Padua. In 1814 he returned to Rome, remaining there the rest of his life. In addition to his duties as abbot and as professor of theology, he served as consultor to the Congregation of Extraordinary Ecclesiastical Affairs, the Holy Office, and other Roman congregations, and as examiner of prospective bishops. Leo XII named him apostolic visitor to four local universities.

Pope Gregory XVI. (Engraving by Henriquel-Dupont, after a drawing by Paul Delaroche.)

Cappellari became vicar-general of the Camaldolese in 1823. After declining the sees of Zante and Tivoli, he was proclaimed a cardinal (March 13, 1826). He acted as consultor to the Congregation for the PROPAGATION OF THE FAITH from 1821 and as prefect from 1826 until his election as pope (Feb. 2, 1831). Between this last date and his enthronement (February 6) he received episcopal consecration.

Previous to 1831 Cappellari was noted for his interest in theology and in the missions. As a theologian he revived the teachings of Augustine and Aquinas in Catholic institutions. In 1799 he published *Il Trionfo della Santa Sede e della Chiesa contro gli assalti dei novatori combattuti e respinti colle stese loro armi* (The Triumph of the Holy See against the Assaults of the Innovators).

At the Congregation for Extraordinary Ecclesiastical Affairs Cappellari sought to establish contact with the new political order created by the FRENCH REVOLUTION. At Propaganda he strove to promote the interests of the Church in the diverse, far-flung countries under the jurisdiction of this congregation, which then had under its charge the Church in Great Britain, Ireland, the Low Countries, Prussia, Scandinavian lands, Africa, Asia, Oceania, and the entire Western Hemisphere.

Profiting by the religious liberty recently inscribed in the Fundamental Law of the Netherlands, he collaborated efficaciously in the conclusion of a concordat with this government (1827). In 1829 he regulated the manner of making episcopal nominations in Ireland. He helped draft the brief of Pius VIII (March 25, 1830) to the German bishops concerning the growing dispute over mixed marriages in Prussia.

These activities revealed Cappellari's apostolic realism. He displayed the same qualities in his dealings with mission territories, where he created numerous vicariates apostolic. In every way open to him he facilitated the administration of the Sacraments, especially Baptism. His decree (July 2, 1827) distinguishing between the religious and purely civil significance of certain rites permitted Catholics in Siam to participate in them by classifying them as merely civil.

The conclave in 1831 remained in session nearly 50 days before selecting Cardinal Cappellari as pope. Two groups among the cardinals, the conservative *zelanti* and the more liberal *politicanti,* opposed one another differing in their appreciation of the relevance to the papacy of the politicoreligious consequences of the French Revolution and the intellectual unrest caused by the ENLIGHTENMENT. Cappellari, who was regarded in the 1829 conclave as papabile, received 33 of the 41 votes and the support of Metternich. Only after receiving an order from his confessor and fellow Camaldolese, Cardinal Zurla, did he accept the papal dignity.

Papal Doctrinal Pronouncements. By temperament he was cold, but his relations with ROSMINI-SERBATI prove his capacity for friendship. All during his pontificate, however, he retained his austere monastic mode of life. ''I am always a monk,'' he declared. At the time he ascended the papal throne, faith was menaced by RATIONALISM and INDIFFERENTISM, and traditional civil authority by LIBERALISM. Gregory XVI attacked their underlying principles. In his solution of the practical problems stemming from these trends he sought accommodations.

One of his dominant views was clearly inscribed in *Il trionfo. . . .* Although written in a heavy style, replete with digressions, it was reprinted several times in Italian between 1831 and 1846, and appeared in a German translation (1833, 1838). The book was directed against the partisans of JANSENISM and those who upheld the power of the state to control religious matters. It repudiated the liberties that these protagonists claimed for the state in opposition to the rights of the Holy See, because Christ established the Church as a monarchy. Although the author insisted that this ecclesiastical monarchy enjoyed full liberty to exercise its power, he did not envision it as a despotism but neither did he regard it as an aristocracy or as a democracy. The pope is unable to alter this form of government, continued the argument, because the Church's constitution is divine in origin and, therefore, unchangeable, unlike civil governments, which are subject to essential modifications.

This fundamental thesis of *Il trionfo* was not, strictly speaking, a doctrine of CHURCH AND STATE; it concerned, rather, the Church's internal life. From this thesis the author concluded that the Church is independent of the civil power and, secondly, that the pope enjoys INFALLIBILITY when he speaks as head of the Church, but does not when he speaks merely as a theologian.

''Mirari vos.'' Some of the essential ideas of *Il trionfo* appeared in *Mirari vos* (Aug. 15, 1832). Two sets of circumstances moved the pope to publish this famous encyclical, forerunner of the SYLLABUS OF ERRORS (1864). The first was the increasing influence of Hugues Félicité de LAMENNAIS, the champion of Catholic liberalism. The other was the political situation in ITALY, particularly in the STATES OF THE CHURCH. Added to this was the continual conservative pressure on the Holy See applied by Metternich.

In his eagerness to effect a religious renovation, Lamennais sought first a reorganization of theological studies. In this program he had the support of Leo XII until 1826. After this date, Lamennais, in his opposition to GALLICANISM and to the *ancien régime* type of government restored in France after the fall of Napoleon I, came to demand liberty for the Church and, consequently, complete separation, at least temporarily, between Church and State. Undoubtedly Lamennais intended to enfranchise the Church from servitude to the civil power. At the same time, his passionate polemics, especially in his journal *L'Avenir,* defended theses that would lead to political democracy, if not to revolution. Around him Lamennais gathered MONTALEMBERT, LACORDAIRE, GERBET, de COUX, and other talented disciples who promoted Catholic liberalism. Outside of France the influence of Lamennais penetrated Belgium, the Rhineland, Italy, Poland, and Ireland. In philosophy Lamennais taught TRADITIONALISM. This combination of philosophical and political concepts in the writings of the French publicist manifested a naturalism that was perhaps unconscious but undoubtedly displeasing to some upholders of ULTRAMONTANISM and to many conservatives.

Gregory XVI became increasingly alarmed by the program of Lamennais because of the serious political unrest current in Italy, especially in his own temporal domain, where revolution broke out in 1831. Demands for civil and national emancipation kept increasing throughout the peninsula. The situation in Italy was a factor that necessarily weighed heavily on the pope's mind as he composed the encyclical.

Mirari vos affirmed rigorously the supernatural character of the Church's constitution and the primacy of its teaching power. But the encyclical, at least insofar as it concerned Italy, confused the Church's divine constitution with the clericalized monarchical institutions of the States of the Church. Gregory XVI seemed to hold that, by reason of the divine origin of papal authority, his own political authority in the Papal States was immutable. Therein could be discerned the ROMAN QUESTION, badly posed.

In *Mirari vos* the pope dealt with principles and abstractions, addressing himself to the entire Catholic world. Before his mind were those countries where the union of throne and altar promoted the Church's supernatural goals and also mission territories in which the union of Church and State could produce great temporal and spiritual advantages. For these reasons the encyclical disapproved separation of the two powers, castigated all revolutionary movements, and demanded support of monarchical regimes. By assuming these positions and by refusing to admit any change in the Church's government, the pope made a frontal attack on modern liberties while resisting political liberalism. He reproved these liberties insofar as they manifested an individualistic and subjective desire for human liberty and affirmed certain rights as belonging to men without taking into account God or the Church. *Mirari vos* contained also a confrontation between the rights demanded by the Church in virtue of its constitution and modern liberties that might conflict in various ways with the Church's rights.

Gregory XVI held that modern liberties were at once the expression and the origin of an indifferentism that admitted as simultaneously true doctrines of the most diverse, even contradictory, kinds. Repeatedly during his pontificate he denounced this intellectual attitude, as in the encyclical *Inter praecipuas machinationes* (May 8, 1844). Moreover, the pope detected in modern liberties the origin of a type of ecclesiastical liberalism that developed in Belgium (1830), Hungary (1841), and Switzerland (1846). In these countries liberalism based itself on natural rights or on rights of citizens, but its effect was to oppose a group of the clergy to the divinely established hierarchy. To him this was an extension of Gallicanism utilized to profit the lower clergy. This tendency received a more explicit papal reproval in the encyclical *Quo graviora* (Oct. 4, 1833).

Rationalism. Naturalism was manifested in rationalism as much as in political liberalism. Rationalism sought to reach satisfactory solutions in matters of FAITH by applying human reason alone, while stripping faith of its rational or its supernatural character. This happened in traditionalism as propounded by Lamenhais, in FIDEISM, ONTOLOGISM, and perhaps in the writings of Louis sa Bautain. HERMESIANISM, as proposed by Georg HERMES and his disciples, also manifested rationalistic tendencies. Gregory XVI revealed his opposition to these ideologies in the encyclicals *Singulari nos* (June 25, 1834) and *Dum acerbissimas* (Dec. 26, 1835).

The papal documents did not mention explicitly which doctrines were held by the different authors. Pope Gregory condemned the fundamental errors inherent in these ideologies, even if not explicitly stated.

Relations with States. In his relations with various governments, Gregory XVI was aided by two conservative secretaries of state, Tommaso BERNETTI and Luigi LAMBRUSCHINI. The papal policy was one of firm opposition to secularizing tendencies of civil authorities, yet it did make some concessions to them that were noticeable in the concordats concluded during these years. State encroachments on the Church were of diverse kinds and occurred as frequently in Protestant countries as in Portugal, Spain, Italy, Latin America, and other Catholic lands. CAESAROPAPISM in Protestant countries acted on the maxim, *cujus regio, eius religio.* Naturalistic liberalism in Catholic nations undoubtedly contributed to LAICISM, but modern, constitutional liberties, supported by Catholic liberals, assured advantages to the Church at the same time. In the United States and Canada, Protestant influence was largely responsible for the adoption of religious freedom.

Gregory XVI strove everywhere to obtain all possible guarantees to permit the Holy See to control episcopal nominations. Continually he insisted on the Holy See's right to appoint bishops. In practice, however, he did not abolish local customs at variance with this ideal. Thus he chose Irish bishops from ternas submitted by local clergies. In France, Spain, Portugal, and Austria nominations continued to be made by the government; in the U.S., bishops were selected from lists drawn up by the resident bishops.

Papal States and Italy. In the States of the Church the papal policy was guided by the desire to maintain papal control and to segregate the area from the influences of political liberalism. To curb insurrections the pope was willing to summon help from Austria but tried to avoid antagonizing France, England, and other European powers. He was eager also to retain clerical control of government administration while introducing a limited amount of administrative innovation. In return for Austrian military support the pope agreed to receive the Memorandum (May 22, 1831) submitted by England, France, Prussia, and Russia demanding changes in the legations, in Rome, and throughout the provinces of the Papal States. The Memorandum further required greater lay participation in administrative and in communal and provincial councils. Gregory XVI did not implement all the contents of the Memorandum, but he did introduce some of the administrative, financial, and judicial reforms that were demanded. Only to a limited extent were breaches made in the traditional clerical monopoly of governmental posts. The most important improvements were in the economic field and concerned insurance, banking, chambers of commerce, and taxation.

These changes did not satisfy the hopes of the supporters of the RISORGIMENTO throughout Italy. Divided as it was between the aims of the NEO-GUELFISM advanced by GIOBERTI and Capponi, and the republican aims of Mazzini and Young Italy, the peninsula remained in the preparatory stage of liberal and political emancipation and unification. Gregory XVI opposed this trend, but his police methods could not reverse it. When he died, the States of the Church were close to the revolution that drove PIUS IX into exile in 1848. The heavy encumbrance of public debt in 1846 and the worsening financial situation served to increase discontent.

Iberian Peninsula. Portugal was the scene of a conflict between the rival claims to the throne made by Don Pedro and Don Miguel (1827–33). Gregory XVI came to an agreement with the latter to ensure the nomination of worthy bishops. By 1833, however, Don Pedro prevailed. Don Miguel fled the country and came to Rome, where the pope received him with great honor for his loyalty to the Church. Diplomatic relations between the Holy See and Portugal were severed in 1833. Despite this, the pope gave his approval to the government's episcopal nominations. When an appeasement was gained (1840), the pope dispatched to Lisbon one of the best papal diplomats, Francesco CAPACCINI, who succeeded in reopening the nunciature (1844).

In Spain dispute broke out between Don Carlos and Maria Cristina after the death of Ferdinand VII (1833). Gregory XVI recalled the nuncio from Madrid (July 31, 1835) and protested (Feb. 1, 1836) against the violations of the Church's liberty and the seizures of ecclesiastical properties. He remained firm in his opposition when Espartero, who came to power in 1840, proceeded along the course of laicism. Not until 1845 were negotiations opened for a concordat, which was concluded only in the following pontificate.

France. France presented a different situation. In Spain and Portugal difficulties arose because the heads of state, inspired by naturalistic liberalism, were intent on monopolizing to themselves the rights of the Church.

In France, where Church-State relations were regulated by the CONCORDAT OF 1801, the government recognized the Church's rights, which were to some extent institutionalized. This situation led to a revival of Gallicanism among the bishops and in the government. Gregory XVI was eager to gain assurance that bishops be nominated from other than political considerations. Thanks to the efforts of the internuncio, Antonio Garibaldi (1797–1853), he was on the whole successful. The Holy See sought also to still the opposition to exempt religious orders manifested by the government and by Abp. QUELEN of Paris and other members of the hierarchy. The pope had been largely instrumental in restoring to France the Dominicans, Benedictines, and Jesuits, but he submitted to governmental pressure and, with apostolic aims in view, permitted the expulsion (1845) of the Jesuits, although they had been in charge of most Catholic schools for young men. The struggle against Gallicanism and the departure of the Jesuits alerted the former disciples of Lamennais. Bishop Parisis and other bishops, together with the Catholic liberal political forces under Montalembert, sought to obtain in the national legislature religious freedom, especially for Catholic schools. Gregory XVI, fearing lest the Catholics demand unlimited freedom of education, did not support them effectively. Soon after the pope's death there was enacted the Falloux Law, whose educational provisions were very favorable to Catholics.

Switzerland and Germany. When Switzerland enacted the Articles of Baden (Jan. 21, 1834), which practically eliminated papal authority over Swiss Catholics, Gregory XVI condemned the law. The papal brief *Commissum divinitus* (May 19, 1835) reiterated the theses on the Church's independence propounded in *Il Trionfo.*

Prussia was the object of considerable concern to Gregory XVI because of the legislation concerning mixed marriages enacted by this Protestant government, which had recently acquired the Catholic Rhineland and Westphalia. Since 1803 Prussia had insisted that children born of mixed marriages must follow the religion of the father. In his briefs of March 27, 1832, and Sept. 12, 1834, Gregory XVI recalled the statements on this matter by Pius VIII, in the drafting of which he had collaborated while prefect of Propaganda. The quarrel was embittered by King Frederick III's protection of the followers of Hermes. When Abp. DROSTE ZU VISCHERING of Cologne was arrested, the pope protested firmly in his consistorial allocution (Dec. 12, 1837). When Frederick William IV succeeded to the Prussian throne, the pope's eagerness for peace induced him to consent to the archbishop's retirement from the see of Cologne. By his previous resistance, however, and perhaps also by his later conciliatory attitude, Gregory XVI contributed to the gaining of spiritual independence by the Rhineland Catholics (*see* COLOGNE, MIXED MARRIAGE DISPUTE IN).

Russia and Poland. The Church suffered severely in Russian territories during this pontificate. Emperor NICHOLAS I was responsible for persecuting the Ukrainian Catholics in an attempt to unite them with the Russian Orthodox Church. He was ruthless also toward Latin Catholics. The pope's efforts to stem the Czar's intolerant absolutism met with some success. He complained vigorously to Nicholas I. When the Czar visited Rome (1845), the pope met him, reproached him to his face, and recalled the duties of conscience that the imperial power itself imposed on him. Negotiations, begun at this time, resulted in the signing of a concordat between the Holy See and Russia in 1847.

Discontent in Poland led to insurrection (1830–31) against Russia. Gregory XVI responded with the encyclical *Cum primum* (June 9, 1832), addressed to the Polish bishops and containing a condemnation of revolutionary movements. The pope took this attitude toward the suffering Polish Catholics mainly because he rejected solutions to problems by recourse to violence. He noted also the duty of subjects to obey legitimate authority, but he did not regard political regimes as immutable. Thus his bull *Sollicitudo ecclesiarum* (Aug. 5, 1831) recognized the *de facto* government of Don Miguel in Portugal. His outlook was similar in 1832 toward the king of Belgium. In countries with a liberal constitution the pope distinguished between abstract principles and concrete realities. In this respect his reaction to the liberal Belgian constitution of 1831 was very significant. He did not condemn the *modus vivendi* arranged between Belgian liberals and Catholics that prepared the way for the famous distinction between the thesis and the hypothesis.

Ireland. Soon after Ireland gained emancipation for Catholics in 1829, Daniel O'CONNELL began another peaceful agitation to repeal the legislative union with Great Britain. The repeal movement won active support from the Catholic priests and from members of the hierarchy, notably Abp. John MACHALE OF TUAM. The British government, which did not have diplomatic relations with the Holy See, was able to bring pressure on the Vatican to condemn the movement and enlisted the support of Metternich to plead its case. Rome refused to issue a public condemnation of the involvement of the clergy in the movement. After considerable urging Cardinal Filippo Fransoni, prefect of Propaganda, wrote a private admonitory letter (Oct. 15, 1844) to Abp. William Crolly of Armagh urging him to counsel the Irish clergy to avoid political and secular concerns.

Missions. The revival of the missions in the 19th century dates from the pontificate of Gregory XVI, who ranks as the greatest missionary pope of his century. During the 18th century, missionary activity plunged into a precipitous decline that could not be reversed in the early decades of the following century. Gregory XVI utilized the more favorable situation to rebuild the missions and to enlarge their sadly depleted personnel. In reorganizing the missions he brought them directly under papal control, where they have remained ever since. This put an end to the enormous power formerly exercised over the Church in mission territories by Spain and Portugal in virtue of their *PATRONATO REAL* and *padroado* privileges. Gregory XVI also worked out sound guiding principles and methods for missionaries. He was active in urging religious orders and congregations to staff the missions and chose the territories each one was to evangelize. The rapid expansion of the missions during these years is indicated by the fact that Gregory XVI created more than 70 dioceses and vicariates apostolic and named 195 missionary bishops. The apostolic letter *In supremo* (Dec. 3, 1839) condemned SLAVERY and the slave trade and forbade all Catholics to propound views contrary to this. The instruction of Propaganda promoting an indigenous clergy and hierarchy in mission lands received the pope's approval (Nov. 12, 1845). To assure financial support for the missions, which no longer could depend on Catholic governments for their material needs, Gregory XVI afforded papal protection to the work of the Society for the Propagation of the Faith and the Pontifical Association of the Holy Childhood, founded in 1843.

India. Indicative of Gregory XVI's firmness and originality in dealing with the missions was his handling of the difficulties that arose in India. When Portugal proved unequal to its obligations as protector of the missions, the pope created a number of vicariates apostolic subject directly to Propaganda rather than to the *padroado.* This move provoked lively Portuguese resentment, particularly after the issuance of the papal brief *Multa praeclare* (April 24, 1838), which suppressed four *padroado* dioceses, confided their territories to the newly created vicariates, and limited the jurisdiction of the Archdiocese of GOA to Portuguese areas. So resentful was the archbishop of Goa that he began what is sometimes called the ''schism'' of Goa.

Western Hemisphere. Latin America, where independence movements were freeing one colony after another from Spanish and Portuguese control, greatly preoccupied Gregory XVI. Illustrative of his policy was the apostolic constitution *Sollicitudo ecclesiarum* (Aug. 5, 1831), which asserted that political vicissitudes must not prevent the Holy See from ministering to the spiritual needs of countries with newly established regimes. While prefect of Propaganda, Gregory XVI had become involved in this problem. Refusing to bow to Spanish demands, he determined in 1826 to establish residential bishops in Latin America. In 1829 he did so in Mexico. At his first consistory (Feb. 28, 1831) he named six residential bishops and soon after (July 2, 1832) raised to this status the vicars apostolic appointed by his predecessors in Buenos Aires, Santiago de Chile, and elsewhere. In this way he demonstrated his determination to establish the hierarchy in these countries. Despite Spanish opposition he favored the national emancipation of the Latin American republics.

North America was the object of special papal solicitude. Although Propaganda retained jurisdiction over this region, it did not enforce it in the same manner as in strictly mission territories. Gregory XVI took into account the political stability of Canada and the United States, their vast extent, and the variety of apostolic needs because of the great influx of immigrants from many European countries. He created four Canadian dioceses between 1834 and 1843 and reorganized the see of Quebec in 1844. In the U.S. he erected ten dioceses and reorganized that of Baltimore (1834). It was perhaps in the U.S. that Gregory XVI manifested to best advantage his sense of adaptation and his religious and political realism, and thereby attained substantial success. In his conversation with Czar Nicholas I (1845) the pope referred to the U.S. thus: ''In this country Catholics are perfectly free to exercise their religion and they are not the less observant of civil laws and constitutions.''

Other Activities. Gregory XVI displayed interest in scholarship and the arts by encouraging and helping Angelo MAI, Giuseppe MEZZOFANTI, Gaetano MORONI, and others. Besides assisting artists such as Johann Overbeck and Bertel Thorvaldsen, the pope opened the Museum of Egyptian and Etruscan Antiquities in the Vatican and furthered the reconstruction of the Roman basilica of St. Paul.

Conclusion. In his opposition to naturalistic liberalism, Gregory XVI did not disassociate it sufficiently from political liberalism. This neglect placed him in the position of trying to block a development that was inevitable. Nonetheless he was impelled by a certain apostolic realism that allowed him to open the way to the future. Even in the political order he prepared for the distinction between the thesis and the hypothesis. He enlarged mission activity and advocated native clergies and hierarchies. His untiring defense of the rights of the Holy See in episcopal nominations promoted the Church's independence in liberal states. His pontificate saw Catholicism solidly established in the Americas. Another service of Gregory XVI was the upholding of the unalterable supremacy of the supernatural. His 15 years on the papal throne marked a milestone in the remarkable 19th-century progress in the effective exercise of the authority of the PAPACY throughout the world.

Bibliography: *Actu Gregorii papae XVI.*, ed. A.M. BERNASCONI, 4 v. (Rome 1901–04), defective. *Bullarii romani continuatio*, ed. A. BARÈRI, 20 v. (Rome 1835–57) v.16–20, to 1835. A. MERCATI, *Raccolta di Concordati . . .* (Rome 1954) 1:724–750. J. SCHMIDLIN, *Papstgeschichte der neuesten Zeit, 1800–1939* (Munich 1933–39) v.1. J. LEFLON, *La Crise révolutionnaire, 1789–1846* (A. FLICHE and V. MARTIN, eds., *Histoire de l'église depuis les origines jusqu'à nos jours* 20; Paris 1949); *Catholicisme* 5:249–251. *Gregorio XVI miscellanea commemorativa*, 2 v. (Rome 1948). K. S. LATOURETTE, *Christianity in a Revolutionary Age: A History of Christianity in the Nineteenth and Twentieth Centuries*, 5 v. (New York 1958–62). E.E.Y. HALES, *Revolution and Papacy*, 1769–1846 (Garden City, N.Y. 1960). R. BELVEDERI, in *I Papi nella storia*, ed. P. PASCHINI and V. MONACHINO, 2 v. (Rome 1961) 2:903–930. É. AMANN, *Dictionnaire de théologie catholique*, ed. A. VACANT et al., 15 v. (Paris 1903–50; Tables générales 1951–) 6.2:1822–36. N. P. WISEMAN, *Recollections of the Last Four Popes and of Rome in Their Times* (London 1858). F. HAYWARD, *Le Dernier siècle de la Rome pontificale*, 1769–1870, 2 v. (Paris 1927–28). H. BASTGEN, *Forschungen und Quellen zur Kirchenpolitik Gregors XVI*, 2 v. in 1 (Paderborn 1929). G. MOLLAT, *La Question romaine de Pie VI à Pie IX* (2d ed. Paris 1932). A. VENTRONE, *L'amministrazione dello Stato Pontificio*, 1814–1870 (Rome 1942). L. PÁSZTOR, ''I cardinali Albani e Bernetti e l'intervento austriaco nel 1831,'' *Rivista de storia della Chiesa in Italia* 8 (Rome 1954) 95–128. E. MORELLI, *La politica estera di Tommaso Bernetti, secretario di stato di Gregorio XVI* (Rome 1953). N. NADA, *L'Austria e la questione romana dalla rivoluzione di luglio alla fine della conferenza diplomatica romana (Agosto 1830-luglio 1831)* (Turin 1953); ''La polemica Fra Palmerston e Metternich sulla questione romana nel 1832,'' *Bollettino storico-bibliografico subalpino* 52 (1954) 89–153; *Metternich e le riforme nello Stato Pontificio: La missione Sebregandi a Roma, 1832–36* (Turin 1957). W. MATURI, ''La convenzione del 29 agosto 1839 tra la S. Sede e il Regno delle Due Sicilie,'' *Archivio storico per le provincie napoletane*, NS 34 (1955) 319–369. R. E. CAMERON, ''Papal Finances and the Temporal Power, 1815–1871,'' *Church History* 26 (Philadelphia 1957) 132–142. A. QUACQUARELLI, *La ricostituzione delle Stato Pontificio* (Bari 1945). D. DEMARCO, *Il tramonto dello Stato Pontificio: Il papato di Gregorio XVI* (Turin 1949). J. P. MARTIN, *La nonciature de Paris . . . (1830–1848)* (Paris 1949). A. SIMON, *Le Cardinal Sterckx et son temps*, 2 v. (Wetteren 1950); *Catholicisme et politique* (Wetteren 1955); ed., *Correspondance du nonce Fornari, 1838–1843* (Brussels 1956); ed., *Documents relatifs à la nonciature de Bruxelles* (Brussels 1958); ed., *Lettres du nonce Pecci, 1843–1846* (Brussels 1959). A. BOUDOU, *Le Saint-Siège et la Russie, 1814–1883,* 2 v. (Paris 1922–25). J. F. BRODERICK, *The Holy See and the Irish Movement for Repeal of the Union with England, 1829–1847* (Analecta Gregoriana 55; Rome 1951). S. DELACROIX, ed., *Histoire universelle des missions catholiques* (Paris 1956–59) v.3. J. SCHMIDLIN, ''Gregor XVI. als Missiospapst,'' *Zeitschrift für Missionswissenschaft und Religionswissenschaft* 21 (1931) 209–228. P. DE LETURIA, ''Gregorio XVI y la emancipación de la América española,'' *Miscellanea historiae pontificiae* 14 (1948) 295–352; ''La primera nunciatura en América y su influencia en las Repúblicas hispanoaméricanos,'' *Razón y Fe* 86 (1929) 28–48; both articles are repr. in his *Relaciones entre la Santa Sede e Hispanoamérica*, 3 v. (Analecta Gregoriana 101–103; Rome 1959–60). G. SCHWAIGER, *Lexikon für Theologie und Kirche*, ed. J. HOFER and K. RAHNER, 10 v. (2d, new ed. Freiburg 1957–65)[2] 4:1190–92. A. REINERMAN, *Austria and the Papacy in the Age of Metternich: Revolution and Reaction, 1830–1838* (Washington, D.C. 1989); ''Metternich, Pope Gregory XVI, and Revolutionary Poland, 1831–1842,'' *The Catholic Historical Review*, v. LXXXVI, n.4 (2000) 603–619. A. M. BERNASCONI, ed. *Acta Gregorii Papae XVI*, 4 v. (Rome 1984). L. GUILLOU, *Le condemnation de Lamennais* (Paris 1982). E. E. Y. HALES, *Revolution and Papacy, 1769–1846* (Notre Dame 1966).

[A. SIMON]

GREGORY IX, DECRETALS OF

The first authentic general collection of papal decretals and constitutions, promulgated by Pope Gregory IX in 1234. When Gregory became pope in 1227 the chief collection of the legal tradition of the church was still the *Decretum* of GRATIAN, then almost 90 years old. Although in the interval the activities of the DECRETISTS, and later of the DECRETALISTS, had resulted in many other collections of papal legislation, notably in the *QUINQUE COMPILATIONES ANTIQUAE*, there was a lack of coherence between these collections that made for confusion. In 1230 Gregory IX, a lawyer of quality himself, called on the Spanish Dominican, RAYMOND OF PEÑAFORT, a former professor of law at Bologna, to remedy the situation. From the bull, *Rex pacificus*, promulgating Raymond's compilation some four years later, it appears that his mandate from Gregory was to ''collect into one volume,'' for ''the use of schools and tribunals,'' the numerous constitutions and decretals of Gregory's predecessors that were scattered through the various collections, as well as Gregory's own constitutions and any decretals ''circulating outside the usual collections'' (''quae vagabantur extra'').

The result of Raymond's labor was a systematic volume based upon the *Quinque compilationes antiquae*. These, indeed, provided him with the division into five books (*iudex, iudicium, clerus, connubia, crimen*), with 179 of 185 titles and with 1,767 of the total 1,971 chapters; of the remaining 204 chapters, 195 are from constitutions of Gregory IX, seven from Innocent III, and two from an unidentified source. Far from verifying the texts taken from the *Compilationes*, Raymond perpetuated their errors, false ascriptions, and mutilations. What is more, in imitation of the compilers' methods, decretals were dissected and then dispersed through various chapters: thus fragments of Innocent III's *Pastorali officio* (A. Potthast, *Regesta pontificum romanorum inde ab a. 1198 ad a. 1304*, 2 v. 2530) occur in 13 chapters (*Corpus iuris canonici*, ed. E. Friedberg (Leipzig 1879–81) X.1.3.14; 1.6.1; 1.29.28; 1.31.11; 2.1.14; 2.22.8; 2.25.4; 2.28.53; 3.10.9; 3.24.7; 3.30.28; 3.38.29; 5.33.19). Obeying Gregory's order to ''eliminate superfluous matter,'' Raymond shortened some passages and modified others; on ambiguous points Gregory provided him with some pithy *ad hoc* decretal letters by way of clarification (*see* REX PACIFICUS and *Corpus iuris canonici,* X.1.13.2; 4.20.8; 5.19.19; "Gregorius IX. Fratri R."; 5.32.4). As a result, the compilation was in reality a fresh edition of decretal law; universal in character, it was also exclusive of all other decretals and collections, to the exception of the *Decretum.* Neither Gregory nor Raymond gave it a title, but it became known as *Liber extravagantium* (*see* EXTRAVAGANTES). It occasioned a host of commentaries, etc., and is the heart of the official CORPUS IURIS CANONICI of 1582 [a modern printing of which is that of A. Friedberg (Leipzig 1881)]. The usual method of citation is by book, title, and chapter, thus: X. (for *Extravagantium*) 1.13.11.

Bibliography: *Corpus iuris canonici,* ed. E. FRIEDBERG (Leipzig 1879–81) 2:IX–XLIV. J. F. VON SCHULTE, *Die Geschichte der Quellen und der Literatur des kanonischen Rechts,* 3 v. in 4 pts. (Stuttgart 1875–80; repr. Graz 1956) 1:243. A. M. STICKLER, *Historia iuris canonici latini: v. 1, Historia jontium* (Turin 1950) 237–251. P. TORQUEBIAU, *Dictionnaire de droit canonique,* ed. R. NAZ, 7 v. (Paris 1935–65) 4:627–632. A. M. STICKLER, *Lexikon für Theologie und Kirche,* ed. J. HOFER and K. RAHNER, 10 v. (2d, new ed. Freiburg 1957–65) 3:66.

[L. E. BOYLE]

GREGORY OF BERGAMO

Theologian and bishop; b. Bergamo, Italy, late 11th century; d. June 9, 1146. A VALLOMBROSAN monk, he was created bishop of Bergamo in 1133. With his friend BERNARD OF CLAIRVAUX he attended the Council of PISA in 1134, and was active in ecclesiastical reform, introducing the CISTERCIAN ORDER into his diocese. He also played an important part in the Eucharistic controversies of the period. In opposition to the teachings of BERENGARIUS OF TOURS, he wrote, between 1130 and 1140, his *Tractatus de veritate corporis et sanguinis Christi,* upholding the Real Presence of Christ in the Sacrament, which he regarded as symbolizing also the Mystical Body of Christ, the Church. Gregory is reported to have suffered a martyr's death.

Bibliography: *Tractatus de veritate corporis et sanguinis Christi,* ed. H. HURTER in *Sanctorum Patrum opuscula selecta,* 48 v. (Innsbruck 1874–85) 39:1–123. J. DE GHELLINCK, *Dictionnaire de théologie catholique,* ed. A. VACANT et al., 15 v. (Paris 1903–50; Tables Générales 1951–) 5.2:1236–37. F. HOLBÖCK, *Der eucharistische und der mystische Leib Christi* (Rome 1941) 33–35.

[M. M. MCLAUGHLIN]

GREGORY OF CERCHIARA, ST.

Abbot; b. Cassano al l'Ionio, Calabria, Italy, *c.* 930; d. Abbey of Burtscheid, Germany, 1002. He became monk and abbot of the BASILIAN monastery of San Andrea at Cerchiara. The Saracen invasion drove him to Rome, where, with the generous endowment of the Empress Theophano (d. 991), he founded the monastery of San Salvatore *c.* 990. At her request Gregory went to Germany and founded at Burtscheid the Greek monastery dedicated to SS. Apollinaris and Nicholas. This place became the center for the diffusion of Byzantine culture in German lands. There Gregory died as abbot and was buried. His life and early cult, fact tangled with fancy, are known only through Latin sources. Nothing certain remains to document his cult, which seems confined to Burtscheid and to his fellow Basilians. His relics are preserved at Burtscheid and at FULDA.

Feast: Nov. 4

Bibliography: *Acta Sanctorum* Nov. 2:463–477. S. HILPISCH, *Lexikon für Theologie und Kirche,* ed. J. HOFER and K. RAHNER, 10 v. (2d, new ed. Freiburg 1957–65) 4:1192. F. RUSSO, "Sulla *vita Gregorii abbatis,*" *Bollettino di badia greca di Grottaferrata* 2 (1948) 193–205. A. M. ZIMMERMANN, *Kalendarium Benedictinum: Die Heiligen und Seligen des Benediktinerorderns und seiner Zweige,* 4 v. (Metten 1933–38) 3:258–260.

[N. M. RIEHLE]

GREGORY OF EINSIEDELN, BL.

Abbot; d. Einsiedeln, Germany, 996. Of an English royal family, Gregory left his virgin wife, with her consent, and became a monk in the Mount Coelius monastery, Rome. In 949 he entered the BENEDICTINE monastery of EINSIEDELN, a foundation not yet 25 years old. Familiar with the English reforms of DUNSTAN OF CANTERBURY, he gave Einsiedeln the norms of its cloistral life along the line of the English *Regularis concordia* when he became the third abbot in 964. The German Emperor OTTO I, related to him by marriage, accorded the abbey great material benefits and confirmed all its privileges. OTTO II and OTTO III also treated Gregory well. His community's reputation caused Gebhard II of Constance to ask him to supply religious for the monastery of PETERSHAUSEN. After his death his tomb near the altar of St. Maurice was the site of miracles. His relics were enshrined in 1609 at Einsiedeln.

Feast: Nov. 8.

Bibliography: P. SCHMITZ, *Histoire de l'ordre de Saint-Benoît,* 7 v. (Maredsous, Belgium 1942–56) 1:180. O. RINGHOLZ, *Geschichte des fürstilichen Benediktinerstiftes U. L. F. von Einsiedeln,* 1 v., no more publ. (Einsiedeln 1904) 43–53. A. M. ZIMMERMANN, *Kalendarium Benedictinum: Die Heiligen und Seligen des Benediktinerorderns und seiner Zweige,* 4 v. (Metten 1933–38) 3:281–283. R. TSCHUDI, *Lexikon für Theologie und Kirche,* ed. J. HOFER and K. RAHNER, 10 v. (2d, new ed. Freiburg 1957–65) 4:1192.

[B. CAVANAUGH]

GREGORY OF ELVIRA, ST.

First known bishop of Elvira (*c.* 357–392); b. Baetica (modern Andalusia), Spain, *c.* 320. An opponent of ARIANISM at the Council of Rimini, Gregory defended the Nicene Creed in action and in writing. Bp. St. EUSEBIUS OF VERCELLI wrote him a letter (*Corpus scriptorum ecclesiasticorum latinorum* 65:46) commending his resistance to Hosius of Córdoba when the latter capitulated at Sirmium in 357, and JEROME praised his *De fide* (*Patrologia Latina,* ed. J. P. MIGNE (Paris 1878–90) 23:703). Gregory is said to have adhered to the schism of LUCIFER OF CAGLIARI in the *Libellus precum* (*Patrologia Latina* 13:89), written by the Luciferians Faustinus and Marcellinus *c.* 383, which hints that Gregory rejected the synod at Alexandria (362), and upon the death of Lucifer, became head of the party.

St. Jerome (*Patrologia Latina* 17:505–506) associates him with Lucifer but concludes only that ''he had nothing to do with the Arian evil.'' No trace of Luciferianism appears in his writings. The literary investigations of A. WILMART restored authorship to Gregory of many Latin homilies and scriptural commentaries, indicating his importance as witness for the early Latin translations of the Bible and the development of Western Christology and ecclesiology. His homilies are marked by a strong anti-Jewish bias, traces of millenarianism, a gradually developing theology of the Holy Spirit, and an insistence on faith and holiness in Christians.

Feast: April 24.

Bibliography: J. COLLANTES LOZANO, *San Gregorio de Elvira* (Granada 1954); *Lexikon für Theologie und Kirche,* ed. J. HOFER and K. RAHNER, 10 v. (2d, new ed. Freiburg 1957–65) 4:1192–93. H. KOCH, ''Zu Gregors von Elvira Schriften und Quellen,'' *Zeitschrift für Kirchengeschicte* 51 (1932) 238–272. F. REGINA, *Il De Fide di Gregorio d'Elvira* (Naples 1942). B. ALTANER, *Patrology,* tr. H. GRAEF from the 5th German ed. (New York 1960) 434–435.

[F. J. BUCKLEY]

GREGORY OF NAZIANZUS, ST.

Bishop of Constantinople (381), Father and Doctor of the Church, called ''the Theologian'' in the Eastern Church; b. Arianzus, near Nazianzus in Cappadocia, *c.* 330; d. Arianzus, *c.* 390.

Career. Gregory was born of well-to-do parents on the family estate in southwest Cappadocia. His father, Gregory Nazianzen the Elder, had been a member of the sect of the Hypsistarians, whose beliefs were an amalgam of Jewish and pagan Gnostic elements, but had been converted to Catholic Christianity under the influence of his wife, Norma, a Christian born of Christian parents. At the time of Gregory's birth, Gregory the Elder was bishop of the nearby city of Nazianzus. An earlier date of birth (*c.* 325) alleged by BARONIUS and others (*Acta Sanctorum*) was based on the erroneous view that celibacy was universal for the episcopacy at this time. A brother, Caesarius, and a sister, Gorgonia, were born later.

Gregory received his early education at Caesarea, the capital and metropolitan city of the Province of Cappadocia, where BASIL OF CAESAREA was a fellow pupil. He continued his studies at Caesarea in Palestine, made famous as a Christian center by both ORIGEN and EUSEBIUS OF CAESAREA, and continued his literary studies in Alexandria before journeying to Athens.

The voyage was a decisive spiritual event in his life. When he was involved in a near shipwreck, the imminent presence of death, especially in the absence of Baptism (he was still a catechumen), had a profound effect on his already devout nature, and he vowed to dedicate the rest of his life to God (*Carm.* 2.1.1:307–338; 2.1.11:124–210). At Athens Gregory pursued his rhetorical studies under the pagan rhetors Himerius and Prohaeresius. There he met Basil again and cemented the intimate friendship that was to have so deep an effect on his life, to both his advantage and his disadvantage. Among his contemporaries were also JULIAN, the later apostate and emperor, and GREGORY OF NYSSA. The idea of a monastic vocation was already taking shape in Gregory's mind when (*c.* 357 or 358) he departed after approximately eight years of study to return to Nazianzus by way of Constantinople.

Baptism and Priesthood. In Cappadocia he received Baptism, which he had probably delayed in order to receive it from his father's hands. For a time he put aside his inclinations to monastic solitude and yielded to the importunities of family and friends to practice rhetoric in his native city, but presently he withdrew to join Basil in his monastic venture on the river Iris in Pontus. There he assisted his friend in the composition of his monastic rules, and it was probably at that time that he and Basil edited the *Philokalia*, an anthology of the sayings of Origen. He was also influential in enlisting Gregory of Nyssa in the venture.

Yielding to his father's entreaties, especially that of failing health, he returned to Nazianzus and received ordination during the Christmas season of 362, but almost at once he regretted the step and withdrew; he was not persuaded to return until Easter, at which time he preached the apologetical oration *On His Flight* (*Orat.* 2). The next ten years were spent in assisting his father in both ecclesiastical affairs and family business matters. Both father and son played an influential role in the eccle-

''St. Gregory of Nazianzus,'' 15th-century baroque oil sketch on panel by Peter Paul Rubens. (©Burstein Collection/CORBIS)

siastical politics of the province, including the election of Basil of Caesarea to the metropolitan see in 370 (*Epistolae* 41). Earlier he had been successful in persuading his brother, Caesarius, to resign his position in Constantinople under Julian and to return home (*Epistolae* 7). Following the Emperor's death, Gregory preached two invectives against him (*Orat.* 4 and 5). The sudden death of Caesarius (*c.* 369) after his return to the imperial service under Jovian affected Gregory deeply and also involved the family in serious financial difficulties (*Carm.* 2.1.11:365–380).

An administrative action by Emperor Valens in 372 was to have disastrous results for Gregory; it divided the Province of Cappadocia into two. Anthimus, the bishop of the new capital city of Tyana, claimed metropolitan rights over the newly created Province of Cappadocia Secunda, and a dispute over territorial jurisdiction arose between him and Basil. The latter, seeking to strengthen his position, erected a new suffragan see at Sasima, a mere posting station of the imperial road system, and prevailed upon Gregory, much against his will and better judgment, to accept consecration as its bishop. Gregory did so, but never took possession of the see; and Anthimus made it quite clear that he was ready to have recourse to violence if necessary to prevent any such attempt. The result of the affair was a rift in the friendship of Gregory and Basil, and the old intimacy was never restored.

Gregory remained at Nazianzus, assisting his father in discharging his episcopal functions; and after his father's death in 374, he continued to do so for a time while declining to accept the see himself and petitioning for a successor to be appointed. When it became evident that none was forthcoming, since Nazianzus lay under the jurisdiction of Tyana, Gregory attempted to bring matters to a head by withdrawing to the shrine of St. Thecla at Seleucia in Isauria. [For an interesting account of the archeological excavations of this shrine and monastic community see R. Devreesse, *Le Patriarcat d' Antioche* (Paris 1945) 144–145.]

Constantinople. Gregory remained in Isauria from 375 until shortly after the death of Emperor Valens in the Battle of Adrianople (Aug. 9, 378). Sometime between that time and January 379, Gregory answered a summons to discharge the episcopal functions for the tiny Nicene minority in the capital city of Constantinople, which had long been without a bishop. The immediate occasion of the summons was, in all probability, the edict of Gratian (autumn 378) confirming earlier steps toward toleration, taken shortly before his death by Valens under the pressure of the Gothic menace, that assured free assembly to all Christian factions. Gregory himself alluded vaguely to the summons as coming from many of the faithful and their shepherds, i.e., the bishops (*Carm.* 2.1.11:595–598). It is not improbable that these bishops represented the adherents of Meletius of Antioch and that they included Basil, who, anticipating a Nicene victory with the change in regime, desired to see someone sympathetic to their cause ultimately installed at Constantinople. Whatever the motive in the minds of the bishops, there was only one in the mind of Gregory, the restoration of the Nicene faith in the city of Constantine, where he arrived sometime before the death of Basil (Jan. 1, 379).

The nearly three years spent at Constantinople were to be the most eventful, and personally the most heartrending, of his life. Upon his arrival Gregory rallied the tiny group of adherents to the Nicene Creed in a small House, located outside the city's walls, that had been converted into a church, the Anastasia, or church of the Resurrection. From the Arian majority under their bishop Demophilus, the Nicenes encountered bitter opposition that reached violence. Further trouble arose from an unforeseen quarter. Maximus, a self-proclaimed Cynic philosopher, actually a crude adventurer acting in connivance with Peter, Bishop of Alexandria, first ingratiated himself as a disciple of Gregory, then had himself stealthily consecrated (380) with the aid of bishops secretly dispatched from Egypt by Peter. Peter apparently preferred to see someone indebted to himself in the capital rather than someone favorable to the See of Antioch, Alexandria's age-old rival. Not only the Nicenes, but also the Arians and pagans, united to expel Maximus, whose pretensions were likewise rejected by Emperor Theodosius I and Pope Damasus. Theodosius himself returned to the city in November 380 and restored the cathedral church of the Holy Apostles and the other churches to Gregory, who refused formal installation.

Shortly thereafter the emperor summoned the bishops of the East to a general council that convened at Constantinople in May 381, although the Macedonian and Egyptian bishops failed to appear. It was presided over by Meletius of Antioch, and its first act was the formal election and installation of Gregory as bishop of the see. This was followed shortly by the unexpected death of Meletius, whose funeral sermon was delivered by Gregory of Nyssa. The death of Meletius proved most untimely, for it plunged the council, now under the presidency of Gregory, into bitter controversy over the succession at Antioch. Gregory ardently urged the recognition of the rival claimant Paulinus, in the hope that it would bring an end to the MELETIAN SCHISM that had so long strained relations between East and West. He failed to prevail, however, and Flavian was elected, thus prolonging the controversy. At this crucial juncture occurred the long-delayed arrival of the Egyptian and Macedonian bishops. They promptly challenged the validity of Gregory's own installation as a violation of the 15th canon of Nicaea, which forbade translation of bishops. Rather than press his claims and see the Church rent asunder by still further schism, Gregory chose voluntarily to resign the see, an act of self-sacrifice that more than any other attests the greatness of his moral stature and spirit.

The Macedonian bishops acted under instructions from Pope Damasus (Dam., *Epistolae* 5), who was following the established, if misguided, Roman policy in the East to support Alexandria and suspect the Meletians. Nectarius of Constantinople succeeded to the see, and Gregory retired to Nazianzus, where he acted as bishop until he finally found a successor in Eulalius (383). His last years were spent upon his estate at Arianzus in literary composition and spiritual direction of the local monastic community. Upon his death he bequeathed his property to the bishopric.

Writings. Orations are the literary productions upon which Gregory's principal claim to fame is founded. Forty-four in number (*Orat.* 35 is spurious), they were published soon after his death and represent only a fragment of the number actually composed and delivered. Best known are the five *Theological Orations* (*Orat.* 27–31) preached at Constantinople. They represent not only a classic exposition of the Nicene Creed, but also a further precision of Trinitarian doctrine. In his development of the personal properties (ἰδιότητες) as distinctive characters of the three Divine Persons (unoriginate for the Father, begottenness for the Son, procession for the Holy Spirit), Gregory also insisted, against the Macedonian heresy, on the divinity of the Holy Spirit. Oration 27 serves as an introduction to the entire group; 28 investigates the existence and nature of the Divine; 29 deals with the oneness of the Trinity; 30 establishes, against the Arians, the true doctrine concerning the Son; and 31, that of the Holy Spirit. The oration on his flight (*Orat.* 2) appears to have been rewritten during his lifetime and constitutes a treatise on the priesthood that influenced both JOHN CHRYSOSTOM in his *Six Books on the Priesthood* and, in Latin translation, GREGORY I's *Pastoral Rule.* Gregory's panegyrical orations are artistically more perfect and give freer scope to his rhetorical style, which has been approvingly characterized by E. Norden as a "restrained Asianism" (*Die antike Kunstprosa,* 564). A good example of this class is the *Oration on the Holy Lights* for Epiphany (*Orat.* 39). Rightly esteemed also are the funeral orations, which are at the same time valuable sources for biographical material (*Orat.* 7 on Caesarius, 8 on Gorgonia, 18 on his father, and 43 on Basil). In these he followed classic models for the *Epitaphios Logos,* but with Christian adaptations. Poignantly moving is his *Final Farewell* in 381 (*Orat.* 42). In all the orations, whether acting as dogmatic theologian, exegete, moralist, spiritual director, or pastor, he remains always the rhetorician.

Letters and Poetry. Gregory's letters were published for the most part during his own lifetime at the request of Nicobulus, grandson of his sister, Gorgonia, and many were written during his retirement with that intent in mind. Of the 244 published by J. P. Migne (*Patrologia Graeca* [1857–66] 37) three are spurious (42 is by Gregory the Elder; 241, by Basil; 243, by Gregory Thaumaturgus). Published separately is one to Basil with his reply. Epistles 51 and 54 set forth his theory of epistolary style: brevity, clarity, charm, and simplicity. Epistles 101 and 102 are refutations of APOLLINARIANISM; 101 was adopted as a doctrinal statement by the Council of CHALCEDON (451) in testimony to the fact that Gregory's CHRISTOLOGY, with its emphasis on the union of the two natures in one Christ, anticipated the later teaching on the HYPOSTATIC UNION.

The poetry (*Patrologia Graeca* 37–38) comprises more than 16,000 lines. It is topically divided in the Migne edition into two books: 1, theological, and 2, historical; and each book is divided into two sections, with further subdivisions in the sections. The books and sections are usually cited accordingly. Thus the *Carmen de vita sua is Carm.* 2.1.11. Among the spurious poems, besides *Christus Patiens,* are 1.1.28; 1.2.18, 20, 23, 32, and 39; 2.2.8; and *Epitaph* 129 (1.1.37). Dubious are 1.1.31 to 35; 1.2.3, and 19; and 2.1.99. Rhythmical poems are 1.1.32 and 1.2.3.

So vast a production, most of it composed between 381 and 390, would automatically give rise to doubts about its artistic merit. The verdict of B. Wyss is a just one. Gregory's productions are not great poetry, but humanistic versifying; yet in particular passages, especially those touched with originality, we encounter, if not great artistry, certainly genuine talent. Most important and most interesting of the entire corpus is the *Carmen de vita sua* (*Carm.* 2.1.11). Here his originality appears in his deft combination of literary forms. Treating his departure from the See of Constantinople as tantamount to his demise (lines 11 and 1919), Gregory adopts the form of a consolatory address (558–589), directed here to his orphaned (spiritual) children of Constantinople, as the basic framework of the poem. He incorporates into it an apology for that demission, maintaining that the canons were not violated and that his resignation was voluntary. He also inserted two lengthy digressions, one didactic (1146–1257), cast in the Christian literary form of *The Two Ways,* and the other an invective against Maximus (736–938). The presence of the consolation is detected in the triple temporal division: introduction (1–50), dealing with the present; main body (51–1918), treating of the past; and conclusion (1919–49), concerned with the future. In the topical development of the main body Gregory discusses his ancestry (51–68); birth (69–81); nature (82–92); training (93–111); education (112–211); conduct (212–262); and deeds (263–1918). The apology concludes with the formal consolation (1919–22) and a final prayer (1947–49); it is characterized by outbursts of grief and protest scattered throughout. The apology itself receives a separate proem (40–50) and conclusion (1923–33). It serves as the norm for selection and emphasis in the topic on his deeds and sets the tone for certain passages with its own rhetorical features (e.g., anticipation of objections, appeal to judges). The two topics are harmoniously united since it is the apology that constitutes the principal element of the consolation (558–561); it is not confined to the brief formal statement (1919–22). The result is an apologetical autobiography constituting an important advance in the development of the autobiographical genre. The poem reveals with striking impact the personality of the author: sensitive, producing the elegiac tone of his finest lines, and passionate, as seen in the four great enthusiasms that successively dominated his life—literature, monasticism, restoration of the faith, harmony in the Church.

Influence. Gregory's theological productions proved a profound force in the East. His works are found in Syriac, Coptic, Ethiopian, Armenian, Slavonic, and Arabic versions. He was considered not only "the Theologian" but also "the Christian Demosthenes"; and in due time scholia began to be composed on his writings. Among the important ones are those of Elias of Crete (tenth century). For the Byzantines, Gregory was a model of style. In the West he enjoyed high prestige because of the laudatory notice accorded him in *De viris illustribus* by his former pupil St. JEROME; but his influence was limited to the translation of nine of the orations by Rufinus (*Corpus scriptorum ecclesiasticorum latinorum* [Vienna 1866–]

46). Rediscovered in the Renaissance, a large selection of Gregory's poetry appeared in volume three of the *Poetae Christiani Veteres* of Aldus Manutius (Venice 1504). The first attempt at a complete edition was that made by Protestant scholars at Basel in 1550; this was superseded by the *Opera Omnia* of J. Billius, with important commentaries (Paris 1609–11), which was in turn superseded by the Benedictine edition (Paris 1778–1840) that is reprinted in Migne. The breadth of Gregory's appeal is seen best in the diversity of his admirers; they included Erasmus, Melanchthon, Gibbon, and J. H. Newman. His relics repose in St. Peter's Basilica, Rome, in the Capella Gregoriana, beneath the altar of Madonna dell Soccorso (Our Lady of Help).

Feast: May 9 in the West; Jan. 25 in the East; commemorated again with St. John Chrysostom and St. Basil the Great on Jan. 30, the ''Feast of Greek Letters.''

Bibliography: Editions: CPG 3010–3125. *Patrologia Graeca* ed. J. P. MIGNE (Paris 1857–66) 35–38. SC (1969–) vols. 149, 208, 247, 250, 270, 284, 309, 318, 358 with French translation and extensive bibliographies. CCSG (Corpus Nazianzenum 1– ; 1988–) vols. 20, 27, 28, 34, 36, 37, 38, 41, 42, 43, 44, 45 Arabic, Armenian, Georgian and Syriac versions and studies. Fontes Christiani (1996) vols. 22 and 75 with German translation. Cambridge Medieval Classics (1996) vol. 6 with English translation. *Poemata Arcana* (Oxford 1997) with English translation. English translations: NPNF 2nd series (1894), vol. 7. LCC (1954) vol. 3. SVC (1991), vol. 13. Literature: R. R. RUETHER, *Gregory of Nazianzus: Rhetor and Philosopher* (Oxford 1969). F. TRISOGLIO, *San Gregorio de Nazianzo in un quarantennio di studi, 1925–1965* (Turin 1974); *Gregorio di Nazianzo: Il teologo* (Milan 1996). D. F. WINSLOW, *The Dynamics of Salvation: A Study in Gregory of Nazianzus*, PMS 7 (Cambridge 1979). G. A. KENNEDY, *Greek Rhetoric under Christian Emperors* (Princeton 1983); *A New History of Classical Rhetoric* (Princeton 1994); *Classical Rhetoric and Its Christian and Secular Tradition from Ancient to Modern Times* (Chapel Hill 1999). F. W. NORRIS, *Faith Gives Fullness to Reason: The Five Theological Orations of Gregory Nazianzen*, SVC 13 (Leiden 1991). Holy Cross Conference on Gregory the Theologian, *Greek Orthodox Theological Review 39* (1994). A. MEREDITH, *The Cappadocians* (Crestwood 1995). K. DEMOEN, *Pagan and Biblical Exempla in Gregory Nazianzen: A Study in Rhetoric and Hermeneutics*, CCLP 2 (Turnhout 1996); J. P. EGAN, ''αἴτοζ/author, αἰτια/cause, ἀρχή/origin: Synonyms in Selected Texts of Gregory Nazianzen,'' *Studia Patristica* 32 (Louvain 1997) 102–107; B. E. DALEY, ''Building a New City: The Cappadocian Fathers and the Rhetoric of Philanthropy,'' *Journal of Early Christian Studies* 7 (1999) 431–461. *Acta sanctorum* May 2:366–457. S. LE NAIN DE TILLEMONT, *Mémoires pour servir à l'histoire ecclésiastique des six premiers siècles* (Paris 1693–1712) v.9, indispensable. J. QUASTEN, *Patrology* (Westminster, Maryland 1950–) 3:236–254, bibliog. and eds. P. GALLAY, *La Vie de Saint Grégoire de Nazianze* (Lyon 1943); *Langue et style de S. Grégoire de Nazianze dans sa correspondance* (Paris 1933). F. LEFHERZ, *Studien zu Gregor von Nazianz* (Bonn 1958), very valuable. *Select Orations and Select Letters of Saint Gregory of Nazianzen*, tr. C. G. BROWNE and J. R. SWALLOW (*A Select Library of the Nicene and Post-Nicene Fathers*, ed. P. SCHAFF and H. WACE [New York 1890–1900] 2d ser. 7; 1894). J. H. NEWMAN, *Historical Sketches* 3 v. (London 1872–73), v.2. M. GUIGNET, *Les Procédés épistolaires de Saint Grégoire de Nazianze* (Paris 1911); *Saint Grégoire de Nazianze et la Rhétorique* (Paris 1911). M. M. HAUSER-MEURY, *Prosopographie zu den Schriften Gregors von Nazianz* (Bonn 1960). B. WYSS, *Museum Helveticum* 6 (1949) 177–210. E. NORDEN, *Die antike Kunstprosa*, 2 v. (3d ed. Leipzig 1915–18). J. PLAGNIEUX, *Saint Grégoire de Nazianze théologien* (Paris 1952). J. MOSSAY, *Questions liturgiques et paroissiales* (Louvain 1921–) 4 (1964) 320–329. S. GIET, *Sasimes, une méprise de Saint Basile* (Paris 1941). G. MISCH, *A History of Autobiography in Antiquity*, tr. E. W. DICKES, 2 v. (London 1950) 2:600–624. L. F. M. DE JONGE, *De S. Gregorii Nazianzeni carminibus* (Amsterdam 1910). J. T. CUMMINGS, ''Towards a Critical Edition of the *Carmen de vita sua*,'' *Studia Patristica* (*Texte und Untersuchungen zur Geschichte der altchristlichen Literatur* 1965). H. WERHAHN, ''Dubia und Spuria unter den Gedichten G. von N.,'' *ibid.*; ed., *Synkrisis Bion* (Wiesbaden 1953), in Gr. F. BOULENGER, ed. and tr., *Discours funèbres* (Paris 1908). A. J. MASON, ed., *The Five Theological Orations* (Cambridge, Eng. 1899). R. KEYDELL, ''Die literarhistorische Stellung der Gedichte G. von N.,'' *Atti del VIII Congresso internazionale di Studi Bizantini* (Rome 1953). H. LECLERCQ, *Dictionnaire d'archéologie chrétienne et de liturgie*,. ed. F. CABROL, H. LECLERCQ, and H. I. MARROU (Paris 1907–53) 6.2: 1667–1711. K. WEITZMANN, *Greek Mythology in Byzantine Art* (Princeton 1951). P. GALLAY, ed. and tr., *Les Lettres*, v.1 (Paris 1964).

[J. T. CUMMINGS/K. B. STEINHAUSER]

GREGORY OF NYSSA, ST.

One of the three Cappadocian Fathers; b. Caesarea, between 335 and 340; d. Constantinople, *c.* 394. His grandmother, Macrina the Elder, was converted to Christianity through the teaching of GREGORY THAUMATURGOS, and his famous Christian family had suffered during the DIOCLETIAN PERSECUTION. Youngest of the three Cappadocian Fathers (sometimes called the Cappadocian Theologians so as to include the eldest sibling MACRINA), he was known as the philosopher and mystic while his brother, Basil of Caesarea, was considered the administrator and GREGORY OF NAZIANZUS the theologian. His sister, MACRINA, who had a formative influence on the education of her brothers, was the teacher and ascetic. Two of his ten brothers were bishops, namely, Basil and Peter of Sebaste.

Destined at first for a career in the church, Gregory was ordained a lector, but apparently he abandoned this vocation to follow that of his father, a rhetorician. He married and, after the death of his wife, was persuaded by Gregory of Nazianzus to enter the monastery founded by Basil in Pontus near the Iris River. At Basil's insistence, he was consecrated bishop of Nyssa, a suffragan of Caesarea in Cappadocia, in 372. Lacking Basil's administrative talents, he was accused of negligence in financial matters and deposed by an Arian dominated synod in 376. However, after the death of the Arian emperor Valens in 378, the pro-Nicene Theodosius I ascended to power and Gregory was able to return to Nyssa. When Basil died in 379, Gregory labored to continue his

Miniature detail of St. Gregory of Nyssa, from "Menologian of Basil II" (Vat. Gr. 1613).

brother's work, essentially becoming his heir. He took part in the Council of Antioch in 379 and was named metropolitan of Caesarea in 380. He played a major role at the Council of Constantinople I in 381, at which he was acknowledged as a pillar of orthodoxy and continuator of the thought of Basil. At the same time he replied to the radical Arian theologian Eunomius. In his last years he was involved in a bitter controversy over Apollinarianism. He died shortly after attending a council in Constantinople in 394.

WORKS

Ascetical Writings. There are problems concerning authenticity in the list of works attributed to Gregory, but they do not involve his major writings, and the authentic list is long and impressive. His letters appear to be incomplete. Written after 370, but perhaps as late at 379, *De Virginitate* was his first published work. In addition, there is the life of his sister, *De vita Macrinae*, and three short treatises, *De perfectione, De instituto Christiano*, and *De castigatione*. His ascetical writings manifest Platonic, Stoic, and Pythagorean influences. The *De anima et resurrectione*, a Christian parallel to Plato's *Phaedo*, is a dialogue with his dying sister, Macrina, that presents Gregory's Christian views of immortality and the future life.

Dogmatic Writings. A number of Gregory's writings were concerned with the refutation of heresies and the clarification of the corresponding orthodox positions. His Trinitarian writings were produced between 380 and 384. Most important among these is *Contra Eunomium*, a lengthy refutation of the writings of the Arian Bishop Eunomius, who asserted that the persons of the Trinity were radically dissimilar from one another. Against the Arians is a short tract, *Ad Simplicium de fide sancta*, addressed to a tribune, Simplicius. There are two pieces directed against the Macedonians, who denied the divinity of the Holy Spirit, *Sermo de Spiritu Sancto adversus Pneumatomachos Macedonianos* and *Ad Eustathium de sancta Trinitate*.

Another major work, *Oratio catechetica magna*, is a summary of catholic teaching, presented in contrast to the teaching of the Jews and the pagans. It stands in the line of systematic works between Origen's *De principiis* and the *De fide orthodoxa* of John Damascene. After 385 Gregory wrote a vigorous refutation of the Christological heresy of Apollinaris, *Antirrheticus adversus Apollinarem*, which quoted frequently from Apollinaris's work.

It is the most important extant writing against Apollinarianism. In *Adversus Apollinaristas* he rejected the Apollinarist charge that he holds there are two sons of God. A small tract, *Contra fatum*, defends the freedom of the will against a pagan philosopher. *Ad Graecos ex communibus notionibus* was written in 397. *Ad Adlabium quod non sint tres dii*, utilizing the distinction between person and nature, explains how one can speak of three persons without asserting the existence of three gods.

Exegetical Writings. A large portion of Gregory's writings is devoted to the exposition of scripture. Two early works (written ca. 379–389), having a scientific intent, that is, attempting to expose the teaching of scripture in harmony with right reason or true philosophy, are the *Explicatio apologetica in Hexaemeron* and the *De opificio hominis*. The first is a continuation of a task undertaken by Basil to explain Genesis in the light of the scientific and philosophical accounts of the formation of the world; the second continues with a concentration on the creation of human beings. The particular exegetical technique which Gregory inherits from Origen is *akolouthia*, that is, connection or sequence of thought, which he utilizes to give meaning and order to the apparently random events of biblical text.

Two short pieces are concerned with theological interpretation, the *De phythonissa* and a homily on 1 Cor 15.28. The other exegetical writings develop the doctrine of Christian perfection and, particularly, the way of mystical union taught by scripture. They include the *De vita Moysis, In psalmorum inscriptiones, In Ecclesiasten homiliae, In Canticum Canticorum*, on the Old Testament; *De oratione dominica, De beatitudinibus* and another homily on 1 Cor 6.18, on the New Testament. Of particular interest is *De vita Moysis*, which describes Moses's mystical ascent to God through the three theophanies recorded in the book of Exodus.

TEACHING

Above all, the intellectual basis of Gregory's theology was Greek. His thought represents the encounter between Greek classical philosophy and Christian biblical revelation. Hellenistic Judaism was the religion of Judea and Galilee during the life of Jesus. Widespread Hellenism had been the environment for the expansion of primitive Christianity, and the New Testament had been written in *koine* or common Greek. However, the Hellenism of the Cappadocians was profoundly different both in form and in content. Gregory's language was in no way common. His writing was more literary and more polished than the language of the New Testament. His thinking was more rational and more sophisticated and especially dependent upon pagan sources. The Cappadocians in general and Gregory in particular were on the forefront of creating a new and genuine Christian culture, namely, a Christian version of classical Greek *paideia*. The philosophy of antiquity is so evident in the works of Gregory that some scholars, not without cause, have considered him more a Neoplatonist than a Christian. The point of view from which to understand Gregory's teaching is precisely this context of Christian *paideia*. In his thinking, scripture and philosophy are in a sense parallel. Both teach a higher doctrine and both have the same goal, the practice of virtue and final union with God. Gregory writes: ''If one can give a definition of Christianity, we shall define it as follows. Christianity is an imitation of divine nature. . . . Christianity, therefore, brings man back to his original good fortune'' (*De Professione*, FC 58, p. 85). The Neoplatonic type and archetype are evident in his definition. The practice of virtue is the imitation of divine nature while salvation is union with God. This salvific union is more precisely a reunion with God or the restoration of human beings to their original state in the garden before the fall.

Allegorical Method. Although Gregory was aware of the Antiochene criticism of the Alexandrian allegorical method of scriptural interpretation and was much more concerned with the literal sense than were the Origenists, he maintained nevertheless that the ultimate purpose of scripture is not its historical teaching, but the elevation of the soul to God. This requires the allegorical method, which makes possible the extension of scripture to include much philosophy that is not directly contained in the historical sense. Within this context Gregory admitted the ability to know God from reason, but vigorously objected, against Eunomius, to the univocal application to God of categories and names derived from creatures. The distinction between creator and creature is fundamental for Gregory, and as a result the creator remains in a realm of mystery. He made much of the incomprehensibility of God and may have been one of the principal sources of the negative theology of Pseudo-Dionysius.

Trinity. Gregory maintained that the Son and Holy Spirit are equally creator and God, although the Son is generated and the Holy Spirit proceeds from the Father and Son. In the fashion that became traditional in the Greek Fathers and Orthodox Christianity, he saw the Holy Spirit as proceeding in a line from the Father through the Son. His attempt to explain the unity of nature and diversity of persons is tinged with a Platonic realism that has difficulties as well as attractiveness. The divine persons are distinct by their relations to each other, correctly enough, but they share one nature in the way that several men share the same human nature. This could suggest tritheism, but Gregory conceived the unity of nature more as the unity of a group than as a nature individually repeated in each member. In his viewpoint ''man'' means the whole human race, which has been inserted into matter in time and which will not be complete until the history of the human race has run its course. He had, as a result, a very strong sense of the unity of all human beings, which suggests a Stoic as well as a Platonic influence. In the Platonic tradition, however, he spoke of two creations of man, an ideal and an historical creation. With regard to the ideal creation, he held the peculiar position that human beings did not have by nature the sexual mode of reproduction. Humans were historically created male and female only because the creator foresaw the fall of the human race.

The Incarnation. This sense of the solidarity of the human race also contributes to the theology of the incarnation. Just as the human spirit made it possible for the physical universe to praise God with its own voice when it entered into matter, so when Christ became incarnate he entered into the whole human race and made it possible for mankind to praise God through his Son. The second person, however, assumes an individual human nature in such a way that there is only one person who is both God and man. Gregory taught the communication of idioms between the two natures in Christ, and accordingly insisted, against the Apollinarists, that Mary was the mother of God (*theotokos*) and not just the mother of man (*anthropotokos*).

Image of God. Part of the creationist pattern as applied to man is the doctrine of man as the image of God. This becomes a central notion in Gregory's anthropology and mystical theology. Man is the image of God as Creator and thus it is as lord of the universe and as a free agent that man's likeness to God is most often found. Because of this freedom man was able to fall into sin, and the image was soiled. It can be recovered through Christ and the practice of virtue. Christian perfection consists in becoming more and more like God. The quality of likeness also makes mystical knowledge possible, for as Greek philosophy taught, like is known by like. The attributes of God can be known through the image that is in man, although the essence of God transcends any knowledge of concepts or qualities.

Human Freedom. Despite the strongly intellectual character of his conception of Christian perfection, Gregory put a high value on human freedom, perhaps in opposition to Manichaeism, and he stressed greatly man's own responsibility and choice, even in the matter of faith and the attainment of the highest perfection. Yet there was a final optimism in Gregory. He did not accept the Origenist theory of the pre-existence of individual human souls, but he did support the doctrine of *apokatastasis* or the ultimate reconciliation of all creatures to God. The metaphysical argument for this rested on the Platonic doctrine of the negative character of evil and on the Platonic doctrine of the dynamism of the good. Evil cannot be absolute and infinite. Neither can there be an unending endurance in evil, for all being is good, and the good must eventually work its way through finite evil. The dynamism of goodness continues even in the final possession of God, and beatitude is conceived as a state of perpetual progress.

Bibliography: Editions: Clavis Patrum Gaecorum 3135–3226; *Patrologia Graeca* ed. J. P. MIGNE (Paris 1857–66) 35–38; W. JAEGER *et al., Gregorii Nysseni Opera* (Leiden 1952–). English translations: A select library of Nicene and Post-Nicine Fathers, 2nd series (1893), vol. 5; Library of Christian Classics (1954) vol. 3; Ancient Christian Writers (1954) vol. 18; Fathers of the Church (1967) vol. 58; Classics of Western Spirituality (1978). **Literature:** M. ALTENBURGER and F. MANN, *Bibliographie zu Gregory von Nyssa: Editionen, Überstezungen, Literatur* (Leiden 1988). J. DANIÉLOU, *Platonisme et théologie mystique: Doctrine spirituelle de saint Grégoire de Nysse* (Paris 1954); "La Chronologie des sermons de Grégoire de Nysse," *Recherches de science religieuse* 29 (1955) 346–372. W. VÖLKER, *Gregor von Nyssa als Mystiker* (Weisbaden 1955). D. L. BALAS, *"Metiousia Theou": Man's Participation in God's Perfections according to Saint Gregory of Nyssa*, Studia Anselmiana philosophica theologica 55 (Rome 1966). E. MÜHLENBURG, *Die Unendlichkeit Gottes bei Gregor von Nyssa: Gregors Kritik am Gottesbegriff der klassischichen Mystik* (Göttingen 1966). M. HARL, *Écriture et culture philosophique dans la pensée de Grégoire de Nysse*, Actes du colloque de Chevetogne, 22–26 septembre 1969 (Leiden 1971). R. E. HEINE, *Perfection in the Virtuous Life: A Study in the Relationship between Edification and Polemical Theology in Gregory of Nyssa's De vita Moysis*, Patristic Monograph Series 2 (Cambridge1975). H. DÖRRIE et al., *Gregor von Nyssa und die Philosophie*, Zweites internationales Kolloquium über Gregor von Nyssa, Freckenhorst bei Münster, 18–23 September 1972 (Leiden 1976). A. SPIRA et al., *The Easter Sermons of Gregory of Nyssa: Translation and Commentary*, Proceedings of the Fourth International Colloquium on Gregory of Nyssa, Cambridge, England, 11–15 September, 1978, Patristic Monograph Series 9 (Cambridge 1981). A. SPIRA, *The Biographical Works of Gregory of Nyssa*, Proceedings of the Fifth International Colloquium on Gregory of Nyssa, Mainz, 6–10 September 1982, Patristic Monograph Series 12 (Cambridge 1984). H. R. DROBNER and C. KLOCK, *Studien zu Gregor von Nyssa und der christlichen Spätantike*, Supplements to Vigiliae christianae 12 (Leiden 1990). M. D. HART, "Gregory of Nyssa's Ironic Praise for the Celibate Life," *Heythrop Journal* 33 (1992) 1–19. V. E. F. HARRISON, *Grace and Human Freedom according to St. Gregory of Nyssa*, Studies in the Bible and Early Christianity 30 (Lewiston 1992). J. PELIKAN, *Christianity and Classical Culture: The Metamorphosis of Natural Theology in the Christian Encounter with Hellenism* (New Haven 1993). S. G. HALL, *Gregory of Nyssa, Homilies on Ecclesiastes: An English Version with Supporting Studies*, Proceedings of the Seventh International Colloquium on Gregory of Nyssa, St. Andrews, 5–10 September 1990 (New York 1993). H. U. VON BALTHASAR, *Presence and Thought: Essay on the Religious Philosophy of Gregory of Nyssa* (San Francisco 1995). M. AZKOUL, *St. Gregory of Nyssa and the Tradition of the Fathers*, Texts and Studies in Religion 63 (Lewiston 1995). D. F. STRAMARA, "Gregory of Nyssa's Terminology for Trinitarian Perichoresis," *Vigiliae Christianae* 52 (1998) 257–263. A. MEREDITH, *Gregory of Nyssa* (New York 1999). J. ZACHHUBER, *Human Nature in Gregory of Nyssa: Philosophical Background and Theological Significance*, Supplements to Vigiliae christianae 46 (Boston 1999). J. P. CAVARNOS, *St. Gregory of Nyssa on the Human Soul: Its Nature, Origin, Relation to the Body, Faculties, and Destiny* (Belmont 2000). H. R. DROBNER and A. VICIANO, *Gregory of Nyssa, Homilies on the Beatitudes: An English Version with Supporting Studies*, Proceedings of the Eighth International Colloquium on Gregory of Nyssa, Paderborn, 14–18 September 1998, Supplements to Vigiliae christianae 52 (Boston 2000). M. R. BARNES, *The Power of God: Dunamis in Gregory of Nyssa's Trinitarian Theology* (Washington, DC 2001).

[R. F. HARVANEK/K. B. STEINHAUSER]

GREGORY OF OSTIA, ST.

Bishop and papal legate; d. Logroño, Navarre, Spain, May 9, 1044. Little is known for certain of Gregory before his election to the See of OSTIA except that he was a BENEDICTINE monk and abbot of the monastery of SS. Cosmas and Damian in Rome from 998 to 1004. He was undoubtedly a man of both learning and holiness and was favored by Pope BENEDICT IX. Under this pope he was elected bishop of Ostia in 1033–34 and was employed either as the librarian of the Roman Church or as chancellor. In 1039 Benedict appointed him papal legate to the Kingdom of Navarre in Spain. He is often invoked against attacks by locusts and other harmful insects, since he reportedly freed the Kingdom of Navarre from a plague of locusts by a simple sign of the cross. His cult was approved for Navarre in 1754.

Feast: May 9.

Bibliography: *Acta Sanctorum* May 2:463–465. *Bibliotheca hagiographica latina antiquae et mediae aetatis* 1:3670. A. MERCATI and A. PELZER, *Dizionario ecclesiastico* 2:262. A. ZIMMERMANN, *Kalendarium Benedictinum: Die Heiligen und Seligen des Benediktinerorderns und seiner Zweige* 2:165.

[R. E. GEIGER]

GREGORY OF RIMINI

Augustinian philosopher and theologian; b. Rimini, Italy, toward the end of the 13th century; d. Vienna, November 1358. Gregory entered the Hermits of St. Augustine and studied in Italy; in Paris, where he received the degree of bachelor of theology (*c.* 1323); and in England. He taught at Paris, and at Bologna, Padua, and Perugia in Italy. He then returned to Paris, where he was given the title of *Magister cathedraticus* (*Chartularium universitatis Parisiensis* 2:557, n. 1097) in 1345.

Gregory returned to Italy. In 1351, he was appointed regent of the Augustinian house of studies at Rimini and prior of the monastery. After the death of the prior general, THOMAS OF STRASSBURG, in 1356, Gregory served as vicar general. A year later, he was unanimously elected prior general. Gregory was considered by his contemporaries to be one of the most subtle philosophers and theologians. Posterity has awarded him the honorary titles of *Doctor authenticus* and *Doctor acutus.*

Gregory was influenced by WILLIAM OF OCKHAM, although he was less prone to skepticism. Gregory admitted the validity of the proofs for the existence of God and held that it is possible to demonstrate philosophically the spirituality of the soul. He opposed Ockham on the question of the plurality of forms. He assigned a great deal of importance to experience, claiming that the intellect knows the singular before the universal, and that intuitive knowledge precedes abstractive knowledge. For him, the universal has no foundation outside the mind; hence, it is only a fictitious concept, formed by the intellect—a sign, arbitrarily instituted (*ad placitum institutum*). The immediate object of knowledge and science is not the object that exists outside the soul but rather the total, overall meaning (*complexe significabile*) of the propositions of a syllogism. His followers not only identified Gregory with NOMINALISM but considered him one of its foremost proponents.

Gregory defended what he believed to be the doctrines of St. AUGUSTINE, including some spurious teachings. He suspected Pelagianism everywhere and fought against it. He overemphasized the corrupt state of human nature, the incapacity of free will, and the need for a special grace in order to perform a morally good act. For him, predestination was entirely gratuitous and independent of the prevision of the good use of free will. He held that children who die unbaptized will never see God and will suffer the punishment of eternal fire, thus earning for himself the nickname of ''infant torturer'' (*tortor infantium*).

Gregory's most important work is his *Lectura in primum et secundum librum sententiarum.* In addition, he is the author of the following: *Epistolarum divi Augustini tabula; Tractatus de imprestantiis Venetorum et de usura* (ed. Reggio Emilia 1522 and 1622); *Tractatus de conceptione B. Mariae Virginis; In omnes divi Pauli epistolas; In divi Iacobi epistolas; De quatuor virtutibus cardinalibus; Tractatus de intensione et remissione formarum corporalium;* and the *Registrum epistolarum sui generalatus.*

Bibliography: É. H. GILSON *History of Christian Philosophy in the Middle Ages* (New York 1955). D. TRAPP, ''Augustinian Theology of the Fourteenth Century,'' *Augustiniana* 6 (1956) 146–274. W. KÖLMEL, ''Von Ockham zu Gabriel Biel. Zur Naturrechtslehre des 14. und 15. Jahrhunderts,'' *Franziskanische Studien* 37 (1955) 218–259. *Analecta Augustiniana* 4–5 (1911–14), 18–23 (1940–54) *passim.* G. LEFF, *Gregory of Rimini* (New York 1961). J. BIARD, ''La science divine entre signification et vision chez Gregoire de Rimini,'' *Vestigia, Imagines, Verba* (Turnhout 1997) 393–408. E. MEI-

Saint Gregory of Tours, engraving after a painting by L. Boulanger. (©Bettmann/CORBIS)

JERING, *Klassieke gestalten van christelijk geloven en denken. Van Irenaeus tot Barth* (Amsterdam 1995) 137–154. K. SMITH, "Ockham's Influence on Gregory of Rimini's Natural Philosophy," *Dialexeis 1996–1997* (Leukosia, Cyprus 1999) 107–144.

[G. GÁL]

GREGORY OF TOURS, ST.

Frankish historian, bishop of Tours from 573 to 594; b. Clermont-Ferrand, probably Nov. 30, 538; d. Tours, Nov. 17, 594. Georgius Florentius Gregorius, the son of Florentius and Armentaria, was related through his mother to Bps. St. Gregory of Langres, St. Tetricus of Langres, St. Nicetius of Lyons, and St. Euphronius of Tours, and through his father to Bp. St. Gallus of Clermont. After Florentius's death Gregory's mother transferred to the vicinity of Cavaillon and Gregory's education was undertaken by his grand-uncle, the future Bishop Nicetius, and by his uncle, Bishop Gallus, and the latter's archdeacon, (St.) Avitus, subsequently bishop of Clermont. Having been ordained to the diaconate apparently at Clermont under Bishop Cautinus (d. 571) in 563, Gregory was chosen bishop of Tours following Euphronius's death in 573 and, after a 19-day vacancy, was consecrated by Bp. Egidius of Reims. Political control of Tours lay first with King Sigebert of Austrasia (561–575), then, during (561–584), with Chilperic of Nuestria, thereafter with Guntram of Burgundy (561–593), who in November 587 relinquished the territory to Childebert II of Austrasia (575–595); although it was Sigebert who authorized Gregory's consecration, Gregory was on intimate terms with all of these rulers.

Gregory assisted at episcopal synods held at Paris in 577, at Berny in 580, and at Poitiers in 590 (*Monumenta Germaniae Historica*, Concilia, I, 151,152,175–6). In his diocese, Gregory put an end to murderous feuds (*Hist. Franc.* 7.47), obtained relief from excessive taxation (*Hist. Franc* 9.30), rebuilt the Tours cathedral, and blessed many churches (*Hist. Franc.* 10.31; see also Fortunatus, *Carm.* 10.5, 6. Gregory's record of these activities appears in the epilogue to his *History,* which he composed in the 21st year of his own episcopacy and the fifth year of Pope Gregory I's pontificate. The *Vita Gregorii,* a tenth-century biography, testifies to the veneration that his name evoked in the Middle Ages.

The following literary works of Gregory are extant: ten books of *Histories,* seven of *Miracles,* the Lives of the Fathers, a commentary on the Psalms, and a treatise on Church Offices (*de cursibus . . . ecclesiasticis*). The first two books of his *Historia Francorum* relate events from Creation to A.D. 511; the remaining eight give the story of the Franks to 591. Books 1–4 were completed by 575; Books 5–6, between 580–584; Books 7–110, in 584–591, with subsequent revision of Books 1–6 and an epilogue (10.31) added in 594. The seven books of *Miracles, Librii IV de virtutibus s. Martini,* fashioned from 574–575 to 591–594, relate the prodigies attributed to the patron of Tours; and the *Liber de passione et virtutibus s. Iuliani* reports the alleged wonders of the fourth-century martyr of Brioude. Its final chapter (50) was penned after 590. The *Liber in gloria martyrum* describes in 106 chapters the miracles worked by Our Lord, His mother, the Apostles, and the Gallic martyrs. The Liber in gloria confessorum gives stories of saints, mostly Gallic; its present preface dates from 593–594, though an earlier prologue (ch. 44) may belong to 584. The Lives of the Fathers in the *Liber vitae patrum* seems to have been composed originally as individual biographies. The concluding 20th chapter of the collection mentions the death of Leobard, which occurred on Jan. 18, 593. Gregory's *In Psalterii tractatum commentarius,* which is fragmentary, and *De cursu stellarum ratio,* with its catalog of the world's wonders and a method for determining the night hours of the Divine Office, belong to his episcopal period.

Gregory states that, with the aid of a Syrian, he had made a Latin version of the legend of the SEVEN SLEEPERS

OF EPHESUS (Glor. Mart. 94). This translation is extant as *Passio ss. martyrum VII dormientium.* F. Dvornik believes the *Liber de miraculis b. Andreae apostoli* was written by Gregory in 591–592 as a Latin adaptation of a Greek original; similarly, the *De miraculis b. Thomae apostoli* may be a work of Gregory.

Without the bishop of Tours, our knowledge of sixth-century Gaul would be incalculably poorer. In large measure, our insight into the history, the geography, the language, and the religion of the period depends on him. While his historical methods are faulty and his credulity concerning the saints is naive, his conviction as to the centrality of the Church for human progress still speaks eloquently to us.

Feast: Nov. 17.

Bibliography: *Opera* in *Patrologia Latina* 71; *Monumenta Germaniae Historica,* Scriptores rerum Merovingicarum 1; 7:707–775; *The History of the Franks,* ed. and tr. O. M. DALTON, 2 v. (Oxford 1927); *Selections from the Minor Works,* tr. W. C. MCDERMOTT (Philadelphia 1949); *Glory of the Confessors*, tr. R. VAN DAM (Liverpool 1988). C. LELONG, *Grégoire de Tours: sa vie et son oeuvre* (Chambray-lès-Tours 1995), selected texts. Literature. H. LECLERCQ, *Dictionnaire d'archéologie chrétienne et de liturgie* 6.2:1711–53. B. ALTANER, *Pathology,* tr. H. GRAEF from 5th German edition (New York 1960) 571–572. S. DILL, *Roman Society in Gaul in the Merovingian Age* (London 1926). S. H. MACGONAGLE, *The Poor in Gregory of Tours* (New York 1936). O. CHADWICK, ''Gregory of Tours and Gregory the Great,'' *Journal of Theological Studies* 50 (1949) 38–49. H. G. J. BECK, *The Pastoral Care of Souls in South-East France during the Sixth Century (Analecta Gregoriana* 51; 1950). J. M. WALLACE-HADRILL, ''The Work of Gregory of Tours in the Light of Modern Research,'' *Transactions of the Royal Historical Society,* 1 (1951) 25–45. M. MANITIUS, *Geschichte der lateinischen Literatur des Mittelalters* 1:216–223. G. DE NIE, *Views from a Many-Windowed Tower: Studies of Imagination in the Works of Gregory of Tours* (Amsterdam 1987). A. H. B. BREREUKELAAR, *Historiography and Episcopal Authority in Sixth-Century Gaul: The Histories of Gregory of Tours Interpreted in Their Historical Context* (Göttingen 1994). *Grégoire de Tours et l'espace gaulois*, Proceedings of Intl. Congress, 3– November 5, 1994, eds. N. GAUTHIER and H. GALINIÉ (Tours 1997). J. SCHMIDT, *Grégoire de Tours: historien des Francs* (Monaco 1998). M. HEINZELMANN, *Gregory of Tours: History and Society in the Sixth Century*, tr. C. CARROLL (New York 2001). F. DVORNIK, *The Idea of Apostolicity in Byzantium and the Legend of the Apostle Andrew* (Cambridge, Mass. 1958) 183–186, 192. G. QUISPEL, ''An Unknown Fragment of the Acts of Andrew,'' *Vigiliae christiannae* 10 (1956) 129–148. H. DELEHAYE, ''Les Recueils antiques de miracles des saints,'' *Analecta Bollandiana* 43 (1925) 305–325. P. R. L. BROWN, *Relics and Social Status in the Age of Gregory of Tours* (Reading 1977). W. A. GOFFART, *The Narrators of Barbarian History* (Princeton, N.J. 1988).

[H. G. J. BECK]

GREGORY OF UTRECHT, ST.

Associate of St. Boniface; b. near Trier, *c.* 707; d. Aug. 25, 776. Born of a leading Merovingian family, he was educated by his grandmother, the abbess of Pfalzel. Gregory met (St.) BONIFACE in 722 and became his devoted follower and constant companion for more than 30 years. In 754, Gregory was made abbot of St. Martin's in Utrecht. The following year Boniface and Bishop EOBAN were martyred and direction of the Frisian mission fell to Gregory; he conducted it for 20 years while administering the Diocese of Utrecht, although he was never consecrated bishop. Building upon WILLIBRORD's early work, Gregory developed a school that became the leading intellectual center of the northern Low Countries, and in it he trained several outstanding religious leaders, the best known being the Frisian, LUDGER. Gregory's head is preserved at Susteren, Netherlands.

Feast: Aug. 25.

Bibliography: *Monumenta Germaniae Scriptores* (Berlin 1825–) 15.1:63–79. A. BUTLER, *The Lives of the Saints,* ed. H. THURSTON and D. ATTWATER, 4 v. (New York 1956) 3:402–403. A. HAUCK, *Kirchengeschichte Deutschlands,* 5 v. (9th ed. Berlin-Leipzig 1958) 2:356–359. T. SCHIEFFER, *Winfrid-Bonifatius und die christliche Grundlegung Europas* (Freiburg 1954). P. VIARD, *Catholicisme* 5:265–266.

[R. BALCH]

GREGORY OF VALENCIA

Theologian; b. Medina del Campo, Spain, March 1549?; d. Naples, March 25 (April 25?), 1603. While a student of law, Gregory entered the Society of Jesus at Salamanca in November 1565. He reviewed philosophy with his fellow student Francisco Suárez, and made his theological studies at Salamanca (1566–68) and then at Valladolid (1568–70). Gregory was ordained at Rome and sent to Germany, where he taught theology at Dillingen (1573–75) and then at Ingolstadt (1575–92). While emphasizing a return to Scripture and the Fathers, philosophical depth, and literary form, Gregory developed a new generation of theology professors (e.g., J. Gretser, A. Tanner). His success as a teacher was crowned by Pope CLEMENT VIII with the title Doctor Doctorum.

During these years of religious ferment in Germany, Gregory wrote more than 40 polemical essays against Lutheran and Calvinistic teachings, especially in defense of the Mass, the Blessed Sacrament, and the veneration of the saints. Their immoderately sharp tone, reflecting the spirit of his times, drew complaints, even from Peter Canisius. In 1591, Gregory collected and published his controversial writings, with additions, in one volume, entitled *De rebus fidei hoc tempore controversis* (Lyons 1591; Paris 1610). Especially noteworthy is the section *Analysis Fidei Catholicae* (Ingolstadt 1585; Waldsassen 1932), in which some of his theses on infallibility anticipate the Vatican definitions of 1870.

As consultant to the dukes of Bavaria and to the Holy See, Gregory was influential in other lively questions of his day. He defended a mutually rescindable rental convention as a moral basis for the "five per cent contract" for interest on loans, which thereafter became the legal norm in Bavaria. However, his defense of the existing laws against witchcraft, at a time when witch hunting in Germany had assumed appalling proportions, lacked the humane approach of his later confrere Friedrich von Spee.

After resigning his professorship in 1592, Gregory focused his energies on completing his principal work, *Commentariorum theologicorum tomi quatuor* (Ingolstadt 1591–97; revised 1603), based on the *Summa* of Thomas Aquinas. This first complete corpus of systematic theology by a Jesuit anticipates the modern return to Scripture and the Fathers as the basis for theological reflection. Herein is found Gregory's "pre-Molinist" theory of free will under grace, called "Valencianism." The work went through 12 editions within 20 years and had a deep and widespread influence.

Called to Rome in 1598 to the leading post at the Roman College, Gregory became actively involved in the famous dispute between Jesuits and Dominicans on grace and free will. In 1602, when Clement VIII personally assumed presidency of the congregations *de auxiliis,* Gregory defended Molina's book and doctrine so competently that all concurred in his praise. Although Clement allowed him to sit during his discourses, Gregory, weakened from illness and overwork, collapsed near the end of his ninth debate. He went to Naples to recover but died there in 1603.

Bibliography: C. SOMMERVOGEL et al, *Bibliothèque de la Compagnie de Jésus* (Brussels-Paris 1890–1932) 8:388–400; 9:897. H. HURTER *Nomenclator literarius theologiae catholicae* (Innsbruck 1926) 3:401–404. W. HENTRICH, "War Gregor von Valencia Prämolinist?" *Scholastik* 4 (1929) 91–106; *Lexikon für Theologie und Kirche*, ed. J. HOFER and K. RAHNER (Freiburg 1957–65) 4:1194–95. B. ROMEYER, *Dictionaire de théologie catholique*, ed. A. VACANT et al. (Paris 1903–50) 15.2:2465–97. B. DUHR, *Geschichte der Jesuiten in den Ländern deutscher Zunge,* 4 v. in 5 (Freiburg 1907–28) 1:665–668.

[G. VAN ACKEREN]

GREGORY SINAITES

Oriental monk, mystic, and ascetical writer; b. Lydia, end of the 13th century; d. Paroria, Bulgaria, Nov. 27, 1346. Gregory became a monk in Cyprus and later on Mt. Sinai. He traveled to Palestine and Crete, where he met the monk Arsenius, who taught him the excellence of mental prayer. Later, he returned to MOUNT ATHOS and gained disciples for his moderate form of HESYCHASM. Forced to flee before the Turkish invasions, he went to Sozopolis on the Black Sea. On Mt. Paroria in Bulgaria, he founded a famous monastery (*c.* 1325) that became the intellectual and spiritual center of the Balkans. Through his writings, Gregory's influence spread in Europe to the whole Orthodox world. His great work, *137 Chapters or Spiritual Meditations*, contains a collection of spiritual aphorisms interspersed with dogmatic opinions, e.g., on the processions of the Holy Spirit, the way of the quietist, and illuminated living. The influence of St. JOHN CLIMACUS is evident.

Gregory wrote shorter tracts on Hesychasm, prayer, and passions that hinder spiritual advancement. His writings are concerned chiefly with the explanation of his method of prayer. His edited works do not contain all of his ascetical writings, and there are many variants in the unedited MSS. He also wrote tropes of the Trinity and liturgical *kanones,* or hymns on the Holy Cross, and on controversial themes such as the FILIOQUE and Christocentricism. His life was written by his disciple, later Patriarch CALLISTUS I.

Feast: Nov. 27 (Greek Church), Aug. 8 (Slavs).

Bibliography: Eds. of the *Life* by P. SYRKOU (Monuments de la Sociéte des amis de l'ancienne littérature et de l'art 174; St. Petersburg 1909), Slavic; and by I. POMYALOVSKY (St. Petersburg 1894), Gr. H. G. BECK, *Kirche und theologische Literatur im byzantinischen Reich* (Munich 1959) 694–695. V. LAURENT, *Catholicisme. Hier, aujourd'hur et demain*, ed. G. JACQUEMET, 5:266–267. V. GRUMEL, *Lexikon für Theologie und Kirche*, ed. M. BUCHBERGER (Freiburg 1930–38) 4:683. M. JUGIE *Theologica dogmatica christianorum orientalium ab ecclesia catholica dissedentium* (Paris 1926–35) 1:432–436. E. TURDEANU, *La Littérature bulgare du XIV siècle* (Paris 1947) 5–15. C. ÉMEREAU, *Échos d'Orient* 22 (1923) 432.

[F. DE SA]

GREGORY THAUMATURGUS, ST.

Bishop of Neocaesarea in Pontus, the Wonderworker; b. Neocaesarea, *c.* 213; d. there, *c.* 270.

He was born Theodore into a well-to-do family, but was called Gregory. He studied rhetoric, Latin, and law. Then, with his brother Athenodorus, he spent five years (probably 233–238) as a disciple of ORIGEN at Caesarea in Palestine. On returning home the brothers were consecrated bishops by Phaedimus of Amasea; however, the bishopric of Athenodorus is unknown. During the Decian persecution Gregory retired into the mountains with a large part of his flock, and after peace was restored instituted feasts in honor of the martyrs. With his brother, he assisted at the first Synod of Antioch (*c.* 264), which condemned PAUL OF SAMOSATA; but he did not assist at the second synod, and died probably under Aurelian (270–275).

The cult rendered him by SS. Basil and Gregory of Nyssa as well as the legends that surround his name testify to his successful apostolic work. Five legendary lives (in Greek, Latin, Syriac, and Armenian) narrate the miracles that merit him the title of *thaumaturgus* (miracle worker). Only the *Vita* by Gregory of Nyssa, whose grandmother was a convert of his, seems trustworthy; but information is supplied on him also by St. Basil in his *De Spiritu Sancto*, Eusebius (*Hist. eccl.* 7.14), and Gregory himself in his *Panegyric for Origen,* a farewell address he preached on separating from the master at the end of his studies. It provides a résumé of Origen's teaching and describes his attitude toward pagan philosophy, the Christian ''philosophy'' that he taught, and the students' admiration for the master. Origen responded with a letter. The *Exposition of Faith* preserved by Gregory of Nyssa in his biography is a brief Trinitarian Creed. Gregory's *Canonical Epistle* answers questions of ecclesiastical discipline raised after the invasion of Pontus by the Goths and the Borades between 254 and 258, and includes decisions regarding violated women and Christians guilty of pillage and apostasy. Canon 11 enumerating different types of penitents is not authentic. His *Metaphrasis of Ecclesiastes* is an adaptation of the Septuagint text in classical Greek; and his *To Theopompus, On the Passible and Impassible in God* is an apologetic dialogue for pagans, giving an explanation of Christ's Passion in view of Hellenistic dogma on the divine impassibility, which was exaggerated to a conception of an ''indolent'' God.

Other works preserved under his name are not authentic: the *Exposition of Faith* is by Apollinaris of Laodicea; and the 12 Chapters *On the Faith* is perhaps of Apollinarist origin. Gregory is also credited falsely with 11 Homilies in several languages and a *Dialogue with Aelian* (Basil, *Epist.* 210). Also doubtfully authentic are: *The Treatise on the Soul for Tatian*; the *Letter to Evagrius* (or Philagrius) in Greek and Syriac, which is disputed; and the letters mentioned by St. Jerome (*De vir. ill. 65; Epist.* 33.4).

Feast: Nov. 17.

Bibliography: *Opera, Patrologia Graeca,* ed. J. P. MIGNE, 161 v. (Paris 1857–66) 10:963–1232; *De passibili et impassibili in Deo,* J. B. PITRA, *Analecta sacra spicilegio Solesmensi parata,* 8 v. (Paris 1876–91) 4:103–120, 363–376; *Address to Origen,* tr. W. METCALFE (Society for Promoting Christian Knowledge; London 1920). GREGORY OF NYSSA, *Vita, Patrologia Graeca,* 46:893–958. H. CROUZEL, *Sciences Ecclésiastiques* 16 (1964) 59–91, panegyric. *L'Homme devant Dieu: Mélanges . . . Henri de Lubac,* 3 v. (Paris 1964) v. 1. B. ALTANER, *Patrology,* tr. H. GRAEF from 5th German ed. (New York 1960) 238–239. J. QUASTEN, *Patrology,* 3 v. (Westminster, Md. 1950–) 2:123–128. W. TELFER, *Journal of Theological Studies* 31 142–155, 354–363; *Harvard Theological Review* 29 (Cambridge, Mass. 1936) 225–334. A. SOLOVIEV, *Byzantion* 19 (Brussels 1949) 263–279. F. J. DÖLGER, *Antike und Christentum* 6 (1940) 74–75 (Logos theology). M. SIMONETTI, *Rendiconti del Instituto lombardo di scienze e léttere* 86 (1953) 101–117, ad Philagrium. C. MARTIN, *Revue d'histoire ecclésiastique* 24 (1928) 364–37 (homilies).

[H. CROUZEL]

GREGORY THE ILLUMINATOR, ST.

Fourth-century apostle of Armenia; b. Valarshapat, or possibly Caesarea in Cappadocia, *c.* 240; d. Armenia, *c.* 332. An Armenian tradition says that Gregory was the son of Anak, a Parthian noble, who assassinated Armenian King Chosroes I. Gregory was saved from the massacre of his family, received a Christian education at Caesarea in Cappadocia, and returned to Armenia to convert his countrymen. According to Agathangelos, he destroyed the temple of the native gods at Ashtishat, was tortured by King TIRIDATES III, and was condemned to incarceration in a grave (*chor virap*), from which he was rescued later. He converted the king and his people and was consecrated a bishop by Leontius of Caesarea (*c.* 315) and enthroned as bishop in Armenia by St. Peter of Sebaste. He evangelized the region of Armenia conquered by the Romans under Galerius (292) and baptized the kings of Caucasian Iberia (*see* GEORGIA, CHURCH IN ANCIENT), Lazes, and Albania.

Gregory consecrated his two sons, Vhartanes and Aristakes, as bishops; the latter took part in the Council of Nicaea I (325). The office of the catholicos or metropolitan of Armenia remained in Gregory's family down to the time of St. ISAAC THE GREAT (d. 438). Nicephorus Callistus asserts that Gregory visited CONSTANTINE I in Rome in the company of Tiridates (*Hist. eccl.* 8.35; *Patrologia Graeca* 146:609). Sometime before his death, Gregory retired to the life of a solitary in the wilderness. The 33 letters and homilies attributed to his authorship are spurious. The principal source for the life of Gregory is the history of Agathangelos, who claimed to be the secretary of King Tiridates. The fifth-century recension of this work is full of legendary material, making it most difficult to sort out the facts in the life of Gregory, who is not mentioned by any contemporary Greek ecclesiastical writers. A vita was written by George the Syrian during the eighth century.

Gregory's relics, which had rested in Naples, were solemnly handed over to the Armenian Apostolic Church on Nov. 10, 2000. He is the patron of Armenia.

Feast: Sept. 30.

Bibliography: *Bibliotheca hagiographica Graeca*, 712–713e. *Bibliotheca hagiographica orientalis*, 76–80. *Acta Sanctorum* Sept. 8:295–413. AGATHANGELOS, *The Teaching of Saint Gregory*, tr. R. W. THOMSON (Cambridge, Mass. 1970); *History of the Armenians*, tr. R. W. THOMSON (Albany, N.Y. 1976). V. G. ZAHIRSKY, *The Conversion of Armenia: A Retelling of Agathangelos' History* (New York 1985). V. LANGLOIS, ed., *Collection des historiens anciens et modernes de l'Arménie*, 2 v. (Paris 1867–69). G. GARITTE, *Lexikon für Theologie und Kirche*, ed. J. HOFER and K. RAHNER (Freiburg 1957–65) 4:1206–07; ed., *Documents pour l'étude du livre d'Agathange* (*Studi e Testi*, 127; 1946). P. DE LAGARDE, *Analecta Syriaca* (Leipzig 1858) 122–128. P. PEETERS, *Analecta Bollandiana* 60 (1942) 91–130. *Dictionnaire de théologie catholique* (Paris 1951), Tables générales 1:1928. O. BARDENHEWER, *Geschichte der altkirklichen Literatur* (Freiburg 1913–32) 5:182–185. V. GRUMEL, *Catholicisme, Hier, aujourd'hui et demain*, ed. G. JACQUEMET, 5:252.

[F. X. MURPHY]

GREMILLION, JOSEPH BENJAMIN

Catholic social justice and ecumenical pioneer, author, educator, and pastor, b. Moreauville, Louisiana, March 11, 1919; d. South Bend, Ind., Aug. 9, 1994.

Gremillion attended Louisiana State University, St. Benedict's College in Covington, Louisiana, Notre Dame Seminary in New Orleans, and The Catholic University of America before being ordained a priest for the diocese of Alexandria, Louisiana, December 1943. Traveling across Louisiana as State Future Farmers of America (FFA) president, he witnessed firsthand the miserable conditions of the black sharecroppers. It led him into the Catholic Rural Life Conference (CRLC), where he became a protégé of CRLC executive director Luigi Ligutti. He became involved with the U.S. Bishops Conference's National Catholic Resettlement Committee to promote resettlement of Europeans displaced by World War II in the rural United States. Gremillion founded and served as pastor of St. Joseph Parish, Shreveport, La. from 1949 to 1958, where he was very involved in civil rights work.

After earning a doctorate in social science at the Pontifical Gregorian University (1960), Gremillion served as director of socio-economic development for Catholic Relief Services (1960–1967), executive secretary of the Pastoral Aid Fund of Latin America (1964–1967), an officer of the Committee for Inter-American Cooperation (C.I.C.O.P.) from 1964 to 1967, and a Vatican observer to WCC Conference (1966). Together with Barbara WARD, James Joseph NORRIS and Arthur McCormick, Gremillion was a leader of the lobbying effort for concrete actions on social justice at the Second Vatican Council. Their lobbying bore fruit in the two paragraphs calling for the creation of an international social justice organization of the Catholic Church that were included in Article 90 of the final version of *Gaudium et Spes*. In early 1967, the Pontifical Commission Justice and Peace (PCJP) was established with Gremillion as its first general secretary (1967–1974) and with Ward and Norris as founding members.

Once the PCJP was securely established, Gremillion established the Society for Development and Peace or SODEPAX, a joint committee of the PCJP and the World Council of Churches (WCC) to promote worldwide ecumenical work for integral human development and social justice. After stepping down as PJCP secretary in 1974, Gremillion became a faculty fellow at the University of Notre Dame (1974–1978). He was the co-founder and coordinator of the Muslim Jewish Christian Conference (1975–1981), Regent's Lecturer at the Boalt School of Law, University of California at Berkeley (spring 1976), director of ecumenical and social ministry for the Diocese of Alexandria-Shreveport (1978–1983), co-director of the Notre Dame Study of Catholic Parish Life and the director of the Institute for Pastoral and Social Ministry (now the Institute for Church Life) (1983–1986). Following his retirement from Notre Dame in 1986 until his death, Gremillion worked with the Research Program on Religion, Church and Society in the Center for the Study of Contemporary Society. The Gremillion Papers are housed at the University of Notre Dame Archives.

Bibliography: Many articles under his own name and the pseudonym of Louis G. Martin as well as nine books including *Continuing Christ in the Modern World: Christian Social Concerns in the Light of Vatican II; Food, Energy, and the Major Faiths; Journal of a Southern Pastor; The Church and Culture Since Vatican II: The Experiences of North and Latin America; and The Gospel of Peace and Justice.*

[P. M. PELZEL]

GRÉTRY, ANDRÉ ERNEST MODESTE

Composer of light opera and sacred works; b. Liège, Belgium, Feb. 8, 1741; d. Montmorency (near Paris), Sept. 24, 1813. His father, a Walloon, was a church violinist, and Grétry was trained as a choirboy at Saint-Denis. At 12 he qualified for more specialized study and was drawn first to instrumental and church compositions, producing six symphonies from 1758 and, *c.* 1759, a solemn Mass. Through the influence of Henri Moreau, Grétry was sent to Liège College in Rome (1760–66). There he composed motets, *De Profundis*; a string quartet, and a flute concerto, among other works. In 1765 he composed his first light opera. He determined then that his career lay in light opera, and by 1767 he was in Paris. Though he found his *forte* late, he had assessed himself well: no contrapuntist, he had vocal, melodic gifts that carried excellently to the theater. He contributed over 60 works to the repertory of the Opéra-Comique, and achieved the success associated with popular theater. Best known of his dramatic pieces are *Le Tableau parlant* (1769), *Zémire et Azor* (1771), *L'Amant jaloux* (1778), and *Richard Coeurde-Lion* (his masterpiece; 1784). Grétry was a diarist of merit, and his observations on the effects of music on the human pulse comprise an early example of experimentation now bearing fruit in music therapy.

Bibliography: Music. *Collection complète*, 49 v. (Leipzig-Brussels 1883–1937). Literary works. *Oeuvres complètes*, ed. L. SOLVAY and E. CLOSSON, 4 v. (Brussels 1919–22). O. STRUNK, ed. *Source Readings in Music History* (New York 1950) 711–727, from the Mémoires. S. CLERCX, *Grétry* (Brussels 1944). G. CHOUQUET, *Grove's Dictionary of Music and Musicians*, ed. E. BLOM 9 v. (5th ed. London 1954) 3:792–797. D. J. GROUT, *A Short History of Opera*, 2 v. (2d, rev. and enl. ed. New York 1965). J. BELLMAN, ''*Aus alten Märchen*: The Chivalric Style of Schumann and Brahms,'' *The Journal of Musicology* 13 (1995) 125–126. D. CHARLTON, *Grétry and the Growth of the Opéra Comique* (Cambridge 1986). Y. LENOIR, ed., *Documents Grétry dans les collections de la Bibliothèque Royale Albert I* (Brussels 1989). L. M. STONES, ''André-Ernest- Modeste Grétry'' in *International Dictionary of Opera* 2 v., ed. C. S. LARUE (Detroit 1993) 553–556; ''*Zémire et Azor*'' in *International Dictionary of Opera* 2 v., ed. C. S. LARUE (Detroit 1993) 1479–1480. P. VENDRIX, ed., *Grétry et l'Europe de l'Opéra-Comique* (Brussels 1992).

[E. BORROFF]

André Ernest Modeste Grétry, engraving. (©Michael Nicholson/CORBIS)

GRETSER, JAKOB

Jesuit theologian, liturgist, polemicist, patristic scholar, philologist, and playwright; b. Markdorf, Baden, March 27, 1562; d. Ingolstadt, Jan. 29, 1625. Gretser entered the Jesuit novitiate at Landsberg (1578), studied humanities at Fribourg (1584–86), and attended the University of Ingolstadt, where he became a professor of metaphysics (1589–92). He succeeded his teacher, Gregory of Valencia, to the chair of scholastic theology (1592–1605) and then taught moral theology (1609–16). During these years, his erudition appeared in a great variety of writings. As a polemicist, Gretser wrote against the Protestants Franciscus Junnius (1545–1602), Aegidius Hunnius (1550–1603), Johannes Pappus (1549–1610), and others. He also defended Robert Bellarmine [*Controversiarum Roberti Bellarmini. . .amplissima defensio* (2 v. Ingolstadt 1607–09)], the Index published by Philip II of Spain [*De jure et more prohibendi. . .libros hereticos et noxios* (Ingolstadt 1603)], pilgrimages, the lives of the saints, the Society of Jesus, ecclesiastical feasts and rites, relics, and the Roman pontiffs. Gretser's *De cruce Christi* (3 v. Ingolstadt 1598–1605) contains a wealth of learning that treats not only Christ's cross, but images of the cross, cross-bearing coins, eulogies of the cross, a defense of veneration of the cross, and the Crusades. Other works include: *Rudimenta linguae graecae* (Inglostadt 1593); *Institutiones graecae* (Ingolstadt 1593); *D. Gregorii episcopi Nysseni commentarius duplex in psalmorum inscriptiones* (Ingolstadt 1600); *Vetera monumenta contra schismaticos* (Ingolstadt 1600). His works total 234 printed books (including 23 dramas) and 46 MSS. The printed works have been edited by P. G. Kolb, *Opera omnia* (17 v. Regensburg 1734–41).

Bibliography: B. DUHR, *Geschichte der Jesuiten in den Ländern deutscher Zunge,* 4 v. in 6 (Freiburg 1907–28), v. 1. C. SOMMERVOGEL et al., *Bibliothèque de la Compagnie de Jesus* (Brussels-Paris 1890–1932) 3:1743–1809. P. BERNARD, *Dictionnaire de théologie catholique*, ed. A. VACANT et al. (Paris 1903–50) 6.2.1866–71. H. LIEBING, *Die Religion in Geschichte und Gegenwart,* (Tübingen 1957–65) 2:1856. T. KURRUS, *Lexikon für Theologie und Kirche*, ed. J. HOFER and K. RAHNER (Freiburg 1957–65) 4:1223.

[E. D. MCSHANE]

GREY NUNS

The Sisters of Charity of Montreal (#0490), commonly called Grey Nuns (SGM), a pontifical congregation of religious women, was founded in 1738 at

Montreal, Canada, by (St.) Marie Marguerite d'YOUVILLE.

Grey Nuns of Montreal. The original foundation developed slowly. On Dec. 31, 1737, Madame d'Youville and three companions, Louise Thaumur, Catherine Cusson, and Catherine Demers, privately professed their dedication to the poor and sick, without any intention, however, of forming a religious community. The following year they began to live together in a rented house in order to receive the destitute and give them better care. This beginning of their community life enraged many citizens, who could not believe that the widow of François d'Youville, confidential agent of the governor-general in illegal trade with the Native Americans, would honestly help the poor. In spite of violence and invective, including their title, *les soeurs grises* (the drunken nuns), the women persisted in their dedication, under the spiritual guidance of a Sulpician priest, Louis Normant du Faradon. In 1745 they made the first formal promises anticipating their rule, when they agreed to live together in charity for the rest of their lives under a superior and according to a rule; to practice entire poverty; to consecrate their time and labor to the care of as many poor persons as they could receive; and, for this purpose, to put their individual resources into a common fund. Moreover, they agreed to wear plain black dresses, uniform only in simplicity.

In 1747 the administrators of the General Hospital of Montreal, established by the Charon Brothers in 1692 for aged men, appealed to Mother d'Youville to take charge of the institution. King Louis XV confirmed the appointment (1753) and authorized the foundation of a religious community. The first papal approval was granted on July 21, 1865. In 1755, when the community numbered 12 members, it was decided to design a habit. Having been called *lex soeurs grises* for 18 years, they chose grey—also *gris* in French—for the color of their costume, thus giving a new meaning to an old title. The General Hospital, now restored, became the first motherhouse of the Grey Nuns, as well as the center of all kinds of work for the blind, the mentally ill, destitute and aged men and women, those suffering from contagious diseases, abandoned children, and needy seminarians. In 1855 a foundation was made in the United States, which later developed into the American province with headquarters at Lexington, Massachusetts.

Grey Nuns of St. Hyacinthe. The first independent foundation, the Sisters of Charity of St. Hyacinthe (SCSH, Official Catholic Directory #0610) was made in 1840 at St. Hyacinthe, near Montreal. From this foundation another was made at Nicolet in 1886, but in 1940 it became a province of the original institute in Montreal. The Sisters of Charity of St. Hyacinthe (SGSH) made their first United States foundation in 1878. The generalate is in St. Hyacinthe, Canada; the United States regional administration is in Lewiston, Maine.

Grey Nuns of Quebec. Another self-governing mission from Montreal was founded in 1849 in the city of Quebec at the request of Bishop Pierre-Flavien Turgeon. These Sisters of Charity (SCQ, Official Catholic Directory #0560) subsequently established provinces in the civil Province of Quebec. In 1890, they established their first foundation in Massachusetts, Massachusetts. The sisters work in schools and hospitals, and care for the elderly.

Grey Nuns of the Cross. In 1845, under the leadership of Mother Elizabeth Bruyère, the Grey Nuns of Montreal founded an autonomous congregation in Ottawa, Ontario. Their rule received pontifical approbation in 1889. Their work includes education, nursing, pastoral work, and care of the aged and orphans. In the United States, the sisters made a foundation in 1857, which eventually became an independent branch, the Grey Nuns of the Sacred Heart in 1921.

Grey Nuns of the Sacred Heart. In 1857 an autonomous congregation was founded from the Grey Nuns of the Cross that became known as the Grey Nuns of the Sacred Heart (GNSH, Official Catholic Directory #1840). At the invitation of Cardinal Dennis Dougherty of Philadelphia, Pennsylvania, they established their motherhouse there in 1921. The sisters are active in schools, hospitals, care for the aged, parochial and pastoral ministries, outreach programs to the homeless, youth ministries, counseling, and campus ministries.

Grey Sisters of the Immaculate Conception. In 1926 a group of English-speaking members of the Grey Nuns of the Cross established a separate motherhouse in Pembroke, Ontario. Besides hospitals, orphanages, and schools (both elementary and secondary), the congregation had also maintained Chinese missions in Canada, which were completely destroyed by communists.

Bibliography: Archives, Grey Nuns of Montreal. T. A. KEEFE, *The Congregation of the Grey Nuns. 1737–1910* (Washington 1942).

[L. R. CAYER/M. P. FITTS/EDS.]

GRIFFIN, BERNARD WILLIAM

Cardinal, archbishop of Westminster, England; b. Birmingham, Feb. 21, 1899; d. New Polzeath, Cornwall, Aug. 20, 1956. Griffin was educated at Cotton College, Oscott, England, and at the English College and the Beda College in Rome. Ordained in 1924, he was secretary to the archbishops of Birmingham from 1927 to 1937. Griffin was chancelor of the archdiocese from 1929 to 1938 and was a notable administrator of archdiocesan charitable homes from 1937 to 1943. He became an auxiliary bishop of Birmingham in 1938, and in 1943 he succeeded Cardinal Arthur HINSLEY as archbishop of Westminster. Griffin was made a cardinal in 1946. His previous association with social welfare helped him to assess and encourage the work of the Labour government whose effect was to change English social life profoundly after World War II. As the leading English Catholic prelate, he often journeyed abroad until the last years of his life, when he suffered from illnesses that severely restricted his activities. *Seek Ye First,* a collection of his sermons and other addresses, was published in 1949.

Bibliography: M. DE LA BEDOYÈRE, *Cardinal Bernard Griffin* (London 1955).

[E. MCDERMOTT]

GRIFFIN, MARTIN IGNATIUS JOSEPH

Journalist, historian; b. Philadelphia, Oct. 23, 1842; d. there, Nov. 10, 1911. Griffin's parents, Terence J. and Elizabeth (Doyle) Griffin, were immigrants from Ireland. Griffin was educated in parochial and public schools. He began his journalistic career as a contributor to Catholic newspapers. Griffin edited a Sunday school journal (1867–70) and served as assistant editor of the newly established *Catholic Standard* (1870–73). An energetic promoter, Griffin organized Philadelphia's first Youths' Catholic Total Abstinence Society. In 1872, he was one of the founders of the Catholic Total Abstinence Union of America. He was secretary of the Irish Catholic Benevolent Union for 22 years. Griffin founded and edited its *I.C.B.U. Journal* (1873–94), continuing its publication as *Griffin's Journal* until 1900. Griffin was also active as a historian and compiler of historical documents. In 1884, he founded the American Catholic Historical Society of Philadelphia. From 1886 to 1911, as proprietor and editor of the *American Catholic Historical Researches*, a quarterly miscellany of documents, comment, and correspondence, Griffin campaigned for authenticity in American Catholic historical writing. His works include a number of parish histories, compilations of documents, and the following books: *History of Rt. Rev. Michael Egan, D.D. First Bishop of Philadelphia* (1893), *Commodore John Barry* (1902), *General Count Casimir Pulaski* (1909), *Stephen Moylan* (1909), and *Catholics and the American Revolution* (1907–11). Despite occasional deficiencies of method and judgment, his work provided a documentary foundation for later historians of American Catholicism.

[F. GERRITY]

GRIFFITH, PATRICK RAYMOND

Missionary bishop; b. Limerick, Ireland, Oct. 1, 15, 1798; d. Cape Town, South Africa, June 18, 1862. After joining the Dominicans and studying in Lisbon and Rome, he was ordained (1821). He then returned to Ireland, where in Dublin and elsewhere he became well known for his oratorical powers, charity, and zeal, and particularly for his work among the stricken during a cholera outbreak. When Pope Gregory XVI created the Vicariate Apostolic of the Cape of Good Hope (1837), he appointed Griffith as the first vicar apostolic. After being consecrated in Dublin as bishop (August 1837), Griffith arrived in Cape Town on April 13, 1838. In 1841 he began the construction of St. Mary's Cathedral, which was opened a decade later. Bishop Griffith established missions at Rondebosch, Wynberg, and Simonstown in the Cape Peninsula, and at Grahamstown and Port Elizabeth in the eastern Cape. Griffith's vicariate was divided in 1847 when the Vicariate Apostolic of the Eastern Districts of the Cape of Good Hope was created. Griffith consecrated Aidan Devereux as its bishop, the first ceremony of episcopal consecration in South Africa. In 1862 Griffith resigned his post after receiving Thomas Grimley as coadjutor in 1861. Between the time of Griffith's arrival in 1838 and his death 24 years later the number of Catholics in the Cape Colony had increased from 700 (mostly military personnel) to more than 30,000. Griffith was buried in St. Mary's Cathedral, the mother church in the present Republic of South Africa.

Bibliography: J. E. BRADY, *Trekking for Souls* (Cedara, Natal 1952). W. E. BROWN, *The Catholic Church in South Africa* (New York 1960).

[J. E. BRADY]

GRIFFITHS, BEDE

Benedictine monk, writer; b. Walton-on-Thames, England, 1906; d. Shantivanam Ashram, Tamil Nadu, India, May 13, 1993. In 1932 Bede Griffiths entered the Roman Catholic Church; a few months later, he joined the Benedictine Abbey of Prinknash. For 15 years he hardly left the cloister and relished the order and peace of monastic life. However, his study of Indian religion and philosophy stirred another level of his search for wholeness, and, in 1955, he left for India "to find the other half of my soul." There he learned Sanskrit and in 1968 took over direction of the Benedictine ashram of Shantivanam, which had been founded by the two great pioneers of an Indianized Christianity, Jules Monchanin and Henri le Saux (Abhishiktananda).

In India Griffiths formed a small, fragile community of great international influence that symbolized his deep-

Prior Dom Bede Griffiths performing silkworm blessing during service at St. Michael's Abbey. (©Hulton-Deutsch Collection/CORBIS)

est beliefs and intuitions. Among these were the need for a truly Asian Christianity reexpressing its faith through the terms of its own philosophy and scriptures. He saw modern Christianity at a crossroads comparable to that faced in the primitive Church when a Jewish framework of ideas and symbols struggled with those of the Gentile world. In his early days in India he met with official and semi-official opposition to his ideas and to his new form of ashramic-monastic life, but toward the end of his life he received official approval. He was always quick to confront and debate the reactionary forces of a eurocentric Christianity, either in India or in the West, and to point out what he saw as general inherent tendencies of all Semitic religions. For him these were the centrality of the dualistic model of seeing God, the domination of male symbolism and leadership, and the intolerance of exclusive claims to truth and salvation. In this spirit, for example, his revision of the psalter for ashram worship excised curses and denunciatory verses.

An anthology of world scriptures published posthumously illustrated Griffiths's belief that all religions originate in an intuition or experience of *advaita* or nonduality. They then decline into excessive rationalism, with its consequent rigidities of dualism and exclusivism, before ascending back through their contemplative traditions to a vision of simplicity and universalism. This latter belief underlies the importance he attributed to the influence of his fellow Benedictine John Main in restoring a method of contemplative meditation to Christianity from within the Christian monastic tradition. Griffiths's last book, *The New Creation in Christ,* takes Main's ideas on contemplation and the modern pursuit of community and personal wholeness as its inspiration for affirming a renewed tradition of lay monasticism. This book dispels any idea that Griffiths's universalist vision of religion resulted in any ultimate syncretism or dilution of Christian specificity.

With characteristic lucidity and elegance of literary style, Bede Griffiths wrote on Indian Christianity, modern Church controversies, Indian scripture, the meeting of East and West, and the encounter of modern science and religious mysticism. Despite his prophetic contemporaneity and inclusivity of vision, Griffiths harbored a deep distrust of modern technological civilization. He believed in the evolutionary movement toward global unity but saw irreconcilable self-contradictions at the core of modern society. He lived and taught from this tension without personal dogmatism and with a growing sweetness of nature that touched the hearts of his listeners around the world during the extensive travels of his last years.

After his stroke in 1990, Griffiths described a personal transformation and affective liberation that he attributed to the awakening of the *muladara chakra.* At Oxford he had struggled through an intellectual journey that took him from fin de siècle aestheticism to twentieth century Romanticism. In this he was accompanied by C.S. Lewis, a friend for 40 years, who described him as ''one of the toughest dialecticians of my acquaintance.'' Yet, it was only after a battle with religious faith and an experiment with utopian living that he accepted the fully spiritual context of his pursuit for truth and wholeness.

Bede Griffiths, in his life and teaching, symbolized the meeting between Christianity and the other world religions, which he considered the most significant event of the twentieth century. As such a symbol (don and sannyasi), he and his writings have continued to inspire the interfaith movement since his death.

Bibliography: Griffiths was the author of a number of books, more than 300 articles, and several audio and video recordings. His books include an autobiography entitled *The Golden String* (London 1954); *Christian Ashram* (London 1966); *Vedanta and Christian Faith* (London 1973); *Return to the Centre* (London 1978); *The Marriage of East and West* (London 1982); *The Cosmic Revelation* (London 1983); *The River of Compassion* (Warwick NY 1987); *A New Vision of Reality* (London 1991); *The New Creation in Christ* (London 1992); *Psalms for Christian Prayer* (Shantivanam 1993); *Pathways to the Supreme* (Shantivanam 1994); *Universal Wisdom* (London 1994). S. DU BOULAY, *Beyond the Darkness: A Biography of Bede Griffiths* (New York 1998).

[L. FREEMAN]

GRIFFITHS, THOMAS

Vicar apostolic of the London District; b. London, June 2, 1791; d. London, Aug. 12, 1847. Griffiths was baptized a Protestant, but became a Catholic while a boy. He was educated at St. Edmund's College, Ware, and lived there (1805–33). Ordained in July 1814, he became president of St. Edmund's at the age of 26. His careful administration saved the college from complete collapse, and he was consecrated there as titular bishop of Olens and coadjutor with right of succession to Bp. James Yorke Bramston of the London District (Oct. 28, 1833). Succeeding Bramston (July 11, 1836), he was the first modern bishop educated wholly in England and the first to introduce ecclesiastical dress for the clergy in place of lay clothes. Griffiths' views tended to be conservative. He did not believe in the possibility of large-scale conversions and distrusted converts from the OXFORD MOVEMENT. He represented the outlook of a Catholic Church that had long suffered under restrictive penal legislation. This outlook was soon dated by the restoration of the English hierarchy (1850). Griffiths was pious, humble, industrious, and capable as an administrator.

Bibliography: B. N. WARD, *The Sequel to Catholic Emancipation*, 2 v. (New York 1915); *The History of St. Edmund's College, Old Hall* (London 1893). T. COOPER, *The Dictionary of National Biography from the Earliest Times to 1900* (London 1885–1900) 8:690.

[B. WHELAN]

GRIGNION DE MONTFORT, LOUIS MARIE, ST.

Founder of the Missionaries of the Company of Mary (Montfort Fathers) and of the Daughters of Wisdom, influential Marian author; b. Montfort-la-Canne, France, Jan. 31, 1673; d. St. Laurent-sur-Sèvre (Vendée), April 28, 1716.

A childlike devotion to the Mother of God was characteristic of Montfort's life from the outset. At confirmation, he took the name of Mary and later dropped his family name, wishing to be called Louis Mary of Montfort. He studied with the Jesuits at Rennes and then at the Sorbonne and Saint-Sulpice. During these years, Montfort became familiar with the French school of spirituality and, as he himself declared, read nearly all of the books that treat devotion to Our Lady. He was ordained at Paris, June 5, 1700, and, in 1710, he was received as a tertiary in the Third Order of St. Dominic.

In the brief 16 years of his priesthood, Louis de Montfort fulfilled a career of founder, missionary, and writer. Two years after his ordination, Montfort organized the nursing and teaching congregation of the Daughters of WISDOM. In 1705, he founded his missionary congregation of men, the MONTFORT FATHERS. Having been named a missionary apostolic by Pope CLEMENT XI, Montfort spent the greater part of his priestly years as a traveling missionary, preaching retreats and missions throughout western France.

St. Louis Marie Grignion de Montfort, sculpture located inside St. Peter's Basilica, Rome.

Montfort was also the author of numerous works inspired by the needs of his apostolate. He composed more than 23,400 verses of hymns and wrote the rules for the two communities he founded. Among his other writings are *The Love of the Eternal Wisdom, The Secret of the Rosary*, and *The Secret of Mary.* However, Montfort's renown as an author and theologian is due primarily to one of his manuscripts, which was discovered in 1842 and called *The True Devotion to the Blessed Virgin Mary* by its first editors. The title is a misnomer, for the work is actually a fuller explanation of what Montfort calls *The Love of the Eternal Wisdom,* the greatest secret of achieving union with Christ, a tender devotion to Mary. He explains that the foundation for devotion to Mary is her role in the economy of salvation as mother and queen. That total consecration accompanies the formal and active recognition of the role that Mary plays in human lives, a recognition that entails the renewal of baptismal promises. Montfort advocates the surrender to Christ, through Mary, of the value of all good actions, past, present, and future, so that they may be used in any way God wishes. Following the authors of his times, he terms this consecration ''Holy Slavery of Love,'' a slavery devoid, of course, of pejorative connotations. PIUS XII sums up the praise of the Church for Montfort's doctrine when he describes it as ''burning, solid, and correct.''

Louis de Montfort is buried in the basilica dedicated to his honor at Saint-Laurent-sur-Sèvre. He was beatified in 1888 and canonized on July 20, 1947.

Feast: April 28.

Bibliography: J. GRANDET, *Vie de messire Louis-Marie Grignion de Montfort* (Nantes 1724). L. LE CROM, *Un Apôtre marial* (Tourcoing 1946). G. RIGAULT, *Saint Louis Marie Grignion de Montfort* (New York 1947). P. J. GAFFNEY, ''The Holy Slavery of Love,'' *Mariology,* ed. J. B. CAROL, 3 v. (Milwaukee 1954–61) 3:143–161. L.-M. CLÉNET, *Grignion de Montfort: le saint de la Vendée* (Paris 1988). L. PÉROUAS, *Grignion de Montfort et la Vendée* (Paris 1989). L. SANKALÉ, *Avec Marie, au pas de l'Esprit: Le secret de Marie de saint Louis-Marie Grignion de Montfort lu aujourd'hui en paroisse* (Paris 1991). B. GUITTENY, *Grignion de Montfort, missionnaire des pauvres* (Paris 1993). R. LAURENTIN, *Dieu seul est ma tendresse* (Paris 1996).

[P. GAFFNEY]

GRIJALVA, JUAN DE

Born in Colima, Mexico, date unknown; died in Mexico City, Nov. 4, 1638. Grijalva joined the Augustinians and made his religious profession on Nov. 5, 1595, at Guayangareo (now Morelia). Later, he studied at the University of Mexico, where he obtained his doctorate in 1612. Grijalva served in various offices in his order, including that of prior in each of the two principal monasteries in Mexico City, San Agustín and the Colegio San Pablo. In 1624, he published *Crónica de la Orden de N.P.S. Agustín en las provincias de la Nueva España en quatro edades desde el año de 1533 hasta el de 1592.* This work is the first published of the Augustinian chronicles and is of major importance for the 16th-century history of the order since the friars spread from New Spain to South America and the Philippines. Many of the sources upon which it was based are no longer extant; therefore, Grijalva's extensive quotations from other documents are especially important. The style is clear and the chronology unusually exact. The chronicle is divided into four books. The first treats the arrival of the first Augustinians in New Spain (1533) and the areas in which they worked; it also includes information on expeditions to the Far East. Mission methods are the topic of book two, which also tells of the *cocoliztli* epidemic among the Native Americans. Book three is primarily concerned with missions to the Philippines and China, though it also covers the founding of the Colegio de San Pablo in Mexico

City and mission work among the Tarascans. Book four contains Augustinian biographies. In general, the account is trustworthy. The original edition is very rare, but an edition published in Mexico City in 1924 is virtually a facsimile reproduction.

Bibliography: G. DE SANTIAGO VELA, *Ensayo de una biblioteca ibero-americana de la Orden de San Agustín*, 7 v. in 8 (Madrid 1913–31) 3:301–307; ''Historiadores de la provincia agustiniana de México,'' *Archivo histórico hispano-agustiniano* 9 (1918) 241–255.

[A. J. ENNIS]

GRILLPARZER, FRANZ

Austrian dramatist; b. Vienna, Jan. 15, 1791; d. there, Jan. 21, 1872. Grillparzer studied law at the University of Vienna, and during that time he wrote his first drama, *Blanka von Kastilien* (1807–09). He entered civil service (1813), advanced to the directorship of the imperial archives (1832), and was pensioned in 1856. Although many circumstances in Grillparzer's life (official displeasure over his historical plays, for example) gave reason for his persistent melancholy, much of Grillparzer's suffering was self-caused by his hypochondria and fear of involvement in life. *Die Ahnfrau* (1817), a fate tragedy, made Grillparzer famous, but his first great drama was *Sappho* (1818). Written in classical Goethean style, it states clearly the thesis that the poet must be ''uncommitted.'' Even in such ''thesis'' plays, however, Grillparzer was fascinated by psychological nuances. If this interest weakened his thesis, it helped shape him into a very modern poet; his plays mark the beginning of the psychological drama in Austria and fully support his reputation as one of the greatest of the Austrian playwrights.

Das goldene Vliess (1821), a powerful trilogy, treats a theme of which Grillparzer never tired—that man upsets not only his own inner equilibrium but that of his environment when he aspires to a status that is not his due. This anti-Faust, quietistic attitude is portrayed quite clearly in *Der Traum ein Leben* (1834). Two tragedies, *König Ottokars Glück und Ende* (1826) and *Ein treuer Diener seines Herrn* (1826), based on Austrian history, provoked governmental censorship. In *Des Meeres und der Liebe Wellen* (1831), a dramatization of the Hero and Leander love tragedy, Grillparzer's dramatic style reached its high point. *Weh dem, der lügt* (1838) was Grillparzer's only comedy. Its failure when produced caused him to withdraw from play-writing.

After his death, his three greatest works were found among his papers: *Libussa, Ein Bruderzwist in Habsburg,* and *Die Jüdin von Toledo. Bruderzwist* is a historical drama; in it Rudolf II (1552–1612) attempts to preserve

Franz Grillparzer.

the Habsburg Empire through highly conservative politics, a policy of inaction. The effect of his failure, telescoped magnificently in the fifth act, is the chaos of the Thirty Years' War. Grillparzer's best prose piece is *Der arme Spielmann* (1847).

Bibliography: *Historisch-kritische Gesamtausgabe,* ed. A. SAUER et al. (Vienna 1909–), 43 v. to date; *Sämtliche Werke: Ausgewählte Briefe, Gespräche, Berichte,* ed. P. FRANK and C. PÖRNBACHER, 4 v. (Munich 1960). Trans. A. BURKHARD of *Medea* (3d ed. Yarmouth Port, Mass. 1956); *King Ottocar: His Rise and Fall* (1962); and *Hero and Leander* (1962). J. NADLER, *Franz Grillparzer* (Vaduz 1948). A. BURKHARD, *Franz Grillparzer in England and America* (pa. New York 1961). C. D. BERND, ed., *Franz Grillparzer's ''Der arme spielmann''* (Camden East 1988). C. H. MUNSCHEN, *Franz Grillparzer* (Regensburg 1960). W. C. REEVE, *The Federfuchser and Penpusher from Lessing to Grillparzer: A Study Focused on Grillparzer's ''Ein Bruderzwist in Habsburg''* (Montreal 1995). I. F. ROE, *Franz Grillparzer: A Century of Criticism* (Camden East 1995). E. WAGNER, *An Analysis of Franz Grillparzer's Dramas: Fate, Guilt, and Tragedy* (Lewiston 1992).

[C. B. GIORDANO]

GRIMBALD, ST.

Monk, teacher under ALFRED THE GREAT; b. Thérouanne (Flanders), *c.* 820–830; d. Winchester, England, July 8, 901. Dedicated when seven years old in the nearby

Benedictine Abbey of SAINT-BERTIN, Grimbald was ordained deacon by 867 and priest *c.* 868 to 873; he was chosen prior there before going to England at King ALFRED's invitation. Arriving *c.* 886, he participated in the Alfredian revival as a devout Churchman, skillful musician, and royal tutor and mass-priest. Grimbald apparently declined the Archbishopric of Canterbury (889). He encouraged Edward the Elder to build New Minster, Winchester, which Alfred had planned. Although said to have been New Minster's first abbot, he died before its dedication and was buried there.

Feast: July 8.

Bibliography: W. HUNT, *The Dictionary of National Biography from the Earliest Times to 1900* (London 1885–1900) 8:695–697. P. GRIERSON, *English Historical Review* 55 (1940) 529–561.

[W. A. CHANEY]

GRIMSTON, RALPH, BL.

Martyr; also known as Ralph Grimstow; b. Nidd, Knaresborough, Yorkshire, England; d. June 15, 1598, hanged at York. Arrested with Fr. Peter SNOW with whom he was traveling to York about May 1, 1598. He was charged with felony for having aided a priest and having attempted to prevent Snow's apprehension. He was beatified by Pope John Paul II on Nov. 22, 1987 with George Haydock and Companions.

Feast of the English Martyrs: May 4 (England).

See Also: ENGLAND, SCOTLAND, AND WALES, MARTYRS OF.

Bibliography: R. CHALLONER, *Memoirs of Missionary Priests,* ed. J. H. POLLEN (rev. ed. London 1924). J. H. POLLEN, *Acts of English Martyrs* (London 1891).

[K. I. RABENSTEIN]

GRISAR, HARTMANN

Church historian; b. Coblenz on the Rhine, Sept. 22, 1845; d. Innsbruck, Austria, Feb. 25, 1932. At the completion of his early studies with the Christian Brothers in Coblenz, Grisar took courses in philosophy and theology at Munster under a renowned Bavarian neo-Thomist, Albert Stockl. Further theological study at the University of Innsbruck led to a doctorate in 1868. That year, Grisar was ordained and joined the Society of Jesus, beginning his Jesuit training in Rome. Returning to Austria after two years, he was appointed unexpectedly to the professorship of Church history at Innsbruck in 1871. At this point, Grisar dedicated himself to the serious study of Church history. His association with the University of Innsbruck continued until 1889. The lifelong influence of Von Rankean historiographical principles upon Grisar's prolific writings had already become evident in this early period of his career (*see* RANKE, LEOPOLD VON; HISTORICISM; HISTORIOGRAPHY, ECCLESIASTICAL). In 1877, Grisar became one of the founders of the *Zeitschrift für katholische Theologie;* and his occasional, lengthy visits to Rome produced several articles for the *Civiltá Cattolica.*

To encourage Grisar's special talents, his superiors relieved him of teaching duties at Innsbruck and transferred him to Rome, where he undertook historical and archeological research. The first fruit of this work was the *Analecta Romana* (Rome 1899), a collection of 15 studies on the early history of Rome. This was followed by his *Geschichte Roms und der Päpste in M.A.* (Freiburg im Breisgau 1901; Eng. tr. 1908), undertaken partly in criticism of the *Geschichte der Stadt Rom im Mittelalter* (1859–72) by Ferdinand Gregorovius. After the publication of the first volume of this classic history of Rome and the popes, Grisar's health forced him to return to Austria, leaving the completion of the work to others. At Innsbruck, he turned his attention to research on Martin Luther that produced *Luther* (3 v. Freiburg im Breisgau 1911–12; Eng. tr. 1913–14), *Lutherstudien* (6 v. Freiburg im Breisgau 1920–23), *Der deutsche Luther im Weltkreig und in der Gegenwart* (Freiburg im Breisgau 1924), and *Martin Luthers Leben und sein Werk* (Freiburg im Breisgau 1926; Eng. tr. 1930). Grisar's analysis of Luther is, by his own description, psychological rather than biographical in orientation. Though intended to be more objective and moderate in tone than previous Catholic studies such as that by Heinrich Seuse DENIFLE in 1903, it tends to emphasize negative qualities in Luther's personality. Contemporary Catholic appraisals of the Reformer appear more balanced than Grisar's without totally replacing it. Among his other works are the publication of addresses given at the Council of Trent by the Jesuit Diego Laínez, *Jacobi Lainez disputationes Tridentinae* (Rome 1886); *S. Gregorio Magno* (Rome 1904); *Das Missale im Licht der römischen Stadtgeschichte* (Freiburg im Breisgau 1925); *Marienblüten. Systematische Marienlehre aus dem grossen Marienwerk des Petrus Canisius* (Freiburg im Breisgau 1930).

Bibliography: An autobiography is found in *Die Religionswissenschaft der Gegenwart in Selbstdarstellungen* (Freiburg 1927) 37–56. Necrologies appear in F. S. BETTEN, *American Catholic Historical Review* 18 (1932) 229–232. *Zeitscrift für katholische Theologie* 56 (1932) 145–147. *La civiltaà cattolica* 1 (1932) 567–571. For the place of Grisar's study on Luther, see E. W. ZEEDEN, *Martin Luther und die Reformation im Urteil des deutschen Luthertums,* 2 v. (Freiburg 1950–52) v. 1, tr. R. M. BETHELL, *The*

Legacy of Luther (Westminster, Md. 1954). A. HERTE, *Das katholische Lutherbild im Bann der Lutherkommentare des Cochläus,* 3 v. (Münster 1943). J. GRISAR, *Lexikon für Theologie und Kirche*, ed. M. BUCHBERGER (Freiburg 1930–38) 4:707–708. R. BÄUMER, *Lexikon für Theologie und Kirche*, ed. J. HOFER and K. RAHNER, (Freiburg 1957–65) 4:1238. K. G. STECK, *Die Religion in Geschichte und Gegenwart* (Tübingen 1957–65) 2:1878–79. A. M. BOZZONE, *Dizionario ecclesiastico* 2:276–277.

[C. SEVILLA]

GRISSOLD, ROBERT, BL.

Lay martyr; also known as Robert Greswold or Griswold; b. at Rowington, Warwickshire, England; d. July 16, 1604, hanged at Warwick under James I. Grissold, who was in the service of Mr. Sheldon of Broadway, was attending Bl. John SUGAR, when they were arrested in his hometown on July 8, 1603. The two martyrs shared a year's captivity before Grissold was charged with refusing to attend church and for assisting Sugar, a seminary priest. He was beatified by Pope John Paul II on Nov. 22, 1987 with George Haydock and Companions.

Feast of the English Martyrs: May 4 (England).

See Also: ENGLAND, SCOTLAND, AND WALES, MARTYRS OF.

Bibliography: R. CHALLONER, *Memoirs of Missionary Priests,* ed. J. H. POLLEN (rev. ed. London 1924). J. H. POLLEN, *Acts of English Martyrs* (London 1891).

[K. I. RABENSTEIN]

GRIVOT, IRMA, ST.

In religion Marie Hermine de Jésus; martyr, religious superior of the Franciscan Missionaries of Mary; b. April 28, 1867, Beaume, France; d. July 9, 1900, Taiyüan, Shanxi, China. Irma, the daughter of a cooper, completed her elementary studies in 1883, then worked as a private tutor. Her parents did not support her religious vocation, perhaps because of her poor health. She joined the Franciscan Missionaries at Vanves near Paris (1894). Then she began her novitiate (July 1894) at Les Châtelets, near Saint Brieuc, where took the name Marie Hermine de Jésus. After making her first vows, she returned to Vanves to serve as bookkeeper. In Marseilles she received training as a nurse in preparation for her assignment to China in 1898. At the time of the Boxer Uprising, she was superior of the mission at Taiyüan. She surprised the bishop by insisting the sisters would rather die for Christ than seek safety. Her offered sacrifice was accepted by God. She and her religious sisters were beatified by Pope Pius XII, Nov. 24, 1946, and canonized, Oct. 1, 2000, by Pope John Paul II with Augustine Zhao Rong and companions.

Feast: July 4.

Bibliography: G. GOYAU, *Valiant women: Mother Mary of the Passion and the Franciscan Missionaries of Mary,* tr. G. TELFORD (London 1936). M. T. DE BLARER, *Les Bse Marie Hermine de Jésus et ses compagnes, franciscaines missionnaires de Marie, massacrées le 9 juillet 1900 à Tai-Yuan-Fou, Chine* (Paris 1947). L. M. BALCONI, *Le Martiri di Taiyuen* (Milan 1945). *Acta Apostolicae Sedis* 47 (Rome 1955) 381–388. L'Osservatore Romano, Eng. Ed. 40 (2000): 1–2, 10.

[K. I. RABENSTEIN]

GROENENDAEL, ABBEY OF

Augustinian monastery located five miles from Brussels in the forest of Soignes, founded in 1350 by two priests, Jan van RUYSBROECK, the Dutch mystic, and Francone de Coudenberg, as a priory of canons regular dependent on the abbey of SAINT-VICTOR of Paris. The site had been a hermitage since 1304, and the founders, after retiring from the collegiate church of St. Gudule in 1343, had lived there under the patronage of John III, Duke of Brabant. The first prior was Ruysbroeck, who held the office until his death in 1381. In 1412 the monastery joined the congregation of WINDESHEIM, remaining a simple priory. Its religious were famous as copyists and writers, and it had a rich library. In the disturbances of the 16th century it was sacked by the Calvinists, but restored by imperial authority. At the time of its suppression by the French revolutionists in 1796, it was in a state of decadence.

Bibliography: É. DE MOREAU, *Histoire de l'Église en Belgique* (Brussels 1945–) v. 3.

[C. FALK]

GROOTE, GERARD

Deacon, preacher of moral reform, author of ascetical and canonical treatises, father of the Devotio Moderna; b. Deventer, Netherlands, Oct. 1340; d. Deventer, Aug. 20, 1384.

Son of patrician parents, Groote took his master of arts degree at the University of Paris in 1358 and specialized further in Canon Law. He held prebends at St. Mary's Cathedral, Aix-la-Chapelle, and St. Martin's Cathedral, Utrecht. In 1374, Groote gave up most of his possessions, resigned his prebends, and withdrew to the Carthusian monastery of Monnikhuizen, near Arnhem, where he stayed more than two years as a guest. Longing for a moral reform of the Church, he left the monastery, became a deacon, and received permission to preach throughout the Diocese of Utrecht. Starting in early 1380,

Groote endeavored to revive the faith and morals of the laity, contributed to monastic reform, and insisted on stricter application of ecclesiastical laws against simony and clerical marriage. He attacked the latter most severely on the occasion of a synod at Utrecht in 1383. Although in large part successful, Groote experienced much opposition, particularly from the higher clergy, and was finally forbidden to preach. An appeal was made to Pope URBAN VI but, before receiving the answer, Groote died of the plague.

Groote attached great importance to apostolic poverty and common life, even when not sanctioned by vows. Changing his house into a hospice for pious women and giving them statutes, he founded the Sisters of the Common Life. Some of his disciples lived together at Deventer and Zwolle and organized themselves as BRETHREN OF THE COMMON LIFE. Groote's plan to establish a community of Canons Regular of St. Augustine, probably inspired by Jan van RUYSBROECK, was forestalled by his death. In 1386, Groote's disciples founded the monastery of WINDESHEIM, which became the center of a spiritual revival, known as DEVOTIO MODERNA.

Groote's spirituality is Christocentric (*Sermo de nativitate Domini; Sermo in die palmarum; Epistola de paciencia*). There is no evidence that Groote wrote the *IMITATION OF CHRIST*, but his ideas influenced its author. Deeply concerned about the WESTERN SCHISM, he stressed the invisible unity of the Church and desired a general council (*Epistola de scismate*). His *De matrimonio* lacks appreciation for marriage. The *De simonia ad beguttas, De locatione ecclesiarum,* and *Sermo contra focaristas* reveal the vehement temperament of the reformer.

Recent editions and studies of his writings include: *Gerardi Magni epistolae,* ed. W. Mulder (Tekstuitgaven van Ons Geestelijk Erf 3; Antwerp 1933); *Tractatus de quatuor generibus meditationum sive contemplationum of Sermo de nativitate Domini;* ed. A. Hyma, *Archief voor de Geschiedenis van het Aartsbisdom Utrecht,* 49 (1924) 296–326; *Geert Groote en het Huwelijk: Uitgave van zijn Tractaat De Matrimonio en Onderzoek naar de Bronnen,* ed. M. H. Mulders (Utrecht 1941); ''Geert Groote's Sermoen voor Palmzondag over de vrijwillige Armoede,'' ed. W. Moll, *Studiën en Bijdragen op het Gebied der historische Theologie* 2 (1872) 425–469; *De simonia ad beguttas: de Middelnederlandse Tekst,* ed. W. de Vreese (The Hague 1940); ''De locatione ecclesiarum,'' ed. J. Clarisse, *Archief voor kerkelijke Geschiedenis* (1937) 119–152; *Sermo magistri Gerardi Magni, dicti Groot, de focariis,* ed. T. A. and J. Clarisse, in article ''Over den Geest en Denkwijze van Geert Groote (Groot, de Groet), kenbaar uit zijne Schriften,'' *Archief voor kerkelijke Geschiedenis* (1829) 355–398, 2 (1830) 245–395 3 (1831); ''Bijlagen,'' 1–90, 8 (1837) 3–383.

Bibliography: K. C. L. M. DE BEER, *Studie over de spiritualiteit van Geert Groote* (Brussels 1938). J. G. J. TIECKE, *De Werken van Geert Groote* (Utrecht 1941). R. R. POST, ''De onderlinge Verhouding van de 4 oude *Vitae Gerardi Magni* en haar Betrouwbaarheid,'' *Studio catholica* 18 (1942) 313–336, 19 (1943) 9–20. T. P. VAN ZIJL, *Gerard Groote: Ascetic and Reformer, 1340–1384* (CUA Studies in Mediaeval Hist., NS 18; 1963). C. C. DE BRUIN, E. PERSOONS, A. G. WEILER, *Geert Grote en de Moderne Devotie* (Zutphen, Germany, 1984). E. F. JACOB, ''Gerard Groote and the Beginnings of the 'New Devotion' in the Low Countries,'' *Journal of Ecclesiastical History* 3 (1952) 40–57.

[T. P. VAN ZIJL]

GROSJEAN, PAUL

Jesuit, Bollandist, and Celtic scholar; b. Uccle, Belgium, May 26, 1900; d. Brussels, June 13, 1964. After brilliant studies at the College of St. Michael, Brussels, Grosjean entered the Society of Jesus (Sept. 23, 1917). He was selected by Hippolyte DELEHAYE for training as a Bollandist in 1921. Grosjean studied at Oxford under C. Plummer and E. A. Lowe, returned to Belgium for military service, and spent two years perfecting his knowledge of Celtic in Dublin. Ordained in 1932, he returned to the College of St. Michael, Brussels, for the rest of his career. He prepared the life of St. Benignus of Armagh for the November 4 volume of the *Acta Sanctorum* and published many unedited *vitae* of Celtic saints in the *Analecta Bollandiana* and the *Irish Texts* series. Grosjean had a gift for solving complicated problems of chronology and enigmas. He contributed numerous articles to the principal journals of history and philology. His studies on the problem of St. Patrick's life and works, the Celtic paschal controversy, the sources of Bede's *Ecclesiastical History,* the *Hisperica famina,* and the Roman Martyrology revealed a tireless and conscientious scholar with a flair for humanist Latin and great generosity in aiding other scholars. He served as chaplain to the Royal Union of St. Raphael and spiritual adviser to the officers of the Belgian Grand Quartier Général. Grosjean was a member of the British and Irish Academies and received a doctorate *honoris causa* from the National University of Dublin.

Bibliography: M. COENS, *Revue d'histoire ecclésiastique* 59 (1964) 1025–26; *Analecta Bollandiana* 82 (1964) 289–318, life and bibliog.

[F. X. MURPHY]

GROSOLI, GIOVANNI

Journalist, senator, Catholic lay leader; b. Carpi (Modena) Aug. 20, 1859; d. Assisi, Feb. 20, 1937. As a young man, after his studies and early religious and charitable activities in his city, he dedicated his life exclusively to the civic, religious, social, and political functions of the Catholic movement. He was among the developers and directors of the Catholic associations of the Romagna, and for several years the communal counselor for Ferrara. In 1902, Pope Leo XIII named him president of the Opera dei Congressi e Comitati Cattolici, which since 1875 had coordinated all public activity of Italian Catholics.

Because of his lively temperament and his origin in a region where social agitation was sharp and far-reaching, Grosoli wanted to bring a new, progressive spirit into the Opera to counteract the more conservative attitude of the group of Venetians who were in control. After the death of Leo XIII (1903), Grosoli's approach did not find favor with the new Pontiff who disbanded the Opera (1904). For the rest of Pius X's pontificate, Grosoli remained outside the Catholic movement, dedicating himself completely to journalism. He organized the Società Editrice Romana, which began and managed the leading Catholic dailies of that time, especially *Il corriere d'Italia* (Rome), *L'Italia* (Milan), and *L'Avvenire d'Italia* (Bologna). This last paper was edited by Cesare Algranati (''Rocca d'Adria''), the principal support of Grosoli during these years. In 1912 Pius X declared the papers under the Societá ''out of conformity with pontifical directives,'' a judgment reversed by the new Pope, Benedict XV, in 1914. In the meantime, however, Grosoli had spent virtually his entire inheritance to maintain the papers abandoned by the bishops.

In 1919, Grosoli was among the founders of the Italian Popular Party (the first political party of Italian Catholics). In 1920 he was its first representative in the Senate, but he abandoned the position in 1924 to found the Italian National Center, which was favorable to fascism. Among his reasons for joining the Fascist movement was his hope of saving the Bank of Rome and with it the Catholic dailies. When the National Center was dissolved following a clearcut reproof from the Holy See, Grosoli abandoned all activity, distributed his means to charitable organizations, and retired to Assisi where he lived his last years in Franciscan poverty. Before his death he destroyed his personal letters and documents.

[E. LUCATELLO]

GROSS, NIKOLAUS, BL.

Lay martyr, journalist; b. Sept. 30, 1898, Niederwenigern (now a suburb of Hattingen near Essen), Ruhr, Germany; d. Jan. 23, 1945, Plotzenzee Prison, Berlin, Germany. After completing his elementary education (1905–12), Nikolaus Gross, the son of a smith, worked in a sheet mill (1912–15) and intensively sought to further his education in his free time. As a coal miner (1915–20), he joined the Christian Miners' Union (1917), the Central Christian Party (Zentrum, 1918), then the Antonius Knappenverein (St. Anthony's Miners Association, 1919). From 1920, he held various union positions in the Ruhr, Schlesien, and Saxony, while acting as assistant editor for the *Bergknappe* (*The Miner*) and as its editor from 1922. On May 24, 1923, he married Elisabeth Koch with whom he had seven children (b. 1924–39).

Thereafter he was assistant editor (1927–29), then editor-in-chief (from 1929), of the Catholic Workers tabloid, the *Westdeutsche Arbeiterzeitung* (later called *Kettelerwacht*). He used his position with the *Kettelerwacht* to awaken the consciences of Christian workers to the evil of National Socialism. For this reason the newspaper was shut down in 1938. Nevertheless, Gross continued to publish pamphlets underground to rally opposition to Nazism. He was arrested by the Gestapo (Aug. 12, 1944) and interred at Ravensbrück concentration camp, then in Berlin's Tegel (from September 1944), where he was tortured. Gross was condemned to death by Roland Freisler on Jan. 15, 1945. Following his execution by hanging, his body was incinerated and its ashes scattered.

Nikolaus's cause for beatification was opened in 1997 in the Diocese of Essen. After the issuance of the decree of martyrdom (July 7, 2001), he was beatified by Pope John Paul II on Oct. 7, 2001.

Bibliography: J. ARETZ, ed., *Nikolaus Gross. Christ—Arbeiterführer—Widerstandskämpfer. Briefe aus dem Gefängnis* (Mainz 1993). V. BÜCKER, B. NADORF, M. POTTHOFF, *Wie sollen wir vor Gott und unserem Volk bestehen? Der politische und soziale Katholizismus im Ruhrgebiet 1927–1949*, (Münster 1999) *Christen an der Ruhr*, ed. A. POTHMANN and R. HAAS (Essen 1998), 200–220; *Martyrologium Germanicum des 20.Jahrhunderts*, ed. H. MOLL, (Cologne 2000), 165–169. B. HERMANS, ed., *Nikolaus Gross und die katholische Arbeiterbewegung in der NS-Zeit Begleitbuch zur Ausstellung des Bistums Essen in der Alten Synagoge* (Essen 1995) 16–25.

[K. I. RABENSTEIN]

GROSS, WILLIAM HICKLEY

Archbishop; b. Baltimore, Md., June 12, 1837; d. Baltimore, Nov. 14, 1898. Gross was the fourth of seven children born to hardware merchant and customs inspector James Gross and Rachel (Haslett) Gross. After attending St. Vincent de Paul parochial school in Baltimore, Gross studied at St. Charles College, Baltimore. Leaving school, he worked as a clerk in his father's store until 1857, when he became a Redemptorist novice. He made

William Hickley Gross.

his profession in 1858 and undertook philosophical and theological studies at the Redemptorist seminary in Annapolis, Md., where he was ordained on March 21, 1863. For a short time, Gross was chaplain at a nearby Civil War prison camp, after which (1863–71) he specialized as a pulpit orator preaching parish ''mission-revivals'' in the eastern U.S. His sympathy for the Confederate cause made him particularly successful in Georgia.

After two years as rector of the Redemptorist Mission Church in Boston, Mass., Gross was named bishop of Savannah, Ga., and was consecrated in Baltimore on April 27, 1873. His diocese contained only 12 priests, and its 20,000 Catholics constituted less than two per cent of Georgia's postwar population. In his episcopate, the progress of Catholicism was not spectacular. However, a new cathedral was erected in Savannah, a combination college and seminary was established in Macon, and the number of Catholics increased by 25 per cent. Gross was an active participant in the Third Plenary Council of Baltimore in 1884, where he contributed to the discussions on the African American apostolate, seminary curriculum, and irremovable pastors. He later supported Cardinal James Gibbons and the ''progressive wing'' of the American hierarchy on such topics as parochial schools, the rights of labor, the problems of immigrants, the Native American apostolate, and the Catholic attitude toward nativist groups.

In February 1885, Gross became the first native American prelate in the Far West when he was appointed archbishop of Portland, Ore. Included in his province were Oregon, Washington, Idaho, Montana, Alaska, and British Columbia. Oregon's 30,000 Catholics were only eight per cent of the state's population, and Gross continued to be a missionary bishop. Special concern for Catholic education, the care of orphans, and the needs of the Native American missions marked his thirteen-year episcopate in Oregon. His successful appeals to religious orders led to the establishment of new parishes and schools. The Benedictines and the Christian Brothers opened two colleges and a seminary, and Gross himself founded the Sisters of St. Mary of Oregon.

Bibliography: J. J. O'CONNELL, *Catholicity in the Carolinas and Georgia 1820–1878* (New York 1879).

[A. H. SKEABECK]

GROSSETESTE, PSEUDO-

A designation for the author(s) of the many spurious writings (more than 65) attributed to ROBERT GROSSETESTE. Of these works only two, both included in L. Baur's *Die philosophischen Werke des Robert Grosseteste* [*Beiträge zur Geschichte der Philosophie und Theologie des Mittelalters* 9 (1912)], are discussed in this article, viz, the *Tractatus de anima* (242–274) and the *Summa philosophiae* (275–643).

Tractatus de anima. This is not a complete treatise, but a series of questions on the nature and powers of the soul. In the only known MS (Oxford, Bodleian Library, Digby 104) it is ascribed in a later hand to ''Blessed Robert Grosseteste, Bishop of Lincoln,'' but this ascription cannot be maintained. Internal and external evidence led its editor to regard it as ''of very doubtful authenticity'' (Prolegomena, 113–120). Later research has conclusively shown that this treatise is a mere borrowing from the *Summa de Bono* (1230–36) of PHILIP THE CHANCELLOR, sometimes literal, sometimes free, with many abbreviations, omissions, and transpositions. Hence neither the assertion that it is ''one of Grosseteste's earliest works, written at Paris *c.* 1208–10,'' nor the conjecture that it is a *reportatio* (a student's notes) of Philip's lectures made by Grosseteste while studying at Paris is tenable. Its date is after 1230. Doctrinal considerations also militate against Grosseteste's authorship.

Summa philosophiae. The question of authorship of this work is still unsolved. Bartholomew of Bologna, ROGER BACON, and ROBERT KILWARDBY have unsuccessfully been proposed. Since many features of the *Summa* seem to indicate an Oxford setting about 1260 to 1270, Bartholomew, suggested by M. Grabmann, is ruled out. Again, although many affinities with some of Bacon's theories are traceable in the *Summa,* they are insufficient to establish his authorship. Further, the praise of ALEXANDER OF HALES and the unmistakable admiration for ALBERT THE GREAT, whom the author quotes with deference even when disagreeing with his views, contrast strikingly with Bacon's genuine works. The conjecture that St. THOMAS AQUINAS wrote the *De ente et essentia* against Kilwardby's *De ortu scientiarum* and that the *Summa* is Kilwardby's riposte to confute *De ente et essentia* and to defend his *De Ortu* [M. Chossat, *Archives de philosophie* 9 (1932) 480] is most unlikely. Two things are certain; that it is not Grosseteste's and that its author is unknown. But whoever the author, the *Summa* ''expresses with remarkable clarity the reaction of a representative of the early Oxonian tradition against the novelties introduced into theology by St. Thomas Aquinas'' (É. H. Gilson, *Les Arts du Beau*, 274). The *Summa* is a systematic and impressive restatement of the main theses of the old school: there is the *binarium famosissimum* (universal hylomorphism and plurality of forms), the soul united to the body by natural inclination rather than by its essence, Intelligences differing individually and not specifically, Platonic Ideas, knowledge by remembrance of innate ideas, denial of distinction of essence and existence, and the rest. The author's estimate of Plato and Aristotle is well balanced: whereas Plato is in many respects superior to Aristotle, Aristotle exceedingly surpasses him in scholarship and is more reliable in philosophy.

Bibliography: *Tractatus de Anima.* S. H. THOMSON, *The Writings of Robert Grosseteste* (Cambridge, Eng. 1940); ''The *De Anima* of R. G.,'' *The New Scholasticism* 7 (1933) 201–202. L. W. KEELER, ''The Dependence of R. G.'s *De Anima* on the *Summa* of Philip the Chancellor,'' *ibid.* 11 (1937) 197–219. D. A. CALLUS, ''Philip the Chancellor and the *De Anima* ascribed to R. G.,'' *Mediaeval and Renaissance Studies* 1 (1941) 105–127; *Recherches de théologie ancienne et médiévale* 13 (1946) 225–229. E. BETTONI, ''Intorno all'autenticità del *De Anima* attribuito a R. G.,'' *Pier Lombardo* 5 (1961) 3–27. *Summa philosophiae.* É. H. GILSON, *History of Christian Philosophy in the Middle Ages* (New York 1955) 265–274, very good. C. K. MCKEON, *A Study of the Summa Philosophiae of the Pseudo-Grosseteste* (New York 1948). E. BETTONI, ''La Dottrina platonica delle idee nella interpretazione dell'autore della S.P.,'' *Mélanges Olgiati* (Milan n.d.) 1–24.

[D. A. CALLUS]

GROTE, FEDERICO

German Redemptorist leader in Catholic social action in Argentina; b. Munster, Wesphalia, July 16, 1853; d. Buenos Aires, April 30, 1940. Grote studied the humanities at the Gymnasium Paulinum and entered the Congregation of the Most Holy Redeemer at the age of 17. As a result of the KULTURKAMPF, he was exiled in 1873, lost his German citizenship, and participated in the Catholic socialist movement. In Luxembourg, he studied philosophy and theology and was ordained in 1877–78. Grote was sent to Ecuador as a missionary in 1879. When transferred to Buenos Aires in 1884, he arrived at a grave time for the Church. Grote joined with José Manuel Estrada, Pedro Goyena, and Emilio Lamarca, outstanding leaders of the Catholic Action movement. To help in this militant work, Grote founded the Convent of San Alfonso in Salta. He went out on missions all over the country, spreading the Argentine Catholic social movement. Grote founded Vincentian conferences in the interior and Catholic workers' groups in Buenos Aires. He gave conferences, organized pilgrimages and workers congresses, and fostered insurance organizations. Grote epitomized the first confrontation of modern social problems by the Argentine Church. With the assistance of Bp. Gregorio Ignacio Romero, he prepared a proposal for Argentine labor legislation. Grote attended the dedication of the statue ''Christ of the Andes'' and on that occasion gave an invocation in Santiago de Chile. In this invocation, he stressed the idea that peace between the two republics was essentially peace between the workers. He founded the Catholic daily *El Pueblo* (1900), the Christian Democratic League, the weekly *Justicia Social* (1907), and El Ahorro, a credit union for all Catholic workers' organizations in the country.

Bibliography: A. SANCHEZ GAMARRA, *Vida del padre Grote, redentorista: Apóstol social cristiano en hispanoamérica* (Madrid 1949).

[V. O. CUTOLO]

GROTIUS, HUGO

Jurist, statesman, humanist, known as the father of international law; b. Delft, Holland, Oct. 10, 1583; d. Rostock, Germany, Aug. 28, 1645. Born into a respectable burgher family, Grotius (Huigh de Groot) was considered a child prodigy. While a boy, he gained international fame for skillful compositions of Latin poetry and was accomplished in the use of Greek and Hebrew. At 15, Grotius had completed not only his studies in jurisprudence at the University of Leiden but also mastery of philosophy, theology, history, and belles lettres.

Career. Grotius began legal practice in 1599 as an advocate at The Hague. In 1604, before the Prize Court of the Dutch Admiralty, he successfully proved the right of a ship commander of the Great United Company of the East Indies to take as a lawful prize the ship and cargo of Portuguese who were harassing Dutch trade in the East Indies. On the basis of this litigation. he wrote his *De iure praedae commentarius* (Commentary on the Law of Prize) in which he developed his initial system of the law of nations. The manuscript remained unpublished until after its accidental discovery in 1868, except for a portion developing the doctrine of freedom of the high seas that was published in 1609 under the title of *Mare liberum.* In 1607, Grotius became attorney general of Holland and, in 1615, he became first magistrate of Rotterdam. The Dutch phase of his career then ended abruptly during the religious strife between the moderate, liberal Calvinists (Arminians), to whom he belonged, and the uncompromising, conservative Calvinists (Gomarians). Grotius was profoundly disturbed by the continuing divisions in Calvinism and strove sincerely for unity among all Christians. In 1619, under Prince Maurice of Orange, Grotius was condemned to life imprisonment. He escaped in 1621 and remained in exile virtually all of his remaining life. In 1625, while in France, he completed his monumental work *De iure belli ac pacis libri tres* (On the Law of War and Peace), which was an immediate success. From 1635 to 1645, he served as the Swedish ambassador to the French court.

Although the hostility of his countrymen was aroused chiefly because of his theological writings, it was Grotius's work in jurisprudence that earned him lasting fame. He wrote several books on Dutch law and history. *De iure belli ac pacis* was the first concise and systematic treatise on international law, although already formed in nucleus in the earlier *De iure praedae.* His political theory and legal system did not represent a break but rather the continuance and summation of ideas that had their origin in the writings of Aristotle and the Stoics and came through the medieval school to the modern age. In particular, Grotius was aware of and in accord with the ideas on the law of nature and the law of nations developed shortly before him by the Spanish theologians, among them Francisco de VITORIA (*c.* 1480–1546) and Francisco SUÁREZ (1548–1617), to whose works he referred.

Natural Law Theory. Grotius held the primary bond between men to be their common rational and social nature. The principles of the latter are known to every mature man and form the basic law governing human relations in all phases, namely, the NATURAL LAW. This law is in conformity with the divine law, although it exists of itself and can be known without revelation. Indeed, Grotius held that it would be the same even if, *per impossibile,* there were no God, thus admitting for subsequent development a principle that, by reducing reason to nature, radically transformed the concept of natural law. In the theory of Grotius, the natural law is a real law, enforceable by men in case of infringement by a wrongdoer. It consists in the first place of certain strict commands and prohibitions. These are self-evident, or can be arrived at by conclusions from self-evident principles. However, principles of the law of nature can also be arrived at in another way, ''in concluding, if not with absolute assurance, at least with every probability, that that is according to the law of nature which is believed to be such among all nations, or among all those that are more advanced in civilization'' (*De iure belli* 1.1.12.42). Acceptance of the broad consensus on principles of right and justice is thus the second method of determining the law of nature.

But the law of nature is not the only law valid in human communities. It can be supplemented by volitional laws, established by the lawgiver within states based on the consent of the governed, or by custom observed as binding among nations: ''For whatever cannot be deduced from certain principles by a sure process of reasoning, and yet is clearly observed everywhere, must have its origin in the free will of man'' (*ibid.*). Thus, according to Grotius, nations are subject in their mutual relations to two laws, the basic law of nature and the supplementary, customary law of nations. It is noteworthy that this distinction was made also by Suárez (*De Legibus ac Deo Legislatore* 2.19).

As real laws, both the law of nature and the law of nations have their outward sanction in force. The use of force is morally permissible in order to vindicate or defend one's rights, or to punish a wrongdoer. Its ultimate form is WAR, which can be waged when there are no authorities or courts above the wrongdoing and suffering parties. Grotius recognized in substance the scholastic doctrine of the just war (*see* WAR, MORALITY OF). Every legal right can eventually form a just cause for war. The bulk of his treatise is the quest for these various rights of nations culminating in a system of the law of nations.

As an observant lawyer and practicing statesman, Grotius had to admit that there exist customs among nations that are not necessarily in conformity with the law of nature. Specifically, wars are not always fought for just causes only. He admitted that inevitable ignorance on the part of statesmen sometimes makes recognition of just causes impossible. Similarly, Vitoria had recognized the *ignorantia invincibilis.* However, Grotius admitted that wars fought between sovereign nations are legal and produce lawful consequences because the customs of nations—sometimes contrary to the law of nature—consider them as such. Thus, he made the important distinction between the ''just war'' and the ''legal, formal, public war.'' According to Grotius, it is a lesser evil to admit the legality of war and to grant legal status to both belligerents when the latter are sovereign nations. The belligerents and third states thus can be subordinated to strict rules of war and neutrality, which is better than to leave application of force without any check. Nations, while entitled to use force, must observe the agreed upon limitations and should introduce certain *temperamenta* or mitigations to avoid unnecessary suffering. It is out of these that subsequent developments produced the body of humanitarian rules applicable to belligerents.

The deemphasis of the necessary agreement that must exist between the law of nature and the law of nations and the emphasis on the voluntaristic principle of the consent of nations that Grotius introduced in his justification for the so-called ''legal, formal, public or lawful war,'' where both belligerent parties are legally equal and lawfully employing force, was slowly taken over into all fields of international law. It was not Grotius's intent that this should be so, but nevertheless his teachings became a source of the later development of the positivist conception of international law. In this view, the consent of nations became the highest criterion and basis of all legal obligations. The criterion of the rational and social nature of man, on which Grotius based his legal system, was slowly lost to sight.

See Also: NATURAL LAW IN POLITICAL THOUGHT.

Bibliography: J. TER MEULEN and P. J. J. DIERMANSE, *Bibliographie des écrits imprimés de Hugo Grotius* (The Hague 1950). H. BASDEVANT, ''Hugo Grotius,'' *Les Fondateurs du droit international* (Paris 1904). A. H. CHROUST, ''Hugo Grotius and the Scholastic Natural Law Tradition,'' *The New Scholasticism* 17 (1943) 101–133. J. KOSTERS, ''Les Fondaments du droit des gens,'' *Bibliotheca Visseriana* 4 (1925). R. FRUIN, ''An Unpublished Work of Hugo Grotius,'' *ibid.* 5 (1925). W. S. M. KNIGHT, *The Life and Work of Hugo Grotius* (London 1925). H. LAUTERPACHT, ''The Grotian Tradition in International Law,'' *British Yearbook of International Law* 23 (1946). P. P. REMEC, *The Position of the Individual in International Law according to Grotius and Vattel* (The Hague 1960).

[P. P. REMEC]

GROTTAFERRATA, MONASTERY OF

A famous abbey about 12 miles southeast of Rome, Italy, an abbey *nullius* since 1939, it has long been a center for Greek Catholic BASILIAN monks in the West.

Early History. It was founded near the site of ancient Tusculum by NILUS OF ROSSANO on the ruins, still visible, of a Roman villa, and near a 5th-century chapel. Work on it progressed under Abbots Paul, Cyril, and Bartholomew the Younger (d. 1055). The last-named finished the construction of the church dedicated to Our Lady in the romanesque style with a narthex and atrium, and Pope JOHN XIX consecrated it on Dec. 17, 1024. Through the centuries the building underwent various alterations that changed its original appearance. The interior was remodeled in 1754 in the baroque style, a far from happy choice, by Cardinal Bernardo Gaetano GUADAGNI, to whom the abbey had been given in COMMENDATION, but in 1930 the exterior was restored to its original design. At the entrance of the church there is a portal with excellent bas-reliefs and a mosaic on the tympanum depicting the *Deësis,* both dating from the 11th century. Within there are lovely mosaics, such as that of Pentecost, from the 12th and 13th centuries, and paintings, such as that of the Trinity, dating from the 13th century, found on the triumphal arch. The icon of the Madonna, dating from the 12th century, is exhibited in a splendid marble shrine by BERNINI. The church is flanked by a small building from the Roman period in the *opus quadratum* style, employed as a Christian chapel in the 5th century, with windows that have double bars, and this accounts for the name *Crypta ferrata* given to the monastery and also to the town. The chapel of SS. Nilus and Bartholomew, built in 1131 by Abbot Nicholas II and restored and enlarged in 1610 by Cardinal Odoardo Farnese (d. 1626), is covered with frescoes by Domenichino (d. 1641). Other important work was done on the church and monastery under the patronage of the commendatory Cardinals Alessandro Farnese (d. 1589), Francesco Barberini (d. 1679), and F. Colonna. In particular, Giuliano della Rovere, later Pope JULIUS II, had the abbey palace built between 1485 and 1490 and fortified the monastery by surrounding it with a moat and towers.

Spiritual and Intellectual Life. Originally, the community of Grottaferrata, composed of about 60 members, was organized to observe Byzantine monastic discipline, and was noticeably influenced by the development of STUDION at Constantinople. The records of the first centuries of its existence reveal an intense ascetic and cultural activity and record the growth of its holdings and of the privileges conferred on it by princes and popes. Among the latter was CALLISTUS II, who exempted the monastery from the jurisdiction of the Tusculan bishop. In its monastic SCRIPTORIUM a group of highly skilled copyists worked on a sizable number of codices, many of which are still preserved *in situ* or in other libraries. Outstanding monks such as Arsenius (fl. 11th century), Luke (fl. 12th century), Sophronius (fl. 12th century), and in particular Bartholomew the Younger, successfully pursued HAGIOGRAPHY and Byzantine HYMNOLOGY. The monastery's vast land holdings made it possible to reclaim some of the wooded and boggy region nearby. A period of decline ensued as a result of the baronial rivalries of COLONNA and ORSINI and coincided with the transfer of the popes to Avignon (*see* AVIGNON PAPACY) and with the WESTERN SCHISM. From 1462 to 1824 the monastery was under abbots who held the abbey in commendation, all but one of whom were CARDINALS. The first of this series was BESSARION, who fostered a return to earlier ascetic and ritual observances and a renewed interest in studies; but because a compact internal organization was lacking, no lasting effects were noted. This need was supplied in part by the Basilian monastic reform in Italy brought about by GREGORY XIII in 1579; the order accorded Grottaferrata first place in the Roman-Neapolitan province, at the same time establishing a novitiate at the abbey. Another consequence of the reform was the revival in 1608 of the post of claustral abbot, which allowed the restoration of the internal organization, thus creating the atmosphere essential to a reflourishing of the religious virtues and a renewed interest in intellectual pursuits.

The Modern Period. The Napoleonic era, during which the community was dispersed, was followed by a slow revival that became more pronounced after LEO XIII; at the request of the monks, Leo decreed in 1881 through the Congregation for the PROPAGATION OF THE FAITH the Byzantine character of the monastery. In 1904 the 9th centenary of the founding of Grottaferrata was celebrated with religious and cultural events and programs that created widespread interest. In 1929 the Latin parish was separated from the Greek parish [*Acta Apostolicae Sedis* 22 (1930) 134–37] and finally in 1937 PIUS XI gave the abbey definitive juridical status, creating it an *abbatia nullius,* or an exarchal monastery [*Acta Apostolicae Sedis* 30 (1938) 183–86]. The monastery was granted a pontifical seminary, erected in 1918 by BENEDICT XV for priests of the ITALO-ALBANIAN CATHOLIC CHURCH [*Acta Apostolicae Sedis* 10 (1918) 419].

The abbey possesses also a specialized library with a valuable collection of Greek codices and a museum with ancient, medieval, and Renaissance works of art, pagan and Christian inscriptions, publications, and coins. Since 1909 it has had its own print shop, which publishes numerous Greek and Slavic liturgical books, and a laboratory for the restoration of old books. Grottaferrata has as dependencies a monastery in Calabria, two in Sicily, and an office in Rome, which serves also as a student center. Two mission houses formerly maintained by the abbey in Albania were closed by the Communist regime in 1945.

Bibliography: A. ROCCHI, *De coenobio cryptoferratensi eiusque bibliotheca . . . commentarii* (Tusculum 1893); *La badia di Grottaferrata* (2d ed. Rome 1904). T. MINISCI, *Santa Maria di Grottaferrata: La chiesa e il monastero* (Grottaferrata 1955). S. KAMBO, *I castelli romani: Grottaferrata e Monte Cavo* (Bergamo 1922). C. CECCHELLI, *L'etimasia criptoferratense* (Rome 1946). H. LECLERCQ, *Dictionnaire d'archéologie chrétienne et de liturgie*, ed. F. CABROL, H. LECLERCQ, and H. I. MARROU, 15 v. (Paris 1907–53) 6.2:1831–42. E. GUAITA BORGHESE, A. MERCATI and A. PELZER, *Dizionario ecclesiastico*, 3 v. (Turin 1954–58) 2:278–79. G. PENCO, *Storia del monachesimo in Italia* (Rome 1961), *passim.*

[M. PETTA]

GROU, JEAN NICOLAS

Jesuit spiritual writer; b. Calais, France, Nov. 23, 1731; d. Lulworth Castle, England, Dec. 13, 1803. He entered the Society of Jesus in November of 1746 and taught humanities at the College of La Flèche from 1751 to 1755. After the suppression of the Jesuits in France, he moved to Lorraine, first to the novitiate house in Nancy and then to the University of Pont-à-Mousson, where he was professor of Greek for two years. During this time he was particularly interested in the study of Plato and Cicero, and produced several important translations of Plato, the *République* (2 v. Paris 1762), the *Lois* (2 v. Paris 1769), and the *Dialogues* (2 v. Amsterdam 1770). With the suppression of the Society in Lorraine in 1766, he returned to Paris and directed a convent of nuns as a secular priest.

After 1770 he turned to the writing of spiritual treatises, for which he is best remembered. His first works were *Caractères de la vraie dévotion* (Paris 1778), *Morale tirée des Confessions de s. Augustin* (2 v. Paris 1786), and *Maximes spirituelles avec des explications* (Paris 1789). Because of the French Revolution, he went to England (1792), where he enjoyed the hospitality of the Thomas Weld family at Lulworth Castle, and remained there the rest of his life. The *Méditations en forme de retraite sur l'amour de Dieu* (London 1796) provoked accusations of QUIETISM. Grou denied the charge but sought for more precise expression in preparing his next work, *L'intérieur de Jésus et de Marie* (2 v. Paris 1815). Along with some other Jesuits who sought to reconstitute the society in England, Grou was able to renew his profession shortly before his death.

Grou's spirituality is reminiscent of that of Pierre de BÉRULLE and was strongly influenced by the teaching of Jean Joseph SURIN. While suspicious of the manifestations and jargon of mysticism, he stressed the idea of pure love of God, untainted by self-love. His teaching on the virtue of hope needs to be properly qualified. Among the voluminous manuscripts left after his death, a number have been subsequently edited and published, including *Le chrétien sanctifié par l'oraison dominicale* (Paris 1832); *Manuel des âmes intérieures* (Paris 1883), perhaps his best known work; *L'école de Jésus-Christ* (2 v. Paris 1885); *Retraite sur les qualités et les devoirs du chrétien* (Paris 1913); and *Retraite spirituelle sur la connaissance et l'amour de Jésus-Christ* (Paris 1920). Very widely read, Grou's works have gone through numerous editions and have been translated into English, German, Italian, Spanish, Flemish, and Polish.

Bibliography: A. A. CADRÈS, *Le Père Jean-Nicolas Grou* (2d ed. Paris 1866). P. POURRAT, *Christian Spirituality,* tr. W. H. MITCHELL et al., 4 v. (Westminster, MD 1922–55) 4:278–284. P. BERNARD, in *Dictionnaire de théologie catholique,* ed. A. VACANT et al., 15 v. (Paris 1903–50; Tables générales 1951–) 6.2:1888–90. E. QUÉLENNEC, *Catholicisme. Hier, aujourd'hui et demain,* ed. G. JACQUEMET (Paris 1947–) 5:313–314. C. SOMMERVOGEL, et al., *Bibliothèque de la Compagnie de Jésus,* 11 v. (Brussels-Paris 1890–1932 v. 12, supplement 1960) 3:1868–82. H. HURTER, *Nomenclator literarius theologiae catholicae,* 5 v. in 6 (3d ed. Innsbruck 1903–13) ; v. 1 (4th edition 1926) 5.1:830.

[J. C. WILLKE]

GRUEBER, JOHANNES

Jesuit missionary to China and explorer; b. Linz (Austria), Oct. 28, 1623; d. Sárospatak, Hungary, Sept. 30, 1680. He entered the Society of Jesus in 1641 and was sent to China in 1656. There, his knowledge of mathematics brought Grueber to the court in Beijing as an assistant to Father Johann Adam SCHALL VON BELL. In 1661, Grueber was commissioned to go to Rome to explain the extent to which Schall's scientific work as chief of the Bureau of Mathematics and Astronomy involved his cooperating with superstitious attitudes of the Chinese. Since the Dutch were blockading Macau, Grueber boldly set out overland from West China through Kokonor, Tibet, and Nepal to India. His companion on the journey, the Belgian Jesuit Albert D'Orville, died at Agra from the rigors of the trip. News that Grueber had traversed Tibet and the mountain passes of the Himalayas caused a sensation in Europe and gave rise to hopes for an all-land route to the Orient. However, Grueber's accounts of Lhasa and the Himalayas seem to have been quite colorless, and his reports concerning the work and manner of life of Schall were considered severe and unsympathetic. In 1664, Grueber tried without success to return overland to China through Russia. It is known that Grueber took sick and returned to Florence, but his later life is clouded in obscurity.

Bibliography: C. WESSELS, *Early Jesuit Travellers in Central Asia* (The Hague 1924) 164–204. L. PFISTER, *Notices biographiques et biographiques sur les Jésuites de l'ancienne mission de Chine 1552–1773* (Shanghai 1932–34) 1:319–322.

[J. H. CAMPANA]

GRUENTHANER, MICHAEL

Scripture scholar; b. Buffalo, N.Y., Oct. 1, 1887; d. St. Marys, Kans., Sept. 14, 1962. Born of German emigrant parents, Gruenthaner completed his elementary and secondary schooling in Buffalo; he entered the Society of Jesus on Aug. 31, 1905, and was ordained on June 27, 1920. He pursued graduate studies in Sacred Scripture at the Pontifical Biblical Institute in Rome, where he earned the doctorate in Sacred Scripture (1928), becoming one of the first Americans to hold this degree.

Gruenthaner's Biblical career coincided with the exciting years of great advancement of Catholic Biblical studies, and his pioneering work contributed much to this movement in the United States. He taught Sacred Scripture and allied subjects at St. Mary's College, St. Marys, Kans. (1931–61), The Catholic University of America (1941–51), and St. Mary's College, South Bend, Ind. (1943–56), where he served also as chancellor of the Graduate School of Sacred Theology for Laywomen. He was one of the founders of the Catholic Biblical Association of America; he served as the second editor (1941–51) of *The Catholic Biblical Quarterly,* to which he contributed many scholarly articles, especially on the Book of Daniel. His diligence, skill, and faith in the competence of his colleagues not only assured this journal's survival, but also raised it to its present recognized status. Gruenthaner died 17 days before his 75th birthday, which was marked by the appearance of a testimonial volume in his honor: *The Bible in Current Catholic Thought.*

Bibliography: F. A. PETRU, *The Bible in Current Catholic Thought,* ed. J. L. MCKENZIE (New York 1962) 1–6. R. NORTH, ''A Frontier Jerome: Gruenthaner,'' *American Ecclesiastical Review* 148 (1963) 289–302; 398–411; 149 (1963) 41–50. F. S. ROSSITER, *The Catholic Biblical Quarterly* 24 (1962) 432–434.

[F. A. PETRU]

GRUNDTVIG, NIKOLAI FREDERIK SEVERIN

Danish writer and theologian whose ideas of education resulted in the folk high school movement; b. Udby, near Vordingborg, Sealand, Sept. 8, 1783; d. Copenhagen, Sept. 2, 1872. His forefathers for generations had been civil servants and clergymen of the Danish State Church, and his father was rector of Udby. Grundtvig won his degree in theology in 1803 but did not take orders immediately, as he was, according to himself, ''without spirit and without faith.'' After a few years as a private tutor, he engaged in studies of Scandinavian mythology and history. *Nordens Mytologi* (1808, Scandinavian Mythology) was a result of this interest, as are his translations of Saxo Grammaticus and Snorri Sturluson. In 1820 he published his translation of *Beowulf,* and in the following years devoted much of his energy to the study of Old English literature. Ordained in 1811, he was for a few years curate to his father, and then briefly rector of Praestø, Sealand.

For the rest of his life Grundtvig lived in Copenhagen, studying and producing an almost endless series of pamphlets and articles on Christianity, history, education, nationalism, and politics. His fearless writings brought him into conflict with ecclesiastical authorities, and he was for some years under censure. In his theology he opposed the Lutheran neorationalism and stressed the importance of the sacraments of baptism and communion. His teaching (known as Grundtvigianism) has had many followers and is still a force in the established church. Related to his pastoral work as minister to an independent congregation in Copenhagen (1839–72) are his *c.* 1,400 hymns, of which 270 can be found in the hymnal of the State Church (the most important contribution by one author). In *Salme-og bønnebog,* the hymnal of the Roman Catholic Diocese of Copenhagen, 27 of Grundtvig's hymns are included. A great number of Danish versions of medieval Latin hymns and sequences are notable. He was, however, an ardent patriot; he emphasized the importance of Danish literature and history over Latin and other traditional academic disciplines in his plans for the folk high schools, which he conceived as schools of "the living word." A church in Copenhagen is dedicated to his memory.

Bibliography: N. F. S. GRUNDTVIG, *Værker i udvalg* (Copenhagen 1940–49). F. V. RØNNING, *N. F. S. Grundtvig,* 4 v. (Copenhagen 1907–14). C. S. PETERSEN and V. ANDERSEN, *Illustreret dansk litteraturhistorie,* 4 v. (Copenhagen 1924–34) 3:141–217, 4:853–855 (references). S. JOHANSEN, *Bibliografi over N. F. S. Grundtvigs skrifter,* 4 v. (Copenhagen 1948–54). H. KOCH, *Grundtvig,* tr. L. JONES (Yellow Springs, Ohio 1952).

[H. BEKKER-NIELSEN]

GRÜNEWALD, MATTHIAS (MATHIS GOTHART NITHART)

A great German religious painter whose works are marked by deep emotional content; b. Würzburg, 1455–80; d. Halle, August 1528. Grünewald spent most of his life in the upper Rhine area and received commissions mainly from the archbishop of Mainz, the Dominicans in Frankfurt, the Antonites at Isenheim, and the cardinal Albrecht of Brandenburg. At the time of his death, he was siding secretly with the Reformation.

The "Portrait of a Young Artist" (*c.* 1495; Art Institute, Chicago), considered by some as an early work of Grünewald, shows affinities with the style of Master WB. With the "Mocking of Christ" (*c.* 1504; Pinakothek, Munich) and his various Crucifixions, Grünewald manifests the intensity of his own style. Fascinated by the subject of the Crucifixion and inspired by the *Revelations* of St. BRIDGET OF SWEDEN, Grünewald created masterpieces that document the spirit of his time. His greatest work, the Isenheim Altarpiece, a polyptych, was commissioned by Guido Guersi, preceptor of the Antonites at Isenheim (1512–17; Unterlindenmuseum, Colmar). It consists of nine painted panels showing the Annunciation, Nativity, Crucifixion, Lamentation, and Resurrection, and scenes from the life of St. Anthony. The Crucifixion is a unique and deeply moving creation that combines horror and mystical elevation. The Resurrection, with its etherealized Christ, probably expresses the concepts of the SPIRITUALISTS. His other masterpiece is the "Meeting of St. Erasmus and St. Maurice" (Pinakothek, Munich). Grünewald's works have provided 20th-century expressionism with a source of inspiration.

Bibliography: H. A. SCHMID, *Mathias Grünewald, Gemälde und Zeichnungen* (Strasbourg 1907–11). H. NAUMANN, *Das Grünewaldproblem* (Jena 1930). G. SCHOENBERGER, *The Drawings of Mathis Gothart Nithart, Called Gruenewald* (New York 1948). N. PEVSNER and M. MEIER, *Grünewald* (New York 1958). A. WEIXLGÄRTNER, *Matthias Grünewald* (Vienna 1962). K. SITZMANN and E. BATTISTI, *Encyclopedia of World Art* (New York 1959–) 7:182–191, extensive bibliog.

[G. GALAVARIS]

GUADAGNI, BERNARDO GAETANO

Cardinal bishop; b. Florence, Sept. 14, 1674; d. Rome, Jan. 15, 1759. He received his doctorate in civil and Canon Law in Pisa in 1694 and was a canon in the cathedral at Florence when he entered the Discalced Carmelite Order in 1700, taking the name John Anthony of St. Bernard. After serving as provincial of the Tuscan Province, he was named bishop of Arezzo in 1724. When Clement XII was elected pope, Guadagni, his nephew, was summoned to Rome, created a cardinal in 1731, and appointed to the Curia. During three pontificates he served as secretary to the Consistory, counselor to many other congregations, and vicar of Rome, from 1732 to 1759. He was made bishop of Frascati in 1750 and of Porto and S. Rufina in 1756. He was a man of eminent virtue, devoted to the reform of morals and the care of the poor; his cause for beatification was introduced in 1761 and 1763. He was the first cardinal of the Discalced Carmelites. (*see* CARMELITES, DISCALCED)

Bibliography: *Bibliotheca Carmelitana,* ed. P. WESSELS (Rome 1927). A. MERCATI and A. PELZER, *Dizionario ecclesiastico* 2:280. V. A. S. MARIA, *Lexikon für Theologie und Kirche*[2] 4: 1256–57.

[P. T. ROHRBACH]

GUADALAJARA (MEXICO), MARTYRS OF, SS.

Also known as Martyrs of the Cristero Movement, or Cristobal Magallanes and 24 Companions; d. 1915–1937, Mexico. Jubilee 2000 was a watershed year for Catholicism in Mexico. In 1992, after 150 years of antireligious laws that forced the Church into near obscurity, laws such as those forbidding the wearing of a religious habit in public were rescinded. In 2000, the first National Eucharistic Congress was convened since just before the latest government persecution (1924–34), which sparked the uprising of the Cristero Rebellion (*see* MEXICO, MODERN). Most of the 22 priests and three lay martyrs (David Roldán Lara, his cousin Salvador Lara Puente, and Manuel Morales) included in this group were victims of that persecution in the area around Guadalajara; however, a few testify to the sufferings of earlier periods. The causes of martyrs from other areas of Mexico have been opened, but are on a different course.

The martyrs by year of their deaths, with their age in parentheses, are:

1915: David GALVÁN BERMÚDEZ (34 years old).

1926: David ROLDÁN LARA (24); Luis BATIZ SAINZ (55); Manuel MORALES (28); and Salvador LARA PUENTE (21).

1927: Agustín (Augustine) CALOCA CORTÉS (29); Cristóbal (Christopher) MAGALLANES JARA (57); David URIBE VELASCO (37); Jenaro SÁNCHEZ DELGADILLO (50); José Isabel Flores VARELA (60); José María Robles HURTADO (39); Julio Alvarez MENDOZA (60); Margarito Flores GARCÍA (28); Mateo Correa MAGALLANES (60); Miguel de la MORA (49); Pedro Esqueda RAMÍREZ (46); Rodrigo Aguilar ALEMÁN (52); Román Adame ROSALES (68); and Sabás Reyes SALAZAR (about 43–47).

1928: Atilano Cruz ALVARADO (26); Jesús Méndez MONTOYA (47); Justino Orona MADRIGAL (51); Toribio Romo GONZÁLEZ (27); and Tranquilino Ubiarco ROBLES (29).

1937: Pedro de Jesús Maldonado LUCERO (44).

These courageous martyrs were beatified Nov. 22, 1992, by Pope John Paul II. He approved a miracle attributed to their intercession on June 28, 1999, and canonized them in Rome during the Jubilee of Mexico, May 21, 2000. Cardinal Juan Sandoval Iñiguez laid the first stone of the ''Shrine of Martyrs,'' Oct. 25, 2000, which will seat 20,000 once it is completed for the 2004 International Eucharistic Congress.

Feast: May 25 (Mexico).

Engraving of Matthias Grünewald.

Bibliography: J. CARDOSO, *Los mártires mexicanos* (Mexico City 1953). D. C. BAILEY, *¡Viva Cristo Rey! The Cristero Rebellion and the Church-State Conflict in Mexico* (Austin 1974). V. CEJA REYES, *Los cristeros: crónica de los que perdieron* (México, D.F. 1981) 2 v. J. DÍAZ ESTRELLA, *El movimiento cristero: sociedad y conflicto en los Altos de Jalisco* (México, D.F. 1979). F. P. DOOLEY, *Los cristeros, Calles y el catolicismo mexicano*, tr. M. E. MARTÍNEZ NEGRETE DEFFIS (México, D.F. 1976). P. GULISANO, *Viva Cristo Re: Cristeros: il martirio del popolo del Messico, 1926–29* (Rimini 1999). V. GARCÍA JUÁREZ, *Los cristeros* (Fresnillo, Zac. 1990). L. LÓPEZ BELTRÁN, *La persecución religiosa en México: Carranza, Obregón, Calles, Portes Gil* (México 1987). J. A. MEYER, *La cristiada*, (México 1997), 4 v.; *La cristiada en Colima* (Colima, México 1993); *La christiade* (Paris 1975), Eng. tr. R. SOUTHERN, *The Cristero Rebellion: The Mexican People between Church and State, 1926–1929* (Cambridge 1976); *Apocalypse et révolution au Mexique* (Paris 1974). Y. PADILLA RANGEL, *El Catolicismo social y el movimiento Cristero en Aguascalientes* (Aguascalientes 1992). J. RODRÍGUEZ INZUNZA, *El mundo de los cristeros campesinos: iglesia y estado en conflicto, México, 1926–1929* (Azcapotzalco, D.F. 1988). M. ROMO DE ALBA, *El gobernador de las estrellas* (México, D.F. 1986)

[K. I. RABENSTEIN]

GUADALUPE, OUR LADY OF

Founded on an old tradition, this image and sanctuary is one of the most famous in all Latin America, and devotion to it has increased in modern times. According to tradition, on Dec. 9, 1531, JUAN DIEGO, a man more

Pilgrims carrying image of the Virgin of Guadalupe to Church of Our Lady of Guadalupe, San Cristobal de las Casas, Mexico. (AP/ Wide World Photos)

than 50 years old, saw the Virgin Mary at Tepeyac, a hill northwest of Mexico City. She instructed him to have the bishop build a church on the site. Three days later in a second appearance she told Juan Diego to pick flowers and take them to the bishop. When he presented them as instructed, roses fell out of his mantle and beneath them was the painted image of the Lady.

Documentary Basis. The oldest documentary evidence of this event comes from the interpreter. Since Juan Diego did not know Spanish and Bishop Zumárraga did not know the Indian language, Juan Gonzáles served as interpreter. González was, at 18, a fortune seeker whom the bishop had sheltered, taught, and ordained, and who became a canon of the cathedral. After Zumárraga died, González gave up his canonry and devoted himself to the evangelization of the native peoples. At the same time he left his papers to Juan de Tovar, whose brief summary of them in Nahuatl was kept in the library of Tepozotlán because Tovar entered the Society of Jesus in 1572. The summary is preserved in the Biblioteca Nacional de México and is of importance as a document based on the evidence given by a witness to the meeting of Juan Diego and Bishop Zūmárraga. However, it is not a detailed account.

A better-known document is the Valeriano Relation, drawn up between 1560 and 1570. It was written by Valeriano and a group of Native Mexicans under the direction of Fray Bernardino de SAHAGÚN. First used by Miguel Sánchez, the document was published by Luis Lazo de la Vega in 1649. There are manuscript copies in several North American libraries, and in Paris a version prepared by Picardo in the 18th century. It has two parts: a direct account of the event, the nucleus of the tradition, and an account of the miracles worked in the sanctuary or through the invocation of the Virgin Mary in this manifestation. The first part, prepared by the students of Tlatelolco under Sahagún's direction, is arranged in a literary fashion, according to Nahuatl stylistics, but the facts coincide with those in the Tovar document. The account of the miracles, also written in Nahuatl, is much later and includes events of the 17th century. Thus it is most important for the study of the progress of the devotion and the cult in that century. Some have attributed this part of the Relation to Carlos de Alva Ixtlilxóchitl. There is little evidence for this, although the document is contemporary with the Texcocan historian.

Among the minor documents are at least 15 *Anales de los Indios.* These give communal testimony of the most notable happenings in the native world and include many references to the Tepeyac apparitions. While it has been stated that Bishop Zumárraga made special reports on this event, none are extant; and it is probable that none were ever written. Reports on such supposed supernatural events were not required until the Council of Trent.

The second archbishop of Mexico, Alonso de Montúfar, was a great promoter of the devotion to Our Lady of Guadalupe. In the Provincial Council of 1555, he, along with other bishops, formulated canons that indirectly approved the apparitions, for the order to abolish and prevent the worship of images and the propagation of traditions not well founded did not mention the Guadalupan image and devotion to it. Canon 72 ordered the examination of songs sung at native feasts and dances for taint of paganism; some testimony indicates that these included songs in honor of the apparition of Mary, but no authentically Guadalupan songs are extant. In 1666 a formal inquiry was made from February 18 to March 22 in order to give authority to the tradition. Information concerning the endurance of the tradition and the general belief in it was given by witnesses, some of them centenarians. References to early events are vague and rather weak. The investigation was not canonical or timely, since it was held 135 years after the event. Another was made in 1723, by order of Archbishop Lanziego y Eguilaz. These have no value except to bear witness to the permanence of the tradition. Of even less value are some of the inquiries that were held during the 19th century.

Cult and Its Extension. The first sanctuary was erected about 1533. It is the little hermitage that rests in the foundations of what was for many years a parish church. In 1556 Archbishop Montúfar began the erection of this second church. In 1695 the first stone of the new sanctuary was laid in the place it now occupies. The sanctuary was solemnly dedicated in 1709. With the additions made in 1893 and the following years, and again in the 1930s, this was the basilica of 1964. However, plans were then being made for a new church.

The image was carried to various parts of the world, particularly after the religious of the Society of Jesus were expelled from the Spanish dominions (1767). But the diffusion had started even earlier. In Italy and France the image and the tradition were already known. In 1564 Andrés De URDANETA carried an image with him on the first formal expedition to the Philippine Islands. One was taken to Puerto Rico. Those who returned from the Indies spread the devotion in Spain. A well-known image is to be found in Trent and another, which made miraculous demonstrations in 1796, is now located in Rome, where it is enshrined in the church of S. Nicola in Carcere Tulliano.

Image of Our Lady of Guadalupe, preserved in the sanctuary of Guadalupe.

In 1746 the knight BOTURINI BENADUCCI promoted the solemn and official coronation of the image. The coronation took place in 1895, with pontifical authority and the attendance of a great part of the episcopate of the Americas. This coronation was made later in various parts of the world: in Santa Fé, Argentina (1928) and later in Los Angeles, Calif., in several places in Europe, and even in Asia, where the image was placed in a Hindu temple.

In 1737 the Most Holy Mary of Guadalupe was chosen as the patroness of the city of Mexico. In the course of the year, other important cities of the country followed suit. In 1746 the patronage was accepted for all of New Spain, which then embraced the regions from Upper California to Guatemala and El Salvador. In 1754 Benedict XIV approved the patronage and granted a Mass and Office proper to the celebration of the feast on December 12. In 1757 the Virgin of Guadalupe was declared patroness of the citizens of Ciudad Ponce in Puerto Rico. In 1910 Pius X declared the Virgin Patroness of Latin

America, and in 1935 Pius XI extended the patronage to the Philippines. Pius XII, speaking in 1945 on the occasion of the 50th anniversary of the coronation, stated that the Virgin of Guadalupe was the "Queen of Mexico and Empress of the Americas" and that she had been painted "by brushes that were not of this world." John XXIII assisted at a coronation in a church in Rome and gave the image special praise in his brief discourse. On January 22, 1999, Pope Paul II declared Our Lady of Guadalupe the Patroness of the Americas. By a decree dated March 25, 1999, the Congregation for Divine Worship and the Discipline of Sacraments mandated the obligatory celebration of the Feast of Our Lady of Guadalupe on December 12 throughout the Americas.

Bibliography: A. M. GARIBAY K., "La maternidad espiritual de María en el Mensaje Guadalupano," *La maternidad espiritual de María* (Mexico City 1961). D. DEMAREST and C. TAYLOR, eds., *The Dark Virgin: The Book of Our Lady of Guadalupe: A Documentary Anthology* (Freeport, Me. 1956). J. GARCÍA ICAZBALCETA, *Investigación histórica y documental sobre la aparición de la Virgen de Guadalupe* (Mexico City 1952). P. F. VELÁZQUEZ, *La aparición de santa María de Guadalupe* (Mexico City 1931). J. RODRIGUEZ, *Our Lady of Guadalupe: Faith and Empowerment among Mexican-American Women* (Austin, Tex. 1994). S. POOLE, *Our Lady of Guadalupe: The Origins and Sources of a Mexican National Symbol, 1531–1797* (Tucson, Ariz 1995). V.P. ELIZONDO, *Guadalupe, Mother of the New Creation* (Maryknoll, N.Y. 1997). L. L. DE LA VEGA, trans. L. SOUSA, S. POOLE, et al. *The Story of Guadalupe: Luis Laso de la Vega's Huei tlamahuiçoltica of 1649* (Stanford, Calif. 1998). D.A. BRADING, *Mexican Phoenix: Our Lady of Guadalupe: Image and Tradition Across Five Centuries* (Cambridge, UK/New York 2001)

[A. M. GARIBAY K./EDS.]

GUAL, PEDRO

Franciscan missionary, apologist, founder and restorer of influential religious institutions in Peru; b. Canet del Mar, Barcelona, Spain, 1813; d. Lima, 1890. Gual was educated in Italy. He arrived at the Peruvian Missionary College of Ocopa in 1845 and, in 1852, he created the famous missionary college of the Descalzos in Lima. Gual became a general commissary of the order, in charge of missionary colleges and visitor of the Franciscan provinces. From the beginning, Gual was the soul of the religious restoration initiated by Andrés HERRERO in the South American Pacific republics. Gual founded or consolidated the string of Colegios de Propaganda Fide that arose in Peru, Bolivia, Chile, Ecuador, and Colombia. He was an untiring promotor and organizer, by his example and writings, of the missions popular among the faithful. He attacked the enemies of the Church, Jansenists, Liberals, Masons, and atheists, with his vigorous lectures and publications, which he directed especially against Renan, Jacolliot, and De Santis. These publications were widely circulated among the educated Peruvians. He also successfully refuted Vigil and other Peruvian writers who spread heretical and demoralizing doctrines in his *Equilibrio entre las dos potestades* (1852), *La Moralizadora del mundo* (1862), *La Vida de Jesús* (1869), *La India cristiana* (1880), and many others.

Bibliography: H. A. BIERCK, *Vida pública de don Pedro Gual* (Caracas 1976).

[O. SAIZ]

GUALA OF BERGAMO, BL.

Dominican bishop; b. Bergamo, Lombardy, Italy, *c.* 1180; d. Astino, Sept. 3, 1244. When (St.) DOMINIC preached at Bergamo in 1217 Guala (Walter) Roni (Romanoni) received from him the habit of the DOMINICANS. In 1221 he became prior of the convent at Brescia. At this time he had a vision of the glory of Dominic, whose death, unknown to Guala, had just occurred. He founded the convent at Bergamo (1222), was associated with the founding of the nuns' convent of St. Agnes at Bologna (1225), and soon after became prior of St. Nicholas in that city. Both HONORIUS III and GREGORY IX recognized his prudence and tact by employing him on difficult missions. In 1229–30 he became bishop of Brescia where he continued his diplomatic activities. Exiled from his see in 1239, Guala spent his last years in penitential retirement with the Benedictines at Astino. Pius IX beatified him in 1868.

Feast: Sept. 3.

Bibliography: *Année Dominicaine,* September 1:67–77 (Lyons 1900). A. MERCATI and A. PELZER, *Dizionario ecclesiastico,* 3 v. (Turin 1954–58) 2:282. A. BUTLER, *The Lives of the Saints,* ed. H. THURSTON and D. ATTWATER, 4 v. (New York 1956) 3:482–483. G. GIERATHS, *Lexikon für Theologie und Kirche,* ed. J. HOFER and K. RAHNER, 10 v. (2d, new ed. Freiburg 1957–65) 4:1258.

[M. J. FINNEGAN]

GUANELLA, LUIGI, BL.

Religious founder; b. Fraciscio di Campodolcino (Sondrio), Italy, Dec. 19, 1842; d. Como, Italy, Oct. 24, 1915. The son of poor parents, Guanella entered the seminary (1854) and was ordained (1866). During his pastoral labors in the village of Savogno, he showed so much concern for the spiritual and temporal needs of his parishioners that they erected a monument in his honor shortly after his death. While pastor in Pianello Lario, Guanella opened a hospice for orphaned and abandoned children (1878) and then transferred its headquarters to Como, where he opened the House of Divine Providence (1886).

He started similar institutions in several other Italian cities. To perpetuate his work, Guanella founded the DAUGHTERS OF ST. MARY OF PROVIDENCE and also a religious congregation for men, the Servants of Charity, originally (1904) known as the Sons of the Sacred Heart. The Servants of Charity (or *Opera Don Guanella*), who received definitive papal approval in 1928, had 600 members in 1963. Both institutes have spread to Switzerland and the Western Hemisphere. Visits to these regions stimulated Guanella to aid Italian immigrants. Through his friendships with Davide ALBERTARIO and Giuseppe TONIOLO, he also became a pioneer leader in solving the social question. Guanella promoted the apostolate of the press and wrote about 50 popular devotional, historical, and pedagogical works. He was beatified Oct. 25, 1964.

Feast: Oct. 24.

Bibliography: L. MAZZUCCHI, *La vita, lo spirito e le opere di don Luigi Guanella* (Como 1920). A. TAMBORINI, *Don Luigi Guanella* (Como 1943). L. CARINI ALIMANDI, *Luigi Guanella: per le vie del quarto mondo* (Rome 1978). P. PELLEGRINI, *Don Guanella inedito: negli scritti di Piero Pellegrini*, ed. A. DI GUEZ and N. MINETTI (Rome 1993).

[V. A. LAPOMARDA]

GUARANTEES, LAW OF

Law of Kingdom of ITALY that was intended to solve the ROMAN QUESTION after the Seizure of the STATES OF THE CHURCH, including Rome itself, by legislating certain guarantees for the dignity and independence of the pope and the Holy See and by separating Church and State in peninsula (May 13, 1871).

Contents. In the preliminary discussions a moderate Catholic group in the Chamber opposed the proposed act as unilateral, injurious to the Church's liberty and lacking in international standing. Laicists among the delegates insisted that concessions to the pope, save very limited ones, would be incompatible with national security, integrity and sovereignty. The final text represented a view moderately liberal, yet hostile to the Church. The principal provisions of its 19 articles follow. The pope's person is declared sacred and inviolable (art. 1). Attempts against his person are punishable and are as serious as those against the king (art. 2). Sovereign honors and the preeminence of honor recognized by Catholic rulers are to be rendered by the Italian government to the pope, who may maintain his customary number of guards (art. 3). The Holy See is to receive in perpetuity an annual, tax-exempt grant of 3,224,000 lire (art. 4). The pope shall continue to enjoy the Vatican and Lateran palaces and the villa at CASTEL GANDOLFO, which are inalienable and tax-exempt, as are the museums, library, art and archeological collections therein; but the Holy See must defray the costs of maintenance and salaries (art. 4, 5). State officials are forbidden to enter the papal palaces or the place of a conclave or ecumenical council, or to examine or seize documents of papal congregations engaged in spiritual functions (art. 7, 8). Foreign envoys to the Holy See are to enjoy all the usual prerogatives and immunities accorded in international law (art. 11). The pope may engage unhindered in correspondence by mail or telegram with the entire episcopate and Catholic world (art. 12). The royal exequatur and placet are abolished, except for acts disposing of ecclesiastical property or benefices outside Roman and its suburbicarian sees. Civil laws concerning ecclesiastical institutions and the alienation of their goods remain in force (art. 16). The conservation and administration of church properties in Italy are to be handled in later laws (art. 18). [For the full Italian text, see H. Bastgen, *Die romische Frage,* 3 v. (Frankfort 1917–19) 1:676–677. For an English translation, see J. Carrere, *The Pope* (London n.d.) 264–268]

Papal Attitude. A very grave defect in this legislation was its unilateral character, its attempt to determine the prerogatives of a sovereign whose rights could not be subject to limits or conditions set by another authority. This flaw resulted from the desire to establish the pope's juridical position ''within the Italian state'' by domestic legislation subject to revocation or suspension at any time at the will of the civil power and bereft of international recognition.

PIUS IX (1846–78) solemnly repudiated the law in the encyclical *Ubi nos* (May 15, 1871) and refused the financial offer. He and his successors abstained from any act implying recognition of the legislation and withdrew into the Vatican as voluntary prisoners. Thereby they avoided the law's application insofar as it involved equality of pope and king in the reception of formal honors. They also escaped the possible reproach of traversing the Eternal City as claimants.

Ineffectiveness. In carrying out the Law of Guarantees the Italian government did not always live up to its promises, as is clear from the incidents at Pius IX's funeral and the criticisms of the popes allowed in the Italian press. The one point in which the law proved operative was in its recognition of the right of active and passive diplomatic representation. Even here grave difficulties arose during World War I. Many jurists and publicists then sought an authoritative act suspending the law, thereby demonstrating the precariousness of prerogatives unilaterally conceded to the papacy. Italy limited the right of representation by insisting that the Holy See suggest to the Central Powers the transference of their diplomatic headquarters to Switzerland.

See Also: ROMAN QUESTION.

Bibliography: H. BASTGEN, *Die romische Frage,* 3 v. (Frankfort 1917–19) 1:676–677. J. CARRERE, *The Pope* (London n.d.) 264–268. F. SCADUTO, *Guarantigie pontificie e relazioni tra Stato e Chiesa* (Turin 1884). A. GALANTE, *Manuale I diritto ecclesiastico* (Milan 1914).

[R. MORI]

GUARDINI, ROMANO

Philosopher of the Christian world view and prolific writer on theological topics; b. Verona, Italy, Feb. 17, 1885; d. Munich, Germany, Oct. 1, 1968. Guardini grew up mostly in Mainz, where his father was Italian consul. His education, however, was German and he decided to stay in Germany as an adult. (His ''European'' rather than nationalist spirit was recognized in the conferral of the Erasmus Prize on him in 1962.) After trying chemistry and economics at the university he turned to theology and the priesthood (1910). From 1923 to 1939 (when he was turned out by the Nazi regime) he occupied a chair created for him at the University of Berlin as ''professor for philosophy of religion and Catholic *Weltanschauung.*'' After the war similar positions were made for him first at Tübingen and then in Munich (1948–63).

Guardini's eminence among leaders and inspirers of Catholic renewal in the years between the two world wars started in 1918 with the publication of *The Spirit of the Liturgy.* There soon followed *The Church and the Catholic* (1923), introduced by words for which he has become famous: ''A religious process of incalculable importance has begun—the Church is coming to life in the souls of men.'' He showed himself perceptive in the extreme in thus picking up and nurturing the elements of spirituality which would characterize all that was best in the life of the Catholic Church of the next decades. In German-speaking lands there is no one who deserves more to be called a precursor of Vatican Council II.

His influence was enormous, not only through his university position in Berlin, but above all by reason of the inspiration he gave to the vigorous German Catholic youth movement as chaplain of the Quickborn. His writings include works on meditation, education, literary figures such as Dante and Rilke, art, philosophy, and theology. His life of Christ, *The Lord* (1937), became his most famous work. *Das Wesen des Christentums* (1939, untranslated) explained the approach he took in *The Lord.* The common background of the immense variety of subjects he treated was his philosophical theory of polar opposition (*Der Gegensatz,* 1925). This proved to be an extraordinarily fruitful starting point from which to bring revelation (*Religion und Offenbarung,* 1950) and worldly reality (*Welt und Person,* 1939; *The End of the Modern World,* 1950; *Power and Responsibility,* 1951) into a synthesis.

Bibliography: A. BABOLIN, *Romano Guardini, Filosofo dell' Alterità* (Bologna 1968–69). H. URS VON BALTHASAR, *Romano Guardini: Reform aus dem Ursprung* (Munich 1970). W. DIRKS in *Tendenzen der Theologie im 20. Jahrhundert,* ed. H. J. SCHULTZ (Stuttgart, Olten 1966) 248–252. H. ENGELMANN and F. FERRIER, *Romano Guardini* (Paris 1966). F. HENRICH, *Die Bünde katholischer Jugendbewegung* (Munich 1968). K. HOFFMAN, ''Portrait of Father Guardini,'' *Commonweal* 60 (Sept. 17, 1954) 575–577. J. LAUBACH in *Theologians of Our Time,* ed. L. REINISCH (Notre Dame 1964) 109–126. H. KUHN, *Romano Guardini. Der Mensch und das Werk* (Munich 1961). B. MONDIN, *I grandi teologi del secolo ventesimo* (Turin 1969) 1.89–120. R. A. KRIEG, *Romano Guardini: A Precursor of Vatican II* (Notre Dame 1997). *Wege zur Wahrheit: Die bleibende Bedeutung von Romano Guardini,* ed. J. CARDINAL RATZINGER (Düsseldorf 1985). *La Weltanschauung cristiana di Romano Guardini,* ed. S. ZUCAL (Trent 1988).

[P. MISNER]

GUARINUS OF PALESTRINA, ST.

Cardinal bishop of Palestrina; b. Bologna, Italy, *c.* 1080; d. Palestrina, Italy, Feb. 6, 1159. Guarinus was already a cleric when he joined the AUGUSTINIANS at Mortara (*c.* 1104). When the bishop of Pavia died (*c.* 1139), Guarinus was elected to the see by popular acclamation. Imprisoned for his steadfast refusal to accept that honor, he managed to escape his confinement only to be required (1144) by order of Pope LUCIUS II, a Bolognese, to become cardinal and bishop of Palestrina, one of the suburbicarian dioceses of Rome. Guarinus's exemplary youth, studious and mortified monastic life, love of the poor, and extraordinary virtue as a bishop prompted Pope ALEXANDER III, another Bolognese, to effect his CANONIZATION immediately after his death. The hospital of St. Job at Bologna reveres him as its founder, and the Canons Regular of the LATERAN honor him as a patron. His life was written by his contemporary, Augustine of Pavia.

Feast: Feb. 6.

Bibliography: *Acta Sanctorum,* Feb. 1 (1863) 923–925. A. BUTLER, *The Lives of the Saints* (New York 1956) 1:264–265.

[N. M. RIEHLE]

GUARINUS (GUÉRIN) OF SION, ST.

Bishop of Sion; b. Pont-à-Mousson, Lorraine, France, *c.* 1065; d. Aulps (near Geneva), Savoy, Aug. 27, 1150. Guarinus entered the BENEDICTINE Order in the Abbey of MOLESME *c.* 1085. In about 1094, he joined a group that had left Molesme for a more retired life at Aulps in Savoy, and he became second abbot of the new foundation *c.* 1110. St. BERNARD OF CLAIRVAUX visited Aulps *c.* 1133–35 and later wrote a fine letter of congratulations to Guarinus, who had his monastery incorporated into the CISTERCIAN Order in 1136. In 1138, Guarinus became bishop of Sion in Switzerland. He died during a visit to Aulps and was buried there. He is still venerated extensively in Savoy and the Valais.

Feast: Jan. 6, Aug. 30 (Diocese of Sion), Jan. 14 (Cistercians).

Bibliography: *Acta Sanctorum* Jan. 1:347–348, 730. J. F. GONTHIER, *Vie de saint Guérin* (Annecy 1896). U. CHEVALIER, *Répetoire des sources historiques du moyen-âge: Topobibliographie* (Paris 1894–1903) 1:1919. A. DIMIER, ''San Guarino, abad de los Alpes y obispo de Sion,'' *Cistercium* 4 (1952) 89–95. M. B. BRARD, *Catholicisme. Hier, aujourd'hui et demain*, ed. G. JACQUEMET. BERNARD OF CLAIRVAUX, *Epistolae* 142 and 254, *Patrologia Latina*, ed. J. P. MIGNE (Paris 1878–90) 182:297–298, 459–462. J. L. BAUDOT and L. CHAUSSIN, *Vies des saints et des bienheureux salon l'ordre du calendrier avec l'historique des fêtes* (Paris 1935–56) 1:125–128. C. LUGON, ''Une Étape vers l'indépendance du Valais. Saint Guérin chef temporel,'' *Bulletin du Diocèse de Sion* 6–7 (1965) 271–302; *Saint Guérin, abbé d'Aulps, évêque de Sion* (Geneva 1970).

[M. STANDAERT]

GUASTALLA, COUNCIL OF

Reform council held under Pope PASCHAL II in Guastalla, a town between Verona and Mantua, in northern Italy. When legates of the new emperor, HENRY V, invited Paschal to Germany to stabilize the Church's position there after the upsets of the INVESTITURE STRUGGLE, the pope held a council in the church of St. Peter near Guastalla on Oct. 22, 1106, attended by Henry's embassy, many bishops, priests, and laymen. The pope renewed the prohibition of lay investiture; granted general pardon to bishops and priests excommunicated during the recent empire-papacy conflicts; confirmed ordinations conferred by schismatic ministers, except in cases of intrusion, SIMONY, and concubinage; and took measures to restore discipline. The council detached from the province of Ravenna the Dioceses of Piacenza, Parma, Reggio, Modena, and Bologna.

Bibliography: C. J. VON HEFELE, *Histoire des conciles d'après les documents originaux,* tr. and continued by H. LECLERCQ, 10 v. in 19 (Paris 1907–38) 5.1:496–497. J. D. MANSI, *Sacrorum Conciliorum nova et amplissima collectio,* 31 v. (Florence-Venice 1757–98); reprinted and continued by L. PETIT and J. B. MARTIN, 53 v. in 60 (Paris 1889–1927; repr. Graz 1960–) 20:1209–16. N. PELICELLI, *Concilio di Guastalla* (Parma 1906). U. BLUMENTAL, ''Some Notes on Papal Policies at Guastalla, 1106,'' MELANGES G. FRANSEN, vol. 1 (Rome 1976), 59–77.

[A. CONDIT]

Capital: Guatemala City.
Size: 42,042 sq. miles.
Population: 12,639,939 in 2000.
Languages: Spanish; more than 20 Amerindian languages are spoken in various regions.
Religions: 7,583,963 Roman Catholics (60%), 4,423,978 Evangelical Protestants (35%); 631,998 other, including indigenous Mayan beliefs.
Archdioceses: Guatemala City, with suffragans Escuintla, Jalapa en Guatemala, Santa Rosa de Lima, Vera Paz, and Zacapa y Santo Cristo de Esquipulas; Los Altos/Quetzaltenango-Totonicapán, with suffragans Huehuetenango, San Marcos, Sololá-Chimaltenango, Suchitepéquez Retalhuleu, and Quiché. There are apostolic vicarates located at El Petén and Izabal.

GUASTO, ANDREA DEL

Founder and superior of the Congregation Centorbi; b. Castrogiovanni, Sicily, Aug. 16, 1534; d. Regalbuto, Sept. 7, 1627. Under the direction of Philip Dulcettus, Guasto joined a group of about 200 hermits on the mountains around Argira. Guasto possessed a reputation of sanctity. At his suggestion, the hermits changed from the Third Order of St. Francis to the First Order of St. Augustine. On Feb. 2, 1579, Pope GREGORY XIII approved the change, but only after the president of Sicily lent his support did Andrea and 12 confreres receive the Augustinian habit on May 22, 1585, from Melchior Testai of Regalbuto, their first moderator. In 1591, the remaining hermits were discalced and led a common life, living from the work of their hands. The *Congregatio heremitarum Siciliae,* called the *Congregatio Centum Urbium,* after Centorbi, their first monastery, from 1602, grew to 19 houses and was united with the order until suppressed in 1873.

Bibliography: *Registers of the Priors General, Rome.* J. LANTERI, *Additamenta ad Crusenii Monasticon,* 2 v. (Valladolid 1890) v. 1. W. RÜGAMER, *Lexikon für Theologie und Kirche*, ed. J. HOFER and K. RAHNER (Freiburg 1957–65) 1:516.

[F. ROTH]

GUATEMALA, THE CATHOLIC CHURCH IN

The Central American Republic of Guatemala borders the North Pacific Ocean on its south, Mexico on its west and north, and Belize, the Caribbean, Honduras and El Salvador on its east. A mountainous region prone to earthquakes and volcanic eruptions, Guatemala derives a quarter of its wealth from coffee, sugar and bananas, and agriculture employs half its labor force. Natural resources include petroleum deposits, fish, chicle, and rare woods

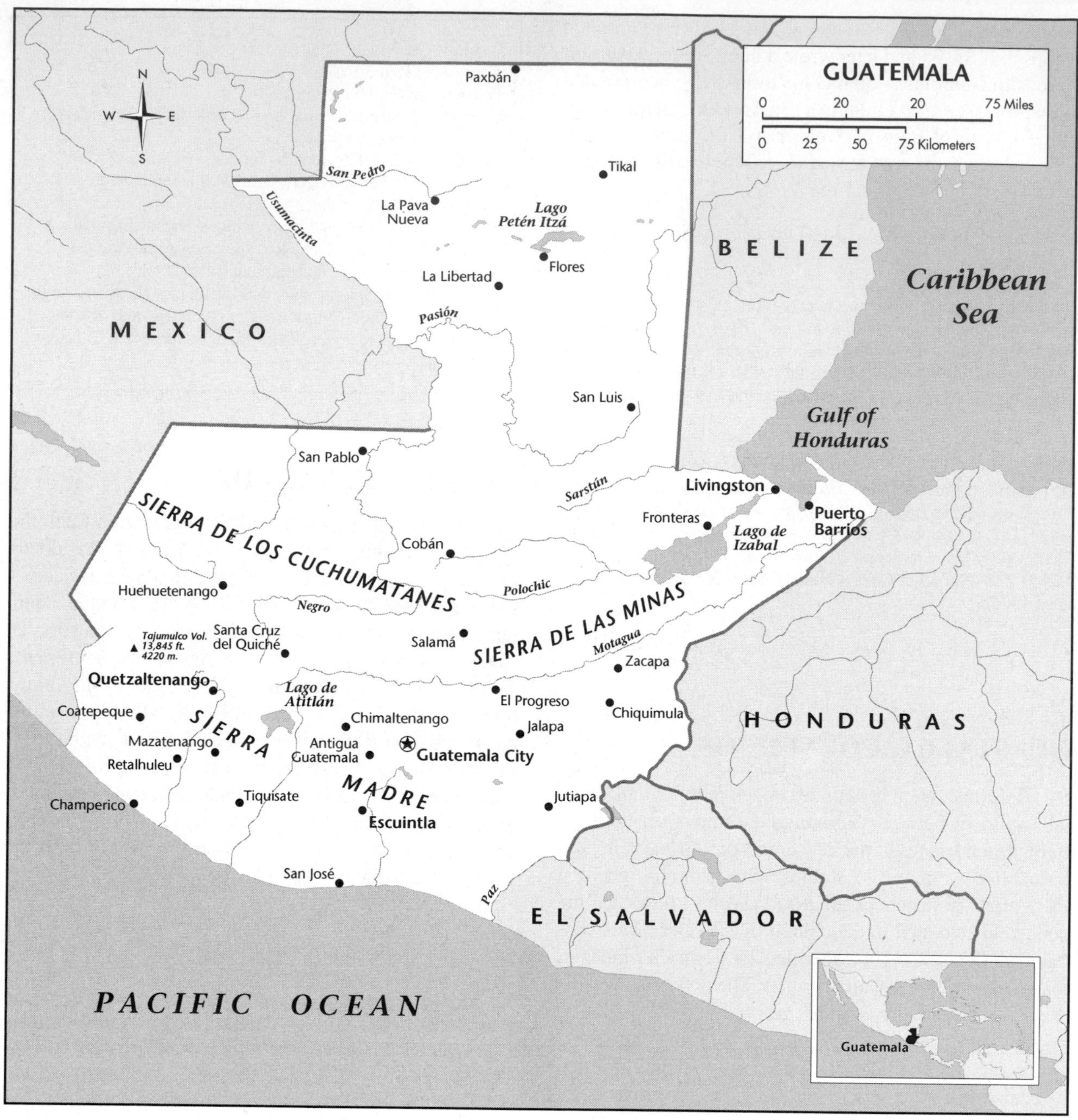

from the country's many forests. A poor country where scarcely more than half the adults are literate, Guatemala's government has waged an ongoing battle against drug trafficking. More than half of all Guatemalans are Mestizo (Amerindian-Spanish), with the remainder predominately Amerindian.

Colonization and Early Christianization. Prior to the coming of the Spanish conquistadores in the 16th century, Guatemala was home to great Mayan cities such as Tikal, Piedras Negras, Uaxactún and Zacualpa. Spaniard Pedro de Alvarado founded the city of Santiago de los Caballeros on July 25, 1524. With Alvarado came the first missionaries: Augustinians, Mercedarians, Franciscans, Dominicans and Jesuits all contributed to the evangelization of the Mayan natives and the fostering of Western culture through schools of various types. Among the early missionaries were Juan Torres, who wrote a catechism in Quitché; Francisco Pontaza, who prepared one in Kakchiquel; Juan Godínez, author of catechisms in both Indian languages; Francisco Parra, who in preparing catechetical material invented five characters not in the

Catholic church, Guatemala. (©Arvind Garg/CORBIS)

European alphabet to express Indian sounds; and Pedro de BETANZOS.

Calling it the ''Audiencia,'' Guatemala's Spanish conquerors transformed the region into a powerful political entity, and it served as a high court for Spain's American outposts. It was also the scene of a special missionary effort by the Dominicans. The Province of Tezulutlán was called the ''land of war'' because of the ferocity of its unconquered inhabitants. A group headed by Bartolomé de LAS CASAS including Rodrigo de Ladrada, Pedro de Angulo, Luis Cáncer and Domingo Antonio de Vico composed poems in the native language telling the biblical accounts of the creation of the world, the life of Jesus and the Redemption, and put them to simple music. These songs were spread by Christian peddlers. The four friars had great success with such methods. An episcopal see was erected in Verapaz in 1599, but it was suppressed in 1607. The missions nevertheless continued in the charge of the Dominicans.

Ecclesiastical Organization. A diocese was erected in Guatemala in 1534, and it was raised to an archdiocese in 1743. The last bishop and the first archbishop was the Peruvian Pedro Pardo de Figueroa, a patron of arts and cultural activities. De Figueroa built the church of Santo Cristo de Esquipulas, which would become a center of pilgrimage for Central America and southern Mexico. This shrine has been erected as a prelature *nullius* in the charge of the Benedictines of North America.

Spanish missionaries and the Church hierarchy firmly reshaped social and family life around Catholicism. Their efforts fostered vocations among men and women of all social classes, gradually enabling the orders and the seminaries to replace those who had come from Spain. The Church also fostered scholarship. Pedro de Lievana, dean of the cathedral at the time of Bishop MARROQUÍN, founded the first literary academy in the Americas, with the assistance of Eugenio de Salazar y Alarcón. Chroniclers and linguists included Antonio REMESAL, Francisco

VÁZQUEZ, Rafael de Landívar y Caballero, Francisco Ximenez and Bachiller Domingo de Juarros. Juarros' *History of the Kingdom of Guatemala* was translated into English and frequently consulted by historians. Scholars of the late colonial period were philosophers Pedro de Zapiain and Miguel Francesch; scientist José Antonio Liendo y Goicoechea; and educator, poet and social writer Matías de CÓRDOVA.

Church and State in Modern Guatemala. In 1821 Guatemala gained independence from Spain and went on to join the short-lived United Provinces of Central America. In 1839 it declared itself an independent republic. In 1853 the country's democratic government signed a concordat with the Holy See. However, the liberal revolution of 1870, led by García Granados and Justo Rufino Barrios, repudiated the concordat, suppressed the religious orders, took possession of all their property and of the seminary, exiled priests and religious, closed the Catholic schools, established civil marriage and divorce, secularized cemeteries and schools, separated the Church from the State and persecuted Catholics. The churches were left without funds and the faithful, without the Sacraments. Protestant evangelicals took advantage of the situation and spread especially among the poorest classes; they continued to make inroads even into the 21st century, albeit within an atmosphere of increased toleration.

In 1951 a liberal government took power, and the Church was allowed to regain independence. Diplomatic relations were eventually resumed with the Holy See. However, the left-wing government was able to enact few reforms under pressure from entrenched conservative powers. For the next three and a half decades the country witnessed continued political upheaval, including guerilla violence, military intervention, manipulation by the U.S. Central Intelligence Agency and numerous government-sponsored human rights violations. The church spoke out constantly against abuses, and was active in efforts to mediate an end to years of civil war. On Dec. 29, 1996 Guatemala achieved peace through a new government, and efforts to rebuild the country's floundering economic base were achieving success by 2000.

During 36 years of civil war, it was estimated that over 140,000 Guatemalans lost their lives through violence, while another 50,000 were listed among the "dissappeared". In an effort to document that violence, the Church created an archdiocesan human rights office to follow up reports of deaths, disappearances and other human rights abuses. Auxiliary Bishop Juan Berardi Conedra led this office, and in late April of 1998 presented his report. The Guatemalan army and other paramilitary organizations came up for criticism, and were cited as responsible for 80 percent of the deaths that occurred; the guerillas were held responsible for the remainder. Tragically, Conedra was found dead two days later, his murder believed to be a political assassination. While several members of the Guatemalan military were arrested in January of 2000, events continued to delay the trial and further investigation.

Following the civil war, the Church saw its core beliefs reflected in the new government, as March 25 was proclaimed the Year of the Unborn Child, according to the country's press office: "to foster the culture of life and the defense of life from the moment of its conception." By 2000 Guatemala had 412 parishes, 340 secular and 576 religious priests, 448 brothers and 1,627 sisters. Religious congregations ran primary and secondary schools, as well as performed other much-needed social works: care of the sick, providing homes for foundlings and orphans, operating psychiatric centers and running reformatories. The Jesuit fathers directed the Rafael Landívar University with the privilege of granting academic titles as respected as those given by the autonomous University of San Carlos. The missions of Huchuetenago remained under the care of the Maryknoll fathers and those of Petén by Spanish missionaries. During his visit to Guatemala in February of 1996, Pope John Paul II reinforced the need for Catholics to continue working among the nation's increasing poor and to continue their "vigorous and dynamic effort to evangelize" in the face of increasing threats from Protestant sects working among Guatemala's rural Amerindian tribes. Following the end of civil war, the Pope prayed that the nation would "enjoy . . . a future of peace and progress, spiritual and material, in which the rights of every person will be respected." Guatemala's president, Alfonso Portillo Cabreras, was a member of a Protestant sect; his first term of office was set to expire in 2004.

Bibliography: C. L. JONES, *Guatemala: Past and Present* (Minneapolis 1940). V. KELSEY and L. DE J. OSBORNE, *Four Keys to Guatemala* (rev. ed. New York 1961).

[B. TRESSERRAS/EDS.]

GUBERNATIS, DOMENICO DE

Franciscan historian; b. Sospitello, Diocese of Turin, date unknown; d. Turin, 1690. Little is known about the life of Gubernatis. His fame as a historian rests on his authorship of the monumental work whose six-line title is usually shortened to *Orbis Seraphicus.* Gubernatis was commissioned to undertake this work about 1670 by the minister general of the Franciscans. As conceived by Gubernatis, it was to be a universal history of the Franciscan Order in 30 volumes. Only seven ever appeared, but the work remains a singular specimen of 17th-century historiography. It is probably the most valuable history of the order, with the single exception of Wadding's *Annales.* The first four volumes, published by Gubernatis himself at Rome and Lyons between 1682 and 1685, concern the internal history of the order. He also published one volume on the missionary history at Rome in 1689. Gubernatis's plan was continued by Sigismundo Cavalli da Cueno, who produced a volume on the history of the provinces at Turin (1741), and by Marcellino da Civezza and Theophil Domenichelli, who authored a second volume of missionary history that was published at Quaracchi in 1886.

Bibliography: A. CHIAPPINI, ''*Orbis Seraphicus:* A Bibliographical Note,'' *The Americas* 8 (1951–52) 77–81. MARCELLINO DA CIVEZZA, *Saggio de bibliografia geografica storica ethnografica sanfrancescana* (Prato 1879) 181. J. H. SBARALEA, *Supplementum et castigatio ad scriptores trium ordinum S. Francisci a Waddingo*, 4:217.

[C. J. LYNCH]

GUDULA, ST.

Virgin, patroness of Brussels; b. Brabant, mid-seventh century; d. *c.* 712. The mother of Gudula (or Goule), St. AMALBERGA, was a niece of Pepin, mayor of the palace. After receiving an education at the abbey of Nivelles under her cousin ST. GERTRUDE, Gudula returned to her home at Ham, near Alast, to lead a life of constant fasting, vigils, and prayers. In gratitude for her abundant alms, a large number of poor and afflicted accompanied her body to burial. Charles, duke of Lower Lorraine, translated her relics to Brussels (977–88). In 1047, her relics were placed in the parish church of St. Michael (now St. Gudule) but they were scattered (1579) by the Calvinists. In art, Gudula is represented holding a lantern. According to legend, a wax taper was miraculously relighted after a jealous demon had extinguished it while she was praying.

Feast: Jan. 8.

Bibliography: *Acta Sanctorum*, Jan. 1:513–530. *Bibliotheca hagiographica latina antiquae et mediae aetatis* (Brussels 1898–1901) 1:3684–86. J. L. BAUDOT and L. CHAUSSIN, *Vies des saints et des bienheureux selon l'ordre du calendier avec l'historique des fêtes* (Paris 1935 56) 1:165–166. É. DE MOREAU, *Histoire de l'Église en Belgique* (2d ed. Brussels 1945) 1:197–200. N. HUYGHEBAERT, *Catholicisme. Hier, aujourd'hui et demain*, ed. G. JACQUEMET, 5:321.

[J. E. LYNCH]

GUDWAL, ST.

Missionary in Brittany also known as Curval, Gurval, and Goal; d. *c.* 640. Probably one of the earliest evangelizers of Brittany, Gudwal is third on the list of the seven pioneer saints of that region, although he was very likely a native of Cornwall in England. He founded the monastery of Plec on the island of Locoal-Mendon, which is still an important center of his cult. Gudwal made other settlements on the neighboring mainland and a more distant one at Guer in western France, which has his holy well. The chapel of St. Stephen at Guer is probably his hermitage. He seems to have died in one of his woodland monasteries, but was buried on Locoal-Mendon. With the 10th-century invasion of Britain by Northmen, his relics were moved first to Picardy and then to Ghent, to the Abbey of St. Peter. He may have been a regional bishop, perhaps of Aleth, but not of Saint-Malo, for the see had not yet been founded. The history of Gudwal presents many problems and has occasioned many conflicting interpretations.

Feast: June 6.

Bibliography: *Acta sanctorum*, June 1 (1863) 716–736. F. DUINE, *Memento des sources hagiographiques de l'histoire de Bretagne* (Rennes 1918) 74, 146, 454, 459. *S. Gudwal, évêque et confesseur* (S. Brieuc 1934). *Bibliotheca hagiographica latina antiquae et mediae aetatis* (Brussels 1898–1901) 1:3687–90. A. M. ZIMMERMANN, *Kalendarium Benedictinum: Die Heiligen und Seligen des Benediktinerorderns und seiner Zweige* (Metten 1933–38) 2:285–286. A. BUTLER *The Lives of the Saints* (New York 1956) 2:489–490. U. CHEVALIER, *Répetorie des sources historiques du moyen-âge* (Paris 1894–1903) 1:1998. G. MARSOT, *Catholicisme. Hier, aujourd'hui et demain*, ed. G.JACQUEMET, 5:432. *The Dictionary of National Biography from the Earliest Times to 1900* (London 1885–1900) 8:759.

[B. CAVANAUGH]

GUELFS AND GHIBELLINES

The words Guelf and Ghibelline are Italianized forms (*Guelfo, Ghibellino*) of the German *Welf* and *Weibelungen.* They are originated from the rivalry in twelfth-century Germany between the Welfs of Saxony and the dominant Hohenstaufens of Swabia (whose rallying cry was ''Weibelungen,'' after a castle at Weibelung). Possibly the words became convenient shibboleths after Welf VI, lord of the German fiefs of Tuscany and Spoleto, had defected in 1162 to join the alliance of the Papacy, Sicily, and the LOMBARD LEAGUE against the Hohenstaufen Emperor FREDERICK BARBAROSSA.

However, the emergence in Italy of a Guelf or papal party as opposed to a Ghibelline or Hohenstaufen party belongs properly to the reign of FREDERICK II (1218–50), grandson of Barbarossa. Elected King of Germany in 1215 and Emperor in 1218, on both occasions with papal support, Frederick II failed to abide by the solemn promise he made at his coronation to resign his kingdom of

Painting depicting mounted fight between Guelfs and Ghibellines, by G. Sabattelli. (©Bettmann/CORBIS)

Sicily. Thus by breaking his promise he provoked a vicious struggle between the Papacy and the Emperor that extended from the pontificate of GREGORY IX (1227–41) onward and in which whole cities from Rome to Milan and Genoa went Guelf (papal) or Ghibelline (imperial), often according as the political wind blew. The Ghibellines, weakened by the deposition of Frederick at the Council of Lyons in 1245 and by his death in 1250, looked for leadership first to Frederick's son CONRAD IV OF GERMANY, and then to his illegitimate son MANFRED. After Pope ALEXANDER IV (1254–61) had secured the backing of the powerful Guelf bankers of Florence, and the French Pope URBAN IV (1261–64) had persuaded Charles of ANJOU to accept the kingdom of Sicily, the Ghibelline cause deteriorated; the mortal blow came in effect with the defeat of Conradin, the son of Conrad IV and the last of the Hohenstaufens, by Charles at Tagliacozzo in 1268. Some Ghibelline strongholds, such as Siena and Pisa, survived for a time, and there was even a brief resurgence of Ghibelline hopes after the successful anti-Angevin revolt of the Sicilian Vespers in 1282; but by 1300 Guelf and Ghibelline by and large represented only local or family, rather than papal and imperial, persuasions.

Bibliography: C. POULET, *Guelfes et Gibelines,* 2 v. (Paris 1922). J. P. TREVELYAN, *A Short History of the Italian People* (4th ed. New York 1956). G. PEPE, *Lo stato ghibellino di Federico II* (2d ed. Bari 1951). A. FLICHE and V. MARTIN, eds., *Histoirede l'église depuis les origines jusqu'à nos jours* (Paris 1935) 10:217–247. S. RUNCIMAN, *The Sicilian Vespers* (Cambridge, England 1958). C. W. PREVITÉ-ORTON, *The Shorter Cambridge Medieval History,* 2 v. (Cambridge, England 1960). G. BARRACLOUGH, *The Origins of Modern Germany* (2d ed. Oxford 1957; pa. New York 1963). D. P. WALEY, *The Papal State in the Thirteenth Century* (New York 1961). R. CELLI, *Pour l'histoire des origines du pouvoir populaire: l'experience des villes-etats italiennes: Xie–XIIe siècles* (Louvain 1980). P. HERDE, *Guelfen und Neoguelfen* (Stuttgart 1986); *Von Dante zum Risorgimento* (Stuttgart 1997). s

[L. E. BOYLE]

GUÉRANGER, PROSPER

Benedictine scholar, liturgist; b. Sablé-sur-Sarthe, France, April 4, 1805; d. Solesmes, Jan. 30, 1875. Guéranger was largely responsible for setting in motion the modern liturgical revival by his prodigious literary campaign in defense of Roman ritual forms. He must also be credited with having had a central role in the rejuvenation of contemporary Benedictine monasticism.

Ordained for the Diocese of Le Mans on Oct. 7, 1827, Guéranger fulfilled several pastoral assignments there. While studying for the secular priesthood, he already had developed a lasting interest in divine worship, convinced that Catholic spirituality must be linked closely and continuously with Catholic worship in order to develop normally and fruitfully. His desire was to unite liturgy and monasticism in order to restore each. Guéranger secured permission from his bishop to devote himself exclusively to this apostolate. In 1833, with the help of friends, he purchased the ancient and long since deserted priory of SOLESMES, just an hour's walk from his birthplace. There, with five other priests, he began to live in strict accordance with the Rule of St. Benedict, in which everything revolved around the daily chanting of the Divine Office in choir.

With the support of his bishop, Guéranger began negotiations with the Holy See to incorporate his community canonically into the Order of St. Benedict and to obtain approval of his new, and somewhat revolutionary, constitutions. His requests were granted by Pope GREGORY XVI in a papal brief, Sept. 1, 1837; by it, Solesmes was constituted an abbey. Guéranger was elected its first abbot on October 30, having already made profession on July 26 of the same year at St. Paul's-Outside-the-Walls in Rome.

Despite financial hardships, the new foundation progressed rapidly. It soon became the center and rallying point for the liturgical revival and kindred movements throughout France and won the esteem of intellectual leaders, both clerical and lay. As the legitimate heir of Cluny, St. Vannes, and St. Maur, Solesmnes dedicated itself to the best scholarly and liturgical traditions of the Order of St. Benedict.

Guéranger was indefatigable in propagating his ideas through the written word. The best-known and most influential of his publications are his *Institutions liturgiques,* 3 v. (Paris 1840–52), a polemic against the prolixity of local diocesan liturgical usages in France, and his *L'année liturgique*, a commentary on the feasts and seasons of the Church year. Despite several incorrect historical arguments that it advanced, the first of these works eventually brought about the elimination of the evil that it attacked. The second treatise, a series of 15 volumes that began to appear in 1841, was completed by L. Fromage in 1866 and has undergone numerous translations and editions.

Guéranger's monastic followers subsequently upheld and propagated the ideals that he stood for, both in the realm of liturgical scholarship and in that of a liturgically oriented Christian life. The influence of his monastic program is exemplified in the Beuronese congregation; along with its many establishments in Germany and Belgium, it owes much to the advice and inspiration Guéranger gave to its founder, Maurus Wolter, in 1860.

Bibliography: P. DELATTE, *Dom Guéranger, abbé de Solesmes* (Solesmes, 1984). C. JOHNSON, *Prosper Guéranger (1805-1875): A Liturgical Theologian: An Introduction to His Liturgical Writings and Work* (Rome 1984). R. W. FRANKLIN, "Guéranger and Pastoral Liturgy: A Nineteenth-Century Context," *Worship* 50 (1976) 146–162. L. SOLTNER, *Solesmes et Dom Guéranger 1805–1875* (Solesmes 1974).

[M. DUCEY]

GUÉRIN, MOTHER THEODORE, BL.

Founder of the SISTERS OF PROVIDENCE OF SAINT MARY-OF-THE-WOODS, Indiana; b. Oct. 2, 1798 at Etables-sur-mer, Brittany, France; d. May 14, 1856 at Saint Mary-of-the-Woods, Indiana.

Christened Anne-Thérèse by her parents, Laurent, a lieutenant in Napoleon's navy, and Isabelle Guérin, she was one of four children, two of whom died tragically by fire in early childhood. Her father was attacked and killed by brigands in 1813 as he was returning home from military service. Taught by her mother as a young child, Anne-Thérèse later attended a local primary school for a brief period. A young seminarian cousin, who lived for some time in the Guérin household, tutored her in theology, history, and philosophy.

At the age of 16, Anne-Thérèse became both the caretaker of her invalid mother and the teacher and guardian of her younger sister Marie Jeanne. After ten years of devoted service to her family, Anne-Thérèse was able to fulfill her cherished desire to enter the Congregation of the Sisters of Providence at Ruillé-sur-Loire, where she received the religious name Sister St. Theodore. Having pronounced her vows on Sept. 8, 1825, she was appointed the following year as superior of a school in the industrial town of Rennes, where she remained for eight years. After being transferred to Soulaines, Sister St. Theodore, in addition to teaching and administering the local school, studied pharmacy and medicine with a local doctor. At this time the Academy of Angers (Université de France) awarded her a medal for excellent teaching methods, especially in the field of mathematics.

In the summer of 1839, the bishop of Vincennes, Indiana, Celestine de Hailandière, came to the sisters' motherhouse in Ruillé seeking volunteers to bring, as he said, "the French religious spirit" to the United States. The superior general, Mother Mary Lecor, agreed to send sisters should any volunteer for this mission. There were five, and Sister St. Theodore was asked to be their leader. She accepted the call and with two professed sisters and three novices left France in July 1840. On Oct. 22, 1840, the six French sisters arrived at the little clearing in the forest already named Saint Mary-of-the-Woods. There they established an academy for girls, the first in Indiana, and began the foundation of a new religious congregation modeled on the one they had left in France. During her 16 years in America, Mother Theodore as she was now called, founded 16 schools, both academies and free schools for the poor as well as two homes for orphans.

Bp. Francis S. Chatard authorized initial proceedings for the cause of the beatification of Mother Theodore, but there were long delays before the apostolic processes were begun in the United States and France in 1956. They were completed in 1958 and the material was forwarded to Rome for examination by the Congregation of Rites. Mother Theodore Guérin was the sixth citizen of the United States and the first in Indiana to be designated as blessed on Oct. 25, 1998 by Pope John Paul II.

Feast: October 3.

Bibliography: *Mother Theodore Guerin, Journals and Letters,* ed. M. T. MUG (Saint Mary-of-the-Woods, Ind. 1937). M. B. BROWN, *History of the Sisters of Providence.* Vol. 1:1806–1856 (New York 1949). K. BURTON, *Faith Is the Substance* (New York 1959). P. B. MITCHELL, *Mother Theodore Guérin: A Woman for Our Time* (Saint Mary-of-the-Woods, Ind. 1998). M. T. MUG, *Life and Life-Work of Mother Theodore Guérin* (New York 1904). J. E. RYAN, *Positio Super Virtutibus ex officio Concinnata* (Rome 1987); *Call to Courage; A Story of Mother Theodore Guérin* (Notre Dame 1968).

[M. R. MADDEN]

GUERRA, ELENA, BL.

Foundress of the Oblate Sisters of the Holy Spirit; b. Lucca, Italy, June 23, 1835; d. there, April 11, 1914. Elena was born of a wealthy, pious family and was educated privately. From an early age, she was active in works of charity. Eventually, she grouped a number of young girls into an association following a common life, calling it the Pious Union of Spiritual Friendship. From these disciples she chose the first members of her congregation, established in 1872 in honor of St. ZITA and dedicated to the spread of devotion to the Holy Spirit. The institute received the approval of the Holy See in 1911 as the Oblate Sisters of the Holy Spirit, but it is more commonly known as the Sisters of St. Zita. In her efforts to promote devotion to the Holy Spirit, Elena wrote frequently to Pope LEO XIII, whose brief of May 5, 1895, and encyclical, *Divinum illud munus* (1897), rewarded her efforts. Elena wrote some short devotional works and was the teacher of St. Gemma GALGANI. Elena was beatified April 27, 1959.

Feast: April 26.

Bibliography: P. SCAVIZZI, *E. G., apostola dello Spirito Santo* (Lucca 1939). L. CRISTIANI, *Apôtre du Saint-Esprit* (Paris 1964). I. TUBALDO, *A ação do Espírito Santo segundo Helena Guerra* (Belo Horizonte 1964). D. M. ABBRESCIA, *Elena Guerra: profetismo e rinnovamento* (Brescia 1974). *Acta Apostolicae Sedis* 51 (1959) 337–342.

[F. G. SOTTOCORNOLA]

GUERRERO GONZÁLEZ, ANGELA DE LA CRUZ, BL.

Foundress of the Sisters of the Cross; b. Jan. 30, 1846, Seville, Spain; d. there March 2, 1932. The growing sanctity of Angela, the uneducated daughter of a simple family, was recognized by Father Torres Padilla as she was working in a shoe factory in Seville. After she was initially rejected by the Carmelites of Seville, accepted, then forced to leave because of illness, Father Torres suggested (Nov. 1, 1871) that she adopt a rule of life to live as a religious in the secular world. Thereafter she professed a private annual religious vow and recruited peasants as sisters in the Company of the Cross to serve the sick and needy in rural areas. Shortly after the founding of the congregation (Aug. 2, 1875), the sisters heroically ministered to victims of an epidemic in Seville (1876). Angela was beatified at Seville by John Paul II, Nov. 5, 1982, for her service to the poorest of the poor, and for her spirituality of the Cross in a life of poverty, detachment, and humility.

Feast: March 2.

Bibliography: ANGELA DE LA CRUZ, *Escritos íntimos*, ed. by J. M. JAVIERRE (Madrid 1974). J. M. JAVIERRE, *Madre dei poveri* (Rome 1969); *Sor Angela de la Cruz* (Madrid 1982).

[K. I. RABENSTEIN]

GUERRIC OF IGNY, BL.

Cistercian spiritual theologian; b. Tournai, *c.* 1070–80; d. monastery of Igny, Diocese of Reims,

France, Aug. 19, 1157. Guerric was initiated into intellectual and ascetical disciplines by Odo of Cambrai. He was first a cathedral canon, the *magister scholarum* at Tournai until his entry into the Cistercian Order at Clairvaux *c.* 1125. Elected abbot of the monastery of Igny in 1138, Guerric demonstrated an astonishing mastery of Scripture and a perfect command of the homily genre in his 53 authentic sermons for the liturgical year (*Patrologia Latina,* ed. J. P. Migne 185:11–214). For Guerric, the spiritual life consists in the formation of Christ in men according to His ''spiritual form,'' i.e., their life of grace in Christ, who by His mysteries is both principle and exemplar of supernatural life. Particularly noteworthy is Guerric's emphasis on Mary's maternal role in this formation of Christ in men. Growth is described by him in terms of an ascent into light, culminating in wisdom and contemplation. Some of his writings have been attributed to St. BERNARD. Guerric's local cultus was approved 1889.

Feast: Aug. 19.

Bibliography: D. DE WILDE, *De beato Guerrico, abbate Igniacensi eiusque doctrina de formatione Christi in nobis* (Westmalle, Belgium 1935), includes an edition of Guerric's curious dialogue, ''De languore animae amantis,'' 189–196. L. BOUYER, *The Cistercian Heritage,* tr. E. A. LIVINGSTONE (Westminster, Md. 1958) 190–203. R. MILCAMP and A. DUBOIS, ''Le bx. Guerric: Sa vie, son oeuvre,'' in *Collectanea ordinis Cisterciensium Reformatorum* 19 (1957) 207–221; quasi-complete bibliography of authentic and spurious works, manuscripts, editions, and studies, 212–221 M. B. BRARD, *Catholicisme* 5:363–364. B. BETTO, *Guerrico d'Igny e i suoi sermoni* (Abbazia di Praglia 1988).

[C. WADDELL]

GUEVARA Y LIRA, SILVESTRE

Fifth archbishop of Caracas, Venezuela, who fought the secularizing laws of Guzmán Blanco; b. Chamariapa, Anzoátegui, Dec. 31, 1814; d. Caracas, Feb. 20, 1882. Having been vicar-general of the old Diocese of Guayana and senator in the National Congress, Guevara was consecrated archbishop of Caracas on Feb. 6, 1853. The first 17 years of his episcopate were characterized by fruitful activity in which he commanded respect and admiration. Guevara completely restored the cathedral, in ruins since the earthquake of 1812. He reorganized the studies and the discipline of the seminary and thus raised the prestige of the clergy. He succeeded in getting the Venezuelan government to accept a concordat with the Holy See and went to Rome to sign it as the representative named by the government. Unfortunately, Venezuela did not ratify that concordat because of a sudden change in government when the federal revolution triumphed. In 1869–70, Guevara attended Vatican Council I.

For the next 12 years, during the regime of Antonio Guzmán Blanco, Guevara was the focus of the most serious political-religious conflicts in the history of Venezuela. A disagreement over the date on which a *Te Deum* requested by the government was to be celebrated was the opportunity and the pretext for the president to expel Guevara from the country on 24 hours' notice. However, the autocratic ruler still had to contend with the courage with which the archbishop sustained the rights of his position during seven years in exile. Other ecclesiastical dignitaries making common cause with the archbishop also suffered exile and severe criticism. Exasperated with the determination of the prelate, President Guzmán began a series of persecuting actions: he closed all of the convents and confiscated the property of the nuns; he closed the seminaries and revoked the autonomy of the university courses in ecclesiastical studies; he secularized the cemeteries; he substituted civil registration for ecclesiastical as a previous condition to Baptism and Matrimony; he established civil marriage, for which he declared priests legally competent; and, finally, he tried to create a national church separate from Rome.

Such a deplorable situation became more serious because the archdiocese was without a pastor. Since Guzmán continued his pressures, the pope, through an apostolic delegate, suggested to Guevara that he make the sacrifice of resigning so that a new archbishop could be named. With great humility and understanding, the archbishop presented his resignation to the pope. In November of 1876, the new archbishop of Caracas was consecrated.

In 1877, with the end of Guzmán's regime, the new president authorized the return of Guevara. The reception that Caracas accorded the famous exile was moving. The prelate spent the last five years of his life surrounded by affection and widespread veneration of the faithful.

Bibliography: H. FANGER, *Silvestre Guevara y Lira* (Washington 1907). *Apoteósis del Ilmo. Silvestre Guevara y Lira* (Caracas 1907). M. WATTERS, *A History of the Church in Venezuela* (Chapel Hill 1933). N. E. NAVARRO, *Anales eclesiásticos Venezolanos* (2d ed. Caracas 1951).

[P. P. BARNOLA]

GUIBERT, JOSEPH DE

Jesuit ascetical and mystical theologian; b. L'Îsle-sur-Tarn, France, Sept. 14, 1877; d. Rome, March 23, 1942. De Guibert studied at the Collège du Caousou in Toulouse before entering the Society of Jesus on Oct. 19, 1895, at Toulouse. His younger brother Bernard followed him into the society. De Guibert pursued his Jesuit studies at Toulouse, Vals-près-Le Puy, France, and Enghien, Belgium, where he was ordained Aug. 26, 1906. In 1899, he received a licentiate in literature from the Sorbonne, and from 1901 to 1903 he studied history at the Sorbonne. De Guibert taught theology at the regional seminary in Lecce, Italy, and at Enghien. From 1914 to 1918, he was an army chaplain. When he founded the *Revue d'ascétique et de mystique* in 1919, it was De Guibert's intention to establish a periodical that would apply the methods demanded by contemporary scientific research to the study of spirituality. From 1922 to 1942, De Guibert taught ascetical and mystical theology at the Gregorian University, Rome, and from 1932 to 1942 he was a consultor to the Congregation of Rites. His writings were primarily the fruit of his teaching. The first edition of *Theologia spiritualis, ascetica et mystica* (Eng. tr. of 3d ed. by Paul Barrett, OFMCap, New York 1953) appeared in Rome in 1937. His posthumous work *La Spiritualité de la Compagnie de Jésus* (Rome 1953; Eng. tr. by W. J. Young, *The Jesuits: Their Doctrine and Practice,* Chicago 1964) is primarily historical and documentary.

Bibliography: J. DE. GUIBERT, *Leçons de théologie spirituelle,* v.1 (Toulouse 1946), preface F. CAVALLERA and M. VILLER. P. GALTIER, in *Revue d'ascétique et de mystique* 26 (1950) 97–120.

[J. F. MULLIN]

GUIBERT OF NOGENT

Historian and ecclesiastical controversialist; b. Clermont-en-Beauvais, 1053; d. Nogent, 1124. Born to noble parents, Guibert was dedicated to the religious life in his infancy. He received his early education at the Benedictine abbey of Flavigny. At first, he was interested in the classical Latin poets. However, under the influence of (St.) Anselm of Bec, he later turned to the study of theology. However, Guibert's literary style shows the influence of his earlier interests. In 1104, Guibert became the abbot of Nogent-sous-Coucy in the Diocese of Laon. He is best remembered today for his writings, especially his autobiography *De vita sua,* which was written toward the end of his life. His work is a prime source for information about life in castle and monastery, educational conditions and methods, and, most especially, about the commune of Laon. Almost as well known is Guibert's history of the first crusade, *Gesta Dei per Francos,* which was written about 1110. This is largely a paraphrase of the anonymous *Gesta Francorum,* but Guibert still manages to impart considerable color to his narrative; he is also often critical of what he recounts. Perhaps Guibert's most controversial work is his treatise on relics, *De pignoribus sanctorum,* in which he was highly critical of the use of relics (*see* RELICS). In addition to the works mentioned, Guibert wrote a treatise on homiletics; ten books of *Moralia in Genesim* based on Gregory's *Moralia;* five books of *Tropologiae* on Hosea, Amos, and Lamentations; a treatise, *De Incarnatione,* against the Jews; and a letter, *De buccella Judae et de veritate Dominici corporis,* which attacked Berengarius's heresy.

Bibliography: *Patrologia Latina* 156; 184:1031–44. *The Autobiography of Guibert, Abbot of Nogent-sous-Coucy,* tr. C. C. S. BLAND (New York 1926). B. MONOD, *Le Moine Guibert et son temps* (Paris 1905). J. C. DIDIER, *Catholicisme. Hier, aujourd'hui et demain,* ed. G. JACQUEMET, 5:367. J. GEISELMANN, ''Die Stellung des G. von N. (—1124) in der Eucharistielehre der Frühscholastik,'' *Theologische Quartalschrift* 110 (1929) 66–84, 279–305. *Histoire littéraire de la France* (Paris 1733–1768) 10:433–500.

[V. L. BULLOUGH]

GUIBERT OF TOURNAI

Franciscan spiritual writer, teacher, preacher; b. Tournai, France, *c.* 1210; d. Tournai, Oct. 7(?), 1284. He was born Guibert (Wibert) Aspiès de Murielporte and was of noble lineage. Guibert had only one brother, Henry, also a teacher, who died before him. After being brought up by Bp. Gautier (Walter) of Marvy (d. 1251), Guibert studied at Paris, where he eventually became a master in theology (*c.* 1256). Attracted to contemplation, Guibert became a Franciscan (*c.* 1235), but his superiors assigned him to teaching. He may have been a participant in the First Crusade of LOUIS IX (1248–54), for it is known through the *De viris illustribus*, attributed to HENRY OF GHENT, that Guibert wrote a history of this Crusade in *Hodoeporicon.* Furthermore, several sermons addressed *Ad crucesignatos* are extant. If Guibert did go, he was back in France preaching (in Latin) before the clergy of Paris in 1250. He published his *Sermones dominicales et de sanctis* (ed. Paris 1518) some time before Aug. 27, 1255, when Pope Alexander IV congratulated him and asked him to give a copy to his *penitentiarius,* Mansueto of Castiglione. In October 1259, Guibert finished *Eruditio regum et principum,* which included three letters, the first dedicated to Louis IX [ed. A. De Poorter (Louvain 1914)]. From 1260 to 1262, Guibert produced *Erudimentum doctrinae,* a work on the four reasons for teaching, followed by *De modo addiscendi* [ed. E. Bonifaccio (Turin 1953)]. Succeeding Eudes of Rosny, Guibert was master regent at Paris from 1260 to 1263; in 1267, he asked Louis IX for a franchise for the city of Tournai. Guibert wrote the *Collectio de scandalis ecclesiae* [ed. A. Stroick, *Archivum Franciscanum historicum* (1931)] in 1274, the treatise *De pace* [ed. E. Longpré (Quaracchi 1925)] in 1275–76. One of his sermons for Ash Wednesday survives (March 3, 1283). His epitaph read: ''Christo servivit qui totum scibile scivit.''

Besides the above works, Guibert was also the author of a commentary on the Sentences, *Quodlibeta,* and *Comm. in epistolas s. Pauli,* but all are lost. Before 1258, he wrote *De officio episcopali et ecclesiae caeremoniis* (ed. 1571, 1677); *Vita s. Eleutherii* (*Acta Sanctorum,* Feb. 3:180–208) and *De miraculis s. Blasii* (lost). His homiletic production included the *Ad varios status* (London 1473), which completed the *De modo addiscendi.* His works on asceticism included *Epistola exhortatoria ad b. Isabellam* [ed. A. De Poorter, *Revue d'ascétique et de mystique* (1931)], *De morte non timenda, De 7 verbis Domini in cruce,* and *De nomine Iesu* (ed. E. Bonelli, 1774). He collected excerpts from the Fathers and Seneca in *Pharetra* (ed. 1866). Guibert's writings are effusive and wander from the main topic. A mystic, he often followed St. BONAVENTURE, but was at times an original thinker.

Bibliography: L. BAUDRY, "Wibert de Tournai," *Revue d'histoire franciscaine* 5 (1928) 23–61. C. BERUBE, "Guibert de Tournai et Robert Grosseteste sources inconnues des Saint Bonaventure: Rudimentum doctrinae de Guibert de Tournai," in *Sanctus Bonaventura 1274–1974,* vol. 2 (Rome 1973), 627–654. P. GLORIEUX, *Répertoire des maîtres en théologie de Paris au XIIIe siècle* (Paris 1933–34) 2:56–59.

[J. CAMBELL]

GUICCIARDINI, FRANCESCO

Italian historian and statesman; b. Florence, 1483; d. Arcetri, May 22, 1540. From his parents, Piero di Jacopo and Simona Gianfigliazzi, he inherited an attachment to the Medici party. He studied law in Ferrara and Padua and gained his doctor's degree at Pisa. He married Maria Salviati in 1508, established a lucrative law practice, and wrote the *Storie fiorentine dal 1378 al 1509,* showing wisdom and judgment beyond his years. Early in 1512, before reaching the statutory age of 30, he was named ambassador to the court of Ferdinand V of Castile, whose portrait he so deftly drew. Upon his return to Italy in 1514, he entered the service of the Medici, who had become rulers of Florence in 1512. In 1516 Leo X appointed him governor of Modena and later of Reggio and Parma, which he successfully defended against the French in 1521. Leo X also named him commissioner general of the papal army, a post Clement VII confirmed. In 1523 he was made president of the Romagna. He fulfilled these offices conscientiously and with ability and firmness. After the battle of Pavia (1525), he was instrumental in forming the League of Cognac against Charles V, and became lieutenant-general of the papal forces. His desire to save Italy was hindered by the dilatory tactics of the Duke of Urbino, commander of the League's troops. During the siege of Florence by Charles V, Guicciardini kept to his villa at Finocchieto to study and write. But after the Medici returned to power in 1530, he served as adviser to Alessandro and even defended him against the Florentine exiles at Naples. His efforts assured the independence of Florence from Charles V, but they did not prevent the assassination of Alessandro by Lorenzino in January 1537. Guicciardini was instrumental in the election of Cosimo de Medici, but his later attempts to check the duke's absolutism led to his political decline. He retired to his villa in Arcetri, spending the leisure of his last years in the composition of the *Storia d' Italia.*

Francesco Guicciardini, by sculptor Luigi Cartei, Florence. (Alinari-Art Reference/Art Resource, NY)

This work, translated into all Western European languages, is an eyewitness account of the period from Charles VIII's expedition (1494) to Clement VII's death (1534). Guicciardini is noteworthy for having broken away from the narrow concept of local municipal chronicles. The era that Guicciardini treated—the time of the Borgias, Leo X, Clement VII, Ferdinand of Spain, Luther, Columbus, Francis I, and Charles V—was also the period of Italy's greatest political intrigues and a time of war.

Guicciardini's attempt at dispassionate narration does not conceal his sorrow at Italy's fate. To him it was clear that the events of history were subordinated to a conflict of interests, in which *la cupidità* was the sole motivating force of the individual protagonists. Emphasis is therefore on political rather than social, cultural, or religious factors. The *Storia d' Italia* was esteemed by Ronsard, Bacon, Raleigh, and others.

Among his other writings in the ten volumes of the *Opere inedite,* ed. G. Canestrini (Florence 1857–67) are many letters; the *Ricordi,* 403 maxims, some duplicated; the *Considerazioni intorno ai discorsi del Machiavelli sopra la prima Deca di Tito Livio*, notes that illustrate the ideological differences between Guicciardini and his contemporary; 16 *Discorsi politici;* the *Dialogo del reggimento di Firenze,* revealing his theory of rule vested in a senate composed of an aristocracy of merit rather than one of class; nine *Discorsi intorno alle mutazioni e riforme del governo fiorentino;* the *Storie fiorentine;* the *Relazione di Spagna;* the *Istruzioni delle cose di Romagna;* and minor works, mostly of an autobiographical nature. Many letters have since been published, as well as his *Diario del viaggio in Spagna* (1932), and *Le cose fiorentine* (1945), a eulogy of the Florentine oligarchy.

Bibliography: *Scrittori d'Italia* (Bari 1910–). R. RIDOLFI, *Vita di Francesco Guicciardini* (Rome 1960). U. SPIRITO, *Machiavelli e Guicciardini* (2d ed. Rome 1945). R. PALMAROCCHI, *Studi Guicciardiniani* (Letteraria 6; Florence 1947). V. DE. CAPRARIIS, *Francesco Guicciardini* (Bari 1950). V. LUCIANI, *Francesco Guicciardini and His European Reputation* (New York 1936). F. GILBERT, *Machiavelli and Guicciardini: Politics and History in 16th-Century Florence* (Princeton 1964). R. RIDOLFI, *Studi Guicciardiani* (Florence 1978). P. BONDANELLA, *Francesco Guicciardini* (Boston 1976). G. SASSO, *Franceso Guicciardini, 1483–1983* (Florence 1984).

[V. LUCIANI]

GUIDO DE BAYSIO

Canonist; b. Reggio d'Emilia; d. Avignon, 1313. He studied in Bologna under the canonist Johannes de Anguissola and the professor of civil law Guido de Suzaria. Guido de Baysio first held ecclesiastical offices in Reggio, and in 1295 he received from Boniface VIII a canonicate and precentorship in Chartres. In 1296 he was made archdeacon of Bologna, from which office he is usually styled *archidiaconus.* He taught Canon Law in Bologna and was installed as professor of the *Decretum* of Gratian in 1301. Among his pupils were Alvarus Pelagius, Mattheus Romanus, and notably, Johannes Andreae. He is mentioned as *auditor litterarum contradictarum* in 1303.

His principal work was the *Apparatus ad Decretum*, called *Rosarium*, completed on Jan. 25, 1300. It is a Canon Law classic and is indispensable for a knowledge of older canonical writings. Guido de Baysio's chief ail in this work was to append material from the DECRETISTS and earlier DECRETALISTS not used in the *glossa ordinaria* on the *Decretum* of Gratian, as well as supplementary material written after the *glossa ordinaria.* His sources for pre-Johannine material on the *Decretum* are HUGUCCIO and the *Glossa Palatina*, which he ascribes in *toto* to Laurentius Hispanus. He also cites, from among the decretists, Bazianus, Bernardus Compostellanus Antiquus, Johannes Faventius, Melendus, P (Petrus Hispanus), and from among the post-Johannine decretists, he cites Bertrandus and Johannes de Phintona.

His *Apparatus ad Sextum*, written between 1306 and 1311, was the third classical commentary on the *Liber Sextus*, after the apparatuses of Johannes Monachus and Johannes Andreae. Following his usual pattern, he made use of the thought of older canonists, especially the early decretalists; the *regulae iuris* are not commented upon. The *Tractatus super haeresi et aliis criminibus in causa templariorum et D. Bonifacii D.P. papae VIII*, written at the time of the Council of Vienne, deals with the question of the Templars and is a defense of Boniface VIII. His *Quaestiones*, written in Reggio between 1283 and 1289, has never been printed.

Bibliography: J. F. VON SCHULTE, *Die Geschichte der Quellen und der Literatur des Kanonischen Rechts,* 3 v. in 4 (Stuttgart 1875–80) 2:186–190. F. GILLMANN, "Die Abfassungszeit der Dekretsumme Huguccios," *Archiv für katholisches Kirchenrecht* 94 (1914) 246, note; "Guido de Baysio und Johannes de Anguissola," *ibid.* 104 (1924) 54–55; "Johannes von Phintona, ein vergessener Kanonist des 13. Jahrhunderts," *ibid.* 116 (1936) 446–484. S. KUTTNER, *Repertorium der Kanonistik* (Rome 1937); *Studi e Testi* 71 (Rome), 87–88. S. KUTTNER, "Bernardus Compostellanus Antiquus," *Traditio* 1 (1943) 309. A. VAN HOVE, *Commentarium Lovaniense in Codicem iuris canonici 1*, v.1–5 (Mechlin 1928–); v.1, Prolegomena (2d. ed. 1945), 1:455, 460. G. MOLLAT, *Dictionnaire de droit canonique,* ed. R. NAZ, 7 v. (Paris 1935–65), 5:1007–08. A. M. STICKLER, "Decretisti Bolognesi dimenticati," *Studia Gratiana* 3 (1955) 386–388. F. LIOTTA, "Appunti per una biografia del canonista Guido da Baisio, arcidiacono de Bologna," *Studi Senesi* 76 (1964) 7–52. S. KUTTNER, introd. to repr. of Venice 1581 ed. of J. KUTTNER, *In quinque decratalium libros: Novella commentaria*, 5 v. in 4 (Turin 1963) 1:xi–xii, also in *Jurist* 24 (1964) 405.

[K. W. NORR]

GUIDO MARAMALDI, BL.

Dominican preacher and inquisitor; b. Naples, Italy, mid-14th century; d. there, *c.* 1391. Born of noble Neopolitan parents, Guido entered the DOMINICANS at San Domenico in Naples, studied philosophy and theology there, and enjoyed a reputation as a pulpit orator. In Ragusa the citizens erected a Dominican convent as a tribute to his preaching, and later he was appointed inquisitor (*see* INQUISITION) for the Kingdom of Naples. He was buried at the chapel of the Rosary in the church of San Domenico, and the popularity of his cult soon caused the chapel to become known as the chapel of Blessed Guido. The cult never received official approbation, but Domenico Marchese (d. 1692) prevailed upon the BOLLANDISTS to insert a brief notice on Guido in the *Acta Sanctorum* in 1612.

Feast: June 25.

Bibliography: *Acta Sanctorum* June 7;130–131. J. QUÉTIF and J. ÉCHARD, *Scriptores Ordinis praedicatorum* 1.2:702. D. M. MARCHESE, *Sagro Diario Domenicano,* 6 v. (Naples 1681–88) 3:333–344. *Année Dominicaine,* 12 v. in 23 (Lyons 1883–1909) 6.2:534–536.

[P. M. STARRS]

GUIDO OF ANDERLECHT, ST.

Confessor, known as St. Wye (in Flemish) and the ''Poor Man of Anderlecht''; d. Anderlecht, Belgium, Sept. 12, 1012. The only details concerning the life of Guido come from a vita composed 100 years after his death. According to this text, Guido was the son of peasant parents in Brabant and become a sexton at the church of Our Lady in Laeken, near Brussels. After engaging in business for some time as a merchant, he undertook a seven-year PILGRIMAGE to Rome and Jerusalem as expiation. After his return, Guido lived out the few remaining days of his life in Anderlecht. He began to be venerated as a result of miracles reputedly worked at his almost forgotten tomb in that city.

Feast: Sept. 12.

Bibliography: *Acta sanctorum,* Sept. 4 (1868) 36–48. J. LECLERCQ, *Saints de Belgique* (new rev. ed. Tournai 1953). F. MORTIER, ''La Légende De S. Guidon à Anderlecht,'' *Folklore brabançon* 10 (1930) 46–55. J. LAVALLAYE, ''Notes sur la culte de S. G. à. A.,'' *Annales de la Societé royale d'archéologie de Bruxelles* 37 (1934) 221–248.

[L. KURRAS]

GUIDO OF AREZZO

Medieval music theorist whose principles prepared the foundation of European music notation; b. Arezzo?, Italy, *c.* 992; d. probably in the Camaldolese monastery at Avellana, 1050. Guido was educated in the Benedictine abbey at Pomposa, where he evidently made great use of the music treatise of Odo of Saint-Maur des Fossés

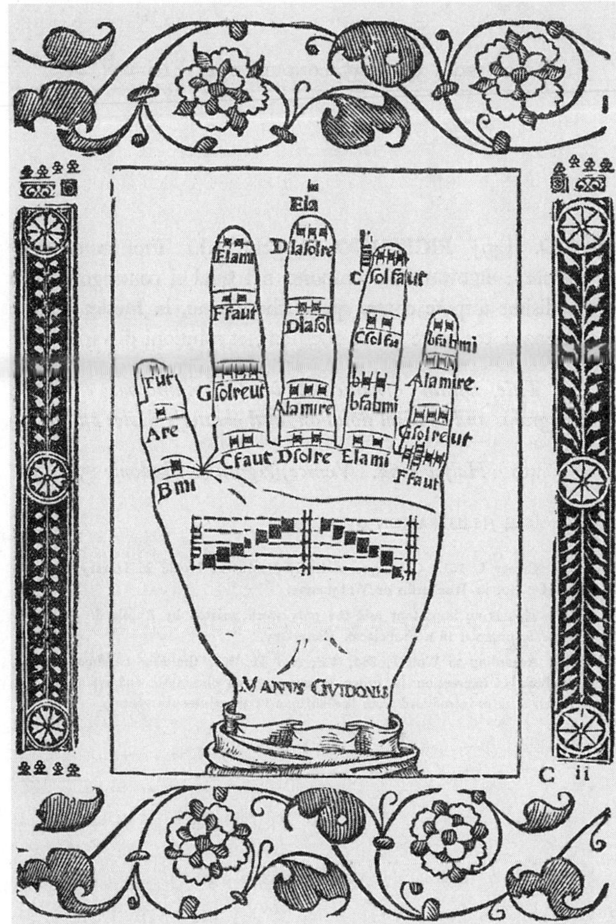

The Guidonian Hand from Picitono, the ''Fra Angelico of Music,'' an illustrated-palm, 11th-century medieval musical scale, first system of learning music by assigning notes to parts of hand, solmization (sightsinging), developed by Guido of Arezzo. (©CORBIS/Bettmann)

(see M. Gerbert, *Scriptores ecclesiastici de musica sacra potissimum,* 1:265–284 and 1:251–264), and also must have developed his principle of staff notation. He left there *c.* 1025 when fellow monks resisted his musical innovations; whereupon Theobald, Bishop of Arezzo (1023–36), appointed him a teacher at his cathedral school and commissioned him to write the *Micrologus de Disciplina Artis Musicae* (c. 1025–26; also versified by Guido for teaching purposes before 1028 under the title *Regulae Rhythmicae*). Theobald also arranged in 1028 for Guido to give Pope John XIX (1024–33) an Antiphonary that he had at least begun in Pomposa. This book (no longer in existence) was probably written in staff notation, and it was accompanied by an explanatory preface to the new method, preserved as the *Aliae Regulae* (*c.* 1020). The prologue to the *Dialogus* of Odo of Saint-Maur (Gerbert, *op. cit.,* 1:251) is probably also by Guido (Oesch, 73–76).

Guido must have returned to Avellana from Rome, where he probably wrote in 1029 the *Epistola de ignoto cantu* to Brother Michael, his friend in Pomposa, and also perhaps a letter condemning the simony of Abp. Heribert II of Milan. No other works attributed to Guido may be regarded as genuine (Gerbert, *op. cit.,* 2:33, 37, 50; *Scriptorum de musica medii aevi nova series,* 2:78, 110, 115). Guido himself and the Camaldolese brought about his future fame, which may be assessed not only in the triumph of his new method of notation, but also in the fact that no medieval treatise is preserved in so many sources spread over so wide an area as the *Micrologus.* Moreover, the oldest MSS notated in this way are of the 11th century and from Camaldolese houses—e.g., MS Florence, Biblioteca Laurenziana, 158 (from Struma), and MS Vallombrosa 247 (from Vallombrosa).

In the new method there are two fundamental innovations: the construction by thirds of the system of lines; and the use of letters as clefs and/or the coloring of certain lines (yellow for C, red for F), indicating with reference to the other lines the position of the semitone. The two innovations together mark the fulfillment of the principle of diastematic writing. Both elements—letters and lines—antedated Guido, but their combination in this manner made possible the first unambiguous notating of neumes. At the same time Guido was developing a second epoch-making technique—that of solmization (see *Harvard Dictionary of Music* 690–691), which enabled one to sing a notated song correctly from the written page through use of the syllables *ut, re, mi, fa, sol,* and *la* (described in *Epistola de ignoto cantu*). In a musical setting, not found earlier than Guido, of the hymn to St. John *Ut queant laxis . . .* (by PAUL THE DEACON?, 8th century), the first syllables of each of the half-lines of the poem fall on tones *c, d, e, f, g,* and *a,* in order. This hymn is intended as a mnemonic aid, enabling students to become familiar with the sound (*proprietas*) of the tones of the hexachord, so that as they read neumes on the staff they would grasp the arrangement of whole and half tones within a section of a melody. There is nothing to suggest that Guido used this mnemonic melody in connection with the principle of solmization (mutation), which appeared at the end of the 11th century (see Oesch, ''Hexachord,'' *Die Musik in Geschichte und Gegenwart,* 6:349; *Harvard Dictionary of Music* 330–332). Hence the ''Guidonian hand'' came into use only after Guido's death. Neither Aribo Scholasticus (*c.* 1078) nor Johannes Affligemensis (*c.* 1100), both of whom discuss Guido, refer to solmization.

Bibliography: H. OESCH, *Guido von Arezzo* (Bern 1954). J. SMITS VAN WAESBERGHE, *De musico-paedagogico et theoretico Guidone Aretino* (Florence 1953); ''The Musical Notation of G. of A.,'' *Musica Disciplina* (Rome 1947–), Yearbook of the History of Music, American Institute of Musicology, 5 (1951) 15–53; ''G. of A. and Musical Improvisation,'' *ibid.,* 55–63; *Die Musik in Geschichte und Gegenwart,* ed. F. BLUME (Kassel-Basel 1949–) 5:1071–78. W. APEL, *Gregorian Chant* (Bloomington, Ind. 1958). G. REESE, *Music in the Middle Ages* (New York 1940). P. H. LÁNG, *Music in Western Civilization* (New York 1941). M. A. LEACH, ''*His ita perspectis:* A Practical Supplement to Guido of Arezzo's Pedagogical Method,'' *Journal of Musicology,* 8 (1990) 82–101. C. V. PALISCA, ''Guido of Arezzo,'' in *The New Grove Dictionary of Music and Musicians,* ed. S. SADIE, v. 7 (New York 1980) 803–807. D. M. RANDEL, ed., *The Harvard Biographical Dictionary of Music* (Cambridge 1996) 339–340. N. SLONIMSKY, ed., *Baker's Biographical Dictionary of Musicians* (8th ed. New York 1992) 682–683.

[H. OESCH]

GUIDO OF CORTONA, BL.

Franciscan priest; b. Cortona, Tuscany, Italy, *c.* 1187; d. Cortona, June 12, 1247. A wealthy young bachelor, in 1210 he welcomed FRANCIS OF ASSISI in his home with such kindness that the saint praised courtesy as one of God's qualities and prayed that Guido would join the new FRANCISCAN order. He did so after seeing Francis in levitation (cf. *FIORETTI* ch. 37 with note in R. Brown ed.). Guido founded the hermitage of Le Celle near Cortona and became an ascetical priest. Usually eating only one meal a day, he acquired fame for miracles reported in his vita: when gravely ill he was cured by water that he had changed into wine; he healed a priest's paralyzed arm; multiplied a widow's flour during a famine; and brought back to life a girl who had drowned in a well. St. Francis appeared to him twice in his last days. His cult was approved in 1583.

Feast: June 16.

Bibliography: U. SERNINI CUCCIATTI, *La leggenda del beato Guido* (Cortona 1900). *Estudios franciscanos* 11 (1913) 43–44. L. DA CORTONA, *Il primo convento francescano* (Florence 1915). N. BRUNI, *Le reliquie del beato Guido da Cortona* (Cortona 1947). O. ENGLEBERT, *St. Francis of Assisi: A Biography,* tr. E. M. COOPER, 2d augm. ed. by I. BRADY and R. BROWN (Chicago 1966). W. FORSTER, *Lexikon für Theologie und Kirche,* ed. J. HOFER and K. RAHNER, 10 v. (2d, new ed. Freiburg 1957–65) 4:1268.

[R. BROWN]

GUIDO OF POMPOSA, ST.

Benedictine abbot; b. Casamari, near Ravenna, Italy, *c.* 1010; d. Borgo San Donnino, March 31, 1046. After living as a hermit for three years in the spirit of St. ROMUALD, he came to the Abbey of POMPOSA, where he was shortly afterward elected abbot. During his tenure, Pomposa became one of the more celebrated monasteries of northern Italy. At Guido's invitation, PETER DAMIAN visited the abbey and for two years (*c.* 1039–41) lectured on Sacred Scripture. When Emperor Henry III entered Italy in 1046 on his way to the Synod of SUTRI, Guido joined the imperial retinue at Henry's request, but he took sick en route and died near Parma, where he was temporarily buried. In 1047 his remains were brought to Speyer, Germany, and they are buried at the present time in the Sankt Guidostift.

Feast: May 4, translation; March 31 in Speyer.

Bibliography: *Acta Santorum*, March 3:912–915, legendary. *Bibliotheca hagiographica latina antiquae et mediae aetatis,* 2 v. (Brussels 1898–1901; suppl. 1911) 8876–78. A. M. ZIMMERMAN, *Kalendarium Benedictinum: Die Heiligen und Seligen des Benediktineorderns und seiner Zweige,* 4 v. (Metten 1933–38) 1:394–396. A. BUTLER, *The Lives of the Saints,* rev. ed. H. THURSTON and D. ATTWATER, 4 v. (New York 1956) 1:709–710. J. E. GUGUMUS, *Lexikon für Theologie und Kirche,* ed. J. HOFER and K. RAHNER, 10 v. (2d, new ed. Freiburg 1957–65) 4:1269.

[O. J. BLUM]

GUIDO THE LOMBARD, BL.

Founder; b. probably Milan, Italy, *c.* 11th century. Two contradictory accounts of Guido's life exist, enabling the historian to affirm little but the fact of his existence and a connection with the HUMILIATI, probably as their founder. The Humiliati, who came into prominence *c.* 1180, were associations of men and women working in the wool trades of the Lombard cities. They were dedicated to an evangelical life, and their status, at first lay, was later that of tertiary religious. One legendary account has it that Guido, *c.* 1134, received the rule of the order from the hands of BERNARD OF CLAIRVAUX. The male branch was suppressed by PIUS V in 1571 for refusing to reform, but a few communities of women still exist in Italy. Besides being revered by these sisters as their founder, Guido is regarded as one of the glories of the Church of Milan.

Feast: Dec. 6.

Bibliography: J. E. STADLER and F. J. HEIM, *Vollständiges Heiligen-Lexikon,* 5 v. (Augsburg 1858–82) 2:549. F. VERNET, *Dictionnaire de théologie catholique*, ed. A. VACANT et al., 15 v. (Paris 1903–50; Tables générales 1951–) 7.1:311–321.

[N. M. RIEHLE]

GUIGO I

Carthusian legislator and spiritual writer; b. 1084; d. July 27, 1136. Guigo entered La Grande-Chartreuse in 1106 and was elected its fifth prior in 1109. After an avalanche destroyed the monastery in 1132, Guigo rebuilt it on the site where it still stands. St. Bernard venerated him as a master of the mystical life; Peter the Venerable considered him one of the most remarkable men of his time.

Between 1121 and 1127, Guigo wrote the *Consuetudines Cartusiae,* a codification of the customs that regulated the life of the earliest Carthusian monks and lay brothers. The main sources of this, after the Scriptures, as Guigo mentions, were the letters of St. Jerome and the Rule of St. Benedict. With regard to the ''other writings of incontestable authority'' to which he refers, recent research has been able to identify many of them and has thus shown that the first Carthusians were widely read in ancient and contemporary literature on the monastic and the eremitical life. The *Consuetudines* of Guigo became the rule of the Carthusian Order, shaping in outline and in many particulars its semi-eremitical character as it is lived to the present day. Subsequent collections of statutes provided for changing circumstances, but the *Consuetudines* remained the backbone of the order's legislation. The first general chapter (1140 or 1141), establishing liturgical uniformity for the whole confederation of charterhouses, made Guigo's codification of the liturgy and the chant of La Grande-Chartreuse normative for all other houses. During the last years of his life, Guigo wrote a life of St. Hugh of Grenoble (d. 1132), the cofounder of La Grande-Chartreuse. In his *Meditationes,* Guigo left us one of the spiritual and literary masterpieces of his century. Nine of his letters are extant.

Bibliography: M. LAPORTE, *Catholicisme. Hier, aujourd'hui et demain,* ed. G. JACQUMET 5:375–376. *Consuetudines Cartusiae, Patrologia Latina* 153:631–760. Critical ed. in *Aux Sources de la Vie Cartusienne,* stenciled Collection to be consulted in Carthusian libraries, v.4 (1962). *Lettres des premiers Chartreux* (*Sources Chrétiennes* 88; Paris 1962) v.1. GUIGUES DU CHASTEL, *Meditationes Guigonis prioris Cartusiae,* ed. A. WILMART (*Études de philosophie médiévale* 22; Paris 1936), critical ed.; *Meditations of Guigo,* tr. J. J. JOLIN (Milwaukee 1951). S. AUTORE, *Dictionnaire de théologie catholique*, ed. A. VACANT et al. (Paris 1903–50) 6.2:1964–66.

[B. DU MOUSTIER]

GUIGO II

Carthusian spiritual writer; d. probably 1188. Guigo was elected ninth prior of La Grande-Chartreuse and general of the order in 1173. He resigned from this office in 1180. Guigo wrote the *Scala Paradisi* (also known as the *Scala Claustralium*) about 1150. The work was variously attributed in the past to St. Augustine, to St. Bernard, and to Guigo I. It distinguishes four stages of spiritual occupation: ''Reading, you should seek; meditating, you will find; praying, you shall call; and contemplating, the door will be opened to you.'' This formula was later borrowed by St. John of the Cross. A Middle English version of the treatise under the title *A Ladder of Four Rungs of Guy II* was published at Stanbrook Abbey in 1953. Guigo also wrote a volume of *Meditationes* (ed. M. M. Davy, *La Vie spirituelle*, supplement 1932–34). Unlike those of Guigo I, these meditations are more effective than profound, and their complicated symbolism makes reading difficult. The *Liber de quadripertito exercitio cellae,* until recently ascribed to Guigo, is now known to have been written by ADAM SCOTUS.

Bibliography: M. LAPORTE, *Catholicisme. Hier, aujourd'hui et deman*, ed. G. JACQUEMET, 5:376. S. AUTORE, *Dictionaaire de théologie catholique*, ed. A. VACANT et al. (Paris 1903–50) 6.2:1966–67. J. M. DÉCHANET, *Dictionnaire de spiritualité ascétique et mystique. Doctrine et histoire.* 2.2:1959–61. Text of Guigo's *Scala* among the works of St. Augustine, *Patrologia latina* ed. J. P. MIGNE (Paris 1878–90) 40:997–1004, and of St. Bernard, *ibid.* 184:475–484.

[B. DU MOUSTIER]

GUIGO DE PONTE

Also known as (Guigue du Pont), Carthusian mystical writer; d. Oct. 29, 1297. He was prior of the Charterhouse of Mont-Dieu from 1290 to 1297. When a monk at La Grande–Chartreuse he wrote a still unedited treatise *De contemplatione* known chiefly, until recently, from the *Contemplationum libri tres* of DENIS THE CARTHUSIAN. Guigo distinguished three main types of contemplation: ''natural,'' which arises from finding the Creator ''mirrored'' in His creation; ''scholastic,'' which is an acquired ''wisdom,'' an experimental knowledge, that results from finding God in the Scriptures; and ''divinely infused,'' which is truly mystical. Denis in his classifications and descriptions was dependent on Hugh of Balma and Guigo, but he assimilated their teaching in his usual personal way. In matters of contemplation Guigo accentuated the affective element rather than the intellectual, though this emphasis is less marked in him than it is in Balma. Real mystical contemplation consisted for him in an *odumbratio caliginis in cubiculo cordis* (an overshadowing of darkness in the chamber of the heart), much as in *The CLOUD OF UNKNOWING.* His dependence on Pseudo-Dionysius is evident.

Bibliography: A. M. SOCHAY, *Catholicisme* 5:374–375. J. P. GRAUSEM, ''Le *De Contemplatione* du Chartreux Guigues du Pont,'' *Revue d'ascétique et de mystiquet* 10 (1929) 259–289. DENIS LE CHARTREUX, *Opera omnia,* 44 v. (Tournai 1896–1935) 41:252–253.

[B. DU MOUSTIER]

GUILDAY, PETER K.

Educator, church historian; b. Chester, Pa., March 25, 1884; d. Washington D.C., July 31, 1947. Guilday was the second of 12 children of Irish-born Peter Wilfred Guilday and Ellen (Keenan) Guilday of Eddyston, Pa. Guilday attended Catholic schools in Chester and Philadelphia. In 1902, he enrolled at St. Charles Borromeo Seminary, Overbrook, Philadelphia, as a candidate for the priesthood of the Archdiocese of Philadelphia. Guilday was awarded a scholarship in 1907 and went to the American College at Louvain, Belgium, for the last two years of theology.

Following his ordination on July 11, 1909, Guilday did graduate work in history at the Catholic University of Louvain. He spent a year of research in the archives of France, Belgium, Spain, and Italy, and another year of study in London. Upon the publication of his dissertation *The English Colleges and Convents in the Catholic Low Countries, 1558–1795* in 1914, Guilday was awarded the doctorate by Louvain. The outbreak of World War I interrupted his labors on a second volume, which was never completed. In 1914, the rector of the Catholic University of America, Thomas J. Shahan, asked for his services. Shortly thereafter, Guilday arrived at the institution with which he was to be associated until his death 33 years later.

In April 1915, the *Catholic Historical Review* was launched, at his instigation. This was a quarterly journal to which Shahan lent the prestige of his name as editor-in-chief; five of the University professors served as editors. Of these, Guilday had the most active role. He continued as the principal editor until 1941, when failing health compelled his practical retirement. During the last six years of his life, Guilday had the title of editor-in-chief, although the editorial work had largely devolved upon the other editors. The AMERICAN CATHOLIC HISTORICAL ASSOCIATION (ACHA), which he founded in Cleveland, Ohio, in December 1919, was designed to further interest in Catholic history through annual meetings of scholars and teachers and the encouragement of research and writing. As the useful character of the ACHA was realized, its membership gradually increased. By the time of its founder's death, the original band of 50 had grown to about 800 members.

Aware of the neglect that had overtaken the history of Catholicism in the U.S. since the death of John Gilmary SHEA, Guilday inaugurated a program of courses in that field leading to the master's and doctor's degrees at the Catholic University of America. For many years, the program he began was unique in American Catholic higher educational circles. Guilday gave tremendous impetus to the revival of American Catholic history through his own writings. Six years before his death, a bibliographical article appeared in the *Catholic Library World* that had an accompanying list of Guilday titles that filled more than two closely printed pages. There was a steady stream of scholarly publications from his pen, beginning with *The Life and Times of John Carroll, First Archbishop of Baltimore, 1735–1815* (1922). His publications also included *An Introduction to Church History* (1925), a manual of historical method for beginners; a two-volume biography of John England, first bishop of Charleston (1927), which was perhaps his best work; and the useful general account, *A History of the Councils of Baltimore, 1791–1884* (1932). Besides these, Guilday edited the joint pastorals of the American hierarchy in 1923 and, later, three volumes containing the papers read at annual meetings of the ACHA. He also wrote a monograph on the lay trustee troubles of the Church in Virginia (1924) and the only real biography of John Gilmary Shea (1926). Moreover, Guilday had gathered a good deal of material and had completed some rough drafts of chapters for a life of John Hughes, first Archbishop of New York. However, he was forced to abandon this project because of ill health.

In 1925, the University of Notre Dame was the first of eight institutions to confer an honorary degree on him; the last of these institutions was Fordham University, which conferred an honorary degree to him in the year of its centennial, 1940. In 1926, Guilday was decorated by the king of the Belgians for efforts on behalf of the restoration of the University of Louvain library. In 1935, Guilday was made a domestic prelate by PIUS XI. Death came to Guilday after a long period of suffering. According to his wishes, his funeral took place from the National Shrine of the Immaculate Conception, and he was buried in the University lot in Mt. Olivet Cemetery in Washington.

Bibliography: J. T. ELLIS, "Peter Guilday: March 25, 1884–July 31, 1947," *American Catholic Historical Review* 33 (1947) 257–268. J. J. KORTENDICK, "Contemporary Catholic Authors: Monsignor Peter K. Guilday, Historian of the American Catholic Church," *Catholic Library World* 12 (May 1941) 263–269, 282.

[J. T. ELLIS]

GUILT

Guilt is the fact or awareness of having done wrong, of violating a norm or prescription. It is a universal phenomenon and a basic trait of human nature. To speak of guilt is to presuppose a world where there are norms and laws and persons with freedom and responsibility who, if they choose, can act against that established order.

Peter K. Guilday. (The Catholic University of America)

There are varying types of guilt relative to the nature of the wrongdoing. Legal or juridical guilt refers to the guilt associated with committing a crime, a violation of law, to which penalties are often attached. Ethical or moral guilt focuses on violation of moral norms. Religious guilt comes from injuring one's relationship with God through breaking divine law. Collective guilt refers to the wrongdoing of a group such as a family or nation. The multidimensioned reality of guilt invites interdisciplinary investigation, especially from the perspectives of theology, psychology, and anthropology.

Subjective and Objective Aspects. Guilt viewed as a subjective reality brings to the fore a person's awareness of having done wrong and the feelings aroused by knowing that one has transgressed in some way. Psychology has given primary attention to guilt feelings which are at times inappropriate or disproportionate responses and not necessarily related to any wrongdoing. Psychology is helpful in sorting out inauthentic guilt feelings from a true consciousness of guilt. Often in a given instance there is a mixture of both authentic and inauthentic guilt.

The degree of awareness, knowledge, freedom, and responsibility has direct bearing on the imputability of guilt but may or may not diminish or eliminate the presence of guilt feelings. Such feelings include unpleasant experiences of distress, such as self-reproach, self-blame, remorse, and anxiety. Guilt feelings typically trigger in the person experiencing them various remedial or expiatory actions such as confession, repentance, and reparation. The positive social role of such feelings is to impel a person to take responsibility and to mend broken relationships.

Objective guilt designates either the condition of the person who has committed the wrong or the behavior which constitutes the violation of the community's values and laws. Thus, in a court of civil law one is pronounced guilty of a particular crime even though one may not feel subjectively guilty or culpable. Objective guilt refers to the misdeed, a true violation of the law, whether or not it was freely intended by the transgressor.

Historical and Phenomenological Perspectives. In primitive societies guilt was related to a disturbance of the social or religious order. To incur guilt was to bring misfortune on oneself and one's community. Various means of expiation developed to restore the former equilibrium. Sacrifices and other ritual actions were efforts to undo the damage and to remove the guilt through various symbolic mediations such as a scapegoat.

Paul Ricoeur's study of the language of confession throws further light on the epigenesis of guilt. He traces a movement from the primitive sense of defilement, characterized by the feeling that one is infected and the experience of dread because of such contamination, to the sense of sin. With the notion of sin the sense of a relationship with God becomes prominent. Sin represents a refusal of God's demand. Guilt internalizes and personalizes the consciousness of having sinned. It anticipates the punishment due to sin by the burden it places on consciousness.

Guilt itself evolves and represents according to Ricoeur a significant advance in human comprehension of fault. In contrast to a simple fear of punishment, guilt acknowledges that an injustice has been done, an interpersonal relationship has been damaged. Guilt ultimately leads to a transformation such as Job experienced where in the face of suffering he surrenders to an order that transcends him. The perceived inescapability of guilt in human life leads to the relinquishing of narcissistic goals and embracing a life focused not on one's own righteousness but on a transcendent Other.

Psychological and Developmental Perspectives. Guilt as a psychological reality has been discussed by Freud and a host of other psychologists. Freud saw guilt feelings as arising when there is tension between a strict superego, the internalized authority of parents and other significant figures, and the ego, the executive agency of the personality. The superego emerges into prominence with the resolution of the Oedipal struggle somewhere around the age of five. Guilt, for Freud, makes its appearance toward the end of early childhood. The sources of such guilt are dread of authority and more specifically a fear of the loss of love of those on whom one depends. Freud saw the positive role that guilt can play in life. He was particularly aware of how it functions in human society as a control on destructive aggression. Freud's attention, however, was focused especially on the unconscious and displaced guilt that often stands behind neurotic symptom formation. According to Freudian psychodynamics, guilt feelings aroused in one area of conflict can be shifted and displaced onto another so that the person remains unaware of the true source of the guilt feelings. Various attempts at atonement are largely ineffective in bringing relief. Sometimes the guilt feelings are not conscious at all but stand behind a person's repeated failures or other self-punishments. Freud's explanation of the origin of religion tries to make comprehensible humanity's need for reparation by postulating a primal parricide for which humans still have guilt even though oblivious of it and its origin.

Erik Erikson, building on Freud's theory, has described a crisis in the life of the play-age child around the issues of initiative and guilt. The child desires to do things like others do but struggles with the awareness that some things are forbidden. Erikson suggests that conscience steps in as the governor of initiative. A healthy resolution of the crisis has the child moving forward unhampered by an excessive sense of guilt and with the sense of initiative prevailing.

Some psychological theories place the emergence of guilt earlier than did Freud or Erikson and see its appearance as an important developmental milestone. Melanie Klein sees the emergence of guilt in the first year of life and links it to the child's growing ability to tolerate ambivalence. According to Klein's formulations, the life of every infant is replete with both gratifications and frustrations. The normal infant responds to frustrations with a desire for retaliation; in other words, he or she would like to respond to the sources of frustration by punishing the inflicting party. In the course of infant development, the child senses that the ''good mother'' who provides food and the ''bad mother'' who frustrates its desire for immediate satisfaction are one and the same person. The child begins to sense its mother is a whole person in which it finds both good and bad. It senses, too, that the very one on whom its well-being depends is the same one it has wished to destroy. But now the child begins to feel concern for the mother and goes through a period of anxiety related to the feeling of almost having lost or destroyed the mother on whom it depends. An experience of guilt over such possible damage signals the ability to tolerate the ambivalence of conflicted feelings of love and hate directed to the same object. The child deals with this guilt through reparation and various restitutive gestures.

The British pediatrician and psychoanalyst D. W. Winnicott, building on Klein's ideas, connects the emerging sense of guilt in the infant with the beginnings of a capacity for concern. He draws attention to the importance of the stable emotional environment provided by the primary care-givers for all this to unfold appropriately. Deprivation in that environment is seen as contributing to the genesis of the antisocial tendency marked by the absence of any sense of guilt.

Guilt Pathologies. Two forms of guilt pathology are commonly recognized. Scrupulosity has to do with an experience of guilt that is too intense and disproportionate or focuses on acts that are not immoral or are beyond the responsibility of the subject. Such excessive guilt feelings seem to arise because of very aggressive, even sadistic, internal monitoring. On the other hand, an absence of appropriate guilt feeling characterizes people with character disorders such as the antisocial or narcissistic personality disorder. In these cases, the etiology often has to do with serious deficiencies in the early interpersonal environment.

Abnormal versus Normal Guilt. In sorting out guilt that has more a psychological origin from guilt in the more properly religious sense, it may be helpful to distinguish between the conscience and the superego. Conscience, in psychoanalytic terms, is an ego function acquired through healthy appropriation of the values and norms of the society to which the individual belongs. As such, it intends love rather than commanding that observance of some rule. It is other-directed, value-oriented, and dynamic in the sense that it looks at the nuances of a particular situation. The experience of guilt engendered by conscience is proportionate to the value at stake.

In contrast, superego is a more primitive agency that censors behavior in terms of past commands. It tends to induce guilt that is often disproportionate to the value at stake. It is more static and does not pay attention to the nuances of situations. It simply enforces past commands of authorities in a blind fashion.

In the average individual, guilt is an ambiguous experience inasmuch as it can respond to a genuine violation of a value or norm as well as to commands internalized during childhood development and still operative in the dynamic unconscious. As Karl Rahner has correctly pointed out, guilt is truly a borderland between theology and psychotherapy, an area where both ministers and psychotherapists may have vital roles to play.

Bibliography: C. BAUDOUIN and L. BEIRNAERT, ''Culpabilité,'' in *Dictionnaire de spiritualité* (Paris 1953) 2:2632–2654. S. FREUD, *Civilization and Its Discontents*, tr. J. STRACHEY (New York 1961). J. W. GLASER, ''Conscience and Superego: A Key Distinction,'' *Theological Studies* 32 (1971) 30–47. M. KLEIN, *Envy and Gratitude and Other Works 1946–1963* (New York 1975). K. RAHNER, ''Guilt and Its Remission: The Borderland Between Theology and Psychotherapy,'' in *Theological Investigations* 2, tr. K.-H. KRUGER (Baltimore 1963) 265–81. P. RICOEUR, *Freud and Philosophy: An Essay on Interpretation*, tr. D. SAVAGE (New Haven, Conn. 1970); *The Symbolism of Evil*, tr. E. BUCHANAN (Boston 1967). A. VERGOTE, *Guilt and Desire: Religious Attitudes and Their Pathological Derivatives*, tr. M. H. WOOD (New Haven, Conn. 1988). D. W. WINNICOTT, *Through Paediatrics to Psycho-Analysis* (New York 1975).

[R. STUDZINSKI]

GUILT (IN THE BIBLE)

In the Bible many Hebrew and Greek words, which are usually translated as ''sin,'' should in many contexts be rendered as ''guilt,'' i.e., the condition that follows upon the act of sin and perdures. This shows that the Israelite and the early Christian did not make much of a distinction between sin and guilt.

In the Old Testament

Connected with a dynamistic concept of SIN was the term *'āwōn,* especially when it was used in the sense of something borne or removed; e.g., in Ps 37(38).5, ''For my iniquities [*'āwōn*] have overwhelmed me'' (i.e., became too great a burden to be borne); in Ps 31(32).2, ''Happy the man to whom the Lord imputes not guilt. . . .'' The original background of the term pictures a twisted body [Is 21.3; Ps 37(38).7]. Traditionally, *'āwōn* was translated as iniquity, connoting something monstrous and intolerable. Thus to bear one's iniquity signified to be guilty. Cain said, ''My punishment is too great to bear'' (Gn 4.13). Here *'āwōn* meant both the misfortune inflicted as punishment and the state of guilt. Suffering brought with itself the sense of guilt. The Septuagint translators used ἀνομία (literally, ''lawlessness'') to translate *'āwōn;* St. Paul and St. John used the same Greek term for the mystery of iniquity or sin.

The word *peša*, a very profound theological term for rebellion, generally indicated a transgression against God and defiance of His rule. In Jb 33.9, however, it signified the guilt accompanying sin: ''I am clean and without transgression; I am innocent; there is no guilt in me.'' The word *ḥeṭ'* often designated the penalty following guilt, e.g., ''Anyone who curses his God shall bear the penalty of his sin'' (Lv 24.15; cf. 19.17; 20.20; 22.9; Nm 9.13; 18.22; Is 53.12; Ez 23.49).

The word *'āšām* quite clearly expressed ideas relative to guilt; however, its use was confined mainly to matters of ritual law and it often connoted a material and objective quality, such as ritual uncleanness. Such guilt did not necessarily involve voluntary sin, but it could be incurred unintentionally. Yet an inadvertent error or mistake (*šᵉgāgā*) still bound one to a voluntary atonement (Lv 4.2; 5.15, 18). Even though one was not aware of the error, he became ritually unclean and guilty (Lv 5.2). The verb *'āšām* (be guilty, condemned) and the noun *'ašmâ* (guilt, guiltiness) referred also to moral guilt, ''And the Chaldean land is full of guilt to be punished by the Holy One of Israel'' [Jer 51.5; cf. Ps 67(68).22]; the wrath of God was upon Juda and Jerusalem because of the *'ašmâ* of the people, i.e., false worship (2 Chr 24.18). The term *'āšām* was used also for a guilt offering (1 Sm 6.3–4, 8, 17 where the golden boils and mice were presented as gifts of reparation). Thus, one and the same word was used for the state of guilt as well as its remedy.

Guilt and Its Consequences. Guilt incurred the wrath of God. Since guilt involved a transgression of the divine will, the wrath of the Holy One of Israel was enkindled. In the early history of Israel the most evident examples of this were the earth's swallowing of the rebels Dathan and Abiram, and their families (Nm 16.32), and the punishment of Achan for appropriating some spoils of Jericho, which had been put under a ban; Achan's guilt was also the reason for the Israelite defeat at Ai (Jos ch. 7). The guilt incurred by the sons of Eli aroused Yahweh's wrath upon the priest and his family (1 Sm 2.27–36; 2.11–14). As a result of his census David, too, incurred the wrath of God; even though he was pardoned, the people were struck by a plague (2 Sm 24.10–17). For the wickedness of Manasseh, Yahweh brought evil upon Jerusalem and Judah (2 Kgs 21.10–15).

The notion of collective guilt was basic in these examples. Yahweh's anger was conceived as not ending with the punishment of the responsible individual but as perduring for generations: ''I will not be quiet until I have paid in full your crimes and the crimes of your fathers as well'' (Is 65.7), and ''We recognize, O Lord, our wickedness, the guilt of our fathers'' (Jer 14.20). The Prophets looked at the misfortunes Yahweh would inflict on His people as a result of the people's guilt, especially of their leaders, the king, nobles, priests, and false prophets.

Sense of Collective Guilt. From their earliest days the Israelites showed a sense of collective guilt (see RESPONSIBILITY [IN THE BIBLE]). Although they considered that God held all responsible for their individual sins, they felt especially bound as a people to the obligations of their COVENANT with YAHWEH. The covenant's blessings were parallel to the guilt that they incurred by breaking it. Solidarity in blessings led to solidarity in guilt. Thus, the individual suffered for the community's sin and the community for the individual's. The expression of this outlook is found in Ex 20.5–6, ''For I the Lord, your God, am a jealous God, inflicting punishment for their father's wickedness on the children of those who hate me, down to the third and fourth generation; but bestowing mercy down to the thousandth generation.'' The family group too was a significant moral entity; its head transmitted guilt to its every member (Jos 7.24–26).

Later, the DEUTERONOMISTS modified this notion: ''Fathers shall not be put to death for their children, nor children for their fathers; only for his own guilt shall a man be put to death'' (Dt 24.16; cf. the application of this rule by Amaziah in 2 Kgs 14.6). Yet during the Exile the older opinion so perdured [''Our fathers, who sinned, are no more, but we bear their guilt'' (Lam 5.7)] that Ezekiel argued against it at length: '''Fathers have eaten green grapes, thus their children's teeth are set on edge?' As I live, says the Lord God: I swear that there shall no longer be anyone among you who will repeat this proverb in Israel. For all lives are mine; the life of the father is like the life of the son, both are mine; only the one who sins shall die'' (Ez 18.2–4 and the rest of ch. 18). Without denying collective guilt, Ezekiel brought personal guilt to the fore and accentuated personal responsibility. Thus, despite national calamity there was hope for the individual.

Because of their deeper knowledge of God and of sin's reality, a more spiritual sense of guilt was developed by the Prophets and the Wisdom literature. Along with the evolving of a profound realization of sin as a personal offense against the loving kindness of the covenant God, these writers linked the sense of guilt with a deep sorrow and shame. Guilt and sin became for them an overwhelming burden: ''There is no health in my flesh because of your indignation; there is no wholeness in my bones because of my sin, for my iniquities have overwhelmed me; they are like a heavy burden, beyond my strength'' [Ps 37(38).4–5; cf. Is 1.5–6; Ezr 9.6].

Prayers for Forgiveness. Mindful of Yahweh as a loving huband and forgiving father, of His justice as equaled by His mercy, of His anger enduring only for a moment whereas His kindness endured forever, the Israelite confessed his guilt and expressed his sorrow in prayer. Examples are numerous: ''As long as I would not speak, my bones wasted away with my groaning all the day, for day and night your hand was heavy upon me; my strength was dried up as by the heat of summer. Then I acknowledged my sin to you, my guilt I covered not. I said, 'I confess my faults to the Lord,' and you took away the guilt of my sin'' [Ps 31 (32).3–5; see also Ps 50(51).11; 24(25).11; 78(79).9]. Isaiah and Jeremiah have other examples: ''Behold you are angry, and we are sinful; all of us have become like unclean men, all our good deeds are like polluted rags; we have all withered like leaves, and our guilt carries us away like the wind'' (Is 64.5); ''Even though our crimes bear witness against us, take action, O Lord, for the honor of your name—even though our rebellions are many, though we have sinned against you'' (Jer 14.7; Ezr 9.6–15). This yearning for forgiveness became even more evident in late Judaism, e.g., in Dn 9.4–19, which ended with these words, ''O Lord, hear! O Lord, pardon! O Lord, be attentive and act without delay, for your own sake, O my God, because this city and your people bear your name!'' Basic to all these concepts was the conviction that adversity was always a sign of guilt for the Israelite, indicating that Yahweh was angry with him and wanted him to beg forgiveness by confessing his guilt.

Guilt as Debt. The Septuagint (LXX) translators apparently introduced a more juridical category of guilt—that of debt, which became prominent in later Judaism. Sin as an act against God Himself belonged to the order of religion and its remission depended solely on God; the consequence of sin was not a stain that man could wash away. By sin, therefore, man incurred a debt that only God could remit. This concept was introduced by the LXX's use of ἀφίημι (to cancel or pardon a debt) in the technical formula for atoning for sins (Lv 4.20; 5.10, 19). In Lv 19.22 and Nm 14.19 the LXX used the same Greek term. Other Hebrew terms for taking away and pardoning sin, never associated with the idea of remitting a debt in the Hebrew, were also translated by this verb. The substantive ἄφεσις was used for the releasing of property to its hereditary owner during the JUBILEE YEAR and for messianic liberation [Is 61.1; Jer 34(42 LXX).8, 15, 17]. In Sir 28.2 ἀφίημι translated forgiving another man's injustice to oneself and not God's forgiveness of the debt of sin. Also, in non-Biblical Judaism the notion of sin and guilt developed as a debt toward God, and God's RETRIBUTION for sin's debt became involved in the concept of guilt.

In the New Testament

The terminology of guilt, its connotations in the Synoptic Gospels, in the Pauline Corpus, in Hebrews and the Catholic Epistles, and in the Johannine literature are of significance in considering guilt in the New Testament.

Terminology. The common New Testament word for sin, ἁμαρτια, was used also for the notion of sinfulness and guilt. Primarily it meant a sinful act, but at times it connoted an internal condition of guilt. St. Paul and St. John used it for a sinful way of life and a state of alienation from God. The word ὀφείλημα (debt) in Mt 6.12 (cf. Lk 11.4) expressed a notion of guilt—the debts that the sinner bore in God's sight. Another term, ἔνοχος, meant guilty of a fault or liable to punishment (e.g., Mk 3.29; Mt 5.22). The term ἀνομία (lawlessness or iniquity) translated the common Hebrew term for guilt, *'āwōn*.

In the Synoptics. A context of FORGIVENESS OF SINS or the remission of guilt or debt was usually the background for the Synoptics' consideration of guilt. The Judaic concept of sin as debt toward God was basic to their thought, although it was not the only notion involved with guilt. In the LORD'S PRAYER, Christ inculcated that charity, in the form of the mutual forgiveness of offenses against one another, was necessary to receive God's forgiveness of the debt of guilt (Mt 6.12). The original meaning of debt signified a financial debt and had been adopted from the language of commerce; but in its religious meaning it signified failure toward God with the consequent burden of guilt. It expressed the totality of man's feeling of indebtedness for having offended God and, in its context, connoted that only the Father's gratuitous love could pardon His children's debts. St. Luke's version of the Lord's Prayer was less Judaic in its use of ἀφρτία in place of ὀφείλημα.

In the parable of the unmerciful servant (Mt 18.21–35), again, in a context of cancelling a debt (18.21 is antithetical to the 70 times 7 vengeance of Lamech, Gn 4.24), the notion of guilt and sin as an enormous debt was implied (18.24: ''one was brought to him who owed him 10,000 talents''—a fantastic debt). The lesson of the parable was that, unless men forgave each other their comparatively small debts (10,000 talents had a relationship to 100 denarii of 600,000 to 1), they would not be forgiven the enormous debt they owed to God. (For being guilty of an everlasting sin in Mk 3.29, *see* SIN AGAINST THE HOLY SPIRIT.)

On the DAY OF THE LORD those guilty of iniquity (ἀνομία) would be excluded from the KINGDOM OF GOD (Mt 7.23) and would be cast into GEHENNA (Mt 13.41). Thus, the lawlessness of evil acts was clearly connected with divine JUDGMENT. The Synoptics further described sin as resulting in slavery to the DEVIL, an idea that entered into their concept of guilt. Thus, Christ's victory over the devil led to freedom from sin and guilt.

Pauline Teaching on Guilt. Paul followed the Judaic concept for sin as a debt in his references to sin's remission and sinful man's REDEMPTION (Col 1.14; Eph 1.7; Rom 3.24–25); his notion of remission, however, included the taking away of sin as well as the paying of a debt. Sin for Paul was not merely an external debt but something very much interior to man, almost natural to him. In Romans, Paul crystallized his doctrine on sinfulness and on the need that it caused in man. All men were subject to sin (Rom 3.9–18, 23) and could be justified only by receiving, through faith, the grace of Redemption won by Christ's propitiatory death (Rom 3.24–25). The believer, once justified, could then be saved through the internal gift of the Spirit and the life that he lived in Christ (Rom 5.1–11). Without the Spirit man could do no good; even though he delighted in the law of God, sin held man back, for he was dominated by sinful flesh. The flesh led to death; the Spirit, to life and peace. Sinfulness, then, brought with it its own condemnation, enmity toward God and death, i.e., a guilt that could be overcome only by a new life vivified by Christ's Resurrection from the dead (Rom 8.1–11).

Guilt in Hebrews and Catholic Epistles. Although specific terms for guilt or debt were scarce in these Epistles, sin and its consequences certainly were not. The notion of sin in Hebrews was that of disobedience, lack of confidence, and failure to follow the way indicated, i.e., faults that had characterized the Israelites in the desert; it was also a stain that had to be washed away and purified (Heb ch. 3). In Heb 2.15 Christ's mission was to deliver those ''who throughout their life were kept in servitude by the fear of death,'' through His own death. As eternal high priest Christ made atonement and took away sin and guilt by offering Himself as a sacrifice: ''But as it is, once for all at the end of the ages, he has appeared for the destruction of sin by the sacrifice of himself'' (Heb 9.26). Because of His sinlessness Christ could do what was beyond the power of the former sacrificial system (10.2–4, 11). With the new covenant sealed by Christ's blood came the means whereby there would no longer be consciousness of sin (10.2). Now there was a ''new and living way'' of access to God (10.20–22).

In the Epistle of St. James sin and guilt had Judaic overtones as in Paul's thought. Man's passions, i.e., his evil desires, were the source of sin (1.14), which led eventually to death. Evil desire, sin, and death followed upon each other. Lack of a loving mercy brought the severest condemnation of guilt (2.8–13). For James, friendship with this world (4.4), a sterile faith (3.14–26), condemnation of brothers (4.11–13), and even the omission of good works (4.17) incurred the guilt of sin. The injustice of the rich was especially condemned by him (5.1–6). The guilt of sin, however, could be removed by turning to God in humble sorrow (4.6–10) and by the prayers and sacramental actions of the community, coupled with the sinner's acknowledgement of guilt (5.14–17).

For 1 Peter, Christ's death and Resurrection were the source of the forgiveness of sin and guilt. The mystery of sin and guilt had been solved by Christ's suffering, although He was innocent; the Christian, even when he was guiltless, had to suffer with Christ (2.18–25). When Christians suffered, therefore, it was no longer because of their personal guilt alone, but because of their part in God's plan for destroying all sin and guilt through Christ's death because of sin (3.17–4.2).

Guilt in Johannine Writings. St. John proclaimed the universality of sin and guilt when he reported John the Baptist's description of Jesus as the lamb of God who was to take away the sin of the world (Jn 1.29, ἁμαρτία in the singular). Sin was the fundamental hostility of the world against God; by succumbing to it, a man rejected Christian vocation, divine filiation, and communion with God, and continued to accept the devil's domination (Jn 8.34–47; 1 Jn 5.18–20).

The consequences of sin led even further to the point of hatred. The worker of evil ''hates the light'' (Jn 3.19). The guilty world hated Christ precisely because His mission was to destroy sin by performing His Father's works (Jn 15.18–25). By the divine paradox, however, the working out of this hatred, namely the Crucifixion, effected the destruction of the devil's domination through sin and guilt (Jn 12.31–33).

Bibliography: *Encyclopedic Dictionary of the Bible*, tr. and adap. by L. HARTMAN (New York 1963), from A. VAN DEN BORN, *Bijbels Woordenboek* 912–18. J. HASTINGS and J. A. SELBIA, eds. *Dictionary of the Bible*, 5 v. (Edinburgh 1942–50) (1963) 354–55. For additional bibliography, *see* SIN (IN THE BIBLE).

[J. LACHOWSKI]

GUILT, THEOLOGY OF

From the standpoint of theology guilt is a willing and knowing violation of a person's relation to God. Such guilt may generate guilt feelings which may be an appropriate response to the perceived violation. To be guilty in a theological sense is to find oneself feeling personally responsible before God and others for the evil that was intended or has been done out of one's freedom. Conditions for real, theological guilt include knowledge and freedom. To the extent that knowledge is lacking or freedom is in some way impaired, guilt is lessened.

Inward and Social Aspects. Theological guilt can be further seen as having both an inward element and a social element. The inward element has to do with the awareness an individual has of personal wrongdoing. The individual may find authentic moral awareness obscured by guilt feelings that have their psychic origin in various types of environmental and social conditioning. Psychological analysis can be helpful in sorting out authentic from inauthentic guilt. The social element of guilt pertains to the consequences that result from someone having posited the evil act. Here it is common to speak of juridical guilt, which implies there is a penalty to be paid or compensation to be made. Juridical guilt may remain after the wrongdoer has dealt with the inward element through a process of repentance. Some of the consequences of guilt include the loss of grace and a wrong frame or mind.

Deed and State. Theological guilt, like sin itself, may be categorized as either a deed or a state. As a deed it is equivalent to what has traditionally been called actual sin. As a state it is equivalent to habitual sin. It is important to avoid conceiving guilt viewed theologically as merely an offence against legal custom or as a wrong action with various unwanted effects. Most radically guilt means a total and definitive decision of the human person against God. It is what makes sin sin. In the concrete this guilt must be weighed according to the degree to which it fully involves the person in his or her freedom. In a radical ''no'' to God who addresses humanity in an ongoing dialogue the person denies the very supporting ground of his or her activity and existence. Guilt is a falsification of the reality of the human person.

Origin of Personal Guilt. Determining or pinpointing the origin of personal guilt in one's life is not as easy as it might seem. Upon reflection people find themselves confronting a cloudy picture in which current acts are always set against a series of decisions already made. In other words, it is impossible to recall a state of complete moral indifference or to trace one's guilt to any one particular act with absolute certainty.

Furthermore, the arena in which human persons live and act is itself an influence on them which is difficult to sort out. It is in fact a realm of interpenetration to which individuals contribute by their actions and in which they receive in turn the impress of other persons' activity—both virtuous and sinful. In analyzing his or her own guilt, the individual is once again in an ambiguous situation. It is difficult to assess the influence various forces have had on one's decision making and the extent to which they may qualify the decision made. Such considerations have made modern Christians aware of how human freedom is limited. Yet over the course of a life freedom orients and shapes who a person will be. Guilt as the ultimate refusal of self to God indicates what the human person can choose to become in virtue of human freedom.

A somewhat different view of the human person and guilt is found within Protestant theology, especially in that branch influenced by existentialism. Paul Tillich found in existentialism an analysis of the human predicament that invited correlation with the classical Christian interpretation of human existence. Human existence for Tillich involves a movement away from humanity's own essential being and from God, the ground of being. Tillich expresses this by speaking of human persons in their existence as being estranged from the ground of being, from other beings, and finally from themselves.

Human persons find themselves in present finitude as beings united with nonbeing; they find themselves separated from that which they ought to be and to which they are strangely related. Here is the duality of essential and existential being as it is concretized in the human person. According to Tillich, human persons as they judge and look over what they have done are struck by a profound ambiguity between good and evil. Just as they experience contradiction within themselves, their own existential being separated from essential being, being limited by nonbeing, so they discover in what they do that a mixture of being and nonbeing emerges and expresses itself in the ambiguity between good and evil. Human persons thus render a negative judgment on themselves and experience this judgment and the ambiguity that occasioned it as guilt. Guilt, for Tillich, is the person's awareness of the ambiguity that characterizes what is done and leads him or her to render a negative judgment on the self. In Tillich's view, what the human person must do in spite of the anxiety of guilt and condemnation is to courageously affirm the self. It is God's acceptance of the person that alone gives courage to take within the self the threat of nonbeing which is at the root of the anxiety of guilt and condemnation. For Tillich all human acts are simply expressions of estrangement; all bring about guilt. It is never possible for humans to perform good and salutary acts for all existence is itself guilty. In contrast, the Catholic position stresses cooperation with grace through good works in the overcoming of guilt and a fuller conversion to God.

In the Catholic perspective the guilty person knows that he or she can repent, be forgiven, repair damage, and continue to grow through good works. In line with the Protestant emphases the guilty likewise should know that they cannot earn God's love but must simply respond to and accept God's gift of forgiveness.

Bibliography: K. RAHNER, ''Guilt—Responsibility—Punishment within the View of Catholic Theology,'' *Theological Investigations* 6, trans. K. H. KRUGER and B. KRUGER (Baltimore 1969) 197–217. P. SCHOONENBERG, *Man and Sin: A Theological View*, trans. J. DONCEEL (London 1965). P. TILLICH, *The Courage to Be* (New Haven 1952). J. D. WHITEHEAD and E. E. WHITEHEAD, *Shadows of the Heart: A Spirituality of the Negative Emotions* (New York 1994).

[R. STUDZINSKI]

Capital: Conakry.
Size: 94,926 sq. miles.
Population: 7,466,200 in 2000.
Languages: French; Malinke, Poulor, and local languages are spoken in various regions.
Religions: 149,530 Catholics (2%), 6,346,290 Sunni Muslims (85%), 223,980 Protestants (3%), 523,450 (7%) follow indigenous beliefs, 222,950 without religious affiliation.
Metropolitan See: Conakry, with suffragans N'Zérékoré and Kankan.

GUINEA, THE CATHOLIC CHURCH IN

The Republic of Guinea is a tropical, largely agricultural country located in western Africa. It borders the North Atlantic Ocean and Guinea-Bissau on the west, Senegal and Mali on the north, the Ivory Coast on the east and Liberia and Sierra Leone on the south. Guinea also includes several islands, including Tombo. Its marshy seacoast rises to hills and an eastern plateau region crossed by several rivers. Guinea's major crops include rice, bananas, coffee, ground nuts and pineapple; natural resources such as iron ore, bauxite, gold and diamonds are also found within its borders. Formerly known as French Guinea, the country left the French community and became an independent republic in 1958.

Dependent on the Vicariate Apostolic of Sierra Leone until 1897, Gambia was created the Prefecture Apostolic of French Guinea (vicariate in 1920), when it numbered 300 Catholics. The hierarchy was established in 1955 when the Vicariate of French Guinea was made the Archdiocese of Conakry and metropolitan see for the country.

History. Beginning in the 5th century and lasting for 300 years, Guinea was part of the kingdom of Ghana. Portuguese traders first explored the area in the mid-15th century, and missionaries occasionally visited the coastal region in their wake. The region became part of the Mali Empire in the 1500s, and Islam was introduced in the 17th century. After the encroachment of the region by the French, Guinea became a French protectorate in 1849, and joined French West Africa in 1895, despite efforts to unite and Islamicize the eastern half of the region by African militant Samori Touré. Meanwhile, organized evangelical efforts had begun in 1877, when the HOLY GHOST FATHERS established a mission in Boffa. Their presence in Guinea was at the invitation of King Katty's sons, who had attended a mission school in Senegal. The White Fathers began to evangelize the northern section in 1896 and established a mission at Bouyé in 1897. By 2000, although Christianity had made headway in the cities, along the coast and in the forest region, little progress was made in the rest of the predominately Muslim country, particularly the central Fouta Jallon region, which remained vehemently Muslim.

Made an overseas territory of France following World War II, Guinea finally achieved independence on Oct. 2, 1958. President Ahmed Séku Touré's repressive and isolating measures led to the nationalization of all schools, the suppression of Catholic youth organizations and the placing of restrictions on missionary activities. When Archbishop Gérard de Milleville protested, he was expelled from the country and replaced by Raymond Tchidimbo, an African, in 1961. Six years later all foreign missionaries were expelled from the country. By 1971 Tchidimbo, too, had proven to be problematic; amid a storm of accusations against Portugal for attempting to topple the government, the archbishop too, was charged with trying to overthrow the government and imprisoned until August of 1979. Touré, who was considered a brutal dictator, died in April of 1984, allowing the more liberal Committee of National Redress to assume power.

During the last decades of the 20th century the military government began to relax, repealing its curbs on missionaries and permitted the minor seminary at Kindia to reopen. One thousand political prisoners were released, several of them Catholics. Major seminarians were allowed to attend the regional seminary in Sebikhotane, Senegal. After 1984 the Church was once again allowed to operate Catholic schools in the country. By 2000 Guinea had 51 parishes, 63 diocesan priests, 18 religious priests, 16 brothers and 91 sisters working within its borders, as well as aiding refugees fleeing the violence spilling over the borders from Sierra Leone and Liberia. The constitution allowed for freedom of religion, and the government extended tax breaks and other subsidies to the Church as a member of its Association of Churches and Missions.

In 1993 free democratic elections were held in Guinea for the first time in over 40 years, although the military government which had been in power since 1984 was elected amid accusations of fraud. By 2000 the sluggish economy, burdened by foreign debt service and the need for humanitarian aid created by hundreds of thousands of refugees, prompted concerns regarding Guinea's political future. Church leaders and religious worked closely in support of United Nations' relief efforts, as well as advocating peaceful resolutions to the political conflicts of neighboring countries.

Bibliography: *Bilan du Monde,* 2:425–429. *Annuario Pontificio.* For additional bibliography *see* AFRICA.

[J. BOUCHAUD/EDS.]

GUINEA-BISSAU, THE CATHOLIC CHURCH IN

Formerly known as Portuguese Guinea, the Republic of Guinea-Bissau is located in west Africa, and is bound by the Atlantic Ocean on the southwest and west, by Senegal on the north, and by Guinea on the east and southeast. With its marshy terrain rising to only 800 feet above sea level in the southeast, Guinea-Bissau's agricultural products include cashews and peanuts, rice, palm oil, timber, fishing, and beeswax, while natural resources consist mainly of phosphates, bauxite, and yet-unexploited deposits of petroleum. The region's tropical climate is punctuated by a long dry season in winter that is characterized by harmattan winds.

In 1951 Guinea-Bissau was made an overseas territory of Portugal. Gaining its independence in 1973, the country held its first multiparty elections in 1994, beginning more than a decade of government instability. Reliant for much of its wealth upon agriculture, the region has been increasingly threatened by overgrazing, deforestation and the desertification caused by the encroachment of the Sahara. By 2000 it was one of the 20 poorest nations on earth. Most of the country's Muslims resided in the interior and the life expectancy of an average citizen of Guinea Bissau was 49 years in 2000.

History. After its discovery by the Portuguese in 1446 Guinea-Bissau became a Portuguese colony. Beginning in 1462 the Franciscans were entrusted with evangelization of the region, which depended ecclesiastically

Capital: Bissau.
Size: 13,948 sq. miles.
Population: 1,285,715 in 2000.
Languages: Portuguese; Crioulo and tribal languages are spoken in various regions.
Religions: 41,320 Catholics (3%), 578,572 Muslims (45%), 24,766 Protestants (2%), 641,057 practice indigenous religions (50%). Most Catholics, as well as other Christians, live in Bissau.
Diocese: Bissau, immediately subject to the Holy See.

on the bishop of the CAPE VERDE ISLANDS. Zealous slave traders who made no distinction between pagan and Christian Africans seriously hampered missionary activity, which was confined to the coastal area. In 1694 Cape Verdean Bishop Vitoriano do Porto became the first bishop to visit the area. Missionary activity remained sporadic until 1866 when a few Portuguese secular priests arrived in an attempt to revive the missions. British claims to the area were withdrawn in 1870, and Guinea-Bissau's boundaries were formalized by 1905.

As late as 1929 there was only one priest in the country. Restoration of the mission began in 1933 when French Franciscans established a mission. Priests from the Milan Foreign Missions Seminary arrived in 1947. After the Portuguese concordat with the Holy See in 1940 the situation improved greatly. The Prefecture Apostolic of Portuguese Guinea, with its seat in Bissau, the capital, was created in 1955 and placed under the Congregation for Extraordinary Ecclesiastical Affairs; it was created a diocese in 1977. Pope John Paul II visited the country in 1990.

During the 1950s a nationalist movement took shape in the region and armed resistance against the Portuguese colonial government began in 1962. The country gained its independence 11 years later, on Sept. 24, 1973, and a new constitution was put into effect in May of 1984. Four years after a new government was put in place during the elections of 1994, a military uprising against the new leaders triggered civil war, despite the efforts of Bissau Bishop Settimio Ferrazzetta to avert the coup. Further violence erupted in June of 1998 when the country was invaded by Senegalese troops. A military junta wrested control in 1999, and appointed a transition government, which ruled until February of the following spring, when Koumba Yalla was elected president. Further efforts to unseat the government were diffused through the efforts of other Church leaders, although nationalist sentiments continued to simmer among members of certain ethnic groups. The country's constitution reflected its political history: modified several times after its initial adoption, it nonetheless continued to provide for freedom of religion and imposed no state church.

During almost a decade of civil war, the Church worked to provide humanitarian aid for the region's growing refugee population. By 2000 there were 29 parishes, 11 secular and 54 religious priests, 15 brothers and 132 sisters at work among Guinea-Bissau's people. Catholic-run schools included 23 primary and four secondary schools. Faced with an economy devastated by a brutal civil war, Guinea-Bissau drew the attention of Pope John Paul II in the late 1990s. In addition to repeated calls for peace and a plea in 1998 to end ''the immense displacement of population,'' the pope asked that nations take steps to put a halt to the trafficking of arms to the region.

Bibliography: R.A. LABBAN *Historical Dictionary of the Republic of Guinea-Bissau* (Metuchen, NJ 1996). R. PATTEE, *Portugal na Africa contemporânea* (Coimbra 1959). R. WILTGEN, *Gold Coast Mission History* (Techny, IL 1956). *Bilan du Monde,* 2:429–430. *Annuario Pontificio* has data on all diocese. For additional bibliography *see* AFRICA.

[R. PATTEE/EDS.]

GUIRAUD, JEAN

French historian, journalist; b. Quillan (Aude), June 24, 1866; d. Saint-Martin-de-Brethencourt, near Paris, Dec. 11, 1953. Jean Baptiste Hippolyte Guiraud, brother of the historian Paul Guiraud (1850–1907), was a brilliant student in Carcassonne and at the Lycée Saint-Louis in Paris. In 1885, he went to the École Normale Superieure. As a member of the École Française in Rome (1885–89), Guiraud specialized in the study of medieval religious history. The École Française had undertaken the publication of the 13th-century papal registers. Guiraud participated in this project by editing the *Registres d'Urbain IV* in four volumes and the *Registres de Grégoire X* in one volume. These researches in Rome permitted Guiraud to become a *docteur ès lettres* in 1896, after he published his main thesis, *L'État pontifical après le Grand Schisme,* and his complementary thesis in Latin (then obligatory) on the Dominican monastery in Prouille: *De Prulianensi monasterio ordinis Praedicatorum incunabilia* (1206–1345). In 1898, he was appointed professor of medieval history on the faculty of letters at Besançon. His *Cartulaire de Notre-Dame de Prouille* (1907) completed his study of the monastery in Prouille. Its lengthy preface contained a very important study of the Albigensian heresy in the 12th and 13th centuries.

Guiraud's scholarly activities were interrupted by the law separating Church and State (1905) and by the other religious difficulties then disturbing France. As an ardent Catholic who opposed the law of separation,

Guiraud published several brochures on *La séparation et les élections* (1906), delivered numerous lectures, and created Catholic associations for heads of families. In 1917, he quit the university and until 1940 he acted as director of *La Croix* in Paris. He contributed much to the high quality of this important Catholic newspaper and exercised great influence on the French Catholic press. Late in his career, Guiraud returned to historical studies and set out to produce a history of the medieval Inquisition to the end of the 15th century, based on a detailed study of documents. However, his two volumes on the *Histoire de l'Inquisition au Moyen Âge* (1935–38) did not complete his project. The first volume was in great part a reproduction of the preface to his *Cartulaire de . . . Prouille.* The second volume did not deal with the period after the 13th century. The work has been criticized for its lack of synthesis and its inexact references.

Guiraud published historical works of a more popular type that gained a wide reception. *Saint Dominique* (1899) and *L'Inquisition médiévale* (1929) were both translated into English. In this class were also *L'Église et les origines de la Renaissance* (1902), *Questions d'histoire et d'archéologie chrétienne* (1906), and *Histoire partiale. Histoire vraie* (4 v. 1911–26). Some of these popularizations, particularly the last one mentioned, were marked by a tone of apologetics that Guiraud's more scholarly books avoided.

Bibliography: J. TOUTAIN, "Jean Guiraud (1886–1953)," *Mélanges d'archéologie et d'histoire* 67 (1955) 341–344.

[Y. DOSSAT]

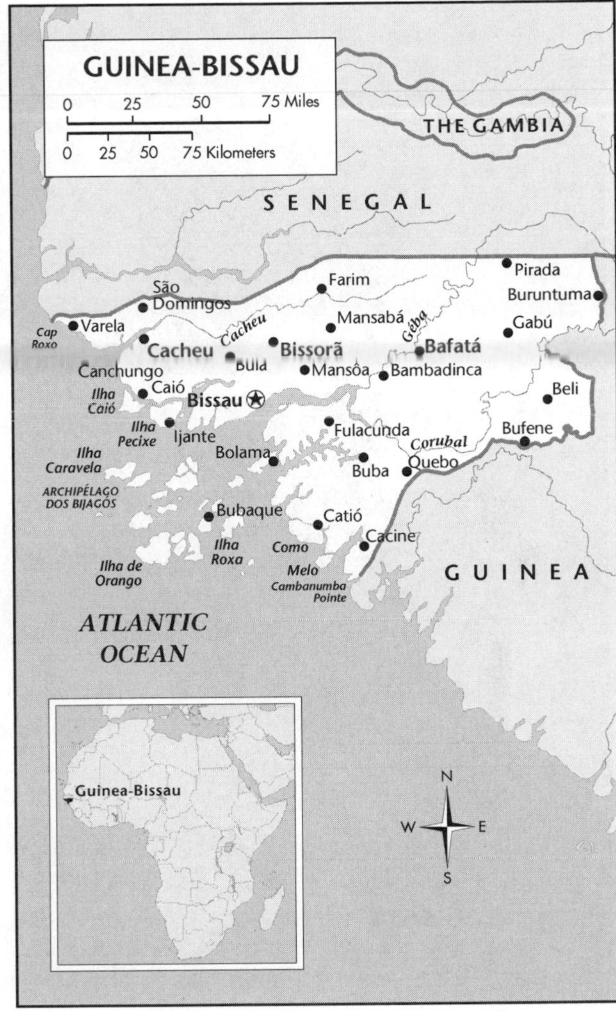

GUISE

The most illustrious branch of the House of Lorraine, named after the town of Guise. It rose to the peak of its power in the 16th century.

Claude, first Duke of Guise, fifth son of René II, Duke of Lorraine; b. Castle of Condé, Oct. 20, 1496; d. Joinville, April 12, 1550. He settled in France as a result of the contest with his elder brother Antoine over the succession to the Duchy of Lorraine. Claude accompanied King Francis I to the war in Italy and received 22 wounds at the battle of Marignano (1515). He defeated the English at Hesdin (1522), drove the Germans from Champagne (1523), and suppressed the peasant revolt in Lorraine (1527). King Francis I created him duke, and he was made governor of Champagne, and distinguished himself in the campaign of 1542 in Luxembourg and in the defense of Landrecies in 1543. It was he who established the eminence of the Guises. In 1513 Claude married Antoinette de Bourbon, sister of Charles, Duke of Vendôme. Among their 12 children were Francis, second Duke of Guise; Charles, Cardinal de Lorraine; Louis, Cardinal de Guise; René, Marquis d'Elbeuf; and Mary, mother of Mary Stuart of Scotland. According to his son Francis, Claude was fatally poisoned.

Mary, daughter of Claude; b. Nov. 22, 1515; d. Edinburgh Castle, June 10, 1560. She married first (1534) Louis II d'Orléans, Count de Longueville, and then in 1538, James V of Scotland, who died in 1542, leaving her with one child, Mary, Queen of Scots. Mary of Guise became regent in 1554.

Francis, second Duke of Guise, one of France's greatest generals, son of Claude; b. Château of Bar, Feb. 17, 1519; d. Orléans, Feb. 24, 1563. He early acquired the reputation of an intrepid soldier; he fought his first battles at Montmédy (1542), Landrecies (1543), and Saint-Dizier (1544) and was scarred by the wound received near Boulogne in 1545 and hence known as "Le Balafré." In 1551 Francis took part in the campaign that won

Francis, the second Duke of Guise, leads the French forces that captured Calais in 1558. (©Bettmann/CORBIS)

Metz, Toul, and Verdun for France; in 1552 to 1553 he defended Metz against Charles V of Germany and distinguished himself at the battle of Renty (1554). Francis later commanded the expedition against Naples (1556), after which he was nominated lieutenant-general of the kingdom by Henry II. He also fought against the English, and his capture of Calais (1558) and other places (Guines, Ham, Thionville, Arlon) led to the Treaty of Cateau Cambrésis (1559). With his brother Claude, Francis became all-powerful during the 16-month reign of Francis II, who married his niece Mary Stuart. The duke lost direct influence over Charles IX, who was dominated by Catherine de' Médicis. He formed a triumvirate (with Constable Anne de Montmorency and Marshal de Saint-André) to oppose the policy of Catherine, who was bent on concessions to the Huguenots. On March 1, 1562, he was involved in the Vassy Massacre of the Huguenots, which began the Wars of Religion. After capturing Rouen (October), he defeated the Huguenots at Dreux (December) and besieged Orléans. He was mortally wounded by a pistol shot fired by the Huguenot Jean Poltrot de Méré (February 18). In 1549 he had married Anne d'Este, daughter of the Duke of Ferrara. His children were Henry, third Duke of Guise; Catherine; Charles de Mayenne; Louis, Archbishop of Reims. Francis was the author of *Memoirs.*

Charles, brother of Francis; b. Joinville, Feb. 17, 1525; d. Avignon, Dec. 26, 1574. Charles was archbishop of Reims (1538) and cardinal (1547), known as Cardinal de Guise until 1550 and as Cardinal de Lorraine thereafter. Extremely intolerant, he tried to bring the Inquisition to France and was responsible for the cruel suppression of the Huguenot conspiracy of Amboise against the Guises (1560). He became head of the family after his brother's assassination (1563) and conducted an ineffectual and cowardly policy. He was a patron of men of letters such as Rabelais and Ronsard and founder of the University of Reims (1547–49). His daughter Anne d'Arne married Besme (Jean Yanowitz), who was responsible for killing Adm. Gaspard de Coligny during the massacre of St. Bartholomew's Day. Charles left many letters and sermons, e.g., *Oraison prononcée au colloque de Poissy* (1562). He also participated in the Council of Trent.

René, Marquis d'Elbeuf, brother of Francis; b. 1536; d. 1566. René took part in the defense of Metz (1552), the battle of Renty (1554), and the recapture of Calais (1558). He was general of the galleys. René was father of Charles de Lorraine, who was later created duke. It is through his line that the House of the Guises has survived to the present day.

Henry I, third Duke of Guise, Prince of Joinville, son of Francis; b. Dec. 31, 1550; d. Blois, Dec. 23, 1588. Scarred by a wound received at Dormans (1575), like his father he was named ''Le Balafré.'' Early in life he participated in campaigns against the Turks (1566) and against the Huguenots at Saint-Denis (1567) and at Jarnac and Moncontour (1569). Henry forced Coligny to raise the siege of Poitiers (1569), directed the massacre of St. Bartholomew's Day (1572), and was instrumental in 1576 in organizing the League, of which he became leader. He had ambitions of becoming King of France. On May 12, 1588 (''Day of the Barricades''), he became the idol of the Parisians and master of the crowds in revolt, but he found circumstances unfavorable for a *coup* against royalty. Guise was assassinated by order of King Henry III at the States-General of Blois. He had married Catherine de Clèves in 1570 and had 14 children, of whom five survived.

Louis, son of Francis; b. Dampierre, July 6, 1555; d. Blois, Dec. 24, 1588. He became archbishop of Reims in 1574 and cardinal in 1578. He supported the League, and like his brother Henry, was assassinated by command of King Henry III.

Charles, Duke of Mayenne, son of Francis; b. March 26, 1554; d. Soissons, Oct. 3, 1611. Charles went to war with his brother Henry and participated in the defense of Poitiers and in the battles of Moncontour and Brouage. He became lieutenant-general of the realm. After the death of his brother Henry, although pressed by relatives (especially his sister Mme. de Montpensier), he refused to contend for the crown; instead he concentrated his ability on giving the League a strong organization. After submitting to King Henry IV in 1596, he served him faithfully. Mayenne married Henriette of Savoy; they had four children, of whom three survived.

Bibliography: H. FORNERON, *Les Ducs de Guise et leur époque,* 2 v. (Paris 1877). R. DE BOUILLÉ, *Histoire de ducs de Guise,* 4 v. (Paris 1849–50). DU TROUSSET DE VALINCOUR, *La Vie de François de Lorraine, duc de Guise* (Paris 1681). A. BAILLY, *Henri le Balafré, duc de Guise* (Paris 1953). H. D. SEDGWICK, *The House of Guise* (Indianapolis 1938). For additional bibliography, *see* WARS OF RELIGION; LEAGUE, THE HOLY; ST. BARTHOLOMEW'S DAY, MASSACRE OF.

[W. J. STANKIEWICZ]

GUITMOND OF AVERSA

Theologian; b. Normandy, at the beginning of the 11th century; d. Aversa, between 1090 and 1095. Guitmond entered the Benedictine monastery of La Croix-Saint-Leufroy (Évreux). He then went to the Abbey of Bec to benefit from the teaching of Lanfranc (d. 1089), by whom he was strongly influenced. During Gregory VII's pontificate (1073–85), Guitmond was on the verge of being nominated a bishop in England by William the Conqueror. URBAN II (d. 1099) named him bishop of Aversa (southern Italy) in 1088, but we know little of his activity as bishop.

Doctrine and Influence. Guitmond's theological importance comes from his work *De corporis et sanguinis Domini veritate,* a controversial and apologetical book that was written as a dialogue with the monk Roger and directed against BERENGARIUS of Tours. The latter was challenged especially by Durand of Troarn, Lanfranc, Guitmond, and Alger of Liège since, invoking certain texts of St. Augustine, he seemed to deny the reality of the Real Presence. Nevertheless, it must not be forgotten that, in the 11th century, sacramental terminology was still defective; the Berengarian controversies corrected it. This is not the place to study Berengarius's beliefs; rather, we will treat only the principal points of Guitmond's exposition. The latter refutes two categories of Berengarius's teaching: the doctrine of the *umbratici* (for whom the Eucharistic Body is only the shadow and the figure of the historical Body of Christ) and that of the *impanatores* (who believe in a hypostatic union of Christ and the bread). Guitmond's arguments are scriptural, patristic (especially St. Augustine and St. Ambrose), and rational; he also appeals to the magisterium. Christ is neither *impanatus* nor *invinatus* by the conversion of the bread and wine to His Body and Blood. After Consecration, the sensible appearances—which Guitmond was the first in the history of Western theology to call *accidentia*—continue to exist, but are ''converted''; the term ''transubstantiation'' is not used yet, but its meaning is implied. For Guitmond, the Eucharistic accidents by God's will remain after the conversion of their substances into the Body and Blood of Christ. Berengarius was also troubled by the paradox of the double presence—historical and Eucharistic—of Christ's Body. Guitmond explains to him that Christ's Eucharistic Body is not subject to the laws of material division and of corruption. It is wholly present in each part of the consecrated Host and is not broken when the Host is. However, Guitmond erred when he declared that the Real Presence remains after the corruption of the species, or their consumption by animals, etc. This doctrinal imperfection can be excused, for the theology of the Sacraments was just beginning to make progress. This treatise, which takes apart and refutes Berengarius's *De sacra caena,* seems to anticipate the scholastic dialectic. Although it borrows its arguments and patristic texts from its ancestors, it contributes to the development of the terminology and the dogma of the Eucharist. It was used later, especially by Alger of Liège and Gregory of Bergamo (d. 1146). Its influence is already noticeable in the canonical collections of the end of the 11th century; the scholastics also quote Guitmond. Thanks to him, we possess a precise exposition of the Eucharistic opinions of the 11th century. Thus, he is one of the principal sources of information about Berengarius of Tours.

Works. Of his *Epistola ad Erfastum* (*Patrologia Latina* 149:1501–08), G. Morin has published the unedited ending [*Revue Bénédictine* 28 (1911) 96–97]. It is an answer to an inquiry from Erfast, Abbot of Lyre (Normandy), about the Trinity; in it, Guitmond lists his other writings: *Confessio de sancta Trinitate, Christi humanitate corporisque ac sanguinis Domini nostri veritate* (*Patrologia Latina* 149:1495–1502), and *De corporis et sanguinis Domini veritate libri tres* (*Patrologia Latina* 149:1427–94). J. Leclercq has found an authentic and unedited gloss on this treatise [*Revue Bénédictine* 57 (1947) 214]. It may have been written between 1075 and 1078; the original title is perhaps that of the manuscript Vat. Reg. lat. 237: *De corporis et sanguinis Christi veritate in eucharistia. The Oratio ad Gulielmum I Anglorum regem,* which was attributed to Guitmond (*Patrologia Latina* 149:1509–12), is very likely an apocrypha that was written by Odoric Vitalis.

Bibliography: G. MORIN, ''La Finale inédite de la lettre de Guitmond d'Aversa à Erfast, sur la Trinité,'' *Revue Bénédictine* 28 (1911) 95–99. J. LECLERCQ, ''Passage authentique inédit de Guitmond d'Aversa,'' *ibid.* 57 (1947) 213–214. P. SHAUGHNESSY, *The Eucharistic Doctrine of Guitmund of Aversa* (Rome 1939). F. VERNET, *Dictionnaire de théologie catholique*, ed. A. VACANT et al. (Paris 1903–50) 6.2:1989–92. J. R. GEISELMANN, *Lexikon für Theologie und Kirche*, ed. J. HOFER and K. RAHNER (Freiburg 1957–65) 4:1272. P. DELHAYE, *Catholicisme. Hier, aujourd'hui et demain*, ed. G. JACQUEMET, 5:422–423.

[R. GRÉGOIRE]

GUÍZAR VALENCIA, RAFAEL, BL.

Bishop of Veracruz, Mexico; b. April 27, 1878, Cotija, Michoacán, Mexico; d. June 6, 1938, Mexico City. Rafael was one of 11 children born to the wealthy hacendados Prudencio Guízar González and Natividad Valencia Vargas. A brother, Antonio, became bishop of Chihuahua. Rafael's studies were begun at home and completed in the seminary of his native Diocese of Zamora; he was ordained on June 1, 1901.

Missionary Work. From the first, the future bishop felt an overwhelming impulse to work as a home missionary. He had physical and spiritual gifts that fitted him for this work, and eight days after his ordination he began his first missionary journey, which lasted almost two years. While assigned to the diocesan seminary as spiritual director, Rafael continued his mission work by founding with his own funds a school for poor girls and on June 3, 1903, a Congregation of Missionaries of Our Lady of Hope with a special college in Jacona, Michoacán, as well as another college for boys in Tulancingo, whose graduates he hoped would enlist in large numbers in his missionary congregation. The missionaries were to dedicate themselves to work in Mexico and the neighboring nations. In June 1910 Guízar was forced to order the dissolution of his foundation of missionaries. Neither the disappointment of the failure of his personal foundation nor the honors that he received dimmed the zeal of this priest for the missions, and by 1910 he had preached innumerable missions in six Mexican states, especially in southeastern Mexico.

The chaos in Mexico consequent on the fall of Porfirio Díaz ended the home missions but opened for the young priest new opportunities to serve the souls of his fellows. Disguised as a peddler, a homeopathic physician, or an accordion player, he traveled with the armies of the revolution, ministering to the wounded and preaching whenever the opportunity presented itself. Often he returned from these missions of mercy with his hat and clothes pierced with bullet holes. Often too, his priestly ministrations would rouse the anger of the revolutionary leaders and on numerous occasions he was condemned to death. His success in escaping this supreme penalty made him a marked man in so many areas that he finally fled to Guatemala in 1916. Under the name of Rafael Ruíz he was able to take up again his life as a home missionary and in one year married 7,000 couples. In 1917 Guízar landed in Cuba and until the end of 1919 he preached 143 missions there. While preaching a mission in the cathedral of Havana in August 1919, Guízar was told that he had been named bishop of Veracruz. His first reaction was to flee to Colombia where he preached for about four months. But on Nov. 30, 1919, he was consecrated bishop in Havana, and on Jan. 4, 1920, he arrived in Veracruz. His arrival coincided with a disastrous earthquake in a number of cities of his diocese and the new bishop immediately went to help his stricken people.

With the permission of his brothers, he sold the beautiful pectoral cross of gold set with precious stones that they had given him, used the money for the poor, and thenceforth wore a cross made of brass.

Reaction to Persecution. During his episcopate, Guízar had to suffer persecution, as did his brother bishops, especially after Plutarco Elías Calles came to power. Guízar had his own particular cross in the person of the governor of Veracruz, Adalberto Tejada, who on June 17, 1931 decreed that he would permit only one priest for each 100,000 inhabitants. Guízar, recognizing that this decree made it physically impossible for the priests to carry out their duties, closed all the churches in the state in order to force the situation on the attention of the people. Tejada answered with a decree ordering that the bishop should be shot wherever he was found in the state. Guízar at the time was in Mexico City but he ordered his secretary to drive as rapidly as possible to the governor's palace in Jalapa. Guízar boldly walked into the governor's office, stating that he respected authority and that he wished to spare the governor's lieutenants the trouble of shooting him. The daring move paid off because the surprised governor did not dare shoot the bishop. Thus, Guízar was free to organize more than 300 Eucharistic centers, where his priests could minister to the people in ever–increasing numbers while the churches were closed. He was even able to maintain a seminary with more than 100 seminarians, who, though forced to move from place to place, were able to complete their studies and be ordained. In this way the diocese counted more priests at the end of the persecution than at its beginning. Worn out with his work, the bishop died in Mexico City.

In 1950 his body was exhumed and found to be incorrupt. Thereafter his remains were transferred to his titular chapel in the cathedral of Veracruz. The cause for his beatification was introduced in Rome Aug. 11, 1958. He was beatified by Pope John Paul II on June 29, 1995.

Bibliography: E. J. CORREA, *Mons. Rafael Guízar Valencia: El obispo santo 1878–1938* (Mexico City 1951). J. DE LA MORA, *Breves apuntes biográficos del Excmo. y Rvmo. Sr. Dr. D. Rafael Guízar Valencia, obispo de Veracruz* (Mexico City 1955). J. A. PEÑALOSA, *Rafael Guízar, a sus órdenes* (Mexico City 1990). E. VALVERDE TÉLLEZ, *Bio bibliografía eclesiástica mexicana, 1821–1943*, 3 v. (Mexico City 1949).

[E. J. CORREA]

Bl. Rafael Guízar Valencia.

GUMBERT OF ANSBACH, ST.

Benedictine abbot bishop, date and place of birth and death unknown. Before 748, Gumbert (or Gundebert) founded St. Mary's Abbey on family lands. In 786, in return for immunity and the free election of abbots, he donated it to CHARLEMAGNE, who *c.* 800 gave it to Bishop Bernwelf of Würzburg in exchange for other possessions. The abbey, called St. Gumbert by 911, was collegiate when the community moved to St. Stefan in WÜRZBURG (and St. Gumbert's feast was moved from March 11 to July 15). The foundation was suppressed in 1563. Data about Gumbert and the early years of Ansbach derive from Charlemagne's document (*Monumenta Germaniae Historica: Diplomats* 12:205–207). A legendary vita *c.* 1110 (*Acta Sanctorum* 4:61) makes him a great lord who renounced the world and gave his possessions to the bishopric of Würzburg and Ansbach. He is not to be confused with Bishop Gumbert of Würzburg (832–842), or with the little-known St. Gumbert (d. *c.* 675; feast: Feb. 21), CHORBISHOP of Sens, who founded (661) the monastery of Senones in the Vosges, to which he retired.

Feast: July 15 (Vilchband).

Bibliography: S. HAENLE, *Ansbach in der deutschen Geschichte* (Berlin 1886). A. PONCELET, *Analecta Bollandiana* 28 (1909) 272–280. L. H. COTTINEAU *Répertoire topobibliographique des abbayes et prieurés* (Mâcon 1935–39) 1:119–120; 2:3006. K. NECKERMANN, *Heimatscholle Vilchband* (Mannheim 1937). A. BAYER, *S. Gumberts Kloster und Stift in Ansbach* (Würzburg 1948).

[P. COUSIN]

GUMMAR, ST.

Hermit and nobleman; b. Emblehem, Belgium, *c.* 717; d. Nivesdonck, *c.* 775. The extant account of his life was written at the end of the 11th century to honor him as the patron saint of Lier. The author, Theobald, claimed that his vita was based on an earlier version, but no earlier life has survived. Gummar (Gomer; in French, Gommaire) is said to have fought in many campaigns under PEPIN III. After building a small oratory at Lier, he divided the rest of his life between solitary prayer and the administration of his estates. He is regarded as one of the outstanding wonder-workers of the Low Countries.

Feast: Oct. 11.

Bibliography: *Acta Sanctorum* Oct. 5:674–697. *Bibliotheca hagiographica latina antiquae et mediae aetatis,* 2 v. (Brussels 1898–1901; suppl. 1911) 1:3694–99. J. L. BAUDOT and L. CHAUSSIN, *Vies des saints et des bienheueux selon l'ordre du calendrier avec l'historique des fêtes* (Paris 1935–56) 10:363–365. É DE MOREAU, *Histoire de l'église en Belgique* (2d ed. Brussels 1945) 1:320–322. T. PAAPS, *De heilige Gummarus in de literatur, de liturgie en de volksvereering* (Antwerp 1944).

[J. E. LYNCH]

GUNDECAR, BL.

Bishop of Eichstätt; b. Aug. 10, 1019; d. Eichstätt, Aug. 2, 1075. He was educated at Eichstätt cathedral school, was canon of Eichstätt cathedral, and *c.* 1045, was the chaplain of the Empress Agnes, under whose influence HENRY IV named Gundecar bishop of Eichstätt (1057). He devoted himself to diocesan affairs, notably education. For his clergy he prepared the so-called *Gundecarianum,* dealing with ritual and liturgy and containing a catalogue of Eichstätt's bishops, which was carried on by successors until 1697. It is important for its miniatures (11th–16th centuries). He undertook the building of the cathedral and consecrated more than 100 churches. Miracles at his grave led to his cult, which spread beyond the diocese after the translation of his relics in 1309.

Feast: Aug. 2.

Bibliography: GUNDECAR, *Liber pontificalis Eichstetensis,* ed. L. C. BETHMANN and G. WAITZ, *Monumenta Germaniae Scriptores* (Berlin 1825–) 7:239–253; 25:590–609. *Acta Sanctorum* August 1:175–189. J. SAX, *Die Bischöfe und Reichsfürsten von Eichstädt, 745–1806,* 2 v. (Landshut 1884–85) v. 1. F. HEIDINGSFELDER, *Die Regesten der Bischöfe v. Eichstätt* (Erlangen 1938). R. GRABER, *Lexikon für Theologie und Kirche,* ed. J. HOFER and K. RAHNER, 10 v. (2d, new ed. Freiburg 1957–65) 4:1274.

[D. ANDREINI]

GUNDLACH, GUSTAV

Social philosopher; b. at Geisenheim (Rheingau), Germany, April 3, 1892; d. Mönchengladbach, June 23, 1963. He entered the Society of Jesus in 1912 and was ordained priest in 1923. After graduate studies at the University of Berlin he became professor at the seminary of Sankt-Georgen in Frankfurt-am-Main. In the first years of the National Socialist regime he transferred his teaching activities to the Pontifical Gregorian University in Rome. At his retirement, he returned to Germany to become director of the Catholic Social Sciences Center, created by the bishops at Mönchengladbach, but died soon after.

Gundlach was a continuator of the school of Heinrich Pesch, founder of solidarism, whose economic and social thought was inspired by natural law and new scholasticism. He had a powerful influence on Catholic social thinking in the 1940s and 1950s and is reputed, not without foundation, to have had a decisive part in the preparation of various social statements of Pope Pius XII. The introduction of the term ''subsidiarity'' is attributed to him. In the postwar years he became particularly involved in discussions in Germany over the relation of Catholic social doctrine to socialism, and related questions such as codetermination. His postulation of an absolute right of self defense, however, met with criticism by contemporary theologians.

Bibliography: *Die Ordnung der menschlichen Gesellschaft,* 2 v. (Cologne 1964–65).

[R. A. GRAHAM]

GUNKEL, HERMANN

Prominent OT scholar; b. Springe (Hanover), Germany, May 23, 1862; d. Halle, March 11, 1932. After teaching NT exegesis for a year at Göttingen (1888), he taught OT exegesis and the history of Israelite literature in Halle (1889–93), Berlin (1894–1907), Giessen (1907–20), and again Halle (1920–27). He was a popular teacher and scholar and had as students Protestant scholars from all over the world. With A. Eichhorn, W. Wrede, and W. BOUSSET, he founded the *Religionsgeschichtliche Schule* (comparative religion school) of interpretation as a reaction and complement to the literary-critical school. He began by freeing the entire Bible from all dogmatic principles; it should be inserted into its proper place in universal human history as an integrating part. In so doing, he concluded that the Bible was the end product of a long preliterary process. He thereby initiated research into the numerous infraliterary stages [*Gattungsforschung* (study of Biblical literary genres) for the OT,

Formenforschung (FORM CRITICISM) for the NT]. He categorized various sayings, legends, and myths, but considered the *Sitz im Leben* (situation in life) as the most important object of research. This method was applied particularly in his *Genesis* (Göttingen 1961), *Schöpfung und Chaos in Urzeit und Endzeit* (Göttingen 1885), and *Die Psalmen* (Göttingen 1926). He did pioneering work also in the determination of Jewish Apocalyptic literature. His research caused a lively discussion and opposition, particularly among theologians, and resulted in much further work by his students and followers. He was the founder, editor, and substantial contributor to the first edition of *Religion in Geschichte und Gegenwart.* With Bousset he initiated the collection of *Forschungen zur Religion und Literatur des A.T. und N.T.* His suggestions for further research in OT worship, prophecy, and law were carried out in the important works of A. Alt, J. Begrich, M. Noth, and G. von Rad.

Bibliography: H. J. KRAUS, *Geschichte der historisch-kritischen Erforschung des Alten Testaments* (Neukirchen 1956) 300–334. L. HENNEQUIN, *Dictionnaire de la Bible,* suppl. ed. L. PIROT, et al. (Paris 1928–) 3:1374–77. K. GALLING, *Die Religion in Geschichte und Gegenwart,* 7 v. (3rd ed. Tübingen 1957–65) 2:1908–09. J. SCHARBERT, *Lexikon für Theologie und Kirche,* ed. J. HOFER and K. RAHNER, 10 v. (2d, new ed. Freiburg 1957–65) 4:1274–75.

[L. A. BUSHINSKI]

GUNTBERT OF SAINT-BERTIN

Monk; b. probably at Cormont (Pas-de-Calais), *c.* 810; d. after 868. He was the son of Goibert, a rich landowner of Morinia, who during a trip to Rome (826) dedicated Guntbert to St. Peter. Upon his return Guntbert entered the monastic school of SAINT-BERTIN as a resident student. In 831 father and son jointly made gifts to the monastery on Sithiu and the collegiate church of Sainte-Marie, which, although separated after 820, remained on good terms. Guntbert copied and illuminated antiphonaries for Sainte-Marie and the abbeys of Bergues-Saint-Winnoc and Saint-Bertin. At Saint-Bertin he founded the scriptorium, which became famous under Odbertus. After being named provost, he was ordained in 844. His relations with the abbey deteriorated and in 868, old and ill, he left for Rome to petition the Pope for justice. There is no further record of him.

Bibliography: G. COOLEN, ''Guntbert de St-Bertin: Chronique des temps carolingiens,'' *Revue du Nord* 40 (1958) 213–224. B. GUÉRARD, ed., *Cartulaire de l'Abbaye de St-Bertin,* 2 pts. (Paris 1840–67).

[G. COOLEN]

GÜNTHER, ANTON

Catholic theologian; b. Lindenau in (what is today) Czechoslovakia, Nov. 17, 1783; d. Vienna, Feb. 24, 1863. His parents were staunch Catholics and quite poor. He attended the village school of Lindenau, secondary schools in Haide and Leitmeritz, and the University of Prague (until 1809). As a student he was frequently obliged to support himself by tutoring children. He was versed in the writings of such philosophers as Descartes, Kant, Fichte, Schelling, and Hegel. At one time he experienced difficulties about his faith, but these were dispelled by his reading of Sacred Scripture and by his association with (St.) Clement HOFBAUER, among others. Subsequently he completed legal studies. Then he undertook the study of theology, and in 1820 he was ordained.

For two years (1822–24) Günther was a Jesuit novice. Leaving the Jesuits, he settled in Vienna for the remainder of his life. He devoted himself to tutoring, assisting in the care of souls, acting as government censor of philosophical and juridical books (until 1848), and writing. His works include the following: *Vorschule zur spekulativen Theologie des positiven Christenthums* (1828–29), *Süd-und Nordlichter am Horizont spekulativer Theologie* (1832), *Der letzte Symboliker* (1834), *Thomas a Scrupulis* (1835), *Die Juste-Milieus in der deutschen Philosophie gegenwärtiger Zeit* (1838), and *Eurysthesus und Herakles* (1843). In addition, he produced a number of books in collaboration with others, as well as articles and book reviews.

In the course of his life, Günther received invitations to join the faculties of such universities as Munich, Bonn, and Breslau, but he refused these, possibly because he hoped to obtain a professorial chair in Vienna, a hope that was never realized. His influence in German theological circles was widespread during his lifetime, not only because of his writings, but also because his pupils occupied chairs in German universities. Nevertheless, Günther also experienced opposition to his theological point of view, especially from Redemptorist and Jesuit theologians. His writings were examined in Rome, and despite the efforts of his friends, some of whom even traveled to Rome, nine of his works were prohibited by the Congregation of the Index on Jan. 8, 1857 (see H. Denzinger, *Enchiridion symbolorum,* ed. A. Schönmetzer 2828–31). The author announced his acceptance of the prohibition of those works Feb. 10, 1857.

See Also: SEMIRATIONALISM for Günther's views.

Bibliography: *Dictionnaire de théologie catholique,* ed. A. VACANT, 15 v. (Paris 1903–50; Tables générales 1951–), Tables générales 1:2005. P. WENZEL, *Lexikon für Theologie und Kirche,* ed. J. HOFER and K. RAHNER, 10 v. (2d, new ed. Freiburg 1957–65) 4:1276–78. G. MARON, *Die Religion in Geschichte und Gegenwart,*

7 v. (3rd ed. Tübingen 1957–65) 2:1902–03. H. THURSTON, J. HASTINGS, ed., *Encyclopedia of Religion & Ethics,* 13 v. (Edinburgh 1908–27) 6:455–456. F. P. KNOODT, *Allgemeine deutsche Biographie* (Leipzig 1875–1910) 10:146–167.

[E. J. GRATSCH]

GÜNTHER OF NIEDERALTAICH, BL.

Monk; b. probably 955; d. Hartmanice, Bohemia, Oct. 9, 1045. A Thuringian nobleman, perhaps of the family of the counts of Schwarzburg, he was more a pagan than a Christian in his youth, but under the spiritual direction of GODARD OF HILDESHEIM he began to reform his life. After a journey to Rome he entered the BENEDICTINE abbey of HERSFELD as a *conversus,* and he later received the TONSURE in the Abbey of NIEDERALTAICH. He was invited to become abbot at Hersfeld or Göllingen but with a few companions turned instead to a hermit's life in the Bavarian forest. He founded Rinchnach, as affiliate of Niederaltaich, and, penetrating even farther through the Bohemian forest, opened up the Golden Ladder, the trade route from Passau to Bohemia. His hermitage became the goal of many pilgrims. He was an adviser to three emperors, a missionary to the Lusatians, and a friend of STEPHEN I of Hungary, in whose territory he founded several monasteries. He obtained the release of German prisoners by his intercession with Duke Bretislav of Bohemia (d. 1055), and he mediated difficulties between Bretislav and HENRY III. He became the patron of the Abbey of Brevnov, where his tomb was located until 1420, when it was destroyed by the HUSSITES.

Feast: Oct. 9.

Bibliography: J. MABILLON, *Acta sanctorum ordinis S. Benedicti,* 9 v. (Paris 1668–1701; 2d ed. Venice 1733–40) 8:419–428. E. HEUFELDER, *1000 Jahre St. Gunther, Festschrift* (Cologne 1955). A. M. ZIMMERMANN, *Kalendarium Benedictinum: Die Heiligen und Seligen des Benediktinerorderns und seiner Zweige,* 4 v. (Metten 1933–38) 3:155–159.

[G. SPAHR]

GUNTHER OF PAIRIS

Cistercian author; d. Abbey of Pairis, Alsace, *c.* 1220. Gunther was a minor literary figure of the late 12th and early 13th century. Probably he came from Basel or near there, and before entering the monastery he lived at the court of FREDERICK I BARBAROSSA, where he taught Conrad, the Emperor's third eldest son. This would indicate considerable knowledge of letters before his entrance into monastic life at the Cistercian Abbey of Pairis. His earliest work, the *Solimarius,* written *c.* 1180 and dedicated to Conrad, is a verse narrative of the First CRUSADE and, in large part, a poetical version of the *Historia Hierosolymitana* of Robert of Reims. Obviously interested in the crusading movement, he wrote another work, *Historia Constantinopolitana,* part prose, part poetry, on the Fourth Crusade, which purports to give an eyewitness account of the expedition supplied by a certain Abbot Martin. His third work, *Liburinus,* is a poetical version of OTTO OF FREISING'S *Gesta Frederici* 2–4. H. O. Taylor praised it as ''still another good example of the long narrative poem,'' and stated that its author ''shows himself widely read in the classics.'' J. Raby claims that he ''was not a mere uninspired imitator'' but asserts that ''he was not a great poet'' but a man who was ''a witness to German patriotism and pride.'' The authenticity of his works, first claimed for Gunther toward the end of the 17th century, was long questioned until two scholars, G. Paris and A. Pannenborg, working independently, established it in 1870.

Bibliography: Works. *Ligurinus,* ed. C. G. DÜMGÉ (Heidelberg 1812); *Solimarius,* ed. G. WATTENBACH, *in Archives de l'Orient latin* 1 (Paris 1881) 555–561; *Historia constantinopolitana* . . . , ed. R. RIANT (Geneva 1875). **Literature.** U. CHEVALIER, *Répertoire des sources historiques du moyen–âge. Biobibliographie,* 2 v. (2d. ed. Paris 1905–07) 1:1832–33. M. MANITIUS, *Geschichte der lateinischen Literatur des Mittelalters,* 3 v. (Munich 1911–31) 3:698–701. J. DE GHELLINCK, *L'Essor de la littérature latine au XII siècle,* 2 v. (Brussels-Paris 1946) 2:128, 217. G. PARIS, *Dissertation critiquesurle poème latin du Ligurinus attribué à Gunther* (Paris 1872). A. PANNENBORG, ''Über den Ligurinus,'' *Forschungen zur deutschen Geschichte* 11 (1871). F. J. E. RABY, *A History of Secular Latin Poetry in the Middle Ages,* 2 v. (2d ed. Oxford 1957). F. BRUNHÖLZI, *Lexikon für Theologie und Kirche,* ed. J. HOFER and K. RAHNER, 10 v. (2d, new ed. Freiburg 1957–65) 4:1276.

[H. MACKINNON]

GUNTHILDIS, SS.

Possibly three saints who bore this name:

Gunthildis of WIMBORNE, England, an Anglo-Saxon nun who with her daughter, Bertgitha, accompanied LIOBA to Germany and became an abbess in Thuringia. One of the letters of BONIFACE (n. 67) is addressed to her as well as to Lioba and Abbess THECLA.

Feast: Dec. 8.

Gunthildis of Eichstätt, an abbess, whom Gundecar II, bishop of Eichstätt (d. 1075) lists in his Pontifical. He transferred her remains from Suffersheim to his cathedral, where she was honored among the 12 founders of Eichstätt.

Feast: Sept. 28.

Gunthildis of Plankstetten, a servant girl venerated at the Abbey of Plankstetten in the Diocese of Eichstätt, though buried at Suffersheim. If it could be proved, as Bauerreiss suggests, that the servant-girl story (which is found only after 1517) was fiction, both the abbess and servant girl might prove to be one and the same saint who in turn might prove to be the follower of Lioba.

Feast: Sept. 22.

Bibliography: *Acta Sanctorum* Sept. 6:530–533. A. M.. ZIMMERMANN, *Kalendarium Benedictinum: Die Heiligen und Seligen des Benediktinerorderns und seiner Zweige,* 4 v. (Metten 1933–38) 3:405–407. J. L. BAUDOT and L. CHAUSSIN, *Vies des saints et des bienheueux selon l'ordre du calendrier avec l'historique des fêtes,* (Paris 1935–56) 9:448–449. R. BAUERREISS, *Kirchengeschichte Bayerns* (2d ed. Munich 1958) 1:56.

[L. MEAGHER]

GURY, JEAN PIERRE

Jesuit moral theologian; b. Mailleroncourt, Haute-Saône, Jan. 23, 1801; d. Mercoeur, Haute-Loire, April 18, 1866. He entered the novitiate of the Society of Jesus at Montrouge on Aug. 22, 1824, and in 1828 was sent to study theology at the Roman College. Upon his return to France he spent a year doing ministerial work in Lyons, and then became professor of moral theology at the scholasticate of Vals, near Le Puy, in 1834. He was called to Rome in 1847 to teach moral theology at the Roman College, but was forced to leave because of the revolution in 1848 and he returned to Vals.

His *Compendium Theologiae Moralis* was published at Lyons in 1850. In it he followed closely the doctrines of Busenbaum and St. Alphonsus Liguori and made use of the works of Cardinal Gousset. Gury aimed especially at the application of general moral principles to contemporary issues. His clarity, careful reasoning, and attention to detail caused his manual to be adopted in many seminaries, including the major ones in Rome. By the time of the author's death, it had reached 17 editions, not to mention adaptations published without his knowledge in Belgium, Germany, Italy, England, Austria, and Spain. Gury was accused of Gallicanism for some of his opinions regarding the obligations binding in France on papal decrees, but replied that he had never called into question the authority of the pope but was merely tolerating the existing situation. Nevertheless he removed certain objectionable paragraphs from the fifth edition of his work. He went to Rome in 1864, and at the bidding of Father Beckx, general of the society, consulted with many outstanding theologians who had been using the *Compendium* as a text. Profiting by their suggestions, he published a definitive edition in 1865.

Gury's other major work, *Casus conscientiae in praecipuas quaestiones theologiae moralis,* published at Le Puy in 1862, enjoyed the same widespread success and fame as his earlier work and together with it exercised a considerable influence on moral theology on into the 20th century. More notable among the many later revised and annotated editions of Gury's works are those made by Dumas in France in 1890, Ballerini and Palmieri in Italy in 1907, Seitz in Germany in 1874, Ferreres in Spain in 1909, and Sabetti and Barret in the U.S. in 1902. Gury's influence contributed much to overcoming remnants of the spirit of Jansenism. He was instrumental in bringing back into vogue the old casuistic method, for which he was criticized by his opponents, especially in Germany.

During his years as professor, Gury kept in close contact with the spiritual life of the people by often preaching and hearing confessions, especially while giving missions in the countryside. He was also active in the spiritual direction of priests and religious communities, and in teaching catechism in the villages.

Bibliography: C. SOMMERVOGEL, *Bibliotèque de la Compagnie de Jésus,* 11 v. (Brussels-Paris 1890–1932) 3:1956–59. H. HURTER, *Nomenclator literarius theologiae catholicae,* 5 v. in 6 (3d ed. Innsbruck 1903–1913) 5.1: 1384–85. P. BERNARD, *Dictionnaire de théologie catholique,* ed. A. VACANT, 15 v. (Paris 1903–50; Tables générales 1951–) 6.2:1993–95.

[J. H. CAMPANA]

GUTENBERG BIBLE, THE

A three-volume, double-column, 1,282-page printed edition of the Latin Vulgate so-called after its printer, Johann Gutenberg (b. 1394–1399, d. 1468), also known as Forty-two-line Bible, or Mazarin Bible. The name "Forty-two-line Bible" derives from the fact that the text was printed in 42-line columns, while "Mazarin Bible" refers to the first catalogued copy in the Paris library of Cardinal Jules Mazarin. Produced *circa* 1452–1455 in Mainz, the Gutenberg Bible is the oldest book printed using the movable-type technique.

Little is known about Gutenberg's early life and career. He achieved fame for his invention of the technique of movable-type, which facilitated the mass printing of books in a quick and efficient manner. Differing from the traditional block printing that necessitated the laborious engraving of type on plates, Gutenberg's technique comprised uniform type that could be mass produced in individual molds and assembled on plates, and books printed using a movable printing press derived from wine-press. He used his previous professional experience as a goldsmith to develop special techniques for cutting punches, stamping matrices, and casting individual pieces of type. He experimented with the use of steel alphabets in a press

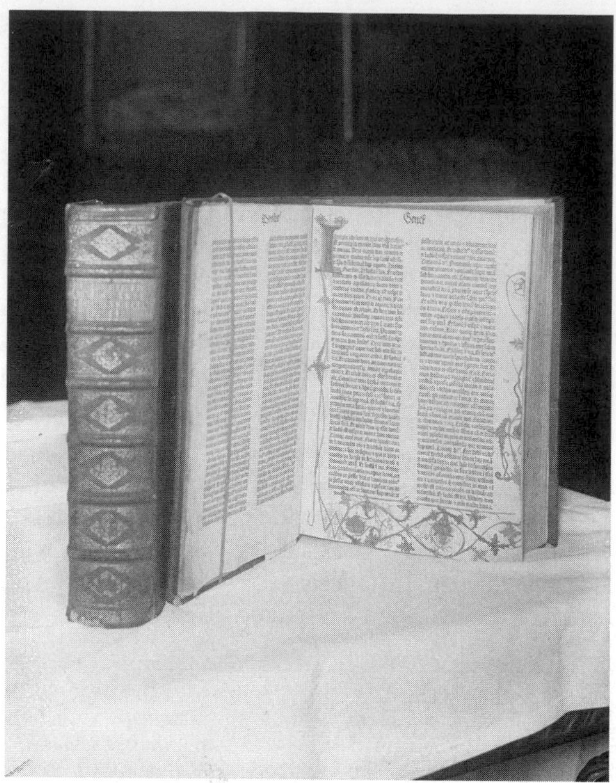

Gutenberg Bible. (©Bettmann/CORBIS)

with iron screws and other contrivances. In an effort to literally ''reproduce'' European books that were hand written by scribes, in a gothic script with many flourishes and ligatures, Gutenberg fashioned a font of over 300 characters. He then invented a variable-width mold and perfected the blend of lead, antimony and tin for casting the type.

While Gutenberg's discovery changed printing history, it did not immediately change his financial situation. The perfection and success of his invention came at enormous expense. Gutenberg formed a partnership with Johann Fust, a lawyer willing to loan him money. Unfortunately Fust later foreclosed on the loan and acquired all of Gutenberg's printing equipment in 1456. Gutenberg died three years later and was buried in the Franciscan church at Mainz.

Approximately 180 copies of the Gutenberg Bible were printed and significant parts of 48 copies still survive. The British Library houses two complete copies of the Gutenberg Bible and a small but important fragment of a third copy. One copy, printed on paper, was transferred in 1829 to the British Library with the library of King George III (1738–1820). The other copy was printed on vellum and was bequeathed by Thomas Grenville (1755–1846). Other perfect vellum copies are held by the Library of Congress and the Bibliotheque Nationale de France. In the United States, near complete copies are in the Huntington, Morgan, New York Public, Harvard University, and Yale University libraries.

Bibliography: J. PELIKAN, *The Reformation of the Bible* (New Haven 1976). J. M. DODU, *The Gutenberg Bible: A Commentary, Historical Background,* trans. J. M. DODU (Paris 1985).

[J. P. HARRELL]

GUTHLAC, ST.

Anglo-Saxon monk, hermit; b. *c.* 667–674; d. April 11, 714. He was of royal stock and the brother of St. Pega (feast: Jan. 8). His vita, written by Felix *c.* 740, the main source of information, states that he began a successful military career at 15, but nine years later took monastic vows at the double MONASTERY of Repton, where his asceticism aroused the dislike of his brethren. There he learned to read and chant, but longing for the spiritual warfare of the hermit's life, he settled on a remote island in the Lincolnshire fens called Crowland, arriving on St. Bartholomew's Day, Aug. 24, *c.* 699. He spent the rest of his life there in meditation and spiritual combat, and had many strange experiences: on one occasion he was attacked by Welsh-speaking devils, on another he was carried by devils to the mouth of hell, whence his patron St. Bartholomew rescued him. Many people came to seek his advice including Ethelbald, afterward king of Mercia. He was ordained priest about eight years before his death. Twelve months after he died, his incorrupt body was elevated and placed in a shrine that Ethelbald later rebuilt. A monastery was eventually established on the site. His relics were twice translated in the 12th century, and are still in CROWLAND ABBEY church. Two Old English poems on Guthlac survive, written *c.* 1100 and both based on Felix's Life. His cult was widespread in the Middle Ages, especially in the Midlands.

Feast: April 11; Aug. 30 (translation).

Bibliography: K. NORGATE, *Dictionary of National Biography from the Earliest Times to 1900,* 63 v. (London 1885–1900; repr. 1908–38) 8:816–817. *Felix's Life of St. Guthlac,* ed. and tr. B. COLGRAVE (Cambridge, Eng. 1956; repr. 1985). J. ROBERTS, ed., *The Guthlac Poems of the Exeter Book* (Oxford 1979). A. H. OLSEN, *Guthlac of Croyland* (Washington, D.C. 1981).

[B. COLGRAVE]

GUTIÉRREZ RODRÍGUEZ, BARTOLOMÉ, BL.

Augustinian missionary in Japan; b. Mexico City, 1580; d. Nagasaki, Japan, Sept. 3, 1632. On June 1, 1597, he pronounced his vows in the Augustinian monastery of his native city. On Feb. 22, 1606, he left for the Philippines. In 1612 he was sent to the Augustinian missions in Japan, and in May 1613 he became prior of Usuki. Because of a decree of banishment, he went into exile in October 1614, but he returned to Japan in 1618. He spent 15 years in Japan in the midst of a bloody persecution. On Nov. 10, 1629, he and his catechist (Bl.) Brother John Shozuburo, were arrested at Kikizu in Arima. After two years of imprisonment at Omura, Gutiérrez was taken with six others, among them two women, to Mt. Unzen to be tortured in the hot sulphur springs for a month. They were then taken to the Cruzmachi prison of Nagasaki. On Sept. 3, 1632, they were carried to the Hill of Martyrs to be burned alive. The firewood was arranged in a wide circle. In the midst were six columns to which one of their fingers was tied with a light string. Many people witnessed the martyrdom. The Christians formed processions and sang psalms. After the fire had died down the charred bodies of the martyrs were burned completely and the ashes thrown into the ocean. Bartolomé was beatified on July 7, 1867.

Bibliography: M. CLAVER, *El admirable y excelente martirio en el Reyno de Japón de los Benditos Padres fray Bartolomé Gutiérrez, fray Francisco de Gracía y fray Tomás de San Agustín, religiosos de la orden de San Agustín nuestro Padre, y de otros compañeros suyos hasta el año de 1637* (Manila 1638). A. HARTMANN, "Blessed Bartholomew Gutiérrez, O.S.A.," *The Tagastan* 22 (1961) 39–52; *The Augustinians in 17th Century Japan* (Louvain 1965).

[A. HARTMANN]

GUY DE MONTPELLIER

Founder of the Order of the HOLY SPIRIT at Montpellier; d. Rome, 1208. Very little is known about him. Some historians credit him with an illustrious birth, but the documents call him only Fra Guido or Master Gui. He founded the hospital and the Order of Hospitalers of the Holy Spirit at Montpellier (*c.* 1180), a lay community for the care of the sick, and wrote for it a rule, which INNOCENT III confirmed (April 23, 1198). This same Pope, having called Guy to Rome (1204), confided to him the hospital of Santa Maria in Saxia, which became the model for similar Holy Spirit hospitals throughout Europe. The order spread into various countries, and soon received not only lay members making simple vows, but also clerics binding themselves by solemn vows. It came to be regarded as a military order, but the religious confined their work to the care of the sick.

Guthlac receiving the tonsure, miniature in a roundel, detail from the "Guthlac Roll," of drawings of scenes from the life of the saint, c.1200.

Bibliography: *Histoire Littéraire de la France* 16:599–600. P. A. J. PAULINIER, *Gui de Montpellier* (Montpellier 1870). P. DE ANGELIS, *L'ospedale di Santo Spirito in Saxia e le sue filiali nel mondo* (Rome 1958).

[J. DAOUST]

GUYANA, THE CATHOLIC CHURCH IN

The Co-operative Republic of Guyana, along with neighboring Suriname and French Guiana, occupies an area in northern South America between the mouth of the Amazon and the Orinoco River that was once known as Guiana. Formerly a colony of Great Britain, Guyana is bordered on the north by the Atlantic Ocean, on the east by Suriname, on the south by Brazil and on the west by Venezuela. The marshy coastal region to the north rises to inland plains and thence to densely forested mountains in the west and south. Numerous rivers run through Guyana, and the climate is tropical, marked by rainy seasons and flooding in summer and winter. Agricultural products include sugar, rice, shrimp and timber, while natural resources include bauxite, gold and diamonds. The population is highly diversified and includes a large proportion of East Indians. Guyanese Catholics are predominately people of Portuguese descent. Hinduism and Islam also have large numbers of followers, the majority being East Indians, though a few blacks are Muslim. Many Guyanese also practice the Caribbean Rastafarianism or Obeah religions, often in conjunction with another faith.

Capital: Georgetown.
Size: 83,000 sq. miles.
Population: 697,286 in 2000.
Languages: English; Amerindian dialects, Creole, Hindi, and Urdu are spoken in various regions.
Religions: 140,455 Catholics (20%), 62,755 Sunni Muslims (9%), 208,226 Protestants (30%), 285,850 Hindus (41%).
Diocese: Georgetown, which is suffragan to the archdiocese of Port of Spain, Trinidad and Tobago. It shares its metropolitan with diocese in Barbados, Suriname, and Aruba.

History. English explorer Sir Walter Raleigh, who in 1595–96 made the first investigations into Guyana, was followed by the Dutch, who also did some exploring in the same decade. The first Dutch colony in Guyana was a trading post established *c.* 1616, while the Dutch West India Company founded the colonies of Berbice in 1624, and Essequibo and Demerara in 1645. The wars of the late 17th century devastated all European colonies in Guiana, and the upheaval continued through the colonial rivalries of the 18th century and the Napoleonic Wars. The division among European powers was regularized in the conventions and treaties of 1814 and 1815, with Great Britain losing its hold over neighboring Suriname but making Guyana a crown colony in 1831.

After the British took control of the region in 1813, only the Church of England and the Church of Scotland were tolerated in Guyana, and in 1825 the parishes were arranged by alternation between the two Churches. After 1899, however, all religions were extended equal legal status and Guyana received her first native bishop in 1971. On May 26, 1966 the region was granted its independence and it became a republic on Feb. 23, 1970. Under the new socialist government, schools were nationalized in 1979, and the economy was heavily controlled. Through the Guyana Council of Churches, a faith-based Christian coalition, Catholic leaders became increasingly outspoken with regard to government policies. A new constitution was implemented on Oct. 6, 1980, after which restrictions on private religious schools were relaxed and eventually abolished. A coalition government elected in the late 1980s implemented a free-market economy designed to promote an upturn in employment and improve the overall standard of living in the country.

Despite government efforts, drought and political instability resulted in continued economic problems through the end of the 20th century. In addition, the country was burdened by interest payments on large amounts of foreign aid loaned by industrialized nations. In 1999, 20 percent of Guyana's foreign debt was forgiven by the nations holding such debt. The Vatican, which had encouraged such an action through its Jubilee 2000 campaign, while noting its gratitude also expressed disappointment that the forgiven amount was not more. However, the release from some debt service, plus other reform measures, signaled an economic upturn by 2001.

Despite an improving economy, at the beginning of the 21st century Guyana remained among the world's poorest nations. However, it maintained a long history of religious tolerance and the government allowed all faiths to worship freely. In 2000 Guyana had 24 parishes tended by four secular and 50 religious priests. Also working among the faithful were 15 brothers and 132 sisters, who served by teaching at the country's 102 primary and 63 secondary schools or providing other humanitarian aid, such as medical efforts to cope with the spread of AIDS. The Church-run newspaper, the *Catholic Standard,* was praised for its continued efforts to promote social and political awareness as well as reinforce Church doctrine. Of concern to Catholics within Guyana was the legalization of abortion in 1995, and the *Catholic Standard* publicized the continued efforts of the nation's churches to overturn that law.

Bibliography: R. T. SMITH, *British Guiana* (New York 1962). B. N. MOORE, *Cultural Power, Resistance, and Pluralism: Colonial Guyana, 1838–1906* (Toronto, 1995).

[J. HERRICK/EDS.]

GUYON, JEANNE MARIE BOUVIER DE LA MOTTE

Spiritual writer, famous for her quietist doctrines and the controversies they provoked; b. Montargis, France, April 13, 1648; d. Blois, June 9, 1717.

Life. Her family belonged to the *petite noblesse,* but the father was old and twice-married, and the mother neglectful, although both were devout; so Jeanne Marie spent most of her childhood in various convents. Her happiness lay largely in the reading first of romances and then of mystical literature, and she developed a strong though unguided attraction for prayer and the interior life. At 16 she was married to Jacques Guyon du Chesnoy, an invalid nearing 40; she was left, after 12 unhappy years, a widow with two children (1676). In 1681, she felt called to the apostolate; she left her son with relatives and took her daughter to Gex, near Geneva, where, at the invitation of the bishop, she assisted in the establishment of a group of converted HUGUENOTS, or *Nouvelles Catholiques.* Here she encountered the Barnabite Father François La Combe (1643–1715), whom she had once met at Montargis. In Rome La Combe had absorbed some of the ideas of QUIETISM propagated by the Spaniard Miguel de

MOLINOS (1640–96), but after becoming Madame Guyon's director, he was before long led by her into a more complete quietism, which she had developed independently and now conceived it to be her mission to spread. From 1681 to 1686 she traveled about Switzerland, Italy, and southern France, often in the company of La Combe. They then went to Paris, under suspicion both as to doctrine and morals. It was known that ever since the Middle Ages, moral degradation had sometimes resulted from the quietist attitude of passivity with respect to virtue or temptation. La Combe was arrested (1687) and imprisoned for life; Madame Guyon was detained in a Visitation convent in Paris (1688). After eight months she was liberated through the interest of Madame de Maintenon (1635–1719), who had secretly married Louis XIV in 1684, and she became the center of devout circles at Court and at Saint-Cyr (Madame de Maintenon's school for girls), and finally the storm center of the quarrel about quietism between Jacques Bénigne Bossuet (1625–1704), Bishop of Meaux, and the Abbé François de Salignac de la Mothe Fénelon (1651–1715), later archbishop of Cambrai. Madame Guyon voluntarily spent some months (1695), at the Visitation convent of Meaux, which she also left freely, but was accused (perhaps through misunderstanding) of fleeing. Now in danger, she hid in Paris, but was arrested and imprisoned at Vincennes (1695–96); then detained at a convent in Vaugirard for two years; later imprisoned in the Bastille (1698–1703). Finally, she was permitted to spend the rest of her life in Blois, at the estate of her son-in-law.

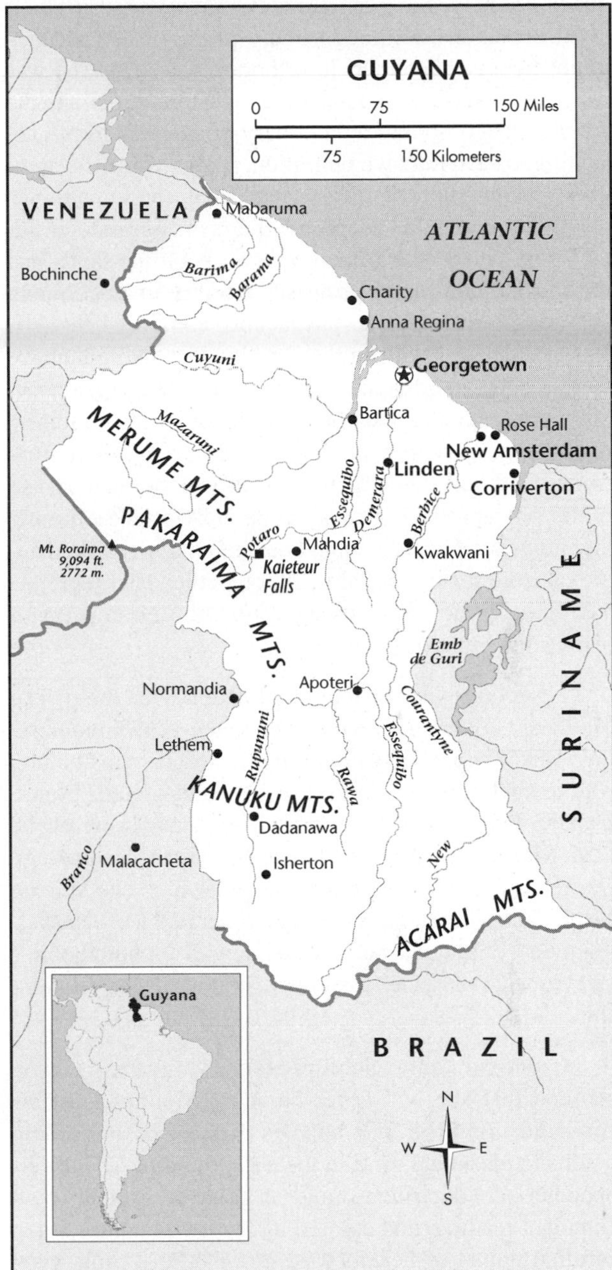

Personal Character. Madame Guyon's personality and history have puzzling aspects. The principal source, her 700-page autobiography, begun in 1687 and concluded just before her death, is revealing but so riddled with contradictions and extravagances that often it cannot be taken at face value. She charmed her hearers, and was quick to find a sympathetic following. Copies of her *Moyen Court* (1685, Short and Easy Method of Prayer) were carried in the pockets of most of the pious aristocracy. Great schemes for universal reform were built up, only to end in conflict or other disappointing eventualities. Historians are hampered by incomplete, inexact, and often contradictory evidence, even apart from Madame Guyon's own account. Further, the whole history of both quietism and orthodox mysticism bristles with moot points, so that it is not surprising that some modern scholars have tended to approve Bossuet's part in the matter, others Fénelon's; or that some are sympathetic toward Madame Guyon, while others are not. However, the main factual lines in the picture stand out fairly clearly. Madame Guyon's virtues are undeniable, though she often went to extremes, as when her charity led her to abandon not only the greater part of her own fortune but that of her children as well. She can hardly be accused of cowardice, for, when freed from one stretch of imprisonment, she straightway risked another through continuation of the activities that had gotten her into trouble. It is even admitted that she had the makings of a saint, and A. Poulain, SJ, is ''led to regard it as probable that she really had the prayer of quiet in her youth'' (*The Graces of Interior Prayer,* 16.38), that is, the first stage of genuine infused contemplation. She has been called half saint, half lunatic, good in heart but weak in mind, and these characterizations appear to be a fair summing-up. In spite of constant apostolic zeal, she lacked prudence and that humility that made the great saints and mystics distrust their own revelations. Although many pages of her writings might find a counterpart in orthodox works (as she was wont to emphasize), the marks of delusion are plain in the whole. She composed a dictionary of mystical terms, assigning to each her own definition, so that while the uninitiated might suppose they were reading the same things the saints had said, adepts of quietism understood her meaning, which was often not at all what the saints had meant. She constantly professed docility to the Church, but was nevertheless so unshakably convinced that she was a prophetess with a great mission that she could have no real understanding of docility. She pushed to strange, often unacceptable, lengths concepts of spiritual motherhood, oneness with her protégés, and her mediation between God and them. Yet so meek was her manner, so subtle her approach, and so apparently wholesome her first influence, that she could boast of having received approval from several prelates, although they later regretted having given it. Even Bossuet found himself in that embarrassing situation.

No proof exists of moral delinquency on the part of Madame Guyon; and La Combe's letter (1698), confessing ''sins'' supposedly committed with her years before, was extracted under duress, if not actual force, from a man on the way to the complete madness in which he died. Madame Guyon repudiated the charge, even though she readily admitted a familiarity in which she saw no harm. Historians have generally exonerated her, especially in view of her constant obsession with ''motherhood,'' and the want of evidence of interest in any other relationship.

Quietism and Semiquietism. Madame Guyon claimed that she had never heard of Molinos until his condemnation (1687). It appears that besides absorbing quietistic ideas that were in the air at the time, she developed her own doctrine from ideas gathered from her own abundant reading, and colored by her own fantasy. Some cardinal points of her doctrine are: (1) Perfection, even in this life, consists in a continual act of contemplation and love, which includes in itself all the acts of religion, and which, once produced, subsists permanently unless expressly revoked. (2) Therefore, a soul that has reached perfection is no longer obliged to specific acts, distinct from charity, and must suppress generally and without exception all acts proceeding from its own industry, as contrary to perfect repose in God. (3) Such a soul must be indifferent to all things concerning either the body or the soul, and either temporal or eternal goods. (4) In the state of perfect contemplation, the soul must repulse all distinct ideas, and consequently even the attributes and mysteries of Christ. Besides the *Moyen Court* and the *Life,* her chief works amplifying these ideas are the *Explanation of the Canticle of Canticles* (1685) and the *Spiritual Torrents,* circulated only in manuscript during her life.

Madame Guyon met Fénelon in October 1688, at Beynes, near Versailles, in the home of the Duchess of Charost. Fénelon, little impressed at first, was soon not only befriending Madame Guyon but following her guidance, and the great drama was underway. He did moderate her rashness of expression, so that later he was really defending a *guyonisme fénelonisé* (Calvet). One key to the Bossuet-Fénelon quarrel is the fact that whereas Fénelon had scarcely bothered to read Madame Guyon's earlier effusions, Bossuet fastened on every detail, frequently with horror. Guyon herself, after seeking pronouncement on her doctrine, took no part in the quarrel, and during most of it was in prison. The chief focal point of the long dispute came to be disinterested love (*pur amour*), pushed to the point of formally giving up any desire for eternal salvation. Orthodoxy was concerned for hope, and would permit such disinterestedness only on condition that it were God's will, a proviso that could not be fulfilled. Historians generally agree that the extent of Madame Guyon's hold on Fénelon is regrettable, especially in view of the so-called ''secret letters'' brought to light by Philippe Dutoit (1767). The authenticity of this correspondence from the first two years of their acquaintance has been questioned, but most scholars accept the ''proof'' of M. Masson. No doubt touches Fénelon on moral grounds; it was a matter of spiritual intimacy, and domination by Madame Guyon, more complete than had been suspected in the lifetime of the principals. On the other hand, it must be admitted that Bossuet knew little about mysticism, at least at the beginning, and was at length carried into a certain violence by the heat of polemics.

Although Fénelon did not see Madame Guyon in their later years, he neither repudiated her as a person nor questioned her good faith. There was some indirect communication between them when members of their respective circles traveled between Cambrai and Blois. She was under the surveillance of a friendly bishop, and entertained visitors, though few were orthodox Catholics, and she went on expounding her ideas of pure love to the end. Her writings spread to other countries, and many Protestants, especially from England and Holland, became interested. They saw in her a victim of ecclesiastical persecution and managed to give some of her teaching a Protestant interpretation. She received all comers as her ''children,'' did not speak of specifically Catholic doctrine or practice, but did keep to the latter in her life, and at her death wrote a testament of adherence to the Church. After her death, she continued to have a following among non-Catholics. Madame Guyon's works have no literary value, and she would almost certainly be unknown to history had she not encountered Fénelon and touched off the great controversy, whose reverberations have not yet entirely subsided.

Bibliography: *Oeuvres,* ed. P. POIRET, 39 v. in 12 (Cologne 1713–32). T. C. UPHAM, *Life and Religious Opinions and Experience of Madame de la Mothe Guyon,* 2 v. (New York 1855), ''interpreted'' translation to make her sound Protestant. R. A. KNOX, *Enthusiasm* (New York 1961). J. CALVET, *La Littérature religieuse de François de Sales à Fénelon* (Paris 1956). A. LARGENT, *Dictionnaire de théologie catholique,* ed. A. VACANT, 15 v. (Paris 1903–50; Tables générales 1951–) 6.2:1997–2006. P. POURRAT, *Christian Spirituality,* tr. W. H. MITCHELL et al., 4 v. (Westminster, Md. 1953–55). A. POULAIN, *The Graces of Interior Prayer,* tr. L. L. Y. SMITH (St. Louis 1950). P. M. MASSON, *Fénelon and Madame Guyon* (Paris 1907). H. BRÉMOND, *Apologie pour Fénelon* (Paris 1910); *Histoire littéraire du sentiment religieux en France,* 12 v. (Paris 1916–36). The last two works favor Fénelon and are sympathetic to Madame Guyon; the last work is epoch-making for the entire period.

[L. TINSLEY]

GUZMÁN Y LECAROS, JOSEPH JAVIER

Franciscan priest and first historian of Chilean independence; b. Santiago, 1759; d. there, 1840. While still very young he entered the Franciscan convent and was distinguished for his culture and intelligence. After his ordination in 1782, he became a teacher of grammar and sacred theology. He took advanced courses in the University of San Felipe, obtaining the bachelor's and doctor's degrees. On the eve of the independence movement his adherence to the doctrines of the Catholic Enlightenment led him to support the cause of the patriots against Spain, and he influenced his colleagues in the order with his preaching. When the republic was proclaimed (1817), he was hailed as a benefactor of the country. His ecclesiastical career was brilliant: he was the Franciscan prior four times, and only his death prevented his being made bishop of Santiago. His literary career began with the simple autobiographical pages *Noticias peculiares a mi* and culminated in 1833, when the government entrusted to him the editing of a history of Chile. This was published in popular editions under the title of *El chileno instruido en la historia, topográfica, civil y política* (Santiago 1834). Modeled after the *Historia* of Abbé Molina, it employed the didactic form of a dialogue between uncle and nephew, with a division into lessons on the following subjects: geographical environment; conquest and colonization of the country; spiritual and temporal government; preliminaries of, and struggle for, independence; and a vigorous defense of the aborigines. The merit of the work rests more in its magnanimous spirit than in its content, which was not based on historical research. The pages devoted to description of the life of the capital in those years are interesting. He died at an advanced age, high in public esteem, as expressed in the obituary notices written by the famous humanist Andrés Bello and by the liberal historians Diego Barros Arana and Miguel Luis Amunátegui.

Bibliography: G. FELIÚ CRUZ, *Historiografía colonial de Chile* (Santiago 1958–).

[E. PEREIRA SALAS]

GWYN, RICHARD (WHITE), BL.

Welsh martyr; b. Llanidloes, Montgomery, date unknown; d. Wrexham, Oct. 17, 1584. Gwyn, descended from Bleddyn, Prince of Powys, who ruled Wales in 11th century, was a poet, schoolmaster, and wit. At 19 or 20, he went for a short time to Oxford, then to St. John's College, Cambridge, where he was supported chiefly by its master, Dr. Bullock. On his return to Wales he became a schoolmaster at Overton in the Maelor, a small district of Flintshire encircled by Denbighshire. There he married and had six children, three of whom died in infancy. As Gwyn's influence spread, Downham, the bishop of Chester, threatened him with imprisonment if he did not attend the Protestant Church. In weakness Gwyn submitted, but he later repented. Leaving Overton, he went to Erbistock, where again he opened a school, meanwhile living with his family in an old barn. In 1579 he was recognized in Wrexham market place, denounced, and imprisoned. The next day he escaped. In June 1580 he was again seized and this time confined in Ruthin Castle. On one occasion he was carried, heavily shackled, into the Protestant church at Wrexham, but he rattled his chains so loudly that the minister was unable to make himself heard; on another he baited a red-nosed minister, who argued that St. Peter had no more been given the keys of the kingdom of heaven than any Protestant minister, by saying, ''The keys you have received are obviously those of the beer cellar.'' In all he was indicted seven times before magistrates, was placed in the stocks, fined heavily, and tortured before October 1584, when he appeared at his eighth assizes at Wrexham and was there indicted for treason on the ground that he had tried to reconcile one Lewis Gronow to the Church and had maintained the supremacy of the Pope. Although the jury had been hand picked, they refused to return a verdict of guilty until, after a night of discussion, they were finally coerced by the judge. The next day when the long sentence was read out, Gwyn said, ''What is all this? Is it more than one death?'' Mrs. Gwyn, brought into court with her baby, was cautioned not to imitate her husband. She retorted,

''If you lack blood, you may take my life as well as my husband's.'' She was imprisoned for her brave words. Gwyn refused an offer of liberty if he conformed. On Oct. 17, 1584, as he left prison for his execution, he said to the sorrowful crowd, ''Weep not for me, I do but pay the rent before the rent-day.'' At the marketplace the hangman knelt to ask his forgiveness. As the executioner tore out his heart, Gwyn said, ''O good God, what is this?'' The hangman replied, ''It is an execution for the Queen's Majesty.'' Gwyn replied ''Jesu, trwgarha wrthyf'' (Jesus, have mercy on me). Gwyn is the protomartyr of Wales. He was beatified by Pius XI on Dec. 15, 1932 (*see* ENGLAND, SCOTLAND, AND WALES, MARTYRS OF).

Feast: Oct. 25.

Bibliography: *Blessed Richard Gwyn* (Postulation Pamphlet; London 1960). R. CHALLONER, *Memoirs of Missionary Priests,* ed. J. H. POLLEN (rev. ed. London 1924). A. BUTLER, *The Lives of Saints,* ed. H. THURSTON and D. ATTWATER, 4 v. (New York, 1956) 4:202–204. T. P. ELLIS, *Catholic Martyrs of Wales* (London 1933).

[G. FITZ HERBERT]

H

HAAS, FRANCIS JOSEPH

Bishop, educator, writer, and labor relations expert; b. Racine, Wis., 18 March 1899; d. Grand Rapids, Mich., Aug. 29, 1953. He was the son of immigrant parents, Peter and Mary L. (O'Day) Haas. After attending (1904–13) St. Francis Seminary, Milwaukee, Wis., he was ordained for the Archdiocese of Milwaukee on June 11, 1913. For two years he served as curate in Holy Rosary parish and then began teaching and study, becoming one of the American priests most closely identified with Catholic ideals of social justice. He was an instructor at St. Francis Seminary, later studied at Johns Hopkins University, Baltimore, Md., and received a Ph.D. (1922) at the Catholic University of America, Washington, D.C. In 1922 he returned to Milwaukee, where he served as professor of sociology at St. Francis Seminary and Marquette University, and from 1922 to 1931 as dean of the college departments of the seminary and editor of the *Salesianum,* the college's quarterly publication. He was rector of the seminary (1935–37), director (1931–35) of the National Catholic School of Social Service, Washington, D.C., and dean (1937) of the School of Social Service of Catholic University.

In June 1933, Pres. Franklin D. Roosevelt named him a member of the Labor Advisory Board of the National Recovery Administration (NRA) and in October of that year called on him to accept appointment to the National Labor Board. He was appointed (1934) labor representative on the General Code Authority of the NRA and member of the National Committee on Business and Labor Standards. Haas won national renown as a strike mediator; he was widely commended for his work as Federal mediator of a Minneapolis, Minn., truck drivers strike (1934), and he was chosen (September 1935) by Secretary of Labor Frances Perkins to be impartial chairman of a board to arbitrate a labor dispute involving 13,000 cigar makers in Tampa, Fla.

In 1943 Fr. Haas was appointed by President Roosevelt as first chairman of the U.S. Committee on Fair Employment Practices. In the same year he was named bishop of the Diocese of Grand Rapids and was consecrated on November 18 by Abp. Amleto G. Cicognani, Apostolic Delegate to the U.S. Haas continued his work on social problems while administering the Diocese of Grand Rapids. In 1945 he was named by Pres. Harry S Truman to serve on a 15 member Committee on Civil Rights. Haas wrote *Shop Collective Bargaining* (1922); *Man and Society, An Introduction to Sociology* (1930); and, as member of the Committee on Long-Range Work Relief of the National Resources Planning Board, *Security, Work and Relief Policies.*

[G. C. HIGGINS]

HABAKKUK, BOOK OF

The Old Testament Book of Habakkuk presents a variety of literary forms in its three chapters. Exegetes have not arrived at any general agreement about these forms. A look at the contents shows reason for the divergence of opinions, which are presented here with the solutions proposed for the date of composition and the unity of authorship. The commentary from Qumram is also considered briefly.

Nothing biographical is known of the Prophet from Scripture, although he is the subject of a midrashic story in Dn 14.33–39.

Contents. The first two chapters of the book contain a twofold complaint against God, whose answer is given in two oracles. The second oracle is developed in the five ''Woes'' of ch. 2. A psalm with liturgical annotations is contained in ch. 3. The psalm, which contains indications of having been adapted from a Babylonian cosmic myth, begins as an ardent prayer of supplication and develops into a hymn of praise whose theme is a THEOPHANY of Yahweh advancing to save His troubled people.

The Prophet is primarily concerned with the mystery of evil. Outraged by the sight of injustice, the Prophet,

Illumination at the beginning of the Book of Habakkuk in the "Great Bible of Demeter Neksei-Lipocz," the prophet Habakkuk kneeling in prayer, c. 1350.

perhaps speaking as a representative of the righteous, complains of God's seeming indifference (1.2–4). God answers that Chaldea is being raised up as His instrument of vengeance on the unjust. Proud, cruel, and rapacious, the CHALDEANS will suddenly descend on their prey and swiftly depart, having carried out the judgment of the Lord on evildoers (1.5–11). Continuing his complaint, the Prophet still demands an explanation of the suffering of the just (1.12–2.1). The response of the Lord is that "the just man, because of his faith, shall live" (2.2–4). As for the unjust, their evil will be turned back onto their heads (2.5–20). The psalm of ch. 3 is the reconciliation of the Prophet to the Lord's wisdom. Like Job, he states that humble trust in the saving God and acceptance of His will is the only answer to the evils that plague the life of the innocent. The Prophet reaches one of the heights of religious sentiment for the Old Testament in ch. 3.17–19. (*See* RETRIBUTION.)

Interpretation. This article treats the book as a unit. Since Chaldea is the instrument of God's vengeance, the evildoers would be the wicked Judaites under King Joachim. The language of the condemnatory oracle reflects that used by other prophets in castigating God's people for violations of the covenant. The prophecy should, on the basis of these factors, be placed around 601 B.C.

Other opinions identify the oppressor as Assyria and hence place the prophecy between 625—the year of the appearance of Chaldea—and 612 B.C.—the year of the capture of Niniveh by the Medes and Chaldeans. Still others, assuming Babylonia to be the tyrant, place the Prophet after 605, when the Babylonians gained control of Palestine, and before 597 B.C., when they took Jerusalem for the first time. Some see the Judaites as the first oppressor; Chaldea is God's instrument of judgment. To this the Prophet adds his second complaint, that the last state of the just man is worse than the first. This again places the prophecy about 601 B.C. Positing a growth similar to that of the PENTATEUCH, others claim that to the first preexilic complaint, a second was added during the Exile, adapting the earlier message to a pre-Persian situation around 550 B.C. Finally, understanding Chaldea in 1.6 as referring to the Greeks, some regard Alexander the Great as the oppressor (*c.* 334). These opinions for the most part consider the psalm to be the work of an editor who lived some time between 600 and 100 B.C.

Qumran Commentary. The *pēšer* or commentary among the DEAD SEA SCROLLS from Qumran (1QpHb), written in Hebrew, applies the first two chapters of Habakkuk to a situation contemporary with the QUMRAN COMMUNITY; the enemy is probably Rome. The absence of the psalm in this commentary is not an argument against the unity of the three chapters, since the Qumran commentaries in general present no continued development of thought. The psalm is found in the Septuagint as well as in the Masoretic Text.

Bibliography: F. HORST, *Die zwölf Kleinen Propheten* (HAT 14; 2d ed. 1954). J. TRINQUET, *Habaquq* (BJ; 1953). C. TAYLOR, JR., G. A. BUTTRICK, ed., *The Interpreters' Bible,* 12 v. (New York 1951–57) 6:973–1003. P. HUMBERT, *Problème du livre d'Habacuc* (Neuchâtel 1944). W. A. IRWIN, "The Psalm of Habakkuk," *Journal of Near Eastern Studies* (1942) 10–40. W. H. BROWNLEE, "The Jerusalem Habakkuk Scroll," *The Bulletin of the American Schools of Oriental Research* 112 (1948) 8–18. M. BURROWS, "Prophecy and the Prophets at Qumran," *Israel's Prophetic Heritage,* ed. B. W. ANDERSON and W. HANELSON (New York 1962).

[D. J. MOELLER]

HABERT, ISAAC

Theologian; b. Paris, *c.* 1598; d. Pont-de-Salars, near Rodez, Sept. 15, 1668. Early in his career Habert tried to carry on the literary tradition of his family by publishing several books of poetry. In 1623 he became a fellow of the Sorbonne, licenciate and doctor in 1626.

About 1639 it was rumored that Cardinal A. J. RICHELIEU was planning to set up a French patriarchate to achieve greater independence from Rome. Against the

Oratorian Charles Hersent, who publicized this idea under the pseudonym of Optatus Gallus, Habert launched his *De consensu hierarchiae et monarchiae adversus paraeneticum Optati Galli schismatum fictoris libri VI* (Paris 1640). Noteworthy is his Latin version of the Greek pontifical entitled 'Αρχιερατικόν *Liber Pontificalis Ecclesiae graecae* (Paris 1643).

After 1626 he was canon theologian of Notre Dame Cathedral and preacher at the royal court. In 1642–43, on Richelieu's orders, he vigorously opposed Cornelius JANSEN's *AUGUSTINUS* in three sermons at the cathedral. In these he compared the book's doctrine with that of Calvin. A. Arnauld attacked these sermons in an apologetic diatribe; Habert responded in his *La défense de la foy de l'Église et de l'ancienne doctrine de Sorbonne* (Paris 1644). Against an expression in the preface of Arnauld's *Fréquente Communion* presenting Peter and Paul as the ''two-fold heads of the Roman Church,'' Habert issued his *De cathedra seu primatu singulari S. Petri* (Paris 1645).

He was named bishop of Vabres in April 1645. The following year at Paris he published against Jansenists and Augustinians his most significant dogmatic work, *Theologiae graecorum patrum vindicatae circa universam materiam gratiae libri III*, an exposition of the Greek Fathers' doctrine of grace.

Bibliography: F. X. BANTLE, *Lexikon für Theologie und Kirche*, ed. J. HOFER and K. RAHNER (Freiberg 1957–65) 4:1297. J. ORCIBAL, ''Le patriarcat de Richelieu,'' in *Jean Duvergier de Hauranne, abbé de Saint-Cyran, Appendices* (Paris 1948), 108–132. L. CEYSSENS, ''L'anijanséniste Isaac Habert,'' *Bulletin de l'Institut historique belge de Rome* [=Jansenistica minora XI] 42 (1972), 237–305

[C. R. MEYER/J. M. GRES-GAYER]

HABIRU (HABIRI)

Certain groups of people located in the Near East during the second millennium B.C. The Habiru first became known to historians with the publication of the Amarna letters at the end of the 19th century. Since that time the available sources of information on them—in Sumerian, Akkadian, Hittite, Ugaritic, and Egyptian—have increased to almost 200 documents. These sources span at least seven centuries and concern the geographical area along the Fertile Crescent from Lower Mesopotamia to Egypt. The earliest certain reference to the Habiru is from Anatolia in the 19th century B.C., the latest from Egypt in the middle of the 12th century B.C. The Habiru must therefore have existed during the second millennium B.C., and the documentation poses two major questions: who were they? And what was their relationship, if any, to the HEBREWS of the Bible?

The Identity of the Habiru. The Habiru are frequently referred to by a Sumerian expression SA.GAZ (with variants) that has been interpreted to mean murderer, tendon-cutter, head-smiter, and the like. The context in which it occurs makes its pejorative sense clear, and this sense also appears in an Akkadian lexical text that translates the Sumerian as *ḫabbātu* (robber).

Etymology. The etymology of Habiru is still uncertain; it is not universally agreed that the word is even of Semitic origin. Ugaritic and Egyptian occurrences, *'prm* and *'pr.w* respectively, resolve the ambiguity of the cuneiform writing with *ḫ,* whence the conventional Habiru, and show that the first consonant is the *'ayin*-sound, a voiced laryngeal. Earlier explanations of Habiru as ''confederate'' or ''Hebronite'' (cf. the biblical city HEBRON), based on a root *ḥbr,* are certainly wrong. The Ugaritic and Egyptian spellings also indicate *p* rather than *b* as the second consonant; likewise, the cuneiform writing with *BI* is ambiguous and can stand for *pi* as well as *bi.* The form *'apiru,* however, is still capable of several interpretations: one provided for (A. Goetze, M. Greenberg; cf. Akkadian *epēru,* to provide for), dusty one, covered with dust (E. Dhorme, R. Borger, R. De Langhe, W. F. Albright according to his latest view; cf. Hebrew *'āpār,* dust), one equipped, and member of a labor gang (Albright according to an earlier view; cf. Egyptian *'pr,* to equip). Moreover, since Semitic *b* occasionally appears as *p* in Egyptian and Ugaritic, J. Lewy believes *'br* is the original root and a Habiru is one who has crossed over, an immigrant.

A Socio-legal Term. Common to these proposals on etymology is the view that Habiru is an appellative without national or ethnic meaning. This view is supported by the wide geographical diffusion of the Habiru, the indications in their personal names of various ethnic origins, the morphology of the term, and the Sumerian equivalent. With the increasing evidence, the much more common opinion is that Habiru is a socio-legal term.

Characteristic of the Habiru is that they are almost always dependents, either on the state, city, or other individuals. In Egypt they perform forced labor for the crown, at Nuzu (Nuzi). In Mesopotamia both male and female Habiru offer their services to a master in exchange for their keep. Most commonly, however, the Habiru serve as soldiers, often organized in special contingents; it is in this role that we find them at Larsa in Babylonia, Mari on the Middle Euphrates, Alalakh in North Syria, and Boghazköy in Anatolia.

Their social status varies from place to place, but with the exception of that of a few individuals, it is an inferior one. In Egypt and at Nuzu they are virtually slaves, although in the latter place they seem to enjoy a higher position than the ordinary slave. At Alalakh, the individual Habiru may occupy a prominent rank, but the majority are inferior to the peasantry. Hittite Habiru are ranked between the freeborn and the slaves.

Very often the Habiru are foreigners. The Nuzu and Alalakh texts are explicit on this point, and it is implied in the Hittite texts, in which the Habiru are frequently placed in parallelism with the Lulaḫi, foreigners from the east. Since the Egyptian Habiru are usually, if not always, prisoners of war, they do not belong to the native population.

The ranks of the Habiru are increased by the presence of fugitives; some scholars, in fact, believe that this is the common characteristic of all Habiru. The Hittite king promises to extradite all subjects of UGARIT who flee to the territory of the Habiru. King Idrimi of Alalakh escapes from his native land and finds refuge with the Habiru in Canaan. A Habiru mentioned at Mari is a fugitive from Eshnunna in the south, and an old Assyrian document perhaps attests a similar flight because of unpaid debts.

Freebooters. The Habiru could constitute a grave threat to the peace. The Mari letters speak of them as endangering a city and engaging in razzias in which men and sheep are carried off (cf. the pejorative SA.GAZ and the Akkadian translation as robber). In the Amarna Letters, to be a Habiru is synonymous with being a rebel against the Egyptian power in Palestine and Syria; it is the Habiru who are most frequently mentioned as supporters of the leaders of revolt, to whom they occasionally bind themselves by a solemn pact. At Alalakh a year is dated by the treaty of peace between the king and the Habiru; this suggests the importance that could be attached to coming to terms with them. They are not, however, to be thought of as marauding nomads, from whom they are at times explicitly distinguished; often too they are found in fixed settlements. The Habiru appear rather as bands of freebooters who, when political authority is strong, are organized as a kind of foreign legion, but who in times of political upheaval or weakness prey on villages or cities and support subversive elements in society. Of course, seminomads may have often joined their ranks.

Outlaws. Since men do not leave their native lands and enter an alien society as dependents, or hover on the fringes of their own society as outlaws and rebels, unless they are forced to, the Habiru must have been men under duress. In the political, social, and economic context of the second millennium the principal sources of their hardship are obvious. The hand of the crown lay heavy on the populace, especially in vassal territories, where the inhabitants not only had to pay tribute to the suzerain, but had to lodge and feed his troops and officials as well; it is not by chance that the principal source of information on the Habiru is the Amarna Letters, written by Egyptian vassals. The oppressive demands of kings in general are well described in 1 Sm 8.11–17, and the accuracy of this passage has been completely confirmed by the administrative texts from the palace archives of Ugarit. A large part of the Syro-Palestinian population were serfs whose lives must often have been a struggle for survival. Because of the precarious nature of the ancient agrarian economy, unpaid debts could accumulate, and the insolvent debtor was subject to personal seizure by his creditor. It should be recalled that legal reforms and general cancellation of debts were constantly necessary in Mesopotamia to redress social and economic imbalances that arose with dangerous regularity.

The motives, therefore, were many for abandoning one's society, and he who did so thereby rejected its political authority and, consequently, forfeited his legal rights. In fact, to judge from the Amarna Letters, in which a whole city may become Habiru, it is not flight that constitutes the essence of a Habiru, although this was usually involved, but it is the refusal to accept any longer the legal power controlling one's society. Ordinarily, only individuals or small groups became Habiru, and in their situation they would naturally tend to band together with others in the same position. They might remain close to home in the less inhabited areas or move on into foreign lands. As the Nuzu texts show, the individual might attach himself to a private master, and these service contracts seem inspired primarily by a concern for protection under a master. This was one way of securing legal rights. Other ways were military service for the state—both parties, king and Habiru, bound themselves by oath according to Hittite sources—or a pact in which the Habiru acquired some legally recognized status. At times, therefore, the Habiru seem to trade one yoke for another, but there is not sufficient information to be able to say whether their new status did not still represent a considerable improvement on their old one; besides, it was not easy to be an outlaw, and for the individual it was virtually impossible.

Unquestionably the term Habiru had particular nuances in different regions and periods that cannot be grasped, and probably many of its social and legal implications still escape modern scholars. But with the present evidence ''outlaw'' seems the best definition of a Habiru.

Reference, however, should be made to Albright's latest view, which unfortunately he has only stated, without elaboration or documentation. He maintains that a Habiru was primarily a donkey driver or caravaneer, whence his name ''the dusty one.'' It was only when he could not make a living at his trade that he entered someone's service, bore arms, banded with others to become a robber, and so forth. While it would be incautious simply to reject this solution of the Habiru problem without first seeing the evidence on which it is based, what immediately strikes one is the anomaly that the sources consistently present of the Habiru as, so to speak, unemployed. Unless this anomaly can somehow be explained away, it is doubtful whether Albright will enlist many followers.

The Habiru and the Hebrews. Until the discovery of the Habiru in the Amarna Letters, two explanations were commonly given to the term Hebrew: (1) ''the one from the other side'' (of the Euphrates), and (2) a descendant of Eber or Heber (Gn 10.21–25; 11.14–26). The Amarna Letters seemed to offer a third possibility, and the invading Israelites of the Conquest were identified by some with the Palestinian Habiru—some even claimed to find the person of JOSHUA, SON OF NUN, in the Amarna Letters—or in some way connected with them. Many objections were raised, and the discovery of the Habiru from Mesopotamia to Egypt necessarily modified earlier and simpler theories. The relationship of Habiru and Hebrew remains a moot question of ancient Near Eastern history.

Reasons for Identification. Favoring the equation of Habiru with Hebrew are a number of considerations. First, Hebrew was almost certainly not originally an ethnic designation. None of the Israelites' neighbors ever refer to them as Hebrews. Their language is never called Hebrew until the late postexilic period (cf. Is 19.18; 2 Kgs 18.26; Neh 13.24; Prologue of Sir). When Moses defends a Hebrew, the author finds it necessary to add ''among his brethren'' (Ex 2.11); a Hebrew, therefore, was not necessarily an Israelite. In 1 Sm 14.21, and perhaps in 1 Sm 13.3, 7; 14.11, the Hebrews are distinguished from the Israelites. The range, too, of usage is too narrow for the term to be an ethnic designation; it is largely confined to the Israelites in Egypt (time of Joseph: Gn 39.14, 17; 41.12; see also 40.15; 43.32; the age of Moses: Ex 1.15–16, 19; 2.6–7, 11, 13, 21; 3.18; 5.3; 9.1, 19; 10.3).

Second, there are many striking correspondences between the Hebrews and the Habiru. Joseph and the people in Egypt are foreigners, and the latter are engaged in forced labor on crown property. Yahweh is the God of Hebrews (Ex 3.18; 5.3; 9.1, 19; 10.3—cf. the gods of the Habiru in Hittite texts), and reference is made to the land of the Hebrews (Gn 40.15), which recalls the territory of the Habiru. In 1 Sm 29.3 the Philistines speak of David and his band as Hebrews. David is a fugitive from his King Saul, and his followers are composed of debtors and malcontents (1 Sm 22.2) and other fugitives (1 Sm 22.20–23). They live in the desert and raid the flocks of others (1 Sm ch. 25). David puts himself and his men at the service of the king of Gath (1 Sm ch. 27). In 1 Sm 14.21 it is said that the Hebrews desert the Philistines and join the Israelites in a shift of loyalties characteristic of the Amarna Habiru. The Hebrews are also men in revolt (1 Sm 4.6, 9). Abraham the Hebrew is a foreigner, capable of surprise attack at the head of his band of followers (Gn ch. 14), and he gains rights through covenant (Gn 14.13; 21.22–24). A Hebrew slave is one who accepts limited service under a master (Ex 21.2–6), and the law on this subject has a number of similarities with the service contracts of the Nuzu Habiru.

Third, like the term Habiru, which disappears in the first millennium B.C., Hebrew is virtually confined to traditions of the second millennium B.C.; it reappears after the Exile as an archaizing ethnolinguistic term.

Objections against Identification. There are objections against equating the two terms. The first is linguistic: *'apiru* and *'ibrī* (the Hebrew form of ''Hebrew'') are too dissimilar to be related. However, for *'apir-'ibr* we have the parallel dialectal variants *malik-milk* (king), and for the change of *p* to *b* we have other examples of the shift of surd to sonant under the influence of sonorous *r.* Popular etymology may also have contributed to this development; *'ipru* may have been connected with being a foreigner and therefore with *'ibru,* ''the other side.'' A few possible occurrences of Habiru in Akkadian texts of the late second millennium B.C. may show the same development: *'apir* to *'abir;* if so, they also provide the only cases of Habiru with a gentilic ending comparable to the Hebrew ending *-ī.*

This leads to the second objection: beside the ending *-ī,* in Gn 10.21–25 (cf. 11.14–26) there is further evidence that *Hebrew* is an ethnic designation, for Eber (Heber, in Hebrew *'ēber*) and the *b*[e]*nê 'ēber* cannot be dissociated from the Hebrews. However, even in Gn ch. 10–11 an awareness is reflected that originally all Hebrews were not Israelites and descendants of Abraham, for Eber (10.25) fathered two sons whose progeny extended far beyond the Israelite line; moreover, it was Sem who was the ancestor of ''all the sons of Heber.'' This cutting across tribal divisions fits the Habiru perfectly. Perhaps too, as seems to have happened in Mesopotamia, in the late second millennium B.C. the Habiru became associated especially with a few interrelated ethnic groups; this would foster a new meaning for the old term now falling into desuetude.

Without therefore denying the value of these objections, the mass of evidence certainly supports the view that ultimately Habiru and Hebrew originally designated the same social class.

Bibliography: J. BOTTÉRO, *Le Problème des Ḫabiru* (Paris 1954). M. GREENBERG, *The Ḫab/piru* (American Oriental Ser. 37; New Haven 1955). M. P. GRAY, "The Ḫâbiru-Hebrew Problem in the Light of the Source Material Available at Present," *Hebrew Union College Annual* 29 (1958) 135–202. J. LEWY, "Origin and Significance of Biblical Term *Hebrew*," *ibid.* 28 (1957) 1–13. M. G. KLINE, "The Ḫa-bi-ru—Kin or Foe of Israel?" *Westminster Theological Journal* 19 (1956) 1–24, 170–184; 20 (1957) 46–70. G. E. MENDENHALL, "The Hebrew Conquest of Palestine," *The Biblical Archaeologist* 25 (1962) 66–87. W. F. ALBRIGHT, "Abram the Hebrew: A New Archaeological Interpretation," *The Bulletinn of the American Schools of Oriental Research* 163 (1961) 36–54. H. OTTEN, "Zwei althethitische Belege zu den Ḫapiru (SA.GAZ)," *Zeitschrift für Assyriologie* 52 (1957) 216–223.

[W. L. MORAN]

HABIT

In common usage, habit designates a person's dress or attire, especially if this is distinctive, as a riding habit or religious habit (*see* RELIGIOUS HABIT). It is used also to describe repetitive physical, mental, and moral behavior, such as nervous habits or habits of thought and action, and in this sense is synonymous with custom, wont, use, and practice. Again, it designates a disposition underlying such behavior. In scholastic philosophy, the word "habit" can designate one of the four post-predicaments, or a special category referred to in English as condition (*see* CATEGORIES OF BEING).

In its most important sense, habit designates one of the species of the category of QUALITY and is defined as a quality difficult to change that disposes a subject well or badly either in itself or in relation to action. In this acceptation, habit is one of the fundamental realities studied in the psychological sciences, and, as such, is discussed in this article. We here consider the general nature of habit, the different kinds of habits, the effects of habits on life, the causes of habit formation, the causes of habit loss, and the physiology of habits. The discussion is based principally on the psychology of St. THOMAS AQUINAS, with additions from modern psychological research.

Nature and Kinds of Habit

As Aquinas observes in his analysis of habit, the word is derived from the Latin *habere* meaning to have (*Summa theologiae* 1a2ae, 49–54). But the "having" signified by the term habit is not the possessing of some object, as the having of a hat or a coat, but an internal having of oneself in a certain state or condition, as when a man holds himself or has himself ready. This having, an internal disposition or orientation by which an organism is ready or prepared for something, furnishes the fundamental notion of habit.

Habit as Quality. Analyzing this concept further, St. Thomas places it in the category of quality, which is the aspect of a thing by which it can be described as such and such. Color, odor, and texture are examples of sensible qualities; the capacities to walk, to fly, and to burn are examples of power qualities; round, square, and oval are examples of qualities as shapes. Habit is the kind of quality that designates the way the parts or elements of a thing are disposed in relation to each other. It implies that the interrelationships of elements are flexible, and that they can assume different positions or proportions among themselves. These various dispositions constitute the habits of a thing, the ways it has itself.

It is evident, therefore, that habits presuppose certain characteristics on the part of their possessor—the subject of a habit must be plastic or potential to different dispositions; it must therefore have several component parts, and these several parts must be capable of various forms of organization among themselves. Given these prerequisites, habits can be formed. Unless, however, the interrelationships that are formed among the component elements of the subject can be fixed and made stable, no true habit is developed, for habits imply a firmness and permanence in structure. Transitory and labile dispositions are merely dispositions, and remain mere dispositions as long as they lack structural rigidity (*see* DISPOSITION).

This notion of habit, which is abstract and generalized, is broader than the modern understanding of the term. It is broad enough to cover what St. Thomas calls entitative habits, namely, habits that affect the disposition of various elements in the nature of a thing, and operative habits, namely, habits that dispose and develop the powers or capacities of a thing. This latter notion is closer to the modern understanding of a habit.

Entitative Habits. Entitative habits comprise all aspects of a thing resulting from various dispositions of its component parts—physical strength and health are entitative habits resulting from good size, proportion, and function of the various organs of the body; weakness and illness are habits resulting from bad interrelationships of bodily organs. TEMPERAMENT is an entitative habit that results from various proportions of energy, emotionality, activity, passivity, etc., in various organisms. In all these cases, several physical or functional elements can be variously disposed among themselves; if the dispositions are firm and stable, they are called entitative habits, but if they are unstable and transitory, they are designated simply as dispositions.

Operative Habits. Entitative habits are of less interest to psychologists than operative habits, and therefore the rest of this treatment concentrates on the latter. Operative habits are acquired dispositions that prepare the powers of an organism for stable patterns of action (*see*

FACULTIES OF THE SOUL). Such habits are theoretically possible in the intellect; in the will and sense appetites; in the imagination, memory, and cogitative sense; in the external senses; and in the muscles and any other organs having a physiological function. In fact, however, not every power has habits, and some powers have many habits; for not every power presents all the prerequisites for the formation of a habit, while some powers have these in abundance.

Habits of Practical Intellect. In Thomistic psychology, the human INTELLECT is the seat of almost numberless habits, which can be subsumed under six general headings: art, prudence, understanding, science, wisdom, and faith.

Art and prudence are habits of the practical intellect, which organizes action and behavior. Art is the right way of making things. It becomes a habit when, after much practice, an individual has tested out the various ways a thing can be made and has learned the right way to make it. The stability of this habit derives from the experience's having proved so successful that the maker would not think of changing his methods. Prudence dictates the right way to behave in order to maintain given moral standards or norms of conduct. Like art, it acquires its stability or fixedness through successful experience (*see* ART [PHILOSOPHY]; PRUDENCE).

Speculative Habits. Three categories of intellectual habit belong to the speculative intellect, which comprehends the natures of things and their relationships. The first of these habits is called UNDERSTANDING (*intellectus*); this grasps the universal and necessary principles of speculative thought, as, for example, whatever comes to be has a cause. The fixedness of such intellectual understanding comes from intrinsic self-evidence. The second such habit is SCIENCE (*scientia*), which deals with demonstrations of truths from evident principles. The stability of scientific conclusions stems from the rigor of DEMONSTRATION. Science thus differs from opinion, which cannot be demonstrated, and hence lacks firmness. The third speculative habit is WISDOM, which views and orders all truths in the light of ultimate truth. The firmness of wisdom depends on the strength by which the intellect is able to grasp ultimate truths and see lesser truths as subsumed under them.

Faith as a Habit. A sixth habit in the intellect, and this can be both speculative and practical, is FAITH. Faith is assent to the truth of a proposition on the basis of an authority that is both competent and veracious. The fixity of beliefs held by faith depends on the trust put in the authority whose word is being accepted; if the authority is thought to be indubitable, faith takes on the firmness of a true habit.

Habits in Will and Appetite. Habits that have their locus in the WILL are, if anything, more numerous than those in the intellect. Wherever there is a stable and firm attachment to some purpose or way of acting to attain a purpose, there is a habit of willing. Devotion to people, nations, and causes can assume the proportions of habits, as can hatreds and fears of them. The determination to be just in all things can generate habits of honesty, fairness in word and deed, truthfulness, patriotism, obedience, courtesy, industriousness, religion, etc. A willingness to take advantage of others can produce habits of dishonesty, cheating, stealing, embezzling, lying, sloth, insolence, disobedience, and so on. A determination to control one's own feelings can lead to habits of continence, by which passions are reined and checked, while an unwillingness to restrain oneself can lead to habitual forms of emotional excess.

If habits such as continence are formed in the will, the passions of sense APPETITE are restrained within bounds, and new habits are formed in the appetites themselves. Habits of sobriety, abstinence, and chastity are formed in the pleasure-seeking concupiscible appetite; habits such as meekness restrain the passion of anger in the irascible appetite; courage and patience restrain tendencies toward cowardice, softness, and timidity; habits of humility govern urges toward arrogance.

Interrelationship of Habits. These four powers, intellect, will, and the two sense appetites, are the major seats of true operative habits. They are the most plastic of human capacities, and therefore subject to the greatest number of variations, but they are also most capable of being formed into the stable modes of action that constitute habits. As is evident from the examples given above, the numerous habits informing these powers are not developed at random, but are able to interlock with each other in fairly well-defined hierarchies. For instance, a habit of understanding is presupposed to habits of science, for understanding gives science its principles. Wisdom in turn presupposes science, for it orders the verities of the various sciences in the light of ultimate verities. Moreover, a habit of moral science (ETHICS) is presupposed to habits of prudence, for moral science establishes the norms toward which prudence orders actual behavior. But prudence in turn is ineffective unless the will has a habit of continence, for if the passions are not governed, a man seldom succeeds in behaving the way he would want to behave, and so on.

Senses and Bodily Processes. St. Thomas did not assign any true operative habits to the internal SENSES, which include IMAGINATION, MEMORY, and the COGITATIVE POWER, nor to muscular power. He did not deny that these powers could be organized so that they would respond with stable patterns of action, e.g., physical skills and well-ordered trains of imagery, memories, and practical estimations. As he conceived them, however, these physical and imaginative activities are assumed into the service of the higher powers, so that the stable modes of action they acquire do not constitute true habits in themselves, but rather quasi habits subordinated to the higher habits of which they are instruments. Thus a good memory of past experiences, a clear imagination about the consequences of a given act, and an accurate estimate of the present situation are necessary components of a prudent act; yet the stable modes of action induced in these internal senses by repeated prudent acts are not so much distinct habits in themselves, as component parts of the higher habit of prudence. Similarly no art can be perfected without some physical skills in handling materials; but these skills are subordinate parts of the higher habit of art, which is essentially a matter of the practical intellect. Another point arguing against the presence of true habits in the internal senses and muscular powers is their susceptibility to disturbances. Habits should be stable and firm; but imagination, memory, and physical skills are subject to disturbances from illnesses, injuries, fatigue, drugs, etc. Contemporary psychology, in treating of habits, treats for the most part of these quasi-habitual dispositions that can be formed in the internal senses and physical powers [Dashiell, 363].

There are no operative habits of any sort in the external senses and simple physiological processes such as digestion and circulation. These operations are simple functions of their organs, without the possibility of being ordered in a variety of ways, and therefore without the need of being organized to operate in one way rather than another. Loosely speaking, one can say that there are habits of visual activity or auditory activity—a doctor naturally notices symptoms, a mother can pick out her baby's cry when no one else can detect it. But such so-called habits are really cases of attention, training, and orientation; they are dispositions of mind and will, rather than developments of visual or auditory powers strictly speaking.

Supernatural Habits. The human SOUL in its substantial aspect is not the subject of natural habits. Since the soul is the ultimate entity in human nature, toward which everything else is ordered, the soul itself is not ordered toward another, and is therefore not susceptible to being disposed or oriented in various ways. Supernaturally, however, the soul can be oriented toward something else, and thus be the seat of habit. Theology treats of this supernatural habit of the soul under the title of sanctifying GRACE [*see* HABIT (IN THEOLOGY)].

Good and Bad Habits. Because habits dispose their subject in relation to something else—entitative habits ordering the subject in reference to its nature, and operative habits disposing the subject for action—habits can be designated as good or bad. An entitative habit that disposes the nature well is good, for example, that of health, whereas sickness is a bad entitative habit because it denotes a defect in the way the nature is disposed. Operative habits such as science or humaneness are good because they orient the intellect and will respectively toward activities that are desirable; error and selfishness on the other hand are bad dispositions because they organize mind and will toward actions that are negative and undesirable. Moral science treats of good and bad habit under the respective titles of VIRTUE and VICE (*see* MORAL THEOLOGY).

Influence and Causes of Habits

The pervading psychological effect of habit is economy of effort. By habit, man performs acts quickly, easily, and with pleasure. He performs acts quickly, because the operative powers are predisposed toward the acts; easily, because habits eliminate false and unnecessary motions; and with pleasure, because successful action without waste of energy gives more immediate satisfaction with less fatigue. Habitual operations become so smooth and effortless that habit is called ''second nature.'' The higher habits, such as art and science in the intellect, and honesty and industriousness in the will, are generally used consciously and deliberately, so that St. Thomas frequently refers to habits as things we use when we want to (e.g., *Summa theologiae* 1a2ae, 50.5). But physical dispositions in the body, and to some extent, dispositions in the imagination, memory, and sense appetites, tend to become unconscious as they become more and more ingrained; and thus a secondary effect of habituation is that one can execute patterns of action and behavior without adverting to their component parts.

The greater part of man's daily routine, as the word routine indicates, is performed by series of acts of which he is almost unaware. This has the great advantage of freeing his mind for more important matters, but it also has disadvantages. If the habit patterns are defective, they are hard to improve, because one has to re-form, along new lines, patterns of behavior formerly executed without thinking, and it is easy to fall back into the former patterns. Moreover, since habituation makes action easier, a tendency toward laziness realizes itself in a reluctance to re-form old habits. Again, people become emotionally attached to familiar ways of behavior and are uneasy with innovations, and therefore many retain poor habits, even when they realize their defects, rather than experience the uneasiness that novelties engender. There is a kind of ''force of habit'' that keeps people treading the familiar paths long after these have lost their effectiveness. Habit thus is a great conservator, keeping men in accustomed ways. The deleterious effects of habit formation emphasize the importance of developing good habits early in life, and of developing a ''habit'' of being flexible about habits.

Causes of Habit Formation. Supernatural habits, such as the infused virtues and gifts, are implanted directly by God, but the study of these pertains to moral theology rather than to psychology. In the natural order, action is the cause of operative habits. The formation of a habit by action presupposes the existence of both active and passive principles in the organism. The active principle moves the passive principle, and in moving it, disposes it to be moved again the same way; after repeated actions, the passive principle becomes completely responsive to being moved. The disposition to respond is the habit.

Generation of Habits. Thus by a deliberate act of will (the active power), a beginner goes through the motions of playing scales and chords on a musical instrument, and his hands (the passive principle) gradually acquire facility in picking out scales and chords; when this is mastered, he goes on to more complex patterns, and gradually builds up the habit of playing the instrument. Similarly, the mind learns the rules of logic, and applies these rules (as an active principle) to various data (the passive principle); as the process of logical thought is strengthened in different areas, habits of science are developed.

If the active principle is dominant in respect to the passive principle, a habit can be generated in a single act; for example, a clear demonstration of a proposition in geometry is so convincing that, once the conclusion has been proved, the mind holds it with the fixity of a habit. But when the passive principle does not receive impressions easily from the active principle, as is the case, for instance, of the concupiscible appetite in relation to the will, habits can be formed only by repeated acts. Hence a habit like chastity is usually the result of a long process of formation. Because the role of the active principle is crucial in the acquisition of habits, the process of learning should be initiated with a strong and decided attack.

Development of Habits. When habits have been begun, they can develop further in two distinctive ways. In one way, they can become more extensive. A person who has learned a dozen demonstrations in geometry has the science of geometry, but can develop it further by learning more demonstrations. One who is friendly with five people can become friendly with five more. Again, habits can retain the same extension but become more intense. A student who knows some demonstrations in geometry, but is slow and awkward in presenting them, can develop facility and ease, and thus the habit becomes more deeply rooted; or a person who is mildly friendly with some people can become more friendly with the same people.

Natural Dispositions. Action is required for the formation of all operative habits, but in some cases, natural dispositions toward such formation are so definite that the habit can be said to be partly from nature. The habit of the understanding of FIRST PRINCIPLES is one such habit. The intellect is so disposed to see self-evident truths that, when they are first presented, they are immediately recognized for what they are. Some people have calmer and more reflective dispositions, for them the acquisition of science is easier, since their memory and imagination tend more naturally to orderly thought. Some have natural dispositions to courage that make it easier to face dangers and develop a habit of courage. Physical dispositions that facilitate acquiring arts and skills also vary greatly in different individuals, giving those with natural tendencies toward dexterity and speed a special advantage. Since people tend to do the things that come easily and naturally, they tend to develop the habits toward which they have a proneness. Conversely, to develop a complete life, most people must take special pains to develop the habits toward which they have no natural leanings.

Time and Habit Formation. Habits are most easily developed early in life, partly because a person then has greater quantities of energy at his disposal, and therefore his active principles are more effective, but principally because he is more plastic and capable of receiving impressions quickly and deeply. In his first few years a child acquires a vast number of highly complex habits, even though he is still too young to undertake habit formation consciously and deliberately. To learn to speak a language, to walk, to eat, to dress and wash oneself, to handle simple tools, to read and write, to do arithmetic, to be familiar with the routine of home, school, church, playground, etc., are only a few examples of the habits children acquire before they are 8 years old. Moreover, deep-seated emotional attitudes, which can persist almost unchanged throughout life and profoundly affect CHARACTER and moral development, can be formed in the earliest years, sometimes in the first year or two. Habits of trustfulness or suspicion, of greediness or generosity, of selfishness or cooperation, of timidity or courage, and many others, are grounded in the experiences of the earliest years. One of the major contributions of modern depth psychology has been its unearthing of such early stages of habit formation.

After the earliest years, habit formation becomes more and more a matter of deliberate choice. Man begins consciously to develop habits of skill, knowledge, attitude, etc. By persistent effort, various actions or modes of behavior become fixed; in typical cases, the improvement is rapid at first, and then gradually tapers off as a given level or plateau of achievement is reached. For the most part, the rate of habit development is a function of the amount of practice and the accuracy of practice. One curious anomaly in habit formation, not satisfactorily explained to date, is that a given amount of spaced practice (i.e., practice with periods of rest in between) is more effective, all else being equal, than an equal amount of uninterrupted practice. It is almost as if the habit becomes fixed in the periods between practice sessions.

Habitual Behavior. Besides operative habits strictly speaking, certain quasi-habitual components of human behavior can loosely be called habits. Psychiatry speaks of ''habit spasms'' such as tics and bed-wetting, which are acquired modes of behavior that serve somehow to release psychological tensions. Some varieties of neurotic symptoms also are fixed modes of action stemming from unconscious psychic factors. Certain drugs, such as alcohol, morphine, and phenobarbital, are called habit-forming because they produce physiological and psychological changes that result in almost uncontrollable cravings for more. These ''habits'' are caused by physiological and psychological factors other than simple repeated actions.

Loss of Habits. Habits can be diminished by the performance of actions contrary to them; for instance, a habit of honesty is corrupted by dishonest actions, and a habit of science by careless observation or reasoning. Habits diminish also by cessation of the actions that generated them, especially if natural tendencies oppose the habit. A scientist who ceases for many years to consider his subject will find he has lost some of it when he returns to practice, but a man who does not restrain his appetites by continence will find he has lost the habit of continence in a very short time. However, it is remarkable how habits of learning and skill can be retained even if neglected for long periods; some psychologists, impressed by this, hold that once formed a habit is never entirely lost [Dashiell, 420].

Injuries that destroy powers destroy also the habits in the powers; athletic skills are lost when muscles are crippled, science may be lost when the brain is injured, and so on. Physiological factors such as use of drugs and fatigue can interfere with the use of habits, as can psychological factors such as repression. In old age there are certain typical patterns of habit deterioration. As perceptiveness and flexibility are diminished, ambition decreases, and more time and effort are required for ordinary activities, an insistent repetition of habitual movements sets in, and the aged person settles down into the use of fewer and simpler behavior patterns. These become crystallized so that even small changes of routine provoke discontent. Similarly mental processes decay, not so much because the component elements are lost—for these seem to remain intact, especially those learned earliest—but because alertness and the energy to activate and sustain the higher, controlling habits are gone.

Physiological Aspects of Habits. The physiological aspects of habit formation constitute a special area of inquiry. The development of physical habits, for example, involves acquired modes of neural organization in the motor parts of the brain and spinal column; the formation of mental habits implies the opening and fixation of new paths of neural communication in the higher parts of the brain; the establishment of emotional and drive patterns involves changes in the brain centers and perhaps also in the nerve systems innervating the viscera. Much research has been done to isolate and specify the parts of the nervous system that are affected by habit formation and the kinds of changes involved, but much remains to be done. Many modern psychologists tend to define habits in terms of their physiology: J. B. Watson considers them as complex, conditioned responses whose basic explanation belongs to physiology [*Behaviorism* (New York 1930) 207]; William JAMES, as ''nothing but a new pathway of discharge formed in the brain, by which certain incoming currents ever after tend to escape'' [*Psychology, Briefer Course* (New York 1908) 134]; and Karl A. Menninger, as the set patterns by which impulses or stimuli entering the brain are resolved into impulses going to muscles and organs [*The Human Mind* (second edition, New York 1937) 164]. The exact delineation of the nature of these neural changes and the modes of path formation constitute the physiological approach to the study of habit formation.

See Also: HUMAN ACT; PERSONALITY.

Bibliography: R. E. BRENNAN, *Thomistic Psychology* (New York 1941). G. P. KLUBERTANZ, *The Philosophy of Human Nature* (New York 1953). *American Handbook of Psychiatry,* ed. S. ARIETI, 2 v. (New York 1959). W. D. COMMINS and B. FAGIN, *Principles of Educational Psychology* (2d ed. rev. New York 1954). J. F. DASHIELL, *Fundamentals of General Psychology* (3d ed. New York 1949). W. JAMES, *The Principles of Psychology,* 2 v. (auth. ed. unabridged, New York 1962). C. T. MORGAN and E. STELLAR, *Physiological Psychology* (2d ed. New York 1950). F. L. RUCH, *Psychology and Life* (6th ed. New York 1963). J. B. WATSON, *Behaviorism* (rev. ed. Chicago 1958).

[M. STOCK]

HABIT (IN THEOLOGY)

In theology the word ''habit'' is used specifically to designate a SUPERNATURAL entity. Although the word is not found in the Scriptures, scholastics borrowed it from philosophy to categorize the realities brought about in the soul by JUSTIFICATION. The intimate nature of these realities transcends man's understanding; however, theology attempts to represent them analogously by means of human concepts and terms. It is in this sense that one speaks of supernatural habits.

Nature. Supernatural habit in general may be defined as a supernatural, internal, permanent quality modifying the soul or its faculties in relation to the supernatural ultimate good. This is a scholastic or Thomistic concept. Aquinas conceives the supernatural structure in man in analogous but parallel lines to the natural structure. Just as in the natural order man is endowed by God with nature, faculties, and dispositions that enable him efficaciously to pursue the natural good, in similar manner, taking for granted man's supernatural elevation, God provides him with supernatural qualities to enable him to attain his ultimate supernatural good (*Summa theologiae* 1a2ae, 110.2–4). The existence of these supernatural realities or qualities in man, described in revelation, and further developed in theology, is amply discussed elsewhere (*see* GRACE). These belong to the realm of entitative and operative supernatural habits. It may be superfluous to add here the qualification of goodness to these habits, since by their very nature they imply an ordination to the Eternal Good. In this respect they fall under the term of VIRTUE in a broad sense.

Division. Catholic theologians consider sanctifying grace to be a supernatural entitative habit of the soul (*Catechism of the Council of Trent* 2.2.50; *Summa theologiae* 1a2ae, 110.3 ad 3). They maintain that in consonance with revelation it must be thought of as a created ACCIDENT that informs the soul, characterizing it or qualifying it supernaturally. It is said to be created, not in the sense that it is produced as a being subsisting in itself and then added to the soul, but in the sense that the soul begins to exist in a new manner because of it, with a new quality of being produced wholly by God without any efficient cooperation or intervention of man. On the other hand, it is an accident truly distinct from the soul, adding a new perfection entirely different from the natural constituents of the soul. Finally, this accident is conceived as a permanent entitative quality because it is a stable principle of supernatural life in man, a second nature so to speak, produced by a regeneration or a REBIRTH (Jn 1.12–13; Ti 3.5). On account of this, man ''has himself'' entitatively or substantially oriented to his supernatural end.

Theology speaks of no other supernatural entitative habit outside of grace. However, it numbers many supernatural operative habits, namely the infused theological and moral virtues (*see* VIRTUE) and the gifts of the Holy Spirit (*see* FAITH; HOPE; CHARITY; HOLY SPIRIT, GIFTS OF). These are permanent qualities or determinations of the soul's faculties that orient them and their activity to the Eternal Good.

Through the theological virtues man is furnished with the fundamental principles that direct his faculties immediately to God as his supernatural end (*see* DESTINY, SUPERNATURAL). They connect him directly with God. Through the supernatural moral virtues man is given the power to render his acts morally right in proportion to his supernatural elevation and in view of his supernatural end. The gifts of the Holy Spirit are also considered supernatural operative habits since they are permanent qualities that perfect the faculties and direct them to supernatural activity. They differ from virtues because they have in them something superior to the common characteristics of virtues, as well as a certain passivity (*Summa theologiae* 1a2ae, 68.1).

Distinctive Characteristics. Supernatural habits differ from natural entitative and operative habits not only because of the very superiority of their constitution but also because of their origin, growth, and effects. Regarding origin and growth, supernatural habits are beyond the capability of nature's activity or nature's repeated acts—a characteristic in which they differ from natural habits (*see* NATURE; GRACE AND NATURE). They are produced and augmented entirely by God alone. They are said to be infused by God, with man remaining totally passive in the process. Aquinas speaks of man's OBEDIENTIAL POTENCY (*De virt. in comm.* 10 ad 13). The Sacraments act merely instrumentally under the power of God. According to present theological opinion, all supernatural habits (grace, virtues, and gifts) are infused by God in man at the moment of justification (see Decrees of the Council of Vienne, H. Denzinger, *Enchiridion symbolorum*, ed. A. Schönmetzer (32d ed. Freiburg 1963) 904; Trent, H. Denzinger, *Enchiridion symbolorum* 1528–1531; *Catechism of the Council of Trent* 2.2.51).

Supernatural habits also differ from natural operative habits in the role they play or the effects they cause in human activity. Natural habits render activity fast, easy, and pleasurable. Supernatural habits merely provide the power to act supernaturally. In this sense they assimilate themselves to faculties rather than to habits; yet they are not faculties, as they presuppose and inform existing faculties. Whether a certain external facility or ease of operation is gradually conferred by the exercise of supernatural habits, and how this facility is conferred, is a matter of discussion. Some theologians explain it only in terms of a natural good disposition and a removal of obstacles on the part of the individual. Others speak of a gradual formation, exercise, and consequent growth of a natural habit alongside the supernatural habit. The natural habit would persist even after the loss of the supernatural habit.

Bibliography: J. HASPECKER et al., *Lexikon für Theologie und Kirche*, ed. J. HOFER and K. RAHNER, 10 v. (2d new ed. Freiburg 1957–65) 4:977–1000. J. AUER, *ibid.* 4:1301. J. VAN DER MEERSCH, *Dictionnaire de théologie catholique*, ed. A. VACANT et al. (Paris 1903–50) 6.2:1554–1687. A. MICHEL, *ibid.* 15.2:2739–99. K. RAHNER and H. VORGRIMLER, *Kleines theologisches Wörterbuch* (Freiburg 1961) 154. C. M. LACHANCE, ''La Grâce est en nous par mode d'habitus entitatif ou l'ontologie de la grâce,'' *Revue de l'Université d'Ottawa* 26 (1956) 23*–51*, 75*–89*. M. LIMBOURG, *Zeitschrift für katholische Theologie* 9 (1885) 643–669; 10 (1886) 107–141, 277–312, 603–628, a series of articles on supernatural habit. M. J. SCHEEBEN, *Nature and Grace*, tr. C. VOLLERT (St. Louis 1954). T. GRAF, *De subiecto psychico gratiae et virtutum secundum doctrinam scholasticorum usque at medium saeculum XIV.* Pt I, *De subiecto virtutum cardinalium,* 2 v. (*Sudia anselmiana* 2, 3, 4; Rome 1934–35).

[R. J. TAPIA]

HADALINUS, ST.

Patron of Visé, Belgium (known also as Adelinus, Hadelin, Haulin); b. Aquitaine; d. Celles, Belgium, mid-seventh century or 690. Of noble parentage, he left home together with his teacher, St. Remaclus (d. 675), to live as a recluse in the wilderness of Cougnon. Later he lived in the Abbey of STAVELOT, founded by Remaclus. Assisted by him and by Pepin of Heristal, Hadalinus founded the monastery of Celles near Dinant-sur-Meuse; its 11th-century Romanesque church is extant. In 1338 the monastery was removed to Visé; it was suppressed in 1797. Hadalinus is invoked against children's ailments; in iconography his attribute is a dove.

Feast: Feb. 3, Oct. 11.

Bibliography: *Acta Sanctorum* Feb. 1:370–381. L. VAN DER ESSEN, *Étude critique et littéraire sur les Vitae des saints mérovingiens de l'ancienne Belgique* (Louvain 1907). D. DE BRUYNE, ''La Translation de s. Hadelin,'' *Analecta Bollandiana* (Brussels 1882–) 42 (1924) 121–125. H. DEMARET, *Notice sur saint Hadelin* (Liège 1928). J. L. BAUDOT and L. CHAUSSIN, *Vies des saints et des bienheueux selon l'ordre du calendrier avec l'historique des fêtes* (Paris 1935–56) 2:70–71. *The Book of Saints* (4th ed. New York 1947) 281. L. RÉAU, *Iconographie de l'art chrétien,* 6 v. (Paris 1955–59) 3.2:631.

[M. CSÁKY]

HADELOGA, ST.

Virgin, monastic foundress (a.k.a. Adeloga, Hadelauga, Halloie); d. Kitzingen (Upper Bavaria), Germany, *c.* 750. According to a 12th-century vita and *laudatio* replete with legend, Hadeloga was the daughter of CHARLES MARTEL. When about to be forced into marriage, she fled from court and founded a double MONASTERY (745?) at Kitzingen in Franconia. St. BONIFACE, who had allegedly inspired Hadeloga's vocation, kept in touch with the foundation; Charles Martel, once reconciled with his daughter, richly endowed it. Hadeloga enjoyed the regard of the whole countryside for her care of the poor. Her body is interred in the church of St. Mary in Kitzingen. Her monastery was secularized in 1544.

Feast: Feb. 2, March 20.

Bibliography: *Acta Sanctorum* Feb. 1:306–311 *Vita,* 952–967 *Laudatio.* J. B. STAMMINGER, *Franconia sancta* (Würzburg 1889) 360–378. A. M. ZIMMERMANN, *Kalendarium Benedictinum: Die Heiligen und Seligen des Benediktinerorderns und seiner Zweige,* 4 v. (Metten 1933–38) 1:156; 4:17. J. L. BAUDOT and L. CHAUSSIN, *Vies des saints et des bienheueux selon l'ordre du calendrier avec l'historique des fêtes* (Paris 1935–56) 2:46. *The Book of Saints* (4th ed. New York 1947) 10.

[M. CSÁKY]

HADES

Hades was originally the name of the Greek god (῞Αιδης, unseen) of the nether world, but later applied to the abode of the dead itself. The Septuagint generally adopted the term to render the Hebrew word *s*[e]*'ôl* (SHEOL), the final resting place of the dead.

In the New Testament, Hades, formerly translated as HELL, has a neutral character in contrast to GEHENNA, which is the place where the wicked are punished. The New Testament, like the Old Testament, locates Hades in the depths of the earth (Mt 11.23; Lk 10.15; 16.23) in contrast to heaven above the earth. Hence, passage to Hades involves a descent (Mt 11.23; Eph 4.9). The expression ''the gates of Hades'' in the well–known Petrine text (Mt 16.18) refers not to diabolical powers but to the kingdom of death. Peter's power reaches even into the kingdom of death; death will never overcome it. The phrase ''gates of the nether world'' occurs also in the Old Testament (Is 38.10; Jb 17.16; Wis 16.13). It shows that Hades was envisaged as a city, which is not so strange in view of the fact that Hades, like Sheol, death, and the rest, lends itself also to personification (Rv 6.8; 20.13–15). From the New Testament it is evident that Hades is not to be equated with Gehenna, for the good as well as the bad descend to Hades (Mt 12.40; Acts 2.27, 31; Rom 10.7; Eph 4.9); Christ, too, descended into Hades (Acts 2.24; 1 Pt 3.19); (*see* DESCENT OF CHRIST INTO HELL). With the resurrection of the dead on the last day, Hades will cease to exist (Rv 20.13–14). There seems to be only one reference in the New Testament to Hades as a place of punishment for the wicked (Lk 16.22), but even here the Hades in which the rich man is in torment may be regarded as merely a general term for the abode of all the dead, even though ''a great chasm'' (16.26) separates him from the other part of Hades where Lazarus is in ABRAHAM's BOSOM.

Bibliography: J. JEREMIAS, G. KITTEL, *Theologisches Wörterbuch zum Neuen Testament* (Stuttgart 1935–) 1:146–150. *Encyclopedic Dictionary of the Bible,* tr. and adap. by L. HARTMAN (New York 1963), from A. VAN DEN BORN, *Bijbels Woordenboek,* 922–923. M. SALLER, *Lexikon für Theologie und Kirche*, ed. J. HOFER and K. RAHNER 10 v. (2d, new ed. Freiburg 1957–65) 4:1305.

[I. H. GORSKI]

HADEWIJCH, BL.

Flemish woman writer of the 13th century. No historical information is available about her, but the language and atmosphere of her writings seem to indicate that she was a lady of noble birth of the Brabant of her time. She probably was the leader of one of many small associations of pious women that had come into existence without any formal organization, and that attracted women intent on works of mercy and on mutual sanctification. These associations, many of which originated at the end of the 12th century, were organized into *béguinages* in the second half of the 13th century (*see* BEGUINES AND BEGHARDS). Hadewijch and her companions had not yet received the status of the *béguines;* she must, therefore, have lived before 1250, and her main literary activity fell most probably between 1230 and 1250.

For her companions Hadewijch committed to writing her 11 *Visions;* she translated her religious experiences into imaginative ''visions'' of genuinely intellectual stature; in a few places she refers to moments of oneness with God, experiences she considers to be of the same nature as the BEATIFIC VISION. Her 31 *Letters* gave her an opportunity to clarify for the benefit of her followers her ideas about God's love of man and man's love of God, though she never tried a systematic treatment. Her mystical vision of love was influenced by the French spirituality of the 12th century, which she recast in the way that characterized the mystical writers of the whole Middle-Dutch period. The 17 *Poems* in rhyming couplets are in fact letters that repeat the same doctrine. With her 45 *Poems in Stanzas* Hadewijch gave rise to the lyric poetry of mystic love; she portrays her yearning for God through the themes, imagery, and technique used by the troubadours to exalt COURTLY LOVE.

Bibliography: *The Complete Works,* tr. C. HART (New York 1980). T. WEEVERS, *Poetry of the Netherlands in Its European Context, 1170–1930* (London 1960) with bibliography and translations. T. M. GUEST, *Some Aspects of Hadewijch's Poetic Form in the ''Strofische gedichten''* (The Hague 1975). F. WILLAERT, *De poëtica van Hadewijch in de Strofische Gedichten* (Utrecht 1984). E. DREYER, *Passionate Women: Two Medieval Mystics* (New York 1989). G. J. LEWIS, *Bibliographie zur deutschen Frauenmystik des Mittelalters* (Berlin 1989). *Der Berg der Liebe: europäische Frauenmystik,* ed. H. UNGER (Freiburg im Breisgau 1991). S. MURK-JANSEN, *The Measure of Mystic Thought: A Study of Hadewijch's Mengeldichten* (Göppingen 1991). J. G. MILHAVEN, *Hadewijch and Her Sisters* (Albany 1993). *Meister Eckhart and the Beguine Mystics,* ed. B. MCGINN (New York 1994).

[N. DE PAEPE]

HADOINDUS, ST.

Bishop of Le Mans; d. August 20, *c.* 653. Reportedly he was born of a noble family, but little else is known about him before he succeeded BERTRAM in the See of Le Mans, *c.* 623. As bishop, Hadoindus founded the abbey at Évron (L. H. Cottineau, *Répertoire topobibliographique des abbayes et prieurés,* 2 v. 1:1089–90) and is said to have aided in the founding of the monastery of St. Lonegisilus (L. H. Cottineau, *Répertoire topobibliographique des abbayes et prieurés,* 2 v. 2:2769). He attended the councils held at Clichy *c.* 627 and at Reims from 627 to 630 (*Monumenta Germaniae Concilia* 1:202; J. D. Mansi, *Sacrorum Conciliorum nova et amplissima collectio* 10:594); but at the council that met at CHALON SUR-SÂONE in 650, he was represented by Abbot Chagnoaldus (J. D. Mansi, *Sacrorum Conciliorum nova et amplissima collectio* 10:1194). On Feb. 6, 643, Hadoindus made his last will and testament, in which he designated the church of Le Mans as his heir, leaving it much property, a large portion of which he had received from a wealthy man named Alan. The bishop also requested that he be buried in the church of Saint-Victor. In the ninth century the cult of Hadoindus is clearly attested by the fact that ALDRIC, bishop of Le Mans, exhumed the relics of the holy bishop and placed them in the cathedral church (*Gesta Aldrici episcopi Cenomannensis* 44).

Feast: Aug. 20 (Diocese of Le Mans).

Bibliography: *Monumenta Germaniae Scriptores* (Berlin 1825–) 15.1:323. *Acta Sanctorum* Jan. 2:1140–43. *Patrologia Latina,* ed. J. P. MIGNE, 217 v. (Paris 1878–90) 80:565–574; 115:850. H. LECLERCQ, *Dictionnaire d'archéologie chrétienneet de liturgie,* ed. F. CABROL, H. LECLERCQ and H. I. MARROU, 15 v. (Paris 1907–53) 10:1521–27. P. VIARD, *Catholicisme* 5:470. *Bibliotheca hagiographica latina antiquae et mediae aetatis,* 2 v. (Brussels 1898–1901; suppl. 1911) 3736. C. DUCHESNAY, *Dictionnaire d'histoire et de géographie ecclésiastiques,* ed. A. BAUDRILLART (Paris 1912–) 16:214–219.

[H. DRESSLER]

HADRIAN, ROMAN EMPEROR

Reigned 117 to 138; b. Publius Aelius Hadrianus, Italica, southern Spain, A.D. 76; d. Baiae, July 10, 138. On

Bust of the Roman Emperor Hadrian found at Tivoli. (Alinari-Art Reference/Art Resource, NY)

the death of his father in 85 he became the ward of Marcus Ulpius Traianus (Trajan), the future Emperor, who was himself childless. After serving in the army, Hadrian became governor of Lower Pannonia in 107, suffect consul the following year, and in 114 governor of Syria. Although he had been designated consul for 118, on the death of Trajan he became emperor (Aug. 11, 117), whereupon he abandoned Trajan's conquests beyond the Euphrates as untenable. He enlarged the civil service, making extensive use of the Roman knights in newly created posts. He traveled through the empire to satisfy his highly curious mind, to organize the defenses of the frontiers, e.g., Hadrian's Wall in Britain (122–128), and to acquaint himself with the provinces. His able administration was marred by the decision to erect a shrine to Jupiter Capitolinus on the site of the temple of Jerusalem. This precipitated a revolt of the Jews under Bar Kokhba (132–135). A rescript that he wrote to Minucius Fundanus on the treatment to be given to Christians in court has been preserved by Eusebius (*Historia ecclesiastica* 4.9.1–3), but its interpretation has been disputed. At best it seems to have been an attempt to protect Christians from popular outcries, insisting that proof be advanced to show that they were ''acting illegally.'' A fair number of Christians suffered for the faith during his reign, the most famous being Pope TELESPHORUS, martyred apparently in 136. Hadrian was buried in the *Moles Hadriana,* preserved as the Castel Sant'Angelo on the right bank of the Tiber.

Bibliography: B. W. HENDERSON, *The Life and Principate of the Emperor Hadrian* (London 1923). *Paulys Realenzyklopädie der klassischen Altertumswissenschaft*, ed. G. WISSOWA et al. 1.1 (Stuttgart 1893): 493–520. S. PEROWNE, *Hadrian* (New York 1960). A. R. BURLEY, *Hadrian: The Restless Emperor* (London 1997). M. T. BOATWRIGHT, *Hadrian and the City of Rome* (Princeton 1987).

[M. J. COSTELLOE]

HADRIAN OF CANTERBURY, ST.

Abbot of ST. AUGUSTINE's Abbey, Canterbury; b. Africa; d. Canterbury, Jan. 9, 709. Hadrian (Adrian) helped to stabilize papal influence and to establish a tradition of sound learning in Anglo-Saxon England. As a BENEDICTINE, perhaps in Africa and certainly at Niridan near Naples, where he became abbot, he was well formed in Greek and Latin secular and sacred literature, as well as in monastic and ecclesiastical discipline. Chosen by Pope VITALIAN to succeed in the See of Canterbury, he demurred, but together with BENEDICT BISCOP and the new archbishop, Theodore of Tarsus (THEODORE OF CANTERBURY), he was sent to England to serve as guide, counselor, and assurer of orthodoxy (670). As abbot of St. Augustine's at Canterbury, he established schools for liberal and ecclesiastical studies to compete with those of the Celts (*Scoti*). These became centers for better instruction in Greek and Latin and were noted for their adherence to the ecclesiastical customs of Rome, especially the form of baptism, tonsure, and the dating of Easter. They promoted close ties with the papacy and unity of the Anglo-Saxon Church with the universal Church. His cult is evidenced in early MARTYROLOGIES of England and Germany.

Feast: Jan. 9.

Bibliography: BEDE, *Ecclesiastical History* 4.1, 2; 5.20, 23; *Historia abbatum in Opera historica,* ed. C. PLUMMER, 2 v. (Oxford 1896; 2d ed. 1956). ALDHELM, *Epistola ad Leutherium, Monumenta Germaniae Auctores antiquissimi* (Berlin 1825–) 15:476–478. A. S. COOK, ''Hadrian of Africa. . . ,'' *Philological Quarterly* 2 (1923) 241–258. E. S. DUCKETT, *Anglo-Saxon Saints and Scholars* (New York 1947). F. M. STENTON, *Anglo-Saxon England* (2d ed. Oxford 1947) 131–132, 180–183. R. H. HODGKIN, *A History of the Anglo-Saxons,* 2 v. (3d ed. London 1952).

[T. A. CARROLL]

HADRIANA COLLECTIO

Dionysio-Hadriana, an official canonical collection of the Roman Church, transmitted by Pope ADRIAN I to

CHARLEMAGNE, at Easter 774, the time of the latter's stay in Rome. It was received officially as the Code of the Frankish Church at the Assembly of Aix-la-Chapelle in 802.

The core of this collection consists in the *DIONYSIANA COLLECTIO.* However, the prefaces of Dionysius are replaced by an epistle in verse addressed by Adrian to Charlemagne. The conciliar series is preceded by a list of titles. It contains the Nicene Creed and the Creed of Constantinople, the *definitio fidei* of Chalcedon, the list of the Fathers of the various councils, and a few canons from them. The canons of Carthage are divided into two groups. The collection of decretals was increased by 15 fragments inserted in chronological order.

Early in the ninth century, the *Hadriana Collectio* was adapted to practical requirements in the *Breviarium ad inquirendas sententias* and in the *Epitome Hadriani.* It was used also by almost all the collections prepared between the ninth and the 11th centuries. As early as the ninth century, it was joined to the *HISPANA COLLECTIO* to form a composite collection, the *Hadriano-hispanica.* It is found in the penitentials of RABANUS MAURUS, the *Capitula episcoporum,* the False Capitularies, the FALSE DECRETALS, the *ANSELMO DEDICATA COLLECTIO,* the *libri de synodalibus causis* of Regino of Prüm, the collection of ABBO OF FLEURY, the collection of Verona, and others. The authors of the great collections of the 11th and 12th centuries, BURCHARD OF WORMS, St. IVO OF CHARTRES, and even the Decretum of GRATIAN reproduced, in many instances, the version of texts given in the *Hadriana Collectio.*

Bibliography: A. M. KOENIGER, *Grundriss einer Geschichte des katholischen Kirchenrechts* (Cologne 1919). C. DE CLERCQ, *La Législation religieuse franque* (Louvain 1936). Maassen 441–452, 965–967. R. NAZ, *Dictionnaire de droit canonique* (Paris 1935–65) 5:1083–84. P. FOURNIER and G. LEBRAS, *Histoire des collections canoniques en occident depuis les fausses décrétales jusqu'au Décret de Gratien* (Paris 1931–32) 1:93–97. P. EWALD, ''Studien zur Ausgabe des Registers Gregors I,'' *Neues Archiv der Gesellschaft für ältere deutsche Geschichtskunde* 3 (1877–78) 433–625.

[J. RAMBAUD-BUHOT]

HADRUMETUM

Hadrumetum, a prosperous Phoenician colony (Sallust, *Jugurtha* 19) with an excellent harbor situated on the eastern coast of modern Tunisia, was founded long before its powerful rival, CARTHAGE, to which it later became subject. After the Punic Wars Hadrumetum was made a free city (*oppidum liberum*) by the Romans. Under Trajan it became a Latin colony and in Diocletian's reorganization of the empire, the capital of the *Provincia Valeria Byzacena.* The Vandals destroyed it *c.* 434 and JUSTINIAN rebuilt it, giving it the name Justinianopolis. Arab invasions in the 7th century left the region of the ancient city desolate. With the arrival of the French in the 19th century the ancient site was rebuilt into the modern Susa (Sousse).

Christianity gained an early foothold in Hadrumetum. Tertullian mentions a certain Mavilus, who suffered martyrdom under the proconsul Scapula (*Ad Scap.* 3.6). Polycarp, Bishop of Hadrumetum, appears third among the 87 bishops listed by seniority who attended the Council of Carthage in 256 at which St. CYPRIAN presided, and he expressed the sentiments of the council briefly and bluntly: ''Whoever admits the validity of baptism conferred by heretics makes void our baptism'' [*Corpus scriptorum ecclesiasticorum latinorum* (Vienna 1866) 3.1:437]. Hadrumetum continued as a center of Christianity and the scene of several important councils until the 7th century. Excavations begun at the ancient site in 1885 yielded rich archeological evidence of the Roman and Christian cultures that flourished in ancient Hadrumetum. Together with Roman burial grounds, five Christian catacombs were discovered, the oldest of which dates back to the last half of the 3rd century.

Bibliography: BÖLTE, *Paulys Realenzklopädie der klassischen Altertumswissenschaft,* ed. G. WISSOWA et al. 7.2 (Stuttgart 1912) 2178–80. H. LECLERCQ, *Dictionnaire d'archéologie chrétienne et de liturgie,* ed. F. CABROL, H. LECLERCQ, and H. I. MARROU 15 v. (Paris 1907–53) 6.2:1981–2010. A. AUDOLLENT, *Dictionnaire d'histoire et de géographie ecclésiastiques,* ed. A. BAUDRILLART et al. (Paris 1912) 10:1460–1500. A. VON HARNACK, *The Mission and Expansion of Christianity in the First Three Centuries,* tr. and ed. J. MOFFATT, 2 v. (2d ed. rev., New York 1908) v.2.

[H. DRESSLER]

HAEC SANCTA

Also called *Sacrosancta,* a decree of the Council of CONSTANCE asserting the authority of ecumenical councils over popes. It was issued April 6, 1415, as a part of the council's effort to end the WESTERN SCHISM. Finding their authority to deal with the schism at issue, the council fathers included language in the decree that has made it the historical high-water mark of CONCILIARISM.

The standard view within the Catholic Church has been that the decree was not valid or universally binding, and after definition of papal authority reached the explicit terms of Vatican I, *Haec sancta* became little more than a matter for academic analysis. In the aftermath of Vatican II, the decree received fresh consideration from some historians who contended that *Haec sancta* was not an aberration but the logical outgrowth of a development in orthodox ECCLESIOLOGY going back several centuries.

Constance was called to reestablish unity in a church whose members were divided by the simultaneous claims of three men to the papal throne. The Council of PISA (1409) sought to deal with the scandal of two men claiming to be pope, but succeeded only in adding one more to the number. At the instigation of Emperor Sigismund, Constance was called by John XXIII (now considered an antipope) of the Pisan line. But when John saw the council would not support his claims, he sought to force its dissolution by leaving—on the assumption that it could not function without a pope. To meet this challenge, the council fathers issued *Haec sancta,* declaring:

> This holy synod of Constance . . . declares in the first place that legitimately convened in the Holy Spirit, forming a general council and representing the militant Catholic Church, it has its powers immediately from Christ, and that each and every one of whatever state or dignity, even if it be papal, is bound to obey it in those things which pertain to faith, the rooting out of the schism and the general reform of the Church of God in head and members.

It made the same claim for any other council legitimately convened.

On July 4, 1415, Gregory XII (now considered to have been the true pope) of the Roman line resigned (through a legate) after having a bull read in which he convened the council. It has subsequently been argued that *Haec sancta* was not valid because it was issued before the council was convened by true papal authority.

John XXIII was deposed by the council on May 29, 1415, and it deposed the third claimant, Benedict XIII of the Avignon line, on July 26, 1417, though Benedict never accepted the action. The council then elected Oddo Colonna as pope, and he served as Martin V, bringing the schism to an end. According to a report of the council, Martin stated that he endorsed its actions, but it has been questioned whether his words applied to *Haec sancta* or whether his verbal statement was in the proper form to give legal standing. However, he did not repudiate the decree, and the validity of his own election and the overall accomplishment of ending the schism depended upon the legitimacy of the council. The condemnation of Hus was also a part of the council's work, and Martin ordered in the bull *Inter cunctas* (Feb. 22, 1418) that anyone suspected of holding Hussite doctrines should be made to swear acceptance of Constance, no exception being made for *Haec sancta.* However, a disputed question is whether *Haec sancta* should be considered a dogma of faith, which if validly defined would be irreformable, or a constitutional enactment, which even if valid at the time would not necessarily be applicable outside the historically unique situation for which it was issued.

In the decades following Constance, the popes reasserted their authority against the conciliarists, and in 1460 Pius II issued the bull *Execrabilis,* forbidding appeals from a pope to a council. The last remnants of conciliarism were thought to have been eliminated by Vatican I. But while contemporary Catholic scholars have not questioned papal primacy, they have begun to give greater attention to collegiality and the role of councils as a balance to papal power. From this standpoint some scholars see *Haec sancta* as support for the position that in extraordinary situations—a pope mentally ill, under the control of a political power, or for some other reason unable to function normally—councils can act independently of papal authority.

Bibliography: R. E. MCNALLY, SJ, ''Conciliarism and the Papacy,'' *Proceedings of the Catholic Theological Society* (1970) 13–30. A. FRANZEN, ''The Council of Constance: Present State of the Problem,'' *Concilium* 7 (1965) 29–68. H. KUNG, *Structures of the Church* (New York 1964). B. TIERNEY, ''Hermeneutics and History: The Problem of Haec Sancta,'' *Essays in Medieval History,* ed. T. A. SANDQUIST and M. R. POWICKE (Toronto 1969). R. E. MCNALLY, ''Conciliarism and the papacy,'' *CTSA Proceedings* (1971) 13–30. T. E. MORRISSEY, ''After Six Hundred Years: The Great Western Schism, Conciliarism, and Constance,'' *Theological Studies* 40 (1979) 495–509. P. H. STUMP, *The Reforms of the Council of Constance, 1414-1418* (Leiden, 1994). For the Latin text see J. ALBERIGO et al., *Conciliorum Oecumenicorum Decreta* (Freiburg 1962) 385–86. For an account of the Council see E. ISERLOH, *Handbook of Church History,* ed. H. JEDIN and J. DOLAN, IV (1970) 448–473.

[T. EARLY]

HAGAR

Egyptian slave girl of Abraham's wife Sarah. When Sarah gave up hope of providing Abraham with an heir, she offered Hagar to her husband, a procedure which, according to marriage contracts found at Nuzi, was expected of a barren wife (see Gordon, 3). In both of the Genesis accounts (Yahwist source in 16.1–16; Elohist source in 21.9–21), Hagar, after incurring Sarah's jealousy, is driven out of the household with her young son, Ishmael. In the desert she is visited by an ANGEL OF THE LORD, who, besides saving her from perishing, promises that Ishmael will grow into a powerful nation. Thus, as mother of the 12 tribes of Ishmael (Gn. 25.12–26; cf. Bar 3.23), Hagar is the first in a series of non-Israelite women (Tamar, Rahab, Ruth) singled out for a special role in salvation history.

In Galatians 4.21–31 St. Paul utilizes the Hagar story ''by way of allegory'' to illustrate the contrast between the Old Law and the New. Just as the offspring of Hagar are slaves, since they are born of a slave, so, too, they who are offspring of the Old Law are slaves. The New

Law, however, like Sarah, gives birth to free offspring. In contrast, Hagar's offspring was ''born according to the flesh,'' i.e., as a purely natural phenomenon, whereas the birth of Sarah's son Isaac was in fulfillment of a divine promise; so, the Jews are but the natural descendants of Abraham, whereas Christians are ''the children of the promise.'' Finally, St. Paul contrasts the Old Covenant given on Sinai, which is ''a mountain in Arabia,'' the land of Ishmael, with the New Covenant, which is bestowed from the New Jerusalem above. These contrasts are climaxed by the Pauline conclusion: ''cast out the slave girl and her son.''

Bibliography: M. NEWMAN, G. A. BUTTRICK, ed., *The Interpreters' Dictionary of the Bible,* 4 v. (Nashville 1962), 2:508–509. *Encyclopedic Dictionary of the Bible,* tr. and adap. by L. HARTMAN (New York 1963) 40–41. J. GABRIEL, *Lexikon für Theologie und Kirche,* ed. J. HOFER and K. RAHNER, 10 v. (2d, new ed. Frieburg 1957–65) 4:1314. G. KITTEL, *Theologisches Wörterbuch zum Neuen Testament* (Stuttgart 1935–) 1:55–56. C. H. GORDON, ''Biblical Customs and the Nuzu Tablets,'' *The Biblical Archaeologist* 3 (1940) 1–12. R. T. O'CALLAHAN, ''Historical Parallels to Patriarchal Social Custom,'' *The Catholic Biblical Quarterly* 6 (1944) 391–405. J. BRIGHT, *A History of Israel* (Philadelphia 1959).

[E. MARTIN]

HAGGADAH

The nonlegal content of Jewish tradition as distinguished from HALAKAH, the legal portion. The term Haggadah (or Aggada), derived from the Hebrew verb *higgîd* (to narrate), denotes narration, story, legend. The material of Haggadah is wide-ranging and includes homilies, ethics, theology, history, science, and folklore. Indeed, whatever cannot be construed as strictly legalistic is subsumed under this term, although Haggadah and Halakah may serve each other for interpretive purposes. Their relationship is often depicted as comparable to that which exists between the emotional heart and logical mind.

Although the TALMUD is the major source of Halakah, about one-third of the Talmud, mainly in the GEMARAH, is devoted to haggadic material. The lengthy and involved deliberations of the Talmudic rabbis on fine points of the law are periodically deflected momentarily through association of ideas into such bypaths as edifying reflections on life's meaning, an incident in the life of some sage, or a discussion of the authorship of the biblical books. One tractate of the MISHNAH, PIRKE AVOTH (Ethics of the Fathers), is devoted exclusively to a presentation of the life philosophies of several generations of Tannaim (rabbis cited in the Mishnah) by means of their pithy maxims.

The largest collection of Haggadot (plural of Haggadah) is in the MIDRASHIC LITERATURE, a term applied to

Haggadahs at a Judaica store. (©Seth Joel/CORBIS)

a number of such collections that serve to interpret the Bible according to its inner meaning rather than its literal purpose, i.e., according to the spirit rather than the letter. Although the midrashic method was used also to establish or validate legal propositions, it found a most fruitful outlet in the uninhibited expositions that sought to derive, from the plain text of Scripture, ideas and ideals not readily apparent or support for notions already accepted. The speculative character of Haggadah is indicative of the disinclination of Judaism for creedal formulas and a systematic theology comparable in definition to Halakah. Whereas the latter ordered the interrelationships of men in the community, for their mutual protection, the former offered guidelines for personal behavior and outlook that were by no means so definitive as to exclude alternate options, as the needs of man and his life view changed.

Haggadah is also the name given both to the Seder (''order'' of the service) of the Passover meal and to the ritual book used for the occasion. In keeping with the biblical prescription (Ex 13.8) that a father should explain to his son the meaning of the observance, the highlight of the celebration lies in the Four Questions asked by the youngest present concerning some of the customs peculiar to the festival: the use of unleavened bread and bitter herbs, the dipping of the latter into the haroseth (relish) and the parsley in salt water, and the reclining at the Seder table. The reply is a lengthy recitation of midrashic interpretations of the kind discussed above, in order to elaborate on the importance of the holy day and the miraculousness of the deliverance of the Israelites from Egyptian bondage. Included are selections from Psalms and the Mishnah, as well as several folk songs. The Haggadah book itself has been, for some centuries, the object of artistic endeavors; it contains, in many of its editions and manuscripts, pictures depicting the conduct of the Seder and the festival's themes.

Illuminated initial of the Book of Haggai in the "Great Bible of Demeter Neksei-Lipocz," c. 1350 (Pre. Acc. MS 1, v. 2, folio 194v).

Bibliography: J. JACOBS, *The Jewish Encyclopedia*, ed. J. SINGER (New York 1901–06) 6:141–146. S. LEVINSON et al., *Universal Jewish Encyclopedia* (New York 1939–44) 5:156–174. A. MARMORSTEIN, *Encyclopaedia Judaica: Das Judentum in Geschichte und Gegenwart* (Berlin 1928–34) incomplete, 1:951–979. R. WISCHNITZER-BERNSTEIN, *Ibid.* 7:788–813. A. COHEN, ed., *Everyman's Talmud* (New York 1949). L. GINZBERG, *Legends of the Jews*, 7 v. (Philadelphia 1947). J. GOLDIN, *The Fathers according to Rabbi Nathan* (Yale Judaica Ser. 10; New Haven 1957). H. SCHAUSS, *The Jewish Festivals*, tr. S. JAFFE (New York 1958) 38–85.

[R. KRINSKY]

HAGGAI, BOOK OF

The tenth of the 12 MINOR PROPHETS according to the biblical arrangement of books, but the first of the postexilic Prophets. His name (spelled Aggaeus in the Vulgate and Aggeus in the Douay Old Testament), is a derivative from the Hebrew *ḥag*, meaning feast. Though probably not a priest himself (Hg 2.11), he may have exercised some official duties at the national sanctuary of Jerusalem, perhaps as a cult prophet or preacher.

A wholly new style of prophetic preaching is discernible in the short compilation of Haggai's sermons. While the earlier Prophets upbraided the nation for excessive concern over Temple ritual and called for a return to strong and sincere morality (Hos 6.4–6; Is 1.11–17; Jer 7.1–8.3), Haggai, instead, was entirely preoccupied with the reconstruction of the Temple and the correct compliance with ceremonial laws (Ezr 5.1; 6.14). Here, as in almost all postexilic writing, the preponderant influence of the priest-prophet Ezekiel is manifest. Not only do Haggai's ideas manifest little or no originality, but his style is prosaic and unimpressive, especially when compared with the poetic rhythm and rich imagery of the earlier Prophets. Attempts to versify his lines remain hypothetical.

An ancient editor of the book indicates that the Prophet spoke four or possibly five times in the second year of DARIUS I, KING OF PERSIA, between Aug. 29 and Dec. 18, 520 B.C. [Hg 1.1; 2.1, 10, 15, 20; conversion of the dates are based on R. A. Parker and W. H. Dubberstein, *Babylonian Chronology 625 B.C.–A.D. 75* (Providence 1956) 30]. The land of the Jews in Palestine had shrunk to about 20 by 25 miles, with a population no greater than 20,000. It belonged to the province of Samaria, which was part of the fifth Persian satrapy of 'Abar Nahara [''across the River'' (Euphrates)]. The country was harrassed with drought and depression (Hg 1.6, 9–11; 2.15–17); grasping, quarreling Jews were guilty of much injustice, even selling their fellow citizens into slavery (Neh 5; Mal 3.5). The neighboring districts, Samaria to the north and Edom to the south, were despised and hated (Ezr 4; Mal 1.3; Ob); and they, in their turn, threatened to invade Judah.

The first discourse (Hg 1.1–15a) presents Haggai's blunt condemnation of the people for living in ''paneled houses, while this house [the Temple] lies in ruin'' (1.4). The prophet attributed the crop failures to the nation's religious laziness and therefore demanded immediate action on the Temple's reconstruction. He obtained a favorable reaction from the people. Some exegetes transfer the speech of 2.15–19 immediately after 1.15a, which is regarded as the date introducing it, on the basis that a date is prefixed to every one of Haggai's discourses. In that case, this short book would contain five instead of four sermons.

The second discourse (1.15b–2.9), the most important of all from a theological point of view, was spoken on the second-last day of the octave of the Feast of BOOTHS (cf. Lv 23.34; Dt 16.13). Haggai's words ring with high messianic hopes, possibly because the feast included a thanksgiving service at the Temple for the year's harvest (Lv 23.39–41; 1 Kgs 8.2). He would have thought of the final harvesting of messianic blessings at the same Temple. The messianic hopes can also be accounted for by international events: Darius's quick seizure of the throne and his repulsive measures against all rebels. God too could act as decisively and quickly as Darius. Although the Vulgate recognizes a personal Messiah in 2.7, e.g., ''the Desired One of all the nations,'' the Hebrew text and the Greek Septuagint refer to ''the treasures,'' i.e., the contributions and talents of all nations flowing into the Temple and having a part in the liturgy.

The third discourse (2.10–14 or 2.10–19) centers on the power of evil to spread and propagate more surely than goodness. Haggai may here be rejecting the Samaritan offer to help on the reconstruction of the Temple (Ezr 4.1–5) for fear that they might contaminate the chosen people.

In the last discourse (2.20–23) Haggai reiterated the hope in a marvelous intervention when Yahweh would save His people through a Davidic king.

Bibliography: P. R. ACKROYD in *Peake's Commentary on the Bible*, ed. M. BLACK and H. H. ROWLEY (New York 1962) 562a–563i. S. BULLOUGH, *Catholic Commentary on Holy Scripture*, ed. B. ORCHARD et al. (London-New York 1957) 543a–544k. T. CHARY, *Les Prophètes et la culte à partir de l'Exil* (Tournai 1955) 118–138. A. GELIN, ''Introduction aux prophètes,'' *Bible de Jérusalem* (Paris 1957—). T. H. ROBINSON and F. HORST, *Die zwölf kleinen Propheten*, [*Handbuch zum Alten Testament*, ed. O. EISSFELDT 14 (Tübingen 1954)]. J. SCHILDENBERGER, *Lexikon für Theologie und Kirche*, ed. J. HOFER and K. RAHNER (Freiburg 1957–65) 1:188. R. BACH, *Die Religion in Geschichte und Gegenwart* (Tübingen 1957–65) 3:25–26. *Encyclopedic Dictionary of the Bible*, tr. and adap. by L. HARTMAN (New York 1963) 42–43.

[C. STUHLMUELLER]

HAGIA SOPHIA

The church of Hagia Sophia (Holy Wisdom in Greek) was commissioned by the Byzantine emperor Justinian I (527–565) and built by the mathematicians Anthemius of Tralles and Isidore of Miletus. The church was inaugurated in 562 after more than five years of labor by over 10,000 workers. It replaced an earlier structure, the Great Church, which was destroyed by fire in the Nika rebellions of 532. The destroyed building was a conventional timber-roofed basilica. In replacing it Justinian and his architects combined elements from basilican—and centrally—planned structures to create a new architectural plan most frequently characterized as a domed basilica. The individual elements used in the building were not new; it was rather their combination that was innovative. Hagia Sophia was originally fronted to the west by a porticoed atrium with a central fountain. Multiple doors then opened onto a double entrance hall, or narthex. This gave access to the great open space of the nave, a rectangle measuring 229 by 245 feet (70 by 77 meters). Above this is the circular dome, 100 feet (30.5 m) in diameter, which rests on pendentives supported by four immense stone piers linked by four massive arches. These supports are not clearly evident, as in classical buildings, but are hidden behind a screen of columns on the north and south walls. On the east and west walls two half-domes are set immediately beneath the main dome; beneath each semidome are three apses. The circular dome thus seems to float unsupported 180 feet (55 m) above the nave floor. Prokopios, a historian in Justinian's court, captured the dome's effect on the viewer: ''It seems not to be founded on solid masonry, but to be suspended from heaven by that golden chain.'' (*De aedif.* I, i, 23).

It is difficult to convey in words the tremendous scale of Hagia Sophia. It is the largest Byzantine church ever built; it was the largest church in medieval Christendom; it encloses a vaulted space larger than that of any building built before it. The scale of the building reflects it importance. Hagia Sophia was in many ways as symbolic of Byzantium as was the nearby Great Palace complex of the Byzantine emperors. It was the showpiece of the empire, proudly displayed to every foreign diplomat, and was equally the object of devout pilgrims and gawking tourists. It gave employment to more than 600 members of the clergy and served as the primary church of the patriarch, whose palace abutted the south facade and connected directly to the gallery. Hagia Sophia was the site of many of the empire's most important celebrations, including the investiture of new emperors. On the major feast days of the Orthodox Church the emperor and patriarch joined together to take part in the liturgy.

The interior decoration matched the splendor of its architectural underpinnings. According to Prokopios, 40,000 pounds of silver was used to decorate the sanctuary. Acres of multicolored marbles were quarried to create the columns and revetments that sheath the walls and floors. Marble was also used for many of the liturgical furnishings, such as the ambo, the elevated platform from which scriptures were read. The upper vaulting was covered with gold tesserae (cubes), which reflected the light streaming in through the tympana and dome windows. Cut marble (*opus sectile*), arranged in the form of vines intertwined with fruit and birds decorated the north and south colonnades at the levels of the aisles and galleries (upper stories). Cloths woven with gold thread covered the solid gold altar and draped the interior doorways. The low screen separating the sanctuary from the nave displayed silver relief icons of Christ, the Virgin, angels, and saints. The full extent of the figural decoration of the building prior to ICONOCLASM is not known. After repairs to the dome in 563, a mosaic depicting a cross was placed in its apex.

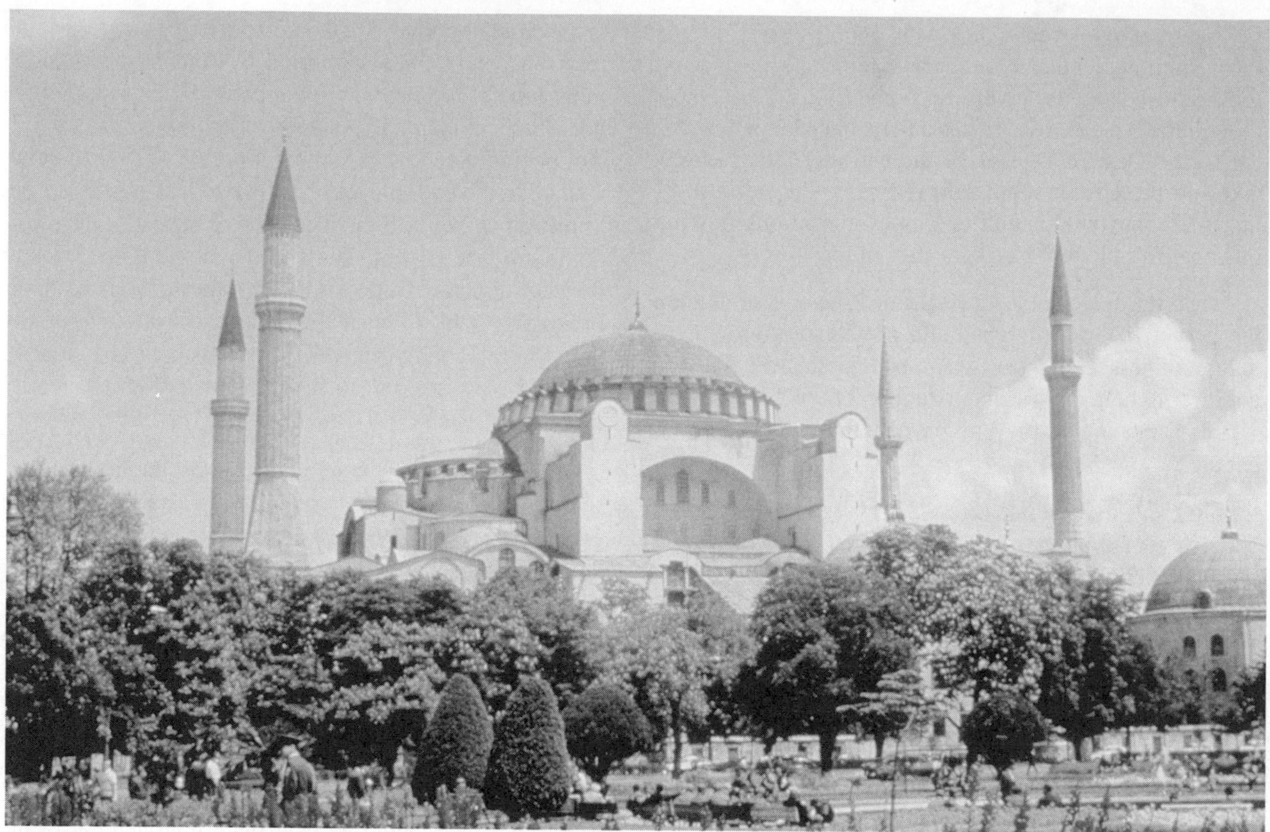

Hagia Sophia, designed by Anthemius of Tralles and Isidorus of Miletus for Emperor Justinian I (532–537), Istanbul. (©Archive Photos)

In 867, after the end of Iconoclasm, Hagia Sophia was the first church to undergo official redecoration. One of the first images to be installed was the mosaic still visible in the eastern apse depicting the enthroned Virgin and Child. It was originally flanked by mosaics of the archangels Michael and Gabriel; only the latter survives today. At the same time mosaic icons of the Church Fathers were placed at the base of the tympanum. In the tenth through twelfth centuries imperial portraits were added to the south gallery and placed above the doors of the narthex, and in the fourteenth century a mosaic of Christ as *Pantokrator* (Ruler of All) was placed in the dome.

The building has of course undergone repairs and alterations. In the Byzantine period frequent earthquakes necessitated repairs to the dome and the strengthening of the exterior buttresses. When Constantinople fell to the Ottoman Sultan Mehmet II in 1453 the church was converted into a mosque. Christian liturgical furnishings were removed and replaced with those necessary for Muslim worship, and four minarets were added to the exterior. The Byzantine buildings that clustered around the church were replaced with Ottoman and, later, Turkish structures. The majority of the Byzantine mosaics were not removed but were painted over in the eighteenth century. Hagia Sophia is now a museum administered by the Turkish government and preserves aspects of both its Christian and Muslim history. In 1930 restoration of the Byzantine mosaics was begun and conservation work continues today on both the Byzantine and Islamic interior decorations.

Bibliography: R. CORMACK and E. J. W. HAWKINS, ''The Mosaics of St. Sophia at Istanbul: The Rooms above the Southwest Vestibule and Ramp'' *Dumbarton Oaks Papers* 31 (1977) 175–251. R. J. MAINSTONE, *Hagia Sophia: Architecture, Structure, and Liturgy of Justinian's Great Church* (London 1988). G. MAJESKA, ''The Emperor in His Church: Imperial Ritual in the Church of St. Sophia'' in *Byzantine Court Culture from 829–1204,* ed. H. MAGUIRE (Washington, DC 1997). C. MANGO, *The Art of the Byzantine Empire 312–1453* (Toronto 1986); *Materials for the Study of the Mosaics of St. Sophia* (Washington, DC 1962). R. MARK and A. ÇAKMAK, eds., *Hagia Sophia from the Age of Justinian to the Present* (New York 1992). T. E. MATHEWS, *The Early Churches of Constantinople: Architecture and Liturgy* (University Park, PA 1971). W. MÜLLER-WEINER, *Bildlexicon zur Topographie Istanbuls* (Tübingen 1977). T. WHITTEMORE, *The Mosaics of Saint Sophia at Istanbul; Preliminary Report on the Year's Work, 1931–32* (Paris 1933).

[L. JONES]

HAGIOGRAPHY

The name given to the branch of learning that has the saints and the worship of them for its object. Writings relating to the worship of the saints may be divided into two categories: (1) those that are the spontaneous product of circumstances or have been called into being by religious needs of one kind or another, and these belong to what may be called practical hagiography; (2) writings devoted to the scientific study of this material, and these constitute critical hagiography.

Practical Hagiography

The cult of the saints has given rise, in both the East and the West, to a very considerable number of documents, varying in form and in tenor with the author's object. In primitive times lists of martyrs were drawn up in particular churches with a view to the celebration of anniversaries; those lists became the nucleus of the MARTYROLOGIES [*see* H. Delehaye, *Cinq leçons sur la méthode hagiographique* (Brussels 1934) ch. 3].

Martyrs and Heroes. Side by side with the martyrologies and calendars there are narratives of martyrdoms and biographies written by contemporaries in memory of the heroes whom the Church celebrates: e.g., in Greek, the Martyrdom of St. POLYCARP and the Life of St. ANTHONY OF EGYPT by St. Athanasius; in Latin, The Passion of the Scillitan Martyrs, the Life of St. Augustine by Possidius, and the Life of St. Martin by Sulpicius Severus. There are accounts composed by writers who lived later than the events recorded and whose object was to edify the faithful or satisfy a pious curiosity. These hagiographers write either in prose, as the author of the Acts of St. CECILIA, or in verse, as PRUDENTIUS and many others. Finally there are texts composed or arranged for liturgical use from historical documents or from artificial compositions.

Hagiographic Collections. The various classes of hagiographic works—historical memoirs, literary compositions, liturgical texts—existed at first as monographs, but soon the need was felt of gathering into a collection separate pieces of the same nature. The most ancient hagiographic collection of which mention is made is EUSEBIUS OF CAESAREA's lost compilation of the Acts of the Ancient martyrs, containing the passions of martyrs previous to the persecution of DIOCLETIAN. Out of this work, Eusebius wrote, in one volume, *On the Martyrs of Palestine,* the story of the last persecution in his own province. THEODORET OF CYR afterward compiled his *Historia religiosa* from a series of 30 monastic biographies that he had previously authored. Thus there are two types of collections, to one or other of which may be attributed all those to be mentioned hereafter—a grouping of pieces from various origin under one title, and a series of narratives from the same pen.

Among the most famous collections of the early Middle Ages were the *In Gloria Martyrum* and *In Gloria Confessorum* of GREGORY OF TOURS, the dialogues of St. GREGORY THE GREAT, *De Vita et Miraculis Patrum Italicorum,* the three books of EULOGIUS OF CÓRDOBA (d. 859) entitled *Memoriale Sanctorum.*

Legendaries. The order in these early collections was dictated by the historical setting of the particular subjects—saints' lives or passions—that they incorporate; later there appear collections of a more artificial character in which the passions and the biographies of the saints follow each other according to the dates of their anniversaries in the calendar. In the West such collections are known as passionaries or legendaries. In time every region came to have its own; the Roman legendary constitutes a common foundation of all with individual additions determined by local cults. The legendaries usually consist of biographies and *passiones* of relatively great length.

Legenda Aurea. Beginning in the 13th century, collections of a more convenient size began to appear, containing the matter of the legendaries in a condensed form. Unquestionably the most famous of these is the *Legenda aurea* of the Dominican JAMES OF VORAGINE, MSS of which were plentiful before printed copies became available. This work was translated during the Middle Ages into several modern languages. A large number of saints' lives in the vernacular, which are now of interest chiefly to students of philology, may be traced to Latin originals. The importance of this body of literature may be estimated by a perusal of Paul Meyer's memoir ''Légendes hagiographiques en français,'' *Histoire Littéraire de la France* 33:328–459; Bossuat 297–322 and Supplement (1955) 73–74; F. Wilhelm, *Deutsche Legenden und Legendare* (Leipzig 1907).

Other hagiographical compilations that date from the Middle Ages are also worthy of mention, even though they have not all enjoyed the same popularity. Such are the Sanctoral of BERNARD GUI, Bishop of Lodève (d. 1331), still unedited (*see* L. Delisle, *Notices et Extraits* 27.2, 1879); the legendary of the Dominican Pierre Calo (d. 1348), also unedited [*see* A. Poncelet, *Analecta Bollandiana* 29 (1910) 5–116]; the *Sanctilogium Angliae* of John of Tynemouth (d. 1366), which became the *Nova legenda Angliae* of John Capgrave (1464), of which there is now a critical edition by C. Horstmann (Oxford 1901); the *Sanctuarium* of B. MOMBRITIUS, printed at Milan before the year 1480, in two folio volumes, and especially precious because it reproduces the lives and the passions of the old MSS without reshaping or rehandling (new ed., Paris 1910); the great compilations of John Gielemans, a Brabantine canon regular (d. 1487), under the titles *Sanctilogium* and *Hagiologium Brabantinum, Novale Sanctorum* [*see Analecta Bollandiana* 14 (1895) 5–88]; and Hilarion of Milan's supplement to James of Voragine (*Legendarium . . . supplementum illius de Voragine,* Milan 1494).

Lippomano and Surius. After the middle of the 16th century, the lives of the saints were collected by Luigi Lippomano, Bishop of Verona [*Sanctorum priscorum patrum vitae* (Venice-Rome 1551–60)], and later by the Carthusian Lawrence SURIUS [*De probatis sanctorum historiis* (Cologne 1570–75)]; both collections were offered as edifying reading and at the same time as a polemic arsenal against the Protestants; they enjoyed a considerable reputation. Surius's *Historae* was several times reprinted. Pedro de RIBADENEYRA's *Flos Sanctorum* (1st ed. Madrid 1599) had a greater popular success and was translated into several languages. It was followed by a large number of lives of the saints for every day in the year.

Alban Butler. Among the most famous of these collections is Alban BUTLER's *Lives of the Fathers, Martyrs and Other Principal Saints,* which first appeared in 1756 and was often reprinted (see the entirely new ed., 4 v. London 1956). Msgr. P. Guérin's *Les petits Bollandistes* is an uncritical collection that has nothing in common with the *Acta sanctorum* or with the publications of the Bollandists. Much better, at least from June on to December, are the *Vies des saints et des bienheureux* edited by the Benedictine Fathers of Paris (13 v. 1935–59). Initiated in 1961, the *Bibliotheca Sanctorum* forms a vast dictionary of the saints, written in Italian and aiming at serious documentation.

Most collections of lives of the saints, particularly those in modern languages, are inspired by the idea of interesting and edifying the reader, without great solicitude for historical truth. There are, finally, isolated biographies, the number of which grew incessantly during the Middle Ages and in later times and served to swell the collections.

Greek Menologies Among the Greeks, the development of hagiography was, at least outwardly, the same as among the Latins. The passions of the martyrs, biographies, and panegyrics of the saints were similarly collected, and were arranged in the order of the calendar, viz, in the menologies mentioned as early as the nineth century, and in the panegyrics. Most famous is the menology of Symeon Metaphrastes (tenth century), on which depend the imperial menologies of the 11th century and several later collections.

The Greeks, in addition, have their shorter menologies, composed of abridged lives. The SYNAXARIES, the use of which is chiefly liturgical, are mainly compositions in which the more extended lives and passions are reduced to the form of brief notices (see H. Delehaye, *Synaxarium ecclesiae Constantinopolitanae, Acta Sanctorum* Nov. Propylaeum, 1902). Neither is there any lack of collections in popular or modern Greek, for the saints' lives of Maximos Margunios, Agapios Landos, NICODEMUS THE HAGIORITE, and others down to the *Megas synaxaristes* of C. Dukakis (14 v. Athens 1889–97) are widely read in Greek-speaking countries.

Slavonic and Oriental Hagiography. Closely connected with Greek hagiography is Slavonic hagiography. The reader is referred, for purposes of orientation, to I. Martinov, *Annus ecclesiasticus graeco-slavicus* in *Acta Sanctorum* Oct. 11, 1863 (repr. Brussels 1963), and the critical edition of the Russian *Menaea* of Macarius (1868–1914; publication interrupted).

The Orient has been the scene of an analogous development. Passions of the martyrs, lives of the saints, collections, and synaxaries are all found in the various Oriental languages; but in spite of the praiseworthy efforts of the specialists, there is still insufficient detailed information. Those desiring a summary account of the hagiography of the different peoples of those regions are referred, for the Armenian, to the *Vitae et Passiones Sanctorum,* published (2 v. 1874) by the MECHITHARISTS of Venice, the great Armenian Synaxary of Ter-Israel (tr. and ed. G. Bayan in the *Patrologia orientalis,* ed. R. Graffin and F. Nau [Paris 1903–]) and the *Acta Sanctorum pleniora* of Aucher (12 v. Venice 1810–35); for the Coptic, to H. Hyvernat, *Actes des martyrs de l'Égypte* (Paris 1886), I. Balestri and H. Hyvernat, *Acta martyrum* in *Corpus scriptorum Christianorum orientalium* (Paris-Louvain 1903), Scriptores Coptici (1907–50), the *Coptic Jacobite Synaxary* (ed. I. Forget in *Corpus scriptorum Christianorum orientalium*, Scriptores Arabici, and R. BASSET in the *Patrologia orientalis*); for the Ethiopian, to E. Pereira, *Acta martyrum,* and C. C. Rossini and B. Turajev, *Vitae Sanctorum indigenarum, Corpus scriptorum Christianorum orientalium*, Scriptores Aethiopici, the *Monumenta Aethiopiae hagiologica* of Turajev, and I. Guidi et al., *Ethiopian Synaxary* in the *Patrologia orientalis* (Eng. tr. by E. A. W. Budge, 4 v. Cambridge 1928); for the Syriac, to S. E. Assemani, *Acta martyrum Orientalium* (2 v. Rome 1748) and P. Bedjan *Acta martyrum et sanctorum* (7 v. Leipzig 1890–97); for the Georgian, to G. Sabinin, *Sakart'hvelos Samot'hkhe* (St. Petersburg 1832), and C. Kekelidze, *Monumenta Hagiographica Georgica* (2 v. Tiflis 1918–46); *see also* G. Garitte, *Le Calendrier palestino-géorgien du Sinaiticus* 34 (Brussels 1958). For fuller details, see the three repertories published by the Bollandists: *Bibliotheca hagiographica latina* (2 v. 1898–1901 and suppl. 1911); *Bibliotheca hagiographica graeca* (3d ed., 3 v. 1957); *Bibliotheca hagiographica orientalis* (1910).

Scientific Hagiography

Criticism of documents belonging to the categories enumerated above is called scientific hagiography. It involves two operations that are hardly separable: the study of written tradition for the purpose of establishing texts, and research into sources to determine the historical value of those texts.

Methodical Criticism. The earliest attempts at methodical hagiographic criticism date from the beginning of the 17th century. It is known that the Jesuit H. Rosweyde (d. 1629) first conceived the project of forming a collection of the *Acta Sanctorum,* which since 1643 has been put into execution by J. Bollandus and his collaborators (*see* BOLLANDISTS) and which has for its essential aim the critical sifting and the publication of all the hagiographic texts that have come down to us relating to the saints venerated everywhere in the world—*quotquot toto orbe coluntur.*

Beginning with the first volumes, Bollandus and his colleagues submitted their documents to a criticism as severe as the means of information and the state of historical science permitted. With the development attained by all branches of science in the course of the 19th century, the importance of archeological discoveries in that period, the progress of philology and paleography, the possibility of using rapid communication and photocopy to obviate the difficulty of scattered material, hagiography could not but take a new orientation.

The Bollandists. Side by side with the compilation of the *Acta Sanctorum,* the Bollandists have been induced to undertake studies that, without modifying the spirit of their work, assure for it a broader and firmer basis and a more rigorous application of the principles of historical criticism. They have not been alone in their devotion to the science of hagiography as constituted since the inauguration of their work; J. MABILLON, in *Acta SS. O.S.B.,* T. RUINART, in *Acta martyrum sincera,* and S. E. Assemani, in *Acta martyrum Orientalium,* have furnished important supplements to the work.

Contemporary Hagiography. After the middle of the 19th century, a host of solid works made their appearance, furthering hagiographic science to a notable extent. Such are the fine editions of the lives of Merovingian and Carolingian saints in the *Monumenta Germaniae Historica* (Berlin 1826–), the *Vitae Sanctorum Hiberniae* ed. C. Plummer (Oxford 1910), the numerous Greek texts brought to light by A. Papadopoulos-Kerameus and other learned Hellenists in various countries, the recent publications of Oriental writers mentioned above, and a mass of labors in minute details that have often opened new paths for the science of criticism.

Of particular value are the researches of R. A. LIPSIUS and M. Bonnet on the apocryphal *Acts of the Apostles* and the studies of P. FRANCHI DE' CAVALIERI on a selection of *Acts of the Martyrs.* The *Bulletin des publications hagiographiques* (of *Analecta Bollandiana*) may fill in for the reader the gaps left by this rapid review. Progress has likewise been made in hagiographical criticism as applied to MARTYROLOGIES, notably, by the edition and commentary of the so-called MARTYROLOGY OF ST. JEROME (*Acta Sanctorum*, Nov. 2, 2 parts, 1894 and 1931). The critical researches on historical martyrologies brilliantly inaugurated by the Bollandist Sollerius (*Martyrologium Usuardi* in *Acta Sanctorum*, June 6–7) have been enlarged and brought into line with modern criticism by H. QUENTIN (*Les martyrologes historiques,* Paris 1908).

Science and Piety. As will be readily understood, the distinction established between practical and scientific hagiography is not always sharply defined. More than one attempt has been made to conciliate science and piety and to supply the latter with nourishment that has been passed through a sieve. The first collection of saints' lives conceived in this spirit is that of A. Baillet, *Les vies des saints* (Paris 1701), the first volumes of which (January 1 to August 31) were put upon the Index. A series of separate saints' lives, edited in France under the title *Les Saints,* was inspired by a similar idea of edifying the reader with biographies that should be irreproachable from the historical point of view. It is hardly necessary to add that more than one hagiographical publication of erudite and critical pretensions possesses no importance from a scientific point of view.

Twentieth Century. In the first half of the 20th century, hagiographical studies profited from the research accomplished in cognate disciplines, known as auxiliary sciences in history and philology. Epigraphy played a crucial part in H. DELEHAYE's *Les origines du culte des martyrs* (1912; 2d ed. 1933); *see also* F. Halkin, ''Inscriptions grecques relative à l'hagiographie,'' *Analecta Bollandiana* 1949–1953. In liturgy, V. Leroquais drew up inventories of Sacramentaries, Pontificals, Psalters, Breviaries, and Missals in MS, and the Henry Bradshaw Society in England as well as M. FÉROTIN, F. CABROL, L. Mohlberg, etc., published editions of the ancient liturgical texts. M. Coens made a study of the ancient litanies in *Recueil d'études bollandiennes* (Brussels 1963).

In HYMNOLOGY, U. Chevalier's monumental *Repertorium hymnologicum* (6 v. 1895–1921) and G. Dreves and C. Blume's *Analecta hymnica* (55 v. 1886–1922) are indispenable. In toponomy, the place name societies of England made precious contributions [*see* H. Delehaye, ''Loca Sanctorum,'' *Analecta Bollandiana* (1930)]. Iconography likewise remained a constant interest of researchers and particularly of art historians in all lands and was well represented by K. Künstle, *Ikonographie der Heiligen* (1926), and G. Kaftal, *Iconography of the Saints in Tuscan Painting* (Florence 1952). Finally for lipsanography, or the study of RELIQUARIES, see H. Delehaye, *Cinq leçons sur la méthode hagiographique,* ch. 4.

Bibliography: R. AIGRAIN, *L'Hagiographie: Ses sources, ses méthodes, son histoire* (Paris 1953). H. DELEHAYE, *The Legends of the Saints,* tr. D. ATTWATER (New York 1962); *Les Passions des martyrs et les genres littéraires* (Brussels 1921); *Sanctus: Essai sur le culte des saints dans l'antiquité* (Brussels 1927). A. EHRHARD, *Überlieferung und Bestand der hagiographischen und homiletischen Literatur der griechischen Kirche von den Anfängen bis zum Ende des 16. Jahrhunderts,* 3 v. (*Texte und Untersucchungen zur Geschichte der altchristlichen Literatur* 50–52; 1937–52).

[F. HALKIN]

HAID, LEO MICHAEL

Bishop; b. near Latrobe, Pa., July 15, 1849; d. Belmont, N.C., July 24, 1924. He was the son of German immigrants. Entering the scholasticate of St. Vincent Abbey, Latrobe, he was admitted in 1868 to the novitiate and made his profession on Sept. 17, 1869. Following ordination on Dec. 21, 1872, he served at St. Vincent College, Latrobe, as professor, chaplain, and secretary. On July 14, 1885, he was elected first abbot of Maryhelp Abbey (Belmont Abbey) in Garibaldi, N.C., which had been a priory since 1876. He received the abbatial blessing on Nov. 26, 1885, in Charleston, S.C. In 1886 he opened a seminary and began construction of buildings for the lay school, which was chartered as St. Mary's College. He persuaded the townsfolk to call their settlement Belmont and in 1913 the school was renamed Belmont Abbey College. On Dec. 7, 1887, Haid was appointed vicar apostolic of North Carolina and titular bishop of Messene. He was consecrated at Baltimore, Md., July 1, 1888, by Cardinal James Gibbons.

The interests of the abbot-bishop were necessarily divided. At Belmont the seminary trained diocesan priests; the college grew; and an abbey church was constructed. Throughout the vicariate churches, schools, and charitable institutions were established. In 1889 Haid was placed in charge of the Florida Benedictine missions, which became St. Leo Conventual Priory in 1894 and an abbey in 1902. From 1890 to 1902 he was president of the American Cassinese Congregation. He founded St. Joseph's Institute near Bristow, Va. (1893), Sacred Heart Priory, Savannah, Ga. (1902), and St. Benedict Priory, Richmond, Va. (1911). On June 8, 1910, Pius X withdrew eight counties from the vicariate to constitute Belmont an abbey *nullius*. Haid was named assistant at the pontifical throne and count of the apostolic palace on July 15, 1914.

Bibliography: T. OESTREICH, *Dictionary of American Biography*, ed. A. JOHNSON and D. MALONE, 10 v. (reissue New York 1957; suppl. 1958) 4.2:88–89.

[A. G. BIGGS]

HAIL MARY

The form of prayer also known as the Angelic Salutation consists of three parts: the words of the Archangel Gabriel (Lk 1.28), ''Hail [Mary] full of grace, the Lord is with Thee, blessed art thou amongst women;'' the words of Elizabeth (Lk 1.42), ''Blessed is the fruit of thy womb [Jesus],'' and a formula of petition, ''Holy Mary, Mother of God, pray for us sinners now and at the hour of our death. Amen.'' The prayer is the result of a gradual development from the sixth century to the 16th when the present wording was adopted as general liturgical usage.

Origins. In the sixth century, the texts of the Archangel and Elizabeth are found as a single formula in the ancient liturgies of St. James, St. Mark, the Ethiopic of the 12 Apostles, and the ritual of Severus of Antioch (d. 538). To the formula have been added the words: ''Because you have conceived Christ, the Redeemer of our souls'' [F. E. Brightman, *Liturgies Eastern and Western* (Oxford 1896) 1:56, 128, 218]. This first part of the prayer appears also in two Egyptian ostraca of the sixth or seventh century (H. Leclercq, *Monumenta Ecclesiae Liturgica* 213, 236). In the seventh century, it is found in the Roman antiphonary as an offertory text for the feast of the Annunciation, the Ember Wednesday of Advent, and the fourth Sunday of Advent. It is in this original form that it was used in the Middle Ages. It is found also in the Church of Santa Maria Antiqua (seventh–eighth century) in a mutilated inscription that accompanies a painting of the Annunciation [W. de Gruneisen, *Sainte-Marie-Antique* (Rome 1911) 433, 445]. Sometimes the combination of both texts as a single formula is ascribed to the Archangel Gabriel, an interpretation derived from the Latin Gospel of the pseudo-Matthew. This interesting adaptation can be seen in the ninth century hymn, *Deus qui mundum crimine jacentem* [G. Dreves, *Analecta Hymnica Medii Aevi* (Leipzig 1886–1915) 50:143]. The same erroneous observation appears in Peter of Celle, about 1157 (PL 202:654, 711, 724).

Popular Devotion. The Hail Mary was not adopted before the 11th century as a popular form of devotion. It was about this time that the practice of reciting the twofold salutation as versicles and responses in the Little Office of the Blessed Virgin Mary developed and became diffused in monastic communities. Peter Damian called it the angelic or evangelical versicle and recommended the practice of its recitation (*De Bono Suffr.* 3; PL 145:564). The oldest prescription relative to the recitation of the Hail Mary is found at the end of the 12th century. Bishop Odo of Siliac in the Synod of 1198 required the clergy to see that the faithful recited not only the Our Father and the Creed but also the Hail Mary (*Statuta Odonis,* n.1; Mansi 22:681). Shortly after, the councils of many other nations made similar prescriptions; the practice attained such popularity that the prayer came to be regarded almost as an appendix to the Our Father.

Later Evolution. The addition of the word ''Jesus'' is attributed by some to Urban IV (1261–64). The second part of the Hail Mary appeared only later. Because the form consisting of the two salutations was considered merely a greeting, the need was felt for an addition of an element of petition, and the second part of the Hail Mary appeared. Through the initiative of individuals there began to appear a paraphrase of the text. St. Bernardine of Siena preached a sermon in 1427 wherein he spoke these words: *''Ave Maria Jesus, Sancta Maria, mater Dei, Ora pro nobis'' [Serm.* 29, ed. Banchi (Siena 1884) 2:429]. The present form was introduced into the canonical hours of the Breviary by the Mercedarians in 1514, the Camaldolese in 1515, and the Franciscans in 1525, and was finally fixed in the reformed Breviary of Pius V in 1568. On March 23, 1955, by the decree *Cum nostra,* the obligation of its recitation in the Breviary was abrogated.

Bibliography: H. LECLERCQ, ''Prière à la Vierge Marie sur un ostraken de Louqsor,'' *Bulletin d'ancienne littérature et d'archéologie chrétienne* 2 (1912) 3–32; *Dictionnaire d'archéologie chrétienne et de liturgie*, ed. F. CABROL, H. LECLERCQ, and H. I. MARROU (Paris 1907–53) 10:2043–62. H. THURSTON, *Dictionnaire de spiritualité ascétique et mystique. Doctrine et histoire*, ed. M. VILLER et al. (Paris 1932) 1 (1932) 1161–65; E. CAMPANA,*Maria nel culto cattolico,* 2 v. (Turin 1933) v.1. G. M. ROSCHINI, ''L'Ave Maria: note storiche,'' *Marianum* 5 (1943) 177–185. J. JUNGMANN, *Lexikon für Theologie und Kirche*, ed. J. HOFER and K. RAHNER (Freiburg 1957–65)1:1141. L. EISENHOFER and J. LECHNER, *The Liturgy of the Roman Rite,* tr. A. J. and E. F. PEELER (New York 1961) 63. P. LAZZARINI, *Il Saluto dell'Angelico: Studio Storico, Critico, Esegetico dell'Ave Maria* (Milan 1972). J. E. MARTINS-TERRA, ''Ave Maria à Luz do Antigo Testamento,'' *A Oraçâo no Antigo Testamento* (Sao Paulo 1974), 191–221. NICHOLAS AYO, *The Hail Mary: A Verbal Icon of Mary* (Notre Dame 1994).

[A. A. DE MARCO]

HAIMO OF AUXERRE

An important medieval exegete; d. *c.* 855. A BENEDICTINE monk, he taught at his Abbey of Saint-Germain in AUXERRE, where his most outstanding student was HEIRIC OF AUXERRE. The 12th-century *Anonymus Mellicensis,* probably also a monk, noted (*Patrologia Latina* 213:977C) that Haimo wrote many works, especially a very large book (*librum infinitae quantitatis*) on St. PAUL, excellent explanations of the Book of REVELATION and of the SONG OF SONGS, as well as a treatise on the 12 Minor Prophets. Through an error in the *Catalogus scriptorum ecclesiasticorum* compiled by Abbot John TRITHEMIUS in 1494, almost all the works of Haimo of Auxerre were attributed to Haimo, Bishop of Halberstadt (d. 853). Recent studies have tended to correct this longstanding error, and the following works are generally regarded as written by Haimo of Auxerre: *In divi Pauli epistolas expositio* (*Patrologia Latina* 117:361–938), *Expositionis in Apocalypsim libri septem* (*Patrologia Latina* 117:938–1220), *Commentarium in Cantica Canticorum* (*Patrologia Latina* 117:295–358), *Homiliae de tempore* (*Patrologia Latina* 118:11–746), and *Homiliae de sanctis* (*Patrologia Latina* 118:747–804). To this list may possibly yet be added the *Homiliae in aliquot epistolas Pauli* (*Patrologia Latina* 118:803C–816) and the *Ennarratio in duodecim prophetas minores* (*Patrologia Latina* 117:11–294).

Bibliography: B. HEURTEBIZE, *Dictionnaire de théologie catholique* 6.2:2068–69. C. SPICQ, *Esquisse d'une histoire de l'exégèse latine au moyen âge* (Paris 1944) 50–51. *Clavis Patrum latinorum*, ed. E. DEKKERS, 873, 902, 910, 1220. P. CLASSEN, *Die Religion in Geschichte und Gegenwart*[3] 3:30. J. GROSS, *Lexikon für Theologie und Kirche* [2] 4:1325. G. MATHON, *Catholicisme* 5:538–539. R. QUADRI, ''Aimone di Auxerre alla luce Dei *Collectanea* di Heiric di Auxerre,'' *Italia Medioevale e Umanistica* 6 (1963) 1–48.

[H. DRESSLER]

HAIMO OF LANDECOP, BL.

Cistercian renowned for his visions and piety and, after his death, for his miracles; b. Landecop (Saint-Êtienne-en-Coglais), in Brittany; d. April 30, 1173. A monk of SAVIGNY, he was friend and confessor to King HENRY II of England and gave advice to King Louis VII of France; in his own monastery he acted as spiritual director to Peter of Avranches. His reputation brought Savigny many gifts that enabled the the community to begin rebuild the abbey church just before Haimo's death. None of his works of edification have survived, but the annals of Savigny include many of his visions and miracles.

Bibliography: *Vitae b. Petri Abrincensis et b. Haimonis,* ed. E. P. SAUVAGE, *Analecta Bollandiana* 2 (1883) 475–560. *Ex libro* *de miraculis sanctorum Savigniacensium,* M. BOUQUET, *Recueil des historiens des Gaules et de la France (Rerum gallicarum et fancicarum scriptores)* (Paris 1738–1904) 23:587–605. *Histoire littéraire de la France* (Paris 1865–) 13:592. C. AUVRY and A. LAVEILLE, *Histoire de la congrégation de Savingny,* 3 v. (Paris 1896–98) 3:194–195.

[M. M. CHIBNALL]

HAINMAR OF AUXERRE, ST.

Martyr, bishop of AUXERRE from *c.* 717 to *c.* 731. The *Historia episcoporum Autisiodorensium* (*Monumenta Germaniae Scriptores* 13:394) styles Hainmar (or Haimarus) ''vocatus episcopus,'' which probably means that, like his predecessor, he was never consecrated bishop. Moreover, the same source presents him more as a military commander than as a bishop. It appears that on two occasions CHARLES MARTEL put him in command of expeditions against the people of Aquitaine. But Hainmar quarreled with the king and was imprisoned in Bastogne, in the Belgian province of Luxembourg. He escaped, but was caught near Toul and executed.

Feast: Oct. 28.

Bibliography: *Acta Sanctorum* Oct. 12:369–371. *Bibliotheca hagiographica latina antiquae et mediae aetatis,* 2 v. (Brussels 1898–1901; suppl. 1911) 1:559. L. DUCHESNE, *Fastes épiscopaux de l'ancienne Gaule,* 3 v. (2d. ed. Paris 1907–15); 2:448–449. A. HAUCK, *Kirchengeschichte Deutschlands,* 5 v. (9th ed. Berlin-Leipzig 1958) 1:381.

[E. BROUETTE]

HAIR SHIRT

A penitential garment woven from the hair of mountain goats or of camels, called in Latin a *cilicium* because the cloth from which it was made originated in Cilicia, where mountain goats abound.

Cloth woven of animal hair was in common use in the Near East from pre-Christian times. It was used for sacking, tents, and bad-weather clothing because of its impermeable quality. Worn next to the skin it becomes a true mortification and was used as such from early Christian times. It became the proper garb for public penitents, and ascetics seeking works of supererogation adopted its use for clothing and bedding.

Ancient and medieval rules of religious communities are silent on the use of the hair shirt. St. JEROME spoke of it as the distinctive sign of the monk in the East. But, in the West, CASSIAN denounced it as a form of monastic exhibitionism, a parading of virtue. However, it appears in the lives of many devout souls, in and out of the cloister. St. GERMAIN slept in a hair shirt and on a pile of ashes. St. Thomas BECKET was found, at his death, to be wearing a hair shirt that covered most of his body. St. LOUIS of France wore one under his regal robes. In the late Middle Ages, the wearing of a hair shirt became standard practice for LENT and ADVENT, but it was reduced in size and form to a narrow strip of hair cloth worn around the waist or as a scapular.

Bibliography: J. VAN DODEWAARD, *Lexikon für Theologie und Kirche,* J. HOFER and K. RAHNER, eds. (Freiburg 1957–65) 2:120–304. H. LECLERCQ, *Dictionnaire d'archéologie chrétienne et de liturgie* (Paris 1907–53) 1:1623–25.

[P. MULHERN]

HAITI, THE CATHOLIC CHURCH IN

One of the poorest and most politically unstable countries in the Western Hemisphere, the Republic of Haiti occupies the western third of the island of Hispaniola in the Greater Antilles, located between Cuba and Puerto Rico. The name Haiti, given to the entire island by the Carib and Arawak Indians, means mountainous land; about 30 percent of the region is over 1,600 feet above sea level, and only 20 percent of its land mass is arable. With the lowest per capita income of any country in Latin America, Haiti's inhabitants live, for the most part, in a subsistence economy. Agriculture produces the export crops of coffee, sugar cane, sisal, cotton, cacao, and bananas. There are virtually no industries. In spite of the beauty of the island and its tropical climate, tourism has not developed because of the unsettled political conditions.

The ethnic composition of the population—95 percent of Haiti's inhabitants are of African descent—reflects its roots as a French colony. Seventy-five percent of Haitians are peasants who work in the towns, speak a dialect called Créole, and understand little French. Five percent of the population, made of French-speaking whites and wealthy people of color, comprise a ruling class whose members have inherited the privileges of the French colonizers. The island's middle class, about 20 percent of the population, consists of people of color ranging economically from a high standard of living to abject poverty. As a group they understand French but usually speak Créole. Beginning in 1957 the middle class began to replace the upper class as the exploiter of the peasants.

The Colonial Era. Christopher Columbus arrived on the island he christened Española on December 6, 1492. Placed under Spanish control from 1492 to 1697, Hispanola was administered under the PATRONATO REAL.

It suffered from the depredations of the Carib people, from the greed of the CONQUISTADORES, and from European diseases. Ultimately the native population was exterminated. African slaves were brought to the island as early as 1512. After the conquest of Mexico the island became a colony of reduced importance to Spain.

While French and English buccaneers began to use the little island of Tortuga to the north of Haiti as their headquarters early in the 17th century, the English were driven out of the area by 1640. At that time a governor was appointed by the king of France and the Catholic religion was reestablished in the area. In 1681 Capuchins came to the island to take charge of evangelization and to found parishes. They succeeded in bringing some order out of the religious chaos. By the time they left in 1704, six parishes had been established. Then the Jesuits took over, to remain until 1763, the date of the suppression of their order in France. The Capuchins returned in 1768 and continued the work of founding parishes.

Haiti was a flourishing French colony until 1804 when it secured its independence, forcing the last prefect apostolic to flee the island for fear of his life. From 1804 to 1860 Haiti remained in schism from Rome, leaving the nation's various governments to attempt to run the Church as they tried to run the state. What few clergy there were were defrocked religious from various countries and seculars driven out of their own dioceses. While the first Protestants made inroads into the island's population, six separate papal delegations also tried to enter Haiti, but were not recognized by the government.

The Church under the Concordat of 1860. On March 28, 1860, a concordat was finally signed by Haitian President Geffrard and Pope Pius IX. The concordat recognized national patronage, which gave the government the privilege of presenting candidates for bishoprics and provided for the establishment in Haiti of an archdiocese and four dioceses. What Haiti likely needed at this time was the establishment of missionary prefectures or vicariates. It was a land where evangelization had to begin again.

In the cities the reestablishment of the Church organization and the presence of priests, together with the almost immediate foundation of schools, extended Catholicism, and a religious veneer was quickly attained by the upper classes. However, at the same time Marxism also was making a strong impression on the same intellectual elite, and the two ideologies would continue to conflict into the next century.

Despite the concordat, in rural areas religious services still consisted largely in the priests' performing baptisms, giving the Last Sacraments, and presiding over burial services. This kind of missionary endeavor, which made little fundamental impression upon the Haitian masses, was largely responsible for the continuance of superstition in the country's interior. What teaching was done was fruitless for the most part. Up to 1951 missionaries still used French catechisms, unintelligible to 75 percent of the people. About 1900 Bishop KERSUZAN wrote a catechism in Créole, but it was never widely used. Forty years later Bp. Robert of Gonaives started a campaign not only for the use of a Créole catechism but also to allow the people to use their own language in hymns. His work would only be partially successful; for the next two decades, when Créole was used at all, churchgoers often sang hymns that were literal translations of French lyrics. In 1959 a much-needed school for the training of lay catechists was opened.

Capital: Port-au-Prince.
Size: 10,714 sq. miles.
Population: 6,867,995 in 2000.
Languages: French; Creole is spoken by many people.
Religions: Catholics 5,493,600 (80%), Protestants 1,098,720 (16%), other 275,675 (4%); approximately 50% of Haitians also practice voodoo.
Metropolitan Sees: Cap-Haïtien, with suffragans Fort-Libcrté, Hinche, Les Gonaïves, and Port-de Paix; Port-au-Prince, with suffragans Jacmel, Jérémie, and Les Cayes.

In 1871 a major seminary was established at Pontchâteau, France, under the direction of the Montfort Fathers, to recruit missionaries for Haiti. In 1893 this establishment was taken over by the secular clergy and transferred to Saint-Jacques-par-Lampaul-Guimiliau. In 1922 the École Apostolique, a seminary for the training of a native clergy, was founded by order of the Holy See in Port-au-Prince. In spite of continued directives from Rome, the ecclesiastics in Haiti were slow to encourage a native clergy. In the 1940s Bishop Collignon began to press for implementation of these wishes of the Holy See, but it took another order from Rome, putting Canadian Jesuits in charge of the seminary in 1953, to get any action. The Jesuits were charged to bring the standards of the seminary up to those in the rest of the Catholic world. By 1962 the institution had received 72 seminarians. However, in February 1964 the Jesuits were expelled by the government, and the seminary was closed. It was opened again in October 1965 under the direction of the Viatorians.

[J. M. SALGADO/EDS.]

The Duvalier Years. In 1957 François "Papa Doc" Duvalier came to power. He quickly established his own private army, the notoriously brutal *Tonton Macoutes,*

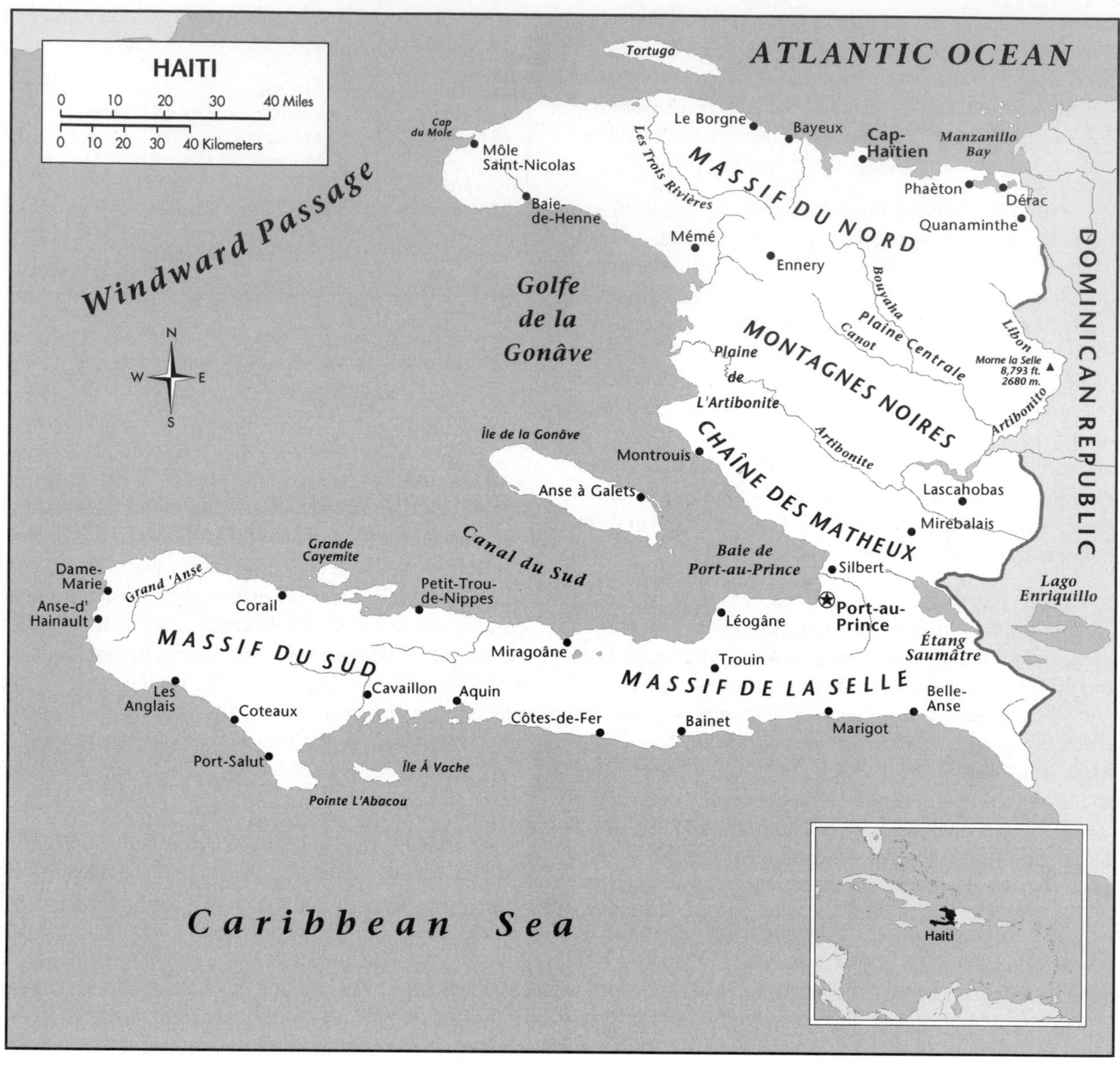

which enabled him to control the military, churches, voodoo priests, and rural sheriffs. Virtually all commercial and agricultural enterprises fell under Duvalier's official and unofficial tax schemes. Upon his death in 1971, he was succeeded by his son, Jean-Claude Duvalier. The younger Duvalier, known as ''Baby Doc'', assumed the title ''president-for-life,'' and thus continued the brutal family dictatorship.

During the period from 1971 to 1986, a new understanding of the Church's mission, involving a prophetic outreach to rural Haitians and away from the urban, mulatto elite was reinforced by Vatican II, LIBERATION THEOLOGY, an increase in native clergy, the growth of the *Ti Legliz* movement (the Haitian version of basic Christian communities), and various spin-off Catholic Action groups. The Church shifted its attention to the countryside, working in education, economic development, health, literacy, and the training of peasant leaders. This changed approach—clearly a preferential option for the poor—included a scripture-based adaptation of Catholic social thought and liberation theology. The use of Créole in the liturgy became more common, and the role and ritual of voodoo and its implications for Catholic sacramental theology were also studied.

In 1983 Pope John Paul II visited Haiti. The Holy Father's cry that ''things must change'' resonated throughout the country and put the dictatorial government on notice. The pope's plea provided cover for the efforts of priests, sisters, and lay leaders. Local Catholic organizations sprang into action, mobilizing the rural sector and urban slums. The Haitian Conference of Religious, Caritas organizations, justice and peace commissions, *Ti Legliz* groups, and peasant organizations were linked together by the Catholic station, *Radio Soleil.* In December 1983, the Haitian bishops outlined their social plan in the *Charte de l'Eglise d'Haïti pour la promotion humaine.* The document, a commitment to solidarity with the poor, announced plans for a massive literacy campaign, *Misyon Alfa.* Another important result of the pope's visit was that the concordat of 1860 was changed, giving Rome full authority to appoint bishops.

Jean-Bertrand Aristide and Democracy. As Church involvement in social change increased, so did the arrest, torture, and exile of Church workers. Although on February 7, 1986, the Duvalier dictatorship fell, and Baby Doc was ushered into exile, ''Duvalierism without Duvalier'' ruled. An overwhelming positive vote on a new constitution on March 29, 1987, was followed by a bloody summer and fall of strikes and killings. In August 1987 a group of priests was brutally attacked after celebrating mass for the victims of the earlier Jean Rebel massacre. The first attempt at democratic elections in Haiti's history on November 29, 1987, ended in a blood bath. The country was then ruled by a series of generals or puppet politicians. It was during these events that a young Salesian priest, Jean-Bertrand Aristide, left his work among urban homeless children to emerge as a major voice for change. On September 11, 1988, forces attacked the church of St. Jean Bosco where Aristide was celebrating mass. Uniformed police and army stood by and watched as at least 12 people were killed and numerous others wounded. Aristide's strong rhetoric was the cause of conflict not only with the dictatorial government but also with the hierarchy. Less than one month after the attack he was expelled from the Salesian order. In an earlier episcopal letter the Haitian bishops, in an obvious reference to Aristide's popularity, had decried a ''people's church'' opposed to the hierarchical church and accused him of inciting the poor to violence.

The events at St. Jean Bosco inspired a curious turn of events. Out of the ashes of the church arose Haiti's first democratically elected president. On December 15, 1990, Aristide was elected with over 67 percent of the vote. A coup attempt in January 1991 by Duvalierist forces almost prevented his inauguration. Moreover, the events increased tension with the hierarchy and the Vatican. During protests in Port-au-Prince in favor of the president-elect, the papal nuncio's residence was attacked. Nonetheless, Aristide was inaugurated and presided over the government for eight months, initiating efforts to reestablish peace, protect rights, and aid the poor. On September 30, 1991, a military coup overthrew the government and President Aristide was forced into exile.

Catholic cathedral, Port-au-Prince, Republic of Haiti, Hispaniola Island. (©Tony Arruza/CORBIS)

Haitians again suffered severe oppression, including an international trade embargo of the country. Military and paramilitary violence claimed over 4,000 lives. During this period community groups, especially the *Ti Legliz,* were severely repressed. Government infrastructure was totally demolished. Priests, nuns, and lay activists were harassed and arrested. Montfort Father Jean-Marie Vincent was murdered, and Bishop Rornélus of Jérémie was attacked. Despite attacks against the Church by the government, the internal controversy between the hierarchy and Aristide supporters continued.

On October 15, 1994, U.S. government troops landed in Haiti to return President Aristide to power and restore the democratic initiative. The president began the process of rebuilding a government and attempting to build a Haitian economy. U.S. forces remained in control until April 1995 when U.N. troops assumed a peacekeeping role. Aristide's restoration to power reminded Haitians of Bishop Laroche's remarks at the *Te Deum* of the mass at the president's inauguration. The then-president of the Bishops' Conference likened ''cher Père Aristide'' to Moses leading his people out of a desert of suffering. Laicized by the Vatican, Aristide was married in January 1996; by the end of the year he had handed over the reins of government to political colleague and former activist Rene Preval, who was elected by a wide margin with Aristide's support.

The Continuing Catholic Presence. For the most part secular clergy took charge of the Church in Haiti during the 20th century. Among the religious orders working there were Oblates of Mary Immaculate, Holy Cross Fathers, Brothers of the Sacred Heart, Montfort Fathers, and Salesians. By 2000 there were 336 secular clergy, a small portion of them Haitians; 257 religious clergy, 323 teaching brothers, and 1,034 sisters.

In 2000 approximately 65,000 pupils were taught in schools conducted under the auspices of the Catholic Church. Following the example of the state-supported lycées, religious establishments provided for the secondary education of young men in two schools in Port-au-Prince, and one each in Cap-Haïtien, Jérémie, and Port-de-Paix. Sisters of St. Joseph and the Filles de la Sagesse each conducted schools for girls in Port-au-Prince; Sisters of St. Francis of Assisi, in Les Cayes; and Sisters of the Holy Cross, in Cap-Haïtien. Normal schools and primary schools, with support from the state, were also conducted by religious congregations. In addition, Salesians directed schools of arts and crafts, financed by the state, in Port-au-Prince and in Cap-Haïtien.

Improving the Quality of Life. In addition to dealing with language differences, Catholic clergy made several attempts to establish social cooperatives, such as credit unions, which numbered ten by 1970. After the expulsion of the Jesuits in 1964, a Jesuit-owned radio station was operated by the episcopacy as *Radio Soleil.* In 1939 Joseph Le Gouaze, Archbishop of Port-au-Prince, founded the daily *La Phalange,* which operated until it was closed by the government in January 1961. More influential was *L'Action Social,* published by a group of lay Catholics; it stopped publication because of lack of funds. Its place was taken by *Rond-Point,* which was closed down by the government in January 1964.

Religious congregations of women served in nine state hospitals and several private hospitals and clinics. Nursing schools were established in connection with the hospital of Father Riou on Tortuga, with the government hospital in Les Cayes, and with several state-supported homes for the elderly. Despite the efforts of the medical profession, the Church, and the government, the fact that many in Haiti continue to subsist in impoverished conditions resulted in an infant mortality rate of 10.2 percent and an average life expectancy of 48.5 years due to the AIDS epidemic by 2000.

Challenges of the Missionary Church. Even apart from the political vicissitudes that began with the Duvalier takeover in 1957, the Church had obstacles to overcome in developing an active Catholic life throughout Haiti. Inroads were made by fostering native vocations and by using Créole for religious instruction. During the second half of the 20th century concubinage still persisted among the peasant class, partly because of the social situation, partly because of economics, and partly because of the shortage of clergy. To remove the social stigma involved in getting these unions regularized, Bishop Collignon organized ''campagnes de mariages,'' which proved quite successful.

Even in the modern world, Haitian freethinkers accepted the practice of voodoo as a ''religion of the race'' and often incorporated a sophisticated version of it into their practice of Catholicism. Missiology demanded that such practices be treated from an ethnological point of view, then combated with both patient catechical work adapted to the level of the people and a living liturgy that takes into account the misery and illness that fosters voodoo.

Although Haiti is officially considered a Roman Catholic nation, the Episcopal, Methodist, and Baptist churches operate long-standing missions. More recently U.S.-based Evangelical and Pentecostal groups have grown significantly. Certain Protestant sects recognized from the beginning of their penetration of Haiti the importance of native recruitment and medical dispensaries as well as an evangelical appeal. Their success is a result of that knowledge: in 1915 there were only 12,000 Protestants, but in 1949 there were 127,000 and by the mid-1960s approximately 400,000.

Beginning the Next Millennium. Entering the 21st century Haiti's future remained uncertain: poverty, illiteracy, unemployment, an unstable government, the flight of boat people, political obstructions to receipt of much-needed economic aid, and devastation of the environment all loomed as major obstacles. At the local level the Haitian Church continued to be a vital force for positive change.

Bibliography: J. M. SALGADO, *Le Culte africain du Vodou et les baptisés en Haiti* (Rome 1963). J. M. JAN, *Collecta: Pour l'histoire du diocèse du Cap-Haitïen,* v.3 (Port-au-Prince 1958). J. B. ARISTIDE, *In the Parish of the Poor* (Maryknoll NY 1990). CONFERENCE EPISCOPALE D'HAITI, Réponse à quelques questions d'actualité dans l'Eglise d'Haïti (Port-au-Prince 1987); Charte fondamentale de l'Eglise catholique sur la promotion humaine (Port-au-Prince 1983). A. GREENE, *The Catholic Church in Haiti: Political and Social Change* (East Lansing 1993). ''Haiti: Security Compromised,'' Human Rights Watch/America and National Coalition for Haitian Refugees publication (New York and Washington DC 1995). C. POPPEN, ed., *Beyond the Mountains, More Mountains: Haiti Faces the Future,* EPICA Report (Washington

Thousands of Muslims gather in the courtyard of the Great Mosque in Mecca for the ḥajj. (©Bettmann/CORBIS)

DC 1994). J. RIDGEWAY, ed., *The Haiti File: Decoding the Crisis* (Washington DC 1994). A. SYLVESTRE, *Ti Kominote Legliz Yo,* LIV-1, 2, 3, 4, (Port-au-Prince n.d.).

[J. P. HOGAN/J. M. SALGADO/EDS.]

ḤAJJ

The ritual pilgrimage to the holy city of MECCA (Makka), called in Arabic *ḥajj* [cf. Hebrew *ḥāg,* a feast of the Lord, from the verbal root *ḥ-gg* (also *ḥ-w-g*), to circle around]. One of the Five Pillars of Islam, and commanded by the Qur'ān: "Pilgrimage to the House of Allah is a duty owed to Allah for those who find a way thereto" (3.91, 97). According to Islamic law every adult Muslim, who is free and of sound mind, and who is able to afford it, is obliged to make the ḥajj at least once in the lifetime. A man who has made the hajj is known as a hajji, and a woman, a ḥajjah. The present Islamic ḥajj generally combines two ancient Arabian rites, viz, the *'umra* and the ḥajj proper, following a precedent set by the Prophet MUḤAMMAD on his "farewell pilgrimage" in the year A.H. 10 (*see* HIJRA), though it is probable that the two had been previously associated in pagan practice.

The ritual begins with the entrance of the pilgrims into the sacral state of ritual purity (*'iḥrām*), either as they first set out for Mecca or as they enter the sacred area (*al-ḥaram*) and pronounces the *talbiya,* i.e., the formula *labbayka* ["we stand here before You (O Lord)"]. Upon their arrival at the sacred mosque they perform seven times the ritual circumambulation (*ṭawâf*) of the Ka'ba; then, going to Ṣafâ, some 50 yards away they make the *sa'y,* which consists in running seven times from Ṣafâ to Marwa, a small hill not far away, praying at each. This much of the ritual belongs properly to the *'umra.*

Thereafter the hajj proper begins. On the eighth day of dhu l-Ḥijja (the *yawm al-tarwiya*) the pilgrims leave the city for the plain of 'Arafāt where, on the ninth day the rites officially begin with the ritual halt (*wuqūf*) or standing before the Lord, from noon till sunset, while the pilgrims listen to homilies and shout out the *talbiya.* After this they make the *'ifāḍa,* a run to Muzdalifa, which is accomplished with much tumult of shouting, shooting, and music, and is followed by the two evening prayers. On the tenth day (*yawm al-naḥr*) another *wuqūf* is made at the mosque before sunrise. After this the pilgrims depart for Minā, where each throws seven stones at the *jamrat al-'aqaba,* one of three heaps of stones found there.

This symbolic stoning of Satan, with the shouting of the *talbiya,* officially ends the ḥajj. There follows the Great Feast (*al-'īd al-kabīr*) or the Feast of the Morning Sacrifice (*'īd al-'aḍḥā*), which is celebrated as an obligation throughout Islam with the sacrifice of goats and sheep and perhaps a few camels by the wealthy. The pilgrim may then shave his head and put off the *'iḥrām.* During the ensuing three days (*'ayyām al-tašrīq*) the pilgrims stay at Minā where they throw seven stones each afternoon at each gamra of the three.

Originally, it would seem, the *'umra* and the ḥajj were quite distinct, the former a spring festival in the month of Rajab (the seventh month of the Islamic calendar), the latter a feast involving a great common fair at the autumnal equinox. However, because of inadequacies in intercalation, the ḥajj fell during the spring in the time of Muḥammad, the original significance having been lost altogether. Since the rise of Islam, because of the use of a strict lunar calendar, the ḥajj may fall at any season of the year.

Bibliography: D. E. LONG, *The Ḥajj Today: A Survey of the Contemporary Makkah Pilgrimage* (Albany, NY 1979). M. WOLFE, *The Ḥadj: A Pilgrimage to Mecca* (London 1994). F. E. PETERS, *The Ḥajj: The Muslim Pilgrimage to Mecca and the Holy Places* (Princeton, N.J. 1994). M. WOLFE, *One Thousand Roads to Mecca: Ten Centuries of Travelers Writing about the Muslim Pilgrimage* (New York 1997). M. W. HOFMANN, *Journey to Makkah* (Beltsville, Md. 1998).

[R. M. FRANK/EDS.]

HALAKAH

Halakah is the legalistic content of Jewish tradition as distinguished from HAGGADAH, the nonlegal portion that comprises largely homiletical, ethical, and folkloristic material. The term Halakah, from the Hebrew verb *hālak* (to walk), means the way to walk, conduct. In the singular it denotes either an individual law or law in the abstract all-inclusive sense; in the plural (Halakot) it refers to collections of laws.

Jewish law begins with the Torah (Pentateuch), upon which the rabbis of Palestine and Babylonia erected a legal superstructure whose main formulation is the TALMUD. The traditional view is that the Sinaitic revelation of the Written Law was accompanied by an equally authoritative Oral Law, which expanded and clarified its often general statements, and that the rabbis, through interpretation, validated for later generations the sources in the former that authenticated the latter. The modern critical opinion, however, is that, as the Torah became firmly established as the constitution of the Jewish people after the institution of the Second Commonwealth in postexilic times, the rabbis, through interpretation and reinterpretation, fulfilled a need to develop its provisions for a different time and other conditions into specific legislative enactments that would comport with new thinking and new problems, though they generally believed that their understanding of the Biblical text conformed with its original intention.

The efforts of the early rabbinical authorities, the Tannaim, were, after sifting and analysis, compiled (*c.* A.D. 200) by Rabbi JUDAH HA-NASI into a code, the MISHNAH. For the next 300 years it became the vehicle of discussion and instruction in the academies of Palestine and Babylonia, where the later sages, the Amoraim, sought to clarify ambiguities and to harmonize Mishnaic statements with other equally authoritative but seemingly contradictory external traditions contained in the Baraitot. The record of these deliberations is the GEMARAH, which together with the Mishnah forms the Talmud. The Babylonian version of the Talmud is considered more authoritative than the Palestinian one.

Subsequent scholars elucidated the Talmudic tradition through juridical replies to specific questions of law arising from practical cases, and the conclusions form a vast Jewish RESPONSA literature, which continues to the present. But the major achievement was in the area of codification of the Talmud's contents, whose rambling discussions and unindexed material made it as unwieldy for the scholar as it certainly was for the layman. Of the various attempts, the codes of Moses MAIMONIDES (the *Mishneh Torah* of the 12th century) and Joseph CARO (the *Shulḥan Aruk* of the 16th century) were among the most successful, with Caro's work becoming for most traditionalists the authoritative statement of the Halakah.

Bibliography: J. Z. LAUTERBACH, *The Jewish Encyclopedia,* ed. J. SINGER, 13 v. (New York 1901–06) 8:569–572. H. FUCHS, *Universal Jewish Encyclopedia,* 10 v. (New York 1939–44) 5:172–175. S. BIALBOCKI, *Encyclopaedia Judaica: Das Judentum in Geschichte und Gegenwart,* 10 v. (Berlin 1928–34) 7:836–848. H. L. STRACK, *Introduction to the Talmud and Midrash,* tr. 5th Ger. ed. (Philadelphia 1931). A. COHEN, *Everyman's Talmud* (New York 1949). S. B. FREEHOF, *The Responsa Literature* (Philadelphia 1955). L. GINZBERG, *On Jewish Law and Lore* (Philadelphia 1955) 77–124, 153–184.

[R. KRINSKY]

HALF-WAY COVENANT

An important doctrinal development in New England Congregationalism in the 17th and 18th centuries. According to the first New England Congregationalists, a true church was composed of those who, having an experience of salvation, were bound together by a covenant.

To enter church membership the applicant related publicly the story and nature of his experience. All such members were entitled to present their sons and daughters for baptism as children of the covenant. The question arose (*c.* 1650) as to whether these children of the covenant, even though they could not relate a personal experience of conversion, could also present their children for baptism. Many churches permitted them to do so if they were of upright character, gave their intellectual assent to the principles of the Gospel, expressed their willingness to submit to the discipline, and promised to promote the welfare of the church; but they were not admitted to the communion and could neither hold office nor vote for church officers. This practice, usually called the half-way covenant, became a warmly debated issue. A majority representing the churches in the conventions of 1657 and 1662 approved the practice, but a minority dissented and held to the original requirements. Eventually many churches administered baptism to children of parents of worthy life. Early in the 18th century the practice spread of admitting to the Lord's Supper all baptized adults who were not leading scandalous lives in the hope that by coming to the communion they might experience conversion. Solomon Stoddard, long the pastor of the church in Northampton, Mass., and the father-in-law of Jonathan EDWARDS, followed this procedure, and from him the custom spread widely in western Massachusetts and the Connecticut Valley. The GREAT AWAKENING in New England, of which Jonathan Edwards was the outstanding figure, led in many churches to the rejection of the half-way covenant and the renewal of an experience of conversion as a prerequisite to church membership. Here, again, divisions occurred between those who held to the new theology, as that which stemmed from Edwards was called, and the practices that were associated with the half-way covenant.

Bibliography: W. WALKER, *History of the Congregational Churches in the United States of America* (New York 1894) 170–182.

[K. S. LATOURETTE]

HALIFAX, CHARLES LINDLEY WOOD

Second Viscount Halifax, Anglo-Catholic leader who worked for reunion of Catholics and Anglicans; b. London, June 7, 1839; d. Hickleton, England, Jan. 19, 1934. His mother was the daughter of Charles Grey, British prime minister. As a student at Christ Church, Oxford, he developed a great interest in the OXFORD MOVEMENT that remained the chief enthusiasm of his long life. Forsaking a promising political career, he accepted in 1868 the presidency of the English Church Union, a society organized to promote Tractarian principles. Retaining the presidency until his death, except for an 8-year interval, he made the Union a powerful force. Under his talented and courageous leadership, it frustrated the attempts of enemies to defeat TRACTARIANISM in the courts. As a Tractarian he was convinced that ANGLICANISM was, despite aberrations, a part of the historically continous Catholic Church and, as such, the possessor of valid orders. He believed it only a matter of time before the entire Church of England would return to the ANGLO-CATHOLIC tradition. In this sanguine frame of mind and with the encouragement of his friend, the French priest E. F. Portal, he submitted the question of the validity of ANGLICAN ORDERS to Pope Leo XIII. A papal commission, after minute investigation, concluded that the continuity of Anglican orders had been broken at the Reformation. This conclusion, officially embodied in the apostolic letter *APOSTOLICAE CURAE* (1896), was a profound disappointment for Halifax.

Several developments induced Halifax and Portal to renew their efforts for reunion after 1920: the progress made by the Anglo-Catholic party in the Church of England, the great appeal for reunion of all the churches made by the Anglican bishops at the Lambeth Conference in 1920, and finally the warm reception given to their ideas by Cardinal MERCIER at a meeting in 1920. Under Mercier's chairmanship representatives of both communions engaged in the MALINES CONVERSATIONS between 1921 and 1925. These terminated with the deaths of Mercier and Portal in 1926 without producing any definite results.

Bibliography: J. G. LOCKHART, *Charles Lindley, Viscount Halifax*, 2 v. (London 1935–36); *The Dictionary of National Biography from the Earliest Times to 1900*, 63 v. (London 1885–1900) 919–921.

[T. S. BOKENKOTTER]

HALLAHAN, MARGARET MARY

Foundress of the English Congregation of St. Catherine of Siena of the Third Order of St. Dominic; b. London, Jan. 23, 1803; d. Stone, Staffordshire, England, May 11, 1868. She was the only child of poor Irish parents who died when she was nine. She received a rudimentary education during the next two years at an orphanage at Somers Town before entering nearly 30 years of service as a maid and nurse. In the employ of a Catholic family, she went to live in Bruges, Belgium (1827), and there became a Dominican tertiary (1837). After failing in her effort, about 1840, to establish a community of tertiaries at Bruges, she was sent in 1842 to work as a schoolmistress under William ULLATHORNE, who was then in charge of the Benedictine mission at Coventry, England. In 1844 she began there a new community of tertiaries. Moving to Clifton (1846), she made another foundation in the Potteries (1851). This was transferred to Stone as the novitiate and motherhouse (1853). John Henry NEWMAN, a close friend, preached at the opening of the church (1854). Mother Hallahan's devotion, energy, and administrative ability led her subsequently to found five convents, several schools and orphanages, four churches, and a hospital for incurables. Her motto was "God alone." Her cause for beatification was introduced in 1936, and the diocesan stage was completed in 1957. Her writings were approved in 1963.

Bibliography: T.COOPER, *The Dictionary of National Biography from the Earliest Times to 1900*, 63 v. (London 1885–1900) 8:980. J. GILLOW, *A Literary and Biographical History or Bibliographical Dictionary of the English Catholics from 1534 to the Present Time*, 5 v. (London-New York 1885–1902; repr. New York 1961) 3:96–102. A. T. DRANE, *Life of Mother Margaret Mary Hallahan* (new ed. London 1929). F. W. GUMBLEY, *Mother Margaret Hallahan* (London 1938). SR. MARY CATHERINE, *Steward of Souls* (London 1952).

[D. MILBURN]

HALLER, JOHANNES

Historian; b. Keinis (Estonia), Oct. 16, 1865; d. Tübingen, Dec. 24, 1947. He studied at Dorpat, Berlin, and Heidelberg. From 1892 to 1897 Haller worked in Rome at the Institute for Prussian History. Having been professor at Marburg (1902), he went to Giessen in 1904 and in 1913 to Tübingen, where he taught until his death. Early in his career Haller demonstrated a profound knowledge of both medieval and modern European history. He acquired fame with the publication of his *Concilium basiliense* (5 v. Basel 1896–1904). However, his reputation rests on his extraordinary history of the papacy, *Das Papsttum, Idee und Wirklichkeit* (3 v. Stuttgart 1934–45; 2d ed. 5 v. 1950–53). *Das Papsttum* is not so much a history as it is a thorough and nearly exhaustive discussion of the papacy as an institution based upon tradition, theology, and law, strongly polemic, often basing its conclusions on challenging hypotheses. In addition Haller wrote *Die Epochen der deutschen Geschichte* (Stuttgart 1923), a provocative work in which he discussed the major epochs of German history. In the later years of his career he turned his attention toward papal officials and decretals, showing their influence upon the history of medieval Germany.

Bibliography: BÄUMER, *Lexikon für Theologie und Kirche*, ed. J. HOFER and K. RAHNER, 10 v. (2d, new ed. Freiburg 1957–65) 4:1334–35. H. DANNENBAUER and J. HALLER, *Das Papsttum*, 5 v. (2d, rev. ed. Stuttgart 1950–53) 5:409–417.

[B. F. SCHERER]

HALLER, LEONHARD

Theologian; b. Denkendorf, Germany, early 16th century; d. Eichstätt, March 23, 1570. He was engaged in the pastoral ministry at Munich in 1533. Shortly afterward he went to Eichstätt, where he distinguished himself as a preacher and served in several posts. In 1540 he was named auxiliary to Moritz von Hutten, Bishop of Eichstätt. Later he served as vicar-general of the diocese under Bp. Martin von Schaumberg. From July 16, 1562, until July 15, 1563, he represented Bishop von Schaumberg at the Council of Trent. At this time the council was considering the possibility of acceding to the demands of Luther to the extent of allowing reception of COMMUNION under both species. Haller strongly opposed any such concession in Germany, although he confessed that he did this on his own authority, and not as the spokesman of the bishop of Eichstätt. Haller was author of *Grund und Kundschaft aus göttlicher Geschrift und den hl. Vätern dass Fleisch und Blut Christi in der hl. Mess wahrhaftiglich geopfert wird* (Eichstätt 1553).

Bibliography: A. FRANZEN, *Lexikon für Theologie und Kirche*, ed. J. HOFER and K. RAHNER, 10 v. (2d, new ed. Freiburg 1957–65) 4:1335.

[C. R. MEYER]

HALLERSTEIN, AUGUSTIN VON

Jesuit missionary in China and scientist; b. Ljubljana, Yugoslavia, Aug. 27 (or 2, or 18), 1703; d. Beijing, Oct. 29, 1774. After finishing his theological studies in Austria, he embarked for China from Lisbon in 1736. He was sent immediately to the court at Beijing, where his reputation as a mathematician had preceded him. The young Emperor Quianlong quickly became fond of him, appointing him to the Bureau of Astronomy and Mathematics in 1739. He succeeded to the presidency in 1746, the last Jesuit to hold this post made famous by Johann Adam SCHALL and Ferdinand Verbiest. For more than 30 years Hallerstein was continually busy with the astronomical observations and computations so esteemed by the Chinese and so necessary to draw up their yearly cycle of holidays and feasts. Although he especially, even more than other Jesuit scientists at the court, had to endure the frequent interference and intrigues of jealous court mandarins as well as the indifference and vagaries of the fickle Quianlong, his scientific work was so highly valued that it gained tolerance for the preaching of Christianity by his fellow missionaries throughout the provinces of the empire. Hallerstein engaged in correspondence with the leading scientists of Europe, and was elected to the Royal Society of London as a foreign associate.

Bibliography: L. PFISTER, *Notices biographiques et bibliographiques sur les Jésuites de l'ancienne mission de Chine 1552–1773*, 2 v. (Shanghai 1932–34) 2: 753–761. C. TESTORE, C. SOMMERVOGEL et al., *Bibliothèque de la Compagnie de Jésus*, 11 v. (Brussels-Paris 1890–1932) 4:49–52.

[J. H. CAMPANA]

HALLINAN, PAUL

First archbishop of Atlanta; b. Painesville, Ohio, April 8, 1911; d. Atlanta, Georgia, March 27, 1968. After elementary and secondary schooling in his native diocese of Cleveland, he graduated from the University of Notre Dame in 1932 and completed theological studies at St. Mary's Seminary, Cleveland. He was ordained to the priesthood on Feb. 20, 1937. Hallinan's ministry as a priest had a threefold aspect: parochial; military chaplain in World War II with the Army Corps of Engineers (winning at New Guinea the Purple Heart); and 11 years as chaplain to the Catholic students at Western Reserve University, Cleveland. On Oct. 28, 1958, the day of Cardinal Roncalli's election to the papacy, Monsignor Hallinan was ordained bishop of Charleston. Twelve years later he was appointed first archbishop of Atlanta. He was installed on March 29, 1962.

As parish priest, military and student chaplain, bishop and archbishop, and even in the singular status of a bishop-graduate student determined to gain an earned doctorate in spite of multiple distracting duties in his episcopal office (Ph. D. from Western Reserve University, 1963), Hallinan instinctively drew others to him by his kindly and considerate manner, his optimistic outlook, and his smile. This combination of talents and traits, plus a discerning and perceptive mind, enabled him to advance the cause of better race relations in Charleston and Atlanta, promote liturgical renewal following the Second Vatican Council, and foster the ecumenical movement. Less than three weeks after the council's opening, Archbishop Hallinan issued a plea for liturgical renewal, declaring, ''The more we can do to render the Mass understandable to all, not just to those equipped by learning or formed by habit, the more we open new avenues to the minds and hearts of Christians who are not Catholic.''

Bibliography: V. A. YZERMANS, ed., *Days of Hope and Promise: The Writings and Speeches of Paul J. Hallinan, Archbishop of Atlanta* (Collegeville 1973). J. T. ELLIS, ''Archbishop Hallinan: In Memoriam,'' *Thought* 43 (1968) 539–572; *Catholic Historical Review* 54 (1968) 407–409. T. J. SHELLEY, *Paul J. Hallinan: First Archbishop of Atlanta* (Wilmington, Del., 1989).

[J. T. ELLIS]

HALLUM, ROBERT

Bishop; b. Warrington, Lancashire, 1362–70; d. Gottlieben Castle (near Constance), Sept. 4, 1417. Educated at Oxford, he had received his doctorate in Canon Law by 1403, when he became chancellor of the university. In 1407, he was consecrated bishop of Salisbury by Gregory XII in Rome. He attended the Council of PISA (1409). Antipope JOHN XXIII created him cardinal, but Hallum declined when Henry IV objected. Hallum served as president of the English nation at the Council of CONSTANCE where he worked closely with the Emperor SIGISMUND to effect Church unity and reform. He was influential in obtaining John XXIII's suspension and served on a committee investigating charges brought against the deposed antipope BENEDICT XIII. He was buried in the cathedral at Constance.

Bibliography: J. LE NEVE, *Fasti ecclesiae Anglicanae*, ed. T. D. HARDY, 3 v. (Oxford 1854) 2:601. R. L. POOLE, *The Dictionary of National Biography from the Earliest Times to 1900* (London 1908) 8:983–985. H. VON DER HARDT, *Magnum oecumenicum Constantiense concilium*, 7 v. (Frankfurt-Leipzig 1697–1742). J. H. WYLIE, *History of England under Henry the Fourth,* 4 v. (London 1884–98). E. F. JACOB, *Essays in the Counciliar Epoch* (rev. ed. Notre Dame, Ind. 1963). A.B. EMDEN, *A Biographical Register of the Scholars of the University of Cambridge before 1500* (Cambridge, Eng. 1963) 2:854–855.

[J. F. JOLLEY]

HALLVARD VEBJÖRNSSON, ST.

Patron of Oslo; d. near Drammen, Norway, 1043. According to legend, a relative of King OLAF II, he was murdered while trying to defend a woman falsely accused of theft. Soon after his death, his relics were enshrined in Oslo. Besides the Latin legend and fragments of an Old Norse life, a Hallvard sequence also is extant. His cult was not widespread outside Norway, except in Iceland and in the Swedish Diocese of Skara. He appears in medieval Norwegian and Swedish iconography, usually bearing a millstone.

Feast: May 15.

Bibliography: *Monumenta historica Norvegiae,* ed. G. STORM (Oslo 1880). *Heilagra manna sögur,* ed. C. R. UNGER, 2 v. (Oslo 1877) v.1. S. UNDSET, *Saga of Saints,* tr. E. C. RAMSDEN (New York 1934). F. PAASCHE, *Norsk biografisk leksikon* (Oslo 1923–)

''Christ Pantocrator,'' detail of the apse mosaic in the royal church of Monreale, Sicily. Christ's halo with cross superimposed denotes divinity, late 12th century.

5:275–276. A. BUTLER, *The Lives of the Saints,* ed. H. THURSTON and D. ATTWATER, 4 v. (New York 1956) 2:322.

[H. BEKKER-NIELSEN]

HALO

Greek ἅλως, in Christian art a symbol of the moral excellence of the person whom it adorns. It is usually a circle of gold surrounding the head, though at times it is shaped as a triangle or square. Gold is ordinarily employed as most expressive of effulgence. When triangular, the halo designates the Holy Trinity or God the Father; when circular, a saint or (with cross superimposed) Our Lord; when square, a living person. This latter form is not now in common usage, though in ancient iconography it frequently was placed behind the head of the donor portrayed in a fresco or painting. The square was used because in symbolism it represents the earth and temporal things and is inferior to the circle, which expresses eternity and heaven. The triangular, or Trinitarian, halo is often composed of three broad rays of light issuing from the head. The halos of the Blessed Virgin are often elaborately decorated, whereas those of the saints are usually simple gold bands. The blessed, those beatified but not yet canonized, are depicted with a halo less explicit, formed by shafts of light radiating from behind the head.

See Also: AUREOLE (NIMBUS).

Bibliography: H. LECLERCQ, *Dictionnaire d'archéologie chrétienne et de liturgie,* 15 v. (Paris 1907–53) 12.1:1272–1312. G. FERGUSON, *Signs and Symbols in Christian Art* (New York 1959). W. LOWRIE, *Arts in the Early Church* (New York 1947), profusely illustrated.

[C. J. CORCORAN]

HAMANN, JOHANN GEORG

German philosopher of faith and of feeling; b. Königsberg, Aug. 27, 1730; d. Münster in Westphalia, June 21, 1788. Known as the ''wise man (Magus) of the North,'' he was associated with J. G. HERDER and F. H. JACOBI and was a precursor of S. A. KIERKEGAARD. Though a friend of I. KANT, Hamann was opposed to the cult of reason of the *Aufklärung* (*see* ENLIGHTENMENT, PHILOSOPHY OF). To him it seemed that the intellect merely succeeds in dissecting the universe into many unities, whereas in reality all is held together in a vital unity and even opposites are brought together in a coincidence of opposition. Hamann adopted this idea from G. BRUNO. It can be traced back from Bruno to NICHOLAS OF CUSA, but Hamann was no more aware of Cusa than were other philosophers who profited from Cusa's thought. To arrive at this unity, Hamann used a concept of experience different from that of Kant, viz, an experience not based on perception and conceptualization but rather on lived experience and intuition, on faith and devotion. The ABSOLUTE, in particular, is accessible only to faith. Man must live in God if he would find Him and the truth. Philosophy must not be directed to intellectual knowledge; rather, wisdom must lead one to see what the wise men from the East saw in the star; hence the title ''Magus of the North.'' Hamann's philosophy can be regarded as a reaction against the rationalism of the Enlightenment, his theology as the foundation of the theology of the irrational (F. D. E. SCHLEIERMACHER, A. RITSCHL), and his literary efforts as a manifestation of the *Sturm und Drang* period. Finally, Hamann's thought was rooted in Lutheran religious sentiment, for which reason G. W. F. HEGEL regarded him as a true Christian philosopher. He was, however, also influenced by D. HUME and Lord Shaftesbury. Whether one sees in Hamann a mystic or a pietist depends on one's definitions; he certainly was not a mystic in the sense of Meister ECKHART and J. TAULER. Perhaps he can be regarded as a proponent of sin mysticism, for he was basically conscious of the ''unclean spirit'' of man in the sense of the Lutheran doctrine of original sin. While he was aware that man is affected in matters of sex, his teaching does not entail a ''philosophy of the Mystical Body of Christ with sex at its center'' (J. Nadler). There is merit in his philosophy of language: reason is language; sense and spirit come together in the word; philosophy is the grammar of the meaning-filled word. To understand Hamann one must read his correspondence, as well as his works; studies of his thought are sometimes colored by the enthusiasm of his followers.

Bibliography: *Sämtliche Werke: Historisch-kritische Ausgabe,* ed. J. NADLER, 6 v. (Vienna 1949–57); *Briefwechsel,* ed. W. ZIESEMER and A. HENKEL, 7 v. (Wiesbaden 1955–), 4 v. to date. Literature. F. C. COPLESTON, *History of Philosophy* (Westminster MD 1946–63) v.6. F. BLANKE and L. SCHREINER, *J. G. Hamanns Hauptschriften erklärt* (Gütersloh 1956–). J. NADLER, *J. G. Hamann: Der Zeuge des Corpus mysticum* (Salzburg 1949). J. C. O'FLAHERTY, *Unity and Language: A Study in the Philosophy of J. G. Hamann* (Chapel Hill, N.C. 1952). ''Hamann in America,'' *Hamann News-Letter* (Winston-Salem, N.C. 1962). H. A. SALMONY, *J. G. Hamanns metakritische Philosophie,* v.1, *Einführung in de metakritische Philosophie* (Zollikon 1958). R. G. SMITH, *J. G. Hamann: A Study in Christian Existence, with Selections from His Writings* (New York 1960). M. SEILS, *Wirklichkeit und Wort bei J. G. Hamann* (Stuttgart 1961). R. KNOLL, *J. G. Hamann und F. H. Jacobi* (Heidelberg 1963).

[J. HIRSCHBERGER]

HAMBLEY, JOHN, BL.

Priest, martyr; b. *c.* 1560 at St. Mabyn, Bodmin, Cornwall, England; d. July 20 (?), 1587, hanged, drawn, and quartered at Salisbury. He was a Protestant who was converted by reading one of Fr. Persons' books in 1582. He took up seminary studies at Rheims, and was ordained at Laon (Sept. 22, 1584). The following year he returned home and worked in the Western Counties. On his way to witness a wedding, he was betrayed and captured around Easter 1586. He was tried and condemned at Taunton, but saved his life for the moment by denying his faith, then managed to break prison, and fled to Salisbury. The following August, however, Hambley was found during a methodical search of Catholic homes on the eve of the Assumption. Again his resolve wavered; he offered conformity and the names of most of his Catholic friends, and was released. Around Easter 1587 he was apprehended a third time and pledged conformity, but recovered quickly, confessed his faith, and suffered ''manfully, and inveighing much against his former fault.'' In this final test, encouragement came from his fellow inmate, Bl. Thomas Pilchard. Hambley was beatified by Pope John Paul II on Nov. 22, 1987 with George Haydock and Companions.

Feast of the English Martyrs: May 4 (England).

See Also: ENGLAND, SCOTLAND, AND WALES, MARTYRS OF.

Bibliography: R. CHALLONER, *Memoirs of Missionary Priests,* ed. J. H. POLLEN (rev. ed. London 1924). J. H. POLLEN, *Acts of English Martyrs* (London 1891). D. DE YEPES, *Historia Particular de la persecución de Inglaterra* (Madrid 1599).

[K. I. RABENSTEIN]

St. John Chrysostom, 12th-century Byzantine mosaic in the Capella Palatina, Palermo, Italy, his halo denoting sainthood.

HAMER, JEAN JÉROME

Cardinal, theologian, Dominican friar; b. June 1, 1916, Brussels, Belgium; d. Dec. 2, 1996, Rome. Upon joining the Order of Preachers in 1934, Hamer took the name of Jérôme and began his studies at the Dominican Studium Generale, La Sarte, at Louvain; he received a doctorate in theology from University of Fribourg, Switzerland. At the beginning of the Second World War he entered the military, and in 1940 spent three months in a prisoner-of-war camp. Following his ordination to the priesthood, Aug. 3, 1941, he continued his theological studies. In 1944 he jointed the faculty of theology at the University of Fribourg; he taught at the Pontifical Angelicum Athenaeum, in Rome (1952–53), and served as rector of the Studium Generale of Saulchoir, France (1956–62). His most influential works from this period were his books *Karl Barth,* a major study of BARTH's dogmatic method, and *The Church Is a Communion,* prompted by Pius XII's encyclical *Mystici corporis.* In 1962 he was appointed secretary general of studies for his order and general assistant for the French Dominican provinces, a position he held till 1966.

Hamer was an expert at the Second Vatican Council for the Secretariat for Christian Unity; in 1966 he was made secretary adjunct for the secretariat, and in 1969 appointed secretary. Shortly after the council he published a commentary on the declaration *Dignitatis humanae* in *La liberté religieuse* (Paris 1967). In 1973 he was named titular archbishop of Lorium and appointed secretary of

Miniature from a 10th-century manuscript of Egbert, Archbishop of Trier, with square halo, indicating that the subject is a living person, in the Stadtsbibliotek, Trier, Germany.

the Congregation for Doctrine of Faith, receiving his episcopal ordination from Pope Paul VI in Vatican City.

Hamer was appointed pro-prefect of the Congregation for Religious and Secular Institutes in 1984 and was elevated to prefect after being made cardinal deacon, with the deaconry of St. Saba, the following year. He attended several assemblies of the Synod of Bishops, including the first special assembly for Europe (1991), before resigning his prefecture in 1992. He died Dec. 2, 1996, in Rome, and is buried in Rome's Campo Verano Cemetery.

[J. A. DICK]

HAMILTON, PATRICK

Patrick, protomartyr of Scottish Protestantism; b. place unknown, *c.* 1504; d. St. Andrews, Scotland, Feb. 29, 1528. He was a younger son of Sir Patrick Hamilton of Kincavel, Linlithgow. He was intended for the Church, but it is uncertain whether he was ordained. He studied at the University of Paris and graduated there in 1520. He left Paris in 1523 to study at Louvain. Later that year he returned to Scotland and became a student at St. Andrews University. Hamilton, who was early attracted to Lutheranism, came before Beaton, Archbishop of St. Andrews, because of his heterodox views. Beaton caused him to be formally accused of heresy, and to avoid further trouble, Hamilton fled in the spring of 1527 to Wittenburg, where he met Luther and Melanchthon. Later that year he enrolled at the new university of Marburg and became acquainted with Tyndale. In the autumn he returned to St. Andrews, but, because of his unorthodoxy, he again appeared before Beaton, who, however, dealt leniently with him. But Hamilton proved to be recalcitrant, and a further examination by Beaton on articles of faith eventually led to his condemnation and execution by burning.

Bibliography: P. LORIMER, *Precursors of Knox: Or, Memoirs of P. Hamilton . . .* (Edinburgh 1857), a scholarly life. J. KNOX, *The Historie of the Reformation of the Church of Scotland . . .*, ed. D. BUCHANAN, 2 pts. (London 1644). J. FOXE, *Actes and Monuments . . .* (London 1563). J. CUNNINGHAM, *The Church History of Scotland . . .*, 2 v. (2d ed. Edinburgh 1882), old but important.

[J. E. PAUL]

HAMILTON, WILLIAM, SIR

Scottish philosopher; b. Glasgow, March 8, 1788; d. Edinburgh, May 6, 1856. He was educated at the universities of Glasgow, Edinburgh, and Oxford, and called to the Scottish bar in 1813. In 1821 he became professor of civil history at Edinburgh and in 1836 was appointed to the chair of logic and metaphysics. In 1844 he suffered a severe stroke that left him partially paralyzed, but his mind was unaffected and he was able to continue his work until he died. Hamilton contributed three important articles on his philosophy to the *Edinburgh Review;* these he republished in *Discussions on Philosophy and Literature, Education and University Reform* (London-Edinburgh 1852). About 1836 he began his edition of Thomas Reid's *Works,* which he published in 1846 without finishing the ''dissertations'' he planned to include in it. After his death the four volumes of his *Lectures on Metaphysics and Logic* (Edinburgh-Boston 1859–60) were published by two of his disciples, H. L. Mansel (1820–71) and J. Veitch (1829–94). Hamilton was a man of extensive learning but not an original thinker, being too eclectic to be equal to the task of constructing the synthesis for which he was working. The great influence he had during his lifetime was short-lived. It never survived J. S. Mill's *Examination of Sir W. Hamilton's Philosophy* (London 1865).

See Also: SCOTTISH SCHOOL OF COMMON SENSE.

Bibliography: V. MATHIEU, *Enciclopedia filosofica* (Venice-Rome 1957) 2:971–973. S. V. RASMUSSEN, *The Philosophy of Sir William Hamilton* (Copenhagen 1925). J. VEITCH, *Hamilton* (Edinburgh 1882). W. H. S. MONCK, *Sir William Hamilton* (New York 1881).

[E. A. SILLEM]

HAMMURABI (HAMMURAPI), KING OF BABYLON

Sixth king of the first dynasty of Babylon, Hammurabi is famous for having established Bablyon as the political center of the Mesopotamia of his time, for his extensive military and building activities, and for the cultural development of his country, typified by his well-known code of laws. His Amorrite name, more exactly Hammurapi (*Hummu-rāpi',* ''the sun-god heals''), was also borne by several lesser known kings.

To establish the precise dates of Hammurabi's reign, most scholars follow the ''low'' chronology, advocated by W. F. Albright and F. Cornelius, that places Hammurabi's reign from 1728 to 1686 B.C. and the first dynasty of Babylon *c.* 1830 to 1530. Another opinion is that of S. Smith who assigns to Hammurabi the period 1792 to 1750 B.C., but a third opinion, expressed by A. Goetze and B. Landsberger using the ''high'' chronology, has placed Hammurabi in the 19th century B.C.

On his accession, Hammurabi found his country threatened by invasion from both the north and the south. His military effectiveness minimized the challenge from his neighbors and began the Babylonian empire that eventually controlled most of the river plain between the Zagros Mountains and the desert, south to the Persian Gulf, and parts of Elam. Scholars assign the famous staged temple tower or ziggurat E-temen-an-ki, ''The House of the Foundation Platform of Heaven and Earth,'' one of the wonders of the world—to Hammurabi's reign. This giant structure influenced the Biblical author in the narrative of the TOWER OF BABEL (Gn 11.4–9). Hammurabi placed MARDUK, a local deity, at the head of the Babylonian pantheon where he remained throughout subsequent centuries.

Hammurabi is also known for economic policies that stabilized wage scales, fostered trade, and improved the canal systems and river navigation. An important product of his reign was a new burst of cultural activity in science and literature. Progress in algebra was unmatched till the Hellenistic period; astronomical observations resulted in valuable compilations; pseudoscience gave attention to astrology, magic, and similar fields. Concerns about literature raised successful efforts to preserve and standardize the great epics of the past, the GILGAMESH EPIC and the ENUMA ELISH.

One of his greatest accomplishments was the Code of Hammurabi, discovered in 1901 at SUSA and now in the Louvre at Paris. It comprises 51 columns of cuneiform text, incised in black diorite stone, that record almost 300 paragraphs of laws pertaining to business, moral, and social life. This code was a new formulation

Statue of Hammurabi, ca. 1792–1750 B.C. (©Gianni Dagli Orti/CORBIS)

of legal traditions stretching back to the third millennium *B.C.* and can be found in the older codes of Ur-nammu, Lipit-Ishtar, and Eshnunna (*see* LAW, ANCIENT NEAR-EASTERN). The once popular identification of Hammurabi as the Amraphel of Gn 14.1, 9 has gone out of favor with Biblical scholars and linguists. There is no evidence that Hammurabi ever campaigned in the West, nor can the equation of the two names be justified linguistically.

See Also: MESOPOTAMIA, ANCIENT.

Bibliography: C. F. JEAN, *Dictionnaire de la Bible*, suppl. ed. L. PIROT, et al. (Paris 1928–) 3:1379–1408. F. M. T. BÖHL, *King Hammurabi of Babylon in the Setting of His Time* (Amsterdam 1946).

[J. B. HUESMAN]

HANDEL, GEORGE FRIDERIC

Baroque composer noted for his oratorios (German form: Georg Friedrich Händel); b. Halle, Germany, Feb. 23, 1685; d. London, April 14, 1759. He was educated at Halle and originally for the law, but became organist at the Domkirche there (1702–03). After a period in Hamburg, working mostly for the opera (1703–06), and at various towns in Italy (1706–10), he was invited to

George Frideric Handel.

London to compose operas (1710–11). In 1712 he returned to England, where he was naturalized in 1727 and remained till his death, apart from a few visits to the Continent. He held appointments at court (having been *Kapellmeister* to George I when he was still elector of Hanover) and for a time under private patrons, but was chiefly engaged in the production of Italian operas (1712–17, 1720–41) and English oratorios (1732–59) in London. He gave one season (1741–42) in Dublin, where the first performances of *Messiah* took place. Handel was primarily a dramatic composer, as his 25 oratorios (written for the theater, not the church) and 100 Italian cantatas demonstrate as clearly as his 40 operas. His church music, though marked by spaciousness and a sense of occasion, is relatively unimportant. He was brought up and died a Lutheran, but composed for the rites of each country in which he lived: for Lutheran Germany two settings of the Passion story; for Catholic Italy a group of Latin psalms and motets (it has been suggested by J. S. Hall that they formed a set of Vespers for the Carmelite church of Santa Maria di Monte Santo in Rome); for the Anglican Church 25 anthems with English words. Many of these were for special occasions such as the Treaty of Utrecht (1713) and the coronation of George II (1727). One or more of his four coronation anthems have been sung at every British coronation since.

The operas, long forgotten on account of their obsolete convention, have recently been revived with considerable success. The oratorios won Handel a great but ill-founded reputation as a sacred composer, since his music reflected an unmystical quality. Two, *Israel in Egypt* and *Messiah* (the only one given in a sacred building during his life), are settings of Biblical words. The majority, based on Old Testament or Apocryphal stories, scarcely differ in spirit or design from similar works (*Semele, Hercules*) in the tradition of Greek tragedy. This tradition he inherited through RACINE, whose plays formed the basis of his first English oratorio (*Esther*) and first masterpiece in the form (*Athalia*). Handel used the chorus in the Greek manner, particularly to draw out the action's moral; this, together with the splendor and variety of the choral counterpoint, gives the oratorios an extra dimension not possible within current operatic conventions. Nevertheless, *Esther* was written with stage action in mind and was so performed. Only a ban by the bishop of London (1732) prevented its transference thus to the opera house. This initiated the tradition of performance in the theater without action, eventually confined to Lent. Even *Messiah,* as the compiler of the text said, was an ''entertainment,'' designed to recall the audience to the limitations and duties of mortality. Handel's spirit speaks clearly through his art; his sympathy embraces the entire human race.

Bibliography: G. F. HANDEL, *Hallische Händel-Ausgabe,* ed. M. SCHNEIDER and R. STEGLICH (Kassel 1955–), 4 ser. in 12 v. pub. to date; *The Sacred Oratorios,* 2 v. (London 1799). R. A. STREATFEILD, *Handel* (2d ed. New York 1964). W. DEAN, *Handel's Dramatic Oratorios and Masques* (New York 1959). G. E. H. ABRAHAM, *Handel: A Symposium* (New York 1954), broad, inclusive study. F. CHRYSANDER, *G. F. Händel,* 3 v. (Leipzig 1858–67). O. E. DEUTSCH, *Handel: A Documentary Biography* (New York 1955). J. MÜLLER-BLATTAU and W. SCHMIEDER, *Die Musik in Geschichte und Gegenwart,* ed. F. BLUME (Kassel-Basel 1949–) 5:1229–86. J. S. HALL, ''Handel among the Carmelites,'' *Dublin Review* 233 (1959–60) 121–131. S. GODDARD, *Grove's Dictionary of Music and Musicians,* ed. E. BLOM, 9 v. (5th ed. London 1954) 4:37–59. J. M. COOPERSMITH, *I. An Investigation of Georg Friedrich Händel's Orchestral Style. II. A Thematic Index of the Complete Works of Georg Friedrich Händel* (Doctoral diss. unpub. Harvard 1932). P. M. YOUNG, *The Choral Tradition* (New York 1962). *Georg Friedrich Händels Werke,* ed. F. CHRYSANDER, 96 v. (Leipzig 1858–94, 1902). M. CHANNON, ''Handel's Early Performances of *Judas Maccabaeus:* Some New Evidence and Interpretations,'' *Music and Letters* 77 (1996) 499–526. G. CUMMINGS, ''Handel's Compositional Methods in His London Operas of the 1730s, and the Unusual Case of *Poro, Rè dell'Indie* (1731),'' *Music and Letters* 79 (1998) 346–367. R. G. KING, ''Classical History and Handel's *Alessandro,*'' *Music and Letters* 77 (1996) 34–63. S. C. LARUE, *Handel and His Singers: The Creation of the Royal Academy Operas, 1720–1728* (Oxford 1995). H. J. MARX, ''Ein Beitrag Händels zur Accademia Ottoboniana in Rom,'' *Hamburger Jahrbuch für Musikwissenschaft* 1 (1975) 69–86. K. NOTT, '''Heroick Vertue': Handel and Morell's *Jephtha* in the Light of Eighteenth-Century Biblical Commentary and Other Sources,'' *Music and Letters* 77

(1996) 194–208. J. A. SADIE, ''Handel: In Pursuit of the Viol,'' *Chelys* 14 (1985) 3–24. J. E. SAWYER, ''Irony and Borrowing in Handel's *Agrippina,*'' *Music and Letters* 80 (1999) 531–559. R. SMITH, *Handel's Oratorios and Eighteenth-Century Thought* (Cambridge, Eng. 1995).

[W. DEAN]

HANDMAIDS OF CHARITY

A religious congregation (Ancillae a Caritate) founded in 1840 in Brescia, Italy, by St. Maria Crocifissa DI ROSA, with Monsignor Faustino Pinzoni and Gabriella Echenos Bornati as cofounders. Approval by the Holy See came in 1847 and 1921. Members take simple perpetual vows and are active mainly in educational and hospital work. During the first few decades after their foundation the Handmaids worked in hospitals in Brescia, Cremona, Mantua, Udine, Trieste, and elsewhere in that region and ran schools in Ragusa and Spalato (Split) in Dalmatia. In 1848 and 1849 the sisters aided the sick and wounded in hospitals and battlefields in northern Italy. The congregation survived the hostility of the government during the early years of the kingdom of Italy.

Bibliography: L. FOSSATI, *Beata Maria Crocifissa di Rosa* (Brescia 1940); *Storia della Congregazione durante il governo di Madre Teresa Pochetti,* v.2 (Brescia 1958) 415–508.

[L. FOSSATI/EDS.]

HANDMAIDS OF THE BLESSED SACRAMENT AND OF CHARITY, SISTERS ADORERS

A religious congregation with papal approval (1859, 1866), whose official title is Instituto de Hermanas Adoratrices Esclavas del Santísimo Sacramento y de la Caridad (AESC). The foundress, St. María DESMAISIÈRES, began her work in Madrid *c.* 1850 by establishing a home for the rehabilitation of the wayward girls with whom she had come into contact through her charitable work in the San Juan de Dios hospital. She founded her congregation to educate and assist them. In the homes established in several Spanish cities her sisters cared for young women between the ages of 14 and 25. As a complement to this work, the sisters established also workshops or trade schools where the girls, after their rehabilitation, might continue to live. Following a period of spiritual formation, they could be admitted to a kind of semireligious life with private vows, and were then called Mínimas de Santa María Miguela del Santísimo Sacramento.

The Handmaids are engaged also in the education of children. In addition to those sisters who devote themselves to the adoration of the Blessed Sacrament and to the works of the congregation, there are coadjutor sisters who do domestic work in the convents. The congregation is active especially in Spain, Portugal, Italy, Argentina, Chile, Bolivia, Venezuela, Colombia, and Japan.

[A. J. ENNIS/EDS.]

HANDMAIDS OF THE SACRED HEART OF JESUS

A religious congregation, Ancillae Sacri Cordis Jesu (ACJ, Official Catholic Directory #1870), with papal approval (1887, 1894), founded in 1877 in Madrid, Spain, by St. Rafaela PORRAS Y AYLLÓN and her sister Dolores. The Handmaids devote themselves to prayer of reparation before the exposed Blessed Sacrament and to various apostolic works. They are also engaged in works relating to education, catechetics, retreats, chaplaincies, and parochial and diocesan ministries. The generalate is in Rome; the United States provincialate is in Haverford, Pennsylvania.

[A. J. ENNIS/EDS.]

HANEBERG, DANIEL BONIFATIUS

Orientalist, Biblical scholar, abbot, and bishop; b. Lenzfried, near Kempten, Bavaria, June 16, 1816; d. Speyer, Rhine Palatinate, May 31, 1876. After his seminary studies at the University of Munich, where he came under the influence of J. J. I. von DÖLLINGER, he was ordained in 1839. During his student years he learned most of the Semitic languages. From 1841 to 1872 he taught OT and Oriental studies at the University of Munich. In 1850 he entered the Benedictine Abbey of St. Boniface in Munich and in 1854 was elected its abbot. Meanwhile he maintained his teaching post and his ties with the German intellectuals, particularly Döllinger, C. M. Brentano, J. J. von GÖRRES's circle, and the Bavarian royal family. Opposed at first to the definition of papal infallibility, he accepted it after VATICAN COUNCIL I. Although he had refused the bishoprics of Trier (1864), Cologne (1865), and Eichstätt (1866), he consented to be consecrated bishop of Speyer (1872). A deeply religious and zealous man, he hastened his death by overwork in his pastoral duties as bishop.

Haneberg is remembered mostly for his theory that the subsequent approbation of the Church constitutes the inspired nature of the books of the Bible, a doctrine that he repudiated after it was condemned by Vatican Council I. He should be remembered rather for his many scholarly works on Biblical and Oriental subjects, among them *Die religiösen Altertümer der Bibel* (Munich 1844, 2d ed. 1869), *Geschichte der biblischen Offenbarung* (Regensburg 1850, 4th ed. 1876), and his edition and Latin translation of the *Canones S. Hippolyti arabice* (Munich 1870).

Bibliography: J. TRINQUET, *Catholicisme* 5:506–507. H. LANG, *Lexikon für Theologie und Kirche*, ed. J. HOFER and K. RAHNER, 10 v. (2d, new ed. Freiburg 1957–65) (1966) 4:1351. P. FUNK, *Lexikon für Theologie und Kirche*, ed. M. BUCHBERGER, 10 v. (Freiburg 1930–38) 4:815–816. S. FURLANI and F. E. GIGOT, *The Catholic Encyclopedia*, ed. C. G. HERBERMANN et al., 16 v. (New York 1907–14; suppl. 1922) 7:127–128.

[M. STRANGE]

HANNA, EDWARD JOSEPH

Archbishop of San Francisco, Calif., scholar, civic leader; b. July 21, 1860, Rochester, New York; d. July 10, 1944, Rome, Italy. He was the first child of Edward Hanna and Anne Clark, both Irish immigrants from Ulster. In 1879 he graduated from the Rochester Free Academy, where he was friends with the future promoter of the ''social gospel,'' Walter RAUSCHENBUSCH. He entered the Urban College in Rome that same year, was ordained at St. John Lateran in 1885, and was awarded a doctorate in sacred theology in 1886 without the need for examination, so impressed was Pope Leo XIII with his academic brilliance.

Hanna returned to Rochester in 1887 and was assigned to St. Andrew's Preparatory School. When the diocese's new seminary, St. Bernard's, opened in 1893 he took up the position of professor of dogmatics. He was a beloved teacher and became an internationally known scholar through contributions to leading journals. In 1907 he was the primary candidate for coadjutor bishop of SAN FRANCISCO, having received the support of his own ordinary, Bernard MCQUAID, and that of the archbishop of San Francisco, Patrick RIORDAN, but accusations of Modernism in his writings—arising most strongly from a series, ''The Human Knowledge of Christ,'' in the *New York Review*; an essay, ''Some Recent Books on Catholic Theology,'' printed in *The American Journal of Theology*; and an entry, ''Absolution,'' in the first edition of the *Catholic Encyclopedia*—delayed his appointment until Dec. 4, 1912 when he was consecrated as auxiliary to Riordan.

Almost immediately after his arrival in the city, and especially after his appointment as archbishop in July 1915, Hanna became well known in the civic arena on city, state, and national levels. He was one of the founding members of the Commission of Immigration and Housing of California, beginning in 1913, and served as president from 1923 to 1935. Noted in the city for his fairness, he was appointed chairman of the Impartial Wage Arbitration Board, which set pay rates from crafts in San Francisco between 1921 and 1923. Between 1931 and 1932 he served as chairman of the California State Unemployment Commission, which sought to gain people employment during the dark days of the Great Depression. In the spring of 1934, at the request of President Franklin Roosevelt, Hanna led a team that negotiated an end to a dock strike that had paralyzed the west coast. His civic presence was noted through his reception in 1922 of the ''Commander of the Crown of Italy'' in recognition for his services toward and sympathy for the people of Italy, especially immigrants, and in 1932 the American Hebrew Medal, for his promotion of understanding between Christians and Jews.

Hanna was equally well respected in Church circles. On the national level he was the founding chairman of the Administrative Committee of the National Catholic Welfare Council, serving from 1919 to his retirement in 1935. During this period he was highly influential in assuring that the Church's view was heard and appreciated in several national issues, including the Oregon School case of 1922, the national immigration acts of 1921 and 1924, the political instability and persecution of the Church in Mexico during the 1920s and 1930s, and the question of American recognition of the Soviet Union in 1933. On March 2, 1935 Hanna resigned as archbishop and retired to a villa outside Rome where he died. His remains were returned to San Francisco in 1947.

Bibliography: R. MCNAMARA, ''Archbishop Hanna, Rochesterian,'' *Rochester History* 25, no. 2 (April 1963): 1–23. J. P. GAFFEY, *Citizen of No Mean City: Archbishop Patrick Riordan of San Francisco (1841–1914)* (Wilmington, N.C. 1976), 275–318. R. GRIBBLE, ''Church, State, and the American Immigrant: The Multiple Contributions of Archbishop Edward J. Hanna,'' *U.S. Catholic Historian* 16, no. 4 (Fall 1998): 1–18; *Catholicism and the San Francisco Labor Movement, 1896–1921* (Lewiston, N.Y. 1993), 119–49, 163–67.

[R. GRIBBLE]

HANNIBALDUS DE HANNIBALDIS

Dominican theologian and cardinal; b. Rome; d. Orvieto, 1272. He was a nephew of Cardinal Richard (1239–74), and entered the Dominican Order at Santa Sabina, Rome. He later studied theology under St. THOMAS AQUINAS at Saint-Jacques in Paris. There he lectured on the *Sentences* (1258–60) and succeeded Thomas as master in the chair for foreign Dominicans (1260–62). His commentary on the *Sentences,* formerly attributed to Aquinas, is one of the earliest expressions of THOMISM, although it includes excerpts from Peter of Tarentaise (Pope INNOCENT V) and St. BONAVENTURE. Returning to Italy, he was created cardinal priest in December 1262 by URBAN IV and given the titular church of the Twelve Apostles. In 1265 he was legate of CLEMENT IV to support the claims of Charles I of Anjou. After the death of Urban IV, Aquinas dedicated the last three books of the *Catena aurea* (1265–68) to his former disciple, who lived to take part in the election of GREGORY X.

Bibliography: J. QUÉTIF and J. ÉCHARD, *Scriptores Ordinis Praedicatorum,* 5 v. (Paris 1719–23) 1.1:261–262. P. GLORIEUX, *Répertoire des maîtres en théologie de Paris au XIII*[e] *siècle* (Paris 1933–34) 1:117. G. GIERATHS, *Lexikon für Theologie und Kirche,* ed. J. HOFER and K. RAHNER, 10 v. (2d new ed. Freiburg 1957–65) 4:1352. A. DUVAL, *Catholicisme* 1:597. F. DU CHESNE, *Histoire de tous les cardinaux français,* 2 v. (Paris 1660) 2:277–278. M. GRABMANN, *Mittelalterliches Geistesleben,* 3 v. (Munich 1925–56) 3:283, 291, 296–299.

[P. GLORIEUX]

HANSE, EVERARD, BL.

Priest, martyr; b. Northamptonshire, England; d. hanged, drawn, and quartered at Tyburn (London), July 31, 1581. The Cambridge-educated Everard Hanse rejected the attempts of his brother William, who had been ordained in 1579, to convert him to Catholicism. Nevertheless, he came to an understanding of the truths of the Faith upon reflection during an illness. Upon his recovery he completed seminary studies at Rheims (1580–81) and was ordained. Shortly after his return to England, he was apprehended while visiting Catholics imprisoned in the Marshalsea because his foreign-made shoes roused the suspicion of the jailer. He was questioned and admitted his priesthood, which was not yet a capital crime. Nevertheless, he was held for closer examination. During his indictment he was tricked into denying the royal supremacy in spiritual matters and admitting that ''I would have all to believe the Catholic faith as I do.'' He was found guilty of persuasion to popery, which was high treason under Elizabeth, sentenced, and executed. Afterwards the Spanish ambassador wrote, ''Two nights after his death, there was not a particle of earth on which his blood had been shed, which had not been carried off as a relic.'' He was beatified by Pope Leo XIII on Dec. 9, 1886.

Feast of the English Martyrs: May 4 (England); July 30 (Diocese of Northampton).

See Also: ENGLAND, SCOTLAND, AND WALES, MARTYRS OF.

Bibliography: B. CAMM, ed., *Lives of the English Martyrs,* (New York 1904–05), II, 249–65. R. CHALLONER, *Memoirs of Missionary Priests,* ed. J. H. POLLEN (rev. ed. London 1924; repr. Farnborough 1969). J. H. POLLEN, *Acts of English Martyrs* (London 1891); ed., *Briefe Historie of the Glorious Martyrdom of Twelve Reverend Priests* (1582; London, 1908), 98–106.

[K. I. RABENSTEIN]

HANTHALER, CHRYSOSTOMUS (JOHANNES ADAM)

Cistercian historian; b. Mehrnbach bei Ried, Austria, Jan. 14, 1690; d. Lilienfeld, Sept. 2, 1754. He joined the Cistercian community of Lilienfeld in 1716 and subsequently studied at the University of Vienna. There he developed an interest in medieval history, numismatics, and genealogy. He returned to Lilienfeld, became librarian, and dedicated his life to the collection and publication of historical documents. At his death his works amounted to 24 volumes in folio, although only a fraction of this material was published in his lifetime. In addition to studies in genealogy and numismatics, his chief work was the *Fasti Campililienses* (3 v., Linz 1747–54), a heavily documented history of Austria from the beginnings to 1500. The continuation of the same history was left in manuscript form until it was edited in Vienna in 1818. His patriotism and professional pride induced him to forge several alleged chronicles of early Austrian history, *Notulae anecdotae* (Krems 1742), which, although cleverly composed, were soon exposed as fabrications.

Bibliography: KRONES, *Allgemeine deutsche Biographie* (Leipzig 1875–1910) 10:547–549. F. LOIDL, *Lexikon für Theologie und Kirche,* ed. J. HOFER and K. RAHNER, 10 v. (2d, new ed. Freiburg 1957–65) 5:3–4.

[L. J. LEKAI]

HANXLEDEN, JOHAN ERNST

Jesuit missionary in India; b. Osterkappeln, near Osnabrück (Germany) 1681; d. Palur, India, March 21, 1732. He entered the Jesuits in 1699, volunteered for the East India Mission, and went through his novitiate on the journey. He started from Augsburg on December 8, 1699, in the company of Fathers Weber and Mayer, both of whom died on the voyage. He was an eminent linguist, knowing East Syrian, Malayâlam, and Sanskrit. To Hanxleden and his confrères, Roberto De Nobili and Heinrich ROTH, belongs the credit of having been the pioneers among Europeans in the study of Sanskrit. Hanxleden compiled a Sanskrit-Portuguese and a Malayâlam-Portuguese lexicon. He composed numerous religious poems and songs in Malayâlam. The Carmelite Paulinus a S. Bartholomaeo brought back Hanxleden's manuscripts and made use of part of them. Most of the writings of Hanxleden are preserved only in manuscripts; a few are extant in the Vatican Library and the library of the University of Coimbra.

Bibliography: A. M. MUNDADAN, ''An 'unknown' Oriental scholar: Ernst Hanxleden,'' *Indian Church History Review* 23 (1989) 39-63.

[J. WICKI]

HAOMA

The sacrificial liquor made of the juice of a plant pounded in a mortar in the course of the principal Parsee or Mazdaean ceremony, during which it was offered and consumed. It was also a god. Sacrifices were offered to this god, and certain parts of the victim were reserved for him. Although a god, he was killed as he was crushed. The *Brāhmanas* in India describe *Soma* in the same way: ''For Soma is a god and they kill him as they press him.'' The sacrifice of Haoma is, therefore, that of a dying god offered to a god. If one recalls that, after the offering, the priest and the faithful swallow the victim and, thereby, partake of the god's immortality, the sacrifice may seem to resemble Catholic Mass. However, the Mazdaean and the Catholic concepts are essentially different. The sacrifice of the Mass, which is the very center of the Catholic liturgy, is hardly surmised in the Mazdaean ritual, which is not based on an historical fact, such as the Crucifixion of Jesus.

Bibliography: J. DUCHESNE-GUILLEMIN, *La Religion de l'Iran ancien* (Paris 1962).

[J. DUCHESNE-GUILLEMIN]

HAPPINESS

Happiness, or beatitude, is the personal possession of a desirable GOOD, ultimately the perfect good of an intellectual nature. Accordingly, God, the sovereign uncreated good, is happiness itself. Inasmuch as creatures participate in the perfect good, they possess created happiness under various forms and in different degrees. Happiness may be considered objectively or subjectively. The good that is capable of giving a person his ultimate perfection by fulfilling his every need is called objective happiness; this is God alone, who by His infinite goodness can satisfy creatures (*see* GOOD, THE SUPREME). The actual perfection experienced by the person through a realization of his potentialities is subjective beatitude; it is the possession of the desirable object. When this actualization is ultimate, the person possesses perfect subjective happiness; until then, it can only be imperfect. Ultimately, man has but one goal: perfect happiness, which is the full realization of his potentialities through intimate, personal union with God in the BEATIFIC VISION (H. Denzinger, *Enchiridion symbolorum,* 1000). In this life, however, a limited participation in the perfect good through human activity (physical, spiritual, SUPERNATURAL, both individual and social) produces a form of happiness, natural and/or supernatural, that, although imperfect, is a beginning of perfect happiness.

Each type of happiness can be discussed further within a philosophical-theological framework according to the historical development of the concepts. While philosophy has generally considered what object constitutes man's happiness, theology has always asked how a person through his intellectual and voluntary activity truly possesses the sovereign good in the beatific vision.

Objective Happiness. Philosophers have frequently placed objective happiness in the goods of this life: material goods—refined pleasure (the HEDONISM of Aristippus, Helvétius), social prosperity (L. BENTHAM, L. S. MILL, K. MARX); spiritual goods—virtue (STOICISM), human perfection (C. WOLFF, F. SCHLEIERMACHER, W. Wundt); or PROGRESS—cultural-moral (J. FICHTE, I. KANT), political (G. HEGEL), positivistic (A. COMTE, H. SPENCER). Others see the object of happiness in God, the supreme good transcending experience—PLATO, all scholastics, some moderns (e.g., R. DESCARTES, N. MALEBRANCHE), and Christian existentialists [e.g., S. KIERKEGAARD, G. Marcel (*see* EXISTENTIALISM)]. For Aristotle, contemplation terminates the successive types of happiness in this life. The systematic Christian approach to objective happiness begins with St. Augustine, who held that God, the true and sovereign good to be loved for Himself alone, and not merely as the object of philosophic contemplation proposed by Plato and PLOTINUS, is the object of happiness. Arguing from imperfect to perfect good in the realm of essences, BOETHIUS further developed the notion of objective happiness by concluding that God is indivisibly one with goodness, whose possession by participation makes man happy. The Platonic and Neoplatonic notion of the transcendent good (especially in PSEUDO-DIONYSIUS) and the Aristotelian concept of happiness as the last end (sovereign good) in the writings of the Fathers prepared the scholastics, notably Thomas Aquinas, for their systematic approach to happiness: only an infinite being can fully satisfy the spiritual faculties whose object is unlimited being and unlimited good; every other finite good, especially temporal goods, is incomplete. Emphasis on Biblical studies has led some contemporary theologians to return to the eschatological aspects of early patristic writings rather than to the philosophical notions of the scholastics in treating man's last end: the victory of Jesus Christ over death (*see* RESURRECTION OF CHRIST, 2).

Subjective Happiness. The actual possession of God in the beatific vision (perfect subjective happiness of the SUPERNATURAL order) essentially requires acts of both INTELLECT and WILL. Augustine indicates this by considering happiness as a person's perfect knowledge of truth, truly enjoyable (*frui*) through apprehension by LOVE. Applying Platonic notions of beatitude, Pseudo-Dionysius focused attention on intuitive vision: beatitude conceived as objective divinization of the intellectual nature, although some Greek Fathers (e.g., Theodoret of Cyr) were reluctant to state that happiness is the vision of the divine essence. More precisely, the scholastics of the medieval period attempted to determine the formal constituency of happiness as the possession of the soverign good: intellectual vision (Thomas Aquinas); voluntarist love (Duns Scotus); vision and love (F. Suárez). The scholastics also attempted to explain how the souls of the elect behold God directly without any created intermediary: God Himself becomes the intelligible form, effecting what is necessary (e.g., the LIGHT OF GLORY) to let reason enter into the possession of its object. Some mid-20th-century theologians (e.g., R. Troisfontaines, SJ) stress a personalistic viewpoint that true happiness consists in perfect dialogue between God and man, in the I-Thou relationship of Sacred Scripture, in which ''to see'' (vision) means to live in conscious, personal union with divine, angelic, and human persons.

Unending joy, rectitude of will, full appreciation of creatures, expansive FRIENDSHIP and ultimate glorification of the body accompany perfect happiness. While each person possessing God in the beatific vision is completely happy by reason of his full actualization of potentials, the degree of participation in the perfect good differs according to merit.

A purely natural happiness after death consisting in an acquired knowledge of God through created things (i.e., analogously) and a natural love, while speculatively possible, does not in fact exist: it cannot be a true termination of the natural DESIRE TO SEE GOD (the opinion held by many scholastics up to the 17th century). In this life, however, man can possess an imperfect natural felicity through virtuous activity in which temporal and spiritual goods, including friendship, are conditionally necessary. The problem, however, is to explain a purely natural happiness in a supernatural economy of SALVATION. In the supernatural order, the wayfarer actually possesses God, but in a manner proper to his state: operations of the theological VIRTUES, the moral virtues, and the gifts of the HOLY SPIRIT are most perfectly manifested in the BEATITUDES, which produce a happiness that is both terrestrial and a beginning of perfect happiness.

See Also: DESTINY, SUPERNATURAL; ELEVATION OF MAN; HEAVEN (THEOLOGY OF); MAN, 3; PURE NATURE, STATE OF; RESURRECTION OF THE DEAD, 2.

Bibliography: A. GARDEIL, *Dictionnaire de théologie catholique,* ed. A. VACANT et al., 15 v. (Paris 1903–50; Tables générales 1951) 2.1:497–515. R. A. GAUTHIER, *Dictionnaire de spiritualitéascétique et mystique. Doctrine et histoire,* ed. M. VILLER et al. (Paris 1932) 4.2:1660–74. G. SIEWERTH, *Lexikon für Theologie und Kirche*[2], ed. J. HOFER and K. RAHNER, 10 v. (Freiburg 1957–65); suppl. *Das Zweite Vatikanische Konzil: Dokumente und Kommentare,* ed. H. S. BRECHTER et al., pt. 1 (1966) 4:973–976. M. and L. BECQUÉ, *Life after Death,* tr. P. HEPBURNE-SCOTT (New York 1960). J. BUCKLEY, *Man's Last End* (St. Louis 1949). R. GUINDON, *Béatitude et théologie morale chez saint Thomas d'Aquin* (Ottawa 1956). S. M. RAMÍREZ, *De hominis beatitudine,* 3 v. (Madrid 1942–47). Collegium Fratrum Discalceatorum . . . , Salamanca, *Cursus theologicus Summam Theologicam angelici doctoris d. Thomae complectens,* 20 v. (Paris 1870–83) v. 5. A. G. SERTILLANGES, *La Fin dernière ou la béatitude* (Paris 1951). R. TROISFONTAINES, ''Le Ciel,'' *Nouvelle revue théologique* 82 (1960) 225–246.

[T. F. MCMAHON]

HAPSBURG (HABSBURG), HOUSE OF

The Hapsburg family (also the House of Hapsburg-Lorraine, the House of Austria) is the most European of the former ruling dynasties of Europe (it played a role in the history of Germany, Switzerland, the Danubian states, the Lowlands, and the Iberian Peninsula) and the one usually associated with Roman Catholicism and the Holy Roman Empire. Its history as a family is the history of the old dynastic Europe in microcosm; it also furnishes an excellent case study of the impact on European affairs of one biological community with its own set of traditions and possessions. A description of that family history will be followed by a brief discussion of Hapsburg relations with the Catholic Church and an assessment of its contributions to European art and culture.

Origins. Though legend would trace its lineage back to the Trojans and the ancient Romans, the actual origins of the family remain obscure. Guntram the Rich (*c.* 950), who may have been one of the Etichonen of Alsace, a great Carolingian noble clan, is usually regarded as the first historical, rather than legendary, member of the family. His descendants flourished in the southwestern section of Germany, and one of them, Bp. Werner of Strassburg, constructed the Habichtsburg (shortened to Habsburg and meaning the ''hawk's castle'') from which the family would take its name. Though they were far less powerful and prestigious than the great local families such as the Hohenstaufen, the Kyburger, and the Zähringer, an early display of the Hapsburg talent for intermarriage and for survival enabled them to inherit large amounts of territory when those families became extinct.

Engraving of the Hapsburgs' Schonbrunn Palace, Vienna, by Fischer von Erlach, 1721. (©Historical Picture Archive/CORBIS)

The resulting concentration of family property was large enough to be partitioned in the years 1232 to 1238; the senior line also recovered the lands of the junior line (Hapsburg-Laufenburg) when it died out in 1408.

The Hapsburgs' first appearance in European politics took place with the election of Count Rudolph IV of Hapsburg as King Rudolph I (1273). This was the beginning of an almost continuous association between the family and the *Reich*—in the process the Hapsburgs provided the Holy Roman Empire with its rulers from 1273 to 1308 and again from 1438 to its dissolution in 1806 (with the brief interim reign of the Bavarian Wittelsbach, Charles VII, 1742–45). Rudolph hoped to restore the central authority in Germany by establishing his *Hausmacht* (family holdings) in southeastern Germany, where he managed to acquire the Babenberg inheritance, chiefly the duchies of Austria and Styria, for his sons Albert and Rudolph (1278–82), thus establishing a family interest in the Danubian area that was to endure for more than 600 years.

This sudden accretion of power and property was quickly followed by a less glorious chapter in the family's history; Rudolph's heir Albert I was murdered by his nephew John the Parricide in 1308 and the imperial title passed out of the family for nearly a century and a half. In this period of retrenchment the family devoted itself to its Austrian lands and to establishing the customary ties of relationship with the dynasties of eastern Europe.

This growing involvement in the east led to a weakening of the family influence in the area of its origin; the Swiss cantons began to assert themselves against their Hapsburg overlords and in the battles of Morgarten (1315) and Sempach (1386) revealed the superiority of their peasant army over the feudal levies of the Hapsburgs. The reign of Duke Rudolph IV, the ''Founder'' (1358–65), was a brief yet promising exception to the general pattern of decline; he rounded out the Austrian possessions (Carinthia and Carniola had been acquired in this period) by the addition of the Tyrol. In 1364 he signed a treaty of mutual succession with his father-in-law, Charles IV of Luxembourg, which provided that the dynasty that outlived the other would inherit fill its territories—an anticipation of the situation at the end of 1437, when the last Luxembourg emperor, Sigismund, was succeded as king of Bohemia and of Hungary by Albert of Austria, Albert II, as Holy Roman emperor.

The Imperial Hapsburgs. The outlines of the Hapsburg monarchy in central Europe were already discernible, but Albert's death in 1439 in the struggle against the Turks and the establishment of George Podiebrad in Bohemia and Matthias Corvinus in Hungary postponed the real foundation of this state until 1527. Emperor Frederick III (1440–93) found it almost impossible to carry out his political program, but he gave an imperishable expression of his faith in the family's historic mission in the motto A.E.I.O.U., variously rendered as *Austria erit in orbe ultimo* (''Austria will exist at the end of the world'') and *Alles erdreich ist österreich unterthan* (''The whole Earth is subject to Austria''); he also gave imperial sanction to the spurious *Privilegium maius* that the equally hopeful Rudolph IV had used to support a claim to the archducal title and to precedence over the other members of the empire's college of princes. This faith in the future was more than justified by the marriage of Frederick's son Maximilian to Mary, the heiress of Charles the Bold of Burgundy in 1477; family interests gravitated then to dynastic and political involvement in western Europe.

Hapsburg-Valois Rivalry. The house of Austria and Burgundy inherited the traditional Burgundian rivalry with the French Valois, and the life and death struggle of the House of Austria and France remained a basic component of European politics until the middle of the 18th century. Maximilian's innumerable, inimitable plans—he dreamed of creating Austrian and Burgundian kingdoms, of becoming pope, of securing for his family the crowns of Bohemia and Hungary, of reforming and reinvigorating the Holy Roman Empire—often remained plans. Yet at his death (1519) his grandson, Charles, fell heir to the largest single inheritance in European history: Castile and Aragon with the Spanish possessions (in Italy and overseas), the Burgundian lands (chiefly the Netherlands), and the Hapsburg lands in Austria now reunited after a partition that had lasted from 1379 to 1496. The relatively unimportant feudal dynasty in southwestern Germany had progressed to the point where it could lay claim to being the first world empire and becoming possibly a ''universal monarchy'' in Europe.

At this zenith of Hapsburg power the magnitude and the diversity of the problems facing Emperor Charles V and his brother Ferdinand I made another partition of the family properties mandatory: Charles retained Spain, the colonies, and the Netherlands, while Ferdinand received the Austrian lands. (The death of Louis II of Hungary at Mohács in 1526 brought about the union of Austria, Bohemia, and Hungary in Ferdinand's person.) Both men remained loyal to the universalistic conceptions of empire and Church (they could be described as old family traditions at this point) and sought to prevent the spread of the Reformation and the rise of newer political and social forces on the European scene. The common family background and the close personal ties, reinforced by excessive intermarriage, did not obscure the fact that there were two houses of Austria rather than one, as dynastic interests often came into conflict with policies dominated by more localized perspectives: the rivalry with France, the affairs of the empire, the war with the Turks, and concessions to the various estates of a measure of religious freedom.

While Hapsburg Spain was widely regarded as the most powerful state in Europe in the reign of PHILIP II (1556–98), the German Hapsburgs played a secondary role in European affairs; there was a tripartite division of the Austrian lands in 1564 and a protracted period of dissension in the family councils on the ways and means of dealing with the Protestants and the estates, which often represented their interests. Emperor Rudolph II (1576–1612) revealed so little appetite for governing that members of the family combined against him in the Treaty of Vienna (1606) and supported his brother Matthias, who it was hoped would provide more effective leadership. This unattractive quarrel of brothers (*Bruderzwist*) ended with the triumph of Matthias and a renewed sense of self-reliance in the various estates, which profiled from these Hapsburg differences.

The Thirty Years' War. Matthias was succeeded in 1619 by FERDINAND II (1619–37), the head of the Hapsburg Styrian line and an exponent of the Counter Reformation and confessional absolutism. The beginning of the THIRTY YEARS' WAR was followed by the defeat of the Bohemian estates and the ''Winter King'' of Bohemia, Frederick V of the Palatinate, at the battle of the White Mountain (1620). It was a decisive victory for the preservation of the Hapsburg dynasty and Roman Catholicism in the Danubian lands, but although possible at that regional level, it could not be repeated for Germany as a whole, for there the territorial princes (Catholic as well as Protestant) and Germany's powerful neighbors, especially Sweden and France, resisted the effort to improve the position of the emperor and the Catholic Church. In the Peace of WESTPHALIA (1648) the German Hapsburgs had to recognize the existence of a constitutional compromise between the emperor and the princes, the Catholic and the Protestant communions.

The Ottoman Empire and Spanish Succession. Disappointed, the German Hapsburgs turned a large portion of their attention to the war against the Turks and to securing for themselves the inheritance of their childless relative, Charles II of Spain. In the reign of Leopold I (1658–1705) the Turks were decisively defeated at the gates of Vienna (1683) and forced to relinquish their hold on Hungary (1699). A heroic period of Austrian arms under the great leadership of Prince Eugene of Savoy assured the Austrian monarchy a place as one of the great powers of Europe.

These striking successes of the *Althabsburger* (the old-Hapsburgs) were paralleled by the decline of the Spanish monarchy evident in the figures of Philip III (1598–1621), Philip IV (1621–65), and Charles II (1665–1700). In the last decades of the 17th century Europe waited expectantly for the death of the childless Charles: both Leopold I and Louis XIV of France laid claim to the Spanish Hapsburg possessions. His death in 1700 and his will, which bequeathed his possessions intact to Louis XIV's grandson Philip, brought the expected Austrian response in the War of the Spanish Succession (1701–13). European statesmen were not at all anxious to see the Spanish dominions joined to the power of France or of Austria, and when Archduke Charles, the Austrian claimant in Spain, succeeded his brother Joseph I in 1711, the maritime powers pressed for a compromise. In the peace settlement Philip received Spain and the colonies; Charles VI received the Spanish Netherlands, Lombardy, and the Two Sicilies.

The Austrian Succession. The family that had once been so blessed with male heirs now found there was only one surviving male Hapsburg—Emperor Charles VI. In the Pragmatic Sanction (1713) he took steps to ensure the succession of male and female heirs by primogeniture to a single and undivided bloc of family possessions. This family law that was also a decisive moment in the constitutional development of the Austrian monarchy received the official recognition of most of the European states. It did not, however, prevent Frederick II of Prussia from invading and occupying Silesia on the death of Charles VI. His daughter MARIA THERESA found herself required now to fight for the continued existence of the Hapsburg state in the War of the Austrian Succession (1740–48). She had married Francis Stephen of Lorraine in 1736, and their numerous progeny would be formally reckoned members of the House of Hapsburg-Lorraine. Francis had exchanged Lorraine for the Grand Duchy of Tuscany (1738), thus establishing a separate Hapsburg line in Tuscany (1738–1859); a similar arrangement would be made for Modena (Hapsburg-Este).

Austria survived the war weakened by the loss of Silesia but strong in Maria Theresa's determination to revamp its government and to bring its society into line with the more advanced states of western and central Europe. Her reign and those of her two sons, JOSEPH II (1780–90) and Leopold II (1790–92), demonstrated a Hapsburg willingness to carry out basic reforms whether in the pragmatic and moderate manner of the mother or the more radical and precipitate manner of Joseph II.

Austria took a vigorous part in the Seven Years' War (1756–63), and though it failed to win back Silesia, its interests had to be reckoned with in the three later partitions of Poland. The Bukovina was also annexed in 1775 without resistance on the part of the Turks. On the eve of the French Revolution the Austrian monarchy could lay justifiable claim to an enlightened public policy and to Hapsburgs who possessed impressive credentials as "enlightened despots."

The French Revolution and Napoleonic Wars. Reform from above, no matter how well intentioned and judicious, could not long delay the confrontation with the notions of nationality and democracy that were powerful moving forces in the revolution. Leopold I and his son Francis II could do little to save the life of their sister and aunt, Marie Antoinette, but Austrians did fight valiantly to contain the Revolution and NAPOLEON's brilliant effort to establish French hegemony in Europe.

In the face of Napoleon's coronation in 1804, Francis II established the Austrian Empire; a combination of French pressure and his own insensitivity to the old imperial traditions of the family led to his formal abdication of the imperial crown (1806). If Francis marked a new decline in the quality of Hapsburg emperors, his gifted brothers, Archduke Charles, the victor at Aspern, Archduke John, one of the most genuinely popular Hapsburg princes of modern times, and Archduke Joseph, who created an impressive reputation as Palatine of Hungary, revealed that there was a creative response to the needs of the dynasty and its subject peoples.

For a few years (1805–09) Austria appealed to the forces of local patriotism and incipient nationalism in preparing for a showdown with Napoleon; its defeat at his hands in 1809 brought Klemens von Metternich to power and with him a more conservative position in foreign and internal affairs. In 1810 Francis I consented to the marriage of his daughter Maria Louisa to Napoleon; in 1814 in rather different circumstances he played host to one of Europe's most brilliant political and social gatherings, the Congress of Vienna. Austria then became synonymous with the preservation of the *status quo* in Europe, the suppression of the national aspirations of its peoples, and the uninspired bureaucratization of society. Such policy or lack of it could not long delay the confrontation between the new and the old, the principle of national self-determination and the principle of dynastic rule.

The Revolutions of 1848. In the revolutionary year of 1848 the peoples of the Austrian Empire experienced the exhilaration of political freedom and national renaissance; in the first months of that year the future of Hapsburg Austria seemed bleak indeed with the general expectation that it would dissolve into its component parts. The Germans, the Magyars, the Italians, and the Slavs looked to their own interests rather than to that of the preservation of the dynasty and the state machine. But the system was still viable enough to defeat the forces of revolution by sheer force of military power and with the support of the army of Czar NICHOLAS I. In the wake of counterrevolution there was a renewed will to recapture Austria's unity, strength, and prestige, and this was the program with which the young Francis Joseph ascended the throne in December of 1848.

Absolutism, even with a modernizing air about it, was a costly business: the huge army and bureaucracy that it required were burdens on an economy already backward by comparison with western Europe and northern Germany. Austria discovered that her pretensions as a great power were more often than not at variance with the facts; in 1859 she was defeated by France and in 1866 by Prussia and thus effectively removed from any further participation in German and Italian affairs. Francis Joseph was then forced to come to terms with the Hungarians and to concede them a large measure of independence in the compromise (*Ausgleich*) of 1867.

The Balkans and World War I. Deprived of their historic base in Germany and their age-old interest in Italian affairs, the Hapsburgs hoped to discover yet another "Austrian mission" in the Balkans, but this led almost inevitably to a collision with nascent South Slav nationalism and Russian interests in the area. Austrian statesmen and military leaders professed to believe that the status of Austrian relations with Serbia constituted the life and death questions for the dual monarchy of Austria-Hungary. The desire to preserve Austrian prestige as a great power at all costs and to eliminate the source of South Slav irredentism (a disruptive force in Bosnia-Herzegovina, which had been annexed in 1908) helped to bring about the war that would seal the fate of the Austrian monarchy; it was the assassination of a Hapsburg, Archduke Francis Ferdinand, the heir apparent at Sarajevo (June 28, 1914) that touched off World War I.

Growing political difficulties were accompanied by troubling signs in the dynasty itself whose members found it more difficult to imitate the selfless devotion to duty of Emperor Francis Joseph. Archduke Ferdinand Maximilian had allowed himself to become involved in the Mexican adventure of Emperor NAPOLEON III of France and with the substantial French support was proclaimed Emperor Maximilian I of Mexico (1864). When the French troops were withdrawn, he made a quixotic effort to save his throne only to be defeated and captured by the forces of Benito Juárez; he was executed at Querétaro on June 19, 1867. Crown Prince Rudolph took his own life at Mayerling (1889); his mother, the Empress Elizabeth, was the victim of an assassin in 1898. A number of archdukes abandoned their titles to seek anonymity as simple citizens abroad. Even Francis Ferdinand, a most militant supporter of the dynastic traditions, married morganatically.

Francis Joseph in his old age came to be the last surviving link between the peoples, an almost ageless symbol of the political anachronism over which he ruled; his death in November of 1916 removed the system's last important prop. The excessive strain of the war had already weakened it beyond repair, and when his youthful successor, Charles I, sought to secure a peace that would permit the monarchy to continue on more democratic and federalistic lines it was already too late; the people were no longer satisfied with a minimal program of that kind. The defeat of the Central Powers in the autumn of 1918 produced an almost instantaneous fragmentation of the Hapsburg *Hausmacht;* the imperial government in its last days was simply charged with the peaceful transfer of its remaining power to the succession states. On Nov. 11, 1918, Charles I renounced any further participation in state affairs and thus brought the long history of the dynasty's involvement in Danubia to a close. In 1920 he attempted on two occasions to prolong that involvement, in this case in Hungary, but pressures from Hungary's neighbors and the lack of real enthusiasm in the country precluded his success. He was then removed to a more remote place of exile (he had originally gone to Switzerland) in the Madeira Islands, where he died in 1922. Dr. Otto Habsburg-Lothringen, Charles' eldest son, applied to return permanently to Austria as a private citizen, but he was denied by the Austrian government (1965). In 1981 his son and heir, Karl von Habsburg (1961–) became a resident of Salzburg. Memories, pleasant and unpleasant, of Hapsburg rule continue to excite lively political controversy in modern Austria.

The Hapsburgs and the Catholic Church. By the 19th century the Hapsburgs had acquired the reputation of being the most Catholic of all European reigning houses. The historical tie with the triumphs of the COUNTER REFORMATION had left an indelible impression on the European consciousness, and as if to give their own expression to it a special form of Hapsburg piety had evolved, the *Pietas Austriaca,* in which family traditions clustered about the devotion to the Blessed Sacrament, the Holy Cross, and the Immaculate Conception. The presence of members of the dynasty at the annual Corpus Christi procession in Vienna testified to the vitality even in the 20th century of such family traditions. But unquestioned piety and filial loyalty to the pope were usually combined with a refusal to make concessions in disputes with the papacy and to regard its requests as unwarranted interventions of the Roman Curia. Throughout the 17th and 18th centuries Habsburg policy often dominated religious affairs, a tendency that reached its zenith in JOSEPHINISM. The Hapsburgs had inherited a conception of state intervention in religious affairs from the Hohenstaufens, and this played a continuing role in their policy. The Catholic Church undoubtedly owed its survival in Danubia and other parts of Europe to the Hapsburgs, but their great zeal in the cause of Catholic Christianity was not without its unfortunate consequences for the inner life of the Church—all too often the Church was regarded as the spiritual arm of dynastic policy.

The Hapsburg Legacy. In their more than 600 years at the center of European affairs the Hapsburgs had revealed more than political gifts and an instinct for survival; they were often generous patrons of the arts and in the process left imperishable monuments to their unique sense of mission and to the greatness of the artists who worked for them. The palace as the center of a dynastic cult took Hapsburg form in the Escorial and Vienna's Hofburg; the character of a number of European cities—Vienna, Innsbruck, and Prague—owed much to Hapsburg builders. Rudolph II was perhaps the most famed of Hapsburg art collectors, but others were quite as active, and the family collections form the core of the great art museums of Madrid and Vienna. The grandeur of the dynasty attracted the musical genius of the classical period of Viennese music, while the portraits of individual members by Dürer, Titian, and Velásquez are a priceless source for the understanding of the family's character and its role in European culture.

Every family eventually acquires its own tone, a set of characteristic traits physical as well as psychic, and the Hapsburgs were no exception. The most obvious and famous of these was the pronounced ''Hapsburg lip'' that appeared in the course of the 15th century and attained to classic proportions in the physiognomies of the last generations of the original Hapsburg line. There were other qualities, too: a love of music, a passion for hunting, a gift of languages easily acquired that assisted them in the family business of ruling so many different peoples, and a predisposition to mildness (*Clementia Austriaca*). Because a Hapsburg ruler had such a compelling sense of the grace of God that had established his family in such a position of authority he tended to be excessively scrupulous in making decisions and in weighing their moral implications; this provided the family with a reputation for lethargy and procrastination. Since the Holy Roman Empire had been virtually a family monopoly for so many centuries, other dynasties seemed to be recent arrivals even when their claim to recognition was beyond doubt. The Hapsburgs had often followed in the wake of other dynastic achievements and had often been most prominent for their ability to husband their resources and to allow intermarriage to take the place of creative political progams—*Bella gerant alii, tu felix Austria nube* (Other nations make war, you, happy Austria, marry). But there had been great visionaries in the family—Rudolph IV, Maximilian I, Joseph II—and individuals whose fame rested on their mastery of practical politics—Rudolph I, Ferdinand I, and Maria Theresa. Though it often seemed that they had been motivated by dynastic interest rather than ideals, the very quest for power had produced as its legitimate consequence a number of political communities in various parts of Europe, and European nations would find shelter and security under Hapsburg rule. The recent tragic experience of the peoples who once composed the most outstanding of these Hapsburg creations, the Austrian monarchy of Danubia, has encouraged observers to take a more nuanced and positive view of the truly unique Hapsburg achievement.

Bibliography: A. WANDRUSKA, *The House of Habsburg,* tr. C. and H. EPSTEIN (Garden City, N.Y. 1964), with convenient genealogical tables. H. RÖSSLER, and G. FRANZ, *Biographisches Wörterbuch zur deutschen Geschichte* (Munich 1952) 289–296. *Gestalter der Geschichte Österreichs,* ed. H. HANTSCH (Innsbruck 1962). A. CORETH, ''Pietas Austriaca: Wesen und Bedeutung habsburgischer Frömmigkeit in der Barockzeit,'' *Mitteilungen des Österreichischen Staatsarchivs* 7 (1954) 90–119. H. HANTSCH, *Die Geschichte Österreichs,* 2 v. (2nd ed. Graz 1947–53). R. A. KANN, *The Multinational Empire: Nationalism and National Reform in the Hapsburg Monarchy, 1848–1918,* 2 v. (New York 1950). A. J. MAY, *The Hapsburg Monarchy,* 1867–1914 (Cambridge, Mass. 1951). O. JÁSZI, *The Dissolution of the Hapsburg Monarchy* (Chicago 1929). Z. A. B. ZEMAN, *The Breakup of the Hapsburg Empire, 1914–1918* (New York 1961). A. WANDRUSZKA, *Lexicon für Theologie und Kirche,* (Freiburg, 1957–66) 4:1301–02. E. CRANSHAW, *The Habsburgs* (London 1971). R.J. EVANS, *The Making of the Habsburg Monarchy, 1500–1700* (New York 1979). P. FICHTNER, *The Habsburg Empire* (Malabar, Fla. 1997). C. INGRAO, *The Habsburg Monarchy 1618–1815,* 2nd ed. (Cambridge 2000). R. A. KANN, *A History of the Habsburg Empire, 1526–1660* (Ithaca, NY 1971). A. WHEATCROFT, *The Habsburgs* (New York 1995).

[W. B. SLOTTMAN]

HARCOURT, WILLIAM, BL.

Jesuit priest and martyr; *vere* Barrow, *alias* Waring; b. Weeton-cum-Prees, Kirkham, Lancashire, England, *c.*1609; d. hanged, drawn, and quartered at Tyburn (London), June 20, 1679. After completing his studies at the Jesuit college in St-Omer, Flanders, William joined the Society of Jesus at Watten (1632). He was ordained (1641) in Flanders. Upon returning to England (1644), he labored in the environs of London for 35 years. On May 7, 1679, the year after he became superior of the Jesuits in London, Harcourt was arrested and committed to Newgate Prison on the charge of complicity in the fictitious Titus Oates Plot to kill the king. Beginning June 13, 1670, he was tried with fellow Jesuits Thomas WHITBREAD, John FENWICK, John GAVAN, and Antony TUR-

NER. Although their accusers were demonstrably guilty of perjury, Justice Scroggs was determined that the jury convict the priests of high treason. Harcourt's cause was introduced by papal decree (Dec. 4, 1886) under the name of William Harcourt. He was beatified by Pius XI on Dec. 15, 1929.

Feast of the English Martyrs: May 4 (England); Dec. 1 (Jesuits).

See Also: ENGLAND, SCOTLAND, AND WALES, MARTYRS OF.

Bibliography: R. CHALLONER, *Memoirs of Missionary Priests,* ed. J. H. POLLEN (rev. ed. London 1924; repr. Farnborough 1969). J. H. POLLEN, *Acts of English Martyrs* (London 1891). J. N. TYLENDA, *Jesuit Saints & Martyrs* (Chicago 1998) 179–81.

[K. I. RABENSTEIN]

HARDESTY, ROBERT, BL.

Lay martyr; b. in Yorkshire, England; d. Sept. 24, 1589, hanged at York. He was arrested for harboring and aiding a seminary priest, Bl. William SPENSER, with whom he was executed following internment at York Castle. Hardesty was beatified by Pope John Paul II on Nov. 22, 1987 with George Haydock and Companions.

Feast of the English Martyrs: May 4 (England).

See Also: ENGLAND, SCOTLAND, AND WALES, MARTYRS OF.

Bibliography: R. CHALLONER, *Memoirs of Missionary Priests,* ed. J. H. POLLEN (rev. ed. London 1924). J. H. POLLEN, *Acts of English Martyrs* (London 1891).

[K. I. RABENSTEIN]

HARDEY, MARY ALOYSIA, MOTHER

Religious superior; b. Piscataway, MD, Dec. 8, 1809; d. Paris, France, June 17, 1886. Her parents were Frederick William and Sarah (Spalding) Hardey, descendants of colonial Maryland Catholics. The family moved to the South, and Mary Ann grew up with her eight brothers and sisters on the Hardey plantation at Opelousas, La. She was educated at the Convent of the Sacred Heart, Grand Coteau, La., and entered the novitiate there in 1825, taking the name Aloysia. She was professed in 1833 and three years later became superior of the convent at St. Michael's, La. where she met (Bl.) Philippine Duchesne, first missionary of the Society of the Sacred Heart in America. Mother Aloysia left the South in 1841 to begin her work on the Atlantic seaboard as foundress and superior of the first house of her society in New York City. The convent on Houston Street later became Manhattanville College, situated at Purchase, NY, since 1955. She was superior at Manhattanville for 25 years, and in 1844 became superior vicar of all the houses of the society in the eastern states and Canada. To the six foundations that she made in New York, Philadelphia, Pa, Buffalo and Albany, N.Y., Detroit, Mich., and Cincinnati, Ohio, she added two in Canada, Montreal and Halifax, and one in Havana, Cuba. She was appointed (1871) assistant general representing the houses of the British Empire and North America and was stationed (1872) at the motherhouse in Paris. Her office obliged her to travel widely and in the following years she returned several times to North America.

Bibliography: M. A. WILLIAMS, *Second Sowing: The Life of Mary Aloysia Hardey* (New York 1942). L. CALLAN, *The Society of the Sacred Heart in North America* (New York 1937).

[M. M. GREEN]

HARDOUIN, JEAN

Jesuit church historian, numismatist, controversialist, philologist, and librarian; b. Quimper, Brittany, Dec. 22 (23?), 1646; d. Paris, Sept. 3, 1729. Hardouin, the son of a book dealer, was admitted to the Jesuit novitiate, Sept. 25, 1660. At the Collège Louis-le-Grand in Paris he served as librarian and taught rhetoric and then theology (1683–1718). During these years he performed extensive research. In his writings on numismatics, which include *Nummi antiqui populorum et urbium illustrati* (Paris 1684), *Numismata aliquot rariora Augustorum . . .* (Luxembourg 1700), and *Chronologia ex nummis antiquis restituta* (2 v. Paris 1697), Hardouin displayed an industrious scholarship, though his works were not free from errors, and his methods of establishing chronology from the dates on coins were criticized. His skill in linguistic science appears in *Themistii orationes XXXIII* (Paris 1684) and *Plini Secundi historiae naturalis libri XXXVII* (Paris 1685).

Hardouin was associated with the publication of the *Journal de Trévoux,* contributing innumerable articles on Scripture, numismatics, history, and patrology, from its first appearance in 1701 until his death. He also engaged in written polemics, notably with the Oratorian Bernard LAMY, over the date of Christ's last paschal supper, *De supremo Domini paschate* (Paris 1685), and with Pierre François Le Courayer on the validity of Anglican orders, *Le Défense des ordinations anglicanes refuteé par le P. J. Hardouin* (2 v. Paris 1727). His fame rests principally on his history of the councils of the Church, *Conciliorum collectio regia maxima: Acta conciliorum et epistolae decretales, ac constitutiones summorum pontificum* (12 v.

Paris 1714–15). It was based on the 18-volume collection by Philippe LABBE and Gabriel Cossart (Paris 1671–72), which it surpassed; it is also conceded to be richer and more reliable than the later 31-volume collection of Giovanni Domenico MANSI (Venice 1757–98). For this work Hardouin was granted a pension by the Assembly of the French Clergy (1687); Louis XIV assumed the expense of its publication. Though it was printed in 1714–15, its distribution was delayed for ten years by order of the French Parlement after a commission of the Sorbonne found that it contained maxims contrary to Gallican Liberties.

Hardouin was a scholar of great erudition, but he held several convictions that caused amazement. He believed that the Cephas rebuked by Paul was not Peter the Apostle; that Christ and the Apostles preached in Latin; that the Alexandrine and Hebrew versions of the OT and many writings of early Christianity (e.g., FACUNDUS OF HERMIANE, Marius Mercator, parts of JUSTIN MARTYR, CASSIODORUS, and ISIDORE) were not authentic; that the odes of Horace, Vergil's *Aeneid,* the orations of Cicero, and a great number of other classics were fabrications of the 13th century; and that Louis THOMASSIN, Cornelius JANSEN, Antoine ARNAULD, Pasquier QUESNEL, Nicolas MALEBRANCHE, Blaise PASCAL, and René DESCARTES were atheists. The appearance of such theses led to the posthumous condemnation of three of his works by the Inquisition: *J. Hardouini . . . opera selecta* (Amsterdam 1709; condemned April 13, 1739), published without consent of Hardouin; *J. Hardouin . . . opera varia* (Amsterdam 1733; condemned April 13, 1739); *Commentarius in Novum Testamentum . . .* (Amsterdam 1741; condemned July 28, 1742).

Bibliography: G. DUMAS, *Histoire du Journal de Trévoux, depuis 1701 jusqu'en 1762* (Paris 1936). P. C. SOMMERVOGEL, *Table méthodique des Mémoires de Trévoux, 1701–1775,* 3 v. (Paris 1864–65). H. QUENTIN, *Jean-Dominique Mansi et les grandes collections conciliaires* (Paris 1900) 38–54. P. MECH, *Catholicisme* 5:510–511. P. BERNARD, *Dictionnaire de théologie catholique*, ed. A. VACANT et al., 15 v. (Paris 1903–50; Tables Générales 1951–) 6.2:2042–46. F. X. BANTLE, *Lexikon für Theologie und Kirche*, ed. J. HOFER and K. RAHNER, 10 v. (2d, new ed. Freiburg 1957–65) 5:5.

[E. D. MCSHANE]

HARE KRISHNA

The Hare Krishna movement, more formally known as the International Society for Krishna Consciousness (ISKCON), was founded in New York City in 1966, one year after the arrival of its charismatic leader, A. C. Bhaktivedanta Swami Prabhupada, from India. The mission of ISKCON's founder was to gain recognition for his Hindu beliefs, which derived from a tradition originating in Bengal, India. While aligned with orthodox Hinduism, the Krishna Consciousness preached by Swami Prabhupada traces its roots to the Krishna *bhakti* movement founded by Sri Caitanya Mahaprabhu in the 16th century. Their beliefs derive from scripture contained in the Vedas, but the movement's central religious text is the *Bhagavad-Gita*, in which the devotional activity of *bhakti* is first fully detailed. Swami Prabhupada preached to his young followers that love for and devotional service to Krishna (God)—the basis of the *bhakti-yoga* tradition—would lead to spiritual realization. To gain this spiritual fulfillment Krishna devotees are required to take part in a number of religious practices: chanting the Hare Krishna mantra and living an austere lifestyle which avoids meat, intoxicants, illicit sex, and gambling.

The initial growth of the Krishna movement during the late 1960s and early 1970s in America was sustained largely by the involvement of middle-class countercultural youth, who were protesting against the traditional values and socio-political structures of American society. Krishna members have joined ISKCON on the basis of a variety of social, psychological, and religious motivations: a search for spiritual enlightenment, the desire for meaningful primary relations, disenchantment with the materialism of contemporary culture, or an attraction to the Krishna lifestyle. The movement gained considerable notoriety during the 1970s as its members were often seen chanting and distributing religious literature in airports and other public settings. Hare Krishna, branded by the public and the media as one of the major ''cults,'' was thought to subject its members to ''mind control'' and various forms of ''exploitation.''

Reorganization. As the counterculture faded from America and other Western countries, ISKCON's membership pattern changed. At its height in the mid-1970s, ISKCON claimed a membership of approximately 5,000 in North America and 10,000 worldwide. Since that time, ISKCON's full-time membership in North America has declined somewhat. However, it has grown worldwide due to an expanding congregation of as many as several million part-time members, many of whom are East Indians. In the mid-1980s, ISKCON had 200 centers and communities on every continent, with over 70 in North America alone.

Following Swami Prabhupada's death in November of 1977, ISKCON was reorganized politically and spiritually. Eleven of Bhaktivedanta's closest disciples were appointed to serve as gurus, responsible for initiating new members into Krishna Consciousness and for helping to oversee the affairs of the movement's communities worldwide. Within a year following the leader's death, however, ISKCON faced a series of succession problems as the authority and legitimacy of the gurus was challenged by many long-time members. In the 1980s ISKCON faced factionalism, schism, the expulsion or defection of four of the original eleven appointed gurus, and the departure of countless other long-time members from the movement. This stabilized somewhat in the 1990s, as the remaining leaders consolidated the movement.

See Also: NEW RELIGIOUS MOVEMENTS; CULTS; SECT.

Bibliography: A. BURR, *I Am Not My Body: A Study of the International Hare Krishna Sect* (New Delhi 1984). F. DANER, *The American Children of Krishna: A Study of the Hare Krishna Movement* (New York 1976). S. J. GELBERG, *Hare Krishna, Hare Krishna* (New York 1983); ''The Catholic Church and the Hare Krishna Movement: An Invitation to Dialogue,'' *ISKCON Review* 2 (1986) 1–63. S. D. GOSWAMI, *Prabhupada* (Los Angeles 1983). G. JOHNSON, ''The Hare Krishna in San Francisco,'' C. GLOCK and R. BELLAH, eds., *The New Religious Consciousness* (Los Angeles 1976). J. S. JUDAH, *Hare Krishna and the Counterculture* (New York 1974). T. H. POLLING and J. F. KENNY, *The Hare Krishna Character Type: A Study of Sensate Personality* (Lewiston, N.Y. 1986). E. B. ROCHFORD, *Hare Krishna in America* (New Brunswick, N.J. 1985). ''Dialectical Processes in the Development of Hare Krishna: Tension, Public Definition and Strategy,'' D. BROMLEY and P. HAMMOND, eds., *The Future of New Religious Movements* (Macon, Ga. 1987). L. D. SHINN, ''The Many Faces of Krishna,'' J. FICHTER, ed., *Alternatives to American Main-Line Churches* (New York 1983).

[E. B. ROCHFORD, JR./EDS.]

Hare Krishnas, c. 1974. (Archive Photos)

HARENT, ÉTIENNE

Theologian; b. Gex, France, Dec. 25, 1845; d. Dôle, Feb. 5, 1927. He entered the Jesuits in 1864, and later taught dogmatic theology at Meld in 1883, at Lyons in 1899, at Canterbury in 1901, and at Ore-Place-Hastings in 1906. His theological treatises *De vera religione, De fide, De ecclesia, De gratia,* and *De ordine* have been published many times. He published also studies in various reviews, and is especially remembered for the important monographs he wrote on belief, faith, hope, and salvation of the infidels for the *Dictionnaire de théologie catholique,* and for his article on the papacy in the *Dictionnaire apologétique de la foi catholique.* Although Harent is chiefly remembered as a scholastic theologian, he took an interest also in history and religious psychology.

Bibliography: B. SCHNEIDER, *Lexikon für Theologie und Kirche*, ed. J. HOFER and K. RAHNER, 10 v. (2d, new ed. Freiburg 1957–65) 5:6. H. RONDET, *Dictionnaire de théologie catholique*, ed. A. VACANT et al., 15 v. (Paris 1903–50; Tables Générales 1951–) Tables Générales 1:2019.

[L. B. O'NEIL]

HÄRING, BERNARD

Moral theologian; professor; Redemptorist priest; b. Böttingen, Germany, November 10, 1912; d. July 3, 1998. It is commonly acknowledged that Häring had a crucial role in the reshaping of moral theology in the twentieth century. From 1941 to 1945, having been conscripted into the German army, he served as a medical orderly in France, Poland, and Russia. From 1949 to 1953 and from 1957 until his retirement in 1988, he was a professor at the Alphonsian Academy in Rome.

In 1964, Paul VI named a papal commission on birth control, of which Häring was a member. The pope issued the encyclical *Humanae vitae* in 1968. Responding to what he saw as an urgent pastoral need, Häring spoke out on the role of conscience. On other occasions also he expressed controversial views that did not escape the attention of ecclesiastical authorities. However, he was never formally censured.

Häring engaged in a critical discussion with Rudolf OTTO, Max SCHELER, and others. He developed a personalist religious ethic based on experience, feeling, and value, rather than on abstract rational analysis. The role of such an ethic is to evoke dispositions and form character, rather than enunciate principles and deduce norms.

In Häring's place in the history of moral theology depends primarily on his early work, *Das Gesetz Christi* [ET *The Law of Christ* (1961)]. Instead of a legalistic system of precepts and sanctions, Häring offered a Christian moral message founded on the Bible. The moral life is empowered by grace, that is, by a new being in Christ. Moral theology, therefore, must be integrated with a theology of the sacraments as historical events of grace. Biblical leitmotifs provide the vision, and Christian virtues the framework. Although subordinate to the Bible, the NATURAL LAW is still normative. Much of the content of *The Law of Christ* is similar to that of the earlier manuals. What is new is the vision and the openness to dialogue with the secular sciences, sociology, and psychology. The biblical orientation provided an opening for ecumenical dialogue, which the author cultivated assiduously. His medical ethics, rather than solving dilemmas, provided a distinctive theological interpretation of life and death.

A major work, *Free and Faithful in Christ* (1978–81) developed the themes of Christian freedom and the liberty and creativity of CONSCIENCE. In saying that conscience is creative he did not mean that it is autonomous or arbitrary; it is bound by fidelity to Christ. While affirming the historicity of natural law, he rejected relativism. This book contributed to developing and popularizing the idea of the FUNDAMENTAL OPTION. Always alert to contemporary issues, the author discussed the ethics of ecology, the media, and peace. Häring's thinking on peace and war continued to develop. By 1986 he was arguing that we must move toward abandoning the just-war theory and replacing it with an ethic of nonviolence. Responsibility is fundamental. The ''goal-commandment,'' as distinct from a negative limit or mere ideal, expresses a summons to organized action toward an end. ''Reciprocity of consciences'' indicates the way in which Christians ought to seek truth, namely through a community endeavor, governed by mutual respect. Responding to controversy, Häring held that there is an intimate connection rather than a dichotomy between a ''faith-ethic'' and an ''autonomous ethic.'' For him, the deontological dimension of ethics means God's call to a loving response, and the teleological, a movement toward sanctity. Moral theology is to be pastoral, personalist, and communitarian; an embodiment of the healing role of faith rather than a system of control by law.

Bibliography: Häring has published over 80 books and hundreds of articles. The following are some of the more significant: *Das Heilige und das Gute: Religion und Sittlichkeit in ihrem gegenseitigen Bezug* (Krailling/Munich 1950); *Das Gesetz Christi* (Freiburg im Breisgau 1954; 8th. ed. 1967); *The Law of Christ* (Westminster 1961–1966); *Medical Ethics* (Slough 1972); *Ethics of Manipulation: Issues in Medicine, Behavior Control and Genetics* (NewYork 1975; *Free and Faithful in Christ* (New York 1978–1981); *The Healing Power of Peace and Nonviolence* (Mahwah 1986); *No Way Out? Pastoral Care of the Divorced and Remarried* (Slough 1990); *My Witness for the Church* (Mahwah 1992).

[B. V. JOHNSTONE]

HARLAY

According to conflicting sources, the Harlay family originated either from the French-Comté (France) or from England, and was extinguished in 1717; it gave to France several distinguished magistrates and prelates.

Achille de, jurist; b. March 7, 1536; d. Oct. 21, 1619. He succeeded his father, Christopher, as court president of the Parlement of Paris in 1572, becoming in 1582 first president of this body. He was among the most respected men of the legal profession of his age and a leader of the Gallican movement. He served faithfully King Henry III and opposed vehemently the Catholic League and the Guise family. After the Day of Barricades (May 12, 1588), when Paris was temporarily taken over by the Guises and the king had fled, Harlay contemptuously rejected an offer of cooperation with the League. After the assassination of Henry of Guise (1588), instigated by Henry III, the prominent jurist was arrested by the League rebels and imprisoned in the Bastille. Liberated a few days after the assassination of Henry III, Harlay joined Henry of Navarre, the Protestant pretender to the vacant throne. When Henry had won the religious-civil war, and had abjured Calvinism, Harlay became one of Henry's most intimate advisers. Under Henry IV he continued his Gallican struggles against papal supremacy in the interest of absolute monarchy. He always disliked Jesuits, and after the assassination of Henry IV, he openly accused them of instigating the crime. As an ardent opponent of ULTRAMONTANISM, he took the initiative in the royal condemnation of the books of Juan de MARIANA and Robert Cardinal BELLARMINE. He resigned in 1611 because of ill health. His only book, entitled *Coutume d'Orléans,* was published in 1585.

Achille de (Baron de Sancy), littérateur, bishop; b. Paris, 1581; d. Paris, Nov. 20, 1646. As a young man he received three abbeys and became bishop of Lavour. After the death of his older brother in 1601, he first became a professional soldier and then served as French ambassador to the Sultan of Turkey (1610–19). He was a protector of the Jesuits against the Turkish persecutions and thus suffered the violent hostility of the Turkish government. He resigned, returned home, and entered the Congregation of the Oratory. He loyally served Louis XIII and Cardinal de RICHELIEU, was confessor of Queen Henrietta of England, and received from Richelieu the bishopric of Saint-Malo (1631). There he acted as one of the ecclesiastical judges who persecuted, on the instruction of Richelieu, several bishops of Brittany involved in the rebellion headed by the Duke of Montmorency. An expert in modern and Oriental languages, his famous collections of ancient Hebrew Bibles are preserved in the National Library of Paris. He also wrote Latin poetry and political tracts, and was editor of Richelieu's *Memoirs.*

François I de, theologian, archbishop of Rouen; b. Paris, 1586; d. Chateau de Gaillon, March 22, 1653. As a brilliant and young student of theology, he received at the age of 17 the benefices of the very rich Abbey of Saint-Victor. His Roman sympathies brought him recognition and some opposition from his Gallican superiors. Appointed coadjutor of Cardinal Joyeuse, Archbishop of Rouen (1614), he succeeded Joyeuse as archbishop (1616). His zealous religious and social reforms soon caused conflict with the Jesuits, resulting in the creation of the theological school in the archiepiscopal palace. When his well-known ambition to become a cardinal was not satisfied, he turned angrily against the papal court with a satirical pamphlet entitled *Ecclesiasticae historiae liber primus.* This pamphlet was considered a complete reversal of the archbishop's previous attitudes in theological matters. He avoided official censure only by a full retraction.

Harlay-Chanvallon, François de, archbishop, nephew of François I; b. Aug. 14, 1625; d. Conflans, Aug. 6, 1696. After a distinguished collegiate career, he began, immediately after graduation, his outstanding career as prelate and courtier. As a graduation gift he received the rich Abbey of Jumièges from his uncle, the archbishop of Rouen. He succeeded upon the latter's resignation (1651) despite the opposition of (St.) Vincent de Paul, who criticized the political ambitions and the private life of the young prelate. He became archbishop of Paris in 1671 and an intimate adviser of Louis XIV in Church matters. The great ambition of his life was to succeed Cardinal Mazarin as prime minister. The archbishop had to be satisfied with an appointment as director of the affairs of the regular clergy. The king, however, transformed the Archdiocese of Paris into a ducal peerage for the archbishop and his successors. Archbishop Harlay-Chanvallon consecrated the secret marriage of Louis XIV and Mme. de Maintenon and had an important part in the revocation of the Edict of Nantes (1685). He was a relentless enemy of Jansenism and Protestantism. He was a brilliant and successful administrator of the most important diocese in France. However, he had many political and ecclesiastical critics, and his private life was much criticized.

Bibliography: F. T. PERRENS, *L'Église et l'état . . . sous Henri IV et la régence de Marie de Médicis,* 2 v. (Paris 1872). A. JEAN, *Les Évêques et archevêques de France depuis 1682 jusqu'à 1801* (Paris 1891). V. MARTIN, *Les Origines du gallicanisme,* 2 v. (Paris 1939). K. HOFMANN, *Lexikon für Theologie und Kirche,* ed. J. HOFER and K. RAHNER, 10 v. (2d, new ed. Freiburg 1957–65) 5:13.

[E. GONDA]

HARMEL, LÉON

French industrialist; b. La Neuville-Lez-Wasigny, Ardennes, Jan. 17, 1829; d. Nice, Nov. 25, 1915. At the age of 25 he was chief of a textile plant that had been founded by his father at Val des Bois, near Reims. Believing that the "most important work of our age is the work of the salvation of our brothers the workers" he transformed his enterprise into a Christian corporation that was also an archconfraternity under the patronage of Our Lady of the Factory (Notre Dame de l'usine). A chapel was placed at the center of the buildings and the principal objective was to maintain the cohesion of the "family" of workers. Committees of workers participated in the management of the project. Harmel lived among the workers with his large family and was known as the "good father." He was encouraged in his endeavors by Abp. Langénieux of Reims and by Father Vincent de Paul BAILLY, Albert de Mun, and C. H. R. de LA TOUR DU PIN, early leaders of Catholic social action. His work became known throughout France and abroad, and it was blessed by Pius IX.

Harmel belonged to the ultramontanist wing of French Catholicism. After he was widowed in 1870, he renounced the idea of the priesthood only after the personal intervention of Pius IX, whose advice he had sought. His bond with Rome was further strengthened under Leo XIII and was not weakened under Pius X. In 1887 he directed the first pilgrimage of French workers to Rome; 100 employers, 1,400 workers, and 300 priests participated. In 1889, a pilgrimage of "France at work" (*la France au travail*), which he had prepared by lecture tours, attracted 10,000 participants. These pilgrimages helped to hasten the publication of the encyclical *RERUM NOVARUM* (1891), which became the charter of the movement led by Harmel.

To make the social doctrine of the Church better known, Harmel established Secrétariats du Peuple, popular lectures, and Christian circles of social studies throughout France. From 1893 on, he organized congresses of Christian workers that exemplified the growing preference given to the action of workers over the action of employers. These organizations were constitutive elements in the formation of French Christian Democracy. Harmel was one of the promoters of the movement, which explains his role at the congress of Reims in 1894, and later, first at Reims, then at Lyons, in 1896. Yet, when plans were made to make Christian Democracy a political party, he joined the national council only with reservations, as he preferred social education to politics. This was prior to the publication of the encyclical *Graves de communi* (1901).

Harmel felt that social education belonged to priests. After 1887, therefore, he organized at Val des Bois annual vacation sessions where seminarians and young priests met men who were involved in social action and where they received appropriate theological instruction. These sessions were forerunners of the Semaines Sociales de France instituted in 1904.

Léon Harmel belonged to the Third Order of St. Francis. As a result a large part of French Catholic social action follows Franciscan spirituality.

Bibliography: G. GUITTON, *Léon Harmel,* 2 v. (Paris 1907). H. ROLLET, *L'Action sociale des catholiques en France,* 1871–1914, 2 v. (Paris 1947–58) v.1.

[J. CARON]

HARNACK, ADOLF VON

Church historian and patrologist; b. Dorpat, Estonia, May 7, 1851; d. Heidelberg, June 10, 1930. Of a staunch Lutheran family, Harnack studied in Dorpat and Leipzig and achieved his doctorate in Church History at Leipzig with a dissertation (*Habilitationsschrift*) on the sources of Gnosticism. During his professorship at Leipzig (1874–79) he produced 90 publications; entered into friendly relations with E. Schürer, W. Graf Baudissin, O. v. Gebhardt, and F. Loofs; and became acquainted with the liberal theology of A. RITSCHL in reaction to the Tübingen school of F. C. BAUR with its application of the Hegelian dialectic to historical and theological studies. Unsympathetic with metaphysics, he judged the influence of Greek philosophy on early Christianity as perverse, and accepted Ritschl's moralistic interpretation of the eschatological quality in Christ's annunciation (kerygma) of the kingdom of God. He taught at Giessen (1879–86) and Marburg (1886–88) and was called to a professorship at the University of Berlin despite the opposition of the Lutheran Church Senate, which felt that his *Lehrbuch der Dogmengeschichte* (3 v. Tübingen 1885–89; 4th ed. 1909) was a betrayal of early Christianity. In 1905 he became an influential member of the Berlin Academy and wrote his *Geschichte der preussischen Akademie der Wissenschaften* (Berlin 1900) for the 200th anniversary of that institution, thereby gaining the friendship of the kaiser and court.

An excellent organizer as well as a meticulous scholar, Harnack participated in many projects for the furtherance of science and knowledge and served as president of the Evangelical Social Congress (1903–11). His primary writings are divided between historical and doctrinal theology. His friendship with Theodore Mommsen led to the formation of the Kirchenväterkommission devoted to the edition of the Greek Fathers of the first three centuries (the Berlin Corpus or *Griechischen Christliche Schriftsteller*) whose foundation he laid in his edition of the *Patrum Apostolicorum Opera* (3 v. Leipzig 1875–77; 2d ed. 1920) with O. v. Gebhardt and T. Zahn, and in his *Geschichte der altchristlichen Literatur: I Überlieferung und Bestand* (2 v. Leipzig 1893); *II Die Chronologie* (Leipzig 1897–1904; 2d ed. 1958). The last, together with O. Bardenhewer's similar work (though a dispute broke out over the title, Bardenhewer opting for Ancient Church writers) is a standard source for a critical approach to the Fathers. He likewise founded a series of publications known as the *Texte und Untersuchungen zur Geschichte der altchristlichen Literatur* (ed. by O. v. Gebhardt and A. v. Harnack, 15 v. Leipzig 1882–97; *Neue Folge,* 15 v. 1897–1906; *Dritte Reihe,* ed. by A. v. Harnack and C. Schmidt, 1907–).

Harnack's *Das Wesen des Christentums* (Leipzig 1900) is a history of the development of Christianity, tracing its evolution from the Old Testament to the Gospels, the recession caused by doctrinal preoccupations introduced with Greek metaphysics, and finally its emancipation through Luther's rejection of dogma, and the modern return to the simplicity of the original Gospel teachings.

In his *Marcion, Das Evangelium vom fremden Gott* (Leipzig 1924) he demonstrates a mépris for the Old Testament, and stripping Marcion of his Gnostic leanings, describes his teaching as a kind of dualism not far removed from Luther's, but concentrating on an ethical approach to the God of goodness. J. WELLHAUSEN judged him devoid of true philological appreciation, and that would account for his distrust of comparative religion concepts. His desire to return to the simplicity of primitive Christianity made him undervalue the institutional Church, the Creed, dogma, Sacraments, miracles, and consecration rites; and he moved closer to R. Bultmann than BARTHIANISM in his final evaluation of early Christianity, adopting an almost traditional approach to the authenticity of the New Testament.

Out of his circle of students developed the influential periodical *Christliche Welt,* and with E. Schürer he founded and edited (1881–1930) the *Theologische Literatur-Zeitung.* As a scholar he resembled Erasmus rather than the German humanists, in the opinion of E. Peterson. As the most learned non-Catholic proponent of early Church history at the turn of the 19th century, he had an incalculable influence on historical scholarship; and although Catholic scholars such as P. BATIFFOL opposed his conception of early Church institutions and doctrines, in many instances his judgments and discoveries have proven a support to Catholic positions.

Bibliography: J. DE GHELLINCK, *Revue d'histoire ecclésiastique* 26 (1930) 962–991. J. DE GHELLINCK, *Patristique et moyen-âge: Études d'histoire littéraire et doctrinale,* v.1 (2d ed. Paris 1949), v.2, 3 (Brussels 1947–48) 3:2–102. A. VON ZAHN-HARNACK, *Adolf v. Harnack* (2d ed. Berlin 1951). W. VÖLKER, *Theologische Zeitschrift* 7 (1951) 209–227. Y. M. J. CONGAR, *Catholicisme* 5:516–519. E. PETERSON, *Theologische Traktate* (Munich 1951). A. SEITZ, "Harnack als Zeuge für die Katholische Kirche," *Die Schönere Zukunft* 5 (1930) 958–959, 962–984. L. DIXON, "Adolf von Harnack," *Historians of the Christian Tradition* (Nashville 1995) 389-409.

[F. X. MURPHY]

HAROLD, FRANCIS

Franciscan historian; b. Limerick, Ireland, early 17th century; d. Rome, 1685. He had five Franciscan relatives: Luke WADDING, uncle; Bonaventure Baron, cousin; and Anthony, Thomas, and Francis (junior) Harold, nephews. After having studied in St. Isidore's College, Rome (from Jan. 9, 1639), he was sent to teach in Prague (Oct. 28, 1642), Vienna, and finally Graz, whence he returned to Rome (1651) to succeed his uncle, Luke Wadding, as annalist of the order (April 12, 1655). Considerably inferior to Wadding as a historian, he collected much but published little.

Bibliography: Franciscan Library, Killiney, MSS D 1, 5, and 17. Archives, St. Isidore's College, Rome, MS W9. J. T. GILBERT, *The Dictionary of National Biography from the Earliest Times to 1900* (London 1885–1900) 8:1310. G. CLEARY, *Father Luke Wadding and St. Isidore's College, Rome* (Rome 1925) 108–112. B. MILLETT, *The Irish Franciscans 1651–1665* (Rome 1964), *passim.,* esp. 124, 127, 467–469. B. JENNINGS, "Miscellaneous Documents," *Archivium Hibernicum* 14 (1949) 5, 7, 11, 12. M. O'N. WALSH, "Irish Books Printed Abroad 1475–1700," *The Irish Book* 2 (1963) 16–17. J. WARE, *The History and Antiquities of Ireland . . . with the History of the Writers of Ireland,* ed. W. HARRIS, 2 v. in 1 (Dublin 1764) 200–201. J. H. SBARALEA, *Supplementum et castigatio ad scriptores trium ordinum S. Francisci a Waddingo,* 2 v. (Rome 1806; new ed. in 4 v. 1906–36) 3:229.

[B. MILLETT]

HAROLD, WILLIAM VINCENT

Missionary; b. Dublin, Ireland, *c.* 1785; d. Dublin, Jan. 29, 1856. He entered the Order of Preachers at the Corpo Santo, Lisbon, Portugal, where he was ordained, and then returned to Ireland. He later immigrated to the U.S. and went to Philadelphia, where Bp. Michael Egan named him copastor of St. Mary's Cathedral in 1808 and later, vicar-general. His unusual eloquence soon made him popular. In 1811, his uncle, Father James Harold, arrived in Philadelphia and became involved in a conflict with the bishop. When Egan attempted to transfer James to Pittsburgh, the younger Harold protested so vehemently that the bishop removed him from the vicar-generalship. The Harolds then resigned, and in April 1813, William returned to Ireland.

After Egan's death, the trustees of St. Mary's petitioned Rome that William Harold be named bishop of Philadelphia. Finally Henry Conwell was named instead. Bishop Conwell invited Harold to Philadelphia, assigned him to St. Mary's, and in 1821 appointed him vicar-general. At the time, the William HOGAN schism at St. Mary's was growing worse, and Harold successfully defended the Church's rights against the Hoganites. However, before long he began to have differences with the senile bishop, who removed him from the vicar-generalship. Harold refused to accept the removal and was suspended. The Haroldites protested to Rome that Harold's removal was a violation of a pact, but the Congregation of the Propaganda procured an order from the master general of the Dominicans transferring Harold to Cincinnati and added its own mandate. He refused to obey and, as a citizen, appealed to the U.S. government against this transfer order from his religious superior.

When James Brown, the U.S. minister to France, discussed the problem with the papal nuncio in France, the nuncio explained that Harold had willingly assumed the vow of obedience and that, in view of his vow, the Holy See had transferred his residence. This closed the case for Washington. Rome then warned Harold that if he remained in Philadelphia he would lose his faculties and be suspended. Harold temporized until he incurred the penalties. A month later he sailed for Ireland, where he was reinstated. He became once more a successful preacher and was provincial of his order from 1840 until 1844.

Bibliography: V. F. O'DANIEL, *The Dominican Province of St. Joseph* (New York 1942). H. J. NOLAN, *The Most Reverend Francis Patrick Kenrick* (Catholic University of America, *Studies in American Church History* 37; Washington 1948).

[H. J. NOLAN]

HAROLD II, KING OF ENGLAND

Reign: January 1066 to October 1066. From his deathbed in January 1066, Edward the Confessor (r.

1042–66) designated his brother-in-law Harold Godwinson his successor. More than one man had looked covetously at the throne the childless Edward would vacate, including his cousin William, duke of Normandy, and Harold's cousin Swein Estrithson, king of Denmark. Edward's sudden choice of Harold met with immediate approval by nobles and church magnates who had gathered around the dying king for the Christmas court and dedication of the newly completed abbey church of Westminster. Harold was duly crowned the same day Edward was interred.

Despite having won Edward's designation and the court's confidence, Harold lacked a royal genealogy linking him to the ruling House of Wessex. Although English preference dictated that a successor be connected by blood to the royal family, election outside it was not without precedent, most notably, for English magnates, the Danish kings who had come to power earlier in the 11th century. Harold had the further advantage of wide support because of the vast amounts of land that he controlled in England.

Harold was well qualified to assume the reins of government. Edward's *subregulus* by 1065, Harold had been an earl since his first appointment to East Anglia in 1045. In 1053 Harold had taken over the administration of the key earldom of Wessex, held by his father Godwin until his death in that year. Able to count on the loyalty of two younger brothers, Gyrth and Leofwine, also earls, Harold could not be as certain of his sister Edith, Edward's widow and queen. She apparently had sided with their brother Tostig when Edward, upon Harold's advice, had removed Tostig from the earldom of Northumbria in the fall of 1065. Harold had recommended that Edward allow the Northumbrians their earl of choice, Morcar, the younger brother of Edwin, who administered Mercia. Tostig, angry and convinced that his loss of Northumbria was Harold's fault, entered exile at his father-in-law's court in Flanders.

Harold had gained a reputation as a formidable opponent in battle that complemented his administrative abilities. He had challenged the Welsh more than once, the last major campaign having occurred in 1063. The outcome brought Harold unprecedented prestige when the Welsh turned against their own King Gruffydd ap Llewelyn and presented Harold with his head to underscore their oaths of loyalty to both Edward and Harold. At some time following Gruffydd's death, Harold married Gruffydd's widow Ealdgyth, sister of Edwin and Morcar. Clearly a political marriage, it probably took place early in 1066. With his brother Tostig no longer earl in Northumbria, Harold needed to forge firm ties with the northern magnate. An alliance through marriage was a well-tried form that had been used before by several of his predecessors, including Aethelred II (r. 978–1016), Edmund Ironside (r. 1016), and Canute (r. 1016–35).

Although Harold was the patron of WALTHAM Abbey, where tradition claims he is buried, his relationship with the Church was of mixed report. As his father before him, Harold may have held some of his lands at the expense of the Church. While Domesday Book describes some of these as disputed or illegally held, without records of the competing claims, Harold's culpability is difficult to assess. He did have the support of leading churchmen including Ealdred, Archbishop of York, and Wulfstan, Bishop of Worcester. Stigand, Archbishop of Canterbury, also was his friend, but since Stigand's legitimacy as archbishop had been questioned, his friendship may have cost Harold as much as it gained. During a pilgrimage to Rome, probably in 1058, Harold had also earned recognition for his generosity to the church.

Those who coveted Harold's crown arrived on England's shores in the fall of 1066. Surprisingly his cousin Swein had stayed at home, but the redoubtable Viking king of Norway Harold III (r. 1045–66) had not. Accompanying him was the still angry Tostig. Harold met and defeated them at Stamford Bridge on September 20. Then, with the knowledge that William, Duke of Normandy, had landed at Hastings, Harold and his men marched across the country to meet this second invader, who, with his troops, carried a papal banner endorsing William's cause. Edwin and Morcar did not arrive in time to participate in the fateful, day-long battle between Harold and his Norman adversary that October 14. At dusk Harold lay dead on the battlefield surrounded by his fallen, loyal troops, including the faithful Gyrth and Leofwine. The very short reign of Harold was over, and William, soon to be called "the Conqueror," was crowned king at London on Christmas Day, 1066.

Bibliography: G. N. GARMONSWAY, *The Anglo-Saxon Chronicle* (Rutland, Vt. 1992) 163–200. R. R. DARLINGTON and P. MCGURK, *The Chronicle of John of Worcester* (Oxford 1995) 543–607. F. BARLOW, *Vita Edwardi Regis* (London 1962) 5–55. H. R. LOYN, *Harold, Son of Godwin* (The Hastings and Bexhill Branch of the Historical Assn. 1966) 3–19. I. W. WALKER, *Harold, the Last Anglo-Saxon King* (Sutton, Eng. 1997).

[P. TORPIS]

HAROLD OF GLOUCESTER, ST.

Alleged martyr; d. March 17, ca. 1160–68, Gloucester, England. Harold was another young boy whose death was attributed to Jewish blood rituals. The story appears to have been handed down orally because many details of the written Peterborough and Brompton accounts are anachronistic. The boy's terribly abused body was retrieved from the Severn River and buried in Gloucester Cathedral. The cultus was permitted locally.

Feast formerly on March 25.

See Also: MEDIEVAL BOY MARTYRS.

[K. I. RABENSTEIN]

HARRINGTON, WILLIAM, BL.

Priest, martyr; b. Mount St. John, Felixkirk, North Riding, Yorkshire, England, 1566; d. hanged, drawn, and quartered at Tyburn (London), Feb. 18, 1594. Inspired by St. Edmund CAMPION, whom his father had entertained in their home in 1581, William Harrington pursued seminary studies at Rheims, even though his family had conformed to Anglicanism. He continued his studies with the Jesuits at Tournai (1582–84) until he contracted a serious illness that kept him home-bound for years. He returned to Rheims in February 1591, where he was ordained before entering the English mission in midsummer 1592. His ministry was interrupted by his arrest in May 1593. After his death he was calumniated by a woman named Friswood or Fid Williams, who falsely claimed he had fathered her child before he became a priest and made many other preposterous accusations against him and other Catholics. Harrington was beatified by Pius XI on Dec. 15, 1929.

Feast of the English Martyrs: May 4 (England).

See Also: ENGLAND, SCOTLAND, AND WALES, MARTYRS OF.

Bibliography: R. CHALLONER, *Memoirs of Missionary Priests,* ed. J. H. POLLEN (rev. ed. London 1924; repr. Farnborough 1969). J. MORRIS, ed., *The Troubles of Our Catholic Forefathers Related by Themselves* (London 1875), 104–107. J. H. POLLEN, *Acts of English Martyrs* (London 1891).

[K. I. RABENSTEIN]

HARRIS, HOWELL

Lay preacher and a key figure in the establishment of METHODISM in Wales; b. Trevacca, Wales, Jan. 23, 1714; d. Trevacca, July 21, 1777. He was the third son of Howell and Susanna Harris. Howell, intended for the ministry, received a good education. At the death of his father in 1730 he opened a school. In 1735 he spent one term at Oxford University. Harris began to conduct worship in his mother's home and his evangelical fervor attracted large crowds. He soon was preaching as often as five times a day. As a result he was deprived of his school in 1737 because of its connection with the Anglican Church. On three occasions he was denied ordination so he had to continue his career as a lay preacher. Harris was encouraged in his work by George Whitefield and later in his life he preached in Whitefield's chapel in London. When Whitefield broke with John Wesley over the issue of predestination Harris sided with Whitefield's Calvinistic concepts. As a result Welsh Methodism was strongly tinged with this doctrine. In 1752 Harris founded a Protestant ''monastery'' that by 1755 contained some 120 disciples. He ministered to this group and to other families that settled in the area to be near him. Harris joined the militia in 1759 during the war with France because he feared a French invasion might bring about the establishment of Catholicism.

Bibliography: W. J. TOWNSEND et al., eds., *A New History of Methodism,* 2 v. (London 1909) v.1. T. REES, *History of Protestant Nonconformity in Wales* (2d ed. London 1883). R. J. JONES, *The Dictionary of National Biography from the Earliest Times to 1900,* 63 v. (London 1885–1900) 9:6–7.

[A. M. SCHLEICH]

HART, WILLIAM, BL.

Priest and martyr; b. Wells, Somerset, England, 1558; d. hanged, drawn, and quartered at York, March 15, 1583. Hart was elected Trappes Scholar at Lincoln College, Oxford, where he took he baccalaureate in June 1574. Thereafter he converted to Catholicism and followed his rector, John Bridgewater, to the seminary at Douai, then Rheims. He finished his studies at the English College, Rome, and was ordained (1581). Almost immediately he entered the English mission, where he labored in Yorkshire. He escaped the priest hunters who arrested Bl. William LACEY only by standing in the chin-high, muddy moat of York Castle. Finally he was betrayed on Christmas Day 1582. After being manacled in double irons in a verminous dungeon, he was examined by the dean of York and Council of the North. He was tried on three counts: (1) under 13 Eliz. c. 2 for bringing papal writings (his certificate of ordination) into the realm; (2) under 13 Eliz. c. 3. for traveling abroad without royal license; and (3) under 23 Eliz. c. 1. for having reconciled others to popery. He was beatified by Pope Leo XIII on December 9, 1886.

Feast of the English Martyrs: May 4 (England).

See Also: ENGLAND, SCOTLAND, AND WALES, MARTYRS OF.

Bibliography: B. CAMM, ed., *Lives of the English Martyrs,* (New York 1905), II, 600–34. R. CHALLONER, *Memoirs of Missionary Priests,* ed. J. H. POLLEN (rev. ed. London 1924; repr. Farnborough 1969). J. H. POLLEN, *Acts of English Martyrs* (London 1891).

[K. I. RABENSTEIN]

HARTFORD, ARCHDIOCESE OF

The Archdiocese of Hartford (*Hartfortiensis*) comprises the counties of Hartford, New Haven, and Litchfield in the state of Connecticut. The area measures 2,288 square miles, and in 2001 had a Catholic population of 745, 069, about 41 percent of the general population of 1.8 million. Established as a diocese Nov. 28, 1843, and raised to an archdiocese Aug. 6, 1953, this see originally embraced the states of Connecticut and Rhode Island. It was restricted to Connecticut alone with creation of the Diocese of Providence, R.I., in 1872, and reduced again when the Dioceses of Bridgeport and Norwich were established within Connecticut in 1953. With Providence, Bridgeport, and Norwich as suffragan sees, the Province of Hartford embraces the same area as the early diocese.

Early History. The first priest known to have visited Connecticut was Gabriel Druillettes, SJ, who went to New Haven from Quebec in September 1651 to plead for the Abenaki Native Americans of Maine against the Iroquois. The earliest Catholic residents included a scattering of Irish convicts and redemptioners deported to America in the 17th and 18th centuries, and 400 Acadian exiles assigned to the colony in 1756. A further trickle of Irish and some German Catholics began to immigrate voluntarily into the state after the American Revolution. The Diocese of Boston was created in 1808 for all New England, and its first bishop, Jean Cheverus, visited the Catholic communities in Hartford and New Haven in 1823. In 1828, Benedict Fenwick, the second bishop, charged Rev. Robert D. Woodley, who resided in Providence, with care of the Catholics in Connecticut, as well as Rhode Island.

Organized church activity in Connecticut began in July 1829, when the first Catholic newspaper in New England, the *Catholic Press,* started weekly publication in Hartford, and the first Sunday school in the state was inaugurated in the newspaper's office. Fenwick visited Hartford in the summer of 1829 to purchase the old Christ Episcopal church and to appoint Bernard O'Cavanagh pastor in Hartford, with jurisdiction throughout Connecticut. The wooden Christ Episcopal church was moved to another site, renamed Holy Trinity, and dedicated as the first Catholic church in Connecticut on June 17, 1830. That fall the pioneer Catholic school in Connecticut, a day school staffed by laymen, opened in the church basement.

In October 1831, James FITTON became pastor in Hartford, and a year later James McDermott was made pastor in New Haven, where there were 200 Catholics, 74 more than in Hartford. In 1834, with the construction of Christ's Church in New Haven, the state had its second Catholic church and, operating in the sacristy, a second day school.

Diocese. At the Fifth Provincial Council of Baltimore, 1843, Fenwick outlined the disadvantages of having Boston the only diocese in New England. The council decided to petition Rome for a division of the diocese, and Gregory XVI established the Diocese of Hartford in 1843.

Tyler. William Tyler was ordained June 3, 1829, at the age of 23, served parishes in Maine and Massachusetts, and was vicar-general in Boston when named first bishop of Hartford. He was consecrated in Baltimore, Md., March 17, 1844, and installed in Holy Trinity, Hartford, on April 14. A census that same year showed that, with 5,180 Catholics in Rhode Island and 4,817 in Connecticut, the population of the diocese was only 2 per cent Catholic. Connecticut had three priests, and parishes in Hartford, New Haven, and Bridgeport, and a mission in Middletown. There were as many priests and churches in Rhode Island. The city of Providence, however, had two parishes with 2,000 members compared to Hartford's one parish with 600 members. Tyler therefore petitioned the Holy See for a transfer of residence and moved to Providence in June 1844. The diocese was so poor that, even there, his residence was a mere shack and his best chalice was made of brass. Within five years, the emigration from Ireland and the rapid growth of industry and railroad construction in New England doubled the Catholic population of the diocese.

O'Reilly. Tyler died June 18, 1849, and was succeeded by Bernard O'Reilly, vicar-general of the Diocese of Buffalo, who was consecrated bishop of Hartford on Nov. 10, 1850. At that time, there were seven priests serving parishes in Hartford, New Haven, Bridgeport, Waterbury, and Norwalk, and numerous missions in Connecticut. Litchfield County was given its first pastor in 1850 when O'Reilly appointed Christopher Moore to Falls Village. The bishop brought the Sisters of Mercy from Pittsburgh to Providence in 1851, and then in 1852, to Connecticut. Four sisters arrived in Hartford on May 11 to staff the school in the basement of St. Patrick's Church (Holy Trinity had been rebuilt and renamed in 1851), and four others traveled to New Haven, May 12, to teach at St. Mary's Church. A girls' academy was soon opened by each group and, eventually, an orphan asylum. Late in 1855, O'Reilly went to Ireland to recruit teaching brothers for the diocese; on Jan. 23, 1856, he set sail for the U.S. on the S.S. ''Pacific'' out of Liverpool. The ship was lost at sea. For two years William O'Reilly, vicar-general and brother of the late bishop, administered the diocese.

McFarland. Francis Patrick McFarland, pastor of St. John's Church in Utica, N.Y., was named third bishop of Hartford on Jan. 8, 1858, and consecrated in Providence,

R.I., on March 14, the first bishop consecrated in New England. During his 16-year episcopate, Hartford experienced an industrial expansion that attracted a constant influx of workers. McFarland arranged for the second community of nuns to enter Connecticut in June 1864, when he brought the Sisters of Charity from Mt. St. Vincent, New York City, to take over the orphan asylum in New Haven. The next year he appointed the Order of Friars Minor, the first religious order of men in the state, to St. Joseph's Church, Winsted. In 1868 the first national parish in Connecticut, St. Boniface, was organized for the Germans of New Haven.

The Diocese of Providence was established in February 1872, with a Catholic population of about 60,000. Connecticut alone had 140,000 Catholics (representing about 23 per cent of its population), 76 churches, 60 chapels and mission stations, and 77 priests. McFarland transferred residence from Providence to Hartford and, upon his arrival, created St. Joseph cathedral parish from the western half of the two parishes in Hartford. A homestead was purchased on Farmington Avenue, and a brownstone and brick convent was consecrated there in 1873 as the Connecticut motherhouse for the Sisters of Mercy. Its chapel was used temporarily as a procathedral. McFarland died on Oct. 12, 1874.

Galberry. Thomas GALBERRY, first provincial of the Augustinians in the U.S., was named fourth bishop of Hartford on Feb. 12, 1875, and was consecrated March 19, 1876, in St. Peter's Church, Hartford. In April 1876 he established the *Connecticut Catholic,* a weekly paper that was taken over by the diocese in 1896. Renamed the *Catholic Transcript* in 1898, it continued to serve the dioceses of Connecticut. Galberry laid the cornerstone of St. Joseph Cathedral on April 29, 1877.

McMahon. Galberry died on Oct. 10, 1878, and was succeeded by Lawrence Stephen McMahon, first vicar-general of the Providence Diocese, who was consecrated bishop of Hartford in St. Joseph's Cathedral basement on Aug. 10, 1879. During his episcopacy, Polish, Lithuanian, Italian, and French-Canadian immigrants swelled the number of Catholics in the state, and among the 48 parishes he created were 13 national parishes and chapels. A second religious order of men entered the diocese in 1886 when the Dominican Fathers took over St. Mary's parish, New Haven. In 15 years of effort, the bishop raised $500,000 for the completion of St. Joseph Cathedral, which, built of local Portland brownstone along French Gothic lines, was dedicated, debt free, on May 8, 1892. McMahon died suddenly at Lakeville, Conn., on Aug. 21, 1893. It was in Bishop McMaon's time that the Reverend Michael McGiveney founded the KNIGHTS OF COLUMBUS, in New Haven in 1882.

Tierney. Michael Tierney, the sixth bishop of Hartford, was ordained May 26, 1866, in Troy, N.Y. He served as McFarland's chancellor and rector of the cathedral at Providence and held pastorates at Norwich, New London, Stamford, Hartford, and New Britain. He was consecrated in St. Joseph Cathedral on Feb. 22, 1894, the first priest of the Hartford Diocese to become its bishop. During his 14-year episcopate, Catholics in the diocese increased from 250,000 to 395,000; parishes from 98 to 167; schools from 48 to 80. Tierney opened St. Thomas Minor Seminary in 1897, with 15 boarding and 22 day students. St. Francis Hospital, Hartford, was founded in 1897 and within 10 years other hospitals were built in Waterbury, Bridgeport, Willimantic, and New Haven. St. Andrew's Home, New Haven, was opened by the Little Sisters of the Poor in 1901, the House of the Good Shepherd was established in Hartford in 1902, and St. John's Industrial Home for Boys was opened in 1904. Tierney also organized the Connecticut Apostolate, a group of diocesan priests who conducted missions for both Catholics and non-Catholics. The bishop's death on Oct. 5, 1908, was followed by a long interregnum, during which John Synott, vicar-general and rector of St. Thomas Seminary, acted as administrator.

Nilan. John Joseph Nilan, pastor of St. Joseph's Church, Amesbury, Mass., was named seventh bishop on Feb. 14, 1910, and consecrated April 28 in Hartford. Nilan strengthened, expanded, and further organized the charitable efforts begun by his predecessor. St. Agnes Infant and Maternity Hospital was founded in West Hartford in 1914. The diocesan bureau of social service, which had begun as a small scale charities office in Bridgeport in 1916, was put on a state-wide basis in 1920. The Connecticut branch of the Council of Catholic Women was organized. During the Depression of 1929, at his own expense, Nilan maintained a house on the cathedral property caring for as many as 80 unemployed men at a time. The first Catholic college for women in the state, ALBERTUS MAGNUS, was opened by the Dominican Sisters at New Haven in 1925. In 1930, a new St. Thomas Seminary was constructed in Bloomfield.

McAuliffe. Nilan died April 13, 1934, and was succeeded by his auxiliary, Maurice Francis McAuliffe, who had been consecrated in 1926 and was installed as Hartford's eighth bishop on May 29, 1934. His major project was renovation of St. Joseph's Cathedral where the foundations needed replacing. A second college for women, ST. JOSEPH'S, which opened in Hartford in 1932, was moved to West Hartford in 1936. The Diocesan Labor Institute was founded to foster Christian social principles; two interracial centers, to promote the work of the Church among Black Americans, were opened—Blessed Martin Center, New Haven, in 1942, and St. Benedict

Center, Hartford, in 1944. During World War II, McAuliffe was the first American bishop to provide Mass in a war plant for the convenience of its workers when he approved the plan for Colt's Fire Arms, Hartford.

Archdiocese. *O'Brien.* Henry Joseph O'Brien was consecrated auxiliary bishop of Hartford on May 15, 1940, and installed as ninth bishop on June 5, 1945, following McAuliffe's death on Dec. 15, 1944. O'Brien immediately set up a diocesan resettlement committee to assist individuals displaced by World War II. In the years immediately following the war, Hartford grew numerically to become the second largest diocese (after Brooklyn, N.Y.) in the U.S. On Aug. 6, 1953, the Dioceses of Bridgeport and Norwich were created and Hartford was made an archdiocese and O'Brien the first archbishop. The old St. Joseph Cathedral was destroyed by fire of unknown origin on Dec. 31, 1956; a new one was begun at the same location on Sept. 8, 1958, and completed in 1962. The archdiocese held its first synod in 1959 (previous diocesan synods had been held previously in 1854, 1878, and 1886), but it was soon overtaken by the Second Vatican Council. Archbishop O'Brien had attended the sessions of Vatican II, and after the Council took initial steps to implement its directives in the archdiocese, but it was left to his successor to deal with change in the Church during the 1970s and 1980s. O'Brien resigned in November 1970 and was given the title "Former Archbishop of Hartford." (He died July 23, 1976.)

Whealon. O'Brien's successor was the bishop of Erie, Pa., John F. Whealon, who had previously served as the seminary rector and appointed auxiliary bishop in Cleveland in 1961. He attended the session of the Second Vatican Council. In his 22 years (1969–1991) as Archbishop of Hartford, Whealon inaugurated, and more often than not, took a hands-on approach to a variety of pastoral programs like the formation programs of permanent deacons, parish renewal, team, ministry involving laity, and the cause of social justice. He was one of the first U.S. bishops to support a ministry to individuals with AIDS. Active in the Christian Conference of Connecticut, the state council of churches, Archbishop Whealon gained a reputation for his ecumenical interest and activities.

Whealon had a indefatigable capacity for and willingness to work that brought him a number of assignments from the National Conference of Catholic Bishops. He chaired the NCCB committee that produced (and is reputed to be the principal author of) the document *Basic Teachings for Catholic Religious Education* in 1972. In 1977 when John Cardinal Deardon's health did not permit him to journey to Rome for the Assembly of the Synod of Bishops on "Catechesis in Our Time," Archbishop Whealon replaced him in the American delegation. It was at this time that Whealon was deeply involved in the production of the National Catechetical Directory *Sharing the Light of Faith.* He both chaired the USCC's ad hoc committee of Policy and Review that had oversight for the project and acted as liaison with working committee that compiled it. The respect that Whealon enjoyed from his fellow bishops and the visibility he had because of his work especially in religious education, made Hartford the focus of national attention. Archbishop Whealon died on Aug. 2, 1991 of cardiac arrest during a routine surgical procedure.

Cronin. In January 1992, Most Reverend Daniel A. Cronin who had been Bishop of Fall River, Mass., since 1970, was installed as the third Archbishop of Hartford. To meet the pastoral needs of the archdiocese whose population is predominantly urban and suburban population, Cronin maintained an Office for Urban Affairs and other offices and agencies for specialized ministries. He created the Office for Hispanic Evangelization under the direction of Auxiliary Bishop Peter A. Rosazza to work with the burgeoning numbers of Spanish speaking Catholics, especially the Puerto Ricans in and around Hartford, Waterbury, Meriden, and New Haven.

Catholic colleges in the archdiocese include Mt. Sacred Heart College, Hamden (sponsored by the Sisters of Community of Apostles of the Sacred Heart of Jesus), Albertus Magnus College, New Haven (sponsored by the Dominican Sisters) and Saint Joseph College, Hartford (sponsored by the Sisters of Mercy). Of these three, Saint Joseph College remains principally a college for women, with a very small population of male students in its weekend coeducational college for working adults and its graduate school. Albertus Magnus College was originally founded as a women's college in 1925, before going coeducational in 1985.

Bibliography: T. S. DUGGAN, *Catholic Church in Connecticut* (New York 1930). A. J. HEFFERNAN, *History of Catholic Education in Connecticut* (Washington 1935). A. F. MUNICH, *Beginnings of Roman Catholic Church in Connecticut* (New Haven 1935). B. L. MARTHALER, *John Francis Whealon (1921–1991): In Memoriam,The Living Light*, 28:2 (Winter 1992):180–182.

[M. J. SCHOLSKY/EDS.]

HARTLEY, WILLIAM, BL.

Priest, martyr; b. *c.* 1557, Wilne (or Wyn), Derbyshire, England; hanged at Shoreditch, Oct. 5, 1588. Having completed his studies at St. John's College, Oxford, the well–born Hartley became the college's Protestant chaplain. Expelled following his conversion to Catholicism (1579) by Vice Chancellor Tobie Mathew, Hartley fled to Rheims on the Continent. He was ordained priest at Châlons (1580), then returned to England, where he assisted Jesuit Frs. Edmund CAMPION and Robert PERSONS in printing and distributing their books. He was arrested Aug. 13, 1581, and sent to Marshalsea Prison, London. There he was discovered saying Mass and was placed in irons (Dec. 5, 1583). Although he was indicted for high treason on Feb. 7, 1584, he was never brought to trial. Instead he was sent into exile the following January. After time for recuperation in Rheims, he made a pilgrimage to Rome then returned to the English mission. He was arrested in Holborn (London) in September 1588 and executed the following month together with Bl. Fr. John HEWETT, son of a York draper; Bl. Robert Sutton, a tutor or schoolmaster in Paternoster Row, London; and John Harrison, *alias* Symons, who had carried letters between the priests. Harrison, unjustly accused of being a spy, has been dropped from the rolls of English martyrs in part because of confusion with Matthias or James Harrison, priests, who suffered martyrdom in 1599 or 1602 respectively. Hartley was beatified by Pius XI on Dec. 15, 1929.

Feast of the English Martyrs: May 4 (England).

See Also: ENGLAND, SCOTLAND, AND WALES, MARTYRS OF.

Bibliography: T. W. BALDWIN, *William Shakespeare Adapts a Hanging* (Princeton 1931) R. CHALLONER, *Memoirs of Missionary Priests,* ed. J. H. POLLEN (rev. ed. London 1924; repr. Farnborough 1969). J. H. POLLEN, *Acts of English Martyrs* (London 1891), 272.

[K. I. RABENSTEIN]

HARTMANN, ANASTASIUS, VEN.

Baptized Alois; bishop, missionary to India; b. Altwis, Lucerne canton, Switzerland, Feb. 20, 1803; d. Patna, Bihar, India, April 24, 1866. He joined the Capuchins at Baden, Germany (1821) and was ordained in 1825. After acting as novice master and teaching philosophy and theology in Switzerland and Rome, he left for India as a missionary, arriving at Agra in 1844. Appointed first vicar apostolic of Patna (1845), he was active in securing additional missionaries and building new schools in Patna and in the Bombay vicariate, to which he was transferred (1849). After obtaining approval for dividing the vicariate by the separation of Poona from Bombay (1854), Hartmann returned to Rome as an adviser on India to the Congregation of Propaganda (1856–58). Having helped to establish the first Capuchin foundation in the U.S. in 1857, he served as the Roman director of Capuchin missions (1858–60). He returned to Patna as vicar apostolic (1860) and helped to promote Church expansion by building new churches and orphanages. In 1865 he successfully sought exemption for Catholics from the Christian Marriage Act. Hartmann's writings included a Hindustani catechism (1853) and New Testament (1864), and two works on pastoral psychology (1907, 1932). The cause for his beatification was introduced in 1906. He was declared venerable on Dec. 21, 1998.

Bibliography: R. STREIT and J. DINDINGER, *Bibliotheca missionum* (Freiburg 1916) 8:134–139. A. JANN, *Monumenta Anastasiana,* 5 v. (Lucerne 1939–48); *Die Autobiographie des A. Hartmann* (Ingenbohl 1917). W. BÜHLMANN, *Pionier der Einheit: Bischof Anastasius Hartmann* (Zürich 1966). E. EBERLE, *Anastasius Hartmann: ein grosser Missionsbischof aus dem Kapuzinerorden* (9th ed., Freiburg, Switz. 1974). FULGENTIUS OF CAMUGNANO, *Bishop Hartmann* (Allahabad, India 1946; rev. ed 1966). L. FÄH, "Die Bibelübersetzungs-Arbeit von Bischof A. Hartmann 1803–66," *Neue Zeitschrift für Missionswissenschaft* 20 (1964) 1–9. *Lexicon Capuccinum* (Rome 1951) 724–726. J. H. GENSE, *The Church at the Gateway of India, 1720–1960* (Bombay 1960).

[E. R. HAMBYE/EDS.]

HARTMANN, EDUARD VON

German philosopher; b. Berlin, Feb. 23, 1842; d. Gros-Lichterfelde (Berlin), June 5, 1906. The son of an army officer, Hartmann himself had a brief military career before retiring and devoting his energies to philosophy. From G. W. F. HEGEL he took the view that a rational idea runs through creation; from A. SCHOPENHAUER he adopted the notion that a blind, irrational will rules the world, forming it into an existent reality. His resulting philosophy is a curious combination of OPTIMISM and PESSIMISM.

From his first work, *Philosophie des Unbewussten* (Berlin 1869), Hartmann was known as the philosopher of the unconscious. In his systematic treatise, *System der Philosophie im Grundriss* (8 v. Bad Sachsa 1906–09), he adopted an inductive metaphysics based on the thought of G. T. Fechner. Hartmann opposed E. Haeckel and his naturalism, and, in general, rejected mechanical explanations of the world; he himself inclined toward VITALISM. He discussed modern science in his *Weltanshauung der modernen Physik* (Leipzig 1902) and wrote a worthwhile history of metaphysics, *Geschichte der Metaphysik* (2 v. Leipzig 1899–1900). Equally significant was his *Kategorienlehre* (Leipzig 1896), which influenced the Neo-Kantian theory of the categories.

In his philosophy of religion Hartmann was an adversary of Christianity, substituting for it a teaching that was decidedly monistic and pantheistic. He made known his views in a series of works published under the general title of *Religionsphilosophie,* among which the more important are *Das Krisis des Christentums in der modernen*

Theologie (Berlin 1880), *Das religiöse Bewusstsein der Menschheit* (Berlin 1882), and *Die Religion des Geistes* (Berlin 1882). These give clear indication of the practical impossibility of constructing a religious philosophy without belief in a personal God.

Bibliography: E. DI CARLO, *Enciclopedia filosofica* 2:980–981. H. WACKERZAPP, *Lexikon für Theologie und Kirche* [2] 5:20. F. J. VON RINTELEN, *Die Religion in Geschichte und Gegenwart* [3] 3:82–83. P. SIWEK, *The Philosophy of Evil* (New York 1951); ''Pessimism in Philosophy,'' *New Scholasticism* (1948) 249–297.

[H. MEYER]

HARTMANN, NICOLAI

German philosopher; b. Riga, Feb. 20, 1882; d. Göttingen, Oct. 9, 1950. The principal features of his philosophy include a ''critical ontology,'' an ethics of material values, and a study of man as creative spirit (demiurge) with Godlike prerogatives. Hartmann moved from the methodological formalism of the Marburg School to a concern, similar to that of PHENOMENOLOGY, with ''things themselves.'' Unlike the phenomenologists, however, he recognized that man's natural consciousness, which he ''critically'' verified through its experience of opposition, was fixed on the real world. Yet, influenced by E. HUSSERL and M. SCHELER, he retained an ideal world and regarded man as a mediator between the spheres of the real and the ideal.

Critical Ontology. In his ''critical ontology,'' Hartmann held that knowledge does not engender the object but is the comprehension of being-in-itself (*Ansichseienden*). Real being (nature) is beyond consciousness in the in-itself (*An-sich*) and is wholly indifferent to being known. The bridging of the two establishes the ''fundamental categorial relation'' by which a partial identity, at least, is established between the categories of knowledge and those of being; this makes possible the grasping of the *An-sich.* Knowledge and being are not comprehended in a common logos, as in the old ontology. Spirit is something in being, the highest level of being, though it is also imbedded in the ''homogeneous'' mass of being. Hartmann's ''new ontology'' lays claim to being critical in that it does not rely on a transcendental insight but is directed to the physical concrete object alone. In the structuring of the real world into levels, one resting on the other but with the higher not derivable from the lower, lies both the strength and the weakness of his physical ontology, which may more properly be termed ''ontics.'' The place that being occupies in the old ontology is taken in critical ontology by the connectedness of things existing in the world.

Ethics. Hartmann's ethics is full of insight into moral values. The domain of values has an ideal *Ansichsein.* For this, man requires a moral faculty, a value sense (*Wertgefühl*). In ethical matters values must be introduced into the real world through volition. But how can values reach into real individual wills? This question is the *experimentum crucis* of Hartmann's ethics. Values are autonomous and unconditional, and the human will has itself an autonomous and absolute freedom. The will has no connaturality for values but is merely an organ for their attainment. Thus, at least in the case of a conflict of values, it can rule effectively against moral values. In this way the unity of morality is disturbed. Nevertheless Hartmann did not undermine the fact that man is by right a moral being or person. As he put it, the solution of this difficulty can be resolved only by answering the question as to the ultimate source of moral being. This, however, is a metaphysical problem and as such is as insoluble as the question of the origin of the world. Hartmann was cognizant of the fundamental metaphysical problems. Yet he so blocked himself off from any solution to them that he displaced value, as he did real being, to the level of *An-sich,* to which neither the person nor the knowing subject is ordered in the interior of his being. The grounding of person and values and of knowledge and being on a common basis would be to point directly to a personal Creator. Hartmann denied himself this view because of the so-called critical boundaries within the world man is able to experience. In his view, the world is, in ultimate analysis, ''absolutely accidental.''

God's Prerogatives. ''In man, the world closes into a unity,'' for man brings together being and value and so establishes a creative sense in the course of history. To look for meaning in being itself is to have recourse to an anthropomorphic subjectivism. Hartmann was a radical opponent of those who saw an indissoluble unity in the concepts of being and meaning (e.g., the *lumen naturale* of St. THOMAS AQUINAS and the *Seinsverständnis* of M. HEIDEGGER). The determination of meaning in absolute freedom is man's privilege. If God existed, man would be neither free nor a moral being (postulational atheism). ''To man falls the metaphysical heritage of God.''

For Hartmann, systems disappear and problems alone live on in history. He distinguished, however, between problems that are neutral and independent of one's particular viewpoint and those that are not. The problem of religion is of the latter type: this no longer lives on—it disappears with time. Although the question of religion continues to cry out against disposal, for Hartmann it does not exist as a true problem.

Hartmann's so-called OBJECTIVITY is oriented toward the natural sciences, and indeed is taken over from them. His theory of the categories in his physical ontics is of value. Philosophy itself, however, can never be restricted merely to categorial analysis.

Bibliography: Works. *Grundzüge einer Metaphysik der Erkenntnis* (4th ed. Berlin 1949); *Das Problem des geistigen Seins* (Berlin 1949); *Ethik* (Berlin 1949); *Zur Grundlegung der Ontologie* (Meisenheim 1948); *Möglichkeit und Wirklichkeit* (Meisenheim 1949); *Der Aufbau der realen Welt* (Meisenheim 1949); *Philosophie der Natur* (Berlin 1950); *Teleologisches Denken* (Berlin 1951); *The New Ways of Ontology,* tr. R. C. KUHN (Chicago 1952). Literature. *Nicolai Hartmann: Der Denker und sein Werk,* ed. H. HEIMSOETH and R. HEISS (Göttingen 1952). A. GUGGENBERGER, *Der Menschengeist und das Sein* (Munich 1942). J. N. MOHANTY, *Nicolai Hartmann and Alfred North Whitehead* (Calcutta 1957). H. HÜLSMANN, *Die Methode in der Philosophie Nicolai Hartmanns* (Düsseldorf 1959). H. BECK, *Möglichkeit und Notwendigkeit* (Pullach 1961). H. M. BAUMGARTNER, *Die Unbedingheit des Sittlichen: Eine Auseinandersetzung mit Nicolai Hartmann* (Munich 1962). G. M. MEYER, *Modalanalyse und Determinationsproblem* (Meisen heim 1962). I. M. BOCHEŃSKI, *Contemporary European Philosophy,* tr. D. NICHOLL and K. ASCHENBRENNER (Berkeley 1956). J. SCHMITZ, *Disput über des teleologische Denken* (Mainz 1960).

[A. GUGGENBERGER]

HARTMANN OF BRIXEN, BL.

Abbot and bishop; b. Polling, near Passau, Germany, *c.* 1090; d. Brixen (Bressanone), Italy, Dec. 23, 1164. Hartmann was educated in Sankt Nikola in Passau, the first AUGUSTINIAN settlement in that area and an important center of reform. When Abp. Conrad of Salzburg decided in 1122 to reform his cathedral clergy according to the Rule of St. AUGUSTINE, he chose Hartmann to lead the new community. In 1128 Hartmann became prior of the Augustinian house at Herren-Chiemsee, also reformed by Conrad, and in 1133 Margrave LEOPOLD III OF AUSTRIA called him to head the new Augustinian community of KLOSTERNEUBURG. Because of his apostolic zeal and saintly life, he was made bishop of Brixen in 1140 or 1141. To renew the spiritual life in his diocese he founded an Augustinian priory at Neustift near Brixen in 1142 and obtained an imperial privilege for it in 1157. Although he always remained loyal to Pope ALEXANDER III and to his metropolitan, Eberhard of Salzburg, FREDERIC I BARBAROSSA respected him for his learning and sanctity. Since 1784 his veneration is permitted in the Diocese of Brixen.

Feast: Dec. 23.

Bibliography: J. L. BAUDOT and L. CHAUSSIN, *Vies des saints et des bienheeux selon l'ordre du calendrier avec l'historique des fêtes,* ed. by The Benedictines of Paris, 12 v. (Paris 1935–56) 12:621–622. A. BUTLER, *The Lives of the Saints,* ed. H. THURSTON and D. ATTWATER, 4 v. (New York 1956) 4:601–602. A. SPARBER, *Leben und Wirken des seligen Hartmann, Bischofs von Brixen, 1140–1164* (Klosterneuburg 1957); *Lexikon für Theologie und Kirche,* ed. J. HOFER and K. RAHNER, 10 v. (2d, new ed. Freiburg 1957–65) 5:19.

[A. A. SCHACHER]

HARTSHORNE, CHARLES

Philosopher, b. June 5, 1897, Kittanning, Pennsylvania; d. October 6, 2000. The son of an Episcopalian minister, Hartshorne left college to serve in the Army Medical Corps in the First World War. After the war, he entered Harvard University, from which he received a Ph.D. in philosophy. He pursued postdoctoral work as a Sheldon Fellow in Germany, with stints in England and Austria, before returning to Harvard in 1925 as instructor and research fellow. At Harvard, he was a teaching assistant to A. N. WHITEHEAD, who exercised enormous influence on his thinking. He edited (with Paul Weiss) the Pierce papers. In 1928, he left Harvard for the University of Chicago where he taught for 27 years. During this time he met and married Dorothy Cooper, with whom he had one daughter. He left Chicago for Emory University in 1955, and upon retirement at the age 65, went to the University of Texas at Austin as Ashbel Smith Professor of Philosophy, becoming emeritus in 1978. He authored more than 20 books and some 500 articles. He is regarded with Whitehead as the foremost representative of PROCESS PHILOSOPHY. Also an accomplished and noted ornithologist, with a specialty in bird songs, he wrote *Born to Sing: An Interpretation and World Survey of Bird Song,* and several articles. He also wrote an intellectual autobiography, *From Darkness to the Light,* which provides useful background to the development of his philosophy and anecdotes connected with his career. He published his last book, *The Zero Fallacy and Other Essays in Neoclassical Metaphysics* at the age of 100.

In a philosophical era that was dominated by an antimetaphysical and to some extent antireligious attitude, Hartshorne persisted in developing, in dialogue with classical theism, his ''neoclassical metaphysics'' which is thoroughly theistic and is most systematically presented in *Creative Synthesis and Philosophic Method.* His effort was to apply logical thinking to religious insights, develop them in dialogue with other philosophical traditions, and systematize them into a coherent and adequate metaphysical system. The result was a major contribution to metaphysics and to philosophical and theological thinking about God. Acknowledging the criticisms of metaphysics made by HUME and the positivists, Hartshorne grounded his metaphysical system in concrete experience, which he regarded as both the departure point and the yardstick for any abstract metaphysical scheme. Developments in contemporary physics also informed his metaphysical thinking. Using modal logic, Hartshorne developed a new version of the ONTOLOGICAL ARGUMENT for the existence of God, set out mainly in *The Logic of Perfection* and in *Anselm's Discovery.* His argument was not intended to produce an actual proof, but rather to reduce the alternatives to atheism or theism.

Insisting that the classical theistic conception of God as absolute and immutable does not do justice to religious claims to a personal God and to the philosophical demand for consistency and adequacy, Hartshorne developed the concept of a dipolar God, particularly in *Man's Vision of God and the Logic of Theism, The Divine Relativity,* and *A Natural Theology for Our Time.* He conceived God as having a concrete pole and an abstract pole. In the abstract pole, God has all the attributes applied by classical theism: absolute, infinite, eternal, immutable, etc.; in the concrete pole, God is said to be relative, finite, temporal, mutable, etc. The predication of these pairs of contrary predicates hinges on the law of polarity, which Hartshorne borrows from Morris Cohen: contraries can be predicated of the same reality at the same time but under different aspects. It is also dependent on a crucial distinction that Hartshorne makes in his metaphysical system between concrete actuality (how something exists) and abstract existence (that something is). Concrete actuality is the more inclusive category; hence, the relationship between the two categories is asymmetrical. The concept of a dipolar God is also premised on the claim that God is not an exception to, but an unrivaled exemplification of, metaphysical categories.

Bibliography: L. E. HAHN, ed., *The Philosophy of Charles Hartshorne* (La Salle, Ill. 1991). S. SIA, ed., *Charles Hartshorne's Concept of God: Philosophical and Theological Responses* (Boston 1990). S. SIA, *God in Process Thought: A Study in Charles Hartshorne's Concept of God* (Boston 1985). J. COBB and F. GAMWELL, eds., *Existence and Actuality: Conversations with Charles Hartshorne* (Chicago 1984). E. PETERS, *Hartshorne and Neoclassical Metaphysics: An Interpretation* (Lincoln 1970).

[S. SIA]

HARTWICH OF SALZBURG, BL.

Archbishop; b. *c.* 955; d. Dec. 5, 1023. The last member of the Aribo-Sponheim family, he was archbishop of Salzburg, 991–1023. His nephew ALBUIN became bishop of Säben-Brixen. Recognizing the abundant charity of Hartwich, OTTO III gave him the rights of market and coinage (996), and from the Emperor HENRY II, Hartwich received large grants of property. Hartwich renovated the cathedral school and a great number of monasteries. He has been venerated as blessed since the 13th century. When the cathedral of Salzburg was destroyed by fire (1598), his remains were lost.

Feast: June 14.

Bibliography: *Acta Sanctorum* June 3:11–20. *Monumenta Germaniae Historica: Scriptores* 11:95–97. *Salzburger Urkundenbuch,* ed. W. K. HAUTHALER and F. MARTIN, 4 v. (Salzburg 1910–33) 1:188–209; 2:113–129, codex Hartwici. P. KARNER, *Austria sancta: Die Heiligen und Seligen Salzburgs* (Vienna 1913). J. WODKA, *Kirche in Österreich* (Vienna 1959). J. OSWALD, *Lexikon für Theologie und Kirche*[2] 5:22.

[V. H. REDLICH]

HARTY, JEREMIAH JAMES

Archbishop; b. St. Louis, Mo., Nov. 5, 1853; d. Los Angeles, Calif., Oct. 29, 1927. He was the son of Andrew and Julia (Murphy) Harty, Irish immigrants. Educated at St. Bridget's Parochial School, St. Louis University, and St. Vincent's Seminary, Cape Girardeau, Mo., he was ordained on April 28, 1878. After he had devoted 25 years to pastoral duties in the St. Louis archdiocese, his name was proposed for auxiliary bishop by Abp. John J. Kain, and in 1902 he was appointed temporary administrator of the archdiocese pending appointment of a coadjutor. In June 1903 he was elected to the Metropolitan See of Manila, Philippine Islands, and was consecrated by Cardinal Francesco SATOLLI in the Church of St. Anthony, Rome, Aug. 15, 1903, although consistorial promotion came only on November 9. En route to Manila, Harty visited Pres. Theodore Roosevelt, who gave assurances of friendly governmental assistance.

Harty took possession of the See of Manila on Jan. 16, 1904. Two of his American suffragans, Bishops Dennis DOUGHERTY and Frederick Rooker, preceded him, while Bp. Thomas A. Hendrick followed shortly afterward. At this time, Church unity was endangered by the Aglipayan schism; Protestant proselytizing was bitterly aggressive; antifriar sentiments divided the faithful; and the native clergy were too few and too badly educated to combat all these attacks. Financial problems arising from change of sovereignty and abolition of the *patronato* privileges further complicated administration. Hospitals administered jointly by the Spanish government and the Church were claimed by the new government; friars' estates were under attack by nationalists; and Church properties seized by schismatics were recovered only through expensive lawsuits. In facing these problems, Harty was handicapped by his ignorance of Spanish and native languages, by misunderstandings with government officials and higher clergy, and especially by the sudden death of the Apostolic Delegate, Abp. John B. Guidi, shortly after calling the first Provincial Council of the Philippines. Nevertheless, Harty reorganized seminaries, rebuilt churches and schools, fought to recover Church property, and stemmed the tide of Aglipayanism before ill-health necessitated his transfer to America as archbishop-bishop of Omaha, Nebr., in May 1916. Installed in Omaha on Dec. 17, 1916, Harty found a diocese that still lacked many agencies incorporated elsewhere. He, therefore, erected 13 parishes and 9 parochial schools; established the first diocesan school board; organized CATHOLIC CHARITIES, NATIONAL COUNCIL OF CATHOLIC WOMEN, NATIONAL COUNCIL OF CATHOLIC MEN, and Society for the Propagation of the Faith; aided Father FLANAGAN with Boys Town; and planned a diocesan seminary. In 1925 continuous illness forced him to leave the diocese, and Bp. Francis J. L. Beckman was appointed diocesan administrator on Nov. 5, 1925.

Bibliography: Archives, Archdiocese of St. Louis. Archives, Archdiocese of Omaha. National Archives, Washington, D.C.

[M. D. CLIFFORD]

HARVEY NEDELLEC (HERVAEUS NATALIS)

Dominican theologian and philosopher, referred to as *Doctor rarus;* b. Brittany, *c.* 1250–60; d. Narbonne, *c.* Aug. 7, 1323. He entered the Order of Preachers in the diocese of Tréguier in 1276. Nothing further is known of him until 1301, when he is listed among those present at the Dominican provincial chapter at Rouen. He was at Saint-Jacques in 1303 and supported King Philip the Fair against Boniface VIII. It is probable that Harvey read the *Sentences* of Peter Lombard at Paris in 1301–02 or 1302–03. He became master of theology in 1307 and occupied one of the magistral chairs at Saint-Jacques until his election as provincial of France, Sept. 17, 1309. On June 10, 1318, he was elected master general of the order at the general chapter in Lyon. During his generalate Harvey worked extensively on behalf of the canonization of THOMAS AQUINAS. His efforts were crowned with success on July 18, 1323, but Harvey was not himself present. On his way from Barcelona to the ceremonies at Avignon he fell sick at the Dominican convent in Narbonne and died there.

Harvey's literary output was not inconsiderable, either in quantity or in breadth of interest. He wrote *Quaestiones super sententias* (Venice 1505; Paris 1647), *Quaestiones disputatae* (Venice 1513), and various Quodlibets. Although the Venice edition (1513) of his Quodlibets contains 11 of these disputes, only Quodlibets 1–4 appear to be authentic. His philosophical works include *In 1 perihermeneias, Quaestiones de praedicamentis, De cognitione primi principii,* and *De secundis intentionibus* (Paris 1489; Venice 1513). He was an almost indefatigable controversialist and polemicist. He was head of a commission appointed to examine the writings of DURANDUS OF SAINT-POURÇAIN, which found 91 objectionable propositions. He attacked JAMES OF METZ in *Correctorium fr. Jacobi* and PETER AUREOLI and directed a long series of treatises against HENRY OF GHENT.

Although Harvey had a wide acquaintance with the works of St. Thomas Aquinas and wrote a valuable *Defensio doctrinae fr. Thomae,* he sometimes adopted positions incompatible with the Thomistic metaphysics of being. In particular, he rejected Aquinas's position on the interrelationship between ESSENCE AND EXISTENCE (*esse*) in creatures. Yet, though Harvey's philosophy may seem more eclectic than Thomistic, he considered himself an ardent follower of Aquinas. And, in this regard, it was the canonization of Thomas, in which Harvey played a major role, that assured the continued influence of Aquinas in the intellectual life of Christendom. (*See* THOMISM.)

Bibliography: É. H. GILSON, *History of Christian Philosophy in the Middle Ages* (New York 1955) 747–748. P. GLORIEUX, *La Littérature quodlibétique,* v.1 (Kain 1925), v.2 (Paris 1935) 1:200–208; 2:138–139. B. HARÉAU, ''Hervé Nédélec: Général des Frères Prêcheurs,'' *Histoire littéraire de la France* 34 (1915) 308–351. C. O. VOLLERT, *The Doctrine of Hervaeus Natalis on Primitive Justice and Original Sin* (*Analecta Gregoriana* 42; 1947). E. ALLEN, ''Hervaeus Natalis: An Early 'Thomist' on the Notion of Being,'' *Mediaeval Studies* 22 (1960) 1–14. A. DE GUIMARÃAES, ''Hervé Noël (1323): Étude biographique,'' *Archivum Fratrum Praedicatorum* 8 (1938) 5–81. E. A. LOWE, *The Dominican Order and the Theological Authority of Thomas Aquinas in the Early Fourteenth Century: The Controversies between Hervaeus Natalis and Durandus of St. Pourcain* (Ph.D. diss., Fordham University, 1999).

[E. B. ALLEN]

HASIDAEANS

Also known as Asidaeans, members of a religious group among the Jews about the middle of the second century B.C. Described in 1 Mc 2.42 as ''the stoutest of Israel, every one that had a good will for the law,'' the Hasidaeans took their name from the Hebrew word *ḥāsîd,* plural *ḥăsîdîm* (Aramaic, *ḥăsîdayyā';* Gr., Ασιδαῖοι), meaning pious. Having been among the first to join with Judas Maccabee in his guerrilla warfare against the Syrian armies of ANTIOCHUS IV EPIPHANES in 166 B.C., the Hasidaeans were still fighting in the time of Demetrius I in 161 B.C., when they were accused to Demetrius by Alcimus, a Hellenistic HIGH PRIEST, of being seditious (2 Mc 14.6). The passage in 1 Mc 1.14, in which they are represented as favorable to Alcimus because he was ''a priest of the seed of Aaron,'' indicates that they were supporters of the legitimate priesthood and were interested in religious rather than political ends. Thus, when the illegitimate high priests, Jason and Menelaus, had been disposed of and Alcimus had been recognized as high priest, the Hasidaeans were ready to make peace. However, they were betrayed by Alcimus and Bacchides, the Syrian commander of Demetrius I (1 Mc 7.15–16), and they may have rejoined Judas to continue the struggle.

Little is known about the Hasidaeans after the time of Judas Maccabee, but it seems that the ESSENES and the PHARISEES continued in different ways the original Hasidaean movement of early Maccabean times. The Essenes, or at least the group of them that formed the QUMRAN COMMUNITY, remaining loyal to the old Sadocite (Zadokite) line of high priests, probably left the main stream of Jewish life after 140 B.C. when Simon Maccabee took for himself and his HASMONAEAN successors the title of high priest (1 Mc 14.41–47). The Pharisees, on the other hand, continued the main line of the Hasidaean movement, opposing all compromise with Hellenism and insisting on a punctilious observance of the Law. The Jewish religious movement of the 18th and 19th centuries called ḤASIDISM has nothing in common with the Hasidaeans except the name.

See Also: MACCABEES, BOOKS OF THE; MACCABEES, HISTORY OF THE.

Bibliography: M. SCHLOESSINGER, *The Jewish Encyclopedia*, ed. J. SINGER (New York 1901–06) 6:250–251. D. B. EERDMANS, ''The Chasidim,'' *Oudtestamentische Studiën* 1 (1942) 176–257. M. J. LAGRANGE, *Le Judaïsme avant Jésus-Christ* (*Études bibliques*; 1931). F. M. CROSS, JR., *The Ancient Library of Qumran and Modern Biblical Studies* (Garden City, N.Y. 1958) 98–107.

[P. F. ELLIS]

ḤASIDISM

A large movement of inner renewal that arose in the 18th century among the poverty-stricken Jews of eastern and southeastern Poland. Ḥasidism was founded by Rabbi ben Eliezer (*c.* 1700–60). It resembled, in some ways, the Franciscan movement of the 13th century.

Historical Background. When, in the aftermath of the plague epidemics of the mid-14th century German Jews had to flee persecution, they were received into Poland. For most of the 15th century their life seemed secure. But as they became economic buffers between the Polish Catholic landlords and the Ukrainian Orthodox peasants in eastern and southeastern Poland (Polkynia and Podolia), they courted the hatred of the oppressed. In the middle of the 17th century Ukrainian cossacks waged a ''holy war'' against the Poles and the ''accursed breed of Jews.'' So cruel was this massacre that an Italian rabbi thought that it was the greatest since the destruction of Jerusalem and indeed, that it was the birth pangs preceding the coming of the Messiah.

Not long after this blood bath there arose in Smyrna an adventurer who fancied himself the royal messiah: triumphantly he would take the Sultan's crown, make him his slave, and change the fate of Jewry. When Shabbatai (Sabbatai) Ṣevi (Tzevi) proved a coward and apostatized to Islam (1666), Jews all over Europe, who for months had lived in eager expectation, fell back into dejection. Devotees continued the fraud and explained his fall as martyrdom necessary for his final rise—a rise that never came. (*See* SHABBATAIÏSM).

Having been fed this travesty of Christianity, the people witnessed also the spectacle of penitents ''pressing'' for the messianic days of glory by the severest mortifications. The rabbis, in the meantime, clung to the study of the minutiae of the law. Thus without comfort in a world of fear, the poor Jews of Poland turned to magic healers who pretended to have power over demons by the shuffling of the letters of YHWH (YAHWEH), the ineffable name. Hence their title Baale Shem, ''Masters of the Name.''

The Founder. Among these healers, yet different from them, was Rabbi Israel. He breathed such kindness that he was called Baal Shem Tov, ''Master of the Good Name'' or ''Kindly Master,'' frequently abbreviated to Besht from the initials (B-SH-T) of this name. He had prepared himself for his work among the downhearted through the study of the Lurianic CABALA (*see* LURIA, ISAAC) and by prayer and solitude in the mountain wilderness. The manner in which he met death tells the man. ''I want to busy myself with God a bit more,'' he said of his desire to pray, and he confessed to those around him, ''Now I know for what I was created.'' Together they asked: ''Let the graciousness of the Lord, our God, be upon us.'' His own final words were: ''Let not the foot of pride overtake me'' [Ps 35(36).12].

The Message. The Besht's main teachings were these. God is everywhere, the darkest corner is not without Him, and the smallest thing is filled with His glory. He loves the simple and unlearned no less than the Talmudic students; even without much knowledge, a Jew can be pure and just and carry the Holy Spirit within him. The heart of God is always open to the penitent, the man who turns from sin and self, and to the humble, the man of prayer who comes before Him like a beggar whose hands are empty. Unavoidable though sadness is in this world, it must ever be a herald of joy. A man should cast away his cares and live in the glad certainty that, as he looks up to his Creator (Blessed be He!), the Creator looks upon him. To serve God, then, is to love, and to love is to rejoice.

The Tzaddik. It was not by tenets but by emphasis and custom that the Ḥasidim, ''men of piety'' (hence the movement is called Ḥasidism), differed from the Orthodox norm. Yet the difference was strong enough to force their withdrawal from the mainstream and their founding of separate congregations. A group would gather around

Ḥasidic men praying at Western Wall, Jerusalem, Israel. (©David Katzenstein/CORBIS)

a charismatic leader, a *tzaddik*, ''just man.'' For miles they would travel to spend the Sabbath with him, eat at his table, listen to his words. They saw to his material needs, while he cared for their spiritual advance. He acted as their mediator with heaven, and they surrendered their lives to him.

The *tzaddik*'s credentials were not learning but communion with the upper world. A cabalistic myth tells that in primeval times some of the vessels of light broke and sparks fell into the world. These long to be freed and return to their sources so that divine harmony may be restored. It is the *tzaddik*'s task and power to end the exile of holy sparks by ''lifting them up.'' Thus he is considered the ''heart of the world,'' one who transfigures and sanctifies the things he touches and the men admitted to his presence.

Song and Dance. Ḥasidic accent on joy, brotherly love, and communal worship made delight in God a corporate experience. Together, the Ḥasidim sought to move closer to God. The *tzaddik*'s table was regarded as an altar that one approached with awe. After the third Sabbath meal, they would sit in a darkened room, listen enraptured to their rebbe's (rabbi's) wisdom, and sing ecstatic songs. Their song and dance was not an amusing pastime but an essential part of their Sabbath and Holy Day celebrations, an expression of their brotherly affection and their craving for God.

On all festive occasions the men took each other by the hand and danced in a circle, while they hummed or sang a wordless melody. Now and then they clapped their hands to rouse their joy and speed their rhythm. Suddenly one of the dancers might burst into prayer or all of them might sing: *Tate ziser, helf!,* ''Sweet Father, help!'' The most famous Ḥasidic song is the ''Song of You'': ''Lord of the world . . . , I will sing You a song of You: You, You, You! . . . Where I wander—You. Where I ponder—You. Only You, You again, always You! You, You, You! . . .''

History. The faster Ḥasidism spread, the fiercer became the opposition. Its adversaries, the Mitnaggedim, ''opponents,'' branded it heretical. The Besht was called an ''empty well,'' his followers ''thorns and thistles to be rooted out,'' ''impure men who had deserted the way of God.'' Appeals to the government asked for their suppression, their books were burned, and repeatedly the great ban of excommunication was pronounced. Later, however, when the existence of both groups, the Ḥasidim and the Mitnaggedim, was threatened by a new movement, the HASKALAH, they made common cause. Soon, with much of their spontaneity gone, Ḥasidism became even more rigid in its orthodoxy than its former opponents in theirs.

The Besht had been fortunate enough to find great and faithful disciples. But in the course of the years, the movement grew into several distinct branches. One is the Ḥabad school (the word is formed from the first letters of the Hebrew words *ḥokmâ, bînâ,* and *dē'â*— wisdom, understanding, and knowledge). It stresses man's intellectuality; hence, it is a faith engaging the mind with the tzaddik acting as teacher. When the charismatic leaders of its early generations gave way to the rulers of hereditary dynasties, the movement declined. Some of the ruling seats even became centers of greed and superstition. Yet, for all its misfortunes, Ḥasidism endured.

Several Ḥasidic leaders escaped even the Nazi extermination machine. They took up residence in the U.S. and Israel: the Lubavitcher rebbe and the Saltmarer rebbe in different parts of Brooklyn, N.Y., the rebbe of Beltz in Tel Aviv, and the rebbe of Ger in Jerusalem. These and others are from eight to ten generations removed from the time of the Besht. The movement, which once embraced half the Jewish population of Europe, has diminished. Yet its influence on Jewish thought and life outweighs its numbers.

Bibliography: E. MUELLER, *A History of Jewish Mysticism,* tr. M. SIMON (Oxford 1946). T. YSANDER, *Studien zum B'eštschen Hasidismus* (Uppsala 1933). S. A. HORODEZKY, *Religiöse Strömungen im Judentum* (Bern 1920). P. P. LEVERTOFF, *Die religiöe Denkweise der Chassidim* (Leipzig 1918). M. BUBER, *The Origin and Meaning of Hasidism,* ed. and tr. M. FRIEDMAN (New York 1960); *The Tales of Rabbi Nachman,* tr. M. FRIEDMAN (New York 1956); *The Tales of the Hasidim,* tr. O. MARX, 2 v. (New York 1964). J. LANGER, *Nine Gates to the Chassidic Mysteries,* tr. S. JOLLY (New York 1961). J. M. OESTERREICHER, ''The Hasidic Movement,'' *The Bridge* (New York 1958) 3:122–186. Z. SCHACHTER, ''How to Become a Hasid,'' *Jewish Heritage* 2 (Spring 1960) 33–40. W. GOODMAN, ''The Hasidim Come to Williamsburg,'' *Commentary* 19 (1955) 269–274. G. SCHOLEM, ''Martin Buber's Hasidism,'' *ibid.* 32 (1961) 305–316; ''Religious Authority and Mysticism,'' *ibid.* 38 (1964) 31–39. H. WEINER, ''The Lubovitcher Movement,'' *ibid.* 23 (1957) 231–241, 316–327; ''The Dead Hasidism,'' *ibid.* 31 (1961) 234–242, 420–427; ''A Wedding in B'nai Brak,'' *ibid.* 40 (1965) 39–46. S. M. DUBNOW, *Geschichte des Chassidismus,* 2 v. (Berlin 1931–32).

[J. M. OESTERREICHER]

HASKALAH

Hebrew term (*haśkālâ,* literally ''the bringing of understanding,'' hence ''enlightenment''), first used by Judah Jeiteles, designating the movement among East-European Jews from *c.* 1750 to *c.* 1880 to add to the traditional Jewish Talmudic studies the knowledge of the literature and culture of Western Europe. As a distinctly Jewish movement, Haskalah resembled only in part the general movement of the ENLIGHTENMENT, with which it was connected. The leaders of the movement, who were called Maskilim (Heb. *maśkîlîm,* those who bring understanding), were convinced that Jewish Emancipation would not be effective unless the Jewish religion were modernized and Westernized. It thus sought a compromise between strict orthodoxy and complete assimilation.

Germany. Although the modernizing movement had forerunners in the 17th century among the Jews of Holland and Italy, the cradle of Haskalah as such was in Berlin, where the Jewish philosopher Moses Mendelssohn (1729–86) in 1750 published a short-lived periodical written in Hebrew but modern in content. In 1778 he established in Berlin a Jewish school that combined the traditional subjects of the ghetto *ḥeder* (elementary school) with the study of German, French, and secular sciences, ''the studies of man,'' as the Maskilim called the humanities. In 1783 he published his German translation (printed in Hebrew characters) of the Pentateuch, accompanied by a rationalistic commentary. In his treatise *Jerusalem* (1783) he stated that Judaism, though a revealed religion, does not contain any truth that could not be attained by rational thinking. Religious observance, not belief, was for Mendelssohn the hallmark of Judaism.

In the reign of FREDERICK II (the Great), King of Prussia, Polish intellectuals who were often tutors in wealthy immigrant Jewish families intermingled with followers of Mendelssohn in Germany, furthering the movement toward Western culture but retaining Jewish orthodoxy in rationalized form. They regarded the modernization of Jewish education as a prerequisite for the emergence of Jewry from its medieval ghetto into the full freedom of European civilization. A group of young Maskilim formed a society for the promotion of the Hebrew language and founded a literary monthly, *Ha-Me'assēf* (The Miscellany), published from 1783 to 1811. Thus Hebrew became the vehicle of the Haskalah movement. The pioneer Maskilim learned to use the holy tongue with ease, a noteworthy achievement because Hebrew had long since degenerated into confused scholastic jargon. Although the Haskalah inspired also a rich literature in Yiddish and other languages, the Maskilim, who opposed assimilation movements and addressed themselves to Jewry as a whole, made a point of using Hebrew.

Russia. The Haskalah reechoed convincingly in the Russian Empire in the early 19th century, where the first generation of Hebrew writers sought to defend the new secular ideas against the fierce opposition of orthodox

Jewry. The outstanding figure of this period was I. B. Levinsohn (1788–1860) in the Ukraine, whose work, *Te'ûdâ be-Yiśra'ēl* (Testimony in Israel), printed in Vilna in 1828, virtually inaugurated the Haskalah movement in Russia. The book was published with a grant of 1,000 rubles from the Russian government, which regarded it as a contribution to their policy of assimilation. In this work, as well as in his *Bêt Yehûdâ* (The House of Judah, 1839), Levinsohn undertook to convince his fellow Jews that the program of the Haskalah, which advocated the study of the Hebrew language and grammar, the acquisition of secular sciences, and the pursuit of handicrafts and agriculture, was not opposed to the Jewish religion. In proposing that at least one-third of the people be encouraged to engage in agriculture, Levinsohn was a forerunner of one aspect of Zionism. Russian Jewry, as a whole, did not support Levinsohn's ideas. The orthodox leadership rejected them outright, considering the Haskalah a dangerous innovation and a threat to the preservation of Judaism, being convinced that it would ultimately lead to atheism or conversion to Christianity.

Two outstanding authors are representative of the second generation of Russian Haskalah, Abraham Mapu (1808–67) and Judah Leib Gordon (1831–92). The former introduced historical romance into Hebrew letters. The subject matter of two of his novels is drawn from biblical times, while his *'Ayiṭ Ṣāvû'a* (The Hypocrite) depicts the life of his own generation, denouncing corrupted community leaders and bigoted rabbis, while presenting in favorable light the young Maskil perplexed between religion and science. With Mapu the Haskalah became militant. The same offensive tone appeared in the work of Gordon, one of the greatest Hebrew poets since the Middle Ages. He attacked the tyrants of the Jewish community as responsible for the backward condition of his beloved people and declared that his desire was not to destroy the Jewish religion, but to seek the golden means to unite pure faith with reason and the needs of the time.

Meanwhile, independently of the Haskalah movement, profound changes had taken place in Russian Jewry. The young generation of the 1860s and 1870s had abandoned not only Jewish practices but Judaism itself. The Maskilim, with their plea for national consciousness, were now considered outdated. Peretz Smolenskin (1842–85), the most representative author of the expiring Haskalah, still struggled for the spread of light and knowledge but recognized that secular knowledge and the mastery of languages were not the panacea for all the ills of the House of Israel. In his opinion, Jews who pretended to be adherents of the Mosaic faith only were no longer Jews. ''In Judaism,'' declared Smolenskin, ''religion and national belonging are inseparable; the Torah is not only the religious guide of the Jews but also the witness of their peoplehood.'' If in an earlier time Maskilim endeavored to save the man in the Jew, Smolenskin wanted to save the Jew in the now enlightened and emancipated man. By asserting the distinctiveness of the Jewish people and by considering the Hebrew language as the mainstay of its national consciousness, Smolenskin paved the way for Zionism

Bibliography: S. BERNFELD, *Encyclopedia Judaica* (Berlin 1928–34) 3:667–681. P. WIERNIK, *Jewish Encyclopedia*, ed. J. SINGER (New York 1901–06) 6:256–258. J. S. RAISIN, *Universal Jewish Encyclopedia* 5:242–245; *The Haskalah Movement in Russia* (Philadelphia 1913). S. HALKIN, *Modern Hebrew Literature* (New York 1950). M. WAXMAN, *A History of Jewish Literature,* 5 v. in 6 (New York 1961) v. 3. L. GREENBERG, *The Jews in Russia,* 2 v. (New Haven 1944–51), bibliog. 1:190–199, esp. 196.

[M. J. STIASSNY]

HASMONAEANS

A Jewish dynasty of the 2d and 1st centuries B.C., the descendants of Mattathias's son Simon and successors of the Maccabees. (*See* MACCABEES, HISTORY OF THE.) The name Hasmonaean is derived from that of Hasmonaeus, who according to Josephus was Mattathias's great-grandfather. Seven members of the dynasty held actual power.

John Hyrcanus (135–104 B.C.). He succeeded his father Simon as king and high priest. In the first year of his reign Antiochus VII Sidetes of the SELEUCID DYNASTY of Syria besieged Jerusalem and forced Hyrcanus to pay tribute for Jewish possessions outside Judea. In 130 B.C. Hyrcanus had to aid Antiochus in a campaign against the Parthians, during which the Syrian king died.

Hyrcanus took advantage of the resulting power vacuum to seize some of the surrounding territory—Medaba (Medeba), SICHEM (SHECHEM), Adora, and Marissa—and to force the Idumeans to accept Judaism; in later years he captured Samaria. Syria's internal problems and wars with Egypt meant effective independence for the Jewish state from 128 B.C. on. Hyrcanus's policies of conquest and national expansion clearly showed the secular character of the Hasmonaean dynasty and brought about a break with the PHARISEES, the successors of the HASIDAEANS, whose religious convictions the Machabees had fought to uphold. Some of the Pharisees whom Hyrcanus persecuted joined the QUMRAN COMMUNITY.

Aristobulus (104–103 B.C.). Known also as Judas, Aristobulus, the eldest of Hyrcanus's five sons, was to have succeeded only to the priesthood; Hyrcanus wished the government to pass to his widow. Instead, Aristobulus put her and three of his brothers in prison; later, because of reports of a plot, Aristobulus had his fourth brother, Antigonus, killed. Aristobulus died, apparently of remorse, soon after. During his reign he had extended his territory northward and Judaized the Ituraeans who lived in Galilee.

Alexander Jannaeus (103–76 B.C.). The eldest of the three remaining sons of Hyrcanus was Alexander Jannaeus, known also as Jonathan. Aristobulus's widow, Salome Alexandra, made him king and high priest and married him. Alexander's reign was occupied with territorial expansion through military campaigns. The first of these, against Ptolemais (Accho), led to defeat through Egyptian interference. More successful were his campaigns against Gadara, east of the Jordan, and, *c.* 96 B.C., the old Philistine cities of Raphia, Anthedon, and Gaza. The Pharisees continued to oppose the warlike Hasmonaean policies of secular nationalism. When Alexander returned to Jerusalem after a campaign in which he had subdued the Moabites and Galaadites but then suffered a reversal from the Nabataean King Obodas I, he met with rebellion. For six years, with the aid of mercenary troops, he fought against civil uprisings; reportedly 50,000 Jews were killed. At last, in 88 B.C., the people appealed for aid to the Seleucid Demetrius III, who defeated Alexander at Sichem. Patriotism, however, brought many Jews back to Alexander, and he was able to expel Demetrius and finally to put down the rebellion. Alexander was pressed by the Nabataeans under Aretas III, but between 83 and 80 B.C. he expanded Jewish territory east and north, as far as Seleucia in Gaulanitis. By the end of his reign Alexander controlled the same territory that had formed the kingdom of David and Solomon. He died in 76 B.C., worn out by excesses, at the age of 51.

Alexandra (76–67 B.C.). She was the widow of Jannaeus and succeeded him as ruler; the heir, Hyrcanus II, became high priest. Though this position satisfied the unambitious Hyrcanus, his younger brother Aristobulus chafed at being subordinate and powerless. Whereas Jannaeus had alienated the Pharisees, Alexandra gave them decisive influence. Aristobulus, however, took the part of the Hellenized, more secular-minded Sadducees. While he was plotting to gain power for himself, Alexandra died at the age of 73.

Aristobulus II (67–63 B.C.). Although Hyrcanus was the rightful heir, his younger brother Aristobulus II, son of Jannaeus and Alexandra, used force to supplant him. In a battle near Jericho, in which many of his troops went over to Aristobulus, Hyrcanus was forced to flee to the citadel of Jerusalem; and there he surrendered himself, the kingship, and the high priesthood to his brother. But a royal official, the Idumean Antipater, persuaded Hyrcanus to seek to regain his rights with the aid of Aretas III, king of the Nabataeans, to whom at Petra Hyrcanus fled. When Aretas besieged Aristobulus in the Temple citadel, the Jews took the part of Hyrcanus. At this point, however, the Romans intervened. Coming from the campaign against Mithridates and Tigranes, Pompey's general Scaurus received delegations from both sides in the dispute, decided in favor of Aristobulus, and ordered Aretas to lift the siege. This decision was subject to reversal by Pompey, however, and when he reached Damascus in 63 B.C., he was met by three delegations. The Jewish people countered the two brothers' arguments by asking that the monarchy be abolished and the priests given power. Pompey postponed a final decision, but Aristobulus defied him and fled to Jerusalem. Although he surrendered there, his partisans would not admit Pompey's general Gabinius to the city. When Pompey himself came, Hyrcanus's followers surrendered the city, but the war party that supported Aristobulus took refuge in the Temple citadel. After a three-month siege Pompey forced his way in, and 12,000 Jews were massacred. Pompey's entrance marked the end of Jewish independence. Judea and Jerusalem were made tributary; and all coastal possessions, Samaria, Scythopolis, and the non-Jewish towns east of the Jordan were lost. These Pompey incorporated into the newly organized province of Syria. Judea now consisted of Juda, Perea, Galilee, the southern districts of Samaria, and Idumea. Aristobulus, with his sons Alexander and Antigonus, was taken to Rome to march in Pompey's triumph of 61 B.C., but Alexander escaped on the way.

Hyrcanus II (63–40 B.C.). Hyrcanus now was high priest, but lacked political power for most of his reign. In 57 B.C., after an attempted rebellion by Alexander, Gabinius divided the land into five districts and placed these under the Roman governor of the province of Syria. The following year Aristobulus and Antigonus escaped from their Roman captivity and led a revolution; after a two-year siege Aristobulus was again captured and taken to Rome. The freedom granted his sons permitted another revolt, led by Alexander, in 55 B.C. Subsequently Gabinius, reversing the five-district division of 57 B.C., decided to strengthen Hyrcanus's position against his rivals and restored the high priest's power. When the Roman civil wars began in 49 B.C., Caesar planned to use Aristobulus to fight for him in Syria, but both he and Alexander were murdered by the Pompeians. Hyrcanus and Antipater joined the Caesarean party after Pompey's defeat at Pharsalia in 48 B.C. and furnished aid in Caesar's Egyptian campaign. For this service Caesar confirmed Hyrcanus as high priest and appointed him ethnarch; Antipater was made Roman procurator of Judea. After Caesar's assassination (44 B.C.) and again after the Battle of Philippi (42 B.C.) Hyrcanus gave his allegiance to the victorious faction, first to Cassius, then to Mark Antony. Antony confirmed Hyrcanus as high priest and made the sons of Antipater, Phasael and HEROD (later known as the Great), tetrarchs.

Antigonus (40–37 B.C.). Antigonus, however, who was known also as Mattathias, took advantage of the Parthian invasion of Syria to have himself installed as king and high priest under the protection of the Parthian garrison in Jerusalem. Phasael and Hyrcanus were captured by a ruse, and Antigonus had his uncle's ears cut off, to make him legally unable to be high priest again, and sent him into exile with the Parthians; Phasael committed suicide. Herod, who had avoided being taken by the Parthians, was himself pronounced king by the Roman Senate at the end of the same year. In 37 B.C. he captured Jerusalem and had Antigonus executed. Hyrcanus was brought back from Babylon, but in 30 B.C. Herod executed him, at the age of 80, to remove his last possible rival for power.

Other members of the Hasmonaean dynasty figured in later Palestinian history. In 37 B.C. Herod married Mariamme, whose parents were Hyrcanus's daughter Alexandra and Alexander, the son of Aristobulus II. At Alexandra's urging Mariamme's brother Aristobulus was appointed high priest by Herod in 36 B.C., but within the year he was murdered by him. In 29 B.C. the jealous Herod had Mariamme herself killed; their sons, Alexander and Aristobulus, he had executed in 7 B.C. Aristobulus's son AGRIPPA I was king of Judea from A.D. 37 to 44. Agrippa I's son, AGRIPPA II (d. A.D. 93–94 or 100), was the last descendant of the Maccabees-Hasmonaeans to have any political power.

Bibliography: F. M. ABEL, *Histoire de la Palestine depuis la conquête d'Alexandre jusqu'à l'invasion Arabe,* 2 v. (*Études bibliques* [Paris 1903–] 1952) v. 1. T. H. ROBINSON and W. O. E. OESTERLEY, *A History of Israel,* 2 v. (Oxford 1932) 2:217–349. E. R. BEVAN, ''Syria and the Jews,'' *The Cambridge Ancient History,* 12 v. (London and New York 1923–39) 8:495–533; ''The Jews,'' *ibid.* 9:397–436. G. H. STEVENSON and A. MOMIGLIANO, ''Rebellion within the Empire,'' *ibid.* 10:850–865. M. J. LAGRANGE, *Le Judaísme avant Jésus-Christ* (*Études bibliques* 1931). R. DE VAUX, *Dictionnaire de la Bible,* suppl. ed. L. PIRTO et al. (Paris 1928–) 4:773–775. D. SCHÖTZ, *Lexikon für Theologie und Kirche,* ed. J. HOFER and K. RAHNER, 10 v. (2d, new ed. Freiburg 1957–65) 5:23.

[J. WALSH]

HASSARD, JOHN ROSE GREENE

Journalist, critic, biographer; b. New York, N.Y., Sept. 4, 1836; d. New York, N.Y., April 18, 1888. The son of Thomas and Augusta Greene Hassard, he was reared as an Episcopalian. He became a Catholic in 1851 and graduated from St. John's College, Fordham, New York City, in 1855. He served as secretary to Abp. John Hughes until the prelate's death in 1864, then wrote a biography (1866) based on the archbishop's private papers. He also compiled articles for the *New American Encyclopedia* and became literary editor of the *New York Tribune.*

In 1865, Hassard became first editor of the *Catholic World,* and helped in forming its distinctly literary character. Later the same year Charles A. Dana persuaded him to join the short-lived *Chicago Republican.* In 1866, Hassard returned to the *Tribune* permanently, working chiefly as music and literary critic and editorial writer, and as managing editor for a time after the death of Horace Greeley in 1872. He was also New York correspondent for the *London Daily News* and wrote essays and reviews for the *Catholic World* and *American Catholic Quarterly Review.* In 1872, he married Isabella Hargous; they had no children. Although restricted by ill health, he traveled extensively, pursuing scholarly interests in English, French, and German literature. He died of tuberculosis and was buried at St. Ann's Church, New York City.

Hassard's *History of the United States* (1878) was long used as a text in Catholic schools. His works include: *The Wreath of Beauty* (1864), *A Life of Pope Pius IX* (1877), *Richard Wagner at Bayreuth* (1877), *A Pickwickian Pilgrimage* (1881), and *New York Tribune's History of the United States* (1887).

Bibliography: I. T. HECKER, ''John R. G. Hassard,'' *Catholic World* 47 (June 1888) 397–400. J. J. WALSH, ''John R. G. Hassard,'' *Catholic World* 97 (June 1913) 349–359.

[J. L. O'SULLIVAN]

HASSE, JOHANN ADOLPH

Composer of opera and church music of the preclassical period; b. Bergedorf (near Hamburg), March 25, 1699; d. Venice, Dec. 16, 1783. He was trained first under his father, and at 18 left for Hamburg to try his musical vocation. After singing in the Hamburg Opera for four seasons and producing his first opera in 1721, he pursued his studies in Naples with PORPORA and A. SCARLATTI and taught in Venice. There he married the noted singer Faustina Bordoni in 1730. In 1731 he was appointed musical director of the Dresden Opera, and remained in Dresden most of his life, taking time for extensive travels. During a stay in London he attempted, unsuccessfully, to challenge HANDEL's domination of the lyric theater. Besides opera he composed instrumental and sacred music (twelve oratorios, including *La conversione di Sant'Agostino*, ten Masses, three Requiems, Psalms, motets, litanies, a *Te Deum*, and a famous *Salve Regina*).

They are operatic in style, with recitatives, arias, and a few choruses, and also, like his operas, melodious and expertly orchestrated.

Bibliography: W. MÜLLER, *J. A. Hasse als Kirchenkomponist* (Leipzig 1911). A. A. ABERT, *Die Musik in Geschichte und Gegenwart*, ed. F. BLUME (Kassel-Basel 1949–) 5:1771–88. H.-B. DIETZ, ''The Dresden-Naples Connection, 1737–1763: Charles of Bourbon, Maria Amalia of Saxony, and Johann Adolf Hasse,'' *International Journal of Musicology* 5 (1996) 95–130. S. HANSELL, ''Johann Adolf Hasse'' in *The New Grove Dictionary of Music and Musicians,* v. 8, ed. S. SADIE (New York 1980) 279–293. W. HOCHSTEIN, ''Wer war Johann Adlof Hasse?,'' *Musik und Kirche* 69 (1999), 99–101. F. L. MILLNER, ''The Operas of Johann Adolf Hasse'' (Ph.D. diss. University of California at Berkeley, 1976); *The Operas of Johann Adolf Hasse* (Ann Arbor 1979). N. SLONIMSKY, ed. *Baker's Biographical Dictionary of Musicians* (New York 1992) 727–728.

[W. C. HOLMES]

HATRED

As a passion or emotion, hatred is the exact opposite of love. It is the reaction of repugnance of an appetite toward an object conceived as an evil. As a sin it is the opposite of Christian love or charity, or, in other words, it is a voluntary hostility to God and the children of God. Since love of others supposes a true love of self (Mt 22.39), hatred of God and of fellow man presupposes a false love of self, which is truly a form of self-hatred. Charity is the highest Christian virtue and the source of every other virtue, and consequently hatred of God is the gravest of sins, for it is directly and immediately corruptive of charity. It is accounted by theologians as a special sin against the Holy Spirit, who is the Spirit of love.

The hatred contrary to charity is an act or habit of will essentially opposed to the benevolence of charity. It is therefore voluntary and deliberate, and should not be identified with feelings of hostility or ANTIPATHY or repugnance that arise spontaneously on the sense level and not infrequently are stubbornly resistant to voluntary control. Feelings of this kind may be quite involuntary, and they are not essentially associated with any malevolence of will. They may exist in persons whose deliberate attitudes and behavior are unexceptionable when measured by the rule of charity.

The formal object of charity is God, first in His own person, and then in His relationship to men. The formal object of hatred, as opposed to charity, is also God, but God as seen under the aspect of evil. God is all good, indeed goodness itself, and seen as He truly is He cannot be hated. He can nevertheless appear to man as an evil, as when He is considered to be the cause of things man sees as odious to himself, or as forbidding sin, or inflicting punishment.

Hatred of neighbor always involves hatred of God, for just as charity toward one's fellows is identifiable with charity toward God because it loves the realization of the divine good in neighbor, so also hatred of neighbor rejects the divine good and its realization. Hence, ''he who says he loves God and hates his neighbor is a liar'' (1 Jn 4.20). One must not hate even his personal enemies or the enemies of the church, since all men in this life are potentially at least members of Christ's Mystical Body (1 Tm 2.4), and hence to hate any other person is to hate Christ (cf. Mt 25.41–46).

Indirectly and by inference there is an element of hatred of God in every mortal sin, for one who sins mortally deforms the image of God. However, this is hatred only in a relative and attenuated sense, for the sinner does not commonly detest the divine good except in the sense that he values it less than he does some created good.

Those with charity hate the evil that deforms, whether it be sin or error. Thus, just as God hates deceit and pride (Prv 6.16–19) and other sins, so do the saints (Ps 96.10). One must, however, love the sinner while he hates the sin, as did Our Lord (Mt 9.11, 13). One must not confuse error with the person who errs, whether in morality, religion, philosophy, or in any other respect.

Bibliography: B. HÄRING, *The Law of Christ*, tr. E. G. KAISER, 3 v. (Westminster, Md. 1961–) v.2. *Encyclopedic Dictionary of the Bible*, tr. and adap. by L. HARTMAN (New York 1963). D. VON HILDEBRAND and A. JOURDAIN, *True Morality and Its Counterfeits* (New York 1955). A. M. HENRY, ed., *Man and His Happiness*, tr. C. MILTNER (Chicago 1957).

[J. M. GIANNINI]

HAUTECOMBE, ABBEY OF

Benedictine monastery of Our Lady in Savoy, France, Archdiocese of Chambéry. Founded in 1121 by Benedictines from Aulps, an abbey affiliated with MOLESME, it joined the Cistercians in 1135 at the suggestion of St. Bernard. St. AMADEUS, later bishop of Lausanne, became abbot in 1139, and the abbey moved to a better location on Lake Bourget donated by the Count of Savoy. From 1184 to 1502 members of the house of Savoy were buried in the abbey, of which they were patrons for many years. From 1439 to 1451 and after 1505 Hautecombe was a commendatory abbey and suffered a decline. It was administered by the government of Savoy from 1700 to 1742. Under Spanish occupation (1742–48) it regained its independence and was rebuilt in baroque style. Suppressed in 1792, it fell into ruin. The restoration begun by King Charles-Felix in 1824 was completed by Maria Christina in 1843; both sovereigns were buried in the abbey. Italian Cistercians from La Consolata in Turin

Abbey of Hautecombe, on the shore of Lake Bourget, Savoie, France. (©Michael Busselle/CORBIS)

were replaced by French from Sénanque in 1864, and in 1922 Benedictines from SOLESMES occupied the abbey, which has edited translations of the Missal.

Bibliography: L. H. COTTINEAU, *Répertoire topobibliographique des abbayes et prieurés,* 2 v. (Mâcon 1935–39) 1:1383–84. R. GAZEAU, *Catholicisme. Hier, aujourd'hui et demain,* ed. G. JACQUEMET 5:531–533. B. GRIESSER, *Lexikon für Theologie und Kirche,* ed. J. HOFER and K. RAHNER, 10 v. (2d, new ed. Freiburg 1957–65) 5:37.

[L. J. LEKAI]

HAUTERIVE, ABBEY OF

Cistercian abbey five miles south of Fribourg, Diocese of Lausanne-Geneva-Fribourg, Switzerland. Founded by William of Glâne (d. 1143) and settled with Cistercians from Cherlieu in Burgundy (1138), it was endowed by William, whose family (Counts of Neuenberg) became *advocati.* Subsequent patrons were the Counts of Aarberg (1299) and the city of Fribourg (1455). Hauterive founded Kappel (1185) and flourished under the protection of the Bishops of Lausanne and the Counts of Zähringen. It was plundered by mercenaries (1387) but revived under Abbot Pierre d'Affry (1405–49), who received pontifical rights (1418). Wars, the rule of weak abbots, and a fire (1578) reduced it to poverty. A revival under Abbots Pierre Python (1604–09), Antoine Du Pasquier (1609–14), and a Guillaume Moënnat (1616–40) was followed by debt and a decline. The abbey was suppressed by Fribourg in 1848 and became an agricultural school and a teachers' college. The archives and library went to Fribourg's cantonal and university library. The church (12th–14th century, restored 1722–84) with its frescoes, stalls (*c.* 1480), and stained glass (1322) was restored along with the cloister as a Swiss art monument (1903–13). In 1939 Cistercians restored Hauterive as a priory under WETTINGEN-MEHRERAU.

Father Bonaventure Loots standing with parishioners outside of grass church in Pua, Hawaii.

Bibliography: L. H. COTTINEAU, *Répertoire topobibliographique des abbayes et prieurés,* 2 v. (Mâcon 1935–39) 1:1385–86. M. REYMOND, *Les Sires de Glâne et leurs possessions* (Fribourg 1918). R. PITTET, *L'abbaye d'Hauterive au moyen âge* (Fribourg 1934). F. KOVÁCS, *Stalles d'Hauterive* (Fribourg 1953). M. H. VICAIRE, *Lexikon für Theologie und Kirche,* ed. J. HOFER and K. RAHNER, 10 v. (2d, new ed. Freiburg 1957–65) 5:37–38.

[A. MAISSEN]

HAWAII, THE CATHOLIC CHURCH IN

The Roman Catholic Church grew from banishment, persecution, and tragedy to become the largest religious body in the state of Hawaii. For most of its history, it was a mission territory administered by missionary personnel from Europe and the United States, until the establishment of the Diocese of Honolulu in 1941, weeks before the United States was plunged into World War II with the bombing of Pearl Harbor on Oahu. Hawaii became the 50th state of the union in 1959, growing rapidly from an economy dominated by agriculture into a major tourist destination and the communications, trading and military hub of the central Pacific. The Diocese of Honolulu, a suffragan see of the Archdiocese of San Francisco, spans the entire state. By the start of the 21st century it had grown into an active multi-ethnic community blending native Hawaiian and American traditions with the cultures and contributions of immigrants from Asia and the South Pacific.

Hawaii is an archipelago of more than 100 islands of which only seven are large enough to sustain permanent populations, stretching through more than 1,500 miles of mid-Pacific Ocean bisecting the Tropic of Cancer in a southeast to northwest arch. Geologically, they are the tips of volcanic mountains resulting from ocean floor eruptions that began perhaps as long as 40 million years ago and which continue today.

The oldest island is Kure Atoll at the archipelago's northwest end. At its southeast tip is the youngest and largest island, Hawai'i, which gives the entire chain its name and is also commonly known as the Big Island. In relative close proximity are the rest of the populated islands—Maui, Molokai, Lanai, Oahu, Kauai and Niihau.

Oahu, the third largest in size after the Big Island and Maui, is the location of the capital city of Honolulu, the center of government and commerce in Hawaii, and home to eight-tenths of the state's population. Honolulu is also where the Catholic Church has its central administrative offices and bishop's residence.

Polynesians from Pacific islands to the south and southwest of Hawaii were the first to populate the Hawaiian Islands, arriving in waves of migration that began as early as 600–800 A.D. When British explorer Captain James Cook arrived in 1778, nearly 300 years after Columbus landed in the new world, he had "discovered" the last significant territory on earth to be visited by Europeans. Captain Cook named his discovery the Sandwich Islands after the Earl of Sandwich in his native England.

In Hawaii, the British explorer found a highly developed, albeit stone-age, civilization with its own unique religion, a complicated caste system, and sophisticated capabilities in open-ocean navigation, featherwork, woodwork, stone carving, fishing and agriculture. He also found a people whose centuries of isolation from the rest of the world had left them free of many of humanity's most common diseases and who consequently lacked any immunity toward them. The result was disastrous. In the first 100 years since Captain Cook's arrival, diseases introduced into Hawaii devastated its population, reducing it from an estimated 250,000 to 40,000.

The first recorded Catholic baptisms in Hawaii, that of two high chiefs, occurred in the summer of 1819, although a Spanish layman and resident of Hawaii named Don Francisco de Paulo Marin claimed to have baptized 300 natives earlier. The more significant of the 1819 baptisms, performed by a chaplain on a visiting French vessel, was conferred on Boki Kamauleule, the governor of Oahu. He would later prove to be a vital supporter of the growing Catholic mission of Hawaii.

It was not until 1827 that the first official Catholic missionaries arrived in the islands. They were members of the French-based Congregation of the SACRED HEARTS OF JESUS AND MARY to whom Rome had given the assignment. The missionaries were Father Alexis Bachelot, Father Patrick Short and Father Abraham Armand, and three religious brothers. They arrived on July 7, 1827, celebrating the first recorded Mass on Hawaiian soil six days later in Honolulu on July 13. They secured mission property in Honolulu which remains in use by the church today as the site of the present Cathedral of Our Lady of Peace.

The Catholic missionaries were not warmly welcomed by the Hawaiian Kingdom. They had been preceded seven years earlier by members of the American Protestant Mission of Massachusetts, whose Congregationalist and Presbyterian ministers had solidly established favor with the Hawaiian royalty. The Protestants had made great progress in a short amount of time, establishing an alphabet for the Hawaiian language which previously had only been spoken, setting up a printing operation, and opening schools. Their influence also resulted in the rulers of Hawaii outlawing the ancient Hawaiian religion with its many idols and stone temples.

The Protestants saw the Catholic priests as rivals. Although the Catholics proceeded peacefully and were nonconfrontational, they faced opposition and disapproval. Because of their statues and crucifixes, they were accused of illegal idol worship. However, as long as Boki was governor of Oahu, they had a faithful defender in a high place. When Boki was lost at sea in 1830, the persecution of Catholics began, led primarily by the powerful Queen Kaahumanu, and later by her successor Kinau.

One of the immediate results of Kaahumanu's hardline policies was the expulsion from the islands of Fathers Bachelot and Patrick Short on December 24, 1831. Father Armand had departed two years earlier because of illness. The Sacred Hearts Brothers were left to maintain the Honolulu mission.

The islands were without a Catholic priest until the arrival of Sacred Hearts Father Robert Arsenius Walsh on Sept. 30, 1836. Being a British subject, he was permitted to stay but prohibited from converting native Hawaiians. Father Walsh's presence in Hawaii prompted the return of Fathers Bachelot and Short on April 17, 1837, and a few months later, the arrival of Sacred Hearts Father Louis Maigret. But all three were met with renewed opposition and were expelled before the year ended. On December 5, the sickly Father Bachelot died at sea and was buried on the tiny reef island Na, off Ponape, in the Caroline Islands.

During this period, the natives were given harsh punishments for the "crime" of being Catholic. Hundreds were imprisoned and forced into hard labor. In December 1837, the Catholic religion was declared illegal by official ordinance. Father Walsh escaped deportation only because he was British.

It took a threat of war to stop the persecution. On July 9, 1839, the French warship *L'Artemise* dropped anchor in Honolulu Harbor. Its captain, Cyril Laplace, demanded religious freedom for Catholics in Hawaii. If not granted, he would retaliate by firing his ship's cannons on the city of Honolulu. That declaration, later called "Laplace's Manifesto," was enough to pressure King Kamehameha III into a concession and he stopped the persecution.

Under the new mantle of religious liberty, the Catholic mission enjoyed a quick revival. Bishop Stephen Rouchouze, vicar apostolic of eastern Oceania of which

Hawaii was a part, arrived with other priests on May 15, 1840. Rouchouze laid the cornerstone for the Cathedral of Our Lady of Peace. It was dedicated, Aug. 15, 1843, and remains one of the oldest Catholic cathedrals in continuous use in the United States. It is also the oldest building structure in downtown Honolulu and the oldest Catholic church in Hawaii.

Rouchouze's efforts to initiate missions through the islands soon suffered a tragic setback. In order to meet the challenge of his expanded mission, Bishop Rouchouze went back to France in 1841 to have a ship built and outfitted, and missionaries recruited for the islands. The ship, the *Marie Joseph,* on its maiden voyage to Hawaii, was lost at sea in March 1843 near the Strait of Magellan, taking with it the bishop, six priests, one seminarian, seven brothers and nine sisters. It would be 16 years before another ship would bring Sacred Hearts Sisters from Europe around Cape Horn to Hawaii.

In 1845, King Kamehameha III gave land in Kahaluu, Oahu, to the Catholic Mission for the building of a school. The following year, Ahuimanu College, the first Catholic school in Hawaii, began operation. Meanwhile, Catholic religious education on the island of Maui was prospering without the benefit of any priest. In a circumstance unique in Hawaii Catholic history, thousands of Maui natives had been instructed in the faith by a young lay catechist named Helio Mahoe and a few others. By the time two priests arrived on the island on April 21, 1846, 4,000 Hawaiians were ready to be baptized.

In 1847, Father Louis Maigret was consecrated a bishop and named the first vicar apostolic of Hawaii. May 4, 1859, marked the arrival of the first nuns in Hawaii, the SACRED HEARTS SISTERS. They established a convent school next to the cathedral, the first of several schools for girls they would eventually open. The Sacred Hearts Academy is the largest Catholic girls school in the state.

Blessed Damien de Veuster. Damien de VEUSTER arrived in Honolulu on March 19, 1864. Born Joseph De Veuster, Jan. 3, 1840, in Tremelo, Belgium, at age 18, he joined his older brother Auguste in the Congregation of the SACRED HEARTS OF JESUS AND MARY (SS.CC.) taking the religious name Damien after the ancient physician-saint. After ordination to the priesthood in the Cathedral of Our Lady of Peace, a few months after his arrival, his first assignment was on the Big Island of Hawaii where he spent ten years.

During this time, Hansen's disease, or leprosy, was ravaging the native Hawaiian people who were particularly susceptible to its virus. The Hawaiian government responded to the dreaded incurable affliction with a solution as old as the Bible—quarantine and isolation. King Kamehameha V decreed that anyone with leprosy would be sent to the small Kalaupapa peninsula on the island of Molokai, inaccessible except by sea or a treacherous cliff trail. There, hundreds of leprosy patients of all ages were left to fend for themselves and to die in squalid and lawless conditions.

Bishop Louis Maigret was extremely concerned about the plight of those abandoned in Kalaupapa but was reluctant to make the place a permanent clergy assignment. Father Damien was the first of four priests who volunteered to go there on rotation. He arrived on Molokai on May 10, 1873, and soon after wrote his bishop that it was "absolutely necessary" for a priest to remain there permanently and that he would be willing to be the one. Father Damien spent the next 16 years bringing dignity to a settlement the rest of the Hawaii had abandoned. He served as priest, doctor, nurse, carpenter, plumber, gravedigger, and coffin maker. Disregarding medical precautions for himself, he ate with the people, accepted them into his house and touched them. He brought normalcy to a condemned world, organizing a choir and a children's band, supervising religious organizations, and directing religious education. He eventually contracted the disease himself and succumbed on April 15, 1889, the Monday of Holy Week, at age 49. He was buried beside his church, St. Philomena. At the request of the Belgian government, his body was returned to his home country in 1936. A cure for Hansen's disease was found in the 1940s and in 1969, the State Board of health ended its policy of segregating those with the disease.

Hawaii received its first major influx of Catholic immigrants with the arrival of the first Portuguese farm laborers from the Azores in 1878. By the end of the 19th century, more than 18,000 would settle in Hawaii. With the decrease of the Hawaiian population, Catholic missionary efforts began shifting their ministry toward these newcomers.

Bishop Maigret died on June 11, 1882, after laboring 42 years in Hawaii, 35 years as its bishop. His administration had seen a Catholic conversion of the Hawaiian people rivaling and exceeding the Protestant efforts. As primary builder of the cathedral, he was buried below its sanctuary. Succeeding him was Bishop Hermann Koeckemann.

The year after Bishop Maigret's death, 1883, saw the arrival of two religious orders that would have a tremendous affect on Hawaii. The first, landing in September, were the educator brothers of the Society of Mary, or MARIANISTS. They opened Catholic boys' schools on Oahu, Maui and the Big Island. Their Honolulu school, St. Louis, continues to be one of the state's most prominent educational institutions.

Two months later, on November 8, six FRANCISCAN SISTERS from Syracuse, NY, led by Mother Marianne COPE, arrived to assist the Hansen's disease patients at the Kakaako Branch Hospital in Honolulu. Marianne Cope had been superior of the Franciscan Sisters of Syracuse, NY, in 1883 when she responded to a plea from King Kalakaua for a nursing order to care for the unattended sick, including 200 leprosy patients, in Honolulu. Not only did Mother Marianne quickly fulfill the Hawaii government's needs, she also opened a hospital on Maui. In 1888, five months before the death of Father Damien, she and two sisters arrived at Kalaupapa to run the settlement's two homes for the sick and homeless.

She remained in Kalaupapa after Father Damien's death. As medical professionals, she and her sisters treated the patients with compassion and without fear, following proper sanitary precautions. She predicted that none of her sisters would ever contract leprosy, and none ever did. She died on August 8, 1918, of natural causes at age 80 and is buried in Kalaupapa.

Church comes of age. Bishop Gulstan Ropert was appointed the mission's third vicar apostolic on June 3, 1892. On April 6, 1903, Bishop Libert Boeynaems was named its fourth vicar apostolic. The fifth vicar apostolic, Bishop Stephen Alencastre, grew up in Hawaii having immigrated to the islands at age five with his family. He was named to head the Catholic mission on May 13, 1926. During his administration, he established Catholic schools and orphanages, launched Honolulu's first Catholic hospital, and set up a small seminary. In 1929, he divided the Honolulu Mission into nine ''quasi-parishes.'' Bishop Alencastre also invited to the islands the MARYKNOLL FATHERS and MARYKNOLL SISTERS who played a large part in the shaping of the island church in the 20th century.

Two events in 1940 forecast the Hawaii mission's coming of age. First was the ordination of the first three local-born ''diocesan'' priests, though the church was not yet a diocese. The second was the unexpected death on Nov. 9, 1940, of the beloved Bishop Alencastre. With his death, the Hawaii Catholic mission era came to an end.

On Sept. 10, 1941, the Catholic Church in Hawaii, at age 114, was elevated to the status of Diocese of Honolulu. Father James J. Sweeney, a priest of the Archdiocese of San Francisco, was consecrated as the first diocesan bishop. At that time, the new diocese had 112 churches, 17 schools, 82 priests, 78 brothers, 250 sisters, and 120,000 faithful.

The Diocese of Honolulu. For its first four years the diocese was in ''war-support-mode'' because of the central role that Hawaii played in the Pacific war effort. But with the war's end in 1945, the fledgling diocese came to life with energy and enthusiasm. In 1946, St. Stephen Diocesan Minor Seminary opened. The late 1940s and early 1950s saw the introduction of Catholic Charities and other new diocesan offices, a flurry of church and school construction, the introduction of new religious orders, and the flourishing of lay organizations, sodalities and societies. In 1957, Bishop Sweeney convened the first diocesan synod.

The diocese continued to grow through the 1960s, conscientiously embracing the renewal introduced by the Second Vatican Council, even as it went through the same social and religious turmoil as the rest of the country. Bishop Sweeney died in 1968 and was succeeded by his auxiliary, Bishop John J. Scanlan.

In 1970, in spite of strong opposition on the part of Bishop Scanlan and the Catholic diocese, Hawaii became the first state in the union to liberalize its abortion laws, predating by one year, the U.S. Supreme Court's Roe vs. Wade decision which essentially legalized abortion for the rest of the nation.

The church of the 1970s responded to the times, welcoming refugees from the Vietnam War, establishing a residence for pregnant unwed mothers, and seeing growth in such groups as the Charismatic renewal movement, MARRIAGE ENCOUNTER and CURSILLO. A drop off in vocations to the priesthood led to the eventual closing of the seminary in the early 1980s. During his administration, Bishop Scanlan also invited a number of religious orders to the islands from Asia, including Carmelite Sisters from Hong Kong and sisters from the Philippines to staff the local parochial schools.

Upon Bishop Scanlan's retirement in 1982, auxiliary Bishop Joseph A. Ferrario was named the third bishop of the Diocese of Honolulu. Bishop Ferrario had come to Hawaii from Scranton, PA, as a seminary professor in 1957 and was incardinated in the diocese in 1966. As bishop, he presided over a maturing of liturgical practice in the diocese, an increase in ecumenical outreach and adult religious education, and a significant expansion of Catholic Charities and parish social ministries. In 1985, Bishop Ferrario renovated and elevated St. Theresa Church in Honolulu to the status of co-cathedral to ease the smaller and less accessible Cathedral of Our Lady of Peace of some of its liturgical burdens. Bishop Ferrario retired because of health reasons in 1993 and was succeeded by Bishop Francis X. DiLorenzo, a Philadelphia native and auxiliary Bishop of Scranton.

As the fourth bishop of Honolulu, DiLorenzo was formally installed on Nov. 30, 1994. He introduced a diocese-wide parish renewal and review program called the

"Welcoming Parish," and in June 2000 convened the diocese's second synod in order to prepare the church in Hawaii for the 21st century. He also increased and strengthened the diocese's ethnic ministries to serve newly arrived immigrants, in particular the Filipinos, Vietnamese, Samoans, Koreans, and Chinese. The Filipinos, who are largely Catholic, were by far the largest of these groups and therefore became the diocese's biggest ethnic ministry challenge. According to the Diocesan Office of Ethnic Ministries, Filipinos make up about one half of the Catholic population of Hawaii.

By the beginning of the 21st century, the Catholic population of Hawaii had grown to 236,688, and it continues to grow with the population. This figure does not include the Catholics in the armed services who fall under the jurisdiction. of the U.S. Military Archdiocese. Routinely the dozen or more Catholic chaplains assigned to the military bases operate independently of the Diocese of Honolulu but enjoy a cooperative relationship with it. The second largest religious group after the Catholic Church is Buddhism, which counted about 100,000 adherents at the end of the 20th century, all sects combined.

The Catholic Church in Hawaii mirrors the multiethnic blend that makes up the local population where no single ethnic group holds a majority. In fact, because of the commonly accepted practice of interracial marriage, one of the largest population groupings belongs to those of mixed ancestry. Other larger racial blocks include part-Hawaiians, Caucasians, and Asians. They are served by 66 parishes, three ethnic Catholic parish communities, and one Eastern Catholic Apostolate.

The Congregation for the Sacred Hearts and the Marianists continue to remain among the largest communities of religious men in Hawaii. In the 1980s, the Capuchin Franciscans added Hawaii to its Guam vice province, and the Philippine province of the La Salette Fathers increased their presence in the islands. On the other hand, the Maryknoll Fathers, who manned a large number of parishes during much of the 20th century reduced their numbers to only a handful by the year 2000. In most places parishes are staffed by at least one or two priests, a small but increasing percentage of whom come from Asia, particularly the Philippines. Hawaii also has 50 active permanent deacons. Among the orders of religious women, the largest are the Sisters of the Sacred Hearts, the Sisters of St. Joseph of Carondelet, the Franciscan Sisters of Syracuse, and the Maryknoll Sisters.

Bibliography: R. SCHOOFS, SS.CC., *Pioneers of the Faith* (Honolulu 1978). M. D. PIRES, SS.CC., *Shrouded in Mystery—The Marie Joseph: A Remarkably Courageous and Tragic Missionary Venture* (Honolulu 2000). L. LUERAS, editor, *Hawaii* (Hong Kong 1981). G. DAWS, *Holy Man* (New York 1973). M. L. HANLEY, O.S.F., and O.A. BUSHNELL, *Pilgrimage and Exile—Mother Marianne of Molokai* (Honolulu 1991).

[P. DOWNS]

HAWKINS, DENIS JOHN BERNARD

English Catholic philosopher; b. Thorntown Heath, London, July 17, 1906; d. Godalming, Surrey, Jan. 16, 1964. He was educated at the Whitgift School, Croydon, and at the Gregorian University, Rome, and received his doctorates in philosophy and theology. Ordained priest for the Diocese of Southwark in 1930, he devoted his life to pastoral as well as to intellectual work. He became rector of Claygate (Surrey) in 1940 and parish priest of Godalming in 1950. In 1956 he was made an honorary canon of the diocese. Canon Hawkins was a Thomist who devoted himself to the task of meeting the challenge of D. Hume and I. Kant to the possibility of metaphysics. He rethought the principles of St. Thomas's metaphysics and presented them anew in the climate of English academic philosophy. His most original works are his *Criticism of Experience* (London 1945) and *Being and Becoming* (New York 1954). *The Essentials of Theism* (New York 1949) and *Sketch of Mediaeval Philosophy* (London 1946) have been the most widely read of his books, but the former suffers from the brevity at which he always aimed in presenting his ideas. In *Crucial Problems of Modern Philosophy* (New York 1957) he discussed the bearing of contemporary ideas on his own critical approach to metaphysics; in *Man and Morals* (New York 1961) he sketched the outlines of a system of ethics. He wrote numerous articles in reviews and symposia and was well known as a lecturer.

[E. A. SILLEM]

HAWKS, EDWARD

Teacher, writer; b. Abergarenny, South Wales, Feb. 17, 1878; d. Philadelphia, Pa., Jan. 22, 1955. He was the son of Edward and Theresa (Hallam) Hawks and lived an uneventful youth in Wales before the family settled in Bristol, England. At 21 he immigrated to Canada to prepare for the Anglican ministry. He studied for a time at Bishop's College, Lennoxville, Canada, and then spent several years as a lay missionary in the mining camps of northern Canada. In 1903 Hawks entered the Episcopal seminary at Nashotah, Wis., where he received orders and became a member of the faculty, teaching Latin and Greek. At Nashotah, Hawks joined the Companions of the Holy Saviour, which had been founded in Philadelphia by William McGarvey, an advocate of clerical celibacy and Anglo-Catholic ideals.

When the Episcopal Church altered its canon law in 1907 to permit non-Episcopalians to preach before its congregations, the Companions regarded this ''open pulpit'' amendment as a denial of the historic priesthood and episcopacy. After resigning his position as instructor at Nashotah, Hawks entered the Catholic Church in 1908, and was soon followed by McGarvey and most of his congregation. In 1911 Hawks became a priest in the Archdiocese of Philadelphia, where he served for several years as a parish curate. During World War I he was a chaplain in the Canadian Army. Upon returning to Philadelphia in 1919, he established the parish of St. Joan of Arc, where he remained until his death. For many years Hawks wrote a column on current events for the diocesan newspaper, the *Catholic Standard and Times.* From 1936 to 1938, after becoming a domestic prelate, he toured Spain to gather accounts of the civil war for his column. His efforts on behalf of the Nationalist cause won him a decoration from the Spanish government.

[D. A. QUAINTANCE]

HAY, GEORGE

Scottish bishop; b. Edinburgh, Aug. 24, 1729; d. Aquhorties, Aberdeenshire, Oct. 15, 1811. An Episcopalian, he trained as a surgeon, a profession then barred to Catholics, and in this capacity accompanied the Jacobite army in 1745. After becoming a Catholic in 1749, he entered the Scots College, Rome (1751). After ordination (1758), he was missioner at Preshome, Banffshire, until his consecration as coadjutor bishop of the Scottish Lowland District (1769). Appointed vicar apostolic (1778), he was chiefly concerned with the welfare of seminaries and with efforts to repeal Scottish anti-Catholic laws. He also wrote a series of instructional works, which influenced English Catholic thought, and was responsible for publication of the first Catholic Bible in English printed in Scotland (1796–97). Hay did much to sustain the Church in Scotland during a period of persecution, riots and repressive penal laws.

Bibliography: A. C. KERR, *Bishop Hay* (London 1927).

[J. QUINN]

HAYDN, FRANZ JOSEPH

Master composer of the classical period; b. Rohrau, lower Austria, March 31, 1732; d. Vienna, May 31, 1806. When the seven-year-old boy's pleasant voice and general musicality aroused the interest of the imperial Kapellmeister Reutter, Haydn was taken to the court chapel at Vienna. As a choirboy he received a thorough general and musical education, with opportunities to sing in the cathedral and at court. In 1749 his voice changed and he was unceremoniously dismissed. Hard years followed, during which he ''barely managed to stay alive by giving music lessons to children,'' as he recalled. At the same time he continued to study and compose. A position as music director at a small court materialized in 1759; two years later he entered the service of the Esterházy family in Eisenstadt. Under Prince Nicholas I (reigned 1762–90) the musical establishment that Haydn directed grew in size and quality; his arduous duties included the composition of sacred music, primarily Masses. For the cathedral of Cádiz, Spain, he wrote the *Seven Words of the Savior on the Cross* (1785), a cycle of seven adagios for string quartet (a later version includes voices and additional instruments).

Franz Joseph Haydn.

Under Prince Anton (1790–94), musical activities in Eisenstadt and at the summer residence, Esterháza, were greatly reduced. For the first time Haydn was free to travel, though he kept the court appointment. His two extensive journeys to England (1791, 1794) brought successes and honors, including a doctorate from Oxford. They also provided opportunities to hear impressive performances of HANDEL's oratorios, in the strong choral-singing tradition of 18th-century England. Partly as a result of these impressions Haydn composed his own oratorios, *The*

Creation (1798) and *The Seasons* (1801), which, despite some critical reviews, established his international fame more than any other works; their rousing choruses in particular achieved widespread popularity. Prince Anton's successor, Nicholas II, showed greater musical interest, particularly in sacred music. Haydn was asked to compose a series of Masses to be performed on the name day of the princess; he responded with his last great Masses: the *Pauken messe* or *Missa in tempore belli* (1796), *Heiligmesse* (1797), *Nelson Mass* (1798), *Theresia Mass* (1799), *Schöpfungsmesse* (1801), and *Harmoniemesse* (1802). His earlier sacred works included a *Missa Brevis* (*c.* 1750), the *Grosse Orgelmesse* (1766), the *Missa Sanctae Ceciliae* (*c.* 1770), *Missa Sancti Nicolai* (1772), *Missa brevis Sti. Joannis de Deo* (*c.* 1775), and *Missa Cellensis* (1782). In most of these the orchestra, though sometimes large, remains in the background. There are many vocal solos, some quite elaborate, others of simple, lyrical beauty. The *Missa Sanctae Ceciliae* is Haydn's longest—a solemn Mass in cantata style in which the subdivisions of the text (especially in the Gloria and Credo) are treated as independent movements. There are several extensive fugues. Among shorter compositions are two *Te Deum* and two *Salve Regina* settings; several motets are of doubtful authenticity.

After the *Missa Cellensis,* Haydn wrote no Masses for 14 years, chiefly because of restrictions imposed on church music during the reign of Emperor JOSEPH II (*see* JOSEPHINISM). The style of the last six Masses reflects his development (aided by his experiences in England) during the intervening years, notably in the handling of the orchestra. Vocal solos are in large part replaced by quartets. Individual movements are more compact, and the general tone tends to be more serious, especially in the *Nelson Mass,* perhaps his most frequently performed Mass today. Yet even in these late works passages occur in which the musical treatment seemed inappropriately gay. For this reason and others the Masses have often been considered inappropriate for the Catholic liturgy, despite their spirit of joy and exuberant faith. Haydn's often quoted reply to this accusation was, ''When I think of the Lord my heart is so full of joy that the notes come running by themselves. Since God gave me a joyful heart He may forgive me for serving Him joyfully.''

Bibliography: K. GEIRINGER, *Joseph Haydn* (rev. ed. New York 1963). R. HUGHES, *Haydn* (London 1950). H. E. JACOB, *Joseph Haydn,* tr. R. and C. WINSTON (New York 1950). R. G. PAULY, *Music in the Classic Period* (New York 1965). C. F. POHL et al., *Grove's Dictionary of Music and Musicians,* ed. E. BLOM, 9 v. (5th ed. London 1954) 4:145–205. J. P. LARSEN et al., *Die Musik in Geschichte und Gegenwart,* ed. F. BLUME (Kassel-Basel 1949–) 5:1858–1934. P. H. LÁNG, *Music in Western Civilization* (New York 1941). *Histoire de la musique,* ed. ROLAND-MANUEL, 2 v. (Paris 1960–63); v. 9, 16 of *Encyclopédie de la Pléiade* v. 2. K. G. FELLERER, *The History of Catholic Church Music,* tr. F. A. BRUNNER (Baltimore 1961). H. BAETEN, ''Auf den Spuren Joseph Haydns: Een bezoek aan de Haydntage in Eisenstadt,'' *Musica Antiqua* 14 (1997) 186–188. D. BARTHA, ''Folk Dance Stylization in Joseph Haydn's Finale Themes,'' *Hungarian Music Quarterly* 6/1–2 (1995) 2–12. A. ESPINOSA, ''Félix Máximo López, Franz Joseph Haydn, and the Art of Homage,'' *Early Keyboard Journal* 16/17 (1999) 133–155. M. HEAD, ''Music with 'No Past?' Archaeologies of Joseph Haydn and *The Creation,*'' *19th Century Music* 23 (2000) 191–217. P. H. KIRBY, ''The Impact of Haydn's Conducted Performances of *The Creation* on the Work and the History of Conducting,'' *Journal of the Conductors' Guild* 13 (1992) 7–22. M. LORBER, ''Das Joseph Haydn zugeschriebene Singspiel *Die reisende Ceres,*'' *Die Musikforschung* 50 (1997) 80–86. N. A. MACE, ''Haydn and the London Music Sellers: Forster v. Longman and Broderip,'' *Music and Letters* 77 (1996) 527–541. L. SOMFAI, *The Keyboard Sonatas of Joseph Haydn: Instruments and Performance Practice, Genres and Styles* (Chicago 1996). G. TABOGA, ''Le relazioni tra A. Luchesi, J. Haydn, e la Spagna,'' *Recerca Musicològica* 13 (1998) 165–200. H. WIRTH, ''Joseph Haydns Symphonie mid dem Paukenwirbel: Ein Betrachtung,'' *Hamburger Jahrbuch für Musikwissenschaft* 1 (1975) 87–99.

[R. G. PAULY]

HAYDN, MICHAEL

Church composer of the classical period; b. Rohrau, Lower Austria, Sept. 14, 1737 (baptized Johann Michael); d. Salzburg, Aug. 10, 1806. Like his older brother, Franz Joseph HAYDN, he began his career with the choristers of St. Stephen's cathedral in Vienna. His three-octave soprano voice won for him the place of soloist in the choir after his brother's voice changed. The training he received at St. Stephen's was supplemented by his mastery of J. J. FUX's *Gradus ad Parnassum,* which proved very influential in his compositional technique. After a period in Hungary and Grosswardein as *Kapellmeister* to Archbishop Count Firmian, he was appointed music director in 1762 to Archbishop Count Schrattenbach, uncle of Count Firmian. This brought him to Salzburg, where he married Maria Magdalena Lipp, daughter of the cathedral organist and herself a noted court singer (she sang the role of Rosina in MOZART's early opera *La Finta Semplice* and the *Regina Caeli,* K. 127, that he wrote for her). Haydn also provided music for the Salzburg Benedictine church, St. Peter's, and much of his music is still in its archives.

With the succession of Hieronymus Collaredo to the Salzburg archbishopric, the course of liturgical music in the Austrian center took a new direction. Collaredo, a prominent clerical figure during the Enlightenment, attempted to simplify the celebration of the liturgy in the light of JOSEPHINISM. After Mozart's departure from Salzburg, Haydn took full responsibility for the archbishop's liturgical music and wrote 117 Graduals and 45 Offertories to reinstate the performance of these liturgical items. His idiom combined the symphonic instrumental emphasis of the classical style with the polyphonic background he had absorbed from the *Gradus ad Parnassum.* In addition to these Mass Propers, he wrote 30 Latin Masses, 4 Vespers, 10 litanies, 6 *Te Deums,* many motets, "German Masses," and other religious music. Symphonic and chamber works number more than 100, and he composed also one opera and several vocal works. His music has been compared frequently and unfavorably to his brother's; yet considered on its own merits, it reveals a craftsmanship of the highest order by a musician who understood well symphonic form, counterpoint, and the happy combination of the two. His religious music was readily admitted by Franz Joseph to be superior to his own in style and treatment. Bound closely to his Salzburg circle, Michael enjoyed friendly relations with the Mozart family and many other musicians, as well as clerics and students, including (briefly) Carl Maria von WEBER.

Bibliography: H. JANCIK, *Michael Haydn* (Zurich 1952); *Die Musik in Geschichte und Gegenwart,* ed. F. BLUME (Kassel-Basel 1949–) 5:1933–44. E. TITTEL, *Österreichische Kirchenmusik* (Vienna 1961). R. G. PAULY, "The Reforms of Church Music under Joseph II," *Musical Quarterly* 43 (1957) 372–382. Most of his music is still unpublished, but his Masses are ed. by A. M. KLAFSKY in *Denkmäler der Tonkunst in Österreich* (1893– ; repr. Graz 1959–) v. 45, 62. R. ANGERMÜLLER, "Geistliche Werke von Michael Haydn in der k. k. Hofkapelle in Wien 1820–1896," *Kirchenmusikalisches Jahrbuch* 78 (1994) 83–93. R. D. MILLER, *The Graduals of Johann Michael Haydn: Performance Editions and Studies of Selected Works* (Ph.D. diss. Texas Tech University 1998). R. G. PAULY, *Michael Haydn's Latin Proprium Missae Compositions* (Ph.D. diss. Yale University 1956). R. G. PAULY and C. H. SHERMAN, "Michael Haydn," in *The New Grove Dictionary of Music and Musicians,* ed. S. SADIE (New York 1980) 8:407–412. D. M. RANDEL, ed., *The Harvard Biographical Dictionary of Music* (Cambridge, Mass. 1996) 369–370. N. SLONIMSKY, ed., *Baker's Biographical Dictionary of Musicians* (8th ed. New York 1992) 740–741.

[F. J. MOLECK]

Silhouette profile of Michael Haydn.

HAYDOCK, GEORGE, BL.

Priest, martyr; b. ca. 1556 at Cottam Hall, Preston, Lancashire, England; hanged, drawn, and quartered Feb. 12, 1584 at Tyburn (London). He was the youngest son of devout Catholics: Evan Haydock and Helen Westby of Mowbreck Hall, Lancashire. About 1574 or 1575, he followed his father and brother to Douai, then continued his studies at the English Colleges in Rome and Rheims. After his ordination at Rheims, Dec. 21, 1581, he returned to England. In February 1582 he was arrested in London and spent 15 months in the Tower, where he was able to administer the Sacraments to his fellow prisoners even through he was suffering from a recurrence of malaria. He was indicted with BB. Wm. DEAN, James Fenn, Thomas Hemerford, John Munden, John Nutter (all beatified 1929), and two other priests on Feb. 5, 1583, on charges of conspiracy against the queen at Rheims. They were found guilty on Feb. 7 and sentenced to death. The other four were shackled to "the pit" in the Tower, but Haydock, still weak from malaria, was sent back to his quarters lest he cheat the executioner by dying in prison. He said Mass early on Wednesday Feb. 12, before being drawn in hurdles to Tyburn and disemboweled while alive. An eyewitness account of the execution, which is included in Pollen's *Unpublished Documents relating to the English Martyrs* (London, Catholic Record Society, 1908, v. 5), describes Haydock as "a man of complexion fayre, of countenance milde, and in professing of his faith passing stoute." He was especially known for his devotion to the successor of Peter and to St. DOROTHY. He was beatified by Pope John Paul II on Nov. 22, 1987 with 84 companions.

Feast of the English Martyrs: May 4 (England).

See Also: ENGLAND, SCOTLAND, AND WALES, MARTYRS OF.

Bibliography: Catholic Record Society publications (London, 1905–), II, V, *passim,* III, 12-15; IV, 74. R. CHALLONER, *Memoirs of Missionary Priests,* ed. J. H. POLLEN (rev. ed. London 1924).

Patrick Joseph Hayes.

H. FOLEY, *Records of the English Province of the Society of Jesus*, 7 v. (London 1877–82) 74, 103. J. H. POLLEN, *Acts of English Martyrs* (London 1891) 252, 253, 304.

[K. I. RABENSTEIN]

HAYES, PATRICK JOSEPH

Cardinal; b. New York City, Nov. 20, 1867; d. New York City, Sept. 4, 1938. His parents, Daniel and Mary (Gleason) Hayes, came from Killarney, Ireland. His mother died when Patrick was five, and he was brought up by her sister and brother-in-law, Ellen and James Egan. After attending Transfiguration School, the De La Salle Institute, and Manhattan College, all run by the Christian Brothers in New York City, he entered St. Joseph's Seminary, Troy, N.Y., in 1888. He was ordained on Sept. 8, 1892, by Abp. Michael A. Corrigan and then went to the Catholic University of America, Washington, D.C., where he received his S.T.L. degree in 1894. On his return to New York City, he was assigned as curate to St. Gabriel's parish, where he became secretary to the pastor, John M. Farley. When Farley was named archbishop of New York in 1902, Hayes was appointed (1903) chancellor of the archdiocese and president of Cathedral College, a new preparatory seminary housed in the chancery building. He retained these offices until Oct. 28, 1914, when Cardinal Farley consecrated him titular bishop of Tagaste. Hayes served as pastor of St. Stephen's parish, New York City, from 1915 until he was appointed military ordinary on Nov. 24, 1917. The U.S. entry into World War I had necessitated rapid expansion of the Chaplain Corps of the U.S. Armed Forces. To meet this need Benedict XV had created a U.S. military ordinariate and named Hayes as its first head. Within a year, the U.S. Army and National Guard increased the number of their chaplains from 25 to nearly 900. Hayes visited military camps in America, but did not get to the European front partly because of the illness of Cardinal Farley, who died Sept. 17, 1918.

On March 10, 1919, Hayes became the fifth archbishop of New York; on March 24, 1924, he was made a cardinal priest. The major concern of his administration was the founding (1920) of Catholic Charities, a widely copied organization that unified and expanded Catholic charitable works. Although he supported temperance and opposed the child-labor amendment on states' rights grounds, Hayes tended to shun controversy and involvement in public issues and restricted his activities mainly to his archdiocese, where he founded 60 new parishes by 1929. Though he was stricken by a severe and lingering illness in 1932, he retained his post as military ordinary until his death. He was one of the four signatories of the *Program of Social Reconstruction* (1919) issued by the National Catholic War Council and gave firm support to its successor, the National Catholic Welfare Conference. He served also as president of the Catholic Near East Welfare Association and attended the National Eucharistic Congress at Cleveland, Ohio, in 1935 as the personal representative of Pius XI. Hayes was the recipient of numerous foreign, papal, and civic awards.

Bibliography: Archives, Archdiocese of New York, St. Joseph's Seminary, Yonkers, N.Y. J. B. KELLY, *Cardinal Hayes* (New York 1940). PARISH VISITORS OF MARY IMMACULATE, ed., *The Cardinal of Charity* (New York 1927). G. J. WARING, *United States Catholic Chaplains in the World War* (New York 1924).

[F. D. COHALAN]

HAYMARUS MONACHUS

Florentine monk, Patriarch of Jerusalem, and poet; d. 1202. He was the author of the *De expugnatione civitatis Acconensis* (*De expugnata Accone liber tetrastichus*), a poem first printed by John Basil Herold in the appendix to his continuation of WILLIAM OF TYRE (Basel 1549). Herold identified the author as Monachus, a Florentine, who was bishop of Acre. Paul Riant gave him the full title of Haymarus Monachus de Florentia. Since Monachus was also a common Florentine name, there has been some disagreement among scholars about his identity. It is generally believed that he was a monk of Corbizzi in Florence, who became chancellor of Jerusalem in 1171, archbishop of Caesarea from 1181 to 1192, and patriarch of Jerusalem from 1192 to 1202. Since Jerusalem was then occupied by the Muslims, Haymarus established his residence in Acre; hence the confusion with Acre. His poem was edited by William Stubbs. Monachus is also credited with the *Narratio patriarchae* or *De viribus Agarenorum,* written in 1199 at the request of Innocent III, and later incorporated into the *De sancta cruce* of JACQUES DE VITRY.

Bibliography: P. É. D. RIANT, *De Haymaro monacho* (Paris 1865). *Chronica Magistri Rogeri de Houedene,* ed. W. STUBBS, 4 v. (Rolls Series 51; 1868–71) 3:cv–cxxxvi. M. MANITIUS, *Geschichte der lateinischen Literatur des Mittelalters*, 3 v. (Munich 1911–31) 3:701–703. J. DE GHELLINCK, *L'Essor de la littérature latine au XIIe siècle*, 2 v. (Brussels-Paris 1946) 2:126, 127, 130.

[V. L. BULLOUGH]

HAYMO OF FAVERSHAM

Franciscan liturgist, the only English minister general; b. probably at Faversham in Kent, England; d. Anagni, Italy, 1244. He was already a priest and a theologian of established reputation when he joined the Franciscan Order in Paris in 1226 or 1228 (*see* FRANCISCANS). From the first he was an influential figure; he held office as custos of Paris and as lector at Bologna, Padua, and Tours, and was a member of a papal mission to the Eastern Church in 1233–34. He became the ringleader of the group of Paris masters who, from 1236, organized opposition to ELIAS OF CORTONA, and he was their spokesman in the chapter in which Elias was deposed in 1239. He succeeded Albert of Pisa as provincial minister in England in 1239, and as minister general in 1240. He was deeply committed to a program of reform that ensured that the new constitutional framework, inaugurated in 1239, became established on a secure basis. He modified some of the new statutes, noting criticisms from other Franciscans and what the Dominicans were doing. His legislation gave the general chapter a clearer control over the minister general, and fundamentally altered the composition of the order by disqualifying lay brothers from holding office and virtually ending their recruitment. His other outstanding achievement was his scholarly revision of the liturgy. The Ordinals he produced were so convenient and comprehensible that they were adopted throughout the Church.

Bibliography: Sources. THOMAS OF ECCLESTON, *De adventu Fratrum Minorum in Angliam,* ed. A. G. LITTLE (2d ed. Manchester 1951). S. J. P. VAN DIJK, ed., *Sources of the Modern Roman Liturgy: The Ordinals by Haymo of Faversham and Related Documents,* 2 v. (Studia et documenta Franciscana 1 and 2; Leiden 1963). **Literature.** A. PISVIN, *Catholicisme* 5:539–540. R. B. BROOKE, *Early Franciscan Government: Elias to Bonaventure* (Cambridge, Eng. 1959). L. HARDICK, *Lexikon für Theologie und Kirche*, ed. J. HOFER and K. RAHNER, 10 v. (2d, new ed. Freiburg 1957–65) 4:1325. S. J. P. VAN DIJK and J. H. WALKER, *The Origins of the Modern Roman Liturgy* (Westminster, Md. 1960).

[R. B. BROOKE]

HAYMO OF HALBERSTADT

Bishop and theologian; b. late 8th century; d. March 28, 853. There are relatively few known details of Haymo's early life, but he was a monk at Fulda and was sent to the celebrated school at Tours (*c.* 802), where he became a fellow pupil of RABANUS MAURUS and was able to attend the lectures of the renowned ALCUIN. Shortly before Alcuin's death (May 8, 804), Haymo returned to Fulda, where he taught in the monastic school as testified by several documents of the years 815 to 820, written probably in his hand. Haymo seems also to have been at the abbey of HERSFELD for some time, and it was while there that he was named bishop of Halberstadt in 840. As bishop he participated in the synods of Mainz in 847 and 852. TRITHEMIUS calls Haymo ''a most learned man, a penetrating interpreter of the Scriptures,'' basing his judgment on the numerous works that have been attributed to him; but the ascribed homiletical and exegetical works are nearly all spurious. Several works formerly attributed to Haymo are now thought to belong to Haymo of Hirschau (d. *c.* 1107), but it is difficult to know which of the two authors composed any particular work that has survived. Some of Haymo's works are: *De corpore et sanguine Christi* (*Patrologia Latina* 118:815–818), a treatise on the dogma of transubstantiation; *De vanitate librorum, sive de amore coelestis patriae libri tres,* a treatise on detachment from the world and the desire of heaven, valuable largely because it is a testimony to the piety of the 9th century; and *Historiae sacrae epitome* (*Patrologia Latina* 118:819–874), which is derived from earlier historians (Eusebius) and records the principal events of Christian times up to the death of Emperor THEODOSIUS (395). A biography of Haymo (*Archiv* 11:285), written *c.* 1000 by Rochus, a monk of Ilsenburg, is no longer extant except for a few fragments. No official cult of Haymo exists, but he is often given the title saint or blessed, and he appears in the Benedictine martyrology for March 27.

Bibliography: *Patrologia Latina*, ed. J. P. MIGNE, 217 v., indexes 4 v. (Paris 1878–90) v.116–118, passim. J. GAUTIER, *Catholicisme* 1:248. M. MÄHLER, *Dictionnaire de spiritualité ascétique et mystique. Doctrine et histoire*, ed. M. VILLER et al. (Paris 1932–) 1:261–262. *Histoire littéraire de la France* (Paris 1733–68)

5:111–126. G. ALLMANG, *Dictionnaire d'histoire et de géographie ecclésiastiques*, ed. A. BAUDRILLART et al. (Paris 1912–) 1:1187–88. M. MANITIUS, *Geschichte der lateinischen Literatur des Mittelalters*, 3 v. (Munich 1911–31) 1:292, 295, 500, 516–517. G. BAADER, *Lexikon für Theologie und Kirche*, ed. J. HOFER and K. RAHNER, 10 v. (2d, new ed. Freiburg 1957–65) 4:1325–26. A. M. ZIMMERMANN, *Kalendarium Benedictinum: Die Heiligen und Seligen des Benediktinerorderns und seiner Zweige*, 4 v. (Metten 1933–38) 1:383. J. MABILLON, *Acta sanctorum ordinis S. Benedicti*, 9 v. (Paris 1668–1701; 2d ed. Venice 1733–40) 5:583–586.

[V. A. SCHAEFER]

HAYNALD, LUDWIG

Cardinal; b. Szécsény, Hungary, Nov. 3, 1816; d. Kalocsa, Hungary, July 4,1891. After studies in Budapest and Vienna he was ordained (1839), taught law and ecclesiastical history, and then acted as secretary to Abp. József Kopácsy of Esztergom (1845–49). In 1851 he became coadjutor bishop, and in 1852 bishop of Alba Iulia in Transylvania. The separation of Transylvania from Hungary, which was then in force, brought Haynald into conflict with the Hungarian government. He had to resign his see and leave the country (1861). When the political situation in Hungary changed, Haynald was recalled from his Roman exile and named archbishop of Kalocsa (1867). At VATICAN COUNCIL I Haynald was a leading opponent of the definition of papal infallibility. He wanted to cast a negative vote in the final ballot ''in the sight of pope, kings, peoples, and of the future.'' On the day of the definition, however, he submitted to the council's decision. Haynald was a zealous bishop and a promoter of education and sciences, especially of his favorite science, botany, which he himself studied.

Bibliography: L. TÓTH, ''Le Cardinale Haynald,'' *Nouvelle Revue de Hongrie* 64 (1941) 11–19. T. V. BOGYAY, *Lexikon für Theologie und Kirche*, ed. J. HOFER and K. RAHNER, 10 v. (2d, new ed. Freiburg 1957–65) 5:42. E. C. BUTLER, *The Vatican Council, 1869–1870,* 2 v. (New York 1930).

[F. MAASS]

HAZE, MARIA THERESIA, BL.

Baptized Jeanne, known in religion as Marie-Thérèse du Sacré-Coeur de Jésus, founder of the Daughters of the Holy Cross of Liège; b. Feb. 27, 1782, Liège, Belgium; d. there, Jan. 7, 1876. Haze experienced considerable hardship in her early life because the French Revolution forced her parents into exile and caused the loss of their property. With the guidance of Canon Jean-Guillaume Habets (d. 1876), the co-founder, Maria founded her religious congregation in Lüttich (1833) with five companions using the Rule of the JESUITS. The sisters conducted schools, nursed the sick, took care of women who were penitents or prisoners, and tended the destitute in public poorhouses. During Maria's lifetime the congregation, which was recognized by the Vatican on Oct. 1, 1845 and approved on May 9, 1851, spread to Germany, India, and England. Her cause for beatification, introduced by Pope Pius IX (1851) and formally opened with the *commissio introductionis causae* by Pope PIUS X (1911), was concluded by Pope John Paul II, who beatified her on April 21, 1991.

Bibliography: L. HUMBLET, *La Vénérable Mère Marie-Thérèse Haze* (Liège 1924). J. DE MARCHI, *The Venerable Mother Marie Thérèse Haze* (1928). M. E. PIETROMARCHI, *La venerabile Maria Teresa Haze, fondatrice delle Figlie delle Croce* (Rome 1946). A. VÄTH, *Unter dem Kreuzesbanner* (2d ed. Düsseldorf 1929).

[M. B. BLISS]

HEALING, CHRISTIAN

The Christian message of salvation presents sickness as connected with sin, if not personal sin (cf. Jn 9.2–3), at any rate with the original Fall. Hence arises the question of a religious approach to its cure. In fact, Christians, besides seeking recovery by means of medical care, have always believed in the help of prayer and religious blessings, or in Christian healing.

History. In the Old Testament the cure of sickness was also sought in prayer and sacrifice. Sick persons seek the blessing of priests or Prophets and implore healing as a grace. Miraculous cures are mentioned in 1 Kgs 17.17–24 (the son of the widow of Sarephta called back to life by Elijah), 2 Kgs 4.18–37 (Elisha raising the son of the Sunamite woman), and 2 Kings ch. 5 (Elisha curing Naaman of his leprosy). Sickness is often attributed to the devil. Together with sin and the reign of the devil it is to be excluded from the last messianic times.

In the New Testament Christ's miraculous healing of the sick is one of the signs that the last messianic times have come (cf. Mt 11.4–5). Not only He Himself but the Apostles also heal the sick (Mt 10.1), sometimes by anointing them (Mk 6.13). Faith or trust on the part of the sick is required as a condition for the cure; it is not its cause (cf. Mt 13.58).

In the nascent Church, the CHARISM of healing shows itself in the miraculous cures wrought by the Apostles (Acts 3.1–16; 8.7; 9.32–42). St. Paul mentions it in his list of charisms (1 Cor 12.9, 28, 30). Besides, there is mentioned in Js 5.14–16 an Anointing of the Sick by the presbyters not only for a bodily cure but also for a spiritual effect (forgiveness of sins). The Church later recognized here the Sacrament of Anointing of the Sick.

"Christ Healing the Paralytic," from the "Predis Codex," 1476 manuscript painting by Cristoforo de Predis. (©Archivo Iconografico, S.A./CORBIS)

In the early centuries St. James's text is invoked to justify both a liturgical anointing of the sick by bishops or priests for spiritual and corporal healing alike (the Sacrament) and a private anointing by the sick person himself or others mainly for recovery (a SACRAMENTAL; cf. H. Denzinger, *Enchiridion symolorum,* ed. A. Schönmetzer 216). The practice of praying for recovery from sickness in private or liturgical prayer is found throughout the Christian centuries. The Church sanctioned prayers and blessings against sickness, whether preventive or curative, and also recourse to PATRON SAINTS against particular diseases. Here, however, superstitious deviations were not always avoided.

When the doctrine of the Sacraments became explicit in the awareness of the Church (11th–12th centuries), the Anointing of the Sick was counted among the seven Sacraments, and bodily healing came to be considered as its subordinate and conditional effect (cf. *Enchiridion symolorum,* 1696).

The presence of the charism of healing in the Church was attested in the miraculous cures effected by saints (modern critical hagiography admits many as authentic). The norms for canonization of saints fixed by Benedict XIV required authentic miracles, usually cures, as signs from heaven confirming their heroic virtue. Another category of miraculous cures are the ones that occur at places of pilgrimage, those in honor of Our Lady in particular, such as LOURDES. The Church after due examination recognizes some of these cures as genuine miracles. Although miraculous cures of this kind are linked to faith, they are not to be confused with the "faith healing" that refuses ordinary means of medical treatment and therapy.

Catholic theology accepting the reality that in human beings body, soul, and spirit constantly interact encourages interdisciplinary cooperation between medical professionals, psychologists, and clergy in the care of individual patients. Most healing is a process involving a time and sequence known only to God. It calls for a community of persons, professional and lay, willing to spend time with those who suffer and love them into wholeness, using the best medical and spiritual means available.

Healing and the Sacraments. The renaming and ritual revision of two important channels of healing, the Sacraments of Reconciliation and of Anointing proposed by the Second Vatican Council, highlight Christ's will for all to become whole in body and spirit. In administering the Sacrament of Reconciliation, the priest has new opportunities to spend time with the penitent, discovering with the help of the Holy Spirit the root causes of sin. He is thus able to encourage penitents to realize the spiritual and emotional healing available to them as they enter into the forgiving love of Jesus and the Father. The Sacrament of Anointing in its new format places more emphasis on the building of faith for direct physical healing in the sick person, as is clear from its ritual formula: ''May the Lord, who frees you from sin, save you and raise you up.'' By making this Sacrament available to persons other than those in imminent danger of death, the Church reaffirms its belief in the restorative power of her anointing, in accordance with Js 5.14–16.

Throughout the centuries the healing Sacrament par excellence has been the Eucharist, an occasion for Christians to enter into greater wholeness on all levels, spiritual, emotional, and physical. Special Masses for healing, sometimes combined with the Sacrament of Anointing for the sick, are held to call the attention of the faithful to the healing power of the Eucharistic Liturgy. Christian healing, which finds its culmination in the Eucharistic celebration of a community gathered in love and prayer, extends beyond personal concerns for bodily and spiritual fulfillment: it calls Christians to work and prayer for the unity of the Body of Christ and the healing of society.

Church-related health services pledge themselves to minister on all levels to the sick and disabled, providing a witness of Gospel values through an environment of love and respect for human dignity, especially important in the experience of death. Entered into with faith and joyful acceptance when it is ultimately seen to be the will of God, a Christian death, graced by the Sacraments, is the most complete healing of all, an entrance into the eternal fullness of life won for all Christians by Christ on Calvary.

In conclusion it should be emphasized that belief in Christian healing does not dispense one from having recourse to medical care. Religious factors do not replace medical care; they help for recovery, not (as medicine does) by directly acting on the level of biological or chemical or physiological realities, but by strengthening the grace life of the sick person or by miracle.

See Also: ANOINTING; ANOINTING OF THE SICK, I (THEOLOGY OF); ANOINTING OF THE SICK, II (LITURGY OF).

Bibliography: J. GIBLET and P. GRELOT, ''Maladie-guérison,'' *Vocabulaire de théologie biblique,* ed. X. LÉON-DUFOUR et al. (Paris 1962) 566–570. *Le Christ et les malades* (Cahiers de la vie spirituelle 6; Paris 1945). Z. ALSZEGHY, ''L'effeto corporale dell'estrema unzione,'' Gregorianum 38 (1957) 385–405. M. KELSEY, *Healing and Christianity* (New York 1973). F. MACNUTT, *Healing* (Notre Dame, IN 1974); *Power to Heal* (Notre Dame, IN 1977). J. SANFORD, *Healing and Wholeness* (New York 1977).

[P. DE LETTER/J. HILL]

HEALY, JAMES AUGUSTINE

Bishop; b. Macon, Ga., April 6, 1830; d. Portland, Me., Aug. 5, 1900. He was born on a plantation in Jones County, Ga. His father, Michael Morris Healy, was an Irish immigrant from County Roscommon. His mother was a Negro slave, Eliza Smith. In 1837 James was placed in a Quaker school at Flushing, Long Island, N.Y. He was sent in 1844 to the College of the Holy Cross in Worcester, Mass., from which he graduated in the first class (1849). After two years in the Sulpician seminary in Montreal, Canada, he entered the Sulpician seminary in Paris. He was ordained in the Cathedral of Notre Dame, Paris, on June 10, 1854. Healy was transferred to the Diocese of Boston, Mass., by Bp. John Bernard Fitzpatrick, and served there for 21 years in various capacities. He was the bishop's secretary, the first chancellor of the diocese, the assistant at St. John's Church, the rector of the cathedral, and the pastor and builder of St. James Church in Boston. Healy, active in welfare work and civic life, played a decisive role in the development of the Home for Destitute Catholic Children, the House of the Good Shepherd, St. Anne's Foundling Home, and the Catholic Laymen's Union.

In February 1875 he was named to the See of Portland, Me., where he was consecrated on June 2, 1875. For 25 years he governed his large diocese, supervising also the founding of the Diocese of Manchester, N.H., when it was cut off from Portland in 1885. His administration added to the diocese more than 60 parishes, 68 mission stations, 18 new schools and convents, and a well-developed series of welfare institutions. Healy also achieved recognition as a pulpit orator and appeared frequently as the featured speaker at civic and ecclesiastical functions in the New England states. Among his other activities were his contributions to American Church law at the Baltimore Council of 1884 and his work as a consultant to the Bureau of Indian Affairs of the Department of the Interior, Washington, D.C. On his silver jubilee as a bishop he was named assistant at the papal throne.

Bibliography: A. S. FOLEY, *Bishop Healy: Beloved Outcaste* (New York 1954). W. L. LUCEY, *The Catholic Church in Maine* (Francestown, N.H. 1957). A. S. FOLEY, *Dream of an Outcast: Patrick F. Healy* (Tuscaloosa 1989). C. DAVIS, *The History of Black Catholics in the United States* (New York 1993).

[A. S. FOLEY]

HEALY, PATRICK JOSEPH

Church historian and educator; b. Waterford, Ireland, July 26, 1871; d. Washington, D.C., May 18, 1937. After ordination (1897) for the Archdiocese of New York, he attended The Catholic University of America, Washington, D.C., for graduate study in Church history (B.Th. 1898, L.Th. 1899, S.T.D. 1903). His unpublished licentiate thesis, ''An Inquiry into the Origin and History of Origen's Allegorical System,'' is available in the Mullen Library of Catholic University. His doctoral dissertation, *The Valerian Persecution: A Study of the Relations between Church and State in the Third Century, A.D.* (New York 1905), received wide acclaim. He did further study at the Universities of Bonn and Heidelberg.

After a short period as an assistant in Holy Innocents' parish in New York City, he returned to Catholic University as an instructor. In 1910 he was elevated to the Patrick Quinn professorship of Church history and was chosen dean of the faculty of theology, a post he held at various times subsequently. He offered courses in early Church history, patrology, the history of monasticism, and the history of Church-State relations. Healy was the editor (1911–14) of the *Catholic University Bulletin* in the final years of its existence as a scholarly publication. He contributed many book reviews to it, as well as articles on monasticism, on Constantine and toleration, on Constantinople, and on Justinian and Charlemagne.

Bibliography: *The Catholic University Bulletin* 5.4 (Aug. 1937) 9. Archives, The Catholic U. of Amer., rector's files.

[A. K. ZIEGLER]

HEART (IN THE BIBLE)

In the Old Testament the word for heart is *lēb* or *lēbāb;* in the New Testament it is καρδία or νοῦς. The definition and use of these terms will be treated in this article.

The Hebrew word *lēb* is derived probably from a root that etymologically means ''agitated motion.'' It is seldom used in the proper sense, referring to the vital organ that pumps blood through the body (1 Sm 25.37; Jb 41.16; etc.). In the Bible the term ''heart'' is used mostly in a transferred sense, referring to the inner resources of the total person as capable of acting, with the accent more specifically on his will or intellect, less often his emotions; it is characteristic of Semitic thought that heart never prescinds from the total person.

In 1 Sm 16.7 heart refers specifically to the invisible inner man: ''man seeth those things that appear; but the Lord beholdeth the heart.'' In Ps 83(84).3 the Psalmist wishes to say that his total being yearns for God, and so he includes his heart together with his flesh and SOUL. Heart in this context is equivalent to the most noble inner part of man, i.e., his SPIRIT (*rûaḥ*), as is the sense of heart in the great commandment of love [Dt 6.5; see also Ps 118(119).2].

Heart appears in the sense of person as source of thought in Nm 16.28: ''Moses said 'This is how you shall know that it was the Lord who sent me to do all I have done and that it was not I who claimed it.''' ''Not I who claimed it,'' is literally ''not from my heart'' (see also Nm 24.13; 1 Kgs 12.33).

Heart is used in the sense of person as the source of volition in 1 Kgs 8.17; ''And David my father would have built a house to the name of the Lord, the God of Israel.'' ''And David my father would have'' is literally ''it was with the heart of David my father.''

Heart is used less often to signify the emotions. In Jer 49.22 heart is used in the sense of courage: ''on that day the hearts of Edom's heroes shall be like the heart of a woman in travail'' (see also Dt 15.10; 28.47).

In the New Testament two words translate the Hebrew *lēb,* καρδία and νοῦς. They both denote the inner person as the source of action; καρδία more specifically denotes volition and emotion while νοῦς denotes intellect.

In Lk 16.15 καρδία specifically denotes the invisible inner man: ''You are they who declare yourselves just in the sight of man, but God knows your heart (cf. 1 Thes 2.4; Rom 8.27). However, καρδία is also used to refer to understanding (2 Cor 4.6; Mt 13.15) and to willing (2 Cor 9.7; Lk 21.14).

In the New Testament νοῦς is used for *lēb* only in Pauline literature with the exceptions of Lk 24.45; Rv 13.18; 17.9. In Rom 7.23 νοῦς, parallel to ''the inner man,'' signifies the higher mental part of the natural man; it is transformed by Baptism to a new mode of being (Rom 12.2; Eph 4.23).

Bibliography: *Encyclopedic Dictionary of the Bible*, tr. and adap. by L. HARTMAN (New York 1963), from A. VAN DEN BORN, *Bijbels Woordenboek* 947–48. J. BEHM, G. KITTEL, *Theologisches Wörterbuch zum Neuen Testament* 3:609–16. J. P. E. PEDERSEN, *Israel: Its Life and Culture,* 4 v. in 2 (New York 1926–40) 1:99–81. R. BULTMANN, *Theology of the New Testament,* tr. K. GROBEL (New York 1951–) 1:190–259. C. TRESMONTANT, *A Study of Hebrew Thought,* tr. M. F. GIBSON (New York 1960) 83–124. M. BAILY, ''Biblical Man and Some Formulae of Christian Teaching,'' *Irish Theological Quarterly* 27 (1960) 173–200.

[W. E. LYNCH]

HEART OF JESUS, INSTITUTE OF THE

A SECULAR INSTITUTE of diocesan priests, founded by Joseph Pierre Picot de Clorivière, SJ, in Paris in 1791 and revived there by Reverend Daniel Fontaine in 1918. This society became a secular institute in 1951 and was introduced in the United States by Reverend Yves M. Guenver in 1957. The priest members remain in their diocesan assignments under the complete authority of their bishops. The purpose of the society, to develop fully the grace of the priesthood and total dedication to priestly work, is accomplished by means of the vows of poverty, chastity, and obedience; a flexible rule of life; regular spiritual direction; and a fraternal community. The spirit of the institute is that of Christ's redemptive love, symbolized by the Sacred Heart, sustained by prayer, and exercised by fraternal and pastoral charity. Members make an hour's daily meditation, report regularly on their spiritual exercises and finances, and meet monthly. Their poverty is marked by simplicity and generosity, and is adapted to their secular state; property ownership is retained, but under the superior's control. Since the society exercises no control over its members' apostolate, obedience is due to the superior only in matters of the spiritual life.

[S. J. PLATT/EDS.]

HEART OF MARY, DAUGHTERS OF THE

(DHM, Official Catholic Directory #0810), a religious community with papal approbation, founded in France in 1790 by Pierre Joseph Picot de Clorivière, a Jesuit priest, and Marie Adelaide de Cicé. The immediate object was the preservation of the religious life, the very existence of which was then threatened by the French Revolution. Following the Rule of St. Ignatius of Loyola, the members of this society take public vows of poverty, chastity, and obedience, but they do not wear a religious habit and they have no cloister. Initial approval of this unique community was granted by Pius VII in 1801; final approbation of the constitutions was given by Leo XIII in 1890.

The work of the sisters varies greatly according to needs and circumstances. Some members live together in common houses (convents) and engage in such organized activities as teaching, retreat work, catechetical instruction, social service, and missionary outreach. Other sisters who are retained in the world by family obligations or apostolic commitments continue to pursue their religious duties and ideals while engaged in professions or other occupations. In this way it is possible for them to exercise a Christian influence in areas that are hostile to religious wearing a habit. The community first established itself in the United States in Cleveland, Ohio, in 1851. Its members in the United States are sometimes referred to as Nardins, a name derived from Miss Ernestine Nardin, a Daughter of the Heart of Mary who founded Nardin Academy in Buffalo, New York, in 1857. The congregation is found throughout Europe, Africa, Asia, and the Americas. The general motherhouse is in Paris; the United States provincial headquarters, in Holyoke, Massachusetts.

[W. J. DONOVAN/EDS.]

HEATH, HENRY, BL.

Franciscan priest, martyr; known in religion as Paul of St. Magdalen; b. *c.* 1599 near Peterborough, Northamptonshire; hanged, drawn, and quartered April 17, 1643 at Tyburn (London) under Charles I. He was the son of the Protestant John Heath. After receiving his degree at Corpus Christi College, Cambridge (1621), he became the college librarian. In 1622, he was received into the Church by George Muscott. After a short stay at the English College at Douai, he entered St. Bonaventure's convent there *c.* 1624–25, where he led a frugal and scholarly existence for many years. Upon obtaining permission to join the English Mission in early 1643, he crossed from Dunkirk to Dover disguised as a sailor, then walked from Dover to London. On the night of his arrival in London, he was arrested as a shoplifter. When papers found in his cap betrayed his religion, he was taken to Compter Prison. The next day he was brought before the lord mayor, and, on confessing he was a priest, was sent to Newgate. Examined by a Parliamentary committee, he was indicted for his priesthood. At his place of execution, Heath reconciled one of the criminals that was to die with him. In an unusual act of mercy, he was allowed to hang until he was dead. He was beatified by Pope John Paul II on Nov. 22, 1987 with George Haydock and Companions.

Feast of the English Martyrs: May 4 (England).

See Also: ENGLAND, SCOTLAND, AND WALES, MARTYRS OF.

Bibliography: R. CHALLONER, *Memoirs of Missionary Priests,* ed. J. H. POLLEN (rev. ed. London 1924), II, 175. J. H. POLLEN, *Acts of English Martyrs* (London 1891). E. M. THOMPSON, *The Carthusian Order in England* (New York 1930).

[K. I. RABENSTEIN]

HEATH, NICHOLAS

Last Catholic archbishop of York; b. London, 1501?; d. Tower of London, December 1578. He was the son of Agnes and William Heath, a "citizen and cutler of London" in comfortable circumstances. Nicholas's family was related to the Heaths of Twickenham in Middlesex and of Apsley, Tamworth. Nicholas was educated at St. Anthony's, London (where Thomas MORE was also a student), Corpus Christi College, Oxford, and Christ's College, Cambridge, where he was elected fellow in 1521. After ordination he was appointed vicar of Hever, Surrey (1531–32), and in 1534 archdeacon of Stafford. The following year he took the degree of D.D. at Cambridge. His witty exposure of the supposed revelations of Elizabeth BARTON, holy maid of Kent, brought him court notice. In December 1535 he was sent on embassy by Henry VIII to the German princes assembled at Schmalkald, where Philipp Melanchthon is said to have admired his learning. Through the patronage of Archbishop CRANMER, he was appointed king's almoner and in 1539 was schismatically elected bishop of Rochester. He was later transferred to the See of Worcester (1543).

Heath's real views on the religious issue became clear in his opposition to the extreme reforms under Edward VI. In 1550 he refused to subscribe to Cranmer's new form of ordination, or to obey the order to take down altars and set up tables in the churches. He was committed to Fleet Prison, March 4, 1550, and shortly afterward was deprived of his see. This was restored to him upon the accession of MARY TUDOR as queen. As he had been appointed bishop during the schism, this restoration was not confirmed by the pope, through Cardinal Pole, until 1555, at which time the queen immediately appointed him archbishop of York. He received the pallium Oct. 3, 1555. Heath procured the restitution of many properties belonging to the see that had been alienated by his reforming predecessor, Robert Holgate. This return of properties was facilitated by Heath's appointment in 1556 as lord chancellor of England. In suppressing heresy under Mary he acted with prudence and advocated moderation, but as lord chancellor he was obliged to issue the writ for execution of his former patron, Archbishop Cranmer. As papal legate, Heath consecrated Cardinal Pole as archbishop of Canterbury, while as chancellor of England he proclaimed ELIZABETH I as queen at the death of Mary in 1558.

Immediately upon Elizabeth's accession, he surrendered the Great Seal, but remained in the Privy Council. Heath's speech in the first Parliament under Elizabeth dissenting from the Bills for Supremacy and changes in religion, still extant, is courageous and clear in principles. On July 5, 1559, having refused the oath of supremacy, he was deprived of his see, and committed to the Tower where he remained until 1571. He was allowed to reside at his own estate at Chobham Park, Surrey. Heath seems to have been recommitted to the Tower shortly before his death. He was buried in Chobham Church, next to his brother William, under a plain marble stone.

"Angels Welcoming the Saved into Heaven," engraving by William Morris from "The Earthly Paradise," 1896. (©Historical Picture Archive/CORBIS)

Bibliography: L. B. SMITH, *Tudor Prelates and Politics* (Princeton 1953). P. HUGHES, *The Reformation in England*, 3 v. in 1 (5th, rev. ed. New York 1963). G. E. PHILLIPS, *The Extinction of the Ancient Hierarchy* (St. Louis 1905). H. N. BIRT, *The Elizabethan Religious Settlement* (London 1907). T. E. BRIDGETT and T. F. KNOX, *The True Story of the Catholic Hierarchy* (London 1889). N. SANDERS, "Report to Cardinal Moroni," ed. J. H. POLLEN in *Catholic Record Society Miscellanea* 1 (1905) 1–56. W. R. TRIMBLE, *The Catholic Laity in Elizabethan England 1558–1603* (Cambridge, Mass. 1964). J. GILLOW, *A Literary and Biographical History or Bibliographical Dictionary of the English Catholics from 1534 to the Present time*, 5 v. (London-New York 1885–1902; repr. New York 1961) 3:242–251.

[J. D. HANLON]

HEAVEN (IN THE BIBLE)

In the Old Testament the word heaven is used both with cosmological significance as part of the physical universe and with religious significance as the dwelling place of God, particularly as the source of His salutary blessings. In the New Testament heaven is, on the one hand, the place from which Christ came and to which He returned and, on the other hand, the ultimate home of the blessed who die in the Lord.

In the Old Testament. Cosmologically the Hebrew word for heaven or the heavens (*šāmayim*) is often used as the equivalent of firmament. In such contexts heaven indicates the solid vault that holds back the waters above the firmament (Gn 1.8; Ps 148.4–6). In this vault are windows or floodgates that open to let rain fall on the earth (Gn 7.11; 2 Kgs 7.2, 19; Mal 3.10). The heavens are like a huge inverted bowl whose rim rests firmly on foundation pillars (2 Sm 22.8; Jb 26.11). The stars of heaven are suspended from this solid dome (Gn 1.14). The Israelites were impressed particularly by the unshakable solidity of the heavens (Ps 148.6; Is 40.22, 44.24, 45.12). At the end of time, however, their structure will be shaken and destroyed (Mt 5.18, 24.29; Mk 13.25; Ap 6.13, 8.10, 9.1). Whereas the firmament (*râqîa'*) is a technical term designating this vault, *šāmayim* has a more general meaning; it often means all that is above the earth. Thus the birds who fly in the air are called the ''birds of heaven'' (Gn 1.26, 1.28, 1.30, 2.19–20). Heaven describes also the region above the firmament where God has built His storehouses for snow, hail, and wind [Jb 37.9, 37.12, 38.22; Jer 49.36; Ps 134(135).7]. Since Hebrew had no single word to express the concept of world [*see* WORLD (IN THE BIBLE)] or universe, the phrase ''heaven and earth'' was used to indicate the sum total of all that God had made (Gn 1.1, 2.4). [*See* COSMOGONY (IN THE BIBLE)].

Heaven is God's abode (Dt 26.15; Ps 2.4). In all the cosmological contexts the heavens are spoken of as God's handiwork, for He spreads them out (Is 40.22, 44.24) and establishes their foundations (2 Sm 22.8). Heaven belongs to God in a special way as His dwelling place. God gives men the earth as their special domain [Gn 1.28; Ps 8.6–10, 113B(115).16], but He reserves heaven for Himself. It would be colossal pride on man's part, such as the pride of Babel (Gn 11.1–9; Is 14.13–14; cf. Lk 10.15; 2 Thes 2.4), to attempt to force one's way up to heaven. God rules all things from His throne in heaven. The throne is pictured as resting upon the firmament (Ex 24.10; Is 66.1); His palace is built above the waters of the heavens [Ps 103(104).3, 13]. There the King is surrounded by His heavenly court (1 Kgs 22.19–22; Jb 1.6; Is 6.1–3). Israelite tradition strove to express in various ways the truth that the transcendent God, dwelling in the heavens, was also Yahweh present and active in the midst of His people upon earth. In the YAHWIST narratives Yahweh ''comes down'' to earth to intervene in the affairs of men (Gn 11.5, 11.7, 19.24; Ex 19.18). He also ''comes down'' to meet with Moses or the people at the tent from time to time (Ex 33.9; Nm 11.17, 11.25, 12.5). The BETHEL narrative (Gn 28.10–12) shows that the earthly sanctuary is the site of God's special presence because it is the point of contact between heaven and earth. When Jacob had a vision at Bethel of angels descending from heaven, he called the place ''the gate of heaven'' (Gn 28.17). The theology of the DEUTERONOMISTS places greater emphasis upon heaven as the dwelling place of God in order to underline the divine transcendence. God sends before the people His angel in whom ''His name'' resides (Ex 23.21); He is present in His temple by ''His name'' (Dt 12.11), but God Himself remains always in heaven. In Deuteronomy Yahweh speaks to His people from heaven (Dt 4.36) rather than from Mt. Sinai itself (Ex 19.11, 18, 20). God cannot dwell upon earth since even ''the heavens and the highest heavens [i.e., the region above the firmament] cannot contain'' Him (1 Kgs 8.27). This transcendence, however, does not result in remoteness, for God dominates all things and knows them intimately [Jer 23.23–24; 2 Chr 2.6, 6.18; Ps 138(139).8–12]. In the later sections of the Old Testament, those dating from the Persian period, ''the God of heaven'' becomes the usual title for Yahweh [Dn 2.18–19, 28, 37, 44; Jon 1.9; Ps 135(136).26; Ezr 1.2; Neh 1.4–5; 2 Chr 3.23].

Israel looked to heaven as the source of salvation and of all blessings (Gn 49.25; Dt 33.13; 1 Kgs 8.35). In the heavens God had established His grace and His salvific word [Ps 88(89).3; 118(119).89]. Israel looked back with nostalgia to the time before man on earth had been shut off from heaven. Man had then enjoyed familiarity with God and the fullness of blessings (Gn 2.8–14; 3.8, 17–19). Israel longed for the day when God would rend the heavens to bring SALVATION to earth (Is 63.19; 45.8). On his part, man expressed the desire that he himself should somehow be lifted up to heaven, where he would find perfect salvation in communion with God [Ps 72(73).23–28]. This special privilege was accorded ENOCH (Gn 5.24) and ELIJAH (2 Kgs 2.11). Salvation would somehow consist not only in a descent of God to earth, but also in a return of man to God in heaven (Is 55.10–11).

In the New Testament. The desire that God would ''rend the heavens and come down'' (Is 63.19) was fulfilled in the coming of Jesus Christ. At the beginning of His ministry ''the heavens were opened'' (Mt 3.16 and parallels) in order that salvation might descend to earth (cf. Acts 2.2) and that God might reveal His Son to men (Mk 1.11, 9.6, 15.38–39). Of himself man could not ascend to heaven to behold the revelation of ''the mystery hidden in God'' (Eph 3.9; Jn 1.18, 3.13; Rom 10.6). God sent His Son to bring this revelation to earth (Mt 11.27;

Jn 1.19, 3.11, 14.9). The Old Testament concept of the sanctuary as the place where earth was opened up to heaven (Gn 28.12) found its full realization in the person of Christ (Jn 1.47–51), who was Himself the new Temple (Jn 2.19–22). Christ returned to the Father in heaven (Jn 6.62, 13.1; Heb 9.11–12) as the first fruits of the Resurrection (1 Cor 15.20), as the firstborn among many brethren (Rom 8.29). As forerunner (Heb 6.20), He enters heaven to prepare a place for his followers (Jn 14.3).

The ASCENSION OF JESUS CHRIST into heaven thus inaugurates a period of eager expectation. The Christian longs for Christ's PAROUSIA from heaven (Mk 14.62; Mt 25.31; 1 Thes 1.10, 4.16; 2 Thes 1.7), when He will seek out His own and raise them up to the clouds of heaven (1 Thes 4.17; Phil 1.23; 2 Cor 5.6–8). Christ will introduce them into the kingdom of His Father (Mt 25.34; 1 Cor 15.24), the new Jerusalem (Rv 3.12, 21.3, 10–14). Heaven is the consummation of SALVATION HISTORY when the world will be transformed into a new heaven and a new earth (Is 65.17; Rom 8.19–23; 2 Pt 3.13; Rv 21.1), and God will be all in all (1 Cor 15.28).

Bibliography: *Encyclopedic Dictionary of the Bible,* tr. and adap. by L. HARTMAN (New York 1963), from A. VAN DEN BORN, *Bijbels Woordenboek* 948–951. J. SCHMID, *Lexikon für Theologie und Kirche*[2], ed. J. HOFER and K. RAHNER, 10 v. (2d, new ed. Freiburg 1957–65) 5:354–355. G. GLOEGE, *Die Religion in Geschichte und Gegenwart*, 7 v. (3d ed. Tübingen 1957–65) 3:331–333. G. VON RAD and H. TRAUB, in G. KITTEL, *Theologisches Wöterbuch zum Neuen Testament* (Stuttgart 1935–) 5:496–535. J. M. FENASSE, "Le Ciel dans la tradition biblique," *La Vie spirituelle* 107 (1962) 604–623. U. E. SIMON, *Heaven in the Christian Tradition* (New York 1958).

[J. PLASTARAS]

HEAVEN (THEOLOGY OF)

This article will deal with heaven as (1) the culmination of SALVATION HISTORY and (2) the state of heavenly glory. The second section will be divided into the essential element in the state of heavenly glory and consummated heavenly glory.

Culmination of Salvation History

Heaven is the state of HAPPINESS of those who have died in Christ. Although it is often thought of as a place, this is of secondary importance. In 1950, Pius XII, defining the ASSUMPTION OF MARY, referred only to her having been "taken up to heavenly glory" without making any express reference to her going to a place. Her Assumption is modeled on the ASCENSION OF JESUS CHRIST into heaven. We understand heaven as the final state of those who die in Christ by reference to the final state of

Ceiling fresco depicting Jesus Christ enthroned in heaven, 18th century. (©Mimmo Jodice/CORBIS)

Christ Himself, who is the SAVIOR and head of His Mystical Body. While this refers first to those who have lived as members of the MYSTICAL BODY OF CHRIST, it must not be thought necessarily to exclude those who have preceded Christ in history, or who have never heard the call of Christ explicitly during their lifetime. We think of heaven as the state of happiness that brings full, lasting satisfaction to the whole of our being through our union with the Holy TRINITY in Christ.

We exist to give God glory and to find our happiness, but we find our happiness only in giving God glory; and it is only in Christ that we can give God glory. Thus the primary purpose of our lives is to give God glory in and through Christ, so to achieve our happiness. Likewise the primary aspect of heaven is that of the members of the *totus Christus* glorifying God by their participation in Christ's glory. Christ is the final temple, heaven its sanctuary in which God is perfectly adored. The picture in Revelation (ch. 4–5, 7–8) of God's glorification in the adoration of the Lamb describes heaven graphically.

Heaven is the fulfillment of the life of GRACE begun already on this earth, that life of union with the Blessed Trinity through Christ. It is the fulfillment of God's salvific plan for the whole world; hence heaven exists in the fullest sense only after the PAROUSIA of Christ at the END OF THE WORLD. Together with this will come the resurrection of the dead now in their GLORIFIED BODIES. (The body that is restored to the damned would hardly be thought of as glorified.) Even the fabric of this world will be restored as a dimension of the final condition.

God's salvific plan is accomplished in two stages: first, in the glorification of Christ, when, having risen from the dead and ascended to heaven, He sits at the right hand of His Father; and, second, when a like glorification has been given to the total community of the redeemed. (Only after Christ had entered heaven in glory was it possible for those who had died before then to pass from the *limbo patrum* to heaven.) The second stage, the process of transforming the human race into a like glorious state, began at the first PENTECOST and is continued through the history of the Church until it is finally achieved at the last day, when Christ comes in glory. The heavenly Jerusalem (Rv 21.2) will then manifest the final application of this SALVATION to humankind: then we human beings, fully glorified in body as well as in soul, shall in Christ share with the angels the beatifying union with the Blessed Trinity. Further theological speculation is difficult since revelation casts no further light on the matter.

State of Heavenly Glory

Theologians teach that the essential element in the state of heavenly glory is the union with the Blessed Trinity in mind and heart (called the intuitive or BEATIFIC VISION, the beatific love) resulting in the beatific joy; they further teach that other factors round off this bliss, notably the glorification of the body and the enjoyment of the renewed universe and the company of the blessed. Although essential glory is possessed by all who die in the state of grace as soon as their purification is completed, the fullness of glory is theirs only afte Christ's Parousia, when they receive back their bodies in the reconstituted universe. We shall speak first of the essential element of heavenly glory and then of its consummated state after the last day.

Essential Element in Heavenly Glory. Heavenly glory is the destiny for which God intends man. Happiness is what the human person desires. Human happiness can be seen to lie in the possession of heavenly bliss.

Human Happiness. Since the attainment of its final end is the attainment of human happiness, heaven must bring a human person to a state of perfect bliss. Humanity's final end must give satisfaction to the person as a whole; it cannot therefore consist primarily in the satisfaction of our corporeal nature but must rather be concerned with our spiritual nature, which is the nobler aspect of human nature. The material aspect enables a person to find pleasure and comfort in purely material things, but the person is aware interiorly that abiding contentment cannot be dissociated from the nobler aspirations of the spirit. Aesthetic and intellectual experiences give a deeper satisfaction than bodily enjoyments, but we find our most satisfying experience in the FRIENDSHIP and LOVE of others. At the same time we have an urge to realize our potentiality to the full, and we gain deep satisfaction when we do so. We are obscurely aware that our potentiality includes even a union with the supreme GOOD itself—God. Thus the human person may be regarded as having a natural desire for union with God.

Man's Natural Desire for God. Is this desire a desire for union with God as He is in Himself? It seems so, although the Church teaches that such a destiny is SUPERNATURAL and, as such, beyond human powers to attain (*see* DESTINY, SUPERNATURAL). By its natural powers alone the human person could attain to a merely indirect union with God corresponding to the kind of knowledge of God that natural reason involves. Such a knowledge does not make the person aware of what God is like in Himself; it merely makes one aware that the maker of a universe containing so much that is good, beautiful, and orderly must Himself be supremely perfect and desirable. Such knowledge is knowledge *about* an unseen God rather than of a God with whom one is in immediate contact. Pius XII taught in *HUMANI GENERIS* (1950) that we may not hold that God could not create human nature without giving it a supernatural destiny and equipping it for this. Hence man has no right to the supernatural destiny that unites him to God; such a destiny is *super*-natural, i.e., above the due of human nature, and so is something that God gratuitously gives. However this does not imply that human nature does not have an aptitude for it and even, as many theologians would hold, a positive desire for it even before one has received the graces that equip one for it. Although some theologians assert that man would have been perfectly content with his natural destiny so as never to hanker after the much greater union with God that the supernatural destiny brings, other theologians hold that history shows humans always to have wanted this closest union with God, even though by their natural powers they are unable to attain it. The best solution, perhaps, to this problem is to say that in point of fact no one has had a destiny other than the supernatural one, since humankind has always been intended for the supernatural union with God. This is as true of man after the Fall as it was before it. Hence one should expect humankind always to have evinced a desire for union with God, even though no one was able to implement that desire until the reception of grace [J. P. Kenny, *Theological Studies* 14 (1953) 280–87; K. Rahner, *Theological Investigations* 1 (Baltimore 1961) ch. 9]. We conclude that the state of heavenly glory brings utter satisfaction to man's deepest desires so that the human person finds full happiness in the union of immediate contact with the Blessed Trinity (*see* DESIRE TO SEE GOD, NATURAL).

Permanence. If this happiness be complete, it follows that it is a happiness that cannot be lost either for a time or permanently; otherwise the mind and heart would not be at rest, fearing its loss; such a condition is incompatible with complete happiness. Thus Scripture (Rv 21.4) says that God wipes away every tear, indicating the absence of anything that can diminish this happiness.

Since this complete happiness is found only in union with God, its permanency involves our permanent avoidance of sin, which would affect that union with God. Theologians differ as to the precise explanation of this IMPECCABILITY of the blessed.

Teaching. Revelation teaches the existence of heavenly glory, and the Church has always taugght that heavenly glory is the final destiny of all members of the KINGDOM OF GOD who live as its members should. This teaching naturally grows in precision, but it is hardly ever obscured by denial or doubt. Western theology seems to have shown more speculative interest in heaven than Eastern, but in both there are many references to our enjoying untold bliss, the possession of God, in the same abode as that of the angels. A natural curiosity prompted more questions than could be answered with likelihood, much less certainty; accordingly, profitless speculations as to the whereabouts of heaven and its internal arrangements were made.

The only divergent stream of thought was that of those who taught that Christ would reign on this earth with the good for 1,000 years before the final casting down to hell of SATAN and the transformation of this world into the new heavens and new earth. This view is known as CHILIASM (from the Greek word for a thousand) or MILLENARIANISM (from the Latin word); it originated in a misunderstanding of Rv 20.4–5, where the earthly phase of the kingdom of God is referred to. In apocalyptic literature numerals often have a special significance other than their literal one; 1,000 meant ''indefinitely large,'' hence ''1,000 years'' referred merely to the long period of the Church's existence on earth. This belief, though held by various early Fathers, was always distinguished by them from the official teaching of the Church; furthermore it did not prevent their acceptance of the orthodox belief in heaven as the final state of the blessed.

As the understanding of the nature of heavenly bliss developed there arose doubts in the minds of some Fathers as to whether it is only at the last day that the good enjoy this intimate union with God; even St. Augustine wavered on this point. The general stream of teaching was that heavenly bliss is granted to the disembodied soul immediately after whatever necessary purification follows death. The matter was finally settled when Benedict XII in 1336 defined that we possess the beatific vision as soon as we are worthy to do so after death (H. Denzinger, *Enchiridion symbolorum,* ed. A. Schönmetzer, 1001–02). This definition was prompted by the private view of his predecessor, John XXII, that we must await the last day for heavenly bliss (*see BENEDICTUS DEUS*).

In one other matter also was there a deviation from Catholic teaching. Eunomius of Constantinople (a fourth-century Arian) thought that a human person unaided by grace could attain to direct, comprehensive knowledge of God. Hesychasts (*see* HESYCHASM), whom Gregory PALAMAS (d. 1359) supported, had an analogous view in that they thought that it was possible by various practices attain to union with God. Both these views, as also those of the BEGUINES AND BEGHARDS and of Michael Baius, do not adequately safeguard the supernatural character of the beatific union with God (*see* BAIUS AND BAIANISM). In opposing Eunomius a few Fathers (Chrysostom, Theodoret, Gregory of Nyssa) seem to go too far in the opposite direction; not only do they oppose the position of Eunomius, but they seem to hold that even with grace we cannot attain direct knowledge of God, so that our union with God is something less than intuitive vision; most theologians excuse them of objective error, but there are those who do not [see V. de Broglie, *De fine ultimo humanae vitae* (Paris 1948) 122]. The followers of Palamas actually agree with this second error since they hold that it is not God's essence but the divine radiance with which we are united; however, in Catholic theology, because of God's simplicity the divine radiance cannot be really distinguished from the divine essence.

These aberrations do not obscure the main stream of Catholic teaching which consistently taught that heavenly bliss is both attained immediately after death (or PURGATORY, as the case might be) and consists in the intuitive vision of God as He is in Himself. Benedict XII's definition is a legitimate conclusion to a steady line of teaching; henceforth the points he defined are a necessary part of the Catholic proposition of Christ's revelation concerning heaven.

Nature of the Beatific Vision. Its basic nature is clear from the above. Clearly, since the beatific union with God occurs before the last day, when the blessed receive back their bodies, the essential part of heavenly bliss does not involve bodily activity; hence neither senses nor imagination are required for it. The beatific vision and love are the activity of the nobler aspect of the human person, namely, the spiritual faculties. Theologians differ as to whether the part played by the intellect or that played by the will is primary, the Thomists favoring the intellect, the Scotists the will; however, the reason why each school follows its view is not so much theological as philosophical: its understanding of human nature. The divergence is of secondary importance since all agree that it is the whole person who receives this glory.

Just as in the earthly phase of the kingdom of heaven man's natural faculties of intellect and will have to be perfected by the supernatural VIRTUES of faith, hope, and charity to make possible the supernatural knowledge and love of God, so too in the heavenly phase of the kingdom of heaven man's faculties will require a similar elevation, only more so. Heavenly bliss is the final consummation of everything that justification on earth leads to; hence an even greater ennoblement and strengthening of the spiritual faculties will be required if a person is to have the closest possible union with the Blessed Trinity. No longer do faith and hope suffice; hope is no longer relevant when the soul is in possession of that for which it hoped; and faith is not so much dispensed with as replaced by the yet higher elevation of the human intellect to perform a still nobler activity. Faith gives true knowledge about God in the form of ideas about the Trinity, but in heavenly glory it is the mystery of the divinity itself, not just ideas concerning God, that is the object of our knowledge. Hence a higher elevation of our intellect than that given by the virtue of faith is necessary; it is the *lumen gloriae* (LIGHT OF GLORY) that brings this about. Hence *lumen gloriae* is the name given to the permanent ennoblement of our intellect by which we are enabled to be united to the Trinity by intuitive vision. The Council of Vienne in 1312 defined the need for the *lumen gloriae* (*Enchiridion symbolorum* 895).

To understand this we must contrast our natural manner of knowing with the way in which we shall know the Trinity in the beatific vision. The normal human method of acquiring knowledge is by forming ideas from the impact that the external world makes on our senses; these sense impressions are the raw material from which our mind abstracts concepts or ideas. Even angels require these ideas, though in their case they are not abstracted from sense impressions (the angels being pure spirits), but are directly infused by God. Hence, short of the beatific vision, both angels and humans can know God only by having ideas about the mystery of the divine. In the beatific vision the divine reality itself replaces these ideas so that God is in direct contact with the human mind. Since the human mind, and angelic intellect likewise, is of itself vastly inferior to such a union, it needs to be elevated by the *lumen gloriae* in order to be capable of this activity. God accordingly is sometimes termed the *species expressa,* i.e., the object immediately actuating the mind of the blessed, in the beatific vision.

Object of the Beatific Vision. The Blessed Trinity is clearly the primary object of the beatific vision. As infinite truth God alone is able to satisfy fully the human and angelic intellect which is made for the possession of truth; also, as infinitely desirable God alone is able to satisfy the desires of the human heart or angelic will. Thus God alone is the primary object of our mind and will in heaven. In heaven we know and love God as He is in Himself, i.e., as the Father, Son, and Holy Spirit, in whose divine life we along with all the other blessed fully share. The infinite perfection of the Blessed Trinity and the infinite love which we shall then fully possess provide a never-ending source of satisfaction to our entire selves. Our restless hearts have at last found rest where alone they can, in the Blessed Trinity. If our imagination is unable to envisage how this happiness does not cloy, it is because we envisage it in human terms that are inadequate to express the divine reality. We are better able to appreciate the absence of those factors that destroy happiness because we can picture that absence. Our imagination cannot help us to envisage a situation in which our potentialities are fully realized so that no unfulfilled element remains. The only happiness that cloys is one that is mixed with material pleasure, which of its nature cannot last; the essentially spiritual nature of the beatific joy excludes cloying.

There is also a secondary object of the beatific vision and love. We are united to God as individuals who take their past history, now purged of imperfection and sinfulness, with them. We are always the children of our parents, we retain our affection for our background and contacts. God does not destroy our past but enables it to contribute to our present happiness. Thus, the secondary object of the beatific joy is our continuing knowledge and love of created beings with whom or which we have a relationship by reason of our earthly life.

Consummated Heavenly Glory. In addition to the essential element of heavenly bliss, theologians speak of certain elements that can differ from one person to another and without which heavenly bliss would remain intact. Thus heavenly bliss varies from one person to another: since heaven is the reward for our good activity while on earth, our degree of heavenly bliss will correspond to our degree of union with God at death; this was defined in 1439 by the Council of Florence (*Enchiridion symbolorum* 1305). Furthermore theologians commonly teach that there is an accidental source of heavenly glory that is given only to some of the blessed, namely to martyrs, virgins, and teachers of the faith. It is called an AUREOLE or special reward that marks the recognition of their special dedication to Christ or His work during their earthly lives.

Other elements additional to essential glory are the company of the other blessed ones, the resurrection of the body, and the renewal of the world. The differing degrees of heavenly glory, the aureoles, and the company of the elect are found in heaven before the last day; the resurrection of the body and the renewal of the world occur only after the last day. From then on the state of the blessed is termed consummated heavenly glory.

Company of the Elect. While union with God is all-sufficient to make the blessed entirely happy, nevertheless, because all the blessed show forth the wonderful works of God in Christ, each one takes delight in coming into contact with other blessed ones. This contact includes all the inhabitants of heaven: Our Lady, the angels, the saints. While one must not envisage these contacts in exactly the same way as human contacts, nevertheless the differences of individuals among themselves as well as their differing formation on earth will explain affinities that unite them with certain of the blessed rather than others, while, however, there is full accord of spirit of all with all. This common union of all in spirit with all others is the natural fruit of the common fulfillment of all within the Mystical Body of Christ: since all in Christ live for the glory of the Blessed Trinity, all are united when the purpose of their existence is attained.

It is sometimes felt that the absence from heaven of individuals to whom one was closely attached on earth will necessarily introduce an element of sadness. However in heaven one clearly perceives, as one does not on earth, that there is no happiness except in God and no sadness except in departing from this complete union with Him. Accordingly we do not, and in fact cannot, maintain an attachment that would take us away from this union with God: all our delight in such an attachment melts away so that we feel no sadness at its obliteration.

Resurrection of the Body. The most notable addition to the essential element of heavenly bliss at the last day is the restoration to the elect of their bodies. This is a mysterious truth raising many questions to which no certain answer can be given, but its truth is manifestly contained in the revelation of humanity's final lot. Here too the principle applies that Christ's glorification is the model for ours, although this does not mean that we shall necessarily have all the perfections that Christ's risen body had.

Two preliminary questions are usually asked. First, will there be a sense of incompleteness in the blessed before the last day, knowing as they do that their bliss is not yet rounded off by the possession of their glorified bodies? The answer is given that since they are completely united in will with God, they fully accept this situation as His will and so are incapable of being saddened at waiting for its fulfillment.

The second question is of greater importance: shall we have the same bodies as those we had on earth? The answer is that we shall, since Scripture and the Fathers clearly teach this. A few theologians do not think that this will entail the restoration of the very same matter into which the mortal body disintegrated; they hold that, since the matter that constitutes our bodies is made into our bodies purely by the presence of our soul in it, it is basically the soul as joined to any matter at all that constitutes such matter as our body. Hence, irrespective of what matter is united to the soul at the resurrection, such bodies as result will be our bodies in exactly the same sense as the body in which we died was ours. This question concerns the mechanics of the resurrection.

All glorified bodies shall have splendor, agility, subtlety, and impassibility. While these qualities do indeed glorify the body and make it quite different from its earthly condition, they do not make it cease to be a body: glorification is not dematerialization. Here lies a difficulty to the attempt to penetrate into the nature of the glorified body: while maintaining the reality of the change in our bodies, we must avoid overspiritualizing them. And revelation gives us little help.

Splendor is that quality which they have whereby they appear beautiful to behold; it gives them a supernatural radiance (as shown in the practice of depicting the saints with HALOS as symbols of their supernatural radiance).

Agility is the property that enables the glorified body to move about without being impeded by the limitations our body imposes on us now; it will probably still have to pass through space to get from one place to another, but an act of will will transfer it with very little lapse of time.

Subtlety has sometimes been identified with the ability to pass through other bodies, as Christ passed through the closed doors of the upper room; this, however, is not certain since many Fathers thought this to be a special miracle of divine power. St. Thomas (*Summa theologiae* 3a suppl., 83.1) has better reason on his side when he identifies it with the complete subordination of the matter of the body to the soul so that both are perfectly integrated; the body henceforth is the perfect manifestation of the soul, fully contributing to, instead of impeding, its life.

Impassibility removes from the glorified body not only its liability to suffer in the way our bodies do now, but also its need to preserve itself from possible harm and wear from either inside or outside. It is generally taught that, as there is no marrying or giving in marriage in heaven, so too there is no vegetative life, i.e., no need to eat or sleep. This was the teaching of the scholastics, and it seems eminently suited to the conditions of an eternal existence such as that of heaven. However the suggestion has been made that, although we need not, we may eat and drink if we wish to (De Broglie, Appendix 6). (*See* RESURRECTION OF THE DEAD.)

Renewal of the World. This, together with the restoration of the body, constitutes the final completion of God's salvific plan. This is the ultimate glorification of Christ, inasmuch as the place He holds at the center of creation and of history is finally acknowledged by the extension of His saving influence throughout the material universe. Revelation (e.g., 2 Pt 3.13) tells us of the renewal of the universe at the end of time as the completion of God's salvific plan. This is what is referred to by the cosmic significance of Christ's work. This renewed universe contributes to the happiness of the blessed; as it finally rounds off Christ's work, so too it finally rounds off our joy in Christ.

See Also: HELL (IN THE BIBLE); HELL (THEOLOGY OF); ESCHATOLOGY, ARTICLES ON; GOD, INTUITION OF; CREATED ACTUATION BY UNCREATED ACT.

Bibliography: P. BERNARD, *Dictionnaire de théologie catholique*, ed. A. VACANT et al., 15 v. (Paris 1903–50) 2.2:2474–2511. A. MICHEL, *ibid.* 6.2:1393–1426; 7.2:2351–94. *Dictionnaire de théologie catholique: Tables générales*, ed. A. VACANT et al. (1951–) 1:609–13. J. RATZINGER, *Lexikon für Theologie und Kirche*, ed. J. HOFER and K. RAHNER, 10 v. (2d, new ed. Freiburg 1957–65) 5:355–58. S. MORENZ and G. GLOEGE, *Die Religion in Geschichte und Gegenwart*, 7 v. (3d ed. Tübingen 1957–65) 3:328–33. L. BILLOT, *Quaestiones de novissimis* (8th ed. Rome 1946). G. C. VAN NOORT and J. P. VERHAAR, *Tractatus de novissimis* . . . (Hilversum, Neth. 1935). C. DAVIS, *Theology for Today* (New York 1962). R. GUARDINI, *The Last Things,* tr. C. E. FORSYTH and G. B. BRANHAM (New York 1954). A. PIOLANTI, ed., *Problems of the Future Life,* tr. T. F. MURRAY (London 1962). A. VONIER, *The Life of the World to Come* in v.3 of *Collected Works,* ed. B. FEHRENBACHER, 3 v. (rev. ed. Westminster, Md. 1952–53). A. WINKLHOFER, *The Coming of His Kingdom,* tr. A. V. LITTLEDALE (New York 1963). J. PAPIN, ed., *The Eschaton: A Community of Love* (Villanova 1971). B. VIVIANO, *The Kingdom of God in History* (Wilmington 1988).

[B. FORSHAW]

HEBBLETHWAITE, PETER

Catholic journalist, broadcaster, author; b. Ashton-under-Lyne, England, Sept. 30, 1930; d. Oxford, Dec. 18, 1994. Hebblethwaite joined the Society of Jesus in 1948. After the novitiate at Manresa, Roehampton, he was sent to Chantilly, France, to study philosophy, mastering the French language in the process. He was ordained a presbyter in 1963.

Shortly after his ordination, Hebblethwaite became assistant editor of the Jesuit journal the *MONTH*, launching a noteworthy career in Catholic journalism. The editor of the *Month,* Ronald Moffat, SJ, sent Hebblethwaite to Rome to report on the final session of Vatican II in 1965. Hebblethwaite was overwhelmingly excited by the promise the council held for renewal, particularly the possibilities for the relationship of the Church with the modern world articulated in the discussion over *Gaudium et spes.*

In 1974 Hebblethwaite left the Society, obtained a dispensation from his vows, and married Margaret Speaight. After his marriage in 1974, Hebblethwaite took up residence in Oxford, where he lectured in French at Wadham College. From 1978 to 1981, he resided in Rome where he served as correspondent for the *National Catholic Reporter* (*NCR*). In 1981, he returned to Oxford, and continued as Vatican affairs writer for the *NCR.* He also produced a steady stream of articles for other newspapers and periodicals. His scholarly acumen, theological training, courageous voice, and loyal Catholic faith aided him in his prodigious contributions. His grasp of the workings of the Vatican and his bold, if often aggressive, criticism of Church affairs and teachings earned him a unique place in English Catholic journalism. In addition to his other writings, Hebblethwaite authored two widely acclaimed biographies, one on John XXIII and the other on Paul VI.

Bibliography: In addition to the articles of Hebblethwaite to be found in the issues of *The Month, The National Catholic Reporter, The Tablet,* and others, Hebblethwaite wrote several books, including: *The Council Fathers and Atheism: The Interventions at the Fourth Session of Vatican Council II* (New York 1966); *Theology of the Church* (Notre Dame IN 1969); *The Runaway Church: Postconciliar Growth or Decline?* (New York 1975); *Christian-Marxist Dialogue: Beginnings, Present Status, and Beyond* (New York 1977); *The Year of Three Popes* (Cleveland 1978); *The New Inquisition?: The Case of Edward Schillebeeckx and Hans Küng* (San Francisco 1979); *The Man Who Leads the Church: An Assessment of Pope John Paul II* (San Francisco 1980) [with J. Wahle]; *The Papal Year* (1981); *Introducing John Paul II: The Populist Pope* (San Francisco 1982); *John XXIII, Shepherd of the Modern World* (Garden City NY 1985); *Synod Extraordinary* (Garden City NY 1986); *In the Vatican*(London 1986); *Paul VI: First Modern Pope* (New York 1993). His last work appeared posthumously, *The Next Pope* (London 1994). On Hebblethwaite himself, see ''Peter Hebblethwaite,'' *The Tablet* 248 (24–31 December 1994) 1676–77; and T. FOX, ''Peter Hebblethwaite Wrote of the Church He Knew and Loved,'' *National Catholic Reporter* (January 6, 1995) 2.

[R. E. MCCARRON]

HÉBERT, MARCEL

Philosopher, proponent of a religious symbolism that denied personality in God; b. Bar-le-Duc, France, April 22, 1851; d. Paris, Feb. 12, 1916. As a priest, educated at Saint-Sulpice, he wrote on modern philosophical questions, Kant, Schopenhauer, Voltaire, and Renan. During his subsequent religious evolution his two most famous works were *Souvenirs d' Assise* (1899) and the article ''La Dernière idole'' (1902). Attacking the Thomistic proof for the existence of God along broadly Kantian lines, he rejected personality in God, which he saw as merely a way of affirming the reality and objectivity of ''the Ideal, the Divine, the Absolute.'' God seemed to him the category of the Ideal, immanent and unknowable. For refusing to retract the ideas in *Souvenirs,* he was suspended from priestly functions. In 1903 he gave up the soutane and went to Brussels, where he dedicated himself to the Belgian workers' party and to "the religion of the human conscience." He held that certainty in a future life was not part of religious belief, but he died "with hope." Hébert was a man of winning personality and of mystic rather than strictly speculative temperament, whose importance lies in his position as perhaps the first philosopher to appear within the phenomenon of MODERNISM.

Bibliography: J. RIVIÈRE, *Le Modernisme dans l'Église* (Paris 1929). A. HOUTIN, *Un Prêtre symboliste, Marcel Hébert* (Paris 1925) includes bibliography of his writings.

[J. J. HEANEY]

HEBREW LANGUAGE

One of the Semitic languages, more precisely a Canaanite dialect among the dialects of Northwest Semitic. The Northwest Semitic branch of the Semitic languages extends over Palestine, Phoenicia, and Syria. In Isaiah 19.18, Hebrew is called "the language [literally, lip] of Canaan," while in Isaiah 36.11 and Nehemiah 13.24 it is referred to as "the language of Judah." Monuments in this language range from the 10th century B.C. (Gezer Calendar) down to the present. This article is limited to a description of Biblical Hebrew.

With the exception of the small sections in Ezra 4.8–6.18; 7.12–26; Jeremiah 10.11; Daniel 2.4b–7.28 that are written in the ARAMAIC LANGUAGE, the protocanonical books of the Old Testament are written in Hebrew. Among the deuterocanonical books, Baruch, Judith, Tobit, 1 Maccabees, and the deuterocanonical parts of Daniel and Esther, written originally in Hebrew or Aramaic, are extant only in Greek versions, apart from the Qumran fragments. Sirach, though composed in Hebrew, was known only in a Greek version until 1896, when about two-thirds of the chapters in Hebrew were discovered.

Script. Hebrew was written in the common Canaanite alphabet that was used alike by the Israelites, the Moabites, the Phoenicians (from whom the Greeks borrowed it *c.* 800 B.C.), and the Aramaeans. The earliest Hebrew examples of writing are in the Phoenician script, but in the postexilic period a transition was made to the Aramaic "square script," which is that generally found at Qumran and in modern printed Hebrew Bibles. The discovery of thousands of fragments of scrolls at Qumran and in the region of the Dead Sea (*see* DEAD SEA SCROLLS) has permitted Hebrew paleography to reach such a point of precision as to make possible the dating of a style of writing to within a generation. Like Arabic, Hebrew is written from right to left.

The alphabet numbers 22 consonants, and as this is less than the 28 of Arabic and Ugaritic, some of the characters, such as *ḥet* and *'ayin,* represent both the harsher and the softer sounds. In certain periods the six consonants *b g d k p t* were aspirated or not according to position (thus *b* and *bh, g* and *gh*), so that the number of sounds in the alphabet was augmented. At first the writing was purely consonantal, but later the consonants *he, waw,* and *yod* were adopted to indicate respectively the pure long vowels *â, û* and *ô,* and *î* and *ê.* These vowel letters are technically known as *matres lectionis.* With the gradual cessation of Hebrew as a living language—the Qumran discoveries show that it was still well understood at the turn of the Christian era—the need was felt to safeguard the pronunciation of the consonantal text, authoritatively fixed toward the end of the 1st Christian century. Thus a vowel system was devised by the Masoretes in about the 5th century and elaborated by them over the following centuries. Two main systems were invented: the Babylonian with mainly superlinear signs, and the Palestinian, or Tiberian, in which the signs were placed mainly under the lines. The Tiberian system is that found in modern Hebrew Bibles generally. The system attained such a degree of precision as to show all the vowel changes occasioned by lengthening, by tone, by laryngals, etc. The rigid uniformity achieved by the Masoretes had the unfortunate side effect of effacing dialectal variations, necessarily existing in the Biblical books that were composed in different places and over a millennium (*c.* 1200–*c.* 200 B.C.); but with the aid of the Ugaritic texts (*c.* 1400–*c.* 1200 B.C.; *see* UGARIT) and the Qumran scrolls, scholars are slowly recovering the dialectal elements that are still identifiable in the Masoretic text.

Morphology and Vocabulary. Hebrew shares the characteristics of the Semitic family of languages, which may be briefly summarized as follows. The roots or basic forms from which the words are derived are usually composed of three consonants, though biliteral roots are very early and important. Vowels do not form parts of the roots but merely serve to express various modifications of the root sense; thus, *mālak* (he ruled), but *melek* (king). The reader conversant with Hebrew does not need written vowels, as these can be supplied mentally from the context. The simple form of the verb is modified by added letters, lengthened vowels, and reduplicated radicals to express intensive, causative, reciprocal, or reflexive action. Prefixes and affixes derived from the independent personal pronouns indicate the person, gender, and number of the verb. The function of the Hebrew verb is still a matter of dispute. One view maintains that the perfect form expresses past time and the imperfect form present and future time. A more widely held opinion considers the verb forms as expressing modes of action; the perfect is the mode of completed action, while the imperfect refers to uncompleted action. Neither view can adequately account for all the data, so a less rigid classification seems called for. What has been considered the imperfect form may more fittingly be described as a universal tense because of its possible past, present, or future reference. On the other hand, the perfect form, hitherto regarded as expressing past or completed action, may equally denote present or future action; the context must be the determining factor.

The vocabulary of Biblical Hebrew is relatively small, only about a tenth of its 5,500 words being found with any frequency. It has been estimated that the known vocabulary cannot represent over a fifth of the total stock of Northwest Semitic words used between 1400 and 400 B.C. The sudden afflux, however, of some 1,800 new words from the Ugaritic tablets has made it possible to identify a good number of obscure words in the Bible, so that the Biblical vocabulary is now judged richer than traditionally assumed.

Modern Study of Hebrew. The modern scientific study of Biblical Hebrew, which began with H. F. Wilhelm Gesenius (d. 1842), has received a fresh impetus from the discovery of the Ugaritic tablets (1929–), which record an ancient Canaanite dialect closely akin to Hebrew. The preservation in this dialect of the three case endings known from Akkadian and Arabic, the four verbal modes, the rich variety of particles, such as vocative *lamed,* emphatic *lamed,* and enclitic *mem,* and the varied prepositions used with multifarious nuances bespeaks a language capable of expressing highly nuanced sentiments. Alerted by these characteristics of Ugaritic, Hebraists have been finding similar phenomena in the Bible that had been concealed by the Masoretic leveling. The gradual reassessment of Hebrew points to the conclusion that the language of the poetical books in particular was much more complex and nuanced than earlier opinion allowed.

See Also: HEBREW STUDIES (IN THE CHRISTIAN CHURCH)

Bibliography: A. SCHALL, *Lexikon für Theologie und Kirche*, ed. J. HOFER and K. RAHNER, 10 v. (2d, new ed. Freiburg) 5:49–51. *Encyclopedic Dictionary of the Bible*, tr. and adap. by L. HARTMAN (New York 1963), from A. VAN DEN BORN, *Bijbels Woordenboek* 951–55. W. GESENIUS, *Hebräische Grammatik* (Halle 1810, 28th ed. rev. E. KAUTZSCH 1909; 29th ed. rev. G. BERGSTRÄSSER 1929; Eng. tr. A. E. COWLEY, Oxford 1910). H. BAUER and P. LEANDER, *Historische Grammatik der hebräischen Sprache des. A.T.* (Hildesheim 1918–22; repr. 1962). P. JOÜON, *Grammaire de l'hébreu biblique* (2d ed. Rome 1947). J. WEINGREEN, *A Practical Grammar for Classical Hebrew* (Oxford 1939; repr. 1955). G. BEER and R. MEYER, *Hebräische Grammatik,* 2 v. (Berlin 1952–55), the first to use, though to a limited degree, the data made available by the Ugaritic discoveries. C. BROCKELMANN, *Hebräische Syntax* (Neukirchen 1956). W. GESENIUS, *Hebräisches und aramäisches Handwörterbuch über das Alte Testament*, ed. F. BUHL (17th ed. Leipzig 1921; repr. 1949). F. BROWN et al., *A Hebrew and English Lexicon of the Old Testament,* ed. W. GESENIUS (Oxford 1906; repr. 1951). L. KOEHLER and W. BAUMGARNTNER, *Lexicon in Veteris Testamenti libros* (2d ed. Leiden 1958). F. ZORELL, *Lexicon Hebraicum et Aramaicum Veteris Testamenti* (Rome 1946–), Latin.

[M. J. DAHOOD]

HEBREW POETRY

Poetry has been defined as patterned speech. This definition is ambiguous and deliberately vague, because the distinction between poetry and prose in any language is difficult and contested. Poetry is an art as well as a science, and the analysis of its patterns and its effects demand the freedom and discipline necessary for any of the arts.

The recognition and analysis of Hebrew poetry has the added difficulty of distance. The poetry of the Hebrew Bible was written more than two thousand years ago in an ancient language only recently restored as a living tongue. In addition the culture, which affects imagery and expectations, is far removed from modern life. On the positive side, the texts have been in constant use since their writing and there is a lengthy tradition of interpretation upon which to draw.

Patterned Speech

The patterns which distinguish Hebrew poetry are found at several levels: sound, meter, word, and imagery.

Sound. The two ways in which sound is brought into play are the repetition of consonants (related to alliteration in English poetry) and the repetition of vowel sounds (related to rhyme or assonance). In Pss 76:4 and 122:6 there are fine examples of the repetition of the consonant sound ''sh.'' In both instances the repetition of the sound reinforces the meaning of the line.

> Ps 76:4: *sh*ammah *sh*ibbar ri*sh*pe-qa*sh*et (There were shattered the flashing arrows). The repetition of ''sh'' echoes the clashing sound of the destruction and fixes the idea of ''shattering'' (*shibbar*) in the hearer's mind.
>
> Ps 122:6: *sh*a'a*l*u *shel*om yeru*shal*aim (Pray for the peace of Jerusalem). The two consonants are repeated in the last half of verse 6 (*yishlayw*) and in verse 7 (*shalom, shalwa*).

Assonance is the repetition of vowel sounds. Note, for example, the repetition of ''i'' in Ps 113:8:

lehoshibi 'im-nedibim / 'im nedibe ammo (to seat them with princes, with the princes of his people).

The repetition of sound may occur through the repetition of the words themselves:

Song of Songs 6:3: *'ani ledodi / wedodi li* (I am my beloved's; my beloved is mine).

In Ps 47:7: *zammeru 'elohim zammeru / zammeru lemalkenu zammeru* (Sing to God, sing; sing to our king, sing).

In Nahum's description of the destruction of Nineveh, the sound of the words—including alliteration, assonance, and rhyme—emphasizes the totality of the devastation. *buqah umebuqah umebulaqah* (devastation and desolation and destruction).

Meter. No element of Hebrew poetry is more contested than that of meter. There is general agreement that meter is important and that it is a feature of Hebrew poetry. The question of analysis of meter, however, is still debated. There are two primary methods: counting syllables and counting accents.

The Hebrew verse unit is very short, often composed of only two or three words. When counting accents, each of these words receives an accent. Introductory or linking words such as conjunctions or prepositions are not counted. The most common meter in a two-unit line is 3 + 3.

Ps 47:7 Sing to-our-God sing / sing to-our-king sing.

Another frequent meter is 3 + 2. Since this meter predominates in Lamentations, it is called *qina* (lament).

Lam 1:3 Judah has-gone-into-exile from-oppression / and-hard servitude.

The meter in Hebrew poetry is not consistent, however. The number of accents in verse units within the same poem will vary.

Another method for analyzing meter involves counting syllables. The standard meter consists of a two-unit verse of around sixteen syllables. In this respect too Hebrew poetry is not consistent.

Word. Words are the tools of the poet's craft. Examples of wordplay, such as puns or paranomasia (the use of similar sounding words), abound in Hebrew poetry. In Ps 88:10 the poet complains: "My eyes (*'eni*) grow dim from trouble (*'oni*). The words for "eyes" and "trouble" have the same consonants. The similarity in sound makes the contrast in meaning surprising in Ps 15:3: "he does no evil (*ra'ah*) to his friends (*re'ahu*). The rhyme in Ps 88:5–6 points out the sufferer's fate: "I am like a man (*geber*) without strength . . . like the slain, lying in the grave (*qeber*)."

A frequent device in Hebrew poetry is the use of the word pair, two words that are frequently linked and usually appear in consecutive lines. Common word pairs are: hand-right hand; sea-river; understand-know. For example:

"Your *hand* will reach all your enemies; your *right hand* will reach those who hate you!" (Ps 21:9)

"God founded it on the *seas*, established it over the *rivers*" (Ps 24:2).

"You *know* when I sit and stand; you *understand* my thoughts from afar" (Ps 139:2).

Imagery. Hebrew poetry is rich in imagery. Almost every verse of the Psalter is an example. In Psalm 1 the faithful are compared to a well-watered tree (Ps 1:3). Even in old age they are full of sap, still producing fruit (Ps 92:13–15). Threatening enemies, however, are wild animals—bulls, lions, dogs—and the sufferer's heart melts like wax (Ps 22:13–15). The believer under attack is a sagging fence or a battered wall (Ps 62:4). Human beings are so inconsequential they weigh less than breath (Ps 62:10). God, on the other hand, is a rock, a tower of strength, a fortress (Pss 18:3; 31:4; 61:4; 62:7–8. The craving for God is like the craving of a deer for water or like the aridity of a dry waterless land (Pss 43:2; 63:2). Security in God's care is like the security of a weaned child on its mother's breast (Ps 131:2).

Structure

The Line. *Parallelism.* The basic unit of Hebrew poetry is the line. Lines are ordinarily broken into two or three parts. In the following discussion "line" will be used to refer to the whole unit, "colon" will refer to a segment of the line. A two-part "line" will be called a "bicolon," a three-part line a "tricolon."

A bicolon:
None among the gods can equal you, O Lord;
nor can their deeds compare to yours (Ps 86:8).

A tricolon: Teach me, Lord, your way
that I may walk in your truth,
single-hearted and revering your name (Ps 86:11)

A basic constituent of Hebrew poetry is the device of parallelism, a technique in which lines are ordinarily end-stopped and balanced according to meaning, syntax, and/or sound. For example:

You who dwell in the shelter of the Most High, who abide in the shadow of the Almighty (Ps 91:1).

The various elements balance each other: you who dwell / who abide; in the shelter / in the shadow; of the Most High / of the Almighty.

The significance of parallelism has been recognized for over a century. Robert Lowth named three types of parallelism by the relationship of the terms in the lines or cola. Synonymous parallelism occurs when the major terms mean basically the same thing:

> Make known to me your ways, Lord;
> teach me your paths (Ps 25:4).
>
> When the major terms are opposites, the result is antithetic parallelism:
>
> They will collapse and fall,
> but we will rise and stand upright (Ps 20:9).
>
> Lines which do not fit either of these patterns Lowth called synthetic:
>
> You win justice for the orphaned and oppressed;
> no one on earth will cause terror again (Ps 10:18).

In the last decades of the twentieth century the discussion turned to the nature of parallelism. James Kugel refined the already existing understanding by pointing out that the essential function of parallelism was not to indicate equivalency (A = B), but rather complementarity, frequently intensification or expansion (''A is so, and what's more B''). For example, one finds complementarity of terms such as ''day'' and ''night'':

> O Lord, my God, by day I cry out,
> at night I clamor in your presence (Ps 88:2).
>
> or expansion in the second colon of a term from the first colon:
>
> The Lord is a great God,
> and a great king above all gods (Ps 95:4).
>
> or the consequence of the first colon in the second:
>
> You are my rock and my fortress;
> for your name's sake you will lead and guide me (Ps 31:4).
>
> or continuation in time:
>
> Weeping stays for the night;
> but at dawn comes rejoicing (Ps 30:6).

Chiasm. A poetic technique related to parallelism is called chiasm. Chiasm is the construction of a line so that the balancing elements in the first colon occur in reverse order in the second colon (ABBA). For example:

> A: Have mercy on me, God, B: in your goodness
> B': in your abundant compassion A': blot out my offense.

The notion of chiasm has been further developed with a consideration of sound as well as meaning. John Kselman named the technique in which one set of balanced elements correspond in meaning and the other set correspond in sound ''semantic-sonant chiasm.'' For example:

> A: My birthright (*bekorati*) B: he took;
> B': now he has taken A': my blessing (*birkati*).
>
> The words ''birthright'' and ''blessing'' are similar in sound and form one leg of the chiasm (A). The word ''took'' is semantically identical in each colon and forms the other leg (B). They are arranged in a chiastic relationship: ABBA.

Grammar. Parallel cola are often balanced grammatically as well as semantically. Examples from Psalms 51 and 131 will illustrate:

> Wash me thoroughly from my guilt;
> from my sin, cleanse me (Ps 51:4).
>
> The imperative ''wash me'' in the first colon is balanced by the imperative ''cleanse me'' in the second; the prepositional phrase ''from my guilt'' is balanced by ''from my sin'' in the second. The parallelism is not slavish. The first colon has an extra word, ''thoroughly.''
>
> Lord, my heart is not proud;
> nor are my eyes haughty (Ps 131:1).
>
> The subject ''my heart'' is balanced by ''my eyes''; the verb ''to be proud'' is balanced by the verb ''to be haughty,'' and both are negated. ''Lord'' is extra in the first colon.

Stanzas. The elements which allow for the division of a Hebrew poem into larger units or stanzas are based on content and grammatical considerations. The simplest division is provided by the refrain. For example, ''The Lord of hosts is with us; our stronghold is the God of Jacob,'' occurs in Ps 46:8 and 12. It is commonly inserted also at the end of verse 4 to provide three balanced stanzas: verses 2–4, 5–8, 9–12. A similar situation occurs in Psalm 67 where the refrain occurs at verses 4 and 6: ''May the peoples praise you, God; may all the peoples praise you!'' This refrain too is commonly added at the end of the psalm to form three stanzas: verses 2–4, 5–6, 7–8.

Refrains also provide other information. The refrain, ''Wait for God, whom I shall praise again, my savior and my God'' (Pss 42:6, 12; 43:5), is a clue that Psalms 42 and 43 really form one poem. In Psalm 136 the refrain, ''God's love endures forever,'' is repeated at the end of each verse, indicating that this psalm is a litany.

An example of grammatical indicators of stanza division is Psalm 76 in which three passive participles—''renowned'' (v. 2), ''awesome'' (v. 5), and ''awesome'' (v. 8)—indicate divisions.

The division of Psalm 88 into stanzas is based on both grammar and meaning. Verses 10b–13 are a series of rhetorical questions, thus a natural grammatical division. Verses 2, 10b, and 14 all state that the suppliant cries out to God. The poem is thus divided into verses 2–10a, 10b–13, 14–19.

The Whole Poem. Hebrew poems are bound together as a whole by several devices. One of the most obvious is the alphabetic poem in which each line or set of lines is begun with a subsequent letter of the alphabet (e.g., Psalms 34, 37, 111, 112). The most extended alphabetic poem is Psalm 119 in which the sets consist of eight lines each. Verses 1–8 begin with the first letter of the Hebrew alphabet, verses 9–16 with the second letter, and so on.

The repetition of key words unites a poem. For example, the word ''heart'' occurs six times throughout Psalm 73. In Psalm 31 the four-fold repetition of the word ''hand'' emphasizes the contrast between falling into God's hands or enemy hands.

Inclusion, the repetition of the same phrase at beginning and end, also binds a poem into unity. For example, Psalm 8 begins and ends with: ''Lord, our Lord, how awesome is your name through all the earth.''

Biblical Hebrew poetry, though difficult because of the distance of time, culture, and language, is well worth the effort. The artistry speaks through the ages.

Bibliography: R. ALTER, *The Art of Biblical Poetry* (New York 1985). J. KSELMAN, ''Semantic-Sonant Chiasmus in Biblical Poetry,'' *Biblica* 58 (1977) 219–23. J. L. KUGEL, *The Idea of Biblical Poetry: Parallelism and its History* (Baltimore 1998). M. O'CONNOR, *Hebrew Verse Structure* (Winona Lake, Ind. 1980). D. L. PETERSEN and K. H. RICHARDS, *Interpreting Hebrew Poetry* (Minneapolis 1992). W. G. E. WATSON, *Classical Hebrew Poetry: A Guide to its Techniques,* Journal for the Study of the Old Testament Supplement Series 26 (Sheffield 1984, 1986, 1995); *Traditional Techniques in Classical Hebrew Verse* (Sheffield 1994).

[I. NOWELL]

HEBREW SCRIPTURES

An alternative designation for that portion of the Bible traditionally called by Christians the ''Old Testament,'' preferred by people sensitive to Christian-Jewish relations.

The term ''Old Testament'' is not recognized by the Jewish tradition, and as it is used in the Christian (in conjunction with ''New Testament'') it has often led the unwary to the unfortunate conclusion that the New Testament has replaced or superseded the Old. The Old is then thought to have lost all permanent value as a source of divine revelation. This conclusion, rising from the juxtaposition of the two terms, contradicts Christian tradition (e.g., *Dei Verbum* 3).

In Judaism, the Bible is normally called *Tanakh,* a vocalized Hebrew acronym that describes its contents: *Torah* (Pentateuch), *Nebi'im* (Prophets), and *Ketubim* (Writings). *Tanakh,* as a Christian alternative to Old Testament, presents a difficulty because of its unfamiliarity. It is also doubtful whether Jewish usage would include those portions that Catholics accept as canonical from the SEPTUAGINT (e.g., Judith, Tobit, Sirach 1–2, Maccabees), but which were not included in the Masoretic canon accepted by rabbinic tradition in the late 2d century. The term ''Jewish Scriptures,'' which is preferred by some Catholic journals, presents similar difficulties.

''Hebrew Scriptures,'' on the other hand, presents the lesser difficulty that not all of the books included in the Catholic canon (e.g., Maccabees) can be shown to have been written originally in the Hebrew language. The term ''Hebrew,'' in the title, therefore needs to be understood as an ethnic or ''peoplehood'' designation rather than as a linguistic one. In this sense, ''Hebrew'' would be taken to refer to ''the Jewish people in the biblical period.''

The terminological dilemma discussed here can be said to be illustrative of Catholic attitudes toward Jews and Judaism encouraged by the Second Vatican Council. While recognizing the above difficulties and even bringing into question the traditional understanding of typology as a means of expressing the essential relationship between the two testaments, the ''Notes on the Correct Way to Present the Jews and Judaism in Preaching and Catachesis,'' issued by the Holy See's Commission for Religious Relations with the Jews (June 24, 1985), opted to ''continue to use the expression 'Old Testament' because it is traditional (cf. already 2 Cor. 3:14) but also because 'Old' does not mean 'out-of-date' or 'outworn''' (Section II). It should be noted, moreover, that the 1984 *Scripture and Christology* promulgated by the Pontifical Biblical Commission speaks of the ''books of the Prior Testament . . . [that] remain the privileged document of those experiences of Israel'' (2.1.4.1). The document of the Biblical Commission consistently uses the term ''prior testament'' instead of ''Old Testament.''

While the phrase ''old covenant'' finds precedent in the Epistle to the Hebrews 7:23, other terms for what the apostolic writers accepted as ''God's Word'' (4:12) can also be found in the New Testament. For example, 2 Tm 3:16 and Heb 11:15 simply use ''Scripture.'' Hebrews, however, does not discuss Judaism as such (whether biblical or rabbinic), but merely the Temple sacrifice, which Christ has replaced (Heb. 8:13) and itself uses the less polemical ''first covenant'' (Heb. 8:7) in introducing the citation from Jeremiah 31:31–34, from which the phrase ''new covenant,'' and hence ''New Testament,'' ultimately derives.

The New Testament thus presents a variety of designations for the Hebrew Scriptures. The issue is to choose one for common usage in the Church that both connotes the continuity between the testaments (covenants) from the Christian point of view and, at the same time, evinces respect for the integrity of Judaism and the Hebrew Bible.

Bibliography: L. BOADT et al., *Biblical Studies: Meeting Ground of Jews and Christians* (New York 1980).

[E. J. FISHER]

HEBREW STUDIES (IN THE CHRISTIAN CHURCH)

Though the constitution of 1311 of Clement V advised that Greek and Hebrew should be taught at every university, it cannot be said that the late medieval Church favored the study of Hebrew by Christians. The fear that the prestige of the Vulgate and the theological exegesis based on it would be impaired by a return to the original languages of the Bible explains much of the opposition of the schoolmen to Hebrew studies. But since the battle cry of the 16th-century humanists was *ad fontes* (back to the sources!), a clash with the traditional view was inevitable. This methodical return to the sources had two important results. By drawing attention to the original texts it was possible to go back to a tradition earlier than that of the schoolmen and thus to adduce testimonies acknowledged by everybody. The second result was the recognition that every interpretation has to start from the original and not from the translation. This assumption, which is still valid today and is one of the lasting achievements of HUMANISM, obviously led to a lowering of the value of the Vulgate. The development of humanistic thought toward a new method of Bible interpretation and translation was mainly the work of two men, Johann REUCHLIN (1455–1522) and Desiderius ERASMUS (1466–1536), whose Bible studies in Hebrew and Greek, respectively, occupied a central place in their lives.

Christian Hebraists of the Renaissance. The victory of the humanist ideal that every man of culture should be *trium linguarum gnarus,* that is, he should know Latin, Greek, and Hebrew, led to the founding of the trilingual colleges. In England Bp. Richard FOXE (*c.* 1448–1528) founded Corpus Christi College, Oxford. In Spain Cardinal XIMÉNEZ DE CISNEROS (1436–1517) established the new University of ALCALÁ, which soon concentrated its attention on trilingual studies. In France Francis I (1494–1547) provided the *noble et trilingue* Académie, the Collège des Lecteurs Royaux, later to be called the Collège de France. In Germany Frederick the Wise of Saxony (1463–1525) endowed the University of Wittenberg with chairs in the three languages. After considerable initial opposition a trilingual college was founded at Louvain. The peculiar problem of Hebrew studies was the suspicion that they all too readily aroused. A monk of Freiburg (where Reuchlin studied) said plainly in 1521, ''Those who speak this tongue are made Jews.'' Jews themselves discovered that they might suffer if they taught Christians Hebrew, for they could be accused of destroying the faith of their pupils. Thus the suspicion they aroused and the fear that the authority of the Vulgate would be undermined were real obstacles to Hebrew studies at the end of the 15th century and the first quarter of the 16th.

Johann Reuchlin. The first Hebrew grammar ever to be published in a European language was by Konrad PELLICANUS (1478–1556), a Franciscan from Alsace, who later was to become a follower of Huldrych ZWINGLI. It was published at Strassburg in 1503 or 1504 and was poor in content, with types neither beautiful nor clear. Pellicanus obtained his knowledge from various sources. In addition to his early instruction from Johannes Pauli (*c.* 1454–1533), a baptized Jew, he had been in contact with Reuchlin and had read the books of PETER NIGRI (SCHWARZ) (1434–83). Pellicanus' grasp of Hebrew was very elementary, since he had not yet understood the basis of Hebrew verb formation. In 1506 Reuchlin's *De rudimentis Hebraicis* was published in Pforzheim, marking the beginning of Hebrew studies in Europe. From this date on, it was possible to learn Hebrew. In fact, Reuchlin could justify his own estimate of himself as the first important Christian Hebrew scholar of the West. Referring to the dictionary contained in his *De rudimentis,* he said, ''Before me among the Latins no one appears to have done this.'' This German layman, doctor of law, and professor of Greek and Hebrew set down in the preface of his *De rudimentis* an account of his work for the world of scholarship in Latin and Greek and complained about the amount of money he had to pay learned Jews for instruction in Hebrew. His book consists of a description of the alphabet, a dictionary in two parts, and a brief but adequate grammar of Hebrew. It is a handsome volume printed so as to be read from the back page forward, like a Hebrew Bible, in the current fashion characteristic of the pedantry of those who published works on Hebrew. It brought him what he wanted: undying fame as a scholar. Not the least of his achievements was the fact that he influenced princes and humanists to establish chairs of Hebrew in the universities of the empires, and through his pupils and correspondence on Hebrew studies, raised up scholars to fill them.

Reuchlin propounded the philological method that traces the meaning of every word in the original Hebrew. No theological argument was ever used by Reuchlin. He was no theologian and openly admitted, ''I do not probe the meaning as a theologian but discuss the words as does the grammarian.'' This thought epitomizes his attitude toward philological studies, and brought him into open conflict with philosophers and theologians throughout his life. His opponents, however, had to face the awkward question whether Hebrew studies should be forbidden.

Yet they could not attack him on that account, for there was the advice of Clement V that Hebrew should be studied.

Other Pioneers. There are other names to record, such as Nicolas Clénard (Cleynaerts) of Louvain (1495–1542) and Santes PAGNINI of Lucca (1470–1536), men who unlike Pellicanus and Wolfgang CAPITO (1478–1541), author of a small Hebrew grammar at Basel in 1518, remained Catholics. But the great name after Reuchlin, who remained a Catholic and died one, is that of Sebastian Münster of Basel (1488–1552). He had Pellicanus as his teacher and dedicated a lifetime to Hebrew studies, producing more than 40 books, which show a capacity for work as prodigious as his range of subjects. In 1527 he published the first Aramaic grammar written by a Christian. He made available to Christian scholars through his Latin translation the best work of Elias Levita (*c.* 1468–1549), the greatest of Jewish grammarians in that age. Münster wrote that ''in the grammatical works written by Christians before Elias had begun his task, the true foundation was missing.'' By his self-effacing devotion, Münster laid this foundation and through Levita learned how to explain the use of the *dagesh* point. Two Protestants might also be mentioned. Paul Fagius of Strassburg (1504–49), who in his early days as schoolmaster at Isny (Allgäu) set up his own Hebrew press, after leaving Strassburg became Regius professor of Hebrew for a time at Cambridge and translated into Latin the PIRKE AVOTH and later the Targum of Onkelos. Of less distinction was Johann Forster of Wittenberg (1496–1558), who issued a Hebrew dictionary in 1557. This did not meet the need for a dictionary of Hebrew that could match the Latin and Greek dictionaries of the ESTIENNES, nor had the similar work of others who preceded him done so. The greatest Christian Hebraist in the post-Reformation period was Johannes Buxtorf the Elder (1564–1629), whose *Praeceptiones Grammaticae de Lingua Hebaea* (later entitled *Epitome Grammaticae Hebraeae*) went through 20 editions between 1605 and 1716.

Christian Hebraists of Modern Times. The first to use Arabic in a scientific way to illustrate Hebrew grammar and to treat Hebrew as a branch of the family of Semitic languages was Albert Schultens of Leiden (1686–1750), who published in 1737 his *Institutiones ad Fundamenta Linguae Hebraeae.* This meant a final break with the rabbinic tradition of the incomparable *lingua sacra.* He placed the comparison of Hebrew and Arabic on a sound basis and so influenced all future lexical study. J. D. Michaelis (1717–91), in his *Supplementa ad Lexicon Hebraicum* (1786), drew out the implications of the work of Schultens for Hebrew philology. Supreme among students of Hebrew grammar was Heinrich Friedrich Wilhelm Gesenius (1786–1842), who published the first edition of his *Hebräische Grammatik* in 1813; the 14th to 18th editions were revised by E. Rödiger (1801–74), the 22d to 28th, by E. F. Kautzsch (1841–1910), and the 29th, by G. Bergsträsser. The 28th edition was translated into English in 1909 by A. E. Cowley. Other widely used teaching instruments have been, in German, the grammars by G. H. A. Ewald (1803–75), J. Olshausen (1800–82), H. Böttcher, B. Stade, E. König, and H. Bauer-P. Leander; in French, by P. Joüon and Mayer Lambert; in English, by A. B. Davidson and S. R. Driver, *Hebrew Tenses.*

Gesenius is considered the father of modern Hebrew lexicography. In 1810 he published his *Hebräisch-Deutsches Handwörterbuch über die Schriften des Alten Testaments,* the basis of his *Thesaurus philologicus Criticus Linguae Hebraeae et Chaldaeae Veteris Testamenti* (1829–42), completed by Rödiger (1853–58). Gesenius's *Lexicon Manuale Hebraicum* of 1833 was translated into English by Edward Robinson, and this formed the basis of the well-known *A Hebrew and English Lexicon of the Old Testament* by F. Brown, S. R. Driver, and C. A. Briggs. Other notable dictionaries are those of Julius Fürst, *Hebräisches und Chaldäisches Handwörterbuch über das Alte Testament* (1867), F. Zorell, *Lexicon Hebraicum et Chaldaicum* (1940–), and L. Koehler-W. Baumgartner, *Lexicon in Veteris Testamenti Libros* (German and English, 1953), with a *Supplementum* (1958) serving as a second edition.

Bibliography: A. E. COWLEY and E. KAUTZSCH, eds., *Gesenius' Hebrew Grammar* (2d ed. Oxford 1910; repr. 1946) 17–23. W. SCHWARZ, *Principles and Problems of Biblical Translation: Some Reformation Controversies and Their Background* (Cambridge, Eng. 1955). S. L. GREENSLADE, ed., *The Cambridge History of the Bible* (Cambridge, Eng. 1963).

[M. J. DAHOOD]

HEBREWS

Term that is found chiefly in the Biblical traditions concerning the 2d millennium B.C., and then, apparently after centuries of desuetude, reappears in the latest books of the OT and roughly contemporary Jewish literature. The English term is derived through the Latin *Hebraeus,* from the Greek Ἑβραῖος, and ultimately from Hebrew *'ibri.* Originally it seems to have been an appellative referring to social or legal status [for details, *see* HABIRU (HABIRI)]. It survived in the later period as an ethnolinguistic designation for the Israelites or Jews and for the Semitic language they spoke before the adoption of Aramaic. The ethnic meaning, though with a much wider application, goes back to the late 10th or early 9th century B.C., appearing in the Yahwistic tradition of the Patriarchs and in the Table of the Nations of Gn 10.21, 25; 11.15–26, where Eber, the eponymous ancestor of the Hebrews is mentioned. The limitation of the term to Israelites first occurs *c.* 500 B.C. (Jon 1.9; yet note the different reading of the Septuagint), and then is well attested in the books of Judith (10.12; 12.11; etc.) and 2 Maccabees (7.31; 11.13; 15.37), both probably compositions of the late 2d or early 1st century B.C. At approximately the same time writers begin to speak of the HEBREW LANGUAGE, for instance, in the Prologue of Sirach.

Hebrew remained a relatively uncommon term and never replaced Israelite or Jew. It connotes the ancient past and is an archaizing expression. This explains why the old language was called Hebrew; why the Phoenician script employed in preexilic times was named Hebrew by the rabbis and was thus distinguished from the later script of Aramaean origin; why Josephus, Philo Judaeus, and other Jewish writers, when speaking of Biblical times, used Hebrew only of the most ancient Israelites. Savoring of the past, Hebrew was used in archaizing or high literary language, particularly where Jew and Gentile confronted each other (as in Judith and 2 Maccabees) and, by implication at least, were contrasted. The association with the national origins inherent in the term also explains why, in a context of ever-increasing Hellenization of culture and mores, Hebrew came to be applied to what was characteristically Jewish and was used even to distinguish one Jew from another. A Hebrew was a Jew who still adhered to old Jewish customs and language; Hebrews, therefore, usually were to be found in Palestine and only rarely in the Diaspora. It is against this background that one should probably explain the struggle between HELLENISTS and Hebrews mentioned in Acts 6.1. It is fidelity to the past that is implied by St. Paul's boast to be a Hebrew as well as an Israelite (2 Cor 11.22), ''a Hebrew of Hebrews'' besides a member of the tribe of Benjamin (Phil 3.5). However, eventually Aramaic became with Hebrew part of the legacy of the past, and the ability to speak it was lost by many Jews, especially those in the Diaspora; hence Aramaic too was called Hebrew (Lk 23.38; Jn 5.2; 10.13, 17, 20; Acts 21.40; 22.2; 26.14).

Bibliography: *Encyclopedic Dictionary of the Bible*, tr. and adap. by L. HARTMAN (New York 1963) 955–959. J. HASPECKER, *Lexikon für Theologie und Kirche*, ed. J. HOFER and K. RAHNER, 10 v. (2d new ed. Freiburg 1957–65) 5:44–45. A. ALT, *Die Religion in Geschichte und Gegenwart*, 7 v. (3d ed. Tübingen 1957–65) 3:105–106. W. GUTBROD et al., in G. KITTEL, *Theologisches Wörterbuch zum Neuen Testament* (Stuttgart 1935–) 3:359–394. (For additional bibliog. *see* HABIRU.)

[W. L. MORAN]

HEBREWS, EPISTLE TO THE

The authorship and circumstances of the composition of the Epistle to the Hebrews remain obscure. Traditionally included in the Pauline corpus, it is unlikely that he is the author. The list of possible authors includes Apollos, Barnabas, Silas, and Priscilla. Modern scholars have proposed new candidates, including Epaphras, a collaborator of Paul mentioned in Colossians 4.12. Yet the arguments for any individual remain inconclusive, and Origen's judgment that ''God only knows'' who wrote the work is justified. The intended audience, which has been conjecturally located throughout the Mediterranean, is now thought more likely to have been at Rome than Corinth, Colossae, or Jerusalem. The problems it addresses were not unique to Jewish Christians, but would have affected any ''third generation'' (2.1–4) Christians of the latter half of the first century.

These problems included external hostility (10.32–34; 12.3; 13.3,13), and internal lassitude, pictured as ''sluggishness'' (5.11) or ''lameness'' (12.13). The addressees may have been attracted by some ''strange teachings'' (13.9), although the warning is conventional and Hebrews mounts no sustained doctrinal polemic. Whatever the causes, and they may have been unclear to the author, there has apparently been some disaffection from the community (10.25), which calls for a series of warnings about the danger of apostasy (2.1; 6.4–8; 10.26–31; 12.13–17). The date of composition can be set only within the broad limits of A.D. 60 to 95, but often repeated arguments for a date prior to the destruction of Jerusalem in 70 A.D. are inconclusive. Hebrews is not interested in the existence or potential attractions of the second temple. It uses the scriptural image of the desert tabernacle primarily as the foundation for its christological exposition.

Genre and Structure. Modern authors generally take Hebrews, a self-described ''word of exhortation'' (13.22), to be a homily. That generic classification has been supported by the recognition that several major pericopes follow a clear homiletic pattern, consisting of introductory comment (3.1–6; 8.1–6); citation of scripture (3.7–11; 8.7–13); exegetical or thematic exposition (3.12–4.11; 9.1–10.10); rhetorical inclusion (4.12–13; 10.11–18); and parenetic application (4.14–16; 10.19–25). The structural significance of these blocks calls into question rigid concentric analyses of the text. The general movement of Hebrews is from Christ to us. In five parts, Hebrews moves from the Son's eschatological, royal, and priestly messiahship, Jesus' covenant fidelity and compassion, and His perfect priestly fulfillment of the Old Testament, to the faith and endurance necessary on our part, and to peace as the reward for pleasing God.

The traditions on which Hebrews relies are diverse and the tensions among them are not explicitly resolved. The exordium (1.1–4) indicates that Christ is understood to be a divine person who pre-existed his incarnation. The catena of scriptural citations which follows (1.5–13) suggests a perspective like that of Romans 1.3, whereby Christ is appointed to his status as Son at His exaltation. Although the text presupposes the exordium's incarnational perspective, it focuses on the exaltation as a decisive christological movement.

A related tension affects the description of Christ as high priest. The title is probably a traditional reference to Christ's function as heavenly intercessor (2.18; 7.25; 8.4). Yet for Hebrews, His chief act as high priest takes place on earth, where He suffers a self-sacrificial death (7.27). Insistence on the latter point is the key interpretive move in handling the imagery of the high-priestly action of the Day of Atonement. Christ's ''entry into the heavenly sanctuary'' and his resultant priestly status are inseparable from his incarnate conformity to the divine will (10.5–10).

Christological reflection grounds the PARENESIS in large part through the motif of the covenant. Because Christ's death is the sort of act it is, earthly by virtue of its shedding of blood, and ''heavenly'' by virtue of its spiritual dimension (9.14) and its conformity to God's will (10.9), it inaugurates the new and ideal covenant promised by Jeremiah (8.8–12). In this relationship between humankind and God, sins are forgiven (10.14–18) and the spiritual dimension of the human self, conscience, is cleansed (9.14). The act by which Christ himself is ''perfected'' (5.9; 7.28), that is, exalted and made fit for his office of High Priest, in turn ''perfects'' his followers who are now being sanctified (10.14). The covenant-inaugurating event provides a way of access (10.19) for believers to the realm where God is truly served (9.14; 12.28); but as Christ's heavenly priesthood is intimately bound up with a very earthly act, so the realm where members of the covenant worship is not the realm of pure spirit, but the earthly arena, where they ''bear Christ's reproach'' (13.13), while offering praise (13.15) and deeds of beneficence (13.16), the true sacrifices of the new covenant's cult. In this arena Christ's followers are called to a life of the cardinal virtues (10.19–24), but especially to fidelity, which was perfectly exemplified by the covenant's inaugurator (12.1–3).

Affinities of Hebrews. Debate about the interpretation of Hebrews continues to be conducted in terms of the religio-historical background of its images and theological concepts. Yet while its Jewish and Judeo-Christian heritage is clear, no precise genealogy for its symbolic world can be found. Parallels with Philo indicate not dependence, but common Hellenistic Jewish interpretations of traditional Biblical categories, and in both the influence of popularized Middle Platonic language can be felt. Parallels with the Dead Sea Scrolls, most striking in the Melchizedek midrash (ch. 7), do not indicate a specific connection, but are part of the general apocalyptic heritage of the early Church. While it contains apocalyptic expectations (9.28; 10.25; 13.14), Hebrews, like many other early Christian texts, emphasizes the decisive eschatological event which has already occurred and which has inaugurated the ''time of correction'' (9.10).

Papyrus roll with Epistle to Hebrews, 3rd–4th century A.D. (©Bettmann/CORBIS)

Hebrews certainly uses a variety of traditions, but it cannot be seen as a simple extension or repudiation of any of them. It is a work of subtlety and sophistication that reflectively engages its heritage in order to make clear the enduring significance of Jesus Christ (13.8), the model (2.10; 12.2) and guarantor (7.22) of a life of covenant fidelity toward God.

Bibliography: H. W. ATTRIDGE, ''The Uses of Antithesis in Hebrews 8–10,'' *Harvard Theological Review* (Cambridge, Mass. 1908–) 79 (1986) 1–9. R. E. BROWN & J. P. MEIER, *Antioch and Rome* (New York 1983). H. BROWN, *An die Hebräer* (Tübingen 1984). G. HUGHES, *Hebrews and Hermeneutics* (Cambridge 1979). R. JEWETT, *Letter to Pilgrims: A Commentary on the Epistle to the Hebrews* (New York 1981). F. LAUB, *Bekenntis und Auslegung: Die paränetische Funktion des Christologie im Hebräerbrief* (Regensburg 1980). W. R. G. LOADER, *Sohn und Hoherpriester: Eine Traditionsgeschichtliche Untersuchung zur Christologie des Hebräerbriefes* (Neukirchen 1981). P. J. KOBELSKI, *Melchizedek and Melchirešac* (Washington, D.C. 1981). D. PETERSON, *Hebrews and Perfection: An Examination of the Concept of Perfection in the ''Epistle to the Hebrews''* (Cambridge 1982). J. SWETNAM, *Jesus and Isaac: A Study of the Epistle to the Hebrews in the Light of the Agedah* (Rome 1981). J. W. THOMPSON, *The Beginnings of Christian Philosophy: The Epistle to the Hebrews, The Catholic Biblical Quarterly* MS 13 (Washington, D.C. 1982).

[H. W. ATTRIDGE/EDS.]

HECKER, ISAAC THOMAS

Founder of the PAULISTS, author, editor; b. New York, N.Y., Dec. 18, 1819; d. New York, Dec. 22, 1888. He was the son of John and Caroline (Freund) Hecker. He left school in his early teens to join his brothers John and George in their rapidly expanding bakery business. Although he had received little formal religious training, in 1842 he became convinced that God was calling him away from all ordinary pursuits of life. He turned for advice to his friend Orestes BROWNSON, who suggested a sojourn at Brook Farm, a new social experiment in West Roxbury, Mass. There, with Ralph W. Emerson, Henry Thoreau, and Bronson Alcott, Hecker and his friends, George Ripley, Charles Dana, George Curtis, and George Bradford, discussed the problem of man's destiny. Hecker was dissatisfied with their answers, and guided by Brownson, he examined the various forms of Protestantism. None satisfied him and he turned to Catholicism, making his profession of faith and receiving Baptism on Aug. 2, 1844. A year later he joined the Redemptorists and was sent to Europe for his novitiate and seminary studies.

Two years after his ordination in England on Oct. 23, 1849, he returned to the U.S. With four other American convert Redemptorists, Augustine F. HEWIT, Clarence A. WALWORTH, George DESHON, and Francis A. BAKER, he gave missions to Catholics throughout the country. Although he was engrossed in the work, the conversion of his non-Catholic countrymen was uppermost in his thoughts. To interest them in the faith he wrote two highly successful books: *Questions of the Soul* (1855), an appeal to the longings of the heart, and *Aspirations of Nature* (1857), an answer to the questionings of the mind. Early in 1857, an opportunity arose for the Redemptorists to open an English-speaking house in New York City for American Redemptorist missionaries. With the encouragement of Abp. John Hughes of New York and Bp. James R. Bayley of Newark, N.J., Hecker went to Rome to plead for the new foundation before the rector major. Three days after his arrival, he was expelled by the rector major for having made the journey without the necessary permission. Convinced that his superior's action was the result of a misunderstanding, Hecker appealed the sentence to the Holy See. After months of litigation, Pius IX released the five Americans from their Redemptorist vows and suggested to Hecker that he begin a new religious community in America. Upon his return, he founded the Society of Missionary Priests of St. Paul the Apostle, or Paulists, with Hewit, Deshon, and Baker as associates; Walworth had withdrawn because of disagreement with the objective and nature of the new community. On July 10, 1858, Hughes approved their Programme of Rule and authorized the establishment of the Paulists in his archdiocese.

With the new community established, Hecker enthusiastically began his work for non-Catholics. To correct misunderstandings and especially to convince men that the Church was not the enemy but the guardian of liberty, he took to the public lecture platform. His warm personality, ringing sincerity, and forthright manner captivated audiences wherever he spoke throughout the country. He utilized the press, which he hailed as ''the most important weapon in modern intellectual and religious warfare.'' In April 1865 he launched a monthly publication, the *Catholic World*, and a year later organized the Catholic Publication Society (later the Paulist Press) to distribute inexpensive literature on a national scale. He pleaded this cause before the Second Plenary Council of Baltimore (1866) with such earnestness that he won the support of many bishops, notably Abp. Martin John Spalding. As the latter's theologian he attended Vatican Council I (1869–70). In 1870 he began the *Young Catholic,* an illustrated monthly for boys and girls, and in 1872 raised necessary funds to buy a secular newspaper and convert it into a first-class Catholic daily. However, failing health prevented the realization of this plan since it forced him to relinquish active work. Until his death he edited the *Catholic World,* wrote in defense and explanation of the Church, and guided the destinies of his community. *The Church and the Age* (1887) was his last book. His remains are interred in a special sarcophagus in the Paulist Fathers' Church in New York City.

Bibliography: V. F. HOLDEN, *The Yankee Paul: Isaac Thomas Hecker* (Milwaukee 1958) bibliog. 415–422. J. MCSORLEY, *Father Hecker and His Friends* (2d ed. St. Louis 1953). W. ELLIOTT, *The Life of Father Hecker* (1891; repr. New York 1972). J. FARINA, *An American Experience of God: The Spirituality of Isaac Hecker* (New York 1981). D. J. O'BRIEN, *Isaac Hecker: An American Catholic* (New York 1992).

[V. HOLDEN]

HEDDA, ST.

Bishop of Wessex; d. July 9, 705. His early life is unknown, but he was a Benedictine monk and abbot before 676, whether at GLASTONBURY rather than WHITBY is not at all certain. He is often confused with Hedda of Lichfield (d. 721) or with Aetla of Whitby. He became the fifth bishop of Wessex in 676 and moved the see from Dorchester to WINCHESTER *c.* 686, at the same time translating the relics of St. BIRINUS, the first bishop of Wessex. The diocese remained undivided until Hedda died, although elsewhere THEODORE, archbishop of Canterbury, sought to subdivide earlier kingdom-centered dioceses. After 705 ALDHELM ruled Sherborne, and Daniel (d. 745) succeeded to Winchester. Hedda worked closely with Theodore and also with King INE, who was often guided by his counsels. After his death many miracles were reported at his tomb, and pilgrims carried so much dust from the grave that a deep ditch developed. His relics may have been translated to Glastonbury and buried under the famous ''Glastonbury pyramids.''

Feast: July 7.

Bibliography: *Acta Sanctorum* July 2:482–483. BEDE, *Ecclesiastical History* 3.7; 4.12, 23; 5.18; *Loeb Classical Library* (London-New York-Cambridge, MA. 1912–), ed., tr. J. E. KING, 2 v. (1930) 2:66, 126, 292. W. HUNT, *The Dictionary of National Biography from the Earliest Times to 1900,* 63 v. (London 1885–1900) 9:361–362; 20:483. A. M.. ZIMMERMANN, *Kalendarium Benedictinum: Die Heiligen und Seligen des Benediktinerorderns und seiner Zweige,* 4 v. (Metten 1933–38) 2:412–414.

[H. E. AIKINS]

HEDONISM

Hedonism, a word derived from the Greek ἡδονή, meaning pleasure, is a name used to refer to at least two different ethical positions. Ethical hedonism is the view that the only thing that is good and ought to be desired is pleasure; we can desire other things but are mistaken when we do so. Among its supporters have been EPICURUS, LOCKE, HOBBES, HUME, BENTHAM, and Sidgwick. Psychological hedonism is the view that we can desire nothing but pleasure; that other things, like learning or virtue, can be sought only as means to pleasure; and that ethical theory consists in showing men how to seek those pleasures that are most intense or lasting. Strictly speaking, this latter view is incompatible with ethical hedonism, for if we *can* desire nothing but pleasure, it is surely pointless to recommend pleasure as the only thing that ought to be desired; nevertheless, some ethicists, such as Epicurus and Bentham, have been both ethical and psychological hedonists. It is also useful to distinguish the individualistic (or egoistic) from the universalistic (or utilitarian) form of hedonism: the first says that one ought to aim at pleasure only for himself; the second says that he ought to aim at pleasure for all.

Historical Survey. The Cyrenaic school of hedonistic philosophy was founded by Aristippus of Cyrene, according to whom the sole good to be desired for its own sake is the enjoyment of the particular pleasure of the moment, and the only moral goal of action is present gratification (*see* CYRENAICS). Primary attention ought to be given to the pleasures of the body since these are the more intense; and one should seize the pleasures of the moment since life is uncertain and one may miss the pleasures put off until tomorrow. Aristippus found a metaphysical basis for this doctrine in the RELATIVISM of Protagoras of Abdera: we can know nothing of things outside us except their impression on ourselves; so the ''smooth motion'' of sense which we call pleasure is the only knowable good (*see* SOPHISTS).

Epicurus agreed with the Cyrenaics that only pleasure is good, and only pain is bad and always bad; the highest wisdom is to learn how to make the wisest choice of pleasures. But, he taught, the highest point of pleasure is to be attained by the mere removal of pain or disturbance, and so the highest form of bodily pleasure is freedom from fear and anxiety; and because of the role of memory and anticipation, mental pleasure is far more valuable than bodily pleasure. It is clear that Epicurus was not an ''Epicurean,'' one given to voluptuous living; for him, one who is wise in his choice of pleasures chooses a virtuous and withdrawn life of study (*see* EPICUREANISM).

With the fairly definitive refutation by Bishop Joseph BUTLER (*Fifteen Sermons,* 1726) of egoistic versions of hedonism, interest tended to center on the defense of universalistic hedonism, or UTILITARIANISM, an ethical theory best known in the form given it by Jeremy Bentham. According to Bentham, actions are to be approved or disapproved according to their tendency to increase the pleasure of all parties concerned by the action; if the whole community is affected, the pleasure of all must be considered. This calls for measuring pleasures and pains, and for comparing those of one person with those of another; and Bentham proposed a ''felicific calculus'' which, he claimed, would make such measurements and comparisons possible.

Though only a few, apart from Kant, would want to deny that some pleasures are intrinsically valuable, the hedonist tends to claim that not only some, or most, but absolutely *all* pleasant experiences are intrinsically valuable; and further, that *only* pleasures are intrinsically valuable; and further that what is ''morally good'' is identical with, or instrumental to, pleasant experience.

Critique. An important source of confusion among hedonists of an empirical cast of mind is their talk of pleasure and pain as occupying opposite ends of the very same scale. Just as the prospect of physical pain makes one avoid some objects, so pleasures are construed as feelings, the prospect of which makes him seek other objects. Yet the counterpart of pleasure in the sense of a pleasurable state of consciousness, the sense that is of interest in ethics, is not pain but displeasure; while both pleasure and pain, in the sense of certain bodily sensations (e.g., ticklings, stingings), are the cause, sometimes, of pleasure in the first sense, and sometimes of displeasure. To attempt an adequate explanation of human likes and dislikes, wants and aversions, by a model of human nature that has pleasure and pain as polar opposites, both of which are capable of precise quantitative variation, is surely a mistake.

One of the major objections that has been raised to hedonism is that it could tend to approve malice, the pleasurable contemplation of another's undeserved misfortune, as intrinsically good; whereas such pleasure is obviously intrinsically bad in direct proportion to its pleasantness.

Further, even if pleasure were somehow involved in our experience of all good things, it would not follow that pleasantness and moral goodness were the same things, any more than it would follow that when one sharpens a pencil the shavings and the sharpened pencil are the same thing. No experience is an experience merely of pleasure, just as nothing is colored without having size and shape; and so even if it be shown that pleasure is a necessary condition of intrinsically valuable experience, this is not to show that it is a sufficient condition. Finally, the hedonist whose whole striving is for pleasure will himself run up against the hedonist paradox: happiness to be got must best be forgot.

See Also: ETHICS, HISTORY OF; EGOISM.

Bibliography: J. WATSON, *Hedonistic Theories from Aristippus to Spencer* (New York 1895). W. J. OATES, ed., *The Stoic and Epicurean Philosophers* (New York 1940). R. D. HICKS, *Stoic and Epicurean* (New York 1910). A. J. FESTUGIÈRE, *Epicurus and His Gods,* tr. C. W. CHILTON (Oxford 1955). H. SIDGWICK, *The Methods of Ethics* (7th ed. 1907; reissued, Chicago 1962). R. M. BLAKE, ''Why Not Hedonism? A Protest,'' *The International Journal of Ethics* 37 (1926) 1–18. G. RYLE, *Dilemmas* (The Tarner Lectures, 1953; Cambridge, Eng. 1954) 54–67.

[R. L. CUNNINGHAM]

HEDWIG OF ANJOU, ST.

Polish: Jadwiga; also known as Hedwig of Lithuania, queen of Poland, married woman; b. 1374 in Buda (now part of Budapest), Hungary; d. July 17, 1399, at Krakow, Poland.

Hedwig was the younger daughter of King Louis I of Hungary and Poland and Elizabeth, princess of Bosnia. At age nine she was betrothed to Duke William of Austria, whom she came to love; however, the Polish parliament vetoed this alliance. She demonstrated her obedience in refusing to elope with the young duke. Upon the death of her father and with the consent of the Polish nobility, ten–year–old Hedwig ascended to the throne of Poland in 1384. Her marriage at age 12 to Grand Duke Władysław Jagiello of Lithuania (thereafter King Ladislaus II of Poland) began a 400–year alliance between Poland and Lithuania and contributed to the growth of Christianity throughout the region. As part of the marriage contract, Jagiello became a Christian, destroyed pagan temples, and required the baptism of the Lithuanian people. The queen used her position to further evangelization by urging a moral reform upon her subjects. In 1397, she received permission from Pope Boniface IX to establish the Theology Faculty of the Jagiellonian University of Krakow. She founded several hospitals at Biecz, Sandomierz, Sacz, and Stradom, and she defended the rights of peasants against the Polish nobility. Queen Hedwig combined contemplation and action. She was a woman of extraordinary piety, personal asceticism, and charity, especially to the poor. Often she would kneel in meditation at the feet of the Crucified Christ on the Black Cross in Wawel cathedral to learn God's generous love from Christ himself. At age 25, she died giving birth to her first child, who did not survive. In 1896 Hedwig was beatified by Pope Leo XIII. In his impassioned homily at her canonization on Blonia Esplanade in Krakow, Poland, on June 8, 1997, Pope John Paul II praised Hedwig for her evangelization of Lithuania, the Ukraine, and Belarus, her heroic charity, and sense of justice rooted in Gospel values. The body of this patron of Poland is now venerated in the cathedral of Krakow, Poland.

Feast: July 17 (formerly Feb. 28 in Poland).

Bibliography: *L'Osservatore Romano,* Eng. ed., no. 26 (1997): 3–5, 7. O. HALECKI, *Jadwiga of Anjou and the Rise of East Central Europe*, ed. T.V. GROMADA (Boulder, Colo. 1991). W. KLUZ, *Jadwiga królowa Polski* (Warsaw 1987). B. PRZYBYSZEWSKI, *Blogoslawiona Jadwiga królowa* (2d ed. Krakow 1996), tr. as *Saint Jadwiga, Queen of Poland*, tr. B. MACQUEEN (Rome 1997). L. RYDEL, *Królowa Jadwiga* (Warsaw 1984). J. STABÍNSKA, *Królowa Jadwiga* (3d ed. Krakow 1997).

[K. I. RABENSTEIN]

HEESWIJK, MONASTERY OF

House of the PREMONSTRATENSIANS, near 's Hertogenbosch, Netherlands—formerly of the Diocese of

St. Hedwig of Anjou, manuscript illumination. (©Francis G. Mayer/CORBIS)

Utrecht, today Diocese of 's Hertogenbosch. It was founded in 1130–31 by Fulco of Berne as a daughter-house of Marienweerd, at Berne, near Heusden; today nothing is left. For almost 300 years after the monastery was destroyed in 1579, the monks lived in various places of refuge without a cloister, the longest recorded exclaustration in the history of the Church. In 1857 it reestablished itself under its old name, Berne, at Heeswijk. The monastery sent to America (1893–1902) a foundation that established St. Norbert Abbey, DePere, Wisconsin, and another to Germany (Windberg) in 1923. Heeswijk has a priory in Essenburgh, maintains a gymnasium, has nine incorporated parishes, and directs a missionary diocese in India (Jubbulpore).

Bibliography: C. L. HUGO, *S. Ordinis Praemonstratensis annales,* 2 v. (Nancy 1734–36) 1:329–335. A. VERSTEYLEN, *Dictionnaire d'histoire et de géographie ecclésiastiques,* ed. A. BAUDRILLART et al. (Paris 1912–) 8:818–821. C. J. KIRKFLEET, *The White Canons of St. Norbert* (Paterson, N.J. 1943). N. BACKMUND, *Monasticon Praemonstratense,* 3 v. (Straubing 1949–56) 2:274–278.

[N. BACKMUND]

HEFELE, CARL JOSEPH VON

Bishop, ecclesiastical historian; b. Unterkochen (Württemberg), Germany, March 15, 1809; d. Rottenburg, June 5, 1893. After studying at Tübingen (1827–32), he was ordained (Aug. 10, 1833). At Tübingen he succeeded J. A. MÖHLER in the chair of Church history, patrology, and Christian archeology as lecturer (*Privatdocent*) from 1836, and as full professor from 1840. As representative for Ellwangen in the Württemberg legislature (1842–45), he supported Bp. Johann von Keller's efforts to free the Church from governmental tutelage. After serving as rector of Tübingen University (1852–53), he began publication of his principal historical writing, a seven-volume *Conciliengeschichte* (1855–74), completed to mid-15th century by him, which treats the provincial and ecumenical synods in their historical milieu, so that this work supplies almost a history of the Church. It displays vast knowledge of ancient and medieval Church history and remains a standard work in the French version revised by Henri LECLERCQ, which is outdated only in some sections. Hefele's numerous learned writings included frequent contributions to the *Theologische Quartalschrift* and more than 150 articles in the first edition of the *Kirchenlexikon.*

Called to Rome in 1868 as a member of the preparatory central commission for VATICAN COUNCIL I, he drafted the council's order of procedure. His hopes for appointment to the committee on faith were disappointed, but he was chosen bishop of Rottenburg (June 17, 1869). At the assembly of German bishops in Fulda, Germany (September 1869), he voiced strong opposition to definition of the doctrine of papal infallibility. In the Vatican Council he was one of the leading opponents of this doctrine. His arguments, mainly historical, made much of the questions concerning Pope HONORIUS I. He voted *non placet* at the decisive session (July 13, 1870) and left Rome to avoid voting in the public session (July 18). He had acted at the council according to his conscience as a theologian, and had repulsed pressures from the OLD CATHOLICS, who falsely claimed him as a supporter, to help the formation of their schism. After a long interior struggle, he published the conciliar decrees in his diocese (April 10, 1871), the last German bishop to do so. Hefele's prudent administration subsequently preserved his diocese from the troubles of the KULTURKAMPF.

Bibliography: Works. *Conciliengeschichte*, v. 1–7 (Freiburg 1855–74), to 1449; v.8–9 by J. HERGENRÖTHER (Freiburg 1887–90), to the Council of Trent; rev. ed. with many corrections and changes by Hefele, v.1–4 (Freiburg 1873–90); v.5–6 rev. by A. KNÖPFLER; Fr. tr. with many additions by H. LECLERCQ et al., 11 v. (Paris 1907–52); Eng. tr. W. R. CLARK, *History of the Councils of the Church,* 5 v. (Edinburgh 1883–96), to 787; *Kardinal Ximenes* (Tübingen 1844), Eng. tr. (London 1860); *Beiträge zur Kirchengeschichte, Archäologie u. Liturgik,* 2 v. (Tübingen 1864). **Literature.** H. HURTER, *Nomenclator literarius theologiae catholicae,* 5 v. in 6 (3d ed. Innsbruck 1903–13) 5:1653–55. *Revue internationale de théologie* 16 (1908) 485–506, 671–694. P. GODET, "Ch.-Jos. Hefele," *Revue du Clergé français* 50 (1907) 449–474. C. BUTLER, *The Vatican Council,* 2 v. (New York 1930). A. HAGEN, "Hefele und das Vatikanische Konzil," *Theologische Quartalschrift* 123 (1942) 223–252; 124 (1943) 1–40; *Gestalten aus dem Schwäbischen Katholizimus,* 3 v. (Stuttgart 1948–54) 2:7–58; *Geschichte der Diözese Rottenburg,* v.2 (Stuttgart 1958). E. MANGENOT, *Dictionnaire de théologie catholique*, ed. A. VACANT et al., 15 v. (Paris 1903–50; Tables Générales 1951–) 6.2:2111–13.

[V. CONZEMIUS]

HEGEL, GEORG WILHELM FRIEDRICH

German idealist philosopher; b. Stuttgart, Aug. 27, 1770; d. Berlin, Nov. 14, 1831. Possessed of great speculative powers, Hegel developed German IDEALISM into an absolute system of knowledge that conceived all of reality as the self-unfolding of the Absolute.

Life and Works. The son of an official in Stuttgart, Hegel was given a stanch Protestant and humanistic education. At 18 he entered the theological school at the University of Tübingen, where he studied philosophy (1788–90) and theology (1790–93). He was a close friend of F. Hölderlin (1770–1843) and F. SCHELLING, and was influenced more by the study of Greek antiquity, contemporary philosophy (I. Kant, F. H. Jacobi, and J. C. F. Schiller), and the stirrings of the French Revolution than by the study of evangelical theology. In 1793 he was a private tutor, first at Bern and later at Frankfurt am Main; at about this time he composed his so-called *Theologischen Jugendschriften* (ed. H. Nohl, Tübingen 1907), in which he opposed the problems of the philosophy of religion to those of religious instruction and clarified his own philosophical position.

In 1801 he went to Jena, where he produced his first published work, *Die Differenz des Fichteschen und Schellingschen Systems der Philosophie* (Jena 1801), and other writings in which he took his stand with Schelling against J. G. FICHTE. Yet, in introducing his dialectical principles, he went far beyond Schelling from the start. The same year he wrote his monograph for habilitation, *De orbitis planetarum.* With Schelling he lectured and worked on the *Kritischen Journal der Philosophie,* in which he discussed contemporary philosophy and worked toward establishing the foundations of his own thought. This he eventually embodied in the introduction of his system [*Jenenser Logik, Metaphysik und Naturphilosophie,* ed. G. Lasson (Leipzig 1923 and 1931–32)]. When Schelling left Jena in 1803, the tenuous collaboration dissolved and the difference in spirit between them grew. It finally became evident that the gap would never narrow when Hegel took a stand against Schelling in the *Phänomenologie des Geistes* (Bamberg and Würzburg 1807), a work that initiated Hegel's own "system" but decreased the chances for a mutual collaboration on a philosophy of the spirit.

After a short period as editor of the *Bamberger Zeitung,* in 1808, he became director of the gymnasium in Nuremberg. Besides a philosophical introduction for school instruction, he composed there his metaphysical masterpiece, *Wissenschaft der Logik* [2 v. (Nuremberg 1812–16) also known as the *Grosse Logik*]. Finally, in 1816 he was invited to become professor at Heidelberg, where he wrote his *Enzyklopädie der philosophischen Wissenschaften* (Heidelberg 1817) to serve as a basic textbook; this proved to be a tightly woven compendium of his entire system.

In 1818 Hegel was invited to the University of Berlin, where he taught until his death, exerting a deep influence upon the whole spiritual and cultural life of Prussia. Here he published his *Grundlinien der Philosophie des Rechts* (Berlin 1821). He lectured on the philosophy of history, of art, and of religion, and also on the history of philosophy. These lectures were first printed after his death. In the midst of his work, Hegel died at 61, evidently of cholera.

Teachings. In his early writings, Hegel showed a tendency to deal with the reconciliation of contradictories, viz, of private devotion and folk religion, of guilt and fate, of particular and general, of finite and infinite. This reconciliation, for him, is accomplished in spirit, where the opposites are dissolved through love. The first and basic opposition is contained in the duality of subject and predicate; it is resolved in the otherness of spirit knowing itself.

Georg Wilhelm Friedrich Hegel, drawing.

Hegel applied this dialectical procedure to the problems of his day. For instance, Kant had unsatisfactorily resolved the relation between subject and object in a transcendental unity. Fichte in turn established unity in the "absolute I," as opposed to the "not-I." This did not actually resolve the duality, but reduced it to the term of a relation, viz, an absolutely given subject that gives rise to the object. To preserve objectivity, Schelling then proffered "absolute identity" as an Absolute whose indifference is both subjective and objective, yet establishes itself in knowledge as the difference between subjectivity and objectivity. Against him, Hegel objected, as had Fichte, that no difference can arise or be understood from absolute identity and indifference. To equate the Absolute with pure identity is sterile, just as "the night, in which all cows are black, means the naïveté of emptiness in knowledge" (*Ausgabe* 2:14). Difference can come from identity only when it is already a component of that identity. Absolute unity is a dialectical unity derived from a thing itself and its contradictory, that is, not as Schelling had assumed, the ''identity of identity,'' but according to Hegel ''the identity of identity and non-identity'' (1:252; 3:68). This implies that spirit becomes the other in knowing itself, but rises above opposition and knows and develops itself in the other. Thus Hegel finds absolute, dialectical unity to consist in the act of knowing, which is thereby able to conceive itself as ''Absolute Knowledge.''

Phenomenology of Spirit. Hegel sought to justify his dialectical ''speculation'' in the *Phenomenology of Spirit,* which constitutes the introduction to his *System of Science.* While Fichte and Schelling started from the immediacy of the ''intellectual intuition'' of an absolute principle in order to grasp therein all a priori deducible notions, Hegel forsook the immediacy of intuition and substituted the rational mediation of Absolute Mind in a reductive manifestation. To this end, he explored all the experiences of consciousness in the *Phenomenology*—from sense knowledge, to perception and understanding, to reason; not only in its theoretical but also in its practical aspects, as in law and morality and in art and religion; and not only subjective experiences but also objective experiences of spirit in its historical development. Here the dialectical law is already in evidence: each achieved degree of consciousness advances through self-contradiction to a higher degree that resolves the contradiction. Thus does Hegel conceive the totality of the experiences of spirit in a dialectically necessary concatenation. The highest ''contradiction of consciousness,'' the duality of subject and object, is finally resolved in Absolute Mind. The knowing spirit attains itself in its own opposition; in the full development of knowledge, what is known as other is raised to the identity of spirit conceiving itself. Mind experiences itself as the Absolute, thereby resolving the opposition between finite and infinite spirit. Finite spirit understands itself as the place where the Absolute comes to self-consciousness and becomes ''spirit.''

Logic. From the vantage point of Absolute Mind, one can reconstruct the Absolute's dialectical unfolding in pure thought and deduce, as a consequence, all knowledge in a purely a priori process, thereby establishing the system of ''absolute science.'' This is the task of the ''science of Logic,'' which for Hegel means ''absolute Logic,'' wherein the order of thought and the order of being, logic and metaphysics, become one and are grasped in the total actuality of their absolute source with logical necessity. The impetus to thought is again the dialectical law. Whereas this notion was explored only empirically in the *Phenomenology,* it here is enforced with logical necessity as an absolute method, as the unfolding rhythm of the Absolute Itself. Each achieved insight displays a contradiction; it grasps a partial and not a whole truth; it displays the ''untrue'' and therefore its negation. The contradiction leads to a higher level, so that the ''immediacy'' of the first notion, through the ''mediation'' of its negation, is resolved in a ''mediated immediacy.'' A thought that avoids contradiction, that abstractly differentiates, and that separates opposites from each other, is for Hegel the product of ''abstract understanding,'' which remains at the level of external empirical representation. When thought accepts the inner contradiction of things but resolves them into a higher unity, it then operates as ''speculative reason,'' which penetrates reality in its most vital movement and conceives it in one, dialectical, and self-interpreting ontological foundation. So Hegel's logic aspires to be not only an ontology, but also a theology—''the representation of God as He is in His eternal essence before the creation of nature and of finite spirit'' (3:36). The absolute system of categories of logic seeks to reconstruct the ideal design of essences and essential laws in the spirit of God. This takes place in three steps from being to essence to idea (*Sein, Wesen, Begriff*) in which the Absolute finally participates in the ''Absolute Idea.''

Total System. Hegel's logic is only the first phase of the total system, which is succinctly treated in the *Encyclopedia* (though considerably enlarged upon in the second edition). Here Hegel considers the triadic development of Idea, Nature, and Spirit, resuming the first step from the science of logic. The latter knows the Absolute in the pure form of Idea; but the Absolute, because it is essentially the absolute dialectic, must emerge from the ideal into reality, and this gives rise to the second phase, which he calls the ''philosophy of nature.'' This describes the externalization of self-estranged Nature in the proximity of space and the continuity of time, but in an unfolding of successively higher forms all the way to that of organic life. The opposition between Idea and Nature is in turn resolved in the ''philosophy of spirit.'' The Absolute as ''Absolute Idea'' mediates itself through the externalization of nature into spirit and attains consciousness in the finite spirit; there it goes beyond the content of human consciousness, of both subjective and objective spirit, and becomes ''Absolute Spirit.''

Philosophy of History. The spiritualization of the Absolute perfects itself in the collective history of man. The universal nature of Hegel's thought provides also for historical reality and attempts to conceptualize it from the Absolute, in the sense that the latter conciliates historical oppositions and incorporates these in its system. One finds the philosophy of history everywhere in Hegel's thought, not only in lectures specifically concerned with the subject but also in his systematic works. Since for

Hegel, however, history is the process by which Absolute Spirit unfolds, it seemed to him that historical progress must involve dialectical oppositions that are resolved in a higher content of historical being. Hegel sought to reconstruct dialectically the whole of history, that is, to comprehend it within the necessity of the Absolute. Thus not only is concrete history interpreted to a great extent in a tortuous way, but freedom as an essential element of history is reduced to absolute necessity.

Political Philosophy. In his philosophy of law and of the state, Hegel was preoccupied in supplying a philosophical basis for the Prussian state; thus he left to posterity the theoretical basis for every form of absolutist and totalitarian government. For in the state the Absolute attains its manifestation. The state is the reality of the moral Idea, of self-unfolding Spirit, and presents the divine will as present, as the real pattern and organizing factor in the world. It is true that Hegel worked for constitutional monarchy, because subjective consciousness is there also granted its right. However, for him the manifestation does not consist in the subjective self-determination of individuals, but in the objective rationality of the structured state as a whole. As elsewhere in Hegel's philosophy, the individual is absorbed into the universal, the individual subject becomes a mere ''moment'' of the universal Spirit; thus the universality of the state transcends the individual as its own subordinated ''moment.'' Nevertheless, for Hegel (as is often overlooked), the state is not the highest manifestation of the Absolute; the state can still evolve in other forms wherein the Absolute is manifested as Absolute Spirit.

Philosophy of Religion. The Absolute Spirit variously manifests itself (1) as art, in the objective form of sensuous manifestation; (2) as religion, in the subjective form of representation; and (3) as philosophy, in the absolute form of pure thought wherein the opposition of objectivity and subjectivity is resolved. The first immediate form of Absolute Spirit is therefore beauty, as this is presented in art. Beauty is the Absolute (Idea) in its sensuous manifestation. Hegel's aesthetic, already sketched in the *Encyclopedia,* was considerably developed in his Berlin lectures. He differentiates between (1) the symbolic art of the ancient Orient in which the Idea (as form) did not entirely penetrate the content; (2) the classical art of Greece, in which the Idea was perfectly embodied in matter; and (3) the romantic art of the Christian Era, in which Idea transcends its sensuous manifestation. In religion, however, Absolute Spirit manifests itself in a higher form than in art—not objectively, but subjectively. Here (as in philosophy) there is an absolute content; that is, the Absolute is its own content. It exists, however, in an imperfect form, not in the pure form of thought but in that of representation. Thus man places God before himself in otherness, outside himself, hence in opposition, presenting a duality and estrangement that must ultimately be resolved in Absolute Mind. Hegel distinguished three phases in the development of religion: the first presents God as an objective power in nature (religion of the ancient East); the second presents Him as a subjective individuality (religion of the Jews, Greeks, and Romans); the third, or ''absolute religion,'' conceives Him as spirit (Christianity). Hegel adopted many elements of Christian belief (from the Protestant point of view), but he interpreted them in terms of his own system. Thus, the doctrine of the Trinity had special significance for him in his absolute dialectic. The level of God-in-Himself is the ''kingdom of the Father'' (expressed in logic); its externalization in the finite world is the ''kingdom of the Son'' (expressed in the philosophy of nature), and the union of God and the faithful (the Church) is the ''kingdom of the Spirit'' (expressed in the philosophy of spirit). The triune Godhead is ''the Father and the Son, and this differentiation in its unity as the Spirit'' (9:393). Religion is for Hegel the highest manifestation of Absolute Spirit short of Absolute Knowledge, superior to everything else in the sphere of consciousness. Yet the imperfect form of religious representation must still be resolved in the purer element of thought, that is, in Absolute Knowledge, in which man grasps himself as one with the Absolute as a ''moment'' of Absolute Spirit. Religion, therefore, is absorbed in philosophy.

Evaluation and Critique. Hegel is certainly one of the most significant philosophers in history. With a lively sense of the fullness of experience, he committed himself to a deeply speculative and boldly constructive thought, which distinguishes him as the unique systematizer of German idealism and perhaps as the greatest systematic philosopher of modern times. His dialectical thought—although historically patterned on Heraclitus, whom he regarded highly, and influenced by Kant, Fichte, and Schelling—gives rise to a true experience of the oppositional aspects of reality, especially in the historical and social domain. This insight is no less verified, even from a Thomistic point of view, in the oppositional structure of finite being and finite spirit. Hegel's dialectic could conveniently have opened up the structures of being, which are meaningful in theology to the extent that they transcend formal-logical thought; in this way, realities that are comprehensible only in the unity and the tension of opposition could have attained fuller realization. Yet, the dialectic of Hegel was eccentric; it failed in consequence of its own one-sidedness. Even Schelling, in his later period, raised the objection (often repeated since) that Hegel's dialectic offers no principle of deduction because it provides no content in its suppositions. Reality is never deduced dialectically, but can be grasped and recognized only in experience, and thus Hegel's thought remains entirely in the logical sphere of possible being. This objection contends that Hegel ''set up'' every opposition in things as a contradiction whether this was required or justified. A dialectic of contradictions yields no new insights, nor does it contribute to the advance of thought.

Again, on deeper reflection, one can see that Hegel's thought is basically a pure and absolute dialectic of reason. Though in the beginning Hegel regarded oppositions as resolved in love, later he dropped this solution and ascribed the resolution to Absolute Knowing alone. With the entrance of practical existential phenomena into the picture, these were resolved in the pure act of Mind. His Absolute (following the Aristotelian νόησις νοήσεως) is Absolute Mind alone, not Absolute Will, Causality, and Love. A tendency toward INTELLECTUALISM, a legacy from the Greeks and an encumbrance on Western philosophy, received its strongest expression in Hegel. Concerned only with what mind can comprehend, he fastened on what could be conceptualized, namely essence, and not on being as such, which cannot be comprehended but only ascertained and acknowledged.

In the last analysis, Hegel's philosophy is rationalistic thought, absolute essentialism in which reality as a whole is derived from the laws of being, a system based on necessity and not on freedom. To the extent that ideal being alone, and not real being, can be ''resolved'' into Mind, absolute idealism is grounded in the absolute fixity of essence, whose entire contents are interpreted as ideal moments in the process of Absolute Spirit.

Though Hegel defended himself against the charge of pantheism, one can hardly understand his spiritual monism as other than pantheistic (or panentheistic). On the one hand, if the finite is resolved in the Infinite and finite spirit in Absolute Spirit, the independence of individuality and of personality is lost. On the other hand, when the Infinite is resolved in the finite, Absolute Spirit develops Itself in Its finite moment. Not only is the ''evil infinite'' not actual, but neither is the ''true infinite,'' as Hegel distinguished these; all that is left is the infinity of dialectical self-unfolding. Again, because the Absolute attains Itself in the mind of finite spirit, Hegel claimed adequate comprehensive knowledge of everything in an absolute way, ''the truth, without outer covering and for itself'' (3:36)—the highest claim for a philosophical system that has ever been made. In this view, not only would religion be absorbed in philosophical knowledge; but since religion is a free person-to-person relationship to God and thus more than philosophy, philosophy should be resolved into religion. The possibility of supernatural revelation and the mystery of divine truth, attainable only through faith and not through reason, is also resolved by Hegel into absolute, rational, and comprehending Mind.

See Also: HEGELIANISM AND NEO-HEGELIANISM; IDEALISM; PANTHEISM; PANENTHEISM.

Bibliography: Works. *Sämtliche Werke: Jubiläumsausgabe,* ed. H. GLOCKNER, 26 v. (Stuttgart 1927–1957); *Sämtliche Werke: Kritische Ausgabe,* ed. G. LASSON and J. HOFFMEISTER (Leipzig-Hamburg 1923–); *Sämtliche Werke: Kritische Ausgabe,,* ed. J. HOFFMEISTER (Leipzig-Hamburg 1949–). For a list of English translations of Hegel's works see J. D. COLLINS, *A History of Modern European Philosophy* (Milwaukee 1954) 658–659. General literature. F. A. STAUDENMAIER, *Darstellung und Kritik des Hegelschen Systems* (Mainz 1844). K. FISCHER, *Hegels Leben, Werke und Lehre,* 2 v. (2d ed. Heidelberg 1911). R. KRONER, *Von Kant bis Hegel,* 2 v. (2d ed. Tübingen 1961). B. HEIMANN, *System und Methode in Hegels Philosophie* (Leipzig 1927). H. FISCHER, *Hegels Methode in ihrer ideengeschichtlichen Notwendigkeit* (Munich 1928). H. NIEL, *De la médiation dans la philosophie de Hegel* (Paris 1945). I. A. IL'IN, *Die Philosophie Hegels als kontemplative Gotteslehre* (Bern 1946). T. LITT, *Hegel: Versuch einer kritischen Erneuerung* (Heidelberg 1953). W. T. STACE, *The Philosophy of Hegel* (New York 1955). J. N. FINDLAY, *Hegel: A Re-examination* (New York 1958). F. GRÉGOIRE, *Études hégéliennes: Les Points capitaux du sysème* (Louvain 1958). W. SEEBERGER, *Hegel* (Stuttgart 1961). Hegel's development. W. DILTHEY, *Die Jugendgeschichte Hegels und andere Abhandlungen zur Geschichte des deutschen Idealismus* (2d ed. Stuttgart 1959). R. HAYM, *Hegel und seine Zeit,* ed. H. ROSENBERG (2d ed. Leipzig 1927). T. HÄRING, *Hegel, sein Wollen und sein Werk,* 2 v. (Leipzig 1929–38). J. SCHWARZ, *Hegels philosophische Entwicklung* (Frankfurt 1938). T. STEINBÜCHEL, *Das Grundproblem der Hegelschen Philosophie* (Bonn 1933), only v.1 publ. G. LUKÁCS, *Der junge Hegel und die Probleme der kapitalistischen Gesellschaft* (Berlin 1954). G. E. MÜLLER, *Hegel: Denkgeschichte eines Lebendigen* (Bern 1959). A. T. B. PEPERZAK, *Le Jeune Hegel et la vision morale du monde* (The Hague 1960). Phenomenology. J. HYPPOLITE, *Genèse et structure de la phénoménologie de l'esprit de Hegel* (Paris 1946). A. KOJÈVE, *Introduction à la lecture de Hegel* (Paris 1947). P. HENRICI, *Hegel und Blondel* (Pullach, Ger. 1958). Logic. G. W. CUNNINGHAM, *Thought and Reality in Hegel's System* (New York 1910). G. R. G. MURE, *An Introduction to Hegel* (Oxford 1940); *A Study of Hegel's Logic* (Oxford 1950). E. CORETH, *Das dialektische Sein in Hegels Logik* (Vienna 1952). J. HYPPOLITE, *Logique et existence* (Paris 1953). B. LAKEBRINK, *Hegels dialektische Ontologie und die Thomistische Analektik* (Cologne 1955). M. HEIDEGGER, *Identität und Differenz* (Pfullingen 1957). Philosophy of history. G. LASSON, *Hegel als Geschichtsphilosoph* (Leipzig 1920). S. VANNI ROVIGHI, *La concezione Hegeliana della storia* (Milan 1942). J. HYPPOLITE, *Introduction à la philosophie de l'histoire de Hegel* (Paris 1948). Political philosophy. G. GIESE, *Hegels Staatsidee und der Begriff der Staatserziehung* (Halle 1926). J. RITTER, *Hegel und die französische Revolution* (Cologne 1957). H. MARCUSE, *Reason and Revolution: Hegel and the Rise of Social Theory* (2d ed. New York 1955). J. BARION, *Hegel und die marxistische Staatslehre* (Bonn 1963). Philosophy of art. F. PUGLISI, *L'estetica di Hegel e i suoi presupposti teoretici* (Padua 1953). G. VECCHI, *L'estetica di Hegel* (Milan 1956). J. KAMINSKY, *Hegel on Art* (Albany, N.Y. 1962). Philosophy of religion. H. GROOS, *Der deutsche Idealismus und das Christentum* (Munich 1927). H. A. OGIERMANN, *Hegels Gottesbeweise* (*Analecta Gregoriana* 49; 1948). J. MÖLLER, *Der Geist and das Absolute* (Paderborn 1951). P. ASVELD, *La Pensée réligieuse du jeune Hegel* (Louvain 1953). E. SCHMIDT, *Hegels Lehre von Gott* (Gütersloh,

Ger. 1952). W. ALBRECHT, *Hegels Gottesbeweis* (Berlin 1958). Other literature. W. KERN, ''Neue Hegel-Bücher: Ein Literaturbericht für die Jahre 1958 bis 1960,'' *Scholastik* 37 (1962) 85–114, 550–578; 38 (1963) 62–90.

[E. CORETH]

HEGELIANISM AND NEO-HEGELIANISM

The term Hegelianism refers to a movement in philosophy usually associated with two sorts of thinkers: (1) followers of G. W. F. HEGEL, in the strict sense of the word who, notwithstanding their personal interpretations, remain faithful to the thought of the German philosopher; (2) philosophers belonging to other schools of thought who have been basically influenced by Hegel. The first usage refers primarily to philosophers of the 19th century, the second to such contemporary movements as French EXISTENTIALISM, Marxism, and even in certain cases, THOMISM (particularly in Germany). The term Neo-Hegelianism, on the other hand, is generally applied to the revival of Hegelian philosophy that began in Europe at the end of the 19th century and then extended to America.

HEGELIANISM

The first school of Hegelian philosophers started during the latter period of Hegel's life, while he was teaching philosophy at the University of Berlin (1818–31). This group founded, in 1827, the *Jahrbücher für wissenschaftliche Kritik.* It encompassed various thinkers who later would separate into ''left'' and ''right'' wings. The most important were G. A. Gabler, who in 1828 published the first commentary on Hegel's *Phänomenologie des Geistes* (pub. 1807); P. K. Marheinecke, who published the first edition of Hegel's lectures on the philosophy of religion, and on the proofs for the existence of God; K. E. Michelet, who later edited Hegel's lectures on the history of philosophy; E. Gans, who taught a course on the philosophy of law that was to have a decisive influence on the young Marx, and who was also the publisher of Hegel's lectures on the philosophy of history; H. Hotho, who edited Hegel's lectures on aesthetics; K. Rosenkranz, who was Hegel's first biographer; B. BAUER, who was to be the leader of the left-wing Hegelians who influenced Marx; and H. F. Hinrichs, whose work on the relation between religion and science (1822) had influenced Hegel's own ideas on philosophy of religion.

Most decisive in the further development of this early Hegelianism was Hegel's own review in the *Jahrbücher* (1823) of a work by K. F. Göschel on the relation between philosophy and faith, proclaiming the complete congruity of his own philosophy with Christian revelation. This profession of orthodoxy, as well as the political conservatism of Hegel's later thought, was responsible for the subsequent division of Hegelianism into a left and a right wing.

Orthodoxy and Liberalism. As long as Hegel was alive, his personal prestige kept all Hegelians together; but shortly after his death the radical split took place. It was occasioned by the publication in 1835 of *Leben Jesu kritisch bearbeitet* by D. F. STRAUSS. Although Hegelian in inspiration, Strauss's work criticizes Hegel's concept of religion on some basic points. For Hegel the contents of religion and philosophy are identical, but whereas philosophy proposes truth in the pure form of reason, religion expresses it in a sensible representation. Such identification favors the theoretical content of religion at the expense of its historical form. Against this thesis Strauss maintained that religious dogmas are irreducible to philosophical concepts, and that, far from being irrelevant, the narratives of the Gospel form the main content of the Christian religion.

These narratives, like all religious doctrines, must be considered not as symbols of rational thought, but as myths expressing the aspirations of the original Christian community. From this viewpoint the historical study of religion becomes essential, but the history of the religious myth is the history of the community that has nurtured it. Very little historical truth is to be found in the narratives themselves. This is not to say that the sacred writings are deprived of truth, but only that their truth is neither historical nor symbolic—it is mythical. Strauss's work preserved the fundamental Hegelian idea of the validity of religious truth, but it destroyed Hegel's ultimate identification of religion with philosophy, as well as the identity of the logical and the historical evolution of truth. Also, by maintaining that the fundamental truth of Christianity, the identity of the divine with the human nature, is realized in not just one exemplar (Christ), but in humanity as a whole, he divorced his brand of Hegelianism from Christian orthodoxy.

Among the many writers who attacked Strauss, the most noteworthy was Bauer, who later was to be convert ed to an even more radical liberalism, denying that the Gospels contained any historical truth. In the controversies over Strauss's *Leben Jesu,* the Hegelian school became divided into a right wing, which considered the unity of God and man to be realized in a unique and historical way (Göschel, Gabler, Marheinecke, and initially, Bauer), and a left wing, which denied the historical and unique value of the Gospel narrations. Strauss's supporters in Berlin organized themselves into the so-called Young Hegelian movement.

Young Hegelians and Feuerbach. Further developments would soon turn the Young Hegelians into a politically leftist group. Over the years Hegel's political views had become more and more conservative, and many considered his lectures in Berlin as merely a philosophical support of the regime of King Frederick William III of Prussia. Hegel justified his attitude on the principle that philosophy must explain what "is," and not what "ought to be." Its task, therefore, is never to anticipate the future. Yet, Hegel's dialectical view of history implied that no historical situation can be final: each stage is to be followed by a new one that negates the present.

The Young Hegelian A. von Cieszkowski concluded from this dialectical necessity that Hegelian philosophy must become a philosophy of action, a means to change the future (*Prolegomena zur Historiosophie,* Berlin 1838). The left-wing Hegelians adopted his view and decided that Hegel's static "system" conflicted with his revolutionary method; the latter alone was to be preserved. Their theories found an outlet in the newly founded *Hallische Jahrbücher für deutsche Wissenschaft und Kunst,* edited by A. Ruge and T. Echtermeyer (1838). This new journal gradually became the liberal counterpart of the conservative *Jahrbücher* of Berlin. It received its definitive bent from an article by L. FEUERBACH, "Zur Kritik der Hegelschen Philosophie" (1839). Feuerbach showed that over and above the contradiction between system and method, Hegel's philosophy suffered from yet another shortcoming that affected the dialectical method itself. The purpose of Hegel's philosophy had been to realize the identity between the real and the ideal, but in trying to achieve it Hegel had placed himself entirely on the side of the ideal. The result was one more idealistic system in which reality was reduced to a moment of thought. To curb this idealistic impetus Feuerbach proposed that the original primacy of reality be restored, and that consciousness be considered as a product of nature rather than the opposite.

Whereas Feuerbach had attacked Hegel's philosophy, Ruge for the first time openly attacked the political conservatism of the Prussian state in an article entitled "Karl Streckfusz und das Preussentum" (1839). The Berlin group of Young Hegelians, mentored by Bauer and Strauss, and recently joined by Marx, accepted the progressive ideas of their Halle colleagues and started contributing to the *Hallische Jahrbücher.* Bauer, now transferred to the University of Bonn, made the link between religious and political liberalism. In his *Kritik der evangelischen Geschichte des Johannes* (Bremen 1840) and *Kritik der evangelischen Geschichte der Synoptiker* (2 v., 2d ed. Leipzig 1841) he defended the view that, at its origin, Christianity was an entirely new manifestation of the World Spirit; yet at present it no longer corresponded to the current stage of universal consciousness. The task of the religious critique, then, was to liberate the State, the highest incarnation of the Spirit, from this antiquated Christian religion. Bauer implied that once the doctrinal changes had taken place, political reforms would follow automatically.

The religious critique of the Young Hegelians reached its apex in Feuerbach's important work, *Das Wesen des Christenthums* (Leipzig 1841). It applied Feuerbach's new principle of philosophy to religion, "an object with universal significance." Rather than start from an infinite and abstract notion, Feuerbach proposed that the Hegelian dialectic start from the concrete reality of man. The real "alienation" in his philosophy is not, as in Hegel's dialectic, the finite appearance of an infinite notion, but the projection of the attributes of human nature into an imaginary religious Being outside man. In religion man is estranged from himself, and the task of philosophical anthropology is to restore man to himself by liberating him from his religious illusions.

In "Vorläufige Thesen Zur Reform der Philosophie" (1843), Feuerbach completed his critique of religion by extending it to Hegel's philosophy. Hegel's Idea is no more than an idol, and his philosophy a pseudotheology. His dialectic, going from the infinite to the finite and back to the infinite, is only a philosophical imitation of man's religious alienation. The final purpose of Feuerbach's dialectic is to overcome this Hegelian Idea, as well as any form of religion.

Marx's Development. What Feuerbach did with the religious aspect of Hegel's philosophy, K. MARX would do with his political views. Initially Marx had shared the speculative viewpoint of Bauer, Feuerbach, and the entire Berlin group. Then, under the influence of Ruge, he became more and more convinced that a change in the established order cannot be effected by a critique of religion, but only by political and social reform.

Philosophy of the State. In his *Kritik des hegelschen Staatsrechts* written in 1842–43 and first published in 1927, Marx applied Feuerbach's reversal of Hegel's dialectic to the philosophy of the State. Whereas for Hegel the spheres of real life, the natural and socioeconomic relations among men, are a mere preparation for the State as Idea, for Marx the real situation is the exact opposite: The State is merely an ideal and empty structure determined by the real spheres of life. Hegel's panlogism, which culminated in his Idea of the State, Marx saw as reducing reality to the simple appearance of an Idea. The only reason why such an illusionist philosophy was successful is that it offered a faithful description of man's actual situation: the real sphere of life has become asocial, and man's status as a social being is preserved only in the ideal sphere of the State. Man's real relations with others in the economic sphere are individualistic and based on the unlimited egoism of private property. The State that is built on these economic relations is merely an ideal illusion of a social reality. Whatever is real in the State structure is, in fact, no more than a legalization of the unlimited right of private property. Marx's critique may be considered as a continuation of Feuerbach's, since he gives the ultimate reason why man creates for himself the religious illusion: being estranged from his full reality in this world, he builds all his expectations upon a better world in an afterlife.

Notion of Alienation. In a series of manuscripts, written in Paris in 1844 and first published in 1932, Marx's critique of Hegel reached the very heart of dialectical philosophy, the notion of alienation. He saw Hegel's basic form of alienation as an alienation of consciousness that consists in the outgoing movement of consciousness toward the material world. But this, according to Marx, is by no means the alienation of man, which consists rather in the fact that man relates himself inhumanly to the material world. Man's alienation is not his relation to the material world—for that is his very essence—but the fact that he is estranged from the product of this relation, from the relation itself (his work), and from the social aspects of the relation (his intercourse with others). The communist society will replace this inhuman relation to nature, exclusively directed to the production of material goods, by an authentic relation to nature in which man is able to realize himself as a free and social being.

It is obvious that in Marx, and even in Feuerbach, Hegelianism has developed into an outright critique of Hegel. Marx's early works are no longer Hegelian in the strict sense; they constitute a new philosophy, strongly influenced by Hegel. This is even more the case for M. Stirner, another Young Hegelian, who in *Der Einzige und sein Eigenthum* (Leipzig 1845), pushes the negative principle of Hegelian dialectic to an extreme. Any moral or social affirmation is to be negated in the next moment; it is therefore false and bound to disappear. Only the process of thought remains constant and this process irresistibly destroys any religious, moral, and political value. But at the end, thought itself is to be destroyed and to be changed into its contrary, the pure, immediate, and individual will. Marx would violently attack this moral and political anarchism in his *Holy Family.*

Other Influences. Among the philosophers on whom Hegel exercised a strong, although negative, influence one should mention A. Trendelenburg and S. A. KIERKEGAARD. In his *Logische Untersuchungen* (2v., Berlin 1840), Trendelenburg attacked Hegel's *Logic* because of the illegitimate intrusion of movement into the realm of logic, which is essentially static. Movement can be perceived, but it can never be thought. That is why Hegel's dialectic cannot be justified within the strictures of logic. Having followed Hegel in his doctoral dissertation, Kierkegaard vehemently criticized his ethical ideas in *Fear and Trembling* (1843), and his logic and philosophy of history in *Philosophical Fragments* (1844) and *Concluding Unscientific Postscript* (1846).

Orthodox Hegelianism went rapidly into decline after the master's death. However, there remained two important interpreters, K. Rosenkranz and J. E. Erdmann. In addition, F. T. Vischer, the aesthetician, and K. Fischer, the historian of philosophy, may be counted as Hegelians, although Vischer was more empirical in his approach than Hegel, and Fischer remained basically a Kantian.

Hegelianism Outside Germany. Around the middle of the 19th century, Hegelianism in the strict sense had almost disappeared from Germany. Yet at about the same time Hegel was introduced into England by H. Stirling's work, *The Secret of Hegel* (London 1865). Stirling used Hegel in his reaction against English EMPIRICISM and DEISM. However imperfect Stirling's study was—it interprets Hegel's philosophy as a mere continuation of Kant's—it remains important for having initiated a school of profound and personal commentators: J. McT. E. McTaggart, who wrote a commentary on Hegel's *Logic*; E. B. McGilvary; W. Wallace, who translated the *Logic;* and J. B. Baillie, who translated the *Phenomenology.*

During the same period Hegel was introduced in Italy through the publications of B. Spaventa and A. Vera. In Denmark Hegel first became popular in theological circles, particularly through J. L. Heiberg, N. Clausen, and H. Martensen. In Russia Hegelianism also split into a right wing, religiously and politically conservative (main representative: V. G. Bielinski in his first period), and a left wing, which inclined toward Stirner's nihilism (Bielinski in his second period), and finally joined forces with populism (Bielinski in his third period) and Marxism (A. Herzen, M. A. Bakunin, G. V. Plekhanov). Russian Hegelians of both right and left connected Hegel's philosophy with some sort of pan-Slavism according to which Russia must fulfill a unique and final role in world history.

NEO-HEGELIANISM

At the end of the 19th century a Hegelian revival started. Various schools in different countries called themselves Neo-Hegelian. Their new approach to Hegel was characterized by a more personal reading of his works than was in vogue among their predecessors.

Holland. Most traditional was probably the Dutch school, in which the study of Hegel's philosophy was associated with a liberal trend in Calvinist theology. Neo-Hegelianism in Holland almost became a religious sect. Its leading figures were V. Bolland (*Collegium Logicum,* 1904) and J. Hessing, who wrote excellent commentaries on Hegel's *Logic* and on the *Phenomenology.* The movement produced two journals, *Annalen van de Critische Philosophie* and *De Idee.* It fell into some disrepute after World War II because of the active Fascism of some of its members, particularly T. Goedewaagen. Its major thinkers of the 1960s were B. Wigersma and the theologian G. A. van den Bergh van Eysinga.

Italy. A similar school, but with a more personal approach, existed in Italy. B. CROCE rejected Hegel's philosophy of nature and proposed an entirely new system based on the philosophy of the spirit: the spirit as individual intuition (aesthetics), as consciousness of the universal (logic), as particular will (economic activity) and as universal will (ethics). G. GENTILE also deviated from Hegelian orthodoxy by his subjective, somewhat Fichtean interpretation of Hegel's Absolute as creative act of the spirit immanent in all reality. By his moral and political activity man participates in this creative act of the spirit. Gentile's work was discredited after the war because of his connection with the Fascist regime.

England. No less personal than the Italians were the English Neo-Hegelians: T. H. Green, F. H. BRADLEY, and B. Bosanquet. Green read in Hegel's philosophy the ultimate answers to the basic questions raised by Hume. Bradley, the most original of the group, combined his IDEALISM with a certain Anglo-Saxon EMPIRICISM. In *Principles of Logic* (London 1883) and *Appearance and Reality* (London 1893) he denies the existence of all external relations, but from this principle he does not conclude, as Hume would, to an atomistic elementarism; on the contrary, for Bradley there is but one reality and its being consists in experience. Reality appears to man in various psychic modes—pleasure, pain, feeling, desire, will, perception, and thought—but each of them is incomplete and calls for the totality of experience. ''In this one whole all appearances come together and in coming together they in various degrees lose their distinctive natures.'' Strangely enough this unity of all experiences, which is experience in its totality, is never directly known.

America. In the U.S. this Anglo-Saxon Hegelianism took a more pragmatic turn: there was a deep concern to connect speculative thought with the requirements of practical life. Its leading figure was J. ROYCE. J. DEWEY also was originally influenced by Hegel's thought, and in his INSTRUMENTALISM one still finds some vestiges of Hegel, particularly his notion of experience as a totality that is both ''spiritual'' and ''material.''

Germany. In Germany the Hegelian renaissance was initiated by W. DILTHEY, who first attracted attention to Hegel's early writings (*Die Jugendgeschichte Hegels,* Berlin 1905). On the basis of this long-neglected material and of his studies of German Romanticists, he interpreted Hegel in a romantic, vitalistic way. Basic for Hegel's thought, according to Dilthey, is the early notion of life.

Dilthey's work initiated a movement toward a more comprehensive understanding of Hegel. In 1907 H. Nohl published Hegel's theological writings. G. Lasson started the first critical edition of Hegel's works, which was later continued by J. Hoffmeister. H. Glockner published a Hegel lexicon in four volumes (1940), earlier having written an authoritative study on the presuppositions and development of Hegel's philosophy (1929). Other major works on Hegel were published by T. Häring (*Hegel: Sein Wollen und sein Werk,* Leipzig 1929–38), R. Kroner (*Von Kant bis Hegel,* Tübingen 1921–24), W. Moog (*Hegel und die hegelsche schule,* Munich 1930), and N. HARTMANN (*Die Philosophie des deutschen: Idealismus II Hegel,* Berlin-Leipzig 1929). But these writers were Hegelian scholars more than Hegelians. Only in the philosophizing of the Neo-Kantian schools (Marburg and Baden) and of Hartmann did Hegel's work stimulate new creative thinking. Hartmann saw in Hegel a return to an authentic ontology. His dialectic is not a purely logical method as are deduction, induction, or analysis—it is the spiritual development of being itself. Yet Hartmann considers Hegel's application of the dialectic to nature a failure: as spiritual principle the dialectic works only in the philosophy of spirit. (*See* NEO-KANTIANISM.)

Indirectly Hegel influenced the DIALECTICAL THEOLOGY of H. E. BRUNNER, K. BARTH, and F. GOGARTEN, and, through Dilthey, Gestalt psychology, according to which the perception of form in its totality is more than (and different from) the perception of its individual elements. German scholasticism also was being enriched by Hegel's thought. Of particular interest are the publications of E. Coreth, B. Welte, J. Möller, and J. Hommes. The influence of Hegel on Catholic thought was likewise noticeable in Belgium and Holland, particularly among students and professors of the University of Louvain (F. Grégoire, L. van der Kerken, A. de Waelhens).

EXISTENTIALIST AND MARXIST INFLUENCES

Apart from the Neo-Hegelians and the Catholic thinkers already mentioned, Hegel's influence on contemporary thought is nowhere as strong as it is in French existentialism and in Marxism.

French Existentialism. In the 19th century Hegel never had a solid foothold in France: P. J. Proudhon, V.

COUSIN, and E. Meyerson showed some influence, but Hegel's work was never seriously studied before J. Wahl introduced his *Phenomenology* to the French public in *Le Malheur de la conscience dans la philosophie de Hegel* (Paris 1929). In the 1930s A. Kojève gave a series of lectures on the *Phenomenology* at the École des Hautes Études, which had an enormous influence both on existentialism and Marxism. Among his auditors were J. P. Sartre, M. MERLEAU-PONTY, J. Hyppolite, and G. Fessard. In an attempt to apply Hegel's ideas to the 20th century, Kojève gave a Marxist and Heideggerian interpretation of the *Phenomenology.* These highly original and provocative lectures were later published as *Introduction à la lecture de Hegel* (Paris 1947). According to Kojève, Marxism and existentialism are the authentic offspring of Hegel's thought. Sartre follows him in this controversial interpretation and, in his philosophy, consolidates the ties between Marxism and existentialism. French existentialists tend to prefer the interpretation of the human condition in the *Phenomenology* to Hegel's later works, where the tragic oppositions of life are too easily reconciled in a panlogical science of the Absolute Spirit. J. Hyppolite, who wrote an excellent commentary on the *Phenomenology* (Paris 1946), reacted against this one-sided separation of Hegel's *Logic* from his early works. His interpretation is less revolutionary, less original, but also less simplistic.

Marxism. Finally, something must be said about the enormous influence of Hegel on contemporary Marxism. After the early works of Marx, Marxism had drifted away from Hegel toward materialism. The first great Marxist to see the importance of Hegel was N. LENIN, who found that Marx's theory was to be completed by a serious study of Hegel's *Logic.* Without Hegel's dialectic Marxism would be unable to defend itself against the attacks of Neo-Kantians and positivists (see H. Lefebvre and N. Gutermann, *Lénine: Cahiers sur la dialectique,* Paris 1938). Hegel's most important commentator in the communist camp was the Hungarian G. Lukacs, who in 1948 published an excellent work on Hegel's political and philosophical evolution until 1807. Lukacs emphasized Hegel's interest in social problems and claimed that his dialectic was originally intended as a philosophy of action. According to Lukacs, Hegel perceived the contradictions of the capitalist society remarkably well, and the only reason he did not preach a social revolution is that the socioeconomic conditions were not ripe for it.

Other important Hegelian Marxists are E. Bloch (*Subjekt-Objekt: Erläuterungen zu Hegel,* 1951), H. Lefebvre (*Le matérialisme dialectique,* Paris 1939), and the excellent historian of left-wing Hegelianism and early Marxism, A. Cornu.

See Also: HEGEL, GEORG WILHELM FRIEDRICH; IDEALISM; DIALECTICS; ABSOLUTE, THE; HISTORY, PHILOSOPHY OF; PHILOSOPHY, HISTORY OF.

Bibliography: K. ROSENKRANZ, *Kritische Erläuterungen des hegel' schen Systems* (Königsberg 1840). J. E. ERDMANN, *Grundriss der Geschichte der Philosophie* (4th ed. Berlin 1896). H. LEVY, *Die Hegel-renaissance in der deutschen Philosophie* (Charlottenburg 1927). H. GLOCKNER, ''Hegelrenaissance und Neuhegelianismus,'' *Logos* 20 (1931) 169–195. G. LASSON, ''Hegel und die Gegenwart,'' *Kant-studien* 36 (1931) 262–276, W. MOOG, *Hegel und die hegelsche Schule* (Munich 1930). I. A. IL'IN, *Die Philosophie Hegels als Kontemplative Gotteslehre* (Bern 1946). H. MARCUSE, *Reason and Revolution* (2d ed. New York 1954). A. CORNU, *Karl Marx et Friedrich Engels: Leur vie et leur oeuvre,* 2 v. (Paris 1955–58) v.1 *Les Années d'enfance et de jeunesse. La Gauche hégélienne, 1818/1820–1844* (Paris 1955). J. KRUITHOF, *Het Uitgangspunt van Hegel's Ontologie* (Bruges 1959). F. C. COPLESTON, *History of Philosophy* 7:159–247.

[L. DUPRÉ]

HEGEMONIUS

4th-century Christian author, of unknown provenance; fl. *c.* mid-4th century. He was the author of the *Acta Archelai,* one of the chief sources for our knowledge of MANICHAEISM. The work is an anti-Manichaean polemic purporting to be a dialogue between Archelaus, Bishop of Kashkar, Mesopotamia, and Manes and his disciple Turbo. The *Acta* are known in their entirety only through a Latin translation; fragments of the original Greek are found in Epiphanius's treatment of Manichaeism (*Panarion* 66). St. Jerome attributed the work to Archelaus and thought that it was composed originally in Syriac and translated into Greek (*De virus illustribus* 72). Heraclianus of Chalcedon, as noted by Photius (*Bibliotheca; Patrologia Graeca,* ed. J. P. Migne, 103:288A), is the first to attribute authorship to Hegemonius, but this statement attracted little attention. Hegemonius was usually credited with being the stenographer who recorded the dialogue. The definitive study by C. Beeson established Hegemonius as the author of the *Acta,* Greek as the original language, and the first half of the 4th century as the date of composition.

Bibliography: HEGEMONIUS, *Acta Archelai,* ed. C. H. BEESON (*Die griechischen christlichen Schriftsteller der ersten drei Jahrhunderte* 16; 1906). G. BAREILLE, *Dictionnaire de théologie catholique*, ed. A. VACANT et al., 15 v. (Paris 1903–50; Tables Générales 1951–) 6.2:2113–16. P. DE LABRIOLLE, *Dictionnaire d'histoire et de géographie ecclésiastiques*, ed. A. BAUDRILLART et al. (Paris 1912–) 3:1542. B. ALTANER, *Patrology*, tr. H. GRAEF from 5th German ed. (New York 1960) 360. E. STOMMEL, *Lexikon für Theologie und Kirche*, ed. J. HOFER and K. RAHNER, 10 v. (2d, new ed. Freiburg 1957–65) 1:115. W. SCHMID and O. STÄHLIN, *Geschichte der griechischen Literatur bis auf die Zeit Justinians* (based on the earlier work of W. CHRIST, *Handbuch der Altertumswissenschaft*), 8 v. (Munich 1920–48) 2.2:1440–41.

[H. DRESSLER]

HEGESIPPUS

Early ecclesiastical writer; d. *c.* 180. According to Eusebius, Hegesippus flourished at the time of Irenaeus (*Historia ecclesiastica* 4.21). He was a master of Hebrew, Syriac, and Greek, and his wide familiarity with Jewish oral traditions made him an important figure. About the middle of the 2d century he set out from his native land (possibly Asia Minor) for Rome. En route he visited many bishops and heard the same doctrine from all of them. At Corinth, he ''was refreshed by the true word'' and learned that the letter of Pope CLEMENT I was still read in the Church (Eusebius, *Hist. Eccl.* 4.22). During the pontificate of Pope ANICETUS he reached Rome, and here too, he found the teaching of the Apostles handed down incorrupt.

As quoted by Eusebius (*Hist. Eccl.* 4.25), Hegesippus says that he made a διαδοχή to the time of Anicetus, and that Soter succeeded (διαδέχεται) Anicetus. The meaning of the Greek noun and verb is disputed. Some scholars take the noun to mean a list of bishops of the Church in Rome (possibly the source on which Irenaeus drew for his account in *Adversus haereses* 3.3.3) and would translate the passage: During my stay in Rome I *made a list* of the bishops down to the time of Anicetus whose deacon was Eleutherius; Soter succeeded Anicetus, and after him came Eleutherius.

More recent research, however, indicates that at the time of Hegesippus διαδοχή had the meaning of transmission of teaching or doctrine, and that the cognate verb did not mean to succeed, but to receive a teaching from another. Consequently, Hegesippus means that while in Rome he ascertained for himself that the genuine apostolic teaching *was transmitted* without interruption down to Anicetus. From Anicetus it was passed on to SOTER, who handed it on to Eleutherius.

After his return from Rome, Hegesippus wrote *Memoirs* in five books to refute the teachings of the Gnostics (*see* GNOSTICISM). This work today is known only through fragments quoted in Eusebius's *Historia ecclesiastica,* although as late as the 17th century the complete work could be found in several Greek monasteries. The traditional account of the death of the Apostle James, ''the brother of the Lord, the rampart of the people and righteousness,'' and scattered bits of information on Simon, second bishop of Jerusalem, are taken from the fragments of Hegesippus.

Bibliography: J. QUASTEN, *Patrology,* 3 v. (Westminster, Md. 1950–) 1:284–287. B. ALTANER, *Patrology,* tr. H. GRAEF from 5th German ed. (New York 1960) 148–150. H. CAMPENHAUSEN, *Kirchliches Amt und geistliche Vollmacht* (Tübingen 1953). L. KOEP, *Reallexikon für Antike und Christentum,* ed. T. KLAUSER (Stuttgart 1941) 2:411. J. LENZENWEGER, *Lexikon für Theologie und Kirche,* ed. J. HOFER and K. RAHNER, 10 v. (2d, new ed. Freiburg 1957–65) 5:60. G. W. H. LAMPE, ed., *A Patristic Greek Lexicon* (Oxford 1961–).

[H. DRESSLER]

HEIDEGGER, MARTIN

Existentialist philosopher; b. Sept. 26, 1889, in Messkirch, Baden, Germany; d. May 26, 1976 and was buried in the place of his birth. Early in life he had intended to become a Catholic priest, but due to a heart condition he ended his theological studies in 1911 and switched to mathematics. He earned a doctorate in philosophy in 1913. From 1915 to 1923, with the exception of his military service, he taught at Freiburg, where he was associated with Edmund HUSSERL, who had a significant impact on Heidegger's thought. He then was professor at Marburg until 1928, when he returned to Freiburg as Husserl's successor. He was rector there from 1933 to 1934, where as a German nationalist and anti-communist he supported Hitler's rise to power and joined the Nazi Party. After the war Heidegger was suspended from teaching until 1950 due to his Nazi sympathies. He retired from teaching in 1952, but continued to publish until his death.

The early influence of *The Many Senses of Being according to Aristotle,* by Franz BRENTANO, and his own habilitation thesis on pseudo-Scotus's *Grammatica speculativa,* foreshadowed Heidegger's lasting concern with the themes of being and speech. In treating these themes, however, Heidegger developed a characteristic style and terminology that resist translation into ordinary language. In fact, attempts to reduce his thought to usual philosophical expressions tend to distort its meaning, if only by conferring upon it a false clarity. For this reason, in what follows Heidegger's thought is rendered in rather literal translation, in many instances accompanied by the German expression itself.

Das Sein. Heidegger develops his philosophy around the difference and interplay between being (*Seiendes*), the ''to be'' (*das Sein*), and *Dasein,* viz, man as the only being who questions the ''to be'' is its presence or thereness (*da*) as differentiated from being. For Heidegger, the question concerning being as being, which characterized classical metaphysics and ontology, must be transcended toward the more radical question concerning the ''to be'' itself, the most questionable theme. The ''dis-coveredness'' of beings in their beingness (*Seiendheit*) presupposes unthematic openness and standing out (*ek-stasis,* ''ex-sistence'') toward the ''to be,'' as opposed to beings; but the ''to be,'' obscured by the beings it illuminates and withdrawn into coveredness by being, is forgotten. The history of the ''to be'' is that of the epochs or difference of ways the ''to be'' sends and withholds itself, goes forth and returns to itself, and promises and loses its name or saying (*Sage*), which is variously rendered as presence out of absence (*physis*), being insofar as it is (*das Sein des Seienden*), object for subject, position (*Setzung*), and construct (*Ge-stell*).

Since the ''to be'' is hidden, what manifest being can one question concerning it? The answer is man himself, the only available being concerned with the ''to be.'' The method of investigation is phenomenological: letting be seen whatever shows itself in the way, as self-manifesting, it uses itself to show itself (*Sein und Zeit*, 7th ed., n.7). Truth as ''un-concealment'' and ''un-forgetting'' (*a-letheia*) is the inseparability of ''disclosedness'' and ''re-collection'' from hiddenness and finitude. One can speak of the veiled ''to be'' only by manifesting oneself as *Dasein.* A neutral or absolute perspective is impossible. The difference between that ''from which'' man questions and the theme ''concerning which'' he questions is constitutive of philosophy.

Dasein. The phenomenological analytic of *Dasein* begins with man as he exists proximally and usually, or in his everydayness. It manifests—through such pretheoretical structures (''the existentials'') as instrumentality, thrownness, call, they (*das Man*), inauthenticity, and fallenness—that man cannot ''catch up with'' (*einholen*) his being as disengaged from being in the world with others. Calling the analysis of the passions in Book 2 of Aristotle's *Rhetoric* the first systematic hermeneutic of the everydayness of being with others (*Sein und Zeit,* 138), Heidegger shows that man's fundamental way of being is disposed attunement (*Gestimmtheit*): man is in concern and dread. But the analytic of *Dasein* is neither of man as man (anthropology), nor of being as being (metaphysics), but of man in his ordinary way of ''being toward'' the ''to be'' as differentiated from beings. Thus concern and dread are neither ontic states nor abstract principles but ontological perspectives (*Sein und Zeit,* 57). Concern is the way in which man finds himself as ''thrown forward toward . . .''; dread is the pathos of ''being toward'' the ''not'' of being as a whole, viz, toward the ''to be'' that makes beings be, but that is not a being. The naught is the ''to be'' differentiated from the perspective of worldliness. Temporality is the unity of being ''already in and with,'' anticipating what is not yet; being-toward-death is being already ''thrown forward toward'' the coming nihilation of being-in-the-world-with-others. The ontological constitution of historicity (*Geschichtlichkeit*) is based on *Dasein's* anticipatory openness to the source: what-is-as-having-been still coming to manifestation through ''re-petition'' (*Wiederholung*). *Dasein*-in-world is before, between, and beyond consciousness of objects. Itself ''ec-static'' toward the ''to be,'' *Dasein* illuminates a purview in which beings can be obvious or show themselves. Projection (*Entwurf*) of and by the ''to be'' frees the ontological space in which beings are encountered—the world.

There being no adequate manifestation of, and speaking about, the ''to be'' in differentiation, the reversal (*Kehre*) that goes beyond the phenomenological analytic of *Dasein* to the limits of a nonphenomenological use of language breaks down before the impossibility of speaking clearly what is most hidden; but this reversal is anticipated in the analysis of *Dasein* as the phenomenon that manifests the ''to be'' by questioning it: *Sein und Zeit,* 38–39; *Ueber den Humanismus* (Klostermann), 17, 41–42; *Holzwege,* 3d ed., 286; *Nietzsche,* 2:353–359, 367–369, 389–390: *Unterkunft der Ankunft des Ausbleibens.* The *logos* of the ''to be'' in differentiation is silence, but to be silent is possible only for a being that can speak.

Heidegger speaks of the absence (*Fehl*) of God and is silent about the relation of God to the ''to be,'' although he does distinguish them. Atheism is the price of considering God the first and highest among beings (*Holzwege,* 240; *Identität und Differenz,* 71).

Heidegger's influence has, for the most part, resulted from the misinterpretation of his earlier work as an anthropology (*Wesen des Grundes,* 4th ed., 43, n. 59; *Vom Wesen der Wahrheit,* 3d ed., 26–27).

Writings. Two-thirds of Heidegger's writings remain unpublished; he made arrangements for the definitive edition, being published by Klostermann; see F.-W. von Herrmann, ''Observations on the Definitive Collected Works of Martin Heidegger,'' *Universitas* 17 n. 1 (1975) 29–37. The edition is divided into four parts: (1) already published works, 1914–76, with Heidegger's marginalia (already available and of special interest are the marginalia to *Sein und Zeit*, also in the Niemeyer edition, 14 Aufl., 1977); (2) the lectures, Marburg, 1923–28, Freiburg, 1928–44, early Frieburg, 1919–23; (3) private monographs and lectures, 1919–67; (4) preparations and sketches, reconsiderations and indications.

Bibliography: M. HEIDEGGER, *Being and Time,* tr. J. MACQUARRIE and E. ROBINSON (New York 1962); *Nietzsche* (Pfullingen, Ger. 1961). A. CHAPELLE, *L'Ontologie phénoménoligique de Heidegger* (Paris 1962). O. PÖGGELER, *Der Denkweg Martin Heideggers* (Pfullingen 1963). R. POLK, *Heidegger: An Introduction* (Ithaca, N.Y. 1999). J. MCCUMBER, *Metaphysics of Oppression: Heidegger's Challenge to Western Philosophy* (Bloomington, Ind. 1999). E. ØVERENGET, *Seeing the Self: Heidegger on Subjectivity* (Boston 1998). H. PHILIPSE, *Heidegger's Philosophy of Being: A Critical Interpretation* (Princeton, N.J. 1998). J. O. PRUDHOMME, *God and Being: Heidegger's Relation to Theology* (Atlantic Highlands, N.J. 1997). D. A. WHITE, *Logic and Ontology in Heidegger* (Columbus 1985).

[T. PRUFER/EDS.]

HEIDELBERG CATECHISM

Next to the Westminster Confession (1646–48), the most important Reformed confession. The Heidelberg Catechism (*Catechesis Palatina*) takes its name from the capital of the Rhenish Palatinate, which became Lutheran in 1546 under Elector Frederick II (1483–1556). The growing influence of the Swiss Reformers toward the end of the reign of Elector Otto Henry (1502–59) precipitated violent controversies, especially about the Sacrament of the Altar. Otto Henry's irenically disposed successor, Frederick III (''the Pious''; 1515–76), while disclaiming any formal knowledge of Calvinism and adhering to the 1540 (''Variata'') edition of the Augsburg Confession, availed himself more and more of Calvinistic theological leadership, staffed the theological faculty of the University of Heidelberg exclusively with Calvinistic professors, and reformed the worship of the church in his domains according to Reformed principles. In 1562 he commissioned his theologians to prepare what became the Heidelberg Catechism, formally adopted by a synod convened in Heidelberg in January 1563.

Since Heinrich Alting (1583–1644), tradition has ascribed the authorship of the catechism to Zacharias URSINUS and Caspar OLEVIANUS (1536–87). Although they are unquestionably the major contributors, available evidence points to the broad cooperation of a considerable number of others as well. The 16th-century rumor that the real authors were Heinrich BULLINGER, the successor of Huldrych ZWINGLI at Zurich, and his associates is unfounded. A second and third edition preceded the authoritative fourth edition, published in November 1563 as part of the Palatine Church Order. Prompted by Olevianus, Frederick ordered the inclusion, in the second edition, of the condemnation of the ''papal mass'' as a ''denial of the once for all sacrifice and passion of Jesus Christ'' (q. 80), presumably as a response to the Tridentine decree on the sacrifice of the Mass; the third edition added the characterization of the Mass as ''an accursed idolatry.''

The Catechism consists of 129 questions and answers, supported by Biblical proofs and divided, after a brief introduction (qq. 1–2), into three parts: man's misery, exposed by the divine law (qq. 3–11); man's redemption—Apostles' Creed, justification, Baptism, the Lord's Supper, the office of the keys (qq. 12–85); and man's gratitude—Decalogue (with four commandments in the first table, six in the second) and Our Father (qq. 86–129). The questions are distributed over 52 parts for annual review on successive Sundays. The tone is warmly devotional, the emphasis primarily ethical, the approach strongly practical; the theology is a mild Calvinism (there is no discussion of predestination), with elements traceable to Philipp MELANCHTHON and to Bullinger. Except in a few places—such as q. 80, the condemnation of excesses in the veneration of the saints and of the use of images, and the moderate but firm disavowal of certain characteristically Lutheran views—the Catechism avoids polemics. Widely adopted in Reformed circles almost from the start, it has been translated into some 40 languages. In 1619 the pan-Reformed Council of Dort gave the Heidelberg Catechism confessional status. In North America both major Reformed bodies, the Reformed Church in America and the Christian Reformed Church, include it among their doctrinal standards; and it is greatly cherished in the former Evangelical and Reformed sectors of the United Church of Christ. Because of difficulties that children had in understanding and learning it, Elector John Casimir (1543–92) of the Palatinate directed the preparation of a simple and popular extract, the ''little Heidelberg Catechism'' (1585).

See Also: CONFESSIONS OF FAITH, PROTESTANT.

Bibliography: W. NIESEL, ed., *Bekenntnisschriften und Kirchenordnungen der nach Gottes Wort reformierten Kirche* (2d ed. Zurich 1938), 148–187, Ger. text. H. A. NIEMEYER, ed., *Collectio confessionum in ecclesiis reformatis publicatarum* (Leipzig 1840) 428–461, Lat. text. A. O. MILLER and M. E. OSTERHAVEN, trs., *The Heidelberg Catechism* (Philadelphia 1962), 400th anniversary Eng. tr. A. PÉRY, *The Heidelberg Catechism with Commentary,* tr. A. O. MILLER and M. B. KOONS (Philadelphia 1963). K. BARTH, *The Heidelberg Catechism for Today,* tr. S. C. GUTHRIE, JR. (Richmond, Va. 1964). D. J. BRUGGINK, ed., *Guilt, Grace and Gratitude* (New York 1963), a comment on the Heidelberg Catechism.

[A. C. PIEPKORN]

HEILIGENKREUZ, ABBEY OF

Cistercian abbey in the Archdiocese of Vienna, Lower Austria; founded (1133) by Margrave LEOPOLD III at the request of his son, OTTO OF FREISING, and settled from MORIMOND. Its name derives from a relic of the Holy Cross received from Leopold VI. Heiligenkreuz founded ZWETTL, Baumgartenberg, Cikádor, MARIENBERG, LILIENFELD, Goldenkron, and Neuberg. Under the first abbot it had 300 monks and lay brothers. GUTOLF (d. *c.* 1300) and Nicholas Vischel (d. 1330) wrote important works. The abbey declined because of wars (1462, 1529, 1532) and the Reformation, but remained Catholic. In the 16th century it assumed the pastoral care of its villages. In the 17th- and 18th-century revival the buildings were partly restored in baroque. United with Heiligenkreuz were the Hungarian monastery of St. Gotthard (1734–

1878) and Neukloster in Wiener Neustadt (1881). The Romanesque church (1187), with the oldest ogives in Austria, and the Gothic cloister (1240) and hall choir (1295) are famous monuments. The school of theology dates from 1802 and the undergymnasium from before 1558. There are 50,000 volumes in the library and 1,300 parchment documents in the archives.

Bibliography: L. H. COTTINEAU, *Répertoire topobibliographique des abbayes et prieurés* 1:1393–94. *Xenia Bernardina III* (Vienna 1891). F. WATZL, *Die Cisterzienser von Heiligenkreuz* (Graz 1898). A. WINKLER, *Die Zisterzienser am Neusidlersee* (Mödling 1923). D. FREY, *Die Denkmäler des Stiftes Heiligenkreuz* (Vienna 1926); *Das Stift Heiligenkreuz* (Vienna 1926). *Festschrift zum 800-Jahrgedächtnis des Todes Bernhards von Clairvaux* (Vienna 1953). B. KLEINSCHROTH, *Flucht und Zuflucht: Tagebuch aus dem Türkenjahr 1683*, ed. H. WATZL (Graz-Köln 1956).

[H. WATZL]

HEILSBRONN, ABBEY OF

Fons Salutis, Cistercian abbey near Ansbach, Germany, in the Diocese of Eichstätt; founded 1132 by Bishop OTTO OF BAMBERG, and secularized in the 16th century. It was the second daughterhouse of EBRACH and the proprietary abbey of the bishops of Bamberg. Heilsbronn reached its peak under Abbot Conrad of Brundelsheim (1308–21), who is probably the Monk of Heilsbronn, a mystical author influenced by St. Bernard of Clairvaux. In 1398, 1402, and 1408 during the Great Western Schism, Cistercian general chapters were held in Heilsbronn. The abbey suffered much damage in the first years of the Reformation and it was under the pressure of neighboring Protestant nobility that it was gradually secularized. The last Catholic abbot died in 1578. In 1581 the buildings were converted into a Lutheran school and several prominent Lutheran leaders thereafter used the abbatial title. The Romanesque church, consecrated in 1149, served from 1297 to 1625 as the burial place of Hohenzollerns. It is somewhat remodeled, and some 14th-century monastic buildings have been converted to a museum. The cloister was destroyed and the rich library is now in the University of Erlangen.

Bibliography: L. H. COTTINEAU, *Répertoire topobibliographique des abbayes et prieurés,* 2 v. (Mâcon 1935–39) 1:1395–96. H. P. EYDOUX, *L'Architecture des églises cisterciennes d'Allemagne* (Paris 1952). A. HEIDACHER, *Die Entstehungs- und Wirtschaftsgeschichte des Klosters Heilsbronn* (Bonn 1955). J. KIST and P. VOLK, *Lexikon für Theologie und Kirche,* ed. J. HOFER and K. RAHNER, 10 v. (2d, new ed. Freiburg 1957–65) 5:147–148.

[L. J. LEKAI]

Vaulted colonnade inside the Cistercian Abbey, Heiligenkreuz, Austria. (©Harald A. Jahn; Viennaslide/CORBIS)

HEIMERAD, ST.

Wandering priest and hermit; b. Messkirch, Baden, Germany; d. Mt. Hasungen, near Kassel, Germany, June 28, 1019. Apparently Heimerad was a serf who became a priest and served as chaplain to the lady of the manor on which he was born. At his request she released him and allowed him to begin his peripatetic career, which took him on pilgrimages to Rome and Jerusalem, and then through western Germany. Heimerad lived a short time at HERSFELD ABBEY but, disliking the routine, departed without taking vows. After further wanderings he built a hermitage on Mt. Hasungen where he lived until death. During his lifetime Heimerad came into contact with Empress KUNIGUNDE, Meinwerk of Paderborn, and ARIBO OF MAINZ. His asceticism and eccentricities attracted attention and respect; miracles were attributed to him even in his lifetime. His cult is popular and unofficial.

Feast: June 28.

Bibliography: *Monumenta Germaniae Scriptores* (Berlin 1825–) 10:595–612. J. L. BAUDOT and L. CHAUSSIN, *Vies des saints et des bienheueux selon l'ordre du calendrier avec l'historique des fêtes* (Paris 1935–56) 6:476–477. A. BUTLER, *The Lives of the Saints,* ed. H. THURSTON and D. ATTWATER, 4 v. (New York 1956) 2:660–662.

[R. H. SCHMANDT]

HEIMO OF MICHELSBERG

Ecclesiastical chronicler; d. Abbey of Michelsberg, Bamberg, Germany, July 3, 1138. He was an AUGUSTINIAN CANON of the church of St. Jakob in Bamberg from 1108 and is to be associated with the historical and chronological studies at Michelsberg during the first half of the 12th century. Among his teachers at Michelsberg he named FRUTOLF, Dudo, and the priest Burchard, to whom he dedicated his *De decursu temporum ab origine mundi* (*c.* 1135). Ebo related in his *Vita Ottonis,* written between 1151 and 1159, that Heimo attributed his extraordinary knowledge of chronology and his skill in reckoning the Church calendar and determining the dates of Easter to another teacher, the Spanish Bishop Bernard, who resided at Michelsberg from 1122 to 1155. Heimo classified the contents of *De decursu temporum* into seven divisions: (1–4) history of the world from Creation to his own day; (5) coordination of the years of the popes and the leaders of the Romans; (6) man's slavery since Adam and Eve's disobedience; (7) proposal of a testament for Christian liberty and the brotherhood of man, to be entered into by virtue of the Precious Blood and confirmed by the glorious Resurrection of Christ. Furthermore Heimo added to the work a table of the Paschal cycles up to 1595. The *De decursu temporum* may not possess real historical merit, but its contents present much material for the researcher in Church history.

Bibliography: P. JAFFÉ, ed., *Bibliotheca rerum Germanicarum,* 6 v. (Berlin 1864–73), v.5 *Monumenta Bambergensia,* ed. E. DUEMMLER, 537–552, 619–620. *Patrologia Latina*, ed. J. P. MIGNE, 217 v., indexes 4 v. (Paris 1878–90) 173:1363–68. *Monumenta Germaniae Historica*: *Scriptores* (Berlin 1826–) 10:1–4. R. CEILLIER, *Histoire générale des auteurs sacrés et ecclésiastiques*, 24 v. (Paris 1729–83) 14.1:182. A. POTTHAST, *Bibliotheca hitorica medii aevi* (2d ed. 1896; repr. Graz 1954) 2:574. M. MANITIUS, *Geschichte der lateinischen Literatur des Mittelalters*, 3 v. (Munich 1911–31) 3:361–363, 320, 351, 354, 598. W. WATTENBACH, *Deutschlands Geschichtsquellen im Mittelalter. Deutsche Kaiserzeit*, ed. R. HOLTZMANN (3d ed. Tübingen 1948; repr. of 2d ed. 1938–43) 1.3:485, 495.

[M. J. KISHPAUGH]

HEINRICH, JOHANN BAPTIST

Neo-Thomist theologian; b. Mainz, April 15, 1816; d. Mainz, Feb. 9, 1891. He studied law at Giessen and on Dec. 27, 1837 received a doctor's diploma in both civil and Canon law. In 1840 he began a teaching career in law at the University of Giessen. He was attracted to the ministry and in 1842–43 pursued a course of theology in the universities of Tübingen and Freiburg im Breisgau. He entered the seminary at Mainz in 1844, was ordained the following year, and was first assigned to the cathedral at Mainz. In 1851 he became professor of dogmatic theology at the seminary of that diocese. While he continued to teach he received other appointments in the diocese: titular canon in the cathedral chapter in 1855, dean in 1867, and vicar-general in 1868. In 1866 he was made a domestic prelate.

From 1850 until 1890 Heinrich was one of the editors of *Der Katholik,* a well-known journal of pastoral theology. He was active in the direction of a lay organization called the Piusverein, dedicated to safeguarding religious freedom in Germany. He published six volumes of a treatise on dogmatic theology. The last four volumes of this work, however, were completed by his friend K. Gutberlet, *Dogmatische Theologie* (10 v. Mainz 1873–1904). Heinrich also wrote a protest against the erroneous teachings of J. DÖLLINGER; a monograph on German movements seeking to restrict religious freedom; and a study of Christ's existence in history in relation to His divine personality, directed against the doctrine of D. F. STRAUSS and J. E. RENAN. Finally he wrote, against Nonweiler, a treatise on the Church as the kingdom of God on earth.

Bibliography: E. MANGENOT, *Dictionnaire de théologie catholique*, ed. A. VACANT et al., 15 v. (Paris 1903–50; Tables Générales 1951–) 6.2:2124–25. L. LENHART, *Lexikon für Theologie und Kirche*, ed. J. HOFER and K. RAHNER, 10 v. (2d, new ed. Freiburg 1957–65) 5:204.

[C. MEYER]

HEIRIC OF AUXERRE

Classicist and hagiographer; b. Héry, France, *c.* 841; d. Auxerre, *c.* 876. A Benedictine, Heiric played an important role in the revival and transmission of ancient learning through the palace and cathedral schools. He studied at AUXERRE, FERRIÈRES, and Laon, and through Lupus of Ferrières and the Irishman, Elias, came into contact with the classical learning of Greece and Rome. This explains the numerous excerpts in his works from later Latin authors such as Persius, SUETONIUS, and Juvenal. At the same time he came under the influence of JOHN SCOTUS ERIGENA. His successful teaching career was pursued mainly at Auxerre, where REMIGIUS OF AUXERRE and possibly HUCBALD OF SAINT-AMAND were his pupils. It is difficult to say exactly where Heiric stood on the question of universals, for although sections of his glosses on the pseudo-Augustinian *Categoriae Decem* have an Aristotelian ring, other sections sound more like Erigena. Heiric's hagiographical work is more widely known. In verse he wrote the *Vita S. Germani Antissiodorensis* (ed. *Monumenta Germaniae Historica, Poetae,* Lat. Carol. 3:428–517), in six books. This was followed by a prose work, the *Miracula* (ed. *Monumenta Germaniae Historica, Scriptores*, 13:401–404), in two books preceded by a prologue. Heiric also collaborated in the writing of the *Gesta Episcoporum Antissiodorensium* (ed. *Monumenta Germaniae Historica, Scriptores*, 13:393–400).

Bibliography: B. HAURÉAU, *Histoire de la philosophie scolastique,* 2 v. in 3 (Paris 1872–80) 1:188–191. *Monumenta Germaniae Historica*: *Poetae* (Berlin 1826–) 3:421–428. M. MANITIUS, *Geschichte der lateinischen Literatur des Mittelalters*, 3 v. (Munich 1911–31) 1:499–504. F. UEBERWEG, *Grundriss der Geschichte der Philosophie*, ed. K. PRAECHTER et al., 5 v. (11th, 12th ed. Berlin 1923–28) 2:177–178, 694–695. D. M. SCHULLIAN, ''The Excerpts of Heiric 'Ex libris Valeriani Maximi''' *Memoirs of the American Academy in Rome* 12 (1935) 155–184. J. DE GHELLINCK, *Littérature latine au moyen-âge*, 2 v. (Paris 1939) 1:117–118. G. MATHON, *Catholicisme* 5:651–652. J. WOLLASCH, ''Zu den persönlichen Notizen des Heiricus von S. Germain d'Auxerre,'' *Deutsches Archiv für Erforschung des Mittelalters* 15 (1959) 211–226.

[L. E. LYNCH]

HEISS, MICHAEL

Archbishop, writer; b. Pfahldorf, Bavaria, April 12, 1818; d. La Crosse, Wis., March 26, 1890. He attended the Latin school at Eichstätt, the gymnasium at Neuburg, and the Georgianum in Munich, and was ordained by Bp. Carl von Reisach of Eichstätt on Oct. 18, 1840. Two years later, Heiss went to the U.S. where he engaged in missionary work for a short time in Kentucky. In 1844 he joined the new Diocese of Milwaukee, Wis., became secretary to Bp. John Henni, and was the first rector of St. Francis Seminary (1856–68).

Heiss played an important part in preparing for the Second Plenary Council of Baltimore (1866). When it recommended two new dioceses for Wisconsin, one at La Crosse and another at Green Bay, he was nominated for the former. After some delay, the Holy See confirmed the nomination and Bishop Henni consecrated him on Sept. 6, 1868. A year later he went to Rome to serve on the committee of discipline of VATICAN COUNCIL I. He consistently favored a definition of papal infallibility even though his friend, Henni, was opposed to such action.

During the last years of the 1870s, spirited opposition along nationalistic lines developed when it became known that Archbishop Henni wanted Heiss as his coadjutor. In the end, the Holy See honored Henni's request and Heiss was named titular archbishop of Hadrianople and coadjutor of Milwaukee. In 1881, he succeeded to that see, but latent hostility disrupted its unity and marred, to some extent, the new archbishop's career. Nationalistic hostilities flared anew in 1883 when John G. Shea published an article in the *American Catholic Quarterly Review* lamenting the absence of ''American'' bishops in the West. Eventually with Heiss's approval, a Milwaukee priest, Peter ABBELEN went to Rome in 1886 to present the case for the Germans. The Abbelen mission was strongly protested by Bps. John IRELAND and John KEANE, and the problem was further embittered by an interview that Heiss granted to the Milwaukee *Sentinel* in 1887. His insistence on the need for more German bishops in the U.S. and the importance of keeping up the German language aggravated the already complicated problem, which was not destined to be solved for a number of years. The BENNETT LAW (1889) conflict, which developed just before he died, underscored the cleavage between himself and his recent suffragan, Ireland. Heiss initiated the campaign to repeal the state law that included provisions for the use of English in schools, but he did not live to see it succeed (*see* KATZER, FREDERICK XAVIER).

Throughout his life, Heiss remained an ardent advocate of parochial schools, but he opposed the founding of a Catholic university, believing rather that the meager resources of the Church should be used to improve seminaries. When he resigned from the university committee established at the Third Plenary Council of Baltimore (1884), he pleaded his many duties in Milwaukee, the great distance he would have to travel to meetings, and the little he could contribute to the university work. Heiss's publications include *De Matrimonio* and *The Four Gospels.* He is buried in the chapel of St. Francis Seminary.

Bibliography: C. J. BARRY, *The Catholic Church and German Americans* (Milwaukee 1953). B. J. BLIED, *Three Archbishops of Milwaukee* (Milwaukee 1955).

[B. J. BLIED]

HEISTERBACH, ABBEY OF

(*Vallis S. Petri*), Cistercian abbey of the Rhineland, Diocese of Cologne; founded 1189; suppressed 1803. Cistercian monks of HIMMEROD, at the request of Archbishop Philip of Cologne in 1189 reclaimed the abandoned house of Augustinian hermits of Petersberg, and a few years later moved to Heisterbach, their new abbey at the foot of the mountain. Heisterbach reached the climax of its history under Abbot Henry (1208–44), builder of the great monastic church and sponsor of the literary activity of CAESARIUS OF HEISTERBACH. In the 14th century economic crisis and rule by unworthy abbots caused a decline. Recovery was hampered during the Reformation and the subsequent wars of religion and of Louis XIV. The 18th century was an era of prosperity, ending with the dissolution of monasteries in 1803 under French occupational authorities. The archives and the rich monastic library of Heisterbach were carried to Düsseldorf, but monastery and church were demolished, only the original apse and choir surviving.

Bibliography: H. PAUEN, *Die Klostergrundherrschaft Heisterbach* (Münster 1913). L. H. COTTINEAU, *Répertoire topobibliographique des abbayes et prieurés,* 2 v. (Mâcon 1935–39) 1:1397–98. H. P. EYDOUX, *L'Architecture des églises cisterciennes d'Allemagne* (Paris 1952) 77–81. J. TORSY, *Lexikon für Theologie und Kirche,* ed. J. HOFER and K. RAHNER, 10 v. (2d, new ed. Freiburg 1957–65) 5:206.

[L. J. LEKAI]

HELEN OF SKÖVDE, ST.

Fl. 12th century, Västergötland, Sweden. Helen (or Elin) became a widow quite young. According to legend she was murdered after a family strife and buried in the church of Skövde, which she had helped build. When later she was venerated as a martyr, the church was named for her. The Office of her feast, written by St. Brynolf Algotsson, bishop of Skara, praises her as the patron saint of Västergötland and all Sweden. She is not to be confused with St. Helen of Tisvilde, Zealand, in Denmark. Her cultus was widespread in medieval Sweden; several paintings and sculptures representing her are extant.

Feast: July 31.

Bibliography: J. A. DUNNEY, *Saint of the Snows: A Chronicle of the Holy Elin of Skövde* (Albany, N.Y. 1937). T. LUNDÉN, *Credo* 25 (1944) 166–182, with bibliog. *Kulturhistorisk leksikon for nordisk middelalder,* ed. A. KARKER et al., v.6 (Copenhagen 1961) 305–308, with bibliog.

[H. BEKKER-NIELSEN]

HELEN OF UDINE, BL.

Augustinian tertiary; b: Udine, *c.* 1396; d. there, April 23, 1458. Helen was of the Valentini family and was given in marriage, at 15, to the nobleman Antonio dei Cavalcanti. The marriage was blessed with many children and was in all respects a happy one. The death of her husband, when she was only 40, grieved Helen deeply. She maintained her home and servants but, enrolling in the Augustinian THIRD ORDER, devoted herself to prayer, penance, and charitable works. Tried much in body and in spirit, she nevertheless experienced an inner joy, often associated with ecstasy. She reputedly obtained miracles for others while she lived and after her death. She was beatified in 1848.

Feast: April 23.

Bibliography: *Acta Sanctorum* April 3:249–260. A. BUTLER, *The Lives of the Saints* 2:155. L. FABRIS, *Vita della Beata Elena Valentinis* (Udine 1849). W. HÜMPFNER, *Lexikon für Theologie und Kirche*[2] 5:208. SIMONE DA ROMA, *Libro over legenda della beata Helena da Udene*, ed. A. TILATTI (Tavagnacco, Udine 1988).

[J. E. BRESNAHAN]

HELENA, ST.

Roman Empress, mother of Constantine I the Great; b. presumably in Drepanon (now Helenopolis), Bithynia, 255; d. Nicomedia, 330. According to St. AMBROSE she was a servant girl who became the concubine of Constantius Chlorus, was abandoned for political reasons, but was named Augusta by her son CONSTANTINE I at the beginning of his reign (306). According to Eusebius she became a Christian under Constantine's influence and in 324 made one of the first pilgrimages to the Holy Land (*Vita Constantini* 3). She exercised an influence on her son's church-building program in Rome (Church of the Holy Cross), in Constantinople (Church of the Apostles), and in Palestine (Church of the Nativity and the Eleona Church on the Mount of Olives). Her body, transported to Rome and originally laid to rest in a splendid mausoleum on the Via Labicana (Tor Pignattara), was later taken to Constantinople. In the ninth century her relics were translated to the Abbey of Hautvilliers. Legend ascribes to her the foundation of the Thebäer Church in Cologne and others in Xanten and Bonn, and the transfer of relics of St. MATTHIAS and St. ROCH to TRIER. The story of the finding of the holy CROSS, first mentioned by St. Ambrose, depends on Eusebius (*Vita Const.* 3.41–47). In Byzantine iconography Helena is depicted together with her son (frequently on coins of the Comneni and Paleologi dynasties) with a crown between them. Since the 15th century she is frequently portrayed with a crown, the model of a church, and the cross and nails; she is honored as a patron in Trier, Bamberg, and Basel.

Feast: Aug. 18 (West); May 21 (East with Constantine).

Bibliography: CYNEWULF, *Elene, an Old English poem,* ed. C. W. KENT (Boston 1889, rep. New York 1973); *Cynewulf's Elene,* ed. P. O. E. GRADON (Rev. ed. Exeter 1996). H. LECLERCQ, *Dictionnaire d'archéologie chrétienneet de liturgie,* ed. F. CABROL, H. LECLERCQ and H. I. MARROU, 15 v. (Paris 1907–53) 6.2:2126–45. O. SEECK, *Paulys Realenzyklopädie der klassischen Altertumswissen-*

schaft, ed. G. WISSOWA, et al. 7.2 (1912) 2820. T. ASHBY and G. LUGLI, "La villa dei Flavi. . . ," *Memorie della Pontificia Accademia Romana di Archeologia,* 3d ser. 2 (1928) 157–192. J. W. DRIJVERS, *Helena Augusta: The Mother of Constantine the Great and the Legend of Her Finding of the True Cross* (Leiden 1992). G. GIANGRASSO, ed., *Libellus de Constantino Magno eiusque matre Helena: la nascita di Costantino tra storia e leggenda* (Florence 1999). G. GIORGIO DI SASSONIA, *Römische Quartalschrift für christliche Altertumskunde und für Kirchengeschichte* suppl. 19 (1913) 255–258. J. MAURICE, *Sainte Hélène* (Paris 1930). H. A. POHLSANDER, *Helena: Empress and Saint* (Chicago 1995). H. VINCENT, *Bethléem* (Paris 1914).

[J. H. GEIGER]

Fresco of Constantine I with St. Helena, Yilan Church, Cappadocia, Central Turkey. (©Chris Hellier/CORBIS)

HELENTRUDIS, ST.

Recluse in Neuenheerse (Westphalia) known also as Helmtrud or Hiltrud; d. *c.* 950. Her name was entered into the martyrology of Bp. Imad of Paderborn in 1052. According to the first Passio of St. URSULA (written *c.* 975), Helentrudis was "visited" by St. Cordula, one of the 11,000 virgins allegedly massacred by the Huns in Cologne. In this vision to Helentrudis, Cordula described her martyrdom so that it might become known to the world. Another Ursula legend, the *Regnante Domino,* relates that pilgrimages were made to Helentrudis's grave and miracles took place there.

Feast: May 31; Oct. 22.

Bibliography: W. LEVISON, "Das Werden der Ursula-Legende," *Bonner Jahrbücher* 132 (1927). J. TORSY, ed., *Lexikon der deutschen Heiligen, Seligen, Ehrwürdigen und Gottseligen* (Cologne 1959) 227.

[S. A. SCHULZ]

HELFTA, CONVENT OF

A former Cistercian establishment near Eisleben, Saxony, Germany, in the former Diocese of Halberstadt. It was founded in 1228 by Count Burchard of Mansfeld in Mansfeld and was moved to Rossbach in 1234 and to Helfta in 1258. The community followed the CISTERCIAN constitutions without belonging to the order, and the spiritual direction of the nuns lay in the hands of DOMINICANS from Halle after 1271. Under Abbess Gertrude of Hackeborn (1251–92), Helfta became the most famous center of German MYSTICISM. The visions and revelations of MECHTILD OF HACKEBORN, Mechtild of Wippra (d. 1299), GERTRUDE THE GREAT, and MECHTILD OF MAGDEBURG represent a transition from the mysticism of BERNARD OF CLAIRVAUX to that of the MENDICANT ORDERS. Steeped in a liturgical life centered around the Eucharist and, especially in Gertrude, the Sacred Heart, these nuns relived their bridal relationship with Christ and praised their mystical union with the bridegroom in emotion-filled revelations that reached incomparable heights of hymnic power in Mechtild of Magdeburg. After having frequently suffered from wars in the area, Helfta was dissolved in 1545.

Bibliography: H. GRUNDMANN, *Religiöse Bewegungen im Mittelalter* (2d ed. Hildesheim 1961). W. MUSCHG, *Die Mystik in der Schweiz, 1200–1500* (Leipzig 1935) 109–113. F. W. WENTZLAFF-EGGEBERT, *Deutsche Mystik zwischen Mittelalter und Neuzeit* (2d ed. Berlin 1947) 48–59, 293–294. E. KREBS, W. STAMMLER, and K. LANGOSCH, eds., *Die deutsche Literatur des Mittelalters: Verfasserlexikon,* 5 v. (Berlin-Leipzig 1933–35) 2:43–44; 3:321–326, bibliog. H. NEUMANN, *ibid.* 5:673–674, bibliography, "Beiträge zur Textgeschichte des *Fliessenden Lichts der Gottheit* und zur Lebensgeschichte Mechthilds von Magdeburg," *Nachrichten der Akademie der Wissenschaften in Göttingen, Phli. hist. Klasse* (1954) 3:27–80. W. BUNKE, *Lexikon für Tbeologie und Kirche*, ed. J. HOFER and K. RAHNER, 10 v. (2d, new ed. Freiburg 1957–65) 5:209–210. J. QUINT, *Reallexikon der deutschen Literaturgeschichte,* ed. P. MERKER and W. STAMMLER (2d ed. Berlin 1955–) 2:547–550. L. H. COTTINEAU, *Répertoire topobibliographique des abbayes et prieurés*, 2 v. (Mâcon 1935–39) 1:1398.

[A. A. SCHACHER]

HELGESEN, POVL (PAULUS HELIAE)

Carmelite controversialist against Lutheranism; b. Varberg, Sweden, *c.* 1485; d. Denmark, after 1534. From 1519 to 1522 he was a professor of theology at the University of Copenhagen, in 1533 and 1534, at the cathedral school of Roskilde. From 1522 to 1534 he was provincial of the Scandinavian Carmelites. As a Biblical humanist after the manner of Erasmus and Lefèvre d'Etaples, he championed a Catholic reform of the Church; in 1522 he came into conflict with King Christian II. This course of action, together with the defection of many of his former students, brought upon him the accusation of being a Lutheran. However, in the years 1524 to 1534 he appeared as their principal adversary, writing several Latin and Danish polemical works against the Danish and Swedish reformers, translating some works of Erasmus, and editing his letters of St. Paul with annotations. In his chronicle of Skiby (1534) he drew a passionate but truthful picture of the religious and political events in Denmark in which he took an active part as adviser of the bishops. His fate after 1534 is unknown.

Bibliography: *Skrifter a Paulus Heliä,* ed. M. KRISTENSEN et al., 7 v. (Copenhagen 1932–48). L. SCHMITT, *Der Karmeliter Paulus Heliä* (Stimmen aus Maria-Laach, Suppl. 60; Freiburg 1893). J. O. ANDERSEN, *Paulus Helie* (Copenhagen 1936). K. VALKNER, *Paulus Helie og Christiern II* (Oslo 1963). W. GÖBELL, *Die Religion in Geschichte und Gegenwart,* 7 v. (3d ed. Tübingen 1957–65) 3:208. A. OTTO, *Lexikon für Theologie und Kirche*, ed. J. HOFER and K. RAHNER, 10 v. (2d, new ed. Freiburg 1957–65) 5:210.

[A. STARING]

HELIAND

The accepted editorial title of a ninth-century Old Saxon alliterative poem of 5,983 lines written, possibly at FULDA, by an unknown monk. The poem is preserved almost completely in two MSS (Munich and London), and fragmentarily in two others (Jena and Vatican). The *Heliand,* meaning Savior, is a product of missionary activity under LOUIS I the Pious (814–840). It is thought to be the Gospel part of a larger project presenting the entire Bible in vernacular verse. References to such a project and to its almost legendary poet survive in a *Praefatio* and *Versus* published in 1562 by the Protestant apologist, FLACIUS ILLYRICUS. Whether the documents, now lost, that he cites are authentic or not, there are extant many verses of an Old Saxon Genesis usually linked with the *Heliand.* Curiously, some of these Genesis verses were translated into Anglo-Saxon and constitute the interpolated Genesis B passage of the Junius MS. The *Heliand* and the Genesis fragments are the most important Old Saxon poetic documents in existence. The literary and scholarly associations of the *Heliand* are rich and broad: in general outline the poem follows the *Diatessaron* (Gospel Harmony) of TATIAN; in theological emphasis it reflects not only the scriptural commentaries of BEDE and ALCUIN but the more contemporary *In Matthaeum* of RABANUS MAURUS; its poetic tradition has two observable sources, the Latin poems of Juvencus and PRUDENTIUS, and the heroic songs and paraphrases of the Anglo-Saxons. Some scholars see considerable Germanization of Biblical materials in the *Heliand*, particularly of Christ and his Apostles, who become heroic figures in a Germanic *comitatus,* and of the countryside of Palestine, which becomes Saxony and northern Europe. Though there is substance to the observation, the poet is still very much the traditional Christian homilist, marking the close rather than the beginning of an era.

Bibliography: Sources. *MS Cgm.* 25, Staatsbibliothek, Munich, (S. IX); MS *Cotton Caligula* A VII, Brit. Mus., London, (S. X). O. BEHAGHEL, ed., *Heliand und Genesis* (6th ed. Halle 1948). Literature. J. K. BOSTOCK, *A Handbook on Old High German Literature* (Oxford 1955). G. EHRISMANN, *Geschichte der deutschen Literatur bis zum Ausgang des Mittelalters,* 2 v. in 4 (Munich 1918–35) 1:150–166.

[L. K. SHOOK]

HÉLINAND OF FROIDMONT

Noted Cistercian writer, chronicler, and poet; b. Pronleroy (Diocese of Beauvais), France, *c.* 1160; d. monastery of Froidmont, after 1229 (feast, May 28). A *trouvère* at the court of Philip II (Augustus) and member of the nobility, Hélinand entered the monastery of Froidmont *c.* 1194, and eventually became prior there. His many works include 28 lively sermons (*Patrologia Latina*, ed. J. P. Migne, 212:481–720), some of which he preached to the students of Toulouse; though often more curious than profound, they reveal the author's grasp of theology, psychological penetration, and familiarity with Scripture and the classics. *De cognitione sui* (*ibid.* 721–736) deals with a favorite Cistercian theme—self-knowledge. *De bono regimine principis* (*ibid.* 735–746) is drawn wholly from JOHN OF SALISBURY's Policraticus. His *Epistola ad Gualterum seu Liber de reparatione lapsi* (*ibid.* 745–760), written to a former novice, contains an exposé of the singular theory that novices are not free to leave their orders. Hélinand's *Vers de la mort* [ed. F. Wulff and E. Walberg, *Les Vers de la Mort par Hélinand de Froidmont,* Paris 1915; *idem.* (including modern Fr. tr.), ed. J. Coppin, Paris 1930], written in Old French, enjoyed immense popularity and belongs to the earliest of the ''Danse macabre'' literature. A *Chronicon* in 49 books, of which only the last five are extant (*Patrologia Latina* 212:771–1082), covers the period 634 to 1204.

Fresco painting depicting the damned consigned to hell, c. 15th century, Chapel of Notre Dame, La Brigue, Arriere, Cote D'Azur, France. (©Charles & Josette Lenars/CORBIS)

Drawn in large part from SIGEBERT OF GEMBLOUX, it was a primary source for VINCENT OF BEAUVAIS. A major commentary on the Canticle of Canticles, discovered by Jean Leclercq, OSB, has not yet been published.

Bibliography: M. DUMONTIER, ''Hélinand de Froidmont et la liturgie,'' *Collectanea ordinis Cisterciensium Reformatorum* 14 (1952) 133–139, 213–215, 295–300; 17 (1955) 49–56, 118–125.

[C. WADDELL]

HELL (IN THE BIBLE)

The English word ''hell'' is derived from the common Teutonic name for the place that was, according to ancient Germanic mythology, the abode of all the dead, like the Hebrew SHEOL and Greek HADES. Nowadays, however, the word is used to signify the place of the damned, corresponding to Hebrew GEHENNA and Greek Tartarus.

Throughout almost the whole Old Testament period it was commonly believed that the dead, whether good or bad, continued to exist in the nether world, a region of darkness, misery, and futility; they lived on as unreal, half-material shades in a land of silence and oblivion [*See* DEAD, THE (IN THE BIBLE)]. The name for this region was rendered as ''hell'' by the older vernacular versions of the Bible (e.g., the Douay Version) and is still used in this sense in speaking of Christ's DESCENT into hell. Toward the end of the Old Testament period, however, the notions of RETRIBUTION and final judgment [*see* JUDGMENT, DIVINE (IN THE BIBLE)] led the Jews to distinguish between the lot of the good and that of the wicked in Sheol; even before the final judgment they were separated by an impassable gulf. In addition to this view of Sheol there developed in postexilic Judaism the idea of an eschatological place of punishment, Gehenna, where apostate Jews and Gentile sinners would be put at the end of the world to suffer everlasting tortures by fire. In time a partial merging of these two originally independent concepts took place; besides the indigenous element of fire in Gehenna, the darkness of Sheol was also present, and ultimately Gehenna becomes a part of Sheol and a place where the wicked suffer even before the RESURRECTION OF THE DEAD.

In the New Testament, the abode of all the dead whether good or wicked is called Hades (Mt 11.23; Lk 10.15; 16.23), whereas the place of punishment for the wicked is generally called Gehenna (Mt 5.22, 29; 10.28; 18.9; 23.15, 33; Mk 9.43, 45, 47; Lk 12.5). Although Jesus made use of the language of His time, He did not necessarily endorse the rabbinic notions of future punishment as physical torment; yet it is impossible to soften the severity of Jesus' warning against unrepented sin, and the sentimentalism that seeks to do so is a distortion of His teaching and that of the New Testament as a whole. The chief characteristic of hell, as depicted in the New Testament, is its fire that is unquenchable (Mt 3.12; Mk 9.43; Lk 3.17) and everlasting (Mt 18.8; 25.41; Jude 7). Whatever may be implied by the terms ''unquenchable fire'' and ''everlasting fire,'' they should not be explained away as meaningless. In the New Testament, hell is also described as a place of ''weeping and gnashing of teeth'' (Mt 8.12; 13.50; 22.13; 24.51; 25.30). Its darkness (Mt 8.12; 22.13; 25.30) is borrowed from the older concept of Sheol.

Bibliography: *Encyclopedic Dictionary of the Bible*, tr. and adap. by L. HARTMAN (New York 1963) 969–970. J. GNILKA, *Lexikon für Theologie und Kirche*, ed. J. HOFER and K. RAHNER (Freiberg 1957–65) 5:445–446. P. ANTOINE, *Dictionnaire de la Bible*, suppl. ed. L. PIROT, et al. (Paris 1928–) 2:1063–76.

[I. H. GORSKI]

HELL (THEOLOGY OF)

This article (1) outlines the theological concept of hell and then traces its development in the fields (2) of dogma and (3) of theology.

Theological Concept. To construct an adequate theological concept of hell is not easy. Christ did not speak of hell to convey information about an object beyond present experience but in the context of the decision to which the human person is called by the proclamation of the gospel. A theological idea of hell is derived from and controlled by other concepts. The ideas of hell that have appeared in the course of Christian theology have varied according to the different concepts from which they have been derived. To elaborate a theological idea of hell that will interpret all the elements, with their priorities, of Christian belief in hell, the concept of the KINGDOM OF GOD is now being used.

The kingdom of God was the dominating concept Jesus used in the proclamation of His gospel (Schnackenburg, 94). This was not a concept created by Jesus but one current, in the form of the kingdom of heaven, in the thought-world of His Jewish contemporaries. But the content Jesus gave to this concept was original (H. L. Strack and P. Billerbeck, *Kommentar zum Neuen Testament* 1:172–84). He used the concept of the kingdom of God as an eschatological metaphor which expressed God's merciful love for the human race and the divine saving will for creation. For Jesus the metaphor of the kingdom of God gathered the whole of the history of SALVATION into a unity, as it was the focal point of the self-manifestation of God. When the theological idea of hell is derived from and controlled by the concept of the kingdom of God, its eschatological character and relation to the mercy and saving will of God receive due priority.

The advantage of deriving the theological idea of hell from the kingdom concept is that its nature as an objective reality is respected. For Christian theology, the kingdom metaphor expresses the conviction that God's saving will is realized in the exalted Jesus and the humiliated Satan. The theological idea of hell is designed to express the second part of this statement, and the construction of the idea should reflect this.

The reality that the theological idea of hell expresses has another form. It expresses a present reality as well as something that is still to come. This too is reflected in the way Jesus used the kingdom metaphor. There is the Lordship of Jesus that will continue until all things are subject to Him (1 Cor 15.27); there is what that Lordship prepares for: that God may be all in all (1 Cor 15.28). To be adequate the theological idea of hell needs to be elaborated in terms of the Lord Jesus (Jn 17.2) and of God all in all.

Given the fact of Christian belief in hell, one of the functions of the theological reflection is to make intelligible the possibility of hell in as far as that is possible. Here too the advantage of deriving the idea of hell from the kingdom metaphor is apparent. Intimately associated with the kingdom is the issue of belief (Mk 1.15). The possibility of hell is made intelligible by the concept of UNBELIEF. The theological idea of hell does not purport to explain unbelief, a problem that involves human freedom and God's will [E. C. Hoskyns, *The Fourth Gospel,* ed. F. N. Davey (London 1947) 295], but it should clearly indicate the eschatological character of the object, the Lord Jesus, and of the testimony, that of the Spirit, involved in unbelief. The theological idea of hell supposes the mystery of the Father sending the Son and the Holy Spirit, with the reality of the saving work within the human race (Eph 2.14) and on the cosmic level (Col 1.20)

Fresco painting depicting scene from hell, 1490, in the Chapel of St. Antoinne, France. (©Charles and Josette Lenars/CORBIS)

that this implies. In this way it puts the question of the understanding of the possibility of hell in its true perspective. Hell is not justified in terms of SIN alone; behind sin is unbelief (Jn 16.9). And yet the concept of sin has its proper function within the theological idea of hell. It is one pole of God's recognition of human historicity, as REPENTANCE is the other. This is the meaning the theological idea of hell is designed to convey.

A technical concept is produced by relating certain ideas according to some model. In this way the theological idea of hell uses SATAN, who ''sins from the beginning. To this end the Son of God appeared that he might destroy the works of the devil'' (1 Jn 3.8). Constructed on this model, the idea of hell indicates what can issue from unbelief: persons like Satan (1 Jn 3.10), since their personal attitude to the God who is disclosed in the Lord Jesus and in the testimony of the Holy Spirit is similar to that of Satan. And by using this model the ultimate meaning of the idea of hell is indicated, the meaning that is metaphorically expressed in the words: ''And the light shines in the darkness'' (Jn 1.5).

The classical theology of the West approached the problem of hell mainly from the angle of retribution for sin. The idea of hell is built up from the analysis of the concept of sin and developed by using analogously the concepts of sanction, perfection, and retribution drawn from morals, metaphysics, and religion. Theology today approaches the problem of hell from the angle of separation from God.

Dogmatic Development. Belief in the possibility of hell has always been present in the Church. For the form in which the primitive Church stated its belief in hell, [*see* HELL (IN THE BIBLE)]. Since New Testament times the doctrinal statement of belief in the mystery of hell is found in the professions of faith. The early *Fides Damasi* states this belief in the context of the retribution that will take place when Christ returns to judge the living and the dead: ''aut poenam pro peccatis aeterni supplicii'' (H. Denzinger, *Enchiridion symbolorum*, ed. A. Schönmetzer, 72); so too the *Quicumque:* ''qui vero mala [egerunt] in ignem aeternum'' (*ibid.* 76). The important profession of faith used in the dialogue between East and West, at the Second Council of Lyons, 1274, and again in 1385, states belief in the mystery of hell in the context of the retribution that takes place immediately after death: ''Illorum autem animas, qui in mortali peccato vel cum solo originali decedunt, mox in infernum descendere, poenis tamen disparibus puniendas'' (*ibid.* 856). Although there is no creedal statement of belief in hell, the creedal statement that Christ will return to judge the living and the dead entails the doctrinal statement of belief in the possibility of hell.

Two points of this statement of belief in hell have been formally defined. In 543, in a definition reflecting the faith of the Church of the East and West, the punishment of the demons and the damned was declared unending. The ninth of the so-called canons against Origen reads: ''Si quis dicit aut sentit, ad tempus esse daemonum et impiorum hominum supplicium, ejusque finem aliquando futurum . . . an. s.'' (*ibid.* 411). And in 1336, the constitution *BENEDICTUS DEUS*, by defining the doctrine that retribution takes place immediately after death, defined that the punishment of the damned begins immediately after death. ''Diffinimus insuper, quod secundum Dei ordinationem communem animae decedentium in actuali peccato mortali mox post mortem suam ad inferna descendunt, ubi poenis infernalibus cruciantur'' (*ibid.* 1002).

These two definitions emerged in the course of the long debate within the Church concerning the content of belief in the return of Christ, the PAROUSIA, for the content of this belief is complex; with the return of Christ are associated other events, such as the END OF THE WORLD, the RESURRECTION OF THE DEAD, and the divine judgment. Eschatology, the understanding of belief concerning the last things, is difficult (*see* ESCHATOLOGY, ARTICLES ON).

To determine the nature of these events and the way they are related to one another and to the return of Christ is not easy. The interpretation of the eschatological statements found in the New Testament and the evaluation of the imagery they employ is beset with difficulties. In the second century Justin held that the punishment of the demons and the damned is delayed until after the final judgment (1 *Apol.* 28; *Dial.* 5.3). The great apologist (*Dial.* 80) deduced this opinion from his interpretation of the Christian doctrine of the resurrection of the body, an interpretation influenced by Jewish eschatology in the form of CHILIASM. Known as the *dilatio inferni* theory, Justin's opinion was widespread in the West until the sixth century, when the teaching of Gregory the Great (*Dial.* 4.27) cause it to be discarded.

Those who understood the return of Christ according to the theory of chiliasm read the eschatological statements of the Scriptures in a purely literal sense. Against these literalist believers Origen reacted strongly (*De prin.* 2.11.2). And in doing this he translates the sufferings of the damned into spiritualized terms (*De prin.* 2.10.4). The real punishment of the damned consists in their sense of separation from God. According to his theory of APOCATASTASIS, Origen (*De prin.* 1.6.2) understands these punishments as remedial and as ending when the final restoration is reached (*In Ezech. hom.* 1.2).

The influence of Origen's opinions on the understanding of belief in hell was considerable. He was largely responsible for the disappearance of chiliasm and so restored the problem of the return of Christ to its eschatological setting. By raising the question of the purpose of the punishment of the damned, he opened the way for the interpretation of scriptural statements about remedial punishment, the FIRE OF JUDGMENT, and PURGATORY. In this way the question of retribution at death appears in connection with the individual, and so belief in hell was stated in this context.

Origen attempted to provide an intelligent understanding of traditional belief in hell. The result at which he arrived was eventually declared by the Church incompatible with that belief. What he attempted remains a problem. His positive contribution to the solution of that problem was, besides showing the folly of relying on the purely literalist reading of scriptural statements about the sufferings of the damned, to place the understanding of belief in hell within Christian belief in the saving work of Christ and in God's merciful love for humankind.

After Origen some attempted to mitigate the unending punishment of the damned by maintaining that these punishments would end for Christians (Jerome, *Ep.* 119.7; Ambrose, *In Ps.* 36.26), or for certain categories of Christians, such as those who always retained belief in Christ, or those who had received the Eucharist. These views, under the influence of the teaching of Augustine (*Enchir.* 112–13), eventually gave way before the traditional belief in the unending punishment of the damned. Others, for whom this belief was incompatible with their belief in the MERCY OF GOD, resolved the problem of the punishment of the demons and the damned by means of the theory of conditionalism, according to which the demons and the damned will be annihilated; or by the theory of universalissm, which postulates the fina restoration of all things, including the demons and the damned. These views are excluded by the dogmatic statement that the punishment of the demons and the damned is unending. But the fact that such views continue to be held by some Christians is a reminder of the problem involved in the understanding of traditional belief in the mystery of hell. The Church has stated that belief in the form of the unending punishment of the demons and the damned, but this form is not to be equated with the total expression of the Church's belief in the mystery of hell; nor can belief in hell in that form alone provide an adequate basis for the elaboration of the theological idea of hell.

Theological Development. The various ideas of hell that have been elaborated in the course of theology have been influenced by the different categories used to integrate the theology of hell within a systematic theology. In terms of his category of apocatastasis, Origen's theological speculations produced the idea of hell as the ultimate stage in the process by which all things return to their primeval order. When Origen's speculations had been hardened by his followers into a doctrine of universalism, this idea of hell was excluded by the Church: ''Si quis dicit . . . restitutionem et redintegrationem fore daemonum aut impiorum hominum, an. s.'' (*Enchiridion symbolorum* 411). The clearer identification of the different eschatological events and states, both at the collective and at the individual level, that resulted from the Church's long reflection on belief in the return of Christ meant that scientific theology, when it emerged in the West during the 12th century, was better placed to work out a theological idea of hell. Peter Lombard integrates the theology of hell into his systematic theology, *Libri 4 sententiarum,* by means of the category of resurrection (*3 Sent.* prol.). This category he linked, by way of the category of Sacrament, to the category of Christ the Samaritan restoring man from the effects of sin: infirmity and death. The theological speculation of Peter Lombard about hell is mainly confined to discussing questions arising from scriptural statements and patristic opinions, especially those of Augustine, about hell (*4 Sent.* 43–50).

The categories used by Peter Lombard were more fully exploited by Thomas Aquinas (*In 2 sent.* prol; *Summa theologiae* 3a, prol.). But he died before completing his own systematic theology (*Summa theologiae*); what is included under the rubric Resurrection (*Summa theologiae* 3a, suppl., 69–99) is taken from his earlier work (*In 4 sent.* 43–50). In his theology of hell, Aquinas traces the horizons within which an intelligent understanding of belief in hell is possible: the place of the will in fault and punishment (*In 4 sent.* prol.), the mutability and fixity of the created will (angels': *Summa theologiae* 1a, 63–64; men's: *Comp. theol.* 174). By working out these horizons in reference to the concrete situation, revealed in FAITH, of the creature's freedom and of God's GRACE, he indicates the mystery of hell. He was aware, too, of the relation of the theology of hell to pneumatology (*Comp. theol.* 147). These possibilities for the development of the theology of hell were little exploited by later theologians. During the 14th and 15th centuries theological interest was chiefly confined to Books 1 and 2 of Peter Lombard's *Libri sententiarum.* And when in the following century the *Summa theologiae* of Aquinas became the text used in the theological faculties, the incomplete state of that work caused eschatology and the theology of hell to be isolated from their traditional place within theology. L. Lessius, *De perfectionibus moribusque divinis* 13.24, inserts the theology of hell under the rubric Judgment and Wrath of God. C. Mazzella, *De Deo creante* (Disp. 6) places it with the theology of man. Until recent times, a similar treatment of the theology of hell was common in the manuals of theology (e.g., A. Tanquerey's). Retribution for sin is the dominant feature of the idea of hell developed by these theologies.

The category of revelation is increasingly used to integrate the theology of hell, and eschatology, within systematic theology (e.g., in Schmaus's work). This category of revelation introduces into the theology of hell the concepts of the kingdom of God and of unbelief. Both concepts express personal realities and entail a concept of freedom: the freedom in which a person rejects the self-giving that another freely makes. In this context separation from God is the theological idea of hell. And by reference to the divine self-giving manifested now in the Lord Jesus and to be manifested when God is all in all, this idea of hell as separation from God is worked out. The consequence of this separation from God is expressed in the idea of hell as retribution for sin; the theological concepts of damnation and hellfire are used to interpret this consequence. While respecting the mystery of God's dealings with the fact of unbelief, this theology of hell endeavors to make a statement of belief in the mystery of hell that is wider in form than the present doctrinal statement of that belief. But it is aware that the truths its idea of hell interpret cannot be held together in logical equilibrium (Jn 17.12).

See Also: ESCHATOLOGY (IN THE BIBLE); ESCHATOLOGY (THEOLOGICAL TREATMENT); GEHENNA; JUDGMENT, DIVINE (IN THE BIBLE); JUDGMENT, DIVINE (IN THEOLOGY); SANCTION, DIVINE.

Bibliography: M. RICHARD, *Dictionnaire de théologie catholique*, ed. A. VACANT et al., 15 v. (Paris 1903–50) 5.1:28–120; *Dictionnaire de théologie catholique: Tables générales* (Paris 1951–) 1.1179–84. J. GNILKA et al., *Lexikon für Theologie und Kirche*, ed. J. HOFER and K. RAHNER, 10 v. (2d, new ed. Freiburg 1957–65) 5:445–50. F. C. GRANT et al., *Die Religion in Geschichte und Gegenwart*, 7 v. (3d ed. Tübingen 1957–65) 3:400–07. A. WINKLHOFER, H. FRIES, ed., *Handbuch theologischer Grundvegriffe*, 2 v. (Munich 1962–63) 1:327–36; *The Coming of His Kingdom,* tr. A. V. LITTLEDALE (New York 1963). P. BERNARD, *Dictionnaire apologétique de la foi catholique*, ed. A. D'ALÈS, 4 v. (Paris 1911–12) 1:1377–99. J. N. D. KELLY, *Early Christian Doctrines* (2d ed. New York 1960). H. DE LAVALETTE, *Eschatologie* in *Handbuch der Dogmengeschichte,* ed. M. SCHMAUS and A. GRILLMEIER (Freiburg 1951–) 5.2. M. SCHMAUS, *Von den letzten Dingen* (his *Katholische Dogmatik* 4.2; 5th ed. Munich 1959). R. SCHNACKENBURG, *God's Rule and Kingdom,* tr. J. MURRAY (New York 1963).

[E. G. HARDWICK]

HELLENIST

In Acts 6.1 Hellenists (Ἑλληνισταί) are Greek-speaking converts from Judaism as distinct from Hebrews (Ἑβραῖοι), converts from Judaism who spoke Hebrew or, rather, Aramaic. The word Ἕλλην (Greek) is used in the NT of Greek-speaking Gentiles (Acts 14.1; 18.4; Rom 1.16; etc.) or Greek-speaking Proselytes. Hellenists were often more fervent in Judaism than the Hebrews. They not only made pilgrimages to Jerusalem, but maintained national synagogues in the holy city (Acts 6.9). It is not surprising, then, that they provided both the greatest impetus and the fiercest opposition to Christianity.

Among the first converts on Pentecost were many Hellenists (Acts 2.5–11). Also the first seven deacons, all of whom had Greek names, were Hellenists. They were men of fiery zeal such as STEPHEN (PROTOMARTYR) and PHILIP THE DEACON, who spread the faith rapidly in Jerusalem, Judea, and Samaria (Acts ch. 6–8). It was Hellenists, too, who began the conversion of the Gentiles at Antioch (Acts 11.20), the base of St. Paul's missionary journeys. At the same time, Hellenists opposed Christianity in Jerusalem and throughout the Roman Empire (e.g., Acts 6.9; 9.29; 13.50). St. Paul, who qualified as both a Hellenist and a Hebrew (Acts 22.3; Phil 3.5), exemplified the roles of both persecutor and missionary of Christianity.

Bibliography: H. WINDISCH, in G.KITTEL, ed., *Theologisches Wörterbuch zum Neuen Testament* (Stuttgart 1935–) 2:508–509. M. SIMON, *St. Stephen and the Hellenists in the Primitive Church* (New York 1958). C. F. D. MOULE, "Once More, Who Were the Hellenists" *Expository Times* 70 (1958–59) 100–102.

[W. F. DICHARRY]

HELLFIRE

In theological discourse hellfire signifies the concept of physical punishment (*poena sensus*) that scholastic theology elaborated, in addition to the concept of punishment of loss (DAMNATION), to interpret the punishment of the demons and the damned. The theological distinction between hellfire and damnation interprets the Church's teaching about the punishment of sin (*Enchiridion symbolorum,* 780). But the nature of the objective reality expressed by the concept of physical punishment has not been clarified by the Church.

The analysis of sin in relation to the last end reveals not only the loss of the last end (*aversio*), which is God, but also, in the same context of the last end, the inordinate estimation of other things (*conversio*). The punishment for this aspect of sin is expressed by the concept of physical punishment (*C. gent.* 3.145). And from the understanding of the relation of sin and punishment to the will (*Comp. theol.* 121), the objective reality interpreted by this concept is seen to be material things (*C. gent.* 4.90).

How material things can inflict punishment on the demons and the damned has been variously understood; the reading of scriptural statements about this punishment and the available scientific knowledge have been reflected. Much of this speculation is now discarded. Aquinas approaches the problem from the metaphysical angle of the relation between spirit and matter (*C. gent.* 4.90) and resolves it in the sense of demons and damned souls being subjected to or constricted by material things (*Comp. theol.* 180). This constrictive action of matter on the damned supposes a special intervention of divine power, so that only analogously can natural knowledge be used to understand it. By this analogous use of natural knowledge, Aquinas justifies the literal reading of scriptural statements about hellfire (*Comp. theol.* 179). Theologians differ about the form of causality involved in the constrictive action of matter on the damned; for some it is physical causality, for others, objective causality. Aquinas understands it as physical and objective (*Comp. theol.* 180).

Theological opinion about what matter constricts the damned has developed considerably. Where earlier views understood this matter as some material things, the trend now is to interpret it as the whole material universe. By this constrictive action the relationship of the damned to the universe and its parts is restricted. This situation of the damned within the universe is understood in terms of the cosmic role of the Holy Spirit manifested in the RESURRECTION OF JESUS; it expresses their humiliated situation within the KINGDOM OF GOD. The material restriction of the demons and the damned, signified by hellfire, articulates their spiritual restriction, signified by damnation. The meaning of the punishment of the demons and the damned in personal terms is that they are the unfree.

See Also: GEHENNA; FIRE OF JUDGMENT; HELL (THEOLOGY OF); SANCTION; SANCTION, DIVINE; ESCHATOLOGY, ARTICLES ON.

Bibliography: A. MICHEL, *Dictionnaire de théologie catholique*, ed. A. VACANT et al., 15 v. (Paris 1903–50; Tables générales 1951) 5.2:2196–2239. A. WINKLHOFER, *The Coming of His Kingdom,* tr. A. V. LITTLEDALE (New York 1963) 77–98.

[E. G. HARDWICK]

HÉLOÏSE

Abbess of the Paraclete; b. *c.* 1098; d. Paraclete, France, May 15, 1164. She was the niece of Canon Fulbert at Paris, and was noted for her learning, her love for Peter ABELARD, and her later devotion to the religious life. As an aftermath of her love affair with Abelard, Héloïse entered a convent and eventually became prioress of the abbey of ARGENTEUIL. In 1128, when Argenteuil was closed, she and the nuns took refuge at the Benedictine abbey, the Paraclete (Diocese of Troyes), built by Abelard. This cloister, of which she became first abbess, flourished and became known for works of piety. At her death she was buried beside Abelard at the Paraclete. Their remains were later (1817) taken to Paris and interred there at Père-Lachaise.

Bibliography: J. T. MUCKLE, ed., ''Historia calamitatum,'' *Mediaeval Studies* 12 (1950) 163–213 Latin text, with review of MSS and editions; ''The Personal Letters between Abelard and Héloise,'' *ibid.,* 15 (1953) 47–94; ''The Letter of Héloise on Religious Life and Abelard's First Reply,'' *ibid.,* 17 (1955) 240–281. E. GILSON, *Héloise and Abelard,* tr. L. K. SHOOK (Chicago 1951). A. M. LANDGRAF, *Lexikon für Theologie und Kirche*, ed. J. HOFER and K. RAHNER, 10 v. (2d, new ed. Freiburg 1957–65) 1:5–6.

[P. KIBRE]

Héloïse. (©Bettmann/CORBIS)

HELPERS OF THE HOLY SOULS

Also known as the Society of Helpers (HHS, Official Catholic Directory #1890), an international missionary congregation of sisters, founded at Paris in 1856 by Blessed Eugénie de SMET. Encouraged by the Curé of Ars (John Baptist VIANNEY), the Society of the Helpers of the Holy Souls early received direction from Pierre OLIVAINT, SJ; the congregation follows the spirit and rules of St. Ignatius. In 1892 the first United States foundation was made in New York City, followed by others in St. Louis, Missouri, and San Francisco and Los Angeles, California. The society's apostolate was later extended to various parts of Asia, Africa, Europe and the Americas. Helpers engage in various ministries, including their traditional ministries of catechetical instruction and the care of the poor, sick and homeless. From the beginning, the foundress envisaged lay collaborators. Training of and retreats for volunteers and recruitment of associate members—clerical, religious, and lay—extend the Helpers' mission. Secular members of the society, sharing fully its spiritual and apostolic formation while living in the world, were approved by Rome in the 1961 revised constitutions. The generalate is in Paris, France. The United States provincialate is in Chicago, Illinois.

[M. A. MCHUGH/EDS.]

HEMERFORD, THOMAS, BL.

Priest, martyr; b. Dorsetshire, England; hanged, drawn, and quartered at Tyburn (London), Feb. 12, 1584. Having completed his studies at St. John's and Hart Hall, Oxford, Hemerford traveled to the English College in Rome for his seminary education. He was ordained in 1583 by Bp. Goldwell at Rheims prior to beginning his work in the English mission. Hemerford was arrested the following year, and indicted on Feb. 5, 1584. Although he pled not guilty, he was sentenced to death two days later and committed to the Tower's ''pit'' to await execution with BB. James FENN, John Munden, and John Nutter. (The sick George HAYDOCK was returned to his cell.) All five were drawn on hurdles to Tyburn. Hemerford, the second of the group to suffer, was hanged, but cut down and disemboweled while still alive. An eyewitness related of Hemerford, ''when the tormentor did cutt off his members, he did cry, 'Oh! A!'; I heard myself standing under the gibbet.'' He was beatified by Pius XI on Dec. 15, 1929.

Ernest Hemingway. (©Bettmann/CORBIS)

Feast of the English Martyrs: May 4 (England).

See Also: ENGLAND, SCOTLAND, AND WALES, MARTYRS OF.

Bibliography: R. CHALLONER, *Memoirs of Missionary Priests,* ed. J. H. POLLEN (rev. ed. London 1924; repr. Farnborough 1969). H. FOLEY, *Records of the English Province of the Society of Jesus,* 7 v. (London 1877–82) 74, 103. GILLOW, *Biblical Dictionary of English Catholicism* (London and New York 1885–1902) III, 202; cf. III, 265; V, 142, 201. J. H. POLLEN, *Acts of English Martyrs* (London 1891) 252, 253, 304.

[K. I. RABENSTEIN]

HEMINGWAY, ERNEST MILLER

Novelist and short-story writer; b. Oak Park, Ill., July 21, 1899; d. Ketchum, Idaho, July 2, 1961. The son of a doctor and a devoutly religious mother, he spent a Tarkingtonian boyhood in a Chicago suburb and enjoyed Huck Finn summers in a still unspoiled, Native American-inhabited upper Michigan. After a job on the *Kansas City Star,* he took part in World War I as an ambulance driver and was wounded when barely 19. Briefly a journalist in Toronto and a correspondent during the Greek-Turkish war, he began his long expatriation in France, Italy, Spain, the West Indies, and Cuba, plus two African safaris and irregular but intimate involvements in both the Spanish Civil War and World War II. His father's suicide (1929) was a profound shock. A convert to Catholicism, Hemingway was apparently a believer to the end, though his marital status after the third of his four marriages precluded formal membership in the Church. He had three sons. He died of a self-inflicted gunshot wound after a protracted illness marked by hypertension and despondency.

The Nobel prize citation's (1954) salute to Hemingway's gift of ''tragic pathos'' seems prophetic in retrospect. All Hemingway's heroes are ''objective correlatives'' of his own attitudes; it is clear that his lifelong literary preoccupation with courage meant, in part, that he constantly dreaded that his own courage would desert him. The fact may well account for the disconcerting Byronic attitudes he struck in public. Underneath these he was a genuine saga figure creating an authentic saga art; his characteristic sardonic irony was a rationalization of his own sense of personal doom.

Classic in technique and romantic in thematics, Hemingway's fictional form is a naturalistic romance utilizing symbols from nature to capture the moral situations of his day. However limited in scope, he is a moralist, a historian of nihilism who takes his text from Ecclesiastes and who realizes in art the ritual inherent in the Catholic ethos, and sets priests and the crucified Christ high among his culture heroes.

For a time Hemingway's celebrated style, the mirror of an apparently straightforward but essentially oblique art, revolutionized world fiction. It is clean, staccato, linear, and vernacular, seeking the visual effects of a Braque, and making a curious Biblical music out of the connective ''and.'' Though he attributes his own derivation to Twain, he displays strong affinities with such far-removed predecessors as the old poet of *Maldon,* and with Stendhal, Hawthorne, Thoreau, Turgenev, and Conrad. The future will probably diagnose his major weaknesses as an oversentimental primitivism and a positively adolescent bravura about sex.

Hemingway's finest work appeared between 1926 and 1936. He was the Froissart of the ''lost generation'' as Fitzgerald was its troubadour, and his best novels are *The Sun Also Rises* (1926), a brilliant, tragicomedy ''Waste Land'' that deploys a freshness of sensibility and incomparably cadenced dialogue; and *A Farewell to Arms* (1929), very possibly the best novel in English to deal with World War I. *To Have and Have Not* (1937) is marred by a gauche technique; and *For Whom the Bell Tolls* (1940) misses the inimitable tension-in-suspension that is his best work's emotional trademark. His only total failure, *Across the River and into the Trees* (1950), breaks down into self-parodying bathos. His single novella, *The Old Man and the Sea* (1952), at once Homeric and deeply Christian, demonstrates a lovely Franciscan empathy with the animal creation and incarnates, in old Santiago, Hemingway's central vision of man ''destroyed but not defeated.'' An unusually high number of his 50-odd short stories are flawlessly executed and may well constitute his chief claim on posterity; such are ''Great Two-Hearted River,'' ''The Undefeated,'' ''Twenty Grand,''

''The Killers,'' ''The Snows of Kilimanjaro,'' and that archetypal parable for its century, ''A Clean, Well-Lighted Place.'' Hemingway's ultimate critical status remains in some debate, but he achieved indubitable literature whose dominant note has been well described as a ''clarity of heart.''

Bibliography: E. HEMINGWAY, *Death in the Afternoon* (New York 1932); *Green Hills of Africa* (New York 1935); *A Moveable Feast* (New York 1964), all contain valuable autobiographical details. C. H. BAKER, *Hemingway: The Writer as Artist* (3d ed. Princeton 1963), best biography and major critical source; ed., *Hemingway and His Critics: An International Anthology* (New York 1961). C. A. FENTON, *The Apprenticeship of Ernest Hemingway* (New York 1954), casts valuable light on the early years. J. K. MCCAFFERY, ed., *Ernest Hemingway: The Man and His Work* (Cleveland 1950). J. ATKINS, *The Art of Ernest Hemingway: His Work and Personality* (New York 1952). P. YOUNG, *Ernest Hemingway* (New York 1952). S. SANDERSON, *Hemingway* (New York 1961). E. ROVIT, *Ernest Hemingway* (New York 1963).

[C. A. BRADY]

HEMMA, BL.

Carolingian queen also known as Emma or Gemma; b. *c.* 808; d. Regensburg, Germany, Jan. 31, 876. Hemma was the sister of Empress Judith, the second wife of Charles II the Bald. The wife of Louis the German, she was the mother of seven children, including Charles III the Fat and Bl. Irmengard. She was patroness and abbess of the Benedictine convent of Obermünster, which has disputed Sankt Emmeram's claim to her body. It seems, however, that she is buried at Sankt Emmeram's, where her tombstone shows some of the best German plastic art of the 13th century.

Feast: June 29; Jan. 31 (Diocese of Regensburg).

Bibliography: *Monumenta Germaniae Historica: Necrologia* 3:305. G. LEIDINGER, ''Bruchstücke einer verlorenen Chronik eines unbekannten Regensburger Verfassers des 12. Jahrhunderts,'' *Sitzungsberichte der Bayerischen Akademie der Wissenschaften zu München* (1933) 1–72. I. WEILNER, *Lexikon für Theologie und Kirche*[2] 5:227.

[A. CABANISS]

HEMMING, BL.

Bishop of Åbo; b. Bälinge, Sweden; d. May 21, 1366. In 1338 he was elected bishop of Åbo (modern Turku, Finland) in what was then a province of medieval Sweden, and the election was confirmed by the archbishop of UPPSALA, who consecrated him. Hemming instituted the office of provost (*praepositus*) at his cathedral in 1340. He obtained two papal letters of indulgence from CLEMENT VI and one from INNOCENT VI. Much reconstruction, especially new windows and portals, was undertaken in the cathedral, and two prebends were established. To his cathedral he willed his library, containing theological works and treatises on canon law; the *De proprietatibus rerum* of BARTHOLOMAEUS ANGLICUS was to be found in this collection. He was much appreciated by St. BRIDGET OF SWEDEN (*nihil timet nec etiam mortem,* bk. 4, ch. 125 of her Revelations says of him) and acted as her messenger to the kings of France and England as well as to the pope. Between 1350 and 1352 he promulgated statutes for the clergy, and for some time he seems to have been kept in custody by King Magnus Eriksson. Hemming was buried in his cathedral. The translation of his relics was authorized by the Holy See in 1514, and the shrine is still extant. He is often called ''saint.''

Feast: May 22.

Bibliography: Sources. BRIDGET, *Extravagantes,* ed. L. HOLLMAN (Uppsala 1956). The important revelation (4.125 in the Latin text), is accessible only in older eds. The documents are ed. in *Finlands Medeltidsurkunder,* 8 v. (Helsinki 1910–35) and *Diplomatarium suecanum* (Stockholm 1829–). Literature. B. KLOCKARS, *Bishop Hemming av Åbo* (Turku 1961). J. GALLÉN, *Lexikon für Theologie und Kirche,* ed. J. HOFER and K. RAHNER, 10 v. (2d, new ed. Freiburg 1957–65) 5:228.

[T. SCHMID]

HENANA

Late 6th-century Syriac theologian; d. Nisibis (Nusaybin, Turkey), *c.* 610. A native of Adiabene, Henana studied in the school of Nisibis under Abraham, successor to Narses, and became director of the school in 572, a position he held until his death in spite of violent opposition. Support from rulers of Nisibis and a large following of disciples enabled him to lead a theological movement that endeavored to abandon NESTORIANISM for Chalcedonian orthodoxy in the Persian Church. He rejected the authority of THEODORE OF MOPSUESTIA, considered an infallible interpreter of Scripture by the Persian Church, and followed JOHN CHRYSOSTOM as a guide in his scriptural exegesis. He accepted the HYPOSTATIC UNION of the two natures in Christ and, as a consequence, the COMMUNICATION OF IDIOMS and THEOTOKOS. He likewise accepted the doctrine of original sin as an explanation of human concupiscence and was consequently accused of Chaldaism or fatalism. He was also considered an Origenist; there is little evidence to support this charge, although the accusation that he denied the resurrection of the body and accepted the Origenistic teaching on the apocatastasis and possibly astral influence on human events led to the charge of fatalism.

Henana is known to have produced commentaries on Genesis, Job, Psalms, Proverbs, Ecclesiastes, the Canticle of Canticles, the lesser Prophets, Mark, and the Epistles of St. Paul; and to have written tracts on the creed, on the Friday after Pentecost called the Golden Friday, and the so-called Fast of the Ninivites. Only fragments of his works have been preserved.

Bibliography: X. DUCROS, *Catholicisme* 5:597–598. A. BAUMSTARK, *Geschichte der syrischen Literatur* (Bonn 1922) 127. J. B. CHABOT, *Littérature syriaque* (Paris 1935) 88–89. R. DUVAL, *La Littérature syriaque* (3d ed. Paris 1907) 348–349. J. LABOURT, *Le Christianisme dans l'empire perse* (Paris 1904) 215–217; 269–280.

[D. M. POSHEK]

HENDRICK, THOMAS AUGUSTINE

Bishop; b. Penn Yan, N.Y., Oct. 29, 1849; d. Cebu, Philippine Islands, Nov. 30, 1909. Born of immigrant Irish parents, Hendrick attended St. John's College (Fordham), N.Y.; Seton Hall University, N.J.; and St. Joseph's Seminary, Troy, N.Y. After ordination on June 7, 1873, he served in several parishes in the Diocese of Rochester, N.Y. His interest in youth and education led to his election as president of the Rochester Society for the Prevention of Cruelty to Children and his appointment to the N.Y. State Board of Regents (1900–04). Hendrick was closely associated with leaders of the Republican Party, including Theodore Roosevelt, and his name was proposed for the archbishopric of Manila after the Spanish American War when Spanish bishops were being supplanted by Americans. Although not named to Manila, Hendrick was consecrated in Rome, Aug. 23, 1903, as bishop of Cebu. Taking possession of a see that had suffered in the transition from Spanish to American rule, Hendrick spent months visiting the many islands that made up his diocese. He reactivated 50 elementary schools and enlisted priests from abroad to help fill the dozens of parishes left vacant by the ravages of war and the withdrawal of many Spanish friars. In criticism of U.S. authorities in the Philippines, the bishop alleged that they had failed to safeguard the rights of the Catholic Church in the Islands. He accused American authorities of favoring Aglipayans for responsible government positions, and his criticism of the occupying authorities for recognizing Aglipayan claims to Catholic Church property was later vindicated by the Philippine Supreme Court's decision sustaining Catholic ownership.

Bibliography: T. A. HENDRICK papers, MSS, Nazareth College, Rochester, N.Y. F. J. ZWIERLEIN, *Theodore Roosevelt and Catholics, 1882–1919* (St. Louis 1956).

[R. M. QUINN]

HENNEPIN, LOUIS

Missionary, explorer; b. Ath, Belgium, May 12, 1626; d. probably Rome, Italy, after 1701. He entered the novitiate of the Récollet Order of Friars Minor at Béthune, France, was ordained, and served as a missionary in Holland (1673–74). On July 14, 1675, he sailed for Canada, where Bp. François de Laval de Montmorency of Quebec appointed him Lenten and Advent preacher. During this time he carefully studied native dialects and customs until appointed to an Iroquois mission at Fort Frontenac on Lake Ontario, near the present site of Kingston. In 1678, Hennepin accompanied René Robert, Sieur de la Salle, on his expedition westward. From a Niagara outpost on Lake Erie, they traveled through both Illinois and Louisiana country, navigated the Detroit and St. Clair Rivers named by La Salle, and founded Fort Crève-Coeur near Lake Peoria. Here La Salle left on foot for Fort Frontenac and Quebec while Hennepin and his companions continued toward the Mississippi River. On April 12, 1681, as they moved northward, they were captured by the Issati Sioux and obliged to accompany them in their wanderings. During one of these journeys, they stopped at a cataract in the Mississippi, which Hennepin named St. Anthony Falls. Through the intercession of the French explorer Daniel Greysolon Du Lhut the missionaries were finally released, and after a long and difficult journey Hennepin returned to Montreal, Canada, to report to Count Louis de Frontenac, the Governor General. At the suggestion of Laval, Hennepin spent the summer at the Franciscan monastery of Our Lady of the Angels, Quebec. In the autumn he returned to France to write *Description de la Louisiana* (1683), an account of his explorations. Experiencing difficulties with his superiors, Hennepin left Artois, where he had been stationed, and established himself in Utrecht, Netherlands. There he published two new versions of his travels, *Nouvelle découverte* (1697) and *Nouvelle Voyage* (1698), which were translated in more than 60 editions. In these books he claimed to have descended the lower Mississippi and discovered the Gulf of Mexico prior to La Salle. Rejecting his claims, historians have since debated his accuracy and originality. At this time Hennepin lost the favor of Louis XIV, and his books were dedicated to King William III of England. In 1698 Hennepin received a grant of money from William, for whom he offered to guide a fleet to the Gulf of Mexico. He did not accompany this fleet, however, but instead made his way to Italy, where his remaining days were spent in a monastery in Rome.

Bibliography: J. DELANGLEZ, *Hennepin's Description of Louisiana* (Chicago 1941) bibliog. 144–156, a leading American authority, who questioned the originality of Hennepin's writings. More recent, and based on documents favorable to Hennepin found in the State Archives, Mons, Belgium, are the writings of A. LO-

UANT, ''Le P. Louis Hennepin: Nouveaux jalons pour sa biographie,'' *Revue d'histoire ecclésiastique* 45 (1950) 186–211; ''Precisions nouvelles sur le Père Hennepin,'' *Academie Royale de Belgique. Bulletin de la classe des lettres . . .* 42 (1956) 215–276; ''Une Confirmation de l'identification du Père Louis Hennepin,'' *Revue d'histoire ecclésiastique* 52 (1957) 871–876. These documents have resulted in some revision of traditional biographical details.

[J. L. MORRISON]

HENNI, JOHN MARTIN

Archbishop, editor; b. Misanenga, Grisons, Switzerland, June 13, 1805; d. Milwaukee, Wis., Sept. 7, 1881. He studied at Saint Gall and Lucerne, Switzerland, and Rome, and in 1829 went to the U.S. to complete his training at the Bardstown, Ky., seminary. He was ordained on Feb. 2, 1829, for the Cincinnati diocese, where he taught philosophy at the minor seminary of the Atheneum for a short time. After taking a census of Germans in Ohio, he rode the circuit out of Canton and earned the title ''Apostle of the Germans.'' In 1834 he became vicar-general and pastor of the Germans in Cincinnati, Ohio.

Because of the cultural void, lack of clergy, and hostility confronting immigrants, he organized the teaching of English for adults, wrote a catechism in German for children, founded a newspaper and library, introduced better Church music, and planned for a bilingual seminary to train a native clergy. Before the Ohio legislature endeavored to assimilate immigrants into American society by permitting bilingual schools in 1838, Henni had inaugurated such a system in Cincinnati. He knew that the scarcity of bilingual teachers permitted them to demand a salary beyond the ability of most places to pay. The result was a compromise allowing each school district to conduct its public schools in either English or German, or both.

One of Henni's greatest benefactions was founding *Der Wahrheitsfreund,* a weekly paper (1837–1907) in Cincinnati, which opposed slavery, prohibition, and autocracy. In it he claimed that Prussian autocracy made the foot fit the shoe, while his ''Creed of Nineteenth Century Citizen'' was a classical expression of belief in equality and tolerance. Like many of his contemporaries, Henni believed that agriculture is the foundation of all the livelihoods of man and the principal support of the state. His contribution to German literature is not excelled by any German liberal in the U.S. In 1835 he was sent to Europe to secure financial aid for the diocese. While there he published *Ein Blick in's Thal des Ohio* (Munich 1836), which outlined the history of the Catholic Church in the U.S.

Ordinary of Milwaukee. Wisconsin became a diocese in 1843 with Milwaukee as headquarters and Henni as bishop. In 1875 he became archbishop when Milwaukee was raised to metropolitan rank. His work there included attracting thousands of Catholic settlers, defending them against anti-Catholic groups, such as the Nativists, Know-Nothingists, and Forty-eighters, and providing them with priests, churches, schools, and institutions. He was opposed to settlement by colonization, because it was generally accompanied by regimentation, excessive land speculation, and restrictions upon industrial initiative and enterprise. Instead, he favored the American system of competitive entry, government land sale, and homesteading as being most conducive to industrial freedom and political liberty. Henni liked to point to the settlements of Catholic Irish and Germans along Lake Michigan and in the interior of Wisconsin as the ideal system of land entry and pattern of settlement. His refutation of a Whig charge that the Catholic hierarchy controlled the vote of alien Catholics appeared in print as *Facts against Assertions* (Milwaukee 1845) and revealed him as a remarkable apologist and historian. He was also successful in fashioning a pattern for successful missionary work with the natives at Wisconsin.

John Martin Henni.

Leader in Education. Henni concerned himself with the recruitment of teaching orders and stimulated the founding of Marquette University and St. Francis Seminary (1856), both in Milwaukee. He considered the cooperative school ventures temporary expedients, justified only in districts where farmers would not or could not support a double school system. He felt that all attempts to harmonize the conflicting views of religious and secular education by omitting the catechism and employing English exclusively produced a sort of hybrid religion that soon deteriorated into paganism. District schools under the control of lay committees that, though Catholic, might change every year jeopardized the pastor's influence. A system of parochial schools conforming to the needs of the parish group seemed far better to Henni, even though it meant supporting a dual system of schools. His policy and program conformed to the legislation of American church councils. He left a tradition of excellence in the German Catholic parochial schools of Cincinnati that was commended by the Second Provincial Council of Cincinnati (1858).

Other Activities. Henni was well known to the European missionary aid societies. Father Joseph Ferdinand Mueller, business manager for the LUDWIG MISSIONSVEREIN, Munich, Germany, was a zealous advocate of Henni's requests to the society and was largely instrumental in settling the Norbertine Canons, Capuchins, Dominican Sisters of Racine, Sisters of St. Francis Assisi, and Notre Dame Sisters in Wisconsin. The Milwaukee Diocese became the largest beneficiary of the society. St. Francis Seminary ensured a supply of clergy not only for Wisconsin but also for the old Northwest and Middle West. Henni wrote that the life and development of the Church throughout that region depended on the seminary. In the school year 1868–69, 36 graduates were ordained for 12 dioceses.

To counter the press of the Forty-eighters, he started two weekly papers, *Der Seebote* (Milwaukee 1852) and *Die Columbia* (Milwaukee 1872). In addition, he sponsored the *Catholic Vindicator* (Monroe, Wis. 1870), the *Star of Bethlehem* (Milwaukee 1869), and merged them with the *Catholic Citizen* (Milwaukee 1870). His pastoral letters stressed history, divine Providence, and the Passion of Our Lord. Synods in 1847 and 1853 were called mainly to promulgate the conciliar decrees of Baltimore. Although against the inclusion of papal infallibility on the conciliar agenda of Vatican Council I, Henni finally voted for its definition. In 1880, when the Holy See honored Henni's request that Bp. Michael HEISS OF LA CROSSE, Wis., be named as his coadjutor, the selection brought on a clash between Irish and Germans.

Bibliography: P. L. JOHNSON, *Crosier on the Frontier: Life of John Martin Henni* (Madison 1959).

[P. L. JOHNSON]

HENOTHEISM

(From Gr. ἕν, ἑνός, one, and θεός, god) is a term introduced by Max Müller (1823–1900) to designate the Vedic religion, which he regarded as a form of polytheism without a firmly fixed hierarchy of divinities. Kathenotheism is employed in practically the same sense. Henotheism signifies a ''monotheism of emotion and mood.'' When the believer devotes all his attention to a given god, this god becomes for him the only god, and for the moment all the other divinities and divine attributes merge in this one divinity. At present, however, henotheism is neither considered to be a stage in the evolution of religion, nor is it applied as an appropriate designation to any particular religion. On the other hand, the concept may be used in a religio-phenomenological sense, since the religious-minded man always meets God under the dominance of a given aspect—His omnipotence, love, or anger.

Bibliography: J. HAEKEL, *Lexikon für Theologie und Kirche*, ed. J. HOFER and K. RAHNER, 10 v. (2d new ed. Freiburg 1957–65) 5:233. W. D. WHITNEY, ''Le Prétendu henothéisme du Véda,'' *Revue de l'histoire des religions* 6 (1882) 129–143. G. VAN DER LEEUW, *Religion in Essence and Manifestation,* tr. J. E. TURNER (London 1938). W. SCHMIDT, *Der Ursprung der Gottesidee* (Münster 1926–). W. HOLSTEN, *Die Religion in Geschichte und Gegenwart*, 7 v. (3d ed. Tübingen 1957–65) 3:225.

[W. DUPRÉ]

HENOTICON

An epistolary decree of Emperor ZENO, prepared in 482 under the inspiration of Acacius, Patriarch of Constantinople (471–489), to restore religious unity between the Monophysites (*see* MONOPHYSITISM) and those who supported the Council of CHALCEDON (451). Chalcedon had solved the theological problem involved in the INCARNATION by defining the doctrine of two natures and one person in Christ; but its terminology was rejected by the Monophysites whose anti-imperial nationalism found an outlet in the Monophysite patriarchs of ALEXANDRIA, ANTIOCH, and JERUSALEM. In an effort to placate the Monophysite leaders, the Henoticon cites the first three ecumenical councils and affirms the consubstantiality of Christ with God and with man, but skillfully avoids the Chalcedonian use of the terms ''nature'' and ''person.'' The decree was sent to all the bishops of the East for their signature, but was rejected by the Egyptian Monophysites, and considered in Rome and the West as a denial of Chalcedonian orthodoxy. It occasioned the first official estrangement between Rome and the East, a disaffection known as the ACACIAN SCHISM (484–519).

Bibliography: Text in *Abhandlungen der Bayerischen Akademie der Wissenschaften* (Münich 1835–) phil. u. hist. Klasse

32.6 (Munich 1927), also in *Patrologia Graeca*, ed. J. P. MIGNE (Paris 1857–66) 86:2620–25. L. SALAVILLE, *Dictionnaire de théologie catholique*, ed. A. VACANT et al., (Paris 1903—50) 6.2: 2153–78. R. HAACKE, ''Die kaiserliche Politik um Chalkedon,'' *Das Konzil von Chalkedon*, ed. A. GRILLMEIER and H. BACHT, 3 v. (Würzburg 1953) v.2. F. STEPHANOU, *Lexikon für Theologie und Kirche*, ed. J. HOFER and K. RAHNER (Freiberg 1957–65) 5:233–234.

[J. VAN PAASSEN]

HENRICUS ARISTIPPUS

Scientist and translator, d. Palermo, Sicily, after 1162. A secular clerk of Norman origin, he became master of the palace school in SICILY and tutor to the future King William I. He was made archdeacon of Catania in 1156, and for a time in 1160 was the principal officer at William's court. After a short while, however, he lost favor and died in prison at Palermo. While royal ambassador to Constantinople in 1158, he brought back to Sicily Greek manuscripts, including a copy of the *Almagest* of PTOLEMY, from the library of Manuel I Comnenus. In 1156 he was the first to translate into Latin PLATO's *Meno* and *Phaedo*, hence his nickname Aristippus (cf. *Meno* 70b; *Phaedo* 59c). His interest in natural sciences led to a hazardous investigation of Mt. Etna and a translation of book four of ARISTOTLE's *Meteorologica*. He may also have translated Diogenes Laértius *De clarorum philosophorum vitis* and the *Opuscula* of GREGORY OF NAZIANZUS, but his work is not extant. His translations are in a distinguished Latin style, showing marked influence of rhetoric and a fondness for alliteration, asyndeton, and parallelism. He has left also some interesting notes on books and libraries in Sicily.

Bibliography: *Corpus Platonicum medii aevi. Plato Latinus,* v.1 *Meno interprete Henrico Aristippo,* ed. V. KORDEUTER and C. LABOWSKY (London 1940), v.2 *Phaedo,* ed. L. MINIO-PALUELLO (1950). C. H. HASKINS, *Studies in the History of Mediaeval Science* (2d ed. Cambridge, Mass. 1927) 159–172. L. MINIO-PALUELLO, *Lexikon für Theologie und Kirche*, ed. J. HOFER and K. RAHNER, 10 v. (2d, new ed. Freiburg 1957–65) 5:234; *Revue philosophique de Louvain* 45 (1947) 206–235.

[T. P. HALTON]

HENRIQUES, HENRIQUE

Missionary; b. Vila Viçosa, Portugal, 1520; d. Punnaikâyal, South India, Feb. 6, 1600. He entered the Society of Jesus, and was ordained at Coimbra probably in 1545 or 1546. That same year he sailed to India, where he worked six months in Goa; then he was sent by Francis Xavier to the Fishery Coast, where he worked for 53 years. He succeeded Antonio CRIMINALI as superior of the mission from 1549 to 1576. His zeal was highly esteemed by Xavier, who described him as ''a very virtuous person and of great edification, who knows how to speak and write Malabar [Tamil] and is loved by the Christians in an amazing manner'' (*Epitolae S. Francisci Xaverii* 2.13). He founded a number of hospitals for the sick. Henriques, probably the first European to write a Tamil grammar and vocabulary, spent many years improving them. Among his works are a catechism, printed in Tamil characters, dated 1578, Quilon, India; a translation of the catechism of Marcos Jorge, printed in Tamil, dated 1579, Cochin; the *Flos sanctorum,* also printed in Tamil (only known copy in Vatican Library), dated 1586; and numerous letters.

Bibliography: J. WICKI, *Studia missionalia* (Rome 1943–) 13 (1963) 113–168; ed., *Documenta indica* (*Monumenta historica Societatis Jesu* 70, 72, 74-; Rome 1948-).

[J. WICKI]

HENRÍQUEZ, ENRIQUE

Jesuit theologian; b. Oporto, Portugal, 1536; d. Tivoli, Jan. 28, 1608. He entered the Society of Jesus in 1552 and early distinguished himself for his learning and ability. He taught philosophy and theology at Córdoba and then at Salamanca, where two of his students were Francisco SUÁREZ and GREGORY OF VALENCIA. His *Theologiae moralis summa* (3 v. Salamanca 1591–93) occasioned serious difficulties with his order. He had earlier taken a leading role in intrigues against the general of the society, Claudius ACQUAVIVA, and in 1593 he refused to accept the changes demanded by the Jesuit censors and ordered by Acquaviva. Henríquez also attacked Suárez, denouncing him without success to the Inquisition at Madrid and at various other places. In 1594 he obtained permission from the pope to leave the Jesuits and enter the Dominicans, whose position on Molina he favored. However, with the persuasion of Gregory of Valencia, he chose to be reinstated with the Jesuits. Henríquez's other major work, *De pontificis romani clave* (Salamanca 1593), was condemned by the Spanish nuncio because of theses concerning ecclesiastical immunities, and was placed on the Index by decree of Aug. 7, 1603, which was later rescinded. Since the book was burned by command of the nuncio, only three or four copies remain as rarities of the Escorial. As a moralist, Henríquez was held in high esteem by St. Alphonsus Liguori.

Bibliography: C. SOMMERVOGEL et al., *Bibliothèque de la Compagnie de Jésus*, 11 v. (Brussels-Paris 1890–1932; v.12, suppl. 1960) 4:275–276. H. HURTER, *Nomenclator literarius theologiae catholicae*, 5 v. in 6 (3d ed. Innsbruck 1903–13) 3:591–592. A. ASTRAIN, *Historia de la Compañia de Jesús,* 7 v. (Madrid 1902–25) 3:360–362; 4:132–134. P. BERARD, *Dictionnaire de théologie*

Henry I, King of England. (Archive Photos)

catholique, ed. A. VACANT et al., 15 v. (Paris 1903–50; Tables Générales 1951–) 6.2: 2197–98.

[F. C. LEHNER]

HENRY I, KING OF ENGLAND

Reigned from 1100 to Dec. 1, 1135; b. Selby (probably), England, 1068; d. Gisors, near Rouen, France. The fourth and youngest son of King WILLIAM I the Conqueror and Matilda of Flanders, he received an education and was literate. Immediately upon the death of his brother, King William II Rufus on Aug. 2, 1100, Henry, accompanied by two of Rufus's chief counselors, the Beaumont brothers, dashed to Winchester, seized the Treasury, and was proclaimed and crowned king of the English. His elder brother, Duke Robert Curthose of Normandy, had not yet returned from the First Crusade. Henry immediately issued his Coronation Charter, confirming the traditional rights of his barons and of the Church in England, and promising to right the wrongs of his brother. The new king also recalled from exile Abp. Anselm of Canterbury, whom Rufus had expelled and exiled from England, and he promised to rule the Church as Anselm wished. With Anselm's support, Henry quelled Curthose's invasion of 1102 without a battle, and the two brothers were reconciled. The king further solidified his rule by marrying Edith-Matilda, daughter of Malcolm and Margaret of Scotland, the latter of the old Anglo-Saxon royal lineage. Henry immediately began a policy of weeding out the most obstreperous of the barons, confiscating their lands and awarding them to more loyal followers.

But Anselm, having heard the decrees of the Papal Court, at once challenged Henry's right to invest clerics and receive their homage, beginning the INVESTITURE contest in England. King and archbishop tried to persuade Pope Paschal II to rescind these decrees for England, with Anselm even traveling to Rome to present his request to the pope in person. When Paschal refused, Henry at once offered him the choice of compliance with England's customs, or exile. Anselm chose exile. Soon thereafter, King Henry launched his attempt to conquer Normandy from his brother, Robert Curthose, but was stymied when Anselm threatened to excommunicate the king, causing some of Henry's allies to desert him. King and archbishop reconciled at a meeting at Laigle in 1105, Henry renouncing his right to investiture but retaining the right of homage of clerics; after papal ratification of the agreement, Henry and Anselm proclaimed their reconciliation publicly at Bec in 1106, and from Bec, now with Anselm's support, Henry proceeded to his victory at Tinchebray. In 1107, Henry and Anselm triumphantly held a great council at London, where king and archbishop appointed new clerics to the many vacancies in England, and Henry received their fealty.

Henry's great achievements were, first, to keep the peace in England for the entire 35 years of his reign; and second, to begin to build a bureaucracy which created the foundation for administrative kingship in England. Finally, he built a strong court of faithful and cooperative barons by judicious rewards of land and privileges, strategic marriage arrangements, particularly of heiresses; and the application of reason and order to a systematic reformulation of the government, but always based on England's Anglo-Saxon heritage. No wars disturbed England's prosperity during Henry's reign, while Normandy, touched by warfare on its borders during three crises—1111–1113, 1118–1119, and 1123–1124—also enjoyed internal peace. Law came to supercede violence as the means of settling property disputes, because of Henry's expansion and reform of the shire courts and use of royal justices in eyre. In Henry's reign began the elaborate records of the newly constituted exchequer, the Pipe Rolls; an avalanche of royal charters preserved the legal records; the first treatise on English Law, the *Leges Henrici Primi*, with its companion *Quadripartitus*, appeared; and the first evidence of a reformed royal household, with an elaborate and complex hierarcy of officials paid by fixed stipends, the *Constitutio Domus Regis*, issued from Henry's court. Henry's highly literate government, transformed by a new systematizing order, clearly underlay and prepared the way for his grandson, HENRY II.

Henry's foreign policy also aided England's peace. One of Henry's greatest triumphs was the marriage of his daughter, Matilda, to Emperor Henry V of Germany, but he also married many of his ''natural'' children to form alliances with many lords on the borders of the Anglo-Norman realm. The king habitually rewarded his loyal courtiers with marriages to heiresses, so that they owed their wealth and prestige to him, assuring their loyalty. The greatest challenge to the peace was the claim of Henry's nephew, William Clito, son of Robert Curthose, to the Anglo-Norman realm—a challenge which Henry's skillful alliances helped to quell.

Henry I's ecclesiastical policies were energetic and benevolent. After he had reconciled with Anselm, Henry founded the sees of ELY (1109) and CARLISLE (1133). He presided over generous and rich benefactions made by his many courtiers to the various abbeys of England and Normandy. Henry himself was the most generous donor to the building of Cluny III, lavishing enormous wealth on it during the building program and involving himself in CLUNY'S building personally. He founded, as his personal foundation, READING ABBEY, and installed Cluniac monks there in cooperation with Abbot PETER THE VENERABLE. Reading enjoyed many liberties and privileges beyond those of other English abbeys. Henry also supported CISTERCIAN and PREMONSTRATENSIAN foundations, which first entered England during his reign, as did GILBERT OF SEMPRINGHAM and his GILBERTINES. In Henry's reign also the traditional rivalry for precedence between the archbishops of CANTERBURY and YORK was definitely settled when York was freed from all subordination to Canterbury. It was as a consequence of this quarrel that Henry permitted papal legates access to England at last in 1125.

Henry was buried in Reading. His insistence that the English barons recognize the EMPRESS MATILDA as his successor would have passed the succession on peacefully, had not his nephew, STEPHEN, seized the throne unexpectedly, violating his own oath of fealty to the empress. There resulted widespread chaos and civil war throughout Normandy and England that threatened to undo all of Henry's constitutional and administrative achievements.

Bibliography: JOHN OF WORCESTER, *The Chronicle of John of Worcester*, ed. tr. R. R. DARLINGTON, P. MCGURK, and J. BRAY 3 v. (Oxford Medieval Texts 1995–2000). *Two of the Saxon Chronicles Parallel*, ed. C. PLUMMER, 2 v. (Oxford 1892–9). EADMER, *Historia Novorum*, ed. M. RULE [*Rerum Britannicarum medii aevi scriptores* (New York 1964—) 81:1884]. WILLIAM OF MALMESBURY, *Gesta Regum Anglorum*, ed. tr. R. A. B. MYNORS, R. M. THOMSON and M. WINTERBOTTOM, v.1 (Oxford Medieval Texts 1998). O. VITALIS, *The Ecclesiastical History of Orderic Vitalis*, ed. tr. M. CHIBNALL, 6 v. (Oxford Medieval Texts 1969–80). HENRY OF HUNTINGDON, *Historia Anglorum*, ed. tr. D. GREENWAY (Oxford Medieval Texts 1996). SYMEON OF DURHAM, *Libellus de Exordio atque Procursu istius hoc est Dunhelmensis Ecclesie*, ed. tr. D. ROLLASON (Oxford Medieval Texts 2000). L. H. PRIMI, ed. tr. L. J. DOWNER (Oxford 1972). *Regesta Regum Anglo-Normannorum*, ed. C. JOHNSON v.2 (Oxford 1956). C. W. HOLLISTER, *Henry I*, ed. and completed by A. C. FROST (New Haven 2001). M. BRETT, *The English Church under Henry I* (Oxford 1975). J. A. GREEN, *The Government of England under Henry I* (Cambridge 1986). C. W. HOLLISTER, *Monarchy, Magnates, and Institutions in the Anglo-Norman World* (London 1986). J. A. GREEN, *The Aristocracy of Norman England* (Cambridge 1997). C. A. NEWMAN, *The Anglo-Norman Nobility in the Reign of Henry I* (Philadelphia 1988). R. W. SOUTHERN, *St. Anselm and His Biographer* (New York 1963). S. N. VAUGHN, *Anselm of Bec and Robert of Meulan* (Berkeley and Los Angeles 1987). R. W. SOUTHERN, *Saint Anselm: A Portrait in a Landscape* (Cambridge 1990). *The Letters of Saint Anselm of Canterbury*, tr. W. FRÖLICH, 3 v. (Kalamazoo 1990–1994).

[S. VAUGHN]

Henry II, King of England.

HENRY II, KING OF ENGLAND

Reigned 1154–89; founder of the English common law; b. Le Mans, March 5, 1133; d. Chinon, July 6, 1189. By inheritance and by his marriage to ELEANOR OF AQUITAINE, Henry was lord of all western France from Normandy to Gascony, and he spent two-thirds of his reign in France. He increased his income by taking money instead of feudal military service. His greatest innovation was to create, out of scattered precedents of his predecessors, the English common law. His system was based on the circuit judge, the legal writ, and the jury. This procedure became so popular that almost all important cases came to his courts, thus increasing his power and income. The judges also sought out royal rights and revenues and checked the growth of other jurisdictions. By the end of the reign the royal courts had developed so rapidly that a formal treatise on the common law could be written.

In trying to increase the jurisdiction of his courts, Henry clashed with his former friend and chancellor, Thomas BECKET. On the issues of criminous clerks and appeals to Rome, precedents were confused, but neither man was willing to compromise. Becket was driven into exile for six years. On his return to England he promptly excommunicated some of Henry's supporters, and Henry, always a bad-tempered man, demanded vengeance. Four of his knights took him at his word and murdered the archbishop in his own cathedral on Dec. 29, 1170.

Henry took refuge in Ireland, where he completed the conquest begun by his vassals. An arrangement was finally made whereby he did public penance, allowed appeals to Rome, and gave clerics immunity from punishment in secular courts. On some other matters dealing with church property, his rules were allowed to prevail.

His last years were unhappy. PHILIP II AUGUSTUS, KING OF FRANCE, in alliance with Henry's own sons, attacked Normandy and Anjou. The old king, discouraged and disheartened, lost some frontier territories, though when he died, his empire was substantially intact. More important, the solid administrative and judicial structure that Henry had built in England continued to function smoothly, preserving the English monarchy during a dangerous quarter century when the king was either an absentee (Richard I), a neurotic (John), or a child (Henry III).

Bibliography: F. POLLOCK and F. W. MAITLAND, *History of English Law,* 2 v. (2d ed. Cambridge, Eng. 1898). A. L. POOLE, *From Domesday Book to Magna Carta, 1087–1216* (2nd ed. Oxford 1955) for sources and older bibliography. R. FOREVILLE, *L'Église et la royauté en Angleterre sous Henri II* (Paris 1943). J. BOUSSARD, *Le Gouvernement d'Henri II Plantagenêt* (Paris 1956). H. G. RICHARDSON and G. O. SAYLES, *The Governance of Medieval England* (Edinburgh 1963).

[J. R. STRAYER]

HENRY VIII, KING OF ENGLAND

Reigned, 1509 to 1547; b. Greenwich, June 28, 1491; d. Windsor, Jan. 28, 1547. Details of his early life are sparse, and not until his accession to the throne can he be seen clearly as an 18-year-old youth who was intelligent, handsome and confident, accomplished in sports (tennis, jousting, wrestling), a fine horseman, fluent in several languages, gifted in music and dancing, and set on a throne so well secured by his father that one could scarcely have begun a reign more propitiously.

Henry did not inherit his father's interest in the day-to-day business of government. Yet throughout his reign he was usually well informed and perceptive in his judgments. Moreover, he was the ultimate source of the major policies of his reign (which is not to deny that other people's ideas and outside events did much to shape them). He was a man with grandiose plans, but without the energy and, perhaps, the skill to execute them. Certainly he had not the character to apply himself to continuous hard work, and hence easily lost interest in business, excepting his own marriage problems. Henry was no working monarch; for two long stretches of his reign (*c.* 1513–29 and *c.* 1532–40), first Cardinal Thomas WOLSEY and then Thomas CROMWELL held sway, and royal government was virtually shed by the king and placed upon the chief minister. Henry always retained ultimate control and could make decisive, sometimes unpredictable, not to say impetuous, interventions. But he had no interest in letter writing; he quickly tired of reading long dispatches and did not worry about accounts. He was therefore a most difficult master to serve—now enthusiastic, cooperating with his servants; now suddenly intervening to halt or reverse a policy; now stricken with headache, bored with government, or absorbed in hunting, miles away from ministers and ambassadors.

Early Years of his Reign. Throughout his reign, but especially as a young man, Henry was hungry for glory and titles. He had been brought up in the chivalrous world of the tournament and the joust, and saw himself first of all as a warrior king. In 1512, the earliest that circumstances would permit, he led England back into her past and reopened the dynastic quarrels with France that had never really been settled in that interminable contest known as the Hundred Years' War (1337–1453). In 1513 he took a large army to Calais to repeat the exploits of Henry V, but won only a few trifling successes. To make war, to assert his title to the throne of France—this was a deep instinct. It came to the surface in the early years of his reign, again in the early 1520s (and after the French collapse in 1525 he seemed to be in sight of huge victory), and finally in the mid-1540s.

But Henry was restless, able and anxious to play several roles. Besides, he was not particularly brave and probably found the victory march more agreeable than the battlefield. By late 1516 he had given up fighting and was ready to appear as peacemaker of Europe, going so far as to preside in London (1518) over an elaborate bit of treaty-making intended to make war impossible. Several other projects occupied his mind. In 1519 he made what was, at least for a while, a serious attempt to be elected Holy Roman Emperor, an extraordinary episode owing as much to his rivalry with Francis I of France as to his taste for the flamboyant. In 1520 he was back in France on the Field of the Cloth of Gold, not this time to fight, but (as befitted his new role) to embrace his French brother and to match the chivalry of England and France in feasting and tilting.

Religions Policies. In 1521 and 1523 Henry was enthusiastic to have Wolsey elected pope. Henry, so to speak, had turned *dévot;* he had also turned theologian. In 1521 he completed a book against Luther, the *Defense of the Seven Sacraments.* Doubtless, he received much help with it; but it was truly his book, that is, put together and shaped by him. The stir caused by the book led Rome to confer upon him the title of DEFENDER OF THE FAITH, which he had been seeking for years. Perhaps the book was simply an intellectual exercise, for it is unlikely that Henry's Catholicism was ever more than nominal. That he heard at least three Masses a day, was generous in his offerings, dutiful to the Holy See and so on, proves little. It seems clear that his religion was formal, external, and ritualistic. Probably Henry would have come into some sort of conflict with the Church even if the problem of his marriage had not arisen. From about 1528 to 1529 he began to put forward growing claims to a responsibility, vested in him as king, for the spiritual welfare of his people. These pastoral claims later grew into the Royal Supremacy and owed their existence more, probably, to his appetite for title and the influence of Protestantism than to the so-called divorce. The divorce was a powerful additional cause of conflict, of course, but the influence of the writings of such men as William TYNDALE and the example of Protestant princes must not be forgotten.

The Divorce Proceedings. In 1527 Henry made the first move to have his marriage to CATHERINE OF ARAGON, whom he had married 18 years previously, declared null. This was not a question of "divorce" in the modern sense of the word. He wanted to be rid of Catherine because she had not produced—and now never would produce—the son whom, as he earnestly and understandably believed, the dynasty and the nation required. For a while he toyed with the idea of bringing forward an illegitimate son, the duke of Richmond, but he recognized that this would not have been a successful venture. Nevertheless, Henry had a second reason for wanting to get rid of Catherine: he had fallen in love with Anne Boleyn.

Two main arguments were adduced against the validity of his marriage: first, he claimed that because Catherine had previously been married to his elder brother Arthur (who had died without issue in 1502) and because the consequent impediment of affinity in the first degree collateral between him and Catherine rested on divine law, as he believed Leviticus showed, the dispensation he had received from Pope Julius II to marry her had been *ultra vires* and his marriage therefore an odious offense against the law of God. Such an argument, besides being intrinsically weak, immediately challenged papal jurisdiction and hence threatened the gravest consequences. It also exposed Henry to the devastating riposte that, since he had committed adultery with Anne's elder sister Mary, and since affinity sprang from illicit as well as licit union, he was related to Anne in exactly the same degree as he was to Catherine; and if he could not take Catherine to wife, no more could he take Anne.

Henry VIII, King of England.

So it was that a second, humbler argument was produced: Henry now claimed not that any papal dispensation of this kind was invalid but that this particular one, for a variety of reasons, was. The two arguments ran side by side for some time until, at the end, the first was paramount. Neither argument was particularly solid, but each precipitated a large volume of polemical literature written by theologians, canonists, and Scripture scholars, Jewish as well as Christian, from all over Europe.

The Papal Commission. Henry's ''great matter'' quickly became a complicated and, because Catherine was the aunt of the Emperor CHARLES V, an international affair. Henry's original plan was to settle the case quietly in England and present the world with a *fait accompli.* But Wolsey and William WARHAM were unwilling to take so grave a step and forced Henry to seek a special commission from Rome. At last, in 1529, a legatine court presided over by cardinals Thomas Wolsey and Lorenzo CAMPEGGIO met at Blackfriars in London to hear the case. But this court failed to grant Henry his urgent desire; to make matters worse, the cause was revoked to Rome, in response to Catherine's appeal; and Henry was called to appear there in person or by proxy. In reply to this disaster, he began, from 1530 onward, to advance claims that the case belonged by law to English jurisdiction, that ancient privileges and customs of the realm forbade CLEMENT VIII's action, and that he was an emperor, subject to no earthly jurisdiction. Pope Clement, caught between Charles and Henry, obeyed his instinct and procrastinated. Maddened by delay and what he assumed was wanton obstinacy, Henry grew bolder in his claims and began to bully the Church in England, partly to frighten Clement, partly to give flesh to those ecclesiastical ambitions already mentioned. For his failure, Wolsey was violently swept aside in late 1529 and shortly afterward the Reformation Parliament met. It began immediately to attack the clerical estate.

Henrician Reform. Brandishing the weapon of praemunire and with the anticlericalism of Parliament at his side, Henry set about bringing the English Church under his control. The first trial of strength came in 1531, and Henry was largely defeated; the second test in 1532 ended with the CONVOCATION OF THE ENGLISH CLERGY yielding to him their legislative independence. This was a vital concession. At the same time, Parliament passed the first overtly antipapal legislation. In May 1532 Lord Chancellor Thomas MORE resigned, and a little later Archbishop Warham died, thus making room for Thomas CRANMER. The following year Henry and Anne were married, in open defiance of Rome. In May 1533, fortified by a solemn judgment given by the English clergy in Convocation, Cranmer declared null Henry's marriage to Catherine. Just before this, Parliament had passed the act in restraint of appeals, which declared the ''imperial'' status of the realm and the king; that is, it had affirmed the jurisdictional self-sufficiency of the sovereign national state and brought to a climax the arguments that Henry had been advancing since 1530. The next year saw the breach with Rome completed.

As the Convocation declared, the bishop of Rome had now no more jurisdiction in England than any other foreign bishop. The supreme head of the Church of England, as it may now be called, is the king, upon whom God has directly bestowed a spiritual authority long usurped by popes but now at last recovered by its rightful owner. So declares the Act of Supremacy (1534). Christ's Church is an assembly of local churches, subject to the prince, who directs the life of his church, guards and declares its teachings, gives its bishops their jurisdiction, and corrects its people. Such is the *Ecclesia Anglicana.* The *plenitudo potestatis* and the *potestas iurisdictionis* have been conferred on the king by God. Parliament has merely declared this fact and laid down penalties for those who deny it.

Henry's Success. Those who did deny it—John FISHER, More, the Carthusians and the others, and later those taking part in the PILGRIMAGE OF GRACE were comparatively few. Henry carried the realm with him not because Englishmen did not understand or accept the papal primacy; they did, though they regarded Rome as the divinely appointed center of government of the Church, rather than as primarily the mouthpiece of the Church's growing understanding of revelation. Englishmen followed Henry into what was evident schism because the alternative was a cruel martyrdom or exile; because of national pride and the loyalty evoked by Tudor monarchy, which often came near to idolatry and was now a religious obedience; because Henry had moved slowly; because Clement had been provocative and negligent, giving neither guidance nor encouragement to his flock; because the case for the royal supremacy was ably backed by propaganda; because the breach with Rome might not be permanent. But above all Henry succeeded because he had allied himself with that discontent with the Church as an institution that was so obvious a feature of early Tudor life. Much of this anticlericalism may have been merely destructive and selfish. But some of it sprang from an altruistic idealism that was shocked by the condition of the Church, its wasteful absorption of so much energy and wealth, its privileges, its spiritual mediocrity (if not sterility) and an idealism that saw that a radical overhaul was necessary for the good of secular society as well as of the Church. Such anti-clericalism was a positive thing, not necessarily unorthodox (for it was present in Fisher and More), though the growing influence of Continental Protestantism would naturally tend more and more to make it so.

Henry had unleashed all this and placed himself at its head; and granted that he was a man of enlightenment, the breach with Rome, so it could be presumed, would not be merely a jurisdictional revolution but a major refashioning of the commonwealth. If Henry had set about cutting back this overgrown, ramshackle Church, there would have been brought back into fertile life an immense amount of wealth and manpower—with which to provide new and small dioceses, schools, colleges, and perhaps a determined attack on poverty. Add to this the hope of a new kind of hierarchy and clergy that was zealous, well-trained, and pastoral; and one glimpses the sort of expectations that some, perhaps only a small minority, had of this climacteric in English history, and doubtless still entertained in 1536 when the first steps were taken toward the greatest transfer of landed wealth since the Norman Conquest, namely, the dissolution of the monasteries.

Meanwhile, the marriage with Anne Boleyn had not produced the much-desired son. Instead Anne had had several miscarriages and only a daughter, the future Elizabeth I, had lived. Anne did not survive this failure for long. In 1536 she was beheaded for witchcraft and adultery. Henry then married Jane Seymour. She bore a son, Edward, but she died 12 days later. This was in late 1537. Two years afterward, Henry made his fourth and least successful essay in matrimony to Anne of Cleves, who, when she arrived in England, was found so disagreeable that the marriage was not consummated. It was quickly dissolved. Anne was dispatched home and replaced by Catherine Howard, who was charged with adultery and beheaded in 1542. The next year Henry married Catherine Parr, who survived him.

Development of Henrician Reformation. During the late 1530s there had been signs that, encouraged by Cranmer and Cromwell, Henry was moving toward Continental Protestantism. The Ten Articles of 1536 and the Bishops' Book of 1537, both, but especially the first, Lutheran in places, were followed by a project for a full alliance with the Lutheran princes of Germany. But by 1539 Henry had retreated from such a step, as the Act of Six Articles of that year showed, and in 1540 Henry completed the *démarche* by destroying Thomas Cromwell. In his eight years or so of power, Cromwell had shown himself a statesman and administrator of outstanding efficiency and versatility. Henry thus removed not only a loyal servant of the Crown but also one who left a deeper imprint on English life than, perhaps, any other minister, by his direction of the Henrician religious revolution, by carrying out widespread administrative changes, but especially by shaping English political life according to a new philosophy of state that owed a good deal to MARSILIUS OF PADUA.

Final Years. The last seven years of Henry's reign, during which ministers of the stature of Stephen GARDINER, rather than of Wolsey and Cromwell, were in power, were comparatively sterile. In the early 1540s Henry, who, thanks to the dissolution of the monasteries and heavy taxation of clergy and laity, enjoyed a huge income, returned to the war he had revived at the outset of his reign. In 1544 he made his last sortie to France and captured Boulogne. As in 1513, this invasion resuscitated the Old Alliance and England found herself engaged in large-scale war on two fronts. This was so expensive that the coinage had to be debased and further spoliation of the Church, especially of chantry lands was envisaged. The war with France lost momentum in 1546, however, and early the next year Henry died at Windsor. For a long time before his death there had been intense jostling for position when the old king should die and his son, a minor, come to the throne. When Henry's reign ended, power passed, according to his will, to a predominantly Protestant council, from which Stephen Gardiner and the duke of NORFOLK (now in the Tower) had been excluded.

Significance of Henry's Reign. Henry's great charm, his power to evoke loyalty (always dangerously close to the meanness and vindictiveness of the egoist), had for years been overlaid by truculence and fickleness. It is difficult to think of anything completely admirable about him at any time of his life, except, perhaps, his friendship with Cranmer; but beginning with the late 1520s, that is, after the divorce proceedings, he proved himself increasingly ruthless. Later on, illness made him yet more aggressive. Whether he suffered from syphilis, a brain disease, or, as lately suggested, gout, is not clear; but his decline seems beyond doubt. Perhaps the debate about his character will never end, but there can be no doubt about the significance of his reign. Henry may have lacked executive skill. He has been accused of being unoriginal and devoid of statesmanship. Though this may well be true and though the important ideas of his reign may have been intuitive or imitative or even supplied by others rather than born of deeply pondered strategy, he was nonetheless the prime mover of momentous change. The two provinces of the English Church had renounced their allegiance to Rome and their visible membership in a unitary Christendom, and had been united under the Crown. Monasticism had been abolished and the clerical estate humiliated.

Even if England had not subsequently undergone further theological change, what Henry accomplished would have left a profound mark on the mind, heart, and face of England. That country acquired a new political unity following the destruction of the greatest ''liberty'' in the land, namely, an independent Church. Between 1534 and 1536 Wales was incorporated into the political life of the kingdom; a determined attempt was made to do the same in Ireland; and the reshaping of the councils in the north and west of England was carried out under the direction of a reformed central government. Meanwhile, important things happened to Parliament. Neither Henry nor Cromwell invented Parliament or the statute; the latter was already the highest form of law-making in the land. But Cromwell proclaimed the omnicompetence of statute law and, whatever Henry may have thought about the matter, firmly placed secular sovereignty in king-in-parliament. And while this was happening, Parliament produced a body of statutes whose size and importance was not surpassed until the 19th or even 20th century. Henry's reign saw England become once more a major power in Europe and finally brought a profound transformation to the English navy.

Many of these things had caused bloodshed, uprooting, and discontent. One manifestation of this discontent was the Pilgrimage of Grace. The resumption of an aggressive European policy and the consequent wars against France and Scotland strike one today as retrogressive folly; they were certainly very costly. The debasement of the coinage necessitated by the wars at the end of the reign was a dubious tactic. Such was his preoccupation with Europe and his own domestic affairs that Henry showed no interest in the new worlds that Iberian ships were now opening up, and to which his father, albeit fitfully, had turned. As a result, when England at last entered this field later in the century, it found itself generations behind the Spanish and Portuguese. But above all Henry had failed to turn to good use the vast new powers and the wealth that the Reformation had brought him. Looking back on his reign one can see that, despite his alleged concern for the *cura animarum* vested in kingship, little was done to revivify the spiritual life of the English people or to cleanse the English Church. A few bishoprics were founded, and a few new professorships. Small endowments went to Oxford and Cambridge. These were steps in the right direction, but such small steps. Very little was done to raise the standard of the secular clergy or to purge the Church of its parasites. Henry had posed as a liberator of the English people from the bonds of the usurped and overbearing authority of the papacy, but the English Church found its new overlord far more exacting than the old and found royal taxation several times heavier than anything the popes had imposed. Worst of all, the great wealth of English monasticism, instead of being used, as some had hoped, for social and educational purposes, was squandered on war. Few kings have had it in their power to do greater good than Henry, and few have done less. Henry was not really interested in education, or social justice, or the spiritual well-being of his subjects and the Church over which he ruled as *summus episcopus.* He was scarcely touched by the ideals of the northern humanists or the reformers.

See Also: REFORMATION, PROTESTANT (IN THE BRITISH ISLES).

Bibliography: J. S. BREWER et al., eds, *Letters and Papers . . . of the Reign of Henry VIII,* 22 v. (London 1862–1932), basic work. G. R. ELTON. *Henry VIII* (London 1962); *Tudor Revolution in Government* (Cambridge, England 1959). A. F. POLLARD, *Henry VIII* (New York 1951); *Wolsey* (New York 1929). P. HUGHES, *The Reformation in England,* 3 v. in 1 (5th, rev. ed. New York 1963). D. KNOWLES, *The Religious Orders in England,* 3 v. (Cambridge, England 1948–60) v.3. C. READ, ed., *Bibliography of British History: Tudor Period, 1485–1603* (2d ed. Oxford 1959), for a complete bibliog. J. D. MACKIE, *The Earlier Tudors, 1485–1558* (New York 1952). J. W. ALLEN, *A History of Political Thought in the Sixteenth Century* (3d ed. rev. New York 1957). S. T. BINDOFF, *Tudor England* (Baltimore 1952). H. M. SMITH, *Henry VIII and the Reformation* (London 1948). F. M. POWICKE, *The Reformation in England* (New York 1941). K. PICKTHORN, *Early Tudor Government: Henry VIII* (Cambridge, England 1934). G. BASKERVILLE, *English Monks and the Suppression of the Monasteries* (London 1940). G. MATTINGLY, *Catherine of Aragon* (Boston 1941). L. B. SMITH, *Tudor Prelates and Politics, 1536–1558* (Princeton 1953). W. G. ZEEVELD, *Foundations of Tudor Policy* (Cambridge, MA 1948). F. HACKETT, *Henry the Eighth* (New York 1929), a psychological study. G. R. ELTON, *Reform and Reformation: England 1509–1558* (Cambridge, MA 1977). J. J. SCARISBRICK, *Henry VIII* (Berkeley 1968). L. B. SMITH, *Henry VIII: The Mask of Royalty* (Boston 1971). R. M. WARNICKE, *The Rise and Fall of Anne Boleyn* (Cambrige 1989).

[J. J. SCARISBRICK]

HENRY IV, KING OF FRANCE

The French king who ended the religious wars and began the Bourbon dynasty; b. Pau (Basses Pyrénées), Dec. 14, 1553; d. Paris, May 14, 1610. Henry, a direct descendant of St. Louis IX, was born to Antoine de Bourbon, the duke of Vendôme, and Jeanne d'Albret, the queen of Navarre. Although baptized a Roman Catholic, Henry was instructed as a Protestant upon his mother's wishes, and in 1568 he joined the Huguenot forces of Gaspard Coligny at La Rochelle. Upon the death of his mother (1572), he became king of Navarre and married Margaret de Valois, the sister of Charles IX. The marriage celebrations were marred by the ST. BARTHOLOMEW'S DAY MASSACRE (Aug. 24, 1572). Henry abjured Protestantism at this time, but in 1576 he rejoined the Huguenot forces, and by the treaty of Beaulieu he was given the government of Guienne. Although he became heir presumptive to the throne in 1584 following the death of the duke d'Anjou, brother of Henry III, he was declared ineligible by the Treaty of Nemours (1585). His exclusion from the succession was also declared by a bull of Sixtus V on Sept. 9, 1585, but *parlement,* reacting against papal interference, refused its publication. The assassination of Henry III on Aug. 1, 1589, brought the succession issue to a climax.

Struggle for the Crown. The Holy League, composed of Catholic nobles, lawyers, bourgeois, and townspeople, and supported by the Guise family and encouraged by Spain, made the reluctant Cardinal Charles de Bourbon, Prince de Condé, King Charles X. Meanwhile, Henry tried to take Paris by force of arms, winning victories at Arques (1589) and at Ivry (1590), but failing before reaching Paris. The cardinal's death on May 9, 1590, undermined opposition to Henry's claims. Actually, few bishops had supported the Holy League, and with growing suspicion of Spanish aims, moderate members of the league hoped that the religious obstacle to Henry's recognition could be removed. On Sept. 21, 1591, an assembly of prelates at Chartres rejected the bull of excommunication sent the preceding March by Sixtus V. Since Henry's conversion to Catholicism was indispensable to his acceptance as sovereign, Jacques Davy DUPERRON, soon to be consecrated bishop of Evreux (1595), instructed him for several months. Renaud de Beaune, Archbishop of Bourges, convened a number of prelates in July of 1593 to give the final instructions and to question Henry on the Catholic religion.

Abjuration of Protestantism. On July 25 at Saint-Denis, amidst great pomp, the king abjured the Protestant religion. Negotiations to remove the last obstacle to Henry's reception into the Church were conducted with the papacy by Duperron, Arnaud d' OSSAT, Cardinal Jean de Gondi, and Alexandre Georges, SJ. On Sept. 17, 1595, Clement VIII gave Henry papal absolution upon the promise that the king's heir would be reared a Catholic, monasteries would be established throughout France in reparation for those destroyed, the Council of Trent would be proclaimed, and Catholic worship would be introduced into Huguenot towns. On April 13, 1598, at Nantes, Henry issued an edict of tolerance designed to resolve the Huguenot question. While not establishing complete equality, the edict granted freedom of conscience, civil liberty, freedom of worship in many areas, and a measure of personal security to Protestants (*see* NANTES, EDICT OF). On Dec. 17, 1599, Henry's marriage to Margaret of Valois was dissolved by papal decree, and on Oct. 5, 1600, he married Marie de Médicis. She gave birth to the future Louis XIII on September 27, 1601. The other royal children were Gaston, the duke of Orléans; Elizabeth, who married Philip IV of Spain; Christine, the duchess of Savoy, and Henrietta, who married Charles I of England.

Policies of State. Henry's greatness rests on his success in restoring order and tranquility to France after years of religious and political strife complicated by foreign interference. Henry's victory over the Spaniards at Fontaine-Française (1595) and his capture of Amiens brought Philip II to sign the peace of Vervins on May 2, 1598. This enabled Henry to devote his full energies to domestic affairs. Maximilien de Béthune, the duke of

Henry IV, King of France.

Sully (1560–1641), a staunch Huguenot and devoted servant of Henry, collaborated on the plan of rebuilding France. Finances were brought into order, taxes collected, a system of careful accounting instituted, and care taken in approving expenditures. Important advances were made in agriculture and industry. Canals and highways were constructed and the overseas explorations into Canada by Samuel de Champlain encouraged.

Henry strengthened royal power through a program that was continued by Cardinal RICHELIEU under Louis XIII and brought to eminence by LOUIS XIV. Determined to concentrate authority in his hands, he cajoled *parlement* into obedience, strictly supervised local administrations, and brought recalcitrant nobles into line. His son inherited a country ready to follow enlightened leadership. In foreign affairs, Henry aimed to make France a power by counterbalancing the Hapsburgs. To this end, alliances were undertaken with Sweden, many Swiss cantons, the duke of Lorraine, and leaders of Protestant states in Germany. To prevent Emperor Rudolf II from occupying the duchies of Cleves and Juliers, he assembled an army of 35,000 men for the campaign that he intended to start on May 19, 1610. On May 14 the king was assassinated by François Ravaillac.

Bibliography: HENRY IV, KING OF FRANCE, *Receuil des lettres missives de Henry IV,* ed. J. BERGER DE XIVREY and J. GUADET, 9

v. (Paris 1843–76); *Oeuvres . . . lettres et harangues* (Paris 1941). LEO XI, *Lettres du Cardinal de Florence sur Henri IV et sur la France,* ed. R. RITTER (Paris 1955). P. DE L'ESTOILE, *Journal pour le règne de Henri IV,* ed. L. LEFÈVRE and A. MARTIN, 2 v. (Paris 1948–58). P. FERET, *Les Grandes figures de l'histoire: Henri IV et l'Église* (Paris 1875). R. RITTER, *Henri IV lui-même: L'Homme* (Paris 1944). C. M. DE LACOMBE, *Henri IV et sa politique* (Paris 1860). F. T. PERRENS, *L'Église et l'État en France sous le règne de Henri IV. . . ,* 2 v. (Paris 1872). A. POIRSON, *Histoire du règne de Henri IV,* 4 v. (2d ed. Paris 1862–67). P. DE VAISSIÈRE, *Henri IV* (Paris 1928). P. F. WILLERT, *Henry of Navarre and the Huguenots in France* (New York 1893). M. REINHARD, *Henri IV, ou la France sauvée* (Paris 1958). P. ERLANGER, *St. Bartholomew's Night . . . ,* tr. P. O'BRIAN (New York 1962). H. PEARSON, *Henry of Navarre . . .* (New York 1963).

[D. R. PENN]

HENRY II, ROMAN EMPEROR, ST.

Reigned from June 7, 1002 until July 13, 1024; b. Bavaria or Hildesheim (?), May 6, 973; d. Grona by Göttingen, Germany. The son of Duke Henry II, the Quarrelsome, of Bavaria, and Gisela, daughter of King Conrad of Burgundy, and the great grandson of King Henry I of Germany, Henry received his earliest education from Bishop Abraham of Freising. Later, he began a clerical education at the cathedral school of Hildesheim, and he finished his education in Bavaria with Bishop Wolfgang of Regensburg, by whom he was introduced to the monastic reform emanating from Lotharingia. In 995, upon his father's death, he became Duke Henry IV of Bavaria and a loyal supporter of his second cousin Emperor Otto III. He married (995–97/1000) Kunigunde, countess of Luxembourg. After Otto III's death, Henry contended for the throne and had himself elected and anointed king in June at Mainz by Archbishop Willigis. Henry II's significance as king lay in his attempts to establish undiminished royal power over secular princes, his complex and manifold relations with the church, his efforts to integrate the realm, and his elevation of a sacral notion of rulership to a new height, which one finds expressed verbally, visually, and liturgically in the sources. He received the imperial coronation in Rome from Benedict VIII on Feb. 14, 1014.

Henry II's elevation to kingship did not come easily. In January 1002, when Otto III died in Italy without an heir, three main candidates emerged for the German throne. Of these, Henry had the strongest hereditary claim to succession, yet a large part of the nobility opposed Henry or did not initially support his candidacy. To fortify his position, Henry seized the *regalia,* including the Holy Lance, from the entourage bearing Otto III's body from Italy to Aachen through Bavaria, and in a series of ritual acts he played the role of next of kin and presumptive successor to the throne. Despite the opposition, Henry managed to have himself elected, anointed, and crowned king at Mainz in June by a small but influential group of nobles and churchmen. Thereafter, he achieved final recognition on the battlefield and made his first royal progress (*Umritt*) through the realm. On this progress, Henry had his election and kingship acclaimed and formally recognized by the peoples of the several duchies through a ritual repetition of ceremonial and constitutive acts.

In Henry II's foreign policy, three areas stand out: his long protracted feud or war with Boleslav Chrobry of Poland, his alterations of Otto III's policies regarding Italy and imperial ambitions, and his efforts to stabilize the West and establish the hereditary claim of the German king to the kingdom of Burgundy. One can argue that under Henry II the eastern borders of the German kingdom began to stabilize, the missionary expansion of the tenth century slowed, and Henry pursued an imperial policy within achievable limits. Henry's hostilities with Boleslav lasted most of his reign and drove him to ally with the heathen Liutizi against the Christian Boleslav. Henry's contemporaries criticized him harshly, and this criticism, coupled with the half-hearted support given Henry by the Saxon nobility, muted his effectiveness. He had to settle for compromises in 1005, 1013, and 1018, which granted Boleslav lands in the East as fiefs, yet curtailed Boleslav's takeover of Bohemia.

Henry's policies in Italy mark a pronounced shift of emphasis, of his rulership in comparison to his Ottonian predecessors. Whereas Otto III spent over fifty percent of his reign in Italy, Henry spent only seven percent of his reign there. He made only three trips to Italy, in 1004 to foil Arduin's usurpation of the Italian kingship, in 1013–14 to support Pope Benedict VIII by reissuing the *Privilegium Ottonianum* and to acquire the imperial coronation, and in 1022 to reassert imperial dominion over Capua and Salerno in the face of Byzantine advances in southern Italy. Despite his infrequent visits to Italy, Henry's charters, regardless of where issued, document intensive rulership activity there. Finally, Henry's initiatives in Burgundy set the stage for the acquisition of that kingdom by his successor, Conrad II.

Henry II's internal policies developed from his concept of a divinely ordained kingship with undiminished royal power in both the secular and the ecclesiastical spheres. Henry strengthened the authority of the king over German dukes, princes, and prelates, systematically augmented the wealth and the political and economic *servitium regis* of bishoprics and royal monasteries, and supported a general reform movement in the Church. Attempting to break up concentrations of princely power,

Henry moved with varying success against dukes and princes alike. He managed to integrate the southern duchies more fully into the realm, to diminish the power of numerous magnates, and often to empower churchmen in their place. Henry's enrichment and empowerment of royal churches, both episcopal and monastic foundations, came with significant increases in royal dominion over these institutions, especially the king's right to invest, sometimes even appoint, bishops, abbots, and abbesses, and to employ candidates from the royal chapel in ecclesiastical positions throughout the realm. Thus, he used the royal church as well as itinerant kingship to bolster his power and to integrate the realm.

Nevertheless, Henry took his divinely conceded obligations seriously. He participated in monastic and episcopal prayer fraternities and became a canon in several cathedral chapters. The reinstatement of the bishopric of Merseburg (1004) and the foundation of the bishopric Bamberg (1007) count as Henry's greatest ecclesiastical achievements. He also founded numerous monasteries and imposed a Lotharingian-based monastic reform on many powerful royal monasteries. Finally, he took active part in numerous German synods and with the pope in general reforming synods of 1014 and 1022. He died in 1024 at the royal residence of Grone and received burial in the cathedral at Bamberg. Soon after his death legends began to circulate about the chastity of his marriage and his religious character. When Pope Eugene III canonized him in 1146, Henry became the sole medieval German king to be so honored.

Feast: July 15; in the diocese of Bamberg, July 13.

Bibliography: ADALBERT, *Die Vita sancti Heinrici regis et confessoris und ihre Bearbeitung durch den Bamberger Diakon Adelbert*, ed. M. STUMPF, *Monumenta Germaniae Historica, Scriptores rerum Germanicarum* 69 (Hanover 1999). ADALBOLD, *Vita Heinrici*, ed. H. VAN RIJ, *Nederlandse Historische Bronnen* 3 (Amsterdam 1983). *Monumenta Germaniae Historica, Diplomata regum et imperatorum Germaniae 3: Heinrici II. et Arduini Diplomata*, ed. H. BRESSLAU (Hanover 1900–03). J. F. BÖHMER, *Regesta Imperii 2 (Sächsisches Haus 919–1024)/4: Die Regesten des Kaiserreiches unter Heinrich II. 1002–1024*, new ed. by T. GRAFF (Vienna 1971). S. HIRSCH, *Jahrbücher des Deutschen Reiches unter Heinrich II.*, 3 v. (Berlin 1862–75 repr. 1975). H. HOFFMANN, *Mönchskönig und rex idiota: Studien zur Kirchenpolitik Heinrichs II. und Konrads II* (Monumenta Germaniae Historica Studien und Texte 8; Hanover 1993). R. KLAUSER, *Der Heinrichs- und Kunigundenkult im mittelalterlichen Bamberg. Historischer Verein Bamberg, Berichte* 95 (Bamberg 1957). B. SCHNEIDMÜLLER and S. WEINFURTER, eds. *Otto III. und Heinrich II.: Eine Wende?*, Mittelalter-Forschungen 1. (Sigmaringen 1997). R. FOLZ, "Le légende liturgique de saint Henri II, empereur et confesseur." *Clio et son regard. Mélanges d'histoire, d'histoire de l'art et d'archéologie offerts à Jacques Stiennon*, ed. R. LEJEUNE and J. DECKERS (Liège 1982), 245–58. A. WOLF, "*Quasi hereditatem inter filios*: Zur Kontroverse über das Königswahlrecht im Jahre 1002 und die Genealogie der Conradiner." *Zeitschrift der Savigny-Stiftung, Germanistische Abteilung* 112 (1995): 64–157. *Kaiser Heinrich II. und seine Zeit* in *Historischer Verein Bamberg, Bericht* 133 (1997). S. WEINFURTER, *Heinrich II. Herrscher am Ende der Zeiten* (Regensburg 1999).

[J. BERNHARDT]

HENRY III, ROMAN EMPEROR

June 4, 1039 to Oct. 5, 1056; son of CONRAD II and Gisella; b. Osterbeck, Oct. 28, 1017. His father named him his successor in 1026, and he was crowned as joint king in 1028. Following a good education, he was married (1036) to Gunhild (d. 1038), the daughter of CANUTE OF ENGLAND AND DENMARK; in 1043, after the death of Gunhild, he married Agnes of Poitou (d. 1077). In 1038 he became Duke of Swabia, and the following year he succeeded his father. During the more than 15 years of his reign, Henry demonstrated his deep concern for the future of the German monarchy and for the reform of the Church. The new king's first task was to enlarge and consolidate the royal domains. He attempted to retain control and to administer personally Swabia, Bavaria, and Carinthia, but he was finally forced to rule through elected dukes. He came to rely upon such ecclesiastical princes of the Empire as ADALBERT OF BREMEN, with the result that he has been blamed for weakening the monarchy, for whose future he had such genuine anxiety. Too often, the bishops he trusted betrayed his confidence and acted from motives as base as those of the turbulent lay nobility. Despite Henry's efforts at enforcing the PEACE OF GOD, private war flourished throughout his reign. Nevertheless, his efforts were rewarded, since Bratislav I did homage for his Duchy of Bohemia in 1041. Subsequently, Henry received the homage of King Peter of Hungary.

Both Henry and his second wife Agnes were persons of deep piety. Agnes' family had founded the monastery of Cluny, where the reform movement of the tenth century began. In 1046 Henry's interest in the reform in the Church took him to Italy to settle the question of papal succession, disputed by three claimants: Benedict IX, Sylvester III, and Gregory VI. For Henry sincerely believed that a healthy papacy was fundamental for a reformed Church. At Piacenza in November, Henry met Gregory, who greeted him with full honors. Nevertheless, Henry brought about the deposition of Gregory and Sylvester in a synod at Sutri and declared Benedict deposed at a later synod in Rome. He then selected a bishop from his retinue, Suidger of Bamberg to the throne of St. Peter. Suidger, who took the name Clement II, crowned Henry and Agnes emperor and empress on Christmas Day 1046. Clement also granted Henry the title *Patricius Romanorum*, which gave ecclesiastical sanction to his role as the defender of the Church. Henry's influence was paramount in the selection of the three popes after Clement II, the most important of whom was LEO IX. At his accession in 1049, the imperial effort at reform was reinforced by vigorous, intelligent pope, who spent most of his five-year pontificate traveling throughout Europe in an attempt to correct ecclesiastical abuses.

Henry's final journey to Italy, in 1055, when be accompanied Pope VICTOR II for his coronation, was marked by his failure to gain the submission of the Count of Tuscany, a failure pregnant with significance for future relations between the papacy and the Empire. Henry died at Bodfeld and was buried in the cathedral of Speyer. His heir was a mere boy; and the great edifice of Empire, which he had defended, had no protector.

Henry's legacy is ambivalent. He certainly succeeded in freeing the papacy from the control of Roman aristocrats, who, if the reformers' reports are to be believed, used the institution only for their own material advantage. In contrast, between 1046 and 1057 there were five German popes, but inspired by the reform movement, which was very strong north of the Alps, the papacy was not about to develop into an imperial chaplaincy. The popes took the opportunity that the minority of his son Henry IV provided to assert their independence of the empire and of lay control. In doing so they struck at the foundation of the very institution that been instrumental in initiating ecclesiastical reform, since control of the Church was integral to the success of the imperial government. In strengthening the papacy, Henry weakened the throne upon which his successors would sit. But the future seems clear only in retrospect. Henry approached his obligations with a high seriousness and fulfilled them with considerable skill. His premature death at the age of 39 and the events that flowed from it were not within his ability to foresee.

Bibliography: E. L. H. STEINDORFF, *Jahrbücher des deutschen Reichs unter Heinrich III,* 2 v. (Leipzig 1874–81). P. F. KEHR, *Vier Kapitel aus der Geschichte Kaiser Heinrichs III* (Berlin 1931). G. LADNER, *Theologie und Politik vor dem Investiturstreit* (Baden bei Wien 1936). T. SCHIEFFER, *Lexikon für Theologie und Kirche*, ed. J. HOFER and K. RAHNER (Freiburg 1957–65) 5:180. M. L. BULST-THIELE, *Kaiserin Agnes* (Hildesheim 1972). K. HAMPE, *Germany under the Salian and Hohenstaufen Emperors* (Oxford 1973). H. FUHRMANN, *Germany in the High Middle Ages, c. 1050–1200,* tr. T. REUTER (Cambridge 1986). J. FLECKENSTEIN, ed., *Investiturstreit und Reichsverfassung* (Sigmaringen 1973). R. SCHIEFFER, *Die Entstehung des päpstlichen Investiturverbots für den deutschen König,* (Stuttgart 1981). U.-R. BLUMENTHAL, *The Investiture Controversy: Church and Monarchy from the Ninth to the Twelfth Century* (Philadelphia 1988).

[J. M. POWELL/T. E. CARSON]

HENRY IV, ROMAN EMPEROR

Reigned 1056 to Aug. 7, 1106; b. Goslar, Germany, Nov. 11, 1050; d. Liège, buried Speyer. In 1056, on the death of his father, HENRY III, he obtained the throne under the regency of his mother, Agnes of Poitou, and of ANNO OF COLOGNE and ADALBERT OF BREMEN. After reaching his majority in 1065, he married Bertha of Saxony and inaugurated a policy aimed at extending the royal power, which had declined during the regency. The INVESTITURE struggle arose out of Henry's concern over the weakening of his power over the German bishops, who exercised broad authority and influence in the empire, and over his unwillingness to accommodate the principles of the GREGORIAN reform.

The revolt of Saxony in 1073 had led to stern measures of repression on Henry's part, including the imprisonment of rebellious Saxon bishops. Moreover, the period of the regency had witnessed the return of open simony. GREGORY VII, elected in 1073, decided to take a firm hand in these matters. In 1075 he promulgated his decree against lay investiture and stated his theory of papal control over the bishops. Henry regarded this act as an invasion of his rights, ignored the pope, and intervened in episcopal elections in Milan. The papal legates summoned Henry to Rome. The emperor's response was the deposition of the Pope at Worms, supported by the majority of the German hierarchy (Jan. 24, 1076), an act later ratified by a meeting of North Italian bishops. Undeterred, Gregory excommunicated the emperor (February 14), forbidding his subjects in Germany and Italy to do him homage, thus virtually inviting the restive German nobility to rebel. This move was successful and Henry was ordered to appear before a German synod to be presided over by the pope and set for February 1077. He anticipated this unwelcome meeting by hastening to Canossa, where he did penance and received the absolution of the pope (Jan. 28, 1077). But the German princes, bent on preventing further growth of royal authority, ignored the reconciliation and elected Rudolf of Swabia as king. Henry faced a civil war. Again excommunicated by Gregory in May 1080, the emperor deposed the pope anew and secured the election of GUIBERT OF RAVENNA as Antipope Clement III. He then turned his attention to Rome. In June 1083 he entered the Leonine City and was crowned emperor in St. Peter's by Clement (Easter 1084). With the arrival of Robert Guiscard and the NORMANS, Henry was forced to suspend operations. He returned to Germany, where Herman of Luxembourg, chosen successor to Rudolf, led the opposition. Henry's war with Gregory continued as a propaganda struggle until the pope died in 1085. After the brief reign of VICTOR III, Henry renewed his quarrel with URBAN II. But revolt by his son Conrad (d. 1101) forced him to abandon Italy and his antipope. His attempt to arrange terms with PASCAL II failed, and he found himself once more excommunicated in 1102. Finally, his son HENRY V revolted successfully in 1104, and Henry died in battle against him. His attempt to increase royal authority in the midst of the Gregorian reform ended in his own defeat and in the weakening of the empire.

Bibliography: G. MEYER VON KNONAU, *Jahrbücher des deutschen Reiches unter Heinrich IV und Heinrich V,* 7 v. (Leipzig 1890–1909). T. LINDNER, *Kaiser Heinrich IV* (Berlin 1881). K. HAMPE, *Deutsche Kaisergeschichte in der Zeit der Salier und Staufer,* ed. F. BAETHGEN (10th ed. Heidelberg 1949). A. FLICHE and V. MARTIN eds., *Histoire de l'église depuis les origines jusqu'à nos jours* (Paris 1935–) v.8. B. SCHMEIDLER, *Kaiser Heinrich IV und seine Helfer im Investiturstreit* (Leipzig 1927). G. TELLENBACH, *Church, State and Christian Society at the Time of Investiture Contest* (Oxford 1959). K. F. MORRISON, ''Canossa: A Revision,'' *Traditio* 18 (1962) 121–148.

[J. M. POWELL]

HENRY V, ROMAN EMPEROR

Reigned Jan. 5, 1106, to May 23, 1125; b. Turin, 1081; d. Utrecht. The son of HENRY IV and Bertha, he was elected German king in 1098 in place of his brother Conrad. He deposed his excommunicated father in 1106 and was crowned emperor in 1111. This scheming, crafty ruler, so adroit in negotiation, was widely respected but loved by none. He pursued his father's policy of intransigence toward the papacy, though in a different fashion. He employed nobles in government and invested even more prelates than his father, meanwhile neglecting the rising communes and the *ministeriales.* In 1111 when he was in Rome for his coronation, his ferocious conduct moved Pope PASCHAL II to decree the Church's abandonment of all REGALIA, although this act was almost immediately repudiated by a Church synod. After Henry suffered crushing defeats by German rebels both lay and ecclesiastical in 1116, he could no longer withstand demands that he negotiate with CALLISTUS II to resolve the empire-papacy struggle (*see* INVESTITURE STRUGGLE). The resulting Concordat of WORMS (Sept. 23, 1122) recognized the validity of the ruler's claim in both the regalian rights and in the ecclesiastical character of the same prelate. The Diet of Bamberg made the concordat imperial law and the LATERAN COUNCIL of 1123 gave it canonical validity. Henry was defeated by the Saxons in his last year, and the electors, headed by his foe, Abp. Adalbert of Mainz, rejected the childless Henry's candidate for king and substituted Duke Lothair of Saxony. This marked the end of Salian monarchy. Thus it was demonstrated that the imperial constitution was now controlled by the aristocracy and that the hereditary principle had yielded to election in choosing the Roman emperor.

Henry V, Roman Emperor.

Bibliography: G. MEYER VON KNONAU, *Jahrbücher des deutschen Reiches unter Heinrich IV. und Heinrich V.,* 7 v. (Leipzig 1890–1909), v.6, 7. *Cambridge Medieval History* 5:154–166. C. W. PREVITÉ-ORTON, *The Shorter Cambridge Medieval History,* 2 v. (Cambridge, Eng. 1952) 1:469–500. A. HOFMEISTER, *Das Wormser Konkordat. Zum Streit um seine Bedeutung, mit einer textkritischen Beilage*, new editon with foreword by R. SCHMIDT (Darmstadt 1962). K. HAMPE, *Germany under the Salian and Hohenstaufen Emperors* (Oxford 1973). H. FUHRMANN, *Germany in the High Middle Ages, c. 1050–1200,* tr. T. REUTER (Cambridge 1986). J. FLECKENSTEIN, ed., *Investiturstreit und Reichsverfassung* (Sigmaringen 1973). R. SCHIEFFER, *Die Entstehung des päpstlichen Investiturverbots für den deutschen König,* (Stuttgart 1981). U.-R. BLUMENTHAL, *The Investiture Controversy: Church and Monarchy from the Ninth to the Twelfth Century* (Philadelphia 1988).

[S. WILLIAMS]

HENRY VII, HOLY ROMAN EMPEROR

Reigned Nov. 27, 1308, to Aug. 24, 1313; b. Henry IV of Luxembourg, between 1269 and 1279. Henry was chosen king of the Romans and emperor-elect after the assassination of Albert of Hapsburg. He was crowned in ceremonies held at Aachen on Jan. 6, 1309. He proved himself an able diplomat north of the Alps and founded his dynasty's fortunes. In Italy Henry failed. Arriving in

Henry VII, Holy Roman Emperor.

October of 1310, he had intended to arbitrate internecine disputes, pacify imperial Italy, and establish imperial rule and administration, as well as be crowned emperor. His attempts to rule, however, generated Italian opposition, especially among dominant northern Guelf lords and cities, and Tuscan communes led by FLORENCE. A lengthy siege of Brescia demonstrated his weakness, because he had to rely on local lords, especially Ghibellines, for military support, and unwillingly assumed a partisan role. Pope CLEMENT V at Avignon turned against Henry, and Robert of Anjou, king of Naples, rebelled. Henry entered Rome by force, and was crowned emperor, June 29, 1312. A six-week siege of Florence ended unsuccessfully on Oct. 31, 1312. In August 1313, Henry left Pisa to invade Naples, but died of malaria at Buonconvento, near Siena. His was the last sincere attempt of a Holy Roman emperor to establish imperial rule in Italy. The medieval Christian Empire had proven unable to defeat the combination of city-states, lay kingdoms, and a secularly oriented Avignon papacy. Henry was the ''alto Arrigo'' (high Henry) of Dante's *Divine Comedy.*

Bibliography: W. M. BOWSKY, *Henry VII in Italy: The Conflict of Empire and City-State, 1310–1313* (Lincoln, NE 1960). F. COGNASSO, ''L'unificazione di Lombardia sotto Milano,'' *Storia di Milano,* ed. G. TRECCANI DEGLI ALFIERI (Milan 1953–) 5:3–99. R. DAVIDSOHN, *Geschiehte von Florenz,* 4 v. (Berlin 1896–1927) 3:345–552.

[W. M. BOWSKY]

HENRY HEINBUCHE OF LANGENSTEIN

Conciliarist and theologian; b. Marburg, Germany, *c.* 1330; d. Vienna, Austria, Feb. 11, 1397. Entering the University of Paris in 1358, he became a master of arts in 1363 and taught and wrote on astronomy until he joined the theological faculty, subsequently becoming doctor of theology in 1375. He remained as a professor of Holy Scripture and became vice chancellor in 1378, the year the WESTERN SCHISM began. His *Epistola pacis* [ed. Von der Hardt, *Magnum oecumenicum Constantiense concilium* (Frankfurt 1697) 2:2–60] of May 1379 appears to be the first treatise to recommend the convocation of a general COUNCIL either by both popes or the cardinals, or by the whole episcopate. During the indecision of the new French monarch, Charles VI (d. 1422), the doctors of the university in a solemn session of May 20, 1384, declared for a general council and may have directed Henry to address all secular princes through his *Epistola concilii pacis* [ed. E. du Pin, *Opera Gersonii* (Anvers 1706) 2:809–840]. He then argued that the plight of the Church passed the norms in Canon Law and required extraordinary measures, for the Church in its totality must make its voice heard in a general council even if it must be summoned, not by papal authority, but by secular princes. The requirement was added, perhaps from the work of another German doctor, CONRAD OF GELNHAUSEN, that the Church must be reformed *in capite et in membris,* or totally and completely. The French political pressure that invaded the university sent Henry into exile, along with others of his fellow doctors, and he settled in a monastery at EBERBACH, from which he was summoned in 1380 by Albert III (d. 1395) to reconstitute the University of Vienna. Henry drew up the constitution of the university, which was established in 1384 by a ducal charter and a bull of URBAN VI. He was its most celebrated professor of theology and also served as its rector (1393–94). Three more works from his Vienna years show his continuing devotion to the cause of the Church and the papacy: *Contra Telesphorum* (1392, in B. PEZ, *Thesaurus anecdotorum novissimus* 26:505–564) against a propaganda prophecy by a Calabrian hermit; a poem *Carmen pro pace* (1393, ed. A. Kneer, *Römische Quartalschrift für christliche Altertumskunde und für Kirchengeschichte*, 1 suppl., 1893, 127–129) against the Avignonese pope; and *Epistola de cathedra Petri* (1395, ed. A. Kneer, *op. cit.* 134–145). Only a portion of

Henry's varied and penetrating works has been printed as indicated (*see* BIBLIOG.) by Pastor, Valois, and Heilig. He was an exegete and commented on Genesis (still unpublished). Some of his writings on ascetical theology and the Immaculate Conception have been printed only in part. He was an early translator of hymns and Psalms into German, and left the first Hebrew grammar known to be composed by a German. He can certainly be counted among the Christian humanists of the dawning Renaissance, and may yet receive other laurels as his work on the natural sciences becomes better known.

Bibliography: C. J. JELLOUSCHEK, *Lexikon für Theologie und Kirche*, ed. J. HOFER and K. RAHNER, 10 v. (2d, new ed. Freiburg 1957–65) 5:190–191. J. ZEMB, *Dictionnaire de théologie catholique*, ed. A. VACANT et al., 15 v. (Paris 1903–50; Tables Générales 1951–) 8.2:2574–76. K. J. HEILIG, *Römische Quartalschrift für christliche Altertumskunde und für Kirchengeschichte* 40 (1932) 105–176. N. VALOIS, *Le France et le grand schisme d'Occident*, 4 v. (Paris 1896–1902). K. HIRSCH, *Die Ausbildung der konziliaren Theorie im XIV. Jahrhundert* (Vienna 1903) 55–76. J. C. DIDIER, *Catholicisme* 5:617–618.

[S. WILLIAMS]

HENRY MURDAC

Cistercian monk, archbishop of York; d. Sherborne, England, Oct. 14, 1153. Henry, who first appears among the clergy of York, was invited to CLAIRVAUX by St. BERNARD, and there he embraced monastic life. In 1135 he was sent to Vauclair in the Diocese of Laon, France, with 12 monks to establish a monastery of which he became abbot. Before long he came into sharp conflict with the abbot of a neighboring Premonstratensian house, thus revealing the pugnacity and contentiousness that were to mar his later years. On the death of the abbot of FOUNTAINS, in England, Bernard dispatched Henry there to advise on the filling of the office. Murdac was himself elected and, on Bernard's instructions, accepted. During his short term of office, Fountains reached a new peak of vigor and fruitfulness: five daughterhouses were founded (four in England and Lysckloster in Norway), greater conformity to the severe discipline of Clairvaux was imposed, and the prosperity of the abbey increased. Intervening vigorously in the disputes that divided the CATHEDRAL CHAPTER and See of York, where the appointment of WILLIAM FITZHERBERT as archbishop had aroused bitter conflict, Murdac found himself attacked by Fitzherbert's party, which sacked and burned his abbey church and reduced the monastery to ruins. Murdac at once set about rebuilding. Present at the council in Paris in 1147, when Pope Eugene III deprived Fitzherbert, Murdac crossed again to France when the chapter's vote proved indecisive. Favored for York by Bernard and the Cistercian pope, he was received with honor at Trier, consecrated on December 7, and presented with the PALLIUM. Upon returning home he met with King STEPHEN's resentment, the confiscation of his prebends, and the hostility of his clergy and the populace. He retired to RIPON; and it was only after several years of fulmination and violence that the parties were reconciled and he was at last enthroned (January 1153). Before long another quarrel broke out, this time with DURHAM. Riots at York drove the archbishop to flight, and though the quarrel was soon patched up, he never returned alive to York. He was buried in York Minster. Murdac was a man of high integrity, personal austerity, and noble ideals, but severe, unyielding, and intolerant. Yet he enjoyed the uninterrupted sympathy and support of St. Bernard and raised the Cistercians in England to new heights of influence and achievement.

See Also: CISTERCIANS.

Bibliography: *Acta Sanctorum* June 2 (1863) 136–144. BERNARD OF CLAIRVAUX, Epistolae 106, 206, 320, 321; *Patrologia Latina*, ed. J. P. MIGNE (Paris 1878–90) v.182. W. H. DIXON, *Fasti Eboracenses*, ed. J. RAINE (London 1863) 310–320, 320–333. *The Dictionary of National Biography from the Earliest Times to 1900*, 63 v. (London 1885–1900) 13:1218–20; 1908) 7:173–176, summary of the conflict in York. D. KNOWLES, *The Monastic Order in England, 943–1216* (2d ed. Cambridge, Eng. 1962) 255–257.

[J. H. BAXTER]

HENRY OF BLOIS

Cluniac monk and bishop of Winchester; b. *c.* 1090–1100; d. Aug. 8, 1171. Henry, the most influential individual in the English Church between ANSELM OF CANTERBURY and Thomas BECKET, exemplified both the virtue and the weakness of CLUNY in his day. He was the fourth son of Stephen, Count of Blois, grandson of William the Conqueror, and brother of King STEPHEN OF ENGLAND. From boyhood he was educated at Cluny, where he formed a lifelong friendship with PETER THE VENERABLE. Henry I invited him to England as abbot of GLASTONBURY in 1126 and appointed him bishop of WINCHESTER in 1129; by papal dispensation he held both offices until his death, and from 1139 he was also dean of St. Martin-le-Grand, London. As abbot and bishop he won the respect of his monks and clergy. He was a remarkable administrator, who reorganized the estates and finances of Glastonbury and Winchester; a GREGORIAN REFORMER on political rather than moral lines; a great builder; and a munificent benefactor. He failed to secure papal consent for his translation to the archbishopric of Canterbury in 1136; but his appointment as papal legate from 1136 to 1143 made him in some ways superior to Archbishop THEOBALD. He attempted unsuccessfully to secure metropolitan status for the See of Winchester. In politics he played a dominant part in the struggle for the throne. He crowned Stephen in 1135 and, apart from a brief defection to Matilda in 1141, gave him powerful support while upholding the independence of the Church. On King HENRY II's accession in 1154 he left England for Cluny, where he reorganized the abbey's finances. After his return in 1158 he exerted a moderating influence, striving especially to keep the peace between Henry II and the new archbishop, Thomas Becket.

Bibliography: ADAM OF DOMERHAM, *Historia de rebus gestis Glastoniensibus,* ed. T. HEARNE, 2 v. (London 1727) 305–331. *The Letters of John of Salisbury,* ed. W. J. MILLOR and H. E. BUTLER, rev. C. N. L. BROOKE (New York 1955–) 1:253–256, *passim. The Historia Pontificalis of John of Salisbury,* ed. and tr. M. CHIBNALL (New York 1956) 78–80, 91–94. L. VOSS, *Heinrich von Blois, Bischof von Winchester, 1129–71* (Historische Studien 210; Berlin 1932). D. KNOWLES, *The Monastic Order in England, 943–1216* (2d ed. Cambridge, Eng. 1962) 282–298. F. L. CROSS, *The Oxford Dictionary of the Christian Church* (London 1957) 624–625.

[M. M. CHIBNALL]

HENRY OF BOLZANO, BL.

Ascetic; b. Bolzano, Italy, *c.* 1250; d. Treviso, Italy, June 10, 1315. Having moved to Treviso with his wife and son, Henry (or Rigo) began, after their deaths, to live in extreme poverty, devoting himself to humble trades, prayer and penance, and also, in his last years, to almsgiving. As he was famed for his holiness at the time of his death, large crowds attended his funeral, and his tomb in the cathedral of Treviso was a constant goal of pilgrimages for more than a year. Many miraculous cures were attributed to him, and a commission of bishops established some 346 of them in the space of a short time on the testimony of eyewitnesses. Among these witnesses was the Paduan Peter of Baone (d. *c.* 1383), later bishop of Treviso, who wrote a biography of Henry in 1381. BENEDICT XIV confirmed the cult for the Diocese of Treviso, and PIUS VII extended it to that of Trent.

Feast: June 10.

Bibliography: B. BONIFACCIO, *Il beato Enrico Trivigiano, panegirico sacro* (Treviso 1653); *Acta Sanctorum* June 2:363–386. I. ROGGER, *Bibliotheca sanctorum* (Rome 1961–) 4:1226–27. *Il beato Enrico da Bolzano nella sua vita e nel suo culto* (Treviso 1915). *Analecta Bollandiana* 45 (1927) 443. A. BUTLER, *The Lives of the Saints,* ed. H. THURSTON and D. ATTWATER, 4 v. (New York 1956) 2:520–521. R. DEGLI AZZONI AVOGARO, *Memorie del beato Enrico,* 2 v. (Venice 1760). A. TSCHÖLL, *Die Heiligen und Seligen Tirols,* v.2 (Austria sancta 6; Vienna 1910).

[M. MONACO]

HENRY OF BONN, BL.

Rhineland noble; b. *c.* 1100; d. Lisbon, 1147. Henry set out from Cologne on April 27, 1147, for the Second CRUSADE. He was among those who en route responded to the plea of Alphonso I of Portugal to help free Lisbon from the Saracens. Henry fell during the siege of Lisbon. After his burial near St. Vincent's church, miracles were reported at his grave, leading to his veneration as a martyr.

Feast: Oct. 18 or 25.

Bibliography: Academia das Sciencias de Lisboa, *Portugaliae monumenta historica* (Lisbon 1856–), *Scriptores* v.1. *Acta Sanctorum* Oct. 8:281. O. PFÜLF, ''Die Heerfahrt des sel. Heinrich von Bonn . . . ,'' *Stimmen aus Maria-Laach* 47 (1894) 24–48. J. TORSY, ed., *Lexikon der deutschen Heiligen . . .* (Cologne 1959).

[D. ANDREINI]

HENRY OF CLAIRVAUX, BL.

Cistercian abbot, cardinal; a.k.a. Henricus Gallus; b. at the Burgundian castle of Marcy; d. Arras, France, Jan. 1, 1189, buried at Clairvaux. He became a CISTERCIAN in 1155, abbot of HAUTECOMBE in 1160, and abbot of CLAIRVAUX in 1176. He served the popes by a mission to Abp. Henry of Reims (1162) and by reconciling King HENRY II OF ENGLAND with the Church of Canterbury (1178). Since 1178 he had been active in reconciling the ALBIGENSES; in 1181—by then cardinal bishop of Albano—he assumed leadership of that mission. He refused election to the papacy in 1187, preferring to dedicate himself to preaching a new CRUSADE. He persuaded FREDERICK BARBAROSSA to take the cross along with thousands of Germans (1188); before his death, he had arranged for treaties between France and England and enrolled Philip Augustus and Henry II in this, the Third Crusade.

Feast: July 4.

Bibliography: Letters and a treatise in *Patrologia Latina,* ed. J. P. MIGNE, 217 v. (Paris 1878–90) 204:215–402; 185:627–628. S. STEFFEN, ''Heinrich, Kardinalbischof von Albano: Ein Kirchenfürst des zwölften Jahrhunderts,'' *Cistercienser-Chronik* 21 (1909) 225–236, 267–280, 300–306, 334–343. G. KÜNNE, *Heinrich von Clairvaux* (Berlin 1909). Y. M. J. CONGAR, ''Henri de Marcy, abbé de Clairvaux, cardinal-évêque d'Albano et légat pontifical,'' *Analecta Monastica* 5 (1958) 1–90.

[J. R. SOMMERFELDT]

HENRY OF FRIEMAR

The Elder; b. *c.* 1245; d. Erfurt, Germany, Oct. 18, 1340. *Magister Parisiensis,* noted theologian, and preacher of the Order of the Augustinian Hermits, he is principally known as the author of numerous ascetical-mystical treatises that had considerable influence on the development of piety among clergy and laity. The popularity of these treatises is attested by their transmission in an extraordinarily large number of manuscripts still preserved, the early translation of some of them into the vernacular, and the fact that several also were repeatedly printed before and after 1500. The following works deserve special mention: *Tractatus de quattuor instinctibus,* a discussion of the four forces moving the human soul (God, angels, the devil, man's own nature) and their characteristics; *Tractatus de decem praeceptis,* a detailed popular explanation of the Decalogue; *Explanatio passionis Dominicae,* a description of the Lord's Passion on the basis of the Gospels, with explanatory additions and short affectionate prayers; *De adventu Verbi in mentem,* a mystical explanation of Lk 1.26–29; *De celebratione missae,* a comprehensive ascetical-mystical explanation of the Mass for the clergy. A great wealth of ascetical and mystical material also is found in Henry's sermons. Henry was the first Augustinian to write a short outline of the origin and development of his order after its establishment in its modern form in 1256, the *Tractatus de origine et progressu ordinis fratrum heremitarum sancti Augustini.*

Bibliography: JORDAN OF QUEDLINBURG, *Liber vitasfratrum* (1357), ed. R. ARBESMANN and W. HÜMPFNER (New York 1943). C. STROICK, *Heinrich von Friemar* (Freiburg 1954). R. ARBESMANN, ''Henry of Friemar's 'Treatise on the Origin and Development of the Order of the Hermit Friars and Its True and Real Title,''' *Augustiniana* 6 (1956) 37–145. A. ZUMKELLER, ''Die Lehrer des geistlichen Lebens unter den deutschen Augustinern vom 13. Jahrhundert bis zum Konzil von Trient,'' *Sanctus Augustinus vitae spiritualis magister,* 2 v. (Rome 1959) v.2. A. ZUMKELLER, ''Manuskripte von Werken der Autoren des Augustiner-Eremitenordens in mitteleuropäischen Bibliotheken,'' *Augustiana* 11 (1961) 285–337. U. STÄRMER, ''Mystik, wo sie niemand erwartet. Beobachtungen am Dekalogtraktat Heinrichs von Friemar und seiner hochdeutschen Übersetzung,'' *Jahrbuch der Oswald von Wolkenstein Gesellschaft* 6 (1991).

[R. ARBESMANN]

HENRY OF GHENT

Secular scholastic philosopher and theologian, known as *Doctor solemnis* and *Summus doctorum;* b. Ghent, *c.* 1217; d. Tournai, June 29, 1293. After early studies at the cathedral school of Tournai, he studied arts at Paris, then theology, probably under WILLIAM OF AUVERGNE and Geoffrey of Bar. As regent master in theology, he lectured at Paris from 1276 to 1292, becoming the most illustrious teacher in the last quarter of the century. Although he was canon of Tournai from 1267, archdeacon of Bruges in 1276 and of Tournai in 1278, he was intimately connected with affairs of the university (*see* PARIS, UNIVERSITY OF). He actively supported the condemnation of Latin AVERROISM in 1277, joined other masters in opposing their chancellor, Philip of Thory, in 1284, and was so violent an opponent of the MENDICANT orders between 1282 and 1290 that he was strongly reprimanded by the future BONIFACE VIII on Nov. 29, 1290. He attended the Council of Lyons in 1274 and took an active part in the synods of Sens, Montpellier, Cologne, and Compiègne. His contemporaries sometimes referred to him under the titles of *Doctor reverendus* and *Doctor digressivus.*

Principal Works. Between 1276 and 1292, Henry held both ordinary disputations and disputations *de quolibet* that were later published as his major contributions to theology. The ordinary disputations were published as a *Summa theologiae* (ed. Paris 1520; Ferrara 1646, etc.) in three parts. Although the prologue announced a complete course in theology dealing equally with God and creatures, the three parts deal exclusively with the nature of theological knowledge (arts. 1–20), the One God (arts. 21–52), and the Trinity (arts. 53–75). Consequently his *Summa* cannot be compared with the more complete and influential *Summa theologiae* of St. THOMAS AQUINAS. The 15 *Quodlibeta,* each consisting of many varied questions posed by students, were held during Advent and Lent from 1276 to 1292 (ed. Paris 1518; Venice 1613, etc.). Henry also wrote questions on the *Metaphysics* of ARISTOTLE and a commentary on the *Physics* (1278). Of the biblical lectures he was obliged to give as master, only an exposition of the first chapter of Genesis is known. Apart from sermons and a few treatises, other works listed by P. Glorieux are doubtful or spurious.

Historical Heritage. Henry was an independent thinker in the Augustinian tradition, equally opposed to the Christian Aristotelianism of St. Thomas Aquinas and to the Averroist Aristotelianism of SIGER OF BRABANT. After the condemnation of Latin Averroism in 1277, Christian thinkers were ready for a new type of PLATONISM and Augustinianism that would replace THOMISM. Consequently, in the last quarter of the 13th century there were at least two Augustinian approaches in Christian thought: the older Platonic Augustinianism of the Franciscan school and the new Avicennian Augustinianism developed by secular masters, notably, by Henry of Ghent. His historical heritage was, therefore, mainly Platonic, Augustinian, and Avicennian. His philosophy might be described as a Christian Avicennism wherein the fatalistic EMANATIONISM of Avicenna was replaced by the Christian concept of free creation in time.

Viewing the relation of faith and reason as distinct but harmonious, Henry did not disagree with St. Thomas essentially on this point. However, for him the notion of divine omnipotence occupies the central position in theology, a position it was to retain, in opposition to Thomistic theology, throughout the 14th century.

Essential Doctrines. Explaining the process of KNOWLEDGE, Henry combined Aristotelian abstraction with Augustinian reflection and illumination. In knowing physical realities, the intellect grasps concrete, existing things, while a higher knowledge reaches the world of possible essences, in themselves indifferent to existence, and of eternal truths that govern them, both being the object of metaphysical knowledge. Possible essences he divided into three primary genera: substance, quality, and quantity; these WILLIAM OF OCKHAM later reduced to two by identifying quantity with material substance. To substance belongs *esse in se;* to quantity and quality belongs *esse in alio.* These may also have an *esse ad aliud,* giving rise, in human thought, to relation and the other six categories (*sex principia*). Thus, the Aristotelian predicaments are no longer CATEGORIES OF BEING, but classification of concepts, later to be developed by NOMINALISM. At the root of Henry's thought is a misconception of ANALOGY that SCOTISM later developed as the univocity of being.

Between real and rational distinctions, Henry introduced a *distinctio intentionalis* to account for essential components, such as animality and rationality in the essence man. This was appropriated by DUNS SCOTUS as a *distinctio formalis* and extended to the whole realm of being.

For Henry, divine causality is exercised in two stages: (1) from all eternity God produced the exemplar ideas, or possible essences (*ideata*) by which His essence may be imitated in various *esse essentiae,* (2) in time, by a free act of will, God decided to give some of these essences actual existence (*esse existentiae*). Thus possible essences proceed from God by an eternal and necessary emanation, as Avicenna taught, while actual existence is a free creation *de novo,* as Christianity teaches. Henry's contemporaries and successors found this doctrine a threat to the Christian concept of creation *ex nihilo.* While he tried to preserve divine omnipotence in the creation of existents, he succumbed to NEOPLATONISM and Avicennism in the explanation of essences.

As all Neoplatonic philosophers, Henry was unable to resolve the duality between ideas and individual reality. Unique among scholastic thinkers, he maintained that there are no divine ideas of individuals, but only of species. Thus metaphysics, which is the science of universal ideas and possible essences, can never reach the individual. Concrete individuals, for him, are known only by the senses and by the intellect working with the data of sense; but this ''physical knowledge'' is not metaphysics. No sincere truth can be expected from sense knowledge alone, but it can be expected from reason judging sense knowledge in the pure light of eternal truth and divine illumination. Henry doubted that man can know truth about anything by his own natural powers alone and without some special divine illumination; at least such truths could not be called ''science.'' Thus, while the rational soul is created to know the rules of eternal truth, man cannot attain the pure truth naturally by his natural powers (*ex puris naturalibus naturaliter*), but must receive them from God, who freely offers Himself to whom He wills (*Sum. theol.* 1.1.2).

For Henry, the distinction between essence and existence is not a real one, since existence is not a thing (*aliqua res*) added to the essence of a creature (*Quodl.* 1.9). However, since an essence as such is something other than an existing essence, their distinction is not purely mental (*ratione*), but also intentional (*intentione*).

In natural philosophy, Henry did not conceive primary matter as a pure potentiality, but as a nature and a substance having its capacity for form from God (*Quodl.* 1.10). The weak and potential being (*esse*) of matter is not derived from form, but from God, who has a specific idea (*propriam ideam*) of it in His mind. Henry insisted on the unicity of form in all creatures other than man (*Quodl.* 4.13). A single natural generation terminates in only one form; yet the rational soul is not the term of generation, but of creation. Therefore the term of human generation is a corporeal form (*forma corporeitatis*) distinct from the rational form created by God.

Widely read, attacked, and defended, Henry had considerable influence on thinkers from the 14th to the 18th centuries, particularly on Platonists who wanted an alternative to Thomism. Though strongly attacked by Duns Scotus, William of Ockham, JAMES OF METZ, and DURANDUS OF SAINT-POURÇAIN, he unmistakably influenced their thought. In the 16th century, the Order of Servites, finding itself without an official doctor, thought that Henry had been a Servite and adopted him. This prompted the numerous editions of his major works.

Bibliography: J. PAULUS, *Henri de Gand: Essai sur les tendances de sa métaphysique* (Paris 1938); ''Les Disputes d'Henri de Gand et de Gilles de Rome sur la distinction de l'essence et de l'existence,'' *Archives d'histoire doctrinale et littéraire du moyen-âge* 15–17 (1940–42) 323–358. A. MAURER, ''Henry of Ghent and the Unity of Man,'' *Mediaeval Studies* 10 (1948) 1–20. R. J. TESKE. *Quodlibetal Questions on Free Will* (Milwaukee 1993). W. VANHAMEL, ed. *Henry of Ghent: Proceedings of the International Colloquium on the Occasion of the 700th Anniversary of his Death (1293)* (Leuven 1996).

[J. PAULUS]

HENRY OF GORKUM

Theologian; b. Gorkum, *c.* 1386; d. Cologne, 1431. In 1418 he was listed as a doctor at the University of Paris. The following year he taught philosophy at Cologne, and from 1420 he was director of a school of arts that apparently he founded in that city at his own expense. Later he was appointed a canon of the basilica of St. Ursula and pro-chancellor of the University of Cologne. He was active on the side of THOMISM in the famous dispute between the followers of St. Albert and those of St. Thomas Aquinas at the university. He left a fairly large number of works, some of them still unedited. Among the most important are his *Conclusiones et concordantiae Bibliorum et canonum in libros Magistri Sententiarum* (Cologne 1489), *Compendium Summae Theologiae sancti Thomae* (Esslingen 1473), *Tractatus consultorii circa divinas et humanas actiones et quorundam Bohemorum errores emergentes* (Cologne 1503).

Bibliography: M. GRABMANN, *Hilfsmittel des Thomasstudiums aus alter Zeit* (Freiburg 1923). H. HURTER, *Nomenclator literarius theologiae catholicae* 2:801–803. P. WILPERT, *Lexikon für Theologie und Kirche*2 5:189.

[C. R. MEYER]

HENRY OF HARCLAY

English theologian and ecclesiastic; b. *c.* 1270; d. Avignon, June 25, 1317. Master of arts at Oxford by 1296, he was ordained for the Diocese of Carlisle in 1297 and before 1310 was a master in theology. From Dec. 11, 1312, until his death, he was chancellor of the University of Oxford and directly involved in the university's dispute with the Dominicans over graduation in theology; as proctor of the university, he went to the Roman Curia at Avignon in 1317 to obtain a settlement of the dispute, but died without having obtained it. His importance as a theologian is represented by a commentary on the *Sentences* (Stegmüller, *Repertorium Commentariorum in Sententias Petri Lombardi* 1:154) and by his *Quaestiones ordinariae* (Worcester, Cath. Lib. MS F. 3), some of which have been published. Strongly rejecting the physical determinism of pagan philosophers, he protested against those ''who tried to make the heretic Aristotle a Catholic'' (F. Pelster, 351). At the height of the controversy between Thomists and Scotists, he wished to remain an independent critic and skeptic. Nevertheless he inclined toward Duns Scotus, whose arguments, distinctions, and solutions he used freely. His commentary on the *Sentences* relied so heavily on Scotus's *Lectura Cantabrigensis* that passages were borrowed verbatim by ALFREDUS GONTERI, a disciple of Scotus.

Bibliography: F. PELSTER, ''Heinrich von Harclay, Kanzler von Oxford, und seine Quästionen,'' *Miscellanea Francesco Ehrle,* 5 v. (Rome 1924) 1:307–356. C. BALIĆ, *Lexikon für Theologie und Kirche*, ed. J. HOFER and K. RAHNER, 10 v. (2d, new ed. Freiburg 1957–65) 5:190; ''Henricus de Harclay et Ioannes Duns Scotus,'' *Mélanges offerts à Étienne Gilson à l'Académie française* (Toronto 1959) 93–121. A. MAURER, ''Henry of Harclay's Questions on Immortality,'' *Mediaeval Studies* 19 (1957) 79–107. É. H. GILSON, *History of Christian Philosophy in the Middle Ages* (New York 1955). A. B. EMDEN, *A Biographical Register of the University of Oxford to A.D. 1500*, 3 v. (Oxford 1957–59) 2:874–875.

[C. BALIĆ]

HENRY OF HEISTERBACH, BL.

Cistercian abbot; b. *c.* 1180; d. *c.* 1244. Henry, born of a noble family and educated in Paris, became a canon of the church of St. Cassius in Bonn; about 1200 he entered the Cistercian Abbey of HEISTERBACH where he later became prior. In 1208 he was unanimously elected abbot. His reign marked the high point in the history of Heisterbach; under him the abbey church was completed (1237), the abbey's land holdings were enlarged, and the daughter house at Marienstatt was founded. He encouraged the important literary activity of CAESARIUS OF HEISTERBACH. Henry served the Church and the secular governments as a counselor, ambassador, and preacher of a CRUSADE.

Feast: Nov. 11.

Bibliography: CAESARIUS OF HEISTERBACH, *Dialogus miraculorum,* ed. J. STRANGE, 2 v. (Cologne 1851), bk. 1, ch. 13; bk. 7, ch. 39, and *passim;* ed. A. HILKA as *Die Wundergeschichten des Cäsarius von Heisterbach,* 3 v. (Bonn 1933–37), and tr. H. VON E. SCOTT and C. S. BLAND as *The Dialogue on Miracles,* 2 v. (London 1929). G. WELLSTEIN, ''Heinrich I, dritter Abt von Heisterbach,'' *Studien und Mitteilungen zur Geschichte des Benediktinerordens und seiner Zweige* 32 (1911) 405–418. A. M. ZIMMERMANN, *Kalendarium Benedictinum: Die Heiligen und Seligen des Benediktinerorderns und seiner Zweige,* 4 v. (Metten 1933–38) 3:290.

[J. R. SOMMERFELDT]

HENRY OF HERP (HARPHIUS VAN ERP)

Dutch mystical writer; b. probably at Erp (North Brabant), *c.* 1405; d. Mechlin, Feb. 22, 1477. He joined the Brethren of the Common Life, was rector of the house at Delft about 1445, and somewhat later was founder and rector of St. Paul's at Gouda. In 1450 he entered the Franciscan Observants while in Rome on pilgrimage. He held the office of guardian at Mechlin several times after 1454, and from 1470 to 1473 was vicar provincial of the Observants of the Cologne province.

His works fall into two groups: oratorical and ascetical-mystical. The oratorical writings are contained in two volumes under the titles *Speculum aureum de praeceptis divinae legis* (sermons on the decalogue) and *Sermones de tempore.* The first of these was published at Mainz (1474), and the latter at Speyer (1484). His ascetical-mystical works were composed between 1450 and 1470. They were written in Latin (with the exception of the *Spieghel*) and in the form of sermons. These include: (1) *Eden, id est Paradisus contemplativorum,* a youthful work showing dependence upon Jan van Ruysbroeck. (2) The *Scala Amoris,* which expounded the nine degrees of charity, and shows dependence upon Rudolph of Biberach and St. Thomas Aquinas, *Summa theologiae* 2a2ae, 23–27. (3) *Collatio I seu Directorium Brevissimum,* a resumé of Herp's doctrine about the prayer of aspiration. Three early manuscripts ascribe this work to John Bourcelli, OFM [see M. Viller, *Harphius ou Bourcelli?* in *Revue d'ascétique et de mystique* 3 (1922) 155–162]. (4) *Soliloquia super Cantica,* sermons describing the whole ascent of the spiritual life. (5) *De processu humani profectus,* sermons about the interior life. (6) *Spieghel der Volcomenheit* (critical edition by L. Verschueren, Antwerp 1931, 2 v.), his chief work, written 1455–60 in Middle Dutch. A complete collection of Herp's mystical writings was edited and published under the title *Theologia Mystica* by Theodoric Loer, OCart (Cologne 1538). This edition was placed on the Index, but a corrected edition was published in Rome in 1586.

The *Spieghel* has four parts. The introduction deals at length with the subject of mortification. The remainder of the work treats of three successive steps of life: the internal-active; the spiritual-contemplative; and the spiritual-superessential. Each life is considered under three aspects—its preparation, its ornamentation, and its ascent—a division borrowed from Ruysbroeck. The preparation of the active life consists in compunction; its ornamentation in the acquisition of the moral virtues; its ascent either in the exercise of the prayer of aspiration, or in the practice of the theological virtues. The preparation of the contemplative life consists in the removal of impediments and in a general refinement of mind and will; its ornamentation in the gifts of the Holy Spirit; its ascent takes place on three levels, namely, in the lower or sensory powers of the soul, in its higher or spiritual powers, and in its very essence. On the occasion of this last phase of ascent the soul is seized by an insatiable desire for God. The spiritual-superessential life (which, according to the uncommon thesis maintained by Herp, has the immediate vision of the divine essence as its final term) has for its preparation a total disengagement from things, and in this Herp distinguished nine differences of degree. In the ornamentation of this life the divine Persons themselves, directly working in the will, the intellect and the memory, effect a final purification and detachment and make the soul able to see the essence of God.

Herp accentuated the importance of the exercise of aspiration, i.e., the frequent raising of the mind to God with ardent sighs, which are not, however, to be conceived as an excitement of the sensitive emotions, but as the fervent tendency of the will to achieve union with God. The general idea was borrowed from Hugh of Balma, but whereas Hugh restricted this exercise principally to the higher phases of spiritual life, Herp saw it as playing a part, though in different forms, in all the phases. He conceived it as the moving force that carries the soul to the highest degrees of union with God.

Herp was especially influential in the 16th and 17th centuries, not only in the Low Countries, but also in Spain, France, and Italy. Though not an original writer, he is one of the most important representatives of Dutch spirituality. He joined a clear and practical précis of Ruysbroeck's mystical teaching with certain ascetical ideas that give him an almost modern air. He felicitously assimilated Hugh of Balma's doctrine about the prayer of aspiration and applied it to the whole progress of the spiritual life.

Bibliography: L. VERSCHUEREN, *Spieghel der Volcomenheit,* 2 v. (Antwerp 1931) v. 1; "De Heraut van Ruusbroec," *Jan van Ruusbroec: Leven en Werken* (Mechlin 1931) 230–262; "Harphius et les capucins français," *Études Franciscaines* 45 (1933) 316–329; 46 (1934) 272–288. D. KALVERKAMP, *Die Vollkommenheitslehre des Franziskaners Heinrich Herp* (Werl, Ger. 1940). M. M. J. SMITS VAN WAESBERGHE, *Het verschijnsel van de opheffing des geestes bij Jan van Ruusbroec en Hendrik Herp* (Nijmegen 1945). C. JANSSEN, "L'Oraison aspirative chez Herp et chez ses prédécesseurs," *Carmelus* 3 (1956) 19–48. K. FREIENHAGEN-BAUMGARDT, *Hendrik Herps Spieghel der Volcomenheit in oberdeutscher Überlieferung: Ein Beitrag zur Rezeptionsgeschichte niederländischer Mystik im oberdeutschen Raum* (Leuven 1998).

[A. EMMEN]

HENRY OF HUNTINGDON

English churchman and chronicler; b. in the vicinity of Lincoln, England, between 1080 and 1085; d. Huntingdon, 1155. Brought up probably in the household of Robert Bloet, Bishop of LINCOLN (1093–1123), and trained by a certain Albinus of Angers as his master, he was ordained a priest before 1110 and was made archdeacon of Huntingdon the following year. At the request of Robert's successor at Lincoln, Alexander (1123–48), Henry began the composition of a *Historia Anglorum* that took BEDE's work as its foundation. In 1134 he accompanied Archbishop THEOBALD OF CANTERBURY to Rome. On this journey he visited the Abbey of BEC, met the Norman chronicler ROBERT OF TORIGNY, then a monk there, and became acquainted with GEOFFREY OF MONMOUTH's *Historia Britonum.* He divided his own history into four periods: Roman, Saxon, Danish, and Norman, utilizing the conventional sources from Roman days down to the Norman period, and at times only his own imagination. However, it should be noted that he put Bede and the *Old English Chronicle* to good use and exhibited no race prejudice in his narrative. Between 1130 and 1154 he brought out five editions of his work, each showing not only continuations but much reworking and change. He eventually added three books, cast in epistolary form, to his *Historia,* viz: *De summitatibus,* letters addressed to high personages including King HENRY I; *De miraculis,* on the miracles of early English saints; and *De contemptu mundi,* a moralizing work in which examples are drawn from his own contemporaries. On the basis of his two extant books of epigrams it can be said that his poetical compositions did not rise above rhetorical flights in verse form. As a chronicler, Henry of Huntingdon is a valuable independent source for the period of his own lifetime, but he is inferior both as a historian and as a stylist to WILLIAM OF MALMESBURY and Robert of Torigny. The best available edition of his *Historia* is that by Thomas Arnold in the Rolls Series (1879).

See Also: ANNALS AND CHRONICLES.

Bibliography: H. R. LUARD, *The Dictionary of National Biography from the Earliest Times to 1900*, 63 v. (London 1885–1900) 9:569–570. M. MANITIUS, *Geschichte der lateinischen Literatur des Mittelalters*, 3 v. (Munich 1911–31) 3:481–485. J. DE GHELLINCK, *L'Essor de la littérature latine au XIIe siècle*, 2 v. (Brussels-Paris 1946) 2: 153–155. F. LIEBERMANN, ''Heinrich von Huntingdon,'' *Forschungen zur deutschen Geschichte* 18 (1878) 267–295.

[M. R. P. MC GUIRE]

HENRY OF KALKAR

Carthusian writer and reformer; b. Kalkar, Duchy of Cleves, 1328; d. Cologne, Dec. 20, 1408. Of a noble family, he studied at Cologne and then at Paris, where he completed his master's degree in 1357. After teaching at Paris, he returned to Cologne, where he became canon at the churches of St. George, Cologne, and St. Swithbert, Kaiserswerth. In 1365 he entered the Cologne Charterhouse. Recognized for his learning and piety, he was made prior of the Charterhouse of Arnheim in 1368, and there exercised decisive influence on the spiritual formation of Gerard GROOTE. He was later prior of Ruremonde (1372–77), of Cologne (1378–84), and of Strasbourg (1384–96), and for 20 years was visitator of the Rhine province. In these positions he promoted a reform that enabled his order to survive the difficulties of the Western Schism.

He wrote extensively on varied topics, sermons, letters, and ascetical and historical tracts, but much of his work remains in manuscript. His published works are *Exercitatorium monachale,* which appeared at Cologne in 1532 under the name of DENIS THE CARTHUSIAN and was also incorporated in the *Theologia mystica* (ch. 1) of HUGH OF BALMA; a chronicle, *Ortus et decursus ordinis Cartusiensis* (ed. H. Vermeer, Wageningen 1929); and *Cantuagium de musica* (ed. H. Hüschen, Krefeld 1952). Henry of Kalkar was for a time proposed as a possible author of the *Imitation of Christ,* but that thesis is no longer accepted. He is, however, recognized as being an important influence in the development of the DEVOTIO MODERNA and upon the writers of that era. He is also referred to as Henry Egher or Eger.

Bibliography: L. LE VASSEUR, *Ephemerides ordinis Cartusiensis,* 2 v. in 4 (Montreuil 1890) 4:540–542. S. AUTORE, *Dictionnaire de théologie catholique*, ed. A. VACANT et al., 15 v. (Paris 1903–50; Tables Générales 1951–) 4.2: 2104–08. P. DOYÈRE, *Catholicisme* 5:621–622.

[F. C. LEHNER]

HENRY OF LAUSANNE

12th-century heretic; d. Toulouse, *c.* 1145. He was of uncertain origin, but St. BERNARD OF CLAIRVAUX thought he was French. He was a black monk who had left his order. Although his theology was compendious and his morality doubtful, his influence was incontestable because of his oratorical talent and convincing external appearance—he presented himself as a prophet and reformer. His doctrine was negative: it was antisacerdotal and antisacramental; it rejected the baptism of children, Holy Eucharist, worship in churches, and probably also the invocation of saints. In 1101 he went from Lausanne to Le Mans, where he was confounded by HILDEBERT OF LAVARDIN, who had returned from Rome, and was expelled. He then preached at Poitiers, at Bordeaux, and in Provence. The Council of Toulouse (1119) denounced him in its 3d and 10th canons. Sometime before 1135 he was refuted by a monk, William. When arrested by the archbishop of Arles, Henry retracted his errors at the Council of Pisa (1135), only to return to his errant life. He then met PETER OF BRUYS and was influenced by his doctrine. PETER THE VENERABLE wrote his *Tractatus adversus petrobrusianos haereticos* (1137–1140) against them (*see* PETROBRUSIANS). The LATERAN COUNCIL OF 1139 condemned them again in canon 23. But subsequently, Henry, protected by Alphonse of St. Gilles, preached so effectively in Languedoc that Bernard himself undertook a successful campaign against him. Henry was seized *c.* 1145, sent to the bishop of Toulouse and condemned to prison, where he died. His disciples, the Henricians, were still in existence in 1236. Though he did not profess the theses later held by the WALDENSES and the ALBIGENSES, his influence cleared the way for them.

Bibliography: HILDEBERT OF LAVARDIN, *Epistolae 23, 24, Patrologia Latina,* ed. J. P. MIGNE, 217 v., indexes 4 v. (Paris 1878–90) 171:237–242. WILLIAM THE MONK, *Contra Henricum scismaticum et hereticum,* ed. R. MANSELLI, *Bullettino dell' Istituto storico italiano* 67 (1953) 1–63. PETER THE VENERABLE, *Tractatus adversus Petrobrusianos, Patrologia Latina* 189:719–850. BERNARD OF CLAIRVAUX, *Epistolae 241, 242, Patrologia Latina* 182:434–437. F. VERNET, *Dictionnaire de théologie catholique*, ed. A. VACANT et al., 15 v. (Paris 1903–50; Tables Générales 1951–) 6.2:2178–83. J. LECLERCQ, *Pierre le Vénérable* (Paris 1946). R. MANSELLI, *Studi sulle eresie del secolo XII.* (Studi storici 5; Rome 1953). E. DELARUELLE, *Catholicisme* 5:622–624.

[F. GLORIEUX]

HENRY OF NEWARK

Archbishop of York; d. Aug. 15, 1299. He was probably a native of Newark, Nottinghamshire, England, and related to several other contemporary clerics of the same family name. Henry began his career *c.* 1270, becoming clerk to King EDWARD I shortly afterward. From then on his advancement was steady, the reward of unspectacular, unremitting service to King and Church. He held the living of Barnby, Nottinghamshire, in 1270, received a prebend in St. Paul's, London, in 1271, and on the death of Abp. WALTER GIFFARD in 1279, was named a guardian of the temporalities of York. In 1218 he became archdeacon of Richmond, with a prebend in York, where in 1290 he was installed as dean. On May 7, 1296, he was elected archbishop of YORK, but the wars prevented him from appearing before Pope BONIFACE VIII. However, his election was confirmed, the temporalities granted (1297), and the PALLIUM sent from Rome, and he was finally consecrated by the bishop of Durham on June 15, 1298. His steady advancement in the Church was accompanied, and perhaps explained, by his lifelong service to King and State. Thus, in 1277 he was at Rome on a mission for Edward; in 1281 he arbitrated in a dispute with subjects of the Count of Holland; in 1283 he was deputed to fix the dues owing to the crown by the northern knights and to collect subsidies in the Diocese of Durham for the Welsh wars; he was a commissioner at Norham, where Edward gave judgment among the claimants to the Scottish crown; in 1296 he was one of those appointed to treat with the Counts of Gelderland and Holland; and in 1297 he called a synod to consider the king's demand for a subsidy. Summoned to Parliament, he became a member of the Council of the Prince of Wales. He was buried in his cathedral church. He appears to have been a man of great competence and wise judgment, faithful in his duties, unambitious, conciliatory, and generous.

Bibliography: W. H. DIXON, *Fasti Eboracenses: Lives of the Archbishops of York,* ed. J. RAINE (London 1863) 349–353. J. LENEVE, *Fasti Ecclesiae Anglicanae 1300–1541*, ed. H. P. F. KING et al. (London 1962–) 2:49, 365; 3:104, 122, 137, 214, 428. W. HUNT, *The Dictionary of National Biography from the Earliest Times to 1900*, 63 v. (London 1885–1900) 14:310–311.

[J. H. BAXTER]

HENRY OF ST. IGNATIUS

Carmelite theologian, whose family name was D'Aumérie; b. Ath, Belgium, *c.* 1630; d. Wandre, near Liège, April 1, 1719. He entered the Carmelites *c.* 1646 and was ordained in 1652. For many years he taught theology, and he also held various administrative positions in the three Carmelite provinces to which at different times he belonged. He vigorously attacked the teaching of the Carmelite Francis Bonne-Espérance (1617–77) and his followers. An indefatigable controversialist, he wrote against the Jesuits and Molinism and roundly condemned the moral laxism he detected in the writings of many who attacked Jansenism. His best-known work, *Ethica amoris, sive theologia sanctorum. . .* (3 v. Liège 1709), was condemned by the bishop of Liège, the Holy Office, and the parlement of Paris. Henry stoutly maintained that his doctrine was in accord with that of Aristotle, Augustine, Aquinas, and the English Carmelite John Baconthorpe (Bacon). The accusation of Jansenism made against Henry is false if understood to mean that he actually propounded Jansenist doctrine.

Bibliography: E. MANGENOT, *Dictionnaire de théologie catholique*, ed. A. VACANT et al., 15 v. (Paris 1903–50; Tables Générales 1951–) 6.2:2195–97. I. ROSIER, *Biographisch en bibliographisch overzicht van de vroomheid in de Nederlandse Carmel van 1235 tot het midden der achttiende eeuw* (Studiën en tekstuitgaven van ons geestelijk erf 10; Tielt 1950) 155–156. L. CEYSSENS, ''Les Deébuts janseénistes du P. Henri de S. Ignace,'' *Analecta Ordinis Carmelitarum Calceatorum* 18 (1953) 56–122, ed. of correspondence, 186–297.

[K. J. EGAN]

HENRY OF UPPSALA, ST.

Bishop and martyr, national saint of Finland; d. Köylio, Finland, *c.* 1156. He is a somewhat enigmatic figure as to date and life, but is believed to have accompanied King ERIC IX of Sweden on his crusade to Finland, where he converted many pagans. However, remaining behind after the king had returned home, he was killed by a Finnish convert. Reputedly, the murderer put on the bishop's *birretum,* but when he tried to take it off his flesh adhered to it. This is noted as one of the saint's outstanding miracles. In another legend, extant in only one manuscript, Henry is linked with Nicholas Breakspear, then legate to Scandinavia, who later became Pope ADRI-

AN IV. The saint's cult spread rapidly in Sweden and Finland, and with the growth of the BRIDGETTINE convents it was carried to the European continent. One *historia rhythmica, Gaude cetus fidelium,* and one *Sequence, Cetus noster,* are known. His epitaph may be found in Nousis, Finland, where his relics were kept, until they were translated in 1300 to the cathedral in Abo (Tartu). He was canonized in 1158.

Feast: Jan. 19; Jan. 20 (Finland).

Bibliography: A. MALINIEMI, *De S. Henrico episcopo et martyre* (Helsinki 1942). J. RINNE, *Pyhä Henrik* (Helsinki 1932). T. SCHMID, *Sveriges kristnande* (Stockholm 1934). U. VENTO, *Piispa Henrikin surmavirsi. The Ballad of the Death of Bishop Henry* (Helsinki 1967). *Analecta hymnica* (Leipzig 1886–1922) 26:92–95; 42:217–218. T. BORENIUS, *Archaeological Journal* 87 (1930) 340–358.

[T. SCHMID]

HENRY OF VITSKÓL, BL.

Abbot; d. February 11, late 12th century. He joined the CISTERCIANS at the Abbey of CLAIRVAUX, where he was listed first among 90 novices on the occasion of a meeting with the saintly Abbot BERNARD, who predicted at that time that one day Henry's spiritual labors would take him far from the monastery. In fact, Henry was sent in 1143 to the Abbey of ALVASTRA in Sweden, and in 1150 he was founder and first abbot of Varnhem. He was forced to leave there because of severe external disorders, and in 1158 he assumed the direction of the monastery of Vitskól in Denmark when it was founded by King Waldemar I (d. 1182). He also undertook from there a new foundation in Oem or Clara-Insula in 1166. Although he is listed in the Cistercian calendar, there is no official cult.

Feast: Feb. 11.

Bibliography: *Scriptores rerum Danicarum medii aevi,* ed. J. LANGEBEK and P. F. SUHM, 9 v. (Copenhagen 1772–1878) 4:458. CONRAD EBERBACENSIS, *Exordium magnum cisterciense* bk. 6.10, ed. B. GRIESSER (Rome 1961) 366. F. ORTVED, *Cistercieordenen og dens klostre i Norden,* 2 v. in 1 (Copenhagen 1927–33) 2:53–141. A. M. ZIMMERMANN, *Kalendarium Benedictinum: Die Heiligen und Seligen des Benediktinerorderns und seiner Zweige,* 4 v. (Metten 1933–38) 1:203; 4:21.

[C. SPAHR]

HENRY OF ZWIEFALTEN, BL.

Benedictine monk; b. *c.* 1200; d. Ochsenhausen, Nov. 4, 1262. His family resided on Mt. Zwiefalten, Germany. As a young man he was a respected knight. From 1238 on he was prior in Ochsenhausen Priory, a dependency of the abbey of SANKT BLASIEN. He is mentioned in the abbey records between 1238 and 1243 and for the last time on Nov. 4, 1262. Henry's chief concern was the expansion of the monastery library; he also managed to mobilize large endowments for the decoration of the church. He was distinguished by great sanctity and miraculous powers. Among other things, he is reported to have miraculously quenched a fire, restored sight to a blind woman, and healed a lame boy. His cult cannot be clearly established for the early period. His vita witnesses to his reputation for sanctity. He is usually designated "blessed," and his memory is held in high esteem.

Feast: Nov. 4.

Bibliography: J. E. STADLER and F. J. HEIM, *Vollständiges Heiligen-Lexikon,* 5 v. (Augsburg 1858–82) v.2. *Die Kunst- und Altertums-Denkmale im Königreich Württemberg: Donaukreis* (Esslingen 1914), see Ochsenhausen. J. L. BAUDOT and L. CHAUSSIN, *Vies des saints et des bienheueux selon l'ordre du calendrier avec l'historique des fêtes,* ed. by The Benedictines of Paris, 12 v. (Paris 1935–56) 11:152–153. A. M. ZIMMERMANN, *Kalendarium Benedictinum: Die Heiligen und Seligen des Benediktinerorderns und seiner Zweige,* 4 v. (Metten 1933–38) 3:259.

[G. SPAHR]

HENRY SUSO, BL.

Dominican preacher and mystic, and leader of the Friends of God; b. Constance, March 21, *c.* 1295; d. Ulm, Jan. 25, 1366.

Life and Works. His father was Count Henry of Berg, a worldly minded man; his mother, a saintly woman of the Süse family (latinized Suso, modern German Seuse) probably of Ueberlingen, from whom Henry took his surname and inherited his religious disposition and tender sympathy. He received the Dominican habit at Constance at the age of 13. After 15 years of mediocre piety, he experienced a "conversion" that marked the beginning of a life of heroic austerity, prayer, and solitude. He studied at Constance, probably at Strassburg, and at the general house of studies at Cologne, sometime between 1322 and 1325, under Meister ECKHART, for whom he developed an intense veneration. About 1326 Suso returned to Constance as professor of the priory school. He wrote the *Little Book of Truth* (*c.* 1327), a speculative treatment of mystical questions, to counter the pantheistic, unsocial, and immoral tenets of the Brethren of the Free Spirit. With marked intellectual vigor, he dealt with profound questions of theology: God's being, Unity and Trinity, creation and Incarnation, man's freedom and moral responsibility, and mystical union with God without loss of personal identity. When the Wild Man whom

Henry used as the personification of the heretical brethren misquoted Eckhart in support of false doctrine, Suso replied by placing obscure passages regarding God's immanence and transcendence, presence and concurrence, into juxtaposition with others, also from Eckhart, that were in full harmony with truth.

Suso's masterpiece, the *Little Book of Eternal Wisdom* (*c.* 1328), is ''the finest fruit of German mysticism'' (Denifle), a judgment corroborated by its unbroken popularity until displaced by the *Imitation of Christ.* It is a practical book containing a minimal discussion of mystical subjects and little theological speculation. ''The thoughts expressed here are simple and the words simpler still, because they are from a simple soul and are intended for simple persons who have bad habits to crush'' (Prol.). In dialogue (used also in the *Little Book of Truth*), Suso spoke ''at one time as a sinner, then as a perfect man, sometimes as a loving soul; or, if the subject requires it, as a servant submissive to Holy Wisdom,'' and is answered by Holy Wisdom, at times by Mary, and once by the soul of one who had died unrepentant. Aiming to rekindle zeal in hearts where it has died, to warm cold hearts, to stir up the lukewarm, to provoke the indevout to devotion, and to awaken the tepid to virtue, Suso leads the reader to the foot of the Cross to ponder the afflictions of Jesus and Mary. He shows him the enormity of sin, the rigor of divine justice, the tawdriness of earthly love and the nobility of the heavenly, and points to the joy of heaven and the treasures hidden in suffering. He instructs how to prepare for death, live inwardly, receive the Sacraments fruitfully, and praise God unceasingly. He concludes with 100 one-sentence meditations on the Passion. Suso's abstruse doctrine and defense of Eckhart in the earlier book brought him a sharp rebuke from a provincial or possibly a general chapter in 1327 or 1330. He also lost his professorship. These events may explain why he sought and obtained approval of the *Little Book of Eternal Wisdom* from the master general, translating it into Latin under the title *Horologium sapientiae,* or *Clock of Wisdom* (*c.* 1334), a free rendition, rearrangement, and fuller presentation of the same material. That the two books are in reverse relationship has also been held (Gröber).

Suso now developed an active ministry, preaching especially to Dominican nuns and the Friends of God of Switzerland and the Upper Rhine region, but he also ranged as far afield as Cologne and Aachen. During 1343–44 he was prior of the Constance community, in exile at Diessenhoven after 1339, owing to its support of the papal cause against Louis of Bavaria. During these years Suso was purified spiritually by physical hardships, the hostility of others, persecution, and calumny. He was shamefully slandered by an evil woman he had befriended. Even friends turned against him. This crisis forced his transfer to Ulm (*c.* 1347), where he died. His tomb was destroyed by Protestants in the 16th century. Henry's veneration began immediately upon his death and has continued without interruption. Gregory XVI approved his cult on April 16, 1831.

The Life of the Servant, ''one of the most charming of Christian biographies'' (Preger), had its origin in correspondence and conversations between Suso and Elsbethe STÄGEL, his spiritual daughter. Suso reworked her notes of the conversations with great literary skill and incorporated some of the letters. More the story of a soul than an autobiography, it recorded his spiritual development (part 1) and instructed Elsbethe how to advance in the spiritual life (part 2). Four extant sermons are attributed to Suso, only two of which are certainly genuine. His 27 or 28 spiritual letters (existing also in an abridged form that constitutes a miniature spiritual treatise) have been judged ''the choicest spiritual letters written during the Middle Ages'' (Preger). The brief *Soul's Love-Book* (in which Christ is the great book of love) is of doubtful authenticity. Suso collected his Middle High German works in an *Exemplar* (*c.* 1362), containing the *Little Book of Truth,* the *Little Book of Eternal Wisdom,* his *Life,* and abridged letters. Some scholars deny that he made the *Exemplar,* composed the *Life,* or abridged the letters, holding that the *Life* contains, besides a nucleus of truth, a large content of fictional anecdote, cloister legend, and hearsay. The traditional view, upheld by other scholars, is still preferred.

Doctrine. Suso's teaching, a milder, more cautious form of Eckhart's speculative doctrine, is corrected by that of Thomas Aquinas and colored by the effective mysticism of Bernard and Bonaventure. He developed a tender personal love for Christ, the Eternal Wisdom, the Eucharist, the Sacred Heart and the Heart of Mary, and the Holy Name, which he cut on his breast. Imitation and contemplation of Christ's sufferings was basic to Suso's doctrine. It leads to conformity with Christ and to the highest reaches of mystical union. Illustrated by constant references to his own experiences, Suso's teaching is psychological, practical, and largely ascetical, but touches at times on profound speculative points. He taught passivity (yet not quietistic) achieved by corporal mortification, acceptance of interior and exterior trials, total detachment from creatures, self-renunciation, and complete abandonment to God's will. Contemplation occurs through an intuition beyond created images in a union with the Divinity beyond comprehension, where the soul, losing all sense of its own identity yet remaining distinct from God, knows and loves Him without knowing that it does so.

Feast: March 15; formerly March 2.

See Also: MYSTICISM; CONTEMPLATION.

Bibliography: Editions. German works. *Heinrich Seuse: Deutsche Schriften,* ed. K. BIHLMEYER (Stuttgart 1907), standard ed. Modern German. N. HELLER, ed., *Des Mystikers Heinrich Seuse deutsche Schriften: Vollständige Ausgabe auf Grund der Handschriften* (Regensberg 1926), Eng. *The Exemplar: Life and Writings of Bl. Henry Suso, O.P.,* tr. SISTER ANN EDWARD, 2 v. (Dubuque 1962). *The Life of the Servant,* abr. tr. J. M. CLARK (London 1952). *The Little Book of Eternal Wisdom* and *The Little Book of Truth,* ed. and tr. J. M. CLARK (New York 1953). *Horologium sapientiae,* ed. J. STRANGE (Cologne 1861); ed. K. RICHSTÄTTER (Turin 1929). Literature. J. ANCELET-HUSTACHE, *Master Eckhart and the Rhineland Mystics,* tr. H. GRAEF (pa. New York 1958). J. BÜHLMANN, *Christuslehre und Christusmystik des Heinrich Seuse* (Lucerne 1942). J. M. CLARK, *The Great German Mystics* (Oxford 1949). H. DENIFLE, *Die deutschen Mystiker des 14. Jahrhunderts. Beitrag zur Deutung ihrer Lehre,* ed. O. SPIESS (Fribourg 1951). C. GRÖBER, *Der Mystiker Heinrich Seuse* (Freiburg 1941). D. PLANZER, ''Des Horologium sapientiae und die Echtheit der Vita des H. Seuse,'' *Archivum Fratrum Praedicatorum* 1 (1930) 181–221; ''Henry Suso on the Spiritual Life,'' *Cross and Crown* 2 (1950) 58–79; *Heinrich Seuses Lehre über das geistliche Leben* (Freiburg 1960). R. SENN, *Die Echtheit der Vita Heinrich Seuses* (Diss. Bern 1930). SISTER MARY CATHERINE, *Henry Suso: Saint and Poet, a Study* (Oxford 1947). U. WEYMANN, *Die Seusesche Mystik und ihre Wirkung auf die bildende Kunst* (Berlin 1938). F. TOBIN, *Henry Suso: The Exemplar, with Two German Sermons* (New York 1989).

[W. A. HINNEBUSCH]

HEORTOLOGY

From Gr. ἑορτή, festival, a branch of LITURGIOLOGY devoted to the history of liturgical feasts and seasons. In the more general liturgiological treatises the Church calendar (*see* CALENDAR, CHRISTIAN) is usually discussed only incidentally. There have been some during the past three centuries, however, who have written special studies on the Church year; among them are: L. de Thomassin, *Traité des festes de l'Église,* v. 2 of *Traités historiques et dogmatiques sur divers points de la discipline de l'Église et de la morale chrétienne* (Paris 1683); Benedict XIV, *De festis Domini Nostri Jesu Christi, beatae Mariae Virginis et quorumdam sanctorum,* v. 10 of *Opera* (Rome 1747–51); and N. Nilles, *Kalendarium manuale utriusque ecclesiae orientalis et occidentalis,* 2 v. (2d ed. Innsbruck 1896–97). In 1900 H. Kellner recommended that heortology be recognized as a separate department of study (H. Kellner, *Heortologie* [3d ed. rev. Freiburg 1911]; English version *Heortology* [London 1908]). The increase since then of heortological treatises, particularly in the form of articles, is doubtless due in a measure to his influence. Broader contemporary studies on the calendar include F. G. Holweck, *Calendarium liturgicum festorum Dei et Dei Matris Mariae* (Philadelphia 1925); W. H. Frere, *Studies in Early Roman Liturgy,* v.1 *The Kalendar* (Alcuin Club Collections 28; London 1930); and F. X. Weiser, *Handbook of Christian Feasts and Customs* (New York 1958). As Weiser indicates, popular customs connected with Church festivals and seasons pertain more properly to folklore than to heortology.

See Also: LITURGICAL YEAR IN ROMAN RITE.

[R. F. MCNAMARA]

HERACLEON

2d-century Italian Gnostic teacher. Almost nothing is known of his life. According to Clement of Alexandria (*Strom.* 4.71) and Hippolytus (*Ref.* 6.29, 35), he was, with Ptolemy, a leader of the Italian school of Valentinian Gnosis. He ranks as the first known commentator on the Fourth Gospel. Origen quotes some 48 passages of Heracleon's work in his own commentary on John, and Clement cites two other passages probably from the same work (*ibid.* and *Eclogae* 25.1). Largely on the basis of doctrinal similarities, H. C. Puech and G. Quispel have very plausibly assigned to Heracleon the *Treatise on the Three Natures* in the Jung Codex from the Chenoboskion manuscripts. At the core of Heracleon's system is the doctrine of the three natures and three classes of men: the material, associated with evil and the devil; the pneumatic, associated with the Father and the Pleroma; the psychic, associated with the Demiurge and capable of some purification by knowledge. The body of Jesus, the Italian Valentinians held, belonged to the psychic category.

See Also: GNOSTICISM.

Bibliography: A. E. BROOKE, ed., *The Fragments of Heracleon* (Cambridge, Eng. 1891). W. VÖLKER, ed., *Quellen zur Geschichte der christlichen Gnosis* (Tübingen 1932) 63–86. W. FOERSTER, ''Von Valentin zur Herakleon'' *Zeitschrift für die neutestamentliche Wissenschaft und die Kunde der älteren Kirche* (1928) Beiheft 7. F. SAGNARD, *La Gnose valentinienne et le témoignage de Saint Irénée* (Paris 1947) 127–134; 480–520. G. BAREILLE, *Dictionnaire de théologie catholique,* ed. A. VACANT et al., 15 v. (Paris 1903–50; Tables Générales 1951–) 6.2: 2198–2205. H. C. PUECH and G. QUISPEL, ''Le Quatrième écrit gnostique du Codex Jung,'' *Vigiliae christianea* 9 (1955) 65–102. R. M. GRANT, *Gnosticism: A Sourcebook . . .* (New York 1961) 195–208.

[G. W. MACRAE]

HERACLITUS

Heraclitus of Ephesus, b. probably in the third quarter of the sixth century B.C. and reported to have died at the age of 60, was the most enigmatic and the most profound of the pre-Socratic thinkers. According to a seemingly reliable tradition, he belonged to a leading family of the Ephesian aristocracy. Nothing else is known definitely of his life.

Scroll Fragments. Most stories about Heraclitus appear to have been invented to illustrate features that emerge from sayings on a scroll handed down under his name. From the scroll there remain well over 100 fragments, as quoted in writers from the 4th century B.C. to the 13th A.D. The exact number is controversial, since in many instances an original Heraclitean saying cannot easily be distinguished from a quoting author's paraphrase. Though one comparatively lengthy fragment (frg. 1, H. DIELS, *Die Fragmente der Vorsokratiker: Griechisch und Deutsch,* 3 v. [10th ed. Berlin 1960–61] 22 B) stood at the beginning and another (frg. 2) followed shortly after, the rest defy modern attempts to rediscover their order on the scroll. In style they are incisive, well rounded, and oracular, as though pointing out truth vividly rather than reasoning to it or analyzing it. They reveal a haughty, aristocratic temperament, mordantly critical of accepted views.

Because the sayings were found to be obscure when approached for teachings on nature, they earned their author in subsequent tradition the epithet of ''dark'' or ''obscure'' (Gr. ὁ σκοτεινός, Lat. *tenebrosus*). The picture of him as ''the weeping philosopher'' cannot be traced further back than late in the 1st century B.C., and may rest on a peripatetic term describing his style as ''impulsive,'' but misunderstood as ''melancholy.''

Teaching. The philosophy contained in the fragments has been interpreted through the centuries in widely differing ways. In PLATO it is seen as an overall doctrine of flux in which nothing is stable, and is summed up (*Crat.* 439C) in the assertion that all things are always flowing (ῥεόντων). This was understood by Plato (*Theaet.* 179E–183C) and ARISTOTLE (*Meta.* 1005b 23–1012a 34) as a denial of being in things and an explanation of all reality in terms only of change, with the consequent rejection of definite meanings for words. From another standpoint, that of material cause, the Greek doxographers looked upon Heraclitus as a philosopher of nature. The view can be traced to Aristotle's brief statement (*Meta.* 984a 7–8) that for Heraclitus the basic material principle—from which all things in the universe developed—was fire. In accord with the doxographical tradition, most interpreters continue to regard Heraclitus as an Ionian cosmologist. A third view handed down from antiquity is that Heraclitus was primarily a moral philosopher, using physical doctrines only to establish his moral teachings (Diogenes Laertius, *Lives,* 9.12, 15).

Perhaps no more than ten of the fragments (frgs. 30, 31, 36, 64, 66, 67, 76, 90, 94, 126) have a patently cosmological meaning, and even these appear readily adaptable to driving home moral considerations. In general the fragments, including the first two, seem concerned predominantly with showing men how to live. Proclaiming that a waking life means solidarity with one's surroundings (frgs. 1, 72), they strive to base human conduct upon what is ''common'' (frgs. 2, 89) and ultimately upon one divine law, which is common to all (frg. 114). They are definite in the meanings they assign to words, and in the assertion of a common, enduring, unified order throughout all things. The order is achieved by maintaining the correct tensions (frg. 51) between ever-changing opposites. Hence its abiding condition is strife or war (frg. 80). Eternal, uncreated, the world order is a living fire that regulates all things according to fixed measures (frgs. 30, 66, 94). In this way fire is a medium of exchange (frg. 90) as it becomes other things (frg. 31) and all other things are exchanged for it. It guides all (frg. 64).

The notion of God or the divine seems merged in the common unity of opposites (frgs. 32, 67, 102) that is the all-pervading direction of things. To understand it is wisdom (frg. 41). By Stoic and patristic writers and by most moderns it is called the logos, in a Stoic sense, though without ground in pre-Stoic tradition and with doubtful support in the fragments. The soul is described as though a material nature (frgs. 117, 118), having depths that can never be penetrated (frgs. 45, 115), and as surviving some time after death (frgs. 26, 27).

Meaning. While there is no general agreement on the meaning of Heraclitus's thought, its vigor and depth are uncontested. Though without a philosophical notion it makes intelligence supreme in the direction of things of the supersensible in regard to either God or the soul, and penetrates deeply into the basic moral problem of the common or universal in the incessantly changing circumstances of life. The fragments continue to inspire philosophers, and can always be pondered over with renewed intellectual profit.

See Also: GREEK PHILOSOPHY.

Bibliography: HERACLITUS, *The Cosmic Fragments,* ed. G. S. KIRK (Cambridge, Eng. 1954). DIOGENES LAERTIUS, *Lives of Eminent Philosophers,* tr. R. D. HICKS, *Loeb Classical Library* (New York 1925; reprint Cambridge, Mass. 1942). P. E. WHEELWRIGHT, *Heraclitus* (Princeton 1959). J. OWENS, ''The Interpretation of the Heraclitean Fragments,'' *An Étienne Gilson Tribute,* ed. C. J. O'NEIL (Milwaukee 1959) 148–168. W. K. C. GUTHRIE, *A History of Greek Philosophy* (Cambridge, Eng. 1962—) 1:403–492. M. MARCOVICH, *Paulys Realenzyklopädie der klassischen Altertumswissenschaft,* suppl. 10 (1965) 246–320.

[J. OWENS]

HERACLIUS, ANTIPOPE

Heraclius was a Roman who in 310 opposed the election of Pope EUSEBIUS (310) and thus earned the title of antipope. Virtually all that is known of Heraclius appears in an epitaph which Pope Damasus I (366–384) wrote for Eusebius. Heraclius apparently headed a faction which favored a harsh treatment for those who had lapsed during persecution. Public disturbances caused by partisans of the two rivals reached such a state that the pagan emperor Maxentius (306–312) exiled both Eusebius and Heraclius to Sicily where the former died and the latter disappeared from history.

Bibliography: A. FERRUA, ed., *Epigrammata Damasiana* (Vatican City 1942), 129–136. G. SCHWAIGER, *Lexikon für Theologie und Kirche*, ed. J. HOFER and K. RAHNER (Freiburg 1957–65) 3:1198–99. H. JEDIN, *History of the Church* (New York 1980) 1:344. J. N. D. KELLY, *Oxford Dictionary of Popes* (New York 1986) 26.

[J. F. KELLY]

HERACLIUS, BYZANTINE EMPEROR

Reigned Oct. 5, 610, to Feb. 11, 641; b. Cappadocia, *c.* 575. Heraclius, son of Heraclius, Exarch of Africa, who was of Armenian origin, played a principal part in his father's revolt against the unpopular Emperor Phocas (602–610). He sailed to Constantinople with an expeditionary force, overthrew and executed Phocas, and was proclaimed emperor. By his first marriage, to Eudoxia, he had a son, Heraclius Constantine, and a daughter, Eudocia. His second marriage, to his niece Martina (631), brought him both two additional sons, Heracleonas and David, and sharp ecclesiastical criticism.

Heraclius spent his entire reign in a struggle against grave external and internal dangers. In 611 the Persians overran successively Syria, Anatolia, Palestine and Egypt; and in 614 they took Jerusalem and removed the Holy Cross to Persia. In a series of brilliant campaigns (622–628), Heraclius broke the Persian power in Anatolia and Armenia, carried the war into Persia (627), and caused the fall of Chrosroes and the accession of Kawadh, who consented (April 628) to restore occupied territory and the Holy Cross to the Byzantine Empire. Heraclius personally returned the Cross to Jerusalem amid popular rejoicing (March 21, 630). However, Heraclius not only was unable to prevent Slavic occupation of much of the Balkans, but also failed to check the Arab conquest of Palestine, Syria, and Egypt in the name of Islam (634–642).

Heraclius may have attempted to generate a renewal of social and cultural aspects of the Byzantine state, including, perhaps, the establishment of the themes, or military districts. To conciliate his Monophysite subjects, he issued an edict (610) that was orthodox in appearance, but that cast doubt upon the Council of CHALCEDON. Patriarch Sergius I of Constantinople induced him to accept monoenergism, which taught a unity of energy and activities in Christ as a consequence of the unity of wills (*c.* 621–622). Heraclius imposed this doctrine upon reconquered Armenia and other eastern provinces in 626–628, and in 631 persuaded the Jacobite bishops in a synod at Mabbug to accept monoenergism. In 633 he forced the Armenian Catholicos Ezras to accept this concept; and in the same year Cyrus, Patriarch of Alexandria, also agreed to this formula. Nevertheless, Monophysite opposition persisted in Egypt and Syria while the Chalcedonian position was strongly reaffirmed by Sophronius of Jerusalem and MAXIMUS THE CONFESSOR. In 634 or 635 Heraclius forbade further discussion of the question.

Recognizing the failure of monoenergism, Heraclius officially proclaimed a new formula in his edict *Ecthesis* (638), asserting the doctrine of Monothelitism, which proclaimed a perfect harmony and unity of the divine and human will in Christ. Pope SEVERINUS refused to accept this explanation; and when, in reprisal, Heraclius's troops seized the papal treasures, Pope JOHN IV openly condemned Monothelitism. The Monophysite Patriarch of Alexandria, Cyrus, accepted the doctrine, but most Copts and Jacobites did not follow him. Heraclius's interventions in ecclesiastical affairs ended in failure.

See Also: MONOTHELITISM.

Bibliography: H. G. BECK, *Kirche und theologische Literatur im byzantinischen Reich* (Munich 1959) 430–432. O. VOLK, *Lexikon für Theologie und Kirche*, ed. J. HOFER and K. RAHNER, 10 v. (2d, new ed. Freiburg 1957–65) 5:237–238. F. DÖLGER, *Corpus der griechischen Urkunden des Mittelalters und der neueren Zeit* (Munich 1924–32) 1:162–217. L. BRÉHIER, A. FLICHE and V. MARTIN eds., *Histoire de l'église depuis les origines jusqu'à nos jours* (Paris 1935–) 5:75–150. A. PERNICE, *L'Imperatore Eraclio* (Florence 1905). G. OSTROGORSKY, *History of the Byzantine State* (New Brunswick NJ 1957) 83–100. A. FROLOW, *Revue des études byzantines* 11 (1953) 88–105, true Cross. P. LEMERLE, *Studi medievali* 3d ser. 1.2 (1960) 347–361.

[W. E. KAEGI, JR.]

HERALDRY

Heraldry, the science of hereditary symbolism, is a discipline of modern origin, deriving from the practice of medieval heralds who put together collections of coats of arms—colored emblems or devices that developed from the decorations on the coats of arms of warriors. They are hereditary when the shield is familial, and uniform or constant if they represent an ecclesiastical person. Soon

Coat of arms depicting the Virgin Mary and the Saints Peter, Magdalena, and Catherine, Bodrum Castle, Bodrum, Turkey, 1472. (©Chris Hellier/CORBIS)

after their origin, armorial bearings were adopted by noncombatants such as ecclesiastics, women, and secular and religious corporations. This article is concerned only with the evolution of ecclesiastical heraldry, its juridical aspect, its characteristics, and its application.

ORIGINS

Heraldry in the Church originated with the seal. Religious seals are nearly contemporary in origin with those of barons, civil officers, and institutions having the right to use seals. The oldest is that of Richard, archbishop of Bourges (1067). The secular lord was generally represented by his arms appearing on the shield and a little later on the caparison of his horse. The ecclesiastic, on the other hand, whether he was a cardinal, bishop, canon, abbot, or priest, appeared in person on his seal, usually without arms.

Obviously the representation of mitered prelates in the act of blessing, with crosier in hand, is of great interest to the historian of ecclesiastical vestments, such as the chasuble, amice, cincture, stole, pallium, maniple, and gloves. As early as the 13th century, however, ecclesiastics are seen bearing armorial devices. Bishops at first had only the heraldic bearings of their rank or see: Miles of Nanteuil (1229), Robert of Cressonsart (1240), and William of Gretz (1261) carried the armorial bearings of the See of Beauvais—a cross cantoned by four keys. But these insignia of ecclesiastical rank were replaced by family arms by, e.g., Guy of Vergy, Bishop of Autun (1223), Guy of Rochefort, Bishop of Langres (1263), and Nicholas of Fontaine, Archdeacon of Valenciennes (1236), who became bishop of Cambray in 1247.

From this time on, the seal and ecclesiastical arms followed a parallel development. Heraldic bearings indicate both the person of the owner of the seal, who is thoroughly identified by the arms, and the date of the document, even though prelates were often designated only by their Christian names. Armorial bearings appear also on currency to identify the authority who had the right to mint and to guarantee its value and weight. Pope MARTIN V'S currency (1417–31) exhibited for the first time his coat of arms topped by the tiara and the keys. Prior to this time, only the tiara and keys were displayed.

Abbeys, priories, and other communities employed seals at the same time that personal seals were being used by churchmen, but special arms for such institutes came into use only at the beginning of the 14th century. Ecclesiastical seals were ordinarily oblong in shape, but sometimes they were round. In the latter form, decoration became more complicated; the hagiographic seal was especially varied, with countless figures of Christ, crucifixes, simple crosses, figures of the Paschal Lamb with halo, of the Trinity, the Blessed Virgin with or without the Child. Of the saints—those appearing most frequently were Peter, Paul, John, Martin, Nicholas, and James.

CHARACTERISTICS OF THE ECCLESIASTICAL COAT OF ARMS

Heraldic bearings, which continued to be part of the decoration of the seal, became a mark of ownership placed on bindings, margins of manuscripts, small chests, sacred vessels, episcopal thrones, and portraits. Arms appearing on these objects are important means of identification. During the 17th century, blazons occupy the entire surface of seals and stamps, and ecclesiastical arms are distinguishable from nonecclesiastical only by such external ornamentation as miters, crosiers, hats, tassels, crosses, or the staff of a prior—placed in pale behind the shield.

HERALDIC CAPACITY

Entitled by Canon Law to use armorial bearing, the prelate had the duty to create a coat of arms if he had no family coat. Following this legislation, ecclesiastical arms were seen everywhere, not only as a mark of authenticity on documents, but as a mark of ownership and ornamentation. They are etched on the façades of churches and episcopal palaces, on altars, tombs, and choir stalls; candlesticks, chalices, Missals, bookbindings, liturgical vestments, stained glass windows, and grillwork were all adorned with ecclesiastical bearings. In more recent times this multiplicity of armorial bearings has been checked by reserving its use only to patrons of churches, to donors, and to funereal monuments. Thus, in general, the right to heraldic devices in the Church was determined by dogmatic, liturgical, and canonical regulations.

It is necessary, however, to note that armorial bearings were the identifying mark not only of the ecclesiastic's person, but also of his rank. For since the rules of religious heraldry are the same as those of lay heraldry, and since the family coat of arms of a pope, bishop, or abbot *nullius* is indistinguishable from that of the other members of the family, his device must exhibit the insignia of his office and rank. To existing family blazons, therefore, and to those that were created for new prelates, were added the hierarchical insignia of the Church.

EMBLEMS OF ECCLESIASTICAL RANK

A variety of conventional heraldic idioms has been employed to distinguish the person and rank of their bearer.

The Tiara. The most exalted symbols were naturally reserved for the pope. Of these, the TIARA has become the emblem of the papacy. The first circlet surrounding the lower band of this headdress did not appear, it would seem, until sometime between the 9th and the 11th century. The second crown was added by BONIFACE VIII (1294–1303), and the third by BENEDICT XI (1303–04) or CLEMENT V (1305–14). Together they make up the *triregnum.*

The Keys. Between the tiara and the shield, the pope's arms bear two keys, one of gold in bend dexter across a silver key in sinister. The keys at first surmounted the shield, but are now placed behind the pope's blazon. They designate the supernatural power of binding and loosing bestowed by Christ on St. Peter and his successors. Moreover, the golden key indicates the power that extends to heaven, the silver key, the power over all the faithful on earth.

The Banner. The banner also is a pontifical emblem. It is the symbol of the Roman Church and its temporal power.

The Miter. The MITER is the mark of episcopal dignity and represents a sacred rank. Certain abbots at times acquired the right to the miter in their heraldic bearings.

The Hat. The most frequently used ecclesiastical crest is the hat. It is a pilgrim's hat, flat and wide-brimmed. The number of tassels (*houppes*) has varied through the years. The use of the hat goes back to the 13th century when INNOCENT IV (1243–54) conferred the red hat on the cardinals to distinguish them from other prelates. The hat is presented to the CARDINAL in a solemn ceremony, at times given to the new dignitary by the chief of state, when, e.g., an apostolic nuncio is promoted to the rank of cardinal.

Following the cardinals, patriarchs, primates, archbishops, and bishops also adopted the hat, but one of different color as shall be seen below.

The Crosier and Miter. The crosier is the most widely used symbol in ecclesiastical heraldry, employed by bishops, abbots, abbesses, and by religious communities. Like the scepter, the crosier is a sign of higher power, the symbol of the Good Shepherd, indicating both temporal power and episcopal jurisdiction. The miter is placed on the shield at the highest line of the chief, as is also done with the upper part of the crosier.

Coronets. The coronet or crown was sometimes placed between the shield and the hat. In France there were six ecclesiastical peerages, three of which had the rank of duchy (the archdiocese of Reims and the Dioceses of Laon and Langres) and three the rank of county (Beauvais, Châlons, and Noyon, all bishoprics). The titulars of these sees wore the respective coronets of the county or duchy. The wearing of such coronets is today forbidden by the Holy See.

Decorations. From his shield the prelate may suspend the knightly orders conferred by the pope, such as the Order of the Holy Sepulcher of Jerusalem with its cross potent gules (red), cantoned by four small crosses of the same, or those conferred by the grand masters of independent orders, such as the Order of St. John of Jerusalem, known as the KNIGHTS OF MALTA or Rhodes, with its eight-pointed white cross (in honor of the beatitudes). Formerly, the king of France conferred the orders of St. Michael and of the Holy Spirit, called the orders of the king, and many prelates were arrayed with their emblems.

The Pallium. The archiepiscopal PALLIUM is placed either above or below the shield. The pallium is of great importance since its appearance distinguishes a residential from a titular archbishop.

The Cross. Patriarchs, archbishops, and bishops are entitled to use the cross, which is placed in pale behind the shield. For patriarchs and archbishops, the cross has a double traverse; for bishops a single.

The Baton or Staff. The staff is the emblem of priors and precentors. Like the crosier, it is derived from the pilgrim's staff.

HIERARCHICAL INSIGNIA

Cardinals customarily crest their arms with a red hat from which hang two red cords, each with 15 tassels. Patriarchs and primates crest their arms with a green hat, the color of chastity and of doctrine, from which hang cords of the same color, again with 15 tassels on either side. For an archbishop, the regulations are the same, except that the number of tassels is 10 on each side. Bishops, abbots, and other prelates *nullius* also are entitled to use the green hat, but with six tassels. For mitered and crosiered abbots and provosts the hat is black with six tassels. Both mitered and nonmitered abbots, however, may top their arms with a black hat having three tassels. The hat of the canon, the vicar, and simple priest also is black, but with a single tassel. The four *prelates di fiocchetto* are entitled to the black hat with six tassels as a part of their armorial bearings. Prothonotaries apostolic may crest their escutcheon with a violet hat from which hang red cords with six red tassels on either side. The arms of domestic prelates include a violet hat with six violet tassels. In short, prelates may bear four rows of red tassels if they are in the service of the papal chamber, and three rows of violet tassels if they are prothonotaries apostolic or domestic prelates of His Holiness. Other ecclesiastics, chamberlains, chaplains, canons, rural deans, minor superiors, and priests, are all entitled to heraldry. The arms of an abbess follow the same rules, although abbesses are without jurisdiction. However, they exercise authority that entitles them to a seal and consequently to armorial bearings. Their arms bear the crosier and the rosary.

COMMUNITIES

The armorial bearings of religious communities are numerous: orders, congregations, fraternities, monasteries, and bishoprics have all had ancient arms which, unfortunately, have often been replaced by pious images with no heraldic significance.

All the major religious orders have their particular arms. The Jesuits use the monogram of Christ, IHS, with the nails of the Passion; the Benedictines of the congregation of Saint-Maur have the word *Pax* in a crown of thorns with one fleur-de-lis in chief and three nails tapering; the Minims bear the word *Charitas;* the Augustinians a flaming heart; the Carmelites have a sable shield powdered with silver, alluding to the colors of their habit and to Mount Carmel; the Premonstratensians have an escutcheon powdered with fleurs-de-lis with two crosiers in saltire; the Dominicans at the chapter of Bogotá (1965) returned to the coat of arms with ''gyronny of eight, sable and argent, over all a cross flory counter-charged''; and the Franciscans bear the arms of Christ and Francis in saltire, surmounted by a cross.

Some armorial bearings can be explained by a historical fact: the Abbey of Saint-Denis, e.g., included in its arms a nail from the Passion, and the Chapter of Chartres has the tunic of Our Lady, both of which are preserved in their treasury. The shield of the chapter of Sens was emblazoned with a cross cantoned with eight crosiers, one for Sens and the seven others for the suffragan sees of Châlons, Auxerre, Meaux, Paris (made an archdiocese in the 17th century), Orléans, Nevers, and Troyes. From the initials of these originated the name Campont, which has led some to believe that there was once an ''Abbey of Campont.'' Several abbeys exhibited fleurs-de-lis in their capacity of royal abbeys, and some Burgundian abbeys, such as Cîteaux, Vézelay, Maizières, and the Sainte Chapelle of Dijon, added the charge of Burgundy impaled with fleurs-de-lis.

As in familial and municipal heraldry, canting arms (armorial devices with a pictorial pun) are employed in ecclesiastical coats of arms. Hence the Abbey of Ourscamp has a bear (*ours*) in its charge; the Abbey of Chelles exhibits a ladder (*échelle*); of Pontigny, a bridge (*pont*); Fontfroide, a fountain (*fontaine*); Thenailles, pliers or tongs (*tenailles*); etc. Abbeys used the characteristic attributes of their patron saint, a key for those dedicated to St. Peter, a sword for St. Paul, shells for St. Michael (Abbey of MONT-SAINT-MICHEL), a perfume box for St. Mary Magdalen of Vézelay; often the instruments of martyrdom, such as a wheel for St. Catherine, a gridiron for St. Lawrence, stones for St. Stephen, and swords for beheadings, appear in the arms. Occasionally, abbots carry an escutcheon impaled with the arms of their abbey or order in the dexter half, and with their family arms in the sinister.

An interesting fact to note for France is that by virtue of an edict of 1696 it was no longer permissible to wear armorial bearings without registering them and paying a fee of 20 pounds. Neither ecclesiastics nor religious communities were exonorated or exempt from this decree. The number of ecclesiastical crests was great. When the arms were not presented for registration the recalcitrant was taxed automatically. In Brittany, for example, 100 curates of poor rural parishes used armorial bearings. The bishop of Avranches was forced to intervene.

CONCLUSION

After nine centuries of existence, ecclesiastical heraldry is still alive and will undoubtedly continue as long as heraldry itself exists. It is as flourishing as familial or municipal heraldry, and at times possesses a binding force that the others lack. The special richness of its symbols and tincture endows the heraldry of the Church with decorative attractiveness, although the function it fulfills is primarily juridical.

Bibliography: D. L. GALBREATH, *Papal Heraldry,* v.1 of *A Treatise on Ecclesiastical Heraldry* (Cambridge, Eng. 1930–). J.

MEURGEY DE TUPIGNY, *Armorial de l'église de France* (Mâcon 1938); "Héraldique" in *L'Histoire et ses methodes* (Paris 1961) 740–767, with good bibliog. B. B. HEIM, *Wappen-Brauch und Wappenrecht in der Kirche* (Olten 1948); *Coutumes et droit héraldiques de l'église* (Paris 1949).

[J. MEURGEY DE TUPIGNY]

HERBERMANN, CHARLES GEORGE

Editor, author, educator; b. Saerbeck, Westphalia, Germany, Dec. 8, 1840; d. New York City, Aug. 24, 1916. He was the oldest of the seven children of George and Elizabeth (Stipp) Herbermann. In 1851 the Herbermann family came to New York City, where Charles attended St. Alphonsus parochial school and in 1858 graduated from St. Francis Xavier College, then affiliated with St. John's College, Fordham. He taught at St. Francis Xavier while continuing to study for his M.A. (St. John's College, 1860) and Ph.D. (St. Francis Xavier, 1865). In 1869 he was appointed professor of Latin at the College of the City of New York, beginning a career that terminated with his retirement in 1915. In 1873 he was also appointed college librarian. The same year he married Mary Theresa Dieter of Baltimore, Md.; after her death in 1876, he wed Elizabeth Schoeb of New York City in 1880.

In 1884 Herbermann joined John Gilmary Shea in founding the United States Catholic Historical Society. The society was inactive from Shea's death in 1892 until 1898 when Herbermann became president, an office he held until his death. During his tenure, there were published nine volumes of *Historical Records and Studies* and such monographs as *Unpublished Letters of Charles Carroll of Carrollton* (1902) and Waldseemuller's *Cosmographiae Introductio* (1907), a facsimile edition of the original (1507). Herbermann also contributed frequent articles to the society's publications. In 1905 he was chosen editor in chief of the *Catholic Encyclopedia.* Although his eyesight was severely impaired at that time, he saw the encyclopedia's 15 volumes to completion in 1913. Recognition of his activities came from Pius X who awarded him a knighthood of St. Gregory and the medal *Pro Ecclesia et Pontifice;* from the University of Notre Dame, Ind., which conferred its Laetare medal; and from Fordham University, New York City, Holy Cross College, Worcester, Mass., and the Catholic University of America, Washington, D.C., which gave him honorary degrees. His published works include editions of Sallust's *Bellum Jugurthinum* (1886) and *Bellum Catilinae* (1900), a translation of Torfason's *History of Ancient Vinland* (1888), and *The Sulpicians in the United States* (1916).

Bibliography: P. CONDON, "Charles George Herbermann," *Historical Records and Studies of the U. S. Catholic Historical Society of New York* 10 (1917) 8–29.

[H. F. HERBERMANN]

HERBERT OF CHERBURY, EDWARD

Religious philosopher, historian, soldier, and diplomatist, elder brother of George Herbert, the religious poet; b. Eyton-on-Severn (Shropshire), March 3, 1583; d. London, Aug. 20, 1648. Of a noble Welsh family, Herbert was educated at University College, Oxford. Shortly after the accession of James I he was created a Knight of the Bath. He went abroad in 1610 for seven years as a soldier of fortune, and made the acquaintance of several scholars, including P. GASSENDI and H. GROTIUS. In 1618 or 1619 he went as ambassador extraordinary to the French court; he was recalled in 1621 owing to differences with De Luynes, but went back the next year as ordinary ambassador. On his return to England he received the Irish peerage of Castle Island, and in 1629 Charles I raised him to the English peerage as Baron Herbert of Cherbury. When the Civil War commenced he sided with the royalists, and in 1644 surrendered his castle at Montgomery to the parliamentarians.

Herbert is remembered as a historian for *The Life and Raigne of King Henry VIII* (1649) and his *Expeditio Buckinghami Ducis* (1656). *The Life of Herbert by Himself* was first printed by Horace Walpole in 1764. His Latin and English poems were published by his son in 1665. His most important work is the *De veritate prout distinguitur a revelatione, a verisimili, a possibili, et a falso* (Paris 1624). The third edition appeared in London in 1645 together with a short treatise *De causis errorum,* a tract *De religione laici,* and an *Appendix ad sacerdotes.* His *De religione gentilium* (Amsterdam 1663) is a kind of pioneer comparative religion.

Herbert held that man is a complex unity of body and soul, but that, while the body is passive, the mind is active in knowing. The senses bring things within the reach of the mind's activities. Presupposing a harmony between the world of things and the mind, he held that truth consists in the harmony between things and analogous mental faculties, which are as innumerable as the things with which they are in harmony. These faculties, though innumerable, can be classified in four groups: natural instinct, internal sense, external sense, and reasoning. Man knows by means of "common notions" or innate ideas, which have the distinctive qualities of apriority, independence, universality, certainty, and necessity. Herbert did not determine the number of these common notions, his main concern being to fix the common notions of religion, viz:

(1) there is a Supreme Being or Deity; (2) this Deity is to be worshiped; (3) the chief part of worship consists in the moral life; (4) man should make expiation for his sins by repentance; and (5) man's deeds will be rewarded or punished in the next life. For him, these five notions determined the character of the natural religion of reason and shaped the primitive religions of mankind before these were corrupted by the sacerdotalism that originated in the self-seeking and craft of men profiteering on religion. They became the five articles of religion held by the English deists of the 18th century; thus Herbert is considered to be the father of English DEISM. His ideas have certain affinities with those of the CAMBRIDGE PLATONISTS and the SCOTTISH SCHOOL OF COMMON SENSE.

Bibliography: Works. *De veritate,* tr. M. H. CARRÉ (Bristol 1937); *De religione laici,* ed. and tr. H. R. HUTCHESON (New Haven 1944), critical study of Herbert's life and work with bibliog. **Literature.** F. C. COPLESTON, *History of Philosophy* (Westminster Md. 1959) 5:53–54. V. SAINATI, *Enciclopedia filosofica,* 4 v. (Venice-Rome 1957) 2:1057–60. M. M. ROSSI, *La vita, le opere, i tempi di Edoardo Herbert di Cherbury,* 3 v. (Florence 1947).

[E. A. SILLEM]

HERBIGNY, MICHAEL D'

Theologian, Orientalist; b. Lille, France, May 8, 1880; d. Aix-en-Provence, Dec. 24, 1957. He joined the Jesuits (1897), was ordained (1910), and became professor of Sacred Scripture and theology at the Jesuit scholasticate in Enghien, Belgium (1912–21), and director of graduate studies at the Gregorian University in Rome (1921–23). As president (1923–26) and then rector (1926–31) of the Pontifical Oriental Institute he developed greatly the school and its library, and founded its semiannual periodical *Orientalia Christiana.* His role in the foundation of the Pontifical Russian College in Rome (1929) was important. He was special consultor for the Congregation of the Oriental Church (1923–37) and a member of the Pontifical Commission for Russia from 1926. During his journeys to Russia he was politically indiscrete, but collected abundant documents, later published in articles or resounding tracts. His activity considerably alleviated suffering during the terrible Russian famine (1922–23). He became titular bishop of Ilium (1926) and assistant at the papal throne (1934), but poor health forced his retirement (1934). His numerous articles and books were devoted to theology, ecumenical apologetics, and contemporary history of Bolshevism. His principal work was *Theologica de Ecclesia* (2 v. 1920–21, 3d ed. 1928).

Bibliography: Y. M. J. CONGAR, *Catholicisme* 5:633. H. BEYLARD, *Dictionnaire de théologie catholique, Tables générales* 2049–50.

[P. GOUBERT]

HERDER

The name of a distinguished international Catholic publishing house owned by the Herder family in Freiburg im Breisgau.

Bartholomew (1774–1839) founded the house in 1801. A colorful and enterprising publisher, he edited, published, and printed the army newspaper and official bulletins of Metternich, whom he served as press liaison in Paris in 1815. Eventually he established an institute for lithography and engraving, which produced highly acclaimed atlases and scholarly publications.

Benjamin (1818–88), who succeeded his father Bartholomew, was the master architect of the Herder image ''Universal-verlag.'' He expanded the firm's scope, emphasizing theological, encyclopedic, and other scholarly works. He published the *Bible for Students* (1848), which was translated into 60 languages. His contributions to Catholic publishing included the production of *Kirchenlexikon* (12 v. 1847–60), a monumental encyclopedia covering every aspect of theology; *Theologische Bibliothek* (31 v. 1882–1930), a theological library; and *Konversations-Lexikon* (5 v. 1853–57), a popular general encyclopedia. He published also *Schott* (1884), a popular layman's missal. Because of his farflung and varied publishing programs, Benjamin was a major influence in the Catholic revival of 19th-century Germany.

Hermann (1864–1937), Benjamin's son, broadened the firm's work into the fields of philosophy, political science, law, and archeology. He published papal encyclicals and initiated the publication of Ludwig von Pastor's *History of the Popes* (16 v. 1886–1933). Hermann also built an impressive new plant in Freiburg, and developed an international network of publishing and distributing divisions in Vienna, Rome, Barcelona, Tokyo, and St. Louis.

Theophil Herder-Dorneich (1898–1987), Hermann's son-in-law, assumed the firm's direction in 1937 at a difficult time. The Nazi regime blocked further expansion and threatened to close the house when the firm, ''for reasons of conscience,'' refused to have articles in an encyclopedia rewritten to conform to Nazi ideology. In November 1944 the publishing house in Freiburg was completely destroyed by bombing, but the plant was reconstructed and modernized after the war. All standard works were reissued; a juvenile division, a book club, and several new magazines were added, a chain of 16 book stores in Germany, Austria, and Switzerland was developed, and branches of the firm were established in Buenos Aires, Santiago de Chile, São Paulo, and Bogotá. Under Herder-Dorneich's direction Herder Verlag has become the world's largest international Catholic publishing house. He also supervised the publication of a Catholic catechism that has been translated into 30 languages, and continued the firm's commitment to publish work to foster the new currents in the Church, especially those devolving from the work of VATICAN COUNCIL II and world ecumenism. (*See* ECUMENICAL MOVEMENT.)

Herder and Herder was established in New York City (1957) to carry on the firm's activities in the English-speaking world. A branch had been set up (1873) in St. Louis, Mo., but as a result of World War I it was incorporated in 1917 as a separate and autonomous firm, the B. Herder Book Company of St. Louis. The initial objective of Herder and Herder was to publish scholarly works from abroad in translation; in keeping with the spirit of the era inaugurated by Pope John XXIII, it successfully embarked upon a new program of publishing original works by U.S. scholars. An important facet of this project is the English-language publication of the ecumenical monthly for the Christian world, *Herder Correspondence.* The firm's affiliated organization, the Herder Book Center (New York City), distributes the publications of 25 other U.S. Catholic publishing houses, including a number of university presses.

[W. M. LINZ]

Johann Gottfried Von Herder.

HERDER, JOHANN GOTTFRIED VON

German critic and philosopher of history; b. Mohrungen, East Prussia, Aug. 25, 1744; d. Weimar, Dec. 18, 1803. He was the third child of Gottfried Herder. After attending Latin school, he began (1762) the study of theology at the University of Königsberg. He went to Riga (1764) as a teacher and there accepted an assignment as preacher in 1767. His first literary and linguistic essays were *Über die neuere deutsche Literatur* (1766) and *Kritische Wälder* (1769). On May 23, 1769, he left Riga by sea to travel in France. His *Journal meiner Reise*, begun after his arrival but published posthumously, reflects the liberating experience of the journey. His time in Nantes and Paris served for the study of the French language and literature. After returning to Germany, he traveled, as companion to Prince Peter von Holstein-Gottorp, to Hanover, Kassel, and Darmstadt. There he met Caroline Flachsland, whom he married in 1773. In Strassburg, Herder resigned as tutor to the prince but remained in that city until the end of 1771 because of a critical eye operation. There he met GOETHE (1770), and from this association came the manifesto of the *Sturm und Drang* movement, *Von deutscher Art und Kunst* (1773), with its contribution to Shakespeare studies. The work also included Goethe's essay on the cathedral of Strassburg. In his own prize essay for the Royal Academy, *Über den Ursprung der Sprache* (1772), Herder developed an organic-genetic interpretation of language. In Bückeburg, where he became court chaplain in 1771, Herder experienced a crisis in his life and a religious turning point. In *Älteste Urkunde des Menschengeschlechtes* (1774) he recognized the Bible as the self-revelation of God. His *Auch eine Philosophie der Geschichte zur Bildung der Menschheit* (1774) attempts to study history as God's action in nature and upon nations and the realization of God's action as successively different among different peoples. The first volume of Herder's collection of folksongs, fairy tales, and myths appeared in 1779. At Wieland's suggestion and Goethe's urging, Herder went to Weimar in 1776, where he published (1778) his study of aesthetics, *Plastik;* it differentiates sculpture from painting and inquires into its representational potentialities. Herder attempted a sociology of poetry in *Über die Wirkung der Dichtkunst auf die Sitten der Völker in alten und neuen Zeiten,* which sees poetry as shaping the tribal community. In 1783, while renewing his friendship with Goethe, Herder wrote *Ideen zur Philosophie der Geschichte der Menschheit* (part 1, 1784; part 2, 1785), a compendium of all his ideas and the most comprehensive treatment of the knowledge of his time. The meaning of world history, he held, consists in the development of humanity, which is both the essence of all human natural tendencies and, at the same time, an ethical ideal. In 1792 Herder reflected on the French Revolution in *Briefe, die Fortschritte der Humanität betreffend,* which opposed to the concept of revolution one of evolution, which would lead to a state government by the people. In *Zerstreute Blätter* (1785) he turned his attention again to poetry. In 1788 Herder traveled to Italy, which, however, he did not regard with classical eyes as Goethe had done. Personal reasons led to a separation from Goethe in 1793, and Herder was left isolated in Weimar. In 1796 Jean Paul (Richter) became a late disciple of Herder, who had made enemies among the other romanticists by his critique of Kant in *Metakritik zur Kritik der reinen Vernunft* (1799) and *Kalligone* (1800). The *Christliche Schriften* (1794–98) contains five collections of theological inquiries with a critique on the handing down of the Gospels. Herder's influence was enormous, especially on the development of Romanticism.

Bibliography: *Sämtliche Werke,* ed. B. SUPHAN, 33 v. (Berlin 1877–1913). R. HAYM, *Herder nach seinem Leben und seinen Werken,* 2 v. (Berlin 1880–85). R. UNGER, *Hamann und die Aufklärung,* 2 v. (Jena 1911; 2d ed. Halle 1925). F. MEINECKE, *Die Entstehung des Historismus,* ed. C. HINRICHS (Munich 1959). F. MCEACHRAN, *Life and Philosophy of Johann Gottfried Herder* (Oxford 1939).

[I. G. MERKEL]

HERDTRICH, CHRISTIAN WOLFGANG

Jesuit missionary and mathematician; b. Graz, Austria, June 25, 1625; d. Hangzhou, China, July 18, 1684. He entered the Society of Jesus in 1641 and departed for the Far East in 1656. He spent two years on the island of Sulawesi before entering the Chinese provinces of Shanxi and Henan in 1660. In 1671 he joined the group of Jesuit mathematicians attached to the imperial court of Kangxi in Beijing. He wrote what is probably the first Chinese-Latin dictionary and collaborated on a Latin translation of the writings of Confucius, *Confucius, Sinarum Philosophus, sive Scientia Sinensis exposita studio et opera Prosperi Intorcetta, Christiani Herdtrich, Francisci Rougemont, Philippi Couplet, P.P. Soc. Jesu* (Paris 1678). From this work European scholars became acquainted with the teachings of the Chinese philosopher. During the last nine years of his life, Herdtrich was superior of the mission at Hangzhou.

Bibliography: L. KOCH, *Jesuiten-Lexikon: Die Gesellschaft Jesu einst und jetzt* (Paderborn 1934); photoduplicated with rev. and suppl., 2 v. (Louvain-Heverlee 1962) E. T. HIBBERT, *K'ang Hsi, Emperor of China* (London 1940). A. H. ROWBOTHAM, *Missionary and Mandarian: The Jesuits at the Court of China* (Berkeley 1942).

[J. V. MENTAG]

HEREFORD, ANCIENT SEE OF

One of the dioceses (Worcester was the other) erected from lands formerly under Lichfield. At some time after 675 and before 680, THEODORE (of Tarsus), Archbishop of Canterbury, brought the huge and unwieldly see of Lichfield under the jurisdiction of Canterbury and, as one of his major administrative reforms, subdivided it. The first bishop of Hereford was probably Putta, Bishop of Rochester (669–686), who had fled to the protection of Seaxwulf, Bishop of Lichfield (i.e., Mercia), after Aethelred, King of Mercia, had devastated Kent and destroyed Rochester (676). The see of Hereford originally corresponded to the area settled by the Anglo-Saxon tribes known collectively as the Magonsaetan, but it also included areas of Celtic occupation, and its boundaries later included all of Herefordshire, southern Shropshire, and a few parishes in other counties.

The cathedral church was dedicated to the Blessed Virgin Mary and to St. ETHELBERT, King of East Anglia (martyred *c.* 793). The present cathedral dates from 1079–1110 and was begun by the learned Robert Losinga (1079–95) and continued by GERARD (1096–1100), who became archbishop of York. The ablest bishop of Hereford in the 12th century was Gilbert FOLIOT (1148–63), better known after his translation as bishop of London (1163–87) and adviser to HENRY II, whom he supported in the quarrel with Archbishop Thomas BECKET. The best known 13th-century bishop of Hereford was St. Thomas of Cantelupe, chancellor of Oxford University and, briefly, royal chancellor (1265) during the baronial ascendancy under Simon de Montfort.

The ''Use of Hereford,'' dating probably from the episcopate of Robert Losinga, was nearer to the Roman rite than the ''Use of SARUM.'' The former was abolished under HENRY VIII. The CATHEDRAL SCHOOL, one of the better educational institutions of the western Midlands, has a continuous history dating from the early 14th century or, probably, earlier. The cathedral has a large collection of MSS, incunabula, and relics.

Bibliography: W. DUGDALE, *Monasticon Anglicanum* (London 1817–30) 6.3:1210–17. W. W. CAPES, ed., *Charters and Records of Hereford Cathedral* (Hereford 1908). A. SCHMITT, *Lexikon für Theologie und Kirche*, J. HOFER and K. RAHNER, eds. (Freiburg 1957–65) 5:244–245. Canterbury and York Society publications, *passim.*

[R. S. HOYT]

HEREFORD, NICHOLAS

Wyclifite, Carthusian; d. Coventry Charterhouse, after 1417. Nothing is known of him until 1369, when he became a fellow at Queen's College, Oxford, where John WYCLIF was a regular resident for the greater part of his Oxford career. It is safe to assume that Hereford's conversion to Lollardy was due to Wyclif's influence (*see* LOLLARDS). About 1380, Hereford was one of the translators of the Lollard Bible, perhaps with John PURVEY. In 1382 he received his doctorate in theology. In the same year, preaching on Ascension Day at the invitation of the chancellor of Oxford, Robert RYGGE, he delivered a sermon in support of Wyclif that resulted in his own condemnation by Church and State. Failing to receive a sympathetic hearing from John of Gaunt, Hereford and Philip REPINGTON appealed to Rome in person, before their excommunication by Abp. William COURTENAY. In Rome Hereford was imprisoned, but the pope saved him from death. During a popular uprising in 1385 he escaped from prison and returned to England. His leadership of Wyclif's disciples was cut short by his renewed excommunication and arrest in 1387. Sometime before December 1391, he recanted and made a full submission. Thereafter he served as chancellor and treasurer of Hereford cathedral. In 1417 he retired to a Coventry charterhouse where he died in old age, date unknown.

Bibliography: C. L. KINGSFORD, *The Dictionary of National Biography from the Earliest Times to 1900*, 63 v. (London 1885–1900; 1908–38) 14:418–420. M. DEANESLY, *The Significance of the Lollard Bible* (London 1951). J. H. DAHMUS, *The Prosecution of John Wyclyf* (New Haven 1952). K. B. MCFARLANE, *John Wycliffe and the Beginnings of English Nonconformity* (New York 1953). A.B. EMDEN, *A Biographical Register of the University of Oxford to A.D. 1500*, 3 v. (Oxford 1957–59) 2:913–915.

[J. E. HEALEY]

HEREFORD USE

Hereford, on the borders of Wales, was founded as a diocese by Putta in 676. St. ETHELBERT (d. *c.* 793), King of East Anglia, was buried in the cathedral and in the 9th century was declared joint patron. The present cathedral was built between 1079 and 1110, a product, like so many others, of the Norman conquest, to which also is owed the organization of the chapter and the liturgical practices there established. With Hereford again it can be said with some certainty that the local use was derived from Rouen and that the borrowing took place during the episcopate of Robert de Bethune (bishop 1131–48), who restored the cathedral (damaged during the civil war that followed the death of Henry I) and reformed the liturgy there. Curiously enough the Use of Hereford penetrated to Savoy where it was adopted in 1267 (persisting until 1580) at the collegiate church of St. Catherine at Aiguebelle; the founder of this church was a former bishop of Hereford.

In the Mass rite the prayers at the foot of the altar were similar to those of the other English uses (that is, in the short form, with Psalm 42, versicles, etc., said while vesting or on the way to the altar). The Officium (Introit) was repeated three times as at Sarum. The bread and wine were set on the altar before the Offertory verse, but both were offered together with a single prayer. At the *Orate fratres* (*et sorores* does not occur at Hereford) there was no answer. At the giving of the kiss of peace the formula was similar to that of York. There were four prayers (as at Rouen) before the celebrant's Communion. A third ablution was taken in water only, and then the chalice was laid horizontally on the paten. Mass ended in the ordinary way, but there was no blessing or Last Gospel.

It is particularly in the HOLY WEEK services that the greatest affinity with Rouen is to be seen. Thus on Palm Sunday the combination of the procession of palms with one of the Blessed Sacrament, the similarities between the *Mandatum* at Hereford and Rouen, the *Exsultet* with its addition *pro rege N. et principe nostro N.* (the original reference being to the king of France and the duke of Normandy) show that Hereford adopted the liturgical practices of Rouen almost en bloc.

Bibliography: W. MASKELL, *The Ancient Liturgy of the Church of England, According to the Uses of Sarum, Bangor, York and Herford, and the Modern Roman Liturgy* (3d ed. Oxford 1882). A. A. KING, *Liturgies of the Past* (Milwaukee 1959). W. H. ST. J. HOPE and E. G. ATCHLEY, *English Liturgical Colours* (London 1918). E. BISHOP, *Liturgica Historica,* ed. R. H. CONNOLLY and K. SISAM (Oxford 1918).W. H. FRERE and L. E. G. BROWN, eds., *The Hereford Breviary* (Henry Bradshaw Society 26, 40, 46; London 1904, 1911, 1915). H. J. FEASEY, *Ancient English Holy Week Ceremonial* (London 1897).

[L. C. SHEPPARD/EDS.]

HERESY

The words ''schism'' (σχίσμα) and ''heresy'' (αἵρεσις) both appear in the NT, but neither is a technical term in the modern canonico-theological sense. While the NT term ''SCHISM'' remains quite undifferentiated and undeveloped, the term ''heresy'' shows the remote beginnings of its later technical orientation.

In Hellenism, heresy (from Gr. αἱρέομαι, to choose) meant (1) a teaching and (2) a school, e.g., a philosophical school such as the Stoics. In Hellenic and rabbinic Jewry heresy designated a religious party within Judaism (e.g., the Pharisees or Sadducees). In these instances the word has a neutral, nonpejorative sense.

This neutral sense of the word appears in Acts, where St. Paul calls the Pharisees ''the strictest sect [heresy] of our religion'' (Acts 26.5; see 5.17; 15.5). Nevertheless, when the Jewish lawyer Tertullus referred to Christianity

Statue of Giordiano Bruno, who in 1600 was burnt at the stake for heresy at this site, Campo dei Fiori, Rome. (©Ted Spiegel/CORBIS)

as ''the Nazarene sect'' (Acts 24.5), making it simply another party within Judaism (cf. Acts 28.22), St. Paul disavowed this sectarian appellation, saying: ''I admit that in serving the God of my forefathers I follow the Way [ὁδός: see W. Michaelis, *Theologisches Wörterbuch zum Neuen Testament* 5:93], which they call a heresy'' (Acts 24.14). For St. Paul Christianity could not be a heresy, or party, in any sense, much less a heretical enclave within Judaism.

When St. Paul uses the term ''heresy'' in a Christian context, the meaning is pejorative, standing for splinter groupings or movements within the Christian community that threaten Church unity (Gal 5.20; 1 Cor 11.19). Paul speaks also of the ''heretical man'' (Ti 3.10), or the sectarian-minded man, in a similar reproving way.

2 Pt 2.1 warns of ''lying teachers who will bring in destructive sects,'' thus marking the start of a sharper delineation of the word ''heresy'' in the direction of the later technical term. Here the heresy, burdened with heterodoxy, seemingly becomes a centrifugal movement dividing the Church.

Patristic Era. From the late 2d century onward the Fathers usually discriminated between heresy and schism. Both were understood not as abstract errors or as individual attitudes but rather as organized bodies or sects outside the Catholic Church. Heresy involved doctrinal error, whereas schism meant orthodox dissent. St. Augustine wrote: ''you are a schismatic by your sacrilegious separation and a heretic by your sacrilegious doctrine'' (*C. Gaud.* 2.9.10; *Corpus scriptorum ecclesiasticorum latinorum* 53:267). ''Heretics violate the faith by thinking falsely about God, while schismatics break away from fraternal love by their wicked separations, although they believe as we do'' (*Fid. et symb.* 8.21; *Corpus scriptorum ecclesiasticorum latinorum* 41:27). The Fathers, however, frequently used the two terms more or less interchangeably. Thus Cyprian called the Novatians schismatics and heretics without any distinction; and the first Council of Toledo (400) spoke of a man returning to the Church "de haereticorum schismate" (*cap.* 12; *Sacrorum Conciliorum nova et amplissima collectio,* 3:1000). To many Fathers it seemed otiose to make a nice distinction between heresy and schism, when, pastorally and religiously, the crucial fact was that both were impious counterfeit communions living outside the true Church (see Cyprian, *Epist.* 69.1; *Corpus scriptorum ecclesiasticorum latinorum* 3.2:749–750). As both issued in corporate separation from the common life of the Church, it did not much matter whether that alienation came from an obdurate persistence in false doctrine or from a crooked desire to live apart from the disciplined life and ordered worship established by the Church.

Some Fathers saw in protracted schism an inbuilt bias toward heresy; there is in schism a latent theological problem that will work its way to the surface, or else some theological ground will be elaborated to bolster up the schism. St. Jerome wrote: "There is no schism which does not invent some heresy for itself in order to justify its departure from the Church" (*In Titum* 3.10–11; *Patrologia Latina* 26:598). St. Augustine also tended to look on heresy as "a long-standing schism" (*C. Cresc.* 2.7.9; *Corpus scriptorum ecclesiasticorum latinorum* 52:367).

But "not all error is heresy" (St. Augustine, *Haer.; Patrologia Latina* 42:19); and "not every error betrays godlessness" (Pope Celestine I, *Epist.* 25.3; *Patrologia Latina* 50:550). Wherever there is simple error or misunderstanding as to the faith, there is no heresy, provided there is fundamental docility to the teaching of the Church. In order to have heresy there must be the stubborn inflexible will, once the falsity of the doctrine in question has become clear to the Church and has been made clear to the erring Christian, to persist in denying the doctrine taught and received by the Catholic Church. Such a willfully obdurate posture, which turns its face against the whole Church and which swarms to form its own conventicle, is the mark of true heresy, which the Fathers reprobated as gravely sinful. Although the presumption of bad faith, wherever heresy was present, strongly influenced the judgment of the Fathers (see J. Korbacher, *Ausserhalb der Kirche kein Heil?* [Munich 1963] 155–164), still St. Augustine held that those who have not fathered the error but received it from others, who do not cling to it pertinaciously but seek the truth, "are by no means to be reckoned among the heretics" (*Epist.* 43.1; *Corpus scriptorum ecclesiasticorum latinorum* 34.2:85).

The Fathers emphasized the religio-moral side of heresy, with its causes and consequences under this aspect; they stressed also its corporate divisive stance.

Middle Ages and After. Augustine, Jerome, and Gregory dominated the thinking of the medieval scholastics on the theme of heresy. Like the Fathers, so too the scholastics delineated only in a very generic way what is, objectively speaking, the heterodox teaching required to constitute heresy; they laid much more stress on the moral aspect of heresy, i.e., on the sin of heresy with its willful, proud isolation from the communion of the faithful, its contemptuous rejection of Church discipline, and its tragic religious consequences for the life of the believer. It was not so much abstract heresy that was cataloged, as the guilty heretic rebuked.

Notwithstanding the scholastics' efforts to systematize the concept of heresy, the term exhibits a notable elasticity in its use. From the Middle Ages until well beyond the time of Trent, the basic correlative concepts, faith and heresy, were often used, both theologically (see St. Thomas Aquinas, *Summa theologiae* 2a2ae, 11.2; 1a, 32.4; *In 1 sent.* 33.1.5) and in Church documents (*Enchiridion symbolorum* 902, 906, 1800) with a less precise content and a wider application than is customary today. Faith was often taken globally to comprise everything of vital significance for a truly Christian and ecclesial way of thinking and for a sound life of faith—everything, therefore, falling within the competence of the Church's discipline of faith. Correspondingly, a heretic was one willfully guilty of a stubborn antagonism to this docile faith-attitude, one whose conduct jeopardized the trueness and soundness of his life of faith. Intractability and pertinacity, coupled with a practical contempt for the teaching authority of the Church, played a decisive role in heresy so conceived. Such a vital and pastoral view of heresy takes in a wider range of reprehensible conduct than the denial of formally revealed truths taught by the Church. It includes every serious threat to the integrity of the life of faith and every stubborn contemptuous rejection of Church discipline.

The medieval scholastics, with their optimistic view of the powers of human reason to achieve the truth, took a correspondingly poor view, morally speaking, of any error, especially heresy. Hence the conviction, long dominant, that heresy's fellow was bad faith; and it was a long while before heresy was reckoned as falling within the ambit of inculpable error.

Since the 17th and 18th centuries, concomitantly with the fuller development of the treatise of theological criteriology, heresy became much more predominantly a doctrinal censure, designating objectively heterodox doctrine as that which contravenes a truth of divine and Catholic faith. In this orientation the religio-moral subjective aspects of heresy are not particularly attended to, although there are indications today that the factor of personal guilt is being reintegrated into the concept of heresy. See *Codex iuris canonici* c. 751 for the modern concept of heresy.

See Also: CENSURE, THEOLOGICAL; RULE OF FAITH; THINKING WITH THE CHURCH, RULES FOR; UNITY OF FAITH; UNITY OF THE CHURCH.

Bibliography: J. BROSCH, *Das Wesen der Häresie* (Bonn 1936). H. E. W. TURNER, *The Pattern of Christian Truth* (London 1954). K. RAHNER, *On Heresy* (New York 1964). M. MEINERTZ, ''σχίσμα und αἵρεσις im N.T.,'' *Biblische Zeitschrift* 1 (1957) 114–118. J. DE GUIBERT, ''La Notion d'hérésie chez Saint Augustin,'' *Bulletin de littérature ecclésiastique* 11 (1920) 368–382. G. W. H. LAMPE, ed., *A Patristic Greek Lexicon* (Oxford 1961–) fasc. 1, p. 51. A. LANG, ''Der Bedeutungswandel der Begriffe 'fides' und 'haeresis' und die dogmatische Wertung der Konzilsentscheidungen von Vienne und Trient,'' *Münchener theologische Zeitschrift* 4 (1953) 133–146.

[F. X. LAWLOR/EDS.]

HERESY (CANON LAW)

In canon law heresy is the offense of one who, having been baptized and retaining the name of Christian, pertinaciously denies or doubts any of the truths that one is under obligation of divine and Catholic faith to believe (cf. *Codex iuris canonici* [Rome 1918; repr. Graz 1955] c. 751). The element of pertinacity distinguishes heresy from inculpable error with regard to a truth of faith, although such error is sometimes called material, as distinguished from formal, heresy. The truth that is denied, or from which assent is deliberately and culpably withheld, must be one of Catholic as well as of divine faith, i.e., it must be explicitly proposed by the Church as a truth of divine faith (*Codex iuris canonici* c. 750 §1; *Codex canonum ecclesiarium orientalium* c. 598).

The term ''heresy'' is no longer used by the Catholic Church in reference to those persons who are outside her visible communion (cf. Vatican II, *Unitatis redintegratio* 3). Total heresy, i.e., the total rejection of faith, is known as APOSTASY.

Pertinacity in error does not require a protracted period. It means simply that, despite certainty that a truth is of Catholic faith, the heretic with culpable obstinacy refuses to assent to it, even if he does not give positive assent to the contrary error. If all the conditions necessary for a deliberate act are verified, this does not demand a lapse of time, and the sin may be committed in the secrecy of the heart, although one is not subject to the canonical penalties unless the heresy has been externally manifested.

Most Catholic moralists agree that heresy destroys the virtue of faith even though the dissent or doubt concerns but a single revealed truth. To refuse assent to anything God has revealed is equivalent to refusing assent to God as revealing and thus to all He has revealed. If a heretic continues to accept other truths of faith, it is because he elects to accept them on his own authority rather than that of God.

Doubt in this context is to be understood as the deliberate suspension or withholding of assent and is by no means to be confused either with indeliberate hesitation of mind that may occur when one considers a particular truth or with temptations, even vehement temptations, to disbelief.

Propositions contrary to divine and Catholic faith are called heretical, and those who profess such doctrine are sometimes referred to as heretics. Most of these, it may be assumed, are heretics only in the material sense of the term and are either in completely inculpable error or their responsibility is attenuated to a greater or lesser degree by ignorance. Formal heresy in the full sense, implying the rejection of a doctrine known certainly to be of faith by one who sees himself as willing to accept the authority of God revealing in other matters, appears somewhat unrealistic and psychologically improbable.

See Also: FAITH, 3; HERESY.

Bibliography: J. A. MCHUGH and C. J. CALLAN, *Moral Theology,* 2 v. (New York 1960), v. 1. B. HÄRING, *The Law of Christ,* tr. E. G. KAISER, v. 1 (Westminster, Md. 1961) 54–57. D. M. PRÜMMER, *Manuale theologiae moralis,* ed. E. M. MÜNCH, 3 v. (12th ed. Freiburg-Barcelona 1955). K. RAHNER, *On Heresy,* tr. W. J. O'HARA (New York 1964).

[G. A. BUCKLEY/EDS.]

HERESY, HISTORY OF

The word αἵρεσις in classical Greek signified a school or party. It was used by the Hellenists to designate a philosophical school and by Josephus to describe the Jewish theological sects.

1. In the Early Church

The primitive Christians were considered at first another school or sect within Judaism (Acts 24.5, 14; 28.22). But among themselves the early Christians quickly distinguished between those who accepted the doctrine as preached by the Apostles and received by the Church, or assembly of the faithful, and those who tried to adapt the Christian message to their own personal, doctrinal, or disciplinary notions (1 Cor 11.19; Gal 5.20). What the Church rejected in thought or deed was heretical. Thus both the doctrines propagated by the Gnostic sects (*see* GNOSTICISM) and the QUARTODECIMAN adherence to the Jewish paschal calendar were condemned as heretical (Hippolytus, *Philos.* 7.18.19).

In the 2d and 3d Centuries. During the 2d century little distinction was made between heresy and SCHISM, and the criterion of true faith and practice appealed to was that of the Roman Church. The earliest collection of heretical doctrines was made by JUSTIN MARTYR in his *Syntagma* against all heresies. This work is mentioned by Justin himself (*1 Apol.* 26.8). Irenaeus in his *Exposé and Refutation of the False Gnosis,* usually quoted as *Adversus haereses,* used the *Syntagma* of Justin and mentions a *Contra Marcionem* that appears to be part of Justin's work (*Adversus haereses* 4.19.9). The exposé concentrates on the Valentinian Gnostics but also gives a résumé of the beginnings of Gnosticism with the teachings of Simon, Menander, and other early sectaries.

During the reign of Pope ZEPHYRINUS (199–217), HIPPOLYTUS OF ROME wrote a *Syntagma* directed against all heresies; it is cited by Eusebius of Caesarea (*Ecclesiastical History* 6.22) and by Photius (*Bibliotheca codex* 121). A fragment of this work, the *Contra Noetum,* has been discovered and published by P. Nautin. Hippolytus wrote also an *Elenchus* or collection of 33 heresies from that of the Naassenians to that of Noetus, together with their refutations. It is known under the incorrect title of the *Philosophumena.* The author traces each doctrinal aberration to a school of false philosophy but in general follows IRENAEUS for his information. The work seems likewise to have been synthesized by TERTULLIAN as an appendix to his *De praescriptione.* Jerome (*De Viris illustribus* 74) attributes an *Adversus omnes haereses* to VICTORINUS OF PETTAU (d. 304).

Treatises of Epiphanius and Augustine on Heresies. Epiphanius of Constantia between 374 and 377 composed a *Panarion* or box of antidotes against all heresies. He names and refutes 80 heresies, relying on Irenaeus and Hippolytus for the older doctrinal errors, and citing the writings of heretics themselves for the more recent heresies. The *Panarion* was used by Filastrius of Brescia (d. 397) for his *Liber de haeresibus* (385–391).

Toward 428 AUGUSTINE wrote a *De haeresibus* for the deacon Quodvultdeus; it is in the main a catalogue of 88 heresies. The last eight cited, however, including Pelagianism (*see* PELAGIUS AND PELAGIANISM), give evidence of his personal study and knowledge. THEODORET OF CYR (d. *c.* 460) wrote a compendium of heretical fables (*c.* 451) in five books, claiming that he culled these false doctrines from his reading of the early Church Fathers. For ARIUS, Eudoxius, NESTORIUS, and EUTYCHES, he cites primary evidence. At the close of the patristic period, JOHN DAMASCENE (d. 749) lists a catalogue of heresies as the second part of his *Source of Knowledge.* Only the three final heresies mentioned, namely, Islam, ICONOCLASM, and the Paulician heresy, are examined from contemporary evidence.

Bibliography: Y. M. J. CONGAR, *Catholicisme. Hier, aujourd'hui et demain,* ed. G. JACQUEMET (Paris 1947–) 5:640–642. H. PETRÉ, "Haeresis, Schisma et leurs synonymes latins," *Revue des études latines* 15 (1936) 316–325. W. BAUER, *Rechtgläubigkeit und Ketzerei im ältesten Christentum* (Tübingen 1934). J. BROSCH, *Das Wesen der Häresie* (Bonn 1936). C. JOURNET, *L'Église du Verbe Incarné,* 2 v. (Paris 1951) 818–823. G. KITTEL, *Theologisches Wörterbuch zum Neuen Testament* (Stuttgart 1935–) 986–987.

[P. ROCHE]

2. Medieval Period

During the Middle Ages both eastern and western Europe were essentially a Christian society. Thus, heresy, a body of doctrine substantially differing in some aspect from the doctrine taught by the Church, was bound to have reverberations in the secular world as well as in the Church. The early Christian community, essentially a minority Church (especially in the West) before Constantine's Edict of Religious Toleration (313), had been shaken in the 4th and 5th centuries by such major heresies as ARIANISM, DONATISM, NESTORIANISM, MONOPHYSITISM, and, in the West, by Pelagianism. In the 6th and 7th centuries, while Europe was absorbed in regrouping after the mass migrations of the barbarian nations, the BYZANTINE EMPIRE was still split over the question of Monophysitism, complicated now by the controversy over the THREE CHAPTERS, and turned to MONOTHELITISM in its attempt to reestablish religious unity throughout the empire.

Earlier Middle Ages. With the West's revival of interest in learning in the 8th and 9th centuries—a phenomenon often labeled the CAROLINGIAN RENAISSANCE, but with its religious facets called the Carolingian Reformation—new study of the inherited theology of late antiquity resulted in the first truly "medieval" heresies. The FILIOQUE controversy had overtones of heresy, as did the contemporary predestination (*see* GOTTSCHALK OF ORBAIS) and Eucharistic Controversies, the latter spearheaded by the opponents PASCHASIUS RADBERTUS and RATRAMNUS. ADOPTIONISM flourished and died. The pantheistic concept of the world, inherent in the Stoic and Neoplatonic philosophy behind Arianism, seems to have received some impetus from the writings of JOHN SCOTUS ERIGENA—although it is probable that this was the result of misunderstanding Erigena's thought. At the same time the BYZANTINE CHURCH and State were convulsed by the great struggle over heretical ICONOCLASM.

High Middle Ages. With the revitalization of all facets of life in Europe in the High Middle Ages, heresy once again became a real issue in the religious and secular worlds. Despite the CLUNIAC and GREGORIAN reforms the 11th century saw the return of the Eucharistic heresy in BERENGARIUS OF TOURS, who adopted the older teachings of Ratramnus. During the 12th century—the century of the CRUSADES, of the CISTERCIANS, and of the nascent medieval universities—occurred the rise of the CATHARI, the most serious heretical threat with which the Middle Ages had to contend. The religious equilibrium of the early 12th century had been thrown off balance by the sporadical heresies of PETER OF BRUYS and his PETROBRUSIANS, of HENRY OF LAUSANNE, and of ARNOLD OF BRESCIA, all of whom advanced certain antisacramental and antisacerdotal ideas, and by AMALRIC OF BÈNE and his AMALRICIANS, who were essentially pantheists. But only the Cathari, with their roots in the DUALISM of the BOGOMILS and PAULICIANS, had a viable doctrinal framework. The heresy, originally Eastern, was brought to Europe after the Second Crusade and by 1175 counted members in northern France, the Rhineland, and Italy, but especially in southern France, the Midi. There the orthodox Christian Church waged spiritual and material war on the strongholds of the Cathari (or ALBIGENSES). The CISTERCIANS, the Albigensian Crusade, the inquisition, the University of Toulouse and, most importantly, the MENDICANT ORDERS finally proved effective, and by 1300 Catharism was defeated in Europe.

The same 12th century also saw the rise of serious non-Manichaean heresies. Although heretical fringe groups, such as the Judaizing Passagini and the followers of radicals, such as ÉON OF STELLA or TANCHELM at Antwerp, were of only passing interest, a number of heresies arose out of the contemporary demand for extreme Church reform in the spirit of apostolic poverty and preaching (*see* POVERTY MOVEMENT). These heresies shook the religious foundations of all Europe. Although the same spirit had motivated orthodox reform interests among the PATARINES, HUMILIATI, and FRANCISCANS, in the WALDENSES the original ideal of evangelical poverty deviated into an antisacerdotal heresy. In 1173 Valdés of Lyons, a layman, renounced all his worldly possessions, took a vow of poverty, and then began preaching to the people. As the ''Poor Men of Lyons'' grew more numerous, Pope LUCIUS III and Emperor FREDERICK I BARBAROSSA agreed at Verona in 1184 that Waldenses who preached without permission or who attacked the Church's hierarchy or Sacraments would be branded as heretics, but that others would be accepted as orthodox. Thus small sects of Waldenses stayed within the Church, although the greater number eventually fell into antihierarchical heresy. The Waldenses were never as strong numerically as the contemporary Cathari, and they were banned from the empire in 1253; from that time on their membership shrank away except in the valleys of the Piedmont and the Briançonnais, where they survive today.

In the 12th, but especially in the 13th, century, groups of heretical spiritualists became discernible in European society. Molded by essentially Catharist ideas wedded to the ideology of JOACHIM OF FIORE, the various groups all adopted an extreme stand on poverty as a protest against the possessions of the Church. Thus the Franciscan SPIRITUALS, as corrupted into the FRATICELLI under ANGELUS CLARENUS, were declared heretical by Pope JOHN XXII. Amalrician ideas, now combined with rejection of the sacramental Church, lived on among the BROTHERS AND SISTERS OF THE FREE SPIRIT who were found in Swabia and along the Rhine from the 12th to the 15th century. A similarly oriented group were the APOSTOLICI, founded by Segarelli of Parma (burned 1300) and his successor Fra DOLCINO (burned 1307).

Later Middle Ages. The major heresy of the 14th century was that initiated by John WYCLIF, who adopted Berengarius's Eucharistic position concerning the permanence of bread and wine after consecration and propounded questionable doctrine concerning the Church and the ownership of property. He was silenced in May 1377 by Pope GREGORY XI and was finally condemned after his denial of TRANSUBSTANTIATION *c.* 1380. The LOLLARDS, who adopted Wyclif's radical views on lordship, grace, the Sacraments, and the temporal power of the papacy, ceased to exist effectively after 1431.

In the meantime, however, Wyclif's teachings had become of primary importance in Bohemia, where they had influenced John HUS, leader of the reform movement in Prague. Although burned as a heretic at the Council of CONSTANCE in 1415, his only heretical deviation was his rejection of the formal and necessary primacy of jurisdiction of the bishop of Rome. His followers, however, the HUSSITES, adopted the full teaching of Wyclif, abandoning orthodoxy as they came to deny transubstantiation and other traditional Catholic teachings. Emperor SIGISMUND led ''crusades'' against the Hussites for 15 years until their defeat in 1436; the Catholic UTRAQUISTS (moderate Hussites), however, survived alongside the orthodox Catholics in Bohemia until the rise of Lutheranism. The radical Hussite ideas were revived in the BOHEMIAN BRETHREN, a group that provided a direct link between the Hussites and the Protestants of the 16th century.

Repression. It is to the medieval concept of ''kingdom'' as a morally unified society that one must turn to understand the cooperation of Church and secular power in the repression of heresy during the Middle Ages. Medieval man believed that civil society, in order to survive, must adhere to a well-defined moral system. When HUGH OF SAINT-VICTOR declared that ''the spiritual power must institute the temporal that it might exist,'' and when Pope BONIFACE VIII asserted in *UNAM SANCTAM* that the Church had both swords, spiritual and temporal, they meant that the contemporary civil powers, deriving their justification from Christian moral doctrine, depended necessarily on the fountainhead of that doctrine. Thus, the temporal power was expected to react against doctrines that undermined its own position. To cite an extreme example, when the Cathari branded pregnancy and normal sexual intercourse as Satan's work, or when they counseled their members to commit suicide (*endura*), contemporary society felt that such action could not go unpunished. In the Church's attitude toward heresy's challenge to the religious *status quo,* there was always much conflict between men, such as the 11th-century Bp. WAZO OF LIÈGE or BERNARD OF CLAIRVAUX, who insisted that faith was a matter of persuasion, and others, such as Pope INNOCENT III or St. DOMINIC, who approved of the Church's part in the effective repression of heresy. Similar tension is found in the two attitudes of St. AUGUSTINE, one stressing the voluntary character of faith and the other underlining the right of society to compel its members to good actions. Prominent medieval Christians realized that the repression of heresy remained essentially a pastoral problem and that a delicate balance was required between justice and charity: leniency in the chastisement of heresy could endanger the faith of others, but excess of zeal in administering justice might become a major impediment to the apostolate. In practice, the Church's medieval antiheresy campaign adopted as its tools the process of legatine inquest and the cooperation of ecclesiastical and civil power (*see* INQUISITION) to stamp out heresy that had gained a popular following.

Bibliography: E. VACANDARD, *The Inquisition,* tr. B. L. CONWAY (New York 1908). J. GUIRAUD, *Histoire de l'inquisition au moyen âge,* 2 v. (Paris 1935–38). H. X. ARQUILLIÈRE, *L'Augustinisme politique* (2d ed. Paris 1955). J. RUPP, *L'Idée de chrétienté* (Paris 1939). M. L. COZENS, *A Handbook of Heresies* (New York 1947). A. C. SHANNON, *The Popes and Heresy in the 13th Century* (Villanova, Pa. 1949). G. SCHNÜRER, *Church and Culture in the Middle Ages,* tr. G. J. UNDREINER (Paterson, N.J. 1956–). K. BIHLMEYER and H. TÜCHLE, *Kirchengeschichte,* 3 v. (17th ed. Paderborn 1962) 1:81–85, 91–96, 207–213, 308–313, 435–444. J. N. GARVIN and J. A. CORBETT, *The Summa contra haereticos Ascribed to Praepositinus* (Notre Dame 1958). H. MAISONNEUVE, *Études sur les origines de l'inquisition* (2d ed. Paris 1960). *Dictionnaire de théologie catholique,* ed. A. VACANT et al., 15 v. (Paris 1903–50; Tables générales 1951–) Tables générales 2051–62. H. GRUNDMANN, *Ketzergeschichte des Mittelalters* (Göttingen 1963). J. RUSSELL, "Interpretations of the Origins of Medieval Heresy," *Mediaeval Studies* (1938–) 25 (1963) 26–53.

[B. CHUDOBA]

3. Modern Period

Heresies upon condemnation do not die but reappear, often with vigorous new growth. Thus the primitivism (the search for a more authentic Christianity in the infancy of the Church) that is found in evangelical Protestantism, as well as Modernism, was already a cry of the Montanists of the 2d century. The Neoplatonist mysticism of the medieval Beghards and Beguines, condemned at the Council of Vienne (1311), appeared once again in the behavior of the Spanish ALUMBRADOS of the 16th century, and the later quietist movement. Conciliarism, formulated at the University of Paris by Conrad of Gelnhausen and Henry of Langenstein, and expressed in an extreme form by PETER OF AILLY and Jean GERSON at the Council of Constance (1414–17), persisted in the many types of Gallicanism. Moreover, the theories of Church and State that appeared during this modern period were influenced by caesaropapist ideas of the Roman emperors, the exaggerated charges of the French legists of Philip the Fair and the equally pretentious claims of the papal curialists, the doctrine of dominion by grace of John Wyclif, the proimperial theses in the *Defensor pacis* (1324) of MARSILIUS OF PADUA, the power politics of Niccolò MACHIAVELLI's *Il principe* (1513), and the Venetian theorist, Paolo Paruta's *Discorsi politici* (1599). Therefore many heresies of this period are more noted for their eclecticism than for their originality.

Protestantism. It is principally on the dogmas of justification, predestination, and sacramental theology that the reformers departed from orthodox belief. Though expressing divergent views on these theological doctrines, they were in agreement in demanding that the Bible be the sole source of faith to the rejection or neglect of tradition.

Lutheranism. The theology of Martin LUTHER as synthesized in the Book of CONCORD (1580) was still creedal, accepting the Apostolic, Nicene, and Athanasian formulas, but avowing Scripture as the sole and constant guide of the Christian. It taught the total depravity of man after the Fall, which left him powerless before indomitable concupiscence to perform deeds of merit, so that he is justified by his faith in Christ alone and the imputation of His merits. This rejection of all forms of synergism whereby the human will can or should cooperate with grace, leaves God the sole agent in the conversion of the soul to justification. Of the Sacraments, only two were sanctioned by Scripture: baptism, incorporating the recipient into membership of a nonhierarchical church, and the Lord's Supper, commemorating the redemptive act. In place of transubstantiation Luther defended consubstantiation in which Christ becomes present in the substance of the elements, not hypostatically, but in a transcendent though real manner.

Reformed Theology. In the doctrines of the Reformed Churches, based upon the tenets and church organization of Huldrych ZWINGLI, Martin BUCER (BUTZER),

Heinrich BULLINGER, and, principally, John CALVIN, are found a similar reliance upon the Bible as sole source of authority, and the fundamental Lutheran doctrine of total human depravity. Calvin established the principles of his system in the *Institutes* (1536), where he teaches that God by divine ordinance disregards the acts of the creature and predetermines him to salvation or doom (*see* INSTITUTES OF CALVIN). It is God's unconditioned will, independent of any foreknowledge of merit or demerit, that determines justification.

This image of an inexorable God was resisted by Jakob Arminius, the Dutch divine, who asserted against Calvin that divine sovereignty is compatible with human will and that grace is not irresistible (*see* ARMINIANISM; INFRALAPSARIANS; SUPRALAPSARIANS). The propositions of this modified conception of CALVINISM were drawn up in the Remonstrance (1610) by Simon Episcopius (1583–1643) and defended unsuccessfully at the Synod of Dort (1618). (*See* CONFESSIONS OF FAITH, PROTESTANT.) Though rejected by Calvinists, Arminianism spread to England and eventually divided Methodism into the moderate party of John WESLEY, and the strict Calvinists, led by George WHITEFIELD.

Zwingli, whose doctrine was formulated in the 67 theses (Zurich 1523) and in Bullinger's First Helvetic Confession (1536), was more insistent on reliance upon Scripture and upon primitivism. To restore the Church to its original simplicity he removed the liturgy and reduced the conduct of his church to congregational direction, and the ultimate control of its revenues to civic tribunals. Zwingli met with Luther, Philipp MELANCHTHON, and Johannes OECOLAMPADIUS at the Colloquy of Marburg (Oct. 1–4, 1529) to attempt a doctrinal compromise, but their theories upon the presence of Christ in the Eucharist were unreconcilable. After Zwingli's death (1531), Calvin, Guillaume FAREL, and Bullinger met in Zurich in 1549, where they formulated the Zurich Consensus on the Eucharistic presence; by 1580 ZWINGLIANISM and Calvinism became the Reformed Church (*see* REFORMED CHURCHES).

Radicalism. The ANABAPTISTS (Zwichau Prophets, Swiss Brethren, Jorists, Hutterian Brethren, Melchiorites, Familists, and MENNONITES) constituted a more radical Protestant motion that appealed to an infallible Scripture and an apocalyptic expectation. Their theories of Christian communism that were put into practice in the polygamic kingdom of Münster made them particularly unloved by conservative Protestants as well as Catholics. The Radicals were characterized by the phenomenon of prophetic charism that had been a by-product of Christian heresies since the primitive Church. It appeared in the hysteria of the Montanist prophetesses, Priscilla and Maximilia, and the Circumcellions of the 5th century who brought Donatism into ridicule; the rantings of the 11th-century Cathars and later medieval mystics; the exhibitionism of the Jansenist *convulsionaires* at the cemetery of St. Médard (1731); the prophecies of the Calvinist CAMISARDS who terrorized 18th-century France; the feats of revivalism of the American frontier; and the glossolalia (speaking in tongues) that has appeared in some 20th-century Protestant sects.

Baianism and Jansenism. The Council of TRENT established a body of dogma, but could not prevent further heresy in the question of grace and human justification. Michael BAIUS and John Hessels, Flemish theologians of the University of Louvain, believed that Catholic reaction to Protestantism had turned too far and that the great villain dividing the Church was scholasticism, especially in its Thomistic expression. For the dialectic of the schoolmen, Baius substituted greater use of scriptural and patristic sources, especially Cyprian, Jerome, Ambrose, and Augustine, since these were most often appealed to by Protestants. Baius's fundamental tenet was God's creation of man in a state of natural integrity, so that after the Fall all his actions were motivated by a nature vitiated toward concupiscence and thus evil to God. Accordingly, after the Redemption, only those actions that proceed from a perfect love of God are of merit. Justification is a continued process of works that merit heaven only if motivated by perfect charity in a triumphant battle over concupiscence. These elements of Baianism as found in the *Opuscula* and the 79 propositions condemned by Pius V in the bull *Ex omnibus afflictionibus,* Oct. 1, 1567, have been criticized as Pelagian, Calvinistic, and Socinian.

Far more reaching in its effect was the theology of Cornelius JANSEN, Louvain professor and bishop of Ypres, who with his friend Jean Duvergier de Hauranne, Abbé of St. Cyran and guide of the consciences of the nuns of PORT-ROYAL from 1636, planned to save the Church from Protestantism, from Jesuits, for whom Jansen had an eminent dislike, and from itself. This was to be achieved again by clearing scholasticism away from the path that led back to Augustine and to the simplicity of the primitive Church. Jansen exposed his doctrine in the *AUGUSTINUS*, published posthumously (1640), and for whose preparation he read the works of Augustine 10 times, and his anti-Pelagian tractates 30 times. Like Baius he asserts man's creation in a state of natural integrity, so that fallen man is radically depraved and at the mercy of concupiscence. In his redeemed state man is still drawn to earthly delectation (*delectatio terrestris*), unless impelled by an irresistible heavenly impulse (*delectatio coelestis*). Thus man is irresistibly attracted to good or evil, depending upon which delectation prevails (*delecta-*

tio victrix). As a corollary came the discouragement of the use of the Sacraments of the Eucharist and Penance. The first was to be received rarely and as a reward for virtue; the second held worthless unless repentance was motivated by perfect love of God. The course of this heresy was a series of ineffectual condemnations, reprisals, insincere submissions, subterfuges, and casuistry that continued even after the sweeping condemnation in the bull *UNIGENITUS* of CLEMENT XI in 1713. In Holland Jansenists were involved in the irregular consecration of Cornelius Steenhoven as archbishop of Utrecht (1723), which led to schism with Rome. These Utrecht Jansenists remained separated and later allied themselves with the Old Catholic party, which declared against papal infallibility in 1870.

Laxism. Contemporary with the Jansenist crisis were the disputes among theologians over the degrees of probability needed for a licit moral action. The theory of probabilism (it is licit to act on a probable opinion even though the opposite is more probable) was accepted and taught by the Jesuits, and attacked by the Jansenist Blaise PASCAL in his *Lettres provinciales* (1657) as dangerous casuistry. This opened an active controversy with George Pirot, SJ (1599–1659), whose *L'Apologie pour les casuistes* (1657) widened the scope of licit probability to the extreme of laxity. The book was proscribed by the Parlement of Paris, the Sorbonne, and censored by the Holy Office in 1659. Laxism was further condemned by Alexander VII by decrees of Sept. 24, 1665; March 18, 1666; and May 5, 1667. Innocent XI condemned 65 laxist propositions on March 2, 1679. Tutiorism (it is not allowed to follow even the most probable among probable opinions) as expressed by the Irish Jansenist John SINNICH in *Saul Exrex* (1662), was also condemned by Alexander VIII on Dec. 7, 1690.

Quietism and Semiquietism. Mysticism is a borderland infrequently traversed, so the expression of the phenomena that occur there cannot be easily touched with precise phrase. Thus the great Rhineland mystic, Meister Eckhart (d. 1327) was accused of being pantheistic and Beghardic; SS. Ignatius Loyola, Teresa of Avila, Francis Borgia, and Joseph Calasanctius were suspected of the Neoplatonic tendencies of the Alumbrados. In the 17th century, however, there was a great revival of quietistic mysticism. Miguel de MOLINOS in his book, *Guía espiritual,* taught a complete contemplative passivity before God. The soul in seeking interior annihilation can allow all license to carnal desire, acts of which are not blameworthy but produce a salutary disinterestedness to sensible devotion as well as personal salvation. Though denounced by the Holy Office (1685), quietism in a modified form became prominent through the Barnabite François Lacombe (*c.* 1640–1715) and his more famous disciple Madame GUYON (Jeanne Marie Bouvier de la Motte). They accepted the doctrine of pure love from Molinos's theology, according to which the soul becomes powerless to act in its own interest. This thesis was expanded in Madame Guyon's *Moyen court et très facile de faire oraison* (1685) and the *Explication des maximes des saints* (1697) of her follower, François FÉNELON, eminent churchman and at the time of the appearance of his book, the governor of Louis XIV's grandson, the duke of Burgundy. Madame Guyon was arrested and imprisoned (1695) at Vincennes, Vaugirard, and the Bastille, where she signed a retractation. Fénelon's book, after two years of bitter controversy with Jacques BOSSUET, was condemned by Innocent XII in the letter *Cum alias,* on March 12, 1699.

Caesarism. From the time of Protestantism, State interference in the affairs of the Church was much more significant than the ancient Byzantine CAESAROPAPISM or the pope-king quarrels of the Middle Ages. Now that Europe contained Christian communities no longer a part of Catholicism, opposition of monarchs to Rome was not only political but touched faith or was founded upon principles that could be destructive of it.

Anglicanism. The divorce proceedings that effected the English schism and set Henry VIII at the head of a national church did not yet place England in heresy. The six Henrician articles (June 1539) attest to the king's demand for orthodoxy. It was during the short reign of his son Edward VI (1547–53) that Continental Protestantism took hold. Peter Martyr Vermigli and Martin Bucer were instrumental in the formation of the Edwardine Ordinal (1550). Thomas CRANMER, long an admirer of the Lutheran movement, produced the revision of the Book of COMMON PRAYER in 1552, and in the next year prevailed on the king to sign the 42 Articles of Religion into the law of the land. Edward's action effectively established England as a Protestant nation, and the king as its religious arbiter, a position that was strengthened by the Stuart claim to authority by divine right within their hereditary line of succession. In the later development of ANGLICANISM, the Erastian (*see* ERASTIANISM) idea of State ascendancy over the Church in ecclesiastical matters took hold in the Westminster Assembly (1643), and in the ideal secularization of the church as conceived by Thomas Hobbes.

Gallican Liberties. In 16th-century France there was a distrust of Rome and its ultramontane foreign policies that sometimes resulted in papal alliances with French enemies, especially the Hapsburg emperor. When the French crown felt oppressed, it appealed to the *libertés de l'Église gallicane,* which it could proudly trace back to King Clovis and his Merovingian successors. The concordat between Leo X and Francis I in 1516 annulled the Pragmatic Sanction of Bourges (1438), which had accepted many of the conciliarist decrees of the Council of Basel (1431–37); GALLICANISM, however, persisted and came to a crisis when Louis XIV attempted to extend the *regalia* (royal right to the revenues of vacant sees) to all the sees of France. Innocent XI (1676–89) repudiated this usurpation of right and threatened ecclesiastical sanction. In reply Louis gathered the clergy of France who adopted the Four Gallican Articles of 1682, which were conciliarist and limited the exercise of papal primacy to the customs of the French Church. Though Louis and Innocent came to terms in 1693, these articles became a formula of anti-Romanism adopted when convenient elsewhere in Europe.

Febronianism and Josephinism. In Germany, the suffragan bishop of Trier, Johann Nikolaus von HONTHEIM, under the pen name of Justinus Febronius, attacked Roman power as compared to papal primacy and as founded upon the False Decretals, and advocated an ecclesiastical order that was regulated as much as possible by episcopal and civic control. These ideas, absorbed by Hontheim from the Gallican canonist of Louvain, Zeger Bernhard van ESPEN, led the archbishops of Mainz, Trier, Cologne, and Salzburg to assert their grievances against Rome at a congress at Bad Ems in Hesse-Nassau, even though Clement XIII had condemned Febronianism in 1764. The Punctation of Ems, issued Aug. 25, 1786, restrained appeals to Rome, and declared papal bulls to be conditioned upon the acceptance of the German episcopate. The force of FEBRONIANISM was felt in the empire and expressed in the policies of Empress MARIA THERESA and her son, JOSEPH II, whose Toleration Edict of 1781 suppressed certain religious orders, placed exempt monasteries under diocesan control, and required civic authorization for the publication of papal documents. Leopold II, Grand Duke of Tuscany and brother of the emperor, introduced Josephinist ideas into northern Italy. In 1786, under the presidency of Scipione de' RICCI, Bishop of Pistoia-Prato, a synod was held that passed reform measures based upon the Gallican articles, 85 of which were condemned by Pius VI in the bull *Auctorem fidei,* Aug. 28, 1794.

The Kulturkampf and Old Catholics. In the 19th century Caesarism appeared in the anti-Romanism of Chancellor Otto von Bismarck. His KULTURKAMPF oppressed the Church, interfered in its educational processes, limited its disciplinary powers by the May Laws (1873), and exiled religious orders. Unexpectedly, this oppression effected a Catholic revival in Germany and strengthened the Catholic political party. The publication of the *Syllabus errorum* by Pius IX on Dec. 8, 1864, and the definition of infallibility by Vatican Council I (1870) aroused the resistance of Johannes J. I. von DÖLLINGER, who met with some professors at Nuremberg and Bonn, where it was agreed that these measures of the pope would paralyze the Church. Despite Döllinger's disapproval, they formed the schismatical church of Old Catholics, receiving episcopal succession from the bishops of the Church of Utrecht, in schism since 1723. The Old Catholics, with affiliated churches in the Netherlands, Poland, and the United States, retain most of the Roman rite (but in the vernacular), allow a married clergy, and make the Sacrament of Penance optional.

Traditionalism. Much Catholic thought in the 19th century grew as a reaction to the philosophies of the Enlightenment or as an attempt at adaptation. Against the *primum mobile,* the depersonalized god of the rationalists, the skepticism as expressed in David Hume's *Treatise of Human Nature* (1738), and the sophistication resulting from new technology and travel abroad, especially during England's Augustan age, some Catholic theologians proposed theories of traditionalism, placing the norm of human certitude in the *sens commun* rather than in distrusted individual intellectual ability. The traditionalists, Casimir Ubaghs, Louis E. BAUTAIN, Augustin BONNETTY, and Hugues Félicité de LAMENNAIS, tried to revive faith, just as the ontologists, Vincenzo GIOBERTI, Antonio ROSMINI-SERBATI, and Jakob Frohschammer, by their central tenet that God is the first object of our intelligence, established a type of optimistic rationalism. Georg HERMES attempted to adjust theology to Kantian philosophy, and Anton GÜNTHER, after studying the pantheistic idealism of Georg HEGEL and Friedrich von SCHELLING, proposed that it was within human power to deduce the mysteries of the Trinity and Incarnation.

All these figures were condemned. Bautain was removed from his chair of philosophy at Strasbourg by Bp. Lepappe de Trévern in 1834; Ubaghs was censored by the Holy Office, Sept. 21, 1864; Bonnetty was denounced by the Congregation of the Index, June 11, 1855; Gioberti's writings were placed on the Index, Jan. 14, 1853; Hermes was condemned by the brief, *Dum acerbissimas,* Sept. 26, 1835; Günther's works were doomed by the Index, Jan. 8, 1857; and propositions from the books of Rosmini-Serbati were condemned by a decree of the Holy Office, Dec. 14, 1887. Frohschammer, professor at the University of Munich, refused to submit to the condemnatory letter of Pius IX, *Gravissimas inter,* which found unorthodox propositions in his *Einleitung in die Philosophie und Grundriss der Metaphysik* (1858), and was suspended. Lammenais believed the future of the Church in post-Napoleonic France would be brighter if its dependent affiliations with the restored monarchy were replaced by a Catholic liberalism. Together with several French intellectuals, such as Charles de MON-

TALEMBERT and Jean B. LACORDAIRE, he published the brilliant *L'Avenir* (1830–31), advocating freedom of the press, of speech, and labor unions; the magazine, however, was suppressed for indifferentism by Gregory XVI in an encyclical *Mirari vos,* Aug. 15, 1832. The adherence to Royalism among many of the French clergy persisted into the 20th century, when a number rallied to the monarchist crusade of Charles MAURRAS and his collaborator, Léon DAUDET. Their publication, *L'Action française* was denounced by Pius XI, Dec. 20, 1926.

Modernism. A more pervading heresy was the complex of movements condemned under the name of MODERNISM by Pius X in the decree, *Lamentabili sane exitu,* July 3, 1903, and the encyclical *Pascendi dominici gregis,* Sept. 8, 1907. Attempting to reconcile the Church with the present, Modernism viewed scholastic Aristotelianism no longer suitable to illustrate and defend Christian belief. The prominent Modernists, Maurice BLONDEL, Lucien LABERTHONNIÈRE, Alfred LOISY, Edouard LE ROY, Eudoxe I. MIGNOT, Antonio Fogazzaro, Romolo MURRI, Friedrich von HÜGEL, and George TYRRELL, composed no theological school or consistent doctrine, but they agreed upon the necessity of reconciling the Church with modern times. From their writings the following beliefs appeared: dogmatic statements have a spirit that is absolute and fixed, and a form that is relative and mutable; Christ's messianic mission and His divinity are not to be sought from Scriptural sources, whose authors were subjected to the limitations of all human historians, but deduced from the *conscientia christiana;* the Christ of history is thus less than the Christ of faith, and it is not important to know whether He instituted a church, since the Holy Spirit guides its progress; and in Christianity there is a religious immanence that effects a continual evolution and pragmatic adaptation to historical situations.

Americanism. By the end of the 19th century the term ''adaptation'' meant a dangerous tampering with faith, as is witnessed in the so-called heresy of AMERICANISM. From a French translation of a biography of Isaac T. HECKER, founder of the Paulists, statements were extracted by Roman theologians that advocated the adaptation of the external form of the Church to modern American life, and extolled the active virtues (humanitarianism, democratic fellowship) to the depreciation of passive virtues (subjection to authority, humility). By an apostolic letter to Cardinal James GIBBONS of Baltimore, *TESTEM BENEVOLENTIAE*, Jan. 22, 1899, Leo XIII cautioned against these notions, and by referring to them as Americanism with the implication that they were widespread, created what F. Klein called a phantom heresy (*Une hérése fantôme, L'Americanisme,* Paris 1949).

The Fathers of Vatican Council II chose not condemn any errors by means of anathemas. At the same time, the pastoral constitution *Gaudium et spes* cited many errors prevalent in modern society. Debates upon the floor of the council and continual written discussions on its schema emphasized the need to consider theological realities in their place in the stream of history. The result, in terms of the understanding of heresy, has been an emphasis on the difference between the rejection of an eternal, unchanging truth and the rejection of its changing historical manifestation.

Bibliography: A. MICHEL, *Dictionnaire de théologie catholique,* ed. A. VACANT et al., 15 v. (Paris 1903–50; Tables générales 1951–) 6.2:2208–57, bibliog. G. CROSS, J. HASTINGS, ed., *Encyclopedia of Religion and Ethics,* 13 v. (Edinburgh 1908–27) 6:614–622. A. DRU, *The Church in the Nineteenth Century: Germany 1800–1918* (London 1963). É. POULAT, *Histoire, dogme et critique dans la crise moderniste* (Paris 1962). M. CREIGHTON, *Persecution and Tolerance* (New York 1895). S. CHÂTEILLON, *Concerning Heretics,* tr. R. H. BAINTON (New York 1935). K. RAHNER, *On Heresy,* tr. W. J. O'HARA (New York 1964). M. NOVAK, *The Open Church* (New York 1964). For extensive bibliographies see J. LECLER, *Toleration and the Reformation,* tr. T. L. WESTOW, 2 v. (New York 1960), and *La Documentation Catholique* 49 (1952) 714–750.

[E. D. MCSHANE]

HERGENRÖTHER, JOSEPH

Ecclesiastical historian and canonist; b. Würzburg, Germany, Sept. 15, 1824; d. Mehrerau Abbey, Bregenz, Austria, Oct. 3, 1890. The son of a professor of medicine, he studied at the University of Würzburg (1842–44) and at the German College, Rome (1844–48), where he was ordained. After receiving a doctorate in theology at the University of Munich (1850), he taught theology there until 1852, when he transferred to Würzburg and became, in 1855, professor of Canon Law and Church history. He was appointed (1868) a consultor for the preparation of VATICAN COUNCIL I. In 1879 he was named cardinal and the first prefect of the VATICAN ARCHIVES, whose treasures he made accessible to scholars of all nations. His scholarly production was voluminous and wide ranging, although his interests centered mainly on early Christian and Byzantine history. *Photius Patriarch von Constantinopel, sein Leben, seine Schriften und das griechische Schisma* (3 v. 1867–69), the fruit of 12 years of research, was an objective and heavily documented study. Only in recent years has this classic study been surpassed by the writings of F. Dvornik, M. Jugie, and S. Salaville. Hergenröther edited the works of PHOTIUS for J. P. MIGNE (*Patrologia Graeca* v. 101–104) and edited separately *Photii Constantinopoli liber de Spiritus Sancti mystagogia* (1857). Hergenröther's history of the Church, *Handbuch der allgemeinen Kirchengeschichte* (3 v. Freiburg 1876–80; 3d ed. 1884–86; 4th ed. 1902–09, ed. J. P. Kirsch, excelled in its wealth and accuracy of information and mastery of sources, but it was not completely free of apologetic tendencies. More a research scholar than a teacher, Hergenröther failed to transmit to students the methods of historical scholarship. He took an active part in German Catholic life and opposed the Church-State policy and theology of the Munich school, being himself a rather moderate exponent of the Roman school. In 1860 he attacked DÖLLINGER for his lectures on the papal temporal power and his opening address at the Munich meeting of Catholic savants (1863). In *Anti-Janus* (1870), Hergenröther refuted the exaggerations of Döllinger written under the pseudonym Janus. His polemics against Döllinger, then considered a demigod by German scholars, exhibited a courageous personality, just as his refusal (1864) to accept the bishopric of Limburg displayed a lofty conception of the scholar's role in the Church. His other works included: *Der Kirchenstaat seit der französischen Revolution* (1860); *Catholic Church and Christian State* (2 v. 1876, tr. from Ger.); and volumes 8 and 9 of C. J. von HEFELE, *Conciliengeschichte* (1887–90). His incompleted *Leonis X Pontificis Maximi regesta* (1884–91) edited the register of Pope Leo X to 1515.

Bibliography: H. HURTER, *Nomenclator literarius theologiae catholicae*, 5 v. in 6 (3d ed. Innsbruck 1903–13) 5:1620–26. J. KIRSCH, *The Catholic Encyclopedia*, ed. C. G. HERBERMANN et al., 16 v. (New York 1907–14; suppl. 1922) 7:262–264. B. LANG, "Zum 50. Todestag des Kardinals Josef Hergenröther, *Theologisch-praktische Quartalschrift* 93 (1940) 302–309. A. BIGELMAIR, *Lexikon für Theologie und Kirche*, ed. J. HOFER and K. RAHNER, 10 v. (2d, new ed. Freiburg 1957–65) 5:245–246.

[V. CONZEMIUS]

HERIBERT OF COLOGNE, ST.

Archbishop of Cologne; b. *c.* 970; d. March 16, 1021. Heribert, son of Count Hugo of Worms, was educated at the CATHEDRAL SCHOOL of Worms and the MONASTIC SCHOOL of GORZE; he was later a canon at Worms and became archbishop of Cologne in 999. Heribert was friend, adviser, and companion of OTTO III, under whom he was made chancellor of Italian affairs in 994, and of German affairs in 998. He was present at Otto's death in Paterno, Italy, on Jan. 23, 1002. While bringing the emperor's body and the imperial insignia to AACHEN, he incurred the enmity of Duke Henry of Bavaria (later Emperor HENRY II), who wished to secure the insignia for himself. They were reconciled shortly before Heribert's death. Though the bull of his canonization by Pope GREGORY VII is almost certainly a forgery, Heribert seems to have led an exemplary life of piety and devotion to the poor. He is buried in the monastery at Deutz, which he founded with the help of Otto III.

Feast: March 16.

Bibliography: Sources. LAMBERT OF DEUTZ, *Vita* and *Miracula, Monumenta Germaniae Scriptores* (Berlin 1825–) 4:740–753; 15.2:1245–60. *Acta Sanctorum* (Paris 1863–) March 2:459–485. RUPERT OF DEUTZ, *Vita Heriberti,*, critical ed. with commentary by P. DINTER (Bonn 1976). Literature. J. KLEINERMANNS, *Die Heiligen auf dem bischöflichen . . . Stuhle von Köln,* 2 v. (Cologne 1896–98) v.2. A. HAUCK, *Kirchengeschichte Deutschlands,* 5 v. (9th ed. Berlin-Leipzig 1958) 3:397–398. W. NEUSS, ed., *Geschichte des Erzbistums Köln,* v.1 (Cologne 1965) 174–180. H. MÜLLER, *Heribert, Kanzler Ottos III. und Erzbischof von Köln* (Cologne 1977).

[M. F. MCCARTHY]

HERIGER OF LOBBES

Ecclesiastical writer; b. Louvain; d. Lobbes, Oct. 31, 1007. Heriger was a monk and scholar at the abbey of LOBBES and was made abbot there Dec. 21, 990. He trained WAZO, future bishop of Liège, and was a friend and collaborator of Bp. Notker of Liège, a fact that explains his sojourns there.

His literary activity was varied. Sometime before 980, he undertook the writing of history in his *Gesta episcoporum Tungrensium, Trajectensium et Leodiensium* (*Monumenta Germaniae Historica:* Scriptores. 7:162–189) that treated of the history of Liège from the fourth to the seventh centuries. In June 980 at the request of Notker, he wrote *S. Landoaldi et sociorum translatio* (*Patrologia Latina*, ed. J. P. Migne, 139:1111–22) for the monks of St. Bavon of Ghent. Only fragments of a *Vita s. Ursmari* (*Patrologia Latina* 139:1125–28), written in hexameters, remain. His *Vita S. Adelini* (*Patrologia Latina* 139:1141–48) and *Vita S. Remacli* (*Patrologia Latina* 139:1147–68) were both written for Notker. Heriger moved into chronology in his *Epistola ad quemdam Hugonem monachum* (*Patrologia Latina* 139:1129–36), probably done in collaboration with Notker. The *Dialogus de dissonantiis ecclesiae de adventu Christi* is lost.

Heriger wrote in the field of mathematics with his *Regulae numerorum super abacum Gerberti* and *Regulae Herberti in abacum* [N. Bübnov, *Gerberti opera mathematicae* (Berlin 1899) 205–225]. In theology he intervened in the eucharistic controversies raised by RATRAMNUS OF CORBIE, not with the *De corpore et sanguine Domini* (*Patrologia Latina* 139:179–188), which was written neither by him nor SYLVESTER II, but through the collection of patristic texts preserved under the title *De Herigeri abbatis exaggeratio plurimorum auctorum de corpore et sanguine Domini,* in the MS Gaud Univ. 909 f. 1–15.

Bibliography: M. MANITIUS, *Geschichte der lateinischen Literatur des Mittelalters* (Munich 1911–31) 2:219–228. G. KURTH, *Biographie nationale de Belgique* v.9. É. AMANN, *Dictionnaire de théologie catholique*, ed. A. VACANT et al., (Paris 1903–50) 11.1:808–809. J. WARICHEZ, *L'Abbaye de Lobbes* (Tournai 1909). J. LEBON, ''Sur la doctrine eucharistique d'Hériger de Lobbes,'' *Studia mediaevalia in honorem . . . R. J. Martin* (Bruges 1948) 61–84. A. CORDOLIANI, ''Abbon de Fleury, Hériger de Lobbes et Gerland de Besançon sur l'ère de l'Incarnation de Denys le Petit,'' *Revue d'histoire ecclésiastique* 44.2 (1949) 463–487. H. PLATELLE, *Catholicisme* 5:652–653.

[P. GLORIEUX]

HERINCX, WILLIAM

Bishop and moral theologian; b. Helmond, Northern Brabant, 1621; d. Ypres, Aug. 17, 1678. Herincx received his preliminary education at 'sHertogenbosch and entered the University of Louvain, where he acquired a doctorate in classical studies. He then entered the Order of Friars Minor Recollect and in 1653 was named letter of theology at Louvain. He was so successful in presenting his matter to students that his superiors ordered him to compose a manual of moral theology for the use of the young friars of his province. The result was *Summa theologiae scholastica et moralis in quatuor partes distributa* (Antwerp 1660–63). By this time Herincx was minister provincial; he was twice elected to this office, and he also served as general definitor of the order and commissary general for northern Europe.

Herincx's *Summa* is remarkable for the clarity and precision with which the doctrine is presented. The section ''De conscientia,'' is worthy of special note. He felt that the study of theology should contribute to the personal sanctification of students and stated in his preface that ''it behooves us to make use of the truth for our own sanctification . . . and above all for kindling and nourishing in ourselves and others the love of God.'' It was necessary for Herincx to make some modifications in his text after the decrees of Alexander VII in 1665 and 1666, and aided by a learned confrere, W. Van Goorlaeken, he brought out a revised edition. Like most Franciscan theologians of his day, he was officially a Scotist, but a moderate one who respected and used the teachings of SS. BONAVENTURE and THOMAS AQUINAS in his own writings.

Herincx was a probabilist; he held that the attack upon PROBABILISM in the 17th century was Jansenist in origin and that the tendency to rigorism was unknown among the theologians of the Middle Ages.

Herincx was named bishop of Ypres and consecrated on Oct. 24, 1677, in the Franciscan church at Brussels. He had barely taken up residence in his diocese and started to visit the places under his care when he died.

''St. Heribert Reconciled with Henry II,'' detail of the reliquary of St. Heribert of Cologne in the abbey church at Deutz, Germany, executed by Godefroy de Hoy before 1170. (Marburg-Art Reference/Art Resource, NY)

Bibliography: H. HURTER, *Nomenclator literarius theologiae catholicae*, 5 v. in 6 (3d ed. Innsbruck 1903–13) 4:48–49.

[A. J. CLARK]

HERKUMBERT, ST.

Bishop; d. June 7, *c.* 805. He is identified with the Ercanbert, first bishop of Minden, mentioned in the necrology of that see and in the medieval episcopal catalogues. He may also be the Herenbert who, according to the chronicle of Pistorianus, was installed as bishop of a great church erected in Minden by CHARLEMAGNE in 780. Most probably he was a monk of Fulda who led the mission sent by that monastery to Minden. The *Acta Sanctorum* notes the scarcity of information regarding him in the first chronicle of the diocese, compiled by Hermann of Lerbecke, and the lack of any mention of him in the Minden *Breviarum,* compiled by Johann Scheffer in 1516.

Feast: July 9.

Bibliography: *Acta Sanctorum* July 2:727–728. K. HONSELMANN, *Lexikon für Theologie und Kirche,* ed. J. HOFER and K. RAH-

NER, 10 v. (2d, new ed. Freiburg 1957–65) 5:248. E. MÜLLER, *Die Entstehungsgeschichte der sächsischen Bistümer unter Karl dem Grossen* (Hildesheim 1938).

[M. B. RYAN]

HERLUIN OF BEC, BL.

Founder and first abbot of Bec; b. Brionne, Normandy, *c.* 995; d. Aug. 26, 1078. At the age of 38 he left the court of Count Gilbert of Brionne, where he had been in service as a knight, and undertook the life of an ascetic and hermit nearby. He then gathered a community of his followers on his own property near Bonneville, and in 1035 Bp. Heribert of Lisieux received his monastic profession, ordained him, and named him first abbot of BEC. Herluin's zeal attracted to the community two Italians, LANFRANC and ANSELM OF CANTERBURY, both of whom served long terms as prior of Bec and whose learning and brilliant careers as archbishops of Canterbury rapidly overshadowed the reputation of the uneducated founder. Lanfranc, who introduced the usages of Bec to England and whom Herluin visited there in 1071, returned to Bec in 1077, just a few months before Herluin's death, to consecrate the abbey church. Three prayers, apparently from a festal Mass, suggest a cult of Herluin; however, his cult has never been formally recognized. When monks returned to Bec in 1948, Herluin's relics were restored to the abbey from the nearby parish church.

Feast: Aug. 26.

Bibliography: GILBERT CRISPIN, ''Vita Herluini'' in J. A. ROBINSON, ed., *Gilbert Crispin, Abbot of Westminster* (Cambridge, England 1911). J. MABILLON, *Annales Ordinis S. Benedicti,* 6 v. (Lucca 1739–45) v.4 *passim.* D. KNOWLES, ''Bec and its Great Men,'' *Downside Review* 52 (1934) 567–585. M. P. DICKSON, ''Introduction à l'édition critique du Coutumier du Bec,'' *Spicilegium Beccense* (Paris 1959–) 1:599–632.

[W. E. WILKIE]

HERLUKA OF BERNRIED, BL.

Nun; b. Swabia, Germany, mid-12th century; d. convent of Bernried, near Augsburg, Germany, 1127. Although little is known about her life, she seems to have been a woman of education, knowledgeable about the affairs of her time and, in a small way, influential within her circle. She first entered the monastery of Epfach, where she lived many years and had WILLIAM OF HIRSAU as her spiritual director. During her stay at Epfach she carried on a vigorous correspondence, especially with Diemoth (d. *c.* 1130), a nun in a nearby convent. She was much concerned with the new spirit of reform in the Church and with the imperial-papal conflicts of the day (*see* GREGORIAN REFORM). Her activities on behalf of the papal cause resulted in her expulsion, along with others, from the convent at Epfach. She went to the convent at Bernried and lived out her days there. Her correspondence, which would have provided a special insight into local history, unfortunately has been lost, as has the unfinished life of her by Paul of Bernried (d. *c.* 1146–50), who knew her well.

Feast: April 18.

Bibliography: *Acta Sanctorum* April 2:549–554. *Analecta Bollandiana* 17 (1898) 159. *Bibliotheca hagiographica latina antiquae ct mediae aetatis,* 2 v. (Brussels 1898–1901; suppl. 1911) 1:3835. L. ROSENBERGER, *Bavaria sancta* (Munich 1948) 181.

[H. MACKINNON]

HERMAN JOSEPH OF STEINFELD, ST.

Premonstratensian mystic and author; b. Cologne, Germany, 1150; d. Hoven convent, near Cologne, April 7, probably 1241. A visionary from a very early age, he joined the PREMONSTRATENSIANS at Steinfeld Abbey in the Eifel when he was 12 years old but, being under age, was sent to one of the order's houses in Frisia for schooling. He then returned to Steinfeld, where he was sacristan and a skilled clockmaker, and also served as chaplain to the CISTERCIAN nuns in the neighborhood. His blameless life as a canon at Steinfeld earned him the epithet ''Joseph,'' which name was most appropriate because of his ''mystical marriage'' to Mary, mother of Jesus. One of the most noteworthy mystics in the history of medieval spirituality, he wrote a treatise on the SONG OF SONGS, now lost as is his life of Elizabeth of Hoven. He may have written the *Summi regis cor aveto* (*Patrologia Latina,* 184:1322–24), the earliest hymn on the Sacred Heart. His modern reputation is based on his surviving prayers and hymns, one in honor of St. URSULA, in both prose and verse. His piety, remarkable for the tender affection it projects, presaged the DEVOTIO MODERNA. He was with the Cistercian nuns at Hoven for Holy Week and Easter when he was taken ill and died. His vita (*Acta Sanctorum* April 1:682–723) was written several months after his death by his prior and friend. His relics are at Steinfeld; his cult was approved in 1958 (*Acta Apostolicae Sedis* 51 [1959] 830) in an action equivalent to canonization.

Feast: April 7.

Bibliography: *Hermanni opuscula,* ed. J. VAN SPIELBECK (Namur 1899). *Bibliotheca hagiographica latina antiquae ct mediae aetatis,* 2 v. (Brussels 1898–1901; suppl. 1911) 1:3845–49. F. PETIT, *Un Mystique rhénan du XIIIe siècle, Le Bx. Hermann-Joseph*

. . . (Juaye-Mondaye 1930); *La Spiritualité des Prémontrés aux 12e et 13e siècle* (Paris 1947) 102–115. A. BUTLER, *The Lives of the Saints,* ed. H. THURSTON and D. ATTWATER, 4 v. (New York 1956) 2:48–49. K. KOCH and E. HEGEL, *Die ''Vita'' des Prämonstratensers Hermann Joseph von Steinfeld* (Cologne 1958). H. J. KUGLER, *Hermann Josef von Steinfeld: im Kontext christlicher Mystik* (St. Ottilien 1992). J. C. DIDIER, *Catholicisme* 5:660–661.

[M. J. HAMILTON]

HERMAN OF SALZA

Grand master of the TEUTONIC KNIGHTS; b. of a ministerial family in Thuringia, Germany, last third of the 12th century; d. Salerno, Italy, March 20, 1239. In 1209 he was elected grand master in Acre, Syria. In 1216 he became the counselor of FREDERICK II with whom he maintained a lasting friendship. Herman served as mediator between Frederick II and Pope HONORIUS III (1220) and influenced the pope in crowning Frederick as emperor. Thereafter he strove to remove the growing tensions between the two heads of Christianity, and worked tirelessly for the welfare of his order. In 1211 he accepted the assignment of King Andrew II of Hungary to patrol the border of Transylvania against pagan nomads; but the order was compelled to leave Hungary in 1225 when it attempted to establish an autonomous territory. Duke Conrad of Masovia (1226) sought the protection of the Knights against the pagan Prussians, and in Rimini, March 1226, Herman received from the emperor the district of Chelmno along the Vistula River and all the territories in Prussia that were still to be subdued and Christianized. The missionary work in these territories began only later, since Herman accompanied the emperor on a crusade to Jerusalem. He again reconciled pope and emperor in 1230. In the same year the conquest of Prussia began, but GREGORY IX (Aug. 3, 1234) placed the new mission country under the patrimony of St. Peter and reserved to the Curia any further political move in that territory. In 1237 the Livonian KNIGHTS OF THE SWORD were incorporated into the Teutonic order with Herman's permission.

Bibliography: E. L. E. CASPAR, *Hermann von Salza und die Gründung des Deutschordensstaats in Preussen* (Tübingen 1924). W. COHN, *H. v. S.* (Breslau 1930). E. E. STENGEL, *Hochmeister und Reich* (Weimar 1938). E. MASCHKE, ''Die Herkunft Hermanns v. S.,'' *Zeitschrift des Vereins für thüringische Geschichte und Altertumskunde,* NS 34 (1940) 372–389. H. HEIMPEL, *Der Mensch in seiner Gegenwart* (Göttingen 1954). W. HUBATSCH, ''Der Deutsche Orden und die Reichslehnschaftüber Cypern,'' *Nachrichten der Akademie der Wissenschaften in Göttingen* (1955) 245–306.

[M. HELLMANN]

HERMAN OF SCHEDA

Abbot and author, called also Herman the Jew; b. Cologne, Germany, *c.* 1107; d. Abbey of Scheda, near Paderborn, Germany, 1170 (or according to some authorities 1198). Of Jewish parentage, he was converted to Christianity *c.* 1128, while on a business trip to Mainz, and entered the PREMONSTRATENSIAN order at the Abbey of Kappenberg. Ordained a priest in 1134, he became abbot of Scheda (1143), one of the houses dependent on Kappenberg. Herman seems to have been singularly impressed by the graces he had received; in his autobiography, *Opusculum de vita sua* (*Patrologia Latina*, ed. J. P. Migne, 170:805–836), he stressed his conversion and traced his own religious development, following his discussions with RUPERT OF DEUTZ, from his entrance into Kappenberg through his days at Scheda. However, the main purpose of the autobiography was a stirring appeal to his fellow Jews to accept Christ. A. Potthast has called it ''a pearl of medieval literature.'' Herman is also credited with the authorship of the *Vita Godefredi* (*Monumenta Germaniae Historica, Scriptores,* 12:513–530), the life of the brother of OTTO OF CAPPENBERG, one of the early supporters of the Premonstratensians in Germany.

Bibliography: R. SEEBERG, *Hermann von Scheda* (Leipzig 1891). *Bibliotheca hagiographica latina antiquae et mediae aetatis,* 2 v. (Brussels 1898–1901; suppl. 1911) 3575–76. M. MANITIUS, *Geschichte der lateinischen Literatur des Mittelalters,* 3 v. (Munich 1911–31) 3:592–593. G. MADELAINE, *Histoire de saint Norbert,* 2 v. (3d ed. Tongerloo Abbey, Belg. 1928) 1:190–209. J. GREVEN, ''Die Schrift des Herimannus quondam Iudaeus *De conversione sua opusculum,'' Annalen des historischen Vereins für den Niederrhein* 115 (1929) 111–131. N. BACKMUND, *Monasticon Praemonstratense,* 3 v. (Straubing 1949–56) 1:190. J. C. DIDIER, *Catholicisme* 5:656–657. K. HONSELMANN, *Lexikon für Theologie und Kirche*, ed. J. HOFER and K. RAHNER, 10 v. (2d, new ed. Freiburg 1957–65) 5:252–253. G. NIEMEYER, ''Das Praemonstratenserstift Scheda im 12. Jahrhundert,'' *Westfälische Zeitschrift* 112 (1962) 309–333.

[L. L. RUMMEL]

HERMAN OF SCHILDESCHE

Or of Westphalia, theologian and administrator; b. Schildesche (Schilditz), Sept. 8, *c.* 1290; d. Würzburg, July 8, 1357. Herman entered the AUGUSTINIAN ORDER at Herford, where he made his novitiate. He did his early studies at Osnabrück; his study of theology, most probably at Erfurt or Magdeburg, though he may have spent the last three of the five years prescribed at the Augustinian *studium* in Paris. He was ordained toward the end of these studies; his winning a lectorship crowned their completion. He taught with distinction at Magdeburg (1317?–24), at Erfurt (1324–28?), and at Paris (1330–35). In the earlier years of his stay in Paris, he obtained first a bachelor's and then a master's degree in theology. He was provincial of his own Augustinian province of Saxony and Thuringia (1337–39); in 1338 he served as one of a commission of three sent by the German bishops to AVIGNON to effect a reconciliation between Pope BENEDICT XII and Louis IV, the Bavarian. He spent his later years (1340–57) in Würzburg, where he not only lectured regularly in theology to the clerics of that diocese but, from 1342 at least, was vicar-general (the first) and *mainor paenitentiarius.* His upright, gentle character won him many friends there. Of the more than 30 works that Herman wrote, only 11 are extant. They dealt with various aspects of theology (dogmatic, moral, pastoral, ascetical, and mystical), and with exegesis, philosophy, and law. Two of them—the pastoral *Speculum manuale sacerdotum* and his *Introductorium iuris,* a lexicon—were widely used.

Bibliography: Sources. A. ZUMKELLER, *Schrifttum und Lehre des Hermann von Schildesche* (Würzburg 1959). JORDAN OF QUEDLINBURG, *Liber vitasfratrum (1357),* ed. R. ARBESMANN and W. HÜMPFNER (New York 1943) 240–241, 476. **Literature.** A. ZUMKELLER, *Hermann von Schildesche, O.E.S.A., †8 Juli 1357* (Würzburg 1957); *Augustiniana* 7 (1957), *passim;* 8 (1958) 113–128; "Wiedergefundene exegetische Werke Hermanns von Schildesche," *Augustinianum* 1 (1961) 236–272, 452–503. O. MAZAL, "Handschriften mittelalterlicher Augustiner-Eremiten in der österreichischen Nationalbibliothek," *ibid.* 4 (1964) 291–296. A. ZUMKELLER, "Manuskripte von Werken der Autoren des Augustiner-Eremitenordens in metteleuropäischen Bibliotheken," *Augustiniana* 11 (1961) 12 (1962) 27–43.

[J. E. BRESNAHAN]

HERMAN THE GERMAN, BL.

DOMINICAN missionary; fl. early 13th century. Together with Bl. Ceslaus of Silesia and St. HYACINTH, he was invested with the habit of the Order of Preachers by St. DOMINIC himself. He was the cofounder of the first Dominican house in Germany (Friesach 1219) and later worked in the apostolate in Silesia. Nothing further is known of his career.

Bibliography: B. ALTANER, *Die Dominikanermissionen des 13. Jh.* (Habelschwerdt 1924).

[O. J. BLUM]

HERMANNUS CONTRACTUS

Monk and polymath (called also Herman the Lame or Herman of Reichenau); b. Saulgau, Württemberg-Hohenzollern, Germany, July 18, 1013; d. Abbey of Reichenau, Germany, Sept. 24, 1054. The son of Count Wolverad II of Altshausen, he was a cripple (hence *contractus*) from birth, and although practically helpless physically, through an iron will he triumphed intellectually over his impairment, becoming skilled in theology, astronomy, mathematics, history, poetry, Arabic, Greek, and Latin. He was entrusted at age seven to BERNO, Abbot of the Benedictine monastery of REICHENAU, and he seems to have lived practically his entire life on the island occupied by the abbey in Lake Constance. He took monastic vows there in 1043 and in time became a noted and remarkably capable teacher, no less by his admirable learning than by his charm and attractiveness of manner. His *Chronicon* is an account of the most important events in history since the birth of Christ, in the tradition of various medieval ANNALS AND CHRONICLES but remarkable for its objectivity and careful CHRONOLOGY (ed. Pertz, *Monumenta Germaniae Historica*, Scriptores, 5:67–133). In astronomy his *De astrolabio* displays wide learning (*Patrologia Latina* 143: 379–412), while his mathematical writings are various and important (see M. B. Cantor, *Vorlesungen über Geschichte der Mathematik* 1:759–889). His lengthy poem *De octo vitiis principalibus* [ed. F. Dümmler, *Zeitschrift für deutsches Altertum* (1867) 13:385–434] is addressed to a group of nuns. His mouthpiece is the muse Melpomene, who converses with Hermannus and the nuns in various skillfully employed meters. Melpomene's burden of address to the nuns is *de contemptu mundi,* and she includes a warning against the seven capital sins. Hermannus is important, too, in the history of the SEQUENCE, though the great *ALMA REDEMPTORIS MATER* and *SALVE REGINA* have been incorrectly ascribed to him. His, however, are the *De sancta cruce* and the *Rex regum Dei agne* (ed. G. Dreves, *Analecta hymnica* 50:308–319), and they are composed basically in the tradition of NOTKER BALBULUS. After his death Hermannus became the object of a local cult, which was confirmed by the Holy See in 1863 and assigned a feast on September 25, although he is not generally regarded as a saint by most authorities.

Bibliography: *Patrologia Latina*, ed. J. P. MIGNE, 217 v., indexes 4 v. (Paris 1878–90) 143:9–458. H. HANSJAKOB, *Herimann, der Lahme von der Reichenau* (Mainz 1875). K. BEYERLE, ed., *Die Kultur der Abtei Reichenau,* 2 v. (Munich 1925), *passim.* A. M. ZIMMERMANN, *Kalendarium Benedictinum: Die Heiligen und Seligen des Benediktinerorderns und seiner Zweige*, 4 v. (Metten 1933–38) 2:482–484. M. MANITIUS, *Geschichte der lateinischen Literatur des Mittelalters*, 3 v. (Munich 1911–31) 2:756–777. F. J. E. RABY, *A History of Christian-Latin Poetry from the Beginnings to the Close of the Middle Ages* (2d ed. Oxford 1953) 225–229. F. KARLINGER, *Lexikon für Theologie und Kirche*, ed. J. HOFER and K. RAHNER, 10 v. (2d, new ed. Freiburg 1957–65) 5:250. J. C. DIDIER, *Catholicisme* 5:663–664.

[W. C. KORFMACHER]

HERMAS, SHEPHERD OF

Second-century Christian apocalyptic work. From personal references it seems that Hermas had been a slave in Rome, was set free, married, and had a family, who because of his indulgence became apostate. He had been prosperous in business, but had lost his wealth and suffered in time of persecution. Some of these details, however, which are given in the first Vision, betray the influence of contemporary romantic literature.

The Muratorian Canon states that Hermas was the brother of Pope PIUS I (d. *c.* 154) and had written during his pontificate. Hermas himself refers to a contemporary Clement of Rome (Vis. 2.4.3) as an authority in the Church, but this is not necessarily Pope CLEMENT I (fl. *c.* 96). Origen's identification of Hermas with Rom 16.14 is regarded as an attempt to provide him with some kind of apostolic background. A date of composition between 140 and 155 fits the period given by the Muratorian Canon, while internal evidence indicates that the work was written after a period of peace.

The Shepherd is in three sections, and comprises five Visions (Vis.), 12 Mandates (Man.), and ten Similitudes (Sim.) or Parables. In the first four Visions, Hermas sees the Church as an elderly matron who grows progressively younger as he carries out her orders. She bids him and his family repent, sends him to the Church authorities with a call to repentance and a warning of imminent persecution; and she shows him a vision of a tower, representing the Church, in process of being built. The different stones used in the building typify varieties of Christians, and stones rejected by the builders may ultimately be used, provided that they repent now, before the tower is finished.

The fifth Vision is clearly intended as an introduction to what follows, for Hermas has a vision of the angel of repentance wearing shepherd dress; the angel dictates the 12 Mandates. The third to the sixth have some affinity with the Qumran Manual of Discipline (iii.13–iv.26), and throughout there are distinct signs of Jewish influence, as in the conflict between the good desire and the evil desire described in the 12th Mandate. Hermas also commends such practices as cheerfulness, patience, continence, and fasting.

In the Similitudes, Hermas continues to receive teaching from the angel, but in the form of parables and more visions, some of which are explained with much allegorical detail. The first five contain moral teaching, and the rest deal with penitence. The ninth Similitude repeats the building of the tower, first described in the third Vision, but with additional details and the important difference that there is a pause in the building to allow men more opportunity for penance. In the Vision, the time had been severely limited.

The most striking and debatable feature of the Shepherd is the teaching about penance. Does Hermas represent a reaction against a current of rigorism that rejected the possibility of forgiveness for any post-Baptismal sin? Is it to counter this that he brings a celestial promise of an exceptional opportunity, referred to by some commentators as a time of jubilee, for penitence? Or is Hermas simply reflecting the penitential discipline current at the time? The first seems the more likely, for the author lays down no formula for reconciliation with the Church, though clearly inclusion within the Church is assumed to be a necessity for salvation.

Hermas was more concerned with morals than with theology, and his Christological thinking is confused. He emphasizes that there is only one God (Man. 1). The Holy Spirit is identified with the Son of God before the Incarnation, and Christ becomes the adopted Son after His humanity is taken up into Heaven (Sim. 5.6.5). Christ is the rock on which the Church is built, the door through which all stones must be carried (Sim. 9), but at times He seems to be no more than an angel.

The Shepherd was regarded as quasi-canonical by St. IRENAEUS, CLEMENT OF ALEXANDRIA, ORIGEN, and Tertullian in his pre-Montanist period. ATHANASIUS set it outside the Canon (probably because of the possibly Arian implications of Man. 1), but valued its moral teaching, as did Eusebius. At Rome, however, the Muratorian Canon expressly denied its inspiration while conceding its value for private reading. Jerome states that it was almost unknown in the West. Yet it is noteworthy that it followed the Epistle of Barnabas in the great 4th-century Codex Sinaiticus.

The incomplete Greek text is based on the Sinaiticus (to Man. 4) and a 15th-century Athos manuscript (to Sim. 9). The rest is known from two Latin versions and one Ethiopic. In this century some Coptic and Greek papyrus fragments and one tiny Persian fragment have been published, and a notable University of Michigan papyrus contains Sim. 2–9, first published in 1934.

Hermas's style is prosaic, and much of his subject matter is repetitive. He is perhaps influenced by Greek literary models in his description of a woman bathing (Vis. 1.1.2), or in situating Sim. 9 in Arcadia, but for the most part his outlook is limited by Jewish and Christian modes of thought. Attempts have been made to differentiate sources, strata, separate authors. The work is indeed diffuse and inconsistent, but that is in the nature of an apocalyptic. A unifying ethos of simple and rather narrow piety characterizes the whole.

Bibliography: Editions. J. B. LIGHTFOOT and J. R. HARMER, eds., *The Apostolic Fathers* (2d ed. London 1912). K. LAKE, ed., *The Apostolic Fathers,* 2 v. (Loeb Classical Library; 1912–13) 2:2–305. M. WHITTAKER, ed. (Griechische Christliche Schriftsteller 48; 1956). R. JOLY, ed. and tr. (Sources Chrétiennes, ed. H. DE LUBAC 53; 1958). Literature. J. QUASTEN, *Patrology,* 3 v. (Westminster, MD 1950–) 1:92–105. B. ALTANER, *Patrology,* tr. H. GRAEF from the 5th German ed. (New York 1960) 84–88. S. GIET, *Hermas et les pasteurs* (Paris 1963).

[M. WHITTAKER]

HERMENEGILD, ST.

Son of Leovigild, Visigothic King of Spain; d. Tarragona, April 13, 585. He married (579) Ingund, daughter of SIGEBERT I, King of Austrasia, and Brunhilde. Since Ingund resisted the efforts of Goisvintha, her grandmother and Leovigild's second wife, to convert her to ARIANISM, Hermenegild was given a separate command centered at Seville. There, Ingund and Bishop LEANDER converted him to Catholicism. Almost simultaneously Hermenegild rebelled against Leovigild, with the support of the Byzantines and some Catholic Hispano-Romans. Hermenegild's rebellion damaged the country but did not spread far, and the threat it raised of intervention by the Sueves, Franks, and Byzantines did not seriously materialize. Leovigild retaliated by holding a council to facilitate conversion to Arianism (580) and, more effectively, by buying off the Byzantines (583), who retained Ingund and Hermenegild's son and sent them to Constantinople. Hermenegild, defeated and captured (*c.* March 584), was beheaded because—according to GREGORY I THE GREAT—he refused Communion from an Arian bishop. Contemporary Catholic authors disapproved of Hermenegild's rebellion. Gregory was the exception, and Hermenegild entered the MARTYROLOGIES from his *Dialogues* (3.31). At the urging of PHILIP II, SIXTUS V authorized the cult of Hermenegild in Spain (1585); URBAN VIII extended it to the whole Church.

Feast: April 13.

Bibliography: L. VÁZQEZ DE PARGA, *San Hermenegildo ante las fuentes históricas* (Madrid 1973). R. GROSSE, *Las fuentes de la época visigoda y bizantinas* (Fontes hispaniae antiquae 9; Barcelona 1947) 161–194. F. GÖRRES, ''Kritische Untersuchungen über den Aufstand und das Martyrium des westgothischen Königsohnes Hermenegild,'' *Zeitschrift für die historische Theologie* 43 (1873) 3–109. K. STROHECKER, ''Leowigild: Aus einer Wendezeit westgothische Geschichte,'' *Die Welt als Geschichte* 5 (1939) 446–485. W. GOFFART, ''Byzantine Policy in the West . . . (579–585),'' *Traditio* 13 (1957) 73–118. E. A. THOMPSON, ''The Conversion of the Visigoths to Catholicism,'' *Nottingham Medieval Studies* 4 (1960) 4–35.

[W. GOFFART]

HERMENEUTICS

In its most general sense hermeneutics refers to the art and theory of interpretation, particularly the interpretation of texts. The history of hermeneutics from antiquity until today has been governed by the universal problem that truth exceeds its expression and that ''discourse always lags behind what one wants or has to say'' (J. Grondin). This gives rise to the parallel recognition that some method is necessary to understand the ''inner truth'' expressed in discourse without thereby delegitimating the expression, which is a necessary precondition for this understanding.

The term is derived from the Greek verb *hermēneuein* (to interpret, to explain, to translate), which in turn has been connected with the messenger of the Greek gods, Hermes, whose role was to proclaim divine oracles that lay beyond human understanding in a form accessible to human intelligence. The earliest uses of *hermēneuein* and its cognates (*hermēneus* [interpreter], *hermēneia* [interpretation, explanation]) carry the wider connotation of a process of bringing something from ambiguity or unintelligibility to understanding, primarily through the use of language. The earliest recorded use of the term ''hermeneutics'' to describe a methodology or a set of ''scientific'' criteria seems to have been in J. C. Dannhauer's *Hermeneutica sacra sive methodus exponendarum sacrarum litterarum* (1654), where it referred to principles and methods of interpretation that were independent of and provided the foundation for the activity of scriptural commentary (exegesis).

Premodern Hermeneutics. In antiquity and in the medieval world the principles of interpretation were understood to apply most often to texts, particularly religious texts, and especially to individual textual cases where the meaning was unclear or difficult to extract. Greek philosophers, for example, employed allegory to interpret difficult passages within the Homeric tradition—i.e., they assumed that there was a ''hidden sense'' within these texts that could be reached only by employing an interpretative strategy from outside the text. PLATO suggests an even broader usage of *hermēneuein:* in *Ion* he calls poets ''the interpreters of the gods'' (*hermēnēs tōn theōn,* 435e) and the rhapsodes who perform their poems ''interpreters of the interpreters'' (*hermēneōn hermēnēs,* 535a), thus bringing hermeneutics in close proximity to divination. Post-Aristotelian philosophy, particularly the Stoics (*see* STOICISM), emphasized the use of allegory to rationalize passages in the mythic traditions that seemed objectionable or offensive. The Stoa in turn influenced Jewish and Christian writers in antiquity. Early Christian theologians developed principles for the ''spiritual'' or ''mystical'' interpretation of biblical texts.

For them, interpretation of the Bible had a twofold purpose: to demonstrate how the eternal word of God was mediated through contingent literary forms, and to display the unity of Scripture despite the fact that there were two different Testaments. The preferred interpretative tool was allegory, especially in the form of typological interpretations that viewed various Old Testament events as types or prefigurements of Christ and His saving actions, thereby interpreting the New Testament as the fulfillment of the prophecies found in the Hebrew Scriptures and appropriating the Hebrew Scriptures for the Christian canon. The allegorical method ultimately derived from the Stoa and more immediately from the Alexandrian school and Jewish writers such as Philo, and was taken up by Origen, Augustine, and Jerome, although the more literal interpretations proposed by the Antiochene school (e.g., Theodore of Mopsuestia, John Chrysostom) also played a role (e.g., both types are present in the Symbol of the Council of Chalcedon [451]). The classic compendium of early Christian interpretative principles is AUGUSTINE's *De doctrina christiana,* which develops the fundamental distinction between *signum* (the material sign) and *res* (the transcendental reality that is prior to and the referent of the sign). In the medieval period the various interpretative principles were codified and often expressed in the form of the famous schema of the fourfold sense of Scripture (literal, allegorical, moral, and anagogical [eschatological]). While allegorical interpretation was dominant earlier in the medieval period, later thinkers tried to rein in the allegorical by associating it more closely with the literal. For example, THOMAS AQUINAS, in his discussion of the fourfold sense (*Summa theologiae* Ia, q. 1, a. 10), is careful to note that the meanings disclosed by the latter three senses (the ''spiritual'' senses) are rooted in the literal sense. Thus, although the Scriptures are not univocal but multivalent, these varied meanings are not contradictory since they are signs pointing to the truth intended by the Scriptures' divine author.

Early Modern Hermeneutics. In early modernity hermeneutics began to develop into an independent discipline dealing with the general principles that governed the authentic interpretation of various types of texts. One major catalyst was the Reformation's rejection of the Catholic use of church authority, tradition, and allegory to interpret Scripture. Following Martin LUTHER's principle of *sola scriptura,* Protestant authors insisted that the Bible was its own interpreter (*sui ipsius interpres*) and developed principles to demonstrate the Bible's self-sufficiency and noncontradictory nature while at the same time helping to decipher difficult passages without recourse to any authority outside the Scriptures. Matthias Flacius Illyricus's *Clavis scripturae sacrae* (1567) is decisive in this regard. Flacius constructed an interpretative key (*clavis*) to the Scriptures by insisting that a thorough linguistic and grammatical training in the biblical languages was necessary for exegesis and by formulating a system of rules (based on the ancient rhetoric, patristic authors, and Augustine) for explicating ambiguous passages in the light of the wholeness of Scripture, thus avoiding any need to appeal to church authority. Renaissance humanist scholars pursued similar goals in their study of classical Greek and Roman texts and legal documents. They devised various philological-critical methods, applicable to wide varieties of texts, in order to assist them in establishing a text's authenticity and determining its correct (for them, the original) version. The development and distillation of hermeneutic principles into a separate humanistic discipline, applicable to religious and nonreligious texts alike, was furthered in the 17th and 18th centuries by Benedictus de Spinoza's insistence on grounding biblical exegesis in natural history and reason rather than faith (*Tractatus theologico-politicus,* 1670) and by authors such as Dannhauer, Johann Martin Chladinius (who defined hermeneutics as ''the art of interpretation'' according to rational rules, aimed at a complete understanding of ''reasonable discourses and writings''), and Johann August Ernesti (who sharply distinguished between the task of general hermeneutics to understand the language and thus the meaning of any text and the task of theology to grasp the content and thus the truth of biblical texts).

Modern Hermeneutics: Schleiermacher and Dilthey. Modern hermeneutics begins with Friedrich SCHLEIERMACHER. While influenced by previous attempts to craft a general hermeneutics, his own theory decisively surpassed them. He departed radically from his predecessors in two ways: (1) by shifting the central focus of hermeneutics from the meaning of texts to the conditions for the possibility of all understanding, thus reenvisioning hermeneutics as philosophy and not merely as technique; (2) by assuming that misunderstanding was not rare but rather was the interpreter's normal situation, and that understanding must be worked out by attempting to overcome obstacles and grasp the whole. Schleiermacher defined hermeneutics as ''the historical *and* divinatory, objective *and* subjective reconstruction of the given utterance'' (*Hermeneutics and Criticism,* introd., #18) and characterized it as an ''art.'' He based his theory upon the reciprocal relationship between thought and speech, and saw the immediate goal of the interpretation to be the reproduction of the author's or speaker's thought that originally gave rise to expression—in other words, the reconstruction of the author's intention. The two necessarily interlocking moments of interpretation are the grammatical (objective), aimed at clarifying the texts' specific linguistic aspects, and the psychological (subjective or ''divinatory'') by which one ''empathetically'' grasps the author's inner life, which gets expressed in the text as a whole. If the goal of discourse is to communicate thought and feeling, then the goal of interpretation is to reproduce and reexperience that thought and feeling. This immediate task is carried out in a circular fashion: ''even within a single text the particular can only be understood from out of the whole'' (*ibid.,* #23) and yet the whole can only be grasped once the parts are understood. The grammatical and psychological are also reciprocally related: the ''divination'' of the author's experience is not independent of the linguistic elements, yet the meaning of a text exceeds what any purely grammatical interpretation may disclose.

Beyond this, Schleiermacher saw that the more fundamental goal of hermeneutics was to examine the overall art of understanding and to articulate its elements. Thought and speech are almost two sides of the same coin: thought is linguistic, and discourse is expressed thought. ''Almost,'' for there is a difference as well: the same thought can be expressed in a variety of ways, and is thus somewhat detachable from language. The hermeneutical problem arises precisely at this juncture of ''same'' and ''different'': how does one understand the other (here, the author) when the other is like myself yet expresses an individuality which is unlike my own? The text, too, is a conjunction of same and different: it is an ''individual universal,'' a network of shared grammatical conventions and linguistic rules applied by the author in a uniquely individual way in order to constitute a new and meaningful whole in a particular ''style,'' which nonetheless communicates to others. The text also expresses the author's individual experience that participates in and clarifies those human experiences shared by all. Schleiermacher argued that interpretation is an infinite task where no absolute understanding of a text (and hence of any author) is ever possible, since the grammatical always deals with the ''infinity'' of linguistic choices and the psychological with the ''infinity'' of the author's intuition. But a high degree of understanding can be reached; indeed, the goal remains ''to understand the utterance at first just as well and then better than its author'' as we ''seek to bring much to consciousness that can remain unconscious'' to the author (*ibid.,* #18). This understanding also takes place in a circular manner: the author's inner life is glimpsed through one particular text, while the particular text is understood as meaningful when interpreted in the context of an author's whole life-experience and the whole of the semantic system within which it has been conceived. Schleiermacher's hermeneutic ''revolution,'' then, consists of seeing hermeneutics as a philosophical ''meta-discipline'' that articulates the circular nature of all understanding, discloses the interplay of the rule-bound and the non-rule-bound in all authentic and meaningful interpretation, and recognizes the necessary risk of empathy in any attempt to understand the other.

Wilhelm DILTHEY developed hermeneutics even further as a philosophical discipline in the service of his ''philosophy of life'' (*Lebensphilosophie*). He widened its focus from textual expressions to historically situated cultural expressions of all kinds. Influenced by his research into Schleiermacher's work, he endeavored to provide a firm methodological basis for the human sciences over against the growing dominance of the natural sciences and to support the objective value of their truth claims over against historical skepticism. He argued that there is a crucial methodological difference between the natural sciences (characterized by the *explanation* of natural phenomena according to a mechanistic model) and the human sciences (which aimed at *understanding* human life from within). The key point is Dilthey's description of ''life'' as a process, a complex mixture of individual lives lived in time, which constitutes the social and historical fabric of humankind and whose truth can be grasped solely through its objective historical expressions. The range of expressions can include gestures, actions, legal codes, historical artifacts, works of art, and whole cultures. Only understanding, rather than explanation, can be adequate to the study of inner human life objectified in these expressions; by deriving its categories from life itself, it is sensitive to the temporal flow of individual experience (*Erlebnis*) that links past (memory) and future (anticipation) with the present. The goal of understanding is the reconstruction and reexperiencing of this individual inner world of experience behind the expression and in turn the overall life-process of which the individual is only a part.

Dilthey's hermeneutics unites these three elements (experience, expression, and understanding) into the methodological foundation of the human sciences. Temporal *lived experience,* as a self-aware, pre-rational act, demands objective historical expression in order to understand itself. *Expressions* are objectifications of lived experience, symbols of inner life that can be adequately understood only when interpreted within their historical context. The highest and fullest expression is art, revealing not simply the artist's personal experience but embodying the deepest aspects of all human experience. The art with the greatest disclosive power is literature, which permanently fixes experience in language. *Understanding* is the reverse of expression: by interpreting these expressions within their historical context, it attempts to reexperience—indeed, to re-create or relive—the lived experience of the other person and thus of the life-process within which they participate. The immediate goal of understanding is to bridge the gap between the other and myself through my empathetic reexperiencing of their ''mental life.'' The ultimate goal is to understand all of human life, of which the individual is only a part. The meaning of the ''whole,'' whether a person's whole life, a whole culture, or the whole of life itself, can be derived only from the study of its individual parts. The parts, moreover, can be understood only in reference to the whole whose unity is presupposed and that determines the function and meaning of the parts. Dilthey explicitly articulates the ''hermeneutic circle'' already alluded to by Schleiermacher and others. The meaning that arises from the circle is the result of a real historical relationship between the interpreter and the objectified expressions of life and is always contextual, changing with one's temporal perspective. Dilthey's hermeneutics is thus left with an inherent dilemma: he abhorred relativism and wanted to render the truths of the human sciences as objectively as those of the natural sciences, yet he demonstrated that self-understanding is never the result of direct introspection but is always indirect, mediated by historical expressions and temporally shifting syntheses.

Contemporary Hermeneutics. Contemporary hermeneutics is dominated by the figures of Martin HEIDEGGER and Hans-Georg GADAMER. Heidegger's early work, especially *Being and Time* (1927), shifted the hermeneutical focus yet again, this time away from texts and cultural expressions to the human person as both interpreted and interpreting. *Being and Time,* among other issues, presents a ''hermeneutics of facticity,'' a phenomenological description of Dasein (Heidegger's term for the human being) that interprets the person's everyday way-of-being in order to reach an understanding of Being as such. Dasein is portrayed as thoroughly hermeneutical, both in the way it lives its ordinary life (interpreting entities as meaningful within a previously constituted ''world'' or ''totality of involvements'' as well as over against a pre-understanding of the meaning of Being) and in the way it understands itself as an incomplete historical ''project,'' constituted in the present by its facticity (past) and its ''projection'' into its possibilities (future). Because Dasein is its own project and because it both constitutes and discloses its being by the actualization of its own possibilities, interpretation and understanding are not actions Dasein chooses to perform but are rather two of Dasein's basic modes of being (''existentials'') from the outset. Heidegger surprisingly changes the traditional polarity: one does not first interpret in order to understand, but rather understands in order to interpret. *Understanding* is the power by which Dasein discloses what its existential choices have already presupposed, namely a grasp of its own future possibilities-for-being and ''of the whole of Being-in-the-world'' (*Being and Time,* §32). Dasein thus understands its own true being as radically temporal and projected over time rather than being merely a present ''object.'' *Interpretation* (*Auslegung*) is the laying-out (*aus-legen*) or the actualizing of the possibilities already disclosed in understanding. Its operation is guided by a threefold ''fore-structure'' of prejudgments: a fore-knowledge of the appropriate context (*Vorhabe*), a ''fore-sight'' or situated point of view (*Vorsicht*), and a pre-understanding of the whole-to-be-actualized (*Vorgriff*). This fore-structure is the pivot upon which the hermeneutic circle turns, guiding the relationship between understanding and interpretation: what is interpreted must be already understood to some degree (to even awaken our interest in interpreting it), while understanding is articulated, actualized, and deepened by interpretation. Understanding is determined by the anticipations of meaning generated by the fore-structure, while interpretation must be guided by the fore-structure provided by understanding. ''Any interpretation which is to contribute understanding, must already have understood what is to be interpreted'' (*ibid.*). This circularity cannot be avoided; it is intrinsic to all human knowing and is itself an expression of one of Dasein's basic modes of being. The necessity of a pre-understanding (*Vorgriff*) means that there is never any presuppositionless understanding or interpretation. Thus the meaning of entities within the world (what *Being and Time* calls their ''as-structure'') and of Dasein itself is the result of a disclosure effected by Dasein, occurring within an interpretation guided by pre-understanding. This Heideggerian version of the hermeneutic circle, which considers the circularity of understanding to be ontological and not merely epistemological, has become extremely influential in both philosophy and theology.

Hans-Georg Gadamer's philosophical hermeneutics draws from several sources, including Schleiermacher's quest for a general hermeneutics, Dilthey's emphasis on historicity and the recuperation of the human sciences, and the Heideggerian themes of the hermeneutics of facticity, the hermeneutic circle, and the ontological basis of understanding. His *magnum opus, Truth and Method* (1960), has become the touchstone for all subsequent approaches to hermeneutics, both pro and con. Behind his overt desire to critique modernity's objectivist methods and rehabilitate the model of understanding promoted by the humanities lies a deeper concern to analyze the process of human understanding itself and to demonstrate its fundamental openness to others and to the past: ''the way we experience one another, the way we experience historical traditions, the way we experience the natural givenness of our existence and of our world, constitute a truly hermeneutic universe, in which we are not imprisoned, as if behind insurmountable barriers, but to which we are opened'' (*Truth and Method,* xxiv).

All understanding begins with *prejudices,* anticipatory prejudgments that are grounded in previous experiences. Prejudices are not disabling, distorting biases (as the Enlightenment claimed) but rather are enabling; they allow us to begin understanding by projecting a meaning upon something (e.g., a text) on the basis of our partial experience of it, and then to either confirm or deny that understanding in the course of further experience. These interpretative projections are both ontological and rooted in the interpreter's situation, which is formed by the *tradition* or *history of effects (Wirkungsgeschichte)* within which the interpreter stands. Thus the present temporal horizon of expectations is constituted by both the past from which it develops (the authoritative tradition that addresses us and ''is already effectual in *finding the right questions to ask*'' [*Truth and Method,* 301]) and the future to which it opens (new understandings that will confirm, expand upon, or deny our prejudgments). The history of effects is constituted by *classics,* works that embody experiences and interpretations that have endured over time and whose significance occurs within history yet appears to be timeless because they are always timely—i.e., their significance applies to situations in historical epochs beyond their own. What allows us to tell the classics from the period pieces is *temporal distance,* which encourages us to test our prejudgments of their enduring significance and thus permits their authoritative and universal nature to appear.

This schema allows Gadamer to make two major claims. First, the true goal of understanding is to have a ''consciousness of being effected by history'' (*ibid.,* 301), the awareness that the present historical horizon is always already effected by the truths disclosed previous to the present in the history of effects. This awareness occurs by the *fusion of horizons,* where ''old and new are always combining into something of living value, without either being explicitly foregrounded from the other'' (*ibid.,* 306). Interpretation is not the attempt to leave one's own historical epoch in order to understand a work from the past and thereby seek to erase the historical difference that plainly exists. Rather, the interpreter's present horizon is tested and expanded by coming into contact with the ''otherness'' that the past horizon represents. Temporality, rather than being an obstacle to understanding, enables understanding to occur: ''it is the supportive ground of the course of events in which the present is rooted'' (*ibid.,* 297) and in which our prejudgments are formed. Secondly, the key to hermeneutical understanding is the *application* that occurs in the fusion of horizons. To interpret a work from the past is to understand it, but ''understanding always involves something such as applying the text to be understood to the interpreter's present situation'' (*ibid.,* 308). The three moments are inseparable and simultaneous. Understanding, which is fundamentally linguistic, thus has the character of a moral decision: just as in ethics the general principle and the particular situation are understood in light of each other in a prudential judgment, so too the truth of a past text is grasped in the moment of application to the present situation, whose truth is disclosed by the difference represented by the past and challenged to expand its expectations in the light of this difference.

In addition to Heidegger and Gadamer, Paul RICOEUR has made important contributions to contemporary hermeneutics. Among these are his emphasis on the productive character of texts, the power of metaphor to evoke new meanings, and the character of narrative, each of which is involved in the disclosure of new possibilities of meaning. The objectifying nature of writing already assures that the finished text is autonomous, distanced from the intention of the author. This ''distanciation'' is productive; the work breaks free of its limited temporal horizon to be recontextualized in any number of new situations of reading, thereby disclosing the multiple possibilities of authentic interpretation (the world ''in front of the text'') beyond the original authorial experience (the world ''behind the text'') and challenging the reader to expand his horizons. Metaphors, by means of the clash of literal meanings that they embody, are a semantic signal of the ''surplus of meaning'' that exceeds the literal meaning and creatively subverts the reader's expectations, disclosing new possibilities of existential meaning for the reader. Narratives, as Ricoeur has claimed in his later work, are the most fundamental form that human activities take and are the necessary mediation of all self and social identity. Fictional narratives configure characters and actions according to a certain emplotted order that, however, plays out over time in unexpected ways with the final meaning intelligible only at the conclusion; the truth of the narrative is available only in a retrospective interpretation. Human identity can be similarly interpreted: it is a temporal ''configuration'' of concordance and discordance, of sedimented identity that is open to innovation and unforeseen responses to others, and thus to constructive ''refiguration'' over time that allows for self-identity to be reinterpreted without being dispersed.

Hermeneutics in Recent Catholic Theology. Hermeneutics has played an extremely important role in contemporary Roman Catholic theology, especially in fundamental or foundational theology. For example, in his Christology Edward Schillebeeckx has employed a fundamental theory of experience and a hermeneutics of tradition very similar to Gadamer's in order to articulate the relationship between divine revelation and the historically situated human experience in which it occurs, and to explain the connections between the disciples' original interpreted experience of the revelation of God in Jesus and the present-day interpreted experience of Jesus as Lord. David Tracy has used the normative status of classics to argue that the Christian tradition is constituted by its religious classics (especially the classic person, Jesus Christ), i.e., historically situated events that disclose a ''radically and finally gracious mystery'' (*Analogical Imagination,* 163). Thus systematic theology is inherently hermeneutical: by interpreting the Christian classics, it seeks to make publically accessible both the meaning of the tradition that mediates this disclosive power and the modes of reception (application) of this power within the present. Francis Schüssler Fiorenza has argued against a foundationalist approach to theology that what is essential to FOUNDATIONAL THEOLOGY is a ''hermeneutical reconstruction'' of the integral Christian tradition, seen as a ''history of effects'' composed of diverse historically situated beliefs and practices. Models of stasis, decay, or unilateral progress which search for a timeless ''essence of Christianity'' fail in the face of this empirical diversity. Only a hermeneutical reconstruction, attuned to the ongoing historical reception of the truth of revelation, can render intelligible the unifying Christian identity that exists in the midst of this diversity and can take into account the varying background theories, retroductive warrants, and various communities of discourse that contribute to the continual constitution and reconstruction of Christian identity over time.

See Also: EXEGESIS.

Bibliography: F. SCHÜSSLER-FIORENZA, *Foundational Theology: Jesus and the Church* (New York 1984); ''History and Hermeneutics,'' in J. C. LIVINGSTON et al., *Modern Christian Thought,* 2d ed. *Volume II: The Twentieth Century,* 341–385 (Upper Saddle River, N.J. 2000). H.-G. GADAMER, *Truth and Method,* 2d rev. ed., tr. J. WEINSHEIMER and D. G. MARSHALL (New York 1989). J. GRONDIN, *Introduction to Philosophical Hermeneutics,* tr. J. WEINSHEIMER (New Haven, Conn. 1994). M. HEIDEGGER, *Being and Time,* tr. J. MACQUARRIE and E. ROBINSON (New York 1962). K. MUELLER-VOLLMER, ed., *The Hermeneutics Reader* (New York 1988). P. RICOEUR, *Hermeneutics and the Human Sciences,* ed. and tr. J. B. THOMPSON (Cambridge 1981); *Time and Narrative,* 3 v., tr. K. MCLAUGHLIN and D. PELLAUER (Chicago 1984–88). J. RISSER, *Hermeneutics and the Voice of the Other: Re-reading Gadamer's Philosophical Hermeneutics* (Albany, N.Y. 1997). E. SCHILLEBEECKX, *Interim Report on the Books ''Jesus'' and ''Christ,''* tr. J. BOWDEN (New York 1981). F. SCHLEIERMACHER, *Hermeneutics and Criticism and Other Writings,* tr. and ed. A. BOWIE (Cambridge/New York 1998). N. H. SMITH, *Strong Hermeneutics: Contingency and Moral Identity* (London 1997). A. C. THISELTON, *New Horizons in Hermeneutics: The Theory and Practice of Transforming Biblical Reading* (Grand Rapids 1992). D. TRACY, *The Analogical Imagination: Christian Theology and the Culture of Pluralism* (New York 1981).

[A. J. GODZIEBA]

HERMENEUTICS, BIBLICAL

The common human experience of seeking the meaning of words, discourses, and events is elevated to a scholarly level in the science of biblical interpretation. The meaning of a text distant by millennia from today's world is not always patent to the modern reader. Moreover, churches claiming a biblical base are constantly confronted with the multiplicity of scriptural interpretations given by other churches, some of them contradictory. Thus interpretation is required, and because the Bible is accepted as the word of God and because of the potential for greater Church unity, there is need to seek the highest degree of objectivity possible.

Development of Hermeneutics. Determining the author's intended meaning was until recently taken to be the role of EXEGESIS, while to HERMENEUTICS was left the task of making a contemporary application. Until the Enlightenment this distinction was virtually unknown, since most analysis of biblical texts was for a pastoral purpose. The arrival of scientific tools of analysis meant that Scripture could be examined like any secular text, with the supposed abstraction from any faith stance. Once that happened, however, the need was felt to find the relevance of the ancient text to contemporary life, whence the science—and some would say the art—of hermeneutics developed. The term actually appears for the first time in the 17th century, apparently by J. C. Dannhauer, *Hermeneutica Sacra, sive methodus exponendarum Sacrarum Litterarum* (Strassburg 1654). Today the distinction has once again become blurred so that exegesis is understood by many, including the Pontifical Biblical Commission (*The Interpretation of the Bible in the Church* [1993]) to be complete only when relevant meaning and application is derived. Hermeneutics in turn normally includes exegesis as an integral part of the interpretive process.

Biblical evidence of the need for interpretation is at least as old as Neh 8:8: ''Ezra read plainly from the book of the law of God, *interpreting* it so that all could understand what was read.'' Indeed, the Bible itself shows later texts interpreting or reinterpreting older ones. This is true already in the Old Testament, as for example when Daniel reinterprets the 70 years Jeremiah prophesied for the duration of the Babylonian exile (Jer 25:11; 29:10) as now extending to 70 weeks of years, i.e., down to the time of the persecution by Antiochus the Illustrious (Dn 9:1–27). It is above all in the New Testament that the Old is interpreted in the light of the new event of the death and resurrection of Jesus Christ. In the gospel of Matthew Jesus says that not only the prophets but the law itself *prophesied* until John (Mt 11:13), reflecting his conviction, widely shared by the Jews of his day, that the biblical texts, even those not expressly prophetic, had a forward-pointing value and thus could be understood to be "fulfilled" in the present ministry of Jesus. This kind of *pesher* reading was common among the sectarians of Qumran, interpreting the texts as fulfilled in their community. They did not think of the texts, particularly the prophetic texts, as having a meaning for the time at which they were written but only as recording a divine secret awaiting interpretation by and application to the later community. While the NT has more respect for the original meaning of the OT, its primary interest is fulfillment in the paschal mystery, that is, in Christ and the Church. This affirmation of fulfillment in Christ, which is the literal sense of the NT, is what the Church understands by the *spiritual* sense. What is distinguished regarding the OT (literal and spiritual senses) becomes identical in the NT.

Spiritual Senses. In some cases the NT sees the OT realties as *types* finding their fulfillment in Christ or the Church. Adam, Moses, David, the Exodus, the paschal lamb, the temple, and Jerusalem are among those explicitly marked as such types. The Church knows certain persons and events to be types because they are so identified in the New Testament or in early Church tradition (e.g., Eve as a type of Mary). Typology alone does not exhaust the spiritual and prophetic potential of the Old Testament, at least according to those who propose a *fuller* sense for many of the OT texts. As a matter of fact, many OT texts, while focusing on a contemporary issue, are expressed in such a way as to be open, of themselves, to greater fulfillment. For example, when Isaiah pronounces his messianic prophecies (in Is 7, 9, and 11), he speaks in hyperbolic terms that the NT finds explicitly fulfilled in Christ. Or the word *almah* ("maiden," 7:14), which could mean nothing more than a young woman of marriageable age, is open, though not compelled, to being narrowed to *parthenos* ("virgin") by the LXX and taken in that narrower sense by Mt 1:23. This "fuller" sense is sometimes described as the sense intended by God but not seen, or not seen clearly, by the human author. Such a definition could, of course, license arbitrary interpretations. It must be qualified by including some intrinsic evidence in the text of such openness to future refinement.

The early Church Fathers were the first to face the question, "Now that we are Christians, what is the place and meaning of the Old Testament?" They did not reject it outright, as did MARCION, for obviously the New Testament appealed to the Old to substantiate its claims about Jesus. It was easy enough for the Fathers to accept the OT typology used by the New Testament, but what to do with other passages that seemed to have no prophetic or typological value, and in fact even seemed scandalous? It is a question that many readers even today have when they begin to read the Hebrew Scriptures for the first time. The Alexandrian Fathers resorted to ALLEGORY, already used extensively by Philo to make the Jewish scriptures attractive to the Hellenistic world. In this they found justification in the method used by Paul in his allegory of Sarah and Hagar (Gal 4:21–31). Though they were aware of the literal sense of the text, they had little appreciation of historical development or progressive revelation in the OT. Rather they sought to find there, in strangely different form, the Gospel itself. Thus in the story of Lot's intercourse with his daughters (an unedifying tale), Origen sees Lot as reason, his wife (who looked back on Sodom) as concupiscence, his daughters vainglory and pride. Through a combination of scripture texts he works up to that wisdom who is Jesus Christ.

If at times the Alexandrian insights are striking, they and those who followed at times elaborated fantastic allegories that were abusive of the text. By the time the Antiochian Fathers reacted to the Alexandrian allegorization, the method was so entrenched it was not abandoned even into the Middle Ages. In the West a distinction was made between what was called the literal or historical sense and the spiritual sense, the latter being divided into three: the allegorical, the tropological or moral, and the anagogical. The allegorical interpretation demonstrated the truths of revelation, the tropological the ethical expectations derived from the text, and the anagogical the ultimate goal of the Christian life, the heavenly realities. For example, the literal Jerusalem was the terrestrial city, the allegorical Jerusalem was the Church, the tropological was the soul called to be the bride of Christ, the anagogical was the heavenly Jerusalem. When medieval authors spoke of the literal or historical sense, they simply meant what was happening in the text or the narrative. They did not mean what modern historians mean who search for "what really happened" according to the canons of modern scientific research. For this reason, even when a biblical author used metaphorical language, this was regularly considered to belong to the spiritual sense.

THOMAS AQUINAS both narrowed the typical sense and expanded the literal sense by shifting the focus to the author's *intention.* The literal sense is what the author intended to convey, whether he used direct or figurative language. This opened the literal sense to the possibility, the fullness of which would be seen only in modern times, of the author's having used various literary forms, including fictive ones, to convey his message. Thus, for example, while it is of interest to know whether Job really existed, the point of the dramatic dialogue, as in Jesus' parables, comes across whether the protagonist existed or not. Or again, John's extensive use of symbols in his Gospel is part of the literal sense, since it was his intention to convey his message in that form. This principle would have wide application in the OT, where modern research has revealed the authors using multiple literary forms. Thomas narrowed the typical sense by pointing out that the spiritual sense (of OT types) is always found somewhere (in the NT) in the literal sense.

A generation earlier JOACHIM OF FIORE had introduced a dispensationalist method of interpretation, which in one form or another has survived until our day. Dividing all of history into three ages or dispensations according to the three persons of the Trinity, Joachim found in Revelation a rich field for imaginative connections with the events, past, present and future, in the history of the Church. Thus the heads of the Beast become the leaders of each of the seven ages of the world and the seven persecutors of the Church. Muḥammad is the beast rising from the earth. The horses in Revelation 19 are the military orders, the ''first resurrection'' is the foundation of the mendicant orders, and so on. This method, which is hardly different from that of QUMRAN convenanters, has had a wide popularity in our day. The mainstream of Catholic tradition, however, has followed Augustine in taking the figures of Revelation either as referring to persons and events of the author's time or as being symbolic of the Church and its enemies of all times.

The Literal Sense, the Reformation, and the Enlightenment. The 14th and 15th centuries were marked by the degeneration of scholastic theology into dialectics with little grounding in the literal sense of Scripture. The aridity of this approach not only brought a reaction in the anti-intellectual *DEVOTIO MODERNA* (e.g., THOMAS À KEMPIS) but laid the ground for Martin Luther's cry to return to the literal sense of the Bible. With the patristic tradition he held that the central theme of the Bible is Christ, but he maintained that Scripture stands above all other authority, be it tradition, the inner witness of the Spirit, Church authority or philosophy. Scripture is its own interpreter—a principle for which the Bible itself offers no textual support. Paul's Epistle to the Romans, with its doctrine of justification by faith, becomes the norm by which the rest of the Bible, even the books of the NT, are to be judged. This, in effect, established a canon within the canon. LUTHER's insistence on the sufficiency of Scripture, and especially CALVIN's stress on the interior witness of the Holy Spirit, would lead to the Catholic accusation that such principles would amount eventually to private interpretation and relativism. On the other hand, if the literal sense of Scripture is the self-determining norm, then scientific exegesis becomes a crucial tool, and ultimately the only tool in arriving at a correct interpretation of Scripture. Thus began the explosion of critical studies and commentaries that has lasted to our times.

With the arrival of the ENLIGHTENMENT, this search for the literal sense, and behind it the historical reference, resulted in establishing the professor's lectern as a parallel pulpit, free from any control save that of the academy. But even there a great deal of disagreement prevailed, especially in the interpretation of the biblical narratives. Although there was a strong conservative wing that took the miracles as happening exactly as narrated, there were others who sought to explain them as natural occurrences that were narrated as supernatural events. Others, such as REIMARUS, maintained that the accounts of the miracles were deceptions. Others interpreted the narratives as religious or moral truths in story form. Still others maintained that the biblical authors were captive of the mythological world view, so that whatever they described was inevitably presented in the clothing of myth. In the 19th century it was common to interpret Jesus as a great teacher of moral living, but nothing more. It was commonly agreed, of course, that no external authority, such as tradition or the Church, should be consulted. In this the positivist were in sync with the mood of the Reformation.

The Catholic Response. The Catholic Church reacted slowly but authoritatively to these developments. Writings of the rationalist critics were put on the Index of Forbidden Books, Pope PIUS IX issued his SYLLABUS OF ERRORS in 1864, and Pope LEO XIII warned of the errors of liberalism in his 1893 encyclical *Providentissimus Deus.* But few Catholic scholars were prepared to meet the historical critics on their own field, nor were they at first encouraged to do so. In 1943, however, Pope PIUS XII issued his encyclical *DIVINO AFFLANTE SPIRITU*, which affirmed the centrality of the literal sense of Scripture, upheld the authority of the original texts, the importance of textual criticism and of taking into account the different literary forms used by the authors, and the contribution of the auxiliary sciences. This encouraged Catholic biblical scholarship and opened the door to a Catholic biblical movement unparalleled in the history of the Church. The Second VATICAN COUNCIL in its Constitution on Divine Revelation (*Dei Verbum*) incorporated many new insights developed since 1943, integrating the achievements of biblical scholarship in an atmosphere that lacked the polemics of the preceding century. Revelation is God's communication not of mere truths but of his very self through words and deeds that are mutually illuminating; the Word of God is Jesus himself, to whom Scripture is the witness; tradition is the *process* by which revelation is handed on; tradition develops, perception of revealed truth grows, and while the magisterium has the final authority in determining the teaching of Scripture, the experience of all the faithful contributes to the process of understanding and transmission of the Word of God.

Meantime, new theories of biblical interpretation were coming onto the field (see below, *Philosophies of*

Interpretation), and meetings of scholarly biblical associations were peppered with presentations using methods that varied from the traditional historical-critical, to text-centered, to reader-centered. Such a diverse array of methods led the PONTIFICAL BIBLICAL COMMISSION in 1993, on the centenary of Leo XIII's biblical encyclical, to publish *The Interpretation of the Bible in the Church*, a comprehensive review and evaluation of past and current methods of interpretation. At the risk of oversimplification in a discipline where there is considerable overlapping, these methods can be organized under the following headings.

The Text as It Stands. These methods look at the text without reference to its prehistory, author, audience, or possible historical reference. *Narrative criticism* first determines where the text begins and ends and then looks at the function of plot, character, setting, and other techniques such as irony. It is interested only in what the text reveals about the implied author and implied reader, not the actual author or the actual reader. This method has been developed on the model of secular literary criticism. It has proved especially helpful in uncovering the theological interest of the text. As a method it is not interested in whether the character or events related actually existed, which is, of course, one of the interests of the believer and the primary interest of the historian. *Rhetorical criticism* assumes that the text wishes to persuade (which most biblical texts do). It then examines the various techniques used. This method can lead to a greater appreciation of the power of the text. The ancients generally did not distinguish between content and expression the way moderns do. They felt that truth should be expressed persuasively. The value of rhetoric is its power to move the emotions and elicit conviction and action. *Structural criticism,* also known as semiotic analysis, considers the relationship of the elements of the text to each other, as binary oppositions, contraries, contradictories, confirmations, etc. It assumes that every text follows a ''grammar,'' that is, a certain number of rules or structures or codes. It is thus useful in showing the internal coherence of texts. Its usefulness is limited to intra-textual analysis, since it has no interest in the extra-textual world, that of the referent, the author or the reader. *Deconstruction,* a form of poststructuralist criticism, is connected with the name of Jaques Derrida. His method is confined to the text itself and opposes any extra-textual concern. He goes beyond structuralism in that he maintains that the meaning of every utterance is indefinitely *deferred* (for which he coins a French word *différance*), i.e., the text provides an unlimited series of signifiers without ever leaving the world of the text. This means that the text has no real-world referent and therefore means nothing. Obviously this system is incompatible with Catholic biblical interpretation or any interpretation that reads a text for its life-transforming message.

The World behind the Text. While the previously discussed methods focused on the text without reference to the text's history, more traditional methods continued to approach the text diachronically, much the way archaeologists move from one level of excavation of a site to another. *Textual criticism* seeks to determine as accurately as possible the original form of the Hebrew or Greek text. This involves comparing and evaluating manuscripts, parchments or papyri, making judgments or at least educated guesses, in cases where readings differ, as to which is the original. Teams of scholars have thus produced critical editions of the Hebrew Bible and the Greek NT with the textual apparatus listing textual variants, and have provided evidence for their judgments, for example in *A Textual Commentary on the Greek New Testament,* edited by Bruce M. Metzger.

Source criticism seeks to determine the written documents a biblical author may have used. The most obvious example of this is in the widely accepted two-source theory for the synoptics, that is, that Matthew and Luke used Mark and a sayings source called *Q* in the composition of their gospels.

Form criticism, on the other hand, is more interested in the oral prehistory of the text and the life-situation (*Sitz-im-Leben*) that occasioned it or shaped it. The method involves first identifying the form of the pericope (miracle story, pronouncement story, apocalyptic saying, etc.) and then tracing its history (*Formgeschichte,* ''history of forms,'' is the word the German scholars used) to its present place in the Bible. Originally introduced in the OT by Hermann GUNKEL, it was applied to the NT notably by Rudolf BULTMANN and Martin DIBELIUS. Bultmann's commitment to ''DEMYTHOLOGIZING'' the NT and ''remythologizing'' it in terms of existentialist philosophy made his project suspect in Catholic and conservative Protestant circles but his highlighting of the role of the early Church in the shaping of the Gospels was a major contribution to NT studies. It is now universally accepted that the Gospels grew out of a long oral tradition in which the deeds and sayings of Jesus were remembered for their usefulness in the ongoing life of the burgeoning communities and were adapted as needed by the new circumstances in which the communities found themselves.

Historical criticism seeks to uncover what facts and events are recoverable by the tools of modern historical research. Here archaeology, epigraphy, papyrology, the study of the history of contemporary peoples, and similar historical disciplines serve as *points de repère* for assessing the historicity of biblical accounts. The Bible was not written according to the norms of modern historiography; it is primarily a religious document, a witness to the faith of the Jewish and the Christian communities. Both communities claim their roots in history (e.g., "suffered under Pontius Pilate" in the Nicene creed). At present there is considerable dispute concerning the historicity of the earlier events narrated in the OT. In NT scholarship, the likelihood of an event or saying of Jesus being original is considered to be enhanced when one or more of the following criteria are present: (1) Multiple attestation: the saying or event appears in more than one source. (2) Dissimilarity: if a saying or an event stands out as unparalleled in contemporary Jewish or Hellenistic sources or is not clearly a development by the later Christian community. (This criterion is a minimalist one, because it finds only a Jesus who is neither Jewish, Hellenist, nor Christian!) (3) Embarrassment: if a saying or event evokes a detectible discomfort in the Gospel tradition, it has likely not been invented by the Christian community. Jesus' baptism by John is frequently cited in this category, since a community bent on exalting the holiness of its hero would not have invented his submission to a baptism of repentance.

Sociocultural criticism, a discipline only recently developed, looks at the environing world in which the text took shape, particularly the values that were at work in the culture(s) of the day, many of which differ remarkably from today's developed world. Thus, for example, honor and shame, patron-client relations, dyadic personality, labeling and deviance, sickness and healing, were viewed in a quite different way in biblical times. These studies have been very helpful in illuminating biblical passages, as long as contemporary sociological models are not imposed on the ancient world.

Redaction criticism looks to the history of the text to see what changes an author may have made of his sources and how he has creatively arranged the pericopes. Like narrative criticism, to which it is closely akin, redaction criticism can highlight the theology of the author by means of the contextual settings in which he has placed stories and sayings. For example, the author of Matthew 18 has gathered sayings of Jesus that have to do with community. By placing in the center Jesus' parable about the shepherd seeking the lost sheep, he has created a powerful mosaic showing how Jesus' pastoral concern is to be shared by the community. Luke delights in diptychs, that is, placing two stories next to each other for their mutual illumination. Redaction criticism thus gives a wider view of the teaching of an evangelist than is available in the isolated pericopes used in the lectionaries of the Roman liturgy.

The World around the Text: Canonical Criticism. If redaction criticism studies the environment in which an author has placed individual passages, canonical criticism points out that the meaning of an entire book is contextualized by the rest of the Bible, that certain books and not others made it into the canon and that even the location of an individual book (and even portions within a book) has significance for the interpretation of that book. It likewise insists that it is the final form of the text, not its presumed "original" pretext that is authoritative. The process by which the canon took shape sheds light on the interpretation given it by the early community. Psalm 50, which calls the people to task for their sins against the covenant, is followed by the famous *Miserere,* Psalm 51, which is a response of confession. The Christian community took over the order of books in the Greek Septuagint rather than the Hebrew Bible, no doubt because the prophetic books were found there last, pointing toward their fulfillment in the NT. The selection of certain books and the rejection of others, an evolving consensus that took at least two centuries, was an interpretive process, meaning that no individual book could claim absolute authority over the others but would be read and heard as part of a symphony of voices, none of which was to be lost. It also implies that the believing community that produced the texts provides the only adequate context for interpreting the text, and, in the Catholic view, this implies the role of the teaching authority of the Church (*Dei Verbum,* 10).

The World in Front of the Text. The Bible is not a book floating in space; from the very beginning it has had an impact on the lives of people more than any other book of world literature. Thus the *history of influence of the text (Wirkungsgeschichte)* is also a discipline of hermeneutical study. Already in Jesus' explanation of the parable of the sower, the seed represents the word (Mk 4:14) but then immediately it becomes people affected in different ways by the word (4:15–20). Saints who have lived the word, religious communities founded on the inspiration of a particular word of Scripture, communities of faith that have been inspired by the word—these are all interpretations of the word, and a study of them gives a fuller insight into the meaning of the written word by a kind of reflux enrichment. The caution, of course, is that some interpretations have been patently false, for example, when used to promote anti-Semitism.

Reader-response criticism presupposes that the text is addressed to readers (or listeners), either the reader(s) to whom the author addresses his work (the implied reader) or the possible actual reader(s), who can belong to multiple worlds. The former really belongs to narrative analysis, the latter to advocacy criticism (see below). The method considered under this rubric is reader, not text, centered. It focuses on what happens in the reading (or listening) process. Some analysts put the reader *over* the text, in the sense that meaning is predetermined by the defenses, expectations, or wishes of the reader—which seems to deny that one can really reach an objective meaning. Others understand the reading process to be an interaction *with* the text, that is, ''Reading is a temporal process of making and revising meaning—the reader develops expectations along the way, and finds them fulfilled, disappointed, or revised as reading continues'' (W. H. Shepherd Jr., *The Narrative Function of the Holy Spirit as Character in Luke-Acts* [1994] 81). Excessive concentration on this method could lead to subjectivism or ''private interpretation,'' but in the Catholic Church this can be avoided by checking one's understanding of the text against the ''reader response'' of the entire Church over the centuries (which is a way of speaking about tradition).

Advocacy criticism focuses on the real readers and the real communities who interact with the text. The poor and the oppressed often see things in a text that others would not, since one's ongoing experience disposes one to find a particular meaning in a text and to favor some texts over others. Thus have emerged various forms of liberationist and notably feminist interpretation, among others. These insights have often alerted other segments of the Christian community to neglected dimensions, thereby enriching the whole Church's understanding of the Bible. The danger comes when experience dominates the word, leading to a selectivity that ignores other texts and mines the Scriptures only for what supports a predetermined stance.

Philosophies of Interpretation. Biblical hermeneutics in the late 19th and 20th centuries came under the influence of general hermeneutics and philosophical theories of interpretation, which were already moving away from the atomizing methods of the Enlightenment. Friedrich SCHLEIERMACHER (1768–1834) reacted to the positivists by insisting that the author's work is not something to be dissected in a laboratory; it is a human work and hermeneutics is the *art* (rather than the science) of getting in touch with the spirit of the author. Notice the Kantian shift from the text as object to the subject, which for Schleiermacher is intersubjectivity. William DILTHEY (1833–1911) emphasized the historicality of both author and interpreter, that is, a biblical text can take on new meaning in light of the individual's or the community's historical perspective. His insistence that both the text and the reader are moving targets and meaning is temporary leads him into historical relativism. Martin HEIDEGGER (1889–1976) insisted there is no presuppositionless understanding (hence it is a pretense to claim total and disinterested objectivity as the positivists did). He also insisted that being encompasses the knower rather than the other way around; it is not the interpreter who interprets being but being that interprets the interpreter, who is virtually passive before being that floods him. Hans-George GADAMER (1900–2002) is indebted to Heidegger for much of his theory, but he finds the process of interpretation more interactive. Language as the ''house of being'' makes possible the ''fusion of horizons'' between the text and the interpreter. Bernard Lonergan offers a corrective to the remnants of passivity in Gadamer by insisting on the critical role of judgment, which the interpreter must exercise. Authentic subjectivity reaches for objectivity. The critical function avoids both the unquestioned hegemony of ''being'' over the subject and the subjectivism of some of the reader-response theories. Paul RICOEUR's position has had a wide impact on biblical interpretation, especially on reader-response theory. In his view, once a discourse is put in human language it has carved out an existence of its own, independent of the author's intention, and can be recontextualized with new meanings. This is what he calls ''the world in front of the text.''

Conclusion. An integral process of interpretation will make discerning use of the various methods, with the exception of deconstruction, which is self-destructing and states in effect that it has nothing to say. The Catholic approach to biblical interpretation assumes that the Bible is the Word of God embedded in human language and therefore subject to the nature of human language, with all its forms and variants. It did not fall out of the sky ready-made but grew out of a centuries-long experience of a people with their God. When the sacred writers took up their pens they believed they were committing to writing not merely their personal faith but the faith of the community, a faith that was Spirit-inspired. Consequently it is only in the continuing community that the expressions of that faith, the Scriptures, can be fully understood, and ultimately only with the assistance of the Holy Spirit who inspired the writings in the first place. That does not exclude, in fact it requires, the work of exegetes and scholars to explore the human face of the word of God. But it gives no authority to interpretations that would be at odds with the common faith of the community, a common faith that is guarded by the ultimate interpretative authority, the magisterium. Does it mean that within the parameters of the Church's faith and tradition the nonspecialist can come to a valid interpretation of the Scriptures? Augustine offers help here. The ultimate goal of all Scripture and its interpretation, he says, is charity: ''If one is deceived in an interpretation that builds up charity, which is the end of the commandments, he is deceived in the same way as a man who leaves the road by mistake but passes through a field toward the same place to which the road itself leads. But he is to be corrected and shown that it is more useful not to leave the road, lest the habit of deviating force him to take a crossroad or a perverse way'' (*De doctrina christiana,* I, xxvi, 41). For this reason even those who use the Bible primarily for devotion should not neglect a serious study of it.

Bibliography: VATICAN COUNCIL II, *Dei Verbum: Constitution on Divine Revelation.* PONTIFICAL BIBLICAL COMMISSION, *The Interpretation of the Bible in the Church* (1993). G. T. MONTAGUE, *Understanding the Bible* (Mahwah, N.J. 1997). E. MCKNIGHT, *What Is Form Criticism?* (Philadelphia 1969). M. A. POWELL, *What Is Narrative Criticism?* (Minneapolis 1990). N. PERRIN, *What Is Redaction Criticism?* (Philadelphia 1969). J. H. ELLIOTT, *What Is Social-Scientific Criticism?* (Minneapolis 1993). E. D. HIRSCH, *Validity in Interpretation* (New Haven, Conn. 1967). S. L. MCKENZIE and S. R. HAYNES, eds., *To Each Its Own Meaning* (Louisville 1999). R. E. PALMER, *Hermeneutics: Interpretation Theory in Schleiermacher, Dilthey, Heidegger, and Gadamer* (Evanston 1969). P. RICOEUR, *Interpretation Theory* (Fort Worth 1976).

[G. T. MONTAGUE]

HERMES, GEORG

Philosopher and theologian whose thought aroused great controversy in nineteenth-century German Catholic theology; b. Dreierwalde, Westphalia, April 22, 1775; d. Bonn, May 26, 1831. During his philosophical studies at the University of Münster (1792–94), Hermes was very much influenced by his reading of Kant and Fichte. This initial contact with philosophy was a disturbing experience that unsettled his own faith and led him to study theology in an attempt to resolve his personal religious difficulties. When, however, his theological studies did not give him the certainty for which he had hoped, he resolved to hold to the fundamental truths of Catholicism, while undertaking what was to be a lifelong attempt to establish the rationality of Christian faith in a way consistent with the thought of the Enlightenment. After teaching for two years at the Gymnasium in Münster, he was ordained a priest in 1799. In 1805 he published his first work, *Untersuchungen über die innere Wahrheit des Christentums,* which was enthusiastically received and which led to his being named in 1807 professor of dogmatic theology at Münster. Both as a priest and as a professor of theology Hermes was highly respected by his students and colleagues, although there were some, notably Clement August Droste zu Vischering, the future archbishop of Cologne, who were disturbed by Hermes's apparent deviations from traditional methods in teaching theology. In 1819 Hermes published the first part of his major theological work, *Einleitung in die christkatholische Theologie: Philosophische Einleitung.* This work, in which he attempted to establish the philosophical presuppositions of religious faith (i.e., the possibility of knowing the truth, the existence and attributes of God, the possibility and knowability of a supernatural revelation), was also enthusiastically received in German academic circles. Shortly after its publication, Hermes accepted a professorship in the theological faculty of the newly established University of Bonn.

Despite the continuing opposition of some professors and bishops, Hermes was greatly respected by the majority of his colleagues at Bonn and was appointed by his friend and patron Archbishop Ferdinand August von Spiegel to important posts in the Diocese of Cologne. By reason of his close association with the archbishop and his acceptability to the Prussian government, his students were, moreover, appointed to theological professorships throughout Germany; after 1826 the faculty at Bonn was staffed almost exclusively by Hermes's followers. While enjoying this academic success, he published in 1829 the second part of his introduction to theology, *Einleitung in die christkatholische Theologie: Positive Einleitung,* in which he sought to work out an apologetic that would establish the factuality of that revelation whose possibility he had established in the earlier, philosophical, part of his work.

The opposition that Hermes's theology had aroused during his lifetime became more effective soon after his death. As a result of a denunciation made by German bishops, his works were examined at length by a group of Roman theologians, including the Jesuit G. Perrone, and in the brief *DUM ACERBISSIMAS* (H. Denzinger, *Enchiridion symbolorum,* 2738–2740), issued on Sept. 26, 1835, Gregory XVI condemned the RATIONALISM judged to be implicit in Hermes's teaching and placed his works (including part of an incomplete work, *Christkatholische Dogmatik,* published in 1834 by Hermes's disciple, J. H. Achterfeldt) on the Index. In the following year a subsequent decree placed on the Index those parts of Hermes's *Dogmatik* that had not been listed in the original decree.

This papal condemnation, which astonished Hermes's followers and which the Prussian government prevented from being published in Bonn, intensified rather than settled the controversy over Hermes's orthodoxy. The controversy became even more bitter when in 1836 Droste zu Vischering succeeded von Spiegel as archbishop of Cologne and required all his candidates for the priesthood to subscribe to 18 anti-Hermesian propositions. In 1837 two of Hermes's most prominent followers, P. J. Elvenich and J. W. Braun, went to Rome to appeal the condemnation. When Roman authorities rejected both this and all subsequent attempts to justify Hermes's orthodoxy, most of the Hermesians accepted the papal brief, and those who did not were removed from teaching. In 1852 the Hermesian *Zeitschrift für Philosophie und katholische Theologie* ceased publication. With that, HERMESIANISM, later to be condemned at VATICAN COUNCIL I, ceased to be an active theological movement.

See Also: SEMIRATIONALISM.

Bibliography: A. THOUVENIN, *Dictionnaire de théologie catholique,* 15 v. (Paris 1903–50) 6.2:2288–2303. R. SCHLUND and E. HEGEL, *Lexikon für Theologie und Kirche,* 10 v. (2d new ed. Freiburg 1957–65) 5:258–261. A. FORTESCUE, *Encyclopedia of Religion and Ethics,* ed. J. HASTINGS, 13 v. (Edinburgh 1908–27) 6:624. H. REUSCH, *Allgemeine deutsche Biographie* (Leipzig 1875–1910) 12:192–196. P. TSCHACKERT, *The New Schaff-Herzog Encyclopedia of Religious Knowledge,* ed. S. M. JACKSON, 13 v. (Grand Rapids, Mich. 1951–54) 5:242–243. R. AUBERT, *Le Problème de l'acte de foi* (3d ed. Louvain 1958) 103–112. E. HOCEDEZ, *Histoire de la the théologie au XIX*e*siècle* (Brussels-Paris 1800–31) 1:177–203.

[J. W. HEALEY]

HERMESIANISM

The theological system developed by Georg HERMES (1775–1831), a German Catholic theologian. The system involves an attempt to defend Catholic dogma by employing the principles of KANT especially. The attempt is unsuccessful, and the writings of Hermes contain many errors that were severely condemned by Pope Gregory XVI in *DUM ACERBISSIMAS* and by the Congregation of the Index (H. Denzinger, *Enchiridion symbolorum* [Freiburg 1963] 2738–40). Some of his ideas may be grouped as follows.

Theological method. Although some have expressed a contrary view, it appears certain that Hermes undertook his theological investigations with the intention of doubting every tenet really and positively, even such facts as the possibility of truth, the existence of God, and the dogmas of faith. He was prepared to admit only those ideas and judgments that could be justified rationally. In this way, he hoped to lay a solid foundation for the whole structure of theology. Hermes escaped from his state of doubt by employing the speculative and practical reasons. The speculative reason is unable to know the essences of things. Nevertheless, it affirms some propositions as true and certain without being able to act otherwise, as in the case of self-evident truths. On the other hand, what the practical reason finds in conformity with human dignity must also be regarded as true and certain.

God. According to Hermes, the best proof, indeed the only certain one, for the existence of God is the argument from contingency. The speculative reason is able to demonstrate to its own satisfaction most of God's attributes, but it cannot demonstrate that God is a pure spirit or that His attributes are infinite in extent. In this latter respect, Hermes differed from the common view of Catholic philosophers.

Apologetics. Hermes maintained that the speculative reason could not acquire certitude about the fact of revelation but must be content with probability (*see* REVELATION, THEOLOGY OF). By this view he opposed the position affirmed by Innocent IX (H. Denzinger, *Enchiridion symbolorum* [Freiburg 1963] 2121) and Pius IX (*ibid.* 2778). Hermes maintained further that the value of miracles as a means of identifying revelation is minimal because one cannot know whether an extraordinary event was caused by God or by the secret forces of nature [*see* MIRACLES (THEOLOGY OF)]. Hermes believed that the means of establishing Christian revelation as true and obligatory is the practical reason with its concern for human dignity. Man must accept Christian revelation because it enables him to realize his human dignity to the highest degree.

Faith. According to Hermes, FAITH is a state of certitude with respect to a particular truth. The certitude may spring either from the speculative or from the practical reason reflecting upon its respective object. As a commentary upon Hermes's conception of faith, it may be noted that faith so conceived does not rest upon the authority of God (the real motive of faith, according to Vatican Council I, H. Denzinger, *Enchiridion symbolorum* [Freiburg 1963] 3008), but upon human understanding. It also follows from such a conception of faith that mysteries of the first order [*see* MYSTERY (IN THEOLOGY)], such as the Trinity or the Incarnation, do not necessarily remain mysteries once a man comes to believe them.

Grace and original sin. According to Hermes, the state of innocence prior to the fall of man consisted in the conformity of man's will to God's. ORIGINAL SIN consists in CONCUPISCENCE, or the rebellion of man's lower nature against his higher one. There are two forms of GRACE, habitual and actual. Habitual, or sanctifying, grace is the intention of God to grant to man, in view of the merits of Jesus Christ, the assistance he needs to vanquish the effects of concupiscence, or original sin. Actual grace is the assistance itself that God grants to man at the right moment for this purpose. Even though concupiscence remains after Baptism, man has regained sanctifying grace because he has regained the favor of God. Thus it is apparent that for Hermes habitual grace is not a supernatural reality modifying man's soul, but rather the permanent disposition of God to help man. By his explanation of original sin and its remission, Hermes approaches Luther's conception that JUSTIFICATION or the regaining of habitual grace is an external imputation on the part of God (*see* IMPUTATION OF JUSTICE AND MERIT).

See Also: FAITH AND REASON; GÜNTHER, ANTON; METHODOLOGY (THEOLOGY); RATIONALISM; SEMIRATIONALISM.

Bibliography: A. THOUVENIN, *Dictionnaire de théologie catholique,* ed. A. VACANT et al. (Paris 1903–50) 6:2:2288–2303, *ibid.* Tables générales 2:2066. R. SCHLUND and E. HEGEL, *Lexikon für Theologie und Kirche,* ed. J. HOFER and K. RAHNER (Freiburg 1957–65) 5:258–261. G. MARON, *Die Religion in Geschichte und Gegenwart* (Tübingen 1957–65) 3:262–264. H. REUSCH, *Allgemeine deutsche Biographie* 12:192–196. A. FORTESCUE, *Encyclopedia of Religion and Ethics,* ed. J. HASTINGS (Edinburgh 1908–27) 6:625–626. G. FRITZ, *Dictionnaire de théologie catholique,* ed. A. VACANT et al. (Paris 1903–50) 14.2:1850–54. P. WENZEL, *Lexikon für Theologie und Kirche,* ed. J. HOFER and K. RAHNER (Freiburg 1957–65) 9:652–653.

[E. J. GRATSCH]

HERMETIC LITERATURE

Hermes Trismegistus (thrice-great) was the Hellenistic Greek name for the Egyptian god of wisdom and letters, Thoth, who was identified with the Greek Hermes or Roman Mercury. In antiquity a vast literature of magic, astrology, alchemy, philosophy, and theology (perhaps better ''theosophy'') was associated with his name. In a narrower sense the Hermetic literature consists of three groups of philosophico-religious materials that originated in Egypt and were first written in Greek, not, as was once thought, in Egyptian. Though the dating of none is certain, it seems safe to assign them to the 2nd and 3rd centuries A.D. with the possibility that some are even earlier. They do not all stem from the same author, though they have a common religious viewpoint. Hermeticism should not, however, be thought of as a school or sect.

Classification of Hermetic writings. The first group of 18 writings, *libelli*, mostly in the form of dialogues between Hermes and one of his sons, Tat, and with Asclepius, is found in manuscripts dating from the late Middle Ages and is called the *Corpus Hermeticum.* It has sometimes been named after the first treatise in it, the *Poimandres*, which does not mention Hermes but is clearly Hermetic. This name probably reflects, not the Greek ποιμὴν ἀνδρῶν, ''shepherd of men,'' but the Coptic *p-eime-n-rē*, ''the knowledge of the Sun-God.'' Poimandres is presented as a semi-divine figure, ''the mind of the sovereignty.''

The second part of the Hermetic literature is the *Asclepius*, a treatise once erroneously assigned to Apuleius and preserved among his works. It is extant in Latin, in which it was known and cited by St. Augustine. Fragments of the Greek original also survive under the title Λόγος τέλειος. The third group of writings is a large collection of excerpts and citation preserved in the works of Stobaeus, including the revelations of Isis called the Κόρη κοσμοῦ.

To this literature we must add several works in Coptic translation that have appeared in Codex VI of the Chenoboskion manuscripts. One of these is a more archaic version of part of the *Asclepius* [J. Doresse, ''Hermès et la Gnose. A propos de l'Asclepius copte,'' *Novum Testamentum* 1 (1956) 54–69].

Evaluation. The Hermetic writings represent on one side the confrontation of Platonic and Stoic philosophy, and on the other the mingling of Greek ideas with Eastern religions, including Judaism. The whole constitutes what can best be described as a pagan form of visionary Gnosticism. The *Hermetica* contain many resemblances to Philo (e.g., the notion of a Logos) and to Christianity, especially to the Fourth Gospel (God as Life and Light, the cosmic role of the Logos, the idea of rebirth, etc.), but most modern scholars deny any direct influence in either direction with regard to either source. Despite some polytheistic and strongly pantheistic passages, the Hermetic writings evidence a doctrine of one transcendent God, who is all good, the Father and Creator of all. The Genesis account of creation is adapted in the *Poimandres* and elsewhere, and sometimes intermediaries such as Nous and the Logos are involved in the process. Salvation for man consists in knowledge (gnosis) of God, the world, and men, i.e., of the Hermetic doctrines. This knowledge leads to liberation and ultimate divinization, characterized as rebirth in *Corpus Hermeticum* XIII.

See Also: CHENOBOSKION, GNOSTIC TEXTS OF; GNOSTICISM.

Bibliography: Texts (very freely emended) and tr. W. SCOTT and A. S. FERGUSON, eds., *Hermetics* 4 v. (Oxford 1934–36). Texts (critical ed.) and Fr. tr. A. D. NOCK, ed. *Corpus hermeticum* tr. A. J. FESTUGIÉRE, 4 v. (Études bibliques Paris 1945–54). R. M. GRANT, *Gnosticism: A Sourcebook* (New York 1961) 209–233. Studies. A. J. FESTUGIÉRE, *La Révélation d'Hermés Trismégiste*, 4 v. (Études bibliques, Paris 1944–54). C. H. DODD, *The Bible and the Greeks* (London 1935; reprint 1954) 99–248; *The Interpretation of the Fourth Gospel* (Cambridge, Eng. 1953) 10–53. H. JONAS, *The Gnostic Religion* (2nd ed. Boston 1963) 147–173. W. KROLL, *Paulys Realenzyklopädie der klassischen Altertumswissenschaft*, ed. G. WISSOWA et al. (Stuttgart 1893) 8.1 (1912) 792–823. H. GUNDEL, *Paulys Realenzyklopädie der klassischen Altertumswissenschaft*, ed. G. WISSOWA et al. (Stuttgart 1893) 21.1 (1951) 1193–1207. G. VAN MOORSEL, *The Mysteries of Hermes Trismegistus* (Utrecht 1955).

[G. W. MACRAE]

HERMITS

Persons who have retired into solitude to lead the religious life. The term is derived through Old French and Latin from the Greek ἐρεμίτης. Although there were probably Christian solitaries before his time, an Egyptian named Paul was the first to popularize the eremitic life. From the beginning of the 4th century, this life was one

Engraving of Odoacer conferring with the hermit Severin. (©Bettmann/CORBIS)

of the standard ways, especially in the East, in which Christian asceticism expressed itself. In the East, after a first period of dramatic and often excessive austerity among hermits, ecclesiastical authority (Chalcedon, 451, and the *Novellae* of Justinian) brought the eremitic life under control and provided that hermits should live adjacent to monasteries and under the control of superiors, as they still do at Mt. Athos and other places in the East. In the West, the 6th-century Rule of St. Benedict (ch. 1) provided for the exceptional case of the ascetic who might be permitted to become a solitary, a provision modeled on the precepts of St. Basil. In the West the cenobitic life has tended to obscure the eremitic life more completely than it has in the East, but several periods of spiritual revival have sent a comparatively large number into the desert places of western Europe; this occurred especially in the 11th century, and again with the mystical movements of the 13th and 14th centuries. From the eremitic impulse of the 11th century sprang the two congregations that have preserved a canonical form of semi-eremitic life into the modern world, the Carthusians and the Camaldolese. In a spiritual climate in which the eremitic life enjoys little popularity, these two groups provide the only institutional possibilities for its practice by Christians of the West. The Augustinian Hermits, formed in the mid-13th century from several Italian societies of hermits, became FRIARS almost immediately upon foundation.

See Also: ANCHORITES.

Bibliography: H. LECLERCQ, F. CABROL, and H. I. MARROU, eds., *Dictionnaire d'archéologie chrétienne et de liturgie* (Paris 1907–53) 5.1:384–386. For additional bibliog. *see* ANCHORITES.

[A. DONAHUE]

HERMITS OF ST. PAUL

Also known as Pauline Fathers (*Ordo Fratrum Sancti Pauli Primi Eremitae;* OSPPE; Official Catholic Directory #1010), a religious order of priests and brothers. It originated in 1250 with the union of a monastery in Patach, Hungary that had been founded in 1215 by Bishop Bartholomew of Pécs with another in Pisilia, Hungary established by Blessed Eusebius of Esztergom (d. 1270). The order received papal approval in 1308 and adopted a strict observance of the rule of St. Augustine (*see* AUGUSTINE, RULE OF ST.). It spread widely in Hungary, Austria, Germany, Sweden, Italy, Prussia, Lithuania, and also in Poland, where the famous sanctuary of the Black Madonna of Czestochowa was founded in 1382. In the 16th and 17th centuries the Reformation and the Turkish invasions caused a serious decline, but a notable revival occurred at the end of the 17th century, when the order expanded to six provinces in Poland, Hungary, Austria, Istria, Swabia, and Croatia. In 1420 Mendo Gomez introduced the Hermits into Portugal, where the membership was always small. Guillaume Callier established the order in France and drew up statutes that received Paul V's approval in 1620. The French group, popularly known as the Brothers of Death, decorated their scapular with a skull and oriented their asceticism toward a constant concern with death. The order was contemplative until the 16th century, when the Holy See assigned to it charitable, educational, and parochial works. Many members became bishops, scholars, and writers. Cardinal Georg Utjesenovich (d. 1551) was famous as a defender of Hungarian independence. Augustin Kordecki is remembered for his defense of Poland and of the shrine at Czestochowa in 1655. Martin Borkowics has been called in Croatia the father of his country. Emperor Joseph II suppressed the houses in his Hapsburg states in 1786. The Portuguese and French houses did not survive the French Revolutionary period. The congregation first arrived in the United States in 1953. The United States provincialate is in Doylestown, Pennsylvania. The generalate is in Czestochowa, Poland.

[V. GELLHAUS/EDS.]

HERMOSILLO, ARCHDIOCESE OF

Mexican ecclesiastical province (*Hermosillensis*); created a diocese in 1779; raised to an archdiocese in 1964; it then had as suffragans the Dioceses of Ciudad Obregón (1959) and Tijuana (1964), recently raised from an apostolic vicariate.

The religious administration of the modern state of Sonora was originally in the care of Franciscan and Jesuit missionaries, who arrived soon after its discovery. There were many illustrious missionaries who evangelized the primitive tribes of this distant region, but the best known is the Jesuit Eusebio Francisco KINO, who occupies an outstanding place in Mexican missiology. When the bishopric of Durango was founded in 1620, the territory of Sonora was under its jurisdiction and was frequently visited by the bishops, as the visitation records in the archives of the cathedral of Durango testify. Since the See of Durango was too large to permit good ecclesiastical administration, Pius VI created the bishopric of Sonora on May 7, 1779. The first bishop, Antonio María de los Reyes, took charge of his diocese in 1782 and made his episcopal residence in Arispe.

The bishopric included the states of Sonora and Sinaloa and the territories of Lower and Upper California, all suffragan to Durango. In 1884 the Diocese of Sinaloa was erected. Lower California was made an apostolic vicariate, and Upper California came under the civil government of the U.S. and was made a separate diocese. Thus the Diocese of Sonora was reduced in size to the modern state of the same name. When the Diocese of Chihuahua was raised to a metropolitan see, Sonora was suffragan to it, and the area then was divided (1959) into the Dioceses of Ciudad Obregón and Hermosillo. Paul VI raised the Diocese of Hermosillo to an archdiocese; the last bishop, Don Juan Navarrete y Guerrero, continued in office as the first archbishop of the see.

[I. GALLEGOS]

HEROD ANTIPAS

The younger son of HEROD THE GREAT and Malthace of Samaria. His education was at the imperial court in Rome. Herod's final will named him tetrarch of Galilee and Perea, and, despite a petition by Antipas to be made king of Judea instead of his older brother Archelaus, Augustus confirmed the will in 4 B.C. The subjects of Antipas's tetrarchy, in large part descended from pagans converted only a few generations before, were zealous and even fanatical Jews. Antipas (who officially used the dynastic name Herod), like his father, checked the nationalistic fervor of his subjects and demanded absolute loyalty to the Roman suzerain; the nobility who supported him in this policy were called HERODIANS (Mt 22.16; Mk 12.13). Antipas's concern to repress any possible disturbance is seen in his imprisonment of JOHN THE BAPTIST and his opposition to Jesus' ministry (Lk 13.31; Mk 3.6). He is the Herod mentioned in the Passion narrative (Lk 23.8–12; *see* PASSION OF CHRIST, I).

Antipas also emulated his father by undertaking building projects; he rebuilt Betharamphtha (modern Tell er-Râmeh) and Sepphoris (modern Suffûriyeh) in Galilee and founded the city of TIBERIAS, whose name testifies to his lifelong close ties with the emperor. A dynastic marriage with the daughter of the Nabataean King Aretas IV gave way to Antipas's infatuation with his half brother Herod's wife, his niece Herodias. The divorce made Aretas his enemy, and in A.D. 36 Aretas attacked Antipas's forces in a boundary dispute; at the time Antipas was absent in Mesopotamia as mediator between the Parthian King Artabanus and the Roman legate Vitellius.

Herodias caused Antipas's final downfall. When Gaius Caligula named Herodias's brother Agrippa king over the former tetrarchy of Philip, the ambitious Herodias urged Antipas to complain to Gaius and seek the title of king himself. Agrippa's response to his uncle's attempt was to follow him to Rome (A.D. 39) and accuse him of treasonous plotting with Artabanus. Antipas was immediately exiled to Gaul, where he and Herodias lived out their days.

Bibliography: J. BLINZLER, *Lexikon für Theologie und Kirche*, ed. J. HOFER and K. RAHNER (Freiberg 1957–65) 5:266; *Herod Antipas and Jesus Christus* (Stuttgart 1947). *Encyclopedic Dictionary of the Bible*, tr. and adap. by L. HARTMAN (New York 1963) 101–102. A. H. M. JONES, *The Herods of Judaea* (Oxford 1938) 176–183. W. G. A. OTTO, *Paulys Realenzyklopädie der klassischen Altertumswissenschaft*, ed. G. WISSOWA et al. Suppl. 2 (1913) 1–200, sep. pub. *Herodes* (Stuttgart 1913) 175–198. F. M. ABEL, *Histoire de la Palestine depuis la conquête d'Alexandre jusqu'à l'invasion Arabe*, 2 v. (*Études bibliques* 1952) 1:438–446.

[J. P. M. WALSH]

HEROD THE GREAT

King of Judea at the time of the birth of Jesus Christ (Mt 2.1). He was born about 73 B.C., the second son of the Idumean Antipater, chief official of the HASMONAEAN king Hyrcanus II; his mother was Cyprus, a Nabataean woman.

Illustration of the Slaughter of the Holy Innocents. (©Bettmann/CORBIS)

Early Life. Throughout his early life, when various factions successively gained dominance in Palestine, Herod, like his father, managed always to align himself with the winning side. He first came to prominence at the age of 25, when as governor of Galilee he overreached his authority by executing some rebellious brigands; Herod escaped condemnation by the Jerusalem Sanhedrin only by leaving Judea and joining the Roman administration of Syria. When in 46 B.C. a follower of Pompey took over the Roman governor's army, Herod, his father, and his elder brother Phasael fought against him on behalf of the party of Julius Caesar. After Caesar's assassination (44 B.C.), however, they supported the republican C. Cassius, who had taken command of Syria, and aided him in preparations for the war against Mark Antony. Soon after, in 43 B.C., a personal enemy, Malichus, had Antipater murdered, and seized the government of Judea. Herod, with Cassius' connivance, had Malichus killed, and Hyrcanus reappointed Phasael governor of Jerusalem. While Cassius joined Brutus for the impending battle against Antony and Octavian, Herod and Phasael had to put down a revolt raised by Malichus's brothers and another raised on behalf of Hyrcanus's nephew and rival Antigonus. With this opposition overcome, Herod then strengthened his position by his betrothal to Hyrcanus's granddaughter Mariamme; thus the Idumean Herod, whose family had been Jewish for barely three generations, was to some extent identified with the legitimate Hasmonaean dynasty.

Tetrarch of Galilee. After the battle of Philippi (41 B.C.), Phasael and Herod ingratiated themselves with the victorious Mark Antony. Despite opposition from Jewish delegations, Antony made Phasael and Herod tetrarchs of Judea and Galilee respectively. In 40 B.C., however, the Parthians invaded Syria, and Antigonus, with the assurance of Parthian support, again marched on Jerusalem. Phasael and Hyrcanus fell into Antigonus's power, but Herod slipped away from Jerusalem with his family and household, and committed them to his brother Joseph's care in the fortress of Masada in southeastern Judea. Phasael seems to have committed suicide; Hyrcanus was mutilated and taken away to Mesopotamia.

Refused asylum with the Nabataean king at Petra, Herod went to Rome in the fall of 40 B.C. to appeal to Antony. In a formal session of the senate Antony and Octavian had Herod named king. After his arrival at Ptolemais (Accho) in the spring of 39 B.C., Herod gathered an army and relieved the besieged Masada, but he was unable to begin the siege of Jerusalem until the spring of 37 B.C., when he also married Mariamme. On taking Jerusalem Herod began his reign with a series of proscriptions, which all but eliminated the Sanhedrin. Antigonus was executed by order of Antony.

Herod faced only three dangers to his power thereafter: Cleopatra of Egypt, the surviving Hasmonaeans, and the fall of his patron, Antony. Cleopatra used her influence with Antony to acquire much of Herod's best land, including Jericho and the port of Joppe (Jaffa); she supported a plot to restore an independent Idumea; at the request of Mariamme's mother, Alexandra, she exerted pressure on Herod to appoint his brother-in-law, the young Aristobulus, high priest. As legitimate successor to the high priesthood and kingship, and as a figure attractive to the people, Aristobulus presented a threat to the parvenu Herod, who accordingly had him killed shortly after his appointment in 36 B.C. Hyrcanus, who had returned from Babylon upon the fall of Antigonus, was also murdered by Herod in 30 B.C., as the last possible rival for power. Antony's defeat at Actium removed Cleopatra as a threat to his kingship, but also put Herod in danger of removal. He quickly changed his allegiance, giving aid to Octavian's forces, and in 30 B.C. Octavian confirmed him as king and even restored the land Cleopatra had taken over, along with other coastal towns and Samaria, Gadara, and Hippos. In 22 B.C. his territory was further enlarged, to include Trachonitis, Batanaea, and Auranitis (Hauran).

King of Judea. Once established as a client king, Herod was occupied with construction projects. He required force to stay in power, and so he built or strengthened many fortresses: Masada, Alexandrium, Hyrcania, Antonia, Phasaelis, Herodium, Machaerus, and Cyprus (at NT Jericho). His army was made up mostly of mercenaries. Besides building for military purposes, Herod lavished money on cities, temples, and theaters. His outstanding achievements were rebuilding the city of Samaria as Sebaste (27 B.C.), his fortress-palace in JERUSALEM (23 B.C.), the port of Caesarea (22 B.C.), and the new Temple of Jerusalem (built between about 20 and 10 B.C.). Herod was a benefactor to many cities of the empire as well, financing expensive projects out of his immense wealth; these had the effect of protecting the interests of Jews in the Diaspora and reducing anti-Jewish feeling in the Hellenistic cities. Throughout his reign, Herod was on good terms with Augustus, until in 9 B.C. a misunderstanding over his actions in a military campaign against the Nabataeans brought him into the emperor's disfavor.

Herod's family life was complex and unhappy, full of intrigue and conflict. He was passionately devoted to his wife, Mariamme, and hence prone to jealousy. Salomé, his sister, out of resentment against the Hasmonaean Mariamme and her sons, Aristobulus and Alexander, poisoned Herod's mind against them. Convinced of Mariamme's unfaithfulness, Herod had her executed in 29 B.C., and her mother, Alexandra, within the year, again at Salomé's instigation. About 23 B.C. Herod married another Mariamme, daughter of Simon of Alexandria, whom he appointed high priest; by her he had a son called Herod, to whom Herodias was first married. Mariamme II was followed by seven other wives; the most important were Malthace, mother of Archelaus and HEROD ANTIPAS, and Cleopatra of Jerusalem, mother of Philip the Tetrarch. Salomé and Herod's brother Pheroras plotted to discredit Alexander and Aristobulus. As a result, in 14 B.C. Herod recalled to the court his first wife, Doris, and her son Antipater, and the latter, out of ambition, became a willing accomplice to the schemes of Salomé and Pheroras. On the basis of their accusations, Herod had Alexander and Aristobulus executed in Sebaste in 7 B.C., and named Antipater heir. But in 4 B.C., when he learned of Antipater's intrigues against his sons and himself, Herod had him executed too; he named Archelaus, Antipas, and Philip joint heirs. Herod himself died a short time later, apparently of cancer.

The account in Mt 2.16 of the slaughter of the Holy INNOCENTS at Bethlehem is entirely in keeping with the king's cruel jealousy.

Bibliography: FLAVIUS JOSEPHUS, *Ant.* 14:19; *Bell Iud.* 17–2.183. S. H. PEROWNE, *The Life and Times of Herod the Great* (Nashville 1959). A. H. M. JONES, *The Herods of Judaea* (Oxford 1938) 1–155. F. M. ABEL, *Histoire de la Palestine depuis la conquête d'Alexandre jusqu'à l'invasion Arabe,* 2 v. *Études Bibliques* 1:310–406. A. MOMIGLIANO, *The Cambridge Ancient History* (London and New York 1923–29) 10:316–339. J. BLINZLER, *Lexikon für Theologie und Kirche,* ed. J. HOFER and K. RAHNER, 10 v. (2d, new ed. Freiburg 1957–65)[2] 5:263–265. W. FOERSTER, *Die Religion in Geschichte und Gegenwart* (3d ed. Tübingen 1957–65) [3] 3:266–268. *Encyclopedic Dictionary of the Bible,* tr. and adap. by L. HARTMAN (New York 1963) from A. VAN DEN BORN, *Bijbels Woordenboek* 988–990.

[J. P. M. WALSH]

HERODIANS

A group of men mentioned in the New Testament as united with the Pharisees against Jesus (Mk 3.6; 12.13; Mt 22.16). The Herodians (ἡρῳδιανοι) did not constitute a religious sect, but probably were members of a small clique of avowed partisans of the Herodian dynasty represented by HEROD ANTIPAS. After the deposition of Archelaus, *c.* A.D. 7, Judea was placed under a Roman procurator. The Jews resented this foreign rule and grew bitter because of the cruelty of many of these governors. Some Jews regarded the reestablishment of the Herodian rule over all of Palestine as necessary for the nation's preservation and for its eventual full independence.

Rock formations viewed from atop Herodian Fortress, Masada, Israel. (©Dave G. Houser/CORBIS)

Bibliography: H. H. ROWLEY, ''The Herodians of the Gospel,'' *Journal of Theological Studies* 41 (London 1940) 14–27. *Encyclopedic Dictionary of the Bible*, tr. and adap. by L. HARTMAN (New York 1963) 990–991.

[J. M. DOUGHERTY]

HERODIAS

The daughter of Aristobulus, the son of HEROD THE GREAT and the HASMONAEAN Mariamme; her mother was Berenice, daughter of Herod's sister Salome and Costobar. Herodias's first husband was her uncle Herod ''Without-land'' (called Philip in Mt 14.3; Mk 6.17), son of Herod the Great and Mariamme II. Some time after the birth of their daughter Salome, Herod's half-brother HEROD ANTIPAS, the tetrarch of Galilee, who had married the daughter of the NABATAEAN King Aretas IV, became infatuated with Herodias. Antipas and Herodias divorced their spouses and married (*c.* A.D. 27). Herodias's motive was probably ambition; Antipas was tetrarch, while Herod had neither power nor the inclination to seek it. It was at the instigation of Herodias that Antipas had St. JOHN THE BAPTIST beheaded for having condemned their marriage (Mt 14.3–11; Mk 6.17–28). When the Emperor Gaius (Caligula) made her brother Agrippa king in A.D. 37, Herodias was humiliated by his success, and in 39 she persuaded Antipas to go to Rome to seek the same title himself. When he was, instead, banished to Lyons, Herodias elected to accompany her husband into exile, where she died.

Bibliography: J. BLINZLER, *Lexikon für Theologie und Kirche,* ed. J. HOFER and K. RAHNER, 10 v. (2d, new ed. Freiburg 1957–65) 5:266–267. *Encyclopedic Dictionary of the Bible,* tr. and adap. by L. HARTMAN (New York 1963), from A. VAN DEN BORN, *Bijbels Woordenboek* 991.

[J. P. M. WALSH]

HERRAD OF LANDSBERG

Abbess, compiler of the *Hortus deliciarum;* b. Chateau of Landsberg, Alsace, *c.* 1130; d. Hohenberg, July 25, 1195. No details are known of her early life. She was abbess of Hohenberg (Mont Sainte-Odile) from 1167 and under her rule the convent prospered materially, spiritually, and intellectually.

Her abbey's cultural level is exemplified by the *Hortus,* which she had compiled for the spiritual benefit of her nuns. Its theme was the history of man from creation to last judgment, told against a Biblical background. Incorporating a wide range of contemporary knowledge, it was a compendium of 12th-century thought. Herrad's personal authorship included only the preface and a few short verses, but selections comprising about 45,000 lines represented sources ranging from the Fathers to her own contemporaries. Its miniatures, numbering at least 344, were its chief claim to distinction. Some of these occupied an entire page of the manuscript, which measured 53 by 37 centimeters. They may have been produced independently of the text and by an organized scriptorium, but exact artistic responsibility is uncertain. The influence of the Canons of MARBACH has been noted in the script, however. The miniatures combined artistic influences of East and West and pictured details of contemporary daily life. The original manuscript was completely destroyed in 1870. Parts of the text have been restored and copies of many of the miniatures are extant. The unpublished portions of the text are in the Bibliothèque Nationale, Paris.

Bibliography: HERRAD OF LANDSBERG, *Notitia et fragmenta,* in PL 194:1537–42; *Hortus deliciarum,* ed. A. STRAUB and G. KELLER (Strasbourg 1879–99), fol. ed. with plates; ed. J. WALTER (Strasbourg 1952), valuable introd. and notes. C. M. ENGLEHARDT, *Herrad von Landsberg* (Stuttgart 1818). L. ECKENSTEIN, *Women under Monasticism* (Cambridge, Eng. 1896). C. WITTMER, *Lexikon für Theologie und Kirche,* J. HOFER and K. RAHNER, eds. (Freiburg 1957–65) 5:269–270. G. WEBB, ''Herrad and Her Garden of Delights,'' *Life of the Spirit* 16 (1961–62) 475–481.

[F. M. BEACH]

HERRERA, BARTOLOMÉ

Peruvian bishop and political theorist; b. Lima, Aug. 24, 1808; d. Arequipa, 1865. By the time he was five, Herrera was orphaned, and he was cared for by his uncles. However, his most important protector was Manuel José Pedemonte, rector of the Colegio de San Carlos, who admitted the young man to that college in 1821 on a full scholarship. Herrera at first studied to become a lawyer and took degrees in civil and canon law. On the advice of Father Pedemonte, and after a year of meditation, he

Bartolomé Herrera.

presented himself for ordination in 1832. Pedemonte wished to retain him on the faculty of San Carlos, but the young priest applied for and received a small parish, far removed from Lima, in Cajacay. Herrera himself says that he wished to have leisure in which to restudy philosophy since he had begun to suspect the orthodoxy of the teachings at San Carlos, especially in its Jansenistic and regalistic aspects. During the next few years Herrera rediscovered St. Thomas and gradually became a scholastic. Archbishop Benavente had him preach the sermon at his installation (1834) and serve as his secretary for the canonical visitation of the archdiocese. Because of his weak health, Herrera requested and was granted a transfer to the parish of Lurín in 1837. He made the acquaintance of a neighboring landlord, whom a revolution made president in 1842. The president appointed Herrera rector of San Carlos, then the first center of intellectual life in Peru and famous since the days of Toribio RODRÍGUEZ DE MENDOZA. By this time, Herrera's own ideas had matured, and in San Carlos he found the medium in which to instill them in the minds of young men who would be the rulers of Peru for many decades. For him sovereignty did not come from the people but from God; the people did not have the capacity or the right to make laws since these emanated from the eternal principles placed by God with the very nature of things. Hence, Herrera wanted a strong government, without congresses or universal suffrage, based on an aristocracy of the most capable and most intelligent. These opinions projected Herrera into the political arena amid the most bitter attacks of the liberals, both ecclesiastic and lay.

In 1849 Herrera was elected deputy to congress from Lima and then elected by his fellow members president of that body. In 1851 he was chosen as member of the president's cabinet, and for a time he discharged the offices of minister of government, foreign affairs, and public instruction. As such he concluded a boundary treaty with Brazil, helped the Sisters of the Sacred Hearts to open the first formal school for girls in Lima, brought Father Pedro GUAL to Lima, sponsored the first groups of Austrian and Irish immigrants, and helped draw up a more judicious law for the election of bishops. His severity irritated the liberals, and the president, under pretext of negotiating a concordat with the Holy See, sent him off to Rome as plenipotentiary in May 1852. Herrera discovered this ruse only when he returned in 1853 for consultation to find that the Lima government had taken no action on his proposed draft of a concordat. For some years his disillusionment and an attack of tuberculosis kept him out of public affairs. He strove to restore the prestige of the Lima archdiocesan seminary and edited a Catholic journal with the help of one of his former students, Juan Ambrosio Huerta. He also began the Conferences of St. Vincent de Paul. In 1858 he returned to congress and was again elected its president. When the congress failed to repeal laws that he thought unfair to the Church, he resigned his seat in 1860.

In 1859 he had been nominated for the bishopric of Arequipa, and now he devoted the remaining years of his life to his see, interesting himself especially in restoring the glory of the diocesan seminary of San Jerónimo and in reforming the diocesan clergy. Tuberculosis was the cause of his premature death. Herrera was the first prominent Peruvian priest after independence who was completely orthodox and ultramontane.

Bibliography: *Bartolomé Herrera: Escritos y discursos*, 2 v. (Lima 1929–34).

[A. S. TIBESAR]

HERRERA, JUAN DE

Architect and scientist who completed the ESCORIAL; b. Mobellan (Asturias), Spain, *c.* 1530; d. Madrid, Jan. 1, 1597. Herrera, the son of small landowners, studied at Valladolid before following Prince Philip (later PHILIP II) to Italy in 1547. In 1563 he was appointed assistant to the royal architect, Juan Bautista de Toledo, who had already projected the Escorial. Upon Toledo's death in May 1567, Herrera gradually assumed direction of the enterprise, received full charge in 1572, and brought it to completion in 1584. He also directed work at royal seats in Madrid, Aranjuez, Segovia, El Pardo, and Toledo. The Exchange in Seville (1584; now the Archivo General de Indias) and the unfinished cathedral of Valladolid (begun in 1585) are also his designs. His work differs from that of his Italian contemporaries, Vignola and Palladio, by its functional severity, as well as by the *estilo desornamentado* inherited from Juan Bautista de Toledo and other military architects of the 1560s, and by the richness of its proportional harmonies. He was the author of *Discurso sobre la figura cubica* (after 1579), and in 1584 he helped to found an academy in Madrid for mathematical studies. He also devised instruments for navigation.

Bibliography: L. CERVERA VERA, *La semblanza de Juan de Herrera* (Madrid 1963). A. RUIZ DE ARCAUTE, *Juan de Herrera: Arquitecto de Felipe II* (Madrid 1936). G. KUBLER and M. SORIA, *Art and Architecture in Spain and Portugal and Their American Dominions, 1500–1800* (Pelican History of Art, ed. N. PEVSNER. Z17; Baltimore, 1959). B. BEVAN, *History of Spanish Architecture* (London 1938). A. L. MAYER, in U. THIEME and F. BECKER, eds., *Allgemeines Lexikon der bildenden Künstler von der Antike bis zur Gegenwart*, 37 v. (Leipzig 1907–38) 16:540–542.

[G. KUBLER]

HERRERA Y TORDESILLAS, ANTONIO DE

Royal chronicler of Spain; b. Cuéllar, Segovia (Spain), 1549?; d. Madrid, March 27, 1625. In Italy *c.* 1570 he entered the service of Vespasian Gonzaga (1532–91), Viceroy of Naples, Navarre, and Valencia, who probably recommended him to King PHILIP II of Spain. Herrera's account of Portugal and the conquest of the Azores in 1582–83 (Madrid 1591) was completed in 1586. Herrera translated Giovanni Minadoi's *Historia della guerra fra Turchi e Persiani,* 1576–85 (Venice 1588), and in 1589 he published a history of Scotland and England during the life of MARY STUART. His translation (Barcelona 1599, Burgos 1603) of Giovanni Botero's anti-Machiavellian study of the State (Milan 1583) and of cities (Venice 1589) was done at the command of Philip II in 1592, and in 1612 Herrera published a work on the disturbances of 1592 in Aragon. His history of the Wars of Religion (*see* THIRTY YEARS WAR) in France (1585–94), from a Spanish point of view, was suppressed on its appearance in 1598, the same year he published an account of the disputes over ecclesiastical and secular jurisdiction in Milan from 1594 to 1598. In 1624 he published a history of Italy from 1281 to 1599. His works, many of which are in MSS in Madrid, include a variety of translations, eulogies, and treatises, which an official might be called on to produce.

Herrera's major work, *General History of the Spanish in the Indies in Eight Decades* (4 v. Madrid 1601–15; 8 v., Madrid 1726–30; 10 v. Asuncion 1944–47), partially translated into French (1621, 1659–71) and English (1725–26, 1740), which caused a dispute with Juan de TORQUEMADA, established a long-lived apologia for Columbus and for Spanish rule in the New World in a detailed but disconnected chronicle of events from 1492 to the conquest of Peru in 1554. It was in great part taken from MSS and published works (some no longer extant) of B. de LAS CASAS, Bp. Juan Bernal y Díaz de Lugo (d. 1566), Francisco Cervantes de Salazar (1514–75), and other authors, to which Herrera had access after he became royal chronicler, May 15, 1596. The *Descripción* of the Indies (Madrid 1601), which accompanied the *History* and has often been reprinted and translated, resembles a text of MS Madrid BN J-15 and has been attributed to Juan López de Velasco, Herrera's predecessor as chronicler.

FARNESE correspondence (ed. C. Pérez Bustamente, Santiago 1934) shows that Herrera *c.* 1607 extorted money from that family to suppress data about Alexander Farnese (1545–92), Governor of the Spanish Netherlands at the time of the 1588 Armada, in the 3d part of his history of the world of Philip II, 1559 to 1598 (3 v. Madrid 1601–12). This work for the most part depended on Italian historians. At this time Herrera translated two works on the spiritual life. In 16 letters or essays (Madrid 1804) Herrera reveals a critical concern about the basic approach of a historian, whose work encompasses geographical, social, chronological, and national (or genealogical) studies; Herrera would judiciously associate historical truth with the divine and ecclesiastical order. Herrera had financial ties in the New World and with the FUGGER bankers and in his last years spent much money in fruitless suits for debts. His imprisonment from 1609 to 1611 is shrouded in secrecy.

Bibliography: A. BALLESTEROS Y BERETTA and A. DE ALTOGUIRRE Y DUVALE, annotated ed. of the *Descripción* and two *Decades of the General History* . . . , 5 v. (Madrid 1934–36), has a study of Herrera, B. SÁNCHEZ ALONSO, *Historia de la historiografía española,* 3 v. (Madrid 1941–50) v.2.

[E. P. COLBERT]

Juan De Herrera.

HERRERO, ANDRÉS

Franciscan missionary, restorer of the Colegios Franciscanos de Propaganda Fide in Bolivia, Peru, and Chile; b. Arnedo, Logroño, Spain, 1782; d. Bolivia, 1838. He arrived in Peru in 1810 at the Apostolic College of Moquegua. For more than 20 years he served as a missionary in the basin of the Madre de Dios and Beni Rivers during the difficult period of the wars for independence. As a firm foundation for his evangelical work, he mastered the native languages and built schools, granges, and art and craft shops in each missionary center. He continued to work under the independent republican regime with a fervor equal to that he had displayed under the patronage of Spain. In view of the almost complete disruption of the Franciscan Order in its provincial organization, missionary colleges, and missions in the South American countries along the Pacific Coast, his greatest aspiration was to bring about its restoration. With the backing of the president of Bolivia, Santa Cruz, he began in 1833 by going to Europe in search of missionaries. He was received kindly by GREGORY XVI, who named him apostolic prefect of all missionary colleges and missions in South America. He returned to Bolivia in 1835 with 12 missionaries. In 1837, he traveled again to Europe, and secured 84 missionaries. With 19 of them, the Colegio de Ocopa in Peru was restored. Furthermore, in Bolivia he promoted national vocations. The work begun by Herrero was consolidated and extended in the following decades by all the South American nations of the Pacific Coast.

Bibliography: P. DOMÍNGUEZ, *El colegio franciscano de propaganda fide de Moquegua* (Madrid 1955).

[O. SAIZ]

HERRISVAD, ABBEY OF

Also called *Herivadum,* oldest Cistercian abbey in Denmark, in the Archdiocese of Lund in Scania, now a part of Sweden. It was founded in 1144 by ESKIL OF LUND, the archbishop; the first monks came directly from CÎTEAUX. The foundation stone of the church was laid in 1158, but it is not known exactly when the church was finished. It was rebuilt wholly or in part early in the 13th century and again, after a great fire, in 1291. The abbey has been demolished but its plan is well known from recent excavations of the site. The importance of Herrisvad was soon recognized, and daughterhouses were founded in Tvis (*Tuta Vallis*) 1163, in Holme (*Insula Dei*) 1172, and in Løgum (*Locus Dei*) *c.* 1173. The church (built *c.* 1200–1350) and part of the monastery in Løgum still exist. After Herrisvad the next Cistercian abbey in Denmark was Esrom (no Latin name), founded *c.* 1153 by Eskil and inhabited by monks from CLAIRVAUX. Esrom was perhaps the wealthiest abbey in Denmark, and from it were founded a number of daughterhouses, including Vitskøl (*Vitae Schola*) 1158, and Sorø (SORA), founded by ABSALON OF LUND (later Archbishop of Denmark) in 1162. Esrom and Sorø had formerly been Benedictine abbeys. The church in Sorø, built soon after the foundation and several times rebuilt (after a fire in 1247 and later), is extant and is regarded as one of the finest specimens of ecclesiastical architecture from medieval Denmark. Øm (*Cara Insula*), founded in 1165 as a daughterhouse of Vitskøl, is remembered from the vivid record of its earliest history in *Exordium Carae Insulae.* Glücksburg Castle in the old Diocese of Schleswig, now a part of Germany, is built on the site of Ryd abbey (*Rus Regis*) founded in 1209. The Cistercian abbeys in Denmark flourished until the 14th century when a serious decline set in. After the Reformation (1536) all abbeys and other religious houses were dissolved.

Bibliography: *Exordium Monasterii Carae Insulae,* ed. M. C. GERTZ in *Scriptores minores historiae Danicae Medii Aevi,* 2 v. (Copenhagen 1917–22) 2:153–264. E. ORTVED, *Cistercieordenen og dens klostre i Norden,* 2 v. in 1 (Copenhagen 1927–33). V. B. LORENZEN, *De danske Cistercienserklostres Bygningshistorie* (Copenhagen 1941). L. GJERLØW and J. GALLÉN, *Kulturhistorisk Leksikon for nordisk middelalder,* v.2 (Copenhagen 1957) 565–573, with bibliog.

[H. BEKKER-NIELSEN]

HERSFELD, ABBEY OF

A former Benedictine abbey (Hirshfeld, Herocampia, Hirsfeldia, Hersfeldense) in the Diocese of Mainz. Sturmius, a pupil of St. Boniface, established a cell there in 736. Lullus, a monk of Malmesbury, the best known of Boniface's companions and later his successor as bishop of Mainz, founded the abbey in 769–770. It was first dedicated to SS. Simon and Thaddeus, but soon after it was renamed to honor the relics of St. Wigbert of Fritzlar. A new church was erected in 850.

When Hersfeld became an imperial abbey under Charlemagne it was already rich in estates in Hesse and Thuringia, and took an active role in the mission to the Saxons. It had one of the great medieval libraries, containing the important annals of the period of Otto II. During the 10th and 11th centuries it was an important spiritual center, particularly under the reforming abbots, Godehard and Arnold. However, as an imperial abbey, Hersfeld opposed the Cluniac reform.

The more important dependencies of Hersfeld were Herrenbreitstein, Göllingen, Memleben, Kreuzberg, and Frauensee. Hersfeld's abbots ranked with the princes of the empire until the mid-12th century, and after the 13th, the abbot received investiture from the emperor. Wealth and worldly living seem to have weakened monastic discipline. Its Vogt (suzerain), the Landgrave of Thuringia and Hesse, greatly reduced its territories in the 14th and 15th centuries. There was, moreover, a bitter quarrel between the abbey and the town. The Bursfeld reform was introduced in 1510, but Abbot Crato brought in the Protestant reform. There were attempts to restore the abbey in the 17th century, but it was given to Hesse as a principality in 1648. Important ruins of the church and frescoes of the Ottonian period remain. (See illustration below.)

Bibliography: H. BÜTTNER, *Lexikon für Theologie und Kirche,* 10v. (2d, new ed. Freiburg 1957–65) 5:281. L. H. COTTINEAU, *Répertoire topo-bibliographique des abbayes et prieurés* 1:1410–11. P. SCHMITZ, *Histoire de l'Ordre de Saint-Benoît,* 7 v. (Maredsous, Bel. 1942–56).

[P. BECKMAN]

HERST, RICHARD, BL.

Lay martyr; name also given as Hurst or Hayhurst; b. Broughton, near Preston, Lancashire, England; d. hanged at Lancaster, Aug. 29, 1628. Richard, a wealthy yeoman who cultivated his own land, was arrested as a recusant Catholic upon the order of the bishop of Chester. In the course of the arrest one of the pursuivant's men, named Dewhurst, broke his leg and later died of the injury. Although Dewhurst himself solemnly swore that the fatal injury was an accident, Herst was indicted for murder. Herst's friends and Queen Henrietta Maria petitioned King Charles I for a reprieve; however the government countered the petition. Although the jury was unwilling to convict Herst of murder, the judge insisted on a verdict of guilt. The following day he was forcibly dragged by the legs to a Protestant church to hear a sermon. Upon the gallows he was offered his life in exchange for swearing allegiance to the king, but he refused because the oath contained attacks upon the Catholic faith. Thereupon he was executed. He was beatified by Pius XI on Dec. 15, 1929.

Feast of the English Martyrs: May 4 (England).

See Also: ENGLAND, SCOTLAND, AND WALES, MARTYRS OF.

Bibliography: R. CHALLONER, *Memoirs of Missionary Priests,* ed. J. H. POLLEN (rev. ed. London 1924; repr. Farnborough 1969), II, 97–101. J. H. POLLEN, *Acts of English Martyrs* (London 1891).

[K. I. RABENSTEIN]

HERTFORD, COUNCIL OF

The first general assembly of the whole English Church (Sept. 26, 672), summoned by THEODORE of Tarsus, Archbishop of Canterbury (669–690), after 3 1/2 years of visitation, reform, and consecration of bishops to fill vacancies throughout England. By its most important canons the Council of Hertford reaffirmed the Roman calculation of Easter (c.1), prohibited bishops from intruding in the affairs of neighboring dioceses (c.2), forbade monks to leave their monasteries without permission of their abbots (c.4), provided for future episcopal synods twice a year if possible, but at least annually (c.7), established the order of precedence among bishops according to dates of consecration (c.8), and recognized adultery as the only basis for divorce while forbidding a divorced man to remarry (c.10). The council marked a new stage in the growth of Christianity in England and the end of the period of regional churches related to each other only tenuously if at all. It inaugurated an established diocesan system under the forms of synodal government to replace the earlier practice of migratory and often ill-disciplined clergy, both regular and secular.

See Also: EASTER CONTROVERSY.

Bibliography: BEDE, *Historia Ecclesiastica* 4.5. A. W. HADDAN and W. STUBBS, eds., *Councils and Ecclesiastical Documents Relating to Great Britain and Ireland,* 3 v. in 4 (Oxford 1869–78) 3:118–122. C. J. GODFREY, *The Church in Anglo-Saxon England* (New York 1962).

[R. S. HOYT]

HERWEGEN, ILDEFONS

Liturgist; b. Junkersdorf, Germany, Nov. 27, 1874; d. Maria Laach Abbey, Sept. 2, 1946. He entered the Benedictine Abbey of Maria Laach in 1895 and studied archeology at Sant' Anselmo, Rome. He was already an ardent supporter of the liturgical movement in 1907. With his election in 1913 as 44th abbot of Maria Laach, he was able to enlist the full force of his monastic community and thus became the revered head of the movement toward liturgical renewal. He brought to this work a profound historical sense as well as rich gifts of personality and oratory.

The extraordinary influence he exerted over his countrymen of all classes was furthered by his use of several media. He gave innumerable retreats and weekend conferences all over Europe; he was the recognized leader of the respected Katholischer Akademikerverband; in 1931 he founded the Benedictine Academy for Liturgical and Monastic Research (since 1948 the Abt-Herwegen-Institut); he also produced both scholarly and popular works. He edited the collections *Beiträge zur Geschichte des alten Mönchtums und des Benediktinerordens* (Münster 1912–), of which 16 volumes have appeared, and *Ecclesia Orans* (Freiburg 1918–), a popular series. Moreover, he published more than 30 books and articles, of which the most famous are: *Der heilige Benedikt* (3d ed. Düsseldorf 1926), which has become a classic; *Antike, Germanentum und Christentum* (Salzburg 1931); *Sinn und Geist der Benediktinerregel* (Einsiedeln-Köln 1944).

Bibliography: *Liturgie und Mönchtum* 1 (1948) 39–44, bibliography. E. V. SEVERUS, *Lexikon für Theologie und Kirche,* ed. J. HOFER and K. RAHNER, 10 v. (2d, new ed. Freiburg 1957–65) 5:284.

[H. A. REINHOLD]

HESS, BEDE FREDERICK

Minister general of the Order Friars Minor Conventual; b. Rome, N.Y., Nov. 16, 1885; d. Assisi, Italy, Aug. 8, 1953. He was the son of Joseph and Catherine (King) Hess. He was educated at St. Mary's School and St. Francis College, Trenton, N.J. In 1900 he entered the Franciscan Order and was professed on Nov. 17, 1901. He was sent to the University of Innsbruck, Austria, where he earned the S.T.D. After being ordained on July 26, 1908, he was given teaching assignments in New York at St. Francis College, Brooklyn, and St. Anthony-on-Hudson Seminary, Rensselaer. From 1912 to 1932 he was director of the mission band and pastor of St. Catherine's Church, Seaside Park, N.J. He founded a monthly magazine, the *Minorite,* later the *Companion,* and was active in promoting the Third Order, both as commissary provincial and chairman of the National Executive Board (1925–32). In 1932 and 1935 he was elected provincial of the Immaculate Conception Province. In 1936 he became the 112th successor of St. Francis and the first native-born American general of a religious order. He was confirmed in this position during World War II by papal appointment, and reelected in 1948, thus functioning as general longer than anyone except St. BONAVENTURE. Under his direction the order expanded its activities, particularly in mission fields. He prevented the destruction of Franciscan provinces behind the Iron Curtain, and by liaison with the Nazi authorities, of Assisi, the birthplace of St. Francis. His writings on the constitutions of his order effected reform in administration and observance; there was a general reorganization of studies, liturgy, and mission norms. Besides numerous articles and a definitive encyclical on the Third Order, his writings include: *The Tertiary Director's Guide* (1926); *De Tertio Ordine Saeculari SPN Francisci* (1938); *De Militia Mariae Immaculatae* (1942); and *Manuale de Regula et Constitutionibus O.F.M.Conv.* (1943).

[A. CLARK]

HESSELBLAD, ELISABETH, BL.

Also known as Maria Hesselblad, apostle of ecumenism, nurse, founder of the Order of the Most Holy Savior of Saint Brigit; b. June 4, 1870, Fåglavik (near Hundene), Alvsborg, Sweden; d. April 24, 1957, Rome, Italy.

Elisabeth was the fifth of the 13 children born to Swedish Lutherans, Augusto Roberto Hesselblad and Cajsa Pettesdotter Dag. She immigrated to the U.S. (1888) to help support her family. She earned a nursing diploma at Roosevelt Hospital, N.Y., where she tended the sick, caring not only for their physical needs but their spiritual needs as well. Here she came in contact with Catholics for the first time. After experiencing a call during a Eucharistic procession in Brussels, she was later received into the Catholic Church in Washington, D.C., in 1902. She noted in her memoirs how significant her devotion to the Eucharist was. Two days later she left for Rome, where she discerned a vocation to promote Christian unity, but then returned to the U.S., where her health deteriorated. Now gravely ill, she went to Rome to the the *Casa di S. Brigida* to die. However, her health improved, and she joined the CARMELITES (March 25, 1904), who were established in that very house of St. BRIDGET, whose writings Maria Elisabeth long admired.

In 1906, Pope PIUS X gave Hesselblad special permission to take the habit of the BRIGITTINE SISTERS. She

Elisabeth Hesselblad. (AP/Wide World Photos)

was unsuccessful in reestablishing a Bridgettine community in Rome with members of existing communities in Europe. On Sept. 9, 1911, she began a new branch of the Brigettines with three English postulants, using the original order's Augustinian Rule. The order received canonical approval in 1920. She exhorted her sisters to work tirelessly for Christian unity throughout the world.

During World War I and especially World War II, Mother Elisabeth worked tirelessly to aid those who needed assistance. She cared for the poor and offered hospitality and a hiding place to Jews and others persecuted by racist laws. In 1947 Mother Elisabeth's longing to build bridges to those of other faiths became reality when she became an enthusiastic collaborator with Fr. Boyer, a worker in the ecumenical field.

At a Vatican ceremony (Nov. 13, 1999) shortly after the signing of a joint Catholic–Lutheran declaration (Augsburg, Oct. 31, 1999), the pope dedicated a statue of St. Bridget, Europe's co–patron, in the presence of the highest Lutheran representatives of Sweden and Finland, as well as the Swedish king and queen. John Paul II recalled that Bridget's "passion for Christian unity sustained her entire life. And, thanks to her witness and the witness of Mother Elisabeth Hesselblad, this commitment has come down to us through the mysterious stream of grace which overflows the bounds of time and space." At Hesselblad's beatification (April 9, 2000) he reiterated: "By constantly meditating on God's word, Sister Elisabeth was confirmed in her resolve to work and pray that all Christians would be one."

Feast: July 4.

Bibliography: *L'Osservatore Romano,* Eng. ed., no. 15 (2000): 2. J. HOGG, *The Carthusian General Chapter and the Spanish Charterhouses*, Analecta Cartusians, v. 164, which includes U. S. OLSEN, "The Revival of the Birgittine Monks in the Twentieth Century," (Salzburg, Austria 2000). M. TJADER, *Mother Elisabeth: The Resurgence of the Order of Saint Birgitta* (New York 1972).

[K. I. RABENSTEIN]

HESYCHASM

A method of prayer in the Oriental Church that depended on the control of physical faculties and concentration on the JESUS PRAYER to achieve peace of soul and union with God. Originally a contemplative, monastic practice, it was popularized in the 13th and 14th centuries and became identified with Palamism.

The earliest descriptions of the hesychastic method of contemplation go back at least to the fifth century: it is mentioned in the vita of the Jerusalem monk, St. John the Hesychast, of the laura of St. Sabas (*Acta Sanctorum* May 3:232–238); Basil of Caesarea (d. 379) seems to have had an equivalent practice in mind in his Rules (*Reg. fus. tract.* 6–8; *Patrologia Graeca* 31:925–941). JOHN CLIMACUS (d. 649) in his *Ladder of Paradise* (ch. 27) described the method as characteristic of the monastery on Mt. SINAI. In this instance only certain monks, after observing the common life for several years, were permitted to retire to a private cell (*celliotes*) under the spiritual guidance of the monastic superior. There they were encouraged to achieve complete control of their bodily movements while seeking an interior peacefulness by banishing thought and concentrating on a short prayer formula involving the name of Jesus. The practitioners were warned frequently against ACEDIA or spiritual listlessness, and they sought the gift of tears.

The Justinian Code (*Novel.* 5.3; 123.36) and the council in Trullo (c.41) warned against false and extravagant versions of this type of ascetical practice; and St. Anastasius, the founder of the laura on Mt. Athos, would allow only five of the more perfect monks in each community of 120 to attempt it. With SYMEON THE NEW THEOLOGIAN (949–1022) the mystical element in the theological foundation of the hesychastic practice became an issue. The goal of this contemplative procedure was set by Nicephorus (fl. *c.* 1260) as an experience of the *photophaneia* or light of glory that surrounded the risen Christ (PG 147:945), whereas GREGORY SINAITES (d. 1346) warned continually that visions were the work of the devil (PG 150:1924), although his ascetical system was based upon the hesychastic method.

Gregory PALAMAS (d. 1359) gave hesychasm its full theological foundation by distinguishing between two concepts of God: the transcendent, indescribable, and uncreated Being, and the experience of God's goodness that He shared with man in creation and in the divinizing process of grace. Palamas made a real distinction between the Being and the energy or outward activity of God that was experienced in the mystical realization of the presence of grace in the form of the light that surrounded Christ in His transfiguration on Mt. Tabor. This theological position was challenged by BARLAAM OF CALABRIA and became the source of a great theological controversy during the 14th century.

In 1342 Palamas's writings were condemned in two Constantinopolitan synods, but under Emperor John VI Cantacuzenus, a synod in 1347 certified the orthodoxy of the Palamite explanation of hesychasm. In 1351 the various opponents of Palamas were excommunicated in the so-called Blachernae Synod, and hesychasm was recognized as an official doctrine of the Orthodox Church with its center on Mt. Athos.

The practice of hesychastic contemplation began with a system of breath control, with the chin resting on the breast and the eyes concentrating on the navel (*omphalopsychia*), while the practitioner ceaselessly repeated the Jesus Prayer. This exercise prepared one for the achievement of absolute quietude of soul and for an experience of divine light; hence its practitioners were referred to also as Taborites.

See Also: TABOR, MOUNT.

Bibliography: I. HAUSHERR, *La Méthode d'oraison hésychaste, Orientalia Christiania Analecta* 9 (1927) 97–209. M. JUGIE, *Dictionnaire de theologie catholique* 11.2:1777–1818. G. WUNDERLE, *Zur Psychologie des hesychastischen Gebets* (Würzburg 1949). A. M. AMMANN, *Die Gottesschau im palamit. Hesychasmus* (Würzburg 1948). J. MEYENDORFF, *Nouvelle revue théologique* 79 (1957) 905–914; *A Study of Gregory Palamas,* tr. G. LAWRENCE (London 1964). H. C. GRAEF, *Lexikon für Theologie und Kirche*, J. HOFER and K. RAHNER, eds. (Freiburg 1957–65) 5:307–308.

[F. X. MURPHY]

HESYCHIUS OF JERUSALEM

Known to Theophanes Confessor [*Chronographia,* ed. C. de Boor, 1 (1883) 83] as a priest of Jerusalem (*c.* 412) who achieved fame as a theologian and preacher; d. probably after 450. CYRIL OF SCYTHOPOLIS records his presence with Bp. Juvenal of Jerusalem at the consecration of the church at the monastery of Euthymius (*Vita S. Euthymii: Patrologia Graeca,* ed. J. P. Migne, 114:629) in 428 or 429. The Greek Menology (*Patrologia Graeca* 117:373) credited him with having commented on the whole of Sacred Scripture, and modern research is gradually showing the justice of that claim.

Hesychius wrote a *Commentary on Leviticus* preserved in the Latin translation of a certain 6th-century Jerome. His *Commentary on Job* (ch. 1–20) has come down in an Armenian version; Hesychius regarded Job as a historical person but explained the book as an allegorical foreshadowing of Christ and the Church. He wrote some 2,680 short glosses on Isaiah in imitation of ORIGEN and scholia on the minor prophets, as well as several works on the Psalms. However, the problem of authorship for both the citations in the *catenae* and the commentaries on the Psalms has not been resolved. The great glosses published among the works of Athanasius (*Patrologia Graeca* 27:649–1344) were actually written by Hesychius, as was a long commentary (*Patrologia Graeca* 93:1179–1340; 55: 711–784). Despite its use of Antiochene theological expressions, a second commentary on the Psalms is also probably of his authorship; so are 147 scholia on 13 Canticles of the Old and New Testament.

Of his sermons only a few have been definitively identified and published. These include a sermon for the Purification, representing the oldest mention of that feast, and discourses on the Annunciation and the Mother of God (*Deipara*). Extant in manuscript are sermons on fasting, a second discourse on the Purification that is interesting for its exegesis of Lk 2.35, two homilies on the resurrection of Lazarus, and encomia of SS. Andrew, Luke, Peter and Paul, Stephen, Anthony the Hermit, and John the Baptist. Sermons on Christmas and the cross and encomia on St. Thomas and St. James have been lost.

After 428 Hesychius wrote a Church history in which he proved himself a strong opponent of NESTORIANISM. The chapter dealing with THEODORE OF MOPSUESTIA was read at the Council of CONSTANTINOPLE II in 553 (J. D. Mansi, *Sacrorum Conciliorum nova et amplissima collectio* 9:248–249). His collection of *Objections and Solutions* deals with apparent discrepancies in the Gospels. It seems to be part of his lost *Evangelica Symphonia* (*Patrologia Graeca* 93:1391–1448).

Hesychius was greatly influenced by the exegetical methods of Origen and went so far as to deny that a literal meaning could be found for every sentence in Scripture (*Patrologia Graeca* 93:791, 1030). He opposed the use of philosophy for solving theological problems, particularly in Christology. He followed Alexandrian thought but preferred scriptural expressions reducing the Christological formula to *Logos sarkotheis* or *Verbum incarnatum,* the Word became flesh. He admitted no possibility of sin, ignorance, or moral progress in Christ and opposed Arian, Apollinarian, and Antiochene doctrine as subordinationist in tendency. He was considered a Monophysite by both Bishop John of Maïuma and the deacon, later pope, PELAGIUS I.

Bibliography: J. QUASTEN, *Patrology*, 3 v. (Westminster, Md. 1950) 3:488–496. G. LOESCHKE, *Paulys Realenzyklopädie der klassischen Altertumswissenschaft*, ed. G. WISSOWA et al. 8.2 (1913) 1328–30. K. JÜSSEN, *Die dogmatischen Anschauungen des Hesychius von Jerusalem,* 2 v. (Münster 1931–34); ''Die Mariologie des Hesychius von Jerusalem,'' *Theologie in Geschichte und Gegenwart: Festschrift M. Schmaus,* ed. J. AUER and H. VOLK (Munich 1957) 651–670. *Bessarione* 22 (1918) 8–46. A. WENGER, *Revue des études augustiniennes* 2 (1956) 457–470. L. SANTIFALLER, *Zentralblatt für Bibliothekswesen* 60 (1943) 241–266. A. SIEGMUND, *Die Überlieferung der griechischen christlichen Literatur* (Munich 1949) 87–88. C. NAHAPETIAN, *Bessarione* 17 (1913) 452–465. M. VON FAULHABER, *Theologische Quartalschrift* 83 (1901) 218–232; ed., *Hesychii Hierosolymitani interpretatio Isaiae prophetae* (Freiburg 1900). G. MERCATI, in *Miscellanea Pio Paschini,* 2 v. (Rome 1948–49) 2:205–211. V. JAGIĆ, *Ein unedierter griechischer Psalmenkommentar* (Vienna 1906). R. DEVREESSE, *Revue biblique* 33 (1924) 498–521. G. BARDY, *ibid.* 42 (1933) 226–229.

[F. X. MURPHY]

HETTINGER, FRANZ

Theologian; b. Aschaffenburg, Jan. 13, 1819; d. Würzburg, Jan. 26, 1890. He was ordained in 1843 and took his doctorate in theology at the German college in Rome in 1845. He taught at the Würzburg seminary until 1856, when he was appointed professor of patrology at the university. His entire life centered around the University of Würzburg to which he and his colleagues J. HERGENRÖTHER and H. J. DENZINGER brought a notable reputation for theological studies. He held the chairs of apologetics and homiletics, filled two terms as rector, and succeeded his friend Denzinger as professor of dogma.

His reputation for learning spread throughout Europe. In 1859 he was made an honorary doctor of philosophy at Würzburg; in 1866, an honorary member of the college of doctors in theology of the University of Vienna; in 1884, an honorary doctor of theology at Louvain; and in the following year, an honorary member of the *Academia religionis Catholicae* of Rome. In 1867 he and

Hergenröther were named consultors for the preparation of VATICAN COUNCIL I. Objections were raised, which resulted in the appointment of other German consultors. These objections, however, were not against either man personally but against the exclusive choice of members of the Würzburg faculty. Yet this incident shows the high regard in which the theological faculty at Würzburg was held especially because of its three distinguished professors, who strongly supported Roman ideas particularly against those espoused by J. J. I. von DÖLLINGER and others at Munich. Hettinger accepted a role at the Vatican Council only on condition that it would not interfere with his teaching. He was named to the dogmatic commission. In 1879 Leo XIII, who called upon him to prepare the German translations of his great encyclicals, named Hettinger a domestic prelate.

Both at the beginning and at the end of his professorial career he wrote practical books for priests: *Das Priesterthum der katholischen Kirche* (Regensburg 1851), *Die Liturgie der Kirche* (Würzburg 1856), *Aphorismen für Predigt und Prediger* (Freiburg 1888), *Timotheus, Brief an einen jungen Theologen* (Freiburg 1891). One of his most popular publications was a collection of essays occasioned by his travels and called *Aus Kirche und Welt* (Freiburg 1885). Throughout his life he was enamored of the works of Dante, concerning which he published numerous articles and important books: *Grundidee und Charakter der Göttlichen Komödie des Dante Alighieri* (Bonn 1876), *Die Theologie der Göttlichen Komödie* (Cologne 1879), *Die Göttliche Komödie des Dante Alighieri nach ihrem wesentlicher Inhalt und Charakter dargestellt* (Freiburg 1880), *Dante und Beatrice* (Frankfurt 1883), and *Dantes Geistesgang* (Cologne 1888).

Hettinger's great contribution to apologetics, *Apologie des Christenthums* (Freiburg), was first published between 1863 and 1867. There were six editions during his lifetime; three more editions after his death, edited by his pupil E. Müller, the latest from 1914 to 1918; and translations into French, English, Spanish, and Portuguese. This is certainly one of the great works of 19th-century apologetics.

Bibliography: H. HURTER, *Nomenclator literarius theologiae catholicae*, 5 v. in 6 (3d ed. Innsbruck 1903–13) 5.2:1433–35. J. HASENFUSS, *Lexikon für Theologie und Kirche*, ed. J. HOFER and K. RAHNER, 10 v. (2d, new ed. Freiburg 1957–65) 5:314. E. MANGENOT, *Dictionnaire de théologie catholique*, ed. A. VACANT et al., 15 v. (Paris 1903–50; Tables générales 1951–) 6.2:2324–25.

[A. ROCK]

HEUSER, HERMAN JOSEPH

Author, editor; b. Potsdam, Germany, Oct. 28, 1852; d. Overbrook, Pa., Aug. 22, 1933. Having been educated in Berlin and in Breslau, Germany, he went in 1870 to Philadelphia, Pa., where he continued his theology at St. Charles Seminary, Overbrook. He was a student teacher in the preparatory department of the seminary from 1870 to 1876. Ordained in Philadelphia on Feb. 2, 1876, he became a professor at Overbrook, teaching languages at first, and then, for most of his years, Sacred Scripture. After serving as assistant editor to Msgr. James Corcoran for the *American Catholic Quarterly Review,* he founded the *American Ecclesiastical Review* in 1899. As its editor (1899–1914, 1919–27), he influenced scholarly circles throughout the world and clerical life in the U.S. In 1897 he began to publicize the novels of Canon Patrick A. Sheehan of Doneraile, Ireland, whose *My New Curate* was written specifically for and appeared serially in Heuser's magazine. Heuser also organized and directed the Dolphin Press of Philadelphia, which printed many ecclesiastical books. From 1900 to 1908 he published the *Dolphin,* a general Catholic literary magazine that had begun as a book supplement to the *American Ecclesiastical Review.*

Heuser's activities were varied. In addition to clerical subjects, he was interested in art, architecture, and music. He was frequently consulted by religious orders, and helped to write the constitutions of the Sisters of Mercy of Merion, Pa., where his sister was for a time superior general, and of Mother M. Katherine Drexel's Sisters of the Blessed Sacrament. He was an adviser to the Pontifical Commission on Anglican Orders in 1896, and received an honorary degree of doctor of sacred theology from (St.) Pius X. In 1907, during the controversy over Modernism, he was appointed by the apostolic delegate as general censor for all Catholic publications in the U.S. He was the author of 15 books, principally on clerical and religious subjects. In 1927 he retired from his editorial and professorial duties, and deeded the *American Ecclesiastical Review* to The Catholic University of America, Washington, D.C.

Bibliography: Historical Collections of the American Catholic Historical Society of Philadelphia, St. Charles Seminary, Philadelphia, Pa. E. J. GALBALLY, *American Ecclesiastical Review* 89 (1933) 337–360. H. T. HENRY, "Some Memories of the Founder of the *Review,*" *ibid.* 100 (1939) 8–21. J. G. HUBBERT, *"For the Upbuilding of the Church": The Reverend Herman Joseph Heuser, D.D., 1851–1933,* 3 vols. (Washington, D.C. 1992).

[B. F. FAIR]

HEWETT, JOHN, BL.

Priest, martyr; sometimes spelled, Hewitt; *alias* Weldon and Sayell; b. York, England; d. hanged at Mile End Green, London, Oct. 5, 1588. From Caius College, Cambridge, Hewett passed to the English College, Rheims. During the course of his seminary studies, he returned to England, where he was captured and banished in 1585. After his ordination the following year, he returned to England and again was captured and exiled (1587) to the Netherlands. He was unsafe even abroad. In the Netherlands he was arrested by the earl of Leicester on a false accusation and sent back to England for trial. In October 1588, he was formally arraigned on the charge of being illegally ordained abroad and entering England to exercise the ministry. The following day he was taken through the streets of London to Mile End Green, where before his execution he held disputes with two preachers. Hewett was beatified by Pius XI on Dec. 15, 1929.

Feast of the English Martyrs: May 4 (England).

See Also: ENGLAND, SCOTLAND, AND WALES, MARTYRS OF.

Bibliography: R. CHALLONER, *Memoirs of Missionary Priests,* ed. J. H. POLLEN (rev. ed. London 1924; repr. Farnborough 1969). J. H. POLLEN, *Acts of English Martyrs* (London 1891).

[K. I. RABENSTEIN]

HEWIT, AUGUSTINE FRANCIS

Associate founder of the PAULISTS, editor, educator; b. Fairfield, Conn., Nov. 27, 1820; d. New York City, July 3, 1897. He was the son of Nathaniel Hewit, a Congregationalist minister, and Rebecca (Hillhouse) Hewit, daughter of U.S. Senator James Hillhouse. After attending Phillips Academy, Andover, and Amherst College, Massachusetts, he entered the Congregationalist seminary at East Windsor, Conn. In March 1843, influenced greatly by the writings of the Oxford theologians, he joined the Episcopal Church and went to study for the ministry under Bp. William Whittingham in Baltimore, Md. He was ordained a deacon in September 1843.

In April 1846, Hewit became a Catholic; he was ordained March 25, 1847, by Bp. Ignatius Reynolds of Charleston, S.C., and taught in the diocesan seminary there. In 1850 Hewit made his profession as a Redemptorist, but he was dispensed from his vows in 1858 in order to found the Paulists, a new society in which he played a part second only to Isaac HECKER. Hewit wrote the first constitutions of the society, trained the candidates, and ruled the society during Hecker's absence for reasons of health. When Hecker founded the *Catholic World* in 1865, Hewit became its principal staff writer, and in 1866, its managing editor. His contribution to U.S. theology and letters led the Holy See to award him a doctorate about 1875.

Hewit was elected second superior general of the Paulists on Jan. 2, 1889. He supported the American hierarchy's effort to open the Catholic University of America in Washington, D.C., and on its grounds started a Paulist house of studies, later St. Paul's College, the first religious house affiliated with the University. He also directed the establishment of the Paulists at San Francisco, Calif. (1894), the inauguration of missions to non-Catholics under Walter ELLIOTT (1893), the founding of the Catholic Missionary Union (1896), and the creation of the Columbus Press (1891), which later became the Paulist Press.

Bibliography: A. F. HEWIT, *Memoir of the Life of the Rev. Francis A. Baker* (7th ed. New York 1889). J. P. FLYNN, *The Early Years of Augustine F. Hewit, CSP* (Washington 1945). J. MCSORLEY, *Father Hecker and His Friends* (2d ed. St. Louis 1953)

[J. P. FLYNN]

HEXAEMERON

The term *hexaemeron* is derived from two Greek words: the numeral ''six'' (ἕξ) and the noun ''day'' (ἡμέραι). It has been used in both the Jewish and the Christian traditions to refer to the opening of the Book of Genesis, where God's creative work brings forth the world and all its non-living and living creatures in a period of six days, followed by the seventh day of Sabbath rest. The term is also used to refer to commentaries on the six days of creation. Such commentaries became a means for patristic authors to offer a critique of cosmogonies that were widespread in the Greco-Roman culture, offering Christian writers the opportunity to present a Christian understanding of humanity and creation.

The first Jewish author to make use of this sort of terminology in reference to the work of creation was Philo, whose interpretation of the text of Genesis reflects the wider cultural context of Greek philosophy and inclines strongly to an allegorical style of interpretation. Philo wished to find some degree of harmony between the Hebrew Scriptures and the Greek philosophy current at that time. Moving from this base, he develops a theology of creation with numerous themes that will reappear in later Christian authors.

In Christian circles, the usage appears already in the second century in the work of Theophilos of Antioch and then in Origen, Basil of Caesarea, and Basil's brother, Gregory of Nyssa, among others. Following his usual, allegorical method of interpretation, Origen attempted to find the moral and allegorical meanings of the creation account, sometimes going so far as to see no real significance in the historical meaning of the text.

Basil used the Genesis text as the basis for a series of Lenten sermons that aim at laying out a Christian understanding of the created world in contrast with the metaphysical dualism of many pagan theories, which related material reality to a lesser, or even evil, principle. Basil presents a picture of the beauty of creation flowing from the work of the good and benevolent Creator. His descriptions of the world reflect the influence of Aristotle, Plato, and Plotinus, among others. He thus displays a theological style that is aware of the best knowledge of the natural science and philosophy of his time. It is this quality that made this work particularly admired during Basil's own time, but that led later critics to find fault with it precisely because of what they saw as its outdated understanding of nature.

While Basil's homilies did not include the work of the sixth day, on which humanity was created, this theme is taken up by Gregory of Nyssa in his *On the Creation of Man*, which Gregory himself describes as the completion of Basil's work. In terms of style, this work is somewhat like a homily; in terms of content, it is above all a reflection on the anthropology involved in Genesis 1:26. Gregory also makes it clear that, on a number of important points concerning creation, such as the doctrine of the pre-existence of human souls, he disagrees with Origen. Here and in his later *Book on the Hexaemeron* Gregory describes the wisdom of God the Creator and defends the writings of the Hebrew Scriptures as well as the work of Basil. Both Basil and Gregory make an explicit point of their intent to explain the biblical text literally and not allegorically.

In Western Christianity, Ambrose of Milan was a significant figure in bringing the influence of Philo and the Greek Christian authors into the Latin tradition. In a series of nine Lenten sermons known as *The Hexaemeron in Six Books*, Ambrose provides remarkable descriptions of the physical world and discusses a number of philosophical theories common at his time. While at one level Ambrose, like Basil before him, deals with the literal meaning of the text, at another level he moves frequently to a form of symbolism and moral teaching that made his work important for the medieval authors. Without using the term *hexaemeron*, Augustine treats the account of the six days at two levels (*On Genesis against the Manichees,* Bk. 1). He acknowledges a literal meaning of the text. But of even greater significance is the spiritual interpretation in which the six days are seen as prophecy showing the six ages of human history, the six stages of human life, and the six stages of growth in the spiritual life. At each level, the seventh day of Sabbath rest symbolizes the reality of heaven.

One of the most complex instances of literature on the six days is found in the *Collations on the Six Days* by Bonaventure. This is a set of 23 collations given to Franciscan students and faculty at the University of Paris in 1273. The work is structured around an allegorical understanding of the six days of creation, culminating in the seventh day of Sabbath rest and an eighth day (repeating the first) of resurrection. The six days provide the framework for discussing a rich theology of history, describing various stages of history and the various levels of knowledge and contemplation that, in principle, would have culminated in the beatific vision of the seventh day. This provides the context for the development of a profound theology of revelation. Because of Bonaventure's appointment to the episcopacy and his work in preparation for the Council of Lyons, the collations were left incomplete, bringing his listeners and later readers to the fourth day and leaving only hints as to what the final two days might represent as stages of history and as levels of contemplative experience.

More recent biblical studies have frequently compared the biblical account of the six days of creation with the Babylonian epic *Enuma Elish.* A critical reading of both leads many to the conclusion that there is no extensive relation between them. The biblical text, with its description of eight acts of creation spread over six days of divine creativity followed by the seventh day of Sabbath rest, reflects a distinctly biblical theology that has virtually no parallel in the Babylonian text.

In nineteenth and twentieth centuries, the six-day account of creation has been the object of much controversy concerning the relation between science and the Bible. Originally much of this was triggered by the theory of Charles Darwin concerning the evolution of species and particularly concerning the origin of the human race. More recently the conflict relates to the wider sense of the nature and development of the cosmos as a whole and not simply to theories of biological evolution. When the biblical text is taken to be a realistic description of the initial phase of cosmic history, it is seen by some to stand in radical contradiction to the contemporary scientific views on cosmic and human origins. But when the same text is read in the light of historical criticism, it is possible to distinguish between the religious message of the Bible and the physical cosmology assumed by the redactor of the present text. From this perspective, there seems to be no necessary conflict between the message of the Bible and the views of the contemporary sciences.

Bibliography: J. QUASTEN, *Patrology,* v. 3 (Westminter, Md. 1986). J. RATZINGER, *The Theology of History in St. Bonaventure,* tr. Z. HAYES (Chicago 1971). R. L. NUMBERS, *The Creationists: The Evolution of Scientific Creationism* (Berkeley 1992).

[Z. HAYES]

HEXAPLA

The body of manuscript evidence compiled by ORIGEN at CAESAREA IN PALESTINE before A.D. 245 for comparison of the existing Greek versions of the OT with the Hebrew text current in his day. The name (τά ἑξαπλᾶ, i.e., βιβλία, the sixfold books) derives from the arrangement given to the pages of this work by Origen. For most of the OT books, he presented in six parallel vertical columns (1) the Hebrew consonantal text in Hebrew letters; (2) a spelling out of the Hebrew as actually pronounced, insofar as that could be represented with the Greek alphabet; (3) the rendering of Aquila; (4) the rendering of Symmachus; (5) the ancient Septuagint (LXX) rendering, modified in the light of the Hebrew and the Greek of the other columns, with critical symbols (see below) to call attention to ways in which the older Greek form and the Hebrew failed to agree; and (6) the early revision of the LXX ascribed to Theodotion. For some books, Origen had available added translations or recensions, so that in the Psalms, for instance, mention is made of a *Quinta* (fifth), a *Sexta* (sixth), and even a *Septima* (seventh) Greek rendering by unknown hands; the number of columns would correspondingly increase from six to at least eight. (The *Septima,* however, may never have been more than marginal notes.) The Hexapla was thus a complex and bulky work; it remained available for consultation at Caesarea until about A.D. 600 and was used by St. Jerome among others. Copies of it were mainly by way of extracts. Origen himself is said to have prepared an abridged edition (*Tetrapla,* fourfold) omitting the two Hebrew columns. The final fate of the complete work is unknown; today it survives only in fragments from the Books of Kingdoms (Samuel and Kings) and the Psalms, along with excerpts in the margins of Greek LXX MSS, citations in the patristic literature in several languages, and extensive portions of the fifth column, especially in Syriac and Arabic translations. The recompiling and critical evaluation of these materials is one of the continuing tasks of students of the LXX; attribution of a particular reading to one or another of the original columns is often either lacking or given incorrectly in the sources.

The Hebrew in Origen's first column was, like all other Hebrew OT texts from the early second Christian century onward, extremely close to the consonantal text as printed in the Hebrew Bibles of today. The second column transliteration is sufficiently consistent in its orthography (*see* G. Mercati, ''Il problema . . .'') so that one must suppose that in this form it was contemporary with Origen. It has been shrewdly conjectured, however, (T. W. Manson, cited by Kahle), that this kind of transcription is at least the heir to a Jewish practice of providing a reader's guide in Greek letters to the liturgical sections to be proclaimed from Hebrew scrolls in the synagogues of the DIASPORA. That the LXX translation was originally made from transliterations of this sort rather than from a Hebrew consonantal text is a quite fanciful theory; the true interest of the second column for modern scholars is its pre-Masoretic evidence for the historical pronunciation of biblical Hebrew. In editing the fifth or LXX column, Origen inserted, marked with an asterisk, usually from ''Theodotion,'' the Greek equivalent of those passages in the Hebrew text not to be found in the older translation. Passages in the LXX for which the Hebrew showed no equivalent were retained, but signaled at the beginning with an obelus. The limits of either type of variant text were marked at the end by a metobelus. There is some question whether this apparatus was employed in the Hexapla itself (the Mercati Psalm fragments do not show it), or whether it was used in a resultant text drawn from the fifth column for separate circulation.

That the Hebrew text of his own day should have served as Origen's exclusive norm leaves something to be desired from the point of view of modern textual criticism; but the invaluable collection of materials is none the less precious on that account. It is simply not true, however, that this was the first critical work done on the OT in Greek; Origen was heir to a continuing process of revision carried on in Jewish circles in Palestine, both in Hebrew and in Greek, during the first century B.C. and the first and early second Christian centuries. Sometimes the basis for the fifth column was not an unrevised LXX, but the product of ''Theodotion,'' or even, for Ecclesiastes, of Aquila. Nor was the arrangement of the columns invariable throughout the OT; in the case of Ecclesiastes, when the ''LXX'' column was occupied by Aquila's work, the third column apparently contained Symmachus, and this has led to faulty attributions by later writers. In the Psalms, the *Quinta* seems to have occupied the customary place of ''Theodotion.'' From 2 Sm 11.2 to 1 Kgs 2.11, ''Theodotion'' stands in the fifth column and a ''Lucianic'' text in the sixth. Abridged transcriptions of the Hexapla after the time of Origen have led to further inconsistencies in the evidence for the content of the various columns.

Bibliography: F. FIELD, *Origenis Hexaplorum quae supersunt,* 2 v. (Oxford 1875). G. MERCATI, *Psalterii hexapli reliquiae* (Vatican City 1958–) v. 1; ''Il problema della seconda colonna dell' Esaplo,'' *Biblica* 28 (1947) 1–30, 173–215. D. BARTHÉLEMY, *Les Devanciers d'Aquila* (*Vetus Testamentum* Suppl. 10; 1963). P. KAHLE, ''Die von Origenes verwendeten griechischen Bibelhandschriften,'' *Studia patristica* 4 (*Texte und Untersuchungen Zur Geschichte der altchristlichen Literatur* 79; 1961) 107–117. H. B. SWETE, *An Introduction to the O.T. in Greek* (rev. ed. Cambridge, Eng. 1914) 59–86.

[P. W. SKEHAN]

HEXATEUCH

A term derived from the Greek, meaning six-roll, and applied to the first six books of the Old Testament. Literary analysis suggested the continuation of the four sources of the PENTATEUCH into the book of JOSHUA. Also, since the theme of the promise of the land is predominant throughout the Pentateuch, a theological truncation would result if those books were isolated from Joshua, where the theme of promise finds its fulfillment in the conquest. More recent studies have cast serious doubts on the theory of a Hexateuch.

Bibliography: D. N. FREEDMAN, *The Interpreters' Dictionary of the Bible*, ed. G. A. BUTTRICK (Nashville 1962) 2:597–598. *Encyclopedic Dictionary of the Bible*, tr. and adap. by L. HARTMAN (New York 1963) 996.

[E. H. MALY]

HEXHAM, MONASTERY OF

Former monastery of BENEDICTINES, then Austin canons, at Hexham, in Northumbria, England. The Benedictine abbey there was founded *c.* 673 by WILFRID, Archbishop of York, and grew rapidly in importance. Five years after the foundation of the abbey, the church of Hexham became the cathedral of the new Diocese of Bernicia, but *c.* 821 this bishopric was united to that of LINDISFARNE. Hexham was destroyed in the course of the Danish invasions in the following century, but was rebuilt, probably in 1113, as a priory of CANONS REGULAR OF ST. AUGUSTINE. The priory was dissolved in 1536 under King HENRY VIII, when the last prior was hanged for his involvement in the PILGRIMAGE OF GRACE. Today the town of Hexham is famous for the priory church, now the parish church of St. Andrew, which is all that remains of the monastery.

Bibliography: W. DUGDALE, *Monasticon Anglicanum* (London 1655–73); best ed. by J. CALEY et al., 6 v. (1817–30) 6.1:179–185. J. RAINE, ed., *The Priory of Hexham, Its Chroniclers, Endowments, and Annals*, 2 v. (Surtees Society 44 and 46; Durham 1864–65). C. C. HODGES, *Ecclesia Hagustaldensis. The Abbey of St. Andrew, Hexham* (privately printed; London 1888). D. KNOWLES and R. N. HADCOCK, *Medieval Religious Houses: England and Wales* (New York 1953) 140. D. KNOWLES, *The Monastic Order in England, 943–1216* (2d ed. Cambridge, Eng. 1962), *passim.* D. KNOWLES, *The Religious Orders in England*, 3 v. (Cambridge, Eng. 1948–60).

[J. BRÜCKMANN]

Hexham Abbey, Northumbria, England. (©Ric Ergenbright/ CORBIS)

HEYTHROP COLLEGE

Heythrop College originated in the Jesuit scholasticates in penal times at Louvain (1614–24) and Liège (1624–1794). In the wake of the French Revolution, the faculties moved to England; eventually the philosophy faculty (St. Mary's Hall, Stonyhurst) and the theology faculty (St. Beuno's, North Wales) were united in 1926 at Heythrop, Oxfordshire, eventually becoming a Pontifical Atheneum (1965–69). This status changed when, by Royal Charter, it became a college of the University of London in 1970, with F. C. Copleston, SJ, as its first principal. It has retained its Jesuit and Catholic identity, with strong ecumenical and interfaith dimensions, within the federal University of London, awarding degrees of the university. Its library, one of the finest in Britain and the property of the British Jesuit province, contains 300,000 volumes; professors number about 35 and students 530. Publications include the *Heythrop Journal, Heythrop Studies in Contemporary Philosophy, Religion and Theology, Bellarmine Series and Commentary, and Heythrop Monographs.*

Bibliography: F. COURTNEY, ''English Jesuit Colleges in the Low Countries 1593–1794,'' *Heythrop Journal* 4 (1963) 254–263.

[J. MCDADE]

HEYWOOD

An English family distinguished for its fidelity to the Catholic Church and for its literary activity, especially during the reigns of the Henrys and Elizabeth I.

John, poet and playwright; b. Coventry, *c.* 1497; d. 1579?. He is the most famous member of this family, and

North facade of the Heythrop Pontifical Athenaeum.

is said to have attended Oxford University, but there are no records. For some years after 1519 he was a singer and musician at court. By 1523 he had married Joan Rastell, the only daughter of John Rastell and niece of Thomas More. They had six children: two sons, Ellis and Jasper, and four daughters, one of whom, Elizabeth, was the mother of John DONNE.

In 1533–34 four of Heywood's plays were printed by William Rastell: *A Play of Love, The Pardoner and the Frere, The Play of the Wether,* and *Johan the husbande, Johan Tyb the wife and Syr Johan the preeste*—these are indisputably Heywood's. Two other plays are attributed to him: *The Foure PP* and *Wytty and Wyttles.*

During the latter part of the reign of Henry VIII and the brief reigns of Edward VI and Mary, Heywood was prominent in dramatic and entertainment activities. At least five interludes, plays, and masques were written by him during this time, but nothing is known of them save the title of one (*King Arthur's Knights*). A certain amount of Heywood's writing was addressed to Queen Mary, whose favorite he was; his graceful ''Description of a Most Noble Lady'' (''Geve place, ye Ladyes'') was written for her in 1534, when she was 18 and under a political cloud. His long poem, *The Spider and the Flie* (an allegory of some 7,600 lines, published in 1556), seems to celebrate Mary's liberation of Catholicism (the entrapped ''flie'') in England; the crushing of the spider perhaps represents Thomas CRANMER, who was burned at the stake in 1556. The allegory is obscure and the work is now little read.

As a result of the Elizabethan Settlement in 1564, Heywood and many other English Catholics went into exile in the Low Countries. In 1576 his son Ellis obtained special permission for him to lodge at the Jesuit college at Antwerp. He lived there through many disturbances in 1578, and seems to have died about 1579 or 1580.

As the author of widely quoted collections of proverbs and epigrams, and a famous wit, John Heywood was well known during the Elizabethan period. His interludes have been produced with success in the 20th century (especially at Birmingham-Malvern, England), and their historical importance in the history of the Tudor interlude, though generally recognized, has only in recent times been adequately understood.

Ellis, son of John; b. London *c.* 1530; d. Louvain, the Low Countries, Oct. 2, 1578. He studied civil law at Oxford, and received the degree of B.C.L. in 1552, having become a fellow of All Souls College (then a center for legal studies) in 1548. Leaving England (*c.* 1554–55) for travel in France and Italy, he served for some time as a secretary to Cardinal Reginald POLE, to whom he dedicated his *Il Moro* in 1556. He entered the Society of Jesus in 1566, and later became spiritual father and preacher in the Jesuit college at Antwerp. As chief executor and beneficiary of William Rastell (d. 1565), Ellis deeded his inheritance to Jesuit educational work at Louvain, Cologne, and Munich.

Jasper, son of John; b. London, 1535; d. Naples, Jan. 9, 1598. He was sent to Oxford in 1547 at the youthful age of 12, and took his B.A. in 1553 and his M.A. in 1558. In 1554 he was made a fellow of Merton College (also, the last Lord of Misrule) and served with distinction there until he was elected a fellow of All Souls in 1558. He resigned from All Souls in 1558 or 1559 because of his recusancy, and in 1561 entered Gray's Inn, but he left within the year to go abroad. Jasper is known for his translations of three Senecan tragedies (published 1559, 1560, 1561); T. S. Eliot has called him ''the first and best of the translators'' of Seneca. This work reveals Jasper as the associate of Thomas Sackville, Thomas North, and William Baldwin, all men of the Inns who were making distinguished contributions to Tudor literature.

After leaving England Jasper was admitted into the Society of Jesus at Rome in 1562. At Dillingen, in Bavaria, he took the degree of doctor of divinity. He was sent into England for missionary work, and arrived in the summer of 1581; he was imprisoned in 1583 and then exiled (1584–85). In 1589 he was sent to Rome, then to Naples, where he died.

See Also: RECUSANTS.

Bibliography: E. HEYWOOD, *Il moro d'Heivodo* (Florence 1556). W. BANG, ''Acta Anglo-Lovaniensia: John Heywood und sein Kreis,'' *Englische Studien* 38 (1907) 234–249. H. DE VOCHT, ed., *Jasper Heywood and His Translation of Seneca's Troas, Thyestes, and Hercules* (Materialen zur Kunde des älteren englischen Dramas 41; Louvain 1913). H. FOLEY, ed., *Records of the English Province of the Society of Jesus,* 7 v. (London 1877–1882) 1:388. R. J. SCHOECK, ''Anthony Bonvisi, the Heywoods and the Ropers,'' *Notes and Queries* 197 (April 26, 1952) 178–179; ''Satire of Wolsey in Heywood's 'Play of Love','' *ibid.,* 196 (March 17, 1951) 112–114. T. S. GRAVES, ''The Heywood Circle and the Reformation,'' *Modern Philology* 10 (1912–13) 553–572; ''On the Reputation of John Heywood,'' *ibid.* 21 (1923–24) 209–213. R. G. W. BOLWELL, *The Life and Works of John Heywood* (New York 1921). I. C. MAXWELL, *French Farce and John Heywood* (Melbourne 1946). A. W. REED, *Early Tudor Drama* (London 1926).

[R. J. SCHOECK]

John Heywood, woodcut in ''The Spider and the Flie,'' 1556.

HIBERNENSIS COLLECTIO

The conventional name of the comprehensive canonical collection of the Irish Church. It is approximately dated 700 by reason of the latest authors it refers to (Theodore of Canterbury, Adamnan of Iona); the absence of references to the Venerable Bede; and the deaths of its (probable) compilers, Rubin of Dair-Inis (d. 725) and Cú-Chuime of Iona (d. 747).

It draws largely on the Bible, especially the Old Testament; on the Fathers of the Church, probably via a collection of *sententiae* [see S. Hellmann, *Sedulius Scottus* (Munich 1906) 136–144], including some Greeks (Origen, Gregory of Nazianzus, Basil, the *Vitae Patrum*); on the *STATUTA ECCLESIAE ANTIQUA* and other conciliar and synodal decrees, but rarely on papal decretals. Native sources include the acts (otherwise unknown) of Irish synods and Irish ecclesiastical writers beginning with St. Patrick. The synods referred to as *Synodus Romana,* or by some other similar term, are probably synods of the Roman faction of the Irish Church in the 7th century as opposed to the Celtic faction [J. B. Bury, *Life of St. Patrick* (London 1905) 235–239].

Contrary to the predominantly chronological arrangement of earlier collections, the 65 chapters of the *Hibernensis* are arranged according to subject matter, but not in a systematic order. The collection treats of the duties and privileges of the ecclesiastical grades; the relations of monks, secular clergy, and laity; liturgy and devotion; morals; ecclesiastical and, to some extent, secular law. The treatment breathes the spirit of reform of morals and discipline that was then strong in Ireland. The compilers attempted also to adjust their authorities to the peculiar pattern of Irish ecclesiastical, political, and social life. There are, e.g., no decrees concerning diocesan episcopal jurisdiction, for this had no place in the predominantly monastic Church of the 7th- and 8th-century Ireland; the Jewish jubilee year is considered as a limit for the validity of uncertain titles, and the parties to a contract are advised to have it made out in writing; the term ''cities of refuge'' refers to monasteries (called *civitates* in Ireland, then a country without towns), and the prerogatives of the monasteries are stated in patristic and canonical terms.

Because of its reformatory spirit, its comprehensiveness, and its practical arrangement, the *Hibernensis* had considerable influence on the Continent of Europe after the 8th century. It was frequently used by the compilers of canonical collections down to the 12th century.

See Also: CANONICAL COLLECTIONS BEFORE GRATIAN.

Bibliography: F. W. H. WASSERSCHLEBEN, *Die irische Kanonensammlung* (2d ed. Leipzig 1885). J. F. KENNEY, *The Sources for the Early History of Ireland* (New York 1929) 247–250, with bibliog. Fournier-LeBras 1:62–64.

[L. BIELER]

HICKEY, ANTONY

Irish Franciscan theologian and historian; b. County Clare, 1586; d. St. Isidore's College, Rome, June 26, 1641. Hickey received his early education in his native place. On Nov. 1, 1607, he entered the Franciscans at St. Anthony's College, Louvain, and studied there under Hugh WARD and Hugh MacCaghwell. After ordination he was a professor of theology at Louvain and at St. Francis, Cologne. In 1619 he was called to Rome to collaborate with the historian Luke WADDING. He resided at the Spanish friary of S. Pietro in Montorio on the Janiculum, but on the founding of St. Isidore's College he moved there on June 22, 1625, and became the college's first lector of theology. He was active on many Roman Congregations and on commissions set up for the revision of the Roman Breviary and of the Greek and Armenian liturgies. A stanch Scotist, he defended the Immaculate Conception with ardor. Wadding's edition of the works of Scotus includes three volumes of commentaries by Hickey on bk. 4 of the *Sentences.* In 1639 he was chosen definitor general of the Franciscan Order, and for a time he was titular provincial of Scotland. His *Nitela Franciscanae Religionis* (Lyons 1627) deals with aspects of the early history of the order.

Bibliography: G. CLEARY, *Father Luke Wadding and St. Isidore's College, Rome* (Rome 1925) 73–78. B. JENNINGS, ed., *Wadding Papers, 1614–1638* (Dublin 1953) 168, 219, 240–241, 269, 557, 558, 573, 606, 610, 614, 622. É. D'ALENÇON, *Dictionnaire de théologie catholique*, ed. A. VACANT et al. (Paris 1903—50) 6.2: 2358–59.

[C. GIBLIN]

HICKEY, JOSEPH ALOYSIUS

Prior general of the Order of St. Augustine; b. Chicago, Ill., May 30,1883; d. Villanova, Pa., July 9, 1955. His parents, James and Margaret (Dawson) Hickey, died while Joseph was a child, and he was raised by Maurice J. Dorney, pastor of St. Gabriel's Church in Chicago. For his secondary and college education Hickey went to Villanova College (now University), where he joined the Augustinians. He made his profession on March 18, 1903, and the following year he was sent to the Augustinian International College of St. Monica in Rome, where he was ordained on Dec. 22, 1906. Two years later he earned the degree of doctor of Canon Law at the Apollinaris. On his return to the U.S., he was assigned briefly to Chicago. Following a provincial chapter in 1910, he went to the principal Augustinian community at Villanova, where between 1910 and 1925, he became rector of postulants, provincial representative at the general chapter in Rome (1913), regent of studies, provincial definitor (counselor), provincial secretary, prior of the seminary Corr Hall, and president of Villanova College. At a general chapter in 1925 in Rome, Hickey was elected fourth assistant general. He held this office for more than 20 years, during which time he also held posts as rector of the International College and professor of Canon Law at The Catholic University of America, Washington, D.C. On April 26, 1947, he was elected prior general, becoming the first U.S. Augustinian to hold that office. As prior general (1947–53) he was responsible for reorganizing the Augustinian Order during the aftermath of World War II, especially in Italy. He performed also numerous services in Rome for both the Holy See and the Augustinian Order, acting as consultor, later as commissary, of the Congregation of the Sacraments, and as apostolic visitator to several religious communities. Upon completion of his term of office he returned to the U.S.

[A. J. ENNIS]

HIDALGO Y COSTILLA, MIGUEL

The father of Mexican Independence; b. at the Hacienda of Corralejo, Guanajuato, May 8, 1753; d. Chihuahua, July 30, 1811. He was educated in Valladolid (now Morelia, Michoacán) in the Colegio de San Francisco Javier. When the Jesuits were expelled in 1767, he went to the Colegio do San Nicolás. He graduated with a bachelor's degree from the University of Mexico in 1773 and, although he had no vocation for the priesthood, was ordained in 1778. Between 1779 and 1782 he taught philosophy and theology at San Nicolás. In 1784 he presented the ''Disertación sobre el verdadero método de estudiar teología,'' in which his revolutionary spirit was already apparent. In 1791 he was rector at San Nicolás. In 1792 he was banished from Valladolid to the distant parish of Colima because of numerous accusations of heretical opinions and scandal. In 1793 he was transferred to the parish of San Felipe, Guanajuato, where he translated and produced the works of Molière and Racine. As a reader of the Encyclopedists and an admirer of the ideas of the Enlightenment, he was tried by the Inquisition in July 1800 but was not sentenced at that time. In October 1808 he received the parish of Dolores, where he devoted his efforts to the economic and intellectual improvement of the people of his parish on the principles of the Enlightenment. He gave parties, organized an orchestra, and established in his house, in the guise of a school of arts and crafts, several small industries. He cultivated silkworms, raised bees, and planted vineyards. He won the affection of his parishioners, and in his constant travels to nearby places he made friends with the most important persons. In July 1807, because of new accusations, the inquisitorial trial was resumed.

In 1810 Hidalgo was the principal figure on the Junta of Querétaro and, early Sunday morning, Sept. 16, 1810, he raised the famous ''Cry of Dolores,'' which marked the beginning of the struggle for independence. That same day, on the way to San Miguel el Grande, in Atotonilco, he gave his troops as standard the image of Our Lady of GUADALUPE. At nightfall he entered San Miguel, where the undisciplined horde accompanying him looted the city, as they later did Celaya, Guanajuato, and Valladolid. On September 21 he arrived in Celaya and was named a general there. September 24 an edict of excommunication was published against Hidalgo and his companions. Yet on they went. Guanajuato was taken on September 28, Valladolid on October 17, and two days later Hidalgo and his forces set out for Mexico City. On October 30 he defeated the royalist forces at Monte de las Cruces, but instead of attacking the capital then, he retreated toward Querétaro. On November 7 he was defeated in Aculco by Gen. Félix María Calleja del Rey. Hidalgo withdrew to Valladolid and then to Guadalajara late in November. There he put on the uniform of a generalissimo and assumed the title of Excellency or Most Serene Highness. He conferred titles and decorations and decreed the abolition of slavery. He started the publication of the periodical *El Despertador Americano* and ordered the secret execution of 400 Spanish prisoners. He appointed Pascasio Ortiz de Letona as ambassador to the U.S. On Jan. 16, 1811, he again met General Calleja in the battle of Puente de Calderón. The insurgents were completely defeated and their troops dispersed. Hidalgo retreated to Aguascalientes, where he was joined by Iriarte's army, and they headed toward Zacatecas. On January 25 Allende caught up with Hidalgo, deprived him of command, and took him prisoner. They then headed north for the frontier, hoping to find refuge in the U.S. They were surprised and arrested by the royalist officer Ignacio Elizondo in Acatita de Baján and sent to Chihuahua.

Hidalgo had two trials, ecclesiastical and military. As a result of the first he was unfrocked July 29, 1811. The military trial sent him to death before a firing squad the next day. The corpse was decapitated and his head and those of Allende, Aldama, and Jiménez were placed in iron cages and taken to Guanajuato, where they were hung in the four corners of the public granary.

Miguel Hidalgo y Costilla.

Bibliography: L. CASTILLO LEDÓN, *Hidalgo: La vida del héroe.* 2 v. (Mexico City 1948–49).

[E. DEL HOYO]

HIDULF, SS.

Name of two saints who lived in the late seventh and early eighth centuries.

Hidulf of Regensburg, founder of MOYENMOUTIER; d. July 11 *c.* 707. He was a monk at Saint-Maximin in Trier, later CHORBISHOP in the diocese, and finally a hermit in the Vosges Mountains around whom other hermits gathered to form the abbey of Moyenmoutier. He was chosen as the secondary patron of the 17th-century Benedictine congregation of Saint-Vanne et Saint-Hydulphe.

Feast: July 11.

Hidulf of Lobbes, count of Hainaut, monk; d. June 23, 707. A Frankish noble and close friend of Pepin of Heristal, he aided SS. LANDELIN and URSMAR in the foundation of the abbey of LOBBES (province of Hainaut, Belgium), where he ended his days as a monk with the consent of his wife, St. Aya (Austregildis or Agia; d. *c.* 714).

Feast: June 23.

Bibliography: *Acta Sanctorum* July 3:211–226. J. MABILLON, *Acta sanctorum ordinis S. Benedicti,* 9 v. (Paris 1668–1701; 2d ed. Venice 1733–40) 4:432–440. *Patrologia Latina,* ed. J. P. MIGNE, 217 v. (Paris 1878–90) 151:587–606. *Monumenta Germaniae Scriptores* (Berlin 1825–) 4:56. *Bibliotheca hagiographica latina antiquae ct mediae aetatis,* 2 v. (Brussels 1898–1901; suppl. 1911) 1:3945–52 (Suppl. 3949b–52b). A. POTTHAST, *Bibliotheca historica medii aevi* (2d ed. 1896; repr. Graz 1954) 2:1369. A. MICHEL, ''Die Frühwerke des Kardinals Humbert-über Hidulf . . . ,'' *Zeitschrift für Kirchengeschichte* 64 (1952–53) 225–259.

[C. DAVIS]

HIERARCHY OF TRUTHS

The term ''hierarchy of truths'' refers to the order and relationship that Christian doctrines have with one another. While the expression came into common theological usage at VATICAN COUNCIL II, the basic idea of a differentiation in the scale and value of individual truths has long been recognized in various ways by theologians.

The *Decree on Ecumenism* of Vatican Council II advised Catholic theologians engaged in ecumenical dialogue: ''when comparing doctrines, they should remember that in Catholic teaching there exists an order or hierarchy of truths, since they vary in their relationship to the foundation of the Christian faith'' (ch. 2.11). This idea originated in a speech given by Archbishop Andrea Pangrazio of Gorizia-Gradisca (Italy):

> . . . to arrive at a fair estimate of both the unity which now exists among Christians and the diversity which still remains, it seems very important to me to pay close attention to the hierarchical order of revealed truths which express the mystery of Christ and those elements which make up the Church.
>
> Although all the truths revealed by divine faith are to be believed with the same divine faith and all those elements which make up the Church must be kept with equal fidelity, not all of them are of equal importance [*Council Speeches of Vatican II,* p. 191].

Distinguishing between truths *on the level of our final goal* (such as the Trinity or Incarnation) and truths *on the level of means toward salvation* (such as the sevenfold number of Sacraments or apostolic succession), Pangrazio thought that

> doctrinal differences among Christians have less to do with these primary truths on the level of our final goal, and deal mostly with truths on the level of means, which are subordinate to those other primary truths.

Since Vatican II did not explain the meaning of hierarchy of truths, its usage has varied since the Council. The second part of the *Ecumenical Directory,* issued by the Secretariat for Promoting Christian Unity (April 16, 1970), identified the hierarchy of truths in terms of the relationship of a particular truth to the foundations of Christian faith, but also distinguished between ''revealed truths'' and ''theological doctrines'' (ch. 2.5). The Secretariat's *Reflections and Suggestions Concerning Ecumenical Dialogue* (Sept. 18, 1970) apparently distinguishes between a hierarchy of truths based on their different relationships to the foundation of Christian faith, and another hierarchy of truths related to the actual life of the Church. Accordingly, the position of a given doctrine in the life of Christians may differ from its theoretical place in relation to Christian foundations (ch. 4.4).

Similarly, a number of different emphases regarding the hierarchy of truths can be found in contemporary theological discussion. For example, some continue to categorize truths on the basis of the degree of their explicitness in scripture or the teaching of the Church. Others evaluate truths on the basis of their necessity for salvation. Still others contrast ''nuclear'' beliefs which are basic to the psychological functioning of a person's belief-system with ''peripheral'' beliefs which have few ramifications in a person's life.

Insofar as various principles of ordering or evaluating truths are available or possible, theologians can construct different hierarchies of truths, so that the position of a particular revelatory truth might then vary from one hierarchy to another.

See Also: TRUTH; ECUMENICAL MOVEMENT.

Bibliography: A. PANGRAZIO, ''The Mystery of the History of the Church,'' in H. Küng, et al., *Council Speeches of Vatican II* (Glen Rock, N.J. 1964) 188–192. G. TAVARD, ''Hierarchi veritatum,'' *Theological Studies* 32 (1971) 278–289. D. CARROLL, '''Hierarchia veritatum': A Theological and Pastoral Insight of the Second Vatican Council,'' *Irish Theological Quarterly* 44 (1977) 125–133. W. HENN, *The Hierarchy of Truths according to Yves Congar, O.P.* (Rome 1987).

[J. T. FORD]

HIERONYMITES (LOS JERÓNIMOS)

Name given to various congregations of the 14th and 15th centuries in Spain and Italy.

The Spanish Congregation of Hermits of St. JEROME, known as Hieronymites or Jerónimos, was organized by Pedro Fernandez Pecha, the royal chamberlain, who died in 1374. On October 18 of the previous year Pope Gregory XI had given his approbation to the order. Soon it established numerous houses throughout Spain. Among the most important were San Bartholomé de Lupiana, near

Toledo; Guadalupe in the province of Cáceres; San Jerónimo el Real in Madrid; Yuste in the province of Guadalajara, to which CHARLES V retired in 1555; San Lorenzo del ESCORIAL, the palace monastery erected by Philip II outside Madrid; and others in Seville and Granada. In 1499 King Manuel of Portugal established the Hieronymites in the monastery of Belen. A community of Hieronymite nuns was founded by María Garcías (d. 1426) in the convent of San Pablo in Toledo and survived until the suppression of 1835 by the Spanish government. The Hieronymites followed the rule of St. AUGUSTINE, under the direction of a general elected every three years by a general chapter. Each convent retained a high degree of autonomy. The observance was quite strict. The habit consisted of a white tunic, a brown scapular, a capuche, and a mantle worn in the choir and outside the monastery. Black was later adopted as the color of the scapular and mantle. The Hieronymites were highly influential in the spiritual and cultural work of the Church during the late 15th and 16th century. They also participated in the evangelization of the New World. One of the most distinguished Hieronymites, Hernando de Talavera, served as confessor to ISABELLA the Catholic and after the conquest of Granada in 1492 became the first archbishop of that city. His conciliatory policy toward the Muslims, however, was unacceptable to more intransigent Spanish clerics. PHILIP II succeeded in uniting all the Hieronymite monasteries in the peninsula under a single superior, but problems of organization and discipline became acute in later days. In 1780 King Charles III obtained from the Holy See broad authority to solve these problems. Suppressed in 1835, together with other religious orders, the Hieronymites began (1957) to reestablish themselves in Segovia.

Entirely independent congregations of hermits of St. Jerome included those of Fiesole, organized by Carlo de Montegranelli (d. 1417); the congregation of Peter Gambacorta of Pisa (d. 1435); and the Observants or congregation of Lombardy, founded by Lope de Olmedo (d. 1433), who was a former general of the Spanish congregation.

Bibliography: P. DE LA VEGA, *Cronica de los frayles de la orden del bienaventurado sant Hieronymo* (Alcalá 1539). F. A. DE MONTALVO, *Historia general de la Orden de San Gerónimo* (Salamanca 1704). IGNACIO DE MADRID, ''La Orden de San Jerónimo en España. Primeros pasos para una historia crítica,'' *Studia monastica* 3 (1961) 409–427.

[J. F. O'CALLAGHAN]

Entrance to the monastery of the Hieronymites, photograph by Eric Dluhosch. (©MIT Collection/CORBIS)

HIGH CHURCH

High Church is a term applied to the party within the Anglican Communion in general, and the Church of England in particular, that has sought to minimize the Protestantism of the Anglican Communion and to stress its continuity with the Catholic Church of the Middle Ages. It has fostered a ''high'' view of the nature of the Church, and especially since the 19th century, a reverence for retrieval of ancient liturgical usages and the acceptance of the sacerdotal nature of the ministerial priesthood. One of their earliest leaders was William LAUD, archbishop of Canterbury (1633–45). In the 17th century this group supported the theory of the DIVINE RIGHT OF KINGS as applied to the Stuarts, and the JACOBITES. Devotion to the latter cause led some into schism in the 18th century as NON–JURORS. In the 19th century the tradition was taken up by followers of TRACTARIANISM and the OXFORD MOVEMENT. The High Church party, successors of the Tractarians, remain a distinctive group. Many of their clerical members have adopted Catholic practices on a large scale. Their Sunday Eucharist, for example, is practically identical to that of a Catholic Mass.

See Also: ANGLICANISM; BROAD CHURCH; LOW CHURCH.

William Laud. (©CORBIS)

Bibliography: G. W. O. ADDLESHAW, *The High Church Tradition: A Study in the Liturgical Thought of the Seventeenth Century* (London 1941). B. E. STEINER, *Samuel Seabury, 1729–1796: A Study in the High Church Tradition* (Athens, Ohio 1971). R. B. MULLIN, *Episcopal Vision/American Reality: High Church Theology and Social Thought in Evangelical America* (New Haven 1986). K. HYLSON-SMITH, *High Churchmanship in the Church of England: From the Sixteenth Century to the Late Twentieth Century* (Edinburgh 1993). R. D. CORNWALL, *Visible and Apostolic: The Constitution of the Church in High Church Anglican and Non–Juror Thought* (Newark/London 1993).

[E. MCDERMOTT/EDS.]

HIGH PRIEST

The High Priest was the head of the priestly hierarchy in postexilic Israel who exercised supreme authority over the Temple, worship, and Temple personnel at Jerusalem. He was the mediator par excellence between God and the people, and the most important of his duties was the carrying out of the expiation rites on the Day of Atonement (Lv 16.1–34); he also shared in the general duties of the priesthood in the Temple. Because of his liturgical position, a more than customary ritual purity was demanded of him (see Lv 21.1–23), and he was expected to remain as close as possible to the Temple; this is probably why his residence was in the Temple area (Neh 3.20). Descriptions of the vestments of the high priest are given in Ex 29.5–9, 39.1–31; Lv 8.7–9; and Sir 45.8–13. Most of this information comes from the postexilic descriptions of ''the sons of AARON'' in the Priestly Code (*see* PRIESTLY WRITERS, PENTATEUCHAL).

In preexilic Israel there was a priest at the head of the Jerusalem clergy, but he was apparently referred to simply as ''the priest'' (e.g., 1 Kgs 4.2; 2 Kgs 11.9), ''head priest'' (2 Kgs 25.18), or ''the priest, the head of the house of Zadoc'' (2 Chr 31.10); cf. the similar terms, ''the great one of the priests'' and ''the head of the priests'' in texts from Ras Shamra and in Phoenician inscriptions. The term high priest (Heb. *hakkōhēn haggādôl*) is found four times in preexilic material (2 Kgs 12.11; 22.4, 8; 23.4); but these occurrences seem to be later modifications of the text (cf. the Septuagint and the parallel texts in Chronicles), and the title high priest appears to be postexilic, being used at first only rarely but coming into common usage in the Greek period. The preexilic head of the priesthood did not have the importance or rank that the high priest had after the exile. The former had control over the clergy of Jerusalem only and was himself responsible to the king (2 Kgs 12.7; 16.10), who had supreme control over the Temple and its clergy.

Immediately after the exile the high priest JESHUA, SON OF JOZADAK, was in charge of the religious affairs of the Jerusalem community; and the Davidic governor Zerubbabel, whom the Persians had appointed, was in charge of temporal affairs. Later the Persians deprived Zerubbabel and his descendants of temporal power at Jerusalem and let the high priest alone administer both religious and temporal matters. From then on into the Greek period the high priest became increasingly a secular prince, regarded as the head of the nation and its representative before God, as the king had been in days gone by. During the period of the HASMONAEANS the high priest even took the title of king. With the end of the Hasmonaean dynasty and the advent of Herod the Great (37–4 B.C.), the office of high priest was at the disposal of the sovereign, who appointed and dismissed nominees at his own caprice. There were no less than 28 high priests between 37 B.C. and A.D. 70, and these and their families formed a priestly aristocracy, the group of CHIEF PRIESTS that is referred to so often in the NT.

Bibliography: *Encyclopedic Dictionary of the Bible,* tr. and adap. by L. HARTMAN (New York 1963), from A. VAN DEN BORN, *Bijbels Woordenboek*, 1002–05. R. ABBA, G. A. BUTTRICK, ed., *The Interpreters' Dictionary of the Bible,* 4 v. (Nashville 1962) 3:878,

886–887. L. GROLLENBERG, *Lexikon für Theologie und Kirche*, ed., J. HOFER and K. RAHNER, 10 v. (Freiburg 1957–65) 5:437–438. R. DE VAUX, *Ancient Israel, Its Life and Institutions,* tr. J. MC HUGH (New York 1961) 378, 397–403. T. J. MEEK, ''Aaronites and Zadokites,'' *American Journal of Semitic Languages and Literatures* 45 (1928–29) 149–166.

[A. G. WRIGHT]

HIGHER CRITICISM

A term first used by the Biblical scholar William Robertson Smith (1846–94) in his book *The Old Testament in the Jewish Church* [(Edinburgh 1881) 105] to distinguish the critical literary and historical study of the books of the Old and New Testaments from textual or lower criticism. Questions of authorship, time of composition, sources, theological content, purpose, and related matters are the concern of higher criticism. Textual, or lower criticism, deals primarily with the establishment of the text itself on the basis of a critical examination and comparison of readings found in MSS written in the original languages and in ancient versions. The new term was soon applied to similar critical, literary, and historical studies in the classics and other fields. However, it should be emphasized that the methods of higher criticism and their underlying principles were not new in themselves. The great classical scholar Richard BENTLEY (1662–1742) had really founded higher criticism in his exhaustive literary and historical investigation of the problems of the authorship and date of composition of the *Epistles of Phalaris.* In the area of Biblical studies, Richard SIMON (1638–1712), Jean ASTRUC, and Alexander GEDDES (1737–1802) were all pioneers in applying the method of higher criticism, at least in part, to the study of the Pentateuch and other parts of the Old Testament. Nineteenth-century scholars greatly elaborated the methods and principles of literary and historical criticism especially in their exhaustive investigations of Homer and the Bible. However, too many in both fields tended to adopt extreme positions that were not warranted by the limited and incomplete data on which they were based. Furthermore, in the case of leading Biblical critics, especially in Germany, many were rationalists whose approach to Biblical problems was often colored, as in the case of J. WELLHAUSEN, for example, by the principles of Hegelian dialectic. The term higher criticism was thus coined precisely at a time when its methods and results were being challenged by more conservative critics, and it acquired the bad reputation that it still has in certain quarters. However, despite its mistakes and its failures, its employment has led to revolutionary and positive advances in both the philological and Biblical fields. Its methods continue to be developed and refined, and, when applied properly, it is an indispensable instrument of literary and historical research. One may cite among its conspicuous successes, the solutions to the problems of the *FALSE DECRETALS,* the *SIBYLLINE ORACLES,* and the time, composition, and character of the works ascribed to Dionysius the Areopagite (*see* PSEUDO-DIONYSIUS). On the Biblical side, it will suffice to mention the great progress made in the interpretation of the Sacred Books by the recognition of their literary genres, their scope, and their purpose. It must be emphasized that the mistakes made in the past by an abuse of the methods of higher criticism have usually been corrected by a proper employment of its own methods.

Bibliography: T. BIRT, ''Höhere Kritik,'' in his *Kritik und Hermeneutik nebst Abriss des antiken Buchwesens* (Munich 1913) 213–242. G. GARRAGHAN, *A Guide to Historical Method* (New York 1946) 168–169. H. CAZALLES and P. GRELOT, ''La Critique littéraire,'' and ''La Critique historique,'' in *Introduction à la Bible*, A. ROBERT and A. FEUILLET, eds. (1959) 1:121–164.

[M. R. P. MCGUIRE]

HIJRA

The Prophet MUḤAMMAD's flight from Mecca (Makka) to Medina (Madna). In Arabic the word is *hiğra;* the related verb *hagara* means, properly, to depart from one's people or tribe, breaking off the ties of mutual obligation with them. The word is applied to Muḥammad's definitive break with Qurayš and his emigration, with his followers, from MECCA to MEDINA in September 622. This event, which followed a period of negotiations with representatives of the factions in Medina, marks the foundation of Islam as an autonomous political community with the prophet as its chief. During the reign of the Caliph 'Umar I (traditionally in the year A.H. 17), after some discussion of the problem of how documents were to be dated, it was decided to reckon from the year of the prophet's establishment at Medina (in Latin, *Annus Hegirae,* abbreviated A.H.). The era, however, was not made to begin with the Hijra itself, which took place in the month of Rabî' I, the third month of the Arabian calendar, but with al-Mu ḥarram, the first month of that year, since the calendar was already fixed.

See Also: CALENDARS OF THE ANCIENT NEAR EAST; ERAS, HISTORICAL.

[R. M. FRANK/EDS.]

HILARION, ST.

Fourth-century ascetic; b. Tabatha, southern Palestine, *c.* 291; d. Cyprus, *c.* 371. He was born of pagan par-

St. Hilarion putting a dragon to flight, detail of a fresco by the 14th-century Sienese artist Pietro Lorenzetti in the Camposanto, Pisa, Italy.

ents, studied with success under a grammarian at Alexandria, and became a Christian. The fame of St. ANTHONY OF EGYPT drew him into the wilderness, where he observed the way of life of that monastic founder. On his return to Palestine he inaugurated the eremitical life in the desert, some seven miles from Maiuma, near Gaza, on the road to Egypt. He progressed in self-conquest and the practice of virtue, and as time went on performed marvels. Through him many embraced the faith and many monasteries sprang up in Palestine, but little is known of their organization. Eventually his followers became so numerous that he sought solitude farther away and traveled to Egypt, Libya, Sicily, Dalmatia, and Cyprus, where he died. He has been especially venerated in Cyprus, Palestine, Venice, Pisa, and France. Much of the available knowledge of Hilarion comes from St. JEROME, who wrote the vita (*c.* 391) on a basis of historical fact but embellished with rhetorical and legendary features. Jerome cites a letter of EPIPHANIUS that mentions Hilarion, and SOZOMEN gives a short account of his life and names some of his companions (*Histoire Ecclesiastique* 3.14; 5.10.15; 6.32).

Feast: Oct. 21.

Bibliography: *Acta Sanctorum* (Paris 1863–) Oct. 9:16–59. *Synaxarium ecclesiae Constantinopolitanae. Propylaeum ad Acta sanctorum novembris,* ed. H. DELEHAYE (Brussels 1902) 153–154, *Bibliotheca hagiographica latina antiquae ct mediae aetatis,* 2 v. (Brussels 1898–1901; suppl. 1911) 1:579–580. *Bibliotheca hagiographica Graeca,* ed. F. HALKIN, 3 v. (Brussels 1957) l:751z–756n. *Patrologia Latina,* ed. J. P. MIGNE, 217 v. (Paris 1878–90) 23:30–54, *vita;* tr. M. L. EWALD in *Early Christian Biographies* (*The Fathers of the Church: A New Translation,* ed. R. J. DEFERRARI et al. 15; 1952) 241–280. H. LECLERCQ, *Dictionnaire d'archéologie chrétienneet de liturgie,* ed. F. CABROL, H. LECLERCQ and H. I. MARROU, 15 v. (Paris 1907–53) 2.2:3157–58. P.T. CAMELOT, *Catholicisme* 5:736. A. BUTLER, *The Lives of the Saints,* ed. H. THURSTON and D. ATTWATER, 4 v. (New York 1956) 4:163–165. R. AIGRAIN, *L'Hagiographie* (Paris 1953). L. RÉAU, *Iconographie de l'art chrétien,* 6 v. (Paris 1955–59) 3.2:649–650.

[F. MEEHAN]

HILARUS OF MENDE, ST.

Also known as Ilerus, Hilarius, bishop; d. *c.* 540. Little credence is to be given to the 10th- or 11th-century vita, according to which Hilarus lived as a hermit on the banks of the Tarn, making periodic visits to LÉRINS. A group of disciples gathered about him for whom he built a monastery, from which he was summoned to the See of Mende (Javols, *Civitas Gabalum*) sometime before 535. Of his episcopal activities the vita says nothing. Fortunatus records an instance of his hospitality in granting shelter to St. LEOBIN OF CHARTRES. The council signatures attest his attendance at the synod of Auvergne (Clermont) in 535.

Feast: Oct. 25.

Bibliography: *Acta Sanctorum* Oct. 11:619–638. *Vita s. Leobini, Monumenta Germaniae Auctores antiquissimi* (Berlin 1825–) 4.2:74. *Monumenta Germaniae Concilia* (Berlin 1825–) 1:70. *Bibliotheca hagiographica latina antiquae et mediae aetatis,* 2 v. (Brussels 1898–1901; suppl. 1911) 1:3910–12. J. L. BAUDOT and L. CHAUSSIN, *Vies des saints et des bienheueux selon l'ordre du calendrier avec l'historique des fêtes* (Paris 1935–56) 10:850–851, gives an extensive bibliog.

[G. M. COOK]

HILARY, POPE, ST.

Pontificate: Nov. 19, 461, to Feb. 29, 468. Hilary, successor to Leo the Great and archdeacon of the Roman Church, was a Sardinian by birth, whose father was Crispinus. As papal legate at the Robber Council of EPHESUS, he barely escaped when pursued by soldiers of DIOSCORUS, Patriarch of Alexandria, who was angered by his support of the Patriarch of Constantinople, FLAVIAN.

His pontificate was relatively quiet; the affairs of the Western Church occupied him. The barbarian Ricimer ruled in Italy, making and unmaking emperors at will. Hilary attempted to reestablish the vicariate of Arles over Gaul as in the days of Patroclus under Pope ZOSIMUS, but without success, as the Bishop Leontius was not eager to assume a vigorous role. When Ascanius, Metropolitan of Tarragona in Spain, appealed a complaint to him against Silvanus of Calahorra, the pope convened a council (Nov. 19, 465) in the church of S. Maria Maggiore. The Spanish bishops were notified by a synodal letter after the rights of the metropolitan were upheld. This was the first such council whose exact minutes, including the pope's allocution and the acclamations of the fathers, have come down to us; according to its regulations a dying bishop was prohibited from appointing his own successor.

Since Hilary attributed his escape at Ephesus to the intervention of St. John the Evangelist, when he became pope he built three chapels adjoining the Lateran Baptistry: one dedicated to St. John the Baptist, another to St. John the Evangelist, and a third to the Holy Cross. The first two are still standing, both with their original bronze doors. He erected a monastery near S. Lorenzo fuori le Mura and was buried in this church "beside the body of blessed Bishop Xystus." The exact location of his tomb is unknown.

The commemoration of Hilary in the MARTYROLOGY OF ST. JEROME on September 10 seems to have been an error.

Feast: Feb. 28.

Bibliography: *Patrologia Latina*, ed. J. P. MIGNE (Paris 1878–90) 58:11–31; *Patrologiae cursus completus, series latina*; suppl. ed. A. HAMMAN (Paris 1957–) 3:379–381, 441–443, editions. *Clavis Patrum latinorum*, ed. E. DEKKERS (Streenbrugge 1961) 1662–63. A. THIEL, ed., *Epistolae romanorum pontificum* (Braunsberg 1868–) 1:126–170. *Liber pontificalis*, ed. L. DUCHESNE (Paris 1886–92, 1958) 1:242–248; 3.86. E. CASPAR, *Geschichte de Papsttums von den Aufängen bis zur Höhe der Weltherrschaft* (Tübingen 1930–33) 2:10–14, 745–746. H. LECLERCQ, *Dictionnaire d'archeologie chretienne et de liturgie,* ed. F. CABROL, H. LECLERCQ and H. I. MARROU (Paris 1907–53) 13.1:1210. G. BARDY, A. FLICHE and V. MARTIN, eds., *Histoire de l'église depuis les origines jusqu'à nos jours* (Paris 1935–) 4:337–338. G. FERRARI, *Early Roman Monasteries* (Rome 1957) 182, 184, 315. R. U. MONTINI, *Le tombe dei Papi* (Rome 1957) 103. G. SCHWAIGER, *Lexikon für Theologie und Kirche,* 3d. ed. (Freiburg 1996).

[J. CHAPIN]

HILARY OF ARLES, ST.

Bishop of Arles (430?–449); b. 401; d. Arles, France, May 5, 449. With the encouragement of his kinsman (St.) HONORATUS, Hilary become a monk at LÉRINS. He served Honoratus briefly during his episcopate at Arles (*c.* 428–*c.* 430), was present at his death (January 14 or 15), and was chosen his successor. GENNADIUS testifies to Hilary's learning (*De vir. ill.* 70), while PROSPER OF AQUITAINE made witness to Hilary's (a variant reads Euladius) concurrence with St. AUGUSTINE'S teaching except in the areas of grace and predestination (Augustine, *Epist.* 225.9). On Prosper's testimony, Hilary is considered a Semi-Pelagian.

Hilary's authentic works include an anniversary *Sermo de vita s. Honorati,* a letter to Eucherius of Lyons, and verses. Several other compositions may also be his. According to Gennadius (*De vir. ill.* 100) the *Vita s. Hilarii* was written by Bp. Honoratus of Marseilles (d. after 492 or 496).

Hilary's episcopacy was marked by strong pastoral action; he presided at several councils, including that of Orange in 441 (J. D. Mansi, *Sacorum Conciliorum nova. Et amplissima collectio* 6:433–452), and engaged in a dispute with Pope LEO I. On July 26, 428, Pope CELESTINE I had apparently restricted the metropolitan jurisdiction of the bishop of Arles to the civil province of Vienne. Hilary acted outside these limits in 443 or 444 by joining other bishops in the deposition of Bp. Chelidonius of Besançon (province of Maxima Sequanorum) and in the replacement of the ailing Bp. Projectus, whose see is unknown. Both prelates appealed to Pope Leo. Although Hilary appeared unexpectedly at a synod in Rome discussing these depositions, he was unable to dissuade the pope from decreeing (probably July 445) the restoration of the two bishops and the suppression of the Arles metropolitanate. Ultimately, a petition to Rome by 19 Gallic prelates moved Pope Leo (May 5, 450) to restore the authority of Arles over all but five bishoprics in the province of Vienne. By this date, Hilary had been dead a year and had been succeeded by Bishop Ravennius (449–452).

Feast: May 5.

Bibliography: S. CAVALLIN, *Vitae sanctorum Honorati et Hilarii* (Lund 1952). HONORAT DE MARSEILLE, *La vie d'Hilaire d'Arles,* tr. P. A. JACOB (Paris 1995). *Clavis Patrum latinorum,* ed. E. DEKKERS (2d ed. Streenbrugge 1961) 500–509. B. KOLON, *Die Vita S. Hilarii Arelatensis* (Paderborn 1925). D. FRANSES, *Paus Leo de Groote en S. Hilarius van Arles* (Bois-le-Duc 1948). J. CHÉNÉ, ''Le semipélagianisme du midi de la Gaule, d'après les lettres . . . d'Hilaire à S. Augustin'' *Recherches de science religieuse* 43 (1955) 321–341. É. GRIFFE, *La Gaule chrétienne à l époque romaine* (Paris 1947–) 2.2. T. G. JALLAND, *The Life and Times of St. Leo the Great* (Society for Promoting Christian Knowledge; 1941). O. CHADWICK, ''Euladius of Arles,'' *Journal of Theological Studies* 46 (1945) 200–205.

[H. G. J. BECK]

HILARY OF CHICHESTER

Canon lawyer, bishop, supporter of King HENRY II against Thomas BECKET; d. Chichester, July 13, 1169. Probably not of high social origin, he appears first in the 1130s as Master Hilary, clerk of HENRY OF BLOIS, Bishop of Winchester, a powerful political figure during Stephen's reign. He was an advocate of some distinction at the papal court and became bishop of CHICHESTER in 1147 through the influence of Pope Eugene III. That he was an able canonist is suggested by the frequency with which Abp. THEOBALD OF CANTERBURY sought his legal assistance or advice, and by the fact that he was often appointed a papal judge-delegate in ENGLAND. As bishop he was remarkable for his record of service to the king; e.g., he acted once as itinerant justice and twice as sheriff of Sussex for Henry II. When he was papal judge-delegate, he would, on occasion, yield to the king as against the pope in a matter of principle. During Henry's controversy with Thomas Becket (1163–64), he emerged as a sharp-tongued opponent of his archbishop. In his diocese Hilary was active in recovering the alienated possessions of his see, favored the regular clergy, and founded the treasurership and chancellorship in his cathedral. In character he has been described as ''an extremely quick-witted, efficient, self-confident, voluble, somewhat shallow man. His talents were great but he used them as an opportunist'' (Knowles).

Bibliography: J. H. ROUND, ''Hilary, Bishop of Chichester,'' *Athenaeum* (Jan.–June 1897) 115–116. D. KNOWLES, *The Episcopal Colleagues of Archbishop Thomas Becket* (Cambridge, Eng. 1951). H. MAYR-HARTING, ''H., Bishop of Chichester, 1147–1169, and Henry II,'' *English Historical Review* 78 (1963) 209–224; *The Bishops of Chichester, 1075–1207* (Chichester 1963).

[H. MAYR-HARTING]

HILARY OF POITIERS, ST.

Bishop and Church Father; b. Poitiers, France, *c.* 315; d. Poitiers, *c.* 367 (feast, Jan. 14). Hilary came of a distinguished family and received a sound training in the classics and philosophy. He was married and the father of a daughter named Abra; he was converted to Christianity in early manhood by reading in the Bible the sublime descriptions of God, which contrasted so strongly with the gross materialism of pagan mythology. His selection as the bishop of Poitiers probably took place in 353. At the council of Béziers (356) he refused to condemn ATHANASIUS, the touchstone of orthodoxy in the Arian controversy (*see* ARIANISM), and was deported to Phrygia by order of the Emperor CONSTANTIUS II. In exile he studied Greek theology, composed two of his most important works, corresponded with the Western bishops, and wrote vigorously to uphold the divinity of Christ. In 360 the emperor refused him permission to debate with the Arian-minded prelates, and in 361 he was released from exile because his enemies regarded him as ''the sower of discord and the troublemaker of the Orient.'' After his return from exile, he allowed MARTIN OF TOURS, the soldier-convert, to inaugurate the monastic movement in Gaul by establishing a hermitage at Ligugé (*see* MONASTICISM). Hilary spent his last years in repairing the damage that Arianism had done in Gaul and Italy.

Works. According to AUGUSTINE, Hilary was a master of Latin eloquence who modeled his style on Quintilian and had begged God to grant him ''beauty of diction'' when writing about the sublime doctrine of the TRINITY. As JEROME pointed out, long and involved sentences obscure his meaning at times, although usually he is more restrained than his contemporaries in employing ornaments of speech. His writings fall into four categories: theology, Scripture, controversial works, and hymns.

Hilary's *De Trinitate* is the first extensive study of this doctrine in Latin; he had to coin new words and expressions to convey his meaning clearly and adequately. Internal evidence indicates that he wrote the first three of the 12 books before 356 and the remaining nine during his exile.

His *De synodis* dates from this same period and explains why the prelates of the East were not satisfied with the term *homoousios,* ''consubstantial,'' which had been approved at the Council of NICAEA (325); it also cites the Oriental professions of faith and tells how they are to be interpreted. He wrote it to give his fellow bishops in Western Europe a more accurate understanding of the religious situation in the East. A *Fragmenta ex opere historico* is also attributed to Hilary. It contains some important documents relating to the Arian heresy that are not found elsewhere.

His *Tractatus super Matthaeum* was written before his exile, and the *Tractatus super Psalmos* after his return. In all probability both were originally sermons. Another scriptural work, *Liber mysteriorum,* is only partially preserved. His principal controversial works are directed against Constantius II, whose religious policy was dividing the Church; and against Auxentius, the Arian bishop of Milan, whom he had failed to depose at a synod in 364. Jerome informs us that Hilary introduced the singing of hymns into the West (*see* HYMNS AND HYMNALS) because he saw how effective they had been in propagating the heresy of Arius among the people. But only three incomplete hymns of his are extant; his hymns were not as well adapted to public singing as were those of St. AMBROSE.

Doctrine. Hilary bases his defense of the dogmas of faith on the testimony of Sacred Scripture. Its authority is unquestioned because it is the word of God Himself. Heretics who appeal to the Bible distort its meaning through ignorance or malice. His fondness for the allegorical interpretation is evident in his scriptural commentaries, and especially in the *Liber mysteriorum,* but he usually uses the literal meaning when citing a text in his dogmatic works.

Catholic Church. Hilary did not write any formal treatise on the Church, but he takes its authority for granted since the Church exhibits unity in Christ. It possesses what all the heretics lack: unity, universality, and indestructibility. Just as certain medicines, he says, can cure all diseases, so the doctrines of the Church provide a remedy against every kind of heresy.

God and the Trinity. Hilary teaches that the existence of God can be known by reason, but that His nature is incomprehensible. The eternal being of God, as expressed in Ex 3.14, *''I Am Who Am,''* had filled him with admiration, even as a pagan, and to it he related all the other divine attributes. This God, who is perfectly happy in Himself, has created angels and men in order that they might share in His happiness. The human soul, according to the better interpretation of Hilary's words, was immediately created by God. The sublime doctrine of the Trinity was in his opinion foreshadowed in the Old Testament but only revealed fully when the Son of God came upon earth.

He marshals his arguments in orderly fashion to show that the proponents of SABELLIANISM are wrong in considering Father, Son, and Holy Spirit as only three names of one and the same divine person and that the Arians are also wrong in speaking of inequality in the Trinity. The doctrine of Trinitarian interaction, later known as circumincession, and its corollary that the Three Divine Persons act inseparably in all works *ad extra* are clearly implied in his explanation of the Trinity. He is often charged, as was his contemporary, St. BASIL, with not giving the name God to the Holy Spirit. One answer to this accusation is that Hilary was concerned with refuting the Arians who denied the divinity of the Son. Another is that in numerous passages he ascribes the same attributes to the Holy Spirit as to the Father and the Son, so that it cannot be seriously maintained that he denied the true divinity of the Third Person of the Trinity.

Hilary's primary purpose in all his writings was to prove that the nature of the Son was consubstantial with that of the Father, and therefore he made no careful study of Christ's human nature. He teaches clearly the two essential doctrines of the Incarnation: that Jesus was only one divine person, and that He had both a divine and a human nature. However, his belief that Christ did not experience interior affliction when He was scourged, crucified, and so on, shows the limitations of his Christological doctrine. He failed to recognize the state of physical weakness to which the Son of God freely subjected Himself when He became a man.

Influence. Hilary was the first Latin writer to acquaint Western Christendom with the vast theological treasures of the Greek Fathers. Augustine and THOMAS AQUINAS cite his authority in their studies of the Trinity. Hilary is rightly called the Athanasius of the West; he preached, wrote, and suffered exile in defense of the divinity of Christ. His role was providential: by strengthening the faith of the clergy and laity of Europe in this fundamental dogma, he prepared the Church for its second struggle against Arianism during the barbarian invasions. In 1851 Pius IX declared Hilary a ''doctor of the Universal Church.''

Feast: Jan. 13 (formerly Jan. 14).

Bibliography: HILARY OF POITIERS, *Tractatus super Psalmos,* ed. A. ZINGERLE in *Corpus scriptorum ecclesiasticorum latinorum* 22 (Vienna 1891); *Tractatus mysteriorum: Hymni Fragmenta, Spuria,* ed. A. FEDER in *Corpus scriptorum ecclesiasticorum latinorum* 65 (Vienna 1916); *The Trinity,* tr. S. MCKENNA in *Fathers of the Church* 25 (New York 1954); *Hilary of Poitiers' preface to his ''Opus historicum,''* tr. P. SMULDERS (Leiden 1995). J. E. EMMENEGGER, *The Functions of Reason and Faith in the Theology of St. Hilary of Poitiers* (Washington 1948). E. P. MEIJERING, *Hilary of Poitiers on the Trinity* (Leiden 1982). M. DURST, *Die Eschatologie des Hilarius von Poitiers: Ein Beitrag zur Dogmengeschichte* *des vierten Jahrhunderts* (Bonn 1987). L. F. LADARIA, *La cristología de Hilario de Poitiers* (Rome 1989).

[S. J. MCKENNA]

HILDA OF WHITBY, ST.

Foundress of Whitby; b. 614; d. 680. The daughter of Hereric and grandniece of King EDWIN OF NORTHUMBRIA, Hilda was baptized by PAULINUS OF YORK on Easter Day, 627. When 33 years old she dedicated herself to the monastic life under St. AIDAN's guidance. She became abbess of a monastery at Hartlepool and later founded the double monastery at WHITBY (657) where, at the famous Council of Whitby (664), the Northumbrian Celtic Church accepted the Roman discipline. She trained many young scholars, five of whom afterward became bishops. She was also responsible for recognizing and cultivating the gift of CAEDMON, the first English Christian poet. A woman of great devotion and ability, she exercised much influence in the Church until her death, which followed a long illness. She was succeeded by St. ELFLEDA. Her relics disappeared after the Vikings destroyed Whitby in 875. BEDE is the main authority for her life.

Feast: Nov. 17.

Bibliography: E. VENABLES, *The Dictionary of National Biography from the Earliest Times to 1900,* 63 v. (London 1885–1900) 9:832–833. BEDE, *Histoire Ecclesiastique* 4.23. N. MOORSOM, *Saint Hilda of Whitby: Historical Notes* (Middlesborough 1970).

[B. COLGRAVE]

HILDEBERT OF LAVARDIN

Archbishop and Latin author; b. Lavardin, France, *c.* 1056; d. Tours, Dec. 18, 1133. After being educated at the cathedral school at LE MANS, he became archdeacon there in 1091. He was elected bishop of Le Mans in 1096 and archbishop of TOURS in 1125. Although he is best known as an important literary figure, his ecclesiastical career was a significant and stormy one. Most notable was his quarrel with King WILLIAM II of England shortly after his election as bishop of Le Mans. The king accused Hildebert of using his cathedral to attack his royal castle at Le Mans and forced him to come to England as a virtual prisoner in 1099. Freed to return in 1100, he proved himself an able administrator and a courageous bishop. He successfully completed the rebuilding of the cathedral, preached with great success in his see, and had the popular but heretical HENRY OF LAUSANNE expelled from the diocese. As archbishop of Tours, he was harshly treated by King LOUIS VI of France, at the time under the influence of the notorious cleric-politician Stephen de Garlande (d. 1150). Hildebert presided at an important provincial synod at Nantes in 1127 and attended the First LATERAN COUNCIL of 1123.

Hildebert's reputation, however, rests in large part on his literary work, for he represents the very pinnacle of the literary achievement of the CATHEDRAL SCHOOLS, and his Latin style has been universally acclaimed by critics of his own day and after. PETER OF BLOIS records that he had to put to memory Hildebert's letters as models of style. He wrote on a variety of topics, both religious and secular, but the collection of his works (*Patrologia Latina* 171:1–1458) contains much that is spurious. Southern cites him as an early influence in the development of political theory.

Bibliography: J. B. HAURÉAU, *Notice sur les mélanges poétiques d'Hildebert de Lavardin* (Paris 1878); *Notices sur les sermons attribués à H. de L.* (Paris 1887). M. MANITIUS, *Geschichte der lateinischen Literatur des Mittelalters*, 3 v. (Munich 1911–31) 3:853–865. J. DE GHELLINCK, *L'Essor de la littérature latine au XIIe siècle*, 2 v. (Brussels-Paris 1946), *passim.* J. DE GHELLINCK, *Littérature latine au moyen-âge*, 2 v. (Paris 1939) 2:118–124. V. BESSE, *Dictionnaire de théologie catholique*, ed. A. VACANT et al., 15 v. (Paris 1903–50; Tables Générales 1951–) 6.2:2466–68. A. WILMART, ''Le *Tractatus theologicus* attribué à Hildebert,'' *Revue Bénédictine* 45 (1933) 163–164; ''Les sermons d'H.,'' *ibid.* 47 (1935) 12–51. R. W. SOUTHERN, *The Making of the Middle Ages* (New York 1953). H. O. TAYLOR, *The Mediaeval Mind,* 2 v. (4th ed. London 1938). F. J. E. RABY, *A History of Secular Latin Poetry in the Middle Ages* 2 v. (2d ed. Oxford 1957) 2. R. R. BOLGAR, *The Classical Heritage and Its Beneficiaries* (Cambridge, Eng. 1954). A. DUMAS, *Catholicisme* 5:737–738. A. HAMMAN, *Lexikon für Theologie und Kirche*, ed. J. HOFER and K. RAHNER, 10 v. (2d, new ed. Freiburg 1957–65) 5:340.

[H. MACKINNON]

HILDEBRAND, DIETRICH VON

Catholic philosopher and moral theologian, outspoken defender of traditional Catholic teaching, b. in Italy, 1889, d. New Rochelle, N.Y., Jan. 30, 1977. His father, Adolph (1847–1921), was a sculptor; his paternal grandfather, Bruno (1812–78), a political economist. Von Hildebrand received his doctorate in philosophy from the University of Göttingen, Germany (1912), was converted to Catholicism in 1914, and was a professor on the faculty of the University of Munich from 1924 to 1933. When Hitler came to power in 1933, von Hildebrand, known to be anti-Nazi, was forced to flee to Florence. Later he joined the faculty of the University of Vienna, but when Austria fell he escaped and joined the faculty of the Catholic University of Toulouse, France. With the fall of France he went to Spain and then to the U.S. where he joined the Fordham University faculty in 1942. He was professor of philosophy there until his retirement in 1960. By the time he had become a professor emeritus he had already written 30 books and more than 100 articles on philosophy and morality. Among his main works *Christian Ethics* (1952) and *True Morality and Its Counterfeits* (1955) were especially praised. In the era of Vatican II in quick succession appeared his *The Sacred Heart* (1965) and *Man and Woman* (1966), as well as two books coauthored by his wife (the former Alice Jourdain), a philosophy teacher at Hunter College: *The Art of Living* (1965) and *Morality and Situation Ethics* (1966). Next came his strong summons to Catholic conservatives. *Trojan Horse in the City of God* (1967), a refutation of secularism and what he described as contemporary errors and horrors. Later he published his defense of Paul VI's encyclical *Humanae vitae* (1969) in his *In Defense of Purity* (1970) and *Celibacy and the Crisis of Faith* (1971).

Von Hildebrand's early writings reflect three dominant influences: the phenomenology of his professor E. HUSSERL, his own conversion to Catholicism, and the ethical approach of M. Schelers. Von Hildebrand's later writings were an attempt to respond to what he considered the most serious crisis in the entire history of the church. In an interview granted to E. Wakin (May 1969) he insisted there could be no change in the revealed doctrine of the church, only development, in Newman's sense of making explicit what was implicit. While von Hildebrand rejoiced over Vatican II's attempts to vivify mere convention and eliminate bureaucratic legalism, he deplored such other results as the loss of a sense of the supernatural and the eagerness to cater to the values of a desacralized, dehumanized, and depersonalized world. Progressives, he maintained, absolutize current views and relativize traditional orthodoxy. The greatest service the church can render the world is to help individual souls progress in sanctity. St. FRANCIS OF ASSISI is the model; he did not set out to change the world, but to follow Christ; by doing that, he did change the world. What is needed are a few great saints who would reverse all secularist and liberal trends and reinstate the true orthodox faith.

Bibliography: E. WAKIN, *U.S. Catholic* 34 (1969) 6–13.

[E. J. DILLON]

HILDEGARD OF BINGEN, ST.

Abbess of Rupertsberg, mystic, and writer; b. Böckelheim, Diocese of Mainz, Germany, 1098; d. Rupertsberg, Sept. 17, 1179. Though sickly from birth, at the age of eight Hildegard was entrusted to Bl. Jutta (d. 1136), sister of Count Meginhard of Spanheim; at 15 she was clothed in the Benedictine habit and instructed in the religious life. At the death of Jutta, Hildegarde, then 38, became abbess. In 1147, accompanied by 18 religious, she transferred the monastery to Rupertsberg, near Bingen, a site that had been revealed to her. She founded a daughter convent at Eibingen prior to 1162.

When the visions she had experienced since childhood increased in later life, she confided in her confessor, Godfrey, and authorized him to submit the matter to the abbot and, later, to the archbishop of Mainz. A committee of theologians gave a favorable verdict on the authenticity of her visions and assigned the monk Volmar to act as her secretary. EUGENE III appointed a committee to review her writings, and again a favorable report followed. Hildegarde's principal work, *Scivias,* is an account of 26 visions treating the relations between God and man in creation, Redemption, and the Church. Other writings include: lives of St. Disibod and St. Rupert; two books of medicine and natural history; hymns and canticles of which she wrote both words and music; 50 allegorical homilies; a morality play; for diversion, a language of her own composed of 900 words and an alphabet of 23 letters; and letters to popes, cardinals, bishops, abbots, kings and emperors, monks and nuns, and men and women of varied levels of society, both in Germany and abroad.

Hildegarde's influence extended beyond her monastery through her extensive correspondence and because of her travels throughout Germany and parts of Gaul. She spoke to people of all classes and walks of life, exhorting them to reform and to heed the prophecies and divine warnings entrusted to her. During her last years she was so ill that she had to be carried from place to place and was unable to stand upright. Nevertheless, she remained available to all who sought her, discussing perplexing questions, encouraging and exhorting her nuns, admonishing sinners, and writing continuously. Her earliest biographer, the monk Theodoric, declared her a saint; miracles, many recorded during her life, increased at her tomb. Twice the process to collect information for canonization was instituted but never completed. She is listed a saint in the Roman MARTYROLOGY, and her cult is honored in several German dioceses. In recent years a considerable literature has grown up dealing with this remarkable mystic and pioneer in science. All manuscripts from the convent of Eibingen have been transferred to the state library at Wiesbaden.

Feast: Sept. 17.

Bibliography: HILDEGARD, *Mystical writings*, ed. F. BOWIE and O. DAVIES, tr. R. CARVER (New York 1990); *The Letters of Hildegard of Bingen*, tr. J. L. BAIRD and R. K. EHRMAN, 2 v. (New York 1994–1998); *Das Speyerer Kräuterbuch mit den Heilpflanzen*

Hildegards von Bingen, ed. B. FEHRINGER (Würzburg 1994); *The "Ordo virtutum" of Hildegard of Bingen*, ed. A. E. DAVIDSON (Kalamazoo, Mich. 1992). GODEFRIDUS and THEODERIC, *The Life of the Holy Hildegard*, tr. Latin to German A. FÜHRKÖTTER, tr. German to English J. MCGRATH (Collegeville, Minn. 1995); ed. including *Canonizatio Sanctae Hildegardis Kanonisation der heiligen Hildegard*, tr. M. KLAES (Freiburg 1998). A. BUTLER, *The Lives of the Saints*, rev. ed. H. THURSTON and D. ATTWATER (New York 1956) 3:580–585. B. WIDMER, *Heilsordnung und Zeitgeschehen in der Mystik Hildegards von Bingen* (Basel 1955). G. HERTZKA, *So heilt Gott* (6th ed. Stein am Rhein 1978), medicine; *Das Wunder der Hildegard-Medizin* (Stein am Rhein 1978) tr. as *Hildegard of Bingen's Medicine*, tr. K. STREHLOW (Santa Fe, N.M. 1988). M. SCHRADER and A. FÜHRKÖTTER, *Die Herkunft der Heiligen Hildegard* (Mainz 1941, rev. 1981); *Die Echtheit des Schrifttums der heiligen Hildegard von Bingen* (Cologne 1956). I. ULRICH, *Hildegard von Bingen: Mystikerin, Heilerin, Gefährtin der Engel* (Munich 1990) tr. as *Hildegard of Bingen: Mystic, Healer, Companion of the Angels*, tr. L. M. MALONEY (Collegeville, Minn. 1993). L. MOULINIER, *Le manuscrit perdu à Strasbourg* (Paris 1995), scientific contributions. *Hildegard von Bingen: Prophetin durch die Zeiten*, ed. E. FORSTER (Freiburg 1997). M. ZÖLLER, *Gott weist seinem Volk seine Wege: die theologische Konzeption des 'Liber Scivias' der Hildegard von Bingen* (Tübingen 1997). C. BURNETT and P. DRONKE, eds., *Hildegard of Bingen: The Context of Her Thought and Art* (London 1998). S. FLANAGAN, *Hildegard of Bingen* (2d ed. London 1998). M. B. MCINERNEY, ed., *Hildegard of Bingen* (New York 1998). R. PERNOUD, *Hildegard of Bingen*, tr. from Fr. P. DUGGAN (New York 1998). W. PODEHL, ed., *900 Jahre Hildegard von Bingen: neuere Untersuchungen und literarische Nachweise* (Wiesbaden 1998). H. SCHIPPERGES, *Die Welt der Hildegard von Bingen* (Freiburg 1997), tr. as *The World of Hildegard of Bingen: Her Life, Times, and Visions*, tr. J. CUMMING (Collegeville, Minn. 1998); *Hildegard von Bingen: Healing and the Nature of the Cosmos*, tr. J. A. BROADWIN (Princeton 1996). M. BERGER, *Hildegard of Bingen: On Natural Philosophy and Medicine* (Cambridge 1999), selections from *Causae et curae*. A. SILVAS, *Jutta and Hildegard: The Biographical Sources* (University Park, Pa. 1999). A. H. KING-LENZMEIER, *Hildegard of Bingen: An Integrated Vision* (Collegeville, Minn. 2001). R. CRAINE, *Hildegard: Prophet of the Cosmic Christ* (New York 1997).

[M. D. BARRY]

HILDEGARD OF KEMPTEN, BL.

Wife of CHARLEMAGNE; b. 758; d. Thionville, Lorraine, France, April 30, 783. She was born of a family allied to the dukes of Swabia and may have been illegitimate. She became the second wife of Charlemagne, to whom she bore four sons and five daughters, including LOUIS I the Pious. In 773, she rebuilt and endowed the Benedictine Abbey of KEMPTEN. She founded many churches and was a close friend of LIOBA. Hildegard was buried at the Abbey of St. Arnulf of Metz, to which she had made a considerable donation. In 872, the nuns of Kempten obtained part of her remains; these were elevated in 963, and since then she has been venerated. Fictitious elements are conspicuous in the accounts of her life.

Feast: April 30.

Bibliography: *Acta Sanctorum* April 3:797–811. J. LECHNER, *Mitteilungen des Instituts für österreichische Geschichtforschung* 21 (1900) 37–75. A. DILGER-FISCHER in *Ulm und Oberschwaben* 34 (1955) 167–170. J. FLECKENSTEIN, *Forschungen zur oberrheinischen Landesgeschichte* 4 (Freiburg 1957) 71–136, esp. 118–. R. GAZEAU, *Catholicisme* 5:740.

[L. MEAGHER]

HILDEGUNDE OF MEER, BL.

Foundress; d. Meer, near Neuss, Germany, Feb. 6, 1183. She was born Countess of Liedberg, and married Count Lothair of Are and Meer. One of her sons, Herman, was the Premonstratensian abbot of Cappenberg from 1171 to 1210. Another son, Theodoric, participated in the sack of Rome with Emperor FREDERICK I BARBAROSSA (1167), burning the church of St. Lawrence. Hildegunde had entered the PREMONSTRATENSIANS after the death of her husband in 1165, and founded the convent of Meer, where she became first prioress. After the sack of Rome she built a replica of St. Lawrence's, at Meer, in expiation for the sacrilege of her son. After her death her daughter Hedwig succeeded as prioress. Though both are recognized as venerable, their cult was never approved.

Feast: Feb. 6.

Bibliography: *Acta Sanctorum*, Feb. 1:925–926; for Hedwig, April 2:263–264. A. BUTLER, *The Lives of the Saints* 1:265–266. J. BREMER, *Das kurkölnische Amt Liedberg* (Möchen-Gladbach 1930) 51–54. N. BACKMUND, *Monasticon Praemonstratense* 1:182–511.

[N. BACKMUND]

HILDEGUNDE OF SCHÖNAU

Cistercian; d. Schönau Abbey, April 20, 1188. She was the daughter of a merchant of Neuss am Rhein who made her cut her hair like a man's, dressed her in man's clothing, and gave her the name Joseph. About 1183 her father took her on a pilgrimage to the Holy Land, where he died. "Joseph" returned to enter the Cistercian Abbey of Schönau near Heidelberg and died there during the novitiate. Only after her death was her true sex discovered; inquiries established her real name and origin. Because of her adventurous life and the unusual way in which she had come to the monastic life, she could not help but attract lively interest, and German Cistercian monasteries especially came to venerate her as a saint. There are pictures of her dating from the 15th century. Her story is so well confirmed by her contemporaries that there is no doubt about the fact that a girl did live and die undetected as a novice in Schönau. Statutes of the general chapter of that time seem to confirm the incident. However, similar happenings date from the first days of Eastern monasticism (cf. Palladius, *c.* 420). The oldest biography of the novice ''Joseph'' was by a confrere from the novitiate, Berthold, who lived later as a monk in Bebenhausen (*Acta Sanctorum* April 2:782–790; probably used by CAESARIUS OF HEISTERBACH, *Dial. mirac.* 1:40).

Bibliography: *Vita A* by Engelhard and metrical *Vita B, Neues Archiv der Gesellschaft für ältere deutsche Geschichtskunde* 6 (1881) 516–521, 533–536. M. HUFFSCHMID, ''Beiträge zur Geschichte der Cisterzienserabtei Schoenao,'' *Zeitschrift für die Geschichte des Oberrheins* 45–46 (1891–92) 430, for sources. K. (C.) SPAHR, *Lexikon für Theologie und Kirche*, ed. J. HOFER and K. RAHNER (Freiburg 1957–65) 5:343. M. SCHAAB, *Die Zisterzienserabtei Schoenau im Odenwald* (Heidelberg 1963) 43. *Cistercienser-Chronik* 71 (1963) 24, for bibliog.

[C. SPAHR]

HILDELIDE, ST.

Hildelitha, Benedictine abbess; b. *c.* 650; d. *c.* 717. She was an Anglo-Saxon princess, who entered the monastery either of CHELLES or of FAREMOUTIERS, France. St. ERCONWALD, Bishop of London, founded BARKING ABBEY for his sister St. ETHELBURGA. He then invited Hildelide to Barking to train Ethelburga in the monastic life. Hildelide became second abbess there *c.* 678 and ruled until her death. She was admired by SS. BEDE, BONIFACE, and ALDHELM; the last-named dedicated to her and her nuns his treatise, *De laudibus virginitatis.* She translated the bodies of the men and women of her abbey from the cemetery to the monastic church.

Feast: Sept. 3, March 24, Dec. 22; translation feasts on March 7 and Sept. 23.

Bibliography: *Acta Sanctorum* March 3:482–485. BEDE, *Ecclesiastical History* 4.6–10. J. L. BAUDOT and L. CHAUSSIN, *Vies des saints et des bienheueux selon l'ordre du calendrier avec l'historique des fêtes* (Paris 1935–56) 3:524–525. A. BUTLER, *The Lives of the Saints,* ed. H. THURSTON and D. ATTWATER, 4 v. (New York 1956) 3:481.

[H. E. AIKINS]

HILDIGRIM, ST.

Bishop and missionary, a.k.a. Hildigrinus; d. Halberstadt, Germany, June 19, 827. (feast, June 19, March 26). Hildigrim was a brother and pupil of St. LUDGER, bishop of Münster, whom he accompanied to Rome (784) and thence to MONTE CASSINO. Later he was abbot of the monastery of WERDEN in the Ruhr Valley. In 802 he became bishop of Châlonssur-Marne; he left there to join his brother in Helmstädt. Later he became bishop of Osterwiek and, finally, in 819, of Halberstadt. Hildigrim was an active missionary bishop among the East Saxons for the last 12 years of his life.

Feast: June 19 and March 26.

Bibliography: *Acta Sanctorum* June 4:742–744. L. DUCHESNE, *Fastes épiscopaux de l'ancienne Gaule,* 3 v. (2d. ed. Paris 1907–15) 3:97. J. L. BAUDOT and L. CHAUSSIN, *Vies des saints et des bienheueux selon l'ordre du calendrier avec l'historique des fêtes* (Paris 1935–56) 6:311. *The Book of Saints* (4th ed. New York 1947) 294. *Sankt Liudger-Festschrift* (Essen 1959), *passim.*

[M. CSÁKY]

HILDUIN OF SAINT-DENIS

Translator of the works of PSEUDO-DIONYSIUS; b. *c.* 775; d. Prüm, Nov. 22, between 855 and 859. Hilduin's father was the Count Udalrich; his aunt, St. Hildegard of Kempten, was the mother of Emperor Louis I the Pious, whence Hilduin's influence at court. He was a student of ALCUIN; he taught HINCMAR OF REIMS, and WALAFRID STRABO. Early in 815, he was made abbot of SAINT-DENIS-EN-FRANCE.

As archchaplain of Louis, 819 to 822, he was involved in all the ecclesiastical questions of the empire. At the Council of Paris (825) he favored the Eastern legates. He was involved in the revolt of the sons of Louis against their father. When they failed in 830, he was exiled to Paderborn, then on Feb. 2, 831, was stripped of his monasteries and banished to the Abbey of CORVEY; but Hincmar obtained his recall. Hilduin then devoted himself to reforming the abbey of Saint-Denis and to study.

At the request of Louis, he wrote a life of St. DENIS OF PARIS that contributed to the identification of this bishop of Paris with Pseudo-Dionysius the Areopagite. Between 831 and 834, Hilduin translated into Latin the *Dionysian Corpus* from the MS (Paris Bib. Nat. Gr. 437) sent by the Byzantine Emperor Michael II to Louis in 827. This rather mediocre translation was taken up and improved *c.* 860 by JOHN SCOTUS ERIGENA. Hilduin became archchancellor of Louis's son, Emperor LOTHAIR I (late 843–855), and accompanied him to Rome. As archbishop designate (never consecrated) he ruled Cologne from 842 to 850.

Bibliography: *Patrologia Latina*, ed. J. P. MIGNE (Paris 1878–90) 106:9–50. *Monumenta Germaniae Historica* (Berlin 1826–) division: Epistolae. 5.1:325–337. DIONYSIUS THE AREOPAGITE, *Dionysiaca*, 2 v. (Bruges 1937). G. THÉRY, *Études dionysiennes,* 2 v. (Études de philosophie médiévale 16, 19; Paris 1932–37). L. LEVILLAIN, ''Études sur l'Abbaye de Saint-Denis,'' *Bibliothèque de l'École Chartes* 82 (1921) 5–116; ''Wandalbert de Prüm et la date de la mort d'Hilduin de Saint-Denis,'' *ibid.*, 108 (1949–50) 5–35. R. J. LOENERTZ, ''La Légende Parisienne de S. Denys l'Aréopagite,'' *Analecta Bollandiana* 69 (1951) 217–237. P. VIARD, *Catholicisme* 5:744–745. J. FLECKENSTEIN, *Lexikon für Theologie und Kirche*, ed. J. HOFER and K. RAHNER (Freiberg 1957–65) 5:346.

[P. GLORIEUX]

HILL, RICHARD, BL.

Priest, martyr; b. in Yorkshire, England; d. May 27, 1590, hanged, drawn, and quartered at Dryburn, Durham. He studied at Rheims (1587–89) and was ordained at Laon (1589) by Bp. Valentine Douglas, OSB. He traveled with BB. Edmund DUKE, John HOGG, and Richard Holiday to England, where they were soon arrested, arraigned, and condemned together. Two Protestants, Robert and Grace Maire, impressed with the courage of the martyrs, were converted. He was beatified by Pope John Paul II on Nov. 22, 1987 with George Haydock and Companions.

Feast of the English Martyrs: May 4 (England).

See Also: ENGLAND, SCOTLAND, AND WALES, MARTYRS OF.

Bibliography: R. CHALLONER, *Memoirs of Missionary Priests,* ed. J. H. POLLEN (rev. ed. London 1924). J. MORRIS, ed., *The Troubles of Our Catholic Forefathers Related by Themselves,* 3 v. (London 1872–77), III, 40. J. H. POLLEN, *Acts of English Martyrs* (London 1891). D. DE YEPES, *Historia Particular de la persecución de Inglaterra* (Madrid 1599).

[K. I. RABENSTEIN]

HILL, WILLIAM JOSEPH

Dominican theologian and editor; b. North Attleboro, Mass., March 30, 1924; d. Washington, D.C., Oct. 12, 2001. Hill was the oldest of seven children of William and Rita (Lanteigne) Hill. He entered the Order of Preachers (Dominicans) in 1943 and graduated from Providence College in 1945. After being ordained a priest in 1950, he was sent to Rome to study at the Angelicum, from which he received an S. T. D. in 1952. On returning to the United States he began teaching at the Dominican House of Studies in Washington, D.C. where he was professor of theology until 1971. The Dominican Order named him a Master of Theology (S. T. M.) in 1967. From 1971 to 1987 he was professor of systematic theology at the Catholic University of America, and from 1987 until his death, professor emeritus. His publications include five books and 44 articles. Hill also was known for his editorial work, serving as editor-in-chief of *The Thomist* for nine years (1975–1983), and on the editorial boards for *The New Catholic Encyclopedia, Communio,* and *Listening*. In 1979–80, he was president of the Catholic Theological Society of America (CTSA), which in 1983 awarded him the John Courtney Murray Award for Outstanding Achievement in Theology. From 1982–1985 he served on the bilateral consultations between Roman Catholics and officials of the Presbyterian and Reformed Churches.

Convinced that Thomism was a living tradition, Hill was best known for his original contributions to trinitarian theology and his creative retrieval of the insights of Thomas Aquinas in dialogue with contemporary culture and diverse theological perspectives. Of particular note are his work on analogy, his efforts to incorporate history and subjectivity into a contemporary theology of God, his original retrieval of an understanding of the Trinity as "Three-Personed God," and his contributions to foundational theology and the theology of preaching. Even in his most speculative reflection on the mystery of inner-trinitarian relations, Hill stressed the salvific significance of doctrine. Likewise, Hill's theology of preaching exemplified the kind of pastoral theology that brings serious and sustained systematic reflection to bear on the ministry of the Church. Referring to the theological task as a ministry of the Word, Hill described the vocation of the theologian in a homily he preached to his colleagues in the Catholic Theological Society of America as "the attempt to show who God will be for us and what humankind must be for God" ("The Theologian: On Pilgrimage with Christ," *CTSA Proceedings* 40 [1985] 230–232).

Bibliography: W. J. HILL, *The Indwelling Trinity* (Somerset, Ohio 1954); *Theological Hope*, v. 33 of the Blackfriars New English *Summa theologiae* (translation, critical notes, and commentary) (New York 1966); *Knowing the Unknown God: An Essay in Theological Epistemology* (New York 1971); *The Three-Personed God: The Trinity as a Mystery of Salvation* (Washington, D.C. 1982); *Search for the Absent God: Tradition and Modernity in Religious Understanding* (New York 1992).

[M. C. HILKERT]

HILTON, WALTER

Spiritual theologian and canon regular of St. Augustine; date and place of birth unknown; d. Thurgarton Priory, Nottinghamshire, England 1395. The day of his death was the vigil either of the Annunciation or of the Assumption. These facts are drawn from various colophons to the MSS of his works. Nothing further is known for certain of his life, though various reasonable conjectures can be made. Among the Latin works ascribed to him is a letter written to a friend, Adam Horsley, an official of the King's Exchequer, who was seriously considering entering religion. In this letter, *De utilitate et prerogativis religionis* (The Advantages and Privileges of Religious Life), Hilton indicated that he was living as a solitary and implied that he himself would welcome the grace of vocation to the religious life; but meantime he must persevere in his solitary life. It has been suggested, with less likelihood, that the autobiographical references here and in another treatise, *De imagine peccati* (The Image of

Sin), to the life of a recluse are merely metaphorical, since Hilton shortly afterward became a canon regular, thus adopting a less strict form of life. A much more probable conclusion is that Hilton was never officially enclosed as an anchorite or blessed as a hermit. The letter to Horsley appears to have been written between 1375 and 1380, and it is reasonable to conclude that he entered the priory at Thurgarton about this time or a little later. There is also evidence that Hilton studied Canon Law: a MS colophon gives him the title of commencer of decrees, which means that he took the degree but never taught the subject; and his letter to a lawyer, ''To one wishing to renounce the world'' (*Ad quemdam saeculo renuntiare volentem*), also suggests that he was a canonist.

Hilton's fame as a doctor of mystical theology and spiritual director of the first rank rests largely on one book, *The Scale of Perfection,* though all the other works ascribed to him, particularly *The Goad of Love,* which is a highly original adaptation into English of the *Stimulus Amoris,* and his *Commentaries on Psalms 90 and 91,* add to his reputation. The ancient claim that Hilton is also the author of *The Cloud of Unknowing* and the other works attributed to that author has never been substantiated; and though the possibility has never been completely excluded, such an attribution seems highly unlikely (*see* CLOUD OF UNKNOWING, THE).

The *Scale* is probably the most complete, lucid, and balanced treatise on the interior life that the late Middle Ages produced. It was highly prized in English Carthusian houses until the dissolution of the monasteries; it was translated into Latin by the Carmelite Thomas Fysshlake before 1400 and was printed by Wynkyn de Worde in 1494; more than 90 MS copies of it are still extant, several in Continental libraries. Perhaps the most significant testimony to Hilton's high reputation as a master of the spiritual life is the fact that the legend that he was the author of the *Imitation of Christ* was so long in dying. It is in the *Scale* that he shows himself the complete master of the long spiritual tradition (christened by Cuthbert BUTLER, ''western mysticism'') whose great exponents are Augustine, Gregory, and Bernard. Hilton is equally at home with the Victorines, particularly HUGH and RICHARD, and with the Dionysians of the 13th and 14th centuries.

The Scale consists of two separate treatises: the first was originally addressed to an anchoress and has survived in two editions, the second of which contains the famous ''Christocentric additions''; by their means Hilton detached himself from the tendency in the 14th century to a dangerous form of Dionysianism akin to pantheism. In the second treatise of the *Scale* Hilton firmly broke away from the medieval tradition that the perfection of the spiritual life can be attained only in the cloister. In this treatise and in his *Letter on the Mixed Life,* Hilton showed that the answer to the spiritual difficulties that times of change and violent unrest throw up is to adapt the Church's spiritual teaching to the life of the Christian in the world. He is perhaps the first person in the whole tradition of medieval western spirituality to see that the perfection of the Christian life is not to be restricted to any particular time or place or circumstance but must always be firmly linked to the fullness of charity. One single quotation from his very free adaptation of the *Stimulus Amoris* will serve to illustrate his preeminent qualities as theologian and spiritual director: ''Many seek after Christ by withdrawing and fleeing from all men, in the belief that he cannot be found except in that way. But it is not so. If you would be a spouse of Jesus Christ and would find him whom your soul loves, I shall tell you where Jesus your spouse is, and where you can find him—in your sick brother who is lame or blind or afflicted with any other disease. Go to the hospital and find Christ there.''

Bibliography: The *Scale* has gone through many eds. since 1494, without there being, as yet, a critical text. The best is still E. UNDERHILL, ed., *Scale of Perfection* (London 1923), though G. SITWELL'S ed. and tr. in the Orchard Ser. (Westminster, Md. 1953), based on Underhill and Wynkyn de Worde, is more immediately available and has a useful introd. D. JONES, ed., *The Minor Works of Walter Hilton* (London 1929), five shorter treatises, including *The Mixed Life* and the *Commentaries on Psalms 90 and 91.* C. KIRCHBERGER, ed., *The Goad of Love* (London 1952), an excellent edition. J. WALSH and E. COLLEDGE, eds., *Of the Knowledge of Ourselves and of God* (London 1961), extracts from the *Scale* and the Psalm commentaries (a Westminster Cathedral MS Florilegium). The Latin works are still unpub. **Studies.** J. M. RUSSEL-SMITH, ''Walter Hilton and a Tract in Defence of the Veneration of Images,'' *Dominican Studies* 7 (1954) 180–214; see also her article on Hilton in *Pre-Reformation English Spirituality,* ed. J. WALSH (New York 1965). H. L. GARDINER, ''Walter Hilton and the Mystical Tradition in England,'' *Essays and Studies of the English Association* 22 (1936) 103–127. E. COLLEDGE, ed., *Mediaeval Mystics of England* (New York 1961). D. KNOWLES, *The English Mystical Tradition* (New York 1961).

[J. WALSH]

HIMMEROD, ABBEY OF

Cistercian abbey in the Rhineland, Diocese of Trier; founded in 1134 by St. Bernard of Clairvaux, whose architect Achard designed the Romanesque basilica (after Clairvaux II); consecrated June 1, 1178 (*see* CLAIRVAUX, ABBEY OF). The abbey first flourished under Abbot Giselbert (1168–86), with more than 70 monks and *conversi* venerated as blessed in the Cistercian Menology. David of Himmerod is venerated by the universal Church.

Abbey of Himmerod.

Abbot Herman I (1188–96) founded the Abbey of HEISTERBACH in 1188, for which lands were acquired through clearing, gifts, and purchase.

In the 13th century the Abbey of Himmerod had 60 monks, 200 *conversi,* and 40 estates. The abbey's boats carried its wine from the Rhine and the Moselle as far as Holland. By 1455 the scriptorium had brought the library's holdings to 2,000 works. Today 145 extant MSS are known. Monks from Himmerod studied in Paris, Cologne, Erfurt, and Heidelberg, and conducted theological studies in the abbey. The change to a money economy, together with a decline in vocations, caused the abbey to lease its holdings in 1228. Himmerod flourished again under Abbot Robert Bootz (1685–1730), historian and friend of the sciences. Abbot Leopold Camp (1731–50) and the architect C. Kretschmar (d. 1768) built the baroque church, with a west façade of 129 feet. After the secularization of 1802, both cloister and church went to ruin. In 1919 the ruins were purchased by the Cistercians, who restored the abbey in 1922; the cloister was rebuilt (1925–27), as was the church (1952–59), according to the old dimensions. Today the abbey is a liturgical and retreat center.

Bibliography: C. WILKES, *Die Zisterzienserabtei Himmerode im 12. und 13. Jahrhundert* (Münster 1924). A. SCHNEIDER, *Die Cistercienserabtei Himmerod im Spätmittelalter* (Himmerod 1954); *Himmerod 1178–1751–1960, Festgabe zur Kirchweihe* (Himmerod 1960); *Lexikon für Theologie und Kirche*, ed. J. HOFER and K. RAHNER, 10 v. (2d, new ed. Freiburg 1957–65) 5:366–367.

[A. SCHNEIDER]

HINAYANA

The name given to a branch of Buddhism primarily by its opponents. Between the first centuries B.C. and A.D., a new set of movements in Buddhism coalesced and came to refer to itself as the ''Mahayana,'' or ''Greater Vehicle,'' and designated its conservative opposition the ''Hinayana,'' or ''Lesser Vehicle.'' Thus, it should be clearly understood that this is a pejorative term that no Buddhist group ever adopted for itself.

The groups so labeled were found objectionable to the newly-arisen Mahayana on both moral and philosophical grounds. On the moral level, they were faulted for a lack of compassion for allegedly teaching that an individual's practice directly benefited only that individual, and that enlightened beings, or buddhas, simply escape the cycle of birth-and-death when their lives end. Mahayanists held that the merits gained from one's religious practice could be transferred to benefit others by an act of intention, and that to withhold such a transfer indicated a lack of concern for others. They also argued that a buddha, having perfected the virtue of compassion, would not simply abandon other suffering beings, but would remain in the world to assist them.

Philosophically, the Mahayanists objected to the "dharma" theory of earlier ontological works. The "dharmas" posited within these systems were much like "atoms" in ancient Greek philosophy: they were indivisible, eternal units that combined and recombined endlessly to create phenomena, thus demonstrating that all things were in flux and so could not be grasped. However, the Mahayanists felt that even these dharmas were not permanent and independent from their surrounding conditions, and so they promoted a philosophy of radical impermanence, stating that everything, even the dharmas of their opponents, were "empty" of any claim to self-existence or independence.

In the past, western scholarship has uncritically accepted the label "Hinayana" as a way of describing the eighteen (or sometimes twenty) schools of early Buddhism, from the Sarvastivadins in the north to the Theravadins in the south. However, in recent times scholars have sought a less offensive designation. One alternative is to use the term "Theravadin," the name of the only surviving school of this group; another is to refer to it as "southern Buddhism" and to call Mahayana "northern Buddhism." All proposed solutions present problems, and so some scholars continue to use the term "Hinayana," at least when referring to the constructed, straw-man opponent of the Mahayanists.

See Also: BUDDHISM; MAHAYANA

[C. B. JONES]

HINCMAR OF LAON

Bishop, d. 879. He was the focal point of a jurisdictional struggle among territorial bishop, metropolitan, king, and pope begun under Bp. Rothad of Soissons and his supporters. They based their opposition to the growing authority of the metropolitan bishop and to the alienation of CHURCH PROPERTY to laymen on the FALSE DECRETALS and the firm support of Pope NICHOLAS I. Hincmar, orphaned at an early age, became the ward of his mother's brother HINCMAR, Archbishop of Reims, who secured his nephew's early appointment as bishop of Laon (858). A worldly and ambitious prelate, Hincmar of Laon soon showed himself an apt student of power politics. In 868 he began his series of challenges against thc king's right to interfere in matters of church property. Seized in 869 by Charles the Bald, he retaliated by forbidding his priests to administer the Sacraments. This interdict, soon removed by the Metropolitan, Hincmar of Reims, led to a falling out of uncle and nephew that reached its climax at the Synod of ATTIGNY (870). Hincmar based his case on the sovereignty of the suffragan bishops and on the right of appeal to the pope (*see* ADRIAN II). The metropolitan's answer came in his *Opusculum 55 capitulorum,* which challenged the authenticity of some of the False Decretals. At the Synod of Douzy (871), Hincmar of Laon was deposed and sent into exile; he was subsequently blinded. At the Council of Troyes, seven years later, he was released by Pope JOHN VIII. A broken man, he died soon afterward.

Bibliography: *Patrologia Latina*, ed. J. P. MIGNE, 217 v., indexes 4 v. (Paris 1878–90) 124:979–1072. *Monumenta Germaniae Historica: Poetae* (Berlin 1826–) 3.2.1:416. J. D. MANSI, *Sacrorum Conciliorum nova et amplissima collectio*, 31 v. (Florence-Venice 1757–98); reprinted and continued by L. PETIT and J. B. MARTIN, 53 v. in 60 (Paris 1889–1927; repr. Graz 1960–) 16:572–864. H. SCHRÖRS, *Hinkmar, Erzbischof von Reims: Sein Leben und seine Schriften* (Freiburg 1884). E. L. DÜMMLER, *Geschichte des ostfränkischen Reiches,* 3 v. (2d ed. Leipzig 1887–88) v.2. H. NETZER, *Dictionnaire de théologie catholique*, ed. A. VACANT et al., 15 v. (Paris 1903–50; Tables Générales 1951–) 6.2:2486–87. A. FLICHE and V. MARTIN eds., *Histoire de l'église depuis les origines jusqu'à nos jours* (Paris 1935–) 6:403–411. J. HALLER, *Das Papsttum*, 5 v. (2d, rev. ed. Stuttgart 1950–53) 2:130–134. J. DEVISSE, *Hincmar et la loi* (Dakar 1962).

[R. B. PALMER]

HINCMAR OF REIMS

Archbishop (845–882), canonist, and theologian; b. probably northern France, *c.* 806; d. Épernay, Dec. 21, 882. He was educated at Saint-Denis, Paris, under Abbot HILDUIN, who in 822 introduced him at the court of LOUIS THE PIOUS. He shared Hilduin's exile at CORVEY (830–831), though he did not support the abbot against the emperor in 833. CHARLES THE BALD gave him the administration of abbeys at Compiègne and Saint-Germer-de-Flay. Already a priest, he was chosen archbishop of Reims (April 845) at the Council of Beauvais and was consecrated by Wenilo of Sens on May 3, 845. Archbishop EBBO OF REIMS, his predecessor, had been deposed on March 4, 835, though for a time after Dec. 6, 840, he had reoccupied the see and had then ordained nine clerics. Sergius II reduced Ebbo to lay communion in June 844, but two years later Emperor LOTHAIR I secured from the pope a directive that a synod at Trier settle the issue of legitimacy between Hincmar and Ebbo. Ebbo refused to go to Trier and died unrestored to Reims in March 851. A council at Soissons on April 22, 853, declared for Hincmar's canonicity and ratified his suspension (June 845) of Ebbo's nine clerics. While LEO IV entertained an appeal from the clerics, succeeding popes gave qualified approval to Soissons. Upon Charles the Bald's decision to appoint Wulfad, one of Ebbo's clerics, to the See of Bourges, NICHOLAS I instructed Hincmar on April 3, 866, to withdraw the censure. Hincmar and a council at Soissons (August 866) declared themselves incompetent to reverse a sentence ratified by Rome, but in September the Crown obtained the installation of Wulfad.

On occasion, Hincmar was at odds with the papacy. On May 23, 851, Leo IV, who had granted him the PALLIUM in 847 and 851, decried Hincmar's treatment of the imperial vassal Fulkrich. When Bp. Rothad II of Soissons (*c.* 832–869) had been deposed by Hincmar and his colleagues, a long series of papal letters ended in Pope Nicholas's restoration of the prelate in January 865. The conflict between the archbishop and his nephew, Bp. HINCMAR OF LAON, occasioned a lengthy dossier and the younger man's deposition in 871. ADRIAN II declined to confirm the sentence until the case had been heard at Rome, but JOHN VIII ratified the judgment on Jan. 5, 876.

Hincmar's *De divortio Lotharii* (*Patrologia Latina*, ed. J. P. Migne 125:623–772) is a defense of a Christian wife against Lorraine's king, LOTHAIR II, and its episcopate, which in 860 had decreed the separation of the monarch from Queen Tetberga. Hincmar protested the installation of Lothair's creature, Hilduin, in the See of Cambrai late in 862; ultimately (July 866) he brought about the consecration of a canonical bishop, John. Over the opposition of the West Frankish kings Louis III (879–882) and Carlomann (879–884) the archbishop was equally successful in securing legitimate prelates for Noyon in 879–880 and Beauvais in 882.

The Council of Mainz (October 848) condemned GOTTSCHALK OF ORBAIS for erroneous teaching on PREDESTINATION and handed him over to Hincmar, who, unable to obtain his recantation at Quiercy (849), imprisoned him at Hautvillers. In 849–850 the archbishop published his *Ad reclusos et simplices,* a refutation of the monk. However, a number of theologians, PRUDENTIUS OF TROYES, LUPUS OF FERRIÈRES, and FLORUS OF LYONS, attacked Hincmar's views and those of his ally, JOHN SCOTUS ERIGENA. The Reims prelate assembled a council at Quiercy in April 853, which asserted but a single predestination to glory or judgment and affirmed that Christ had died on behalf of all. When interprovincial councils at Valence (855) and at Langres (859) and counter *capitula* by Prudentius in 856 (*Patrologia Latina* 125: 64–65) took issue with Hincmar, he composed a second treatise on predestination in 856–857 (*Monumenta Germaniae Historica*: Epistolae 8, n.99) and a third in 859–860 (*Patrologia Latina* 125:55–474). The attempt by the Council of Thuzey (October 860) to reconcile the opposing theologies reflects a limited victory for the archbishop. He proved his loyalty to Charles the Bald in 858 and 875 against the machinations of King Louis the German (840–876); yet in June 876 he stoutly resisted Charles's project for obtaining a papal vicariate for Abp. Ansegis of Sens. Hincmar died in flight before Norse invaders.

The *De jure metropolitanorum* (*Patrologia Latina* 126:189–210) reveals Hincmar's concern for archiepiscopal authority. The question of his possible authorship of the *Lex Salica* has been diversely viewed by S. Stein [*Speculum* 22 (1947) 113–134, 395–418] and by J. M. Wallace-Hadrill [*Tijdschrift voor rechtsgeschiedenis* 21 (1953) 1–29]. More recently Devisse has argued that Hincmar mentioned the FALSE DECRETALS only after 875 and that he showed them scant respect. The archbishop's works fall into many categories: canonical (*Opusculum LV capitulorum*), pastoral (*Capitula synodica*), historical (*Annales Bertiniani, 861–882; Vita s. Remigii*), political (*De ordine palatii; De institutione regia*), dogmatic (*De una et non trina deitate;* the predestination *opera*), moral (*De cavendis vitiis*), and philosophical (*De diversa animae ratione*), along with some verse and letters, the latter of high interest.

Bibliography: Works. *Opera omnia, Patrologia Latina*, ed. J. P. MIGNE, 217 v., indexes 4 v. (Paris 1878–90) v.125–126; projected ed. in *Corpus Christianorum*; *De ordine palatii,* ed. M. PROU (Paris 1884); *Collectio de ecclesiis,* ed. W. GUNDLACH in *Zeitschrift für Kirchengeschicte* 10 (1889) 93–144; *Ad reclusos et simplices,* ed. W. GRUNDLACH in *ibid.* 258–309; *Vita Remigii episcopi Remensis, Monumenta Germaniae Historica: Scriptores* rerum Merovingicarum (Berlin 1826–) 3: 239–341; verse, *Monumenta Germaniae Historica: Poetae* (Berlin 1826–) 3.1:409–420; letters, *Monumenta Germaniae Historica: Epistolae* (Berlin 1826–) v.8; *Annales Bertiniani,* 867–882 A.D., ed. R. RAU in *Quellen zur karolingischen Reichsgeschichte* 2 (Berlin 1958) 104–286. **Literature.** H. SCHRÖRS, *Hinkmar, Erzbischof von Reims* (Freiburg 1884). É. LESNE, ''H. et l'Empereur Lothaire,'' *Revue des questions historiques* 78 (1905) 5–58. G. EHRENFORTH, ''H. von Rheims und Ludwig III. von Westfranken,'' *Zeitschrift für Kirchengeschicte* 44 (1925) 65–98. F. ARNOLD, *Das Diözesanrecht nach den Schriften H. s von Reims* (Vienna 1935). F. M. CAREY, ''The Scriptorium of Reims during the Archbishopric of H.,'' *Classical and Mediaeval Studies in Honor of Edward Kennard Rand,* ed. L. W. JONES (New York 1938) 41–60. K. WEINZIERL, ''Erzbischof H. von Reims als Verfechter des geltenden Rechts,'' *Episcopus: Festschrift Kardinal Faulhaber* (Regensburg 1949) 136–163. M. ANDRIEU, ''Le Sacre épiscopal d'après H. de Reims,'' *Revue d'histoire ecclésiastique* 48

(1953) 22–73. H. G. J. BECK, ''Canonical Election to Suffragan Bishoprics According to H. of Rheims.'' *American Catholic Historical Review* 43 (1957–58) 137–159; ''The Selection of Bishops Suffragen to H. of Rheims, 845–882,'' *ibid.* 45 (1959–60) 273–308. J. DEVISSE, *Hincmar et la loi* (Dakar 1962). E. S. DUCKETT, *Carolingian Portraits: A Study in the Ninth Century* (Ann Arbor 1962) 202–264.

[H. G. J. BECK]

HINDEMITH, PAUL

Leading contemporary composer and theorist; b. Hanau, Germany, Nov. 16, 1895; d. Frankfurt, Dec. 28, 1963. He learned to play violin as a child; and after attending a conservatory in Frankfurt, he became experienced as concertmaster, soloist, and quartet player, all fruitful for his composing career. From 1927 he taught composition at the Berliner Hochschule für Musik and in 1937 he published his influential *Unterweisung im Tonsatz* (translated by A. Mendel as *The Craft of Musical Composition* [New York 1941; rev. 1945]). In keeping with its principles he revised some of his own works, notably *Das Marienleben* (1923, 1948), a song cycle based on R. M. Rilke's poetry. When his activities were curtailed by the Nazis, he moved to Switzerland in 1938 and in 1940 to the U.S., becoming a citizen in 1946. He taught at Yale University from 1940, then at the University of Zurich (1953–56). In later years he was attracted to Catholicism, and in 1963 he wrote a Mass for unaccompanied mixed choir. In 1962 he shared the Balzan Prize—one of his numerous honors—with Pope John XXIII. His prolific output includes music in almost every category. Best known are the symphonic *Mathis der Maler* (1934), derived from his opera inspired by Matthias GRÜNEWALD's Isenheim altarpiece, and the parallel opera-into-symphony *Die Harmonie der Welt* (1951). His theories as well as his style constitute a rallying point for neoclassicists, although his interest in contrapuntal forms, German folk songs, and chant evoke the baroque or earlier periods. Strongly opposed to 12-tone composition, he recognized the force of tonality and assigned central importance to the major triad.

Paul Hindemith. (Archive Photos)

Bibliography: *Paul Hindemith: Catalogue of Published Works and Recordings* (Schott; London 1954: suppl. 1962). N. DEL MAR, ''Paul Hindemith,'' *European Music in the Twentieth Century,* ed. H. HARTOG (New York 1957). E. PREUSSNER, *Die Musik in Geschichte und Gegenwart,* ed. F. BLUME (Kassel-Basel 1949–) 6:439–451. N. CAZDEN, ''Hindemith and Nature,'' *Music Review* 15 (1954) 288–306. M. BREIVIK, ''Arnold Schönberg og Paul Hindemith: Individualister på funksjonalistisk grunn,'' *Svensk tidskrift för musikforskning* 78 (1996) 11–24. A. FORTE, ''Paul Hindemith's Contribution to Music Theory in the United States,'' *Journal of Music Theory* 42 (1998) 1–14. P. HINDEMITH, *Selected Letters of Paul Hindemith,* ed. and tr. G. SKELTON (New Haven, Conn. 1995). M. KUBE, ''Paul Hindemiths Jazz-Rezeption: Stationen einer Episode,'' *Musiktheorie,* 10 (1995) 63–72. J. C. SANTORE, ''Attitudes toward Sexuality and the Tonal Structure of Hindemith's *Sancta Susanna,*'' *Opera Journal* 30/2 (1997) 2–10. P. THALHEIMER, ''Hindemith heute: Anmerkungen zur Aufführungspraxis seines Trios für Blockflöten,'' *Tibia: Magazin für Holzbläser* 20 (1995) 586–593. M. VENUTI, ''Morire per la bellezza: una metafora dell'artista moderno nel capolavoro di Paul Hindemith,'' *Rassegna Musicale Curci* 52 (1999) 16–19.

[H. BRAUNLICH]

HINDERER, ROMAN

Missionary and cartographer; b. Reiningen, Alsace, Sept. 21, 1669; d. Changzhou, China, Aug. 26, 1744. He entered the Society of Jesus in Mainz, Sept. 29, 1686. His first task after his arrival in China in 1707 was to work with other Jesuits at the order of the Emperor Kangxi in a mapping expedition to several provinces. Afterward, the emperor wanted him at court because of his mathematical talents, but he was allowed to preach Christianity throughout the empire: Zhejiang, Jiangsu, Guangdong, Yunnan, and Shanxi. He was austere in his personal life and had a great devotion to the Sacred Heart, to which he attributed his apostolic success. He was visitor of the missions in China, Japan, and Tonkin in 1722 and 1730, difficult times for missions. He wrote works in Chinese on the Rosary and on the Mass.

Bibliography: L. PFISTER, *Notices biographiques et bibliographiques,* 2 v. (Shanghai 1932–34). J. DEHERGNE, *Catholicisme* 5:752–753.

[B. LAHIFF]

HINDUISM

The word "Hindu" is derived from *sindhu,* the name that the Persians gave to the land watered by the Indus River. The inhabitants of this land were a pre-Aryan people, possibly related to the Dravidians of South India, who had developed a high civilization, akin to that of Mesopotamia, in the 3d millennium B.C., and of which the remains have been excavated at Mohenjo-Daro and Harappa in the Punjab. Toward the middle of the 2d millennium B.C., this civilization was overwhelmed by Aryan invaders from the North, who spoke Sanskrit. The invaders brought with them a new religion, of which the sacred books, written in Sanskrit, were known as the Vedas. In the course of time, the religion of the Aryan newcomers blending with the cults of the pre-Aryan population spread all over India and developed into what is known as Hinduism. Nothing in the nature of Hinduism determines a strictly logical approach to the study of it, but the present article will survey its sacred writings, schools of thought, religious teachers, popular religion, relation to the caste system, major reformers, and relation to Christianity.

It is important to note that the "Aryan invasion theory" is now being questioned by scholars. Many scholars have suggested that there is no archaeological evidence that the cities of Harappa and Mohenjo-Daro were destroyed by Aryan invaders. More significantly, archaeologists have discovered "Harappan sites" dating back to the same period in the Northwestern parts of India.

SACRED WRITINGS

They include the VEDAS with their different parts known as the *Brāhmaṇas,* the *Āraṇyakas,* and the UPANISHADS; *dharmashāstras* or collections of "remembered" traditions; and two major epics, the *Rāmāyaṇa* and the *Mahābhārata* with its subsequently added *Bhagavad Gītā.*

Vedic Scriptures. Hindus speak of their religion as the "eternal religion" (*sanātana dharma*), asserting that the Vedas are the expression of eternal truth, made known to the "seers" (*rishis*) of ancient times. Veda means literally knowledge or wisdom, and the Vedas are said to be *śruti* (literally, "that which has been heard") to signify that they came as revelation. The acceptance of this revelation is the test of Hindu "orthodoxy." All systems of philosophy based on the Vedas, however much they may differ in their interpretation, are considered to be orthodox (*āstika*), while those that reject the authority of the Vedas, such as Buddhism and Jainism, are regarded as unorthodox (*nāstika*).

Originally the Vedas came down by word of mouth, and it is impossible to say exactly when they took their present shape. The earliest collection of hymns, known as the *Rig Veda,* was probably completed by 900 B.C. Later a collection of verses (*mantras*) from these hymns, arranged for chanting at the sacrifices, was added and known as the *Sāma Veda.* Another collection of prose formulas followed; it was used in the ritual of sacrifice and known as the *Yajur Veda.* Finally at a much later date a further compilation appeared, namely, the *Atharva Veda,* containing magic spells and incantations. To these original four books of the Vedas three additions were made between 900 and 500 B.C.: first the *Brāhmaṇas,* a kind of prose commentary explaining the symbolic significance of the rites; then the *Araṇyakas* (or "forest-books"); and finally the Upanishads, in which a mystical commentary on the rites was developed into profound and original philosophical speculation. Each Veda eventually consisted of four parts: a hymn (*mantra*), a *brāhmaṇa,* an *āraṇyaka,* and an *Upanishad,* and these together form the corpus of sacred doctrine or *śruti.*

The hymns of the *Rig Veda* were addressed to gods who represented different powers of nature, such as Sūrya, the sun-god; Agni, the fire-god; Indra, the god of thunder; and Uṣas, the goddess of the dawn. They reflect a stage of religion not unlike that of the early Greeks, and many of them have a poetic character, which is reminiscent of the poems of Homer. Moreover, behind the lesser gods there is to be discerned the figure of a creator-god, who was known at first as Dyaus-pita (the equivalent of the Greek Zeus and the Latin Jupiter), but later his place was taken by Varuna, whom some have connected with the Greek Uranos. Varuna was a sky-god, who was worshiped as the sovereign Lord and guardian of the cosmic order (*zita*). Unlike that of the other gods his character was moral, and he officiated as the supreme judge who sees all and punishes the sinner. Although for a while his place was taken by Prajāpati, the "lord of creatures" and by Viṣvakarman, the "all-creator," the image of the creator-god gradually disappeared in the course of time and retained no hold over the Hindu mind. The tendency of Hindu thought, present already in the *Rig Veda,* was rather to see all the gods as different forms or manifestations of one divine being. In the later hynms of the *Rig Veda* there are signs even of speculation on the nature of God and the universe. In one hymn, the *Puruṣa Sūkta,* the universe is said to have been formed by the sacrifice of *Puruṣa,* the primeval or cosmic Person, and to have been produced from the different parts of his body.

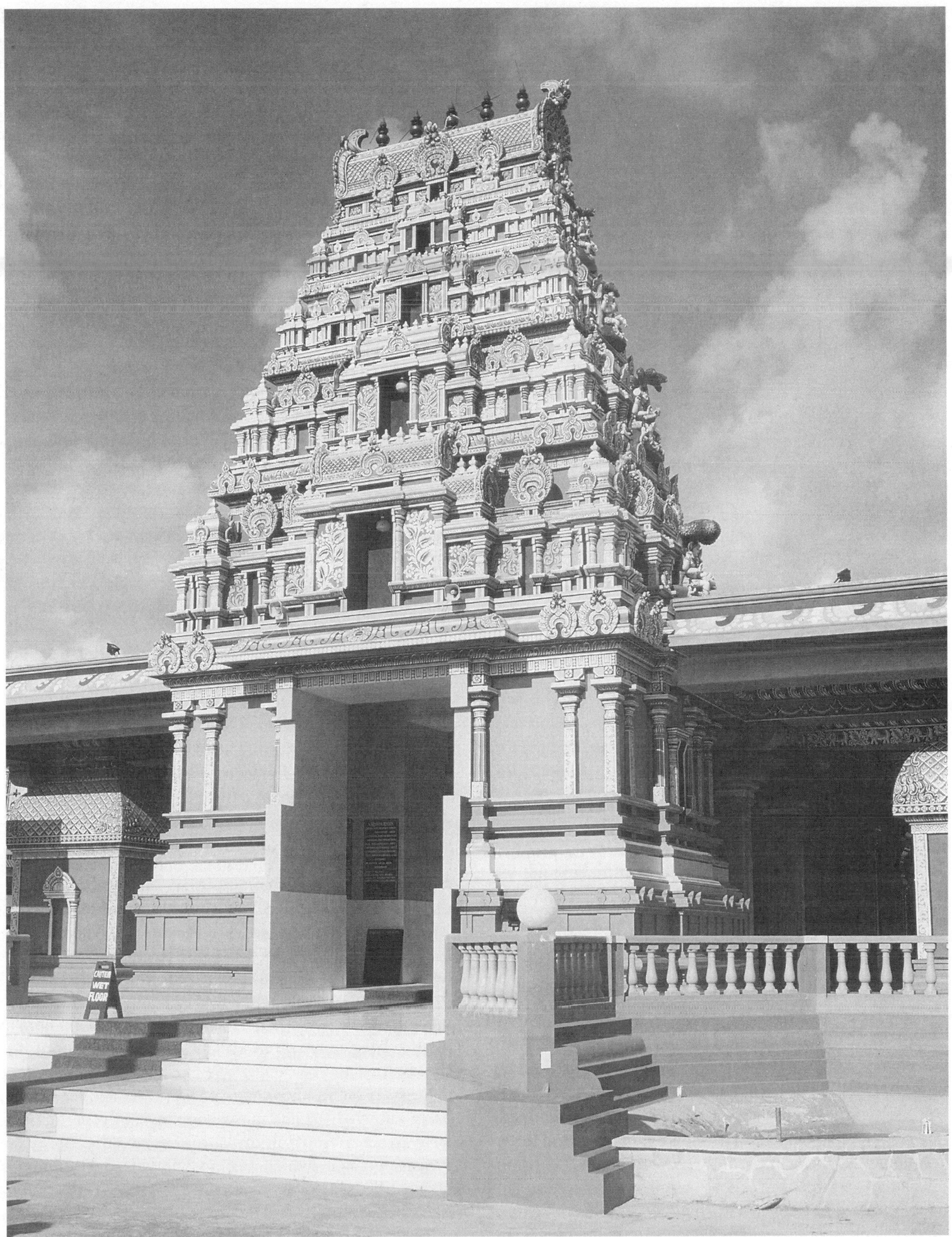

A Hindu Temple in Nandi, Viti Levu, Fiji. (©Jon Sparks/CORBIS)

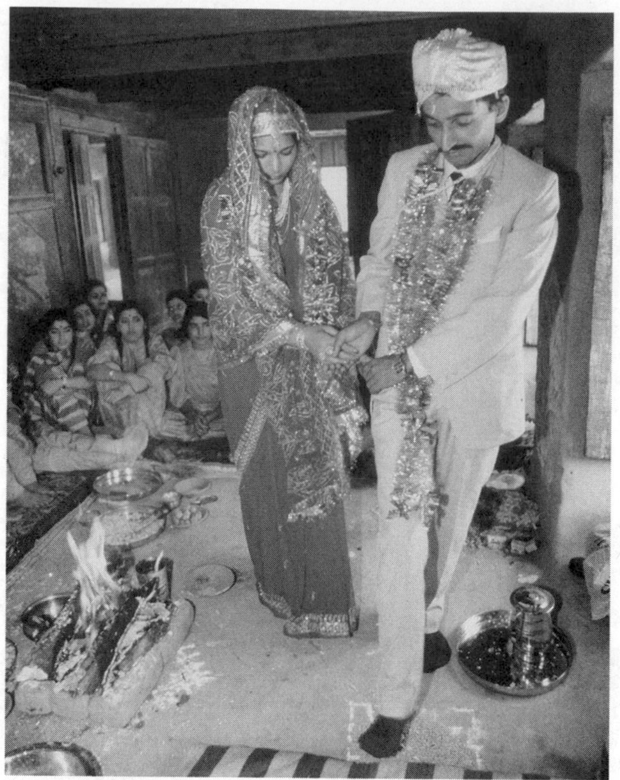

During a Hindu wedding ceremony, the bride and groom circle a ceremonial fire three times to formalize their union, Mattan, Kashmir. (©Earl & Nazima Kowall/CORBIS)

The Brāhmaṇas. The center of the ancient Vedic religion was sacrifice. At public sacrifices animals were slaughtered and an intoxicating drink called *soma* was drunk, to obtain from the gods such favors as success in war, offspring, increase of cattle, and long life. Behind this lay a deeper conception than that of seeking favors. Every sacrifice was held to be a repetition of the primeval sacrifice by which the world was brought into being; the continuation of the world was believed to depend on the exactness of the performance of the ritual of sacrifice, a concept developed in that part of the Veda called the *Brāhmaṇas*. The sacrifice came to be conceived as having power in itself; even the gods were believed to be dependent on it. Thus the position of the priest, the Brahmin, who offered the sacrifice was of supreme importance. He alone knew the sacrificial words and actions, and he therefore was possessed of supreme power. As the sacrificing priest was known as the Brahmin, so the power that was held to be inherent in the sacrifice was known as the *Brahman*. The *Brahman* came to be regarded as the supreme power that sustains the universe. This idea, already present in the *Brāhmaṇas,* was developed in the Vedic writings called *Āraṇyakas* and in the Upanishads, and became the most fertile concept of Hindu philosophy.

The Āraṇyakas. Sacrifice lost its importance with the *Āraṇyakas,* which mark a new stage in the growth of the Vedas and in Hindu religion. They were the work of the ''forest-dwellers,'' ascetics who retired to the forest to meditate in silence on the mystery of the universe. For ritual sacrifice they substituted meditation and asceticism (*tapas*), developing the idea that the power in the sacrifice, the *Brahman,* was found in the spiritual sacrifice of the inner man. A new conception of the meaning and purpose of life began to take form with the introduction of the doctrine of transmigration, according to which the souls of all living things, plants and animals and human beings, even the gods, are subject to a perpetual cycle of rebirth (*sàmsāra*). The condition of a soul in the present life is rigorously conditioned by the actions of its past life (*karma*); by its good deeds the soul ascends in the scale of being, and by its evil deeds it descends; in either case there is no finality. Even the gods must die and be reborn, and though the performance of good works, especially the ritual of sacrifice, could lead to heaven, even heaven is not permanent. Against this background of belief arose the idea of liberation (*moksa*). Instead of the perpetuation of the round of rebirth by sacrifice, liberation from rebirth altogether, and deliverance not only from this world but also from the world of the gods with its promised blessings was sought. The goal to reach was the ultimate source of life, the *Brahman.*

The Upanishads. The word ''upanishad'' means literally to ''sit near to,'' and was used to signify secret doctrine containing the key to life, handed on from master to disciple. The earliest Upanishads, written in prose, were composed not later than the 6th century B.C. They were followed by others, many of them in verse, until eventually a collection of 108 was made. Of these, the original and fundamental texts numbered only 11. They contain all those profound ideas that were to germinate in the Indian soul and to inspire Hindu religion and philosophy down to the present day.

The teaching of the Upanishads is of a mystical nature. Although in Greek philosophy there is a mystical strain, the Greek genius had a bent for speculative thought; its achievement marks the triumph of human reason. The genius of India on the other hand is for mystical experience. The seers of the Upanishads were seeking not a speculative knowledge of truth attained by reason, but a knowledge that transcends reason, giving an intimate experience of ultimate truth. Their question was, ''What is that which, being known, everything is known?'' The answer was in the knowledge of the *Brahman.* Thus from being conceived as the power in the sacrifice that upholds the world, the *Brahman* had come to be regarded as the supreme power in the universe, to be known by meditation and asceticism. This knowledge of the *Brahman* was sought in the Upanishads, a knowledge of the ultimate being that is beyond this world and the world of the gods, beyond sense and reason, and that confers liberation (*moksa*) and bliss (*ānanda*).

The path of this progression of thought is traceable in India's search for the ultimate reality or ground of the universe, first, in the elements of earth, air, fire, and water; then in space (*ākāśa*), which embraces all matter. Then they turned to human nature, seeking its essence, the true Self (*Ātman*) in breath (*prāna*) or life or thought. Finally the discovery was made that the ultimate reality is beyond all these; it is ''not this, not this'' (*neti, neti*). It is a mystery beyond human understanding, which can be known only by direct intuition. Then the supreme discovery of the Upanishads was made. The ultimate ground of reality in nature (*Brahman*) is one with the ultimate ground of being in the soul (*Ātman*). The *Brahman* is the *Ātman*, or as it is said in one of the great sayings of the Upanishads, ''Thou art That.'' When the ultimate reality is known, it is not by sense or reason but by the soul's direct intuition of itself. In this experience there is no more distinction of subject and object, no ''duality.''

The conception of the identity of the *Brahman* and the *Ātman* was essentially a mystical intuition, one that underlies all Hindu philosophy. The interpretation of it gave rise to many diverse schools of thought. The difficulty is that the Upanishads expressed profound intuitions that were not worked out logically; different systems could be derived from them. Their purpose was not to lead to systematic reasoning but to awaken the intuition of ultimate truth in the heart, and so to lead the hearer to final liberation. There appeared to be conflicting statements in the Upanishads: they declared that the *Brahman* is not only the source but also the substance of all being: ''all this (world) is *Brahman.*'' It was said that just as the spider comes out with its thread or as small sparks come from the fire, so the world comes forth from *Brahman.* Or again, as all clay pots are the same clay and differ only in their forms, so all things in the universe are *Brahman* and differ only in their names and forms (*nāmarūpa*). Yet again it was said that the Brahman is not to be identified with anything in the universe; it is the ''subtle essence'' that is in all things but is distinct from them. It is like the soul in the body, the principle of being, life, and thought, yet apart from these.

What the seers of the Upanishads reached was an intuition of an absolute spiritual reality. The *Brahman* was the principle alike of being and of knowing. It was the plenitude of being, and when all the worlds came forth from it, it was not diminished. It was also the plenitude of knowing, not as that which is known but rather as that which knows. ''Who,'' it was asked, ''shall know the knower?'' It could not be known by any method of human reason; it could be known only to him to whom it made itself known. As such it was the ''controller,'' the ''dweller-within,'' the inner Self (*Ātman*). It was that which was ''dearer than all,'' for the sake of which all other things were to be desired, the bestower of joy and immortality. Thus in the later Upanishads, especially the *Svetāṣvatara* (4.11; 6.7), the *Brahman* took a distinctly personal character. It was known as the Lord (*īsā*), the great Person (*puruṣa*), and was even given the name of Śiva (the gracious).

Because the Upanishads brought to an end the revelation (*śruti*) of the Vedas, they are known as *Vedānta* (literally, the ''end'' of the Veda). Although they contain profound insights into the mystery of being, they do not propound a system of thought. They leave unresolved the question of the relation between the personal and the impersonal character in the *Brahman* and the relation between the world and the *Brahman.* These questions therefore became the subject of subsequent debate, giving rise to the differing schools of the *Vedānta.* But in the meantime Hindu religion was to undergo a profound transformation. In the period following the Upanishads—between 500 B.C. and A.D. 500—their religion was gradually modified by the influence of the local cults. At the same time ''unorthodox'' doctrines of BUDDHISM and JAINISM became rivals of Hinduism, and it was only at the end of this period that Hinduism emerged as the religion of the greater part of India.

The Darmashāstras. The writings of this period were known as *smrti* (literally ''that which is remembered'') or ''tradition'' as distinguished from *śruti* or ''revelation.'' Among them were the law-books (*dharmaśāstraś*), above all the laws of Manu, which laid down the basic principles on which Hindu society was to be governed. Society was divided into four castes, or more properly ''classes'' (*varṇa,* meaning literally ''color''), from which the caste system later developed. The first three classes, the Brahmins (priests), *kshatriyas* (warriors), and *vaishyas* (merchants) were known as the ''twice-born,'' because they alone could be initiated into the wisdom of the Vedas. The fourth class, the *śūdras* (workers), had no right to learning. Yet it was they who in the end were to transform the Hindu religion.

In the *dharmaśāstras* appeared also the division of an individual's life into four stages (*āśramas*). In the first, the student (*brahmachārin*) had to study the Vedas at the feet of a master and to observe chastity. The second stage was that of the householder (*grhastha*), who was to marry and bring up a family. The third phase was that of the ''forest-dweller'' (*vānaprastha*), which began when a man's hair began to turn grey. He was supposed to leave his home and his wife and go to live in the forest to meditate and do penance for the good of his soul. The last stage was that of the *sannyāsi* (literally "one who has renounced all"), when he was expected to break all attachments to the world and live as a wanderer begging his way. A great number neglected to put this ideal into practice, but all Hindu society recognized the ideal of complete detachment from the world for the sake of attaining liberation (*moksa*). The doctrines of the *Āranyakas* and the Upanishads had thus been incorporated into the framework of Hindu life.

Four ends of life. The same principle governed the four "ends" of life as they were formulated at this time. The first was pleasure (*kāma*) and the second wealth (*artha*), both frankly recognized as natural goods and meriting elaborate treatises; the third end was *dharma,* translated as "law," the basic principle of order in human society. Every man was held to have his proper place with its rights and duties determined largely by his position in the framework of the four classes. The happiness both of the individual and of society was held to depend on the observance of *dharma,* and the whole of human society was held to be subject to divine law; human activity, economic, social, political, and religious, was given a divine sanction. It was this above everything that stamped a religious character on Hindu society. The fourth end of life was *moksa,* or liberation from this world. However important the place of worldly pleasure or wealth or worldly duty, the supreme end of life was liberation from this world and enjoyment of the supreme bliss of *Brahman.* The ideal of the Upanishads thus influenced the whole of Hindu life.

Epics. Of the same period as the *dharmaśāstras* and reflecting the same order of society were the two great Hindu epics (*Itihāsas*), the *Rāmāyaṇa* and the *Mahābhārata.* The original poems were composed probably soon after 500 B.C., but both received numerous interpolations in the course of time and were not completed until the 4th century A.D. They hold a place in literature not unlike that of the *Iliad* and the *Odyssey.*

The Rāmāyaṇa. Written traditionally by the sage Vālmāki, the *Rāmāyaṇa* is the story of the prince Rāma, who was exiled in the forest with his wife Sītā; she was kidnaped by the demon king, Rāvaṇa. After many adventures, Rāma killed Rāvaṇa, rescued Sītā, and returned to reign in his kingdom. It is probable that Rāma was a historical person, who lived in the 7th or 8th century B.C. In the original story he was represented as a brave and noble king and Sītā, as a devoted wife. The whole story was impressed with the idea of *dharma* as the ruling principle of life and with moral idealism. In the later versions of the epic, Rāma was conceived as a divine being, an incarnation of the god Viṣṇu, and with this change the story was translated in later times into all the languages of India; the divine hero became the object of a universal cult. To this day Rāma remains one of the names of God to the devout Hindu, and his name was the last word uttered by Mahātmā Gāndhi.

The Mahābhārata. This epic, composed traditionally by Vyasa, is the story of a great battle between the Pāndavas and Kauravas, two families descended from Bharata, one of the ancient kings of North India. In the course of time the epic grew to vast proportions, through the addition of myths and legends, moral stories, fables, and long didactic discourses. In its present form it is said to be the longest poem in the world, consisting of 100,000 stanzas (*ślokas*), the whole being more than three times as long as the Bible. In this form it was a kind of encyclopedia of early Hinduism, reflecting the profound changes of the period. The ancient gods of the Vedas had faded into insignificance and two gods, Viṣṇu and Śiva, who had been obscure in ancient times, became the principal objects of worship. Not only the object but also the manner of worship had changed. Instead of the ancient Vedic sacrifices of slaughtered animals, offerings of fruit and flowers were made to the images of the temple gods, possibly because of the influences of Buddhism and Jainism. From this time, too, the ideal of never taking life (*ahiṁsā*) became a ruling principle of Hinduism. But the most notable change was that the worship of the gods began to take a more personal form.

The Bhagavad Gītā. In the later Upanishads, the *Brahman* conceived in a personal form had been worshiped under the name of Śiva. Now in the *Bhagavad Gītā* ("the Song of the Lord"), which was added to the *Mahābhārata* perhaps around the 2d century B.C., this devotion to a personal God was raised to a high level. The Supreme Being, the *Brahman,* was represented as Bhagavān, the Lord, to be worshiped not by sacrifices but by personal love and devotion (*bhakti*). He was conceived under the name of Viṣṇu, who became incarnate, or more exactly "descended" in the form of an *avatāra,* to deliver the world from unrighteousness (*adharma*) and restore righteousness (*dharma*). In the original story of the *Mahābhārata,* Krishna like Rāma was an epic hero, but by the time the *Gītā* was added he, like Rāma, had come to be regarded as an incarnation of Viṣṇu. Krishna in the *Bhagavad Gītā,* was represented as the Supreme Being (*parabrahma*) governing the universe; he was beyond all human conception, and at the same time the Supreme Self (*parātman*) dwelling in the heart of every man and manifesting himself by his grace (*prasāda*) to those who devoted themselves to him. Thus the *Brahman* of the Upanishads was transformed into a supreme personal god. Yet just as in the Upanishads there was no clear distinction made between the creator and the creature, so in the *Gītā*, Krishna was never clearly distinguished from nature and the souls in which he dwelt. This was the problem that was to occupy different schools of the *Vedānta* in their interpretation of both the Upanishads and the *Gītā*.

The *Bhagavad Gītā* became the most popular of all the sacred writings of Hinduism not only for its beautiful conception of a personal god, but also for its ethical teaching. The great lesson of the *Gītā* was that the knowledge of the *Brahman*, which had been the goal of the Upanishads, was to be reached not merely by the ascetic who renounced the world but also by the householder living in the world. It was to be attained by action (*karma*) no less than by meditation. Every action in accord with *dharma,* that is with a man's state in life, could become a means of salvation, if it was done with ''detachment'' and its ''fruit'' was renounced. Every action could become a true sacrifice, if it was offered to God in a spirit of devotion (*bhakti*) and thus became a means of union with God. Thus the *Gītā* marked a further stage on the path of ascent to the *Brahman;* the goal was to be attained not merely by sacrifice (*yajña*) as in the Vedas, or by knowledge (*jñāna*) as in the Upanishads, but by love (*bhakti*). It was the conception of love (*bhakti*) that was to work so wonderful a transformation in Hindu religion and to lead to its greatest achievements.

SCHOOLS OF THOUGHT

The metaphysical doctrine of the *Bhagavad Gītā* was based on the *Sāṅkhya*, which was one of the schools (*darśanas*) of philosophy that arose during the period when the *Mahābhārata* and the *dharmaśāstras* were being composed. *Darśana* means literally ''point of view,'' and the six *darśanas* were not systems of philosophy so much as different points of view within orthodox Hindu doctrine.

Nyāya. The first school, *Nyāya* (analysis), was a system of logical realism which, although it was similar to that of Aristotle, was quite independent of it. *Nyāya* maintained the existence of an external world independent of the mind and sought to establish this view by logical reasoning. It never gained popularity, but the study of logic came to be regarded as a discipline for the study of philosophy and by a characteristically Indian turn of thought as a means of salvation, the end of all philosophy.

Vaiśeṣika. The second school, *Vaiśeṣika* (individual characteristics), was a system of philosophy based on atomism; it taught that the universe consists of five elements—earth, air, fire, water, and space (*ākāśa*)—each of which is composed of a number of atoms. The influence of these theories was slight, their principal interest being the remarkable fact that they had a place in Hindu thought.

Sāṅkhya. More characteristic and more influential was the *Sāṅkhya* (the ''school of the Count''), the basis of the doctrine of the *Bhagavad Gītā*, tracing its origin probably to the time of the Upanishads. It was a metaphysical doctrine that the universe was derived from two principles called *Purusha* and *Prakrti*. *Purusha,* which may be translated Spirit, was the principle of Being, corresponding in some ways with Aristotle's ''form'' or essence. *Prakrti* was the principle of Becoming, corresponding to Aristotle's ''matter'' or, more generally, ''substance.'' From these two principles all the elements in human nature and the natural world were derived. What was peculiar to the *Sāṅkhya* was the doctrine that all activity came not from *Purusha* but from *Prakrti.* The universe evolved from *Prakrti*, while *Purusha* remained above all action in a state of pure consciousness. In man *Purusha* became identified with *Prakrti* through ignorance, although in itself eternal and unchanging. The ultimate state of man as pure spirit was considered to transcend this world altogether.

Yoga. Sāṅkhya formed the basis of the fourth school of philosophy known as YOGA. Yoga was a system of practical philosophy, whose purpose was to teach the way to separate *Purusha* from *Prakrti* and so to attain liberation (*moksa*). In a sense, it may be said that this was the goal of all the different schools, since the ultimate end of all life and thought was to attain liberation, but Yoga was distinguished by concern with practical method. The word ''Yoga,'' akin to the English ''yoke,'' meant a discipline or method of union. The principles of Yoga were known to the writers of the Upanishads and were probably older, but the classical school of Yoga originated in the Yoga *sūtras* or sayings of Patañjali, around A.D. 500. It was a system of physical and spiritual discipline by which the mind was set free from all bodily and mental states dependent upon matter (*Prakrti*) and realized its nature as a pure spirit (*Purusha*). One respect in which the Yoga philosophy differed from the Sāṅkhya was that it recognized the existence of a god (Iśvara) who was conceived as a pure spirit, who was able to assist souls on the path of liberation. Yoga was to have an incalculable influence on all Hindu life and thought and to develop many different schools that continue even to the present day.

Pūrva Mīmāṁsā, Uttara Mīmāṁsā. The other two schools of philosophy, called *Mīmāṁsā*, were concerned exclusively with the interpretation of the Vedas. The first, called *Pūrva Mīmāṁsā*, was based on the *Brāhmanās* and dealt with the laws of sacrifice and the duties of religion (*dharma*). It endeavored by rational argument to establish the validity of the Vedas as an eternal revelation, which was valid in itself and was the supreme authority in matters of religion. The second school, *Uttara Mīmāṁsā*, was what became generally known as the *Vedānta;* for the term *Vedānta*, ''end of the Vedas,'' applied originally to the Upanishads themselves, was later to be used for philosophical systems based on them. *Uttara Mīmāṁsā* was concerned with the interpretation of the Vedas not as a way of action (*karma*) but of knowledge (*jñāna*), and was based on the Upanishads. The basic text was the *Brahma-sūtras* of Bādarāyaṇa, written early in the Christian Era. It consisted of short aphorisms, summarizing the doctrine of the Upanishads on the subject of the *Brahman.* This together with the Upanishads themselves and the *Bhagavad Gītā* formed the ''triple foundation'' of the *Vedānta*, and the principal works of the doctors of the *Vedānta* consisted in commentaries on these texts.

RELIGIOUS TEACHERS

In the interpretation of the Upanishads, religious teachers (usually Brahmins) formed systems of thought that represented stages of the development of Hinduism within the orthodox framework of the *Vedānta.*

Śaṅkara. Śaṅkara (b. Kaladi, Malabar, Kerala, 8th century A.D.) was the great master of the *Vedānta.* In his time Buddhism, Jainism, and other ''unorthodox'' systems of philosophy were flourishing, but through him Hindu ''orthodoxy'' was firmly established as the religion of the greater part of India. Śaṅkara himself was a disciple of Gaudapāda, whose commentary on the *Māndūkya Upanishad* bears clear traces of Buddhist influence. Thus one of the reasons for the triumph of Hinduism over Buddhism may well have been its ability to incorporate the basic insights of Buddhist philosophy into its own system. Śaṅkara himself regarded the Vedas as a revelation of absolute truth and the sole source of that supreme knowledge, which brings liberation. However, in his interpretation of the Vedas he introduced a distinction between the different kinds of knowledge to be found in them. He regarded the knowledge of ritual action (*karma*) found in the *Pūrva Mīmāṁsā* to be of no value for liberation, any more than knowledge in the Vedas, which was derived from ordinary human experience. The supreme knowledge (*parāvidyā*) to be found in the Vedas was contained rather in certain ''great sayings'' (*mahāvākya*), which revealed the true nature of the *Brahman.* In comparison with this knowledge, all other knowledge was to be classed as ignorance (*avidyā*).

The doctrine which Śaṅkara upheld was called *Advaita* (nonduality) because it affirmed that the *Brahman* was one, ''without a second.'' Its nature was pure Being (*sat*), pure knowledge (*chit*), and pure bliss (*ānanda*), and this one absolute Being was identical with the Self, the *Ātman*. The true knowledge of the *Brahman* could not be attained by any method of reasoning, but only by a direct intuition (*anubhava*), in which the soul knew itself in its identity with the *Brahman.* It followed that all distinctions of being, as they appeared to the rational mind, based on the evidence of the senses were an illusion (*māyā*). They were like the figures of a dream or like the forms conjured up by a magician. It was, to use his famous illustration, as when a rope was mistaken for a snake: the form of the snake was ''superimposed'' on that of the rope; when the ''superimposition'' was removed, it was seen that there was nothing but a rope. So it was that all the different forms of being were superimposed on the pure being of the *Brahman.* True knowledge was simply the knowledge of the *Brahman.* All the revelation of the Vedas and all the reasoning based upon it had no other purpose than to lead the soul to this supreme knowledge, which was also supreme bliss. Such a state of perfect knowledge and bliss was liberation (*moksa*). It was a liberation from the illusion (*māyā*) of this world and an experience of real being in pure consciousness.

Thus the doctrine of Śaṅkara, like that of the Upanishads, was based on a mystical experience, but it was distinguished by the rigorous logic by which he refuted every argument that could be used against it; his teaching succeeded in unifying the whole body of Hindu doctrine in the light of this central intuition. Śaṅkara did not deny the validity of reason and sense experience in their own spheres; on the contrary, he firmly upheld against the Buddhists a realistic view of nature. Nor did he ever suggest that the soul (*jīva*), which was a relative being, was divine. But he maintained that from the point of view of the absolute, all such knowledge and all such distinctions were illusory. Thus he used reason with a rigorous logic as far as it would go, but he maintained the possibility of a knowledge transcending reason, revealed in the Vedas and apprehended by mystical intuition.

There were many who opposed Śaṅkara's view, even though he had succeeded in giving a coherent form to Hindu doctrine. The debate turned especially on the relation of the personal god, as revealed in the *Bhagavad Gītā*, to the *Brahman.* According to Śaṅkara, the idea of a personal god with attributes or qualities (*saguna*), though it could be helpful to the believer on the way to truth, was itself a product of ignorance (*avidyā*). It belonged to the sphere of *māyā* and had to be transcended, if the soul was to reach the supreme knowledge of the *Brahman* without attributes (*nirguna*).

Rāmānuja. In this matter Śaṅkara was opposed by Rāmānuja, a Tamil Brahmin (b. near Madras, 11th century A.D.; d. at the famous temple of Sri Rangam near Tricinopoli, 1137). His doctrine was known as *Viśiṣṭāvaita* or ''qualified'' *Advaita* to distinguish it from the pure *Advaita* of Śaṅkara. Rāmānuja was a Vedantin who, like Śaṅkara, claimed to interpret the true meaning of the Vedas and on the authority of the same texts of the *Brahma-sūtras* and the *Bhagavad Gītā*. But his doctrine was influenced also by another current of religious thought in which the Supreme Being was worshiped under the name of Viṣṇu Nārāyaṇa or Vāsudeva, later identified with Krishna as Bhagavān or Lord. The followers of Rāmānuja's sect were known as Bhāgavatas, and their doctrine developed in a school known as Pāñcarātra, one of the sources of Ramanuja's theology. The *Bhagavad Gītā* itself was an early expression of the doctrine, but it was in the Tamil country (Madras State) in the period between A.D. 500 and 1000 that the great flowering of devotion to a personal god took shape in the hymns of the Ālvārs, the poet-saints of South India.

Inspired by this school, Rāmānuja contended that the Supreme Being, the *Brahman,* had essentially a personal character and a personal relationship to his worshipers. In opposition to Śaṅkara, he maintained that the way of knowledge (*jñāna-mārga*) was inferior to the way of devotion (*bhakti-mārga*) and that in the highest state of bliss the individual soul was united with God but never wholly identified with Him. Further, while Śaṅkara had taught that the knowledge of the *Brahman* depended on the soul itself, which had only to realize its essential identity with the *Brahman,* Rāmānuja contended that the soul was assisted in its ascent to God by divine grace (*prasāda*).

Rāmānuja asserted the personal nature of the *Brahman* and the real distinction between God and nature (*Prakṛti*) and souls (*Ātman*). He maintained that the nature of the *Brahman* is ''qualified.'' It is not the absolutely simple being that Śaṅkara had conceived, but a being with many different attributes. Rāmānuja supported this view by maintaining that as a substance and its attributes are essentially one yet different, so the *Brahman* was essentially one but had different attributes. Nature and souls he considered to be ''modes'' of the divine being, which stood to them in the relation of the soul to the body. Thus nature and souls were essentially divine and had lost the knowledge of their true nature due to ignorance. The work of divine grace was to restore them to the knowledge of their true nature and to unite them with God in the love of total self-surrender (*prapatti*). In this state, souls were one with the divine being but did not lose their individual self-consciousness.

Madhva. A third school of *Vedānta,* known as *dvaita* (duality), arose in opposition to both Śaṅkara and Rāmānuja. Its founder was Madhva (b. South Canara, Kerala, 12th century A.D.). Against all forms of *Advaita* he maintained the real diversity of being. ''Diverse are all the things of the world and they possess diverse attributes.'' Above all he conceived of God as Viṣṇu-Nārāyaṇa, a personal being, possessed of an infinite number of qualities, a being absolutely transcendent, the supreme cause of all things and eternally distinct from them. God alone has being in Himself; all other beings are dependent on Him. Whether the world depends on God for its existence does not seem to be clear, for Madhva held that nature or matter (*Prakṛti*) is eternal like God; but in all other respects he maintained that nature and souls depend entirely on God. The beatitude of the soul when it attains liberation consists precisely in realizing its entire dependence on God for its being, its knowledge, and its activity. Further, the liberation of the soul depends on the grace of God, first by His revealing Himself in the Vedas and then by His giving it a teacher (*guru*) to instruct it in the knowledge of the Vedas; finally in giving it an interior light. There were several features in the doctrine of Madhva and in the stories told about him, suggesting that he might have been influenced by Christian doctrine. This is not certain, however.

Niṁbārka. A new doctrine, called *dvaitādvaita,* which held that the *Brahman* is both different and not different (*bhedābheda*) from the world, was introduced by Niṁbārka (13th century?). His illustration was that of a clay pot, which is both different and not different from the clay of which it is made; again, that of the waves of the sea, which are both different and not different from the sea. In other words, *Brahman* and the world are essentially the same, differing only accidentally.

Vallabha. A fifth innovator in the interpretation of the *Vedānta,* Vallabha (1473–1531), went further than Niṁbārka and declared that *Brahman* and the world are identical and not different in anything. He called his doctrine *suddhādvaita* or pure nonduality, but he stood at the opposite pole to Śaṅkara. Whereas Śaṅkara, to maintain the absolute ''nonduality'' of the *Brahman,* had maintained that the world was *émāyā* and had no real being, Vallabha held that the world is no less real than the *Brahman* and is simply a manifestation of the *Brahman.* The *Brahman* is being, knowledge, and bliss. In the world he reveals his being but hides his knowledge and bliss. In souls he reveals his being and knowledge and hides his bliss. Only in his own form, identified with that of Krishna, does he reveal his perfect being, knowledge and bliss.

One of the most remarkable elements in the doctrine of Vallabha was his conception of divine grace. With the growth of devotion (*bhakti*) to a personal god the idea of divine grace (*anugraha*) had steadily developed. The idea had its origin in the Upanishads in a famous text where it is said that "Self" (*Ātman*) cannot be attained by the Vedas, or by intelligence or by much learning; by him it is attained whom it chooses" (*Katha Up.* 1.2.23). Although it was characteristic of Śaṅkara to translate this passage differently, since he rejected the doctrine of grace, it was eagerly accepted by those who worshiped a personal god. By Rāmānuja the worship of God was conceived of rather as the devotion of a servant to his Lord, and divine grace was conceived of as an act of condescension. But with the growth of popular devotion in later times, devotion came to be conceived more and more in terms of love (*prema*). The attitude of the devotee was that of total surrender (*prapatti*) in love. With this grew the idea that love itself is a gift of God. There were two schools of thought on the subject, the schools of "Monkey-Logic" and "Cat-Logic," which were developed respectively by *Vadakalai* ("Northern") and *Tentakalai* ("Southern") Vaisnavism in the Tamil regions of South India. According to the first school, the soul has to cooperate with divine grace, as the young monkey clings to its mother; but according to the other, grace is wholly an act of God as a cat carries its young.

Vallabha described divine grace as *pushṭi,* a state in which the soul feels itself to be absolutely helpless and abandons itself entirely to God. God is to be loved for His own sake, and the soul itself and the world for the sake of God. The union with God, which is sought, is one in which the soul participates in the very being and knowledge and bliss of God and loves with God's own love. Yet the soul is held to be essentially divine; it does not receive a new nature from God, but it discovers the reality of its own nature.

POPULAR RELIGION

While this great doctrinal synthesis was being built on the *Vedānta,* Hindu religion had undergone a profound transformation. The Vedic tradition continued to be preserved by the Brahmins, but popular religion introduced new elements into it. It is to be noticed that all the great doctors of the *Vedānta* came from South India, and to them is due also the fusion of the Vedic tradition with the popular religion. Popular religion found expression in a new literature, and in the worship of numerous deities.

Legends and manuals. Popular religion was represented in legends, especially those of the *Purāṇas;* and in manuals of doctrine and ritual, known as *Āgamas,* which were concerned especially with the cult of Viṣṇu, Śiva, and *Śakti.*

Purāṇas were the most important books of the new literature. These were collections of the myths and stories of the gods of popular devotion, confined not to the upper classes alone, but spread among people of all castes. The most notable of the *Purāṇas* were the *Viṣṇu* and *Bhāgavata Purāṇas,* telling the story of the *avatāras* or incarnations of Viṣṇu. An indication of the importance of this story was its inclusion by the later teachers of the *Vedānta,* such as Madhva, Niṁbārka, and Vallabha, with the Upanishads, the *Brahma-sūtras,* and the *Bhagavad Gītā* as one of the bases of their philosophy.

The *Āgamas* were manuals not only of doctrine but especially of ritual regulating the worship of the different sects. Although the *Brahman* was universally recognized as one, eternal, absolute being, whose nature is Being, knowledge, and bliss (*saccidānanda*), nevertheless *Brahman* was thought to be manifested in three forms (*trimūrti*), Brahmā (in the masculine as distinguished from the neuter *Brahman*), Viṣṇu, and Śiva.

Brahmā. Brahmā was the form of the creator, Viṣṇu the form of the preserver, and Śiva that of the destroyer of the universe. In practice however, scarcely any worship was given to Brahmā; Viṣṇu and Śiva each came to be regarded as the supreme God, who is at once creator, preserver, and destroyer of the world. The followers of Viṣṇu were known as Vaisnavaites, and those of Śiva, as Shaivites. Each sect had its own *Āgamas,* on which were based its doctrine and worship.

Viṣṇu. He was a solar deity of little importance in the Vedas, who came to be identified with Vāsudeva, and also with Nārāyaṇa, a cosmic deity of uncertain origin. As such, he was represented as sleeping in the primeval ocean on the thousand-headed serpent (Seṣa), while Brahmā, the world-creator was born of a lotus coming from his navel. This was an interesting reversal of the role of Brahmā, who was originally conceived as the supreme creator, not subject to Viṣṇu.

Viṣṇu, by his "descent" in different forms to save the world, had become incarnate. The first six incarnations, in the forms of a fish, a tortoise, a boar, a man-lion, a dwarf, and the hero Paraśurāma, were purely mythological and had little religious importance. But the incarnation of Viṣṇu as Rāma and Krishna, the heroes of the *Rāmāyaṇa* and the *Mahābhārata,* had a profound influence on Hindu religion.

Rāma. The cult of Rāma was comparatively late in developing. From the early Middle Ages, Rāma was represented in literature as an incarnation of Viṣṇu, but it was not until the 11th century that a cult seems to have developed. From this time, Rāma began to be represented not merely as an incarnation of Viṣṇu but as himself the supreme god. His cult was carried from South to North India in the 14th century by Ramananda, a disciple of Rāmānuja. It inspired some of the greatest religious poetry of India. One of his disciples was Kabīr (1440–1518), whose poems were later translated by Rabīndranāth Tagore. There is evidence in his work of Muslim influence on Hinduism, a more exalted conception of the transcendence of God, and a greater universality. But the poet who more than anyone else was responsible for the spread of devotion to Rāma was Tulsī Das (1532–1623), whose version of the *Rāmāyaṇa,* written in Hindi, is regarded as one of the great masterpieces of religious literature. The cult of Rāma was organized in the 17th century by Rāmdās (1608–81), who established many temples and monasteries (*maṭhs*), besides writing poetry. A contemporary of Rāmdās, Tukārām (1608–49), contributed some of the most moving poems to this cult. On the whole, the cult of Rāma was remarkable for its moral purity, in which it often compares favorably with that of Krishna.

Krishna. The cult of Krishna, although it began with the *Bhagavad Gītā,* reached its culmination in the Bhāgavata Purāṇa (10th century A.D.), one of the most popular works of Hindu piety, placed by later writers on a level with the Vedas. It tells the story of Krishna's infancy, which was full of miraculous incidents and many charming stories that endeared him to the people as the child-god. But of even greater importance was the story of Krishna as a young cowherd (*gopā*), who won the love of all the milkmaids (*gopīs*). Drawing wives from their husbands, he danced with them to the music of his flute in the moonlight. The story was intended to have a mystical significance and as such it was interpreted by all the great poets and philosophers of the cult. It represented the love of God, which draws men to forsake home and family and to surrender themselves to the joy of loving God. The extreme emotionalism of this cult often led to abuse. In later times Krishna, like Rāma, came to be regarded not so much as an incarnation of Viṣṇu, as the very person of God. Just as Viṣṇu was represented with his consort, the goddess Laksmī, so Krishna was worshiped with his consort Rādhā, the favorite among the *gopīs,* and the model of total surrender to the love of God. The conception was found in Niṁbārka and in Vallabha, but it reached its highest expression in the doctrine of Caitanya (1485–1553), a contemporary of Vallabha from Bengal, where the cult has continued to the present day in the emotional form which he gave to it, accompanied by singing and dancing.

Other Incarnations of Viṣṇu. These were ten in number and of a different nature from incarnations as Rāma and Krishna. The first was his incarnation in the form of the Buddha. This was added late in the Middle Ages in the spirit of "comprehension" so typical of Hinduism. It marks the fact that Buddhism had ceased to be a rival of Hinduism in India, and its great founder could now be safely introduced into the Hindu pantheon, but the cult of the Buddha never attained popularity. The last incarnation is to be that of Kalki, the *avatāra* of the end of time, when Viṣṇu will appear riding on a white horse with a flaming sword in his hand to destroy the wicked and restore the age of gold.

Śiva. The other great god of Hinduism was Śiva, often known as Maheśvara, the "great god." While Viṣṇu was a god of the ocean and the sky of wholly beneficent aspect, Śiva was originally a non-Vedic god later identified with Rudra, the Vedic god of mountain and storm. Śiva had his dark side in which he was represented as the "destroyer" of the world, wearing a garland of skulls and haunting the burning grounds of corpses; but he was also an ascetic (*mahāyogi*), living in solitude on Mt. Kailasa, holding the world in being by the power of his asceticism (*tapas*). He was represented with the "third eye," the sign of supreme wisdom, with matted locks, his body smeared with ashes—like his devotees today—and with snakes, of which he was Lord, encircling his neck and arms. But while in one aspect he was the Yogi, wrapped in meditation, in another he was lord of the Dance (*nātarāja*), who held the world in being in the cosmic dance and would finally bring it to an end.

This strange and rather fierce deity, with his ambivalent nature and marks of many different origins, captured the imagination of India and was gradually transformed into a god of supreme beauty with dominant characteristics of grace and love. As the dance of Krishna with the *gopīs* became a symbol of divine love, so the linga of Śiva, a cylindrical pillar with a rounded top, seen in countless temples all over India, became a symbol of the pure godhead "without form" and the creative source of life. In South India in the Tamil country the cult of Śiva developed its most beautiful features. While, in the Middle Ages between the 5th and 10th century, the Ālvārs were celebrating Viṣṇu in their poetry, a school of Shaivite poets arose called the Nāyāṇars; of these the most famous was Māṇikka Vāchakar, one of the greatest religious poets of all time. He celebrated Śiva as a god of pure love, who yet punishes the sinner to teach him to mend his ways. Thus the worship of Śiva developed a pure moral character; the god was seen as the Lord of all, full of compassion and mercy, bestowing his grace on the sinner and drawing him by his love.

The cult also developed its own distinctive theology called the *Shaiva Siddhānta.* Though it recognized the authority of the Vedas, it had its own distinctive scriptures that took the form of *Āgamas.* Śiva was represented as the supreme God, who was being, knowledge, and bliss, as in the *Vedānta.* But the Shaiva Siddhānta introduced another principle, the *Śakti* or power of Śiva, by which he brought the world into being. By this means, the pure transcendence of Śiva as lord (*pati*) was preserved, and matter (*paśa*) and the soul (*pāśu*) were held to be really distinct from him. The soul was liberated from the bonds of matter by the grace of Śiva and in its final state enjoyed not absorption but self-realization in the perfect bliss of Śiva. There were other forms of Śivism, notably Kāshmīra Śivism, said to have been introduced into Kashmir in the 9th century A.D., and Vīra Śivism, introduced by Basava into Kannada (Mysore State) in the 12th century A.D. Basava's followers were called Liṅgāyats, from their custom of wearing the liṅga on their person. But neither of these cults had a distinctive doctrine.

The Śakti of Śiva. In the course of time, the *Śakti* of Śiva, conceived as a feminine principle, became the object of a separate cult originating probably in the worship of the Mother Goddess, according to the evidence furnished by the prehistoric culture of Harappā and Mohenjo-Daro. It was not until the Middle Ages that it appeared in orthodox Hinduism. From the 4th century onward, the mother goddess made an appearance as consort of the great gods. Thus Brahmā was represented with his consort Sarasvatī, the goddess of wisdom; Viṣṇu with Lakṣmī, the goddess of wealth; and Śiva with Pārvatī, daughter of the Himalaya Mountain. The consort of Śiva was also known as Durgā or KĀLĪ, and in this form she received worship in a special cult as *Śakti.* The peculiarity of the *Śakti* doctrine was that Śiva, who was pure being and pure consciousness, was regarded as wholly transcendent and inactive; all the activity of the world came from the power of his *Śakti.* Thus, *Śakti* was the moving principle of the universe, the source of all life and energy. She was the womb of nature, the Mother of all creation. Ultimately indeed, she was regarded as one with the supreme principle of Being, the source of the life not only of nature but also of the gods.

As Mother Nature, *Śakti* had two aspects, one fierce and terrible, representing the destructive aspect of nature, the other gentle and loving, the source of joy and liberation. The doctrine and worship of the *Śakti* cult was based on scriptures known as the *Tantras* (*see* TANTRISM). Through these writings, the tradition of the old fertility cults entered Hinduism. Since some of these rites involved orgiastic practices, the breaking of all taboos, the reputation of the cult suffered as a whole. But essentially the cult was based on the recognition of the divine power inherent in matter and the processes of nature, on the sacramental value of the body and its powers to lead the soul on the path of liberation. Its most characteristic doctrine was that of Kundalinī Yoga. According to this doctrine *Śakti,* the divine energy, lies coiled up like a serpent at the base of the spine in the form of Kundalinī. The purpose of this Yoga is to lead the *Śakti* through the different centers of consciousness (*chakras*) in the body, from the base of the spine to the top of the head, until *Śakti* unites with Śiva or pure consciousness and attains to the perfect bliss of liberation.

Worship. In addition to the great gods of Hinduism, there were innumerable lesser deities; indeed it is said in the *Purāṇas* that there are 333 million deities in the Hindu pantheon. These include local gods and goddesses, spirits and demigods of all kinds. India never lost the primitive sense of the "sacred," of a divine mystery present in the world of nature. Hills and mountains, rivers and streams, plants and animals, have a sacred character and may be worshiped as manifestations of the divine being. Persons of all kinds, parents and teachers, husband and wife, above all the *guru,* the spiritual teacher, may be worshiped as God, because they are invested with divine authority. This gives a special character to the worship of the gods. It would not be correct to describe it simply as polytheism, in spite of the multitude of gods, since each god or goddess is regarded as but a "form" or manifestation of the one Universal Being. The danger of polytheism, even among the simple people in the villages, is less evident than the sense of the divine as one infinite power extending everywhere.

Temples. From the time of the Middle Ages when the Vedic sacrifice (*yajña*) lost its importance, worship (*pūjā*) has been offered to the gods in temples. The temple itself is a mark of the later popular religion. Worship is offered by the placing of fruit and flowers before an image of the god set in a shrine (*mūlasthānam*) around which the temple is built. The Hindu temple is not a place of congregational worship; it is essentially the shrine of a deity, and offerings are made by the priest (*pūjarī*) for individuals or small family groups. The great Hindu temples have a multitude of such shrines, where different gods are worshiped, but the temple centers on the principal shrine. This is usually dark and low, representing the hidden dwelling place of the divine mystery at the heart of the universe, of which the temple is an image.

An image that is worshiped is consecrated by a special ceremony, and after its consecration it is believed that the god is really present in it. It is treated as a living being, awakened from sleep in the morning, washed and dressed and arrayed with garlands of flowers; lamps are waved before it, and it is given food to eat, the "essence" being taken by the god and the material part being given to the worshipers or distributed to the poor. This worship of idols is one of the principal elements in Hindu religion; yet it would be a mistake to regard it simply as idolatry. Generally speaking, such worship is rather the expression of a profound sacramental sense. It is not the idol as such that is worshiped, but the god who is believed to dwell in the idol, and above any particular god, Divine Being itself, which thus manifests itself to its worshipers. The true nature of this worship is expressed in a remarkable text of the 13th century: "God when present in the inanimate idol becomes in all respects subject to his devotee. Though omniscient, he seems to be without knowledge; though alive and conscious he appears to be inanimate; though independent, he appears to be entirely dependent on others; though omnipotent, he seems to be powerless; though perfect, he appears needy; the protector of the universe, helpless he is the Lord, but he hides his Lordship; the invisible makes himself an object for our senses to perceive, the inapprehensible brings himself within our easy reach." Nothing could express more clearly the sacramental character of Hindu popular worship, when it is properly understood.

Although the temple is in a sense the center of religious worship and the temples are crowded with worshipers on the great festivals and visited by pilgrims from all over India, yet the home remains, as in Vedic times, the place where most of the sacred rites are performed. An orthodox Brahmin house has a room set apart for the daily prayers, which are offered at sunrise, and almost every religious home has a small shrine in a corner of a room set apart for prayer. Every stage of life, moreover, is accompanied by sacramental rites (*saṁskāras*) from birth, or rather before birth, to death. There are three rites prescribed during the pregnancy of the mother and three after birth. Not all these are observed in modern times, but a special importance continues to be attached to the ceremony of the thread (*upanayana*), by which the Brahmin boy is initiated as a full member of his community and becomes one of the "twice-born." This is accompanied by the recital of the *gāyatrī*, a verse of the *Rig Veda,* considered to be supremely sacred and used on many occasions. A Hindu marriage is performed in the home and is invested with a solemn character. According to tradition, marriage is indissoluble and a widow is never permitted to marry again. However, divorce was introduced by the State. Marriages were arranged by the family and normally took place in childhood until recently, when it was forbidden by law.

According to Vedic tradition, the dead are cremated, but burial is common among many of the lower castes. There are elaborate funeral rites, renewed up to 30 days after the death, and offerings of rice are made to the souls of the dead at regular intervals.

HINDUISM AND THE CASTE SYSTEM

Though abolished by law, caste remains in force to a large extent, especially in regard to marriage. It is quite distinct from the four "classes" (*varṇa*) of ancient India, and appears merely to have been grafted on to them, having been derived from the tribal customs.

Crafts and Castes. Caste was determined partly by religious and social customs and partly by craft or trade. It was by means of the caste system that the innumerable tribal and racial groups of ancient India with their different religions and social customs were integrated into Hinduism, while preserving their own traditions. At the same time, the different craftsmen, whose work was the glory of ancient India and was always stamped with a religions character, formed themselves into guilds, which gradually formed distinct castes. In the course of time, the number of castes grew to be more than 2,000, and the restrictions on intercourse between castes grew more and more rigid. At the same time certain tribal groups and certain trades came to be regarded as base and unclean and were held to be "untouchable," so that they could not approach within a certain distance of a person of a higher caste. The caste system has undoubtedly been responsible for many injustices in Hindu life, especially as it was held to be based on *karma,* so that a man's position in society was determined by the actions of his former life. On the other hand, the caste system enabled each group to retain its own individuality and distinctive traditions, gave each person a clearly defined status in society, and provided a kind of social security for widows and orphans, the aged, and the poor, who would otherwise have had no one to care for them.

Persistence of the caste system. The caste system retains a strong hold over Hindu society, especially in the villages, but it has begun to break down as a result of contact with modern habits of life in the towns. The State abolished "untouchability" by law, and efforts were made to secure equality of status for all classes. A transformation in Hindu society is evident in the suppression of such customs as the immolation of widows on the funeral pyre of their husbands (*satī*) and temple prostitution. Child marriage is illegal and divorce is permitted. But these are changes in the social structure. Hinduism, far from having lost its hold over the people, has rather undergone a reformation and emerged stronger than before.

REFORM IN HINDUISM

In the 19th and 20th centuries, Hinduism was purified in a variety of ways by the influence of learned or saintly Hindus.

Sen, Sarasvati. The first movement of reform in Hinduism began with the foundation of a school of rational theism on the basis of the Upanishads, the Brāhma Samāj, by Rām Mohan Roy (1772–1833), a Brahmin from Bengal. It was an attempt to free Hinduism from polytheism and image worship and to construct a pure monotheism in the light of Christian and Muslim doctrine. Though the Brāhma Samāj had some influence for a time and the work was continued by Debendra Nāth Tagore (1817–1905), the father of the poet, who gave it a more Indian character, it became divided under its next leader, Keshab Chandra Sen (1838–84), on the question of the relation between the Christian and Hindu elements within it. This led to another movement of reform by Dayānand Sarasvatī (1824–83), who founded the Ārya Samāj, another attempt to abolish polytheism, image worship, and caste practices. Based on what its founder believed to be the pure religion of the Vedas, it was opposed alike to Christianity and to Islam. It continues to form a militant group within Hinduism, but its influence is not extensive.

Parahaṁsa. The greatest portent in modern Hinduism was Rāmakrishna Parahaṁsa (1834–86). He was a poor and almost unlettered Brahmin, who spent most of his life as a devotee of the Mother Goddess at the Dakshineswar temple outside Calcutta. He summed up in himself all that was best in Hinduism. A devotee of the Mother Goddess, who practiced all the tantric rites of her cult, he was at the same time a Vedantin, who worshiped God "without form" no less than "with form." He was an ascetic, who realized the ideal of Hindu *sannyāsi,* and a mystic, who manifested the Hindu ideal of a "holy man" who had "realized" God. His mind was open to other religions, and for some time he deliberately meditated as a Christian and a Muslim in order to enter into the spirit of each religion. Finally he was led to the belief that "all religions are one." His influence was extended by his disciple Vivekānanda (1862–1902), who founded the Rāmakrishna Mission, introducing a new element of social service into Hinduism and giving it a missionary character that extended its influence to Europe and America.

Gāndhi. While these movements of reform affected only a cultured minority, it was Mahātmā Gāndhi (1869–1948) more than anyone who was responsible for bringing the reform to the masses of the people. Through him untouchability was abolished and many caste barriers were removed. He introduced the ideal of nonviolence (*ahiṁsa*) as the basic principle of social and political life, and by this India was able eventually to obtain her independence. Gāndhi was deeply influenced by the teaching and example of Christ, as well as by the writings of Tolstoi, but he remained a devout Hindu at heart, accepting all Hinduism's basic principles. Through him Hindu religion acquired a new moral character, which affected the whole mass of the people.

Ghose. The doctrine of the *Vedānta* received further development at the hands of Aurobindo Ghose (1872–1950), who in 1910 founded an *ashram,* or hermitage, at Pondicherry, where he lived for 40 years. He had read modern Western philosophy, and in his great work, *The Life Divine,* he sought to reconcile an evolutionary view of the universe with the traditional doctrine of the *Vedānta.* According to his theory, both being and becoming are essential aspects of the one *Brahman;* the world of becoming, of time and evolution, is a manifestation of the eternal *Brahman.* There is a movement of descent from the divine being into the world, and a corresponding movement of ascent by which the world returns to the divine being, by becoming conscious in man of its identity with the divine nature.

Maharishi. Perhaps the most authentic expression of the doctrine of the *Vedānta* in modern times is to be found in Ramana Maharishi (1879–1950) of South India, who left his home at the age of 17 to live in a cave as a *sannyāsī* on the holy hill of Aruṇācala at Tiruvaṇṇāmalai, near Madras. Without any training in the *Vedānta* he reached the state of absolute "identity" with the *Brahman,* which had always been the goal of the Hindu religious quest. He taught the doctrine of pure "nonduality" (*Advaita*) as it was held by Śaṅkara, but with him it was not so much a theory as an experience; he showed in his life the example of perfect detachment and at the same time sympathy and understanding, which is the Hindu's mark of the "holy man." Thus in different ways Hinduism showed itself capable of new life, satisfying the religious, moral, and social ideals of the majority of its adherents.

HINDUISM AND CHRISTIANITY

Hinduism was called by the theologian P. Johanns, SJ, "the most searching quest in the natural order for the Divine that the world has known." In common with Christianity, it has its own idea of Trinity and Incarnation, of sin and salvation, of revelation and inspiration, of sacrifice and sacrament, of law and morality, of the ascetic and mystical ife, of grace and love, and of man's ultimate goal of union with God. It is impossible not to admire the profundity of its conception of God as *saccidānanda,* being, knowledge, and bliss and the degree of intimacy with God to which it declares that the soul is called.

Lack of a clear concept of creation. According to Johanns, this is its principal weakness. As a result of it, Hinduism has never been able to define a relation between God, the soul, and the world. To preserve the divine simplicity and transcendence, it must say with Śaṅkara that the world is *māyā,* that is, without ultimate reality; or with Rāmānuja and his school, it must say that the world itself is divine. Nor has it ever been able to clarify the true nature of personality in God. It is true that in the dualist system of Madhva and in the *Shaiva Siddhānta,* a real distinction between God, the soul, and the world is established, but there is no creation, properly speaking, and matter and souls are conceived as eternal like God.

Soul's union with God. Another limitation is that, the soul being never clearly distinguished from God, union with God is always conceived in terms of identity. Thus grace in Hindu doctrine is not a pure gift of God by which the soul is raised to a participation in the divine being, but a divine assistance by which it is enabled to know its true and eternal being as one with God. Hinduism's rootedness in mythology, moreover, can easily result in an unworthy conception of the divine nature and a practical polytheism. The caste system, also, with its concept of untouchability, child marriage, and polygamy, the cult of images, which may easily lead to idolatry, and such customs as ritual prostitution and the burning of widows (*satī*), have in practice often led to degradation. Modern Hinduism, however, has reacted against such abuses. Its profound philosophy has succeeded in effectually purifying the tangle of mythology and in constructing a noble ethical ideal in the face of corrupt practices.

See Also: INDIAN PHILOSOPHY.

Bibliography: Translations. W. T. DE BARY et al., comps., *Sources of Indian Tradition* (*Records of Civilization* 56; New York 1958). S. RADHAKRISHNAN and C. A. MOORE, *A Source Book in Indian Philosophy* (Princeton 1957). S. RADHAKRISHNAN, ed. and tr., *The Principal Upanishads* (New York 1953). General. A. L. BASHAM, *The Wonder That Was India: A Survey of the Culture of the Indian Sub-Continent before the Coming of the Muslims* (London 1954) ch. 7. T. M. P. MAHADEVAN, *Outlines of Hinduism* (Bombay 1956). S. RADHAKRISHNAN, *Indian Philosophy,* 2 v. (2d ed. rev. London 1941); ed., *History of Philosophy, Eastern and Western,* 2 v. (London 1952–53) v. 1 *Indian Thought.* S. DASGUPTA, *A History of Indian Philosophy,* 5 v. (Cambridge, Eng. 1932–55). H. LOSCH, *Die Religion in Geschichte und Gegenwart* (Tübingen 1957–65) 3:340–349. W. CROOKE and J. HASTINGS, ed., *Encyclopedia of Religion and Ethics* (Edinburgh 1908–27) 6:686–715. J. FINEGAN, *The Archeology of World Religions* (Princeton 1952) 123–181. C. SHARMA, *A Critical Survey of Indian Philosophy* (London 1960). K. K. KLOSTERMAIER, *A Survey of Hinduism,* 2d ed (Albany, NY 1994). Catholic. C. REGAMEY, *Lexikon für Theologie und Kirche,* ed. J. HOFER and K. RAHNER (Freiburg 1957–65) 5:368–372. G. DANDOY, *An Essay on the Unreality of the World in the Advaita* (Calcutta 1919), tr. L. M. GAUTHIER (Paris 1932), excellent survey by Catholic scholars with bibliog. P. JOHANNS, *A Synopsis of "To Christ through the Vedanta"* (*Light of the East* series 4, 7, 9, 19; Ranchi 1942–44); *La Pensée religieuse de l'Inde,* tr. L. M. GAUTHIER (Namur 1952). M. QUÉGUINER, *Catholicisme* 5 (1960) 1463–82. P. MASSON-OURSEL, "Les Religions de l'Inde," *Histoire des religions,* eds. M. BRILLANT and R. AIGRAIN (Paris 1953—) 2:85–163. A. KRÄMER, *Christus und Christentum im Denken des modernen Hinduismus* (Bonn 1958). On the relations between Hinduism and Christianity, see the systematic bibliog. in E. BENZ and M. NAMBARA, *Das Christentum und die nicht-christlichen Hochreligionen* (Beihefte der Zeitschrift für Religions- und Geistesgeschichte 5; Leiden 1960) 33–46.

[B. GRIFFITHS/K. R. SUNDARARAJAN]

Arthur Hinsley.

HINSLEY, ARTHUR

Cardinal, fifth archbishop of Westminster, England; b. Carlton, Yorkshire, England, Aug. 25, 1865; d. Buntingford, near London, March 17, 1943. He was the son of Thomas, a carpenter, and Bridget (Ryan) Hinsley. He was educated at the Catholic school in Carlton; at Ushaw College, Durham, England, receiving his A.B. (1889); and at the English College, Rome. After ordination (1893) he lectured on philosophy at Ushaw until 1897. He was headmaster (1899–1904) of St. Bede's Grammar School, which he founded at Bradford, England. After acting as pastor in Sutton Park (1904–11) and Sydenham (1911–17), he served as rector of the English College, Rome (1917–28). He was visitor apostolic to Africa (1929) and first apostolic delegate there (1930–34). Though elderly and infirm, he was recalled from retirement to fill the See at WESTMINSTER (1935). He became a cardinal in 1937. Active in diocesan affairs, he was largely responsible for the establishment in 1941 of the SWORD OF THE SPIRIT, a movement to encourage a return to Christian principles in public and private life.

Bibliography: D. NEWTON, *The Dictionary of National Biography from the Earliest Times to 1900*, 63 v. (London 1885–1900; repr. with corrections, 21 v., 1908–09, 1921–22, 1938; suppl. 1901–) (1941–50) 394–395. J. C. HEENAN, *Cardinal Hinsley* (London 1944).

[D. MILBURN]

HIPPO REGIUS

Ancient North African bishopric, modern Bone, Algeria. The Phoenicians are believed to have had a settlement there in the 10th century B.C. The title Regius was used to distinguish it from Hippo Diarrhytus, because it both formed part of the kingdom of Numidia and apparently served as a residence for Numidian kings. On the defeat of Pompey and his allies, including the Numidian King Juba, at Thapsus, Caesar annexed Hippo to the Roman Empire (46 B.C.). Under St. AUGUSTINE it formed part of the civil *Africa proconsularis* and belonged to the ecclesiastical Province of Numidia. In 431 it was taken by the Vandals and in 533 was reconquered by Justinian's army. In the 7th century the Arabs took possession and founded Bona-el-Hadida in a naturally protected area about a mile distant. This is the location of the modern port of Bone, which extends to the site of the ancient city. Lybian, Punic, Greek, Latin, Vandal, and Byzantine rulers and settlers gave the city its population and cultural pattern. Its geographical locale made it an important port, with roads running up and down the coast and into the hinterlands.

Christianity appears to have been brought to Hippo from Italy and from the East. The Christian quarter was in the port area, within the pre-Roman settlement on the outskirts of the Roman city and its forum. Its first known bishop bore a Greek name; Augustine's immediate predecessor, Valerius, still spoke Greek and had difficulty with Latin. Bishop Theogenes (*Sent. episc.* 87.14; *Corpus scriptorum ecclesiasticorum latinorum* 3.1:443) was a martyr under VALERIAN; another bishop, Fidentius, was one of the 20 martyrs in the DIOCLETIAN persecution (Aug., *Serm.* 148; 257; 325; *Civ.* 22.8). Its cathedral was built by Bishop Leontius (not a martyr) and named after him (Aug., *Serm.* 260, 262; *Epist.* 29). Under Emperors Constantius II and Julian, the Donatists formed a majority of citizens, particularly under their bishop, Faustinus (Aug., *C. Petil.* 2.83.184). Bishop Valerius, in 395, consecrated Augustine as his auxiliary bishop. Augustine became bishop of Hippo in 396, and in 411, after the religious debate at Carthage, he succeeded in restoring religious unity to the city. His successor, Heraclius, is the last bishop whose name is known (Aug., *Serm.* 213). The latest information on the diocese comes from the 8th and 9th centuries.

Synods, Churches, and Monasteries. An African plenary synod was held in Hippo in 393 and presided over by Bp. Aurelius of Carthage in the *secretarium* of the basilica of Peace (J. D. Mansi, *Sacrorum Conciliorum nova et amplissima collectio,* 3:849; Possidius, *Vita* 7). Augustine, though still a priest, addressed the assembly (*Retract.* 1.17). A plenary synod was held also, probably in 427, in the basilica of St. Leontius (Mansi 3:859; 4:441; 539). Augustine gives information regarding the basilica of Leontius that was apparently the same as the basilica Maior (*Serm.* 260; 258; 325.2) and perhaps also identical with the basilica Pacis (Mansi 3:730; *De actis c. Fel.* 2.1; *Epist.* 213). He speaks of a Donatist church (*Epist.* 29.11) that (after 411) was taken over by the Catholics; of an ''old church'' that is difficult to identify (*Epist.* 99.3); a memoria of St. Theogones (Mai., *Serm.* 158.2); and of another in honor of the 20 martyrs (*Serm.* 148). Heraclius the priest built a chapel attached to the main church for the relics of St. Stephen in 425 at the request of Augustine; and miracles took place there (*Serm.* 318–324, 356.7; *Civ.* 22.8). Another priest, Leporius, constructed a basilica in honor of the eight martyrs and a hospice for strangers (*Serm.* 356.10).

On his arrival in Hippo after his conversion, Augustine had built a small monastery for his lay monks in the garden of the community (*Vita* 5); and on his election as bishop, he turned the bishop's house into a residence for his clergy, so that they lived a common life (*Serm.* 355.2). There were other monasteries in the vicinity of Hippo founded by Leporius and Barnabas (*Serm.* 356.10, 15); and Augustine's sister presided over a convent for nuns (*Serm.* 355.3, 6; Possidius, *Vita* 26).

Archeology. Excavations have unearthed a small but important part of Hippo with pre-Roman and Roman settlements, including a large forum, a theater, public baths in the north and south, temples, a market place, a port, villas, many mosaics, inscriptions, sculptures, lamps, jewelry, and coins. A five-sided island (*insula*), or quarter, occupied by Christian buildings bordered the seacoast about one-eighth of a mile east of the forum, somewhat south of the northern baths and the temple and close to the market place. It contained a three-aisled, pillared basilica whose nave was about 107 feet long by 49 feet wide and had an elevated half-rounded apse, about 27 by 21 feet; it was preceded by a narthex. At the back of the apse are the positions of the bishop's *cathedra* and the benches for the priests. The altar with its surrounding chancel was located before the apse. The baptistery, with an anteroom and *consignatorium* (for Confirmation), was located on the east side near the main entrance. Around the basilica were grouped administration and living rooms, a chapel with three apses, and apparently a *secretarium* (sacristy, a reception room, and an assembly hall for synods). It was decorated with an apse and peristyle and contained a library. Beneath the basilica are ruins probably of a pre-Constantinian house church. Despite the group of buildings, mosaics, and graves, particularly from the time of the Vandals, it is not possible to say whether this was originally a Catholic or Donatist church. It is thought to have been the basilica of the Catholics that served as the bishop's church in Augustine's day and that the annexed chapel was that of St. Stephen, with living quarters of the bishop and the monastery in the garden (*Serm.* 318–324, 356–357). East of this *insula,* E. Marec believes he has discovered another five-aisled basilica; the graves found in the atrium might point to this, but the view has not won acceptance. It could be the ''old church'' mentioned by Augustine (*Epist.* 99.3). After 411 all the churches belonged to the Catholic community. Augustine mentions many places and holy sites, such as the *Castellum Fussala (Epist.* 209; 224.1) and the *Municipium Tulliense (Cur. mort.* 12.15), both of which became dioceses.

Bibliography: J. MESNAGE, *L'Afrique chrétienne . . .* (Paris 1912) 263–267. H. LECLERCQ, *Dictionnaire d'archéologie chrétienne et de liturgie*, ed. F. CARROLL, H. LECLERQ, and H. I. MARROU, 15 v. (Paris 1907–53) 6.2:2483–2531. W. H. C. FREND, *The Donatist Church* (Oxford 1952). O. PERLER, ''L'Église principale et les autres sanctuaires chrétiens d'Hipponela-Royale,'' *Revue des études augustiniennes* 1 (1955) 299–343; 2 (1956) 435–446. C. LAMBOT, *Revue des sciences religieuses* 30 (1956) 230–240. E. MAREC, *Hippone la Royale* (Algiers 1954). *Monuments chrétiens d'Hippone* (Paris 1958), cf. T. W. PHELAN, *Theological Studies* 20 (1959) 422–431. H. I. MARROU, *Revue des études augustiniennes* 6 (1960) 109–154. J. LASSUS,''L'Archéologie Algerienne en 1958: Hippone,'' *Libyca* 7 (1959) 306–323; *Fasti Archeologici* 15 (1963) 315–316. G. CAMPS, ''. . . Massinissa,'' *Libyca* 8 (1960) 1–320.

[O. PERLER]

HIPPOCRATES

Ancient Greek physician; b. Cos, 460(?) B.C.; d. probably at Larissa, Thrace, 377(?) B.C. He is generally referred to as the ''Father of Medicine,'' but recent scholarship has rendered this a doubtful appellation. According to his biographer, Soranus (A.D. 98–138), Hippocrates was a descendant of Asclepius, a physician mentioned in the *Iliad.* It is thought that he learned medicine from his father, who is believed to have been a priest physician attached to the temple of Asclepius on Cos. He is thought to have traveled widely and to have taught and practiced his art at Thrace, Thessaly, Delos, and possibly Athens. His age at death is variously estimated between 85 and 110 years.

Not much is accurately known about the details of his life, and it seems likely that none of the works attributed to him, i.e., in the *Corpus Hippocraticum,* were actually written by him. Nevertheless, these writings laid down logical principles upon which the practice of medicine as a science took a firm foundation.

Hippocrates.

The first collection of writings attributed to Hippocrates was made about the 3rd century B.C. for the library at Alexandria. The most ancient extant manuscripts, dating from the 10th to the 12th century A.D., are found in the Vatican Library, in St. Mark's in Venice, in the state libraries of Vienna and Paris, and in the Laurentian Library in Florence.

According to Plato, he separated medicine from superstition and primitive religion. He differentiated kinds of diseases, whereas prior to that time, all illness was thought to be just one disease. He taught that diseases had natural causes and denied that disease was the work of the gods; he taught that disease was a natural process and the symptoms of a disease were due to reactions of the body to that disease. He stressed bedside observation of the patient, recording what he observed and then making logical deductions from these observations.

The description of some diseases in the *Corpus* are so accurate and complete that they could, with but minimal change, still be used in teaching medicine. Actually, the methods advocated for reduction of dislocation of the shoulder are practically those of modern orthopedics.

Hippocrates and his followers possessed a deep respect for the patient as a human being. In their view the chief function of the physician was to aid the natural forces of the body to rid itself of disease.

The oath attributed to Hippocrates elevated the practice of medicine and gave it an altruistic code of ethics. The oath, with only minor changes, is taken by many graduating medical students today.

Bibliography: *The Genuine Works of Hippocrates,* ed. and tr. F. ADAMS (London 1849). W. A. HEIDEL, ''Hippocratea'' in *Harvard Studies in Classical Philology* 25 (1914). F. H. GARRISON, *Introduction to the History of Medicine* (4th ed. Philadelphia 1929). D. GUTHRIE, *A History of Medicine* (Philadelphia 1946). C. J. SINGER, *Greek Biology and Greek Medicine* (Oxford 1922). L. EDELSTEIN, in *The Oxford Classical Dictionary,* ed. M. CARY et al. (Oxford 1949) 430.

[R. A. OSBOURN]

HIPPOCRATIC OATH

The pledge traditionally affirmed by physicians upon entering their profession. It embodies the general ethical principles governing relations of a physician to his profession and to his patients. Variant readings of its text frequently represent Christian or non-Christian modifications.

The earliest form of the oath is found among a corpus of some 70 ancient Greek medical writings that have been associated with the name of HIPPOCRATES of Cos (460–377 or 359 B.C.) and have been referred to as the Hippocratic Collection. This short work shares in historical, textual, and hermeneutical difficulties besetting the general Hippocratic literary question.

Hippocrates was held in such regard, even by PLATO, his junior contemporary, that the ethos inspired by his idealized image—namely, deep medical insight and high performance of duty—accounts for the association made by history between his name and the writings included today in the Hippocratic corpus. The texts reflect a Grecian setting. The importance of these writings, however, described by some as the library of the School of Cos, composed and collected over a span of five centuries, is measured by the value consistently placed on them in succeeding ages. The present text of the oath is thought to be probably post-Hippocratic. One opinion finds a pre-Hippocratic source in Pythagorean tradition. Erotian, living in Nero's time, considered the oath to be genuine. Thus, whether from his hand or spirit, the oath is worthily deemed Hippocratic.

In addition to the usual division of the text's teaching into duties to the healing art and to the patient, there is a statement of the goal of medicine. The physician practices his art for the benefit of the patient in the form of health, a human good. Thus is it linked with the science of human good, or ethics. Hence, the second half of the oath is suitably directed to ethical matters in medicine. A further unfolding of the temperate virtues, becoming to a physician, is found in other works of the collection, for example, in ''On the Physician'' and ''On Decorum.''

Some things in the oath are difficult to interpret. The precise meaning of ''oath'' and ''indenture'' in the text, the professional import of ''the craft of the knife,'' and the ethical connotation in ancient Greece of forswearing abortive procedures and of the giving of harmful drugs present goading questions. Despite such obscurities the physician who would use this pre-Christian document as a venerable source will find it consistent with later professional ethical principles.

The oath's hardy medical affinity has made it a symbolic vehicle for medical ideals. A professional pledge is not only written; it is also lived. The literal meaning therefore is secondary to the moral signification as this has come to be understood through doctor-patient experience acquired over centuries. With appropriate modification the ethical burden of the Hippocratic Oath has been found compatible with both Christian and non-Christian thought. Its binding force has been variously estimated from that of an obligatory promise to that of exemplary counsel. In general it has been the traditional formula pledged during graduation exercises at medical schools.

A nostalgic simplicity characterizes its presence among the modern national and international codes of medical ethics. In the face of problems arising from technical medical advance and mankind's stockpiling of scientific means that function both for human destruction and for the deterrence of aggression, ethical principles with a greater degree of explication have had to be formulated. Modern medical codes proclaim the humanistic goal of medicine and protect physicians from untoward pressures to have them participate in genocide or in the aggressive activities of ABC warfare or in certain inhumane uses of psychological skills. Although the medical practice of Hippocrates is long outmoded, his ideals are enduring.

Bibliography: HIPPOCRATES, ''The Oath,'' ed. and tr. W. H. S. JONES, *Hippocrates* v.1 (Loeb Classical Library; London-New York-Cambridge, Mass. 1948) 291–301. L. EDELSTEIN, *The Hippocratic Oath: Text, Translation, and Interpretation* (Baltimore 1943). C. J. SINGER and E. A. UNDERWOOD, *A Short History of Medicine* (2d ed. New York 1962).

[A. W. MURPHY]

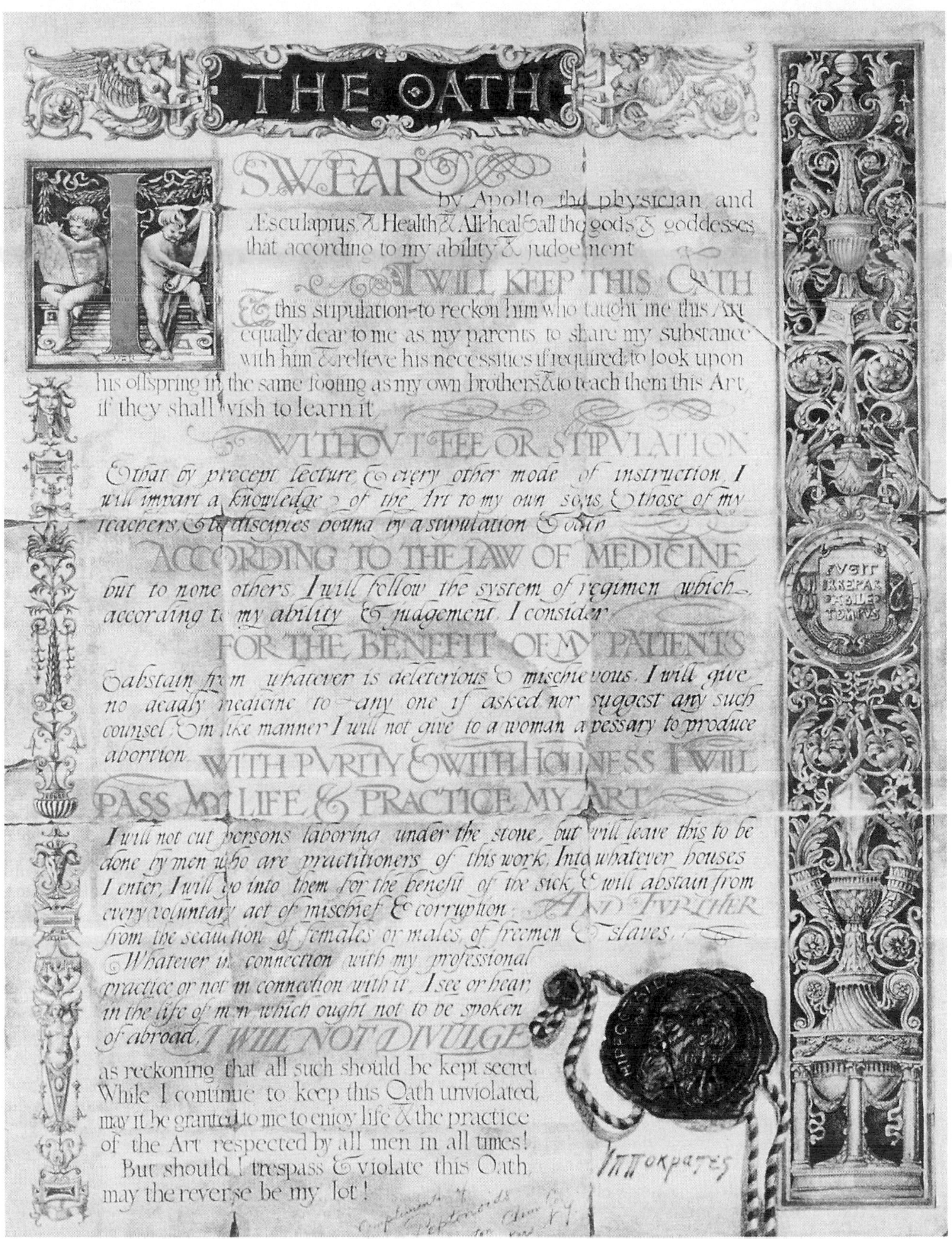

THE OATH

I SWEAR by Apollo the physician and Esculapius & Health & All-heal & all the gods & goddesses, that according to my ability & judgement

I WILL KEEP THIS OATH

& this stipulation—to reckon him who taught me this Art equally dear to me as my parents, to share my substance with him & relieve his necessities if required; to look upon his offspring in the same footing as my own brothers & to teach them this Art, if they shall wish to learn it

WITHOUT FEE OR STIPULATION

& that by precept, lecture & every other mode of instruction, I will impart a knowledge of the Art to my own sons & those of my teachers & to disciples bound by a stipulation & oath

ACCORDING TO THE LAW OF MEDICINE

but to none others. I will follow the system of regimen which according to my ability & judgement I consider

FOR THE BENEFIT OF MY PATIENTS

& abstain from whatever is deleterious & mischievous. I will give no deadly medicine to any one if asked nor suggest any such counsel & in like manner I will not give to a woman a pessary to produce abortion.

WITH PURITY & WITH HOLINESS I WILL PASS MY LIFE & PRACTICE MY ART

I will not cut persons laboring under the stone, but will leave this to be done by men who are practitioners of this work. Into whatever houses I enter, I will go into them for the benefit of the sick & will abstain from every voluntary act of mischief & corruption; AND FURTHER from the seduction of females or males, of freemen & slaves.

Whatever in connection with my professional practice or not in connection with it, I see or hear, in the life of men which ought not to be spoken of abroad, I WILL NOT DIVULGE as reckoning that all such should be kept secret. While I continue to keep this Oath unviolated, may it be granted to me to enjoy life & the practice of the Art respected by all men in all times!

But should I trespass & violate this Oath, may the reverse be my lot!

The Hippocratic Oath. (©CORBIS)

St. Hippolytus of Rome.

HIPPOLYTUS OF ROME, ST.

Ecclesiastical author, presbyter, antipope, and martyr; b.*c.* 170; d. Sardinia, 235 or 236. The identity, life, and writings of Hippolytus continue to pose challenges to scholars.

Life

Probably of Eastern extraction, although the exact place of his origin is unknown, Hippolytus became a member of the Roman clergy and distinguished himself as the foremost writer of the Roman church in the third century. His learning and talent for writing won him the admiration and support of a rigorist faction within the church at Rome who encouraged him as a rival claimant to that see. His education and intellectual abilities exceeded those of contemporary Roman bishops whom he despised and denounced. Hippolytus charged Zephyrinus (198/9–217) with ineptness and avarice. He unjustly accused Callistus I (217–222) of Sabellianism, or Modalism, and disciplinary laxity. In the last years of the pontificate of Callistus I, Hippolytus and his supporters went into formal schism, asserting his claim to the see of Rome. He persisted in this claim throughout the pontificates of Urban I (223–230) and Pontian (230–235). In the persecution launched by Emperor Maximus the Thracian (235–238), Pontian and Hippolytus were exiled to hard labor in the mines of Sardinia where the two rivals became reconciled. Hippolytus renounced his claim to the Roman see, and Pontian likewise abdicated the pontificate in order to end the schism and to ensure an unhindered succession. The newly reunited community of Rome elected Anteros (235–236) and, upon his death, Fabian (236–250). After Hippolytus and Pontian died in exile, Fabian had their bodies brought to Rome, where he buried both of them with solemnity as martyrs: Pontian in the crypt of the popes in the catacomb of St Callistus, and Hippolytus on the Via Tiburtina.

As early as the middle of the third century, the *Liberian Catalogue* lists Hippolytus among the Catholic martyrs and identifies him as a presbyter rather than a bishop. Later legends obscure his identity. Pope Damasus I, and later Prudentius, portray him as a Novatianist schismatic. Roman Passionals of the seventh and eighth centuries present him as a soldier converted by St Lawrence. Other legends confuse him with a martyred bishop of the same name, buried at Porto.

In 1551, a badly damaged statue of a figure, seated in magisterial pose, was discovered near the Via Tiburtina in Rome. The upper part of the body and the head were missing at the time of the discovery. A list of works, carved in Greek characters into the lower part of the chair, led to its identification with Hippolytus and to its restoration in the likeness of a bearded man, even though it originally was a female figure, possibly a Muse or an allegory of one of the sciences. The statue is now on display at the entrance of the Vatican Library.

Writings

Anti-heretical expositions. *Philosophumena* or *Refutation of All Heresies* is the chief work of Hippolytus. Written in ten books, the treatise describes Greek philosophy and religion (books 1 to 4, of which books 2 and 3 are missing) and various systems of Gnosticism that arose from these pagan sources (books 5 to 9). Book 10, a summary of the preceding sections, also presents a chronology of Jewish history, and outlines orthodox Christian faith. Owing to poor sources, the section on Greek philosophy is inferior to the more astute analysis of Gnosticism. In the *Refutation*, Hippolytus decries the mitigation of the penitential system brought about by the vast influx of pagan converts into the Church. This work is not listed on the statue.

The following works have been commonly ascribed to Hippolytus, although his authorship cannot be proven. In fact, Pierre Nautin has suggested that differences in style and theology, particularly between the *Refutation* and the *Contra Noetum*, point to two different authors between whom the works may be divided.

Syntagma or *Against All Heresies*. This refutation of 32 heresies no longer survives in the original. Any attempt at reconstruction depends upon the fragments and references to it that do survive thanks to its recurrent citation by later writers.

Contra Noetum, or *Discourse against the Heresy of Noetus*, formerly regarded as a large fragment of an antiheretical treatise, is now recognized as a fine example of a Christian adaptation of classical diatribe.

Dogmatic and Exegetical Treatises. *Antichrist*, preserved in Greek, Old Slavonic, and Georgian versions, remains his sole extant dogmatic work. It consititutes the most thorough patristic treatment of the topic. Of his many scriptural commentaries, the following survive either whole or in fragments: *Commentary on Daniel*, preserved in an Old Slavonic version as well as in various Greek fragments, is the oldest extant Christian exegesis; *Commentary on the Song of Songs*, preserved in a Georgian version and fragments in Old Slavonic, Armenian, and Syriac translations; *On the Blessings of Jacob*, extant in the original Greek plus Armenian and Georgian versions; *On the Blessings of Moses*, extant in Armenian and Georgian versions; and *On the Psalms*, a work preserved only in several Greek fragments and treating only a limited number of psalms. Seventeen other commentaries are known, but chiefly by title alone. Jerome, in *De viris illustribus*, 61, is the only witness that Hippolytus delivered the exegetical homily *On the Passover* in the presence of Origen on the latter's visit to Rome. As an exegete, Hippolytus shows little influence of Alexandrian allegorical method.

Chronological Works. The *Chronicle*, extant no longer in the original Greek, but in three independent Latin translations, treats the history of the world from creation until his own period. Although it treats the nature of the universe, its chief aim was to show that the end of the world, calculated to have a term of six thousand years, was not imminent. A large fragment of the *Paschal Table*, devised in 222, was inscribed on the side of the chair of the 'Hippolytus' statue.

Liturgical and Canonical Writings. The *Apostolic Tradition*, preserved not in the original Greek, but in Latin, Ethiopic, and Coptic versions, has long been associated with Hippolytus, owing in part to its mention on the statue list. Although the attribution of this work to him enjoyed widespread currency in the twentieth century, toward the end of that century scholars have been increasingly reluctant to ascribe this work to Hippolytus. Paul Bradshaw, Marcel Metzger, and Maxwell Johnson all have challenged this attribution. According to Bradshaw, there were perhaps three distinct stages in the development of the document that has come down to us. The sections dealing with initiation reflect at least two different sources: an older Roman core with its emphasis on the bishop and a later North African source providing more specific directions for the deacons and presbyters.

The works of Hippolytus enjoyed wider currency in the East than in Rome itself. The growing dominance of Latin and the decline of Greek in the Roman church may account in part for his lack of later influence in Rome. Association with a schismatic movement also may have compromised the subsequent appeal of his writings within such a prestigious local church. His final reconciliation with the church, however, and his sufferings in persecution and exile, prepared the way for his liturgical cultus.

Feast: Aug. 13.

Bibliography: Primary Sources: J.-P. MIGNE, *Patrologiae Graeca*, 10 (Paris 1857–1866) cols. 261–962. H. ACHELIS, with G. N. BONWETSCH and others. 4 v. *Die griechischen christlichen Schriftstellar der ersten drei Jahrhunderte.* (Leipzig 1897 [Critical edition]). *Ante-Nicene Christian Library*, v. 6 and 9, pt. 2; M. MARKOVICH, *Patristiche Texte und Studien*, 25 (Berlin 1986). F. LEGGE, *Refutation of All Heresies*, 2 v. (London New York 1921). M. LEFÈVRE, with G. BARDY. *Sources Chrétiennes* 14 (Paris 1947), [with French trans.] P. NAUTIN, *Hippolyte contre les heresies* (Paris 1949). R. BUTTERWORTH, *Contra Noetum* (Heythrop Monographs, 2; London 1977) [with English trans.] P. NAUTIN, *Homélies Pascales*, 1 (Sources Chrétiennes, 27; Paris 1947). G. VISONÀ, *Studia Patristica Mediolanensia*, 15 (Milan 1988). B. BOTTE, *La Tradition apostolique: d'après les anciennes versions avec introduction, traduction, et notes* (Sources chrétiennes, 11; Paris 1968) [Reprinted with revisions, 1984]. *La Tradition apostolique de saint Hippolyte* (Münster, Westfalen 1963) [critical edition.]. G. J. CUMING, *Hippolytus: A Text for Students* (Grove Liturgical Study, 8; Bramcote, Nottingham 1976). [best English trans. currently available.]. J. M. HANSSENS, *La liturgie d'Hippolyte: ses documents, son titulaire, ses origines et son charactère* (*Orientalia Christiana Analecta*, 155; Rome 1959). *La liturgie d'Hippolyte: Documents et Études* (Rome 1970). **Studies on Hippolytus:** A. ZANI, *La Cristologia di Ippolito* (Ricerche di Scienze Teologiche, 22; Brescia 1984). C. OSBORNE, *Rethinking Early Greek Philosophy: Hippolytus of Rome and the Presocratics* (Ithaca, N. Y. 1987). J. FRICKEL, *Das Dunkel um Hippolyt von Rom: Ein Lösungsversuch: Die Schriften Elenchos und contra Noëtum* (Grazer Theologische Studien, 13; 1988). J. MANSFELD, *Heresiology in Context: Hippolytus'* Elenchos *as a Source for Greek Philosophy* (Philosophia Antiqua, 56; Leiden and New York 1992). G. MAURICE, and F. GLORIE, ed. *Clavis Patrum Graecorum*, 1 (Turnhout 1983). G. J. CUMING, *Essays on Hippolytus* (Grove Liturgical Study 15; Nottingham 1978). R. CABIÉ, ''L'Ordo de l'Initiation chrétienne dans la 'Tradition apostolige' d'Hippolyte de Rome,'' in *Mens concordet voci pour Mgr. A. G. Martimort* (Paris 1983), pp. 543–558. M. METZGER, ''Nouvelles perspectives pour la prétendue *Tradition apostolique*,'' *Ecclesia Orans* 5 (1988) 241–259; ''Enquêtes autour de la prétendue *Tradition apostolique*,'' *Ecclesia Orans* 9 (1992) 7–36; ''A propos des règlements ecclésiastiques et de la prétendue *Tradition apostolique*,'' *Revue des sciences religieuses* 66 (1992) 249–261. P. F. BRADSHAW, ''Re-dating the Apostolic Tradition: Some Preliminary

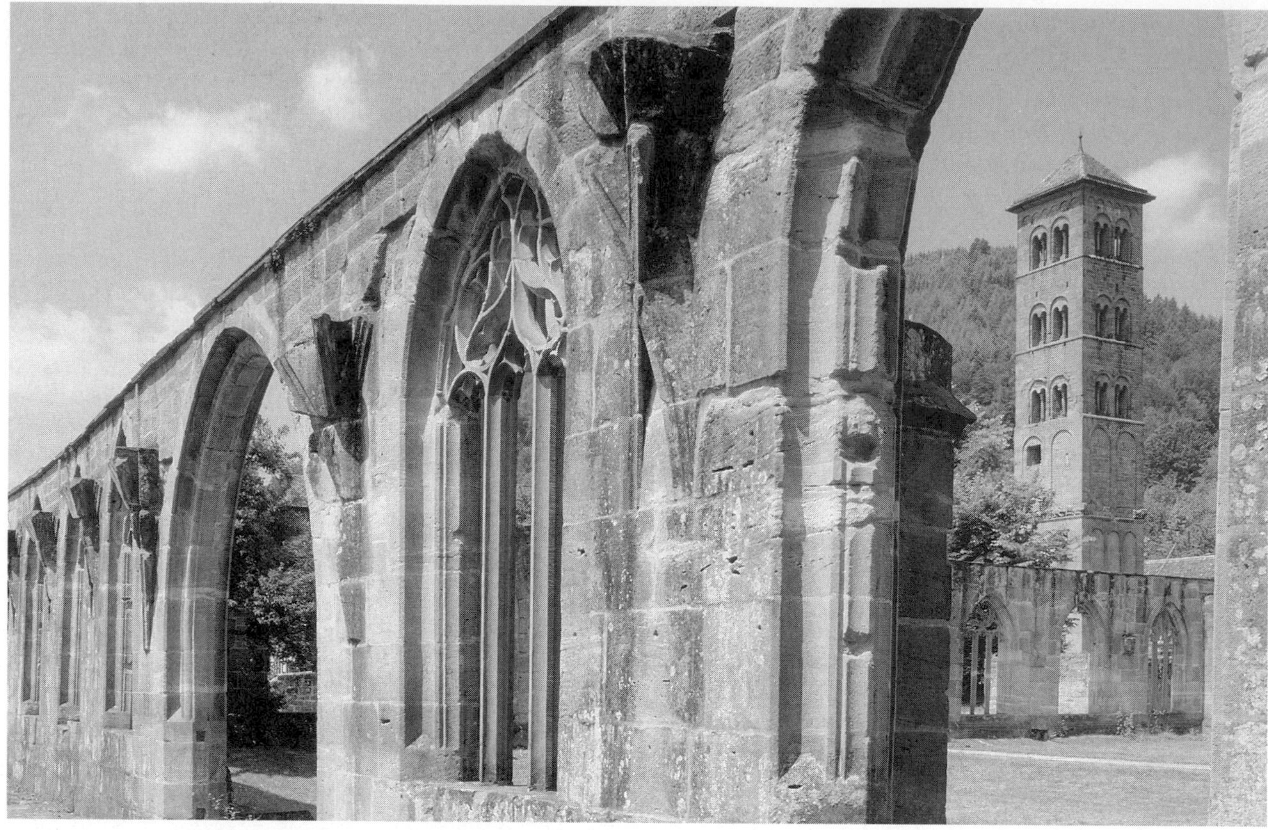

Ruins of Hirsau Monastery, Germany. (©Werner H. Muller/CORBIS)

Steps,'' in *Rule of Prayer, Rule of Faith: Essays in Honour of Aidan Kavanagh, O. S. B.*, ed. J. BALDOVIN and N. MITCHELL (Collegeville 1996) 3–17, [this work surveys recent scholarship on the *Apostolic Tradition*]. M. JOHNSON, *The Rites of Christian Initiation: Their Origins and Development* (Collegeville 1999) 80–85.

[N. ROY]

HIRSAU, ABBEY OF

The former Benedictine abbey of SS. Peter and Paul near Calw, Würtemberg, in the Black Forest, in the Diocese of Speyer. Originally founded in 830 and dedicated to St. Aurelius, it was not a permanent foundation until Pope Leo IX urged his nephew Count Adalbert II of Calw to construct a new abbey, staffed by monks from Einsiedeln in 1065. The fame of Hirsau (Hirsaugia) is connected almost exclusively with the name of Abbot William, who came from St. Emmeram in Regensburg.

Abbot William reversed the secular trend particularly noticeable in imperial abbeys and revitalized monastic life. He rejected lay investiture, breaking the attachment to the state. He suppressed the numerous lay officials and inaugurated reforms. Gregory VII granted immunity to the abbey in 1075, and in the investiture struggle Hirsau was a center of ecclesiastical reform and resistance to Henry IV.

Abbot William adapted the Cluniac usages to Germany (*Consuetudines Hirsaugienses,* 1079). The Hirsau reform represented a final blend of the 10th-century reform movements; it was rapidly diffused among the monasteries of southern and eastern Germany and in Austria. The formation of a congregation was opposed by the bishops, but more than 100 houses belonged to the loose confederation when it was at its peak.

In William's time the community numbered about 150 monks. Its library, its style of manuscript illumination, and its music were well known. The abbey church of SS. Peter and Paul was prototype of German Romanesque and fathered a school of architecture.

The direction given to Hirsau's monastic life by Abbot William survived for little more than half a century after his death. The abbey was unable to maintain its independence. It was forced to cede a large part of its possessions to the Emperor in 1215, and ten years later elected him its *Vogt.* In the 15th century Hirsau took part in the restoration of regular life, and joined the Congregation of Bursfeld in 1458. However, in the next century, its Protestant prince secularized it and made it a school. For practical purposes, 1535 marks the end of the abbey, although the fluctuating fortunes of the religious wars awarded it first to one side, then to the other; the monks were finally banished in 1648.

Bibliography: S. HILPISCH, *Lexikon für Theologie und Kirche*, ed. J. HOFER and K. RAHNER, 10 v. (2d, new ed. Freiburg 1957–65) 5:381–382. L. H. COTTINEAU, *Répertoire topobibliographique des abbayes et prieurés*, 2 v. (Mâcon 1935–39) 1:1421–22. P. SCHMITZ, *Histoire de l'Ordre de Saint-Benoît,* 7 v. (Maredsous, Bel. 1942–56).

[P. BECKMAN]

HIRSCHER, JOHANN

Theologian; b. Altergarten, Württemberg, Jan. 20, 1788; d. Freiburg, Sept. 4, 1865. Hirscher studied at the Weissenau monastery school, the lyceum of Constance, and the University of Freiburg. He was ordained in 1810 and was a curate in Rehlingen until 1812, when he became a tutor in the theology school of Ellwangen. In 1817 he occupied the chair of moral and pastoral theology at Tübingen University, and in 1837 he became professor of moral theology and catechetics in the University of Freiburg. He became a canon in 1839 and dean of the chapter in 1850. Frequently he served as delegate of the University of Freiburg to the First Chamber of the Grand Duchy of Baden. He retired in 1863. Hirscher was a prolific writer on theological subjects, especially in the area of homiletics and catechetics, and a cofounder of the review *Theologische Quartalschrift.*

In an early work, *De genuina missae notione,* he proposed sweeping changes in the liturgy of the Mass. He demanded the suppression of private Masses, the use of the vernacular, and Communion under both species for the laity. To this work he appended two suggested texts of the Mass in German. This work was placed on the Index in 1823, two years after its composition.

Much of his writing was concerned with preaching. He wished to replace the long, abstract moral considerations, which were popular in the Germany of his day, with brief homilies based on the text of the Mass for the day. In 1829 he published a commentary on the Lenten Gospels, and in 1837 a commentary on the Gospels and Epistles for the entire year, both of which were reprinted several times.

Hirscher wrote also a three-volume course in moral theology, *Die christliche Moral als Lehre von der Verwirklichung des göttlichen Reiches in der Menschheit,* which was reprinted five times between 1835 and 1851. He considered Christian morality as the realization of the kingdom of God in mankind. Thus his moral course differed from other manuals of his time and consisted mostly of pious meditations on the Christian life.

Despite much criticism by scholars, his many works on catechetics, especially his catechisms, were well received and were very popular. His 1842 catechism (*Katechismus der christkatholischen Religion*) and *Der kleinere Katechismus der christkatholischen Religion* were reprinted in many editions between 1845 and 1862. Through these works Hirscher exercised a strong influence on pastoral theology in Germany, and through translations of them, in France.

He also wrote, if less happily, on some of the social questions of his time, especially on the relation of Church and State in Germany. His spirit of conciliation toward the State was excessive and his proposals for Church reform were sharply criticized. A collection of his works on these matters was placed on the Index in 1849. He submitted to the condemnation of the Holy See and retracted the errors, but wrote replies to those who attacked them.

Hirscher in his own time was a controversial figure because of his very liberal views with regard to the liturgy and clerical celibacy and because of the suspicion that he was aiming at a German national church. Hence, when he was mentioned as a possible coadjutor for the Diocese of Freiburg, there was an outcry against his appointment in *Schweizerische Kirchenzeitung* and *Revue Sion.* When the government of Württemberg asked for the appointment, Rome refused. He has been referred to as an intellectual adventurer, but in some of his ideas he was only ahead of his time. This can be seen from the fact that a number of his suggestions, especially with regard to ecumenism and the liturgy, were discussed and acted upon by VATICAN COUNCIL II.

Bibliography: E. MANGENOT, *Dictionnaire de théologie catholique*, ed. A. VACANT et al., 15 v. (Paris 1903–50; Tables Générales 1951–) 6.2:2512–14. F. X. ARNOLD, *Lexikon für Theologie und Kirche*, ed. J. HOFER and K. RAHNER, 10 v. (2d, new ed. Freiburg 1957–65) 5:383–384. F. LAUCHERT, *Revue internationale de théologie* 2 (1894) 627–656; 3 (1895) 260–280, 723–738; 4 (1896) 151–174. F. KÖSSING in *Badische Biographien,* ed. F. VON WEECH, v.1 (Karlsruhe 1881) 372–377. F. X. THALHOFER, *Entwicklung des katholischen Katechismus in Deutschland von Canisius bis Deharbe* (Freiburg 1899).

[F. C. LEHNER]

HISPANA COLLECTIO (ISIDORIANA)

The most extensive and important canonical collection of the first ten centuries; it gathers and classifies all the traditional legislation in two parts: that of councils and that of papal decretals. The number of decretals, 103, is almost invariable in all the manuscripts and includes decretals from Popes Damasus (366–384) to Gregory I (604). The conciliar part, however, has met with three recensions: the Isidorian, to the Fourth Council of Toledo (633), with no manuscript in existence; the Ervigian, to the Twelfth Council of Toledo (685), in six manuscripts, three Spanish and three Gallican in form; the Vulgate, to the Seventeenth Council of Toledo (694), in eight Spanish and two foreign manuscripts. The *Hispana* recension, the lengthiest, comprises in geographical order, 11 Greek councils, eight African councils, 17 French councils, and 30 Spanish councils, setting in strict chronological order all the councils of the same city, thus meriting the name of *Hispana Collectio.*

COMPILER.

Although the oldest recension (633–35) of the Spanish collection is from the Isidorian era, there are reasons to date it to the Leandrine era, before 600 (M. Díaz y Díaz). A controversy as to whether St. ISIDORE OF SEVILLE was the author of this collection dates to the 16th century. On the affirmative side are P. Sejourné and J. Madoz; on the doubtful side, without considering it a proved fact, is G. Le Bras. The medieval manuscript tradition never attributed to Isidore the genuine *Hispana,* but it did ascribe to him the FALSE DECRETALS, basing its belief on the preface of Isidorus Mercator. The author is still unknown, although it seems probable that it was St. Isidore of Seville.

ORIGIN AND DEVELOPMENT.

The Isidorian, Ervigian, and Vulgate recensions were either written by the hierarchy or under the immediate control of the hierarchy, so that it can be called the official collection of the Spanish Church, making other collections obsolete. The three were used exclusively for almost 500 years, until the Gregorian reform.

The *Hispana Collectio* appeared at the beginning of the eighth century in Gaul, where it spread rapidly, representing the traditional, universal, and ecclesiastical law against the particularistic disintegration of the penitential literature. Being transcribed by itself, as in the *Codex Rachionis,* copied in 787 for the bishop of Strasbourg, or combined with other collections—*Hispana-Adriana, DACHERIANA*—it served for a century as juridical support of the Carolingian attempt at reform. Its authority served in the ninth century to conceal the greatest literary fraud of the history of Canon Law, the false decretals.

Using the *Hispana Chronologica* as the basis, the so-called *Excerpta* came into existence in Spain around 656. These *Excerpta* included the canons of the Isidorian recension (Fourth Council of Toledo) and the canons of the Fifth to Tenth Councils of Toledo systetematically ordered in ten books according to subject matter, each one summarized in a line. They were transcribed at the beginning of the Spanish manuscripts of the *Hispana,* both in the Ervigian and the Vulgate recensions.

The *Hispana Systematica* was formed by substituting the summary of each canon of the *Excerpta* for the complete text. Although preserved in three French manuscripts, it is considered Spanish in origin, since it was used by the Mozarabs of the south of Spain, a fact evidenced by the Arabic version (Madrid, B.N. 4879, s. XI).

Bibliography: P. SÉJOURNÉ, *Le Dernier pére de l'Église: Saint Isidore de Séville* (Paris 1929). P. ARIÑO ALAFONT, *Colección canónica hispana* (Avila 1941). C. GARCÍA-GOLDÁRAZ, *El Codice Lucense de la colección canónica hispana,* 2 v. (Madrid 1954). F. A. GONZÁLEZ, ed., *Collectio canonum ecclesiae hispanae,* 2 v. (Madrid 1808–21). M. C. DÍAZ Y DÍZ, ''Pequeñas aportaciónes para el estudio de la Hispana,'' RevEspDC 17 (1962) 373–390. J. MADOZ, *San Isidoro de Sevilla* (Madrid 1960). G. LE BRAS, ''Sur la part d'Isidore de Séville et des Espagnols dans l'histoire des collections canoniques, à propos d'un livre récent,'' *Revue des sciences religieuses* 10 (1930) 218–257.

[G. MARTÍNEZ DÍEZ]

HISPANA VERSIO

A canonical collection dated between 419 and 451 in Rome. The collection is known in Africa as *Corpus canonum Africanum.* It is known in three collations: the *Antiqua-originalis* contains the canons of the Councils of Nicaea (except for the last canon), Ancyra, Neocaesarea, Gangra, Antioch, Laodicea—all of these under the same enumeration—as well as those of Constantinople, Sardica, and the African Council of 419, and is preserved in the collections of Freising and Würzburg; the *Vulgata* contains all the canons of Nicaea, Ancyra, Neocaesarea, and Gangra, and is preserved most completely in the collections of St. Blaise, St. Maurus, and in the *QUESNELLIANA*; the *Isidoriana-gallica* (following the plan of the *Antiqua*) is preserved in the Gallic collections. According to W. M. Peitz, the *Hispana Versio* is the work of DIONYSIUS EXIGUUS.

Bibliography: C. H. TURNER, ed., *Ecclesiae occidentalis monumenta iuris antiquissima* (Oxford 1899–1939) 1.1.2:154–243; 2.1:33–142; 2.2:161–214, 218–316, 323–392, 402–420. E. SCHWARTZ, *Zeitschrift der Savigny-Stiftung für Rechtgeschichte, Kanonistische Abteilung* 56 (1936) 83–95. W. M. PEITZ, *Dionysius Exiguus-Studien* (Berlin 1960). H. WURM, *Studien und Texte zur Dekretalensammlung des Dionysius Exiguus* (Bonn 1939).

[C. VOGEL]

HISTORICAL BOOKS OF THE OLD TESTAMENT

The value of classifying certain books of the Old Testament as historical depends on a correct understanding and definition of ancient Hebrew historiography. The aims and methods of the writers of the Old Testament books have been studied and grasped more adequately during the first half of the 20th century than they had been earlier. Documents of the Catholic Church's magisterium, especially the PONTIFICAL BIBLICAL COMMISSION's decrees of June 30, 1909 [*Acta Apostolicae Sedis* 1 (Rome 1909) 567–569; *Enchiridion biblicum* (4th ed. Rome 1961) 324–331], and the same commission's letter to Cardinal Suhard of Jan. 16, 1948 [*Acta Apostolicae Sedis* 40 (1948) 45–48; *Enchiridion biblicum* (4th ed. Rome 1961) 577–581] reflect this development.

Although the classical Hebrew division of the Old Testament into the Law, the Prophets, and the Writings gives no explicit recognition of history-writing in the Bible, it has long been the custom among Christian scholars to categorize some books of the Old Testament as historical, or histories. St. CYRIL OF JERUSALEM (*c.* A.D. 348) divided the Old Testament into four sections: the Law, the historical books, the poetic books, and the Prophets [*Patrologia Graeca*, ed. J. P. Migne, 161 v. (Paris 1857–66) 33:500]. In the second category, the historical books, he listed Joshua, Judges, Ruth, 1 and 2 Samuel, 1 and 2 Kings, 1 and 2 Chronicles, Ezra, Nehemiah, and Esther. Pope St. INNOCENT I (*c.* A.D. 405) added to these, in his category of histories, the books of Job, Tobit, Judith, and 1 and 2 Maccabees [H. Wurm, *Apollinaris* 12 (1939) 75–76]. This listing of the historical books may find some support in the Septuagint.

Modern introductions to the Bible differ among themselves when they classify certain Old Testament books as historical. Some keep the Pentateuch distinct from the category of history, while others label it historical. Some dispense with the category of history altogether and prefer the ancient Hebrew divisions of the Law, the Prophets, and the Writings, with a fourth section for the deuterocanonical books. (*see* CANON, BIBLICAL 2, HISTORY OF OLD TESTAMENT.)

Modern study has shown that there is real historiography in the Old Testament, but that the classification of specific books as historical is a delicate task. Many qualifications have to be made regarding the historical character of the individual books and passages. Many distinctions have to be made between ancient and modern historiography and between ordinary historiography and the writing of SALVATION HISTORY among ancient writers of history.

There is a wide range of historicity in the Old Testament, from the chronicle-like writing in parts of the Books of SAMUEL and KINGS to the highly imaginative story of the Book of TOBIT. The literary form of the Book of JUDITH, which many in the past have designated as historical, is certainly nonhistorical.

See Also: HISTORY AND HISTORICITY (GESCHICHTLICHKEIT).

Bibliography: M. REHM, *Lexikon für Theologie und Kirche*, ed. J. HOFER and K. RAHNER, 10 v. (2d new ed. Freiburg 1957–65) 4:791–792. *Encyclopedic Dictionary of the Bible*, tr. and adap. by L. HARTMAN (New York 1963) 1007–12. A. ROBERT and A. TRICOT, *Guide to the Bible*, tr. E. P. ARBEZ and M. P. MCGUIRE, 2 v. (Tournai-New York 1951–55; v.1 rev. and enl. 1960) 1:282–314. A. LEMONNYER, *Dictionnaire de la Bible*, suppl. ed. L. PIROT, et al. (Paris 1928–) 1:588–596.

[M. STRANGE]

HISTORICAL JESUS

The term ''historical Jesus'' refers to Jesus of Nazareth in so far as the course of his earthly life can be reconstructed by historical critical methods. The use of historical critical methods has led biblical scholars to recognize the character of the Gospels as theological interpretations of Jesus' religious significance. Directly, then, the Gospels document the beliefs of the 1st-century Christian communities for which they were composed; they are not historical biographies in the modern sense of the term. Thus a question arises: what can be known, by historical means, about the one whose religious significance the Gospels proclaim?

The ''Old Quest'' for the Historical Jesus. The discipline of critical history itself emerged within the context of the Enlightenment, and those who first urged the distinction between the Gospels as articulations of Christian belief and what can be known about Jesus on historical grounds exploited that difference in the service of various agendas. Albert Schweitzer conducted a magisterial survey of the first phase of historical Jesus research in *The Quest of the Historical Jesus* (1906). Among the writings he reviewed, three tendencies were operative.

At one extreme were authors who, representing an emerging fundamentalist rejection of modernity, persisted in reading the Scriptures as simply true in every respect. Opposite them were writers like H. S. REIMARUS, D. F. STRAUSS, and B. BAUER, who seized upon historical research as a weapon to wield against the Christian church. On their respective accounts, Jesus was either (1) a failed messianic revolutionary whose followers spiritualized his message, clumsily concocted the story of the

Jesus of Nazareth appearing before Pilate, 6th century mosaic.

resurrection, and on this fraudulent basis kept his movement alive (Reimarus); (2) the human being whose personality inspired the myth of God-manhood recounted in the Gospels (Strauss); or (3) an hypothesis rendered superfluous to explain the origin of Christianity, since the earliest Gospel, that of Mark, can be accounted for as the result of the confluence of Jewish and Hellenistic religious streams (Bauer).

Between these two extremes were Protestant liberals like A. von Harnack, who played their version of the historical Jesus and his simple message off against traditional doctrine in order to render Christianity appealing to their contemporaries. Schweitzer's own account built on the work of Johannes Weiss, according to which Jesus conceived his central theme, the coming of the KINGDOM OF GOD, in apocalyptic terms: at the Kingdom's approach the righteous would suffer; a final conflict, both cosmic and earthly, would erupt; and God's victory would bring the end of the world and the resurrection of the dead. For Schweitzer, Jesus believed that all this was imminent and that he himself had a role in its occurrence. Indeed, Jesus entered upon his passion and death in order to force God's hand, but as the continuing course of history demonstrates, this was a mistake; the Kingdom failed to come. Schweitzer's work marked the close of the so-called old quest; the apparent outcome was a gulf expressed in the title of a book by M. Kähler, *The So-called Historical Jesus and the Historic, Biblical Christ* (Leipzig 1892) or, as an earlier work by Strauss had more simply put it, *The Historical Jesus and the Christ of Faith* (Berlin 1865).

The Decline of Historical Jesus Research. There followed a hiatus in historical Jesus research that lasted until 1953. The interim period saw, theologically, the dominance of the neo-orthodox theology introduced by Karl BARTH in 1919, and, with respect to historical method, the introduction of form criticism into NT studies with the practically simultaneous publication in 1919 and

1920 of works by Rudolf BULTMANN, M. DIBELIUS, and K.-L. Schmidt. These two developments conspired to reinforce the skepticism regarding the possibility of knowledge of Jesus by historical means already articulated in W. Wrede's *The Messianic Secret in the Gospel of Mark* (1910). Wrede had argued that the notion of the messianic secret around which the Gospel of Mark is organized was an apologetic device invented by the author, so that even Mark, the earliest of the Gospels, offers data not on Jesus but on the community for which it was written. Wrede thus challenged the common-sense assumption that because Mark was the earliest Gospel, it must be closest to the facts and thus historically most reliable.

Skepticism like Wrede's was reinforced in the next generation when Bultmann, for example, argued theologically that any attempt to ascertain historically whether the biblical call to faith had a historical basis in Jesus and his ministry amounted to an effort to win salvation by intellectual works, while as a form critic Bultmann also judged the attempt to reconstruct Jesus' ministry practically impossible because of the nature of the sources. On this view the religious beliefs animating the Gospels formed an impenetrable barrier blocking any attempt at historical reconstruction of Jesus and his ministry.

The "New Quest." The quest for the Jesus of history took a new turn in 1953. Ernst Käsemann delivered a paper at a gathering of Bultmann's former students in which he argued that a "new quest" for the historical Jesus was legitimate, necessary, and possible: legitimate, because it cohered with the evangelists' intention to inform us about Jesus; necessary, because otherwise Christians would have no response to those who charged their religion with being simply a myth bereft of any demonstrable relation to the historic personage of Jesus; possible, because of the availability of a method, form criticism, fostered by Bultmann himself. Even Bultmann's analysis of *The History of the Synoptic Tradition,* Käsemann could point out, not infrequently traced some saying or deed found in the Gospels back to Jesus himself.

The "new quest" differed from its predecessor in two major respects. On the one hand, it had a positive goal, namely, to ascertain what continuity might be found to underlie the discontinuity, so stressed by participants in the "old quest," between Jesus as viewed through a historian's lens and the Christ portraits of the NT. This goal was by no means a matter of proving the validity of the latter, but it did involve an effort to show that the Christian faith expressed in the Gospels was at least one possible response to Jesus' earthly career. But if the goal was more positive, the "new quest" also assumed a far more critical attitude toward its sources than did its predecessor. From the vantage point of form criticism, nothing in the Gospels is to be acknowledged as historical simply by its presence in the texts. Rather, only those sayings and deeds ascribed to Jesus that meet a set of stringent criteria are to be accorded historical probability. The "new quest" makes no promise of achieving a full-blown biography of Jesus, but it does claim with some confidence that Jesus' characteristic manners of speaking and acting can be recovered.

Three years after Käsemann delivered his paper, another member of the Bultmannian circle, Günther Bornkamm, published *Jesus of Nazareth.* This first major contribution to the "new quest" established the contours of an historical image of Jesus that would enjoy consensus status for almost three decades. On Bornkamm's account, Jesus' contemporaries might have perceived him as a prophet because of his message about the Kingdom of God, or as a rabbi, because he expounded God's will. In each case, however, there was something unique about Jesus' exercise of the role. Whereas prophets spoke a word of the Lord that came to them, Jesus spoke on his own authority: "Amen, I say to you." In Bornkamm's reconstruction, by announcing the imminence of the Kingdom, Jesus also claimed that people's response to his ministry in the present would be decisive for their status when the SON OF MAN, a figure whom Jesus regarded as other than himself, came as eschatological judge.

The rabbis, for their part, expounded God's will through casuistic commentary on the text of Scripture, a role they assumed only after years of study as disciple to another rabbi to whom they presented themselves. Jesus, however, possesses no scholarly credentials, he chooses his disciples, not they him, and there is no notion that they might someday equal, much less surpass, him. In contrast to the rabbis, his style of teaching is direct and almost secular, presuming no prior knowledge of learned debates but appealing, in parables, directly to his hearers' experience. In the content of his teaching, Jesus contradicts the normative interpretation of the Law, making light, for example, of the Sabbath obligation to abstain from work. Even more audaciously, he proceeds to contradict the letter of the Law itself, abrogating the dietary regulations in favor of interior purity. Exercising the power to forgive sin, as both prophet and rabbi Jesus arrogates to himself an authority greater than Moses' and thus sets himself beyond the pale of Judaism. Unique in addressing God with filial tenderness and familiarity as ABBA, Jesus stands in sharp contrast to the casuistic legalism and ritualistic formalism of his contemporaries. Implicit in Jesus' speech and actions was a claim to authority that rendered him a blasphemer liable to death in the eyes of his fellow Jews. That same implicit claim was, Christians believe, vindicated when God raised

Jesus from the dead, and its meaning becomes explicit when they resort to titles like MESSIAH, SON OF GOD, Son of Man, or LORD to articulate his significance. Thus for Bornkamm and the many authors who followed him, the implicit claim operative in Jesus' uniquely authoritative manner of speaking and acting and vindicated by the resurrection provides the continuity between the "historical Jesus" and the "Christ of faith."

Critique and Revision of the New Quest. In time this image of Jesus became the object of severe critique and ongoing revision. The critique, laid out by scholars like E. P. Sanders in *Jesus and Judaism* (1985) and Paula Fredriksen in *From Jesus to Christ* (1988), uncovered first of all a theological bias operative in the historical portrait of Jesus that draws his features into focus by heightening the contrast between him and the Judaism of his day. The unrelieved legalism and formalism of that Judaism stem more from the confessional heritage of Bornkamm and his fellow post-Bultmannians than from the historical reality of Jesus' time. Bornkamm's Jesus emerges from a line of German Protestant scholarship that consistently historicized Luther's Law/Gospel dialectic. Scholars in this line, extending back at least as far as Bultmann's teacher, Wilhelm BOUSSET, portray a Judaism which, as a religion of works and ritual, comes to resemble the Catholicism Luther opposed and against which Jesus could be claimed as a champion of the gospel of free grace. This negative image of Judaism, the distorted result of projecting a theological a priori onto an historical situation, has traveled beyond its originally Protestant context, being put to use by European Catholics critical of their church's central administration (H. Küng) and by Latin American liberation theologians eager to parallel their context with that of Jesus. That negative stereotype of Judaism unfortunately contributes to the continuance of anti-Semitism.

Beyond this critique of the theological bias operative in the "new quest," several sources fed an ongoing process of revision of the historical image of Jesus. Archeological investigations combined with literary findings like the DEAD SEA SCROLLS to yield a considerably nuanced picture of Second Temple Judaism. In light of the pluralism extant among the Jews of Jesus' day, the notion of a monolithic, "official," normative Judaism to which Jesus can be contrasted has lost plausibility. Geographical differences also now assumed significance: Jesus was born to and exercised his ministry among Galilean villagers remote from the influence of both Temple and PHARISEES and not kindly disposed to an urban center that imposed and benefitted from a crushing burden of taxation.

Jewish scholars like David Flusser and Geza Vermes responded to the "new quest" by advancing the recovery of Jesus' own Jewishness. They highlighted his affinities with Pharisaism, denied the uniqueness of his Abba-usage, and argued that his intensification of the demands of Torah and declarations of the forgiveness of sin lie well within the parameters of Judaism. Vermes, in a series of studies beginning with his *Jesus the Jew* (1973), located Jesus within the tradition of Galilean wonder-working Hasidim or holy men whose model was the prophet Elijah; this Jesus was a wandering charismatic who, taking his place among the poor and outcasts, healed and cast out demons in enthusiastic expectation of the imminent arrival of God's Kingdom. Vermes used a social scientific category when he focused on Jesus as a charismatic, and thus he reflects the interdisciplinary turn biblical studies took with the addition of sociology and anthropology to their resources. That turn favored a retrieval of the full dimensions of Jesus' activity, rescuing him from the Enlightenment's relegation of religion to the private and individual sphere and allowing consideration of the social and political ramifications of his ministry as exercised concretely in the context of Roman-dominated Palestine.

Recent Approaches. Much of the ferment fostered by these developments came to a head in the work of the Jesus Seminar organized within the Society of Biblical Literature in 1985. The novel approach taken by this group of scholars to determine the historicity of sayings attributed to Jesus in the NT and other early Christian documents has received notoriety. They voted on each saying, casting colored beads coded according to degree of probability. They published the results, again color-coded: sayings in red are most probably those of Jesus, sayings in black are least probable. The Jesus Seminar also takes a novel approach to historical Jesus research by expanding the core of what it takes as basic data. In addition to the four canonical gospels, members of the Jesus Seminar argue, some of the GNOSTIC material discovered at Nag Hammadi in 1945 ought also to be taken into account. Maintaining that documents like the Gospel of Peter, the Apocryphon of James, and especially the collection of sayings known as the Gospel of Thomas enshrine early and independent data on the formation of the Christian tradition, seminar members particularly prize the latter document as preserving authentic sayings of Jesus. Some of these sayings are unknown to the gospels while, for others, the Gospel of Thomas provides the more original version. Seminar members also greatly expand the significance of the Q-source, the hypothetical collection of sayings of Jesus, the existence of which is deduced from the occurrence of these sayings in both Matthew and Luke but not Mark. This hypothetical collection is promoted to become the Sayings Gospel Q, and stages in its composition are discerned to yield an earliest layer which, like the Thomas material, says nothing of Jesus' death or resurrection, betrays no tincture of apocalyptic eschatology, but rather resonates with wisdom movements within and outside Israel. Indeed, the wisdom sayings of Q-source are found to bear marked similarities to contemporary traditions of Greco-Roman Cynicism.

John Dominic Crossan draws these threads together in *The Historical Jesus: The Life of a Mediterranean Jewish Peasant* (1991), subsequently popularized in *Jesus: A Revolutionary Biography.* In Crossan's account, Jesus changed his mind about John the Baptist's message of the imminence of an apocalyptically conceived kingdom, rejecting the apocalyptic in favor of the immediate, unbrokered accessibility of God which, shattering a social hierarchy based on honor and shame, called for a radically egalitarian way of life. This was the Kingdom of God, which Jesus acted out in an itinerant ministry to the villages of Galilee. His journeys were similar to the counter-cultural wanderings of the Cynics, whom Crossan likens to the hippies of the Greco-Roman world. What Jesus offered was healing, and, in a context where much illness both physical and mental was attributable to the poverty and systemic violence imposed to maintain the hegemony of the Temple and the Romans, such healing had political significance. In the eyes of the Jerusalem establishment, whose control over the definition of illness and over the means of relief Jesus challenged, his healings and exorcisms cast him in the role of magician or sorcerer. On one point Jesus differs from the Cynics: while they supported themselves by begging, Jesus deliberately sent his followers out without a bag for provisions. By this stratagem Jesus ensured the dependence of his itinerant ministry on the hospitality of those who would receive him. Offering healing, he sought the practice of open-table fellowship, by which he again subverted the social rankings of the day and acted out the egalitarianism consonant with the presence of the Kingdom. All of this set Jesus and his socially revolutionary movement on a collision course with the power structure of the day, centered in the Temple. Thus, Jesus' actions, symbolic of the destruction of the Temple, happening at Passover, could easily have brought about his arrest and execution. Regarding the details of Jesus' last days, Crossan invokes the Gospel of Peter to mount an argument that the passion narratives are spun for the most part from a Christian reading of the OT.

Far less iconoclastic than the work of Crossan and the Jesus Seminar is John P. Meier's multi-volume study *A Marginal Jew.* Meier's first volume, appearing in 1991, set the stage by considering sources, method, Jesus' background and education, and the chronology of Jesus' life. Notably, he concurs with Joseph Fitzmyer in rejecting the Jesus Seminar's claims for the early and independent provenance of material preserved in the Gnostic writings from Nag Hammadi and thus sweeps aside Crossan's strictly sapiential, non-eschatological reading of Jesus' message. Rather, in his second volume, Meier emphasizes John the Baptist's perduring influence as Jesus' mentor. While Jesus may have shifted his emphasis away from John's prospect of imminent fiery judgment to stress the glad news of the nearness of a saving God, undertones of judgment were never totally absent from his preaching, which, like John's preaching, proclaimed the imminence of God's decisive act. Centering his message on the symbol of Kingdom of God, Jesus both announced the futurity of the coming of the Kingdom and also claimed that it was in some sense already present in his own ministry, a claim that he acted out by performing not magic but miracles, especially healings and exorcisms. From this consideration of Jesus' mentor, message, and miracles, the figure of Jesus emerges as an Elijah-like eschatological prophet of a Kingdom both future and yet already in some fashion present, especially in Jesus' miracles. Meier proposes in his third volume to reconstruct Jesus' authoritative interpretation of the Law and guidance for concrete behavior, as well as the individuals and groups with whom he interacted: the Twelve and other disciples, tax collectors and sinners, Sadducees and Pharisees.

By 2000, the lines of division among those pursuing the question of the historical Jesus corresponded roughly to earlier positions on Jesus' eschatology. Weiss' and Schweitzer's construct of a Jesus for whom the coming of an apocalyptically envisaged Kingdom lay wholly in the future met its counterpoint in C. H. Dodd's assertion that for Jesus the Kingdom was wholly present in his own ministry, to which J. Jeremias responded with a Kingdom which was for Jesus both already and not-yet. In similar fashion, E. P. Sanders more recently emphasized the futurity of Jesus' expectation, while Crossan's and Marcus Borg's sapiential Jesus knows only a present Kingdom, to which Meier responded with a Jesus for whom the Kingdom is both outstanding and yet proleptically present. On all their accounts, however, Jesus is to be understood historically as a 1st-century Jew concerned in some fashion with the renewal of his people, and none would deny that such renewal involved more than a purely religious realm; for Jesus, as for the ancient world generally, religion, society, and politics formed a seamless garment.

Theological Significance. Beyond the question of the historical Jesus lies the further question of the theological significance of the results of historical Jesus research. The very nature of that research sheds some light on the issue. Inquiry into Jesus by historical means involves the historian in a subtle interplay between initial interpretive hypothesis and data, the factual status of which is to be determined; the outcome will be a set of more or less probable facts rendered coherent and intelligible by some more or less comprehensive master image or hypothesis. Historical constructs of Jesus thus involve both degrees of probability in their various components and perspectival definition of their unifying hypotheses; hence, such constructs are in principle always subject to revision. Negatively, this would preclude according foundational significance for Christian faith to anyone's particular version of the historical Jesus. It would rule out as naive and simplistic moves like Harnack's, common though such maneuvers have again become, whereby one appeals to a historical construct as the ''real Jesus'' who ought to take precedence over the interpretive products of Scripture and tradition. On the other hand, the limits intrinsic to the practice of history do not render that discipline's results merely arbitrary or purely subjective.

The results of historical Jesus research become significant for Christian faith in at least two ways. Most generally, they counter recurring temptations to docetism by presenting Christians with images of Jesus as fully human and historically situated. Second, when the perspectives from which historical data on Jesus are evaluated and interpreted includes Christian faith, that faith may, among other things, illumine the significance those data hold for the present. From this enlarged perspective an interpreter may move beyond a strictly historical account to produce a historically informed theological narrative. Such theological readings of historical interpretations of Jesus are distinctively modern artifacts that continue the christological process from which the Gospels emerged; they may function for contemporary Christians much as the gospels did for their original addressees, even while they serve the ongoing proclamation of those same gospels.

See Also: JESUS CHRIST, BIOGRAPHICAL STUDIES OF; JESUS CHRIST AND WORLD RELIGIONS; JESUS CHRIST (THEOLOGY).

Bibliography: M. BORG, *Jesus, A New Vision. Spirit, Culture, and the Life of Discipleship* (San Francisco, Calif. 1987); *Meeting Jesus Again for the First Time* (San Francisco, Calif. 1994). G. BORNKAMM, *Jesus of Nazareth* (Eng. trans.; New York 1960). J. D. CROSSAN, *The Historical Jesus: The Life of a Mediterranean Peasant* (San Francisco, Calif. 1991). R. A. HORSLEY, *Jesus and the Spiral of Violence: Popular Jewish Resistance in Roman Palestine* (San Francisco, Calif. 1987). J. P. MEIER, *A Marginal Jew: Rethinking the Historical Jesus,* Volume One: *The Roots of the Problem and the Person* (New York 1991). E. P. SANDERS, *Jesus and Judaism* (Philadelphia, Pa. 1985). A. SCHWEITZER, *A Quest of the Historical Jesus* (Eng. trans.; New York 1968). J. SOBRINO, *Jesus The Liberator: A Historical-Theological Reading of Jesus of Nazareth* (Eng. trans.; Maryknoll, N.Y. 1993). G. VERMES, *The Religion of Jesus the Jew* (Minneapolis, Minn. 1993).

[W. P. LOEWE]

HISTORICAL THEOLOGY

Historical theology as a scholarly discipline is difficult to define. An acceptable working definition might be ''the genetic study of Christian faith and doctrine'' (Pelikan xiii). But such study has been differently designated in recent centuries, with varying content and consequent confusion. The time-honored term for the genetic history of faith and doctrine is *history of dogma,* where ''dogma'' is sometimes restricted to basic orthodox affirmations of the Christian Church (e.g., Trinity), sometimes used more loosely to include less central doctrines. In the latter sense, *history of theology* is a term consecrated by long usage. *History of Christian thought* adds to dogmas and doctrines what we call ethics, as well as Christian reflection on other problems both of thought and of society (e.g., politics or such philosophical issues as the problem of universals). *Historical theology* itself has been used not only for the genetic study of faith and doctrine, but for the entire study of the history of the Church, and occasionally for all those theological and paratheological disciplines whose method is historical. One understanding of *positive theology* has been the study of Scripture and church history. Some see *history of Christian doctrine* as the clearest term; for it distinguishes the field from general church history and from other branches of church history, e.g., history of liturgy or of Canon Law.

Development of the Discipline. The development of the discipline has been influenced from two quarters: (1) the movement of theology, especially its stances toward doctrinal continuity and change; (2) the evolution of the historical method. If the definitive Word God spoke in Christ has been deposited with the Church, then, as early orthodoxy saw it, doctrinal change could only be distortion. In consequence, historical theology in the patristic period is largely a matter of documenting the apostolic succession of dioceses and dogmas, and the cataloguing of sects and heresies, rather than the genetic study of the mainstream of Christian doctrine (cf., e.g., the works of Irenaeus, Eusebius, Epiphanius). In this context the prevailing theological attitude came to be enshrined in the classic axiom of VINCENT OF LÉRINS: ''one must take the greatest possible care to believe what has been believed everywhere, ever, by everyone (*quod ubique, quod semper, quod ab omnibus creditum est*)'' (*Commonitoria* 2). Tradition was the touchstone, innovation the automatic enemy. ''Let nothing be innovated,'' Stephen I wrote to Cyprian, ''beyond what has been handed down'' (Cyprian, *Ep.* 74).

In the Middle Ages the *Sic et non* theological method (e.g., in ABELARD and in its refinement by Aquinas) uncovered apparent contradictions in what had been accepted as patristic consensus. But the method is more important for the questions it raised than for the answers it proposed. It did not make use of historical criteria to account for the theological variations it was attempting to explain.

The REFORMATION controversies, while confronting the crucial allegation of a cleavage between primitive Christianity and the Catholic tradition, still pursued history polemically and evaluated change dogmatically. The task of historical scholarship was to prove that the adversary was guilty of innovation, had broken from authoritative Scripture or unvarying tradition, and therefore was doctrinally in error. In this sense the Reformation and COUNTER-REFORMATION outlook was closer to patristic and medieval than to modern historiography. On the other hand, a new temper and method were beginning to show: a more profound probing of the past and a growing sense of the pluralism of the past. In addition, the more objective methodology of Renaissance HUMANISM, especially in the area of secular history, could not but affect, if only gradually, the confessional search for the Church's historical and doctrinal roots.

In the ENLIGHTENMENT climate of the 18th century, both on the Continent and in Great Britain, the scholarly study of church history increasingly emancipated itself from ecclesiastical sponsorship and began to define itself as an academic discipline. But the golden age of historical theology was the 19th century. This for two reasons. First, research in Christian theology came to be dominated by the modern historical method, particularly by the historical investigation of the New Testament and of the development of dogma. Here some of the more influential figures, for all their recognized inadequacies, are Ferdinand Christian BAUR, Johann Adam MÖHLER, John Henry NEWMAN, and the most erudite and eloquent spokesman for historical theology, Adolf von HARNACK, with his utter commitment to the historical method as the primary means for analyzing Christian doctrine. Each faced frankly and knowledgeably the inevitable tension between history and tradition or faith commitment. Second, critical editions of the source material, e.g., patristic texts, built more extensively and profoundly upon the remarkable editions produced in the previous three centuries, stimulated in part by many discoveries of lost works, particularly from the earliest period and in Oriental languages (e.g., Syriac, Georgian, Coptic). Such editions and discoveries have increased at a remarkable rate in the 20th century and historical research has been intensified through comprehensive study of individual writers and the history of individual words and ideas.

Vatican II. The Council did not explicitly espouse any particular philosophy or theology which attempts to expose a design for the course of history. Nonetheless, the official documents of the Council take more notice of history than those of any previous council, and, hence, they at least implicitly deal with the process of the story of mankind. The Constitution on the Church, though it never loses sight of the transcendent nature of the Church, insists that the Church truly enters human history (*Lumen gentium* 8, 9). The introductory paragraphs of the Constitution on the Church in the Modern World even attempt an assessment of the current historical situation and venture the judgment that the human race has entered ''a new age of history'' (*Gaudium et spes* 4). This judgment concurs with, and probably reflects, the conviction Pope JOHN XXIII expressed in *Humanae salutis*, his apostolic constitution, Dec. 25, 1961, convoking the Council, which stated that human society was ''on the edge of a new era.'' Other documents of the Council, especially when they deal with real or seeming changes in doctrine and discipline, evince a similar awareness of historical context and process. The desire to bring the Church up to date and to make it more effective in the contemporary world was the pervasive theme of the Council, as the term *aggiornamento* suggests. Such a desire in itself indicated an awareness of historical and cultural change and made possible the Council's adoption of ''accommodation to the times'' as its theme. Previous councils tended to assess change negatively and, in principle, to resist it in the Church.

Vatican II's attention to history was a response to the more general application of historical methods and categories to the kind of study of religion that had gained great momentum in the 19th century, especially in Protestant circles, and that in the 20th century characterized biblical, patristic, and liturgical scholarship also among Catholics. The impetus for the Council's attention to history was, in fact, derived from such scholarship rather than from systematic theology, where a rather ahistorical NEO-THOMISM prevailed for the most part. Simply by taking account of history, the Council virtually assumed the obligation to make some statements about its course or design. The pastoral nature of the Council and the fact that its decrees were documents formulated in committee precluded the possibility that any single point of view would prevail to the exclusion of others. Nonetheless, certain features of the Council's appreciation of history can be singled out as more typical than others.

First of all, the Council assesses the course of history and the current ''age'' with considerable optimism, speaking of its social, scientific, technological ''progress'' (cf. *Gravissimum educationis* Introd. and 1; *Apostolicam actuositatem* 1; *Gaudium et spes* 57. For qualification of this optimism cf. *Apostolicam actuositatem* 7; *Presbyterorum ordinis* 17 and 22; *Gaudium et spes* 10, 15, and 37). Although it recognizes the ambiguities and ambivalence of the human condition, it gives relatively little support to those philosophies or theologies of history that view the story of mankind as a decline from an earlier and better condition. Secondly, the Council consistently maintains that the course of history is under providential guidance (*Lumen gentium* 23) and it occasionally employs the Eusebian description of the historical process as a "preparation for the Gospel" (*Lumen gentium* 16), as an unfolding of a divine plan, which presumably has a beginning, middle, and end (*Dei Verbum* 2–3, 11, 14). The Council asserts, for instance, that Christ is the key, the center, and the purpose of the whole of human history (*Gaudium et spes* 10). Eschatological expectations for history are expressed in that same document (ibid. 39, 45). Thirdly, Vatican II evidences a strong sense of continuity with the past and a desire to remain faithful to it. Continuity of faith, of spiritual gift, and of evangelical tradition from the primitive Church to the present is often asserted, despite recognition that considerable change has taken place through the centuries (*Lumen gentium* 9, 21, 23, 33, 39, 50, 51; *Perfectae caritatis* 1, 9; *Apostolicam actuositatem* 8; *Ad gentes* 5). Fourthly, the Council often makes use of forward-looking terms like progress, evolution, and maturation to describe how continuity has been maintained while change has occurred (*Gaudium et spes* 6, 54; cf. above on optimism). When these terms are applied to doctrine, (*Lumen gentium* 12; 55; *Unitatis redintegratio* 24; *Optatam totius* 11; *Dei Verbum* 7; *Apostolicam actuositatem* 3; *Dignitatis humanae* 1, 9, 12; *Gaudium et spes* 63) they quite inevitably suggest the viewpoint of scholars influenced by Newman's essay on the *Development of Christian Doctrine* and by the renewed interest in the doctrine of the MYSTICAL BODY OF CHRIST, which was widespread in Catholic circles for several decades before the convocation of the Council. In both instances, an organic model of change is implied. The evolutionary model for the development of the cosmos expounded by TEILHARD DE CHARDIN was probably also an influence (cf. *Gaudium et spes* 39, 45).

Thus there is considerable effort in the documents of the Council to break away from a style of historical thinking which would see the Church as immune to process or change, as if it moved through history unaffected by history. This effort in some instances even intimates a breakdown of the traditional dichotomy in ecclesiastical documents between the Church and the Christian people, which allowed the Church to be without fault and untouched by history while the Christian people sinned and were subject to the "injuries of time." The use of terms like "the People of God" to designate the Church, especially in *Lumen gentium*, is seen by some scholars as indicating this change in mentality.

Present Views: Content and Method. The present task of historical theology is not easily expressed. The basic issues are content and method. For some, the subject matter is what the Church has believed, taught, and confessed on the basis of the Word of God. Besides admitted ambiguities ("Church," "Word of God"), such a definition restricts the discipline unduly to what the various confessions regard as dogmas or their equivalent. It is hard to see how historical theology can disregard the genetic study of theologoumena (e.g., speculations on the human knowledge or ignorance of Christ, on religious freedom, on the human person as image of God) and moral issues (e.g., abortion, social justice). Historical theology's subject matter should be broad enough to embrace whatever in thought, belief, and life can properly be termed Christian and has a history.

Equally controversial is the discipline's methodology. For some scholars, the one legitimate demand on historical theology is that it be sound history, that it follow the canons of acceptable historical method, presumably determined nontheologically. Others would accept this for a *history of theology*, but are persuaded that a discipline which calls itself *historical theology* cannot disregard theological presuppositions that make for a ceaseless dialectical interaction between faith and history and in fact affect one's interpretation of the past.

The issue so put involves the relationship between historical and systematic or dogmatic theology. Contemporary reflection sees them as inseparable, yet distinct. For Gerhard Ebeling, these are two aspects of the same hermeneutic task of theology: their common concern is the concrete event of the Word of God; their common task to foster effective contemporary proclamation. Historical theology is primarily concerned to determine the *traditum*: what was handed down and how. DOGMATIC THEOLOGY focuses on the contemporary observance of the tradition, participates in the *actus tradendi*, the tradition of a present and continuous event. As essentially systematic, it must show how all genuine theological statements are necessarily related to one another and to the reality they bring to understanding. Historical theology exercises a "disturbing" function: it upsets established prejudices, forces the dogmatic theologian to face uncomfortable facts and forgotten truths.

Wolfhart Pannenberg argues that, since Christianity is essentially a process, a history, the tasks involved in describing the essence and truth of Christianity can only be performed within a historical theology, provided that, while remaining historical, it adopt a systematic approach. Such a historical theology, he believes, would end "the opposition between historical and systematic theology." In the present theological situation, however, a ''special'' systematic theology is necessary in addition to the historical disciplines.

Bibliography: G. EBELING, *Theology and Proclamation: Dialogue with Bultmann* (Philadelphia 1966) 22–31. W. PANNENBERG, *Theology and the Philosophy of Science* (Philadelphia 1976) 371–381, 418–420. J. PELIKAN, *Historical Theology: Continuity and Change in Christian Doctrine* (New York 1971). J. RATZINGER, *Das Problem der Dogmengeschichte in der Sicht der katholischen Theologie* (Cologne 1966). G. H. WILLIAMS, ''Church History: From Historical Theology to the Theology of History,'' in A.S. NASH, ed., *Protestant Thought in the Twentieth Century: Whence and Whither?* (New York 1951) 145–178. L. J. O'DONOVAN, ''Was Vatican II Evolutionary?'' *Theological Studies* 36 (Woodstock, Md. 1975) 493–502. J. W. O'MALLEY, ''Reform, Historical Consciousness, and Vatican II's Aggiornamento,'' *Theological Studies* 32 (Woodstock, Md. 1971) 573–601.

[W. J. BURGHARDT/J. W. O'MALLEY]

HISTORICISM

A tendency to accord a primacy to history in the explanation of facts, akin to the tendencies of LOGICISM and SCIENTISM to give primacy to logic and science respectively. First used in 1879 to describe the thought of Giambattista VICO (Cecil Currie), the term is currently used in two senses.

In the first sense, historicism may be defined as a preoccupation with the individual, unique, ascertainable historical situation, without any attempt to judge the situation by any epistemological or theological presuppositions. Facts are considered in their multiplicity and totality, not as amenable to systematic interpretation, but as expressive of the endless variety of historical forms in constant transformation. All individual historical manifestations are in Leopold von RANKE's phrase ''immediate to God.'' Thought structures, institutions, and cultures themselves are to be judged, not in terms of an evolving meaningful plan of universal validity, but solely in terms of their relativistic value to a given time and place. Historicism in this sense is opposed in theory to any of the classical philosophies of history that would try to discern intelligible patterns in the historical process as a whole.

As opposed to this, Maurice Mandelbaum sees historicism as a philosophical effort to explain the fact of change. He distinguishes a historicity of values, i.e., a belief that cultural values are indigenous to the age that produces them, from a historicism of knowledge, which maintains that truth and falsity must be judged with reference to the time in which they are formulated. To Martin D'ARCY, on the other hand, historicism is identical with the philosophy of history—any broad interpretative effort to assemble facts into a meaningful pattern. He considers three types of historicism: the first attempts to explain history in terms of physical laws (biological or economic); the second sees history as a meaningful drama with a beginning and end created by man's own efforts; the third sees history in terms of divine Providence.

Karl R. POPPER is perhaps the most articulate of recent critics of historicism in this latter sense of interpretative history. He questions both the logic and methodology of a historicism that would discover a key to history through laws of historical development.

See Also: HISTORY, PHILOSOPHY OF; HISTORY, THEOLOGY OF.

Bibliography: M. H. MANDELBAUM, *The Problem of Historical Knowledge* (New York 1938). M. C. D'ARCY, *The Meaning and Matter of History* (New York 1959). D. E. LEE and R. N. BECK, ''The Meaning of 'Historicism','' *American Historical Review* 59 (1953–54) 568–577. N. PETRUZZELLIS, *Enciclopedia filosofica,* 4 v. (Venice-Rome 1957) 4:997–1005. A. MIRGELER, *Lexikon für Theologie und Kirche,* ed. J. HOFER and K. RAHNER, 10 v. (2d, new ed. Freiburg 1957–65) 5:393–394. H. G. GADAMER, *Die Religion in Geschichte und Gegenwart,* 7 v. (3rd ed. Tübingen 1957–65) 3:369–371.

[R. P. MOHAN]

HISTORIOGRAPHY, ECCLESIASTICAL

The development of ecclesiastical historiography depends both on the formal recognition of its object, the Church, and on the methods by which the investigator examines and presents the role of the Church in time and space. The study of this discipline may center on four distinct periods: (1) the beginnings in Christian antiquity; (2) the expansion of historical insight, both sacred and profane, in the Middle Ages; (3) Church history from the 16th to the 18th century; and (4) the modern science of Church history in the 19th and 20th centuries.

Early Christianity

If the first Pentecost is accepted as the Church's birthdate, the ACTS of the Apostles should be credited with the distinction of being the first fruits of historiography in the Church. Nevertheless EUSEBIUS of Caesarea bears the title ''Father of Church History'' by reason of his *Historia ecclesiastica*, which in its earliest form (in seven books) appeared prior to the persecution of the Emperor DIOCLETIAN. After the conversion of CONSTANTINE he continued his account to 324, expanding it into ten books. It was Eusebius's purpose to report ''on the times which transpired from Our Savior's day to our own,'' especially on the most distinguished Christian communities

Denis Pétau, by Jacques Lubin.

and their leaders, on the rise of heresies and on the persecutions with which the Church was harassed. Accordingly, he began with the work of Christ and the Apostles (books 1–3), published the lists of bishops in the apostolic churches of Rome, Alexandria, Antioch and Jerusalem (books 4–7), included a catalogue of ecclesiastical and heretical writer as well as a discussion of the persecutions of the Church and concluded with the ''persecution of our time'' (books 8–9) and the victory of Christianity (book 10). Because of the citation of numerous texts from official acts and of excerpts from documents no longer extant (for example, from PAPIAS of Hieropolis), the work of Eusebius is considered to be the most important historical source for the first three centuries of the Church's existence. In the judgment of Eusebius, the universal Church lived pre-eminently in the local churches of apostolic origin.

EUSEBIUS was fortunate in his three continuators. Of these, the best was the lawyer and historian SOCRATES of Constantinople, who, depending on excellent sources, described events from 305 to 439; in covering the period 325 to 439, SOZOMEN was superior to his collaborator in narrative skill but not in reliability. THEODORET OF CYR wove into his text many sources for the years 324 to 428, but is inaccurate in chronology and lacked impartiality as a native of Antioch. THEODORE LECTOR coordinated the three accounts and continued the relation of events to 527. Of his work, however, only an epitome has survived. The Church history of EVAGRIUS SCHOLASTICUS, down to the year 594, presents a severely orthodox account of the CHRISTOLOGICAL CONTROVERSIES of that age. From this work and from the epitome of Theodore, later Byzantine annalistic historians, for example, THEOPHANES THE CONFESSOR (d. 817) and Nicephorus Callistus XANTHOPULUS (d. *c.* 1335), drew their inspiration, but they considered Church history to be connected in the strictest fashion with the history of the Byzantine Empire and its rulers.

In the West, the *Church History* of Eusebius exerted its influence through the free Latin rendering and additions of RUFINUS OF AQUILEIA (403); his three continuators lived on in the *Historia tripartite,* translated by Epiphanius under the direction of CASSIODORUS. Western historical interpretation during the Middle Ages, however, while it was indebted to these works, was more deeply influenced by the creation of a Christian SALVATION HISTORY, drawn from Old Testament and New Testament sources, appearing in the world chronicles that began as early as the third century with Sextus JULIUS AFRICANUS and HIPPOLYTUS OF ROME. The somewhat free Latin recasting of the world chronicle of Eusebius by St. JEROME became both the prototype and the point of departure for Christian historiography in the medieval West. In the same category, the *Chronicon* of ISIDORE OF SEVILLE (to 615) was highly esteemed. The chronicles of SULPICIUS SEVERUS and of PROSPER OF AQUITAINE were also held in esteem though to a lesser degree. Employing the history of the Roman emperors as their chronological frame of reference, these chroniclers projected a profane history in the guise of a Biblically oriented salvation history. It remained for St. AUGUSTINE, however, to present salvation history in the grand manner in the 22 books of *De civitate Dei,* composed between 413 and 426. The City of God, identified with the Church as a sacramental society, stands in unending conflict with the Earthly City (*civitas terrena*). The latter Augustinian concept is not to be identified with the Roman state, but with the society of men concerned with earthly values. The struggle between faith and unbelief is the master theme of world history. Augustine sought to demonstrate that Christianity bore no guilt for the current miseries with which the Roman world was afflicted. A similar apologetic theme was pursued by Paul OROSIUS of Braga in his *Historiae adversus paganos,* a work inspired by Augustine, written between 417 and 418. The central focus of both profane and salvation history is the Incarnation of the Logos. In placing the birth of Christ in the year 754 *ab Urbe condita,* cited in his Easter table for 532, DIONYSIUS EXIGUUS became the founder of Christian chronology.

Middle Ages

Medieval historiography in the West cannot be labeled Church history; it is, rather, a combination of salvation and profane history, embellished with individual historical accounts of dioceses, monasteries and saints. The divine economy of redemption, proceeding according to medieval thought, from the creation of man through the Old down to the New Dispensation, found its ultimate expression in the last things, the *Eschata.* It was customary to distinguish three stages in the history of the world (*ante legem, sub lege, sub gratia*), or six world epochs corresponding to the six days of creation in Genesis (Aug., *Civ.* 22.30; *Trin.* 4.4). Furthermore, the organization of time periods into four world empires, associated with Daniel 2.36, suggested for the Christian Era the succession of the Roman emperors as a chronological framework.

CHRONICLES AND ANNALS

The more important chronicles of the Middle Ages depended on Eusebius and Jerome and their continuators for their reconstruction of the earlier period. But the closer they approached their own day, the more they depended on personal experience for knowledge of contemporary events. Thus, the *Chronicon* of REGINO OF PRÜM, a mere compilation down to the time of Louis the Pious, becomes a reliable source for the later Carolingian period. Similarly, the world chronicles of HERMANNUS CONTRACTUS of Reichenau (d. 1054) and of SIGEBERT OF GEMBLOUX (ending in 1105) were expanded into histories of the German Empire. OTTO OF FREISING (d. 1158), on the other hand, in his *Historia de duabus civitatibus,* follows Augustine rather than the work of Eusebius and Jerome.

During the age of the evangelization of the German peoples, GREGORY OF TOURS (d. 594) described the acceptance of Christianity by the Franks; somewhat later, in his *Historia ecclesiastica*, BEDE (d. 735) wrote on the Anglo-Saxons and how ''they were converted to the Church of Christ.'' The *Chronicon Bohemorum* of COSMAS OF PRAGUE (d. 1125) was similarly motivated. Monastic and diocesan ANNALS, however, were to become more significant than ethnic histories in developing the history of the Church in the Middle Ages. Year by year in every great monastery (for example, FULDA, SANKT GALLEN, and LINDISFARNE), the chronicler recorded the most important events. Outstanding among the diocesan annals, which developed somewhat later, were such works as the history of the church of Reims by FLODOARD (d. *c.* 966) and the *Gesta Hammaburgensis ecclesiae pontificum* by ADAM OF BREMEN (d. after 1081).

Daniel Papebroch.

VITAE

Perhaps the most popular form of medieval historical writing—with the exception of the ubiquitous annals—was the vita, a biography devised to serve the purposes of edification. With notable exceptions, the vita was generally the life of a saint, fashioned on classical models such as the *Lives* of Sallust or Suetonius and on the Christian pattern of Sulpicius Severus. Although in the later Middle Ages hagiographical writing showed a marked degree of restraint, when compared to the legendary fabrications that abounded in the Merovingian lives of the saints, they nevertheless maintained the same inspirational objective. Thus the monk Ruotger, in his life of St. BRUNO OF COLOGNE (composed 967–969), projected the model bishop of the Empire, successful in achieving both spiritual and temporal goals; EADMER accented the sanctity of ANSELM OF CANTERBURY (d. 1106), not by regaling the reader with miracles but by stressing his subject's fidelity to the monastic ideal. WILLIAM OF SAINT-THIERRY and Gaufridus composed a life of St. BERNARD OF CLAIRVAUX based on their intimate familiarity with that great Cistercian. The lives of the great religious founders, for example, of FRANCIS OF ASSISI by BONAVENTURE and of DOMINIC by JORDAN OF SAXONY, were influenced by the concern of each order for a standardized portrait of its founder.

EMINENTISSIMO DOMINO

D CÆSARI ESTRÆO

S· R· E· ÇARDINALI·

NTER præcipuos studiorum nostrorum, immo & totius Congregationis nostræ patronos ac fautores, cùm te jam dudum in primis suspiciamus, EMINENTISSIME DOMINE; *nemini mirum videri debet, quòd S. Hilarii Opera, quæ novis recognita curis, & pro modulo à nobis illustrata in lucem denuo prodeunt, Eminentiæ tuæ nuncupemus & offeramus. Nam post tot honorifica testimonia, quibus non modò universum cœtum nostrum, verùm etiam quorumdam è sodalibus nostris, tum in sanctorum Patrum scriptis recensendis, tum in eruendis veneranda antiquitatis monumentis labores summis Pontificibus, sacro Collegio, totique Romanæ curiæ approbare dignatus es; sane committendum non erat, ut tam propensa in nos benevolentia & humanitas debitâ grati animi testificatione fraudaretur. Quod repugnante æquitate ne eveniret, nihil opportu-*

a ij

''Works of St. Hilary, Bishop of Poiters,'' dedication page, published by Pierre Coustant.

History. With the emergence of HUGH OF FLEURY and ORDERICUS VITALIS in the 12th century, the use of the title *Historia ecclesiastica* began anew. Their work, however, was hardly Church history after the fashion of Eusebius. Toward the close of the century the *Historia pontificalis* by JOHN OF SALISBURY (d. 1180) attempted to assign to papal history the function of universal Church history, an effort that was repeated in the *Historia ecclesiastica nova* by the Dominican BARTHOLOMEW OF LUCCA (d. 1326). The chronicle of the Dominican MARTIN OF TROPPAU (d. 1278) was widely used as a textbook and frequently translated and continued, as was that of the Dominican BERNARD GUI (finished in 1331). While these works may be classified as valuable late medieval chronicles of the popes, they cannot be considered as Church history in the strict sense. They failed to satisfy the requirements of the genre because, in basic structure, they conformed to the pattern of the world chronicle. And finally, neither the continuations of the *LIBER PONTIFICALIS* down to B. Platina nor the *Lives of the Popes of Avignon* provided a proper substitute for a genuine history of the Church.

The theology of history, elaborated by the Calabrian Cistercian JOACHIM OF FIORE (d. 1202), exerted a profound influence on historical thought in the High Middle Ages and succeeding centuries. Joachim distinguished three periods of salvation history: (1) the age of the Father, in which Old Testament law prevailed; (2) the current age of the Son, dominated by faith and grace; and (3) the future age of the Holy Spirit, producing the reign of love, during which the *Evangelium aeternum* would be announced. In the course of the last prophetic period of salvation history the Johannine Church of the spirit would replace the current Petrine Church. Despite the Fourth LATERAN COUNCIL's condemnation of Joachim's Trinitarian teachings, his ideas continued unabated among the FRANCISCAN SPIRITUALS (for example, PETER JOHN OLIVI), in late medieval APOCALYPTIC movements in the literature of reform, and, surprisingly, in the writings of NICHOLAS OF CUSA.

Related to Joachimism was the ''theory of decline, which held that the Church in the current age had fallen from the high estate of the primitive Church and was in need of reform. The descent from the ideal of early Christianity had proceeded through several stages: the golden age of the martyrs had been followed by the silver era of Constantine, then by an age of bronze and finally by an iron age, in which both clerical and lay indifference and immorality provoked the judgment of God. Influenced by the theory of decline, Dietrich of NIEHEIM in the 15th century wrote his *History of the Great Schism* (*see* WESTERN SCHISM), and the Viennese professor Thomas EBENDORFER produced his several tracts on the same theme. During the age of religious dissension in the 16th century, however, the theory of decline was given a completely new interpretation.

Church History, 16th to 18th Century

The historical image of the Church as it appeared to Martin LUTHER was formed by the conviction that the true Biblical doctrine of salvation had been falsified by the influence of ARISTOTELIANISM on theology and the connivance of the papacy during the previous 400 years. He concluded that the repeated efforts toward the reform of the Church in the late Middle Ages—never actually implemented—demanded, as a presupposition, a return to the primitive doctrines of Redemption and justification and the removal of intervening ''human institutions.'' Matthias FLACIUS (Vlačich) and his collaborators attempted a vindication of Luther's view in their historical project (1559–74), which was organized according to centuries and based on a systematic marshaling of the sources. They tried to prove that, in its teaching and organization, Lutheranism rather than the Roman Church corresponded more closely to the early Church and that it was, in consequence, the true Church. As a result of this position, the history of theology was compelled to assume the burden of proof and to furnish historical evidence that the Roman Catholic Church, in its teaching, liturgy and institutions, was in conformity with primitive Christianity. Simultaneously, systematic theology developed the doctrine of the MARKS OF THE CHURCH (*notae ecclesiae*), and through the efforts of Robert BELLARMINE and Maximilian Sandaeus (Van der Sandt, d. 1656) ECCLESIOLOGY became an integrating factor in APOLOGETICS. The need for a more precise definition of the concept of the Church and the pressure to defend it against Protestant attack actually contributed to the return of Christian historiography to the tasks of general Church history.

Obviously, both Catholics and Protestants were able to rely on the preparatory work supplied by the humanists. The published editions of the great Fathers of the Church (Ambrose, Augustine, Jerome) and of the early Church historians (Eusebius) in Latin, 1523, and in Greek, 1544, by ERASMUS of Rotterdam and his collaborators; the conciliar collections of J. MERLIN, Peter Crabbe and L. SURIUS; the editions of the ancient liturgies (for example, the liturgy of St. Basil by Georg WITZEL, 1546 and the *APOSTOLIC CONSTITUTIONS* by Francisco TORRES, 1563); and the collected sources for the history of the papacy and of the Roman Church by the Augustinian Onofrio PANVINIO (d. 1569)—all provided a wealth of material for the *Annales ecclesiastici* of Caesar BARONIUS (d. 1607), an elaboration of the lectures that he had delivered in the Oratory of St. Philip NERI. The work of Baronius, appearing in 12 volumes between 1588 and 1605, covered the history of the Church down to the pontificate of INNOCENT III and was based on both printed and manuscript sources with copious citation of pertinent texts. The objective was patently apologetic: ''against the innovators of our day, and in defense of the authority and of the antiquity of the sacred traditions of the Roman Church.'' The *Annales,* continued by many authors, especially Abraham Bzovius (d. 1637) and Odoricus Raynaldus (d. 1671), remained the standard work of general Church history into the 19th century.

The same period saw the emergence of the history of Christian literature. The catalogues of authors, compiled by GENNADIUS OF MARSEILLES (*c.* 480), Isidore of Seville, ILDEFONSUS OF TOLEDO and their medieval continuators, SIGEBERT OF GEMBLOUX and Johannes TRITHEMIUS, were reedited and enlarged (1580) by a fresh review of Christian literary production. Similar works appeared at short intervals: the *Epitome* of the Augustinian Angelo ROCCA (1594), the voluminous *Apparatus sacer* of the Jesuit Antonio POSSEVINO (1606) and the little work of R. Bellarmine, *De scriptoribus ecclesiasticis* (1613). At the same time the Belgian Albert Le Mire (d. 1640) carried on the catalogue of Trithemius and founded the study of ecclesiastical statistics.

John Bolland.

The advance of Church history in the 17th and 18th centuries can be studied under three headings: (1) the broadening of the documentary foundation of Church history by the edition of numerous texts, improved through the application of a critical method; (2) the appearance of monumental historicostatistical works on the papacy, the dioceses and religious orders, which were to remain authoritative for centuries; and (3) the rise of professional instruction in Church history in schools of theology toward the end of the period.

EDITIONS AND METHODOLOGY

By employing Greek texts for the first time, the Roman edition of the general councils (1608–12), prepared under the direction of PAUL V, surpassed all of its predecessors in the 16th century. The *Sacrosancta concilia* (17 v. 1671–72), edited by the Jesuits Philippe LABBÉ and G. Cossart, included both ecumenical and provincial councils and synods—as the *Collectio regia*

(Paris 1644) had previously done. Their work was later expanded by Étienne BALUZE (1683), Nicola and Sebastiano Coleti (1728–33) and Giovanni Domenico MANSI (1748–52). Mansi's later work, the *Amplissima collectio* (31 v. 1759–98), is the most complete and the most frequently consulted conciliar collection. Between 1899 and 1927, L. PETIT and J. B. Martin, continued Mansi's work down to VATICAN COUNCIL I. Though inferior to Mansi in volume, the *Collectio maxima* of the Jesuit J. HARDOUIN (1714–15), commissioned by the ASSEMBLY OF THE FRENCH CLERGY, surpassed it in the use of critical method. The appearance of national conciliar collections paralleled the great conciliar editions of G. Loaysa (1593) and J. Catalani's second edition of the work of J. Sáenz de Aguirre (1693–95) for Spain; of J. SIRMOND (1629) for France; of H. Spelman (1639–64) and D. Wilkins (1737) for Ireland and England; of J. F. Schannat and J. Hartzheim (1759–90) for Germany.

The methodological advance that characterized the editing of conciliar documents was applied with equal success to the hagiographical collections, whose objective was the vindication of Catholic veneration of the saints. The *Lives of the Saints*, calendared by L. Lippomano (d. 1559) and L. Surius (d. 1578), were not only brought to completion by the *Acta sanctorum* (ActSS) of the Jesuits John Bolland and Gottfried Henskens but—more importantly—were superseded by the use of historical criticism. The first two volumes of the *Acta sanctorum*, containing the saints for the month of January, appeared in 1643. The most renowned successor of Bolland, Daniel Papebroch (d. 1714), defended the method of the BOLLANDISTS against the attack of the Benedictines and the Spanish INQUISITION. The Jesuit Denis PÉTAU (Petavius, d. 1652) founded the science of CHRONOLOGY, and the Benedictine Jean MABILLON (d. 1707) founded the sciences of PALEOGRAPHY and DIPLOMATICS. In preparing reliable texts for the Fathers of the Church, the MAURISTS refined the methods of textual and literary criticism, systematically investigated manuscript collections and solved problems of authenticity.

The edition of the works of St. Augustine by the Maurists Thomas Blampin and Pierre COUSTANT, and the edition of John Chrysostom by Bernard de MONTFAUCON surpassed all previous efforts as a result of the meticulous care employed in emending the text and by the critical approach to questions of authenticity. The *De antiquis ecclesiae ritibus* (1700–02), the work of the Maurists Mabillon and Edmond Martène, marked the beginning of the science of LITURGICS. Somewhat earlier, the Oratorian L. THOMASSIN, in his *Vetus et nova ecclesiae disciplina* (1688), had begun the scientific study of the history of Canon Law. In the field of the history of Christian literature, the *Nouvelle bibliothèque des auteurs ecclésiastiques* (1684–91) by the Jansenist L. E. DUPIN, replaced all earlier works because of the expanse of its coverage.

PAPAL, DIOCESAN AND INSTITUTIONAL HISTORY

Among the 17th and 18th century historical works of reference emphasizing the statistical approach, the most outstanding was the *Vitae et res gestae pontificum Romanorum et S. R. E. cardinalium* (1601–02) by the Dominican Alfons Chacon (Ciaconius). The revised and expanded edition by A. Oldoini is still useful. For its time, the *Italia sacra* (1643–62) of the Cistercian Ferdinando Ughelli was a monumental work of reference for the diocesan history of Italy. Later improved by the edition of N. Coleti (1717–22), it served as the model for the *Gallia Christiana*, edited by Scévole and Louis Sainte-Marthe. In 1710, by order of the Assembly of the French Clergy, this work was revised by the Benedictine Martène and his collaborators and became the most perfect work of its kind. Somewhat later came the *España sagrada* by the Augustinian Enrique FLÓREZ (begun in 1754) and the *Illyricum sacrum* by the Jesuit D. FARLATI (begun in 1751). The plan of Abbot Gerbert of Sankt Blasien to produce a similar work, the *Germania sacra,* was never carried out.

All of the great orders provided for the publication of source collections and encyclopedic works on their own history: the Franciscans, in the *Annales Ordinis Minorum* by the Irish friar Luke WADDING (d. 1657); the Benedictines, in the *Annales Ordinis Sancti Benedicti* by the Maurist Mabillon, preceded by his *Acta sanctorum O.S.B.;* the Dominicans, the *Scriptores Ordinis Praedicatorum* (1719–21), an outstanding catalogue of authors made through the efforts of J. QUÉTIF and J. ÉCHARD. The Carmelites, with C. de Villiers (1752), and the Augustinians, with J. F. Ossinger (1768), published similar works. The 18th century was the age of great documentary collections, of which the most distinguished was the *Bullarium Ordinis Praedicatorum* by P. Ripoll and A. Brémond (1729–40). The Franciscan H. Hélyot attempted to write the first general history of all religious orders (1714–19).

General Church history, however, failed to keep pace with the publication of new source material and works of a historicostatistical character. The *Historia ecclesiastica* of the Dominican Natalis Alexander (1699) was a collection of 230 monographs, hardly a work of historical narrative. The mosaic-like but orderly and accurate mélange of selections from the sources, the *Mémoirs pour servir à l'histoire ecclésiastique* by L. S. de TILLEMONT (1693–1712), ends suddenly with 513. C. FLEURY, on the other hand, brought his *Histoire ecclésiastique* (1691–1720) down to the Council of CONSTANCE, but his work was marred by Gallican views, which were opposed by G. A. ORSI, OP, in his *Istoria ec-*

clesiastica (1747–62). All of these multivolumed enterprises, however, lacked the necessary penetration and organization of material, which generally result from formal instruction and training.

PROFESSIONAL STUDIES IN CHURCH HISTORY

Although there was no dearth of planning during the 17th century to place Church history in the curriculum, it was nevertheless excluded from the program of studies in Catholic universities. In Protestant centers, however, and for the first time in Helmstedt in 1650, the new field of Church history was introduced successfully. The *Summarium historiae ecclesiasticae*, prepared for instructional purposes by the Leipzig professor A. Rechenberg (1697), who continued to labor under the preoccupations of the Magdeburg CENTURIATORS, abandoned their systematic divisions by centuries and substituted five distinct periods: (1) *Ecclesia plantata* (organization of the Church), (2) *Ecclesia libertate gaudens* (the Church in liberty), (3) *Ecclesia pressa et obscurata* (the Church oppressed and benighted), (4) *Ecclesia gemens* (the Church in travail), and (5) *Ecclesia repurgata* (the Church purified), that is, since the 16th century.

In Catholic circles, Church history was not introduced into the curriculum of theological schools until the 18th century, and even then not universally. A chair of Church history was founded at the Collegium Romanum in 1741 and Austrian schools of theology began lectures in ''religious (*geistliche*) history'' in 1752. Protestant leadership in the field was apparent in that Catholic textbooks prepared for instruction in history followed either the standard Protestant models, especially the work of J. L. von Mosheim (d. 1755), the ''father of Protestant Church history,'' or fell under the influence of the ENLIGHTENMENT, following, for example, such works as the *Institutiones historiae ecclesiasticae* and the *Leitfaden in der Kirchengeschichte* (1790) by M. Dannenmeyer. A progressive note appeared in the attempt, evident in the leading texts of the period, to achieve a periodization of history determined by content. Most texts, however, labored under a severe disadvantage: they were generally written from the viewpoint of a state-controlled Church, were anti-Roman in their interpretation and failed to grasp the supernatural character of the Church. Before a new advance could be made, Church history first had to purge itself of the values and outlooks of the Enlightenment that had vitiated its study. A clear reaction to rationalist Church history was already apparent in the *History of the Church of Christ* (1794–1809) by the Anglican I. Milner and in the *General History of the Christian Church* by the American Unitarian J. A. Priestley (1802–03). The decisive movement, however, was to develop on the Continent.

Scientific Church History

Two tasks presented themselves to the Church historian during the 19th and 20th centuries: a reevaluation of the Church in the light of its origins and the development of a scientific methodology to cope with its sources and their interpretation.

NEW INTERPRETATION

The distinction of having overcome the regalistic and rationalist concepts of the Church and of winning respect for its independence from the state and the acceptance of its supernatural character belongs to many authors working in the period from the French Revolution to the Restoration, some of whom were actually not Church historians. In 1799, while Pius VI was being taken to France as a prisoner, B. A. Cappellari, later Pope GREGORY XVI, wrote his *Trionfo della s. sede e della chiesa*, in which he predicted that both the Church and the papacy, as institutions founded by Christ, were indestructible and that they would shortly be revitalized. F. R. de CHATEAUBRIAND and J. de MAISTRE opened the perspective of the Church's great tradition and of its cultural contributions in the Middle Ages. Meanwhile, the young H. F. R. de LAMENNAIS refuted GALLICANISM and the German Romantics steeped themselves in the piety of the much-abused MIDDLE AGES. F. L. Stolberg (d. 1819), attempted to confirm the tenets of faith, in the several volumes of his *Geschichte der Religion Jesu Christi*, by recourse to history and identified himself as a proponent of Augustine's and Bossuet's interpretation of Church history as salvation history. J. T. KATERKAMP, also a member of the Münster circle of historians, wrote his history of the Church (1823–34) in the spirit of Stolberg. The decisive influence, however, in the reorientation of ecclesiastical historiography was the University of Tübingen Church historian, J. A. MÖHLER (1796–1838). Establishing the historicity of Christianity in the fact of the Incarnation, Möhler elaborated the distinction between Christian history and the history of the Church founded by Christ. His *Symbolik* sharply contrasted the doctrinal differences existing between Catholics and Protestants, thereby overcoming and rejecting the confessional indifferentism engendered by the Enlightenment. The Tübingen school, founded by Möhler and Johann Sebastian DREY (d. 1853), inspired the *Conciliengeschichte*, written by the future bishop C. J. HEFELE, which in its French edition and continuation by H. LECLERCQ is still the indispensable work in its field. The Munich school, founded by J. J. I. DÖLLINGER (1799–1890), was equally illustrious, exerting its influence on both France (C. F. MONTALEMBERT) and England (Lord J. E. ACTON)

In England, J. LINGARD's *Antiquities of the Anglo-Saxon Church* (1806) had already appeared, presenting a just interpretation of the Christian Middle Ages. The *History of Latin Christianity down to the Death of Pope Nicholas V*, by the Anglican H. MILMAN (1854–55), followed in the same vein and was praised by A. Froude as the ''finest historical work in the English language.'' The OXFORD MOVEMENT rediscovered the Fathers of the Church, producing J. H. NEWMAN, who, in his *Essay on the Development of Christian Doctrine* (1845), while summarizing the results of his historical studies, concluded that the Roman Catholic Church had preserved intact the DEPOSIT OF FAITH committed to it, and in consequence consistently returned to its communion. By frankly acknowledging, however, the religious values to be found in the churches not united with Rome, Newman laid the foundation for a Catholic ecumenical interpretation of Church history.

CRITICAL SOURCE COLLECTIONS

Insight into the supernatural character of the Church and the removal of the Enlightenment's indifferentism and prejudice against the Middle Ages were only one prerequisite for the flowering of Church history in the 19th century. The other was the discovery and availability of new sources, the emendation of the texts of sources already known and the application of historical criticism to their investigation. The *Patrologia latina* and the *Patrologia graeca* by J. P. MIGNE (d. 1875) merely reproduced the best existing texts of Latin ecclesiastical writers down to Innocent III and of the Greek writers to Cardinal Bessarion. Since 1903 supplementary texts have appeared in the *Patrologia orientalis.* The *Corpus scriptorum ecclesiasticorum latinorum*, under the auspices of the Vienna Academy of Sciences (since 1860), has provided modern critical texts for the Latin Christian writers and since 1897 the Berlin Academy of Sciences has published the *Griechischen christlichen Schriftsteller der ersten drei Jahrhunderte* (including some writers of the 4th and 5th centuries as well). Many other works of the Fathers of the Church have appeared in bilingual editions with French or English translations. Special mention should be made of the *Sources chrétiennes.*

Medieval and modern Church history has been especially enriched by the publication of great national source collections: in Germany, the *Monuments Germaniae historica* (since 1819) and the *Reichstagsakten* (since 1867) edited under the auspices of the Historical Commission of Munich; in France, the continuation of the *Rerum Gallicarum et Franciarum scriptores* (begun in 1728) and the *Collection de documents inédits* (since 1835); in England, the *Rerum Britannicarum medii aevi scriptores* [*Rerum Britannicarum medii aevi scriptores,* 224 v. (London 1858–96)] and the *State Papers* (1856); in Spain, the *Colección de documentos inéditos* (1847); in Italy, the *Fonti per la storia d'Italia* (1887) and the new edition of the *Rerum Italicarum scriptores* by L. A MURATORI [since 1900; for contents, see *Repertorium fontium Historiae medii aevii primum ab Augusto Potthast digestum, nunc cura collegii historicorum e pluribus nationum emendatum et auctum:* v.1, Series collectionum, Instituto Storico Italiano per il Medico Evo (Rome 1957—) 509–522].

The history of the popes in the Middle Ages was advanced by the admirable surveys of papal documents in the *Regesta pontificum Romanorum* by P. Jaffé (1851; 2d ed. 1885–88) and their continuation by A. POTTHAST (1873–75). Far superior to the above, however, is the collection of all papal documents to 1198, arranged by country, begun by P. KEHR and refined by new techniques of diplomatics developed by the École des Chartes in Paris and by the School of the Diplomatics in Vienna. The opening of the secret VATICAN ARCHIVES by Leo XIII in 1884 was a monumental event, marking a new era in the study of papal history and of Church history generally. Following Leo's action, French scholarship undertook the publication of the papal registers of the 14th century and the GÖRRES-GESELLSCHAFT edited the sources for the history of papal financial administration and the *Acta* of the Council of TRENT. Next came the publication of the 16th- and 17th-century nunciature reports from Germany, France, Belgium, Poland and Spain; the status reports of dioceses prescribed by SIXTUS V; and the records pertaining to the investigation of episcopal candidates. The archives of the Congregation for the PROPAGATION OF THE FAITH provided a wealth of material for Catholic history in Protestant and mission countries. All the major religious orders exploited the Vatican archives in the interest of their own history, gradually publishing the sources pertinent to their own development, for example, in the *Monumenta ordinis praedicatorum* and in the *Monumenta historica societatis Jesu.*

REFERENCE WORKS AND PERIODICALS

The investigation of new source material was facilitated by new historical tools and works of reference. While the *Series episcoporum* (1873) of the Benedictine P. GAMS depended solely on printed sources, the *Hierarchia Catholica* (since 1898) by the Conventual K. EUBEL and his successors could draw on documents recently made available in the Vatican archives for statistical records pertinent to episcopal history. Indispensable for medieval Church history were the *Répertoire des sources historiques du moyen-âge* of U. CHEVALIER (1877- 88; 2d ed. 1903–07) and the *Bibliotheca historica medii aevi* of A. Potthast (1862–88; new ed. 1962—). H. Biaudet (1910), L. Karttunen (1912) and G. De Marchi (1957) assembled lists of apostolic nuncios from the beginning of permanent nunciatures down to the present. The *Bibliotheca missionum* (since 1916), begun by R. Streit, is a basic treatment of the sources and bibliography of mission history. All modern theological encyclopedias give attention to the history of the Church, the most exhaustive being the *Realenzyklopädie für protestantische Theologie und Kirche* (3d ed. 1896–1913) and the excellent though somewhat less comprehensive *Religion in Geschichte und Gegenwart* (3d ed. 1957–62); *The Catholic Encyclopedia* (1908–14); the *Lexikon für Theologie und Kirche* (2d ed. since 1957); the *Dictionnaire de théologie catholique* (1902–50); and the *Dictionnaire d'archéologie chrétienne et de liturgie* (1924–53). The *Dictionnaire d'histoire et de géographie ecclésiastiques* (since 1912), however, is devoted exclusively to Church history. All national bibliographies, for example, that of Dahlmann- Waitz for Germany and the *Bibliography of British History* (C. Gross: C. Read, 2d ed. 1959; G. Davies) for England, take into account the Church history of their respective countries.

To accommodate the ever-growing number of special studies appearing in the field, Church history journals began to make their appearance. The *Zeitschrift für Kirchengeschichte*, founded in 1876 by the Protestant theologian T. Brieger, was shortly followed (1880) by the *Historisches Jahrbuch* by the Görres-Gesellschaft and in 1887 by the *Römische Quartalschrift für Christ-liche Archäologie und Kirchengeschichte.* In 1900 the *Revue d'histoire ecclésiastique*, founded at Louvain by A. Cauchie, developed into the indispensable clearing house of international research, providing a full bibliography of all important works in the field of Church history. In France the growth of studies in ecclesiastical history were indebted to the *Revue d'histoire de l'église de France* (1910); those in the United States were under similar obligation to the *Catholic Historical Review*, founded in 1917 by P. GUILDAY. Important new journals of the 1940s and 1950s were the following: in the United States, *Traditio* (1943); in Italy, the *Rivista di storia della chiesa in Italia* (1947); in Spain, *Hispania sacra* (1948); and in England, the *Journal of Ecclesiastical History* (1950). Before World War I several reviews specializing in the history of religious orders made their appearance: the *Studien und Mitteilungen aus dem Benediktinerund Zisterzienserorden* (1880), the *Revue Mabillon* (1905) and the *Archivum Franciscanum historicum* (1908). Many others were begun some years later and published as organs of their own institutes, for example, the *Archivum Fratrum Praedicatorum* (1931) and the *Archivum historicum Societatis Jesu* (1932).

This renaissance in the study of Church history would not have been possible without the introduction and concomitant development of basic instruction in Church history, evident almost everywhere in the theological faculties of universities and seminaries. The constitution of Pius XI, *DEUS SCIENTIARUM DOMINUS* of May 24, 1931, moreover, prescribed the introduction of seminars for the study of historical method. About the same time many universities, for example, Louvain and The Catholic University of America in Washington, began publishing notable series comprising dissertations in Church history.

TEXTBOOKS AND SPECIAL MONOGRAPHS

Instruction and research in Church history were constantly in need of textbooks and scholarly handbooks or works of reference. The voluminous production in the first half of the 19th century, for example, Priestley's *General History of the Christian Church* (1802–03) and R. F. ROHRBACHER'S *Histoire universelle de l'église* (1842–49), had paid scant attention to research and were unsatisfactory for scientific work in the field. At the start, Protestants had the advantage with such excellent texts as those of J. K. L. Gieseler (1824–57), F. C. BAUR (1853–63), W. Möller and G. Kawerau (1889–1907). But they were soon matched by the texts of I. Ritter (1826–35), Döllinger (1836) and J. ALZOG (1841; 10 eds.), but especially by the *Handbuch der allgemeinen Kirchengeschichte* (1876–80; 5 eds., tr. into several languages) by (later cardinal) J. HERGENRÖTHER and the shorter texts by F. X. KRAUS (1872–75), F. X. FUNK (1886; later eds. by K. BIHLMEYER and H. Tüchle), A. Knöpfler (1895), and J. P. KIRSCH (1930–49). These works were distinguished for their exact presentation of facts, but in their earlier editions were rigid and categorical in tendency.

After the turn of the 19th century several first-rate texts and manuals made their, appearance in France: L. DUCHESNE, *Histoire ancienne de l'église* (1906–10)—an epoch-making work; F. MOURRET, *Histoire générale de l'église* (1909–21); and the projected 24 volume *Histoire de l'église* by A. FLICHE and V. MARTIN (since 1936). In Italy texts were prepared by L. Todesco (1922–30), A. Saba (1938–43) and P. Paschini (1931); in England, by P. Hughes, *A History of the Church* (1934–49) and O. Chadwick, *The History of the Church* (London 1962); and in Holland, by (later cardinal) J. de JONG. The monumental works by Hughes, *The Reformation in England* (3 v. 1950–54) and by M. D. Knowles, *The Monastic Order in England* (2d ed. 1962) and *The Religious Orders in England* (3 v. 1948–60), are models of scholarship.

The numerous histories of the popes that made their appearance in this period were of great significance for general Church history. The brilliant *Römischen Päpste in den letzten vier Jahrhunderten* by L. RANKE (1838), written before the opening of the Vatican Archives, was superseded by the wealth of new material found in the *Geschichte der Päpste* by L. von PASTOR (1885–1933), a work that has been translated into many languages and that might well be considered a history of the Church from the 15th to the 18th century. Pastor's work is supplemented by E. Caspar, *Geschichte des Papsttums* (1930–33), for the early Christian centuries and by J. HALLER, *Papsttum, Idee und Wirklichkeit* (2d ed. 1950–55), for the Middle Ages—both works of Protestant scholarship. J. SCHMIDLIN (1933–39) continued the history of the papacy into the 19th and 20th centuries. The best comprehensive treatment of papal history is that of F. X. Seppelt; and the number of popular histories of the popes is legion.

The histories of the Church in various countries form to some extent a counterpart to the history of the popes: for Belgium, the work of E. de Moreau; for Germany, that of A. Hauck; for England, W. HUNT, G. Stephens and J. R. H. Moorman; for Austria, E. Tomek; for Spain, Z. GARCÍA VILLADA; and for the United States, J. G. SHEA.

SPECIAL AREAS OF CHURCH HISTORY

One result of the constantly growing trend toward specialization was the splitting off of large segments of Church history into independent fields of study and research. The history of Christian literature, which, together with Church history, developed into an integral part of the theological curriculum at many 18th-century universities, became delimited in time and was put on a sounder basis and defined as patrology. The Oxford movement was distinguished for its study of the Fathers of the Church (*Library of the Fathers,* 1838–80). The German Protestant school of A. von Harnack and K. Holl improved on the methods employed by the Maurists and was rivaled by such Catholic scholars as A. EHRHARD (d. 1940), O. Bardenhewer (*Geschichte der altkirchlichen Literatur,* 5 v. 1913-32) and B. ALTANER (*Patrologie,* 6th ed. 1960).

In France the most prominent, patrologists were G. BARDY, A. Puech and F. Cayré; in Italy, A. Casamassa and U. Moricca. In the United States the most significant work is the *Patrology* (3 v. 1950–60) by J. Quasten. Research in Christian Latin has been ably served by the journal *Vigiliae Christianae* (since 1947), and the advance in the study of medieval Literature has been due partly to the studies in medieval Latin language and literature by L. TRAUBE, M. Manitius, P. Lehmann, J. de Ghellinck, the journal *Speculum* and other journals and partly due to the research in the history of scholasticism by H. DENIFLE, F. EHRLE, P. MANDONNET and M. GRABMANN. In the field of medieval EXEGESIS, until recently a largely uncultivated area, works by F. Stegmüller, B. Smalley and H. de Lubac are important.

Through the work of G. B. de ROSSI (d. 1894) Christian archeology was raised to the status of a philological science. The strictly limited Roman orientation given to the field by J. WILPERT (d. 1940) in his monumental works on the art of the CATACOMBS, Christian SARCOPHAGI, and Roman mosaics was greatly extended by excavations in the Middle East (DURA-EUROPOS and Ephesus), the study of early Christian architecture (R. Krautheimer) and the integration of the relations between pagan antiquity and Christianity by F. J. DÖLGER and T. Klauser.

In the field of HAGIOGRAPHY the reestablished institute of the Bollandists (1837) easily surpassed all other efforts, especially under the direction of such scholars as C. de SMEDT (d. 1911), H. DELEHAYE (d. 1941), P. Peeters (d. 1950) and P. GROSJEAN (d. 1964). The journal of this enterprise, the *Analecta Bollandiana* (since 1882), is also unsurpassed.

The history of dogma has been conspicuously advanced through the monographic publications of eminent Catholic scholars, such as P. BATIFFOL, A. d' ALÈS and J. LEBRETON. But despite the effort of L. J. TIXERONT, whose *Histoire des dogmes de l'antiquité chrétienne* (1905–12) was an exceptional work for its time, no comprehensive survey of the history of dogma exists today that can equal the great Protestant works by A. von HARNACK, R. SEEBERG and F. Loofs. However, the *Handbuch der Dogmengeschichte* by M. Schmaus, J. R. Geiselmann and A. Grillmeier was begun in 1951.

The history of the BYZANTINE CHURCH and of the other Oriental Churches, which goes back to the work of L. Allatius and J. Assemani in the 17th and 18th centuries, has become a distinct area of study. Recent Byzantine studies were pioneered, particularly by German and French scholars (A. Ehrhard, K. Krumbacher; currently, H. G. Beck); A. Baumstark's *Geschichte der syrischen Literatur* (1922) and the *Geschichte der christlichen arabischen Literatur* (5 v. 1944–55) by G. Graf (d. 1955) opened up relatively unknown areas of investigation. In 1917 Benedict XV founded the Istituto Pontificio Orientale, which since 1935 has published the *Orientalia Christiana periodica.*

The foundations for the history of liturgy were laid by the editions of the sources by the Maurists E. Martène and E. RENAUDOT. It became a distinct discipline, however, through the efforts of L. Duchesne, P. Batiffol, E. BISHOP and K. MOHLBERG, among others. Important texts were published by the Henry Bradshaw Society (since 1890), the *Analecta hymnica* (since 1886) by M. Dreves and C. Blume and the editions of the *Ordines Romani* and the *Pontificale Romanum* by M. ANDRIEU (d. 1956). The history of liturgy has contributed greatly to the current liturgical movement.

The history of CANON LAW was able to build on the efforts of L. THOMASSIN and BENEDICT XIV. It continued to develop during the 19th century through the contributions of such Protestant scholars as E. Friedberg, P. Hinschius and his successor U. Stutz (d. 1938) and the Old Catholic historian J. F. Schulte (d. 1914). Their efforts were matched by Catholic canonists such as J. B. Sägmüller (d. 1942), P. Fournier (d. 1935), G. Le Bras, A. Stickler and S. G. Kuttner. In 1955 Kuttner founded the Institute of Research and Study in Mediaeval Canon Law at The Catholic University in Washington (moved to Yale University, 1964).

MISSIOLOGY and SPIRITUAL THEOLOGY were introduced only recently into theological curriculums as formal disciplines. Mission history and the history of asceticism and mysticism have thus become independent studies. J. Schmidlin (1925) prepared the first serviceable textbook of Catholic mission history, later expanded and improved by A. Mulders and S. Delacroix. The best history of the missions is that of the American Protestant historian K. S. Latourette. The *Revue d'histoire des missions* began publication in 1924, but the general missiological journals have also from time to time carried historical articles. In 1932 Pius XI established a faculty of missiology at the Gregorian University in Rome. A similar development is to be noted respecting the history of asceticism and mysticism, which had been cultivated consistently by the contemplative orders, for example, by the Benedictines (C. BUTLER) and by the Carmelites (*Études carmélitaines*, 1913). Its most recent growth, however, has been the result of the introduction of the subject into the area of formal theological instruction.

The growth of all these fields of specialization, branching out of general Church history, has not, however, rendered the latter superfluous; on the contrary, modern ecclesiology requires a sound historical foundation. More than ever, Church history is an integrating component of theology.

Bibliography: General. F. C. BAUR, *Die Epochen der kirchlichen Geschichtschreibung* (Tübingen 1852; repr. Hildesheim 1962). W. NIGG, *Die Kirchengeschichtsschreibung* (Munich 1934). P. BREZZI, *La storiografia ecclesiastica* (Naples 1959). Early Christianity. R. A. LAQUEUR, *Eusebius als Historiker seiner Zeit* (Berlin 1929). A. WACHTEL, *Beiträge zur Geschichtstheologie des Aurelius Augustinus* (Bonn 1960). J. DANIÉLOU, ''La Typologie millénariste de la semaine dans le christianisme primitif,'' *Vigiliae christianae,* 2 (1948) 1–16. A. D. VON DEN BRINCKEN, ''Weltaeren,'' *Archiv für Kulturgeschichte,* 39 (1957) 133–149. B. STICKER, ''Weltzeitalter und astronomische Perioden,'' *Saeculum,* 4 (1953) 241–249. R. SCHMIDT, ''*Aetates mundi.* Die Weltalter als Gliederungsprinzip der Geschichte,'' *Zeitschrift für Kirchengeschicte,* 67 (1955–56) 288–317. Middle Ages. J. SPÖRL, *Grundformen hochmittelalterlicher Geschichtsanschauung* (Munich 1935). W. LEVISON, ''Bede as Historian,'' *Aus rheinischer und fränkischer Frühzeit* (Düsseldorf 1948) 347–382. W. KAEGI, *Chronica mundi* (Einsiedeln 1954). A. D. VON DEN BRINCKEN, *Studien zur lateinischen Weltchronistik bis in das Zeitalter Ottos von Freising* (Düsseldorf 1957). H. LÖWE, *Von Theoderich dem Grossen zu Karl dem Grossen. Das Werden des Abendlandes im Geschichtsbild des frühen Mittel-alters* (Darmstadt 1956). W. GOEZ, *Translatio Imperii. Ein Beitrag zur Geschichte des Geschichtsdenkens und der politischen Theorien im Mittelalter und in der frühen Neuzeit* (Tübingen 1958). H. ZIMMERMANN, *Ecclesia als Objekt der Historiographie* (Vienna 1960). *Ausgewählte Aufsätze und Arbeiten aus den Jahren 1933 bis 1959,* ed. W. LAMMERS, (Darmstadt 1961). H. VOGT, *Die literarische Personenschilderung des frühen Mittelalters* (Leipzig 1934). G. MISCH, *Geschichte der Autobiographie,* v.2–3 (3d ed. Frankfurt a.M. 1955–62). W. KAMLAH, *Apokalypse und Geschichtstheologie* (Berlin 1935). N. R. C. COHN, *The Pursuit of the Millennium* (London 1957). M. W. BLOOMFIELD, ''Joachim of Flora: A Critical Survey,'' *Traditio,* 13 (1957) 249–311. From 16th to 18th century. E. MENKE-GLÜCKERT, *Die Geschichtschreibung der Reformation und Gegenreformation* (Leipzig 1912). P. POLMAN, *L'Élément historique dans la controverse religieuse du 16e siècle* (Gembloux 1932). B. A. VERMASEREN, *De katholicke Nederlandsche Geschiedschrijving in de 16e en 17e eeuw over den Opstand* (Maastricht 1941). A. HERTE, *Das katholische Lutherbild im Bann der Lutherkommentare des Cochläus,* 3 v. (Münster 1943). H. QUENTIN, *Jean-Dominique Mansi et les grandes collections conciliaires* (Paris 1900). P. PEETERS, *L'Oeuvre des Bollandistes* (new ed. Brussels 1961). K. VÖLKER, *Die Kirchengeschichtschreibung der Aufklärung* (Tübingen 1921). E. C. SCHERER, *Geschichte und Kirchengeschichte an den deutschen Universitäten* (Freiburg 1927). P. DE LETURIA, ''L'insegnamento della storia ecclesiastica nella Roma dell'Umanesimo e del Barocco,'' *La civiltà cattolica,* 96.4 (1945) 393–402; ''El P. Filippo Febei S.I. y la fundación de la cátedra de historia eclesiástica en el Colegio Romano, 1741,'' *Gregorianum,* 30 (1949) 158–192. P. PASCHINI, ''La Conferenza dei Concili a Propaganda Fide,'' *Rivista di storia della Chiesa in Italia,* 14 (1960) 371–382. The 19th and 20th centuries. H. VON SRBIK, *Geist und Geschichte vom deutschen Humanismus bis zur Gegenwart,* 2 v. (Munich 1950–51). F. WAGNER, *Geschichtswissenschaft* (Freiburg 1951). H. BUTTERFIELD, *Man on His Past* (Cambridge, Eng. 1955; pa. Boston 1960). K. BIHLMEYER, ''J. A. Möhler als Kirchenhistoriker,'' *Theologische Quartalschrift,* 100 (1919) 134–198. H. BRESSLAU, ''Geschichte der MGH,'' *Neues Archiv der Gesellschaft für ältere deutsche Geschichtskunde,* 42 (1921) 326–330. K. A. FINK, *Das vatikanische Archiv* (2d ed. Rome 1951). H. JEDIN, ''Die *Hierarchia catholica* als universalgeschichtliche Aufgabe,'' *Saeculum,* 12 (1961) 169–180. R. AUBERT, ''Un Demisiècle de *Revues d'histoire ecclésiastique,*'' *Rivista di storia della Chiesa in Italia,* 14 (1960) 173–202. *Rerum Britannicarum medii aevi scriptores,* 224 v. (London 1858–96).

[H. JEDIN]

HISTORY, PHILOSOPHY OF

In its most general sense, the philosophy of history is interpretative history; it deals with the basic or ultimate causes of the historical process as a whole, and attempts to see a discernible purposive plan in the multitude of events. Some authors equate the philosophy of history with metahistory, which ''has for its end the determination of laws regulating historical facts and the place of such facts in an explanatory view of the world'' (P.

Foulquié and R. Saint-Jean, *Dictionnaire de la langue philosophique* [Paris 1962] 437). Since the historian is not merely a statistician, he too concerns himself with more than the recording of fact, but his historical explanations, usually influenced by his epistemological presuppositions, may emphasize or minimize factors of remote or proximate causation as these affect the factual data.

In view of the great diversity of views on the subject, this article treats first of various interpretations and usages that are current regarding the philosophy of history, and then sketches the origin of the expression and various factors affecting the growth and development of philosophies of history since the 18th century.

Various Interpretations

The principal understandings of the expression ''philosophy of history,'' as used by theologians, philosophers, and social scientists, may be grouped under six headings: classical cyclicism, providential history, explanatory laws, interpretative history, philosophically oriented history, and progressivist theories.

Classical Cyclicism. The first general category of historical interpretation is classical cyclicism, which envisions an eternal universe featuring a continuous recurrence of historical experience. Arnold Joseph Toynbee (1889–1975) considers cyclicism to have had its probable origin in ancient Chaldean astronomy, but it derived much of its force in the ancient world as an intellectually naive extrapolation from a world of nature that exhibited observably recurrent daily and seasonal changes. Linear creationism was practically unknown in the ancient world, and even the *Timaeus* of PLATO and scattered references in EPICURUS make no case for a genuine *creatio ex nihilo* in the Christian sense of the term. Ancient cyclicism had its psychological counterpart in the theories of METEMPSYCHOSIS that pictured successive psychic existences in historically repetitive patterns.

Karl Löwith (1897–1973) cites the main sources for the classical view of eternal recurrence as certain fragments of HERACLITUS and of EMPEDOCLES; most of the myths of Plato; Aristotle's astronomical teaching (*Metaphysics* 1073a 13–1074b 14; *Cael.* 269b 18–271a 35); a fragment of Eudemus; and the *Epist. ad Lucilium* 24 of Seneca. Early Christian sources are Justin's *Dialogue with Trypho* 1 and Origen's *Against Celsus* 4.67 and *De principiis* 2.3.

St. Augustine's *City of God* is Christianity's most famous protest against a cyclicism that would confine history within itself in a series of endless repetitions. While a mode of cyclicism appeared in the medieval Aristotelianism of SIGER OF BRABANT and in the *Paradiso* of Dante, the cyclic theme was to have its greatest modern vogue in the philosophy of F. W. NIETZSCHE, for whom eternal recurrence was basic.

Providential History. A second general area of inquiry, considered by some as the philosophy of history, is providential history, such as that written by St. AUGUSTINE and J. B. BOSSUET. Providential history sees the historical process as initiated by a divine creative act and proceeding meaningfully to a conclusion. It is teleological, but not deterministic, as man's free will is a part of the PROVIDENCE OF GOD rather than a competing dynamic principle. Such a theologically oriented eschatology is not, strictly speaking, a philosophy, but as it is broadly interpretative, it is included for consideration in most works in philosophy of history. Christopher Dawson (1889–1970) quite correctly observes that the Christian vision of history is essentially theological in character, reflecting an integral part of divine revelation rather than a philosophical effort elaborated by Christian scholars. (*See* THEOLOGY, HISTORY OF.)

Augustinian history is inevitably universal, and, as it envisages an eternal goal beyond the temporal order, it is metahistorical. As R. G. Collingwood has pointed out, Greco-Roman ecumenical history is not universal in the Christian sense, having, as it does, the particularist center of gravity that is Greece or Rome. Augustinian history, on the other hand, has a pivotal event, the Incarnation, toward which the pre-Christian era moves, and by which the Christian era is transfigured. Thus EUSEBIUS OF CAESAREA sees in his *Preparatio evangelica* human events as preparatory to the coming of Christ, and colored, as it were, by that event. Such a Christian vision of history involves a restructuring of thought as well as a liberation from cyclicism. Although a secular scholar such as J. B. Bury sees in providential history external control rather than liberation, St. Augustine's *City of God* does herald a new linear dimension in historical experience, in which free human activity, moving into an unknown future, acquires a unique meaning not destined for inevitable repetition. (See P. Henry, ''The Christian Philosophy of History,'' *Theological Studies* 13 [1952] 419–432.)

Explanatory Laws. A third species considered as a philosophy of history is a type of interpretative history that claims the existence of laws or keys revealing the metaphysic of the historical process. In its extreme form either it replaces causation itself by destiny (as with O. SPENGLER); or it overemphasizes single causative elements and sees all history determined by such factors as race, geography, climate, and economics; or it views history as given new impulses and directions by what Collingwood calls ''apocalyptic'' events, such as the Renaissance, the invention of printing, the Reformation, the Enlightenment, the French Revolution, or the sociopolitical liberal movements of the 19th century. Interpretative extremism also features history as prophecy, for if the major cosmic impulse, deterministic in character, can be sufficiently identified, then the future as well as the past can be expected to yield its secrets.

Needless to say, it is this unwarranted Gnosticism in history to which the critical historian most vehemently and justifiably objects. He may consider the insight of a Spengler or a Toynbee ingeniously formulated and reflective of a deeply felt personal view of the historical process, but he is understandably hesitant to accord this objectivity. Yet he too can forget, as Ernst Bernheim (1850–1942) has suggested, that the philosophy of history is by no means a superfluous luxury for the historian (see *Einleitung in die Geschichtswissenschaft* [3d ed., Berlin-Leipzig 1926]). Norman Sykes has also observed in this regard that even the most conservative of scientific historians have found it impossible to restrain their steps from divagations into the pastures of philosophy. Facts, far from speaking for themselves, are agile performers, and their performance is largely determined by the meaningful context in which they are assembled. Factual history is POSITIVISM manifesting itself in historical writing. It may well be true that the Battle of Hastings occurred in 1066 irrespective of the ideological background of the historian who records the event; but the mere recording of the event is not history, and the material selected or suppressed in judging the significance of the event inevitably involves one in value judgments.

Interpretative History. A fourth possibility is interpretative history, or history integrally taken as nondeterministic in character. While recognizing the unpredictable character of free human choice, this discerns various patterns or trends in the historical process as a whole. Jacques MARITAIN speaks of axiomatic formulas, by which he means formulas that reveal the endurance of basic relations or fundamental characteristics. He distinguishes these functional laws from what he calls typological or vectorial laws, i.e., more particularized descriptions of historical growth and development that exhibit a typical direction.

Philosophically Oriented History. A fifth category of the philosophy of history is simply philosophically oriented history. While not neglecting the factual, this is more preoccupied with relations and causes, general as well as specific, epistemological positions antecedent to investigation, and a philosophy of man with particular emphasis on human freedom. This type of philosophical history is a matter of general orientation in which philosophical factors take precedence over the methodology and the specific content of historical investigation.

Progressivist Theories. A final area of inquiry in the philosophy of history are the secular philosophies of progress produced by the RATIONALISM of the 18th and 19th centuries. History and cultural institutions came to be judged in the light of an ascending progressive evolution. Nietzsche was quite correct in seeing the philosophies of progress, which he despised, as a ''trivialization'' and secularization of Christian linearism, which he also despised. But the new Jerusalem of the progressivists was an earthly city that envisioned no transcendent goal. As has been generally observed, this trend to the secular had been abetted by both the Renaissance and the Reformation, and by the scientism of empiricists desirous of extending natural science to philosophy.

Bury (*The Idea of Progress* [London 1920, New York 1932]) and Dawson (*Progress and Religion* [London 1929]) have examined progressivist theory in its secular and religious forms. It is important to note that the Christian rejects, not the possibility of progress, but its inevitability. Believing that man possesses neither the naturally good nature as taught by J. J. ROUSSEAU, nor a vitiated nature as taught by M. LUTHER, but a nature wounded by original sin, the Christian recognizes the possibility of retrogression as well as the possibility of progress. Rectilinear progress had its psychological variant in the turn-of-the-century Couéism, which assured increasingly insecure man that ''every day in every way he was getting better and better.''

General theories of progress are associated particularly with the writings of B. B. de Fontenelle (1657–1757); C. I. Castel, Abbé de Saint-Pierre (1658–1743); the Marquis de CONDORCET; VOLTAIRE; J. B. J. Fourier (1768–1830); C. H. SAINT-SIMON; A. R. J. Turgot (1727–81); C. DARWIN; and A. COMTE. Latent in progressivist theory is the idea that progress is a law of nature, and that such a law applies both to the processes of the natural order and the cultural development of man. The theory finds much to substantiate it in the order of technology, where the accumulated intellectual capital of the past is immediately at the service of contemporary experimentation. Academic capital is also added in each successive generation, although it is questionable to suggest that the available knowledge is acquired by successive generations with increasing skill.

Voltaire's prejudice in favor of contemporary history, and the belief that history exhibited a constant progress from a barbarous primitive era to his own day was not only reflective of an arbitrary conviction that the only meaningful history was modern history, but it was also the consequence of a limited knowledge of the age that was held to be primitive. N. A. BERDIAEV (*The Meaning of History* [New York 1936]) was perhaps the progressivist's most formidable modern adversary. He considered the philosophy of progress to be a secularized Messianism, a divinization of the future at the expense of the past and present, that had not the slightest philosophical, scientific, or moral justification. But the idea of progress was a comfortable and optimistic illusion that endured until the early years of the 20th century, when the static and peaceful Newtonian universe began to collapse as empirical science expanded its frontiers, and a devastating worldwide conflict reminded free man that he was capable of going in more than one forward direction.

Were one to seek to reduce the ways of understanding history to their essential forms, one might, following the lead of Löwith, Collingwood, and H. Stuart Hughes, list cyclical recurrence and eschatological direction. It would seem advisable, however, on the basis of the influence of progressivist theories, to include secular futurism as a third possibility.

Origin and Development

The growth and development of the philosophy of history perforce is traceable to the origin of the expression itself; from this point it is affected by the various influences and climates of opinion in which philosophers of history labored, notably by Romanticism and positivism, idealism, neoidealism, and more recent movements such as those of cyclic history and modern synthesis.

Origin of the Expression. Concerning the origin of the expression, ''philosophy of history,'' several observations are to be made. Juan Donoso Cortés refers in his *Ensayo sobre el catolicismo, el liberalismo y el socialismo . . .* (Madrid 1851) to St. Augustine's *City of God* as a ''Catholic philosophy of history.'' In his essay on G. VICO, however, he refers to Bossuet as the ''first philosopher of history.'' Vico himself is called by H. P. Adams ''the founder of philosophy of history.'' Löwith, in referring to a period of crisis at the end of the 17th century, when, as he says, ''Providence was replaced by progress,'' insists that Voltaire's essay on the manners and mind of nations is the first philosophy of history (cf. *La Philosophie de l'histoire* [Geneva 1765]); and Löwith considers this event the inauguration of an epoch of historical evaluation that is basically antireligious. M. C. Swabey (*The Judgment of History* [New York 1954]) rejects this identification of philosophical history with figures such as Voltaire, C. de MONTESQUIEU, or I. Kant, and prefers to consider the problem in terms of general orientation. W. H. Walsh claims that philosophy of history first gained recognition in 1784 with the publication of the first part of J. G. Herder's *Ideen zur Philosophie der Geschichte der Menschheit* (Leipzig 1784–91). Collingwood maintains that the name at least ''was invented by Voltaire, who meant by it no more than critical or scientific history.'' S. J. Case concedes that Voltaire may be said to have coined the phrase, but considers that the technique of evaluation involved is current in the thought of the ancient Hebrews. Father Gilbert Garraghan (*A Guide to Historical Method* [New York 1946]), considering philosophy of history ''essentially a theological concept,'' claims that Augustine was the first to state a philosophy of history, in his *City of God.* Raymond Aron's use of the term in his *Introduction à la philosophie de l'histoire* (Paris 1938) is more like that of Case and Swabey. He is concerned with a philosophical conception of the historical process as a whole, in opposition to positivism and *rationalisme scientiste.*

From such a variety of opinion some basic facts emerge. The name at least, originates with Voltaire, who summarizes his position in the dictum: *Il faut écrire l'histoire en philosophe.* Secondly, there is no general agreement as to the role philosophy should play in historical interpretation. This difference is reflected in an oscillation between extremes of factual and philosophical history that seems to take place over the years.

Romanticism and Positivism. Interpretative history in the late 19th century was as indebted to romanticism as factual history was to positivism (*see* ROMANTICISM, PHILOSOPHICAL). Particularly in German HISTORICISM did the romantic spirit flourish in the attempt to capture a living sense of the past in its indigenous cultural setting. The historicists found an ideal image for this attempt in plant morphology. J. Burckhardt and Spengler could see the historical value of art forms as veritable mirrors of culture. They could explore historical change in its growth and decay by an organic metaphor that the 19th-century preoccupation with Darwinian science would render understandable. Yet evolutionism, implying as it did a linear theory of progress, was clearly at variance with such a theory as Spengler's, whose discontinuous cultures with their relative value systems were nevertheless explained as subject to the laws of plant morphology. Positivism's contribution to critical history was a respect for fact and the methodology that would lead to it, although it had a built-in inhibition about interpreting facts. Romanticism's contribution was more imaginative and profound. Although more prone to error by reason of increased subjectivity, it did attempt to penetrate the surface of fact to discover the inner dynamics of the historical process. In this it was more inferential than descriptive.

Idealism. Of particular interest to the philosopher of history is historical IDEALISM, which envisions historical knowledge as a reliving of the past in the mind of the historian. Idealism aims at capturing the spirit of an age by intellectual re-creation rather than by an excessive preoccupation with factual minutiae; its principal proponents are J. G. FICHTE, F. W. J. von SCHELLING, and G. W. F. HEGEL.

Fichte has perhaps gained his greatest fame as a systematizer of Kantian philosophy, but he is significant in German Romanticism in providing a philosophical framework within the self for analyzing historical experience. In his lectures, *Die Grundzüge des gegenwärtigen Zeitalters* (Berlin 1806), he sees the self's awareness of its own time as prefatory to an understanding of the past, and he sees a given culture as the living embodiment of an idea. An integral understanding of history is not derived from a study of given cultures, but from the meaningful logical relation of ideas that articulate themselves progressively and dialectically in the historical process. Being is in a sense reduced to thought, and history is therefore the history of ideas, especially the idea of freedom. The world of "representations" is the periodic unfolding of Absolute Ego, and the individual self is but part of the embracing Ego.

Schelling, a colleague of Fichte at Jena, developed a similarly far-fetched system of transcendental idealism. Schelling distinguishes nature and history, both of which manifest the ABSOLUTE. Nature is the sum total of extramental realities and their observable relationships, but history is seen as the developed phase of the Absolute—a development involving free human enterprise and providential plan. The Absolute as mind is a continuous process of self-awareness, and history is the very process by which the Absolute realizes itself as both knower and known.

Philosophical history reaches perhaps its most sophisticated formulation in the work of Hegel. Hegel's implicative philosophy is historically oriented and posits a monistic Absolute working toward the State as the objective manifestation of the divine upon Earth. History is there vaguely defined as the rediscovery of Absolute Spirit through human consciousness and time. Philosophy rather than theology is seen by Hegel as the means of demonstrating a providential plan to which man unwittingly contributes.

Neoidealism. The idealist theory of history continued to receive considerable attention in the pre-Spengler period of German historical thought in the late 19th century; of particular importance then was the work of Georg Simmel (1858–1918) and Wilhelm DILTHEY. Simmel questions the positivist's notion of historical objectivity, insisting that while the facts of nature may be subject to empirical scrutiny, the facts of history must inevitably be a spiritual reconstruction of the past from documents and external evidence. Although admittedly a subjective construction, such history is felt by Simmel to have a valid objectivity. Dilthey also was influential in the neoidealist critique of factual history, seeing in the wealth of the historian's intellectual and spiritual resources the means of interpreting the lifeless data of the past. Both Simmel and Dilthey have a common problem in establishing satisfactorily the objectivity of historical knowledge, emphasizing as they do the subjectivity of a psychological experience far removed in time from the data of the past.

Benedetto CROCE, the greatest exponent of the Italian neoidealist tradition, also considers history a spiritual re-creation of the past, but like Voltaire, he sees the significance of the past in terms of its relevance to the present. He not only combines the idealistic with the pragmatic, but sees history, not as the investigation of the general truths proper to science, but as a cognitive vision of individuality proper to his definition of art.

Cyclic History. Cyclic history finds its foremost proponents in Vico, Nietzsche, and Spengler. Vico, to whom Goethe referred as a patriarch of modern thought, combines in his *Principij di una Scienza Nuova* (Naples 1725) a providential cyclicism and an anti-Cartesian critical method of appraising developing human societies. He sees not only similar periods in history, but a regularity of recurrence that he identifies as the divine, heroic, and human periods. The spiral rather than the circle is a better figure by which to identify Vico's Christian, but non-scholastic, approach, because he sees society moving forward and differentiated by previous experience. As Collingwood indicates, this is obviously not the old classical Greco-Roman cyclicism found in Plato, Polybius, and in Renaissance historians such as Campanella and Machiavelli.

Nietzsche rejects Christian linearism entirely and sees the world as an eternal cosmos affirming itself in periodic recurrence. Eternal recurrence is fundamental to Nietzsche's thought; but, though he was a trained classical philologist and a great admirer of Greek classicism, his cyclicism is not the classic form. He attempts to give it a scientific foundation by seeing the finite realities of matter and energy eternally reassembling themselves in space, and therefore destined to repeat historical configurations.

Spengler's *Decline of the West* presents the most imaginative and controversial of cyclic theories. History is there seen as a series of discontinuous cultures, each of which has its own value system and develops along strictly predictable lines of plant morphology. Before a given culture degenerates into a "civilization" preparatory to its death, its progress can be continuously charted by comparison with other cultures whose history exhibits comparable phenomena at all levels. Spengler was greatly influenced by Goethe and Nietzsche, and predicted that his work would become "the philosophy of our time." The work is historically inaccurate, but it did spark the revival of philosophical history after World War I.

Modern Syntheses. The greatest of the modern syntheses is *A Study of History* (New York 1934–61) by Toynbee. Toynbee's first six volumes represent a comparative analysis of intelligible units of historical study that he calls civilizations. These advanced societies, 21 in number, are studied in terms of genesis, growth, breakdown, and disintegration, and only five are seen to have survived disintegration. As Dawson has observed, what Toynbee starts as a relativist phenomenology of equivalent cultures, becomes, in volumes 7 to 10, a unitary philosophy of history comparable to those of the idealist philosophers of the 19th century. A syncretic faith of the future composed of the "higher religions" (Christianity, Mahayana Buddhism, Hinduism, and Islam) replaces civilization as the intelligible unit of study. This new world religion he analyzes in terms of Jung's psychological types, and sees it as satisfying man's diverse spiritual needs.

Although Toynbee accepts the fact of human freedom and emphasizes the importance of religion in the human experience, his point of view is not authentically Christian, and he has a pronounced bias against a theology based exclusively on Judeo-Christian sources of revelation (see M. R. P. McGuire, "Fruitful Failure on the Grand Scale," *American Catholic Historical Review* 42 [1956] 322–329). Dawson and Jacques Maritain, to a lesser extent, have contributed to a basic Augustinian vision of history in recent times, and interpretative history in general endured throughout the 20th century.

See Also: HEGELIANISM AND NEO-HEGELIANISM; MATERIALISM, DIALECTICAL AND HISTORICAL; PHILOSOPHY, HISTORY OF.

Bibliography: R. G. COLLINGWOOD, *The Idea of History* (London 1946). K. LÖWITH, *Meaning in History* (Chicago 1949). M. C. D'ARCY, *The Meaning and Matter of History* (New York 1959). H. MEYERHOFF, ed., *The Philosophy of History in Our Time* (New York 1959). S. J. CASE, *The Christián Philosophy of History* (Chicago 1943). W. H. WALSH, *An Introduction to Philosophy of History* (New York 1951). M. H. MANDELBAUM, *The Problem of Historical Knowledge* (New York 1938). H. I. MARROU, *De la Connaissance historique* (3d ed. Paris 1959); "Qu'est-ce que l'histoire?" *L'Histoire et ses méthodes,* ed. C. SAMARAN (Encyclopédie de la Pléiade 11; Paris 1961) 1–33; "Comment comprendre le métier d'historien," *ibid.,* 1465–540.

[R. P. MOHAN]

HISTORY, THEOLOGY OF

The notion of a theology of history, or the *Weltanschauung* based on the providential action of God in human affairs, is here discussed in terms of its concept, its relation to Holy Scripture, and its historical developments.

CONCEPT

The concept of a theology of history as distinct from a philosophy of HISTORY raises problems that affect our understanding of the field. Loose, ambivalent use of both terms is not uncommon. Several reasons may account for the confusion: (1) there is some question about the claims of each field to be properly a science; (2) both are phases of the larger problem that concerns the relationship of philosophy and theology, reason and faith; and (3) the historical development of comprehensive theories of history has occasioned fluctuations and ambiguities, such as the still prevalent tendency to include plainly theological interpretations under the loose heading of philosophies of history. On the other hand, defensible opinions hold that the key concepts of modern philosophies of history are secularized forms of older, theological concepts.

A nice, theoretical delimitation of the two fields will not exorcise concrete, historic ambiguities that are disregarded because of a passionate absorption in the central problem of history and its ultimate meaning. The driving concern, however unspoken and unacknowledged, seems to be deeply religious, and even theological.

With this preamble it may be said that the theology of history, as conceived today, is that branch of theology that studies both the uniqueness and the universality of God's providential action in history, and the various phases of the divine plan. More precisely, it inquires into the divine action on behalf of, and in relation to, the human race and attempts to interpret this action from the human point of view. As SALVATION HISTORY, the theology of history embraces the whole of time and tries to clarify its ultimate meaning. It draws into its domain the entire sweep of history in order to discover how it comports with the intentions of God as discoverable in revelation. Theology of history necessarily regards the whole of reality, hence also the progress of cultures, but it is not concerned with the progress of cultures as such. True to its own inner principle it aims to focus the action of God in history as revealed to man and the ongoing understanding and free response of mankind to the divine action.

It is customary to contrast cyclical theories of history as typical of pagan antiquity with the linear concept of history characteristic of OT Judaism and Christianity—a concept involving a beginning in creation, an end divinely appointed, and a precarious progression of events in between through the exercise of human freedom and the governance of Divine Providence.

It is unfair and inaccurate to label all ancient cyclical theories as pessimistic and despairing subjections of man to blind fate. The ancient cyclicisms also existed in a hopeful, if vague, religious matrix. The idea of an everlasting recurrence, probably taking a leaf from nature, implied possibilities of renewal, rebirth, redemption in some sense, and salvation from frustration and meaninglessness. Pessimism and despair come later with a culture that had lost the primitive religious conception and had come to be haunted by the horror of blind DETERMINISM and meaningless repetition. To this weary culture the linear conception of Christian thought signified a new sense of purpose and meaning.

The people of Israel experienced their historical situation as God's action guiding them to the promised goal of salvation and the Messianic kingdom. Christian doctrine also is grounded in historical fact: the Incarnation, the death, and Resurrection of Christ (1 Cor 15.14). But the Christian message, going beyond the historical distinction of Jews and Greeks, extends to all mankind. Christian theology, moreover, has set itself from the beginning to think out the historical implications of the faith. The procedure has nothing in common with that of the Enlightenment philosophers who rejected revelation, secularized theological concepts, and reduced Christian teaching to a hard core of rationally accepted truths.

HOLY SCRIPTURE AND THEOLOGY OF HISTORY

Holy Scripture contains not only the fact of God's action in history but also first reflections on its meaning. In the OT God is the lord of history. He holds the nations in His hand; He chose Israel out of them to be His people and the instrument of His purposes (PROVIDENCE). He intervened to free them from Egypt. He used the Gentiles to discipline His faithless people, but the election of Israel (COVENANT) was part of a comprehensive plan for all men and the entire world. The beginning of this divine action was creation itself, a consideration that draws all of nature into the historical perspective. The Prophets speak of God's great deeds of the past in order to awaken confidence in still greater things to come at the end of ages (Is 43.18–19; *see* ESCHATOLOGY). In contrast to pagan religions, which reduced time to a lingering, fading shadow of a vanished golden age, the OT endows time with positive meaning and grounds a strong, forward-looking expectation. The apocalyptic writings (Ezekiel; Zechariah, ch. 9–14; Joel, ch. 3–4; Daniel) expand this eschatology into a veritable theology of history moving surely to the ultimate triumph of God over the powers of evil.

The NT emphasizes the same themes: God as lord of history, providence, freedom of divine action, and eschatology, but it adds a new element—the end of the ages and their fulfillment have come with the Incarnation and Resurrection of Christ. God's action is essentially completed in Christ, all that the Prophets had proclaimed: Judgment, Resurrection, the kingdom, the eternal covenant, the new creation. In Christ the plan of God is substantially fulfilled, God is fully glorified, and human nature has become fully participant in the divine riches. What in essence has been accomplished must now be extended to all mankind before the great day of Christ's second coming (PAROUSIA) and the final judgment. This ''time-in-between'' is a period of divine action that is now mainly sacramental and draws the events of profane history into its saving purpose.

This destiny of the Church seems to be the dominant theme of the Revelation of St. John and the recurrent subject of the Pauline Epistles. Romans, ch. 11 on the fate of Israel after Christ and 2 Peter on the deferment of the Parousia contribute important elements. The Parousia, the resurrection of the dead, and the final judgment will be part of this history, constituting its final phase, which according to St. Paul, will be but the cosmic unfolding of Christ's Resurrection and the full revelation of what has already been substantially accomplished in Christ and the Church.

Some theologians see a typological similarity between various phases of the history of salvation and in this typology a revelation of the constant aspects of God's action. In these constant aspects they see certain universal laws of divine action, which in their view constitute the object of a theology of history as science in the strict sense of the word (TYPOLOGY).

HISTORICAL DEVELOPMENT

It will be convenient to discuss the theology of history during the several periods of Christian history.

Early Fathers and Apologists. In controversy with Jewish religionists, pagans, and Gnostics the early Fathers and apologists utilized the theology of history to establish continuity of God's action between the OT and NT Christianity. JUSTIN MARTYR outlined a theology of history. IRENAEUS considered history as a cosmic week of seven millenniums during which mankind, like a child, gradually grows up to understand the glory of God. Christ came, not to restore a primordial state of perfection, but to complete what was germinally present from the beginning. In the doctrine of his disciple HIPPOLYTUS and others this scheme implied CHILIASM, the reign of Christ for 1000 years in the 7th millennium (*see* MILLENARIANISM). CLEMENT OF ALEXANDRIA in his broad doctrine of the

LOGOS spoke of the preparation of both Jews and pagans for the coming of the True Logos, Christ. ORIGEN continued the ideas of Irenaeus and Clement, but introduced a compromising cyclicism with his notions of the preexistence of souls and the APOCATASTASIS. EUSEBIUS OF CAESAREA injected a political note: monotheism makes for world unity and peace whereas polytheism favors a fragmentation into nations, and consequently warfare.

St. Augustine and the Middle Ages. In the *City of God* AUGUSTINE developed a theology of history that dominated Western thinking on the subject until the 18th century. Taken as one vast effort of intellect and faith, this was theology of history in the grand style and on a grand scale. Nowhere else is there a comparable combination of sustained sublimity of theological vision with an almost harshly realistic appraisal of human events. As a theology of history Augustine's work has never been superseded; it still calls for thorough theological analysis and development.

The first ten books wrestle with a historical problem—the fall of Rome in 410 that shook the civilized world and brought public outcries against the Christians. Both the attack on the Church and Augustine's apologetic involve a total theology of history—Christian vs. pagan. Augustine's exposition proceeds along practical rather than abstract theological lines of argumentation. In books 11 to 22 the implicit theology becomes explicit. His simple, vast conception is of the ''Two Loves'' building two cities or commonwealths, both existing side by side as invisible protagonists from beginning to end of history (and beyond), both locked in conflict and competition throughout the ages and providing the dynamic of historical development until the issue shall be decided between them in the grand denouement of the Parousia, the Last Judgment, and the triumph of Christ and the Church. This basic conceptual framework supports the exposition and provides the theme from start to finish. Not surprisingly, as in the *City of God,* the problem of evil in the world serves as one of the mainsprings of theological speculation on history; it was one of the chief issues in Augustine's own intellectual evolution and conversion. It stimulated many historians to discuss Divine Providence and the role of man's FREE WILL in the dynamics of history (*see* FREE WILL AND PROVIDENCE). It presented the recurrent temptation, wisely resisted by Augustine but perhaps too easily indulged by Eusebius and others, to discover signs of providential favor in current political events and structures or to embody the City of God in a definite political reality such as the HOLY ROMAN EMPIRE. None of this is in the work of Augustine; there is no identification of the Messianic kingdom with any earthly kingdom or any earthly culture. The City of God, an invisible spiritual polity, now grows through this new era of history, but will not stand fully revealed until the end of time. The earthly kingdom is essentially ambivalent: in justice, peace, and prosperity it will serve the City of God when it bows to the rule of Christ; but it may also be an instrument of evil to oppose that reign. On this issue Augustine allowed himself no facile optimism, nor did the evidence of political history as he knew it, or as it developed for the next 1,000 years, encourage such illusion. Soberly comprehensive, large and free of all presumptuous attempts to read the mind of Providence in political events, Augustine's theology of history does not seek assurance of divine approval from the events of history. The same reserve governs his treatment of the Chiliast controversy and similar attempts to establish a prophetic chronology of the last days. History moves on steadily toward its God-appointed goal. Worldly events and transcendent goal are distinct but related in the striving of the faithful toward the supreme objective. The attitude and position of the true Christian is always precarious, always a courageously trustful commitment to the sublimely inscrutable will of Providence in faith, hope, and love.

Augustine's work had no fully authentic continuators. His pupil OROSIUS, who wrote at his behest in 418 (*Seven Books of History against the Pagans*), maintained the providential principle and the apologetic purpose of Augustine, but for the rest followed the more pedestrian, political line of Eusebius. He stated that the *Pax Romana* at the birth of Christ was a special providence and that political events developed to favor Christianity, which in turn promoted human culture. OTTO OF FREISING in *The Two Cities: A Chronicle of Universal History to the Year 1146* (1157) identified the Church with the City of God and affirmed that Christianity always moves westward. This Eusebian tendency to turn history into a theodicy seems to have continued as a subtle ingredient of medieval consciousness together with its large acceptance of Augustine's theology of history (*see* HISTORIOGRAPHY, ECCLESIASTICAL). JOACHIM OF FIORE introduced an apocalyptic theology of history that announced the coming age of the Holy Spirit, superseding the Petrine Church and inaugurating a spiritual interpretation of the Scripture and the ''Eternal Gospel'' (Rv 14.6)—a doctrine that THOMAS AQUINAS gently refuted (ST 1a2ae, 106.4) but which reverberated through the politics, civil and ecclesiastical, of the next century and possibly echoes in all the later utopias of history.

Early Modern Period. J. B. BOSSUET's *Discourse on Universal History* centered in the theological concept of God's providence, which he sought to justify by detailed reference to the facts of history. He assigned a special place to the French monarchy as heir to the Holy Roman Empire, to serve the ultimate triumph of the Church. His theology of history was more in the spirit of

Eusebius than of Augustine, and in attempting to prove too much apologetically, he laid himself open to later refutations.

Giambattista VICO in his *La scienza nuova* represented the critical transition point between Bossuet and Voltaire. Abstracting from divine revelation (which Vico faithfully accepted), he was the first to point the way to a philosophy of history by adopting the philosophical principle of an eternal law of providential development to be examined empirically. His work may well be called a rational theology of divine providence. Adapting the Cartesian approach to the historical and social sciences, Vico equated the *verum* and the *factum,* because history is the creation of man who both creates and describes the fact. Through secondary causes providence operates to establish forms of order beyond human discernment or intent. Vico's work, remarkable as it was, had no influence until a century later. C. de MONTESQUIEU's *Spirit of the Laws* was probably the first influential attempt at a philosophy of history.

The period from the 18th century ENLIGHTENMENT to the 20th century is difficult to analyze in terms of a theology of history. The Enlightenment rejected revelation, but the old theological concepts remained in secularized form. Reason, for example, took the place of Providence, but was given the same governing function in history, now as a kind of natural law. The eschatological tension was transmuted into the idea of progress, and later, into evolution. Eternal reward became ''posterity'' and fame; the Parousia was reduced to some distant utopian triumph on earth. VOLTAIRE's *Essay on the Manners and Mind of Nations* signaled the radical shift to an antireligious interpretation of history. The work was conceived as a continuation of Bossuet's but became an attack on the traditional theology of history. Voltaire objected that Bossuet's universal history was not universal and that providence cannot be demonstrated from the empirical course of history. Voltaire's critique offered no constructive solution to the problem of historical meaning, but set the tone for the rest of the century. This development of a philosophy of history (or secularized and disguised theology) through the period of KANT to the grandiose construction of HEGEL, through COMTE's POSITIVISM and the era of German HISTORICISM down to a history-conscious EXISTENTIALISM goes beyond the scope of the theology of history.

While philosophers went their own way, sweeping transformations occurred in the theology of history. Protestant theology from the beginning seemed intensely conscious of history. At first, this occurred possibly because of the tension between LUTHER's and CALVIN's views. The former saw this world as the city of wicked man; the latter gave it importance only as the place where the Christian has a mission to help build the kingdom of God. Then in the Enlightenment one tradition emphasized God's transcendence; the other became increasingly antisupernatural and moved with the philosophic currents of empiricism, KANTIANISM, historicism, positivism, evolutionism, existentialism. This liberal Protestantism prevailed through the 19th century up to World War I. Catholic theology, facing GALLICANISM, JANSENISM, FEBRONIANISM, and JOSEPHINISM, seems to have stressed the juridical concept of the Church until J. MÖHLER, followed by C. PASSAGLIA, K. SCHRADER, M. SCHEEBEN, J. B. FRANZELIN, and K. Adam, revived the truth of the Church as the Mystical Body of Christ.

In view of these developments the theology of history generated two tendencies or preferred emphases: the eschatological and the incarnational—both orientations rooted in doctrines that are integral to the gospel and mutually complementary. The incarnational trend stresses the Christian's engagement in this world; the eschatological his disengagement. The former concentrates on the person of Christ and the Church, His Mystical Body, and the importance of man's work here and now to build up the Body of Christ, pointing up the value of God's creation and of human culture. The latter looking rather to the final outcome, the Judgment and Parousia, tends to discount the value of the present, the ''time-in-between,'' as essentially transitory, and to be less than sympathetic to the value of human culture and man's work in the world. On the whole it is probably true that most Protestant theologians of history have been somewhat partial to the eschatological, while most Catholic theologians have favored the incarnational approach. Nevertheless, the distinction need not be overstressed, since both doctrines—the Incarnation and the Second Coming—are recognized as integral to Christianity.

Recent Protestant Theologians. *Neo-Orthodoxy.* In the period after World War I the relevancy of Christian faith began to erode under the impact of the historical consciousness of liberal Protestantism, in which the being of man is understood as essentially temporal and self-determinative, autonomous vis-à-vis the past and so oriented creatively towards the future. This precipitated the Neo-Orthodoxy movement in Protestantism, which capitulated to the modern notion of history as entirely secular and of itself devoid of any sacral dimension. God's act above time, however, intersects each moment and event, but in a time-transcending way hidden to the world and available only on the basis of faith in the Christ-event. This initial ahistorical cast, in which faith is rescued from historical criticism by being reduced to existential decision (BULTMANN), was later compromised by allowing for a hidden sovereignty of God over the world (e.g. in Karl BARTH's *Church Dogmatics*). But still history (and along with it, nature) was relativized to the point that it was no longer itself a bearer of divine purposes, but only an occasion in which God's Word confronts individuals. The inadequacies of this view appear in its ahistorical character, its fideism, and its individualism. Two major attempts to meet this objection have been Oscar Cullmann's doctrine of *Heilsgeschichte*, a sacred history superimposed upon world history in which the purposes of God are unfolded; and the advocacy by the post-Bultmannians of a revised notion of New Testament history as the existential life-commitment of Jesus undergirding the events recounted.

The Eschatological View. Reaction began with an emphasis upon ESCHATOLOGY, understood now not as the vertical dimension of eternity in every temporal moment (Neo-Orthodoxy), but as a thrust within history itself towards its own consummation and occurring within the present course of history rather than at the end of time. Divine revelation is universal history (Pannenberg), whose unity appears only from its end, anticipated in the destiny of Jesus. Reality is thus structured as time, in which the future is accorded ontological priority and impinges efficaciously upon the present. Thus, the transformation of history occurs not developmentally out of the past but in novel ways out of the future. This is not the *telos* of Aristotle and Aquinas, in which the end preexists in divine intentionality, because the mode of God's being is also future. Nor is it Hegelianism, since the future lacks all logical determination and remains open, giving rise to the religious response of hope. For Jürgen Moltmann, God's action in history continually contradicts man's own achievements (*Theology of Hope*, 1967); thus the Church is summoned to the cause of liberation under the Holy Spirit as the divine power of futurity (*The Church in the Power of the Spirit*, 1977). This emphasis upon eschatology as the decisive element in Christianity is motivated in part by a desire to meet the charges of contemporary ATHEISM, especially in dialogue with Marxists (e.g. Ernst Bloch). Questionable in all this are the ontologizing of history, the conceiving of God in terms of futurity so that he ceases to be a God of the present, an arbitrary identifying of the future with freedom and the past with sin.

Process Thought. A radical alternative is operative in the theological use of Whitehead's ontology of process, represented by C. HARTSHORNE, S. Ogden, J. Cobb, L. Ford, D. D. Williams, N. Pittenger, and a host of younger American, mostly Protestant, theologians. Here, the basic category is becoming, applicable not just to history but to all reality, which ultimately consists of a plurality of "occasions" that are self-creative actualizations of eternal ideas. God himself is dipolar, at once temporal (necessarily interacting with the world in time) and eternal (in the sense that nothing of his being perishes in his becoming). History thus becomes God's supplying of subjective aims to actual occasions, by way of his envisioning of infinite possibilities, luring them to maximum actualization. A Catholic approximation to this, in some respects only, appears in TEILHARD DE CHARDIN's theology within an evolutionary worldview. Serious reservations towards this thought arise because of its dismissal of the events of history in their particularity, which, collapsing into pure becoming, possess no perduring significance. The centrality of Christ and his resurrection are necessarily relativized and lose all claim to uniqueness.

Recent Catholic Thought. Catholic thinking likewise continues to intensify its interest in the theology of history. The preponderant effort centers on the relationship of the Christian to the world; on the Church as the Body of Christ committed to the transformation of all human history and culture, to a positive appreciation of natural and human values, and to a like engagement in human events; and on the extension of the Incarnation by building the Body of Christ and by making of this world an anticipation of the world to come. There is a cautionary attitude toward eschatology, lest man lose a sense of responsibility toward the present economy of salvation. So H. de LUBAC sees the meaning of history in the Church as the extension of the Incarnation of Christ. The Christian's conscientious involvement in the work of the world he calls the "law of the Incarnation." P. Teilhard de Chardin grasps history in an enlarged evolutionary concept by which all creation moves toward "Christogenesis," i.e., the integration of human personality with Christ as the triumph of cosmogenesis, the Parousia. Rightly understood, there is, then, nothing profane to the Christian's view.

In England C. BUTLER and M. D'ARCY deplore a misanthropic unworldliness and call for a joyous, generous transfiguration of human history in Christ. C. DAWSON focuses this transformative effort on a new recognition of the spirit of vocation and individual responsibility. At Louvain G. Thils' theology of history centers on the concept of the progressive unity between the orders of nature and of grace, and their eventual, eschatological identity in the kingdom of God.

Gradually, theologians have enlarged their view to balance this predominantly incarnational theology of history with eschatological elements from Holy Scripture. A decidedly eschatological position emerges among certain Biblical scholars of the NT. Thus, for example, L. Bouyer, influenced by K. Barth and O. Cullmann, insists that Christianity is essentially eschatological, resting on belief in the end of time, and that human history will end in a catastrophe to be interrupted by the return of Christ, the Universal Judgment, and the Resurrection. The incarnational attitude, in his opinion, tends to forget the mystery of the Cross and could easily become a pagan apotheosis of created things. E. Beaucamp, W. Bulst, H. M. Feret, and to some extent R. Guardini lean to the eschatological pole and envision a theology of history in apocalyptic terms. In the Revelation of St. John, Feret finds three elements of a theology of history: MESSIANISM; identification of Christ and truth in history; and the victory of Christ as pledge of the Christian's victory, stirring profound longing for the final consummation of the kingdom and urging action to hasten this consummation. Similarly F. X. Durrwell constructs his theology of history around the Resurrection; in the course of history the Church moves toward the splendor of the eternal Easter. This full accomplishment of the Resurrection in the Parousia is the goal of history. The Church as the Body of Christ in history still exists in a state of incomplete evolution of her resurrection in Christ.

Out of this chorus of many theological tongues, all more or less talking the language of Scripture, there rises a need, ever more strongly felt, to balance the equation if possible, and to unify all legitimate insights fairly into a comprehensive theology of history.

Thus Y. M. J. CONGAR and L. Malevez seek a harmony between one-sided incarnationalism and excessive eschatologism. The problem for Congar turns on a valuation of the ''time-in-between.'' Is it a mere accident or is it a part of a plan? The solution, then, lies in the higher concept: God's will and plan that the Christian be in the world (incarnationalism) but not of it (eschatologism). From this resolution of the tension emerges, for Congar, the concept of the Christian's full vocation. Against an extreme eschatological disdain of the world Malevez urges: ''But seek first the kingdom of God'' (Mt 6.33); against an extreme incarnational valuation of human activity he invokes the cross of Christ. J. C. Murray recognizes the theoretical necessity of both positions and indicates the practical human risks attached to each. The problem and the tension lie in the practical sphere, i.e., in the often dubious capacity of man to live his faith.

In his *Theology of History* (2d ed. New York 1959), Hans urs von BALTHASAR begins with the uniqueness of Christ as both God and man, and hardly lets the aforesaid problem arise. The special Christian fact, viz, Christ's uniqueness, is so constituted as to be, in all its historical singularity, the concrete norm for the abstract norm itself. In Christ the factual and the normative coincide not only in fact, but necessarily, because the fact is both the manifestation of God and the divine-human pattern of true humanity in God's eyes. ''In Jesus Christ, the Logos . . . is himself history . . . the source of history, the point whence the whole of history before and after Christ emanates: Its center.''

He expands this original and somewhat startling approach by developing the notion of Christ as the mode of time and the norm of history. By freely obeying the Father in heaven, the Son fulfills and includes in His task the whole historical dimension, conferring upon it its ultimate meaning. It was in view of Him that the venture of having any such thing as a world and world history could be undertaken at all. From the point of view of a theology of history, at least, no life or age has its own self-contained meaning. The meaning of the past and of individual destinies is not irrevocably fixed; they can always be newly defined and transformed with the passage of time.

Through the action of the Holy Spirit in a threefold process, Christ becomes the relevant norm for all of history, always involving, in new and surprising ways, the μετανοεῖτε that lies at the heart of the gospel. The whole of history, then, transformed by the hypostatic union, has its ultimate justification and meaning in Christ. But this truth does not mean that created nature has no immanent meaning, no intelligibility of its own —else there could be no true Incarnation. World history, then, is not coextensive (invisibly) with the history of the kingdom of God. The two forms of Christian existence manifest the tension between natural and supernatural, plant the Cross in the structure of the Church, but do not split the unity of Christian existence. Man's act of corresponding to what God wills for world history as grace is the central core that makes history happen. Since Christ all history is basically sacred, because of the Church's presence and testimony within an all-inclusive world history. The external battle of history between the Church and the powers of evil is only the outward echo of a more essential battle fought within the womb of the Church. The historical battle is not between Jerusalem and Babylon but a deeper, more hard-fought, more crucial struggle against the Babylon within us.

Similarly, K. RAHNER's ideas on a theology of history exist only in brief sketches, or as a set of broad directives and profound intimations, and as a series of specialized relevant investigations. Even so, one senses everywhere the rich suggestiveness and the strong vitality of genuine theological thought.

Basic is his penetrating analysis of the relationship of nature and grace and his concept of a SUPERNATURAL EXISTENTIAL in man as consequence of his God-given, supernatural destiny. This ''existential'' is more than a negatively conceived OBEDIENTIAL POTENCY; rather it is a positive supernatural orientation of man's being to God, an unexacted supernatural ordination to the Trinity. Rahner conceives of revelation as a saving happening and not merely the communication of certain propositions. Revelation reaches its climax and end in Jesus Christ. The beginning and the end of history are revealed data. The entire course of history obeys the plan of God, which becomes manifest only in the progressive events of history. God enters the world in Christ and reveals Himself to man, but only the man who willingly hears the Eternal Word in faith can form a concept of salvation history distinct from profane history. Revelation and covenant are important concepts for a theology of history, which can in turn support a theological history of the Church and a genuine pastoral theology.

The unfolding divine plan of history does not destroy human freedom, is not some rigid, predetermined unchanging pattern, even though it sets a goal for man that is infallibly pursued and attained. In history man receives power to respond freely to God's Word, and God's further word freely adapts itself to this free response of man. In this revelation and response history proceeds.

Nevertheless, as Rahner suggests, many questions remain uninvestigated or even unrecognized—e.g., the theological meaning of a theology of history, heresies as opinions and as churches in the light of the theology of history, the temporal mode of created being, a theology of time, the purposive unity of human history, the theology of human history before Christ, tradition as history and as the development of revelation, the sanctification of the whole sphere of the profane through the Church, and others. We are, indeed, poor in the theology of history. This complex, subtle, and crucial study touches every part of theology—and history. Many tentatives abound, and bold initiatives, and there is much that is merely personal intuition and construction, requiring a deep and solid foundationing, and many scattered valid insights. But with all of this one detects currents of genuine theological vitality and a growing sense of the theological and historical urgency of these problems.

Bibliography: C. L. BECKER, *The Heavenly City of the Eighteenth-century Philosophers* (New Haven 1932). N. A. BERDYAEV, *The Destiny of Man,* tr. N. DUDDINGTON (New York 1960); *The Meaning of History,* tr. G. REAVEY (New York 1936); *The Beginning and the End,* tr. R. M. FRENCH (New York 1952). P. TILLICH, *The Interpretation of History* (New York 1936). B. CROCE, *History as the Story of Liberty,* tr. S. SPRIGGE (New York 1941). C. DAWSON, *The Judgement of the Nations* (New York 1942). G. B. VICO, *The New Science,* tr. T. G. BERGIN and M. H. FISCH from 3d ed., 1744 (Ithaca 1948). R. AUBERT, ''Discussions récentes autour de la théologie de l'histoire,'' in *Collectanea Mechliniensia* 33 (1948) 129–149. E. C. RUST, *The Christian Understanding of History* (London 1947); *Salvation History: A Biblical Interpretation* (Richmond, Va. 1962); *Towards a Theological Understanding of History* (New York 1963). R. NIEBUHR, *Faith and History* (New York 1949). L. MALEVEZ, ''Deux théologies catholiques de l'histoire,'' *Bijdragen: Tijdschrift voor filosophie en theologie* 10 (1949) 225–240. K. LÖWITH, *Meaning in History* (Chicago 1949). H. DE LUBAC, *Catholicism,* tr. L. C. SHEPPARD (New York 1950); *La Pensée religieuse du Pierre Teilhard de Chardin* (Paris 1962). G. THILS, ''Bibliographie sur la théologie de l'histoire,'' *Ephemerides theologicae Lovanienses* 26 (1950) 87–95. O. CULLMANN, *Christ and Time,* tr. F. V. FILSON (rev. ed. Philadelphia 1964). W. H. WALSH, *An Introduction to Philosophy of History* (New York 1951). E. CASSIRER, *The Philosophy of the Enlightenment,* tr. C. A. KOELLN and J. P. PETTEGROVE (Princeton 1951). R. SHINN, *Christianity and the Problem of History* (New York 1953). M. SCHMAUS, *Von den letzten Dingen* (His *Katholische Dogmatik* 4.2; 5th ed. Munich 1953). P. CHIOCCHETTA, *Teologia della storia* (Rome 1953). E. CASTELLI, *Les Présupposés d'une théologie de l'histoire* (Paris 1954). R. GUARDINI, *The Lord,* tr. E. C. BRIEFS (Chicago 1954). J. PIEPER, *The End of Time,* tr. M. BULLOCK (London 1954). K. ADAM, *Spirit of Catholicism,* tr. J. MCCANN (pa. Garden City, N.Y. 1954). H. R. NIEBUHR, *Christ and Culture* (New York 1951; repr. pa. 1956). R. G. COLLINGWOOD, *The Idea of History* (London 1946; pa. New York 1956). J. MCINTRYE, *The Christian Doctrine of History* (Grand Rapids 1957). J. MARITAIN, *On the Philosophy of History,* ed. J. W. EVANS (New York 1957). R. BULTMANN, *History and Eschatology* (Edinburgh 1957). H. W. BARTSCH, ed., *Kerygma and Myth,* tr. R. H. FULLER, 2 v. (New York 1953; rev. ed. 1961), tr. of selections from *Kerygma und Mythos,* ed. H. W. BARTSCH, 5 v. (Hamburg 1948–62), containing discussions of Bultmann and his critics from 1948–55. J. DANIÉLOU, *The Lord of History,* tr. N. ABERCROMBIE (Chicago 1958). C. MICHALSON, *The Hinge of History* (New York 1959). D. E. ROBERTS, *Existentialism and Religious Belief,* ed. R. HAZELTON (New York 1959). M. C. D'ARCY, *The Meaning and Matter of History* (New York 1959). G. FESSARD, *De l'actualité historique,* 2 v. (Paris 1960). J. C. MURRAY, *We Hold These Truths* (New York 1960). W. J. ONG, ''Evolution and Cyclicism in Our Time,'' in *Darwin's Vision and Christian Perspectives,* ed. W. J. ONG (New York 1960) 125–148. J. MACQUARRIE, *The Scope of Demythologizing* (New York 1960). K. RAHNER, *Theological Investigations,* tr. C. ERNST and K. H. KRUGER (Baltimore 1961–64) v.1, 2; *Nature and Grace: Dilemmas in the Modern Church,* tr. D. WHARTON (New York 1964). J. MUILENBURG, ''The Biblical View of Time,'' *Harvard Theological Review* 54 (1961) 225–252. A. H. JOHNSON, *Whitehead's Philosophy of Civilization* (New York 1962). J. MOUROUX, *The Mystery of Time,* tr. J. DRURY (New York 1964). J. BARR, *Biblical Words for Time* (Naperville, Ill. 1962). W. DILTHEY, *Pattern and Meaning in History,* ed. H. P. RICKMAN (New York 1962). G. E. CAIRNS, *Philosophies of History* (New York 1962). I. KANT, *On History,* ed. L. W. BECK; tr. L. W. BECK et al. (Indianapolis 1963). J. M. ROBINSON and J. B. COBB, eds., *The Later Heidegger and Theology* (New Frontiers in Theology 1; New York 1963). G. A. BUTTRICK, *Christ and History* (New York 1963). A. RICHARDSON, *History Sacred and Profane* (Philadelphia 1964). T. A. O'MEARA and C. D. WEISSER, *Paul Tillich in Catholic Thought* (Dubuque 1964). J. M. CONNOLLY, *Human History and the Word of God* (New York 1965). B. HÄRING, *The Law of Christ,* tr. E.G. KAISER (Westminster, Md. 1961) v.1. J. DANIÉLOU et al., *Lexikon für Theologie und Kirche,* ed. J. HOFER and K. RAHNER (Freiburg 1957–65) 4:793–799. P. RIGA, ''The Ecclesiology of Johann Adam Möhler,'' *Theological Studies* 22 (1961) 563–587. R. ANDERSON, *Historical Transcendence and the Reality of God* (Grand Rapids, Mich. 1975). H. URS VON BALTHASAR, *A Theology of History* (New York 1963). L. GILKEY, *Reaping the Whirlwind* (New York 1976). J. B. METZ, *Theology of the World* (New York 1969). W. PANNENBERG, *Theology and the Kingdom of God* (Philadelphia 1969). K. RAHNER, ''The Hermeneutics of Eschatological Assertions,'' *Theological Investigations* 6, tr. K. H. and B. KRUGER (Baltimore 1969). D. SOELLE, *Po-*

litical Theology (Philadelphia 1971). E. SCHILLEBEECKX, "The Interpretation of Eschatology," in L. COGNET, ed., *Post-Reformation Spirituality. Concilium* 41 (1969).

[P. L. HUG/W. J. HILL]

HISTORY AND HISTORICITY (GESCHICHTLICHKEIT)

Standard English dictionaries have not furnished a definition of historicity corresponding even roughly to that given the term *Geschichtlichkeit* by German existentialists. Owing to the diversity in German existentialist thought, the terms *geschichtlich* (historical) and *Geschichtlichkeit* (historicity) exhibit a fairly wide semantic range. However, it may be said in general that, from the existentialist point of view, the historically significant is not necessarily identified completely with the factually historical. Thus, because of their impact on the individual believer, the Crucifixion and Resurrection of Christ are to be regarded as historically significant, whether factually established or not. *Geschichtlichkeit* may be described approximately as the full, authentic, active, and durative expression of a belief or movement in terms of personal participation and in relation to a given time. It can be used in an absolute sense, but also in a relative sense as well. It has application to the general as well as to the particular, and to the individual in relation to the community. It often involves contrasts and paradoxes. *Geschichtlichkeit* implies a rejection of traditional metaphysics, but, despite its opposition to certain aspects of historicism on the factual side, it likewise reflects, in some of its representatives at least, a relativistic concept of truth.

See Also: HISTORY, PHILOSOPHY OF; HISTORY, THEOLOGY OF; EXISTENTIALISM.

Bibliography: A. DARLAPP, *Lexicon für Theologie und Kirche*, ed. J. HOFER and K. RAHNER (Freiburg 1957–65) 4:780–783, with bibliog. A. BRUNNER, *Geschichtlichkeit* (Bern-Munich 1961). W. KAMLAH, *Christentum und Geschichtlichkeit* (2d ed. Stuttgart 1951), esp. 7–30. G. HASENHÜTTL, *Geschichte und existenziales Denken* (Wiesbaden 1965).

[M. R. P. MCGUIRE]

HITTITE AND HURRIAN RELIGIONS

Since the religion of the HITTITES had much in common with that of the Hurrians, those elements common to both religions will be treated here in connection with Hittite religion. The elements peculiar to Hurrian religion will then be treated separately.

Hittite Religion. The Hittite conception of divinity was deeply anthropomorphic (*see* ANTHROPOMORPHISM). Survivals of more primitive thought are apparent in the representation of the storm-god as a bull, in the worship of mountains, rivers, and springs, and in a few other features such as certain divine images not in human form, but these are exceptional. In general the gods are very much like men: sexually differentiated, forming families, requiring sustenance, swayed by passions, etc. They are thus consistently represented in literature and art.

Hittite Pantheon. The gods, however, were immortal. They had, too, a quality called *para handandatar,* which they occasionally "showed" to men in extraordinary events. This is a specifically and, for us, virtually undefinable conception of numinous power. One text translates it by Sumerian *nig.si.sá,* "equity," and however inadequate this equation unquestionably is, it is important as indicating the ethical nature of the numinous.

The gods themselves were legion. Not only were the same gods in numerous local cults recognized as distinct, but the gods of the different peoples of Anatolia and neighboring countries, preceding and during the time of the Hittites, were worshiped with little effort at syncretism. These gods were even addressed in their "native languages." There were Hattic gods whom the Hittites inherited from the Hatti, their predecessors in the land, Indo-European gods of the Hittites, Hurrian and Babylonian gods, and a primitive group called Asianic.

The most important, even in the classical period of the Hittites (*c.* 1400–1200 B.C.), were Hattic, who were worshiped either under their Hattic names or in Hittite translations of their names, e.g., the Hattic goddess of healing, Katahzipuris, who was called Kamrusipas in Hittite. Supreme was the sun-goddess of Arinna, a city not far from the capital Hattusa. She was "the mistress of the Hatti lands, the queen of heaven and earth . . . queen of all the countries." Her Hattic name was Wurusemu, her Hittite name is unknown. Her husband, probably Hattic Taru, was the storm-god, worshiped as the god of rain and fertility, either under the image of a bull or as a human figure with the bull his pedestal (*cf.* Jupiter Dolichenus). The couple's sons, the storm-gods of Nerik and Zippalanda, had cult centers north of Hattusa like Arinna and were probably local forms of Taru. Another important Hattic god was Telepinus, a vegetation or agricultural deity. The sun-god Istanus, "the sun-god of heaven," also had his cult; in fact, in the lists of divine witnesses to treaties, the sun-god is the first to be mentioned. He is the god of justice, a conception possibly connoting Babylonian influence.

Hurrian Pantheon. The next most important group of gods is the Hurrian. In the eastern part of the Hittite kingdom, the Hurrian cults of the goddess Hebat and her consort Teshub flourished in many centers. Within the of-

Relief detail, 10th century B.C., depicting weather god of Hatti receiving libation from King Shulumeli of Melid, Eastern Asia Minor.

ficial religion there was a tendency to identify Hebat with the sun-goddess of Arinna and Teshub with Taru. King Hattusili III honored as his special protectress Shaushka, the Hurrian Ishtar of Shamuha.

Hurrian gods were adopted into the Hittite pantheon; for example, Sheri and Hurri, perhaps ''Day and Night,'' who were Teshub's two bulls, and the sacred mountains Namni and Hazzi, the latter being Mt. Casius in north Syria near the mouth of the Orontes. Shaushka with her maids, Ninatta and Kulitta, regularly appear among the divine witnesses of the treaties, and besides other gods, such as Shimegi, the sun-god, and Kushuh, the moon-god, the Hurrians transmitted to the Hittites a number of Babylonian deities.

Relations of Gods and Men. The fundamental relationship of gods to men was that of masters to servants. It finds its clearest expression in the cult. Each day, like masters of a household, the gods must be washed, clothed, and given their food and drink. As the real rulers of the land they must also receive their tribute in the form of first fruits, unblemished animals, etc. This was done in a fixed cycle of religious FEASTS, which in general were seasonal. At the most important feasts the king himself officiated as chief priest. This was one of his most important duties, and annually he had to make a tour of the principal sanctuaries. To perform their religious duties kings are known to have interrupted even a military campaign.

The cult took place in temples, although open-air sanctuaries also existed. To judge from the temples at Hattusa, the cella containing the cult-statue was so located that it was accessible only to the priests and usually was invisible to the general body of worshipers. However, there were processions of statues, and in the entertainment of the gods, for example, the mock battle performed before the war-god Yarris, the statues must often have been visible to general view. The cult was not without its risks. The participants and all else had to be pure (*see* PURE AND IMPURE). Therefore, before the cult began, rites of purification were necessary, but neglect was possible, and the god could be offended with dire results for the guilty.

The Hittite conception of sin and divine punishment is well illustrated by the plague prayers of King Mursili II. The plague, which had raged for 20 years, is first explained as due to failure to make regular offerings to the Euphrates River. This was concluded from the fact that consultation of an ancient tablet revealed that earlier kings had made these offerings, but they were discontinued in the time of Mursili's father, during which period the plague began. This Mursili promises to correct; to do so, he is on his way now to the Euphrates. Beyond this, another tablet was discovered which showed that Mursili's father had violated the oath of a treaty. Although he gained a military victory in doing so, he brought back prisoners with the plague. To remedy the evil, Mursili confesses:

> The father's sin falls upon the son. So, my father's sin has fallen upon me. Now, I have confessed before the Hattian storm-god, my lord, and before the gods, my lords (admitting): "It is true, we have done it. . . ." This is what I have to remind thee: The bird takes refuge in its nest, and the nest saves its life. Again: if anything becomes too much for a servant, he appeals to his lord. His lord hears him and takes pity on him. Whatever had become too much for him, he sets right for him. Again: if the servant has incurred guilt, but confesses his guilt to his lord, his lord may do with him what he pleases. But, because he [the servant] has confessed his guilt to his lord, his lord's soul is pacified, and his lord will not punish his servant. I have now confessed my father's sin.

This beautiful prayer shows the basic concepts, the tensions, and the occasional heights of Hittite religion.

Relief detail depicting Hittite King Tudhaliya IV in embrace of tutelary deity, Hurrian god Sharruma, Yazilikaya, Turkey.

A less attractive, but very characteristic, element in this religion was its alliance with MAGIC. Black magic was absolutely forbidden and punishable by death. Where genuine sin was involved, reliance on magic was never complete; prayer, too, was needed, and the mercy of the gods was implored. Magic was seen as distinct from religion and, at least on the official level, not considered its surrogate. Magic removed impurity, which could be contracted from sexual intercourse, from contact with impure objects like corpses, from curses effected by black magic, etc. It cured impotence, drove ghosts out of houses, and gave specific form and power to a curse. In general it was governed, like all magic, by analogy. Thus, in the soldier's oath, salt was placed in his hands, and he heard the fate of the disloyal: "Just as salt has no seed, even so let that man's name, seed, house, cattle, and sheep perish"; and to this he said "Amen." Uncleanness is compared to darkness, and so the ailing, "impure" person is made to don black clothes only to be stripped of them.

Guidance might come from extraordinary divine intervention through a dream or a prophet. Usually, however, it was sought by DIVINATION: extispicy, augury, and a third means, which was probably some use of lots. The first was borrowed from the Babylonians; the techniques were elaborate, the tradition behind them long and complex. By a series of omens with their "favorable" or "unfavorable" responses, the precise information sought could finally be acquired.

Myths. In the *purulliyas* festival, probably the New Year festival, which honored the storm-god, the Illuyankas myth was recited. Illuyankas, a dragon, and the storm-god meet one day and engage in combat. The dragon wins. Inaras, a Hattic goddess, helps the storm-god take his vengeance. First she gives her love to a mortal who in return promises his assistance. Then she entices Illuyankas to a feast and gets him drunk. Her lover binds the drunken dragon, then the storm-god easily disposes of him. In another and more recent version, Illuyankas first deprives the storm-god of his heart and eyes. The storm-god marries a mortal by whom he has a son; the son then marries the daughter of Illuyankas. At his father's advice he requests the return of the heart and eyes. This granted, the reinvigorated storm-god sets out for battle against Illuyankas. His son, now part of the dragon's household, sides with his father-in-law, and at his request is killed together with the dragon by his father.

The interpretation of this *hieros logos* of the *purulliyas* festival is obscure, but its similarity to the myth of Typhon in Greek sources should be noted. In a fight the monster Typhon overcomes Zeus, whose strength, however, is restored with the help of Typhon's daughter. Zeus then kills the monster. Zeus lives on Mt. Casius, Typhon on the Cilician coast. The myth, therefore, was originally at home in the neighborhood of the Hittites.

Myths, besides being used in the cult, were also employed in magical rituals (*see* MYTH AND MYTHOLOGY). One such was the myth of Telepinus, the disappearing god. Because he disappears, he has been compared with TAMMUZ, Adonis, and other ''dying gods.'' However, Telepinus does not die; he hides. The myth was not recited seasonally in the cult, but in a magical rite to appease an angered god. According to the myth, Telepinus disappears in a fit of anger with the result that vegetation withers (Telepinus is the vegetation god), men and animals become sterile, etc. In this calamity all search proves futile until the goddess Hannahanna sends a bee, which finds Telepinus, but only makes matters worse by stinging the god and angering him the more. Magic is required; it is successfully applied by Kamrusipas (in another version by a man). Telepinus returns, and nature is restored.

Hurrian Religion. Although our knowledge of Hurrian religion is still imperfect, owing partly to the unsolved difficulties of the Hurrian language, the broad outlines are clear. To the principal gods of the Hurrian pantheon, which have already been mentioned, might be added the gods of war, Ashtabi and Nubadig, the latter appearing as Lubadagash in the third millennium.

Distinctive of the Hurrian pantheon is the presence of many Sumero-Akkadian gods (*see* MESOPOTAMIA, ANCIENT, 3.): Aya, the wife of Shimegi; Nikkal, Sumerian Ningal and wife of the moon-god; Shala, in Akkadian sources the wife of the storm-god Adad, but in Hurrian religion the wife of Kumarbi, ''father of the gods.'' In fact, as an organized pantheon, that of the Hurrians is Sumero-Akkadian, but adapted to the supremacy of the storm-god Teshub and his consort Hebat. Similar borrowings and adaptations are evident in the cult practices.

The myths of Kumarbi also illustrate the Sumero-Akkadian influence, and, more interestingly, they show Hurrian influence on Greek myths. In one myth the Hurrian god Kumarbi is preceded as king of heaven by Alalu and Anu, each having reigned for nine years. Anu is the Sumero-Akkadian god of heaven, and Alalu in the god-lists is one of his ancestors. Kumarbi is equated with Enlil; thus, in the myth, Kumarbi betakes himself to Nippur, Enlil's city; outside the myth there are also many indications of this equation. According to the myth, Kumarbi gains the kingship by biting off Anu's membrum. Whether he thereby impregnates himself or, by spitting it out, impregnates the earth is not clear, but eventually three gods are born, one of whom is Teshub who deposes Kumarbi.

In another myth, which presupposes that Teshub is ruling, Kumarbi sleeps with a huge rock, which gives birth to the diorite monster Ullikummi. Placed in the sea, it grows and grows until it threatens all the gods of heaven; only the intervention of Ea, the Babylonian god of wisdom and magic, saves Teshub his kingship. In Hesiod's *Theogony* Uranos, ''Heaven,'' is emasculated and deposed by Kronos, who in turn is overcome by Zeus; the similarity with Kumarbi's victory over Anu, ''Heaven,'' is obvious. In the Ullikummi myth, in which the conflict of Ullikummi and Teshub takes place by Mt. Casius, one is again struck by a certain similarity to the Zeus-Typhon myth. Probably it was the Phoenicians who transmitted these Hurrian myths to the Greek mythographers.

Bibliography: L. DELPORTE, *Dictionnaire de la Bible* suppl. ed. L. PIROT, et al. (Paris 1928–) 4:60–78. A. GOETZE, J. B. PRITCHARD, *Ancient Near Eastern Texts Relating to the Old Testament* (Princeton 1955); *Kleinasien*[2] *Kulturgeschichte des alten Orients* 3.1 (Handbuch der Altertumwissenschaft; Munich 1957) 130–171. H. G. GUETERBOCK, ''Hittite Religion,'' *Forgotten Religions*, ed. V. FERM (New York 1950) 83–107. O. R. GURNEY, *The Hittites* (Baltimore 1952).

[W. L. MORAN]

HITTITES

An Indo-European group, probably Aryans, who crossed over the Caucasus Mountains into Armenia and Cappadocia. Historians point out two eras, the Old or Proto-Hittite Kingdom (1700–1530 B.C.) and the New Kingdom (*c.* 1420–1200 B.C.). Internationally the Hittites reached their peak in the 13th century, only to see their empire collapse shortly afterwards. In the realm of religion and literature, the Hittites betray no striking originality but proved to be quite adept in assimilating the cultures of their neighbors.

Old Kingdom. Scholars do not agree on the precise area from which the Hittites migrated or the approximate time of their departure. Evidence found in the cuneiform documents of the Assyrian merchant colony at Kültepe reveals numerous Indo-European names. Hence it is clear that the Hittites were established in the area by 1900 B.C., when the Assyrian colony was flourishing. On arrival in Asia Minor they took for themselves the name of an indigenous group, the Hatti, or Hitti.

At first, the new invaders were organized in a loose system of city-states, such as Kusara, Zalpa, and Hattusa. By the 17th century B.C., however, determined efforts at unification resulted in the establishment of a Hittite kingdom. Though credited to Labarna (early 16th century?), this work of unification had its beginnings much earlier. The first efforts at spreading the Hittite power were pursued by Hattusili, the successor of Labarna, who pushed south into Syria and actually laid siege to Yamkhad (Alep). Not until the advent of Mursili (*c.* 1535 B.C.) did Aleppo actually fall under Hittite control. This ambitious monarch even swept eastward to sack Babylon in 1530 and put an end to its first dynasty. The destruction of Babylon, however, proved to be simply a passing raid by the Hittites, and Babylonia never became a part of the Hittite Empire.

After the death of Mursili an era of turmoil began, during which succession to the throne usually entailed violence. Simultaneously the Hurrians to the east began to exert pressure on Hittite borders. As a result of these factors, Hittite power retreated into Asia Minor and was unimportant for 100 years.

New Kingdom. Shortly before 1400 B.C. new vitality began to show itself. Expansionist pressure was directed against northern Syria, but the alliance of Egypt and Mitanni held the Hittites in check. However, when in 1375 the able politician and general Suppiluliuma came to the Hittite throne, a period of decline began for Egypt. Suppiluliuma moved south and took most of Syria and northern Phoenicia from Egypt. When the weak and vacillating Egyptians failed to help Mitanni, it too fell to the Hittites as a vassal state. On the international scene, the fall of Mitanni was the prelude to the resurgence of Assyria under Ashur-uballit. I (1354–1318; *see* MESOPOTAMIA, ANCIENT, 2).

So weak had Egypt become that the young widow of Tutankhamun petitioned Suppiluliuma for one of his sons as her consort in an effort to provide some stability after the chaos of the Amarna Age (*see* EGYPT). However, the young Hittite prince was murdered by the Egyptians. War was averted for a time by a plague that was ravaging Hittite lands, but open conflict came when the 19th Egyptian dynasty tried to restore Egyptian control over Syria. In 1286 Ramses II (1290–1224) led his forces against those of Muwattili (1306–1282) at Kadesh on the Orontes. Although Egyptian hieroglyphs tell of the brilliant victory of the pharaoh, Hittite reports of a savage slaughter of the Egyptian troops are closer to the truth. Confirmation of the Hittite account is the fact that Egyptian forces never ventured into Syria again, though the fighting south of Syria dragged on for another 15 years. It was only the rise of a new menace to the East, Assyria, that led the Egyptians and the Hittites to make peace. In 1270, then, Ramses II and the new Hittite monarch Hattusili III made a treaty that was sealed by the marriage of a daughter of Hattusili to Ramses.

From its position as a great world power, the Hittite Empire came to a swift collapse before the 13th-century tide of vigorous Aegean peoples migrating into western

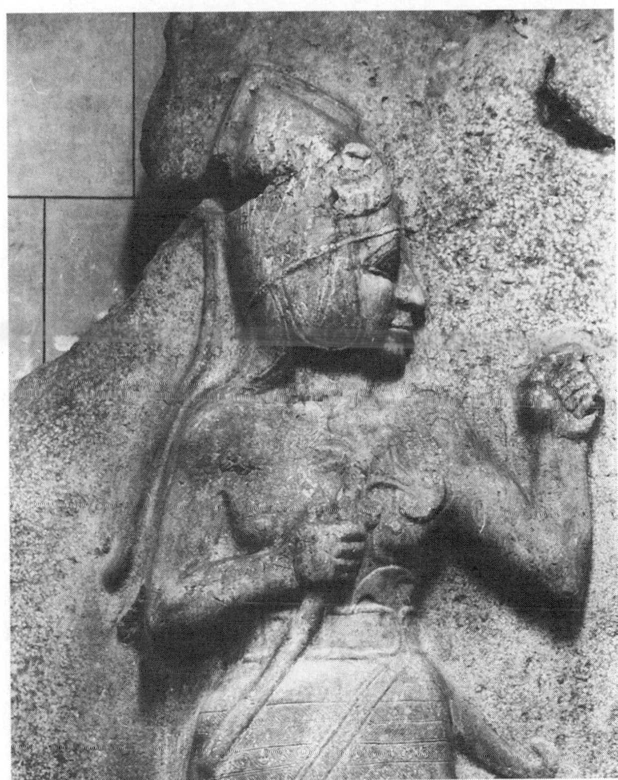

Relief detail, Gate god, 14th-century B.C., Hattusa.

Asia Minor. But responsibility for this collapse rests principally with the ''Sea Peoples,'' who were next to challenge Egypt and eventually settle the coastal plain of Palestine. Some city-states did manage to survive, among them Carchemish, Zinjirli, and Karatepe, but even these bowed completely out of history in the 8th century, when Sargon II, king of Assyria seized Carchemish.

Culture. Culturally the Hittites lagged far behind the great civilizations of the 2d millennium B.C. Study, even of their era of international prominence, shows little cultural initiative. They strove, rather, to imitate and assimilate the contributions of their neighbors. Moreover, one can point to no single Hittite religion. There was a host of national and local cults. Sumero-Akkadian deities came to the Hittites through the mediation of the Hurrians. From Nineveh came the cult of Ishtar. Egypt too was to contribute to the conglomeration of Hittite practices. And a pervading syncretism led to a refashioning of these cults in their new homeland.

Hittite legal codes belong to the same class of secular laws as those contained in the Code of Hammurabi. Their formula for overlord-vassal treaties has provided a better understanding of the important OT concept of covenant [see G. E. Mendenhall, ''Ancient Oriental and Biblical Law'' and ''Covenant Forms in Israelite Tradition'' *The*

Hieroglyphic inscription from Aleppo, c. 1354 B.C. (©Gianni Dagli Orti/CORBIS)

Biblical Archaeologist 17 (1954) 26–46; 50–76]. The social order founded on Hittite law was actually more humane than the earlier codes from which it borrowed. The law of retaliation (*lex talionis*), ''An eye for an eye, a tooth for a tooth, a life for a life,'' was not in vogue. Nor were the various classes inseparably divided; even the rights of a slave were recognized.

It is the opinion of some scholars that the Hittites probably learned the secret of making iron as early as 1600 B.C., but it is doubtful when they first employed it for military purposes. Its first uses seem to have been for ornaments, not weapons. Perhaps the first effective military use of iron was by the Sea Peoples, who effected the breakup of the Hittite Empire near the close of the 13th century. Allusion to the iron monopoly of these Sea Peoples, known to Bible readers as the PHILISTINES, is to be found in 1 Sm 13.19–22.

From ancient times Hittite lands were well known for their horses. Biblical reference to this fact is seen in 2 Kgs 10.28–29, where we learn that the enterprising SOLOMON imported horses from Asia Minor and chariots from Egypt and sold both ''to all the kings of the Hittites and Aram.'' Hittites are mentioned in the OT under the name of Hethites.

Bibliography: O. R. GURNEY, *The Hittites* (Baltimore, Md. 1952). K. W. MAREK, *The Secret of the Hittites: The Discovery of an Ancient Empire,* tr. R. and O. WINSTON (New York 1956). G. CONTENAU, *La Civilisation des Hittites et des Hurrites du Mitanni* (new ed. rev. Paris 1948). A. GOETZE, *Hethiter, Churriter und Assyrer* (Cambridge, Mass. 1936). C. L. WOOLLEY, *A Forgotten Kingdom* (Baltimore, Md. 1953). E. NEUFELD, tr., *The Hittite Laws* (London 1951).

[J. E. HUESMAN]

HITTORP, MELCHIOR

Liturgist; b. Cologne, *c.* 1525; d. Cologne, 1584. He contributed to the preservation of the faith of the people of Cologne by publishing an edition of the writings of various medieval liturgists and an ancient Roman Ordinal, *De Divinis Catholicae Ecclesiae Officiis ac Ministeriis* (Cologne 1568). This Ordinal, as M. Andrieu has shown, is a part of the Romano-German Pontifical compiled at Mainz about 950, which formed the basis for our modern Roman Pontifical. This entire edition is still the most complete collection of medieval liturgists.

Bibliography: *Allgemeine deutsche Biographie* (Leipzig 1875–1910) 12:507. A. FRANZEN, *Lexikon für Theologie und Kirche*, ed. J. HOFER and K. RAHNER, 10 v. (2d, new ed. Freiburg 1957–65) 5:394–395. M. ANDRIEU, ''Melchior Hittorp et l'*Ordo Romanus Antiquus,*'' *Ephemerides liturgicae* 46 (1932) 3–21. M. ANDRIEU, *Les ''Ordines Romani'' du haut moyen-âge*, 5 v. (Louvain 1931–61) 1:494–525.

[B. NEUNHEUSER]

HLOND, AUGUSTYN

Polish cardinal; b. Brzeczkowice (Upper Silesia), June 5, 1881; d. Warsaw, Oct. 22, 1948. Following his early school years in his native district, he continued his education under the SALESIANS at Turin and entered their congregation in 1897. He received his doctorate at the Gregorian University in Rome in 1899 and was ordained in Cracow Sept. 23, 1905. He was appointed director of a Salesian school in Cracow (1907) and later was a schoolmaster in Vienna. From 1919 to 1922 he was head of the newly founded German-Austrian province of the Salesians.

In the reorganization of ecclesiastical affairs in Poland after World War I, he was made apostolic administrator (1922) and became the first bishop of Katowice (Dec. 14, 1925; consecrated Jan. 3, 1926). He played a major part in the negotiations leading to the concordat between the Holy See and Poland (1925). In 1926 he was made archbishop of Gniezno-Poznań and primate of Poland, and in 1927, cardinal. His able leadership in Polish episcopal synods, pastoral letters, development of CATHOLIC ACTION, and promotion of the missionary apostolate of the press, imparted new life to the care of souls in Poland. At the outbreak of World War II he traveled by way of Rumania to Rome. From the fall of 1940 he resided in southern France. On Feb. 3, 1944, he was arrested by the Gestapo and, in September, was taken to Wiedenbrück (in Westphalia), where, on April 1, 1945, he was freed by American troops. By way of Rome and Prague he returned to Poznań (July 20, 1945) and began the reorganization of ecclesiastical life in Poland, having received special authority for this work from the Holy See. In the ''Western Polish'' districts, belonging to the East German ecclesiastical province, he established five apostolic administrators. On March 4, 1946, Pius XII dissolved the personal union of Gniezno and Poznań. Cardinal Hlond remained archbishop of Gniezno and, in addition, was made archbishop of Warsaw. Owing to his initiative, Catholicism recovered its strength after the suppression it suffered under National Socialism during the German occupation. To the end of his life, the cardinal-archbishop defended the Church against all limitations on its freedom imposed by the Communist government. On Jan. 22, 1959, his remains were transferred to the new primate's chapel in the Cathedral of St. John in Warsaw. Monuments in the cathedrals of Poznań and Warsaw manifested the gratitude of Polish Catholics for his labors on their behalf.

Bibliography: Works. *The Persecution of the Catholic Church in German-Occupied Poland* (New York 1941); *Na straży sumienia narodu, wybór pism i przemówień z przedmowem O. Haleckiego* (Ramsey, N.Y. 1951). **Literature.** B. STASIEWSKI, *Lexikon für Theologie und Kirche*, ed. J. HOFER and K. RAHNER, 10 v. (2d, new ed. Freiburg 1957–65) 5:395–396. W. SUCKER, *Die Religion in Geschichte und Gegenwart*, 7 v. (3d ed. Tübingen 1957–65) 3:371. K. M. ŻYWCZYŃSKI, ''A. Hlond,'' *Polski słownik biograficzny* 9 (Wrocław-Warsaw-Cracow 1961) 545–546. W. MALEJ, ''Kardynał A. Hlond, 1881–1948,'' *Wiadomości archidiecezji warszawskiej* 40 (Warsaw 1958) 510–520.

[B. STASIEWSKI]

HOBBES, THOMAS

British empiricist noted for his political philosophy; b. Malmesbury (Wiltshire), April 5, 1588; d. Hardwick, Dec. 4, 1679.

Life. Hobbes's schooling was at Magdalen Hall, Oxford. After graduation he became the private tutor of William Cavendish, later the first earl of Devonshire; this early association with the Cavendish family proved to be extremely helpful throughout his life. It provided him, for instance, with the opportunity to travel extensively through Europe, where he came to know R. DESCARTES, M. Mersenne, and G. GALILEI.

Thomas Hobbes. (Archive Photos)

By temperament Hobbes was a classicist. His first published work was a translation of Thucydides, and fully half his literary output he rendered in Latin. But by conviction Hobbes was a man of his age, and he felt the philosophical speculations and metaphysical suppositions of antiquity to be of little value in seventeenth-century Europe.

Endangered by his radical political ideas, Hobbes fled from England in 1640 and sought refuge in Paris. During an 11-year stay in the French capital, he was hired as tutor to a fellow exile, the then Prince of Wales. Later as Charles II, the former pupil ensured Hobbes a measure of safety and independence by granting him a life-long pension.

In 1651 Hobbes aroused the ire of French authorities by his remarks about the papacy, and he quickly returned to England. Commanding little if any popular support, he lived out his years with few interests save writing. But the quiet and detached life of the scholar was not to be his. Even with the relative protection afforded by his royal pension, Hobbes's later years were stormy and hectic. His godlessness was attacked in pulpit and pamphlet; the House of Commons condemned his masterwork, *Leviathan,* in 1666, and several of his other writings were subject to proscription and censorship.

Thought. Although there is a superficial development of Hobbes's political ideas out of a mechanistic or empirical theory of nature, the nexus is perhaps more convenient than crucial. This is a disputed point among Hobbes's present-day commentators. This issue can remain open, however, while the relevance of the political theory is examined.

Hobbes postulates a "state of nature" from which man emerges as he builds his political and social world. In this state of nature man is free, absolutely free, but his freedom is something to be quickly rid of in the SOCIAL CONTRACT. It is not an initial condition or franchise for further progress and attainment. Rather, in the state of nature freedom implies lack of order, and without order life is in dire jeopardy. So man barters freedom for security. And a social contract once entered carries strong sanctions. Indeed, the only moral imperative in Hobbes's system states that man must not break the contract, for to do so risks a return to the dangers of the state of nature.

Out of individual social contracts develops a new entity, the state. Men pool their freedoms in the construction of an artificial commonwealth, and then they find themselves totally subject to its rigid and monolithic order.

Thus Hobbes did not consider the motivation that prompts man to the building of a body politic as the seeking of a good. Indeed, man himself is not a creature who seeks to do good. He is moved to act only out of fear, especially and archetypically the fear of violent death. Life itself, sheer life, is the only good or value that Hobbes recognized, and to its protection all human enterprises are oriented. Again, for Hobbes there is no objective order of values to be recognized and implemented; there is merely a subjective desire to be fulfilled, or more properly, preserved. But even this subjective desire is not an optimistic longing to achieve any positive concept of self-identity; it is nothing but a pessimistic fear of destruction.

Assessment. Hobbes's understanding of the nature of man strikes at the very heart of any classical, much less Christian, interpretation. Devoid of any hope of seeking positive values, indeed with the denial of any notion of moral virtue, man would indeed find freedom a terrible specter. There is, perhaps, a degree of similarity between Hobbes's state of nature and the anguish of contemporary EXISTENTIALISM. Each would deny that man has any positive or intelligible essence, and each would likewise deny that man seeks to discover an external order in his political and philosophical activity. Whereas Hobbes finds nothing to do with freedom except surrender it to an artificial leviathan, the existentialist clings to his freedom but despairs of finding a solution to the very questions he has raised.

The end product of Hobbes's analysis is a state ripe for totalitarianism. Stripped of the radical individuality that Christianity won for him, gripped with a fear of violence and disorder, and blind to any vision of positive social and moral values, man held tight to the state itself, awkwardly pieced together with forfeited freedom (cf. H. Arendt).

Hobbes did not generate a school of followers, and it is very questionable whether his thought has had any direct positive influence at all. Many took strong issue with both his political and natural speculations. Benjamin Whichcote and the CAMBRIDGE PLATONISTS led a religious movement against the teachings of Hobbes. But perhaps his final significance lies in his having given expression to an ever-present possibility in thought—one that has been resisted in philosophy since Plato, and against which man must remain forever on guard.

Bibliography: Works. *The English Works of Thomas Hobbes,* ed. W. MOLESWORTH, 11 v. (London 1839–45); *Opera philosophica quae Latine scripsit omnia,* ed. W. MOLESWORTH, 5 v. (London 1839–45); *Leviathan,* ed. M. OAKESHOTT (Oxford 1957); *De cive, or The Citizen,* ed. S. P. LAMPRECHT (New York 1949). Literature. M. A. PACCHI, "Bibliografia hobbesiana dal 1840 ad oggi," *Rivista critica di storia della filosofia* 17 (1962): 528–547. L. STRAUSS, *The Political Philosophy of Hobbes,* tr. E. M. SINCLAIR (Chicago 1952); *Natural Right and History* (Chicago 1953). H. ARENDT, *The Origins of Totalitarianism* (New York 1951). R. POLIN, *Politique et philosophie chez Thomas Hobbes* (Paris 1953).

[B. J. CUDAHY]

HOCEDEZ, EDGAR

Theologian; b. Ghent, Belgium, July 1, 1877; d. Fayt-lez-Manage, Sept. 5, 1948. Entering the Society of Jesus in 1895, he combined a profound religious life with an eagerness for scientific work and a passionate interest in the history of ideas. At first, his superiors planned the career of a Bollandist for him and had him spend one year under the direction of H. Delehaye and P. Peeters, publishing articles of hagiography in the *Analecta Bollandiana.* He showed so marked an ability in theology, however, that his superiors assigned him to teach the subject. He taught successively at Kurseong, Bengal (1908–12); Louvain (1912–14); and Hastings, England. Returning to Louvain in 1919, he taught fundamental theology. Hocedez enriched his classes with his knowledge of medieval scholasticism, especially the work of St. Thomas, and his acquaintance with modern apologetic thought. His private study on the history of medieval philosophy and theology yielded such works as *Richard de Middleton* (Louvain 1925) and *Aegidii Romani Theoremata de Esse et Essentia* (Louvain 1930). He also published many magazine articles and was editor of the

Nouvelle Revue Théologique from 1920 until 1926. From 1928 on, he was in charge of theology courses preparatory to the doctorate at the Gregorian University. Two or three years before World War II he conceived the project that was the culmination of his scientific work, the *Histoire de la théologie au XIXe siècle,* 3 volumes (Brussels 1949–52). The war forced him to leave Rome hurriedly in 1940; he completed his masterwork in Belgium. He was a man of constant religious fervor, with remarkable zeal for work, and with a cordial and delicate charity. All these were expressed in his stimulating book provoked by the war, *L'Évangile de la souffrance* (Tournai 1946).

Bibliography: J. LEVIE, *Nouvelle revue théologique* 70 (1948) 786–793. C. MARTIN, *Catholicisme* 5:817.

[J. LEVIE]

HODGE, CHARLES

American Presbyterian theologian; b. Philadelphia, Pa., Dec. 28, 1797; d. Princeton, N.J., June 19, 1878. His father, a surgeon in George Washington's army, died in Hodge's childhood. Hodge attended Princeton and Princeton Theological Seminary, where he studied under Archibald ALEXANDER. In 1822 he was appointed professor of Oriental and Biblical literature at the seminary, a post he held until 1840. On a leave of absence (1826–28) he studied at the University of Berlin under the historian John A. W. Neander and became acquainted with Otto von Gerlach's circle.

In 1840 Hodge succeeded Alexander as professor of didactic and polemic theology, holding this chair until his death. His class lectures were the basis of his *Systematic Theology* (1872), the most generally used seminary text of the late 19th century. Hodge carried on the theological tradition of Alexander, a blend of 17th-century Calvinist scholasticism and Scottish realism that stressed both the power of reason and a verbally inspired, inerrant Bible as the basis of faith. Although he contributed to the original division, Hodge worked actively to reunite the Old and New School Presbyterians after the Civil War, and his efforts were instrumental in effecting union in 1869. He personally taught more than 3,000 ministers, and by the time of the general assembly in 1890, his theology was almost universally held among Presbyterians.

Bibliography: A. A. HODGE, *The Life of Charles Hodge* (New York 1880). W. THORP, ed., *Lives of Eighteen from Princeton* (Princeton 1946). H. T. KERR, ed., *Sons of the Prophets* (Princeton 1963).

[R. K. MACMASTER]

Charles Hodge.

HODGSON, SYDNEY, BL.

Lay martyr; hanged at Tyburn (London), Dec. 10, 1591. Hodgson, a convert to Catholicism, demonstrated the depth of his passion for the Eucharist. He was assisting at a Mass said by St. Edmund GENNINGS in the home of St. Swithun WELLS when Topcliffe broke into the house searching for priests. Hodgson and other men of the congregation prevented their entry into the ''sanctuary'' until the conclusion of the Mass. Thereafter all surrendered, were tried (Dec. 4, 1591), and condemned for relieving priests and being reconciled to the Roman Church. He was beatified by Pius XI on Dec. 15, 1929.

Feast of the English Martyrs: May 4 (England).

See Also: ENGLAND, SCOTLAND, AND WALES, MARTYRS OF.

Bibliography: R. CHALLONER, *Memoirs of Missionary Priests,* ed. J. H. POLLEN (rev. ed. London 1924; repr. Farnborough 1969), I, 180, 190. J. MORRIS, ed., *The Troubles of Our Catholic Forefathers Related by Themselves* (London 1877), III. J. H. POLLEN, *Acts of English Martyrs* (London 1891).

[K. I. RABENSTEIN]

St. Clement Mary Hofbauer.

HOFBAUER, CLEMENT MARY, ST.

Redemptorist priest; b. Tasswitz, Moravia, Dec. 26, 1751; d. Vienna, Austria, March 15, 1820. He was the youngest of 12 children of Paul, a grazier and butcher, and Mary (Steer) Hofbauer (German equivalent of Dvořák, the original family name). His father's death (1757) caused him to defer his early desire for the priesthood and to work as a baker until 1780, except for a period when he lived as a hermit. He changed his baptismal name John to Clement Mary. Financial help from three elderly Viennese ladies enabled him to prepare for the priesthood at the University of Vienna (1780–84). He and Thaddeus Hübl went to Rome, joined the recently founded REDEMPTORISTS (The Congregation of the Most Holy Redeemer) in 1784, and were ordained (1785). The two priests were then sent to Austria. Since JOSEPHINISM made it impossible to establish a house in Vienna, Hofbauer went to Warsaw (1787–1808) where he engaged in pastoral work, opened schools, introduced the order into Switzerland and southern Germany, and acted as its vicar-general for the regions north of the Alps. When NAPOLEON I caused him to leave Warsaw, he returned to Vienna for the remainder of his life. He worked for a time in the Franciscan church, served as chaplain to the Ursulines and as pastor of St. Ursula's Church from 1813, and established the Redemptorists in the city (1819). He gained renown for his influence over the populace, students, learned persons, artists, and writers. Especially notable was his influence over leading Romanticists such as Karl von Schlegel, Adam Müller, and their numerous friends. Hofbauer won many converts and effected a spiritual rejuvenation of the capital and of Austria. He was called the apostle of Vienna and was named patron saint of the city by PIUS X (1914). He was beatified Jan. 29,1888, and canonized May 20, 1909.

Feast: March 15.

Bibliography: J. HOFER, *St. Clement Maria Hofbauer,* tr. J. B. HAAS (New York 1926). J. L. BAUDOT and L. CHAUSSIN, *Vies des saints et des bienheueux selon l'ordre du calendrier avec l'historique des fêtes,* ed. by the Benedictines of Paris, 12 v. (Paris 1935–56) 3:333–342. E. HOSP, *Lexikon für Theologie und Kirche,* ed. J. HOFER and K. RAHNER, 10 v. (2d, new ed. Freiburg 1957–65); suppl., *Das ZweiteVatikanische Konzil: Dokumente und kommentare,* ed. H. S. BRECHTER, pt. 1 (1966) 5:413–414. E. DUDEL, *Klemens Hofbauer* (Bonn 1970). K. FLEISCHMANN, *Klemens Maria Hofbauer: sein Leben und seine Zeit* (Graz 1988). J. HEINZMANN, *Preaching the Gospel Anew: Saint Clement Maria Hofbauer,* tr. B. J. MCGRADE (Liguori, Mo. 1998).

[D. J. SHARROCK]

HOFFMAN, MELCHIOR

Furrier and laypreacher who joined the ANABAPTISTS, contributing an esoteric-enthusiastic interpretation of Scripture that influenced both revolutionary and pacifist groups; b. Schwäbisch Hall, before 1500?; d. Strassburg, 1543. While traveling across northern Europe practicing his trade, Hoffman preached wherever opportunity presented itself. Distrusted by the clergy because of his lack of theological education, he went to Wittenberg (1525) to obtain Luther's approval. In possession of a recommendation, he returned to the Baltic countries, but his theology remained suspect. Everywhere his preaching created disorder, forcing him to flee. In 1529 he made contact with Anabaptists in Strassburg, was rebaptized, and became a spokesman of this movement in northern Europe. He returned in 1533 to Strassburg, where he was arrested and imprisoned until his death.

A prolific writer, Hoffman considered himself one of the promised two witnesses (Ap 11.3), empowered to understand and proclaim the hidden meaning of Scripture. He promised the millennial rule of the saints, profoundly influencing the revolutionary Anabaptists. The Melchiorites were named after him. His Christology, which denies the true motherhood of the Blessed Virgin Mary, influenced Menno Simons.

Bibliography: P. KAWERAU, *Melchior Hoffman als religiöser Denker* (Haarlem 1954); *Die Religion in Geschichte und Gegenwart,* 7 v. (3d ed. Tübingen 1957–65) 3:422–423. G. H. WILLIAMS, ed., *Spiritual and Anabaptist Writers* (Philadelphia 1957); *The Radical Reformation* (Philadelphia 1962). W. SCHATZ, *Lexikon für Theologie und Kirche*, ed. J. HOFER and K. RAHNER, 10 v. (2d, new ed. Freiburg 1957–65) 5:426.

[G. W. FORELL]

HOFINGER, JOHANNES

Scholar, catechist; b. Tyrol, Austria, March 21, 1905; d. New Orleans, La., Feb. 14, 1984. At age 11 Hofinger entered the minor seminary in Salzburg. He studied philosophy at the Gregorian University in Rome, entered the Society of Jesus on Sept. 7, 1925, studied theology under Josef A. JUNGMANN, SJ in Innsbruck, and in 1937 completed his doctoral dissertation on the history of the catechism in Austria and Germany from the time of St. Peter Canisius. In that year he went to China and taught in a regional seminary at Kinghsien. There he produced his second book, in Latin and Chinese, *Our Good News* (1946). In 1949 he went with the seminarians to Manila, where he continued to teach until 1958.

Hofinger's major contribution was to reform the Church's methods in catechesis and religious education; he called for adopting insights from the Biblical and liturgical movements and from cultural anthropology. In addition to writing several books and many articles, he founded influential periodicals: ''Good Tidings'' (1962) and ''Teaching All Nations'' (1964). These merged into the ''East Asian Pastoral Review'' (1979).

From 1953 to 1970 he circled the globe 16 times, lecturing on the ''kerygmatic approach,'' proclaiming the good news of salvation history which reached its climax in Jesus Christ, and stressing God's loving gift of self and the invitation to respond.

He organized a series of international congresses in Nijmegen (1959), Eichstätt (1960), Bangkok (1962), Katigondo (1964), Manila (1967), Medellin (1968), and San Antonio (1969), bringing together Biblical, liturgical, and catechetical experts from every continent. These meetings influenced the Constitution on the Sacred Liturgy, the Decree on Missionary Activity of the Church, and the Declaration on the Relationship of the Church to Non-Christian Religions at the Second Vatican Council. They also prepared the way for the International Catechetical Congress in Rome in 1971 and contributed to the Synods of Bishops on Evangelization (1974) and Catechesis (1977) and to the resulting Apostolic Exhortations of Paul VI, *Evangelii nuntiandi* (1975) and JOHN PAUL II, *Catechesi tradendae* (1979).

Hofinger was a prolific writer. Among his major works are the following: *Nuntius Noster seu Themata Predicationis Nostrae* (Tientsin 1964); *Der priesterlose Gemeindegottesdienst in den Missionen,* with J. Kellner (Schöneck 1956); *The Art of Teaching Christian Doctrine* (South Bend 1957); *Liturgische Erneurung in der Weltmission,* with J. Kellner (Innsbruck 1957); *Worship: the Life of the Missions,* (Notre Dame 1958); *The ABC's of Modern Catechetics, with W. J. Reedy* (New York 1964); *The Good News and its Proclamation,* with F. J. Buckley (Notre Dame 1968); *Our Message is Christ: the More Outstanding Elements of the Christian Message* (Notre Dame 1974); *Evangelization and Catechesis: Are We Really Proclaiming the Gospel?* (New York 1976); *You Are My Witnesses: Spirituality for Religion Teachers* (Huntington 1977); *Pastoral Life in the Power of the Spirit* (New York 1982).

A man of tremendous energy and zealous enthusiasm, in 1963 he organized in Manila the East Asian Pastoral Institute, which became a center for inculturation. He briefly taught at the Fiji Islands in Oceania. Then at age 66, in spite of failing eyesight, he learned Spanish to be able to bring the ''good news'' to Latin America, where he lectured, taught, and wrote. In his final years he was active in the charismatic movement, integrating that with catechetics, especially in its Biblical basis. Eventually he became Associate Director at the Archdiocesan Office of Religious Education in New Orleans. He died the day before he would have become a naturalized citizen of the United States.

Bibliography: A. MARIA DE LA CRUZ, ''Johannes Hofinger Remembered: 1905–1984,'' *The Living Light* 20 (June 1984) 345–347. F. J. BUCKLEY, et al., ''Panel Honors Pioneering Catholic Educator,'' *Religious Education Association Clearing House* 12 (Spring 1982) 3–6. F. X. CLARK, ''Johannes Hofinger, S.J., (1905–1984). Life and Bibliography.'' *East Asian Pastoral Review* 21 (2 1984) 103–120. A. M. NEBREDA, ''Johannes Hofinger: Catalyst and Pioneer,'' *ibid.,* 120–127. R. R. EKSTROM, ''He is Much Missed,'' *Catechist* 18 (Feb. 1985) 56.

[F. J. BUCKLEY]

HOGAN, JOHN BAPTIST

Sulpician rector; b. near Ennis, County Clare, Ireland, June 24, 1829; d. Paris, France, Sept. 29, 1901. With the help of an uncle who was a priest in the Diocese of Périgueux, Hogan went to France at 15 and studied for the priesthood in the minor and major seminaries of Bordeaux. When he finished theology in 1849, he was sent to Paris for two years of postgraduate work in the Seminary of Saint-Sulpice at Issy. In September 1851 he began his novitiate for the Sulpicians and was ordained June 5, 1852. The following September, at 23, Hogan began to teach dogmatic theology at Issy, where he continued to teach it and several other subjects until he turned to moral theology and liturgy in 1863. In 1884 he was sent to the U.S., where as Abbé Hogan he served as first president of St. John's Seminary, Brighton, Mass. (1884–89), as president of Divinity College, The Catholic University of America, Washington, D.C. (1889–94), and again as president of St. John's Seminary for his last seven years. Failing health brought about his resignation and return to France, where he died suddenly. Hogan prepared occasional articles for periodicals and wrote two books, *Clerical Studies,* which first appeared as a series of articles in the *Ecclesiastical Review* (1891–95), and *Daily Thoughts,* a series of short meditations for seminarians and priests. Both have been translated into French.

[C. M. CUYLER]

HOGAN, JOHN JOSEPH

Bishop; b. County Limerick, Ireland, May 10, 1829; d. Kansas City, Mo., Feb. 21, 1913. He received his classical education in Ireland and came to the U.S. in 1848 for his theological course. Ordained on April 10, 1852, by Abp. Peter Richard Kenrick, he filled parochial assignments in St. Louis, Mo., from 1852 to 1857. In 1857 Hogan volunteered for northern Missouri and, with a base at Chillicothe, took up a life of travel by horseback and on the newly built railroad. In 1865 he was indicted for refusing to take a test oath required of clergy by the Missouri Constitution, but he won a victory when the U.S. Supreme Court declared this requirement to be unconstitutional. When the city of St. Joseph in northwestern Missouri became an episcopal see, Hogan was appointed bishop (March 3, 1868) and was consecrated on September 13 by Kenrick. At this time there were some 3,000 Catholics in the territory. In 1880 the Diocese of Kansas City was erected, and Hogan was transferred there while continuing to administer the Diocese of St. Joseph. He governed the two dioceses until 1893, when Bp. Maurice F. Burke of Cheyenne, Wyo., was transferred to St. Joseph. During Hogan's episcopate at Kansas City, the number of priests and Catholics increased sharply, new religious communities came to the diocese, and new churches, including the Cathedral of the Immaculate Conception, were built. In 1896 John J. Glennon, a priest of the Diocese of Kansas City, was appointed coadjutor. Among Hogan's published works were *On the Mission in Missouri* (1892) and *Nautical Distances and How to Compute Them* (1903).

Bibliography: J. J. SCHLAFLY, *A History of the Catholic Church in the Diocese of Kansas City* (Kansas City 1955).

[W. W. BAUM]

HOGAN, WILLIAM

Schismatic; b. Ireland, 1788; d. Nashua, N.H., Jan. 3, 1848. Little is known of his early years except that he was ordained in Ireland and functioned as a priest in the Diocese of Limerick. According to his cousin, Rev. George Hogan, William was suspended five years before he arrived in the U.S., and had declared his intention of becoming a Protestant clergyman. Hogan first settled in the New York Archdiocese, but in 1820, without the permission of Bp. John Connolly of New York, he moved to St. Mary's Cathedral, Philadelphia, Pa. There he ingratiated himself with the lay trustees, conducted himself in an unpriestly manner, and publicly attacked Bp. Henry CONWELL. Despite warnings, Hogan refused to reform and was suspended by Conwell. There followed a series of recriminations aired in the public press and the state courts. In the course of the dispute, Hogan proposed the founding of an American Catholic Church in which the congregation would choose its own pastor. This doctrine, known as ''Hoganism,'' was struck down by the Pennsylvania Supreme Court in 1822, but the rebellious trustees, persisting in their claim to control Church property, closed the cathedral. Hogan himself was obliged to resign because of publicity concerning his moral life. As a former priest, he was twice ''married'' and worked as a lecturer and author of such anti-Catholic pamphlets as *Popery as It Was and Is* and *Nunneries and Auricular Confession.* In 1843 he was appointed U.S. consul at Nuevitas, Cuba. There is no record of his having been reconciled to the Church before he died.

Bibliography: M. I. J. GRIFFIN, ''The Life of Bishop Conwell of Philadelphia,'' rev. and ed. L. B. NORTON, *Records of the American Catholic Historical Society of Philadelphia* 24–29 (1913–18), see Indexes. F. E. TOURSCHER, *The Hogan Schism . . .* (Philadelphia 1930).

[H. J. NOLAN]

HOGER OF BREMEN-HAMBURG, ST.

Archbishop; d. Dec. 20, 916? His origins and early life are unknown. He became a monk at the Abbey of CORVEY, and from there was called to assist the aging Archbishop ADALGAR OF BREMEN (d. 909), whom he succeeded. Although his diocese was much troubled by invasions of Slavs and Magyars, Hoger scrupulously upheld diocesan and monastic discipline. Little else is known of his episcopal career, but ancient tradition testifies to his sanctity. He was buried in the Church of St. Michael, and *c.* 1036 his remains were transferred to the main basilica.

Feast: Dec. 20 or 29.

Bibliography: J. MABILLON, *Acta sanctorum ordinis S. Benedicti,* 9 v. (Paris 1668–1701; 2d ed. Venice 1733–40) 5:24. ADAMUS

BREMENSIS, *Gesta Hammaburgensis ecclesiae pontificum,* ed. B. SCHMEIDLER in *Monumenta Germaniae Scriptores rerum Germanicarum* (Berlin 1825–), bk. 1, ch. 50–52; *History of the Archbishops of Hamburg-Bremen,* tr. F. J. TSCHAN (New York 1959).

[F. BEHRENDS]

HOGG, JOHN, BL.

Priest, martyr; b. at Cleveland, North Riding, Yorkshire, England; d. May 27, 1590, hanged, drawn, and quartered at Durham. He studied at Rheims from Oct. 15, 1587, and was ordained with his fellow martyrs BB. Richard Holiday and Richard HILL on Sept. 23, 1589. They were all arrested while taking up their posts in the north of England and condemned for treason as seminary priests. He was beatified by Pope John Paul II on Nov. 22, 1987 with George Haydock and Companions.

Feast of the English Martyrs: May 4 (England).

See Also: ENGLAND, SCOTLAND, AND WALES, MARTYRS OF.

Bibliography: R. CHALLONER, *Memoirs of Missionary Priests,* ed. J. H. POLLEN (rev. ed. London 1924). J. H. POLLEN, *Acts of English Martyrs* (London 1891).

[K. I. RABENSTEIN]

HOHENBAUM VAN DER MEER, MORITZ

Benedictine historian; b. Spörl, near Belgrade, June 25, 1718; d. Abbey of Rheinau, near Schaffhausen, Switzerland, Dec. 18, 1795. He had been a student at Rheinau since 1730 when he was professed there in 1734; he was ordained in 1741, became professor in 1744, and served as prior of the abbey from 1758 to 1794. From 1759 until his death he was monastic archivist, and during the last 19 years of his life he functioned as secretary of the Swiss Benedictine Congregation. Besides several theological works he wrote a great number of historical treatises, mostly about his abbey, the Benedictine Order, and Switzerland. Without personal contact with the MAURISTS, he nevertheless followed their historical method, stressing, however, the actual writing of history rather than historical research. One Swiss scholar considered him the ''Swiss MABILLON.''

Bibliography: G. MAYER, ''Leben und Schriften des Pater Moriz Hohenbaum van der Meer,'' *Freiburger Diöcesan Archiv* 11 (1877) 1–34. G. PFEILSCHIFTER, *Die St. Blasianische Germania Sacra* (Munich 1921). G. HEER, *Johannes Mabillon und die Schweizer Benediktiner* (St. Gallen 1938); *Lexikon für Theologie und Kirche,* ed. J. HOFER and K. RAHNER, 10 v. (2d, new ed. Freiburg 1957–65) 5:428.

[O. L. KAPSNER]

ISBN 0-7876-4010-7